ANTIQUE MAP PRICE GUIDE No. 24

All the maps from Price Guides No. 1-23 listed alphabetically by Map Maker. More than

Prices: All prices in this catalogue are the current values for maps in 'fine' condition i.e. maps that are undamaged this is because maps are so rare that pricing becomes too speculative.

Dates: These often refer to the first date of publication. However, this is not guaranteed. The collector is advised to further information about individual maps. **Sizes:** These refer to the printed image not the sheet size and are appro.

Map Makers: These are listed alphabetically. When two names appear together, such as Mercator-Hondius, the first ... .ap maker and the second is the publisher. If a map maker is not known, either the publisher's or engraver's name is listed, or it is listed under 'Anon .

Titles: Titles of maps are listed in alphabetic order, ignoring hyphens, apostrophes. Untitled maps or English translations of foreign scripts are bracketed and listed first. Titles appearing within a map are preferred to titles appearing above or below a map. Titles in more than one language are often printed on the same map. However, sometimes only one of these titles is listed.

Comments: These sometimes appear before or after a title, in brackets, and are taken from the 23 regional illustrated Price Guides.

Exclusions: Antique maps that have not been selected for this reference work include diagrammatic route maps, antique maps of parts of counties or parts of cities, reprints of the same map unless of historical interest, maps made in the Far East, maps of proposed developments, globe gores, puzzle maps, Ptolemaic maps printed after the year 1570 and antique maps of such rarity that none are known to exist in private hands. Topographical views of cities are not included unless they give 'birds eye' information about a whole city.

Disclaimer: While reasonable steps have been taken to ensure the accuracy of information in this catalogue, the author/publisher accept no responsibility or liability for any damages arising for whatever reason from the information in the catalogue or from errors or omissions.

Acknowledgment: 'Antique Map Price Record' published by Jeremy Pool, 2009 edition.

AMPG REFERENCE	REGION	DATE	MAP MAKER	PRICE (UK£)	VERT. (cm.)	HOR. (cm.)	TITLE OF MAP (Comments by the editor in brackets)
mwm0076	mediterranean	1798	ABEL	450	24	50	Charte vom Mittellaendschen Meer
mwm0248	mediterranean malta	1772	ABELA	2000	30	71	Malta colle sue Citta, Fortificazioni, Terre, Villaggi ... con le sue Isole Adiacenti
mwjk0149	japan	1852	ACKERMAN LITHO	100	20	16	Island of Great Lew-Chew
mwuk0474	scotland	1736	ADAIR	2000	48	69	A Map of East Lothian
mwuk0475	scotland	1737	ADAIR	2000	50	66	A Map of West Lothian
mwuk0471	scotland	1731	ADAIR	2000	49	69	A New and Exact Map of the River Clyde
mwuk0749	uk	1689	ADAIR	1800	57	47	A New Mapp of ye Kingdom of England
mwuk1567	england islands	1703	ADAIR	480	36	47	Holy-Island Fairn-Islands with the Many Rocks & Hazards
mwuk0427	scotland	1688	ADAIR	2000	44	67	The Mapp of Straithern Stormount, and Cars of Gourie with the Rivers Tay
mwca0553	canada quebec	1826	ADAMS	1200	71	93	... This Map of Quebec and its Environs
mwca0583	canada quebec montreal	1825	ADAMS	7500	80	186	Map of the City and Suburbs of Montreal
mwuk0675	uk	1590	ADAMS R.	15000	52	76	(Untitled map showing the route of the Spanish Armada)
mwuk0931	england	1677	ADAMS, J		202	188	Angliae Totius Tabula cum Distantijs Notioribus in Itinerantium Usum Accommodata
mwuk0935	england	1680	ADAMS, J	10000	70	99	Angliae Totius Tabula cum Distantijs Notioribus in Itinerantium Usum Accommodata (1st reduced version of 1677 map)
mwuss1383	pennsylvania	1792	ADLUM & WALLIS	12000	88	96	A Map Exhibiting a General View of the Roads and Inland Navigation of Pennsylvania, and Part of the Adjacent States
mwme0447a	jerusalem	1629	ADRICHOM	5000	40	49	Abrisz der Stadt Jerusalem wie sie furnemlich zur Zeit desz Herrn Christi beschaffen gewesen. (Plan after Adrichom 1584. Vignettes after Villalpando)
mwme0184a	holy land	1682	ADRICHOM	300	22	45	Dimidia Tribus Manasse hoc est, ea Terrae Sanctae Pars (first edition 1590)
mwme0441a	jerusalem	1590	ADRICHOM	15000	49	73	Gierusalemme, et i Borghi suoi come fiori nel tempo di Christo (based on Adrichom 1584)
mwme0465	jerusalem	1682	ADRICHOM	5000	51	74	Ierusalem et suburbia eius (see first edition 1584; several other editions until 1682 with minor differences)
mwme0440a	jerusalem	1584	ADRICHOM		51	74	Ierusalem, et suburbia eius, sicut tempore Christi floruit, cum Locis in quibus Christ Passus ... Descripta per Christianum Adrichom Delphum (see also 1590 and 1682)
mwme0092	holy land	1631	ADRICHOM		35	101	Situacion de la Tierra de Promision para la Inteligencia de los Libros Sagrados segun la Description de Christiano Adrichomio (Spanish re-issue of Adrichom 1590. Illustrated is c1800 re-engraving)
mwme0185	holy land	1682	ADRICHOM	1800	36	101	Situs Terrae Promissionis. S.S. Bibliorum Intelligentiam Exacte Aperiens (first edition 1590)
mwme0186	holy land	1682	ADRICHOM	300	22	38	Tribus Aser, id est, Portio illa Terrae Sanctae, quae Tribui Aser in Divisione Regionis Attributa Fuit (first edition 1590. Illustration from 1628 edition)
mwme0187	holy land	1682	ADRICHOM	300	38	46	Tribus Ephraim, Beniamin et Dan (first edition 1590)
mwme0188	holy land	1682	ADRICHOM	300	18	36	Tribus Gad nempe ea Terrae Sanctae Pars
mwme0189	holy land	1682	ADRICHOM	300	33	42	Tribus Iuda, id est, Pars illa Terrae Sancta, quam in Ingressu Tribus Iuda Consecuta Fuit
mwme0190	holy land	1682	ADRICHOM	300	21	36	Tribus Neptalim videlicet, ea Terrae Sanctae
mwme0191	holy land	1682	ADRICHOM	300	23	47	Tribus Ruben hoc est, ea Terrae Sanctae
mwme0192	holy land	1682	ADRICHOM	300	18	36	Tribus Simeon nempe ea Terrae Sanctae Portio
mwme0193	holy land	1682	ADRICHOM	300	36	40	Tribus Zabulon, Isachar, et, Dimidia Manasse (first edition 1590)
mwme0194	holy land	1682	ADRICHOM	450	42	53	Tribuum Ephraim, Benaimin et Dimidae Manasse intra Jordanem Partes Occidentales et Partes Septentrionales Dan et Juda

AMPG REFERENCE	REGION	DATE	MAP MAKER	PRICE (UK£)	VERT. (cm.)	HOR. (cm.)	TITLE OF MAP (Comments by the editor in brackets)
mww0259a	world	1696	AEFFERDEN	1800	18	28	(Untitled double hemisphere map)
mwaf0005	africa	1556	AFRICANUS	2000	28	38	(Untitled close copy of Ramusio 1554)
mwuk1171	england london	1737	AGAS-VERTUE	5000	69	190	Civitas Londinum (Re-issue of a birds-eye view supposedly made by Agas c1560. Various reduced size versions of this re-issue were made during the 18th and 19th centuries)
mwit0537	italy milan	1698	AGNELLI	2000	41	55	La Gran Citta di Milano
mwuk0539	scotland	1782	AINSLIE	480	46	57	(Edinburgh)
mwuk0570	scotland	1804	AINSLIE	4000	114	80	(Untitled map of Edinburgh. Text reads:) To the Right Honourable the Lord Provost ... this Plan of the Old and New Town of Edinburgh and the Proposed Docks is Most Humbly Inscribed
mwuk0542	scotland	1785	AINSLIE	2800	57	52	A Chart of Part of Scotland from Berwick upon Tweed to Skateraw Harbour in the County of Kincardine ... Surveyed and Engraved by John Ainslie 1785 (in 4 sheets, each 57x52cm.)
mwuk0551a	scotland	1789	AINSLIE	2000	118	133	A Chart of the West Coast of Scotland and Northern Ireland
mwuk0559	scotland	1794	AINSLIE	2400	119	105	Map of the County of Forfar or Shire of Angus, from an Actual Survey
mwuk0586	scotland	1821	AINSLIE	2000	125	169	Map of the Environs of Glasgow, Paisley, Ayr, Lanark, Sanquhar, Wigton, Kirkcudbright &c. / The Environs of Edinbugh, Haddington, Dunse, Kelso, Jedburgh, Hawick, Selkirk, Peebles, Langholm and Annan
mwuk0552	scotland	1790	AINSLIE	550	59	44	Scotland
mwuk0550	scotland	1789	AINSLIE	2400	179	164	Scotland Drawn and Engrav'd from a Series of Angles and Astronomical Observations
mwuk0520	scotland	1775	AINSLIE	3600	62	49	The Counties of Fife and Kinross with the River Forth and Tay Survey'd & Engraved by John Ainslie (in 6 sheets, each 62x49cm.)
mwuss1642	virginia	1776	AITKEN	1500	25	28	Map of the Maritime Parts of Virginia Exhibiting the Seat of War and of L. Dunmore's Depredations in that Colony
			AITZINGER, SEE VON AITZING				
mwp0520	pacific south	1818	AKERLAND	500	34	42	Karta ofver Australien eller Polynesien
mwaf0308a	africa	1818	AKERLAND	240	34	42	Karta ofver Africa (illustrated is 1828 edition)
mwuss1027	new hampshire	1839	AKERMAN	750	45	44	Plan of Portsmouth, N.H.
mwsc0744	scandinavia sweden	1785	AKREL	650	57	49	Charta ofver Stockholms och Upsala ...
mwam0607	america north	1817	ALABERN	250	36	42	America Septentrional
mwam0606	america north	1817	ALABERN	500	29	41	Estados Unidos de la America Septentrional
mww0731	world	1845	ALABERN	350	25	43	Mapa Mundi en Dos Hemisferios
mwgm0286	mexico	1820	ALABERN	250	29	38	Mejico
mwit0255a	italy abruzzo	1567	ALBERTI	400	17	25	(Tremiti Islands, shown below left)
mwf0462	france corsica	1588	ALBERTI	1000	25	17	L'Isola di Corsica
mwit0774c	italy sardinia	1567	ALBERTI	720	25	17	Sardegna (wood block)
mwit1208	italy venice	1568	ALBERTI	1000	17	25	Venetia
mwit0679	italy piedmont	1729	ALBERTS	450	46	52	Casal dit de St. Vas ... 1695
mwit0680	italy piedmont	1729	ALBERTS	450	51	60	Theatre de la Guerre en Piemont en Savoye & dans le Dauphine (copy of Blaeu 1682 with different title)
mwaf0191a	africa	1750	ALBRIZZI	480	33	43	Carta Generale dell' Africa
mwit0515c	italy lombardy	1750	ALBRIZZI	300	33	43	Carta Geografica dei Territori di Pavia di Lodi e di Piacenza
mwsam0370	south america brazil	1740	ALBRIZZI	450	33	43	Carta Geografica del Bresil
mwca0065a	canada	1750	ALBRIZZI	720	33	43	Carta Geografica del Canada nell America Settentrionale
mwaf0929a	africa south	1750	ALBRIZZI	400	33	43	Carta Geografica del Capo di Buono Speranza
mwaf0917a	africa south	1740	ALBRIZZI	350	34	43	Carta Geografica del Congo o Bassa Guinea della Caffraria e del Monopotapa (reduced version of De L'Isle 1708)
mwit0515b	italy lombardy	1750	ALBRIZZI	350	33	43	Carta Geografica del Ducato di Mantua
mwit0685a	italy piedmont	1740	ALBRIZZI	250	33	43	Carta Geografica del Ducato di Savoja
mwf0352	france brittany	1750	ALBRIZZI	250	32	41	Carta Geografica del Governo della Bretagna
mwf0589b	france ile de france	1750	ALBRIZZI	200	33	43	Carta Geografica del Governo dell' Isola di Francia
mwit0440	italy liguria	1750	ALBRIZZI	250	33	43	Carta Geografica del Governo della Liguria o sia Dello Stato della Republica di Genova
mwf0623a	france languedoc	1750	ALBRIZZI	250	33	43	Carta Geografica del Governo della Linguadocca
mwf0790	france normandy	1750	ALBRIZZI	250	33	42	Carta Geografica del Governo della Normandia
mwf1065a	france provence	1750	ALBRIZZI	300	34	45	Carta Geografica del Governo della Provenza.
mwf0269	france aquitaine	1750	ALBRIZZI	250	33	43	Carta Geografica del Governo di Guienne e Guascogna
mwit1122a	italy tuscany	1750	ALBRIZZI	500	33	43	Carta Geografica del Gran Ducato di Toscana
mwgm0212a	mexico	1750	ALBRIZZI	550	33	42	Carta Geografica del Messico o sia della Nuova Spagna
mwf0503a	france corsica	1750	ALBRIZZI	600	33	43	Carta Geografica del Regno di Corsica
mwf0127a	france	1750	ALBRIZZI	300	33	37	Carta Geografica del Regno di Francia
mwit1036a	italy south	1750	ALBRIZZI	400	33	43	Carta Geografica del Regno di Napoli
mwsp0093b	portugal	1750	ALBRIZZI	300	40	33	Carta Geografica del Regno di Portogallo
mwit0315	italy central	1750	ALBRIZZI	350	33	43	Carta Geografica del Stato della Chiesa
mwit0515a	italy lombardy	1750	ALBRIZZI	350	33	43	Carta Geografica del Territorio Bresciano
mwit1199b	italy veneto	1750	ALBRIZZI	400	33	43	Carta Geografica del Territorio Padovano
mwit1122	italy tuscany	1750	ALBRIZZI	320	33	43	Carta Geografica del Territorio Senese (Siena)
mwit1199a	italy veneto	1750	ALBRIZZI	350		43	Carta Geografica del Territorio Trevigiano

AMPG REFERENCE	REGION	DATE	MAP MAKER	PRICE (UK£)	VERT. (cm.)	HOR. (cm.)	TITLE OF MAP (Comments by the editor in brackets)
mwit0813	italy sardinia	1750	ALBRIZZI	550	33	43	Carta Geografica dell' Isola di Sardegna
mwit0947	italy sicily	1750	ALBRIZZI	600	33	43	Carta Geografica dell' Isola di Sicilia
mwit1199c	italy veneto	1750	ALBRIZZI	400	33	43	Carta Geografica dell' Stato Veneto in Italia
mwsam0070a	south america	1750	ALBRIZZI	400	34	43	Carta Geografica della America Meridionale
mwe0686	europe dalmatia	1753	ALBRIZZI	220	34	44	Carta Geografica della Dalmazia
mwuss0412	america florida	1750	ALBRIZZI	800	33	43	Carta Geografica della Florida nell'America Settentrionale
mwit0373a	italy friuli	1750	ALBRIZZI	350	33	43	Carta Geografica della Provincia del Friuli
mwit0288	italy campagna	1750	ALBRIZZI	400	33	43	Carta Geografica della Terra di Lavora o sia della Campagna Felice
mwam0401	america north	1750	ALBRIZZI	600	33	43	Carta Geografica dell'America Settentrionale
mwit0183	italy	1750	ALBRIZZI	400	33	43	Carta Geografica Generale dell'Italia
mwit0685	italy piedmont	1750	ALBRIZZI	250	33	43	Carta Geografica dello Stato del Piemonte
mwsc0357	scandinavia denmark	1740	ALBRIZZI	220	28	33	Carta Nuova del Regno di Danimarca ... in Amsterdam da Isac Tirion (also issued in 1740 with the title 'Regno di Danimarca')
mwme0617	arabia etc	1740	ALBRIZZI	650	28	35	Carta Nuova dell'Arabia
mwe0155a	europe	1740	ALBRIZZI	300	28	34	Carta Nuova dell Europa
mwbh0637	belgium holland	1740	ALBRIZZI	250	28	33	Carta Nuova ed Accurata delle XVII Provincie de Paesi Bassi
mwe1155a	europe south east	1740	ALBRIZZI	200	30	36	Europa Turchesca ... apresso Isaak Tirion (also issued in 1740 with the title 'Nuova Carta del Europa Turchesca Seconde l'Ultime Ossevazioni Fata in Amesterdam Apresso Isaak Tirion'
mwg0123a	germany	1740	ALBRIZZI	240	28	34	Germania Divisa i Dieci Circoli
mwjk0095a	japan	1740	ALBRIZZI	650	25	32	Imperio del Giappone
mwin0200	india	1740	ALBRIZZI	500	29	36	Impero del Gran Mogol
mwas0832	asia south east siam	1750	ALBRIZZI	550	28	36	India di la Fiume Ganges Overo di Malacca Siam Cambodia Chiampa Kochinkina Laos Pegu Ava &c.
mwuk0996a	england	1750	ALBRIZZI	320	38	33	Inghilterra
mwme0740	iraq etc	1740	ALBRIZZI	240	27	33	Irak Arabi Kurdistan Diarbek Turcomarnia Siria e Palestina
mwuk0173a	ireland	1750	ALBRIZZI	350	38	32	Irlanda (re-issue of Weigel 1720 with different title)
mwin0046	ceylon	1740	ALBRIZZI	350	28	35	Isola Ceilon
mwas0475	asia south east	1740	ALBRIZZI	450	28	37	Isole di Sunda Borneo Sumatra Iava Grande &c.
mwas0769	asia south east philippines	1740	ALBRIZZI	450	29	33	Isole Filippine Ladronese Moluccos Isole Della Spezairie Come Anco Celebes &c. (also issued with the title 'Nuova et Accurata Carta dell' Isole Filippine, Ladrones, e Moluccus o Isole delle Speziarie como anco Celebes &c.')
mww0375a	world	1740	ALBRIZZI	1650	30	36	Mappamondo, o sia Descrizione Generale del Globo Terrestre ed Acquatico
mwru0185a	russia	1740	ALBRIZZI	200	29	34	Moscovia o Russia
mwsw0149a	switzerland	1750	ALBRIZZI	250	27	33	Nuova Carta dei XIII Cantoni degli Suizzeri insieme coi lora Alleati e Sudditi
mwg0383	bavaria	1750	ALBRIZZI	240	28	33	Nuova Carta del Circolo di Franconia, e di Suevia
mwg0825	westphalia	1750	ALBRIZZI	220	28	33	Nuova Carta del Circolo di Westfalia Diviso ne' suoi Vescovadi, Principat
mwbh0864a	luxembourg	1740	ALBRIZZI	320	28	32	Nuova Carta del Ducato di Lucemburgo e della Contea di Namur
mwaa0125	arctic	1740	ALBRIZZI	300	28	33	Nuova Carta del Polo Artico Secondo l'Ultime Osservazioni
mwe0569	europe czech republic (bohemia)	1740	ALBRIZZI	250	28	33	Nuova Carta del Regno di Boemia, Ducato di Slesia, Marchesato di Moravia, e Lusazia. In Amsterdam da Isac Tirion (also issued with title 'Regno di Boemia ...')
mwbp0421	poland	1740	ALBRIZZI	400	29	34	Nuova Carta del Regno di Polonia Diviso nei suoi Palatinati (Tirion's 1733 map. Re-engraved in 1740 with a new title 'Regno di Polonia')
mwsc0136	scandinavia	1740	ALBRIZZI	300	28	34	Nuova Carta del Regno di Suezia (also issued in 1740 with the title 'Regno di Suezia')
mwas0163	asia continent	1740	ALBRIZZI	375	28	35	Nuova Carta dell' Asia Secondo le Ultime Osservazioni
mwas0458a	asia south east	1740	ALBRIZZI	500	28	36	Nuova Carta dell' India di la del Fiume Ganges overo di Malacca Siam Cambodia Chiampa Kochinchina Laos Pegu Ava &c.
mwuk0832	uk	1750	ALBRIZZI	350	28	33	Nuova Carta dell' Isole Britanniche Divise nei Tre Regni d'Inghilterra de Scozia et d'Irlanda
mwbh0637	belgium holland	1750	ALBRIZZI	250	28	33	Nuova Carta della Contea di Olanda
mwbh0691	belgium holland	1750	ALBRIZZI	235	28	32	Nuova Carta delle Contea di Flandra Artois et Hannonia
mwbh0691a	belgium holland	1750	ALBRIZZI	300	28	32	Nuova Carta delle Provincie Unite Data in Luce in Amsterdam da Isac Tirion
mwru0522	ukraine	1740	ALBRIZZI	720	35	45	Nuova Carta Geografica per servire all storia della Guerra
mwsp0271a	spain	1750	ALBRIZZI	320	28	36	Nuovo Carta della Spagna
mwme0820	persia etc	1740	ALBRIZZI	450	29	36	Regno di Persia
mwe09340	europe hungary	1740	ALBRIZZI	220	28	32	Regno di Ungheria e Della Transilvania
mwuk0492a	scotland	1750	ALBRIZZI	350	37	32	Scozia
mwme0617a	arabia etc	1740	ALBRIZZI	300	28	34	Stati del Turco situati Nell' Europa Asia ed Affrica
mwit0515d	italy lombardy	1750	ALBRIZZI	350	33	43	Stato di Milano e suoi Confini
mwru0449	russia tartary	1740	ALBRIZZI	240	28	34	Tartaria (close copy of Tirion 1732. Also issued with the title 'Nuova Carta della Tartary')
mwam0763	america north	1845	ALDEN	2000	104	134	Alden's Pictorial Map of the United States of North America
mwuss0146	california	1860	ALDEN - COAST SURVEY	1250	66	99	San Francisco Harbour

AMPG REFERENCE	REGION	DATE	MAP MAKER	PRICE (UK£)	VERT. (cm.)	HOR. (cm.)	TITLE OF MAP (Comments by the editor in brackets)
mwgr0274b	greece athens	1837	ALDENHOVEN	480	32	35	Athenes
mwf0009a	france	1513	ALDINE	2000			(Untitled map of France, Belgium, Germany)
mwam0640a	america north	1825	ALES	550	43	53	États-Unis d'Amérique
mwca0012	canada	1624	ALEXANDER	10000	25	34	(Untitled map centred on 'New Scotlande' from his book 'An Encouragement to Colonies'. Illustration shows re-issue by Samuel Purchas, 1625, with page nos. top left and right.)
mwuss0354	washington DC	1838	ALEXANDRIA CANAL CO.	350	49	91	Chart of the Head of Navigation of the Potomac River Shewing the Route of the Alexandria Canal.
mwsc0017	scandinavia	1562	ALGOET		76	102	Terrarum Septentrionalium Exacta Novissimaque Descriptio Per Livinum Algoet ... 1562
mwuk0752	uk	1690	ALLARD	2500	51	59	Accuratissima Angliae Scotiae et Hiberniae
mwe0101	europe	1690	ALLARD	1200	50	59	Accuratissima Europae Tabula Multis Locis
mwg0087	germany	1700	ALLARD	400	49	57	Accuratissima Germaniae Tabula
mwaf0085	africa	1679	ALLARD	3500	50	59	Africae Nova Discriptio
mwam0080	america continent	1679	ALLARD	2400	44	54	Americae Nova Descriptio
mwbh0479a	belgium holland	1697	ALLARD	500	50	58	Antverpiae Marchionatus et Dominium Mechliniae
mwas0064	asia continent	1679	ALLARD	1200	44	54	Asiae Nova Discriptio
mwbh0479	belgium holland	1697	ALLARD	700	48	57	Comitatus Hollandiae Tabula Pluribus ...
mwsp0692	gibraltar	1704	ALLARD	1600	50	59	De Haven en Straat van Gibraltar
mwbh0399	belgium holland	1680	ALLARD	450	50	59	Dioecesis Leodiensis Accurata Tabula
mwsp0212	spain	1700	ALLARD	2000	50	59	Division Generale des Royaumes d'Espagne & de Portugal (4 sheets, each 50x59cm)
mwbh0486	belgium holland	1700	ALLARD	450	60	50	Ducatus Geldriae Batavae et Hispanicae, in Tetrarchias Noviomagi, Arnhemii, Ruremondae & Zutphaniae Comitatus Distinctae
mwg0709	schleswig-holstein	1660	ALLARD	500	44	52	Ducatus Holsatiae
mwaf1152	africa west	1695	ALLARD	12500	46	60	Effigies Ampli Regni Auriferi Guineae in Africa (Originally published by Claesz, 1602)
mwm0023	mediterranean	1690	ALLARD	1500	43	105	Europa / Tooneel des Oorlogs in't Zuider Deel van Europa
mwe0086	europe	1679	ALLARD	950	44	54	Europae Nova Descriptio
mwas0081	asia continent	1690	ALLARD	900	50	58	Exactissima Asiae Delineatio in Praecipuasa Regionis
mwbh0337	belgium holland	1660	ALLARD	850	46	54	Foederatae Belgicae Tabula in Multis Locis Emendata
mwbh0445	belgium holland	1690	ALLARD	550	47	56	Foederatum Belgium nec non Ducatus Bremensis ac etiam Pars Fluminis Albis
mwbh0474	belgium holland	1696	ALLARD	720	51	58	Frisia Dominium vernacule Friesland
mwbh0480	belgium holland	1697	ALLARD	550	46	56	Frisiae Orientalis. Amstelodami
mwsc0677a	scandinavia sweden	1660	ALLARD	600	44	52	Hallandia Nova et Accurata Descriptio
mwgr0082	greece	1665	ALLARD	1000	45	56	Hellas seu Graecia Universa
mwsp0213	spain	1700	ALLARD	480	45	56	Hispaniae et Portugalliae Regna
mwuk0103	ireland	1690	ALLARD	1800	59	51	Hyberniae Regni in Provincias Ultoniam, Connachian, Lageniam, Momoniamq Divisi Tabula Accuratissima
mwit0111a	italy	1685	ALLARD	960	42	51	Italia et Insulae Circumjacentes: Sicilia, Sardinia, Corsica (This map credits Sanson but bears the signature Carel Allardt (lower left). Perhaps it was originally prepared by Carel's father Hugo but issued in Carel's name when he took over his father's business. Carel issued his own map of Italy in 1705.)
mwit0135	italy	1705	ALLARD	1200	50	59	Italia in suos quoscunq Status divisus ... Auctore Carolo Allard (inset of Sicily)
mwsc0278	scandinavia denmark	1660	ALLARD	400	44	52	Jutia Meridionalis et Fionia
mwsc0279	scandinavia denmark	1660	ALLARD	400	43	52	Jutia Septentrionalis
mwf0605	france languedoc	1690	ALLARD	1100	53	86	La Basse Partie du Gouvernement de Languedoc
mwf0679a	france lorraine	1695	ALLARD	450	50	60	Le Duche de Lorraine & de Bar, le Gouvernt. de Champagne et une Partie de celui di L'Isle de France &c. (illustration shows an additional right-hand section of Alsace, which increases its value to £900)
mwbh0371	belgium holland	1665	ALLARD	25000	43	56	Leo Belgicus (re-issue of Gerritsz' map, lion faces left.)
mwf0606	france languedoc	1695	ALLARD	900	50	60	Les Bas Sevennes dans le Languedoc ou le Diocese de Montpelier (illustrated is the Covens & Mortier re-issue)
mwuk1109	england london	1645	ALLARD	2500	28	38	London (panorama)
mwuk0724	uk	1665	ALLARD	2500	45	56	Nieuwe en Perfecte Caarte, van Engeland Schotland en Yrland
mwaf0064	africa	1660	ALLARD	2400	45	56	Nova Africa (title above map 'Nova Africae Geographica et Hydrographica Descriptio'. Shown above left)
mwe0068	europe	1660	ALLARD	1500	45	57	Nova et Accurat Totius Europae Tabula
mwbh0476	belgium holland	1696	ALLARD	550	46	54	Nova et Accurata Comitatus Zelandiae Tabula
mwsp0186	spain	1662	ALLARD	5000	46	56	Nova et Accurata Tabula Hispaniae (4 carte-a-figure borders)
mwg0088	germany	1700	ALLARD	300	48	57	Nova et Denuo Correcta Germaniae Tabula, Comprehendens X Circulos, Regnum Bohemiae, ac Universam Helvetiam, cum Coeteris Regionibus iis Annexis
mwas0050	asia continent	1660	ALLARD	1400	45	57	Nova et Exacta Asiae Geographica Descriptio
mwf0064	france	1660	ALLARD	600	45	57	Nova Galliae et Accurata Descriptio
mwme0559	arabia etc	1660	ALLARD	1200	51	59	Nova Tabula et Accurata Turcicum Imperium
mwas0395	asia south east	1660	ALLARD	3500	46	57	Nova Tabula India Orientalis Hugo Allardt Excudit inde Kalverstraet inde Werrelt Caerte

AMPG REFERENCE	REGION	DATE	MAP MAKER	PRICE (UK£)	VERT. (cm.)	HOR. (cm.)	TITLE OF MAP (Comments by the editor in brackets)
mwin0419	indian ocean	1680	ALLARD	4800	42	53	Nova Tabula Indiae Orientalis
mwbh0446	belgium holland	1690	ALLARD	750	47	56	Nova Tabula Totius Frisiae Orientalis Emendata ab, H. Allardo
mwam0062	america continent	1660	ALLARD	4000	45	57	Nova Totius Americae sive Novi Orbis Tabula (title above map)
mwbp0280	poland	1670	ALLARD	1200	39	51	Nova Totius Regni Poloniae, Magniq. Ducatus Lithuaniae, cum suis Palatinatibus ac Confinis
mwbh0374	belgium holland	1666	ALLARD	1100	38	53	Nova XVII Provinciarum Descriptio
mwuss1075	new york	1660	ALLARD	2000	47	55	Novi Belgii Novaeque Angliae nec non Partis Virginiae Tabula
mwaf0106	africa	1696	ALLARD	1200	49	57	Novissima et Perfectissima Africae
mwuk0441	scotland	1695	ALLARD	1600	51	59	Novissima Regni Scotiae Septentrionalis et Meridionalis Tabula
mwru0075	russia	1680	ALLARD	720	46	56	Novissima Russiae vulgo Moscoviae Tabula
mww0220	world	1683	ALLARD	5500	50	59	Novissima Totius Orbis Tabula, per Carolum Allard (copy of De Wit 1670)
mww0219a	world	1682	ALLARD	15000	45	56	Novissima Totius Tarrarum Orbis Tabula. Auctore Hugonis Allardi (illustration shows De Ram's re-issue 1685 with 'terrarum' instead of 'tarrarum' and his name instead of Allard's)
mwin0415	indian ocean	1668	ALLARD		70	91	Oost Indien
mww0159	world	1650	ALLARD	6000	40	55	Orbis Terrarum Typus de Integro Multis in Locis Emendatus. Auctore Petro Plancio (updated re-issue of Plancius 1594)
mwg0081	germany	1689	ALLARD	960	47	94	Pars Germaniae Gallorum Armis Hodie Conquassata (also issued with the 'Theatrum Belli' cartouche removed etc., as below)
mww0260	world	1696	ALLARD	5000	52	60	Planisphaerium Terrestre, sive Terrarum Orbis
mwsp0038	portugal	1660	ALLARD	675	45	56	Portugallia et Algarbia quae olim Lusitania Novissima Descriptio
mwsp0061	portugal	1700	ALLARD	650	26	62	Portugalliae Meridionalis Plagae
mwe0552	europe czech republic (bohemia)	1695	ALLARD	300	22	27	Praga
mwam0102	america continent	1700	ALLARD	2000	50	58	Recentissima Novi Orbis sive Americae Septentrionalis et Meridionalis Tabula
mwuk0946	england	1689	ALLARD	1800	50	59	Regni Angliae et Walliae Principatus Tabula, Divisa in LII Regiones, Anglice Shire, Dictas
mwsc0280	scandinavia denmark	1660	ALLARD	750	45	56	Regni Daniae, Novissima et Accuratissima Tabula
mwbp0331	poland	1697	ALLARD	950	50	59	Regni Poloniae, Magni Ducatus Lithuaniae
mwuk0759	uk	1695	ALLARD	2500	51	59	Regnorum Magnae Brittaniae, sive Angliae Scotiae nec non Hibernia
mwsc0677	scandinavia sweden	1660	ALLARD	650	44	52	Scania; vulgo Schonen
mwru0501b	ukraine	1710	ALLARD	1350	53	87	Sedes Belli in Polonia et in Moscoviae Turciae (illustration shows Covens & Mortier re-issue c1730)
mwsc0281	scandinavia denmark	1660	ALLARD	650	44	52	Selandiae in Regno Daniae Insulae Chorographica Descriptio
mwit0349	italy emilia-romagna	1700	ALLARD	500	50	60	Status et Ducatus Mediolanensis et Parmensis
mwe1014	europe rhine	1700	ALLARD	1200	52	62	Superioris et Inferioris Rheni
mwg0062	germany	1660	ALLARD	650	47	55	Tabula Germaniae Emendata Recens
mwsc0095	scandinavia	1700	ALLARD	850	45	57	Tabula Regnorum Sveciae et Norvegiae
mwbh0533	belgium holland	1708	ALLARD	2000	46	56	Tabula Roterodami Novissima
mwru0437	russia tartary	1690	ALLARD	650	51	60	Tartaria sive Magni Chami Imperium
mwuss1078	new york	1674	ALLARD	20000	46	51	Totius Neobelgii Nova et Accuratissima Tabula (first state of Restitutio view of New York)
mwe0998	europe rhine	1660	ALLARD	750	46	51	Totius Rheni Albeius ... Novissima Descriptio
mwit1230	italy venice	1700	ALLARD	350	16	21	Venetia ...
mwsp0214	spain	1700	ALLARD	675	49	57	Weg-Wyzer der Legertogten in Spanje en Portugaal
mwuss1563	vermont	1798	ALLEN	1200	44	53	A Map of the State of Vermont
mwc0292	china	1847	ALLEN	960	126	95	Chart to the Coast of China from the Canton River, to the Yang Tze Keang
mwf0541	france corsica	1800	ALLEZARD	200	13	19	Golfe et Rade de Ajaccio
mwf0542	france corsica	1800	ALLEZARD	500	13	19	Plan de la Baye de Calvi sur l'Isle de Corse
mwuss0806	massachusetts	1775	ALMON	750	19	25	Map of the Environs of Boston, Drawn at Boston in June 1775
mwsp0587	spain regions	1780	AMBROSI	3000	34	48	Barcellona (view)
mwsp0588	spain regions	1780	AMBROSI	2000	33	48	Sevilla (view)
mwbp0470a	poland	1760	AMBROSI	1000	17	28	Warsovia (view)
mwuss0147	california	1866	AMERICAN LITHO. CO.	400	33	39	Railroad Map of the City of San Francisco California 1866
mwaa0181	arctic / antarctic	1564	AMMAN	20000	30	20	Globus Terrestris
mwme0428	holy land	1845	ANDERSON	750	117	168	Map of the Countries Mentioned in the Holy Scriptures
mwuss1299	ohio	1829	ANDERSON	2000	37	32	Ohio. Corrected and Improved from the Best Authorities
mwuk1675	north sea	1785	ANDREWS	180	17	27	A Chart of the German Ocean, or North Sea
mwuk1227a	england london	1772	ANDREWS	875	39	67	A New and Accurate Plan of the Cities of London and Westminster, including the New Roads & New Buildings
mwp0023a	australia	1787	ANDREWS	3000	36	36	A New Chart of New Holland on which are delineated New South Wales, and a plan of Botany Bay

AMPG REFERENCE	REGION	DATE	MAP MAKER	PRICE (UK£)	VERT. (cm.)	HOR. (cm.)	TITLE OF MAP (Comments by the editor in brackets)
mwuk1022	england	1785	ANDREWS	1000	159	130	A New Physical, Historical & Political Map of England & Wales from Actual Surveys & Astronomical Observations of the Royal Society
mwec0555	uk england hertfordshire	1766	ANDREWS	750	43	57	A Plan of Hartford
mwuk1224	england london	1771	ANDREWS	600	17	36	A Plan of the Cities of London and Westminster …
mwbh0722	belgium holland	1771	ANDREWS	180	18	26	A Plan of the City of Amsterdam
mwg0392	bavaria	1776	ANDREWS	200	17	22	A Plan of the City of Augsburg
mwas0663	asia south east java	1774	ANDREWS	140	17	23	A Plan of the City of Batavia
mwsam0531	south america colombia	1772	ANDREWS	300	18	23	A Plan of the City of Carthagena
mwit0447	italy liguria	1776	ANDREWS	200	19	26	A plan of the City of Genoa
mwg0668	saxony	1776	ANDREWS	200	18	27	A Plan of the City of Hanover
mwjk0157	japan tokyo	1771	ANDREWS	400	17	16	A Plan of the City of Jedo
mwsam0775	south america peru	1772	ANDREWS	180	17	24	A Plan of the City of Lima
mwru0392a	russia moscow	1771	ANDREWS	375	18	25	A Plan of the City of Moscow
mwit1069	italy naples	1776	ANDREWS	200	17	26	A plan of the City of Naples
mwru0245a	russia	1771	ANDREWS	320	18	27	A Plan of the City of St. Petersburg
mwca0528	canada quebec	1771	ANDREWS	300	18	24	A Plan of the City of Quebec
mwas0838	asia south east siam	1771	ANDREWS	400	14	23	A Plan of the City of Siam or Juthia
mwuk1243	england london	1782	ANDREWS	650	58	61	Andrew's new and accurate map of the country thirty miles round London
mwuk0215	ireland	1781	ANDREWS	675	76	54	Andrew's New and Accurate Travelling Map, of the Kingdom of Ireland
mwca0649	canada st lawrence	1852	ANDREWS	500	89	191	Map of the Basin of the St. Lawrence Showing also the Natural and Artificial Routes between the Atlantic Ocean and the Interior of North America
mwam1268	america north (east)	1853	ANDREWS	500	67	117	Map of the Eastern Portion of British North America Including Gulf of St. Lawrence, and Part of New England States Compiled from the Latest Surveys and Charts by Henry F. Perley
mwuss0489	florida	1852	ANDREWS	400	67	87	Map of the Straits of Florida and Gulf of Mexico
mwme1022	turkey etc	1771	ANDREWS	200	17	25	Plan of the City of Constantinople
mwuk1509	uk english channel (all)	1785	ANDREWS	180	18	30	The British Channel Including the Coasts of England and France
mwas0510	asia south east	1785	ANDREWS	180	18	29	The East Indies, Distinguishing the Empires and Kingdoms on the Continent Commonly Called India
mwuk1234	england london	1777	ANDREWS & DURY	250	50	67	A Map of the Country Sixty Five Miles round London; from Actual Survey, by John Andrews and Andrew Dury
mwuk1233	england london	1776	ANDREWS & DURY	550	103	126	A New Travelling Map of the Country round London
mwec1255	uk england wiltshire	1773	ANDREWS & DURY	3000	270	180	A Topographical Map of Wiltshire on a Scale of 2 Inches to a Mile from an Actual Survey, by John Andrews and Andrew Dury
			SEE ALSO UNDER 'DURY'				
mwsam0163	south america	1849	ANDRIVEAU-GOUJON	280	94	66	Amerique du Sud
mwam0675	america north	1832	ANDRIVEAU-GOUJON	150	50	38	Carte de l'Amerique du Nord
mwsam0155	south america	1837	ANDRIVEAU-GOUJON	180	50	38	Carte de l'Amerique du Sud
mwam0746	america north	1841	ANDRIVEAU-GOUJON	200	38	51	Carte des Etats-Unis d'Amerique Comprenant une Partie des Districts de l'Ouest et de la Nouvelle Bretagne
mwaf0565	africa egypt etc	1845	ANDRIVEAU-GOUJON	100	50	38	Carte du Cours du Nil
mwas0545	asia south east	1837	ANDRIVEAU-GOUJON	150	38	51	Carte Generale des Indes Orientales Indiquant les Possessions Anglaises
mwf0196	france	1834	ANDRIVEAU-GOUJON	150	60	74	Carte Generale des Routes de France a l'Usage des Voyageurs
mwit0251	italy	1850	ANDRIVEAU-GOUJON	300	121	96	Carte Physique et Routiere de l'Italie Indiquant les Distances d'un Relais a l'Autre
mwit0249	italy	1846	ANDRIVEAU-GOUJON	400	82	60	Esquisse d'une Carte Geologique d'Italie
mww0708	world	1836	ANDRIVEAU-GOUJON	2000	89	137	Mappemonde en Deux Hemispheres
mwf0926	france paris	1838	ANDRIVEAU-GOUJON	400	59	88	Nouveau Plan Itineraire de la Ville de Paris
mwf0933	france paris	1845	ANDRIVEAU-GOUJON	600	66	86	Plan de Paris Fortifie, 1845
mwf0938	france paris	1850	ANDRIVEAU-GOUJON	1200	100	132	Plan Geometral de la Ville de Paris. Par X. Girard. Geographe des Postes
mwuss0875	massachusetts	1833	ANDRUS & JUDD	500	43	52	The States of Massachusetts, Connecticut and Rhode Island from the Best Authorities
mwsc0390	scandinavia denmark	1805	ANGELO	750	57	81	Kort over Tonder og Lugumcloster Amter Samt Deele af Haderslebhuus Apenrade Flensborg og Bredsted Amter Udi Hertzgdommet Schleswig
mww0131	world	1628	ANGELOCRATOR	4500	28	54	Novum Orbis Terrarum Schema, in Plano sic Descriptum … ad Inventum Daniele Angelocratore
mwe0381	europe austria	1774	ANICH & HUEBER	2950	220	210	Tyrolis Sub Felice Regimine Mariae Theresiae
mwuss0871	massachusetts	1832	ANNIN & SMITH	400	46	64	Map of Bridgewater, Mass.
mwam0633	america north	1823	ANNIN & SMITH	240	26	43	United States
mwjk0122	japan	1793	ANON	1000	47	35	(Guide to the Capital, Kyoto, in Japanese)
mwc0227a	china	1799?	ANON	40000	97	121	(Plan of Beijing in 4 woodcut sheets, in Chinese script)
mwru0403b	russia moscow	1813	ANON	1800	39	48	(Plan of the City of Moscow, Cyrillic. Shows the extent of the fire)
mwsc0441	scandinavia finland	1788	ANON	2000	66	73	(Title in Russian script. Sveaborg. Environs and view of Helsinki. Produced by Naval Academy, St. Petersburg?)

AMPG REFERENCE	REGION	DATE	MAP MAKER	PRICE (UK£)	VERT. (cm.)	HOR. (cm.)	TITLE OF MAP (Comments by the editor in brackets)
mwru0408a	russia moscow	1838	ANON	12000	72	69	(Topographical Plan of Moscow, in Cyrillic script. In 16 sheets, each 72x69cm)
mww0009	world	1485	ANON		18		(Untitled circular map, the most advanced geographically for its time, with a roughly correct south-western Africa, which includes the supposed source of the Nile. But it still represents the earth as a flat disc.)
mwsc0463b	scandinavia greenland	1744	ANON	200	20	28	(Untitled map from Churchill's Voyages)
mwuk1130	england london	1690	ANON	4500	49	60	(Untitled map. Howgego 39).
mwuk1440	england thames	1780	ANON	1800	41	61	A Map of the Thames from Osney Lock to Teddington Lock (in 25 sheets, bound)
mwin0253	india	1775	ANON	250	26	34	A Plan of the Town & Fortress of Garlah … on the coast of Mallabar
mwe1065b	europe serbia	1719	ANON	350	28	37	Accurate Situation, und Marches der Kaijl: Armee wie solche 1717, den 9. Junij nacher Bellgrad marchiret
mwaf0343	africa	1850	ANON	150	20	18	Africa (anthropomorphic map)
mwme0736a	iraq etc	1680	ANON	400	29	35	Bagdad
mwbp0106a	baltic states	1701	ANON	300	38	26	Carte du cours de la Duna, de la descente glorieuse de Charles XII, et de la Victoire remportée sur les Saxons le 9 Juillet 1701
mwf0689a	france nord pas-de-calais	1558	ANON	1500	26	35	Chales (Calais)
mwaf0846a	africa north west	1810	ANON	320	30	41	Charte von Nord - Africa. Nach den neusten Entdeckungen. Prag 1810
mwbh0225	belgium holland	1630	ANON		46	55	Comitatus Hollandia (illustrated is 1680 edition)
mwme0996a	turkey etc	1720	ANON	1000	31	37	Constantinopel
mwc0237	china	1810	ANON	40000	132	223	Da Qing Wannian Yitong Dili Quantu
mwe1072b	europe serbia	1739	ANON	1500	61	41	Descrizione Della Fortezza, e Citta di Belgrado (2 views and plan on one sheet)
mwe1164	europe south east	1790	ANON	1000	35	46	Die Graenzen Oesterreichs, Russlands, und der Turkey
mwaf0629a	africa islands mauritius	1745	ANON	200	17	22	Die Insel Moritz, nachher Isle de France oder die Insel Frankreich genannt
mwe1062	europe serbia	1700	ANON	400	34	42	Eigentliche Entwurf der Weltberuhmtem Stadt und Vestung Belgrad
mwgr0100	greece	1686	ANON	5000	42	33	Eigentlicher Entwurss des Heutigen Griechenlandes. Insonderheit Moreae oder Peloponnesi, sambt seinen Vestungen und Jetzigen Progressien der Venetianer Daselbst Anno 1686
mwaf0191	africa	1750	ANON	1200	48	58	El Africa dividida en todos (publ. in London. See also under 'World maps')
mwas0162	asia continent	1750	ANON	1200	48	55	El Asia con Toda la Extension de sus Reinos y Provincias segun las Ultimas y Nuevas Observationes de las Accademias y de Paris, y de Londres. En Londres (See 'World Maps')
mwaf0568a	africa islands bourbon	1661	ANON	450	18	21	l'Isle de Bourbon Anciennement dicte Isle de Mascaregne
mwit0022	italy	1554	ANON	15000	41	57	Italia Nuova.
mwbh0886	luxembourg	1840	ANON	400	31	24	Kaart van het Groot Hertogdom Luxemburg
mwsc0654a	scandinavia norway	1852	ANON	2500	49	57	Kart over Christiania Byes ældre Deel og de Indtil bestemte Gadeanlæg i de nyere Dele, især med Hensyn til disse Gaders Navne. 1852
mwsp0671a	balearic islands	1760	ANON	800	38	29	L'Isola di Minorca / Pianta Del Porto, F Della Città Di Maone (2 maps on one sheet)
mwam0165	america continent	1750	ANON	1350	46	51	La America Dispuesta segun las Ultimas, y Nuevas Observationes de las Accademias (publ. in London. See also under 'World maps')
mwaf0543a	africa egypt etc	1808	ANON	200	18	20	Landungen der Franzosen im Jahr 1798 und der Engländer 1801, in der Nähe von Alxandria vor der Belagerung dieser Stadt - Débarquement des Francais l'an 1798 et des Anglais 1801, prés d'Alexandrie et avant le Siège de cette ville.
mww0692	world	1830	ANON	2500	51	77	Le Monde ou Panorama Geographique du Monde … apres Mr. De Humbold (a central half-globe with a fictitious land mass gives technical terms)
mwit0821b	italy sardinia	1795	ANON	300	10	7	L'Isola di Sardegna Divisa ne' suoi Distretti
mww0411	world	1750	ANON	2000	45	53	Mapa Mundi o Descripcion del Globo Terrestre … en Londres (publ. in London, possibly engraved by E. Bowen. Based on a map by Pedro Gendron c1670)
mww0662a	world	1820	ANON	480	26	40	MappeMonde Revue et Corrigee
mwec0621	uk england kent	1719	ANON	150	40	35	Mappa Thaneti Insule (based on a medieval mss, in Harris' History of Kent)
mwit1052a	italy naples	1600	ANON	250	12	18	Mare Puteolanum (shown above left)
mwwi0663a	hispaniola	1792	ANON	750	32	37	Neue Karte der Insel San Domingo in West-Indien (engr. By J. Lange. Title above map)

AMPG REFERENCE	REGION	DATE	MAP MAKER	PRICE (UK£)	VERT. (cm.)	HOR. (cm.)	TITLE OF MAP (Comments by the editor in brackets)
mwru0563a	ukraine	1788	ANON	750	40	62	Neue Karte von den gegenwärtigen Kriegs-Schauplatze zwischen den Kaiserl. Königl. oder Österreichischen, Russisch Kayserl. und Türkischen Armeén, welche vorzüglich den grösten Theil der Europäischen Türkey, die Krim... Dalmatien, Ungarn
mwam0413	america north	1755	ANON	1200	19	24	North America (image courtesy Altea Gallery)
mwf1171a	france lyon	1789	ANON	450	45	42	Nouveau Plan Géométral de la Ville de Lyon
mwf0760a	france nord pas-de-calais	1786	ANON	1200	56	85	Plan de Dieppe avec le projet général des ouvrages... approuvé en Mars 1786
mwf0760b	france nord pas-de-calais	1787	ANON	1000	31	44	Plan de l'Agrandissement de la Ville du Havre et de l'amélioration de son port. Ces ouvrages ont été commencés le 3 mai 1787 (title above map and continued below map)
mwbh0842a	luxembourg	1690	ANON	300	22	29	Plan de la Ville de Luxembourg Assiegee
mwf0760a	france nord pas-de-calais	1784	ANON	850	55	77	Plan de Lille de la Citadelle et Banlieue de la Ville et de ses environs
mwru0300	russia	1792	ANON	1600	58	93	Plan der Haupstadt St. Petersburg
mwe1078	europe serbia	1790	ANON	720	26	40	Plan von Belgrad und Pantschoura ... (publ. by the Beyreuth Comptoir. Size does not include 5 insets below map, printed from a separate plate)
mwru0401	russia moscow	1808	ANON	720	60	47	Plan von Moskwa Prag 1808
mwbp0553	poland	1810	ANON	600	52	58	Polens Auflosung durch Dreymalige Theilung 1773-1796
mwf0965a	france poitou	1630	ANON	875	49	34	Portraict de La Rochelle (shows the siege)
mwe0429b	europe austria vienna	1750	ANON	720	39	48	Prospect der Kaijserl. Königl. Haupt=und Residenz=Stadt Wien, und ihrer Vorstädten
mwsc0605a	scandinavia norway	1716	ANON	500	33	40	Regni Norvegiae Nova et Accurata descriptio
mwbp0479	poland	1770	ANON		172	203	Regni Poloniae, Magni Ducatus Lithuaniae ... dedicata a Joanne Jacobo Kanter (in 16 sheets, joined)
mwit0756a	italy rome	1790	ANON	500	19	36	Roma (view. Text in German)
mwm0252a	mediterranean malta	1798	ANON		50	70	Situation de l'Isle de Malte a L'egard du Ciel
mwf0245a	france alsace	1750	ANON	350	20	33	Strasburg (view)
mww0181a	world	1664	ANON	600	24	33	Tabula Geographico-Horologica Universalis
mwe1061a	europe serbia	1690	ANON	500	31	42	Veduta di Belgrado
mwaf0326	africa	1838	ANSART	150	33	45	Afrique avec ses divisions
mwas0772	asia south east philippines	1748	ANSON	800	70	54	A Chart of the Channel in the Phillipine Islands through which the Manila Galeon Passes together with the Adjacent Islands
mwp0405a	pacific (north)	1748	ANSON	240	27	88	A Chart of the Pacific Ocean from the Equinoctial to the Latitude of 39 1/2 D No.
mwsam0682a	south america magellan	1748	ANSON	400	50	48	A Chart of the Southern Part of South America; with the Track of the Centurion
mww0400	world	1748	ANSON	600	23	41	A Chart Shewing the Track of the Centurion round the World
mwsam0482	south america juan fernandez	1748	ANSON	250	24	50	A Plan of Juan Fernandes Island in the South Seas in Lat. of 33 D 40' S.
mwas0773	asia south east philippines	1748	ANSON	250	20	25	A Plan of the Bay of Manilla
mwgm0209	mexico	1748	ANSON	150	22	49	A Plan of the East End of the Island of Quibo
mwgm0210	mexico	1748	ANSON	150	25	49	A Plan of the Harbour of Chequetan or Seguataneo
mwas0778	asia south east philippines	1750	ANSON	650	54	43	Carte du Canal des Iles Philippines par lequel Passe le Galion de Manille et les Iles Voisines de ce Canal (illustrated is De Pretot's re-issue of 1787)
mwuss0735	maine	1843	ANSON	850	59	36	Map of Maine, constructed from the Most Correct Surveys
mwas0773	asia south east philippines	1751	ANSON	650	20	38	Plan du Port d'Acapulco - Plan de la Baye de Manille
mwsam0459	south america chile	1748	ANSON	150	27	35	Plan of a Bay and Harbour on the Coast of Chile ... 1741
mwuss1473	rhode isl	1823	ANTHONY	2000	58	86	Map of the Town of Providence from Actual Survey by Daniel Anthony 1823
mwp0271	pacific (all)	1802	ANTILLON	1500	46	57	Carta Esferica del Grande Oceano: con un Analisis en que se Manifiestan los Fundamentos Sobre que se ha Construido
mwam0555	america north	1802	ANTILLON	2500	59	70	La America Septentrional
mwgm0367	mexico	1849	ANTOINE	100	22	29	Mexique
mwam0294	america continent	1834	ANTONELLI	200	46	35	Carta dell America
mwgr0010	greece	1524	APIAN	1200	9	10	(Untitled map of Greece, naming Corfu and Crete. 16 editions until 1589)
mww0039	world	1544	APIAN	6000	19	28	Carte Cosmographicque, ou Universelle Description du Monde, avecq les Ventz (size excl. text borders)
mww0072	world	1583	APIAN	3500	19	28	Charta Cosmographica, Cum Ventorum Propria Natura Et Operatione (one of several re-issues of Apian's 1553 map)
mww0045	world	1553	APIAN	5000	19	28	Charta Cosmographica, cum Ventorum Propria Natura et Operatione (size excl. text borders)
mww0026	world	1520	APIAN	60000	30	43	Tipus Orbis Universalis iuxta Ptolemei Cosmographi Traditionem et Americi Vespucii Aliorque Lustrationes a Petro Apiano Leysnico Elucbrat An. Do. MDXX
mwp0146	australia	1843	ARAGON	1500	18	38	Mapa de la Ciudad de Sydney en 1840
mwam0757	america north	1843	ARCHER	100	23	28	British and Russian America. Drawn & Engraved by J. Archer

AMPG REFERENCE	REGION	DATE	MAP MAKER	PRICE (UK£)	VERT. (cm.)	HOR. (cm.)	TITLE OF MAP (Comments by the editor in brackets)
mwca0191	canada	1842	ARCHER	75	23	29	Canada, New Brunswick, Nova Scotia, etc.
mwuk1889	wales	1850	ARCHER	30	18	23	Cardiganshire
mwwi0387	barbados	1842	ARCHER	200	27	21	Diocese of Barbados
mwwi0758	jamaica	1842	ARCHER	100	22	27	Diocese of Jamaica
mwaa0173	arctic	1834	ARCHER	120	15	23	Map of the Polar Regions, Shewing All Discoveries Made by British Officers, Ross, Parry & Scoresby to 1833
mwuss1514	texas	1841	ARCHER	200	23	28	Mexico & Texas
mwgm0339	mexico	1842	ARCHER	100	23	29	Mexico. Drawn & Engraved by J. Archer
mwuk1314	england london	1833	ARCHER	850	34	51	New Plan of London
mwsam0158	south america	1842	ARCHER	50	28	23	South America. Drawn & Engraved by J. Archer
mwam0729	america north	1840	ARCHER	100	28	23	United States
mwwi0201	west indies	1838	ARCHER	80	23	28	West Indies, Guatimala, etc. Drawn & Engraved by J. Archer
mwme0041	holy land	1572	ARIAS MONTANUS	2500	34	52	Tabula Terrae Canaan
mwme0042	holy land	1572	ARIAS MONTANUS	2500	34	50	Terrae Israel Omnis ante Canaan
mwit0458a	italy liguria	1846	ARMANINO	720	80	71	Genova Massa in Pianta Topgrafica
mwec0752	uk england lincolnshire	1779	ARMSTRONG	1600	51	74	A Map of Lincoln-Shire, Comprehending Lindsay, Kesteven & Holland, Surveyed in the Years 1776, 7, &8, by Capt. Andrew Armstrong (map in 8 sheets, each 51x74cm.)
mwuk0516	scotland	1771	ARMSTRONG	1600	74	105	A Map of the County of Berwick Taken from an Actual Survey and Laid Down from a Scale of an Inch to a Mile
mwec0891	uk england northumberland	1769	ARMSTRONG	2000	61	47	A Map of the County of Northumberland with that Part of the County of Durham that is North of the River Tyne, also the Town of Berwick Taken from an Actual Survey ... Engraved by Thos. Kitchin Geog. 1769 (map in 9 sheets, each 61x47cm.)
mwec0378	uk england durham	1768	ARMSTRONG	1800	95	124	The County Palatine of Durham ... engraved by Thomas Jefferys
mwuk0517	scotland	1773	ARMSTRONG	1500	43	51	To the Nobility, Gentry & Clergy ... this Map of the Three Lothians (map in 6 sheets, each 43x51cm.)
mwuk0521	scotland	1775	ARMSTRONG	960	83	65	To the Right Honourable William Douglas, Earl of March and Ruglen ... this Map of the County of Peebles, or Tweedale is Most Humbly Inscribed
mwuk0546	scotland	1787	ARMSTRONG-SAYER	1600	128	109	A New Map of Scotland or North Britain
mwp0113	australia	1836	ARROWSMITH	2500	33	43	(Port Phillip)
mwam1138	america north (east)	1800	ARROWSMITH	3000	51	79	A Chart of Part of North America, from Cape Hatteras to Cape Canso (map in 2 sheets)
mwsam0568	south america galapagos	1798	ARROWSMITH	1200	76	57	A Chart of the Galapagos Surveyed in the Merchant Ship Rattler, and Drawn by Capt: James Colnett, of the Royal Navy in 1793 1794
mww0564	world	1790	ARROWSMITH	1800	74	120	A Chart of the World on Mercator's Projection, Exhibiting All the New Discoveries to the Present Time with the Tracks of the Most Distinguished Navigators since the Year 1700
mww0563a	world	1790	ARROWSMITH	20000	133	210	A Chart of the World upon Mercator's Projection, Exhibiting All the New Discoveries to the Present Time: with the Tracks of the Most Distinguished Navigators since the Year 1700
mwca0122	canada	1796	ARROWSMITH	15000	91	169	A Map Exhibiting All the New Discoveries in the Interior Parts of North America. Inscribed by Permission to the Honorable Governor and Company of Adventurers of England Trading into Hudsons Bay (1st edition 1795. The 5th issue, 1802, is 125x146cm and valued at £40000)
mwaf0542	africa egypt etc	1807	ARROWSMITH	680	121	155	A Map of Lower Egypt
mwsam0247	south america argentina	1806	ARROWSMITH	2200	100	54	A Map of Part of the Viceroyalty of Buenos Ayres 1806.
mwme1041	turkey etc	1801	ARROWSMITH	4200	127	159	A Map of the Environs of Constantinople
mwam1118a	america north (east)	1796	ARROWSMITH	14000	122	140	A Map of the United States of North America Drawn from a Number of Critical Researches
mwaf0543	africa egypt etc	1807	ARROWSMITH	680	97	66	A Map of Upper Egypt
mwgr0236	greece	1799	ARROWSMITH	1500	80	129	A new chart of the Greek Islands and adjacent Coasts
mwgm0271	mexico	1810	ARROWSMITH	15000	128	158	A New Map of Mexico and Adjacent Provinces Compiled from Original Documents
mwam0513	america north	1791	ARROWSMITH	200	20	24	A New Map of North America Shewing All the New Discoveries, 1791
mwuk0639a	scotland	1846	ARROWSMITH	900	181	143	A Skeleton Map of Scotland (map by J. Basire)
mwme0393a	holy land	1815	ARROWSMITH	2000	133	66	A Sketch of the Countries between Jerusalem and Aleppo. By A. Arrowsmith 1814.
mwp0134	australia	1841	ARROWSMITH	900	62	49	A Trigonometrical Survey of the Country at Moreton Bay
mwaf0323	africa	1834	ARROWSMITH	350	61	49	Africa
mwaf0296	africa	1807	ARROWSMITH	200	25	32	Africa
mwam0299	america continent	1840	ARROWSMITH	350	64	53	America. London, Pubd. 15 Feby. 1840
mwas0232	asia continent	1801	ARROWSMITH	2350	122	142	Asia
mwas0249	asia continent	1832	ARROWSMITH	280	48	59	Asia
mwas0540	asia south east	1832	ARROWSMITH	400	48	60	Asiatic Archipelago
mwsam0432	south america brazil	1842	ARROWSMITH	450	60	47	Brazil

AMPG REFERENCE	REGION	DATE	MAP MAKER	PRICE (UK£)	VERT. (cm.)	HOR. (cm.)	TITLE OF MAP (Comments by the editor in brackets)
mwuk0582	scotland	1817	ARROWSMITH	100	20	25	British Isles: Orkney and Shetland; Channel Islands; Scilly Islands
mwca0186	canada	1840	ARROWSMITH	950	47	60	British North America. By Permission Dedicated to the Honble. Hudsons Bay Company
mwas0854	asia south east siam	1842	ARROWSMITH	450	61	48	Burmah, Siam and Cochin China
mwme0394	holy land	1817	ARROWSMITH	100	25	20	Canaan, Illustrating the Books of Joshua
mwca0146	canada	1823	ARROWSMITH	150	20	25	Canada
mwaf1022	africa south	1842	ARROWSMITH	400	46	61	Cape of Good Hope
mwaf0990	africa south	1807	ARROWSMITH	240	25	39	Cape of Good Hope
mwaf1000	africa south	1820	ARROWSMITH	100	21	25	Cape of Good Hope
mwaf1015	africa south	1836	ARROWSMITH	550	50	60	Cape of Good Hope (size excl. right-hand margin extension to Delagoa Bay pasted on by publisher)
mwc0231	china	1802	ARROWSMITH	200	25	40	Central Asia
mwin0358	india	1834	ARROWSMITH	450	48	72	Central Asia Comprising Bokhara, Cabool, Persia, the River Indus and Countries Eastward of it
mwin0499	pakistan etc.	1834	ARROWSMITH	300	49	73	Central Asia: Comprising Bokhara, Cabool, Persia
mwme0852	persia etc	1834	ARROWSMITH	300	49	73	Central Asia: Comprising Bokhara, Cabool, Persia
mwin0071	ceylon	1817	ARROWSMITH	200	25	20	Ceylon
mwp0135	australia	1841	ARROWSMITH	200	36	29	Chart of Forestiers and Tasmans Peninsulas
mwam1347	america north (west)	1805	ARROWSMITH	1200	52	43	Chart of Pulo Penang, now Prince of Wales's Island: Compiled from Various Surveys (today, part of Alaska)
mwsam0404	south america brazil	1809	ARROWSMITH	650	79	65	Chart of the Coast of Brazil, from Cape St. Roque to C. Castellanos
mwaf0530	africa egypt etc	1798	ARROWSMITH	900	48	70	Chart of the Coast of Egypt, from Alexandria to the Western Branch of the Nile; with the Bay of Abou-kir Shewing the Position of the French and English Fleets, at the Battle of the Nile, August 1st 1798
mwsam0644	south america guyana	1809	ARROWSMITH	850	64	98	Chart of the Coast of Guyana from Cayenne to Essequebo
mwas0535	asia south east	1824	ARROWSMITH	3000	132	194	Chart of the East India Islands, Exhibiting the Several Passages between the Indian and Pacific Oceans
mwp0268	pacific (all)	1798	ARROWSMITH	15000	68	87	Chart of the Pacific Ocean Drawn from a Great Number of Printed and MS. Journals (9 sheets, each 68x87cm. 1st edition)
mwsam0403	south america brazil	1806	ARROWSMITH	100	12	20	Chart of the Rio de la Plata. Drawn and Engraved by Arrowsmith. London Published Octr. 31st, 1806, by J. Gold, Shoe Lane, Fleet Street
mwwi0150	west indies	1803	ARROWSMITH	6000	123	190	Chart of the West Indies and Spanish Dominions in North America. By A. Arrowsmith. 1803 (re-issued smaller in 1810, 121x141cm)
mwaf1261	africa west	1849	ARROWSMITH	1200	105	130	Chart Prepared with a View to Shew the Present State of the Slave Trade on the West Coast of Africa
mwin0067	ceylon	1803	ARROWSMITH	150	33	21	Charte von Ceylon. Nach A. Arrowsmith
mwc0263	china	1832	ARROWSMITH	350	48	60	China
mwsam0552	south america colombia	1834	ARROWSMITH	375	48	61	Colombia, Dedicated to Colonel Belford Hinton Wilson, Late Aid de Camp to the Liberator Simon Bolivar
mwgm0443	panama	1825	ARROWSMITH	150	23	30	Darien
mwsc0403	scandinavia denmark	1840	ARROWSMITH	250	60	48	Denmark
mwaf0345	africa	1857	ARROWSMITH	350	29	64	Detailed Map of the Revd. Dr. Livingstone's Route across Africa
mwp0103	australia	1833	ARROWSMITH	2400	50	60	Discoveries in Western Australia from the Documents Furnished to the Colonial Office by J.S. Roe
mwas0532	asia south east	1817	ARROWSMITH	100	20	25	East Indies Islands
mwaf1028	africa south	1848	ARROWSMITH	500	49	59	Eastern Frontier of the Colony of the Cape of Good Hope, (and Part of Kaffirland) from Algoa Bay to the Great Kei River
mwaf0557	africa egypt etc	1828	ARROWSMITH	100	28	22	Egypt
mwjk0134	japan	1807	ARROWSMITH	350	25	40	Empire of Japan
mwe0267	europe	1832	ARROWSMITH	300	48	60	Europe
mwgr0255	greece	1832	ARROWSMITH	250	61	48	Greece and the Ionian Islands
mww0646b	world	1814	ARROWSMITH	8000	153	259	Hydrographical Chart of the World: According to Wrights, or Mercators Projection Delineated by A. Arrowsmith 1811... Additions to 1814
mwin0357	india	1832	ARROWSMITH	350	60	48	India
mwuk0250	ireland	1811	ARROWSMITH	2000	182	142	Ireland
mwuk0282	ireland	1842	ARROWSMITH	350	60	47	Ireland
mwuk0241	ireland	1798	ARROWSMITH	150	39	24	Ireland
mwme0395	holy land	1817	ARROWSMITH	100	25	20	Judah & Israel: Illustrating the Books of Kings
mwca0174	canada	1834	ARROWSMITH	350	61	48	Lower Canada, New Brunswick, Nova Scotia, Prince Edwards Id., Newfoundland, and a Large Portion of the United States
mwam0252	america continent	1804	ARROWSMITH	2500	120	144	Map of America
mwam0279	america continent	1822	ARROWSMITH	30000	198	163	Map of America By A. Arrowsmith Hydrographer to His Majesty 1822.
mwme1061	turkey etc	1834	ARROWSMITH	350	50	50	Map of Asia Minor
mwme1063	turkey etc	1837	ARROWSMITH	400	49	64	Map of Asia Minor to Illustrate the Journeys of W. I. Hamilton Esq.

AMPG REFERENCE	REGION	DATE	MAP MAKER	PRICE (UK£)	VERT. (cm.)	HOR. (cm.)	TITLE OF MAP (Comments by the editor in brackets)
mwsam0650	south america guyana	1842	ARROWSMITH	250	41	46	Map of British Guiana from the Latest Surveys ... Shewing the Parochial Divisions as Well as the Present Extent of Cultivation of the Staple Productions; & the Tracts of Such that Have Been Abandoned within the Last 30 Yrs.
mwaf0547	africa egypt etc	1818	ARROWSMITH	540	126	76	Map of Egypt
mwuk1100	england and scotland	1848	ARROWSMITH	300	104	66	Map of England and Scotland, Shewing the Amalgamation of Railways, Returned to Orders of the House of Commons
mwe0231	europe	1798	ARROWSMITH	2400	123	145	Map of Europe
mwgm0109	guatemala	1820	ARROWSMITH	1800	66	81	Map of Guatemala Reduced from the Survey in the Archives of that Country / Chart of the Isthmus of Darien, Principally Copied from the Spanish Charts (2 maps)
mwwi0759	jamaica	1842	ARROWSMITH	360	33	61	Map of Jamaica Compiled Chiefly from Manuscripts in the Colonial Office and Admiralty
mwuss0616	kentucky	1839	ARROWSMITH	1800	97	128	Map of Kentucky & Tennessee Exhibiting the Post Offices, Post Roads, Canals, Railroads
mwp0119	australia	1837	ARROWSMITH	700	64	43	Map of New South Wales
mwuk0572	scotland	1807	ARROWSMITH	420	90	71	Map of Scotland Constructed from Original Materials Obtained under the Authority of the Parliamentary Commissioners for Making Roads and Building Bridges in the Highlands of Scotland
mwuk0579	scotland	1813	ARROWSMITH	300	58	49	Map of Scotland from Original Materials Obtained by the Parliamentary Commissioners
mwit1044	italy south	1807	ARROWSMITH	1500	131	164	Map of South Italy and Adjacent Coasts
mwme0889	syria etc	1823	ARROWSMITH	1500	83	135	Map of Syria ... 1818, by Captn. Armar L. Corry R.N.
mwuss1514a	texas	1843	ARROWSMITH	15000	60	51	Map of Texas, Compiled from Surveys Recorded in the Land Office of Texas, and other Official Surveys ... Recognized as an Independent State by Great Britain 16th Novr. 1840
mwsw0243	alps	1800	ARROWSMITH	1500	121	150	Map of the Alpine Country in the South of Europe. To Charles Viscount Newark, Baron Pierrepont of Holmepierrepont L.L.D. this Map is Respectfully Inscribed
mwwi0356	bahamas	1848	ARROWSMITH	1200	55	65	Map of the Bahama Islands from Official Documents Compiled by John Arrowsmith
mwca0153	canada	1827	ARROWSMITH	250	40	67	Map of the British Possessions in North America Compiled from Documents in the Colonial Dept.
mwp0217	new zealand	1842	ARROWSMITH	1100	61	50	Map of the Colony of New Zealand
mwme0841a	persia etc	1813	ARROWSMITH	3000	100	132	Map of the Countries lying between the Euphrates and Indus on the East and West, and the Oxus and Terek and Indian Ocean on the North and South. Inscribed to Brigadier General Sir John Malcolm Knight of the Royal Persian Order of the Lion and Sun By John Macdonald Kinneir.
mwp0106	australia	1834	ARROWSMITH	400	48	60	Map of the Discoveries in Australia Copied from the Latest M.S. Surveys in the Colonial Office, by Permission Dedicated to the Right Hon. Viscount Goderich
mwca0192	canada	1842	ARROWSMITH	1000	61	102	Map of the Eastern Townships of Lower Canada, Drawn Principally from Actual Survey for the British American Land Company by A. Wells
mwuk1054	england	1826	ARROWSMITH	1250	96	76	Map of the Hills, Rivers, Canals and Principal Roads of England and Wales
mwm0261	mediterranean malta	1844	ARROWSMITH	450	61	51	Map of the Ionian Islands and Malta Compiled from Surveys & Original Documents in the Colonial Office, the Ordnance Department &c.
mwin0069	ceylon	1805	ARROWSMITH	2000	93	61	Map of the Island of Ceylon
mwin0068	ceylon	1803	ARROWSMITH	600	53	36	Map of the Island of Ceylon, Reduced from a Drawing in the Possession of the Right Honorable the Commissioners for the Affairs of India
mwjk0136a	japan	1811	ARROWSMITH	5000	133	174	Map of the Island of Japan, Kurile &c. with the Adjacent Coasts of the Chinese Dominions and a Sketch of the River Amoor and the Baikal Lake Including the Trading Posts of Russia and China and their relative situations with Peking.
mwwi0273	west indies (east)	1839	ARROWSMITH	350	46	58	Map of the Leeward Islands Comprising Antigua, Montserrat, Barbuda, St. Christopher, Nevis, Anguilla, Virgin Islands & Dominica under the Administration of Lieut. Colonel Sir. Wm. M.G. Colebrook
mwin0379	india	1849	ARROWSMITH	450	74	69	Map of the Punjab, Kashmir, Iskardu & Ladak. Comprising the Dominions of Ranjeet Singh. Compiled from Original Documents, Particularly from the Detailed MS Map of Baron Hugel
mwsp0128	portugal	1811	ARROWSMITH	850	59	132	Map of the Roads of Portugal
mwp0101	australia	1832	ARROWSMITH	300	33	42	Map of the South East Portion of Australia, Shewing the Progress of Discovery, in the Interior of New South Wales
mwp0136	australia	1841	ARROWSMITH	600	32	77	Map of the Southern Coast of Australia, from Encounter Bay to King George's Sound, Shewing Mr. Eyre's Track in the Years 1839, 1840 & 41 in his Attempt to Penetrate into the Interior
mwaf1256	africa west	1843	ARROWSMITH	400	61	51	Map of the West Coast of Africa

AMPG REFERENCE	REGION	DATE	MAP MAKER	PRICE (UK£)	VERT. (cm.)	HOR. (cm.)	TITLE OF MAP (Comments by the editor in brackets)
mwwi0274	west indies (east)	1842	ARROWSMITH	300	60	47	Map of the Windward Islands Comprising Barbados, St. Vincint, Grenada, Tobago, St. Lucia & Trinidad under the Administration of Major Genl. Sir. E.I. Murray Macgregor, Compiled Principally from Documents in the Colonial Office and Admiralty
mww0621	world	1804	ARROWSMITH	12000	100	187	Map of the World on a Globular Projection
mwp0120	australia	1837	ARROWSMITH	500	58	43	Map of Van Diemens Land
mwp0137	australia	1841	ARROWSMITH	1250	69	52	Map Shewing the Surveyed Lands at Port Phillip from the Government Surveys Made in 1840
mww0608	world	1800	ARROWSMITH	280	23	39	Mappe Monde par Arrowsmith
mwgm0341b	mexico	1842	ARROWSMITH	2250	48	60	Mexico (first publ. 1832)
mwgm0284	mexico	1817	ARROWSMITH	200	20	24	Mexico
mwec1182	uk england sussex	1847	ARROWSMITH	100	48	32	Newhaven 1846
mwam0556	america north	1802	ARROWSMITH	200	25	20	North America
mwca0157	canada	1828	ARROWSMITH	200	23	30	North America. London
mwaf0846b	africa north west	1835	ARROWSMITH	240	48	60	North Western Africa
mwru0362	russia	1842	ARROWSMITH	240	47	59	Northern Asia, from the Himilaya Mountains to the Arctic Ocean
mwca0206	canada	1848	ARROWSMITH	300	49	73	Nova Scotia, New Brunswick & Part of Canada Shewing the Explored Route for the Proposed Trunk Line of Railway from Halifax to Quebec
mwaf0432a	africa east	1842	ARROWSMITH	250	51	60	Nubia and Abyssinia
mwgr0245	greece	1819	ARROWSMITH	2500	181	199	Outlines of Greece and Adjacent Countries, with Modern and Antient Names
mwme0670	arabia etc	1816	ARROWSMITH	2000	158	287	Outlines of the Countries between Delhi and Constantinople
mwsam0131	south america	1811	ARROWSMITH	2500	200	240	Outlines of the Physical and Political Divisions of South America
mwp0281	pacific (all)	1832	ARROWSMITH	400	48	60	Pacific Ocean
mwme0678	arabia etc	1828	ARROWSMITH	100	23	30	Persia and Arabia
mwsam0790	south america peru	1820	ARROWSMITH	250	50	60	Peru & Bolivia
mwwi0389	barbados	1851	ARROWSMITH	400	40	50	Plan of Carlisle Bay, Barbados / Refuge at Bridgetown
mwp0169	australia	1848	ARROWSMITH	850	61	47	Plan of Port Curtis, by Captain Owen Stanley R.N. H.M.S. Rattlesnake. Novr. 1847
mwgm0263	mexico	1798	ARROWSMITH	300	37	52	Plan of the Anchoring Place at the Island Quibo by Capt. James Colnett, Royal Navy
mwas0621	asia south east cocos isl	1798	ARROWSMITH	350	36	50	Plan of the Island Cocos Surveyed and Drawn by Capt. James Colnett of the Royal Navy 1793
mwaf0539	africa egypt etc	1802	ARROWSMITH	600	89	42	Plan of the Operations of British & Ottoman Forces in Egypt (large inset shows the Battle of Alexandria)
mwp0269	pacific (all)	1798?	ARROWSMITH	1500	63	80	Reduced Chart of the Pacific Ocean from the one published in Nine Sheets
mwp0138	australia	1841	ARROWSMITH	2000	52	42	Route from Yass Plains by the Australian Alps and Gipps Land to Port Phillip by E.P. Strelski
mwru0363	russia	1842	ARROWSMITH	200	44	61	Russia & Poland
mwuk0627	scotland	1840	ARROWSMITH	200	60	48	Scotland
mwca0140	canada	1817	ARROWSMITH	200	29	32	Sketch of Part of the Hudson's Bay Company's Territory
mwru0364	russia	1842	ARROWSMITH	300	46	57	Sketch of the Acquisitions of Russia Since the Accession of Peter 1st
mwp0139	australia	1841	ARROWSMITH	250	33	21	Sketch of the Lower Part of the River Glenelg
mwin0344	india	1822	ARROWSMITH	500	82	63	Sketch of the Outline and Principal River of India
mwp0140	australia	1841	ARROWSMITH	600	54	40	Sketch Shewing the Relative Positions of the Lands under Survey to the Northward of Port Macquarie
mwaf0997	africa south	1815	ARROWSMITH	600	61	94	South Africa, Delineated from Various Documents (inset of Delagoa Bay, Mozambique)
mwsam0154	south america	1834	ARROWSMITH	250	60	48	South America
mwp0149	australia	1844	ARROWSMITH	800	61	50	South Australia shewing the division into Counties of the settled portions of the Province
mwca0673	canada west	1859	ARROWSMITH	400	30	37	South East Part of Vancouver Island Showing Proposed Sites for Light Houses
mwgm0435	panama	1791	ARROWSMITH	800	57	76	Survey of the Harbour of Panama by the Sloops Descubierta and Atrevida
mwsc0212	scandinavia	1832	ARROWSMITH	240	60	48	Sweden & Norway
mwme0887	syria etc	1817	ARROWSMITH	100	25	20	Syria
mwas0327	asia caspian sea	1841	ARROWSMITH	400	63	53	The Caspian Sea Khivah And The Surrounding Country
mwgm0113	guatemala	1839	ARROWSMITH	300	37	50	The Coasts of Guatemala and Mexico from Panama to Cape Mendocino, with the Principal Harbours of California
mwp0126	australia	1839	ARROWSMITH	1500	52	61	The Colony of Western Australia (illustrated is 1863 edition with added right-hand sheet. Acknowledgement to National Library of Australia).
mwin0470	indian ocean maldives	1837	ARROWSMITH	120	33	20	The Head of the Maldives from the Late Survey by Comr. Moresby I.N.
mwuk1060	england	1834	ARROWSMITH	360	62	51	The Inland Navigation, Rail Roads, Geology and Minerals of England & Wales
mwwi0913	trinidad & tobago	1842	ARROWSMITH	750	47	60	The Island of Trinidad from the Latest Surveys by Joseph Basanta

AMPG REFERENCE	REGION	DATE	MAP MAKER	PRICE (UK£)	VERT. (cm.)	HOR. (cm.)	TITLE OF MAP (Comments by the editor in brackets)
mwp0132	australia	1840	ARROWSMITH	600	50	61	The Maritime Portion of South Australia, from Captn. Flinders & from More Recent Surveys Made by the Survr. Genl. of the Colonies
mwsam0815	south america uruguay	1840	ARROWSMITH	400	62	50	The Provinces of la Plata, the Banda Oriental del Uruguay and Chile, Chiefly from M.S. Documents Communicated by Sir. Woodbine Parish
mwp0124	australia	1838	ARROWSMITH	800	52	64	The South Eastern Portion of Australia Compiled from the Colonial Surveys and from Details Furnished by Exploratory Expeditions
mwp0173	australia	1849	ARROWSMITH	300	52	46	The South Western Or Unexplored Portion of V.D. Land
mwsam0257	south america argentina	1834	ARROWSMITH	350	61	48	The United Provinces of la Plata, the Banda Oriental & Chile
mww0704	world	1835	ARROWSMITH	350	49	60	The World on Mercators Projection
mww0623	world	1805	ARROWSMITH	280	24	39	The World on Mercators Projection
mwsam0258	south america argentina	1834	ARROWSMITH	400	60	48	This Map of the United Provinces of la Plata, the Banda Oriental, & Chile
mwaf0983	africa south	1805	ARROWSMITH	2500	124	143	To Captain Carmichael Smith of the Corps of Royal Engineers who Obligingly Furnished Many of the Materials. This Chart of the Cape of Good Hope is Inscribed
mwaf0288	africa	1802	ARROWSMITH	2000	125	144	To the Committee and Members of the British Association for Discovering the Interior Parts of Africa, this Map is with their Permission Most Respectfully Inscribed
mwin0338	india	1816	ARROWSMITH	3500	192	274	To the Honble. the Court of Directors of the East India Company this Improved Map of India
mwwi0888	st lucia	1847	ARROWSMITH	400	44	32	Topographical Map of Saint Lucia Executed by Order of His Excellency Lt. Col. Reid
mwp0141	australia	1841	ARROWSMITH	450	35	45	Trigonometrical Survey of Part of the Country between Melbourne and the River Glenelg by C.J. Tyers, Survr. & T.S. Townsend Asst. Survr. Feby. 1840
mwme1058	turkey etc	1832	ARROWSMITH	400	48	60	Turkey in Asia
mwam0565	america north	1805	ARROWSMITH	350	28	43	United States
mwca0185	canada	1838	ARROWSMITH	750	63	101	Upper Canada &c., Lower Canada, New Brunswick, Nova Scotia, Prince Edwards Id., Newfoundland, and a Large Portion of the United States (left-hand sheet illustrated)
mwp0108	australia	1834	ARROWSMITH	250	61	50	Van Diemens Land ... From Surveys of the Colonial Office and the Van Diemen's Land Company Office
mwwi0172	west indies	1825	ARROWSMITH	200	24	30	W. Indies
mwwi0187	west indies	1832	ARROWSMITH	400	48	60	West Indies
mwp0145	australia	1842	ARROWSMITH	350	24	32	Western Australia, from the Government Surveys
mwam0566	america north	1806	ARROWSMITH & LEWIS	100	15	19	A Map of North America from the Latest Discoveries
mwp0521	pacific south	1819	ARROWSMITH & LEWIS	350	20	24	Australasia
mwca0134	canada	1812	ARROWSMITH & LEWIS	200	22	27	British Possessions in America
mwaf0984	africa south	1805	ARROWSMITH & LEWIS	180	20	24	Colony of the Cape of Good Hope
mwuss0304	connecticut	1804	ARROWSMITH & LEWIS	200	20	24	Connecticut
mwuss0374	delaware	1804	ARROWSMITH & LEWIS	200	25	20	Delaware
mwuss0512	georgia	1804	ARROWSMITH & LEWIS	200	22	27	Georgia
mwjk0131	japan	1804	ARROWSMITH & LEWIS	400	22	27	Japan
mwuss0600	kentucky	1804	ARROWSMITH & LEWIS	200	22	26	Kentucky
mwuss0652	louisiana	1804	ARROWSMITH & LEWIS	400	25	20	Louisiana
mwuss0711	maine	1804	ARROWSMITH & LEWIS	200	21	26	Maine
mwuss0767	maryland	1804	ARROWSMITH & LEWIS	200	21	26	Maryland
mwuss0856	massachusetts	1804	ARROWSMITH & LEWIS	200	20	25	Massachusetts
mwuss1014	new hampshire	1804	ARROWSMITH & LEWIS	200	24	20	New Hampshire
mwp0041	australia	1804	ARROWSMITH & LEWIS	600	21	25	New Holland (shows Tasmania complete but Australia incomplete
mwuss1050	new jersey	1804	ARROWSMITH & LEWIS	200	27	22	New Jersey
mwuss0254	carolinas	1804	ARROWSMITH & LEWIS	200	20	24	North Carolina
mwuss1276	ohio	1804	ARROWSMITH & LEWIS	200	26	21	Ohio
mwuss1396	pennsylvania	1804	ARROWSMITH & LEWIS	200	20	25	Pennsylvania
mwuss1465	rhode isl	1804	ARROWSMITH & LEWIS	200	20	25	Rhode Island
mwuss0253	carolinas	1804	ARROWSMITH & LEWIS	200	20	24	South Carolina
mwam0561	america north	1804	ARROWSMITH & LEWIS	200	20	25	Spanish Dominions in North America
mwuss1488	tennessee	1804	ARROWSMITH & LEWIS	200	22	27	Tennessee
mwuss1565	vermont	1804	ARROWSMITH & LEWIS	200	25	20	Vermont
mwuss1673	virginia	1804	ARROWSMITH & LEWIS	200	19	24	Virginia
mwru0345	russia	1828	ARTARIA	1600	160	120	Carte de la Partie Europeene de l'Empire de Russie, avec l'Indication des Chemins de Poste Nouvellement Revue et Corrigee d'apres la Carte du Depot Topographique Militaire a St. Petersbourg (12 sheets, joined)
mwbp0556	poland	1813	ARTARIA	1800	50	59	Carte du ci-devant Royaume de Pologne dans son Etat Actuel. Dressee d'apres les Cartes de Gilly, Liesgang, Mayer, Schroetter et Textor (in 9 sheets)
mwe0975	europe hungary	1867	ARTARIA	950	107	168	Carte Generale des Postes du Royaume de Hongrie y Compris la Transylvanie, l'Esclavonie, la Croatie ... Reduite d'apres la Grande Carte de Lipszky par E. de Zuccheri
mwe1075	europe serbia	1788	ARTARIA	500	48	68	Karte der Gegend um Belgrad

AMPG REFERENCE	REGION	DATE	MAP MAKER	PRICE (UK£)	VERT. (cm.)	HOR. (cm.)	TITLE OF MAP (Comments by the editor in brackets)
mwe0808	europe east	1769	ARTARIA	1000	50	61	Mappa Novissima Regnorum Hungariae, Croatiae, Slavoniae nec non Magni Principatus Transilvaniae Juxta Adcuratissimas Observationes, Adhibitisque Certissimis Veritatis Fontibus Descripta (in 4 sheets)
mwe0833	europe east	1790	ARTARIA	500	58	83	Neue und Volkommene Postkarte durch Ganz Teutschland nach Italien ... Polen, und Ungarn
mwg0165a	germany	1799	ARTARIA	480	61	95	Neue und Vollständigste Postkarte von ganz Deutschland, Niederlanden Schweiz Pohlen Ungarn ... Italien
mwe0433a	europe austria vienna	1808	ARTARIA	1500	62	98	Neuester Grundriss der Haupt und Residenzstadt Wien und der Umliegenden Gegenden
mwru0327	russia	1810	ARTARIA	1500	77	170	Neueste Karte des Russischen Reichs. Mit der Eintheilung in die Neu Erreichteten Statthalterschaften und Kreise (in 3 sheets)
mwbp0528	poland	1794	ARTARIA	650	49	69	Neueste Karte von Polen und Litauen samt den Oesterrichischen, Russischen und Preussischen Antheile
mwe0239	europe	1807	ARTARIA	1500	124	144	Neueste Post und General Karte von Europa mit der Neuesten Lander Abtheilung des Letzten Frieden Tractats nach Arrowsmith's Grosser Karte
mwg0169	germany	1806	ARTARIA	1000	220	205	Neueste Special Karte von Deutschland in 24 Blattern. Nach den Letzten Veranderungen ... nach Chauchards Grosser Karte
mwe0440	europe austria vienna	1832	ARTARIA	450	44	58	Neuester Plan der Haupt und Residenz Stadt Wien und dessen Vorstaedten
mwe0438	europe austria vienna	1829	ARTARIA	850	64	92	Neuester Plan der Haupt und Residenz Stadt Wien und dessen Vorstaedten, nach der Neuesten Nummerirung der Haeuser nebst Angabe der Verschoerungen mit Hochster Bewilligung nach dem Original-Plane
mwe0439	europe austria vienna	1830	ARTARIA	550	60	74	Neuester Plan Der Haupt- und Residenzstadt Wien mit Allen von seiner Majestat Allerhochst Genehmigten Verschonerungen nebst dem Glacis und Eingang in die Vorstadte
mwit1264	italy venice	1850	ARTARIA	650	50	68	Nuova Pianta della Città e Porto Franco di Venezia
mwe1074	europe serbia	1788	ARTARIA	300	24	30	Plan von Belgrad, Semlin und den Umliegenden Gegenden
mwbp0548	poland	1807	ARTARIA	500	39	53	Topographische Karte der Gegend um Warschau
mwuk1225	england london	1771	ASHBY	1200	42	69	A New Plan of London Westminster and Southwark
mwca0493	canada prince edward isl.	1798	ASHBY	800	18	35	Prince Edward Island
mwme0697	bahrain	1939	ASHRAF	500	15	11	Bahrain Is. (publ. by Ashram Bros. Bahrain)
mwaf0546	africa egypt etc	1816	ASPIN	100	18	24	Lower Egypt with Part of Canaan Arabia &c.
mwam0281	america continent	1823	ASPIN	250	34	43	North and South America for the Elucidation of the Abbe Gaultier's Geographical Games
mwca0154	canada	1827	ASPIN	250	33	43	Recent Discoveries in the Arctic Regions
mwme0405	holy land	1828	ASSHETON	960	109	73	A Historical Map of Palestine, or the Holy Land
mwuss0712	maine	1808	ATCHESON	350	31	23	A Map of Passamaquoddy Bay, from Actual Survey
mwuss0611	kentucky	1828	ATKINSON	250	20	27	Kentucky with the Latest Improvements
mwuss1286	ohio	1820	ATWATER	800	49	42	Map of the State of Ohio Drawn by A. Bourne
mwuss1513	texas	1840	AUSTIN	50000	73	59	Genl. Austins Map of Texas with Parts of the Adjoining States
mwuss1503	texas	1830	AUSTIN	100000	75	60	Map of Texas with Parts of the Adjoining States
mwf0076	france	1690	AUVRAY	720	50	50	La France ou l'un des douze Grands Estats de L'Europe
mwf1021	france provence	1690	AVELINE	500	19	31	Aix Ville Capitale du Comte de Provence
mwf1023	france provence	1690	AVELINE	300	19	31	Avignon Ville Capitale du Comtat
mwf0405	france burgundy	1690	AVELINE	300	16	27	Dijon
mwsp0473a	spain regions	1690	AVELINE	650	22	32	Grenade
mwf1135a	france rhone-alpes	1690	AVELINE	400	22	32	Grenoble, Ville Capitale de Dauphiné et Siège de Parlement
mwme0474b	holy land	1700	AVELINE	1400	34	52	Ierusalem comme elle est a Present
mwsc0313	scandinavia denmark	1690	AVELINE	400	19	31	Koppenhague Hafnia Ville Capitale du Royaume de Danemarck
mwm0188	mediterranean malta	1660	AVELINE	500	21	31	La Nouveau Ville de Malte Nommee Vallette
mwuk1133	england london	1700	AVELINE	4800	37	50	Londinum Urbs Praecipua Regni Anglae
mwf1022	france provence	1690	AVELINE	500	19	31	Nice, Ville Capitale du Comte de Meme Nom, que etait Autrefois de la Provence en France
mwf0829	france paris	1676	AVELINE	2800	52	74	Paris
mwf0839	france paris	1700	AVELINE	900	36	50	Paris
mwit0662	italy piedmont	1690	AVELINE	300	19	31	Pignerol, Ville du Piemont, a la France
mwbp0099	baltic states	1690	AVELINE	500	20	31	Riga Capitale de la Province de Livonie
mwf0778	france normandy	1690	AVELINE	300	18	32	Rouen
mwit1235	italy venice	1710	AVELINE	1500	32	52	Venise
mwf0485	france corsica	1732	AYROUARD	300	30	45	Carte de la Baye et du Port de la Hiace en Corse
mwit0804	italy sardinia	1732	AYROUARD	750	54	66	Carte du Golfe de Caillery en l'Isle de Sardaigne
mwf0486	france corsica	1732	AYROUARD	300	46	60	Carte d'une Partie de la Cote de l'Isle de Corse Contenant de puis le Cap de Fen jusque au Golfe de Ste. Manza
mwsp0537a	spain regions	1732	AYROUARD	300	29	46	Plan de la Baye d'Alicant
mwf1055	france provence	1732	AYROUARD	280	30	46	Plan de la Baye de Bandol en Provence
mwf0487	france corsica	1732	AYROUARD	320	29	45	Plan de la Baye de Calvi en Corse
mwsp0537	spain regions	1732	AYROUARD	300	29	45	Plan de la Baye de la Selue en Catalogne
mwit0806	italy sardinia	1732	AYROUARD	360	29	45	Plan de la Baye de Loristan
mwf1196	monaco	1732	AYROUARD	800	30	45	Plan de la Baye de Monaco

AMPG REFERENCE	REGION	DATE	MAP MAKER	PRICE (UK£)	VERT. (cm.)	HOR. (cm.)	TITLE OF MAP (Comments by the editor in brackets)
mwsp0538	spain regions	1732	AYROUARD	400	29	45	Plan de la Baye de Rose et des Cotes des Environs depuis le Port de Cadequie jusques au Cap St. Sebastien
mwsp0539	spain regions	1732	AYROUARD	300	29	45	Plan de la Baye de Salo en Catalogne
mwsp0659b	balearic islands	1732	AYROUARD	360	29	45	Plan de la Baye de St. Antoine en lisle d'Ivice
mwsp0541a	spain regions	1732	AYROUARD	300	29	44	Plan de la Baye de St. Philiou en Catalogne
mwf1056	france provence	1732	AYROUARD	300	30	46	Plan de la Baye des Isles d'Hieres
mwit0805	italy sardinia	1732	AYROUARD	360	29	45	Plan de la Baye du Cap Carbonaire en Sardaigne
mwf1057	france provence	1732	AYROUARD	300	30	45	Plan de la Baye du Gourien et des Isles Ste. Marguerite
mwsp0659b	balearic islands	1732	AYROUARD	360	29	45	Plan de la Baye et Port de Mayorque
mwf1058	france provence	1732	AYROUARD	240	30	46	Plan de la Baye et Port de Toulon
mwf1059	france provence	1732	AYROUARD	240	30	45	Plan de la Rade du Brusc ou des Embiez.
mwf0488	france corsica	1732	AYROUARD	300	29	45	Plan de Porto Vecchio en l'Isle de Corse
mwsp0540	spain regions	1732	AYROUARD	300	29	45	Plan des Rades de Saufa en Catalogne
mwit0807	italy sardinia	1732	AYROUARD	360	30	46	Plan du Canal et Port des Isles de la Madelaine en Sardaigne (south to the top)
mwf0489	france corsica	1732	AYROUARD	300	30	46	Plan du Golfe de St. Fiorenzo en Lisle de Corse
mwf0490	france corsica	1732	AYROUARD	320	29	42	Plan du Golfe de Talane et de la Baye de Campe Moro en l'Isle de Corse
mwf1060	france provence	1732	AYROUARD	400	30	46	Plan du Golfe et des Caps de St Tropez
mwsp0541	spain regions	1732	AYROUARD	200	29	45	Plan du Passage du Fort Brescon / Plan de la Rade de Peniscola en Valence /Plan de la Rade de Carpi / Plan de la Rade de Benidorme en Valence
mwit0808	italy sardinia	1732	AYROUARD	360	29	45	Plan du Passage entre lisle Azinara et le Cap Azinara de Sardaigne
mwf1061	france provence	1732	AYROUARD	300	30	45	Plan du Port d'Antibe
mwf0491	france corsica	1732	AYROUARD	320	29	46	Plan du Port de Boniface en Corse
mwf1062	france provence	1732	AYROUARD	300	30	45	Plan du Port de Bouc a la Cote du Martigues
mwsp0542	spain regions	1732	AYROUARD	400	30	43	Plan du Port de Cadequie en Catalogne
mwf1063	france provence	1732	AYROUARD	400	30	46	Plan du Port de Cassis en Provence
mwf0492	france corsica	1732	AYROUARD	300	30	46	Plan du Port de la Bastide en Lisle de Corse
mwf1064	france provence	1732	AYROUARD	300	30	45	Plan du Port de la Ciota
mwit0809	italy sardinia	1732	AYROUARD	360	29	45	Plan du Port de Longo Sardo en Sardaigne
mwf1065	france provence	1732	AYROUARD	300	30	45	Plan du Port de Porte Crose
mwit0823b	italy sardinia	1803	AZUNI	400	52	31	Karte von der Insel Sardinien (German edition of Azuni's map in French 1802. Shown above left)
mwg0173	saxony	1817	BACH	500	61	57	Plan des Schlachtfeldes um Leipzig
mwbp0551a	poland	1809	BACH	1350	69	79	Plan Miasta Warszawy
mwwi0263	west indies (east)	1785	BACHIENE	200	32	21	Aanhangzel tot de Antilles Eilanden
mwme0330	holy land	1750	BACHIENE	280	38	47	Afbeelding de Oostersche Landen
mwme1009	turkey etc	1748	BACHIENE	360	39	51	Afbeelding van Alle de Landen Gelegen tusschen de Middleandsche, Zwarte, Caspische, Persische en Rode Zeen
mwaf0514	africa egypt etc	1750	BACHIENE	240	49	39	Afbeelding van Egypte, de Woestyne der Schelf-Zee, en 't Land Kanaan
mwme0332	holy land	1750	BACHIENE	250	38	47	Afbeelding van t' Joodsche Land Toen het aan de Heerschappy der Romeinen Onderworfen ... der Geschiedenis van Christus
mwme0327	holy land	1749	BACHIENE	280	48	39	Afbeelding van 't Land van Israel, naar deszelfs Natuurlyke Gesteltheid
mww0405	world	1749	BACHIENE	350	37	50	Afbeeldinge der Oude Waereld
mwme0501	jerusalem	1750	BACHIENE	280	38	49	Afbeeldinge der Stad Jerusalem
mwaf0251	africa	1785	BACHIENE	350	34	41	Africa
mwme0333	holy land	1750	BACHIENE	280	39	48	Aftbeelding van 't Koningryk Israels, Benevens de door 't Zelve Overheerde Landen; Gedurende de Regering der Koningen Saul, David, en Salomo
mwwi0119	west indies	1785	BACHIENE	200	20	32	De Antilles Eilanden en de Golf van Mexico
mwme0336	holy land	1750	BACHIENE	280	37	48	De Beyde Koningryken Juda en Israel
mwme0337	holy land	1750	BACHIENE	220	37	47	De Landen van 't Romeinische Gebied
mwaf0719	africa north	1785	BACHIENE	100	32	22	Het Westelijk Gedeelte van het Oude Vaste Land, van Lisbon tot ann de River Sierra Leona; Benevens de Madera, Kanarische en Kaap Verdesche Eilanden
mwaf0250	africa	1785	BACHIENE	250	21	32	Kaart van Afrika
mwsam0468	south america chile	1785	BACHIENE	180	32	21	Kaart van Chili
mwwi0120	west indies	1785	BACHIENE	220	31	21	Kaart van de Antilles of Eil. boven den Wind met het Oostelyk Gedeelte der Eil. beneden den Wind
mwwi0558	guadeloupe	1785	BACHIENE	100	21	32	Kaart van de Eilanden Guadeloupe, Marie Galante, Desirade en de Saintes
mwg0154a	germany	1785	BACHIENE	150	21	32	Kaart van Duitschland, Bohemen, Hongaryen, en een Gedeelte van Poolen
mwsam0637	south america guyana	1785	BACHIENE	100	33	22	Kaart van Fransch Guijane, met een Gedeelte van Hollandsch Guijane
mwwi0468	cuba	1785	BACHIENE	250	22	31	Kaart van het Eiland Cuba
mwwi0736	jamaica	1780	BACHIENE	200	21	31	Kaart van het Eiland Jamaika
mwwi0801	martinique	1785	BACHIENE	100	33	22	Kaart van het Eiland Martinique
mwca0112	canada	1785	BACHIENE	200	22	32	Kaart van het Eiland Terre Neuve, van Nieuw Schotland, het Eiland St. Jan en het Oostelyk Gedeilte van Kanada

AMPG REFERENCE	REGION	DATE	MAP MAKER	PRICE (UK£)	VERT. (cm.)	HOR. (cm.)	TITLE OF MAP (Comments by the editor in brackets)
mwaf0960	africa south	1785	BACHIENE	240	21	32	Kaart van het Kanaal van Mosambique Bevattende het Eiland Madagascar en de Oostkust van Afrika, van de Kaap de Goede Hoop tot Melinde
mwsam0638	south america guyana	1785	BACHIENE	100	21	32	Kaart van het nieuw Koningrijk Grenada, Nieuw Andalusie en Guyane
mwaf0722	africa north	1790	BACHIENE	100	21	32	Kaart van het Noordlijk Gedeelte van Afrika, of Barbarye; Bevattende de Koninkryken Tripoli, Tunis, Algiers, Fez en Marokko
mwsam0396	south america brazil	1785	BACHIENE	150	21	32	Kaart van het Noordlijk Gedeelte van Bresil
mwam0489	america north	1785	BACHIENE	300	21	32	Kaart van het Noordlyk Gedeelte der Vereenigde Staaten van Nord Amerika
mwca0113	canada	1785	BACHIENE	200	21	32	Kaart van het Oostelijke Gedeelte van Kanada
mwca0658	canada west	1785	BACHIENE	200	21	32	Kaart van het Westelyk Gedeelte van Kanada, Bevattende de Vyf Groote Meiren, met de Omleggende Landen
mwgm0253	mexico	1785	BACHIENE	220	22	32	Kaart van het Zuidelyk Gedeelte van Oud Mexiko of Nieuw Spanje
mwuss0650	louisiana	1785	BACHIENE	240	32	21	Kaart van Louisiana, en Florida
mwgm0254	mexico	1785	BACHIENE	220	21	32	Kaart van Nieuw Mexiko, met het Noordelyk Gedeelte van Oud Mexiko of Nieuw Spanje
mwam0488	america north	1785	BACHIENE	300	21	32	Kaart van Noord Amerika
mwsam0781	south america peru	1785	BACHIENE	150	33	21	Kaart van Peru met een Gedeelte
mwsam0101	south america	1785	BACHIENE	100	32	21	Kaart van Zuid Amerika
mwme0338	holy land	1750	BACHIENE	280	41	50	Koninkrijk Israels
mwam0213	america continent	1783	BACHIENE	350	35	43	Nieuwe en Algemeene Kaart van America, Getrokken uit Verscheiden Naauwkeurige Byzondere Landkarten door Eman. Bowen
mww0480	world	1772	BACHIENE	350	36	44	Nieuwe en Naukeurige Kaart des Geheelen Aardbolems, Opgemaakt mit de Echste Beschryvingen en de Beste Heedendaagsche Land en Zeekaarten ... Jaare 1744. Door E. Bowen Verbeterald door W. Bachiene
mwe0821	europe east	1785	BACHIENE	240	34	42	Nieuwe en Naukeurige Kaart van Europeesch Turkye Beneven de Aangrenzende Landen Hongaryen, Zevenbergen, Klein Tartarye
mwaf1225	africa west	1780	BACHIENE	200	34	42	Nieuwe en Naukeurige Landkaart van Nigritie, en Aangrenzende Landen; als meede van Opper Guinee
mwc0186	china	1775	BACHIENE	300	34	41	Nieuwe Kaart van China
mwaf0417	africa east	1785	BACHIENE	300	35	42	Nubie en Abissinie
mwas0503	asia south east	1780	BACHIENE	280	23	41	Oost-Indischen Eilanden
mwgm0255	mexico	1785	BACHIENE	220	21	32	Oud Mexico of Nieuw Spanje
mwin0282	india	1785	BACHIENE	350	34	42	Rijk der Indien aan Weerzijden des Ganges
mwme0339	holy land	1750	BACHIENE	250	49	38	t Land Kanaan
mwaf0720	africa north	1785	BACHIENE	180	42	34	Westelijk en Oostelijk Gedeelte van Barbarye
mwwi0497b	cuba	1851	BACHMANN	3000	54	79	Birds' Eye View of Havana
mwam0968a	america north (east)	1755	BACK	3000	51	48	A Map of the British Empire in America with the French Spanish and the Dutch Settlements Adjacent thereto by Henry Popple (copy of Popple's 1733 key map)
mwam1003	america north (east)	1759	BACK	500	18	29	Carte des Possessions des Anglois en Amerique, par Rapport a leurs Differends avec la France
mwme0480	jerusalem	1716	BACK	960	37	48	Die heylige und weitberuhmte Stadt Jerusalem
mwgr0189	greece	1750	BACK	180	8	15	La Grece et Ionie
mwca0248	canada arctic	1836	BACK	600	38	48	Map of the Discoveries and Routes of the Arctic Land Expedition, in the Years 1833 & 1834 (below is a 'Sketch of the Route of the recent Arctic Land Expedition 1835')
mwuk0992	england	1742	BADESLADE	200	15	15	A Chart Shewing the Sea Coast of England & Wales, with ye Fortifications
mwec0043	uk england berkshire	1742	BADESLADE	80	14	15	A Map of Berk Shire
mwec0071	uk england buckinghamshire	1742	BADESLADE	80	14	15	A Map of Buckingham Shire
mwec0100	uk england cambridgeshire	1742	BADESLADE	100	14	15	A Map of Cambridge Shire
mwec0141	uk england cheshire	1742	BADESLADE	80	14	15	A Map of Cheshire
mwec0183	uk england cornwall	1742	BADESLADE	150	14	15	A Map of Cornwall
mwec0231	uk england cumbria	1742	BADESLADE	80	14	15	A Map of Cumberland
mwec0264	uk england derbyshire	1742	BADESLADE	80	14	15	A Map of Derby Shire
mwec0294	uk england devon	1742	BADESLADE	80	14	15	A Map of Devon Shire
mwec0335	uk england dorset	1742	BADESLADE	80	14	15	A Map of Dorset Shire
mwec0448	uk england gloucestershire	1742	BADESLADE	80	14	15	A Map of Glocester-Shire
mwec0478	uk england hampshire	1742	BADESLADE	100	14	15	A Map of Hamp Shire
mwec0522	uk england herefordshire	1742	BADESLADE	80	14	15	A Map of Hereford Shire
mwec0627	uk england kent	1742	BADESLADE	140	14	15	A Map of Kent
mwec0722	uk england leicestershire	1742	BADESLADE	80	14	15	A Map of Leicester Shire
mwec0747	uk england lincolnshire	1742	BADESLADE	80	14	15	A Map of Lincoln Shire
mwuk1829	wales	1742	BADESLADE	80	14	15	A Map of Monmouth Shire
mwec0828	uk england norfolk	1742	BADESLADE	80	14	15	A Map of Norfolk
mwuk1830	wales	1742	BADESLADE	80	14	15	A Map of North Wales
mwec0862	uk england northamptonshire	1742	BADESLADE	80	14	15	A Map of Northampton Shire

AMPG REFERENCE	REGION	DATE	MAP MAKER	PRICE (UK£)	VERT. (cm.)	HOR. (cm.)	TITLE OF MAP (Comments by the editor in brackets)
mwec0888	uk england northumberland	1742	BADESLADE	80	14	15	A Map of Northumberland
mwec0915	uk england nottinghamshire	1742	BADESLADE	80	14	15	A Map of Nottingham Shire
mwec0988	uk england rutland	1742	BADESLADE	80	14	15	A Map of Rutland Shire
mwec1043	uk england somerset	1742	BADESLADE	80	14	15	A Map of Somerset Shire
mwuk1831	wales	1742	BADESLADE	80	14	15	A Map of South Wales
mwec1073	uk england staffordshire	1742	BADESLADE	80	14	15	A Map of Stafford Shire
mwec1107	uk england suffolk	1742	BADESLADE	80	14	15	A Map of Suffolk
mwec1140	uk england surrey	1742	BADESLADE	100	14	15	A Map of Surrey
mwec1169	uk england sussex	1742	BADESLADE	100	14	15	A Map of Sussex
mwec0371	uk england durham	1742	BADESLADE	100	14	15	A Map of the Bishoprick of Durham
mwec0782	uk england middlesex	1742	BADESLADE	100	14	15	A Map of the County of Middlesex
mwec1013	uk england shropshire	1742	BADESLADE	80	14	15	A Map of the County of Salop
mwec1200	uk england warwickshire	1742	BADESLADE	80	14	15	A Map of Warwick Shire
mwec1227	uk england westmorland	1742	BADESLADE	80	14	15	A Map of Westmorland
mwec1281	uk england worcestershire	1742	BADESLADE	80	14	15	A Map of Worcester Shire
mwec1333	uk england yorkshire	1742	BADESLADE	100	14	15	A Map of York Shire
mwec0013	uk england bedfordshire	1742	BADESLADE	80	14	15	Bedford Shire
mwec0410	uk england essex	1742	BADESLADE	80	14	15	Essex
mwec0687	uk england lancashire	1742	BADESLADE	80	14	15	Lancashire
mwec0955	uk england oxfordshire	1742	BADESLADE	100	14	15	Oxford-Shire
mwec1250	uk england wiltshire	1742	BADESLADE	80	14	15	Wilt Shire
mwe0723a	europe danube	1735	BAECK	750	32	126	Accurat Aufgezeichneter Donau-Strom ... allwo Jezo das Kriegs-Theatrum Eroffnet Worden (in 28 sheets)
mwit0922	italy sicily	1710	BAECK	450	15	22	Das Konigreich Sicilien
mwf0481	france corsica	1730	BAECK	500	15	21	Die Insel und das Reich Corsica
mwuk0824	uk	1746	BAECK	250	17	23	Engelland Schottland u.Irland
mwsc0109	scandinavia	1710	BAECK	240	15	19	La Scandinavie
mwe0783	europe east	1710	BAECK	200	16	22	La Turquie en Europe, ou sont, les Etats Possedez par les Turcs jusqu en l'An 1690
mwam0366	america north	1710	BAECK	600	17	22	L'Amerique Septentrionalle
mwuk0789	uk	1710	BAECK	280	16	21	Les Isles Britanniques
mwww0308a	world	1710	BAECK	600	16	22	Mapemonde Planisphere Ou Carte Generale Du Monde. - Welt-Charte oder die Haupt-Charte der gantzen Welt.
mwe1072a	europe serbia	1739	BAECK	720	29	39	Neu accurater Plan der Haupt Vestung Belgrad
mwe0582	europe czech republic (bohemia)	1744	BAECK	600	28	40	Plan Generale de la Ville de Prague, Fait par le Fameux Ingenieur F. de P. dans le Royaume de Boheme
mwe0920	europe hungary	1710	BAECK	300	16	24	Ungarn
mwit0181	italy	1747	BAECK	1200	47	66	Wahrhaffter Grund-Riss der Stadt Genua, wie solche 1747
mwbp0392	poland	1730	BAECK	2750	31	106	Warsovia
mwuss1540	texas	1849	BAEDEKER	18000	29	36	Karte des Staates Texas (aufgenommen in die Union 1846) nach der Neuesten Eintheilung
mwam0790	america north	1848	BAEDEKER	150	20	27	Noord Amerika
mwuss0087	california	1772	BAEGERT	800	23	20	California per P. Ferdinandum Consak S.I. et Alios
mwin0100	india	1619	BAFFIN		39	49	A Description of East India Conteyning the Empire of the Great Mogoll (first western survey of North India. Baffin also discovered Baffin Bay, Canada in 1616. Illustrated is a later edition.)
mwin0101	india	1625	BAFFIN-PURCHAS	1250	28	36	A Description of East India Conteyning the Empire of the Great Mogoll (reduced size version of the 1619 edition)
mwf1071a	france provence	1750	BAILLEUL	875	48	70	Carte de Provence divisée par ses Vigueries et Baillages
mwit0596a	italy north	1710	BAILLEUL	900	50	96	Carte Nouvelle du Milanez pour l'Intelligence de la Guerre Tiree su les Memoires d'Hollande et Corrige sur les Lieux. Les Duchez de Milan, Parme, Plaisance, Modene et Mantoue
mwaf0194	africa	1752	BAILLEUL	500	47	61	L'Afrique Divisee selon l'Etendue de Tous ses Etats
mwg0139	germany	1761	BAILLEUL	480	48	55	l'Allemagne (size excl. side text borders)
mwam0167	america continent	1752	BAILLEUL	15000	76	100	L'Amerique Divisee en ses Principales Parties ou sont Distingues les Uns des Autres les Estats selon qu'ils Appartiennent Presentement aux Differents Souverains de l'Europe (publ. by J. Daudet)
mwam0162	america continent	1748	BAILLEUL	1600	48	69	L'Amerique Septentrionale et Meridionale Divisee solon les Possesions
mwsp0087	portugal	1735	BAILLEUL	1000	109	71	Le Portugal et ses Frontieres
mwww0419a	world	1752	BAILLEUL	15000	78	100	Mappe Monde Dressee sur les Observations ...
mwww0409	world	1750	BAILLEUL	7500	52	72	Nouvelle Mappe-Monde avec la Representation des deux Emispheres Celestes, les Disques du Soleil, et de la Lune, et les Differents Sentiments sur le Mouvement des Planetes
mwf0856	france paris	1730	BAILLEUL	5500	104	150	Nouveau Plan de la Ville et Fauxbourgs de Paris
mwbh0848	luxembourg	1695	BAILLIEU	950	38	50	Plan de la Ville de Luxembourg forte et capitale ... fut Prise en 1684
mwuk0826	uk	1747	BAILLIE	3000	100	69	A General Map of Great Britain; wherein are Delineated the Military Operations in that Island during the Years 1745 and 1746, and Even the Secret Routs of the Pr after the Battle of Culloden until his Escape to France
mwuk0532a	scotland	1777	BAILLIE	500	63	37	A Plan of Loch Lomond in the Shire of Dumbarton
mwg0747a	thuringia	1715	BAILLIE	1200	52	55	Nova Territorij Erfordiensis in suas praefecturas Accurata Descriptio cum Terris Vicinis

AMPG REFERENCE	REGION	DATE	MAP MAKER	PRICE (UK£)	VERT. (cm.)	HOR. (cm.)	TITLE OF MAP (Comments by the editor in brackets)
mwm0156	mediterranean east	1800	BAILLOU	600	73	49	Carta Comparativa della Geografia Antica e Moderna dell' Egitto e della Siria Assoggettata alle piu Recenti Osservazioni Astronomiche
mwgm0370	mexico	1850	BAILY	900	66	95	Map of Central America Including the States of Guatemala, Salvador, Honduras, Nicaragua & Costa-Rica, the Territories of Belise & Mosquito, with parts of Mexico, Yucatan & New Granada
mwec1353	uk england yorkshire	1817	BAINES	120	25	24	A Map of Near 10 Miles round Leeds
mwec1359	uk england yorkshire	1831	BAINES	800	57	59	A Map of the Country Extending Ten Miles round Leeds, Including Wakefield, Bradford, Dewsbury, Otley, Harewood, Aberford & Castleford ... By Joshua Thorp; and Re-Surveyed & Corrected to January 1st. 1831. By S.D. Martin, Surveyor, Leeds
mwam0601a	america north	1816	BAINES	200	24	34	United States of America Exhibiting the Seat of War on the Canadian Frontier from 1812 to 1815
mwwi0299	antigua	1749	BAKER, R.	12500	110	138	A New and Exact Map of the Island of Antigua in America, According to an Actual and Accurate Survey Made in the Years 1746, 1747 & 1748. Describing the Limits & Boundaries of the Several Parishes, with the Churches
mwec0494	uk england hampshire	1801	BAKER	120	56	43	A Plan of the Roads, Gentlemens Seats, &c Twelve Miles Round Southampton with the Isle of Wight
mwec0113	uk england cambridgeshire	1830	BAKER	1800	109	85	Baker's New Map of the University and Town of Cambridge. To His Royal Highness William Frederick, Duke of Gloucester, K.G.G.C.B., Chancellor of the University of Cambridge, this Map Delineated from Actual Survey
mwec0111	uk england cambridgeshire	1821	BAKER	1800	154	119	Map of the County of Cambridge and Isle of Ely. Surveyed by R.G. Baker, in the Years 1816, 17, 18, 19 & 20.
mwuss0143	california	1854	BAKER	2500	27	22	Map of the Mining Region of California, 1854
mwuss1234	new york	1838	BAKER	300	43	52	Map of the State of New York Showing the Location of Public Improvements
mwam0549	america north	1800	BAKER	180	19	23	North America from the Best Authorities
mwme0511	jerusalem	1807	BAKER	120	22	28	The Kingdom of Jerusalem with its Environs at the Time of the Crusades
mwwi0130	west indies	1794	BAKER	120	19	23	West Indies from the Best Authorities
mwaf0182a	africa	1745	BAKEWELL	6000	59	95	Africa a new and most exact map laid down according to the observations communicated to the English Royall Society, the French Royall Academy of Sciences and those made by the latest travellers, to this present year 1745.
mwam0147	america continent	1740	BAKEWELL		60	95	America a new and most exact Map laid down according to the observations communicated to the Royall Society (insets incl: Porto Bello. Many other views etc in borders. California shown as an island.)
mwuk1197	england london	1760	BAKEWELL-PARKER	1800	28	55	The city guide or a pocket plan of London, Westminster and Southwark with the new buildings
mwit0226	italy	1810	BALATRI	600	45	64	Piata dell Citta di Firenze e sue Principali Vedute
mwe0545	europe czech republic (bohemia)	1677	BALBINUS	2000	39	27	Bohemiae Rosa Omnibus Saeculis Cruenta in qua Plura quam 80 Magna Pratia Commissa sunt nunc Primum hac Form Excusa
mwin0021	ceylon	1672	BALDAEUS	600	29	35	Colombo (north to the left)
mwin0115	india	1672	BALDAEUS	450	29	36	Description Nova Imperii Malabar Canara Decan et Aliarum Provinciarum
mwin0398	india goa	1672	BALDAEUS	500	28	35	Goa
mwin0020	ceylon	1672	BALDAEUS	750	30	38	Insula Ceylan olim Taprobana
mwin0116	india	1672	BALDAEUS	450	29	36	Regionum Choromandel Golconda et Orixa Nova et accurata descriptio
mwam0442	america north	1769	BALDWIN	240	17	10	A Map of that Part of America where a Degree of Latitude was Measured for the Royal Society: By Cha. Mason, & Jere. Dixon
mwuss1635	virginia	1754	BALDWIN	350	20	12	A Map of the Western Parts of the Colony of Virginia
mwam0967	america north (east)	1755	BALDWIN	250	22	26	A Map of Virginia, North and South Carolina, Georgia, Maryland with Part of New Jersey, &c.
mww0539	world	1786	BALDWIN	1100	29	46	A New and Accurate Map of the World, Comprehending All the New Discoveries in Both Hemispheres Carefully Brought Down to the Present Time
mwca0509	canada quebec	1758	BALDWIN	240	11	18	A Plan of the Fort and Bay of Frontenac with the Adjacent Countries
mwaf0272	africa	1794	BALDWIN	250	34	38	Africa
mwuss0528	georgia	1837	BALDWIN	4250	50	85	City of Brunswick, State of Georgia. Showing the Recent Additions as Located in 1837
mwuss1086	new york	1757	BALDWIN	240	19	10	Plan of the Forts Ontario and Oswego, with Part of the River Onondago and Lake Ontario
mwwi0520	grenada	1762	BALDWIN	240	23	18	Plan of the Town & Fort of Grenada. by Mr. de Caylus, Engineer General of the French Islands (publ. in London Magazine)

AMPG REFERENCE	REGION	DATE	MAP MAKER	PRICE (UK£)	VERT. (cm.)	HOR. (cm.)	TITLE OF MAP (Comments by the editor in brackets)
mwam0289	america continent	1830	BALDWIN & CRADOCK (Also publisher of SOCIETY D.U.K. maps)	800	126	96	America in Eight Sheets Shewing the Latest Discoveries
mwsam0479	south america chile	1826	BALDWIN & CRADOCK	240	25	43	Map of a Portion of Chile with the Intermediate Mountain Ranges and Passes over the Cordillera between Valparaiso & Mendosa
mwsam0253	south america argentina	1826	BALDWIN & CRADOCK	450	25	60	Map of the Country between Rio de la Plata and the Pacific Ocean, between Parallels 29 & 36 S. Lat.
mwme0990b	turkey etc	1711	BANDURI	400	35	41	Anaplus Bospori Thracii a Domino de Combes ... Anselmus Bandurius
mwme0990a	turkey etc	1711	BANDURI	450	24	43	La Ville et le Port de Constantinople (view)
mwam0516	america north	1792	BANKES	400	31	43	A Correct Map of the United States of North America, Including the British and Spanish Territories, Carefully Laid down Agreeable to the Treaty of 1784
mwuk0231	ireland	1790	BANKES	150	29	19	A New and Accurate Map of Ireland Drawn from the Best Authorities
mwwi0124	west indies	1787	BANKES	150	19	28	The West Indies
mwsw0197	switzerland	1790	BANKES	150	11	18	View of Zurich Principal City of Zurich, One of the Cantons of Switzerland
mwme0211	holy land	1695	BAR YAAQOV	5000	26	48	(Untitled map with Hebrew script.)
mwe1124a	europe slovenia	1778	BARAGA	2000	44	67	(untitled map of Krainska)
mwit0274	italy campagna	1616	BARATTA	3750	38	52	Campaniae Felicis Typus
mwit0474a	italy lombardy	1628	BARATTERI	3000	35	52	Ducato di Mantova con sui Confini (illustrated is the 1641 edition)
mwuk0206	ireland	1776	BARBER	300	37	34	A Map of Ireland
mwuss0324	connecticut	1845	BARBER	200	19	23	Connecticut
mwf0143	france	1776	BARBER	300	34	37	France with the Netherlands Corrected and Improved
mwam0764	america north	1845	BARBER	200	26	22	Map of the United States Exhibiting the Principal Rail Road & Steam Boat Routes
mwam0693	america north	1835	BARBER	1500	72	107	Map of the United States of America with its Territories & Districts. Including also a Part of Upper & Lower Canada and Mexico
mwgr0207	greece	1776	BARBER	300	34	37	Turky in Europe and Hungary
mwaa0203a	arctic / antarctic	1808	BARBIELLINI	350	22	39	Regioni Polari Paragonate Secondo gli Ultimi Viaggi
			FOR BARBIE DU BOCAGE, SEE 'DU BOCAGE'.				
mwuk0010	ireland	1596	BARENTSZ	9000	36	51	Beschrivinge der Zee Custen van de Zuijdtsijde ende de Oost-Sijde van Irlandt Beginnende van Cabo Vello of Doude Hoeck, Alle de Havenen tot Waterfor ende Voorts tot Dubling ende Dondalck (first printed sea chart of Ireland)
mwm0264a	mediterranean west	1607	BARENTSZ	8000	34	53	Description des Costes Marines d'Espagne; des Cales Malis par les Destoict de Gibraltar, jusques Cap de Gata
mwm0265	mediterranean west	1607	BARENTSZ	8000	34	53	Hydrographica descriptio ... (text in cartouche)
mwit0991a	italy south	1593	BARENTSZ	8000	34	53	Hydrographica descriptio, in quo orae maritimae Italiae a monte Argentato Napolim
mwat0133a	atlantic canary isl.	1594	BARENTSZ	4800	39	54	Tabula Hispaniae Intra promontorium S. Vincenty et premontorium Bagador, ut et Canarie insulae (illustrated is the Jansson re-issue of 1654)
mwat0133	atlantic canary isl.	1594	BARENTSZ	4800	39	54	Tabula Hydrographica, in qua Hispaniae Orae Maritimae a Civitate Setubal ... Insularum item Canariarum Orae Maritimae
mwsp0441a	spain regions	1654	BARENTSZ-JANSSON	2400	34	53	Ora Maritima Granadae et Barbarie
mwsp0441b	spain regions	1654	BARENTSZ-JANSSON	3000	38	52	Tabula Hispaniae a promontorio de Gato
mwaa0065	arctic	1598	BARENTSZ-LINSCHOTEN	15000	42	57	Deliniatio Cartae Trium Navigationum per Batavos ad Septentrionalem Plagam, Norvegiae Moscoviae et Novae Semblae (below is a 1599 re-engraved version with minor differences)
mwsam0296	south america brazil	1647	BARLAEUS	2000	29	38	Mauritiopolis Reciffa, et Circumiacentia Castra
mwuss1443	pennsylvania	1848	BARNES	3500	64	93	Map of Pennsylvania Constructed from the County Surveys Authorized by the State; and other Original Documents. Revised and Improved under the Supervision of Wm. E. Morris
mwuss0311	connecticut	1824	BARNUM	785	43	54	A Map of Bridgeport
mwc0218	china	1796	BARROW	300	50	42	A Chart of Part of the Coast of Cochin-China Including Turon Harbour and the Island Callao
mwc0220	china	1797	BARROW	650	74	53	A General Chart, on Mercator's Projection, Containing the Track and Soundings of the Lion, the Hindustan and Tenders, from Turon-Bay in Cochin-China to the Mouth of the PeiHo River in the Gulph of Pe-Tche-Lee or Pekin
mwin0444	indian ocean	1796	BARROW	300	57	94	A General Chart, on Mercator's Projection, to Shew the Track of the Lion and Hindustan from England to the Gulph of Pekin in China
mwc0221	china	1797	BARROW	1200	69	53	A Plan of the City and Harbour of Macao, a Colony of the Portugueze Situated at the Southern Extremity of the Chinese Empire

AMPG REFERENCE	REGION	DATE	MAP MAKER	PRICE (UK£)	VERT. (cm.)	HOR. (cm.)	TITLE OF MAP (Comments by the editor in brackets)
mwc0213	china	1793	BARROW	250	69	50	A Sketch by Compass of the Coast of the Promontory of Shan-Tung with the Track of the Ships
mwaf0987	africa south	1806	BARROW	250	25	43	Algoa Bay. Surveyed by Lieut. Wm. Mcpherson Rice, Royal Navy
mwc0224	china	1797	BARROW	300	56	93	General Chart ... to the Gulph of Pekin in China 1796
mwaf0978	africa south	1800	BARROW	450	47	69	General Chart of the Cape of Good Hope Constructed ... in the Years 1797-1798
mwaf0988	africa south	1806	BARROW	250	32	46	General Chart of the Colony of the Cape of Good Hope Constructed ... During the Years 1797 & 1798
mwaf0989	africa south	1806	BARROW	550	55	23	Military Plan of the Cape Peninsula Drawn by Order of the Dutch Government by Captn. Bridges (illustrated left)
mwam0419	america north	1759	BARROW	400	22	29	Part of North America; Comprehending the Course of the Ohio, New England, New York, New Jersey, Pensilvania, Maryland, Virginia, Carolina and Georgia. From the Sr. Robert, with Improvements
mwc0222	china	1797	BARROW	500	68	49	Sketch of a Journey from Hang-Tchoo-Foo to Quang-Tchoo-Foo or Canton in China
mwuk1351a	england east	1845	BARTHOLOMEW	100	47	32	Ports & Harbours on the East Coast of England
mwam0803	america north	1853	BARTLETT	350	39	49	General Map Showing the Countries Explored & Surveyed by the United States & Mexican Boundary Commission, in the Years 1850, 51, 52 & 53, under the Direction of John R. Bartlett
mwuk1316	england london	1834	BARTLETT	3000	114	97	Topographical Survey of the Borough of St. Marylebone, as Incorporated & Defined by an Act of Parliament 1832 Embracing & Marking the Boundaries of the Parishes of St. Marylebone, St. Pancras & Paddington
mwit0178	italy	1744	BARTON	250	20	30	Italy as Divided into Regions by C. Augustus
mwuss1019	new hampshire	1824	BARTON	800	49	58	To the Citizens of New Hampshire, Generally; but More Particularly to those Living in the Counties of Cheshire and Merrimack
mwuss0234	carolinas	1793	BARTRAM	600	35	28	Esquisse des Operations du Siege de Charleston, Capitole de la Caroline Meridionale, en 1780
mwit0364	italy emilia-romagna	1758	BARUFFALDI	1600	66	91	Corografia del Ducato di Ferrara
mwaf1198	africa west	1745	BASIRE	150	22	15	A Map of the Coast and Country about Sierra Lione and Sherbro River (engraved by Basire)
mwg0355	bavaria	1710	BASIRE	480	38	47	Battle of Donawert 1704
mwp0121	australia	1837	BASIRE	2500	31	39	Plan of Sydney with Pyrmont, New South Wales: The Latter the Property of Edwd. Macarthure Esqre. Divided into Allotments for Building, 1836
mwf0750	france nord pas-de-calais	1745	BASIRE	240	39	49	Plan of the City and Citadel of Dunkirk
mwf0751	france nord pas-de-calais	1745	BASIRE	240	36	47	Plan of the City and Citadel of Lisle (Lille)
mwsp0709	gibraltar	1745	BASIRE	500	37	59	Plan of the Town and Fortifications of Gibraltar, Exactly Taken on the Spot in the Year 1738
mwsp0662	balearic islands	1745	BASIRE	600	35	62	Plan of the Town and Harbour of Mahon, St. Philip's Castle, and its Fortifications
mwf1072	france provence	1750	BASIRE	400	39	46	Plan of Toulon
mwit0687a	italy piedmont	1751	BASIRE	300	38	48	Plan of Turin as Besieged in 1706
mwit0929	italy sicily	1720	BASIRE	200	20	30	Sicilia
mwme0499	jerusalem	1745	BASIRE	300	35	43	The City of Jerusalem
mwc0138a	china	1745	BASIRE	280	21	33	The City of Pekin from Nieuhof (re-issued in 1780, slightly smaller in size)
mwme0727	caucasus	1747	BASIRE	200	20	30	The Kingdoms of Armenia, Pontus, Cappadocia, Media &c.
			SEE ALSO UNDER 'RAPIN' AND 'TINDAL' (Basire was the engraver of Rapin/Tindal's maps				
mwit0084	italy	1638	BASSANO	2800	40	50	Italia Nova di Gio. Antonio Magino
mwam0290	america continent	1831	BASSET	300	52	73	Carte d'Amerique, Dressee par Pierre Tardieu
mwf0182	france	1814	BASSET	600	48	68	Carte de la France Tracee d'apres les Nouvelles Limites
mwam0676	america north	1832	BASSET	500	52	73	Carte de l'Amerique Septentrionale
mwam0210	america continent	1780	BASSET	1000	51	76	Carte de l'Amérique Septentrionale et Meridionale Ou se trouvent les Découvertes les plus nouvelles, et les trois Voyages de Cook (Map by Herisson, Bonne. Illustrated is 1795 edition)
mwas0223	asia continent	1795	BASSET	300	53	77	Carte Generale de Asie, ou se Trouvent les Decouvertes des Iles, de Bougainville, Surville et Dampierre
mww0586	world	1795	BASSET	875	46	76	Mappe Monde en Deux Hemispheres, ou sont Marquees les Decouvertes les Plus Recentes et les Routes des Trois Voyages de Cook
mwf1079	france provence	1780	BASSET	300	26	40	Vue Perspective de la Ville de Nice
mwbh0162	belgium holland	1603	BAST	720	40	49	Leeuwerden de Hooft Stadt van Frisslant
mwbh0216	belgium holland	1630	BAST	6000	44	44	Lugdunum Batavorum. Die Stadt Leyden
mwg0573a	germany saxony	1598	BAST	1500	29	37	Wahrhafftige Contrafactur, der Grafflichen Stadt Oldenburgh
mww0663	world	1820	BATELLI & FANFANI	450	34	64	Mappa-Mondo in Due Emisferi
mww0664	world	1820	BATELLI & FANFANI	300	29	38	Mappa-Mondo per Indicare la Principale Costruizione ... de Due Continenti
mwit0218	italy	1797	BATES	150	18	21	Italy
mwam0535	america north	1797	BATES	250	20	23	United States of America Agreeable to the Peace of 1783

AMPG REFERENCE	REGION	DATE	MAP MAKER	PRICE (UK£)	VERT. (cm.)	HOR. (cm.)	TITLE OF MAP (Comments by the editor in brackets)
mwec0619	uk england kent	1711	BATTELY	350	19	33	(Untitled)
mwgm0334	mexico	1838	BAUDIN	600	41	38	Attaque et Prise de la Fortresse de St. Juan d'Ullua, par la Division Navale aux Ordres de Mr. le Contre-Amiral Baudin. Le 27 Novemb. 1838
mwgr0524	greece rhodes	1640	BAUDOIN	235	15	21	Rhodes
mwit0105a	italy	1672	BAUDRAND	500	43	52	Italia Divisa Ne Suoi Regni Principati Ducati
mwit0132	italy	1700	BAUDRAND	600	45	56	L'Italie sur les nouv. Observation (inset of Sicily)
mwww0166	world	1658	BAUDRAND	12000	57	92	Nova Et Essata Tavola Del Mondo O Terra Universale
mwgr0095	greece	1682	BAUDRAND	1400	44	57	La Grece tiree de memoires de Monsieur l'Abbe Baudrand
mwgr0103	greece	1688	BAUDRAND-DESGRANGES	3600	65	80	La Grece tiree de memoires de Monsieur l'Abbe Baudrand ... Profil des principales villes de la Grece (21 town views have been added to the borders of Baudrand's 1682 map of Greece)
mwuk1324a	england london	1841	BAUERKELLER	3000	61	107	Bauerkeller's New Embossed Map of London (3 edition to 1844)
mwg0185	germany	1850	BAUERKELLER	300	50	38	Geographisch-Statistische Post und Reisekarte zu den Besuchsten Rhein- und Main-Gegenden
mwe0273	europe	1845	BAUERKELLER	600	53	66	Hydrogr. Karte von Europa
mwat0336	atlantic st helena	1850	BAUERKELLER	400	20	24	Ile Ste. Helene en Relief
mwe0441a	europe austria vienna	1843	BAUERKELLER	1200	56	70	Neuester Plan von Wien (shown above left)
mwf0932	france paris	1842	BAUERKELLER	750	56	69	Nouveau Plan de Paris en Relief
mwuss1653	virginia	1782	BAUMAN	60000	64	45	To His Excellency Genl. Washington ... this Plan of the Investment of York and Gloucester has been Surveyed and Laid Down
mwwi0614	hispaniola	1753	BAUMGARTEN	300	22	29	Die Insel Hispaniola, oder San Domingo
mwwi0615	hispaniola	1753	BAUMGARTEN	300	20	29	Die Insel Hispaniola, von den Indianern Genant Hayti
mwgm0215	mexico	1753	BAUMGARTEN	300	24	36	Gegend um die Mexicanische See / Die Provinzen Mexico, Panuco, und Tlascala
mwec0482	uk england hampshire	1756	BAUR	1000	30	42	A Correct Plan of the City of Winchester the adjacent Parts with the Hessian Camp, by Order of his Excellency Lieutenant General Count Isenburg. Plan de la Ville & des Environs de Winchester avec le Comp des Trouppes Hessoises aux ordres S: Excellencie Monseigneur Le Lieutenant General Comte d'Isenburg.
mwsam0858a	south america venezuela	1829	BAUZA	900	60	90	Carta que Comprehende las Costas del Seno Mejicano Construida con las Observaciones Astronomicas, y Cronometricas Hechas por Varios Oficiales de la Marine Real Espanola y Ynglesa
mwsam0557	south america colombia	1841	BAUZA	550	75	128	Mapa de una Parte del Territorio de Colombia en la America Meridional
mwsp0604	spain regions	1789	BAUZA	900	58	87	Plano del Puerto de Cadiz
mwas0506	asia south east	1782	BAYLY	100	22	32	A New Map of the East Indies
mwuk0188	ireland	1763	BAYLY	480	55	48	A New Map of the Kingdom of Ireland
mwww0515	world	1782	BAYLY	450	24	43	A New Map of the World in Three Sections; wherein the Several Tracks and Discoveries of the British Navigators, to the Present Time, are Distinctly and Accurately Laid Down (close copy of Phipps 1776)
mwme1017	turkey etc	1767	BAYLY	650	39	42	A Plan of Constantinople, Places Adjacent and Canal of the Black Sea
mwwi0121	west indies	1785	BAYLY	350	29	53	West Indies, Drawn from the Best Authorities
mwuk0232	ireland	1792	BEAUFORT	720	110	88	A New Map of Ireland Civil and Ecclesiastical
mwgr0406	greece crete	1680	BEAULIEU	900	45	54	Candia Capitale du Royaume
mwm0184a	mediterranean malta	1650	BEAULIEU	3600	50	63	Carte et Plan de l'Isle de Malthe et des Villes et Forts avec les Nouvelles Fortifications ainsy quelle sont a Present
mwg0339	bavaria	1646	BEAULIEU	2500	117	91	La Bataille de Nordlingen Donnee le Troisiesme Jour d'Aoust 1645
mwgr0396	greece crete	1669	BEAULIEU	1200	50	55	La Ville de Candie pour la 3.e Fois Attaquee de l'Armee Ottomane
mwbh0829	luxembourg	1644	BEAULIEU	1200	68	59	Plan de la Ville de Theonville au Duche de Luxembourg. Assiegee ... 1643
mwgr0402	greece crete	1670	BEAULIEU	1600	45	54	Plan de l'Isle de Candie iadis Crete et des Isles Voisines
mwf0676	france lorraine	1662	BEAULIEU	400	45	54	Plan des Villes de Vic Moyenvic et Marsal en Lorraine
			BEAURAIN: See under DE BEAURAIN				
mwp0387	pacific new guinea	1804	BEAUTEMPS-BEAUPRE	250	75	50	Carte de Detroit de Dampier, Situe entre la Nouvelle Guinee et la Nouvelle Bretagne
mwp0372	pacific new caledonia	1804	BEAUTEMPS-BEAUPRE	250	49	75	Carte de la Nouvelle Caledonie (New Caledonia)
mwp0485	pacific solomon isl	1806	BEAUTEMPS-BEAUPRE	250	49	76	Carte de la Partie Meridionale de l'Archipel des Iles Salomon de Mendana, Reconnue par le Lieutenant Shortland en 1788, Bruny Dentrecasteaux en Mai et Juin 1793
mwp0388	pacific new guinea	1806	BEAUTEMPS-BEAUPRE	250	46	72	Carte de la Partie Septentrionale de la Nouvelle Guinee depuis le Cap de Goede Hoop (Bonne Esperance) jusqu au Detroit de Dampier
mwp0042	australia	1807	BEAUTEMPS-BEAUPRE	2000	50	76	Carte Generale de la Nouvelle Hollande et des Archipels du Grand Ocean

AMPG REFERENCE	REGION	DATE	MAP MAKER	PRICE (UK£)	VERT. (cm.)	HOR. (cm.)	TITLE OF MAP (Comments by the editor in brackets)
mww0593	world	1796	BEAUTEMPS-BEAUPRE	400	38	75	Carte Hydrographique des Parties Connues du Globe, entre le Soixante-Dixieme Parallele au Nord et le Soixantieme au Sud
mwf0375	france brittany	1825	BEAUTEMPS-BEAUPRE	300	94	65	Carte Particuliere des Cotes de France (Entree du Port de Lorient, Presqu'ile de Quiberon et Partie Septentle. de Belle-Ile)
mwf0376	france brittany	1825	BEAUTEMPS-BEAUPRE	300	66	98	Plan des Entrees du Morbihan et de la Riviere de Crac'h
mwwi0922	virgin isl	1754	BECK	6000	47	73	Tilforladelig Kort over Eylandet St. Croix udi America
mwsc0441a	scandinavia finland	1789	BECKMAN	600	42	72	Charta ofver Aland
mwuss0047	alaska	1830	BEECHEY	800	44	33	Chart of Part of the North West Coast of America. From Point Rodney to Point Barrow.
mwbh0538a	belgium holland	1709	BEECK	1100	59	75	Le Véritable Plan de la Ville et Citadelle de Tournay (north to the left)
mwsp0503a	spain regions	1706	BEECK	1350	45	59	Plan de la Ville de Barcelone et Château de Montjuy
mwaf0372	africa east	1679	BEER	200	12	10	Abissinia sive Aethiopia
mwam0081	america continent	1679	BEER	550	11	13	America
mwuk0951	england	1690	BEER	200	10	12	Anglia
mwme0576	arabia etc	1690	BEER	400	10	12	Arabia
mwas0078	asia continent	1690	BEER	250	10	12	Asia
mwsam0320	south america brazil	1679	BEER	300	10	12	Brasilia
mwca0031	canada	1679	BEER	300	10	12	Canada
mwgr0415	greece crete	1690	BEER	235	10	12	Candia
mwec0611a	uk england kent	1690	BEER	150	17	13	Canterburn. Cantuaria
mwsam0503	south america colombia	1679	BEER	200	10	12	Castilla Doro
mwsam0452	south america chile	1679	BEER	200	12	10	Chili
mwc0062	china	1679	BEER	250	13	10	China
mwec0441	uk england gloucestershire	1690	BEER	120	16	13	Claudio Cestria - Glocester
mwaf1134	africa west	1679	BEER	200	10	12	Congo
mwuss0398	florida	1678	BEER	500	9	12	Florida
mwuss0490	georgia	1679	BEER	450	10	13	Georgia
mwsam0586	south america guyana	1679	BEER	200	10	12	Guaiana
mwuk0104	ireland	1690	BEER	375	29	25	Hiberniae Das Konigreich Irland. Regnum
mwjk0042	japan	1679	BEER	400	10	12	Iaponia
mwin0120	india	1679	BEER	200	10	13	Impery Magni Mogolis
mwin0121	india	1679	BEER	235	9	13	India intra Gangem
mwin0022	ceylon	1679	BEER	235	12	10	Insula Ceilon
mwsc0493	scandinavia iceland	1679	BEER	300	11	13	Insula Islandia
mwwi0030	west indies	1679	BEER	280	10	12	Insulae Antilles
mwuk0753	uk	1690	BEER	235	10	12	Insulae Britanniae
mwat0149	atlantic canary isl.	1679	BEER	200	10	12	Insulae Canariae
mwat0191	atlantic cape verde isl.	1679	BEER	180	10	12	Insulae Capo Viridis
mwin0459	indian ocean maldives	1679	BEER	180	13	10	Insulae Maldivae
mwas0717	asia south east moluccas	1679	BEER	200	10	12	Insulae Moluccae
mwas0754	asia south east philippines	1679	BEER	350	10	12	Insulae Philippinae alias Manhilhae dictae
mwas0408	asia south east	1679	BEER	200	10	12	Insulae Sindae
mwat0083	atlantic azores	1679	BEER	250	10	13	Insulae Tercerae alias Acores
mwuk0105	ireland	1690	BEER	235	10	12	Irlandia
mwit0114	italy	1690	BEER	235	10	12	Italiae Tabula
mwuk1127	england london	1690	BEER	1200	16	26	Londinum London
mwm0209	mediterranean malta	1690	BEER	375	10	12	Maltha
mwgm0183	mexico	1690	BEER	250	10	12	Mexico sive N. Hispania
mwuss0073	california	1679	BEER	600	9	12	Nova Mexico
mwaf0373	africa east	1679	BEER	200	10	12	Nubia
mwme0795	persia etc	1690	BEER	200	10	12	Persia
mwec0611	uk england kent	1690	BEER	120	16	13	Rochesstria - Rochester
mwf1136	france rhone-alpes	1690	BEER	150	10	12	Sabaudiae
mwuk0430	scotland	1690	BEER	250	10	12	Scotia
mwit0905	italy sicily	1690	BEER	235	10	12	Sicilia
mwaa0010	antarctic	1679	BEER	350	10	12	Terra Antarctica
mwaa0099	arctic	1690	BEER	250	10	12	Terra Arctica
mwsam0673	south america magellan	1679	BEER	200	10	12	Terra Magellanica
mwsam0220	south america argentina	1679	BEER	235	10	12	Tucuman
mwme0179	holy land	1679	BEER	200	10	13	Turcicu Imperium in Asia
mww0240	world	1690	BEER	400	10	12	Typus Orbis Terrarum
mwuss1616	virginia	1679	BEER	700	10	12	Virginia
mwaf0374	africa east	1679	BEER	300	13	10	Zanguebar
mwuk1141	england london	1707	BEEVERELL	500	12	16	London
mwec1198	uk england warwickshire	1729	BEIGHTON	200	37	38	A map of Knightlow-Hundred
mwec1199	uk england warwickshire	1729	BEIGHTON	200	40	37	A mapp of Warwickshire
mwe0507	europe croatia	1802	BEISCHLAG	400	57	96	(Croatia) Comitatus Varasdinensis Ichnographice Delineatus per Ignatium Bejschlag Ejusdem Comitatis Juratum Geometram. Anno MDCCCI
mwe1114	europe slovak republic (moravia)	1735	BEL	750	66	56	Mappa Comitatus Posoniensis Accuratione Astronomico-Geometrico Concinnata
mwe1113	europe slovak republic (moravia)	1731	BEL	400	44	33	Terrae seu Comitatus Scepusiensis Tabula

AMPG REFERENCE	REGION	DATE	MAP MAKER	PRICE (UK£)	VERT. (cm.)	HOR. (cm.)	TITLE OF MAP (Comments by the editor in brackets)
mwp0352	pacific hawaii	1843	BELCHER	250	11	20	View of Honolulu, Oahu, Sandwich Islands
mwuss1067	new jersey	1850	BELDING	1800	125	92	Map of Essex County, New Jersey, with the Names of Property Holders &c
mwgr0393	greece crete	1668	BELGRANO	1600	37	50	Dissegno di Candia Attaccata dal Turco sotto il Commando del Primo Visir et Diffesa dall' Eccmo. Sigr. Marchese Villa, dal Principio del Attacco li 24 Maggio 1667, sino li 21 Aprile 1668
mwuss1004	new hampshire	1792	BELKNAP	500	38	28	New Map of New Hampshire by Jeremy Belknap
			BELLEFOREST, SEE DE BELLEFOREST				
mwam0004	america continent	1554	BELLERE	5000	17	13	Brevis Exactaque Totius Novi Orbis eiusque Insularum Descriptio
mwjk0086	japan	1736	BELLIN	280	20	28	(Azuchi) Plan de la Ville et Chateau D'Anzuquiama
mwjk0088	japan	1736	BELLIN	320	20	29	(Osaka) Plan de la Ville D'Ozaca et de son Chateau
mwf0369	france brittany	1773	BELLIN	400	58	80	4me Carte Particuliere des Costes de Bretagne depuis l'Anse de Goulven jusqu'a l'Isle d'Ouessant
mwf0352b	france brittany	1753	BELLIN	450	58	80	7me Carte Particuliere des Costes de Bretagne depuis L'Isle de Groa
mwf0352a	france brittany	1753	BELLIN	450	58	80	8me Carte Particuliere des Costes de Bretagne Qui comprend l'entrée de la Loire et lIsle de Noirmoustier
mwgm0227a	mexico	1764	BELLIN	300	23	33	Acapulco (view, based on Valentyn 1724)
mwsam0071	south america	1750	BELLIN	240	44	33	Amerique Meridionale
mwsam0079	south america	1760	BELLIN	150	20	15	Amerique Meridionale
mww0412	world	1750	BELLIN	1800	55	71	An Essay of a New and Compact Map Containing the Known Parts of the Terrestrial Globe (English edition of Bellin 1748)
mwsam0525	south america colombia	1764	BELLIN	300	22	35	Baye de Carthagene dans l'Amerique Meridionale
mwca0083	canada	1763	BELLIN	200	23	36	Baye de Hudson et Pays Voisins
mwwi0448	cuba	1764	BELLIN	200	22	16	Baye de Matance dans l'Isle de Cube
mwgm0420	panama	1764	BELLIN	250	21	17	Baye de Porto Bello
mwgm0421	panama	1764	BELLIN	200	20	27	Baye de Porto-Bello et Costes Voisines
mwuss1096	new york	1764	BELLIN	1200	22	17	Baye et Port d'Yorc Capitale de la Nouvelle Yorc
mwwi0626	hispaniola	1764	BELLIN	250	23	35	Baye et Ville de Bayaha ou Port Dauphin dans l'Isle de Saint-Domingue
mwca0388	canada nova scotia	1764	BELLIN	300	22	33	Baye Ste. Anne ou le Port Dauphin dans l'Isle Royale
mwin0239	india	1763	BELLIN	140	21	17	Baye, Ville et Forst d'Andarajapour a la Coste de Malabar
mwgm0047	gulf of mexico and surrounding regions	1781	BELLIN	450	27	37	Carta del Golfo del Messico
mwat0167	atlantic canary isl.	1781	BELLIN	240	20	25	Carta dell' Isola Canarie
mwjk0105	japan	1751	BELLIN	450	21	28	Carta dell' Isole del Giappone e la Penisola de Corea con le Coste della China da Pekin sino a Canton
mwas0784	asia south east philippines	1760	BELLIN	250	21	16	Carta dell' Isole Filippine di Mr. Bellin Ingegnere della Marina Foglio 1.mo / Carta dell' Isole Filippine
mwuss1145	new york	1781	BELLIN	450	20	29	Carta della Nuova Inghilterra, Nuova Yorc, e Pennsilvania
mwuss1084	new york	1750	BELLIN	350	22	32	Carta della Nuova Inghilterra, Nuova Yorke, Pensilvania
mwuss1647	virginia	1781	BELLIN	350	18	28	Carta della Virginia della Baja Chesapeack
mwwi0866	st kitts	1780	BELLIN	200	19	30	Carte de de l'Isle St. Christophe pour Servir a l'Histoire Generale des Voyages
mwca0094	canada	1773	BELLIN	200	22	29	Carte de la Baie de Hudson
mwaf0605	africa islands madagascar	1764	BELLIN	200	22	18	Carte de la Baye d'Antongil
mwuss0800	massachusetts	1764	BELLIN	250	22	17	Carte de la Baye de Baston Situee dans la Nouvelle Angleterre
mwuss0748	maryland	1757	BELLIN	250	20	29	Carte de la Baye de Chesapeack et Pays Voisins
mwuss0744	maryland	1750	BELLIN	300	28	38	Carte de la Baye de Chesapeak et Pays Voisins
mwc0157	china	1756	BELLIN	240	21	30	Carte de la Baye de Chin-Chew ou Chang-Chew avec les Isles d'Emowi et de Quemowi
mwsp0567	spain regions	1764	BELLIN	200	21	17	Carte de la Baye de Corcubion
mwsp0740	gibraltar	1790	BELLIN	550	42	58	Carte de la Baye de Gibraltar Dressee au Depost des Cartes de la Marine pour le Service de Vaisseaux de Roy ... Par le S. Bellin Ingenieur de la Marine Ceuseur Royal &a. 1762
mwca0075	canada	1757	BELLIN	200	22	30	Carte de la Baye de Hudson, pour Servir a l'Histoire Generale des Voyages
mwaf0924	africa south	1748	BELLIN	200	18	17	Carte de la Baye de la Table et Rade du Cap de Bonne Esperance
mwit0816	italy sardinia	1764	BELLIN	140	22	17	Carte de la Baye de l'Oristan
mwaf1051	africa south east	1752	BELLIN	150	21	16	Carte de la Baye de Mosambique
mwgm0422	panama	1764	BELLIN	250	22	17	Carte de la Baye de Panama dans l'Amerique Meridionale
mwaf0923	africa south	1748	BELLIN	100	21	16	Carte de la Baye de Sainte Helene
mwsam0378	south america brazil	1764	BELLIN	200	22	17	Carte de la Baye de Tous les Saints
mwsp0568	spain regions	1764	BELLIN	180	22	17	Carte de la Baye de Vigo et Isles de Bayone
mwc0163	china	1759	BELLIN	180	20	27	Carte de la Baye d'Hocsieu et des Entrees de la Riviere de Chang Situees dans la Province de Fokyen
mwaf0925	africa south	1748	BELLIN	200	23	28	Carte de la Baye Saldane
mwuss0088	california	1777	BELLIN	550	30	20	Carte de la Californie
mwuss0189	carolinas	1773	BELLIN	350	19	28	Carte de la Caroline et Georgie pour Servir a l'Histoire Philosophique & Politique des Etablissemens et du Commerce des Europeens dans les Deux Indes

AMPG REFERENCE	REGION	DATE	MAP MAKER	PRICE (UK£)	VERT. (cm.)	HOR. (cm.)	TITLE OF MAP (Comments by the editor in brackets)
mwsam0631	south america guyana	1773	BELLIN	200	21	41	Carte de la Colonie de Surinam
mwme0614a	arabia etc	1740	BELLIN	350	22	25	Carte de la Coste d'Arabie Mer Rouge et Golfe de Perse ... 1740 (illustrated left is the van der Schley 1745 edition)
mwuss0421	florida	1764	BELLIN	350	22	34	Carte de la Coste de la Floride depuis la Baye de la Mobile jusqu'aux Cayes de St. Martin
mwaf1193	africa west	1739	BELLIN	250	20	25	Carte de la Coste Occidentale d'Afrique, depuis le XIIe Degre de Latitude Septentrionale
mwaf0405	africa east	1750	BELLIN	120	25	23	Carte de la Coste Orientale d'Afrique, depuis le Cap de Bonne Esperance, jusqu'au Cap del Gada
mwaf0406	africa east	1750	BELLIN	200	25	20	Carte de la Coste Orientale d'Afrique, depuis le XIIIe Degre de Latitude Meridionale jusqu'au XVIe Degre de Latitude Septentrionale
mwru0534a	ukraine	1750	BELLIN	180	21	17	Carte de la Crimee
mwuss0413	florida	1757	BELLIN	320	22	30	Carte de la Floride, de la Louisiane et Pays Voisins. Pour Servir a l'Histoire Generale des Voyages
mwf0128	france	1755	BELLIN	650	54	90	Carte de la France Divisee en Archevesches et Evesches ou l'on a Marque les Benefices qui Dependent de l'Ordre de Cluny
mwgr0195	greece	1764	BELLIN	280	18	23	Carte de la Grece et de la Moree
mwsam0613	south america guyana	1763	BELLIN	300	42	60	Carte de la Guyane Francoise et l'Isle de Cayenne Francoise et l'Isle de Cayenne
mwam0948	america north (east)	1744	BELLIN	900	39	56	Carte de la Louisiane Cours du Mississipi et Pais Voisins Dediee au M. le Comte de Maurepas, Ministre et Secretaire d'Etat
mwuss0628	louisiana	1750	BELLIN	1800	48	62	Carte de la Louisiane et des Pays Voisins
mwuss0643	louisiana	1773	BELLIN	450	22	30	Carte de la Louisiane et Pays Voisins pour Servir a l'Histoire des Etablissemens Europeens
mwas0325	asia caspian sea	1764	BELLIN	250	22	17	Carte de la Mer Caspienne et ses Environs
mwme1015	turkey etc	1764	BELLIN	250	23	36	Carte de la Mer de Marmara
mwm0058	mediterranean	1745	BELLIN	2400	52	74	Carte de la Mer Mediterranee (set of 3 maps; 2 maps 52x74cm, central map 78x55cm)
mwgr0206	greece	1771	BELLIN	320	24	30	Carte de la Moree et partie de la Grece
mwru0238	russia	1764	BELLIN	180	29	23	Carte de la Moscovie Europeene
mwam0997	america north (east)	1757	BELLIN	300	21	30	Carte de la Nouvelle Angleterre Nouvelle York et Pensilvanie
mwam1016	america north (east)	1764	BELLIN	1000	32	38	Carte de la Nouvelle Angleterre New York Pensilvanie et Nouveau Jersay
mwuss0495	georgia	1764	BELLIN	300	22	15	Carte de la Nouvelle Georgie
mwuss1087	new york	1757	BELLIN	400	20	29	Carte de la Nouvelle Yorck et Pensilvanie
mwgr0190	greece	1751	BELLIN	240	24	32	Carte de la partie meridionale de la Grece
mwca0057	canada	1744	BELLIN	1000	40	56	Carte de la Partie Orientale de la Nouvelle France ou du Canada Dediee a Monseigneur le Comte de Maurepas (illustrated is Homann Heirs 1755 re-issue)
mwjk0164	korea	1760	BELLIN	650	27	22	Carte de la Province de Quantong ou Lyau-Tong et du Royaume de Kau-Li ou Coree
mwaf1205	africa west	1748	BELLIN	140	20	28	Carte de la Rade de Benguela
mwsam0807	south america uruguay	1755	BELLIN	250	19	28	Carte de la Riviere de la Plata
mwuss1547	vermont	1744	BELLIN	300	30	14	Carte de la Riviere de Richelieu et du Lac Champlain
mwru0226	russia	1757	BELLIN	250	28	46	Carte de la Siberie et des Pays Voisins
mwru0227	russia	1757	BELLIN	250	23	32	Carte de la Tartarie Occidentale, pour Servir a l'Histoire Generale des Voyages
mwru0455a	russia tartary	1758	BELLIN	200	20	28	Carte de la Tartarie Orientale, pour Servir a l'Histoire Generale des Voyages
mwuss1633	virginia	1747	BELLIN	400	19	30	Carte de la Virginie Mari-Land &c. Tiree de Meilleures Cartes Angloises
mwuss1637	virginia	1757	BELLIN	400	20	30	Carte de la Virginie, de la Baye Chesapeack, et Pays Voisins
mwuss1640	virginia	1770	BELLIN	450	19	29	Carte de la Virginie, Maryland and Bai de Chesapeack
mwgm0216	mexico	1754	BELLIN	150	22	15	Carte de Lac de Mexico et de ses Environs Lors de la Conquete
mwca0396	canada nova scotia	1773	BELLIN	200	21	32	Carte de l'Acadie
mwca0397	canada nova scotia	1773	BELLIN	200	20	32	Carte de l'Acadie, Isle Royale et Pais Voisins
mwaf0184	africa	1747	BELLIN	200	21	17	Carte de l'Afrique
mwam0187	america continent	1764	BELLIN	300	46	30	Carte de l'Amerique et des Mers Voisines 1763
mwam0410	america north	1755	BELLIN	1400	55	86	Carte de l'Amerique Septentrionale depuis le 28 Degre de Latitude jusqu'au 72
mwam0390	america north	1743	BELLIN	400	28	36	Carte de l'Amerique Septentrionale pour Servir a l'Histoire de la Nouvelle France 1743
mwaf0606	africa islands madagascar	1764	BELLIN	200	22	35	Carte de l'Ance Dauphine
mwp0363	pacific marianas	1750	BELLIN	300	23	15	Carte de l'Archipel de St. Lazare ou les Isles Marianes
mwaf1206	africa west	1748	BELLIN	120	22	17	Carte de l'Embouchure de la Riviere de Congo ou de Zayre
mwsam0627	south america guyana	1773	BELLIN	140	21	16	Carte de l'Embouchure des Rivieres de Copename et Sarameca
mwjk0089	japan	1736	BELLIN	2400	42	54	Carte de l'Empire du Japon
mwjk0111	japan	1757	BELLIN	450	20	32	Carte de l'Empire du Japon pour Servir a l'Histoire Generale des Voyages
mwgm0218	mexico	1754	BELLIN	180	21	29	Carte de l'Empire du Mexique pour l'Histoire General des Voyages

AMPG REFERENCE	REGION	DATE	MAP MAKER	PRICE (UK£)	VERT. (cm.)	HOR. (cm.)	TITLE OF MAP (Comments by the editor in brackets)
mwsam0628	south america guyana	1773	BELLIN	140	21	17	Carte de l'Entree de la Riviere de Berbice Suivant les Plans des Hollandois
mwc0170	china	1764	BELLIN	300	27	22	Carte de l'Entree de la Riviere de Canton
mwsam0629	south america guyana	1773	BELLIN	140	21	17	Carte de l'Entree de la Riviere de Corentyn sur ce que les Anglois et les Hollandois en ont Publie
mwsam0611	south america guyana	1762	BELLIN	140	22	17	Carte de l'Entree de la Riviere de Kourou
mwsam0612	south america guyana	1762	BELLIN	140	21	16	Carte de l'Entree de la Riviere de Marony
mwsam0615	south america guyana	1764	BELLIN	140	22	17	Carte de l'Entree de la Riviere de Poumaron
mwin0208a	india	1750	BELLIN	250	22	17	Carte de L'Entrée du Gange (inset of River Aracam mouth)
mwsam0460	south america chile	1764	BELLIN	180	22	17	Carte de l'Entree du Golphe du Chilos et du Port de Cachao au Chili
mwaa0036	antarctic	1780	BELLIN	600	56	56	Carte de l'Hemisphere Austral Montrant les Routes des Navigateurs les Plus Celebres par le Capitaine Jacques Cook
mwas0834	asia south east siam	1757	BELLIN	280	28	28	Carte de l'Inde au-dela du Gange comprenant les Royaumes de Siam, de Tunquin, Pegu, Ava, Aracan &c.
mwin0214	india	1752	BELLIN	200	23	34	Carte de l'Inde en deca du Gange Comprenant l'Indoustan &c.
mwin0215	india	1752	BELLIN	250	22	33	Carte de L'Indoustan
mwuk0176	ireland	1757	BELLIN	200	19	14	Carte de L'Irlande
mwsc0507	scandinavia iceland	1770	BELLIN	300	30	38	Carte de l'Islande pour Servir a la Continuation de l'Histoire Generale des Voyages
mwsc0505	scandinavia iceland	1764	BELLIN	250	21	16	Carte de l'Islande Situee entre le 64 et 66 Deg. de Lat. Sept.
mwas0613	asia south east celebes	1760	BELLIN	180	20	15	Carte de l'Isle Celebes ou Macassar
mwwi0301a	antigua	1764	BELLIN	280	21	13	Carte de L'Isle d'Antigue
mwaf0571	africa islands bourbon	1763	BELLIN	800	56	72	Carte de l'Isle de Bourbon
mwaf0570	africa islands bourbon	1750	BELLIN	240	20	23	Carte de l'Isle de Bourbon autrefois Mascareigne
mwsam0603	south america guyana	1753	BELLIN	180	22	28	Carte de l'Isle de Caienne et de ses Environs (Dutch edition illustrated)
mwsam0618	south america guyana	1764	BELLIN	200	20	28	Carte de l'Isle de Cayenne et de ses Environs
mwin0054	ceylon	1764	BELLIN	160	26	20	Carte de l'Isle de Ceylan
mwc0164	china	1759	BELLIN	200	21	31	Carte de l'Isle de Cheu-Chan ou Isle de Chusan
mwgr0507	greece cyprus	1764	BELLIN	1000	17	21	Carte de l'Isle de Chypre
mwf0508	france corsica	1764	BELLIN	300	40	23	Carte de l'Isle de Corse
mwf0517	france corsica	1768	BELLIN	960	59	86	Carte de l'Isle de Corse
mwaf0633	africa islands mauritius	1764	BELLIN	350	22	35	Carte de l'Isle de France
mwaf0632	africa islands mauritius	1763	BELLIN	1500	57	88	Carte de l'Isle de France ... M.DCC.LXIII
mwwi0373	barbados	1750	BELLIN	200	20	15	Carte de l'Isle de la Barbade
mwwi0376	barbados	1758	BELLIN	800	56	40	Carte de l'Isle de la Barbade Dressee au Depost des Cartes et Plans de la Marine pour le Service des Vaisseaux du Roy
mwwi0518	grenada	1760	BELLIN	850	89	56	Carte de l'Isle de la Grenade Dressee au Depost des Cartes et Plans de la Marine pour le Service des Vaisseaux du Roy
mwwi0517	grenada	1758	BELLIN	200	22	17	Carte de l'Isle de la Grenade, pour Servir a l'Histoire Generale des Voyages ... 1758
mwwi0553	guadeloupe	1770	BELLIN	180	21	30	Carte de l'Isle de la Guadeloupe. Pour Servir a l'Histoire Generale des Voyages. Par M.B. Ing'r de la Marine. 1758
mwwi0714	jamaica	1758	BELLIN	220	21	32	Carte de l'Isle de la Jamaique ... 1758
mwwi0777	martinique	1753	BELLIN	200	17	23	Carte de l'Isle de la Martinique
mwwi0794	martinique	1770	BELLIN	240	20	30	Carte de l'Isle de la Martinique. Pour Servir a l'Histoire Generale des Voyages ... 1758
mwaf0608	africa islands madagascar	1765	BELLIN	900	55	89	Carte de l'Isle de Madagascar
mwaf0607	africa islands madagascar	1764	BELLIN	350	22	35	Carte de l'Isle de Madagascar et du Canal de Mozambique
mwm0246a	mediterranean malta	1764	BELLIN	500	22	17	Carte de L'Isle de Malte
mwwi0541	guadeloupe	1758	BELLIN	450	22	16	Carte de l'Isle de Mari-Galante
mwca0570	canada quebec montreal	1744	BELLIN	550	24	31	Carte de l'Isle de Montreal et de ses Environs Dressee sur les Manuscrits du Depost des Cartes Plans et Journaux de la Marine
mwwi0816	nevis	1764	BELLIN	480	22	17	Carte de l'Isle de Nieves
mwec0484	uk england hampshire	1764	BELLIN	200	21	15	Carte de l'Isle de Portsey, et Havre de Portsmouth
mwwi0626	hispaniola	1764	BELLIN	960	56	90	Carte de l'Isle de Saint Domingue
mwwi0617	hispaniola	1758	BELLIN	235	19	29	Carte de l'Isle de Saint Domingue pour Servir a l'Histoire Generale des Voyages
mwwi0891	st vincent	1764	BELLIN	175	21	16	Carte de l'Isle de Saint Vincent
mwwi0923	virgin isl	1764	BELLIN	450	22	17	Carte de l'Isle de Sainte Croix au Sud des Isles des Vierges / carte de l'Isle de Saint Jean de Portorico
mwwi0878	st lucia	1763	BELLIN	950	57	87	Carte de l'Isle de Sainte Lucie Dressee au Depost des Cartes et Plans de la Marine pour le Service des Vaisseaux du Roy ... Par le Sr. Bellin Ingenieur de la Marine 1763.
mwwi0875	st lucia	1758	BELLIN	250	20	30	Carte de l'Isle de Sainte Lucie, pour Servir a l'Histoire Generale des Voyages
mwwi0862	st kitts	1764	BELLIN	250	20	33	Carte de l'Isle de St. Christophe
mwas0882	asia south east sumatra	1750	BELLIN	240	25	29	Carte de l'Isle de Sumatra
mwat0159	atlantic canary isl.	1746	BELLIN	250	23	17	Carte de l'Isle de Tenerife Suivant les Observations Astronomiques et les Journaux de Navigateurs
mwca0306	canada newfoundland	1744	BELLIN	250	29	36	Carte de l'Isle de Terre-Neuve

AMPG REFERENCE	REGION	DATE	MAP MAKER	PRICE (UK£)	VERT. (cm.)	HOR. (cm.)	TITLE OF MAP (Comments by the editor in brackets)
mwwi0637	hispaniola	1771	BELLIN	200	23	33	Carte de l'Isle d'Hayti Aujourd'hui l'Espagnole, ou l'Isle de St. Domingue avec les Isles Voisines
mwca0591	canada st lawrence	1744	BELLIN	200	19	28	Carte de l'Isle d'Orleans et du Passage de la Traverse dans le Fleuve St. Laurent
mwgr0329	greece corfu	1771	BELLIN	450	21	31	Carte de l'isle et canal de Corfu
mwc0309	china formosa	1764	BELLIN	650	22	17	Carte de l'Isle Formose aux Costes de la Chine
mwca0352	canada nova scotia	1744	BELLIN	400	23	27	Carte de l'Isle Royale
mwca0651	canada st pierre & miquelon	1763	BELLIN	500	59	90	Carte de l'Isle Saint Pierre Dressee au Depost des Cartes et Plans
mwca0654	canada st pierre & miquelon	1764	BELLIN	250	22	16	Carte de l'Isle St. Pierre
mwwi0924	virgin isl	1764	BELLIN	600	22	36	Carte de l'Isle St. Thomas l'une des Vierges
mwgm0423	panama	1764	BELLIN	235	22	30	Carte de l'Isthme de Panama
mwgm0412	panama	1754	BELLIN	250	20	29	Carte de l'Isthme de Panama et des Provinces de Veragua, Terre Ferme, et Darien pour l'Histoire Generale des Voyages
mwat0037	atlantic ocean (all)	1746	BELLIN	350	33	46	Carte de l'Ocean Occidental Dressee pour Servir a l'Histoire Generale des Voyages
mwam0947	america north (east)	1744	BELLIN	300	24	37	Carte de l'Ocean Occidental et Partie de l'Amerique Septentrionale Dressee pour l'Intelligence du Journal du Voyage que le R.P. de Charlevoix de la Compagnie de Jesus a Fait en 1720 au Canada, a la Louisiane & a St. Domingue
mwas0478	asia south east	1753	BELLIN	300	35	47	Carte de l'Ocean Oriental, ou Mer des Indes
mwwi0627	hispaniola	1764	BELLIN	150	21	32	Carte des Bayes du Mesle des Flamands et de Cavaillon
mwca0307	canada newfoundland	1744	BELLIN	200	21	30	Carte des Bayes, Rades et Port de Plaisance dans l'Isle de Terre Neuve
mwf0509	france corsica	1764	BELLIN	200	22	17	Carte des Bouches de Boniface entre la Corse et la Sardaigne
mwam1287	great lakes	1764	BELLIN	550	23	33	Carte des Cinq Grands Lacs du Canada
mwc0183	china	1773	BELLIN	150	20	14	Carte des Costes de Cochin Chine, Tunquin, et Partie de celles de la Chine
mwuss0410	florida	1744	BELLIN	250	20	14	Carte des Costes de la Floride Francoise Suivant les Premieres Decouvertes
mwin0225	india	1757	BELLIN	250	24	20	Carte des Costes de Perse, Gusarat, et Malabar. Tiree de la Carte Francoise de l'Ocean Oriental
mwuss0942	mississippi	1744	BELLIN	450	20	28	Carte des Embouchures du Mississipi
mwuk1436	england thames	1759	BELLIN	500	58	87	Carte des Entrees de la Tamise
mwuk1437	england thames	1764	BELLIN	120	22	18	Carte des Entrees de la Tamise
mwsam0616	south america guyana	1764	BELLIN	140	21	17	Carte des Entrees des Rivieres de Demerary et d'Essequebo Suivant les Plans des Hollandois
mwas0662	asia south east java	1773	BELLIN	180	21	28	Carte des Environs de Batavia
mwgm0219	mexico	1754	BELLIN	150	21	16	Carte des Environs de la Ville de Mexico
mwsc0363	scandinavia denmark	1750	BELLIN	180	21	15	Carte des Environs de Tornea
mwit1246	italy venice	1764	BELLIN	200	22	17	Carte des Environs de Venise
mwit1249	italy venice	1771	BELLIN	800	57	83	Carte des Environs de Venise
mwwi0608	hispaniola	1749	BELLIN	200	20	31	Carte des Environs du Cap Francois et des Paroisses qui en Dependent
mwwi0715	jamaica	1758	BELLIN	500	25	37	Carte des Havres de Kingstown et de Port Royal
mwwi0917	turks & caicos isl.	1768	BELLIN	250	22	16	Carte des Isles a l'Est des Isles Turques
mwat0122	atlantic bermuda	1764	BELLIN	550	20	33	Carte des Isles Bermudes ou de Sommer Tire de l'Anglois
mwat0160	atlantic canary isl.	1746	BELLIN	200	22	29	Carte des Isles Canaries Dressee sur les Journaux des Navigateurs
mwwi0330	bahamas	1773	BELLIN	250	21	16	Carte des Isles d'Aklin de la Fortune de Kroo-Ked
mwaf0577b	africa islands comores	1757	BELLIN	120	19	23	Carte des Isles de Comore
mwuk0513	scotland	1764	BELLIN	200	23	17	Carte des Isles de Hetland ou Shetland
mwas0482	asia south east	1757	BELLIN	300	25	30	Carte des Isles de Java, Sumatra, Borneo &c., les Detroits de la Sonde Malaca et Banca Golphe de Siam &c.
mwat0240	atlantic madeira	1746	BELLIN	350	18	24	Carte des Isles de Madere et Porto Santo Dressee sur les Journaux des Plus Habiles Navigateurs
mwsp0660	balearic islands	1740	BELLIN	750	42	57	Carte des Isles de Maiorque Minorque et Yvice
mwca0655	canada st pierre & miquelon	1764	BELLIN	250	22	16	Carte des Isles de Miquelon et de St. Pierre et la Coste de Terre-Neuve Voisine
mwp0383	pacific new guinea	1756	BELLIN	280	32	35	Carte des Isles de Papous
mwf0981	france poitou	1750	BELLIN	400	88	56	Carte des Isles de Re et d'Olleron - avec Partie des Costes de Poitou Aunis et Saintonge
mwit0837	italy sardinia and corsica	1764	BELLIN	280	24	34	Carte des Isles de Sardaigne et Du Corse
mwwi0925	virgin isl	1764	BELLIN	600	20	24	Carte des Isles des Vierges
mwat0197	atlantic cape verde isl.	1746	BELLIN	150	20	28	Carte des Isles du Cap Verd
mwjk0090	japan	1736	BELLIN	550	33	28	Carte des Isles du Japon ... Pays de Kamtschatka
mwjk0097	japan	1746	BELLIN	500	21	29	Carte des Isles du Japon et la Presqu'Isle de Coree, avec les Costes de la Chine depuis Pekin jusqu'a Canton
mwjk0110	japan	1754	BELLIN	550	25	36	Carte des Isles du Japon Terre de Jesso et Pays Voisins, 1752
mwjk0107	japan	1753	BELLIN	200	24	26	Carte des Isles Kouriles d'apres la Carte Russe Dressee et Gravee par Laurent
mwwi0322	bahamas	1764	BELLIN	400	22	27	Carte des Isles Lucayes
mwin0466	indian ocean maldives	1750	BELLIN	140	22	15	Carte des Isles Maldives, pour Servir a l'Histoire des Etablissemens Europeens

AMPG REFERENCE	REGION	DATE	MAP MAKER	PRICE (UK£)	VERT. (cm.)	HOR. (cm.)	TITLE OF MAP (Comments by the editor in brackets)
mwat0219	atlantic falkland isl.	1760	BELLIN	250	21	30	Carte des Isles Malouines ou Isles Nouvelles que les Anglois Noment Aujourd'hui Isles de Falkland
mwas0780	asia south east philippines	1752	BELLIN	400	21	17	Carte des Isles Philippines ... 1re Feuille / Carte des Isles Philippines Dressee sur la Carte Espagnole ... 2e Feuille (2 maps, different sizes)
mwas0774	asia south east philippines	1748	BELLIN	240	22	15	Carte des Isles Philippines Celebes et Moluques
mwc0158	china	1756	BELLIN	240	21	32	Carte des Isles qui sont a l'Embouchure de la Riviere de Canton
mwwi0915	turks & caicos Isl.	1764	BELLIN	300	23	38	Carte des Isles Situees au Nord de St. Domingue
mwwi0323	bahamas	1764	BELLIN	200	23	38	Carte des Isles Situees au Nord de St. Domingue avec les Passages pour le Retour Appelles Debouquemens 1763
mwwi0916	turks & caicos Isl.	1768	BELLIN	300	22	16	Carte des Isles Turques
mwas0742	asia south east moluccas	1757	BELLIN	160	20	30	Carte des Isles Voisines des Moluques, Ceram, Bouro Amboine, Banda, Neyra &ca.
mwam1277	great lakes	1744	BELLIN	3000	28	44	Carte des Lacs du Canada Dressee sur les Manuscrits du Depost des Cartes, Plans et Journaux de la Marine et sur le Journal du RP. de Charlevoix ... 1742
mwam1284	great lakes	1757	BELLIN	400	20	29	Carte des Lacs du Canada pour Servir a l'Histoire Generale des Voyages
mwca0216	canada arctic	1753	BELLIN	200	21	27	Carte des Parties du Nord-Ouest de l'Amerique Suivant les Voyages de Middleton et d'Ellis en 1742 et 1746. Pour Chercher un Passage dans la Mer du Sud
mwsam0838	south america venezuela	1770	BELLIN	240	19	29	Carte des Provinces de Caracas, Comana et Paria Situees dans l'Amerique Meridionale
mwsam0833	south america venezuela	1754	BELLIN	180	20	29	Carte des Provinces de Cartagene, S. Marthe et Venezuela
mwgm0375	nicaragua	1754	BELLIN	150	20	17	Carte des Provinces de Nicaragua et Costa Rica
mwgm0224	mexico	1759	BELLIN	200	21	34	Carte des Provinces de Tabasco, Chiapa, Verapaz, Guatimala, Honduras et Yucatan
mwsam0519a	south america colombia	1756	BELLIN	200	21	26	Carte des Provinces de Tierra Firme, Darien, Cartagene et Nouvelle Grenade
mwaf1216	africa west	1757	BELLIN	180	24	30	Carte des Royaumes de Congo, Angola et Benguela
	asia south east siam	1750	BELLIN	280	28	28	Carte des Royaumes de Siam, de Tunquin, Pegu, Ava, Aracan
mww0463	world	1765	BELLIN	1350	55	88	Carte des Variations de la Boussole et des Vents Generaux que l'on Trouve dans les Mers les Plus Frequentees
mwsam0375	south america brazil	1757	BELLIN	200	25	33	Carte du Bresil Prem. Partie depuis la Riviere des Amazones jusqu'a la Baye de Tous les Saints
mwwi0325	bahamas	1768	BELLIN	650	21	31	Carte du Canal de Bahama
mwsam0463	south america chile	1764	BELLIN	200	24	18	Carte du Chili
mwec0636	uk england kent	1759	BELLIN	480	56	84	Carte du Comte de Kent et du Pas de Calais pour Servir aux Vaisseaux du Roy
mwas0912	asia south east vietnam	1747	BELLIN	250	21	14	Carte du Cours de la Riviere de Tunquin, depuis Cacho jusqu'a la Mer (environs of Hanoi)
mwca0505	canada quebec	1744	BELLIN	300	20	29	Carte du Cours de la Riviere du Saguenay Appellee par les Sauvages Pitchitaouichetz
mwca0612	canada st lawrence	1771	BELLIN	180	19	30	Carte du Cours du Fleuve de St. Laurent depuis son Embouchure jusqu'au Dessus de Quebec
mwsam0209	south america amazon	1773	BELLIN	200	17	37	Carte du Cours du Maragnon ou de la Grande Riviere des Amazones
mwas0836	asia south east siam	1764	BELLIN	180	22	16	Carte du Cours du Menam depuis Siam jusqu'a la Mer
mwsp0710	gibraltar	1750	BELLIN	250	22	17	Carte du Detroit de Gibraltar
mwsp0721	gibraltar	1761	BELLIN	800	60	91	Carte du Detroit de Gibraltar Dressee au Depost des Cartes et Plans de la Marine pour le Service des Vaisseaux du Roy
mwsam0683	south america magellan	1753	BELLIN	200	18	27	Carte du Detroit de la Maire, dressee sur les Journaux des Navigateurs
mwru0228	russia	1757	BELLIN	180	20	30	Carte du Detroit de Waeigats ou de Nassau
mwam1278	great lakes	1744	BELLIN	400	21	16	Carte du Detroit entre le Lac Superieur et le Lac Huron, avec le Sault Sainte Marie et le Poste de Michillimakinac
mwin0234	india	1760	BELLIN	180	30	31	Carte du District de Tranquebar
mwca0058	canada	1744	BELLIN	400	43	29	Carte du Fonds de la Baye de Hudson que les Anglois Appellent Baye James / Carte de la Baye de Hudson
mwme0882a	syria etc	1764	BELLIN	200	22	17	Carte du Golphe d'Alexandrette (north to the left)
mwin0388	india bay of bengal	1760	BELLIN	220	22	27	Carte du Golphe de Bengale
mwsc0734	scandinavia sweden	1756	BELLIN	235	21	16	Carte du Golphe de Bothnie
mwin0240	india	1763	BELLIN	140	22	18	Carte du Golphe de Cambaye
mwca0613	canada st lawrence	1773	BELLIN	180	19	28	Carte du Golphe de St. Laurent et Pays Voisins pour Servir a l'Histoire des Etablissemens Europeens
mwca0597	canada st lawrence	1757	BELLIN	180	22	35	Carte du Golphe de St. Laurent et Pays Voisins pour Servir a l'Histoire Generale des Voyages
mwgm0032	gulf of mexico and surrounding regions	1754	BELLIN	500	27	37	Carte du Golphe du Mexique et des Isles de l'Amerique
mwc0314	china tibet	1749	BELLIN	280	22	31	Carte du Grande Thibet
mwsc0468	scandinavia greenland	1770	BELLIN	240	20	25	Carte du Groenland Dressee et Gravee par Laurent
mwca0314	canada newfoundland	1764	BELLIN	150	21	16	Carte du Havre de Saint Jean dans l'Isle de Terre-Neuve (north to the left)
mwru0455	russia tartary	1757	BELLIN	300	52	30	Carte du Kamtchatka Dressee et Gravee par Laurent (see Laurent 1705)

AMPG REFERENCE	REGION	DATE	MAP MAKER	PRICE (UK£)	VERT. (cm.)	HOR. (cm.)	TITLE OF MAP (Comments by the editor in brackets)
mwjk0162	korea	1750	BELLIN	400	21	31	Carte du Katay, ou Empire de Kin, pour Servir a l'Historie de Jenghiz Khan
mwgm0212	mexico	1750	BELLIN	200	21	15	Carte du Lac de Mexico et de ses Environs lors de la Conqueste des Espagnols
mwgm0220	mexico	1754	BELLIN	200	21	29	Carte du Mexique
mwsam0484	south america juan fernandez	1752	BELLIN	240	20	28	Carte du Nord Est de l'Isle de Juan Fernandez / Vue de la Baye de Cumberland
mwsam0718	south america paraguay	1756	BELLIN	220	46	30	Carte du Paraguay et des Pays Voisins pour Servir a l'Histoire Generale des Voyages
mwsam0762	south america peru	1755	BELLIN	200	37	20	Carte du Perou. Pour l'Histoire Generale des Voyages
mwsc0628	scandinavia norway	1764	BELLIN	200	22	30	Carte du Spits-Berg Suivant les Hollandois (rarer variant 22x18cm shown far left above)
mwam1006	america north (east)	1760	BELLIN	400	36	46	Carte d'une Partie de l'Amerique Septentrionale, pour Servir a l'Intelligence du Memoire sur les Pretentions des Anglois au Sujet des Limites a Regler avec la France
mwsam0836	south america venezuela	1764	BELLIN	220	21	29	Carte d'une Partie du Cours de l'Orenoque / Carte du Bras Principal de la Riviere d'Orenoque
mwaf0517	africa egypt etc	1764	BELLIN	150	22	17	Carte Exacte du Cours du Nile
mwaf1211	africa west	1750	BELLIN	480	55	89	Carte Generale de la Coste de Guinee depuis la Riviere de Sierra Leona jusqu'au Cap de Lopez Gonsalvo
mwuk0201	ireland	1770	BELLIN	850	61	88	Carte Generale des Costes d'Irelande et des Costes Occidentales d'Angleterre
mwsp0563	spain regions	1762	BELLIN	800	56	88	Carte Hydrographique de la Baye de Cadix
mwwi0434	cuba	1762	BELLIN	600	43	59	Carte Hydrographique de la Baye de la Havane avec le Plan de la Ville et de ses Forts pour Joindre a la Carte de l'Isle de Cube
mwsam0242	south america argentina	1770	BELLIN	450	39	56	Carte Hydrographique de la Riviere de la Plata (illustration shows Spanish edition)
mwm0100	mediterranean adriatic	1771	BELLIN	875	50	86	Carte Hydrographique du Golphe de Venise (inset: whole Mediterranean)
mwas0733	asia south east moluccas	1750	BELLIN	160	18	27	Carte Particuliere de l'Isle d'Amboine
mwsam0485	south america juan fernandez	1757	BELLIN	240	20	28	Carte Particuliere de l'Isle de Juan Fernandes. Tiree du Voyage de l'Amiral Anson
mwwi0716	jamaica	1758	BELLIN	750	60	88	Carte Particuliere de l'Isle de la Jamaique Dressee au Depost des Cartes ... pour le Service des Vaisseaux du Roy par Ordre de M. le Marquis de Massaic
mwbh0702b	belgium holland	1753	BELLIN	450	61	81	Carte Particuliere des Costes de Flanders de Picarde et de Normandie depuis Nieuport jusqu'a Dieppe. Avec les Costes d'Angleterre aux Environs de Pas de Calais (Map by C. Berey. North to the left)
mwf0796	france normandy	1770	BELLIN	400	60	86	Carte Particuliere des Costes de Normandie depuis Dieppe jusqu'a la Pointe de la Percee en Bessin
mwuk1389	england south	1756	BELLIN	600	61	87	Carte Particuliere des Costes Meridionales d'Angleterre qui Comprend l'Isle de Wight, et le Havre de Portsmouth
mwas0741	asia south east moluccas	1757	BELLIN	180	23	15	Carte Particuliere des Isles Moluques
mwsam0630	south america guyana	1773	BELLIN	140	19	27	Carte Particuliere d'une Partie des Rivieres de Berbice et de Caroje, pour l'Intelligence de la Relation Touchant la Revolt des Negres en 1763
mwas0831	asia south east siam	1750	BELLIN	500	48	34	Carte Plate du Golfe de Siam avec une Partie des Cotes de Malaye et de Camboje, depuis l'Isle Timor jusqu'a celle Condor
mwru0193	russia	1744	BELLIN	240	23	35	Carte pour les Voyages de Rubruquis, Marco Polo, Jen-kin-son, &c.
mwat0124	atlantic bermuda	1768	BELLIN	200	18	24	Carte pour Marquer la Position des Isles Bermudes
mwsam0685	south america magellan	1764	BELLIN	220	20	35	Carte Reduite de Detroit de Magellan. Dresses sur les Journaux des Navigateurs
mwme1026	turkey etc	1772	BELLIN	800	59	89	Carte Reduite de la Mer de Marmara et du Canal des Dardanelles
mwp0252	pacific (all)	1753	BELLIN	400	20	36	Carte Reduite de la Mer du Sud
mwm0065a	mediterranean	1764	BELLIN	450	24	51	Carte Reduite de la Mer Mediterranee
mwru0549	ukraine	1772	BELLIN	960	53	81	Carte Reduite de la Mer Noire, dressee pour le service des vaisseaux du Roy. Par Ordre de M. de Boynes, Secretaire d'Etat
mwsam0238	south america argentina	1760	BELLIN	200	21	17	Carte Reduite de la Partie la Plus Meridionale de l'Amerique (title also in Dutch)
mwca0315a	canada newfoundland	1764	BELLIN	450	60	79	Carte Reduite de la Partie Septentrionale de l'Isle de Terre Neuve Dresse au Depost des Cartes et Plans de la Marine ... M.DCC.LXIV
mwin0244	india	1766	BELLIN	800	62	88	Carte Reduite de la Presque Isle de l'Inde
mwec0634	uk england kent	1757	BELLIN	400	58	41	Carte Reduite de la Rade des Dunes
mwgr0628	greece islands	1751	BELLIN	650	66	53	Carte reduite de l'Archipel
mwsc0506	scandinavia iceland	1767	BELLIN	800	54	83	Carte Reduite de l'Islande et des Mers qui en sont Voisines
mwwi0300	antigua	1758	BELLIN	950	57	42	Carte Reduite de l'Isle d'Antigue Dressee au Depost des Cartes Plans et Journaux de la Marine pour le Service des Vaisseaux du Roy

AMPG REFERENCE	REGION	DATE	MAP MAKER	PRICE (UK£)	VERT. (cm.)	HOR. (cm.)	TITLE OF MAP (Comments by the editor in brackets)
mwwi0435	cuba	1762	BELLIN	1200	57	88	Carte Reduite de l'Isle de Cube Dressee au Depot des Cartes et Plans de la Marine, pour le Service des Vaisseaux du Roy par Ordre de Mle. Duc de Choiseul
mwwi0778	martinique	1758	BELLIN	875	58	90	Carte Reduite de l'Isle de la Martinique
mwwi0861	st kitts	1758	BELLIN	1350	58	89	Carte Reduite de l'Isle de Saint Christophe Dressee au Depost des Cartes Plans et Journaux de la Marine
mwwi0611	hispaniola	1750	BELLIN	1200	56	88	Carte Reduite de l'Isle de Saint Domingue et de ses Debouquements pour Servir aux Vaisseaux du Roy
mwat0042	atlantic ocean (all)	1757	BELLIN	1200	57	88	Carte Reduite de l'Ocean Occidental
mwat0034	atlantic ocean (all)	1742	BELLIN	1500	57	88	Carte Reduite de l'Ocean Occidental ... 1742 (see also Bellin 1757)
mwin0426a	indian ocean	1740	BELLIN	900	55	87	Carte Reduite de l'Ocean Oriental ou Mer des Indes
mwp0415	pacific north	1766	BELLIN	1350	56	85	Carte Reduite de L'Ocean Septentrional
mwat0279	atlantic north	1768	BELLIN	800	58	88	Carte Reduite de Partie de la Mer du Nord comprise entre L'Ecosse, Le Dannemark, La Norwege et l'Islande
mwbh0712	belgium holland	1763	BELLIN	550	56	86	Carte Reduite des Costes de Flandre et de Hollande
mwsam0609a	south america guyana	1760	BELLIN	850	56	88	Carte Reduite des Costes de la Guyane depuis la Riviere d'Orenoque jusqu'au Cap de Nord à l'Entrée de la Riviere des Amazones
mwuss0422	florida	1764	BELLIN	2500	57	85	Carte Reduite des Costes de la Louisiane et de la Floride
mwsp0272	spain	1751	BELLIN	600	86	53	Carte Reduite des Costes d'Espagne et de Portugal (mainly Portugal)
mwaf0844b	africa north west	1753	BELLIN	550	59	89	Carte Reduite Des Costes Occidentales d'Afrique Depuis Premier Feuille
mwaf1215a	africa west	1753	BELLIN	550	89	55	Carte Reduite des Costes Occidentales d'Afrique. Seconde Feuille depuis le Cap Bojador jusqu'a la Riviere de Sierra Leona
mwam0996	america north (east)	1757	BELLIN	2400	54	88	Carte Reduite des Costes Orientales de l'Amerique Septentrionale
mwwi0328	bahamas	1768	BELLIN	800	58	89	Carte Reduite des Debouquemens de St. Domingue Dressee pour le Service des Vaisseaux du Roy par Ordre de Duc de Choiseul
mwuss0021	alaska	1764	BELLIN	400	20	28	Carte Reduite des Decouvertes des Russes entre l'Asie et l'Amerique
mwas0690	asia south east malacca	1755	BELLIN	1500	58	90	Carte Reduite des Detroits de Malacca Sincapour et du Gouverneur
mwat0093a	atlantic azores	1755	BELLIN	720	56	90	Carte Réduite des Isles Açores Pour servir aux Vaisseaux du Roy
mwwi0246	west indies (east)	1758	BELLIN	1250	87	55	Carte Reduite des Isles Antilles (inset: Virgin Isl.)
mwuk0503a	scotland	1757	BELLIN	800	56	86	Carte Reduite des Isles Britanniques (sheets 3 and 4, Scotland)
mwuk0176a	ireland	1757	BELLIN	850	86	54	Carte Reduite des Isles Britanniques Cinquieme Feuille Contenant l'Irlande (first edition, no Rhumb lines)
mwuk0839a	uk	1757	BELLIN	850	87	55	Carte Reduite des Isles Britanniques Dressee au Depost des Cartes, Plans et Journaux de la Marine
mwuk1001a	england	1757	BELLIN	1200	55	87	Carte Réduite des Isles Britanniques en cinq feuilles ... premiere feuille Partie Meridionale/seconde feuille Partie Septentrionale de l'Angleterre (2 sheets, each 55x87cm)
mwuk1584	channel islands	1757	BELLIN	900	57	42	Carte Reduite des Isles de Jersey Grenesey et d'Aurigny avec les Costes de Normandie et de Bretagne
mwwi0543	guadeloupe	1759	BELLIN	750	58	86	Carte Reduite des Isles de la Guadeloupe Marie Galante et les Saintes
mwat0225	atlantic falkland isl.	1771	BELLIN	1000	63	92	Carte Reduite des Isles Malouines ou Isles Nouvelles que les Anglois Nomment Aujourhui Isles de Falkland ... sur les Observations Memoirs et Journaux des Francois et des Anglois. 1771
mwas0781	asia south east philippines	1752	BELLIN	1500	87	54	Carte Reduite des Isles Philippines
mwp0248	pacific (all)	1742	BELLIN	1600	57	85	Carte Reduite des Mers Comprises entre l'Asie et l'Amerique Apelees par les Navigateurs Mer du Sud ou Mer Pacifique
mwat0275	atlantic north	1751	BELLIN	1000	55	88	Carte Reduite des Mers du Nord
mwat0277	atlantic north	1758	BELLIN	280	33	45	Carte Reduite des Mers du Nord pour Servir a l'Histoire Generale des Voyages
mwca0078	canada	1759	BELLIN	280	20	34	Carte Reduite des Parties Septentrionales du Globe, Situees entre l'Asie et l'Amerique
mwp0012	australia	1753	BELLIN	1350	20	28	Carte Reduite des Terres Australes (illustrated below is 1758 edition, same size)
mwaf0404a	africa east	1749	BELLIN	850	59	87	Carte Reduite du Canal de Mozambique
mwsc0465a	scandinavia greenland	1765	BELLIN	550	55	87	Carte Reduite du Detroit de Davids (north to the right)
mwsam0684	south america magellan	1760	BELLIN	200	19	34	Carte Reduite du Detroit de Magellan Dressee sur les Journaux des Navigateurs ... 1753
mww0461	world	1764	BELLIN	550	22	34	Carte Reduite du Globe Terrestre
mwca0594	canada st lawrence	1754	BELLIN	650	54	86	Carte Reduite du Golphe de St. Laurent Contenant l'Isle de Terre-Neuve et Partie de la Coste des Esquimaux l'Isle Royale, l'Isle St. Jean et celle d'Anticosti ... M.DCC LIV

AMPG REFERENCE	REGION	DATE	MAP MAKER	PRICE (UK£)	VERT. (cm.)	HOR. (cm.)	TITLE OF MAP (Comments by the editor in brackets)
mwgm0035	gulf of mexico and surrounding regions	1765	BELLIN	320	24	32	Carte Reduite du Golphe du Mexique et des Isles de l'Amerique
mwwi0143	west indies	1798	BELLIN	1200	53	80	Carte Reduite du Golphe du Mexique et des Isles de l'Amerique
mwca0315	canada newfoundland	1764	BELLIN	600	57	82	Carte Reduite du Grand Banc et d'une Partie de l'Isle de Terre Neuve Dressee au Depot des Cartes Plans et Journaux de la Marine ... MDCCLXIV
mwaf0938	africa south west	1754	BELLIN	800	90	58	Carte Reduite d'une Partie des Costes Occidentales et Meridionales de l'Afrique depuis Cabo Frio ou Cap Froid ... jusqu'a la Baye S. Blaise
mwsam0614a	south america guyana	1764	BELLIN	500	55	73	Carte Reduite pour la Navigation de Cayenne a la Martinique
mwin0242	india	1764	BELLIN	180	23	18	Coste de Coromandel et les Pays de Tonda, Mandalum et Tanjaor
mwaf1194	africa west	1740	BELLIN	200	25	20	Coste Occidentale d'Afrique depuis le Detroit de Gibraltar jusqu'au XIe Degre de Latitude Septentrionale
mwaf1078	africa south west	1739	BELLIN	200	26	26	Coste Occidentale d'Afrique depuis le XIe Degre de Latitude Meridionale jusqu'au Cap de Bonne Esperance
mwaf0517b	africa egypt etc	1764	BELLIN	200	22	36	Costes d'Egypte, depuis Alexandrie jusqu'a Rosette (illustrated above left, south to the top)
mwuk1502	uk english channel (all)	1764	BELLIN	160	22	35	Costes de France depuis Brest jusqu'a Dunkerque
mwsam0837	south america venezuela	1764	BELLIN	350	23	44	Cours de l'Orenoque depuis ses Sources jusqu'a le Mer avec des Rivieres que cy Deschargent
mwuss0947	mississippi	1764	BELLIN	400	22	35	Cours du Fleuve Saint Louis depuis ses Embouchures jusqu'a la Riviere d'Iberville et Costes Voisines
mwc0306	china formosa	1750	BELLIN	650	23	28	Das Eyland Formosa (German edition of Bellin)
mwgm0409	panama	1750	BELLIN	200	18	26	De Stad en Haven van Porto-Bello
mwsam0759	south america peru	1748	BELLIN	200	22	36	Der Hafen von Callo
mwwi0326	bahamas	1768	BELLIN	720	61	92	Description Geographique des Debouquemens qui sont au Nord de L'Isle de Saint Domingue
mwuss0946	mississippi	1764	BELLIN	400	22	17	Embouchures du Fleuve St. Louis ou Mississippi 1763
mwaf1054	africa south east	1757	BELLIN	150	21	27	Empire du Monomotapa et Etats Voisins
mwwi0449	cuba	1764	BELLIN	140	22	16	Entree de la Baye de St. Yago dans l'Isle de Cube
mwwi0628	hispaniola	1764	BELLIN	200	23	36	Environs de Leogane et du Port au Prince dans l'Isle de St. Domingue
mwwi0549	guadeloupe	1764	BELLIN	180	22	17	Environs du Fort Louis de la Guadeloupe
mww0401	world	1748	BELLIN	2000	50	69	Essay d'une Carte Reduite Contenant les Parties Connues du Globe Terrestre
mwsam0237	south america argentina	1756	BELLIN	200	18	28	Flusse de la Plata
mwf0510	france corsica	1764	BELLIN	180	21	18	Golphe de Campo-Moro et Valinco
mwf0511	france corsica	1764	BELLIN	180	22	16	Golphe de la Baye de Calvi
mwp0260	pacific (all)	1780	BELLIN	200	20	25	Grande Oceano ouvero Quinta Parte de Monde
mwsam0764	south america peru	1757	BELLIN	180	20	35	Grond-Tekening van de Stad Paita in 't Koningryk Sanata-Fe
mwsam0607	south america guyana	1757	BELLIN	140	20	31	Guyana
mwsam0617	south america guyana	1764	BELLIN	180	20	46	Guyane Portugaise et Partie du Cours de la Riviere des Amazones
mwca0606	canada st lawrence	1764	BELLIN	180	20	17	Idee de la Rade du Mingan Suivant le Journal de la Fregate du Roy la Diane en 1755
mwas0502	asia south east	1780	BELLIN	180	18	31	Indie Occidentali
mwas0560	asia south east bali	1761	BELLIN	350	19	23	Isle de Baly ou Petite Java (re-issued in smaller format, engraved by Louise Tardieu)
mwwi0450	cuba	1764	BELLIN	300	21	32	Isle de Cube
mwwi0500	curacao	1764	BELLIN	250	21	17	Isle de Curacao ou Corassol
mwwi0790	martinique	1764	BELLIN	200	20	36	Isle de la Martinique
mwaf0602	africa islands madagascar	1747	BELLIN	280	30	23	Isle de Madagascar autrement Isle de St. Laurent
mwsam0461	south america chile	1764	BELLIN	180	23	18	Isle du Chiloe et Environs
mwin0050	ceylon	1750	BELLIN	140	27	35	Jaffenapatam
mwuss0186	carolinas	1764	BELLIN	450	22	35	La Caroline dans l'Amerique Septentrionale Suivant les Cartes Angloises
mwc0156	china	1755	BELLIN	250	33	35	La Chine avec la Koree
mwsam0385	south america brazil	1773	BELLIN	250	17	37	La Grande Riviere des Amazones
mwuss0640	louisiana	1764	BELLIN	300	22	34	La Louisiane et Pays Voisin
mwca0085	canada	1764	BELLIN	250	20	35	La Nouvelle France ou Canada
mwwi0630	hispaniola	1764	BELLIN	200	22	35	La Partie Francoise de l'Isle de Saint Domingue
mwuss0900	michigan	1764	BELLIN	1500	21	32	La Riviere du Detroit depuis le Lac Sainte Claire jusqu'au Lac Erie (first map of Detroit)
mwgm0227	mexico	1764	BELLIN	200	22	17	La Vera-Cruz, Ville du Mexique
mwca0316	canada newfoundland	1764	BELLIN	250	22	16	Le Detroit de Belle-Isle
mwca0317	canada newfoundland	1764	BELLIN	200	21	34	Le Golphe de Saint Laurent et l'Isle de Terre-Neuve
mwaf0927	africa south	1748	BELLIN	450	24	34	Le Pays des Hottentots aux Environs du Cap de Bonne Esperance
mwwi0631	hispaniola	1764	BELLIN	180	23	17	Le Port au Prince dans l'Isle de St. Domingue
mwwi0451	cuba	1764	BELLIN	200	23	16	Le Port Marianne dans l'Isle de Cube
mwsp0099	portugal	1762	BELLIN	500	88	55	Le Portugal
mwc0141	china	1748	BELLIN	400	30	42	L'Empire de la Chine

AMPG REFERENCE	REGION	DATE	MAP MAKER	PRICE (UK£)	VERT. (cm.)	HOR. (cm.)	TITLE OF MAP (Comments by the editor in brackets)
mwsam0769	south america peru	1764	BELLIN	200	22	36	Lima et ses Environs Port du Callao avec la Cote et les Isles Voisines
mwsp0676	balearic islands	1770	BELLIN	350	24	35	L'Isle de Maiorque / L'Isle de Minorque / Carte de l'Isle d'Yvice et des Fromentieres
mwca0579	canada quebec montreal	1764	BELLIN	500	23	37	L'Isle de Montreal et ses Environs
mwit0817	italy sardinia	1764	BELLIN	400	22	17	L'Isle de Sardaigne
mwc0305	china formosa	1750	BELLIN	720	23	28	L'Isle Formose et Partie des Costes de la Chine
mwca0353	canada nova scotia	1744	BELLIN	300	22	30	L'Isle Royale Situee a l'Entree du Golphe de Saint Laurent
mww0485	world	1773	BELLIN	500	25	38	Mappe Monde
mwp0253	pacific (all)	1754	BELLIN	550	36	55	Neue und Richtige Karte von dem Stillen Meere oder Mar del Sur
mwas0661	asia south east java	1760	BELLIN	300	21	44	Nouvelle Carte de l'Isle de Java
mwp0301	pacific caroline isl.	1752	BELLIN	240	20	39	Nouvelle Carte des Isles Carolines
mwin0251	india	1773	BELLIN	250	28	35	Nouvelle Carte du Royaume de Bengale
mwuk1496a	uk english channel (all)	1749	BELLIN	1000	58	88	Nouvelle Carte Reduite de la Manche
mwsam0717	south america paraguay	1756	BELLIN	200	20	29	Paraguay
mwuss0639	louisiana	1764	BELLIN	450	20	44	Partie de la Coste de la Louisiane et de la Floride depuis le Mississipi jusqu'a St. Marc. d'Apalache
mwru0233	russia	1758	BELLIN	140	22	35	Partie de la Mer Glaciale Contenant la Nouvelle Zemle et le Pais des Samoiedes
mwca0603	canada st lawrence	1761	BELLIN	1350	56	86	Partie du Cours du Fleuve de Saint Laurent depuis Quebec jusqu'au Cap aux Oyes / Carte du Cours du Fleuve Saint Laurent depuis Quebec jusqu'a la Mer … 1761 (2 sheets, each 56x86cm)
mwca0607	canada st lawrence	1764	BELLIN	180	24	30	Partie du Fleuve St. Laurent avec le Passage de la Traverse et les Isles Voisines
mwca0524	canada quebec	1764	BELLIN	300	21	32	Partie du Fleuve St. Laurent depuis Quebec jusqu'au Lac St. Francois / Carte du Lac Champlain
mwwi0791	martinique	1764	BELLIN	200	22	36	Partie Meridionale de la Martinique
mwam1279	great lakes	1745	BELLIN	3000	48	61	Partie Occidentale de la Nouvelle France ou Canada
mwwi0550	guadeloupe	1764	BELLIN	200	23	36	Partie Orientale de l'Isle de la Guadeloupe Appellee la Grande-Terre
mwat0094	atlantic azores	1764	BELLIN	200	21	17	Partie Orientale des Isles Acores
mwwi0792	martinique	1764	BELLIN	200	22	36	Partie Septentrionale de la Martinique
mwwi0251	west indies (east)	1764	BELLIN	200	22	32	Petites Antilles ou Isles du Vent 3e Partie
mwsam0462	south america chile	1764	BELLIN	180	22	18	Pinco ou Port de la Conception au Chili
mwsp0569	spain regions	1764	BELLIN	320	23	18	Plan de Barcelone, Capitale de Catalogne
mwf0271	france aquitaine	1764	BELLIN	140	22	33	Plan de Bayonne
mwin0211	india	1751	BELLIN	240	19	26	Plan de Bombay et de ses Environs
mwf0759	france nord pas-de-calais	1764	BELLIN	160	23	28	Plan de Calais
mwsc0372	scandinavia denmark	1764	BELLIN	240	22	18	Plan de Copenhague
mwsam0767	south america peru	1763	BELLIN	140	18	15	Plan de Cusco lors de la Conqueste des Espagnols
mwf0758	france nord pas-de-calais	1764	BELLIN	160	21	34	Plan de Dunkerque
mwsam0379	south america brazil	1764	BELLIN	200	22	17	Plan de Fernambouc a la Coste de Bresil
mwuk0190	ireland	1764	BELLIN	95	21	18	Plan de Galloway et ses Environs
mwin0207	india	1750	BELLIN	250	20	35	Plan de Goa
mwin0404	india goa	1764	BELLIN	200	20	35	Plan de Goa
mwbh0713	belgium holland	1764	BELLIN	180	20	27	Plan de Gravelines a la Coste de Flandres
mwaf0404	africa east	1748	BELLIN	180	23	15	Plan de Isle et Ville Quiloa
mwjk0153	japan tokyo	1736	BELLIN	400	25	25	Plan de Jedo (shown left is c1752 re-issue, with minor changes)
mwaf0718	africa north	1764	BELLIN	240	23	35	Plan de la Baye d'Alger et ses Environs
mwsp0570	spain regions	1764	BELLIN	180	22	17	Plan de la Baye de Cadix
mwca0354	canada nova scotia	1744	BELLIN	550	20	28	Plan de la Baye de Chedabouctou Aujourd'hui Havre de Milfort
mwca0387	canada nova scotia	1763	BELLIN	450	22	35	Plan de la Baye de Chibouctou Nommee par les Anglois Halifax 1763
mwf0512	france corsica	1764	BELLIN	180	21	17	Plan de la Baye de La Hiace
mwas0790	asia south east philippines	1764	BELLIN	300	22	17	Plan de la Baye de Manille Situee dans l'Isle de Lucon
mwuss0409	florida	1744	BELLIN	400	19	17	Plan de la Baye de Pansacola
mwsam0380	south america brazil	1764	BELLIN	300	21	32	Plan de la Baye de Rio-Janeiro
mwsam0382	south america brazil	1765	BELLIN	600	51	34	Plan de la Baye de Rio-Janeiro
mwwi0452	cuba	1764	BELLIN	220	21	16	Plan de la Baye de St. Yago dans l'Isle de Cube
mwgm0410	panama	1750	BELLIN	250	19	32	Plan de la Baye et Ville de Portobelo en 1736
mwsam0524	south america colombia	1764	BELLIN	200	23	18	Plan de la Baye et Ville de Sainte Marthe et de la Coste aux Environs
mwat0331	atlantic st helena	1750	BELLIN	200	22	17	Plan de la Forteresse et Bourg, de Lisle de Ste. Helene
mwuss0638	louisiana	1764	BELLIN	400	19	28	Plan de la Nouvelle Orleans
mwaf0513	africa egypt etc	1750	BELLIN	200	20	28	Plan de la partie septentrionale du Golfe arabique et de la ville Sues (title below map. North to the right.)
mwsam0770	south america peru	1764	BELLIN	200	22	17	Plan de la Rade de Pisco a la Coste du Perou
mwme0882	syria etc	1764	BELLIN	140	22	17	Plan de la Rade de St. Jean d'Acre
mwca0656	canada st pierre & miquelon	1764	BELLIN	200	22	33	Plan de la Rade et Port de l'Isle St. Pierre
mwsp0571	spain regions	1764	BELLIN	320	23	18	Plan de la Rade et Ville d'Alicant

AMPG REFERENCE	REGION	DATE	MAP MAKER	PRICE (UK£)	VERT. (cm.)	HOR. (cm.)	TITLE OF MAP (Comments by the editor in brackets)
mwgm0221	mexico	1754	BELLIN	180	21	15	Plan de la Rade et Ville de la Vera-Cruz Situee par 19 Deg. 10 Min. de Lat. Sep. et 100 D, 15m, a l'Occid. de Paris
mwwi0632	hispaniola	1764	BELLIN	200	22	30	Plan de la Rade et Ville du Petit Goave
mwf0987	france poitou	1764	BELLIN	160	22	33	Plan de la Rochelle
mwru0239	russia	1764	BELLIN	250	22	18	Plan de la Ville d'Astracan
mwuss0799	massachusetts	1764	BELLIN	450	21	15	Plan de la Ville de Boston
mwuss0796	massachusetts	1760	BELLIN	550	19	29	Plan de la Ville de Boston et ses Environs
mwsam0236	south america argentina	1750	BELLIN	400	18	28	Plan de la Ville de Buenos-Ayres
mwsp0572	spain regions	1764	BELLIN	200	23	33	Plan de la Ville de Cadiz
mwsam0519	south america colombia	1754	BELLIN	300	19	32	Plan de la Ville de Carthagene des Indes ... 1735 (map by A. de Ulloa)
mwsam0619	south america guyana	1764	BELLIN	200	22	18	Plan de la Ville de Cayenne
mwf0513	france corsica	1764	BELLIN	180	22	18	Plan de la Ville de Corte dan l'Isle de Corse
mwf0795	france normandy	1764	BELLIN	180	22	33	Plan de la Ville de Dieppe
mwuk0191	ireland	1764	BELLIN	200	21	29	Plan de la Ville de Dublin
mwwi0721	jamaica	1764	BELLIN	180	20	30	Plan de la Ville de Kingston Suivant le Projet Donne par le Colonel Christian Lilly
mwsam0766	south america peru	1760	BELLIN	240	22	35	Plan de la Ville de Lima ou Des Rois Capitale du Perou
mwit1123	italy tuscany	1764	BELLIN	200	21	17	Plan de la Ville de Livourne
mwuk1206	england london	1764	BELLIN	600	23	17	Plan de la Ville de Londres et ses Fauxbourgs
mwca0389	canada nova scotia	1764	BELLIN	280	20	34	Plan de la Ville de Louisbourg dans l'Isle Royale
mwas0829	asia south east siam	1748	BELLIN	250	24	32	Plan de la Ville de Louvo Demeure Ordinaire des Roi de Siam
mwjk0091	japan	1736	BELLIN	320	20	27	Plan de la Ville de Meaco
mwaf0797	africa north morocco	1764	BELLIN	180	22	17	Plan de la Ville de Mellila
mwf0362	france brittany	1764	BELLIN	180	22	33	Plan de la Ville de Nantes
mwsam0620	south america guyana	1764	BELLIN	200	21	17	Plan de la Ville de Paramaribo Suivant les Plans Hollandois
mwc0146	china	1750	BELLIN	180	22	17	Plan de la Ville de Peking Capitale de l'Empire de la Chine
mwin0212	india	1764	BELLIN	235	19	15	Plan de la Ville de Pondicheri
mwca0505a	canada quebec	1744	BELLIN	400	20	28	Plan de la Ville de Quebec
mwsam0459a	south america chile	1748	BELLIN	200	18	24	Plan de la Ville de Santiago
mwas0835	asia south east siam	1757	BELLIN	400	20	28	Plan de la Ville de Siam Capitale du Royaume de ce nom (illustration shows Dutch edition)
mwsam0373	south america brazil	1754	BELLIN	375	18	30	Plan de la Ville de St. Salvador / Vue de la Ville
mwaf0823	africa north tunisia	1764	BELLIN	200	22	18	Plan de la Ville de Tunis et ses Environs
mwit1247	italy venice	1764	BELLIN	400	27	36	Plan de la Ville de Venise
mwsam0561	south america ecuador	1748	BELLIN	400	18	36	Plan de la Ville et Cite de St. Francois de Quito
mwas0657	asia south east java	1750	BELLIN	200	22	30	Plan de la Ville et de Chateau de Batavia
mwuss0801	massachusetts	1764	BELLIN	12500	49	68	Plan de la Ville et du Port de Boston Capitale de la Nouvelle Angleterre
mwc0172	china	1764	BELLIN	240	21	17	Plan de la Ville et du Port de Macao
mwas0691	asia south east malacca	1753	BELLIN	180	22	17	Plan de la Ville et Forteresse de Malaca
mwuss0425	florida	1768	BELLIN	300	20	29	Plan de la Ville et Port de St. Augustin
mwru0238a	russia	1764	BELLIN	280	21	17	Plan de la Ville et Port de St. Petersbourg
mwaf0754	africa north algeria	1780	BELLIN	150	21	17	Plan de la Ville Fort et Port d'Alger
mwas0833	asia south east siam	1750	BELLIN	250	21	28	Plan de la Ville Louvo (Lopburi)
mwwi0633	hispaniola	1764	BELLIN	150	21	17	Plan de l'Isle a Vache a la Coste du Sud de S. Domingue
mwit0330	italy elba	1764	BELLIN	180	22	17	Plan de l'Isle d'Elbe
mwwi0327	bahamas	1768	BELLIN	400	21	16	Plan de l'Isle d'Inague / Carte de la Partie Occidentale d'Inague (2 maps)
mwin0226	india	1757	BELLIN	200	22	18	Plan de Madras a la Coste de Coromandel
mwin0227	india	1757	BELLIN	250	19	31	Plan de Madraz et du Fort St. Georges
mwit0952	italy sicily	1764	BELLIN	140	22	17	Plan de Milazzo dans l'Isle de Sicile
mwf1197	monaco	1764	BELLIN	400	22	18	Plan de Monaco
mwsp0573	spain regions	1764	BELLIN	140	21	17	Plan de Palamos
mwuss1355	pennsylvania	1764	BELLIN	350	21	17	Plan de Philadelphie et Environs
mwsam0686	south america magellan	1764	BELLIN	120	16	22	Plan de Plusieurs Bayes decouvertes aux Terres de Fer
mwuk1843	wales	1757	BELLIN	350	50	66	Plan de Port de Milford
mwca0375	canada nova scotia	1754	BELLIN	300	19	14	Plan de Port Royal et de ses Environs Situe dans la Baye de Campeche
mwf0514	france corsica	1764	BELLIN	180	22	18	Plan de Porto Vecchio
mwf0988	france poitou	1764	BELLIN	140	22	33	Plan de Rochefort
mwf0792	france normandy	1764	BELLIN	140	22	33	Plan de Rouen et des Environs
mwit0953	italy sicily	1764	BELLIN	140	22	17	Plan de Siracuse
mwsp0574	spain regions	1764	BELLIN	180	23	18	Plan de St Sebastien
mwwi0619	hispaniola	1760	BELLIN	200	19	23	Plan de Ville du Cap, a la Cote Septentrionale de Saint Domingue
mwe0504a	europe croatia	1764	BELLIN	200	22	18	Plan de Zara, Capitale de la Dalmatie
mwwi0722	jamaica	1764	BELLIN	180	20	15	Plan des Havres de Port Antonio et de Saint Francois
mwm0246	mediterranean malta	1764	BELLIN	500	22	18	Plan des Port et Ville de Maltha (illustration below left)
mwaf0517a	africa egypt etc	1764	BELLIN	200	22	18	Plan des Ports et Ville d'Alexandrie
mwas0793	asia south east philippines	1775	BELLIN	350	49	33	Plan des Principaux Portes de la Cote d'Illocos
mwca0506	canada quebec	1744	BELLIN	250	20	28	Plan du Bassin de Quebec et de ses Environs
mwwi0876	st lucia	1758	BELLIN	200	22	17	Plan du Carenage ou Petit Cul de Sac de l'Isle Se. Lucie
mwwi0877	st lucia	1763	BELLIN	200	22	17	Plan du Cul de Sac des Roseaux dans l'Isle de Ste. Lucie
mwwi0793	martinique	1764	BELLIN	150	17	21	Plan du Cul de Sac Royal de la Martinique
mwaf0941	africa south	1760	BELLIN	250	20	25	Plan du Fort et de la Ville du Cap de Bonne Esperance

AMPG REFERENCE	REGION	DATE	MAP MAKER	PRICE (UK£)	VERT. (cm.)	HOR. (cm.)	TITLE OF MAP (Comments by the editor in brackets)
mwit1067	italy naples	1764	BELLIN	200	22	35	Plan du Golphe, Ville et Environs de Naples
mwec1172	uk england sussex	1764	BELLIN	200	22	18	Plan du Havre de Rye et de ses Environs
mwf0793	france normandy	1764	BELLIN	140	22	33	Plan du Havre et des Environs
mwf0794	france normandy	1764	BELLIN	100	23	17	Plan du Mont St. Michel
mwaf0572	africa islands bourbon	1764	BELLIN	240	22	17	Plan du Port Bourbon
mwgm0228	mexico	1764	BELLIN	200	21	16	Plan du Port d'Acapulco sur la Cote du Mexique dans la Mer du Sud (north to the left)
mwca0355	canada nova scotia	1744	BELLIN	240	20	28	Plan du Port Dauphin et de sa Rade avec l'Entree de Labrador
mwsp0575	spain regions	1764	BELLIN	200	22	17	Plan du Port de Ferrol
mwca0356	canada nova scotia	1744	BELLIN	200	20	28	Plan du Port de la Haive Situe a la Cote d'Accadie
mwjk0106	japan	1752	BELLIN	200	20	34	Plan du Port de la Ville de Nagasaki
mwsp0108	portugal	1764	BELLIN	200	22	17	Plan du Port de Lisbonne
mwsp0096	portugal	1756	BELLIN	800	45	64	Plan du Port de Lisbonne et des Costes Voisines
mwe0504	europe croatia	1764	BELLIN	140	23	17	Plan du Port de Pole dans l'Istrie
mwuss0420	florida	1764	BELLIN	350	22	16	Plan du Port de St Augustin dans la Floride
mwsam0464	south america chile	1764	BELLIN	200	22	16	Plan du Port de Valparaiso
mwwi0634	hispaniola	1764	BELLIN	200	23	36	Plan du Port du Cap dans l'Isle de St. Domingue
mwjk0092	japan	1736	BELLIN	350	19	34	Plan du Port et de la Ville de Nangasaki
mwwi0890	st vincent	1758	BELLIN	250	18	23	Plan du Port et du Carenage de Cariacoua Situe dans la Partie du Sud de l'Isle de St. Vincent
mwf0515	france corsica	1764	BELLIN	180	22	18	Plan du Port et Ville de Boniface dans l'Isle de Corse
mwf0361	france brittany	1764	BELLIN	140	25	36	Plan du Port et Ville de Brest
mwsp0576	spain regions	1764	BELLIN	140	22	34	Plan du Port et Ville de Cartagene en Espagne
mwit0406	italy lazio	1764	BELLIN	140	22	17	Plan du Port et Ville de Civita-Vecchia
mwca0380	canada nova scotia	1757	BELLIN	250	23	28	Plan du Port et Ville de Louisbourg dans l'Isle Royale
mwsp0672	balearic islands	1764	BELLIN	350	22	17	Plan du Port et Ville de Mahon avec ses Forts
mwca0357	canada nova scotia	1744	BELLIN	200	19	28	Plan du Port Royal dans l'Accadie Appele Aujourd'hui par les Anglois Annapolis Royale
mwsam0687	south america magellan	1764	BELLIN	120	15	24	Plan Geometrique de Plusieurs Bayes situees au Detroit de Magellan
mwsam0771	south america peru	1764	BELLIN	280	19	32	Plan Scenographique de la Cite des Rois ou Lima Capitale du Royaume de Perou
mwwi0453	cuba	1764	BELLIN	280	22	16	Port de la Havane dans l'Isle de Cube
mwwi0522	grenada	1764	BELLIN	200	22	17	Port et Fort Royal de la Grenade
mwgm0424	panama	1764	BELLIN	200	22	17	Port et Ville de Chagre
mwuss0185	carolinas	1764	BELLIN	400	22	15	Port et Ville de Charles-Town dans la Caroline
mwwi0828	puerto rico	1764	BELLIN	300	22	32	Port et Ville de Porto-Rico dans l'Isle de ce Nom
mwsam0565	south america ecuador	1764	BELLIN	200	23	34	Province de Quito au Perou
mwsam0768	south america peru	1764	BELLIN	180	22	17	Rade d'Arica et Environs. Situee a la Coste du Perou
mwgm0425	panama	1764	BELLIN	200	22	16	Rade du Darien et les Isles Voisines
mwaf0796	africa north morocco	1764	BELLIN	140	21	17	Rade et Ville de Ceute
mwp0251	pacific (all)	1750	BELLIN	250	15	30	Representation du Cours Ordinaire des Vents de Traverse qui Regnent sur les Costes, dans la Grande Mer du Sud
mwru0454a	russia tartary	1757	BELLIN	250	24	25	Suite de la Carte de la Siberie et le Pays de Kamtschatka
mwin0217	india	1752	BELLIN	180	22	25	Suite de la Carte de l'Indoustan, Ile Feuille, Comprenant la Presqu'Isle de l'Inde
mwca0595	canada st lawrence	1754	BELLIN	450	86	54	Suite de la Carte Reduite du Golphe de St. Laurent Contenant les Costes de Labrador depuis Mecatina jusqu'a la Baye des Esquimaux le Detroit de Belle-Isle … Costes de l'Isle de Terre Neuve Connues sous le Nom du Petit Nord
mwaf1207	africa west	1748	BELLIN	150	20	27	Suite de la Coste de Guinee depuis la Riviere de Volta jusqu'a Jakin ou sont les Royaumes de Koto, de Popo, de Whidah ou Juida, et d'Ardra
mwaf1209	africa west	1750	BELLIN	200	23	43	Suite de la Coste de Guinee depuis le Cap Apollonia
mwsam0565a	south america ecuador	1764	BELLIN	200	23	34	Suite de la Province de Quito au Perou (shown above left)
mwas0467	asia south east	1746	BELLIN	150	29	30	Suite de l'Ocean Oriental Contenant les Isles de la Sonde les Costes de Tunquin et de la Chine les Isles du Japon les Philippines Moluques
mwwi0249	west indies (east)	1764	BELLIN	200	22	16	Suite des Isles Antilles 1 Partie
mwwi0250	west indies (east)	1764	BELLIN	200	22	17	Suite des Isles Antilles 2 Partie
mwsam0374	south america brazil	1756	BELLIN	240	24	17	Suite du Bresil pour Servir a l'Histoire Generale des Voyages. Villages d'Indiens et Missions Ruinees. Tire de la Carte d'Amerique de M. Danville
mwca0510	canada quebec	1758	BELLIN	250	19	30	Suite du Cours du Fleuve de St. Laurent depuis Quebec jusqu'au Lac Ontario
mwuss0945	mississippi	1764	BELLIN	400	22	36	Suite du Cours du Fleuve St Louis depuis la Riviere d'Iberville jusqu, a celle des Yasous et les Parties Connues de la Riviere Rouge et le Riviere Noire
mwsc0735	scandinavia sweden	1758	BELLIN	235	21	16	Suite du Golphe de Bothnie
mwsam0773	south america peru	1771	BELLIN	150	22	30	Suite du Perou Audience de Charcas
mwsam0765	south america peru	1760	BELLIN	200	21	29	Suite du Perou Audience de Lima
mwaf0521	africa egypt etc	1770	BELLIN	180	19	28	Tabula Itineraria a Sues (north to the left)
mwin0208	india	1750	BELLIN	150	33	26	Theatre de la Guerre sur la Coste de Coromandel
mwsam0240	south america argentina	1764	BELLIN	250	20	16	Ville de Buenos-Ayres
mwsam0526	south america colombia	1764	BELLIN	300	22	17	Ville de Cartagene dans l'Amerique Meridionale

AMPG REFERENCE	REGION	DATE	MAP MAKER	PRICE (UK£)	VERT. (cm.)	HOR. (cm.)	TITLE OF MAP (Comments by the editor in brackets)
mwuss1095	new york	1764	BELLIN	1500	21	16	Ville de Manathe ou Nouvelle-Yorc
mwwi0635	hispaniola	1764	BELLIN	180	22	16	Ville de S. Domingue dans l'Isle de ce Nom
mwsam0381	south america brazil	1764	BELLIN	300	17	32	Ville de Saint Salvador, Capitale du Bresil
mwas0830	asia south east siam	1749	BELLIN	280	16	20	Ville de Siam ou Juthia
mwwi0636	hispaniola	1764	BELLIN	250	22	36	Ville du Cap dans l'Isle de St. Domingue
mwaf0926	africa south	1748	BELLIN	220	22	17	Ville et Fort du Cap de Bonne Esperance
mwjk0113	japan	1773	BELLIN-RAYNAL	400	21	29	Carte des Isles du Japon et la Presqu'Isle de Coree avec les Costes de la Chine (re-engraving of Bellin's 1746 map)
mwf1085	france provence	1833	BELLUE	200	43	59	Plan des Environs de Toulon
mwit0473	italy lombardy	1627	BELLUS	250	25	36	Abriss der Landschafft Veltlin, vom Frantzosischen General Marquis di Covure den Spanischen wieder Abgenommen Worden
mwg0512	rheinland-pfalz	1627	BELLUS	350	27	32	Abriss der Stadt Franckenthal, Wie Solche von dem Vice General Don Go ... alo Fernandes de Cordova Belagert Worden. 1621
mwg0776	westphalia	1627	BELLUS	350	26	32	Abriss der Vestung Gulch, wie Dieselbe von den Spanischen Eingenommen Worden Ist 1621
mwg0257	baden-wurttemberg	1627	BELLUS	600	27	32	Belagerung und Einnehmun der Stadt und Vestung Mannheim. Anno 1622
mwg0585	saxony	1627	BELLUS	300	26	31	Descriptio Saxoniae Superioris Lusatiae Misniaeove
mwg0586	saxony	1627	BELLUS	350	26	31	Dess Andern Theils dess Nider Sachsischen Kreyses
mwg0328	bavaria	1627	BELLUS	300	27	31	Franconia vulgo Franckenlandt
mwit0076	italy	1627	BELLUS	400	27	31	Italia Nova et Exacta Descriptio
mwe1095	europe slovak republic (moravia)	1627	BELLUS	300	26	31	Moravia Merhern
mwg0513	rheinland-pfalz	1627	BELLUS	350	26	30	Palatinatus Rheni
mwaf0455a	africa egypt etc	1553	BELON	1200			Portraict de la Ville D'Alexandrie en Egypte
mwf0353	france brittany	1754	BELPREY	1500	82	124	Plan General des Deux Ville de Nancy
mwat0030	atlantic ocean (all)	1722	BENARD	250	27	26	A Chart of the Western and Southern Oceans Describing the Course of Sir John Narbrough's Voyage to the South Sea (copy of Robinson 1711)
mwam1324	america north (west)	1785	BENARD	350	23	30	Carte de la Riviere de Cook, dans la Partie N.O. de l'Amerique
mwaa0037	antarctic	1780	BENARD	850	54	54	Carte de l'Hemisphere Austral Montrant les Routes des Navigateurs les Plus Celebres par le Capitaine Jacques Cook
mwat0224	atlantic falkland isl.	1770	BENARD	350	23	30	Carte de Maideland ou de la Virginie de Hawkins, Decouverte par Sir Richard Hawkins 1574. et du Canal Falkland Ainsi Appelle par le Cap. Jean Strong 1689
mwme0647	arabia etc	1780	BENARD	650	62	50	Carte du Golfe d'Arabie depuis Suez a Bab-el-Mandeb
mwam0810	america north (central)	1782	BENARD	850	32	43	Carte d'une Partie de l'Amerique Septentrionale, qui Contient Partie de la Nle. Espagne, et de la Louisiane
mww0516	world	1782	BENARD	500	27	34	Carte Reduite du Globe Terrestre
mwm0040	mediterranean	1720	BENARD	550	28	72	Les Quatre Grandes Monarchies des Assiriens, des Perses, des Grecs et des Romains
mwjk0118	japan	1785	BENARD	200	25	20	Partie du Japon ou Nipon
mwit0753	italy rome	1773	BENEDETTI	1000	46	67	La Topografia di Roma
mwe0391	europe austria	1798	BENEDICTI	650	59	89	Grundriss der Landesfurstlichen Stadt Baaden
mwuss0122	california	1849	BENTLEY	180	19	24	Map of California: from the Latest Authorities, as Published in the United States
mwuss1423	pennsylvania	1833	BENTON	450	41	53	The States of Pennsylvania New Jersey and Delaware from the Latest Authorities
mwe0761	europe east	1663	BEREY	800	37	53	Carte de Haute et Basse Hongrie Transilvanie Sclavonie, Croatie, et Dalmatie
mwaf0061	africa	1658	BEREY	960	40	51	Carte de l'Afrique Corrigee et Augmentee
mwas0046	asia continent	1658	BEREY	1200	40	51	Carte de l'Asie Corrigee et Augmentee (re-issue of Bertius 1629)
mwe0064	europe	1658	BEREY	2400	40	52	Carte de l'Europe Corrigee et Augmentee (illustrated is the Jaillot re-issue of 1671)
mwm0230b	mediterranean malta	1726	BEREY	1000	23	50	Carte des Isles de Malte du Goze et du Cuming
mwm0221	mediterranean malta	1720	BEREY	650	23	49	Carte des Isles de Malte, du Goze et du Cuming avec la Position des Batteries et des Redoutes Faites pour la Deffence de la Coste
mwf0058	france	1640	BEREY	1800	40	52	Carte Generale de Toute les Poste et Traverse de France (carte-a-figures borders on three sides. Re-issued by Langlois 1670)
mwbh0258	belgium holland	1640	BEREY	1800	42	53	Carte Generale des Dixsept Provinces des Pais Bas
mwsw0068	switzerland	1654	BEREY	1650	40	52	Carte Generale des Treze Cantons de Suisse (close copy of Jansson 1630)
mwf0785a	france normandy	1715	BEREY	3000	136	157	Carte Particuliere du Diocese de Rouen
mwme0474a	jerusalem	1700	BEREY-LAMY	750	28	38	Descriptio Urbis Jerusalem
mwe0719	europe danube	1703	BEREY	1800	46	159	Le Cours du Danube
mwf0820	france paris	1641	BEREY	1500	32	43	Le Plan De La Ville Cite Univercite Et Fauxbourgs De Paris
mwm0007	mediterranean	1650	BEREY	2500	46	77	Nouvelle Carte Marine de tous les Ports de l'Europe sur l'Ocean et sur la Mediterranée... (Berey was the engraver of this map, which was re-published until c1730)

AMPG REFERENCE	REGION	DATE	MAP MAKER	PRICE (UK£)	VERT. (cm.)	HOR. (cm.)	TITLE OF MAP (Comments by the editor in brackets)
mwe0142	europe	1723	BEREY	1400	52	75	Nouvelle Carte Marine de Tous les Ports de l'Europe sur l'Ocean et sur la Mediterranee
mwme0215a	holy land	1700	BEREY-LAMY	500	28	38	Nova Descriptio Judaeae et totius Terrae Israel
mww0150	world	1640	BEREY	6000	38	55	Nova Totius Terrarum Orbis Geographica ac Hydpographica Tabula Auct: Iud Hondio
mwf0823	france paris	1654	BEREY	15000	101	125	Plan de la Ville de Paris (in 6 sheets, joined)
mwme0226	holy land	1700	BEREY	1000	32	43	Plan et Distribution de la Terre de Chanaan
mwsp0342	spain madrid	1700	BERGE	650	36	50	Mantua Carpetanorum, sive Madritum, Urbs Regia, ad Guadarammam Amnem
mwuk1220	england london	1770	BERGER	900	32	50	Accurater Plan der Stadt London nebst Westminster, Southwar und den Neu Angebaueten Haeusern vom Jahr 1767
mwbp0286	poland	1676	BERGER	900	51	57	Delineatioem Liberae in Silesia Dynastiae Drachenberg
mwsam0433a	south america brazil	1844	BERGHAUS	600	48	70	To his Royal Highness William Adalbert Prince of Prussia, this chart of the approaches of Rio de Janeiro
mwit0248	italy	1845	BERLETTI	1200	117	90	Carta Postale ed Itineraria d'Italia
mwf0002	france	1482	BERLINGHIERI	15000	39	53	Gallia Novella (1st printed 'modern' map of France, in the 'Florence' Ptolemy atlas. Although this map was based on a 13th century manuscript, the coastline is much closer to reality than Ptolemy's ideas, who lived in the first century AD. This is also demonstrated in Berlinghieri's 'modern' maps of Italy and Spain and his Ptolemaic world map, which is the first to show curved lines of longitude, implying his belief that the earth was spherical not flat and circular.)
mwsp0140	spain	1482	BERLINGHIERI	18000	39	53	Hispania Novella (1st 'modern' printed map of Spain, in the Ptolemy atlas (Florence). Although this map was based on a 13th century manuscript, the coastline is much closer to reality than Ptolemy's, who lived in the first century AD. This is also demonstrated in Berlinghieri's 'modern' maps of France and Italy and also his Ptolemaic world map, which is the first to show curved lines of longitude, implying his belief that the earth was spherical not flat.)
mwit0003	italy	1482	BERLINGHIERI	25000	41	53	Novella Italia (1st printed 'modern' map of Italy by Berlinghieri included in his atlas of Ptolemy's maps (Florence). Although this map was based on a 13th century manuscript, the coastline is much closer to reality than Ptolemy's ideas, who lived in the first century AD. This is also demonstrated in Berlinghieri's 'modern' maps of France and Spain and his Ptolemaic world map, which is the first to show curved lines of longitude, implying his belief that the earth was spherical not flat.)
mwme0003	holy land	1482	BERLINGHIERI	18000	29	49	Palestina Moderna Et Terra Sancta (one of 4 'modern' maps in the Florence Ptolemy atlas, the others being France, Spain and Italy).
			FOR BERLINGHIERI'S PTOLEMAIC MAPS, SEE UNDER 'PTOLEMY - FLORENCE'				
mwsam0351	south america brazil	1722	BERNARD	80	13	7	Baie de Tous les Sains
mwgm0395	panama	1722	BERNARD	250	21	31	Baye et Forts de Porto Belo
mwwi0424	cuba	1722	BERNARD	250	21	31	Baye et Ville de la Havana ou de S. Christoval
mwsam0510	south america colombia	1722	BERNARD	300	21	31	Cartagene avec ses Ports et ses Forts
mwuss0623	louisiana	1720	BERNARD	2000	35	40	Carte de la Louisiane et du Cours du Mississipi Dressee sur un Grand Nombre de Memoires entrau tres sur ceux de Mr. le Maire par Guillaume. De l'Isle (reduced version of De L'Isle's 1718 map. For illustration, see under America North East)
mwp0498	pacific south	1774	BERNARD	750	38	67	Carte d'une Partie de la Mer du Sud Contentant les Decouvertes de Vaisseaux de sa Majeste le Dauphin, Commodore Byron, la Tamar, Capitne. Mouats, 1765, le Dauphin, Capitne. Wallis, le Swallow, Capitne. Cartaret, 1767, et l'Endeavour, Lieutenant Cook 1769
mwin0276a	india	1782	BERNARD	200	24	41	Carte d'une partie des Cotes de L'Inde depuis Bombay... faits par M. de Pages
mwaa0116	arctic	1715	BERNARD	650	33	57	Carte du Nord Est & du Nord West du Pole (copy of Pitt 1680 but excl. the decorative cartouches, etc.)
mwru0169	russia	1732	BERNARD	300	15	29	Carte du Waeigatz ou Detroit de Nassau Suivant la Relation de Linschooten (south to the top)
mwsam0679	south america magellan	1722	BERNARD	500	42	51	Detroit du Magellan
mwsam0352	south america brazil	1722	BERNARD	180	13	7	Entree de Rio Janeiro
mwam0386b	america north	1737	BERNARD	1500	37	44	Le Cours du Fleuve Missisipi, selon les Relations les Plus Modernes (based on Hennepin 1737)
mwuss0491	georgia	1734	BERNARD	750	19	26	New Map of Georgia
mwsam0230	south america argentina	1722	BERNARD	200	21	32	Plan de la Riviere de la Plate
mwsam0353	south america brazil	1722	BERNARD	200	13	26	S. Salvador
mwsam0354	south america brazil	1722	BERNARD	200	13	26	S. Sebastien
mwin0113	india	1670	BERNIER	400	14	20	Carte nouvelle de Royaume de Kachemire
mwin0112	india	1670	BERNIER	300	19	26	L'Empire du Grand Mogol (copied from Sanson)

AMPG REFERENCE	REGION	DATE	MAP MAKER	PRICE (UK£)	VERT. (cm.)	HOR. (cm.)	TITLE OF MAP (Comments by the editor in brackets)
mwuk0095	ireland	1689	BERRY	1350	85	53	A General Mapp of Ireland, Surveyed By Sr. William Petty (2 maps, joined)
mww0211	world	1680	BERRY	5000	57	88	A Mapp of All the World
mwuk0942	england	1685	BERRY	2500	59	88	A New Mapp of the Kingdome of England and Dominion of Wales (title above map)
mwe1196	europe west	1679	BERRY	1600	56	43	A New Mapp of the Sea Coasts of England, France & Holland
mwaf0087	africa	1680	BERRY	1400	54	89	Africa divided according to the extent of its principall parts (English copy of Jaillot 1674)
mwam0326	america north	1681	BERRY	5000	58	90	North America Divided into its Principall Parts where are Distinguished the Severall States which Belong to the English, Spanish, and French (English language version of Jaillot 1674)
mwe0334	europe austria	1686	BERRY	420	56	86	Part of the Circle of Austria viz. The Archdukedom of Austria
mwm0189	mediterranean malta	1662	BERRY	3000	58	104	Plan des Fortresse de Vallete Bourg et Sangle de Malte
mwbp0307	poland	1683	BERRY	1200	56	87	Poland Subdivided According to the Extent of its Severall Palatinates (based on Jaillot 1674. Illustrated is Bowles re-issue, c1744)
mwsp0199	spain	1682	BERRY	520	57	89	Spain Divided into its Severall Kingdoms and Principalities (English version of Jailot 1672)
mwwi0695b	jamaica	1678	BERRY	3500	44	63	Tabula Jamaicae Insulae per Edwd Slaney 1678. Published by His Majestyes Especiall Command. Sold by Robert Morden at the Atlas in Cornhill
mwbh0433	belgium holland	1683	BERRY	380	57	88	The Catholick Provinces of the Low-Countries
mwg0808	westphalia	1689	BERRY	380	89	56	The Circle and Electorat of the Rhine
mwg0347	bavaria	1686	BERRY	550	56	86	The Circle of Swabia Subdivided into All the Territories
mwg0806	westphalia	1686	BERRY	380	87	56	The Circle of Westphalia Divided into it's States
mwe1002	europe rhine	1685	BERRY	750	87	57	The Course of the River Rhine from its Fountain ... to the Sea
mwru0087	russia	1682	BERRY	1200	57	88	The Dominions of the Czar of Russia
mwg0413	brandenburg	1685	BERRY	420	56	88	The Dukedom and Electorat of Brandenbourg
mwg0079	germany	1685	BERRY	500	58	89	The Empire of Germany
mwuk0933	england	1679	BERRY	1200	47	40	The Grand Roads of England
mwsc0311	scandinavia denmark	1686	BERRY	450	56	87	The Kingdom of Denmark Subdivided into its Principal Provinces
mwgr0025	greece	1568	BERTELLI	1500	15	20	(Untitled map of Morea)
mwat0009	atlantic ocean (all)	1565	BERTELLI	15000	24	36	Al Molto Mag:Co Sig:Or Marco del Sole Sig:Or Mio Osser.Mo...D.V. Servitore, Fernando Bertelli (based on the 1560 Camocio-Forlani map)
mwit1160	italy veneto	1568	BERTELLI	3000	44	55	Al Rmo. Mons. Gio. Delfino, Meritissimo. Vescovo di Torcello ... Nova Disegno del Territorio Padoano
mwgr0030	greece	1571	BERTELLI	2000	30	44	Anzaijgung wie die Tirckhen auff die Cristen Armada in der Flucht Ghallten haben am 7.te Octobris im 71.
mwuk0666	uk	1562	BERTELLI	20000	48	35	Britania Insula Quae Duo Regna Continet Angliam Et Scotiam Cum Hibernia Adiacente (close copy of Lily-IHS, 1556)
mwsc0028	scandinavia	1588	BERTELLI	9000	39	52	Caelator Candido Lectori Salutem. Accipe Candide Lector Absolutissimam Septentrionalium Regionum, Suetiae, Gotiae, Norvegiae, Prussiae, Pomeraniae, Ducatus Megapolensis, Frisiae, Geldriae, Altae Marchiae, Lusatiae
mwgr0341	greece crete	1562	BERTELLI	7200	18	25	Candido Lectori haec est illa insignis insula Creta (Cut from part of a map that also includes Cyprus. See below for details.)
mwgr0438	greece cyprus	1560	BERTELLI	7500	23	34	Cyprus Insula olim Macharia
mwgr0441	greece cyprus	1569	BERTELLI	20000	50	34	Cyprus, que olim (Macaria)
mwsc0475	scandinavia iceland	1566	BERTELLI	4800	26	19	De Islanda Insula
mwsp0640	balearic islands	1569	BERTELLI	2500	26	19	De Maiorica Insula
mwsp0639	balearic islands	1569	BERTELLI	2500	25	20	De Minorica Insula
mwgr0023	greece	1567	BERTELLI	8000	39	51	Descriptio della Geographia Moderna de Tutto la Gretia ... Opera di Iacomo Gastaldo Cosmographo
mwgr0024	greece	1567	BERTELLI	12000	49	68	Descrittione della geografia moderna di tutta la Grecia (based on Gastaldi 1566)
mwbp0174	poland	1563	BERTELLI	4500	25	33	Ducatus Oswieczimen et Zatoriensis Descriptio
mwwi0397	cuba	1564	BERTELLI	2500	18	24	El Vero et Nuovo Disegno di Tutta la Isola di Candia (Camocio's map with imprint changed)
mwuk0310b	scotland	1560	BERTELLI	2400	24	19	Estland (Shetland Isles)
mwg0425b	hessen	1568	BERTELLI	500	15	25	Franckfort
mwbh0021	belgium holland	1565	BERTELLI	3000	35	47	Galliae Belgichae Romae MDLXIIIII Ferando Berteli Excudebat
mwg0019	germany	1564	BERTELLI	2000	25	37	Germania del Gastaldo (date approx.)
mwe0742	europe east	1562	BERTELLI	6000	37	50	Germaniae Omniumque eius Provinciarum, atque Austriae, Boemiae, Ungaricae, Carinthiae, Coruatiae, Poloniae, Moraviae, Bosinae, Serviae, Prussiae, Masoviae, Transulvaniae, Lithuaniae, Russiae
mwsc0655a	scandinavia sweden	1566	BERTELLI	2000	25	19	Gotlandia
mwit0381	italy lazio	1566	BERTELLI	500	18	21	Il Vero Disegno de Forti fatti Intorno ad Ostia dalli Essercisi del Papa
mwit0323	italy elba	1560	BERTELLI	2000	24	18	Ilba sive Ilva Insula est

AMPG REFERENCE	REGION	DATE	MAP MAKER	PRICE (UK£)	VERT. (cm.)	HOR. (cm.)	TITLE OF MAP (Comments by the editor in brackets)
mwgr0439	greece cyprus	1562	BERTELLI	20000	18	25	Isola di Cipro, Cyprus Insula olim Macharia / Candia. Candido Lectori haec est illa Insignis Insula Creta (2 maps on one sheet, each 18x25cm.)
mwgr0299	greece corfu	1574	BERTELLI	1000	21	16	Isola di Corfu
mwgr0520	greece rhodes	1574	BERTELLI	1500	21	16	Issola de' Rhodi
mwit0028	italy	1565	BERTELLI	15000	39	57	Italia Novamente Posta in Luce et da Molti Errori Emendata
mwit0986	italy south	1567	BERTELLI	2000	21	35	La Descriptione de la Puglia
mwaf0460a	africa egypt etc	1569	BERTELLI	2400	22	34	La Gran Citta del Cairo
mwgr0026	greece	1570	BERTELLI	650	17	13	L'Arcipelago con il Stretto di Constantinopoli
mwit0863	italy sicily	1566	BERTELLI	5000	34	44	Li Nomi Antichi e Moderni de l'Isola d'Sicilia
mwf1162b	france lyon	1570	BERTELLI	800	20	29	Lion (view)
mwit0462	italy lombardy	1565	BERTELLI	3500	31	46	Lombardia. La Vera et Ultima Discrittione della Lombardia
mwm0174a	mediterranean malta	1599	BERTELLI	550	12	17	Malta (Valetta)
mwit0465a	italy lombardy	1599	BERTELLI	350	13	19	Mantova
mwgr0037	greece	1575	BERTELLI	800	15	20	Morea Peninsula Anticamete della Peloponesso, Apia, e Palagia
mwit1049	italy naples	1564	BERTELLI	5000	38	52	Napoli (date approx.)
mwit1054	italy naples	1629	BERTELLI	200	11	17	Napoli (map by Francesco Bertelli)
mwru0015	russia	1566	BERTELLI	4000	26	37	Nova Descripcione de la Moscovia
mwe0489	europe croatia	1565	BERTELLI	3000	29	40	Nova Discrittione dela Dalmatia et Crovatia
mwit0409a	italy liguria	1567	BERTELLI	4000	30	45	Nova descrittione di tutto il Ducado di Milano, del Piamonte, del paese de Suizzeri, et gran parte di altre regioni confinanti
mwit0092	italy	1648	BERTELLI	10000	41	57	Nuovo Italia (by Francesco Bertelli)
mwme0030	holy land	1563	BERTELLI	15000	37	48	Palestinae sive Tere Sancte Descriptio
mwaf0008a	africa	1565	BERTELLI	3500	29	38	Prima Tavola - Nelle presenti tre Tavole sono descritte le Marine secondo le Carta da navicar... (shown below left)
mwit0774a	italy sardinia	1562	BERTELLI	5000	30	19	Sardinia insula
mwgr0021	greece	1564	BERTELLI	12000	40	63	Totius Graecia Descriptio
mww0058	world	1568	BERTELLI	120000	42	75	Universale Descrittione di Tutta la Terra Conosciuta Fin Qui (nearly the same as Forlani no. 3 but slightly smaller)
mwit1208a	italy venice	1568	BERTELLI	2000	21	30	Venetia (shown below left)
mwgr0292	greece corfu	1564	BERTELLI-FORLANI	2000	37	27	Vogliono Alcuni che l'Isola di Corfu ... 1564 (text in panel top-right)
mwit0064	italy	1610	BERTELLI-PITTONI	1250	20	26	L'Italia con la descritione delle provincie
mwit0594	italy north	1704	BERTERHAM	950	45	60	Viage del Rey Catholico N.S. Phelipe V. de Milan a Cremona Cuyo de Strito Comprende este Mapa
mwm0250	mediterranean malta	1785	BERTHAULT	750	22	34	Vue a Vol d'Oiseau de la Ville & du Port de Malte Prise du Fond du Port, et dessus les Hauteurs des Rochers du Corradin
mwam0656	america north	1826	BERTHE	500	56	79	Carte de L'Amerique Septentrionale
mwam0291	america continent	1832	BERTHE	300	74	52	Nouvelle Carte des Ameriques Septentrionale et Meridionale avec les Plans des Possessions Francaises en ces Pays, Redigee et Presentee a l'Academie des Sciences
mwm0028	mediterranean	1700	BERTHELOT	5500	55	83	Nouvelle Carte de la Mer Mediterranee (2 sheets each 55x83cm)
mwas0228	asia continent	1799	BERTHOLON	120	18	22	Carte d'Asie
mwam1127	america north (east)	1799	BERTHOLON	320	18	23	Carte de la Nouvelle Angleterre, Nouvelle York, Nouvelle Jersey et Pensilvanie
mwuss1670	virginia	1799	BERTHOLON	280	17	22	Carte de la Virginie et du Mariland
mwam0543	america north	1799	BERTHOLON	240	18	22	L'Amerique Septentrionale Divisee en ses Principaux Etats
mww0604	world	1799	BERTHOLON	200	17	22	Mappe-Monde ou Description du Globe Terrestre
mwaf0466	africa egypt etc	1600	BERTIUS	250	9	13	Aegyptus
mwaf0031	africa	1600	BERTIUS	300	9	12	Africa
mwaf0857	africa south	1600	BERTIUS	300	9	13	Africae Pars meridionalior
mwwi0578	hispaniola	1600	BERTIUS	300	9	12	Aity sive Spaniola
mwf0210a	france alsace	1600	BERTIUS	150	9	12	Alsatia
mwsp0390	spain regions	1600	BERTIUS	180	9	12	Andaluzia
mwuk0911	england	1600	BERTIUS	300	9	12	Anglia (shown on the left is the 1616 edition)
mwuk0682	uk	1600	BERTIUS	350	9	13	Anglia, Scotia et Hibernia
mwf0646	france loire	1600	BERTIUS	150	9	12	Aniou
mwit0995	italy south	1600	BERTIUS	200	9	12	Aprutium
mwme0543	arabia etc	1600	BERTIUS	400	9	12	Arabia
mwas0280	asia burma	1600	BERTIUS	280	9	12	Aracam (north to the left. See also 'Asia - Siam' for 1609 edition, which extends farther south.)
mwas0816	asia south east siam	1609	BERTIUS	250	9	12	Aracam et Pegu (See also 'Asia Burma' for 1600 1st edition, which does not extend as far south. North to the left)
mwf0707	france nord pas-de-calais	1600	BERTIUS	150	9	12	Artesia
mwas0021	asia continent	1600	BERTIUS	350	9	12	Asia
mwe0302	europe austria	1600	BERTIUS	200	9	13	Austria
mwaf0680	africa north	1600	BERTIUS	200	9	13	Barbaria
mwin0095	india	1600	BERTIUS	200	9	12	Bengala
mwsc0530	scandinavia norway	1616	BERTIUS	350	14	19	Bergen in Norwegen (view)
mwf0424	france central	1600	BERTIUS	150	9	12	Biturigum
mwe0522	europe czech republic (bohemia)	1600	BERTIUS	200	9	12	Bohemia

AMPG REFERENCE	REGION	DATE	MAP MAKER	PRICE (UK£)	VERT. (cm.)	HOR. (cm.)	TITLE OF MAP (Comments by the editor in brackets)
mwas0580	asia south east borneo	1600	BERTIUS	250	9	12	Borneo
mwbh0142	belgium holland	1600	BERTIUS	200	9	12	Brabantia
mwg0411	brandenburg	1600	BERTIUS	200	9	13	Brandenburg
mwsam0277	south america brazil	1600	BERTIUS	300	9	13	Brasilia
mwf0306	france brittany	1600	BERTIUS	180	9	12	Britannia
mwf0387	france burgundy	1600	BERTIUS	150	9	12	Burgundiae Com (north to the left)
mwf0388	france burgundy	1600	BERTIUS	150	9	12	Burgundiae Ducatus
mwf0708	france nord pas-de-calais	1600	BERTIUS	150	9	12	Caletensium et Bononiesium des. (north to the left)
mwin0096	india	1600	BERTIUS	200	9	12	Cambaia
mwuk1698	wales	1600	BERTIUS	250	9	13	Cambria
mwgr0364	greece crete	1600	BERTIUS	200	9	12	Candia
mwaf0042	africa	1627	BERTIUS	1600	38	50	Carte de l'Afrique Corrigee et Augmentee, dessus Toutes les Aultres cy devant Faictes (French edition of Hondius 1619. See Hondius 1631)
mwaf0049	africa	1639	BERTIUS	1000	27	36	Carte de L'Afrique Corrigee et Augmentee, dessus Toutes les Aultres cy devant Faictes ... 1639 (reduced size version of Bertius' 1627 map)
mwam0034	america continent	1624	BERTIUS	2800	38	48	Carte de l'Amerique Corrigee et Augmentee dessus Toutes les Aultres cy devant Faictes (derived from Hondius' map of 1618 but lacking the carte-a-figure borders. Illustrated is the 1627 Tavernier re-issue with changed cartouche. See also 1640 Van Lochom revised edition with original cartouche and 1662 for reduced size map)
mwas0031	asia continent	1629	BERTIUS	1400	38	51	Carte de l'Asie (publ. by M. Tavernier)
mwe0036	europe	1627	BERTIUS	1400	38	50	Carte de l'Europe corrigee et augmentee
mwaf0817	africa north tunisia	1600	BERTIUS	200	9	12	Carthaginensis Sinus
mwsp0399	spain regions	1616	BERTIUS	200	10	13	Catalonia et Aragonia
mwgr0281	greece cefalonia	1600	BERTIUS	350	9	13	Cefalonia
mwsam0266a	south america bolivia	1600	BERTIUS	150	9	12	Cerro de Potosi (view)
mwsam0441	south america chile	1600	BERTIUS	160	9	13	Chili et Patagonum Regio
mwc0006	china	1600	BERTIUS	450	9	12	China (illustrated below is 1616 edition, 10x14cm, north to the right)
mwg0774	westphalia	1616	BERTIUS	200	15	19	Cleve et Murs
mwg0765	westphalia	1600	BERTIUS	80	9	12	Clivia Ducatus
mwaf1094	africa west	1600	BERTIUS	200	9	12	Congi Regni Christiani in Africa Nova Descriptio
mwuk0023	ireland	1616	BERTIUS	180	12	14	Connatia
mwgr0302	greece corfu	1600	BERTIUS	300	9	13	Corfu
mwuk1380	england south	1610	BERTIUS	120	9	13	Cornub. Devonia, Somerset, etc.
mwf0463	france corsica	1600	BERTIUS	250	9	12	Corsica
mwit0466	italy lombardy	1600	BERTIUS	140	9	12	Cremonensis. Ager.
mwwi0404	cuba	1600	BERTIUS	480	9	12	Cuba Insula (shown far left is the 1618 edition with title 'Cuba et Jamaica')
mwgr0467	greece cyprus	1600	BERTIUS	650	9	13	Cyprus
mwsc0246	scandinavia denmark	1600	BERTIUS	180	9	12	Dania
mwsc0527	scandinavia norway	1606	BERTIUS	240	9	13	Delineatio Spitsbergiae
mwam0023	america continent	1600	BERTIUS	480	9	12	Descriptio Americae
mwsam0009	south america	1600	BERTIUS	250	9	12	Descriptio Americae Australis
mwbh0140	belgium holland	1600	BERTIUS	150	9	12	Descriptio Arcis Britannicae (Roman ruins near Katwijk. Signature P.Keere.)
mwg0579	saxony	1606	BERTIUS	160	9	13	Descriptio Comitatus Embdani
mwf0038	france	1600	BERTIUS	240	9	12	Descriptio Gadium. (Incorrect title above map. Same map as 'Descriptio Galliae'.)
mwf0037	france	1600	BERTIUS	160	9	12	Descriptio Galliae. (title above map)
mwsc0665	scandinavia sweden	1600	BERTIUS	180	9	12	Descriptio Insulae Gothland
mwaf1095	africa west	1600	BERTIUS	140	9	12	Descriptio Insulae S. Thomae
mwat0134	atlantic canary isl.	1600	BERTIUS	250	9	12	Descriptio Insularum Canariarum (title above map. Inset of Portus Canaria. 1618 edition shown left with title 'Canariae I.')
mwsc0481	scandinavia iceland	1600	BERTIUS	300	9	12	Descriptio Islandiae
mwgm0142	mexico	1600	BERTIUS	400	9	12	Descriptio Novae Hispaniae
mwgr0047	greece	1600	BERTIUS	200	9	12	Description Peloponnesi (title above map)
mwat0076	atlantic azores	1600	BERTIUS	200	9	12	Descriptio Tercerae
mwaa0004	antarctic	1616	BERTIUS	650	9	13	Descriptio Terrae Subaustralis. (title above map)
mwbh0143	belgium holland	1600	BERTIUS	200	9	12	Die Zyp
mwit0328	italy elba	1600	BERTIUS	250	9	12	Elba
mwe0024	europe	1600	BERTIUS	300	9	12	Europa
mwbh0144	belgium holland	1600	BERTIUS	200	9	12	Flandria
mwit0372	italy friuli	1600	BERTIUS	150	9	12	Forum Iulii
mwsam0652	south america magellan	1600	BERTIUS	400	9	12	Fretum Magellanicum (first map to focus on the Magellan Straits. North to the right)
mwbh0145	belgium holland	1600	BERTIUS	200	9	12	Frisia
mwbh0141	belgium holland	1600	BERTIUS	180	9	13	Galliae Belgicae
mwf1089d	france pyrenees	1600	BERTIUS	120	9	12	Galliae Narbonensis descriptio (south to the top)
mwf0597	france languedoc	1600	BERTIUS	150	9	12	Gasconia
mwbh0146	belgium holland	1600	BERTIUS	200	9	12	Geldria
mwg0035	germany	1600	BERTIUS	150	9	12	Germania

AMPG REFERENCE	REGION	DATE	MAP MAKER	PRICE (UK£)	VERT. (cm.)	HOR. (cm.)	TITLE OF MAP (Comments by the editor in brackets)
mwg0050	germany	1632	BERTIUS	250	15	20	Germania
mwg0041	germany	1620	BERTIUS	180	16	20	Germaniae Descriptio Ptolemaica
mwsc0666	scandinavia sweden	1600	BERTIUS	200	9	12	Gotia
mwgr0046	greece	1600	BERTIUS	300	9	12	Graecia
mwsc0450	scandinavia greenland	1616	BERTIUS	300	10	14	Groenland
mwaf1093	africa west	1600	BERTIUS	200	9	12	Guinea
mwbh0147	belgium holland	1600	BERTIUS	200	9	12	Hannonia
mwg0433a	hessen	1600	BERTIUS	180	9	12	Hassiae Descriptio
mwsw0032	switzerland	1600	BERTIUS	220	9	12	Helvetia
mwuk0012	ireland	1600	BERTIUS	300	9	13	Hibernia
mwsp0169	spain	1600	BERTIUS	200	9	12	Hispania
mwe0493h	europe croatia	1600	BERTIUS	200	9	12	Histria
mwbh0148	belgium holland	1600	BERTIUS	250	9	12	Hollandia
mwbh0149	belgium holland	1600	BERTIUS	200	9	12	Hollandia Sept. (north Holland)
mwe0862	europe hungary	1600	BERTIUS	250	9	13	Hungaria
mwaf0583	africa islands madagascar	1600	BERTIUS	280	9	12	I. S. Lauretij
mwjk0007	japan	1600	BERTIUS	600	9	12	Iapan
mwas0627	asia south east java	1600	BERTIUS	250	9	12	Iava Maior
mwe1122a	europe slovenia	1600	BERTIUS	180	9	12	Illyricum (shown below left)
mwas0370	asia south east	1600	BERTIUS	450	9	12	India Orientalis
mwbh0150	belgium holland	1600	BERTIUS	250	9	12	Inferior Germania
mwru0022	russia	1600	BERTIUS	240	9	12	Ins. Vaygats (Novaya Zemla. See also Bertius 1606)
mwaf1039	africa south east	1600	BERTIUS	200	9	12	Insulae & Ars Mosambique
mwat0178	atlantic cape verde isl.	1600	BERTIUS	140	9	13	Insulae Capitis Viridis
mwwi0004	west indies	1602	BERTIUS	320	9	12	Insularum Cubae, Hispaniolae. Yucatanae & circumajacentium describtio
mwit0273	italy campagna	1600	BERTIUS	150	9	13	Ischia Insula
mwit0052	italy	1600	BERTIUS	300	9	13	Italia
mwgm0143	mexico	1600	BERTIUS	250	9	12	Iucatana
mwbh0151	belgium holland	1600	BERTIUS	200	9	12	Leodiensis Dioecesis
mwf0631	france limousin	1600	BERTIUS	150	9	12	Limania
mwbp0073	baltic states	1600	BERTIUS	300	9	13	Livoniae Descrip.
mwbh0817	luxembourg	1600	BERTIUS	250	9	12	Lutzenburg
mwuk1094a	england and scotland	1616	BERTIUS	200	9	13	Magna Britannia
mwsp0644	balearic islands	1600	BERTIUS	350	9	12	Majorcae et Minorcae Descrip.
mwin0097	india	1600	BERTIUS	200	9	12	Malabar (north to the left)
mwas0679	asia south east malacca	1600	BERTIUS	300	9	12	Malacca
mwin0458	indian ocean maldives	1600	BERTIUS	240	9	12	Maldivae Insulae
mwm0175	mediterranean malta	1600	BERTIUS	350	9	12	Malta
mwit0565	italy north	1600	BERTIUS	200	9	12	Marcha Anconae, olim Picenum. 1572.
mwme0544	arabia etc	1600	BERTIUS	300	9	12	Maris Rubrum (see illustration below left)
mwuk0014	ireland	1600	BERTIUS	140	10	14	Media (historical map of northern Ireland)
mwgm0146	mexico	1609	BERTIUS	260	9	13	Mexicana
mwgm0147	mexico	1616	BERTIUS	260	9	13	Mexico (view)
mwas0710	asia south east moluccas	1600	BERTIUS	250	9	12	Moluccae Insulae
mwbh0152	belgium holland	1600	BERTIUS	200	9	12	Namur
mwin0098	india	1600	BERTIUS	250	9	12	Narsinga et Ceylon
mwme0934	turkey etc	1600	BERTIUS	240	9	12	Natolia
mwf0766	france normandy	1600	BERTIUS	150	9	12	Normandia
mwsc0036	scandinavia	1600	BERTIUS	300	9	12	Nortcaep (north to the right)
mwsc0037	scandinavia	1600	BERTIUS	240	9	12	Norvegia et Suecia
mwsc0528	scandinavia norway	1602	BERTIUS	3500	9	12	Norwegia (first printed map of the whole of Norway)
mwp0374	pacific new guinea	1600	BERTIUS	300	9	12	Nova Guinea et In. Salomonis
mwru0026	russia	1606	BERTIUS	200	9	12	Novae Zemlae Delineatio
mwe0864	europe hungary	1616	BERTIUS	200	14	19	Ofen (view of Budapest)
mwaa0184	arctic / antarctic	1628	BERTIUS	1200	15	20	Orbis Stans Sectus Per Aequatorem (2 polar projections)
mwme0545	arabia etc	1600	BERTIUS	300	9	12	Ormus
mwit1148	italy umbria	1600	BERTIUS	200	9	12	Orvietum
mwbp0209	poland	1600	BERTIUS	100	9	13	Oswieczimesis et Zatoriensis Duc
mwme0060	holy land	1600	BERTIUS	300	9	12	Palaestina
mwg0509	rheinland-pfalz	1600	BERTIUS	150	9	12	Palatinatus Rheni
mwit1165	italy veneto	1600	BERTIUS	200	9	12	Patavinum
mwit0633	italy piedmont	1600	BERTIUS	140	9	12	Pedemontii descriptio
mwme0765	persia etc	1600	BERTIUS	200	9	12	Persicum Regnum
mwsam0733	south america peru	1600	BERTIUS	200	9	12	Peru (north to the right)
mwit1149	italy umbria	1600	BERTIUS	200	9	12	Perusia
mwas0747	asia south east philippines	1600	BERTIUS	850	9	12	Philippinae Insulae
mwf0943	france picardy	1600	BERTIUS	150	9	12	Picardia
mwf0963	france poitou	1600	BERTIUS	150	9	12	Poictou
mwbp0210	poland	1600	BERTIUS	250	9	12	Polonia
mwbp0211	poland	1600	BERTIUS	150	9	12	Pomerania
mwsp0016	portugal	1600	BERTIUS	180	9	12	Portugallia (north to the right)
mwf0998	france provence	1615	BERTIUS	150	10	14	Provence
mwbp0215a	poland	1606	BERTIUS	240	9	12	Prussia (shown left is the 1618 edition)
mwaa0073	arctic	1616	BERTIUS	450	9	12	Regionis Hyperboreae
mwgr0521	greece rhodes	1600	BERTIUS	300	9	12	Rhodi

AMPG REFERENCE	REGION	DATE	MAP MAKER	PRICE (UK£)	VERT. (cm.)	HOR. (cm.)	TITLE OF MAP (Comments by the editor in brackets)
mwit0391	italy lazio	1600	BERTIUS	140	9	13	Romanum territorium
mwru0023	russia	1600	BERTIUS	240	9	12	Russia
mwe0304	europe austria	1600	BERTIUS	150	9	13	Salisburgensis Dioecesis
mwat0321	atlantic st helena	1600	BERTIUS	300	9	13	Sancta Helena
mwe0493e	europe croatia	1600	BERTIUS	200	9	12	Sara et Zebenic
mwit0779	italy sardinia	1600	BERTIUS	300	9	12	Sardinia
mwg0590	saxony	1632	BERTIUS	150	15	19	Saxoniae Superioris Lusatiae Misniaeque Descriptio
mwgr0578	greece islands	1600	BERTIUS	200	9	13	Scio (Chios)
mwuk0320	scotland	1600	BERTIUS	250	9	12	Scotia
mwuk0333	scotland	1618	BERTIUS	350	10	14	Scotia Australis / Scotia Septentrion (2 maps, each 10x14cm.)
mwbh0153	belgium holland	1600	BERTIUS	200	9	12	Selandia
mwsc0038	scandinavia	1600	BERTIUS	350	9	12	Septentrionalum Regionu
mwat0012	atlantic ocean (all)	1602	BERTIUS	250	9	13	Septentrionalum Regionu Descrip. Petrus Kaerius Fecit et Caelavit
mwit0875	italy sicily	1600	BERTIUS	300	9	13	Sicilia
mwit1098	italy tuscany	1600	BERTIUS	200	9	12	Siena
mwg0581	saxony	1616	BERTIUS	200	14	19	Staden
mwas0875	asia south east sumatra	1600	BERTIUS	300	9	12	Sumatra Insula (north to the left. Shown far left is the 1616 edition, Singapore named, north to the right)
mwuk1555	england islands	1616	BERTIUS	160	10	14	Tab VII. Angliae, in qua Insulae (4 maps on one sheet)
mwru0419a	russia tartary	1600	BERTIUS	350	9	12	Tartaria (1616 edition shown left)
mwca0281	canada newfoundland	1600	BERTIUS	500	9	12	Terra Nova (first map to focus on Newfoundland)
mwg0694	schleswig-holstein	1600	BERTIUS	180	9	12	Thietmarsia
mwit1095a	italy tuscany	1600	BERTIUS	200	9	12	Thuscia
mwit0566	italy north	1600	BERTIUS	200	9	12	Tirolis Comita
mwe0989	europe rhine	1616	BERTIUS	120	14	20	Tractus Rheni in Germania Inferiore ad IV & V Historiarum C. Cornelii Taciti (historical map)
mwe1042a	europe romania	1600	BERTIUS	180	9	12	Transilvania
mwme0546	arabia etc	1600	BERTIUS	300	9	12	Turcicum Imperium
mww0105	world	1600	BERTIUS	750	9	13	Typus Orbis Terrarum
mwbh0154	belgium holland	1600	BERTIUS	200	9	12	Ultrajectum
mwsp0390a	spain regions	1600	BERTIUS	180	9	12	Valentia
mwit1166	italy veneto	1600	BERTIUS	200	9	12	Veronensis Ager.
mwuss1592	virginia	1616	BERTIUS	750	9	13	Virginia et Nova Francia
mwec1187a	uk england warwickshire	1616	BERTIUS	150	10	14	Warwicum Northapton. Hunting. etc. (south east England)
mwuk1354	england north	1616	BERTIUS	150	10	14	Westmorlad Lancastris Cestria
mwg0764	westphalia	1600	BERTIUS	80	9	12	Westphalia
mwsw0033	switzerland	1600	BERTIUS	150	9	12	Wiflispurgergow
mwgr0539	greece zante (zakynthos)	1600	BERTIUS	250	9	12	Zante Insula
mwbh0155	belgium holland	1600	BERTIUS	200	9	12	Zuyd Holland
							Petrus BERTIUS was the author of the text of 'Tabularum Geographicarum Contractarum Libri Quatuor' first edition 1600 (publ. by Claesz. The maps were engraved by Van Den Keere or Hondius. Maps listed here with later dates were not published in the 1600 edition)
mwam0045	america continent	1640	BERTIUS-VAN LOCHOM	2800	38	50	Carte de l'Amerique Corrigee et Augmentee dessus Toutes les Aultres cy devant Faictes (As Bertius 1624 but with the NW coastline removed)
mwm0003b	mediterranean	1630	BERTIUS-PICART	1500	64	98	Imperium Caroli Magni cum Vicinis Regionibus
mwam0068a	america continent	1662	BERTIUS-TAVERNIER	1200	27	37	Carte de l'Amerique ... 1662 (reduced size version of Bertius 1624)
mwit1258	italy venice	1831	BERTOJA	1500	51	57	Pianta della Regia Citta di Venezia Rinnovata l'An 1831
mwf0825	france paris	1657	BERTRAND	4800	40	41	Plan de la Ville Citte et Universite et Fauxbourgs de Paris (3 borders with 65 portraits of kings of France)
mwp0062	australia	1816	BERTUCH	800	32	42	Charte des Austral-Landes (German edition of Flinders' map of 1814)
mwg0120	germany	1732	BESSEL	600	64	89	Germania in Priscas suas Provinces Ducatus ... Nominibus Locorum ad Medii Aevi Dialectum Expressis ex Diplomatibus Chartis et Tabulis Medii Aevi Descripta 1729
mww0067	world	1578	BEST	20000	22	40	(Untitled woodcut)
mwuss0523	georgia	1831	BETHUNE	7500	52	67	A Map of that Part of Georgia Occupied by the Cherokee Indians
mwp0529	pacific south	1848	BETTS	280	37	64	Australia and Polynesia
mwuk1074	england	1848	BETTS	1200	66	58	Betts Tour through England & Wales
mwuk1075	england	1848	BETTS	250	75	64	Betts's New Map of England and Wales
mwca0205	canada	1848	BETTS	350	67	65	British America
mwgm0363	mexico	1848	BETTS	300	39	31	Mexico including California and Texas
mwp0218	new zealand	1843	BETTS	300	37	29	New Zealand
mwam0712	america north	1838	BETTS	220	29	37	North America
mwp0170	australia	1848	BETTS	300	30	37	South Eastern Australia
mww0748	world	1850	BETTS	450	44	76	The World on Mercator's Projection
mwam0694	america north	1835	BETTS	220	30	37	United States
mwam0688	america north	1834	BETTS	220	30	38	United States, Canada & New Brunswick
mwp0148	australia	1843	BETTS	300	29	38	Western Australia

AMPG REFERENCE	REGION	DATE	MAP MAKER	PRICE (UK£)	VERT. (cm.)	HOR. (cm.)	TITLE OF MAP (Comments by the editor in brackets)
mwit0458	italy liguria	1846	BEUF	500	42	53	Nouveau Plan de la Ville de Genes Corrige de Tous les Changemens Faits jusqu'a ce Jour 1846 (engraved by Zucoli)
mwuss0446	florida	1781	BEW	450	27	37	A Map of East and West Florida, Georgia and Louisiana, with the Islands of Cuba, Bahama, and the Countries Surrounding the Gulf of Mexico, with the Tract of the Spanish Galleons, and of our Fleets thro' the Straits of Florida
mwgm0251	mexico	1782	BEW	400	27	36	A Map of Mexico or New Spain, from the Latest Authorities
mwsam0634	south america guyana	1781	BEW	180	27	37	A Map of the Dutch Settlements of Surinam, Demerary, Issequibo, Berbices, and the Islands of Curassoa, Aruba, Bonaire, &c. with the French Colony of Cayenne, and the Adjacent Spanish Countries
mwwi0115	west indies	1781	BEW	300	27	36	A Map of the English, French, Spanish, Dutch & Danish Islands, in the West Indies, Taken from an Improved Map of the Geographer to the King of France; with the Track of the Last West India Fleet, through the Windward Passage
mwin0279	india	1783	BEW	250	39	28	A Map of the Peninsula of India and the Island of Ceylon
mwuss0842	massachusetts	1782	BEW	350	23	17	A New and Accurate Chart of the Harbour of Boston, in New England. In North America
mwuk0217	ireland	1782	BEW	250	36	33	A New and Accurate Map of the Kingdom of Ireland, with the Roads
mwuss1456	rhode isl	1780	BEW	400	27	38	An Accurate Map of Rhode Island, Part of Connecticut and Massachusetts, Shewing Admiral Arbuthnot's Station in Blocking up Admiral Ternay
mwin0278a	india	1782	BEW	150	34	25	An Accurate Map of the Coast of Coromandel from Fort St. David to Cape Comorin
mwuss0212	carolinas	1780	BEW	450	27	36	Chief Parts of South Carolina and Georgia
mwf1080	france provence	1781	BEW	180	19	25	The Roads of Toulon with the Adjacent Country
mww0664a	world	1820	BIANCO	600	27	26	Planisferio Antico di Andrea Bianco (copy of the 15th century map)
mwec0296a	uk england devon	1750	BICKHAM	500	26	14	A Map of Devonshire (bird's eye view)
mwuk0168	ireland	1748	BICKHAM	180	15	14	A Map of Ireland Divided into the Provinces and Counties.
mwec0630	uk england kent	1750	BICKHAM	160	15	23	A Map of Kent. South from London … (view)
mwuk0997a	england	1751	BICKHAM	240	26	15	A Map of the South Part of Great Britain, called England and Wales (size incl. title above map)
mwuk0820	uk	1744	BICKHAM	400	24	32	A New and Accurate Chart of the Sea-Coasts, of Great Britain
mwc0298	china	1850	BIDWELL	1500	168	213	Missionary Map of China Embracing Chiefly the Eighteen Provinces from the Latest and Best Authorities
mwin0376	india	1846	BIDWELL	1250	210	210	Missionary Map of India, Embracing Hindustan, Burmah, Siam and Adjacent Provinces
mwas0258a	asia	1846	BIDWELL	650	210	210	Missionary Map of Western Asia, and Adjacent Countries
mwuk0919	england	1626	BILL	400	10	13	A Tipe of England
mwec0084	uk england cambridgeshire	1626	BILL	200	9	13	Cambridge Shire and Isle of Ely
mwec0600	uk england kent	1626	BILL	720	9	13	Kent
mwec1125	uk england surrey	1626	BILL	650	9	12	Surrey
mwec1217	uk england westmorland	1626	BILL	160	9	13	West Morland
mwam0730	america north	1840	BILLER	150	20	25	Vereinigte Staaten
mwat0335b	atlantic st helena	1841	BINET	650	46	68	Ile Ste Hélène
mwgm0345	mexico	1844	BINET	100	24	19	Mexique
mwam0155	america continent	1744	BION	240	16	20	L'Amerique
mwe0146	europe	1728	BION	150	16	20	L'Europe
mww0309	world	1710	BION	350	17	20	Mappe-Monde, ou Carte Generale du Monde en Deux Plans Hemisphere
mwuss0545	illinois	1818	BIRKBECK	800	30	41	Map of Part of the United States of North America, with the Territories of the Illinois on the Ohio
mwam0052	america continent	1647	BISSEL	400	7	12	Tabula In Argonautica Victoriae
mwc0242	china	1815	BITCHURIN	12500	122	96	Plan de la Ville de Peking Levee en 1817
mwsc0733a	scandinavia sweden	1752	BIURMAN	550	48	56	Charta ofwer Skane
mwsc0733	scandinavia sweden	1751	BIURMAN	1200	57	50	Charta ofwer Stockholm med des Malmar och Forstader
mwsc0732a	scandinavia sweden	1750	BIURMAN	800	48	56	Charta ofwer Stockholms Stads Belagenhet
mwsc0733b	scandinavia sweden	1753	BIURMAN	450	48	56	Charta ofwer Upland och Soder Torn
mwbp0042	baltic sea (east)	1742	BIURMAN	750	49	57	Regiones ad Sinum Finnicum (incl. 8 town views incl. St. Petersburg)
mwsc0730a	scandinavia	1747	BIURMAN	480	55	47	Svea ock Gota Riken med Finland ock Norland Afritade
mwuk1689	north sea	1829	BLACHFORD	450	93	124	A New and Correct Chart of the North Sea on Mercators Projection from the Most Recent Authorities
mwat0057	atlantic ocean (all)	1810	BLACHFORD	1800	94	127	A New Chart of the Atlantic or Western Ocean
mwsam0426	south america brazil	1835	BLACHFORD	850	70	93	A New Chart of the Coast of Brazil from Cape Frio to the River Plate
mwsc0449	scandinavia finland	1837	BLACHFORD	800	66	190	A New Chart of the Gulf of Finland, upon the Largest Scale Published from the Several Surveys Recently Made by Orders of the Russian and Swedish Governments

AMPG REFERENCE	REGION	DATE	MAP MAKER	PRICE (UK£)	VERT. (cm.)	HOR. (cm.)	TITLE OF MAP (Comments by the editor in brackets)
mwm0083	mediterranean	1828	BLACHFORD	2000	81	183	Blachford's New Chart of the Mediterranean Sea, Adriatic Archipelago & Black Sea from the Surveys of Capt. W.H. Smyth
mwsam0265	south america argentina	1848	BLACHFORD	800	92	160	The East and West Coasts of South America from the River Plate Round Cape Horn to Valparaiso ... from the Celebrated Surveys & Remarks of Capt'ns Malespina & Heywood, J. Warner, Master, R.N. & Several South Sea Traders ... 1848
mwuk1525	uk english channel (all)	1839	BLACHFORD	800	91	183	The English Channel
mwin0452	indian ocean	1848	BLACHFORD	800	98	181	To the Merchants and Ship Owners of the United Kingdom of Great Britain & Ireland, this Chart of the Indian & Pacific Oceans
mwuk0290	ireland	1846	BLACHFORD	800	98	193	To the Right Honorable the Master Wardens and Elder Bretheren of the Trinity House this Chart Reduced from the Trigonometrical Surveys
mwp0150	australia	1844	BLACK	240	27	39	Australasia
mwuk0628	scotland	1840	BLACK	280	85	62	Black's Road & Railway Travelling Map of Scotland
mwca0196	canada	1844	BLACK	180	26	37	Canada, New Brunswick &c.
mwsam0556	south america colombia	1840	BLACK	180	37	27	Columbia, Peru &c.
mwuss0621	kentucky	1850	BLACK	200	27	38	Kentucky and Tennessee
mwgm0336	mexico	1840	BLACK	180	25	37	Mexico
mwgm0364	mexico	1848	BLACK	200	27	38	Mexico, California & Texas
mwp0147	australia	1843	BLACK	235	28	38	New South Wales and South Australia
mwp0219	new zealand	1843	BLACK	300	38	28	New Zealand
mwam0783	america north	1847	BLACK	200	39	29	North America
mwme0427	holy land	1844	BLACK	120	38	25	Palestine According to its Ancient Divisions
mwp0154	australia	1844	BLACK	235	27	38	Part of Australia Comprising the Settled Portions of New South Wales and South Australia
mwaf1030	africa south	1850	BLACK	235	41	56	South Africa
mwam0782	america north	1847	BLACK	200	49	37	United States. Engraved by S. Hall
mwp0156	australia	1844	BLACK	235	27	39	Victoria, New South Wales and South Australia
mwaf0329	africa	1840	BLACKIE & SON	80	31	37	Africa
mwme0892	syria etc	1840	BLACKIE & SON	400	33	51	Syria North Division / Syria South Division
mww0737	world	1846	BLACKIE & SON	250	34	51	The World on Mercator's Projection
mwam0731	america north	1840	BLACKIE & SON	250	48	37	United States
mwgm0277	mexico	1812	BLACKWOOD	100	18	11	Viceroyalty of Mexico
mwbh0303	belgium holland	1649	BLAEU	900	41	52	(Amersfoort) Amisfurtum
mwg0794	westphalia	1649	BLAEU	350	16	24	(Erkelenz Fortification Plan)
mwbh0360	belgium holland	1662	BLAEU	800	41	49	(Gent) Hanc Veteris Burgis novam tabulam (inset: Petra Comitis)
mwuk1572	channel islands	1612	BLAEU	1500	25	54	(untitled sea chart of the coast-line of Brittany, south to the top)
mwbh0361	belgium holland	1662	BLAEU	2000	41	51	Nova et Exacta Geographica Salae et Castellaniae (Ypres)
mwit0261	italy abruzzo	1640	BLAEU	300	38	50	Abruzzo Citra et Ultra
mwuk0354	scotland	1654	BLAEU	500	37	52	Aebudae Insulae sive Hebrides
mwaf0859	africa south	1635	BLAEU	800	39	50	Aethiopia Inferior vel Exterior
mwaf0356a	africa east	1630	BLAEU	720	38	50	Aethiopia Superior vel Interior; vulgo Abissinorum sive Presbiteri Ioannis Imperium
mwsc0254	scandinavia denmark	1623	BLAEU	350	26	36	Afbeeldinge der Zeecusten van Iutlandt tussche Schagen en Refhorn
mwsp0022	portugal	1608	BLAEU	1500	25	54	Afbeeldinge der Zeecusten, tusschen C. de S. Vincete Ende de Strate van Gibraltar
mwbp0007	baltic sea (east)	1608	BLAEU	1600	25	55	Afbeeldinghe der Zeecusten van Coerlant en Lijflant ... tusschen Memel en Revel (north to the left)
mwf0722	france nord pas-de-calais	1634	BLAEU	450	44	69	Afbeeldinghe vande Vermaerde Seehaven ende Stadt van Duynkercken met de Omliggende Plaetsen Sanden ende Droochten
mwsc0666a	scandinavia sweden	1608	BLAEU	2000	25	54	Afbeeldinghe vande Wonderlijcke Gebrooken Zeecusten van Sweden Ende van Schoonen, van Benoorden Stockholm af Tot Verbij Valsterboen
mwaf0044	africa	1630	BLAEU	4000	42	56	Africae Nova Descriptio
mwf0575	france ile de france	1640	BLAEU	600	38	50	Ager Parisiensis vulgo l'Isle de France
mwbh0259	belgium holland	1640	BLAEU	400	37	47	Agri Biemstrani Descriptio a L.I.S.
mwit0648	italy piedmont	1682	BLAEU	550	52	61	Alba Pompeia sub Ditione Reg. Cels. in Ducatu Montisferrati
mwg0335	bavaria	1640	BLAEU	400	39	50	Alemannia sive Suevia Superior
mwsw0051	switzerland	1630	BLAEU	400	38	50	Alpinae seu Foederatae Rhaetiae Subditarumque ei Terrarum Nova Descriptio
mwf0216	france alsace	1635	BLAEU	900	40	80	Alsatia Landgraviatus, cum Suntgoia et Brisgola
mwam0041	america continent	1631	BLAEU	5500	41	56	Americae Nova Tabula (carte-a-figure borders on three sides. Earlier states of this map are rare. First publ. in 1617)
mwbh0298	belgium holland	1648	BLAEU	5000	43	54	Amstelodami Celeberrimi Hollandiae Emporii Delineatio Nova
mwsp0426	spain regions	1640	BLAEU	400	38	50	Andaluzia Continens Sevillam et Cordubam
mwit0649	italy piedmont	1682	BLAEU	650	51	112	Andurni Marchionatus Pars versus Meridiem
mwuk0921	england	1634	BLAEU	850	38	50	Anglia Regnum
mwuk0355	scotland	1654	BLAEU	550	41	50	Annandiae Praefectura, vulgo the Stewartrie of Annandail

AMPG REFERENCE	REGION	DATE	MAP MAKER	PRICE (UK£)	VERT. (cm.)	HOR. (cm.)	TITLE OF MAP (Comments by the editor in brackets)
mwg0795	westphalia	1649	BLAEU	400	42	52	Aquisgranum. Gallis Aix la Chapelle. Germans et Belgis Aken
mwme0561	arabia etc	1662	BLAEU	2500	42	52	Arabia
mwsp0420	spain regions	1634	BLAEU	500	39	50	Aragonia et Navarra
mwuk0356	scotland	1654	BLAEU	500	38	51	Arania Insula in Aestuario Glottae. The Yle of Arren in the Fyrth of Clyd (Isle of Arran)
mwf0734	france nord pas-de-calais	1663	BLAEU	450	40	50	Archiepiscopatus Cameracensis. Archevesche de Cambray
mwg0600	saxony	1647	BLAEU	400	38	50	Archiepiscopatus Maghdeburgensis, et Anhaltinus Ducatus
mwg0515	rheinland-pfalz	1640	BLAEU	400	42	50	Archiepiscopatus Trevirensis
mwsw0059	switzerland	1635	BLAEU	400	39	49	Argow cum Parte Merid. Zurichgow (map by Mercator)
mwf0727	france nord pas-de-calais	1645	BLAEU	350	38	48	Armentieres
mwbh0304	belgium holland	1649	BLAEU	240	42	52	Arnemuiden
mwsp0427	spain regions	1640	BLAEU	400	42	52	Arragonia Regnum
mwf0728	france nord pas-de-calais	1647	BLAEU	250	38	50	Artesia, Comitatus. Artois
mwas0032	asia continent	1630	BLAEU	4000	41	56	Asia Noviter Delineata (3 carte-a-figure borders)
mwe0322	europe austria	1642	BLAEU	650	37	54	Austria Archiducatus Auctore Wolfgango Lazio
mwf1011	france provence	1663	BLAEU	800	42	54	Avenio Vulgo Avignon
mwaf0692	africa north	1662	BLAEU	480	48	56	Barbaria
mwec0006	uk england bedfordshire	1645	BLAEU	800	41	51	Bedfordiensis Comitatus, Anglis Bedford Shire / Buckinghamiensis Comitatus, Anglis Buckingham Shire
mwbh0359	belgium holland	1662	BLAEU	960	43	52	Belgica Foederata
mwec0035	uk england berkshire	1645	BLAEU	650	40	51	Bercheria vernacule Bark Shire.
mwsp0428	spain regions	1640	BLAEU	400	39	50	Biscaia et Guipuscoa Cantabriae Veteris Pars
mwf0428	france central	1640	BLAEU	240	38	50	Bituricum Ducatus. Duche de Berri
mwe0529	europe czech republic (bohemia)	1620	BLAEU	900	38	50	Bohemia (early issue with Blaeu's 'Guiljel Janssonius' imprint. Shown below is the later issue, 41x55cm.)
mwf0285	france auvergne	1647	BLAEU	250	39	51	Borbonium, Ducatus. Bourbonnois
mwbh0260	belgium holland	1640	BLAEU	1200	38	50	Brabantia Ducatus
mwsam0291	south america brazil	1643	BLAEU	1250	39	50	Brasilia
mwf1106	france rhone-alpes	1630	BLAEU	300	38	51	Bressia vulgo Bresse
mwf0311	france brittany	1635	BLAEU	500	38	52	Britannia Ducatus. Duche de Bretaigne
mwuk1095	england and scotland	1645	BLAEU	3500	42	53	Britannia Prout Divisa fuit Temporibus Anglo-Saxonum, Praesertim Durante Illorum Heptarchia
mwbh0261	belgium holland	1640	BLAEU	1500	46	57	Bruxella (ilustrated is Jansson 1657 edition)
mwf0400	france burgundy	1660	BLAEU	400	44	57	Burgundia Comitatus vulgo la Franche Comte
mwf0401	france burgundy	1662	BLAEU	600	43	57	Burgundia Ducatus
mwuk0357	scotland	1654	BLAEU	500	38	49	Buthe Insula vulgo the Yle of Boot
mwsc0669	scandinavia sweden	1630	BLAEU	800	26	36	Caarte der Schoonse en Zeelandsche Kust (the Sound between Sweden and Denmark. North to the left.)
mwsc0667	scandinavia sweden	1630	BLAEU	1200	26	36	Caarte van't Stochholmse liet
mwf1093	france pyrenees	1635	BLAEU	350	38	49	Cadurcium vernacule Querci
mwit1012	italy south	1645	BLAEU	300	38	50	Calabria Citra olim Magna Graecia
mwit0396	italy lazio	1640	BLAEU	500	39	50	Campagna di Roma, olim Latium: Patrimonio di S. Pietro; et Sabina
mwru0474	ukraine	1631	BLAEU	1500	75	32	Campus Inter Bohum et Borysthenem ('Hunc Borysthenis tractum ...' text at foot. Dnieper River, publ. separately and also as part of 'Magni Ducatus Lithuaniae'. See also 'Baltic States' 1613)
mwgr0374	greece crete	1640	BLAEU	500	38	53	Candia, olim Creta
mwwi0230	west indies (east)	1663	BLAEU	1100	42	53	Canibales Insulae
mwec0089	uk england cambridgeshire	1645	BLAEU	750	42	53	Cantabrigiensis Comitatus; Cambridge Shire.
mwec0604	uk england kent	1645	BLAEU	1000	38	52	Cantium vernacule Kent.
mwuk0358	scotland	1654	BLAEU	600	40	49	Cantyra Chersonesus, Cantyr a Demie-Yland
mwit1010	italy south	1640	BLAEU	280	38	50	Capitanata olim Mesapiae et Iapygiae Pars
mwuk0359	scotland	1654	BLAEU	350	41	51	Caricta Borealis vulgo the Northpart of Carrick
mwuk0360	scotland	1654	BLAEU	350	41	51	Carricta Meridionalis. The South Part of Carrick
mwru0383	russia moscow	1662	BLAEU	3000	38	50	Carstvajuscoi Grad Moskva Nacal'noi Gorod useh Moskovskih Gosudarstu ... Urbis Moskvae (title in Cyrillic script)
mwf0258	france aquitaine	1635	BLAEU	300	39	50	Carte du Bourdelois, du Pais de Medoc, et de la Prevoste de Born / Principatus Benearnia. La Principaute de Bearn
mwf0578	france ile de france	1662	BLAEU	280	42	52	Carte du Pays et Forest d'Yveline, que quelques uns Mettent pour la Partie Septentrionale de l'Hurepois
mwf0576	france ile de france	1640	BLAEU	650	44	50	Carte du Pays Vexin Francois
mwsp0422	spain regions	1635	BLAEU	450	38	50	Catalonia
mwuk0361	scotland	1654	BLAEU	550	37	51	Cathensia - Caithness
mwg0186	elbe river	1628	BLAEU	350	31	53	Celeberrimi Fluvii Albis Nova Delineatio
mwf0650	france loire	1640	BLAEU	350	38	50	Cenomanorum Galliae Regionis Typus: vulgo Le Mans
mwuk1748	wales	1645	BLAEU	280	38	51	Ceretica sive Cardiganensis Comitatus; Anglis Cardigan Shire.
mwec0131	uk england cheshire	1645	BLAEU	750	38	50	Cestria Comitatus Palatinus.
mwf0441	france champagne	1635	BLAEU	400	38	50	Champagne Latine Campania Comitatus
mwc0030	china	1655	BLAEU	650	40	49	Chekiang, Imperii Sinarum Provincia Decima
mwc0017	china	1635	BLAEU	2000	41	50	China Veteribus Sinarum Regio nunc Incolis Tame Dicta
mwg0783	westphalia	1640	BLAEU	300	41	52	Circulus Westphalicus, sive Germaniae Inferioris
mwit0650	italy piedmont	1682	BLAEU	400	36	54	Civitatis Bennarum Scenographia (view of Bene Vagienna)
mwg0781	westphalia	1635	BLAEU	400	38	51	Clivia Ducatus et Ravestein Dominium

AMPG REFERENCE	REGION	DATE	MAP MAKER	PRICE (UK£)	VERT. (cm.)	HOR. (cm.)	TITLE OF MAP (Comments by the editor in brackets)
mwuk0362	scotland	1654	BLAEU	550	45	56	Coila Provincia. The Province of Kyle
mwg0778	westphalia	1630	BLAEU	240	37	48	Coloniensis Archiepiscopatus
mwf0951	france picardy	1650	BLAEU	240	41	51	Comitatus Bellovacum vernacule Beauvais
mwuk1749	wales	1645	BLAEU	250	38	50	Comitatus Brechiniae, Breknoke.
mwuk1750	wales	1645	BLAEU	500	38	51	Comitatus Caernarvoniensis; Vernacule Carnarvon-Shire et Mona Insula vulgo Anglesey.
mwec0324	uk england dorset	1645	BLAEU	550	39	51	Comitatus Dorcestria, sive Dorsettia; vulgo Anglice Dorset Shire.
mwbp0243	poland	1640	BLAEU	400	41	50	Comitatus Glatz Authore Jona Sculteto
mwbh0169a	belgium holland	1608	BLAEU		49	62	Comitatus Hollandia t'Graefschap Hollandt van nieus verbetert ... door Willem Ianszoon... 1608
mwg0801	westphalia	1662	BLAEU	500	38	50	Comitatus Marchia et Ravensberg
mwec0851	uk england northamptonshire	1645	BLAEU	400	42	50	Comitatus Northantonensis; vernacule Northamton Shire.
mwec0878	uk england northumberland	1645	BLAEU	400	41	50	Comitatus Northumbria. Vernacule Northumberland.
mwec0906	uk england nottinghamshire	1645	BLAEU	600	38	50	Comitatus Nottinghamiensis; Nottingham Shire.
mwec1004	uk england shropshire	1645	BLAEU	600	38	50	Comitatus Salopiensis. Anglice Shrop Shire.
mwf0726	france nord pas-de-calais	1643	BLAEU	280	38	50	Comitatuum Boloniae et Guines Descriptio
mwbh0367	belgium holland	1663	BLAEU	300	39	50	Comitatuum Hannoniae et Namurci Descriptio
mwuk0058	ireland	1654	BLAEU	600	38	50	Connachtia vulgo Connaughty
mwit0261b	italy abruzzo	1640	BLAEU	400	38	50	Contado di Molise et Principato Ultra
mwec0169	uk england cornwall	1645	BLAEU	800	39	50	Cornubia sive Cornwallia (11 coats of arms)
mwf0471	france corsica	1662	BLAEU	960	39	52	Corsica Insula
mwf0468	france corsica	1634	BLAEU	240	18	24	Corsica Insula
mwec0222	uk england cumbria	1645	BLAEU	600	41	50	Cumbria; vulgo Cumberland.
mwuk0363	scotland	1654	BLAEU	550	41	55	Cuninghamia. Ex schedis Timotheo Pont
mwgr0581	greece islands	1659	BLAEU	750	49	58	Cyclades Insulae in Mare Aegeo Hodie Archipelago
mwgr0475	greece cyprus	1634	BLAEU	1800	39	51	Cyprus Insula
mwsc0262	scandinavia denmark	1640	BLAEU	400	43	53	Dania Regnum
mwe0704	europe danube	1635	BLAEU	1350	42	97	Danubius, Fluvius Europae Maximus, a Fontibus ad Ostia
mwec0256	uk england derbyshire	1645	BLAEU	600	38	50	Darbiensis Comitatus. Vernacule Darbie Shire.
mwsw0055	switzerland	1634	BLAEU	400	38	50	Das Wiflispurgergow
mwuk1380a	uk england south	1623	BLAEU	800	26	36	De Cust van Engelandt tusschen de Singels en de Drooghten van Weembrugh
mwaf0686	africa north	1625	BLAEU	650	26	36	De Custen van Barbarien van C. Cantin Tot de C de Geer
mwuk1637	north sea	1623	BLAEU	2500	26	36	De Custen van Engelandt, Nederlandt, Iutlandt en Noorwegen ... Noordzee
mwg0799	westphalia	1660	BLAEU	600	43	55	De Hertochdommen Gulick, Cleve, Berghe en de Graefschappen vander Marck en Ravensbergh
mwuk1354a	england north	1623	BLAEU	800	26	36	De Noord-Cust van Enghelandt tusschen Flamburger Hoost en de Rivier van Nicasteel
mwsc0668	scandinavia sweden	1630	BLAEU	1200	26	36	De Zeecusten van Gotlandt
mwsc0531	scandinavia norway	1623	BLAEU	1200	26	36	De Zeecusten van Noorwegen tusschen de Langesondt en Pater Nosters
mwbh0308	belgium holland	1649	BLAEU	900	38	49	Delfi Batavorum vernacule Delft
mwbh0356	belgium holland	1661	BLAEU	550	38	50	Delflandia, Schielandia, et Insulae trans Mosam
mwit0651	italy piedmont	1682	BLAEU	750	45	69	Delinea Civitatis Fossani in Principatu Pedemontii (view of Fossano)
mwf1121	france rhone-alpes	1644	BLAEU	350	38	49	Delphinatus vulgo Dauphine avec ses Confins des Pais et Provinces Voisines
mwuk1751	wales	1645	BLAEU	240	38	50	Denbigiensis Comitatus et Comitatus Flintensis. Denbigh et Flintshire.
mwg0802	westphalia	1663	BLAEU	1000	38	53	Descriptio Agri Civitatis Coloniensis
mwf0804	france north	1645	BLAEU	300	38	52	Descriptio Veromanduorum Gallice Vermandois / Gouvernement de la Cappelle
mwf0803	france north	1608	BLAEU	1200	25	55	Description des Costes ... Picardie et Normandie
mwec0285	uk england devon	1645	BLAEU	650	39	50	Devonia vulgo Devon Shire.
mwat0238	atlantic madeira	1625	BLAEU	2000	43	54	d'Eylanden Madera en Porto Santo / De Raade van Punto del Gada int eylandt S. Michaels
mwf0443	france champagne	1640	BLAEU	320	42	52	Diocese de Rheims, et le Pais de Rethel
mwsc0561	scandinavia norway	1662	BLAEU	600	44	54	Dioecesis Bergensis Tabula
mwf0774	france normandy	1662	BLAEU	280	43	53	Dioecesis Ebroicensis, vulgo l'Evesche d'Evreux
mwf1186	france south west	1640	BLAEU	240	38	50	Dioecesis Sarlatensis, vernacule le Dioecese de Sarlat
mwsc0541	scandinavia norway	1640	BLAEU	720	41	50	Dioecesis Stavangriensis & Partes aliquot Vicinae
mwsc0562	scandinavia norway	1662	BLAEU	600	43	53	Dioecesis Trundhemiensis Pars Australis
mwit0652	italy piedmont	1682	BLAEU	1250	43	104	Dissegno della Citta di Mondovi in Piemonte (view)
mwit1103	italy tuscany	1640	BLAEU	500	38	50	Dominio Fiorentino
mwit1175	italy veneto	1635	BLAEU	500	39	50	Dominio Veneto nell'Italia
mwbh0262	belgium holland	1640	BLAEU	500	38	53	Drentia Comitatus. Transiselaniae Tabula II
mwit0343	italy emilia-romagna	1640	BLAEU	300	38	50	Ducato di Ferrara
mwit0478	italy lombardy	1640	BLAEU	350	38	49	Ducato di Mantova
mwit0344	italy emilia-romagna	1640	BLAEU	280	40	46	Ducato di Modena, Regio et Carpi, col Dominio della Carfagnana
mwit0345	italy emilia-romagna	1640	BLAEU	320	38	50	Ducato di Parma et di Piacenza
mwit0553	italy marches	1640	BLAEU	500	38	50	Ducato di Urbino
mwit0479	italy lombardy	1640	BLAEU	600	38	51	Ducato, overo Territorio di Milano

AMPG REFERENCE	REGION	DATE	MAP MAKER	PRICE (UK£)	VERT. (cm.)	HOR. (cm.)	TITLE OF MAP (Comments by the editor in brackets)
mwf0651	france loire	1640	BLAEU	280	37	50	Ducatus Andegauensis, Aniou
mwbp0270	poland	1662	BLAEU	450	42	55	Ducatus Breslanus sive Wratislaviensis
mwg0611	saxony	1680	BLAEU	400	41	52	Ducatus Brunsuicensis fereq Lunaeburgensis, cum Adjacentibus Episcopatibus, Comit. Domin. etc.
mwsw0087	switzerland	1682	BLAEU	500	38	60	Ducatus Chablasius et Lacus Lemanus
mwec1300	uk england yorkshire	1645	BLAEU	600	41	53	Ducatus Eboracensis Anglice York Shire.
mwec1301	uk england yorkshire	1645	BLAEU	650	38	50	Ducatus Eboracensis Pars Borealis. The North Riding of Yorkshire.
mwec1302	uk england yorkshire	1645	BLAEU	750	39	50	Ducatus Eboracensis Pars Occidentalis; The Westriding of Yorke Shire.
mwec1303	uk england yorkshire	1645	BLAEU	400	38	51	Ducatus Eboracensis Pars Orientalis; The Eastriding of Yorkeshire.
mwg0700	schleswig-holstein	1630	BLAEU	550	38	51	Ducatus Holsatiae Nova Tabula (based on Hondius, 1629)
mwbp0275	poland	1664	BLAEU	720	41	52	Ducatus Oswieczensis, et Zatoriensis
mwbp0244	poland	1640	BLAEU	350	42	51	Ducatus Silesiae Glogani Vera Delineatio
mwbp0264	poland	1660	BLAEU	450	39	53	Ducatus Silesiae Grotganus cum Districtu Episcopali Nissensi
mwbp0243a	poland	1640	BLAEU	400	42	51	Ducatus Silesiae Ligniciensis (shown above left)
mwbp0271	poland	1662	BLAEU	350	42	53	Ducatus Silesiae Schwidnicensis
mwbp0273	poland	1663	BLAEU	350	42	53	Ducatus Silesiae Wolanus
mwsc0283	scandinavia denmark	1662	BLAEU	220	43	55	Ducatus Sonderborg cum Adjacentibus Territoriis Alssen, Sundewitt et Luxburgh
mwf0654	france loire	1647	BLAEU	250	39	51	Ducatus Turonensis Touraine
mwsc0671	scandinavia sweden	1640	BLAEU	500	39	50	Ducatus Uplandia
mwuk0364	scotland	1654	BLAEU	350	41	54	Duo Vicecomitatus Aberdonia & Banfia / A Description of the Two Shyres Aberdene and Banf
mwru0056	russia	1660	BLAEU	500	42	54	Dwina Fluvius (Dvina river)
mwit0329	italy elba	1640	BLAEU	450	20	26	Elba Isola olim Ilva
mwf1096	france pyrenees	1662	BLAEU	450	47	59	Episcopatus Albiensis - Evesche d'Alby
mwec0361	uk england durham	1645	BLAEU	600	38	50	Episcopatus Dunelmensis. Vulgo The Bishoprike of Durham.
mwg0597	saxony	1643	BLAEU	320	41	50	Episcopatus Hildesiensis Descriptio Novissima
mwsc0556	scandinavia norway	1662	BLAEU	720	42	53	Episcopatus Stavangriae Pars Australis
mwsc0557	scandinavia norway	1662	BLAEU	720	39	50	Episcopatus Stavangriae Pars Borealis
mwec0400	uk england essex	1645	BLAEU	750	42	52	Essexia Comitatus.
mwe0038	europe	1630	BLAEU	4000	41	56	Europa Recens Descripta (3 carte-a-figure borders)
mwuk0365	scotland	1654	BLAEU	550	41	51	Evia et Escia Scotis, Eusdail et Eskdail (Dumfries)
mwuk0366	scotland	1654	BLAEU	550	40	51	Extima Scotiae Septentrionalis Ora, ubi Provinciae sunt Rossia, Sutherlandia, Cathenesia, Straithnaverniae cum Vicinis
mwca0023	canada	1662	BLAEU	1600	45	56	Extrema Americae Versus Boream, ubi Terra Nova Nova Francia, Adiacentiaq.
mwf0307	france brittany	1608	BLAEU	1200	25	55	Eygentlijcke Afbeeldinge ... Zee Custen van Bretaigne Poicto
mwsc0529	scandinavia norway	1608	BLAEU	2500	24	54	Eygentlycke Beschryvinghe der Zeecusten van Noorweghen tusschen der Neus en de Paternosters (part of Blaeu's first atlas, re-issued by Jansson from 1625)
mwaf0777	africa north morocco	1635	BLAEU	550	39	50	Fezzae et Marocchi Regna Africae Celeberrima
mwuk0367	scotland	1654	BLAEU	450	41	53	Fifae Pars Occidentalis. The West Part of Fife
mwuk0368	scotland	1654	BLAEU	450	41	52	Fifae Pars Orientalis, the East Part of Fife
mwuk0369	scotland	1654	BLAEU	720	41	51	Fifae Vicecomitatus. The Sherifdome of Fyfe
mwsc0563	scandinavia norway	1662	BLAEU	500	40	55	Finmarchia
mwsc0263	scandinavia denmark	1640	BLAEU	350	38	50	Fionia vulgo Funen
mwbh0235	belgium holland	1634	BLAEU	400	42	53	Flandria et Zeelandia Comitatus
mwbh0236	belgium holland	1634	BLAEU	400	41	52	Flandriae Partes Duae, quarum Altera Proprietaria, Altera Imperialis vulgo Dicitur
mwbh0237	belgium holland	1634	BLAEU	250	38	49	Flandriae Teutonicae Pars Orientalior
mwc0041	china	1655	BLAEU	800	40	49	Fokien Imperii Sinarum Provincia Undecima
mwg0778a	westphalia	1630	BLAEU	400	39	51	Fossa Sanctae Mariae, quae et Eugeniana dicitur vulgo De Nieuwe Grist (first issued in 1627 with only the lower right cartouche and title 'Fossa quae a Rheno ad Mosam Duci Coepta est Anno 1627')
mwbh0263	belgium holland	1640	BLAEU	600	38	49	Franconatus, vulgo het Vrye
mwg0331	bavaria	1634	BLAEU	240	38	50	Franconia vulgo Franckenlandt
mwsam0663	south america magellan	1630	BLAEU	1500	38	49	Freti Magellanici ac Novi Freti vulgo Le Maire Exactissima Delineatio
mwru0066	russia	1664	BLAEU	900	25	56	Fretum Nassovium vulgo de Straet Nassou
mwbh0264	belgium holland	1640	BLAEU	450	38	50	Frisia Occidentalis
mwsp0423	spain regions	1635	BLAEU	500	38	50	Gallaecia, Regnum
mwf0046	france	1631	BLAEU	720	38	50	Gallia - Le Royaume de France
mwf0052	france	1634	BLAEU	400	39	50	Gallia Vetus, ad Iul. Caesaris Commentaria
mwf0045	france	1630	BLAEU	3000	43	57	Gallia. Nova Galliae descriptio (3 carte-a-figure borders. Signed 'Janssonius'.)
mwf0730	france nord pas-de-calais	1650	BLAEU	650	38	51	Galloflandria, in qua Castellaniae Lilana, Duacena, & Orchiesia, cum Dependentibus; necnon Tornacum, & Tornacesium
mwuk0370	scotland	1654	BLAEU	550	41	52	Gallovidia vernacule Galloway

AMPG REFERENCE	REGION	DATE	MAP MAKER	PRICE (UK£)	VERT. (cm.)	HOR. (cm.)	TITLE OF MAP (Comments by the editor in brackets)
mwuk0371	scotland	1654	BLAEU	500	42	53	Gallovidiae Pars Media, quae Deam et Cream Fluvios interjacet. The Middle Part of Galloway
mwuk0372	scotland	1654	BLAEU	500	41	52	Gallovidiae Pars Occidentalior, in qua Vicecomitatus Victoniensis cum Regalitates Glenlucensi
mwf0652	france loire	1640	BLAEU	600	38	50	Gastinois et Hurepois
mwf0649	france loire	1630	BLAEU	550	38	51	Gastinois et Senonois
mwit0653	italy piedmont	1682	BLAEU	350	57	60	Gattinara
mwbh0265	belgium holland	1640	BLAEU	400	39	50	Geldria Ducatus, et Zutfania Comitatus
mwe1185	europe west	1623	BLAEU	2400	26	36	General Paskaert vande Oostersche Noordsche en Westersche Schipvaert
mwit0416	italy liguria	1634	BLAEU	700	37	50	Genovesato. Serenissimae Reipublicae Genuensis Ducatus et Dominii Nova Descriptio
mwg0067	germany	1662	BLAEU	650	49	56	Germania vulgo Teutschlandt
mwg0038	germany	1607	BLAEU	6000	42	57	Germania, non ea Tantum quae Rheno (3 carte-a-figure borders. Illustrated is the 3rd state of this map c1630.)
mwg0049	germany	1631	BLAEU	4000	45	56	Germaniae Post Omnes in hac Forma Editiones Exactissima Locupletissimaq. Descriptio (1st publ. 1608?)
mwg0045	germany	1630	BLAEU	350	38	48	Germaniae Veteris Typus
mwuk1752	wales	1645	BLAEU	450	38	51	Glamorganensis Comitatus; Vulgo Glamorgan Shire.
mwec0434	uk england gloucestershire	1645	BLAEU	720	42	50	Glocestria Ducatus; vulgo Glocester Shire.
mwuk0373	scotland	1654	BLAEU	550	38	52	Glottiana Praefectura Inferior, cum Baronia Glascuensi. The Nether Warde of Clyds-Dail, and Baronie of Glasco
mwuk0374	scotland	1654	BLAEU	550	38	52	Glottiana Praefectura Superior
mwg0796	westphalia	1649	BLAEU	300	37	49	Gochum vernacule Goch (view)
mwsc0672	scandinavia sweden	1640	BLAEU	650	42	53	Gothia Auctore Andrea Bareo Sueco
mwf0262a	france aquitaine	1662	BLAEU	550	45	60	Gouvernement de la Guienne & Gascogne (re-issued by Wolfgang c1688 no text on verso)
mwf0433	france central	1660	BLAEU	200	47	60	Gouvernement General du Pays Orleanois
mwgr0067	greece	1643	BLAEU	720	41	52	Graecia
mwsp0438	spain regions	1650	BLAEU	400	38	50	Granata, et Murcia Regna
mwf0728a	france north pas-de-calais	1649	BLAEU	480	41	52	Gravelinga Gallis Gravelines dicta
mwbh0309	belgium holland	1649	BLAEU	1000	41	53	Groeninga
mwbh0266	belgium holland	1640	BLAEU	400	38	50	Grolla Obsessa et Expugnata
mwbh0267	belgium holland	1640	BLAEU	400	38	49	Groninga Dominium
mwaf1100	africa west	1634	BLAEU	875	39	53	Guinea
mwbh0310	belgium holland	1649	BLAEU	1500	38	50	Haga Comitis, vulgo 's Graven-Hage (view)
mwec0468	uk england hampshire	1645	BLAEU	720	41	50	Hantonia sive Southantoniensis Comitatus vulgo Hantshire.
mwg0442a	hessen	1634	BLAEU	480	39	50	Hassia Landgraviatus (1662 edition 45x56cm shown below)
mwg0710	schleswig-holstein	1662	BLAEU	450	43	28	Helgelandia A. 1649 / Helgeladt in Annis Christi 800, 1200 & 1649
mwsw0056	switzerland	1634	BLAEU-MERCATOR	400	39	51	Helvetia, cum Finitimis Regionibus Confoederatis
mwec0513	uk england herefordshire	1645	BLAEU	300	41	50	Herefordia Comitatus. Herefordshire.
mwec0542	uk england hertfordshire	1645	BLAEU	750	39	50	Hertfordia Comitatus. Vernacule Hertfordshire.
mwuk1452	uk english channel (all)	1640	BLAEU	1500	26	36	Het Canael tusschen Engelandt en Vranckryk (English edition)
mwsc0532	scandinavia norway	1623	BLAEU	800	26	36	Het Liet van Bergen
mwuk0044	ireland	1634	BLAEU	1000	39	50	Hibernia Regnum Vulgo Ireland
mwbh0164a	belgium holland	1604	BLAEU	12000	42	57	Hollandia
mwbh0234	belgium holland	1634	BLAEU	1000	39	52	Hollandia Comitatus
mwbh0225a	belgium holland	1631	BLAEU	3000	39	48	Hollandia Comitatus (first edition, with 32 shields in lower border. This is a re-issue of Blaeu's rare 1608 map with title: 'Comitatus Hollandia T'Grafschap Hollandt ...', size 49x62cm, but without the 4 outer borders and with a new title. Shown left is another re-issue by Blaeu without the 4 borders and 32 shields but with the original title!)
mwbh0283	belgium holland	1642	BLAEU	550	39	50	Hollandiae Pars Septentrionalis, vulgo Westvriesland en 't Noorder Quartier
mwc0032	china	1655	BLAEU	800	39	47	Honan, Imperii Sinarum Provinciae Quinta
mwe0878	europe hungary	1650	BLAEU	550	42	51	Hungaria Regnum
mwec0575	uk england huntingdonshire	1645	BLAEU	600	39	50	Huntingdonensis Comitatus. Huntington Shire.
mwc0033	china	1655	BLAEU	650	40	48	Huqvang, Imperii Sinarum Provinciae Septima
mwjk0024	japan	1655	BLAEU	2500	42	57	Iaponia Regnum
mwit1176	italy veneto	1640	BLAEU	500	38	50	Il Bellunese con il Feltrino
mwit1177	italy veneto	1640	BLAEU	500	38	50	Il Cadorino
mwuk0375	scotland	1654	BLAEU	550	39	52	Ila Insula, ex Aebudarum Majoribus Una. The Yle of Ila, being one of the Biggest of the Westerne Yles
mwe0495b	europe croatia	1680?	BLAEU	3000	45	52	Illyricum Hodiernum
mwm0265b	mediterranean west	1634	BLAEU	1200	64	98	Imperii Caroli Magni et Vicinarum Regionum Descriptio
mwc0027	china	1655	BLAEU	2000	46	61	Imperii Sinarum Nova Descriptio (illustrated is Covens & Mortier re-issue of 1720. See below.)
mwas0384	asia south east	1635	BLAEU	2250	41	50	India quae Orientalis Dicitur et Insulae Adiacentes
mwru0054a	russia	1659	BLAEU	250	16	21	Ingria
mwsp0444	spain regions	1662	BLAEU	500	38	50	Insula Gaditana, vulgo Isla de Cadiz
mwsc0282	scandinavia denmark	1662	BLAEU	960	41	52	Insula Hvaena, sive Venusia, a Guiljelmo Blaeu, cum sub Tychone, Astronomiae Operam daret, Delineata

AMPG REFERENCE	REGION	DATE	MAP MAKER	PRICE (UK£)	VERT. (cm.)	HOR. (cm.)	TITLE OF MAP (Comments by the editor in brackets)
mwsc0517	scandinavia jan mayen isl.	1662	BLAEU	700	44	55	Insula quae a Ioanne Mayen Nomen Sortita est
mwaf0585	africa islands madagascar	1662	BLAEU	900	42	55	Insula S. Laurentii, vulgo Madagascar
mwuk1558	england islands	1645	BLAEU	300	39	47	Insula Sacra; vulgo Holy Iland; et Farne.
mwf0729	france nord pas-de-calais	1649	BLAEU	550	38	47	Insula Vulgo Lille
mwat0079	atlantic azores	1660	BLAEU	550	38	50	Insulae Acores Delineante Ludovico Teisera
mwwi0009	west indies	1634	BLAEU		47	54	Insulae Americanae in Oceano Septentrionali, cum Terris Adiacentibus (part of his much larger 1630 chart of the Atlantic Ocean, but printed separately with a pasted-on title)
mwwi0010	west indies	1635	BLAEU	1650	38	52	Insulae Americanae in Oceano Septentrionali, cum Terris Adiacentibus (replaces his 1634 map)
mwsp0645	balearic islands	1634	BLAEU	800	38	50	Insulae Balearides et Pytiusae
mwat0143	atlantic canary isl.	1662	BLAEU	800	38	50	Insulae Canariae alias Fortunatae Dictae
mwat0186	atlantic cape verde isl.	1665	BLAEU	550	43	55	Insulae de Cabo Verde, olim Hesperides, sive Gorgades: Belgice de Zoute Eylanden
mwf0970	france poitou	1635	BLAEU	600	39	53	Insulae Divi Martini et Uliarus vulgo l'Isle de Re et d'Oleron
mwat0184	atlantic cape verde isl.	1662	BLAEU	480	38	50	Insulae Promontorii Viridis, Hispanis Islas de Cabo Verde, Belgis de Soute Eylanden
mwuk0376	scotland	1654	BLAEU	300	39	52	Insulae quaedam minores ex Abebuda Quae Mulam et Skiam Insulas interjacent. Some of the Smaller Westerne Yles, Lying betweene the Yles of Mull and Skye
mwit0261a	italy abruzzo	1640	BLAEU	500	38	50	Insulae Tremitanae, olim Diomedeae dictae
mwit0277	italy campagna	1640	BLAEU	600	38	49	Ischia Isola, olim Aenaria
mwit0790	italy sardinia	1650	BLAEU	720	38	50	Isola di Sardegna
mwe0494	europe croatia	1640	BLAEU	400	38	50	Istria olim Iapidia
mwit0082a	italy	1635	BLAEU	1000	42	52	Italia
mwit0059	italy	1606	BLAEU		41	56	Italiae, Sardiniae, Corsicae et Confinium Regionum Nova Tabula, Effigies Praeciparum Urbiu et Habituum Inibi Final Complectens (Carte-a-figure borders on three sides)
mwg0780	westphalia	1634	BLAEU	280	38	50	Iuliacensis et Montensis Ducatus. De Hertoghdomen Gulick en Berghe
mwg0797	westphalia	1649	BLAEU	350	42	53	Iuliaci Obsidio Ao. MDCXI (view of Julich)
mwc0028	china	1655	BLAEU	1200	41	49	Iunnan, Imperii Sinarum Provincia Decimaquinta
mwuk0377	scotland	1654	BLAEU	350	40	51	Iura Insula. The Ile of Iura one of the westerne Iles of Scotland
mwsc0285	scandinavia denmark	1662	BLAEU	400	44	58	Iutia, olim Cimbrica Chersonesus
mwit0654	italy piedmont	1682	BLAEU	900	45	61	Ivrea (view)
mwe0495	europe croatia	1650	BLAEU	350	39	51	Karstia, Carniola, Histria et Windorum Marchia
mwc0029	china	1655	BLAEU	1200	40	50	Kiangsi, Imperii Sinarum Provincia Octava
mwuk0378	scotland	1654	BLAEU	550	41	52	Knapdalia Provincia, que sub Argathelia Consetur. The Province of Knapdail which is Accounted a Member of Argyll
mwru0384	russia moscow	1662	BLAEU	3200	38	48	Kremlenagrad, Castellum Urbis Moskvae
mwf1005	france provence	1638	BLAEU	350	38	50	La Principaute d'Orange et Comtat de Venaissin par Iaques de Chieze Orangeois. 1627
mwf1119	france rhone-alpes	1635	BLAEU	300	50	38	La Souverainete de Dombes
mwsw0050	switzerland	1630	BLAEU	600	41	52	Lacus Lemanni Locorumque Circumiacentium Accuratissimo Descriptio (Lake Geneva)
mwuk0059	ireland	1654	BLAEU	600	38	50	Lagenia; Anglis Leinster
mwsc0286	scandinavia denmark	1662	BLAEU	350	39	52	Lalandia, Falstria et Mona Insulae in Mari Balthico
mwec0678	uk england lancashire	1645	BLAEU	400	40	50	Lancastria. Palatinus Anglis Lancaster et Lancashire.
mwsc0284	scandinavia denmark	1662	BLAEU	800	43	56	Landtcarte von dem Ambte Flensborg
mwsc0291	scandinavia denmark	1662	BLAEU	500	24	30	Landtcarte Von dem Daenischen Walde
mwsc0290	scandinavia denmark	1662	BLAEU	960	43	55	Landtcarte von dem Furstenthumb Sonderborg
mwf0599	france languedoc	1635	BLAEU	600	44	54	Languedoc
mwsc0562a	scandinavia norway	1662	BLAEU	500	41	52	Lapponia Auct. Andrea Buraeo Sueco
mwuk0379	scotland	1654	BLAEU	650	38	49	Laudelia sive Lauderdalia Scotis vulgo Lauderdail
mwf0573	france ile de france	1635	BLAEU	450	38	50	Le Gouvernement de l'Isle de France
mwf0574	france ile de france	1635	BLAEU	550	39	50	Le Pais de Brie
mwbh0311	belgium holland	1649	BLAEU	1500	44	80	Legia, sive Leodium; vulgo, Liege
mwsp0429	spain regions	1640	BLAEU	400	39	50	Legionis Regnum et Asturiarum Principatus
mwec0713	uk england leicestershire	1645	BLAEU	450	39	51	Leicestrensis Comitatus. Leicester Shire.
mwf0634	france limousin	1645	BLAEU	400	38	50	Lemovicum - Lymosin / Topographia Limaniae
mwbh0268	belgium holland	1640	BLAEU	350	38	50	Leodiensis Dioecesis (Liege)
mwuk0380	scotland	1654	BLAEU	650	38	51	Leogus et Haraia, Insulae ex Aebudarum Numero, quae, quamquam Isthmo Cohaerant, pro Diversis Habentur. Lewis and Harray
mwf0395	france burgundy	1640	BLAEU	250	37	50	Les Environs de l'Estang de Longpendu, Comprenant une Grande Partie du Comte de Charolois
mwf0673	france lorraine	1645	BLAEU	280	38	50	Les Souverainetez de Sedan et de Ravcourt et la Prevoste de Doncheri
mwuk0381	scotland	1654	BLAEU	550	39	52	Levinia Vicecomitatus. The Province of Lennox, called the Shyre of Dun-Britton
mwuk0382	scotland	1654	BLAEU	550	40	51	Lidalia vel Lidisdalia regio. Lidisdail
mwit0418	italy liguria	1640	BLAEU	650	38	53	Liguria, o Stato della Republica di Genova
mwec0738	uk england lincolnshire	1645	BLAEU	600	42	50	Lincolnia Comitatus. Anglis Lincoln-Shire.
mwf1120	france rhone-alpes	1640	BLAEU	400	37	50	Lionnois, Forest, Beaviolois et Masconnois

AMPG REFERENCE	REGION	DATE	MAP MAKER	PRICE (UK£)	VERT. (cm.)	HOR. (cm.)	TITLE OF MAP (Comments by the editor in brackets)
mwbp0082	baltic states	1640	BLAEU	900	38	50	Livonia, vulgo Lyefland
mwuk0383	scotland	1654	BLAEU	650	38	52	Lorna cum Insulis Vicinis et Provinciis eidem Conterminis
mwf0670	france lorraine	1640	BLAEU	400	38	51	Lotharingia Ducatus; vulgo Lorraine
mwuk0384	scotland	1654	BLAEU	800	37	55	Lothian and Linlitquo
mwf0966	france poitou	1630	BLAEU	350	38	51	Loudonois. Laudunum / Mirebalais
mwbh0830	luxembourg	1649	BLAEU	1500	43	52	Luceburgum (view)
mwbh0312	belgium holland	1649	BLAEU	1200	43	54	Lugdunum Batavorum vernacule Leyden (view)
mwg0595	saxony	1640	BLAEU	320	42	53	Lusatia Superior
mwbh0828	luxembourg	1640	BLAEU	480	38	50	Lutzenburg Ducatus
mwbh0831	luxembourg	1649	BLAEU	1000	39	50	Lutzenburgum
mwgr0069	greece	1644	BLAEU	500	42	51	Macedonia, Epirus et Achaia
mwuk0696	uk	1631	BLAEU	1500	39	50	Magnae Britanniae et Hiberniae Tabula (as the 1630 map but without the four decorative borders)
mwbp0076	baltic states	1631	BLAEU	3500	75	106	Magni Ducatus Lithuaniae Caeterarumque Regionum illi Adiacentium Exacta Descriptio (incl. Dnieper river section, also publ. separately. See 'Russia-Ukraine', 1631.)
mwbp0077	baltic states	1631	BLAEU	2000	75	74	Magni Ducatus Lithuaniae Caeterarumque Regionum illi Adiacentium Exacta Descriptio (without Dnieper river section, publ. separately. See 'Russia-Ukraine', 1631.)
mwbp0084	baltic states	1648	BLAEU	1400	45	53	Magni Ducatus Lithuaniae et Regionum Adiacentium Exacta Descriptio
mwin0102	india	1638	BLAEU	800	42	52	Magni Mogolis Imperium (based on Hondius)
mwsc0415	scandinavia finland	1662	BLAEU	1500	44	52	Magnus Ducatus Finlandiae Auct. Andrea Buraeo Sueco
mwit0475	italy lombardy	1634	BLAEU	350	35	47	Mantua Ducatus
mwat0105	atlantic bermuda	1630	BLAEU	2000	41	53	Mappa Aestivarum Insularum, alias Barmudas Dictarum ... Accurate Descripta
mwit0554	italy marches	1640	BLAEU	280	42	51	Marca d'Ancona olim Picenum
mwg0412	brandenburg	1659	BLAEU	350	39	53	Marchionatus Brandenburgici Partes Duae, Nova Marchia et Uckerana. Auctore Olao Joannis Gotho
mwg0207	germany north east	1659	BLAEU	400	48	55	Marchionatus Brandenburgicus (shown left is Jansson version)
mwgr0582a	greece islands	1660	BLAEU	600	49	58	Maris Aegaei, quod hodie Archipelago nuncupatur, Pars Septentrionalis
mwbh0269	belgium holland	1640	BLAEU	450	38	50	Mechlinia Dominium, et Aerschot Ducatus
mwit0477	italy lombardy	1635	BLAEU	720	38	49	Mediolanum Ducatus
mwg0482	mecklenburg	1640	BLAEU	300	37	49	Meklenburg Ducatus
mwm0190	mediterranean malta	1662	BLAEU	2000	45	56	Melite Insula, vulgo Malta
mwuk0385	scotland	1654	BLAEU	650	37	48	Mercia vulgo Vicecomitatus Bervicensis
mwec0769	uk england middlesex	1645	BLAEU	720	39	41	Middle-Sexia.
mwas0711	asia south east moluccas	1630	BLAEU	600	37	48	Moluccae Insulae Celeberrimae (The 'Spice Islands'. Inset of Bachian Island. North to the right.)
mwuk0060	ireland	1654	BLAEU	600	38	50	Momonia, Hibernice Moun et Woun; Anglice Mounster
mwuk1603a	isle of man	1645	BLAEU	550	38	28	Mona
mwg0784	westphalia	1640	BLAEU	300	38	50	Monasteriensis Episcopatus
mwuk1754	wales	1645	BLAEU	400	38	50	Montgomeria Comitatus et Comitatus Mervinia.
mwit0636	italy piedmont	1634	BLAEU	450	37	48	Montisferrati Ducatus
mwuk1755	wales	1645	BLAEU	650	38	51	Monumethensis Comitatus. Vernacule Monmouth Shire.
mwe1100	europe slovak republic (moravia)	1643	BLAEU	480	38	49	Moravia Marchionatus (below is the Jansson re-issue with changed cartouche etc.)
mwuk0386	scotland	1654	BLAEU	650	40	54	Moravia Scotiae Provincia (Murry Firth)
mwgr0066	greece	1643	BLAEU	400	42	51	Morea olim Peloponnesus
mwuk0387	scotland	1654	BLAEU	650	42	53	Mula Insula, quae ex Aebudarum Numero Una est, et Lochabriae ad Occasum Praetenditur. The Yle of Mul
mwbh0318	belgium holland	1650	BLAEU	600	41	52	Namurcum Comitatus
mwc0031	china	1655	BLAEU	1200	41	49	Nanking, sive Kiangnan, Imperii Sinarum Provincia Nona
mwg0449	hessen	1650	BLAEU	300	38	48	Nassovia Comitatus
mwme0943	turkey etc	1640	BLAEU	650	40	51	Natolia, quae olim Asia Minor
mwsp0430	spain regions	1640	BLAEU	400	43	53	Navarra Regnum
mwf1013	france provence	1668	BLAEU	1200	48	63	Nicaea ad Varum cum Novo Urbis Incremento
mwf1014	france provence	1668	BLAEU	1200	46	59	Nicaea Civitas
mwuss1073	new york	1650	BLAEU	6000	7	31	Nieuw Amsterdam op t Eylant Manhattans (earliest known engraving of New York)
mwbh0169	belgium holland	1607	BLAEU	1650	25	36	Nieuwe beschrijvinghe van alle de Eylande ... langs de custen van Vrieslandt (north to the left)
mwbh0205	belgium holland	1622	BLAEU	80000	104	161	Nieuwe ende Waarachtighe Beschrijvinghe der Zeventien Nederlanden, na hare Rechte Gheleghentheyt, Volcomender ende Breeder als oyt voor desen is Ghedaen, nu Nieulijcx met Grooten Vlijt Aldus Verbetert ende Ghemeerdert, Anno MDCXXII (only three known examples)
mwaf1107a	africa west	1650	BLAEU	1000	38	57	Nigritarum Regio
mwuk0388	scotland	1654	BLAEU	550	38	52	Nithia Vicecomitatus. The Shirifdome of Nidis-dail
mwf0396	france burgundy	1640	BLAEU	600	38	51	Nivernium Ducatus, Gallice Duche de Nevers
mwbh0362	belgium holland	1662	BLAEU	720	46	57	Nobiliss Prudentiss Syndico Civitatis Zirizeae
mwsc0678b	scandinavia sweden	1662	BLAEU	720	41	48	Nordlandiae et quibies Gestricia et Helsingicae Regiones Auct. Andrea Buraeo Sueco
mwf0769	france normandy	1635	BLAEU	350	38	52	Normandia Ducatus

AMPG REFERENCE	REGION	DATE	MAP MAKER	PRICE (UK£)	VERT. (cm.)	HOR. (cm.)	TITLE OF MAP (Comments by the editor in brackets)
mwec0812	uk england norfolk	1645	BLAEU	720	41	53	Nortfolcia. Norfolke.
mwsc0564	scandinavia norway	1662	BLAEU	2000	42	50	Norvegia Regnum vulgo Nor-Ryke
mwaf0475	africa egypt etc	1662	BLAEU	800	45	54	Nova Aegypti Tabula
mwam0856	america north (east)	1634	BLAEU	3500	39	50	Nova Belgica et Anglia Nova (north to the right)
mwsam0313	south america brazil	1667	BLAEU	1500	50	59	Nova et Accurata Brasiliae Totius Tabula
mwgr0087	greece	1672	BLAEU	720	46	56	Nova et Accurata Moreae, olim Peloponnesus Dictae, Delineatio
mwww0178	world	1663	BLAEU	16000	41	54	Nova et Accuratissima Totius Terrarum Orbis Tabula
mwe0082	europe	1673	BLAEU	25000	102	141	Nova et Acurata Totius Europae Tabula Auct Blaeu
mwgm0157	mexico	1635	BLAEU	650	39	50	Nova Hispania, et Nova Galicia (close copy of Hondius 1630)
mwit0078	italy	1630	BLAEU	6000	48	60	Nova Italiae Delineatio (4 carte-a-figure borders. Re-issue of Hondius 1620)
mwit0079	italy	1631	BLAEU	1500	38	50	Nova Italiae Delineatio (no carte-a-figure borders)
mwf0950a	france picardy	1649	BLAEU	320	39	54	Nova Picardiae Tabula (1st edition)
mwww0256	world	1695	BLAEU-VALK	5500	40	54	Novus Planiglobii Terristris Per Utrumque Polum Conspectus (2 polar hemispheres. Blaeu's final world map, produced in 1672 just before a fire destroyed his stock. This plate survived and was published in 1695)
mwsp0172	spain	1605	BLAEU	4800	40	54	Nova Regni Hispaniae Descriptio, de Novo Multis in Locis Aucta et Emendata (inset city views in corners)
mwg0048	germany	1631	BLAEU	550	38	48	Nova Totius Germaniae Descriptio
mwww0139	world	1630	BLAEU	13500	41	55	Nova Totius Terrarum Orbis Geographica Ac Hydrographica Tabula (Blaeu's classic world map, first produced in 1606 and re-issued with minor changes until 1662. The illustration shows the least rare 4th and final state, issued from 1630.)
mwww0203	world	1676	BLAEU-SCOLARI		104	159	Nova Totius Terrarum Orbis Sive Nova Orbis Tabula
mwuss1598	virginia	1631	BLAEU	2500	38	48	Nova Virginiae Tabula
mwru0059	russia	1662	BLAEU	500	38	50	Nova Zemla
mwg0446	hessen	1640	BLAEU	1200	46	55	Novam hanc Territorii Francofurtensis Tabulam
mwsam0283	south america brazil	1630	BLAEU	1000	38	50	Novus Brasiliae Typus
mwbh0169b	belgium holland	1608	BLAEU	12000	48	62	Novus XVII Inferioris Germaniae Provinciarum Typus (with decorative borders; see also 1630)
mwbh0217	belgium holland	1630	BLAEU	2800	40	50	Novus XVII Inferioris Germaniae Provinciarum Typus (1st state 1608)
mwbh0319	belgium holland	1650	BLAEU	1200	41	52	Obsidio et Expugnatio Sylvaeducis-'s-Hertogenbosch
mwg0598	saxony	1643	BLAEU	400	38	50	Oldenburg Comitatus
mwit0422	italy liguria	1682	BLAEU	750	47	61	Onelia vulgo Oneglia (view of Imperia)
mwuk0389	scotland	1654	BLAEU	500	40	52	Orcadum et Schetlandiae Insularum Accuratissima Descriptio
mwec0941	uk england oxfordshire	1645	BLAEU	750	39	51	Oxonium Comitatus, vulgo Oxford Shire.
mwg0785	westphalia	1640	BLAEU	320	38	50	Paderbornensis Episcopatus Descriptio Nova
mwg0516	rheinland-pfalz	1640	BLAEU	350	41	50	Palatinatus ad Rhenum
mwg0332	bavaria	1635	BLAEU	240	38	50	Palatinatus Bavariae
mwbp0276	poland	1664	BLAEU	800	42	53	Palatinatus Posnaniensis, in Maiori Polonia Primarii Nova Delineatio
mwsam0706	south america paraguay	1662	BLAEU	720	45	55	Paraquaria vulgo Paraguay. Cum Adjacentibus
mwsc0289	scandinavia denmark	1662	BLAEU	400	44	58	Pars Australior Iutiae Septentrionalis, in qua Dioeceses Ripensis et Arhusiensis
mwsc0288	scandinavia denmark	1662	BLAEU	400	44	58	Pars Borealitor Iutiae Septentrionalis
mwbh0338	belgium holland	1660	BLAEU	400	40	50	Pars Flandriae Teutonicae Occidentalior
mwg0712a	schleswig-holstein	1662	BLAEU	500	43	57	Pars Meridionalis Wagriae, cum partes Stormariae
mwsc0292	scandinavia denmark	1664	BLAEU	350	41	54	Pars Occidentalis Praefecturae Hadersleben cum Adjacentibus Ripen et Lohmcloster Praefecturis
mwsc0287	scandinavia denmark	1662	BLAEU	220	41	54	Pars Orientalis Praefecturae Hadersleben vulgo Dictae Baringsijssel
mwit0479a	italy lombardy	1640	BLAEU	450	38	50	Parte Alpestre dello Stato di Milano, con il Lago Maggiore di Lugano, e di Como
mwuk1638	north sea	1623	BLAEU	800	26	36	Pascaart vande Noord-Zee, van het Tessel tot de Hoofden (illustrated is the 1652 edition)
mwe1184a	europe west	1621	BLAEU	40000	69	87	Pascaarte van alle de Zecuften van Europa. (North to the right)
mwat0135a	atlantic canary isl.	1623	BLAEU	1100	26	36	Pascaarte van Barbarische cust mitsgaders van de Canarische en Vlaemsche Eylanden
mwsc0533	scandinavia norway	1623	BLAEU	800	25	39	Pascaarte van de Westcuste van Noorwegen en Spitsberge
mwuk1546	bristol channel	1608	BLAEU	1800	25	56	Pascaarte van het vermaert Canael van Bristou
mwec0163	uk england cornwall	1608	BLAEU	4500	25	56	Pascaarte van het Vermart Canael van Bristou / Eygentlijck Beworp nae 't Leven van alle Havenen, Gaten en Reeden (2 charts, each 25x56cm. covering the coastline of Cornwall)
mwsc0262	scandinavia denmark	1608	BLAEU	2400	25	56	Pascaarte van 't Schagerrack Vertoonende Schaghen en Maesterlandt of Door de Sond Tot om Valsterboen
mwsc0059	scandinavia	1658	BLAEU	1000	26	37	Pascaarte vande Custen van Noorwegen Denemarcken Holsten Mekelenborg en Pomeren
mwat0135	atlantic canary isl.	1608	BLAEU	1650	25	56	Pascaarte vande Eijlanden van Canarien
mwsc0534	scandinavia norway	1623	BLAEU	600	27	36	Pascaarte vande Noorweegsche Cust van Olde tot Stemmersheft

AMPG REFERENCE	REGION	DATE	MAP MAKER	PRICE (UK£)	VERT. (cm.)	HOR. (cm.)	TITLE OF MAP (Comments by the editor in brackets)
mwg0697	schleswig-holstein	1625	BLAEU	1200	25	55	Pascaarte vande Westcuste van Iuthlant en Holsterlant
mwru028a	russia	1608	BLAEU	1500	25	55	Pascaarte vande witte Zee …
mwsp0022a	portugal	1608	BLAEU	1500	25	54	Pascaarte vande Zeecuste van Portugal tußchen de Baerlenges en de C. de S. Vincente geleghen… vande vermaerde Riviere Lisbona
mwuk1419	england thames	1623	BLAEU	1000	25	36	Pascaarte Verrthoonende de Mont vande Teemse de Rivier van Londen met Alle Gronden Diepten en Ondiepten daer voor Gelegen
mwe1189	europe west	1666	BLAEU	20000	68	86	Paskaarte Vertonende Alle de Zekusten van Europa. Nieulvez Aldus Uytgegeven, door P. Goos (re-issue by Goos. First publ. 1621)
mwit0373	italy friuli	1662	BLAEU	550	42	50	Patria del Friuli olim Forum Iulii
mwc0035	china	1655	BLAEU	1600	40	48	Pecheli, sive Peking Imperii Sinarum Provincia Prima (incl. Beijing)
mwit0638	italy piedmont	1635	BLAEU	300	38	50	Pedemontana Regio cum Genvensium Territorio et Montisferrati Marchionatu
mwit0656	italy piedmont	1682	BLAEU	960	50	59	Pedemontium et Reliquae Ditiones Italiae
mwuk1756	wales	1645	BLAEU	450	41	53	Penbrochia Comitatus et Comitatus Caermaridunum.
mwf0434	france central	1662	BLAEU	300	38	23	Perchensis Comitatus. La Perche Comte / Comitatus Blesensis, Auctore Ioanne Temporio. Blaisois
mwme0773	persia etc	1640	BLAEU	720	38	49	Persia sive Sophorum Regnum
mwf0948	france picardy	1640	BLAEU	400	38	54	Picardia Regio Belgica
mwf0972	france poitou	1640	BLAEU	400	38	53	Pictaviae Ducatus Descriptio, vulgo le Pais de Poictou
mwit0639	italy piedmont	1640	BLAEU	400	42	52	Piemonte et Monferrato
mwbh0270	belgium holland	1640	BLAEU	350	43	53	Plan du Fort de Watten (Waettene, Belgium. Inset map and view)
mwf0671	france lorraine	1640	BLAEU	500	42	52	Plan et Siege Damvillers, 1637
mwit1178	italy veneto	1640	BLAEU	550	38	50	Polesino di Rovigo
mwbp0236	poland	1634	BLAEU	1000	41	51	Polonia Regnum, et Silesia Ducatus
mwbp0231	poland	1630	BLAEU	500	38	49	Pomeraniae Ducatus Tabula Auctore Eilhardo Lubino
mwf1015	france provence	1668	BLAEU	400	48	55	Porto di Villafranca (view)
mwsp0026	portugal	1635	BLAEU	500	38	50	Portugallia et Algarbia quae olim Lusitania
mwf0723	france nord pas-de-calais	1635	BLAEU	550	45	70	Pourtraict de la Fameuse Ville et Havre de Duynckercke et Places Voisines
mwf0288	france bay of biscay	1608	BLAEU	1000	24	55	Pourtraict des Costes … de France … Biscaje
mwsam0307	south america brazil	1662	BLAEU	2000	41	53	Praefectura de Ciriii, vel Seregippe del Rey cum Itapuama
mwg0711	schleswig-holstein	1662	BLAEU	600	43	57	Praefectura Flensburgensis absque Nordgoes Herde
mwuk0390	scotland	1654	BLAEU	720	42	53	Praefectura Kircubriensis, qua Gallovidiae Maxime Orientalis Pars Est. The Steuartrie of Kircubright
mwuk0391	scotland	1654	BLAEU	600	38	52	Praefectura Renfroana vulgo dicta Baronia. The Baronie of Renfrow
mwg0712	schleswig-holstein	1662	BLAEU	950	44	59	Praefectura Tondern sine Lundtofft Herde Anno 1648 Christian Rothgiesser Husum. Sculps.
mwsam0308	south america brazil	1662	BLAEU	2000	41	53	Praefecturae de Paraiba, et Rio Grande
mwsam0309	south america brazil	1662	BLAEU	2000	41	53	Praefecturae Paranambucae Pars Borealis, una cum Praefectura de Itamaraca
mwsam0310	south america brazil	1662	BLAEU	2000	42	54	Praefecturae Paranambucae Pars Meridionalis
mwbh0320	belgium holland	1650	BLAEU	1000	41	52	Prima Pars Brabantiae cuius Caput Lovanium
mwit0278	italy campagna	1640	BLAEU	350	38	50	Principato Citra olim Picentia
mwf1007	france provence	1642	BLAEU	480	38	54	Provincia Auctore Petro Joanne Bompario. Provence
mwbp0237	poland	1635	BLAEU	800	39	50	Prussia Accurate Descripta a Gasparo Henneberg Erlichensi
mwbp0238	poland	1635	BLAEU	800	38	50	Prussiae Nova Tabula Auctore Gasparo Henneberg Erlichensi
mwc0034	china	1655	BLAEU	650	38	47	Quangsi, Imperii Sinarum Provinciae Decimatertia
mwc0036	china	1655	BLAEU	1600	40	48	Quantung, Imperii Sinarum Provincia Duodecima (incl. Hong Kong)
mwbh0241	belgium holland	1634	BLAEU	1800	42	53	Quarta Pars Brabantiae cujus Caput Sylvaducis (also available is a proof state, below)
mwc0037	china	1655	BLAEU	800	39	48	Queicheu, Imperii Sinarum Provincia Decimaquarta
mwuk1757	wales	1645	BLAEU	450	41	53	Radnoria Comitatus. Radnor Shire.
mwuk1339	england east	1645	BLAEU	600	44	55	Regiones Inundatae in finibus Comitatus Norfolciae, Suffolciae, Cantabrigiae, Huntingtoniae, Northamtoniae, et Lincolniae.
mwaa0085	arctic	1639	BLAEU	1200	41	53	Regiones Sub Polo Arctico
mwaf1111	africa west	1662	BLAEU	875	45	54	Regna Congo et Angola
mwit1003	italy south	1634	BLAEU	950	38	50	Regno di Napoli
mwsp0176	spain	1630	BLAEU	600	38	49	Regnorum Hispaniae nova descriptio
mwg0713	schleswig-holstein	1662	BLAEU	500	41	61	Rendsburgum, Chilonium et Bordesholma, sive Holsatia Propria
mwbh0242	belgium holland	1635	BLAEU	600	40	50	Rhenolandiae et Amstellandiae Exactissima Tabula
mwe0994	europe rhine	1635	BLAEU	1250	42	96	Rhenus Fluviorum Europae celeberrimus, cum Mosa, Mosella, et Reliquis, in illum se Exonerantibus, Fluminibus (north to the right)
mwe0993	europe rhine	1634	BLAEU	2200	77	49	Rhenus Mosella, Vahalis, Mosa, & Reliqui qui in illos se Exonerant Fluvii
mwit0417a	italy liguria	1640	BLAEU	550	38	50	Riviera di Genova di Levante

AMPG REFERENCE	REGION	DATE	MAP MAKER	PRICE (UK£)	VERT. (cm.)	HOR. (cm.)	TITLE OF MAP (Comments by the editor in brackets)
mwit0417b	italy liguria	1640	BLAEU	550	39	50	Riviera di Genova di Ponente (shown above left)
mwit0719	italy rome	1663	BLAEU	600	49	55	Roma Vetus
mwit0346	italy emilia-romagna	1640	BLAEU	550	38	49	Romagna olim Flaminia
mwbh0313	belgium holland	1649	BLAEU	2000	42	53	Rotterdam (view)
mwg0478	mecklenburg	1631	BLAEU	300	38	50	Rugia Insula ac Ducatus Accuratissime Descripta
mwru0040b	russia	1640	BLAEU	600	39	49	Russiae, vulgo Moscovia Dictae, Pars Occidentalis
mwru0040	russia	1640	BLAEU	600	39	53	Russiae, vulgo Moscovia, Pars Australis
mwru0040a	russia	1640	BLAEU	600	39	49	Russiae, vulgo Moscovia, Partes Septentrionalis et Orientalis
mwec0981	uk england rutland	1645	BLAEU	550	38	49	Rutlandia Comitatus. Rutland Shire.
mwf1111	france rhone-alpes	1631	BLAEU	450	38	48	Sabaudia Ducatus. Savoye
mwe0320	europe austria	1640	BLAEU	600	38	50	Saltzburg Archiepiscopatus et Carinthia Ducatus
mwit0786	italy sardinia	1634	BLAEU	550	18	24	Sardinia Insula
mwuk1573	channel islands	1645	BLAEU	600	39	47	Sarnia Insula, vulgo Garnsey: et Insula Caesarae, vernacule Jarsey
mwg0599	saxony	1644	BLAEU	400	39	51	Saxonia Superior, cum Lusatia et Misnia
mwsc0679	scandinavia sweden	1662	BLAEU	450	49	51	Scania vulgo Schoonen
mwe1122e	europe slovenia	1635	BLAEU	400	38	50	Sclavonia, Croatia, Bosnia cum Dalmatiae Parte
mwuk0392	scotland	1654	BLAEU	800	40	53	Scotia Antiqua : qualis priscis temporibus, Romanis
mwuk0342	scotland	1634	BLAEU	720	38	50	Scotia Regnum
mwuk0353	scotland	1654	BLAEU	900	40	53	Scotia Regnum cum Insulis adjacentibus
mwuk0393	scotland	1654	BLAEU	600	41	51	Scotiae Provinciae Mediterraneae inter Taum Flumen et Cararis Aestuarium: Sunt autem Braid-Allaban, Atholia, Marria Superior, Badenocha, Strath-Spea, Lochabria cum Chersoneso
mwbh0243	belgium holland	1635	BLAEU	600	41	53	Secunda Pars Brabantiae cuius Urbs Primaria Bruxellae
mwit0885	italy sicily	1634	BLAEU	1350	38	50	Sicilia Regnum
mwf0674	france lorraine	1645	BLAEU	500	44	54	Siege et Prise de Thionville, 1643
mwit0640	italy piedmont	1640	BLAEU	400	41	50	Signoria di Vercelli
mwbp0239	poland	1635	BLAEU	450	38	49	Silesia Ducatus
mwbp0248	poland	1644	BLAEU	450	42	51	Silesia Inferior Noviter et Accurata Delineata a Jona Sculteto Sprotta Silesio
mwsam0306	south america brazil	1662	BLAEU	1350	39	50	Sinus Omnium Sanctoru (inset: San Salvador)
mwuk0394	scotland	1654	BLAEU	550	40	51	Skia vel Skiana. The Yle of Skie
mwec1033	uk england somerset	1645	BLAEU	900	39	50	Somersettensis Comitatus. Somersetshire.
mwuk0395	scotland	1654	BLAEU	500	38	52	Southerlandia
mwsc0565	scandinavia norway	1662	BLAEU	600	38	49	Spitsberga
mwec1063	uk england staffordshire	1645	BLAEU	600	41	50	Staffordiensis Comitatus; vulgo Stafford Shire.
mwit0641	italy piedmont	1640	BLAEU	400	39	50	Stato del Piemonte
mwit0297	italy central	1635	BLAEU	550	39	50	Stato della Chiesa con la Toscana
mwit1104	italy tuscany	1640	BLAEU	400	38	50	Stato della Republica di Lucca
mwit0480	italy lombardy	1640	BLAEU	400	42	53	Stato di Milano
mwuk0396	scotland	1654	BLAEU	650	40	51	Sterlinensis Praefectura. Sterlin-Shyr
mwe0321	europe austria	1640	BLAEU	300	38	51	Stiria Steyrmarck
mwe0318	europe austria	1638	BLAEU	450	38	50	Stiria vulgo Steyrmarck
mwg0710a	schleswig-holstein	1662	BLAEU	500	40	55	Stormaria Ducatus
mwuk0397	scotland	1654	BLAEU	600	40	49	Strath-Navernia Strath-Navern
mwc0038	china	1655	BLAEU	650	41	49	Suchuen, Imperii Sinarum Provincia Sexta
mwsc0679a	scandinavia sweden	1662	BLAEU	1200	43	48	Suecia Regnum, Auct. Andrea Buraeo Sueco
mwsc0049	scandinavia	1634	BLAEU	960	43	53	Suecia, Dania, et Norvegia, Regna Europae Septentrionalia
mwsc0678c	scandinavia sweden	1662	BLAEU	720	41	48	Sueonia Proprie sic Dicta
mwg0259	baden-wurttemberg	1640	BLAEU	400	37	48	Sueviae Nova Tabula
mwec1095	uk england suffolk	1645	BLAEU	720	38	50	Suffolcia. Vernacule Suffolke.
mwec1129	uk england surrey	1645	BLAEU	1000	39	50	Surria vernacule Surrey.
mwec1158	uk england sussex	1645	BLAEU	900	38	52	Suthsexia, vernacule Sussex.
mwru0065	russia	1664	BLAEU	720	16	21	t Hertogdom Ingrien oft Ingermannien
mwbh0314	belgium holland	1649	BLAEU	720	40	50	Tabula Castelli ad Sandflitam, qua Simul Inundati Agri, Alluviones, Fossae, Alvei, quae Bergas ad Zomam et Antverpiam interjacent, Annotantur
mwbh0218	belgium holland	1630	BLAEU	500	38	50	Tabula Castelli ad Sandflitam, qua Simul Inundati Agri, Alluviones, Fossae, Alvei, quae Bergas ad Zomam et Antverpiam interjacent, Annotantur
mwsc0486	scandinavia iceland	1630	BLAEU	900	38	49	Tabula Islandiae Auctore Georgio Carolo Flandro
mwsam0666	south america magellan	1635	BLAEU	850	42	49	Tabula Magellanica, qua Tierrae del Fuego, cum Celeberrimis Fretis a F. Magellani et I. Le Maire Detectis Novissima et Accuratissima Descriptio Exhibetur
mwbh0315	belgium holland	1649	BLAEU	600	41	52	Tabula Praelii Prope Neoportum commissi. 1600 (2 maps on one sheet, battle of Nieuwpoort.
mwru0037	russia	1634	BLAEU	1500	43	55	Tabula Russiae ... M.DC.XIIII
mwru0423	russia tartary	1640	BLAEU	720	39	50	Tartaria sive Magni Chami Imperium
mwru0475	ukraine	1635	BLAEU	500	38	49	Taurica Chersonesus nostra Aetate Przecopsca, et Gazara Dicitur (copy of Hondius 1609)
mwit1006	italy south	1640	BLAEU	500	38	51	Terra di Bari et Basilicata (illustrated is Jansson's 1652 re-issue)
mwit0281	italy campagna	1642	BLAEU	450	38	50	Terra di Lavoro, olim Campania Felix
mwit1011	italy south	1640	BLAEU	400	38	49	Terra di Otranto olim Salentina et Iapigia

AMPG REFERENCE	REGION	DATE	MAP MAKER	PRICE (UK£)	VERT. (cm.)	HOR. (cm.)	TITLE OF MAP (Comments by the editor in brackets)
mwsam0497	south america colombia	1650	BLAEU	1000	37	48	Terra Firma et Novum Regnum Granatense et Popayan
mwme0096	holy land	1635	BLAEU	750	38	50	Terra Sancta quae in Sacris Terra Promissionis olim Palestina
mwit0279	italy campagna	1640	BLAEU	600	38	50	Terre de Labeur ou Campagne Felix
mwbh0363	belgium holland	1662	BLAEU	720	42	55	Territorii Bergensis Accuratissima Descriptio
mwit0481	italy lombardy	1640	BLAEU	240	38	24	Territorio Cremasco
mwit0482	italy lombardy	1640	BLAEU	500	38	49	Territorio di Bergamo
mwit0347	italy emilia-romagna	1640	BLAEU	400	44	54	Territorio di Bologna
mwit0483	italy lombardy	1640	BLAEU	600	38	50	Territorio di Brescia et di Crema
mwit0484	italy lombardy	1640	BLAEU	280	38	50	Territorio di Cremona
mwit1152	italy umbria	1640	BLAEU	280	38	50	Territorio di Orvieto
mwit0485	italy lombardy	1640	BLAEU	300	38	50	Territorio di Pavia, Lodi, Novarra, Tortona, Alessandria et Altri Vicini dello Stato di Milano
mwit1105	italy tuscany	1640	BLAEU	550	39	51	Territorio di Siena et Ducato di Castro
mwit1082	italy trentino-alto	1631	BLAEU	400	37	48	Territorio di Trento
mwit1179	italy veneto	1640	BLAEU	600	38	50	Territorio di Verona
mwit1180	italy veneto	1640	BLAEU	550	43	51	Territorio di Vicenza
mwit1181	italy veneto	1640	BLAEU	500	38	50	Territorio Padovano
mwit1153	italy umbria	1640	BLAEU	280	38	50	Territorio Perugino
mwit1182	italy veneto	1645	BLAEU	550	38	51	Territorio Trevigiano
mwg0448	hessen	1643	BLAEU	350	38	50	Territorium Abbatiae Heresfeldensis. 't Stift Hirszfeldt
mwsw0077	switzerland	1662	BLAEU	600	41	52	Territorium Basileense
mwf0217	france alsace	1640	BLAEU	400	39	50	Territorium Metense. Le Pais Messin
mwg0336	bavaria	1640	BLAEU	350	37	48	Territorium Norimbergense (inset plan of Nuremburg)
mwbh0296	belgium holland	1647	BLAEU	650	42	53	Tertia Pars Brabantiae qua Continetur Marchionat. S.R.I. Horum Urbs Primaria Antverpia
mwbh0364	belgium holland	1662	BLAEU	650	41	53	Tetrarchia Ducatus Gelriae Arnhemiensis sive Velavia
mwbh0335	belgium holland	1659	BLAEU	800	38	52	Tetrarchia Ducatus Gelriae Neomagensis
mwbh0368	belgium holland	1663	BLAEU	650	41	53	Tetrarchia Ducatus Gelriae Ruraemundensis
mwuk0398	scotland	1654	BLAEU	500	41	52	Teviotia vulgo Tivedail
mwg0739	thuringia	1640	BLAEU	300	42	53	Thuringia Landgraviatus
mwru0479	ukraine	1662	BLAEU	550	47	55	Tractus Borysthenis vulgo Dniepr et Niepr Dicti, a Chortika Ostro ad Urbem Oczakow ubin in Pontum Euxinum se Exonerat
mwe0705	europe danube	1635	BLAEU	2000	41	89	Tractus Danubii, Fluminis in Europa Maximi, a Fontibus, per Germaniam et Hungariam, Belgradum usque
mwe0995	europe rhine	1640	BLAEU	400	39	50	Tractus Rheni et Mosae totusq Vahalis a Rhenoberca Gorcomium usque cum Terris Adjacentibus Ducatus Cliviae Regno Noviomagensi et Bommelerwaert Parte Insuper Veteris Bataviae
mwbp0265	poland	1660	BLAEU	500	42	52	Tractuum Borussiae, circa Gedanum et Elbingam
mwbh0316	belgium holland	1649	BLAEU	1400	38	50	Trajectum Utrecht
mwbh0271	belgium holland	1640	BLAEU	400	42	52	Transiselania Dominum vernacule Over-Yssel
mwe1043a	europe romania	1666	BLAEU	550	38	50	Transylvania Sibenburgen
mwbh0826	luxembourg	1635	BLAEU	750	38	50	Trevirensis Archiepiscopatus, et Lutzenburgi Ducatus
mwuk0399	scotland	1654	BLAEU	650	41	50	Tuedia cum Vicecomitatu Etterico Forestrae etiam Selkirkae Dictus. Twee-Dail with the Sherifdome of Etterik-Forrest called also Selkirk
mwme0550a	arabia etc	1635	BLAEU	800	41	52	Turcicum Imperium
mwbh0272	belgium holland	1640	BLAEU	650	38	48	Typus Frisiae Orientalis
mwru0487	ukraine	1670	BLAEU	1250	46	58	Ukrainae Pars quae Barclavia vulgo Dicitur (later re-issued by Covens & Mortier)
mwru0484	ukraine	1670	BLAEU	1250	41	57	Ukrainae Pars quae Kiovia Palatinatus vulgo Dicitur (later re-issued by Covens & Mortier)
mwru0485	ukraine	1670	BLAEU	1250	45	54	Ukrainae Pars quae Podolia Palatinatus vulgo Dicitur (later re-issued by Covens & Mortier)
mwru0486	ukraine	1670	BLAEU	1250	45	53	Ukrainae Pars quae Pokutia vulgo Dicitur (later re-issued by Covens & Mortier)
mwuk0061	ireland	1654	BLAEU	600	38	50	Ultonia; Hibernis Cui-Guilly; Anglis Ulster
mwbh0219	belgium holland	1630	BLAEU	400	38	50	Ultraiectum Dominium
mwit1154	italy umbria	1640	BLAEU	400	38	50	Umbria overo Ducato di Spoleto
mwbh0365	belgium holland	1662	BLAEU	650	43	56	Utraque Bevelandia, & Wolfersdyck, Insulae Orientaliores Zelandiae Cisscaldinae
mwf0397	france burgundy	1640	BLAEU	350	39	51	Utriusque Burgundiae, tum Ducatus tum Comitatus Descriptio
mwsp0431	spain regions	1640	BLAEU	400	42	51	Utriusque Castiliae Nova Descriptio
mwit0397	italy lazio	1640	BLAEU	600	34	56	Utriusque Portus Ostia Delineatio
mwsp0432	spain regions	1640	BLAEU	400	39	50	Valentia Regnum
mwf0949	france picardy	1640	BLAEU	280	39	50	Valesium Ducatus - Valois
mwuk1618	isle of wight	1645	BLAEU	450	38	50	Vectis Insula. Anglice The Isle of Wight.
mwit1232	italy venice	1704	BLAEU-MORTIER	6500	45	102	Venetia (close copy of Jansson 1657)
mwf1016	france provence	1668	BLAEU	300	49	57	Villarium Oppidu (view of Villars-sur-Var)
mwuss1602	virginia	1638	BLAEU	1500	38	50	Virginiae Partis Australis, et Floridae Partis Orientalis, interjacentiumq. Regionum Nova Descriptio
mwuk0400	scotland	1654	BLAEU	650	44	57	Vistus Insula, vulgo Viist, cum Aliis Minoribus ex Aebudarum Numero ei ad Meridiem Adjacentibus

AMPG REFERENCE	REGION	DATE	MAP MAKER	PRICE (UK£)	VERT. (cm.)	HOR. (cm.)	TITLE OF MAP (Comments by the editor in brackets)
mwg0712b	schleswig-holstein	1662	BLAEU	500	43	55	Wagriae pars Septentrionalis (shown above left)
mwe0758	europe east	1635	BLAEU	550	38	50	Walachia Servia, Bulgaria, Romania
mwbh0366	belgium holland	1662	BLAEU	720	45	55	Walachria, Zelandiae Cisscaldinae Insula Occidentalis
mwg0445	hessen	1640	BLAEU	300	39	50	Waldeck Comitatus
mwuk1746	wales	1645	BLAEU	900	39	50	Wallia Principatus. vulgo Wales.
mwat0013	atlantic ocean (all)	1630	BLAEU	120000	78	98	West Indische Paskaert waerin de Graden der Breedde over Weder Zijden vande Middellijn Wassende (re-issued by Goos-Loots, 1695. Goos imprint cartouche shown below)
mwec1221	uk england westmorland	1645	BLAEU	600	38	50	Westmoria Comitatus; Anglice Westmorland.
mwg0786	westphalia	1640	BLAEU	280	38	50	Westphalia Ducatus
mwec1273	uk england worcestershire	1645	BLAEU	720	41	51	Wigorniensis Comitatus et Comitatus Warwicensis; nec non Coventrae Libertas. Worcester, Warwik Shire and the Liberty of Coventre.
mwec1240	uk england wiltshire	1645	BLAEU	785	42	50	Wiltonia sive Comitatus Wiltoniensis; Anglis Wil Shire.
mwg0260	baden-wurttemberg	1640	BLAEU	300	41	50	Wirtenberg Ducatus
mwf0971	france poitou	1635	BLAEU	350	39	50	Xaintonge et Angoumois (now Saintonge)
mwc0039	china	1655	BLAEU	800	39	48	Xansi, Imperii Sinarum, Provincia Secunda
mwc0040	china	1655	BLAEU	1200	40	48	Xantung. Sinarum Imperii Provincia Quarta
mwc0042	china	1655	BLAEU	800	41	49	Xensi, Imperii Sinarum Provincia Tertia
mwgm0164	mexico	1662	BLAEU	1200	42	52	Yucatan Conventus Iuridici Hispaniae Novae Pars Occidentalis, et Guatimala Conventus Iuridicus
mwuk0030	ireland	1623	BLAEU	1500	26	36	Zeekaarte van Yerlandt
mwbh0284	belgium holland	1642	BLAEU	500	39	53	Zeelandia Comitatus
mwsc0277	scandinavia denmark	1659	BLAEU	600	44	53	Zeelandia Insula Danicarum Maxima
mwsw0058	switzerland	1634	BLAEU	400	38	50	Zurichgow et Basiliensis Provincia
mwbh0226	belgium holland	1631	BLAEU	250	22	27	Zutphania Comitatus
mwbh0336	belgium holland	1659	BLAEU	600	41	53	Zutphania Comitatus, sive Ducatus Gelriae Tetrarchia Zutphaniensis / Zutphania Comitatus (2 maps)
mwbh0288	belgium holland	1645	BLAEU	400	38	51	Zuydhollandia Stricte Sumta
			SEE ALSO VAN DER KEERE / BLAEU MINIATURE MAPS				
mww0088	world	1596	BLAGRAVE	25000	30	27	Novis Orbis Terrarum Descriptio (north polar projection)
mwuk1012	england	1773	BLAIR	375	43	58	A Map of England and Wales from the Latest Authorities and Observations
mwg0148	germany	1773	BLAIR	200	43	58	A Map of Germany Divided into its Circles
mwuk0852	uk	1773	BLAIR	375	43	57	A Map of Great Britain and Ireland from the Latest Authorities and Observations
mwas0489	asia south east	1773	BLAIR	450	42	56	A Map of the East Indies from the Latest Authorities and Observations
mwwi0103	west indies	1773	BLAIR	400	42	58	A Map of the West Indies and Middle Continent of America from the Latest Observations
mww0504	world	1779	BLAIR	1000	41	70	A Map of the World with the Latest Discoveries (shows Cook's discoveries)
mwgr0198	greece	1768	BLAIR	380	42	57	Grecia Antiqua
mwme0363	holy land	1773	BLAIR	250	43	58	Palaestinae sive Terrae Promissionis in Duodecim Tribus Partitae Facies Vetus
mwit0954	italy sicily	1773	BLAIR	400	43	58	Sicilia Antiqua quae et Sicania et Trinacria Dicta
mwit0199a	italy	1773	BLAIR	350	43	58	Tabula Italiae Antiquae in Provincias et Populos Divisa
mwas0490	asia south east	1773	BLAIR	450	42	57	The East Indies Including More Particularly the British Dominions on the Continent of India
mwuss0998	new hampshire	1761	BLANCHARD & LANGDON	20000	79	70	An Accurate Map of His Majesty's Province of New-Hampshire in New England
mwjk0012	japan	1617	BLANCUS		42	67	Iaponia
mwaf0059	africa	1652	BLANKAART	480	37	53	Africae Antiquae, ed quarundam Europae Asiaeque Adiacentium Regionum, Accurata Delineatio, ad Historiarum Lucem (excl. southernmost 1/3 of Africa)
mwas0044	asia continent	1652	BLANKAART	1600	37	55	Asia Antiqua cum Finitimis Africae et Europae Regionibus Nicolaus Blancardus Belga, Leidensis, ad Lucem Aevi Veteris Delineabat
mwe0062	europe	1652	BLANKAART	400	37	51	Europa Antiqua cum Finitimus Africae & utriusque Asiae Regionibus
mwe0847	europe east	1847	BLASCHNEK	1500	179	233	Karte des Konigreichs Ungarn der Konigreiche Croatien, Slavonien, Dalmatien, des Grossfrustenth. Siebenburgen, des Kustenlandes und der Militar Grenze
mwe0973	europe hungary	1835	BLASCHNEK	600	43	51	Plan der K. Ung. Freyen Stadte Ofen und Pesth
mwuss1614	virginia	1672	BLOME	1200	20	25	A Draught of the Sea Coast and Rivers of Virginia, Maryland and New England. Taken from the Latest Surveys
mwec0326	uk england dorset	1673	BLOME	550	27	31	A General Mapp of Dorsetshire
mwec1007	uk england shropshire	1673	BLOME	500	27	31	A General Mapp of Shrop Shire
mwec0225	uk england cumbria	1673	BLOME	400	32	26	A General Mapp of the Countie of Cumberland
mwas0400	asia south east	1667	BLOME	720	40	34	A General Mapp of the East Indies Comprehending the Estats or Kingdoms of the Great Mogol
mwsp0191	spain	1670	BLOME	480	29	41	A General Mapp of the Kingdom of Spaine
mwme0563	arabia etc	1670	BLOME	1200	28	41	A Generall Mapp of Arabia with the Red Sea and Circumjacent Lands (title below map)

AMPG REFERENCE	REGION	DATE	MAP MAKER	PRICE (UK£)	VERT. (cm.)	HOR. (cm.)	TITLE OF MAP (Comments by the editor in brackets)
mwas0056	asia continent	1669	BLOME	1600	39	55	A Generall Mapp of Asia
mwuss0155	carolinas	1678	BLOME	1200	15	22	A Generall Mapp of Carolina. Describeing its Sea Coast and Rivers
mwuk0727	uk	1667	BLOME	720	31	21	A Generall Mapp of England, Scotland, Ireland, Ye Isles of Orkney & Shetland (title below map)
mwuk1765	wales	1673	BLOME	450	34	47	A Generall Mapp of North Wales
mwuk1766	wales	1673	BLOME	450	34	47	A Generall Mapp of South Wales
mwaf0694a	africa north	1670	BLOME	1000	35	106	A Generall Mapp of the Coast of Barbarie, where are the Kingdoms and Estates of Morocco, Fez, Algier, Tunis and Tripolis
mwec0944	uk england oxfordshire	1673	BLOME	600	32	28	A Generall Mapp of the County of Oxford
mwg0075	germany	1682	BLOME	300	28	41	A Generall Mapp of the Empire of Germany - Designed by Monsieur Sanson - by Richard Blome (1st issued 1670)
mwuk0727a	uk	1670	BLOME	950	40	52	A Generall Mapp of the Isles of Great Brittaine, Designed by Monsieur Sanson
mwf0066	france	1670	BLOME	650	29	41	A Generall Mapp of the Kingdom of France
mwru0069	russia	1673	BLOME	500	25	39	A Generall Mapp of the Kingdom of Tartaria
mwsc0069	scandinavia	1670	BLOME	720	33	41	A Generall Mappe of Scandinavia, where are the Estates and Kingdomes of Danemark, Norway and Sweden
mwme0342	holy land	1753	BLOME	500	36	41	A Map of the Holy Land Divided into the XII Tribes of Israel wherein is Exactly Mark'd ye Travells of Jesus Christ
mwec0037	uk england berkshire	1673	BLOME	500	27	31	A Mapp of Barkshire
mwec0007	uk england bedfordshire	1673	BLOME	500	27	31	A Mapp of Bedfordshire
mwec0063	uk england buckinghamshire	1673	BLOME	500	27	31	A Mapp of Buckinghamshire
mwec0091	uk england cambridgeshire	1673	BLOME	600	30	27	A Mapp of Cambridgeshire with the Ile of Ely
mwec0287	uk england devon	1673	BLOME	550	27	31	A Mapp of Devon Shire
mwe0087	europe	1680	BLOME	900	40	55	A Mapp of Europe
mwec0438	uk england gloucestershire	1673	BLOME	400	33	28	A Mapp of Glocestershire
mwec0472	uk england hampshire	1673	BLOME	720	30	25	A Mapp of Hantshire
mwec0543	uk england hertfordshire	1673	BLOME	550	27	31	A Mapp of Hartfordshire
mwec0577	uk england huntingdonshire	1673	BLOME	350	32	26	A Mapp of Huntingtonshire
mwit0103	italy	1669	BLOME	800	32	40	A Mapp of Italy
mwec0610	uk england kent	1673	BLOME	600	27	33	A Mapp of Kent
mwec0908	uk england nottinghamshire	1673	BLOME	400	32	26	A Mapp of Nottingham Shire
mwec1065	uk england staffordshire	1673	BLOME	550	33	23	A Mapp of Stafford Shire
mwec1133	uk england surrey	1673	BLOME	720	27	31	A Mapp of Surrey
mwec0171	uk england cornwall	1673	BLOME	500	27	31	A Mapp of the County of Cornwal
mwec0258	uk england derbyshire	1673	BLOME	550	32	25	A Mapp of the County of Darbye
mwec0715	uk england leicestershire	1673	BLOME	400	25	31	A Mapp of the County of Leicester
mwec0817	uk england norfolk	1673	BLOME	500	27	30	A Mapp of the County of Norfolck
mwec0854	uk england northamptonshire	1673	BLOME	450	26	32	A Mapp of the County of Northampton
mwec0982	uk england rutland	1673	BLOME	350	32	29	A Mapp of the County of Rutland
mwec1036	uk england somerset	1673	BLOME	500	27	31	A Mapp of the County of Somerset
mwec1099	uk england suffolk	1673	BLOME	550	27	31	A Mapp of the County of Suffolk
mwec1162	uk england sussex	1673	BLOME	650	27	31	A Mapp of the County of Sussex
mwme0783	persia etc	1669	BLOME	500	29	40	A Mapp of the Empire of the Sophie of Persia, with its Severall Provinces
mwru0068	russia	1669	BLOME	550	28	40	A Mapp of the Estates of the Great Duke of Russia, Blanch, or Moscovia
mwme0959	turkey etc	1670	BLOME	750	28	43	A Mapp of the Estates of the Turkish Empire in Asia, and Europe
mwaf0867	africa south	1669	BLOME	750	30	40	A Mapp of the Higher and Lower Aethiopia Comprehending ye Several Kingdomes ... the Empire of the Abissines, the Coast of Zanguebar (re-issued 1683 with a different dedication and signed R.B.)
mwwi0360	barbados	1672	BLOME	800	18	17	A Mapp of the Island of Barbados. Taken from the Latest Survey. 1672
mwuk1561	england islands	1673	BLOME	550	28	38	A Mapp of the Isles of Wight, Jarsey, Garnsey, Sarke, Man, Orcades, and Shetland
mwsc0294	scandinavia denmark	1670	BLOME	300	30	40	A Mapp of the Kingdome of Dennmarke
mwuk0076	ireland	1673	BLOME	900	38	39	A Mapp of the Kingdome of Ireland
mwuk0413	scotland	1673	BLOME	900	38	41	A Mapp of the Kingdome of Scotland
mwm0135	mediterranean east	1687	BLOME	600	30	46	A Mapp of the Travels and Voyages of the Apostles in their Mission and in Particular of Saint Paul
mwec1312	uk england yorkshire	1673	BLOME	600	27	32	A Mapp of the West Riding of Yorke Shire
mwec1191	uk england warwickshire	1673	BLOME	550	27	31	A Mapp of Warwickshire
mwec1243	uk england wiltshire	1673	BLOME	550	32	26	A Mapp of Wiltshire
mwec1276	uk england worcestershire	1673	BLOME	550	27	32	A Mapp of Worchestershire
mwec0364	uk england durham	1673	BLOME	450	27	32	A Mapp of ye Bishoprick of Durham
mwec1222	uk england westmorland	1673	BLOME	450	32	26	A Mapp of ye Countie of Westmorland
mwec0403	uk england essex	1673	BLOME	600	26	32	A Mapp of ye County of Essex
mwec0741	uk england lincolnshire	1673	BLOME	550	33	27	A Mapp of ye County of Lincolne
mwec0772	uk england middlesex	1673	BLOME	650	29	32	A Mapp of ye County of Midlesex
mwuk1767	wales	1673	BLOME	450	32	25	A Mapp of ye County of Mounmouthshire

AMPG REFERENCE	REGION	DATE	MAP MAKER	PRICE (UK£)	VERT. (cm.)	HOR. (cm.)	TITLE OF MAP (Comments by the editor in brackets)
mwec0880	uk england northumberland	1673	BLOME	450	26	32	A Mapp of ye County of Northumberland with ye isles of Farne & Holy Island
mwec0681	uk england lancashire	1673	BLOME	500	27	31	A Mapp of ye County Palatine of Lancaster
mwec1313	uk england yorkshire	1673	BLOME	600	27	32	A Mapp of ye East Rideing of Yorkshire
mwuk0926	england	1667	BLOME	785	21	32	A Mapp of ye kingdome of England
mwru0435b	russia tartary	1688	BLOME	500	26	39	A Mapp of ye Kingdome of Tartary
mwec1314	uk england yorkshire	1673	BLOME	600	27	32	A Mapp of York Shire
mww0189	world	1670	BLOME	4200	39	52	A Mapp or Generall Carte of the World Designed in Two Plaine Hemispheres by Monsieur Sanson Geographr to the French King and Rendered into English
mwwi0690	jamaica	1672	BLOME	1500	28	33	A New & Exact Mapp of ye Isle of Iamaica as it was Lately Surveyed by Order of S. Thomas Mediford Bar. Late Gover. Divided into Precincts, or Parishes with its Ports, Bayes, etc.
mwaf0076	africa	1669	BLOME	1500	39	55	A New Mapp of Africa Designed by Mounsr. Sanson ... 1669 (see also under 'Africa South')
mwsam0025	south america	1662	BLOME	1200	39	54	A New Mapp of America Meridionale Designed by Monsieur Sanson Geographer ... and Rendered into English & Illustrated by Richard Blome by His Maiestie Especiall Command
mwam0320	america north	1668	BLOME	2800	38	55	A New Mapp of America Septentrionale Designed by Monsieur Sanson ... Rendered into English, and Illustrated by Richard Blome
mwc0055	china	1669	BLOME	900	30	38	A New Mapp of ye Empire of China with its Severall Provinces or Kingdomes, Together with the Adjacent Isles of Japon or Niphon, Formosa, Hainan, &c
mwaf1118	africa west	1670	BLOME	600	33	41	Africa or Libia Ulteriour where are the Countries of Saara Desert the Countrie of Negroes and Guine with the Circumjacent Countries and Kingdoms
mwsam0033	south america	1690	BLOME	1200	39	53	America Meridionale
mwme0201	holy land	1687	BLOME	650	26	45	Canaan Commonly Called the Holy Land or the Land of Promise Being ye Possession of ye Israelites & Traveled through by Our Lord
mww0206	world	1678	BLOME	650	38	24	Geography
mwme0475	jerusalem	1701	BLOME	720	41	48	Jerusalem
mwuk1119	england london	1667	BLOME	1400	17	28	London (4 editions with changes in the late 1600s)
mwec0134	uk england cheshire	1673	BLOME	450	26	31	The County Palatine of Chester
mwme0154	holy land	1660	BLOME	750	27	44	The Forty Years Travels of the Children of Israel out of Egypt through the Red Sea and the Wilderness into Canaan or the Land of Promise
mwec1315	uk england yorkshire	1673	BLOME	500	27	32	The North Ridinge of York Shire
mwaf0280	africa	1796	BLONDEAU	100	18	22	Afrique
mwam0567	america north	1806	BLONDEAU	200	19	23	Amerique Septentrionale
mwuss0455	florida	1803	BLONDEAU	720	19	41	Basse-Louisiane et Floride Occidentale
mwuss0857	massachusetts	1804	BLONDEAU	120	19	11	Boston y sus Alrededores-Boston et ses Environs
mwgr0242	greece	1814	BLONDEAU	1000	60	107	Carte de la Moree Dressee et Gravee au Depot Gl. de la Guerre
mwam0608	america north	1817	BLONDEAU	200	18	20	Etats Unis de l'Amerique
mwas0513	asia south east	1790	BLONDEAU	250	19	32	Indes Occidentale
mww0587	world	1795	BLONDEAU	235	18	25	Mappe-Monde Reduite
mwuss1168	new york	1800	BLONDEAU	160	14	10	Plan de la Baie de New-York
mwam1257	america north (east)	1850	BLUNT	1200	66	94	(Coast from Cape Fear to Cape Hatteras)
mwuss0284	carolinas	1845	BLUNT	650	66	95	(North Carolina Coast)
mwam1246	america north (east)	1842	BLUNT	2250	64	92	(United States: East Coast from Cape Fear to St. Augustine)
mwgm0079	gulf of mexico and surrounding regions	1845	BLUNT	800	91	206	(Yucatan to Orinoco)
mwgm0080	gulf of mexico and surrounding regions	1845	BLUNT	3000	69	215	Chart of the Gulf of Mexico, West Indies, and Spanish Main
mwgm0307	mexico	1827	BLUNT	300	21	29	Chart of the Harbour of Vera Cruz
mwat0065	atlantic ocean (all)	1844	BLUNT	450	114	150	Chart of the North Atlantic Ocean from the Equator to 65 North Latitude
mwsam0164	south america	1849	BLUNT	650	94	185	Chart of the South Atlantic Ocean
mwuss1683	virginia	1827	BLUNT	240	18	21	Chesapeake Bay Entrance
mwam1251	america north (east)	1846	BLUNT	3500	74	333	Coast of North America, from Port Judith to Cape St. Antonio, (Island of Cuba) Including the Bahama Banks
mwwi0496	cuba	1850	BLUNT	2000	205	105	Cuba and the Windward Passage
mwuss0517	georgia	1822	BLUNT	150	18	18	Doboy Sound
mwca0463	canada nova scotia	1832	BLUNT	180	11	18	Isle of Sable
mwuss0721	maine	1827	BLUNT	120	23	19	Isles of Shoals
mwuss1222	new york	1833	BLUNT	280	23	48	Long Island Sound
mwuss1212	new york	1830	BLUNT	5000	56	203	Long Island Sound from New York to Montock Point, Surveyed in the Years 1828, 29 & 30
mwuss1181	new york	1815	BLUNT	200	10	18	New York
mwuss1189	new york	1822	BLUNT	200	25	19	New York Harbour
mwuss1248	new york	1844	BLUNT	500	39	42	New York Harbour and Entrance
mwam1241	america north (east)	1840	BLUNT	600	196	97	North-Eastern Coast of North America from New York to Cape Canso

AMPG REFERENCE	REGION	DATE	MAP MAKER	PRICE (UK£)	VERT. (cm.)	HOR. (cm.)	TITLE OF MAP (Comments by the editor in brackets)
mwuss0715	maine	1822	BLUNT	200	18	10	Plan of Portland Harbour
mwuss1025	new hampshire	1837	BLUNT	120	18	19	Plan of Portsmouth Harbour
mwuss0536	georgia	1847	BLUNT	180	18	23	Sapello Island, Cabarita Is. & Doboy Sound
mwuss0525	georgia	1833	BLUNT	180	18	23	Sapello Island, Doboy Sound
mwuss0520	georgia	1827	BLUNT	150	20	43	Savannah River from its Mouth to the City of Savannah by John LeConte ... 1821
mwwi0347	bahamas	1827	BLUNT	3000	100	125	The Bahama Banks and Gulf of Florida (re-issued 1848)
mwuss0375	delaware	1804	BLUNT	200	18	22	The Bay and River of Delaware
mwgm0078a	gulf of mexico and surrounding regions	1844	BLUNT	1500	63	99	The North Coast of the Gulf of Mexico, from St. Marks to Galveston
mwuss0485	florida	1846	BLUNT	1800	67	248	The Tortugas: Florida and Carysfort Reefs and Keys, with Additions and Corrections to 1855
mwam1191	america north (east)	1826	BLUNT	3500	74	307	To the Members of the Nautical Institution and Shipmasters Society, of the City of New York; this Chart, Extending from Lat. 40 15 N. Long: 72 15" W. to Lat 22 35" N. Long: 80 25" W.
mwuss0532	georgia	1841	BLUNT	150	20	25	Tybee Bay, and Savannah River
mwuss0120	california	1848	BLUNT	1200	57	89	West Coast of North America from the Gulf of Dulce to San Francisco. From Spanish & Other Authorities
mwf0522	france corsica	1769	BOASSO	2000	38	67	Carta dell'Isola di Corsica
mwit0820a	italy sardinia	1777	BOASSO	300	12	10	Regno di Sardegna
mwat0177	atlantic cape verde isl.	1588	BOAZIO		43	56	Hoc Opidum Divi Jacobi eo Nomine quo Insula Vocat, et Comercium habet cum Guynea (view of Santiago published 1588 in an account of Francis Drake's expedition.)
mwat0011	atlantic ocean (all)	1589	BOAZIO		41	54	The famous West Indian voyadge made by the Englishe fleet of 23 shippes
mwgr0580a	greece islands	1646	BOCHARD	1000	29	38	Aegei Maris Insulae (several insets showing the voyages of the Phoenicians)
mwm0268	mediterranean west	1681	BOCHART	400	29	35	Hispania et Africae pars Occidentalis / Baeticae partis / Italiae pars (3 maps on one sheet)
mwwi0699	jamaica	1684	BOCHART & KNOLLIS	8000	56	130	A New & Exact Mapp of the Island of Jamaica
mwaa0169	arctic	1824	BOCK	240	37	39	Laender um den Nordpol-Die Bergegran van H. Bock
mwme0165	holy land	1670	BOCKLER	800	26	39	Eygentliche Delineatio ... der Kinder Israel Auszug aus Egypten (illustration damaged)
mwme0460	jerusalem	1670	BOCKLER	800	26	40	Eygentlicher Situs und Grundt Riss ... Statt Jerusalem
mwme0166a	holy land	1670	BOCKLER	800	26	40	Geographische Beschreibung der Landt-Schafften welche die Apostel
mwme0166	holy land	1670	BOCKLER	600	26	40	Land Tafel darinnen die Gegendt des Paradys
mwam0180	america continent	1760	BOD	800	32	36	Amerika (Hungarian map of America)
mwe0787	europe east	1720	BODENEHR	200	16	22	(Bendery, Moldavia) Bender, Sonsten auch Tekin Genant
mwg0273	baden-wurttemberg	1720	BODENEHR	350	19	30	(Lake Constance)
mwe1066	europe serbia	1720	BODENEHR	200	17	25	(Nis) Plan von der Turckischen Graenz Vestung Nissa, und den Situation im Konigreich Servien
mwaf0702	africa north	1700	BODENEHR	250	27	39	Abris der Verstung Tripoli in Barbarien
mwf1032	france provence	1700	BODENEHR	350	16	20	Abriss die Dreyen Gegeneinander Correspondierenden Bessungen Monaco, Capo di Sant Spirito, und Niza di Provenza
mwbh0600	belgium holland	1727	BODENEHR	240	16	27	Amstelodamum Amsterdam
mwbh0570	belgium holland	1720	BODENEHR	240	16	27	Antwerpen
mwf0747	france nord pas-de-calais	1720	BODENEHR	180	16	30	Arras mitt Nahe Anliegender Gegend
mwg0360	bavaria	1720	BODENEHR	240	16	26	Augusta Vindelicorum. Augspurg wie es vom Konig Gustavo Adolpho aus Scweden Ao. 1632 Bevestiget Werden Sollen
mwe1067	europe serbia	1720	BODENEHR	200	16	20	Belgrad
mwg0233	berlin	1700	BODENEHR	400	18	27	Berlin und Colln an der Spree vor Dero Erweiterung
mwe0348	europe austria	1720	BODENEHR	350	17	32	Bregentz wie Statt und Schlos und Claussen Ao. 1647 den 5. Jenner von dem Schwedichen Feldmarschal Wrangeln mitt Sturm Orobert Worden
mwg0274	baden-wurttemberg	1720	BODENEHR	200	17	33	Breisach wie Es Ao. 1697 bey Schliessung des Ryswyckischen Fridens Gestanden
mwg0631a	saxony	1720	BODENEHR	300	16	27	Bremen
mwbp0371	poland	1720	BODENEHR	350	16	27	Breslau
mwbh0573	belgium holland	1720	BODENEHR	240	16	29	Brussel
mwsp0497	spain regions	1705	BODENEHR	250	17	51	Cadiz nach Malaga durch die Straasse oder Meer-Enge von Gibraltar aus dem Ocean in dass Mittellaendische Meer
mww0297	world	1704	BODENEHR	600	15	24	Carta Hydrographica oder Algemeine Welt und Commercien Carte
mwg0266	baden-wurttemberg	1680	BODENEHR	720	48	56	Circulus Suevicus (shown below left)
mwsp0232	spain	1710	BODENEHR	200	15	21	Compendiosa Hispaniae Repraesentatio Die Konigreich Spanien u Portugall mit ihren Provincien
mwit0154	italy	1720	BODENEHR	200	16	21	Compendiosa Italie Repraesentatio / Italien mitt Angrentzenden Landern
mwsc0352	scandinavia denmark	1727	BODENEHR	250	16	27	Copenhagen
mwgr0320	greece corfu	1720	BODENEHR	400	14	31	Corfu (view)

AMPG REFERENCE	REGION	DATE	MAP MAKER	PRICE (UK£)	VERT. (cm.)	HOR. (cm.)	TITLE OF MAP (Comments by the editor in brackets)
mwbp0372	poland	1720	BODENEHR	350	16	35	Dantzig, die Hauptstatt in dem Koniglich Polnischen Preussen
mwsp0520	spain regions	1715	BODENEHR	200	15	24	Das Furstenthum Catalonien
mwit0737	italy rome	1720	BODENEHR	200	17	27	Das Heutige Rom nach dero XIV. Rionen
mwit1030a	italy south	1720	BODENEHR	150	16	28	Das Konigreichs Napoli Sud=Theil
mwm0055a	mediterranean	1740	BODENEHR	350	17	24	Das Mittelaendische Meer
mwsp0697a	gibraltar	1727	BODENEHR	900	46	56	Das Von Denen Spaniern in Anno 1727 Belagerte Gibraltar (view)
mww0310	world	1710	BODENEHR	600	15	27	Der Neuen Welt Begriff / Der Alte Welt Begriff (2 hemispheres on 1 sheet)
mwsc0345	scandinavia denmark	1720	BODENEHR	200	17	30	Der Nordischen Konigreiche Sud-West Theil Begreiffende Dennemarck und Gothland
mwg0488	mecklenburg	1720	BODENEHR	200	16	23	Der Pass Neu Fehr zwische der Insul Rugen u. d. Stadt Stralsund
mwbp0373	poland	1720	BODENEHR	240	17	35	Der Weixelstroom von Danzig bis zum Auslauf in die Oost See
mwit1035	italy south	1748	BODENEHR	180	16	29	Des Konigreichs Napoli Nord=Theil
mwit1061	italy south	1720	BODENEHR	150	16	28	Des Konigreichs Napoli Sud=Theil
mwg0235	berlin	1720	BODENEHR	1500	16	52	Die Churfurstliche Brandenburgisch nun Koniglich Preussische Residenz Statt Berlin - Berlin und Colln an der Spree sampt Fridrichswerder und Dorotheen Statt
mwg0719	schleswig-holstein	1720	BODENEHR	280	17	21	Die Festung Harburg unweit Hamburg
mwf1037	france provence	1705	BODENEHR	250	17	31	Die Gegend von Toulon bis Marsilien und S. Tropez
mwru0507	ukraine	1720	BODENEHR	300	17	30	Die Gegend zwischen Pultava und Bender mitt Angraenzenden Polnisch, Turckisch und Tartarischen Landschafften
mwit0502	italy lombardy	1720	BODENEHR	180	16	28	Die Obere oder Westliche Lombardia
mwg0631	saxony	1720	BODENEHR	200	19	31	Die Stadt Stade
mwsp0489	spain regions	1700	BODENEHR	280	16	22	Die Sud Cust von Andaluzien von Cadiz durch die Meer Enge Gibraltar
mwme0216	holy land	1700	BODENEHR	550	19	38	Eigentliche Abriss des Heyligen oder Belobten Lands (north to the left)
mwg0749	thuringia	1720	BODENEHR	150	15	27	Erfurt
mwe0131	europe	1715	BODENEHR	180	15	20	Europae Compendiosa Representatio
mwg0453	hessen	1720	BODENEHR	250	16	34	Frankfurt am Main wie es Ao 1719 zwischen den 26 u. 27. luny den Grausamen Brand Erlitten
mwg0275	baden-wurttemberg	1720	BODENEHR	200	16	29	Freiburg im Brisgow
mwsw0112	switzerland	1720	BODENEHR	250	15	28	Genff oder Genev
mwit0426a	italy liguria	1720	BODENEHR	450	17	46	Genua oder Genova
mwuk0777	uk	1704	BODENEHR	375	17	30	Geographische Vorstellung der Konigreiche Grosbritannien und Irland
mwe0926	europe hungary	1720	BODENEHR	180	13	20	Giula
mwg0720	schleswig-holstein	1720	BODENEHR	450	17	30	Hamburg
mwsw0095	switzerland	1698	BODENEHR	2500	52	74	Helvetia Rhaetia, Valesia
mwg0721	schleswig-holstein	1720	BODENEHR	400	16	28	Homburg Stad und Schloss wie es von denen Frantzosen von Neuem Bevestiget Worden
mwf0477a	france corsica	1710	BODENEHR	180	17	30	Insul und Konigreich Corsica mitt Angraenzen den Custen
mwit0798	italy sardinia	1715	BODENEHR	300	15	24	Insul und Konigreich Sardinien
mwit0149	italy	1715	BODENEHR	250	16	30	Italien fur die Reisende
mwg0717	schleswig-holstein	1720	BODENEHR	300	15	23	Kiel. Chilonium
mwru0146	russia	1720	BODENEHR	350	16	21	Konigsberg im Grundriss (Kaliningrad)
mwg0530	rheinland-pfalz	1720	BODENEHR	150	16	22	Landau
mwg0531	rheinland-pfalz	1720	BODENEHR	250	16	19	Landau von Ihro Rom. Konigl. Maj. Ao. 1704 den 26. Nov. zum Andernmahl Erobert
mwsw0113	switzerland	1720	BODENEHR	300	17	30	Lindau im Boden See
mwg0632	saxony	1720	BODENEHR	350	16	30	Lipsia. Leipzig
mwsp0076	portugal	1720	BODENEHR	300	16	23	Lissabon mitt dero Gegend auff 10. Stundt
mwuk1143	england london	1710	BODENEHR	875	16	71	Londen, Westmunster u: Soudwark (size incl. text panels at sides)
mwbh0855	luxembourg	1720	BODENEHR	500	17	28	Luxemburg mit dero Gegend auff 2 Stunde
mwsp0343b	spain madrid	1720	BODENEHR	300	17	38	Madrit
mwsp0659a	balearic islands	1730	BODENEHR	400	16	20	Maiorca
mwm0222	mediterranean malta	1720	BODENEHR	400	18	28	Malta eine Insul
mwit0505	italy lombardy	1720	BODENEHR	240	16	25	Mantova
mwit0506	italy lombardy	1720	BODENEHR	240	18	22	Mantova mitt dero Gegend
mwit0512	italy lombardy	1734	BODENEHR	900	41	57	Mappa Geographica Continens Ducatum Mantuanum
mwbh0578	belgium holland	1720	BODENEHR	280	16	25	Mecheln
mwsp0651	balearic islands	1700	BODENEHR	240	16	19	Minorca, eine von den Balearischen Insulen
mwru0389	russia moscow	1725	BODENEHR	400	16	23	Moscow des Grossen Zaars Residenz
mwit1060	italy naples	1720	BODENEHR	350	16	28	Napoli
mwwi0423	cuba	1720	BODENEHR	400	17	26	Neuer Plan der Stadt u. Hafens Havana
mwe0935	europe hungary	1730	BODENEHR	720	49	59	Nova et Accurata Tabula Regnorum Sup. et Inf. Hungariae
mwit0918	italy sicily	1704	BODENEHR	200	15	19	Palermo
mwf0850	france paris	1720	BODENEHR	250	15	19	Paris die Haupt Stadt in Franckreich
mwsw0114	switzerland	1720	BODENEHR	400	19	30	Plan der ober Ostr. Stadt Constanz am Boden-See
mwbp0374	poland	1720	BODENEHR	280	16	26	Posen die Haupt Stadt in Gros Polen

AMPG REFERENCE	REGION	DATE	MAP MAKER	PRICE (UK£)	VERT. (cm.)	HOR. (cm.)	TITLE OF MAP (Comments by the editor in brackets)
mwe0559	europe czech republic (bohemia)	1720	BODENEHR	400	15	26	Praag
mwsp0521	spain regions	1720	BODENEHR	200	17	29	Roses eine Vestung ... in Catalonien Gelegen
mwe0352	europe austria	1720	BODENEHR	400	16	27	Saltzburg
mwe0928	europe hungary	1720	BODENEHR	240	17	26	Sigeth
mwit0931	italy sicily	1720	BODENEHR	120	16	24	Siracusa, in Sicilien Gelegen
mwf0748	france nord pas-de-calais	1720	BODENEHR	120	17	27	St. Omer mitt Nahe Anliegender Gegend
mwg0489	mecklenburg	1720	BODENEHR	150	16	27	Stralsund
mwbp0375	poland	1720	BODENEHR	300	17	37	Thorn mit Ao. 1658 Erlittener Belagerung (Torun)
mwg0265	baden-wurttemberg	1678	BODENEHR	950	24	38	Topographia Alsatiae, Sungoiae
mwit1083	italy trentino-alto	1720	BODENEHR	250	16	27	Trient oder Trento
mwit0676	italy piedmont	1720	BODENEHR	280	17	34	Turin
mwg0276	baden-wurttemberg	1720	BODENEHR	550	17	27	Ulma. Ulm
mwit1242	italy venice	1730	BODENEHR	720	15	36	Venetia - Venedig
mwe0572a	europe czech republic (bohemia)	1742	BODENEHR	400	29	33	Wahrer Grundriß von der Königl. Haupt-Stadt Prag in Böhmen, wie selbe von den Ungar: u. Oesterreichischen Völckern belagert und beschoßen worden Ao. 1742
mwbp0376	poland	1720	BODENEHR	500	16	24	Warschau (view)
mwbp0377	poland	1720	BODENEHR	300	16	25	Wie es Ao 1700 aus dem Polnischen Lager Comunicirt Worden
mwe0422	europe austria vienna	1720	BODENEHR	250	16	34	Wien mit Naechst Anliegender Gegend und denen Neuen Linien
mwbp0112	baltic states	1720	BODENEHR	300	16	24	Wilna oder Wilda die Haupt-Stadt in Littauen
mwg0490	mecklenburg	1720	BODENEHR	150	16	23	Wismar
mwg0633	saxony	1720	BODENEHR	280	16	34	Wittenberg eine ihrer Universitaet Halber Weith Beruhmte Statt im Chur Furstenthum Ober-Saxen
mwbh0579	belgium holland	1720	BODENEHR	280	16	30	Ypra Ypern / Ypra oder Ypern wie es von der Cron Franckreigh Bevestiget Worden (map and view)
mwec0105	uk england cambridgeshire	1786	BODGER	1250	47	67	Chart of the Beautiful Fishery of Whittlesea Mere (printed on silk)
mwe0553	europe czech republic (bohemia)	1700	BOENER	1800	44	62	Bohemia in suas Partes Geograph: Distincta (publ. by J.Zieger)
mwe0910	europe hungary	1690	BOETHIUS	1200	42	54	Belager- und Eroberung der Konigl: Ungarischen Haupt-Stadt Ofen durch die Kayserl: und dero Hohen Allirten Gluckseelige Waffen
mwuss0709	maine	1798	BOHN	3500	64	44	Maine Entworfen von D.F. Sotzman
mwas0894	asia south east sumatra	1783	BOHN	800	47	57	Nieuwe Kaart van het Eyland Sumatra
mwuk1210	england london	1765	BOHN	950	32	64	Plan von London, Westmunster en Southwark
mwaf0051	africa	1642	BOISSEAU	1200	38	50	Africae Nova Tabula. Auct: Jud: Hondio
mwam0047	america continent	1642	BOISSEAU	2250	38	50	America Noviter Delineata Auct. Judoco Hondius (copy of Hondius 1633)
mwas0036	asia continent	1642	BOISSEAU	1800	38	50	Asia Recens Summa Accura Delineata
mwsw0065b	switzerland	1646	BOISSEAU	2000	25	77	Aspect ou Profil Oriental de la Grande et Petitte Ville de Basle Canton des Suisses
mwf0060	france	1642	BOISSEAU	500	36	49	Carte de la France Divisee par les Provinces de l'Esglise Galicane
mwf0282	france auvergne	1642	BOISSEAU	750	39	49	Carte de la Haute Auvergne - Carte Generale des Montagnes de la Haute Auvergne par le Sr. de Clerville
mwf0279	france auvergne	1635	BOISSEAU	550	38	48	Carte du Diocese d'Aire Nouvellement Deseignee (Jean Boisseau's first map)
mwbh0244	belgium holland	1636	BOISSEAU	1350	39	49	Carte Generale des Pays Bas
mwuk0703	uk	1644	BOISSEAU	1800	38	51	Carte Generalle de la Grande Bretagne, jadis Albion, et du Royaume d'Irlande ou Hybernie, avec les Isles Circonvoisins Despandantes desdits Royaumes; avec Plusiers Observations 1644
mwgr0479	greece cyprus	1643	BOISSEAU	400	14	18	Cypre (illustrated is Jollain re-issue of 1667. Close copy of Hondius 1607)
mwam1269	great lakes	1643	BOISSEAU	25000	35	55	Description de la Nouvelle France ou sont Remarquees les Diverse Habitations des Francois (first map to name the great lakes)
mwf0724	france nord pas-de-calais	1640	BOISSEAU	750	38	47	Description de la Vicomte de Bourbourg
mwme0450	jerusalem	1642	BOISSEAU	3500	24	74	Description de la Ville de Jerusalem avec les Noms des Saints Lieux ou Antiquitez qui sont Visitez par les Pellerins et Voiageurs (view)
mwe0537	europe czech republic (bohemia)	1642	BOISSEAU	2000	27	67	Description de la Ville de Prague Siege et Metropolitaine du Royaume de Boheme (view)
mwgr0375	greece crete	1645	BOISSEAU	900	32	47	Description de IIsle de Candie et des Isles Voisines de la Grece
mwwi0537a	guadeloupe	1645	BOISSEAU	1350	37	50	Description de L'Isle de Gadeloupe Habitee des Francois depuis L'An 1634
mwit1223	italy venice	1646	BOISSEAU	3000	28	70	Description de Lopulente et Manifique Ville de Venise (a copy of Merian's map with title across the top.)
mwit0487	italy lombardy	1643	BOISSEAU	1600	34	46	Description du Pais de la Valetolinne
mwe0052	europe	1642	BOISSEAU	1500	38	50	Europa Exactissime Descripta
mwe0051	europe	1641	BOISSEAU	2800	43	58	Europe Francoise ou Description Generalle des Empires Royaumes, Estats, et Grandes Seigneuries

AMPG REFERENCE	REGION	DATE	MAP MAKER	PRICE (UK£)	VERT. (cm.)	HOR. (cm.)	TITLE OF MAP (Comments by the editor in brackets)
mwit1131a	italy florence	1646	BOISSEAU	1800	27	73	Florence la Belle Ville Capitale de Lestat du Grand Duc de Toscane
mwgr0068	greece	1643	BOISSEAU	875	36	49	Graecia Sophiani (title also in Greek)
mwe0875	europe hungary	1643	BOISSEAU	350	13	17	Hongrie
mwsc0491	scandinavia iceland	1646	BOISSEAU	2500	34	48	Islandia (copy of Ortelius)
mwf0260a	france aquitaine	1641	BOISSEAU	1350	33	71	La Description de la Ville de Bourdeaux, Cappitalle de la Guienne et Grand Port de Mer
mwaf0360a	africa east	1643	BOISSEAU	400	14	19	Le Royaume Abyssin ou l'Empire du Preste Iean 1643
mwf0577	france ile de france	1650	BOISSEAU	1200	36	49	Nouvelle Description de la Forest Royale de Fontaine Belleau
mww0154	world	1641	BOISSEAU	18000	46	82	Nouvelle Description De La Terre Universelle (in 2 sheets, joined)
mwm0183	mediterranean malta	1645	BOISSEAU	2250	35	54	Nouvelle Description de l'Isle de Malte jadis Melite, et des Isles de Comin et Cominot, avec l'Esle et Principaute de Goze
mwaa0185	arctic / antarctic	1640	BOISSEAU	9000	29	29	Nouvelle Description de Toute la Terre Universelle (2 maps, each with dimensions shown)
mwf0600	france languedoc	1639	BOISSEAU	350	34	45	Nouvelle Description du Comte de Roussillon Ensemble d'une Parte des Mons Pirenees ou Confinent la France et l'Espagne
mww0143	world	1636	BOISSEAU	8000	39	55	Nouvelle et Exacte Description de la Terre Universelle
mww0156b	world	1645	BOISSEAU		105	198	Nouvelle et Exacte Description Geographique et Hydrographique de la Terre Universelle Diligemmet Receuillie Sur Plusieurs Relations des Plus Fidels Voyageurs De Nostre Temps (1st publ. without title or text panels. Image courtesy of B. Ruderman, from the 1672 edition. Size excludes text panels. Shirley 362)
mwit0085	italy	1639	BOISSEAU	1800	38	49	Nuova Descrittione dell'Italia Sicilia
mwf0821	france paris	1642	BOISSEAU	2000	27	69	Paris (view)
mwf0822	france paris	1648	BOISSEAU	8000	99	98	Plan General de la Ville Cite Universite Isles et Faubourgs de Paris
mwf0653	france loire	1642	BOISSEAU	1000	24	81	Profil de la Ville Archiepiscopal de Tours Appellee Vulgairement le Jardin de France
mwme0944	turkey etc	1643	BOISSEAU	2400	25	84	Profil de la Ville de Constantinople Nomee des Turcs Stamboul (view)
mww0155a	world	1643	BOISSEAU	1200	15	20	Typus Orbis Terrarum Description de la Terre Universelle
mwe0410c	europe austria vienna	1644	BOISSEAU	2500	26	68	Vienne en Austriche
mwbh0715	belgium holland	1768	BOLSTRA	600	18	70	Kaart van de Beneeden Rivier de Maas en de Merwede, van de Noord Zee tot Gorinchem (2 sheets, joined)
mwin0252	india	1773	BOLTS	400	38	55	Carte du Bengale et de ses dependances
mwit0536	italy milan	1697	BONACINA	4000	76	81	La Gran Citta di Milano
mwam0276	america continent	1821	BONATTI	550	38	70	L'America Settentrionale / ... Meridionale (2 sheets)
mwit0256	italy abruzzo	1587	BONIFACIO	10000	36	50	Abruzzo Ulteriore
mwgr0358	greece crete	1586	BONIFACIO	280	9	13	Candia
mwgr0461	greece cyprus	1586	BONIFACIO	900	9	12	Cipro
mwgr0442	greece cyprus	1570	BONIFACIO	10000	27	41	Cyprus insula in Pamphylio mare
mwgr0442a	greece cyprus	1570	BONIFACIO	12500	21	16	Isola di Cipro
mwgr0276	greece cefalonia	1568	BONIFACIO	1500	21	16	Isola.de Zafalonia
mwgr0462	greece cyprus	1586	BONIFACIO	450	9	12	Mediterraneo e Golfo de Setelia
mwit1215	italy venice	1586	BONIFACIO	500	9	12	Venetia
mwgr0537	greece zante (zakynthos)	1586	BONIFACIO	300	9	12	Zante
mwaf1221	africa west	1770	BONNE	160	44	32	(Untitled map of Guinee / Congo)
mwaf0239	africa	1780	BONNE	280	24	34	Afrique
mwsam0104	south america	1787	BONNE	200	33	24	Amerique Meridionale
mwme0653	arabia etc	1787	BONNE	320	24	39	Arabie, Mer Rouge, et Golfe Persique
mwme1033	turkey etc	1787	BONNE	200	24	34	Asia Minor
mwsam0393	south america brazil	1780	BONNE	250	30	44	Bresil et Pays des Amazones
mwsam0391	south america brazil	1780	BONNE	150	24	36	Bresil et Pays des Amazones. 1re. Feuille
mwsam0398	south america brazil	1787	BONNE	150	24	36	Bresil et Pays des Amazones. 2eme. Feuille
mwca0114	canada	1787	BONNE	180	24	33	Canada
mwca0092	canada	1771	BONNE	300	30	45	Canada IIe Feuille (Eastern Canada)
mwf0797	france normandy	1771	BONNE	200	30	43	Carte ... Normandie avec celui Maine et Perche
mwp0434	pacific north	1787	BONNE	400	23	34	Carte de la Cote N.O. de l'Amerique et de la Cote N.E. de l'Asie Reconnues en 1778 et 1779
mwuss0414	florida	1757	BONNE	280	23	30	Carte de la Floride de la Louisiana
mwbh0748	belgium holland	1787	BONNE	120	22	32	Carte de la Hollande Prise en General Contenant les Sept Provinces Unies des Pays Bas
mwuss0646	louisiana	1780	BONNE	280	32	20	Carte de la Louisiane, et de la Floride
mwm0063	mediterranean	1763	BONNE	720	32	68	Carte de la Mer Mediterranee
mwp0185a	new zealand	1780	BONNE	900	34	23	Carte de la Nouvelle Zeelande
mwin0436	indian ocean	1780	BONNE	280	21	31	Carte de la Partie Inferieure de l'Inde
mwsam0392	south america brazil	1780	BONNE	240	30	44	Carte de la Partie Meridionale du Bresil, avec les Possessions Espagnoles Voisines qui en sont a l'Ouest
mwam1009	america north (east)	1762	BONNE	200	22	32	Carte de la Partie Nord, des Etats Unis, de l'Amerique Septentrionale

AMPG REFERENCE	REGION	DATE	MAP MAKER	PRICE (UK£)	VERT. (cm.)	HOR. (cm.)	TITLE OF MAP (Comments by the editor in brackets)
mwam1095a	america north (east)	1787	BONNE	300	21	32	Carte de la Partie Sud des Etats Unis de l'Amerique Septentrionale
mwin0273	india	1780	BONNE	240	21	32	Carte de la Partie Superieure de l'Inde en deca du Gange Comprise entre la Cote du Concan et celle d'Orixaa avec l'Empire du Mogol, le Bengale le Re. d'Asham, Partie de ceux d'Ava et de Pegu
mwme0830	persia etc	1780	BONNE	250	22	34	Carte de la Perse, de la Georgie et de la Tartarie Independante
mwuss0025	alaska	1784	BONNE	400	23	34	Carte de la Riviere de Cook, dans la Partie N.O. de l'Amerique
mwc0180	china	1771	BONNE	280	29	41	Carte de la Tartarie Chinoise Projettee et Assujettee aux Observations Astronomiques
mwas0344	asia central	1770	BONNE	300	31	44	Carte de la Tartarie Independante qui Comprend le Pays des Calmuks, des Usbeks et Turkestan
mwsam0182	south america north	1771	BONNE	280	31	43	Carte de la Terre Ferme, de la Guyane et du Pays des Amazones
mwp0024	australia	1787	BONNE	280	23	36	Carte de la Terre Van-Diemen
mwme1024	turkey etc	1771	BONNE	200	30	43	Carte de la Turquie d'Asie presque Entiere Contenant l'Anatolie, la Georgie, l'Armenie, la Curdistan, l'Alge-Zira, l'Irak-Arabi
mwme0652	arabia etc	1785	BONNE	400	31	46	Carte de l'Arabie qui se Divise en Arabie Petree, Deserte et Heureuse
mwas0207	asia continent	1787	BONNE	1500	72	101	Carte de l'Asie Divisee en ses Principaux Etats
mwaf0516	africa egypt etc	1762	BONNE	150	44	30	Carte de l'Egypte Ancienne et Moderne
mwaf0524	africa egypt etc	1781	BONNE	80	21	32	Carte de L'Egypte Moderne
mwc0182	china	1772	BONNE	250	32	22	Carte de l'Empire de la Chine, de la Tartarie Chinoise, et du Royaume de Coree: avec les Isles du Japon
mwme0825	persia etc	1771	BONNE	200	32	43	Carte de l'Empire de Perse
mwru0267	russia	1780	BONNE	200	20	30	Carte de l'Empire de Russie en Europe et en Asie
mwp0435	pacific north	1787	BONNE	280	24	30	Carte de l'Entree de Norton et du Detroit de Bhering, ou l'on Voit le Cap le Plus Oriental de l'Asie, et la Pointe la Plus Occidentale de l'Amerique
mwwi0729	jamaica	1774	BONNE	180	21	32	Carte de l'Isle de la Jamaique
mwwi0796	martinique	1774	BONNE	120	34	23	Carte de l'Isle de la Martinique, Colonie Francoise dans les Isles Antilles
mwwi0643	hispaniola	1782	BONNE	280	21	32	Carte de L'Isle de St. Domingue une des Grandes Antilles
mwp0534	pacific tahiti	1787	BONNE	300	24	34	Carte de l'Isle O-Taiti
mwuss1043	new jersey	1782	BONNE	240	24	33	Carte de Pensylvanie et du Nouveau Jersey
mwsam0774	south america peru	1771	BONNE	200	43	31	Carte de Perou ou se Trouvent les Audiences de Quito, Lima et la Plata
mwm0278	mediterranean west	1771	BONNE	280	30	43	Carte des Cotes de Barbarie ou les Royaumes de Maroc, de Fez, d'Alger, de Tunis, et de Tripoli, avec les Pays Circonvoisins par M. Bonne, Hydrographe du Roi
mwme0359	holy land	1770	BONNE	280	31	44	Carte des Douze Tribus d'Israel
mwf1076	france provence	1771	BONNE	180	41	29	Carte des Gouvernemens de Dauphine et de Provence avec le Comtat Venaissin et la Princte. d'Orange
mwf0627	france languedoc	1783	BONNE	180	41	31	Carte des Gouvernemens de Languedoc, de Foix et de Roussillon avec la Partie Orientale du Gouvernement de Guienne
mwf0438	france central	1771	BONNE	120	41	30	Carte des Gouvernemens du Berri, du Nivernois, de la Marche, du Bourbonnis, du Limosin et de l'Auvergne
mwin0277	india	1782	BONNE	235	32	22	Carte des Indes en deca et au dela du Gange
mwgm0053	gulf of mexico and surrounding regions	1786	BONNE	2000	65	142	Carte des Isles Antilles et du Golfe du Mexique; avec la Majeure Partie de la Nouvelle Espagne (3 sheets, joined)
mwwi0253	west indies (east)	1770	BONNE	150	32	21	Carte des Isles Antilles ou du Vent, avec la Partie Orientale des Isles sous le Vent
mwuk0857	uk	1780	BONNE	200	32	21	Carte des Isles Britanniques
mwat0168	atlantic canary isl.	1784	BONNE	200	32	21	Carte des Isles Canaries, avec l'Isle de Madere, et Celle de Porto Santo
mwp0477	pacific society isl.	1787	BONNE	150	24	33	Carte des Isles de la Societe
mwas0501	asia south east	1780	BONNE	280	21	32	Carte des Isles de la Sonde et des Isles Moluques
mwp0318	pacific friendly isl.	1787	BONNE	300	23	34	Carte des Isles des Amis
mwp0331	pacific hawaii	1787	BONNE	500	24	37	Carte des Isles Sandwich
mwme0360	holy land	1771	BONNE	235	30	44	Carte des Regions et des Lieux dont il est Parle dans le Nouveau Testament
mwuk0858	uk	1780	BONNE	235	32	21	Carte des Royaumes d'Angleterre, d'Ecosse et d'Irlande
mwsp0284	spain	1770	BONNE	235	23	34	Carte des Royaumes d'Espagne et de Portugal
mwbh0734	belgium holland	1781	BONNE	160	34	23	Carte des Sept Provinces-Unies des Pays-Bas
mwuk0203	ireland	1771	BONNE	300	30	42	Carte d'Irlande Projettee et Assujettie aux Observations Astronomiques
mwaf0951	africa south	1780	BONNE	280	22	32	Carte du Canal de Mosambique, Contenant l'Isle de Madagascar avec les Cotes d'Afrique, depuis le Cap de Bonne Esperance, jusqu'a Melinde
mwsam0466	south america chile	1780	BONNE	200	32	21	Carte du Chili Depuis le Sud du Perou jusqu'au Cap Horn, avec Partie des Regions qui en sont a l'Est

AMPG REFERENCE	REGION	DATE	MAP MAKER	PRICE (UK£)	VERT. (cm.)	HOR. (cm.)	TITLE OF MAP (Comments by the editor in brackets)
mwgm0052	gulf of mexico and surrounding regions	1785	BONNE	350	15	27	Carte du Golfe du Mexique
mwf0367	france brittany	1771	BONNE	200	29	41	Carte du Gouvernement de Bretagne
mwf0453	france champagne	1771	BONNE	200	41	29	Carte du Gouvernment de Champagne et Brie
mwf0275	france aquitaine	1785	BONNE	235	41	29	Carte du Gouvernement de Guienne et Gascogne, avec celui de Bearn et Basse Navarre
mwf0590	france ile de france	1770	BONNE	200	41	30	Carte du Gouvernment de l'Isle de France et de celui de l'Orleanois
mwsc0469	scandinavia greenland	1770	BONNE	240	19	25	Carte du Groenland Dressee et Gravee par Laurent
mwgm0036	gulf of mexico and surrounding regions	1771	BONNE	400	30	41	Carte du Mexique ou de la Nlle. Espagne Contenant aussi le Nouveau Mexique, la Californie, avec une Partie des Pays Adjacents
mwsam0181	south america (north)	1762	BONNE	180	21	32	Carte du Nouv. Rme. de Grenade, de la Nou'le Andalousie, et de la Guyane
mwsp0596	spain regions	1783	BONNE	180	21	32	Carte du Nouv. Rme. de Grenade, de la Noule. Andalousie, et de la Guyane, avec les Pays Limitrophes qui en sont au Sud
mwsam0721	south america paraguay	1783	BONNE	240	42	32	Carte du Paraguay et Partie des Pays Adjacants
mwaf0259	africa	1788	BONNE	280	23	33	Carte Generale de l'Afrique
mwam0471	america north	1781	BONNE	400	21	32	Carte Generale de l'Amerique Septentrionale (later west coast correction and title 'Amerique ...' shown left)
mww0517	world	1782	BONNE	350	24	36	Carte Generale de Toutes les Parties Connues de la Surface de la Terre en Carte Reduite (revised 1780 edition, with title 'Planisphere ...')
mwc0181	china	1771	BONNE	180	32	43	Carte Hydro-Geographique des Indes Orientales
mwas0488	asia south east	1771	BONNE	750	60	83	Carte Hydro-Geo-Graphique des Indes Orientales en Deca et au Dela du Gange avec leur Archipel
mwuk1587	channel islands	1764	BONNE	250	12	15	Carte Particuliere des Iles Jersey, Grenesey et Aurigny
mwsam0089	south america	1774	BONNE	200	32	46	Carte pour Servir a l'Histoire Philosophique et Politique des Etablissemens et du Commerce dans les Deux Indes (incl. the Atlantic Ocean)
mww0518	world	1782	BONNE	350	23	33	Carte Reduite des Terres et des Mers du Globe Terrestre
mwwi0931	virgin isl	1787	BONNE	280	24	33	Cartes de supplement pour les Isles Antilles
mwaf0637	africa islands mauritius	1780	BONNE	450	22	33	Cartes Generale des Isles de France, de Bourbon, et de Rodrigue
mwsp0589	spain regions	1780	BONNE	200	24	34	Castille Nouvelle, et Rme. de Valence
mwg0395	bavaria	1787	BONNE	180	32	22	Cercle de Baviere
mwsam0694	south america magellan	1787	BONNE	240	23	34	Detroit de Magellan avec les Plans des Principaux Ports, Bayes &c.
mwme0368	holy land	1781	BONNE	200	33	23	Duodecim Tribus Israelis, sive Terra Sancta
mwaf0419	africa east	1787	BONNE	160	36	23	Egypte, Nubie et Abissinie
mwc0207	china	1787	BONNE	280	24	36	Empire de la Chine, Rme. de Coree et Isles du Japon
mwp0190	new zealand	1785	BONNE	350	23	34	Equise de la Baye Dusky dans la Nouvelle Zelande
mwaf0721	africa north	1787	BONNE	100	21	32	Etats du Roy du Maroc-Alger/Tunis/Tripoli
mwe0218	europe	1788	BONNE	240	24	34	Europe
mwsam0695	south america magellan	1787	BONNE	280	23	34	Extremite Meridionale de l'Amerique (5 insets)
mwg0160	germany	1790	BONNE	120	24	34	Germania Vetus
mwf0273	france aquitaine	1780	BONNE	120	25	35	Gouvernement de Guienne et Gascogne
mwf0688	france lorraine	1787	BONNE	150	25	36	Gouvernement de Lorraine et celui d'Alsace
mwgr0211	greece	1779	BONNE	280	33	45	Graeciae Antiquae
mwsp0302	spain	1787	BONNE	120	24	34	Hispania Vetus
mwuk0868	uk	1790	BONNE	250	23	36	Iles Britanniques Contenant les Royaumes d'Angleterre, d'Ecosse, et d'Irlande
mwas0267	asia (from turkey to india)	1787	BONNE	300	35	23	Imperia Antiqua, Pars Occidentalis / Imperia Antiqua, Pars Media / Imperia Antiqua, Pars Orientalis (3 sheets)
mwm0069	mediterranean	1783	BONNE	350	60	84	Imperii Romani Tabula
mwin0248	india	1770	BONNE	240	29	41	Indes IVe. Feuille
mwuk0865	uk	1787	BONNE	160	34	24	Insulae Britannicae Veteres
mwwi0802	martinique	1787	BONNE	120	24	36	Isle de la Martinique / Isles de la Guadeloupe, de Marie Galante, de la Desirade, et celles des Saintes
mwca0337	canada newfoundland	1787	BONNE	200	24	36	Isle et Banc de Terre Neuve, Isle Royale et Isle St. Jean; avec l'Acadie ou la Nouvelle Ecosse
mwat0097	atlantic azores	1787	BONNE	200	23	35	Isles Acores
mwwi0260	west indies (east)	1782	BONNE	250	32	21	Isles Antilles ou du Vent avec les Isles sous le Vent (as Bonne 1770 but with an inset)
mwat0169	atlantic canary isl.	1787	BONNE	200	23	36	Isles Canaries
mwit0839	italy sardinia and corsica	1780	BONNE	200	35	23	Isles de Corse et de Sardaigne
mwca0659a	canada west	1787	BONNE	140	23	34	Isles de la Reine Charlotte
mwat0244	atlantic madeira	1780	BONNE	300	24	39	Isles de Madere, de Porto Santo et celles des Salvages / Plan de la Rade de Funchal / Isle de Goree Situee a la Cote Sud du Cap Verd
mwp0400	pacific new hebrides	1787	BONNE	250	24	33	Isles des Nouvelles Hebrides et celle de la Nouvelle Caledonie
mwat0201	atlantic cape verde isl.	1780	BONNE	160	23	34	Isles du Cap-Verd
mwat0229	atlantic falkland isl.	1780	BONNE	350	23	34	Isles Maidenland, de Hawkins, et le Detroit de Falkland, ces Isles sont Nommes Malouines, par les Francois

AMPG REFERENCE	REGION	DATE	MAP MAKER	PRICE (UK£)	VERT. (cm.)	HOR. (cm.)	TITLE OF MAP (Comments by the editor in brackets)
mwsp0686	balearic islands	1787	BONNE	240	24	33	Isles Mayorque, Minorque et Yvice
mwit0207	italy	1787	BONNE	150	34	24	Italia Vetus
mwaf1236	africa west	1788	BONNE	200	24	34	La Basse Guinee Contenant les Royaumes de Loango, de Congo, d'Angola et de Benguela, avec la Cafrerie Occidentale et la Meridionale ... [in set with] Le Canal de Mosambique, l'Isle de Madagascar, les Etats du Monomotapa et les Royaumes Voisins
mwas0511	asia south east	1787	BONNE	300	35	24	La Presqu'Isle de l'Inde au dela du Gange
mwin0287	india	1787	BONNE	240	39	24	La Presqu'Isle de l'Inde au dela du Gange, avec l'Archipel des Indes. Partie Occidentale
mwsw0177	switzerland	1771	BONNE	180	30	44	La Suisse Divisee en ses Treize Cantons et ses Allies
mwsw0168	switzerland	1767	BONNE	650	47	64	La Suisse Divisee en ses XIII Cantons et ses Allies
mwm0154	mediterranean east	1774	BONNE	200	21	32	La Turquie d'Europe et celle d'Asie hors la Partie Situe dans l'Arabie
mwaf0237	africa	1778	BONNE	960	70	98	L'Afrique divisee en ses principaux etats (insets of Southern Africa, Isles Bourbon, Mauritius. See also Herission 1818 re-issue)
mwgm0225	mexico	1762	BONNE	600	35	24	L'Ancien et le Nouveau Mexique, avec la Floride et la Basse Louisiane. Partie Occidentale / L'Ancien et le Nouveau Mexique, avec la Floride et la Basse Louisiane. Partie Orientale (2 maps, each 35x24cm.)
mww0496	world	1776	BONNE	720	21	41	L'Ancien Monde et le Nouveau en Deux Hemispheres
mwas0186	asia continent	1770	BONNE	200	24	34	L'Asie
mwas0209	asia continent	1787	BONNE	180	21	32	L'Asie
mwaf1057	africa south east	1787	BONNE	180	24	36	Le Canal de Mosambique, l'Isle de Madagascar, les Etats du Monomotapa et les Royaumes Voisins
mwsc0164	scandinavia	1780	BONNE	120	21	31	Le Nord de l'Europe (incl. western Russia)
mwgm0250	mexico	1781	BONNE	200	23	33	Le Nouveau Mexique, avec la Partie Septentrionale de l'Ancien, ou de la Nouvelle Espagne
mwaf0412	africa east	1780	BONNE	240	34	23	Le Royaume d'Adel: Les Cotes d'Ajan et de Zanguebar avec les Etats qu'elles Comprenent
mwc0200	china	1781	BONNE	375	31	45	L'Empire de la Chine
mwc0165	china	1760	BONNE	400	32	46	L'Empire de la Chine d'apres l'Atlas Chinois, avec les Isles du Japon
mwru0283	russia	1787	BONNE	785	35	24	L'Empire de Russie en Europe et en Asie (3 sheets)
mwin0288	india	1787	BONNE	200	36	24	L'Empire du Mogol, et la Presqu'Isle de l'Inde en deca du Gange
mwam1074	america north (east)	1781	BONNE	300	32	22	Les Etats Unis de l'Amerique Septentrionale, Contenant en Outre, les Isles Royale, de Terre Neuve, de St. Jean et l'Acadie; avec Partie du Canada, de la Louisiane et de la Floride
mwam1066a	america north (east)	1780	BONNE	450	39	24	Les Etats Unis de l'Amerique Septentrionale, Partie Occidentale / ... Partie Orientale (two maps, each 39x24cm)
mwas0507	asia south east	1783	BONNE	350	32	45	Les Indes Oriental Orientales et leur Archipel
mwas0492	asia south east	1774	BONNE	350	32	45	Les Indes Orientales et leur Archipel
mwgm0034	gulf of mexico and surrounding regions	1762	BONNE	240	20	32	Les Isles Antilles, et le Golfe du Mexique (inset of Bermuda)
mwwi0557	guadeloupe	1780	BONNE	120	22	33	Les Isles de la Guadeloupe, de Marie Galante, de la Desirade, et celles des Saintes: Colonie Francoise dans les Antilles
mwc0179	china	1770	BONNE	350	23	33	Les Isles Philippines, celle de Formose, le Sud de la Chine, les Royaumes de Tunkin, de Cochinchine, de Camboge, de Siam, des Laos; avec Partie de ceux de Pegu et d'Ava
mwwi0254	west indies (east)	1771	BONNE	235	24	35	Les Petites Antilles ou les Isles du Vent avec celles de sous le Vent
mwsc0171	scandinavia	1787	BONNE	180	36	24	Les Royaumes de Suede, de Danemark et de Norwege
mwe0202	europe	1780	BONNE	180	20	31	L'Europe
mwwi0464	cuba	1780	BONNE	240	21	31	L'Isle de Cuba et de la Jamaique
mwwi0638	hispaniola	1771	BONNE	300	24	35	L'Isle de St. Domingue et celle de Porto-Rico
mwca0330	canada newfoundland	1783	BONNE	300	21	32	L'Isle de Terre-Neuve, l'Acadie, ou la Nouvelle Ecosse, l'Isle St Jean et la Partie Orientale du Canada
mwit0204	italy	1786	BONNE	220	31	20	L'Italie
mww0500	world	1778	BONNE	9000	70	100	Mappe Monde ou Description du Globe Terrestre (re-issued by Delamarche 1804)
mww0512	world	1781	BONNE	400	22	33	Mappe-Monde en deux Hemispheres L'Oriental et L'Occidental
mwaa0039a	antarctic	1785	BONNE	300	24	34	Mappe-Monde sur le Plan de l'Equateur. Hemisphere Meridionale
mww0547	world	1787	BONNE	800	24	34	Mappe-Monde, sur le Plan d'un Meridien. Hemisphere Oriental / Hemisphere Occidental (2 sheets)
mwaa0148	arctic	1780	BONNE	350	23	36	Mappe-Monde, sur un plan horisontal, situe a 45d de latitude nord (Offset polar projection)
mwsam0633	south america guyana	1780	BONNE	160	30	44	Meridionale Guiane Divisee du Bresil en Guiane et Caribane
mwp0026	australia	1788	BONNE	300	35	24	Nlle. Galles Meridle. ou Cote Orientale de la Nouvelle Hollande (4 insets)

AMPG REFERENCE	REGION	DATE	MAP MAKER	PRICE (UK£)	VERT. (cm.)	HOR. (cm.)	TITLE OF MAP (Comments by the editor in brackets)
mwsam0533	south america colombia	1780	BONNE	200	24	35	Nouveau Royaume de Grenade, Nouvelle Andalousie et Guyane
mwaf0414	africa east	1782	BONNE	250	29	41	Nubie et Abissinie
mwme0369	holy land	1781	BONNE	200	32	22	Palestina et Syria
mwaf0413	africa east	1780	BONNE	280	29	41	Partie de la Cote Orientale d'Afrique avec l'Isle de Madagascar et les Cartes Particulieres des Isles de France et de Bourbon
mwam1022a	america north east	1771	BONNE	900	30	43	Partie de l'Amerique Septentrionale, qui Comprend le Canada, la Louisiane, le Labrador, le Groenland, la Nouvelle Angleterre, la Floride &c. (2 sheets each 29x44cm.)
mwam0447	america north	1775	BONNE	240	33	24	Partie du Nord de l'Amerique Septentrionale pour Servir a l'Histoire Philosophique et Politique des Etablissemens et du Commerce des Europeens dan les Deux Indes
mwgr0214	greece	1781	BONNE	280	24	35	Partie Meridionale de la Turquie d'Europe
mwit1070	italy naples	1780	BONNE	200	24	34	Partie Meridionale du Royaume de Naples
mwgm0252	mexico	1783	BONNE	180	21	32	Partie Meridionale, de l'Ancien Mexique ou de la Nouvle. Espagne
mwaf1227	africa west	1780	BONNE	200	34	23	Partie Occidentale de l'Afrique
mwru0244	russia	1771	BONNE	400	44	62	Partie Occidentale de l'Empire de Russie, Extrait de l'Atlas Russien et d'autres Cartes / Partie Orientale (2 maps, joined)
mwam1289	great lakes	1775	BONNE	500	21	31	Partie Occidentale du Canada, Contenant les Cinq Grands Lacs, avec les Pays Circonvoisins
mwsam0783	south america peru	1787	BONNE	160	34	24	Perou et Pays Circonvoisins
mwc0202	china	1782	BONNE	240	36	23	Plan de la Baye d'Awatska ... Kamtschatka / Partie du Japon ou Nipon [and] Plan du Typa ou de Macao
mwc0187	china	1775	BONNE	280	35	24	Plan du Typa ou de Macao
mwsp0721a	gibraltar	1762	BONNE	300	23	35	Plan Geometral de Gibraltar de la Montagne et de la Ville de Gibraltar (3 maps on one sheet)
mww0505	world	1780	BONNE	375	21	32	Planisphere Suivant la Projection de Mercator
mwsp0590	spain regions	1780	BONNE	180	24	34	Royaume d'Aragon et de Navarre avec la Principaute de Catalogne
mwe0608	europe czech republic (bohemia)	1780	BONNE	200	34	23	Royaume de Boheme et Marquiseat de Lusace
mwme0833	persia etc	1787	BONNE	250	24	34	Royaume de Perse et Georgie
mwbp0503	poland	1784	BONNE	200	23	34	Royaume de Pologne, et Duche de Lithuanie
mwbp0489	poland	1774	BONNE	140	23	34	Royaume de Prusse
mwuk0196	ireland	1766	BONNE	240	35	24	Royaume d'Irlande
mwaf1226	africa west	1780	BONNE	160	24	36	Royaumes Etats et Pays de la Haute Guinee
mwwi0929	virgin isl	1778	BONNE	280	32	21	Supplement pour les Isles Antilles Extrait des Cartes Angloises
mwc0209	china	1787	BONNE	280	23	36	Tartarie Chinoise, Roy. de Coree et Isles du Japon
mwru0460	russia tartary	1787	BONNE	280	23	36	Tartarie Independante
mwin0456	indian ocean kerguelen isl	1788	BONNE	240	23	35	Terre de Kerguelen, Appellee par M. Cook, Isle de la Desolation
mwam1038a	america north east	1776	BONNE	850	67	43	Theatre de la Guerre en Amerique - Partie de l'Amerique Septentrionale (as Bonne 1771 but with an additional lower strip added)
mwam1066	america north (east)	1779	BONNE	900	68	43	Theatre de la Guerre en Amerique, avec les Isles Antilles
mwme1032	turkey etc	1787	BONNE	200	24	36	Turquie d'Asie; a l'Exception des Enclaves Situees en Arabie
mwe0817	europe east	1780	BONNE	200	24	35	Turquie d'Europe
mwuss0793	massachusetts	1743	BONNER	120000	43	60	A New Plan of ye Great Town of Boston in New England in America
mwuss0537	georgia	1847	BONNER	2000	132	149	Map of the State of Georgia under the Direction of his Excellency George W. Crawford
mwam1361	america north (west)	1837	BONNEVILLE	400	42	39	A Map of the Sources of the Colorado & Big Salt Lake, Platte, Yellow-Stone, Muscle-Shell, Missouri; & Salmon & Snake Rivers, Branches of the Columbia River
mwam1360	america north (west)	1837	BONNEVILLE	500	44	41	Map of the Territory West of the Rocky Mountains
mwam1386	america north (west)	1850	BONNEVILLE	280	28	45	Map to Illustrate Capt. Bonneville's Adventures among the Rocky Mountains
mwf0910	france paris	1814	BONNISEL	2800	92	117	Plan de la Ville et Faubourgs de Paris avec ses Monuments. Divise par Quartiers et Arrondissements (with decorative border)
mwuss0890	massachusetts	1844	BORDEN	1000	127	193	Topographical Map of the State of Massachusetts
mwit0620a	italy north	1811	BORDIGA	1000	129	109	Carta Amministrativa del Regno d'Italia
mwas0243	asia continent	1820	BORDIGA	350	52	75	Carta Generale dell'Asia
mwjk0130	japan	1800	BORDIGA	280	20	25	Giappone
mwam0262	america continent	1810	BORDIGA	600	52	73	L'America Settentrionale e Meridionale
mwgr0545	greece islands	1528	BORDONE	550	16	34	(Untitled map of Negroponte. North to the right. 'Constantinopoli' on verso.)
mwgr0545a	greece islands	1528	BORDONE	960	30	40	(Aegean Islands. Shown above left)
mwaf0345a	africa east	1528	BORDONE	400	14	8	(Africa - East coast islands: Madagascar, Zanzibar)
mwat0132	atlantic canary isl.	1528	BORDONE	600	8	14	(Canary Islands)
mwat0131	atlantic canary isl.	1528	BORDONE	600	14	15	(Canary Islands. On verso: Madeira 8x14cm)
mwf0455	france corsica	1528	BORDONE	1000	8	15	(Corsica. On verso, Palmosa and Elba)

AMPG REFERENCE	REGION	DATE	MAP MAKER	PRICE (UK£)	VERT. (cm.)	HOR. (cm.)	TITLE OF MAP (Comments by the editor in brackets)
mwru0468	ukraine	1528	BORDONE	500	8	15	(Crimea: Taurica Chersoneso)
mwgr0435	greece cyprus	1528	BORDONE	2800	16	33	(Cyprus)
mwe0628	europe dalmatia	1528	BORDONE	200	9	15	(Dalmatian Coast, Curzola, Lissena)
mwwi0275	west indies islands	1528	BORDONE	600	10	15	(Dominica, Monserrat, Martinique & Antigua)
mwat0236	atlantic madeira	1528	BORDONE	600	8	14	(Madeira. On verso: Canary Islands 14x15cm)
mwsp0638	balearic islands	1528	BORDONE	600	8	14	(Majorca and Minorca. On verso: Ibiza)
mwgr0012	greece	1528	BORDONE	500	14	15	(Morea)
mwe0629	europe dalmatia	1528	BORDONE	200	9	15	(Dalmation coast, Vegia, Arbe)
mwsp0350	spain regions	1528	BORDONE	450	8	15	('Regno de Castiglia', incl. Cadiz, Straits of Gibraltar)
mwit0770	italy sardinia	1528	BORDONE	400	9	14	(Sardinia)
mwme0907	turkey etc	1528	BORDONE	550	8	15	(Sea of Marmora. On verso 'Negroponte'.)
mwsam0170b	south america north	1528	BORDONE	650	9	15	(Untitled map incl. Jamaica and Hispaniola)
mwsp0351	spain regions	1528	BORDONE	450	8	15	(Untitled map of Galicia. Incl. Atlantic islands.)
mwgr0011	greece	1528	BORDONE	1800	30	40	(Untitled map of Greece and part of Turkey)
mwgr0545	greece islands	1528	BORDONE	550	16	34	(Untitled map of Negroponte. North to the right)
mwsc0006	scandinavia	1528	BORDONE	1500	14	15	(Untitled map of Scandinavia. NE America on verso.)
mwgr0266	greece athens	1528	BORDONE	450	8	14	(Untitled map of the environs of Athens. On verso: Cerigo.)
mwit0265	italy south	1528	BORDONE	250	9	15	(Untitled map of the environs of Naples incl. Ischia)
mwam0842	america north (east)	1528	BORDONE	1500	9	15	(Untitled map with little recognizable detail. Map of Scandinavia on verso, 14x15cm)
mwwi0393	cuba	1528	BORDONE	600	8	15	(untitled map)
mwat0072	atlantic azores	1528	BORDONE	300	8	14	(Untitled map)
mwat0176	atlantic cape verde isl.	1528	BORDONE	300	8	14	(Untitled map)
mwgr0337	greece crete	1528	BORDONE	800	14	34	(Untitled map. 'Scarpanto' on verso.)
mwe0002	europe	1528	BORDONE	1500	14	15	(Untitled map. NE America on verso)
mwgr0291	greece corfu	1528	BORDONE	600	9	14	(Untitled map. North to the right.)
mwe0003	europe	1528	BORDONE	1500	28	38	(Untitled map.)
mww0031	world	1528	BORDONE	6000	22	38	(Untitled oval projection)
mwjk0001	japan	1528	BORDONE	2500	9	15	Ciampagu (on verso, Java etc)
mwwi0537	guadeloupe	1528	BORDONE	300	8	15	guadalupe (Leeward Islands on verso)
mwwi0568	hispaniola	1528	BORDONE	1000	8	15	Hispaniola
mwwi0687	jamaica	1528	BORDONE	600	8	15	Iamaiqua
mwas0626	asia south east java	1528	BORDONE	400	8	15	Iava Minore
mwuk0001	ireland	1528	BORDONE	1200	9	15	Irlanda (Incl. part of England. Iceland on verso)
mwsc0472	scandinavia iceland	1528	BORDONE	1200	8	15	Islanda (North to the left. On verso: Ireland.)
mwgm0128	mexico	1528	BORDONE	1000	16	16	La Gran Citta di Temistitan (Mexico City. Title below map.)
mwwi0763	martinique	1528	BORDONE	400	8	14	matinina
mwit0858	italy sicily	1528	BORDONE	1650	16	33	Sicilia secondo tolomeo / sicilia secondo moderni (2 maps on one sheet, Ptolemaic and modern)
mwuk0899	england	1528	BORDONE	900	14	14	Tavola secondo moderni (title below map.)
mwit1204	italy venice	1528	BORDONE	2000	29	38	Vinegia
mwgr0275	greece cefalonia	1528	BORDONE	500	8	14	Zafalonia (Zante on verso)
mwaf0123	africa	1704	BORGHESI	600			Tavola della Navigazione ...
mwam1351	america north (west)	1817	BORGHI	450	22	29	(United States: Western)
mwam0612	america north	1819	BORGHI	300	23	30	America Settentrionale
mwgr0243	greece	1817	BORGHI	200	23	31	La Morea l'Isola di Candia con l'Isole dell'Arcipelago
mwuk1870	wales	1820	BORGHI	250	23	31	La Provincie ... al Ouest
mwuk1395	england south	1820	BORGHI	250	23	31	La Provincie ... al Sud Est
mwuk1396	england south	1820	BORGHI	250	23	31	La Provincie ... al Sud Ouest
mwuk1348	england east	1820	BORGHI	250	23	31	La Provincie ... dell'Est 1818 (East Anglia)
mwit0825a	italy sardinia	1817	BORGHI	200	31	23	La Sardegna
mwsc0201	scandinavia	1816	BORGHI	200	31	23	La Svezia Come era nella sua prima divisione
mwsc0753g	scandinavia sweden	1816	BORGHI	200	31	23	...La Svezia Meridionale
mwwi0290a	west indies (west)	1817	BORGHI	600	22	30	Le Grandi Antille e l'Isole Lucaje (inset of Virgin Isl.)
mwam0272	america continent	1819	BORGHI	200	24	33	Mappa Mondo Emisfero Nuovo
mwc0243	china	1817	BORGHI	300	23	30	Parte Settentrionale dell'Impero Chinese
mwit0968	italy sicily	1819	BORGHI	140	23	31	Sicilia Antiqua
mww0595	world	1797	BORGIA	10000	107	76	Apographon Descriptionis Orbis Terrae Figuris et Narratiunculis Distinctae Manu Germanica Opere Nigellari Discoloris Circa Medium Saec. XV Tabulae Aeneae Musei Borgiani Velitris Consignatae (copy of 15th century circular map)
mwit0819	italy sardinia	1772	BORGONIO-STAGNON	9600	152	203	Carta Corografica degli Stati di S.M. il re di Sardegna (illustrated is c1801 edition issued in 4 sections)
mww0227	world	1685	BORMEESTER	5000	46	55	Nova Totius Terrarum Orbis Tabula. A.J. Bormeester (close copy of Visscher 1658)
mwgr0381	greece crete	1651	BOSCHINI	1800	41	55	Citta di Candia Assediata
mwgr0377	greece crete	1645	BOSCHINI	5000	33	82	Il regno di Candia
mwgr0382	greece crete	1651	BOSCHINI	2500	24	43	Il regno di Candia
mwgr0383	greece crete	1654	BOSCHINI	1600	19	28	Regno di Candia
mwgr0525	greece rhodes	1650	BOSCHINI	300	17	12	Rhodi
mwit0520	italy lombardy	1796	BOSELLI	2500	69	102	Carta Topografica della citta e territorio di Mantova
mwaf0154	africa	1722	BOSSUET	250	13	17	Afrique
mwam0134	america continent	1722	BOSSUET	280	13	17	Amerique
mwuk0805	uk	1722	BOSSUET	240	13	16	Isles Britanniques

AMPG REFERENCE	REGION	DATE	MAP MAKER	PRICE (UK£)	VERT. (cm.)	HOR. (cm.)	TITLE OF MAP (Comments by the editor in brackets)
mwas0129	asia continent	1722	BOSSUET	300	13	16	L'Asie
mwuk0466	scotland	1722	BOSSUET	200	13	16	Le Royaume d'Escosse
mwuk0160	ireland	1738	BOSSUET	200	13	16	Le Royaume D'Irlande Divise en Ses Grandes Provinces
mww0347	world	1725	BOSSUET	500	9	17	Mappe-Monde ou Carte Generale du Globe Terrestre
mwsp0389	spain regions	1598	BOTERO	180	8	11	Andaluzia
mwe0521	europe czech republic (bohemia)	1598	BOTERO	150	8	11	Bohemia. Regni Bohemiae Descriptio
mwgr0362	greece crete	1598	BOTERO	200	8	11	Candia olim Creta
mwm0174	mediterranean malta	1598	BOTERO	350	7	10	Malta Olim Melita Insula
mwme0931	turkey etc	1592	BOTERO	650	15	20	Natoliae Quae Olim Asia Minor Nove Descriptio (south to the top)
mwme0057	holy land	1598	BOTERO	200	8	11	Palaestina
mwme0764	persia etc	1598	BOTERO	200	8	11	Persici
mwru0419	russia tartary	1599	BOTERO	350	8	10	Tartariae sive Magni Chami Regni Tipus (shown above left)
mww0090	world	1596	BOTERO	1800	19	30	Typus Orbis Terrarum (nearly the same as Quad 1596. Shown below left)
mwit1137	italy florence	1755	BOUCHARD	3000	51	67	Pianta della Citta di Firenze (1st publ. 1731)
mwam1097a	america north (east)	1787	BOUCHER	650	54	45	Carte réduite du Sud des Etats-Unis avec l'intérieur du Pays
mwca0634	canada st lawrence	1829	BOUCHETTE	240	21	16	Figurative Plan and Views of the Island of St. Paul. Entrance to Gulf of St. Lawrence
mwca0548	canada quebec	1815	BOUCHETTE	200	13	20	Fort Chambly
mwca0478	canada ontario	1832	BOUCHETTE	200	18	26	Plan and Elevation of the Union Bridges-Ottawa River, near the Falls of Chaudiere in 1827
mwuss1182	new york	1815	BOUCHETTE	200	21	12	Plan of Oswego Harbour, by Joseph Bouchette
mwca0479	canada ontario	1832	BOUCHETTE	200	19	20	Plan of the Town of Goderich, Upper Canada. Founded by the Canada Company 1829
mwca0480	canada ontario	1832	BOUCHETTE	200	19	20	Plan of the Town of Guelf, Upper Canada. Founded by the Canada Company 1827
mwca0474	canada ontario	1815	BOUCHETTE	450	13	23	Plan of York Harbour (publ. by W. Faden)
mwca0555a	canada quebec	1831	BOUCHETTE	10000	128	230	Topographical Map of the Districts of Quebec, Three Rivers, St. Francis and Gaspe, Lower Canada (publ. by Wyld)
mwca0160	canada	1831	BOUCHETTE	10000	101	197	To His Most Excellent Majesty King William IVth, this Map of the Provinces of Lower & Upper Canada, Nova Scotia, New Brunswick, Newfoundland & Prince Edward Island, with a Large Section of the United States (publ. by Wyld. See also Sherman & Smith 1846)
mwca0556	canada quebec	1832	BOUCHETTE	200	13	21	Village of St. Hyacinthe. Co. of St. Hyacinthe
mwam1090	america north (east)	1785	BOUDET	1600	47	63	Etats-Unis de l'Amérique Septentrionale
mwme0373	holy land	1786	BOUDET	750	46	56	La Judee depuis le Retour de la Captivite
mwp0420a	pacific north	1774	BOUDET	300	20	28	Nouveau Systeme Geographique … les Pays nord-ouest de l'Amerique
mwam0702	america north	1836	BOUFFARD	250	30	38	Carte des Etats-Unis d'Amerique
mwat0174	atlantic canary isl.	1835	BOUFFARD	750	43	52	Carte Phytostatique de l'Ile de Teneriffe
mwsam0243	south america argentina	1773	BOUGAINVILLE	300	31	49	A Chart of Rio de la Plata
mwsam0810	south america uruguay	1773	BOUGAINVILLE	350	19	24	A View and a Plan of the Town of St. Philip of Monte Video
mwsam0689a	south america magellan	1771	BOUGAINVILLE	350			Carte de Detroit de Magellan
mwat0221	atlantic falkland isl.	1768	BOUGAINVILLE	400	19	33	Carte des Iles Malouines Nommees par les Anglois Iles Falkland
mwp0256	pacific (all)	1771	BOUGAINVILLE	500	21	53	Development de la Route faite autour du Monde par les Vaissaux Du Roy La Boudeuse et L'Etoile
mww0478	world	1771	BOUGAINVILLE	500	21	53	Development de la Route Faite autour du Monde par les Vaisseaux du Roy la Boudeuse et l'Etoile
mwp0121a	australia	1837	BOUGAINVILLE	1400	51	55	Plan du Port Jackson Leve a bord de la Fregate la Thetis commande par M. Le Baron de Bougainville (shows Sydney)
mwat0226	atlantic falkland isl.	1773	BOUGAINVILLE	250	26	24	Plan of Acarron Bay Situated at the East Point of the Malouine Islands / A View of Fort St. Louis at Accaron Bay
mwe0196	europe	1774	BOULTON	550	69	79	A Correct Map of Europe Divided into its Empires Kingdoms &c.
mwaf1220	africa west	1766	BOULTON	400	38	48	A New and Correct Map of the Coast of Africa from Cape Blanco … to the Coast of Angola … 1753
mwaf0195	africa	1752	BOULTON	900	97	96	Africa Performed by the Sr. D'Anville
mwaf0254	africa	1787	BOULTON	2500	104	122	Africa with All its States, Kingdoms, Republics, Regions, Islands &c. Improved and Inlarged from D'Anville's Map: To which have been Added a Particular Chart of the Gold Coast, wherein are Distinguished All the European Forts and Factories
mwas0191	asia continent	1774	BOULTON	650	74	77	First Part of Asia, Being Turkey, Arabia, Persia, Most of India and Tartary
mwam0438	america north	1766	BOULTON	1800	83	86	North America. Performed under the Patronage of Louis Duke of Orleans … By the Sieur d'Anville. Greatly Improved by Mr. Bolton (4 sheets, joined)
mwsam0088	south america	1774	BOULTON	650	122	76	South America Performed under the Patronage of Louis Duke of Orleans

AMPG REFERENCE	REGION	DATE	MAP MAKER	PRICE (UK£)	VERT. (cm.)	HOR. (cm.)	TITLE OF MAP (Comments by the editor in brackets)
mwsw0244	alps	1811	BOURCET	1100	117	83	Carte des Alpes Francaises Reduite d'apres celles du Gal. Bourcet Comprenant le Cidt. Haut Dauphine et le Comte de Nice
mwaf0249	africa	1784	BOURGOIN	350	34	42	Carte de l'Afrique
mwam0443	america north	1770	BOURGOIN	480	34	42	Carte de l'Amerique Septentrionale
mwe0192	europe	1770	BOURGOIN	400	33	41	Carte de L'Europe divisee en ses Grands Etats
mwuk0833	uk	1750	BOURGOIN	300	34	42	Carte des Isles Britanniques
mwbh0683	belgium holland	1748	BOURGOIN	200	35	43	Carte des Pays Bas
mwsc0375	scandinavia denmark	1784	BOURGOIN	180	34	43	Carte du Royaume de Dannemarck
mwf0137	france	1765	BOURGOIN	180	34	41	Carte du Royaume de France Divisee par Provinces
mwsc0169	scandinavia	1784	BOURGOIN	300	35	44	Carte du Royaume de Suede Norwege et Partie du Dannemarck
mwsp0298	spain	1784	BOURGOIN	250	34	42	Carte du Royaume d'Espagne et de Portugal
mwf0148	france	1779	BOURGOIN	720	95	95	Carte Itineraire de la France
mwas0151	asia continent	1740	BOURGOIN	150	14	15	Le Commerce des Europeens en Asie
mwaf0224	africa	1770	BOURGOIN	80	14	7	Le Port d'Ophir et l'Ancienne Route de Tarsis
mwam0148	america continent	1740	BOURGOIN	120	14	7	Les Colonies des Europeens en Amerique
mww0436	world	1756	BOURGOIN	1200	31	44	Mappe Monde Carte Universelle de la Terre
mwwi0495	cuba	1845	BOURRELIER	350	29	36	Plano Topografico de los Barrios Estramuros de la Habana
mwg0742	thuringia	1670	BOUTTATS	450	32	41	(Erfut) Erphordia
mwgr0407	greece crete	1680	BOUTTATS	720	22	66	Carte dell Regno di Candia
mwg0610	saxony	1674	BOUTTATS	160	14	25	De Stadt Lingen
mwbp0262a	poland	1659	BOUTTATS	400			Dissegno di Stettin in Pomerania assediato (text lower left)
mwsc0295	scandinavia denmark	1670	BOUTTATS	180	36	46	Fionia Isola
mwjk0031	japan	1663	BOUTTATS	1500	15	20	Nova delineatio Japoniae Regnis
mwgr0084	greece	1670	BOUTTATS	4800	50	75	Peloponnesus Hodiae Moreae Regnum (14 town views in 3 borders)
mwuss0868	massachusetts	1830	BOWEN	250	31	31	A Map of Boston County of Suffolk and the Adjacent Towns
mwsam0368	south america brazil	1747	BOWEN, E.	500	35	42	(Brazil)
mwuk1813	wales	1720	BOWEN, E.	70	11	11	(Brecknockshire)
mwec0068	uk england buckinghamshire	1720	BOWEN, E.	70	11	11	(Buckinghamshire)
mwm0148	mediterranean east	1736	BOWEN, E.	250	31	39	(Eastern Mediterranean and Middle East)
mwuk1814	wales	1720	BOWEN, E.	70	11	11	(Flintshire)
mwec0446	uk england gloucestershire	1720	BOWEN, E.	70	11	11	(Gloucestershire)
mwuk1815	wales	1720	BOWEN, E.	70	11	11	(Montgomeryshire)
mwec1070	uk england staffordshire	1720	BOWEN, E.	70	11	11	(Staffordshire)
mwp0010	australia	1744	BOWEN, E.	4000	38	48	A Complete Map of the Southern Continent. Survey'd by Capt. Abel Tasman & Depicted by Order of the East India Company in Holland in the Stadt House at Amsterdam
mwuk1495	uk english channel (all)	1744	BOWEN, E.	400	38	48	A Correct Chart of the English Channel from the North Foreland to the Lands End on the Coast of England, and from Calais to Brest on the Coast of France
mwaa0129	arctic	1748	BOWEN, E.	480	39	43	A Correct Draught of the North Pole and of All the Countries Hitherto Discovered, Intercepted between the Pole and the Parallel of 50 Degrees. Exhibiting the Most Remarkable Tracts of our English Navigators
mwg0230	germany north west	1755	BOWEN, E.	250	34	42	A Correct Map of the South East Part of Germany
mwit0836d	italy sardinia and corsica	1740	BOWEN, E.	180	20	27	A Map of Great Greece and of the Islands of Sardinia and Corsica (shown above)
mwin0241	india	1764	BOWEN, E.	240	32	23	A Map of India on the West Side of the Ganges
mwas0266	asia (from turkey to india)	1764	BOWEN, E.	240	20	26	A Map of Marco Polo's Voyages & Travels in the 13th Century through a Great Part of Asia, All Tartary, the East India Islands & Part of Africa
mwsc0464	scandinavia greenland	1747	BOWEN, E.	320	33	23	A Map of Old Greenland or Oster Bygd & Wester Bygd / An Improved Map of Iceland / A Map of the Islands of Ferro / A Draught of the Whirlpool on the South East of Sumbo Rocks
mwsam0066	south america	1746	BOWEN, E.	350	47	37	A Map of South America with All the European Settlements & Whatever else is Remarkable from the Latest & Best Observations
mwam0965	america north (east)	1754	BOWEN, E.	375	22	27	A Map of the British American Plantations, Extending from Boston in New England to Georgia; Including All the Back Settlements in the Respective Provinces, as Far as the Mississipi
mwp0381	pacific new guinea	1744	BOWEN, E.	300	20	32	A Map of the Discoveries Made by Captn. Willm. Dampier in the Roebuck in 1699
mwme0322	holy land	1748	BOWEN, E.	240	28	28	A Map of the Divisions & Situations of the Tribes of the Canaanites, Moabites, Ammonites, Midianites, Edomites, Amalekites &c. before & at ye Time of ye Exodus of ye Children of Israel, According to this History
mwme0329	holy land	1750	BOWEN, E.	400	28	25	A Map of the Journey in the Wilderness, and of the Conquest and Partition of the Land of Canaan by the Children of Israel
mwuk0164	ireland	1744	BOWEN, E.	600	48	38	A Map of the Kingdom of Ireland from ye Latest & Best Observations

AMPG REFERENCE	REGION	DATE	MAP MAKER	PRICE (UK£)	VERT. (cm.)	HOR. (cm.)	TITLE OF MAP (Comments by the editor in brackets)
mwat0036	atlantic ocean (all)	1744	BOWEN, E.	400	37	44	A New & Accurate Chart of the Western or Atlantic Ocean Drawn from Surveys and Most Approved Maps & Charts
mww0383	world	1744	BOWEN, E.	1350	36	45	A New & Accurate Chart of the World. Drawn from Authentic Surveys, Assisted by the Most Approved Modern Maps & Charts & Regulated by Astronl. Observations (Mercator's projection. Also issued with minor changes and title: 'A New & Correct Chart of all the Known World ...')
mww0395a	world	1747	BOWEN, E.	1600	32	53	A New & Accurate Map of All the Known World
mwas0157	asia continent	1747	BOWEN, E.	400	35	43	A New & Accurate Map of Asia Drawn from Actual Surveys
mwat0120	atlantic bermuda	1747	BOWEN, E.	1100	35	45	A New & Accurate Map of Bermudas or Sommer's Islands, Taken from an Actual Survey / An accurate map of the Island of St Christopher (2 maps on one sheet)
mwsam0369	south america brazil	1747	BOWEN, E.	550	35	43	A New & Accurate Map of Brasil. Divided into its Captainships (inset: Island of St. Katharine)
mwc0139	china	1747	BOWEN, E.	500	35	42	A New & Accurate Map of China Drawn from Surveys Made by the Jesuit Missionaries, by Order of the Emperor
mwg0128	germany	1747	BOWEN, E.	180	32	23	A New & Accurate Map of Germany, Divided into its Circles
mwbp0437	poland	1747	BOWEN, E.	180	32	22	A New & Accurate Map ... Germany / Breslaw
mwam0954	america north (east)	1747	BOWEN, E.	800	34	42	A New & Accurate Map of Louisiana, with Part of Florida and Canada, and the Adjacent Countries
mwgm0031	gulf of mexico and surrounding regions	1747	BOWEN, E.	650	36	43	A New & Accurate Map of Mexico or New Spain (inset of Galapagos Isl.)
mwru0206	russia	1747	BOWEN, E.	340	32	22	A New & Accurate Map of Moscovy, or Russia in Europe, with its Acquisitions
mwaf1208	africa west	1748	BOWEN, E.	350	34	43	A New & Accurate Map of Negroland and the Adjacent Countries; also Upper Guinea
mwme0820	persia etc	1747	BOWEN, E.	350	35	43	A New & Accurate Map of Persia, with the Adjacent Countries
mwuk0490	scotland	1747	BOWEN, E.	450	43	35	A New & Accurate Map of Scotland or North Britain
mwsp0269	spain	1747	BOWEN, E.	400	36	44	A New & Accurate Map of Spain and Portugal
mwsw0147	switzerland	1747	BOWEN, E.	350	32	23	A New & Accurate Map of Switzerland with its Allies and Subjects, Composed from ye Most Approv'd Maps &c. and Regulated by Astronoml. Observatns.
mwwi0432	cuba	1747	BOWEN, E.	400	34	42	A New & Accurate Map of the Island of Cuba / Hispaniola or St. Domingo, Porto Rico (2 maps on one sheet)
mwwi0712	jamaica	1747	BOWEN, E.	400	34	42	A New & Accurate Map of the Island of Jamaica. Divided into its Principal Parishes (insets: Port Antonio, Kingston)
mwca0063	canada	1747	BOWEN, E.	450	35	43	A New & Accurate Map of the Islands of Newfoundland, Cape Breton, St. John and Anticosta; Together with the Neighbouring Countries of Nova Scotia, Canada, &c.
mwgr0185	greece	1747	BOWEN, E.	375	35	43	A New & Accurate Map of the Islands of the Archipelago, together with the Morea, and the Neighbouring Countries in Greece
mwit0945	italy sicily	1747	BOWEN, E.	280	33	22	A New & Accurate Map of the Kingdoms of Naples & Sicily
mwaa0128	arctic	1747	BOWEN, E.	480	38	43	A New & Accurate Map of the North Pole, with All the Countries Hitherto Discovered Situated Near or Adjacent to it as Well as some others More Remote
mwg0222	germany north west	1747	BOWEN, E.	140	32	23	A New & Accurate Map of the North West Part of Germany
mwuss0179	carolinas	1744	BOWEN, E.	750	35	43	A New & Accurate Map of the Provinces of North & South Carolina, Georgia &c.
mwaf0922	africa south	1747	BOWEN, E.	480	33	43	A New & Accurate Map of the Southern Parts of Africa
mwaf0715	africa north	1747	BOWEN, E.	280	35	43	A New & Accurate Map of the Western Parts of Barbary / A New & Accurate Map of the Eastern Parts of Barbary
mwru0207	russia	1747	BOWEN, E.	400	35	47	A New & Accurate Map of the Whole Russian Empire, as Contain'd both in Europe and Asia
mwe0800	europe east	1747	BOWEN, E.	350	35	42	A New & Accurate Map of Turky in Europe, with the Adjacent Countries of Hungary, Little Tartary &c
mwbh0669	belgium holland	1747	BOWEN, E.	300	35	43	A New & Correct Map of the Netherlands or Low Countries
mwas0158	asia continent	1748	BOWEN, E.	400	37	45	A New & Exact Map of Asia
mwwi0079	west indies	1744	BOWEN, E.	685	37	45	A New and Accurate Chart of the West Indies with the Adjacent Coasts of North and South America
mwaf0185	africa	1747	BOWEN, E.	480	35	43	A New and Accurate Map of Africa
mwam0163	america continent	1748	BOWEN, E.	550	35	44	A New and Accurate Map of America ... Exhibiting the Course of the Trade Winds both in the Atlantic & Pacific Oceans
mwme1008	turkey etc	1747	BOWEN, E.	360	35	43	A New and Accurate Map of Anatolia or Asia Minor with Syria and such other Provinces of the Turkish Empire
mwsam0458	south america chile	1747	BOWEN, E.	480	37	44	A New and Accurate Map of Chili, Terra Magellanica, Terra del Fuego &c. (insets of Saint Jago, Magellan)
mwsc0362	scandinavia denmark	1747	BOWEN, E.	180	32	23	A New and Accurate Map of Denmark
mwuk0986	england	1734	BOWEN, E.		63	137	A New and Accurate Map of England & Wales
mwe0165	europe	1748	BOWEN, E.	350	37	45	A New and Accurate Map of Europe
mwuk0827	uk	1747	BOWEN, E.	400	34	41	A New and Accurate Map of Great Britain & Ireland
mwuk0161	ireland	1740	BOWEN, E.	320	32	23	A New and Accurate Map of Ireland

AMPG REFERENCE	REGION	DATE	MAP MAKER	PRICE (UK£)	VERT. (cm.)	HOR. (cm.)	TITLE OF MAP (Comments by the editor in brackets)
mwit0182	italy	1747	BOWEN, E.	300	32	22	A New and Accurate Map of Italy Drawn from the Latest and Best Authorities, and Regulated by the Most Approved Astronl. Observations
mwuss1036	new jersey	1744	BOWEN, E.	1350	34	42	A New and Accurate Map of New Jersey, Pensilvania, New York and New England with the Adjacent Countries
mwaf0403	africa east	1747	BOWEN, E.	320	35	42	A New and Accurate Map of Nubia & Abissinia, Together with All the Kingdoms Tributary thereto
mwsam0716	south america paraguay	1747	BOWEN, E.	450	35	43	A New and Accurate Map of Paraguay, Rio de la Plata, Tucumania Guaria &c.
mwsam0758	south america peru	1747	BOWEN, E.	450	35	42	A New and Accurate Map of Peru, and the Country of the Amazones. Drawn from the Most Authentick French Maps &c.
mwbp0436	poland	1747	BOWEN, E.	350	33	42	A New and Accurate Map of Poland, Lithuania &c. Divided into its Palatinats
mwsp0091	portugal	1747	BOWEN, E.	280	32	22	A New and Accurate Map of Portugal Composed from the Latest Improvemts. and Adjusted by the Most Authentic Astronl. Observats.
mwit0609	italy north	1747	BOWEN, E.	380	35	43	A New and Accurate Map of Savoy, Piemont, and Montferrat, Exhibiting the Present Seat of War
mwsc0141	scandinavia	1747	BOWEN, E.	280	32	23	A New and Accurate Map of Scandinavia or the Northern Crowns of Sweden, Denmark, and Norway
mwuk1851a	wales	1766	BOWEN, E.	4500	113	158	A New and Accurate Map of South Wales
mwsc0731	scandinavia sweden	1747	BOWEN, E.	280	32	22	A New and Accurate Map of Sweden
mwsam0832	south america venezuela	1747	BOWEN, E.	500	36	43	A New and Accurate Map of Terra Firma and the Caribbe Islands Drawn from the Most Approved Modern Maps & Charts
mwas0321	asia caspian sea	1747	BOWEN, E.	320	31	23	A New and Accurate Map of the Caspian Sea, Laid down from the Memoirs of Soskam Sabbas a Georgian Prince
mwas0468	asia south east	1747	BOWEN, E.	675	35	43	A New and Accurate Map of the East India Islands
mwjk0098	japan	1747	BOWEN, E.	1000	35	44	A New and Accurate Map of the Empire of Japan Laid down from the Memoirs of the Portuguese and Dutch and ... the Jesuit Missionaries
mwin0205	india	1747	BOWEN, E.	500	35	42	A New and Accurate Map of the Empire of the Great Mogul
mwwi0298	antigua	1747	BOWEN, E.	400	32	23	A New and Accurate Map of the Island of Antigua or Antego ... Containing all the Towns, Parish Churches, Forts, Castles, Windmills, Roads &c.
mwe0947	europe hungary	1747	BOWEN, E.	360	32	42	A New and Accurate Map of the Kingdom of Hungary and Principality of Transilvania with the Bordering Countries Drawn from the Best Authorities Assisted by the Most Approved Modern Maps. The whole being adjusted by Astronomical Observations
mwbh0670	belgium holland	1747	BOWEN, E.	180	32	22	A New and Accurate Map of the Netherlands of Low Countries (inset plan of Mons)
mwit0608	italy north	1747	BOWEN, E.	260	32	23	A New and Accurate Map of the Northern Parts of Italy / A Draught of the Road of Leghorn
mwbh0671	belgium holland	1747	BOWEN, E.	180	32	22	A New and Accurate Map of the Seven United Provinces Compiled from the Most Approv'd Maps & Charts, and Adjusted by Astronoml. Observations
mwg0229	germany north west	1752	BOWEN, E.	180	32	21	A New and Accurate Map of the South East part of Germany
mww0414	world	1750	BOWEN, E.	650	29	38	A New and Accurate Map of the World Drawn from the Best Authorities and Regulated by Astronomical Observations: Describing the Course of Each of the Following Circum-Navigators vizt. Ferdinand Magellan, Sr. Francis Drake and Commodore Anson
mwme0622	arabia etc	1750	BOWEN, E.	500	35	43	A New and Accurate Map of Turkey in Asia, Arabia, &c.
mwuss1634	virginia	1747	BOWEN, E.	800	33	23	A New and Accurate Map of Virginia & Maryland Laid Down from Surveys and Regulated by Astronl. Observatns.
mwaf0187	africa	1748	BOWEN, E.	450	36	44	A New and Correct Map of Africa Drawn from the Most Approved Modern Maps and Charts
mwg0232	germany north west	1763	BOWEN, E.	250	34	42	A New and Correct Map of the South West Part of Germany Containing the Archbishopricks and Electorates of Mentz and Triers; also that of the Palatinate of the Rhine; the Duchy of Wirtemberg, Franconia, Swabia, Alsace, Lorrain, &c.
mwuk0994	england	1747	BOWEN, E.	400	34	42	A New and very Accurate Map of South Britain or England & Wales
mwat0041	atlantic ocean (all)	1755	BOWEN, E.	320	31	42	A New Chart of the Vast Atlantic Ocean; Exhibiting the Seat of War, both in Europe and America, Likewise the Trade Winds & Course of Sailing from One Continent to the other; with the Banks Shoals and Rocks
mwam0161	america continent	1747	BOWEN, E.	400	35	43	A New General Map of America, Drawn from Several Accurate Particular Maps and Charts
mwat0278a	atlantic north	1763	BOWEN, E.	250	18	28	A New Geographical Map or Chart of the Atlantic Ocean (publ. in the 'General Magazine of Arts & Science')
mwec0189	uk england cornwall	1750	BOWEN, E.	900	54	70	A New Improved Map of Cornwall

AMPG REFERENCE	REGION	DATE	MAP MAKER	PRICE (UK£)	VERT. (cm.)	HOR. (cm.)	TITLE OF MAP (Comments by the editor in brackets)
mwec0480	uk england hampshire	1751	BOWEN, E.	850	54	70	A New Improved Map of Hampshire
mwec0553	uk england hertfordshire	1750	BOWEN, E.	450	69	52	A New Improved Map of Hertfordshire
mwec0889	uk england northumberland	1750	BOWEN, E.	500	69	52	A New Improved Map of Northumberland from the Best Surveys & Intelligences, Divided into its Wards
mwec0957	uk england oxfordshire	1750	BOWEN, E.	400	71	53	A New Improved Map of Oxfordshire
mwam0956	america north (east)	1748	BOWEN, E.	3200	36	48	A New Map of Georgia with Part of Carolina, Florida, and Louisiana. Drawn from Original Draughts Assisted by the Most Approved Maps and Charts
mwwi0095	west indies	1761	BOWEN, E.	250	24	18	A New Map of the Caribbee Islands in America 1761
mwat0272a	atlantic north	1740	BOWEN, E.	400	34	31	A New Map or Chart of the Western or Atlantic Ocean, with Part of Europe, Africa & America; Shewing the Course of the Galleons, Flota &c. to & from the West Indies
mwgm0206	mexico	1740	BOWEN, E.	300	14	17	A Plan of the City and Harbour of La Vera Cruz and the Castle of San Juan de Ulua Being the Key of Traffick and the Principal Port of New Spain Lat: 19°:10'
mwme0504	jerusalem	1760	BOWEN, E.	200	40	41	A Plan of the City of Jerusalem According to the Description thereof in the Books of the Old Testament but More Especially in that of Nehemiah
mwm0060	mediterranean	1748	BOWEN, E.	550	29	59	An Accurate Chart of the Mediterranean and Adriatic Seas with the Archipelago and Part of the Black Sea
mwuk1081	england and france	1757	BOWEN, E.	300	30	30	An Accurate Map of 460 Miles round London
mwme1007	turkey etc	1747	BOWEN, E.	200	33	23	An Accurate Map of Asia Minor, as Divided into its Provinces, before it became Possess'd by the Turks
mwec0046	uk england berkshire	1756	BOWEN, E.	350	53	69	An Accurate Map of Berkshire
mwec0073	uk england buckinghamshire	1756	BOWEN, E.	350	70	53	An Accurate Map of Buckingham Shire
mwec0102	uk england cambridgeshire	1753	BOWEN, E.	400	70	52	An Accurate Map of Cambridgeshire Divided into its Hundreds
mwuk1836	wales	1754	BOWEN, E.	280	70	53	An Accurate Map of Carmarthenshire / Glamorganshire
mwc0152	china	1754	BOWEN, E.	180	18	22	An Accurate Map of China Laid down from Late Surveys
mwec0296	uk england devon	1750	BOWEN, E.	450	53	68	An Accurate Map of Devon Shire
mwec0527	uk england herefordshire	1770	BOWEN, E.	280	52	69	An Accurate Map of Hereford Shire
mwec0585	uk england huntingdonshire	1777	BOWEN, E.	200	52	41	An Accurate Map of Huntingdon
mwuk0192	ireland	1764	BOWEN, E.	180	17	22	An Accurate Map of Ireland
mwit0194	italy	1764	BOWEN, E.	180	24	22	An Accurate Map of Italy
mwec0749	uk england lincolnshire	1750	BOWEN, E.	350	71	53	An Accurate Map of Lincolnshire, Divided into its Wapontakes
mwam0448	america north	1775	BOWEN, E.	3500	106	117	An Accurate Map of North America. Describing and Distinguishing the British and Spanish Dominions on this Great Continent; According to the Definitive Treaty Concluded at Paris 10th Feb. 1763. Also the West India Islands (close copy of Bowles 1763)
mwec0863	uk england northamptonshire	1752	BOWEN, E.	300	70	53	An Accurate Map of Northampton Shire. Divided into its Hundreds
mwec0917	uk england nottinghamshire	1760	BOWEN, E.	320	69	53	An Accurate Map of Nottingham Shire
mwsam0715	south america paraguay	1746	BOWEN, E.	320	28	42	An Accurate Map of Paraguay, Tucumania, Chaco, Rio de la Plata, &c. with Part of Brasil from 20 to 37 Degrees South Latitude
mwuk1837	wales	1754	BOWEN, E.	280	70	53	An Accurate Map of Radnorshire / Brecknockshire
mwec1016	uk england shropshire	1753	BOWEN, E.	400	52	70	An Accurate Map of Shropshire Divided into its Hundreds Drawn and Compiled from the Most Approved Maps & Surveys
mwec0723	uk england leicestershire	1778	BOWEN, E.	280	53	69	An Accurate Map of the Counties of Leicester & Rutland
mwec0015	uk england bedfordshire	1760	BOWEN, E.	400	70	52	An Accurate Map of the County of Bedford, Divided into its Hundreds
mwec0192	uk england cornwall	1764	BOWEN, E.	1000	42	50	An Accurate Map of the County of Cornwall
mwec0266	uk england derbyshire	1758	BOWEN, E.	320	69	53	An Accurate Map of the County of Derby
mwec0413	uk england essex	1750	BOWEN, E.	420	53	71	An Accurate Map of the County of Essex
mwec0583	uk england huntingdonshire	1750		250	70	52	An Accurate Map of the County of Huntingdon Divided into its Hundreds
mwec0639	uk england kent	1763	BOWEN, E.	300	40	49	An Accurate Map of the County of Kent
mwec0631	uk england kent	1751	BOWEN, E.	600	51	70	An Accurate Map of the County of Kent, Divided into its Lathes
mwec0688	uk england lancashire	1753	BOWEN, E.	580	51	69	An Accurate Map of the County of Lancaster Divided into its Hundreds
mwec0830	uk england norfolk	1750	BOWEN, E.	375	53	72	An Accurate Map of the County of Norfolk, Divided into Hundreds, and Drawn from Surveys
mwec1109	uk england suffolk	1750	BOWEN, E.	450	53	71	An Accurate Map of the County of Suffolk, Divided into its Hundreds
mwec1142	uk england surrey	1750	BOWEN, E.	750	53	71	An Accurate Map of the County of Surrey, Divided into its Hundreds
mwec1171	uk england sussex	1750	BOWEN, E.	650	51	69	An Accurate Map of the County of Sussex. Divided into its Rapes, Deaneries, and Hundreds
mwec1201	uk england warwickshire	1750	BOWEN, E.	600	67	53	An Accurate Map of the County of Warwickshire
mwec1284	uk england worcestershire	1770	BOWEN, E.	450	53	70	An Accurate Map of the County of Worcester, Divided into its Hundreds

AMPG REFERENCE	REGION	DATE	MAP MAKER	PRICE (UK£)	VERT. (cm.)	HOR. (cm.)	TITLE OF MAP (Comments by the editor in brackets)
mwec1335	uk england yorkshire	1750	BOWEN, E.	500	53	70	An Accurate Map of the County of York Divided into its Ridings, and Subdivided into Wapontakes
mwec0144	uk england cheshire	1753	BOWEN, E.	580	54	70	An Accurate Map of the County Palatine of Chester Divided into its Hundreds
mwec0375	uk england durham	1752	BOWEN, E.	720	51	69	An Accurate Map of the County Palatine of Durham
mwas0484	asia south east	1764	BOWEN, E.	500	37	48	An Accurate Map of the East Indies Exhibiting the Course of the European Trade Both on the Continent and Islands
mwec1336	uk england yorkshire	1750	BOWEN, E.	360	53	66	An Accurate Map of the East Riding of York Shire
mwme0318	holy land	1747	BOWEN, E.	250	33	23	An Accurate Map of the Holy Land Divided into the XII Tribes of Israel. Accomodated to Sacred History & Describing the Travels of Jesus Christ
mwwi0372	barbados	1747	BOWEN, E.	650	35	43	An Accurate Map of the Island of Barbadoes Drawn from an Actual Survey Containing All the Towns Churches
mwgr0186	greece	1747	BOWEN, E.	240	22	32	An Accurate Map of the Morea Together with the Neighbouring Countries in Greece, also the Islands in the Archipelago and Aegean Seas
mwec1337	uk england yorkshire	1750	BOWEN, E.	550	52	70	An Accurate Map of the North Riding of Yorkshire, Divided into its Wapontakes
mwwi0082	west indies	1747	BOWEN, E.	675	35	43	An Accurate Map of the West Indies. Drawn from the Best Authorities, Assisted by the Most Approved Modern Maps and Charts, and Regulated by Astronomical Observations (also issued with the title: 'A New & Accurate Chart of the West Indies ...')
mwec1338	uk england yorkshire	1750	BOWEN, E.	580	53	71	An Accurate Map of the West Riding of Yorkshire Divided into its Wapontakes
mwru0194	russia	1744	BOWEN, E.	250	18	33	An Exact Chart of All the Countries through which Capt. Behring Travelled from Tobolski Capital of Siberia, to the Country of Kamtschatka
mwec1044	uk england somerset	1750	BOWEN, E.	480	52	70	An Improved Map of the County of Somerset Divided into its Hundreds
mwec1075	uk england staffordshire	1756	BOWEN, E.	250	71	54	An Improved Map of the County of Stafford Divided into its Hundreds
mwec1251	uk england wiltshire	1750	BOWEN, E.	400	54	69	An Improved Map of Wilt Shire, Divided into its Hundreds
mwec0018	uk england bedfordshire	1767	BOWEN, E.	200	32	22	Bedford Shire Divided into Hundreds
mwec0193	uk england cornwall	1767	BOWEN, E.	240	24	34	Cornwall Divided into Hundreds
mwsc0369	scandinavia denmark	1758	BOWEN, E.	80	11	8	Denmaark
mwec0338	uk england dorset	1760	BOWEN, E.	300	55	71	Dorset Shire Divided into its Hundreds
mwwi0540	guadeloupe	1749	BOWEN, E.	250	19	23	Guadeloupe, One of the Caribbee Islands in the West Indies from the Latest Discovery
mwec0558	uk england hertfordshire	1767	BOWEN, E.	200	23	32	Hartford Shire Divided into Hundreds
mwca0398	canada nova scotia	1774	BOWEN, E.	300	10	6	Island of Cape Breton
mwec0691	uk england lancashire	1767	BOWEN, E.	200	32	22	Lancashire Divided into Hundreds
mwgm0223	mexico	1758	BOWEN, E.	250	10	6	Mexico or New Spain
mwca0321	canada newfoundland	1774	BOWEN, E.	200	10	6	New Found Land
mwec0832	uk england norfolk	1767	BOWEN, E.	200	33	23	Norfolk Divided into its Hundreds
mwec0919	uk england nottinghamshire	1767	BOWEN, E.	150	33	23	Nottingham Shire, Describing its Wapentakes &c.
mwca0399	canada nova scotia	1774	BOWEN, E.	300	10	6	Nova Scotia
mwe0363	europe austria	1740	BOWEN, E.	550	56	85	Part of the Circle of Austria in which are the Dukedoms of Stiria, and Carinthia, of Carniola, and other Hereditary Countrys of the House of Austria
mwam0398	america north	1747	BOWEN, E.	650	36	43	Particular Draughts and Plans of Some of the Principal Towns and Harbours Belonging to the English, French, and Spaniards, in America and West Indies
mwuss1349	pennsylvania	1758	BOWEN, E.	240	6	10	Pensilvania, Maryland & Virginia
mwit0942	italy sicily	1740	BOWEN, E.	500	30	38	Sicily
mwsp0290	spain	1777	BOWEN, E.	180	18	22	Spain and Portugal
mwg0823	westphalia	1741	BOWEN, E.	350	87	57	The Circle of Westphalia Divided into All its States and Soveranities (based on Berry 1686, publ. by Bowles)
mwg0123	germany	1740	BOWEN, E.	650	102	120	The Empire of Germany, in which are Distinguished According to All the States, Principalities and Sovereignties
mwme0321	holy land	1747	BOWEN, E.	250	21	36	The Expedition of the Shalmaneser King of Assyria Against the Syrians and the Ten Tribes of Israel
mwsam0567	south america galapagos	1744	BOWEN, E.	400	32	20	The Gallapagos Islands Discovered and Described by Capt. Cowley in 1684
mww0395	world	1747	BOWEN, E.	650	19	37	The World, According to the Latest Discoveries
mwme0636	arabia etc	1774	BOWEN, E.	240	9	6	Turky in Asia
mwit0167	italy	1732	BOWEN, E.-WILLDEY	2500	64	106	A New & Correct Map of Italy Done from the Latest Discoveries & Observations Communicated to the Royal Society of London & the Royal Academy of Paris ... with 18 Views of ye Principal Cities and Places of Note
mwf0116	france	1732	BOWEN, E.-WILLDEY	2000	63	103	A New & Exact Map of France Corrected from the Observations made by the Royal Academy of Sciences at Paris &c. (side panels show 10 ports and cities)
mwf0124	france	1747	BOWEN, E.-WILLDEY	280	36	44	A New and Accurate Map of France with its Acquisitions
mwsc0132	scandinavia	1732	BOWEN, E.-WILLDEY	3000	59	98	A New and Exact Map of Sweden and Norway

AMPG REFERENCE	REGION	DATE	MAP MAKER	PRICE (UK£)	VERT. (cm.)	HOR. (cm.)	TITLE OF MAP (Comments by the editor in brackets)
mwas0140	asia continent	1732	BOWEN, E.-WILLDEY	2400	62	97	Asia Corrected According to ye Latest Discoveries & Observations
mwe0149	europe	1732	BOWEN, E.-WILLDEY	1500	63	91	Europe Corrected According to ye Latest Discoveries & Observations by Eman Bowen
mwe0936	europe hungary	1732	BOWEN, E.-WILLDEY	2400	63	100	Hungary ... Corrected from ye Observations Communicated to the Royal Society at London & the Royal Academy at Paris
mwe1149	europe south east	1715	BOWEN, E.-WILLDEY	1800	92	63	Turkey in Europe ... 1715
mwuk1230	england london	1775	BOWEN, M.	350	49	55	A Topographical Survey of the Country, from Thirty Five to Forty Miles, round London
mwme0357	holy land	1770	BOWEN, T.	200	29	18	A Correct Map of the Countries Surrounding the Garden of Eden or Paradise with the Course of Noah's Ark During the Flood
mwme0645	arabia etc	1780	BOWEN, T.	250	32	42	A Correct Map of the Ottoman Empire, Including all the Countries Possess'd by, or Tributary to the Turks, in Europe, Asia and Africa, with Part of the Adjacent Territories
mwam0490	america north	1785	BOWEN, T.	550	34	47	A Correct Map of the United States of North America, Including the British and Spanish Territories, Carefully Laid down Agreeable to the Treaty of 1784
mwam0411	america north	1755	BOWEN, T.	800	38	49	A Map of the British and French Settlements in North America (2 maps on one sheet)
mwwi0509	dominica	1778	BOWEN, T.	240	24	20	A Map of the Island of Dominica, Taken from an Actual Survey: Also Part of Martinico & Guadaloupe Shewing their True Bearing & Distance from each other
mwwi0903	trinidad & tobago	1779	BOWEN, T.	300	19	24	A Map of the Island of Tobago, Drawn from an Actual Survey, by Thos. Bowen, 1779
mwme0744	iraq etc	1780	BOWEN. T.	200	19	23	A Map of the Situation of the Garden of Eden and also of Mount Ararat
mwaa0030	antarctic	1776	BOWEN, T.	800	22	22	A Map of the South Pole, with the Track of His Majesty's Sloop Resolution in Search of a Southern Continent (the first map to show all Capt. Cook's discoveries in the Antarctic, publ. in the Gentleman's Magazine)
mww0501	world	1778	BOWEN, T.	400	34	46	A Mercator Chart of the World
mwp0262	pacific (all)	1790	BOWEN, T.	650	45	34	A New & Accurate Chart of the Discoveries Made by the Late Capt. J. Cook ... Latitudes of 80 Degs. North and 50 Degs. South and Extending to 260 Degs. East Long. from the Meridian of Greenwich (engraved by J. Lodge)
mwas0195	asia continent	1780	BOWEN, T.	400	32	40	A New & Accurate Map of Asia
mwam0509	america north	1790	BOWEN, T.	400	26	43	A New & Accurate Map of North America Including Nootka Sound: with the New Discovered Islands on the North East Coast of Asia (publ. by C. Cooke)
mwuk0492	scotland	1750	BOWEN, T.	180	32	22	A New & Accurate Map of that Part of Great Britain, Called Scotland
mwat0054	atlantic ocean (all)	1790	BOWEN, T.	240	21	27	A New and Accurate Chart of the Western or Atlantic Ocean, Drawn from the Most Approved Modern Maps
mwaf0236	africa	1777	BOWEN, T.	250	34	41	A New and Accurate Map of Africa, Drawn from the Best Authorities by Thos. Bowen
mwuk0209	ireland	1778	BOWEN, T.	200	29	19	A New and Accurate Map of Ireland
mww0565	world	1790	BOWEN, T.	400	33	45	A New and Complete Chart of the World
mwuk1221	england london	1770	BOWEN, T.	400	32	36	A New and Correct Map of the Countries Twenty Miles round London. By Thos. Bowen
mwuk0211a	ireland	1779	BOWEN. T.	250	19	29	A Plan of the Grand Canal from the City of Dublin to the River Shannon
mwme0358	holy land	1770	BOWEN, T.	200	29	18	An Accurate Map of the Holy Land with the Adjacent Countries
mwe0956	europe hungary	1780	BOWEN, T.	235	32	39	Hungary with Part of the Adjoining Principalities
mwsc0640	scandinavia norway	1791	BOWEN, T.	280	33	41	Norway from the Best Authorities
mwec0958	uk england oxfordshire	1767	BOWEN, T.	200	32	23	Oxford Shire Divided into its Hundreds
mwwi0881	st lucia	1779	BOWEN, T.	235	19	25	Plan of St. Lucia, in the West Indies: Shewing the Positions of the English & French Forces with the Attacks Made at its Reduction in Decr. 1778
mwgm0123	honduras	1780	BOWEN, T.	250	23	19	Plan of the Harbour of Omoa, by Capt. J.S. Speer. Latde. 15°. 50'. N. Long. 89. 50. W. / Plan of the Fortification Now Erecting at Omoa
mwca0659	canada west	1785	BOWEN, T.	280	33	22	Sketch of Nootka Sound. A Ship Cove ... 1778
mwsc0740a	scandinavia sweden	1780	BOWEN, T.	280	33	41	Sweden from the Best Authorities
mwme0510	jerusalem	1780	BOWEN. T.	200	17	27	The Ancient City of Jerusalem and Places Adjacent
mwme0348	holy land	1760	BOWEN, T.	200	23	19	The Distances of Places in Palestine Reduced to Roman Miles
mww0519	world	1782	BOWEN, T.	600	29	47	The World Including the Discoveries Made by Capt. Cook
mww0519a	world	1782	BOWEN, T.	1100	27	45	The World Including the late Discoveries, by Capt. Cook
mwat0222	atlantic falkland isl.	1770	BOWLES	1200	45	69	A Draught of Falklands Islands
mwam0425a	america north	1762	BOWLES	1650	48	58	A Map of North America by J. Palairet
mwca0358	canada nova scotia	1745	BOWLES	400	25	31	A Map of Royal Island or Cape Breton Drawn by N. Bellin Engineer of the Marine

AMPG REFERENCE	REGION	DATE	MAP MAKER	PRICE (UK£)	VERT. (cm.)	HOR. (cm.)	TITLE OF MAP (Comments by the editor in brackets)
mwam1319	america north (west)	1754	BOWLES	1100	46	61	A Map of the Discoveries Made by the Russians on the North West Coast of America. Published by the Royal Academy of Sciences at Petersburg
mwam1017	america north (east)	1765	BOWLES	6000	64	52	A Map of the Most Inhabited Part of New England, Containing the Provinces of Massachusets Bay and New Hampshire, with the Colonies of Conecticut and Rhode Island, Divided into Counties and Townships
mwam0445	america north	1771	BOWLES	2000	47	51	A New and Accurate Map of North America, Drawn from the Famous Mr d'Anville with Improvements from the Best English Maps; and Engraved by R.W. Seale; also the New Divisions According to the Late Treaty of Peace, by Peter Bell, Geor.
mwuk0202	ireland	1770	BOWLES	1200	119	90	A New and Complete Map of the Kingdom of Ireland
mwas0142a	asia continent	1733	BOWLES	2000			A New and Correct Map of Asia (12 views in right-hand border)
mwaf0231	africa	1775	BOWLES	650	48	57	A New and Correct Map of the Coast of Africa ... with Explanatory Notes of All the Forts and Settlements Belonging to the Several European Powers.
mwuk1175	england london	1740	BOWLES	2800	64		A New and Correct Map of Thirty Miles round London Showing All the Towns, Villages, Roads &c with the Seats of the Nobility & Gentry and whatever else is Remarkable ... Together with an Alphabetical Table for the Ready Finding of All the Places (circular map)
mwwi0858	st kitts	1753	BOWLES	10000	115	142	A New and Exact Map of the Island of St. Chistopher in America According to an Actual and Accurate Survey Made in the Year 1753. Describing the Several Parishes, with their Respective Limits, Contents & Churches (map by S. Baker)
mwbh0638	belgium holland	1740	BOWLES	1350	62	102	A New and Exact Map of the United Provinces, or Netherlands
mwuk1207	england london	1764	BOWLES	4000	58	98	A new and exact plan of the Cities of London
mwuk1150	england london	1719	BOWLES	6000	67	198	A New and Exact Plan of ye City of London and Suburbs thereof (6 editions to 1731. A new edition entitled 'London Surveyed' was published in 1736. See below.)
mwat0046	atlantic ocean (all)	1771	BOWLES	400	46	56	A New Chart of the Vast Atlantic or Western Ocean Including the Sea Coast of Europe, Africa, America and the West India Islands
mwwi0727	jamaica	1771	BOWLES	650	48	56	A New Map of Jamaica in which the Several Towns, Forts & Settlements are Accurately Laid down ... by Mr. Sheffield & Others
mwec0235	uk england cumbria	1760	BOWLES	480	67	51	A New Map of the Counties of Cumberland and Westmoreland divided into their respective Wards
mwe0951	europe hungary	1754	BOWLES	1000	65	100	A New Map of the Kingdom of Hungary and of the Countries, Provinces &c. Bordering thereupon
mwuk1166	england london	1733	BOWLES	1200	38	57	A Plan of London as in Q. Elizabeths Time
mwme0489	jerusalem	1730	BOWLES	2500	36	41	A Plan of the City of Jerusalem & Places adjacent
mwuk1159	england london	1723	BOWLES	1750	27	41	A pocket map of the cities of London & Westminster (a larger edition published in 1725 and later)
mwuss1098	new york	1768	BOWLES	13500	35	50	A Southwest View of the City of New York in North America. Drawn on the Spot by Capt. Thomas Howdell, of the Royal Artillery / A South East View of the City of New York in North America. Drawn on the Spot by Capt. Thomas Howdell (2 views on one sheet)
mwuss1356	pennsylvania	1768	BOWLES	2500	32	51	A View of Bethlem, the Great Moravian Settlement in the Province of Pennsylvania
mwuss0188	carolinas	1768	BOWLES	15000	37	52	A View of Charles Town the Capital of South Carolina in North America
mwca0392	canada nova scotia	1768	BOWLES	2000	36	51	A View of Louisburg in North America, Taken Near the Light House when that City was Besieged in 1758
mwwi0505	dominica	1768	BOWLES	950	31	50	A View of Roseau in the Island of Dominique, with the Attack Made by Lord Rollo & Sr. James Douglas, in 1760
mwuss0802	massachusetts	1768	BOWLES	8750	36	52	A View of the City of Boston the Capital of New England, in North America
mwuk1844	wales	1760	BOWLES	320	50	66	An Accurate Map of North Wales
mwec0449	uk england gloucestershire	1760	BOWLES	900	52	68	An Accurate Map of the Counties of Gloucester and Monmouth
mwec0827a	uk england norfolk	1735	BOWLES	2000	55	70	An Actual Survey of the County of Norfolk (map by J. Corbridge)
mwec1110	uk england suffolk	1763	BOWLES	800	51	69	An Actual Survey of the County of Suffolk, to which is Added Great Part of ye County of Norfolk
mwuk1438	england thames	1774	BOWLES	650	20	88	Bowle's Draught of the River Thames, from its Spring in Gloucester-Shire, to its Influx into the Sea; with a Table of All the Locks, Wears, and Bridges Thereupon; Shewing the Tolls Payable at Each and their Distance by Water from One Another

AMPG REFERENCE	REGION	DATE	MAP MAKER	PRICE (UK£)	VERT. (cm.)	HOR. (cm.)	TITLE OF MAP (Comments by the editor in brackets)
mwam0430	america north	1763	BOWLES	2500	101	115	Bowles' New Map of North America and the West Indies
mwaf0225	africa	1770	BOWLES	500	49	56	Bowles' New One-Sheet Map of Africa Divided into its Empires, Kingdoms, States and Subdivisions
mwe0191	europe	1770	BOWLES	1500	48	68	Bowles's European Geographical Amusement, or Game of Geography; Designed from the Grand Tour of Europe, by Dr. Nugent
mwam1031	america north (east)	1776	BOWLES	2400	64	53	Bowles's Map of the Seat of War in New England Comprehending the Provinces of Massachusetts Bay, and New Hampshire; with the Colonies of Connecticut and Rhode Island; Divided into their Townships; Together with an Accurate Plan of the Town ... of Boston
mwuk1019	england	1782	BOWLES	960	131	104	Bowles's New and Accurate Map of England and Wales, Comprehending All the Cities, Boroughs, Markets and Sea-Port Towns ... with the Roads Described by Daniel Paterson
mwec0789	uk england middlesex	1785	BOWLES	280	23	32	Bowles's New Medium Map of Middlesex
mwam0205	america continent	1780	BOWLES	650	58	57	Bowles's New One-Sheet Map of America
mwas0175	asia continent	1794	BOWLES	550	49	57	Bowles's New One-sheet Map of Asia Divided into its Empires, Kingdoms, States and Other Sub-Divisions (illustrated below is the c1800 re-issue with inset of Australia)
mwuk1032a	england	1796	BOWLES	450	59	51	Bowles's New One-Sheet Map of England & Wales
mwam1119	america north (east)	1796	BOWLES	6000	64	52	Bowles's New One-Sheet Map of New England Comprehending the Provinces of Massachusetts Bay Connecticut & Rhode Island; Divided into their Couties, Townships, &c.
mwam0532	america north	1796	BOWLES	750	47	58	Bowles's New One-Sheet Map of North America, Divided into its Provinces, Colonies, States, &c.
mwam1121	america north (east)	1797	BOWLES	2000	48	64	Bowles's New One-Sheet Map of the Independent States of Virginia, Maryland, Delaware, Pensylvania, New Jersey, New York, Connecticut, Rhode Island &c ... also the Habitations & Hunting Countries of the Confederate Indians. By Lewis Evans
mwam1133	america north (east)	1799	BOWLES	2000	47	51	Bowles's New One-Sheet Map of the United States of America: With the Territories Belonging to Great Britain and Spain
mwwi0144	west indies	1798	BOWLES	500	51	69	Bowles's New One-Sheet Map of the West Indies, Laid Down from the Observations of the Most Celebrated Geographers
mwam0216	america continent	1784	BOWLES	500	52	56	Bowles's New Pocket Map of America, Divided into its Provinces, Colonies, States, Governments, &c. Exhibiting the British & Spanish Empires Shown Together with the Territories Belonging to the French, Dutch, Danes & Portuguese
mwwi0745	jamaica	1792	BOWLES	750	48	56	Bowles's New Pocket Map of Jamaica
mwam0426	america north	1762	BOWLES	1500	47	58	Bowles's New Pocket Map of North America Divided into its Provinces, Colonies, States, etc., by J. Palairet, Geographer, Lately Revised and Improved with Many Additions from d'Anville, Michel, & Bellin, by J. Delarochette
mwsam0102	south america	1785	BOWLES	300	49	60	Bowles's New Pocket Map of South America
mwsw0201	switzerland	1792	BOWLES	450	51	67	Bowles's New Pocket Map of Switzerland Comprehending the Thirteen Cantons with their Allies and Subjected Territories
mwp0425a	pacific north	1780	BOWLES	1250	45	62	Bowles's New Pocket Map of the Discoveries Made by the Russians on the North West Coast of America (close copy of Jefferys 1761)
mwru0224	russia	1755	BOWLES	350	50	56	Bowles's New Pocket Map of the East Part of the Russian Empire in Asia, from the Sr. d'Anville of the Academy of Sciences at Petersburg
mwam1083	america north (east)	1784	BOWLES	2800	50	64	Bowles's New Pocket Map of the Following Independent States of North America, viz. Virginia, Maryland, Delaware, Pensylvania, New Jersey, New York, Connecticut & Rhode Island
mwbp0491	poland	1775	BOWLES	350	46	54	Bowles's New Pocket Map of the Kingdom of Poland, and Grand Dutchy of Lithuania
mwme0377	holy land	1792	BOWLES	720	47	58	Bowles's New Pocket Map of the Land of Canaan, or Holy Land, which God Promised to Abraham and his Seed, as Divided among the Twelve Tribes of Israel together with their Forty Years Sojournment thro the Wilderness to the said Land
mwam1029	america north (east)	1775	BOWLES	3000	51	66	Bowles's New Pocket Map of the Middle British Colonies, in America, viz. Virginia, Maryland, Delaware, Pensylvania, New Jersey, New York, Connecticut & Rhode Island (reprint of Lewis Evans' 1755 map)

AMPG REFERENCE	REGION	DATE	MAP MAKER	PRICE (UK£)	VERT. (cm.)	HOR. (cm.)	TITLE OF MAP (Comments by the editor in brackets)
mwam1038	america north (east)	1776	BOWLES	4000	64	52	Bowles's New Pocket Map of the Most Inhabited Part of New England; Comprehending the Provinces of Massachusets Bay and New Hampshire; with the Colonies of Connecticut & Rhode Island ... Environs of Boston
mww0548	world	1787	BOWLES	1500	38	71	Bowles's New Pocket Map of the World ... Comprehending the New Discoveries to the Present Time, Particularly those Lately Made in the Southern Seas by Byron, Wallis, Cook, Bougainville and Others
mww0510a	world	1780	BOWLES	2000	38	74	Bowles New Pocket Map of the World laid down from the latest observations and comprehending The New Discoveries to the present Time, particularly those lately made in the Southern Seas By Byron, Wallis, Cook, Bougainville, and others . . . 1780
mwuk1246	england london	1786	BOWLES	2800	44	89	Bowles's New Pocket Plan of cities of London and Westminster (14 editions until 1814)
mwuk1015	england	1777	BOWLES	400	48	35	Bowles's New Traveller's Guide through the Principal Direct and Cross Roads of England and Wales
mwuk1025	england	1788	BOWLES	500	61	54	Bowles's New Travelling Map of England and Wales Exhibiting All the Direct and Principal Cross Roads; with the Distances in Measured Miles
mwec0019	uk england bedfordshire	1785	BOWLES	160	15	11	Bowles's Reduced Map of Bedfordshire
mwec0104	uk england cambridgeshire	1785	BOWLES	180	18	14	Bowles's Reduced Map of Cambridgeshire
mwec0559	uk england hertfordshire	1785	BOWLES	160	14	18	Bowles's Reduced Map of Hertfordshire
mwec0694	uk england lancashire	1785	BOWLES	240	29	25	Bowles's Reduced Map of Lancashire
mwec0833	uk england norfolk	1785	BOWLES	200	21	29	Bowles's Reduced Map of Norfolk
mwec0961	uk england oxfordshire	1785	BOWLES	180	19	17	Bowles's Reduced Map of Oxfordshire
mwuk1611	isle of man	1785	BOWLES	180	13	20	Bowles's Reduced Map of the Isle of Man
mwuk1635	scilly isles	1785	BOWLES	240	14	19	Bowles's Reduced Map of the Isles of Scilly
mwuk1229	england london	1773	BOWLES	1200	39	55	Bowles's Reduced New Pocket Plan of the Cities of London and Westminster, with the Borough of Southwark, exhibiting the New Buildings (17 editions to 1799)
mwuk1018	england	1780	BOWLES	400	59	52	Bowles's Road Director through England and Wales
mwuss1158	new york	1794	BOWLES	4000	14	20	Fort George with the City of New York from the SW (view)
mwuk0149	ireland	1728	BOWLES	280	28	26	Ireland Divided into its Provinces and Counties
mwuk1170	england london	1736	BOWLES	4000	63	145	London Surveyed, or A New Map of the Cities of London and Westminster and the Borough of Southwark Shewing the several Streets and Lanes with most of ye Alleys & Thorough Fairs: with the additional new buildings to the present year
mwec0643	uk england kent	1773	BOWLES	600	42	54	New Map of Kent
mwuk1251	england london	1790	BOWLES	3000	100		New Plan of London (circular map) (5 editions until 1806)
mwsp0112	portugal	1778	BOWLES	500	65	48	New Pocket Map of Portugal
mwbp0281	poland	1670	BOWLES	500	34	43	Polonia Regnum
mwsc0128	scandinavia	1724	BOWLES	800	57	86	Scandinavia or the Seat of War in the Kingdoms of Sweden, Denmark and Norway
mwsam0067	south america	1748	BOWLES	400	49	59	South America from the Latest Discoveries Showing the Spanish & Portuguese Settlements According to Mr D'Anville
mwam0412	america north	1755	BOWLES	1000	43	56	The British & French Dominions in North America
mwbp0407	poland	1734	BOWLES	1500	49	57	The City of Dantzick
mwuk1226	england london	1771	BOWLES	1350	31	51	The London Directory, or a new & improved plan of London (8 editions until 1802)
mwe1018	europe rhine	1720	BOWLES	550	94	58	The Seat of War on the Rhine being a New Map of the Course of the River from Strasbourg to Bonn with the Adjacent Countries
mwuk1222	england london	1770	BOWLES	1200	45	90	The Traveller's Guide through London, Westminster, and Borough of Southwark; with their Liberties: Exhibiting the Streets, Roads, Churches, Palaces, Public Buildings, &c., as they have been lately extended and improved
mwat0273	atlantic north	1746	BOWLES	1800	59	96	To Arthur Dobbs ... This Chart of the Seas Straits &c
mwm0040a	mediterranean	1720	BOWLES	800	58	98	To the Right Honourable ... This Sea Chart of all the Sea Ports of Europe (2 text columns in borders)
mwe0220	europe	1789	BOWLES-CARVER	1500	104	120	Bowles's New Four-Sheet Map of Europe, Divided into it's Empires, Kingdoms, States, Republicks and Principalities
mwuk0507	scotland	1760	BOWLES-SAYER	400	55	48	A Map of North Britain or Scotland from the Newest Surveys & Observations
mwuk0508	scotland	1760	BOWLES-SAYER	400	55	48	A Map of North Britain or Scotland from the Newest Surveys & Observations
mwuk1260	england london	1796	BOWLES-CARVER	2000	45	94	Bowles's Two Sheeet Plan of the Cities of London & Westminster; with the Borough of Southwark (13 editions until 1825)
mwam1023	america north (east)	1771	BOWLER-EVANS	2400	49	64	A General Map of the Middle British Colonies in America, viz. Virginia, Maryland, Delaware, Pensilvania, New Jersey, New York, Connecticut & Rhode Island ... Carefully Copied from the Original Publish'd at Philadelphia by Mr. Lewis Evans (First publ. 1755)

AMPG REFERENCE	REGION	DATE	MAP MAKER	PRICE (UK£)	VERT. (cm.)	HOR. (cm.)	TITLE OF MAP (Comments by the editor in brackets)
mwru0338	russia	1815	BOWYER	200	38	25	A Map Exhibiting the Retreat of the French Army from Moscow to Paris
mwit0331	italy elba	1815	BOWYER	400	34	22	Map of the Island of Elba
mwru0404	russia moscow	1814	BOWYER	650	28	52	Moscow
mwuk1443	england thames	1795	BOYDELL	450	32	60	(Thames River, through London into King's Channel)
mwam0747	america north	1841	BOYNTON	1000	64	61	A Map of the United States, from the Latest Surveys, with the Height of Mountains and Length of the Principal Rivers. Patent. Printed by Joseph W. Tuttle Boston (printed on linen)
mwuss0893	massachusetts	1845	BOYNTON	350	46	39	A New & Complete Map of the City of Boston, with Part of Charlestown, Cambridge & Roxbury. From the Best Authorities
mwuss0891	massachusetts	1844	BOYNTON	120	24	29	City of Boston
mwam1308	great lakes	1835	BOYNTON	250	20	25	Michigan and the Great Lakes
mwuss1482	rhode isl	1850	BOYNTON	200	15	11	Rhode Island
mwam0613	america north	1819	BRADBURY	300	31	41	Map of the United States of America, Comprehending the Western Territory with the Course of the Missouri
mwaf0324	africa	1835	BRADFORD	100	19	25	Africa
mwuss0014	alabama	1838	BRADFORD	150	37	28	Alabama
mwuss0060	arkansas	1838	BRADFORD	150	28	37	Arkansas
mwat0064	atlantic ocean (all)	1842	BRADFORD	150	37	30	Atlantic Ocean
mwuss0781	maryland	1838	BRADFORD	240	29	36	Baltimore
mwuss0883	massachusetts	1838	BRADFORD	200	28	37	Boston
mwca0177	canada	1835	BRADFORD	80	20	25	British America
mwc0269	china	1835	BRADFORD	60	20	25	China, Japan &c.
mwuss0322	connecticut	1838	BRADFORD	150	29	36	Connecticut
mwuss0320	connecticut	1835	BRADFORD	150	20	25	Connecticut and Rhode Island
mwuss0383	delaware	1838	BRADFORD	175	37	28	Delaware
mwuss0350	washington DC	1835	BRADFORD	200	25	20	District of Columbia
mwuss0477	florida	1838	BRADFORD	225	37	28	Florida
mwf0197	france	1835	BRADFORD	60	20	25	France
mwuss0530	georgia	1838	BRADFORD	200	37	28	Georgia
mwuss0558	illinois	1838	BRADFORD	150	37	28	Illinois
mwuss0555	illinois	1835	BRADFORD	120	25	20	Illinois & Missouri
mwuss0577	indiana	1838	BRADFORD	150	37	28	Indiana
mwuss0575	indiana	1835	BRADFORD	120	20	25	Indiana & Ohio
mwuss0582	iowa	1838	BRADFORD	280	37	28	Iowa and Wisconsin
mwit0246	italy	1835	BRADFORD	80	25	20	Italy
mwuss0615	kentucky	1838	BRADFORD	150	28	37	Kentucky
mwuss0677	louisiana	1838	BRADFORD	150	28	37	Louisiana
mwuss0676	louisiana	1835	BRADFORD	100	25	20	Louisiana and Part of Arkansas
mwca0183	canada	1838	BRADFORD	150	29	36	Lower Canada and New Brunswick
mwuss0730	maine	1838	BRADFORD	150	37	28	Maine
mwam0723	america north	1839	BRADFORD	240	27	45	Map of the United States and Texas
mwuss0780	maryland	1838	BRADFORD	180	29	36	Maryland
mwuss0882	massachusetts	1838	BRADFORD	150	28	37	Massachusetts
mwgm0071	gulf of mexico and surrounding regions	1835	BRADFORD	200	20	25	Mexico, Guatemala and the West Indies
mwuss0920	michigan	1838	BRADFORD	225	37	28	Michigan
mwuss0914	michigan	1835	BRADFORD	150	20	25	Michigan and the Great Lakes
mwuss0966	mississippi	1838	BRADFORD	150	36	28	Mississippi
mwuss0964	mississippi	1835	BRADFORD	100	20	25	Mississippi & Alabama
mwuss0988	missouri	1838	BRADFORD	150	28	37	Missouri
mwuss0985	missouri	1835	BRADFORD	150	25	20	Missouri, Illinois and Iowa
mwuss1026	new hampshire	1838	BRADFORD	150	37	28	New Hampshire
mwuss1024	new hampshire	1835	BRADFORD	150	25	19	New Hampshire & Vermont
mwuss1061	new jersey	1838	BRADFORD	150	37	28	New Jersey
mwuss1235	new york	1838	BRADFORD	300	37	28	New York
mwam0714	america north	1838	BRADFORD	180	37	28	North America
mwuss0277	carolinas	1838	BRADFORD	150	28	37	North Carolina
mwuss0275	carolinas	1835	BRADFORD	100	20	25	North Carolina, South Carolina, and Georgia
mwaf0730	africa north	1835	BRADFORD	60	20	25	Northern Africa
mww0705	world	1835	BRADFORD	200	15	24	Northern Hemisphere-Southern Hemisphere
mwp0525	pacific south	1835	BRADFORD	120	20	25	Oceanica or Oceania
mwuss1315	ohio	1838	BRADFORD	100	36	29	Ohio
mwp0283	pacific (all)	1835	BRADFORD	100	20	25	Pacific Ocean
mwme0417	holy land	1837	BRADFORD	80	25	19	Palestine or the Holy Land
mwuss1428	pennsylvania	1838	BRADFORD	150	28	36	Pennsylvania
mwuss1426	pennsylvania	1835	BRADFORD	150	20	25	Pennsylvania & New Jersey
mwuss1430	pennsylvania	1838	BRADFORD	150	37	28	Philadelphia
mwam0696	america north	1835	BRADFORD	120	25	20	Railroad Map of the United States
mwuss1479	rhode isl	1838	BRADFORD	150	37	28	Rhode Island
mwuss0276	carolinas	1838	BRADFORD	180	29	36	South Carolina
mwaf1014	africa south	1835	BRADFORD	100	20	25	Southern Africa
mwuss1496	tennessee	1838	BRADFORD	150	28	37	Tennessee
mwuss1495	tennessee	1835	BRADFORD	120	20	25	Tennessee & Kentucky

AMPG REFERENCE	REGION	DATE	MAP MAKER	PRICE (UK£)	VERT. (cm.)	HOR. (cm.)	TITLE OF MAP (Comments by the editor in brackets)
mwuss1507	texas	1838	BRADFORD	2500	37	28	Texas
mwsam0259	south america argentina	1835	BRADFORD	80	25	20	United Provinces Chili & Patagonia
mwam0713	america north	1838	BRADFORD	400	37	57	United States
mwam0695	america north	1835	BRADFORD	180	19	25	United States, Exhibiting the Railroads & Canals
mwca0179	canada	1835	BRADFORD	120	20	25	Upper and Lower Canada
mwca0184	canada	1838	BRADFORD	235	28	37	Upper Canada
mwuss1578	vermont	1838	BRADFORD	150	37	28	Vermont
mwuss1686	virginia	1838	BRADFORD	180	28	37	Virginia
mwuss1688	virginia	1840	BRADFORD	150	35	50	Virginia, Maryland and Delaware
mwuss0355	washington DC	1838	BRADFORD	250	29	36	Washington / Cincinnati / Louisville / New Orleans
mwwi0202	west indies	1838	BRADFORD	150	28	37	West Indies
mww0706	world	1835	BRADFORD	240	24	19	Western Hemisphere / Eastern Hemisphere (2 maps)
mwam1148	america north (east)	1804	BRADLEY		98	132	Map of the United States, Exhibiting the Post-Roads (shown left is 1st edition, 1796)
mwuk0893	uk	1839	BRADSHAW	3000	162	100	Map & Sections of the Railways of Great Britain (first railway map. Illustrated is 1841 re-issue)
mwuk1399	england south	1830	BRADSHAW	2000	186	95	Map of the Canals, Navigable Rivers, Railways, &c. in the Southern Counties of England
mwit0527	italy milan	1589	BRAMBILLA	2500	38	52	La Gran Citta di Milano
mwsp0378	spain regions	1585	BRAMBILLA	2400	48	72	Toledo
mwit0709	italy rome	1582	BRAMBILLA	3000	41	54	Urbis Romae Descriptio
mww0011	world	1491	BRANDIS	35000	31		(Circular map - 5 further editions until c1555. A reduced size version of the 1489 map.)
mww0010	world	1489	BRANDIS		37		(Circular map, slightly reduced version of the 1475 map, publ. by Brandis)
mww0002	world	1475	BRANDIS		38		(Circular untitled map, north to the left. From the first travel book 'Rudimentum Novitiorum'. The first printed map to be more than a diagram, publ. by Lucas Brandis. See also under 'Middle East'.)
mwme0001	holy land	1475	BRANDIS		41	58	(Text top left: Cedar et tabernacla eius Aras wecha unde baldach in Job. (From the book 'Rudimentum novitiorum sive chronicarum historiarum epitome', publ. by Lucas Brandis. The first printed modern map, north to the left.)
mwme0009	holy land	1491	BRANDIS		31	43	Cedar et ses tabernacles (reduced size version of the 1475 map).
mwg0757	westphalia	1576	BRAUN & HOGENBERG	480	32	39	(Aachen) Aquisgranum, vulgo Aich
mwit0705	italy rome	1572	BRAUN & HOGENBERG	1200	38	51	(Ancient Rome) Urbis Romae Situs cum iis quae adhuc Conspiciuntur Veter. Monumet Reliquiis Pyrrho Ligorio Neap. Invent. Romae M.D.LXX
mwbh0043	belgium holland	1572	BRAUN & HOGENBERG	1000	34	48	(Antwerp) Anverpia, nobile in Brabantia oppidum
mwg0303	bavaria	1572	BRAUN & HOGENBERG	600	33	47	(Augsburg) Augusta Iuxta Figuram
mwf0382	france burgundy	1580	BRAUN & HOGENBERG	600	36	50	(Besancon) Vesontio Sequanorum Gallis Besanson Germanis Byzantz
mwf0639	france loire	1575	BRAUN & HOGENBERG	400	31	45	(Blois) Bloys
mwsp0012	portugal	1594	BRAUN & HOGENBERG	600	36	50	(Braga) Nova Bracarae Auguste Descriptio
mwg0560	saxony	1580	BRAUN & HOGENBERG	500	37	49	(Bremen) Brema
mwbp0195	poland	1588	BRAUN & HOGENBERG	1200	36	48	(Breslau) Wratislavia
mwec1154	uk england sussex	1581	BRAUN & HOGENBERG	720	35	44	(Bristol) Brightstowe
mwbh0067	belgium holland	1575	BRAUN & HOGENBERG	800	33	48	(Bruges) Brugae, Flandricarum Urbium Ornamenta
mwsp0354	spain regions	1572	BRAUN & HOGENBERG	750	37	49	(Cadiz) Gades ab Occiduis Insulae Partibus
mwin0091	india	1572	BRAUN & HOGENBERG	1000	34	48	(Calcutta) Calechut Celeberrimum Indiae Emporium / Ormus / Canonor / S. Georgii Oppidum Mina
mwec0080	uk england cambridgeshire	1575	BRAUN & HOGENBERG	1200	33	45	(Cambridge) Cantebrigia, Opulentissimi Angliae Regni
mwaf0675	africa north	1572	BRAUN & HOGENBERG	250	10	23	(Casablanca) Anfa, Quisbusdam Anaffa
mwf0379	france burgundy	1572	BRAUN & HOGENBERG	500	33	23	(Chalon sur Saone) Cabillinum, Indigenis, Chalon, ut Agri Uberrimi, ita Saluberrimi Coeli, ac Proinde Eximie Felix Burgundiae Opp.
mwsp0003	portugal	1574	BRAUN & HOGENBERG	600	29	46	(Coimbra) Illustris Civitatis Conimbirae in Lusitania
mwg0755	westphalia	1572	BRAUN & HOGENBERG	1000	34	48	(Cologne) Colonia Aggrippina
mwgr0456	greece cyprus	1574	BRAUN & HOGENBERG	850	16	23	Famagusta (part of a map of Cagliari, Valletta, Rhodus, Famugusta. Price is for the complete map)
mwbh0088	belgium holland	1580	BRAUN & HOGENBERG	800	34	48	(Ghent) Gandavum, Aplissima Flandriae Urbs
mwe0861	europe hungary	1597	BRAUN & HOGENBERG	400	36	51	(Gyor) Iaverinum vulgo Rab Anno 1594
mwsc0234	scandinavia denmark	1588	BRAUN & HOGENBERG	800	34	48	(Hven) Topographia Insulae Huenae in Celebri Porthmo Regni Daniae, quem vulgo Oersunt Vocant
mwe0301	europe austria	1598	BRAUN & HOGENBERG	650	36	51	(Innsbruck) Elegantissimus a Parte Orientali Oenipontis Prospectus
mwe0284	europe austria	1575	BRAUN & HOGENBERG	720	34	44	(Innsbruck) Oenipons, sive Enipontus vulgo Insspruck, Tirolensis Comitatus Urbs Amplissima MDLXXV
mwbp0218	poland	1617	BRAUN & HOGENBERG	960	33	45	(Kalwarya) Mons Calvariae
mwg0688	schleswig-holstein	1580	BRAUN & HOGENBERG	550	33	48	(Kiel) Chilonium, vulgo Kyell
mwe1091	europe slovak republic (moravia)	1595	BRAUN & HOGENBERG	500	37	48	(Komarno) Comorra
mwg0548	saxony	1572	BRAUN & HOGENBERG	500	27	46	(Leipzig) Lipsiae Insignis Saxoniae Urbis et Celeberrimi Emporij Vera Effigies
mwbh0044	belgium holland	1572	BRAUN & HOGENBERG	650	33	48	(Liege) Leodium

AMPG REFERENCE	REGION	DATE	MAP MAKER	PRICE (UK£)	VERT. (cm.)	HOR. (cm.)	TITLE OF MAP (Comments by the editor in brackets)
mwg0763	westphalia	1590	BRAUN & HOGENBERG	720	35	44	(Lippstadt) Lippe / Dortmund
mwbh0045	belgium holland	1572	BRAUN & HOGENBERG	500	35	49	(Louvain / Leuven) Lovanium, Brabanticarum Urbium Caput
mwbp0219	poland	1617	BRAUN & HOGENBERG	960	33	49	(Lowicz) Lovicensis Civitas
mwf1163	france lyon	1575	BRAUN & HOGENBERG	800	33	48	(Lyon) Lugdunum
mwbh0064	belgium holland	1575	BRAUN & HOGENBERG	1000	37	50	(Maastricht) Traiectum ad Mosam
mwg0582	saxony	1617	BRAUN & HOGENBERG	400	33	45	(Meissen) Marienberg Misniae Civitas
mwg0551	saxony	1572	BRAUN & HOGENBERG	500	33	48	(Meissen) Misena Hermundurorum Urbis
mwg0313	bavaria	1588	BRAUN & HOGENBERG	1000	30	49	(Munich) Monachium Utriusque Bavariae Civitas Primar
mwe0858	europe hungary	1595	BRAUN & HOGENBERG	720	33	46	(Neuhausel) Owar Germanice Nieuhuisel / Vizzegrad, Germanice Plindeburg
mwec0801	uk england norfolk	1575	BRAUN & HOGENBERG	800	29	42	(Norwich) Nordovicum, Angliae Civitas
mwe0754	europe east	1617	BRAUN & HOGENBERG	800	34	46	(Oradea, in Romania) Varadinum vulgo Gros Wardein
mwf0815	france paris	1572	BRAUN & HOGENBERG	2500	34	48	(Paris) Lutetia vulgari Nomine Paris, Urbs Galliae Maxima, Sequana Navigabili Flumine Irrigatur
mwg0473	mecklenburg	1572	BRAUN & HOGENBERG	720	35	48	(Rostock) Rostochium Urbs Vandalica Anseatica et Megapolitana
mwe0865	europe hungary	1617	BRAUN & HOGENBERG	500	32	44	(Saros-Patak) Zaros Superioris Hungariae Civitas
mwg0584	saxony	1617	BRAUN & HOGENBERG	400	39	51	(Stade) Staden
mwaf0812	africa north tunisia	1572	BRAUN & HOGENBERG	720	32	42	(Tunis, Tunisia) Tunes Urbs - Tunetis Urbis, ac Novae Eius Arcis, et Guletae, quae Philippo Hispan Regi Parent
mwg0761	westphalia	1580	BRAUN & HOGENBERG	480	34	42	(Werden) / (Essen)
mwbh0066	belgium holland	1575	BRAUN & HOGENBERG	450	34	32	(Ypres) Hypra Flandriarum Civitas Munitissima
mwaf0348	africa east	1582	BRAUN & HOGENBERG	800	33	47	Aden / Mombaza / Quiloa / Cefala
mwme0536	arabia etc	1572	BRAUN & HOGENBERG	800	34	48	Aden, Arabiae Foelicis Emporium Celeberrimi Nominis, quo ex India, Aethiopia / Mombaza / Quiloa / Cefala
mwaf0461	africa egypt etc	1572	BRAUN & HOGENBERG	1000	37	49	Alexandria, Vetustissimum Aegypti Emporium, Amplissima Civitas
mwaf0736	africa north algeria	1600	BRAUN & HOGENBERG	1000	35	49	Algerii Saracenorum Urbis Fortissimae
mwsp0362	spain regions	1575	BRAUN & HOGENBERG	450	34	46	Alhama
mwbp0180	poland	1572	BRAUN & HOGENBERG	720	34	48	Alten Stettin
mwbh0046	belgium holland	1572	BRAUN & HOGENBERG	1800	34	49	Amstelredamum, Nobile Inferioris Germaniae Oppidum
mwit0548	italy marches	1578	BRAUN & HOGENBERG	600	33	48	Ancona Civitas Piceni Celeberrima, ad Mare Adriaticum Posita
mwit0710	italy rome	1588	BRAUN & HOGENBERG	2400	36	49	Antiquae Urbis Romae Imago Accuratiss (2 sheets of 36x49cm.)
mwbh0137	belgium holland	1598	BRAUN & HOGENBERG	3400	45	71	Antverpia. Depingbat Georgi Hoefnag.
mwf0208	france alsace	1580	BRAUN & HOGENBERG	500	34	42	Argentoratum Strasburg
mwg0762	westphalia	1588	BRAUN & HOGENBERG	480	33	44	Arnsberg
mwf0992	france provence	1575	BRAUN & HOGENBERG	600	31	47	Avignon
mwg0324	bavaria	1617	BRAUN & HOGENBERG	600	37	51	Bambergae
mwsp0355	spain regions	1572	BRAUN & HOGENBERG	400	32	47	Barcelona, Barcino, que vulgo Barcelona Dicitur / Ecija
mwg0567	saxony	1588	BRAUN & HOGENBERG	450	38	51	Bardewick
mwsw0018a	switzerland	1575	BRAUN & HOGENBERG	720	37	37	Basilea.
mwsc0523	scandinavia norway	1588	BRAUN & HOGENBERG	2400	33	48	Bergen
mwsp0356	spain regions	1572	BRAUN & HOGENBERG	500	25	49	Bilvao. En, Spectator Benevole, Magnifica Hispaniae Civitas Bilbao
mwit0333	italy emilia-romagna	1572	BRAUN & HOGENBERG	720	33	50	Bononia Alma Studior Mater
mwbh0047	belgium holland	1572	BRAUN & HOGENBERG	1400	33	48	Bruxella, Urbs Aulicorum Frequentia, Fontium Copia, Magnificentia Principalis Aulae
mwe0866	europe hungary	1617	BRAUN & HOGENBERG	1400	32	48	Buda Citerioris Hungariae Caput ... vulgo Ofen
mwme0922	turkey etc	1572	BRAUN & HOGENBERG	2400	32	48	Byzantium, nunc Constantinopolis
mwaf0463	africa egypt etc	1583	BRAUN & HOGENBERG	1400	34	48	Cairus, quae olim Babylon; Aegypti Maxima Urbs
mwm0159	mediterranean islands	1572	BRAUN & HOGENBERG	900	33	47	Calaris / Malta / Rhodus / Famagusta
mwf0704	france nord pas-de-calais	1597	BRAUN & HOGENBERG	450	32	39	Caletum, sive Calesium, vulgo Cales, Janua, Frenum, et Clavis Galliae
mwgr0350	greece crete	1575	BRAUN & HOGENBERG	1000	38	49	Candia / La Cita de Corphu
mwec0594	uk england kent	1588	BRAUN & HOGENBERG	1200	29	43	Cantuarbury
mwit0869	italy sicily	1580	BRAUN & HOGENBERG	720	37	49	Catana Urbs Siciliae Clarissima Patria Scte. Agathae Virginis et Mart
mwec0120	uk england cheshire	1580	BRAUN & HOGENBERG	1200	32	44	Cestria vulgo Chester, Angliae Civitas
mwgr0577	greece islands	1588	BRAUN & HOGENBERG	750	33	47	Chios
mwg0428	hessen	1572	BRAUN & HOGENBERG	900	34	48	Civitas Francofordiana ad Moe.
mwg0754	westphalia	1572	BRAUN & HOGENBERG	600	35	49	Cliviam, Ducatus Clivensis / Duisburgum, Oppidum Antiquissimum Vetus / Embrica, Clivensis Ditionis Oppidum /Gennapium, Ducatus Clivensis
mwg0507	rheinland-pfalz	1572	BRAUN & HOGENBERG	750	34	48	Colonia Agrippina
mwsp0402	spain regions	1618	BRAUN & HOGENBERG	600	33	50	Corduba
mwbp0225	poland	1618	BRAUN & HOGENBERG	6000	37	110	Cracovia Metropolis Regni Poloniae
mwbp0220	poland	1617	BRAUN & HOGENBERG	2500	31	55	Cracovia Minoris Poloniae Metropolis
mwe0527	europe czech republic (bohemia)	1617	BRAUN & HOGENBERG	500	37	47	Czaslavium vulgo Czasla Bohemiae Civitas / Commoda vulgo Comethau Bohemiae Civitas
mwme0862	syria etc	1575	BRAUN & HOGENBERG	1000	32	36	Damascus, Urbs Nobilissima ad Libanum Montem, Totius Syriae Metropolis
mwsc0231	scandinavia denmark	1585	BRAUN & HOGENBERG	1800	38	46	Danorum Marca, vel Cimbricum, aut Daniae Regnum (map, not view)
mwbp0181	poland	1572	BRAUN & HOGENBERG	1400	33	48	Dantzigt (Gdansk)

AMPG REFERENCE	REGION	DATE	MAP MAKER	PRICE (UK£)	VERT. (cm.)	HOR. (cm.)	TITLE OF MAP (Comments by the editor in brackets)
mwsw0017	switzerland	1572	BRAUN & HOGENBERG	800	37	47	Decem et Tria Loca Confoederatorum Helvetiae
mwg0196	germany north east	1572	BRAUN & HOGENBERG	800	20	41	Die Furstliche Hauptt Statt Konigssbergk in Preussen
mwbp0192	poland	1580	BRAUN & HOGENBERG	600	34	46	Die Stat Swybuschin in Nider Schlesien
mwg0559	saxony	1580	BRAUN & HOGENBERG	400	34	48	Dresden - Dresa Florentissimum Misniae Opp. Illust: Saxoniae Ducum Sedes / Leibzigk - Lipsia Litterarum Studiis et Mercatura Celebre Misniae Oppidum
mwuk0317	scotland	1581	BRAUN & HOGENBERG	1200	35	46	Edenburg - Edenburgum, Scotiae Metropolis
mwit1051	italy naples	1572	BRAUN & HOGENBERG	750	36	49	Elegantissimus ad Mare Tyrrhenum ex Monte Pausilipo Neapolis Montisque Vesuvius Prospectus
mwsc0245a	scandinavia denmark	1598	BRAUN & HOGENBERG	600	34	47	Elsenor / Ripen
mwg0561	saxony	1580	BRAUN & HOGENBERG	600	35	49	Emuda vulgo Embden Urbs Frisiae Orientalis Primaria
mwsc0236	scandinavia denmark	1588	BRAUN & HOGENBERG	800	33	48	Freti Danici or Sundt Accuratiss Delineatio. (north to the right. Incl. Copenhagen)
mwit0991	italy south	1585	BRAUN & HOGENBERG	300	37	51	Gallipolis
mwuk0024	ireland	1617	BRAUN & HOGENBERG	1200	31	44	Galwaye / Dubline / Lymericke / Corcke
mwit0410	italy liguria	1572	BRAUN & HOGENBERG	1000	33	48	Genua Ligurum / Florentia Urbs (2 views on one sheet)
mwin0393	india goa	1572	BRAUN & HOGENBERG	720	33	46	Goa fortissima Indiae urbs in Christianorum Potestatem Anno Salutis 1509 Devenit / Diu /Azaamurum / Anfa
mwsp0358	spain regions	1572	BRAUN & HOGENBERG	650	33	51	Granada 1563
mwsp0386	spain regions	1598	BRAUN & HOGENBERG	800	37	50	Granata. Effigiebat Georgius Houfnaglius, Anno MDLXV
mwit1050	italy naples	1572	BRAUN & HOGENBERG	1200	34	41	Haec est Nobilis, & Florens Illa Neapolis
mwsc0235	scandinavia denmark	1588	BRAUN & HOGENBERG	1350	37	42	Hafnia vulgo Kopenhagen (2 views on one sheet)
mwg0685	schleswig-holstein	1572	BRAUN & HOGENBERG	1200	37	48	Hamburgum
mwsp0387	spain regions	1598	BRAUN & HOGENBERG	350	37	48	Hardales / Cartama
mwme0438	jerusalem	1575	BRAUN & HOGENBERG	2000	33	42	Hierosolyma Urbs Sancta, Iudeae, Totiusque Orientis Longe Clarissima
mwme0438a	jerusalem	1575	BRAUN & HOGENBERG	1400	34	49	Hierosolyma, Clarissima totius Orientis Civitas Iudaee Metropolis (text top left. Maps of old and new Jerusalem)
mwme0441	jerusalem	1588	BRAUN & HOGENBERG	4000	37	49	Ierusalem, et Suburbia eius, sicut Tempore Christi Floruit, cum Locis in quibus Christ Passus ... Descripta per Christianum Adrichom Delphum (in 2 sheets, each 37x49cm, based on Adrichom)
mwsp0388	spain regions	1598	BRAUN & HOGENBERG	600	34	49	La Muy Noble y Muy Leal Civdas de Cadiz [on sheet with] Almodrava de Caditz sive Thynnorum Piscatio apud Cades
mwf0694	france nord pas-de-calais	1581	BRAUN & HOGENBERG	400	33	43	Lille - Insula
mwe0283	europe austria	1572	BRAUN & HOGENBERG	720	36	49	Linsum Austriae vulgo Lintz
mwsp0006	portugal	1580	BRAUN & HOGENBERG	1200	35	48	Lisbona. Olisipo ... vulgo Lisbona Florentissimum Portugalliae Emporiv. / Cascale Lusitaniae Opp.
mwuk1101	england london	1572	BRAUN & HOGENBERG	7500	34	49	Londinum Feracissimi Angliae Regni Metropolis
mwg0689	schleswig-holstein	1580	BRAUN & HOGENBERG	500	33	47	Lubeca Urbs Imperialis ... Inclytae Hanseaticae Societatis Caput / Hamburga, Florentissimum Inferioris Saxoniae Emporium
mwit1090	italy tuscany	1572	BRAUN & HOGENBERG	800	36	53	Luca
mwbh0812	luxembourg	1580	BRAUN & HOGENBERG	1500	36	46	Lucenburgum Urbs eiusdem Nominis Ducatus Primaria
mwf1163a	france lyon	1598	BRAUN & HOGENBERG	600	34	48	Lugdunum vulgo Lion / Vienna vulgo Vienne
mwbh0813	luxembourg	1581	BRAUN & HOGENBERG	1000	35	42	Lutzenburgum, Ducatus eiusdem Nominis, Vetus et Primaria Urbs
mwit1164	italy veneto	1588	BRAUN & HOGENBERG	750	36	47	Magnifica Illa Civitas Verona (view) / Colonia Augusta Verona Nova Galieniana Verona, Celeberrima, Amplissimaque Cenomanorum Urbs, Ptolemaeo
mwit0463	italy lombardy	1575	BRAUN & HOGENBERG	720	36	50	Mantua
mwg0427	hessen	1572	BRAUN & HOGENBERG	800	34	48	Marpurg. - Martpurgum Urbs Hassiae Metropolis, Universitate Clara / Cassel. - Cassula, Communiter Cassel, Florentissimu Lanigerae Oppidum
mwf0993	france provence	1575	BRAUN & HOGENBERG	500	32	36	Marseille
mwbh0077	belgium holland	1578	BRAUN & HOGENBERG	500	34	46	Mechelen - Nittidissimae Civitatis Mechlineensis in Meditulli Brabantiae Sitae, Exactis, Delineatio
mwit0525	italy milan	1572	BRAUN & HOGENBERG	1000	33	48	Mediolanum
mwit0870	italy sicily	1580	BRAUN & HOGENBERG	900	34	48	Messinae
mwgm0133	mexico	1572	BRAUN & HOGENBERG	1600	27	48	Mexico, Regia et Celebris Hispaniae Novae Civitas / Cusco, Regni Peru in Novo Orbe Caput
mwru0377	russia moscow	1575	BRAUN & HOGENBERG	3000	35	49	Moscauw
mwru0379	russia moscow	1617	BRAUN & HOGENBERG	3000	35	46	Moscovia Urbs Metropolis Totius Russiae Albae
mwbh0051	belgium holland	1572	BRAUN & HOGENBERG	450	35	44	Namurcum Elegantissima ad Mosae Flume Civatis
mwbp0182	poland	1572	BRAUN & HOGENBERG	1200	33	45	Nissa Silesior Sedes Episcopalis / Liginicium
mwg0306	bavaria	1575	BRAUN & HOGENBERG	1000	34	47	Nurnberg - Norenberga, Urbs Nobilissima
mwsp0017	portugal	1600	BRAUN & HOGENBERG	1400	36	47	Olissippo quae nunc Lisboa, Civitas Amplissima Lusitaniae
mwit1144	italy umbria	1572	BRAUN & HOGENBERG	600	36	48	Orivetum vulgo Orvieto Thusciae, Noblissimae Italiae Regionis Opp. / Lavretum, Agri Recenaten in Italia Celebre Opp: A D. Mariae Antiquissima ibi Sita Aede Illustratum
mwf0638	france loire	1575	BRAUN & HOGENBERG	400	37	47	Orleans / Bourges
mwbh0188	belgium holland	1617	BRAUN & HOGENBERG	600	35	47	Ostenda
mwit0383	italy lazio	1572	BRAUN & HOGENBERG	600	35	50	Ostia
mwec0933	uk england oxfordshire	1575	BRAUN & HOGENBERG	1200	37	49	Oxonium Nobile Anglie Oppidum [on sheet with] Vindesorium Celeberrimum Angliae Castrum

AMPG REFERENCE	REGION	DATE	MAP MAKER	PRICE (UK£)	VERT. (cm.)	HOR. (cm.)	TITLE OF MAP (Comments by the editor in brackets)
mwe0519	europe czech republic (bohemia)	1588	BRAUN & HOGENBERG	2000	36	50	Palatium Imperatorum Pragae quod vulgo Ratzin Appellatur / Praga Regni Bohemiae Metropolis
mwit0872	italy sicily	1580	BRAUN & HOGENBERG	800	32	49	Palermo - Panormus Corona Regis et Urbium Sicularum Maxima, Emporium Celebratissimum
mwe0867	europe hungary	1617	BRAUN & HOGENBERG	800	33	49	Papa, Inferioris Hungariae Oppidum
mwit1145	italy umbria	1588	BRAUN & HOGENBERG	800	37	44	Perusia Gratumusis in Tuscia Domicilium (Perugia)
mwe0526	europe czech republic (bohemia)	1616	BRAUN & HOGENBERG	500	32	49	Polna vulgo Polm Insign. Bohemiae
mwe0515	europe czech republic (bohemia)	1572	BRAUN & HOGENBERG	800	33	46	Praga, Bohemiae Metropolis Accuratissime Expressa / Egra, Urbs a Fluvio
mwe1089	europe slovak republic (moravia)	1588	BRAUN & HOGENBERG	1000	30	49	Pressburg
mwit0879a	italy sicily	1620	BRAUN & HOGENBERG	1000	32	49	Prospectus Freti Siculi, vulgo il Faro de Messina
mwit0267	italy campagna	1585	BRAUN & HOGENBERG	500	29	49	Puteoli / Baiae
mwf0763	france normandy	1572	BRAUN & HOGENBERG	500	30	38	Rhotomagus, Galliae Lugdunensis ... Rouen
mwit0706	italy rome	1572	BRAUN & HOGENBERG	1800	34	49	Roma
mwbh0122	belgium holland	1588	BRAUN & HOGENBERG	1400	29	40	Roterodamum
mwf0962	france poitou	1598	BRAUN & HOGENBERG	450	36	46	Saintes
mwe0292	europe austria	1580	BRAUN & HOGENBERG	800	33	51	Saltzburgk. Recens et Accuratissima Urbis Salisburgensis Delineatio
mwe0855	europe hungary	1572	BRAUN & HOGENBERG	350	33	45	Sanctonicolaum vulgo S. Nicolas Oppidum in Superiore Hungaria
mwsp0364	spain regions	1575	BRAUN & HOGENBERG	400	32	35	Santander
mwbp0221	poland	1617	BRAUN & HOGENBERG	900	32	45	Sendomiria / Biecz
mwit1163	italy veneto	1585	BRAUN & HOGENBERG	600	33	49	Seravallum Celeberrimum Marchiae Tarusiniae
mwsp0380	spain regions	1588	BRAUN & HOGENBERG	1200	38	50	Sevilla
mwe0646	europe dalmatia	1575	BRAUN & HOGENBERG	550	35	49	Sibinium, Ptolemeo Sicum vulgo Sibenicho. Dalmatie Opp. / Parens, sive Parentium vulgo, Parenzo Histriae Opp. / Modon, sive Modona, quondam Methone, Civitas est Littoralis Pelopponesi, in Morea
mwsc0661	scandinavia sweden	1588	BRAUN & HOGENBERG	1600	33	49	Stockholm / Stocholm (2 views on one sheet)
mwe0859	europe hungary	1595	BRAUN & HOGENBERG	600	35	51	Strigonium. Gran
mwaf0676	africa north	1572	BRAUN & HOGENBERG	600	33	48	Tingis Lusitanis Tangiara / Tzaffin / Septa / Arzilla / Sala
mwbp0222	poland	1617	BRAUN & HOGENBERG	1800	31	50	Tipus Civitatis Lublinesi in Regno Poloniae
mwsp0359	spain regions	1572	BRAUN & HOGENBERG	850	38	50	Toletum
mwsp0360	spain regions	1572	BRAUN & HOGENBERG	850	33	47	Toletum / Vallisoletum
mwit1081	italy trentino-alto	1588	BRAUN & HOGENBERG	600	37	46	Tridentum. Trient
mwaf0813	africa north tunisia	1575	BRAUN & HOGENBERG	450	33	47	Tunes, Oppidum Barbarie & Regia Sedes 1535 / Africa olim Aphrodisum / Penon de Veles
mwf0644	france loire	1590	BRAUN & HOGENBERG	400	35	46	Turones vulgo Tours. Le Jardin de France / Andegavum vulgo Angiers.
mwf0668a	france lorraine	1617	BRAUN & HOGENBERG	400	34	46	Urbis Nancei Lotharingiae Metropolis
mwbp0223	poland	1617	BRAUN & HOGENBERG	4000	32	47	Varsovia
mwit1212	italy venice	1572	BRAUN & HOGENBERG	2500	34	48	Venetia
mwe0410	europe austria vienna	1572	BRAUN & HOGENBERG	1000	31	47	Vienna Austria Metropolis, Urbs Toto Orbe Notissima Celebratissimaq, Unicum Hodie in Oriente contra Saevissimum Turcam Invictum Propugnacvium / Buda, vulgo Ofen (2 views on one map)
mwe0410b	europe austria vienna	1617	BRAUN & HOGENBERG	2000	34	49	Vienna Austriae (after Hoefnagel)
mwbp0070	baltic states	1588	BRAUN & HOGENBERG	1200	37	50	Vilna Lituaniae Metropolis
mwg0737	thuringia	1580	BRAUN & HOGENBERG	500	35	48	Weinmar - Winmaria, Fertiliss. Thuringiae Urbs Praestantissima vulgo Weinmar
mwbp0224	poland	1617	BRAUN & HOGENBERG	1200	35	46	Zamoscium
mwsw0023	switzerland	1580	BRAUN & HOGENBERG	2000	36	48	Zurych - Tigurum, sive Turegum, Caesari, ut Plerique Existimant, Tigurinus Pagus, vulgo Zurych, Urbs in Helvetijs
mwit0291a	italy campagna	1801	BREISLAK	675	66	56	Carte Physique de la Campanie
mwit0522	italy lombardy	1833	BRENNA	300	69	85	Carta Topografica dei Contorni di Milano
mwca0022	canada	1657	BRESSANI	100000	51	75	Novae Franciae Accurata Delineatio 1657
mwf0863	france paris	1739	BRETEZ-TURGOT	15000	250	320	Plan de Paris (20 sheets)
mwuss0143a	california	1854	BRIDGENS	20000	104	186	Map of the City of San Francisco Compiled from Records & Surveys by R.P. Bridgens, C.E. Respectfully Dedicated to the Citizens by the Publisher M. Bixby 1854
mwit0281a	italy campagna	1649	BRIET	200	19	15	Campania et Samnium Descriptio
mwit0831a	italy sardinia and corsica	1648	BRIET	240	14	19	Corsica seu Cyrnus / Sardinia Vetus (2 maps on one sheet, shown below left)
mwgr0378	greece crete	1648	BRIET	300	19	14	Creta
mwe0057	europe	1648	BRIET	300	15	20	Europae Antiquae Delineatio
mwit0418b	italy liguria	1649	BRIET	180	16	20	Gallia Cispadana (shown above left)
mwuk0055	ireland	1648	BRIET	300	19	15	Hibernia seu Britannia Minor cum aliqt Insulis (inset of Orkneys)
mwit0093	italy	1649	BRIET	200	16	20	Italia Antiqua
mwit0579	italy north	1649	BRIET	250	16	20	Italiae Antiquae pars Septentrionale
mwit0093a	italy	1649	BRIET	200	16	20	Italiae Divisio per Augustum in XI regiones
mwit0261c	italy abruzzo	1649	BRIET	280	15	19	L'Abruzzo et Le Conte de Molisse
mwam0053	america continent	1648	BRIET	600	18	14	La Division de l'Ocean du Nouveau Monde
mwit0578	italy north	1649	BRIET	250	15	20	La Partie Septentrionale d'Italie

AMPG REFERENCE	REGION	DATE	MAP MAKER	PRICE (UK£)	VERT. (cm.)	HOR. (cm.)	TITLE OF MAP (Comments by the editor in brackets)
mwru0045a	russia	1649	BRIET	200	16	20	La Russie ou Moscovie
mwsp0032	portugal	1649	BRIET	300	19	15	Le Royaume de Portugal
mwuk0057	ireland	1653	BRIET	200	15	19	Le Royaume d'Irlande (shown above left)
mwm0184	mediterranean malta	1649	BRIET	1000	14	19	L'Isle de Malte avec ses Voisines / Les Isles Occidentales de Sicile / Les Isles de Lipari au desus de Sicile / La Valete Forte Place de Malte
mwgr0071	greece	1649	BRIET	180	16	20	Macedonia, Thessalia, Epirus
mwm0007a	mediterranean	1640	BRIET	600	31	51	Roma Gentium Domina
mwjk0027	japan	1658	BRIET	2400	37	52	Royaume du Iapon
mwe0446	europe bosnia	1740	BRIFFAUT	2000	61	91	Le Royaume de Bosnie (title text above map)
mwam0312	america north	1625	BRIGGS-PURCHAS	15000	29	35	The North Part of America Conteyning Newfoundland, New England, Virginia, Florida, New Spaine, and Nova Francia, wth ye Riche Iles of Hispaniola, Cuba, Jamaica, and Porto Rico on the South, and upon ye West the Large and Goodly Iland of California
mwas0237	asia continent	1806	BRIGHTLY KINNERSLEY	75	19	23	Asia from the latest Authorities
mwf0174	france	1806	BRIGHTLY KINNERSLEY	50	18	21	France Divided into Circles and Departments
mww0629	world	1807	BRIGHTLY KINNERSLEY	200	18	35	Map of the World from the Best Authorities
mwam0568	america north	1806	BRIGHTLY KINNERSLEY	135	18	22	North America from the Best Authorities
mwsw0220	switzerland	1807	BRIGHTLY KINNERSLEY	50	17	22	Switzerland
mwwi0152	west indies	1806	BRIGHTLY KINNERSLEY	120	20	33	West Indies from the Best Authorities
mwm0192	mediterranean malta	1665	BRIGONCI	300	12	12	Malta Malta Citta
mwjk0112	japan	1770	BRION	450	25	35	Carte de la Coree et du Japon
mwaf0192	africa	1750	BRION DE LA TOUR	220	28	27	Afrique (text panels at sides, not incl. in dimensions)
mwam0480	america north	1783	BRION DE LA TOUR	950	49	64	Amerique Septentrionale Divisee en ses Principales Parties, ou sont Distingues les Uns des Autres les Estats
mwc0197a	china	1780	BRION DE LA TOUR	550	40	49	Carta della Tartaria Cinese e dei Paesi Limitrofi
mwbp0494	poland	1776	BRION DE LA TOUR	500	36	40	Carte Curieuse des Nouvelles Limites de la Pologne de l'Empire Ottoman, et des Etats Voisins
mwc0178	china	1770	BRION DE LA TOUR	280	35	34	Carte de la Chine, avec la Tartarie Chinoise, les Pays Conquis depuis 25 a 30 Ans, et les Etats Tributaires de cet Empire
mwam0958	america north (east)	1750	BRION DE LA TOUR	240	23	32	Carte de la Nouvelle Angleterre, Comprenant les Etats de Massachusets Bay, N. Hamp Shire, Connecticut et Rhode Island
mwgm0056	gulf of mexico and surrounding regions	1788	BRION DE LA TOUR	250	22	27	Carte de la Partie de l'Amerique Septentrionale, Comprenant les Possessions Espagnoles
mwg0174	germany	1818	BRION DE LA TOUR	250	53	75	Carte de l'Allemagne, Comprenant la Confederation Germanique l'Empire d'Autriche, les Royaumes Prusse, Hanovre, Bavare
mwp0264	pacific (all)	1790	BRION DE LA TOUR	280	23	23	Carte de Toutes les N.les Decouvertes dans la Mer du Sud, ou est Tracee la Route du Celebre Capitaine Cook, dans son Dernier Voyage
mwuss0950	mississippi	1790	BRION DE LA TOUR	550	23	27	Carte des Etats-Unis d'Amerique et du Cours du Mississipi
mwam0486	america north	1784	BRION DE LA TOUR	3500	51	70	Carte des Etats-Unis d'Amerique et du Cours du Mississipi; Redigee d'apres Differentes Cartes et Relations Anglaises, et les Operations de la Derniere Guerre
mwam0470	america north	1780	BRION DE LA TOUR	450	29	31	Carte des Etats-Unis de l'Amerique Septentrionale, Dressee d'apres des Cartes Anglaises
mwwi0117	west indies	1782	BRION DE LA TOUR	1200	52	75	Carte des Isles Antilles dans l'Amerique Septentrionale, avec la Majeure Partie des Isles Lucayes, Faisant Partie du Theatre de la Guerre entre les Anglais et les Americains
mwwi0126	west indies	1790	BRION DE LA TOUR	180	22	25	Carte des Isles Antilles et Lucayes, dans l'Amerique Septentrionale
mwuk0856	uk	1779	BRION DE LA TOUR	600	73	50	Carte des Isles Britanniques et de la Manche
mwas0801	asia south east philippines	1780	BRION DE LA TOUR	480	25	36	Carte des Isles Philippines
mwme0351	holy land	1766	BRION DE LA TOUR	150	27	29	Carte des Pays et Principaux Lieux Connus dans les Premiers Ages du Monde
mwuk0838a	uk	1756	BRION DE LA TOUR	650	50	62	Carte des Places Fortes et des Principaux Ports des Isles Britanniques et des Etats d'Hanovre
mwsp0313	spain	1808	BRION DE LA TOUR	720	73	82	Carte D'Espagne et de Portugal
mwca0110	canada	1784	BRION DE LA TOUR	4000	51	76	Carte du Canada et des Contrees Limitrophes, Formant la Suite du Theatre de la Guerre dans l'Amerique Septentrionale ... 1784
mwe1031	europe rhine	1792	BRION DE LA TOUR	720	86	56	Carte du Cours du Rhin depuis sa Source ... avec Tous les Pays qu'il Traverse
mwam1053a	new york	1778	BRION DE LA TOUR	2500	74	50	Carte du Theatre de la Guerre entre les Anglais et les Americains: Dressee d'apres les Cartes Anglaises les Plus Modernes
mwat0044	atlantic ocean (all)	1760	BRION DE LA TOUR	550	39	55	Carte Reduite de l'Ocean Occidental, Contenant les Cotes Occidentales de l'Europe et ... Cotes Orientales de l'Amerique
mwe0380	europe austria	1766	BRION DE LA TOUR	140	28	31	Cercle d'Autriche, Divise en Toutes ses Provinces, tant Civiles qu'Ecclesiastiques
mwg0397	bavaria	1792	BRION DE LA TOUR	240	28	30	Cercles de Baviere, de Franconie, et de Souabe
mwg0666	saxony	1766	BRION DE LA TOUR	320	36	51	Cercles de Haute et Basse Saxe Divises en Toutes les Principautes et Provinces

AMPG REFERENCE	REGION	DATE	MAP MAKER	PRICE (UK£)	VERT. (cm.)	HOR. (cm.)	TITLE OF MAP (Comments by the editor in brackets)
mwsam0103	south america	1786	BRION DE LA TOUR	240	27	31	Chili, Paraguay, Bresil, Amazones et Perou
mwc0205	china	1786	BRION DE LA TOUR	280	27	30	Chine et Indes avec les Isles
mwit1038	italy south	1766	BRION DE LA TOUR	220	27	29	Etat du Roi des Deux Siciles, avec les Metropoles Ecclesiastiques et Tous leurs Suffragans
mwe0602	europe czech republic (bohemia)	1766	BRION DE LA TOUR	240	27	31	Etats de Boheme Divises en Toutes leurs Provinces tant Civiles qu' Ecclesiastiques
mwit0320	italy central	1766	BRION DE LA TOUR	240	27	31	Etats de l'Eglise, de Toscane, Modene et Luques
mwbp0516	poland	1790	BRION DE LA TOUR	280	27	31	Etats de Pologne et de Lithuanie
mww0476	world	1770	BRION DE LA TOUR	400	44	56	Globe Terrestre. Globe Celeste
mwf0798	france normandy	1771	BRION DE LA TOUR	240	44	56	Gouvernemens de Normandie et du Havre (text panels at sides)
mwf0365	france brittany	1769	BRION DE LA TOUR	220	23	25	Gouvernement de Bretagne
mwf1077	france provence	1771	BRION DE LA TOUR	280	41	55	Gouvernement de Provence, et Generalite d'Aix avec le Comtat Venaisein (text panels at sides)
mwf0248	france alsace	1771	BRION DE LA TOUR	240	44	56	Gouvernement et Generalite d'Alsace avec les Grandes Routes a Paris
mwc0175	china	1766	BRION DE LA TOUR	250	28	48	Grande Tartarie et Isles du Japon (text panels at sides)
mwsam0623	south america guyana	1769	BRION DE LA TOUR	220	24	27	Guayane, Terre Ferme, Isles Antilles et Nlle. Espagne
mww0465	world	1766	BRION DE LA TOUR	500	36	39	Hemisphere Occidental / Hemisphere Oriental
mwas0181	asia continent	1766	BRION DE LA TOUR	300	30	33	Hemisphere Oriental
mwme0353	holy land	1766	BRION DE LA TOUR	220	36	51	Histoire-Sainte depuis l'An 3029 jusqu'a l'An 3050
mwam0240	america continent	1795	BRION DE LA TOUR	400	60	23	Iere Feuille de l'Amerique Meridionale / IIeme Feuille de l'Amerique Meridionale
mwf0159	france	1790	BRION DE LA TOUR	140	27	31	La France Divisee en 83 Departemens avec leurs Chef-Lieux
mwe0954	europe hungary	1766	BRION DE LA TOUR	220	28	31	La Hongrie avec les Provinces Adjacentes
mwme0352	holy land	1766	BRION DE LA TOUR	150	27	29	La Judee ou Palestine
mwru0279	russia	1786	BRION DE LA TOUR	220	27	30	La Russie Europeenne Conformement a l'Atlas de cet Empire
mwsw0165	switzerland	1766	BRION DE LA TOUR	220	27	29	La Suisse, Divisee en ses Cantons, ses Allies et Sujets
mwaf0219	africa	1766	BRION DE LA TOUR	300	23	26	L'Afrique Dressee pour l'Etude de la Geographie (size excl. text panels outside map)
mwam0214	america continent	1783	BRION DE LA TOUR	15000	110	132	L'Amerique Divisee en Septentrionale et Meridionale ... 1783
mwam0218	america continent	1786	BRION DE LA TOUR	550	30	48	L'Amerique Dressee pour l'Etude de la Geographie
mwsam0108	south america	1788	BRION DE LA TOUR	550	73	50	L'Amerique Meridionale
mwam0467	america north	1779	BRION DE LA TOUR	3000	51	76	L'Amerique Septentrionale ou se Remarquent les Etats Unis (first map to name 'United States'?)
mwas0200b	asia continent	1784	BRION DE LA TOUR	650	51	76	L'Asie Divisee en ses Principaux Etats
mwas0200	asia continent	1783	BRION DE LA TOUR	480	45	62	L'Asie Divisee en ses Principales Regions
mwas0180	asia continent	1765	BRION DE LA TOUR	400	28	31	L'Asie Dressee pour l'Etude de la Geographie (incl. 'Mer de Coree')
mwsc0376	scandinavia denmark	1786	BRION DE LA TOUR	220	27	30	Le Danemark Divise par Provinces et Dioceses sous une Metropole
mwbh0717	belgium holland	1770	BRION DE LA TOUR	280	44	56	Le Pays Bas Francois, Austrichiens, et Hollandois
mwuk0545	scotland	1786	BRION DE LA TOUR	200	28	48	L'Ecosse (with text side panels)
mwf0591	france ile de france	1771	BRION DE LA TOUR	180	37	55	Les Gouvernemens de l'Isle de France et de Champagne
mwit0838	italy sardinia and corsica	1766	BRION DE LA TOUR	280	23	26	Les Isles de Sardaigne et de Corse Divisees par Provinces
mwsp0300	spain	1786	BRION DE LA TOUR	200	27	31	L'Espagne et le Portugal
mwit0613	italy north	1766	BRION DE LA TOUR	220	27	31	L'Etat de Venise et le Duche de Mantoue, avec leurs Provinces Ecclesiastiques
mwe0199	europe	1779	BRION DE LA TOUR	785	50	74	L'Europe divisee en tous ses Principaux Etats ou Pays
mwe0222	europe	1790	BRION DE LA TOUR	180	27	31	L'Europe Dressee pour l'Etude de la Geographie
mwuk0194	ireland	1765	BRION DE LA TOUR	280	27	31	L'Irlande assujettie aux Observations Astronomiques
mwuk0197	ireland	1766	BRION DE LA TOUR	280	27	31	L'Irlande Divisee par Provinces Civiles et Ecclesiastiques
mwit0205	italy	1786	BRION DE LA TOUR	200	27	31	L'Italie Divisee en Tous ses Etats
mww0466	world	1766	BRION DE LA TOUR	800	24	27	Mappe-Monde Dresse pour l'Etude de la Geographie ... d'apres les Nouvelles Observations Astronomiques de M. Tchirikcow et De L'Isle (G. de l'Isles's son J.N. Size does not include text panels and decorative border)
mww0526	world	1783	BRION DE LA TOUR	4800	54	77	Mappemonde Ou Sont Marquees Les Nouvelles Decouvertes
mwam0439	america north	1766	BRION DE LA TOUR	480	28	48	Nouveau Mexique, Louisiane, Canada et Nlle. Angleterre
mwf0894	france paris	1784	BRION DE LA TOUR	1250	57	80	Nouveau Plan de Paris Avec les Augmentations
mwin0286	india	1786	BRION DE LA TOUR	240	27	31	Nouvelle Carte de la Partie des Indes Orientales, qui Comprend, entr'autres Etats, les Vastes Possessions des Anglais
mwbp0490	poland	1774	BRION DE LA TOUR	180	24	27	Nouvelle Carte de la Pologne Demembree
mwp0303	pacific caroline isl.	1790	BRION DE LA TOUR	240	24	34	Nouvelle Carte des Isles Carolines et des Marianes ou Isles des Larons
mwf0354	france brittany	1757	BRION DE LA TOUR	320	28	36	Partie de la Bretagne
mwf0983	france poitou	1757	BRION DE LA TOUR	320	28	36	Partie de la Saintonge
mwaf0961	africa south	1786	BRION DE LA TOUR	280	24	34	Partie de l'Afrique au dela de l'Equateur Comprenant le Congo, la Cafrerie &c. (text panels at sides)
mwit0614	italy north	1766	BRION DE LA TOUR	220	28	31	Partie de l'Italie Comprenant les Etats du Roy de Sardaigne, de Milan, Parme, et Genes avec leurs Provinces Ecclesiastiques
mwf0984	france poitou	1757	BRION DE LA TOUR	320	28	36	Partie du Poitou et de l'Aunis

AMPG REFERENCE	REGION	DATE	MAP MAKER	PRICE (UK£)	VERT. (cm.)	HOR. (cm.)	TITLE OF MAP (Comments by the editor in brackets)
mwme0632	arabia etc	1766	BRION DE LA TOUR	240	28	32	Perse, Turquie Asiatique et Arabie
mwaf0756	africa north algeria	1784	BRION DE LA TOUR	480	45	65	Plan des Defenses de la Ville d'Alger
mwas0896	asia south east sumatra	1790	BRION DE LA TOUR	250	24	34	Premiere Carte des Isles de la Sonde
mwin0274	india	1780	BRION DE LA TOUR	240	24	35	Carte de la Partie Septentrionale de la Presqu'Ile des Indes Orientales en deca du Gange
mwgm0048	gulf of mexico and surrounding regions	1782	BRION DE LA TOUR	12000	74	51	Suite du Theatre de la Guerre dans l'Amerique Septentrionale y Compris le Golfe du Mexique
mwuk0862	uk	1783	BRION DE LA TOUR	480	52	73	Tableau General des Isles Britanniques (incl. 3 text borders)
mwam0200	america continent	1775	BRION DE LA TOUR	785	52	74	Tableau Generale de l'Amerique Comprenant les Principales Regions qui Composent cette Partie du Monde; leur Population et leur Commerce; avec des Notes Aussi Curieuses (map surrounded by text)
mwe1159	europe south east	1780	BRION DE LA TOUR	180	28	48	Turquie Europeenne avec les Etats
mwaa0163	arctic	1818	BRITISH ADMIRALTY	1600	61	61	(Arctic Regions)
mwit0332	italy elba	1845	BRITISH ADMIRALTY	400	48	61	(Elba & adjacent islands)
mwwi0843	puerto rico	1830	BRITISH ADMIRALTY	280	25	37	(Mayaguex, Aguadilla & Puerto de Guarnica)
mwca0560	canada quebec	1837	BRITISH ADMIRALTY	1400	46	62	(St. Lawrence River. Point des Monts to Quebec. Set of 7 sheets)
mwca0237	canada arctic	1824	BRITISH ADMIRALTY	1600	61	46	A Chart of Baffin's Bay, with Davis & Barrow Straits; by Captn. Ross & Lieut. Parry R.N. in 1818, 19 & 20, and the Discoveries of Captn. Parry in 1822 and 23; & Captn. Lyon in 1824
mwca0459a	canada nova scotia	1826	BRITISH ADMIRALTY	300	94	62	A Chart of Grand Manan, Passamaquody Bay &c. in the Bay of Fundy, Principally Taken from a Survey by Captn. Thos. Hurd R.N
mwwi0840	puerto rico	1824	BRITISH ADMIRALTY	800	46	61	A Geometrical Plan of the Principal Harbour in the Island of Porto Rico Surveyed in 1794
mwsam0412	south america brazil	1823	BRITISH ADMIRALTY	2000	82	54	A New and Correct Chart of the Entrance and Harbour of Rio de Janeiro, from a Survey Made by Order of the Portuguese Government
mwsam0435	south america brazil	1846	BRITISH ADMIRALTY	1500	61	95	A New General Chart of the Coast of Brazil from the River Amazon to the River Plate
mwaf1249	africa west	1828	BRITISH ADMIRALTY	500	61	94	A Plan of the Establishment of Clarence in the Island of Fernando Po
mwaf0659	africa islands seychelles	1828	BRITISH ADMIRALTY	400	44	59	A Plan of the Port and Bay in the Island of Mahe
mwwi0566	guadeloupe	1830	BRITISH ADMIRALTY	300	30	47	A Plan of the Saintes
mwwi0938	virgin isl	1816	BRITISH ADMIRALTY	1200	29	46	A Survey of Culebra or Passage Island
mwwi0909	trinidad & tobago	1820	BRITISH ADMIRALTY	400	30	20	A Survey of Great Courland Bay in the Island of Tobago
mwaf1007	africa south	1828	BRITISH ADMIRALTY	350	28	22	A Survey of Hout Bay, Cape of Good Hope
mwec0310	uk england devon	1822	BRITISH ADMIRALTY	600	94	61	A Survey of Plymouth Sound
mwsam0858	south america venezuela	1828	BRITISH ADMIRALTY	400	28	41	A Survey of Port El Roque, Coast of Terra Firma
mwwi0873	st kitts	1820	BRITISH ADMIRALTY	300	29	22	A Survey of the Channel Called the Narrows
mwec0203	uk england cornwall	1810	BRITISH ADMIRALTY	1000	95	62	A Survey of the Coasts of Cornwall and Devonshire ... From St. Agnes Head to Hartland Point
mwwi0908a	trinidad & tobago	1816	BRITISH ADMIRALTY	1500	49	49	A Survey of the Island of Trinidad
mwwi0348	bahamas	1828	BRITISH ADMIRALTY	400	30	46	A Survey of the Keys and Shoals in the Mira-Por-Vos Passage
mwam1305	great lakes	1828	BRITISH ADMIRALTY	1200	58	28	A Survey of the River Detroit from Lake Erie to Lake Clair by Capt. W.F.W. Owen & Assistants in 1815
mwec0202	uk england cornwall	1809	BRITISH ADMIRALTY	1000	64	95	A Survey of the South Coast of England from Plymouth to the Lizard
mwuk1394	england south	1808	BRITISH ADMIRALTY	500	62	95	A Survey of the South Coast of England from St. Alban's Head to Abbotsbury
mwwi0762	marie galante	1824	BRITISH ADMIRALTY	400	31	22	A Survey of the West Side of Mariagalante
mwin0365	india	1840	BRITISH ADMIRALTY	300	36	60	A Trigonometric Survey of the Bay of Coringa
mwin0502	pakistan etc.	1844	BRITISH ADMIRALTY	1500	64	69	A Trigonometrical Survey of Kurachee Harbour, on the Coast of Sinde, by Lieutt. T.G. Carless. Indian Navy
mwuk0634	scotland	1843	BRITISH ADMIRALTY	400	48	61	Aberdeen Harbour
mwuss0461	florida	1823	BRITISH ADMIRALTY	7500	60	79	An Accurate Chart of the Coast of West Florida and the Coast of Louisiana
mwuss0473	florida	1835	BRITISH ADMIRALTY	6000	60	74	An Accurate Chart of the Tortugas and Florida Kays (3 charts 60x74cm.)
mwit0970	italy sicily	1823	BRITISH ADMIRALTY	200	62	46	Anchorages and Shoals in the Vicinity of Trapani
mwas0605	asia south east borneo	1846	BRITISH ADMIRALTY	500	46	62	Api Point to the River Sarawak (one of 6 maps of the NW coast)
mwat0100	atlantic azores	1849	BRITISH ADMIRALTY	600	47	63	Atlantic Ocean. Azores or Western Isles Surveyed by Captain A.T.E. Vidal R.N. 1843-4
mwwi0350	bahamas	1843	BRITISH ADMIRALTY	550	46	61	Bahama Bank Racoon Cut Surveyed by Cmdr. R. Owen 1834
mwwi0351	bahamas	1843	BRITISH ADMIRALTY	480	47	61	Bahama Bank the Nurse Channel Surveyed by Cmdr. E. Barnett 1841
mwgm0092	belize	1842	BRITISH ADMIRALTY	350	32	44	Bahama Bank, Great Stirrup Cay Berry Islands by Comd. Richard Owen, 1835
mwwi0355	bahamas	1845	BRITISH ADMIRALTY	150	27	28	Bahama Bank, Highborne Cut by Comr. Edward Barnett
mwwi0352	bahamas	1843	BRITISH ADMIRALTY	200	48	63	Bahama Bank, Ragged Island Harbour Surveyed by Cmdr. R. Owen 1834

AMPG REFERENCE	REGION	DATE	MAP MAKER	PRICE (UK£)	VERT. (cm.)	HOR. (cm.)	TITLE OF MAP (Comments by the editor in brackets)
mwwi0353	bahamas	1843	BRITISH ADMIRALTY	250	48	65	Bahamas, Douglas Road or Cochrane Anchorage East of New Providence by Anthony Demayne Master R.N.
mwp0152	australia	1844	BRITISH ADMIRALTY	1200	64	95	Bass Strait
mwwi0683	hispaniola	1831	BRITISH ADMIRALTY	350	27	22	Bay and Harbour of Port Au Prince, in the Island of Haiti
mwwi0814	martinique	1845	BRITISH ADMIRALTY	650	25	30	Bay of la Trinite / Cul-de-Sac Marin / Fort Royal Bay (3 charts)
mwca0639	canada st lawrence	1838	BRITISH ADMIRALTY	400	46	60	Bay of the Seven Islands
mwgm0126	honduras	1831	BRITISH ADMIRALTY	800	61	45	Belize Harbour on the Coast of Honduras
mwaf0761	africa north algeria	1846	BRITISH ADMIRALTY	120	47	62	Cape Ferrat to Cape Carbon
mwwi0685	hispaniola	1845	BRITISH ADMIRALTY	450	47	60	Cape Haiti Harbour
mwat0206	atlantic cape verde isl.	1822	BRITISH ADMIRALTY	400	62	77	Cape Verd Islands
mwsam0544	south america colombia	1823	BRITISH ADMIRALTY	800	56	43	Carthagena and the Adjacent Coast from Point Canoa to Point Gigante Compiled from Two Spanish MSs. Communicated by Commissioner Woodriff and Capt. Cumby RN
mwgm0380	nicaragua	1849	BRITISH ADMIRALTY	350	48	61	Central America, Nicaragua, Port Culebra Surveyed by Captn. Sir Edwd. Belcher, 1838
mwaf0444	africa east coast etc	1847	BRITISH ADMIRALTY	500	63	48	Chala Point to Kwyhoo Bay
mwca0497	canada prince edward isl.	1845	BRITISH ADMIRALTY	2000	48	52	Charlottetown Harbour
mwam1304	great lakes	1828	BRITISH ADMIRALTY	550	47	62	Chart of Part of the North Coast of Lake Superior from Small Lake Harbour to Peninsula Harbour. Surveyed by Lieut. Henry Wy. Bayfield ... 1823
mwc0291	china	1847	BRITISH ADMIRALTY	3000	68	105	Chart of the Coast of China, from the Canton River to the Yang Tze Keang, by John Walker, Geographer to the Honourable East India Company (2 sheets, each 68x105cm.)
mwf1178	france south	1826	BRITISH ADMIRALTY	200	44	60	Chart of the Coast of France from Banduff to Riou Isle
mwin0377	india	1848	BRITISH ADMIRALTY	1000	64	77	Chart of the Coromandel Coast from Latitude 16°30' to 18°05' North, Including Coringah Bay & Santipilly Shoal ... No.1 /Coromandel Coast Sheet No.2, from Latitude 15° to 16°30'N / Coromandel Coast Sheet No.3, from Latitude 13° to 16°N (in 3 sheets, each roughly 64x77cm.)
mwin0070	ceylon	1814	BRITISH ADMIRALTY	600	58	69	Chart of the Harbour of Point de Galle
mwsam0255	south america argentina	1828	BRITISH ADMIRALTY	1200	66	163	Chart of the River la Plata from Cape St Mary to Buenos Ayres, Surveyed by John Warner
mwaf0660	africa islands seychelles	1828	BRITISH ADMIRALTY	500	48	65	Chart of the Seychelle Islands by the Officers of H.M. Ships Leven & Barracouta
mwaa0054	antarctic	1845	BRITISH ADMIRALTY	2500	62	62	Chart of the South Polar Sea
mwas0575	asia south east banda	1828	BRITISH ADMIRALTY	400	30	50	Chart of the Track and Discoveries of the East India Company's Cruizers Panther & Endeavour under the Command of Lieut. John McCluer, 1790, 1791 & 1792
mwaf1246	africa west	1827	BRITISH ADMIRALTY	240	61	95	Chart of the West Coast of Africa between Latitudes of 15ºN & 2ºS and the Longitudes of 17ºW & 10ºE
mwas0619	asia south east celebes	1845	BRITISH ADMIRALTY	400	30	57	Chart of the West Coast of Celebes
mwsam0480	south america chile	1841	BRITISH ADMIRALTY	200	62	47	Chile, Maitencillo to Herradura
mwc0278a	china	1841	BRITISH ADMIRALTY	400	61	46	China Sheet V East Coast From the Kwesan Islands to Whang-Ho Gulf, The Yang-Tse Kiang by Capt. R.D.Bethune R.N.. Chusan &c. by Lieut. Collinson R.N.1840
mwc0286a	china	1843	BRITISH ADMIRALTY	600	63	98	China Sheet V Eastern Coast from Port Matheson to Ragged Point
mwc0286	china	1843	BRITISH ADMIRALTY	500	50	68	China, East Coast. Amoy Harbours and Approaches. By Captns. Kellett & Collinson, R.N. 1843. Additions by A.F. Boxer, Commanding H.M.S. St. Hesper, 1862
mwc0310	china formosa	1849	BRITISH ADMIRALTY	250	92	61	China, Pescadores Islands
mwc0274a	china	1840	BRITISH ADMIRALTY	600	47	64	China South Coast Chou Kiang or Canton River from the Second Bar to Canton by Capt. D. Ross (sheet 3. Inset of Canton)
mwc0274	china	1840	BRITISH ADMIRALTY	400	62	48	China South Coast from Hainan Id to Macao (sheet 1)
mwgm0447	panama	1847	BRITISH ADMIRALTY	300	64	94	Chiriqui Lagoon
mwgm0448	panama	1847	BRITISH ADMIRALTY	400	47	62	Chiriqui Lagoon, Tiger Channel Surveyed by Commander E. Barnett 1839
mwit0971	italy sicily	1823	BRITISH ADMIRALTY	250	62	46	City and Bay of Palermo
mwit0972	italy sicily	1823	BRITISH ADMIRALTY	250	62	46	City and Harbour of Augusta
mwit0973	italy sicily	1823	BRITISH ADMIRALTY	450	62	46	City and Harbour of Messina
mwit0974	italy sicily	1823	BRITISH ADMIRALTY	240	62	46	City, Bay and Promontory of Milazzo
mwit0975	italy sicily	1823	BRITISH ADMIRALTY	200	62	46	City, Environs and Anchorages of Girgenti
mwec0900	uk england northumberland	1847	BRITISH ADMIRALTY	300	94	61	Coquet Road and Channel
mwwi0912	trinidad & tobago	1838	BRITISH ADMIRALTY	600	24	34	Dragons Mouths
mwsam0263	south america argentina	1840	BRITISH ADMIRALTY	400	47	62	East Coast of South America Sheet VI from the Rio de la Plata to the Rio Negro
mwca0633	canada st lawrence	1828	BRITISH ADMIRALTY	240	26	22	Ellis Bay in the Island of Anticosti by Commander H.W. Bayfield ... 1828
mwuk1351	england east	1845	BRITISH ADMIRALTY	350	64	48	England East Coast Sheet III Form Southwold to Cromer
mwec0841	uk england norfolk	1843	BRITISH ADMIRALTY	300	48	64	England East Coast Sheet IV from Cromer to Trusthorpe
mwec1367	uk england yorkshire	1842	BRITISH ADMIRALTY	400	64	47	England East Coast Sheet V from Trusthorpe to Flamborough Head [in set with] England East Coast Sheet VI from Flamborough Head to the Tees

AMPG REFERENCE	REGION	DATE	MAP MAKER	PRICE (UK£)	VERT. (cm.)	HOR. (cm.)	TITLE OF MAP (Comments by the editor in brackets)
mwuk1350	england east	1842	BRITISH ADMIRALTY	150	48	60	England East Coast Sheet VII from the Tees to Blyth
mwec0352	uk england dorset	1848	BRITISH ADMIRALTY	360	48	64	England South Coast Sheet IV Portland to Portsmouth
mwec0314	uk england devon	1839	BRITISH ADMIRALTY	300	62	46	England West Coast Sheet II Padstow to the Bristol Channel
mwuk1884	wales	1842	BRITISH ADMIRALTY	240	47	62	England West Coast Sheet V Wales Bristol Channel to New Quay
mwuk1885	wales	1842	BRITISH ADMIRALTY	240	62	46	England West Coast Sheet VI Wales New Quay to Bardsey
mwuk1886	wales	1842	BRITISH ADMIRALTY	240	62	46	England West Coast Sheet VII Wales Bardsey Island to Point Lynus
mwwi0311	antigua	1848	BRITISH ADMIRALTY	600	60	46	English Harbour
mwc0278	china	1840	BRITISH ADMIRALTY	700	47	62	Entrance to the Chou-Kiang or Canton River from the Outer Islands to Lintin / Chou-Kiang or Canton River from Lintin to the Second Bar (2 maps, Hong Kong)
mwwi0354	bahamas	1843	BRITISH ADMIRALTY	200	30	41	Exuma Sound, Wax Cay Cut by Comdr. R Owen
mwwi0312	antigua	1850	BRITISH ADMIRALTY	550	62	46	Falmouth and English Harbours
mwat0247a	atlantic madeira	1845	BRITISH ADMIRALTY	500	49	64	Funchal Bay, Madeira
mwca0640	canada st lawrence	1838	BRITISH ADMIRALTY	240	59	46	Gaspe and Mal Bays
mwat0066	atlantic ocean (all)	1844	BRITISH ADMIRALTY	650	95	125	General Chart of the Atlantic Ocean; According to the Observations, Surveys & Determinations, of the Most Eminent Navigators ... by John Purdy
mwwi0946	virgin isl	1850	BRITISH ADMIRALTY	1000	47	63	Gorda Sound
mwgm0376	nicaragua	1833	BRITISH ADMIRALTY	240	21	25	Greytown Formerly San Juan de Nicaragua by Mr. George Peacock
mwca0641	canada st lawrence	1838	BRITISH ADMIRALTY	350	28	20	Gulf of St. Lawrence Bradore Bay and Harbour. Surveyed by Captn. W.H. Bayfield ... 1834
mwca0642	canada st lawrence	1838	BRITISH ADMIRALTY	350	27	20	Gulf of St. Lawrence Coacoacho Bay Surveyed by Captn. W.H. Bayfield ... 1834
mwca0643	canada st lawrence	1838	BRITISH ADMIRALTY	350	46	61	Gulf of St. Lawrence Little Mecattian Id. &c. Surveyed by Captn. W.H. Bayfield ... 1834
mwca0647	canada st lawrence	1845	BRITISH ADMIRALTY	450	47	62	Gulf of St. Lawrence Miramichi Bay and River Sheet II Surveyed by Captn. W.H. Bayfield
mwca0648	canada st lawrence	1850	BRITISH ADMIRALTY	800	60	96	Gulf of St. Lawrence Prince Edward Island, Cardigan Bay Surveyed by Captn. W.H. Bayfield ... 1844
mwca0644	canada st lawrence	1838	BRITISH ADMIRALTY	350	29	38	Gulf of St. Lawrence Wapitagun Harbour Surveyed by Captn. W.H. Bayfield ... 1835
mwca0645	canada st lawrence	1838	BRITISH ADMIRALTY	350	61	45	Gulf of St. Lawrence Watagheistic Sound, Mary Islands &c. Surveyed by Captn. H.W. Bayfield ... 1834
mwuk1887	wales	1843	BRITISH ADMIRALTY	240	46	62	Gynfelin Patches, Aberystwith and New-Quay
mwec0390	uk england durham	1847	BRITISH ADMIRALTY	300	91	61	Hartlepool Bay
mwc0282	china	1843	BRITISH ADMIRALTY	8000	67	98	Hong Kong - Surveyed by Captn. Sir Edward Belcher, in H.M.S. Sulphur 1841
mwec0315	uk england devon	1839	BRITISH ADMIRALTY	120	25	22	Ilfracombe Harbour
mwc0275	china	1840	BRITISH ADMIRALTY	240	64	48	Index to the Charts of the Coast of China
mwin0352	india	1829	BRITISH ADMIRALTY	720	104	68	India, West Coast. Bombay Harbour
mwin0451	indian ocean	1833	BRITISH ADMIRALTY	600	69	101	Indian Ocean. Ceylon, South Coast. Surveyed by Mr. T.H. Twynam, Master Attendant at Point de Galle, 1833
mwit0624	italy north	1826	BRITISH ADMIRALTY	400	44	61	Italy Sheet I West Coast from Ventimiglia to Piombino
mwaf0428a	africa east	1828	BRITISH ADMIRALTY	300	66	87	Juba or Dundas Islands on the East Coast of Africa, by Captain A.T.E. Vidal and the Officers of H.M. Sloop Barracouta, under the Orders of Captn. W.F.W. Owen, 1824 & 5
mwgr0264	greece	1848	BRITISH ADMIRALTY	450	25	25	Kastro / Port Moudros and Port Kondia / Pournea Bay
mwuk0283	ireland	1843	BRITISH ADMIRALTY	200	61	47	Kingstown Harbour
mwsam0805	south america peru	1848	BRITISH ADMIRALTY	500	66	79	La Laguna De Titicaca and the valleys of Yucay, Collao and Desaguadero in Peru and Bolivia (inset: Cuzco)
mwas0676	asia south east labouan	1848	BRITISH ADMIRALTY	800	47	60	Labouan Island
mwca0482	canada ontario	1838	BRITISH ADMIRALTY	400	60	93	Lake Ontario and the Back Communication with Lake Huron
mwaf1259	africa west	1846	BRITISH ADMIRALTY	200	48	64	Lekki to River Forcados
mwca0646	canada st lawrence	1838	BRITISH ADMIRALTY	400	45	61	Little Mecattina Id. &c.
mwuk0642	scotland	1849	BRITISH ADMIRALTY	180	50	69	Loch Inver and Loch Roe
mwuk0286	ireland	1844	BRITISH ADMIRALTY	200	89	56	Lough Ree on the River Shannon
mwp0158	australia	1845	BRITISH ADMIRALTY	200	47	61	Macquarie Harbour (Tasmania)
mwas0622	asia south east floris	1845	BRITISH ADMIRALTY	350	29	37	Mangrove Harbour on Floris
mwas0293	asia burma	1848	BRITISH ADMIRALTY	200	64	48	Maulmain River
mwaf0638	africa islands mauritius	1831	BRITISH ADMIRALTY	720	50	34	Mauritius or Isle of France
mwuk1876	wales	1831	BRITISH ADMIRALTY	240	48	62	Milford Haven
mwme0693	arabia etc	1849	BRITISH ADMIRALTY	550	47	60	Mocha Road
mwca0585	canada quebec montreal	1838	BRITISH ADMIRALTY	1200	61	46	Montreal Harbour Surveyed by Captain H.W. Bayfield, R.N., R.A.S., 1834
mwgm0378	nicaragua	1843	BRITISH ADMIRALTY	400	62	47	Mosquito Coast, Blewfields Lagoon Surveyed by Capt. Rich. Owen, 1836
mwca0280	canada new brunswick	1848	BRITISH ADMIRALTY	300	48	63	New Brunswick - Bay of Fundy - L'Etang Harbour
mwgm0381	nicaragua	1849	BRITISH ADMIRALTY	400	48	60	Nicaraqua, Port Culebra Surveyed by Captn. Sir Edwd. Belcher 1838
mwam1234	america north (east)	1836	BRITISH ADMIRALTY	350	48	62	North America East Coast ... Sheet III
mwam1227	america north (east)	1834	BRITISH ADMIRALTY	350	46	62	North America East Coast ... Sheet IV

AMPG REFERENCE	REGION	DATE	MAP MAKER	PRICE (UK£)	VERT. (cm.)	HOR. (cm.)	TITLE OF MAP (Comments by the editor in brackets)
mwam1233	america north (east)	1836	BRITISH ADMIRALTY	350	48	62	North America East Coast ... Sheet VII
mwuss0488	florida	1847	BRITISH ADMIRALTY	350	64	49	North America. East Coast. Sheet VIII. Cumberland Sound to the Florida Channel
mwat0207	atlantic cape verde isl.	1822	BRITISH ADMIRALTY	400	66	86	North Atlantic Ocean. Cape Verde Islands Surveyed by Lieuts. Vidal and Mudge, R.N. of H.M. Ship Leven, Captain D.E. Bartholomew
mwec0901	uk england northumberland	1847	BRITISH ADMIRALTY	280	62	47	North Sunderland Harbour
mwec0216	uk england cornwall	1846	BRITISH ADMIRALTY	350	94	64	Padstow Harbour
mwec0496	uk england hampshire	1808	BRITISH ADMIRALTY	800	64	95	Part of the Channel between the Isle of Wight and Hampshire
mwaf0428b	africa east	1828	BRITISH ADMIRALTY	400	22	28	Part of the North East Coast of Africa, in the Gulph of Aden, from Cape Kurrum to Burburra / A Survey of Port Burburra on the North East Coast of Africa
mwas0547	asia south east	1840	BRITISH ADMIRALTY	250	62	47	Penang or Prince of Wales Island
mwsam0802	south america peru	1840	BRITISH ADMIRALTY	350	48	62	Perus Cape Lobos to Pescadores Point
mwgr0634	greece islands	1847	BRITISH ADMIRALTY	400	48	64	Petali Islands and Anchorages
mwsam0405	south america brazil	1811	BRITISH ADMIRALTY	200	29	33	Plan and View of the Island Fernando Noronha
mwin0073	ceylon	1845	BRITISH ADMIRALTY	400	32	41	Plan of Batacalao Road
mwaf1080	africa south west	1796	BRITISH ADMIRALTY	300	29	15	Plan of Spencer's Bay on the West Coast of Africa (Namibia)
mwaf0425a	africa east	1811	BRITISH ADMIRALTY	200	29	22	Plan of the African Islands from the Observations of Lieut Campbell of H.M. Schooner Spitfire by Chas. Shakleton / Plan of the African Islands Taken on Board the French Frigate, La Chiffonne, Capt. Guieysse (2 maps on same sheet)
mwwi0808	martinique	1814	BRITISH ADMIRALTY	300	39	64	Plan of the Bay, Town, Fortifications, and Environs, of St. Pierre, in the Island of Martinique. Survey'd by Order of Sr. G.B. Rodney in 1763 by Captn. John Stott of the Royal Navy
mwit0976	italy sicily	1823	BRITISH ADMIRALTY	320	62	46	Plan of the City and Harbour of Augusta
mwit0977	italy sicily	1823	BRITISH ADMIRALTY	350	32	55	Plan of the City and Harbour of Messina
mwaf0566	africa egypt etc	1845	BRITISH ADMIRALTY	250	28	22	Plan of the Harbour and Road of Suez
mwec0204	uk england cornwall	1813	BRITISH ADMIRALTY	320	76	58	Plan of the Harbour of Fowey Laid Down from Actual Survey by Mr. George Thomas
mwm0259	mediterranean malta	1823	BRITISH ADMIRALTY	1200	65	50	Plan of the Harbours and Fortifications of Valetta
mwsp0631	spain regions	1823	BRITISH ADMIRALTY	240	44	56	Plan of the Inlets of Ferrol Coruna and Betanzos (Galicia)
mwas0745	asia south east moluccas	1840	BRITISH ADMIRALTY	450	29	44	Plan of the Island of Amboina from a M.S. at the East-India-House
mwm0258	mediterranean malta	1823	BRITISH ADMIRALTY	1200	50	63	Plan of the Maltese Islands
mwsp0632	spain regions	1823	BRITISH ADMIRALTY	400	49	79	Plan of the Mouth and Harbour of Ferrol
mwsp0620	spain regions	1810	BRITISH ADMIRALTY	300	60	46	Plan of the Port of Santander / Plan of the Entrance to Bilbao
mwsp0618	spain regions	1809	BRITISH ADMIRALTY	300	60	46	Plan of the Port of Santona (Cantabria)
mwas0813	asia south east philippines	1845	BRITISH ADMIRALTY	450	33	30	Plan of the Port of Subec near Manila ... 1766
mwme1044	turkey etc	1808	BRITISH ADMIRALTY	200	29	27	Plan of the Port of Tchesme in the Strait of Scio
mwas0871	asia south east solor	1845	BRITISH ADMIRALTY	400	48	64	Plan of the Straits of Solor
mwwi0532	grenada	1821	BRITISH ADMIRALTY	900	92	63	Plan of the Town and Heights and a Survey of the Bay, Carenage and Lagoon of St. George's, Grenada
mwsp0619	spain regions	1809	BRITISH ADMIRALTY	300	64	48	Plan of the Town and Port of San Sebastian / Plan of the Port Passages
mwwi0494	cuba	1844	BRITISH ADMIRALTY	450	41	53	Plan the of Harbour and City of Havana Surveyed by Don Joseph Del Rio, Captain in the Spanish Navy
mwuk1888	wales	1843	BRITISH ADMIRALTY	240	47	61	Plans of Ports in Wales
mwca0636	canada st lawrence	1837	BRITISH ADMIRALTY	1000	46	64	Plans of the River St. Lawrence below Quebec Sheet 1 from Point de Monts to Bersimis River / Sheet 2 between the Rivers Bersimis and Saguenay Including Bic and Green Islands / Sheet 3 from Green Island to the Pilgrims
mwec0353	uk england dorset	1849	BRITISH ADMIRALTY	240	64	94	Poole Harbour
mwgr0633	greece islands	1843	BRITISH ADMIRALTY	400	48	61	Poros Island
mwsam0800	south america peru	1837	BRITISH ADMIRALTY	300	60	44	Port and Road of Marseille / The Position of la Cassidaigne Rock
mwp0300	pacific bonin isl.	1833	BRITISH ADMIRALTY	350	42	58	Port Lloyd on the Western Side of Peel Island, One of the Arzobispo or Bonin Islands
mwgm0442	panama	1820	BRITISH ADMIRALTY	1000	61	46	Porto Bello and Adjacent Coast from a Spanish M.S. Communicated by Captn. Taite R.N.
mwme1062	turkey etc	1836	BRITISH ADMIRALTY	280	51	64	Ports in the Gulf of Smyrna
mwsp0635	spain regions	1836	BRITISH ADMIRALTY	300	62	48	Portugalete and Bilbao with the Channel of the River Nervion
mwwi0684	hispaniola	1831	BRITISH ADMIRALTY	400	34	23	Puerto de Plata
mwas0291	asia burma	1835	BRITISH ADMIRALTY	300	36	23	Rangoon River
mwsam0436	south america brazil	1847	BRITISH ADMIRALTY	1200	94	63	Rio de Janeiro Harbour
mwgm0114	guatemala	1839	BRITISH ADMIRALTY	400	47	61	River Dulce in Guatemala
mwaf1018	africa south	1839	BRITISH ADMIRALTY	240	29	23	Saldanha Bay
mwgm0377	nicaragua	1833	BRITISH ADMIRALTY	400	20	25	San Juan de Nicaragua
mwec1371	uk england yorkshire	1847	BRITISH ADMIRALTY	300	65	48	Scarborough
mwec0389	uk england durham	1846	BRITISH ADMIRALTY	240	61	47	Seaham Harbour
mwuk1449	england thames	1844	BRITISH ADMIRALTY	480	62	94	Sheet II of the River Thames from Ramsgate to the Nore

AMPG REFERENCE	REGION	DATE	MAP MAKER	PRICE (UK£)	VERT. (cm.)	HOR. (cm.)	TITLE OF MAP (Comments by the editor in brackets)
mwit1047	italy south	1827	BRITISH ADMIRALTY	300	46	61	Sheet III Coast of Italy from Civita Vecchia to the Bay of Naples
mwas0678	asia south east lombok	1845	BRITISH ADMIRALTY	300	29	20	Sketch of the West Coast of Lombok from a Draught of Raddin Tomoongoong Communicated by John Marsden Esq
mwsam0262	south america argentina	1840	BRITISH ADMIRALTY	200	62	47	South America East Coast, Patagonia Cape Three Points to the Strait of Magellan
mwsam0157	south america	1841	BRITISH ADMIRALTY	250	62	47	South America West Coast Sheet X
mwsam0801	south america peru	1840	BRITISH ADMIRALTY	200	63	47	South America West Coast Sheet XIV
mwuk1631	isle of wight	1846	BRITISH ADMIRALTY	360	33	45	South Yarmouth Surveyed by Commr. Sheringham
mwsp0636	spain regions	1839	BRITISH ADMIRALTY	400	48	62	Spain South Coast from Gibraltar to Alicante and North Coast of Barbary to Cape Ferrat / Spain South Coast from Alicante to Palamos and the Baleares
mwat0333	atlantic st helena	1816	BRITISH ADMIRALTY	480	45	61	St. Helena Island
mwwi0811	martinique	1825	BRITISH ADMIRALTY	200	58	43	St. Pierre Roadstead
mwaf0801	africa north morocco	1844	BRITISH ADMIRALTY	240	46	61	Suirah or Mogador Harbour
mwec0201	uk england cornwall	1808	BRITISH ADMIRALTY	300	64	95	Survey of Falmouth Harbour and the Coast to the Manacles with Helford River
mwam1303	great lakes	1828	BRITISH ADMIRALTY	750	90	62	Survey of Lake Superior. By Lieut. Henry W. Bayfield, R.N. assisted by Mr. Philip Ed. Collins, Mid. (3 sheets each 90x62cm.)
mwec0497	uk england hampshire	1808	BRITISH ADMIRALTY	900	95	65	Survey of Part of the Isle of Wight with the Coast of Hampshire from Gillkicker Point to Calshot Castle with the Mother Bank
mwec0498	uk england hampshire	1808	BRITISH ADMIRALTY	800	95	64	Survey of Southampton River the Brambles and Cowes Road with the Adjacent Parts
mwaf1008	africa south	1828	BRITISH ADMIRALTY	600	59	43	Survey of the Cape of Good Hope
mwec0341	uk england dorset	1785	BRITISH ADMIRALTY	500	63	95	Survey of the South Coast of England ... Blackwood ... St. Alban's
mwuk1883	wales	1839	BRITISH ADMIRALTY	240	29	42	Swansea and Neath
mwaf1029	africa south	1849	BRITISH ADMIRALTY	750	48	63	Table Bay
mwaf0658	africa islands seychelles	1827	BRITISH ADMIRALTY	300	22	29	The Bay of Curieuse, Seychelles Islands
mwru0373	russia	1854	BRITISH ADMIRALTY	1200	51	66	The Bay of St. Petersburg
mwsam0804	south america peru	1848	BRITISH ADMIRALTY	400	51	68	The Boqueron of Callao Surveyed by Captains Fitzroy and Belcher
mwat0175	atlantic canary isl.	1848	BRITISH ADMIRALTY	600	50	66	The Canary Islands
mwuk1526	uk english channel (all)	1844	BRITISH ADMIRALTY	400	65	97	The English Channel
mwc0277	china	1840	BRITISH ADMIRALTY	300	46	61	The Entrance to the River Min
mwat0231	atlantic falkland isl.	1841	BRITISH ADMIRALTY	1000	64	98	The Falklands Surveyed by Captain Robert Fitzroy R.N., Commander William Robinson, and Captain Bartholomew James Sulivan, 1838-1845
mwf0373	france brittany	1817	BRITISH ADMIRALTY	350	62	94	The Glenan Isles and Penmark Rocks with the Adjacent Coast of France from Penmark Point to Point Keabras
mwwi0357	bahamas	1850	BRITISH ADMIRALTY	1000	63	94	The Great Bahama Bank with its Islands, Bays and Channels Sheet II. Surveyed by Commanders R. Owen, E. Barnett and T. Smith in H.M.S. Thunder and Lark 1836-1943
mwca0637	canada st lawrence	1837	BRITISH ADMIRALTY	350	48	64	The Gulf of St. Lawrence Sheet III from Lake Island to Pashasheeboo Point Surveyed by Captn. H.W. Bayfield ... 1832-1834
mwca0638	canada st lawrence	1837	BRITISH ADMIRALTY	350	48	63	The Gulf of the St. Lawrence Sheet IV from Pashasheeboo Pt. to Magpie Bay
mwsam0407	south america brazil	1817	BRITISH ADMIRALTY	200	27	22	The Harbour and Road of Pernambuco
mwsam0540	south america colombia	1818	BRITISH ADMIRALTY	400	38	30	The Harbour of Santa Marta
mwca0279	canada new brunswick	1846	BRITISH ADMIRALTY	1000	48	62	The Harbour of St. John
mwuk0298	ireland	1847	BRITISH ADMIRALTY	450	95	64	The Irish Channel
mwwi0390	barbados	1814	BRITISH ADMIRALTY	400	29	20	The Island of Barbuda
mwwi0752	jamaica	1821	BRITISH ADMIRALTY	480	59	76	The Island of Jamaica from Observations Taken on the Principal Headlands by Anthony de Mayne R.N. 1821
mwwi0942	virgin isl	1831	BRITISH ADMIRALTY	2000	40	59	The Island of Sainte Croix, from the Danish Survey of General Oxholm 1799
mwat0247	atlantic madeira	1843	BRITISH ADMIRALTY	600	67	87	The Islands of Madeira, Porto Santo and Dezertas
mwaf0639	africa islands mauritius	1836	BRITISH ADMIRALTY	900	64	47	The Isle of France or Mauritius from a French MS.
mwjk0172	korea	1840	BRITISH ADMIRALTY	1000	62	46	The Peninsula of Korea
mwgm0298	mexico	1825	BRITISH ADMIRALTY	200	60	79	The Port of Veracruz, and Anchorage of Anton Lizardo
mwaf1247	africa west	1827	BRITISH ADMIRALTY	300	30	46	The River Congo
mwwi0310	antigua	1845	BRITISH ADMIRALTY	720	58	69	The Road and Harbour of St. John, in the Island of Antigua
mwme1060	turkey etc	1833	BRITISH ADMIRALTY	250	48	62	The Sea of Marmora with the Dardanells
mwsam0701	south america magellan	1841	BRITISH ADMIRALTY	400	62	94	The South-Eastern Part of Tierra del Fuego with Staten Island, Cape Horn and Diego Ramirez Islands
mwas0908	asia south east timor	1814	BRITISH ADMIRALTY	600	46	64	Timor and some Neighbouring Islands
mwuk0641	scotland	1848	BRITISH ADMIRALTY	200	61	47	Tobermory Harbour
mwwi0945	virgin isl	1836	BRITISH ADMIRALTY	2000	46	62	Tortola Road or Sir Francis Drake Bay in the Virgin Islands by R.H. Schomburgh F.R.G.S. 1835
mwf1088	france provence	1845	BRITISH ADMIRALTY	250	46	60	Toulon and the Adjacent Coast
mwgm0127	honduras	1843	BRITISH ADMIRALTY	600	46	63	Utilla Island
mwuk1881	wales	1835	BRITISH ADMIRALTY	400	47	63	Wales, North Coast Sheet VII, Point Lynus to Abergele
mwp0133	australia	1840	BRITISH ADMIRALTY	750	34	21	Warnbro Sound / Peel Harbour

AMPG REFERENCE	REGION	DATE	MAP MAKER	PRICE (UK£)	VERT. (cm.)	HOR. (cm.)	TITLE OF MAP (Comments by the editor in brackets)
mwca0635	canada st lawrence	1834	BRITISH ADMIRALTY	400	61	45	Watagheistic Sound, Mary Islands &c.
mwaf1250	africa west	1830	BRITISH ADMIRALTY	3000	47	64	West Coast of Africa Sheet I to Sheet 20 inclusive
mwwi0198	west indies	1837	BRITISH ADMIRALTY	400	61	48	West Indies from Los Roques to Cabo la Vela Chiefly from Spanish Documents
mwsam0554	south america colombia	1837	BRITISH ADMIRALTY	300	48	62	West Indies Sheet X from the Cabo la Vela to Cayos Ratones
mwgm0077	gulf of mexico and surrounding regions	1844	BRITISH ADMIRALTY	300	48	62	West Indies Sheet XI from Cayos Ratones to San Juan de Nicaragua
mwwi0209	west indies	1844	BRITISH ADMIRALTY	300	62	47	West Indies Sheet XII from San Juan de Nicaragua to C. Gracias
mwgm0093	belize	1843	BRITISH ADMIRALTY	550	48	62	West Indies Sheet XIII from Cape Gracias a Dios to Belize (insets incl. Roatan)
mwgm0335	mexico	1839	BRITISH ADMIRALTY	320	62	47	West Indies Sheet XIV from Belize to Cape Catoche
mwgm0074	gulf of mexico and surrounding regions	1840	BRITISH ADMIRALTY	400	46	64	West Indies. Bonacca Island
mwgm0379	nicaragua	1844	BRITISH ADMIRALTY	350	62	47	West Indies. Sheet XII San Juan de Nicaragua to C. Gracias
mwec0354	uk england dorset	1850	BRITISH ADMIRALTY	360	49	63	Weymouth and Portland Roads
mwec0247	uk england cumbria	1844	BRITISH ADMIRALTY	300	64	48	Whitehaven
mwc0285	china	1843	BRITISH ADMIRALTY	300	61	94	Yang-Tse-Kiang River
mwuss0634	louisiana	1760	BRITISH MAGAZINE	400	19	22	An Accurate Map of Louisiana and the Territory in Dispute between the English & French
mwuk0275	ireland	1835	BRITISH ORDNANCE SURVEY	3600	66	99	(Donegal, 21 sheets, early issues)
mwuk1039	england	1805	BRITISH ORDNANCE SURVEY	7500	75	64	(England and Wales complete. Price for the first 58 sheets ever published, between 1805 and 1833)
mwec0418	uk england essex	1804	BRITISH ORDNANCE SURVEY	1200	64	88	A Topographical Map of the County of Essex. Constructed from the Trigonometrical Survey Made by Order of the Board of Ordnance (first edition)
mwec0656	uk england kent	1801	BRITISH ORDNANCE SURVEY	1500	121	177	General Survey of England and Wales. An Entirely New & Accurate Survey of the County of Kent, with Part of the County of Essex (first Ordnance Survey map published)
mwgr0274a	greece athens	1835	BROCKHAUS	480			Plan von Athen
mwbh0731	belgium holland	1780	BROEN	4000	95	117	Amsterdam (first published c1732)
mwsc0763b	scandinavia sweden	1769	BROLIN	600	50	56	Charta ofwer Upstaden Linkoping / Charta ofwer Stopelstaden Soderkoping
mwaf0277	africa	1795	BROOKES	100	19	28	A Map of Africa from the Sieur Robert, Geographer to the French King with Improvements
mwam0569	america north	1806	BROOKES	200	20	27	A Map of the United States and Part of Louisiana
mww0588	world	1795	BROOKES	280	15	28	A Map of the World from the Best Authorities
mwas0239	asia continent	1809	BROOKES	80	20	24	Asia from the Best Authorities
mwas0529	asia south east	1809	BROOKES	80	19	30	East Indies from the Best Authorities
mwam0586	america north	1812	BROOKES	150	20	25	The Eastern States with Part of Canada
mwam1349	america north (west)	1812	BROOKES	240	19	24	The Northwestern Territories of the United States
mwme0347	holy land	1759	BROUCKNER	300	22	26	Cette Carte pour le Nouveau Testament
mww0406	world	1749	BROUCKNER	12500	45	52	Nouvel Atlas de Marine (in 12 sheets, each 45x52cm. From 82 degrees north to 60 degrees south)
mww0077	world	1590	BROUGHTON	1000	16	22	A map of the earth with names (the most) from scriptures
mwaa0061	arctic	1590	BROUGHTON	5000	55		A mapp of the north part of the equinoctial, with the ancient seates of the families mentioned in genesis (polar projection to the equator)
mwjk0168	korea	1804	BROUGHTON	400	24	41	Sketch of Thosan Harbour on the S.E. Coast of Corea / The Sketch of Napachan Roads, in the Island of Lieuchieux
mwjk0132	japan	1805	BROUGHTON-VASHON	480	49	47	Neue Karte von der Nordost Kuste von Asien und den Japanischen Inseln (German version of Broughton's map of his voyage)
mwuk0558	scotland	1793	BROWN	375	56	46	A New Accurate Travelling Map of Scotland with the Distances Marked between Each Stage in Measured Miles
mwsc0379	scandinavia denmark	1790	BROWN	75	28	33	A New and Accurate Map of Denmark & Holstein from the Best Authorities
mwf0171	france	1801	BROWN	75	28	33	A New and Accurate Map of France Divided into Departments, &c., from the Best Authorities
mwuss0329	connecticut	1850	BROWN & PARSONS	1000	51	56	Map of Connecticut from Actual Survey
mwuss0736	maine	1845	BROWN & PARSONS	400	39	50	Map of Maine, New Hampshire, and Vermont, from the Most Authentic Sources
mwuss0884	massachusetts	1838	BROWN & PARSONS	400	39	50	Massachusetts, Connecticut & Rhode Island
mww0570	world	1792	BROWN, T.	800	36	60	A New and Accurate Chart of the World According to Mercator's Projection
mwam0510	america north	1790	BROWN, T.	500	27	34	A New and Accurate Map of the United States of America, &c. from the Best Authorities
mwwi0131	west indies	1794	BROWN, T.	150	27	36	A New and Accurate Map of the West Indies from the Best Authorities
mwf0742	france nord pas-de-calais	1708	BROWNE	800	40	47	A New and Exact Plan of the Town and Citadel of Lille
mwf0741	france nord pas-de-calais	1706	BROWNE	1000	48	60	A New and Exact Plan of ye Towne and Port of Dunkirk, together with the Citadel Castles of Risbanck and other Forts at the Entrance of the Mole or Harbour, and All ye Outworks Lately Added

AMPG REFERENCE	REGION	DATE	MAP MAKER	PRICE (UK£)	VERT. (cm.)	HOR. (cm.)	TITLE OF MAP (Comments by the editor in brackets)
mwwi0713	jamaica	1755	BROWNE	4500	75	140	A New Map of Jamaica ... from Actual Surveys Made by Mr. Sheffield and Others, from the Year 1730 to the Year 1749
mwit0734	italy rome	1710	BROWNE	900	49	58	A New Map of Rome Showing its Ancient and Present Situation
mwam0913	america north (east)	1712	BROWNE	24000	50	60	A New Mapp of New England and Annapolis with the Country's Adjacent
mwuk0962	england	1700	BROWNE	8000	156	166	A New Mapp of the Kingdom of England Showing its Antient and Present Government
mwuk0110	ireland	1691	BROWNE	900	59	48	A New Mapp Of The Kingdome Of Ireland Done from Sr William Petty's Survey
mwuk0956	england	1693	BROWNE	2000	61	86	A Newe Map of England
mwaf0709	africa north	1710	BROWNE	400	59	57	Barbaria
mwaf0423	africa east	1799	BROWNE	400	37	37	Carte de la Route ... Sudan ... au Dar-Four
mwaf0424	africa east	1799	BROWNE	400	44	35	Carte du Dar-Four
mww0676	world	1826	BROWNE	720	87	67	H. Browne's Chart of Empires Chronologically and Geographically Arranged
mwit0121	italy	1695	BROWNE	1000	51	88	H. Jaillot's Map of the Seat of War in Italy
mwru0439	russia tartary	1700	BROWNE	720	54	65	Magnae Tartariae Magni Mogolis Imperii Japoniae et Chinae
mwuk0455	scotland	1708	BROWNE	1350	56	48	North Britain or Scotland 1708. A New Mapp of Scotland, the Western, Orkney, and Shetland Islands. Begun by Appointment of Rob.t Morden, Finished at ye Charge and by Direction of C. Browne
mwme0582	arabia etc	1700	BROWNE	720	47	55	Nova Persiae Armeniae Natoliae et Arabiae (map by F. de Wit c1680).
mwsam0711	south america paraguay	1690	BROWNE	800	45	55	Paraquaria vulgo Paraguay. Cum Adjacentibus
mwaf0421	africa east	1790	BRUCE	300	67	31	... this Map Shewing the Tract of Soloman's Fleet in their Three Years Voyage from Elanitic Gulf to Ophir and Tarshishi
mwaf0420	africa east	1790	BRUCE	300	51	29	... this Plan of Two Attempts to Arrive at the Source of the Nile
mww0452	world	1761	BRUCKNER	550	23	34	Carte General du Globe Terrestre
mwme0406	holy land	1828	BRUE	140	51	36	Carte de la Palestine sous la Domination Romaine
mwru0347	russia	1830	BRUE	200	36	51	Carte de la Russie D'Asie
mwp0078	australia	1826	BRUE	400	36	52	Carte de l'Australie (Partie Sud-Ouest de l'Oceanie) (2 insets)
mwp0523	pacific south	1820	BRUE	300	36	50	Carte de L'Oceanie
mwf0913	france paris	1820	BRUE	400	94	132	Carte des Environs de Paris
mwsam0418	south america brazil	1826	BRUE	400	51	36	Carte du Bresil et d'une Partie des Pays Adjacent. Redigee ... d'apres les ... des Portugais, des Espagnols, des Francais, des Anglois et un Grand Nombres de Cartes Publiees ou Inedites. 1826
mwbh0790	belgium holland	1821	BRUE	150	51	37	Carte du Royaume des Pays-Bas
mwam0598	america north	1815	BRUE	1500	111	142	Carte Encyprotype de l'Amerique Septentrionale
mwam0597	america north	1815	BRUE	500	55	69	Carte Encyprotype de l'Amerique Septentrionale Reduite de la Carte sur 4 Feuilles de Meme Auteur
mwe0247	europe	1816	BRUE	1400	110	150	Carte Encyprotype de l'Europe
mwsam0137	south america	1818	BRUE	900	111	142	Carte Encyprotype, de l' Amerique Meridionale
mwsam0548	south america colombia	1830	BRUE	240	36	51	Carte Generale de Colombie, de la Guyane Francaise, Hollandaise et Anglaise. Redigee ... 1826
mwaf0549	africa egypt etc	1822	BRUE	200	51	37	Carte Generale de Egypte et de l'Arabie Petree
mwam0660a	america north	1828	BRUE	300	37	51	Carte Generale de l'Amerique Septentrionale, et des Iles qui en Dependent
mwas0244	asia continent	1820	BRUE	280	36	51	Carte Generale de l'Asie
mwc0247	china	1821	BRUE	300	37	51	Carte Generale de l'Empire Chinois et du Japon
mwam0642	america north	1825	BRUE	450	38	51	Carte Generale des Etats-Unis de l'Amerique Septentrionale
mwgm0299	mexico	1825	BRUE	400	57	36	Carte Generale des Etats-Unis Mexicains (inset of Central America)
mwam0641	america north	1825	BRUE	300	38	51	Carte Generale des Etats-Unis, du Canada
mwwi0188	west indies	1832	BRUE	750	62	93	Carte Generale des Iles Antilles des Isles et Bancs de Bahama, des Etats-Unis de l'Amerique-Centrale, de la Mer du Mexique
mwuk0883	uk	1820	BRUE	150	51	36	Carte Generale des Iles Britanniques
mwin0345	india	1824	BRUE	280	36	51	Carte Generale Des Indes en dec et au dela du Gange
mwin0342	india	1821	BRUE	240	36	51	Carte Generale des Indes en-deca et au-dela de Gange
mwsam0797	south america peru	1830	BRUE	180	51	38	Carte Generale du Perou, de Haut-Perou, du Chile et de la Plata
mwwi0183	west indies	1830	BRUE	280	36	51	Carte Particuliere des Iles Antilles
mwaf0313	africa	1822	BRUE	350	57	87	Carte Physique et Politique de l'Afrique
mwam0657	america north	1827	BRUE	1100	58	87	Carte Physique et Politique de l'Amerique Septentrionale
mwe0255a	europe	1821	BRUE	500	58	86	Carte Physique et Politique de l'Europe
mwf0193	france	1828	BRUE	300	51	71	Carte Physique et Routiere de la France de la Suisse
mwit0245	italy	1834	BRUE	400	83	61	Carte Routiere de l'Italie Indiquant les Divisions Politiques de ses Divers Etats
mwit1048	italy south	1835	BRUE	120	37	51	Italie, Partie Sud
mww0683	world	1828	BRUE	6000	100	190	Mappe Monde en deux Hemispheres
mww0688	world	1830	BRUE	280	38	51	Mappe Monde en Deux Hemispheres

AMPG REFERENCE	REGION	DATE	MAP MAKER	PRICE (UK£)	VERT. (cm.)	HOR. (cm.)	TITLE OF MAP (Comments by the editor in brackets)
mww0650	world	1816	BRUE	2400	109	152	Mappe-Monde sur la Projection de Mercator Carte Encyprotype
mwsam0161	south america	1843	BRUE	1500	180	127	Nouvelle Carte de l'Amerique Meridionale et des Isles qui en Dependent
mwgm0323	mexico	1834	BRUE	12500	93	63	Nouvelle Carte du Mexique, du Texas et d'une Partie des Etats Limitrophes (illustrated is the 1839 revised edition)
	pacific west	1816	BRUE	300	53	77	Oceanie ou Cinquieme Partie du Monde Comprenant l'Arcipel d'Asie, l'Australasie la Polynesie &c. par M. Brue Carte Encyprotype Reduite de celle sur 4 Feuilles ... revue et Augmente en 1816
mwsc0204	scandinavia	1822	BRUE	200	51	36	Suede, du Norwege et de Danemark
mwru0515	ukraine	1737	BRUGGEN	400	26	32	Podolia et Bessarabia
mwam1128	america north (east)	1799	BRUN	2500	56	84	Carte Reduite des Cotes Orientales de l'Amerique Septentrionale Contenant Partie du Nouveau Jersey, le Pensylvanie, le Mary-Land, la Virginie, la Caroline Septentrionale, la Caroline Meridionale et la Georgie
mwg0053b	germany	1639	BRUN-AUBRY	4000	46	55	Nova Germaniae Descriptio (4 carte-a-figure borders)
mwec0024	uk england bedfordshire	1826	BRYANT	1400	69	48	Map of the County of Bedford from Actual Survey by A. Bryant, in the Years 1825 and 1826 (4 sheets)
mwec0076	uk england buckinghamshire	1825	BRYANT	2000	201	112	Map of the County of Buckingham, from Actual Survey by A. Bryant in the Year 1824
mwec0454	uk england gloucestershire	1824	BRYANT	1400	121	85	Map of the County of Gloucester from Actual Survey, by A. Bryant in the Years 1823 & 1824
mwec0839	uk england norfolk	1826	BRYANT	2800	240	198	Map of the County of Norfolk
mwec0870	uk england northamptonshire	1827	BRYANT	1500	187	192	Map of the County of Northampton from an Actual Survey
mwec0970	uk england oxfordshire	1824	BRYANT	1500	191	149	Map of the County of Oxford from Actual Survey by A. Bryant in the Year 1823 Described by Permission of the Earl of Macclesfield
mwec1118	uk england suffolk	1821	BRYANT	2500	151	195	Map of the County of Suffolk
mwec1148	uk england surrey	1823	BRYANT	2500	132	159	Map of the County of Surrey from Actual Survey by A. Bryant, in the Years 1822 and 1823
mwuk0482	scotland	1744	BRYCE	3000	50	70	A Map of the North Coast of Britain from Row Stoir of Assynt to Wick in Caithness
mwsc0385	scandinavia denmark	1801	BRYDON	1500	25	55	Plan and Disposition of the Danish Force, Moored for the Defence of the City of Copenhagen, with the British Squadron, Placed under the Command of Vice Admiral Lord Nelson
mwaf0183	africa	1745	BUACHE	650	49	62	Carte d'Afrique (re-issue of De L'Isle's 1722 map)
mwam0156	america continent	1745	BUACHE	750	48	61	Carte d'Amerique, Dressee pour l'Usage du Roy. Par Guillaume Delisle Premier Geographe de sa Majeste
mwas0212	asia continent	1788	BUACHE	600	49	62	Carte d'Asie Dressee pour l'Usage du Roy sur ce que les Arabes nous ont Laissee
mwwi0510	dominica	1778	BUACHE	1000	61	48	Carte de la Dominique Prise par les Francois le 7 Septembre 1778. Avec le Plan du Debarquement et de l'Attaque des Forts et Batteries par les Troupes et Les Fregates de sa Majeste
mwam0950	america north (east)	1745	BUACHE	2500	48	65	Carte de la Louisiane (re-issue of De L'Isle's 1718 map)
mwuss0627	louisiana	1745	BUACHE	2500	48	65	Carte de la Louisiane (re-issue of De L'Isle's 1718 map)
mwat0305	atlantic south	1737	BUACHE	500	50	65	Carte de la Partie de l'Ocean vers l'Equateur entre les Cotes d'Afrique et d'Amerique (large inset of Fernando de Noronha)
mwsam0178	south america (north)	1730	BUACHE	600	50	57	Carte de la Terre Ferme, du Perou, du Bresil, et du Pays des Amazones (copy of the northern sheet of De L'Isle's 1703 map of South America)
mwsp0304	spain	1789	BUACHE	375	48	60	Carte De L'Espagne dressee paar Guillaume Delisle ... augmente et verifie en 1789
mwe0204	europe	1782	BUACHE	480	48	60	Carte de L'Europe
mwjk0109	japan	1754	BUACHE	450	37	25	Carte de l'Isle de Ieso et de ses Environs pour Servir a Concilier les Differentes Idees que l'on a eue jusqu'a Present. Dressee par Philippe Buache
mwwi0710	jamaica	1740	BUACHE	350	24	32	Carte de l'Isle de la Jamaique aux Anglois avec les Passages entre cette Isle et celles de St. Domingue
mwru0199	russia	1745	BUACHE	720	96	64	Carte de Moscovie
mwwi0252	west indies (east)	1769	BUACHE	650	65	38	Carte des Antilles Francoises et des Isles Voisines
mwca0305	canada newfoundland	1741	BUACHE	750	25	34	Carte des Cotes Meridionales de l'Isle de Terre Neuve Comprenant les Isles Royale et de Sable avec la Partie du Grand Banc ... et Comparee avec le Plan de ces Memes Cotes et Isles de la Carte de Mr. Popple
mww0375	world	1739	BUACHE	750	51	65	Carte des Lieux ou les Differentes Longueurs du Pendule a Secondes ont ete Observees / Carte du Globe Terrestre ou les Terres de l"hemisphere Meridl. / Carte des Terres Australes (2 world maps on one sheet)

AMPG REFERENCE	REGION	DATE	MAP MAKER	PRICE (UK£)	VERT. (cm.)	HOR. (cm.)	TITLE OF MAP (Comments by the editor in brackets)
mwp0406	pacific north	1752	BUACHE-DE L'ISLE	4000	46	64	Carte des Nouvelles Decouvertes au Nord de la Mer du Sud, tant a l'Est de la Siberie et du Kamtchatka, qu'a l'Ouest de la Nouvelle France (this map was a collaboration between J. Buache and G. de L'Isles's son Joseph-Nicholas)
mwas0320	asia caspian sea	1745	BUACHE	550	46	62	Carte des Pays Voisins de la Mer Caspiene Dressee pour l'Usage du Roy sur la Carte de cette Mer Faite par l'Ordre du Czar, sur les Memoire Manuscrits de Soskam-Sabbas Prince de Georgie
mwaa0025	antarctic	1757	BUACHE	600	24		Carte des Terres Australes entre le Tropique du Capricorne et le Pole Antarctique (size is diameter of circle. See also Buache's map of the Pacific, 1757, with an inset of the Antarctic.)
mwbh0661	belgium holland	1745	BUACHE	350	64	64	Carte du Brabant
mwca0060	canada	1745	BUACHE	1200	50	65	Carte du Canada ou de la Nouvelle France et des Decouvertes qui y ont ete Faites Dressee sur Plusieurs Observations ... par Guillaume Del'Isle (re-issue of De L'Isle's 1703 map)
mww0392	world	1746	BUACHE	750	25	33	Carte du Globe Terrestre ou les Terres de l'Hemisphere Meridl. sont Supposees etre Vues a Travers celles de l'Hemisphere Septentl (2 polar projections superimposed on one another)
mwgm0045	gulf of mexico and surrounding regions	1780	BUACHE	1650	49	93	Carte du Golphe du Mexique et des Isles Antilles Reduite de la Grande Carte Angloise de Popple, par Ph. Buache 1er Geographe du Roi, Corrigee et Augmentee en 1780
mwam0949	america north (east)	1745	BUACHE	1400	48	65	Carte du Mexique et de la Floride des Terres Angloises et des Isles Antilles du Cours et des Environs de la Riviere de Mississipi (re-issue of De L'Isle 1703)
mwsam0757b	south america peru	1739	BUACHE	400	22	30	Carte du Pérou pour servir à l'histoire des Incas
mwit0689	italy piedmont	1775	BUACHE	320	49	64	Carte du Piemont et du Monferrat
mwwi0073	west indies	1740	BUACHE	1650	49	93	Carte d'une Partie de l'Amerique pour la Navigation des Isles et du Golfe du Mexique
mwsw0152	switzerland	1752	BUACHE	240	26	34	Carte Mineralogique de la Suisse
mwam0405	america north	1752	BUACHE	800	28	32	Carte Mineralogique ou l'on Voit la Nature des Terreins du Canada et de la Louisiane
mwam1007a	america north (east)	1761	BUACHE	600	27	31	Carte Mineralogique, ou l on voit la Nature des Terreins de Canada et de la Louisiane, Dressee par Philippe Buache...1752
mwaa0136	arctic	1754	BUACHE	250	21	21	Carte Phisique de la Mer Glaciale Arctique
mwp0255	pacific (all)	1757	BUACHE	1500	31	43	Carte Physique de la Grande Mer ci-devant Nommee Mer du Sud ou Pacifique; ou se Volent les Grandes Chaines de Montagnes
mwas0265	asia (from turkey to india)	1754	BUACHE	400	30	35	Carte Physique de la Mer des Indes (incl. Australia)
mwaa0028	antarctic	1771	BUACHE	1200	46	46	Hemisphere Meridional pour Voir Plus Distinctement les Terres Australes
mww0389	world	1745	BUACHE	1200	51	50	Hemisphere Occidental / Hemisphere Oriental (2 maps)
mwaa0140	arctic	1770	BUACHE	750	46	45	Hemisphere Septentrional pour Voir Plus Distinctement les Terres Arctiques
mwbp0430	poland	1745	BUACHE	550	48	62	La Pologne
mww0432	world	1755	BUACHE	2400	44	68	Mappemonde a l'Usage du Roy par Guillaume Delisle (see Dezauche re-issue for illustration, 1785)
mwit0688	italy piedmont	1770	BUACHE	320	49	64	Partie Meridionale du Piemont et du Monferrat
mwsam0362	south america brazil	1737	BUACHE	600	49	65	Plan de L'Isle de Fernand de Noronha - Carte de la Partie de L'Ocean
mwf0870	france paris	1745	BUACHE	180	20	28	Plan de Paris
mww0438	world	1756	BUACHE	720	34	44	Planisphere Physique ou l'on Voit du Pole Septentrionale ce que l'on Connoit de Terres et de Mers avec les Grandes Chaines du Montagnes (size incl. text borders. Illustration is 1780 Dezauche reprint.)
mwaa0137	arctic	1756	BUACHE	720	34	44	Planisphere Physique ou l'on Voit du Pole Septentrionale ce que l'on Connoit de Terres et de Mers avec les Grandes Chaines du Montagnes (size incl. text borders. Illustration: see 'World'.)
mwaa0132	arctic	1750	BUACHE	650	34	44	Planisphere Physique ou l'on Voit du Pole Septentrionale ce que l'on Connoit de Terres et de Mers avec les Grandes Chaines du Montagnes ... Dressee par Phil. Buache
mwp0407	pacific north	1754	BUACHE-VERDUN	1000	32	38	Kaart der Nieuwe Ontdekkingen benoorden de Zuyd Zee ... (reduction of Buache's 1752 map)
mwam0059	america continent	1658	BUCELINI	375	6	11	Americae Nova Descriptio
mwaf0062	africa	1658	BUCELINI	250	7	11	Africae Descriptio
mwas0045	asia continent	1658	BUCELINI	300	7	11	Asiae Superficialis Descriptio
mwc0046	china	1658	BUCELINI	300	6	11	Chinae Compendiosa Descriptio
mwsc0273	scandinavia denmark	1658	BUCELINI	240	7	11	Daniae Typus
mwe0065	europe	1658	BUCELINI	250	7	11	Europa
mwbh0333	belgium holland	1658	BUCELINI	120	7	11	Flandriae Compendiosa Delineatio
mwgr0078	greece	1662	BUCELINI	300	7	11	Graecia olim Hellas

AMPG REFERENCE	REGION	DATE	MAP MAKER	PRICE (UK£)	VERT. (cm.)	HOR. (cm.)	TITLE OF MAP (Comments by the editor in brackets)
mwuk0063	ireland	1658	BUCELINI	300	7	11	Hiberniae Insulae Miraculis Naturalibus pro digiosae delineatio
mwbh0332	belgium holland	1658	BUCELINI	250	6	10	Hollandiae
mwas0388	asia south east	1650	BUCELINI	375	6	10	India Orientalis
mwjk0025	japan	1658	BUCELINI	450	6	11	Japoniae Descripto
mwme0948	turkey etc	1658	BUCELINI	200	7	11	Natolia
mwit1015	italy south	1658	BUCELINI	200	6	10	Neapolitani Regni Compendiosa Descriptio
mwme0779	persia etc	1658	BUCELINI	200	6	11	Persarum Regni Descriptio
mwsp0037	portugal	1658	BUCELINI	200	7	11	Portugalliae Descriptio
mwit0891	italy sicily	1658	BUCELINI	200	7	11	Siciliae Superficialis Adiumbratio
mwru0428	russia tartary	1658	BUCELINI	200	6	11	Tartaria sive Magni Chami Imperium
mwme0149	holy land	1658	BUCELINI	200	11	7	Terra Sancta, sive Palaestina
mwme0949	turkey etc	1658	BUCELINI	200	7	11	Turci Impery Adumbratio
mwg0634	saxony	1720	BUCHNER	550	36	36	Accurate Geographische Delineation der Hochgrafl. Solmischen Herrschaft Wildenfels
mwam0644	america north	1825	BUCHON	300	44	65	Americae Septentrionale
mwam0643	america north	1825	BUCHON	400	37	64	Carte de l'Adjonction Progressive des Divers Etats au Territoire et a l'Union Constitutionelle des Etats-Unis de l'Amerique du Nord
mwsam0143	south america	1825	BUCHON	200	46	64	Carte de l'Amerique Meridionale
mwuss0041	alaska	1825	BUCHON	350	47	64	Carte des Possessions Russes Dressee par Pierron d'Apres le Carte de Mr. Brue
mwuss0055	arkansas	1825	BUCHON	400	36	36	Carte du Territoire d'Arkansas et des Autres Territoires des Etats-Unis
mwuss0008	alabama	1825	BUCHON	450	29	23	Carte Geographique, Statistique et Historique d'Alabama
mwsam0252	south america argentina	1825	BUCHON	200	22	32	Carte Geographique, Statistique et Historique de Buenos Ayres (size excludes surrounding text)
mwwi0483	cuba	1825	BUCHON	400	48	64	Carte Geographique, Statistique et Historique de Cuba / Ile de Cuba Dressee par Pierron d'apres la Carte de Humboldt
mwgm0110	guatemala	1825	BUCHON	450	41	60	Carte Geographique, Statistique et Historique de Guatimala
mwwi0680	hispaniola	1825	BUCHON	300	47	61	Carte Geographique, Statistique et Historique de Haity. Grave Par B. Beaupre
mwuss0265	carolinas	1825	BUCHON	300	26	45	Carte Geographique, Statistique et Historique de la Caroline du Nord
mwuss0464	florida	1825	BUCHON	350	28	24	Carte Geographique, Statistique et Historique de la Floride
mwuss0519	georgia	1826	BUCHON	400	46	61	Carte Geographique, Statistique et Historique de la Georgie d(size incl. text borders)
mwwi0565	guadeloupe	1827	BUCHON	400	50	64	Carte Geographique, Statistique et Historique de la Guadeloupe - Ile de la Guadeloupe Dressee par Pierron d'apres la Carte Publiee par le Colonel Boyer-Peyreleau
mwwi0755	jamaica	1825	BUCHON	200	46	61	Carte Geographique, Statistique et Historique de la Jamaique
mwuss0671	louisiana	1825	BUCHON	280	29	32	Carte Geographique, Statistique et Historique de la Louisiane
mwwi0812	martinique	1825	BUCHON	280	47	61	Carte Geographique, Statistique et Historique de la Martinique
mwuss1407	pennsylvania	1825	BUCHON	300	29	44	Carte Geographique, Statistique et Historique de la Pensylvanie
mwsam0545	south america colombia	1825	BUCHON	280	46	61	Carte Geographique, Statistique et Historique de la Republique Colombienne
mwuss1680	virginia	1825	BUCHON	350	30	45	Carte Geographique, Statistique et Historique de la Virginie
mwam0283	america continent	1825	BUCHON	280	24	40	Carte Geographique, Statistique et Historique de l'Amerique
mwuss0550	illinois	1825	BUCHON	400	43	61	Carte Geographique, Statistique et Historique de l'Illinois
mwuss0570	indiana	1825	BUCHON	400	28	22	Carte Geographique, Statistique et Historique de l'Indiana
mwuss1291	ohio	1825	BUCHON	350	46	61	Carte Geographique, Statistique et Historique de l'Ohio
mwuss0865	massachusetts	1825	BUCHON	300	46	63	Carte Geographique, Statistique et Historique de Massachusetts
mwuss0906	michigan	1825	BUCHON	450	46	61	Carte Geographique, Statistique et Historique de Michigan
mwuss1195	new york	1825	BUCHON	350	46	61	Carte Geographique, Statistique et Historique de New York
mwuss1021	new hampshire	1825	BUCHON	200	28	22	Carte Geographique, Statistique et Historique de New-Hampshire
mwwi0841	puerto rico	1825	BUCHON	400	25	42	Carte Geographique, Statistique et Historique de Porto-Rico et des Iles Vierges
mwwi0175	west indies	1827	BUCHON	350	46	59	Carte Geographique, Statistique et Historique des Indes Occidentales
mwuss0040	alaska	1825	BUCHON	350	37	44	Carte Geographique, Statistique et Historique des Possessions Russes
mwsam0413	south america brazil	1825	BUCHON	180	28	28	Carte Geographique, Statistique et Historique du Bresil (map surrounded by text)
mwuss0314	connecticut	1825	BUCHON	350	46	61	Carte Geographique, Statistique et Historique du Connecticut
mwuss0381	delaware	1825	BUCHON	450	46	61	Carte Geographique, Statistique et Historique du Delaware
mwuss0349	washington DC	1825	BUCHON	400	46	61	Carte Geographique, Statistique et Historique du District de Colombie
mwuss0608	kentucky	1825	BUCHON	200	28	43	Carte Geographique, Statistique et Historique du Kentucky
mwuss0718	maine	1825	BUCHON	280	46	61	Carte Geographique, Statistique et Historique du Maine

AMPG REFERENCE	REGION	DATE	MAP MAKER	PRICE (UK£)	VERT. (cm.)	HOR. (cm.)	TITLE OF MAP (Comments by the editor in brackets)
mwuss0773	maryland	1825	BUCHON	350	28	47	Carte Geographique, Statistique et Historique du Maryland
mwuss0959	mississippi	1825	BUCHON	300	29	24	Carte Geografique, Statistique et Historique du Missouri
mwuss1058	new jersey	1825	BUCHON	500	54	69	Carte Geographique, Statistique et Historique du New-Jersey
mwsam0727	south america paraguay	1825	BUCHON	240	42	25	Carte Geographique, Statistique et Historique du Paraguay
mwsam0792	south america peru	1825	BUCHON	200	46	64	Carte Geographique, Statistique et Historique du Perou
mwuss1474	rhode isl	1825	BUCHON	280	46	61	Carte Geographique, Statistique et Historique du Rhode-Island
mwuss1493	tennessee	1825	BUCHON	200	29	45	Carte Geographique, Statistique et Historique du Tennessee
mwuss1573	vermont	1825	BUCHON	350	46	61	Carte Geographique, Statistique et Historique du Vermont
mwuk1186	england london	1749	BUCK	6000	32	80	(Panorama of London & Westminster in 5 sheets, each 32x80cm.)
mwe0168	europe	1750	BUFFIER	135	19	22	Carte de l'Europe
mwam0145a	america continent	1737	BUFFIER	200	18	14	L'Amerique Suivant les Dernieres Observations de l'Academie Royale des Sciences
mwin0437a	indian ocean	1788	BUFFON	300	51	58	Carte des Declinaisons et Inclinaisons de L'Aquille Aimantee (map by La Perouse)
mwp0261	pacific (all)	1788	BUFFON	3000	42	55	Carte des Declinaisons et Inclinaisons de l'Aiguille Aimantee Redigee d'apres la Table des Observations Magnetiques Faites par les Voyageurs depuis l'Annee 1775 (4 sheets, the smallest 42x55cm, incl. Capt. Cook's discoveries. Maps by La Perouse)
mwaa0195	arctic / antarctic	1760	BUFFON	450	22	45	Carte des Deux Regions Polaires jusqu'au 45e Degre de Latitude
mwaa0201a	arctic / antarctic	1788	BUFFON	800	48	98	Carte Magnetique des Deux Hemispheres (incl. discoveries by La Perouse)
mwuss1657	virginia	1787	BUISSON	500	29	38	Plan d'York en Virginie ... Amerique
mwit0907	italy sicily	1692	BULIFON	600	22	32	Regno et Isola di Sicilia
mwam0765	america north	1845	BULLA FRERES & JOUY	150	27	37	Estados-Unidos
mwme0053	holy land	1594	BUNTING	650	16	25	Reisen der Kinder Israel aus Egypten
mwaf0016	africa	1581	BUNTING	960	27	34	Africa Tertia Pars Terrae
mwas0012	asia continent	1592	BUNTING	3000	27	34	Asia Secunda Pars Terrae in Forma Pegasi (stylized in the form of a winged horse)
mwme0052	holy land	1592	BUNTING	650	27	17	Beschreibung des gelobten Landes Canaan (other versions shown far left)
mwme0045	holy land	1581	BUNTING	960	28	37	Beschreibung des Heiligen Landes
mwme0062	holy land	1605	BUNTING	400	16	25	Dese Caerte des Heylighen Landts
mwaf0022	africa	1594	BUNTING	1200	16	25	Dese Derde Caerte van Aphrica (reduced size version of 1581 map)
mwas0026	asia continent	1605	BUNTING	800	17	26	Dese Tweede Caerte van Asia
mwm0128	mediterranean east	1663	BUNTING	550	16	25	Deze Caerte van den Uittocht der Kinderen Israels
mwas0009	asia continent	1581	BUNTING	2000	27	36	Die Eigentliche und Warhafftige Gestalt der Erden und des Meers. Cosmographia Universalis (shows W. Australia correctly!)
mww0070	world	1581	BUNTING	6500	27	36	Die Gantze Welt in ein Kleberblat / welches in der Stadt Hannover / meines Lieben Vaterlandes Wapen (the world in the form of a clover leaf)
mwe0015	europe	1592	BUNTING	2500	26	35	Europa Prima Pars Terrae in Forma Virginis (stylized in the form of a queen)
mwme0439	jerusalem	1582	BUNTING	200	27	39	Gestalt des Tempels Salomonis mit seinen Dreyen Vorhoffen
mwme0440	jerusalem	1582	BUNTING	500	27	36	Jerusalem die Heilige Viereckete Stadt, in Grund Gelegt und Eigentlich Abgemalet
mwme0045a	holy land	1581	BUNTING	960	28	36	Reisen der Kinder Israel aus Egypten
mwm0112	mediterranean east	1585	BUNTING	720	30	38	Taffel der Lender darin der Apostel Paulus Geprediget hat
mwme0054	holy land	1594	BUNTING	720	27	19	Taffel des Heiligen Landes zu dem Newen Testament Dienlich
mwas0174	asia continent	1760	BURCKHARDT	1200	33	38	Asia (Hungarian text)
mwe0180	europe	1760	BURCKHARDT	1200	33	37	Europa (Hungarian text)
mwme0512	jerusalem	1810	BURDER	500	35	43	Old Jerusalem
mwec0269	uk england derbyshire	1786	BURDETT	450	76	53	A New Map of Derbyshire, Describing the Noblemen and Gentlemen's Seats, Borough and Market Towns, Villages, Canals, Rivers, Moors, Hills, Watering Places, &c.
mwsc0043a	scandinavia	1626	BURE		56	42	Orbis Arctoi Nova et Accurata Delineatio (In 6 sheets, each 56x42cm)
mwuk0973a	england	1714	BURGHERS	90	18	27	Magna Britannia et Hibernia Antiqua et Nova (M. Burghers was the engraver)
mwe0316	europe austria	1629	BURGKLEHNER	1800	160	155	Die Fr. Graffschafft Tirol
mwuss0099	california	1803	BURNEY	350	26	26	(California Peninsula)
mwgm0265	mexico	1803	BURNEY	200	25	25	(Lower California)
mwgm0266	mexico	1803	BURNEY	200	25	25	(Mexico)
mwc0244	china	1818	BURNEY	250	44	39	Chart of the Coast of China and of the Sea Eastwards from the River of Canton to the Southern Islands of Japan
mwsam0427	south america brazil	1835	BURR	150	33	27	Brazil with Guiana & Paraguay
mwru0184	russia	1740	BUSCH	1200	47	67	Grundriß der Festung Statt und Situation St: Petersburg
mwm0145a	mediterranean east	1730	BUSCH	400	34	50	Tabula Geographica Pertinens ad Acta Apostolorum

AMPG REFERENCE	REGION	DATE	MAP MAKER	PRICE (UK£)	VERT. (cm.)	HOR. (cm.)	TITLE OF MAP (Comments by the editor in brackets)
mwca0148	canada	1824	BUSHNAN	180	17	23	Plan of Hurd Channel
mww0645	world	1813	BUTTE	3000	62	95	Mappemonde Physico-Climatologique (incl. human statistics)
mwwi0535	grenadines	1776	BYRES	7500	62	94	Plan of the Island of Bequia Laid Down by the Actual Survey under the Direction of the Honourable the Commissioners for the Sale of Lands in the Ceded Islands
mwwi0507	dominica	1776	BYRES	20000	153	90	Plan of the Island of Dominica Laid down by Actual Survey under the Direction of the Honourable the Commissioners for the Sale of Lands in the Ceded Islands (publ. by Faden)
mwwi0893	st vincent	1776	BYRES	10000	94	62	Plan of the Island of St. Vincent Laid Down by Actual Survey
mwwi0900a	trinidad & tobago	1776	BYRES	10000	61	92	Plan of the Island of Tobago, Laid down by Actual Survey under the Direction of the Honorable the Commissioners for the Sale of Lands in the Ceded Islands
mwuss0225	carolinas	1787	CADELL	650	25	29	Plan of the Siege of Charlestown in South Carolina
mwuk1598a	channel islands	1811	CADELL & DAVIES	200	18	26	(Untitled map, north to the left)
mwme0513	jerusalem	1812	CADELL & DAVIES	200	25	20	A New Plan of Jerusalem, in which Some Attempt is Made to Reconcile Historical Documents
mwsp0621	spain regions	1814	CADELL & DAVIES	400	42	30	A Plan of the Battle of the Arapiles near Salamanca with the Previous Movements of the Armies from the Douro to the Tormes
mwaf0985	africa south	1805	CADELL & DAVIES	280	36	24	Chart of Table Bay at the Cape of Good Hope, as Taken in the Year 1786 by Order of the Governor van de Graaff.
mwaf0986	africa south	1805	CADELL & DAVIES	675	20	28	Chart of the Knysna, an Arm of the Sea Seven Leagues to the Westward of Plettenberg's Bay, Surveyed by Mr James Callender
mwc0232	china	1802	CADELL & DAVIES	100	25	20	China
mwme0385	holy land	1797	CADELL & DAVIES	100	20	27	Palaestina
mwru0273	russia	1784	CADELL & DAVIES	240	31	24	Plan of the Canal of Vishnei Voloshok, which Unites the Baltic and the Caspian / Plan of the Ladoga Canal
mwaf0757	africa north algeria	1817	CADELL & DAVIES	250	23	34	Plan of the Town and Mole of Algiers and it's Vicinity, with the Disposition of the British and Netherland Fleets; Augt. 27: 1816
mwaf0555	africa egypt etc	1827	CAILLIAUD	280	61	43	Carte Generale de l'Egypte et de la Nubie
mww0048	world	1555	CALAPODA-ANON	50000	21	29	(Untitled oval projection, surrounded by ornate border with 6 portraits)
mwbh0212	belgium holland	1628	CALLOT	6750	120	140	Sige de Breda. Israel Silvestre ex Parisijs
mwm0231	mediterranean malta	1728	CALMET	450	29	43	Ancien Plan de l'Isle de Malte, ou S. Paul Aborda apres son Naufrage
mwme0293	holy land	1730	CALMET	500	32	46	Carte de la Terre Promise
mwme0276	holy land	1722	CALMET	300	24	20	Carte du Paradis Terrestre (2 maps)
mwme0277a	holy land	1724	CALMET	500	23	35	Carte du Voiage des Israelites dans le Desert (reduced size 1707 map plus decorative borders)
mwme0237	holy land	1707	CALMET	750	34	46	Carte du Voyage et Routes des Israelites dans le Desert (engr. By P. Starckman)
mwm0145	mediterranean east	1730	CALMET	450	33	45	Carte Particuliere des Pais que les Apotres ont Parcourus, et des Lieux les Plus Renommez ou ils ont Preche
mwme0485	jerusalem	1722	CALMET	480	30	44	Description de l'Ancienne Jerusalem selon Villalpand
mww0349	world	1725	CALMET	550	33	44	Geografische Kaarte van de Oude Weereld Volgens de Verdeeling der Kinderen van Noach
mwme0277	holy land	1722	CALMET	150	35	19	Plan et Distribution de la Terre de Chanaan, Suivant le Vision d'Ezechiel Chap.XLVIII, laquelle ne Fut jamais Executee a la Lettre
mwf0531	france corsica	1771	CAMBIAGI	3500	39	66	Isola di Corsica
mwuk1735	wales	1637	CAMDEN	300	27	20	Anglesey Comitatus, olim Mona Insula Druidum Sedes Britannia Tir Mon
mwec0005	uk england bedfordshire	1637	CAMDEN	375	27	33	Bedford Comitatus olim Pars Cathisuclanorum
mwuk1736	wales	1637	CAMDEN	180	27	31	Brecknoc Comitatus Pars olim Silurum
mwuk1699	wales	1607	CAMDEN	650	27	34	Breknoc comitatus.
mwuk1093	england and scotland	1607	CAMDEN	500	26	16	Britannia (enlarged copy of Rogers' 1600 map)
mwec0057	uk england buckinghamshire	1607	CAMDEN	600	27	28	Buckingha comitatus
mwuk1737	wales	1637	CAMDEN	350	27	32	Caermardi Comitatus in quo Dimetae olim Habitarunt
mwuk1738	wales	1637	CAMDEN	350	25	31	Caernarvo Comitatus Pars olim Ordovicum
mwec0088	uk england cambridgeshire	1637	CAMDEN	400	28	32	Cambridge Comitatus quem olim Iceni Insederunt
mwec0596	uk england kent	1607	CAMDEN	450	28	38	Cantium quod nunc Kent
mwuk1739	wales	1637	CAMDEN	350	27	31	Cardigan Comitatus Pars olim Dimetarum
mwec0123	uk england cheshire	1607	CAMDEN	720	28	38	Cestria comitatus
mwec0031	uk england berkshire	1607	CAMDEN	720	28	38	Comitatus Bercheriae.
mwec0162	uk england cornwall	1607	CAMDEN	900	28	38	Cornwall.
mwec0217	uk england cumbria	1607	CAMDEN	720	28	38	Cumbria sive Cumberlandia.
mwuk1700	wales	1607	CAMDEN	650	26	32	Denbigh comitatus.
mwec0280	uk england devon	1607	CAMDEN	720	28	38	Devoniae comitatus
mwec0318	uk england dorset	1610	CAMDEN	600	27	39	Dorcestriae Comitatis vulgo Dorsett ubi olim Durotriges Insederunt
mwec0356	uk england durham	1607	CAMDEN	720	27	32	Dunelmensis episcopatus.
mwec1291	uk england yorkshire	1607	CAMDEN	720	28	38	Eboracensis comitatus ... vulgo East Riding.

AMPG REFERENCE	REGION	DATE	MAP MAKER	PRICE (UK£)	VERT. (cm.)	HOR. (cm.)	TITLE OF MAP (Comments by the editor in brackets)
mwec1292	uk england yorkshire	1607	CAMDEN	720	28	38	Eboracensis comitatus … vulgo North Riding.
mwec1293	uk england yorkshire	1607	CAMDEN	720	28	38	Eboracensis comitatus … vulgo West Riding.
mwuk0914	england	1607	CAMDEN	1000	28	33	Englalond Anglia Anglosaxonum Heptarchia
mwec0394	uk england essex	1607	CAMDEN	720	28	38	Essexia comitatus.
mwuk1740	wales	1637	CAMDEN	350	26	33	Flint Comitatus, quem Ordovices olim Incoluerunt
mwec0508	uk england herefordshire	1607	CAMDEN	600	29	31	Frugiferi ac Amaeni Herefordiae comitatus
mwuk1741	wales	1637	CAMDEN	350	27	34	Glamorgan Comitatus qui olim Pars Silurum
mwec0429	uk england gloucestershire	1607	CAMDEN	720	28	38	Glocestriae comitatus
mwec0462	uk england hampshire	1607	CAMDEN	800	28	38	Hamshire.
mwec0536	uk england hertfordshire	1607	CAMDEN	800	28	38	Hertfordiae comitatus
mwuk0016	ireland	1607	CAMDEN	800	27	33	Hiberniae
mwec0574	uk england huntingdonshire	1637	CAMDEN	280	28	34	Huntington Comitatus
mwec0671	uk england lancashire	1607	CAMDEN	720	29	30	Lancastriae Comitatus Palatinus olim Pars Brigantum
mwec0712	uk england leicestershire	1637	CAMDEN	350	29	36	Lecestriae Comitatus
mwec0732	uk england lincolnshire	1607	CAMDEN	720	29	36	Lincolniae comitatus.
mwuk1742	wales	1637	CAMDEN	350	26	33	Merioneth Comitatus olim Pars Ordiwicum
mwec0764	uk england middlesex	1607	CAMDEN	900	28	38	Middlesex.
mwuk1743	wales	1637	CAMDEN	350	26	30	Mongomery Comitatus qui olim Pars Ordovicum
mwuk1701	wales	1607	CAMDEN	650	28	34	Monumenthensis comitatus.
mwec0805	uk england norfolk	1607	CAMDEN	720	28	36	Norfolciae comitatus
mwec0850	uk england northamptonshire	1637	CAMDEN	320	28	36	Northamtoniae Comitatus
mwec0874	uk england northumberland	1607	CAMDEN	685	28	38	Northumbriae comitatus.
mwec0902	uk england nottinghamshire	1607	CAMDEN	650	28	38	Notingamiae comitatus.
mwec0935	uk england oxfordshire	1607	CAMDEN	800	28	38	Oxoniensis comitatus
mwuk1744	wales	1637	CAMDEN	350	28	34	Penbrok Comitatus olim Pars Demetarum
mwuk1702	wales	1607	CAMDEN	650	27	34	Radnor comitatus.
mwec0977	uk england rutland	1607	CAMDEN	650	28	34	Rutlandiae omnium in Anglia comitatuum minimus.
mwec0997	uk england shropshire	1607	CAMDEN	650	27	34	Salopiae comitatus.
mwuk0323	scotland	1607	CAMDEN	800	26	31	Scotia Regnum
mwec1031	uk england somerset	1637	CAMDEN	420	28	39	Somersettensis Comitatus
mwec1057	uk england staffordshire	1607	CAMDEN	685	28	38	Staffordiae comitatus.
mwec1090	uk england suffolk	1607	CAMDEN	800	28	39	Suffolciae comitatus
mwec1128	uk england surrey	1637	CAMDEN	600	29	38	Surrey olim Sedes Regnorum
mwec1157	uk england sussex	1637	CAMDEN	500	22	40	Sussexia sive Southsex, olim pars Regnorum
mwec0251	uk england derbyshire	1607	CAMDEN	685	28	38	Universi Derbiensis comitatus
mwec1186	uk england warwickshire	1607	CAMDEN	720	29	35	Warwici comitatus.
mwec1220	uk england westmorland	1637	CAMDEN	450	26	30	Westmorlandiae Comitatus qui olim Spectavit ad Brigantas
mwec1268	uk england worcestershire	1607	CAMDEN	720	28	38	Wigorniensis comitatus.
mwec1236	uk england wiltshire	1607	CAMDEN	650	27	36	Wiltoniae comitatus.
mwe0979	europe montenegro	1570	CAMOCIO	750	16	22	(Bar) Antivari Cita in Confine della Dalmatia et Albania
mwat0010	atlantic ocean (all)	1572	CAMOCIO	1200	17	20	(Europe, Africa & Eastern Canada)
mwit0032	italy	1575	CAMOCIO	1500	17	22	(Italy)
mwe0636	europe dalmatia	1570	CAMOCIO	600	15	19	(Korcula) Curciola Insula
mwgr0554	greece islands	1572	CAMOCIO	600	22	16	(Lesbos) Metelin Mitilene
mwgr0550	greece islands	1572	CAMOCIO	400	17	24	(Levkas) Sancta Maura Scopulus Antichame Detta
mwe0492	europe croatia	1572	CAMOCIO	500	14	18	(Osor on Cres isl.) Osero
mwgr0551	greece islands	1572	CAMOCIO	500	21	16	(Patmos) Palmosa Patmo Antiquame … Dominato da Turchi
mwe0491b	europe croatia	1572	CAMOCIO	550	14	18	(Pula) Polla Querrner
mwe0491a	europe croatia	1571	CAMOCIO	400	18	22	(Sibenik) Sebenico
mwe0491c	europe croatia	1572	CAMOCIO	600	15	20	(Split) Spallato
mwgr0560	greece islands	1575	CAMOCIO	720	16	20	(Tinos) Tine insula e citta antiqua
mwe0978	europe montenegro	1570	CAMOCIO	1200	16	21	(Untitled map focussing on Kotor and Dubrovnik)
mwbh0023	belgium holland	1566	CAMOCIO	6000	51	40	Brabantiae Belgarum Provinciae Recens Exactaque Descriptio
mwuk0667	uk	1563	CAMOCIO	15000	50	36	Britania Insula quae Duo Regna Continet Angliam et Scotiam cum Hibernia Adiacente (close copy of Lily, 1556)
mwsc0019	scandinavia	1562	CAMOCIO	12000	39	52	Caelator Candido Lectori Salutem. Accipe Candide Lector Absolutissimam Septentrionalium Regionum, Suetiae, Gotiae, Norvegiae, Prussiae, Pomeraniae, Ducatus Megapolensis, Frisiae, Geldriae, Altae Marchiae, Lusatiae (close copy of Tramezini 1556)
mwgr0348	greece crete	1575	CAMOCIO	1200	20	16	Candia vel Creta Insula
mwe0976	europe montenegro	1570	CAMOCIO	600	15	21	Castel Novo
mwgr0277	greece cefalonia	1572	CAMOCIO	650	15	21	Cefalonia. Insula Posta sopra il Mare Adriatico
mwgr0552	greece islands	1572	CAMOCIO	400	16	21	Cerigo Insula
mwgr0451a	greece cyprus	1571	CAMOCIO	2000	20	16	Cipro insula nobiliss.
mwgr0553	greece islands	1572	CAMOCIO	800	17	23	Citta di Scio
mwe0274c	europe albania	1572	CAMOCIO	650	18	22	Colfo de Lodrin con Parte di Albania
mwme0923	turkey etc	1572	CAMOCIO	1200	15	20	Constantinopoli Citta Principale del Gran Turcho (map by D. Zenoi)
mwgr0296	greece corfu	1572	CAMOCIO	1100	20	15	Corfu Insula Antiquamente detta Malena
mwf0460	france corsica	1574	CAMOCIO	1100	15	20	Corsica
mwgr0349	greece crete	1575	CAMOCIO	2500	28	21	Creta Insula, hodie Candia
mwgr0440	greece cyprus	1566	CAMOCIO	25000	26	41	Cyprus Insula Nobilissima

AMPG REFERENCE	REGION	DATE	MAP MAKER	PRICE (UK£)	VERT. (cm.)	HOR. (cm.)	TITLE OF MAP (Comments by the editor in brackets)
mwme0919	turkey etc	1570	CAMOCIO	600	16	22	Dardanelo
mwme0924	turkey etc	1572	CAMOCIO	300	16	23	Dardanelo Fortezza dala Parte dela Gretia
mwsc0476	scandinavia iceland	1570	CAMOCIO	4000	26	18	De Islandia Insula
mwe0977	europe montenegro	1570	CAMOCIO	600	15	20	Dulcigno
mwe0274a	europe croatia	1570	CAMOCIO	600	14	17	Durazzo Antiquamente Dette Epidamna Citta (Albania)
mwm0001	mediterranean	1568	CAMOCIO	8500	27	38	Europae Brevis, ac Novissima Descriptio
mwgr0451	greece cyprus	1571	CAMOCIO	1500	17	22	Famagosta (view of the siege)
mwbh0024	belgium holland	1566	CAMOCIO	3500	48	38	Frisiae Antiouissimae trans Rhenum Provinc. et Adiacentum Regionu Nova et Exacta Descriptio
mwme0925	turkey etc	1575	CAMOCIO	500	17	22	Galipoli
mwgr0033	greece	1572	CAMOCIO	400	16	21	Golfo della Prevesa
mwgr0034	greece	1572	CAMOCIO	400	16	21	Golfo di Lepanto
mwuk0005	ireland	1570	CAMOCIO	7500	25	18	Hibernia sive Irlanda ... apud Camocium (south to the top)
mwaf0811	africa north tunisia	1572	CAMOCIO	800	23	17	Il Vero Disegno della Cita di Tunisi e Biserta
mwgr0035	greece	1572	CAMOCIO	400	18	23	Il Vero Ritrato del Sito di Modone et Navarino nella Provincia della Morea
mwit0325	italy elba	1574	CAMOCIO	1500	24	18	Ilba sive Ilva Insula
mwuk1091	england and scotland	1575	CAMOCIO	2500	22	18	Inghilterra Et Scotia
mwuk0006a	ireland	1575	CAMOCIO	3000	14	19	Irlanda (re-issue of Bertelli)
mwsc0477	scandinavia iceland	1574	CAMOCIO	1500	24	18	Islanda
mwe0491	europe croatia	1569	CAMOCIO	4000	31	42	Istria sotto il Dominio Veneto
mwe0492c	europe croatia	1575	CAMOCIO	1000	18	24	Istria sotto il dominio Veneto (shown below left)
mwit0461	italy lombardy	1562	CAMOCIO	6000	31	48	La Vera Descritione di Tutta la Lombardia
mwgr0561	greece islands	1575	CAMOCIO	1500	17	13	L'Arcipelago
mwgr0562	greece islands	1575	CAMOCIO	720	20	15	Milo Insula posta del mare del Arcipelago
mwgr0027	greece	1570	CAMOCIO	1250	21	15	Morea Peninsula Provinc.a Principale della Grecia ... Fertile di Ogni Cosa
mwgr0554a	greece islands	1572	CAMOCIO	600	21	16	Negroponte Insula
mwgr0440a	greece cyprus	1569	CAMOCIO	1000	18	24	Nicosia
mwgr0452	greece cyprus	1571	CAMOCIO	2000	20	28	Nicossia (showing the siege by the Ottomans)
mwgr0547	greece islands	1570	CAMOCIO	750	20	15	Nicsia Nacso Antiquame detta Isola Posta nello Arcipelago
mwe0490	europe croatia	1566	CAMOCIO	2400	29	40	Novo Dissegno della Dalmatia et Crovatia
mwe0274b	europe albania	1572	CAMOCIO	1200	18	23	Provincia di Albania
mwme0917	turkey etc	1566	CAMOCIO	6000	43	59	Questo Disegno Rapresenta il Naturale della Provincia della Natolia, et Caramania ... l'Isola di Candia, et quella di Cipro (map by Gastaldi)
mwgr0517	greece rhodes	1572	CAMOCIO	1500	21	15	Rhodi Insula et Citta Memorabile
mwgr0518	greece rhodes	1572	CAMOCIO	1000	16	20	Rodi Citta
mwgr0548	greece islands	1570	CAMOCIO	750	21	15	Samo nello Arcipelago che dal Nome
mwit0774d	italy sardinia	1570	CAMOCIO	1200	17	20	Sardegna (shown above left)
mwgr0555	greece islands	1572	CAMOCIO	480	21	16	Scarpanto, Carpanto Antiquamente Detta
mwgr0556	greece islands	1572	CAMOCIO	800	22	16	Scio Chio Antiquame Detta
mwit0866	italy sicily	1574	CAMOCIO	1500	15	22	Sicilia Insula
mwme0033	holy land	1566	CAMOCIO	16000	28	49	Situs Terre Sancte iuxta Numeru Filior Israel per Apices, seu Pucta Divisus
mwgr0563	greece islands	1575	CAMOCIO	650	14	20	Stalimene
mwit0378	italy lazio	1559	CAMOCIO	3000	33	49	Territorio di Roma
mwm0170	mediterranean malta	1570	CAMOCIO	1800	17	13	Valletta Nova Citta di Malta
mwit1207	italy venice	1562	CAMOCIO	4000	48	35	Venice
mwe0410a	europe austria	1575	CAMOCIO	1200	15	20	Vienna
mwgr0534	greece zante (zakynthos)	1572	CAMOCIO	1000	16	21	Zante Insula Posta nel Mare Mediterraneo
mwe0638	europe dalmatia	1570	CAMOCIO	1200	27	20	Zarra
mwgr0342	greece crete	1564	CAMOCIO-BERTELLI	2400	27	38	El Vero et Nuovo Disegno di Tutta la Isola di Candia
mwat0006	atlantic ocean (all)	1560	CAMOCIO-FORLANI	25000	24	36	Navigationi dil mondo novo (close copy of De Nicolay's 1554 map)
mwaf0071	africa	1662	CAMOCIO-SCOLARI	40000	98	105	Nova et Acurata Totius Africae Tabula auct G.I. Blaeu (3rd state of a map originally engraved c1569)
mwam0067	america continent	1662	CAMOCIO-SCOLARI	80000	98	105	Nova et Acurata Totius Americae Tabula auct: G.I. Blaeu (3rd state of c1569 map)
mwas0052	asia continent	1662	CAMOCIO-SCOLARI	40000	98	105	Nova et Acurata Totius Asiae Tabula, Auct: G.I. Blaeu (3rd state of c1569 map)
mwe0075	europe	1662	CAMOCIO-SCOLARI	40000	98	105	Nova et Acurata Totius Europae Tabula Auct. G.I. Blaeu (3rd state of c1569 map)
mwuk1874b	wales	1827	CAMPBELL	1250	120	123	A Map of the County of Pembroke ... 1826
mwbp0152a	baltic states	1812	CAMPE	720	53	81	Neue militairische Situations und Postkarte von West-Rußland (title also in French)
mwf1083	france provence	1810	CAMPEN	1600	62	91	Plan Routier de la Ville de Marseille
mwsp0732	gibraltar	1780	CAMPIONS	1200	48	61	Plan des Attaques Combinees de Terre et de Mer pour Prendre d'Assaut la Forteresse de Gibraltar. Fait par un Ingenieur de l'Armee
mwit0304	italy central	1699	CANALI	900	49	66	Latium Campania et Samnium
mww0269	world	1699	CANALI	2800	39	59	Mappamondo o Vero Carta Generale del Globo Terrestre
mwit0455b	italy liguria	1830	CANIANI	350	53	44	Carta Militare di Genova
mwit0544a	italy milan	1801	CANIANI	1200	78	57	Pianta della citta di Milano
mwit0763	italy rome	1832	CANINA	650	95	135	Pianta Topografica di Roma Antica con i Principali Monumenti

AMPG REFERENCE	REGION	DATE	MAP MAKER	PRICE (UK£)	VERT. (cm.)	HOR. (cm.)	TITLE OF MAP (Comments by the editor in brackets)
mwit0493a	italy lombardy	1701	CANTELLI	800	45	64	Lombardia Alta et Bassa e Stati ad essa Circonuicini
mwp0509	pacific south	1795	CANZLER	1250	45	57	Karte vom Funften Erdtheil oder Polynaesien-Inselwelt oder Australien od. Sudindien (later editions omit the words 'oder Polynaesien-Inselwelt' from the title)
mwit0616	italy north	1782	CAPELLARIS	1500	62	70	Carte delle Contee di Gorizia, di Grandisca, Distretto di Trieste, e del Friuli Veneto
mwsc0650	scandinavia norway	1845	CAPPELEN	1250	61	74	Kart over det Sydlige Norge (2 sheets 61x74cm.)
mwe0434	europe austria vienna	1811	CAPPI	600	59	67	Grundriss der Kaiserl. Konigl. Haupt und Residenz Stadt Wien mit ihren Vorstadten in Viertel Eingetheilt
mwe0248	europe	1816	CAPPI	1200	122	140	Neueste Post-Karte von Europa mit der Neuesten Laender-Abtheilung des Letzten Frieden-Tractats
mwit1141	italy florence	1810	CAPPIARDI	500	48	41	Pianta della Citta di Firenze
mwf1000a	france provence	1634	CAPUCINS	550	22	32	Provincia S. Ludovici vel Provinciae cum confinis
mwjk0020	japan	1646	CARDIM	12000	27	40	Iapponiae. Nova & Accuraa Descriptio per R.P. Antonium Franciscum Cardim Societatis Iesu ad Elogia Iapponica
mwbh0780	belgium holland	1810	CARDON	1350	70	104	Carte Topographique des Franches Forets de Merdael Mollendael et Heverlez
mww0594	world	1796	CAREY	875	37	47	A Chart of the World According to Mercator's Projection.
mwuss1676	virginia	1814	CAREY	300	33	49	A Correct Map of Virginia
mwsam0406	south america brazil	1814	CAREY	250	45	35	A Map of Brazil Now Called New Portugal
mwuk0239	ireland	1796	CAREY	120	36	34	A Map of Ireland According to the Best Authorities
mwam1332	america north (west)	1796	CAREY	3500	49	64	A Map of Part of the N:W: Territory of the United States: Compiled from Actual Surveys, and the Best Information, by Samuel Lewis 1796
mwsam0117	south america	1795	CAREY	100	33	36	A Map of South America According to the Best Authorities
mwsam0846	south america venezuela	1814	CAREY	140	31	52	A Map of the Caracas
mwaa0153	arctic	1795	CAREY	350	26	25	A Map of the Countries Situate about the North Pole as Far as the 50th Degree of North Latitude
mwp0444	pacific north	1794	CAREY	200	20	28	A Map of the Discoveries Made by Capts. Cook & Clerke in the Years 1778 & 1779 between the Eastern Coast of Asia and the Western Coast of North America
mwuss1483	tennessee	1794	CAREY	1200	24	52	A Map of the Tennassee Government, Formerly Part of North Carolina, Taken Chiefly from Surveys by Genl. D. Smith & Others
mwam0525	america north	1795	CAREY	2000	62	89	A Map of the United States: Compiled Chiefly from the State Maps and other Authentic Information by Saml. Lewis, 1795
mwp0054	australia	1814	CAREY	175	27	22	A New and Accurate Map of New South Wales, with Norfolk and Lord Howe's Islands, Port Jackson, &c. from Actual Surveys
mwuk1044	england	1814	CAREY	140	36	32	An Accurate Map of England and Wales with the Principal Roads from the Best Authorities
mwin0335	india	1814	CAREY	480	40	41	An Accurate Map of Hindostan or India from the Best Authorities
mwme0396	holy land	1820	CAREY	500	42	52	Canaan with Part of Egypt during the Residence of the Israelites in the Desert / Canaan, Subsequent to its Conquest by the Israelites, and its Division among the Tribes
mwwi0667	hispaniola	1800	CAREY	400	38	47	Carte de la Partie Francoise de St. Domingue Faite par Bellin Ingr. de la Marine et depuis Augmentee par P.C. Varle
mwsam0474	south america chile	1814	CAREY	140	39	24	Chili and Part of the Viceroyalty of la Plata
mwc0217	china	1795	CAREY	200	34	36	China, Divided into its Great Provinces According to the Best Authorities
mwuss0299	connecticut	1795	CAREY	650	30	37	Connecticut from the Best Authorities
mwuss0373	delaware	1801	CAREY	240	20	15	Delaware
mwuss0371	delaware	1795	CAREY	1000	41	23	Delaware from the Best Authorities
mwe0242	europe	1814	CAREY	140	40	46	Europe
mwf0183	france	1814	CAREY	120	40	45	France, Divided into Circles and Departments
mwit0232	italy	1820	CAREY	120	36	29	Geographical and Statistical Map of Italy
mwuss0604	kentucky	1822	CAREY	300	43	53	Geographical, Statistical, and Historical Map of Kentucky
mwuss0507	georgia	1796	CAREY	240	15	19	Georgia
mwuss0506	georgia	1795	CAREY	1250	23	40	Georgia from the Latest Authorities
mwg0171	germany	1814	CAREY	120	40	45	Germany
mwit0230	italy	1814	CAREY	135	37	38	Italy and Sardinia from the Best Authorities
mwuss0599	kentucky	1801	CAREY	350	15	20	Kentuckey
mwuss0603	kentucky	1818	CAREY	600	26	47	Kentucky
mwuss0594	kentucky	1795	CAREY	1000	25	49	Kentucky, Reduced from Elihu Barker's Large Map
mwuss0659	louisiana	1814	CAREY	350	32	36	Louisiana
mwru0340	russia	1820	CAREY	200	27	38	Map of the Russian Empire, Intended for the Elucidation of Lavoisne's Historical Atlas
mwam0593	america north	1814	CAREY	320	33	44	Map of the United States of America
mwuss0768	maryland	1814	CAREY	450	28	43	Maryland
mwuss0854	massachusetts	1801	CAREY	200	15	19	Massachusetts
mwuss0954	mississippi	1814	CAREY	650	31	36	Mississippi Territory
mwuss0513	georgia	1805	CAREY	240	15	18	Mississippi Territory and Georgia

AMPG REFERENCE	REGION	DATE	MAP MAKER	PRICE (UK£)	VERT. (cm.)	HOR. (cm.)	TITLE OF MAP (Comments by the editor in brackets)
mwuss0972	missouri	1814	CAREY	1200	30	35	Missouri Territory Formerly Louisiana
mwuss0932	minnesota	1801	CAREY	650	20	15	N.W. Territory (incl. Wisconsin)
mwuss1049	new jersey	1801	CAREY	200	19	14	New Jersey
mwuss1277	ohio	1805	CAREY	400	20	15	Ohio and N.W. Territory (incl. Indiana territory)
mwsam0787	south america peru	1814	CAREY	160	39	27	Peru
mwuss1273	ohio	1796	CAREY	800	61	34	Plat of the Seven Ranges of Townships Being Part of the Territory of the United States N.W. of the River Ohio
mwbp0557	poland	1814	CAREY	200	31	37	Poland
mwuss0707	maine	1796	CAREY	200	19	14	Province of Maine
mwuss1464	rhode isl	1801	CAREY	200	19	15	Rhode Island
mwuk0562	scotland	1795	CAREY	120	36	28	Scotland with the Principal Roads from the Best Authorities
mwuss0249	carolinas	1801	CAREY	200	15	19	South Carolina
mwsp0319	spain	1814	CAREY	400	37	44	Spain and Portugal
mwsc0198	scandinavia	1814	CAREY	125	33	36	Sweden, Denmark, Norway and Finland from the Best Authorities
mwsw0222	switzerland	1814	CAREY	350	22	29	Switzerland According to the Best Authorities
mwuss1489	tennessee	1804	CAREY	400	15	20	Tennessee: Lately the S.Wn. Territory
mwuss1491	tennessee	1814	CAREY	1000	22	50	Tennessee
mwca0138	canada	1814	CAREY	300	38	43	The British Possessions in North America from the Latest Authorities
mwuss0713	maine	1814	CAREY	350	39	29	The District of Maine
mwam0815	america north (central)	1812	CAREY	200	20	25	The Middle States and Western Territories of the United States Including the Seat of the Western War
mwuss0703	maine	1795	CAREY	550	38	25	The Province of Maine, from the Best Authorities by Samuel Lewis 1794
mwru0306	russia	1794	CAREY	120	20	28	The Russian Empire in Europe and Asia
mwuss0515	georgia	1814	CAREY	1250	43	38	The State of Georgia
mwuss0758	maryland	1795	CAREY	900	28	42	The State of Maryland, from the Best Authorities. By Samuel Lewis
mwuss0860	massachusetts	1814	CAREY	500	31	46	The State of Massachusetts
mwuss0847	massachusetts	1795	CAREY	900	36	48	The State of Massachusetts. Compiled from the Best Authorities by Samuel Lewis
mwuss0956	mississippi	1818	CAREY	1000	30	36	The State of Mississippi and Alabama Territory
mwuss1013	new hampshire	1801	CAREY	240	20	15	The State of New Hampshire by Saml. Lewis
mwuss1005	new hampshire	1794	CAREY	400	46	29	The State of New Hampshire Compiled Chiefly from Actual Surveys. By Samuel Lewis, 1794
mwuss1045	new jersey	1795	CAREY	650	47	30	The State of New Jersey, Compiled from the Most Authentic Information
mwuss1162	new york	1795	CAREY	950	41	50	The State of New York, Compiled from the Best Authorities, by Samuel Lewis. 1795
mwuss0239	carolinas	1795	CAREY	550	28	47	The State of North Carolina from the Best Authorities, &c. By Samuel Lewis
mwuss1279	ohio	1814	CAREY	1000	37	35	The State of Ohio with Part of Upper Canada, &c.
mwuss1387	pennsylvania	1795	CAREY	800	29	46	The State of Pennsylvania. Reduced with Permission from Reading Howells Map, by Samuel Lewis
mwuss1459	rhode isl	1795	CAREY	450	34	24	The State of Rhode-Island; Compiled, from the Surveys and Observations of Caleb Harris. By Harding Harris
mwuss1490	tennessee	1814	CAREY	1350	24	52	The State of Tennessee
mwuss1666	virginia	1795	CAREY	800	45	49	The State of Virginia from the Best Authorities, by Samuel Lewis. 1794
mwam1300	great lakes	1814	CAREY	900	41	32	The Upper Territories of the United States
mwam1299	great lakes	1814	CAREY	400	20	15	Upper Territories of the United States
mwuss1567	vermont	1814	CAREY	800	37	31	Vermont from Actual Survey
mwuss1672	virginia	1801	CAREY	400	15	20	Virginia
mwp0100	australia	1832	CAREY & LEA	200	9	14	Australia
mwas0852	asia burma	1832	CAREY & LEA	60	14	9	Birman Empire with Anam, Siam & Cochin China (copy of Starling 1831)
mwuss0309	connecticut	1822	CAREY & LEA	450	42	53	Geographical, Historical, and Statistical Map of Connecticut
mwuss0862	massachusetts	1822	CAREY & LEA	350	42	53	Geographical, Historical, and Statistical Map of Massachusetts
mwuss0005	alabama	1822	CAREY & LEA	600	42	53	Geographical, Statistical, and Historical Map of Alabama
mwuss0053	arkansas	1822	CAREY & LEA	950	42	53	Geographical, Statistical, and Historical Map of Arkansas Territory
mwsam0408	south america brazil	1822	CAREY & LEA	200	42	53	Geographical, Statistical, and Historical Map of Brazil
mwsam0543	south america colombia	1822	CAREY & LEA	280	42	53	Geographical, Statistical, and Historical Map of Colombia
mwwi0481	cuba	1822	CAREY & LEA	650	42	53	Geographical, Statistical, and Historical Map of Cuba and the Bahama Islands
mwuss0379	delaware	1822	CAREY & LEA	400	42	53	Geographical, Statistical, and Historical Map of Delaware
mwuss0460	florida	1822	CAREY & LEA	550	42	53	Geographical, Statistical, and Historical Map of Florida
mwuss0518	georgia	1822	CAREY & LEA	200	42	53	Geographical, Statistical, and Historical Map of Georgia
mwwi0677	hispaniola	1820	CAREY & LEA	350	42	53	Geographical, Statistical, and Historical Map of Hayti, Formerly Hispaniola or St. Domingo
mwuss0546	illinois	1822	CAREY & LEA	950	42	53	Geographical, Statistical, and Historical Map of Illinois
mwuss0567	indiana	1822	CAREY & LEA	300	42	53	Geographical, Statistical, and Historical Map of Indiana
mwwi0753	jamaica	1822	CAREY & LEA	320	42	53	Geographical, Statistical, and Historical Map of Jamaica

AMPG REFERENCE	REGION	DATE	MAP MAKER	PRICE (UK£)	VERT. (cm.)	HOR. (cm.)	TITLE OF MAP (Comments by the editor in brackets)
mwuss0667	louisiana	1822	CAREY & LEA	450	42	53	Geographical, Statistical, and Historical Map of Louisiana
mwuss0716	maine	1822	CAREY & LEA	450	42	53	Geographical, Statistical, and Historical Map of Maine
mwuss0771	maryland	1822	CAREY & LEA	550	42	53	Geographical, Statistical, and Historical Map of Maryland
mwgm0291	mexico	1822	CAREY & LEA	375	42	53	Geographical, Statistical, and Historical Map of Mexico
mwuss0904	michigan	1822	CAREY & LEA	650	42	53	Geographical, Statistical, and Historical Map of Michigan Territory
mwuss0957	mississippi	1822	CAREY & LEA	300	42	53	Geographical, Statistical, and Historical Map of Mississippi
mwuss0973	missouri	1822	CAREY & LEA	650	42	53	Geographical, Statistical, and Historical Map of Missouri
mwuss1017	new hampshire	1822	CAREY & LEA	350	42	53	Geographical, Statistical, and Historical Map of New Hampshire
mwuss1054	new jersey	1822	CAREY & LEA	375	42	53	Geographical, Statistical, and Historical Map of New Jersey
mwuss0258	carolinas	1822	CAREY & LEA	300	42	53	Geographical, Statistical, and Historical Map of North Carolina
mwuss1288	ohio	1822	CAREY & LEA	400	42	53	Geographical, Statistical, and Historical Map of Ohio
mwuss1403	pennsylvania	1822	CAREY & LEA	350	42	53	Geographical, Statistical, and Historical Map of Pennsylvania
mwwi0838	puerto rico	1822	CAREY & LEA	450	42	53	Geographical, Statistical, and Historical Map of Porto Rico and the Virgin Islands
mwuss1471	rhode isl	1822	CAREY & LEA	300	42	53	Geographical, Statistical, and Historical Map of Rhode Island
mwuss0257	carolinas	1822	CAREY & LEA	550	42	53	Geographical, Statistical, and Historical Map of South Carolina
mwuss0256	carolinas	1822	CAREY & LEA	550	42	53	Geographical, Statistical, and Historical Map of the District of Columbia
mwsam0140	south america	1823	CAREY & LEA	200	42	53	Geographical, Statistical, and Historical Map of the United Provinces of South America
mwwi0170	west indies	1823	CAREY & LEA	300	42	53	Geographical, Statistical, and Historical Map of the West Indies
mwwi0167	west indies	1822	CAREY & LEA	280	42	53	Geographical, Statistical, and Historical Map of the Windward Islands
mwca0145	canada	1822	CAREY & LEA	240	42	53	Geographical, Statistical, and Historical Map of Upper and Lower Canada, and the Other British Possessions in North America
mwuss1570	vermont	1822	CAREY & LEA	350	42	53	Geographical, Statistical, and Historical Map of Vermont
mwuss1678	virginia	1822	CAREY & LEA	550	42	53	Geographical, Statistical, and Historical Map of Virginia
mwbp0567	poland	1832	CAREY & LEA	75	9	14	Poland, Previous to its Partition in 1795 between Russia, Austria & Prussia, Showing also its Present Extent of Territory
mwaf1011	africa south	1832	CAREY & LEA	60	9	53	Southern Africa
mwam0630	america north	1822	CAREY & LEA	1000	43	53	United States of America
mwwi0484	cuba	1825	CAREZ	500	48	64	Ile de Cube Dressee par Pierron d'apres la Carte de M. de Humboldt et celle du Depot de la Marine
mwc0295	china	1850	CARLES	1250	46	31	Description Entiere de la Ville Imperiale (Plan de Pe-king)
mwam0570	america north	1806	CARLETON	15000	120	139	A New Map of the United States of America Including Part of Louisiana Drawn from the Latest Authorities. Revised and Corrected
mwuss0851	massachusetts	1796	CARLETON	2000	36	21	A Plan of Boston, from Actual Survey; by Osgood Carleton. 1796
mwuss0848	massachusetts	1795	CARLETON	12500	90	121	An Accurate Map of the Commonwealth of Massachusetts Exclusive of the District of Maine
mwuss0704	maine	1795	CARLETON	9500	137	98	An Accurate Map of the District of Maine Being Part of the Commonwealth of Massachusetts: Compiled Pursuant to an Act of the General Court, from Actual Surveys of the Several Towns, &c. Taken by their Order: Exhibiting the Boundary Lines of the District
mwuss0855	massachusetts	1801	CARLETON	9500	79	122	Map of Massachusetts Compiled from Actual Surveys Made by Order of the General Court
mwru0299a	russia	1790	CARLI	200	25	33	I Governi d'Arcangelo
mwit0821a	italy sardinia	1795	CARLI	350	31	23	La Sardegna (shown above, far left)
mwgr0224	greece	1788	CARLI	250	33	25	La Turchia Europea
mwsp0687	balearic islands	1791	CARLI	500	26	34	Le Isole di Majorca Minorca ed Ivica
mwp0123	australia	1837	CARMICHAEL	600	19	38	Map of the Town of Sydney 1837
mwg0291	baden-wurttemberg	1790	CARMINE	1800	94	116	Totius S.R.I. Circuli Suevici
mwg0073	germany	1680	CAROLI	550	49	58	Accuratissima Germaniae Tabula Denuo in Lucem Edita a Francisco Caroli (re-issued by F. de Wit with different cartouche etc. as below)
mwbh0446a	belgium holland	1690	CAROLI	550	45	55	Comitatus Hollandiae Tabula Pluribus Locis Recens Emendata a Francisco Caroli (illustrated is re-issue by P. Schenk. Also copied by F. de Wit, below)
mwjk0030	japan	1663	CARON	2000	15	23	Die Rechte See-Karte von der Zelegenheit der Landes Iapan
mwjk0029	japan	1661	CARON	5000	25	38	Perfeckte Kaert vande gelegenheydt des Landis van Iapan
mwsc0753c	scandinavia sweden	1817	CARPELAN	720	33	55	Karta ofver Belagenheten omkring Stockholm
mwuk0927	england	1668	CARR	720	34	39	A Description of the postroads in England (text title)
mwgm0029a	gulf of mexico and surrounding regions	1740	CARRANZA-SMITH	1000	28	39	A New and Correct Chart or Map of the West Indies. &c. (the mapmaker is unknown. The map is bound with an English translation of a Spanish manuscript by Carranza)

AMPG REFERENCE	REGION	DATE	MAP MAKER	PRICE (UK£)	VERT. (cm.)	HOR. (cm.)	TITLE OF MAP (Comments by the editor in brackets)
mwuss1015	new hampshire	1816	CARRIGAIN	8000	154	118	New Hampshire by Recent Survey Made under the Supreme Authority and Published According to Law
mwgr0344	greece crete	1570	CARTARO	2000	22	32	... Haec est illa insignis insula Creta (Map engraved by Forlani)
mwca0542	canada quebec	1788	CARVER	350	51	69	A New and Correct Map of the Province of Quebec
mwam0459	america north	1778	CARVER	400	33	33	A New Map of North America from the Latest Discoveries, 1778, Engraved for Carver's Travels
mwam1291	great lakes	1781	CARVER	1200	26	34	A Plan of Captain Carver's Travels in the Interior Parts of North America in 1766 and 1767
mwam1296	great lakes	1784	CARVER	1200	27	34	Carte des Voyages du Cape. Carver
mwec0237	uk england cumbria	1789	CARY	250	39	51	(Cumberland)
mwec0271	uk england derbyshire	1789	CARY	350	40	52	(Derby)
mwec0561	uk england hertfordshire	1789	CARY	360	40	52	(Hertfordshire)
mwec0587	uk england huntingdonshire	1789	CARY	280	40	52	(Huntingdon)
mwec0726	uk england leicestershire	1789	CARY	200	39	51	(Leicester)
mwec0922	uk england nottinghamshire	1789	CARY	280	40	52	(Nottingham)
mwec1259	uk england wiltshire	1789	CARY	400	40	52	(Wiltshire)
mwat0049	atlantic ocean (all)	1780	CARY	300	30	43	A Chart of the Atlantic Ocean Exhibiting the Seat of War Both in Europe & America
mwec0149	uk england cheshire	1789	CARY	350	39	51	A Map of Cheshire from the Best Authorities
mwec0343	uk england dorset	1789	CARY	450	37	52	A Map of Dorset-Shire from the Best Authorities
mwe0253	europe	1819	CARY	1350	129	149	A Map of Europe, Exhibiting its Present Political Divisions, Drawn from the Most Authentic Authorities
mwec0452	uk england gloucestershire	1789	CARY	450	48	42	A Map of Glocestershire from the Best Authorities
mwuk1866	wales	1805	CARY	280	40	52	A Map of North Wales from the Best Authorities / A Map of South Wales from the Best Authorities (2 maps)
mwec1176	uk england sussex	1789	CARY	550	36	51	A Map of Sussex, from the Best Authorities
mwec1348	uk england yorkshire	1789	CARY	450	41	51	A Map of the East Riding of Yorkshire with Ainsty Liberty
mwuk1593a	channel islands	1789	CARY	300	50	38	A Map of the Island of Jersey / Garnsey ot Sarina / Aldernay / Isle of Man (4 maps on one sheet. Illustrated is re-issue by Stockdale, 1805)
mwec1204	uk england warwickshire	1789	CARY	400	52	43	A Map of Warwickshire from the Best Authorities
mww0617	world	1801	CARY	600	47	52	A New Chart of the World, on Mercator's Projection, Exhibiting the Tracks & Discoveries of the most Eminent Navigators, to the Present Period.
mwaf0294	africa	1814	CARY	2000	132	151	A New Map of Africa, Exhibiting its Natural and Political Divisions Delineated from the Most Recent Authorities
mwaf0318a	africa	1828	CARY	1000	92	86	A New Map of Africa Exhibiting Its Natural and Political Divisions Drawn from the Most Recent Materials
mwaf0293	africa	1805	CARY	450	46	53	A New Map of Africa, from the Latest Authorities
mwam0265	america continent	1811	CARY	400	51	59	A New Map of America
mwam0272a	america continent	1819	CARY	4000	130	152	A New Map of America exhibiting its natural and political divisions
mwme0667	arabia etc	1804	CARY	550	47	52	A New Map of Arabia Including Egypt, Abyssinia the Red Sea &c.
mwas0236	asia continent	1806	CARY	350	47	53	A New Map of Asia, from the Latest Authorities
mwec0050	uk england berkshire	1801	CARY	240	51	56	A New Map of Berkshire Divided into Hundreds, Exhibiting its Roads, Rivers, Parks &c. By John Cary, Engraver, 1801
mwe0613	europe czech republic (bohemia)	1801	CARY	280	46	52	A New Map of Bohemia and Moravia
mwec0150	uk england cheshire	1809	CARY	300	48	54	A New Map of Cheshire, Divided into Hundreds
mwc0229	china	1801	CARY	350	47	53	A New Map of China, from the Latest Authorities
mwc0235	china	1806	CARY	300	47	53	A New Map of Chinese & Independent Tartary from the Latest Authorities
mwec0240	uk england cumbria	1809	CARY	200	53	48	A New Map of Cumberland, Divided into Hundreds
mwec0272	uk england derbyshire	1809	CARY	300	54	49	A New Map of Derbyshire, Divided into Hundreds, Exhibiting its Roads, Rivers, Parks &c.
mwec0275	uk england derbyshire	1831	CARY	280	60	51	A New Map of Derbyshire, Divided into Hundreds, Exhibiting its Roads, Rivers, Parks &c.
mwec0309	uk england devon	1809	CARY	200	48	54	A New Map of Devonshire, Divided into Hundreds
mwaf0541	africa egypt etc	1805	CARY	175	51	59	A New Map of Egypt, from the Latest Authorities
mwe0235	europe	1804	CARY	350	46	51	A New Map of Europe, from the Latest Authorities
mwf0175	france	1806	CARY	200	46	52	A New Map of France agreeable to its Divisions into Provinces
mwf0170	france	1799	CARY	240	46	51	A New Map of France, Divided into Departments as Decreed by the National Assembly 1790
mwg0166	germany	1799	CARY	240	46	52	A New Map of Germany, Divided into its Circles
mwgr0244	greece	1817	CARY	2000	139	100	A New Map of Greece, Exhibiting the Provinces Governed by Ali Pacha and his Children, viz South Albania, Thessaly, Part of Macedonia, Livadia and the Morea
mwec0530	uk england herefordshire	1809	CARY	200	54	48	A New Map of Herefordshire, Divided into Hundreds
mwin0328	india	1806	CARY	375	46	51	A New Map of Hindoostan, from the Latest Authorities
mwe0969	europe hungary	1799	CARY	280	46	52	A New Map of Hungary, with its Divisions into Gespanchafts or Counties; the Principality of Transylvania, Croatia &c.
mwuk0243	ireland	1799	CARY	350	46	52	A New Map of Ireland, Divided into its Provinces and Counties

AMPG REFERENCE	REGION	DATE	MAP MAKER	PRICE (UK£)	VERT. (cm.)	HOR. (cm.)	TITLE OF MAP (Comments by the editor in brackets)
mwit0220	italy	1799	CARY	320	46	51	A New Map of Italy Including the Islands of Sicily, Sardinia and Corsica with the Post Roads from the Latest Authorities
mwec0699	uk england lancashire	1809	CARY	300	54	48	A New Map of Lancashire, Divided into Hundreds
mwec0728	uk england leicestershire	1809	CARY	240	54	49	A New Map of Leicestershire, Divided into Hundreds
mwec0757	uk england lincolnshire	1809	CARY	200	54	49	A New Map of Lincolnshire, Divided into Hundreds
mwec0790	uk england middlesex	1801	CARY	320	49	54	A new map of Middlesex divided into Hundreds
mwam0571	america north	1806	CARY	675	51	57	A New Map of North America
mwec0924	uk england nottinghamshire	1809	CARY	250	54	49	A New Map of Nottinghamshire, Divided into Hundreds
mwca0456	canada nova scotia	1807	CARY	300	46	51	A New Map of Nova Scotia, Newfoundland &c. from the Latest Authorities
mwec0966	uk england oxfordshire	1809	CARY	250	54	48	A New Map of Oxfordshire, Divided into Hundreds
mwam1151	america north (east)	1806	CARY	900	46	52	A New Map of Part of the United States of North America, containing those of New York, Vermont, New Hampshire, Massachusetts … and Virginia
mwuss0255	carolinas	1806	CARY	800	46	52	A New Map of Part of the United States of North America, Containing the Carolinas and Georgia, also the Floridas and Part of the Bahama Islands &c.
mwam0813a	america north (central)	1805	CARY	960	46	51	A New Map of Part of the United States, Exhibiting the North West, Michigan, Indiana, and Illinois Territory, the States of Kentucky, Ohio, Virginia, Maryland and Pennsylvania. From the Latest Authorities
mwme0839	persia etc	1801	CARY	300	47	52	A New Map of Persia
mwit0693	italy piedmont	1799	CARY	240	46	51	A New Map of Piedmont, the Duchies of Savoy and Milan; and the Republic of Genua
mwbp0539	poland	1799	CARY	240	46	51	A New Map of Poland and the Grand Duchy of Lithuania Shewing their Dismemberments and Divisions between Austria, Russia and Prussia, in 1772, 1793 & 1795
mwec0991	uk england rutland	1801	CARY	240	48	54	A New Map of Rutlandshire, Divided into Hundreds
mwuk0568	scotland	1801	CARY	600	89	102	A New Map of Scotland
mwec1019	uk england shropshire	1809	CARY	300	54	48	A New Map of Shropshire, Divided into Hundreds
mwsam0128	south america	1807	CARY	450	90	52	A New Map of South America from the Latest Authorities
mwsp0311	spain	1801	CARY	280	46	51	A New Map of Spain and Portugal
mwec1080	uk england staffordshire	1809	CARY	300	55	49	A New Map of Straffordshire, Divided into Hundreds
mwsc0192	scandinavia	1801	CARY	240	46	52	A New Map of Sweden, Denmark and Norway
mwsw0211	switzerland	1799	CARY	350	46	52	A New Map of Swisserland, Divided into its Cantons and Dependencies, Including the Grisons &c. &c.
mwuk0880	uk	1807	CARY	350	46	52	A New Map of the British Isles
mwe0392	europe austria	1801	CARY	240	50	56	A New Map of the Circle of Austria
mwg0398	bavaria	1799	CARY	280	45	51	A New Map of the Circle of Bavaria
mwg0406	bavaria	1811	CARY	280	46	52	A New Map of the Circle of Franconia, from the Latest Authorities. By John Cary, Engraver, 1811
mwg0399	bavaria	1799	CARY	280	46	51	A New Map of the Circle of Swabia
mwg0674	saxony	1801	CARY	240	46	52	A New Map of the Circle of Upper Saxony with the Duchy of Silesia and Lusatia
mwg0851	westphalia	1799	CARY	240	46	52	A New Map of the Circle of Westphalia, from the Latest Authorities, by John Cary, Engraver, 1799
mwec0963	uk england oxfordshire	1797	CARY	3000	62	46	A New Map of the County of Oxford … by Richard Davis of Lewknow (in 16 sheets of 62x46cm.)
mwit0621	italy north	1811	CARY	240	46	52	A New Map of the County of Tyrol, and the Republic of Venice; Duchy of Mantua &c.
mwas0526	asia south east	1801	CARY	450	46	51	A New Map of the East India Isles, from the Latest Authorities
mwsc0386	scandinavia denmark	1801	CARY	200	46	51	A New Map of the Kingdom of Denmark, Comprehending North and South Jutland, Zeeland, Fyen, Laaland, and Part of Holstein
mwsp0124	portugal	1801	CARY	250	45	51	A New Map of the Kingdom of Portugal Divided into its Provinces from the Latest Authorities
mwbp0540	poland	1799	CARY	200	45	51	A New Map of the Kingdom of Prussia
mwbh0774	belgium holland	1804	CARY	280	46	51	A New Map of the Netherlands
mwuk1874a	wales	1825	CARY	750	99	59	A New Map of the Principality of Wales
mwru0320	russia	1799	CARY	850	46	101	A New Map of the Russian Empire, Divided into its Governments; from the Latest Authorities
mwbh0769	belgium holland	1799	CARY	200	46	51	A New Map of the United Provinces
mwam1160	america north (east)	1806	CARY	720	46	52	A New Map of the United States of America
mwwi0151	west indies	1803	CARY	400	46	51	A New Map of the West India Isles from the Latest Authorities
mwme1046	turkey etc	1811	CARY	280	46	52	A New Map of Turkey in Asia, Divided into its Provinces, from the Best Authorities
mwca0131	canada	1807	CARY	550	52	61	A New Map of Upper and Lower Canada from the Latest Authorities by John Cary, Engraver
mwec1206	uk england warwickshire	1809	CARY	300	54	48	A New Map of Warwickshire, Divided into Hundreds
mwec1286	uk england worcestershire	1809	CARY	300	48	54	A New Map of Worcestershire, Divided into Hundreds
mwec1356	uk england yorkshire	1825	CARY	300	54	60	A New Map of Yorkshire
mwaf0299	africa	1813	CARY	90	23	29	Africa
mwam0260	america continent	1808	CARY	200	28	23	America

AMPG REFERENCE	REGION	DATE	MAP MAKER	PRICE (UK£)	VERT. (cm.)	HOR. (cm.)	TITLE OF MAP (Comments by the editor in brackets)
mwwi0868	st kitts	1782	CARY	350	31	39	An Accurate Map of the Islands of St. Christophers and Nevis in the West Indies by an Officer with the Position of the English and French Fleets February 7th. 1782
mwme0668	arabia etc	1808	CARY	120	23	28	Arabia
mwec0020	uk england bedfordshire	1787	CARY	200	21	27	Bedfordshire
mwec0020a	uk england bedfordshire	1790	CARY	80	14	9	Bedfordshire
mwec0049	uk england berkshire	1787	CARY	200	21	27	Berkshire
mwec0049a	uk england berkshire	1790	CARY	80	14	9	Berkshire
mwec0075	uk england buckinghamshire	1787	CARY	200	21	27	Buckinghamshire
mwec0075a	uk england buckinghamshire	1790	CARY	80	14	9	Buckinghamshire
mwec0106	uk england cambridgeshire	1787	CARY	240	21	27	Cambridgeshire
mwec0107	uk england cambridgeshire	1789	CARY	120	14	9	Cambridgeshire
mwca0132	canada	1808	CARY	180	28	23	Canada (reduction of previous map)
mwaf0996	africa south	1813	CARY	120	23	28	Cape of Good Hope
mwuk1247	england london	1786	CARY	1000	77	89	Cary's Actual Survey of the Country Fifteen Miles round London
mwuk1248	england london	1787	CARY	4000	73	123	Cary's New and Accurate Plan of London and Westminster, the Borough of Southwark and Parts Adjacent (20 editions until 1825)
mwuk1030	england	1794	CARY	2400	228	178	Cary's New Map of England and Wales, with Part of Scotland (illustrated is 1820 re-issue)
mww0681	world	1828	CARY	6000	90	172	Cary's New Map of the Eastern and Western Hemispheres
mwuk1294	england london	1820	CARY	1600	62	82	Cary's New Plan of London and it's Vicinity (15 editions until 1848)
mwuk1252	england london	1790	CARY	750	40	60	Cary's New Pocket Plan of London, Westminster and Southwark (18 editions to 1836)
mwuk1057	england	1830	CARY	950	135	103	Cary's Six Sheet Map of England and Wales, with Part of Scotland: On which are Carefully Laid down All the Direct and Principal Cross Roads, the Course of the Rivers and Navigable Canals, Cities, Markets
mwuk0273	ireland	1832	CARY	550	78	65	Cary's Travelling Map of Ireland
mww0665	world	1820	CARY	240	23	36	Chart of the World, on Mercator's Projection
mwec0148	uk england cheshire	1787	CARY	200	21	27	Cheshire
mwec0149a	uk england cheshire	1790	CARY	100	14	9	Cheshire
mwec0196	uk england cornwall	1787	CARY	200	21	27	Cornwall
mwec0196a	uk england cornwall	1790	CARY	120	14	9	Cornwall
mwec0237a	uk england cumbria	1790	CARY	80	14	9	Cumberland
mwec0270	uk england derbyshire	1787	CARY	200	21	27	Derbyshire
mwec0271a	uk england derbyshire	1790	CARY	80	14	9	Derbyshire
mwec0303	uk england devon	1787	CARY	200	21	27	Devonshire
mwec0303a	uk england devon	1790	CARY	100	14	9	Devonshire
mwec0342	uk england dorset	1787	CARY	200	21	27	Dorsetshire
mwec0344	uk england dorset	1789	CARY	100	14	9	Dorsetshire
mwec0380	uk england durham	1789	CARY	320	39	51	Durham
mwec0380a	uk england durham	1790	CARY	80	14	9	Durham
mwec0381	uk england durham	1793	CARY	100	21	27	Durham
mwec1344	uk england yorkshire	1787	CARY	200	21	27	East Riding of Yorkshire
mwuk1028a	england	1790	CARY	75	14	9	England and Wales (from Cary's Traveller's Companion, reprinted until 1828)
mwec0416	uk england essex	1787	CARY	200	21	27	Essex
mwec0416a	uk england essex	1790	CARY	80	14	9	Essex
mwec0451	uk england gloucestershire	1787	CARY	200	21	27	Glocestershire
mwec0452a	uk england gloucestershire	1790	CARY	80	14	9	Glocestershire
mwec0487	uk england hampshire	1787	CARY	200	21	27	Hampshire
mwec0489a	uk england hampshire	1790	CARY	80	14	9	Hampshire
mwec0528	uk england herefordshire	1787	CARY	140	21	27	Herefordshire
mwec0528a	uk england herefordshire	1790	CARY	80	14	9	Herefordshire
mwec0560	uk england hertfordshire	1787	CARY	200	21	27	Hertfordshire
mwec0561a	uk england hertfordshire	1790	CARY	80	14	9	Hertfordshire
mwec0586	uk england huntingdonshire	1787	CARY	200	21	27	Huntingdonshire
mwec0587a	uk england huntingdonshire	1790	CARY	80	14	9	Huntingdonshire
mwuk0254	ireland	1813	CARY	90	28	23	Ireland
mwit0826	italy sardinia	1825	CARY	150	23	28	K.dom of Sardinia According to the Treaties of 1814-15
mwec0646	uk england kent	1787	CARY	200	21	27	Kent
mwec0647a	uk england kent	1790	CARY	100	14	9	Kent
mwec0697	uk england lancashire	1787	CARY	200	21	27	Lancashire
mwec0697a	uk england lancashire	1790	CARY	80	14	9	Lancashire
mwec0727	uk england leicestershire	1789	CARY	80	14	9	Leicestershire
mwec0754	uk england lincolnshire	1787	CARY	150	21	27	Lincolnshire
mwec0754a	uk england lincolnshire	1790	CARY	80	14	9	Lincolnshire

AMPG REFERENCE	REGION	DATE	MAP MAKER	PRICE (UK£)	VERT. (cm.)	HOR. (cm.)	TITLE OF MAP (Comments by the editor in brackets)
mwuk1244	england london	1782	CARY	650	42	54	London, Westminster and Southwark ... Accurately Delineated ... Now First Added a Correct List of Upwards of 350 Hackney Coach Fares from the Principal Stands, to the Most Frequented Places in and about the Metropolis (6 edtions to 1787)
mwin0297	india	1790	CARY	200	17	23	Madras and Fort St. George, Taken by the French under the Command of M. Mahe de la Bourdonnais the 21st Sept. 1746
mww0660	world	1819	CARY	10000	93	166	Map of the World upon Mercator's Projection (illustrated is the 1835 edition)
mwec0789a	uk england middlesex	1790	CARY	80	14	9	Middlesex
mwuk1861c	wales	1790	CARY	75	14	9	Monmouthshire
mwec0834a	uk england norfolk	1790	CARY	80	14	9	Norfolk
mwam0602	america north	1816	CARY	240	23	29	North America
mwam0576	america north	1808	CARY	240	28	23	North America (reduction of his 1806 map)
mwec1345	uk england yorkshire	1787	CARY	200	21	27	North Riding of Yorkshire
mwuk1861a	wales	1790	CARY	75	14	9	North Wales (re-issued until 1828)
mwec0867	uk england northamptonshire	1787	CARY	200	21	27	Northamptonshire
mwec0867a	uk england northamptonshire	1790	CARY	80	14	9	Northamptonshire
mwec0892	uk england northumberland	1787	CARY	200	21	27	Northumberland
mwec0892a	uk england northumberland	1790	CARY	80	14	9	Northumberland
mwec0922a	uk england nottinghamshire	1790	CARY	80	14	9	Nottinghamshire
mwca0139	canada	1816	CARY	140	23	28	Nova Scotia, Newfoundland &cc.
mwca0457	canada nova scotia	1808	CARY	120	28	23	Nova Scotia, Newfoundland (reduction of previous map)
mwec0962	uk england oxfordshire	1787	CARY	240	21	27	Oxfordshire
mwec0962a	uk england oxfordshire	1790	CARY	100	14	9	Oxfordshire
mwme0840	persia etc	1808	CARY	100	23	28	Persia
mwf0761	france nord pas-de-calais	1790	CARY	200	17	24	Plan of Dunkirk, with the Canal of Mardick
mwec0990a	uk england rutland	1790	CARY	80	14	9	Rutlandshire
mwec1018	uk england shropshire	1787	CARY	180	21	27	Shropshire
mwec1018a	uk england shropshire	1790	CARY	80	14	9	Shropshire
mwit0967	italy sicily	1813	CARY	180	23	28	Sicily
mwin0331	india	1808	CARY	95	28	23	Sindetic Hindoostan or the countries occupied by the Sinde or Indus
mwec1047	uk england somerset	1787	CARY	200	21	27	Somersetshire
mwec1048	uk england somerset	1789	CARY	100	14	9	Somersetshire
mwuk1861b	wales	1790	CARY	75	14	9	South Wales (re-issued until 1828)
mwec1076	uk england staffordshire	1787	CARY	200	21	27	Staffordshire
mwec1076a	uk england staffordshire	1790	CARY	80	14	9	Staffordshire
mwec1114a	uk england suffolk	1790	CARY	80	14	9	Suffolk
mwec1145	uk england surrey	1787	CARY	200	21	27	Surry
mwec1145a	uk england surrey	1790	CARY	100	14	9	Surry
mwec1175	uk england sussex	1787	CARY	200	21	27	Sussex
mwec1176a	uk england sussex	1790	CARY	80	14	9	Sussex
mwme0886	syria etc	1808	CARY	120	28	23	Syria
mwec1348a	uk england yorkshire	1790	CARY	300	31	36	The Turnpike Roads of Yorkshire (from Cary's 'Traveller's Companion', publ. until 1828)
mwam1161	america north (east)	1808	CARY	280	28	23	The United States of America (reduction of previous map)
mwwi0154	west indies	1808	CARY	150	23	28	The West India Islands
mww0616	world	1801	CARY	900	50	89	The Western Hemisphere / The Eastern Hemisphere (2 maps)
mwsam0249a	south america argentina	1808	CARY	200	28	23	Vice Royalty of La Plata and Government of Chili
mwec1203	uk england warwickshire	1787	CARY	200	21	27	Warwickshire
mwec1204a	uk england warwickshire	1790	CARY	80	14	9	Warwickshire
mwec1346	uk england yorkshire	1787	CARY	200	21	27	West Riding of Yorkshire
mwec1229	uk england westmorland	1787	CARY	200	21	27	Westmoreland
mwec1258	uk england wiltshire	1787	CARY	200	21	27	Wiltshire
mwec1259a	uk england wiltshire	1790	CARY	80	14	9	Wiltshire
mwec1285	uk england worcestershire	1787	CARY	180	21	27	Worcestershire
mwec1285a	uk england worcestershire	1790	CARY	80	14	9	Worcestershire
mwec1347	uk england yorkshire	1787	CARY	240	21	27	Yorkshire
mwe0508	europe croatia	1802	CASSAS	675	44	60	Plan General de la Ville et des Environs de Spalatro (Split)
mwbh0765a	belgium holland	1795	CASSINI	1800	37	50	Carta Generale de Paesi Bassi (in 6 sheets, each 37x50cm with a separate title)
mwam0273	america continent	1820	CASSINI	3600	105	122	Carta Generale dell'America con Porzione della Polinesia o Parte Orientale dell'Oceanica Secondo le Nuove Scoperte ed Osservazioni
mwit0215	italy	1793	CASSINI	2500	202	194	Carta Generale dell'Italia Divisa ne' suoi Stati e Provincie
mwme0665a	arabia etc	1800	CASSINI	1350	50	69	Gli Imperi Antichi Parte Occidentale / Gli Imperi Antichi Parte Orientale
mwin0319	india	1797	CASSINI	480	50	37	Gli Stati del Mogol e la Penisola delle Indie di qua dal Gange Delineati sulle Ultime Osservazione

AMPG REFERENCE	REGION	DATE	MAP MAKER	PRICE (UK£)	VERT. (cm.)	HOR. (cm.)	TITLE OF MAP (Comments by the editor in brackets)
mwam1121a	america north (east)	1797	CASSINI	4000	37	50	Gli Stati Uniti dell'America /Primo Foglio (Great Lakes) /Secondo Foglio (East & Maritimes)/ Terzo Foglio (Mississippi & Ohio) /Quarto Foglio (East Coast) / Quinta Foglio (Florida & Gulf Coast) / Sesto Foglio (Newfoundland Inset) (in all 6 sheets, publ. in 'Nuovo Atlante Geografico')
mwsam0402	south america brazil	1798	CASSINI	720	50	37	Il Brasile ed il Paese delle Amazzoni col Paraguai Delineati sulle Ultime Osservazioni
mwsam0470	south america chile	1798	CASSINI	400	48	34	Il Chili, con le Contrade Vicine, ed il Paese de'Patagoni
mwg0673a	saxony	1796	CASSINI	300	33	47	Il Circolo della Bassa Sassonia
mwru0312	russia	1796	CASSINI	350	47	33	Il Governo di Arcangelo
mww0609	world	1800	CASSINI	720	36	49	Il Mondo Noto agli Antichi
mwsam0785	south america peru	1798	CASSINI	375	50	37	Il Peru con I Paesi Circonvicini Delineato
mwsp0688b	balearic islands	1798	CASSINI	480	36	48	Il Regno di Valenza con le Isole di Majorica, Minoricae e Ivica
mwsc0511a	scandinavia iceland	1798	CASSINI	420	37	50	Islanda
mwe0824	europe east	1788	CASSINI	450	33	46	La Bessarabia e Parte della Moldavia e della Vallachia con le Provincie Confinanti della Polonia e della Russia
mwsp0604c	spain regions	1798	CASSINI	320	33	47	La Castiglia nouva e l'Estremadura
mwc02276a	china	1798	CASSINI	850	35	47	La Cina
mwf0166	france	1794	CASSINI	450	34	48	La Francia Delineata sulle Ultime Osservazione
mwme0390a	holy land	1800	CASSINI	400	50	37	La Giudea ovvero Terra Santa divisa nelle sue Dodici Tribù
mwgr0237	greece	1799	CASSINI	350	35	48	La Grecia antica divisa nei suoi stati.
mwgr0223	greece	1788	CASSINI	480	35	49	La Morea, la Livadia
mwsc0641	scandinavia norway	1796	CASSINI	350	47	34	La Norvegia Divisa
mwaf0422	africa east	1798	CASSINI	350	37	50	La Nubia ed Abissinia
mwp0038	australia	1798	CASSINI	3000	37	49	La Nuova Olanda e la Nuova Guinea (1st map of Australia on its own to include Capt. Cook's discoveries.)
mwp0193	new zealand	1793	CASSINI	1800	45	31	La Nuova Zelanda delineata sulle osservazione del Capitan Cook
mwru0310	russia	1795	CASSINI	400	35	47	La Parte Occidentale della Russia Asiatica (see also 'Eastern' half under 'Russia Tartary'
mwgm0263a	mexico	1798	CASSINI	1800	50	37	La Parte Occidentale dell'Antico, e Nuovo Messico, con la Florida e la Bassa Luigiana / La Parte Orientale dell'Antico, e Nuovo Messico con la Florida e la Bassa Luigiana Dellineata sulle Ultime Osservazioni (on 2 sheets, each 50x37cm)
mwuk0236	ireland	1795	CASSINI	480	47	34	La Parte Orientale della Irlanda / La Parte Occidentale della Irlanda (2 sheets, each 47x34cm.)
mwru0461	russia tartary	1796	CASSINI	750	34	47	La Parte Orientale della Russia Asiatica Delineata sulle Ultime Osservazioni
mwgm0059	gulf of mexico and surrounding regions	1798	CASSINI	1200	48	35	La Parte Orientale dell'Antico, e Nuovo Messico con la Florida e la Bassa Luigiana Dellineata sulle Ultime Osservazioni
mwas0705	asia south east malacca	1798	CASSINI	1500	47	34	La Penisola delle Indie di la dal Gange con Parte delle Isole della Sonda
mwme0838	persia etc	1797	CASSINI	400	37	50	La Persia Delineata sulle Ultime Osservazioni
mwbp0536	poland	1797	CASSINI	1000	34	47	La Polonia (4 sheets, each 34x47cm.)
mwbp0536a	poland	1797	CASSINI	300	34	47	La Slesia Superiore
mwc0226	china	1798	CASSINI	400	36	49	La Tartaria Cinese
mwsam0843	south america venezuela	1798	CASSINI	480	37	50	La Terra Ferma e la Guiana co' suoi Dipartimenti
mwaf0260	africa	1788	CASSINI	600	32	46	L'Africa Secondo le Ultime Osservazioni Divisa ne' suoi Stati Principali
mwe0692	europe dalmatia	1788	CASSINI	400	35	48	L'Albania e la Macedonia con porzione della Dalmazia, Servia, Vallachia Bulgaria e Romania
mwam0225	america continent	1788	CASSINI	875	33	46	L'America Secondo le Ultime Osservazioni Divisa ne suoi Stati Principali
mwme0665	arabia etc	1797	CASSINI	1000	35	49	L'Arabia Delineata sulle Ultime Osservazioni
mwsp0604a	spain regions	1798	CASSINI	320	37	50	L'Aragona e La Catalogna
mwas0213	asia continent	1788	CASSINI	875	33	46	L'Asia Secondo le Ultime Osservazioni Divisa ne'suoi Stati Principali
mwaf0846	africa north west	1799	CASSINI	350	36	49	Le Coste di Barbaria ouvero i Regni di Marocco, di Fez, di Algeri, di Tunisis, e di Tripoli
mwp0450	pacific north	1797	CASSINI	480	36	50	Le Coste Nord Ouest dell'America e Nord Est dell'Asia
mwin0320	india	1797	CASSINI	480	37	50	Le Indie Orientali (illustrated above)
mwwi0145	west indies	1798	CASSINI	750	35	48	Le Isole Antille Delineate sulle Ultime Osservazioni
mwat0099a	atlantic azores	1798	CASSINI	500	37	50	Le Isole Azoridi
mwuk0873	uk	1796	CASSINI	350	50	36	Le Isole Britanniche o Sieno li Regni di Inghilterra, Scozia ed Irlanda
mwat0171	atlantic canary isl.	1798	CASSINI	480	37	50	Le Isole Canarie Delineate sulle Ultime Osservazioni
mwp0320	pacific friendly isl.	1798	CASSINI	600	48	36	Le Isole degli Amici Delineate sulle Ultime Osservazioni del Cap. Cook
mwjk0126	japan	1797	CASSINI	1350	31	45	Le Isole del Giappone e la Corea Delineate
mwp0479	pacific society isl.	1798	CASSINI	720	36	49	Le Isole della Societa e di Noel Delineate sulle Ultime Osservazioni del Capitan Cook
mwas0520	asia south east	1797	CASSINI	1000	50	36	Le Isole della Sonda, Molucche, e Filippine
mwat0205	atlantic cape verde isl.	1798	CASSINI	400	36	50	Le Isole di Capo Verde
mwp0340	pacific hawaii	1798	CASSINI	3000	36	48	Le Isole di Sandwich Delineate sulle Osservazione del Cap. Cook (cartouche shows the death of Capt. Cook)

AMPG REFERENCE	REGION	DATE	MAP MAKER	PRICE (UK£)	VERT. (cm.)	HOR. (cm.)	TITLE OF MAP (Comments by the editor in brackets)
mwp0401	pacific new hebrides	1798	CASSINI	450	50	37	Le Nuove Ebridi e la Nouova Caledonia Delineate sulle Osservazioni del Cap. Cook
mwaf0537	africa egypt etc	1800	CASSINI	240	52	38	L'Egitto Antico
mwaf0531	africa egypt etc	1798	CASSINI	350	50	37	L'Egitto Antico e Moderno
mwe0219	europe	1788	CASSINI	785	33	46	L'Europa Secondo le Ultime Osservazioni
mwit0759	italy rome	1801	CASSINI	480	34	48	Li Contorni Antichi di Roma
mwsp0604b	spain regions	1798	CASSINI	320	37	48	Li Regni di Galizia, Asturie e Leon (shown above left)
mwit0840	italy sardinia and corsica	1792	CASSINI	1250			L'Isola di Corsica / Parte dell'Isola di Sardegna (2 maps)
mwf0538	france corsica	1792	CASSINI	720	47	33	L'Isola di Corsica Divisa nelle sue Provincie, o Giurisdizioni e Parte dell'Isola di Sardegna
mwp0535	pacific tahiti	1798	CASSINI	800	36	48	L'Isola O-Taiti Scoperta dal Cap. Cook, con le Marchesi di Mendoza
mwit0210	italy	1790	CASSINI	550	34	46	L'Italia Secondo
mww0555	world	1788	CASSINI	2000	34	47	Mappa Mondo o Descrizione Generale del Globo
mwru0311	russia	1795	CASSINI	280	48	35	Moscoviae Woronez
mwaf0977	africa south	1798	CASSINI	375	37	50	Parte dell'Africa che Comprende la Bassa Guinea e la Cafreria
mwaf1241	africa west	1797	CASSINI	350	36	50	Parte dell'Africa che comprende L'Alta Guinea
mwf0155	france	1785	CASSINI DE THURY	40000			Carte De France (in 182 sheets, various sizes)
mwf0147	france	1778	CASSINI DE THURY	1800	150	147	Carte de France divisee en XXX1 Gouvernements Militaires
mwf0414	france burgundy	1763	CASSINI DE THURY	3500	282	234	Carte Particuliere du Duche de Bourgogne
mwf0130	france	1760	CASSINI DE THURY	1500	137	126	Carte qui Comprend Toutes les Lieux de la France qui ont etes Determines par les Operations Geometriques
mwuk1592	channel islands	1780	CASSINI DE THURY	850	60	92	Isle de Gersey (part of an 18-sheet map of France)
mwf0122a	france	1744	CASSINI DE THURY	3000	141	126	Nouvelle Carte Qui Comprend les principaux Triangles qui servent de Fondement a la Description Geometrique de la France (1st map of France to use triangulated measurements)
mww0717	world	1840	CASTELLINI	550	51	51	Il Nuova Mondo
mwsam0856	south america venezuela	1825	CASTILLA	1600	46	64	Carta de las Costas de Tierra Firma Deade el Rio Orinoco hasta Yucatan y de las Islas Antillas y Lucayas con las Derrotas que Siguio Dn. Cristobal Colon en sus Descubrimientos por Estos Mares
mwat0060	atlantic ocean (all)	1825	CASTILLA	250	46	65	Carta del Oceano Atlantico Setentrional, con las Derrotas que Siguio Dn. Cristobal Colon hasta su Recalada a las Primeras Islas que Descubrio en el Nuevo Mundo
mwca0590	canada st lawrence	1723	CATALOGNE	25000	37	51	Partie Haute et Occidentale du Fleuve de Canada ou de St. Laurent depuis le Lac Ontario jusqu'a la Ville de Quebec / Basse Partie et Orientale du Fleuve de St. Laurent depuis l'Isle aux Lievres jusqu'a son Embouchure (2 maps)
mwam0968	america north (east)	1755	CATESBY	4000	43	59	Carolinae Floridae nec non Insularum Bahamensium ... Ioh. Michael Seligmann (German edition of Catesby's 1743 map 'A Map of Carolina, Florida and the Bahama Islands with Adjacent Parts')
mwam0766	america north	1845	CATLIN	300	49	35	Localities of All the Indian Tribes of North America in 1833 / Present Localities of the Indian Tribes West of the Mississippi
mwin0167	india	1715	CATROU	450	30	36	L'Empire du Mogol sur les Memoires de Mr. Manouchi
mwca0477	canada ontario	1832	CATTLIN	400	18	21	(Plan of Ottawa) Sketch of Bytown, Ottawa River Founded in 1826
mwf0613	france languedoc	1703	CAVALIER	1350	77	55	Carte et Description Generale de Languedoc avec les Confins des Pais et Provinces Voizines (in 3 sheets of 77x55cm.)
mww0155	world	1642	CAVAZZA	8000	35	55	Nova Totius Terrarum Orbis Geographica ac Hydrographica Tabula
mwit1056	italy naples	1665	CAVAZZA	5500	33	84	Prospetiva della Nobillisima Citta di Napoli Metropoli
mwaf0168	africa	1732	CELEBI	1200	15	20	(Africa, published in Constantinople by Katib Celebi)
mwc0110	china	1732	CELEBI	1000	20	15	(China, published in Constantinople by Katib Celebi)
mwaf0388	africa east	1706	CELLARIUS	180	20	30	Africa Interior
mwaf0765	africa north libya	1706	CELLARIUS	180	20	30	Africa Propria
mwaf0494	africa egypt etc	1706	CELLARIUS	200	20	30	Egypti Delta et Nili
mwgr0139	greece	1701	CELLARIUS	180	21	31	Graeciae Antiquae et insularum conspectus
mwgr0139a	greece	1701	CELLARIUS	150	21	31	Macedonia, Thessalia, Epirus
mwaf0841	africa north west	1706	CELLARIUS	200	20	30	Mauritania et Numidia
mwme0738a	iraq etc	1706	CELLARIUS	200	21	31	Mesopotamia et Babylonia
mwme0800	persia etc	1706	CELLARIUS	200	21	30	Oriens Persia, India
mwit0915	italy sicily	1701	CELLARIUS	240	20	31	Sicilia Antiqua
mwme0872	syria etc	1706	CELLARIUS	300	20	30	Syria
mww0284	world	1701	CELLARIUS	480	21	31	Veteris Orbis Climata ex Strabone
mwit0494	italy lombardy	1703	CERRUTI	1650	57	130	Corso del Po per la Lombardia dalle sue Fonti sino al Mare
							CHABERT, SEE 'DE CHABERT'.
mwf0410	france burgundy	1735	CHAFFAT	675	51	71	(Belfort) Besfort dessen Situation und Construction Profile und Grund-Riss nach des Herren G.L. de Vaubans Manier
mwf0626	france languedoc	1774	CHALMANDRIER	1350	52	328	Carte du Canal Royal de la Province de Languedoc depuis Trebes jusqu'a Capestang
mwf0625a	france languedoc	1771	CHALMANDRIER	650	48	209	Carte Générale du Canal Royal de la Province de Languedoc

AMPG REFERENCE	REGION	DATE	MAP MAKER	PRICE (UK£)	VERT. (cm.)	HOR. (cm.)	TITLE OF MAP (Comments by the editor in brackets)
mwsw0173	switzerland	1770	CHALMANDRIER	1500	47	63	Plan de la Ville de Geneve
mwsp0345a	spain madrid	1761	CHALMANDRIER	8000	100	141	Plan Geometrico y Historico de la Villa de Madrid y sus contornos - Plan Geometrique et Historique de la Ville de Madrid et de ses environs / gravé par N. Chalmandrier.
mwca0568	canada quebec montreal	1613	CHAMPLAIN	8000	12	17	(Montreal) le grand sautl st. louis
mwca0014	canada	1632	CHAMPLAIN	145000	53	87	Carte de la Nouvelle France, Augmentee depuis la Derniere, Servant a la Navigation Faicte en son Vray Meridien, par le Sr. de Champlain Capitaine pour le Roy en la Marine
mwca0011	canada	1613	CHAMPLAIN	20000	26	34	Carte Geographique de la Nouvelle Franse et son vray mondia
mwca0009	canada	1612	CHAMPLAIN	225000	44	77	Carte Geographique de la Nouvelle Franse Faictte par le Sieur de Champlain Saint Tongois Cappitaine Ordinaire pour le Roy en la Marine Faict len 1612
mwuss0390	florida	1613	CHAMPLAIN	2400	15	25	Isle de Sainte Croix
mwuss0789	massachusetts	1613	CHAMPLAIN	2400	15	25	Le Beau Port (Gloucester)
mwuss0788	massachusetts	1613	CHAMPLAIN	3000	15	24	Port Fortune (Stage Harbour near Chatham)
mwca0348	canada nova scotia	1613	CHAMPLAIN	2400	15	25	Port Royal
mwca0498	canada quebec	1613	CHAMPLAIN	8000	15	25	Quebec
mwuss0685	maine	1613	CHAMPLAIN	2000	12	16	Qui Ni Be Quy (Kennebec River)
mwca0019	canada	1653	CHAMPLAIN-DUVAL	20000	35	54	Le Canada Faict par le Sr. de Champlain, ou sont la Nouvelle France, la Nouvelle Angleterre, la Nouvelle Hollande, la Nouvelle Suede, la Virginie &c. (re-working of an uncompleted and unpublished copper plate engraved c1616, by Champlain. Illustrated is the 1677 edition, which also includes 2 cartouches).
mwwi0472	cuba	1798	CHANLAIRE	600	33	43	Carte de l'Isle de Cuba et des Isles Lucayes
mwsp0310	spain	1799	CHANLAIRE	1200	97	126	Carte d'Espagne et de Portugal en Neuf Feuilles
mwf0536	france corsica	1790	CHANLAIRE	720	64	50	Departement de l'Isle de Corse
mwf1081	france provence	1790	CHANLAIRE	280	46	60	Departement des Alpes Maritimes
mwf0543	france corsica	1801	CHANLAIRE	280	23	18	Departement du Golo et du Liamone
mwf1161	france rhone-alpes	1794	CHANLAIRE	500	57	51	Departement du Mont Blanc. Departement du Leman ... Decrete le 29. Janvier 1793 par la Convention Nationale
mwf0251	france alsace	1800	CHANLAIRE	235	51	53	Haut Rhin
mwuk0244	ireland	1799	CHANLAIRE	280	32	43	Isles Britanniques. Cinquieme Carte. Irlande.
mww0598	world	1798	CHANLAIRE	650	32	42	Mappemonde en Deux Hemispheres ou l'on Indique les Nouvelles Decouvertes
mww0626	world	1806	CHANLAIRE	450	32	45	Mappe-Monde Suivant la Projection des Cartes Reduites ou l'on a Trace les Routes de Mr. de Bougainville, et les Deux Derniers Voyages du Captaine Cook
mwru0403a	russia moscow	1812	CHANLAIRE	2000	96	89	Plan de la Ville et des faubourgs de Moscou
mwas0522	asia south east	1798	CHANLAIRE	400	32	42	Presqu'lle au dela du Gange et Archipel de l'Inde
mwe0835	europe east	1807	CHANLAIRE	720	38	59	Valakie, Brancovani
			SEE ALSO UNDER 'MENTELLE'				
mwuss1214	new york	1831	CHAPIN	1500	37	32	Plan of the City of New York for the Use of Strangers
mwuss1225	new york	1834	CHAPIN	800	73	53	Squire's Map of the State of New York, Containing All the Towns in the State
mwam0767	america north	1845	CHAPIN & TAYLOR	2000	117	144	Chapin's Ornamental Map of the United States, with Plans of the World, British Possessions, West Indies, and Columbia
mwec0921	uk england nottinghamshire	1778	CHAPMAN	1800	84	64	Nottinghamshire Survey'd in 1774 by John Chapman
mwec0414	uk england essex	1777	CHAPMAN & ANDRE	3000	45	59	A Map of the County of Essex from an Actual Survey (in 25 sheets, each 45x59cm)
mwuk1073	england	1847	CHAPMAN & HALL	400	62	43	England & Wales, with Railways and Electric Telegraph
mwuss1432	pennsylvania	1840	CHAPMAN & HALL	200	38	30	Philadelphia
mwsam0159	south america	1842	CHAPMAN & HALL	160	39	30	South America
mwas0553	asia south east	1848	CHAPMAN & HALL	200	32	41	South Eastern Asia Birmah-China-Japan
mwec1084	uk england staffordshire	1833	CHAPMAN & HALL	60	26	20	Staffordshire
mwam1255	america north (east)	1849	CHAPMAN & HALL	275	32	41	United States North East. Sharpe's Corresponding Maps No.46. Divisional Series. Engraved by J. Wilson Lowry. London Published by Chapman and Hall 186 Strand-1848
mwuss1311	ohio	1835	CHARDON	300	13	17	Cincinnati
mwf0202	france	1845	CHARLE	180	61	52	Nouvelle Carte de la France indiquant les Routes de Poste
mww0647	world	1814	CHARLES	500	33	43	A General Chart of the World on Mercator's Projection Exhibiting the New Discoveries
mwwi0159	west indies	1814	CHARLES	350	35	47	The West Indies
mwm0243a	mediterranean malta	1760	CHARPENTIER	1800	33	51	Les Villes Forts et Châteaux de Malte (view)
mwuk1179	england london	1745	CHASSEREAU	650	50	54	An Actual Survey of the Parish of St Leonard in Shoreditch Middlesex
mwec1339	uk england yorkshire	1750	CHASSEREAU	1200	43	63	Plan de la Ville et Foubourgs de York Capitale de la Comte du Meme Nom
mwwi0648	hispaniola	1787	CHASTENET-PUISEGUR	850	60	94	Carte Reduite de l'Isle de St. Domingue
mwwi0334a	hispaniola	1787	CHASTENET-PUISEGUR	1000	61	91	Carte Reduite des Debouquemens de St. Domingue, Levee, Dressee et Publiee par Ordre du Roi ... d'apres les Observations Faites sur la Corvette le Vautour en 1784

AMPG REFERENCE	REGION	DATE	MAP MAKER	PRICE (UK£)	VERT. (cm.)	HOR. (cm.)	TITLE OF MAP (Comments by the editor in brackets)
mwme0988	turkey etc	1719	CHATELAIN	375	37	43	Bosphore de Thrace (3 views of Constantinople surrounded by text)
mwuk0130	ireland	1708	CHATELAIN	320	36	46	(Ireland) Carte Ancienne et Moderne
mwsw0115	switzerland	1720	CHATELAIN	400	35	44	Carte Ancienne de la Suisse
mwe0720a	europe danube	1708	CHATELAIN	300	36	46	Carte Ancienne et Moderne des Differents Etats et Pais Situez au Long du Danube, pour Servir a l'Intelligence de l'Histoire
mwgm0023	gulf of mexico and surrounding regions	1719	CHATELAIN	960	41	52	Carte Contenant le Royaume du Mexique et la Floride
mwm0096	mediterranean adriatic	1708	CHATELAIN	650	50	62	Carte de Geographie des Differents Etats de la Republique de Venise
mwaf1179	africa west	1719	CHATELAIN	400	40	51	Carte de la Barbarie, Nigritie et de la Guinee avec les Pays Voisins
mwe0125	europe	1708	CHATELAIN	300	34	44	Carte de la Germanie et les Diferents Etats ou ses Peuples ont Porte leurs Conquestes
mwgr0148	greece	1708	CHATELAIN	250	39	44	Carte de la Grece contenant l'etat present de l'Eglise Grecque
mwsc0707	scandinavia sweden	1714	CHATELAIN	300	34	21	Carte de la Laponie Suedoise
mwam0372	america north	1719	CHATELAIN	1800	42	48	Carte de la Nouvelle France, ou se Voit le Cours des Grandes Rivieres de S. Laurens & de Mississipi ... de la Floride, de la Louisiane, de la Virginie, de la Marie-Lande, de la Pensilvanie, du Nouveau Jersay, de la Nouvelle Yorck (reduced version of De Fer 1718)
mwsc0110	scandinavia	1710	CHATELAIN	550	39	45	Carte de la Partie Septentrionale du Royaume de Suede avec une Table des Provinces et Villes Principales / Carte de la Partie Meridionale du Royaume de Suede avec une Table des Provinces et des Villes Principales (2 maps)
mwsam0176a	south america north	1720	CHATELAIN	350	40	52	Carte de la Terre Ferme, du Perou, du Bresil, et du Pays des Amazones ...
mwme0262	holy land	1719	CHATELAIN	375	37	49	Carte de la Terre Sainte Divisee dans Toutes ses Parties selon le Nombre des Tribus d'Israel
mwaf0147	africa	1719	CHATELAIN	220	38	49	Carte de l'Afrique selon les Auteurs Anciens Enrichie de Remarques Historiques (map surrounded by text)
mwme0263	holy land	1719	CHATELAIN	300	38	43	Carte de L'Asie Inferieure Selon les Auters Anciens
mwas0120a	asia continent	1719	CHATELAIN	300	38	48	Carte de L'Asie selon des auters anciens
mwme0601	arabia etc	1719	CHATELAIN	500	40	52	Carte de L'Empire des Turcs
mwme0604	arabia etc	1720	CHATELAIN	800	50	120	Carte de l'Empire Othoman
mwe0342	europe austria	1708	CHATELAIN	240	38	47	Carte de L'Etat de la Cour Imperiale ... D'Autriche
mwsc0337	scandinavia denmark	1714	CHATELAIN	300	35	45	Carte de L'Etat du Royaume de Dannemark
mwe0121	europe	1705	CHATELAIN	480	46	59	Carte de l'Europe Suivant les Plus Nouvelles Observations de Messieurs de l'Academie
mwas0642	asia south east java	1719	CHATELAIN	1400	38	87	Carte de l'Ile de Java: Partie Occidentale, Partie Orientale, Dressee tout Nouvellement
mwaf0599	africa islands madagascar	1719	CHATELAIN	450	38	43	Carte de l'Ile de Madagascar, dite Aujourd'hui l'Ile Daufine
mwbp0354	poland	1710	CHATELAIN	1250	50	60	Carte de Pologne
mwwi0241a	west indies (east)	1719	CHATELAIN	650	49	34	Carte des Antilles Francoises et des Isles Voisines Dressee sur les Memoires Manuscrits
mwsc0708	scandinavia sweden	1714	CHATELAIN	480	51	60	Carte des Estats de la Couronne de Suede avec des Remarques et des Tables Tres Instructives
mwsw0102	switzerland	1708	CHATELAIN	320	35	48	Carte des Grisons
mwas0446	asia south east	1719	CHATELAIN	720	51	49	Carte des Indes, de la Chine & des Iles de Sumatra, Java &c.
mwbp0362	poland	1714	CHATELAIN	450	35	45	Carte des Trois Ordres ... Pologne (views of Warsaw, Cracow, Wilna)
mwsp0228	spain	1705	CHATELAIN	380	34	44	Carte d'Espagne et des Principaux Etats Appartenans a cette Monarchie
mwca0047	canada	1719	CHATELAIN	875	40	52	Carte du Canada ou de la Nouvelle France, & des Decouvertes qui y ont ete Faites, Dressee sur les Observations les Plus Nouvelles
mwru0387	russia moscow	1714	CHATELAIN	450	34	44	Carte du Gouvernement Civil et Eclesiastique de Moscovie, l'Etat des Revenus et l'Ordre de la Justice et des Officiers de la Cour (small plan of Moscow with text)
mwuk0131	ireland	1708	CHATELAIN	320	36	46	Carte du Gouvernement Civil et Militaire ... Royaume d'Ireland
mwam0114	america continent	1708	CHATELAIN	240	33	44	Carte du Gouvernement de l'Amerique (small map and 4 illustrations on a page of text)
mwuk0783	uk	1708	CHATELAIN	240	35	46	Carte du Gouvernement Militaire de l'Angleterre ou l'on Represente l'Etat des Officiers de Guerre et celui des Forces de Terre et de Mer (small map surrounded by text)
mwg0094	germany	1708	CHATELAIN	250	47	61	Carte du Gouvernement Militaire de l'Empire
mwsam0229	south america argentina	1720	CHATELAIN	400	40	52	Carte du Paraguai, du Chili, de Detroit de Magellan &c.
mwit1234	italy venice	1708	CHATELAIN	900	20	46	Carte du Plan de Venise, l'Etat de sa Noblesse
mww0334	world	1720	CHATELAIN	500	38	47	Carte du Premier Periode de Monde depuis Adam
mwe0554	europe czech republic (bohemia)	1708	CHATELAIN	450	47	62	Carte du Royaume de Boheme, la Chronologie de ses Rois, les Etats de Silesie, Moravie, et Lusace
mwaf0900	africa south	1719	CHATELAIN	550	41	53	Carte du Royaume de Congo, du Monomotapa et de la Cafrerie

AMPG REFERENCE	REGION	DATE	MAP MAKER	PRICE (UK£)	VERT. (cm.)	HOR. (cm.)	TITLE OF MAP (Comments by the editor in brackets)
mwe0784	europe east	1714	CHATELAIN	550	38	95	Carte Genealogique des Ducs et Rois de Boheme et de Hongrie qui ont Regne ou Governe ces Diferents Etats avec des Instructions pour Conduire a l'Histoire de Pologne
mwbp0363	poland	1714	CHATELAIN	500	38	92	Carte Genealogique Des Princes et Rois de Pologne (illustration chopped on right hand side)
mwit1029	italy south	1720	CHATELAIN	550	37	91	Carte Genealogique des Rois de Naples et de Sicile
mwsp0522	spain regions	1720	CHATELAIN	300	41	98	Carte Genealogique des Rois de Navarre, de Castille, d'Arragon, de Portugal et de Grenade
mwsc0115	scandinavia	1714	CHATELAIN	550	39	96	Carte Genealogique pour Conduire a l'Historique des Rois du Nord, la Carte de leurs Etats, leurs Armes et des Remarques pour Conduire a l'Intelligence de l'Histoire du Nord
mwsw0103	switzerland	1708	CHATELAIN	450	47	62	Carte Generale des Treize Cantons de Suisse
mwm0143	mediterranean east	1720	CHATELAIN	320	34	45	Carte Historique et Geographique ... St. Paul
mwgr0149	greece	1708	CHATELAIN	400	34	44	Carte Historique et Geographique de l'Ancienne Grece
mwsp0245	spain	1719	CHATELAIN	450	43	56	Carte Historique et Geographique des Royaumes d'Espagne et de Portugal, Divises selon leurs Royaumes et Provinces
mwit0670	italy piedmont	1708	CHATELAIN	250	36	48	Carte Historique et Geographique pour Introduire a l'Intelligence de l'Histoire de Savoye, et a la Connoissance du Gouverment de cet Etat (inset plan of Turin)
mwm0034	mediterranean	1705	CHATELAIN	350	33	44	Carte Historique, Cronologique, Geographique de l'Empire Grec, avec des Remarques sur les Conquestes d'Alexandre le Grand, Fondateur de cette Empire
mwm0045	mediterranean	1721	CHATELAIN	350	34	45	Carte Historique, Cronologique, Geographique de l'Empire Romain
mwru0446a	russia tartary	1719	CHATELAIN	550	41	51	Carte Nouvelle de la Grande Tartarie ou de l'Empire du Grand Cham
mwaf0500	africa egypt etc	1719	CHATELAIN	480	40	51	Carte Particuliere de l'Egypte, de la Nubie et de l'Abyssinie
mwca0048	canada	1720	CHATELAIN	400	37	46	Carte Particuliere du Fleuve Saint Louis
mwam1276	great lakes	1719	CHATELAIN	1000	36	44	Carte Particuliere du Fleuve Saint Louis Dressee sur les Lieux avec les Noms des Sauvages du Pais
mwsam0756	south america peru	1719	CHATELAIN	500	49	38	Carte Particuliere du Perou, Plan de la Ville de Lima
mwme0264	holy land	1719	CHATELAIN	320	40	47	Carte pour Conduire a l'Intelligence de l'Histoire Sacree
mwuk1080	england and france	1708	CHATELAIN	250	47	62	Carte pour l'Intelligence de l'Histoire d'Angleterre ou on Remarque les Conquestes de cette Monarchie dans la Plus Part des Etats de l'Europe
mwf0681	france lorraine	1708	CHATELAIN	240	35	45	Carte pour L'Intelligence de L'Histoire de Lorraine
mwuk0784	uk	1708	CHATELAIN	375	51	59	Carte pour l'Introduction a l'Histoire d'Angleterre ou l'on Voit son Premier Gouvernement et l'Etat Abrege de cette Monarchie sous les Empereurs Romains, et sous les Rois Saxons (map surrounded by text and many portraits in borders)
mwe1202	europe west	1720	CHATELAIN	350	50	58	Carte pour servir a L'Histoire de L'Empire d'Occident
mwm0041	mediterranean	1720	CHATELAIN	400	39	50	Carte pour servir D'Introduction a l'Histoire Romain
mwam0376	america north	1719	CHATELAIN	550	41	52	Carte qui contient une description des Iles & Terres que Les Anglois possedent dans L'Amerique Septentrionale (text and 8 small maps on one sheet incl. Bermuda, Barbados and Jamaica)
mwam0125	america continent	1719	CHATELAIN	13500	80	140	Carte tres Curieuse de la Mer du Sud, Contenant des Remarques Nouvelles et tres Utiles non Seulement sur les Ports et Iles de cette Mer, mais aussy sur les Principaux Pays de l'Amerique tant Septentrionale que Meridionale
mwin0168	india	1720	CHATELAIN	450	38	43	Cartes Nouvelle des Terres de Cucan, de Canara, de Malabar, de Madura, et de Coromandel
mwaf0901	africa south	1719	CHATELAIN	550	38	44	Coutumes Moeurs & Habillemens des Peuples qui Habitent aux Environs du Cap de Bonne Esperance
mwgr0150	greece	1708	CHATELAIN	250	33	44	Cronologie Historique ... D'Ancienne Grece
mwaf0497	africa egypt etc	1719	CHATELAIN	250	34	48	Description de la Ville D'Alexandrie
mwgm0394	panama	1719	CHATELAIN	450	37	43	Description de l'Isthme de Darien, des Proprietez du Pays et de la Ville de Panama; a la quelle on a Joint une Description Curieuse des Diverses Plantes, Oiseaux Poissons les Plus Rares qui se Trouvent dans la Nouvelle Hollande (inset map of Panama)
mwaf0498	africa egypt etc	1719	CHATELAIN	250	37	49	Description du Nil
mwgm0200	mexico	1719	CHATELAIN	850	37	44	Description, Situation & Vue de la Ville de Mexique, des Deux Lacs sur lesquels elle est Batie, du Grand Temple de cette Ville, des Sacrifice d'Homme qu'on y Faisoit, de l'Idole des Mexicains
mwru0446	russia tartary	1719	CHATELAIN	250	37	43	Genealogie des Anciens Empereurs Tartares, Descendus de Genghiscan
mwin0169	india	1720	CHATELAIN	300	37	43	Genealogie des Empereurs Mogols
mwjk0151	japan tokyo	1719	CHATELAIN	800	29	88	Jedo Capitale du Japan (view)
mwas0822	asia south east siam	1715	CHATELAIN	600	37	43	Le Royaume de Siam avec les Royaumes qui luy sont Tributaires et les Isles de Sumatra Andemaon
mwjk0068	japan	1719	CHATELAIN	1600	36	44	L'Empire du Japon Tire des Cartes des Japonnois
mwit1157	italy vatican	1708	CHATELAIN	300	33	44	L'Idee Generale du Conclave

AMPG REFERENCE	REGION	DATE	MAP MAKER	PRICE (UK£)	VERT. (cm.)	HOR. (cm.)	TITLE OF MAP (Comments by the editor in brackets)
mww0298		1705	CHATELAIN	950	34	44	Mappemonde ou Description Generale du Globe Terrestre
mww0299		1705	CHATELAIN	950	33	45	Mappe-Monde pour Connoitre les Progres & les Conquestes les Plus Remarquables des Provinces-Unies, ainsy que celles des Compagnies d'Orient et d'Occident, et les Pais quelles Possedent dans l'un et dans l'autre Hemisphere
mww0332	world	1719	CHATELAIN	1500	48	68	Nouvaux Mappemonde ou Globe Terrestre avec des Tables et des Remarques pour Conduire a la Connoissance de la Geographie et de l'Histoire
mwit0732	italy rome	1708	CHATELAIN	400	33	42	Nouveau Plan de la Ville de Rome Tire par Ordre du Pape par Matteo Gregoria de Romans Tres Utille pour les Voiageurs
mwuk0785	uk	1708	CHATELAIN	650	48	62	Nouvelle Carte d'Angleterre, d'Ecosse, et d'Irlande, avec des Instructions pour Connoitre les Differents Etats de la Couronne d'Angleterre en Europe, Asie, Afrique, et Amerique
mwsam0053	south america	1713	CHATELAIN	550	46	60	Nouvelle Carte de Geographie de la Partie Meridionale de l'Amerique Suivant les Plus Nouvelles Observations
mwe0917	europe hungary	1708	CHATELAIN	480	47	63	Nouvelle Carte de la Hongrie, Divisee selon ses Differents Etats
mwaf0162	africa	1730	CHATELAIN	750	47	58	Nouvelle Carte de l'Afrique avec des Remarques et des Tables pour Trouver sans Peine les Differents Peuples de cette Partie du Monde
mwg0105	germany	1720	CHATELAIN	350	47	62	Nouvelle Carte De L'Alemagne avec des Tables des Branches de la Noblesse
mwam0360	america north	1705	CHATELAIN	1650	49	62	Nouvelle Carte de l'Amerique Septentrionale Dressee sur les Plus Nouvelles Observations
mwuk0967	england	1708	CHATELAIN	600	48	63	Nouvelle Carte de l'Angleterre dans laquelle l'on Observe les Comtez, les Archeveschez, les Eveschez, les Universitez, les Villes, et les Bourgs
mwas0120	asia continent	1719	CHATELAIN	480	47	58	Nouvelle Carte de l'Asie, avec des Tables Alphabetiques pour Trouver sans Paine les Etats des Principaux Princes de cette Partie du Monde
mwit0159	italy	1721	CHATELAIN	600	34	66	Nouvelle Carte de L'Etat de L'Italie
mwin0035	ceylon	1719	CHATELAIN	400	39	44	Nouvelle Carte de l'Ile de Ceylon avec des Remarques Historiques
mwru0145	russia	1719	CHATELAIN	450	50	58	Nouvelle Carte de Moscovie ou sont Representes les Diferents Etats de sa Maieste Czarienne en Europe et en Asie et le Chemin d'un de ses Ambassadeurs a Peking Ville
mwsc0116	scandinavia	1714	CHATELAIN	500	50	59	Nouvelle Carte de Scandinavie ou des Etats du Nord Dressee sur les Observations les Plus Nouvelles des Meilleurs Geographes avec les Armes des Provinces de la Suede
mwuk0460	scotland	1719	CHATELAIN	450	36	46	Nouvelle Carte d'Ecosse ou l'on Fait Observer l'Etat de la Noblesse: les Villes et les Bourgs qui Deputent au Parlement
mwm0044	mediterranean	1721	CHATELAIN	300	49	55	Nouvelle Carte des Conciles Generaux et Particuliers qui se sont Tenus en Europe, en Asie, en Afrique, et en Amerique
mwg0416	brandenburg	1720	CHATELAIN	400	37	48	Nouvelle Carte des Differents Etats du Roi Prusse et de ceux des autres Princes de la Maison de Brandenbourg
mwbh0592	belgium holland	1721	CHATELAIN	450	47	45	Nouvelle Carte des Dix-Sept Provinces des Pays-Bas
mwru0138	russia	1717	CHATELAIN	550	37	48	Nouvelle Carte des Etats du Grand Duc de Moscovie en Europe. Partie Septentrionale / Partie Meridionale (2 maps. Northern map illustrated.)
mwuk0132	ireland	1708	CHATELAIN	450	37	47	Nouvelle Carte d'Irlande, ou on Remarque l'Etat Present de cette Isle, l'Ordre du Gouvernement Ecclesiastique et Politique
mwuk1151	england london	1720	CHATELAIN	360	35	46	Nouvelle Carte du Gouvernement Civil d'Angleterre et de celuy de la Ville de Londres (small inset plan of London)
mwbp0378	poland	1720	CHATELAIN	450	50	58	Nouvelle Carte du Royaume de Pologne
mwsc0338	scandinavia denmark	1714	CHATELAIN	480	50	59	Nouvelle Carte Geographique du Royaume de Dannemarck avec une Table des Villes les Plus Remarquables
mwm0042	mediterranean	1720	CHATELAIN	350	50	58	Nouvelle Carte pour servir a L'Histoire de L'Empire D'Occident
mww0300	world	1705	CHATELAIN	500	33	44	Plan de l'Histoire Universelle, ou l'on Voit les Quatre Monarchies du Monde, et Tous les Anciens Etats aussi bien que ceux qui Subsistent Aujourdhuy
mwit0741	italy rome	1721	CHATELAIN	250	33	43	Plan des Antiquities de Rome
mwit0733	italy rome	1708	CHATELAIN	450	34	44	Rome Ancienne et Moderne (plan surrounded by key)
mwaf0792	africa north morocco	1719	CHATELAIN	400	37	43	Singularitez Curieuses des Royaumes de Maroc et de Fez dans la Barbarie
mwjk0069	japan	1719	CHATELAIN	650	38	44	Succession des Empereurs du Japon avec une Description du Meutre de l'Empereur Cubo et la Reception des Ambassadeurs Hollandois ... Carte du Japon
mwme0269	holy land	1720	CHATELAIN	350	38	47	Suite de la Genealogie ou Chronologie des Rois Patriarches et Prophetes
mwaf1177	africa west	1719	CHATELAIN	300	38	43	Vue & Description de la Ville de Lovango
mwaf1178	africa west	1719	CHATELAIN	300	37	43	Vue & Description des Forts - La Cote de Guinee

AMPG REFERENCE	REGION	DATE	MAP MAKER	PRICE (UK£)	VERT. (cm.)	HOR. (cm.)	TITLE OF MAP (Comments by the editor in brackets)
mwaf0499	africa egypt etc	1719	CHATELAIN	350	37	43	Vue de la Ville du Grand Cairo
mwas0823	asia south east siam	1719	CHATELAIN	400	38	49	Vue et Description de la Ville de Siam
mwme0724	caucasus	1719	CHATELAIN	450	37	49	Vue et Description Des Principales Villes de L'Armenie et de la Georgie.
mwg0153	germany	1784	CHAUCHARD	1200	180	210	Carte Generale de l'Empire d'Allemagne
mwg0167	germany	1801	CHAUCHARD	240	62	74	Carte Reduite de la Carte Generale d'Allemagne
mwwi0239	west indies (east)	1713	CHAUFOURIER	2000	64	91	Plan de la Martinique, la Guadeloupe, Marie Galande, et la Grenade
mwbh0884	luxembourg	1792	CHAUMIER	480	43	55	Carte du Duche de Luxembourg … Jaillot
mwf0181	france	1813	CHAUMIER	720	128	144	Tableau General et Itineraire de l'Empire Francais Divise en 130 Departemens
mwwi0620	hispaniola	1760	CHEDEL, F.	300	18	26	Ville de St. Domingue
mwuk1068a	uk england	1841	CHEFFINS	220	68	68	Cheffins's Map of the English & Scotch Railways …
mwuk1063	england	1835	CHEFFINS	3000	76	155	London & Birmingham Railway. Plan of the Line and Adjacent Country / Map of the Principal Railways in England / Map of the Grand Junction Railway and Adjacent Country (3 maps of different sizes folding into case)
mwaf0750a	africa north algeria	1760	CHEREAU	1200	34	51	Alger ville capitale d'Afrique (view)
mwsp0552	spain regions	1750	CHEREAU	3500	34	52	Barcelone, Ville Capitale de la principaute Catalogne (view)
mwsp0556a	spain regions	1760	CHEREAU	1500	34	51	Cadiz
mwf0755	france nord pas-de-calais	1760	CHEREAU	250	16	25	Cambray
mwgr0428a	greece crete	1760	CHEREAU	1800	35	51	Candie, Ville Capitale de l'Isle du même nom (view)
mwf1157	france rhone-alpes	1760	CHEREAU	250	15	25	Chambery Ville Capitale de Savoye Siege d'un Senat et Chambre des Comptes
mwbp0466a	poland	1760	CHEREAU	2000	35	52	Cracovie (view)
mwuk0493	scotland	1750	CHEREAU	480	16	22	Edimbourg Ville Capitale du Royaume d'Ecosse Evesche et Universite
mwuss0626	louisiana	1740	CHEREAU	2000	16	23	Le Missisipi ou la Louisiane dans l'Amerique Septentrionale
mwm0239	mediterranean malta	1750	CHEREAU	2500	35	51	Les Villes forts et chateaux de Malte (view)
mwsp0096a	portugal	1760	CHEREAU	1500	35	52	Lisbone
mwuk1189	england london	1750	CHEREAU	480	16	22	Londres Capitale du Royaume d'Angleterre Evesche et Celebre Port de Mer
mwit0504	italy lombardy	1720	CHEREAU	480	13	18	Mantoue Ville de la Lombardie Transalpine
mwit0948	italy sicily	1750	CHEREAU	3000	34	50	Messine (view)
mwf0686	france lorraine	1760	CHEREAU	300	14	22	Nancy Ville Capitale du Duche de Lorraine
mwit1065	italy naples	1750	CHEREAU	3500	34	51	Naples, Ville de la Province de Labour (view)
mwf0881a	france paris	1760	CHEREAU	1200	34	52	Paris (view)
mwf0624	france languedoc	1760	CHEREAU	300	15	25	Perpignan Ville Capitale de Comte de Rousillon
mwsp0553	spain regions	1750	CHEREAU	2500	35	51	Seville. Ville Archiepiscopale et Capitale du Raume d'Andalusie en Espagne (view)
mwaf0795a	africa north morocco	1760	CHEREAU	1500	34	51	Tanger
mwf0625	france languedoc	1760	CHEREAU	300	15	24	Toulouse Ville Capitale du Languedoc
mwaf0765a	africa north libya	1760	CHEREAU	1500	34	51	Tripoli (view)
mwit0686	italy piedmont	1750	CHEREAU	3750	34	52	Turin. Ville Capitale du Piedmont (view)
mwit1244	italy venice	1750	CHEREAU	3500	50	65	Venise.
mwe0430a	europe austria vienna	1760	CHEREAU	1500	34	50	Vienne en Autriche
mwaf0075	africa	1666	CHETWIND	700	34	42	Africae Descriptio Nova Impensis (re-issue of Seile 1652)
mwam0068b	america continent	1666	CHETWIND	900	34	42	Americae Descriptio Nova (re-issue of Seile 1752)
mwe0077a	europe	1666	CHETWIND	550	33	41	Europae Descriptio Nova Impensis (re-issue of Seile 1652)
mwam0833	america north (central)	1841	CHEVALIER	720	46	62	Plan Topographique du Terrain Traverse par le Canal de la Chesapeake a l'Ohio
mwam0748	america north	1841	CHEVALIER	480	61	64	Voies de Communication des Etats-Unis - Carte General des Etats-Unis 1840
mwc0147a	china	1752	CHEVIGNY	120	14	17	Chine
mwme0615	arabia etc	1740	CHILD	180	22	25	A Chart of the Coast of Arabia, the Red Sea, & Persian Gulf, Drawn from the Chart of the Eastern Ocean
mwaf1201	africa west	1745	CHILD	300	25	26	A Chart of the West Coast of Africa
mwc0315	china tibet	1752	CHILD	300	17	23	A Map of Great Tibet Drawn from that Made by Lama Mathematicians in 1717
mwaf0929	africa south	1750	CHILD	650	25	37	A Map of the Country of the Hottentots, towards the Cape of Good Hope
mwaf1199	africa west	1745	CHILD	180	24	30	A Map of the Kingdoms of Kongo, Angola & Benguela with the Adjacent Countries
mwaf1200	africa west	1745	CHILD	200	22	14	A Particular Map of the River Sanaga, from its Mouth, to the Desert
mwat0162	atlantic canary isl.	1753	CHILD	300	23	15	Island of Teneriffe
mwaf0928	africa south	1750	CHILD	280	20	15	Prospect of the Cape of Good Hope (2 insets)
mwru0447b	russia tartary	1730	CHILD	300	29	46	The Eleventh Sheet of Chinese Tartary, Containing ye Country West of Nipcha, Subject to Russia … by P. Jartoux, Fridelli & Bonjour in 1711
mwit0152	italy	1719	CHIQUET	300	16	22	Carte Generale d'Italie
mwsc0118	scandinavia	1719	CHIQUET	280	17	22	Estats de la Couronne de Suede dans la Scandinavie, ou sont Suede, Gotlande, Lapponie Suedoise, Finlande, Ingrie et Livonie. Subdivisees en leurs Provinces
mwme0482	jerusalem	1719	CHIQUET	350	16	22	Estats de l'Empire du Grande Seigneur dit Sultan et Ottomans Empereur des Turcs

AMPG REFERENCE	REGION	DATE	MAP MAKER	PRICE (UK£)	VERT. (cm.)	HOR. (cm.)	TITLE OF MAP (Comments by the editor in brackets)
mwgr0422	greece crete	1719	CHIQUET	200	16	22	Isle et Royaume de Candie
mwgr0163	greece	1719	CHIQUET	240	17	22	La Grece
mwaf0148	africa	1719	CHIQUET	300	17	22	L'Afrique Dressee Suivant les Auteurs les Plus Nouvea et sur les Observations de Messieurs de l'Academie Royale des Sciences
mwsam0055	south america	1719	CHIQUET	240	16	22	L'Amerique Meridionale qui Fait l'autre Partie des Indes Occidentales, Dressee tres Exactement Suivant les Observations
mwam0373	america north	1719	CHIQUET	550	17	22	L'Amerique Septentrionale qui Fait Partie des Indes Occidentales
mwas0119	asia continent	1719	CHIQUET	280	17	22	L'Asie Dressee Selon les Observations Mrs. de l'Academie Royale des Sciences
mww0354	world	1729	CHIQUET	550	16	22	Le Globe Terrestre Represente en Deux Plans-Hemispheres
mwsc0344	scandinavia denmark	1719	CHIQUET	200	17	22	Le Royaume de Danemark
mwf0104	france	1719	CHIQUET	160	16	22	Le Royaume de France Suivant les Nouvelles Observations
mwsc0607	scandinavia norway	1719	CHIQUET	400	22	16	Le Royaume de Norwege
mwg0104	germany	1719	CHIQUET	160	16	22	L'Empire d'Allemagne Divise en ses Dix Cercles et Autres Estats
mwe0681	europe dalmatia	1719	CHIQUET	240	17	22	Les Isles et Coste de la Dalmatie
mwuk0800	uk	1719	CHIQUET	240	17	22	Les Royaumes d'Angleterre, d'Ecosse et d'Irlande
mwsp0075	portugal	1719	CHIQUET	200	22	17	Les Royaumes de Portugal et d'Algarve
mwbh0568	belgium holland	1719	CHIQUET	180	22	17	Les XVII Provinces des Pays-Bas
mwe0135	europe	1719	CHIQUET	200	17	22	L'Europe Dressee sur les Observations
mwit0922b	italy sicily	1710	CHIQUET	350	14	21	Palerme Ville Capitale de Sicile
mwuk1142	england london	1707	CHISWELL	1500	32	57	A new map of the cityes of London, Westminster and the Burrough of Southwark
mwbp0569	poland	1840	CHODZKO	500	44	55	Carte Generale Routiere Historique et Statistique des Etats de l'Ancienne Republique de Pologne
mwgr0632	greece islands	1809	CHOISEUL-GOUFFIER	550	44	62	Carte de l'Ile de Lemnos, Levee sur les Lieux, et Assujettie aux Observations Astronomiques
mww0488	world	1774	CHRYSOLOGUE	1500	64	123	Hemisphere Superieur de la Mappemonde Projettee - Hemisphere Inferieur de la Mappemonde Projettee
mww0713	world	1838	CHURCH MISSIONARY SOC	1800	74	151	Missionary Map of the World Distinguishing the Stations of All the Protestant Missionary Societies
mwat0270a	atlantic north	1727	CHURCHILL	200	20	28	(North Atlantic)
mwsc0462	scandinavia greenland	1704	CHURCHILL	250	14	30	A Map of Greenland (from Churchill's 'Collection of Voyages' publ. between 1704 and 1730. Shown left is a later version with title 'the Map of Greenland')
mwin0144	india	1704	CHURCHILL	400	28	35	A Map of the Coast of Malabar Madura & Cormandel (copy of Baldaeus 1672)
mwas0635	asia south east java	1705	CHURCHILL	400	28	36	A Mapp of Batavia
mwaf0891b	africa south	1704	CHURCHILL	500	28	36	A Mapp of the Cape of Good Hope with its true Situation
mwas0635a	asia south east java	1705	CHURCHILL	250	13	17	A Mapp of the Islands before Batavia
mwgm0190	mexico	1704	CHURCHILL	300	18	22	An Hidrographicall Draught of Mexico, as it Lies in its Lakes
mwsam0367	south america brazil	1746	CHURCHILL	450	28	36	Brasilia
mwin0032a	ceylon	1704	CHURCHILL	250	29	36	Regnum Jafnapatnam cum Insulis Adjacentibus
mwwi0270	west indies (east)	1811	CHURRUCA	1650	41	55	Carta Esferica de los Canales que Forma la Isla San Martin, con las de San Bartolome y Anguila
mwwi0833	puerto rico	1794	CHURRUCA	2400	47	61	Plano Geometrico del Puerto Capital de la Isla de Puerto Rico Levantado en 1794 (San Juan. Re-issued by Faden in 1805)
mwsam0180a	south america (north)	1751	CIGNI	2400	64	91	Provincia Quitensis Societatis Iesu in America Topographice Exhibita
mww0056	world	1566	CIMERLINO	150000	52	59	(Untitled close copy of Fine's 1534 map)
mwit0727a	italy rome	1692	CINGOLANI-DE ROSSI	6000	92	195	Topografia Geometrica dell'Agro Romano
mwm0169	mediterranean malta	1567	CIRNI	2500	17	26	(Untitled woodcut)
mwam0025	america continent	1602	CLAESZ		106	146	Americae Tabula Nova Multis
mwsam0006a	south america	1594	CLAESZ	15000	39	56	Meridionalis Americae pars in quinq: regiones ab Hispanis dividitur
mwca0003	canada	1594	CLAESZ	25000	38	55	Nova Francia alio nomine dicta Terra Nova
mwuss0036	alaska	1798	CLARET DE FLEURIEU	720	23	17	Plan de la Baie de Tchinkitane (La Baia de Guadalupa des Espagnols en 1775, et Norfolk-Bay des Anglais en 1787) a la Cote N.O. de l'Amerique. Leve par le Cap. Prosper Chanal 1791
mwuss0503	georgia	1790	CLARK	18000	63	41	Chart of the Coast of America from St. Helens Sound St Johns River. Boston. Published & Sold by Matthew Clark
mwru0342	russia	1821	CLARK	100	23	18	Russia
mwuss0296	connecticut	1789	CLARK, M.	24000	43	62	Chart of the Coast of America from New York to Rhode Island
mwuk1358	england north	1789	CLARKE	1950	44	26	A Survey of the Lakes of Cumberland, Westmoreland, and Lancashire (11 maps and 2 plates)
mwsw0192a	switzerland	1786	CLAUSNER	600	76	62	Carte en perspective du Nord au Midi
mwru0397	russia moscow	1790	CLAUSNER	350	30	33	Plan von Moskav (copy of Kitchin 1784)
mwsc0748a	scandinavia sweden	1790	CLAUSNER	280	32	28	Plan de Stockholm

AMPG REFERENCE	REGION	DATE	MAP MAKER	PRICE (UK£)	VERT. (cm.)	HOR. (cm.)	TITLE OF MAP (Comments by the editor in brackets)
mwgm0249a	mexico	1781	CLAVIGERO	1200	29	40	Anahuac o sia l'Impero Messicano i Regni d'Acolhuacan, e di Michuacan etc: Siccom' erano nell' anno 1521 per servire alla Storia antica del Messico delineati dallo stesso Autore della suddetta Storia nel 1780
mwuss0090a	california	1789	CLAVIGERO	1500	37	30	Carta della California suo Golfo e Contracoste della Nuova Spagna
mwm0072	mediterranean	1785	CLERC	1500	51	103	Carte de la Mer Mediterranee
mwbp0054	baltic sea (east)	1785	CLERC	960	77	60	Carte Reduite de la Mer Baltique (2 sheets, each 77x60m.)
mwuss0342	washington DC	1798	CLERK	720	22	28	Plan of the City of Washington
mwuk1508	uk english channel (all)	1781	CLERMONT	1350	74	105	Carte du Canale ou de la Manche (incl. SE Ireland)
mwsw0194	switzerland	1788	CLERMONT	400	33	44	Carte du Canton de Schafhausen
mwsw0186	switzerland	1781	CLERMONT	480	32	44	Carte Generale de la Suisse
mwec0663	uk england kent	1829	CLIFFORD	500	45	45	A Sketch of the Roads within Fourteen Miles of Tunbridge Wells
mwaf0355	africa east	1630	CLOPPENBURG	280	17	24	Abissinorum, sive, Pretiosi Iannis, Imperium
mwaf0045	africa	1630	CLOPPENBURG	350	19	25	Africae Nova Tabula
mwsam0016	south america	1630	CLOPPENBURG	350	17	24	America Meridionalis
mwam0037	america continent	1630	CLOPPENBURG	600	18	24	America Noviter Delineata
mwsp0413	spain regions	1630	CLOPPENBURG	250	18	25	Andaluzia
mwuk1556	england islands	1630	CLOPPENBURG	200	18	25	Anglesey / Wight Vectis olim / Garnesay / Jarsay
mwuk0920	england	1630	CLOPPENBURG	300	19	25	Anglia Regnum
mwuk0694	uk	1630	CLOPPENBURG	400	20	26	Anglia Scotia et Hibernia
mwas0033	asia continent	1630	CLOPPENBURG	500	19	26	Asia
mwf0717	france nord pas-de-calais	1630	CLOPPENBURG	200	18	25	Bolonia & Guines Comitatus
mwuk1539a	uk english channel (west)	1630	CLOPPENBURG	240	18	25	Bretania et Normandia
mwf1092	france pyrenees	1632	CLOPPENBURG	150	19	24	Cadurcium
mwuk1734	wales	1630	CLOPPENBURG	320	18	25	Cambriae Typus Auctore Humeredo Lhuydo Denbigiense Cambrobritanno
mwsp0414	spain regions	1630	CLOPPENBURG	250	17	24	Catalonia
mwin0018	ceylon	1630	CLOPPENBURG	375	20	25	Ceilan
mwc0016	china	1630	CLOPPENBURG	500	18	25	China
mwuk1383	england south	1630	CLOPPENBURG	220	20	26	Cornubia, Devonia, Somersetus, Dorcestria, Wiltonia, Glocestria, Monumetha, Glamorgan, Caermarden, Penbrok, Breknoke, et Herefordia
mwit0830a	italy sardinia	1630	CLOPPENBURG	240	19	26	Corsica / Sardinia (2 maps on one sheet)
mwsc0258a	scandinavia denmark	1630	CLOPPENBURG	300	18	25	Daniae Regnum (shown below left)
mwwi0006	west indies	1630	CLOPPENBURG	450	18	26	De Groote ende Kleyne Eylanden van West-Indien
mwat0103	atlantic bermuda	1630	CLOPPENBURG	1500	19	26	Description des Isles Bermudas - Mappa Aestivarum Insularum
mwsam0664	south america magellan	1630	CLOPPENBURG	400	19	25	Du Destroit de Magellan (title above map)
mwaf0775	africa north morocco	1630	CLOPPENBURG	240	17	24	Fessae et Marocchi Regna
mwsp0415	spain regions	1630	CLOPPENBURG	250	18	25	Gallicia
mwg0051	germany	1632	CLOPPENBURG	200	19	25	Germania
mwaf1099	africa west	1632	CLOPPENBURG	280	19	25	Guineae Nova Descriptio
mwgm0152	mexico	1630	CLOPPENBURG	400	19	25	Hispaniae Novae Nova Descriptio
mwsp0175	spain	1630	CLOPPENBURG	250	19	25	Hispaniae Novae Nova Descriptio
mwjk0014	japan	1630	CLOPPENBURG	720	18	24	Iaponia ... Petrus Kaerius Coelavit
mwas0381	asia south east	1630	CLOPPENBURG	450	18	24	Indiae Orientalis
mwuk0040	ireland	1630	CLOPPENBURG	400	19	26	Irlandiae Regnum
mwsc0487	scandinavia iceland	1630	CLOPPENBURG	300	18	25	Islandia
mwbh0825	luxembourg	1630	CLOPPENBURG	350	18	25	Lutzenburgensis Ducatus Jacobo Surhonio Montensi Auctore
mwbh0220	belgium holland	1630	CLOPPENBURG	200	19	26	Mechlinia Dominium
mwe1096	europe slovak republic (moravia)	1630	CLOPPENBURG	200	18	25	Moravia
mwf0054	france	1635	CLOPPENBURG	4000	46	55	Nova Galliae Tabula
mwuss1599	virginia	1632	CLOPPENBURG	600	19	25	Nova Virginiae Tabula
mwme0768	persia etc	1630	CLOPPENBURG	250	19	26	Persici vel Sophorum Regni Tipus
mwsam0738	south america peru	1630	CLOPPENBURG	240	18	25	Peru
mwbp0232	poland	1630	CLOPPENBURG	200	19	26	Polonia et Silesia
mwsp0025	portugal	1630	CLOPPENBURG	240	17	24	Portugallia et Algarve (North to the left)
mwe0660	europe slovenia	1630	CLOPPENBURG	200	19	25	Sclavonia Croatia Bosniacum Dalmatiae Parte
mwuk0339	scotland	1630	CLOPPENBURG	320	19	25	Scotia Regnum
mwsc0296	scandinavia denmark	1676	CLOPPENBURG	200	18	25	Selandia in Regno Daniae
mwaa0081	arctic	1630	CLOPPENBURG	600	19	25	Septentrionalium Terrarum descriptio (later editions had a longer title '... juxta Mentem Veterum Geographorum')
mwme0103	holy land	1643	CLOPPENBURG	1000	30	50	Tabula Geographica, in qua Israelitarum, ab Aegypto ad Kenahanaeam (re-issue of Plancius 1609)
mwsam0491	south america colombia	1632	CLOPPENBURG	280	19	25	Terra Firma et Novum Regnum Granatense et Popaian
mwf0633	france limousin	1630	CLOPPENBURG	200	17	23	Totius Lemovici
mwme0549a	arabia etc	1630	CLOPPENBURG	400	19	25	Turcici Imperii Imago
mww0137	world	1630	CLOPPENBURG	3000	19	26	Typus Orbis Terrarum (1st map to show parts of the Australian coastline; the extreme west and north east. Illustration: Professor Robert Clancy)
mwuk0077	ireland	1673	CLOPPENBURG	150	18	25	Udrone Irlandiae in Caterlagh Baronia

AMPG REFERENCE	REGION	DATE	MAP MAKER	PRICE (UK£)	VERT. (cm.)	HOR. (cm.)	TITLE OF MAP (Comments by the editor in brackets)
mwuss1597	virginia	1630	CLOPPENBURG	600	19	25	Virginiae Item et Floridae Americae Provinciarum, Nova Descriptio
mwg0439	hessen	1630	CLOPPENBURG	150	18	25	Waldeck Comitatus
mwbh0221	belgium holland	1630	CLOPPENBURG	235	19	25	Zeelandiae Comitatus
mwam1020	america north (east)	1767	CLOUET	550	32	56	(Eastern North America)
mwaf0233	africa	1776	CLOUET	10000	98	123	Carte d'Afrique Divisee en ses Principaux Etats
mwam0201	america continent	1776	CLOUET	13500	95	122	Carte d'Amerique Divisee en ses Principaux Pays
mwam0187	america continent	1764	CLOUET	900	46	62	Carte D'Amerique divisee en ses principaux Pays
mwas0179	asia continent	1764	CLOUET	685	48	64	Carte d'Asie Divisee en ses Principaux Etats
mwas0192	asia continent	1776	CLOUET	12000	98	123	Carte d'Asie Divisee en ses Principaux Etats
mwe0198	europe	1776	CLOUET	7200	96	124	Carte d'Europe Divisee en ses Empires et Royaumes
mww0497	world	1776	CLOUET	25000	96	121	Carte Generale de la Terre ou Mappe Monde avec les Quatres Principaux Systemes
mwam0182a	america continent	1760	CLOUET	250	32	56	De L'Amerique en general (shows New Zealand as part of Antarctica etc.)
mwam1093	america north (east)	1787	CLOUET	480	31	56	Des Possessions Francoises Aujourd'hui sous la Domination Angloises
mwgr0212	greece	1780	CLOUET	150	12	13	Graeciae descriptio
mwam0206	america continent	1780	CLOUET	720	31	54	Isles, Caps et Ports de Mer de l'Amerique
mwaf0271	africa	1793	CLOUET	200	41	39	Lacs, fleuves, rivieres et principales montagnes de L'Afrique (size excl. text panels at sides of map)
mww0464	world	1765	CLOUET	3800	43	65	Mappemonde ou Globe Terrestre
mww0473a	world	1769	CLOUET	500	31	55	Mappe-Monde Suivant les Nouvelles Observations
mwgr0119	greece	1697	CLUVER	150	20	24	Achaia
mwaf0067	africa	1661	CLUVER	300	13	13	Africa
mwaf0069	africa	1661	CLUVER	280	22	26	Africa Antiqua et Nova
mwaf0068	africa	1661	CLUVER	250	15	20	Africae Descriptio
mwam0065	america continent	1661	CLUVER	480	21	26	America
mwam0061	america continent	1659	CLUVER	240	12	12	Americae sive Indiae Occidentalis Tabula Generalis (reduced version of De Laet 1630)
mwme0560	arabia etc	1661	CLUVER	400	16	21	Arabia
mwme0712	caucasus	1661	CLUVER	150	14	19	Armenia, Syria, Mesopotamia
mwas0051	asia continent	1661	CLUVER	280	14	20	Asia
mwas0079	asia continent	1690	CLUVER	360	21	26	Asia Antiqua et Nova
mwbh0357	belgium holland	1661	CLUVER	160	15	20	Belgii sive Germaniae Inferioris
mwuk0719	uk	1661	CLUVER	250	15	20	Britannicarum Insularum Typus
mwit1019	italy south	1697	CLUVER	180	26	22	Campanie, Samnii Apuliae
mwme0975	turkey etc	1697	CLUVER	280	20	25	Chersonesi quae hodie Natolia Descriptio
mwc0048	china	1661	CLUVER	300	13	19	China (copy of Hondius 1607, north to the top)
mwc0071	china	1686	CLUVER	600	27	34	China Veteribus Sinarum Regio nunc Incolis Tame Dicta
mwit0832	italy sardinia and corsica	1661	CLUVER	250	12	13	Corsica Antiquae Tabula / Sardiniae Antiquae Tabula (later editions 27x11cm)
mwgr0388	greece crete	1661	CLUVER	240	13	20	Creta ex Deliniatione Ubonis Emmii
mwgr0482	greece cyprus	1661	CLUVER	785	13	20	Cyprus ex Delination Ubonis Emmii
mwe0760c	europe east	1661	CLUVER	150	15	19	Daciarum, Moesiarumque, Vetus Descriptio
mwgr0120	greece	1697	CLUVER	150	20	26	Epirus hodie Canina cum Mares Ionii Insulis
mwit0302	italy central	1695	CLUVER	200	20	25	Etruriae Lati Umbriae
mwe0074	europe	1661	CLUVER	240	13	13	Europa
mwf0084	france	1697	CLUVER	300	27	33	Gallia Antique et Nova
mwg0066	germany	1661	CLUVER	180	15	20	Germania
mwbh0471	belgium holland	1695	CLUVER	200	24	25	Germaniae Cisrhenanae
mwgr0077	greece	1661	CLUVER	240	16	20	Graecia, Sophiani
mwgr0054	greece	1624	CLUVER	720	24	27	Hellas seu Graecia Universa
mwgr0123	greece	1697	CLUVER	180	24	26	Hellas seu Graecia Universa
mwsw0083	switzerland	1680	CLUVER	200	20	25	Helvetia
mwsp0211	spain	1697	CLUVER	280	27	32	Hispaniae Veteris et Novae Descriptio
mwbh0481	belgium holland	1697	CLUVER	280	20	25	Hodiernae Belgicae sive Germaniae Inferioris Tabula
mwc0086	china	1697	CLUVER	350	21	26	Imperii Sinarum, Nova Descriptio
mwas0396	asia south east	1661	CLUVER	280	14	20	India Orientalis
mwas0394	asia south east	1659	CLUVER	350	11	13	India Orientalis Nova
mwin0109	india	1661	CLUVER	240	14	19	India Vetus
mwas0421	asia south east	1697	CLUVER	350	22	26	Indiae Orientalis et Insularum Adiacentium
mwit0073	italy	1624	CLUVER	300	28	34	Italia Antiqua
mwit0581	italy north	1661	CLUVER	200	15	20	Italia Gallica, sive Gallia Cisalpina, Ligures, Taurini
mwit0125	italy	1697	CLUVER	280	26	31	Italia Nova
mwit0096a	italy	1660	CLUVER-JANSSON	550	35	49	Italiae Antiquae Noua Descriptio
mwit0398	italy lazio	1661	CLUVER	200	16	20	Latium, Vestini, Campani.
mwbp0090	baltic states	1661	CLUVER	280	14	20	Lithuania
mwgr0121	greece	1697	CLUVER	150	20	25	Macedoniae et Thessaliae
mwaf0701	africa north	1697	CLUVER	150	13	22	Mauritana et Africa Propria nunc Barbaria
mwme0951	turkey etc	1661	CLUVER	240	15	19	Natolia, quae olim Asia Minor
mww0176	world	1661	CLUVER	500	12	23	Orbis Terrarum Typus
mwme0155	holy land	1661	CLUVER	240	15	20	Palaestinae sive Totius Terrae Promissionis
mwe0667b	europe dalmatia	1661	CLUVER	150	15	20	Pannoniae et Illyrici Veteris Tabula
mwgr0122	greece	1697	CLUVER	180	21	26	Peloponnesus nunc Morea

AMPG REFERENCE	REGION	DATE	MAP MAKER	PRICE (UK£)	VERT. (cm.)	HOR. (cm.)	TITLE OF MAP (Comments by the editor in brackets)
mwme0780	persia etc	1660	CLUVER	280	20	26	Persia sive Sophorum Regnum cum Armenia Assyria Mesopotamia et Babilonia
mwbp0332	poland	1697	CLUVER	280	27	34	Prussiae Nova Tabula
mwsc0316	scandinavia denmark	1697	CLUVER	240	20	25	Regni Daniae Accuratissima Delineatio
mwru0058	russia	1661	CLUVER	240	14	20	Russia cum Confinijs
mwru0105	russia	1697	CLUVER	180	21	30	Scythia et Serica
mwme0245	holy land	1711	CLUVER	240	14	21	Situs Chorographia et Flumina Paradisi
mwme0782	persia etc	1661	CLUVER	200	15	19	Sophorum Regnum
mwsc0094	scandinavia	1697	CLUVER	280	21	25	Suecia Dania et Norvegia
mwe0106	europe	1697	CLUVER	250	20	25	Summa Europae Antiquae Descriptio
mwg0344	bavaria	1661	CLUVER	180	16	20	Sweviae Circulus
mwme0870	syria etc	1697	CLUVER	240	20	25	Syriae sive Soriae Descriptio
mwit0097	italy	1661	CLUVER	240	15	20	Tabula Italiae Corsicae, Sardiniae, et Adjacentium Regnorum
mwru0429	russia tartary	1661	CLUVER	200	14	20	Tartaria
mww0152	world	1641	CLUVER	1500	14	28	Typus Orbis Terrarum (illustrated above is 1697 edition)
mwe0776	europe east	1697	CLUVER	280	20	24	Veteris et Nova Pannoniae et Illyrici Descriptio
mwuk0765	uk	1697	CLUVER	300	22	25	Veteris et Novae Britanniae Descriptio
mwbp0266	poland	1660	CLUVER	350	21	25	Veteris et Novae Regni Poloniae Magniq Ducatus Lithuaniae cum suis Palatinatibus ac Confinus Descriptio
mwam0609	america north	1818	COBBETT	550	32	42	United States
mwme0486	jerusalem	1722	COCCEJO	500	33	41	Jerusalem Niewlicks uyte de Schriften Iosephus Afgebeeld (publ. by Weigel)
mwsp0156a	spain	1553	COCK		76	95	Nova Descriptio Hispaniae (re-issued by De La Hoove 1601. Hieronymus Cock 1518-1570 was a printer, publisher)
mwgm0029	gulf of mexico and surrounding regions	1735	COCKBURN	720			A Map of that Part of ye Kingdom of Mexico Travers'd by Jn. Cockburn & his Companions
mwwi0497	cuba	1851	COELLO	2400	75	112	Isla de Cuba. Medias Hojas Estremas Oriental y Occidental o de Derecha e Izquierda
mwwi0847	puerto rico	1851	COELLO	1350	79	106	Isla de Puerto Rico
mwas0814	asia south east philippines	1849	COELLO	1350	78	104	Islas Filipinas
mwaf0846c	africa north west	1850	COELLO	350	74	104	Posesiones de Africa (Spanish possessions shown in 20 small maps on one sheet)
mwuss0876	massachusetts	1833	COFFIN	10000	85	58	Map of the Town of Nantucket, in the State of Massachusetts
mwuk1320	england london	1836	COGHLAN	600	25	40	A New Map of London, Westminster, Southwark, and their Suburbs, for Coghlan's Picture of London
mwuk0739a	uk	1680	COHRS	320	13	13	Britannicarum Insularum Typus
mwgm0310	mexico	1828	COLBURN	500	54	68	Mexico
mwgr0251	greece	1828	COLBURN	250	20	25	The Harbour of Navarin, with a Plan of the Battle on the 20th Octr. 1827
mwam0925	america north (east)	1724	COLDEN	650	18	23	A Map of the Country of the Five Nations, Belonging to the Province of New York; and of the Lakes near which the Nations of the Far Indians live, with Part of Canada
mwme0040	holy land	1572	COLE	3000	47	52	(Untitled map based on Ortelius, made for Richard Jugge's Bishops' Bible. The first map to be engraved in England by an Englishman.)
mwwi0782	martinique	1760	COLE	300	20	25	A Map of the Island Martinico
mwec0659	uk england kent	1806	COLE	140	18	23	Canterbury
mwec0149b	uk england cheshire	1806	COLE	100	19	24	Chester
mwec0239a	uk england cumbria	1805	COLE	60	24	18	Cumberland
mwec0965a	uk england oxfordshire	1806	COLE	120	19	23	Oxford
mwec1285b	uk england worcestershire	1806	COLE	80	24	19	Worcester
mwec1350	uk england yorkshire	1808	COLE, G.	150	17	22	Yorkshire: West Riding
mwuk1193	england london	1756	COLE-MAITLAND	400	23	36	A New and Accurate Plan of the City of Westminster the Duchy of Lancaster and Places Adjacent
mwuk1194	england london	1756	COLE-MAITLAND	280	24	29	A New Map of the Counties Ten Miles Round the Cities of London Westminster and Borough of Southwark
mwuk1195	england london	1756	COLE-MAITLAND	280	20	34	London Restored or Sir John Evelyn's Plan for Rebuilding that Antient Metropolis after the Fire in 1666
mwgr0397	greece crete	1669	COLLIGNON	1200	30	46	Isola di Candia Anticamente Creta
mwf0205	france	1848	COLLIN	3000	185	284	Carte Geologique de la France
mwam0558	america north	1802	COLLIN	350	24	36	Louisiane et Pays Voisins, d'apres les Relations et les Cartes les Plus Recentes
mwuk0431	scotland	1690	COLLINS	280	45	56	(Approaches to Dundee)
mwec1164	uk england sussex	1693	COLLINS	320	44	28	(Approaches to Rye)
mwuk0116a	ireland	1693	COLLINS	650	45	55	(Belfast Lough. Inset: Prospect of Carreck-Fergus)
mwec0300	uk england devon	1779	COLLINS	480	44	56	(Bigberry to Exmouth)
mwec0818	uk england norfolk	1693	COLLINS	450	28	44	(Blakeney)
mwp0037	australia	1798	COLLINS	720	19	24	(Botany Bay, Port Jackson and Broken Bay)
mwuk1775	wales	1693	COLLINS	600	44	56	(Cardigan Bay)
mwuk0116	ireland	1693	COLLINS	400	42	32	(Carlingford Lough)
mwuk0117	ireland	1693	COLLINS	720	45	58	(Dublin Bay. Below is shown a later state with plan of Dublin)
mwuk0433	scotland	1693	COLLINS	950	44	55	(Dungeness to Edinburgh)

AMPG REFERENCE	REGION	DATE	MAP MAKER	PRICE (UK£)	VERT. (cm.)	HOR. (cm.)	TITLE OF MAP (Comments by the editor in brackets)
mwuk0434	scotland	1693	COLLINS	400	45	56	(Firth of Forth)
mwuk0302	irish sea	1693	COLLINS	500	46	58	(Irish Sea)
mwuk1606	isle of man	1693	COLLINS	600	44	56	(Isle of Man, north to the right.)
mwuk1620	isle of wight	1693	COLLINS	600	46	58	(Isle of Wight)
mwuk0435	scotland	1693	COLLINS	500	44	55	(Leith)
mwuk0436	scotland	1693	COLLINS	400	44	55	(Moray Firth)
mwuk1661	north sea	1693	COLLINS	875	45	57	(North Sea south)
mwec0882	uk england northumberland	1693	COLLINS	300	44	55	(Northumberland, Cocket Island, Amble, Warksworth)
mwuk1812	wales	1720	COLLINS	300	45	57	(Part of the Isle of Anglesey, south to the top)
mwuk0464a	scotland	1781	COLLINS	350	46	57	(Part of the Maine Island of Shetland)
mwec1037	uk england somerset	1693	COLLINS	600	45	56	(The Severn or Channell of Bristoll)
mwuk1477	uk english channel (all)	1693	COLLINS	2000	59	136	(Untitled chart in 3 sheets, joined)
mwuk1549	bristol channel	1693	COLLINS	400	46	58	(Untitled chart)
mwuk1478	uk english channel (all)	1693	COLLINS	1800	46	56	… This Chart of the Channel …
mwec0638	uk england kent	1763	COLLINS	720	44	55	A Large Draught of the Downes
mwuk1536	uk english channel (east)	1760	COLLINS	400	42	54	A Large Draught of the Downes (Dover Castle to N. Foreland. North to the right.)
mwec0135	uk england cheshire	1693	COLLINS	950	44	55	A New & Exact Survey of the River Dee or Chester-Water
mwuk0178	ireland	1759	COLLINS	600	44	52	A New and Correct Chart of the Harbour of Corke by the Revd. J. Lindsay (publ. by Mount & Page)
mwec1316	uk england yorkshire	1693	COLLINS	550	44	55	Burlington Bay, Scarbrough & Hartlepoole
mwec0329	uk england dorset	1693	COLLINS	320	45	57	Chart of Portland
mwuk1632a	scilly isles	1693	COLLINS	450	45	57	Chart of the Islands of Scilly
mwec0297	uk england devon	1763	COLLINS	720	44	55	Dartmouth. To the Right Honorable George Lord Dartmouth
mwec0190	uk england cornwall	1763	COLLINS	720	44	55	Falmouth
mwec0191	uk england cornwall	1763	COLLINS	720	44	55	Fowey & Mounts-Bay
mwuk1341	england east	1686	COLLINS	650	44	56	Harwich, Woodbridge and Handfordwater, with the Sands from the Nazeland to Hosely Bay
mwec0883	uk england northumberland	1693	COLLINS	300	43	56	Holy Island Staples and Barwick is Most Humbly Dedicated and Presented to Capt. Will Davies
mwec0667	uk england kent	1850	COLLINS	280	36	44	Kent with its Railways
mwuk1859	wales	1779	COLLINS	300	44	56	Milford Haven and the Islands Adjacent
mwuk1845	wales	1760	COLLINS	360	45	57	Milford-Haven
mwec0288	uk england devon	1693	COLLINS	600	45	56	Plymouth
mwuk1391	england south	1760	COLLINS	750	44	57	Plymouth.
mwuk0477	scotland	1740	COLLINS	450	44	56	The Chiefe Harbours in the Islands of Orkney (north to the right)
mwuk0437	scotland	1693	COLLINS	300	44	56	The East Coast of Scotland with the Isles of Orkney and Shetland
mwuk0118a	ireland	1693	COLLINS	650	43	52	The Harbour of Corke
mwuk1632	scilly isles	1693	COLLINS	900	45	57	The Islands of Scilly.
mwuk1550	bristol channel	1760	COLLINS	800	40	92	The River Avon from the Severn to the City of Bristol
mwuk1342	england east	1693	COLLINS	550	46	57	The River Humber
mwuk1430a	england thames	1693	COLLINS	1200	59	92	The River of Thames from London to the Buoy of the Noure (north to the right)
mwuk0438	scotland	1693	COLLINS	350	44	56	The South Part of the Isles of Shetland
mwuk0118	ireland	1693	COLLINS	650	45	58	This Chart of Kingsale Harbour ... by Capt. Greenvile Collins
mwec0328	uk england dorset	1690	COLLINS	320	44	56	To Captain George St. Lo. (approaches to Portland Bill)
mwuk1607a	isle of man	1742	COLLINS	960	45	55	To the Rt. Honorable William E.le of Derby, Lord of Ye Isle of Man &c
mwam0732	america north	1840	COLLINS	320	48	28	United States (early railroad map)
mwec0212	uk england cornwall	1840	COLLINS, H.	280	38	45	Cornwall with its Railways
mwuk0629	scotland	1840	COLLINS, H.	280	36	29	Scotland with its Railways
mwuss1295	ohio	1826	COLLOT	950	30	49	A General Map of the River Ohio. Plate the First
mwam0651	america north	1826	COLLOT	6000	61	86	General Map of North America (re-issue)
mwuss0539	illinois	1796	COLLOT	7200	37	60	Map of the Country of the Illinois
mwam1353	america north (west)	1826	COLLOT	20000	48	45	Map of the Missouri; of the Higher Parts of the Mississipi; and of the Elevated Plain, where the Waters Divide
mwuss1294	ohio	1826	COLLOT	600	28	20	Plan d'un Ancien Camp Retranche Decouvert sur les Bords du Muskinghum et Dessine par John Hart Capitaine du 1er. Regiment des Etats Unis
mwuss0977	missouri	1824	COLLOT	1500	16	27	Plan of Cape Girardo
mwuss0669	louisiana	1824	COLLOT	4000	17	28	Plan of Fort Baton Rouge
mwuss0976	missouri	1824	COLLOT	6000	16	27	Plan of St. Lewis with the Project of an Intrenched Camp French
mwuss1409	pennsylvania	1826	COLLOT	2000	19	28	Plan of the Town of Pittsbourg
mwuss0961	mississippi	1826	COLLOT	4000	20	28	Town and Fort of Natchez
mwam0866	america north (east)	1663	COLOM	24000	55	64	(Untitled map, New England to Virginia)
mwbh0339	belgium holland	1660	COLOM	240	16	23	Baroniam Bredanam
mwbh0340	belgium holland	1660	COLOM	240	16	22	Beemster
mwgr0384	greece crete	1657	COLOM	1600	39	51	Candia met de Omleggende Eylanden
mwbh0341	belgium holland	1660	COLOM	240	17	24	Comitatus Flandria
mwaf1107	africa west	1648	COLOM	650	24	28	Cust van Barbaria van C. de Geer tot verby C. Verde by Iacob Colom
mwwi0016	west indies	1654	COLOM	7500	55	64	De Carybsche Eylanden van de Barbados tot de Bocht van Mexico Toe Nu Eerst Uytgegeven

AMPG REFERENCE	REGION	DATE	MAP MAKER	PRICE (UK£)	VERT. (cm.)	HOR. (cm.)	TITLE OF MAP (Comments by the editor in brackets)
mwsc0411	scandinavia finland	1650	COLOM	1350	32	41	De Cust van Oost Finlandt tusschen Cuma en de Noordtbodem / De Zeecusten van Godtlandt met de Omleggende Eylandekens
mwsp0418	spain regions	1633	COLOM	1650	38	54	De Custe van Hispangen vande Riviere van Sivilien tot Malaga ende de Custe van Barbarien van out Mamora tot Penon de Velez
mwsc0546	scandinavia norway	1649	COLOM	1500	39	53	De Custe van Noorwegen Tusschen Schaersondt en Schuijtenes
mwsc0545	scandinavia norway	1649	COLOM	1800	37	53	De Custe van Noorwegen van Bergen tot Stemmeshest Nieulyx Beschreven
mwsc0569	scandinavia norway	1668	COLOM	960	55	64	De Custen van Noorwegen vande Patemosters tot Schutenes
mwsc0558	scandinavia norway	1660	COLOM	1200	38	53	De Custen van Noorwegenen Finmarken tusschen Drontem en de Noort Caap
mwat0137	atlantic canary isl.	1632	COLOM	2000	38	52	De Eylanden Lancerota Forteventur Groot Canarien Teneriffa en I. Gomera
mwsc0678	scandinavia sweden	1660	COLOM	1350	39	54	De Kusten van Sweden / Caarte van't Stocholmse Liet. (Based on Blaeu)
mwsc0274	scandinavia denmark	1658	COLOM	2500	55	62	De Sondt en Belt (inset view of Copenhagen)
mwbh0342	belgium holland	1660	COLOM	240	16	22	De Veluwe
mwbh0343	belgium holland	1660	COLOM	240	15	23	De Vier Ambachten
mwat0141	atlantic canary isl.	1658	COLOM	1800	55	64	De Vlaemsche en Canarische Eylanden
mwbp0021	baltic sea (east)	1662	COLOM	1000	38	53	De Zee Custen van Courlant en Pruyssen tussen Derwinde en Rygshooft Nieuelyx Beschreven
mwit0889	italy sicily	1650	COLOM	1350	38	53	De Zee Custen van Secilien en Calabria
mwuk1530	uk english channel (east)	1669	COLOM	500	44	53	De Zee Custen van Vrancryck tusschen Swartenes en C. de la Hague als mede de Custen van Engelandt (south to the top)
mwbh0344	belgium holland	1660	COLOM	240	16	23	De Zeeven Wolden
mwbh0345	belgium holland	1660	COLOM	240	16	24	Diocesis Leodiensis Accurata Tabula
mwbh0346	belgium holland	1660	COLOM	240	16	22	Drentiae
mwaf1113	africa west	1663	COLOM	2500	44	48	Guinea
mwas0715	asia south east moluccas	1663	COLOM	2200	39	53	Insularum Moluccarum
mwg0800	westphalia	1660	COLOM	240	16	22	La Fosse de S Marie Appelle aussi Eugeniene
mwbh0347	belgium holland	1660	COLOM	240	16	23	La Rhinlande Amstellande et Terres Circonvosines
mwbh0348	belgium holland	1660	COLOM	240	15	22	Le Comte de Zutphen
mwp0230	pacific (all)	1658	COLOM	6500	54	61	Mar del Zur Hispanis Mare Pacificum (illustration shows the Colom-Doncker c1700 edition, the only one with New Zealand coastline)
mwm0009	mediterranean	1654	COLOM	2500	54	63	Middel-landtsche Zee Nieuwlix uytgegewen (in 2 horizontal sections)
mwbp0022	baltic sea (east)	1668	COLOM	2250	54	64	Nieuw Verbeterde Oost-Zee (untitled inset of the eastern Baltic Sea)
mwwi0228	west indies (east)	1654	COLOM	3000	54	63	Nieuwe Carybsche Pascaart - The Carybes Islands Newly setforth and amendid - Pascaarte Nieuwelyx Uytgegeven door Arnold Colom (south to the top)
mwsc0057	scandinavia	1654	COLOM	1650	55	64	Nieuwe Pascaart (incl. arctic regions. Inset: Jan Mayen Isl.)
mwe1192	europe west	1668	COLOM	9000	61	64	Nieuwe Pascaarte op hare rechte Distantie
mww0162	world	1655	COLOM	14000	56	62	Nova Delineatio Totius Orbis Terrarum Auctore A. Colom
mww0160	world	1650	COLOM	6500	39	54	Nova Totius Terrarum Orbis Geographica ac Hydrographica Tabula Auct. Iacobus Colom
mwin0474	indian ocean west	1658	COLOM	3000	55	63	Oost Indien van Cabo de Bona Esperanca tot Ceilon
mwbp0020	baltic sea (east)	1658	COLOM	2000	55	64	Oost Zee door Arnold Colom (based on Jacobsz 1644)
mwas0393	asia south east	1658	COLOM	6000	64	55	Oosterdeel van Oost Indien
mwbp0023	baltic sea (east)	1668	COLOM	2250	55	65	Oosterdeel van de Oost-Zee (inset: Oostfinlandt)
mwuk1529a	uk english channel (east)	1668	COLOM	1250	55	65	Ooster-Deel van 't Canaal
mwbh0349	belgium holland	1660	COLOM	240	16	22	Ooster-Goe
mwbh0350	belgium holland	1660	COLOM	240	15	23	Partie de la Flandre Orientale
mwam0863	america north (east)	1656	COLOM	25000	57	65	Pas caarte van Nieu Nederlandt
mwsc0459	scandinavia greenland	1668	COLOM	2500	38	52	Pas caerte van GroenLand
mwca0024	canada	1663	COLOM	5000	38	54	Pas Caerte van Terra Nova Nova Francia Niew Engelandt en de Grote Rivier van Canada
mwat0339	atlantic west	1663	COLOM	1000	42	53	Pas-Caarte van de Canarise, Vlaemse, en Groen-Eylanden, tot de Caribse Ey-Landen (north to the left)
mwuk1646	north sea	1654	COLOM	3000	55	63	Pascaarte van de Noord Zee
mwuk1651	north sea	1668	COLOM	2500	54	63	Pas-Caarte van de Noord-Zee Nieulijx Verbetert
mwaf1063	africa south west	1654	COLOM	1500	64	55	Pascaarte van Guinea van Capo Verde tot Capo de bon Esperance.
mwsp0181	spain	1654	COLOM	2000	54	64	Pascaarte van Hispangien van de Nooryd Zyde van Yrlandt tot de Straet (north to the left)
mwat0080a	atlantic azores	1668	COLOM	900	42	53	Pascaert vande Vlaemsche Eylanden
mwgr0579	greece islands	1644	COLOM	1350	25	30	Pascaarte vande Zee Archipelagus (13 insets of individual islands)
mwat0338	atlantic west	1654	COLOM	2500	55	64	Pascaerte van Brazil en Nieu Nederlandt van Cuorvo en Flores tot de Barbados

AMPG REFERENCE	REGION	DATE	MAP MAKER	PRICE (UK£)	VERT. (cm.)	HOR. (cm.)	TITLE OF MAP (Comments by the editor in brackets)
mwuk0043a	ireland	1632	COLOM	2000	38	54	Pascaerte van het Canael tusschen Vranckryck, en Engelant van de West-Zijde van Schotlant als mede van Ierlandt (first edition. North to the right.)
mwuk1639	north sea	1640	COLOM	2250	42	55	Pascaerte vande Noord-Zee Nieulix Uitgegeven
mwg0591	saxony	1632	COLOM	650	37	52	Pascaerte vande Wester en Ooster Eemsen, de Weser, Elve, de Eyder met de ander Seegaten tusschen Amelandt en de Eyder
mwru0049	russia	1651	COLOM	1000	37	52	Pascaerte vande Witte-Zee
mwuk1422	england thames	1647	COLOM	1350	38	53	Pascaerte Vertoonende de Mont vande Teemse en Voort de Custe van Engelandt tot Crammer
mwgr0306	greece corfu	1657	COLOM	1250	39	51	Paskaarte vande Eijlanden Corfu
mwuk0711	uk	1654	COLOM	2000	42	56	Paskaarte vant Canaal (north to the right)
mwsam0026a	south america	1663	COLOM	1650	40	53	t Suyder Deel van America
mwuk0412	scotland	1668	COLOM	1500	54	64	West Cust van Schotlandt
mwuk1540a	uk english channel (west)	1668	COLOM	1250	54	64	Wester-Deel van 't Canaal
mwbh0351	belgium holland	1660	COLOM	240	16	24	Wester-Goe
mwsam0023	south america	1654	COLOM	1500	54	63	Zuyder Deel van America (Chart of the southern part of South America; 2 insets: NW coast, La Plata. Illustrated is Doncker re-issue c1696)
mwuss1504	texas	1835	COLORADO R.R.L CO.	30000	50	64	Map of Texas Shewing the Grants in Possession of the Colorado & Red River Land Compy. N.B. the Tracts Possessed by the Company are the Wilson & Exeter 1st Grant and the Milam Grant
mwuss1236	new york	1839	COLTON	150	14	15	A Description of the Cities, Townships, and Principal Villages and Settlements within Thirty Miles of the City of New York: Being a Guide to the Most Fashionable Resorts, and Watering Places in the Vicinity
mwuss1316	ohio	1839	COLTON	650	46	56	Burr's Map of the State of Ohio
mwuss1262	new york	1850	COLTON	600	51	51	Colton's Map of New York
mwam1259	america north (east)	1850	COLTON	800	46	62	Colton's Map of the States of New England & New York, with Parts of Pennsylvania, New Jersey, the Canadas &c. Showing the Rail Roads, Canals and Stage Roads
mwam1258	america north (east)	1850	COLTON	1000	65	76	Colton's Map of the United States, the Canadas, &c. Showing the Rail Roads, Canals, & Stage Roads, with Distances from Place to Place
mwuss1577	vermont	1836	COLTON	1000	61	81	Map of Burlington in Vermont
mwam1384	america north (west)	1849	COLTON	4800	53	46	Map of California, Oregon, Texas and the Territories Adjoining with Routes &c.
mwuss1510	texas	1839	COLTON	20000	80	59	Map of Texas Compiled from Surveys on Record in the General Land Office of the Republic, to the Year 1839, by Richard S. Hunt and Jesse F. Randel
mwuss1257	new york	1846	COLTON	1200	54	54	Map of the Country Thirty Three Miles around the City of New York
mwuss0885	massachusetts	1838	COLTON	9000	60	85	Map of the Island of Nantucket, Including Tuckernuck. Surveyed by Wm. Mitchell. 1838
mwuss1226	new york	1834	COLTON	2000	117	142	Map of the State of New-York with Parts of the Adjacent Country. Embracing Plans of the Cities ... by David A. Burr
mwam0784	america north	1847	COLTON	2500	92	118	Map of the United States of America, the British Provinces, Mexico and the West Indies
mwam0795	america north	1849	COLTON	3500	84	102	Map of the United States, the British Provinces, Mexico &c. Showing the Routes of the U.S. Mail Steam Packets to California and a Plan of the Gold Regions
mwuss1586	vermont	1849	COLTON	960	73	58	Map of Vermont & New Hampshire
mwuss1576	vermont	1835	COLTON	2500	86	97	Map, Survey and History in Brief of the Town of Bennington, Vt. from an Actual Survey, Surveyed Designed & Executed by Joseph N. Hinsdill. 1835
mwme0429	holy land	1845	COLTON	720	71	96	New Map of Palestine from the Latest Authorities Cheifly from the Maps and Drawings of Robinson & Smith
mwuss1223	new york	1833	COLTON	1000	47	57	New York
mwam0305	america continent	1850	COLTON	1250	81	57	North & South America
mwuss0879	massachusetts	1835	COLTON	1000	80	63	Plan of Springfield
mwuss1313	ohio	1836	COLTON	1600	54	77	Portsmouth on the Ohio River
mwam0839	america north (central)	1847	COLTON	950	51	68	Guide through Ohio, Michigan, Indiana, Illinois, Missouri, Wisconsin & Iowa. Showing the Township Lines of the United States Surveys
mwuss1382	pennsylvania	1788	COLUMBIAN MAG	4000	31	54	To the Patrons of the Colombian Magazine this Map of Pennsylvania
mwaf0861	africa south	1646	COMMELIN	400	14	22	(Untitled map of the earliest Dutch voyage to the Cape in 1595)
mwbh0321	belgium holland	1650	COMMELIN	750	27	34	Amsterdam
mwaf0584	africa islands madagascar	1646	COMMELIN	400	14	22	Insula de S. Lauretij
mwaf1106a	africa west	1646	COMMELIN	250	14	21	Insulae St. Thomae (north to the right)
mwc0021a	china	1646	COMMELIN	800	15	19	Macao (illustration shows 1706 De Renneville re-issue, below left, courtesy of Wattis Fine Art)

AMPG REFERENCE	REGION	DATE	MAP MAKER	PRICE (UK£)	VERT. (cm.)	HOR. (cm.)	TITLE OF MAP (Comments by the editor in brackets)
mwc0020a	china	1646	COMMELIN	1000	16	20	Mont van der Rivier Chincheo in China (Map of the Bay of Amoy in Fujien Province. The earliest printed chart to depict any Western observed part of the coast of China - Zeyger van Rechteren in his voyage in 1632)
mwin0018a	ceylon	1646	COMMELIN	1000	23	15	Zelon (illustrated is the De Renneville 1706 copy)
mwgm0353a	mexico	1845	CONDE	40000	92	125	Carta Geografica General de la Republica Mexicana, formada el ano de 1845 con los datos que reunio la seccion de Geografia del Ministerio de la Guerra
mww0531a	world	1784	CONDER	750	33	49	A General Chart Exhibiting the Discoveries of Capt. James Cook in this and his two preceeding Voyages (reduced size version of Cook's 1784 map)
mwam0526	america north	1795	CONDER	650	35	33	A Map of the Western Part of the Territories Belonging to the United States of America. Drawn from the Best Authorities
mwec0379	uk england durham	1784	CONDER	160	16	21	A New and Correct Map of Durham
mwaf0238	africa	1779	CONDER	280	33	37	Africa, agreeable to the most approved maps and charts
mww0506	world	1780	CONDER	720	29	48	An Accurate Map of the World, Comprehending All the Discoveries in Both Hemispheres Carefully Drawn from the Best Authorities
mwuss0027	alaska	1785	CONDER	250	20	32	Chart of Norton Sound and of Bherings Strait Made by the East Cape of Asia and the West Point of America
mwam0505	america north	1789	CONDER	450	39	37	Map for the Interior Travels through America, Delineating the March of the Army
mwuss1003	new hampshire	1788	CONDER	600	35	33	New Hampshire, Vermont, &c.
mwuss1156	new york	1788	CONDER	450	27	17	New York Island, & Parts Adjacent
mwam0460	america north	1778	CONDER	475	34	37	North America Agreeable to the Most Approved Maps and Charts
mwuss1151	new york	1782	CONDER	350	38	25	Plan of the Harbour of New-York / Boston / Philadelphia / Charleston / Havana
mwuss0232	carolinas	1790	CONDER	650	35	36	The Carolina's with Part of Georgia
mwam1101	america north (east)	1790	CONDER	320	20	23	The United States of America Drawn From The Latest Authorities
mwgm0208	mexico	1747	CONSAG	1200	29	30	Seno de California, y su Costa Oriental Nuevamente Descubierta, y Registrada desde el Cabo de las Virgenas, hasta su Termino, que es el Rio Colorado Ano 1747
mwg0466	hessen	1783	CONTGEN	600	27	25	Carte von der Nieder Grafschaft Cazenelnbogen / Carte von der Ober Grafschaft Cazenelnbogen (2 sheets)
mwuk1406a	uk geological	1822	CONYBEARE	750	28	22	Geological Map of England & Wales
mwp0017	australia	1773	COOK	650	13	33	Entrance of Endeavour River, in New South Wales / Botany Bay in New South Wales
mwp0466	pacific pitcairn isl.	1773	COOK	240	21	27	A Chart and Views of Pitcairns Island
mwp0016	australia	1773	COOK	1350	37	80	A Chart of New South Wales or the East Coast of New Holland Discover'd and Explored by Lieutenant J. Cook
mwsam0692	south america magellan	1777	COOK	400	43	51	A Chart of the Southern Extremity of America 1775
mwaa0032	antarctic	1777	COOK	1500	57	54	A Chart of the Southern Hemisphere Showing the Tracks of Some of the Most Distinguished Navigators
mwca0319	canada newfoundland	1770	COOK	6000	49	172	A Chart of the West Coast of Newfoundland
mwca0601	canada st lawrence	1760	COOK	28000	85	232	A New Chart of the River St. Laurence, from the Island of Anticosti to the Falls of Richelieu
mwp0179	new zealand	1774	COOK	2400	51	40	Carte de la Nle. Zelande Visitee en 1769 et 1770 par le Lieutenant J. Cook Commandant de l'Endeavour Vaisseau de sa Majeste (French edition)
mwaa0033	antarctic	1778	COOK	900	53	53	Carte de l'Hemisphere Austral Montrant les Routes des Navigateurs les Plus Celebres par le Capitaine Jacques Cook (French edition)
mwat0227	atlantic falkland isl.	1774	COOK	500	22	30	Carte de Maidenland ou de la Viginie de Hawkins...et du Canal Falkland
mwp0385	pacific new guinea	1774	COOK	300	22	61	Carte des Decouvertes du Cap. Carteret dans la Nle. Bretagne avec une Partie du Passage du Cap. Cook a Travers les Detroits Endeavour et de la Route ed des Decouvertes du Cap. Dampierre dans la Nle Guinee et la Nle. Bretagne en 1699 et 1700
mwp0398	pacific new hebrides	1774	COOK	500	35	45	Carte des Decouvertes Faites dans la Mer Pacifique sur le Vaisseau de Roi la Resolution (north to the right)
mwat0231a	atlantic georgia	1775	COOK	250			Carte des Decouvertes Faites dans L'Ocean Atlantique du Sud (South to the top. French edition)
mwp0181	new zealand	1774	COOK	350	27	28	Carte du Detroit de Cook dans la Nle. Zelande
mwp0018	australia	1774	COOK	650	29	34	Carte d'une Partie de la Cote de la Nle Galles Meridle depuis le Cap Tribulation jusqu'au Detroit de l'Endeavour par le Lieut. J. Cook 1770
mwp0178	new zealand	1773	COOK	3000	51	41	Chart of New Zealand Explored in 1769 and 1770 by Lieut: I. Cook, Commander of His Majesty's Bark Endeavour ... 1772
mwp0432	pacific north	1784	COOK	800	27	38	Chart of Norton Sound and of Bherings Strait Made by the East Cape of Asia and the West Point of America

AMPG REFERENCE	REGION	DATE	MAP MAKER	PRICE (UK£)	VERT. (cm.)	HOR. (cm.)	TITLE OF MAP (Comments by the editor in brackets)
mwp0015	australia	1773	COOK	400	33	37	Chart of Part of the Coast of New South Wales, from Cape Tribulation to Endeavour Straits by Lieut. J. Cook, 1770
mwp0317	pacific friendly isl.	1784	COOK	500	24	35	Chart of the Friendly Islands
mwp0533	pacific tahiti	1774	COOK	480	23	41	Chart of the Island Otaheite by Captn. Cook 1769 (1st French edition)
mwp0431	pacific north	1784	COOK	1000	39	66	Chart of the NW Coast of America and the NE Coast of Asia Explored in the Years 1778 & 1779. The unshaded parts of the Coast of Asia are Taken from a M.S. Chart Received from the Russians
mwp0327	pacific hawaii	1784	COOK	2500	28	45	Chart of the Sandwich Islands. (First chart of the Sandwich Islands, with inset 'Karakakooa Bay'. Illustration shows 1784 Irish edition.)
mwp0305	pacific christmas isl.	1784	COOK	800	18	21	Christmas Island
mwsam0693	south america magellan	1777	COOK	120	21	16	Christmas Sound on the S.W. coast of Terra Del Fuego
mwp0309	pacific easter isl.	1784	COOK	300	21	20	Easter Island. Latitude 27.05.30, So. Longitude 109.46.20, Wt. of Greenwich
mwp0308	pacific cook isl.	1784	COOK	200	24	20	Harvey's Eiland / Eiland Palmerston / Schildpad Eiland / Wild Eiland
mwca0657a	canada west	1774	COOK	200	24	39	Isles de la Reine Charlotte (French edition. First edition in English publ. 1773)
mwuss0032	alaska	1795	COOK	200	23	30	Kaart van Cook's Rivier, in Het N.O. Gedeelte van Amerika
mwru0266	russia	1779	COOK	200	25	20	Kaart van de Awatska-Baai op de Oost Kust van Kamtschatka
mwaa0041	antarctic	1795	COOK	800	53	53	Kaart Van Het Zuider Halfrond vertoonende de koersen van enige der beroemdste zee reizigers door Kapitein James Cook (from a Dutch edition of Cook's voyages)
mwin0455	indian ocean kerguelen isl	1784	COOK	280	25	28	Kerguelen's Land Called by C. Cook Island of Desolation
mwp0402	pacific norfolk isl.	1784	COOK	200	20	18	Norfolk Isle
mwp0180	new zealand	1774	COOK	350	20	38	Plan de la Baye Duskey
mwp0020	australia	1778	COOK	300	22	14	Plan de la Terre de Van Diemen Reconnue par le Cap.e Furneaux en Mars 1773
mwp0476	pacific society isl.	1774	COOK	120	20	25	Plan des Havres qu'on Trouve au Cote N. d'Eimeo
mwp0177	new zealand	1773	COOK	500	33	44	River Thames and Mercury Bay in New Zealand / Bay of Islands in New Zealand / Tolaga Bay in New Zealand (3 maps on one sheet. Illustration shows 1774 French edition.)
mwc0198a	china	1784	COOK	300	26	21	Sketch of the Typa and Macao
mwp0316	pacific friendly isl.	1784	COOK	500	22	40	Sketch of Tongataboo Harbour
mwp0357	pacific iwo jima	1784	COOK	300	26	21	Sulphur Island
mwas0614	asia south east celebes	1774	COOK	100	17	30	Vue de la Baye de Bonthain … SE de Macassar
mwp0497a	pacific south	1772	COOK-BANKS	80000	37	40	(Untitled chart of the South Pacific and Antarctica)
mwp0435a	pacific north	1787	COOK-FRITZSCH	600	39	66	Charte von der Nord-Westlichen Kuste von America und der Nord-Ostlichen Kuste von Asien n Samt der Durchfahrth zwischen diesen beyden Welttheile
mww0531	world	1784	COOK-ROBERTS	2000	57	91	A General Chart Exhibiting the Discoveries of Capt. James Cook in this and his two preceeding Voyages (illustrated is the Irish edition, also first publ. 1784)
mwp0431a	pacific north	1784	COOK-ROBERTS	8000	39	68	Chart of the N.W. Coast of America and the N.E. Coast of Asia Explored in the Years 1778 and 1779. Prepared by Lieut. Heny. Roberts under the immediate Inspection of Capt Cook (publ. separately by W. Faden)
mwaf0303	africa	1817	COOKE	140	27	22	Africa
mwuss0119	california	1846	COOKE	240	29	58	Sketch of Part of the March & Wagon Road of Lt. Colonel Cooke, from Santa Fe to the Pacific Ocean, 1846-7
mwuk1444	england thames	1795	COOKE	200	30	58	The Course of the River Thames, from it's Source to the Sea
mwuss0141	california	1852	COOKE & LICOUNT	7800	55	69	A Complete Map of San Francisco Compiled from the Original Map from the Latest Surveys. Containing All the Latest Extentions and Improvements
mwsam0514	south america colombia	1741	COOPER	400	16	28	A New Plan of the Harbour, City & Forts of Cartagena; with the Progress of the British Fleet in their Several Stations & Attacks from the 4th of March 1741, till the 1st of April
mwuk1078	england	1849	COOPER	360	78	63	England, Wales, and the Southern Part of Scotland
mwuk0895	uk	1840	COOPER	150	159	152	Map of the British Isles Compiled from Government Surveys
mwca0133	canada	1810	COOPER	240	19	25	Map of the North Part of America, on which is Laid down Mackenzie's Track from Montreal to the North Sea
mww0635	world	1809	COOPER	280	24	38	Map of the World Exhibiting the Principal Features in Natural Geography
mwaa0161	arctic	1810	COOPER	240	25	20	North Part of the Globe, Corrected from the Latest Voyages
mwam0768	america north	1845	COPLEY	450	44	58	Map of the United States, and Texas
mwuk0656	uk	1524	COPPO		27	36	(Untitled portolan-style map, a channel separating Scotland and England)
mwit0013	italy	1524	COPPO		30	43	Italia Illyricum Epirus Gretia et Mare Aegeum (title above map of Italy and Greece)

AMPG REFERENCE	REGION	DATE	MAP MAKER	PRICE (UK£)	VERT. (cm.)	HOR. (cm.)	TITLE OF MAP (Comments by the editor in brackets)
mww0030	world	1524	COPPO		24	43	Orbicularis totius terrae et maris figuratio impressa MDXXIIII
mwuk0247a	ireland	1808	CORBET	400	27	35	New & Improved Plan of the City of Dublin laid down 1808 (Title above map. The 1817 edition has the title 'New Map of the City of Dublin' within the map)
mwaa0020	antarctic	1722	COREAL	600	28	28	Hemisphere, Meridional ou Terres Australes
mwsam0757a	south america peru	1722	COREAL	600			Lima
mwf0607	france languedoc	1695	CORONELLI	500	45	61	(Canal du Midi) Disegno Idrografico del Canale Reale
mwaf0821	africa north tunisia	1691	CORONELLI	300	23	31	(Djerba) Isola, e Castello di Gerbi
mwbh0456	belgium holland	1692	CORONELLI	480	45	60	(Overijssel) Tran-Siselana
mwp0379	pacific new guinea	1695	CORONELLI	1500	23	27	(Untitled map of New Guinea and Northern Australia, part of a globe gore)
mwe0912	europe hungary	1691	CORONELLI	1200	61	44	(Untitled map)
mwgr0417	greece crete	1690	CORONELLI	650	45	60	(Untitled. 9 views of Crete)
mwaf0383	africa east	1692	CORONELLI	1200	45	60	Abissinia dove sono le Fonti del Nilo (1st map to show a reasonably correct source of the Nile. An inset shows the classical view.)
mwgr0494	greece cyprus	1691	CORONELLI	1800	46	61	Acamantis Insula hoggidi Cipro, Posseduta dalla Republica Veneta sin'all'Anno 1571
mwit0282a	italy campagna	1691	CORONELLI	500	28	42	Aenaria Ins. hoggidi Ischia
mwas0084	asia continent	1691	CORONELLI	500	45	61	Aevi Veteris usque ad Annum Salutis non Agesimum supra Milles Quadringentos
mwf0226	france alsace	1691	CORONELLI	550	44	62	Alsacia Superiore / Alsacia Inferiore (2 maps)
mwsam0034	south america	1690	CORONELLI	3600	62	88	America Meridionale
mwam0334	america north	1691	CORONELLI	9000	61	46	America Settentrionale colle Nuove Scoperte sin all' Anno 1688 (2 sheets, each 61x46cm)
mwuk1797	wales	1700	CORONELLI	400	23	30	Anglesey Isola
mwgr0267	greece athens	1687	CORONELLI	1000	47	62	Antica, e Moderna Citta d'Atene
mwwi0036	west indies	1688	CORONELLI-NOLIN	1400	45	60	Archipelague du Mexique, ou sont les Isles de Cuba, Espagnole, Iamaique, etc. avec les Isles Lucayes, et les Isles Caribes, Connues sous le Nom d'Antilles. Par le P. Coronelli
mwas0091	asia continent	1697	CORONELLI	4500	61	88	Asia Divisa nelle sue Parti (2 maps)
mwe0336	europe austria	1690	CORONELLI	400	45	60	Austria Superiore
mwas0636	asia south east java	1705	CORONELLI	100	12	18	Batavia
mwbh0514	belgium holland	1705	CORONELLI	180	13	18	Belgio Descritto
mwuk1431	england thames	1705	CORONELLI	250	13	18	Bocca del Fiume Tamigi
mwat0193	atlantic cape verde isl.	1690	CORONELLI	960	45	60	Bocche del Fiume Negro et Isole di Capo Verde
mwbh0458a	belgium holland	1692	CORONELLI	1200	46	61	Brabante, Parte Settentrionale / Meridionale (shown above left, in 2 sheets, each 46x61cm)
mwca0293	canada newfoundland	1696	CORONELLI	1350	45	61	Canada Orientale nell'America Settentrionale
mwme0972	turkey etc	1690	CORONELLI	650	27	44	Canale di Costantinopoli
mwme0974	turkey etc	1696	CORONELLI	150	13	17	Canale di Costantinopol (in a page of text)
mwm0136	mediterranean east	1698	CORONELLI	1800	40	53	Carta Maritima dell' Isola Cypri
mwgr0495	greece cyprus	1698	CORONELLI	1800	40	53	Carta Maritima dell' Isola Cypri
mwit0423	italy liguria	1696	CORONELLI	600	40	52	Carta Marittima della Costa Ligustica fra C. della Melle, e M. Argentato con Isola di Corsica, e altre Circonvicine
mwc0077	china	1692	CORONELLI	1200	46	62	Chekiang, e Kiangsi, Provincie della China
mwgr0530	greece rhodes	1696	CORONELLI	200	13	17	Citta de Rodi (in a page of text)
mwit0424	italy liguria	1700	CORONELLI	720	36	53	Citta di Genova
mwit1227	italy venice	1693	CORONELLI	5500	50	77	Citta di Venetia
mwgr0418b	greece crete	1692	CORONELLI	500	32	41	Citta, e Fortezza di Candia
mwf0323	france brittany	1690	CORONELLI	720	61	45	Citta, Porto, e Rada di Brest, e Luoghi Convicini nella Bretagna
mwe0678	europe dalmatia	1691	CORONELLI	960	46	60	Contado di Zara, Parte della Dalmatia Descritto
mwbh0457	belgium holland	1692	CORONELLI	600	46	60	Contado di Zelanda
mwbh0458	belgium holland	1692	CORONELLI	1200	62	89	Contado d'Ollanda Parte Settentrionale / Contado d'Ollanda Parte Meridionale
mwsam0203a	south america amazon	1690	CORONELLI	650	29	46	Corso del Fiume dell'Amazoni
mwe0715	europe danube	1690	CORONELLI	3000	60	270	Corso del Danubio da Vienna sin' a Nicopoli e Paesi Adiacenti
mwe1009	europe rhine	1695	CORONELLI	900	45	61	Corso del Reno Parte Settentrio / Corso del Reno Partie Meridionale (2 maps. Northern map illustrated.)
mwe0775	europe east	1690	CORONELLI	720	45	61	Corso delli Fiumi Drino, e Boiana nella Dalmatia Descrito
mwg0526a	rheinland-pfalz	1690	CORONELLI	720	61	88	Del Palatinato et Elettorato del Reno Parte Occidentale / Del Palatinato et Elettorato del Reno Parte Orientale
mwe0980	europe montenegro	1688	CORONELLI	1000	43	60	Disegno Topografico del Canale di Cattaro
mwbh0845	luxembourg	1691	CORONELLI	750	45	61	Ducato di Luxembourgo
mwit0348b	italy emilia-romagna	1690	CORONELLI	650	46	60	Ducati di Modena e Regio, Principato di Carpi, e Val di Carsagnana
mwf0779	france normandy	1692	CORONELLI	450	46	61	Ducato di Normandia
mwgr0489	greece cyprus	1688	CORONELLI	650	13	17	Famagosta
mwuk1432	england thames	1706	CORONELLI	350	10	32	Fiumi Tamigi
mwsc0461a	scandinavia greenland	1692	CORONELLI	550	23	31	Frislanda, Scoperta da Nicolo Zeno Patritio Veneto Creduta Favolosa, o nel Mare Somersa
mwg0085	germany	1692	CORONELLI	1000	58	45	Germania, Parte Occidentale / Parte Orientale della Germania Divisa ne suoi Stati (2 maps, each 58x45cm)

AMPG REFERENCE	REGION	DATE	MAP MAKER	PRICE (UK£)	VERT. (cm.)	HOR. (cm.)	TITLE OF MAP (Comments by the editor in brackets)
mwgr0110	greece	1690	CORONELLI	650	46	60	Golfo della Prevesa
mwm0090	mediterranean adriatic	1692	CORONELLI	1800	43	60	Golfo di Venezia
mwc0083	china	1694	CORONELLI	800	44	60	Hunouang, e Sucuhen, Provincie della China
mwp0307	pacific cocos/horn isl.	1705	CORONELLI	120	12	18	I.Cocos - I. Horn
mwf1138	france rhone-alpes	1692	CORONELLI	360	45	61	Il Delfinato
mwit0660a	italy piedmont	1690	CORONELLI	900	46	60	Il Monferrato
mwin0137	india	1690	CORONELLI	2000	46	61	Impero del Gran Mogol / Peninsola dell' Indo (2 maps)
mwuk0966	england	1705	CORONELLI	200	13	18	Inghilterra
mwit0283	italy campagna	1695	CORONELLI	900	22	28	Is. di Capri
mwas0722	asia south east moluccas	1705	CORONELLI	120	12	18	Isles Molucche (incl. 2 views of Batavia)
mwuk1811	wales	1705	CORONELLI	240	13	18	Isola Anglesey
mwwi0415	cuba	1692	CORONELLI	500	22	29	Isola Cuba Descritta dal P. Mro. Coronelli Lettore Publica e Cosmografo della S.S. Republica di Venetia
mwwi0278a	west indies (islands)	1696	CORONELLI	1200	46	62	Isola Cuba / Isola de James / Isola D'Island / La Spanuola Descritta
mwwi0704	jamaica	1696	CORONELLI	375	22	29	Isola de Iames o Giamaica Posseduta dal Re Britannico Divisa in Parrocchie (from a larger map of 4 islands)
mwgr0529	greece rhodes	1696	CORONELLI	250	13	17	Isola de Rodi
mwjk0051	japan	1692	CORONELLI	2400	46	62	Isola del Giapone e Penisola di Corea
mwca0349	canada nova scotia	1696	CORONELLI	300	13	17	Isola di Capo Breton (map of Cartagena on verso)
mwgr0285	greece cefalonia	1692	CORONELLI	550	23	29	Isola di Cefalonia
mwgr0493	greece cyprus	1690	CORONELLI	800	13	17	Isola di Cipro
mwgr0313	greece corfu	1690	CORONELLI	1800	47	62	Isola di Corfu
mwf0474	france corsica	1692	CORONELLI	1600	61	46	Isola di Corsica
mwe0498	europe croatia	1690	CORONELLI	300	13	17	Isola di Lissa (map of Citta di Curzola nella Dalmatia on verso)
mwaf0593	africa islands madagascar	1690	CORONELLI	1250	60	45	Isola di Madagascar, o di S. Lorenzo
mwsp0650	balearic islands	1695	CORONELLI	550	17	24	Isola di Maiorca (in page of text, south to the top)
mwm0208	mediterranean malta	1689	CORONELLI	3000	46	62	Isola di Malta, olim Melita
mwwi0761	marie galante	1696	CORONELLI	400	22	30	Isola di Maria Galante nelle Antilli Posseduta da S.M. Christianissima
mwsc0520	scandinavia jan mayen isl.	1692	CORONELLI	300	23	31	Isola di Mayen, Scoperta l'Anno 1614 (part of a larger map of 4 islands)
mwca0292	canada newfoundland	1690	CORONELLI	480	24	30	Isola di Terra Nuova Scoperta da Gio: Cabota Veneto con suo Figliuolo Sebastiano l'An: 1596 24 Giugno a'Hore 12 (part of a larger map of 4 islands)
mwe0499	europe croatia	1690	CORONELLI	360	26	33	Isola di Veglia
mwuk1623	isle of wight	1700	CORONELLI	300	23	30	Isola di Wight (part of a larger map of 4 islands)
mwuk1563	england islands	1692	CORONELLI	675	47	62	Isola di Wight / Jarsey Isola / Mona Insula / Anglesey Isola
mwsc0499	scandinavia iceland	1692	CORONELLI	900	23	30	Isola d'Islanda (part of a larger map of 4 islands)
mwf0975	france poitou	1690	CORONELLI	300	28	44	Isola d'Oleron
mwsam0505	south america colombia	1696	CORONELLI	450	22	12	Isola e Citta di Cartagena nell America
mwit0794	italy sardinia	1695	CORONELLI	1000	62	47	Isola e Regno di Sardegna
mwgr0416a	greece crete	1690	CORONELLI	750	27	43	Isola e Regno di Candia ol Creta (2 maps on one sheet)
mwgr0414	greece crete	1689	CORONELLI	2250	45	120	Isola, e Regno di Candia
mwwi0039	west indies	1692	CORONELLI	750	26	44	Isole Antilli, la Cuba, e la Spagnuola Descritto e Dedicata dal Padre Maestro Coronelli
mwat0087	atlantic azores	1690	CORONELLI	1200	48	60	Isole Azzori, o Azzoridi
mwuk0778	uk	1705	CORONELLI	280	13	19	Isole Britanniche
mwat0156	atlantic canary isl.	1695	CORONELLI	1200	45	60	Isole Canarie
mwat0154	atlantic canary isl.	1690	CORONELLI	600	22	30	Isole Canarie gia dette Fortunatae Ins
mwaf1148	africa west	1690	CORONELLI	280	22	31	Isole della Guinea
mwas0418	asia south east	1691	CORONELLI	2000	45	61	Isole Dell'Indie
mwgm0011	gulf of mexico and surrounding regions	1695	CORONELLI	800	23	29	Isole nelle Piagge della Nuova Spagna de Cartagena sino a S. Gio: d'Ulua
mwit0124	italy	1696	CORONELLI	2000	62	45	Italia, Parte Occidentale/ Parte Orientale (2 sheets)
mwc0074	china	1690	CORONELLI	600	45	60	Iunan, Queicheu, e Quangsi Provincie della China
mwf1181	france south east	1696	CORONELLI	550	41	51	La Costa di Linguadocha, Provenza, et una Parte d'Italia da C. Dragonis fino a Cabo delle Mollo
mwf0077	france	1692	CORONELLI	1400	62	89	La Francia Antica e Moderna (in 2 sheets. Size is joined)
mwgr0111	greece	1690	CORONELLI	800	46	62	La Grecia
mwf0263	france aquitaine	1690	CORONELLI	600	61	46	La Guienna, Medoc, Saintonge, Aunis e Paesi Convicini (inset plan of Bordeaux)
mwam1272	great lakes	1695	CORONELLI	2400	26	43	La Louisiana, Parte Settentrionale, Scoperta sotto la Protettione di Luigi XIV
mwwi0588	hispaniola	1696	CORONELLI	400	23	30	La Spagnuola Descritta dal P. Cosmografo Coronelli Dedicata all Illustris: Sig. Guistimiano Lorenzo Cocco
mwaf0100	africa	1691	CORONELLI	3600	61	45	L'Africa Divisa nelle sue Parti secondo le piu moderne relationi (2 maps, each 61x45cm.)
mwam0330	america north	1689	CORONELLI	4500	45	59	L'Amerique Septentrionale, ou la Partie Septentrionale des Indes Occidentales ou se trouve Le Canada (publ. by Nolin)
mwat0233	atlantic islands	1696	CORONELLI	960	46	62	Le Bermude / Isola di Mayen / Frislanda / Isola di Terra Nuova (4 islands on one sheet)
mww0241	world	1690	CORONELLI-NOLIN	3000	45	60	Le Globe Terrestre Represente en Deux Plans-Hemispheres, et en Diverses autres Figures
mwas0720	asia south east moluccas	1690	CORONELLI	280	24	32	Le Molucche

AMPG REFERENCE	REGION	DATE	MAP MAKER	PRICE (UK£)	VERT. (cm.)	HOR. (cm.)	TITLE OF MAP (Comments by the editor in brackets)
mwsw0240	alps	1690	CORONELLI	500	45	60	Le Quattro Valli, di Lucerne, Angrogna, S. Martino, e la Perosa
mwuk0947	england	1689	CORONELLI-NOLIN	1500	45	59	Le Royaume d'Angleterre
mwuk0108	ireland	1690	CORONELLI-NOLIN	960	60	46	Le Royaume d'Irlande Divise en Provinces Subdivisees en Comtez et en Baronies
mwe0676	europe dalmatia	1690	CORONELLI	900	45	60	Le Royaume de Dalmacie, Divise en ses Comtez, Territoires ect.
mwit0136	italy	1705	CORONELLI	1200	36	46	L'Italia con le sue poste
mwbp0100	baltic states	1690	CORONELLI	2000	45	61	Lituania Dedicata all'Illustrissimo Signore
mwuk1126	england london	1689	CORONELLI	800	36	49	Londra
mwbh0842	luxembourg	1689	CORONELLI	1000	26	43	Luxembourgo
mwe1105	europe slovak republic (moravia)	1690	CORONELLI	720	46	61	Marcomania, hoggidi Marchesato de Moravia
mwat0265	atlantic north	1690	CORONELLI	1200	46	61	Mare del Nord Auttore Il P.M. Coronelli
mwp0238	pacific (all)	1696	CORONELLI	2400	46	61	Mare del Sud, detto Altrimenti Mare Pacifico. Auttore Il P.M. Coronelli
mwuk1774	wales	1691	CORONELLI	360	23	31	Mona Insula
mwru0104	russia	1696	CORONELLI	1500	60	88	Moscovia Parte Occidentale / Moscovia Parte Orientale
mwc0082	china	1692	CORONELLI	800	46	61	Nanking e Honan, Provincie della China
mwp0176	new zealand	1692	CORONELLI	1200	11	15	Nuova Zelandia
mwgr0112	greece	1690	CORONELLI	1500	46	61	Parallelo Geografico dell'Antico col Moderno Arcipelago / Parte Meridionale dell' Arcipelago (2 maps)
mwgm0185	mexico	1695	CORONELLI	800	45	60	Parte della Nuova Spagna, o del Mexico dove sono le Provincie di Guadalaira Xalisco Mecoacan e Mexico
mwuk0955	england	1691	CORONELLI	900	46	61	Parte Meridionale del Regno d'Inghilterra / Parte Settentrionale (2 maps, each 46x61cm.)
mwgr0612	greece islands	1690	CORONELLI	1650	46	61	Parte Meridionale dell'Arcipelago / Parte Settentrionale dell'Arciepelago (2 maps)
mwe0103	europe	1691	CORONELLI	3500	60	48	Parte Occidentale dell' Europa / Parte Orientale dell' Europa (2 sheets, each 60x48cm.)
mwc0076	china	1690	CORONELLI	8000	46	61	Parte Occidentale della China / Parte Orientale della China (2 maps, each 46x61cm.)
mwsp0206	spain	1690	CORONELLI	1800	61	89	Parte Occidentale della Spagna / Parte Orientale della Spagna
mwf0579b	france ile de france	1690	CORONELLI	800	88	60	Parte Occidentale delli Contorni di Parigi/Parte Orientale ... (2 maps)
mwuk0119	ireland	1693	CORONELLI	1800	92	61	Parte Settentrionale dell'Irlanda Descritta / Irlanda Parte Meridionale
mwam1271	great lakes	1688	CORONELLI	11000	44	59	Partie Occidentale du Canada ou de la Nouvelle France ou sont les Nations des Ilinois, de Tracy, les Iroquois, et Plusieurs autres Peuples; avec la Louisiane Nouvellement Decouverte etc.
mwca0034a	canada	1689	CORONELLI	4000	45	60	Partie Orientale du Canada ou de la Nouvelle France... Avec la Nouvelle Angleterre, la Nouvelle Ecosse, la Nouvelle Yorck, et la Virgine
mwgr0113	greece	1690	CORONELLI	600	45	60	Peloponneso hoggidi Morea
mwgr0269	greece athens	1695	CORONELLI	1000	45	61	Pianta della Citta e Fortezza d'Atene
mwgr0416	greece crete	1690	CORONELLI	950	45	60	Pianta della Real Fortezza, e Citta di Candia (Heraklion)
mwe0911	europe hungary	1690	CORONELLI	500	45	60	Pianta du Buda Citta Reale nell' Ungharia Inferiore
mwam0093	america continent	1691	CORONELLI	2500	45	61	Planisfero del Mondo Nuovo (2nd state shown, with decorative astrological symbols in side borders)
mww0245	world	1691	CORONELLI	4800	45	61	Planisfero del Mondo Nuovo / Planisfero del Mondo Vecchio (2 maps. Second state shown, with decorative astrological symbols)
mwaa0014	antarctic	1690	CORONELLI	600	37		Polo Australe, o Meridionale, & Antartico
mwaa0103	arctic	1695	CORONELLI	600	37		Polo Settentrionale
mwbp0317	poland	1690	CORONELLI	2500	61	46	Polonia Parte Occidentale / Polonia Parte Orientale (2 sheets, each 61x46cm)
mwc0081	china	1692	CORONELLI	1400	46	61	Quantung, e Fokien, Provincie della China
mwgr0613	greece islands	1690	CORONELLI	800	46	62	Regno di Negroponte Descritto e Dedicato al Reverendis P. Maestro Felice Rotondi
mwsp0056	portugal	1690	CORONELLI	480	45	60	Regno di Portogallo
mwm0029	mediterranean	1700	CORONELLI	3750	46	118	Ristretto del Mediterraneo / Parte Orientale del Mediterraneo
mwe0677	europe dalmatia	1690	CORONELLI	2000	45	122	Ristretto della Dalmazia Divisa ne suoi Contadi
mwaf0094	africa	1687	CORONELLI	3000	43	72	Route Maritime de Brest a Siam, et de Siam a Brest, Faite en 1685 et 1686
mwas0820	asia south east siam	1687	CORONELLI	4000	61	45	Royaume de Siam avec les Royaumes qui luy sont Tributaires
mwuk0432	scotland	1690	CORONELLI	1500	89	63	Scotia Parte Settentrionale [in set with] Scotia Parte Meridionale
mwas0821	asia south east siam	1696	CORONELLI	800	27	43	Siam, o Iudia
mwbp0318	poland	1690	CORONELLI	1250	46	61	Silesia Inferiore
mwe0500	europe croatia	1690	CORONELLI	675	45	60	Stato di Ragusi. Bocca del Fiume Narenta, Isole di Lessina e Curzola nella Dalmazia

AMPG REFERENCE	REGION	DATE	MAP MAKER	PRICE (UK£)	VERT. (cm.)	HOR. (cm.)	TITLE OF MAP (Comments by the editor in brackets)
mwaa0100	arctic	1690	CORONELLI	1350	45	61	Terre Artiche Descritte dal P.M. Coronelli M.C. Cosmografo della Sereniss. Republica di Venetia
mwit0906	italy sicily	1691	CORONELLI	1200	47	62	Trinacria Hoggidi Sicilia
mwe0417	europe austria vienna	1692	CORONELLI	720	28	41	Vienna Metropoli dell'Austria Descritta
mwsc0594	scandinavia norway	1695	CORONELLI	500	39	25	Voraigne di Moskestroom / Onde Formate dalla Voraigne di Moskestrom
mwc0084	china	1695	CORONELLI	600	47	61	Xansi e Xensi, Provincie della China
mwc0085	china	1695	CORONELLI	1000	45	60	Xantung, e Peking Provincie della China
mwgm0001	gulf of mexico and surrounding regions	1524	CORTES		31	46	(No title. The main part of the map shows a plan of the Aztec capital Temixtitan)
mwgm0234c	mexico	1771	COSTANZO	60000	83	80	Carta Reducida Del Oceano Asiatico, Ó Mar Del Sur, Que Comprehende La Costa Oriental Y Occidental De La Peninsula De La California, Con El Golfo De Su Denominacion Antiguamente Conocido Por La De Mar De Cortés, Y De Las Costas De La América (first map to name San Francisco)
mwe0755	europe east	1619	COTOVICUS	200	9	12	Colpho con l'Italia (Adriatic and N.E. Mediterannean)
mwgr0303	greece corfu	1619	COTOVICUS	1200	19	12	Corcyra Corfu
mwgr0368	greece crete	1619	COTOVICUS	500	13	18	Creta Candia
mwgr0470	greece cyprus	1619	COTOVICUS	3500	13	18	Cypri Insulae Descriptio
mwm0119	mediterranean east	1619	COTOVICUS	400	9	12	Mediteraneo e Colfo de Setelia
mwgr0523	greece rhodes	1619	COTOVICUS	500	19	12	Rhodus
mwam1364	america north (west)	1843	COTTA	600	46	60	Wegweiser durch die Staaten Ohio, Michigan, Indiana, Illinois, & Missouri; u. die Territorien Wisconsin & Iowa
mwin0404a	india goa	1831	COTTINEAU	500	25	27	A Figurative Plan of the City of Goa
mwit0842	italy sardinia and corsica	1846	COULIER	180	43	38	Carte d'Ensemble des Phares (sea chart)
mwgm0093a	belize	1844	COULIER	280	21	28	Carte du Phare de Belize, d'après celle de M. Barnett, de 1839.
mwgm0379a	nicaragua	1844	COULIER	200	21	28	Plan du Fanal accid.el de S. Juan de Nicaragua, par G. Peacock, de 1832.
mwgm0446	panama	1844	COULIER	300	20	28	Plan du Fanal proposé de Porto Bello, d'après un plan Espagnol.
mwgm0127a	honduras	1844	COULIER	250	28	21	Plan du Phare d'Omoa, d'après celui de M. de Candé, de 1841.
mwuss1104	new york	1776	COURIER DE L'EUROPE	650	27	40	Theatre de la Guerre en Amerique - Seat of War in America (Courier publ. London, no. XXXII)
mwme0938	turkey etc	1624	COURMENIN	240	20	23	(North West Anatolia)
mwme0939	turkey etc	1624	COURMENIN	180	21	30	Helespont a Present Destroit de Galipoli
mwru0399a	russia moscow	1805	COURTENER (KURTENER)	4800	108	99	(Plan of Moscow, in Cyrillic and French)
mwe1063	europe serbia	1717	COUTT	1200	52	61	Belgradi
mwbh0730a	belgium holland	1778	COVENS	1800	59	69	Niewe Kaart van de Wydberoemde Koopstat Amsteldam (copy of P. Mol's map of 1770)
mwbh0755b	belgium holland	1792	COVENS	900	87	58	Nieuwe Kaart van Noord Holland (shown above left)
mwg0537	rheinland-pfalz	1745	COVENS & MORTIER	1200	46	65	(Mainz) Plan de Mayence de ses Nouvelles Fortifications et de ses Environs / Platte Grond van de Stadt Mentz met deszelfs Nieuwe Werken en Omleggende Landen
mwuss1552	vermont	1780	COVENS & MORTIER	15000	51	62	A Chorographical Map of the Northern Department of North-America
mwuss1352	pennsylvania	1760	COVENS & MORTIER	2500	30	32	A Chorographical Map, of the Country, round Philadelphia (title above map, also in French)
mwam0941	america north (east)	1740	COVENS & MORTIER	15000	111	102	A Map of the British Empire in America with the French, Spanish and Hollandish Settlements Adjacent thereto by Henry Popple (reduction of Popple's 1733 map)
mwas0154a	asia continent	1744	COVENS & MORTIER	750	43	54	Accuratissima Totius Asiae Tabula in Omnes Partes Divisa, de Novo Correcta
mwgr0176	greece	1730	COVENS & MORTIER	550	49	57	Achaiae Descriptio (title above map)
mwaf0511	africa egypt etc	1746	COVENS & MORTIER	550	59	37	Aegypti (title above map: Carte de L'Egypte et Le Cours du Nil)
mwaf0399	africa east	1730	COVENS & MORTIER	500	42	55	Aethiopia Superior vel Interior; vulgo Abissinorum sive Presbiteri Ioannis Imperium
mwaf0124	africa	1704	COVENS & MORTIER	10000	111	130	Afrique - L'Afrique Dressee sur les Observations de Mrs de l'Academie Royale des Sciences
mwam0415	america north	1757	COVENS & MORTIER	785	45	59	Amerique Septentrionale dresse
mwaf0711a	africa north	1727	COVENS & MORTIER	350	37	50	Antiquorum Africae Episcopatuum Geographica Descriptio
mwf0240	france alsace	1730	COVENS & MORTIER	500	48	58	Argentorati Territorium, vulgo Strasburger Gebiet
mwam0133	america continent	1721	COVENS & MORTIER	800	39	55	Atlantis Insula, a Nicolao Sanson Antiquitati Restituta; nunc demum Majori Forma Delineata, et in Decem Regna (copy of Sanson 1669)
mwf0749	france nord pas-de-calais	1730	COVENS & MORTIER	280	49	61	Carte D'Artois et des Environs
mwaf1188	africa west	1730	COVENS & MORTIER	400	49	61	Carte de la Barbarie de la Nigritie et de la Guinee
mwgr0177	greece	1730	COVENS & MORTIER	500	46	59	Carte de la Grece
mwam0931	america north (east)	1730	COVENS & MORTIER	2800£	44	60	Carte de la Louisiane et du Cours du Mississipi Dressee sur un Grand Nombre de Memoires entr'autres sur ceux de Mr. le Maire par Guillme. de l'Isle

AMPG REFERENCE	REGION	DATE	MAP MAKER	PRICE (UK£)	VERT. (cm.)	HOR. (cm.)	TITLE OF MAP (Comments by the editor in brackets)
mwuss0625	louisiana	1730	COVENS & MORTIER	2800	44	60	Carte de la Louisiane et du Cours du Mississipi Dressee sur un Grand Nombre de Memoires entr'autres sur ceux de Mr. le Maire par Guillme. de l'Isle
mwam1000	america north (east)	1758	COVENS & MORTIER	1000	42	58	Carte de la Louisiane, Maryland, Virginie, Caroline, Georgie, avec une Partie de la Floride
mwuk1490	uk english channel (all)	1740	COVENS & MORTIER	750	59	80	Carte de la Manche
mwuk1667	north sea	1740	COVENS & MORTIER	1000	60	84	Carte de la Mer d'Allemagne ... depuis Bergen et les Isles Schetland jusques au Pas de Calais
mwme0292	holy land	1730	COVENS & MORTIER	450	40	47	Carte de la Situation du Paradis Terrestre, et des Pais Habitez par les Patriarches (based on Senex 1720)
mwme0608a	arabia etc.	1720	COVENS & MORTIER	650	51	58	Carte de la Turquie de l'Arabie et de la Perse
mwaf0400	africa east	1730	COVENS & MORTIER	500	49	56	Carte de l'Egypte de la Nubie de l'Abissinie &c.
mwin0033	ceylon	1705	COVENS & MORTIER	550	46	57	Carte de l'Isle de Ceylan Dressee sur les Observations de Mrs. de l'Academie Royale des Sciences
mwru0160	russia	1730	COVENS & MORTIER	500	49	62	Carte de Moscovie Dressee par Guilaume de l'Isle / Partie Meridionale de Moscovie Dressee par G. de l'Isle (2 maps)
mwme0813	persia etc	1730	COVENS & MORTIER	900	52	62	Carte de Perse
mwf1054	france provence	1730	COVENS & MORTIER	300	50	60	Carte de Provence et des Terres Adjacentes
mwwi0243a	west indies (east)	1730	COVENS & MORTIER	600	59	45	Carte des Antilles Francoises
mwas0450	asia south east	1720	COVENS & MORTIER	3000	57	86	Carte des Costes de l'Asie sur l'Ocean (re-issue of Mortier 1696)
mwin0189	india	1733	COVENS & MORTIER	500	46	57	Carte des Cotes de Malabar et de Coromandel
mwsc0111	scandinavia	1710	COVENS & MORTIER	550	89	60	Carte des Courones du Nord qui Comprend les Royaumes de Danemark, Suede, & Norwege, &c. / Seconde Carte des Courones du Nord qui Comprend le Royaume de Danemark &c. (2 maps, north and south)
mwe0155	europe	1739	COVENS & MORTIER	500	48	60	Carte d'Europe
mwca0052	canada	1730	COVENS & MORTIER	1200	49	56	Carte du Canada ou de la Nouvelle France et des Decouvertes qui y ont ete Faites Dressee sur Plusieurs Observations ... par Guillaume Del'Isle (sl. reduced size version of De L'Isle's 1703 map)
mwbh0608	belgium holland	1730	COVENS & MORTIER	550	49	63	Carte du Comte de Flandre.
mwaf0916	africa south	1730	COVENS & MORTIER	550	48	61	Carte du Congo et du Pays des Cafres (re-issue of De L'Isle 1708)
mwf0618	france languedoc	1730	COVENS & MORTIER	450	47	58	Carte du Diocese de Beziers
mwf0619	france languedoc	1730	COVENS & MORTIER	450	47	58	Carte du Diocese de Narbonne
mwgm0025	gulf of mexico and surrounding regions	1722	COVENS & MORTIER	1500	49	60	Carte du Mexique et de la Floride des Terres Angloises et des Isles Antilles du Cours et des Environs de la Riviere de Mississipi ... par Guillaume Del'Isle (slightly reduced copy of De L'Isles' 1703 map)
mwsam0231	south america argentina	1730	COVENS & MORTIER	550	50	57	Carte du Paraguay du Chili du Detroit de Magellan &c. Dressee sur les Descriptions des PP. Alfonse d'Ovalle, et Nicolas Techo
mwsc0354	scandinavia denmark	1730	COVENS & MORTIER	400	48	60	Carte du Royaume de Danemarc Par Guill. de l'Isle a Amsterdam Chez Iean Covens et Corneille Mortier Geographes
mwas0452	asia south east	1721	COVENS & MORTIER	1200	59	50	Carte d'une Partie de la Chine, les Isles Philippines, de la Sonde, Moloques, de Papoesi &c.
mwin0171	india	1721	COVENS & MORTIER	450	53	49	Carte d'une partie des Isles Orientales
mwe0462	europe central	1730	COVENS & MORTIER	400	46	59	Carte Exacte des Postes et Routes de l'Empire d'Allemagne Divisee en ses Cercles
mwuss0171	carolinas	1720	COVENS & MORTIER	3500	57	46	Carte Generale de la Caroline
mwru0208	russia	1748	COVENS & MORTIER	800	50	49	Carte Generale de l'Empire de Russie (2 sheets, each 50x49cm. English version of De L'Isle 1745)
mww0335	world	1720	COVENS & MORTIER	4000	58	50	Carte Generale de Toutes les Costes du Monde ... Amerique / Partie Orientale du Monde (2 maps, each 58x50cm)
mwam1088	america north (east)	1785	COVENS & MORTIER	1200	41	57	Carte Generale des Treize Etats Unis, de l'Amerique Septentrionale
mwe1114a	europe slovak republic (moravia)	1757	COVENS & MORTIER	400	51	64	Carte Generale du Marquisat de Moravie
mww0357	world	1730	COVENS & MORTIER	650	40	47	Carte Generale du Monde, ou Description du Monde Terrestre & Aquatique (re-issue of Mortier 1700)
mwit0509	italy lombardy	1730	COVENS & MORTIER	540	59	46	Carte Nouvelle du Bergamasco Faisant Partie des Etats de la Republique de Venise
mwit0508a	italy lombardy	1730	COVENS & MORTIER	550	49	58	Carte Nouvelle du Duché de Mantoue
mwit0358	italy emilia-romagna	1725	COVENS & MORTIER	550	50	58	Carte Nouvelle du Duche de Modene, de Regio et de Carpi; avec la Seigneurie de la Cafargnana
mwit0358a	italy emilia-romagna	1730	COVENS & MORTIER	600	47	56	Carte Nouvelle du Duche et Legation de Ferrare a l'Eglise
mwit1195b	italy veneto	1720	COVENS & MORTIER	600	46	56	Carte Nouvelle du Padouan, et le Polesin de Rovigo, de la Pepublique de Venise
mwit1195a	italy veneto	1720	COVENS & MORTIER	550	48	56	Carte Nouvelle du Territoire de Verone
mwit1198	italy veneto	1725	COVENS & MORTIER	450	51	58	Carte Nouvelle du Territoire de Vicenza, ou sont Marquees Toutes les Vallees, Cols, Passages et Mines d'Argent
mwbh0684	belgium holland	1748	COVENS & MORTIER	2400	41	111	Carte particuliere ... l'Isle de Walcheren (2 charts, each 41x111cm)

AMPG REFERENCE	REGION	DATE	MAP MAKER	PRICE (UK£)	VERT. (cm.)	HOR. (cm.)	TITLE OF MAP (Comments by the editor in brackets)
mwe0948	europe hungary	1749	COVENS & MORTIER	400	48	56	Carte Particuliere de la Hongrie de la Transilvanie de la Croatie et de la Sclavonie Dressee sur les Observations de Mr. le Comte Marsilli et sur Plusieurs autres Memoires
mwaf0601	africa islands madagascar	1730	COVENS & MORTIER	750	57	85	Carte Particuliere de l'Isle Dauphine ou Madagascar et St. Laurens (copy of Mortier 1705)
mwbh0612a	belgium holland	1730	COVENS & MORTIER	400	46	56	Carte Particuliere des Environs de Bruges, Ostende …
mwbh0662	belgium holland	1745	COVENS & MORTIER	550	42	55	Carte Particuliere des Environs de Bruxelles avec le Bois de Soigne et d'une Partie de la Flandre jusques a Gand
mwit0507	italy lombardy	1725	COVENS & MORTIER	550	58	51	Carte Particuliere du Bressan Faisant Partie des Etats de la Republique de Venise
mwbh0609	belgium holland	1730	COVENS & MORTIER	650	46	54	Comitatus Zelandiae Tabula
mwuss0294	connecticut	1780	COVENS & MORTIER	10000	52	59	Connecticut, and Parts Adjacent (Map incl. Long Island)
mwgr0323	greece corfu	1735	COVENS & MORTIER	500	27	36	Corfou ou Corcyre, Ile de la Mer Ionienne, avec une partie de la Gréce (map by Van Der Aa)
mwgr0423	greece crete	1720	COVENS & MORTIER	400	38	53	Creta Insula hodie Candia
mwgr0496	greece cyprus	1705	COVENS & MORTIER	1100	38	50	Cyprus Insula
mwsp0699	gibraltar	1727	COVENS & MORTIER	720	50	59	De Haven en Straat van Gibraltar (copy of Allard 1704 plus a 3rd inset)
mwg0493	mecklenburg	1730	COVENS & MORTIER	250	49	57	Ducatus Meklenburgicus in quo sunt Ducatus Vandaliae et Meklenburgi Ducatus et Comitatus Swerinensis (re-issue of De Wit 1680)
mwbp0117	baltic states	1730	COVENS & MORTIER	550	42	50	Ducatuum Livoniae et Curlandiae Nova Tabula
mwaf0505	africa egypt etc	1721	COVENS & MORTIER	375	28	35	Egypte, partie d'Afrique
mwbh0610	belgium holland	1730	COVENS & MORTIER	500	58	51	Episcopatus et Principatus Leodiensis et Namurcensis Comitatus
mwit0312	italy central	1725	COVENS & MORTIER	400	61	45	Estats de l'Eglise et de Toscane
mwsp0530	spain regions	1730	COVENS & MORTIER	2400	90	118	Exacta Principatus Cataloniae Tabula
mwit0508	italy lombardy	1725	COVENS & MORTIER	400	38	50	Haute Partie du Duche de Milan
mwgr0170	greece	1725	COVENS & MORTIER	750	44	56	Hellas seu Graecia Universa
mww0358	world	1730	COVENS & MORTIER	1350	48		Hemisphere Oriental Dresse en 1720 / Hemisphere Occidental Dresse en 1720 (2 circular maps, re-issue of De l'Isle 1714)
mwme0280	holy land	1725	COVENS & MORTIER	500	39	46	Het Heylige Land Verdeeld in de Twaalf Stammen Israel
mwuk0143	ireland	1720	COVENS & MORTIER	900	58	50	Hyberniae Regni in Provincias Ultoniam, Connachiam, Lageniam, Momoniamq
mwjk0062	japan	1715	COVENS & MORTIER	1200	31	45	Iaponia Regnum
mwme0488	jerusalem	1728	COVENS & MORTIER	720	32	40	Ierusalem Niewlicks uyt de de Schriften Iosephus Afgebeeld door J.H. Coccejus
mwat0195	atlantic cape verde isl.	1720	COVENS & MORTIER	450	38	48	Iles du Cap Verd, Hispanis Islas de Cabo Verde Belgis des Soute Eylanden
mwc0096	china	1720	COVENS & MORTIER	1200	46	61	Imperii Sinarum Nova Descriptio
mwaf0711	africa north	1727	COVENS & MORTIER	350	39	53	In Notitiam Ecclesiasticam Africae Tabula Geographica Auctore G. de l'Isle (copy of De L'Isle 1700)
mwf0495	france corsica	1737	COVENS & MORTIER	1200	56	48	Insula Corsica olim Regni Titulo Insignis
mwm0226	mediterranean malta	1721	COVENS & MORTIER	960	44	54	Insularum Melitae vulgo Maltae
mwme0281	holy land	1725	COVENS & MORTIER	550	46	61	Iudae, sive Terra Sancta
mwjk0055	japan	1700	COVENS & MORTIER	2800	42	57	Japonia Regnum
mwbp0114	baltic states	1721	COVENS & MORTIER	350	29	36	La Livonie avec les Frontieres de Courlande et de Finlande (map by Van Der Aa)
mwbp0393	poland	1730	COVENS & MORTIER	550	48	62	La Pologne
mwit0605	italy north	1733	COVENS & MORTIER	675	43	50	La Source du Po et les Passages de France en Piemont / Le Cours du Po dans le Piemont et le Montferrat / Le Cours du Po dans le Milanez (3 maps)
mwsw0117	switzerland	1721	COVENS & MORTIER	1350	59	85	La Suisse Divisee en ses Treze Cantons, ses Alliez & ses Sujets (3 borders decorated with crests)
mwaf0163	africa	1730	COVENS & MORTIER	800	46	58	L'Afrique Dressee sur les Observations (re-issue of De L'Isle's 1700 map)
mwg0118	germany	1730	COVENS & MORTIER	450	49	62	L'Allemagne Dressee sur les Observations de Tycho Brahe de Kepler de Snellius
mwsam0060	south america	1730	COVENS & MORTIER	600	49	59	L'Amerique Meridionale Dressee sur les Observations de Mrs. de l'Academie Royale des Sciences … Par G. de l'Isle
mwam0383	america north	1728	COVENS & MORTIER	1500	45	58	L'Amerique Septentrionale Dressee sur les Observations de Mrs. de l'Academie Royale des Sciences … Par G. de l'Isle (title also in Latin above map: America Septentrionalis)
mwam0128	america continent	1720	COVENS & MORTIER	15000	112	130	L'Amerique, Dresse sur les N:Observations Faites en Toutes les Parties de la Terre
mwg0418	brandenburg	1750	COVENS & MORTIER	480	47	60	Land-Charte des Chur-Furstenthums Brandenburg
mwas0171	asia continent	1757	COVENS & MORTIER	650	47	58	L'Asie Divisee en ses Principales Regions
mwas0124	asia continent	1720	COVENS & MORTIER	10000	109	129	L'Asie Dressee sur les Observations de Mrs de l'Academie Royale de Sciences
mwit1195	italy veneto	1720	COVENS & MORTIER	250	38	50	Le Bellunese et le Feltrino
mwca0050a	canada	1722	COVENS & MORTIER	900	55	79	Le Canada ou Partie dela Nouvelle France (title above map)
mwe1021	europe rhine	1730	COVENS & MORTIER	600	142	63	Le Cours du Rhin au dessus de Strasbourg (etc.) jusqu'a Bonne
mwg0821	westphalia	1730	COVENS & MORTIER	300	42	56	Le Duche de Berg, le Comte de Homberg, les Seigneuries de Hardenberg, et de Wildenborg

AMPG REFERENCE	REGION	DATE	MAP MAKER	PRICE (UK£)	VERT. (cm.)	HOR. (cm.)	TITLE OF MAP (Comments by the editor in brackets)
mwf0621	france languedoc	1733	COVENS & MORTIER	240	58	46	Le Gouvernement General de Languedoc, Partie Occidentale
mwit0600	italy north	1721	COVENS & MORTIER	2000	96	117	Le Grand Teatre de la Guerre en Italie
mwe0581	europe czech republic (bohemia)	1744	COVENS & MORTIER	480	47	55	Le Royaume de Boheme Divisee en ses Douze Cercles (reduced size version of Muller's map of 1722. Title above map: Mappa Totius Regni Bohemia.)
mwe0932	europe hungary	1730	COVENS & MORTIER	480	48	59	Le Royaume de Hongrie sur les Memoires les plus nouveaux
mwg0648	saxony	1745	COVENS & MORTIER	600	62	52	L'Electorat de Hannover ou les Domaines du Roi de la Grande Bretagne en Allemagne
mwg0457c	hessen	1745	COVENS & MORTIER	375	62	52	L'Electorat de Mayence
mwg0111	germany	1721	COVENS & MORTIER	500	57	88	L'Empire D'Allemagne (copy of Jaillot 1692)
mwuk1180	england london	1745	COVENS & MORTIER	800	48	56	Les Environs de Londres
mwam0386	america north	1735	COVENS & MORTIER	720	51	61	Les Principales Forteresses Ports &c. de l'Amerique Septentrionale
mwbh0623a	belgium holland	1735	COVENS & MORTIER	7500	102	122	Les Provinces Confederees Du Pais-Bas (map by Van Der Aa)
mwsp0260	spain	1735	COVENS & MORTIER	450	49	61	L'Espagne
mwaa0126	arctic	1740	COVENS & MORTIER	550	46	51	L'Hemisphere Septentrional pour Voir Plus Destinctement les Terres Arctiques par Guillaume de Lisle de l'Academie Rle. des Sciences (see also Antarctic)
mwc0301	china formosa	1721	COVENS & MORTIER	1200	29	35	L'Ile de Formosa (re-issue of Van der Aa's map, north to the left)
mwit0157	italy	1720	COVENS & MORTIER	550	49	60	L'Italie, Dressee sur les Observations de Mrs. de l'Academie Royale des Sciences
mwru0448	russia tartary	1730	COVENS & MORTIER	600	43	55	Magnae Tartariae, Magni Mogolis Imperii, Iaponiae et Chinae, Nova Descriptio (copy of De Wit c1688)
mwbp0116	baltic states	1730	COVENS & MORTIER	550	45	53	Magni Ducatus Lithuaniae Tabula
mww0350	world	1725	COVENS & MORTIER	1800	50	64	Mappe-Monde Dresse sur les Observations de Mrs de l'Academie Royale des Sciences (re-issue of De l'Isle 1700)
mww0315	world	1711	COVENS & MORTIER	5000	57	96	Mappe-Monde Geo-Hydrographique, ou Description Generale du Globe Terrestre et Aquatique en Deux Plans Hemispheres
mww0374a	world	1735	COVENS & MORTIER	960	23	33	Mappe Monde Suivant les Nouvelles Observations (close copy of Van der Aa 1720)
mwm0046a	mediterranean	1721	COVENS & MORTIER	1800	43	103	Mare Mediterraneum
mwme0996	turkey etc	1725	COVENS & MORTIER	500	38	53	Natolia - Asia Minor Auctore Ph. de la Rue
mwbh0799	belgium holland	1830	MORTIER, COVENS	240	41	51	Nieuwe Kaart der Residentie 's Gravenhage, waarop zyn Gebbagt
mwbh0796	belgium holland	1829	MORTIER, COVENS	400	62	91	Nieuwe Kaart der Stad Amsterdam
mwsp0699a	mediterranean	1727	COVENS & MORTIER	720	51	57	Nouveau Plan de Gibraltar avec ses Fortifications &c.
mwbh0872	luxembourg	1744	COVENS & MORTIER	1200	40	49	Nouveau Plan de la Ville de Luxembourg
mwsw0116	switzerland	1720	COVENS & MORTIER	5000	99	116	Nouvelle Carte de la Suisse (based on Scheuchzer's map of 1715)
mwam0943	america north (east)	1741	COVENS & MORTIER	15000	111	102	Nouvelle Carte Particuliere de l'Amerique (Reduction of Popple's 1733 map)
mwaf0506	africa egypt etc	1730	COVENS & MORTIER	450	44	52	Nova Aegypti Tabula
mwe0933	europe hungary	1730	COVENS & MORTIER	300	46	56	Nova et Accurata Regni Hungariae Tabula, ad Usum Serenissimi Burgundiae Ducis (title above map. Title in cartouche: Le Royaume de Hongrie et des Pays qui en Dependoient Autrefois. Shown above left)
mwsc0712	scandinavia sweden	1721	COVENS & MORTIER	1200	50	59	Nova et Accurata Scaniae et Maximae Partis Zeelandiae Tabula (re-issue of De Wit's c1680 map, but with an additional inset view top left).
mwe0141	europe	1721	COVENS & MORTIER	600	43	53	Nova et Accurate Divisa in Regna et Regiones Praecipuas Europae Descriptio ... F. de Witt
mwsc0713	scandinavia sweden	1721	COVENS & MORTIER	500	49	59	Nova Gothiae Australis sive Scaniae, Blekingiae et Hallandiae
mwsw0125	switzerland	1730	COVENS & MORTIER	500	47	61	Nova Helvetiae, Foederatarumque cum ea, nec non Subditarum Regionum Tabula
mwru0161	russia	1730	COVENS & MORTIER	450	50	67	Nova Tabula Imperii Russici
mwsc0428	scandinavia finland	1721	COVENS & MORTIER	800	44	52	Nova Tabula Magni Ducatus Finlandiae (copy of De Wit)
mwf0588	france ile de france	1730	COVENS & MORTIER	250	54	64	Nova Territorii Parisiensis Tabula ad Usum Serenissimi Burgundiae Ducis
mwgr0178	greece	1730	COVENS & MORTIER	500	46	53	Novantiqua Epirus quae hodie Albania
mwgr0176a	greece	1730	COVENS & MORTIER	450	49	55	Novantiquae Thessaliae Descriptio
mwsp0256	spain	1730	COVENS & MORTIER	500	49	57	Novissima et Accuratissima Regnorum Hispaniae et Portugalliae Tabula Auctore F. de Witt
mwsp0246	spain	1720	COVENS & MORTIER	500	46	59	Novissima et Accuratissima Tabula Regnorum Hispaniae et Portugalliae ... per Carolo Allard
mwuk0823	uk	1745	COVENS & MORTIER	12000	104	125	Novissima nec non Perfectissima Regnorum Angliae, Scotiae, et Hiberniae, Tabula
mwsc0125	scandinavia	1721	COVENS & MORTIER	600	50	57	Novissima nec non Perfectissima Scandinaviae Tabula Comprehendens Regnorum Sueciae, Daniae et Novegiae
mwuk0467	scotland	1728	COVENS & MORTIER	900	50	59	Novissima Regni Scotiae Septentrionalis et Meridionalis Tabula Divisee in Ducatus, Comitatus, Vice-Comitatus, Provincias, Dominia et Insulas
mwe0790	europe east	1730	COVENS & MORTIER	400	46	60	Orbis Romani Descriptio seu Divisio per Themata

AMPG REFERENCE	REGION	DATE	MAP MAKER	PRICE (UK£)	VERT. (cm.)	HOR. (cm.)	TITLE OF MAP (Comments by the editor in brackets)
mwg0376	bavaria	1740	COVENS & MORTIER	550	48	64	Partie Meridionale de la Souabe / Partie Septentrionale de la Souabe (2 maps)
mwas0139	asia continent	1730	COVENS & MORTIER	750	59	50	Partie Orientale du Monde
mwaf0506a	africa egypt etc	1730	COVENS & MORTIER	450	35	50	Patriarchatus Alexandrini Geographica descriptio ... N. Sanson
mwme0295	holy land	1730	COVENS & MORTIER	450	35	50	Patriarchatus Hierosolymitani Geographica Descriptio Parisiis apud M. Tavernier Sculptorem ... Autore N. Sanson
mwgr0179	greece	1730	COVENS & MORTIER	500	48	54	Peloponnesi quae hodie Morea Descriptio
mwbp0423	poland	1740	COVENS & MORTIER	480	50	54	Plan de la Celebre Ville Marchante de Dantzig, et de ses Environs, par Mr. Homan, et Corrigee de Nouveau sur les Lieux par un Curieux Tres Renomme
mwru0162	russia	1730	COVENS & MORTIER	1500	48	56	Plan de la Ville & du Fort de St. Petersbourg (copied from Homann 1718)
mwbh0611	belgium holland	1730	COVENS & MORTIER	500	50	58	Plan de la Ville de Brusselles (copy of Fricx 1710)
mwbh0569	belgium holland	1720	COVENS & MORTIER	750	44	56	Plan de la Ville et Citadelle d'Anvers
mwf0752	france nord pas-de-calais	1747	COVENS & MORTIER	600	40	47	Plan de la Ville et Citadelle de Valenciennes
mwbh0873	luxembourg	1745	COVENS & MORTIER	1200	65	54	Plan de Luxembourg de ses Nouvelles Fortifications et de ses Environs
mwf1067	france provence	1744	COVENS & MORTIER	800	44	48	Plan de Toulon
mwsam0515	south america colombia	1741	COVENS & MORTIER	900	51	60	Plan du Port de la Ville et des Forteresses de Carthagene
mwbh0608a	belgium holland	1730	COVENS & MORTIER	7500	123	162	Platte-Grondt van de Oude en Nieuwe Royinge Der Stat Amsterdam (Daniel Stalpaert drew this map in 1662)
mwsam0364	south america brazil	1740	COVENS & MORTIER	1200	41	53	Praefecturae de Paraiba, et Rio Grande
mwsam0360	south america brazil	1730	COVENS & MORTIER	850	41	53	Preafectura de Ciriii, vel Seregippe Delrey cum Itapuama (copy of Blaeu 1662)
mwca0504	canada quebec	1737	COVENS & MORTIER	450	12	27	Quebec
mwit0735	italy rome	1710	COVENS & MORTIER	2000	67	87	Recentis Romae Ichnographia et Hypsographia
mwit0403a	italy lazio	1740	COVENS & MORTIER	350	45	62	Regionum Italiae Mediarum Tabula Geographica Pernoscendis Historiae Romanae Primordiis Paresertim
mwuk0984	england	1728	COVENS & MORTIER	500	50	59	Regni Angliae et Walliae Principatus Tabula, Divisa in LII Regiones, Anglice Shire, Dictas
mwsc0714	scandinavia sweden	1721	COVENS & MORTIER	400	42	53	Regni Gothiae, Tabula Generalis
mwuk0807	uk	1728	COVENS & MORTIER	675	50	59	Regnorum Magnae Britanniae, sive Angliae, Scotiae, nec non Hiberniae Nuperrima Delineatiop; Geographice Constructa et in Lucem Edita
mwsp0082	portugal	1721	COVENS & MORTIER	750	58	48	Regnorum Portugalliae et Algarbiae Tabula
mwsc0126	scandinavia	1721	COVENS & MORTIER	7200	102	125	Regnorum Sueciae Daniae et Norvegiae (copy of Gerritsz 1630, but different cartouche and title)
mwbp0037	baltic sea (east)	1714	COVENS & MORTIER	400	47	61	Seconde Carte des Courones du Nord qui Comprend le Royaume de Danemark &c.
mwru0507a	ukraine	1720	COVENS & MORTIER	350	49	62	Seconde Partie de la Crimee la Mer Noire &c. Rectifies par Diverses Observations Faite par Guillaume de l'Isle
mwsam0359	south america brazil	1730	COVENS & MORTIER	850	38	50	Sinus Omnium Sanctoru (copy of Blaeu 1662)
mwbp0425	poland	1741	COVENS & MORTIER	450	48	57	Sup.s et Inferioris Ducatus Silesiae (inset plan of Breslau)
mwe1020	europe rhine	1725	COVENS & MORTIER	785	95	116	Teatre de la Guerre sur le Rhein, Moessele, Mayn, & le Necker. Sur les Memoires du Sr. Sanson
mwme0296	holy land	1730	COVENS & MORTIER	650	40	52	Terra Promissa
mwme0274	holy land	1721	COVENS & MORTIER	450	36	48	Terre de Canaan, a present la Palestine (north to the right)
mwit1196	italy veneto	1720	COVENS & MORTIER	250	38	49	Territoire de Trevigiano
mwru0520	ukraine	1740	COVENS & MORTIER	960	92	62	Theatre de la Guerre dans la Petite Tartarie, la Crimee, la Mer Noire (in 2 sheets, total size given)
mwbh0612	belgium holland	1730	COVENS & MORTIER	800	96	120	Theatre de la Guerre en Flandre, & Brabant, les Pays Conquis, et le Bas-Rhein, &c.
mwru0178	russia	1737	COVENS & MORTIER	400	48	66	Theatre de la Guerre Faite en 1737 / Carte Exacte de la Chersonese Taurique ... avec la Route de l'Armee Russienne
mwsp0256a	spain	1730	COVENS & MORTIER	3000	96	118	Theatre de la guerre en Espagne et en Portugal
mwe0793	europe east	1738	COVENS & MORTIER	400	46	63	Theatre de la Guerre sur les Rivieres de Dnieper, Tira et Danube
mwru0525b	ukraine	1740	COVENS & MORTIER	850	49	64	Theatrum Belli a.o MDCCXXXVII (copy of Du Chaffat's map)
mwe0794	europe east	1738	COVENS & MORTIER	750	49	63	Theatrum Belli ad Borysthenem Tyram & Danubium
mwaf0164	africa	1730	COVENS & MORTIER	720	43	54	Totius Africae Accuratissima (re-issue of De Wit's 1680 map)
mwgr0425	greece crete	1721	COVENS & MORTIER	280	27	35	Vesting van Retimo
mwgm0103	guatemala	1721	COVENS & MORTIER	800	41	50	Yucatan Conventus Iuridici Hispaniae Novae Pars Occidentalis, et Guatimala Conventus Iuridicus
mwuk0815	uk	1740	COWLEY	650	43	52	A Hydrographical Description or Chart of the Sea Coasts of Great Britain
mwam0385	america north	1734	COWLEY	550	23	39	A Map of North America from the Best Authorities
mwam0387	america north	1740	COWLEY	550	11	13	A Map of the British Plantations in Canada, Florida &c.
mww0453	world	1761	COWLEY	400	15	25	A Map of the World from the Best Authorities
mwec0295a	uk england devon	1744	COWLEY	140	14	18	An Improved Map of Devon-Shire
mwec0628	uk england kent	1744	COWLEY	140	12	17	An Improved Map of Kent
mwec1141	uk england surrey	1744	COWLEY	180	14	19	An improved Map of the County of Surrey
mwuss0831	massachusetts	1780	COWLEY	200	24	15	Battle at Bunkers Hill
mwec0014	uk england bedfordshire	1744	COWLEY	200	17	14	Bedfordshire
mwuk1832	wales	1744	COWLEY	80	17	14	Breconshire

AMPG REFERENCE	REGION	DATE	MAP MAKER	PRICE (UK£)	VERT. (cm.)	HOR. (cm.)	TITLE OF MAP (Comments by the editor in brackets)
mwec0101	uk england cambridgeshire	1744	COWLEY	240	17	14	Cambridgeshire
mwec0372	uk england durham	1744	COWLEY	240	17	14	Durham
mwec0479	uk england hampshire	1744	COWLEY	180	14	18	Hampshire
mwec0748	uk england lincolnshire	1744	COWLEY	240	17	14	Lincolnshire
mwgm0238	mexico	1777	COWLEY	360	7	13	Mexico or New Spain, New Mexico &c.
mwec0829	uk england norfolk	1744	COWLEY	240	17	14	Norfolk
mwec0916	uk england nottinghamshire	1744	COWLEY	160	14	18	Nottinghamshire
mwec0956	uk england oxfordshire	1744	COWLEY	280	17	14	Oxfordshire
mwuk1833	wales	1744	COWLEY	160	17	14	Pembrokeshire
mwec1074	uk england staffordshire	1744	COWLEY	240	17	14	Staffordshire
mwec1334	uk england yorkshire	1744	COWLEY	200	14	18	Yorkshire
mwuss0213	carolinas	1780	COWLEY, R.	450	19	19	Charles Town, South Carolina, with a Chart of the Bars & Harbour
mwgm0354c	mexico	1846	COWPERTHWAIT	960	20	27	Map of Mexico including Yucatan
mwuss1542	texas	1850	COWPERTHWAIT, DESILVER	500	32	40	Map of the State of Texas from the Latest Authorities
mwsw0198	switzerland	1790	COXE	375	52	76	Carte de la Suisse, ou l'on Marque les Routes Suivies par Mre. Wil. Coxe, dans ses Quatre Voyages en 1776, 1779, 1785 et 1786
mwru0266b	russia	1780	COXE	235	13	34	Chart of Shalaurof's Voyage. Northern or Frozen Ocean
mwsw0242	alps	1789	COXE	500	41	50	Mont Blanc, and the Adjacent Alps
mwru0393	russia moscow	1780	COXE	480	30	33	Plan de Moskow
mwru0266a	russia	1780	COXE	375	26	30	Plan de St. Petersbourg
mwaf1257	africa west	1845	COYLE	80	44	61	Map of Liberia Compiled from Data on File in the Office of the American Colonization Society
mwam1168	america north (east)	1813	CRADDOCK & JOY	480	38	38	Map of the British Settlements and the United States of North America, from the Coast of Labrador to Florida
mwme1059	turkey etc	1832	CRAMER	785	61	95	Asia vulgo Minor Dicta Antiqua et Nova cum Insulis Adjacentibus
mwgr0249	greece	1827	CRAMER	1500	125	99	Graecia Antiqua et Nova una cum Insulis Circumjacentibus
mwsc0466	scandinavia greenland	1767	CRANTZ	300	18	25	Nova Groenlandiae Tabula a 59° Gradu usque ad 73°
mwsc0467	scandinavia greenland	1767	CRANTZ	360	17	23	The Western Coast of Greenland, from Ball's River to the Ice Glance
mwwi0719	jamaica	1763	CRASKELL & SIMPSON	3000	97	122	Map of the County of Middlesex in the Island of Jamaica
mwwi0720	jamaica	1763	CRASKELL & SIMPSON	5000	96	230	To the Right Honorable ... this Map of the Island of Jamaica
mwit0646	italy piedmont	1668	CRASSUS	960	32	46	Carta del le tre Valli di Piemonte (north to the right)
mwuk1068	england	1840	CREIGHTON	280	105	89	A Map of England & Wales
mwuk1310	england london	1831	CREIGHTON	750	35	47	A Plan of London and its Environs (4 editions until 1848)
mwam0144	america continent	1735	CREPY	2400	52	65	Amerique
mwf0989	france poitou	1767	CREPY	550	49	68	Carte de la Province de Poitou le Pays d'Aunis
mwf1158	france rhone-alpes	1767	CREPY	300	50	71	Carte du Dauphine le Duche de Savoye Principaute de Piemont
mwit0512a	italy lombardy	1735	CREPY	800	52	68	Carte du Theatre de la Guerre en Italie qui comprend les Duchées de Milan, de Mantoue, de Parme
mwam0944	america north (east)	1742	CREPY	1250	52	51	Carte Generale de l'Amerique Septentrionale avec les Possessions Angloises dans cette Partie du Nouveau Monde, Dressee sur la Carte de Pople, Publiee a Londres en 20 Feuilles, pour Servir a l'Intelligence de la Guerre Presente
mwas0143	asia continent	1735	CREPY	675	53	67	Cartes de l'Asie avec lEttendue de ses Principaux Pais qui sont la Turquie Asiatique lArabie la Perse la Georgie la Grande Tartarie la Chine lInde et les Isles
mwbp0129	baltic states	1759	CREPY	240	20	28	Curlande Partie Occidentale
mwme1027	turkey etc	1780	CREPY	400	21	30	Destroit des Dardanelles ou des Chateaux Appelle encor Gallipoli (view)
mwbh0879	luxembourg	1767	CREPY	300	21	28	Duche de Luxembourg
mwg0385	bavaria	1759	CREPY	180	21	28	Environs de Munich
mwbp0487	poland	1773	CREPY	200	21	28	Etat Present du Royaume de Pologne, avec les Possessions Nouvelles de l'Empereur, de l'Imperatrice de Russie, et du Roy de Prusse
mwg0831	westphalia	1759	CREPY	300	28	21	Eveche de Munster
mwg0658	saxony	1759	CREPY	180	24	21	Eveche de Osnabruck
mwwi0726	jamaica / bermuda	1767	CREPY	280	20	27	La Jamaique aux Anglois / La Bermude aux Anglois (2 maps on one sheet)
mwaf0221	africa	1767	CREPY	200	23	29	L'Afrique Suivant les Nouvelles Observations
mwam0440	america north	1767	CREPY	550	27	20	L'Amerique Septentrionale
mwf0364	france brittany	1767	CREPY	350	48	63	Le Duche de Bretagne Divisee en Haute et Basse et en ses Neuf Eveches
mwbh0630a	belgium holland	1735	CREPY	400	50	63	Les Comtez de Hainaut
mwuk0816	uk	1740	CREPY	800	52	68	Les Isles Britanniques Comprenant les Royaumes d'Angleterre, Ecosse et Irlande
mwe0188	europe	1767	CREPY	200	20	28	L'Europe
mww0471	world	1767	CREPY	950	23	30	Mappe Monde qui Comprend les Nouvelles Decouvertes Faites jusqua ce Jour (copy of Le Rouge 1748)

AMPG REFERENCE	REGION	DATE	MAP MAKER	PRICE (UK£)	VERT. (cm.)	HOR. (cm.)	TITLE OF MAP (Comments by the editor in brackets)
mwf0891	france paris	1775	CREPY	600	29	40	Nouveau Plan de la Ville et Faubourg de Paris
mwf0868	france paris	1741	CREPY	8000	100	145	Nouveau Plan de Paris et ses Nouvelles Limites
mwf0876	france paris	1750	CREPY	1250	52	68	Nouveau Plan Routier de la Ville et Faubourg de Paris
mwbh0857	luxembourg	1730	CREPY	420	33	42	Plan de Luxembourg
mwf0886	france paris	1767	CREPY	300	22	28	Plan de Paris et de ses Faubourgs
mwit0174	italy	1740	CREPY	1000	49	64	Premiere Planche de l'Italie Contenant ... des Remarques Historiques et Chronologiques des Personnes
mwca0508	canada quebec	1755	CREPY	1200	18	22	Quebec
mwca0252	canada arctic	1854	CRESSWELL	1800	36	46	(first chart of the complete Northwest Passage, by artist Samuel Cresswell on HMS Investigator)
mwgr0403a	greece crete	1670	CREUZ	650	31	39	Candia (view. Title above: 'Die Uhralte Christen= aber nun von dem Türcken überwundene Stat Candia')
mwuss0136	california	1850	CROCKER	7200	38	91	(San Francisco view)
mwp0343	pacific hawaii	1825	CROCKER & BREWSTER	480	19	15	Hawaii. The Outline from Vancouver; Improved by the Deputation
mwf0594	france ile de france	1785	CROISEY	1685	57	98	Nouveau Plan de Versailles
mwin0249	india	1770	CROISEY	1650	58	91	Theatre de la Guerre dans l'Inde sur la Coste de Coromandel (north to the right)
mwe0205	europe	1782	CROME	850	54	71	Neue Carte von Europa, welche die Merkwurdigsten Producte und Vornehmsten Handelsplatze ... Enthalt
mwuk0939	england	1682	CROSS	350	25	29	An Exact Map of England with the Roads from London
mwp0086	australia	1827	CROSS	9000	94	63	Chart of part of New South Wales with Plans of the Harbours.
mww0674a	world	1825	CROSS	1250	18	22	Chart of the World, on Mercator's Projection. Illustrative of the Impolicy of Slavery
mwp0077a	australia	1826	CROSS	3000	80	76	Chart of Van Dieman's Land Compiled from the most authentic documents extant
mwuk1322	england london	1837	CROSS	650	43	68	Cross's London Guide (4 editions until 1851)
mwuk1306	england london	1828	CROSS	900	63	98	Cross's New Plan of London (15 editions until 1864)
mwp0077	australia	1825	CROSS	9000	78	61	Map of Part of New South Wales (incl. inset views)
mwp0089	australia	1828	CROSS	2000	107	68	Plan of the Australian Agricultural Company's Grant at Port Stephens, New South Wales
mwaf0334	africa	1841	CRUCHLEY	100	37	44	Africa
mwas0255	asia continent	1841	CRUCHLEY	100	36	44	Asia
mwme0421	holy land	1841	CRUCHLEY	100	43	36	Canaan or the Land of Promise as Divided among the Tribes
mwuk1299	england london	1824	CRUCHLEY	800	87	89	Cruchley's Environs of London Extending Thirty Miles from the Metropolis (13 editions until 1894)
mwuk1067	england	1838	CRUCHLEY	600	99	70	Cruchley's Improved Geographical Companion throughout England and Wales Including Part of Scotland
mwuk0888	uk	1832	CRUCHLEY	720			Cruchley's New Map of the British Isles, showing the present state of the Parliamentary Representation
mwuk1307	england london	1828	CRUCHLEY	5000	120	144	Cruchley's New Plan of London and its environs (15 editions until 1851. Illustrated is 1847 edition.)
mwuk1302	england london	1826	CRUCHLEY	960	44	61	Cruchley's new plan of London improved to ...(2 editions, 1826/1827)
mwuk1303	england london	1826	CRUCHLEY	2000	44	91	Cruchley's new plan of London improved to ... Including the East and West India Docks (14 editions until 1846)
mwuk1320a	england london	1836	CRUCHLEY	2400	51	136	Cruchley's New Plan of London Improved to 1836 (incl. separate 48pp index, 8vo.)
mwuk1304	england london	1827	CRUCHLEY	850	36	53	Cruchley's New Plan of London Shewing All the New and Intended Improvements to the Present Time (25 editions until 1856)
mwec0213	uk england cornwall	1840	CRUCHLEY	400	102	130	Cruchley's Reduced Ordnance Survey Map of Parts of Cornwall and Devon
mwp0130	australia	1840	CRUCHLEY	100	30	24	New South Wales
mwru0365	russia	1842	CRUCHLEY	100	47	37	Russia in Europe
mwme0894	syria etc	1841	CRUCHLEY	150	44	35	Syria
mww0689	world	1830	CRUCHLEY	450	52	64	The World
mwwi0203	west indies	1842	CRUCHLEY	100	37	44	West Indies
mwbh0621a	belgium holland	1734	CRUQUIUS	720	65	54	Het Eylandt West-Voorn of Goedereede (shown above left)
mwbh0776	belgium holland	1808	CRUTTWELL	100	34	39	Belgium, or the Netherlands
mwbh0777	belgium holland	1808	CRUTTWELL	100	34	39	Holland.
mwsc0195	scandinavia	1808	CRUTTWELL	120	42	34	Sweden, Denmark, and Norway
mww0633	world	1808	CRUTTWELL	300	26	46	The World
mwam1128a	america north (east)	1799	CRUTTWELL	450	35	40	United States of America
mwgm0370b	mexico	1858	CUBAS	960	49	63	Carta General de la Republica Mexicana formada para el estudio de la configuracion y division interior de su territorio.
mwit0769	italy rome	1848	CUCCIONI	650	54	64	Pianta Topografica della Citta' di Roma coll' Aggiunta delle Antichita' Recentemente Scoperte
mwgm0259	mexico	1787	CULLEN	500	25	34	Lakes of Mexico
mwam0581	america north	1810	CUMMINGS & HILLIARD	300	27	20	North America
mwam0589	america north	1813	CUMMINGS & HILLIARD	300	23	27	The United States of America

AMPG REFERENCE	REGION	DATE	MAP MAKER	PRICE (UK£)	VERT. (cm.)	HOR. (cm.)	TITLE OF MAP (Comments by the editor in brackets)
mwuss1230	new york	1835	CURRIER	600	41	10	(Hudson River)
mwe0869	europe hungary	1625	CUSTODIS	650	28	38	Abriss dess Konigreichs Ober und Nider Ungern sampt den Angrentzenden Landen zur Nachricht der Kriegslaufften
mwuk0692	uk	1627	CUSTODIS	1250	27	31	Angliae Scotiae et Hiberniae sive Britannicarum Insularum (updated version of Deutecum's 1605 map)
mwf0044	france	1627	CUSTODIS	550	27	31	Descriptio Galliae cum Confinys Regionibus. 1626
mwbh0210	belgium holland	1627	CUSTODIS	550	27	32	Flandria Comitatus
mwit0075	italy	1626	CUSTODIS	550	23	31	Italiae Nova et Exacta Descriptio
mwuk1106	england london	1623	CUSTODIS	1800	27	32	Lunden (view)
mwbp0228	poland	1625	CUSTODIS	550	27	32	Prussia Lat - Preussen Ger
mwjk0002	japan	1586	CYSAT		27	41	Der Grossen Namhafften Neuwlicherfurenen Iapponischen Insel
mwe1120	europe slovak republic (moravia)	1762	CZAKI	1800	44	56	(Spis) Mappa Geographica Repraesentans Partem Hungariae Nempe sic Dictum Comitatum de Zips qua Starostia Spisk
mwit0038	italy	1582	DA PALMA		39	51	Italia (re-issued 1610 by Ferrante)
mwam1270	great lakes	1672	DABLON	36000	34	46	Lac Superieur et Autres Lieux ou Sont les Missions des Peres de la Compagnie des Iesus Comprises sous le Nom d'Outaovacs
mwuss0327	connecticut	1848	DAGGETT	520	49	55	Map of Connecticut (first published c1827)
mwsc0684a	scandinavia sweden	1667	DAHLBERG	1800	28	264	(Stockholm. Panoramic view in 12 joined sheets)
mwsc0696b	scandinavia sweden	1693	DAHLBERG	1000	24	78	Stokholmia
mwsc0093	scandinavia	1696	DAHLBERG	600	27	33	Veteris Orbis Arctoi Typus
mwf0475	france corsica	1700	DAL RE	1800	49	75	(Untitled map of Corsica)
mwm0270	mediterranean west	1700	DAL RE	1200	41	32	Coste del Mediteraneo dello Stretto di Gibilterra sino a Tolone, con l'Isola di Minora, a Pianta di Porto Mahone (3 maps on one sheet)
mwp0030	australia	1791	DALRYMPLE	450	30	23	(Tasmania) Plan of Oyster Bay and Part of Marias Islands by Capt. J.H. Cox 1789
mwc0179	china	1771	DALRYMPLE	750	50	55	A Chart of Part of the Coast of China and the Adjacent Islands from Pedro Blanco to the Mizen
mwc0184	china	1775	DALRYMPLE	1350	66	48	A Chart of the China Sea Inscribed to Monsr. d'Apres de Mannevillette the Ingenious Author of the Neptune Oriental: As a Tribute Due to his Labours for the Benefit of Navigation
mwc0219	china	1796	DALRYMPLE	500	54	34	A Chart of the Islands to the Southward of Tchu-San on the Eastern Coast of China Generally Laid down from one Published by Alexander Dalrymple Esqre. with Additions and Alterations by J. Barrow
mwas0521	asia south east	1798	DALRYMPLE	450	29	22	A Chart of the Strait of Allass Constructed from Observations made in March 1796
mwas0593	asia south east borneo	1769	DALRYMPLE	900	47	62	A Mar of Part of Borneo and the Sooloo Archipelago: Laid down Chiefly from Observations Made in 1761, 2, 3, and 4 by A. Dalrymple ('Mar' for 'Map' in title)
mwgm0259b	mexico	1790	DALRYMPLE	10000	56	48	Chart of California by Miguel Costansó 1770 entitled Carta Reducida del Oceano Asiático ó Mar del Súr
mwas0594	asia south east borneo	1770	DALRYMPLE	600	61	47	... Chart of Felicia and Plan of the Island of Balambangan
mwas0893	asia south east sumatra	1783	DALRYMPLE	350	29	18	Chart of Part of the Islands of Pora ... and Poggys
mwp0187	new zealand	1781	DALRYMPLE	1200	29	37	Plan of the Bay of Lauriston on New-Zeland (first British Admiralty chart of NZ, based on a French manuscript drawn in 1769) (NW part of North Island)
mwjk0120	japan	1788	DALRYMPLE	450	29	32	Plan of the Harbour of Nangasaky in Japan ... in 1762 by Capt. Alexander Hume
mwp0022	australia	1780	DALRYMPLE		30	21	Plan of the Island Rottenest ... the West Coast of New Holland, based on Van Keulen 1753 (view and map on one sheet).
mwas0677	asia south east lombok	1784	DALRYMPLE	450	29	19	Sketch of the West Coast of Lombok from a Draught of Raddin Tomoongoong Communicated by John Marsden Esq
mwin0438	indian ocean	1790	DALRYMPLE	300	29	22	Sketch of Vlamingo Road on the East Side of Amsterdam Island
mwas0792	asia south east philippines	1771	DALRYMPLE	875	46	61	The Sooloo Archipelago, Laid down Chiefly from Observations in 1761, 1762, 1763 & 1764
mwuss1183	new york	1815	DAMERUM	8000	58	71	Map of the Southern Part of the State of New York Including Long Island, the Sound, the State of Connecticut
mwwi0067	west indies	1729	DAMPIER	600	15	29	A Map of the Middle Part of America
mwp0380	pacific new guinea	1740	DAMPIER	400	17	41	A View of the Course of Capt. Wil. Dampiers Voyage from Timor round Nova Britannia
mwc0192a	china	1779	DALRYMPLE	200	30	21	Plan of Tien-Pe-Hien on the Coast of China / Gallong or Gelang Bay ... On South Coast of Hainan...
mwin0424	indian ocean	1703	DAMPIER	450	17	29	Capt. Dampier's New Voyage to New Holland &c in 1699
mwas0099	asia continent	1703	DAMPIER	450	17	29	Capt. Dampiers New Voyage to New Holland &c. in 1699 &c.
mwgm0189	mexico	1701	DAMPIER	300	15	27	Carte de la Baye de Campeche
mwgm0393	panama	1715	DAMPIER	200	16	16	Carte de l'Isthme de Darien et du Golfe de Panama
mwas0681	asia south east malacca	1699	DAMPIER	240	15	28	Carte du Detroit de Malacca (re-issue of Moll 1697)

AMPG REFERENCE	REGION	DATE	MAP MAKER	PRICE (UK£)	VERT. (cm.)	HOR. (cm.)	TITLE OF MAP (Comments by the editor in brackets)
mwaf0110	africa	1699	DAMPIER	400	16	30	Een Schets van de Algemeene Passaad-Winden in de Atlantische en Indianshce Zeen
mwas0433	asia south east	1703	DAMPIER	400	15	28	Kaart van Oost Indie
mwp0239	pacific (all)	1699	DAMPIER	400	16	30	Representation du Cours Ordinaire des Vents de Traverse qui Regnent sur les Cotes, dans la Grande Mer du Sud
mwsam0358	south america brazil	1729	DAMPIER	240	15	21	The Great and Small Bay of le Grande. Part of Brazile &c.
mwgm0096	costa rica	1729	DAMPIER	450	17	21	The Gulf of Nicoya, by Some Call'd the Gulf of Salinas
mww0268	world	1698	DAMPIER	800	17	29	Werreld-Kaart Aanwyzende de Koers, van Mr. Dampier Reystogt Rondom den Aardkloot van't Jaar 1679 tot 1691
mwaf0017	africa	1582	D'ANANIA	1500	18	25	Africa (re-issued by Botero in 1596 and by Porro in 1598 with an engraved rule surrounding the entire country)
mwam0011	america continent	1582	D'ANANIA	2500	18	25	America (re-issued by Botero in 1596 and by Porro in 1598 with an engraved rule surrounding the entire continent)
mwas0010	asia continent	1582	D'ANANIA	850	18	25	Asia (re-issued by Botero in 1596)
mwe0014	europe	1582	D'ANANIA	800	18	25	Europa (re-issued by Botero in 1596)
mwam0008	america continent	1573	D'ANANIA	10000	25	19	Peru (but North and South America complete)
mwam0019	america continent	1596	D'ANANIA - MAGINI	500	14	18	America (reduced version of D'Anania 1582)
mwgm0235a	mexico	1772	D'AUTEROCHE	1500	39	52	Plan de la Ville de Mexico (illustration shows reduced size English edition of 1778, 19x25cm)
mwuss1280	ohio	1815	DANBY	1200	32	26	Plan of Cincinatti
mwuk1111	england london	1647	DANCKERTS		45	231	(Panorama of London, engraved by Hollar. A copy was made by Martin in 1832.)
mwgr0125	greece	1700	DANCKERTS	1200	51	61	Accurata totius Archipelagi et Graciae tabula
mwuk0963	england	1700	DANCKERTS	720	53	52	Accuratissima Angliae Regni et Walliae Principatus Descriptio
mwbp0291	poland	1680	DANCKERTS	550	50	57	Accuratissima Ducatus Silesiae
mwme0567a	arabia etc	1680	DANCKERTS	750	49	57	Accuratissima et Maxima Totius Turcici Imperii Tabula
mwe0112	europe	1700	DANCKERTS	1000	49	58	Accuratissima Europae Tabula
mwg0077	germany	1684	DANCKERTS	500	48	56	Accuratissima Germaniae Tabula (re-issue of Caroli-De Wit 1680)
mwm0024	mediterranean	1690	DANCKERTS	3200	50	57	Accuratissima Occidentalioris Districtus Maris Mediterranei Tabula / Accuratissima Orientalioris Districtus Maris Mediterranei Tabula (2 maps)
mwsc0091	scandinavia	1696	DANCKERTS	720	51	59	Accuratissima Regnorum Sueciae, Daniae, et Norvegiae
mwe0997	europe rhine	1660	DANCKERTS	785	99	58	Accuratissima Rheni Inferioris Mosae et Mosellae Tabula / Accuratissima Rheni Superioris Mosae et Mosellae
mwas0077	asia continent	1690	DANCKERTS	700	50	58	Accuratissima Totius Asiae Tabula Recens Emendata per I. Danckerts
mwsp0229	spain	1706	DANCKERTS	2400	50	86	Accuratissima Totius Regni Hispaniae Tabula
mwsp0182	spain	1660	DANCKERTS	960	48	56	Accuratissima Totius Regni Hispaniae Tabula
mwme0272	holy land	1721	DANCKERTS	450	35	51	Afbeeldinge van de Veertich-Iaarige Reyse der Kinderen Israels uyt Egypten door de Roode Zee
mwaf0088	africa	1680	DANCKERTS	1600	43	52	Africae Noviss: Cateres Tabula
mwg0187a	germany elbe river	1660	DANCKERTS	450	39	49	Albis Fluvius. Germaniae Celebris, a Fontibus ad Ostia
mwam0096	america continent	1696	DANCKERTS	2500	43	53	Americam Utramque Aliis Correctiorem
mwbh0469	belgium holland	1694	DANCKERTS	2400	47	57	Amstelodamum cum Antiquis et Nuperrimis Pomoeriis
mwm0126	mediterranean east	1660	DANCKERTS	450	34	48	Asiae Minoris Nova Descriptio ... Geographische Beschryvinge Aller Landen, Staden en Plaetzen (historical)
mwe0319	europe austria	1640	DANCKERTS	400	36	53	Austria Archiducatus
mwf0446	france champagne	1700	DANCKERTS	280	59	51	Comté et Gouvernment Generale de Champagne
mwg0353	bavaria	1700	DANCKERTS	350	50	58	Circulus Bavaricus in quo sunt Ducatus Electoratus et Palatinatus Bavariae
mwg0352	bavaria	1696	DANCKERTS	350	50	59	Circulus Franconicus in quo sunt Episcopatus Wurtzburg, Bamberg et Aichstet
mwg0269	baden-wurttemberg	1700	DANCKERTS	300	48	57	Circulus Suevicus in quo sunt Ducatus Wirtenbergensis
mwf0406	france burgundy	1700	DANCKERTS	400	60	50	Comitatus Burgundiae, vulgo la Franche Comte
mwbh0243a	belgium holland	1635	DANCKERTS	650	41	51	Comitatus Flandriae Nova Tabula (based on Hondius)
mwbh0400	belgium holland	1680	DANCKERTS	800	45	54	Comitatus Hollandiae Tabula Pluribus Locis Recens Emendata a Iusto Danckerts
mwsc0312a	scandinavia denmark	1690	DANCKERTS	600	50	59	Dania Regnum (close copy of De Wit 1680)
mwsc0272	scandinavia denmark	1657	DANCKERTS	750	38	49	Daniae Regni Typus
mwme0273	holy land	1721	DANCKERTS	400	35	51	De Gelegentheyt van 't Paradys en 't Landt Canaan (based on Moxon 1671. First issued by Danckerts 1710. This issue publ. by Wetstein. Shown below left)
mwme0484	jerusalem	1721	DANCKERTS	550	35	51	De Stadt Jerusalem
mww0270	world	1700	DANCKERTS	3800	36	51	De Werelt Caart
mwit0584	italy north	1690	DANCKERTS	685	50	60	Dominii Veneti in Italia in Partes
mwg0619	saxony	1690	DANCKERTS	600	49	57	Ducatus Bremae & Ferdae Maximaeque Partis Fluminus Ulsurgis Descriptio per Cornelium Danckerts
mwbh0245	belgium holland	1636	DANCKERTS	450	39	50	Ducatus Geldriae Novissima Descriptio. Auct. Balth. Flor. a Berkenrode
mwbh0273	belgium holland	1640	DANCKERTS	400	38	49	Ducatus Limburg
mwg0622	saxony	1700	DANCKERTS	400	49	59	Ducatus Luneburgensis ... Pars Septentrionalis Germaniae
mwbh0843	luxembourg	1690	DANCKERTS	800	51	59	Ducatus Lutzenburgi Nova et Accurata Tabula
mwit0492	italy lombardy	1700	DANCKERTS	600	50	57	Ducatus Mantuensis
mwit0493	italy lombardy	1700	DANCKERTS	600	48	58	Ducatus Mediolanensis Parmensis et Montisferrati

AMPG REFERENCE	REGION	DATE	MAP MAKER	PRICE (UK£)	VERT. (cm.)	HOR. (cm.)	TITLE OF MAP (Comments by the editor in brackets)
mwbp0337	poland	1700	DANCKERTS	450	49	57	Ducatus Pomeraniae Tabula Generalis
mwbp0325	poland	1696	DANCKERTS	500	46	59	Ducatus Prussiae tam Polono Regiae quam Ducalis Brandenburgo Novissima Descriptio
mwbp0104	baltic states	1700	DANCKERTS	875	49	58	Ducatuum Livoniae et Curlandiae
mwe1011	europe rhine	1700	DANCKERTS	1000	45	57	D'Voornaamste Fortresse aen de Rivier den Rhyn (shows 20 town plans)
mwe0778	europe east	1700	DANCKERTS	800	43	59	D'Voornaamste Fortressen van Hungaria
mwgr0126	greece	1700	DANCKERTS	1500	44	59	D'Voornaamste Fortresses van Morea
mwg0814	westphalia	1700	DANCKERTS	350	60	50	Episcopatus Monasteriensis et Osnabrugensis nec non Comitatuum Bentheim Teckelenburg Stenford Lingen Diepholt Delmenhorst Ritberg etc. Tabula
mwas0073	asia continent	1685	DANCKERTS	750	47	50	Exactissima Asiae Delineatio
mwe0717	europe danube	1700	DANCKERTS	650	50	50	Exactissima Totius Danubii Fluvii Tabula
mwf0229	france alsace	1696	DANCKERTS	350	59	50	Exactissima Totius Mosellae
mwit0421	italy liguria	1660	DANCKERTS	2000	37	52	Genoa
mwg0054b	germany	1642	DANCKERTS	4000	46	56	Germania Nova ac accurata (map by J. Cloppenburgh, close copy of Visscher)
mwme0260	holy land	1718	DANCKERTS	400	35	50	Het Beloofde Landt Canaan
mwbh0330	belgium holland	1656	DANCKERTS	1000	39	51	Hollandia Comitatus
mwwi0041	west indies	1696	DANCKERTS	2000	50	58	Insulae Americanae, Nempe: Cuba, Hispaniola, Jamaica, Pto Rico, Lucania, Antillae vulgo Caribae, Barlo-et Sotto-Vento, etc.
mwit0087a	italy	1640	DANCKERTS	6000	41	56	Italiae, Sardiniae, Corsicae et Confinium Regionum Nova Tabula, Effigies Praeciparum Urbiu et Habituum Inibi Final Complectens (Carte-a-figures borders on three sides. Re-issue of Blaeu's 1606 map.)
mwme0213	holy land	1696	DANCKERTS	950	51	58	Iudaea sive Terra Sancta quae Israelitarum
mwf0225	france alsace	1690	DANCKERTS	350	57	48	Landgraviatus Alsatiae Superioris et Inferioris Tabula qua Simul Sundgovia Brisigovia et Ortenavia
mwg0451a	hessen	1690	DANCKERTS	400	49	62	Landgraviatus Hassiae
mwf0608a	france languedoc	1696	DANCKERTS	580	63	53	Le Theatre de la Guerre dans les Sevennes avec les Montagne et les Plaines des environs de Languedoc
mwsp0039	portugal	1660	DANCKERTS	1200	40	51	Lisbona (view)
mwg0635	saxony	1720	DANCKERTS	300	50	59	Marchionatus Misniae
mwit1055b	italy naples	1660	DANCKERTS	1200	40	51	Neapolis
mwsc0590	scandinavia norway	1690	DANCKERTS	785	59	51	Norvegia Regnum
mwbh0329	belgium holland	1653	DANCKERTS	650	38	48	Nouvelle et Exacte Carte du Duche de Brabant, l'Annee 1635. A Amsterdam, Chez Corneille Dankert
mwf0784	france normandy	1700	DANCKERTS	400	50	58	Nova et Accurata Normandiae Ducatus Tabula
mwsp0180e	spain	1650	DANCKERTS	2800	41	56	Nova et Accurata Tabula Hispaniae Praecipuis Urbibus Vestitu Insignibus, et Antiquitatibus Exornata per Cornelium Dankerum (carte-a-figure borders on three sides)
mwe0071	europe	1660	DANCKERTS	720	47	56	Nova et Accurata totius Europae
mwe0879	europe hungary	1657	DANCKERTS	2800	39	53	Nova et Recens Emendata Totius Regni Ungariae una cum Adjacentibus et Finitimis Regionibus Excudebat C. Dankertz (two views of Budapest at top).
mwe0054	europe	1643	DANCKERTS	1400	45	56	Nova Europae Descriptio. Auctore Cornelis Dankertz
mwsc0700	scandinavia sweden	1700	DANCKERTS	400	51	61	Nova Gothiae Australis sive Scaniae
mwme0798	persia etc	1700	DANCKERTS	720	47	56	Nova Persiae, Armeniae, Natoliae et Arabiae Descriptio
mwuk0745	uk	1685	DANCKERTS	24000	87	105	Nova Totius Angliae, Scotiae, et Hiberniae, Tabula
mwbp0282	poland	1670	DANCKERTS	1200	39	51	Nova Totius Regni Poloniae Magniq. Ducatus Prussiae et Lithuaniae, cum suis Palatinatibus ac Confiniis
mww0228	world	1685	DANCKERTS	6500	49	58	Nova Totius Terrarum Orbis Tabula Amstelodami per I. Danckerts cum Privil. (updated version of De Wit 1770 ref. mww0190)
mwe0760	europe east	1645	DANCKERTS	850	48	58	Nova Transilvaniae Principatus Tabula
mwam0893	america north (east)	1690	DANCKERTS	9000	46	55	Novi Belgii Novaeque Angliae nec non Pennsylvaniae et Partis Virginiae Tabula
mwuk1481	uk english channel (all)	1700	DANCKERTS	1100	51	60	Novissima et Accuratissima Canalis inter Angliae et Galliae Tabula
mwsw0092	switzerland	1690	DANCKERTS	720	49	57	Novissima et Accuratissima Helvetiae, Rhaetiae, Valesiae et Partis Sabaudiae Tabula
mwbh0400b	belgium holland	1680	DANCKERTS	400	50	58	Novissima et Accuratissima Namurci (shown above left)
mwam0078	america continent	1675	DANCKERTS	1600	49	57	Novissima et Accuratissima Totius Americae Descriptio
mwuk0746	uk	1685	DANCKERTS	1200	50	58	Novissima et Accuratissima Totius Angliae, Scotiae et Hiberniae Tabula
mwit0115	italy	1690	DANCKERTS	720	50	58	Novissima et Accuratissima Totius Italiae Corsicae et Sardiniae Desc.
mwru0102	russia	1690	DANCKERTS	600	49	57	Novissima et Accuratissima Totius Russiae vulgo Muscoviae Tabula
mwbh0400a	belgium holland	1680	DANCKERTS	800	48	56	Novissima et Accuratissima XVII Provinciarum Germaniae Inferioris Tabula
mwaf0112	africa	1700	DANCKERTS	675	49	57	Novissima et Perfectissima Africae Descriptio (close copy of De Wit 1680)
mwbh0447	belgium holland	1690	DANCKERTS	550	51	58	Novissima Flandriae Comitatus Tabula

AMPG REFERENCE	REGION	DATE	MAP MAKER	PRICE (UK£)	VERT. (cm.)	HOR. (cm.)	TITLE OF MAP (Comments by the editor in brackets)
mwsp0040	portugal	1660	DANCKERTS	500	41	53	Novissima Regnorum Portugalliae et Algarbiae Descriptio
mwsp0047	portugal	1680	DANCKERTS	785	58	50	Novissima Regnorum Portugalliae et Algarbiae Descriptio
mww0167	world	1658	DANCKERTS	9000	31	47	Orbis Terrarum Typus de Integro in Plurimis Emendatus, Auctus et Icunculis Illustratus
mwgr0127	greece	1700	DANCKERTS	2000	60	89	Peloponnesus hodie Moreae Regnum ...
mwgr0099b	greece	1685	DANCKERTS	720	51	60	Peloponnesus hodie Moreae Regnum ...
mwsp0041	portugal	1660	DANCKERTS	650	43	54	Portugallia et Algarbia quae olim Lusitania Novissima Descriptio
mwe0540	europe czech republic (bohemia)	1660	DANCKERTS	1400	40	51	Praga
mwsp0481	spain regions	1696	DANCKERTS	900	46	56	Principatus Cataloniae et comitatus Ruscinonis
mwbh0488	belgium holland	1700	DANCKERTS	720	49	58	Provinciae Belgii Regii Distincte
mwe1144	europe south east	1690	DANCKERTS	550	50	58	Regni Hungariae, Graeciae, et Moreae
mwbp0326	poland	1696	DANCKERTS	800	49	58	Regni Poloniae et Ducatus Lithuaniae
mwbp0338	poland	1700	DANCKERTS	720	51	59	Regni Poloniae et Ducatus Lithuaniae, Voliniae, Podoliae, Ucraniae, Prussiae et Curlandiae
mwit0913	italy sicily	1700	DANCKERTS	1350	48	57	Regni Siciliae et insulae Maltae et Gozae (inset of Malta)
mwe0550	europe czech republic (bohemia)	1690	DANCKERTS	550	50	59	Regnum Bohemia eique Annexae Provinciae
mwsp0523	spain regions	1720	DANCKERTS	685	48	56	Regnum Castellae Novae Andalusiae, Granadae et Algarbiae nec non Maxime Partis Portugalliae et Extremadurae
mwit1017	italy south	1695	DANCKERTS	800	57	49	Regnum Neapolis Siciliae et Lipariae Insulae Multis Locis Correctae Novissima Descriptio (inset of Sicily)
mwit0718	italy rome	1660	DANCKERTS	1200	40	51	Roma
mwf1036	france provence	1702	DANCKERTS	1000	50	59	Sedes Belli in Dauphinae et Provincae
mwit1112	italy tuscany	1700	DANCKERTS	720	49	60	Status Ecclesiasticus et Magnus Ducatus Thoscanae
mwbh0489	belgium holland	1700	DANCKERTS	550	50	58	Tabula Episcopatuum Leodiensis et Coloniensis Trevirensis ut et Ducatuum Juliacensis et Montensis
mwg0716	schleswig-holstein	1700	DANCKERTS	500	50	59	Tabula Generalis Holsatiae
mwit0123	italy	1695	DANCKERTS	800	50	58	Tabula Italiae Corsicae, Sardiniae et adjacentium regorum nova et accurata descriptio
mwuk1107	england london	1633	DANCKERTS	4800	33	42	The Cittie of London (3 revised editions until 1710 with changed titles)
mwaf0099	africa	1690	DANCKERTS	720	49	58	Totius Africae Accuratissima Tabula (copy of De Wit 1680)
mwe1006	europe rhine	1690	DANCKERTS	500	50	58	Totius Fluminus Rheni Novissima Descriptio
mwit1225	italy venice	1661	DANCKERTS	3000	41	51	Venetia
mwbh0274	belgium holland	1640	DANCKERTS	875	40	51	Zeelandia Comitatus
mww0134	world	1628	DANCKERTS & TAVERNIER	60000	52	91	Charte Universelle de Tout le Monde
mwg0706a	schleswig-holstein	1652	DANCKWERTH	950	44	59	Das Ambt Tondern ohne Lundtofft Herde
mwg0059	germany	1652	DANCKWERTH	480	41	57	Germania Antiqua Australis
mwg0704	schleswig-holstein	1650	DANCKWERTH	2000	43	59	Newe Landtcarte von denbeiden Hertzogthumbern Schleswieg und Holstein zusamen ... 1650 (18 town plans at sides. Illustrated is Blaeu 1662 re-issue.)
mwg0705	schleswig-holstein	1652	DANCKWERTH	650	43	58	Newe Landtcarte von der Insull Helgelandt Anno 1649 / Helgeladt in Annis Christi 800, 1200 & 1649 (2 maps on one sheet)
mwg0706	schleswig-holstein	1652	DANCKWERTH	500	42	62	Nova & Accuratissima Ducatus Holsatiae Tabula
mwsc0056	scandinavia	1652	DANCKWERTH	480	43	53	Germania Antiqua Septentrionalis cum Finitimis Regionibus Scythicis et Sarmaticis
mwas0040a	asia	1651	DANCKWERTH	1200	43	53	Orbis Vetus cum Origine Magnarum in Eo Gentium a Filiis et Nepotibus Noe
mwit0684	italy piedmont	1745	DANET	800	40	51	Attaques de Turin par l'Armee du Roy Commandee par le Duc de la Feuillade en 1706 le 30 Juin
mwm0229	mediterranean malta	1723	DANET	2400	45	53	Carte et Plan de l'Isle de Malthe et des Villes et Forts avec les Nouvelles Fortifications ainsy quelle sont a Present
mww0355	world	1729	DANET	5500	49	72	Carte Generale de la Terre ou Mappemonde
mwbh0582	belgium holland	1720	DANET	650	40	53	La Hollande ou les Provinces Unies des Pays Bas ... avec leurs Conquestes sur les Etats Voisins du Roy Catholique et de l'Empire
mwaf0169	africa	1732	DANET	1800	48	71	L'Afrique Dressee sur les Relations & Nouvelles Decouvertes de Differens Voyageurs Conformes aux Observations Astronomiques
mwam0142	america continent	1731	DANET	2500	48	70	L'Amerique Meridionale et Septentrionale (see also revised version by Desnos 1766)
mwas0141	asia continent	1732	DANET	2000	52	73	L'Asie Dressee Sur de nouveaux Memoires Assujetis aux Observations Astronomiq par J. Luillier
mwme0630	arabia etc	1760	DANET	600	49	57	L'Empire des Turcs, en Europe, en Asie, et en Afrique (copy of De Fer 1715)
mwsp0255a	spain	1730	DANET	800	49	61	L'Espagne (map by De Fer)
mwf0114	france	1728	DANET	500	45	49	Les Routes des Postes du Royaume de France
mwe0150	europe	1732	DANET	1800	50	72	L'Europe
mwbp0408	poland	1734	DANET	800	45	55	Plan de Dantzick avec ces Nouvaux Ouvrages
mwuk1162	england london	1727	DANET	2400	43	76	Plan de la Ville de Londres et de Westminster avec le Bourg de Southwark, leurs Faubourgs et leurs Environs

AMPG REFERENCE	REGION	DATE	MAP MAKER	PRICE (UK£)	VERT. (cm.)	HOR. (cm.)	TITLE OF MAP (Comments by the editor in brackets)
mwm0228	mediterranean malta	1723	DANET	1650	40	49	Plan de la Ville de Malthe ses Forts, ses Nouvelles Fortiffications
mwbh0860	luxembourg	1734	DANET	2400	45	53	Plan de Luxembourg Ville Forte Capitale du Duche de Meme Nom
mwwi0001	west indies	1511	D'ANGHIERA		19	28	(No title. First map of the West Indies and the Americas. Ref: 'The Mapping of North America', by Philip Burden.)
mwam0881a	america north east	1685	DANIEL	15000	50	60	A Map of ye English Empire in ye Continent of America (publ. by R. Morden)
mwf0928a	france paris	1841	DANLOS	800	56	79	Carte Routiere des Environs de Paris Indiquant les Differentes Especes de Routes et les Distances
mwaf1263	africa west	1852	D'ANVILLE	120	19	34	A Map of the Gold Coast, from Issimi to Alampi
mww0556	world	1788	D'ANVILLE	600	40	72	A Map of the World, Drawn and Engraved from d'Anville's Two-Sheet Map with Improvements for J. Harrison
mwin0243a	india	1765	D'ANVILLE	250	48	36	Ad Antiquam Indiae Geographicam Tabula
mwaf0519	africa egypt etc	1765	D'ANVILLE	200	49	31	Aegyptus Antiqua Mandato Serenissimi Delphini Publici Juris Facta
mwaf0190	africa	1749	D'ANVILLE	1200	100	97	Afrique Publiee sous les Auspices de Monseigneur le Duc d'Orleans Premier Prince du Sang
mwsam0077	south america	1755	D'ANVILLE	400	42	76	Amazonia Terra Firma, Part Brasil & Peru, Revised by Mr. Bolton
mwsam0068	south america	1748	D'ANVILLE	800	125	77	Amerique Meridionale Publiee sous les Auspices de Monseigneur le Duc d'Orleans
mwam0396	america north	1746	D'ANVILLE	1500	83	86	Amerique Septentrionale Publiee sous les Auspices de Monseigneur le Duc d'Orleans ... MDCCXLVI
mwme1016	turkey etc	1764	D'ANVILLE	375	50	62	Asiae, quae vulgo Minor Dicitur, et Syriae, Tabula Geographica
mwca0069a	canada	1755	D'ANVILLE	2250	87	113	Canada Louisiane et Terres Angloises par le Sr. d'Anville
mwam0198	america continent	1774	D'ANVILLE	450	52	61	Carte d'Amerique Divisees en ses Principales Parties, par G. Delisle
mwaf1185	africa west	1729	D'ANVILLE	200	20	39	Carte de la Coste de Guinee et du Pays autant qu'il est Connu depuis la Riviere de Sierre Leone jusuq'a celle de Camarones
mwsam0632	south america guyana	1773	D'ANVILLE	200	23	32	Carte de la Guiane
mwsam0594	south america guyana	1729	D'ANVILLE	150	34	34	Carte de la Guiane Francoise ou du Gouvernement de Caienne depuis le Cap de Nord jusqu'a la Riviere de Marconi
mwsam0608	south america guyana	1757	D'ANVILLE	200	24	32	Carte de la Guyane
mwuss0629	louisiana	1752	D'ANVILLE	1250	52	92	Carte de la Louisiane par le Sr. d'Anville. Dressee en Mai 1732, Publiee en 1752
mwwi0598	hispaniola	1731	D'ANVILLE	250	24	33	Carte de la Partie de Saint-Domingue Habitee par les Francois
mwaf0397	africa east	1727	D'ANVILLE	500	64	41	Carte de l'Ethiope Orientale Situee sur la Mer des Indes entre le Cap Gaurdafoin et le Cap de Bonne Esperance
mwin0213	india	1752	D'ANVILLE	900	88	104	Carte de l'Inde Dressee pour la Compagnie des Indes par le Sr. d'Anville
mwsam0595	south america guyana	1729	D'ANVILLE	300	32	43	Carte de l'Isle de Caienne et des Rivieres Voisines
mwwi0596	hispaniola	1730	D'ANVILLE	350	29	43	Carte de l'Isle de Saint Domingue avec Partie des Isles Voisines. Dressee sur Diverses Pieces et Instructions ... sur la Derniere Carte de Mr. Frezier, et sur les Memoires de Mr. Buttet
mwwi0068	west indies	1731	D'ANVILLE	300	30	43	Carte des Isles de l'Amerique et de Plusieurs Pays de Terre Ferme
mwru0179	russia	1737	D'ANVILLE	550	24	53	Carte des Pays Traverses par le Cap.ne Beerings depuis Tobolsk jusqu'a Kamtschatka
mwsam0527	south america colombia	1764	D'ANVILLE	200	21	26	Carte des Provinces de Tierra Firme, Darien, Cartagene et Nouvelle Grenade
mwam1032	america north (east)	1776	D'ANVILLE	950	48	65	Carte Generale du Canada, de la Louisiane, de la Floride, de la Caroline, de la Virginie, de la Nouvelle Angleterre etc. par le Sr. d'Anville
mwaf1214	africa west	1751	D'ANVILLE	600	100	70	Carte Particuliere de la Cote Occidentale de l'Afrique depuis le Cap Blanc jusqu'au Cap de Verga, et du Cours des Rivieres de Senega et de Gambie
mwaf1186	africa west	1729	D'ANVILLE	300	55	28	Carte Particuliere de la Partie Principale de la Guinee
mwsam0511	south america colombia	1730	D'ANVILLE	200	20	34	Carte Particuliere de l'Ishtme de Panama, Golfe de Darien, Cote de Carthagene jusqu'a Ste. Marthe
mwaf1190	africa west	1731	D'ANVILLE	200	26	34	Carte Particuliere des Royaumes d'Angola de Matemba et de Benguela
mwin0218	india	1753	D'ANVILLE	450	50	51	Coromandel. Par le Sr. d'Anville
mwaf0520	africa egypt etc	1765	D'ANVILLE	350	67	41	Egypte Nomme dans le Pays Missir
mwas0323	asia caspian sea	1754	D'ANVILLE	450	51	25	Essai d'une nouvelle carte de la Mer Caspienne
mwf0131	france	1760	D'ANVILLE	100	45	57	Gallia Antiqua ex Aevi Romani Monumentis Eruta, et Serenissimi Carnutum Ducis
mwe1205	europe west	1782	D'ANVILLE	250	51	47	Germanie, France, Italie, Espagne, Isles Britanniques (historical map)
mwme0826	persia etc	1776	D'ANVILLE	300	28	44	Golfe Persique
mwgr0194	greece	1762	D'ANVILLE	350	54	51	Graeciae Antiquae Specimen Geographicum

AMPG REFERENCE	REGION	DATE	MAP MAKER	PRICE (UK£)	VERT. (cm.)	HOR. (cm.)	TITLE OF MAP (Comments by the editor in brackets)
mww0454	world	1761	D'ANVILLE	1200	65	118	Hemisphere Occidental ou du Nouveau Monde / Hemisphere Oriental ou de l'Ancien Monde
mwit0184	italy	1750	D'ANVILLE	240	27	24	Italy
mwe0805	europe east	1752	D'ANVILLE	250	33	33	La Dace conquise par Trajan
mwgr0183a	greece	1741	D'ANVILLE	240	30	28	La Grece Proprement dite pour l'Hist. Romaine de Mr. Rollin … 1741
mwme0305	holy land	1740	D'ANVILLE	200	34	29	La Palestina per l'Istoria de gl Imperatori Romani del Sigr. Crevier
mwme0371	holy land	1784	D'ANVILLE	250	41	46	La Palestine
mwme0355	holy land	1767	D'ANVILLE	360	39	43	La Palestine … MDCCLXVII en Juin
mwsam0714	south america paraguay	1733	D'ANVILLE	200	30	30	Le Paraguay ou les R.R.P.P. de la Compagnie de Jesus ont Repandu leurs Missions
mwgr0192	greece	1756	D'ANVILLE	480	55	71	Les Cotes de la Grece et l'Archipel par le Sr. d'Anville
mwaf0401	africa east	1732	D'ANVILLE	250	29	39	L'Ethiopie Occidentale
mwme0745	iraq etc	1783	D'ANVILLE	450	42	50	L'Euphrate et le Tigre
mwwi0599	hispaniola	1731	D'ANVILLE	250	19	29	L'Isle Espagnole sous le Nom Indien d'Hayti
mwit0176	italy	1743	D'ANVILLE	850	84	67	L'Italie Publiee sous les Auspices de Monseigneur le Duc d'Orleans
mwme0306	holy land	1740	D'ANVILLE	150	27	36	L'Orient pour l'Histoire Ancienne de Mr. Rollin
mww0459	world	1763	D'ANVILLE	450	53	74	Orbis Veteribus Notus Auspiciis Serenissimi Principis Ludovici Philippi Aurelianorum Ducis Publici Juris Factus (illustrated is Laurie & Whittle 1794 reprint)
mwme0356	holy land	1767	D'ANVILLE	400	38	42	Palaestina by Mons. d'Anville of the Royal Academy
mwme0393	holy land	1814	D'ANVILLE	300	52	66	Palestine
mwuss0644	louisiana	1776	D'ANVILLE	1200	46	57	Partie Meridionale de la Louisiane, avec la Floride, la Caroline et la Virginie
mwca0097	canada	1775	D'ANVILLE	1250	48	57	Partie Orientale du Canada / Partie Occidentale du Canada et Septentrionale de la Louisiane avec une Partie de la Pensilvanie (2 sheets)
mwwi0600	hispaniola	1733	D'ANVILLE	250	17	20	Plan du Petit Goave, et de l'Acul
mwme0624	arabia etc	1751	D'ANVILLE	600	76	78	Premiere Partie de la Carte d'Asie Contenant la Turquie, l'Arabie, la Perse, l'Inde en deca du Gange et de la Tartarie
mwc0148	china	1752	D'ANVILLE	800	96	69	Seconde Partie de la Carte d'Asie Contenant la Chine et Partie de la Tartarie, l'Inde au Deca du Gange, les Isles Sumatra, Java, Borneo, Moluques, Philippines, et du Japon … M.DCCLII (re-issued in English by Bolton in 1755)
mwe0177	europe	1758	D'ANVILLE	600	69	100	Seconde Partie de la Carte d'Europe Contenant le Danemark et la Norwege, la Suede et la Russie (a l'Exception de l'Ukraine)
mwsam0272	south america bolivia	1771	D'ANVILLE	150	22	30	Suite de Perou Audience de Charcas
mwme0881	syria etc	1760	D'ANVILLE	150	26	19	Syrie et Palestine
mwit0195	italy	1764	D'ANVILLE	400	62	50	Tabula Italiae Antiquae Geographica
mwru0221	russia	1753	D'ANVILLE	480	51	108	Troisieme Partie de la Carte d'Asie, Contenant la Siberie, et quelques autres Parties de la Tartarie … par le Sr. d'Anville
mwc0129	china	1738	D'ANVILLE-CAVE	1500	47	69	A General Map Comprizing China, Chinese Tartary & Tibet (based on D'Anville's map for Cave's translation of Du Halde)
mwc0131	china	1738	D'ANVILLE-CAVE	480	38	54	A General Map of Eastern and Western Tatary, Commonly Call'd Tartary, Drawn from the Particular Maps of the Jesuit Missionaries
mwc0130	china	1738	D'ANVILLE-CAVE	750	46	55	A Map of China, Drawn from those of the Particular Provinces Made on the Spot by the Jesuit Missionaries (based on D'Anville's map of China, for Cave's translation of Du Halde)
mwjk0161	korea	1738	D'ANVILLE-CAVE	1800	51	35	The Kingdom of Korea (based on D'Anville's map, for Cave's translation of Du Halde)
			SEE ALSO DU HALDE-D'ANVILLE.				
mwaf0782	africa north morocco	1670	DAPPER	350	26	35	(Marrakech) Het Koninklyk Hof met een Gedeelte der Stadt Marokko
mwsam0451	south america chile	1673	DAPPER	140	13	15	(Santiago) St. Jago
mwgr0590	greece islands	1677	DAPPER	300	26	32	(Untitled map of Negroponte)
mwgr0528	greece rhodes	1689	DAPPER	300	27	32	Afbeelding der Oude Stad Rhodus (3 maps on one sheet)
mwaf0078	africa	1670	DAPPER	800	44	55	Africae Accurata Tabula ex Officina Jacobum Meursium
mwgr0591	greece islands	1677	DAPPER	450	30	36	Archipelagi Meridionalis seu Cycladum
mwuss0397	florida	1673	DAPPER	320	28	35	Arx Carolina (view of Jacksonville)
mwaf0695	africa north	1670	DAPPER	350	27	33	Barbaria Biledulgerid o: Libye et Pars Nigritarum Terra
mwgr0413	greece crete	1688	DAPPER	320	24	37	Creta Candia
mwgr0490	greece cyprus	1688	DAPPER	1200	29	38	Cyprus insula
mwme0866a	syria etc	1677	DAPPER	500	29	38	Damascus
mwaf0481	africa egypt etc	1671	DAPPER	400	24	35	De Stadt Cairus
mwaf0764	africa north libya	1686	DAPPER	300	27	36	De Stadt Tripolis
mwme0173	holy land	1677	DAPPER	1500	56	120	Dimidia Tribus Manasse ultra Jordanem (in 6 sheets. Reduced size version of Jansson 1658)
mwaf0787	africa north morocco	1686	DAPPER	350	26	35	Fezzae et Marocchi Regna Africae Celeberrima
mwaf1146	africa west	1686	DAPPER	400	27	37	Guinea

AMPG REFERENCE	REGION	DATE	MAP MAKER	PRICE (UK£)	VERT. (cm.)	HOR. (cm.)	TITLE OF MAP (Comments by the editor in brackets)
mwme0959a	turkey etc	1677	DAPPER	150	12	16	Het Kanaal van Constantinopolen (incl. an explanation for the current between the Black Sea and the Sea of Marmara)
mwme0472	jerusalem	1689	DAPPER	1200	29	71	Ierusalem (based on Hollar 1660)
mwat0147	atlantic canary isl.	1670	DAPPER	650	26	34	Insulae Canariae alias Fortunatae Dictae
mwat0189	atlantic cape verde isl.	1670	DAPPER	350	25	32	Insulae Promontorii Viridis, Hispanis Islas de Cabo Verde, Belgis de Soute Eylanden
mwgr0592	greece islands	1677	DAPPER	450	30	37	Insularum Archipelagi Septentrionalis seu Maris Aegei
mwme0204	holy land	1688	DAPPER	400	29	36	Jaffa vulgo Joppen Volgens de Asteeckening Gedasen in t Inet 1668
mwme0471	jerusalem	1688	DAPPER	450	28	37	Jerusalem
mwaf1066	africa south west	1670	DAPPER	400	28	50	Loanda S. Pauli (view of the island of Luanda)
mwm0193	mediterranean malta	1670	DAPPER	1200	56	37	Melite Insula vulgo Malta / Valetta Civitas Nova Maltae olim Millitae
mwbh0369	belgium holland	1663	DAPPER	720	28	36	Nette Aftekening van d'Oude en Nieuwe Roojingh der Stadt Amsterdam
mwaf1120	africa west	1670	DAPPER	500	27	37	Nigritarum Regio
mwgr0610	greece islands	1688	DAPPER	250	26	34	Nisari / Le Simie / Carchi e Limonia / Piscopia
mwaf0478	africa egypt etc	1670	DAPPER	280	29	37	Nova Aegypti Tabula
mwme0205	holy land	1688	DAPPER	650	28	36	Pars Maxima Tribus Juda versa Orientem
mwas0306	asia caspian sea	1672	DAPPER	720	29	35	Paskaert vande Caspise Zee
mwme0176	holy land	1677	DAPPER	300	39	47	Perigrinatie ofte Veertich Iarige Reyse der Kinderen Israels. Uyt Egypten door de Roode Zee ende de Woestyne tot in't Beloofde Landt Canaan ... door Jacop Van Muers
mwaf0786	africa north morocco	1686	DAPPER	200	22	29	Salee
mwme0867	syria etc	1677	DAPPER	400	30	36	Syriae sive Soriae Nova et Accurata descriptio
mwme0714	caucasus	1672	DAPPER	280	29	35	Tabula Colchidis Hodie Mengrelie
mwaf1119	africa west	1670	DAPPER	200	26	34	The City of Lovango / De Stadt van Lovango
mwaf0819	africa north tunisia	1670	DAPPER	300	26	35	Thunis
mwm0206	mediterranean malta	1686	DAPPER	1500	57	36	Valetta Civitas Nova / Melite Insula vulgo Malta
mwm0198	mediterranean malta	1680	DAPPER	600	28	37	Valetta Civitas Nova Maltae olim Millitae
mwgm0173	mexico	1673	DAPPER	500	29	37	Yucatan / Guatimala
mwgr0611	greece islands	1688	DAPPER	900	45	52	Zee Kaerte van de Archipel en Archipelische Eylanden
mwuss0662	louisiana	1816	DARBY	28000	79	114	A Map of the State of Louisiana with Part of the Mississippi Territory from Actual Survey
mwuss0902	michigan	1818	DARBY	350	28	17	Environs of Detroit
mwf1173	france lyon	1830	DARMET	400	55	89	Plan de la Ville de Lyon, et ses Environs, Reduit d'apres les Meilleurs Leves, Corrige, Augmente et Grave d'apres des Plans Particuliers et des Reconoissances Faits sur les Lieux
mww0639	world	1811	DARTON	240	23	36	A New Chart of the World on Mercator's Projection
mwec1117	uk england suffolk	1816	DARTON	240	35	44	A New Map of the County of Suffolk, Divided into Hundreds, by Mr. Thos. Dix
mwuk1288	england london	1817	DARTON	1400	43	73	An Entire New Plan of the Cities of London (3 editions until 1827, also issued with an eastern section, 43x89cm)
mwuk1047	england	1819	DARTON	350	60	51	Brooke's Travelling Companion through England and Wales
mwuk1284	england london	1814	DARTON	1400	44	76	London, Westminster and Southwark with the East and West India Docks
mwec0796	uk england middlesex	1822	DARTON	280	35	43	Middlesex divided into Hundreds
mwuk1052	england	1823	DARTON	400	78	67	New and Improved Map of England & Wales, Including the Principal Part of Scotland
mwme0400	holy land	1822	DARTON	90	23	20	Palestine
mwsam0134	south america	1812	DARTON	90	27	23	South America, from the Latest Authorities. Engraved by Willm. Darton, No.58 Holborn Hill. Published Jany. 26, 1812 by William Darton
mwuk1363	england north	1846	DARTON	600	58	48	The Circuit of the Lakes, in the Counties of Cumberland, Westmoreland and Lancashire
mwuk1295	england london	1820	DARTON	480	42	53	The City of London; in the Time of the Saxon Dynasty, abouth the Year One Thousand: Compiled from the Most Authentic Documents, Public and Private
mwuk1278	england london	1807	DARTON	600	36	56	The Stranger's Guide through the Streets of London and Westminster &c. (8 editions until 1823)
mwwi0158	west indies	1812	DARTON	90	24	29	The West India Islands. London Published August 27th 1811, by W. Darton, Junr., 58 Holborn Hill
mww0651	world	1816	DARTON	3000	50	49	Walker's Geographical Pastime Exhibiting a Complete Voyage round the World in Two Hemispheres (2 maps)
mwuk1040	england	1809	DARTON	1800	50	43	Walker's Tour through England and Wales, a New Pastime
mwuk0253	ireland	1812	DARTON	720	53	38	Walker's Tour through Ireland. A New Geographical Pastime
mwwi0136	west indies	1796	DARTON	240	19	31	West Indies
mww0596	world	1797	DARTON	350	18	36	World. ... Engraved for Walker's Geography
mwuk1324	england london	1841	DARTON & CLARK	800	43	66	Darby's London Guide (3 editions until 1844)
mwam0715	america north	1838	DARTON & CLARK	200	18	23	United States
mwec0205	uk england cornwall	1820	DARTON & DIX	300	36	44	Cornwall, Divided into Hundreds, and the Parliamentary Divisions

AMPG REFERENCE	REGION	DATE	MAP MAKER	PRICE (UK£)	VERT. (cm.)	HOR. (cm.)	TITLE OF MAP (Comments by the editor in brackets)
mwuk1360	england north	1798	DARTON & HARVEY	900	63	75	A Map of Ninety Miles by Seventy Five, in which Chesterfield is the Center, Comprising the Counties of Derby and Nottingham Part of the Counties of York, Lincoln, Rutland, Leicester, Stafford, Salop, Chester, and Lancaster
mwec1355	uk england yorkshire	1820	DARTON & HARVEY	90	57	74	A New Map of the County of York, Divided into its Ridings with their Subdivisions, Exhibiting the Whole of the Mail, Direct and Principal Cross Roads, Navigable Canals, Rivers &c. &c.
mwuk1256	england london	1792	DARTON & HARVEY	1400	30	53	A new pocket plan of London
mwuk1268	england london	1800	DARTON & HARVEY	1400	36	53	London Westminster and Southwark (3 editions until 1805)
mwuss0723	maine	1830	DASHIELL	200	42	39	Map of the Northern Part of the State of Maine and of the Adjacent British Provinces, Shewing the Portion of that State to which Great Britain Lays Claim. Reduced from the Official Map
mwam1240a	america north (east)	1838	DAUBENY	200	17	23	Map of the United States and Canada (map to accompany 'Sketch of the Geology of North America')
mwf1159	france rhone-alpes	1767	DAUDET	400	53	70	Gouvernement General des Provinces du Lyonnois Forez et Beaujolois
mwsw0178	switzerland	1771	DAUDET	650	49	64	La Suisse qui Comprends les XIII Cantons
mwaf0196	africa	1752	DAUDET	8000	78	100	L'Afrique Divisee (4 carte-a-figure borders. Map by N. de Bailleul)
mwas0164	asia continent	1752	DAUDET	6000	78	101	L'Asie Divisee selon Tous ses Etats Empires et Royaume &c. (4 carte-a-figure borders)
mwe0170	europe	1752	DAUDET	6000	79	101	L'Europe Divisee selon l'Etendue de ses Principaux Estates et Subdivisees en leurs Principales Provinces
mwat0276	atlantic north	1752	DAUSSEY	400	62	91	Carte de l'Ocean Atlantique septentrionale
mww0204	world	1676	DAVIDSZOON	4500	40	58	Nova Totius Terrarum Orbis Tabula Auctore D.D.
mwbh0351a	belgium holland	1660	DAVIDSZOON	3000	43	94	Paskaert van de Zeeusche en Vlaemsche Kusten (south to the top. Illustrated below is the Goos 1666 copy, with different title cartouche)
mwuk1298	england london	1823	DAVIES	350	25	39	A New Map of London, Westminster, Southwark, and their Suburbs
mwuk1332a	england london	1848	DAVIES	650	67	92	Davies's Map of the British Metropolis (2 editions)
mwuk1323a	england london	1840	DAVIES	450	57	73	London and its Environs (9 editions to 1854)
mwec0964	uk england oxfordshire	1797	DAVIS	5000	57	39	A New Map of the County of Oxford, from an Actual Survey; on which are Delineated; the Course of the Rivers and Roads, the Parks, Gentlemens Seats, Heaths, Woods, Forests, Commons (16 maps plus index sheet)
mwec0456	uk england gloucestershire	1832	DAWSON	80	32	20	Gloucester (town plan)
mwuk1312	england london	1832	DAWSON	720	59	82	Jurisdiction of the Metropolitan Police
mwaf1032a	africa south	1854	DAY	750	32	40	Plan of Cape Town, Cape of Good Hope. 1854
mwuss1515	texas	1841	DAY & HAGHE	3600	42	39	A New Map of Texas, 1841
mwsp0125	portugal	1808	DE ALMEIDA	850	72	136	Carta Militar das Principaes Estradas de Portugal
mwsam0725	south america paraguay	1809	DE AZARA	350	88	45	Carte Generale du Paraguay et de la Province de Buenos-Ayres
mwsam0250	south america argentina	1809	DE AZARA	720	26	47	Plan de la Ville de Buenos-Ayres
mwsam0726	south america paraguay	1809	DE AZARA	600	26	47	Plan de la Ville de l'Assomption dans le Paraguay
mwsam0812	south america uruguay	1809	DE AZARA	250	19	27	Plan du Port de Maldonado sur la Cote Septentrionale et a l'Embouchure de la Rivere de la Plata
mwsam0813	south america uruguay	1809	DE AZARA	400	22	27	Plan du Port Montevideo sur la Cote Septentrionale de la Riviere de la Plata Leve en 1789
mwit1203a	italy venice	1500	DE BARBARI		134	282	Venetie MD (image courtesy Daniel Crouch)
mwin0099	india	1615	DE BARROS	3000	29	19	Descripcao do Reino de Guzarate (first western survey of a small part of India)
mwg0144	germany	1765	DE BEAURAIN	1500	105	130	Carte d'Allemagne pour Servir a l'Intelligence de l'Histoire de la Guerre
mwbp0451	poland	1757	DE BEAURAIN	800	39	50	Carte de la Basse Partie du Duche de Silesie / Carte de la Haute Partie du Duche de Silesie
mwbh0705	belgium holland	1760	DE BEAURAIN	650	74	66	Carte de la Hollande et d'une Partie des Etats Voisins, pour Servir a l'Intelligence de la Campagne de 1672
mwbh0706	belgium holland	1760	DE BEAURAIN	650	74	66	Carte de la Hollande et d'une Partie des Etats Voisins, pour Servir a l'Intelligence de la Campagne de 1672
mwuk1506	uk english channel (all)	1778	DE BEAURAIN	1200	50	107	Carte de la Manche ou du Canal qui Separe les Cotes de France d'avec celles d'Angleterre
mwam1042	america north (east)	1777	DE BEAURAIN	16000	43	62	Carte de l'Amerique Septle. pour Servir a l'Intelligence de la Guerre entre les Anglois et les Insurgents
mwaa0201	arctic / antarctic	1782	DE BEAURAIN	300	19	28	Carte des deux regions Polaires jusqu'au 45 degre de Latitude
mwsp0728	gibraltar	1770	DE BEAURAIN	450	37	44	Carte du Detroit de Gibraltar son Plan Particulier et sa Vue en Perspective et ceux de Cadix & Ceuta
mwuss0818	massachusetts	1776	DE BEAURAIN	20000	57	70	Carte du Port et Havre de Boston avec les Cotes Adjacentes, dans laquelle on a Tracee les Camps et les Retrenchmens Occupes, tant par les Anglois que par les Americains

AMPG REFERENCE	REGION	DATE	MAP MAKER	PRICE (UK£)	VERT. (cm.)	HOR. (cm.)	TITLE OF MAP (Comments by the editor in brackets)
mwe0596	europe czech republic (bohemia)	1760	DE BEAURAIN	750	48	55	Carte du Royaume de Boheme
mwuk1585	channel islands	1757	DE BEAURAIN	800	51	46	Carte Generale des lisles Grenesy, Jersey, Aurigny, Chausey, &c.
mwru0190a	russia	1741	DE BEAURAIN	1500	47	57	Carte Particulière des Environs de St. Peters-bourg, du Cours de la R. de Neva, depuis cette Ville jusqu'au Lac de Ladoga, avex partie du Golfe de Finlande et du Lac Ladoga
mwsam0516	south america colombia	1741	DE BEAURAIN	1000	44	59	Carte Topographique de la Baye Ville et Faubourg de Cartagene
mwit0511a	lombardy	1734	DE BEAURAIN	850	57	71	Carte Topographique de la Plus Grande Partie du Duche de Mantoue
mwf1074	france provence	1757	DE BEAURAIN	750	51	48	Carte Topo-Graphique de l'Isle d'Aix
mwsp0666a	balearic islands	1756	DE BEAURAIN	900	37	52	Carte topographique de l'isle Minorque
mwf0986	france poitou	1758	DE BEAURAIN	500	50	58	Carte Topographique des Environs de La Rochelle
mwsp0726	gibraltar	1765	DE BEAURAIN	650	44	69	Carte Topographique des Payes et Cotes Maritimes qui Formet le Detroit de Gibraltar
mwuk1586	channel islands	1757	DE BEAURAIN	650	38	67	Carte Topo-Hidro-Graphique des Isles d'Aurigny, de Burhou et des Casquets
mwf0245	france alsace	1750	DE BEAURAIN	300	43	51	Combat de Turckheim dans la Haute-Alsace, Gagne le 5. Janvier 1675
mwsp0697	gibraltar	1720	DE BEAURAIN	150	25	33	Le Detroit de Gibraltar et les Environs de Cadis / Les Ports de Lisbonne
mww0379	world	1741	DE BEAURAIN	720	24	34	Mappe-Monde Dressee sur les Nouvelles Decouvertes
mwf0420	france burgundy	1790	DE BEAURAIN	1000	52	70	Nouveau Plan de la Ville et des Environs de Dijon
mwit0938	italy sicily	1730	DE BEAURAIN	600	40	50	Nouveau Plan de Messine avec ses Chateaux
mwsp0525	spain regions	1725	DE BEAURAIN	1200	27	34	Plan de Barcelone, du Fort de Montjouy, et Leurs Environs ; Ville Capitale de la Catalogne
mwf0745	france nord pas-de-calais	1710	DE BEAURAIN	350	27	34	Plan de Dunkerque en Flandre
mwf0754	france nord pas-de-calais	1750	DE BEAURAIN	350	24	32	Plan de la Haute et Basse Ville de Boulogne sur Mer Capital du Comte Boulonnois
mwbp0410a	poland	1734	DE BEAURAIN	1350	30	37	Plan de la Ville, Faubourg, et Environs de Dantzick
mwf1045	france provence	1710	DE BEAURAIN	350	27	33	Plan de Mons, Ville Capitale du Comte d'Haynaut
mwsp0666b	balearic islands	1756	DE BEAURAIN	1800	44	63	Plan du fort Saint Philippe dans L'Isle Minorque
mwsp0714	gibraltar	1756	DE BEAURAIN	720	33	54	Plan Geometral de Gibraltar
mwuk1498	uk english channel (all)	1760	DE BEAURAIN	850	50	70	Tableau Hidrographique ... de la Manche
mwsp0132	portugal	1821	DE BEAUVOISIN	750	51	84	Plan de Lisbonne
mwaf0010	africa	1575	DE BELLEFOREST	2000	37	50	Africae Tabula Nova (woodcut based on Ortelius)
mwgr0351	greece crete	1575	DE BELLEFOREST	1400	29	42	Candia olim Creta (size includes text below map)
mwgr0457	greece cyprus	1575	DE BELLEFOREST	1800	29	42	Cyprus Insula (size includes text below map)
mwuk0671	uk	1575	DE BELLEFOREST	600	18	28	Des Isles de Bretagne la Grand Albion
mwf0024	france	1575	DE BELLEFOREST	800	34	50	Description Generale de Toute la France
mwe0010	europe	1575	DE BELLEFOREST	1600	34	47	Europae (woodblock copy of Ortelius)
mwin0394	india goa	1575	DE BELLEFOREST	600	13	41	Goa Fortissima Indiae Urbs
mwe0516a	europe czech republic (bohemia)	1575	DE BELLEFOREST	300	23	34	La Ville d'Eger
mwuk1103	england london	1575	DE BELLEFOREST	5000	32	49	La Ville de Londres. Londinum Feracissimi Angliae Regni Metropolis
mwf0640	france loire	1576	DE BELLEFOREST	1100	37	50	La Ville, Cite, et Universite d'Angers
mwf0816	france paris	1575	DE BELLEFOREST	2000	42	54	La Ville, Cite, Universite, & Faux-Bourgs de Paris
mwit0334	italy emilia-romagna	1575	DE BELLEFOREST	500	28	36	La Ville, et Cite de Parme.
mwf0253a	france aquitaine	1575	DE BELLEFOREST	650	34	44	Le vif pourtraict de la Cité de Bourdeaux
mwit0526	italy milan	1575	DE BELLEFOREST	1000	41	51	Mediolanum (wood cut copy of Braun & Hogenberg)
mwit0775a	italy sardinia	1575	DE BELLEFOREST	400	23	10	Sardinia
mww0065	world	1575	DE BELLEFOREST	6000	34	50	Typus Orbis Terrarum - Description universelle de tout le Monde (woodcut verson of Ortelius)
mwf0163	france	1791	DE BELLEYME	1800	116	160	Carte de la France, Divisee en 85 Departements et Subdivisee en Districts
mwf0192	france	1827	DE BELLEYME	750	64	81	Carte Itineraire de France
mww0446	world	1760	DE BOISJERMAIN	1750	59	84	Carte des Parties Principales du Globe Terrestre pour Servier a l'Histoire des Deux Premiers Siecles depuis la Creation du Mond (very decorative but lacking in detail)
mwbh0795	belgium holland	1828	DE BOUGE	2400	195	130	(Belgium) Carte Chorographique du Royaume des Pays Bas. Comprenant la Division Territoriale en Provinces et Arrondissements ... Carte de la Belgique, la Frise et Batavie du Tems des Romains
mwbh0751	belgium holland	1789	DE BOUGE	280	49	64	Carte Generale des Bureaux et Tenances des Postes des Pays-Bas-Autrichens
mwe0228	europe	1797	DE BOUGE	2500	213	233	Carte de l'Europe (en 50 Feuilles)
mwit0820g	italy sardinia	1793	DE BOUGE	650	76	69	Nouvelle Carte Chorographique des Etats du Roi de Sardaigne (shown below left)
mwbh0752	belgium holland	1789	DE BOUGE	1600	125	160	Nouvelle Carte Chorographique des Pays Bas Autrichiens
mwuss0181	carolinas	1757	DE BRAHM	15000	135	122	A Map of South Carolina and a Part of Georgia, Containing the Whole Sea Coast; All Boroughs, Roads and Bridges
mwru0385	russia moscow	1698	DE BRUYN	2800	30	190	(Moscow view)
mwme0977	turkey etc	1700	DE BRUYN	1200	28	98	(Smyrna view)
mwme0301	holy land	1740	DE BRUYN	450	28	54	A Map of ye Holy Land

AMPG REFERENCE	REGION	DATE	MAP MAKER	PRICE (UK£)	VERT. (cm.)	HOR. (cm.)	TITLE OF MAP (Comments by the editor in brackets)
mwme0976	turkey etc	1698	DE BRUYN	1500	29	98	Constantinopolen
mwme0979a	turkey etc	1698	DE BRUYN	480	23	30	Constantinopolen
mwme0473a	jerusalem	1698	DE BRUYN	1500	28	124	Ierusalem
mwm0137	mediterranean east	1698	DE BRUYN	600	31	58	Tabula Geographica ... Maritimi quam Terrestri
mwsp0011	portugal	1592	DE BRY	500	16	19	(Lisbon Harbour)
mwin0015	ceylon	1599	DE BRY	600	28	19	(Untitled 1st edition in German. Illustration shows the 1609 edition in Latin.)
mww0103	world	1599	DE BRY	800	8	15	(Untitled oval projection, from a title page)
mww0104	world	1599	DE BRY	1800	12	23	(Untitled reduction of Hondius' 1595 map)
mwsam0286a	south america brazil	1634	DE BRY-MERIAN	1000	36	44	(Untitled view of Pernambuco coast. North to the right. Inset with title 'Das Norder Theil ... ' shows northern part of Brazil)
mwin0014	ceylon	1599	DE BRY	600	28	36	(Untitled view-plan of Candy)
mwuss0387	florida	1590	DE BRY	720	15	21	(View of Fort Caroline, on St. John's River)
mwwi0896	trinidad & tobago	1599	DE BRY	300	14	18	(View of Port of Spain)
mwat0075	atlantic azores	1598	DE BRY	1100	39	55	A Cidade de Angra na Ilha de Iesu Xpo da Tercera
mwin0396	india goa	1598	DE BRY	1600	38	43	A Ilhae Cidade de Goa Metropolitana da Indiae Partes Orientalis que Esta en 15 Graos da Banda do Norte
mwc0005	china	1598	DE BRY	1000	26	33	Amacao (view of Macao)
mwam0018	america continent	1596	DE BRY	8500	33	40	America sive Novuus Orbis Respectu Europaeorum Inferior Globi Terrestris Pars 1596
mwsam0005	south america	1592	DE BRY	6500	37	44	Americae Pars Magis Cognita. Chorographia Nobilis & Opulentae Peruanae Provinciae, atque Brasiliae (incl. the southern part of N. America)
mwuss1588	virginia	1590	DE BRY	16000	31	42	Americae Pars, Nunc Virginia Dicta, Primum ab Anglis Inventa Sumtibus Dn. Walteri Raleigh Equestris Ordinis Viri Anno Dni. M.DLXXXV
mwit0711a	italy rome	1597	DE BRY	550	31	38	Antiquae Urbis Perfecta Imago (north to the left)
mwgm0153	mexico	1630	DE BRY	480	15	18	Aquapolque (view of Acapulco)
mwuss0148	carolinas	1591	DE BRY	960	16	21	Arcis Carolinae Delineatio
mwas0581	asia south east borneo	1602	DE BRY	400	14	22	Borneo Insula
mwsam0659	south america magellan	1620	DE BRY	480	17	21	Caarte vande Nieuwe Passagie Bezuiden de Strate Magellani Ontdect ... 1616 door Willem Schouten va Hoor
mwas0856	asia south east singapore	1603	DE BRY	3000	33	26	Contrafactur des Scharmutz els der Hollender wider die Portigesen in dem Flus Balusabar
mwas0557	asia south east bali	1600	DE BRY	650	25	18	Contrafaytung der Insel Baly
mwsam0730	south america peru	1596	DE BRY	720	29	40	Cusco Urbs Nobilissima et Opuletissima Peruani Regni
mwas0746	asia south east philippines	1599	DE BRY	550	14	17	De Sinu Baye la Baye
mwaf0625	africa islands mauritius	1600	DE BRY	800	14	17	Delineatio Insulae do Cerne, alias Mauritius Dictae (illustrated is the close copy by Coronelli, 1705.)
mwaf0855	africa south	1598	DE BRY	1200	14	17	Delineatio Sinus Illius, Quem Hollandi mensalem, sualingua Taffel Baje, nominarunt. (incl. the first delineation of Table Bay and Table Mountain)
mwaa0066	arctic	1599	DE BRY	3000	28	36	Deliniatio Cartae Trium Navigationum per Batavos ad Septentrionalem Plagem Norvegia Moscovia et Novae Zembla (Reduced size version of previous map)
mwsam0735	south america peru	1617	DE BRY	400	16	23	Descripcion del Destieto del Audiencia de Lima
mwwi0005	west indies	1623	DE BRY	720	19	22	Descriptio del Districto del Audiencia dela Espanola
mwc0014	china	1628	DE BRY	2500	30	36	Descriptio Chorographica Regni Chinae
mwsam0658	south america magellan	1620	DE BRY	480	17	21	Descriptio Freti le Maire a Guilhemo Schouten Hornano
mwin0406	indian ocean	1601	DE BRY	6500	35	67	Descriptio Hydrographica accommodata ad Battavorum navigatione (copy of Linschoten 1599)
mwp0375a	pacific new guinea	1619	DE BRY	550	15	27	Eine Carte von Nova Guinea neulich im ihar 1616 gesegelt undt beschrieben durch Wilhelm Schouten von Hoorn
mwuss0388	florida	1591	DE BRY	13500	37	45	Floridae Americae Provinciae Recens & Exactissima Descriptio Auctore Iacobo Le Moyne cui Cognomen de Morgues, qui Laudonierum
mwwi0400	cuba	1591	DE BRY	13500	37	45	Floridae Americae Provinciae Recens & Exactissima Descriptio Auctore Iacobo Le Moyne cui Cognomen de Morgues, qui Laudonierum
mwsam0489	south america colombia	1599	DE BRY	400	15	21	Franciscus Draco Carthagenam Civitatem Expugnat (view of Carthagena)
mww0127	world	1619	DE BRY	800	17	21	Guilhelmi Schouten in australem oceanum expeditio. (Title above map)
mwgm0137	mexico	1595	DE BRY	650	33	44	Hispaniae Novae sive Magnae, Recens et Vera Descriptio. 1595
mwas0625	asia south east guam	1624	DE BRY	550	23	18	I. Ladrones und Volken
mwas0556	asia south east bali	1598	DE BRY	550	14	17	Insula Bali (south to the top. Re-issued with German title)
mwat0317	atlantic st helena	1589	DE BRY	500	21	28	Insula D. Helenae Sacra Coeli Clementia et Aequabilitate
mwaf0582	africa islands madagascar	1594	DE BRY	400	15	20	Insula de S. Laurety
mwp0311	pacific fiji	1624	DE BRY	400	18	30	Insula Horn
mwaf1037	africa south east	1598	DE BRY	450	21	27	Insulae et Arcis Mocambique Deschriptio ad Fines Melinde, Sitae Ebano Puriss, Auro et Ambare Odorate Affluentis
mwit0045	italy	1596	DE BRY	2000	33	42	Italia
mwas0369	asia south east	1598	DE BRY	4200	37	43	Nova Tabula Insularum Iavae, Sumatrae, Borneonis et Aliarum Mallaccam usquae

AMPG REFERENCE	REGION	DATE	MAP MAKER	PRICE (UK£)	VERT. (cm.)	HOR. (cm.)	TITLE OF MAP (Comments by the editor in brackets)
mwwi0003	west indies	1594	DE BRY	9500	33	44	Occidentalis Americae Partis, vel, Earum Regionum quas Christophorus Columbus Primu Detexit Tabula Chorographicae Multorum Auctorum Scriptis, Praesertim Vero ex Hieronymi Benzoni ... M D XCIIII
mwsam0285	south america brazil	1631	DE BRY	800	15	17	Rio Iauero
mwaf1090	africa west	1592	DE BRY	400	28	37	Tabula Geogra: Regni Congo
mwsam0572	south america guyana	1599	DE BRY	3000	34	46	Tabula Geographica Nova Omnium Oculis Exhibens et Proponens Venissimam Descriptionem Potentissimi et Aurifen Regni ... Guiana
mwp0488	pacific south	1619	DE BRY	1200	17	40	Tabula Hydrographica Maris Australis vulgo del Zur, Ductum Navigationis Wilhelm Schouten et Terras ac Insulas ab eo Ibiden Detectas Demostrans
mwat0249	atlantic north	1613	DE BRY	2500	15	33	Tabula Nautica qua Repraesentatur Orae Maritimae Meatus ac Freta, Noviter a H Hudsono Anglo ad Caurum supra Novam Franciam Indagata Anno 1612 (reduced size copy of Gerritsz 1612)
mwru0031	russia	1613	DE BRY	1200	13	33	Tabula Septemtrionalis Russiae, Samoithiae et Tingosiae, Quemadmodum ea ab Universali Russia Separata et ab Isaaco Massa Descripta est
mwru0025a	russia	1601	DE BRY	600	18	24	Tabula Terrae Novae Zemblae, in qua Fretum Sinusq Waigats item Ora Littorlis Tartariae atq Russiae
mwas0019	asia continent	1598	DE BRY	600	12	21	Typus Expeditionis Nauticae Battavorii in Javam, Absolutae 1597
mwsc0042	scandinavia	1613	DE BRY	1200	14	33	Vera Delineatio Totius Tractus ex Hollandia Septentrionem versus per Fretrum Nassovicum, ad Fluvium Oby Ducentes, ex Annotatione Iohannis Hugouis Lintschottani, de Annis 1594 et 1595, etc.
mwat0068	atlantic ascension isl.	1598	DE BRY	300	15	22	Vera Effigies et Delineatio Insulae, Ascensio Nuncupatae Sitae in Altitudine 8 Graduum
mwe0860	europe hungary	1595	DE BRY	900	30	48	Vetustissimi potentissimique Hungariae Regni ...
mwuss1591	virginia	1613	DE BRY	1000	16	22	Von der Ankunsst der Engellander in Virginia (German edition of 'The arrival of the Englishemen in Virginia', 1590)
mwsc0408a	scandinavia faroe isl.	1676	DEBES	500	22	15	A Mapp of the Land of Feroe containing XVII Inhabited Islands
mww0147	world	1639	DE CAMOENS	3500	24	39	Hoc quod Continet Omnia Scientia habet Vocis
mwit0820b	italy sardinia	1779	DE CAROLI	1800	75	87	Carta degli stati di S.M. il Re di Sardegna e parte de paesi ad essi confinanti rettificata nella Regia Topografia
mwca0372	canada nova scotia	1753	DE CHABERT	800	57	87	Carte Reduite des Costes de l'Acadie de l'Isle Royale et de la Partie Meridionale de l'Isle de Terre-Neuve (publ. by M. Bellin)
mwjk0158	korea	1736	DE CHARLEVOIX	750	29	16	Carte de la Coree
mwwi0601	hispaniola	1733	DE CHARLEVOIX	200	19	25	Plan de la Rade du Port-Paix a la Cote Septentrionale de Saint Domingue
mwwi0602	hispaniola	1733	DE CHARLEVOIX	200	18	23	Plan de la Ville du Cap a la Cote Septentrionale de Saint Domingue
mwwi0603	hispaniola	1733	DE CHARLEVOIX	200	17	20	Plan de Leogane et de la Cote depuis l'Esler jusqu'au Cul de Sac
mwwi0604	hispaniola	1733	DE CHARLEVOIX	200	16	21	Plan du Cul de Sac de Leogane ou le Port au Prince
mwwi0605	hispaniola	1733	DE CHARLEVOIX	200	17	20	Plan du Petit Goave, et de l'Acul
mwwi0606	hispaniola	1733	DE CHARLEVOIX	200	19	13	Plan du Port de Bayaha a la Cote Septentrionale de Saint-Domingue
mwsam0696a	south america magellan	1788	DE CORDOBA	800	58	62	Carta Esferica de la Parte Sur de la America Meridional.
mwuss1541a	texas	1849	DE CORDOVA	35000	83	76	J. De Cordova's Map of the State of Texas Compiled from the Records of the General Land Office of the State, by Robert Creuzbaur (1st printing of official map of the state of Texas)
mwam0554	america north	1801	DE CREVECOEUR	750	36	50	Carte de la Partie Septentrionale des Etats-Unis / Carte de la Partie Meridionale des Etats-Unis (2 maps, each 36x50cm.)
mwuss0845	massachusetts	1787	DE CREVECOEUR	1650	22	26	Carte de l'Ile de Martha's Vineyard avec ses Dependances
mwuss0844	massachusetts	1787	DE CREVECOEUR	720	20	27	Carte de l'Ile de Nantucket pour les Lettres d'un Cultivateur Ameriquain
mwuss1658	virginia	1787	DE CREVECOEUR	1200	48	65	Carte Generale des Etats de Virginie, Maryland, Delaware, Pensilvanie, Nouveau-Jersey, New-York, Connecticut et Isle de Rhodes ... d'apres la Carte Ameriquaine de Louis Evans
mwuss1271	ohio	1787	DE CREVECOEUR	300	24	51	Esquisse du Muskinghum / Esquisse du Sioto / Esquisse de la Riviere du Grand Castor (3 maps on one sheet)
mwbh0515	belgium holland	1705	DE FER	240	23	59	(Namur) Les Environs de Dinant, de Philippeville, et de Charlemont
mwbp0367	poland	1715	DE FER	700	24	34	(Untitled plan of Warsaw)
mwaf0102	africa	1693	DE FER	240	23	28	Afrique
mwaf0107	africa	1696	DE FER	15000	90	117	Afrique, Divisee selon l'Etendue de ses Principales Parties - L'Afrique ou Tous les Points Principaux (also issued without 3 text borders, as here. Total size 106x161cm. Illustrated is the Desnos 1770 re-issue)

AMPG REFERENCE	REGION	DATE	MAP MAKER	PRICE (UK£)	VERT. (cm.)	HOR. (cm.)	TITLE OF MAP (Comments by the editor in brackets)
mwam0356	america north	1704	DE FER	480	13	16	Amerique Septentrionale
mwbh0516	belgium holland	1705	DE FER	400	22	33	Amsterdam, Fameux Port de Mer
mwbh0455	belgium holland	1691	DE FER	235	20	27	Anvers, Antwerpen en Flamand Belle et Grande Ville des Pais Bas
mwsw0093	switzerland	1691	DE FER	280	20	26	Basle Ville Capitale du Canton du Meme Nom Situee sur le Rhein
mwwi0417	cuba	1702	DE FER	360	22	32	Baye et Ville de Havana ou S. Christoval
mwbh0517	belgium holland	1705	DE FER	360	22	31	Bruselles Ville des Pais Bas Capitale du Brabant
mwsp0498	spain regions	1705	DE FER	400	24	34	Cadis son Port, sa Rade, et ses Environs
mwaf0892	africa south	1705	DE FER	600	25	35	Cap de Bonne Esperance
mwam0120	america continent	1713	DE FER	40000	102	189	Carte de la Mer du Sud, et des Costes d'Amerique et d'Asie, Situees sur cette Mer / Carte de la Mer du Nord, et des Costes d'Amerique, d'Europe et d'Afrique, Situees sur cette Mer ... 1713
mwam0374	america north	1719	DE FER	3750	51	55	Carte de la Nouvelle France, ou se Voit le Cours des Grandes Rivieres de S. Laurens & de Mississipi ... de la Floride, de la Louisiane, de la Virginie, de la Marie-Lande, de la Pensilvanie, du Nouveau Jersay, de la Nouvelle Yorck
mwf0343	france brittany	1705	DE FER	200	20	28	Carte de la Rade et des Environs de Brest
mwme0261	holy land	1719	DE FER	450	47	23	Carte de la Terre Promise Dressee sur le Plan de l'Auteur du Comentaire sure Iosue
mwbp0103	baltic states	1700	DE FER	960	43	70	Carte des Estats de Suede, de Dannemarq, et de Pologne
mww0265	world	1697	DE FER	450	21	28	Carte Generale du Globe Terrestre et Aquatiques ou Mappemonde en Deux Plans-Hemispheres
mwru0130	russia	1711	DE FER	720	53	57	Carte pour l'Intelligence des Affaires Presente des Turcs ... et des Moscovites aux Environs de la Mer Noire et de la Mer Baltique
mwuss0078	california	1700	DE FER	950	22	34	Cette Carte de Californie et du Nouveau Mexique est Tiree de celle qui a ete Envoyee par un Grande d'Espagne pour etre Communiquee a Mrs. de l'Academie Royale des Sciences
mwsc0329a	scandinavia denmark	1705	DE FER	250	23	34	Copenhague Ville Capitale du Royaume de Dannemarq
mwme0238	holy land	1707	DE FER	800	48	72	Descriptio Acurata Terrae Promissae per Sortes XII / Terre Sainte Moderne que les Turcs
mwsp0074	portugal	1715	DE FER	320	17	41	Embouchere de la Riviere du Tage
mwf0840	france paris	1705	DE FER	240	24	35	Environs de Paris
mwf0234	france alsace	1705	DE FER	140	19	24	Environs de Strasbourg
mwsp0223	spain	1705	DE FER	350	24	34	Espagne et Portugal Divises en ses Principales Parties ou Royaumes
mwsp0221a	spain	1704	DE FER	9000	100	128	Espagne Triomphante sous le Regne de Philippe V
mwbp0339	poland	1700	DE FER	140	14	16	Estats de la Couronne de Pologne
mwsc0103	scandinavia	1705	DE FER	1000	44	35	Estats des Couronnes de Dannemark, Suede, et Pologne sur la Mer Baltique (2 maps, each 44x35cm.)
mwru0118	russia	1702	DE FER	240	18	30	Etats du Grand Duc de Moscovie
mwf0583	france ile de france	1705	DE FER	300	43	42	Forest de Biere ou de Fontaine-Bleau
mwit0424a	italy liguria	1702	DE FER	350	20	27	Genes
mwru0440	russia tartary	1700	DE FER	200	14	16	Grande Tartarie
mwgr0141	greece	1705	DE FER	250	23	33	Grece Moderne, ou Partie Meridionale de la Turquie en Europe
mwe0779a	europe east	1700	DE FER	180	13	18	Hongrie
mwf0841	france paris	1705	DE FER	800	45	56	Huitieme Plan de Paris Divise en ses Vingts Quartiers
mwbh0511	belgium holland	1703	DE FER	850	44	68	Il Theatro della Guerra ... Paesi Bassi
mww0345	world	1722	DE FER	1200	46	69	Introduction a la Geographie de la Corespondance du Globe Terrestre ou Mappe-Monde avec la Sphere Celeste par les Cercles, les Lignes et les Points qui sont Imagines dans celle cy, et ceux que se Decrivent sur l'Autre
mwit0914	italy sicily	1701	DE FER	300	22	33	Isle et Royaume de Sicile
mwuk0106	ireland	1690	DE FER	1500	60	47	Isle et Royaume d'Irlande
mwuk0779	uk	1705	DE FER	200	13	16	Isles Britaniques ou sont les Royaumes d'Angleterre, d'Escosse et d'Irlande
mwru0497	ukraine	1691	DE FER	480	21	29	Kamienic Podolski Ville Forte des Estats de Pologne et de la Haute Podolie
mwf0849	france paris	1717	DE FER	1200	47	61	La Banlieue de Paris
mwuss0080	california	1720	DE FER	6000	45	66	La Californie ou Nouvelle Caroline, Teatro de los Trabajos, Apostolicos de la Compa. e Jesus en la America, Septe. Dresse sur celle que le Viceroy de la Nouvelle Espagne Envoya il y a Peu d'Annees a Mrs. de l'Academie des Sciences
mwf1034	france provence	1700	DE FER	350	17	37	La Citta di Nizza Capitale della Contea di Nizza
mwam0370	america north	1718	DE FER	48000	97	106	La France Occidentale dans l'Amerique Septentrionale ou le Cours de la Riviere de St. Laurens aux Environs de la quelle se Trouvent le Canada, l'Acadie ... la Virginie, la Marie-Lande, la Pensilvanie, le Nouveau Jersay
mwf0080	france	1693	DE FER	18000	105	155	La France Triomphante (illustrated is the 1722 re-issue)
mwf0113	france	1725	DE FER	585	49	65	La France, dans Toute son Etandue

AMPG REFERENCE	REGION	DATE	MAP MAKER	PRICE (UK£)	VERT. (cm.)	HOR. (cm.)	TITLE OF MAP (Comments by the editor in brackets)
mwca0588	canada st lawrence	1695	DE FER	2400	61	96	La Grande Riviere de Canada Appellee par les Europeens de St. Laurens
mwgr0161	greece	1715	DE FER	1500	53	69	La Grece ou La Partie Meridionale de la Turquie en Europe
mwru0503a	ukraine	1714	DE FER	400	23	33	La journée de Poltawa en Ukraine, le 8e juillet 1709
mwuk0964	england	1701	DE FER	960	69	51	La Manche ou Le Canal Au Septentrion du quel se trouve Le Royaume D'Angleterre
mwsam0176	south america (north)	1719	DE FER	685	48	64	La Partie de l'Amerique Appellee Terre Ferme ... 1719
mwc0090	china	1705	DE FER	480	23	34	La Partie Orientale de l'Asie ou se Trouvent le Grand Empire des Tartares Chinois et celuy du Iapon
mwme0609	arabia etc	1724	DE FER	850	42	56	La Perse, la Georgie, la Natolie, les Arabies, l'Egipte et le Cours du Nile
mwsp0519d	spain regions	1714	DE FER	900	47	65	La Principaute De Catalogne Divisee en Vigueries
mwsc0084	scandinavia	1690	DE FER	450	30	18	La Suede et La Norvege
mwme0232	holy land	1703	DE FER	300	23	31	La Terre Sainte Tiree des Memoires de M. de la Rue
mwf0824	france paris	1654	DE FER	8000	85	83	La Ville Cite et Universite de Paris
mwaf0113	africa	1700	DE FER	400	23	32	L'Afrique Dressee selon les Dernieres Relat. et Suivant les Nouvelles Decouvertes
mwaf0114	africa	1700	DE FER	1800	46	60	L'Afrique Dressee selon les Dernieres Relations et Suivant les Nouvelles Decouvertes
mwam0099	america continent	1698	DE FER	50000	108	157	L'Amerique Divisee selon l'Etendue de ses Principales Parties et dont les Points Principaux sont Placez sur les Observations de Mes.rs de l'Academie Royale des Sciences (The first 'Beaver' map. Size incl. text panels at sides and bottom.)
mwam0337	america north	1693	DE FER	1000	20	28	L'Amerique Septentrionale et les Terres Polaires Arctique
mwam0124	america continent	1717	DE FER	750	23	34	L'Amerique, Meridionale et Septentrionale Dressee selon les Dernieres Relations et Suivant les Nouvelles Decouvertes
mwam0100	america continent	1699	DE FER	1800	47	60	L'Amerique, Meridionale, et Septentrionale Dressee selon les Dernieres Relations et Suivant les Nouvelles Decouvertes (illustrated is 1726 edition with minor cartouche differences)
mwf0584	france ile de france	1708	DE FER	550	40	47	L'Archeveche de Paris Divise en ses Trois Archidiaconez et en ses Deux Archipretrez et Sept Doyennez Ruraux
mwas0085	asia continent	1693	DE FER	280	20	28	L'Asie
mwas0104	asia continent	1705	DE FER	900	46	59	L'Asie Dresse selon les Dernieres Relations et Suivant les Nouvelles Decouvertes
mwas0105	asia continent	1705	DE FER	300	22	32	L'Asie Suivant les Nouvelles Decouvertes dont les Point Principaux sont Placez sur les Observations de Mrs. de l'Academie Royale des Sciences
mwas0090	asia continent	1696	DE FER	25000	107	158	L'Asie, Divisee selon l'Etendue de ses Principales Parties et dont les Points Principaux sont Placez sur les Observations de Mesrs. de l'Academie Royale des Sciences (illustrated is 1724 edition publ. by Danet. See also Petrini 1700, largely copied, but lacking the text borders)
mwg0113	germany	1723	DE FER	5000	116	151	L'Empire d'Allemagne Dressee et Dediee a Monseigneur le Dauphin par N. De Fer (as De Fer 1705 but with additional borders of text panels etc.)
mwg0092	germany	1705	DE FER	3600	94	120	L'Empire d'Allemagne Dressee et Dediee a Monseigneur le Dauphin par N. De Fer
mwme0599	arabia etc	1715	DE FER	800	49	57	L'Empire des Turcs, en Europe, en Asie, et en Afrique
mwe0102	europe	1690	DE FER	1000	49	60	L'Europe
mwe0113	europe	1700	DE FER	200	13	16	L'Europe
mwe0105	europe	1695	DE FER	20000	103	158	L'Europe ou Tous les Points Principaux
mwe0115	europe	1700	DE FER	300	22	33	L'Europe Suivant les Nouvelles Observations de Mrs. de l'Academie Royale des Sciences
mwe0131a	europe	1716	DE FER	1000	48	59	L'Europe suivant les nouvelles observations de M. de l'Academie Royale des Sciences
mwuk0097	ireland	1689	DE FER	300	18	30	L'Irlande Suivant les dernieres Relations
mwsp0068	portugal	1705	DE FER	360	24	33	Lisbonne
mwwi0705	jamaica	1714	DE FER	300	23	35	L'Isle de la Jamaique, Divisee par Paroisses
mwwi0767	martinique	1704	DE FER	250	26	36	L'Isle de la Martinique
mwm0213	mediterranean malta	1694	DE FER	400	18	29	L'Isle de Malthe
mwm0227	mediterranean malta	1722	DE FER	1800	38	52	L'Isle de Malthe et celles de Goze et de Comino
mwuk1622	isle of wight	1700	DE FER	300	36	32	L'Isle de Wight
mwsp0657	balearic islands	1715	DE FER	375	24	34	L'Isle Mayorque
mwwi0592	hispaniola	1715	DE FER	375	23	33	L'Isle St. Domingue ou Espagnole Decouverte en 1492 par les Espagnols Dressee sur les Memoires de Dessunt Mr. De Cussy
mwwi0593	hispaniola	1723	DE FER	960	43	58	L'Isle St. Domingue ou Espagnole Decouverte l'An 1492. Par les Espagnols
mwit0141	italy	1706	DE FER	3000	86	101	L'Italie divisee en ses Estats
mwit0141a	italy	1707	DE FER	850	47	62	L'Italie divisee en ses Estats
mwit0119	italy	1693	DE FER	275	21	28	L'Italie divisee en ses Principaux Estats
mwsam0349	south america brazil	1719	DE FER	1000	42	54	Le Bresil dont les Cotes sont Divisees en Capitaineries Dresse sur les Dernieres Relations des Filibustiers et Fameux Voyageurs

AMPG REFERENCE	REGION	DATE	MAP MAKER	PRICE (UK£)	VERT. (cm.)	HOR. (cm.)	TITLE OF MAP (Comments by the editor in brackets)
mwca0042	canada	1705	DE FER	650	24	34	Le Canada, ou Nouvelle France, la Floride, la Virginie, Pensilvanie, Caroline, Nouvelle Angleterre et Nouvelle Yorck, l'isle de Terre Neuve, la Louisiane et le cours de la rivière de Misisipi.
mwg0267	baden-wurttemberg	1694	DE FER	1500	94	91	Le Cercle de Souabe
mwg0269b	baden-wurttemberg	1705	DE FER	180	19	29	Le Cercle de Souabe
mwg0269c	baden-wurttemberg	1705	DE FER	450	47	60	Le Cercle de Souabe et partie de celuy de Franconie
mwsam0225	south america argentina	1705	DE FER	300	23	34	Le Chili et les Provinces qui Composent celle de Rio de la Plata avec les Terres Magellanique
mwf0407	france burgundy	1708	DE FER	300	67	50	Le Comte de Bourgogne dit Franche-Comte
mwf1028	france provence	1692	DE FER	800	44	44	Le Comte de Nice Le Marquisat de Salusse et Principaute de Monaco (one sheet of a four-sheet map: mwit0586. See below under De Fer 'Principaute ...')
mwf1043	france provence	1708	DE FER	650	44	57	Le Comte de Provence
mwe0713	europe danube	1688	DE FER	4000	66	45	Le Cours du Danube (3 sheets, each 66x45cm.)
mwaf0395	africa east	1720	DE FER	350	47	65	Le Cours du Nil Suivant les Auteurs Modernes et les Dernieres Relations
mwe1008	europe rhine	1691	DE FER	650	59	49	Le Cours du Rhein ou se Trouvent les 17 Provinces des Pays-Bas
mwsc0326	scandinavia denmark	1700	DE FER	120	18	14	Le Danemark Suivant Dernier Relations
mwsam0677	south america magellan	1705	DE FER	300	23	34	Le Detroit de Magellan
mwf0657	france loire	1723	DE FER	240	49	61	Le Duche d'Anjou Dresse sur les Memoires de Jean de Loyer
mwit0596	italy north	1705	DE FER	785	46	66	Le Duche de Milan et les Etats du Duc de Savoye ... avec les Diverses Routes de France et d'Allemagne en Italie par les Alpes
mwsp0693	gibraltar	1705	DE FER	300	24	30	Le Fameux Detroit de Gibraltar
mwgm0022	gulf of mexico and surrounding regions	1717	DE FER	1500	46	60	Le Golfe de Mexique, et les Provinces et Isles qui l'Environe comme sont la Floride au Nord, le Mexique ou Nouvelle Espagne a l'Ouest, la Terre-Ferme au Sud, les Is. Antilles, Lucayes, St. Domingue et Jamaique a l'Est ... 1717
mwm0097	mediterranean adriatic	1716	DE FER	1350	52	59	Le Golfe de Venise aux environs
mwf0615	france languedoc	1712	DE FER	675	45	68	Le Gouvernement General de Languedoc
mwf0785	france normandy	1710	DE FER	900	47	66	Le Gouvernement General de Normandie Divisee en Haute et Basse
mwf0447	france champagne	1710	DE FER	320	61	52	Le Gouvernment General de Champagne et la Province de Brie
mwe0779	europe east	1700	DE FER	140	14	16	Le Gran Royaume de Hongrie ou Partie Septentrionale de la Turquie en Europe, Divisee par Grands Gouvernements, Suivant Ricaut Anglois
mwbh0518	belgium holland	1705	DE FER	300	39	50	Le Pais d'Entre Sambre et Meuse et les Environs de Namur, Dinant, Charles-Roy, Mons, Ath, Brusseles, Louvain et Huy. Par N. de Fer, 1705. C. Inselin Sculp.
mwsam0757	south america peru	1719	DE FER	900	48	58	Le Perou dans l'Amerique Meridionale Dresse sur les Divers Relations des Filibustiers et Nouveaux Voyageurs
mwf0853	france paris	1724	DE FER	280	22	28	Le Plan de la Ville, Cite, et Universite de Paris
mwf0843	france paris	1707	DE FER	1800	55	75	Le Plan de Paris ses Faubourgs et ses Environs
mwf0980	france poitou	1737	DE FER	300	42	65	Le Poitou et le Pays d'Aunis
mwsp0656	balearic islands	1715	DE FER	300	23	33	Le Port et de la Ville de Mahon
mwsp0504	spain regions	1706	DE FER	800	40	54	Le Roussillon ... Partie de la Catalogne
mwf0620	france languedoc	1730	DE FER	550	40	54	Le Roussillon Subdivise en Cerdagne, Capsir, Conflans, Vals de Carol et de Spir ou se Trouve Encore le Lampourdan, Faisant Partie de la Catalogne
mwsp0510	spain regions	1708	DE FER	450	44	47	Le Royaume de Galice
mwit1022	italy south	1705	DE FER	300	22	33	Le Royaum de Naples (large inset of Sardinia)
mwe0786	europe east	1717	DE FER	675	48	63	Le Theatre de la Guerre sur les Frontieres des Deux Empires depuis Vienne jusques a Constantinople ou se Trouvent la Hongrie
mwgm0017	gulf of mexico and surrounding regions	1705	DE FER	650	23	33	Le Vieux Mexique ou Nouvelle Espagne avec les Costes de la Floride Faisant Partie de l'Amerique Septentrionale
mwsp0499	spain regions	1705	DE FER	250	27	38	Les Asturies et la Biscaye, les Royaume de Navarre, d'Arragon et de Leon, et celuy de la Vielle Castille
mwam0804	america north (central)	1705	DE FER	900	22	33	Les Costes aux Environs de la Rivière de Misisipi. Découvertes par Mr. de La Salle en 1683 et reconnues par Mr. le Chevallier d'Iberville en 1698 et 1699
mwf0682	france lorraine	1708	DE FER	240	58	58	Les Duchez de Lorraine et de Bar. Les Evechez de Metz Toul et Verdun
mwit0497	italy lombardy	1705	DE FER	235	24	35	Les Duchez de Mantoue et de la Mirandole. Avec la Plus Grande Partie des Territoire de Verone Brescia, et de Cremone
mwf1146	france rhone-alpes	1709	DE FER	550	53	41	Les Duchez de Savoye, de Chablais, et de Genevois, les Comtez de Maurienne, et de Tarantaise, et la Baronie de Fausigny
mwit0284	italy campagna	1700	DE FER	280	23	34	Les Environs de la Ville de Naples, dans la Province de Labour, avec la Routte de Cette Ville a Rome
mwe0341	europe austria	1705	DE FER	320	16	51	Les Environs de Vienne en Austriche

AMPG REFERENCE	REGION	DATE	MAP MAKER	PRICE (UK£)	VERT. (cm.)	HOR. (cm.)	TITLE OF MAP (Comments by the editor in brackets)
mwbp0369	poland	1716	DE FER	720	47	58	Les Etats de la Couronne de Pologne, sous les quels sont Compris la Grande et la Petite Pologne, le Grand Duche de Lithuanie, les Prusses et la Curlande
mwit0309	italy central	1719	DE FER	650	52	58	Les Etats de l'Eglise et de Toscane
mwru0151	russia	1722	DE FER	875	42	65	Les Etats du Czar ou Empereur des Russes en Europe et en Asie
mwe1004	europe rhine	1689	DE FER	18000	139	104	Les Frontieres de France et d'Allemagne, dessus et aux Environs du Rhein, de la Meuse, de la Moselle et de la Saare
mwf1099	france pyrenees	1694	DE FER	400	50	60	Les Frontieres de France et d'Espagne tant deca que de la les Monts Pirenees
mwf0805	france north	1705	DE FER	600	67	96	Les Frontieres de France et des Pays Bas...Le Bas Rhein...
mwsp0064	portugal	1703	DE FER	675	57	42	Les Frontieres d'Espagne et de Portugal
mwin0154a	india	1709	DE FER	1500	62	47	Les Indes Orientales sous le Nom desquels est Compris l'Empire du Grand Mogol, les Deux Presqu'Isles de ca et de la le Gange, les Maldives, et l'Isle de Ceylan (re-issued by Danet in 1721)
mwuk0780a	uk	1706	DE FER	550	46	48	Les Isles Britanique ou se trouvent les Royaumes d'Angleterre, d'Ecosse et d'Irlande
mwuk0792	uk	1714	DE FER	2400	107	85	Les Isles Britanniques
mwuk0773	uk	1701	DE FER	350	22	32	Les Isles Britanniques, ou sont les Royaumes d'Angleterre, d'Escosse et d'Irlande
mwwi0049	west indies	1705	DE FER	480	23	33	Les Isles de l'Amerique Connues sous le Nom d'Antilles, ou sont les Isles de Cuba, St Domingue et Jamaique les Lucayes, les Caribes et celles du Vent
mwas0432	asia south east	1702	DE FER	400	23	34	Les Isles Philippines et celles des Larrons ou de Marianes, les Isles Moluques et de la Sonde, avec la Presquisle de l'Inde de la Gange ou Orientale
mwas0430	asia south east	1700	DE FER	280	14	17	Les Isles Philippines, Molucques et de la Sonde
mwf0287	france auvergne	1712	DE FER	240	47	58	Les Provinces et Gouvernemens du Lionnois, Forez et Beaujelois, de la Haute et Basse Auvergne, et du Bourbonois
mwf0093	france	1705	DE FER	550	44	49	Les Routes des Postes du Royaume de France
mwit1025	italy south	1708	DE FER	1000	55	40	Les Royaume de Naples et de Sicile
mwsp0507	spain regions	1707	DE FER	480	44	48	Les Royaumes de Grenade et d'Andalousie
mwsp0067	portugal	1705	DE FER	360	36	25	Les Royaumes de Portugal et d'Algarve
mwsw0118	switzerland	1721	DE FER	900	52	74	Les Suisses Leurs Sujets Et Leurs Alliez
mwin0143	india	1703	DE FER	320	23	32	Les Vrays Indes dits Grands Indes ou Indes Orientales
mwsw0100	switzerland	1703	DE FER	280	23	33	Les XIII Cantons des Suisses
mwf1167a	france rhone-alpes	1702	DE FER	250	22	32	Lion Ville
mwbh0847	luxembourg	1693	DE FER	280	20	27	Luxembourg
mwsp0343a	spain madrid	1705	DE FER	1800	59	92	Madrid
mwsp0343	spain madrid	1705	DE FER	400	23	33	Madrid, Ville Considerable de la Nouvelle Castille
mwit0498	italy lombardy	1705	DE FER	350	23	34	Mantoue
mww0271	world	1700	DE FER	900	44	30	Mappe Monde ou Carte Gen.le / Planisphere Celeste (terrestrial and celestial hemispheres)
mww0274	world	1700	DE FER	960	23	34	Mappe-Monde ou Carte Generale De La Terre (also publ. by Mortier)
mww0273	world	1700	DE FER	720	23	34	Mappe-Monde ou Carte Universelle (Mercator's projection)
mww0250	world	1694	DE FER	48000	99	150	Mappe-Monde, ou Carte Generale de la Terre Divisee en Deux Hemispheres Suivant la Projection la Plus Commune ou Tous les Points Principaux sont Placez sur les Observations de Mrs. de l'Academie Royale des Sciences (map includes text borders)
mww0272	world	1700	DE FER	3500	45	71	Mappe-Monde, ou Carte Generale de la Terre, Divisee en Deux Hemispheres Suivant la Projection la Plus Commune ou Tous les Points Principaux sont Placez sur les Observations de Mrs. de l'Academie Royale des Siences
mwaf0706	africa north	1705	DE FER	200	20	31	Mauretania et Numidia
mwit0538	italy milan	1700	DE FER	350	22	33	Milan
mwin0145	india	1705	DE FER	200	13	16	Mogul par N. De Fer
mwit1056d	italy naples	1702	DE FER	400	23	34	Naples
mwf1036a	france provence	1702	DE FER	200	21	27	Nice Ville Capitale du Comte de Meme Nom
mwsp0698	gibraltar	1727	DE FER	650	40	49	Nouveau Plan de la Ville de Gibraltar
mwit0168	italy	1733	DE FER	600	45	56	Nouvelle Carte pour la Guerre d'Italie
mwit0540a	italy milan	1702	DE FER	350	23	35	Novara du Duché de Milan
mwsp0524	spain regions	1720	DE FER	300	18	30	Palamos Ville de Catalogne en Espagne Petit Port de la Mediterranee avec une Citadelle
mwf0837	france paris	1696	DE FER	650	24	30	Paris
mwf0324	france brittany	1690	DE FER	200	22	32	Partie de la Coste de Bretagne
mwf1024	france provence	1690	DE FER	200	22	32	Partie de la Coste de Provence
mwg0523	rheinland-pfalz	1689	DE FER	675	49	73	Partie des Pays Bas Catholiques
mwsam0225a	south america argentina	1709	DE FER	900	49	63	Partie la Plus Meridionale de l'Amerique, ou se Trouve le Chili, le Paraguay, et les Terres Magellaniques avec les Fameux Detroits de Magellan et de Le Maire

AMPG REFERENCE	REGION	DATE	MAP MAKER	PRICE (UK£)	VERT. (cm.)	HOR. (cm.)	TITLE OF MAP (Comments by the editor in brackets)
mwaf0888	africa south	1701	DE FER	400	22	32	Partie Meridionale d'Afrique ou se Trouvent le Bassee Guinee, la Cafrerie, le Monomotapa, le Monoemugi, le Zanguebar et l'Isle de Madagascar
mwam0805	america north (central)	1718	DE FER	8000	46	64	Partie Meridionale de la Riviere de Missisipi, et ses Environs, dans l'Amerique Septentrionale (illustrated is 1723 edition)
mwaf1158	africa west	1700	DE FER	280	23	33	Partie Occidentale d'Afrique
mwbh0513	belgium holland	1704	DE FER	235	25	35	Partie Septentrionale du Duche de Brabant
mwgr0141a	greece	1705	DE FER	1200	42	52	Peloponeses aujourd'huy La Moree ... (12 small insets showing fortified towns)
mwme0799	persia etc	1703	DE FER	200	13	16	Perse par N. De Fer
mwgm0197a	mexico	1715	DE FER	400	23	33	Plan de la Fameuse et Nouvelle Ville de Mexique
mwru0139	russia	1717	DE FER	2400	38	47	Plan de la Nouvelle Ville de Petersbourg
mwit0729	italy rome	1702	DE FER	400	23	30	Plan de la Ville de Rome
mwf0835	france paris	1694	DE FER	2400	59	88	Plan de la Ville, Cite, Universite et Fauxbourgs de Paris
mwsp0658	balearic islands	1715	DE FER	450	24	35	Plan de Palma Ville Capitale
mwin0146	india	1705	DE FER	360	24	35	Plan de Pondicherry a la cote de Coromandel Occupe par la Compagnie Royale des Indes Orientales
mwf0338	france brittany	1697	DE FER	240	47	60	Plan des Villes & Places Importantes qui sont dans la Carte du Duche de Bretagne avec leurs Fortifications
mwuk1134	england london	1700	DE FER	450	23	34	Plan des Villes de Londres et de Westminster et de leurs Faubourgs avec le Bourg de Southwark
mwsam0507	south america colombia	1700	DE FER	350	23	32	Plan des Villes, Forts, Port, Rade et Environs de Cartagene
mwin0204	india	1746	DE FER	200	14	16	Presqu'isle de l'Inde de ca le Golfe du Gange / Presqu'isle de l'Inde de la le Golfe du Gange (2 maps, each 14x16cm.)
mwsp0500	spain regions	1705	DE FER	240	24	34	Principaute de Catalogne
mwit0586	italy north	1692	DE FER	2250	98	80	Principaute de Piemont, Seigneurie de Verceil, Duche ou Val d'Aoust / Le Comte de Nice, le Marquisat de Salusse et Principaute de Monaco / Principaute d'Oneglia Marquisat de Final / Partie du Piemont, du Montferrat et de la Republique de Genes
mwe1045c	europe east	1704	DE FER	650	45	49	Principaute de Transilvanie Divisee en Cinq Nations Subdivisee en Quartiers et Comtez
mwsp0508	spain regions	1707	DE FER	400	31	42	Principaute des Asturies
mwbh0633	belgium holland	1737	DE FER	600	47	62	Provinces des Pais Bas Divisees Suivant les Traites ... Faits en 1713, 1714 et 1716
mwca0501	canada quebec	1696	DE FER	400	21	31	Quebec, Ville de l'Amerique Septentrionale dans la Nouvelle France avec Titre d'Eveche. Situee sur le Fleuve de St. Laurent ... Elle fut Assiegee par les Anglois sur les Francois
mwit0139	italy	1705	DE FER	650	46	50	Routes des Postes d'Italie
mwsp0501	spain regions	1705	DE FER	275	24	32	Royaume de Galice Province d'Espagne
mwsp0062	portugal	1700	DE FER	180	18	14	Royaume de Portugal
mwru0106	russia	1700	DE FER	140	14	16	Russie Blanche ou Moscovie
mwf0842a	france paris	1705	DE FER	800	48	56	Sixième Plan de la Ville de Paris, et son accroissement, depuis le commencement du Regne de Charles VII l'an 1422, jusqu'a la fin du règne d'Henry III l'an 1589 (map by La Mare)
mwf0230	france alsace	1696	DE FER	240	20	27	Strasbourg Ville Fameuse Situee sur la Petite Riviere
mwme0229	holy land	1701	DE FER	15000	91	119	Terre-Sainte Ancienne, Moderne, et Historique
mwit0666a	italy piedmont	1702	DE FER	350	20	26	Turin Ville Capitale de Piemont
mwme0583	arabia etc	1700	DE FER	200	13	16	Turquie en Asie
mwit1233a	italy venice	1705	DE FER	480	23	35	Venise (shown below left)
mwit1228	italy venice	1695	DE FER	2000	45	68	Venise, Ville Capitale de la Plus Celebre, et Illustre Republique de l'Europe
mwme0978	turkey etc	1700	DE FER	400	21	28	Veue de Constantinople
mwf1036b	france provence	1702	DE FER	250	14	21	Veue de Nice
mwme0984a	turkey etc	1705	DE FER	200	24	34	Veue des Dardanelles de Constantinople
mwaf0156	africa	1724	DE FER - DANET	15000	111	164	L'Afrique Divisee selon l'Etendue de Ses Principal Parties
mwsw0174	switzerland	1770	DE FER-DESNOS	720	47	67	Les Suisses Leurs Sujets Et Leurs Alliez
mwp0029	australia	1790	DE FLEURIEU	800	21	35	A Reduced Chart of the French Discoveries to the South East of New-Guinea in 1768 and 1769 (incl. NE coast of Australia)
mwat0094a	atlantic azores	1774	DE FLEURIEU	400	39	49	Carte Réduite des îles Açores Dressée sur de Nouvelles Observations
mwat0162a	atlantic canary isl.	1772	DE FLEURIEU	450	39	49	Carte Reduite des Iles Canaries, Madere
mwjk0059	japan	1708	DE FONTENAY	500	14	24	Nangasaki appelle par les Chinois Tchangki
mwam0202	america continent	1776	DE GROOT	180	13	6	De Europische Volkplantingen in America
mwaf0234	africa	1776	DE GROOT	80	13	6	De Haven van Ophir en de Oude van Tarsis
mwas0193	asia continent	1776	DE GROOT	100	13	14	De Koophandel der Europeaanen in Asia
mwm0068	mediterranean	1776	DE GROOT	80	13	6	De Ommevaart der Middelandsche Zee
mwit0436	italy liguria	1747	DE GROOT	800	50	58	Plan de l'Enceinte de la Ville de Genes avec ses environs
mwam0032	america continent	1622	DE HERRERA	2000	29	19	(Untitled 1st map depicting California as an Island, on the title page of De Herrera's work. Size is for the printed page)
mwsam0661	south america magellan	1622	DE HERRERA	480	21	29	Charte du Destroict Trouve et Passe par Iacq. Le Maire au dela du Destroict de Magallanes vers le Zudest

AMPG REFERENCE	REGION	DATE	MAP MAKER	PRICE (UK£)	VERT. (cm.)	HOR. (cm.)	TITLE OF MAP (Comments by the editor in brackets)
mwsam0442	south america chile	1601	DE HERRERA	400	15	29	Descripcion de la Provincia de Chile
mwas0372	asia south east	1601	DE HERRERA	1350	20	28	Descripcion de las Indias del Poniente
mwam0137	america continent	1723	DE HERRERA	1000	23	32	Descripcion de las Indias Ocidentalis (incl. climatic regions)
mwam0033	america continent	1622	DE HERRERA	1250	22	31	Descripcion de las Indias Ocidentalis (shows the 1494 Papal lines of demarcation between Spanish and Portuguese territories)
mwsam0015	south america	1622	DE HERRERA	800	22	30	Descripcion de las Yndias de Mediodia
mwam0310	america north	1601	DE HERRERA	1250	21	30	Descripcion de las Yndias del Norte
mwgm0101	guatemala	1622	DE HERRERA	500	20	27	Descripcion del Audiencia de Guatimala
mwsam0267	south america bolivia	1622	DE HERRERA	400	21	30	Descripcion del Audiencia de los Charcas
mwsam0490	south america colombia	1622	DE HERRERA	400	22	30	Descripcion del Audiencia del Nuevo Reino
mwsam0560	south america ecuador	1622	DE HERRERA	400	21	30	Descripcion del Audiencia del Quito
mwsam0736	south america peru	1622	DE HERRERA	400	22	30	Descripcion del Destieto del Audiencia de Lima
mwgm0148	mexico	1622	DE HERRERA	400	22	29	Descripcion del Destricto del Audiencia de la Nueva Galicia
mwgm0149	mexico	1622	DE HERRERA	500	22	29	Description del Destricto de Nueva Espana
mwp0490	pacific south	1622	DE HERRERA	800	22	53	Tabula, Dictum Navigationis, quem in Mari Australi Tenuit Iacobus Le Maire
mwgm0382a	panama	1623	DE HERRERA-DE BRY	400	22	29	Descripcion del Audiencia de Panama
mwgm0002	gulf of mexico and surrounding regions	1623	DE HERRERA-DE BRY	2000	17	23	Descriptcion De Las Yndias Del Norte
mwit0819a	italy sardinia	1773	DE HOCHSTEIN	550	45	30	Sardegna ed isole aggiacenti secondo lo stato presente (above)
mwe0595	europe czech republic (bohemia)	1758	DE HONDT	450	42	50	Plan de la Bataille de Chotzenitz
mww0234	world	1687	DE HOOGHE	1200	36	47	(Untitled map of the ancient world)
mwf1125	france rhone-alpes	1675	DE HOOGHE	750	47	59	Arx et Oppidum Montismeliani
mwme0298	holy land	1736	DE HOOGHE	600	36	46	Beschryvinge van den Oorsprong der Volkeren, uit de Drie Sonen van Noah na den Sondvloed, en Voorts vande Reysen der Eerste Vaderen in Canaan
mwuk1388	england south	1693	DE HOOGHE	4000	58	95	Carte Maritime de l'Angleterre depuis les Sorlingues jusques a Portland (The map was engraved by De Hooghe and publ. by Jaillot-Mortier)
mwf0265	france aquitaine	1693	DE HOOGHE	1200	60	45	Carte Maritime depuis la Riviere de Bordeaux jusques a St. Sebastien
mwf0976	france poitou	1693	DE HOOGHE	1200	59	47	Carte Maritime des Environs de L'Isle d'Oleron
mwm0025	mediterranean	1694	DE HOOGHE-MORTIER	24000	58	141	Carte Nouvelle de la Mer Mediterranee ou sont Exactement Remarques Tous les Ports, Golfes, Rochers, Bancs de Sable &c. (38 insets of ports)
mwuk1387	england south	1693	DE HOOGHE	3500	58	95	Carte Nouvelle des Costes d'Angleterre, depuis la Riviere de la Tamise jusques a Portland
mwuk1533	uk english channel (east)	1693	DE HOOGHE	2400	59	95	Carte Nouvelle des Costes de Hollande ... avec une partie des costes D'Angleterre
mwf0781a	france normandy	1693	DE HOOGHE	1800	59	95	Carte Nouvelle des Costes De Normandie Et De Bretagne despuis le Havre De Grace jusques a Morlaix (publ. by P. Mortier)
mwm0046	mediterranean	1721	DE HOOGHE	600	32	47	De Reysen Christi des Heyland en Pauli met andere syne Bloedgetuygen
mwme0490	jerusalem	1730	DE HOOGHE	400	30	38	Hierusalem
mwme0231	holy land	1702	DE HOOGHE	800	32	46	Historische Kaert der Landen en Saecken int Oude en Nieuwe Testament
mwbh0442	belgium holland	1688	DE HOOGHE	8000	211	221	Hoogheymraadschap van Rhynland
mww0324	world	1715	DE HOOGHE	850	33	47	Orbis per Creationem Institutus / Orbis per Diluvium Destitutus
mwbh0470	belgium holland	1694	DE HOOGHE-DE VOU	20000	166	234	Rotterdam met al syn Gebouwen ... 1694
mwe0901	europe hungary	1686	DE HOOGHE	1000	45	56	Verovering der Sterke Stad, Buda of Offen, doo de Keyserlyke en Geallieerde Machten. 1686
mwbp0287a	poland	1677	DE HOOGHE	950	42	54	Verovering van Stettin
mwbh0020a	belgium holland	1565	DE HOREN?	4000	38	52	Hollandt
mwaf0752	africa north algeria	1771	DE HUYSER	300	20	35	Algiers (view)
mwgr0577a	greece islands	1593	DE JODE	2000	37	51	(6 maps on one sheet - Sicily, Cyprus, Corsica/Sardinia, Crete, Balearic Isl, Malta/Mitylene)
mwaf0013	africa	1578	DE JODE	7200	34	48	Africae ut Terra Mariq Lustrata est
mwaf0021	africa	1593	DE JODE	6000	33	45	Africae Vera Forma, et Situs
mwam0308	america north	1593	DE JODE	25000	37	50	Americae Pars Borealis, Florida, Baccalaos, Canada, Corterealis. A Cornelio de Iudaeis in Luce Edita
mwsam0004	south america	1578	DE JODE	16000	37	46	Americae Peruvi (2 insets)
mwuk0673	uk	1578	DE JODE	2400	35	50	Angliae Scotiae et Hibernie Nova Descriptio
mwf0702	france nord pas-de-calais	1593	DE JODE	720	37	47	Artois. Atrebatum Regionis Vera Descriptio
mwas0013	asia continent	1593	DE JODE	7500	37	46	Asia, Partium Orbis Maxima
mwas0008	asia continent	1578	DE JODE	8000	35	44	Asiae Novissima Tabula
mwe0289	europe austria	1578	DE JODE	2000	38	52	Austriae Ducatus seu Pannoniae Superioris
mwaf0679	africa north	1593	DE JODE	1200	36	46	Barbaria Pars Africa (2 maps on one sheet, north east and north west)
mwsw0021	switzerland	1578	DE JODE	960	39	48	Basileae Inclytae Rauracorum Urbis (inset: Valesia. South to the top.)

AMPG REFERENCE	REGION	DATE	MAP MAKER	PRICE (UK£)	VERT. (cm.)	HOR. (cm.)	TITLE OF MAP (Comments by the editor in brackets)
mwg0311	bavaria	1578	DE JODE	1500	35	45	Bavariae Utriusque cum Inferioris tu Superioris Vera et ad Amus Sim Descriptio
mwbh0080	belgium holland	1578	DE JODE	2000	35	49	Brabantiae Belgarum
mwsam0006	south america	1593	DE JODE	10000	36	43	Brasilia et Peruvia
mwc0003	china	1593	DE JODE	12000	36	45	China Regnum
mwe0518	europe czech republic (bohemia)	1578	DE JODE	2000	32	51	Chorographia Insignis Regni Bohemiae
mwf0380	france burgundy	1578	DE JODE	800	35	47	Comitatus Burgundiae
mwe0493	europe croatia	1593	DE JODE	1000	34	41	Croatiae & Circumiacentiu Regionu versus Turcam Nova Delineatio
mwsc0228	scandinavia denmark	1578	DE JODE	3000	33	51	Danorum Marchiae seu Cimbrici Regnum Continentis Iutiae Ducatum / Chorographica Ducatum Holsatiae Schleswicae et Stormariae (2 maps on one sheet)
mwme0052a	holy land	1593	DE JODE	4000	33	51	Descriptio et Situs Terrae Sanctae Alio Nomine Palestina
mwme0079	holy land	1617	DE JODE-CAIMOR	7200	60	55	Descriptio et Situs Terrae Sanctae, Alio Nomine Palaestina
mwbh0131a	belgium holland	1593	DE JODE	1500	32	50	Episcopatus Leodiensis (compass directions in corners. West and East are misplaced.)
mwbh0079	belgium holland	1578	DE JODE	1000	34	52	Episcopatus Leodiensis Provincia / Trevirensis Episcopatus Exactissimo Descriptio (2 maps on one sheet)
mwe0012	europe	1578	DE JODE	8000	36	47	Europae Totius Orbis Partitum (illustration below shows 1593 edition, same size, different map and title 'Nova Totius Europae Tabula')
mwf0641	france loire	1578	DE JODE	900	35	44	Exacta Novaque Descriptio Ducatus Andegavensis quem Vulgari Nomine le Duche d'Anjou Indigitant
mwbh0084	belgium holland	1578	DE JODE	2000	36	48	Exactissima Flandriae Descriptio
mwit0371	italy friuli	1578	DE JODE	1000	37	51	Fori Iulii / Tusciae / corfu (3 maps on one sheet)
mwbh0081	belgium holland	1578	DE JODE	3000	39	51	Frisiae Antiquissimae trans Rhenu Provinc: et Adiacentium Regionum Nova et Exacta Descriptio
mwg0570	saxony	1593	DE JODE	1000	36	49	Frisiae Orientalis Nova et Exacta Descriptio
mwf0026	france	1578	DE JODE	1500	36	50	Gallia tuxta veterum Romanorum
mwf0030	france	1593	DE JODE	1800	31	44	Galliae Amplissimi Regni Tabula
mwbh0078	belgium holland	1578	DE JODE	1500	37	48	Geldria
mwg0023	germany	1578	DE JODE	1500	39	50	Germania universa
mwbh0085	belgium holland	1578	DE JODE	3000	31	48	Germaniae Inferioris Galliae Belgicae
mwg0028	germany	1593	DE JODE	900	38	53	Germaniae Totius, Nostrae Europae Celeberrimae Regionis, Descriptio Singularis
mwsw0020	switzerland	1578	DE JODE	1500	40	52	Helvetiae seu Suiciae
mww0082	world	1593	DE JODE	40000	32	52	Hemispheriu ab Aequinoctiali Linea, ad Circulu Poli Arctici / Hemispheriu ab Aequinoctiali Linea, ad Circulu Poli Atarctici
mwg0429	hessen	1578	DE JODE	800	36	46	Hessiae seu Cattorum Noblissimorum ac Bellicosissimorum
mwbh0131	belgium holland	1593	DE JODE	3500	37	51	Holla diae Integra Comita
mwe0857	europe hungary	1578	DE JODE	2400	30	49	Hungariae Totius uti ex Compluribus Aliorum Geographicis Chartis
mwe1121b	europe slovenia	1578	DE JODE	2000	30	52	Illirici seu Sclavoniae, Continentis
mwit0034	italy	1578	DE JODE	4800	37	52	Italiae Totius Orbis olim Domatricis Nova Exactis Descriptio Iacobo Castaldo Auctore. Antwerpiae Celabat Gerardus de Jode Anno 77 cum Privilegio
mwbp0069	baltic states	1578	DE JODE	800	33	50	Livoniae / Moscovie (2 maps on one sheet)
mwf0663	france lorraine	1593	DE JODE	900	35	49	Lotharingia Ducatus
mwbh0810	luxembourg	1578	DE JODE	2500	37	45	Lutzenburgii
mwg0758	westphalia	1578	DE JODE	1500	34	50	Mansfeldiae Comitatus / Clivensis et Iuliacensis Ducatum
mwe1090	europe slovak republic (moravia)	1593	DE JODE	1600	37	46	Maravaniae seu Moraviae Marchionatus
mwe1088	europe slovak republic (moravia)	1578	DE JODE	1600	37	51	Maravaniae seu Moraviae Marchionatus / Silesiae Ducatus Typice
mwme0929	turkey etc	1578	DE JODE	6500	38	51	Natoliam moderni - Turcia
mwit0990	italy south	1578	DE JODE	3000	38	52	Neapolitani Regni exacta ac didligens delineatio (inset view of Napoli)
mwsp0164	spain	1578	DE JODE	4500	38	50	Nova Descriptio Hispaniae (no title cartouche. Reprinted 1593)
mwbh0083	belgium holland	1578	DE JODE	3000	37	51	Nova et Castigator Comitatus Hollandiae Descriptio
mwsp0365	spain regions	1578	DE JODE	1000	35	26	Nova Et Exactissima Descriptio nobilis provinciae Guipuscovae in partibus Hispaniae sitae
mwf0645	france loire	1593	DE JODE	720	35	47	Nova et Integra Caenomaniae Descriptio vulg: la Mans
mwe0702	europe danube	1578	DE JODE	5000	35	50	Nova Exactissimaque Descriptio Danubii (in 2 sheets, each 35x50cm)
mww0061	world	1571	DE JODE		34	52	Nova Totius Terrarum Orbis Descriptio
mwp0373	pacific new guinea	1593	DE JODE	14000	35	22	Novae Guineae Forma, & Situs
mwit1161	italy veneto	1578	DE JODE	1600	38	52	Paduani Agri eiusque Urbium Vicorum Castorum Montium Fluminum ad Vivum Expressio / Urbis Romane Territorium Praeter circumacentium (2 maps on one sheet)
mwit0335	italy emilia-romagna	1578	DE JODE	2400	39	49	Parmae Ac Plaisantiae Amoenissimi (2 insets)
mwbp0189	poland	1578	DE JODE	2500	39	50	Poloniae Amplissimi Regni Typus Geographicus
mwbp0190	poland	1578	DE JODE	1800	32	45	Pomeraniae utriusq Continentis / Thietmarsorum Simbricae Schersonesi Populorum / Prussiae seu Pruteniae Chorographia

AMPG REFERENCE	REGION	DATE	MAP MAKER	PRICE (UK£)	VERT. (cm.)	HOR. (cm.)	TITLE OF MAP (Comments by the editor in brackets)
mwsp0005	portugal	1578	DE JODE	2000	32	52	Portugalliae quae olim Lusitania Vernando Alvaro Secco Autore Recens Descriptio
mwme0759	persia etc	1578	DE JODE	2500	30	51	Primae Partis Asiae acurata delineatio
mwbp0198	poland	1593	DE JODE	2000	37	50	Prussiae Regionis Sarmatiae Europae Nobibilissimae Nova et Vera Descriptio
mwam1310	america north (west)	1593	DE JODE	8000	35	24	Quivirae Regnu cum Alijs versus Borea
mwg0759	westphalia	1578	DE JODE	600	35	45	Reiterata Episcopatus Monasteriensis Geographica Descriptio cui Addita est et Osnabrugensis
mwe0297	europe austria	1593	DE JODE	1400	35	25	Saltzburgensis Episcopatus
mwg0556	saxony	1578	DE JODE	1000	33	45	Saxonum Regionis Quatenus eius Gentis Imperium Nomenque
mwme0538	arabia etc	1578	DE JODE	5500	32	50	Secundae Partis Asiae (close reduced size copy of Gastaldi 1561)
mwsc0025	scandinavia	1578	DE JODE	12500	37	50	Septentrionaliu Regionum Suetiae, Gothiae, Norvegiae, Daniae
mwm0160	mediterranean islands	1578	DE JODE	6000	37	51	Sicilia Insula Maris / Cyprus Insula Maris Syriaci / Corsica, Sardinia / Candia / Maiorica et Minorica / Melita, Mitylene
mwbp0199	poland	1593	DE JODE	720	35	53	Silesiae Ducatus Typice / Ducatus Oswieczime et Zatoriesis
mwe0290	europe austria	1578	DE JODE	2000	36	52	Stiraemarchiae Ducatus / Carinthiae Ducatus
mwg0310	bavaria	1578	DE JODE	1500	37	42	Sueviae utriusq. cum Germanicae tum Rheticae Martianorumque Nemoru Typus Chorographicus versus ac Germanus
mwru0416	russia tartary	1578	DE JODE	6500	33	51	Tartariae Partis Asiae
mwme0044	holy land	1578	DE JODE	7200	31	51	Terrae Sanctae quae Promissionis terra, est Syria pars ea, quae Palestina vocatur descriptio Tylmannu Stellam
mwas0366	asia south east	1578	DE JODE	6000	33	50	Tertiae Partis Asiae quae modernis Indi orientalis dicitur acurata delineatio.
mwe0288	europe austria	1578	DE JODE	1000	35	51	Tirolensis Comitatus / Carniolae Chaziolaeq. Ducatus, nec non, et, Goritiae Comitatus (2 maps on one sheet)
mww0075	world	1589	DE JODE	25000	35	50	Totius Orbis Cogniti Universalis Descriptio ... M.D.Lxxxix
mwe0987	europe rhine	1578	DE JODE	4500	35	45	Tractus Rheni Prima Tabula /... Secunda Tabula /... Tertia Tabula (3 maps, each 35x45cm)
mwg0734	thuringia	1578	DE JODE	1000	30	51	Turingiae Comitatus Provincialis / Misniae Marchionatus (2 maps on one sheet)
mww0068	world	1578	DE JODE	80000	34	52	Universi Orbis seu Terreni Globi in Plano Effigies cum Privilegio (similar to 1571 map but with title changed.)
mwsw0028	switzerland	1593	DE JODE	960	38	48	Valesiae Provinciae Montanae / Basileae Inclytae Rauracorum Urbis ac eiusdem Circum Vicini Agri Situs Exactissima Delineatio Authore Sebastino Munstero
mwgr0039	greece	1578	DE JODE	7500	39	51	Videbis totius Grecia limites divisos
mwbh0082	belgium holland	1578	DE JODE	3000	36	48	Zelandia
mwf0736	france nord pas-de-calais	1670	DE JONGE	650	41	51	Duynkercken (view)
mwf0068	france	1675	DE JONGE	960	45	55	Gallia, Nova et Accurata descriptio
mwuk1116	england london	1666	DE JONGE	3500	40	52	Londinum Celeberrimum Anglia Emporium / Another Prospect of the Sayd City (view)
mwit1075	italy naples	1826	DE JORIO	320	48	54	Plan de la Ville de Naples
mwit0292	italy campagna	1831	DE JORIO	650	37	55	Plan de Pompei de M. le Chanoine
mwgm0058	gulf of mexico and surrounding regions	1795	DE LA BASTIDE	1800	46	53	Plan pour Ouvrir une Communication de la Mer du Nord a la Mer du Sud
mwaf0931	africa south	1752	DE LA CAILLE	250	16	12	Carte du Cap de Bonne Esperance et de ses Environs (first triangulation of this region)
mwsam0562	south america ecuador	1744	DE LA CONDAMINE	300	23	99	Carte de la Meridiene Mesuree au Royaume de Quito
mwsam0563	south america ecuador	1751	DE LA CONDAMINE	400	59	35	Carte de la Province de Quito au Perou (shows triangulation sites to determine the curvature of the earth)
mwsam0207	south america amazon	1745	DE LA CONDAMINE	300	18	38	Carte du Cours du Maragnon
mwaf0096	africa	1688	DE LA CROIX	235	14	16	Afrique
mwe0133	europe	1717	DE LA CROIX	140	14	20	L'Europe
mwam0361	america north	1705	DE LA CROIX	800	19	28	Noorder America
mwsam0090	south america	1775	DE LA CRUZ	8000	170	145	Mapa Geografico De America Meridional
mwjk0119	japan	1788	DE LA CRUZ BAGAY	1500	21	28	Japonia
mwbh0510	belgium holland	1702	DE LA FEUILLE	400	18	25	Afbeelding van het Fort de Knoque
mwbh0539	belgium holland	1710	DE LA FEUILLE	8000	51	99	Amstelodami Veteris et Novissimi Delineatio (publ. by G. van Keulen)
mwbh0527	belgium holland	1706	DE LA FEUILLE	3000	49	57	Amstelodami Veteris et Novissimi Delineatio
mwsp0545	spain regions	1735	DE LA FEUILLE	450	15	27	Barcelona
mwf0622	france languedoc	1735	DE LA FEUILLE	180	18	24	Caart van Languedoc (north to the right)
mwf1039	france provence	1706	DE LA FEUILLE	400	17	25	Carte de Provence avec ses Confins et ses Fortereses
mwf0680a	france lorraine	1706	DE LA FEUILLE	280	17	25	Carte du Duche de Lorraine
mwbh0624	belgium holland	1735	DE LA FEUILLE	250	17	25	Carte Generale Des 17 Provinces des Pais Bas
mwuk0469	scotland	1729	DE LA FEUILLE	400	18	27	Carte Nouvelle D'Ecosse
mwe1049a	europe romania	1735	DE LA FEUILLE	250	17	25	Carte Nouvelle de Transilvanie
mwsw0135	switzerland	1735	DE LA FEUILLE	250	17	26	Carte van Neuchatel et Valangin
mwbh0625	belgium holland	1735	DE LA FEUILLE	150	16	23	Dioecesis Leodiensis Accurata Tabula
mwg0375	bavaria	1735	DE LA FEUILLE	300	18	26	Duche de Baviere het Hertogdom Byerum
mwbh0626	belgium holland	1735	DE LA FEUILLE	150	18	26	Duche de Brabant
mwe0164	europe	1747	DE LA FEUILLE	250	15	20	Europa Selon les Auth. Les plus Modernes

AMPG REFERENCE	REGION	DATE	MAP MAKER	PRICE (UK£)	VERT. (cm.)	HOR. (cm.)	TITLE OF MAP (Comments by the editor in brackets)
mwbh0627	belgium holland	1735	DE LA FEUILLE	200	16	23	Groninga Dominium
mwsc0134	scandinavia	1735	DE LA FEUILLE	350	18	26	Kaart van Sweden
mwbh0628	belgium holland	1735	DE LA FEUILLE	200	18	25	Kaart van't Hertogdom Brabant
mwwi0069	west indies	1735	DE LA FEUILLE	350	18	29	Kaarte van de Golf van Mexico
mwf0097	france	1710	DE LA FEUILLE	350	17	25	La France Moderne avec ses 12 Anciens Gouvernement
mwbp0109	baltic states	1710	DE LA FEUILLE	280	15	22	La Livonie
mwbh0629	belgium holland	1735	DE LA FEUILLE	150	15	23	La Rhinlande Amstellande et Terres Circovosines
mwbh0863	luxembourg	1735	DE LA FEUILLE	300	12	18	La Ville de Luxembourg
mwaf0133	africa	1710	DE LA FEUILLE	400	16	21	L'Afrique selon les Autheurs les Plus Modernes (engraved by Elias Baeck)
mwg0122	germany	1735	DE LA FEUILLE	180	14	20	L'Allemagne avec ses Confins et ses Dependances
mwam0347	america north	1701	DE LA FEUILLE	450	14	19	L'Amerique Septentrionale
mwas0110	asia continent	1710	DE LA FEUILLE	240	13	19	L'Asie
mwbh0490	belgium holland	1700	DE LA FEUILLE	150	15	22	Le Duche de Gueldres
mwbp0355	poland	1710	DE LA FEUILLE	280	15	21	Le Royaume de Pologne avec ses Confins
mwsp0092	portugal	1747	DE LA FEUILLE	250	17	25	Le Royaume de Portgual et Algarve
mwsp0233	spain	1710	DE LA FEUILLE	240	15	23	Le Royaume d'Espagne avec ses Confins
mwuk0790	uk	1710	DE LA FEUILLE	280	15	22	Les Iles Britanniques ou les Royaumes d'Angleterre d'Ecosse et d'Irlande
mwit0145	italy	1710	DE LA FEUILLE	400	17	22	L'Italie Avec Les Iles (14 crests in side borders. Engraved by Elias Baeck)
mwuk1144	england london	1710	DE LA FEUILLE	375	12	17	Londres Ville Capitale de l'Angleterre
mww0285	world	1701	DE LA FEUILLE	450	15	22	Mapemonde Planisphere ou Carte Generale du Monde
mwe0802	europe east	1747	DE LA FEUILLE	250	17	42	Nieuwe Kaart van Bosnien, Servien, Bulgarien, Romanien
mwru0501a	ukraine	1709	DE LA FEUILLE	200	20	32	Nieuwe Kaart van de Crim, de Zwarte Zee, en Omleggende Landen
mwsp0706	gibraltar	1735	DE LA FEUILLE	400	17	46	Nieuwe Paskaart van t Naauw van de Straat
mwru0173	russia	1735	DE LA FEUILLE	80	18	26	Niewe Kaart van Moscovien
mwe0801	europe east	1747	DE LA FEUILLE	350	17	25	Nouvelle Carte de Transilvanie
mwit0170	italy	1735	DE LA FEUILLE	500	17	25	Nouvelle Carte D'Italie
mwbh0630	belgium holland	1735	DE LA FEUILLE	250	18	26	Nouvelle Carte du Comte de Flandre
mwit0681	italy piedmont	1735	DE LA FEUILLE	280	18	26	Nouvelle Carte du Piedmont
mwe0919	europe hungary	1710	DE LA FEUILLE	350	17	26	Nouvelle Carte du Royaume de Hongrie avec ses Forteresses
mwit0738	italy rome	1720	DE LA FEUILLE	950	50	59	Novissima et Accuratissima Delineatio Romae Veteris
mwam0103	america continent	1700	DE LA FEUILLE	1650	45	57	Novissima et Accuratissima Totius Americae Descriptio (close copy of De Ram)
mww0301	world	1705	DE LA FEUILLE	6000	45	56	Novissima Totius Terrarum Orbis Tabula
mwbp0120	baltic states	1735	DE LA FEUILLE	200	15	27	Oorlog van Nerva
mwf0845	france paris	1710	DE LA FEUILLE	280	11	17	Paris
mwsp0544	spain regions	1735	DE LA FEUILLE	300	17	26	Principaute de Catalogne
mwit0736	italy rome	1710	DE LA FEUILLE	350	11	17	Rome Ville Capitale de l'Etat de l'Eglise en Italie
mwsp0514	spain regions	1710	DE LA FEUILLE	350	18	26	Royaume d'Andalousie et de Grenade
mwaf0791	africa north morocco	1710	DE LA FEUILLE	180	16	24	Royaume de Maroc Divise en Sept Provinces &c.
mwit1236	italy venice	1710	DE LA FEUILLE	280	11	17	Venise Ville Capitale de la Republique de Venise
mwsam0049	south america	1710	DE LA FEUILLE	350	14	19	Zuid America. L'Amerique Meridionale.
mwme0367	holy land	1780	DE LA HAYE	400	49	34	Carte de la Phoenicie et des Environs de Damas
mwaa0142	arctic	1774	DE LA HAYE	600	59		Hemisphere Superieur de la mappemonde (polar projection showing most of the world)
mwe0166	europe	1749	DE LA HAYE	600	47	56	L'Europe divisee en ses Empires, Royaumes et Republiques
mwbh0161b	belgium holland	1601	DE LA HOUVE		82	78	Nova Celeberrimi Ducatus Geldriae, Comitatusque Zutphaniae
mwit0874a	italy sicily	1600	DE LA HOUVE		41	54	Nova et Exactissima Insulae Siciliae
mwsc0127	scandinavia	1723	DE LA MOTRAYE	480	31	37	(Untitled map, engraved by S. Parker)
mwca0049	canada	1722	DE LA POTHERIE	600	12	16	Carte de la Baye et Detroit d'Hudson
mwca0569	canada quebec montreal	1722	DE LA POTHERIE	720	13	8	Carte du Gouvernement du Montreal
mwca0503	canada quebec	1722	DE LA POTHERIE	720	13	16	Quebec
mwca0050	canada	1722	DE LA POTHERIE	600	13	24	The Siege of Fort Nelson (Hudson Bay)
mwam0437	america north	1764	DE LA ROCHETTE	3500	99	117	A New Map of North America wherein the British Dominions in the Continent of North America, and on the Islands of the West Indies are Carefully Laid Down from All the Surveys (close copy of Bowles 1763)
mwuk1253	england london	1790	DE LA ROCHETTE	685	51	55	De la Rochette's map of the Country, Twenty Miles round London
mwg0134	germany	1759	DE LA ROCHETTE	1200	102	122	Map of the Empire of Germany, Including All the States Comprehended under that Name: with the Kingdom of Prussia, &c.
mwsc0203	scandinavia	1821	DE LA ROCHETTE	400	72	50	Scandia or Scandinavia Comprehending the Kingdom of Sweden Including Norway. With the Addition of Denmark & Finland
mwme0723	caucasus	1694	DE LA RUE	500	38	51	Armenia Vetus In Quattuor Partes
mwme0143	holy land	1651	DE LA RUE	400	39	54	Assyria Vetus
mwaf0472	africa egypt etc	1650	DE LA RUE	600	41	46	Egypte Moderne dict Chibet Aujour-Dhuy
mwme0947	turkey etc	1652	DE LA RUE	675	38	53	Natolia - Asia Minor
mwme0139	holy land	1651	DE LA RUE	500	40	53	Pinax Geographicus Patriarchatus Hierosolymitani (illustrated below is 1720 Mortier re-issue)

AMPG REFERENCE	REGION	DATE	MAP MAKER	PRICE (UK£)	VERT. (cm.)	HOR. (cm.)	TITLE OF MAP (Comments by the editor in brackets)
mwme0140	holy land	1651	DE LA RUE	500	40	52	Regnum Iudeorum in Filios Herodis Magni per Tatrarchias Divisum ad Tempora Christi Domini
mwme0141	holy land	1651	DE LA RUE	500	39	53	Regnum Salomonicum seu Tabula Digesta ad Libros Judicum Regnum par Eparchias XII Mox Regna Duo
mwme0142	holy land	1651	DE LA RUE	500	39	54	Sourie ou Terre Saincte Moderne
mwme0144	holy land	1651	DE LA RUE	500	41	55	Terra Chanaan ad Abrahami Tempora per Populos XI
mwme0145	holy land	1651	DE LA RUE	500	39	52	Terra Promissa in Sortes seu Tribus XII
mwca0668	canada west	1791	DE LABORDE	1100	44	88	Carte de la Cote Nord-Est de la Mer du Sud. Par M. de Laborde (5 maps on one sheet showing 5 depictions of the same coastline)
mwp0484	pacific solomon isl	1791	DE LABORDE	200	31	39	Carte de l'Isle des Arsacides, pour servir aux Voyages de Messieurs de Bougainville, de Surville et Shortland
mwm0073	mediterranean	1785	DE LABORDE	400	33	66	Carte Des Pays qu'occupe maintenant la Mer Mediterranee
mwca0663	canada west	1791	DE LABORDE	320	20	36	Carte du Voyage du Capitaine Cook
mwp0507	pacific south	1791	DE LABORDE	1100	85	62	Carte d'une Partie de la Mer du Sud avec des Details sur les Principles Isles de cette Mer (incl. New Zealand 46 insets of islands)
mwp0031	australia	1791	DE LABORDE	500	94	57	Carte d'une Partie de la Nouvelle Holland, de l'Isles des Arsacides Decouverte par Mrs. De Bougainville de Surville et Shortland et de quelques Cotes de la Mer Sud
mwsw0187	switzerland	1781	DE LABORDE	480	42	57	Carte Generale de la Suisse
mwit1043	italy south	1786	DE LABORDE	550	76	77	Ombria, Etruria, Latium
mwsp0633	spain regions	1827	DE LABORDE	200	44	25	Plan de la Cuidad ... Tarragona
mwam0038	america continent	1630	DE LAET	1600	28	36	Americae sive Indiae Occidentalis Tabula Generalis
mwsam0444	south america chile	1630	DE LAET	600	28	35	Chili
mwam0854	america north (east)	1630	DE LAET	3500	28	36	Florida, et Regiones Vicinae.
mwsam0573	south america guyana	1625	DE LAET	750	28	36	Guaiana sive Provinciae intra Rio de las Amazonas atque Rio de Yviapari sive Orinoque
mwwi0007	west indies	1630	DE LAET	2400	28	36	Maiores Minores que Insulae. Hispaniola, Cuba, Lucaiae et Caribes
mwam0853	america north (east)	1630	DE LAET	6000	28	36	Nova Anglia, Novum Belgium et Virginia (1st map to name Manhattan and New Amsterdam or New York, founded in 1626)
mwca0013	canada	1630	DE LAET	3000	29	37	Nova Francia et Regiones Adiacentes
mwgm0156	mexico	1633	DE LAET	600	28	36	Nova Hispania, Nova Galicia, Guatimala
mwsam0704	south america paraguay	1630	DE LAET	750	28	36	Paraguay, o Prov. de Rio de la Plata
mwsam0739	south america peru	1633	DE LAET	750	28	36	Peru
mwsam0282	south america brazil	1630	DE LAET	750	28	36	Provincia de Brasil cum Adiacentibus Provinciis
mwsam0212	south america argentina	1630	DE LAET	750	28	36	Provinciae Sitae ad Fretum Magallanis itemque Fretum le Maire (north to the right)
mwsam0492	south america colombia	1633	DE LAET	600	28	36	Tierra Firma item Nuevo Reyno de Grenada atque Popayan
mwsam0819	south america venezuela	1630	DE LAET	750	28	36	Venezuela ende het Westelyckste Gedeelte van Nueva Andalusia
mwas0771	asia south east philippines	1747	DE LAT	750	24	17	Caart van de Philippynsche Eilanden
mwaa0023	antarctic	1747	DE LAT	750	18	28	De Zuid Pool
mwit0180	italy	1747	DE LAT	180	18	24	Kaart van Italie
mwme0821	persia etc	1747	DE LAT	250	18	25	Kaart van Persien
mwaf0175	africa	1740	DE LAT	400	18	24	Kaarte van Africa
mwc0135	china	1742	DE LAT	500	17	24	Kaartje van de Chineese Tarters en het Land van Jeso Opgestelt door I. Matheis Hasi Math. en Gelegen na de Stelling van de Heer Guil. de l'Isle
mwjk0099	japan	1747	DE LAT	750	17	24	Kaartje van het Keizer-Ryck Japan
mwp0011	australia	1747	DE LAT	1800	17	24	Kaartje van Nieu Holland Carpentarie en A. van Diemens Land
mwas0469	asia south east	1747	DE LAT	400	18	24	Kaartje van Oost-Indien
mwme0319	holy land	1747	DE LAT	250	17	24	Kaartje van t' Heilige Land
mwgr0504	greece cyprus	1747	DE LAT	5000	17	24	Kaartje van't Eiland Cyprus
mwsw0146a	switzerland	1747	DE LAT	220	18	24	Kaartjen van Zwitzerland (inset of Bern)
mwm0150	mediterranean east	1747	DE LAT	200	17	28	t Oosterdeel van de Middelandse Zee
mwgr0187	greece	1747	DE LAT	160	24	18	t Zuyder Deel van Turks Europa Genaamt Griekenland
mwsam0598	south america guyana	1737	DE LAVAUX	4800	97	109	Algemeene Kaart van de Colonie of Provintie van Suriname me de Rivieren, Districten, Ontekkingen door Militaire Togten, en de Grootte Vergemeeten Plantagien (re-issued in reduced size)
mwec0142	uk england cheshire	1745	DE LAVAUX	1500	63	80	Plan of the City & Castle of Chester
mwru0410	russia moscow	1850	DE LAVEAU	1200	56	64	Nouveau Plan de Moscou (In French and Cyrillic)
mwru0406	russia moscow	1826	DE LAVEAU	1600	51	62	Nouveau Plan de Moscou 1826 (in French and Cyrillic)
mwuk1177	england london	1743	DE LETH	980	33	50	A Pocket Map of London, Westminster and Southwark, with ye New Buildings to the Year 1739
mwbh0639	belgium holland	1740	DE LETH	200	20	23	Afbeeldinge van Rhynlands Waterstaat ... Haarlemmer of Leydse
mwru0534	ukraine	1750	DE LETH	720	42	49	Carte de la Petite Tartarie
mwaf0919	africa south	1745	DE LETH	850	51	58	Carte de l'Afrique Meridionale ou Pays Entre la Ligne et le Cap Esperance et l'Isle de Madagascar. Par le Veuve de Nicolas Visscher

AMPG REFERENCE	REGION	DATE	MAP MAKER	PRICE (UK£)	VERT. (cm.)	HOR. (cm.)	TITLE OF MAP (Comments by the editor in brackets)
mwaf0402	africa east	1740	DE LETH	550	48	56	Carte de l'Egypte de la Nubie de l'Abissinie &c. (copy of Covens & Mortier 1730)
mwp0247	pacific (all)	1730	DE LETH	9000	58	93	Carte Nouvelle de la Mer du Sud
mwaf0743a	africa north algeria	1725	DE LETH	900	51	50	De Stat Algiers (view and map below)
mwsw0126	switzerland	1730	DE LETH	120	16	22	La Suisse
mwam0402	america north	1750	DE LETH	280	16	22	L'Amerique Septentrionale
mwas0149	asia continent	1740	DE LETH	2000	48	59	L'Asie Divisee en ses Principales Parties
mww0376	world	1740	DE LETH	4000	45	66	Mappe Monde or Description du Globe Terrestre Vu en Concave ou Creux en Deux Hemispheres
mwsam0600	south america guyana	1741	DE LETH	3500	58	86	Naaukeurige Plate Grond vanden Staaten den Loop van Rio de Berbice met derselver Plantagien in de Geoctroyeerde Colonie de Berbice Gelegen
mwbh0640	belgium holland	1740	DE LETH	300	20	22	Nieuwe en Accurate Kaart van de Balluage van Amstelland
mwsp0701	gibraltar	1728	DE LETH	900	46	55	Nieuwe Paskaart van t Naauw van de Straat. Opgedragen aan den Hoog Edel:Geboren Heer F. van Aerssen van Sommelsdyk ... door syn Onderdanige Dienaar Hendrik Lynslager Capityn ter Zee Anno 1726
mwbh0621	belgium holland	1733	DE LETH	960	41	48	Nieuwe Platte Grond vande Stad Rotterdam (illustrated is 1768 re-issue)
mwm0052	mediterranean	1730	DE LETH	3000	46	113	Nouvelle Carte de la Mer Mediterrenee
mwca0368	canada nova scotia	1750	DE LETH	2400	58	46	Plan des Fortifications de la Ville de Louisbourg dans l'Isle de Cap-Breton
mwbp0424	poland	1740	DE LETH	1400	36	50	Plan en Profil der Beroemde Stadt Dantzig, derzelver Werders, en Omleggende Landen
mwbh0631	belgium holland	1736	DE LETH	1800	60	93	Plan Tres Exact de la Fameuse Ville Marchande d'Amsterdam
mwsam0606	south america guyana	1755	DE LETH	550	60	89	Suriname
mwru0200a	russia	1745	DE L'ISLE	1200	100	168	(Untitled map of Russia in 6 sheets, publ. in St. Petersburg) Partis Fluviorum Petschorae, Obii et Jenisae / Pars Maris Ostiumique Fluvii Lenae cum Territorio Septentrionali Jacutensi / Territorii Jacutensis Pars Orientalior / Ostium Fluvii Amur cum Parte Australiori Kamtschatrae / Urkutensis Vice Praefectura cum Mari Baikal et Fonte Fluvii Lenae / Tractus Fluviorum Irtisch, Tobol et Jeniseae
mwe0127	europe	1709	DE L'ISLE	550	48	116	An Historical Map of the Roman Empire and the Neighbouring Barbarous Nations to the Year of Our Lord Four Hundred, when the Empire Began to be Rent with Foreign Invasions
mwbh0519	belgium holland	1705	DE L'ISLE	720	63	63	Caarte van Brabant - Carte du Brabant
mwaf0155	africa	1722	DE L'ISLE	900	50	64	Carte d'Afrique, Dressee pour l'Usage du Roy (title above map 'Africa Accurate in Imperia Regna ...'. Updated version of De L'Isle 1700, publ. by Covens & Mortier)
mwam0135	america continent	1722	DE L'ISLE	1200	48	61	Carte d'Amerique, Dressee pour l'Usage du Roy (illustrated is 1739 re-issue by Covens & Mortier)
mwas0129a	asia continent	1723	DE L'ISLE	720	48	63	Carte D'Asie Dressee ... (illustrated is Buache re-issue of 1745.)
mwf0111	france	1721	DE L'ISLE	720	49	62	Carte de France
mwe0142a	europe	1724	DE L'ISLE	720	49	61	Carte de l'Europe
mwaf1167a	africa west	1712	DE L'ISLE	600	50	58	Carte de la Barbarie de la Nigritie et de la Guinee
mwgr0147	greece	1707	DE L'ISLE	720	45	64	Carte de la Grece
mwe0780	europe east	1703	DE L'ISLE	450	47	65	Carte de la Hongrie et des Pays qui en Dependoient Autrefois
mwe0795	europe east	1739	DE L'ISLE	450	45	49	Carte de la Hongrie, de la Transilvanie, et de la Sclavonie
mwuss0622	louisiana	1718	DE L'ISLE	12000	49	65	Carte de la Louisiane et du Cours du Mississipi Dressee sur un Grand Nombre de Memoires entrautres sur ceux de Mr. le Maire
mwsw0120	switzerland	1722	DE L'ISLE	400	48	64	Carte de la Souverainete de Neuchatel et Valangin
mwsam0044	south america	1703	DE L'ISLE	1200	88	65	Carte de la Terre Ferme, du Perou, du Bresil, et du Pays des Amazones / Carte du Paraguay, du Chili, du Detroit du Magellan (2 maps of 45x67cm.)
mwme0591a	arabia etc	1707	DE L'ISLE	875	48	62	Carte de la Turquie, de l'Arabie et de la Perse (illustrated with Buache's revised 1770 edition.)
mwaf1182	africa west	1726	DE L'ISLE	550	49	62	Carte de l'Afrique Francoise ou du Senegal
mwaf0495	africa egypt etc	1707	DE L'ISLE	550	49	62	Carte de l'Egypte de la Nubie
mwin0037	ceylon	1722	DE L'ISLE	720	42	56	Carte de l'Isle de Ceylan
mwwi0772	martinique	1730	DE L'ISLE	720	46	58	Carte de l'Isle de la Martinique Colonie Francoise de l'une des Isles Antilles de l'Amerique (illustrated is Covens & Mortier reprint)
mwwi0595	hispaniola	1725	DE L'ISLE	800	48	62	Carte de l'Isle de Saint Domingue Dressee en 1722 pour l'Usage du Roy sur les Memoires de Mr. Frezier (re-issued by Covens & Mortier, Buache, Dezauche)
mwru0120	russia	1706	DE L'ISLE	750	96	60	Carte de Moscovie
mwme0811a	persia etc	1724	DE L'ISLE	1200	48	62	Carte de Perse (copy of De L'Isle 1724)
mwf1046	france provence	1715	DE L'ISLE	720	48	60	Carte de Provence
mwsw0109	switzerland	1715	DE L'ISLE	650	49	64	Carte de Suisse

AMPG REFERENCE	REGION	DATE	MAP MAKER	PRICE (UK£)	VERT. (cm.)	HOR. (cm.)	TITLE OF MAP (Comments by the editor in brackets)
mwru0445	russia tartary	1706	DE L'ISLE	850	49	64	Carte de Tartarie Dressee sur les Relations de Plusieurs Voyageurs de Differentes Nations
mwwi0241	west indies (east)	1717	DE L'ISLE	750	64	37	Carte des Antilles Francoises et des Isles Voisines. Dressee sur les Memoires Manuscrits de Mr. Petit Ingenieur du Roy
mwbh0528	belgium holland	1706	DE L'ISLE	600	47	67	Carte des Comtez de Hainaut, de Namur et de Cambresis. Par Guillaume de l'Isle ... Paris, 1706 et Amsterdam, Chez Louis Renard
mwin0174	india	1723	DE L'ISLE	600	44	57	Carte des Cotes de Malabar et de Coromandel
mwsc0105	scandinavia	1706	DE L'ISLE	720	45	61	Carte des Courones du Nord Dediee au Tres Puissant et Tres Invincible Prince Charles XII Roy de Suede, des Gots et Vandales Grand Duc de Finlande &c. (2 maps, each 45x61cm)
mwas0434a	asia south east	1706	DE L'ISLE	1200	63	65	Carte des Indes et de la Chine
mwm0048	mediterranean	1726	DE L'ISLE	550	22	53	Carte des Pays ou les Chevaliers de St. Jean de Jerusalem ont Porte leurs Armes
mwas0313	asia caspian sea	1723	DE L'ISLE	750	46	62	Carte des Pays Voisins de la Mer Caspiene Dressee pour l'Usage du Roy sur la Carte de cete Mer Faite par l'Ordre du Czar, sur les Memoire Manuscrits de Soskam-Sabbas Prince de Georgie
mwbh0506	belgium holland	1702	DE L'ISLE	480	47	62	Carte des Pays-Bas Catholiques ... Paris, Chez l'Auteur, sur le Quay de l'Horologe a l'Aigle d'Or
mwbh0507	belgium holland	1702	DE L'ISLE	1000	47	62	Carte des Provinces Unies des Pays Bas
mwca0040	canada	1703	DE L'ISLE	10500	50	65	Carte du Canada ou de la Nouvelle France et des Decouvertes qui y ont ete Faites Dressee sur Plusieurs Observations (first edition, first issue. Illustrated is 5th issue, c1718. The only change is De L'Isle Paris address)
mwaf0894	africa south	1708	DE L'ISLE	800	48	61	Carte du Congo et du Pays des Cafres (illustrated is Covens & Mortier 1730 re-issue)
mwf0954	france picardy	1710	DE L'ISLE	350	47	60	Carte du Diocese de Beauvais
mwgm0015	gulf of mexico and surrounding regions	1703	DE L'ISLE	7500	50	66	Carte du Mexique et de la Floride des Terres Angloises et des Isles Antilles du Cours et des Environs de la Riviere de Mississipi (1st edition, 1st issue. Illustrated is the 1783 close copy by Dezauche with title 'Carte du Mexique et des Etats Unis d'Amerique, Partie Meridionale', value: £1350)
mwsam0224	south america argentina	1703	DE L'ISLE	650	50	64	Carte du Paraguay du Chili du Detroit de Magellan &c. Dressee sur les Descriptions des PP. Alfonse d'Ovalle, et Nicolas Techo
mwit0669	italy piedmont	1707	DE L'ISLE	800	48	64	Carte du Piemont et du Monferrat
mwsc0332	scandinavia denmark	1710	DE L'ISLE	800	49	64	Carte du Royaume de Danemarc Par Guill. de l'Isle
mwme0883	syria etc	1764	DE L'ISLE, J.N.	900	36	50	Carte Generale de la Syrie, de la Palestine
mwp0406a	pacific north	1753	DE L'ISLE, J.N.	1200	29	38	Carte Generale des Decouvertes de l'Amiral de Fonte et autres Navigateurs Espagnols, Anglois et Russes pour la Recherche du Passage a la Mer du Sud (copied by R. de Vaugondy for Diderot)
mwas0312	asia caspian sea	1722	DE L'ISLE	1250	93	63	Carte Marine de la Mer Caspiene Levee Suivant les Ordres de S.M. Czarienne, par Mr. Carl Vanverden en 1719, 1720, et 1721. Et Reduite au Meridien de Paris par Guillaume Delisle / Coste de Perse sur la Mer Caspiene et Partie de celles de Tartarie (2 sheets, joined)
mwf0953	france picardy	1709	DE L'ISLE	450	47	65	Carte Topographique du Diocese de Senlis
mwgr0147a	greece	1707	DE L'ISLE	720	48	64	Graeciae Antiquae Tabula Nova (2 maps Meridionalis / Septentrionalis, each 48x64cm.)
mww0323a	world	1714	DE L'ISLE	2000	47	47	Hemisphere Septentrional pour Voir Plus Distinctement les Terres Arctiques / Hemisphere Meridional (2 sheets. Re-issued by Covens & Mortier c1730 sl. smaller 46x46cm)
mwam0138	america continent	1724	DE L'ISLE	800	51	51	Hemisphere Occidental Dresse en 1720 pour l'Usage Particulier du Roy sur les Observations Astronomiques et Geographiques
mwme0993	turkey etc	1722	DE L'ISLE	500	48	64	Imperii Orientalis et Circumjacentium Region
mwaf0703	africa north	1700	DE L'ISLE	400	49	65	In Notitiam Ecclesiasticam Africae Tabula Geographica Auctore G. de l'Isle
mwru0174a	russia	1735	DE L'ISLE	1000	60	46	Karta Ingermanlandii i Karelii (Russian script)
mwbp0347	poland	1702	DE L'ISLE	750	48	63	La Pologne (first edition)
mwaf0115	africa	1700	DE L'ISLE	1200	45	59	L'Afrique Dressee sur les Observations de Ms. de l'Academie Royal des Sciences
mwg0090a	germany	1701	DE L'ISLE	650	50	61	L'Allemagne Dressee sur les Observations de Tycho Brahe de Kepler de Snellius
mwsam0037	south america	1700	DE L'ISLE	2000	46	61	L'Amerique Meridionale Dressee sur les Observations de Mrs. de l'Academie Royale des Sciences (1st issue illustrated, Rue des Canettes, with western distortion, corrected ln later editions)
mwam0343	america north	1700	DE L'ISLE	10000	45	60	L'Amerique Septentrionale Dressee sur les Observations de Mrs. de l'Academie Royale des Sciences ... Par G. de l'Isle (price is for the first issue of this much re-issued map)

AMPG REFERENCE	REGION	DATE	MAP MAKER	PRICE (UK£)	VERT. (cm.)	HOR. (cm.)	TITLE OF MAP (Comments by the editor in brackets)
mwas0097	asia continent	1700	DE L'ISLE	900	45	58	L'Asie Dressee sur les Observations de l'Academie Royale des Sciences et quelques Autres (first edition)
mwe1016	europe rhine	1704	DE L'ISLE	1200	142	63	Le Cours du Rhin ... jusqu'a Bonne (re-issued by Covens & Mortier in 1730)
mwf0850b	france paris	1720	DE L'ISLE	2400	57	76	Le Plan de Paris, ses Faubourgs et ses Environs / Platte Grond van Parys, zyn Voorburgen en Omleggende Plaatse (publ. by Covens & Mortier; shown above left)
mwuk0775	uk	1702	DE L'ISLE	1200	47	62	Les Isles Britanniques ou sont le Rme. d'Angleterre Tire de Sped celuy d'Ecosse Tire de Th. Pont &c. et celuy d'Irlande Tire de Petti (first edition)
mwsp0218	spain	1701	DE L'ISLE	600	44	62	L'Espagne Dressee sur la Description qui en a ete Faite par Rodrigo Mendez Sylva
mwit0130	italy	1700	DE L'ISLE	800	50	63	L'Italie Dressee sur les Observations de l'Academie Royale des Sciences
mwru0200	russia	1745	DE L'ISLE	1600	55	96	Mappa Generalis Totius Imperii Russici (in 2 sheets, published in St. Petersburg)
mww0275	world	1700	DE L'ISLE	2250	43	66	Mappe-Monde Dresse sur les Observations de Mrs. de l'Academie Royale des Sciences et quelques Autres
mwg0269a	baden-wurttemberg	1704	DE L'ISLE	600	48	64	Partie Septentrionale / Meridionale de la Souabe (2 maps each 48x64cm. Titles above maps. Northern map illustrated)
mwf0871	france paris	1745	DE L'ISLE	1200	50	64	Plan de la Ville et Fauxbourgs de Paris
mwc0174	china	1765	DE L'ISLE, J.N.	960	38	49	Plan de la Ville Tartare de Peking (map engr. By Lattre)
mwit0402a	italy lazio	1711	DE L'ISLE	400	46	62	Regionum Italiae Mediarum Tabula Geographica pernoscendis Historiae Romanae Primordiis Paresertim
mwme0994	turkey etc	1723	DE L'ISLE	400	44	57	Retraite des Dix Mille Tabula Conspectum Exhibens Regionum Omnium quas Cyrus Junior, Artaxerxi Fratibellum Illaturus ac Cyro in Acie Caeso
mwbh0491	belgium holland	1700	DE L'ISLE	720	46	55	s-Gravenhage
mwit0924	italy sicily	1714	DE L'ISLE	650	46	63	Siciliae Antiquae quae et Sicania et Trinacria dicta Tabula Geographica
mwf1147	france rhone-alpes	1711	DE L'ISLE	350	49	62	Tabula Delphinatus
mwme0369a	holy land	1782	DE L'ISLE, J.N.	750	66	49	Terrae Sanctae Tabula (issued posthumously by the author's brother)
mwm0034a	mediterranean	1705	DE L'ISLE	600	48	116	Theatrum Historicum ad Annum Christi Quadringentesimu in quo tum Imperii Romani tu Barbarorum ... pars Occidentalis / pars Orientalis
mwam0805	america north (central)	1737	DE L'ISLE-BERNARD	1500	35	40	Carte de la Louisiane de du Cours du Mississipi
mwbp0495a	poland	1780	DE L'ISLE-BUACHE	650	48	62	La Pologne dressee (showing boundary changes)
mww0261	world	1696	DE L'ISLE-MORTIER	4000	50	64	Mappe-Monde Dresse sur les Observations de Mrs. de l'Academie Royale des Sciences et quelques autres et sur les memoires les plus recens Par M. Sanson (This map is usually found with Sanson's name. However, the shape of South America is unmistakeably De L'Isle's. Later, Sanson's name was replaced with De L'Isle's by Mortier, the publisher, presumably when De L'Isle's reputation as a cartographer supplanted Sanson's. The illustration has De L'Isle's imprint.)
mwam0365	america north	1710	DE L'ISLE-WOLF	1200	45	60	America Septentrionalis (close copy of De L'Isle 1700)
mwas0802a	asia south east philippines	1790	DE LUQUE	1500	37	44	Plan de Manila su Bahia
mwaf0410	africa east	1775	DE MANNEVILLETTE	300	50	33	(Kenya, Lamu / Mozambique, Ibo. 2 charts)
mwas0595	asia south east borneo	1775	DE MANNEVILLETTE	400	46	65	A Map of Part of Borneo and the Sooloo Archipelago: Laid down Chiefly from Observations Made in 1761, 2, 3, and 4 by A. Dalrymple
mwin0056	ceylon	1775	DE MANNEVILLETTE	400	49	65	Carte de la Baye et du Port de Trinquemalay dans l'Isle de Ceylan Levee Exactement en 1762 par le Sr. Ge. Neichelson
mwc0137a	china	1745	DE MANNEVILLETTE	2500	60	45	Carte de la Coste orientale de la Chine depuis Amoy, jusqu'à Chusan avec une partie de l'Isle Formose
mwaf0948	africa south	1775	DE MANNEVILLETTE	400	48	67	Carte de la Cote d'Afrique depuis le Cap Blanc jusques et Compris la Riviere de Gambie
mwin0254	india	1775	DE MANNEVILLETTE	350	66	48	Carte de la Cote de Guzerat, du Golfe de Cambaye et des Cotes de Concan et de Canara
mwas0844	asia south east siam	1781	DE MANNEVILLETTE	300	34	48	Carte de la Cote de Pegou et de Celle de Martagan
mwas0839	asia south east siam	1775	DE MANNEVILLETTE	300	33	48	Carte de la Cote de Pegu
mwin0386b	india bay of bengal	1745	DE MANNEVILLETTE	250	48	33	Carte de la Cote du Golfe de Bengale
mwas0885	asia south east sumatra	1775	DE MANNEVILLETTE	400	66	49	Carte de la Cote Occidentale de l'Isle Sumatra depuis la Ligne Equinoctiale jusqu'au Detroit de la Sonde
mwaf0411	africa east	1775	DE MANNEVILLETTE	400	66	48	Carte de la Cote Orientale d'Afrique depuis l'Isle de Patte jusques a Mocambique, avec les Isles Adjacentes
mwaf0614	africa islands madagascar	1775	DE MANNEVILLETTE	400	67	49	Carte de la Cote Orientale de Madagascar depuis Mananzari ... Fort Dauphin
mwaf0615	africa islands madagascar	1775	DE MANNEVILLETTE	400	67	49	Carte de la Cote Orientale de Madagascar, depuis la Pointe de l'Est ... Lac Nossi
mwin0255	india	1775	DE MANNEVILLETTE	400	48	33	Carte de la Cote Orientale du Golfe du Bengale
mwme0639	arabia etc	1775	DE MANNEVILLETTE	480	48	66	Carte de la Mer Rouge depuis Moka jusqu'a Gedda

AMPG REFERENCE	REGION	DATE	MAP MAKER	PRICE (UK£)	VERT. (cm.)	HOR. (cm.)	TITLE OF MAP (Comments by the editor in brackets)
mwas0596	asia south east borneo	1775	DE MANNEVILLETTE	400	35	51	Carte de la Partie Comprise entre la Sortie du Detroit de Malac le Detroit de Banca et l'Isle Borneo
mwme0638	arabia etc	1775	DE MANNEVILLETTE	275	33	49	Carte de l'Entree du Golfe de la Mer Rouge
mwas0664	asia south east java	1775	DE MANNEVILLETTE	600	48	67	Carte de l'Isle de Java, avec les Isles de Banca, de Billiton, et une Partie de celles de Sumatra et de Borneo
mwaf0650	africa islands seychelles	1775	DE MANNEVILLETTE	800	48	66	Carte de l'isle Mahé ou Seychelle avec les isles circonvoisines.
mwaf0655	africa islands seychelles	1781	DE MANNEVILLETTE	600	48	66	Carte de l'Isle Mahe ou Seychelles avec les Isles Circonvoisines Decouvertes par M.M. du Roslan et de la Bioliere
mwf0142	france	1775	DE MANNEVILLETTE	300	48	66	Carte des Cotes Occidentales de France et d'une Partie de celles d'Espagne, d'Angleterre et d'Irlande
mwat0095	atlantic azores	1775	DE MANNEVILLETTE	300	48	34	Carte des Isles Acores et des Isles Canaries, Dressee pour le Neptune Oriental
mwat0200	atlantic cape verde isl.	1774	DE MANNEVILLETTE	200	48	33	Carte des Isles du Cap-Verd
mwaf0621	africa islands madagascar	1781	DE MANNEVILLETTE	300	34	50	Carte des Isles et Dangers Situes au Nord-Est de l'Isle Madagascar
mwin0256	india	1775	DE MANNEVILLETTE	300	46	30	Carte des Isles Nicobar
mwas0692	asia south east malacca	1775	DE MANNEVILLETTE	400	66	48	Carte du Detroit de la Sonde depuis la Pointe de Winerou jusques a l'Isle du Nord
mwme0639a	iraq etc	1775	DE MANNEVILLETTE	675	48	66	Carte du Golfe Persique depuis Bassora jusqu'au Cap Rasalgate
mwas0840	asia south east siam	1775	DE MANNEVILLETTE	400	48	33	Carte d'une Partie des Cotes de Cochinchine depuis l'Isle Cham-Collan jusqu'a la Rive du Roi / Plan de l'Isle Condor
mwc0185	china	1775	DE MANNEVILLETTE	3500	34	49	Carte d'une Partie des Cotes de la Chine et des Isles Adjacentes ... Tracee sur les Observations Faites ... par Mr. Alexandre Dalrymple (first Western representation of Hong Kong)
mwaf0611	africa islands madagascar	1775	DE MANNEVILLETTE	300	48	33	Carte Plate de la Cote Occidentale de l'Isle de Madagascar depuis la Baye de St. Augustin jusqu'au Cap St. Andre
mwas0693	asia south east malacca	1775	DE MANNEVILLETTE	600	48	70	Carte Plate de la Partie Septentrionale du Detroit de Malac, depuis la Rade d'Achem jusqu'a Malac
mwas0841	asia south east siam	1775	DE MANNEVILLETTE	450	50	36	Carte Plate du Golfe de Siam avec une Partie des Cotes de Malaye et de Camboje, depuis l'Isle Timor jusqu'a celle Condor
mwin0057	ceylon	1775	DE MANNEVILLETTE	500	51	69	Carte Plate qui Comprend l'Isle de Ceylon et une Partie des Cotes de Malabar et de Coromandel
mwas0694	asia south east malacca	1775	DE MANNEVILLETTE	400	66	49	Carte pour Aller du Detroit de la Sonde ou de Batavia au Detroit de Banca
mwin0389	india bay of bengal	1745	DE MANNEVILLETTE	450	49	67	Carte Reduite de Golfe de Bengale
mwaf0949	africa south	1775	DE MANNEVILLETTE	600	50	68	Carte Reduite de la Cote Meridionale d'Afrique depuis la Baye de Saldagne jusqu'au Cap des Courans
mwas0464	asia south east	1745	DE MANNEVILLETTE	800	58	80	Carte Reduite de l'Archipel des Indes Orientales avec les Cotes du Continent depuis le Golfe de Manar jusqu'a Emoui a la Chine
mwaf0612	africa islands madagascar	1775	DE MANNEVILLETTE	300	46	66	Carte Reduite de l'Archipel du Nord-Est de l'Isle Madagascar, depuis la Ligne Equinoctiale jusqu'au 21d. 30m. de Latitude Meridional
mwin0429	indian ocean	1771	DE MANNEVILLETTE	1000	56	84	Carte Reduite de l'Ocean Oriental
mwas0465	asia south east	1745	DE MANNEVILLETTE	1200	60	85	Carte Reduite de l'Ocean Oriental depuis le Cap de Bonne Esperance, jusqu'au Japon
mwas0493	asia south east	1775	DE MANNEVILLETTE	600	48	66	Carte Reduite de l'Ocean Oriental Septentrional
mwin0485	indian ocean west	1775	DE MANNEVILLETTE	600	48	67	Carte Reduite de l'Ocean Orientale qui Contient la Cote d'Afrique, depuis le 9e. Degre de Latitude Meridionale jusqu'au 30e. avec l'Isle Madagascar et les Isles Adjacentes
mwin0257	india	1775	DE MANNEVILLETTE	600	49	67	Carte Reduite du Golfe de Bengale
mwas0597	asia south east borneo	1775	DE MANNEVILLETTE	400	61	47	Chart of Felicia and Plan of the Island of Balambangan
mwaf0613	africa islands madagascar	1775	DE MANNEVILLETTE	300	49	34	Cote Orientale de Madagascar depuis la Riviere d'Ivondrou jusqu'a Mananzari
mwas0666	asia south east java	1775	DE MANNEVILLETTE	400	48	33	Nouveau Plan des Detroits, Situes a l'Est de Java et de Madura, Nommes Communement les Detroits de Bali et d'entre Pondi et Respondi
mwas0687	asia south east malacca	1750	DE MANNEVILLETTE	850	50	67	Nouvelle Carte des Mers Comprises entre le Detroit de Banca et Po. Timon, avec la Partie Orientale du Detroit de Malac
mwaf0610	africa islands madagascar	1775	DE MANNEVILLETTE	180	47	33	Plan de la Baye de St. Augustin en l'Isle de Madagascar / Plan du Port de l'Isle Ste. Marie Situe pres la Cote Orientale de Madagascar
mwsam0387	south america brazil	1775	DE MANNEVILLETTE	1500	49	32	Plan de la Baye et du Port de Rio Janeiro ... Verifie par l'Auteur en 1751
mwas0886	asia south east sumatra	1775	DE MANNEVILLETTE	300	48	33	Plan de la Rade d'Achem et des Isles Circonvoisines
mwme0637	arabia etc	1775	DE MANNEVILLETTE	250	48	33	Plan de la Rade de Gedda, Situee a la Cote d'Arabie sur la Mer Rouge
mwas0842	asia south east siam	1775	DE MANNEVILLETTE	500	33	48	Plan de l'Archipel de Merguy / Plan de l'Isle Junkseilon et de son Port
mwaf0574	africa islands bourbon	1775	DE MANNEVILLETTE	500	48	33	Plan de l'Isle de Bourbon, Situee sur l'Ocean Oriental

AMPG REFERENCE	REGION	DATE	MAP MAKER	PRICE (UK£)	VERT. (cm.)	HOR. (cm.)	TITLE OF MAP (Comments by the editor in brackets)
mwaf0635	africa islands mauritius	1775	DE MANNEVILLETTE	1500	50	72	Plan de l'Isle de France
mwaf0644	africa islands rodrigues	1775	DE MANNEVILLETTE	450	33	48	Plan de l'Isle Rodrigues
mwas0577a	asia south east bantam	1775	DE MANNEVILLETTE	400	33	48	Plan de Port de Rio / Plan du Detroit du Gouverneur
mwas0695	asia south east malacca	1775	DE MANNEVILLETTE	250	48	33	Plan de Salangor et de la Cote de Malaye depuis la Pointe de Caran jusqu'au Mont Parcelar
mwaf0650a	africa islands seychelles	1775	DE MANNEVILLETTE	400	34	49	Plan des Isles Mahe
mwas0696	asia south east malacca	1775	DE MANNEVILLETTE	250	49	32	Plan des Principaux Ports de la Cote d'Illocos en l'Isle de Lucon
mwaf0932	africa south	1752	DE MANNEVILLETTE	350	48	33	Plan du Cap de Bonne-Esperance et de ses Environs Levee Geometriquement en 1752
mwas0565	asia south east banca	1745	DE MANNEVILLETTE	400	48	33	Plan du Detroit de Banca
mwas0795	asia south east philippines	1775	DE MANNEVILLETTE	250	48	33	Plan du Port de Subec en l'Isle de Lucon
mwaf0634	africa islands mauritius	1775	DE MANNEVILLETTE	900	49	33	Plan du Port-Louis et de l'Orient
mwas0794	asia south east philippines	1775	DE MANNEVILLETTE	335	46	60	The Sooloo Archipelago, Laid down Chiefly from Observations in 1761, 1762, 1763 & 1764, by A. Dalrymple
mwas0598	asia south east borneo	1775	DE MANNEVILLETTE	400	47	60	To His Majesty George the Third, King of Great Britain, &c. this Chart of Felicia, and Plan of the Island Balambangan, is Humbly Presented by His Majesty's Faithful Subject, Dalrymple
mwas0670	asia south east java	1785	DE MARRE	500	18	46	Batavia in der Gestalt die Es im Iahr 1731 Hatte
mwit1113	italy tuscany	1700	DE MARTINEZ	950	44	64	Topografia dela Plaza de Orvitelo
mww0040	world	1545	DE MEDINA	4800	12		(Untitled circular map)
mwat0003a	atlantic ocean (all)	1545	DE MEDINA		15	25	Nuevo Mundo (North America, North Atlantic, Western Africa and Europe. See also 'America Continent' 1548)
mwam0003	america continent	1548	DE MEDINA	20000	22	25	Nuevo Mundo / Andaluzia (2 maps, overall size 22x25cm. The maps were first published in 1545 without the southern part of South America)
mwat0008	atlantic ocean (all)	1561	DE MEDINA-EDEN	5000	15	24	The Newe Worlde (woodcut derived from De Medina'a map of 1545)
mwat0004	atlantic ocean (all)	1554	DE MEDINA-PEDREZANO	10000	13	18	Mundo Novo (based on De Medina's 1545 map but reduced size)
mwaf0131	africa	1709	DE MEDRADO	280	15	18	Afriquae
mwat0005	atlantic ocean (all)	1554	DE NICOLAY	15000	25	36	Nouveau Monde (Updated version of De Medina's 1545 map)
mwgm0250a	mexico	1782	DE PAGES	1350	33	43	Carte d'une Partie de l'Amerique Septentrionale qui Contient Partie de la Nle. Espagne et de la Louisiane
mww0520a	world	1782	DE PAGES	550	28	34	Carte Reduite du Globe Terrestre
mwm0241	mediterranean malta	1752	DE PALMEUS	5000	57	133	Carte Generale de la Principaute Souveraine des Isles de Malte et du Goze
mwm0242	mediterranean malta	1757	DE PALMEUS	1500	43	75	Plan de la Cite Neuve de Chambray dans l'Isle de Goze
mwm0240	mediterranean malta	1751	DE PALMEUS	3000	58	89	Plan General de la Ville Capitale de Malte
mwit1219	italy venice	1600	DE PAOLI	5500	39	52	Venetia (3 insets below map)
mwsc0063	scandinavia	1664	DE PIENE	800	28	36	La Gran Penisola della Scandia (north to the right)
mwf1143	france rhone-alpes	1700	DE PIENNE	3500	61	61	Carte Generale des Estats de S.A.R. tant deca que dela les Monts. Et du Royaume de Chypre (inset of Cyprus)
mwin0288a	india	1787	DE PRETOT	320	38	54	Carte de Bengale (shown below left)
mwat0228	atlantic falkland isl.	1775	DE PRETOT	350	24	36	Carte de Isles Malouines Nomme par les Anglois, Isles Falkland
mwp0497	pacific (all)	1767	DE PRETOT	500	19	47	Carte de la Partie Meridionale de la Mer du Sud qui Represente les Decouvertes Faites avant 1764
mww0479	world	1771	DE PRETOT	650	29	42	Carte de l'Ancien et du Nouveau Monde
mwaf0255	africa	1787	DE PRETOT	250	26	32	Carte Nouvelle d'Afrique
mwam0194	america continent	1770	DE PRETOT	400	27	39	Carte Nouvelle d'Amerique
mwas0208	asia continent	1787	DE PRETOT	235	26	32	Carte Nouvelle d'Asie
mwe0214	europe	1787	DE PRETOT	235	26	32	Carte Nouvelle d'Europe
mwe0609	europe czech republic (bohemia)	1787	DE PRETOT	240	26	40	Chorographie de Royaume de Boheme (incl. adjacent territories)
mwg0290	baden-wurttemberg	1787	DE PRETOT	235	26	34	Chorographie du Cercle de Souabe
mwuk1010	england	1770	DE PRETOT	300	27	40	L'Angleterre
mwuk0847	uk	1767	DE PRETOT	320	27	40	Les Isles Britanniques
mwam0223	america continent	1787	DE PRETOT	400	34	36	Nouvelle Carte des Parties Occidentales du Monde Servant a Indiquer les Navigations Decouvertes et Etablissements des Hollandois en Amerique Suivant les Dernieres Observations
mwm0234	mediterranean malta	1729	DE PUTTER	800	30	43	D'oude schets van het eyland Malta, alwaer, Paulus na zyn schipbreuk aenlandde (title below map)
mwbh0398	belgium holland	1677	DE RAM	6500	82	125	(Plan of Delft)
mwg0524	rheinland-pfalz	1689	DE RAM	800	50	60	(Triers environs) Archiepiscopatus Trevirensis Recentissima Delineatio
mwaf0099a	africa	1690	DE RAM	720	44	56	Africae Accurata Tabula (reduced size close copy of De Wit 1680)
mwin0030	ceylon	1690	DE RAM	1000	50	59	Insula Ceilon et Madura
mwuk1128	england london	1690	DE RAM	5000	50	59	Londini Angliae Regni Metropolis Novissima & Accuratissima

AMPG REFERENCE	REGION	DATE	MAP MAKER	PRICE (UK£)	VERT. (cm.)	HOR. (cm.)	TITLE OF MAP (Comments by the editor in brackets)
mwf0834	france paris	1686	DE RAM	2400	50	59	Lutetiae Parisiorum Universae Galliae Metropolis Novissima & Accuratissima Delineatio (updated by F. de Witt c1690 {illustrated} and J. De La Feuille in 1696)
mwe0090	europe	1680	DE RAM	1400	44	55	Nova Europae Tabula
mwsp0048	portugal	1680	DE RAM	785	50	59	Nova Regni Portugalliae et Algarbiae Descriptio
mwas0083	asia continent	1690	DE RAM	700	45	57	Nova Totius Asiae Tabula per Ioannem de Ram
mwam0087	america continent	1685	DE RAM	2000	44	56	Novissima et Accuratissima Totius Americae Descriptio
mww0229	world	1685	DE RAM	12500	45	56	Novissima Totius Terrarum Orbis Tabula. Auctore Ioannes de Ram (copy of Allard 1682)
mwuk0948	england	1689	DE RAM	1200	50	58	Regni Angliae Nova Tabula
mwbp0319	poland	1690	DE RAM	1250	54	63	Regni Poloniae et Ducatus Lithuaniae, Volhyniae
mwe0550a	europe czech republic (bohemia)	1690	DE RAM	600	51	60	Regnum Bohemiae
mwe0893	europe hungary	1680	DE RAM	875	48	57	Regnum Hungariae
mww0455a	world	1762	DE REDERN	2250	45	56	Hemisphere Septentrionale / Hemisphere Meridionale (2 maps)
mwp0494	pacific south	1725	DE RENNEVILLE	280	14	36	(Reduced version of Van Spilbergen 1619)
mwas0588	asia south east borneo	1726	DE RENNEVILLE	280	14	21	Borneo Insula (copy of Commelin 1646)
mwaf0904	africa south	1725	DE RENNEVILLE	280	14	16	Cabo de Bona Esperanca (based on Commelin 1646)
mwas0647	asia south east java	1726	DE RENNEVILLE	150	15	20	Iava Maior
mwas0764	asia south east philippines	1726	DE RENNEVILLE	400	14	16	Manila (view)
mwsam0680	south america magellan	1725	DE RENNEVILLE	350	14	36	Typus Freti Magellanici quod Giorgius Spilbergius
mwas0765	asia south east philippines	1726	DE RENNEVILLE	450	14	22	Typus Freti Manilensis. Detroit de Manilles
mwsc0603a	scandinavia norway	1702	DE RENNEVILLE	250	16	20	delineatio Spitsbergiae (based on Commelin)
mwru0118a	russia	1702	DE RENNEVILLE	200	13	17	Nova Zemla (based on Commelin 1646, in turn based on Van Doetecum 1598)
mwas0910a	asia south east vietnam	1651	DE RHODES	1000			Regnu Annam (north to the right)
mwam0733	america north	1840	DE RIENZI	200	19	25	Amerique Septentrionale
mwf0829a	france paris	1679	DE ROCHEFORT	2000	55	70	Paris et ses Environs
mww0670a	world	1823	DE ROQUEFEUIL	480	33	63	Mappe-Monde Pour servir au Voyage au tour du Monde (illustrated below left)
			DE ROSSI, SEE UNDER ROSSI.				
mwbh0655	belgium holland	1743	DE ROY	3000	119	185	Nieuwe Kaart van den Lande van Utrecht
mwe0069	europe	1660	DE SANDRART	720	48	56	Nova et Accurata totius Europae delineatio Vulgata
mwsw0241	alps	1786	DE SAUSSURE	580	41	50	Carte de la Partie des Alpes qui Avoisine le Mont-Blanc
mwit1021	italy south	1703	DE SILVA	240	20	28	Calabria Citra
mwit1021a	italy south	1703	DE SILVA	240	20	28	Calabria Ult. (shown above left)
mwgm0201a	mexico	1724	DE SOLIS	350	20	33	(Untitled map)
mwgm0204	mexico	1730	DE SOLIS	150	16	12	(Untitled map showing Indian settlements)
mwaf0028	africa	1598	DE SOLIS	2000	37	50	Africa (based on Ortelius 1570)
mwas0025a	asia continent	1603	DE SOLIS	1800	36	48	Asiae Nova Descriptio (copy of Ortelius 1570)
mwgm0201	mexico	1724	DE SOLIS	200	20	16	The Lake of Mexico and Parts Adjacent
mww0109	world	1603	DE SOLIS	4500	34	50	Tipus Orbis Terrarum
mwam0027	america continent	1603	DE SOLIS	5000	35	47	Americae sive Novi Orbis Nova Descriptio
mwe1053	europe romania	1771	DE STRICKER	875	90	64	Plan de l'Expedition de M. 'le General-Major de Veismann de l'Autre Cote du Danube, sur les Camps Ennemis pres de Somow, Tultscha, Isaktschi & sur la Camp du Grand-Visir ... 1771 (Titles also in Russian and German)
mwbp0471a	poland	1762	DE TIRREGAILLE	40000	76	106	Plan de la Ville de Varsovie
			DE ULLOA: SEE 'ULLOA'				
mwit0647	italy piedmont	1677	DE VAL	480	44	39	Le Piemont et Le Monferrat
mwaf0205	africa	1759	DE VAUGONDY	720	50	66	Afrique Divisee en ses Principaux Empires et Royaumes
mwam0400	america north	1748	DE VAUGONDY	240	15	19	America Settentrionale
mwsam0071a	south america	1750	DE VAUGONDY	375	48	59	Amérique Méridionale
mwam0204a	america continent	1778	DE VAUGONDY	800	50	64	America ou Indes Occidentales
mwam0403	america north	1750	DE VAUGONDY	750	48	59	Amerique Septentrionale Dressee sur les Relations les Plus Modernes des Voyageurs et Navigateurs, et Divisee Suivant les Differentes Possessions des Europeans (shown below is the 1775 update with inset of the NW)
mwme0627	arabia etc	1753	DE VAUGONDY	400	47	62	Antiquor? Imperiorum Tabula, in qua Prae Caeteris, Macedonicum seu Alexandri Magni Imperium et Expeditiones Exarantur
mwas0476	asia south east	1752	DE VAUGONDY	720	48	58	Archipel des Indes Orientales qui Comprend les Isles de la Sonde, Moluques et Philippines
mwas0194a	asia continent	1778	DE VAUGONDY	550	50	65	Asie Divisee en ses Principaux Etats, Empires & Royaumes (illustrated is the 1791 Delamarche re-issue)
mwca0064	canada	1749	DE VAUGONDY	180	17	17	Bayes d'Hudson et de Baffins, et Terre de Labrador
mwuk0834	uk	1750	DE VAUGONDY	350	48	53	Britannicae Insulae in quibus Albion seu Britannia Major, et Ivernia seu Britannia Minor juxta Ptolemaei Mentem Divisae ... Sanson
mwam0473	america north	1782	DE VAUGONDY	280	24	29	Canada, Louisiane, Etats-Unis
mwsw0172	switzerland	1769	DE VAUGONDY	650	50	65	Carte de la Suisse ou sont les Treize Cantons
mwme0314	holy land	1745	DE VAUGONDY	650	50	70	Carte de la Terre des Hebreux
mwuss1636	virginia	1755	DE VAUGONDY	3600	47	63	Carte de la Virginie et du Maryland Dressee sur la Grande Carte Angloise de Mrs. Josue Fry et Pierre Jefferson
mwas0161	asia continent	1750	DE VAUGONDY	720	47	52	Carte de l'Asie Dressee sur les Relations les Plus Nouvelles

AMPG REFERENCE	REGION	DATE	MAP MAKER	PRICE (UK£)	VERT. (cm.)	HOR. (cm.)	TITLE OF MAP (Comments by the editor in brackets)
mwaf0515	africa egypt etc	1753	DE VAUGONDY	550	64	46	Carte de l'Egypte Ancienne et Moderne
mwg0132	germany	1756	DE VAUGONDY	300	48	55	Carte de L'Empire D'Allemagne
mwf1071	france provence	1748	DE VAUGONDY	280	16	17	Carte de l'Etat de Genes ou se Trouvent Nice, Vintimille, S. Remo, &c.
mwf0499	france corsica	1748	DE VAUGONDY	220	21	17	Carte de l'Isle de Corse
mwwi0609	hispaniola	1749	DE VAUGONDY	720	46	60	Carte de l'Isle de Saint-Domingue Dressee d'apres la Carte Originale de Mr. Frezier
mwit0188	italy	1756	DE VAUGONDY	450	48	54	Carte de L'Italie ... les routes des Postes
mwsc0149	scandinavia	1759	DE VAUGONDY	1500	50	112	Carte des Couronnes du Nord qui comprehend la Suede, la Norwege, le Danemarc, les I.s Britaniques et la Russie Europeenne
mwru0538	ukraine	1769	DE VAUGONDY	1350	52	92	Carte des Environs de la Mer-Noire ou se Trouvent l'Ukrayne, la Petite Tartarie, la Circassie, la Georgie, et les Confins de la Russie Europeenne, et de la Turquie
mwuk1217	england london	1769	DE VAUGONDY	650	47	66	Carte des environs de Londres qui comprehend Le cours de la Thamise
mwuk0839	uk	1757	DE VAUGONDY	480	47	58	Carte des Grandes Routes d'Angleterre, d'Ecosse ... d'Irlande
mwuk0860	uk	1780	DE VAUGONDY	550	54	60	Carte des Isles Britanniques qui renferment
mwm0238	mediterranean malta	1748	DE VAUGONDY	480	10	13	Carte des Isles de Malte et de Goze ... 1748
mwp0383a	pacific new guinea	1756	DE VAUGONDY	280	29	35	Carte des Isles de Papous (close copy of Tirion 1753)
mwca0069	canada	1753	DE VAUGONDY	2000	50	65	Carte des Pays Connus sous le Nom de Canada (re-issued in 1778 with the title 'Carte du Canada et des Etats-Unis' after American Independence)
mwsp0275	spain	1757	DE VAUGONDY	400	48	57	Carte des Royaumes d'Espagne et de Portugal dans laquelle sont Tracees les Routes de Postes
mwme0320	holy land	1747	DE VAUGONDY	400	46	59	Carte des Voyages de Notre Seigneur Jesus-Christ (insets of Judea, Jerusalem)
mwam1054	america north (east)	1778	DE VAUGONDY	2000	48	66	Carte du Canada et des Etats-Unis (inset of Newfoundland. First publ. in 1753 with the title 'Carte des Pays Connus sous le Nom de Canada')
mwbh0877	luxembourg	1757	DE VAUGONDY	375	48	53	Carte du Duche de Luxembourg dans laquelle on Trouve la Partie Meridionale & Limitrophe de la Seigneurie de Lyege
mwf0132	france	1762	DE VAUGONDY	300	47	51	Carte du Royaume de France ou sont Tracees Exactement les Routes des Postes
mwru0280	russia	1786	DE VAUGONDY	1200	47	121	Carte Generale de l'Empire des Russes en Europe et en Asie, Dressee d'apres les Cartes de l'Atlas Russien
mww0437	world	1756	DE VAUGONDY	720	24	64	Carte Generale qui Represente les Mers des Indes, Pacifique, et Atlantique, et Principalement, le Monde Austral, Divise en Australasie, Polynesie, et Magellanie pour Servir a l'Histoire des Terres Australes. (Shows from 40N to 60S only.)
mwp0496	pacific south	1756	DE VAUGONDY	600	24	64	Carte Generale qui represente les Mers des Indies, Pacifique et Atlantique
mwf0523	france corsica	1769	DE VAUGONDY	550	57	44	Carte Nouvelle de l'Isle de Corse
mwm0243	mediterranean malta	1758	DE VAUGONDY	1800	50	55	Carte Occidentale de la Mer Mediterranee / Carte de L'Empire de Grand-Seigneur (2 maps, each 50x55cm)
mwca0217	canada arctic	1772	DE VAUGONDY	200	31	39	Carte qui Represente les Differentes Connoissances que l'on a Eues des Terres Arctiques Depuis 1650 Jusqu'en 1747
mwp0014	australia	1756	DE VAUGONDY	1200	23	27	Carte Reduite de l'Australasie, pour Servir a la Lecture de l'Histoire des Terres Australes
mwaf0942	africa south	1761	DE VAUGONDY	235	24	28	Congo, Cafrarie (inset: Horn of Africa)
mwaf0408	africa east	1766	DE VAUGONDY	240	19	16	Cote de Zanguebar
mwuss0943	mississippi	1760	DE VAUGONDY	400	24	18	Cours du Mississipi et la Louisiane
mwf0119	france	1738	DE VAUGONDY	400	51	69	Description des Gaules Tiree des Cartes Imprimees et Manuscrites des Srs. Sanson, Corrigee sur les Remarques de Dom Bouquet Benedictin, et sur les Dissertations de Mr Lebeuf, Chanoine d'Auxerre
mwc0142	china	1749	DE VAUGONDY	160	16	20	Empire de la Chine
mwaa0143	arctic	1774	DE VAUGONDY	1200	50	49	Essai d'une Carte Polaire Arctique Construite d'apres Toutes les Connoissances les Plus Nouvelles
mwbp0477	poland	1769	DE VAUGONDY	1250	92	121	Estats de la Couronne de Pologne ou sont les Royaume de Pologne, Duches et Provinces de Prusse, Cuivaie, Mazovie, Russie Noire &c. Duches de Lithuanie, Volhynie Podolie &c. de l'Ukranie &c. (re-issue of Sanson 1676)
mwsc0433	scandinavia finland	1741	DE VAUGONDY	450	44	49	Estats de la Couronne de Suede dans la Scandinavie
mwme0628	arabia etc	1753	DE VAUGONDY	600	43	55	Etats du Grand-Seigneur en Asie Empire de Perse, Pays des Usbecs, Arabie et Egypte
mwf0121	france	1740	DE VAUGONDY	400	50	67	Franciae Status sub Regibus Primae Stirpis
mwca0592	canada st lawrence	1749	DE VAUGONDY	200	16	18	Golfe de St. Laurent, Isle et Bancs de Terre Neuve
mwf0791	france normandy	1751	DE VAUGONDY	280	49	58	Gouvernement General de Normandie
mwgr0191	greece	1752	DE VAUGONDY	450	48	55	Graecia Vetus
mwm0060a	mediterranean	1750	DE VAUGONDY	350	39	53	Gulielmi Sanson Nicolai Filii Geographia Patriarchalis Tabula ...

AMPG REFERENCE	REGION	DATE	MAP MAKER	PRICE (UK£)	VERT. (cm.)	HOR. (cm.)	TITLE OF MAP (Comments by the editor in brackets)
mwaa0029	antarctic	1773	DE VAUGONDY	2500	65	61	Hemisphere Australe ou Antarctique Projette sur un Horizon dont le Zenith est Situe a 140 Degres de Longit. (first map to include track of Cook's first voyage. An English edition was also publ. in 1773. Illustration shows c1776 edition.)
mwsp0276	spain	1757	DE VAUGONDY	375	47	54	Hispania Antiqua
mwf1082	france provence	1799	DE VAUGONDY	280	15	18	I. Carte de l'Etat de Genes ou se Trouvent Nice, Vintimille, S. Remo, &c. / II. Carte des Confins de l'Etat de Genes ou se Trouve une Partie du Cie. de Nice (2 maps of 15x18cm.)
mwm0277a	mediterranean west	1757	DE VAUGONDY	375	48	59	Imperii Romani Occidentis
mwin0235	india	1761	DE VAUGONDY	200	24	28	Indostan, Presqu'Isles de l'Inde Chine, Tartarie Independante
mwaf0603	africa islands madagascar	1748	DE VAUGONDY	180	17	18	Isle de Madagascar ou de St, Laurent et Isles de la Reunion, Sechelles et Rodrique
mwca0308	canada newfoundland	1749	DE VAUGONDY	200	16	18	Isle de Terre-Neuve
mwuk0170	ireland	1749	DE VAUGONDY	175	17	16	Isle et Royaume d'Irlande
mwit0812a	italy sardinia	1748	DE VAUGONDY	175	21	16	Isle et Royaume de Sardaigne (shown below left)
mwca0363	canada nova scotia	1749	DE VAUGONDY	150	16	19	Isle Royale (Cape Breton Isl.)
mwwi0612	hispaniola	1750	DE VAUGONDY	600	47	51	Isles de Saint Domingue ou Hispaniola, et de la Martinique par le Sr. Robert ... 1750
mwas0776	asia south east philippines	1749	DE VAUGONDY	280	20	27	Isles Philippines
mwit0186	italy	1751	DE VAUGONDY	350	48	55	Italia Antiqua cum Insulis Sicilia, Sardinia et Corsica
mwme0365	holy land	1778	DE VAUGONDY	180	24	21	Judee ou Terre Sainte sous les Turcs
mwuss0411	florida	1749	DE VAUGONDY	280	16	17	La Floride Divisee en Floride et Caroline
mwme0340	holy land	1750	DE VAUGONDY	500	48	59	La Judee ou Terre Sainte, divisee en ses douze Tribus
mwbp0446a	poland	1752	DE VAUGONDY	500	49	61	La Prusse Divisee
mwsc0736a	scandinavia	1762	DE VAUGONDY	200	23	19	La Suede
mwaf0207	africa	1760	DE VAUGONDY	1600	100	112	L'Afrique Divisee en ses Empires, Royaumes et Republiques (an updated edition of this map also publ. by Delamarche 1790)
mwaf0188	africa	1748	DE VAUGONDY	150	16	19	L'Afrique Divisee en ses Principales Parties
mwaf0202	africa	1756	DE VAUGONDY	500	48	58	L'Afrique Dressee, sur les Relations les Plus Recentes, et Assujettie aux Observations Astronomiques
mwaf0211	africa	1761	DE VAUGONDY	150	24	28	L'Afrique par Robert
mwf0246	france alsace	1754	DE VAUGONDY	140	48	69	L'Alsace Divisee en Haute et Basse et le Sundgau (2 maps on one sheet)
mwam0164	america continent	1749	DE VAUGONDY	650	52	65	L'Amerique Septentrionale et Meridionale Divisee en ses Principales Parties par les Srs. Sanson
mwam0181	america continent	1760	DE VAUGONDY	2500	97	113	L'Amerique Septentrionale et Meridionale Divisee Suivant ses Differens Pays (illustrated is revised edition, c1786 by Delamarche)
mwas0216	asia continent	1791	DE VAUGONDY	2400	98	113	L'Asie Divisee en ses Empires et Royaumes
mwjk0101	japan	1749	DE VAUGONDY	280	16	16	Le Japon
mwam0149	america continent	1740	DE VAUGONDY	720	49	65	Le Nouveau Continent
mwsam0719	south america paraguay	1766	DE VAUGONDY	200	16	19	Le Paraguay
mwuk0998	england	1753	DE VAUGONDY	300	48	51	Le Royaume d'Angleterre, Divise Selon les Sept Royaumes, ou Heptarchie des Saxons, avec la Principaute de Galles et Subdivise en Shires ou Comtes
mwe0588	europe czech republic (bohemia)	1751	DE VAUGONDY	350	48	55	Le Royaume de Boheme, le Duche de Silesie, et les Marquisats de Moravia et Lusace
mwbp0446	poland	1752	DE VAUGONDY	500	48	54	Le Royaume de Pologne, Divise en ses Duches et Provinces, et Subdivise en Palatinats
mwuk0500	scotland	1751	DE VAUGONDY	500	48	57	Le Royaume d'Ecosse Divise en Shires et Comtes
mwe0371	europe austria	1753	DE VAUGONDY	235	48	55	Le Tyrol sous le Nom duquel l'on Comprend le Comte de Tyrol, les Comtes Annexes de Bregentz, Feldkirck, Monfort, Pludentz, &c. et les Eveches de Trente, et de Brixen
mwg0125	germany	1745	DE VAUGONDY	300	50	71	L'Empire d'Allemagne Divise en ses Dix Cercles
mwc0159	china	1757	DE VAUGONDY	720	48	52	L'Empire de la Chine Dresse d'apres les Cartes de l'Atlas Chinois
mwjk0104	japan	1750	DE VAUGONDY	750	49	55	L'Empire du Japon, Divise en Sept Principales Parties
mwsp0268a	spain	1747	DE VAUGONDY	600	46	68	L'Espagne divisee en tous ses Royaumes et Principautes
mwas0475a	asia south east	1751	DE VAUGONDY	650	48	56	Les Indes Orientales
mwwi0083	west indies	1749	DE VAUGONDY	200	16	23	Les Isles Antilles
mwuk0854	uk	1778	DE VAUGONDY	675	54	80	Les Isles Britannicques (copy of an anonymous Spanish map c1750)
mwuk0837	uk	1754	DE VAUGONDY	500	48	60	Les Isles Britanniques qui Comprennent les Royaumes d'Angleterre, d'Ecosse et d'Irlande
mwas0492a	pacific west	1775	DE VAUGONDY	240	24	26	Les Isles de la Sonde, Moluques, Philippines, Carolines, et Marianes
mwat0199	atlantic cape verde isl.	1766	DE VAUGONDY	150	16	19	Les Isles du Cap Verde
mwam1280	great lakes	1749	DE VAUGONDY	500	16	21	Les Lacs du Canada et Nouvelle Angleterre
mwsc0148	scandinavia	1756	DE VAUGONDY	450	48	57	Les Royaumes de Suede et de Norwege, Divises en leurs Provinces ou Gouvernemens
mwsam0682b	south america magellan	1749	DE VAUGONDY	180	19	16	Les Terres Magellaniques
mwe0225	europe	1791	DE VAUGONDY	1800	98	113	L'Europe Divisee en ses Principaux Etats, Empires, Royaumes et Republiques

AMPG REFERENCE	REGION	DATE	MAP MAKER	PRICE (UK£)	VERT. (cm.)	HOR. (cm.)	TITLE OF MAP (Comments by the editor in brackets)
mwwi0775	martinique	1749	DE VAUGONDY	140	16	19	L'Isle de la Martinique
mwwi0610	hispaniola	1749	DE VAUGONDY	150	17	22	L'Isle St. Domingue
mwit0185	italy	1750	DE VAUGONDY	450	48	54	L'Italie
mwit0200	italy	1778	DE VAUGONDY	450	51	68	L'Italie et ses Isles Circonvoisines Sicilie Sardaigne Corse (first edition 1743)
mww0542	world	1786	DE VAUGONDY	2500	104	119	Mappe Monde ou Carte Generale du Globe Terrestre Dessinee Suivante les Regles de la Projection des Cartes Reduites. Par Robert de Vaugondy (shows Cook's voyages)
mww0402	world	1748	DE VAUGONDY	500	16	30	Mappe Monde ou Description du Globe Terrestre
mww0571	world	1792	DE VAUGONDY	1350	47	74	Mappe-Monde Dressee Suivant les Nouvelles Relations et Assujettie aux Observations Astronomiques (publ. by Delamarche)
mww0420	world	1752	DE VAUGONDY	2200	47	74	Mappemonde ou Description du Globe Terrestre, Dressee sur les Memoires les Plus Nouveaux, et Assujettie aux Observations Astronomiques
mwam0957	america north (east)	1748	DE VAUGONDY	300	19	16	Nouvelle Angleterre Nlle. York Nlle. Jersey Pensilvanie Mariland et Virginie
mwgm0033	gulf of mexico and surrounding regions	1761	DE VAUGONDY	400	24	31	Nouvelle Espagne, Nouveau Mexique, Isles Antilles
mwp0418	pacific north	1772	DE VAUGONDY	350	30	38	Nouvelle Representation des Cotes Nord et Est de l'Asie pour Servir d'Eclaircissement aux Articles du Supplement de l'Encyclopedie qui Concernent le Passage aux Indes par le Nord. Gravee sous la Direction de Mr. de Vaugondy en 1772
mwam0153	america continent	1741	DE VAUGONDY	720	40	61	Novus Orbis Potius Altera Continens sive Atlantis Insula
mwaf0407	africa east	1766	DE VAUGONDY	150	16	18	Nubie Abissinie et Cote d'Ajan
mww0421	world	1752	DE VAUGONDY	1800	47	74	Orbis Vetus in utraque Continente juxta Mentem Sansonianam Distinctus, nec non Observationibus Astronomicis Redactus
mwca0093	canada	1772	DE VAUGONDY	240	30	49	Partie de la Carte du Capitaine Cluny Auteur d un Ouvrage Anglois Intitule American Traveller Publie a Londres en 1769
mwwi0086	west indies	1750	DE VAUGONDY	685	49	59	Partie de la Mer du Nord, ou se Trouvent les Grandes et Petites Isles Antilles, et les Isles Lucayes
mwam1281	great lakes	1755	DE VAUGONDY	900	48	60	Partie de l'Amérique Septent? qui comprend la Nouvelle France ou le Canada (large inset of the Great Lakes)
mwam0984	america north (east)	1755	DE VAUGONDY	750	48	62	Partie de l'Amerique Septentrionale, qui Comprend le Cours de l'Ohio, la Nlle. Angleterre, la Nlle. York, le New Jersey, la Pensylvanie, le Maryland la Virginie, la Caroline (inset of Carolinas)
mwgm0211	mexico	1749	DE VAUGONDY	200	16	24	Partie du Mexique ou de la Nlle. Espagne ou se Trouve l'Audience du Mexique
mwgm0106a	guatemala	1749	DE VAUGONDY	200	17	24	Partie du Mexique ou de la Nouvelle Espagne où se trouve l'audience de Guatimala
mwbh0702	belgium holland	1752	DE VAUGONDY	235	47	61	Partie Meridion. du Duche de Brabant
mwit0946a	italy sicily	1748	DE VAUGONDY	140	16	20	Partie Meridionale du Royaume Naples ... La Sicile
mwit0946b	italy sicily	1750	DE VAUGONDY	450	47	59	Partie Meridionale du Royaume De Naples ... et Royaume de Sicile (inset of Malta)
mwru0213	russia	1750	DE VAUGONDY	650	47	59	Partie Occidentale de l'Empire de Russie, ou se Trouve Distinguee la Russie Europeenne / Partie Orientale de l'Empire de Russie en Asie (in 2 sheets, each 47x59cm)
mwsp0554	spain regions	1752	DE VAUGONDY	200	48	58	Partie Septentrionale de la Couronne de Castille ou se Trouvent les Royaumes de Castille Vieille de Leon, de Gallice, des Asturies, la Biscaye et la Navarre, en Partie
mwru0222	russia	1753	DE VAUGONDY	650	47	58	Partie Septentrionale de la Russe Europeenne / Partie Meridionale (in 2 sheets)
mwe0372	europe austria	1755	DE VAUGONDY	450	48	62	Partie Septentrionale du Cercle D'Autriche / Partie Meridionale du Cercle D'Autriche (2 maps, each 48x62cm.)
mwg0661a	saxony	1760	DE VAUGONDY	350	48	58	Partie Septentrionale du Cercle de Haute Saxe
mwf0411	france burgundy	1740	DE VAUGONDY	180	47	56	Partie Septentrionale du Comte de Bourgogne ou Franche-Comte
mwsp0095	portugal	1751	DE VAUGONDY	600	48	51	Partie Septentrionale du Royaume de Portugal / Partie Meridionale du Royaume de Portugal (2 maps)
mwbh0702a	belgium holland	1752	DE VAUGONDY	235	48	56	Pays-Bas Catholiques
mwf0882	france paris	1760	DE VAUGONDY	1250	58	85	Plan de la Ville et des Faubourgs de Paris Divise in ses Vingt Quartiers
mwin0228	india	1758	DE VAUGONDY	900	47	62	Presqu'Isle des Indes Orientales, Comprenant l'Indostan ou Empire de Mogol
mwsc0364	scandinavia denmark	1750	DE VAUGONDY	350	49	58	Royaume de Danemarck qui Comprend le Nort-Jutland Divise en ses Quatre Dioceses, le Sud-Jutland Divise en ses Deux Duches de Sleswick et de Holstein, et les Isles de Fionie, Selande, Laland, &c.
mwe0949	europe hungary	1751	DE VAUGONDY	350	47	55	Royaume de Hongrie Principaute de Transilvanie, Sclavonie, Croatie, et Partie de la Principaute de Valaquie de la Bosnie, de la Servie de la Bulgarie

AMPG REFERENCE	REGION	DATE	MAP MAKER	PRICE (UK£)	VERT. (cm.)	HOR. (cm.)	TITLE OF MAP (Comments by the editor in brackets)
mwsc0624	scandinavia norway	1747	DE VAUGONDY	650	51	51	Royaume de Norwege Subdivise en ses Principaux Gouvernements (size incl. left hand text border)
mwbp0438	poland	1749	DE VAUGONDY	200	16	19	Royaume de Pologne Divise en Haute et Basse Pologne, et Subdivise en Palatinats
mwbp0438a	poland	1749	DE VAUGONDY	150	16	19	Royaume de Prusse
mwuk0171	ireland	1750	DE VAUGONDY	550	49	55	Royaume d'Ireland Divise en ses Quatre Provinces et Sub Divise en Comtes (illustrated is 1780 edition)
mwsp0271b	spain	1750	DE VAUGONDY	400	48	58	Royaumes d'Espagne et de Portugal
mwuk0995	england	1748	DE VAUGONDY	150	16	16	Royme. d'Angleterre Divise par Provinces et Shires ou Comtes
mwme0366	holy land	1778	DE VAUGONDY	550	42	55	Terre de Canaan ou Terre Promise a Abraham et a sa Posterite ou a Chiffre les Noms des Onze Fils de Chanaan selon leur Ordre ... Dressee sur les Manuscrits de G. Sanson
mwe1155b	europe south east	1760	DE VAUGONDY	350	49	51	Turquie Europeenne
mwaf0510	africa egypt etc	1743	DE VAUGONDY	450	60	46	Veteris Egypti Tabula
mwf0503	france corsica	1750	DE VEZOU	875	59	45	Carte de l'Isle de Corse
mww0447	world	1760	DE VEZOU	3500	50	75	Mappe-Monde Geo Spherique ou Nouvelle Carte Ideale du Globe Terrestre
mwsp0711	gibraltar	1756	DE VEZOU	550	44	56	Plan Topo-Hydrographique de la Baye de Gibraltar
mwsp0712	gibraltar	1756	DE VEZOU	550	45	52	Plan Topo-Hydrographique du Detroit de Gibraltar
mwsc0591	scandinavia norway	1694	DE WIT	1600	32	47	(View of Bergen) Berga Noorwegiae (re-issue of Braun & Hogenberg, 1588)
mwbp0323	poland	1695	DE WIT	900	35	46	(Zamosc) Zamoscium, Nova Poloniae Civitas
mwsc0692a	scandinavia sweden	1680	DE WIT	550	49	58	Accurata Scaniae, Blekingiae et Hallandiae Descriptio (see illustration above left)
mwgr0091	greece	1680	DE WIT	750	44	53	Accurata Totius Archipelagi et Graeciae Universae Tabula
mwit0582	italy north	1680	DE WIT	350	50	62	Accuratissima Dominii Veneti in Italia, Ducatus Parmae, Placentiae Modenae Regii et Mantuae Episcopatusq. Tridentini Tabula quae Est Lombardia Inferior
mwf0070	france	1680	DE WIT	550	48	57	Accuratissima Galliae Tabula Gallis vulgo Dicta le Royaume de France
mwsp0448	spain regions	1665	DE WIT	650	49	57	Accuratissima Principatus Cataloniae, et Comitatuum Ruscinonis, et Cerretaniae Descriptio
mwas0066	asia continent	1680	DE WIT	800	49	57	Accuratissima Totius Asiae Tabula Recens Emendata per Fredericum de Wit Amstelodami
mwsp0204	spain	1688	DE WIT	600	50	59	Accuratissima Totius Regni Hispaniae Tabula (also issued with title: 'Accuratissima Totius Regni Hispaniae Portugalliae Tabula)
mwuk0936	england	1680	DE WIT	675	58	49	Anglia Regnum in Omnes suos Ducatus, Comitatus, et Provincias Divisum
mwbh0401	belgium holland	1680	DE WIT	1650	46	79	Antverpia
mwgr0593	greece islands	1680	DE WIT	600	48	55	Archipelagi Meridionalis, seu Cycladum Insularum (re-issue of Jansson plate)
mwbh0403	belgium holland	1680	DE WIT	875	45	40	Arnhem (inset view at top)
mwas0049	asia continent	1660	DE WIT	3000	44	56	Asiae Nova Descriptio (carte-a-figure borders on three sides)
mwaf1129	africa west	1675	DE WIT	800	49	57	Barbariae et Guineae Maritimi a Freto Gibraltar ad Fluvium Gambiae (north to the left)
mwbh0404	belgium holland	1680	DE WIT	550	47	54	Belgii Regii Accuratissima Tabula Pluribus Locis Recens Emen: A F De Wit
mwbh0405	belgium holland	1680	DE WIT	800	47	55	Belgium Foederatum
mwbh0407a	belgium holland	1680	DE WIT	500	47	55	Brabantiae pars Septentrionalis
mwuk1465	uk english channel (all)	1675	DE WIT	1500	48	56	Canalis inter Angliae et Galliae Littora - Pascaert van 't Canaal tusschen Engeland en Vranckryck
mwit0581a	italy north	1671	DE WIT	450	47	55	Carta Nova accurata del passagio et strada ... 1671
mwaf0875	africa south	1680	DE WIT	1350	43	53	Cimbebas et Caffariae Littora a Catenbela ad Promontorium Bonae Spei - Pascaerte van Cimbebas en Caffares Streckende van Catembela tot Cabo de Bona Esperanca
mwg0616a	saxony	1680	DE WIT	300	49	57	Circuli Saxoniae Superiorae pars Meridionalis
mwg0345b	bavaria	1680	DE WIT	450	49	57	Circulus Bavaricus
mwe0999	europe rhine	1680	DE WIT	350	57	50	Circulus Electorum Rheni sive Rhenanus Inferior
mwg0345c	bavaria	1680	DE WIT	350	49	57	Circulus Franconicus (shown above left)
mwbh0406	belgium holland	1680	DE WIT	350	46	56	Comitatus Flandriae Tabula
mwbh0428	belgium holland	1681	DE WIT	15000	162	290	Comitatus Hollandiae et Dominii Ultraiectini Tabula
mwbh0408	belgium holland	1680	DE WIT	450	47	56	Comitatus Namurci Tabula (shown above left)
mwsp0224a	spain	1705	DE WIT	2000	50	69	Corona Portugalliae cum ei affinibus Regnis Hispanicis / Exactissima et plane Nova Tabula, in qua summa cura delineate invetus Arragoniae Regissima et Navarrae, una cum Cataloniae Principatu; utque Galliae conterminis / Hispaniae utque Portugalliae / Curiosa Nova Tabula Complectens Regnum Valentiae et Murciae (4 sheets 50x59cm each, based on Allard 1700)
mwsc0302	scandinavia denmark	1680	DE WIT	1500	49	57	Daniae, Frisiae, Groningae et Orientalis Frisiae Littora
mwsc0301a	scandinavia denmark	1680	DE WIT	600	51	59	Dania Regnum (see also close copy by Danckerts 1690. Illustrated is Covens & Mortier re-issue)
mwe1138	europe south east	1670	DE WIT	600	50	61	Danubii Fluvii sive Turcici Imperii in Europa

AMPG REFERENCE	REGION	DATE	MAP MAKER	PRICE (UK£)	VERT. (cm.)	HOR. (cm.)	TITLE OF MAP (Comments by the editor in brackets)
mwit0582a	italy north	1680	DE WIT	550	49	61	Dominii Veneti in Italia
mwbp0093	baltic states	1680	DE WIT	600	42	50	Ducatum Livoniae et Curlandiae, Nova Tabula, Descripta, Divisa, et Edita per F. De Witt Amstelodami
mwbh0844	luxembourg	1690	DE WIT	800	46	56	Ducatus Lutzenburgici Tabula Nuperrime in Lucem Edita
mwg0482a	mecklenburg	1680	DE WIT	350	49	57	Ducatus Meklenburgicus in quo sunt Ducatus Vandaliae et Meklenburgi Ducatus et Comitatus Swerinensis
mwsc0696c	scandinavia sweden	1690	DE WIT	480	38	48	Ducatus Uplandiae cum Westmanniae
mwf0320	france brittany	1680	DE WIT	600	49	60	Duche et Gouvernement General de Bretagne
mwf0776	france normandy	1680	DE WIT	600	49	59	Duche et Gouvernement General de Normandie
mwsc0577	scandinavia norway	1675	DE WIT	1200	49	57	Finmarchiae et Laplandiae Maritimae
mwit1133	italy florence	1700	DE WIT	2000	44	72	Florentia Pulcherrima Etruriae Civitas
mwe1017	europe rhine	1710	DE WIT	1400	50	89	Fluviorum Rheni Mosae Mosellae Moeni Neccaris (illustrated is Covens & Mortier 1730 re-issue)
mwbh0407	belgium holland	1680	DE WIT	800	46	55	Foederatae Belgicae Tabula in Multis Locis Emendata et in Lucem Edita a F. de Wit
mwf0264	france aquitaine	1690	DE WIT	350	44	59	Gouvernement de la Guienne & Gascogne
mwf1144	france rhone-alpes	1700	DE WIT	350	41	58	Gouvernement General du Lyonnois
mwaf1136a	africa west	1680	DE WIT	550	42	53	Guinea (close copy of Blaeu 1634)
mwsp0205	spain	1690	DE WIT	1200	49	57	Hispaniae et Portugalliae Maritimi Tractus, a' S. Andero, ad Malagam - Pascaert van Spangiae, en Portugal
mwgr0398	greece crete	1669	DE WIT	2500	62	54	Ignographia Candiae Tertia Vice a Turcis Obsessae in Lucem Edita a F. De Wit
mwru0076	russia	1680	DE WIT	1000	44	55	Imperii Russici sive Moscoviae
mwas0416	asia south east	1690	DE WIT	1500	46	56	Indiae Orientalis nec non Insularum Adiacentium Nova Descriptio (re-issue of De Wit's 1662 map)
mwwi0032	west indies	1680	DE WIT	2800	48	56	Indiarum Occidentalium Tractus Littorales cum Insulis Caribicis - Pascaert van Westindien ende Caribise Eylanden
mwgr0408	greece crete	1680	DE WIT	1500	46	55	Insula Candia Ejusque Fortificatio
mwm0199	mediterranean malta	1680	DE WIT	2000	44	54	Insula Malta Accuratissime Delineata, Urbibus et Fortalitiis (shown left is the 1707 edition, 46x57cm, with title 'Insularum Melite vulgo Maltae, Gozae et Comini correctissima descripte')
mwit0896	italy sicily	1680	DE WIT	1800	50	59	Insula sive Regnum Siciliae Urbibus Praecipuis Exornatum et Novissime Editum
mwsp0649	balearic islands	1670	DE WIT	720	40	51	Insulae Balearides et Pytiusae
mwgr0594	greece islands	1680	DE WIT	600	48	57	Insularum Archipelagi Septentrionalis seu Maris Aegaej Accurata Delineatio
mwsc0302a	scandinavia denmark	1680	DE WIT	400	49	60	Insularum Danicarum qua sunt Zeelandiae, Fioniae
mwm0217	mediterranean malta	1707	DE WIT	1500	46	56	Insularum Melitae vulgo Maltae Gozae et Comini Correctissima Descriptio
mwit0834	italy sardinia and corsica	1680	DE WIT	800	58	49	Insularum Sardiniae et Corsicae Descriptio
mwsc0312	scandinavia denmark	1688	DE WIT	350	59	48	Jutiae Tabula in quae sunt Dioeceses Alburgensis, Wiburgensis, Ripensis et Arhusiensis
mwf1026	france provence	1690	DE WIT	785	48	59	Le Comte et Gouvernement General de Provence
mwf0579a	france ile de france	1680	DE WIT	350	41	52	Le Gouvernement de L'Isle de France
mwsam0318	south america brazil	1675	DE WIT	2000	49	57	Littora Brasiliae. Pascaert van Brasil
mwsp0341a	spain madrid	1697	DE WIT	2400	40	55	Madrid (view)
mwru0433	russia tartary	1680	DE WIT	720	43	55	Magnae Tartariae, Magni Mogolis Imperii, Iaponiae et Chinae, Nova Descriptio (copy of De Wit 1670. The revised map below has the same title, c1688)
mwbp0098	baltic states	1688	DE WIT	785	45	53	Magni Ducatus Lithuanie Tabula
mwin0123	india	1680	DE WIT	720	41	51	Magni Mogolis Imperium (illustrated is Covens & Mortier reprint)
mwp0234	pacific (all)	1675	DE WIT	3500	49	60	Magnum Mare del Zur cum Insula California. De Groote Zuyd-Zee en 't Eylandt California
mwuk1654	north sea	1675	DE WIT	2000	49	57	Mare Germanicum ac Tractus Maritimus retro Hiberniam et Scotiam - Pascaert vande Noort Zee om Achter Yrland en Schotland om te Seylen (illustrated is the updated Renard 1715 issue).
mwit0897	italy sicily	1680	DE WIT	1200	39	51	Messina
mwbp0026	baltic sea (east)	1675	DE WIT	2000	50	56	Nieuwe Pascaert van de Oost Zee
mwbh0409	belgium holland	1680	DE WIT	450	45	55	Noordt Hollandt
mwsc0693	scandinavia sweden	1680	DE WIT	550	41	47	Nordlandia Sive Regni Sueciae Propriae
mwsc0579	scandinavia norway	1680	DE WIT	1000	60	51	Norvegia Regnum Divisum in suos Dioeceses Nidrosiensem, Bergensem, Opsloensem, et Stavangriensem et Praefecturam Bahusiae
mwsc0578	scandinavia norway	1675	DE WIT	1800	49	56	Norvegiae Maritimae ab Elf-Burgo ad Dronten. Pascaert van Noorwegen Strekende van Elf-Burg tot Dronten (north to the left)
mwaf0065	africa	1660	DE WIT	3200	44	55	Nova Africa Descriptio (carte-a-figure borders on three sides)
mwbh0410	belgium holland	1680	DE WIT	350	44	54	Nova atque Emendata Descriptio Suydt Hollandiae
mwaf0484	africa egypt etc	1680	DE WIT	800	42	51	Nova Egypti Tabula
mwaf0081	africa	1672	DE WIT	40000	119	163	Nova et Accurata Totius Africae Tabula emendata a F. de Wit
mwe0089	europe	1680	DE WIT	1000	48	58	Nova et Accurata Totius Europae Tabula

AMPG REFERENCE	REGION	DATE	MAP MAKER	PRICE (UK£)	VERT. (cm.)	HOR. (cm.)	TITLE OF MAP (Comments by the editor in brackets)
mwe0116	europe	1700	DE WIT	40000	100	124	Nova et Accurata Totius Europae Tabula (3rd edition)
mwe0099	europe	1688	DE WIT	1000	48	58	Nova et Accurate Divisa in Regna et Regiones Praecipuas Europae Descriptio
mwit0348a	italy emilia-romagna	1680	DE WIT	500	50	61	Nova et prae Caeteris Aliis Status et Ducatus Mediolanensis, Parmensis et Montis Ferrati
mwe0070	europe	1660	DE WIT	3000	45	56	Nova Europae Descriptio (carte-a-figure decorative borders on three sides)
mww0191	world	1670	DE WIT	7000	48	56	Nova Orbis Tabula, in Lucem Edita (later editions are updated and have a thin decorative border etc. as shown)
mwme0788	persia etc	1680	DE WIT	960	47	56	Nova Persiae, Armeniae, Natoliae et Arabiae Descriptio
mwsc0424	scandinavia finland	1700	DE WIT	1200	44	52	Nova Tabula Magni Ducatus Finlandiae
mwam0063	america continent	1660	DE WIT	3500	45	57	Nova Totius Americae Descriptio ... 1660 (carte-a-figure borders on three sides)
mwam0076	america continent	1672	DE WIT	100000	121	168	Nova et Accurata Totius Americae Tabula
mwuk0732	uk	1675	DE WIT	785	48	57	Nova Totius Angliae, Scotiae et Hiberniae Tab.
mwe0765	europe east	1668	DE WIT	450	44	57	Nova Totius Hungariae, Transilvaniae, Serviae, Romaniae, Bulgariae, Walachiae, Moldaviae, Sclavoniae, Croatiae, Bosniae, Dalmatiae, Maximaeq. Partis Danubii Fluminis Descriptio
mww0179a	world	1663	DE WIT	10000	54	62	Nova Totius Terrarum Orbis Tabula (revised version of Colom 1655. Image courtesy of B.L. Ruderman)
mww0190	world	1670	DE WIT	7500	48	55	Nova Totius Terrarum Orbis Tabula
mww0171	world	1660	DE WIT	9000	43	55	Nova Totius Terrarum Orbis Tabula Auctore F. de Wit
mww0210a	world	1680	DE WIT		125	188	Nova Totius Terrarum Orbis Tabula (image courtesy of D. Crouch)
mwbh0366b	belgium holland	1662	DE WIT	8000	44	56	Nova XVII Provinciarum Inferioris Germaniae Descriptio (updated version of Van Den Keere 1607)
mwsam0193	south america (north west)	1675	DE WIT	1200	49	56	Novae Hispaniae, Chili, Peruviae, et Guatimalae Littorae (north to the left. Illustrated is the c1680 edition, including the names of the seas.)
mwuk0092a	ireland	1680	DE WIT	1600	71	50	Novissima ac Prae Caeteris Aliis Accuratissima Regni et Insulae Hiberniae Delineato
mwsp0471	spain regions	1688	DE WIT	480	45	55	Novissima Arragoniae Regni Tabula
mwg0803a	westphalia	1680	DE WIT	300	49	58	Novissima et Accuratissima Archiepiscopatus et Electoratus Coloniensis Ducatuum Iuliacensis et Montensis et Meursiae Comitatus tabula descriptae
mwsp0224	spain	1705	DE WIT	480	48	58	Novissima et Accuratissima Regnorum Hispaniae et Portugalliae Tabula
mwam0084	america continent	1680	DE WIT	1800	49	58	Novissima et Accuratissima Septentrionalis ac Meridionalis Americae Descriptio (his 1670 map with different title and minor differences)
mwam0072	america continent	1670	DE WIT	1800	49	58	Novissima et Accuratissima Totius Americae Descriptio
mwit0105	italy	1671	DE WIT	650	49	56	Novissima et Accuratissima totius Italiae Corsicae et Sardiniae
mwe0886	europe hungary	1670	DE WIT	2500	40	52	Novissima Et Emendata Delineatio Hungariae
mwsc0083	scandinavia	1688	DE WIT	720	50	57	Novissima nec non Perfectissima Scandinaviae Tabula Comprehendens Regnorum Sueciae, Daniae et Novegiae
mwuk0755	uk	1690	DE WIT	1000	59	50	Novissima Prae Caeteris aliis Accuratissima Regnorum Angliae, Scotiae, Hiberniae
mwsp0049	portugal	1680	DE WIT	785	58	49	Novissima Regnorum Portugalliae et Algarbiae Descriptio
mwin0477	indian ocean west	1675	DE WIT	1350	44	54	Occidentalior Tractus Indiarum Orientalium a Promontorio Bonae Spei
mwm0016	mediterranean	1675	DE WIT	4800	48	59	Orientalior Districtus Maris Mediterranei. t'Ooster Gedeelte van de Middelandse Zee / Occidentalior Tractus (2 charts)
mwuk0937	england	1680	DE WIT	800	58	50	Orientalior Districtus Regni Angliae ... / Occidentalior Districtus Regni Angliae ... (2 sheets, each 58x50cm)
mwas0409	asia south east	1680	DE WIT	4000	46	55	Orientaliora Indiarum Orientalium cum Insulis Adjacentibus a Promontorio C. Comorin ad Iapan - Pascaert van t'Ooster Gedeelte van Oost Indien van C. Comorin tot Iapan
mwuk1660	north sea	1690	DE WIT	1200	48	59	Pascaert van de Noord Zee van Ameland tot de Hoofden - Mare Germanicum ab Amelandia ad Promontoria Caleti et Doverae
mwgr0092	greece	1680	DE WIT	2800	49	76	Peloponnesus hodie Moreae Regnum Distincte Divisum, in Omnes suas Provincias, Hodiernas atque Veteres, cui et Adiunguntur Insulae Cefalonia, Zante, Cerigo et St. Maura (with border of 14 insets)
mwuk1117	england london	1666	DE WIT	4000	58	53	Platte Grondt der Stadt London met de Aenwysinghe hoe die Afgebrandt is (size incl. text below map describing the great fire. Shown below is a proof copy)
mwaa0092	arctic	1675	DE WIT	2000	44	50	Poli Arctici, et Circumiacentium Terrarum Descriptio Novissima
mwbp0267	poland	1660	DE WIT	650	44	54	Poloniae et Silesiae Descriptio
mwaa0011	antarctic	1680	DE WIT	1800	43	48	Polus Antarcticus
mwam0090	america continent	1690	DE WIT	1600	50	58	Recentissima Novi Orbis sive Americae Septentrionalis et Meridionalis Tabula
mwsc0275	scandinavia denmark	1659	DE WIT	600	45	55	Regni Daniae Accuratissima Delineatio

AMPG REFERENCE	REGION	DATE	MAP MAKER	PRICE (UK£)	VERT. (cm.)	HOR. (cm.)	TITLE OF MAP (Comments by the editor in brackets)
mwsc0691	scandinavia sweden	1680	DE WIT	480	42	53	Regni Gothiae, Tabula Generalis
mwe0774	europe east	1688	DE WIT	900	50	88	Regni Hungariae, et Regionum, quae ei quondam Fuere Unitae, ut Transilvaniae, Valachiae, Moldaviae Serviae ... Maximaeq Partis Danubii Fluminis, Novissima Delineatio
mwbp0292	poland	1680	DE WIT	850	48	56	Regni Poloniae et Ducatus Lithuaniae, Voliniae, Podoliae, Ucraniae, Prussiae, Livoniae et Curlandiae Descriptio
mwbp0292a	poland	1680	DE WIT	650	46	59	Regni Prussiae et Prussiae Polonicae
mwsc0423	scandinavia finland	1690	DE WIT	900	50	57	Regni Sueciae Tabula Generalis
mwsp0472	spain regions	1688	DE WIT	450	50	58	Regnorum Castellae Veteris, Legionis, et Gallaeciae, Principatuumq Biscaiae, et Asturiarum Accuratissima Descriptio per F. de Wit
mwe0547	europe czech republic (bohemia)	1680	DE WIT	720	48	57	Regnum Bohemia, eique Annexae Provinciae, ut Ducatus Silesia, Marchionatus Moravia, et Lusatia
mwuk0079	ireland	1680	DE WIT	1000	58	49	Regnum Hiberniae
mwe0891	europe hungary	1680	DE WIT	750	48	58	Regnum Hungaria in Omnes suos Comitatus Accurate Divisum et Editum (illustrated is the Mortier re-issue 1710)
mwit1015a	italy south	1680	DE WIT	600	58	49	Regnum Neapolis in quo sunt Aprutium Ulterius et Citerius
mwbp0313	poland	1688	DE WIT	850	47	54	Republicae et Status Generalis Poloniae Nova Tabula (new title, but close copy of De Wit 1680)
mwbp0105	baltic states	1700	DE WIT	1000	39	49	Riga
mwbh0484	belgium holland	1698	DE WIT	2000	40	50	Rotterdam
mwru0071	russia	1675	DE WIT	800	49	57	Russiae et Novae Zemlae Maritimae (illustrated is Ottens re-issue of 1745. Also re-issued by Renard in 1715.)
mwsc0692	scandinavia sweden	1680	DE WIT?	650	49	51	Scania Vulgo Schoonen
mwuk0420	scotland	1680	DE WIT	875	57	50	Scotia Regnum Divisum in Partem Septentrionalem et Meridionalem
mwca0212	canada arctic	1680	DE WIT	1250	49	57	Septemtrionaliora Americae a Groenlandia, per Freta Davidis et Hudson, ad Terram Novam - De Noordelyckste Zee Kusten van America van Groenland door de Straet Davis ende Straet Hudson tot Terra Neuf
mwsc0096	scandinavia	1700	DE WIT	650	41	52	Suecicae Lapponiae et Norvegicae Nova Tabula
mwsc0691a	scandinavia sweden	1680	DE WIT	675	41	48	Sueonia sive Regni Sueciae Propriae Pars Meridionalis, Comprehendens Uplandiae, Westmanniae, Sudermanniae
mwas0398a	asia south east	1662	DE WIT	1500	46	56	Tabula Indiae Orientalis Emendata
mwsp0050	portugal	1680	DE WIT	550	47	57	Tabula Portugalliae et Algarbia
mwsc0070	scandinavia	1670	DE WIT	850	44	56	Tabula Regnorum Sueciae et Norvegiae
mwru0077	russia	1680	DE WIT	800	45	56	Tabula Russia vulgo Moscovia
mwru0430	russia	1670	DE WIT	600	44	55	Tabula Tartariae et Majoris Partis Regni Chinae
mwat0341	atlantic west	1680	DE WIT	1500	48	56	Terra Nova, ac Maris Tractus circa Novam Franciam, Angliam, Belgium, Venezuelam Novam Andalusiam, Guianam et Brasiliam - Terra Neuf, en de Custen van Nieuw Vranckryck, Nieu Engeland, Nieu Nederland, Nieu Andalusia, Guiana en Venezuela (north to the left)
mwme0206	holy land	1688	DE WIT	650	46	56	Terra Sancta, sive Promissionis, olim Palestina recens delineata (re-issue of Visscher 1659)
mwaf0089	africa	1680	DE WIT	900	49	58	Totius Africae Accuratissima Tabula
mwe1194	europe west	1675	DE WIT	7200	49	89	Totius Europae Littora Novissime Edita. Pascaert Vertoonende Alle de See-Custen van Europa
mwe1000	europe rhine	1680	DE WIT	480	50	53	Totius Fluminis Rheni Novissima Descriptio
mwsp0195	spain	1680	DE WIT	800	46	56	Totius Regnorum Hispaniae Tabula
mwsam0219	south america argentina	1675	DE WIT	1350	48	55	Tractus Australior Americae Meridionalis, a Rio de la Plata per Fretum Magellanicum ad Toraltum - Nieuwe Perfecte Pascaert van 't Suyderlyckste Deel van Suyt America, van Rio de la Plata door de Straet Magellaen tot Toral
mwaf1136	africa west	1680	DE WIT	960	49	57	Tractus Littorales Guineae a Promontorio Verde usque ad Sinum Catenbelae (illustrated is the Ottens 1745 re-issue. Also see Renard 1715)
mwuk1357	england north	1680	DE WIT	600	48	58	Tractus Regni Angliae Septentrion. in quo Ducatus Eboracensis, Episcopatus Dunelmensis, Comitatus Northumbriae, Cumbriae, Westmoriae, et Lancastriae cum Mona Insula
mwbh0485	belgium holland	1698	DE WIT	1800	42	52	Traiectum - Utrecht
mwme0568	arabia etc	1680	DE WIT	750	45	55	Turcicum Imperium
mwru0489	ukraine	1680	DE WIT	900	42	53	Typus Generalis Ukrainae
mwf0224	france alsace	1680	DE WIT	550	49	57	Utriusquae Alsatiae, Ducatus
mwuss1173	new york	1804	DE WITT	3500	56	69	A Map of the State of New York ... Contracted from his Large Map of the State (1802)
mwuss1171	new york	1802	DE WITT	8000	58	67	A Map of the State of New York by Simon de Witt, Surveyor General MDCCCII (6 sheets of 58x67cm.)
mwuss1159	new york	1794	DE WITT	4800	50	39	A Plan of the City of Albany Surveyed at the Request of the Mayor Alderman and Commonalty
mwsw0233	switzerland	1840	DE WYHER	550	53	53	Panorama du Mont-Righi ... vom Rigiberg (view and map)
mwca0175	canada	1834	DEAN & MUNDAY	300	25	41	Map of the Eastern Townships of Lower Canada
mwuss0897	massachusetts	1848	DEARBORN	300	41	46	A New & Complete Map of the City of Boston, and Precincts, Including Part of Charlestown, Cambridge & Roxbury

AMPG REFERENCE	REGION	DATE	MAP MAKER	PRICE (UK£)	VERT. (cm.)	HOR. (cm.)	TITLE OF MAP (Comments by the editor in brackets)
mwuss0861	massachusetts	1814	DEARBORN	3000	52	44	Boston and its Vicinity
mwuk1223	england london	1770	DECREMPS	1200	32	44	Plan de Londres contenant les rues et les places principales
mwuk1520	uk english channel (all)	1810	DEGAULLE	1600	94	61	Nouvelle Carte Reduite de la Manche de Bretagne
mwe0435	europe austria vienna	1820	DEGEN	2000	178	176	Grundriss der Haupt- un Residenzstadt Wien
mwf0884	france paris	1763	DEHARME	2400			Plan de la Ville et Fauxbourgs de Paris
mwsc0160	scandinavia	1780	DELAFOSSE	720	52	63	Carte des Royaumes de Suede et Norwege Divisee en ses Differents Etats Suivant les Nouvelles Observations
mwsp0113	portugal	1778	DELAFOSSE	1500	51	62	Les Royaumes de Portugal et des Algarves
mwf0866	france paris	1740	DELAGRIVE	4500			Environs de Paris Leves Geometriquement
mwf0860	france paris	1735	DELAGRIVE	1600	62	84	Neuvieme Plan de Paris ses Accroissemens sours le Regne de Louis XV
mwf0869	france paris	1744	DELAGRIVE	1350	60	88	Plan de Paris Divise en Seize Quartiers
mwf0879	france paris	1756	DELAGRIVE	1800	58	88	Plan de Paris Divise en Seize Quartiers (1st edition 1744)
mwf0589	france ile de france	1746	DELAGRIVE	1500	62	92	Plan de Versailles
mwf0861	france paris	1735	DELAGRIVE	720	55	58	Plan des Fontaines de la Ville et des Faubourgs de Paris
mwin0233	india	1760	DELAHAYE	450	48	33	Carte de la Cote Orientale du Golfe de Bengale
mwsw0179	switzerland	1776	DELAHAYE	1000	47	70	Carte des Environs de Geneve Comprenant le Territoire de cette Republique, et les Frontiers de France, de Savoye, et de Suisse, entre Lesquelles
mwf0534	france corsica	1783	DELAHAYE	1000	50	80	Carte Particuliere de l'Isle de Corse
mwme0518	jerusalem	1840	DELAHAYE	1000	74	104	Plan de Jerusalem et de ses Faubourgs
mwaf0526	africa egypt etc	1790	DELAMARCHE	150	28	36	Aegyptus Antiqua
mwaf0282	africa	1798	DELAMARCHE	480	50	66	Afrique Divisee en ses Principaux Empires et Royaumes (re-issue of De Vaugondy 1759)
mwsam0146	south america	1827	DELAMARCHE	75	28	32	Amerique Meridionale
mwam0232	america continent	1792	DELAMARCHE	720	53	64	Amerique ou Indes Occidentales avec les Nouvelles Decouvertes du Capite. Cook
mwam0658	america north	1827	DELAMARCHE	200	28	33	Amerique Septentrionale
mwam0475	america north	1782	DELAMARCHE	250	18	25	Amerique Septentrionale divisee
mwam0474	america north	1782	DELAMARCHE	200	19	22	Amerique Septentrionale Dressee d'apres les Decouvertes du Cap. Cook
mwme0404	holy land	1827	DELAMARCHE	280	28	40	Carte de la Dispersion des Peuples avant le Deluge
mwme0403	holy land	1825	DELAMARCHE	400	51	61	Carte de la Geographie Sacre pour l'Ancien Testiment
mwit0619	italy north	1796	DELAMARCHE	800	66	100	Carte de la Republique Cisalpine, Suivant le Traite Conclu entre la Republique Francaise et l'Empereur, Divisee en 20 Departments
mwsw0236	switzerland	1843	DELAMARCHE	180	29	43	Carte de la Suisse ou Helvetie
mwme0384	holy land	1797	DELAMARCHE	450	49	61	Carte de la Terre des Hebreux ou Israelites Partagee selon l'Ordre de Dieu aux Douze Descendantes des Douze Fils de Jacob
mwe0473	europe central	1806	DELAMARCHE	250	50	72	Carte de l'Allemagne Contenent les Etats de la Confederation du Rhin le Royaume de Prusse le Grand Duche de Warsovie et l'Empire d'Autriche
mwgm0078	gulf of mexico and surrounding regions	1844	DELAMARCHE	320	43	29	Carte de l'Amerique Septentrionale et des Antilles
mwp0531	pacific south	1850	DELAMARCHE	235	29	43	Carte de l'Oceanie
mwp0528	pacific south	1837	DELAMARCHE	180	29	39	Carte de l'Oceanie Contenant l'Australie, la Polynesie et les Iles Asiatiques
mwuk0878	uk	1804	DELAMARCHE	480	53	72	Carte Des Isles Britanniques (copy of De Vaugondy 1780)
mwuk0885	uk	1824	DELAMARCHE	300	51	64	Carte des Isles Britanniques
mwam0271	america continent	1818	DELAMARCHE	500	53	59	Carte Generale de l'Amerique Divisee en ses Principaux Etats ... par Fx. Delamarche Successeur de Robert de Vaugondy
mwbp0546	poland	1805	DELAMARCHE	2000	92	121	Carte Generale de l'Ancien Royaume de Pologne ... avec la Prusse Ducale Erige en Royaume en 1701
mwgr0428	greece crete	1760	DELAMARCHE	400	40	54	Creta Insula pleriumq. Deum Natalibus, Iovis Incunabulis Sepulchroq. Inclyta (re-issue of Sanson 1676)
mwe0834	europe east	1790	DELAMARCHE	250	23	28	Dacia, Moesia, Thracia, Macedonia
mwf0190	france	1825	DELAMARCHE	350	51	61	Description des Gaules Tiree des Cartes Imprimees et Manuscriptes
mwam0491	america north	1785	DELAMARCHE	960	48	63	Etats-Unis de l'Amerique Septentrionale avec les Isles Royale, de Terre Neuve de St. Jean, l'Acadie &c.
mwbp0517	poland	1790	DELAMARCHE	150	23	27	Germano-Sarmatia
mwm0155	mediterranean east	1799	DELAMARCHE	280	49	58	Imperii Romani Occidentis Scilicet et Orientis Tabula
mwam0249	america continent	1800	DELAMARCHE	720	50	65	L'Amerique Divisee dans les Principaux Etats avec les Nouvelles Decouvertes du Capit. Cook ... et du Capit. Jean Meares dan les Annees 1788 et 1789
mwas0234	asia continent	1804	DELAMARCHE	80	24	27	L'Asie
mwuk0563	scotland	1795	DELAMARCHE	100	24	23	L'Ecosse
mwsc0183	scandinavia	1792	DELAMARCHE	650	88	60	Les Couronnes du Nord, le Danemarcke ... (2 sheets joined)
mwas0517	asia south east	1793	DELAMARCHE	140	18	29	Les Indes Orientales
mwww0577	world	1793	DELAMARCHE	200	18	25	Mappe Monde ou Description du Globe Terrestre
mwww0652	world	1816	DELAMARCHE	1200	48	74	Mappe-Monde Dressee Suivant les Nouvelles Relations et Assujettie aux Observations Astronomiques

AMPG REFERENCE	REGION	DATE	MAP MAKER	PRICE (UK£)	VERT. (cm.)	HOR. (cm.)	TITLE OF MAP (Comments by the editor in brackets)
mww0738	world	1846	DELAMARCHE	250	29	43	Mappe-Monde en Deux Hemispheres
mwsc0207	scandinavia	1826	DELAMARCHE	75	29	28	Norwege, Suede et Danemark
mwgm0051	gulf of mexico and surrounding regions	1784	DELAMARCHE	250	24	31	Nouvelle Espagne, Nouveau Mexique, Isles Antilles
mwf0903	france paris	1797	DELAMARCHE	2000	64	94	Plan Geometral de Paris et de ses Fauxbourgs
mwbp0531	poland	1795	DELAMARCHE	80	24	29	Royaume de Pologne par Robert de Vaugondy. Divise et Corrige selon les Partages faits en 1772, 1793 et 1795, entre la Russie la Prusse et l'Autriche
mwuss0046	alaska	1828	DELAMARCHE	800	49	74	Russie d'Asie ou Siberie Russie Americaine
mwme1054	turkey etc	1828	DELAMARCHE	140	30	43	Tableau de la Retraite des Dix Mille
mwme0380	holy land	1795	DELAMARCHE	450	42	56	Terre de Chanaan, ou Terre Promise a Abraham et a sa Posterite (2 maps on one sheet)
mwsw0242a	alps	1793	DELAVAL	500	57	50	Département du Mont Blanc - du Léman
mwsc0753e	scandinavia sweden	1819	DELEEN	600	53	45	Wagvisare I Stockholm (illustrated is 1829 edition)
mwe1035	europe rhine	1830	DELKESKAMP	800	271	19	Delkeskamp's Panorama of the Rhine and the Adjacent Country from Cologne to Mayence
mwe1037	europe rhine	1839	DELKESKAMP	1000	277	25	Nouveau Panorama du Rhin depuis Mayence jusqu'a Cologne
mwe1038	europe rhine	1840	DELKESKAMP	900	221	23	Panorama des Rheins und seiner Nachsten Umgebungen von Mainz bis Coln
mwme0027	holy land	1557	DELLA GATTA	16000	38	55	Palestinae sive Terra Sanctae Descriptio Apud Iannen Fransisium vulgo Della Gatta
mwf1084	france provence	1830	DEMAREST	200	27	36	Plan de la Ville de Marseille
mwf0416	france burgundy	1776	DEMIEGE	1000	113	132	Carte du Pays et Comte du Maconnois Comprenant le Diocese et Bailliage de Macon
mwuk1507a	uk english channel (all)	1780	DENIS	750	49	72	Carte de la Manche
mwgm0046	gulf of mexico and surrounding regions	1780	DENIS	800	50	71	Carte du Golphe du Mexique dressee (4 island insets)
mwuss1136	america north (east)	1779	DENIS	3500	66	50	Carte du Theatre de la Guerre Presente en Amerique Dressee d'apres les Nouvelles Cartes Anglaises
mwm0279	mediterranean west	1780	DENIS	720	52	77	Carte Reduite de la Partie Occidentale de la Mer Mediterranee (2 insets of Gibraltar)
mwm0280	mediterranean west	1782	DENIS	1250	54	87	La Mer Mediterranee (based on Sanson-Jaillot)
mww0520	world	1782	DENIS	4500	55	89	Mappe-Monde Geo-Hydrographique ou Description Generale du Globe Terrestre ... Par Le Sr. Sanson (incl. Cook's tracks and discoveries)
mwsp0593	spain regions	1782	DENIS	650	45	63	Principaute de Catalogne
mwf0250	france alsace	1778	DENIS	720	18	62	Route de Belfort a Strasbourg par Colmar, Dressee et Dessinee sur les Lieux en 1778
mwf0592	france ile de france	1776	DENIS	500	15	58	Route de Paris a Amiens, Desinee sur les Lieux par Louis Denis, Geographe, en Juin 1776
mwuss1562	vermont	1796	DENISON	600	19	23	A Map of the States of New Hampshire and Vermont by J. Denison
mwp0192	new zealand	1793	DENTRECASTEAUX	600	25	35	Carte de l'extremite Septentrionale de la Nouvelle Zeelande
mwp0358	pacific kermadec Isl.	1793	DENTRECASTEAUX	350	50	35	Carte des Iles Kermadec, situees dans le grand Ocean Austral entre la Nle. Zeelande et les Iles des Amis
mwp0298	pacific bismarck archipelago	1807	D'ENTRECASTEAUX	180	24	75	Carte Contenant les Parties de la Nouvelle Irlande, de la Nouvlle Hanovre, et des Isles de l'Amiraute
mwp0299	pacific bismarck archipelago	1807	D'ENTRECASTEAUX	240	49	75	Carte de la Partie Septentrionale de la Nouvelle Bretagne, Decouverte par Dampier en 1700
mwas0524	asia south east	1800	D'ENTRECASTEAUX	1350	48	70	Carte Reduite des la Mer des Indes
mwp0044	australia	1807	D'ENTRECASTEAUX	650	47	33	Plan de la baie de l'Adventure
mwwi0934	virgin isl	1804	DEPOSITO HIDROGR.	3000	58	90	(Virgin Islands)
mwuk1588	channel islands	1770	DEPOT DE LA MARINE	1800	60	81	2me Carte Particuliere des Costes de Normandie ... ou sont Comprises les Isles de Jerzey, Grenzey, Cers, & Aurigny
mwsc0644	scandinavia norway	1812	DEPOT DE LA MARINE	550	60	86	A l'Est de Flekkeroe et Christiansand avec Partie de la Cote de Suede jusqua Saelo Baak
mwwi0686	hispaniola	1852	DEPOT DE LA MARINE	350	62	43	Baie des Gonaives Ile Haiti
mwuss0752	maryland	1778	DEPOT DE LA MARINE	4000	58	87	Carte de la Baie de Chesapeake et de la Partie Navigable des Rivieres James, York, Potoumack, Patuxen, Patapsco, North-east, Choptank et Pocomack
mwsp0744	gibraltar	1805	DEPOT DE LA MARINE	500	60	44	Carte de la Baie de Gibraltar Reduite du Plan Leve en 1786 par D. Vincent Tofino
mwca0618	canada st lawrence	1780	DEPOT DE LA MARINE	400	61	43	Carte de la Baie des Chaleurs a la Cote Occidentale du Golfe de St. Laurent
mwbp0048	baltic sea (east)	1750	DEPOT DE LA MARINE	1000	61	90	Carte de la Baltique. Contenant les Bancs, Isles et Costes
mwec0347	uk england dorset	1824	DEPOT DE LA MARINE	500	64	94	Carte de la Cote Meridionale d'Angleterre depuis Plymouth jusqu'au Cap Lizard
mwaf1252	africa west	1833	DEPOT DE LA MARINE	300	60	88	Carte de la Cote Occidentale d'Afrique Partie Comprise entre les Isles de Los et le Cap Lopez
mwp0163	australia	1847	DEPOT DE LA MARINE	550	61	91	Carte de la Cote Orientale de la Nouvelle Hollande Comprise entre les 20-36 Degrees Latitude Meridionale, et des Terres Environnantes (Nouvelle Caledonie, Iles Loyalty, Partie Septentle de la Nouvelle Zelande, Mer du Corail) ... M.C.A. Vincendon-Dumoulin

AMPG REFERENCE	REGION	DATE	MAP MAKER	PRICE (UK£)	VERT. (cm.)	HOR. (cm.)	TITLE OF MAP (Comments by the editor in brackets)
mwam1226	america north (east)	1834	DEPOT DE LA MARINE	720	60	88	Carte de la Cote Orientale de l'Amerique Septentrionale Partie Comprise entre la Baie de Gaspee et New York (inset Boston harbour)
mwam1225	america north (east)	1834	DEPOT DE LA MARINE	1200	61	89	Carte de la Côte Orientale de l'Amérique Septentrionale partie comprise entre New-York et la rivière Saint Jean
mwwi0650	hispaniola	1788	DEPOT DE LA MARINE	480	58	89	Carte de la Gonave, Dressee sur les Operations Geometriques Faites en 1787
mwuk1503	uk english channel (all)	1765	DEPOT DE LA MARINE	750	60	82	Carte de la Manche
mwuk1673	north sea	1770	DEPOT DE LA MARINE	750	61	85	Carte de la Mer d'Allemagne Contenant les Bancs Isles et Costes Comprises depuis Bergen et les Isles Schetland justues au Pas de Calais
mwsc0373	scandinavia denmark	1773	DEPOT DE LA MARINE	600	60	88	Carte de la Mer de Dannemark et des Entrees dans la Mer Baltique Contenant les Bancs, Passes, Isles et Costes Comprises depuis Norden et le Cap Der-Neus jusques a Rostock et Valsterbon (north to the left. Based on Jaillot.)
mwp0164	australia	1847	DEPOT DE LA MARINE	550	59	90	Carte de la Mer du Corail et des Terres Environnantes
mwin0072	ceylon	1825	DEPOT DE LA MARINE	400	49	70	Carte de la Partie Meridionale de la Presqu'Isle de l'Inde qui Comprend l'Isle de Ceylan. 1798
mwwi0290	west indies (west)	1801	DEPOT DE LA MARINE	800	60	89	Carte de la Partie Occidentale des Iles Antilles Comprenant St. Domingue, la Jamaique, Cuba et les Iles et Bancs de Bahama
mwp0162	australia	1846	DEPOT DE LA MARINE	550	58	88	Carte de la Partie Sud-Ouest de la Nouvelle-Hollande Dressee par Mr. Daussy, Ingenieur Hydrographe en Chef
mwp0221	new zealand	1846	DEPOT DE LA MARINE	1000	59	87	Carte de la presqu'ile de Banks
mwec0657	uk england kent	1803	DEPOT DE LA MARINE	300	57	44	Carte de la Rade des Dunes ... l'An XII
mwsam0246	south america argentina	1801	DEPOT DE LA MARINE	500	58	88	Carte de la Riviere de la Plata depuis son Embouchure jusqu'a Buenos-Ayres (insets of Maldonado and Monte-Video)
mwp0165	australia	1847	DEPOT DE LA MARINE	1200	61	90	Carte de la Tasmanie et des Terres Environnantes (Partie Meridionale de la Nouvelle Hollande, Comprise entre le Port Macquarie et la Baie Fowlers) Par M.C.A. Vincendon-Dumoulin
mwaf0801a	africa north morocco	1848	DEPOT DE LA MARINE	400	80	102	Carte de l'Empire de Maroc
mwuss1144	new york	1780	DEPOT DE LA MARINE	2250	57	85	Carte de l'Entree de la Riviere d'Hudson ... 1778 / Carte de la Baye et Riviere de Delaware ... 1778 (2 maps on one sheet)
mwaf1260	africa west	1848	DEPOT DE LA MARINE	450	89	61	Carte de l'Entree du Rio Nunez
mwuk1545	uk english channel (west)	1825	DEPOT DE LA MARINE	480	62	96	Carte de L'Extrêmité Occidentale D'Angleterre Levée par le Lieutenant Mackenzie en 1772, et des Sorlinges Levée par Graeme Spence en 1792
mwca0339	canada newfoundland	1792	DEPOT DE LA MARINE	400	62	91	Carte de l'Ile de Fogo a la Cote Orientale de Terre-Neuve: Levee par Ordre de Vice-Amiral Campbell ... Par le Lieutenant Michael Lane en 1785. Publiee par Ordre du Ministre pour le Service des Vaisseaux Francais
mwwi0744	jamaica	1786	DEPOT DE LA MARINE	1000	58	86	Carte de l'Ile de la Jamaique Extraite des Cartes Topographiques Angloises de Thos. Craskell Ingenieur et de Jas. Simpson Arpenteur ... en 1786
mwuk1627	isle of wight	1803	DEPOT DE LA MARINE	650	61	90	Carte de l'Ile de Wight et de la Cote Adjacente de Hampshire Contenant une Description Particuliere des Rades de Ste. Helene Spithead &c.
mwf0360	france brittany	1761	DEPOT DE LA MARINE	600	58	87	Carte de l'Isle de Belle-Isle
mwwi0906	trinidad & tobago	1804	DEPOT DE LA MARINE	1800	57	43	Carte de l'Isle de la Trinite / Plan de la Presque Ile et du Port de Chaguaramas
mwec1174	uk england sussex	1786	DEPOT DE LA MARINE	720	94	91	Carte de Selsea-Bill, des Owers, et des Ports de Chichester et Emsworth / Carte des Rades Ste Helene et Spithead (2 sheets of 94x91cm.)
mwp0486	pacific solomon isl	1807	DEPOT DE LA MARINE	500	47	73	Carte des Archipels des Iles Salomon, de la Louisiade et de la Nouvle. Bretagne. 1806
mwas0674	asia south east java	1846	DEPOT DE LA MARINE	200	43	58	Carte des Atterrages de Batavia
mwaf1081	africa south west	1833	DEPOT DE LA MARINE	650	88	58	Carte des Cotes d'Afrique depuis le Cap Frio jusqua la Baie d'Algoa
mwin0347	india	1825	DEPOT DE LA MARINE	350	69	48	Carte des Cotes de Guzerat, de Concan et de Canara. 1798
mwgr0235	greece	1797	DEPOT DE LA MARINE	500	60	91	Carte des Cotes de la Grece depuis Navarin en Moree jusqu'au Cap Doro au Se de Negroponte avec la Partie de l'Archipel qui Comprend les Iles Cyclades
mwsam0246	south america argentina	1800	DEPOT DE LA MARINE	1500	92	62	Carte des Cotes de l'Amerique Meridionale (copy of Spanish map, 1798, publ. by Direccion Hydrogr.)
mwsp0099a	portugal	1762	DEPOT DE LA MARINE	650	59	88	Carte des Costes de Portugal et de Partie d'Espagne depuis le Cap de Finisterre jusques au Detroit de Gibraltar
mwsp0121a	portugal	1797	DEPOT DE LA MARINE	300	85	57	Carte des Costes d'Espagne et de Portugal
mwgm0060	gulf of mexico and surrounding regions	1800	DEPOT DE LA MARINE	3000	60	90	Carte des Cotes du Golfe du Mexique Compris entre la Pointe Sud de la Presqu'Ile de la Floride et la Pointe Nord de la Presqu'Ile d'Yucatan (close copy of Spanish chart, 1799)
mwc0280	china	1842	DEPOT DE LA MARINE	720	88	59	Carte des Cotes Orientales de Chine

AMPG REFERENCE	REGION	DATE	MAP MAKER	PRICE (UK£)	VERT. (cm.)	HOR. (cm.)	TITLE OF MAP (Comments by the editor in brackets)
mwas0675	asia south east java	1850	DEPOT DE LA MARINE	500	60	94	Carte des Detroits a l'Est de Java (Detroits de Sourabaya, Bali, Lombok et Allas) Dressee par Mr. J. de la Roche-Poncie
mwas0899	asia south east sumatra	1850	DEPOT DE LA MARINE	400	90	60	Carte des Detroits de Banca et de Gaspar (sea chart)
mwbh0703a	belgium holland	1753	DEPOT DE LA MARINE	650	61	84	Carte des Entrées de l'Escaut et de la Meuse entre Gravelines et Rotterdam (south to the top)
mwwi0290b	west indies (west)	1843	DEPOT DE LA MARINE	800	58	88	Carte des Grandes Antilles Cuba, Haiti, Jamaique, Archipel de Bahama
mwin0471	indian ocean maldives	1841	DEPOT DE LA MARINE	500	88	60	Carte des Iles Maldives. Levée en 1835 par MMR Moresby et FT Powell
mwp0370	pacific marquesas	1842	DEPOT DE LA MARINE	720	86	58	Carte des Iles Marquises. (Archipel de Mendana ou de Nou-Ka-Hiva). Levee et Dressee en 1838 a Bord de la Venus, sous les Ordres de Mr. A. Du-Petit Thouars
mwuk0553	scotland	1790	DEPOT DE LA MARINE	450	61	89	Carte des Iles Orcades et de la Cote Nord Ecosse depuis le Cap Wrath jusqu'au Cap Duncansby Reduite des Plans de Mackenzie
mwp0342	pacific hawaii	1825	DEPOT DE LA MARINE	2000	55	77	Carte des Iles Sandwich
mwuk0554	scotland	1790	DEPOT DE LA MARINE	450	61	89	Carte des Iles Shetland d'apres le Plan du Capne Anglais Preston Rectifie par M. De Loweorn en 1787
mwaf0623	africa islands madagascar	1845	DEPOT DE LA MARINE	300	86	58	Carte des Iles Situees a l'Est et Nord-Est de Madagascar
mwat0163	atlantic canary isl.	1776	DEPOT DE LA MARINE	550	59	87	Carte des Isles Canaries et d'une Partie des Cotes Occidentale d'Afrique
mwaf0640	africa islands mauritius	1849	DEPOT DE LA MARINE	720	60	89	Carte des Isles de France et de la Reunion
mwca0652	canada st pierre & miquelon	1763	DEPOT DE LA MARINE	900	56	87	Carte des Isles de Saint Pierre et Miquelon Levee par Ordre de M. le Duc de Choiseul ... Par le Sr. Bellin
mwat0208	atlantic cape verde isl.	1831	DEPOT DE LA MARINE	400	58	88	Carte des Isles du Cap Verd
mwas0859	asia south east singapore	1745	DEPOT DE LA MARINE	1200	59	45	Carte des Mers Comprises entre le Detroit de Banca et Po. Tilmon
mwuk0246b	ireland	1803	DEPOT DE LA MARINE	300	67	52	Carte d'Irlande Divisee en Provinces (shown above left)
mwaf1060	africa south east	1838	DEPOT DE LA MARINE	350	86	58	Carte du Canal de Mozambique et de l'Ile de Madagascar
mwsam0700	south america magellan	1838	DEPOT DE LA MARINE	600	60	89	Carte du Detroit de Magellan
mwsc0382	scandinavia denmark	1793	DEPOT DE LA MARINE	500	58	88	Carte du Detroit du Sond Contentant les Costes de l'Isle de Zelande Comprises entre Nicopen et l'Isle de Meun, et celles du Schonen (map originally publ. by Mortier)
mwc0251	china	1825	DEPOT DE LA MARINE	500	69	49	Carte d'une Partie de la Mer de Chine. 1798 (Hainan)
mwam0807	america north (central)	1778	DEPOT DE LA MARINE	3000	39	58	Carte d'une Partie des Cotes de la Florida et la Louisiane Contenant le Cours du Mississippi
mwgm0042	gulf of mexico and surrounding regions	1778	DEPOT DE LA MARINE	1800	39	58	Carte d'une Partie des Cotes de la Floride et de la Louisiane Contenant le Cours du Mississipi
mwwi0813	martinique	1831	DEPOT DE LA MARINE	400	95	66	Carte Generale de la Martinique pour la Topographie
mwme0676	arabia etc	1825	DEPOT DE LA MARINE	1600	60	87	Carte Generale de la Mer Rouge. 1798 (3 sheets of 60x87cm.)
mwf0546a	france corsica	1821	DEPOT DE LA MARINE	650	92	61	Carte Générale de l'Isle de Corse
mwat0052	atlantic ocean (all)	1786	DEPOT DE LA MARINE	450	61	88	Carte Generale de l'Ocean Atlantique ou Occidental
mwuk0175	ireland	1753	DEPOT DE LA MARINE	720	61	88	Carte Generale des Costes d'Irelande, et des Costes Occidentales d'Angleterre avec une Partie de celles d'Ecosse (copy of Jaillot, 1693)
mwas0847	asia south east siam	1800	DEPOT DE LA MARINE	720	54	86	Carte Generale des Cotes de la Cochinchine et du Camboge par M. Dayot
mwwi0274a	west indies	1844	DEPOT DE LA MARINE	400	86	58	Carte Generale des Iles Antilles Comprises entre la Trinite et Porto-Rico
mwgm0061	gulf of mexico and surrounding regions	1807	DEPOT DE LA MARINE	720	59	88	Carte Generale du Golfe du Mexique et de l'Archipel des Antilles
mwaf1212	africa west	1750	DEPOT DE LA MARINE	360	42	60	Carte Particuliere de la Coste d'Or pour Servir aux Vaisseaux Francais
mwsc0644a	scandinavia norway	1812	DEPOT DE LA MARINE	450	61	90	Carte Particuliere de la Cote de Norwege
mwuk0555	scotland	1790	DEPOT DE LA MARINE	500	61	89	Carte Particuliere de la Cote Occidentale d'Ecosse depuis la Pointe Ardnamurchan jusq. Mull de Galloway
mwuk0246c	ireland	1803	DEPOT DE LA MARINE	400	77	53	Carte Particuliere de la Cote Ouest d`Irlande depuis Sligo jusqu`a l`Embouchure du Shannon
mwuk1349	england east	1820	DEPOT DE LA MARINE	600	89	61	Carte Particuliere de la Cote Orientale d'Angleterre depuis Cap Gibraltar jusqu'au Golfe d'Edinbur
mwuk0308	irish sea	1798	DEPOT DE LA MARINE	900	90	61	Carte Particuliere de la Mer d'Irlande
mwwi0671	hispaniola	1803	DEPOT DE LA MARINE	850	55	91	Carte Particuliere de l'Ile de Saint Domingue Dressee d'apres Divers Plans Manuscrits Communiques par le Cen. Sorrel Ingenieur des Colonies
mwf0374	france brittany	1824	DEPOT DE LA MARINE	400	59	88	Carte Particuliere des Cotes de France (Entree de la Rade de Brest et Partie Meridionale du Chenal du Four)
mwuk1552a	bristol channel	1797	DEPOT DE LA MARINE	500	57	87	Carte Particuliere du Canal de Bristol
mwas0707	asia south east malacca	1846	DEPOT DE LA MARINE	400	42	58	Carte Particuliere du Detroit de la Sonde
mwuss0832	massachusetts	1780	DEPOT DE LA MARINE	3600	58	86	Carte Particuliere du Havre de Boston
mwsam0410	south america brazil	1823	DEPOT DE LA MARINE	450	61	91	Carte Reduite de la Baie de Todos os Santos et de ses Atterages Situes a la Cote du Bresil
mwsam0409	south america brazil	1822	DEPOT DE LA MARINE	450	61	91	Carte Reduite de la Cote de Bresil Comprise entre l'Ile Santa Catharina et le Cap Frio

AMPG REFERENCE	REGION	DATE	MAP MAKER	PRICE (UK£)	VERT. (cm.)	HOR. (cm.)	TITLE OF MAP (Comments by the editor in brackets)
mwgm0293	mexico	1823	DEPOT DE LA MARINE	500	65	98	Carte Reduite de la Cote du Mexique sur la Mer du Sud depuis le Golfe Dulce jusqu'au Cap Corrientes
mwsam0411	south america brazil	1823	DEPOT DE LA MARINE	450	61	91	Carte Réduite de la Còte Meridionale du Brésil Comprise Porto Seguro et Pernambuco
mwgm0444	panama	1825	DEPOT DE LA MARINE	500	85	56	Carte Reduite de la Cote Occidentale de l'Amerique depuis 9 de Latitude Nord jusqu'a 7 de Latitude Sud. 1821
mwbp0055	baltic sea (east)	1785	DEPOT DE LA MARINE	960	77	120	Carte Reduite de la Mer Baltique
mwsc0753a	scandinavia sweden	1815	DEPOT DE LA MARINE	600	60	94	Carte Reduite de la Mer Baltique (sheet 3)
mwuk1684	north sea	1807	DEPOT DE LA MARINE	600	119	91	Carte Reduite de la Mer du Nord
mwsam0475	south america chile	1821	DEPOT DE LA MARINE	800	94	64	Carte Reduite de la Partie de la Cote du Chili Comprise entre le 22e et le 38e Degre de Latitude Sud. 1821
mwsam0791	south america peru	1821	DEPOT DE LA MARINE	800	84	55	Carte Reduite de la Partie de la Cote du Perou Comprise entre le 7e, et le 21e Degre de Latitude Sud
mwc0252	china	1825	DEPOT DE LA MARINE	250	43	57	Carte Reduite de la Partie Meridionale de l'Ile d'Hainan Parcouroe en 1817 par la Fregate du Roi la Cybele 1819
mwgm0305a	mexico	1826	DEPOT DE LA MARINE	550	57	88	Carte Réduite de la Partie Meridionale du Golfe du Mexique
mwsam0728	south america paraguay	1833	DEPOT DE LA MARINE	500	58	88	Carte Reduite de la Riviere de la Plata depuis les Caps Sainte Marie et Saint Antoine jusqu'aux Iles de Hornos et Buenos-Ayres
mwsam0254	south america argentina	1826	DEPOT DE LA MARINE	450	61	91	Carte Réduite de la Rivière de La Plata depuis les Caps Sainte Marie et Saint Antoine jusqu'aux Iles de Hornos et Buenos-Ayres
mwca0424	canada nova scotia	1779	DEPOT DE LA MARINE	600	58	89	Carte Reduite de l'Acadie ou Nouvelle Ecosse Comprenant une Partie de l'Ile Royale, de l'Ile St. Jean et du Canada Dressee au Depot General des Cartes, Plans et Journaux de la Marine. Pour le Service des Vaisseaux du Roi par Ordre de M. de Sartine
mwam1129	america north (east)	1799	DEPOT DE LA MARINE	2000	57	84	Carte Reduite de l'Amerique Septentrionale
mwgr0627	greece islands	1738	DEPOT DE LA MARINE	600	64	52	Carte Reduite de l'Archipel
mwuk0308a	irish sea	1798	DEPOT DE LA MARINE	500	61	91	Carte Reduite de l`Entre de la Mer d`Irlande et du Canal du Bristol (shown above left)
mwca0331	canada newfoundland	1784	DEPOT DE LA MARINE	600	86	59	Carte Reduite de l'Ile de Terre-Neuve Dressee d'apres les Plans Anglois de James Cook et Michael Lane
mwca0440	canada nova scotia	1780	DEPOT DE LA MARINE	480	40	58	Carte Reduite de l'Ile Royale
mwat0306	atlantic south	1739	DEPOT DE LA MARINE	600	62	78	Carte Reduite de l'Ocean Meridionale
mwat0309	atlantic south	1753	DEPOT DE LA MARINE	500	55	88	Carte Reduite de l'Ocean Meridionale Contenant Toutes les Costes de l'Amerique Meridionale depuis l'Equateur jusqu'au 57 Degre de Latitude et les Costes d'Afrique
mwat0272	atlantic north	1738	DEPOT DE LA MARINE	800	53	78	Carte Reduite de l'Ocean Occidental Comprenant les Cotes d'Europe et d'Afrique ... et les Cotes d'Amerique Opposees
mwca0332	canada newfoundland	1784	DEPOT DE LA MARINE	600	57	85	Carte Reduite des Bancs et de l'Ile de Terre-Neuve avec les Cotes du Golfe de St. Laurent et de l'Acadie ... Au Depot General des Cartes Plans et Journaux de la Marine ... 1784
mwam1010	america north (east)	1762	DEPOT DE LA MARINE	1000	54	87	Carte Reduite des Costes Orientales de l'Amerique Septentrionale. 1re Feuille Contenant l'Isle Royale, l'Accadie, la Baye Francoise, la Nouvelle Angleterre et la Nouvelle Yorc
mwsam0644a	south america guyana	1817	DEPOT DE LA MARINE	960	78	58	Carte Reduite des côtes de la Guyane entre les Bouches de la riviere des Amazones et celles du Maroni / ... depuis Cayenne (2 sheets, second sheet 91x62cm)
mwuss0444	florida	1780	DEPOT DE LA MARINE	2500	58	39	Carte Reduite des Cotes et de l'Interieur de la Presqu'ile de la Floride, avec le Detroit de Cette Presqu'ile et le Canal de Bahama
mwuss0102	california	1826	DEPOT DE LA MARINE	800	84	57	Carte Reduite des Cotes et du Golfe de Californie depuis le Cap Corrientes jusqu'au Port St. Diego
mwam1055	america north (east)	1778	DEPOT DE LA MARINE	3000	62	90	Carte Reduite des Cotes Orientales de l'Amerique Septentrionale Contenant celles des Provinces de New-York et de la Nouvelle Angleterre / Partie du Nouveau Jersey, Le Pensylvanie (2 maps, each roughly 62x90cm)
mwam1067	america north (east)	1780	DEPOT DE LA MARINE	2250	58	86	Carte Reduite des Cotes Orientales de l'Amerique Septentrionale Contenant celles des Provinces de New-York et de la Nouvelle Angleterre celles de l'Acadie ou Nouvelle Escosse de l'Ile Royale et l'Ile St. Jean
mwat0098	atlantic azores	1791	DEPOT DE LA MARINE	650	56	86	Carte Reduite des Isles Acores
mwaa0133	arctic	1751	DEPOT DE LA MARINE	600	55	89	Carte Reduite des Mers du Nord
mwsc0395	scandinavia denmark	1813	DEPOT DE LA MARINE	400	84	58	Carte Reduite du Cattegat
mwf0297	france bay of biscay	1784	DEPOT DE LA MARINE	600	85	90	Carte Reduite du Golfe de Gascogne (first edition 1756)
mwp0266	pacific (all)	1798	DEPOT DE LA MARINE	900	61	90	Carte Reduite du Grand Ocean Compris entre l'Asie et l'Amerique
mwat0281	atlantic north	1775	DEPOT DE LA MARINE	800	58	89	Carte Réduite d'une Partie de l'Océan Atlantique ou Occidental
mwwi0474	cuba	1801	DEPOT DE LA MARINE	600	59	92	Carte Reduite d'une Partie du Vieux Canal de Bahama et des Bancs Adjacent depuis la Pointe de Maternillos jusqu'a celle d'Ycacos
mwgm0375a	nicaragua	1818	DEPOT DE LA MARINE	200	19	26	Costa de Mosquitos - Puerto y Boca del Rio de S. Juan de Nicaragua

AMPG REFERENCE	REGION	DATE	MAP MAKER	PRICE (UK£)	VERT. (cm.)	HOR. (cm.)	TITLE OF MAP (Comments by the editor in brackets)
mwsp0741	gibraltar	1793	DEPOT DE LA MARINE	600	56	88	Cote Meridionale d'Espagne depuis Cadiz jusqu Cap de Palos et Cote Septentrionale d'Afrique depuis le Cap Spartel jusqu Cap de Tenez
mwaf1262	africa west	1849	DEPOT DE LA MARINE	300	60	90	Cote Occidentale d'Afrique Partie Comprise entre le Cap Ghir et le Cap Bojadar
mwuk1678	north sea	1797	DEPOT DE LA MARINE	450	61	89	Cote Orientale d'Angleterre depuis Lowestoft jusques et Compris l'Embouchure de l'Humber
mwuk1446	england thames	1797	DEPOT DE LA MARINE	600	62	91	Cote Orientale d'Angleterre depuis South Foreland, jusqu'a Lowestoft Comprenant les Entrees de la Tamise
mwc0253	china	1825	DEPOT DE LA MARINE	250	43	57	Plan de la Baie de Gaalong (Hainan)
mwc0254	china	1825	DEPOT DE LA MARINE	250	43	57	Plan de la Baie de Lyeoung-Soy (Hainan)
mwuss0110	california	1844	DEPOT DE LA MARINE	800	59	88	Plan de la Baie de Monterey (Haute Californie) Leve et Dressee en 1837, a Bord de la Venus
mwuss1455	rhode isl	1780	DEPOT DE LA MARINE	2500	58	41	Plan de la Baie de Narraganset dans la Nouvelle Angleterre
mwsam0421	south america brazil	1829	DEPOT DE LA MARINE	1000	88	59	Plan de la Baie de Rio-Janeiro. Leve en 1826 et 1827. Par M. Barral ... au Depot-General de la Marine en 1829
mwc0255	china	1825	DEPOT DE LA MARINE	250	43	57	Plan de la Baie d'Yu-Lin-Kan et du Mouillage de Sanghia (Hainan)
mwuss0700	maine	1780	DEPOT DE LA MARINE	800	41	58	Plan de la Baie et du Havre de Casco et des Iles Adjacentes par le Cape. Cyprian Southack
mwaf0656	africa islands seychelles	1790	DEPOT DE LA MARINE	500	61	44	Plan de la Baie et du Port de Mahé
mwuss0208a	carolinas	1778	DEPOT DE LA MARINE	1500	42	58	Plan de la Barre et du Havre de Charles-Town d'apres un plan Anglois leve en 1776
mwas0806	asia south east philippines	1798	DEPOT DE LA MARINE	450	48	30	Plan de la Bay de Manille et de ses Environs Verifie sur le Fregate la Meduse en 1789 et Corrige Particulierement pour les Positions du Banc de St. Nicholas et de la Pointe de Capponne
mwca0336	canada newfoundland	1785	DEPOT DE LA MARINE	400	27	57	Plan de la Baye de St. Lunaire a la Cote du Nord-Est de Terre-Neuve Leve Geometriquement en 1784
mwf0561	france corsica	1830	DEPOT DE LA MARINE	400	46	62	Plan de la Cote de Bastia et du Mouillage de la Pointe d'Arco
mwuk1398	england south	1824	DEPOT DE LA MARINE	450	62	94	Plan de la Cote Meridionale d'Angleterre depuis la Pte Blackwood de l'Ile de Wight jusqu'a St. Albans. Leve en 1785 par le Lieutenant Murdoch Mackenzie
mwf0547	france corsica	1825	DEPOT DE LA MARINE	500	47	60	Plan de la Mouillage de Propriano / Plan de Porto-Polo / Plan de Campo-Moro
mwec0501	uk england hampshire	1824	DEPOT DE LA MARINE	720	61	94	Plan de la Partie Occidentale du Canal qui Separe l'Ile de Wight de la Cote de Hampshire
mwme0686	arabia etc	1843	DEPOT DE LA MARINE	500	43	58	Plan de la Rade de Moka
mwca0656a	canada st pierre & miquelon	1818	DEPOT DE LA MARINE	400	68	52	Plan de la Rade et du Baraquois des Iles St. Pierre et Miquelon
mwec0500	uk england hampshire	1823	DEPOT DE LA MARINE	720	94	61	Plan de la Riviere de Southampton ... et de la Rade de Cowes
mwuss0208	carolinas	1778	DEPOT DE LA MARINE	2500	61	89	Plan de la Riviere du Cap Fear depuis la Barre jusques a Brunswick / Plan de la Barre et du Havre de Charles-Town (2 maps on one sheet)
mwas0846	asia south east siam	1795	DEPOT DE LA MARINE	600	59	44	Plan de la Ville de Saigon Fortifiee en 1790 par le Colonel Victor Olivier ... No 3
mwca0431	canada nova scotia	1779	DEPOT DE LA MARINE	600	45	61	Plan de la Ville et du Port de Louisbourg leve en 1756. Suivant l'Original ... par Ordre de M. De Sartine
mwsam0645a	south america guyana	1822	DEPOT DE LA MARINE	350	58	89	Plan de l'Embouchure de la Rivière de Cayenne et des Mouillages Extérieurs
mwg0677	saxony	1821	DEPOT DE LA MARINE	800	60	89	Plan de l'Embouchure de l'Ems
mwuss0443	florida	1779	DEPOT DE LA MARINE	1400	60	43	Plan de l'Ile d'Amelia / Plan de la Barre et du Port d'Amelia (2 maps on one sheet)
mwca0653	canada st pierre & miquelon	1763	DEPOT DE LA MARINE	600	70	88	Plan de l'Ile de Saint Pierre au Sud de Terre-Neuve Leve en 1763 par le St. Fortin Ingenieur
mwca0490	canada prince edward isl.	1778	DEPOT DE LA MARINE	600	43	58	Plan de l'Ile de St. Jean au Nord de l'Acadie ... Suivant l'Arpentage du Capitaine Anglois Holland ... par Ordre de M. De Sartine
mwuss0201	carolinas	1778	DEPOT DE LA MARINE	1800	89	61	Plan de Port Royal et de la Riviere et du Detroit d'Awfoskee ... 1778
mwsam0792	south america peru	1824	DEPOT DE LA MARINE	400	52	68	Plan de Quilca
mwp0212	new zealand	1840	DEPOT DE LA MARINE	480	43	60	Plan des Baies de Tokolabo et de Koko-Rarata
mwc0294	china	1848	DEPOT DE LA MARINE	550	44	60	Plan des Bouches du Tigre (Riviere de Canton)
mwca0333a	canada newfoundland	1784	DEPOT DE LA MARINE	600	66	96	Plan des Cotes de Terre Neuve IIIe. Feuille Contenant la Partie Meridionale depuis les Iles de Burgeo jusqu'au Cap de Raye, avec l'Entree de Golfe de St. Laurent ... Tire des Plans Anglois de J. Cook et M. Lane ... 1784
mwca0333	canada newfoundland	1784	DEPOT DE LA MARINE	600	93	64	Plan des Cotes de Terre-Neuve Ve. Feuille. Contenant la Partie Occidentale depuis le Cap de St. Gregoire jusqu'a la Pointe de Ferolle. Tire des Plans Anglois de J. Cook et M. Lane ... 1784
mwca0334	canada newfoundland	1784	DEPOT DE LA MARINE	600	65	96	Plan des Cotes de Terre-Neuve VIe. Feuille. Contenant la Partie Septentrionale, depuis la Pointe de Ferolle jusqu'a l'Ile de Quirpon, avec le Detroit de Bell'-Ile et les Cotes de Labrador ... Tire des Plans Anglois de J. Cook et M. Lane

AMPG REFERENCE	REGION	DATE	MAP MAKER	PRICE (UK£)	VERT. (cm.)	HOR. (cm.)	TITLE OF MAP (Comments by the editor in brackets)
mwca0335	canada newfoundland	1784	DEPOT DE LA MARINE	600	93	64	Plan des Cotes de Terre-Neuve. IVe. Feuille. Contenant la Partie Occidentale depuis le Cap de Ray jusqu'au Cap de St. Gregoire: Tire des Plans Anglois de J. Cook et M. Lane
mwca0340	canada newfoundland	1792	DEPOT DE LA MARINE	600	91	59	Plan des Cotes de Terre-Neuve: IXe. Feuille Contenant la Partie Orientale depuis le Cap de Bonavista, jusqu'au Cap Broyle: Levee par Ordre des Gouverneurs Anglois de Terre-Neuve en 1774 et 1775. Par Michael Lane
mwe0509b	europe croatia	1820	DEPOT DE LA MARINE	600	93	63	Plan des Environs de Raguse. Leve en 1809 (Dubrovnik)
mwe0509c	europe croatia	1820	DEPOT DE LA MARINE	600	92	62	Plan des Environs de Sebenico. Leve en 1806
mwf0556	france corsica	1829	DEPOT DE LA MARINE	400	47	62	Plan des Golfes de Calvi et de Revellata
mwf0551	france corsica	1827	DEPOT DE LA MARINE	400	60	47	Plan des Iles Cerbicale et du Canal qui les Separe
mwf0550	france corsica	1826	DEPOT DE LA MARINE	400	47	60	Plan des Iles Sanguinaires
mwwi0562	guadeloupe	1818	DEPOT DE LA MARINE	450	41	56	Plan des Isles des Saintes Leve en 1803 par Pre. Gautier Enseigne de Vaisseau
mwf0548	france corsica	1825	DEPOT DE LA MARINE	400	47	61	Plan des Moines ou Monachi et de la Partie Adjacente de la Cote S.O. de l'Ile de Corse
mwaf0578	comores	1849	DEPOT DE LA MARINE	480	41	58	Plan des mouillages situés à la côte sud de Mohéli
mwf0549	france corsica	1825	DEPOT DE LA MARINE	400	47	60	Plan des Mouillages Situes au Fond du Golfe d'Ajaccio
mwe0509c	europe croatia	1821	DEPOT DE LA MARINE	600	92	62	Plan des Ports de Molonta Leve en 1809
mwuk1630	isle of wight	1824	DEPOT DE LA MARINE	650	95	61	Plan des Rades Ste Helene, Spithead, et des Ports Portsmouth et Langstone
mwca0432	canada nova scotia	1779	DEPOT DE LA MARINE	600	40	61	Plan du Bassin et de la Riviere du Port Royal ou Annapolis, dans l'Acadie sur la Cote Orientale de la Baie Francoise … par Ordre de M. De Sartine
mwsam0793	south america peru	1825	DEPOT DE LA MARINE	400	59	43	Plan du Callao de Lima / Plan de l'Anse et Port de Valparaiso
mwf0557	france corsica	1829	DEPOT DE LA MARINE	400	45	60	Plan du Danger de l'Algajola / Plan du Port de Malfalco [and] Plan du Port et de la Cote de Centuri
mwe0982	europe montenegro	1820	DEPOT DE LA MARINE	800	84	92	Plan du Golfe de Cattaro Leve en 1808
mwf0562	france corsica	1830	DEPOT DE LA MARINE	400	61	47	Plan du Golfe de Lava / Plan du Golfe et du Port de Girolata
mwf0552	france corsica	1828	DEPOT DE LA MARINE	850	47	60	Plan du Golfe de Pinarello / Plan du Port de Favone / Plan de Porto Nuovo et de la Calangue del Gionco
mwf0553	france corsica	1828	DEPOT DE LA MARINE	500	46	59	Plan du Golfe de Porto Vecchio
mwf0558	france corsica	1829	DEPOT DE LA MARINE	400	59	46	Plan du Golfe et du Port de Galeria
mwf0559	france corsica	1829	DEPOT DE LA MARINE	400	46	59	Plan du Mouillage de l'Ile Rousse
mwf0560	france corsica	1829	DEPOT DE LA MARINE	400	47	60	Plan du Mouillage de Sagone
mwp0213	new zealand	1840	DEPOT DE LA MARINE	480	88	59	Plan du Port Akaroa dans la Presqu'ile de Banks
mwca0422	canada nova scotia	1778	DEPOT DE LA MARINE	400	44	61	Plan du Port Dauphin, de la Rade de Ste. Anne, de l'Entree de Labrador et de la Baie de Niganiche … Par Order de M. De Sartine
mwsam0476	south america chile	1825	DEPOT DE LA MARINE	350	57	41	Plan du Port de Baldivia / Plan de la Rade de Sn Juan Bautista a la Pointe N.E. de l'Ile de Juan Fernandez. 1821
mwas0845	asia south east siam	1790	DEPOT DE LA MARINE	720	48	70	Plan du Port de Candiu Situe a la Cote de Tsiompa / Plan d'une Partie du Cours de la Riviere de Saigon depuis cette Ville jusqu'a son Embouchure
mwec0206	uk england cornwall	1824	DEPOT DE LA MARINE	500	93	58	Plan du Port de Fowey
mwaf1058	africa south east	1809	DEPOT DE LA MARINE	300	35	24	Plan du Port de Mozambique et de Pays Adjacent (map by H. Salt)
mwec0308	uk england devon	1803	DEPOT DE LA MARINE	450	58	43	Plan du Port de Plymouth … l'An XII
mwsam0477	south america chile	1825	DEPOT DE LA MARINE	350	56	42	Plan du Port de Sn Carlos Situe a la Partie du Nord de l'Ile de Chiloe. 1821
mwuss0042	alaska	1825	DEPOT DE LA MARINE	500	50	69	Plan du Port des Francais 1786
mwm0264	mediterranean malta	1850	DEPOT DE LA MARINE	500	86	58	Plan du Port et de Fortifications de la Valette
mwwi0475	cuba	1801	DEPOT DE LA MARINE	900	42	53	Plan du Port et de la Ville de la Havanne Leve en 1798 par Jose del Rio Capitaine
mwca0433	canada nova scotia	1779	DEPOT DE LA MARINE	600	60	41	Plan du Port Toulouse / Plan de la Baie Nerichac
mwwi0834	puerto rico	1794	DEPOT DE LA MARINE	1500	40	56	Plan du Principal Port de l'Ile de Porto Rico Leve en 1794 par D. Cosme de Churruca … par Ordre du Ministre de la Marine et des Colonies
mwuk1629	isle of wight	1823	DEPOT DE LA MARINE	650	94	61	Plan d'une Partie de l'Ile de Wight et de la Cote de Hampshire
mwas0686	asia south east malacca	1745	DEPOT DE LA MARINE	800	57	74	Plan Particuliere du Detroit de Malaca avec une Partie de la Coste de l'Ouest de Sumatra
mwgm0264	mexico	1800	DEPOT DE LA MARINE	450	41	57	Port de la Vera Cruz a la Cote Occidentale du Golfe du Mexique d'apres la Plan Leve par Dn. Bernardo de Orta … en l'An XI
mwas0848	asia south east siam	1825	DEPOT DE LA MARINE	350	48	69	Premiere Feuille des Cotes de la Cochinchine. 1798
mwas0849	asia south east siam	1825	DEPOT DE LA MARINE	350	70	49	Seconde Feuille des Cotes de la Cochinchine. 1798
mwas0850	asia south east siam	1825	DEPOT DE LA MARINE	350	70	49	Troisieme Feuille des Cotes de la Cochinchine. 1798
mwf0178	france	1807	DEPOT GUERRE	400	65	103	Carte de l'Empire Francois avec ses Etablissements Politiques, Militaires, Civils, et Religieux
mwme0672	arabia etc	1822	DEPOT GUERRE	400	93	110	Carte de l'Empire Ottoman en Europe, en Asie et en Afrique, avec les Pays Limitrophes; Dressee par le Chevalier Lapie
mwe0392	europe austria	1801	DEPOT GUERRE	1600	55	83	Carte du Tyrol Verifie et Corrige sur les Memoires de Dupuis et La Luzerne et Reduite d'apres celle d'Anich et Hueber (map in 6 sheets)

AMPG REFERENCE	REGION	DATE	MAP MAKER	PRICE (UK£)	VERT. (cm.)	HOR. (cm.)	TITLE OF MAP (Comments by the editor in brackets)
mwas0548	asia south east	1842	DERFELDEN VAN HINDERSTEIN	1600	66	85	Algemeene Kaart van Nederlandsch Oostindie ... door G.F. Baron von Derfelden van Hinderstein (8 sheets, 66x85cm.)
mwca0620	canada st lawrence	1781	DES BARRES	950	58	79	(Bay of Chaleurs)
mwca0406a	canada nova scotia	1776	DES BARRES	2250	70	207	(Bay of Fundy, South East Part)
mwca0621	canada st lawrence	1781	DES BARRES	1100	76	55	(Bay of Seven Islands)
mwca0273	canada new brunswick	1779	DES BARRES	900	78	61	(Bay Verte to Buctush)
mwuss0840	massachusetts	1775	DES BARRES	6000	71	104	(Boston Bay)
mwuss0808	massachusetts	1775	DES BARRES	17500	71	104	(Boston Harbour)
mwuss0839	massachusetts	1781	DES BARRES	2500	74	105	(Cape Anne to Boston to Plymouth, with Outer Cape Cod)
mwuss0697	maine	1776	DES BARRES	1200	74	106	(Casco Bay)
mwca0441	canada nova scotia	1781	DES BARRES	500	52	64	(Chedabucto Bay with Lenox or Petit Passage)
mwca0268	canada new brunswick	1776	DES BARRES	550	76	160	(Chignecto Bay)
mwuss0696	maine	1776	DES BARRES	2250	74	158	(Coast from Gouldsborough to Moose Harbor)
mwuss0695	maine	1776	DES BARRES	1500	107	74	(Coast from Musketo Harbour to Frenchman Bay)
mwuss0694	maine	1776	DES BARRES	1800	107	75	(Coast from Pemaquid Point to Owls Head Bay)
mwuss0693	maine	1776	DES BARRES	2500	75	107	(Coast from Salter Island to Portland Head)
mwuss1367	pennsylvania	1777	DES BARRES	4800	77	106	(Environs of Philadelphia - Delaware river)
mwuss0698	maine	1777	DES BARRES	2250	74	53	(Falmouth Harbour)
mwuss1147	new york	1781	DES BARRES	5000	74	105	(From Great Bay, Long Island to Pt. Judith, Rhode Island)
mwuss0838	massachusetts	1781	DES BARRES	3200	105	75	(From Great Boars Head to Marblehead)
mwuss0699	maine	1778	DES BARRES	1600	150	120	(Grand Manan Island & Passamaquody Bay)
mwca0540	canada quebec	1781	DES BARRES	1500	153	77	(Harbour and Bay of Gaspe and Mal Bay)
mwuss0692	maine	1776	DES BARRES	1500	74	104	(Maine Coast)
mwuss0820	massachusetts	1776	DES BARRES	6000	105	74	(Martha's Vineyard, Elizabeth Islands, Buzzards Bay)
mwuss0807	massachusetts	1775	DES BARRES	1800	27	78	(Martha's Vineyard, Rhode Island, Block Island Coastal Profiles)
mwuss0819	massachusetts	1776	DES BARRES	5000	74	105	(Massachusetts Bay)
mwca0270	canada new brunswick	1777	DES BARRES	500	54	75	(Miramichy Bay)
mwuss0691	maine	1776	DES BARRES	1500	107	76	(Mount Desert Island & Adjacent Coast)
mwuss0837	massachusetts	1781	DES BARRES	6500	74	106	(Nantucket and Eastern Martha's Vineyard)
mwuss0836	massachusetts	1781	DES BARRES	6500	74	107	(Nantucket, Martha's Vineyard, Elizabeth Islands, Upper & Middle Cape Cod, Buzzards Bay & Narragansett Bay)
mwuss1146	new york	1781	DES BARRES	3000	79	115	(New York City, Hell Gate and Western Long Island)
mwuss0690	maine	1776	DES BARRES	2500	75	105	(Newbury Harbor to Cape Elizabeth)
mwca0413	canada nova scotia	1777	DES BARRES	2000	74	158	(Nova Scotia, Northeast Coast)
mwuss0689	maine	1776	DES BARRES	3600	77	106	(Penobscot Bay Entrance) / (Penobscot Bay, Upper Part) (2 charts, each 77x106cm.)
mwuss0445	florida	1780	DES BARRES	1800	74	210	(Pensacola to Apalachicola)
mwuss1371	pennsylvania	1777	DES BARRES	6500	78	104	(Philadelphia and Environs)
mwuss1000	new hampshire	1781	DES BARRES	3000	106	74	(Piscataqua Harbour)
mwuss0835	massachusetts	1781	DES BARRES	1250	66	48	(Plymouth Bay & Town)
mwca0274	canada new brunswick	1779	DES BARRES	750	74	53	(Port Shediack & Cocagne)
mwca0275	canada new brunswick	1781	DES BARRES	600	77	54	(Rishibucto & Buctush Harbors)
mwca0489	canada prince edward isl.	1778	DES BARRES	1500	75	52	(St. Peters Bay with Inset View of Cape Round)
mwuss0645	louisiana	1777	DES BARRES	9000	74	104	(United States: Gulf Coast)
mwca0400	canada nova scotia	1775	DES BARRES	650	69	50	(Untitled chart of Canso harbour)
mwca0442a	canada nova scotia	1781	DES BARRES	750	60	71	A Chart of Cape Breton and St. John's Island &c. in the Gulph of St. Lawrence
mwuss0367	delaware	1779	DES BARRES	4500	78	57	A Chart of Delawar Bay, with Soundings and Nautical Observations - Taken by Capt. Sir Andrew Snape Hammond
mwuss1379	pennsylvania	1780	DES BARRES	10000	52	74	A Chart of Delawar River from Bombay Hook to Ridley Creek, with Soundings &c / A Plan of Delawar River from Chester to Philadelphia. Shewing the Situation of His Majesty's Ships &c.
mwwi0737	jamaica	1780	DES BARRES	1000	75	53	A chart of Montego Bay on the north west shore of the island of Jamaica
mwuss1137	new york	1779	DES BARRES	20000	82	61	A Chart of New York Harbour with the soundings
mwca0401	canada nova scotia	1775	DES BARRES	2500	73	150	A Chart of Nova Scotia, Surveyed by Frederick Wallet des Barres Esqr ... 1775
mwwi0738	jamaica	1780	DES BARRES	1500	74	104	A Chart of Port Royal and Kingston Harbours, in the Island of Jamaica
mwca0442	canada nova scotia	1781	DES BARRES	1500	51	74	A Chart of the Harbour of Louisbourg in the Island of Cape Breton. October 1, 1781
mwuss1449	rhode isl	1776	DES BARRES	9000	107	75	A Chart of the Harbour of Rhode Island and Narraganset Bay. Surveyed in Pursuance of Directions from the Lords of Trade to His Majesty's Surveyor General ... Published at the Request of the Right Honourable Lord Viscount Howe
mwca0443	canada nova scotia	1781	DES BARRES	850	69	57	A Chart of the Island of Cape Breton
mwca0444	canada nova scotia	1781	DES BARRES	2000	76	156	A Chart of the N.E. Coast of Cape Breton Island, from St. Ann Bay to Cape Morien (illustrated is the 1st state, without the date October 1, 1781)
mwca0538	canada quebec	1779	DES BARRES	12000	73	152	A Plan of Quebec and Environs, with its Defenses and the Occasional Entrenched Camps of the French Commanded by Marquis de Montcalm ... During the Siege of that Place in 1759

AMPG REFERENCE	REGION	DATE	MAP MAKER	PRICE (UK£)	VERT. (cm.)	HOR. (cm.)	TITLE OF MAP (Comments by the editor in brackets)
mwuss1448	rhode isl	1776	DES BARRES	9000	72	52	A Plan of the Town of Newport in the Province of Rhode Island
mwuss0214	carolinas	1780	DES BARRES	2000	55	39	A Sketch of the Environs of Charlestown in South Carolina
mwuss1119	new york	1777	DES BARRES	6000	80	58	A Sketch of the Operations of His Majesty's Fleet and Army under the Command of Vice Admiral the Rt. Hble. Lord Viscount Howe and Genl. Sr. Wm. Howe, K.B. in 1776
mwuss0999	new hampshire	1778	DES BARRES	1600	18	25	A View of New Castle with the Fort and Light House on the Entrance of Pisquataqua River
mwuss1118	new york	1777	DES BARRES	7500	69	47	A View of the Highland of Neversink / The South Shore of Long Island / New York / The Light House on Sandy Hook / The Narrows
mwca0414	canada nova scotia	1777	DES BARRES	1200	79	53	A. Cape Prospect /C. The High Lands of Haspotagoen / The Ovens at the Entrance of Lunenburg Bay /D. Cape Sable /F. Cape Sable Bearing N.E.
mwca0405	canada nova scotia	1776	DES BARRES	2000	73	104	Annapolis Royal. St. Mary's Bay
mwca0406	canada nova scotia	1776	DES BARRES	1500	75	105	Barrington Bay. Publish'd According to Act of Parliament by J.F.W. Des Barres Esq. April 6, 1776
mwuss0823	massachusetts	1777	DES BARRES	4200	55	79	Boston, Seen between Castle Williams and Governors Island / The Entrance of Boston Harbour / Boston Bay / Appearance of the High lands of Agamenticus
mwca0407	canada nova scotia	1776	DES BARRES	1500	71	102	Charlotte Bay ... 1776
mwca0408	canada nova scotia	1776	DES BARRES	2000	69	102	Chart of Port Campbell
mwca0409	canada nova scotia	1776	DES BARRES	720	53	70	Conway Harbour - Port Aylesbury
mwca0425	canada nova scotia	1779	DES BARRES	600	27	24	Crow Harbour, on the South Shore of Chedabuctou Bay
mwca0426	canada nova scotia	1779	DES BARRES	1500	81	61	Egmont Harbor
mwca0446	canada nova scotia	1781	DES BARRES	7200	75	134	Halifax Harbour
mwuss1126	new york	1778	DES BARRES	5000	78	53	Hell Gate / Oyster Bay and Huntington / Huntington Bay
mwca0416	canada nova scotia	1777	DES BARRES	1350	72	102	Keppell Harbour / Knowles Harbour / Tangier Harbour / Saunder's Harbour / Deane Harbour
mwca0427	canada nova scotia	1779	DES BARRES	1350	68	98	King's Bay and Lunenburg
mwca0428	canada nova scotia	1779	DES BARRES	1350	75	100	Leith Harbour / Prospect Harbour / Bristol Bay / Sambro Harbour
mwca0417	canada nova scotia	1777	DES BARRES	1600	74	53	Liverpool Bay
mwca0410	canada nova scotia	1776	DES BARRES	2000	71	102	Mecklenburgh Bay
mwca0429	canada nova scotia	1779	DES BARRES	2000	76	56	Milford Haven
mwuss0949	mississippi	1779	DES BARRES	12000	160	58	Mississipi River from Iberville to Yazous
mwca0404	canada nova scotia	1775	DES BARRES	800	75	56	Port Amherst. Port Haldimand.
mwca0411	canada nova scotia	1776	DES BARRES	1000	67	45	Port Hood Situated on the North-Western Extremity of the Island of Cape Breton
mwca0434	canada nova scotia	1779	DES BARRES	500	74	52	Port Jackson
mwca0447	canada nova scotia	1781	DES BARRES	1400	73	209	Port Mills, Port Mansfield, Gambier Harbour
mwuss0195	carolinas	1777	DES BARRES	3000	82	61	Port Royal in South Carolina Taken from Surveys Deposited at the Plantation Office
mwca0616	canada st lawrence	1777	DES BARRES	6000	83	241	River of St. Lawrence (1st state in 4 sheets. Illustration shows western-most sheet. Later editions in 8 sheets, incl. upper river.)
mwca0418	canada nova scotia	1777	DES BARRES	1350	74	53	South Entrance of Grand Passage / Cape St. Mary N: E: One Mile / St. Mary's Bay
mwca0435	canada nova scotia	1779	DES BARRES	1200	73	103	Spry Harbour / Port Pallisser / Port North / Port Parker / Beaver Harbour / Fleming River
mwam1056	america north (east)	1778	DES BARRES	2000	106	74	The Coast of New England
mwca0419	canada nova scotia	1777	DES BARRES	1600	81	120	The Coast of Nova Scotia, New England, New York, Jersey, the Gulph and River of St. Lawrence, the Islands of Newfoundland, Cape Breton, St. John, Antecosty, Sable &c.
mwuss0499	georgia	1780	DES BARRES	7500	58	74	The Coast, Rivers and Inlets of the Province of Georgia, Surveyed by Joseph Avery
mwca0448	canada nova scotia	1781	DES BARRES	400	52	74	The Environs of Fort Cumberland in the Bay of Fundy
mwca0437	canada nova scotia	1779	DES BARRES	1350	66	158	The Gut of Canso
mwuss0194	carolinas	1777	DES BARRES	10000	84	62	The Harbour of Charles Town in South-Carolina from the Surveys of Sr. Jas. Wallace Captn in His Majestys Navy & Others with a View of the Town from the South Shore of Ashley River
mwca0272	canada new brunswick	1778	DES BARRES	1350	78	51	The Harbours of Rishibucto & Buctush on the West Shore of the Gulph of St. Lawrence
mwca0420	canada nova scotia	1777	DES BARRES	1350	107	77	The Isthmus of Nova Scotia
mwca0627	canada st lawrence	1781	DES BARRES	800	73	54	The Magdalen Isles in the Gulph of St. Lawrence. September 1, 1781
mwca0269	canada new brunswick	1776	DES BARRES	1400	54	76	The River St. John
mwca0449	canada nova scotia	1781	DES BARRES	2000	76	210	The South East Coast of Cape Breton Island Surveyed under the Direction of the Right Honble. Lords Commissioners of Trade and Plantations. By Samuel Holland Esqr. Survr. Genl. of the Lands of the Northern District of N. America

AMPG REFERENCE	REGION	DATE	MAP MAKER	PRICE (UK£)	VERT. (cm.)	HOR. (cm.)	TITLE OF MAP (Comments by the editor in brackets)
mwca0491	canada prince edward isl.	1781	DES BARRES	2000	102	77	The South East Coast of the Island of St. John, Surveyd under the Direction of the Right Honourable the Lords of Trade and Plantations: by Saml. Holland ... 1781
mwca0412	canada nova scotia	1776	DES BARRES	3000	70	207	The South West Coast of the Peninsula of Nova Scotia Surveyed by Captain Des Barres. By Order of the Right Honourable the Lords Commissioners of the Admiralty
mwca0271	canada new brunswick	1777	DES BARRES	1200	53	79	The Wolves / Grand Manan Island / A View of the Shore Westward of the River St. John / A View of the Coast at the Entrance of the River St. John / A View of the Entrance to Pasamaquady Bay
mwca0438	canada nova scotia	1779	DES BARRES	1500	76	56	White Haven
mwin0032	ceylon	1700	DESBORDES	400	23	15	Isle de Zeilan ou Ceilon
mwas0463	asia south east	1745	DESBRUSLINS	300	22	30	Carte des Voyages de Mr. Tavernier, dans les Indes
mwg0149	germany	1774	DESBRUSLINS	100	19	25	Carte Generale ... de l'Empire d'Allemagne
mwuk0750	uk	1689	DESGRANGES	2800	45	56	La Carte des Royaumes d'Angleterre d'Ecosse et d'Irlande (in editions after 1693, Desgranges' name is erased and the map is attributed to Baudrand)
mwuss0137	california	1850	DESILVER	250	38	30	A New Map of the State of California, the Territories of Oregon, Washington, Utah & New Mexico
mwuss1475	rhode isl	1826	DESILVER	400	23	17	Map of Rhode-Island Published in 1826
mwuss1201	new york	1826	DESILVER	300	18	20	The State of New York from the Best Information 1826
mwuss1402	pennsylvania	1819	DESILVER	6000	65	65	This Plan of the City of Philadelphia and Environs is Respectuflly Inscribed
mwam0154	america continent	1741	DESING	320	13	11	Haupt Karte America oder West-Indien oder die Neue Welt
mwuk0812	uk	1734	DESING	280	13	11	Hauptkarte Engelland Schottland Irland
mwuk1216	england london	1767	DESNOS	500	20	28	(Plan de Londres)
mwaf0212	africa	1762	DESNOS	320	39	53	Afrique
mwf0154	france	1783	DESNOS	500	64	66	Carte des Postes de France pour l'Annee 1783. Revue, Corrigee et Augmentee pour l'Annee 1783
mwbh0740	belgium holland	1784	DESNOS	450	47	61	Carte du Theatre de la Guerre, Comprenant les Pays-Bas et Partie des Provinces Unies avec l'Eve. de Liege
mwsam0624	south america guyana	1769	DESNOS	300	38	55	Carte Particulaire de l'Isle et des Environs de Cayenne, Colonie Francaise
mwsam0110	south america	1790	DESNOS	200	28	48	Chili, Paraguay, Bresil, Amazones et Perou
mwas0486	asia south east	1766	DESNOS	320	39	52	Chine, et Indes avec les Isles
mwru0456	russia tartary	1766	DESNOS	350	24	27	Grande Tartarie et Isles du Japon (size excludes text panels and decorative borders)
mwam0191	america continent	1766	DESNOS	450	39	52	Hemisphere Occidental
mww0455	world	1761	DESNOS	550	36	52	Histoire de la Decouverte des Monde Nouveau et Inconnu
mww0468	world	1766	DESNOS	400	29	46	Histoire de la Decouverte des Mondes Nouveau et Inconnu (for illustration, see 'Arctic-Antarctic')
mwf0153a	france	1782	DESNOS	750	49	56	La France, Divisée en ses Principaux Gouvernements. Avec toutes les Routes de ce Royaume
mwsc0153	scandinavia	1766	DESNOS	280	39	52	La Suede et la Norwege avec l'Islande
mwsw0163	switzerland	1764	DESNOS	400	39	56	La Suisse divisee en ses Cantons
mwaf0226	africa	1770	DESNOS	6000	97	102	L'Afrique Dressee selon l'Etendue de ses Principales Parties (reduced copy of De Fer 1696)
mwaf0220	africa	1766	DESNOS	2000	48	71	L'Afrique Dressee sur les Relations & Nouvelles Decouvertes des Differens Voyageurs
mwam0190	america continent	1766	DESNOS	2000	48	70	L'Amerique Meridionale et Septentrionale (revised version of Danet 1731)
mwas0189	asia continent	1772	DESNOS	10000	91	118	L'Asie Dressee selon l'Etendue de ses Principales Parties (title above map. Title in cartouche: 'Nou.le Asie')
mwas0182	asia continent	1766	DESNOS	2000	50	72	L'Asie Dressee sur de Nouveaux Memoires Assujetis aux Observations Astronomiques, Corrigee et Augmentee
mwit1039	italy south	1770	DESNOS	60	10	9	Le Royaume de Naple et de Sicile
mwbh0741	belgium holland	1784	DESNOS	400	44	57	Les Dix-Sept Provinces des Pays-Bas
mwbp0501	poland	1782	DESNOS	450	47	59	Les Etats de la Couronne de Pologne
mwuk0845	uk	1766	DESNOS	280	39	52	Les Isles Britanniques, Assujetties aux Observations Astronomiques, Combinees avec les Itineraires tant Anciens que Modernes
mwsp0294	spain	1782	DESNOS	450	46	65	L'Espagne Divisee en Tous ses Royaumes et Principautes ou sont Exactement Recueillies et Observees Toutes les Routes des Postes d'Espagne
mwe0187	europe	1766	DESNOS	2000	50	72	L'Europe Divisee dans ses Principaux Etats
mwe0194	europe	1772	DESNOS	6000	94	101	L'Europe Divisee selon l'Etendue de ses Principales Parties
mwuk0855	uk	1778	DESNOS	850	103	86	Les Isles Britanniques
mww0566	world	1790	DESNOS	250	23	27	Mappe-Monde Dressee pour l'Etude de la Geographie
mww0467	world	1766	DESNOS	5600	52	76	Mappemonde Dressee sur les Relations les Plus Nouvelles
mww0521	world	1782	DESNOS	7500	76	136	Mappe-Monde Geo-Hydrographique, ou Description Generale du Globe Terrestre et Aquatique en Deux Plans-Hemispheres
mww0567	world	1790	DESNOS	1600	47	64	Mappe-Monde Geo-Hydrographique, ou Description Generale du Globe Terrestre et Aquatique en Deux Plans-Hemispheres

AMPG REFERENCE	REGION	DATE	MAP MAKER	PRICE (UK£)	VERT. (cm.)	HOR. (cm.)	TITLE OF MAP (Comments by the editor in brackets)
mww0481	world	1772	DESNOS	15000	79	118	Mappe-Monde ou Carte Generale de la Terre Divisee en Deux Hemispheres Suivant la Projection la Plus Commune ou Tous les Points Principaux sont Placez sur les Observations de Mrs. de l'Academie Royale des Sciences
mwam0195	america continent	1770	DESNOS	13500	112	117	Nle. Carte d'Amerique Dressee sur les Memoires les Plus Recens et Assujetie aux Dernieres Observations Astronomiques
mwam0511	america north	1790	DESNOS	550	28	48	Nouveau Mexique, Louisiane, Canada et Etats Unis
mwf0885b	france paris	1766	DESNOS	1100	54	100	Nouveau Plan de Paris, ses Faubourgs et ses Environs
mwe0466	europe central	1774	DESNOS	550	77	87	Nouvelle Carte Geographique des Postes et Autres Routes d'Allemagne, Poussees jusques dans les Pays Bas, en Suisse, en Italie, en Hongrie, en Pologne, en Prusse, en Denemarck, &c.
mwaf0962	africa south	1786	DESNOS	265	28	48	Partie de l'Afrique au dela de l'Equateur Comprenant le Congo, la Cafrerie &c.
mwf1171	france lyon	1767	DESNOS	400	36	49	Plan de Lion
mwf0900	france paris	1790	DESNOS	480	32	42	Plan General de la Ville et Faubourg de Paris (size incl. decorative border)
mwf0530	france corsica	1770	DESNOS	200	10	10	Royaume de Corse
mwit0818	italy sardinia	1770	DESNOS	100	10	9	Royaume de Sardaigne
mwuk0198	ireland	1766	DESNOS	280	37	53	Royaume d'Irlande ... 1760
mwf0883	france paris	1762	DESNOS	480	29	41	Sixieme Plan de la Ville de Paris (size incl. decorative border)
mwe0181	europe	1761	DESNOS	320	39	52	Souverainetes de l'Europe
mwuss1314	ohio	1836	DESOBRY	1200	77	55	Portsmouth on the Ohio River / Map of Ohio (2 maps)
mwbh0732	belgium holland	1780	DESOER	800	36	45	Plan de Spa (avec ses Principaux Edifices)
mwf0854	france paris	1726	DESPREZ	1200	62	85	Plan de Paris pour Servir a l'Histoire de la ditte Ville Composee par D Michel Felibien
mwme0254	holy land	1715	DETLEFFSEN	400	37	48	Die Gelegenheit des Paradeis und des Lands Canaan
mwme0256	holy land	1715	DETLEFFSEN	450	36	48	Geographische Beschreibung von der Wanderschaft der Apostelen und Reisen des H. Apostels Pauli
mww0330	world	1716	DETLEFFSEN	1500	33	48	Orbis Terrarum Typus de Integro Plurimis
mwbh0541a	belgium holland	1710	DEUR	650	34	42	Plan of Brussels the Capital of Brabant
				DEUTECUM. SEE VAN DOETECUM			
mwf1074a	france provence	1758	DEVOUX	1500	71	106	Carte Geographique, Historique, Chronologique de Provence
mwg0542	rheinland-pfalz	1794	DEWARAT	1800	60	80	Kriegs Theater der Teutschen und Franzoesischen Graenzlanden zwichen dem Rhein und der Mosel (6 sheets, each 60x80cm.)
mwg0292	baden-wurttemberg	1795	DEWARAT	1200	25	36	Special Carte des Rheinlaufes von Speier bis Bingen / Special Carte des Rheinlaufes von Lauterburg bis Speyer nebst den Angraenzenden Gegenden von Beiden Ufern bis an die Gebirge (in 3 sheets)
mwaf0217	africa	1765	D'EXPILLY	150	10	12	Afrique 1765
mwam0196	america continent	1770	D'EXPILLY	200	13	9	Amerique Septentrionale et Meridionale
mwas0188	asia continent	1772	D'EXPILLY	150	15	18	Asiae
mwf0140	france	1771	D'EXPILLY	80	10	13	La France
mwe0193	europe	1771	D'EXPILLY	150	10	13	L'Europe
mww0441	world	1758	D'EXPILLY	550	15	19	Mappemonde dont les Poles sont au Centre de l'Horizon
mwaf0295	africa	1805	DEZAUCHE	300	51	66	Carte d'Afrique Dressee pour l'Instruction par Guil. De L'Isle
mwas0211	asia continent	1788	DEZAUCHE	480	49	62	Carte d'Asie Dressee pour l'Instruction (shown is 1817 edition by Dezauche)
mwe0816	europe east	1780	DEZAUCHE	350	47	65	Carte de la Hongrie et des Pays qui en Dependoient Autrefois
mwf0689	france lorraine	1790	DEZAUCHE	400	86	68	Carte de la Lorraine ... Metz, Toul, et Verdun
mwuss0648	louisiana	1782	DEZAUCHE	1600	48	65	Carte de la Louisiane et du Cours du Mississipi. Avec les Colonies Anglaises. Revue, Corrigee et Considerablemt. Augmentee en 1782 (updated map originally by De L'Isle 1718)
mwru0564	ukraine	1788	DEZAUCHE	750	69	97	Carte de la Mer Noire, Comprenant la Plus Grande Partie de l'Empire Otoman, Partie des Etats de l'Empereur de la Russie
mwit0617	italy north	1791	DEZAUCHE	675	44	78	Carte de la Partie Septentrionale de l'Italie
mwf0628a	france languedoc	1785	DEZAUCHE	400	73	62	Carte de la Province du Languedoc, divisée suivant ses différens diocèses
mwf0628	france languedoc	1785	DEZAUCHE	300	45	66	Carte de la Province du Languedoc. Partie Meridionale du Languedoc ... le Roussillon et le Comte de Foix
mwme0383	holy land	1797	DEZAUCHE	450	50	65	Carte de la Terre Sainte ou des Douze Tribus d'Israel
mwme0643	arabia etc	1780	DEZAUCHE	550	47	63	Carte de la Turquie de l'Arabie et de la Perse
mwam0285	america continent	1827	DEZAUCHE	450	49	61	Carte de l'Amerique Dressee par G. Delisle et Ph. Buache ... Revue, Corrigee et Augmentee (inset of Alaska etc)
mwe0259	europe	1827	DEZAUCHE	300	49	61	Carte de l'Europe
mwwi0795	martinique	1770	DEZAUCHE	450	46	59	Carte de l'Isle de la Martinique Colonie Francoise de l'une des Isles Antilles de l'Amerique
mwsw0199	switzerland	1790	DEZAUCHE	450	49	62	Carte de Suisse ... De L'Isle ... Buache
mwas0505	asia south east	1781	DEZAUCHE	800	63	65	Carte des Indes et de la Chine

AMPG REFERENCE	REGION	DATE	MAP MAKER	PRICE (UK£)	VERT. (cm.)	HOR. (cm.)	TITLE OF MAP (Comments by the editor in brackets)
mwp0425	pacific north	1780	DEZAUCHE	1350	45	63	Carte des Nouvelles Decouvertes au Nord de la Mer du Sud, tant a l'Est de la Siberie et du Kamtchatka, qu'a l'Ouest de la Nouvelle France. Dressee sur les Memoires de Mr. Del'Isle (originally publ. by Buache 1750)
mwca0106	canada	1781	DEZAUCHE	1200	50	65	Carte du Canada ou de la Nouvelle France et des Decouvertes qui y ont ete Faites Dressee sur Plusieurs Observations ... par Guillaume Del'Isle (revised edition of De L'Isle's 1703 map)
mwsw0189	switzerland	1782	DEZAUCHE	400	50	66	Carte du Lac de Geneve et des Pays Circonvoisins
mwsam0778	south america peru	1780	DEZAUCHE	400	39	31	Carte du Perou (map originally by Buache, 1739)
mwin0449	indian ocean	1815	DEZAUCHE	600	50	70	Carte Reduite de l'Ocean Oriental, depuis le Cap de Bonne Esperance jusqu'a l'Isle Formose
mwsc0175	scandinavia	1788	DEZAUCHE	400	45	61	Cartes des Courones du Nord
mwgr0213	greece	1780	DEZAUCHE	250	49	67	Graeciae Antiquae Tabula Nova
mww0522	world	1782	DEZAUCHE	2500	51	50	Hemisphere Occidentale Dresse pour l'Usage Particuliere du Roy sur les Observations Astronomiques et Geographiques / Hemisphere Orientale Dresse pour l'Usage Particuliere du Roy sur les Observations Astronomiques et Geographiques (2 maps, each 51x50cm. Incl. Cook's discoveries)
mwf0151	france	1781	DEZAUCHE	720	86	114	La France Ecclesiastique (map originally by Jaillot)
mwbh0880	luxembourg	1781	DEZAUCHE	900	105	123	Le Duche de Luxembourg Divise en Quartier Walon, et Allemand (copy of Jaillot's map)
mwsp0116a	portugal	1792	DEZAUCHE	650	68	46	Le Portugal par le P. Placide (see Placide 1695)
mwuk0850	uk	1772	DEZAUCHE	450	47	61	Les Isles Britanniques ou sont le Rme. d'Angleterre Tire de Sped celuy d'Ecosse Tire de Th. Pont &c. et celuy d'Irlande Tire de Petti
mwsp0293	spain	1781	DEZAUCHE	1200	44	56	L'Espagne suivant l'Etendue de Tous les Royaumes et Principautes Compris sous les Couronnes de Castille, d'Aragon et de Portugal (in 4 sheets, each 44x56cm.)
mwit0202	italy	1780	DEZAUCHE	350	49	63	Tabula Italiae Antiquae in Regiones XI ab Augusto divisae
mww0534	world	1785	DEZAUCHE	2000	45	65	Mappemonde a l'Usage du Roi, par Guillaume Delisle et Philippe Buache (illustrated is 1808 edition)
mww0680	world	1828	DEZAUCHE	720	46	67	Mappemonde Dressee par G. Delisle et Ph. Buache Premiers Geographes du Roi et de l'Academie Royale des Sciences
mwp0429a	pacific north	1782	DEZAUCHE	550	26	33	Nouvelle Carte de la Partie Septentrionale du Globe, comprise entre le Kamtchatka et la Californie
mwf0791a	france normandy	1758	DEZAUCHE	900	35	55	Nouveau Plan de la Rade de Cherbourg
mwsp0683	balearic islands	1782	DEZAUCHE	720	42	56	Nouveau Plan du Port Mahon et du Fort St. Philippe avec les Campemens et les Differentes Attaques des Troupes Francoises et Espagnoles (2 insets)
mwsam0397	south america brazil	1785	DEZAUCHE	1800	73	51	Plan de la Baye et Port de Rio Janeiro, Situe a la Coste de Bresil ... Levee Geometriquement par le Capassi
mww0507	world	1780	DEZAUCHE	600	34	44	Planisphere Physique ou l'on Voit du Pole Septentrionale ce que l'on Connoit de Terres et de Mers avec les Grandes Chaines du Montagnes
mwuss0757	maryland	1786	DEZOTEUX	550	18	27	Carte pour Servir au Journal de Mr. le Marquis de Chastellux Redigee
mwas0661a	asia south east java	1760	DHEULLAND	600	56	69	(Untitled sea chart)
mwm0054	mediterranean	1737	DHEULLAND	3000	60	51	Carte Reduite de la Mer Mediterranee pour servir aux Vaisseaux
mwbh0685	belgium holland	1748	DHEULLAND	800	51	65	Carte Topographique des Environs de la Ville de Maestrich
mwit0434a	italy liguria	1747	DHEULLAND	240	23	31	Environs de Gênes, Savone, et Finale
mwsp0702	gibraltar	1730	DHEULLAND	800	63	47	Plan Topographique de la Ville Port, et Baye de Gibraltar
mwf0885c	france paris	1766	DHEULLAND	1500	67	81	Ville Cite et Universite de Paris
mwit0611	italy north	1748	DHEULLAND & JULIEN	4000	21	30	Theatre de la Guerre en Italie ou Carte Nouvelle (in 24 sheets)
mwaf0032	africa	1600	DI ARNOLDI	4000	38	49	Africa (close copy of Ortelius 1570)
mwam0024	america continent	1600	DI ARNOLDI	10000	37	48	America
mwas0022	asia continent	1600	DI ARNOLDI	4000	37	48	Asia (close copy of Ortelius 1570)
mwe0023	europe	1600	DI ARNOLDI	2000	37	49	Europa (close copy of Ortelius 1570, publ. by M. Florimi)
mwit1097	italy tuscany	1600	DI ARNOLDI	2400	38	49	Stato di Siena
mww0106	world	1601	DI ARNOLDI		50	80	Universale Descrittione Del Mondo (2-sheet reduction of his 1600 large map)
mww0186	world	1669	DI ARNOLDI-PETRUCCI	400000	104	185	Descrittione Universale Della Terra Con L'Uso Del Navigare (re-issue by Petrucci of the 1600 edition, in 10 sheets)
mwuk0825	uk	1746	DICEY	2000	50	59	A Correct Map of Great Brittain and Ireland
mwuk1211	england london	1765	DICEY	3200	60	105	A New & accurate Plan of the Cities of London (8 editions until 1803)
mwuss0086	california	1772	DIDEROT	320	29	36	Carte de la Californie et des Pays Nord-Ouest Separes de l'Asie par le Detroit d'Anian
mwuss0085	california	1767	DIDEROT	650	29	38	Carte de la Californie Suivant I. La Carte Manuscrite de l'Amerique de Mathieu Neron Pecci Olen Dresse a Florence en 1604, II. Sanson 1656, III. De L'Isle Amerique Sept. 1700, IV. Le Pere Kino Jesuite en 1705, V. La Societe des Jesuites en 1767

AMPG REFERENCE	REGION	DATE	MAP MAKER	PRICE (UK£)	VERT. (cm.)	HOR. (cm.)	TITLE OF MAP (Comments by the editor in brackets)
mwp0416	pacific north	1770	DIDEROT	500	30	38	Carte des Nouvelles Decouvertes Dressee par Phil. Buache ... Aout 1752 / Extrait d'une Carte Japonaise de l'Univers Apportee en Europe par Kaempfer
mwru0458	russia tartary	1779	DIDEROT	400	30	39	Carte des parties Nord et est de L'Asie
mwam1321	america north (west)	1772	DIDEROT	450	29	37	Carte des Parties Nord et Ouest de l'Amerique Dressee d'apres les Relations les Plus Authentiques ... en 1764
mwca0089	canada	1769	DIDEROT	450	28	48	Partie de la Carte du Capitaine Cluny Auteur d'un Ouvrage Anglois Intitule American Traveller Publie a Londres en 1769
mwg0187b	germany elbe river	1750	DIELHELM	200	18	31	Delineatio Fluminis Superioris Partis Albis / Fluvii Albis Partis Inferioris (2 maps)
mwe1029	europe rhine	1750	DIELHELM	250	19	36	Der Gantze Rheinstrom
mwat0335	atlantic st helena	1819	DIEN	480	35	41	(Ile) Ste. Helene (size excl. text)
mwe0836	europe east	1807	DIEN	720	50	119	Carte Generale du Theatre de la Guerre Comprenant les Etats Prussiens, la Pologne et Tous les Pays depuis le Rhin jusqu'en Russie
mwf0885	france paris	1764	DIEN	4800	100	125	Plan de la Ville et Faubourgs de Paris avec les Armes de Mrs. les Prevots des Marchands (Reissue of 1656 map by Berey)
mwme0880	syria etc	1729	DIETELL	200	27	26	Die Land-Schaft Syrien Gezeichnet von denen Missionarijs Soc. Jesu
mwe0357	europe austria	1728	DIETELL	720	49	66	Geographischer Entwurff des Hertzogthums Steyermarck nach der Neuen Eintheilung
mwe0615a	europe czech republic (bohemia)	1818	DIEWALD-FEMBO	300	47	58	Das Königreich Böhmen, nach Davids astronomischen Bestimmungen und den zuverlässigsten Spezialkarten
mwe0616	europe czech republic (bohemia)	1829	DIEWALD-FEMBO	500	93	112	Topographische Karte vom Konigreiche Bohmen
mwaf0429	africa east	1836	DIEZ	750	107	40	Carte de l'Egypt / Carte de la Nubie Dressee pour le Voyage de M. Mrs. de Cadalvene et de Breuvery
mwe0481	europe central	1825	DIEZ	450	93	98	Post- und Reise-Karte von Deutschland und den Anliegenden Landern
mwam0492	america north	1785	DILLY	400	36	40	A Map of the United States of America Agreeable to the Peace of 1783
mwam1026a	america north (east)	1798	DILLY	400	19	38	Map of the Southern Part of the United States of America
mwit0337	italy emilia-romagna	1597	DINOVO	6500	41	52	(Untitled map inlcuding Ferrara and Bologna. Illustrated is the 1602 edition by Orlandi)
mwuss0004	alabama	1809	DIRECCION HIDROGRAFICA MADRID	1200	18	27	(Mobile Bay) Plano de la Bahia de Movila
mwsam0538	south america colombia	1809	DIRECCION HIDROGR.	300	18	23	Bahia de Candelaria en el Golfo del Darien
mwwi0807	martinique	1809	DIRECCION HIDROGR.	300	23	28	Bahia de Fte. Real de Martinica
mwuss1500	texas	1809	DIRECCION HIDROGR.	2000	18	26	Bahia de S. Bernardo
mwuss0459	florida	1818	DIRECCION HIDROGR.	375	18	26	Bahia de Tampa
mwuss0456	florida	1809	DIRECCION HIDROGR.	375	18	27	Bahia y Puerto de Sn. Agustin
mwuss0458	florida	1818	DIRECCION HIDROGR.	375	17	26	Boca y Bahia del Rio Nasau
mwwi0488	cuba	1832	DIRECCION HIDROGR.	2800	63	188	Carta de Isla de Cuba con las Islas, Cayos, Bancos y Canales Adyacentes, Canal Viejo de Bahama, y la Parte Corografica del la Isla
mwgm0083	gulf of mexico and surrounding regions	1846	DIRECCION HIDROGR.	7200	63	97	Carta de las Costas de la Escambia, Alabama y Bocas del Rio Misisipi, la Luisiana, Tejas, con la Provincia del Nuevo Santander en el Golfo de Mejico
mwwi0349	bahamas	1838	DIRECCION HIDROGR.	2250	56	87	Carta de los Canales de Bahama, Providencia y Santaren, Costas de la Florida e Isla de Cuba
mwgm0355	mexico	1847	DIRECCION HIDROGR.	350	61	100	Carta de Parte de las Costas del Nuevo Santander, las de Vera Cruz, Tabasco y Yucatan
mwru0343	russia	1824	DIRECCION HIDROGR.	680	95	100	Carta del Mar Negro, de Azof y de Marmara, Construida en la Direccion Hidrografica
mwwi0479	cuba	1821	DIRECCION HIDROGR.	500	58	90	Carta Esférica De Una Parte De La Costa Septentrional y Meridional De La Isla De Cuba
mwwi0844	puerto rico	1840	DIRECCION HIDROGR.	1250	62	92	Carta Esferica de la Isla de Puerto-Rico y las Adyacentes, que a la Misma Pertenecen, Vieques, Culebra, Caja-de-Muertos, Mona Monito y Desecheo, con Parte de las Islas de Santo Domingo y Saona
mwsam0434	south america brazil	1845	DIRECCION HIDROGR.	750	73	60	Carta Esferica de la Rada de Pernambuco y sus Immediaciones en la Costa del Brasil Levantada en 1819
mwm0281	mediterranean west	1838	DIRECCION HIDROGR.	480	63	93	Carta Esferica de las Costas de Francia, Cerdena, Luca y Toscana con las Yslas de Elba, Corega y Parte Septentrional de la Cerdena
mwsam0472a	south america chile	1798	DIRECCION HIDROGR.	3500	98	61	Carta Esferica De Las Costas de la America Meridional desde el Paralelo de 36° 30' de Latitud S. Hasta el Cabo de Hornos
mwsam0472b	south america chile	1799	DIRECCION HIDROGR.	1500	87	58	Carta Esferica De Las Costas del Reyno de Chile Comprendidas Entre Los Paralelos de 38° y 22° de Latitud Sur Levantada
mwgm0072	gulf of mexico and surrounding regions	1836	DIRECCION HIDROGR.	2500	63	94	Carta Esferica de las Costas del Seno Mexicano, con Parte de la Isla de Cuba y Canales Adyacentes

AMPG REFERENCE	REGION	DATE	MAP MAKER	PRICE (UK£)	VERT. (cm.)	HOR. (cm.)	TITLE OF MAP (Comments by the editor in brackets)
mwam1182	america north (east)	1820	DIRECCION HIDROGR.	720	61	65	Carta Esferica de las Costas Orientales de la America Setentrional desde el Rio San Juan hasta Nueva York Construida en la Direccion Hidrografica
mwam1192	america north (east)	1826	DIRECCION HIDROGR.	2000	62	91	Carta Esferica de las Costas Orientales de los Estados Unidos en la America Setentrional desde el Rio San Juan hasta Nueva York Construida en la Direccion Hidrografica (includes Bermuda)
mwwi0267	west indies (east)	1802	DIRECCION HIDROGR.	750	91	61	Carta Esferica de las Islas Antillas con Parte de la Costa del Continente de America. Trabajada de Orden del Rey por los Capitanes de Navio de Su Rt. Armada Dn. Cosme Churruca y Dn. Joaquin Franco Fidalgo
mwwi0491	cuba	1837	DIRECCION HIDROGR.	500	62	90	Carta Esferica de una Parte de la Costa Setentrional y Meridional de la Isla de Cuba desde Punta Icacos y Cayo de Piedras hasta el Cabo San Antonio, con la Isla de Pinos y Cayos Adyacentea
mwwi0340	bahamas	1799	DIRECCION HIDROGR.	1000	60	93	Carta Esferica de une Parte del Canal Viego de Bahama
mwas0810	asia south east philippines	1816	DIRECCION HIDROGR.	600	62	94	Carta Esferica del Estrecho de S. Bernardino
mwgm0064	gulf of mexico and surrounding regions	1810	DIRECCION HIDROGR.	600	66	99	Carta Esferica del Mar de las Antillas y de las Costas de Tierra Firme, desde las Bocas del Rio Orinoco hasta el Golfo de Honduras
mwc0294a	china	1849	DIRECCION HIDROGR.	3000	99	67	Carta Esférica del Rio Chou-Kiang ó Canton, Desde su Embocadura con los Canales de S.Y So. É Isla de Hong-Kong, Hasta la Ciudad de Canton.
mwsam0260	south america argentina	1838	DIRECCION HIDROGR.	1000	57	89	Carta Esferica del Rio de la Plata desde su Embocadura hasta Buenos Ayres (insets: Plano del Puerto de Montevideo/Plano del Pto. De Maldonado)
mwwi0476	cuba	1805	DIRECCION HIDROGR.	600	91	61	Carta Esferica que Comprehende desde el Rio Guaurabo hasta Boca-Grande en la Parte Meridional de la Isla de Cuba Leventada en 1803
mwsam0197a	south america (north west)	1800	DIRECCION HIDROGR.	1000	88	58	Carta Esferica Que Comprehende La Costa Occidental de America Desde Sieto Grados de Latitude sur Hasta Nueve Grados de Latitude Norte
mwwi0342	bahamas	1802	DIRECCION HIDROGR.	1500	66	101	Carta Esferica que Comprehende los Desemboques al Norte de la Isla de Sto. Domingo y la Parte Oriental del Canal Viejo de Bahama. Construida de Orden del Rey en la Direccion Hidrografica ... Ano de 1802
mwgm0084	gulf of mexico and surrounding regions	1846	DIRECCION HIDROGR.	3000	63	94	Carta Esferica que comprehende todas las costas del Seno Mexicano Golfo de Honduras Islas de Cuba Sto. Dominigo Jamaica y Lucayas (1st edition 1808)
mwwi0291	west indies (west)	1846	DIRECCION HIDROGR.	3000	61	92	Carta Esferica que Comprehende Todas las Costas del Seno Mexicano Golfo de Honduras, Islas de Cuba, Sto. Domingo Jamaica y Lucayas (Texas referred to as 'Republic de Tejas)
mwwi0289	west indies (west)	1799	DIRECCION HIDROGR.	1500	58	89	Carta Esferica que Comprehende una Parte de las Islas Antillas las de Puerto Rico, Santo Domingo, Jamayca y Cuba con Bancos y Canales Adyacentes
mwwi0480	cuba	1821	DIRECCION HIDROGR.	500	58	90	Carta Esferica que Comprende la Costa Meridional, Parte de la Setentrional e Islas Adyacentes de la Isla de Cuba, desde la Punta de Maisi hasta Cabo S. Antonio, Levantada de Orden Superior en 1795
mwas0809	asia south east philippines	1808	DIRECCION HIDROGR.	1000	117	90	Carta General del Archipelago de Filipinas Levantada
mwat0291	atlantic north	1825	DIRECCION HIDROGR.	500	57	90	Carta General del Oceano Atlantico Septentrional
mwgm0062	gulf of mexico and surrounding regions	1807	DIRECCION HIDROGR.	5000	58	88	Carta Particular de las Costas Setentrionales del Seno Mexicano que Comprehende las de la Florida Ocidental las Margenes de la Luisiana
mwwi0845	puerto rico	1842	DIRECCION HIDROGR.	1250	61	89	Carta Particular Esferica y Corografica de la Isla de Puerto Rico y las Adyacentes que a la Misma Pertenecen Vieques, Culebra, Culebrita, Caja de Muertos, Mona, Monito y Desecheo
mwsam0860	south america venezuela	1836	DIRECCION HIDROGR.	600	18	23	Ensenadas de Pto Santo / Ensenada de la Esmeraldo / Plano Del ... Laguna Grande del Obispo / Ensenada de San Juan (4 maps)
mwwi0343	bahamas	1805	DIRECCION HIDROGR.	1500	64	97	Florida Oriental ... 1792 / Nueva Carta del Canal de Bahama que Comprehende tambien los de Providencia y Santaren con los Bajos Islas y Sondas al Este y al Oeste de la Peninsula de la Florida
mwwi0344	bahamas	1805	DIRECCION HIDROGR.	2000	58	89	Nueva Carta del Canal de Bahama que Comprehende tambien los de Providencia y Santaren con los Bajos Islas y Sondas al Este y al Oeste de la Peninsula de la Florida
mwaf1034	africa south	1860	DIRECCION HIDROGR.	2000	88	55	Plano de la Bahia de Tablas (Cape Town and harbour)
mwgm0445	panama	1836	DIRECCION HIDROGR.	250	18	25	Plano de la Boca de Rio de Chagres Situado el Castillo de S. Lorenzo
mwwi0490	cuba	1836	DIRECCION MAP HIDROGR.	450	46	59	Plano de la Gran Bahia de Cardenas y de los Fondeaderos do Cayo de Piedras, Mono y Monillo en la Costa Setentrional de la Isla de Cuba
mwwi0531	grenada	1808	DIRECCION HIDROGR.	350	24	18	Plano de la Rada y Carenero de San Jorge

AMPG REFERENCE	REGION	DATE	MAP MAKER	PRICE (UK£)	VERT. (cm.)	HOR. (cm.)	TITLE OF MAP (Comments by the editor in brackets)
mwsam0539	south america colombia	1809	DIRECCION HIDROGR.	400	18	26	Plano de las Islas de Sta. Catalina y Providencia
mwgm0063	gulf of mexico and surrounding regions	1808	DIRECCION HIDROGR.	400	18	25	Plano de las Islas de Sta. Catalina y Providencia Latitud N. de 13°26'
mwwi0936	virgin isl	1809	DIRECCION HIDROGR.	550	18	24	Plano del Pto. de San Tomas
mwgm0283	mexico	1816	DIRECCION HIDROGR.	300	46	60	Plano del Puerto de Veracruz. Levantado en 1807
mwwi0473	cuba	1800	DIRECCION HIDROGR.	300	22	31	Plano del Puerto de Yaguaneque / Plano del Puerto de Cebollas (2 charts, each 22x31cm)
mwwi0937	virgin isl	1809	DIRECCION HIDROGR.	550	18	24	Plano del Puerto Principal de la Tortola
mwwi0477	cuba	1809	DIRECCION HIDROGR.	200	20	30	Puerto del Guantanamo
mwgm0441	panama	1817	DIRECCION HIDROGR.	1500	64	97	Quarta Hoja que Comprehende las Costas de la Provincia de Cartagena, Golfo del Darien y Provincia de Porto Velo, con el Golfo de Panama y Archipielago de las Perlas
mwwi0307	antigua	1809	DIRECCION HIDROGR.	450	23	27	Rada y Puerto de S. Juan de Antigua
mwsam0539a	south america colombia	1816	DIRECCION HIDROGR.	1500	61	94	Tercera Hoja Que Comprende la parte de Costa De Tierra Firme Islas adyacentes (Third of four sheets. Maps by D. Churruca and J. Fidalgo)
mwit0767	italy rome	1840	DIREZIONE GENERALE	960	129	174	Carta Topografica di Roma e Comarca Disegnata ed Incisa nell' Officio del Censo
mwit0764a	italy rome	1833	DIREZIONE GENERALE	200	35	46	Pianta di Roma incisa nel Dicastero Generale del Censo nell'anno MDCCXXXII
mwp0516	pacific south	1807	DIRWALD-MOLLO	600	33	46	Australien nach den neuesten astronomischen Bestimungen und Entdeckungs-Reisen.
mwgm0356	mexico	1847	DISTURNELL	3500	62	49	A Correct Map of the Seat of War in Mexico. Being a Copy of Genl. Arista's Map, Taken at Resaca de la Palma with Additions and Corrections; Embellished with Diagrams of the Battles of the 8th & 9th May and Capture of Monterey
mwam0796	america north	1849	DISTURNELL	300	54	47	Map of North America, by J. Calvin Smith
mwuss1224	new york	1833	DISTURNELL	720	30	25	Map of the City of New York. Drawn ... Expressly for New York as it is in 1833
mwuss1237	new york	1839	DISTURNELL	1800	56	55	Map of the Country Thirty Miles round the City of New York
mwuss1252	new york	1845	DISTURNELL	480	48	62	Map of the State of New York Showing the Boundaries of Counties & Townships, the Location of Cities, Towns and Villages: and the Courses of Rail Roads, Canals & Stage Roads
mwgm0356a	mexico	1847	DISTURNELL	2000	38	45	Map of the Valley of Mexico, and the Surrounding Mountains (based on Oltmanns/Von Humboldt's map publ. 1811)
mwgm0355a	mexico	1847	DISTURNELL	30000	75	104	Mapa de los Estados Unidos de Méjico, segun lo organizado y definido por las varias actas del Congreso de dicha República: y construido por las mejores autoridades (copy of White's 1828 map)
mwuss1233	new york	1837	DISTURNELL	1250	60	11	Routes between New York and Washington
mwam0791	america north	1848	DISTURNELL	500	46	59	Traveller's Map of the Middle, Northern, Eastern States, and Canada, Showing All the Railroad, Steamboat, Canal, and Principal Stage Routes (9th edition)
mwuk1871	wales	1820	DIX	650	56	68	A New Map of North Wales Divided into its Six Counties or Shires
mwuk1872	wales	1820	DIX	650	56	68	A New Map of South Wales
mwec0309a	uk england devon	1816	DIX	350	36	45	A New Map of the County of Devon (1st publ. by W. Darton in 1822)
mwec0153	uk england cheshire	1820	DIX	400	41	50	A New Map of the County Palatine of Chester, Divided into Hundreds
mwuk0577	scotland	1811	DIX	80	13	17	Scotland
mwsc0155	scandinavia	1769	DIXON	500	40	52	A Chart of the Sea Coast and Islands near the North Cape
mwuss0028	alaska	1788	DIXON	300	25	32	Montague Island / Staten Land / C. St. Hermogenies
mwp0122	australia	1837	DIXON	2000	120	72	This Map of the Colony of New South Wales
mwam1328	america north (west)	1788	DIXON	3600	59	88	To the Right Honorable the Lords Commissioners ... this Chart of the North West Coast of America, with the Tracks of the King George and Queen Charlotte in 1786 & 1787
mwp0332	pacific hawaii	1788	DIXON	350	20	28	Yam Bay Oneeheow ... 1786
mwp0503	pacific south	1780	DJURBERG	1500	47	71	Karta over Polynesien (first Swedish map showing Cook's voyages)
mwuk1412a	uk geological	1843	DOBBS	5000	55	45	Geological Map of England & Wales
mwsam0720a	south america paraguay	1780	DOBRIZHOFER	1200	42	35	Mappa Paraquariae
mww0572	world	1792	DOBSON	600	23	42	A Map of the World in Three Sections Describing Polar Regions to the Tropics
mwuss0764	maryland	1799	DOBSON & COBBETT	3500	56	75	A Map of the Head of Chesapeake Bay and Susquehanna River Shewing the Navigation of the Same with a Topographical Description of the Surrounding Country from an Actual Survey by C.P. Hauducoeur
mwuk1200	england london	1761	DODSLEY	1500	35	66	A New and Correct Plan of London, Westminster and Southwark with Several Additional Improvements not in any Former Survey
mwuk1178	england london	1744	DODSLEY	875	20	40	A Plan of the Cities of London and Westminster with the Borough of Southwark

AMPG REFERENCE	REGION	DATE	MAP MAKER	PRICE (UK£)	VERT. (cm.)	HOR. (cm.)	TITLE OF MAP (Comments by the editor in brackets)
mwsc0030	scandinavia	1589	DOEDSZ		54	40	Tabula hydrographica tum maris Baltici
mwru0277	russia	1785	DOETSCH	600	56	71	Imperium Russicum part Occidentalis cum Adjacentibus Provinciis
mwuk0918	england	1623	DOGLIONI	400	8	11	Anglia
mww0046	world	1553	DOLCE	2000	11	12	(No title. Circular map surrounded by wind cherubs)
mwin0413	indian ocean	1659	DONCKER	8000	54	86	(Untitled pair of charts of the Indian Ocean. Illustration shows 2nd edition with titles added: 't Wester Deel van Oost Indien Streckende van C. de Bona Esperance tot Ceylon / 't Ooster Deel van Oost Indien Streckende van Ceyon tot Iapan en Hollandia Nova')
mwbh0327a	belgium holland	1652	DONCKER	3000	46	56	Afbeeldinge der Stadt Groningen met de omliggende Fortressen. 1652.
mwaf0742	africa north algeria	1689	DONCKER	450	38	50	Barbarien tusschen C. de Tenes en C. de Rosa
mwat0145	atlantic canary isl.	1665	DONCKER	1000	42	52	Canarische Eylanden Canaria Tenerifa, Forteventura (re-issue of Goos 1660)
mwgr0309	greece corfu	1664	DONCKER	960	40	52	Corfu en by-Leggende plaatsen
mwsp0054a	portugal	1686	DONCKER	675	40	51	Cust van Andaluzia en Algarve, van Zizembre tot aen het Clif
mwwi0027	west indies	1676	DONCKER	6000	55	64	De Carybsche Eilanden van de Barbados tot de Bocht van Mexico (based on Colom's chart of 1656)
mwaf0838	africa north west	1659	DONCKER	1200	43	53	De Cust van Barbaria, Gualata, Arguyn en Geneheo van Capo S. Vincent tot Capo Verde (Variant shown below)
mwf0317	france brittany	1664	DONCKER	500	43	52	De Cust van Bretaigne, van Heysandt tot aan't Eylant Boelyn
mwsc0576	scandinavia norway	1669	DONCKER	750	44	55	De Custen van Noorwegen, Finmarken, Laplandt, Spitzberen ... gedeelte van Schotlandt
mwf1194	france west	1664	DONCKER	500	43	53	De Custen van Poictou, Xaintonge en een Gedeelt van Bretaigne van Boelyn tot aen de Rivier van Bourdeaux
mwin0385	india bay of bengal	1669	DONCKER	1600	44	52	De Golf van Bengala
mwsc0518	scandinavia jan mayen isl.	1670	DONCKER	600	40	30	De Noordwest Hoec van Ian Mayen Eylandt
mwat0148	atlantic canary isl.	1676	DONCKER	1000	52	62	De Vlaamsche en Canarische Eylanden (re-issue of Colom 1658)
mwuk1339c	england east	1685	DONCKER	1350	42	52	De Zee-kust van Engelandt tusschen Welles en 't Eylandt Coket (inset: 'The River of Tyne'. Shown above left)
mwsc0068b	russia	1670	DONCKER	500	43	51	De Zee kust van Laplandt tußchen de Rivier van Kola en de eylanden van Swetenoes
mwuk1339a	england east	1670	DONCKER	550	43	53	Du Cust van Engeland tusschen Welles en't Eyland
mwgr0584	greece islands	1664	DONCKER	1200	42	53	Golf van Constantinopolen / Paskaarte van 't Eylant Metelino / Lemnos / Tenedos
mwin0416a	indian ocean	1670	DONCKER		71	92	India Orientalis - Pascaerte van Oost Indien
mwm0104	mediterranean central	1664	DONCKER	1000	50	52	Italien tusschen Caap della Mella en Ostia
mwf0603	france languedoc	1664	DONCKER	800	40	52	Languedoc tusschen C. de Creos en C. delle Melle
mwp0235	pacific (all)	1676	DONCKER	4800	53	61	Mar del Zur Hispanis Mare Pacificum (updated Colom 1658)
mwgr0585	greece islands	1664	DONCKER	1400	41	52	Negroponte en Omleggende Eylanden / Archipelago en Negroponte
mwat0145a	atlantic canary isl.	1665	DONCKER	1000	43	53	Nieuwe Pas-Caart: Vertoonende hoemen uyt De Canaal, de Custen van Portugael, Barbaryen, de Canarische en Vlaemsche Eylanden (shown above left)
mwsc0068a	russia	1670	DONCKER	500	43	51	Nieuwe Pas Caert van de Witte Zee
mwru0435c	russia tartary	1688	DONCKER	900	45	55	Noordoost Cust van Asia van Iapan tot Nova Zemla
mww0238	world	1689	DONCKER	10000	54	63	Nova Totius Terrarum Orbis Tabula (based on Colom 1655)
mwm0017	mediterranean	1676	DONCKER	4000	54	62	Ooster Deel der Middelantse Zee Streckende van het Eyland van Sicilia tot het Eyland Cipres en Alexsandria / Wester Deel der Middelandsche Zee Streckende van het Naeu van de Straat tot Sicilia (2 maps)
mwm0267a	mediterranean west	1680	DONCKER	2000	54	62	Ooster Deel de Middelansche Zee
mwbp0026a	baltic sea (east)	1676	DONCKER	1500	53	62	Oost Zee Vertoonende Alle de gelegentheyt tusschen 't Eylant Rugen en Wyborg (copy of Colom 1658)
mwbh0370	belgium holland	1664	DONCKER	720	43	52	Pas Caaart van de Zuyder-Zee Texel (close copy of Van Loon 1661)
mwuk1458	uk english channel (all)	1661	DONCKER	2000	43	53	Pas Caart van de Canaal Tusschen Engeland en Vrancrijck
mwat0086a	atlantic azores	1686	DONCKER	1000	44	52	Pas Caart van de Vlaemsche Eylanden
mwuk1647	north sea	1658	DONCKER	2000	44	54	Pas Caart van de Noort Zee
mwuk1339b	england east	1685	DONCKER	1500	43	54	Pas Caart van Engelandt van 't Voorlandt tot aen Blakeney waer in te sien is de mont van de Teems
mwaf1122	africa west	1670	DONCKER	800	44	53	Pas Caert van Congo en Angola Streckende van C. de Lopo Gonzalves tot C. de Bras
mwsc0696a	scandinavia sweden	1686	DONCKER	1100	44	52	Pas Caert van Sweden van Oelandt tot Stockholm (north to the right)
mwuk1539c	uk english channel (west)	1660	DONCKER	1250	43	53	Pas Caert van't in Komen van de Canael
mwm0014	mediterranean	1670	DONCKER	3000	43	54	Pas Kaert van 't Oostelycke Deel der Middelandsche Zee / Paskaert van 't Westelycke Deel der Middelandsche Zee (2 maps)
mwaf1064	africa south west	1659	DONCKER	800	43	54	Pascaart van de Zee Custen van Angola en Cimbebas ... C. de Bona Esperance
mwsc0554	scandinavia norway	1659	DONCKER	2000	44	55	Pascaart van de Zee-Custen van Ruslant, Laplant, Finmarcken, Spitsbergen en Nova-zemla

AMPG REFERENCE	REGION	DATE	MAP MAKER	PRICE (UK£)	VERT. (cm.)	HOR. (cm.)	TITLE OF MAP (Comments by the editor in brackets)
mwsp0190	spain	1669	DONCKER	1250	45	56	Pas-Caart van Hispangien (north to the left)
mwuk0717	uk	1658	DONCKER	1500	44	54	Pas-Caart van 'T Canaal, Vertoonende in 't Geheel Engelandt Schotlandt, Yrlandt
mwuk0723	uk	1665	DONCKER	1250	44	53	Pas-Caart van 'T Canaal, Vertoonende in 't Geheel Engelant Schotlant, Yrlant (illustration shows c1670 edition)
mwp0232	pacific (all)	1669	DONCKER	2400	43	51	Pas-Caart van Zuyd-Zee tusschen California en Ilhas de Ladrones
mwat0188	atlantic cape verde isl.	1669	DONCKER	750	43	52	Pas-Caart vande Soute Eylanden ofte Ilhas de Cabo Verde
mwuss0072	california	1669	DONCKER	3500	43	55	Pascaart Vertoonende de Zeecusten van Chili, Peru, Hispania Nova, Nova Granada, en California (north to the left, California shown as an island)
mwm0129	mediterranean east	1664	DONCKER	1200	41	51	Pas-Caert van de Levant ofte de Zee Kusten van Aegypten, Soria, Caramania en t' Eylandt Cyprus
mwsc0519	scandinavia jan mayen isl.	1670	DONCKER	600	43	53	Pas-Caert van Ian Mayen Eylandt / Pas Caert van Spitsbergen
mwam0864	america north (east)	1660	DONCKER	16500	44	55	Pascaert van Nieu Nederland, Virginia en Nieu Engelant
mwca0027	canada	1669	DONCKER	2500	43	52	Pas-Caert van Terra Nova, Nova Francia, Nieuw-Engeland en de Groote Rivier van Canada. t'Amsterdam. By Hendrick Doncker (close copy of Van Loon 1661 but lacking 2 ships)
mwwi0020	west indies	1659	DONCKER	4000	44	54	Pas Caert vande Caribische Eylanden, vande Barbados tot Aende Bocht van Mexico
mwin0476	indian ocean west	1669	DONCKER	2000	43	52	Pas-Caert van't Westelyckste Deel van Oost-Indien
mwsam0302	south america brazil	1659	DONCKER	1200	43	55	Pascaerte van Brazil, en Nieu Nederlandt van Corvo en Flores tot de Barbados
mwsc0457	scandinavia greenland	1660	DONCKER	1800	43	53	Pas-caerte van GroenLand
mwat0257	atlantic north	1659	DONCKER	1800	43	53	Pas-Caerte van Groenlandt, Yslandt, Straet Davids en Ian Mayen Eylant; Hoeman de Selvige van Hitlant en de Noord Kusten van Schotlandt en Yrlandt Beseylen Mach
mwwi0019	west indies	1658	DONCKER	2000	44	54	Pascaerte vande Caribes Eylanden
mwe1188	europe west	1665	DONCKER	4000	43	52	Pas-Kaart van Europa ... 1665
mwaf1121	africa west	1670	DONCKER	550	43	53	Paskaart van Gambia Vertoonende Rio Senega
mwaf1117	africa west	1669	DONCKER	650	42	53	Paskaart van Guinea van C. Verde tot R. de Galion
mwuk0069	ireland	1665	DONCKER	1200	44	54	Paskaarte achter Yrland om te Zeylen, van Hitlandt Tot aen Heyssant (shown left is the Robijn 1683 version, 52x60cm)
mwsam0218	south america argentina	1669	DONCKER	1500	43	53	Paskaarte van't Zuydelyckste deel van America
mwsam0321	south america brazil	1680	DONCKER	1200	43	54	Paskaert van Brasilia van Pernambuco tot C. de S. Antonio
mwsam0826	south america venezuela	1688	DONCKER	2800	42	54	Paskaert van de Rivieren van Suriname en Comnewyne met Verschyde Creken (north to the left)
mwuk1659	north sea	1688	DONCKER	1000	52	59	Paskaert van een Gedeelte vande Noort Zee Streckende van Harwitz en Egmon tot Stavanger
mwwi0229	west indies (east)	1658	DONCKER	2000	44	54	Pascaerte vande Caribes Eylanden
mwit0833	italy sardinia and corsica	1664	DONCKER	1400	40	53	Sardinia en Corsica
mwgr0586	greece islands	1664	DONCKER	600	40	52	Smyrne en de Eylanden Scio en Metelino
mwgr0484	greece cyprus	1664	DONCKER	2500	40	52	t Eylandt Cyprus Begrypende de Zuydelicste Zee Custen (copy of Goos 1662)
mwin0413	indian ocean	1660	DONCKER	1200	56	46	t Wester Deel van Oost Indien Streckende van C. de Bona Esperance tot Ceylon
mwsp0445	spain regions	1664	DONCKER	1200	40	56	Valentien, ende Catalonia tusschen C. d. S. Martin ende C. de Creos. Als mede de Eylanden van Majorca, Minorca ende Yvica
mwuk1663	north sea	1705	DONCKER	600	53	58	Wassende Grade Paskaart van de Noort Zee Beginnende van de Hoofden tot t'Land van Noorwegen met de Geheelen Oostkust van Engeland ... Fero en Lewys Eylanden
mwat0014	atlantic ocean (all)	1659	DONCKER		76	97	West-Indische Paskaert. Waer in de Graden der Breedde over Weder Zyden
mwec1257	uk england wiltshire	1781	DONN	750	41	45	A Plan of the City of Salisbury with the Adjacent Close
mwec0299	uk england devon	1765	DONN	4000	183	189	A Map of the County of Devon, with the City & County of Exeter (12-sheet map)
mwf0187	france	1817	DONNET	1400	279	250	Carte Topographique, Mineralogique et Statistique de la France, Reduite de celle de Cassini
mwca0118a	canada	1793	DOOLITTLE	650	32	41	A Map of the Northern and Middle States: Comprehending the Western Territory and the British Dominions in North America
mwuss1283	ohio	1818	DOOLITTLE	7200	43	57	City of Sandusky
mwuss1558	vermont	1795	DOOLITTLE	600	38	30	Vermont from Actual Survey
mwuk1118	england london	1666	DOORNICK	4500	29	53	Platte Grondt der Verbrande Stadt London (2 editions. Size excl. text panel below map)
mww0380a	world	1742	DOPPELMAYR	1000	49	59	Basis Geographiae Recintioris Astronomica (shown above left)
mwgr0510	greece cyprus	1766	DORN	1350	24	33	Cypri Facies Antiqva
mwgr0511	greece cyprus	1766	DORN	2000	37	48	Cypri Facies Hodierna
mwgr0205	greece	1771	DORN	400	20	27	Graeciae et Provinciarum Adjacentium Nova
mwuss0886	massachusetts	1839	DORR, HOWLAND	450	18	30	Massachusetts
mwuk0492b	scotland	1750	DORRET	3000	178	137	A General Map of Scotland and Islands
mwuk0509	scotland	1761	DORRET	650	58	53	An Accurate Map of Scotland
mwbh0393	belgium holland	1675	DOU	12000	164	179	(Leiden) Lugdunum Batavorum Ano. 1670

AMPG REFERENCE	REGION	DATE	MAP MAKER	PRICE (UK£)	VERT. (cm.)	HOR. (cm.)	TITLE OF MAP (Comments by the editor in brackets)
mwbh0441	belgium holland	1687	DOU	7200	46	59	t Hoogh-Heemraetschap vande Uytwaterende Sluysen in Kennemerlandt ende West-Friesland (map in 16 sheets, each 46x59cm.)
mwuss1209	new york	1829	DOUGHERTY	280	16	22	Cammeyer's Plan of the City of Albany
mwuss1227	new york	1834	DOUGHTY	2400	54	76	Map Showing a Division of Part of the Real Estate Late of Nicholas Stuyvesant, Dec'd, among his Heirs Situated in the 11th Ward of the City of New York
mwas0294	asia burma	1850	DOWER	120	26	21	Burman Empire and Hindoo-Chinese States
mwuss0111	california	1844	DOWER	450	21	25	California, Mexico, Guatimala &c.
mwp0097	australia	1831	DOWER	400	35	42	Colony of New South Wales
mwsam0550	south america colombia	1833	DOWER	120	33	42	Columbia
mwit0457	italy liguria	1840	DOWER	135	22	27	Genoa
mwuk0610	scotland	1830	DOWER	240	24	32	Glasgow
mwuk0607	scotland	1828	DOWER	650	89	117	Map of the Counties of Fife and Kinross Made on the Basis of the Trigonometrical Survey of Scotland. Surveyed in the Years 1826 and 1827
mwgm0342	mexico	1843	DOWER	100	20	25	Mexico & Guatimala
mwgm0340	mexico	1842	DOWER	1500	34	42	Mexico and Guatimala
mwp0223a	new zealand	1849	DOWER	280	26	21	New Zealand
mwam0734	america north	1840	DOWER	150	25	21	North America
mwme0415	holy land	1836	DOWER	50	27	21	Palestine
mwsam0799	south america peru	1835	DOWER	150	34	41	Peru & Bolivia
mwru0353	russia	1835	DOWER	120	42	34	Russia in Europe
mww0749	world	1850	DOWER	120	20	28	The World in Mercator's Projection
mwam0703	america north	1836	DOWER	200	26	21	United States
mwp0098	australia	1831	DOWER	400	34	41	Van Dieman's Land
mwit1259	italy venice	1836	DOWER	200	21	26	Venice
mwwi0220	west indies	1850	DOWER	100	21	26	West Indies. Drawn & Engraved by J. Dower
mwam0300	america continent	1840	DOWER	100	20	20	Western Hemisphere
mwec1106	uk england suffolk	1741	DOWNING	2500	52	69	A New and Accurate Plan of the Ancient Borough of Bury Saint Edmunds in the County of Suffolk (1st printed map of this town)
mwuk0160a	ireland	1738	DOYLE	2400	57	73	A Chart of Waterford Harbour
mwec1332	uk england yorkshire	1736	DRAKE	180	35	45	(Environs of York)
mww0076a	world	1590	DRAKE	60000	25	45	La Heroike Interprinse Faict Par Le Signeur Draeck D'Avoir Cirquit Toute La Terre
mwuss0481	florida	1840	DRAKE	280	41	27	Map of East Florida, Reduced from the Map Compiled by Capt. John Mackay & Lieut. J.E. Blake (1839)
mwec1000	uk england shropshire	1622	DRAYTON	750	25	33	(Shropshire)
mwec0002	uk england bedfordshire	1622	DRAYTON	750	25	33	Bedfordshire, Huntingdonshire, Parte of Cambridgeshire
mwec0059	uk england buckinghamshire	1612	DRAYTON	750	25	33	Buckinghamshyre, Oxfordshyre and Barckshyre
mwec0082	uk england cambridgeshire	1622	DRAYTON	1200	25	33	Cambridgeshire and Parte of Huntingdonshire
mwuk1711	wales	1612	DRAYTON	400	25	33	Cardyganshyre, Radnorshyre, Mountgomeryshyre
mwuk1712	wales	1612	DRAYTON	500	26	33	Carnarvanshyre, Merionethshyre and the Ile of Anglesey
mwec0126	uk england cheshire	1622	DRAYTON	1200	25	33	Chesshyre
mwec0166	uk england cornwall	1622	DRAYTON	1200	25	33	Cornwal, Devonshyre
mwec0219	uk england cumbria	1622	DRAYTON	600	25	33	Cumberlande, Westmorlande
mwec0253	uk england derbyshire	1622	DRAYTON	750	25	31	Darbyshyre, Lecestershyre, Nottinghamshyre
mwuk1713	wales	1612	DRAYTON	400	26	33	Denbighshyre and Flintshyre
mwec0319	uk england dorset	1612	DRAYTON	750	26	33	Dorsetshere, Hampshere
mwec0396	uk england essex	1622	DRAYTON	900	23	32	Essex, Parte of Suffolk
mwuk1714	wales	1612	DRAYTON	400	23	32	Flintshyre, Denbighshyre, Parte of Carnarvanshyre
mwuk1715	wales	1612	DRAYTON	1200	24	32	Glamorganshyre and Monmouthshyre
mwec0431	uk england gloucestershire	1622	DRAYTON	750	25	33	Glocestershyre, Parte of Worcestershyre
mwec0463	uk england hampshire	1612	DRAYTON	900	25	33	Hampshire and Dorsetshere
mwec0537	uk england hertfordshire	1612	DRAYTON	900	25	33	Hartfordshyre and Middlesex
mwec0510	uk england herefordshire	1622	DRAYTON	600	25	33	Herefordshyre with Parte of Glocestershyre and Parte of Worcestershyre
mwec0571	uk england huntingdonshire	1622	DRAYTON	650	24	30	Huntingdonshire and Parte of Cambridgeshire
mwec0598	uk england kent	1612	DRAYTON	1200	23	33	Kent
mwec0673	uk england lancashire	1622	DRAYTON	1200	24	30	Lancashyre, The Ile of Man
mwec0734	uk england lincolnshire	1622	DRAYTON	850	24	30	Lincolnshyre
mwec0766	uk england middlesex	1612	DRAYTON	1200	24	30	Midlesex, Hartforshyre
mwec0808	uk england norfolk	1622	DRAYTON	850	24	31	Norfolke, the North Parte of Suffolk
mwec0847	uk england northamptonshire	1622	DRAYTON	750	24	30	Northamptonshyre, Parte of Rutlandshyre, Parte of Bedfordshyre
mwec0876	uk england northumberland	1622	DRAYTON	900	24	30	Northumberlande, The Bishoprick of Durham
mwec0936	uk england oxfordshire	1612	DRAYTON	1200	24	30	Oxfordshyre, Barckshyre, Buckinghamshyre
mwuk1716	wales	1612	DRAYTON	600	25	33	Permbrokshyre and Carmardenshyre
mwuss1424	pennsylvania	1833	DRAYTON	400	38	44	Plan of the City of Philadelphia
mwec0979	uk england rutland	1622	DRAYTON	650	24	30	Rutlandshyre, Parte of Northamptonshyre
mwec1027	uk england somerset	1612	DRAYTON	720	25	33	Somersetshyre and Wiltshere
mwuss0251	carolinas	1802	DRAYTON	650	42	48	South Carolina
mwec1058	uk england staffordshire	1612	DRAYTON	650	25	33	Staffordshyre and Parte of Shropshyre on the East of the Severne

AMPG REFERENCE	REGION	DATE	MAP MAKER	PRICE (UK£)	VERT. (cm.)	HOR. (cm.)	TITLE OF MAP (Comments by the editor in brackets)
mwec1123	uk england surrey	1612	DRAYTON	1100	24	33	Surrey, Sussex
mwec0083	uk england cambridgeshire	1622	DRAYTON	720	24	33	The Isle of Ely, Cambridgeshire, Parte of Huntingdonshire
mwec0998	uk england shropshire	1612	DRAYTON	650	25	33	The Parte of Shropshyre on the West of Severne
mwam0724	america north	1839	DRAYTON	200	23	27	United States of America
mwec1187	uk england warwickshire	1612	DRAYTON	720	25	33	Warwickshyre ... Parte of Lestershyre
mwec1295	uk england yorkshire	1622	DRAYTON	1350	24	30	Yorkeshyre
mwuk1265	england london	1799	DREW	900	41	52	Drew's New and Correct Plan of the Cities of London and Westminster, the Borough of Southwark &c., Including the Latest Improvements
mwuk1613	isle of man	1826	DRINKWATER	1800	94	62	Isle of Man ... from a Trigonometrical Survey by Mr. Benjamin Smythe
mwru0281	russia	1786	DROUET	400	33	48	Mapa General del Imperio Ruso Ano 1788 (incl. Alaska)
mwgr0506	greece cyprus	1754	DRUMMOND	4000	49	75	To George Wakeman Esqr. ... this Map of the Island of Cyprus
mwgr0240	greece	1811	DU BOCAGE	450	47	71	Carte Generale de la Grece (incl. Southern parts of Italy)
mwuk0245	ireland	1801	DU BOCAGE	280	38	32	L'Irlande, Par J.D.Barbie Du Bocage
mwgr0271b	greece athens	1791	DU BOCAGE	250	19	28	Plan d'Athenes (close copy of Zatta)
mwgr0271a	greece athens	1785	DU BOCAGE	250	17	22	Plan of the Environs of Athens (illustrated is Italian edition)
mwru0523	ukraine	1740	DU CHAFFAT	400	26	31	Plan veritable de la fameuse Forteresse d'Oczakov
mwru0524	ukraine	1740	DU CHAFFAT	1200	58	73	Provinciarum Turcico Tartaricum
mwru0525	ukraine	1740	DU CHAFFAT	1000	47	64	Theatrum Belli a.o. MDCCXXXVII
mwuss1135	new york	1779	DU CHESNOY	15000	74	64	Carte du Theatre de la Guerre dans L'Amerique Septentrionale, pendant les annees 76, 77, 78 et 79
mwam0865	america north (east)	1660	DU CREUX	7200	33	43	Tabula Novae Franciae Anno 1660
mwe0258	europe	1826	DU FOUR	200	35	42	Carte de l'Europe
mwjk0159	korea	1735	DU HALDE	2500	52	36	Royaume du Coree (illustrated with the 1737 re-issue by D'Anville)
mwru0447b	russia tartary	1730	DU HALDE	300	29	46	The Eleventh Sheet of Chinese Tartary, Containing ye Country West of Nipcha, Subject to Russia ... by P. Jartoux, Fridelli & Bonjour in 1711 (explorations around Lake Baikal)
mwc0313	china tibet	1737	DU HALDE-D'ANVILLE	2400	29	48	(Tibet. Set of 9 regional maps, various sizes. Size given for map 1, illustrated) 1/ L'Extremite Occidentale ... Pays aux environs de Hami 2/ Le Pays ... couchant de Tourfan 3/ Environs de Kashgar 4/ Pais de Tartares de Hoho-Nor 5/ Le Si-Fan et Pais Limitrophe 6/ Pays qui est du Levant de Lasa 7/ Du Tsanpou au couchant de Lasa 8/ Du Tsanpon de Du Gange 9/ Latac)
mwru0448c	russia tartary	1738	DU HALDE-D'ANVILLE	360	22	51	A Map of Capt. Beering's Travels
mwc0114	china	1737	DU HALDE-D'ANVILLE	800	59	51	Carte Generale de La Chine Dressee sur les Cartes Particulieres que l'Empereur Cang-Hi a Fait Lever
mwc0112	china	1737	DU HALDE-D'ANVILLE	750	51	79	Carte Generale de la Tartarie Chinoise
mwc0312	china tibet	1737	DU HALDE-D'ANVILLE	1200	46	58	Carte Generale du Thibet ou Bout-Tan et des Pays de Kashgar et Hami Dressee sur les Cartes et Memoires des Jesuites de la Chine
mwc0111	china	1737	DU HALDE-D'ANVILLE	3000	47	69	Carte la Plus Generale et qui comprend la Chine, la Tartarie Chinoise, et le Thibet
mwc0113	china	1737	DU HALDE-D'ANVILLE	600	39	24	Carte Particuliere de l'Entree de Canton
mwc0115	china	1737	DU HALDE-D'ANVILLE	480	29	48	I.e Feuille de la Tartarie Chinoise ... Leao Tong
mwc0116	china	1737	DU HALDE-D'ANVILLE	480	29	48	II.e Feuille Particuliere de la Tartarie Chinoise ... les environs de Nimgouta
mwc0117	china	1737	DU HALDE-D'ANVILLE	480	29	48	IV.e Feuille Particuliere de la Tartarie Chinoise ... partie du Cobi ou Cha-Mo Desert
mwc0118	china	1737	DU HALDE-D'ANVILLE	480	36	23	Province de Chan-Si
mwc0119	china	1737	DU HALDE-D'ANVILLE	800	40	34	Province de Fo-Kien (incl. Formosa)
mwc0120	china	1737	DU HALDE-D'ANVILLE	480	31	30	Province de Ho-Nan
mwc0121	china	1737	DU HALDE-D'ANVILLE	480	27	40	Province de Quang-Si
mwc0122	china	1737	DU HALDE-D'ANVILLE	480	26	24	Province de Kiang-nan
mwc0123	china	1737	DU HALDE-D'ANVILLE	480	34	27	Province de Kiang-Si
mwc0124	china	1737	DU HALDE-D'ANVILLE	480	26	30	Province de Koei-Tcheou
mwc0125	china	1737	DU HALDE-D'ANVILLE	600	38	29	Province de Pe-Tche-Li
mwc0126	china	1737	DU HALDE-D'ANVILLE	2000	43	54	Province de Quang-Tong
mwc0127	china	1737	DU HALDE-D'ANVILLE	600	41	49	Province de Se-Tchuen
mwc0128	china	1737	DU HALDE-D'ANVILLE	480	26	24	Province de Tche-Kiang
mwme0436b	jerusalem	1569	DU PERAC	10000	32	66	Hierusalem
mwme0914	turkey etc	1564	DU PINET	1500	28	34	Constantinoble (based on Munster)
mwe0007	europe	1564	DU PINET	1200	26	34	La Carte & Description d'Europe
mwit0774b	italy sardinia	1564	DU PINET	400	16	13	Sardinia Insula (reduced version of Munster 1550)
mwuk0813	uk	1734	DU SAUZET	350	20	25	Anglia, Scotia et Hibernia
mwuk0987	england	1734	DU SAUZET	280	20	25	Angliae Regnum (based on Cloppenburg 1630)
mwaf0714	africa north	1734	DU SAUZET	235	19	25	Barbarie
mwaf0747	africa north algeria	1734	DU SAUZET	235	17	23	Carte du Royaume d'Alger
mwru0512	ukraine	1735	DU SAUZET	500	19	25	Descriptio Ukraniae sive Palatinatuum Podoliae Kioviensis et Braczlaviensis
mwbh0862	luxembourg	1734	DU SAUZET	200	18	25	Le Duche de Luxembourg
mwwi0070	west indies	1735	DU SAUZET	350	19	26	Les Antilles
mwsc0724	scandinavia sweden	1734	DU SAUZET	200	18	25	Scania vulgo Schonen

AMPG REFERENCE	REGION	DATE	MAP MAKER	PRICE (UK£)	VERT. (cm.)	HOR. (cm.)	TITLE OF MAP (Comments by the editor in brackets)
mwsam0180	south america (north)	1735	DU SAUZET	350	19	26	Terre Firme et Nouv. Royaume de Granade
mwuss1632	virginia	1735	DU SAUZET	400	18	25	Virginiae Item et Floridae Americae Provinciarum, Nova Descriptio (late edition)
mwwi0920	virgin isl	1671	DU TERTRE	1350	22	31	L'Isle de Ste. Croix
mwgr0592a	greece islands	1677	DU VAL	240	24	16	(Unitled map of the Archipelago)
mwm0132a	mediterranean east	1677	DU VAL	400	17	24	(Untitled map, showing Cyprus and Mer de Levant)
mwm0132b	mediterranean east	1677	DU VAL	375	17	24	(Untitled map, showing Malta and Mer de Tunis)
mwme0172	holy land	1675	DU VAL	720	33	42	A Map of the Holy Land Delineated for the Better Understanding of the History of Iosephus
mwaf0375	africa east	1682	DU VAL	200	12	10	Abissinie ou Haute Ethiopie
mwaf0474a	africa egypt etc	1660	DUVAL	480	37	51	Aegyptus Antiqua Divisa in Nomos
mwaf0072	africa	1663	DU VAL	300	10	13	Afrique par P. Du Val Geogr. du Roy
mwam0064	america continent	1660	DU VAL	375	10	13	Amerique par P. Du Val Geogr. du Roy
mwuk0923a	england	1661	DU VAL	140	10	12	Angleterre
mwuk0715	uk	1657	DU VAL	280	14	18	Angleterre, Ecosse et Irlande
mwme0562	arabia etc	1663	DU VAL	375	10	12	Arabie
mwit0098	italy	1662	DU VAL	300	10	13	Archeveschez d'Italie
mwe0879b	europe hungary	1662	DU VAL	180	11	13	Archeveschez et Eveschez de Hongrie de Transilvanie &c
mwbp0272	poland	1662	DU VAL	235	10	13	Archeveschez et Eveschez de Pologne
mwsp0186a	spain	1662	DU VAL	200	10	13	Archeveschez et Eveschez d'Espanie et de Portugal
mwbh0366a	belgium holland	1662	DU VAL	160	10	13	Archeveschez et Eveschez du Pays Bas
mwru0062	russia	1662	DU VAL	200	10	12	Archeveschez et Eveschez Schismatiques de Moscovie
mwas0053	asia continent	1663	DU VAL	300	10	12	Asie par P. Du Val
mwsam0322	south america brazil	1682	DU VAL	250	10	12	Bresil
mwaf0865	africa south	1663	DU VAL	320	10	13	Cafrerie et Monomotapa
mwca0028	canada	1672	DU VAL	350	10	12	Canada
mwgr0410	greece crete	1682	DU VAL	250	10	13	Candie
mwme0868	syria etc	1677	DU VAL	240	16	24	Carte d'Assyrie et de Syrie.
mwe0541	europe czech republic (bohemia)	1665	DU VAL	450	41	53	Carte de Boheme Moravie Silesie et Lusace
mwru0063	russia	1663	DU VAL	720	41	51	Carte de la Grande Russie ou Moscovie
mwe0880	europe hungary	1664	DU VAL	400	37	53	Carte de La Hongrie a l'Autriche
mwme0164	holy land	1668	DU VAL	850	33	45	Carte de la Terre Sainte, dressee
mwuss1609	virginia	1663	DU VAL	500	10	12	Carte de la Virginie
mwg0071	germany	1678	DU VAL	650	41	43	Carte de L'Empire D'Alemagne
mwm0012	mediterranean	1663	DU VAL	650	32	55	Carte de l'Empire Romain Dressee sur Appian Alexandrin
mwaf0587	africa islands madagascar	1666	DU VAL	750	37	55	Carte de l'Isle Madagascar Dite Autrement Madecase et de S. Laurens et Aujourdhui l'Isle Dauphine avecque les Costes de Cofala et du Mozambique en Afrique
mwit0113	italy	1688	DU VAL	875	37	48	Carte de L'Italie
mwaf1109	africa west	1653	DU VAL	650	39	55	Carte de Nigritie et Guinee
mwbp0312	poland	1685	DU VAL	785	40	52	Carte de Pologne et des Etats qui en Dependent
mwin0414	indian ocean	1665	DU VAL	2500	39	54	Carte des Indes Orientales
mwuk0725	uk	1665	DU VAL	960	48	35	Carte des Isles Britanniques
mwbh0836	luxembourg	1664	DU VAL	720	38	49	Carte du Duche de Luxembourg et Souverainete de Sedan
mwaf0741	africa north algeria	1677	DU VAL	400	37	53	Carte du Roiaume d'Alger
mwsc0296a	scandinavia denmark	1676	DU VAL	550	41	55	Carte du Royaume Danemarq, et de la partie Méridionale de la Gotie
mwas0062	asia continent	1677	DU VAL	200	16	23	Carte du Voyage de Mr l'Evesque de Beryte Vicaire Apostolique au Royaume de la Cochin-Chine &c.
mwc0051	china	1665	DU VAL	250	23	16	Carte du Voyage des Ambassades de la Campagnie Orientale des Provinces Unies vers la Tartare Empereur de la Chine des Annees 1655, 1656 et 1657, Tiree de cette de Jean Nieuhoff
mwit0489	italy lombardy	1650	DU VAL	600	34	56	Carte Generale de Lombardie
mww0197	world	1674	DU VAL	2800	37	53	Carte Universelle du Commerce, c'est a dire Carte Hidrographique
mww0210	world	1679	DU VAL	15000	70	113	Carte Universelle du Monde Vulgairement dite la Mappemonde avec de Nouvelles Observations ... par P. Du-Val Geographe Ordinaire du Roy
mwsam0499	south america colombia	1663	DU VAL	240	10	12	Castile d'Or
mwsam0447	south america chile	1663	DU VAL	180	12	10	Chili
mwc0066	china	1682	DU VAL	300	12	10	Chine
mwaf1114	africa west	1663	DU VAL	150	11	13	Congo
mwsam0585	south america guyana	1677	DU VAL	450	26	34	Coste de Guayane autrement France Equinoctiale en la Terre-Ferme d'Amerique
mwaf1128	africa west	1671	DU VAL	650	34	53	Costes de Guinee avec les Royaumes qui y sont Connus des Europeens
mww0196	world	1674	DU VAL	550	12	18	Description de la Terre Universelle
mwuk0404a	scotland	1661	DU VAL	450	41	54	Description des Isles Britaniques
mwme0197	holy land	1685	DU VAL	200	15	19	Divisio Palaestinae Secundum Provincias
mwaf0476	africa egypt etc	1663	DU VAL	150	13	11	Egypte
mwin0109a	india	1661	DU VAL	200	10	12	Empire du Mogol
mwuk0405	scotland	1663	DU VAL	200	10	13	Escosse par P. Du Val Geogr. D. R.
mwe0076	europe	1663	DU VAL	200	11	14	Europe
mwme0715	caucasus	1676	DU VAL	200	10	13	Georgie

AMPG REFERENCE	REGION	DATE	MAP MAKER	PRICE (UK£)	VERT. (cm.)	HOR. (cm.)	TITLE OF MAP (Comments by the editor in brackets)
mwaf1139	africa west	1682	DU VAL	160	11	13	Guinee
mwe0879a	europe hungary	1661	DU VAL	140	11	13	Hongrie
mwuk0068	ireland	1661	DU VAL	200	13	11	Irlande par P. Du Val G.D.R.
mwgr0392a	greece crete	1667	DU VAL	1200	51	39	Isle de Candie (2 maps on one sheet)
mwin0026	ceylon	1682	DU VAL	200	12	10	Isle de Ceilan
mwaf0586	africa islands madagascar	1663	DU VAL	240	10	12	Isle de Madagascar dite de St Laurens
mwm0191	mediterranean malta	1663	DU VAL	400	10	12	Isle de Malthe p. P. Du Val G.O.D.R.
mwwi0021	west indies	1663	DU VAL	250	10	12	Isles Antilles
mwuk0720	uk	1661	DU VAL	250	10	12	Isles Britanniques par P. Du Val Geogr. du Roy
mwat0144	atlantic canary isl.	1663	DU VAL	200	10	12	Isles Canaries par P. Du Val Geogr. du Roy
mwwi0231	west indies (east)	1664	DU VAL	600	33	26	Isles d'Amerique dites Caribes ou Cannibales et de Barlovento
mwas0405	asia south east	1676	DU VAL	300	10	13	Isles de la Sonde
mwat0185	atlantic cape verde isl.	1663	DU VAL	200	10	12	Isles du Cap Verd
mwjk0029a	japan	1661	DU VAL	500	10	12	Isles du Iapon (illustrated is the 1694 re-engraved edition publ. by Hoffmann, with the title 'Japonia')
mwin0460	indian ocean maldives	1682	DU VAL	100	12	10	Isles Maldives
mwas0716	asia south east moluccas	1676	DU VAL	180	10	12	Isles Molucques
mwas0753	asia south east philippines	1663	DU VAL	600	10	13	Isles Philippines dites autrement de Manilhe
mwat0080	atlantic azores	1663	DU VAL	200	11	13	Isles Terceres dites Acores
mwme0564	arabia etc	1670	DU VAL	240	16	23	Itineraire du Caire a la Mecque
mwf0604	france languedoc	1667	DU VAL	600	33	47	La Carte des Eaux de la Montagne Noire, du Lers, du Fresquel, de l'Aude, et autres Rivieres Emploiees pour le Nouveau Canal de Languedoc et pour la Ionction des Deux Mers Oceane, et Mediterranee
mwf0065a	france	1661	DU VAL	550	40	54	La Carte Generale de France et de ses nouvelles Acquisitions (publ. by N. Berey)
mww0185	world	1668	DU VAL	3600	39	53	La Carte Generale du Monde Dressee sur les Relations les Plus Recentes par P Du Val
mwc0070	china	1684	DU VAL	1250	39	52	La Chine avec l'Empire du Mogol, les Presqu-Isles et les Isles de l'Asie (half of a map of South Asia)
mwe0670	europe dalmatia	1675	DU VAL	675	44	56	La Dalmatie
mwuss0154	carolinas	1677	DU VAL	1200	16	23	La Floride Francoise Dressee sur la Relation des Voiages que Ribaut, Laudonier, et Gourgues y ont Faits en 1562, 1564, et 1567
mwuss0396	florida	1672	DU VAL	375	10	11	La Floride par P Du Val G.O.D.R.
mwsam0312	south america brazil	1665	DU VAL	300	16	23	La France Antarctique autrement le Rio Ianero Tiree des Voyages que Villegagnon et Jean de Leri ont Faits au Bresil les Annees 1557 & 1558
mwf0074	france	1688	DU VAL	1200	40	55	La France avec ses Anciennes, et ses Nouvelles Bornes (4 sheets, each 41x56cm.)
mwf0078	france	1692	DU VAL	600	40	52	La France en toute son estendue sous le Roy Louis XIV
mwf0092a	france	1704	DU VAL	1200	73	109	La France par Pierre Duval... Reveüe et Augmentée sur les manuscrits de l'Auteur et selon les Nouvelles Observations. Par le R.P. Placide
mwgr0089	greece	1677	DU VAL	1000	35	44	La Grece, ou partie meridionale de l'empire des Turcs (size excl. text in 3 borders)
mwsam0580	south america guyana	1668	DU VAL	1200	38	48	La Guaiane ou Coste Sauvage, autrement El Dorado
mwsam0577	south america guyana	1661	DU VAL	160	10	12	La Guaiane ou France Equinoctiale
mwm0018	mediterranean	1677	DU VAL	2000	38	49	La Mer Mediterranee (in 2 sheets, each 38x49cm)
mwsam0707	south america paraguay	1663	DU VAL	180	10	12	La Plata
mwsp0473	spain regions	1688	DU VAL	720	40	45	La Principaute de Catalogne et le Comte de Roussillon
mwuk0945	england	1688	DU VAL	1500	41	46	La Royaume d'Angleterre
mwf1126	france rhone-alpes	1677	DU VAL	350	39	53	La Savoye Divisee en ses Grandes Parties
mwsc0678a	scandinavia sweden	1661	DU VAL	120	13	11	La Suède et tous les estats qui en dépendent
mwsw0078	switzerland	1664	DU VAL	960	41	52	La Suisse
mwme0160	holy land	1665	DU VAL	280	10	12	La Terre Saincte est auiourdhuy entre les mains du Turc,
mwme0953	turkey etc	1663	DU VAL	200	10	12	La Turquie en Asie
mwaf0073	africa	1664	DU VAL	1100	41	52	L'Afrique
mwaf0092	africa	1684	DU VAL	3500	40	53	L'Afrique ou sont Exactement Decrites (4 sheets, each 40x53cm.)
mwam0057	america continent	1655	DU VAL	2400	37	39	L'Amerique Autrement Nouveau Monde et Indes Occidentales
mwam0066	america continent	1661	DU VAL	3000	40	48	L'Amerique par P. Du Val Geographe du Roy (18 small maps on one sheet)
mwam0082	america continent	1679	DU VAL	9500	41	53	L'Amerique Suivant les Dernieres Relations ... avec les Routes que l'on Tient pour les Indes Orientales (in 4 sheets)
mwas0072	asia continent	1684	DU VAL	3200	41	53	L'Asie ou sont Exactement Decrites Toutes les Costes de la Mer (in 4 sheets, each 41x53cm)
mwas0060	asia continent	1676	DU VAL	1100	41	53	L'Asie Revue et Augmente par P. Du Val
mwe0710	europe danube	1684	DU VAL	300	40	52	Le Cours du Danube ou sont la Baviere, l'Austriche et la Boheme
mwbh0838	luxembourg	1679	DU VAL	675	38	54	Le Duche de Luxembourg, et le comte de Namur
mwe0768a	europe east	1677	DU VAL	720	39	53	Le Grand Royaume de Hongrie qui est aujourdhuy La Turquie Septemtrionale en Europe
mww0179	world	1663	DU VAL	550	11	13	Le Monde en Planisphere par P. Du-Val Geograp. du Roy

AMPG REFERENCE	REGION	DATE	MAP MAKER	PRICE (UK£)	VERT. (cm.)	HOR. (cm.)	TITLE OF MAP (Comments by the editor in brackets)
mww0171a	world	1660	DU VAL	5500	41	81	Le Planis(phere) Autrement La Carte Du Monde Terrestre
mwsc0071	scandinavia	1676	DU VAL	720	40	53	Le Royaume de Suede
mwg0078	germany	1684	DU VAL	1500	40	53	L'Empire d'Alemagne (4 sheets, each 40x53cm.)
mwme0786	persia etc	1677	DU VAL	280	16	23	L'Empire des Perses
mwme0571	arabia etc	1686	DU VAL	1200	39	53	L'Empire des Turcs, en Europe, en Asie, et en Afrique
mwaf0693	africa north	1664	DU VAL	400	21	76	Les Costes des Royaumes de Fez, Alger, Tunis et Tripoli en Barbarie (2 maps)
mwuk0738	uk	1680	DU VAL	2800	41	54	Les Isles Britanniques (in 4 sheets, each 41x54cm.)
mwm0197	mediterranean malta	1677	DU VAL	2000	40	53	Les Isles de Malthe, Goze, Comin, Cominot ... 1677
mwat0078	atlantic azores	1654	DU VAL	600	32	44	Les Isles Terceres
mwbh0440a	belgium holland	1687	DU VAL	650	54	42	Les Provinces des Pays Bas
mwbp0088	baltic states	1660	DU VAL	800	40	55	Les Royaumes du Nort c'est a Dire le Danemarq la Suede et la Pologne
mwbh0411	belgium holland	1680	DU VAL	200	12	10	Les XVII Provinces des Pais Bas
mwsp0187	spain	1663	DU VAL	720	39	51	L'Espagne divisee en ses principaux Royaumes
mwe0077	europe	1664	DU VAL	1000	39	51	L'Europe ... dediee a Monsieur le colonel de Vatteuille
mwe0095	europe	1684	DU VAL	2800	40	50	L'Europe par P. Duval (4 sheets, each 40x50cm)
mwsc0496	scandinavia iceland	1682	DU VAL	280	11	13	L'Islande
mwit0097a	italy	1661	DU VAL	200	10	13	L'Italie
mwit0110	italy	1683	DU VAL	2250	42	54	L'Italie (in 4 sheets, each 42x54cm.)
mwat0213c	atlantic east	1666	DU VAL	720	47	34	L'Ocean pres d'Europe, avec les Costes de France, d'Espagne, de Portugal, d'Angleterre, de Hollande, de Danemarc &c. Suivant les Cartes Marines les Plus Nouvelles
mwsam0674	south america magellan	1680	DU VAL	200	11	13	Magellanique
mwgm0165	mexico	1663	DU VAL	240	10	12	Mexique ou Nle Espagne
mwru0088	russia	1682	DU VAL	450	40	51	Moscovie dite autrement Grande et Blanche Russie
mwaf1138	africa west	1682	DU VAL	140	11	13	Nigritie
mwgm0166	mexico	1663	DU VAL	600	10	12	Nouveau Mexique
mwe0909	europe hungary	1690	DU VAL	720	39	47	Novissima et Accuratissima Totius Hungariae Tabula ... Gedruckt by Justus Danckers
mwaf0365a	africa east	1663	DU VAL	180	10	12	Nubie
mwm0010	mediterranean	1655	DU VAL	350	24	37	Patriarchatus Romanus, Constantinopolitanus, Alexandrinus, Antiochenus, et Hierosolimitanus
mwme0789	persia etc	1680	DU VAL	240	10	13	Perse
mww0182a	world	1666	DU VAL	3600	33	58	Planisphere, ou Carte Generale du Monde (illustrated is a close copy issued by Du Val's granddaughter in 1684)
mwas0406	asia south east	1676	DU VAL	300	13	10	Presqu'Isle de Linde de la le Gange
mwm0125	mediterranean east	1657	DU VAL	720	29	43	Pyrrhi Regis Epirotarum Expeditiones; per Macedoniam, Italiam, Siciliam et Peloponesum ex Plutarcho
mwgr0118	greece	1694	DU VAL	400	28	42	Pyrrhi regis Epirotorum (a larger slightly different version of this map also exists, 35x56cm, also by Du Val, with the title 'Alcibiadis Expeditionum'; illustrated below).
mwit0834a	italy sardinia and corsica	1686	DU VAL	500	16	19	Republique de Genes et les Isles de Corse et Sardaigne (illustrated above)
mwsp0193	spain	1661	DU VAL	180	11	13	Royaume d' Espagne
mwsp0046	portugal	1676	DU VAL	675	52	38	Royaume de Portugal
mwsp0042a	portugal	1661	DU VAL	140	13	10	Royaume de Portugal
mwit0893	italy sicily	1663	DU VAL	320	10	12	Sicile
mwm0131	mediterranean east	1665	DU VAL	300	16	23	Tabula Geographica ex Eusebii Pamphili Historical Ecclesiastica
mwme0962	turkey etc	1680	DU VAL	480	41	49	Tabula Itineris Decies Mille Graecorum sub Cyro contra Fratrem suum Artaxerxem, Regem Persarum
mwru0434	russia tartary	1682	DU VAL	160	10	12	Tartarie
mwaa0009	antarctic	1661	DU VAL	350	10	12	Terres Antarctiques
mwme0162	holy land	1666	DU VAL	1200	37	52	Terra Sancta quae et Terra Chanaan, Terra Promissionis (in 2 sheets, each 37x52cm.)
mwme0156	holy land	1662	DU VAL	240	13	19	Terre Sainte jadis Terre Promise ou Palestine
mwaa0090	arctic	1661	DU VAL	280	11	13	Terres Arctiques
mwe1042c	europe romania	1661	DU VAL	120	11	13	Transilvanie, Valaquie et Moldavie
mwsam0215	south america argentina	1663	DU VAL	120	11	13	Tucuman
mwgr0096	greece	1682	DU VAL	100	10	13	Turquie en Europe
mwuss1608	virginia	1660	DU VAL	600	10	12	Virginia et Insulae Bermudes
mwaf0365	africa east	1663	DU VAL	240	12	10	Zanguebar. Par P. Duval G.O.D.R.
mwbh0443	belgium holland	1688	DU VIVIER	600	42	54	Le Comte de Namur. Par F. Du Vivier
mwaf0737	africa north algeria	1600	DUCHETO	1500	39	60	Algier Fortificato l'Anno MDLXXVIII (view)
mwf0709	france nord pas-de-calais	1602	DUCHETO	1000	34	37	Chales (view of the French attack on the English garrison)
mwme0918	turkey etc	1570	DUCHETO	5000	29	44	Costatinopoli
mwgr0343	greece crete	1570	DUCHETO	2000	28	22	Creta Insula, hodie Cadia
mwgr0443	greece cyprus	1570	DUCHETO	5000	22	29	Cyprus quae olim
mwit1130a	italy florence	1580	DUCHETO	2500	32	44	Fiorenza
mwit0037	italy	1582	DUCHETO	10000	39	50	Geographia moderna de tutta la Italia con le sue.
mwme0437	jerusalem	1570	DUCHETO	8000	29	42	Hierusalem
mwaf0014	africa	1579	DUCHETO	20000	43	59	Il disegno della Geografia moderna de tutta la parte dell'Africa (Title: text panel in cartouche. A close copy of Forlani 1562).
mwgr0293	greece corfu	1570	DUCHETO	2400	21	30	Isola de Corfu

AMPG REFERENCE	REGION	DATE	MAP MAKER	PRICE (UK£)	VERT. (cm.)	HOR. (cm.)	TITLE OF MAP (Comments by the editor in brackets)
mwit1052	italy naples	1585	DUCHETO	3500	39	51	La Citta de Napoli Gentile
mwit0392	italy lazio	1602	DUCHETO	3000	32	47	La Descrittione della Campagna di Roma, detta Dagli Antichi Latium (1st edition 1564)
mwaf0763a	africa north libya	1602	DUCHETO-ORLANDINI	1000	29	43	Tripoli Citta di Barbaria (view of the siege)
mwin0105	india	1646	DUDLEY	1000	48	37	(Untitled sea chart incl. the Maldives and most of Ceylon)
mwsam0821	south america venezuela	1647	DUDLEY	3000	47	73	Al Sermo. Ferdinando II Granduca di Toscana suo Signore Don Roberto Dudleo Duca di Northumbria
mwsam0575	south america guyana	1646	DUDLEY	2000	47	72	Alla Serma Sigra Principsa. d'Urbino Granduchessa di Toscana sua Sigra D: Roberto Dudleo Duca di Northumbria
mwjk0018	japan	1646	DUDLEY	6000	43	56	Asia Carta Diciasete piu Moderna
mwat0179	atlantic cape verde isl.	1646	DUDLEY	1600	48	75	Carta dell Isole di Capo Verde con l'Isole dell Indie Occidentale, et Parte della Terra Ferma di Guiana
mwsc0559	scandinavia norway	1661	DUDLEY	1200	50	36	Carta di Norvegia piu Moderna
mwsc0544	scandinavia norway	1646	DUDLEY	1200	38	48	Carta nonna Generale di Europa (northern coastline of Norway etc.)
mwaf1061	africa south west	1646	DUDLEY	650	46	34	Carta Particolare che Comincia con il Capo Aldea e Finisce con il Capo Degortam
mwme0553	arabia etc	1648	DUDLEY	4000	48	73	Carta Particolare che Comincia con il Capo Baduis e Finisce con il Capo Cumana e Mostra la Bocca del Mare Russo / Carta Particolare che Comincia con il Capo Dofar in Arabia e Finisce con il Capo Cintapora nell Indie (2 charts)
mwaf0863	africa south	1646	DUDLEY	5000	46	74	Carta Particolare che Comincia con il Capo Degortam e con il Capo Buona Speranza e Finisce in Gradi 27 di Latitudine Australe (South Africa)
mwsp0435	spain regions	1646	DUDLEY	2000	48	76	Carta Particolare che Comincia con il Capo di Coriano e Finisce con il Capo di Aviles in Ispagnia (Galicia)
mwsp0436a	spain regions	1646	DUDLEY	1000	48	38	Carta Particolare che Comincia con il Capo di Oringan in Biscaia e Finisce con la Costa di Alcason in Francia
mwaf0361	africa east	1646	DUDLEY	1250	46	36	Carta Particolare che Comincia con il Capo e l'Isola Mombazza e Finisce con il Capo Baduis
mwsp0043	portugal	1661	DUDLEY	1200	46	33	Carta Particolare che Comincia con il Capo Mogera in Portogallo e Finisce con il Capo di Coriano in Ispagna
mwaf1105	africa west	1646	DUDLEY	1200	46	74	Carta Particolare che Comincia con il Fiume Iuntas nella Guinea e Finisce con il Capo di S: Dara e con l'Isola di S: Tomaso
mwsc0268c	scandinavia denmark	1646	DUDLEY	1600	48	75	Carta particolare che Comincia con il Gran Fiume Albis e Contene Parte dell Mare Baltico e Lentrata al Sondo di Danemarca
mwsc0267	scandinavia denmark	1646	DUDLEY	2800	49	75	Carta Particolare che Comincia con la Iutlandia e Contiene Parte della Costa di Suetzia e della Norvegia
mwaf0778a	africa north morocco	1646	DUDLEY	1000	48	76	Carta Particolare che Comincia con li Stretto di Gibilterro e Finisce con il Capo Gruer nella Barberia Occidele
mwaf1104	africa west	1646	DUDLEY	1000	46	34	Carta Particolare che Comincia con l'Isola di S: Tomasso o Tome e C: d' S. Clara e Finisce con il C: d'Aldeas
mwaf1062	africa south west	1646	DUDLEY	3000	46	76	Carta Particolare che Mostra il Capo Buona Speranza con il Mare verso Ponete e con l'Isole di Tristan d'Acunha e di Martn. Vaz
mwgr0580	greece islands	1646	DUDLEY	3600	46	76	Carta Particolare del Arcipelago
mwp0491	pacific south	1646	DUDLEY	1250	47	75	Carta Particolare del Mare del Sur che Comincia con l'Isole di Salamone e Finisice con la Costa di Lima nel' Peru
mwat0323	atlantic st helena	1646	DUDLEY	800	48	75	Carta particolare del Mare di Ethiopia con l'Isola di S. Elena e Parte della Costa
mwsam0495	panama	1646	DUDLEY	1350	49	75	Carta particolare del' mare duZur ... capo S. Francesco nel' Peru e finisce con il capo S. Lazaro nella nuova Spagnia
mwe0667a	europe dalmatia	1661	DUDLEY	800	43	33	Carta Particolare del Mare Mediterraneo che comincia con Budua in Dalmatia ... Corfu
mwaf0763b	africa north libya	1646	DUDLEY	1800	46	74	Carta Particolare del Mare Mediterraneo che Comincia con il Capo Teti e Finisce con Folselli in Barberia
mwm0102	mediterranean central	1646	DUDLEY	2500	49	76	Carta Particolare del Mare Mediterraneo che Comincia con il Porto di Tre Croce e Finisce con il Capo Araso
mwf1177	france south	1646	DUDLEY	2800	46	74	Carta Particolare del Mare Mediterraneo, che Comincia con il Capo Dragone, in Ispagna e Finisce con il Capo Melle nella Rivera di Genova
mwru0043	russia	1646	DUDLEY	2000	48	76	Carta Particolare del Mare Settentrionale di Moscovia e Russia con Listreto di Wigats e Finisce con il Fiume Oby
mwsp0029	portugal	1646	DUDLEY	1500	47	38	Carta Particolare del Oceano che Comincia con il Capo S: Vincentio e Finisce con il Capo Roxo in Portogallo
mwsp0030	portugal	1646	DUDLEY	720	47	38	Carta Particolare del Oceano che Comincia con la Costa di C. Roxo e Finisce con il Capo di Mogera ni Portogallo
mwas0900	asia south east sunda	1646	DUDLEY	2000	46	33	Carta Particolare del Stretto di Sunda fra l'Isole di Sumatra e Iavamaggre
mwin0384	india bay of bengal	1661	DUDLEY	2400	48	75	Carta Particolare del'Golfo di Bengala e Pegu che Comincia con il Capo Masulipatan e Finisce con la Punta Domurco
mwsam0496	south america colombia	1646	DUDLEY	3600	46	76	Carta Particolare dell'India Occidentale che Comincia con il Capo S: Romano nel'Mare del'Nort, e Finisce con il Rio Coquele

AMPG REFERENCE	REGION	DATE	MAP MAKER	PRICE (UK£)	VERT. (cm.)	HOR. (cm.)	TITLE OF MAP (Comments by the editor in brackets)
mwgm0160	mexico	1646	DUDLEY	2500	48	75	Carta Particolare dell'India Occidentale che Contiene il Golfo di Veragua, la Baia di Honduras nel' Mare del' Noort e Parte del' Mare di Zur
mwas0607	asia south east celebes	1646	DUDLEY	3000	46	74	Carta Particolare dell'Isola Mindano Parte Australe con Celebes e Gilolo Parte Tramontana e con l'Isole di Molucchi e altre Isolette Intoro
mwas0629	asia south east java	1646	DUDLEY	4500	48	75	Carta Particolare dell'Isole di Iava Maggre. e Minore con la Parte Austrle. del Isole di Sumatra e Burneo
mwuk1539b	uk english channel (west)	1646	DUDLEY	3000	49	74	Carta Particolare dell Canale fra Inghilterra e Francia che Comincia con l'Isole di Sorlinges e Finisce con l'Isola di Garnsey
mwbp0012	baltic sea (east)	1646	DUDLEY	2000	48	75	Carta particolare dell Fine del Mare Baltico in Sino all Narve
mwbp0013	baltic sea (east)	1646	DUDLEY	2000	48	76	Carta particolare dell Mare Baltico che Comincia con il Capo di Eleeholm in Suezia e Finisce con Padus in Liflandia
mwaf0648	africa islands seychelles	1661	DUDLEY	1800	48	38	Carta Particolare dell Mare dell Indie con le Secaie e Alcqune Isolle
mwuk0054	ireland	1647	DUDLEY	5000	48	76	Carta Particolare dell Mare di Ierlandia e Parte di Inghilterra e della Iscotia
mwp0315	pacific friendly isl.	1646	DUDLEY	1350	48	75	Carta particolare dell' mare e Isole scoperte dal Iacomo Maier Olandese nel 1617 ...
mwat0298	atlantic south	1646	DUDLEY	1200	48	73	Carta particolare dell Mare Oceano fra la Costa di Guinea e la Brasilia
mwuss0068	california	1646	DUDLEY	6000	47	75	Carta Particolare della America e Parte Maestrale dal C: di Cedros
mwgm0004	gulf of mexico and surrounding regions	1646	DUDLEY	24000	48	76	Carta Particolare della Baia di Messico con la Costa
mwaf1106	africa west	1646	DUDLEY	1000	48	76	Carta Particolare della Barberia Australe che Comincia con il Capo Matas e Finisce con il. C. Himilas con l'Isole di Capo Verde
mwaf0837a	africa north west	1646	DUDLEY	3500	48	76	Carta Particolare della Barberia Occidentale che Comincia con il Capo Gruer e Finisce con il Capo Matas
mwuk1421	england thames	1646	DUDLEY	1500	46	34	Carta Particolare della Bocca del Tamigi in Inghita. e Finisce a Leystof nella Provincia di Suffoleh
mwsam0292	south america brazil	1646	DUDLEY	800	46	34	Carta Particolare della Brasilia Australe che Comincia dal' Poro. del' Spirito. Santo e Finisce con il Capo Bianco
mwsam0293	south america brazil	1646	DUDLEY	1200	46	76	Carta Particolare della Brasilia Settentrionale
mwsam0294	south america brazil	1646	DUDLEY	1600	46	74	Carta Particolare della Brasilia, che Comincia con il Capo S: Antonio et Finisce con il Porto del'Spirito Sancto
mwf0312	france brittany	1646	DUDLEY	1200	46	74	Carta Particolare della Brittania Bassa in Francia che Comincia con il Capo Armentice e Finisce con il Capo Forne
mwp0002	australia	1646	DUDLEY	8000	38	47	Carta Particolare della Costa Australe Scoperta dall' Olandesi (north Australia and New Guinea)
mwsam0742	south america peru	1661	DUDLEY	600	48	37	Carta Particolare della Costa del'Peru Parte Australe con Parte di Cili
mwsam0445	south america chile	1646	DUDLEY	600	46	34	Carta Particolare della Costa di Chilve e di Chica e Parte Australe di Cili
mwsc0410	scandinavia finland	1646	DUDLEY	1800	48	39	Carta Particolare della Costa di Finlandia con il Capo dell Norto
mwuss0393	florida	1647	DUDLEY	9600	48	39	Carta Particolare della Costa di Florida e di Virginia
mwf0261	france aquitaine	1646	DUDLEY	1200	46	34	Carta particolare della Costa di Guasconnia in Francia che Comincia con il Fiume di Burdeaux e Finisce con l'Isola di Heys
mwuk1643	north sea	1646	DUDLEY	1000	46	34	Carta Particolare della Costa di Inghilterra che Comincia con Orfordness e Finisce con Flamborow Heade
mwru0044	russia	1646	DUDLEY	2000	48	76	Carta Particolare della Costa di Nuova Zembla
mwuk0346	scotland	1646	DUDLEY	800	46	34	Carta Particolare della Costa di Scozia che Comincia con il C: di S: Tabs e Finisce con il C: di Comar
mwuk0347	scotland	1646	DUDLEY	800	49	38	Carta particolare della costa di Scozia che comincia con il C:di Cromar à¨ Finisce con l'Isole di Orcades
mwbh0289	belgium holland	1646	DUDLEY	2000	48	76	Carta Particolare della Costa di Zelanda e Frislanda e Olanda che Comincia con il Porto di Newport e Finisce con Messelward
mwuk1527	uk english channel (east)	1646	DUDLEY	1500	46	34	Carta Particolare della Costa d'Inghilterra e Francia che Comincia con l'Isola di Garnesy e Finisce con il C: di Fecam nella Costa di Normandia
mwbp0014	baltic sea (east)	1646	DUDLEY	1800	48	38	Carta particolare della Entrata del Mare Botnico o Boddico
mwjk0019	japan	1646	DUDLEY	12000	48	75	Carta Particolare della Grande Isola del'Giapone e di Iezo con il Regno di Corai et Altre Isole Intorno
mwit0831	italy sardinia and corsica	1646	DUDLEY	2850	48	34	Carta Particolare della Isola di Sardinia e Parte della Corsica
mwas0387	asia south east	1646	DUDLEY	14000	48	75	Carta Particolare della Mallaca con la Costa sin'al Pegu e Comboia con l'Isole di Sumatra / Carta Particolare dell'Isole di Iava Maggre. e Minore con la Parte Austrle. del Isole di Sumatra e Burneo (2 charts)
mwca0017	canada	1646	DUDLEY	1800	46	34	Carta Particolare della Meta Incognita Australe con una Parte della America Settentrionale (1st map to focus on the Davis Straits. Illustrated is the 1661 re-issue)

AMPG REFERENCE	REGION	DATE	MAP MAKER	PRICE (UK£)	VERT. (cm.)	HOR. (cm.)	TITLE OF MAP (Comments by the editor in brackets)
mwsc0452	scandinavia greenland	1646	DUDLEY	3000	46	75	Carta Particolare della Meta Inconita con la Gronlandia Occidentale e dell'Estotiland Scopto. dall'Inglesi
mwam0860	america north (east)	1646	DUDLEY	18000	47	38	Carta particolare della Nuova Belgia e parte della Nuova Anglia
mwsc0544b	scandinavia norway	1646	DUDLEY	1200	49	37	Carta particolare della parte Australe della Norvegia
mwaf1041	africa south east	1646	DUDLEY	1400	48	76	Carta Particolare della Parte Australle della Isola S: Lorenzo con la Terra Ferma Dirinpetto e Finisce con Gradi: 6: di Latitudine Australe
mwgm0161	mexico	1647	DUDLEY	2500	48	76	Carta Particolare della Parte Occidentale della Nuova Spagnia, e del la California
mwuss0067	california	1646	DUDLEY	5500	46	74	Carta Particolare della Parte Orientale dell'Isola di Iezo con li Stretto fra America e la detta Isola
mwaf1041a	africa south east	1646	DUDLEY	1400	48	76	Carta Particolare della parte Tramontana dell Isola di San Lorenzo con la coasta diripetto sino à Monbazza con l'Isola di San Lorenzo con la coasta diripetto sino à Monbazza con l'Isole à¨ Seccagne interno
mwaf0362	africa east	1646	DUDLEY	2000	48	76	Carta Particolare della Parte Tramontana dell Isola di San Lorenzo con la Costa Diripetto sino a Monbazza con l'Isole e Seccagne Intno.
mwsc0453	scandinavia greenland	1646	DUDLEY	2000	49	74	Carta Particolare della Terra di Grenlande Gia Incognita fu Scoperta da Inglesi sino a Gradi 80: da Latitudine
mwca0283	canada newfoundland	1646	DUDLEY	4200	46	76	Carta Particolare della Terra Nuova con la Gran Baia et il Fiume Grande della Canida
mwuss1605	virginia	1646	DUDLEY	18000	46	34	Carta Particolare della Virginia Vecchia e Nuova
mwsc0410a	scandinavia finland	1646	DUDLEY	900	48	38	Carta particolare delle entrata del mare Botnico à Boddico
mwas0713	asia south east moluccas	1646	DUDLEY	1600	46	34	Carta Particolare delle: 6: Isole de Molucchi
mwat0108	atlantic bermuda	1646	DUDLEY	9000	48	74	Carta Particolare dell'Isola di Bermuda sin all'India Occidentale et al'Capo S: Romano della Florida
mwwi0407	cuba	1646	DUDLEY	8000	46	76	Carta Particolare dell'Isola di Cuba
mwwi0580	hispaniola	1646	DUDLEY	4200	48	76	Carta Particolare dell'Isola Ispaniola e S: Gioni. nel'India Occidentle, con l'Isole Intorno
mwas0608	asia south east celebes	1646	DUDLEY	1600	46	34	Carta Particolare dell'Isole Celebes e Giliolo Parte Austrle. di Butto, Batuliar, Timor, Seram, Banda, e Amboina e altre Isolete
mwat0212	atlantic east	1646	DUDLEY	1600	48	76	Carta Particolare dell'Isole d'Asores con l'Isola di Madera
mwsc0492	scandinavia iceland	1646	DUDLEY	5000	48	76	Carta Particolare dell'Isole di Islandia e Frislandia, con l'Isolette di Fare
mwas0750	asia south east philippines	1646	DUDLEY	4500	49	38	Carta Particolare dell'Isole Fillipine e di Luzon
mwca0018	canada	1646	DUDLEY	3600	71	48	Carta particolare dello Istreto e Mare Iscoperto da Heno. Hudson Ingilese nel. 1611
mwsam0669	south america magellan	1646	DUDLEY	3000	48	76	Carta particolare dello Stretto de Magellano e di Maire
mwam1313	america north (west)	1648	DUDLEY	3000	48	39	Carta Particolare dello Stretto di Iezo fra l'America e l'Isola Iezo
mwuk1528	uk english channel (east)	1646	DUDLEY	1500	46	34	Carta Particolare dello Stretto di Inghilterra fra Dovere e Cales con la Costa Intorno
mwas0752	asia south east philippines	1661	DUDLEY	2400	47	75	Carta Particolare dello Stretto di Manilia nel Isole Filippine
mwsam0295	south america brazil	1646	DUDLEY	1500	34	46	Carta Particolare dell'Rio d'Amazone con la Costa sin al'Fiume Maranhan
mwsam0213	south america argentina	1646	DUDLEY	1500	48	74	Carta Particolare dell'Rio della Plata che Comincia con la Costa in Gradi 31 di Latine. Australe, e Finisce con il Capo S: Andrea
mwsam0495	south america colombia	1646	DUDLEY	1350	49	75	Carta Particolare del'Mare del'Zur che Comincia con il'Capo S: Francesco nel'Peru e Finisce con il'Capo S: Lazaro nella Nuova Spagnia
mwc0021	china	1646	DUDLEY	3600	46	33	Carta particolare del'Mare di Cocincina con la Parte Australe della China
mwat0252a	atlantic north	1646	DUDLEY	1800	46	34	Carta Particolare del'Mare Oceano dal'Isole d'Asores di Flores, e Corvo sin alla Terra Nuova in America
mwbp0015	baltic sea (east)	1646	DUDLEY	2000	46	34	Carta particolare di Livonia cor una Particella della Costa che Comincia con Lockston e Finisce con il Pto. Derliven
mwc0299	china formosa	1646	DUDLEY	3600	48	76	Carta Particolare d'una parte della Costa di China con L'Isola de Pakas (Taiwan)
mwc0020b	china	1646	DUDLEY	3600	47	76	Carta Particolare d'una Parte della Cota. di China con l'Isola di Pakas, e altre Isole, sino alla Parte Piu Australe del'Giapone
mwat0299	atlantic south	1647	DUDLEY	1200	45	70	Carta Prima Generale d'Affrica e Pare. d'America
mwgm0005	gulf of mexico and surrounding regions	1646	DUDLEY	4000	49	70	Carta Prima Generale d'America dell' India Occidentale e Mare del Zur (inset of NW America)
mwin0408	indian ocean	1646	DUDLEY	8000	46	76	Carta Prima Generale dell'Asia
mwuk1455	uk english channel (all)	1646	DUDLEY	1650	39	48	Carta Quinta Generale di Europa
mwp0377	pacific new guinea	1646	DUDLEY	3000	48	37	Carta Secona. Generale del'Asia (shows the Philippines and New Guinea)
mwaf0862	africa south	1646	DUDLEY	3500	48	75	Carta Seconda Generale d'Affrica (southern africa)
mwam0858	america north (east)	1646	DUDLEY	12000	45	38	Carta Seconda Generale del America
mwuk0348	scotland	1646	DUDLEY	1500	48	34	Carta Sesta Generale del'Europa
mwsam0167	south america (central)	1646	DUDLEY	2500	47	75	Carta Terza Generale d'America (inset of Magellan)

AMPG REFERENCE	REGION	DATE	MAP MAKER	PRICE (UK£)	VERT. (cm.)	HOR. (cm.)	TITLE OF MAP (Comments by the editor in brackets)
mwp0228	pacific (all)	1646	DUDLEY	3000	46	38	Carta Terza Generale del'Asia (New Guinea shown lower left)
mwat0213	atlantic east	1646	DUDLEY	1000	34	44	Carta Terza Generale di Europa
mwin0106	india	1646	DUDLEY	2400	48	76	Questa Carta Contiene la Costa dell'India Orientale con la Costa di Coromandell e l'Isola di Zeilan e Finisce con la Parte Tramontna di Sumatra
mwsc0544a	scandinavia norway	1646	DUDLEY	2000	48	76	Questa Carta Contiene l'Isolle di Fero e di Shutland con la Norvegia Settentrionale
mwsp0436	spain regions	1646	DUDLEY	1600	47	68	Una Carta del Mare Oceano, che Comincia con il Capo S: Vincenzio in Portogallo, e Finisce con lo Streto di Gibilterra
mwm0127	mediterranean east	1661	DUDLEY	2800	42	37	Una Carta dell'Arcipelago con Parte del Mare Mediterraneo verso Levante
mwm0005	mediterranean	1646	DUDLEY	6000	43	109	Una Carta General del Mare Mediterranio / Una Carta dell'Arcipelago con Parte del Mare Mediterraneo verso Levante
mwuss0123	california	1849	DUFLOT DE MOFRAS	550	28	38	Carte de la Californie Extrait de la Grande Carte de l'Exploration du Territoire de l'Oregon des Californiens
mwp0464	pacific north	1844	DUFLOT DE MOFRAS	200	29	40	Carte de l'Ocean Pacifique au Nord de l'Equateur
mwuss0117	california	1844	DUFLOT DE MOFRAS	650	55	41	Carte Detaillee du Mouillage du Fort Ross et du Port de la Bodega ou Romanzoff dans la Nouvelle Californie
mwuss1693	washington	1844	DUFLOT DE MOFRAS	450	23	41	Carte du Rio Colombia depuis son Embouchure jusqu'au Fort Vancouver, a 17 Myriametres de la Mer
mwgm0346	mexico	1844	DUFLOT DE MOFRAS	100	32	36	Isthme de Tehuantepec
mwuss0116	california	1844	DUFLOT DE MOFRAS	550	23	18	Mouillage de San Pedro / Mouillage de la Mission de Sta. Barbara
mwuss0115	california	1844	DUFLOT DE MOFRAS	650	23	18	Plan de l'Embouchure du Rio Colorado dans la Mer Vermeille / Plan du Port de S. Diego Situe sur la Cote Septentrionale de la Californie
mwgm0347	mexico	1844	DUFLOT DE MOFRAS	100	24	18	Plan de Mazatlan / Plan de San Blas
mwgm0348	mexico	1844	DUFLOT DE MOFRAS	100	18	23	Plan du Port d'Acapulco sur la Cote Occidentale du Mexique
mwgm0349	mexico	1844	DUFLOT DE MOFRAS	100	23	18	Plan du Port de Guaymas sur la Mer Vermeille / Plan de la Baie de la Paz et du Port de Pichilingue
mwuss0114	california	1844	DUFLOT DE MOFRAS	400	23	18	Plan du Port de S. Diego Situe sur la Cote Septentrionale de la Californie
mwgm0350	mexico	1844	DUFLOT DE MOFRAS	100	18	23	Plan du Port del Manzanillo dans le Territoire de Colima / Plan du Port d'Acapulco sur la Cote Occidentale du Mexique
mwuss0113	california	1844	DUFLOT DE MOFRAS	650	23	18	Plan du Port et de la Baie de Monte-Rey / Baie de la Trinidad
mwca0672	canada west	1844	DUFLOT DE MOFRAS	450	23	18	Port de Quadra ou de la Decouverte / Plan du Port de Nutka Cala de los Amigos (2 maps on one sheet)
mwuss0112	california	1844	DUFLOT DE MOFRAS	1650	45	26	Port de San Francisco dans la Haute Californie / Entree du Port de San Francisco et des Mouillages del Sausalito et de la Yerba Buena
mwgr0514	greece cyprus	1827	DUFOUR	500	20	28	(Untitled map of ancient Cyprus)
mwme1065	turkey etc	1839	DUFOUR	300	26	34	(Untitled plan of Constantinople)
mwsp0338a	spain	1861	DUFOUR	1000	95	126	Carte Administrative, Physique et Routière de L'Espagne et du Portugal: Indiquant les Canaux, les Rivieres navigables, les Routes de Poste
mwme0409	holy land	1830	DUFOUR	400	46	42	Carte de la Palestine
mwme0432	holy land	1850	DUFOUR	100	31	23	La Terre Sainte
mwsam0358a	south america brazil	1730	DUGAY-TROUIN	400	21	28	Plan de la Baye et de la Ville de Rio Janeiro prise par l'Escadre Commandee par Mr. Duguay Trouin, et Armee par des particuliers de St. Malo en 1711
mwit0673	italy piedmont	1720	DUMONT	400	47	59	Plan de la Bataille de Turin Gagnee par le Duc de Savoye & le Pr. Eugene le 7 Sept. 1706
mwit0674	italy piedmont	1720	DUMONT	500	46	59	Plan de la Ville et Citadelle de Turin
mwe1070a	europe serbia	1729	DUMONT & ROUSSET	350	34	43	Plan de Belgrade Assiégé par l'Armee Imperiale (shown above left)
mwe1049	europe romania	1729	DUMONT & ROUSSET	720	68	93	(Timisoara) Plan de Temiswar et des ses Environs avec l'Attaque dans la Palanque
mwe1070	europe serbia	1729	DUMONT & ROUSSET	450	51	69	Plan de la Glorieuse Bataille le 16e. Aout, 1717. Proche de Belgrade
mwbh0607	belgium holland	1729	DUMONT & ROUSSET	800	50	59	Plan van Brussel
mwp0210	new zealand	1835	DUMONT D'URVILLE	500	35	23	Carte de la Nouvelle-Zelande
mwp0211	new zealand	1840	DUMONT D'URVILLE	480	89	60	Carte de la Partie Orientale des Iles Tavai-Pounamou et Stewart
mwp0197	new zealand	1827	DUMONT D'URVILLE	480	58	86	Carte de la Partie Orientale du l'Ile Ika-Na-Mawi (North Island)
mwas0617	asia south east celebes	1828	DUMONT D'URVILLE	240	39	58	Carte de la Partie Septentrionale de l'Ile Celebes
mwp0397a	pacific new guinea	1840	DUMONT D'URVILLE	400			Carte de la Route des Corvettes l'Astrolabe et de la Zélée à travers le Detroit de Torres (inset 'Plan du Canal Mauvais')
mwp0355	pacific hawaii	1847	DUMONT D'URVILLE	750	61	91	Carte des Iles Hawaii (Sandwich) et des Isles Environnantes ... par Mr. C.A. Vincendon-Dumoulin
mwp0349	pacific hawaii	1834	DUMONT D'URVILLE	400	22	33	Carte des Iles Hawaii pour Servir au Voyage Pittoresque autour du Monde (engr. By A. Tardieu)
mwp0359	pacific loyalty isl.	1828	DUMONT D'URVILLE	180	59	88	Carte des Iles Loyalty

AMPG REFERENCE	REGION	DATE	MAP MAKER	PRICE (UK£)	VERT. (cm.)	HOR. (cm.)	TITLE OF MAP (Comments by the editor in brackets)
mwp0539	pacific tahiti	1834	DUMONT D'URVILLE	280	22	33	Carte des Iles Taiti pour le Voyage autour du Monde de Dumont Durville
mwp0323	pacific friendly isl.	1834	DUMONT D'URVILLE	280	33	22	Carte des Iles Tonga
mwp0395	pacific new guinea	1828	DUMONT D'URVILLE	450	58	87	Carte générale de la côte septentrionale de la Nouvelle Guinée et de la côte meridionale de la Nouvelle Bretagne / reconnues par le Cap.ne de frégate Dumont d'Urville ; levée et dressée par M. Lottin... ; Gravé par Ambroise Tardieu
mwp0216	new zealand	1842	DUMONT D'URVILLE	1200	59	88	Carte generale de la Nouvelle-Zelande (21 insets)
mwp0198	new zealand	1827	DUMONT D'URVILLE	750	59	44	Carte Generale de la Partie de la Nouvelle Zelande Reconnue par le Capitaine de Fregate Dumont d'Urville, Dressee par Mr. Lottin, Enseigne de V. au Expedition de la Corvette de S.M. l'Astrolabe
mwp0282	pacific (all)	1834	DUMONT D'URVILLE	250	34	51	Carte Generale de l'Ocean Pacifique
mwp0199	new zealand	1827	DUMONT D'URVILLE	600	59	89	Carte Particuliere de la Baie Shouraki et du Canal de l'Astrolabe Ile Ika-Na-Mawi, Nlle. Zelande
mwp0200	new zealand	1827	DUMONT D'URVILLE	600	87	60	Carte Particuliere de la Baie Tasman Ile Tavai-Pounamou, Nouvelle Zelande
mwp0396	pacific new guinea	1833	DUMONT D'URVILLE	900	58	87	Carte Particuliere de la Nouvelle Guinee (3 sheets, each 58x87cm.)
mwp0201	new zealand	1827	DUMONT D'URVILLE	600	59	87	Carte Particuliere de la Partie Nord de l'Ile Ika-Na-Mawi
mwp0202	new zealand	1827	DUMONT D'URVILLE	600	59	43	Carte Particuliere de la Partie Sud-Est de l'Ile Ika-Na-Mawi (North Island)
mwp0203	new zealand	1827	DUMONT D'URVILLE	480	42	58	Carte Particuliere du Canal de l'Astrolabe Ile Ika-Na-Mawi, Nlle. Zelande
mwp0204	new zealand	1827	DUMONT D'URVILLE	480	57	87	Carte Particuliere du Detroit de Cook
mwp0205	new zealand	1827	DUMONT D'URVILLE	350	57	41	Plan de la Baie Houa-Houa / Plan de la Baie Wangari
mwp0206	new zealand	1827	DUMONT D'URVILLE	350	58	42	Plan de l'Anse de l'Astrolabe dans la Baie de Tasman (Detroit de Cook)
mwp0474	pacific santa cruz isl.	1828	DUMONT D'URVILLE	400	59	88	Plan des Iles Vanikoro ou de la Perouse
mwp0207	new zealand	1827	DUMONT D'URVILLE	350	43	59	Plan du Bassin des Courants, Detroit de Cook
mwas0744	asia south east moluccas	1828	DUMONT D'URVILLE	240	58	43	Routes de la Corvette l'Astrolabe au Travers des Iles Moluques
mwp0475	pacific santa cruz isl.	1828	DUMONT D'URVILLE	250	43	58	Vanikoro / Kapogo / Partie Septentrionale de l'Ile Celebes et des Iles Banka
mwp0397	pacific new guinea	1838	DUMOULIN	350	42	54	Carte de la Cote Sud-Ouest de la Nouvelle Guinee
mwp0313	pacific fiji	1838	DUMOULIN	200	43	53	Carte de l'Archipel Viti. (inset: Solomon Isl.)
mwas0604	asia south east borneo	1839	DUMOULIN	500	54	41	Carte de l'Ile Borneo Dresse en l'Annee 1835
mwaa0052	antarctic	1841	DUMOULIN	400	59	88	Carte des Explorations Executees par les Corvettes l'Astrolabe et la Zelee dans les Regions Circum-Polaires ... Janvier et Fevrier 1841
mwp0487	pacific solomon isl	1838	DUMOULIN	200	42	54	Carte des Iles Solomon
mwp0366	pacific marianas	1847	DUMOULIN	720	61	90	Carte des Isles Mariannes et des Terres Environnantes (Iles Philippines, Formose, Madjico-Sima, Lou-Chou, Bonin-Sima)
mwme0363a	holy land	1774	DUNN	600	65	48	A Compleat Map of the Holy Land (publ. by Sayer)
mwwi0132	west indies	1794	DUNN	375	30	44	A Compleat Map of the West Indies Containing ... Florida, Louisiana, New Spain and Terra Firma: with All the Islands
mww0482	world	1772	DUNN	8000	104	122	A General Map of the World, or Terraqueous Globe, with all the New Discoveries and Marginal Delineations, Containing the Most Interesting Particulars in the Solar, Starry and Mundane System (publ. by Jefferys. Various editions, incl. one with the title 'Scientia Terrarum'. The 1799 edition is illustrated, publ. by Laurie & Whittle.)
mwaf0409	africa east	1774	DUNN	200	28	38	A Map of Abyssinia and Nubia
mwam0451	america north	1776	DUNN	550	48	30	A Map of the British Empire in North America; by Samuel Dunn, Mathematician
mwme0374	holy land	1786	DUNN	240	30	44	A Map of the Countries and Places, Mentioned in the New Testament
mww0549	world	1787	DUNN	1650	40	58	A Map of the World on a New Projection with a Delineation of the Various Parts and Phaenomena of the Solar System, to Facilitate the Principles and Study of Geography and Astronomy by Benj. Martin. With Improvements and the Additions
mwam0496	america north	1786	DUNN	650	47	31	A New Map of the United States of North America with the British Dominions on that Continent &c.
mwam0237	america continent	1794	DUNN	350	31	44	America North and South and the West Indies; with the Atlantic, Aethiopic and Pacific Ocean: wherein are Distinguished All the Discoveries Lately Made
mwme0664	arabia etc	1794	DUNN	300	31	44	Arabia According to its Modern Divisions
mwuk1012a	england	1774	DUNN	200	41	44	England, or the South Part of Great Britain
mwuk0204	ireland	1774	DUNN	280	37	34	Ireland, divided into its Four Provinces

AMPG REFERENCE	REGION	DATE	MAP MAKER	PRICE (UK£)	VERT. (cm.)	HOR. (cm.)	TITLE OF MAP (Comments by the editor in brackets)
mww0483	world	1772	DUNN	8000	104	122	Scientia Terrarum et Coelorum: or, the Heavens and Earth Astronomically and Geographically Delineated and Display'd. Containing the Most Curious & Useful Particulars in the Solar, Starry, & Mundane Systems, Faithfully Enumerated ... by S. Dunn (as 'A General Map of the World' but publ. by Sayer. Re-issued, updated, in 1781)
mwsam0105	south america	1787	DUNN	250	30	44	South America as Divided amongst the Spaniards and the Portugese, the French and the Dutch
mwsw0192	switzerland	1786	DUNN	250	27	37	Switzerland Divided into Thirteen Cantons with their Subjects and their Allies
mwas0491	asia south east	1774	DUNN	350	30	43	The East India Islands, Comprehending the Isles of Sunda the Moluccas and the Philippine Islands (publ. by Sayer)
mwsc0143	scandinavia	1750	DUNN	650	48	57	The Northern States Comprehending the Kingdoms of Denmark, Norway and Sweden with their Divisions
mwf0152	france	1781	DUPAIN-TRIEL	500	94	93	Carte Generale des Fleuves, des Rivieres, et des Principaux Ruisseaux de la France avec les Canaux Actuellement Construits: A l'Usage de la Navigation Interieure du Royaume
mwf0153	france	1782	DUPAIN-TRIEL	375	52	57	Carte Physique et Hydrographique de la France
mwf0593	france ile de france	1782	DUPAIN-TRIEL	600	47	57	Diocese de Paris
mwf0149	france	1780	DUPAIN-TRIEL	1600	58	90	Plan Topographique de la Ville de Toulouse et de ses Environs
mwit0707	italy rome	1573	DUPERAC	4000	47	61	De Vestigitis Urbis Antiquae
mwit0727	italy rome	1691	DUPERAC-DE ROSSI	20000	106	157	Urbis Romae Sciographia ex Antiquis Monumentis Accuratiss Delineata (Re-issue by De Rossi plus 12 views in side borders. Dimensions excl. views)
mwp0194	new zealand	1824	DUPERREY	400	47	74	Carte de la Baie des Iles
mwp0391	pacific new guinea	1827	DUPERREY	250	50	77	Carte de la Cote de la Nouvelle Guinee depuis le Havre de Doreri jusqu'aux Iles Mispalu
mwp0195	new zealand	1824	DUPERREY	400	50	36	Carte de la Cote Meridionale de l'Ile de Tawai-Poenammou / Carte de l'Ile Ika-Na-Mauwi / Plan du Havre Chalky (3 maps on one sheet)
mwp0480	pacific society isl.	1826	DUPERREY	750	46	73	Carte des Iles de la Societe Dressee d'apres les Observations Faites dans les Trois Voyages de Cook et dans l'Expedition de la Corvette de S.M. la Coquille
mwsam0570a	south america galapagos	1826	DUPERREY	350	50	36	Carte des îles Gallapagos
mwas0616	asia south east celebes	1827	DUPERREY	150	48	74	Carte du Detroit de Wangi-Wangi
mwsam0419	south america brazil	1827	DUPERREY	400	52	37	Carte d'une Partie de la Cote du Bresil Comprise entre le Rio Guaratuba et la Laguna del Gurupaba / Plan de l'Ile Santa Catharina
mwp0340	pacific hawaii	1826	DUPERREY	900	34	50	Plan de la Baie de Kohai-Hai.
mwp0326	pacific guam	1826	DUPERREY	200	34	50	Plan de la Baie d'Umata
mwat0071	atlantic ascension isl.	1825	DUPERREY	600	36	50	Plan de l'Ile de l'Ascension
mwp0392	pacific new guinea	1827	DUPERREY	250	50	77	Plan du Havre de Doreri
mwp0393	pacific new guinea	1827	DUPERREY	250	50	77	Plan du Havre Offak
mwp0481	pacific society isl.	1826	DUPERREY	250	50	37	Plan du Port de l'Ile Borabora Leve par M.M. les Officiers de la Corvette de S.M. la Coquille ... 1823
mwp0341	pacific hawaii	1826	DUPERREY	900	34	50	Plan du Port d'Onorourou
mwp0196	new zealand	1824	DUPERREY	400	47	74	Plan du Port Manawa (Baie des Iles)
mwp0394	pacific new guinea	1827	DUPERREY	250	50	77	Plan d'une Partie des Iles des Papous
mwam0540	america north	1798	DUPONT-BUISSON	650	33	51	Carte des Etats-Unis Provinces Septentrionalis
mwf0862	france paris	1738	DUPRE	1400	42	59	Nouveau Plan de la Ville de Paris et de ses Faubourgs
mwgm0248	mexico	1780	DUPUIS	480	44	35	(Baja California and Sonora)
mwm0070	mediterranean	1785	DUPUIS	1200	55	107	Carte de la Mer Mediterranee
mwgr0222	greece	1785	DUPUIS	550	49	63	Carte de la Morée Anciennement Peloponnèse 1785
mwp0441	pacific north	1790	DUPUIS	400	26	37	Carte de la Partie Septentrionale de la Mer du Sud
mwbh0729	belgium holland	1777	DUPUIS	800	57	90	Plan Topographique de la Ville de Bruxelles
mwwi0431	cuba	1741	DURELL	4000	47	57	A Plan of Cumberland Harbour on ye So. Side of Cuba Formerly Call'd Walltenam Bay (now Guantanamo Bay)
mwsam0517	south america colombia	1741	DURELL	2000	52	75	A Plan of the Harbour Town & Castles of Carthagena
mww0023a	world	1515	DURER		66	86	(Untitled map, printed from 4 wood blocks. No original has survived but the blocks were discovered in 1780 and printed in 1781 - illustrated here.)
mwuss0364	delaware	1776	DURY	3500	47	71	A Chart of Delaware Bay and River; Containing a Full and Exact Description of the Shores, Creeks, Harbours, Soundings, Shoals, Sands and Bearings, of the Most Considerable Land Marks, from the Capes to Philadelphia ... by Joshua Fisher
mwec0642	uk england kent	1769	DURY, ANDREWS	350	49	71	A Map of the County of Kent (key to his 1769 map in 25 sheets)
mwuss1120	new york	1777	DURY	4000	142	92	A Map of the Province of New York, with Part of Pensilvania, and New England, from an Actual Survey by Captain Montresor

AMPG REFERENCE	REGION	DATE	MAP MAKER	PRICE (UK£)	VERT. (cm.)	HOR. (cm.)	TITLE OF MAP (Comments by the editor in brackets)
mwuk1235	england london	1777	DURY	1200	80	69	A New and Accurate Map of the Country Fifteen Miles round Richmond. On which are Delineated from an Actual Survey his Majesty's Palaces, Noblemen and Gentlemen's Seats, Cities, Market Towns, Villages, Churches, Cottages, Rivers, Mills
mwuss0821	massachusetts	1776	DURY	27500	46	65	A Plan of Boston and its Environs, Shewing the True Situation of His Majesty's Army. And also those of the Rebels
mwuk1207a	england london	1764	DURY	240	10	19	A Plan of the Cities of London & Westminster (size excl. text panels)
mwec0640a	uk england kent	1768	DURY	750	49	61	A Plan of the City of Canterbury
mwuss1366	pennsylvania	1776	DURY	9500	50	67	A Plan of the City of Philadelphia, the Capital of Pennsylvania, from Actual Survey by Benjamin Easburn ... 1776
mwca0488	canada prince edward island	1775	DURY	1200	36	69	A Plan of the Island of St. John with the Divisions of the Counties, Parishes, & the Lots as Granted by the Government ... Surveyed by Capt. Holland, 1775
mwec0556	uk england hertfordshire	1766	DURY	2400	153	207	A Topographical Map of Hartford-shire, from an Actual Survey
mwec0557	uk england hertfordshire	1766	DURY	250	53	70	A Topographical Map of Hartford-shire, Taken from an Actual Survey (key for larger map, 1766)
mwec0641	uk england kent	1769	DURY, ANDREWS	6000	227	332	A Topographical-Map of the County of Kent (engraved by John Andrews in 25 sheets)
mwam0425	america north	1761	DURY	300	10	12	North America.
mwca0081	canada	1761	DURY	140	11	24	Canada
mwuk1003	england	1760	DURY	250			England and Wales, With the Post & Cross Roads
mwuk0186	ireland	1761	DURY	95	12	10	Ireland.
mwaf1196	africa west	1742	DURY	120	12	13	Map of Senegal, with part of the Coast of Africa
mwuk1013	england	1775	DURY	685	57	48	The Post Roads through England and Wales (re-issue of Jefferys 1765)
mwuss1105	new york	1776	DURY	600	71	39	To Sir Jeffery Amherst ... this Map of the Province of New York
mwuk1218	england london	1769	DURY & BELL	1200	65	86	Environs of London
mwam0776	america north	1846	DUSSIEUX	300	28	38	Carte des Etats-Unis
mwgm0365	mexico	1848	DUVAL LITHO.	450	31	32	Plan of Santa Cruz de Rosales & Operations of U.S. Troops under Gen. S. Price during the Siege 16th Mar. 1848
			SEE ALSO DU VAL, ABOVE				
mwgm0343	mexico	1843	DUVOTENAY	100	18	23	Anahuac Comprenant les Royaumes de Mexico d'Acalhuacan, de Mechoacan et les Republiques Tlascala
mwwi0217	west indies	1848	DUVOTENAY	100	23	31	Antilles ou Indes Occidentales
mwas0603	asia south east borneo	1835	DUVOTENAY	160	18	23	Esquisse d'une Carte Geographique et Ethnographique de L'Isle Kalemantan ou Borneo
mwm0263a	mediterranean malta	1850	DUVOTENAY	120	17	11	Iles de Malte et du Goze
mwm0263	mediterranean malta	1846	DUVOTENAY	250	26	34	Malte
mwuss1521	texas	1843	DUVOTENAY	750	26	18	Mexique
mwgm0343a	mexico	1843	DUVOTENAY	100	18	23	Mexico et Guatemala
mwm0263b	mediterranean malta	1850	DUVOTENAY	120	11	17	Plan Géométral de la Ville & du Port de Malte
mwsam0816	south america uruguay	1850	DUVOTENAY	200	23	18	Provinces Unies du Rio de la Plata, Paraguay, Uruguay and Chili
mwuss0308	connecticut	1821	DWIGHT	300	28	34	Map of the Southern Part of New England Compiled for Prest Dwight's Travels by George Gillet Esq. 1821
mwuss1191	new york	1823	DWIGHT	300	29	30	Map of the State of New York
mwf0929	france paris	1841	DYONNET	950	80	90	Plan de Paris (4 decorative borders)
mwec0053	uk england berkshire	1825	EBDEN	400	36	45	Ebden's New Map of the County Berkshire; Divided into Hundreds Laid down from Trigonometrical Observations
mwec0077	uk england buckinghamshire	1825	EBDEN	400	46	37	Ebden's New Map of the County Buckinghamshire; Divided into Hundreds Laid down from Trigonometrical Observations
mwec1287	uk england worcestershire	1825	EBDEN	400	37	45	Ebden's New Map of the County of Worcestershire; Divided into Hundreds Laid down from Trigonometrical Observation
mwec0836	uk england norfolk	1811	EBDEN	500	73	59	Laurie & Whittle's New Map of Norfolk and Suffolk, Divided into Hundreds; Exhibiting the Whole of the Mail, Direct, and Principal Cross Roads, Gentlemen's Seats, Rivers, &c.
mwec0564	uk england hertfordshire	1825	EBDEN	400	37	45	Map of the County of Hertfordshire; Divided into Hundreds Laid down from Trigonometrical Observations
mwg0545	rheinland-pfalz	1822	EBERHARD	1800	51	214	Panorama der Stadt Mainz
mww0168	world	1658	ECKEBRECHT	40000	38	68	Nova Orbis Terrarum Delineatio Singulari Ratione Accommodata Meridiano Tabb. Rudolphi Astronomicarum (the map is dated 1630 but published in 1658 or later)
mww0611	world	1800	ECKER-SCHRAEMBL	2500	68	61	Die Obere oder Nordliche Halbkugel der Erde auf den Horizont von Wien, Sterographisch Entworfen / Die Untere oder Sudliche Halbkugel der Erde auf den Horizont von Wien, Stereographisch (2 circular polar maps)
mwaf1243a	africa west	1816	EDDY	200			A Map of part of Africa ... Captain James Riley

AMPG REFERENCE	REGION	DATE	MAP MAKER	PRICE (UK£)	VERT. (cm.)	HOR. (cm.)	TITLE OF MAP (Comments by the editor in brackets)
mwuss1180	new york	1811	EDDY	1400	58		A Map of the Country Thirty Miles Round the City of New York (circular folding map)
mwuss0142	california	1852	EDDY	3000	58	51	A Topographical & Complete Map of San Francisco. Compiled from the Original Map
mwuss1179	new york	1811	EDDY	1400	28	53	Map of the Western Part of the State of New York
mwuss0124	california	1849	EDDY	1250	64	51	Official Map of San Francisco Compiled from the Field Notes of the Official Re-Survey Made by William M. Eddy
mwuss0892	massachusetts	1844	EDDY	1250	58	88	Plan of East Boston, Exhibiting the Land & Water Lots & other Improvements
mwuss1186	new york	1818	EDDY	3000	97	110	The State of New York with Part of the Adjacent States
mwit0821c	italy sardinia	1796	EDER	400	35	30	Karte von der Insel und dem Königreiche Sardinien (shown above left)
mwuk0480	scotland	1742	EDGAR	550	32	60	The Plan of the City and Castle of Edinburgh
mwg0472	hessen	1850	EDLER	960	40	56	Plan der Stadt Hanau
mwuss1506a	texas	1836	EDWARD	3000	32	22	Map of Texas, Containing the Latest Grants and Discoveries by E.F. Lee. Published by J.A. James & Co. Cincinnati 1836
mwwi0746	jamaica	1794	EDWARDS	500	31	61	A Map of the Island of Jamaica, Divided into Counties and Parishes for the History of the British West Indies by Bryan Edwards Esqr. 1794
mwwi0668	hispaniola	1800	EDWARDS	500	45	91	A Map of the Island of St. Domingo
mwwi0128	west indies	1793	EDWARDS	1250	69	112	A New Map of the West Indies for the History of the British Colonies
mwp0368	pacific marquesas	1798	EDWARDS	250	24	19	Hergest's Islands Discovered by the Daedalus Store Ship, Lieut. Hergest Commdr.
mwwi0306	antigua	1794	EDWARDS	240	18	23	Map of the Island Antigua for the History of the West Indies, by Bryan Edwards Esqr.
mwwi0383	barbados	1794	EDWARDS	300	24	19	Map of the Island of Barbadoes for the History of the West Indies
mwwi0513	dominica	1794	EDWARDS	180	22	17	Map of the Island of Dominica for the History of the West Indies
mwwi0529	grenada	1794	EDWARDS	250	24	18	Map of the Island of Grenada, for the History of the West Indies
mwwi0870	st kitts	1794	EDWARDS	240	19	23	Map of the Island of St. Christopher's, for the History of the West Indies
mwwi0904	trinidad & tobago	1794	EDWARDS	250	20	24	Map of the Island of Tobago for the History of the West Indies
mwwi0932	virgin isl	1794	EDWARDS	250	18	23	Map of the Virgin Islands, for the History of the West Indies by Bryan Edwards Esqr.
mwuss0037	alaska	1798	EDWARDS	250	18	23	Port Dick, near Cook's Inlet
mwuk0251	ireland	1811	EDWARDS & SAVAGE	8750	133	224	The County of Cork
mwsc0470a	scandinavia greenland	1785	EGEDE	350	39	29	Kort over Grönland
mww0372	world	1735	EHMANN	1000	42	57	Universal-Historie auf der Land-Karten
mwaf1080a	africa south west	1806	EHRMANN	250	42	31	Charte von Nieder-Guinea (publ. by Weimar)
mwuss0653	louisiana	1804	EHRMANN	250	22	17	Louisiana
mwam1074a	america north (east)	1781	ELIOT	4500	70	52	Carte du Theatre de la Guerre Actuel entre Les Anglais et les Treize Colonies Unies
mwuss1431	pennsylvania	1839	ELLET	3750	85	149	A Map of the County of Philadelphia from Actual Survey
mwuss0952	mississippi	1803	ELLICOTT	300	38	30	(Mississippi River)
mwuss1275	ohio	1803	ELLICOTT	300	30	44	(Ohio River, from Cincinnati to Pittsburgh)
mwuss1174	new york	1804	ELLICOTT	3500	51	66	Map of Morris's Purchase or West Geneseo in the State of New York: Exhibiting Part of the Lakes Erie and Ontario, the Straights of Niagara, Chautauque Lake and All the Principal Waters
mwuss0332	washington DC	1792	ELLICOTT	16000	22	26	Plan of the City of Washington (publ. in the Columbian Magazine)
mwuss0335	washington DC	1793	ELLICOTT	2000	24	29	Plan of the City of Washington (publ. in the Literary Magazine)
mwuss0333	washington DC	1792	ELLICOTT	24000	52	71	Plan of the City of Washington in the Territory of Columbia, Ceded by the States of Virginia and Maryland to the United States of America, and by them Established as the Seat of their Government, after the Year MDCCC
mwuss0336	washington DC	1793	ELLICOTT	2000	27	34	Plan of the City of Washington; Now Building for the Metropolis of America, and Established as the Permanent Residence of Congress after the Year 1800 (publ. in the Universal Magazine)
mwuss0003	alabama	1803	ELLICOTT	1500	27	51	Southern Boundary of the United States
mwuss0334	washington DC	1793	ELLICOTT	20000	58	55	Territory of Columbia
mwuss0351	washington DC	1835	ELLIOT	1500	41	46	Plan of the City of Washington, Seat of Government of the United States
mwec0925	uk england nottinghamshire	1825	ELLIS	1400	58	44	A Map of the County of Nottingham ... Made from an Actual Survey by T.J. Ellis in the Years 1824 and 1825 (4 sheets of 58x44cm.)
mwec0146	uk england cheshire	1766	ELLIS	100	20	25	A Modern Map of Cheshire
mwec0486	uk england hampshire	1766	ELLIS	100	20	25	A Modern Map of Hampshire
mwec0526	uk england herefordshire	1766	ELLIS	100	25	20	A Modern Map of Herefordshire

AMPG REFERENCE	REGION	DATE	MAP MAKER	PRICE (UK£)	VERT. (cm.)	HOR. (cm.)	TITLE OF MAP (Comments by the editor in brackets)
mwec0690	uk england lancashire	1766	ELLIS	100	24	19	A Modern Map of Lancashire
mwec0890	uk england northumberland	1766	ELLIS	100	25	20	A Modern Map of Northumberland
mwec1112	uk england suffolk	1766	ELLIS	100	20	25	A Modern Map of Suffolk
mwec1254	uk england wiltshire	1766	ELLIS	100	25	19	A Modern Map of Wiltshire
mwec1283	uk england worcestershire	1766	ELLIS	100	25	19	A Modern Map of Worcestershire
mwsc0465	scandinavia greenland	1750	ELLIS	480	27	36	Alt Groenland (from the German edition of Ellis' Voyage to Hudson's Bay, first publ. 1748)
mwec0023	uk england bedfordshire	1819	ELLIS	75	18	27	Bedfordshire
mwec0109	uk england cambridgeshire	1819	ELLIS	75	18	27	Cambridgeshire
mwf0517a	france corsica	1768	ELLIS	600	42	21	Carte de l'Isle de Corse...
mwec0423	uk england essex	1819	ELLIS	75	18	27	Essex
mwuk1609	isle of man	1768	ELLIS	235	26	19	Isle of Man
mwec0865	uk england northamptonshire	1766	ELLIS	100	25	19	Modern Map of Northampton-Shire
mwca0065	canada	1750	ELLIS	400	17	44	Neue Karte, von den Gegenden wo eine Nordwest Durchfahrt in den Iahren 1746, 1747 Gesucht ward, nebst dem Laufe der Schiffe auf Dieser Ganzen Reise
mwec0838	uk england norfolk	1819	ELLIS	100	18	27	Norfolk
mwec0968	uk england oxfordshire	1819	ELLIS	75	18	27	Oxfordshire
mwuss1695	wisconsin	1836	ELLIS	5500	43	60	Plat of Navarino Green Bay, Wisconsin Territory 1836
mwec1147	uk england surrey	1819	ELLIS	75	18	27	Surrey
mwam0634	america north	1823	ELLIS	200	30	23	United States
mwp0346	pacific hawaii	1826	ELLIS-FISHER	450	18	24	Chart of the Sandwich Isles
mwp0347	pacific hawaii	1826	ELLIS-FISHER	450	23	19	Map of Hawaii, the Largest of the Sandwich Islands. Improved from Vancouver's Survey
mwec0640	uk england kent	1765	ELLIS-SAYER	120	19	24	A Modern Map of Kent
mwuk0484	scotland	1745	ELPHINSTONE	1000	67	53	A New & Correct Mercator's Map of North Britain Carefully Laid down from the Latest Surveys and Most Approved Observations
mwuk0819	uk	1743	ELPHINSTONE	1000	45	56	To his Excellency John Earl of Stair ... This Map of Great Britain & Ireland
mww0097	world	1598	ELSHEIMER	7500	23	30	(No title. Map illustrates the first Dutch expedition to the Cape and the East, led by Houtman)
mwaf0174	africa	1739	ELSWORTH	200	18	25	Viro Optimo Maximoque, Minorum Gentium Patricio, Philippo Sydenham - Africa
mwam0517	america north	1792	ELWE	900	47	58	Amerique Septentrionale Divisee en ses Principales Parties
mwaf1238a	africa west	1792	ELWE	400	49	57	Carte de la Barbarie de la Nigritie et de la Guinee (copy of De L'Isle 1712)
mwme0834	persia etc	1792	ELWE	600	48	56	Carte de la Perse, de l'Armenie, de la Natolie & de l'Arabie (re-issue of De Wit 1680 with changed title)
mwaf0965	africa south	1792	ELWE	685	51	58	Carte de l'Afrique Meridionale ou Pays entre la Ligne & le Cap de Bonne Esperance (re-issue of Visscher 1710)
mwaf0421a	africa east	1792	ELWE	500	49	57	Carte de l'Egypte, de la Nubie, de l'Abissine (copy of De L'Isle)
mwsc0184	scandinavia	1792	ELWE	450	51	60	Carte des Courones du Nord (copy of De L'Isle)
mwbh0755a	belgium holland	1792	ELWE	450	50	59	Carte Generale des Provincies Unies des Pais Bas (copy of Husson 1706)
mwru0301	russia	1792	ELWE	550	41	55	Carte Nouvelle de Moscovie Represente la Partie Septentrionale / Carte Nouvelle de Moscovie Represente la Partie Meridionale (2 maps, each 41x55cm.)
mwbh0755a	belgium holland	1792	ELWE	500	50	59	Carte Nouvelle des Pays Bas Catholiques
mwf0156	france	1788	ELWE	500	49	59	Carte Nouvelle du Royaume de France Divise en Toutes les Provinces et ses Acquisitions (re-issue of Husson 1708 without title above map)
mwgm0057a	gulf of mexico and surrounding regions	1792	ELWE	1200	48	58	De Golf van Mexico, de Eilanden en het Omleggende Land (reprint of Jaillot/Ottens)
mwme0658	arabia etc	1788	ELWE	500	45	61	Estats de l'Empire du Grand Seigneur des Turcs, en Europe, en Asie, et en Afrique, Divise en Tous ses Beglerbeglicz, ou Gouvernements (copy of Jaillot / Ottens)
mwe0212	europe	1787	ELWE	720	49	59	Europe, Compossee par G. de l'Isle et Correge selon les Plus Nouvelle Observations
mwme0378	holy land	1792	ELWE	600	50	59	Generale Kaart van het Beloofde Land tot Verlichting voor de Geschiedenisse, Vervat in den Bybel (copied from De Wit 1686 with a different title)
mwbp0521	poland	1792	ELWE	600	48	60	La Pologne Divisee en Royaume de Pologne et les Etats y Apartenans la Pologne Prussienne Autrichienne & Russienne (copied from Jaillot 1694)
mwaf0268	africa	1792	ELWE	550	46	58	L'Afrique Divisee en ses Empires, Royaumes et Etats (re-issue of Jaillot 1694)
mwsam0113	south america	1792	ELWE	550	47	61	L'Amerique Meridionale Divisee en ses Principales Parties (re-issue of Jaillot 1694)
mwas0219	asia continent	1792	ELWE	600	47	58	L'Asie Divisee en ses Empires, Royaumes, et Etats, Corrigee (uncorrected copy of Jaillot 1692)
mwe0822	europe east	1787	ELWE	600	43	55	Le Royaume de Hongrie et les Estats qui ont este Unis a sa Couronne Chez Elwe & Langeveld (re-issue of Jaillot 1717 with cartouches reversed etc.)

AMPG REFERENCE	REGION	DATE	MAP MAKER	PRICE (UK£)	VERT. (cm.)	HOR. (cm.)	TITLE OF MAP (Comments by the editor in brackets)
mwsp0306	spain	1792	ELWE	450	50	58	Les Royaumes d'Espagne et de Portugal (copy of Allard 1700)
mwit0214	italy	1792	ELWE	450	46	55	L'Italie Dressee sur les Observations ... (reduced size copy of De L'Isle 1700)
mww0573	world	1792	ELWE	2400	49	61	Mappe Monde ou Description du Globe Terrestre & Aquatique (copy of Jaillot 1694 with no title above map)
mwaf0251a	africa	1785	ELWE	200	18	22	Nieuwe Generale Kaart van Afrika
mwam0217	america continent	1785	ELWE	300	18	22	Nieuwe Generale Kaart van Amerika
mwas0202a	asia continent	1785	ELWE	200	18	22	Nieuwe Generale Kaart van Asia (engraved by Krevelt)
mwe0207a	europe	1785	ELWE	200	18	22	Nieuwe Generale Kaart van Europa
mwru0571a	ukraine	1787	ELWE	800	51	60	Nouvelle Carte de la Petite Tartarie ou Taurie, Montrant les Frontieres de l'Imperatrice de Russie et l'Empereur des Turcs, tant en Europe qu'en Asie
mwas0516a	asia south east	1792	ELWE	2800	50	60	Nouvelle Grande Carte des Indes Orientales ... (set of 4 maps, each 50x60cm. Re-issue of Ottens 1725)
mwin0301	india	1792	ELWE	900	50	60	Partie de la Nouvelle Grande Carte des Indes Orientales, contenant les Terres du Mogol (re-issue of sheet 1 from a 4-part set by Ottens. See Ottens 1725 for the complete set)
mww0574	world	1792	ELWE	960	43	27	Planisphere Representant Toute l'Etendue du Monde (re-issue of Renard's 1715 frontispiece map)
mwbp0522	poland	1792	ELWE	600	44	60	Regni Borussiae Secundum Observationes Novissima, Acuratissima Descriptio (title also in French. Copy of Ottens)
mww0535	world	1785	ELWE	450	13	21	Universele of Waereld-Kaart Volgens de Laatste Ontdekkingen van Capt. Cook
mwme0418	holy land	1839	ELY	350	64	41	The Holy Land. A New Map of Palestine
mwuss1427	pennsylvania	1836	ELY & HAMMOND	1800	55	58	Map of Pennsylvania
mwbh0187a	belgium holland	1616	EMMIUS	1500	42	55	Typum hunc Frisiae Orientalis ... 1595 (inset of Embden)
mwuss0052	arizona	1854	EMORY	400	20	25	Map of the Valleys of the Rio Grande and Rio Gila
mww0549a	world	1787	ENDASIAN	4000	46	64	(World map with Armenian/Amharic script)
mwam0222	america continent	1787	ENDASIAN	3000	46	64	(Map of America with Armenian/Amharic script)
mwas0204	asia continent	1787	ENDASIAN	1500	46	64	(Map of Asia with Armenian/Amharic script)
mwaf0255a	africa	1787	ENDASIAN	1500	46	64	(Map of Africa with Armenian/Amharic script)
mwe0211a	europe	1787	ENDASIAN	1500	46	64	(Map of Europe with Armenian/Amharic script)
mwbp0448	poland	1753	ENDERSCH	1800	46	56	Mappa Geographica Trium Insularum in Prussia
mwbp0450	poland	1755	ENDERSCH	1800	51	57	Tabula Geographica Episcopatum Warmiensem in Prussia Exhibens
mwam0799	america north	1850	ENDICOTT	400	38	42	Map of the Sites of the Indian Tribes of North America when First Known to the Europeans about 1600 A.D. along the Atlantic and about 1800 A.D. on the Pacific
mwuss0125	california	1849	ENDICOTT	8000	34	82	San Francisco 1849 (view)
mwas0898	asia south east sumatra	1847	ENDICOTT	500	96	109	The West Coast of Sumatra from Analaboo to Sinkel (sea chart, first edition 1833)
mwin0323	india	1800	ENDNER	450	35	34	Charte von Indostan
mwam1320	america north (west)	1764	ENGEL	1200	48	74	Carte de la Partie Septentrionale et Occidentale de l'Amerique
mwp0414a	pacific north	1764	ENGEL	950	48	69	Carte de la Partie Septentrionale et Orientale de L'Asie
mwsc0633	scandinavia norway	1779	ENGEL	960	41	56	Nouvelle Carte des Isles de Spizbergue et des environs
mwg0822	westphalia	1740	ENGELBRECHT	500	18	30	Dusseldorpium Dusseldorff (view)
mwit0542a	italy milan	1735	ENGELBRECHT	2000	37	41	Mediolanum Mayland (view)
mwsam0270	south america bolivia	1740	ENGELBRECHT	100	27	37	Potosi (view)
mwit0680a	italy piedmont	1735	ENGELBRECHT	2000	38	41	Taurinum Turin. (view)
mwbp0441	poland	1750	ENGELBRECHT	800	37	42	Uratislavia Bresslau (view)
mwbp0444	poland	1751	ENGELBRECHT	800	18	30	Warsovia. Warschau (view)
mwbp0554	poland	1812	ENGELHARDT	1800	88	93	Carte du Duche de Varsovie et des Etats qui l'Environnent en IV Feuilles
mwuk1361	england north	1828	ENGELMANN	5000	69	632	A Plan & Section of an Intended Railway or Tram Road from the Town & County of Newcastle upon Tyne to the City of Carlisle
mww0689a	world	1830	ENGELMANN	450	31	46	Welt-karte der Mission
mwuk0887	uk	1828	ENOUY	600	71	60	The United Kingdom of Great Britain & Ireland, with the Adjacent Parts of the Continent, from Amsterdam, to Paris and Brest
mwuss1253	new york	1845	ENSIGN	4500	64	112	City of New York by T. & E.H. Ensign. 36 Ann Street. 1845
mwuss1254	new york	1845	ENSIGN	1000	54	72	Distance Map of the State of New York, Containing All the Towns in the State
mwam0768a	america north	1845	ENSIGN	2000	61	104	Ensign's Travellers' Guide and Map of the United States, Containing the Roads, Distances, Steam Boat and Canal Routes &c 1845
mwuss1533	texas	1846	ENSIGN	2400	15	12	Map of Texas and Part of Mexico Reduced and Compiled from the Congressional Map and other Recent Authorities ... 1846
mwam0775	america north	1846	ENSIGN	2000	89	105	Map of the United States from the Latest Authorities
mww0727a	world	1844	ENSIGN	1500	75	109	Map of the World on Mercator's Projection
mwuss0898	massachusetts	1848	ENSIGN & THAYER	685	64	85	Map of Massachusetts, Rhode-Island & Connecticut
mwam0785	america north	1847	ENSIGN & THAYER	600	72	57	Map of New England

AMPG REFERENCE	REGION	DATE	MAP MAKER	PRICE (UK£)	VERT. (cm.)	HOR. (cm.)	TITLE OF MAP (Comments by the editor in brackets)
mwuss1263	new york	1850	ENSIGN & THAYER	800	41	51	Map of the City of New York, with Adjacent Cities of Brooklyn and Jersey City, & the Village of Williamsburg
mwuss0126	california	1849	ENSIGN & THAYER	3500	71	52	Map of the Gold Regions of California. Showing the Routes via Chagres and Panama, Cape Horn, &c. (large inset of the Americas)
mwgm0357	mexico	1847	ENSIGN & THAYER	1800	72	54	Map of the Seat of War (map and text)
mwam1378	america north (west)	1848	ENSIGN & THAYER	1500	45	58	Map of the Western States
mwam0789	america north	1848	ENSIGN & THAYER	1500	75	54	Ornamental Map of the United States & Mexico - Map of the United States and Mexico Including Oregon, Texas and the Californias
mwam1379	america north (west)	1848	ENSIGN & THAYER	2000	79	60	Pictorial Map of the Great West. Ohio, Michigan, Illinois, Indiana, Wisconsin, Missouri, & Iowa (map and text)
mwam0786	america north	1847	ENSIGN & THAYER	1500	72	101	Pictorial Map of the United States
mwww0742	world	1847	ENSIGN & THAYER	500	53	73	World at One View
mwam0431	america north	1763	ENTICK	350	19	23	A New & Accurate Map of North America, Including the British Acquisitions Gain'd by the Late War
mwwi0100	west indies	1763	ENTICK	200	20	23	A New & Accurate Map of the Seat of the Late War in the West Indies with a Plan of the City and Harbour of Havannah
mwwi0789	martinique	1763	ENTICK	200	18	23	A New and Accurate Map of the Island of Martinico
mwin0237	india	1763	ENTICK	200	24	20	A New and Accurate Map of the Seat of the Late War on the Coast of Choromandel in the East Indies
mwca0609	canada st lawrence	1766	ENTICK	200	17	24	A New and Accurate Plan of the River St. Lawrence, from the Falls of Montmorenci to Sillery; with the Operations of the Seige of Quebec 1763
mwca0384	canada nova scotia	1758	ENTICK	250	18	24	A Plan of the Harbour and Town of Louisbourg in the Island of Cape Breton, Drawn on the Spot
mwsp0673	balearic islands	1764	ENTICK	320	25	20	New Accurate Map of Minorca with Town and Harbor of Mahon
mwm0254	mediterranean malta	1799	EPHEM	550	16	27	Die Insels Malta, Gozzo und Cumino
mwm0255	mediterranean malta	1799	EPHEM	450	21	27	Plan von La Valetta
mwsc0509	scandinavia iceland	1780	ERIKSSON	1800	44	56	Nouvelle Carte d'Islande d'apres celle des Professeurs Erichsen et Schoenning
mwsc0508	scandinavia iceland	1771	ERIKSSON	1800	45	57	Nyt Carte over Island
mwf0554	france corsica	1828	ERSCH & GRUBER	240	22	17	Corsika
mwaf0369	africa east	1674	ESCHINARDI	2500	71	92	Imperii Abassini Tabula Geographica
mwf0895a	france paris	1784	ESNAUTS	600	51	76	Nouveau Plan des Environs de Paris
mwf0895	france paris	1784	ESNAUTS	900	55	79	Nouveau Plan Routier de la Ville et Fauxbourgs de Paris (first issue 1776)
mwuss1654	virginia	1784	ESNAUTS ET RAPILLY	28000	46	60	Carte de la Partie de la Virginie ou l'Armee Combinee de France & des Etats-Unis de l'Amerique a Fait Prisonniere l'Armee Anglaise
mwgm0210a	mexico	1748	ESPINOSA	2000	37	43	Mapa de las Aguas que por el circulo de 90 leguas uienen a la Laguna de Tescuco y de la estension que esta y la de Chalco tenian sacado del que en el siglo antecedente deligneò Carlos de Siguenza
mwsp0689	balearic islands	1812	ESPINOSA Y TELLO	750	62	92	Carta Esferica de las Yslas Baleares y Pithyusas, Arreglada a la que se Construyo en 1807
mwgm0094	costa rica	1699	ESQUEMELING	240	11	18	A Description of Golfe Dulce
mwsam0030	south america	1685	ESQUEMELING	1000	33	25	A Description of the South Sea & Coasts of America Containing ye Whole Navigation and All those Places at which Capt: Sharp and his Companions were in the Years 1680 & 1681
mwgm0385	panama	1695	ESQUEMELING	300	14	11	A Description of ye Laguna or Gulf of Ballona
mwgm0383	panama	1684	ESQUEMELING	500	17	28	A Map of the Countrey and Citty of Panama
mwgm0095	costa rica	1699	ESQUEMELING	180	11	18	Gulf of Nicoya Described
mwsam0481	south america juan fernandez	1684	ESQUEMELING	240	13	10	Isla de Juan Fernandez
mwgm0387	panama	1699	ESQUEMELING	875	18	28	The Battle between the Spaniards and the Pyrates or Buccaneers before the Citty of Panama
mwgm0386	panama	1695	ESQUEMELING	400	14	13	The Bay of Panama and Gulf of Ballona
mwsam0825	south america venezuela	1684	ESQUEMELING	450	17	27	The Spanish Armada Destroyed by Captaine Morgan
mwwi0412	cuba	1684	ESQUEMELING	280	16	11	Towne of Puerto del Principe Cuba Taken by Buccaneers
mwwi0489	cuba	1835	ESTRUC	9000	127	381	Carta Geogro. Topografica de la Isla de Cuba Dedicanla a la Reyna nuestra Senora Dona Isabel II
mwin0048	ceylon	1745	ESVELDT & HOLTROP	200	10	13	Het Eiland Ceilon, Volgens de Nieuwste Waarneminge
mwuk0999	england	1753	EULER	200	37	32	Anglia et Wallia
mwww0415	world	1750	EULER	1200	34	38	Carte des Differentes Operations Faites pour Determiner la Figure de la Terre
mwbh0703	belgium holland	1753	EULER	200	31	36	Mappa Geograph. Circuli Westphalici, Rhenani Superioris, Belgii Foederati et Catholici
mwam0404	america north	1750	EULER	1800	34	35	Mappa Geographica Americae Septentrionalis ad Emendatiora Exemplaria adhuc Edita (4 maps of 34x35cm.)
mwuk0172	ireland	1750	EULER	320	37	32	Mappa Geographica Regni Hiberniae

AMPG REFERENCE	REGION	DATE	MAP MAKER	PRICE (UK£)	VERT. (cm.)	HOR. (cm.)	TITLE OF MAP (Comments by the editor in brackets)
mww0424	world	1753	EULER	650	32	38	Mappa Mundi Generalis ad Emendatiora Exempla adhuc Edita
mwas0165	asia continent	1753	EULER	400	33	38	Tab. Geogr. Asiae
mwru0220	russia	1753	EULER	240	32	36	Tab. Geogr. Imperii Russici
mwme0343	holy land	1753	EULER	450	32	37	Tab. Geogr. Palaestinae
mwam0170	america continent	1753	EULER	500	31	36	Tab: Geogr. Americae ad Emendatiora
mwuk0836	uk	1753	EULER	240	31	37	Tabula Geograph. Magnae Britanniae
mwe0171	europe	1753	EULER	450	60	69	Tabula Geographica Europae ad Emendatiora Exempla adhuc Edita
mww0425	world	1753	EULER	1200	31		Tabula Geographica Hemispherii Borealis / Australis (2 circular maps, 31cm. diameter)
mwp0412	pacific north	1760	EULER	1200	32	37	Tabula Geographica Partis Septentrionalis Maris Pacifici cum Adjacentibus Regionibus Superime tam a Russis Orientem (reduced size re-issue of Buache's map, 1750)
mwuk0501	scotland	1753	EULER	200	38	30	Tabula Geographica Scotiae
mww0426	world	1753	EULER	650	32	37	Tabula Geographica utriusque Hemisphaerii Terrestris
mwam0482	america north	1783	EUROPEAN MAG.	350	21	25	A Map of the United States of America, as Settled by the Peace of 1783
mwit0228	italy	1814	EUSTACE	240	43	10	Italy
mwam0969	america north (east)	1755	EVANS	80000	50	67	A General Map of the Middle British Colonies, in America; viz. Virginia, Mariland, Delaware, Pensilvania, New-Jersey, New-York, Connecticut and Rhode Island ... and Part of New France (for illustration see Bowles re-issue of 1771)
mwam1036a	america north	1776	EVANS	16000	50	81	A Map of the Middle British Colonies in North America. First Published by Mr. Lewis Evans, of Philadelphia, in 1755; and Since Corrected and Improved, as also Extended, with the Addition of New England, and Bordering Parts of Canada
mwuk1266	england london	1799	EVANS	2500	56	103	A New & Accurate Plan of the Cities of London & Westminster & Borough of Southwark with the New Roads & New Buildings
mww0605	world	1799	EVANS	5500	56	104	A New Map of the World. with All the New Discoveries. By Capt. Cook and Other Navigators Ornamented with the Solar System the Eclipses of the Sun Moon & Planets &c. (copy of Kitchin 1794)
mwp0070	australia	1823	EVANS	1350	57	44	Carte de la Terre de Van Diemen Dressee par G.W. Evans, Arpenteur General d'Hobart-Town 1822 (Illustrated is the French edition publ. in 1823. The first edition, in English, was publ. in 1822)
mwuss1037	new jersey	1747	EVANS	11000	43	35	Map No. II (central and northern New Jersey incl. New York city)
mwam0716	america north	1838	EVANS	350	28	23	N. America & the West Indies
mwuk1863	wales	1795	EVANS	2000	52	59	To Sir Watkin Williams Wynn ... This Map of the Six Counties of North Wales (map in 9 sections, each 52x59cm.)
mwuk1864	wales	1797	EVANS	450	73	62	To Sir Watkin Williams Wynn, Bart. this Map of North Wales is Respectfully Inscribed
mwp0173a	australia	1849	EWALD	240	36	45	Australien (incl. New Zealand)
mwwi0460	cuba	1774	EXSHAW	250	18	18	Plan of the City and Harbour of Havanna
mwbh0282	belgium holland	1641	FABIUS	500	33	45	Nova Antiquae Flandriae Geographica Tabula
mwe1085	europe slovak republic (moravia)	1569	FABRICUS		98	83	Chorographia Marchionatus Moraviae (1st modern map of Moravia)
mwe1158	europe south east	1772	FACIUS	800	87	80	Carte de la Turquie Europeene avec un Precis des Evenemens de la Guerre en 1769 et 1770
mwe1156a	europe south east	1769	FACIUS	2000	102	82	Carte exacte d'une Partie de L'Empire de Russie et la Pologne Meridionale
mwme0666	arabia etc	1804	FADEN	1000	76	62	(Red Sea)
mwuss0363	delaware	1776	FADEN	4000	47	71	A Chart of Delaware Bay and River, Containing a Full and Exact Description of the Shores, Creeks, Harbours, Soundings, Shoals, and Bearings of the Most Considerable Land Marks from the Capes to Philadelphia
mwwi0262	west indies (east)	1784	FADEN	800	54	47	A Chart of the Antilles, or Charibbee, or Caribs Islands, with the Virgin Isles, by L.S. de la Rochette
mwme0649	arabia etc	1781	FADEN	1500	118	88	A Chart of the Arabian Gulf or Red Sea ... Composed Chiefly from the Journals ... of Colonel James Capper
mwat0287	atlantic north	1807	FADEN	800	60	91	A Chart of the Atlantic or Western Ocean ... the Latest Observations of the English, French and Spanish Astronomers wherein ... the Track of His Majesty's Fleet, by the Late Viscount Nelson ... in Pursuit of the Combined Fleets of France and Spain 1805
mwuk1511	uk english channel (all)	1794	FADEN	500	54	89	A Chart of the British Channel and the Bay of Biscay, with a Part of the North Sea, and the Entrance of St. George's Channel
mwsp0291	spain	1780	FADEN	720	53	72	A Chart of the Coasts of Spain and Portugal, with the Balearic Islands, and Part of the Coast of Barbary. By L.S. de la Rochette.

AMPG REFERENCE	REGION	DATE	MAP MAKER	PRICE (UK£)	VERT. (cm.)	HOR. (cm.)	TITLE OF MAP (Comments by the editor in brackets)
mwat0312	atlantic south	1808	FADEN	450	60	90	A Chart of the Ethiopic or Southern Ocean, & Part Pacific Ocean
mwwi0335	bahamas	1794	FADEN	6000	56	71	A Chart of the Gulf of Florida or New Bahama Channel, Commonly Called the Gulf Passage
mwin0447a	indian ocean	1803	FADEN	2000	58	110	A Chart of the Indian Ocean improved from the Chart of M. D'Apres De Mannevillette; with the Addition of a Part of the Pacific Ocean (incl. Australia and New Zealand)
mwuk1593	channel islands	1781	FADEN	650	72	53	A Chart of the Islands of Jersey and Guernsey, Sark, Herm and Alderney; with the Adjacent Coast of France. By L.S. de la Rochette MDCCLXXXI
mww0550	world	1787	FADEN	1000	38	45	A Chart of the World upon Mercator's Projection, with the New Discoveries. Printed for W. Faden, Geographer to the King Charing Cross 1787
mwuss1138	new york	1779	FADEN	15000	185	140	A Chorographical Map of the Province of New-York in North America, Divided into Counties, Manors, Patents and Townships ... By Claude Joseph Sauthier Esqr
mwf0176	france	1806	FADEN	1000	126	118	A Correct Map of France According to the New Divisions into Metropolitan Circles, Departments and Districts; as Decreed by the National Assembly, January 15th, 1790, from a Reduced Copy of Monsr. Cassini's Large Map
mww0606	world	1799	FADEN	1250	54	91	A General Chart Exhibiting the Discoveries Made by Captn. James Cook in this and his Two Preceeding Voyages; with the Tracks of the Ships under his Command (copy of Cook 1784)
mwbp0062	baltic sea (east)	1803	FADEN	550	80	61	A General Chart of the Baltic or East Sea, Including the Gulfs of Botnia and Finland (2 insets, St. Petersburg and Revel)
mwwi0137	west indies	1796	FADEN	1200	54	78	A General Chart of the West India Islands with the Adjacent Coasts of the Spanish Continent
mwgm0063a	gulf of mexico and surrounding regions	1808	FADEN	3500	123	191	A General Chart of the West Indies and Gulf of Mexico, Describing the Gulf and Windward Passages, Coasts of Florida, Louisiana and Mexico, Bay of Honduras
mwgm0259a	mexico	1787	FADEN	3500	53	80	A Map of a Part of Yucatan Part of the Eastern Shore within the Bay of Honduras Allotted to Gt. Britain for the Cutting of Logwood in Consequence of the Convention Signed 14 July 1786.
mwgm0090	belize	1787	FADEN	3500	52	90	A Map of a Part of Yucatan, Part of the Eastern Shore within the Bay of Honduras Allotted to Gt. Britain for Cutting of Logwood in Consequence of the Convention Signed 14 July 1786 (column of text on left)
mwam0245	america continent	1797	FADEN	650	59	53	A Map of America, or the New World, wherein are Introduced All the Known Parts of the Western Hemisphere, from the Map of D'Anville; with the Necessary Alterations, and the Addition of the Discoveries Made since the Year 1761
mwin0285	india	1786	FADEN	800	71	105	A Map of Bengal, Bahar, Oude & Allahabad with Part of Agra and Delhi Exhibiting the Course of the Ganges from Hurdwar to the Sea by James Rennell, R.F.S.
mwuk1098a	england	1801	FADEN	500	75	62	A Map of England, Wales & Scotland Describing All the Direct and Principal Cross Roads in Great Britain, with the Distances Measured between Market Towns and from London (illustration shows Wyld 1838 update)
mwuk0242	ireland	1798	FADEN	450	72	55	A Map of Ireland Divided into Provinces and Counties, Showing the Great and Cross Roads with the Distances of the Principal Towns from Dublin
mwuk0626	scotland	1839	FADEN	600	117	102	A Map of Scotland Drawn Chiefly from the Topographical Surveys of Mr. John Ainslie and from those of the Late General Roy &c. &c.
mwuss0215	carolinas	1780	FADEN	12000	135	121	A Map of South Carolina and a Part of Georgia, Containing the Whole Sea Coast; All Boroughs, Roads and Bridges (reprint of De Brahm's map, 1757)
mwbh0753	belgium holland	1789	FADEN	600	55	69	A Map of the Austrian Possessions in the Netherlands or Low Countries, with the Principalities of Liege and Stavelo
mwuss1139	new york	1780	FADEN	1500	58	28	A Map of the Country in which the Army Under Lt. General Burgoyne Acted in the Campaign of 1777, Shewing the Marches of the Army & the Places of the Principal Actions
mwwi0935	virgin isl	1809	FADEN	2400	43	76	A Map of the Danish Island of St. Croix
mwg0730	schleswig-holstein	1804	FADEN	300	47	58	A Map of the Duchy of Holstein, with the Territories of the Imperial Towns Hamburg & Lubeck also the Bishoprick of Eutin
mwca0101	canada	1777	FADEN	1400	56	84	A Map of the Inhabited Part of Canada from the French Surveys; with the Frontiers of New York and New England from the Large Survey by Claude Joseph Sauthier
mwsc0380	scandinavia denmark	1790	FADEN	280	72	51	A Map of the Kingdom of Denmark with the Duchy of Holstein

AMPG REFERENCE	REGION	DATE	MAP MAKER	PRICE (UKE)	VERT. (cm.)	HOR. (cm.)	TITLE OF MAP (Comments by the editor in brackets)
mwbp0541	poland	1799	FADEN	550	55	62	A Map of the Kingdom of Poland and Grand Dutchy of Lithuania Including Samogitia and Curland, Divided According to their Dismemberments with the Kingdom of Prussia
mwca0470	canada ontario	1813	FADEN	1350	85	114	A Map of the Located Districts in the Province of Upper Canada
mwm0071	mediterranean	1785	FADEN	1600	62	182	A Map of the Mediterranean Sea with the Adjacent Region and Seas in Europe, Asia and Africa
mwf0809	france north	1795	FADEN	300	54	79	A Map of the Northern Part of France with the Adjacent Netherlands
mwin0298	india	1792	FADEN	1000	102	84	A Map of the Peninsula of India from the 19th Degree North Latitude to Cape Comorin
mwg0164	germany	1795	FADEN	480	77	94	A Map of the Post Roads of Germany, and the Adjacent States
mwuss1106	new york	1776	FADEN	4400	72	57	A Map of the Province of New-York, Reduc'd from the Large Drawing of that Province … to which is Added New Jersey, from Topographical Observations of C.J. Sauthier & B. Ratzer
mwbh0762	belgium holland	1794	FADEN	350	73	55	A Map of the Seven United Provinces, with the Land of Drent, and the Generality Lands
mwec0422	uk england essex	1809	FADEN	720	66	63	A Military Plan of the District of Colchester
mwca0628	canada st lawrence	1790	FADEN	4000	125	105	A New Chart of the Gulf of St. Lawrence, Compiled from the Original Drawings of Actual Surveys; Preserving the Natural Configurations of the Several Coasts & Headlands; the Whole Adjusted by Astronomical Observations, by Thos. Wright
mww0551	world	1787	FADEN	1250	44	60	A New General Chart of the World
mwsp0316	spain	1810	FADEN	1200	116	161	A New Map of Spain and Portugal, Exhibiting the Chains of Mountains with their Passes the Principal & Cross Roads, with Other Details Requisite for the Intelligence of Military Operations Compiled by Jasper Nantiat
mwwi0901	trinidad & tobago	1779	FADEN	2000	44	59	A New Map of the Island of Tobago (copy of Kitchin 1762)
mwg0193	germany north	1789	FADEN	480	60	52	A New Map of the King of Great Britain's Dominions in Germany
mwca0546	canada quebec	1813	FADEN	800	59	87	A New Map of the Province of Lower Canada, Describing All the Seigneuries, Townships, Grants of Land, &c
mwme1039	turkey etc	1794	FADEN	320	51	71	A New Map of Turkey in Asia
mwwi0528	grenada	1780	FADEN	7200	85	64	A New Plan of the Island of Grenada, from the Original French Survey of Monsieur Pinel; Taken in 1763 by Order of Government, and Now Published with the Addition of English Names, Alterations of Property … by Lieut. Daniel Paterson
mwuk1249	england london	1787	FADEN	2400	43	88	A New Pocket Plan of the Cities of London & Westminster; with the Borough of Southwark: Comprehending the New Buildings and Other Alterations to the Year 1787 (12 editions until 1815)
mwuk1281	england london	1810	FADEN	1000	75	78	A new Topographical map of the country in the vicinity of London, describing all the new improvements (13 editions until 1864)
mwec0489	uk england hampshire	1789	FADEN	2800	55	58	A Plan of His Majesty's Forest, Called the New Forest in the County of Southampton (8 maps, each 55x58cm.)
mwuk1289	england london	1817	FADEN	2000	44	89	A Plan of London and Westminster with the Borough of Southwark (3 editions to 1819)
mwuss1107	new york	1776	FADEN	15000	47	42	A Plan of New York Island, with Part of Long Island, Staten Island & East New Jersey, with a Particular Description of the Engagement of the Woody Heights of Long Island … on the 27th of August 1776
mwuss0822	massachusetts	1776	FADEN	9000	50	43	A Plan of the Action at Bunkers Hill, on the 17th of June 1775, between His Majesty's Troops under the Command of Major General Howe, and the Rebel Forces. By Lieut. Page of the Engineers, who Acted as Aide de Camp to General Howe in that Action
mwuss0191	carolinas	1776	FADEN	6000	28	37	A Plan of the Attack of Fort Sullivan, Near Charles Town in South Carolina, by a Squadron of His Majesty's Ships, on the 28th of June 1776, with the Disposition of the King's Land Forces
mwuk1290	england london	1818	FADEN	2250	45	102	A Plan of the cities of London & Westminster, the Borough of Southwark
mwuk1231	england london	1775	FADEN	160	32	55	A Plan of the Cities of London and Westminster (8 editions until 1788)
mwuss1378	pennsylvania	1779	FADEN	20000	59	48	A Plan of the City and Environs of Philadelphia, with the Works and Encampments of His Majesty's Forces under the Command of Lieutenant General Sir William Howe, K.B.

AMPG REFERENCE	REGION	DATE	MAP MAKER	PRICE (UK£)	VERT. (cm.)	HOR. (cm.)	TITLE OF MAP (Comments by the editor in brackets)
mwsc0392	scandinavia denmark	1807	FADEN	1200	56	80	A Plan of the City of Copenhagen, with the Adjacent Ground. Shewing the Positions of the Several Batteries, Erected by the British During the Siege in September 1807
mwuk0240a	ireland	1797	FADEN	1000	51	77	A Plan of the City of Dublin Surveyed for the Use of the Divisionl: Justices
mwuss1648	virginia	1781	FADEN	8000	41	50	A Plan of the Entrance of Chesapeak Bay, with James and York Rivers; wherein are Shewn the Respective Positions
mwca0472	canada ontario	1815	FADEN	800	19	60	A Plan of the New Townships on the Grand or Ottawa River in which Lands Have Been Granted
mwuss1121	new york	1777	FADEN	10000	72	49	A Plan of the Operations of the King's Army under the Command of General Sr. William Howe, K.B. in New York and East New Jersey, against American Forces Commanded by General Washington, from the 12th of October to the 28th of November 1776
mwuss1153	new york	1784	FADEN	4000	50	70	A Plan of the Surprise of Stoney Point by a Detachment of the American Army Commanded by Brigr: Genl. Wayne
mwuss0825	massachusetts	1777	FADEN	5000	57	38	A Plan of the Town of Boston, with the Intrenchments &c. of His Majestys Forces in 1775 from the Observations of Lieut. Page
mwuss1450	rhode isl	1777	FADEN	3600	33	36	A Plan of the Town of Newport in Rhode Island
mwaf0973a	africa south	1795	FADEN	3000	50	38	A Plan of the Town of the Cape of Good Hope and its Environs, taken by Monsr. Bourset in December 1770
mwuss0216	carolinas	1780	FADEN	14000	51	68	A Plan of the Town, Bar, Harbour and Environs of Charlestown in South Carolina, with All the Channels, Sounding, Sailing-Marks, &c
mwuss1655	virginia	1785	FADEN	9600	54	71	A Plan of Yorktown and Gloucester, in the Province of Virginia, Shewing the Works Constructed for the Defense of those Posts by the British Army under the Command of Lt. Genl. Earl Cornwallis
mwuss1451	rhode isl	1777	FADEN	8000	93	63	A Topographical Chart of the Bay of Narraganset in the Province of New England
mwsp0127	portugal	1810	FADEN	800	59	91	A Topographical Chart of the Entrance of the River Tagus Describing the Coast from Cape Roca to Sacavem with the Harbour and Environs of Lisbon
mwuss1108	new york	1776	FADEN	4800	81	56	A Topographical Map of Hudson's River ... Sandy Hook ... Fort Edward
mwuk1254	england london	1790	FADEN	900	56		A Topographical Map of the Country Twenty Miles round London (circular map, 3 editions to 1818)
mwec0419	uk england essex	1804	FADEN	350	64	88	A Topographical Map of the County of Essex. Constructed from the Trigonometrical Survey Made by Order of the Board of Ordnance
mwec0835	uk england norfolk	1797	FADEN	2000	122	183	A Topographical Map of the County of Norfolk Surveyed and Measured in the Years 1790, 91, 92, 93 and 94
mwuk1599a	channel islands	1816	FADEN	4500	71	130	A Topographical Map Of The Islands Of Guernsey, Sark, Herm & Jetho
mwuss1122	new york	1777	FADEN	5500	47	26	A Topographical Map of the Northn. Part of New York Island, Exhibiting the Plan of Fort Washington, Now Fort Knyphausen, with the Rebel Lines to the Southward which were Forced by the Troops under the Command of the Rt. Honble. Earl Percy
mwuss1002	new hampshire	1784	FADEN	24000	59	79	A Topographical Map of the Province of New Hampshire, Surveyed Agreeably to the Orders and Instructions of the Right Honourable the Lords Commissioners for Trade and Plantations
mwm0253	mediterranean malta	1799	FADEN	3000	52	113	A Topographical Map, Describing the Sovereign Principality, of the Islands of Malta and Goza
mwaf0289	africa	1803	FADEN	600	51	57	Africa ... 1782. London: Published April 25th, 1803, by Wm. Faden, Charing Cross
mwuss1549	vermont	1775	FADEN	7200	75	47	An Account of the Expedition of the British Fleet on Lake Champlain
mwwi0305	antigua	1793	FADEN	8000	100	101	Antigua in the West Indies America (in 4 sheets, joined. Map by J. Luffman)
mwuk0576	scotland	1810	FADEN	1600	148	120	Argyllshire
mwas0229	asia continent	1800	FADEN	650	48	55	Asia Divided into its Empires, Kingdoms, States and other Subdivisions
mwuss1373	pennsylvania	1778	FADEN	5500	56	46	Battle of Brandywine in which the Rebels Were Defeated, September the 11th 1777 ... under the Command of General Sr. Willm. Howe
mwuss0828	massachusetts	1778	FADEN	8750	45	63	Boston, its Environs and Harbour, with the Rebel Works Raised against that Town in 1775
mwuss1374	pennsylvania	1778	FADEN	9000	25	40	British Camp at Trudruffrin from the 18th to the 21st of September 1777. With the Attack made by Major General Grey against the Rebels near White Horse Tavern. On the 20th of September. Drawn by an Officer on the Spot. ... 1778

AMPG REFERENCE	REGION	DATE	MAP MAKER	PRICE (UK£)	VERT. (cm.)	HOR. (cm.)	TITLE OF MAP (Comments by the editor in brackets)
mwf0808	france north	1793	FADEN	200	34	27	Chart of the Coast of France, from Neville to the Isles de Brehat with Jersey and Guernsey
mwuk1393	england south	1799	FADEN	300	64	54	Chart of the Coast of Hampshire from Portsmouth to Southampton Water with Part of the Isle of Wight from Culver Cliff to West Cowes Including the Roads of Spithead, St. Helens, Stokes Bay &c.
mwuk1347	england east	1807	FADEN	400	62	60	Chart of the East Coast of England
mwf0539	france corsica	1793	FADEN	250	32	22	Chart of the Island of Corsica from the Topographic Survey Made by Order of the Marquis de Cursay with Several Emendations from Bellin's Charts
mwp0446	pacific north	1794	FADEN	12500	39	67	Chart of the N.W. Coast of America and the N.E. Coast of Asia, Explored in the Years 1778 and 1779. Prepared by Lieut. Henr. Roberts under the Immediate Inspection of Capt. Cook (state 1)
mwp0447	pacific north	1794	FADEN	1200	43	70	Chart of the N.W. Coast of America and the N.E. Coast of Asia, Explored in the Years 1778 and 1779. Prepared by Lieut. Henr. Roberts under the Immediate Inspection of Capt. Cook (state 2)
mwuk1519	uk english channel (all)	1808	FADEN	350	54	69	Chart of the Strait of Dover
mwsc0193	scandinavia	1801	FADEN	600	61	38	Chart of the Straits between Denmark and Sweden, Shewing the Passage from the Kattegat through the Sound, to Copenhagen Road, and thence through the Grounds to the Entrance of the Baltic
mww0598a	world	1798	FADEN	150	11	17	Chart of the World on Mercator's Projection
mwsp0119	portugal	1797	FADEN	300	73	51	Chorographical Map of the Kingdom of Portugal Divided into its Grand Provinces
mwf1182	france south east	1805	FADEN	250	23	31	Coast of France and Italy from La Napoule to Villafranca
mwf0810	france north	1805	FADEN	150	31	23	Coast of France from Cape La Hague to Isle Brehat with All the Adjacent Islands and Dangers
mwf0811	france north	1805	FADEN	150	23	36	Coast of France from the River Seine to the Loire with the Entrance of the English and St. George's Channels
mwsam0130	south america	1811	FADEN	900	110	79	Colombia Prima or South America Drawn from the Large Map in Eight Sheets By Louis Stanislas D'Arcy Delarochette (reduced version of the previous map)
mwsam0129	south america	1807	FADEN	2800	244	168	Colombia Prima or South America, in which has been Attempted to Delineate the Extent of our Knowledge ... Louis Stanislas D'Arcy De La Rochette
mwe0224	europe	1791	FADEN	450	54	68	Europe, Exhibiting its Principal States, &c.
mwe1168	europe south east	1795	FADEN	350	55	73	European Dominions of the Ottomans, or Turkey in Europe
mwf0164	france	1792	FADEN	275	52	61	France Divided into Metropolitan Circles Departments & Districts; as Decreed by the National Assembly Jany. 15th 1790
mwf0160	france	1790	FADEN	350	53	61	France Divided into Provinces
mwm0082	mediterranean	1821	FADEN	875	47	91	General Chart of the Mediterranean Sea Including the Gulf of Venice, Archipelago and Part of the Black Sea
mwat0244a	atlantic madeira	1791	FADEN	2250	59	116	Geo-Hydrographic Survey of the Isle of Madeira
mwit1072	italy naples	1793	FADEN	200	23	36	Geometrical Survey of the Gulf of Naples Made by Order of the King of the Two Sicilies
mwgr0229	greece	1791	FADEN	450	53	74	Greece, Archipelago and Part of Anadoli. By L.S. de la Rochette
mwec0490	uk england hampshire	1791	FADEN	3000	50	69	Hampshire, or the County of Southampton, Including the Isle of Wight, Surveyed by Thomas Milne in the Years 1788, 89 & 90, Executed and Published at the Private Expense of the Proprietor, W. Faden (6 sheets, each 50x69cm.)
mwin0295	india	1797	FADEN	550	69	53	Hind, Hindoostan, or India. By L.S. De La Rochette
mwwi0665	hispaniola	1796	FADEN	900	47	74	Isle of St. Domingo or Hispaniola
mwit0222	italy	1800	FADEN	800	128	110	Italy with the Addition of the Southern Parts of Germany as Far as Pettau in Stiria; Murlakia, Dalmatia, the Adjacent Countries
mwuk1291	england london	1818	FADEN	2250	45	102	London and Westminster with the Borough of Westminster (22 editions to 1846)
mwaf0540	africa egypt etc	1802	FADEN	350	56	77	Lower Egypt and the Adjacent Deserts, with a Part of Palestine; to which has been Added the Nomenclature of the Roman Age, MDCCCII
mwca0459	canada nova scotia	1815	FADEN	200	13	32	Map and Elevation of the Shubenacadie Navigation from Halifax Harbour to the Basin of Mines
mwam0617	america north	1820	FADEN	15000	37	55	Map of North America from 20 to 80 Degrees North Latitude, Exhibiting the Recent Discoveries, Geographical and Nautical (in 6 sheets)
mwsp0321	spain	1820	FADEN	1350	128	184	Map of the Kingdom of Spain and Portugal, Including Algarve
mwsw0224	switzerland	1820	FADEN	400	58	60	Map of the Republic of Switzerland

AMPG REFERENCE	REGION	DATE	MAP MAKER	PRICE (UK£)	VERT. (cm.)	HOR. (cm.)	TITLE OF MAP (Comments by the editor in brackets)
mwwi0168	west indies	1822	FADEN	550	52	77	Map of the West India & Bahama Islands with the Adjacent Coasts of Yucatan, Honduras, Caracas &c. (illustration shows 1847 edition, publ. by Wyld)
mwam0541	america north	1798	FADEN	150	10	11	North America, Including the West Indies
mwsw0212	switzerland	1799	FADEN	700	64	86	Nouvelle Carte de la Suisse dans laquelle sont Exactement Distingues les Treize Cantons ... Londre Chez W. Faden Charing Cross 1799 (copy of Schraembl 1789)
mwme0382	holy land	1796	FADEN	150	10	12	Palestina quae et Chanaan et Terra Promissionis vel Terra Sancta
mwuk1285	england london	1814	FADEN	200	39	27	Plan of a Street Proposed from Charing Cross to Portland Place Designed by J. Nash Esq.
mwwi0884	st lucia	1798	FADEN	1200	42	63	Plan of Morne Fortune and Environs from Choc Bay to Morne Petit, Showing the Disposition and Attack of the British Army Commanded by his Excellency Ralph Abercrombie
mwuss1553	vermont	1780	FADEN	1200	28	34	Plan of the Action at Huberton under the Brigadier Genl. Frezer, Supported by Major Genl. Reidesel, on the 7th July 1777
mwuss1154	new york	1784	FADEN	4000	68	53	Plan of the Attack of the Forts Clinton & Montgomery upon Hudsons River, which were Stormed by His Majestys Forces under the Command of Sir Henry Clinton, K.B. on the 6th of Octr. 1777
mwsp0737	gibraltar	1783	FADEN	480	53	73	Plan of the Bay, Rock and Town of Gibraltar from an Actual Survey ... the Spanish Army on 19th. Oct. 1782 the Position of the Combined Fleet
mwca0533	canada quebec	1776	FADEN	1500	44	62	Plan of the City and Environs of Quebec, with its Siege and Blockade by the Americans
mwuk1293	england london	1819	FADEN	3000	64	152	Plan of the City of London, Distinguishing the Several Wards as Sketched from Maitlands History of London
mwca0473	canada ontario	1815	FADEN	350	23	25	Plan of the Different Channels Leading from Kingston to Lake Ontario; Surveyed by Jos. Bouchette 1796
mwca0550	canada quebec	1815	FADEN	2000	43	50	Plan of the District of Gaspe by Joseph Bouchette Surveyor General
mwsp0616	spain regions	1805	FADEN	600	56	86	Plan of the Harbour of Cadiz; Surveyed by Brigadier Don Vincente Tofino de San Miguel, Director of the Naval Academies for Cadets, 1789
mwit0452	italy liguria	1793	FADEN	350	20	31	Plan of the Harbour of Genoa
mwwi0803	martinique	1795	FADEN	1000	88	70	Plan of the Harbour, Fort, Town and Environs of Fort Royal in Martinique. Drawn by Lieut. William Booth Royl. Engrs.
mwuss1038	new jersey	1777	FADEN	8000	31	41	Plan of the Operations of General Washington, against the King's Troops in New Jersey
mwuss1140	new york	1780	FADEN	1500	22	47	Plan of the Position which the Army under Lt. Genl. Burgoine Took at Saratoga on the 10th of September 1777, and in which it Remained till the Convention was Signed
mwec1261	uk england wiltshire	1794	FADEN	1400	50	197	Plan of the Proposed Navigable Canal between the River Kennet at Newbury in the County of Berks: and the River Avon at Bath in the County of Somerset: whereby a Navigable Communication will be Opened between the Cities of London and Bristol
mwuss0502	georgia	1784	FADEN	3000	62	84	Plan of the Siege of Savannah, with the Joint Attack of the French and Americans on the 9th October 1779, in which they were Defeated by His Majesty's Forces under the Command of Major Genl. Augustin Prevost
mwuss0431	florida	1775	FADEN	1200	21	29	Plan of the Town of St. Augustine the Capital of East Florida. Printed for W. Faden Charing Cross. T. Jefferys Sculp.
mwuss1554	vermont	1780	FADEN	650	28	34	Position of the Detachment under Lieut. Col. Baum, at Walmscock Near Bennington Shewing the Attacks of the Enemy on the 16th August 1777
mwf0762	france nord pas-de-calais	1805	FADEN	120	22	32	Road of Dunkirk
mwsc0186	scandinavia	1794	FADEN	550	71	49	Scandia or Scandinavia Comprehending Sweden and Norway with the Danish Islands
mwwi0882	st lucia	1781	FADEN	1250	38	48	Sketch of Part of the Island of Ste. Lucie Compiled at about 2500 Feet to an Inch
mwuss1381	pennsylvania	1784	FADEN	7000	47	54	Sketch of the Surprise of German Town by the American Forces Commanded by General Washington, October 4th 1777. By J. Hills
mwaa0040	antarctic	1790	FADEN	900	35		Southern Hemisphere (circular map)
mwaa0202	arctic / antarctic	1790	FADEN	720	35		Southern Hemisphere, Northern Hemisphere (2 maps, each 35cm. diameter)
mwsp0309	spain	1796	FADEN	350	51	72	Spain and Portugal Divided into their Respective Kingdoms and Provinces

AMPG REFERENCE	REGION	DATE	MAP MAKER	PRICE (UK£)	VERT. (cm.)	HOR. (cm.)	TITLE OF MAP (Comments by the editor in brackets)
mwsam0198	south america (north west)	1805	FADEN	900	87	57	Spherical Chart Comprehending the West Coast of America, from the Seventh Degree of South latitude to the Ninth Degree of North Latitude (copy of Madrid 1800)
mwuss0432	florida	1775	FADEN	600	20	26	The Bay of Espiritu Santo, on the Western Coast of East Florida. Printed for W. Faden Charing Cross. T. Jefferys Sculp.
mwam1041a	america north (east)	1777	FADEN	3600	53	63	The British Colonies in North America
mwsam0635	south america guyana	1783	FADEN	400	53	70	The Coast of Guyana from the Oroonoko to the River of Amazons and the Inland Parts as Far as they have been Explored by the French & Dutch Engineers, with the Islands of Barbadoes, Tobago &ca from the Observations of Captain Edward Thompson
mwuk1270	england london	1802	FADEN	1800	104	126	The Country Twenty-Five Miles round London planned from a scale of one mile to an inch (12 edtions to 1850)
mwec0866	uk england northamptonshire	1779	FADEN	1200	128	132	The County of Northampton as Surveyed and Planned by the Late Mr. Thomas Eyre of Kettering, Revised by the Late Mr. Thomas Jefferys
mwec1113	uk england suffolk	1783	FADEN	2400	64	50	The County of Suffolk, Surveyed (6 sheets, each 64x50cm.)
mwec0695	uk england lancashire	1786	FADEN	2000	204	132	The County Palatine of Lancaster
mwuss1375	pennsylvania	1778	FADEN	8500	44	68	The Course of Delaware River from Philadelphia to Chester, Exhibiting the Several Works Erected by the Rebels to Defend its Passage with the Attacks made upon them by His Majesty's Land & Sea Forces
mwaf0958	africa south	1782	FADEN	650	50	33	The Dutch Colony of the Cape of Good Hope by L.S. De La Rochette
mwru0307	russia	1794	FADEN	1200	46	126	The European Part of the Russian Empire from the Maps Published by the Imperial Academy at St. Petersburg, with the New Provinces of the Black Sea / The Asiatic Part of the Russian Empire .. .with the New Discoveries of Captn. Cook, &c.
mwca0338	canada newfoundland	1791	FADEN	1200	73	60	The Island of Newfoundland, Laid down from Surveys Taken by Order of the Right Honourable the Lords Commissioners of Admiralty, by Lieut. Michael Lane
mwwi0852	st eustatia	1795	FADEN	1600	46	53	The Island of St. Eustatius Corruptly St. Eustatia
mwam1096	america north (east)	1787	FADEN	4800	67	51	The Marches of Lord Cornwallis in the Southern Provinces, Now States of North America; Comprehending the Two Carolinas, with Virginia and Maryland and the Delaware Counties
mwuk1677	north sea	1796	FADEN	800	66	61	The North Sea with the Kattegat from the Chart of Messrs de Verdun, de Borda, and Pingre, Made Public, in 1777, by Order of Louis XVI; Constructed on a Larger Scale, and with Considerable Additions and Emendations by L.S. De La Rochette, MDCCXCVI
mwuss1039	new jersey	1777	FADEN	16000	76	55	The Province of New Jersey, Divided into East and West, Commonly Called the Jerseys
mwf0991	france poitou	1805	FADEN	120	32	22	The Road of Basque, or the Bay of Rochefort, Including the Isles of Re and Olleron
mwru0325	russia	1808	FADEN	720	107	91	The Russian Dominions in Europe ... with the Post Roads & New Governments from the Russian Atlas of 1806 by Jasper Nantiat
mwam0533	america north	1796	FADEN	1800	54	64	The United States of North America: With the British Territories and those of Spain, According to the Treaty of 1784
mwwi0392	cayman isl.	1790	FADEN	2500	57	39	The West End of the Island of Cuba, and Part of the Colorados / The Grand Caymans (2 maps on one sheet)
mwuk0226	ireland	1786	FADEN	1800	36	46	To his Grace the Duke of Rutland, Lord Lieut. General and Genl. Governor of Ireland; This Survey of the Lakes of Killarney, is Most Humbly Dedicated by Wm. Faden
mwam1333	america north (west)	1796	FADEN	240	10	12	Western Coast of North America with Berhing's Straits
mww0491	world	1775	FADEN	1500	36	71	Western Hemisphere / Eastern Hemisphere (2 circular maps on one sheet)
mwwi0848	st barts	1786	FAHLBERG	1200	33	41	Charta ofver Oen St. Barthelemi
mwwi0849	st barts	1801	FAHLBERG	2000	51	71	Charta ofver On St. Barthelemy
mwbh0768	belgium holland	1797	FAIRBURN	800	32	46	A Chart of the Coast of Holland Exhibiting the Situation of the Dutch Fleet at the Time of the Engagement with Admiral Duncan, also the Opposite Coast of England Including Yarmouth &c
mwme0389	holy land	1800	FAIRBURN	2400	61	130	A New Mapp of the Land of Promise and the Holy Citty
mwuk1296	england london	1820	FAIRBURN	1200	64		Fairburn's circular plan of London
mwuk1263	england london	1798	FAIRBURN	800	50		Fairburn's Map of the Country Twelve Miles Round London (revised editions of this circular map in 1800 and 1831)
mwbh0763	belgium holland	1794	FAIRBURN	400	28	38	Fairburn's New Map of the Seat of War in Holland and the Netherlands

AMPG REFERENCE	REGION	DATE	MAP MAKER	PRICE (UK£)	VERT. (cm.)	HOR. (cm.)	TITLE OF MAP (Comments by the editor in brackets)
mwaf0532	africa egypt etc	1798	FAIRBURN	2000	32	27	Fairburn's Plan of the Position of Adml. Nelson's Squadron and the French Fleet [on sheet with] A Chart of the Mouths of the Nile, Alexandria, &c.
mwuk1258	england london	1795	FAIRBURN	2000	44	79	London and Westminster (8 editions until 1806)
mwsc0387	scandinavia denmark	1801	FAIRBURN	3000	52	42	Passage of the Sound to Copenhagen & Draco, Exhibiting the Track of the British Fleet
mwec0177	uk england cornwall	1709	FAIRLOVE	950	55	44	Plan of the City of Exeter
mwit0722	italy rome	1676	FALDA	20000			Nuova Pianta et Alzata della Citta di Roma
mwit0721	italy rome	1667	FALDA	4000	68	86	Recentis Romae Ichnographia et Hypsographia sive Planta et Facies (publ. by De Rossi)
mwit0720	italy rome	1663	FALDA	1800	55	56	Roma
mwit0702	italy rome	1561	FALETI	2500	35	55	Roma
mwbh0613	belgium holland	1730	FALKEN	300	43	52	Frisiae Antiquae et Veteris Brabantiae Pars in Pagos Distributa
mwuk1331	england london	1846	FAMILY TIMES	1500	86		Twelve miles round St. Pauls (circular map)
mwuss0917	michigan	1836	FARMER	2000	54	79	An Improved Edition of a Map of Surveyed Part of Territory of Michigan
mwuss0908	michigan	1829	FARMER	1500	51	76	An Improved Map of the Surveyed Part of the Territory of Michigan
mwuss0915	michigan	1835	FARMER	4000	36	56	Map of the City of Detroit in the State of Michigan (in 4 sheets, each 36x56cm)
mwuss0926	michigan	1844	FARMER	3000	81	58	Map of the State of Michigan and the Surrounding Country, Exhibiting the Sections and the Latest Surveys
mwuss0922	michigan	1840	FARMER	3000	84	58	Map of the Surveyed Part of Michigan
mwuss0909	michigan	1831	FARMER	1500	76	81	Map of the Territories of Michigan and Ouisconsin
mwuss0918	michigan	1836	FARMER	2000	52	86	Map of the Territories of Michigan and Ouisconsin on a Scale of 50 Geographical Miles to an Inch
mwuss1538a	texas	1847	FARMER	2500	27	23	Texas eine geographische Skizze bearbeitet nach Berghaus Länderkunde und den neuesten Forschungen des Prinzen Carl zu Solms Braunfels und anderer Reisenden
mwam1370	america north (west)	1846	FARNHAM	450	28	27	Mexico, Texas & California
mww0416	world	1750	FAURE	480	23	35	Carte Generale du Globe Terrestre Construite sur les Dernieres Observations des Geographes de la M.T.C. et Publiee pour Plus Grand Ecclarsisement du Dictionnaire Geographique Portatif, et de la Geographie Moderne
mww0624	world	1805	FAUVET	450	33	51	Nouvelle Mappe-Monde ... aux Dernieres Observations Astronomiques
mwuss0936	minnesota	1835	FEATHERSTONHAUGH	375	60	99	A Reconnoisance of the Minnay Sotor Watapah or St. Peter's River to its Sources
mwam0725	america north	1839	FEATHERSTONHAUGH	180	32	27	Part of the United States, Lower Canada & New Brunswick
mwbh0206	belgium holland	1622	FEDDES	1200	40	52	Nieuwe end Heerlycke Beschryvinghe der Ghelegentheyt van Vrieslandt
mwsp0505	spain regions	1706	FEHR	550	24	34	Barcelona (view)
mwe0568	europe czech republic (bohemia)	1740	FELSECKER	685	33	39	Des Konigreich Bohmen
mwe0792	europe east	1737	FELSECKER	685	37	57	Des Neu Eroffneten Kriegs Theatri in Ungarn Zweyter Theil Enthaltend die Kriegs Operationes in der Walachey, Moldau, Servien, Bosnien, und Bulgarien
mwbp0409	poland	1734	FELSECKER	800	29	37	Geographischer Plan der Stadt Dantzig mit der Rusischen Belagerung u. Attaque 1734 Benebenst des Dantziger Werders
mwe0939	europe hungary	1739	FELSECKER	800	39	55	Kayserlich-Turckischen Friedens-Theatrum in Ungarn worinen de Bedungene Fridensgrantze von Verschiedenen Friedens Schlussen Deutlich Angezeiget werden
mwe1073	europe serbia	1750	FELSECKER	500	39	57	Plan der Gegend und Grundriss der Vestung Belgrad in Servien
mwbh0529	belgium holland	1706	FELSECKERS	750	57	36	Ligentliche Abbildung Menin ... Dendermonde / Den 5. September (Flanders ... British successes in the war of Spanish Succession)
mwuss0287	carolinas	1848	FELTON	1250	62	81	Plan of the City of Charleston, Made by Order of the City Council from Actual Survey
mwam0670	america north	1831	FENNER	350	25	39	A Geological Map of the United States
mwec0662	uk england kent	1825	FENNER	480	32	38	A Plan of the City of Canterbury & the Adjoining Suburbs; A.D. MDCCCXXV. Shewing the Several Precincts and Liberties within it which are Exempt from Jurisdiction
mwin0353	india	1830	FENNER	50	14	12	Hindoostan
mwuss0726	maine	1832	FENNER	360	36	25	Map of Maine, New Hampshire and Vermont
mwuss0962	mississippi	1831	FENNER	350	41	27	Map of Mississippi, Louisiana, and the Arkansas Territory
mwuss0469	florida	1832	FENNER	300	20	25	Map of the State of Florida
mwuss0991	missouri	1842	FENNER	550	25	37	Map of the State of Missouri (dated 1832)
mwuss1219	new york	1832	FENNER	240	24	39	Map of the State of New York
mwuss1213	new york	1830	FENNER	240	24	39	Map of the State of New York with Part of Upper Canada
mwuss0012	alabama	1831	FENNER	550	25	40	Map of the States of Alabama and Georgia
mwuss0572	indiana	1831	FENNER	350	25	40	Map of the States of Indiana and Ohio, with Part of Michigan Territory
mwuss0612	kentucky	1831	FENNER	550	25	39	Map of the States of Kentucky and Tennessee

AMPG REFERENCE	REGION	DATE	MAP MAKER	PRICE (UK£)	VERT. (cm.)	HOR. (cm.)	TITLE OF MAP (Comments by the editor in brackets)
mwuss0872	massachusetts	1832	FENNER	300	19	25	Map of the States of Massachusetts, Connecticut and Rhode Island
mwuss0272	carolinas	1832	FENNER	320	25	40	Map of the States of North & South Carolina
mwuss1422	pennsylvania	1832	FENNER	400	25	38	Map of the States of Pennsylvania and New Jersey
mwuss1684	virginia	1832	FENNER	400	25	38	Map of the States of Virginia and Maryland
mwgm0316	mexico	1830	FENNER	240	11	14	Mexico & Guatemala
mwam0677	america north	1832	FENNER	500	50	41	North America
mwme0845	persia etc	1830	FENNER	80	12	14	Persia and Arabia
mwuss0777	maryland	1832	FENNER	400	36	51	Southern States of America Comprehending Maryland, Virginia, Kentucky, Territorys of the Ohio, N & S. Caroline, Tennessee & Georgia
mwam0645	america north	1825	FENNER	400	31	39	United States
mwwi0184	west indies	1830	FENNER	80	12	15	West Indies
mwuk1006	england	1765	FENNING	180	20	29	A New Map of England and Wales Divided into Counties Drawn from the Best Authorities
mwe0379	europe austria	1765	FENNING	160	19	29	A New Map of the Circle of Austria from the Best Authorities
mww0477	world	1770	FERGUSON	280	20	36	A Map of the Earth upon which are Marked the Hours and Minutes of True Times of the Entrance and Exit of Venus, in its passage over the Sun's Disc, June 6th, 1761 (double hemisphere polar projections)
mwbh0730	belgium holland	1777	FERRARIS	2000	280	370	Carte Chorographique des Pays-Bas Autrichiens (25-sheet map of Belgium)
mwgr0355	greece crete	1580	FERRETTI	500	13	9	Ragionevoe' Forma et Vera Postura del' Isola di Candia
mwm0173	mediterranean malta	1580	FERRETTI	1200	14	9	Ragionevol' Forma et Vera Postura del' Isola di Malta
mwit0778	italy sardinia	1580	FERRETTI	800	14	9	Ragionevol Forma et vera postura del Isola di Sardegna
mwit0868	italy sicily	1580	FERRETTI	800	14	9	Ragionevol Forma et vera postura del Isola di Sicilia
mwgr0459	greece cyprus	1580	FERRETTI	2250	13	9	Ragionevol' Forma et Vera Postura dell'Isola di Cipro
mwf0461	france corsica	1580	FERRETTI	1000	13	9	Ragionevol' Forma et Vera Postura dell'Isola di Corsica
mwit0326	italy elba	1580	FERRETTI	600	14	9	Ragionevol' Forma et Vera Postura dell'Isola di Elba
mwuk1092a	uk	1580	FERRETTI	875	13	9	Ragionevol' Forma et Vera Postura dell'Isola di Ingliterra
mwsp0643	balearic islands	1580	FERRETTI	1000	13	9	Ragionevol' Forma et Vera Postura dell'Isola di Maiorica
mwuss0138	california	1850	FERRY	450	39	50	Carte de la Nouvle. Californie Dressee d'apres les Travaux Geographiques de Mr. Duflot de Mofras et du Colonel Fremont
mwsam0751a	south america peru	1714	FEUILLET	720	20	30	Plan de la Ville de Lima Capitale du Perou
mwsam0849	south america venezuela	1818	FIDALGO	300	18	24	Ensda. de Carupano
mwsam0850	south america venezuela	1818	FIDALGO	300	18	24	Ensena. de Unare
mwsam0854	south america venezuela	1818	FIDALGO	300	17	23	Fondeadero de la Guayra
mwsam0852	south america venezuela	1818	FIDALGO	300	23	18	Pampatar ... Margarita
mwgm0439	panama	1809	FIDALGO	480	19	26	Plano del Puerto de Naos y sus Adyacentes-Istmo de Panama
mwsam0541	south america colombia	1818	FIDALGO	300	18	26	Plano del Puerto y Ciudad de Santa Marta
mwsam0851	south america venezuela	1818	FIDALGO	300	18	23	Pto. Santo
mwsam0853	south america venezuela	1818	FIDALGO	300	18	27	Puerto Cabello
mwp0504	pacific south	1786	FIELDING	550	20	35	A General Chart of New Holland, including New South Wales & Botany Bay, with the Adjacent Countries and New Discovered Islands
mwme0844	persia etc	1823	FIELDING	150	23	27	Persia
mwit0823a	italy sardinia	1802	FILETI	800	40	62	Isola di Sardegna (2 sea charts on one sheet)
mwit0376a	italy friuli	1811	FILIASI	1000	52	72	Venetia Superior et Inferior (shown above)
mwuss0592	kentucky	1785	FILSON	2500	36	32	Carte de Kentucke
mwg0344a	bavaria	1663	FINCKH	1600	115	87	S. Rom. Imperii Circuli Et Electoratus Bavariae Tabula Chororaphia ... Maximiliano Emmanueli ... Georg Philippus Finckh (dissected into 56 sections. Re-issued 1671)
mwuss0058	arkansas	1836	FINDLAY	250	18	23	Arkansaw
mwca0208	canada	1850	FINDLAY	80	22	26	Canada
mwc0268	china	1835	FINDLAY	80	20	24	China
mwme1067	turkey etc	1840	FINDLAY	100	25	20	Constantinople and Bosphorus
mwgm0341	mexico	1842	FINDLAY	100	19	25	Mexico & Guatemala
mwp0115	australia	1836	FINDLAY	100	24	19	New South Wales
mwam0750	america north	1842	FINDLAY	135	26	21	North America
mww0709	world	1836	FINDLAY	180	21	33	The World on Mercator's Projection
mww0625	world	1805	FINDLAY	240	23	43	The World with the Tracks & Discoveries of the Latest Navigators
mwam0704	america north	1836	FINDLAY	200	19	24	United States
mwwi0204	west indies	1842	FINDLAY	80	20	25	West Indies
mwaf0316	africa	1824	FINLEY	140	29	22	Africa
mwuss0011	alabama	1829	FINLEY	300	29	22	Alabama
mwca0151	canada	1826	FINLEY	140	22	28	Canada
mwc0259	china	1827	FINLEY	140	22	28	China
mwuss0312	connecticut	1824	FINLEY	240	23	29	Connecticut
mwuss0382	delaware	1831	FINLEY	300	29	22	Delaware
mwaf0551	africa egypt etc	1825	FINLEY	100	29	22	Egypt
mwuk1056	england	1829	FINLEY	180	35	26	England and Wales
mwe0264	europe	1831	FINLEY	140	22	29	Europe

AMPG REFERENCE	REGION	DATE	MAP MAKER	PRICE (UK£)	VERT. (cm.)	HOR. (cm.)	TITLE OF MAP (Comments by the editor in brackets)
mwuss0522	georgia	1830	FINLEY	300	28	21	Georgia
mwuss0549	illinois	1824	FINLEY	280	28	22	Illinois
mwuss0571	indiana	1826	FINLEY	300	29	22	Indiana
mwuk0263	ireland	1824	FINLEY	120	29	22	Ireland
mwuss0607	kentucky	1824	FINLEY	240	22	29	Kentucky
mwuss0670	louisiana	1824	FINLEY	240	22	28	Louisiana
mwuss0722	maine	1828	FINLEY	240	28	22	Maine
mwuss0465	florida	1826	FINLEY	450	42	25	Map of Florida According to the Latest Authorities / Comparative Elevations of Mountains in North and South America
mwuss0609	kentucky	1826	FINLEY	1200	43	52	Map of Kentucky and Tennessee Compiled from the Latest Authorities
mwuss0672	louisiana	1826	FINLEY	1500	43	52	Map of Louisiana, Mississippi and Alabama Constructed from the Latest Authorities
mwuss0720	maine	1826	FINLEY	1200	43	56	Map of Maine, New Hampshire and Vermont, Compiled from the Latest Authorities
mwuss0866	massachusetts	1826	FINLEY	1200	43	55	Map of Massachusetts, Connecticut and Rhode Island Constructed from the Latest Authorities
mwam0653	america north	1826	FINLEY	900	56	44	Map of North America Including All the Recent Geographical Discoveries
mwuss0269	carolinas	1826	FINLEY	1500	43	53	Map of North and South Carolina and Georgia Constructed from the Latest Authorities
mwuss1310	ohio	1834	FINLEY	900	48	33	Map of Ohio and the Settled Parts of Michigan
mwuss1410	pennsylvania	1826	FINLEY	1200	41	51	Map of Pennsylvania, New Jersey and Delaware Constructed from the Latest Authorities
mwuss0979	missouri	1826	FINLEY	1200	43	55	Map of the State of Missouri and Territory of Arkansas Compiled from the Latest Authorities
mwuss1202	new york	1826	FINLEY	900	42	54	Map of the State of New York
mwuss1296	ohio	1826	FINLEY	1500	43	55	Map of the States of Ohio, Indiana & Illinois and Part of Michigan Territory Compiled from the Latest Authorities
mwam0652	america north	1826	FINLEY	500	45	56	Map of the United States
mwam0647	america north	1825	FINLEY	3500	135	159	Map of the United States of North America Compiled from the Latest and Most Authentic Information by David H. Vance
mwaf1251	africa west	1831	FINLEY	100	20	28	Map of the West Coast of Africa from Sierra Leone to Cape Palmas
mwuss1682	virginia	1826	FINLEY	1500	43	56	Map of Virginia and Maryland Constructed from the Latest Authorities
mwuss0775	maryland	1829	FINLEY	240	21	28	Maryland
mwuss0869	massachusetts	1831	FINLEY	240	22	27	Massachusetts
mwgm0295	mexico	1824	FINLEY	200	22	29	Mexico
mwuss0963	mississippi	1832	FINLEY	240	27	22	Mississippi
mwuss0980	missouri	1831	FINLEY	240	29	22	Missouri
mwbh0793	belgium holland	1825	FINLEY	80	22	28	Netherlands
mwuss1020	new hampshire	1824	FINLEY	240	28	22	New Hampshire
mwuss1057	new jersey	1824	FINLEY	240	29	22	New Jersey
mwuss1196	new york	1825	FINLEY	550	33	46	New York
mwam0638	america north	1824	FINLEY	180	29	22	North America
mwuss0270	carolinas	1829	FINLEY	300	22	28	North Carolina
mwuss1300	ohio	1829	FINLEY	300	28	21	Ohio
mwme0401	holy land	1824	FINLEY	100	28	22	Palestine
mwuss1413	pennsylvania	1829	FINLEY	375	32	47	Pennsylvania
mwuss1476	rhode isl	1831	FINLEY	240	29	22	Rhode Island
mwm0082a	europe mediterranean	1827	FINLEY	100	28	43	Romanum Imperium
mwuk0587	scotland	1824	FINLEY	120	29	22	Scotland
mwsam0150	south america	1831	FINLEY	120	29	22	South America
mwuss0264	carolinas	1824	FINLEY	240	22	29	South Carolina
mwsc0210	scandinavia	1832	FINLEY	100	26	21	Sweden, Denmark & Norway
mwuss1494	tennessee	1828	FINLEY	240	22	29	Tennessee
mww0682	world	1828	FINLEY	200	22	28	The World on Mercator's Projection
mwam0646	america north	1825	FINLEY	180	28	23	United States
mwuss1572	vermont	1824	FINLEY	240	28	22	Vermont
mwuss1681	virginia	1826	FINLEY	1500	32	47	Virginia
mwwi0173	west indies	1825	FINLEY	140	23	28	West Indies
mwit1016a	italy south	1691	FIORE	3500	37	43	Calabria Citeriore ed Vlteriore
mwc0100a	china	1721	FISCHER	400	27	43	Perspectivscher GrundRiß und Auffzug der Sinesischen Kaiserl: Burg zu Peking
mwme0402	holy land	1825	FISHER	120	37	23	Canaan Subsequent to its Conquest by Joshua, and Division among the Twelve Tribes of Israel
mwuss1204	new york	1827	FISHER	180	18	20	City of Albany, in the State of New York
mwwi0487	cuba	1829	FISHER	150	15	21	Havannah
mwgm0296	mexico	1824	FISHER	200	19	23	Mexico &c.
mwam0599	america north	1815	FISHER	150	18	23	North America
mwbp0558	poland	1814	FISHER	75	18	21	Poland
mwca0557	canada quebec	1833	FISHER	150	15	22	Quebec
mwat0315	atlantic south shetland isl.	1821	FISHER	150	19	23	Sketch of New South Shetland

AMPG REFERENCE	REGION	DATE	MAP MAKER	PRICE (UK£)	VERT. (cm.)	HOR. (cm.)	TITLE OF MAP (Comments by the editor in brackets)
mww0685	world	1829	FISHER	240	25	41	The World on Mercator's Projection with the New Discoveries by Capt. Parry
mwam1325	america north (west)	1785	FITCH	90000	71	53	A Map of the North West Parts of the United States of America
mwuss1264	new york	1850	FITCH	180	36	13	Map of Washington County by Asa Fitch
mwaa0200	arctic / antarctic	1782	FLECHEUX	720	77	53	Carte Generale de la terre
mwam0624	america north	1821	FLEISCHER	400	35	42	Karte von dem Vereinten Freistaaten Nordamericas
mwme0477a	jerusalem	1708	FLEISCHMANN	1350	38	48	Erste Abriss der Stadt Jerusalem
mwca0207	canada	1850	FLEMMING	120	31	39	Britisches Nord-America
mwuss0121	california	1848	FLEMMING	480	41	36	Californien, Oregon, Utah und Neu-Mejico
mwc0288	china	1845	FLEMMING	120	30	39	Chinesisches Reich und Japan
mwam1380	america north (west)	1848	FLEMMING	275	43	33	Das Oregon-Gebiet
mwgr0262	greece	1845	FLEMMING	100	33	42	Griechenland und die Ionischen Inseln
mwuk0289	ireland	1845	FLEMMING	100	37	30	Ireland
mwuss1517	texas	1842	FLEMMING	550	35	44	Mexico, Mittel America, Texas
mwp0142	australia	1842	FLEMMING	150	40	33	Neu Sud-Wales
mwaf1031	africa south	1850	FLEMMING	120	32	39	Sud-Africa
mwuss1528	texas	1845	FLEMMING	1500	39	32	Texas
mwaf0824a	africa north tunisia	1845	FLEMMING	80	36	32	Tunis u. Westl. Theil von Tripoli
mwuss1583	vermont	1845	FLETCHER	350	56	24	A New Map of Lake Champlain (size excl. text panels at sides)
mwp0055	australia	1814	FLINDERS	4800	66	46	Chart of Terra Australis by M. Flinders 1798-9. South Coast. Sheet VI. (first circumnavigation and map of Tasmania. Inset of Storm Bay.)
mwp0056	australia	1814	FLINDERS	4800	60	89	Chart of Terra Australis by M. Flinders, Commr. Of H.M. Sloop Investigator, South Coast Sheet V 1798, 1802 & 3 (Bass Strait, Melbourne, Victoria)
mwp0057	australia	1814	FLINDERS	4800	60	89	Chart of Terra Australis. Sheet III, South coast (Spencers Gulf, South Australia)
mwp0058	australia	1814	FLINDERS	10000	66	94	General chart of Terra Australis or Australia showing the parts explored between 1798 and 1803 (Only published in 1814 as Flinders was imprisoned on Mauritius by the French for nearly seven years)
mwp0041a	australia	1805	FLINDERS-HONKOOP	5000	70	48	Kaart van Basses Straat, tusschen Nieuw Zuid Wales en Van Diemens-Land ... 1798 1799 (The engraver was C. van Baarsel. It combines sheets V and VI of Flinders' charts, first publ. in 1814)
mww0049	world	1555	FLORIANO	100000	55	88	(This untitled map consists of globe gores laid out radially as 2 polar hemispheres)
mwaf0738	africa north algeria	1600	FLORIMI	800	40	51	Algeri (view)
mwbh0179	belgium holland	1610	FLORIMI	2500	34	44	Belgii Inferioris Descriptio Emendata cum Circuiacentiu Regionu Confiniis
mwaf0467	africa egypt etc	1600	FLORIMI	1200	34	47	Cairus quae olim Babylon; Aegypti Maxima Urbs (view)
mwme0933	turkey etc	1600	FLORIMI	1650	34	48	Costantinopoli (view)
mwe0023	europe	1600	FLORIMI	900	37	49	Europa
mwf0036	france	1600	FLORIMI	1000	44	50	Gallia
mwit0041	italy	1590	FLORIMI	6000	40	50	Geographia moderna de tutta la Italia con le sue (copy of Ducheto's 1582 map)
mwg0034	germany	1600	FLORIMI	1000	33	46	Germania, Regnum Totius Europae Amplissimum ac Florentissimum, Sedes Imperatoria
mwsp0170a	spain	1600	FLORIMI	1500	39	51	Hispaniae Nova Descriptio
mwe0861b	europe hungary	1600	FLORIMI	1000	37	45	Hungaria (shown above left)
mwit0529	italy milan	1600	FLORIMI	2000	41	54	La Gran Citta di Milano (close copy of Rascicotti)
mwit0338	italy emilia-romagna	1600	FLORIMI	960	34	46	La Nobilissima Citta di Parma
mwf0818a	france paris	1600	FLORIMI	2500	49	51	La Nobilissima et Grande Citta di Parigi
mwme0442a	jerusalem	1600	FLORIMI	4000	40	51	L'Antichissima Citta Di Gierusalemme come era nei Tempo sin.s. Gisv Christo con le sve Dechiaratione (reduced size version of Adrichom 1590)
mwf0996	france provence	1600	FLORIMI	900	41	52	Marsilia
mwit0876	italy sicily	1600	FLORIMI	1000	37	46	Messina
mwru0378	russia moscow	1600	FLORIMI	2250	36	50	Moscovia - Questa Citta e la Principale de la Provincia di Russia (view)
mwit0712	italy rome	1599	FLORIMI	3200	37	53	Novissima Urbis Romae Descriptio
mwit1167	italy veneto	1600	FLORIMI	4000	42	55	Padoa
mwit0871	italy sicily	1580	FLORIMI	2250	40	53	Palermo (close copy of Braun & Hogenberg 1580)
mwit0877	italy sicily	1600	FLORIMI	2400	37	46	Palermo Citta principalissima nella Sicilia (close copy of Braun & Hogenberg 1580)
mwit1096	italy tuscany	1600	FLORIMI	1500	38	51	Sena Vetus Civitas Virginis
mwit0877a	italy sicily	1600	FLORIMI	1000	34	48	Siciliae Regnum (close copy of Mercator)
mwsp0390c	spain regions	1600	FLORIMI	1500	39	54	Toledo (reduced version of Brambilla)
mwme0059	holy land	1600	FLORIMI	4500	43	65	Totius Terre Promissionis (north to the left. Based on Duchetti, 1572)
mwit1217a	italy venice	1598	FLORIMI	4500	39	51	Venetia
mwuk1223a	england london	1770	FLYN	900	29	50	A New and Correct Plan of London Westminster and Southwark with the New Buildings to the Year 1770
mwbh0352	belgium holland	1660	FOCKEN	2250	41	50	Gent (view)

AMPG REFERENCE	REGION	DATE	MAP MAKER	PRICE (UK£)	VERT. (cm.)	HOR. (cm.)	TITLE OF MAP (Comments by the editor in brackets)
mwuss1385	pennsylvania	1794	FOLIE	6000	66	67	To Thomas Mifflin Governor and Commander in Chief of the State of Pennsylvania this Plan of the City and Suburbs of Philadelphia is Respectfully Inscribed by the Editor
mwgm0341a	mexico	1842	FOLSOM	600	24	26	Mexico and Texas in 1842
mwwi0363	barbados	1681	FORD	6000	48	56	A New Map of the Island of Barbadoes wherein Every Parish, Plantation, Watermill & Cattlemill is Described with the Name of the Present Possessor, and All Things Els Remarkable (publ. by Mr Overton. Illustrated is the 1710 re-issue)
mwuk1250	england london	1789	FORES	950	31	56	A New Plan of London (second edition 1807)
mwuk1308	england london	1829	FORES	1350	43	79	Fores's New Plan of London Including all the late Improvements (second edition 1836)
mwf0349	france brittany	1726	FORESTIER	1350	51	61	Plan de la Ville de Rennes Leve par F. Forestier apres l'Incendie Arrivee le 22 Xbre 1720
mwbh0035	belgium holland	1569	FORLANI	1200	20	27	(Antwerp) Anversa
mwsw0015	switzerland	1569	FORLANI	1000	20	27	(Geneva) Ginevra
mwme0035	holy land	1569	FORLANI	2400	20	27	(Holy Land)
mwgm0132	mexico	1569	FORLANI	1200	20	27	(Mexico City)
mwit0110a	mediterranean east	1571	FORLANI	20000	33	43	(Untitled map)
mwit0030	italy	1568	FORLANI	20000	53	78	(Untitled map based on Gastaldi's 1561 map)
mwsp0160	spain	1567	FORLANI	12000	44	55	(Untitled map of Spain and Portugal, publ. by Bertelli)
mww0083	world	1594	FORLANI	60000	30	54	(Untitled map, 1st of 4 world maps by Forlani, 1st publ in 1560. This is the 3rd state.)
mwg0298a	bavaria	1570	FORLANI	1500	29	36	A Benigni Lettori, Ecoui la descrittione del Ducato di Bauiera
mwbp0067	baltic states	1568	FORLANI	8000	37	51	A Benigni Lettori ... Rapresenta la Prima Parte della Descrittione del Regno di Polonia, con la sua Scale di Miglia (close copy of Gastaldi 1562)
mwaf0007	africa	1563	FORLANI	30000	43	63	Africa a veteribus (title: text panel in cartouche. Map extends farther east than previous map.)
mwaf0006	africa	1562	FORLANI	30000	45	61	Al Ecc,mo Philosopho, Mathematico, Medico, et Cauallier aureato ... la descrittione dell'Africa (title: text panel in cartouche)
mwam0006	america continent	1570	FORLANI		51	65	Al Mag. Sig. Antonio Tognale Sig. Mio Osser.
mwit0460	italy lombardy	1561	FORLANI	5000	29	43	Al Molto Magco. Sigor. Daniel dana Sigor. suo Sempre Osservandissimo Pauli di Forlani de Verona ... Disegno di Tutta la Descrition e Region di Lombardia
mwme0918	turkey etc	1569	FORLANI	1500	19	25	Costantinopoli
mwit0629a	italy piedmont	1562	FORLANI	3000	33	44	Descrittione del Ducato di Savoia
mwbh0025	belgium holland	1567	FORLANI	2400	27	36	Descrittione Particulare di Fiandra
mwit1085	italy tuscany	1563	FORLANI	3000	32	44	Descrittione tutta la Toscana ... Bellamarto
mwit0630	italy piedmont	1567	FORLANI	3500	35	49	Essendomi Venuta Occasione d'Intagliare la Descrittione del Piemonte
mwit1129	italy florence	1569	FORLANI	1500	21	28	Fiorenza
mwbh0019	belgium holland	1563	FORLANI	3500	49	39	Gelriae, Cliviae, Iuliae, nec non Alliarum Regionum Adiacentium Nova Descriptio
mwam0306	america north	1565	FORLANI	150000	28	40	Il Disegno del Discoperto della Nova Franza, il quale s'e havuto Ultimamente dalla Novissima Navigatione de' Franzesi in quel Luogo: nel quale si Vedono Tutti l'Isole, Porti, Capi et Luoghi fra Terra che in quella sono (second state illustrated here, with Zaltieri's name and date 1566 inserted into title cartouche)
mwm0089	mediterranean adriatic	1568	FORLANI	7500	23	43	Il Golfo di Venetia
mwit0524	italy milan	1568	FORLANI	450	20	25	Il vero disegno della pianta di Milano si come veramente oggi di' si ritrova 1567 (shows fortifications)
mwit1087	italy tuscany	1569	FORLANI	550	19	28	Il vero disegno et ritratto di Siena
mwe1040a	europe romania	1566	FORLANI	4000	63	106	La Discrittione della Transilvania, et Parte del' Ungaria et il Simile della Romania
mwsam0003	south america	1562	FORLANI	35000	52	37	La Descrittione Di Tutto Il Peru.
mwit0864	italy sicily	1569	FORLANI	1200	21	29	La Nobile Citta di Messina
mwme0031	holy land	1566	FORLANI	5000	26	34	La Nuova et Esatta Descrittione della Soria, e dela Terra Santa
mwbp0175	poland	1568	FORLANI	12000	38	50	la Prima Parte della Descrittione del Regno di Polonia / Il Vero Disegno della Seconda Parte dil Regno di Polonia (2 maps, 38x50cm, close copies of Gastaldi 1562)
mwwi0398	cuba	1564	FORLANI	3000	18	25	L'Isola Cuba e Piu Settentrional della Spagnola
mwwi0573	hispaniola	1564	FORLANI	3000	17	24	L'Isola Spagnola una delle Prime che Colombo Trovasse, hoggi e dette l'Isola di S. Dominico ... 1564
mwit1049a	italy naples	1569	FORLANI	900	17	26	Napoli
mwit0368	italy friuli	1564	FORLANI	3500	28	38	Nova Descrittione del Friuli
mwit0380	italy lazio	1563	FORLANI	2000	32	47	Nova Discrittione di Tutto il Territorio de Roma (engraved by P. Forlani)
mwaf0460	africa egypt etc	1566	FORLANI	3000	27	36	Nuova, et Copiosa, Descrittione di Tutto l'Egitto
mwf0814	france paris	1569	FORLANI	2000	19	26	Parise
mwit0704	italy rome	1569	FORLANI	960	18	27	Roma (engraved by P. Forlani)
mwf0019	france	1566	FORLANI	6000	46	62	Totius Galliae Exactissima Descriptio
mwaf0761b	africa north libya	1569	FORLANI	1000	19	26	Tripoli de Barbaria

AMPG REFERENCE	REGION	DATE	MAP MAKER	PRICE (UK£)	VERT. (cm.)	HOR. (cm.)	TITLE OF MAP (Comments by the editor in brackets)
mww0053	world	1562	FORLANI		40	66	Universale Descrittione di Tutta la Terra Conosciuta Fin Qui (2nd world map by Forlani, reprinted in 1564 and 1576)
mww0059	world	1570	FORLANI	100000	41	74	Universale Descrittione di Tutta la Terra Conosciuta Fin Qui (4th world map by Forlani)
mwit1209	italy venice	1569	FORLANI	1500	20	27	Venetia
mwe0744	europe east	1566	FORLANI	3000	35	48	Very et Ultima Discrittione di Tutta l'Austria, Ungheria, Transilvania, Dalmatia, et Altri Paesi
mwe0409	europe austria vienna	1569	FORLANI	1000	20	26	Vienna - Il Vero Ritrato della Fortezza di Vienna Citta Nobilissima in Austria, si Veramente come Ogi di si Ritrova L'Anno 1567.
mwuk0311	scotland	1566	FORLANI?		25	34	Regno di Scotia (1st map of Scotland on its own. Only one example known.)
mww0055	world	1565	FORLANI-BERTELLI	150000	44	78	Universale Descrittione di Tutta la Terra Conosciuta Fin Qui (3rd state of Forlani's 3rd world map, 1st publ in 1563?)
mwuk0584	scotland	1818	FORREST	2500	178	128	The County of Lanark from Actual Survey (folding, dissected map)
mwsc0753b	scandinavia sweden	1815	FORSELL	2400	231	163	Karta ofver Sodra Delen af Sverige och Norrige eller det fordna sa Kallade Skandinavien
mwaa0031	antarctic	1777	FORSTER	2500	67	64	A Chart of the Southern Hemisphere According to the Latest Discoveries: with the Tracks of the Resolution (Forster traveled with Cook on his 2nd voyage and published this map weeks before Cook's official map.)
mwas0495	asia south east	1777	FORSTER	300	23	27	Chart Shewing the Track of the French Ships through the Moluccas to Batavia in 1768
mwam1331	america north (west)	1791	FORSTER	1000	50	65	Karte des Nordens von America, zur Beurtheilung der Wahrscheinlichkeit einer Nord=Westlichen Durchfahrt
mwuss1414	pennsylvania	1830	FORSTER	500	30	41	Map of a Part of the South Shore of Lake Erie in the Vicinity of Twenty Mile Creek, Jan. 1830
mwaa0151	arctic	1784	FORSTER	600	33	32	Neue und Verbesserte Carte der um den Nordpol Gelegen Lander bis zum 50 Grade; aus den Zuverlassigsten und Neusten Nachrichten Entworfen ...
mwec0376	uk england durham	1754	FORSTER	1200	50	72	To the ... Right Reverend Richard Lord Bishop of Durham ... this Plan of the City of Durham
mwf0146	france	1776	FOSSE	1500	94	119	Carte de la France, divisee en ses Provinces
mwam0877	america north (east)	1677	FOSTER	80000	30	39	A Map of New-England, Being the First that was Here Cut, and Done by the Best Pattern that Could be had, which Being in Some Places Defective, it Made the other Less Exact: Yet does it Sufficiently Shew the Scituation of the Country
mwuk0989	england	1737	FOSTER	4800	59	106	A New & Correct Map of England and Wales
mwam0145	america continent	1735	FOSTER	2500	54	47	A New and Correct Map of America Laid Down According to the Accurate Improvements of Senex, Moll
mwuk1172	england london	1738	FOSTER	3500	57	102	A New and Exact Plan of the Cities of London and Westminster & the Borough of Southwark (6 editions to 1775)
mwuk1174	england london	1739	FOSTER	1800	25	50	A Pocket Map of London Westminster and Southwark (4 editions to 1770)
mwuss0127	california	1849	FOSTER	240	12	23	Map of the Gold Region in Upper California
mwwi0074	west indies	1740	FOSTER	1650	40	47	The Seat of War in the West Indies
mwaa0082	arctic	1635	FOXE		32	44	(Untitled polar projection showing Foxe's unsuccessful attempt to find a north-west passage)
mwaf0001	africa	1508	FRACANZANO		20	30	(Untitled woodblock)
mwe1064	europe serbia	1717	FRANCESCHINI	1000	27	37	La Vera Pianta della Citta e Fortezza di Belgrado (shows the siege of 1717)
mwaa0060	arctic	1587	FRANCO	80000	45	46	Cosmographia Universalis Ab Orontio Olim Descriptio (based on Fine-Cimerlino but slightly smaller)
mwe1136a	europe south east	1597	FRANCO	900	16	21	Descrittione di quello che i Turchi possedono in Europa con i confini de' Papi
mwe0493b	europe croatia	1597	FRANCO	1000	14	18	Istria
mwit1216	italy venice	1597	FRANCO	5000	39	53	Venetia
mwf0852	france paris	1721	FRANCUS	960	33	37	Parys (9 insets).
mwp0117	australia	1837	FRANKLAND	350	29	37	Chart of Forestier's and Tasman's Peninsulas
mwca0227	canada arctic	1823	FRANKLIN	300	81	48	A Chart of the Discoveries & Route of the North Land Expedition, under the Command of Capt. Franklin, R.N. in the Years 1820 & 21
mwca0228	canada arctic	1823	FRANKLIN	400	26	46	An Outline to Shew the Connected Discoveries of Captains Ross, Parry & Franklin in the Years 1818, 19, 20, 22 & 23
mwca0245	canada arctic	1828	FRANKLIN	700	69	126	The Discoveries of the Expedition under the Command of Capt. Franklin R.N. near the Mouth of the Mackenzie River, and on the Sea Coast East & West A.D. 1825-6
mwp0440	pacific north	1790	FRASER	480	16	25	Bhering's Straits with the Adjacent Coasts of Asia & America
mwuk1310a	england london	1831	FRASER	1350	41	55	Fraser's Panoramic Plan of London (size incl. borders of views; 3 editions)
mwuk1257	england london	1794	FRAZER	850	49	64	A Correct Ground Plan of the Dreadful Fire at Ratcliff (Stepney, East End)
mwme0264a	holy land	1720	FREDERICH	180	21	16	(Untitled map of 'Das Paradies')

AMPG REFERENCE	REGION	DATE	MAP MAKER	PRICE (UK£)	VERT. (cm.)	HOR. (cm.)	TITLE OF MAP (Comments by the editor in brackets)
mwuss1059	new jersey	1828	FREEMAN	1200	59	48	(Patterson)
mwam0735	america north	1840	FREMIN	140	22	30	Amerique Septentrionale
mwam0297	america continent	1836	FREMIN	720	86	60	Carte de l'Amerique
mwam0618	america north	1820	FREMIN	800	53	80	Carte des Etats-Unis de l'Amerique Septentrionale Comprenant aussi les Territoires a l'Ouest du Mississipi ... et un Parte de la Nouvelle Espagne
mwaa0165	arctic	1820	FREMIN	200	30	29	Carte des Regions Polaires Boreales ou se Trouvent Tracees la Route et les Decouvertes du Cap. Parry en 1819 et 1820
mwsp0332	spain	1840	FREMIN	350	55	73	Carte Itineraire Physique Politique et Routiere de l'Espagne et du Portugal Indiquant let Trois Grandes Regions Geographiques
mwru0336	russia	1814	FREMIN	1200	46	65	Nouveau Plan de Saint Petersbourg
mwf0206	france	1850	FREMIN	650	81	115	Nouvelle Carte Routiere des Empre de France, de Belgique, de Sardaine et de la Suisse (borders of 28 town views)
mwme0420	holy land	1840	FREMIN	80	25	20	Palestine
mwf1167b	france lyon	1714	FREMONT, M.	2400	76	93	Description au Naturel de la Ville de Lyon et Paisages Alentour D'icelle (first publ. in 1659 by F. Demasso)
mwam1368	america north (west)	1845	FREMONT	1500	80	131	Map of an Exploring Expedition to the Rocky Mountains in the Year 1842 and to Oregon & North California in the Years 1843-44
mwuss1336	oregon	1848	FREMONT	1500	85	67	Map of Oregon and Upper California from the Surveys of John Charles Fremont and other Authorities
mwuss1337	oregon	1848	FREMONT	500	50	43	Map of Oregon and Upper California from the Surveys of John Charles Fremont and other Authorities
mwam0838	america north (central)	1845	FREMONT	800	50	71	Map Showing the Route Pursued by the Exploring Expedition to New Mexico and the Southern Rocky Mountains
mwam1365	america north (west)	1843	FREMONT	450	36	84	Map to Illustrate an Exploration of the Country, Lying between the Missouri River and the Rocky Mountains, on the Line of the Nebraska or Platte River
mwam1383	america north (west)	1848	FREMONT-PREUSS	800	50	43	Map of Oregon and Upper California From the Surveys of John Charles Fremont And other Authorities.
mwam1371	america north (west)	1846	FREMONT-PREUSS	5000	39	65	Topographical Map of the Road from Missouri to Oregon Commencing at the Mouth of the Kansas in the Missouri River and Ending at the Mouth of the Wallah-Wallah in the Columbia. In VII Sections ... from the Field Notes and Journal of Capt. J. C. Fremont (map in 7 sections, each 39x65cm.)
mwaa0149	arctic	1781	FRENTZEL	500	47		Nordliche Oberflaeche der Erde (polar projection excl. the European sector)
mwaa0038	antarctic	1781	FRENTZEL	650	47		Sudliche Oberflaeche der Erde (polar projection excl. the Atlantic sector)
mwwi0031	west indies	1680	FRESCHOT	650	5	5	Antille (7) Isole nel. America
mwp0049	australia	1812	FREYCINET	4800	75	49	Carte de la Baie des Chiens-Marins (Shark's Bay de Dampier) al la Terre d'Endracht; Nouvelle-Hollande
mwas0536	asia south east	1825	FREYCINET	160	32	23	Carte de la Partie Orientale du Gran Archipel d'Asie
mwsam0417	south america brazil	1825	FREYCINET	720	31	54	Carte de la Province de Rio de Janeiro
mwp0050	australia	1812	FREYCINET	4800	75	49	Carte Generale de la Cote Orientale de la Terre de Diemen
mwp0046	australia	1811	FREYCINET	8000	49	75	Carte Generale de la Nouvelle Hollande
mwp0047	australia	1811	FREYCINET	4000	49	75	Carte Generale de la Terre Napoleon (land areas are shaded)
mwp0051	australia	1812	FREYCINET	4800	49	75	Carte Generale du Detroit de Bass
mwsam0414	south america brazil	1825	FREYCINET	400	33	24	Plan de la Baie de Rio de Janeiro
mwat0230a	atlantic falkland isl.	1826	FREYCINET	600	51	77	Plan de la Baie Francaise
mwsam0814	south america uruguay	1825	FREYCINET	240	20	30	Plan de la Ville de Montivideo ... 1820
mwsam0415	south america brazil	1825	FREYCINET	720	23	32	Plan de la Ville de S. Sebastiao de Rio de Janeiro 1820
mwp0048	australia	1812	FREYCINET	4000	33	47	Plan de la Ville de Sydney (made in 1802)
mwsw0142a	switzerland	1742	FREYTAG	500	36	41	Nova et accurata Agri Tigurini
mwsam0678a	south america magellan	1716	FREZIER	300	19	29	Carte Reduite de l'Extremite de l'Amerique Meridionale dans la Partie du Sud
mwwi0594	hispaniola	1724	FREZIER	2000	41	60	Isle de S. Domingue et Debouquemens Circonvoisins
mwsam0455	south america chile	1716	FREZIER	320	18	29	Plan de la Baye de la Conception Situee a la Cote du Chily
mwsam0752	south america peru	1716	FREZIER	320	18	29	Plan de la Rade de Arica
mwsam0753	south america peru	1716	FREZIER	320	18	29	Plan de la Rade de Ylo situee a la Cote du Perou
mwsam0754	south america peru	1716	FREZIER	400	23	30	Plan de la Vile de Lima Capitale du Perou (sic)
mwsam0456	south america chile	1716	FREZIER	400	18	29	Plan de la Ville Santiago Capital du Royaume de Chili
mwat0092	atlantic azores	1716	FREZIER	240	19	30	Plan du Port, Ville, Citadelle, et Fortresses d'Angra
mwbh0540	belgium holland	1710	FRICX	350	47	61	(Ghent) Plan de la Ville et Citadelle de Gand
mwaf0166	africa	1730	FRICX	685	48	61	Carte d'Afrique
mwbh0874	luxembourg	1745	FRICX	350	41	53	Carte des Environs de Luxembourg
mwf0748a	france nord pas-de-calais	1725	FRICX	350	44	56	Carte Particuliere des Environs de Dunkerque, Bergues, Furnes, Gravelines, Calais
mwbh0530	belgium holland	1706	FRICX	350	43	57	Carte Particuliere des Environs de Lier et d'une Partie de la Campine

AMPG REFERENCE	REGION	DATE	MAP MAKER	PRICE (UK£)	VERT. (cm.)	HOR. (cm.)	TITLE OF MAP (Comments by the editor in brackets)
mwbh0534	belgium holland	1708	FRICX	350	43	57	Carte Particuliere des Environs de Maestricht, Partie de Liege, Fauccquemont, et Pays d'Outremeuse
mwas0136	asia continent	1730	FRICX	685	44	58	L'Asie
mwf0955	france picardy	1710	FRICX	350	42	57	Les Embouchures de la Somme et de Bresle Riv. ou est Sr. Valeri, eu et Dieppe
mwbh0541	belgium holland	1710	FRICX	1000	50	58	Plan de la Ville de Brusselles
mwf0743	france nord pas-de-calais	1709	FRICX	650	45	56	Plan de la Ville et Citadelle de Lille
mwg0098	germany	1711	FRICX	500	47	58	Postarum seu Veredariorum Stationes per Germaniam et Provincias Adiacentes
mwe0461	europe central	1711	FRICX	600	48	57	Postarum seu Veredariorum Stationes per Germaniam et Provincias Adiacentes (postal map)
mwbh0537	belgium holland	1709	FRICX	2000	42	56	Table des cartes des Pays-Bas et des frontieres de France (24-sheet map, each 42x56cm.)
mwgr0245a	greece	1824	FRIED	550	82	115	Carte Comparative de la Grèce Ancienne & moderne
mwe0843	europe east	1829	FRIED	1200	122	109	Carte de la Plus Grande Partie de la Turquie d'Europe Contenant la Moldavie, la Bessarabie, la Valachie, la Bulgarie et la Roumelie
mwe0837	europe east	1811	FRIED	1200	41	69	Carte de la Valachie et de la Moldavie Comprenant aussi la Bessarabie, la Transilvanie (4 sheets, each 41x69cm.)
mwe0838	europe east	1811	FRIED	600	45	63	Carte Generale de la Valachie - Generalcharte de Walachey
mwe1084	europe serbia	1812	FRIED	500	41	59	Generalcharte von Servien und Bosnien
mwe0398	europe austria	1823	FRIED	450	62	80	Karte der Umgebungen Wiens
mwe0974	europe hungary	1842	FRIED	450	53	75	Magyar-Orszag General- Post- und Strassen-Karte des Konigreichs Ungarn und des Grossfurstenthums Siebenburgen
mwme1051	turkey etc	1821	FRIED	600	74	56	Plan de Constantinople du Bosphore & du Canal de la Mer Noire
mwe0399	europe austria	1823	FRIED	450	60	78	Topographische Karte der Umgebungen Wien's nach den Neuesten und Besten Hulfsquellen
mwf0660	france lorraine	1522	FRIES	4500	30	44	(Lotharingia. Printed on the verso of Fries' map of Scandinavia)
mwin0081	india	1522	FRIES	5000	33	44	Indiae Tabula Moderna (reprinted 1525, 1535, 1541)
mww0027	world	1522	FRIES	7200	34	48	Orbis.Typus.Universalis.Juxta.Hydrographoru.Traditionem.Exactissime.Depicta.1522.L.F. (reprinted 1525, 1535 and 1541)
mwc0001	china	1522	FRIES	6000	33	46	Ta Superioris Indiae (title on verso. 1st printed map of China, reprinted 1525,1535,1541)
mwsc0005	scandinavia	1522	FRIES	4500	34	48	Tab Nova Nor & Goti (reprinted 1525, 1535, 1541 with different titles)
mwit0848	italy sardinia and sicily	1522	FRIES	1200	31	40	Tab. Mo. Italiae Corsice et Sardinie (title on verso. Reprinted 1525, 1535, 1541, titles vary. Illustrated is the 1535 edition)
mwme0904	turkey etc	1522	FRIES	2250	30	38	Tabu Minor. Asiae (reprinted 1525,1535, 1541)
mwme0014	holy land	1522	FRIES	2500	29	42	Tabu Mo.ter Sanctae (reprinted 1525, 1535, 1541)
mwe0734	europe east	1522	FRIES	2400	31	37	Tabu Mode. Vvala. (reprinted 1525, 1535, 1541)
mwbp0161	poland	1522	FRIES	2400	31	37	Tabu Mode. Vvala. (reprinted 1525, 1535, 1541)
mwsp0148	spain	1522	FRIES	2500	33	43	Tabu Moder Hispa (reprinted 1525, 1535, 1541)
mwgr0336	greece crete	1522	FRIES	2000	32	46	Tabu Nova Can (reprinted 1525, 1535, 1541. Illustrated: 1535 edition)
mwit0011	italy	1522	FRIES	4000	30	34	Tabu Nova Itali. (reprinted 1525, 1535 and 1541)
mwe0983	europe rhine	1522	FRIES	1500	30	43	Tabu Provi. Rhen (reprinted 1525,1535, 1541)
mwsw0003	switzerland	1522	FRIES	2000	34	42	Tabu. Heremi Helvetiorum (reprinted 1525, 1535, 1541. Illustrated is 1535 edition with different title. South to the top.)
mwuk0654	uk	1522	FRIES	3500	31	41	Tabu. Hiberniae.. Sco. (reprinted 1525, 1535, 1541. The 1535 edition shown.)
mwf0010	france	1522	FRIES	2500	31	39	Tabu. Moder. Galie (reprinted 1525, 1535, 1541)
mwg0009	germany	1522	FRIES	2500	34	33	Tabu. Moder. Germ. (reprinted 1525, 1535, 1541)
mwg0500a	rheinland-pfalz	1535	FRIES	720	27	43	Tabu. Nova Provin. Rheni
mwe1132	europe south east	1522	FRIES	1500	32	40	Tabula Mo Bossin (Balkans & Greece, reprinted 3 times. 1541 edition illustrated.)
mwgr0009	greece	1522	FRIES	3000	36	41	Tabula Mo. Bossin T. P R E. ('Modern Greece'. Illustrated is the 1525 edition. Also reprinted 1535 and 1541)
mwaf0848	africa south	1522	FRIES	3000	35	43	Tabula Moderna Aphrice (reprinted 1525, 1535 and 1541. Illustrated is 1535 edition)
mwe0850	europe hungary	1525	FRIES	1200	28	36	Tabula Moderna Hungariae, Poloniae ... (title on verso)
mwas0359	asia south east	1522	FRIES	6000	31	43	Tabula Moderna Indiae Orientalis (title on verso. 1st modern printed map of the East Indies, reprinted 1525,1535, 1541)
mwaf1084	africa west	1522	FRIES	3000	32	41	Tabula Moderna Portionis Aphrice (reprinted 1525, 1535 and 1541. Illustrated is the 1535 edition. This is a reduced size version of Waldseemuller. Although it is a map of North Africa, the Western parts are for the first time shown in 'modern' form by Waldseemuller.)

AMPG REFERENCE	REGION	DATE	MAP MAKER	PRICE (UK£)	VERT. (cm.)	HOR. (cm.)	TITLE OF MAP (Comments by the editor in brackets)
mwat0002	atlantic ocean (all)	1522	FRIES	12000	33	44	Tabula Terre. Nova (reprinted 1525, 1535, 1541, with different titles. Reduced size version of Waldseemuller map.)
							SEE ALSO 'PTOLEMY-FRIES' AND 'WALDSEEMULLER-FRIES'
mwru0562	ukraine	1787	FRIESEMAN	2000	40	45	Carte de la Crimee (4 sheets, each 40x45cm. Map by JH van Kinsbergen)
mwsam0204	south america amazon	1707	FRITZ	500	21	34	Strom Maragnon
mwuk1325	england london	1842	FROGGETT	2000	84		Froggett's Map of the Country Fifteen Miles round London (circular map)
mwuk1311	england london	1831	FROGGETT	1800	112	137	Froggett's Survey of the Country Thirty Miles round London (5 editions until 1841)
mwuss1640a	virginia	1775	FRY-JEFFERSON	20000	80	125	A Map of the most Inhabited part of Virginia containing the whole Province of Maryland
mwg0188	elbe river	1835	FUCHS	1200	10	850	Panorama des Rechten Elb-Ufers von Hamburg bis Blankenese
mwuk1878	wales	1833	FULLARTON	40	24	19	(Monmouthshire)
mwuk1061	england	1834	FULLARTON	300	56	44	A Map of England and Wales Taken from the Government Map Made by Order of the Board of Ordnance. Engr'd. by R. Scott
mwaf0340	africa	1847	FULLARTON	50	25	20	Africa
mwam0678	america north	1832	FULLARTON	160	20	25	British North America
mwgm0087	gulf of mexico and surrounding regions	1850	FULLARTON	160	24	15	Central America Shewing the Proposed Junctions of Atlantic and Pacific Oceans
mwgm0081	gulf of mexico and surrounding regions	1845	FULLARTON	180	52	41	Central America, Namely the (Late) Confederated States of Central America: The Mexican States of Chiapa, Tabasco & Yucatan; and British Honduras
mwc0289	china	1846	FULLARTON	240	41	52	China
mwsam0558	south america colombia	1847	FULLARTON	120	19	24	Colombia
mwec0209	uk england cornwall	1833	FULLARTON	100	19	24	Cornwall
mwsc0405	scandinavia denmark	1845	FULLARTON	100	50	41	Denmark and the Duchies by G.H. Swanston
mwsam0648	south america guyana	1840	FULLARTON	160	47	32	Dutch Possessions in South America and the West Indies
mwas0551	asia south east	1847	FULLARTON	100	21	26	East India Islands
mwjk0147	japan	1846	FULLARTON	240	47	31	Japan, Mandshuria, (Showing the Course of the Amur River) the Kurile Isles &c. According to the British & Russian Admiralty Surveys, Krusenstern, Siebold &c.
mwme0519	jerusalem	1848	FULLARTON	60	13	23	Jerusalem or the City of the Lord
mwp0166	australia	1847	FULLARTON	160	19	24	Map of Australia
mwam1385	america north (west)	1849	FULLARTON	160	24	15	Oregon and California
mwp0292	pacific (all)	1847	FULLARTON	80	21	27	Pacific Ocean
mwgm0449	panama	1849	FULLARTON	160	23	14	Panama Shewing the Proposed Junction by Railway
mwca0200	canada	1845	FULLARTON	200	23	14	Principal Cities and Ports in Canada
mwaf1024	africa south	1845	FULLARTON	240	40	52	South Africa from Official & other Authorities
mwaf1027	africa south	1847	FULLARTON	80	20	25	Southern Africa
mwg0184	germany	1845	FULLARTON	120	53	42	States of the German Confederation
mwsw0229a	switzerland	1836	FULLARTON	120	20	25	Switzerland (incl. 'Sardinian State')
mwaa0176	arctic	1850	FULLARTON	200	46	32	The Arctic Regions, Showing the North-West Passage as Determined by Cap. R. Mc.Clure and other Arctic Voyagers. Compiled by J. Hugh Johnson F.R.G.S.
mwam0800	america north	1850	FULLARTON	200	42	52	United States North America
mwec1210	uk england warwickshire	1841	FULLARTON	140	24	19	Warwickshire
mwme0113	holy land	1650	FULLER	350	28	33	(Caesarea, Manasseh)
mwme0106	holy land	1648	FULLER	350	28	33	(Gilead)
mwme0114	holy land	1650	FULLER	875	74	35	(Holy Land)
mwme0115	holy land	1650	FULLER	350	30	36	(Holy Land, Arabian Desert and Mesopotamia)
mwme0076	holy land	1614	FULLER	350	28	37	A Description of the Land of Gosen and Moses's Passage through the Deserts
mwaf0473	africa egypt etc	1650	FULLER	350	29	34	Aegyptus Antiqua
mwme0116	holy land	1650	FULLER	350	28	33	Assher
mwme0117	holy land	1650	FULLER	350	28	33	Benjamin
mwme0118	holy land	1650	FULLER	550	28	33	Canaan
mwme0119	holy land	1650	FULLER	350	30	35	Confina Palestinae cum Incolis as Orientem
mwme0120	holy land	1650	FULLER	350	24	30	Dan
mwme0121	holy land	1650	FULLER	350	29	37	Desertum Paran. (Sinai)
mwme0122	holy land	1650	FULLER	350	28	34	Ephraim Vitula est Edocta Amans Triturare
mwme0108	holy land	1648	FULLER	350	29	33	Gad
mwme0123	holy land	1650	FULLER	350	28	34	Galileae
mwme0455	jerusalem	1650	FULLER	650	28	37	Ierusalem Qualis (ut Plurimum) Extitit Aetate Solomonis
mwme0124	holy land	1650	FULLER	350	28	32	Issachar
mwme0125	holy land	1650	FULLER	350	29	34	Juda
mwme0126	holy land	1650	FULLER	350	28	33	Lectori en Tibi Antiquam Canaan (Qualis Tempore Abrahae, et Ante Adventum Jushuae Exitit) in Tredecim Nationes Divisam
mwme0127	holy land	1650	FULLER	350	28	33	Libanus et Ejus Vicinia
mwme0128	holy land	1650	FULLER	350	27	32	Manasse Trans-Jordanicam
mwme0129	holy land	1650	FULLER	350	30	35	Manasseh Ramus Faec Undus
mwme0130	holy land	1650	FULLER	350	29	34	Manassen cis Jordanicam

AMPG REFERENCE	REGION	DATE	MAP MAKER	PRICE (UK£)	VERT. (cm.)	HOR. (cm.)	TITLE OF MAP (Comments by the editor in brackets)
mwme0131	holy land	1650	FULLER	350	28	38	Napthali
mwme0132	holy land	1650	FULLER	350	28	33	Pars Regni Moab
mwme0133	holy land	1650	FULLER	350	28	33	Reuben
mwme0134	holy land	1650	FULLER	350	27	32	Simeon
mwme0135	holy land	1650	FULLER	350	28	34	Terra Moria Jerusalem
mwme0456	jerusalem	1650	FULLER	650	27	33	Terra Moriath sive Solymarum Ager Suburbanus
mwme0136	holy land	1650	FULLER	650	34	50	Terrae Israel
mwme0137	holy land	1650	FULLER	350	28	32	Tribe of Issachar
mwme0138	holy land	1650	FULLER	350	28	34	Zebulon ad Portum Marium ipse ad Portu Marium Habitabit
mwsw0096	switzerland	1700	FUNCKE	600	46	55	Exactissima Helvetiae, Rhaetiae, Valesiae
mwit0911	italy sicily	1700	FUNCKE	1200	48	57	Infelicis Regni Siciliae Tabula in Tres Valles Divisa Demonae, Notae et Mazarae ex Officina Davidis Funcke
mwgr0419	greece crete	1700	FUNCKE	1200	54	60	Insula & Regnum Candia olim Creta Edita
mwg0745	thuringia	1690	FUNCKE	480	42	51	Landgraviatus Thuringia
mwbp0340	poland	1700	FUNCKE	960	47	55	Magnae Prussiae Ducatus Tabula
mww0276	world	1700	FUNCKE	6000	48	56	Novissima & Exactissima Totius Orbis Terrarum Tabula
mwsc0097	scandinavia	1700	FUNCKE	800	50	58	Novissima et Accuratissima Scandinaviae Tabula Complectens Regnorum Sueciae, Daniae et Norwegiae
mwme0225	holy land	1700	FUNCKE	650	46	55	Novissima Totius Terrae Sanctae sive Promissionis Descriptio
mwit0376	italy friuli	1798	FURLANETTO	2500	60	69	Carta Topografica di Tutto il Territorio del Friuli Goriziano ed Udinese (1st edition 1780)
mwit1250	italy venice	1780	FURLANETTO	8000	73	136	Laguna Veneta
mwe0826	europe east	1788	FURLANETTO	720	40	92	Nuova Carta Geografica della Guerra Presente tra i due Imperj e la Porta Ottomana
mwm0101	mediterranean adriatic	1796	FURLANETTO	7200	55	151	Nuova Carta Marittima del Golfo di Venezia
mwe0981	europe montenegro	1785	FURLANETTO	550	44	57	Nuova Carta Topografica delle Bocche di Cattaro, Monte-Negro e Parte dell'Albania
mwit1248	italy venice	1770	FURLANETTO	5500	57	98	Nuova Pianta Elevata della Nobile e Cospicua Citta di Venezia
mwe0762	europe east	1665	FURST	1200	36	86	Abbildung des Konigreich Ungarn durch Turckey bis nach Constantinopel
mwme0956	turkey etc	1665	FURST	500	22	37	Bildnus der Statt Constantinopel in Turckey (view)
mwgr0399	greece crete	1669	FURST	720	31	39	Die Uhralte Christen- aber nun von dem Turcken Uberwundene Stat Candia (view)
mwsw0245	swiss alps	1814	FUSSLI	450	16	190	Panorama prise ou sommet du Mont Rigi
mwca0277	canada new brunswick	1835	GAGE	1000	65	88	A Plan of the City & Harbour of St. John, N.B. with the Adjoining Country
mwgm0186	mexico	1695	GAGE	300	21	14	Environs du Lac de Mexique
mwec0705	uk england lancashire	1836	GAGE	1500	102	168	This Trigonometrical Plan of the Town and Port of Liverpool
mwec1325	uk england yorkshire	1712	GALE	480	45	52	Richmondiae Comitatus et Alvertunae Schira
mwsp0675	balearic islands	1770	GALIANI	280	34	23	L'isola di Minorica / Plano ... Mahone
mwuss0097	california	1802	GALIANO & VALDES	1200	36	34	Carta de los Reconocimientos Hechos in 1602 por el Capitan Sebastian Vizcayno Formada por los Planos que Hizo el Mismo durante su Comision
mwca0665	canada west	1795	GALIANO & VALDES	3000	58	88	Carta Esferica de los Reconocimientos Hechos en la Costa No. De America desde la parte en que empiezan á angostar Los Canales De La Entrada De Juan De Fuca
mwca0664	canada west	1795	GALIANO & VALDES	10000	57	89	Carta Esferica de las reconocimientos hechos en 1792 en la Costa N.O. de America para Examinar la Entrada de Juan Fuca, y la internacion de sus Canales navigables...
mwca0669	canada west	1800	GALIANO & VALDES	1500	48	36	Carta Esferica de los Reconocimientos Hechos en la Costa N.O. de America en 1791 y 92 por las Goletas Sutil, y Mexicana y otros Buques de S.M.
mwuss0098	california	1802	GALIANO & VALDES	600	55	44	Plano del Puerto de S. Diego en la Costa Setentl. de Californs. Levantado por el 2o. Piloto de la Armada D. Juan Pantoja Ano 1782
mwf0939	france paris	1850	GALIGNANI	300	41	55	Galignani's Plan of Paris and Environs
mwp0174	australia	1851	GALL & INGLIS	350	44	56	Australian Colonies and New Zealand
mwca0209	canada	1850	GALL & INGLIS	250	43	56	Canada and Arctic Regions of North America
mwas0555	asia south east	1850	GALL & INGLIS	300	44	55	Gall & Inglis' Map of Asiatic Islands
mwuk0301	ireland	1850	GALL & INGLIS	200	53	44	Gall & Inglis' Map of Ireland with the Railways
mwaf0344	africa	1850	GALL & INGLIS	200	57	46	Map of Africa
mwme0695	arabia etc	1850	GALL & INGLIS	200	27	46	Map of Arabia
mwp0532	pacific south	1851	GALL & INGLIS	350	44	56	Map of Asiatic Islands.
mwc0297	china	1850	GALL & INGLIS	240	46	57	Map of China, and Japan
mwin0382	india	1850	GALL & INGLIS	240	55	43	Map of Hindostan
mwit0252	italy	1850	GALL & INGLIS	150	57	46	Map of Italy
mwme1069	turkey etc	1850	GALL & INGLIS	250	45	54	Map of Modern Asia Minor
mwam0801	america north	1850	GALL & INGLIS	300	44	54	Map of North America
mwme0857	persia etc	1850	GALL & INGLIS	160	45	54	Map of Persia
mwbp0573	poland	1850	GALL & INGLIS	200	45	55	Map of Poland

AMPG REFERENCE	REGION	DATE	MAP MAKER	PRICE (UK£)	VERT. (cm.)	HOR. (cm.)	TITLE OF MAP (Comments by the editor in brackets)
mwuk1364	england north	1850	GALL & INGLIS	200	46	59	Map of Roman Wall / Map of Britannia Antiqua (2 maps on one sheet)
mwru0370	russia	1850	GALL & INGLIS	240	44	55	Map of Russia in Asia
mwuk0643	scotland	1850	GALL & INGLIS	160	57	47	Map of Scotland
mwsw0238	switzerland	1850	GALL & INGLIS	200	47	57	Map of Switzerland
mwam1260	america north (east)	1850	GALL & INGLIS	240	53	43	Map of the United States
mwwi0221	west indies	1850	GALL & INGLIS	240	46	57	Map of the West Indies
mwsam0165	south america	1850	GALL & INGLIS	160	43	54	South America
mww0750	world	1850	GALL & INGLIS	300	45	52	The World on Mercators Projection
mww0751	world	1850	GALL & INGLIS	400	46	57	Western Hemisphere / Eastern Hemisphere (2 maps)
mwbh0096	belgium holland	1581	GALLE	3000	38	52	Antverpia. Antwerpiae Celeberrimi
mwbh0209b	belgium holland	1625	GALLE	2000	37	48	Nieuwe beschrijvinge van Oost en West Vrieslant door Davidt Fabricio
			FOR ORTELIUS-GALLE SEE ORTELIUS (MINIATURE)				
mwgm0268	mexico	1807	GARCIA CONDE	25000	148	198	Plano General de la Ciudad de Mexico (illustrated below is the reduced size Mogg, 1811 edition, 51x59cm.)
mwit1260	italy venice	1838	GARLATO	550	54	72	Pianta della Regia Citta di Venezia e sue Isole Vicine
mwuk0414	scotland	1675	GARRETT	1100	40	50	The Kingdome of Scotland
mwuk1138	england london	1703	GASCOYNE	7200	125	110	An Actuall Survey of the Parish of St. Dunstan Stepney
mwe0741	europe east	1560	GASTALDI	6000	35	103	(Southeastern Europe)
mwbp0066	baltic states	1562	GASTALDI	12000	37	53	(Untitled northern sheet of 2 maps. For southern sheet see 'Poland')
mwaf0454	africa egypt etc	1548	GASTALDI	400	13	17	Aegyptus Nova Tabula
mwaf0849	africa south	1548	GASTALDI	800	13	17	Africa Nova Tabula
mwuk0660	uk	1548	GASTALDI	650	13	18	Anglia E Hibernia Nova
mwme0529	arabia etc	1548	GASTALDI	1000	13	18	Arabia Felix Nova Tabula
mwin0084	india	1548	GASTALDI	600	13	17	Calecut Nova Tavola
mww0042	world	1548	GASTALDI	1600	14	18	Carta Marina Nova Tabula
mwe0632	europe dalmatia	1548	GASTALDI	450	13	17	Dalmacia Nova Tabula
mwru0011	russia	1550	GASTALDI	6000	27	38	Descriptione de la Moscovia
mwit0859	italy sicily	1545	GASTALDI	9000	37	54	Descrittione della Sicilia con le sue Isole
mwbh0006	belgium holland	1548	GASTALDI	600	13	17	Flandria, Barbantia e Holanda Nova
mwf0015	france	1548	GASTALDI	450	13	17	Gallia Nova Tabula
mwe1133	europe south east	1560	GASTALDI	12000	83	107	Geografia Particolare d'una Gran Parte dell'Europa, Nuovamente Descritta
mwg0014	germany	1548	GASTALDI	400	13	17	Germania Nova Tabula MDXXXXII
mwgr0016	greece	1548	GASTALDI	550	13	17	Graetia Nova Tabula
mwsp0154	spain	1548	GASTALDI	450	13	17	Hispania Nova Tabula
mwbp0173	poland	1562	GASTALDI	18000	80	53	Il Disegno de Geografia Moderna del Regno di Polonia … e Parte del Ducado di Moscovia (Publ. by Tramezini)
mwaf0008	africa	1564	GASTALDI		106	142	Il disegno della Geografia moderna de tutta la parte dell'Africa (title: text panel top right)
mwit0025	italy	1561	GASTALDI	25000	53	78	Il Disegno della Geografia Moderna de Tutta la Provincia de la Italia
mwme0531	arabia etc	1561	GASTALDI	12000	63	74	Il Disegno Della Seconda Parte Dell'Asia.
mwas0362	asia south east	1561	GASTALDI	40000	76	76	Il Disegno della Terza Parte dell'Asia
mwme0915	turkey etc	1564	GASTALDI	8000	40	52	Il Disegno d'Geografia Moderna della Provincia di Natolia, et Caramania … l'Isola di Candia, et quella di Cipro
mwg0014a	germany	1552	GASTALDI	3000	25	36	Il vera ritratto di tutta d'Alamagna (shown above left)
mwme0920	turkey etc	1570	GASTALDI	6000	34	45	Il vero disegno della provincia della Natolia et Caramania
mwas0360	asia south east	1548	GASTALDI	1500	13	17	India Tercera Nova Tabula
mwwi0394	cuba	1548	GASTALDI	1500	14	17	Isola Cuba Nova
mwaf0579	africa islands madagascar	1567	GASTALDI	1250	24	18	Isola di San Lorenzo. In questo Isola Visono Elefanti e Boschi
mwwi0570	hispaniola	1548	GASTALDI	750	13	17	Isola Spagnola Nova
mwit0020	italy	1548	GASTALDI	550	12	16	Italia Nova Tavola
mwas0003	asia continent	1561	GASTALDI	36000	45	71	La Descrittione dell Prima Parte dell'Asia (middle east) / Il Disegno della Seconda Parte dell'Asia (SW asia) / Il Disegno della Terza Parte dell'Asia (SE Asia) (3 maps, each roughly 45x71cm)
mwme0710	caucasus	1561	GASTALDI	6000	43	74	La Descrittione Della Prima Parte Dell'Asia.
mwf0457	france corsica	1560?	GASTALDI	3000	31	21	L'Isola di Corsica, con i Territori, Citta, et Castelle Forti
mwit1158	italy veneto	1548	GASTALDI	350	13	18	Marcha Trevisana Nova Tavola
mwaf1085	africa west	1548	GASTALDI	500	13	17	Mauritania Nova Tabula
mwru0009	russia	1548	GASTALDI	550	14	17	Moschovia Nova Tavola
mwme0909	turkey etc	1548	GASTALDI	600	13	18	Natolia Nova Tabula
mwgm0129	mexico	1548	GASTALDI	2400	13	17	Nueva Hispania Tabula Nova
mwme0754	persia etc	1548	GASTALDI	450	13	17	Persia Nova Tabula
mwit0626	italy piedmont	1548	GASTALDI	450	13	18	Piamonte Nova Tav.
mwbp0168	poland	1548	GASTALDI	450	13	18	Polonia et Hungaria Nova Tabula
mwbp0169	poland	1548	GASTALDI	450	13	18	Prussia e Livonia Nova Tabula
mwsp0152	spain	1544	GASTALDI	36000	69	95	Questa e la Vera Descrittione di Tutta la Spagna (Gastaldi's first map?)
mwsc0010	scandinavia	1548	GASTALDI	1250	13	17	Schonladia Nova
mwit0851	italy sardinia and sicily	1548	GASTALDI	450	13	16	Sicilia, Sardinia Nova Tabula

AMPG REFERENCE	REGION	DATE	MAP MAKER	PRICE (UK£)	VERT. (cm.)	HOR. (cm.)	TITLE OF MAP (Comments by the editor in brackets)
mwme0860	syria etc	1548	GASTALDI	650	13	17	Soria e Terra Sancta Nova Tabula
mwbp0064a	baltic states	1548	GASTALDI	500	13	17	Tavola Nuova di Prussia et di Livonia (illustrated below left is enlarged re-issue by Ruscelli)
mwsam0001	south america	1548	GASTALDI	1000	13	18	Tierra Nova
mwam0843	america north (east)	1548	GASTALDI	2500	13	17	Tierra Nueva
mwca0001	canada	1548	GASTALDI	2500	13	18	Tierra Nueva
mww0043	world	1548	GASTALDI	2500	14	18	Universale Novo
mww0057	world	1567	GASTALDI-CAMOCIO		63	105	Cosmographia universalis et exactissima … MDLXIX (based on Gastaldi's map of c1561 but smaller in size)
mwgr0022	greece	1566	GASTALDI-CAMOCIO	15000	49	68	Descrittione della geografia moderna di tutta la Grecia
mwjk0102	japan	1750	GAUBIL	400	17	21	Carte des Isles de Lieou-kieou (shows Okinawa)
mwuss0451	florida	1790	GAULD	28000	61	225	An Accurate Chart of the Tortugas and Florida Kays or Martyrs, Surveyed by George Gauld
mwam0246	america continent	1797	GAULTIER	75	38	32	A Plain Map of America
mwam0263	america continent	1810	GAULTIER	250	43	34	Amerique Septentrionale et Meridionale, pour Servir aux Lecons de Geographie
mwit1065a	italy naples	1754	GAULTIER	450	43	48	Cratere Maritimo, o Parte del Golfo di Napoli
mwf0417	france burgundy	1782	GAUTHEY	280	22	44	Carte du Canal de Communication des Mers par le Charollois Joignant la Loire al la Saone, le Long des Rivieres de Bourbince de Dheune et de Thalie
mwme0508a	jerusalem	1764	GAVIN	240	18	23	The Ancient City of Jerusalem and Places Adjacent
mww0448	world	1760	GAVIN	500	19	38	The World Agreable to the Latest Discoveries
mwam1261	america north (east)	1850	GAVIT & DUTHIE	420	28	43	Map of the Frontiers of the Northern Colonies with the Boundary Line Established between them and the Indians at the Treaty Held by S. Will Johnson at Ft. Stanwix in Nov'r 1768.
mwuss1093	new york	1763	GAZZETTIERE AMERIC.	280	24	18	Caduta di Niagara
mwsam0208	south america amazon	1763	GAZZETTIERE AMERIC.	240	22	32	Carta del Corso del Maragnone o Sia del Gran Fiume dell' Amazzoni
mwam1012	america north (east)	1763	GAZZETTIERE AMERIC.	300	22	32	Carta della Nuova Inghilterra, Nuova Iork, e Pensilvania
mwsam0809	south america uruguay	1763	GAZZETTIERE AMERIC.	240	23	26	Carta Esatta Rappresentante il Corso del Fiume Paraguay e di Paesi ad esso Vicini
mwwi0556	guadeloupe	1777	GAZZETTIERE AMERIC.	320	22	30	Carta Esatta Rappresentante l'Isola della Guadalupa
mwwi0379	barbados	1777	GAZZETTIERE AMERIC.	450	23	18	Carta Esatta Rappresentante l'Isola di Barbados
mwwi0446	cuba	1763	GAZZETTIERE AMERIC.	750	26	32	Carta Esatta Rappresentante l'Isola di Cuba Estratta dalle Carte del Sig. Poppler
mwwi0525	grenada	1777	GAZZETTIERE AMERIC.	180	23	18	Carta Esatta Rappresentante l'Isola di Granata
mwwi0624	hispaniola	1763	GAZZETTIERE AMERIC.	300	26	32	Carta Esatta Rappresentante l'Isola di S. Domingo o sia Hispaniola
mwam1286	great lakes	1763	GAZZETTIERE AMERIC.	600	26	20	Carta Rappresentante i Cinque Laghi del Canada
mwca0605	canada st lawrence	1763	GAZZETTIERE AMERIC.	240	25	19	Carta Rappresentante il Golfo del Fiume S. Lorenzo
mwuss0798	massachusetts	1763	GAZZETTIERE AMERIC.	375	21	18	Carta Rappresentante il Porto di Boston
mwgm0239	mexico	1777	GAZZETTIERE AMERIC.	250	24	22	Carta Rappresentante la Baia di Campeggio e l'Jucatan
mwuss0417	florida	1763	GAZZETTIERE AMERIC.	300	23	22	Carta Rappresentante la Penisola della Florida
mwsam0096	south america	1777	GAZZETTIERE AMERIC.	200	21	18	Carta Rappresentante l'America Meridionale
mwsam0835a	south america venezuela	1763	GAZZETTIERE AMERIC.	200	21	29	Carta Rappresentante le Provincie di Cartagena, S. Marta, e Venezuela (copy of Bellin 1754)
mwwi0733	jamaica	1777	GAZZETTIERE AMERIC.	400	20	32	Carta Rappresentante l'Isola della Giammaica
mwwi0798	martinique	1777	GAZZETTIERE AMERIC.	350	22	30	Carta Rappresentante l'Isola della Martinicca
mwgm0417	panama	1763	GAZZETTIERE AMERIC.	400	24	21	Carta Rappresentante l'Istmo di Darien o' sia di Panama
mwca0084	canada	1763	GAZZETTIERE AMERIC.	150	21	27	Carta Rappresentante una Parte dlla Baja d'Hudson, e le Regioni a Maestro dell'America Settentrle
mwgm0240	mexico	1777	GAZZETTIERE AMERIC.	300	28	37	Messico o Nuova Spagna
mwwi0108	west indies	1777	GAZZETTIERE AMERIC.	350	30	37	Nuova e Corretta Carta dell'Indie Occidentali
mwam0186	america continent	1763	GAZZETTIERE AMERIC.	550	35	27	Nuova ed Esatta Carta della America Ricavata dalle Mappe, e Carte Piu Approvate
mwca0313	canada newfoundland	1763	GAZZETTIERE AMERIC.	300	23	17	Nuova, e Corretta Carta dell'Isola di Terra Nuova
mwgm0241	mexico	1777	GAZZETTIERE AMERIC.	240	17	25	Nuovo Messico (view of Mexico City)
mwuss0434	florida	1777	GAZZETTIERE AMERIC.	300	20	27	Piano del Porto, e degli Stabilimenti di Pensacola
mwca0523a	canada quebec	1763	GAZZETTIERE AMERIC.	450	24	24	Piano della Citta di Quebec
mwwi0625	hispaniola	1763	GAZZETTIERE AMERIC.	200	18	26	Piano della Citta di S. Domingo
mwwi0463	cuba	1777	GAZZETTIERE AMERIC.	400	22	27	Piano della Citta e Porto dell' Havana
mwuss0435	florida	1777	GAZZETTIERE AMERIC.	300	20	29	Piano della Citta, e Porto di Sant' Agostino
mwsam0532	south america colombia	1777	GAZZETTIERE AMERIC.	320	35	48	Piano della Citta, e Sobborghi di Cartagena
mwgm0418	panama	1763	GAZZETTIERE AMERIC.	200	25	20	Piano della Citta, Rada, e Porto di Chagre
mwgm0226	mexico	1763	GAZZETTIERE AMERIC.	240	23	17	Piano della Rada, e della Citta della Vera Cruz
mwwi0447	cuba	1763	GAZZETTIERE AMERIC.	350	26	20	Piano di Guantanimo Chiamato dagl' Inglesi Porto di Cumberland
mwgm0419	panama	1763	GAZZETTIERE AMERIC.	300	20	25	Piano di Porto Bello
mwsam0777	south america peru	1777	GAZZETTIERE AMERIC.	300	26	27	Piano Scenografico della Citta dei Re, o sia di Lima Capitale del Regno del Peru
mwgm0242	mexico	1777	GAZZETTIERE AMERIC.	240	23	15	Pianta del Porto d'Acapulco sopra la Costa de Messico nel Mar del Sud
mwsam0377	south america brazil	1763	GAZZETTIERE AMERIC.	350	19	29	Pianta della Citta di S. Salvadore
mwsam0465	south america chile	1777	GAZZETTIERE AMERIC.	300	23	20	Pianta della Citta di Sant' Iago Capitale del Regno del Chili

AMPG REFERENCE	REGION	DATE	MAP MAKER	PRICE (UK£)	VERT. (cm.)	HOR. (cm.)	TITLE OF MAP (Comments by the editor in brackets)
mwsam0776	south america peru	1777	GAZZETTIERE AMERIC.	200	20	18	Pianta di Cusco nel Tempo della Conquista che ne Secero gli Spagnola
mwuss1094	new york	1763	GAZZETTIERE AMERIC.	550	20	16	Porti della Nuova York e Perthamboy
mwsam0271	south america bolivia	1763	GAZZETTIERE AMERIC.	300	25	18	Veduta della Citta, e della Montagna del Potosi
mwam0393	america north	1745	GEBAUER	750	33	42	America das Mitternachtige nach der Zeichnung des Herren Wilhem Delisle
mwsam0074	south america	1753	GEBAUER	350	32	41	America das Sudliche nach der Zeichnung des Herrn Wilhelm Delisle
mwme0629a	arabia etc	1759	GEBAUER	500	21	30	Arabia
mwit0450	italy liguria	1782	GEBAUER	550	38	44	Carta Topografica de Contorni di Genova e delle Due Valli di Polcevera e Bisagno con sue Adiacente
mwme0621a	arabia etc	1749	GEBAUER	200	20	30	Die Königreiche in Armenien, Pontvs, Cappadocien, Medien, Bactriana
mwit0201	italy	1778	GEBAUER	500	32	43	Tabula Italiae Medii Aevi Graeco-Langobardico-Francici Accurante Societate Palatina
mwit0765	italy rome	1834	GELL	600	72	98	Rome and its Environs, from a Trigonometrical Survey
mwme0681	arabia etc	1835	GELLATLY	150	26	32	Arabia
mwp0109	australia	1835	GELLATLY	240	27	34	Australia with the British Settlements
mwgm0330	mexico	1836	GELLATLY	400	29	34	Mexico & Guatimala (incl. Texas)
mwam1235	america north (east)	1836	GELLATLY	250	27	33	United States
mwam1249	america north (east)	1845	GELLATLY	180	20	25	United States
mww0429	world	1754	GENDRON	400	16	30	Carta General de el Mundo
mwaf0198	africa	1754	GENDRON	240	16	19	El Africa
mwas0168	asia continent	1754	GENDRON	200	16	19	El Asia
mwam0408	america north	1754	GENDRON	280	15	20	Mapa de la Principal Parte de la America Septentrional
mwam0970	america north (east)	1755	GENERAL MAG.	350	20	18	A Map of New England & ye Country Adjacent, Extending Northward to Quebec, & Westward to Niagara, on Lake Ontario; Shewing Gen: Shirley and Gen: Iohnson's Routs, & Many Places Omitted in other
mwam0971	america north (east)	1755	GENERAL MAG.	800	19	48	A Map of the British and French Settlements in North America … Containing Canada, Nova Scotia, New Found Land, New England / Part of New York, Pensilvania, New Jersey, Mary Land (2 maps, each 19x48cm.)
mwca0383	canada nova scotia	1758	GENERAL MAG.	200	18	11	A Plan of the City and Fortifications of Louisburg. Taken from a Survey Made by Mr Gridley Lieut Coll. of Artillery in 1745 / A View of Fort St Louis on the East Side of ye Isle of Senegal.
mwas0481	asia south east	1757	GENERAL MAG.	235	17	29	An Accurate Map of the East Indies, in which ye European Forts, Factories, and Settlements are Inserted & Distinguished
mwwi0101	west indies	1763	GENERAL MAG.	280	18	25	An Accurate Map of the West Indies, Containing the Bahamas & Caribbe Islands; the Great & Little Antilles; with the Leward and Windward Islands & Part of the American Continent
mwf0807	france north	1759	GENERAL MAG.	100	12	19	The River Seine from Rouen to the Sea, with the Road and Town of Havre de Grace.
mwam1013	america north (east)	1763	GENTLEMAN'S MAG.	300	18	24	(Louisiana, Virginia & Carolina. Map by J. Gibson)
mwuss0368	delaware	1779	GENTLEMAN'S MAG.	500	18	23	A Chart of Delaware Bay and River, from the Original by Mr. Fisher of Philadelphia, 1776
mwbp0047	baltic sea (east)	1748	GENTLEMAN'S MAG.	150	24	26	A Chart of the Baltic Sea, Gulfs of Finland and Bothnia, with the Sound, Drawn from the Best Maps & Charts by T. Jefferys
mwg0135	germany	1759	GENTLEMAN'S MAG.	150	29	34	A Complete Map of Germany Comprehending in One View the Different Seats of the Present War 1759
mwuk0305	irish sea	1760	GENTLEMAN'S MAG.	120	23	18	A Correct Chart of the Irish Sea, &c. Exhibiting a View of the Several Islands & Bays, Lately Touch'd at by M. Thurot, in his Attempt upon Ireland
mwf0355	france brittany	1757	GENTLEMAN'S MAG.	120	18	44	A Draught of the Road and Harbour of Brest with the Adjacent Coast
mwp0408	pacific north	1754	GENTLEMAN'S MAG.	400	20	27	A General Map of the Discoveries of Admiral de Fonte & Others, by M. De l'Isle
mwuss0810	massachusetts	1775	GENTLEMAN'S MAG.	550	23	24	A Map of 100 Miles round Boston
mwuss0293	connecticut	1776	GENTLEMAN'S MAG.	375	17	23	A Map of Connecticut and Rhode Island, with Long Island Sound, &c.
mwat0223	atlantic falkland isl.	1770	GENTLEMAN'S MAG.	240	17	24	A Map of Falkland Islands in the Latitude of 51°, 22' South, Longitude 64°, 30' West; from the Latest Observations
mwwi0780	martinique	1759	GENTLEMAN'S MAG.	180	19	25	A Map of Martinico, from the Latest and Best Authorities
mwuss0001	alabama	1772	GENTLEMAN'S MAG.	300	20	36	A Map of Part of West Florida, from Pensacola to the Mouth of the Iberville River, with a View to Shew the Proper Spot for a Settlement on the Mississipi
mwbp0480	poland	1772	GENTLEMAN'S MAG.	120	17	20	A Map of Poland with its Appendages; Shewing the Late Partition of that Kingdom.
mwbp0459	poland	1759	GENTLEMAN'S MAG.	60	19	26	A Map of Pomerania and Brandenburg with the Frontiers of Poland

AMPG REFERENCE	REGION	DATE	MAP MAKER	PRICE (UK£)	VERT. (cm.)	HOR. (cm.)	TITLE OF MAP (Comments by the editor in brackets)
mwuss0362	delaware	1769	GENTLEMAN'S MAG.	250	16	10	A Map of that Part of America where a Degree of Latitude was Measured for the Royal Society: By Cha. Mason, & Jere. Dixon
mwam0998	america north (east)	1757	GENTLEMAN'S MAG.	400	22	33	A Map of that Part of America which was the Principal Seat of War, in 1756
mwaf0940	africa south	1755	GENTLEMAN'S MAG.	180	18	11	A Map of the Cape of Good Hope & the Country Adjacent. 1752 (copied from De La Caille's survey of 1752)
mwwi0088	west indies	1756	GENTLEMAN'S MAG.	200	33	21	A Map of the Caribbee Islands; Shewing which Belong to England, France, Spain, Dutch & Danes, Collected from the Best Authorities; by Thos. Jefferys
mwec0232	uk england cumbria	1746	GENTLEMAN'S MAG.	350	21	27	A Map of the Countries Adjacent to Carlisle Shewing the Route of the Rebels with their Principal Fords over ye Rr. Eden
mwuss1092	new york	1759	GENTLEMAN'S MAG.	150	19	11	A Map of the Country between Crown Point and Fort Edward
mwuss1363	pennsylvania	1776	GENTLEMAN'S MAG.	320	18	22	A Map of the Country round Philadelphia Including Part of New Jersey New York Staten Island & Long Island
mwf0504	france corsica	1757	GENTLEMAN'S MAG.	320	20	11	A Map of the Island of Corsica (by Jefferys)
mwwi0718	jamaica	1762	GENTLEMAN'S MAG.	150	13	18	A Map of the Island of Jamaica
mwca0513	canada quebec	1759	GENTLEMAN'S MAG.	200	11	19	A Map of the Island of Orleans with the Environs of Quebec
mwuk1591	channel islands	1779	GENTLEMAN'S MAG.	200	23	17	A Map of the Islands of Guernsey, Jersey, Alderney & Sark. Situated in the English Channel, with the Sands, Rocks & Soundings
mwsp0100	portugal	1762	GENTLEMAN'S MAG.	140	32	19	A Map of the Kingdom of Portugal
mwam0174	america continent	1758	GENTLEMAN'S MAG.	250	21	17	A Map of the New Continent According to its Greatest Diametrical Length from the River la Plata to beyond the Lake of the Assiniboils
mwuss0418	florida	1763	GENTLEMAN'S MAG.	875	19	25	A Map of the New Governments, of East & West Florida
mwg0539	rheinland-pfalz	1759	GENTLEMAN'S MAG.	200	19	27	A Map of the Seat of War on the Rhine, and Part's Adjacent, in Germany, 1759
mww0433	world	1755	GENTLEMAN'S MAG.	350	18	28	A Map of the World, on Mercators Projection
mwg0654	saxony	1757	GENTLEMAN'S MAG.	100	20	25	A Map of Upper Saxony Comprehending that Part of Germany which is the Present Seat of War
mwca0660	canada west	1790	GENTLEMAN'S MAG.	240	20	23	A Map Shewing the Communication of the Lakes and the Rivers between Lake Superior and Slave Lake in North America
mwuk0304a	irish sea	1757	GENTLEMAN'S MAG.	180	35	22	A New and accurate Map of the Parts of England, Scotland, & Ireland, bordering on St. George's Channel
mwe0809	europe east	1770	GENTLEMAN'S MAG.	100	22	25	A New and Accurate Map of Turkey in Europe, Drawn from the Best Authorities
mwuss0811	massachusetts	1775	GENTLEMAN'S MAG.	300	26	19	A New and Correct Plan of the Town of Boston
mwca0062	canada	1746	GENTLEMAN'S MAG.	500	34	47	A New Chart of the Coast of New England, Nova Scotia New France or Canada, with the Islands of Newfoundld. Cape Breton St. John's &c. Done from the Original Publish'd in 1744. At Paris. By Monsr. N. Bellin
mww0498	world	1776	GENTLEMAN'S MAG.	350	21	23	A New Projection of the Western Hemisphere of the Earth on a Plane (Shewing the Proportions of its Several Parts Nearly as on a Globe) / A New Projection of the Eastern Hemisphere of the Earth on a Plane (set of 2 maps)
mwca0574	canada quebec montreal	1760	GENTLEMAN'S MAG.	200	18	23	A Particular Map, to Illustrate Gen. Amhersts, Expedition, to Montreal; with a Plan of the Town & Draught of ye Island
mww0439	world	1757	GENTLEMAN'S MAG.	400	31	29	A Physical Planisphere wherein are Represented All the Known Lands and Seas wth. the Great Chains of Mountains wch. Traverse the Globe from the North Pole (reprint of Buache's 1756 north polar or 'flat earth' projection)
mwwi0378	barbados	1776	GENTLEMAN'S MAG.	100	11	19	A Plan of Bridge Town, in the Island of Barbadoes
mwsam0512	south america colombia	1740	GENTLEMAN'S MAG.	180	10	18	A Plan of Carthagena
mwbh0672	belgium holland	1747	GENTLEMAN'S MAG.	200	26	22	A Plan of Maestricht, with the Adjacent Villages, where the Battle was Fought June 21. By T. Jefferys
mwuk0485	scotland	1745	GENTLEMAN'S MAG.	80	11	18	A Plan of the City of Edinburgh
mwe0572	europe czech republic (bohemia)	1742	GENTLEMAN'S MAG.	250	30	37	A Plan of the City of Prague, with the French and Austrian Camps / City of Egra. Describ'd in Octr. Mag. P.530 / Southern View of Prague / Maria Teresa Q. of Hungary Born May 13th. 1717
mwca0367	canada nova scotia	1750	GENTLEMAN'S MAG.	450	22	27	A Plan of the Harbour of Chebucto and Town of Halifax (the 'porcupine' map)
mwuss1656	virginia	1785	GENTLEMAN'S MAG.	240	22	19	A Plan of the Investment of York & Gloucester, by the Allied Armies; in Sept. & Oct. 1781
mwam1285	great lakes	1761	GENTLEMAN'S MAG.	400	23	32	A Plan of the Straits of St. Mary, and Michilimakinac, to Shew the Situation & Importance of the Two Westernmost Settlements of Canada for the Fur Trade (1st detailed map of this area)
mwuss0812	massachusetts	1775	GENTLEMAN'S MAG.	350	26	33	A Plan of the Town and Chart of the Harbour of Boston Exhibiting a View of the Islands Castle Forts and Entrances into the Said Harbour
mwaf0750	africa north algeria	1749	GENTLEMAN'S MAG.	180	20	10	Algiers, and Parts Adjacent

AMPG REFERENCE	REGION	DATE	MAP MAKER	PRICE (UK£)	VERT. (cm.)	HOR. (cm.)	TITLE OF MAP (Comments by the editor in brackets)
mwg0191	germany north	1761	GENTLEMAN'S MAG.	120	28	34	An Accurate Map of All His Majesty's Dominions in Germany, with the Adjacent Countries
mwit0319	italy central	1764	GENTLEMAN'S MAG.	60	19	25	An Accurate Map of His R.H. the Duke of York's Journey thro' Italy in 1763 & 1764
mwam1011	america north (east)	1762	GENTLEMAN'S MAG.	280	21	23	An Accurate Map of the British Empire in Nth. America as Settled by the Preliminaries in 1762
mwuk1208	england london	1764	GENTLEMAN'S MAG.	400	41	41	An Accurate Map of the Country Sixteen Miles Round London Drawn and Engrav'd from an Actual Survey
mwgr0199	greece	1770	GENTLEMAN'S MAG.	100	19	19	An Accurate Map of the Seat of War in the Mediterranean Including the Morea and Archipelago
mwwi0075	west indies	1740	GENTLEMAN'S MAG.	400	29	39	An Accurate Map of the West Indies. Exhibiting Not Only All the Islands Possess'd by the English, French, Spaniards & Dutch, but also All the Towns and Settlements on the Continent of America Adjacent thereto
mwca0599	canada st lawrence	1759	GENTLEMAN'S MAG.	120	10	19	An Authentic Plan of the River St Laurence, from Sillery to the Falls of Montmorency
mwgm0404	panama	1740	GENTLEMAN'S MAG.	160	14	18	An Exact Draft of the Castle of San Lorenzo
mwgm0399	panama	1740	GENTLEMAN'S MAG.	100	14	17	An Exact Draught of the Castle of San Lorenzo ye Village and River of Chagre with the Situation of Adml Vernon's Ships in ye Attack of the Fort March 24. 1740. by R.T. & Sent over in the Diamond Man of War
mwru0182	russia	1739	GENTLEMAN'S MAG.	200	22	32	An Exact Map of the Crim, (Formerly Taurica Chersonesus) Part of Lesser Tartary, the Sea of Asoph, and the Adjacent Country of the Kuban Tartars
mwaa0027	antarctic	1763	GENTLEMAN'S MAG.	350	20	22	Chart of the Antarctic Polar Circle, with the Countries Adjoining, According to the New Hypothesis of M. Buache. From the Memoirs of the Royal Accademy at Paris
mww0486	world	1773	GENTLEMAN'S MAG.	600	25	62	Chart of the Track of the Dolphin, Tamar, Swallow & Endeavor, through the South Seas; & the Track of M. Bougainville, round the World (excludes polar regions)
mwf0125	france	1747	GENTLEMAN'S MAG.	160	23	28	France with its Acquired Territories in Germany, and the Netherlands. By T. Jefferys
mwit0179	italy	1747	GENTLEMAN'S MAG.	160	27	23	Italy by Mr. d'Anville Geographer to the French King Drawn and Engrav'd from the Original Publish'd at Paris, at the Expence of the Duke of Orleans
mwec0234	uk england cumbria	1751	GENTLEMAN'S MAG.	240	20	24	Map of the Black Lead Mines &c. in the Cumberland
mwuss1109	new york	1776	GENTLEMAN'S MAG.	350	20	32	Map of the Progress of His Majesty's Armies in New York, during the Late Campaign Illustrating the Accounts Publish'd in the London Gazette
mwwi0743	jamaica	1785	GENTLEMAN'S MAG.	160	18	32	Old Pt. Royal
mwp0499	pacific south	1776	GENTLEMAN'S MAG.	60	21	12	Part of the Tropical Discoveries of the Resolution Sloop, Captain J. Cook in 1774
mwf0757	france nord pas-de-calais	1763	GENTLEMAN'S MAG.	200	19	29	Plan of Dunkirk, with the Canal of Mardick, as they were in 1757
mwuss0687	maine	1755	GENTLEMAN'S MAG.	300	19	11	Plan of Fort Hallifax / Plan of Fort Franckfort / Plan of Fort Western, Built in 1754
mwsp0722	gibraltar	1762	GENTLEMAN'S MAG.	240	17	45	Plan of Gibraltar
mwru0209	russia	1749	GENTLEMAN'S MAG.	350	19	25	Plan of St Petersburg; with it's Fortifications, Built by Peter the Great in 1703 / The Harbour of Crownslot River Neva, Canal Made from the Said River to the R. Wolschowa
mwuss1088	new york	1757	GENTLEMAN'S MAG.	320	21	13	Plan of the Forts Ontario and Oswego, with Part of the River Onondago and Lake Ontario
mwca0365	canada nova scotia	1749	GENTLEMAN'S MAG.	200	10	15	Plan of the New Town of Halifax in Nova Scotia
mwgm0400	panama	1740	GENTLEMAN'S MAG.	280	10	10	Plan of the Towm of Porto Bello
mwuss1110	new york	1776	GENTLEMAN'S MAG.	300	20	32	Sketch of the Country Illustrating the Late Engagement in Long Island
mwsam0070	south america	1749	GENTLEMAN'S MAG.	160	25	23	South America Drawn from the Best Maps, by T. Jefferys, Geographer to His Royal Highness the Prince of Wales
mwsp0095a	portugal	1756	GENTLEMAN'S MAG.	100	23	18	Spain and Portugal / A Map of the Mouth of the River Tagus, or Harbour of the City of Lisbon
mwat0202	atlantic cape verde isl.	1781	GENTLEMAN'S MAG.	160	16	25	Station of the Ships in Port Praya Bay. When the Engagement Began between Come Johnstone & M. de Suffrien
mwp0073	australia	1824	GENTLEMAN'S MAG.	300	9	17	Sydney, New South Wales, S. View
mwuss0809	massachusetts	1775	GENTLEMAN'S MAG.	650	11	13	The Attack of the Lines on Bunkers Hill
mwbh0657	belgium holland	1744	GENTLEMAN'S MAG.	120	11	20	The Austrian & French Netherlands Agreeable to the Barrier Concluded at Antwerp, and Relative to the Present War
mwam1014	america north (east)	1763	GENTLEMAN'S MAG.	500	20	24	The British Governments in Nth. America Laid down Agreeable to the Proclamation of Octr. 7. 1763
mwas0473	asia south east	1748	GENTLEMAN'S MAG.	350	23	26	The East Indies Drawn from the Latest Discoveries, by T. Jefferys, Geographer, to His Royal Highness the Prince of Wales
mwin0245	india	1767	GENTLEMAN'S MAG.	140	24	20	The Moguls Empire Divided into its Principal Governments.

AMPG REFERENCE	REGION	DATE	MAP MAKER	PRICE (UK£)	VERT. (cm.)	HOR. (cm.)	TITLE OF MAP (Comments by the editor in brackets)
mwsam0761	south america peru	1753	GENTLEMAN'S MAG.	100	21	36	The Port of Callao, in the South Sea; with the Adjacent Islands, Rocks & Coasts, to the Windward and Leeward, and the Soundings in Fathoms: Drawn by Order of His Catholic Majesty
mwf1075	france provence	1759	GENTLEMAN'S MAG.	160	20	27	The Roads, of Toulon, with the Adjacent Country (south to the top)
mwg0827	westphalia	1757	GENTLEMAN'S MAG.	60	20	25	The Seat of War in the Circle of Westphalia
mwuss1454	rhode isl	1779	GENTLEMAN'S MAG.	200	13	22	The Siege of Rhode Island, Taken from Mr. Brindley's House, on the 25th of August, 1778
mwam0204b	america continent	1779	GENTOT	800	47	65	L'Amerique divisée selon qu'elle est possedée par les Puissances Européennes (map by Delafosse)
mwam0226	america continent	1788	GENTY	300	33	36	Nouvelle Carte des Parties Occidentales du Monde Servant a Indiquer les Navigations Decouvertes et Etablissements des Hollandois en Amerique
mwsc0728a	scandinavia sweden	1745	GERINGIUS	450	49	57	Charta ofver Sodermanland
mwbh0183	belgium holland	1611	GERRITSZ	35000	44	56	(Leo Belgicus) Nova XVII Provinciarum Germaniae Inferioris Tabula, Leonis effigie, accurate delineata. (First issued by Hondius, then by Visscher etc.)
mwwi0008	west indies	1631	GERRITSZ		51	72	De Eylanden Ende Vastelanden Van Westindien Op De Noordzee
mwwi0225	west indies (east)	1631	GERRITSZ		53	75	Pascaert vande Caribes Eylenden, curiouslyck betrocken ... (north to the right)
mwsc0044	scandinavia	1630	GERRITSZ		107	125	Serenissimae Potentissimae Principi ac Dominae ... Regni Sueciae Tabulam ... dedicatq Henricus Hondius
mwca0010	canada	1612	GERRITSZ	25000	24	52	Tabula Nautica
mwru0033	russia	1614	GERRITSZ	2400	43	55	Tabula Russiae ... M.DC.XIIII (re-issued after 1630 with Blaeu's imprint)
mwuss0134a	california	1849	GERSTACKER	1500	20	15	Kaliforniens Gold- U. Quecksilber-District. Nach: the California-Herald ... 1849
mwuss0797	massachusetts	1760	GERSTMAYR	240	24	18	Boston
mwuss0183	carolinas	1760	GERSTMAYR	240	24	18	Charlestown
mwe0578	europe czech republic (bohemia)	1743	GEYER	650	42	34	Neuester Grund-Riess von Prag ... nebst denen Umligenten Gegend, welche 1742 Erobert, aber 1743
mwit0956	italy sicily	1779	GHISI		49	70	Nuova ed esatta carta corografica della Sicilia (in 4 sheets, each 49x70cm)
mwam0198a	america continent	1774	GHISIUS	900	30	45	America Septentrionalis et Meridionalis
mwit1256	italy venice	1813	GIAMPICCOLI	1500	31	72	Piano Elevato dell'Inclita Citta di Venezia (view, first published 1797)
mwam0414	america north	1755	GIBSON	250	18	24	(United States)
mwsp0273	spain	1755	GIBSON	450	45	59	3.e Carte d'Espagne & 2.e Carte de Portugal
mwme0317	holy land	1747	GIBSON	350	25	36	A Map of Paradise, Mount Ararat, and the City of Babel
mwca0385	canada nova scotia	1760	GIBSON	120	19	11	A Map of the Island of Cape Breton
mwca0487	canada prince edward isl.	1758	GIBSON	250	11	19	A Map of the Island of St. John, near Nova Scotia Lately Taken from the French, 1758
mwme0350	holy land	1764	GIBSON	120	24	21	A Map to Explain the History of the Assyrians. Babylonians, Medes, & Persians
mwe0190	europe	1770	GIBSON	120	20	29	A New & Accurate Map of Europe
mwc0162	china	1759	GIBSON	280	19	29	A New & Accurate Map of the Empire of China, from the Sieur Robert's Atlas with Improvements
mwbp0462	poland	1760	GIBSON	120	21	30	A New & Accurate Map of the Kingdom of Prussia and Polish Prussia
mwsp0285	spain	1770	GIBSON	120	21	30	A New & Accurate Map of the Kingdom of Spain and Portugal from the Sieur Robert's Atlas, with Improvements
mwaf0227	africa	1771	GIBSON	200	20	23	A New and Accurate Map of Africa Drawn & Engraved from the Best Authorities
mwam1024	america north (east)	1771	GIBSON	1350	57	76	A New and Accurate Map of Part of North America
mwsam0072	south america	1750	GIBSON	95	15	19	A New and Accurate Map of South America Drawn & Engrav'd from the Best Authorities
mwwi0542	guadeloupe	1758	GIBSON	160	12	20	A New and Accurate Map of the Isles of Guadeloupe, Marie-Galante &c. from the Best Authorities
mwuss1354	pennsylvania	1762	GIBSON	450	27	34	A New and Accurate Map of the Provinces of Pensilvania, Virginia, Maryland and New Jersey
mwuk1204	england london	1763	GIBSON	875	30	51	A New and Correct Plan of the Cities and Suburbs of London (5 revised editions until 1771)
mwas0322	asia caspian sea	1753	GIBSON	450	35	55	A Plain Chart of the Caspian Sea
mwca0527	canada quebec	1769	GIBSON	200	6	11	A Plan of the City of Quebec and its Fortifications
mwca0520	canada quebec	1759	GIBSON	160	11	18	A Plan of the Seat of War at and near Quebec, with the Line of Battle
mwaf0197	africa	1752	GIBSON	400	28	33	Africa
mwam0199	america continent	1774	GIBSON	240	22	17	An Accurate Map of America, from the Latest Discoveries
mwwi0096	west indies	1762	GIBSON	280	18	29	An Accurate Map of the West Indies, with the Adjacent Coast
mwas0225	asia continent	1798	GIBSON	95	6	10	Asia
mwas0169a	asia continent	1755	GIBSON	250	29	33	Asia
mwsam0399	south america brazil	1792	GIBSON	95	10	7	Brasil

AMPG REFERENCE	REGION	DATE	MAP MAKER	PRICE (UK£)	VERT. (cm.)	HOR. (cm.)	TITLE OF MAP (Comments by the editor in brackets)
mwca0077	canada	1758	GIBSON	150	6	10	Canada or New France
mwuss0182	carolinas	1758	GIBSON	200	6	10	Carolina and Georgia
mwsc0144	scandinavia	1755	GIBSON	350			Carte de Norwege et 1e. De Suede 1755
mwc0211	china	1792	GIBSON	95	7	10	China
mwas0514	asia south east	1792	GIBSON	95	7	10	East India Islands
mwe0176	europe	1758	GIBSON	100	10	7	Europe
mwgr0196	greece	1764	GIBSON	120	20	18	Greece with the Northern Provinces near the Danube
mwe0950	europe hungary	1752	GIBSON	240	27	32	Hungary
mwe0964	europe hungary	1792	GIBSON	95	7	10	Hungary
mwin0299	india	1792	GIBSON	95	7	10	India on Both Sides the Ganges
mwuk0233	ireland	1792	GIBSON	95	10	7	Ireland
mwca0393	canada nova scotia	1768	GIBSON	95	10	6	Island of Cape Breton
mwat0241	atlantic madeira	1750	GIBSON	300	22	15	Island of Madera (and The Dragon Tree)
mwit0213	italy	1792	GIBSON	95	10	7	Italy
mwec0637	uk england kent	1759	GIBSON	120	6	11	Kent
mwwi0783	martinique	1760	GIBSON	160	19	24	Martinico
mwam1103	america north (east)	1792	GIBSON	120	10	7	New England
mwuss1089	new york	1758	GIBSON	200	6	10	New York and Pensilvania
mwca0311	canada newfoundland	1758	GIBSON	200	9	6	New-Found Land
mwam0406	america north	1752	GIBSON	450	28	32	North America
mwam0519a	america north	1792	GIBSON	180	9	6	North America
mwsam0723	south america paraguay	1792	GIBSON	95	7	10	Paraguay and Tucuman
mwuss1350	pennsylvania	1758	GIBSON	200	6	10	Pensilvania, Maryland and Virginia
mwme0835	persia etc	1792	GIBSON	95	10	7	Persia
mwuss1353	pennsylvania	1760	GIBSON	200	7	11	Plan of the City of Philadelphia with the Country Adjacent
mwbp0523	poland	1792	GIBSON	95	7	10	Poland
mwru0225	russia	1755	GIBSON	200	27	32	Russia
mwru0314	russia	1798	GIBSON	95	9	6	Russia in Europe
mwuk0557	scotland	1792	GIBSON	95	10	7	Scotland
mwsam0075	south america	1753	GIBSON	240	28	33	South America
mwsp0307	spain	1792	GIBSON	100	7	10	Spain and Portugal
mww0417	world	1750	GIBSON	720	27	46	The World
mwme0661a	arabia etc	1792	GIBSON	240	10	6	Turky in Asia
mwwi0089	west indies	1758	GIBSON	95	6	10	West Indies
mwuk1079	england	1849	GILBERT	280	81	65	Gilbert's New Map of England & Wales, Drawn from the Best Authorities
mwuss1584	vermont	1848	GILBERT	280	60	136	Map & Profile of the Rutland & Burlington Railroad
mwuss1518	texas	1842	GILBERT	300	23	28	Mexico & Texas
mwam0697	america north	1835	GILBERT	200	28	24	North America
mww0732	world	1845	GILBERT	200	31	48	The World on Mercator's Projection
mww0722	world	1841	GILBERT	300	26	49	The World.
mwp0144	australia	1842	GILBERT	100	28	23	Van Diemen's Land
mwec1352	uk england yorkshire	1815	GILES	850	64	84	Plan of the Town of Leeds and its Environs
mwam1186	america north (east)	1824	GILLET	240	21	36	Map of the Northern Part of New England
mwgm0354	mexico	1846	GILLIAM	300	48	47	Map of Gilliam's Travels in Mexico, Including Texas and Part of the United States
mwbp0543a	poland	1803	GILLY	2000	57	74	Special Karte von Südpreussen (in 12 sheets, each 57x74cm)
mwam0792	america north	1848	GILMAN	450	35	84	(United States. Size incl. text at sides)
mwjk0017	japan	1641	GINNARO	10000	27	41	Nuova Descrittione Del Giappone (Based on Blancus)
mww0050	world	1556	GIRAVA	25000	29	41	Typo de la Carta Cosmographica de Gaspar Vopellio Medeburgense
mwam0146	america continent	1739	GIUSTINIANI	350	15	18	America
mwas0144	asia continent	1739	GIUSTINIANI	160	15	18	Asiae
mwc0132	china	1739	GIUSTINIANI	180	13	15	La Chine
mwas0768	asia south east philippines	1739	GIUSTINIANI	240	14	16	Les Isles Philippines, Moluques et de la Sonde
mwp0502	pacific south	1780	GLASSBACH	400	35	65	Carte d'une Partie de la Mer du Sud Contenant les Decouvertes des Vaisseaux de sa Majeste le Dauphin
mwe0343	europe austria	1710	GLOTSCH	480	29	36	Ducat. Nobillissim. Tirolensis
mwbp0566a	poland	1832	GLUCKSBERG	250	25	36	Plan Ogólny Miasta Stołecznego Warszawy - Plan Général de la Ville de Varsovie
mwf0915a	france paris	1825	GODET-LEROND	650	68	96	Nouveau Plan Routier de la Ville et des Faubourgs de Paris où se trouvent tous les changements, augmentations et embellissements
mww0242	world	1690	GOEREE	350	27	17	(Creation of the Earth)
mwme0248	holy land	1714	GOEREE	180	18	13	Conspectus Palaestinae Divisae in Primam, Secundam et Tertiam
mwme0249	holy land	1714	GOEREE	180	18	13	Conspectus Palaestinae et Regionum, in quas Distributa suit Stante Templo Secundo, et aliquo Tempore Post ejus Excidium
mww0277	world	1700	GOEREE	350	17	29	De Aard-Kloot Volgens de Hedendaagse Gedaante
mww0278	world	1700	GOEREE	350	17	29	De Bekende Weereld der Ouden; Volgens Strabo, in Zeven Klimaten Afgebakend
mww0243	world	1690	GOEREE	450	21	42	Den Aardbodem na de Zundvloed door Noachs Dri Soonen en Hare Nakomelingen Bevolkt Gen. 10

AMPG REFERENCE	REGION	DATE	MAP MAKER	PRICE (UK£)	VERT. (cm.)	HOR. (cm.)	TITLE OF MAP (Comments by the editor in brackets)
mww0244	world	1690	GOEREE	550	28	15	Den Aardkloot nade Zondvloed, in Haar Gebroken Stand, met Bergen en Dalen, Groote Zee-Boesem, en der Selver Eilanden en Ondiepten Vertoond
mwbh0767	belgium holland	1796	GOETHALS	750	52	73	Plan van Gend
mwru0402	russia moscow	1812	GOETZ & DIETRICH	2000	50	93	Plan de Moscou / Plan von Moskau nach der Neuesten Russichen Original Aufnahme samt einer Erklaerung in Rusischer, Franzosischer und Deutscher Sprache (2 parts, both 50x93cm.)
mwaf0993	africa south	1812	GOLD	150	16	12	Cape of Good Hope
mwf0546	france corsica	1812	GOLD	180	16	12	Corsica
mwca0455	canada nova scotia	1803	GOLD	150	15	23	Entrance into Halifax Harbour
mwp0537	pacific tahiti	1815	GOLD	120	13	17	Otaheite
mwwi0674	hispaniola	1808	GOLD	200	15	23	Platform Bay, near Cape Nicola, Mole, St. Domingo, Hamilton, Invt. Hall, Sculpt. Published July 30th, 1808, by Joyce Gold, 103, Shoe Lane, Fleet Street
mwuss0660	louisiana	1815	GOLD	300	13	20	Sketch of the Position of the British and American Forces, during the Operations against New Orleans, from 23d. Decr. 1814, to 18th. Jany 1815
mwam0751	america north	1842	GOLDTHWAIT	280	27	33	Miniature County Map of the United States
mwam1262	america north (east)	1850	GOLDTHWAIT	350	61	50	Rail Road Map of New England, Canada & Eastern N.Y., Compiled from the Most Authentic Sources
mwam1256	america north (east)	1849	GOLDTHWAIT	500	60	50	Railroad Map of New England & Eastern New York Compiled from the Most Authentic Sources
mwme0866	syria etc	1673	GONSALES	250	17	13	Syria
mwme0171	holy land	1673	GONSALES	300	17	13.	Terra Promisionis
mwuss1205	new york	1827	GOODRICH	4000	97	61	A Map of the City of New York
mwuss0018	alabama	1844	GOODRICH	200	36	28	Alabama
mwuss0061	arkansas	1841	GOODRICH	250	30	37	Arkansas
mwat0063	atlantic ocean (all)	1841	GOODRICH	150	37	30	Atlantic Ocean
mwuss0783	maryland	1841	GOODRICH	200	30	37	Baltimore
mwuss0887	massachusetts	1841	GOODRICH	250	30	37	Boston
mwuss0323	connecticut	1841	GOODRICH	200	30	37	Connecticut
mwuss0318	connecticut	1833	GOODRICH	80	11	15	Connecticut
mwuss0385	delaware	1841	GOODRICH	250	37	30	Delaware
mwuss0482	florida	1841	GOODRICH	300	38	33	Florida
mwuss0533	georgia	1841	GOODRICH	150	37	30	Georgia
mwuss0562	illinois	1841	GOODRICH	200	37	30	Illinois
mwuss0578	indiana	1841	GOODRICH	200	37	30	Indiana
mwuss0580	indiana	1848	GOODRICH	80	16	11	Indiana
mwuss0583	iowa	1841	GOODRICH	300	37	30	Iowa and Wisconsin
mwuss0618	kentucky	1841	GOODRICH	150	30	37	Kentucky
mwuss0679	louisiana	1841	GOODRICH	250	30	37	Louisiana
mwuss0732	maine	1841	GOODRICH	150	38	30	Maine
mwuss1187	new york	1820	GOODRICH	2000	119	22	Map of the Hudson between Sandy Hook & Sandy Hill with the Post Road between New York and Albany
mwuss0784	maryland	1841	GOODRICH	250	30	37	Maryland
mwuss0888	massachusetts	1841	GOODRICH	200	30	37	Massachusetts
mwuss0894	massachusetts	1845	GOODRICH	50	11	15	Massachusetts
mwgm0352	mexico	1845	GOODRICH	50	11	16	Mexico, Texas, Guatimala & West Indies
mwuss0923	michigan	1841	GOODRICH	150	37	30	Michigan
mwam0826	america north (central)	1834	GOODRICH	80	15	11	Middle States
mwuss0968	mississippi	1841	GOODRICH	200	37	30	Mississippi
mwuss0990	missouri	1841	GOODRICH	250	30	37	Missouri
mwam1218	america north (east)	1833	GOODRICH	80	15	11	New England
mwuss1028	new hampshire	1841	GOODRICH	120	37	30	New Hampshire
mwuss1022	new hampshire	1833	GOODRICH	80	15	11	New Hampshire
mwuss1062	new jersey	1841	GOODRICH	160	37	30	New Jersey
mwuss1241	new york	1841	GOODRICH	160	30	37	New York
mwam0749	america north	1841	GOODRICH	200	38	30	North America
mwam0708	america north	1837	GOODRICH	80	15	11	North America
mwuss0279	carolinas	1841	GOODRICH	200	30	37	North Carolina
mwuss1319	ohio	1841	GOODRICH	120	30	37	Ohio
mwp0287	pacific (all)	1841	GOODRICH	120	30	37	Pacific Ocean
mwuss1434	pennsylvania	1841	GOODRICH	150	30	37	Pennsylvania
mwuss1435	pennsylvania	1841	GOODRICH	200	30	37	Philadelphia
mwsam0152	south america	1833	GOODRICH	80	15	11	South America
mwuss0280	carolinas	1841	GOODRICH	200	30	37	South Carolina
mwuss1516	texas	1841	GOODRICH	1500	37	30	Texas
mwuss1543	texas	1850	GOODRICH	80	11	16	Texas - New Mexico
mwam0654	america north	1826	GOODRICH	550	32	47	United States
mwca0485	canada ontario	1841	GOODRICH	250	30	37	Upper Canada
mwuss1580	vermont	1841	GOODRICH	150	37	30	Vermont
mwuss1689	virginia	1841	GOODRICH	200	30	37	Virginia
mwbh0204	belgium holland	1621	GOOS	10000	43	56	Belgium, sive Inferior Germania Post Omnes in hac Forma, Exactissime Descriptia. Auct. Abrahamo Goos. 1621 (3 carte-a-figure borders; 1631 edition illustrated.)

AMPG REFERENCE	REGION	DATE	MAP MAKER	PRICE (UK£)	VERT. (cm.)	HOR. (cm.)	TITLE OF MAP (Comments by the editor in brackets)
mwat0142	atlantic canary isl.	1660	GOOS	1200	43	53	Caarte voor en Gedeelte der Canarise Eylanden als Canaria, Tenerifa, Forteventura, etc.
mwbh0372	belgium holland	1665	GOOS	600	42	53	Cust van Hollant tusschen de Maes ende Texel
mwaf0694	africa north	1666	DONCKER	550	43	52	De Cust van Barbaria, Gualata, Arguyn en Geneheo van Capo S. Vincent tot Capo Verde
mwaf0839	africa north west	1666	GOOS	1000	44	53	De Cust van Barbaryen van out Mamora tot Capo Blanco / De Cust van Barbaryen van Capo Blanco tot Capo de Geer / De Reede van Punte del Gada / De Reede voor de Stadt Angra int Eylandt Tercera / De Eylanden van Madera en Porto Santo (5 maps on one sheet)
mwbh0376	belgium holland	1666	GOOS	1200	43	54	De Cust van Zeelandt, Begrypende in sich de Gaten, als vande Wielingen, ter Veere, Ziericzee, Brouwershaven, Goeree, en de Maes
mwuk1574	channel islands	1650	GOOS	1350	43	53	De Custen van Bretaigne, Waer in vertoont wort alle gelegentheyt tuschen Caap de Hague en t'Eylant Heyssant (south to the top)
mwsp0183	spain	1660	GOOS	1500	43	53	De Custen van Hispania
mwat0258	atlantic north	1669	GOOS	800	43	53	De Custen van Noorwegen, Finmarcken, Laplandt, Spitsbergen, Ian Mayen Eylandt, Yslandt, als mede Hitlandt, en een Gedeelte van Schotlandt
mwsp0648	balearic islands	1662	GOOS	1000	40	52	De Custen van Valencia en Catalonia ... Als meede de Eylanden van Majorca, Minorca en Yvica
mwbh0238	belgium holland	1634	GOOS	1500	39	60	De Heerlicheyt van Over. Yssel
mwsc0567	scandinavia norway	1666	GOOS	800	45	54	De Kusten van Noorwegen, Finmarken, Laplandt, Spitzbergen, Ian Mayen Eylandt, Yslandt
mwbh0380	belgium holland	1669	GOOS	800	43	53	De Texel Stroom met de Gaten vant Marsdiep / Caarte van de Mase, ende net Goereesche Gat
mwru0066a	russia	1666	GOOS	1250	45	55	De Zee Custen van Ruslant, Laplant, Finmarcken, Spitsbergen en Nova Zemla
mwgr0389	greece crete	1662	GOOS	720	40	52	De Zeecusten van 't Yland Candia
mwuk1460	uk english channel (all)	1666	GOOS	1800	43	55	Het Canaal tusschen Engeland en Vrancriick
mwsp0185	spain	1660	GOOS	1000	42	53	Kust van Biscayen tusschen Orio ende Rio de Sella / tusschen Rio de Sella en t'Eylant van S. Cyprian
mwru0429a	russia tartary	1666	GOOS	2000	45	55	Noordoost Cust van Asia van Iapan tot Nova Zemla
mwin0412	indian ocean	1658	GOOS		62	89	Oost Indien / Wassende-Graade Paskaart, Vertoonende nevens het Oostelykste van Africa, meede de Zeekusten van Asia (for illustration see re-issue by Van Keulen, 1680.)
mww0094	world	1597	MAGINI	1000	18	25	Orbis Terrae Compendiosa Descriptio
mww0183	world	1666	GOOS	14000	44	54	Orbis Terrarum Nova et Accuratissima Tabula Auctore Petro Goos / Nieuwe Werelt Kaert uyt Gegeven tot Amsteldam by Pieter Goos
mwam0867	america north (east)	1666	GOOS	5500	43	53	Pas Caerte van Nieu Nederlandt en de Engelsche Virginies van Cabo Cod tot Cabo Canrick
mwm0013a	mediterranean	1666	GOOS	2400	44	55	Pas-caart van de Middellandsche Zee, Vertoonende in twee deelen
mwuk1648	north sea	1661	GOOS	2500	44	55	Pascaart van de Noord Zee van Texel, Tot de Hoofden
mwuk1649	north sea	1662	GOOS	2000	45	55	Pascaart van de Noort Zee Verthoonende in zich Alle de Custen en Havens daer rontom Gelegen (copied by Van Keulen 1666)
mwe1190	europe west	1666	GOOS	2250	43	53	Pascaart van Europa, als mede een Gedeelt vande Cust van Africa
mwaf1116	africa west	1666	GOOS	1000	44	54	Pas-Caart van Guinea en de Custen daer aen Gelegen van Cabo Verde tot Cabo de Bona Esperanca (north to the left)
mwuk0717a	uk	1660	GOOS	1500	44	53	Pascaart vant Canaal Begrypende in sich Engelandt, Schotlandt en Ierlandt
mwru0057	russia	1660	GOOS	800	26	36	Pascaarte van de Mont van de Witte Zee
mwuk1423	england thames	1665	GOOS	750	43	54	Pascaarte van Engelant van t' Voorlandt tot aen Blakeney waer in te Sien is de Mont vande Teemse
mwbp0024	baltic sea (east)	1669	GOOS	2000	43	53	Pascaarte vande Oost-Zee van 't Eylandt Rugen, ofte Bornholm tot aen Wyborg
mwbh0381	belgium holland	1669	GOOS	1200	43	53	Pascaarte vande Zuyder-Zee, Texel ende Vlie-Stroom, als mede 't Amelander-Gat. t'Amsterdam, by Pieter Goos op 't Water inde Vergulde Zee Spiegel. Anno 1666 (copy of Van Loon 1661)
mwwi0232	west indies (east)	1666	GOOS	1500	45	54	Pascaert vande Caribes Eylanden (north to the right)
mwm0013	mediterranean	1666	GOOS	4800	41	52	Pascaerte van de Levant ... t'Eylandt Cyprus / Paskaerte van 't Westelyckste der Middelandsche Zee (2 charts)
mwat0254	atlantic north	1650	GOOS	2000	43	53	Pascaerte van Groen-Landt, Yslandt, Straet Davids en Ian Mayen Eylandt; Hoemen de Selvige van Hitlandt en de Noortcusten van Schotlandt en Yrlandt Beseylen Mach
mwsam0192a	south america (north west)	1666	GOOS	1350	44	54	Pascaerte van Nova Hispania, Chili, Peru, en Guatimala
mwin0475	indian ocean west	1666	GOOS	2500	44	54	Pascaerte van 't Westelycke Deel van Oost Indien, van Cabo de Bona Esperanca, tot C. Comorin
mwin0475	indian ocean west	1666	GOOS	1500	44	54	Pascaerte van 't Westelycke Deel van Oost-Indien
mwwi0022	west indies	1666	GOOS	2800	46	55	Pascaerte van Westindien de Vaste Kusten en de Eylanden

AMPG REFERENCE	REGION	DATE	MAP MAKER	PRICE (UK£)	VERT. (cm.)	HOR. (cm.)	TITLE OF MAP (Comments by the editor in brackets)
mwat0190	atlantic cape verde isl.	1676	GOOS	750	42	53	Pascaerte vande Soute Eylanden ofte Ilhas de Cabo Verde
mwat0340	atlantic west	1668	GOOS	1200	44	54	Pascaerte vande Vlaemsche, Soute, en Caribesche Eylanden, als mede Terra Nova, en de Custen van Nova Francia, Nova Anglia, Nieu Nederlandt, Venezuela, Nueva Andalusia, Guiana, en een Gedeelte, van Brazil
mwp0231	pacific (all)	1666	GOOS	2500	45	55	Pascaerte vande Zuyd-Zee tussche California, en Ilhas de Ladrones
mwgr0483	greece cyprus	1662	GOOS	4000	40	52	Paskaarte van't Eylant Cyprus (inset: coast of Egypt)
mwsam0304	south america brazil	1660	GOOS	1350	45	56	Paskaart van Brasil van Rio de los Amazones, tot Rio de la Plata
mwuk0075	ireland	1669	GOOS	1200	44	55	Paskaarte om Achter Yrlandt om te Zeylen van Hitlant tot aen Heyssat Nieuwlycx Uytgegeven (copy of Doncker 1665)
mwgr0622	greece islands	1720	GOOS	675	40	52	Paskaarte van de Golfe van Smyrne als meede het Eylandt Scio
mwaf0866	africa south	1666	GOOS	1500	30	53	Pas-Kaarte van de Zuyd-west-Kust van Africa; van Cabo Negro tot beoosten Cabo de Bona Esperanca (north to the left)
mwaf1065	africa south west	1666	GOOS	1600	30	53	Pas-Kaarte van de Zuyd-West-Kust van Afrika; van Cabo Negro tot Beoosten Cabo de Bona Esperanca
mwsam0216	south america argentina	1666	GOOS	1500	44	55	Paskaarte van het Zuydelijckste van America van Rio de la Plata, tot Caap de Hoorn, ende inde Zuyd Zee, tot B. de Koquimbo
mwgr0307	greece corfu	1662	GOOS	1250	40	51	Paskaarte vande Eijlanden Corfu
mwbh0382	belgium holland	1669	GOOS	2000	44	93	Paskaert van de Zeeusche en Vlaemsche Kusten, tonende Alle Drooghten, Diepten, en Ondiepten, tusschen t'Eylandt Schouwen en de Hoofden, Curieuselyck Beschreven door Dirck Davidsz
mwaf1130	africa west	1676	GOOS	1500	42	51	Paskaert vande Gout Cust, van Rio Volta tot Cabo Lagoa
mwca0211a	canada arctic	1666	GOOS	3000	45	54	Paskaert Zijnde de Noordelijckste Zeekusten van America van Groenland door de Straet Davis en de Straet Hudson tot Terra Neuf
mwuss1033	new jersey	1666	GOOS	15000	52	62	Paskaerte van de Zuydt en Noordt Revier in Nieu Nederlant Streckende van Cabo Hinloopen tot Rechkewach (for illustration see 'America North East')
mwuss0071	california	1666	GOOS	17500	44	54	Paskaerte van Nova Granada, en t'Eylandt California (close copy of Van Loon 1661, but omits P. de Monte Rey. For illustration, see under 'America North [West]')
mwf0290	france bay of biscay	1669	GOOS	1000	43	53	Paskaerte vande Bocht van Vranckrijck Biscajen en Galisen tusschen Heysant en C. de Finisterre
mwsp0460	spain regions	1670	GOOS	800	45	54	Paskaerte Vande Bocht van Vranckryck Biscajen
mwuk1540b	uk english channel (west)	1669	GOOS	875	43	53	Paskaerte van't in Comen van 't Canaal, Hoemen dat Sal aen Doen, als men uyt de West Comt
mwm0131a	mediterranean east	1670	GOOS	950	40	52	Paskaerte van't Oostelyckste der Middelandsche Zee
mwas0399	asia south east	1666	GOOS	6000	45	54	Paskaerte Zynde t'Oosterdeel van Oost Indien, met Alle de Eylanden daer Ontrendt Geleegen van C. Comorin tot aen Japan
mwuss1060	new jersey	1828	GORDON	5000	142	84	A Map of the State of New Jersey, with Part of the Adjoining States, Compiled under the Patronage of the Legislature of the Said State
mww0373	world	1735	GORDON	350	15	29	A New and Correct Map of the World from the Latest Observations
mwuk0159	ireland	1737	GORDON	140	15	20	A New Map of Ireland from the Latest Observations
mwit0169	italy	1735	GORDON	140	15	19	A New Map of Italy from the Latest Observations
mwru0174	russia	1735	GORDON	140	15	18	A New Map of Moscovy from the Latest Observations
mwbp0412	poland	1735	GORDON	140	15	19	A New Map of Poland from the Latest Observations
mwsc0135	scandinavia	1735	GORDON	140	15	22	A New Map of Scandinavia, Containing ye Kingdoms of Sweden, Denmark and Norway
mwuk0473	scotland	1735	GORDON	140	15	19	A New Map of Scotland from the Latest Observations
mwam1099	america north (east)	1789	GORDON	800	27	41	A New Map of the States of Pensylvania New Jersey New York Connecticut Rhode Island Massachusets and New Hampshire Including Nova Scotia and Canada from the Latest Authorities
mwme1001	turkey etc	1735	GORDON	140	15	18	A New Map of Turkey in Europe from the Latest Observations
mwec0012	uk england bedfordshire	1736	GORDON	1800	96	66	An Accurate Map of the County of Bedford Actually Surveyed after a New Method by William Gordon Gent. 1736
mwec0582	uk england huntingdonshire	1731	GORDON	2400	49	59	An Accurate Map of the County of Huntingdon, Actually Survey'd after a New Method, in the Years 1730 & 1731 (6 sheets)
mwuss0843	massachusetts	1785	GORDON	300	23	32	Boston with its Environs
mwe0152	europe	1735	GORDON	140	15	18	Europe According to the Latest Observations
mwam1100	america north (east)	1789	GORDON	800	31	37	New Map of the States of Georgia, South and North Carolina, Virginia and Maryland, Including the Spanish Provinces of West and East Florida

AMPG REFERENCE	REGION	DATE	MAP MAKER	PRICE (UK£)	VERT. (cm.)	HOR. (cm.)	TITLE OF MAP (Comments by the editor in brackets)
mwam0382	america north	1728	GORDON	200	15	18	North America According to the Latest Observations
mwuss0220	carolinas	1781	GORDON	300	16	29	Plan du Havre de Charleston, Montrant la Disposition de la Flotte Britannique
mwuss1649	virginia	1781	GORDON	600	21	20	Plan du Siege d'York et de Gloucester par les Armees Alliees en Septembre et Octobre 1781
mwsam0059	south america	1728	GORDON	120	16	20	South America
mwuss1044	new jersey	1788	GORDON	225	31	23	The Jerseys, &c.&c.
mwuss1662	virginia	1788	GORDON	350	18	26	The Part of Virginia which was the Seat of Action
mwam0501	america north	1788	GORDON	350	29	29	The United States of America
mwuss1663	virginia	1788	GORDON	350	29	21	York Town, and Gloucester Point, as Besieged by the Allied Army
mwg0835	westphalia	1762	GOSSE & PINET	450	64	62	Plan de la Bataille de Vellinghausen Gagnie le 16 Juillet 1761
mwg0842	westphalia	1766	GOSSE & PINET	785	54	91	Plan des Mouvements de l'Armee depuis le 26 jusqu'au 31 de May de Meme depuis le 12. d'Aout jusqu'au Sept. 1758
mwg0464	hessen	1763	GOSSE & PINET	1000	86	60	Plan du Siege de Cassel avec les Traveaux et les Tranchees des Allies devant cette Place depuis de 18 d'Aout jusqu'au 1. Novembre 1762 (map by Lt. Gerlach)
mwg0592	saxony	1632	GOTTFRIED	200	27	38	Delineatio Praelii inter ser. Suecorum Regem
mwg0442	hessen	1632	GOTTFRIED	400	18	30	Francfurt am Mayn
mwg0701	schleswig-holstein	1632	GOTTFRIED	200	7	13	Lubec
mwgm0159	mexico	1640	GOTTFRIED	200	15	18	Mexico
mwg0480	mecklenburg	1632	GOTTFRIED	200	8	14	Rostock
mwbp0078	baltic states	1632	GOTTFRIED	120	7	13	Wittenstein (Estonia)
mwit0841	italy sardinia and corsica	1801	GOTZE	600	45	61	Charte von der Insel Corsica nach den Bewahrtesten Hulfsmitteln / Charte von Sardinien nach den Bewahrtesten Hulfsmitteln (publ. by Weimar)
mwf0917a	france paris	1831	GOUJON	1200	59	87	Nouveau Plan Itinéraire de la Ville de Paris divisé en 12 arr. avec tous les édifices publics (map by N. Maire)
mwf0916a	france paris	1826	GOUJON	1800	65	105	Plan de la Ville de Paris, divisé en 12 arrondissements et 48 quartiers (map by X. Girard)
mwca0144	canada	1821	GOURLAY	1200	35	49	Map of Upper Canada Engraved for a Statistical Account
mwbh0535	belgium holland	1708	GOURNAY	500	41	63	Plan du Siege de Namur
mwca0512	canada quebec	1759	GRAND MAG.	150	16	23	A Map of the Country round Quebec, with the Camps of the English & French, at the Siege thereof.
mwam1001	america north (east)	1758	GRAND MAG.	585	25	33	A New and Accurate Map of the English Empire in North America
mwuk1198	england london	1760	GRAND MAG.	1000	30	43	A New and Accurate Survey of the Country about the Cities of London, and Westminster and the Borough of Southwark. For 15 Miles in Length, & 12 in Depth in which is Contain'd All the Main & Cross Roads &c. to this Present Year 1760
mwam0176	america continent	1759	GRAND MAG.	500	26	33	America Drawn from the Latest and Best Observations, Describing All the European Settlements &c by R. Bennett Engraver.
mwp0362	pacific marianas	1748	GRAND MAG.	150	19	11	Chart of the Ladrones or Marianne Islands
mwuss0749	maryland	1758	GRAND MAG.	300	19	12	Map of the Country between Wills Creek and Fort du Quesne.
mwit0263	italy abruzzo	1743	GRANDI	600	39	26	Diocesi di Larino Posta per la Magior Parte di nella Provincia di Abruzzo Citra e per l'Altra nel Contado di Molise
mwuk0830a	uk	1749	GRANTE	4000	63	40	A Chart Wherein are mark'd all the different Routs of P. Edward in Great Britain and the Marches of his Army and the English.
mwuk0828	uk	1747	GRANTE		159	108	Carte ou sont tracees toutes les differentes routes, que S.A.R. Charles Edward Prince de Galles, a suivies dans la grande Bretagne
mwuk0583	scotland	1817	GRASSOM	2000	118	182	To the Noblemen and Gentlemen of the County of Stirling, this Map from Actual Survey
mwaf0330	africa	1840	GRATTAN & GILBERT	75	23	28	Africa
mwp0114	australia	1836	GRATTAN & GILBERT	250	25	30	Australia
mwaf1020	africa south	1840	GRATTAN & GILBERT	200	23	28	Cape Colony
mwme0888	syria etc	1820	GRATTAN & GILBERT	95	29	24	Syria
mwam1236	america north (east)	1836	GRATTAN & GILBERT	200	29	23	United States
mwme0848	persia etc	1831	GRATZ	75	21	17	Persien mit den Rusischen Besitzungen am Kaukasus
mwe0456	europe bulgaria	1831	GRATZ	100	16	16	Plan von Shumla
mwit0450a	italy liguria	1784	GRAVIER	3500	107	184	A Topographical Map of the Republick of Genua taken from the Celebrated Spanish map by Chaffrion with many additions & improvements, 1784 (title also in French, Italian, German)
mwit0449	italy liguria	1781	GRAVIER	750			Genova
mwit1068a	italy naples	1770	GRAVIER	950	46	72	Pianta della Citta di Napoli (re-issue of Jolivet 1755)
mwit0455a	italy liguria	1829	GRAVIER	750	52	73	Plan de la Ville de Genes en 1829
mwit0451	italy liguria	1789	GRAVIER	1100	41	56	Topografia del Porto, e Citta di Genova
mww0508	world	1780	GRAVIUS	400	17	30	Kaart van de Twee Platte Warelds Bollen

AMPG REFERENCE	REGION	DATE	MAP MAKER	PRICE (UK£)	VERT. (cm.)	HOR. (cm.)	TITLE OF MAP (Comments by the editor in brackets)
mwaf0240	africa	1780	GRAVIUS	150	18	23	Kaartje van Africa
mwas0198	asia continent	1780	GRAVIUS	150	18	23	Kaartje van Asia Verbatero Vitgegeren
mwe0201	europe	1780	GRAVIUS	150	18	23	Kaartje van Europe
mwam0207	america continent	1780	GRAVIUS	350	18	24	Kaartje van het Noorder-Deel van America / Kaartje van het Zuider-Deel van America (2 maps)
mwbh0714	belgium holland	1765	GREEBE	4000	47	64	Amsterdam. (The illustrated map does not include a text panel pasted onto the lower border of the map entitled 'Explicatie', total size: 53x64cm.)
mwuk0093	ireland	1686	GREENE	1200	45	54	A Mapp of Ireland with the Roads and Baronies
mwuk0940	england	1682	GREENE		46	56	The Royal Map of England
mwuk0417	scotland	1679	GREENE & BERRY	1200	47	55	A New Map of Scotland with the Roads
mwam1366	america north (west)	1844	GREENHOW	300	58	65	Map of the Western & Middle Portions of North America, to Illustrate the History of California, Oregon and the Other Countries on the North-West Coast of America
mwam1363	america north (west)	1840	GREENHOW	300	41	55	The Northwest-Coast of North America and Adjacent Territories
mwuss1245	new york	1843	GREENLEAF	280	28		(Circular) Map of the Country Twenty Five Miles round the City of New York
mwuss0017	alabama	1842	GREENLEAF	100	33	28	Alabama
mwuss0062	arkansas	1843	GREENLEAF	100	28	36	Arkansas
mwsam0433	south america brazil	1842	GREENLEAF	100	32	27	Brazil with Guiana & Paraguay
mwuss0386	delaware	1843	GREENLEAF	100	28	33	Delaware and Maryland
mwuss0534	georgia	1843	GREENLEAF	100	36	28	Georgia
mwuss0563	illinois	1843	GREENLEAF	100	33	28	Illinois
mwuss0579	indiana	1842	GREENLEAF	250	33	28	Indiana
mwuss0619	kentucky	1842	GREENLEAF	180	30	33	Kentucky and Tennessee
mwuss0680	louisiana	1842	GREENLEAF	275	28	33	Louisiana
mwca0562	canada quebec	1840	GREENLEAF	160	27	31	Lower Canada
mwca0564	canada quebec	1842	GREENLEAF	160	27	31	Lower Part of Canada
mwuss0733	maine	1842	GREENLEAF	150	32	27	Maine
mwuss0725	maine	1832	GREENLEAF	3500	127	107	Map of the State of Maine with the Province of New Brunswick (first edition 1829)
mwuss0483	florida	1843	GREENLEAF	240	33	28	Map of the Territory of Florida
mwuss0924	michigan	1842	GREENLEAF	250	30	27	Michigan
mwuss0969	mississippi	1842	GREENLEAF	140	32	27	Mississippi
mwuss0992	missouri	1842	GREENLEAF	120	27	32	Missouri
mwp0143	australia	1842	GREENLEAF	180	28	34	New Holland and New Zealand
mwuss1063	new jersey	1843	GREENLEAF	100	32	27	New Jersey
mwuss1243	new york	1842	GREENLEAF	160	27	32	New York
mwca0193	canada	1842	GREENLEAF	160	27	32	Newfoundland, Nova Scotia, and New Brunswick
mwuss0282	carolinas	1843	GREENLEAF	100	28	32	North and South Carolina
mwaa0174	arctic	1842	GREENLEAF	120	27	27	Northern Hemisphere
mwuss1320	ohio	1843	GREENLEAF	120	28	36	Ohio
mwuss1333	oregon	1843	GREENLEAF	300	28	33	Oregon Territory
mwme0423	holy land	1842	GREENLEAF	160	32	27	Palestine or the Holy Land or the Land of Canaan
mwuss1437	pennsylvania	1842	GREENLEAF	140	27	33	Pennsylvania
mwaa0053	antarctic	1842	GREENLEAF	360	27	27	Sothern Hemisphere
mwsam0160	south america	1842	GREENLEAF	80	33	28	South America
mwuss1519	texas	1842	GREENLEAF	1500	33	30	Texas Compiled from the Latest and Best Authorities
mwgm0344	mexico	1843	GREENLEAF	100	33	28	The United States of Mexico
mwam0736	america north	1840	GREENLEAF	250	27	32	United States
mwca0484	canada ontario	1840	GREENLEAF	200	27	31	Upper Canada
mwuss1581	vermont	1842	GREENLEAF	240	32	26	Vermont and New Hampshire
mwuss1687	virginia	1840	GREENLEAF	200	27	32	Virginia
mwwi0205	west indies	1842	GREENLEAF	200	28	33	West Indies
mww0726	world	1842	GREENLEAF	300	33	28	Western Hemisphere / Eastern Hemisphere (2 maps)
mwuss1697	wisconsin	1843	GREENLEAF	200	28	36	Wisconsin and Iowa
mwuk1305	england london	1827	GREENWOOD	13500	126	186	Map of London, from Actual Survey Made in the Years 1824, 1825 and 1826 (9 editions to 1854)
mwec0026	uk england bedfordshire	1834	GREENWOOD	280	58	69	Map of the County of Bedford
mwec0115	uk england cambridgeshire	1834	GREENWOOD	320	57	72	Map of the County of Cambridge from an Actual Survey Made in the Years 1832 & 1833
mwuk1879	wales	1834	GREENWOOD	280	58	69	... Cardigan, Pembroke & Carmarthen
mwec0207	uk england cornwall	1827	GREENWOOD	2950	181	186	Map of the County of Cornwall, Made from an Actual Survey in the Years 1826-27
mwec0243	uk england cumbria	1823	GREENWOOD	1350	183	154	Map of the County of Cumberland, from an Actual Survey Made in the Years 1821 & 1822
mwec0245	uk england cumbria	1831	GREENWOOD	320	62	69	A Map of the County of Cumberland, from an Actual Survey
mwec0273	uk england derbyshire	1825	GREENWOOD	1000	154	122	Map of the County of Derby, from an Actual Survey Made in the Years 1824 & 1825
mwec0311	uk england devon	1827	GREENWOOD	1500	193	198	Map of the County of Devon, from an Actual Survey, Made in the Years 1825 & 1826
mwec0348	uk england dorset	1826	GREENWOOD	1400	56	51	A Map of the County of Dorset from an Actual Survey Made in the Years 1825 and 1826 (6 sheets, each 56x51cm.)

AMPG REFERENCE	REGION	DATE	MAP MAKER	PRICE (UK£)	VERT. (cm.)	HOR. (cm.)	TITLE OF MAP (Comments by the editor in brackets)
mwec0350	uk england dorset	1834	GREENWOOD	280	58	69	Map of the County of Dorset
mwec0424	uk england essex	1825	GREENWOOD	1200	131	156	Map of the County of Essex, from an Actual Survey Made in the Year 1824
mwec0453	uk england gloucestershire	1823	GREENWOOD	1600	150	127	A Map of the County of Gloucester
mwec0457	uk england gloucestershire	1834	GREENWOOD	280	58	69	Map of the County of Gloucester
mwec0566	uk england hertfordshire	1834	GREENWOOD	320	58	69	Map of the County of Hertford
mwec0590	uk england huntingdonshire	1830	GREENWOOD	200	63	73	Map of the County of Huntingdon
mwec0664	uk england kent	1829	GREENWOOD	320	58	70	Map of the County of Kent
mwec0661	uk england kent	1821	GREENWOOD	1500	123	191	Map of the County of Kent made from an actual survey in 1819 and 1820
mwec0797	uk england middlesex	1829	GREENWOOD	360	54	65	Map of the County of Middlesex
mwec0795	uk england middlesex	1819	GREENWOOD	1850	126	130	Map of the County of Middlesex, from an Actual Survey Made in the Years 1818 & 1819
mwuk1880	wales	1834	GREENWOOD	280	58	69	Map of the County of Monmouth
mwec0897	uk england northumberland	1834	GREENWOOD	280	58	69	Map of the County of Northumberland
mwec0926	uk england nottinghamshire	1826	GREENWOOD	1400	142	108	Map of the County of Nottingham, from an Actual Survey Made in the Years 1824 & 1825
mwec0973	uk england oxfordshire	1834	GREENWOOD	360	58	69	Map of the County of Oxford
mwec0993	uk england rutland	1834	GREENWOOD	300	58	69	Map of the County of Rutland
mwec1021	uk england shropshire	1830	GREENWOOD	300	62	72	Map of the County of Salop
mwec1052	uk england somerset	1822	GREENWOOD	1400	62	129	Map of the County of Somersetshire, from Actual Survey Made in the Years 1820 & 1821
mwec0502	uk england hampshire	1826	GREENWOOD	1350	158	147	Map of the County of Southampton from an Actual Survey Made in the Years 1825 & 1826 (in 6 folding sheets, each 52x74cm.)
mwec1081	uk england staffordshire	1820	GREENWOOD	800	154	114	Map of the County of Stafford
mwec1085	uk england staffordshire	1834	GREENWOOD	280	58	69	Map of the County of Stafford
mwec1119	uk england suffolk	1825	GREENWOOD	1500	137	164	Map of the County of Suffolk from an Actual Survey Made in the Years 1823 & 1824
mwec1149	uk england surrey	1823	GREENWOOD	1800	101	125	Map of the County of Surrey from an Actual Survey Made in the Years 1822 and 1823
mwec1180	uk england sussex	1834	GREENWOOD	320	58	69	Map of the County of Sussex
mwec1207	uk england warwickshire	1822	GREENWOOD	1200	154	114	Map of the County of Warwick
mwec1230	uk england westmorland	1821	GREENWOOD	1500	100	120	Map of the County of Westmorland
mwec1263	uk england wiltshire	1834	GREENWOOD	280	63	73	Map of the County of Wilts.
mwec1354	uk england yorkshire	1817	GREENWOOD	2000	183	217	Map of the County of York, Made on the Basis of Triangles in the County.
mwec0152	uk england cheshire	1815	GREENWOOD	1500	116	151	Map of the County Palatine of Chester
mwec0384	uk england durham	1820	GREENWOOD	1200	104	126	Map of the County Palatine of Durham, from Actual Survey Made in the Years 1818 & 1819 (4 sheets, each 52x62cm.)
mwec0704	uk england lancashire	1834	GREENWOOD	400	58	69	Map of the County Palatine of Lancaster
mwec0700	uk england lancashire	1818	GREENWOOD	1500	203	137	Map of the County Palatine of Lancaster from an Actual Survey Made in the Year 1818
mwec1360	uk england yorkshire	1834	GREENWOOD	250	58	69	Map of the North Riding of the County of York
mwuk1877	wales	1831	GREENWOOD	280	61	69	Map of the South East Circuit of the Principality of Wales. Glamorgan, Brecon & Radnor
mwec1357	uk england yorkshire	1828	GREENWOOD	2000	64	41	To the Nobility, Gentry & Clergy of Yorkshire, this Map of the County Constructed from Survey Commenced in the Year 1817, & Corrected in the Years 1827 and 1828 (9 sheets, each 64x41cm.)
mwuss1527	texas	1844	GREGG	600	31	38	A Map of the Indian Territory Northern Texas and New Mexico Showing the Great Western Prairies
mwaf0654	africa islands seychelles	1779	GREGORY	800	42	55	A Plain Chart of the Seychelles, Praslin and other Adjacent Islands
mwas0600	asia south east borneo	1780	GREGORY	350	59	36	Chart of some Islands between Borneo and Banca
mwe0396	europe austria	1809	GREIPEL	650	95	104	Neueste General Karte des Erzherzoghtums Osterreich ob der Enns. Nach der Verbesserten Bonnischen Projektion
mwin0430	indian ocean	1776	GRENIER	250	33	61	Carte des Isles et Bancs Nommes Adu et Candu, Chagas
mwit0077	italy	1630	GREUTER		117	212	Italia (12 sheets joined)
mwwi0244	west indies (east)	1730	GRIERSON	785	43	53	A Chart of the Caribe Islands
mwf0296	france bay of biscay	1749	GRIERSON	500	45	55	A Chart of the Sea Coast Biscay and Gallicia between Cape Machicaco and Cape de Pinas and from Cape de Pinas to Cape de Finisterre
mwuk1666a	north sea	1730	GRIERSON	600	43	53	A Chart of the Seacoasts of England Flanders & Holland
mwuk1497	uk english channel (all)	1750	GRIERSON	1600	48	86	A Correct Chart of the Channell between England & France from the Newest and Best Surveys with the Flowing of the Tides & Setting of the Current as Observed by Dr. Ed. Halley
mwsam0601	south america guyana	1749	GRIERSON	450	55	44	A Draught of the Coast of Guiana from the River Oronoque to the River Amazones
mwwi0084	west indies	1749	GRIERSON	1000	44	56	A Generall Chart for the West Indies
mwuk0831	uk	1749	GRIERSON	1200	43	53	A New and Correct Chart of the Sea Coast of England Scotland & Ireland.
mwwi0085	west indies	1749	GRIERSON	2000	49	82	A New and Correct Large Draught of the Tradeing Part of the West Indies

AMPG REFERENCE	REGION	DATE	MAP MAKER	PRICE (UK£)	VERT. (cm.)	HOR. (cm.)	TITLE OF MAP (Comments by the editor in brackets)
mww0361	world	1730	GRIERSON	6000	69	118	A New and Correct Map of ye Whole World. By H. Moll Geor. (copy of Moll 1719)
mwwi0320	bahamas	1749	GRIERSON	1000	43	52	A New Chart of the Bahama Islands and the Windward Passage
mwe0463	europe central	1757	GRIERSON	800	59	98	A New Map of Germany, Hungary, Transilvania and the Suisse
mwuss0792	massachusetts	1730	GRIERSON	2000	41	53	A New Survey of the Harbour of Boston in New England
mwam0937	america north (east)	1735	GRIERSON	600	20	27	New England, New York, New Jersey and Pensilvania
mwam0423	america north	1760	GRIERSON	300	15	17	North America According to the Latest Observations
mwca0309	canada newfoundland	1749	GRIERSON	600	41	49	The Coast of New Found Land from Salmon Cove to Cape Bonavista Sold by George Grierson Dublin
mwuss0686	maine	1749	GRIERSON	800	43	52	The Harbour of Casco Bay and Islands Adjacent by Capt. Cyprian Southicke
mwwi0371	barbados	1745	GRIERSON	400	29	35	The Island of Barbadoes Divided into its Parishes
mwas0142	asia continent	1733	GRIERSON	1000	57	95	This Map of Asia According to ye Newest & Most Exact Observations
mwuk0279	ireland	1838	GRIFFITHS	4000	181	146	A General Map of Ireland to Accompany the Report of the Railway Commissioners Shewing the Principal Physical Features and Geological Structure of the Country
mwuss0759	maryland	1795	GRIFFITH	50000	74	130	Map of the State of Maryland Laid Down from an Actual Survey of All the Principal Waters, Public Roads, and Divisions of the Counties therein ... June 20th 1794
mwe0433	europe austria vienna	1803	GRIMM	4500	137	139	Grundriss der K: K: Haupt und Residenzstadt Wien mit ihren Vorstadten nach den Neuen Hausnumern 1797 - Plan de la Ville de Vienne et de ses Fouxbourgs avec le Denombrement des Maisons Fait en 1797 (new edition publ. 1810)
mwc0266	china	1833	GRIMM	450	75	97	Karte von Hoch-Asien zu C. Ritter's Erdkunde, Buch II Asien, Th. 1 & 2
mwbh0741a	belgium holland	1785	GRIMM	400	31	26	Plan der Stadt Antwerpen an der Schelde in Oesterreichischen Niederlanden
mwru0191	russia	1741	GRIMMEL	4000	50	64	Canalis Ladogensis (title also in Russian script. One of a set of 6 maps. Other titles are: "Lacus Ladoga et Sinus Finnicus" - "Der Sinus Finnicus von Cronstadt bis St. Petersburg" - "Fluvius Newa e Lacu Ladoga Petropolin versus procurrens" - "Karta Ingermanlandii i Karelii" - "Magnus Ducatus Finlandiae".)
mwam1089	america north (east)	1785	GRISELINI	900	29	36	Mappa Dell'America Settentrionale
mwe0591a	europe czech republic (bohemia)	1757	GRISELINI	480	28	34	Teatro della Guerra fra S. M. I' Imperatrice Regina d' Ungheri e S. M. Prussiana
mwwi0664	hispaniola	1795	GRIWTONN	500	43	65	Carte de l'Isle de Saint Domingue avec les Routes
mwe1116a	europe slovak republic (moravia)	1750	GROENEWOUD	250	35	40	Nieuwe Kaart van het Markgraafschap Moravia
mwuk1852	wales	1775	GROSE	120	15	12	(Brecknockshire)
mwec0268	uk england derbyshire	1775	GROSE	150	15	12	(Derby)
mwec0235a	uk england cumbria	1777	GROSE	80	14	12	Cumberland (updated version of Seller 1695)
mwuk1590	channel islands	1775	GROSE	100	12	15	Guernsey (based on Seller, 1694)
mwec0960	uk england oxfordshire	1775	GROSE	160	15	12	(Oxford)
mwec1256	uk england wiltshire	1775	GROSE	80	15	12	(Untitled)
mwme1070	turkey etc	1850	GROSS	240	21	28	Constantinople (key in right-hand border)
mwsp0348a	spain madrid	1844	GROSS	140	13	19	Plan von Madrid
mwbp0123	baltic states	1747	GROT	1200	50	58	Ducatuum Curlandiae et Semigalliae nec non Districtus Regii Piltensis Tabula Geographia
mwuk0991	england	1741	GRUNDY	600	42	53	A Map of the River Trent as it Runs from Farndon Ferry to Holme Meadow in its Two Branches by Kellum & Newark. Survey'd Level'd and Delineated by John Grundy Junr. Surveyor
mwme1013	turkey etc	1760	GUDENUS	20000	54	425	Vue de la Ville de Constantinople Capitale de l'Empire Ottoman
mwbp0262	poland	1658	GUDICANUS	3000	31	33	Nova Descriptio Totius Regni Polonici nec non Magni Ducatus Lithuaniae cum suis Palatinatibus Castellaniis ac Confiniis
mwf1068	france provence	1744	GUERARD	750	43	61	Carte Particuliere des Environs de Nice, et de Ville-Franche, depuis Ville-Neuve en Provence, jusqu'a Monaco
mwit1206	italy venice	1553	GUEROULT	1800	16	26	La Ville de Venise
mwit1126	italy tuscany	1828	GUERRAZZI	1500	58	76	Pianta Topografica della Citta ... Livorno
mwg0793	westphalia	1648	GUICCIARDINI	250	23	31	(Aachen) Aquisgranum vulgo Aich per Antiqua Imperij Urbs, Monumento Caroli Magni, Therma Prestantia et Memorablis
mwbh0097	belgium holland	1581	GUICCIARDINI	350	23	32	(Ghent) Gandavum
mwf0731	france nord pas-de-calais	1652	GUICCIARDINI	100	11	13	(Valenciennes) Valentiniana
mwbh0098	belgium holland	1581	GUICCIARDINI	550	24	27	Amstelredam
mwbh0033	belgium holland	1568	GUICCIARDINI	950	25	35	Amsterdam
mwbh0026	belgium holland	1567	GUICCIARDINI	850	28	35	Antverpia (woodcut)
mwf0713	france nord pas-de-calais	1612	GUICCIARDINI	180	23	31	Artois Atrebatum Regionis Vera Descriptio
mwbh0105	belgium holland	1582	GUICCIARDINI	400	24	31	Brabantia. (north to the left)
mwbh0093	belgium holland	1580	GUICCIARDINI	400	23	31	Brugae Flandicarum Urbium Decus

AMPG REFERENCE	REGION	DATE	MAP MAKER	PRICE (UK£)	VERT. (cm.)	HOR. (cm.)	TITLE OF MAP (Comments by the editor in brackets)
mwbh0099	belgium holland	1581	GUICCIARDINI	450	23	32	Bruxella Fontium
mwf0695	france nord pas-de-calais	1581	GUICCIARDINI	350	23	32	Cambray
mwg0580	saxony	1612	GUICCIARDINI	200	25	36	Civitas Embda
mwbh0027	belgium holland	1567	GUICCIARDINI	550	23	32	Descrittione Particulare et del Paese d'Utrecht
mwf0696	france nord pas-de-calais	1581	GUICCIARDINI	350	23	31	Duacum
mwbh0100	belgium holland	1581	GUICCIARDINI	400	24	32	Graven Hage, 't Hof van Hollant
mwbh0178	belgium holland	1609	GUICCIARDINI	875	36	49	Hollandiae Cattorum Regionis Typus
mwbh0106	belgium holland	1582	GUICCIARDINI	400	23	31	Liege
mwbh0028	belgium holland	1567	GUICCIARDINI	550	25	35	Liege (woodcut)
mwf0714	france nord pas-de-calais	1612	GUICCIARDINI	300	23	30	Lille
mwbh0820	luxembourg	1612	GUICCIARDINI	500	24	31	Lutzenbourg - Lutzenburgu ...
mwbh0102	belgium holland	1581	GUICCIARDINI	400	24	32	Nymmegen
mwbh0029	belgium holland	1567	GUICCIARDINI	550	26	34	Particuliere et Geographique Description du Duche de Brabant
mwbh0103	belgium holland	1581	GUICCIARDINI	400	25	34	Rotterdam
mwbh0128	belgium holland	1590	GUICCIARDINI	350	24	32	Zelandiae Typus
mwam1263	america north (east)	1850	GUIZOT	200	38	51	Carte des Etats-Unis
mwsc0515a	scandinavia iceland	1849	GUNNLAUGSSON	3000	56	69	Uppdráttr Islands (reduced version of his 4-sheet map publ. in 1848)
mwg0161	germany	1790	GURSCH	120	26	30	(Untitled map of Germany)
mwbh0749	belgium holland	1787	GUSSEFELD	200	57	46	Carte von Over-Yssel und Drenthe
mwg0541	rheinland-pfalz	1789	GUSSEFELD	280	46	56	Charte das Erzstift u. Churfurstenthum Trier
mwam1139	america north (east)	1800	GUSSEFELD	720	47	52	Charte der XV Vereinigten Staaten von Nord-America nach Murdochischer Projection Entworfen
mwg0223	germany north west	1798	GUSSEFELD	280	48	60	Charte uber den Nordlichen Theil des Ober Sachsischen Kreises Enthaltend die Mark Brandenburg u. d. Hrz. Pommern
mwbh0883	luxembourg	1791	GUSSEFELD	720	68	73	Charte vom Herzogthum Luxemburg
mwaf0425	africa east	1804	GUSSEFELD	300	59	45	Charte vom Nil Strome, Aegypten, Nubien und Habesch
mwaf0281	africa	1797	GUSSEFELD	400	47	52	Charte von Africa
mwam0244	america continent	1796	GUSSEFELD	480	58	44	Charte von America nach Astronomischen Bestimmungen, den Neuesten Nachrichten und Charten
mwam0241	america continent	1795	GUSSEFELD	480	66	50	Charte von Amerika aus der Altesten noch Unedirten Weltcharte des Diego Ribero
mwg0753	thuringia	1775	GUSSEFELD	800	86	61	Charte von dem Furstenhume Weimar
mwe0820	europe east	1785	GUSSEFELD	350	46	57	Charte von der Moldau und Walachey
mwbp0520	poland	1791	GUSSEFELD	350	45	57	Charte von Gros Polen
mwg0420	brandenburg	1789	GUSSEFELD	400	58	47	Charte von Neumarck Neu Entworfen
mwsam0120	south america	1797	GUSSEFELD	400	57	47	Charte von Sud America: Nach den Bewahrtesten Astronomischen Bestimmungen
mwwi0148	west indies	1800	GUSSEFELD	650	44	61	Charte von West Indien nach der Grossen Charte des B. Edwards
mwww0557	world	1788	GUTHRIE	275	23	28	A Chart of the World Shewing the latest Discoveries of Capt. Cook
mwam0502	america north	1788	GUTHRIE	240	19	23	A General Map of North America
mwaf0261	africa	1788	GUTHRIE	150	19	23	Africa from the best authorities
mwas0512a	asia south east	1788	GUTHRIE	180	19	28	East Indies from the Best Authorities
mwuk1026	england	1788	GUTHRIE	150	19	23	England and Wales
mwe0217	europe	1788	GUTHRIE	150	19	23	Europe from the best Authorities
mwf0157	france	1788	GUTHRIE	100	20	23	France from the latest Authorities
mwg0157	germany	1788	GUTHRIE	60	19	22	Germany and the Netherlands
mwuk0229	ireland	1788	GUTHRIE	180	19	23	Ireland from the latest Authorities
mwit0208	italy	1788	GUTHRIE	150	19	23	Italy from the best Authorities
mwbp0511a	poland	1788	GUTHRIE	120	19	22	Poland Lithuania and Prussia
mwru0289	russia	1788	GUTHRIE	120	19	21	Russia or Muscovy in Europe
mwuk0549	scotland	1788	GUTHRIE	180	20	23	Scotland from the best Authorities
mwsam0109	south america	1788	GUTHRIE	120	19	23	South America from the best authorities
mwsp0303	spain	1788	GUTHRIE	180	19	23	Spain and Portugal from the latest Authorities
mwww0558	world	1788	GUTHRIE	400	20	37	The World from the Best Authorities
mwe1161b	europe south east	1788	GUTHRIE	120	20	26	Turkey in Europe and Hungary
mwwi0055a	west indies	1788	GUTHRIE	280	18	35	West Indies from the latest Authorities
mwsw0027	switzerland	1588	GYGER	400	12	16	Die Eydgnoschafft mit dero Grentzen
mwsw0088	switzerland	1683	GYGER	4000	57	82	Helvetiae Rhaetiae et Valesiae, Caeterorumque
mwsw0088B	switzerland	1685	GYGER	8000	93	98	Nova Descriptio Ditionis Tigurinae (shown above left)
mwsw0213	switzerland	1799	HAAS	400	37	49	Die Helvetische Republik
mwit0219	italy	1797	HAAS	550	31	47	Nouvelle Carte de l'Italie d'apres des Traitees de Paix de Paris ... An 4, (1796) et de Campo Formio ... An 6, (1797)
mwsc0623	scandinavia norway	1746	HAAS	480	38	46	Vorstellung der Feldzuge welche der Konig Carl XII in den Letzteren Jahren in einer Theile des Konigreichs Norwegen Gethan (incl. Christiania - Oslo, top left)
mwit0954a	italy sicily	1777	HAAS, G.	1500	46	60	Carte de la Sicile
mwaa0183	arctic / antarctic	1628	HABRECHT	2000	20		(No titles; 2 maps, polar projections. Illustrated is the Sturm 1667 re-issue with 26cm. diameter)

AMPG REFERENCE	REGION	DATE	MAP MAKER	PRICE (UK£)	VERT. (cm.)	HOR. (cm.)	TITLE OF MAP (Comments by the editor in brackets)
mwgm0388	panama	1699	HACKE	1800	59	48	A Draft of the Golden & Adjacent Islands, with Part of ye Isthmus of Darien as it was Taken by Capt. Ienefer where ye Scots West India Company were Settled / A New Map of ye Isthmus of Darien in America, the Bay of Panama (2 maps on one sheet)
mww0286	world	1701	HACKE	1200	22	48	A New & Correct Sea Chart of the Whole World Shewing the Variations of ye Compass as they were Found Ano 1700
mwaa0086	arctic	1640	HAFENREFFERUM	500	20		(Untitled north polar projection, showing most of the world)
mwme0720	caucasus	1686	HAFFNER	600	29	35	Armenia seu Turcomania Georgia Commania
mwas0074	asia continent	1686	HAFFNER	960	29	36	Asia
mwsw0127	switzerland	1730	HAFFNER	800	27	62	Basel - Basilea (view)
mwg0235b	berlin	1730	HAFFNER	2000	27	65	Berolinum (view)
mwme1004	turkey etc	1740	HAFFNER	2000	22	66	Constantinopolis. Constantinopel (view)
mwme0793a	persia etc	1686	HAFFNER	600	28	35	Das Konigreich Persien (incl. view of Isphahan)
mwin0134	india	1686	HAFFNER	750	29	36	Das Reich des Grossen Mogols (incl. view of Delhi)
mwg0348	bavaria	1686	HAFFNER	280	37	32	Der Hochloblich Schwabische Circul ... nach der, de Ao. 1563, Verfasten und Publicirten Craisordnung
mwin0135	india	1686	HAFFNER	600	29	36	Die Halb Insul Indiens Disseit des Ganges mit den Konigreichen Decan, Golconda, Bisnagar und den Kusten Malabar und Coromandel
mwas0412	asia south east	1686	HAFFNER	875	29	35	Ein Theil von Indien Auserhalb des Ganges / Die Halb-Insul von Indien auser dem Ganges
mwf0857	france paris	1730	HAFFNER	2000	27	64	Paris Paris (view)
mwit0742a	italy rome	1740	HAFFNER	1600	23	65	Roma Rom
mwsc0644b	scandinavia norway	1816	HAGELSTAM	5000	53	42	Karta öfver Staden Christiania i Norrige
mwbh0394	belgium holland	1675	HAGEN	3500	79	88	(Leiden) Lugdunum Batavorum
mww0574a	world	1792	HAHN	500	11	22	Globus oder Erd-Kugel
mwme0408	holy land	1828	HAINES	4000	60	150	A New Map of the Land of Promise and the Holy City of Jerusalem Describing the Most Important Events in the Old and New Testaments
mwam1193	america north (east)	1826	HALE	2750	112	99	A Map of the New England States; Maine, New Hampshire, Vermont, Massachusetts, Rhode Island & Connecticut, with the Adjacent Parts of New York and Lower Canada
mwuss0877	massachusetts	1833	HALES	2000	62	79	Map of Boston and its Vicinity from Actual Survey by John G. Hales. With Corrections in 1833
mwca0460	canada nova scotia	1829	HALIBURTON	120	10	17	Plan of the Harbour and Fortifications of Louisburg
mwca0461	canada nova scotia	1829	HALIBURTON	120	10	17	Plan of the Town of Louisburg
mwca0462	canada nova scotia	1829	HALIBURTON	150	11	37	Shubenacadie Canal Line
mww0718	world	1840	HALL	300	46	56	(No title. Mercator's Projection)
mww0110	world	1605	HALL	800	16	19	(No title. From 'Mundus Alter et Idem Sive Terra' . Delineates a speculative Antarctica)
mwam0507	america north	1789	HALL	600	27	43	A New & Accurate Map of North America Including Nootka Sound; with the New Discovered Islands on the North East Coast of Asia
mwaf0319	africa	1829	HALL	250	50	41	Africa
mwp0125	australia	1839	HALL	235	25	38	Australasia
mwp0160	australia	1845	HALL	350	41	51	Australia
mwas0287a	asia burma	1829	HALL	450	51	41	Birmah with Part of Anam and Siam
mwsam0420	south america brazil	1828	HALL	400	51	41	Brazil and Paraguay
mwca0155	canada	1828	HALL	450	41	51	British North America
mwca0156	canada	1828	HALL	350	42	52	Canada, New Brunswick and Nova Scotia
mwc0261	china	1830	HALL	275	41	51	China
mwsam0546	south america colombia	1828	HALL	250	42	51	Colombia
mwp0087	australia	1828	HALL	400	51	41	Colony of New South Wales
mwsc0398a	scandinavia	1828	HALL	180	51	41	Denmark.
mwas0538	asia south east	1830	HALL	300	41	50	East India Islands
mwuk0261	ireland	1823	HALL	80	24	18	Ireland
mwwi0757	jamaica	1841	HALL	240	26	35	Jamaica
mwuk1098	england and scotland	1800	HALL	300	100	75	Leigh's New Road Map of England, Wales and Scotland, Drawn ... by Sidney Hall
mwgm0311	mexico	1828	HALL	200	40	56	Map of Routes to the Principal Mining Districts in the Central States of Mexico
mwp0072	australia	1824	HALL	450	52	40	Map of the Settlements in New South Wales Including All the Discoveries yet Made both Eastward & Westward of the Blue Mountians
mwgm0337	mexico	1840	HALL	350	41	50	Mexico and Central States Corrected from Original Information Communicated by Simon A.G. Bourne Esq.
mwgm0312	mexico	1828	HALL	500	40	51	Mexico and Guatimala
mwgm0287	mexico	1820	HALL	160	21	27	Mexico or New Spain, in which the Expedition of Cortes may be Traced
mwam0661	america north	1829	HALL	350	51	41	North America
mwuk0581a	scotland	1817	HALL	90	21	25	Orkney and Shetland Islands /Jersey, Guernsey &c. / Scilly Islands
mwp0279	pacific (all)	1830	HALL	240	42	51	Pacific Ocean

AMPG REFERENCE	REGION	DATE	MAP MAKER	PRICE (UK£)	VERT. (cm.)	HOR. (cm.)	TITLE OF MAP (Comments by the editor in brackets)
mwme0407	holy land	1828	HALL	240	51	41	Palestine
mwsam0794	south america peru	1828	HALL	140	41	51	Peru
mwuk0260a	ireland	1821	HALL	720	39	54	Plan of the City of Dublin
mwuk0630	scotland	1840	HALL	180	48	37	Scotland
mwsam0147	south america	1827	HALL	240	51	43	South America.
mwaf1009	africa south	1828	HALL	240	42	52	Southern Africa
mwru0346	russia	1828	HALL	300	27	37	St. Petersburgh
mwuss0326	connecticut	1847	HALL	350	43	26	The Principal Part of Norwalk in the Year 1847, with a Plan of the Ancient Settlement
mww0733	world	1845	HALL	200	22	39	The World. ... by S. Hall
mww0672a	world	1823	HALL	200	15	28	The World.
mwam1201	america north (east)	1828	HALL	500	41	51	United States
mwp0096	australia	1830	HALL	400	52	41	Van Diemen's Land
mwsam0862	south america venezuela	1838	HALL	200	38	28	Venezuela, New Granada, Equador, Peru
mwuss1601	virginia	1636	HALL	2400	16	24	Virginia
mwbp0564b	poland	1828	HALL	300	11	16	Warsaw
mwwi0177	west indies	1828	HALL	280	41	51	West Indies
mwaf1255	africa west	1840	HALL	200	41	51	Western Africa
mwam0298	america continent	1838	HALL	250	42	42	Western Hemisphere
mwaa0039	antarctic	1785	HALLE	2000	36	36	Der Funfte Weltheil nach den Neusten Entdeckingen ('The fifth continent according to the latest discoveries')
mww0232	world	1686	HALLEY	1500	15	49	(Untitled map, from 35N to 35S)
mwgr0624	greece islands	1728	HALLEY	720	51	60	A Chart of the Archipelago with the Island of Candia
mwam0927	america north (east)	1728	HALLEY	2400	51	58	A Chart of the Atlantick Ocean from Buttons Island to Port Royall
mwaf0398	africa east	1728	HALLEY	600	50	61	A Chart of the Coast of Africa from Mozambique to the Straits of Babelmandel and the Adjoyning Ocean
mwsam0357	south america brazil	1728	HALLEY	1000	51	60	A Chart of the Coast of Brazil and Guiana, in America with Part of the Caribbe Islands
mwc0106	china	1728	HALLEY	1000	50	60	A Chart of the Coast of China from Cambodia to Namquam with Part of Japan
mwin0183	india	1728	HALLEY	550	50	60	A Chart of the East Indian Ocean
mwat0033	atlantic ocean (all)	1728	HALLEY-SENEX	1000	50	60	A Chart of the Great Western Ocean with the Coast of Europe, Africa & America
mwuk0150	ireland	1728	HALLEY	850	58	50	A Compleat Chart Of The Coast Of Ireland
mwuk1549a	bristol channel	1728	HALLEY	600	46	55	A Draught of the Bristol Channel from the Holmes to King Road
mwbp0040	baltic sea (east)	1728	HALLEY	1200	50	56	A Draught of the Sound or Fuer to Dram and Christiana / A Draught of the Harbour of Revel / The Coast from Rose Head to Dantzick and Koningsberg
mwaa0121	arctic	1728	HALLEY	720	48	49	A Globular Draught from the North Pole to the Latitude of 60 Degrees
mwat0270b	atlantic ocean (north)	1728	HALLEY	800	51	58	A New and Correct Chart of the Atlantick Ocean Reduced Describing Part of the Coasts of Europe, Africa and America with their Adjacent Islands
mwuk1486a	uk english channel (all)	1728	HALLEY	1600	50	120	A New and Correct Chart of the Channel
mwm0051	mediterranean	1728	HALLEY	3000	51	122	A New and Correct Chart of the Mediterranean Sea
mwgm0027	gulf of mexico and surrounding regions	1728	HALLEY	1800	50	116	A New and Correct Chart of the Trading Part of the West Indies /A Chart of the Atlantick Ocean from Oronoque River to the River May with the Caribbee & Bahama Is. (lower half of a 4-sheet map)
mww0287	world	1701	HALLEY	18000	55	145	Nova et Accuratissima Totius Terrarum Orbis Tabula Nautica Variationum Magneticarum Index juxta Observationes Anno. 1700 (shown is the 1745 re-issue by Renard)
mwsam0168	south america (central)	1728	HALLEY	500	51	59	The Coast of Chili and Peru from Baldivia to Lima
mwca0300	canada newfoundland	1728	HALLEY	720	46	24	The Coast of Newfoundland from Placencia to Cape Bonavista
mwsc0200	scandinavia	1815	HALLSTROM	550	94	61	Karta ofver Sverige och Norrige
mwbh0565	belgium holland	1718	HALMA	720	53	81	(Beetsterzwaag) Opsterlandt de Achste Grietenije van Zevenwolden
mwme0874	syria etc	1717	HALMA	250	20	33	Damascus in Syrien Volgens de Afteekening Gedaen in 't Jaer 1668
mwme0876	syria etc	1717	HALMA	200	13	20	De Stadt Beroot, bij Oudts Berijtus (view)
mwme0481	jerusalem	1717	HALMA	1000	28	35	De Stadt Jerusalem als zy Hedendaeghs Bevonden wordt (view)
mwme0241	holy land	1709	HALMA	240	21	33	Descriptio Paradisi, et Terrae Canaan, Regionumque a Patriarchis Primum Habitatarum
mwme0242	holy land	1709	HALMA	240	21	33	Descriptio Terrae Canaan
mwbh0566	belgium holland	1718	HALMA	550	52	60	Frisiae Dominium
mwsp0070	portugal	1708	HALMA	720	49	66	Nouvelle Carte du Portugal
mwru0118b	russia	1704	HALMA	1500	51	68	Nova Tabula Imperii Russici (copy of Witsen 1687)
mwit0400a	italy lazio	1697	HALMA	250	35	42	Partis Latii a Roma Labicum usque descriptio
mwme0875	syria etc	1717	HALMA	240	24	34	Syriae sive Soriae Nova et Accurata Descriptio

AMPG REFERENCE	REGION	DATE	MAP MAKER	PRICE (UK£)	VERT. (cm.)	HOR. (cm.)	TITLE OF MAP (Comments by the editor in brackets)
mwme0271	holy land	1709	HALMA	600	38	112	Tabula Geographica Terrae Sanctae Auctore J. Bonfrerio (north to the left. Also re-engraved and signed 'Franciscus Halma' as below)
mwme0478	jerusalem	1709	HALMA	280	21	33	Vera Hierosolymae Veteris Imago
mwit0499	italy lombardy	1705	HALMA	240	20	29	Zetel des Oorlogs in Italien
mwin0181	india	1727	HAMILTON	300	19	23	A Map of the East Coast of the Bay of Bengall with the Islands
mwas0825	asia south east siam	1727	HAMILTON	450	19	31	A Map of the Sea Coasts of Siam, Cambodia, Couchin China and Tonquin with the Islands to the Eastward of them as Far as Luconia
mwgm0308	mexico	1827	HAMILTON	350	24	29	Mexico
mwca0662	canada west	1790	HANNA	250	24	19	A Plan of Sea Otter Harbour and St. Patricks Bay Taken by Capt. James Hanna
mwuss0673	louisiana	1827	HANSARD	400	30	37	Land District North of Red River in the State of Louisiana, Actual Survey by Charles Gordon. Surveyed to March 1823 by Maxfield Ludlow
mwe1143	europe south east	1688	HAPPEL	4000	32	82	(European cities of the Turkish wars)
mww0235	world	1687	HAPPEL	2400	29	29	(Set of two hemisphere maps)
mwsc0276	scandinavia denmark	1659	HAPPEL	200	30	36	Das Ao. 1658 den 1 Novemb. zwischen den Schweden und Hollandern Vorgegangene Zeetreffen (sea battle at Sjaelland)
mwit0668	italy piedmont	1706	HAPPEL	800	32	39	Das Glucklich Entsetzte Turin
mwe0416	europe austria vienna	1688	HAPPEL	800	29	36	Die Belagerung und Entsatzung der Stadt Wien 1683 (view)
mww0200	world	1675	HAPPEL	1500	21	30	Die Ebbe und Fluth auff Einer Flachen Landt-Karten Furgestelt
mwgr0400	greece crete	1669	HAPPEL	280	31	36	Die Statt Candia wie Solche Ao. 1667 und 1668 von den Turken ist Belagert und den 28 Augusti 1669 Denselben uber Geben Worden
mwe0908	europe hungary	1688	HAPPEL	800	29	52	Eigentlicher Entwurff der Grossen und Kleinen Insul Schutt sampt denen Umbher Liegenden Christlichen und Turkischen Vestungen
mwe0773	europe east	1688	HAPPEL	500	25	51	Eine Newe Land Karte von Wien biss nach Constantinopel und Angrantzenden Landern
mwca0043	canada	1705	HAPPEL	240	11	15	General-Carte von Canada
mwuk0111	ireland	1691	HAPPEL	300	26	19	Land=Charte von Irrlandt:
mwgm0314	mexico	1829	HARDY	300	33	43	A Map of Sonora, and Gulf of California (first mention of 'Arizona')
mwca01432a	canada	1820	HARMON	500	19	46	A Map of the Interior of North America
mwam1208	america north (east)	1830	HARPER	240	14	15	Map of the Routes in New York, New England and Pennsylvania Drawn for the Northern Traveller
mwam0760	america north	1844	HARPER	450	46	56	Map of the United States, and Texas
mwbh0475	belgium holland	1696	HARREWYN	3000	58	94	Bruxella nobilissima Brabantiae civitas
mwbh0744	belgium holland	1786	HARREWYN	200	14	19	La Ville d'Amsterdam
mwbh0745	belgium holland	1786	HARREWYN	200	14	19	La Ville d'Utrecht
mwbh0881	luxembourg	1785	HARREWYN	200	14	19	Luxembourg
mwbh0492	belgium holland	1700	HARREWYN	500	36	46	Palatium Bruxellense Ducis Brabantiae
mwbh0482	belgium holland	1697	HARREWYN	6000	78	98	Plan de la Ville de Bruxelles avec la Situation des Retranchements et Campemens des Armees de Allies sous le Commandement de Sa Majeste Britannique au Mois d'Aout 1697 (printed on silk)
mwbh0746	belgium holland	1786	HARREWYN	200	14	19	Plan de Rotterdam
mwas0154	asia continent	1744	HARRIS	280	19	30	A Map of Marco Polo's Voyages & Travels in the 13th Century through a Great Part of Asia, All Tartary, the East India Islands & Part of Africa
mwuss0933	minnesota	1805	HARRIS	800	33	23	A Map of the Alleghany, Monongahela and Yohiogany Rivers
mwec0823	uk england norfolk	1701	HARRIS	500	29	40	A Map of the Great Levell of the Fenns Extending into ye Countyes of Norfolk, Suffolke
mww0385	world	1744	HARRIS	1100	34	55	A New and Accurate Map of the World. Drawn from the Best Authorities and Regulated by Astronomical Observations: Describing the Course of Each of the Following Circumnavigators Vizt: Ferdinand Magellan, Sr. Francis Drake and Commodore Anson
mwuk1237	england london	1779	HARRIS	950	32	50	A New and Accurate Plan of London, Westminster and the Borough of Southwark (11 editions until 1801) ('Harris's Plan ...' added to beginning of title in 1791)
mwuk1148	england london	1714	HARRIS	1800	53	62	A New and Exact Map of the Diocese of London (incl surrounding counties)
mww0303	world	1705	HARRIS	650	29	53	A New Map of the World Shewing the Course of Sr. Francis Drake, William Schouten and Capt. William Dampiers Voyages round it (copy of Heylyn 1703. See also Harris 1744)
mwsam0772	south america peru	1764	HARRIS	240	36	22	A Plan of Lima / Potosi
mwc0173	china	1764	HARRIS	300	28	21	A Plan of the City of Canton on the River Ta Ho

AMPG REFERENCE	REGION	DATE	MAP MAKER	PRICE (UK£)	VERT. (cm.)	HOR. (cm.)	TITLE OF MAP (Comments by the editor in brackets)
mwuss1278	ohio	1805	HARRIS	400	15	26	A Plat of that Part of the State of Ohio which Is Appropriated for Military Services Surveyed under the Direction of Rufus Putnam, Surveyor General
mww0266	world	1697	HARRIS	15000	47	57	A View of the World in Divers Projections by J: Harris
mwc0137	china	1744	HARRIS	350	34	20	Plans of the Old and New City of Peking ye Metropolis of China
mwuk1676	north sea	1785	HARRISON	300	47	37	A Correct Chart of the German Ocean
mww0527	world	1783	HARRISON	250	14	19	A General Stereographic Map on the Plane of the Meridian
mwaf0267	africa	1791	HARRISON	400	50	71	A Map of Africa Drawn and Engraved from D'Anville's Two Sheet Map
mwec0488	uk england hampshire	1788	HARRISON	720	33	46	A Map of Hampshire engraved from an Actual Survey
mwin0292	india	1788	HARRISON	500	52	62	A Map of India Drawn from D'Anville's two Sheet Map. With Improvements (see 1752)
mwam0514	america north	1791	HARRISON	750	51	71	A Map of North America Published under the Patronage of the Duke of Orleans
mwuk1236	england london	1777	HARRISON	1000	25	50	A New and Complete Plan of London
mwp0328	pacific hawaii	1784	HARRISON	1000	21	33	A New Chart of the Sandwich Islands, including Owhyhee, where Captn. Cooke was killed
mwuk0227	ireland	1787	HARRISON	280	41	36	A New Map of Ireland Divided into Provinces and Counties
mww0552	world	1787	HARRISON	785	26	42	A New Map of the World with the Latest Discoveries
mwam1101a	america north (east)	1790	HARRISON	800	51	73	A Particular Map of the American Lakes, Rivers etc. par le Sr. D'Anville
mwuk1238	england london	1780	HARRISON	375	19	32	A Plan of the City and Environs of London
mwme0656	arabia etc	1788	HARRISON	280	46	33	Arabian Gulf or Red Sea
mwp0433	pacific north	1784	HARRISON	550	19	32	Chart of the N.W. Coast of America and the N.E. Coast of Asia. Explored by Capt. Cook, in the Years 1778 and 1779. The Unshaded Parts of the Coast of Asia are Taken from a M.S. Chart Received from the Russians ... Harrison & Co. Aug. 1, 1784
mwin0294	india	1788	HARRISON	350	72	34	Coromandel from d'Anville's Atlas
mwec0708	uk england lancashire	1849	HARRISON	320	63	46	Harrison & Sale's Guide to the East Lancashire Railway
mwuss0651	louisiana	1788	HARRISON	1000	30	50	Map of Louisiana from d'Anville's Atlas
mwam0498	america north	1787	HARRISON	550	34	39	North America Drawn from the Latest and Best Authorities
mww0559	world	1788	HARRISON	300	37	50	Orbis Veteribus Notus Drawn and Engraved from d'Anville's Map of the Antient World
mwaf1237	africa west	1788	HARRISON	235	50	35	Particular Map of the Western Coast of Africa from Cape Blanco to Cape de Verga and of the Course of the Rivers Senaga and Gambia
mwme0659	arabia etc	1788	HARRISON	280	29	43	Persian Gulph. From the Original by d'Anville
mwc0210	china	1791	HARRISON	400	72	50	Second Part of a Map of Asia, Containing China, Part of Tartary and India beyond the Ganges, with the Isles of Sunda, Philippines, Moluccas and Japon
mwaa0150	arctic	1783	HARRISON	175	14	18	Stereographic Map & Orthographic Map on Plane of the Equator
mwgr0225	greece	1788	HARRISON	175	30	46	The Coasts of Greece and the Archipelago
mwme0746	iraq etc	1788	HARRISON	200	33	39	The Euphrates and the Tigris from d'Anville's Atlas
mwca0619	canada st lawrence	1780	HARRISON	250	33	42	The River St. Lawrence
mwam0671	america north	1831	HART	250	37	33	Map of North America
mwuss1215	new york	1831	HART	250	33	37	Map of the State of New York
mwbp0311	poland	1684	HARTKNOCH	400	30	38	Prussia Accurate Descripta
mwbp0290	poland	1679	HARTKNOCH	200	28	32	Prussia Vetus
mwbp0555	poland	1812	HARTL	375	50	58	Generalcharte von dem Herzogthume Warschau nebst dem Konigreiche Preussen unde den Angranzenden Landern
mwru0285	russia	1787	HARTL	720	58	73	Imperium Russicum Pars Occidentalis
mww0346	world	1722	HASELDEN	15000	38	61	A Mapp of the Known World, According to Mercator's Projection, with a New Scale to Measure Distances thereon (publ. by Mount & Page)
mwuss1255	new york	1845	HASSLER	1200	86	60	Map of New York Bay and Harbor
mwec0654	uk england kent	1798	HASTED	180	20	33	A map showing Kent and the adjacent territories during Roman times (one of 25 maps from 'The History and Topographical Survey of Kent')
mwec0655	uk england kent	1800	HASTED	400	30	38	A Plan of the City of Canterbury
mwec0645	uk england kent	1783	HASTED	720	49	69	An Accurate Map of the County of Kent
mwg0138	germany	1760	HAUPT	300	32	39	Besondere Post und Reise Carte der Wege dur Teutschland (west/east: paris/venice)
mwe0724	europe danube	1737	HAUPT	2750	56	68	Danubii Fluminis pars Infima in qua Transylvania, Walachia, Moldavia, Bulgaria, Servia, Thracia et Bessarab Accurate Distincta (4 decorative borders incl. 13 city views)
mwsam0179	south america (north)	1730	HAUPT	2000	49	57	Mappa Geographica in qua Terra Firma
mwru0185	russia	1740	HAUPT	2000	56	68	Nova et Accurata Tartariae Europaeae seu Minoris et in Specie Crimeae Delineatio Geographica (decorative borders with 10 city views)
mwru0526	ukraine	1740	HAUPT	1000	38	47	Tartaria Minor - Calendarium Perpetuum ...

AMPG REFERENCE	REGION	DATE	MAP MAKER	PRICE (UK£)	VERT. (cm.)	HOR. (cm.)	TITLE OF MAP (Comments by the editor in brackets)
mwru0527	ukraine	1740	HAUPT	1500	39	47	Tartaria Minor oder der Jenige Theil der Praecobenischen Tartarn
mwg0258	baden-wurttemberg	1636	HAUTT	5500	31	41	Icon Totius Sueviae Wurttemberg
mwg0289a	baden-wurttemberg	1777	HAUTT	3500	39	52	Lacus Acroniani Terraeque adiacentis Tabula Geographica iam olim regnante Leopoldo Magno C.A. a. David Nic. Hauttio
mwam0777	america north	1846	HAVEN	600	37	39	Map of the United States and Mexico, Including Oregon, Texas, and the Californias
mwam0778	america north	1846	HAVEN	900	58	44	Map of the United States, Including Oregon, Texas, and the Californias, Showing the Boundary Claimed by the United States, Boundary Offered as Compromise, Boundary Proposed by Great Britain … Battles of the Texian Revolution
mwuss1123	new york	1777	HAWKES	9000	63	48	The Country Twenty Five Miles round New York, Drawn by a Gentleman from that City (size incl. text below map)
mwsam0689b	south america magellan	1774	HAWKESWORTH	900	56	79	A Chart of the Straights of Magellan, in which are Inserted the Observations and Discoveries, of Captn. Byron, Captn. Wallis and Captain Carteret (Capt. Cook was also present on this voyage. Illustration shows slightly reduced size French edition of the same year)
mwca0559	canada quebec	1834	HAWKINS	500	30	28	The Environs of Quebec, Compiled for A. Hawkins
mwjk0066	japan	1716	HAYASHI	5000	160	120	(Kyoto) Shinsen Daizoho Kyo O-Ezu
mwuss1246	new york	1843	HAYWARD	600	34	49	Hayward's Map of the City of Brooklyn
mwam0797	america north	1849	HAYWARD	350	61	104	The United States from the Latest Authorities for Hayward's Gazetteer
mwp0215	new zealand	1841	HEAPHY	350	36	52	Part of Lambton Harbour in Port Nicholson, New Zealand
mwca0220	canada arctic	1795	HEARNE	1800	53	74	A Map exhibiting Mr. Hearne's Tracks in his two Journies for the discovery of the Copper Mine River, in the Years 1770, 1771 and 1772 under the direction of the Hudson's Bay Company (Hearne discovered the Arctic Ocean. Also publ. in French the same year)
mwec1351	uk england yorkshire	1812	HEATHER	350	77	62	(Flamborough Head to Holy Island)
mwsp0615	spain regions	1802	HEATHER	140	18	14	(Port Alfaques, Catalonia)
mwsc0643	scandinavia norway	1811	HEATHER	800	79	124	A New and Accurate Chart of the Coast of Norway (large inset of the White Sea)
mwuk0310	irish sea	1804	HEATHER	1200	80	189	A New and Correct Chart of St George's Channel
mwwi0185	west indies	1831	HEATHER	1800	79	122	A New and Correct General Chart of the West Indies
mwaf0974	africa south	1796	HEATHER	900	65	79	A New and Improved Chart of the Cape of Good Hope, the Mozambique Passage, &c. Taken from the Latest & Best Authorities
mwuk1685	north sea	1807	HEATHER	1200	94	126	A New and Improved Chart of the North Sea or the German Ocean Constructed on Mercator's Projection
mwwi0265	west indies (east)	1795	HEATHER	1500	79	63	A New and Improved Chart of the West Indies or Carribbee Islands Drawn from the Best Authorities by William Heather
mwam1136	america north (east)	1799	HEATHER	5000	64	155	A New Chart of America with the Harbours of Port Royal, Savannah
mwam1137	america north (east)	1799	HEATHER	7200	63	155	A New Chart of America with the Harbours of New York, Boston &c.
mwbh0773	belgium holland	1802	HEATHER	750	63	79	A New Chart of Holland with the Entrances to the Scheld, &c.
mwbp0059	baltic sea (east)	1801	HEATHER	1000	94	126	A New Chart of the Cattegat and Baltic or East Sea
mwam1172	america north (east)	1815	HEATHER	8000	78	250	A New Chart of the Coast of America from Philadelphia to the Gulf of Florida
mwas0523	asia south east	1800	HEATHER	1200	65	93	A New Chart of the Eastern Straits to China Drawn from the Best Authorities
mwbp0061	baltic sea (east)	1802	HEATHER	1500	64	152	A New Chart of the Gulf of Finland Surveyed by Order of the Emperor of Russia and King of Sweden with Additions and Improvements by William Heather 1802
mwm0079	mediterranean	1812	HEATHER	2500	79	190	A New Chart of the Mediterranean Sea
mwas0602	asia south east borneo	1807	HEATHER	1000	63	92	A New Chart of the Sooloo Archipelago, Exhibiting All the Islands and Passages between the Islands of Borneo & Magindanao, Together with those Between Borneo and Palawan (illustration shows 1820 edition with updates by J. Norie)
mwwi0288c	west indies (west)	1797	HEATHER	3000	78	187	A New Chart of the West Indies Including the Florida Gulf and Stream, Drawn from the Latest Authorities
mww0640	world	1812	HEATHER	1600	92	122	A New Chart of the World on Mercator's Projection
mwaf0538	africa egypt etc	1801	HEATHER	1100	65	93	A New Plan of Egypt. Shewing the Entrances to the Nile, etc.
mwc0227	china	1799	HEATHER	1800	93	126	Chart of the China Seas
mwuk1514	uk english channel (all)	1797	HEATHER	1800	80	192	Chart of the English Channel
mwat0129	atlantic bermuda	1814	HEATHER-NORIE	2400	62	38	Heathers Improved Chart of the Bermudas.
mwuk1683	north sea	1805	HEATHER	1200	79	124	Heather's New Chart of the Coast of England and Holland from the Latest Surveys
mwsc0388	scandinavia denmark	1801	HEATHER	850	63	77	Sous's Chart of the Cattegat, improved (north to the left. Inset of Copenhagen environs. North to the left.)

AMPG REFERENCE	REGION	DATE	MAP MAKER	PRICE (UK£)	VERT. (cm.)	HOR. (cm.)	TITLE OF MAP (Comments by the editor in brackets)
mwe0508a	europe croatia	1802	HEATHER	100	15	18	The Harbour of Spalmadore
mwwi0756	jamaica	1837	HEATHER	600	67	98	The Island of Jamaica
mwuk0241a	ireland	1798	HEATHER	1200	118	129	... This Chart of St George's Channel
mwuk1537	uk english channel (east)	1797	HEATHER	720	65	82	... This Chart of the Downs and Margate Roads
mwuk1681	north sea	1798	HEATHER	720	62	77	To the Merchants and Masters of Vessels Employed in the Coasting Trade, &c. this Chart of the East Coast of England and Scotland from the Humber to Aberdeen is Most Respectfully Dedicated
mww0649a	world	1815	HEATHER-NORIE	1500	66	120	To the Officers in the Honourable East India Company's Service This Outline Chart Intended for their Use to Prick Off a Ship's Track
mwuk1682	north sea	1799	HEATHER	750	64	77	To the Right Honorable Lord Duncan ... this Chart of the Coasts of Holland and England
mwec0653	uk england kent	1797	HEATHER	480	65	79	To the Right Honorable the Master, Wardens, & Elder Brethren of the Trinity House, this Chart of the Downs
mwec0493	uk england hampshire	1797	HEATHER	1350	63	77	This Chart of Spithead
mwuk1397	england south	1821	HEBNER	375	100	178	The Grand Southern Tour of England, Including a Principal Part of the East, West, & Inland Countries, Patronised by Her Majesty the Queen ... By M. Phillips, Civil Engineer & Surveyor.
mwuk0301a	ireland	1861	HEFFERNAN	2000	63	94	Dublin in 1861.
mwe0470	europe central	1795	HEGER & BORS	480	78	95	A Map of the Post Roads of Germany, and the Adjacent States
mwsw0200	switzerland	1790	HEIDEGGER	240	17	23	(Untitled map)
mwgm0370a	mexico	1853	HELLER	400	48	34	Karte von Yucatan nach der Handschriftlichen Karte von Juan Jose de Leon
mwme0686a	arabia etc	1843	HELLERT	650	30	32	Arabie (2 insets, Mecca, Medina. From 'Nouvel Atlas physique ... de l'Empire Ottoman'.)
mwbp0417	poland	1738	HELWIG	800	67	81	M. Martin Helwigs Erste Charte von Herzoghum Schlesien
mwam0341	america north	1698	HENNEPIN	2400	43	53	Amerique Septentrionalis Carte d'un Tres Grand Pays entre le Nouveau Mexique et la Mer Glaciale (illustrated is 1699 German edition)
mwam0327	america north	1683	HENNEPIN	7200	30	48	Carte de la Nouvelle France et de la Louisiane (one of the few mapmakers who resisted the idea of California as an island)
mwam0342	america north	1698	HENNEPIN	3000	29	47	Carte d'un Nouveau Monde, entre le Nouveau Mexique et la Mer Glacialle
mwam0342a	america north	1698	HENNEPIN	2800	38	45	Carte d'un Tres Grand Pais Nouvellement Decouvert dans l'Amerique Septentrionale entre le Nouveau Mexique et la Mer Glaciale avec le Cours du Grand Fleuve Meschasipi (re-issued by Van Der Aa in 1704)
mwam0386a	america north	1737	HENNEPIN	2500	37	44	Le Cours du Fleuve Missisipi, selon les Relations les Plus Modernes
mwec0701	uk england lancashire	1830	HENNET	1000	163	129	A Map of the County Palatine of Lancaster Divided into Hundreds and Parishes from an Accurate Survey Made in the Years 1828 and 1829 (published by H. Teesdale)
mwe0620	europe czech republic (bohemia)	1850	HENNIG & TEMSKY	900	65	86	General-Uibersichts-Karte des Konigreiches Bohmen
mwf0940	france paris	1850	HENRIOT	600	86	58	Nouveau Plan Compleat de Paris
mwf0936	france paris	1848	HENRIOT	650	38	85	Nouveau Plan Complet de Paris avec ses Fortifications Divise en 12 Arrondissements & 48 Quartiers
mww0707	world	1835	HENRY	600	32	46	Monde Entier par J. Henry ... 1835
mwru0010	russia	1549	HERBERSTEIN	5500	28	20	(Title page for 'Rerum Moscovitarum commentarii' incl. map 7x9cm.)
mwru0012	russia	1551	HERBERSTEIN	4000	26	38	Moscovia Sigismundi Liberi Baronis in Herberstein Neiberg et Gutenhag Anno M.DXLIX (1571 edition illustrated)
mwru0374	russia moscow	1556	HERBERSTEIN	3000	24	32	Moscovia, Quatenus Moenibus Includitur, Arx Vocatur (title above map)
mwru0375	russia moscow	1557	HERBERSTEIN	2000	24	32	Mosqua so vil der Maur einfangen (1st German edition of previous map)
mwin0390	india bay of bengal	1780	HERBERT	450	60	64	(Bay of Bengal)
mwas0284	asia burma	1780	HERBERT	450	43	58	(Burma Coast)
mwas0843	asia south east siam	1780	HERBERT	600	59	44	(Cambodia)
mwc0197	china	1780	HERBERT	900	56	45	(China & Formosa)
mwin0486	indian ocean west	1779	HERBERT	450	42	59	(Gulf of Aden)
mwas0837	asia south east siam	1767	HERBERT	750	53	67	(Gulf of Thailand)
mwin0270	india	1780	HERBERT	300	60	40	(India, East Coast)
mwin0271	india	1780	HERBERT	600	45	56	(India, Northeast Coast)
mwin0272	india	1780	HERBERT	500	50	50	(India, West Coast)
mwin0434	indian ocean	1779	HERBERT	685	59	89	(Indian Ocean)
mwas0669	asia south east java	1779	HERBERT	500	56	78	(Java)
mwas0700	asia south east malacca	1779	HERBERT	1200	56	71	(Malacca Strait)
mwme0827	persia etc	1779	HERBERT	750	59	99	(Persian Gulf to India)
mwas0701	asia south east malacca	1779	HERBERT	650	54	67	(South China Sea)
mwas0888	asia south east sumatra	1779	HERBERT	350	44	44	(Southwest Sumatra)
mwin0061	ceylon	1779	HERBERT	685	58	86	(Sri Lanka and Extreme Southern India)

AMPG REFERENCE	REGION	DATE	MAP MAKER	PRICE (UK£)	VERT. (cm.)	HOR. (cm.)	TITLE OF MAP (Comments by the editor in brackets)
mwas0890	asia south east sumatra	1780	HERBERT	350	44	43	(Sumatra, West Coast)
mwas0906	asia south east sunda	1779	HERBERT	175	50	74	(Sunda Strait)
mwaf0944	africa south	1767	HERBERT	900	69	57	A Chart of False Bay, with the Appearances of the Land; also of Simon's Bay
mwas0592	asia south east borneo	1765	HERBERT	400	59	37	A Chart of Some Islands between Borneo and Banca Seen by the "Osterly" in her Passage Outward and Homeward 1758 & 1759
mwaf0609	africa islands madagascar	1767	HERBERT	720	50	82	A Chart of St. Augustin's Bay, on the Island Madagascar, as Surveyed by Wm. Nichelson (Master of His Majesty's Ship 'Elizabeth') in the Year 1758
mwaf0950	africa south	1779	HERBERT	900	47	33	A Chart of the Cape of Good Hope, and Parts Adjacent, Taken Geometrically in the Year 1752
mwas0667	asia south east java	1777	HERBERT	1000	52	84	A Chart of the Coast of Java from Bantam to Batavia Delineated and Translated from a Dutch Original Manuscript
mwin0428	indian ocean	1759	HERBERT	1200	56	84	A Chart of the Eastern Ocean from C. Good Hope to the Islands of Japan; Drawn from the Journals and Remarks of the Most Skilful Navigators, More Especially from Those of M d'Apres de Mannevillette
mwas0482	asia south east	1758	HERBERT	1500	57	79	A Chart of the Easternmost Part of the East Indies
mwme0828	persia etc	1780	HERBERT	1000	45	60	A Chart of the Gulf of Persia According to the Latest Observations
mwaf0636	africa islands mauritius	1779	HERBERT	2500	58	74	A Chart of the Island Mauritius in the Indian Ocean According to the Latest Observations
mwaf0575	africa islands bourbon	1780	HERBERT	720	55	71	A Chart of the Island of Bourbon in the Indian Ocean
mwaf0647	africa islands rodrigues	1779	HERBERT	600	40	55	A Chart of the Island of Diego Roiz or Rodrigues in the Indian Ocean (map surveyed by Capt. Nichelson)
mwin0435	indian ocean	1779	HERBERT	600	49	73	A Chart of the Islands in the Middle Part of the Indian Ocean
mwaf0411a	africa east	1779	HERBERT	400	55	41	A Chart of the Isles of Patte on the East Coast of Africa / A Chart of the Islands Querimbo, Oybo and Natemo on the East Coast of Africa / A Chart of the North Part of the Island Madagascar in the Indian Ocean
mwin0453a	andaman/nicobar isl.	1777	HERBERT	300	45	30	A Chart of the Nicobar Islands and other Islands Situated to the NNW and to the Northwards of them
mwas0702	asia south east malacca	1780	HERBERT	1250	58	44	A Chart of the Seas between the Strait of Banca and P. Timou with the Eastern Part of the Straits of Malacca
mwaf1055	africa south east	1779	HERBERT	900	45	64	A Chart of the South East Coast of Africa from Cape of Good Hope to Delagoa Bay According to Wrights Projection
mwas0563	asia south east bali	1779	HERBERT	450	57	41	A Chart of the Straits of Bali with the Soundings and the Northern Adjacent Islands
mwas0907	asia south east sunda	1780	HERBERT	550	44	60	A Chart of the Straits of Sunda with Part of the North Coast of the Island of Java as Far as Batavia
mwas0703	asia south east malacca	1780	HERBERT	750	45	108	A Chart of the Streights of Dryon, Containing Those Lands Only, that were Seen on Board the Ship Bute ... 1765
mwc0177	china	1770	HERBERT	900	60	78	A Correct Chart of the China Seas Containing the Coasts of Tsiompa, Cochin, China, the Gulf of Tonquin, Part of the Coast of China and the Philippine Islands
mwin0266	india	1779	HERBERT	800	59	84	A Correct Map and Chart of the Peninsula of India, Done from the Plans and Journals Deposited in the Marine Office
mwas0591	asia south east borneo	1763	HERBERT	400	41	62	A Draught of the Bay on the S W Side of the Island Timoan
mwas0789	asia south east philippines	1764	HERBERT	4800	62	108	A Draught of the Great Bay of Manilla and Harbour of Cavita (2 sheets of 62x108cm.)
mwin0053	ceylon	1762	HERBERT	960	45	98	A Draught of the Great Bay, Black Bay and Harbour of Trincomaly off the Island of Zeloan, Describing the Island, Rivers, Rocks and Dangerous Shoals (2 sheets, 45x98cm.)
mwaf0620	africa islands madagascar	1779	HERBERT	550	44	51	A Mercator's Chart of the East Coast of Africa, Madagascar Isle, the Inner Passage and Adjacent Islands ...
mwe0185	europe	1763	HERBERT	1800	62	79	A New Map, or Chart in Mercators Projection of Part of Europe, Asia and Africa
mwat0311a	atlantic south	1780	HERBERT	960	59	79	A New Map, or Chart in Mercators Projection of The Ethiopic Ocean with Part of Africa and South America
mwas0842b	asia south east siam	1779	HERBERT	550	72	57	A Particular Plan of Junk-Seilon and the Adjacent (Phuket)
mwas0891	asia south east sumatra	1780	HERBERT	300	49	40	A Particular Plan of the Acheen Road with the Islands Adjacent
mwas0800	asia south east philippines	1779	HERBERT	850	57	40	A Plan of Pulo Condore, Situated at the East End of the Gulf of Siam / A Plan of the Bay of Manilla
mwaf0618	africa islands madagascar	1779	HERBERT	350	44	59	A Plan of the Principal Harbour & Town of the Isl. S. Maries, Laying off the East Coast of the Isl. Madagascar / The Bay of Antongall on the N.E. Part of the Island Madagascar
mwin0267	india	1779	HERBERT	2500	49	81	A Reduced Chart of Bombay Harbour
mwaf0643	africa islands rodrigues	1770	HERBERT	720	85	129	Draft of Mathewern Bay, on the North Side of the Island of Diego Rayes (map surveyed by Capt. W. Nichelson)
mwin0111	india	1670	HERBERT	200	17	14	India on this Side Ganges
mwaf0619	africa islands madagascar	1779	HERBERT	350	58	42	Part of the East Coast of Madagascar from Manghabey Bay to Plumb Island

AMPG REFERENCE	REGION	DATE	MAP MAKER	PRICE (UK£)	VERT. (cm.)	HOR. (cm.)	TITLE OF MAP (Comments by the editor in brackets)
mwas0892	asia south east sumatra	1780	HERBERT	350	59	44	The Straits of Banca According to the Best Memoirs and Extracts from Journals
mwas0688	asia south east malacca	1752	HERBERT	3500	135	69	To the Honble. the Court of Directors for the United Company of Merchants of England, Trading to the East Indies, this Chart of the Straits of Malacca
mwam0972	america north (east)	1755	HERBERT & SAYER	10000	43	85	A New and Accurate Map of the English Empire in North America (7 insets)
mwg0404	bavaria	1809	HERDEGEN	650	53	64	Konigreich Baiern 1809
mwca0582	canada quebec montreal	1807	HERIOT	200	13	19	City of Montreal
mwca0630	canada st lawrence	1807	HERIOT	200	23	38	Map of the River St. Lawrence
mwsw0214	switzerland	1799	HERISSON	550	52	76	Carte de la Suisse divisee en ses 13 Cantons
mwaf0317	africa	1825	HERISSON	350	50	54	Carte de l'Afrique Divisee en ses Principaux Etats pour Servir a l'Instruction de la Jeunesse
mwam0280	america continent	1822	HERISSON	480	52	62	Carte de l'Amerique Septentrionale et Meridionale avec les decouvertes Faites dans les derniers Voyages ... 1822
mwam0261	america continent	1809	HERISSON	550	52	77	Carte de l'Amerique Septentrionale et Meridionale ou se Trouvent les Decouvertes les Plus Nouvelles et les Trois Voyages de Cook Mackenzie et Vancouver
mwme0696	arabia etc	1854	HERISSON	500	52	77	Carte de l'Empire de Turquie en Europe et en Asie
mwp0280a	pacific (all)	1832	HERISSON	900	54	76	Carte de l'Oceanie Comprenant l'Australie, la Polynesie et du Grand Archipel d'Asie (Inset 'Plan de la Riviere des Cignes' i.e. Swan River, Perth, Australia shown above left)
mwuk1021	england	1785	HERISSON	400	76	52	Carte de Royaume d'Angleterre
mwsc0213	scandinavia	1833	HERISSON	250	79	56	Carte des Couronnes du Nord Comprenant les Royaumes de Suede, Norwege et de Denemark ... Chez Jean, Paris 1833
mwam0292	america continent	1832	HERISSON	300	51	69	Carte des Deux Ameriques, avec leurs Nouvelles Divisions Politiques: Dressee d'apres les Decouvertes Recentes
mwaa0164	arctic	1819	HERISSON	135	20	22	Carte des Regions Arctiques
mwsc0190	scandinavia	1799	HERISSON	500	76	52	Carte du Royaume de Suede
mwaf0307a	africa	1818	HERISSON	850	86	118	Carte Générale de l'Afrique Divisée en Plusieurs Royaumes (3 insets)
mwaf0318a	africa	1795	HERISSON	500	54	77	Carte Générale de l'Afrique Divisée en plusieurs royaumes contenant aussi les pays et états voisins (illustrated below left is the 1828 re-issue with different cartouche, publ. by Basset)
mwe0241	europe	1814	HERISSON	450	53	77	Carte Generale de l'Europe, ou l'on Voit le Depart et le Retour du Capne. Cook dans ses Differents Voyages
mwam0655	america north	1826	HERISSON	550	51	76	Carte Generale des Etats-Unis d'Amerique avec Plans des Principales Villes
mwuk0876	uk	1798	HERISSON	480	77	52	Carte Generale des Isles Britanniques
mwf0185	france	1816	HERISSON	1200	131	186	Carte Generale et Routiere du Royaume de France
mwaf0241	africa	1780	HERISSON	120	18	21	L'Afrique
mww0710	world	1836	HERISSON	1500	92	129	Mappe Monde ou Globe Terrestre
mww0698	world	1832	HERISSON	500	46	70	Mappe-Monde Divisee en Deux Hemispheres Oriental et Occidental
mwf0191	france	1826	HERISSON	120	36	41	Nouvelle Carte de France
mwe0240	europe	1809	HERISSON	950	95	125	Nouvelle Carte de l'Europe dans son Etat Actuel
mwec0608	uk england kent	1661	HERMANNIDES	180	16	13	Dower - Dover
mwuk1115	england london	1661	HERMANNIDES	2000	13	26	Londinum London
mwsc0444	scandinavia finland	1799	HERMELIN	800	55	64	Charta ofver Sawolax och Karelens eller Kuopio Hofdeingedome
mwsc0445	scandinavia finland	1799	HERMELIN	960	55	59	Charta ofver Storfurstendomet Finland
mwsc0446	scandinavia finland	1799	HERMELIN	800	59	62	Charta ofver Uleaborgs
mwsc0447	scandinavia finland	1799	HERMELIN	800	57	63	Charta ofver Wasa Hofdingedome
mwsc0751a	scandinavia sweden	1800	HERMELIN	450	57	61	Charta öfver Wästerås Höfdingedöme
mwsc0751a	scandinavia sweden	1805	HERMELIN	550	90	58	Karta ofver Gottland eller Wisby Hofdingdome
mwas0202	asia continent	1785	HERTEL	240	19	25	Asia (incl. Australia)
mwme0493	jerusalem	1735	HERZ	3000	80	120	(Untitled imaginary reconstruction of biblical Jerusalem)
mwp0420b	pacific north	1774	HEYDINGER	500	20	27	An Account of the New Northern Archipelago, lately discovered by the Russians in the Seas of Kamtschatka and Anadir (map by J. von Staehlin first publ. in St. Petersburg 1774. This edition publ. in London, engraved by T. Kitchin. Also publ. in Germany 1774 with French title!)
mwaf0181	africa	1744	HEYDT	480	22	28	(Africa)
mwaa0127	arctic	1744	HEYDT	480	22	25	(Arctic Regions)
mwas0461	asia south east	1744	HEYDT	785	23	28	(Southeast Asia)
mwin0047	ceylon	1744	HEYDT	400	23	28	Accurater Plan u See-Charte von der Insul Ceylon, sambt der Kuste Coromandel, Madura, und der Malabar
mwas0655	asia south east java	1744	HEYDT	360	24	28	Particular See-Charte der Strass Sunda
mwas0654	asia south east java	1739	HEYDT	200	22	26	Plan oder Grundriss der Stadt und derer Vorstatte, wie auch des Castels Batavia
mww0386	world	1744	HEYDT	875	22	26	Welt Charten, Worauf die Reife nach Indien
mww0295	world	1703	HEYLYN	720	29	53	A New Map of the World
mwit0221	italy	1799	HEYMANN	1500	109	108	Italia coie Tutte le Grandi e Picciole Sovranita e Republiche d'Italia Divisi nelli Nuovi loro Confini

AMPG REFERENCE	REGION	DATE	MAP MAKER	PRICE (UK£)	VERT. (cm.)	HOR. (cm.)	TITLE OF MAP (Comments by the editor in brackets)
mwe0474	europe central	1806	HEYMANN	450	106	168	Post Karte von Deutschland und den Angraenzenden Laendern Gezeichnet und Herausgegeben von Ignaz Heymann K.K. Oberpostamts Offizier in Triest
mwaf0029	africa	1598	HEYNS	500	15	17	Africa
mwuk0681a	uk	1598	HEYNS	1000	18	14	Anglia, Scotia et Hibernia (title outside right-hand border)
mwam0022	america continent	1598	HEYNS	800	15	17	America
mwas0018	asia continent	1598	HEYNS	550	14	17	Asia
mwgr0465a	greece cyprus	1598	HEYNS	1350	15	17	Cyprus (shown above left)
mww0098	world	1598	HEYNS	1200	11	20	De Generale Kaerte des Aerdtbodems
mwg0032	germany	1598	HEYNS	300	16	20	Germania
mwas0619a	asia south east celebes	1848	HEYSE	500	59	44	Carte de l'île de Célèbes par le Baron P. Melvill de Carnbee
mwsw0204	switzerland	1795	HIENZMANN	480	49	62	Carte des Principales Routes de la Suisse
mwuss0846	massachusetts	1791	HILL	1800	32	27	A Map of Cape Cod, and the Parts Adjacent
mwuss1152	new york	1782	HILLIARD D'AUBERTEUIL	720	23	32	Carte de la Nouvelle York, y Compris les Terres Cedees du N. Hamp-Shire, sous le Nom d'Etat de Vermont
mwam1076	america north (east)	1782	HILLIARD D'AUBERTEUIL	1200	23	41	Plan de la Bataille de Montmouth ou le Gl. Washington Commandait l'Armee Americaine et le Gl. Clinton l'Armee Anglaise, le 28 Juin 1778
mwaf0309	africa	1820	HILLIARD, GRAY	200	28	22	Africa
mwuss1397	pennsylvania	1810	HILLS	12500	105	104	A Plan of the City of Philadelphia and Environs (Circular map)
mwuss1395	pennsylvania	1798	HILLS	6850	71	97	This Plan of the City of Philadelphia and its Environs
mwsw0175	switzerland	1770	HILTENSPERGER	8000	85	101	Helvetia Rhaetia, Valesia (copy of Bodenehr's 1698 map plus 4 borders of 52 town and historical views)
mwsw0176	switzerland	1770	HILTENSPERGER	1500	56	85	Helvetiae Rhaetiae et Valesiae ... 1657
mwru0331	russia	1812	HINRICHS	300	36	88	Neue Karte von Ganzen Russischen Reiche den Turkischen und Oesterreichischen Kaiserstaaten
mwec0295c	uk england devon	1749	HINTON	160	17	20	A Map of Devon-Shire
mwam0432	america north	1763	HINTON	400	26	34	A New and Accurate Map of North America
mwuss0833	massachusetts	1780	HINTON	480	27	33	A New and Accurate Map of the Colony of Massachusetts Bay, in North America from a Late Survey
mwam1043	america north (east)	1777	HINTON	720	37	28	A New and Accurate Map of the Present Seat of War in North America, Comprehending New Jersey, Philadelphia, Pensylvania, New-York &c.
mwca0581	canada quebec montreal	1775	HINTON	480	16	25	A Perspective View of Montreal in Canada
mwuss0423	florida	1764	HINTON	450	15	25	A Perspective View of Pensacola
mwuss0470	florida	1832	HINTON	375	20	42	Florida
mwuss0727	maine	1832	HINTON	200	25	20	Maine, New Hampshire & Vermont
mwuss0981	missouri	1832	HINTON	300	28	37	Map of the States of Missouri and Illinois
mwam0679	america north	1832	HINTON	200	25	39	Map of the United States of America and Nova Scotia
mwam1209	america north (east)	1830	HINTON	250	19	25	New England and New York in 1697 from the "Magnalia Americana"
mwam0679a	america north	1832	HINTON	300	51	41	North America
							J. Hinton was the founder of the Universal Magazine. See below.
mwe0888	europe hungary	1680	HIPSCHMANN	2000	41	53	Eigentlicher Grundtriess der Inssel Schiedt in Ungern sambt den Herumbgrentzenten Haupt Vestungen und Orter, gegen den Turcken
mwsw0043a	switzerland	1616	HIRTZGARTER	2000	39	42	Raetiae Veteris, Exterae, et Hodiernae (5 sheets, each 39x42cm)
mwuss0873	massachusetts	1832	HITCHCOCK	400	46	71	Geological Map of Massachusetts
mwwi0846a	puerto rico	1846	HOBBS	4000	66	99	A Chart of Porto Rico and the Virgin Islands, &c. (illustrated is the 1850 edition)
mwuk0310a	irish sea	1843	HOBBS	1500	126	121	A Chart of St. George`s Channel and Coasts of Ireland, &c. Constructed & Drawn from the latest Observations and Surveys, by J. S. Hobbs, Hydrographer (illustrated is 1882 edition)
mwas0870	asia south east singapore	1852	HOBBS	2500	65	95	A Chart showing the navigation through the Straight of Malacca, to Singapore, &c.
mwec0387	uk england durham	1840	HOBSON	1000	81	102	This Map of the County Palatine of Durham
mwec1368	uk england yorkshire	1844	HOBSON	1600	129	163	This Map of Yorkshire, is Most Respectfully Dedicated to the Nobility, Clergy, Gentry, Landowners and Manufacturers of the County
mwme0403a	holy land	1826	HOCQUART	500	71	52	Tableau de l'Histoire Sainte
mwwi0711	jamaica	1740	HODGES	550	25	53	A New Map of the Island of Jamaica
mwec1231	uk england westmorland	1828	HODGSON	8000	140	161	Plan of the County of Westmorland, Describing the Boundaries of Wards, Parishes, and Townships ... Turnpike, Carriage, Bridle and Roman Roads, also the Positions of Towns, Villages, Seats & Farm Houses, Commons, Parks, Woods, Lakes, Mountains, &c.
mwec1114	uk england suffolk	1787	HODSKINSON	600	137	164	The County of Suffolk, Reduced from the Large Map in Six Sheets Surveyed by Joseph Hodskinson & Planned from a Scale of Half an Inch to One Mile
mwgr0433a	greece crete	1823	HOECK	120	18	42	Kreta (shown above left)
mwe0410b	europe austria vienna	1609	HOEFNAGEL				Vienna Austriae (illustrated is the Visscher 1640 reprint)
mwuk1672	north sea	1769	HOEG	1200	80	96	Et Nyt Forbedret Retwisend Soe-kaart over Nord-Soen (north to the right)

AMPG REFERENCE	REGION	DATE	MAP MAKER	PRICE (UK£)	VERT. (cm.)	HOR. (cm.)	TITLE OF MAP (Comments by the editor in brackets)
mwbh0212a	belgium holland	1628	HOEYE	6000	46	57	Germania Inferior
mwe1015	europe rhine	1703	HOFFMANN	1800	46	159	Alsatiae Superioris et Inferioris
mwam0331	america north	1690	HOFFMANN	4000	56	87	America Septentrionalis Divisa in suas Principales Partes
mwuk0932	england	1678	HOFFMANN	180	7	12	Anglia
mwgr0401	greece crete	1669	HOFFMANN	1000	41	49	Candia
mwg0348a	bavaria	1686	HOFFMAN	550	40	54	Das Bisthum Wurtzburg in Francken
mwg0070	germany	1675	HOFFMANN	2500	58	88	Das Heyl Romische Reich Teutsche Nation
mwe0338	europe austria	1697	HOFFMANN	1350	67	42	Das in dam Ertzhertzogtumb Unter Osterreich ... (4 sheets, each 67x42cm incl. text.)
mwf0067	france	1674	HOFFMANN	600	55	87	Das Konigreich Franckreich (German edition of Sanson-Jaillot map with title 'Le Royaume de France')
mwe0546	europe czech republic (bohemia)	1680	HOFFMANN	400	39	51	Delineatio Regni Bohemiae. Das Konigreich Bohmen
mwe0329	europe austria	1677	HOFFMANN	2400	53	86	Ein Theil dess Oesterreichische Craises, oder das Ertzhertzoghtum Oesterreich, Abgetheilet in das Obere und Untere oden in das Land ob und unter der Ens
mwgr0403	greece crete	1670	HOFFMANN	1500	41	49	Geometrisch-Grundrichtige Zuvor Nie Gesehne Abbildung der Welt Beruffene Real-Vestung Candia
mwe0772	europe east	1686	HOFFMANN	300	19	31	Hungaria, Transylvania, Wallachia, Moldavia, Croatia, Dalmatia, Bosnia, Servia, & Thracia
mwit0591	italy north	1701	HOFFMANN	650	39	52	Lombardia oder Land-Carte Jeziges Krigs in Italien 1701
mww0201	world	1675	HOFFMANN	4000	54	89	Mappe-Monde Geo-Hydrographique, ou Description Generale du Globe Terrestre et Aquatique en Deux Plans-Hemispheres (copy of Jaillot 1674)
mwgr0084a	greece	1670	HOFFMANN	1350	41	56	Morea una Cum Adjacentib. Insulis, Graecia et Universo Archipelago
mwe0882	europe hungary	1664	HOFFMANN	1800	42	54	Neue und Richtige Abbildung dess Gantzen Konigreichs Ungern
mwe0763	europe east	1666	HOFFMANN	1400	42	71	Neue Ungararisch und Turckische Grosse Land Charle Nebendt
mwuss1207	new york	1828	HOFFMANN	280	14	8	New York und Umgebungen
mwme0497	jerusalem	1740	HOFFMANN	300	19	28	Nova Delineatio Urbis et Templi Hierosolymarum
mwg0618	saxony	1686	HOFFMANN	300	26	36	Ober Sachsen Lausnitz und Meissen
mwuss1298	ohio	1828	HOFFMANN	150	25	20	Ohio
mwg0349	bavaria	1686	HOFFMANN	400	20	29	Palatinatus Bavariae
mwuss1411	pennsylvania	1828	HOFFMANN	300	36	44	Plan von Philadelphia
mwuss1412	pennsylvania	1828	HOFFMANN	180	30	26	Plan von Pittsburg und Umgebungen
mwe0484	europe central	1834	HOFFMANN	280	54	75	Reise-, Post- und Zoll-Karte von Deutschland, mit Angabe der Eilwagen-Kurse
mwg0612	saxony	1680	HOFFMANN	1400	40	54	Territorium Norimbergensie
mwg0744	thuringia	1686	HOFFMANN	400	26	34	Thuringia
mwg0065a	germany	1660	HOFFMANN	3000	41	55	Nova Totius Germaniae Descriptio (4 carte-a-figure borders)
mwe0767	europe east	1675	HOFFMANN	2500	37	90	Ungarn, Siebenburgen, Wallachey, Moldau und Angrentzende Turckische Lander biss nacher Constantinopel (24 border views and plans of towns)
mwam0013	america continent	1589	HOGENBERG		34	47	Americae et Proximarum
mwg0311a	bavaria	1579	HOGENBERG	1200	14	19	Bavaria Baiern Baviere
mwbh0179a	belgium holland	1610	HOGENBERG	960	24	33	Descriptio Germaniae Inferioris
mwg0021	germany	1576	HOGENBERG		31	49	Deutschlanndt - Germaniae Typus (illustration shows the first Ortelius re-issue, 1603)
mwbh0164b	belgium holland	1604	HOGENBERG	550	22	34	Flandria Borealis
mwjk0124	japan	1795	HOGG	100	30	22	(West Coast of Honshu. Cook's 3rd voyage)
mwp0386	pacific new guinea	1790	HOGG	240	15	36	A Chart of Captn. Carteret's Discoveries at New Britain, with Part of Captn. Cook's Passage thro Endeavour Streights & of Captn. Dampier's Track & Discoveries in 1699 & 1700 at New Guinea & New Britain
mwsam0698	south america magellan	1795	HOGG	100	22	34	A Chart of the S.E. Part of Terra del Fuego Including Strait le Maire / a Plan of Success Bay in Strait le Maire
mwas0615	asia south east celebes	1795	HOGG	140	20	33	A Draught of Bonthain Bay
mwec0302	uk england devon	1780	HOGG	140	15	20	A Modern Map of Devonshire Drawn from the Latest Surveys Corrected and Improved by the Best Authorities
mwuk0221	ireland	1784	HOGG	200	29	21	A New and Correct Map of the Province of Connaught
mwuk0222	ireland	1784	HOGG	200	30	20	A New and Correct Map of the Province of Leinster Drawn from the Latest and Best Authorities
mwuk0223	ireland	1784	HOGG	240	22	32	A New and Correct Map of the Province of Munster
mwuk0224	ireland	1784	HOGG	280	20	32	A New and Correct Map of the Province of Ulster
mwp0034	australia	1794	HOGG	150	20	26	A View of Port Jackson in New South Wales
mwp0329	pacific hawaii	1784	HOGG	300	23	36	An Island View in Atooi, one of the Sandwich Islands
mwp0468	pacific pitcairn isl.	1784	HOGG	80	20	33	Chart and Views of Pitcairns Island (copy of Cook 1783)
mwuss0023	alaska	1780	HOGG	480	21	32	Chart of Cook's River in the N.W. Part of America
mwp0188	new zealand	1784	HOGG	350	22	33	Chart of Cook's Strait in New Zealand
mwp0319	pacific friendly isl.	1790	HOGG	200	30	20	Chart of Friendly Islands
mwp0330	pacific hawaii	1784	HOGG	720	21	34	Chart of the Sandwich Isles (with inset 'Karakakooa Bay')
mwp0478	pacific society isl.	1790	HOGG	100	21	35	Chart of the Society Isles Discovered by Capt. Cook 1769
mwp0306	pacific christmas isl.	1790	HOGG	500	22	30	Christmas Island

AMPG REFERENCE	REGION	DATE	MAP MAKER	PRICE (UK£)	VERT. (cm.)	HOR. (cm.)	TITLE OF MAP (Comments by the editor in brackets)
mwam1108	america north (east)	1794	HOGG	480	31	22	Part of North America, Comprehending the Course of the Ohio, New England, New York, New Jersey, Pennsylvania, Maryland, Virginia, Carolina, Georgia
mwp0023	australia	1780	HOGG	480	33	21	Plan of Adventure Bay on Van Diemens Land
mwuk1239	england london	1780	HOGG	200	18	28	Sir John Evelyn's Plan for Rebuilding the City of London, after the Great Fire in the Year 1666
mwuss0026	alaska	1784	HOGG	200	20	33	Sketch of the Harbour of Samganooda, on the Island of Oonalaska ... T. Bowen
mwam1326	america north (west)	1785	HOGG	200	20	33	The North Side of Largest of Queen Charlotte's Islands
mwaf1033	africa south	1854	HOLDEN	150	21	26	Sketch of the Sovereignty beyond the Orange River
mwme0516	jerusalem	1836	HOLDSWORTH	180	22	30	Jerusalem and Places Adjacent
	asia south	1614	HOLE	320	25	38	(Caspian Sea to Malaysia)
mwme0072	holy land	1614	HOLE	450	30	35	(Cyprus to Persian Gulf)
mwme0073	holy land	1614	HOLE	500	31	39	(Greece to Persia)
mwme0074	holy land	1614	HOLE	450	25	36	(Palestine)
mwme0075	holy land	1614	HOLE	450	30	35	(Travels of Abraham from Vr to Canaan)
mwit0065	italy	1614	HOLE	500	30	38	(Untitled map of Italy)
mwme0077	holy land	1614	HOLE	350	28	37	A Description of the Land of Gosen and Moses's Passage through the Deserts
mwaf0074a	africa	1666	HOLLAR	1500	37	48	A New and Exact Map of Africa and the Ilands
mwas0053a	asia continent	1666	HOLLAR	1200	38	49	A New and Exact Map of Asia
mwuk0921a	england	1644	HOLLAR	4000	38	48	A New and Exacte Mappe of England (illustrated above left is the 1653 edition)
mwme0146a	holy land	1657	HOLLAR	750	37	50	Chorographica Terrae Sanctae Descriptio
mwme0458	jerusalem	1660	HOLLAR	4000	39	109	Ierusalem - Hierusalem veteris imago vera
mwuss0361	delaware	1702	HOLM	720	13	12	(Trefalldigheet or Trinity Fort. Now New Castle)
mwuss0360	delaware	1702	HOLM	2400	13	13	Christinae Skantz och Staden Christinae Hamns Belagringh af Hollanderne 1655 (Wilmington)
mwuss1342	pennsylvania	1702	HOLM	3000	27	13	Novae Suecia Hodie dicta Pensylvania
mwam0108	america continent	1702	HOLM	300	19	14	Totius Americae Descriptio
mwuss1622	virginia	1702	HOLM	360	13	13	Virginiae N. Angliae N. Hollandiae nec non Novae Sueciae Delineatio
mwuss1341	pennsylvania	1690	HOLME	36000	53	39	A Mapp of ye Improved Part of Pensilvania in America, Divided into Countyes Townships and Lotts Surveyed by Tho: Holme. Sold by P. Lea at ye Atlas and Hercules in Cheapside (Reduced version of Holme's 6-sheet map of 1683)
mwme0657	arabia etc	1788	HOLTROP	180	10	12	Arabie
mwam0503	america north	1788	HOLTROP	300	9	11	De Vereenigde Staten von Noord-America
mwam1107	america north (east)	1793	HOLTROP	120	9	12	Het Noord-Ooster Gedeelte van Zuid-America Inhoudende Guiana, Bresil en 't Land de Amazoonen
mwme1036	turkey etc	1788	HOLTROP	100	10	13	Het Turksche Rijk in Europa
mwam0227	america continent	1788	HOLTROP	300	10	12	L'Amerique
mwe0310	europe austria	1612	HOLTZWURM	20000	39	72	Archiducatus Carinthiae Fertilissimi, Carantania olim Carnia, Dicte ex Diligenti Omnium Locorum Perlustratione et Dimensione, Nova, Vera, et Exactissima Geographia
mwme0989	turkey etc	1720	HOMANN	1800	48	58	(Istanbul) Accurate Vorstellung der Orientalisch Kayserlichen Haupt- und Residenz-Stadt Constantinopel samt ihrer Gegend und Zweyen Beruhmten Meer-Engen, Bosphoro Thracio und Hellesponto, oder dem Freto der Dardanellen
mwsc0710	scandinavia sweden	1720	HOMANN	1000	49	58	(Stockholm) Accurater Grundriss und Prospect der Kon. Schwed. Reichs u. Haupstadt Stockholm
mwg0455	hessen	1720	HOMANN	550	50	58	Abbildung der Keysrl. Freyen- Reichs- Wahl und Handelstatt Franckfurt am Mayn mit ihrem Gebiet und Grantzen
mwsc0720	scandinavia sweden	1730	HOMANN	1200	49	57	Accurate Carte der Uplandischen Scheren mit der Situation und Gegend umb die Konigle Schwedische Haupt und Residentz Stadt Stockholm
mwsc0348	scandinavia denmark	1720	HOMANN	1000	49	57	Accurate Vorstellung der Beruhmten Meer-Enge Zwischen der Nord und Ost See der Sund Genannt, mit der Berumliegenden Gegend von Seeland und Schonen nebst der Koniglich-Danischen Haupt und Residentz Stadt Copenhagen
mwg0371a	bavaria	1723	HOMANN	720	50	58	Accurate Vorstellung der... Residenz und Haupt-Stadt Würtzburg
mwsp0344	spain madrid	1720	HOMANN	1200	49	57	Accurater Grundris der Konigl. Spanischen Haupt und Residentz Stadt Madrit
mwuk1145	england london	1710	HOMANN	1350	50	59	Accurater Grundriss u: Gegend der Konigl: Gross Brittannischen Haupt und Residenz-Stadt London
mwbh0601	belgium holland	1727	HOMANN	1350	49	58	Accurater Grundriss und Prospect der Weltberuhmten Hollandische Haupt und Handels-Stadt Amsterdam
mwuk1139	england london	1705	HOMANN	2500	48	57	Accurater Prospect und Grundris der Konigl: Gros-Britannisch: Haupt und Residenz Stadt London
mwgr0166	greece	1720	HOMANN	360	50	59	Achaia Vetus et Nova
mwaf0501	africa egypt etc	1720	HOMANN	480	56	46	Aegyptus Hodierna (title above map)

AMPG REFERENCE	REGION	DATE	MAP MAKER	PRICE (UK£)	VERT. (cm.)	HOR. (cm.)	TITLE OF MAP (Comments by the editor in brackets)
mwf0585	france ile de france	1716	HOMANN	300	57	48	Agri Parisiensis. Tabula Particularis, qua Maxima Pars Insulae Franciae, seu Regiae Celeberrimaeq Parisiorum Urbis Vicina Regio in suas Castellanias Accurate Divisa Exhibetur
mwam0920	america north (east)	1720	HOMANN	2000	48	58	Amplissimae Regionis Mississipi seu Provinciae Ludovicianae a R.P. Ludovico Hennepin Francisc Miss in America Septentrionali Anno 1687. Detectae, Nunc Gallorum Coloniis et Actionum Negotiis Toto Orbe Celeberrimae
mwe0347	europe austria	1716	HOMANN	375	48	57	Archiducatus Austriae Inferioris
mwg0818a	westphalia	1720	HOMANN	320	48	57	Archiepiscopatus et Electoratus Coloniensis ut et Ducatuum Iuliacensis et Montensis nec non Comitatus Meursiae
mwbh0561	belgium holland	1716	HOMANN	320	48	56	Arena Martis in Belgio, qua Provinciae X. Catholicae
mwas0122	asia continent	1720	HOMANN	720	49	58	Asiae Recentissima Delineatio, qua Status et Imperia Totius Orientis Unacum Orientalibus Indiis Exhibentur
mww0336	world	1720	HOMANN	900	50	59	Basis Geographicae Recentioris Astronomica
mwbh0583	belgium holland	1720	HOMANN	800	48	56	Belgii Pars Septentrionalis Communi Nomine vulgo Hollandia
mwit0603	italy north	1730	HOMANN	280	47	55	Belli Typus in Italia
mwg0358	bavaria	1716	HOMANN	400	55	48	Circuli Franconiae Pars Occidentalis, Exhibens Simul Integrum Fere Electoratum Moguntinum quem unacum Tractu Totius Moeni Fluminis / Circuli Franconiae pars Orientalis (2 maps)
mwg0629	saxony	1716	HOMANN	300	48	57	Circulus Saxoniae Superioris in quo Ducatus & Electoratus Saxoniae Marchionatus Misniae et Landgraviatus Thuringiae cum Insertis et Finitimis Regionibus Exhibentur
mwf0409	france burgundy	1720	HOMANN	350	57	48	Comitatus Burgundia tam in Primarias ejus Praefacturas quam in Minores
mwbh0584	belgium holland	1720	HOMANN	280	48	57	Comitatus Hannoniae
mwe0349	europe austria	1720	HOMANN	400	49	58	Comitatus Principalis Tirolis in quo Episc. Tridentin et Brixensis, Comitatus Brigantinus, Feldkirchiae Sonnebergae et Pludentii
mwe0722	europe danube	1720	HOMANN	1100	50	59	Danubii Fluminis a Fontibus Prope Doneschingam usq Posonium Urbem Designati Pars Superior / Danubii Fluminis ... Pars Media / Danubii Fluminis ... Pars Infima (3 sheets)
mwg0236	berlin	1730	HOMANN	1500	48	57	Die Konigl. Preus. U. Churf. Brandenburg, Residenz-Stadt Berlin
mwam0930	america north (east)	1730	HOMANN	600	51	56	Dominia Anglorum in America Septentrionali. Specialibus Mappis Londini Primum a Mollio Edita, Nunc Recusa ab Homannianis Hered. (4 maps on one sheet: Newfoundland, New England, Virginia, Carolina)
mwit1197	italy veneto	1724	HOMANN	600	47	57	Dominii Veneti cum Vicinis Parmae Mutinae Mantuae et Mirandoli
mwbh0585	belgium holland	1720	HOMANN	360	58	50	Ducatus Brabantiae
mwg0630	saxony	1716	HOMANN	375	49	57	Ducatus Bremae et Ferdae Nova Tabula
mwg0636	saxony	1720	HOMANN	280	48	58	Ducatus Brunsuicensis in ejusdem Tres Principatus Calenbergicu
mwg0366	bavaria	1720	HOMANN	450	49	58	Ducatus Franciae Orientalis ... Principatus et Episcopatus Herbipolensis vulgo Wurtzburgensis
mwg0637	saxony	1720	HOMANN	320	50	58	Ducatus Luneburgici et Comitatus Dannebergensis
mwbh0854a	luxembourg	1720	HOMANN	675	47	57	Ducatus Luxembourg tam
mwg0491a	mecklenburg	1720	HOMANN	300	49	58	Ducatus Meklenburgici
mwit0503	italy lombardy	1720	HOMANN	420	47	57	Ducatus Mediolani una cum Confinys Accurata Tabula
mwbp0356	poland	1710	HOMANN	550	50	57	Ducatus Pomeraniae Novissima Tabula in Anteriorem et Interiorem Divisa, quatenus susunt Coronis Sueciae et Borussiae
mwg0718a	schleswig-holstein	1720	HOMANN	400	48	57	Ducatus Slesvicensis in omnes ...
mwe0358a	europe austria	1730	HOMANN	480	48	56	Ducatus Stiriae Novissima Tabula
mwg0270	baden-wurttemberg	1710	HOMANN	960	59	98	Ducatus Wurtenbergici cum Locis Limitaneis utpote Maxima Parte Circuli Suevici Praesertim utroque Marchionatu Badensi et Sylva vulgo Nigra
mwbp0113	baltic states	1720	HOMANN	550	48	57	Ducatuum Livoniae et Curlandiae cum Vicinis Insulis
mwg0456	hessen	1730	HOMANN	280	58	51	Electoratus Moguntinus ut et Palatin: Infer. Hassiae & Fluminis Moeni Aliqua
mwg0638	saxony	1720	HOMANN	400	50	57	Episcopatus Hildesiensis nec non Vicinorum Statuum Delineatio Geographica (inset plan and view of Hildersheim)
mwe0128	europe	1710	HOMANN	600	48	57	Europa Christiani Orbis Domina
mwg0532b	rheinland-pfalz	1730	HOMANN	350	49	57	Exactissima Palatinatus ad Rhenum
mwe1148a	europe south east	1715	HOMANN	450	49	57	Fluviorum in Europa principis Danubii... Graeciae et Archipelagi Novißima Tabula
mwru0123	russia	1707	HOMANN	600	48	56	Generalis Totius Imperii Moscovitici Novissima Tabula Magnam Orbis terrarum artem a Polo Arctico (the illustration below shows a revised version of this map. The revised version was also publ. with the title 'Generalis Totius Imperii Russorum Novissima...')

AMPG REFERENCE	REGION	DATE	MAP MAKER	PRICE (UK£)	VERT. (cm.)	HOR. (cm.)	TITLE OF MAP (Comments by the editor in brackets)
mwg0367	bavaria	1720	HOMANN	400	50	57	Geographica Descriptio Montani Cuiusdam Districtus in Franconia
mwas0317	asia caspian sea	1730	HOMANN	720	50	59	Geographica Nova ex Oriente Gratiosissima, Duabus Tabulis Specialissimis Contenta quarum una Mare Caspium / Kamtzadaliam seu Terram Jedso Curiose Exhibet (2 maps on one sheet. Title above map: Das Caspische Meer / Das Land Kamtzadalie)
mwaa0118	arctic	1715	HOMANN	1250	48	57	Geographische Universal-Zeig und Schlag-Uhr (polar map on a clock face, showing time zones)
mwg0221	germany north west	1730	HOMANN	2000	47	58	Geographische Vorstellung der Wasser-Flutt in Nieder-Teutschland
mwe0353	europe austria	1720	HOMANN	400	48	56	Germania Austriaca Complectens S.R.I. Circulum Austriacum ut et Reliquas in Germania
mwbp0348	poland	1705	HOMANN	900	49	57	Hanc Regni Poloniarum Magnique Ducatus Lithuaniae
mwuk1152	england london	1720	HOMANN	650	48	58	Haupt und Residenz Stadt London
mwuk0144	ireland	1720	HOMANN	685	57	48	Hiberniae Regnum tam in Praecipuas Ultoniae, Connaciae, Laceniae et Momoniae quam in Minores Earundem Provincias
mwg0109	germany	1720	HOMANN	480	49	59	Hydrographia Germaniae (rivers)
mwit1240	italy venice	1729	HOMANN	1800	47	55	Iconografica Rappresentatione della Inclita Citta di Venetia
mwme0806	persia etc	1720	HOMANN	550	48	57	Imperii Persici in Omnes suas Provincias
mwas0308	asia caspian sea	1716	HOMANN	720	49	58	Imperii Persici in omnes suas provincias (not strictly a map of the Caspian Sea, but one of the first to show it with a reasonably correct shape)
mwg0103	germany	1716	HOMANN	400	48	57	Imperii Romano-Germanici in suos Status et Circulos Divisi Tabula Generalis in Ustus Iuventutis Erudiendae
mwme0606	arabia etc	1720	HOMANN	800	49	56	Imperium Turcicum in Europa, Asia et Africa Regiones Proprias, Tributarias, Clientelares
mwgr0424	greece crete	1720	HOMANN	450	50	59	Insula Creta hodie Candia in sua IV Territoria Divisa
mwsc0342	scandinavia denmark	1716	HOMANN	280	48	57	Insulae Danicae in Mari Balthico Sitae utpote Zeelandia, Fionia, Langelandia, Lalandia, Falstria, Fembria Mona
mwm0223	mediterranean malta	1720	HOMANN	2000	49	58	Insularum Maltae et Gozae
mwit0156	italy	1720	HOMANN	480	49	57	Italia Cursoria
mwme0239	holy land	1707	HOMANN	650	48	56	Iudaea seu Palaestina ob Sacratissima Redemtoris Vestigia Hodie dicta Terra Sancta Prout olim in Duodecim Tribus Divisa Separatis ab Invicem Regnis Iuda et Israel
mwf0236	france alsace	1716	HOMANN	280	58	48	Landgraviatus Alsatiae tam Superioris quam Inferi cum utroque Marchionatu Badensi
mwsc0120	scandinavia	1720	HOMANN	600	48	57	Les Trois Couronnes du Nord. Scandinavia Complectens Sueciae, Daniae & Norvegiae Regna
mwf0685	france lorraine	1720	HOMANN	375	49	58	Lotharingiae Tabula Generalis in qua Ducatus Lotharingiae et Barri nec non Metensis, Tullensis et Verdunensis Episcopatus
mwuk0782	uk	1707	HOMANN	875	48	58	Magna Britannia complectens Angliae, Scotiae et Hiberniae Regna (with portrait of Queen Anne. After 1714 this changed to George 1.)
mwuk0974	england	1715	HOMANN	650	57	48	Magnae Britanniae Pars Meridionalis in qua Regnum Angliae tam in Septem Antiqua Anglo-Saxonum Regna
mwuk0461	scotland	1720	HOMANN	675	58	48	Magnae Britanniae Pars Septentrionalis qua Regnum Scotiae
mwe1110	europe slovak republic (moravia)	1720	HOMANN	280	47	57	Marchionatus Moraviae circuli Znoymensis et Ignaviensis (illustration left)
mwe1109	europe slovak republic (moravia)	1720	HOMANN	280	47	57	Marchionatus Moraviae Circulus Hradistiensis
mwe1111	europe slovak republic (moravia)	1720	HOMANN	560	47	57	Marchionatus Moraviae Circulus Preroviensis Pars Borealis / Australis (2 maps)
mwg0531a	rheinland-pfalz	1720	HOMANN	350	48	57	Mosellae Fluminis
mwg0102	germany	1716	HOMANN	375	48	57	Neu Vermehrte Post Charte durch Gantz Teutschland
mwe1068	europe serbia	1720	HOMANN	720	48	58	Neu-Geographisch Vorgestelltes Ungarisches Kriegs-Theatrum in Servien und dem Bannat Temeswar ... 1716 und 1717
mwam0916	america north (east)	1716	HOMANN	1600	49	58	Nova Anglia Septentrionali Americae Implantata Anglorumque Coloniis Florentissima Geographice Exhibita
mwe0350	europe austria	1720	HOMANN	480	50	59	Nova et Accurata Carinthiae Ducatus (shown below left)
mwg0272a	baden-wurttemberg	1720	HOMANN	350	48	57	Nova et accurata Territorii Ulmensis
mwsc0709	scandinavia sweden	1716	HOMANN	500	48	57	Nova Tabula Scaniae, quae est Gothia Australis Provincias Scaniam, Hallandiam, et Blekingiam
mwg0751	thuringia	1729	HOMANN	720	48	58	Nova Territorii Erfordien in suas Praefecturas Accurate Divisi Descriptio
mwit1024	italy south	1707	HOMANN	450	58	49	Novissima & Exactissima Totius Regni Neapolis Tabula
mwg0368	bavaria	1720	HOMANN	240	47	55	Palatinatus Bavariae vulgo die Obere Pfaltz
mwg0487	mecklenburg	1720	HOMANN	400	50	58	Particulier Carte der Gegend von Wismar nebst der Insel Poel (north to the left)
mwgr0167	greece	1720	HOMANN	550	48	58	Peloponesus hodie Moreae Regnum in Omnes suas Provincias Veteres et Hodiernas Accurate Divisum

AMPG REFERENCE	REGION	DATE	MAP MAKER	PRICE (UK£)	VERT. (cm.)	HOR. (cm.)	TITLE OF MAP (Comments by the editor in brackets)
mwgr0317	greece corfu	1716	HOMANN	650	49	56	Plan de la Place de Corfu avec ses Environs (shows the siege of 1716)
mwsc0608	scandinavia norway	1720	HOMANN	1000	49	58	Plan der Belagerung von Fridrichshall Angefangen von Carl XII
mwgr0318	greece corfu	1716	HOMANN	960	48	56	Plan du Siege de Corfu
mww0305a	world	1707	HOMANN	2800	48	54	Planiglobii Terrestris cum utroq Hemisphaerio Caelesti Generalis Exhibitio
mwsp0078	portugal	1720	HOMANN	685	48	54	Portugalliae et Algarbiae (inset of Brazil)
mwsw0104	switzerland	1710	HOMANN	400	50	57	Potentissimae Helvetiorum Reipublicae Cantones Tredecim cum Foederatis et Subjectis Provinciis Exhibiti
mwsp0515	spain regions	1710	HOMANN	450	49	58	Principatus Cataloniae nec non Comitatuum Ruscinonensis et Cerretanaie Nova Tabula
mwg0748	thuringia	1716	HOMANN	280	49	56	Principatus Isenacensis
mwe1046	europe romania	1716	HOMANN	500	48	57	Principatus Transilvaniae
mwe1046a	europe romania	1720	HOMANN	400	47	57	Principatus Transilvaniae in Quinque Nationes
mwsc0721	scandinavia sweden	1730	HOMANN	1250	49	58	Prospect der Königl: Schwed: Haupt und Stadt Stockholm (panorama and 12 views of buildings)
mwbp0370a	poland	1720	HOMANN	800	49	57	Prospect, Grundris und Gegend der Polnischen Reichs und Handels-Stadt Dantzig und ihrem Werder
mwg0369	bavaria	1720	HOMANN	550	48	58	Prospect und Grundris der des Heil: Rom Reichs-Stadt Nurnberg samt ihren Linien und Gegend
mwg0724	schleswig-holstein	1730	HOMANN	1200	49	57	Prospect und Grundris der Keiserl Freyn Reichs und Ansee Stadt Hamburg
mwe0421	europe austria vienna	1720	HOMANN	875	48	57	Prospect und Grund-Riss der Kayserl. Residenz-Stadt Wien
mwf0858	france paris	1730	HOMANN	1800	49	57	Prospect und Grundriss der Weltberuhmten Konigliche Haubt-Stadt Paris
mwg0638b	saxony	1720	HOMANN	600	49	58	Prospect und Grunris der Keiserl. Freyen Reichs und Ansee Stadt Bremen samt ihrer Gegend
mwg0491	mecklenburg	1720	HOMANN	600	49	58	Prospect, Grundris und Gegent der Konigl. Schwed. Vestung Stralsund
mwe0359	europe austria	1730	HOMANN	480	50	58	Prospectus Elegantiores Splendidissimae Archiepiscopatis Urbis Salisburgensis (views of Salzburg)
mwf1047	france provence	1720	HOMANN	450	48	57	Provincia Indigenis dicta la Provence
mwas0316	asia caspian sea	1728	HOMANN	685	49	58	Provinciarum Persicarum Kilaniae nempe Chirvaniae Dagestaniae
mwas0138	asia continent	1730	HOMANN	950	48	57	Recentissima Asiae Delineatio qua Imperia, ejus Regna et Status
mwit0675	italy piedmont	1720	HOMANN	320	51	58	Regiae Celsitudinis Sabaudicae Status in quo Ducatus Sabaudiae, Principatus Pedemontium et Ducatus Montisferrati
mwsc0333	scandinavia denmark	1712	HOMANN	360	48	57	Regni Daniae in quo sunt Ducatus Holsatia et Slesvicum Insulae Danicae Provinciae Iutia Scania Blekingia Nova Tabula
mwe0934	europe hungary	1730	HOMANN	500	47	57	Regni Hungariae Tabula Generalis
mwgm0021	gulf of mexico and surrounding regions	1710	HOMANN	1500	48	57	Regni Mexicani seu Novae Hispaniae Floridae, Novae Angliae, Carolinae, Virginiae, et Pensylvaniae nec non Insularum Archipelagi Mexicani in America Septentrionali Accurata Tabula (illustrated is the updated edition post-1716 with 'Floridae' removed from the title)
mwsc0609	scandinavia norway	1720	HOMANN	720	58	50	Regni Norvegiae Accurata Tabula in qua Praefecturae Quinque Generales Aggerhusiensis, Bergensis Nidrosiensis, Wardhusiensis et Bahusiensis (close copy of De Wit 1680)
mwbp0349	poland	1705	HOMANN	720	48	55	Regni Poloniae Magnique Ducat9 Lithuaniae Nova et Exacta Tabula (Ducatus wrongly engraved)
mwsc0710a	scandinavia sweden	1720	HOMANN	500	49	57	Regni Sueciae in Omnes suas Subjacentes Provincias Accurate Divisi Tabula Generalis
mwsp0239	spain	1715	HOMANN	550	47	55	Regnorum Hispaniae et Portugalliae Tabula Generalis ... ad usum scholarum (another edition with title in Spanish above map shown below)
mwsp0225	spain	1705	HOMANN	600	48	56	Regnorum Hispaniae et Portugalliae Tabula Generalis
mwe0785	europe east	1715	HOMANN	720	96	114	Regnorum Hungariae, Dalmatia, Croatiae, Sclavoniae, Bosniae, Serviae et Principatus Transilvaniae
mwit0857	italy sardinia and sicily	1720	HOMANN	800	50	58	Regnorum Siciliae et Sardiniae nec non Melitae seu Maltae Insula cum Adjectis Italiae et Africae Litoribus Nova Tabula
mwit0911a	italy sicily	1700	HOMANN-FUNCKE	1200	49	57	Regnorum Siciliae et Sardiniae nova & accurata Tabula proposita a Io. Baptista Homanno
mwbp0368	poland	1715	HOMANN	720	48	57	Regnum Borussiae
mwsp0089	portugal	1736	HOMANN	450	59	45	Regnum Portugalliae Divisum in Quinque Provincias Majores ... Regno Algarbiae
mwg0532	rheinland-pfalz	1720	HOMANN	280	48	57	S. R. I. Circulus Rhenanus Superior in quo sunt Landgraviatus Hasso-Casselensis Darmstadiensis et Rhenofeldensis Abbatia Fuldensis ... Urbes Imperiales: Franckfurt, Fridberg, Wetzlar et Gelenhausen
mwg0359	bavaria	1716	HOMANN	240	48	56	S. R. I. Circulus Sueviae Continens Ducatum Wirtenbergensem Novissime Propositus & Exhibitus

AMPG REFERENCE	REGION	DATE	MAP MAKER	PRICE (UK£)	VERT. (cm.)	HOR. (cm.)	TITLE OF MAP (Comments by the editor in brackets)
mwit0598	italy north	1720	HOMANN	400	47	55	S. R. I. Feudum Ducatus Mediolanensis in suas Principales Partes Exacte Divisus Ostenditur
mwe0351	europe austria	1720	HOMANN	785	49	58	S. R. I. Principatus et Archiepiscopatus Salisburgensis
mwg0640	saxony	1729	HOMANN	500	47	54	Saxoniae Tractus Ducatum Magdeburgcensem
mwsc0122	scandinavia	1720	HOMANN	600	48	57	Scandinavia Complectens Sueciae, Daniae & Norvegiae Regna ex Tabulis Ioh. Bapt. Homanni. Norimbergae. cum Privilegio Sac. Caes. Maj.
mwit0307a	italy central	1730	HOMANN	600	48	58	Status Ecclesiastici Magnique Ducatus Florentini Nova Exhibitio
mwit0428a	italy liguria	1730	HOMANN	1200	48	55	Status Reipublicae Genuensis nec non Prospectuum
mwaf0794	africa north morocco	1728	HOMANN	550	49	55	Statuum Maroccanorum, Regnorum nempe Fessani, Maroccani, Tafiletani et Segelomessani
mwit0158	italy	1720	HOMANN	650	48	57	Statuum Totius Italiae Novissima Repraesentatio Geographica
mwg0486	mecklenburg	1716	HOMANN	350	47	56	Stralsund / Stettin / Wismar / Der Pass Neu Fehr zwischen der Insul Rugen und der Stadt Stralsund
mwbp0352	poland	1707	HOMANN	475	48	56	Superioris et Inferioris Ducatus Silesiae in suos XVII Minores Principatus et Dominia Divisi Nova Tabula (incl. plan of Breslau)
mwsam0177	south america (north)	1728	HOMANN	480	48	56	Tabula Americae Specialis Geographica Regni Peru, Brasiliae, Terrae Firmae et Reg. Amazonum (below is more decorative version, 1740+)
mwf0268	france aquitaine	1716	HOMANN	450	48	57	Tabula Aquitaniae Complectens Gubernationem Guiennae et Vasconiae
mwf1149	france rhone-alpes	1720	HOMANN	280	49	58	Tabula Delphinatus vulgo Gouvernement General du Dauphine in suos Ballifiatus et Regiones Divisus per S'r Tillemon
mwf0347	france brittany	1720	HOMANN	320	48	58	Tabula Ducatus Britanniae. Gallis le Gouvernement General de Bretagne
mwe0682	europe dalmatia	1720	HOMANN	480	49	58	Tabula Ducatus Carnioliae, Vindorum Marchiae et Histriae
mwg0220	germany north west	1730	HOMANN	650	50	58	Tabula Frisiae Orientalis
mwg0718	schleswig-holstein	1720	HOMANN	480	50	60	Tabula Generalis Holsatiae Complectens Holsatiae, Dithmarsiae, Stormariae, et Vagriae Ducatus
mwsc0343	scandinavia denmark	1716	HOMANN	280	56	49	Tabula Generalis Iutiae, Continens Dioeceses Quatuor, Alburgensem, Wiburgensem, Ripensem et Arhusiensem quae et sunt Divisae in Omnia sua Dominia
mwe1107	europe slovak republic (moravia)	1716	HOMANN	450	48	57	Tabula Generalis Marchionatus Moraviae in Sex Circulos Divisae
mwf0450	france champagne	1720	HOMANN	300	57	49	Tabula Geographica Campaniae (insets of Reims, Troyes)
mwit0254	italy and central europe	1720	HOMANN	875	48	56	Tabula Geographica Europae Austriacae Generalis
mwg0750	thuringia	1720	HOMANN	350	49	58	Tabula Geographica in qua ... Principatus Gotha, Coburg et Altenburg
mwru0505	ukraine	1716	HOMANN	800	58	48	Tabula Geographica qua Pars Russiae Magnae Pontus Euxinus seu Mare Nigrum et Tartaria Minor
mwg0213	germany north east	1720	HOMANN	320	49	56	Tabula Marchionatus Brandenburgici et Ducatus Pomeraniae quae sunt Pars Septentrionalis Circuli Saxoniae Superioris
mwg0108	germany	1720	HOMANN	1500	94	113	Tabula Novissima Totius Germaniae
mwe1019	europe rhine	1720	HOMANN	400	58	50	Theatrum Belli Rhenani
mwru0142	russia	1718	HOMANN	1800	50	58	Topographische Vorstellung der Neuen Russischen Haupt-Residenz und See-Stadt St. Petersburg samt ihrer zu Erst Aufgerichten Vestug
mwaf0146	africa	1715	HOMANN	960	48	57	Totius Africae Nova Repraesentatio qua Practer Diversos in ea Status et Regiones
mwam0115	america continent	1710	HOMANN	1800	49	57	Totius Americae Septentrionalis et Meridionalis Novissima Repraesentatio (illustrated is later version without insular California)
mwf0102	france	1715	HOMANN	650	48	56	Totius Regni Galliae sive Franciae Tabula (Issue with privilege, re-engraved cartouche)
mwsc0718	scandinavia sweden	1729	HOMANN	750	48	55	Tractus Norvegiae Suecicus Praefecturam Bahusiae Finitimaeque Daliae Provinciae Partem (insets incl. Goteborg)
mwsc0611	scandinavia norway	1729	HOMANN	1000	48	55	Tractus Norvegiae Danicus Magnam Dioeceseos Aggerhusiensis
mwru0506	ukraine	1716	HOMANN	850	48	57	Ukrania quae et Terra Cosaccorum cum Vicinis Walachiae, Moldaviae, Minorisq., Tartariae Provinciis Exhibita
mwit0739	italy rome	1720	HOMANN	1200	48	58	Urbis Romae Veteris ac Modernae Accurata Delineatio
mwme0808	persia etc	1720	HOMANN	1200	48	56	Verschiedene Prospecte der Vornemsten Stadten in Persien (16 views of towns)
mwuss1627	virginia	1714	HOMANN	1800	49	58	Virginia Marylandia et Carolina in America Septentrionali Britannorum Industria Excultae Repraesentatae
mwbp0452	poland	1757	HOMANN HEIRS	800	41	55	(Breslau) Ichnographica Urbis Wratislaviensis Delineatio
mwbh0634	belgium holland	1739	HOMANN HEIRS	950	51	57	(The Hague) Haga Comitum
mwsp0708	gibraltar	1740	HOMANN HEIRS	650	49	57	Accurate Vorstellung der Beruhmten Meers-Enge bey Gibraltar mit denen Herumliegenden See-Haefen
mwaf0171	africa	1737	HOMANN HEIRS	720	45	54	Africa Secundum legitimas Projectionis Stereographicae

AMPG REFERENCE	REGION	DATE	MAP MAKER	PRICE (UK£)	VERT. (cm.)	HOR. (cm.)	TITLE OF MAP (Comments by the editor in brackets)
mwe1028	europe rhine	1750	HOMANN HEIRS	550	111	43	Alsatia tam Superior, quam Inferior una cum Sundgovia ... Delineata
mwam0991a	america north (east)	1756	HOMANN HEIRS	800	46	51	America Septentrionalis a Domino d'Anville in Galliis Edita Nunc in Anglia Coloniis in Interiorem Virginiam Deductis nec non Fluvii Ohio Cursu
mwam0158	america continent	1746	HOMANN HEIRS	750	46	53	Americae Mappa Generalis Secundum Legitimas Projectionis Stereographicae Regulas ... Concinnata et Delineata ab Aug. Gott Boehmio Phil. Magistro ... MDCCXXXXVI
mwas0155	asia continent	1744	HOMANN HEIRS	1200	48	55	Asia Secundum Legitimas Projectionis Stereographicae
mwme1005	turkey etc	1743	HOMANN HEIRS	550	50	57	Asiae Minoris Veteris et Novae, Itemque Ponti Euxini et Paludis Maeotidis (title also in French)
mwsp0605	spain regions	1798	HOMANN HEIRS	650	43	56	Asturiae Principatus (inset: Oviedo)
mwbh0673	belgium holland	1747	HOMANN HEIRS	300	47	53	Belgii Universi seu Inferioris Germaniae Nova Tabula
mwbh0674	belgium holland	1747	HOMANN HEIRS	300	47	56	Belgium Catholicum seu Decem Provinciae Germaniae Inferioris
mwe0566a	europe czech republic (bohemia)	1733	HOMANN HEIRS	300	47	55	Bohemiae Regnum
mwme1014	turkey etc	1764	HOMANN HEIRS	1000	79	50	Bosphorus Thracicus. Der Kanal des Schwartzen Meers oder die Meer-Enge bey Constantinopel sambt denen an Beiden Ufern
mwsw0169a	switzerland	1767	HOMANN HEIRS	480	49	58	Canton Basel
mwsw0169	switzerland	1767	HOMANN HEIRS	480	49	58	Canton Freiburg sive Pagus Helvetia Friburgensis
mwsw0170	switzerland	1768	HOMANN HEIRS	480	44	54	Canton Glarus
mwsw0162	switzerland	1763	HOMANN HEIRS	360	46	55	Canton Lucern
mwsw0166	switzerland	1766	HOMANN HEIRS	280	48	57	Canton Solothurn
mwsw0169b	switzerland	1768	HOMANN HEIRS	400	49	56	Canton Uri sive Pagus Helvetiae Uriensis
mwit0433	italy liguria	1743	HOMANN HEIRS	1100	48	56	Carta Geographica la quale Rappresenta lo Stato della Republica di Genova / Der Staat von der Republic Genova, nach seiner Eintheilung in die Ost- u. West-Revier
mwas0785	asia south east philippines	1760	HOMANN HEIRS	1650	93	54	Carta Hydrographica y Chorographica de las Ysles Filipinnas
mwsp0670	balearic islands	1757	HOMANN HEIRS	650	42	53	Carta Topographique de l'Isle Minorque (map by De Beaurain)
mwgm0030	gulf of mexico and surrounding regions	1740	HOMANN HEIRS	1200	23	28	Cartagena in Terra Firma Americae Sita / Havana / Portus Pulchri ex Isthmo Panamensi / Portobello (4 plans on one sheet, each 23x28cm.)
mwf0760	france nord pas-de-calais	1765	HOMANN HEIRS	280	48	56	Carte d'Artois et des Environs vel Mappa Specialis Comitatus Artesiae
mwme0334	holy land	1750	HOMANN HEIRS	720	50	58	Carte de la Terre Sainte divisee selon les Douze Tribus d'Israel (title above map. Title: 'Palaestina ....' in lower cartouche)
mwme1023	turkey etc	1771	HOMANN HEIRS	480	46	53	Carte de la Turquie Asiatique Contenant la Natolie Moderne Divisee en ses Beglerbeys, &c.
mwme1006	turkey etc	1743	HOMANN HEIRS	550	49	58	Carte de l'Asie Mineure ou de la Natolie et du Pont Euxin
mwwi0787	martinique	1762	HOMANN HEIRS	500	47	56	Carte de l'Isle de la Martinique Dressee par Mr. Bellin, Ingr. du Roy ... Par les Heritiers de Homann
mwg0379a	bavaria	1743	HOMANN HEIRS	450	44	52	Carte des Environs de Munich
mwas0470	asia south east	1748	HOMANN HEIRS	1250	50	86	Carte des Indes Orientales Dessinee Suivant les Observations ... des Cartes Hydrographiques de Mr. d'Apres de Mannevillette Dediee a Monsgr le Prince Guillaume Charles Henry Friso Souverain Prince d'Orange
mwsp0667	balearic islands	1756	HOMANN HEIRS	650	41	56	Carte des Isles de Maiorque, Minorque et Yvice par Mr. Bellin
mwe0944	europe hungary	1744	HOMANN HEIRS	350	47	60	Carte d'Hongrie en general
mwe0577a	europe czech republic (bohemia)	1742	HOMANN HEIRS	400	47	55	Carte du Territoire d'Egra, & du Cercle d'Elnbogue (title also in Latin)
mwg0155	germany	1786	HOMANN HEIRS	480	95	77	Carte Geographique des Postes d'Allemagne
mwm0277	mediterranean west	1756	HOMANN HEIRS	400	56	48	Carte nouvelle de l'Isle de Cadix & du Detroit de Gibraltar
mwsp0556	spain regions	1757	HOMANN HEIRS	375	56	48	Carte Nouvelle de l'Isle de Cadix & du Detroit de Gibraltar
mwf0864	france paris	1739	HOMANN HEIRS	1200	53	61	Carte Topographique des Environs & du Plan de Paris
mwsp0715	gibraltar	1757	HOMANN HEIRS	600	46	56	Carte Topographique des Pays et Cotes Maritimes qui Forment le Detroit de Gibraltar / Topographische Carte der Lander und Kusten welche die Meer-Enge von Gibraltar Eigentlich Formiren (Straits of Gibraltar)
mwsp0591	spain regions	1781	HOMANN HEIRS	320	52	44	Castiliae Novae Parts Orientalis Provincias Ceunca et Guadalaxara
mwsp0546	spain regions	1740	HOMANN HEIRS	500	50	57	Catalonie
mwg0498	mecklenburg	1781	HOMANN HEIRS	280	48	59	Charta Ducatus Megapolensis
mwsp0612	spain regions	1800	HOMANN HEIRS	550	45	53	Charta Geografica Regnum Galaeciam
mwsp0613	spain regions	1801	HOMANN HEIRS	480	46	62	Charta Geographica Provinciam Soriam (La Rioja, with inset of Minorca)
mwsp0614	spain regions	1801	HOMANN HEIRS	350	45	54	Charta Provinciam Salamanticam Salamanca
mwsp0606	spain regions	1798	HOMANN HEIRS	375	53	44	Charta Regni Aragoniae

AMPG REFERENCE	REGION	DATE	MAP MAKER	PRICE (UK£)	VERT. (cm.)	HOR. (cm.)	TITLE OF MAP (Comments by the editor in brackets)
mwru0282	russia	1786	HOMANN HEIRS	600	46	60	Charte das Russische Reich und die von den Tatarn Bewohnte Lander in Europa und Asia Enthaltend (Also issued with the title 'Tartariae Maioris'. Title above map: 'Carte de L'Empire de Russie')
mwsc0750	scandinavia sweden	1793	HOMANN HEIRS	300	57	43	Charte uber das Konigreich Schweden
mwam1084	america north (east)	1784	HOMANN HEIRS	1200	46	58	Charte uber die XIII Vereinigte Staaten von Nord-America
mwg0847	westphalia	1777	HOMANN HEIRS	480	44	55	Charte vom Herzogthum Cleve Worauf Zugleich das Furstenthum Meurs nebst den Konigl. Preussie
mwsc0638	scandinavia norway	1789	HOMANN HEIRS	450	57	46	Charte vom Konigreich Norwegen
mwg0218	germany north east	1805	HOMANN HEIRS	400	47	56	Charte vom Konigreich Preussen
mwas0221	asia continent	1793	HOMANN HEIRS	375	48	57	Charte von Asien
mwg0468	hessen	1806	HOMANN HEIRS	500	47	56	Charte von den Staaten des Herzogs von Nassau-Usingen
mwbh0755	belgium holland	1791	HOMANN HEIRS	480	57	45	Charte von Holland (partly Zuyder Zee)
mwam0536	america north	1797	HOMANN HEIRS	750	49	59	Charte von Nord America
mwbp0135	baltic states	1775	HOMANN HEIRS	600	56	44	Charte von Russisch Litauen, welche die von Polen an Russland Abgetretene Woiewodschaften, Liefland, Witepsk, Mscislaw, und einem Theil der Woiewodschaften Polock und Minsk Enthalt
mwe0428	europe austria vienna	1748	HOMANN HEIRS	480	46	56	Chorographia VI. milliarium Regionis circa Urbem Viennam
mwg0284a	baden-wurttemberg	1743	HOMANN HEIRS	350	52	55	Circuli Sueviae Mappa
mwe0368	europe austria	1747	HOMANN HEIRS	400	49	55	Circulus Austriacus
mwbh0675	belgium holland	1747	HOMANN HEIRS	300	47	56	Circulus Burgundicus Prout ille pro nunc Continet Partes Ducatus Brabantiae, Luxemburgensis, Limburgensis et Geldriae
mwbh0665	belgium holland	1746	HOMANN HEIRS	280	50	58	Comitatus Namur Tabula Geographica ex Mappis Frixianis Depromta
mwe1118	europe slovak republic (moravia)	1757	HOMANN HEIRS	450	66	55	Comitatus Posoniensis Germanis Presburg dicti Delineatio Geographica
mwg0663	saxony	1761	HOMANN HEIRS	400	51	51	Comitatuum Oldenburg et Delmenhorst
mwit0606	italy north	1735	HOMANN HEIRS	1000	51	116	Cursus Fluminis Padi vel Po per Langobardiam
mwe1030	europe rhine	1753	HOMANN HEIRS	900	148	64	Cursus Rheni a Basilea usque ad Bonnam
mwbp0410	poland	1734	HOMANN HEIRS	800	48	57	Das Belagerte Danzig eine Weltberuhmte Haupt und Handelstatt des Polnischen Preussens ... wie solche vom 14. Febr. 1734 von denen Russen Eingeschlossen
mwe0393	europe austria	1803	HOMANN HEIRS	600	52	50	Das Chur-Furstenthum Salzburg
mwg0405	bavaria	1809	HOMANN HEIRS	320			Das Ehemalige Furstenthum Passau
mwbp0551	poland	1809	HOMANN HEIRS	350	56	82	Das Furstenthum Munsterberg oder der Munsterbergsche und Frankesteinsche Kreis
mwg0458	hessen	1754	HOMANN HEIRS	950	45	54	Delineatio Geographica Generalis, Comprehendens VI. Foliis Singulos Principatus, Comitatus, Ditiones, Dynastias Omnes (6 maps, each 45x54cm.)
mwg0374	bavaria	1733	HOMANN HEIRS	240	46	56	Delineatio Nordgoviae Veteris
mwsw0171	switzerland	1768	HOMANN HEIRS	320	48	58	Der Furstliche Abt von St. Gallen und die Stadt St. Gallen samt dem Toggenburg und denen Angraenzenden Orten Appenzell, Thurgeu und Rheinthal
mwas0651	asia south east java	1733	HOMANN HEIRS	2000	47	55	Der Hollaendisch-Ostindianischen Compagnie Weltberuhmte Haupt-Handels und Niederlags-Stadt Batavia in Asien auf dem Grossen Eyland Java
mwg0727	schleswig-holstein	1762	HOMANN HEIRS	1200	50	57	Des Heil. Rom. Reichs Freye Handels- u. Hansee Stadt Hamburg (title above map. Also in French)
mwe0573	europe czech republic (bohemia)	1742	HOMANN HEIRS	480	51	59	Die Gegend um Prag oder der Alte Prager Kreys - Les Environs de Prague
mwg0652	saxony	1753	HOMANN HEIRS	400	50	60	Die Grafschaft Pyrmont mit den Umliegenden Hanoverischen, Braunschweig, und Lippischen auch Paderbornischen Graenzlaendern
mwg0725	schleswig-holstein	1735	HOMANN HEIRS	875	55	47	Die Herzogl. Holstein Gottorp Residenz-See und Handelsstadt Kiel
mwm0257	mediterranean malta	1808	HOMANN HEIRS	2000	50	59	Die Inseln Malta und Gozzo
mwe0429	europe austria vienna	1748	HOMANN HEIRS	785	49	54	Die Kays. Residenz u. Haubt-Stadt Wien
mwbp0420	poland	1739	HOMANN HEIRS	1000	48	55	Die Konigl. Polnische u. Preusische Hansee- und Handels-Stadt Dantzig
mwbh0864	luxembourg	1735	HOMANN HEIRS	1350	52	60	Die Stadt u. Vestung Luxemburg
mwwi0279	west indies islands	1737	HOMANN HEIRS	600	49	55	Dominia Anglorum in Praecipuis Insulis Americae ut sunt Insula S. Christophori Antegoa Iamaica Barbados ex Insulis Antillicanis nec non Insulae Bermudes vel Sommers Dictae (maps of 5 islands: St Kitts, Antigua, Barbados, Bermuda, Jamaica)
mwit0610	italy north	1747	HOMANN HEIRS	500	49	58	Dominii Veneti cum Vicinis Parmae Mutinae Mantuae et Mirandoli
mwbp0124	baltic states	1747	HOMANN HEIRS	960	49	78	Ducatus Curlandiae / Semgalliae (in 2 sheets)
mwg0642	saxony	1731	HOMANN HEIRS	650	56	93	Ducatus Electorat. et Principat. Ducum Saxoniae
mwbp0434a	poland	1747	HOMANN HEIRS	400	46	55	Ducatus Glaciencis
mwbh0865	luxembourg	1740	HOMANN HEIRS	800	48	58	Ducatus Luxemburgi
mwg0643	saxony	1732	HOMANN HEIRS	480	48	58	Ducatus Saxoniae Superioris (set of 2 historical maps)
mwbp0433	poland	1746	HOMANN HEIRS	450	40	56	Ducatus Silesiae Tabula Altera Superiorem Silesiam
mwbp0439	poland	1749	HOMANN HEIRS	450	46	54	Ducatus Silesiae Tabula geographica generalis

AMPG REFERENCE	REGION	DATE	MAP MAKER	PRICE (UK£)	VERT. (cm.)	HOR. (cm.)	TITLE OF MAP (Comments by the editor in brackets)
mwbp0431	poland	1745	HOMANN HEIRS	450	40	57	Ducatus Silesiae Tabula Geographica Prima
mwsw0148	switzerland	1748	HOMANN HEIRS	650	45	47	Eigentliche Vorstellung fer Schlacht und Gegend bey St. Iacob vor Basel
mwg0533	rheinland-pfalz	1735	HOMANN HEIRS	685	33	176	Ein Theil des Hundsrucks
mwe0158	europe	1740	HOMANN HEIRS	3000	94	110	Europa in Partes suas X Methodicas a Primariis Regnis Denominatas Divisa ... et Exhibita Projectionis Steregraphicae Leges
mwe0161	europe	1743	HOMANN HEIRS	400	47	55	Europa Secundum Legitimas Projectionis Stereographicae Regulas
mwf0120	france	1738	HOMANN HEIRS	500	48	57	Gallia Benedictina
mwg0280	baden-wurttemberg	1734	HOMANN HEIRS	500	47	55	Gegend des Neckar Stroms von Lauffen bis Wimpfen
mwru0175	russia	1735	HOMANN HEIRS	550	49	57	Generalis Totius Imperii Russorum Novissima Tabula
mwg0121	germany	1732	HOMANN HEIRS	650	46	56	Germania Benedictina
mwsp0594	spain regions	1782	HOMANN HEIRS	500	47	58	Granadae, Cordovae et Gienensis Regna
mwg0373	bavaria	1732	HOMANN HEIRS	720	49	58	Grundris der des Heil. Rom. Reichs Freyen Stadt Nurnberg
mwg0650a	saxony	1749	HOMANN HEIRS	720	52	54	Grundriss der Stadt Leipzig
mwe0566	europe czech republic (bohemia)	1733	HOMANN HEIRS	785	49	58	Grundriss und Prospect des Weltberuhmten Carlsbad
mwf0623	france languedoc	1742	HOMANN HEIRS	360	50	60	Gubernatio Generalis Languedociae
mwaf1197	africa west	1743	HOMANN HEIRS	600	50	56	Guinea Propria, nec non Nigritiae vel Terrae Nigrorum Maxima Pars ... Aethiopia Inferior
mwg0457a	hessen	1742	HOMANN HEIRS	350	49	57	Hassiae Superioris
mwsw0150	switzerland	1751	HOMANN HEIRS	550	43	55	Helvetia Tredecim Statibus Liberis quos Cantones Vocant Composita
mwsp0271	spain	1750	HOMANN HEIRS	450	45	52	Hispania Benedictina
mwg0288	baden-wurttemberg	1762	HOMANN HEIRS	550	49	58	Hodierna Sedes Electoris Palatini Manheimium
mwg0651	saxony	1752	HOMANN HEIRS	350	38	57	Hohe Heer-Strasse durch das Chur Furst Sachsen
mwe0799	europe east	1744	HOMANN HEIRS	320	47	59	Hungariae Ampliori Signifcatu et Veteris vel Methodicae, Complexae
mwit1135	italy florence	1731	HOMANN HEIRS	1250	49	58	Ichnographia Urbis in Tuscia Primariae Florentiae
mwe1117	europe slovak republic (moravia)	1752	HOMANN HEIRS	720	59	70	Ichnographica Urbis Wratislaviensis Delineatio
mwru0183	russia	1739	HOMANN HEIRS	720	48	55	Imperii Russici et Tatariae Universae tam Majoris et Asiaticae quam Minoris et Europaeae Tabula (other editions, with title in French and with portrait of Anna Iwanowa, below, and with different cartouches, left)
mwm0149	mediterranean east	1741	HOMANN HEIRS	350	49	57	Imperii Turcici Europaei Terra in Primis Graecia
mwru0214	russia	1750	HOMANN HEIRS	250	16	25	Imperium Russicum tam in Europa quam Asia
mwru0170	russia	1734	HOMANN HEIRS	960	50	59	Ingermanlandiae seu Ingriae Novissima Tabula Luci Tradita
mwf0494	france corsica	1735	HOMANN HEIRS	800	56	49	Insulae Corsicae Accurata Chorographia Tradita
mwf0493	france corsica	1732	HOMANN HEIRS	1350	52	44	Insulae Corsicae olim Cyrnus dictae Novissima Facies Chorographice Tradita
mwsc0504	scandinavia iceland	1761	HOMANN HEIRS	500	48	59	Insulae Islandiae Delineatio
mwsp0688a	balearic islands	1798	HOMANN HEIRS	500	28	43	Insularum Mallorca & Cabrera / Murcia Regnum (2 maps by Lopez on one sheet)
mwit0190	italy	1760	HOMANN HEIRS	450	48	55	Italia Benedictina Delineata A.P.R.C.P.W.
mwit0175	italy	1742	HOMANN HEIRS	550	49	58	Italia in suos Status Divisa
mwwi0138	west indies	1796	HOMANN HEIRS	375	53	57	Karte von Mittel-America oder Westindien
mwe0579	europe czech republic (bohemia)	1743	HOMANN HEIRS	350	56	59	Kriegs Expeditions Carte
mwe0579a	europe czech republic (bohemia)	1743	HOMANN HEIRS	450	51	57	Kriegs-Expeditions-Carte in Böhmen I. Blat
mwit0362	italy emilia-romagna	1754	HOMANN HEIRS	300	39	30	Kriegs Karte von denen Operationen ... in Italien 1746
mwg0823a	westphalia	1742	HOMANN HEIRS	550	63	49	La Westphalie
mwit0404	italy lazio	1745	HOMANN HEIRS	375	47	56	Latium cum Omnibus suis Celebrioribus Viis quo ad Antiquum & Novuum Statum
mwg0652a	saxony	1756	HOMANN HEIRS	400			Le Cercle de Basse Saxe
mwit0857a	italy sardinia and sicily	1762	HOMANN HEIRS	500	47	57	Li Regni di Sicilia, e Sardegna, colle Adiacenti Isole di Corsica, Elba, Malta, e Liparee, o di Vulcano (title above map)
mwbp0492	poland	1775	HOMANN HEIRS	400	45	59	Lubomeriae et Galliciae Regni Tabula Geographica Imperiss Homannianorum Haeredum 1775
mwbp0125	baltic states	1749	HOMANN HEIRS	450	47	54	Magn. Ducatus Lutaniae
mwbp0126	baltic states	1749	HOMANN HEIRS	480	47	54	Magni Ducatus Lituaniae
mwsc0442	scandinavia finland	1789	HOMANN HEIRS	600	44	44	Magni Principatus, ceu Provinciae Regni Sueciae, Finnlandiae Mappa Generalis Geographica
mwg0380	bavaria	1744	HOMANN HEIRS	300	49	53	Mappa Geographica Comitatus Oettingensis
mwgm0028	gulf of mexico and surrounding regions	1732	HOMANN HEIRS	800	58	49	Mappa Geographica Complectens I. Indiae Occidentalis Partem Mediam Circum Isthmum Panamensem II. Ipsumq. Isthmum III. Ichnographiam Praecipuorum Locorum & Portuum
mwe0276	europe albania	1770	HOMANN HEIRS	400	46	58	Mappa Geographica Graeciae Septentrionalis Hondiernae sive Macedoniae, Thessaliae et Albaniae
mwuss1127	new york	1778	HOMANN HEIRS	1400	71	56	Mappa Geographica Provinciae Novae Eboraci ab Anglis New York Dictae ex Ampliori Delineatione ad Exactas Dimensiones Concinnata in Arctius Spatium Redacta Cura Claudii Josephi Sauthier cui Accedit Nova Jersey

AMPG REFERENCE	REGION	DATE	MAP MAKER	PRICE (UK£)	VERT. (cm.)	HOR. (cm.)	TITLE OF MAP (Comments by the editor in brackets)
mwbp0488	poland	1773	HOMANN HEIRS	400	46	53	Mappa Geographica Regni Poloniae ex Novissimis quot quot sunt Mappis Specialibus Composita et ad LL. Stereographica Projectionis Revocata
mwit0439	italy liguria	1749	HOMANN HEIRS	350	48	56	Mappa Geographica Status Genuensis
mwwi0076	west indies	1740	HOMANN HEIRS	720	59	49	Mappa Geographica, complectens Indiae Occidentalis (4 inset plans and view of Mexico City)
mwe1116	europe slovak republic (moravia)	1744	HOMANN HEIRS	650	48	60	Marchionatus Moraviae Circulus Brunnensis / Circuli Brunnensis Pars Meridionalis (2 sheets)
mwm0066	mediterranean	1770	HOMANN HEIRS	375	38	61	Mare Mediterraneum unacum suis Insulis et Vicinis Maribus Minoribus
mwit0543	italy milan	1734	HOMANN HEIRS	1350	49	56	Mayland die Haupt-Stadt des Herzogthumbs Gleiches Nahmens nebst Beygefugten Plans der Ubrigen Furnehmsten Vestungen
mwwi0429	cuba	1739	HOMANN HEIRS	400	24	29	Neu und verbesserter Plan der St. u. Hafens Havana auf der Ins. Cuba mit den Wasser Tiefen, Sandbaencken und Klippen
mwg0143	germany	1764	HOMANN HEIRS	720	76	93	Neu und Vollstandige Postkarte durch ganz Deutschland
mww0532	world	1784	HOMANN HEIRS	1200	48	57	Neue Welt Karte welche auf Zwoo Kugelflaechen die Haupt-Theile der Erde
mwsp0705	gibraltar	1733	HOMANN HEIRS	875	48	57	Neuester und Exacter Plan und Prospect von der Stadt Vestung, Bay und Fortification von Gibraltar
mwf0789	france normandy	1740	HOMANN HEIRS	400	49	58	Normannia Galliae Celebris Provincia
mwg0378	bavaria	1740	HOMANN HEIRS	750	50	59	Nova Comitatus Pappenheimensis Tabula
mwsw0167	switzerland	1766	HOMANN HEIRS	600	42	55	Nova Landgraviatus Turgoviae
mwas0318	asia caspian sea	1735	HOMANN HEIRS	750	48	57	Nova Maris Caspii et Regionis Usbeck
mwm0109	mediterranean central	1762	HOMANN HEIRS	720	46	56	Novissima et Accuratissima Regnorum et Insularum Siciliae et Sardiniae ... 1762
mwf0437	france central	1762	HOMANN HEIRS	240	40	55	Novissima Totius Aureliani Generalitatis Exhibitio in suas XII Electiones Stereographico More Divisa
mwsw0165a	switzerland	1766	HOMANN HEIRS	500	48	59	Novissima totius Lavsonii sive Lemani Lacvs cum Regionibus circumjacentibus Chorographia Repraesentatio
mwme0312	holy land	1744	HOMANN HEIRS	750	46	55	Palaestina seu Terra olim Sancta
mwam1282	great lakes	1755	HOMANN HEIRS	2500	44	55	Partie Occidentale de la Nouvelle France ou du Canada (sl. reduced size reprint of Bellin's map of 1745)
mwit0405	italy lazio	1745	HOMANN HEIRS	375	47	56	Patrimonium Petri olim Tuscia Suburbicaria
mwin0194	india	1733	HOMANN HEIRS	550	55	48	Peninsula Indiae citra Gangem, hoc est Orae Celeberrimae Malabar & Coromandel. Cum Adjacente Insula non Minus Celebratissima Ceylon
mwg0285	baden-wurttemberg	1750	HOMANN HEIRS	5000	140	130	Per Inclyti Circuli Suevici ... Sueviae Universae Descriptionem
mwgr0324	greece corfu	1735	HOMANN HEIRS	2400	80	75	Plan de Corfu (inset view of Kerkira)
mwbh0859	luxembourg	1733	HOMANN HEIRS	1350	49	57	Plan de la Ville & Forteresse de Luxembourg
mwsp0668	balearic islands	1756	HOMANN HEIRS	1000	45	90	Plan de la Ville et du Port Mahon et du Fort Philippe
mwsc0436a	scandinavia finland	1750	HOMANN HEIRS	400	42	54	Plan der fürnehmsten Finnischen Vestungen aus Russischen u. Schwedischen Urkunden hergenommen (title above map)
mwg0457	hessen	1742	HOMANN HEIRS	550	50	57	Plan der Hochfurstl. Residenz- und Haubt-Stadt Cassel in Nieder-Hessen nebst dem Hochfurstl. Lust-Garten auf der Aue
mwru0215	russia	1750	HOMANN HEIRS	785	51	55	Plan des Castels Cronslot im Finnischen Meer Busen nebst den Furnehmsten Vestungen an den Beiden Kusten Derselben
mwsc0436	scandinavia finland	1750	HOMANN HEIRS	785	42	54	Plan des Fortresses les plus celebres situees dans la Finnland (Neustadt)
mwg0535	rheinland-pfalz	1740	HOMANN HEIRS	720	57	48	Plan du Mayence, Ville Fort de l'Archeveche ... avec ses Nouveaux Ouvrages Exterieurs 1735
mww0394	world	1746	HOMANN HEIRS	2000	47	56	Planiglobii Terrestris Mappa Universalis utrumque Hemisphaerium Orient et Occidentale Repraesentans ex IV. Mappis Generalibus / Mappe-Monde qui Represente les Deux Hemispheres Savoir celui de l'Orient et celui de l'Occident
mwbp0445	poland	1751	HOMANN HEIRS	280	43	34	Polnische Reise Karte uber die Vornehmsten Passagen von Dresden nach Warschau
mwbp0481	poland	1772	HOMANN HEIRS	400	41	48	Polonia Propria
mwgm0401	panama	1740	HOMANN HEIRS	800	48	30	Portus Pulchri in Isthmo Panamensi / Scenographia Portus Pulchri (map and view of Porto Bello under siege in 1739, on one sheet)
mwuss1141	new york	1780	HOMANN HEIRS	2800	35	45	Position der Konigl: Grosbrittanschen und derer Vereinigten Provincial Armee in New York und dem Jerseys in Nord America im Jahr 1780
mwbp0412a	poland	1735	HOMANN HEIRS	1000	49	57	Potentissimo Borussorum Regi Friderico Wilhelmo Majestate Fortitudine Clementia Augustissimo Hanece Lithuaniam Borussicam (2 sheets, each 49x57cm.)
mwbp0413	poland	1736	HOMANN HEIRS	480	55	82	Princip. Silesiae Iavoriensis
mwsp0607	spain regions	1798	HOMANN HEIRS	400	43	53	Principatus Cataloniae ... D.T. Lopez
mwbp0418	poland	1739	HOMANN HEIRS	600	56	81	Principatus Silesiae Glogoviensis Novissima Tabula Geographica
mwbp0414	poland	1736	HOMANN HEIRS	480	56	82	Principatus Silesiae Lignicensis

AMPG REFERENCE	REGION	DATE	MAP MAKER	PRICE (UK£)	VERT. (cm.)	HOR. (cm.)	TITLE OF MAP (Comments by the editor in brackets)
mwbp0413a	poland	1736	HOMANN HEIRS	480	55	82	Principatus Silesiae Saganensis
mwbp0415	poland	1736	HOMANN HEIRS	480	56	82	Principatus Silesiae Schwidnicensis
mwbp0416	poland	1736	HOMANN HEIRS	480	56	83	Principatus Silesiae Wolani
mwbp0414a	poland	1736	HOMANN HEIRS	600	56	82	Principatus Silesiae Wratislaviensis exactissima tabula
mwf1170	france lyon	1762	HOMANN HEIRS	280	47	57	Propriae Lugudunensis Generalitatis Mappa Chorographica Insuas V. Electiones
mwsp0116	portugal	1791	HOMANN HEIRS	480	45	47	Provinciae Extremadura
mwsp0122	portugal	1800	HOMANN HEIRS	550	55	44	Provincias Meridiones Regni Portugalliae
mwuk1176	england london	1741	HOMANN HEIRS	585	49	57	Regionis quae est circa Londinum / Ausfuhrliche Geographische Vorstellung der Gegend um London
mwit0944	italy sicily	1747	HOMANN HEIRS	650	46	54	Regni & Insulae Siciliae Tabula Geographica
mwe0604a	europe czech republic (bohemia)	1776	HOMANN HEIRS	350	50	59	Regni Bohemiae Circulus Bechinensis
mwe0603	europe czech republic (bohemia)	1769	HOMANN HEIRS	350	49	55	Regni Bohemiae Circulus Pilsnensis
mwe0567	europe czech republic (bohemia)	1737	HOMANN HEIRS	350	48	57	Regni Bohemiae, Duc. Silesiae, Marchionatus Moraviae et Lusatiae. Tabula Generalis (illustrated is the 1748 edition)
mwme0316	holy land	1745	HOMANN HEIRS	350	46	32	Regni Davidici et Salomonaei Descriptio Geographica cum Vicinis Regionibus Syriae et Aegypti
mwf0122	france	1741	HOMANN HEIRS	500	48	57	Regni Galliae seu Franciae et Navarrae
mwbp0419	poland	1739	HOMANN HEIRS	720	48	56	Regni Poloniae Magnique Ducatus Lithuaniae Nova et Exacta Tabula
mwsp0123	portugal	1800	HOMANN HEIRS	500	54	44	Regni Portugalliae Provincias Tres Septentrionales Beiram
mwc0134	china	1740	HOMANN HEIRS	450	59	53	Regni Sinae vel Sinae Propriae Mappa et Descriptio Geographica (close copy of D'Anville 1737)
mwsp0295	spain	1782	HOMANN HEIRS	400	46	57	Regnorum Hispaniae et Portugalliae Tabula Generalis (also issued without the cartouche, as below)
mwuk0830	uk	1749	HOMANN HEIRS	650	47	54	Regnorum Magnae Britanniae et Hiberniae Mappa Geographica
mwe0444	europe bosnia	1738	HOMANN HEIRS	1200	51	112	Regnum Bosniae, una cum Finitimis Croatiae, Dalmatiae, Slavoniae, Hung. et Serviae Partibus / Regni Serviae Pars, una cum Finitimis Valachiae & Bulgariae Partibus
mwit0810	italy sardinia	1734	HOMANN HEIRS	800	57	48	Sardiniae Regnum et Insulae
mwsc0158	scandinavia	1776	HOMANN HEIRS	550	47	54	Scandinavia Complectens Sueciae, Daniae & Norvegiae Regna
mwbh0688b	belgium holland	1748	HOMANN HEIRS	350	47	53	Septem Provinciae seu Belgium Foederatum
mwsp0592	spain regions	1781	HOMANN HEIRS	450	44	56	Sevilla Regnum in suos Archiepiscopatos Episcopatos et Praefecturas Divisum
mwsc0437	scandinavia finland	1751	HOMANN HEIRS	800	46	81	Sinus Finnici Delineatio Geographica
mwg0500	mecklenburg	1797	HOMANN HEIRS	350	46	56	Special Charte von Mecklenburg Strelitz aus der Grossen Schmettauischen Charte Gezogen
mwg0286	baden-wurttemberg	1752	HOMANN HEIRS	400	47	57	Special Post Karte durch den Schwaebischen Kreis
mwf0241	france alsace	1734	HOMANN HEIRS	900	50	59	Stadt und Vestung Strasburg samt dem Fort Kehl in einem Sehr Accuraten u. Gantz Neuen Grundriss u. Prospect
wmit1121b	italy tuscany	1748	HOMANN HEIRS	350	47	49	Status Ecclesiastici nec non Magni Ducatus Toscanae (shown above left)
mwit0360	italy emilia-romagna	1731	HOMANN HEIRS	650	46	55	Status Parmensis sive Ducatus Parmensis et Placentinus una con Ditione Buxetana et Valle Tarae
mwit0515	italy lombardy	1749	HOMANN HEIRS	280	49	58	Statuum Italiae Superioris vulgo olim Lombardia
mwbh0622	belgium holland	1734	HOMANN HEIRS	600	58	49	Tabula Comitatus Hollandiae cum Ipsuis Confinijs, Dominii Nimirum Ultraiectini nec non Geldriae et Frisiae
mwbh0676	belgium holland	1747	HOMANN HEIRS	450	49	57	Tabula Generalis Totius Belgii qua Provinciae XVII. Infer. Germaniae
mwe1124	europe slovenia	1745	HOMANN HEIRS	400	50	58	Tabula Geographica Exhibens Regnum Sclavoniae cum Syrmii Ducatu
mwbp0493	poland	1775	HOMANN HEIRS	500	50	58	Tabula Regni Borussiae Borussiam Orientalem
mwru0453	russia tartary	1749	HOMANN HEIRS	750	50	79	Tartariae Sinensis (title above map: Carte Generale de la Tartarie Chinoise et des Royaumes de Coree et de Iapan. In 2 sheets, joined)
mwc0143	china	1749	HOMANN HEIRS	1500	50	78	Tatariae Sinensis Mappa Geographica (in 2 sheets. Title above map: 'Carte Generale de Tartarie Chinoise et des Royaumes de Corée et de Japan'
mwsw0153	switzerland	1753	HOMANN HEIRS	480	45	56	Territorium Reipublicae Liberae Helveticae Scaphusiensis (Schaffhausen)
mwe1022	europe rhine	1734	HOMANN HEIRS	550	55	46	Theatrum Belli ad Rhenum Superior
mwg0281	baden-wurttemberg	1734	HOMANN HEIRS	350	55	47	Theatrum Belli ad Rhenum Superior
mwe0445	europe bosnia	1740	HOMANN HEIRS	1200	60	112	Theatrum Belli inter Imperat. Carol VI et Sult. Achmet IV … Serviae et Bosniae
mwaf0745	africa north algeria	1732	HOMANN HEIRS	550	46	54	Topographica Repraesentatio Barbarici Portus et Urbis Munitae Oran
mwe1156	europe south east	1766	HOMANN HEIRS	475	46	55	Totius Danubii cum Adjacentibus Regnis nec non Totius Graeciae et Archipelagi Novissima Tabula
mwsw0151	switzerland	1751	HOMANN HEIRS	480	45	57	Tredecim Statibus Liberis, quos Cantones Vocant

AMPG REFERENCE	REGION	DATE	MAP MAKER	PRICE (UK£)	VERT. (cm.)	HOR. (cm.)	TITLE OF MAP (Comments by the editor in brackets)
mwf0136	france	1764	HOMANN HEIRS	360	48	59	Tres Nouvelle Carte du Royaume de France Divise en Toutes ses Provinces et Gouvernements Dressee sur une Nouvelle Observation Astronomique Faite aux Environ du Globe
mwme0335	holy land	1750	HOMANN HEIRS	450	31	40	Typus Aetiologicus
mwsam0233	south america argentina	1733	HOMANN HEIRS	650	48	56	Typus Geographicus Chili Paraguay, Freti Magellanici &c. (inset of Magellan Str.)
mwsam0457	south america chile	1733	HOMANN HEIRS	650	48	56	Typus Geographicus Chili Paraguay, Freti Magellanici &c. (inset of Santiago)
mwit1063	italy naples	1734	HOMANN HEIRS	1200	49	58	Urbis Neapolis cum Praecipus Eius Aedificiis Secundum Planitiem Exacte Delineatio
mwit0748	italy rome	1755	HOMANN HEIRS	900	71	96	Urbis Romae Ichnografia
mwuk1169	england london	1736	HOMANN HEIRS	3500	51	168	Urbium Londini et West-Monasterii nec non Surburbii Southwark Accurata Ichnographia ... Neuester Grundris der Staedte London und West-Munster, Samt der Vorstadt Southwark
mwsw0171a	switzerland	1769	HOMANN HEIRS	400	49	58	Vallesia Superior
mwin0327	india	1804	HOMANN HEIRS	480	51	53	Vorder=Indien oder Hindostan
mwca0377a	canada nova scotia	1756	HOMANN HEIRS	875	46	50	Vorstellung Einiger Gegenden und Plaetze in Nord-America unter Franzoesisch und Englische Jurisdiction Gehoerig zu Finden bey den Homaennischen Erben in Nurnberg Ao. 1756 (Plans of Quebec, Halifax and Louisbourg).
mwsp0669	balearic islands	1756	HOMANN HEIRS	750	56	46	Wahrer und Accurater Plan der Vestung Saint Philippe auf der Balearischen Ins. Minorca
mwg0238	berlin	1737	HOMANN HEIRS - VON SCHMETTAU	3600	85	60	Plan de la Ville de Berlin Leve et Dessine ... sous la Direction du Marechall Comte de Schmettau (4 sheets, each 85x60cm.)
mwuss0584	iowa	1841	HOME MISSIONARY MAG.	240	35	28	Iowa
mwm0002	mediterranean	1569	HOMEM-FORLANI	35000	50	82	Al Molto Magco. S. il S. Giacomo Murari ... la Carta di Navigare (The first printed sea chart, engraved by Paolo Forlani from Diego Homem's manuscript Portolan chart.)
mwbh0254	belgium holland	1639	HONDIUS	480	37	49	(Antwerp) Santvliet: Tabula Castelli Ad Sandfliatum ... Apud Ioan. Ianssonium
mww0079	world	1592	HONDIUS	1500	9	12	(Double hemisphere map with the word 'Jehova' as title. Illustrated is the Wolfe-Rogers close copy of 1598)
mwsw0045	switzerland	1619	HONDIUS	250	36	47	(Untitled map of Argow)
mwec0810	uk england norfolk	1632	HONDIUS	750	44	56	A General Plott and Description of the Fennes and Surounded Grounds in the six Counties of Norfolke, Suffolke, Cambridge, with in the Isle of Ely, Huntington, Northampton and Lincolne etc.
mwuk0341	scotland	1631	HONDIUS	1200	37	54	A New Description of the Shyres Lothian and Linlitquo. By T. Pont. Henricus Hondius Excudit
mwg0440	hessen	1630	HONDIUS	400	42	54	Abbatia Heresfeldensis vulgo t'Stifftt Hirsfeldt. Amstelodami Sumptibus Henrici Hondy
mwaf0356	africa east	1630	HONDIUS	900	35	50	Abissinorum sive Pretiosi Ioannis Imperiu
mwaf0353	africa east	1607	HONDIUS	150	14	19	Abissinorum sive Pretiosi Ioannis Imperium
mwit0260a	italy abruzzo	1639	HONDIUS	500	38	49	Abruzzo Citra et Ultra
mwsam0289	south america brazil	1638	HONDIUS	1000	38	49	Accuratissima Brasiliae Tabula
mwaf0469	africa egypt etc	1607	HONDIUS	200	15	18	Aegyptus
mwf0719	france nord pas-de-calais	1631	HONDIUS	550	44	52	Pascaert vande Custe van Vlaenderen, van Walcheren tot Cales en Bouloigne in Vranckrijck / Afbeeldinghe vande Vermaerde Seehaven ende Stadt van Duynckercken met der Omliggende Plaetsen Sanden, ende Droochten (2 maps on one sheet)
mwaf0034	africa	1602	HONDIUS	4000	36	48	Africa Tabula (A close copy of Ortelius, but incl. figure of Neptune)
mwaf0039	africa	1609	HONDIUS	280	15	20	Africae Descriptio
mwaf0038	africa	1606	HONDIUS	9000	47	61	Africae nova Tabula (carte-a-figures on all borders. Illustrated below is the 1623 edition, sl. smaller with an additional cartouche lower left etc.)
mwaf0047	africa	1632	HONDIUS	3600	41	56	Africae nova Tabula (carte-a-figures on three borders. Hondius' 1606 map was re-engraved slightly smaller in 1623. This map was re-issued in 1632 with the lower border removed.)
mwaf0046	africa	1631	HONDIUS	1350	38	50	Africae nova Tabula Auct. Hen. Hondio 1631 (first issued in 1619 undated, as shown below)
mwf0212a	france alsace	1607	HONDIUS	100	14	19	Alsatia Inferior
mwam0028	america continent	1606	HONDIUS	5500	37	51	America (with Brazilian liquor-making illustration)
mwsam0014	south america	1607	HONDIUS	400	14	19	America Meridionalis (1625 edition by Purchas illustrated)
mwam0031a	america continent	1618	HONDIUS		48	61	America noviter delineata Auct. Judoco Hondio (4 carte-a-figure borders)
mwam0033a	america continent	1623	HONDIUS-JANSSON	18000	46	56	America noviter delineata Auct: Judoco Hondio (also with Jansson signature. Slightly reduced version of Hondius 1618 with revised cartouche and lower border)

AMPG REFERENCE	REGION	DATE	MAP MAKER	PRICE (UK£)	VERT. (cm.)	HOR. (cm.)	TITLE OF MAP (Comments by the editor in brackets)
mwam0042	america continent	1632	HONDIUS-JANSSON	5500	41	56	America Noviter Delineata Auct: Judoco Hondio (state 3, with 3 carte-a-figure borders instead of 4, the lower border having been removed from the 1623 map.)
mwam0044	america continent	1633	HONDIUS	3000	38	50	America noviter delineata (all 4 carte-a-figure borders removed from 1618 map)
mwam0313	america north	1636	HONDIUS	4800	47	55	America Septentrionalis (Illustrated is the c1695 edition by Valk & Schenk. The first edition has a blank cartouche lower left and no dotted boundary lines)
mwam0029	america continent	1607	HONDIUS	500	15	19	Americae Descrip. (Illustrated is 1625 edition by Purchas)
mwsp0393	spain regions	1606	HONDIUS	400	36	51	Andaluziae Nova Descript.
mwuk0915	england	1607	HONDIUS	280	15	19	Anglia
mwuk0686	uk	1607	HONDIUS	320	14	18	Anglia Scotia et Hibernia
mwuk1083	england and ireland	1592	HONDIUS		53	80	Angliae et Hiberniae Nova Descriptio
mwuk1084	england and ireland	1592	HONDIUS		53	80	Angliae Et Hiberniae Nova Descriptio Veteribus Et recentioribus
mwf0254a	france aquitaine	1608	HONDIUS	150	14	19	Aquitania
mwsw0036	switzerland	1608	HONDIUS	100	14	20	Argow
mwf0720	france nord pas-de-calais	1631	HONDIUS	135	12	18	Artesia Comitatus
mwas0027	asia continent	1607	HONDIUS	400	15	19	Asia
mwas0029a	asia continent	1619	HONDIUS	8000	47	61	Asia recens summa cura delineata (carte-a-figures on 4 borders)
mwas0034	asia continent	1631	HONDIUS	4000	41	56	Asia recens Summa cura delineata (carte-a-figures on 3 borders)
mwas0035	asia continent	1631	HONDIUS	1500	38	50	Asia recens Summa cura delineata (re-issue without 3 carte-a-figures borders, present when it was first publ. in 1619.)
mwas0028	asia continent	1613	HONDIUS	1650	38	50	Asiae Nova Descriptio Auctore Jodoco Hondio
mwe0308	europe austria	1608	HONDIUS	200	15	18	Austria Archiduc
mwaf0685	africa north	1608	HONDIUS	150	14	18	Barbaria
mwaf0684	africa north	1607	HONDIUS	650	35	47	Barbaria (3 maps on one sheet)
mwbh0227	belgium holland	1631	HONDIUS	8000	48	61	Belgii sive Germaniae Inferioris accuratissima tabula. Auctore Henrico Hondio 1631 (carte-a-figures on all borders)
mwbh0248	belgium holland	1638	HONDIUS	800	39	50	Belgii sive Germaniae Inferioris accuratissima tabula. Auctore Henrico Hondio 1631 - Amstelodami, Sumptibus Henrici Hondii (decorative borders removed)
mwe0525a	europe czech republic (bohemia)	1607	HONDIUS	150	14	19	Bohemia
mwf0278a	france auvergne	1619	HONDIUS	300	38	50	Borbonium, Ducatus. Bourbonnois
mwf0259	france aquitaine	1636	HONDIUS	500	38	50	Bourdelois, Pays de Medoc, et la Prevoste de Born (Valk & Schenk re-issue illustrated)
mwf0802	france north	1607	HONDIUS	150	13	18	Britania et Normadia cum Confinijs
mwf0390a	france burgundy	1608	HONDIUS	150	14	19	Burgundia Comitatus
mwit0782	italy sardinia	1627	HONDIUS	375	18	25	Caliaris
mwuk1703	wales	1607	HONDIUS	240	15	20	Cambria sive Wallia
mwgr0366	greece crete	1607	HONDIUS	200	14	19	Candia
mwin0017	ceylon	1608	HONDIUS	280	15	18	Ceilan Insula (illustrated is Jansson 1628 re-issue with different title.)
mwsam0443	south america chile	1629	HONDIUS	900	36	48	Chili (north to the left. Illustration shows Blaeu re-issue. Also re-issued by Jansson.)
mwc0009	china	1606	HONDIUS	3000	34	46	China
mwc0009a	china	1607	HONDIUS	550	15	19	China (also issued with north to the top)
mwbp0241	poland	1639	HONDIUS	400	38	46	Comitatus Glatz Authore Iona Sculteto
mwbh0249	belgium holland	1638	HONDIUS	900	40	51	Comitatus Hollandiae novissima descriptio Designatore Balthazaro Florentio a Berckenrode. Anno Domini 1629
mwg0588	saxony	1630	HONDIUS	320	38	50	Comitatus Mansfeldia
mwit0260b	italy abruzzo	1639	HONDIUS	320	39	49	Contado di Molise et Principatum Ultra
mwwi0276	west indies islands	1608	HONDIUS	280	15	20	Cuba Insul. / Hispaniola / Havana Portus / I. Iamaica / I. S. Ioannis / I. Margareta
mwwi0277	west indies islands	1609	HONDIUS	800	35	50	Cuba Insula / Hispaniola Insula / Insula Iamaica / Ins. S. Ioannis / I.S. Margareta cum Confiniis
mwgr0468a	greece cyprus	1607	HONDIUS	600	15	19	Cyprus (6 insets of islands)
mwsw0037	switzerland	1608	HONDIUS	200	14	20	Das Wiflispurgergou
mww0114	world	1607	HONDIUS	600	15	19	Designatio Orbis Christiani
mwit0338a	italy emilia-romagna	1607	HONDIUS	450	38	48	Ducato di Parma et di Piacenza
mwbp0245	poland	1640	HONDIUS	550	40	49	Ducatus Breslanus sive Wratislaviensis
mwg0589	saxony	1630	HONDIUS	320	40	50	Ducatus Brunsuicensis
mwg0698	schleswig-holstein	1629	HONDIUS	650	38	51	Ducatus Holsatiae Nova Tabula
mwbh0819a	luxembourg	1608	HONDIUS	400	13	18	Ducatus Lutzemburgicus
mwf0309	france brittany	1630	HONDIUS	550	38	50	Duche de Bretaigne
mwe0039	europe	1630	HONDIUS	250	15	20	Europa
mwe0044	europe	1638	HONDIUS	1000	38	51	Europa Exactissime Descripta ... 1631
mwsam0653	south america magellan	1606	HONDIUS	1000	34	46	Exquisita & Magno Aliquot Mensium Periculo Lustrata et Iam Retecta Freti Magellanici Facies (south to the top)
mwaf0774	africa north morocco	1618	HONDIUS	200	15	20	Fessae Regnum
mwaf0776	africa north morocco	1633	HONDIUS	650	36	48	Fessae et Marocchi Regna
mwsc0260	scandinavia denmark	1638	HONDIUS	400	36	40	Fioniae Nova et Acurata Descriptio

AMPG REFERENCE	REGION	DATE	MAP MAKER	PRICE (UK£)	VERT. (cm.)	HOR. (cm.)	TITLE OF MAP (Comments by the editor in brackets)
mwsam0662	south america magellan	1629	HONDIUS	1350	38	49	Freti Magellanici ac novi Freti vulgo Le Maire exactissima delineatio
mwsam0662a	south america magellan	1630	HONDIUS	300	13	18	Freti Magellanici ac novi Freti vulgo Le Maire exactissima delineatio (shows the whole of Terra del Fuego)
mwsam0654	south america magellan	1607	HONDIUS	240	13	18	Fretum Magellani
mwbh0201	belgium holland	1620	HONDIUS	150	13	18	Frisia Occidenta
mwbh0230a	belgium holland	1632	HONDIUS	500	39	50	Frisia Occidentalis
mwsp0411	spain regions	1628	HONDIUS	400	36	41	Gallaecia Regnum
mwf0056	france	1639	HONDIUS	650	37	50	Galliae supra Omnes in hac Forma Editiones Locu Pletissima et Exactissima Descriptio
mwf0042	france	1618	HONDIUS	450	39	49	Galliae Veteris Typus
mwbh0214a	belgium holland	1628	HONDIUS, JANSSON	6000	42	57	Gelriae Ducatus Descriptio Nova (4 carte-a-figure borders)
mwg0039	germany	1607	HONDIUS	12000	42	56	Germania (4 carte-a-figure borders)
mwg0038b	germany	1607	HONDIUS	200	15	19	Germania (illustrated is the 1628 re-issue by Jansson)
mwg0043	germany	1625	HONDIUS	6000	46	56	Germaniae Nova ac Accurata Descriptio (4 carte-a-figure decorative borders. Close copy of Visscher's 1621 map. Re-issued by Cloppenburg in 1642, the map dated 1630. Note: Visscher's map of 1621 has slightly different wording top left, as shown below)
mwg0049a	germany	1631	HONDIUS	500	36	49	Germaniae nova et accurata delineatio ... 1631
mwsc0674	scandinavia sweden	1649	HONDIUS	480	39	49	Gothia
mwgr0052	greece	1607	HONDIUS	200	15	18	Graecia
mwsam0574	south america guyana	1630	HONDIUS	1000	38	48	Guiana sive Amazonum Regio (re-issued 1631 unchanged by Blaeu, illustrated here, and later by Jansson)
mwaf1097	africa west	1608	HONDIUS	180	14	18	Guinea
mwaf1096	africa west	1606	HONDIUS	960	35	49	Guineae Nova Descriptio
mwsp0173b	spain	1625	HONDIUS-PURCHAS	240	15	19	Hispania (Shown above)
mwsp0173a	spain	1607	HONDIUS	200	13	19	Hispania nova Descript.
mwsp0173	spain	1606	HONDIUS	800	37	51	Hispaniae Nova Descriptio, de Integro Multis in Locis, Secundum Hydrographicas, Desc. Emendata
mwbh0170	belgium holland	1608	HONDIUS	240	15	18	Hollandia
mwjk0010	japan	1606	HONDIUS	1600	35	45	Iaponia
mwjk0011	japan	1607	HONDIUS	450	13	17	Iaponia (incl. Korea as an island)
mwas0376	asia south east	1609	HONDIUS	1800	36	49	India Orientalis
mwas0374	asia south east	1607	HONDIUS	300	15	20	India orientalis
mwas0385	asia south east	1638	HONDIUS	2000	39	49	India quae Orientalis Dicitur, et Insulae Adiacentes
mwbh0171	belgium holland	1608	HONDIUS	150	15	18	Inferior Germania
mwwi0227	west indies (east)	1650	HONDIUS	1500	41	51	Insula S. Juan de Puerto Rico Caribes, vel Canibalum Insulae (illustrated is Jansson re-issue)
mwas0375	asia south east	1607	HONDIUS	400	14	20	Insulae Indiae Orientalis
mwas0377	asia south east	1609	HONDIUS	3000	35	48	Insulae Indiae Orientalis Praecipuae, in quibus Moluccae Celeberrimae sunt
mwuk0017	ireland	1607	HONDIUS	280	14	19	Irlandia
mwsc0483	scandinavia iceland	1608	HONDIUS	300	14	19	Island
mwit0062a	italy	1608	HONDIUS	240	15	19	Italia
mwit0080	italy	1631	HONDIUS	1350	39	50	Italia Nuovamente Piu Perfetta che Mai per Inanzi Posta in Luce
mwf0598	france languedoc	1633	HONDIUS	750	37	48	La Partie Meridionale du Languedoc / La partie Septentrionale (2 maps. Re-issued by Jansson, sold by M. Tavernier)
mwf1000	france provence	1633	HONDIUS	450	38	50	La Principaute d'Orange et Comtat de Venaissin (south to the top)
mwbh0255	belgium holland	1639	HONDIUS	480	41	51	La Seigneurie de Malines. Mechlinia Dominium et Aerschot Ducatus. Auctore Michaele Flor. A Langren. Apud Ioannem Ianssonium
mwsw0052	switzerland	1630	HONDIUS	550	38	49	Lacus Lemani Vicinorumq. Locorum Nova et Accurata Descriptio
mwsw0038	switzerland	1608	HONDIUS	150	14	20	Lacus Lemannus
mwuk1354c	uk england north	1628	HONDIUS	150	15	20	Lancastria, Cestria, Caernarvan, Denbich, Flint, Merionidh, Montgomery, Salopia, Cardigan, Radnor, Wigornia, et Ins. Anglesey
mwsp0412	spain regions	1628	HONDIUS	480	35	47	Legionis, Biscaiae et Guipiscoae Typus
mwbh0221a	belgium holland	1630	HONDIUS	60000	44	56	Leo Belgicus (illustrated is the Visscher 1641 re-issue)
mwbp0075	baltic states	1607	HONDIUS	250	14	18	Lithuania
mwbp0074	baltic states	1607	HONDIUS	250	15	19	Livonia
	greece	1607	HONDIUS	150	15	18	Macedonia, Epir. et Achaia
mwuk0691	uk	1625	HONDIUS	18000	47	55	Magnae Britanniae et Hiberniae Tabula (close copy of Visscher 1623)
mwbp0081	baltic states	1639	HONDIUS	900	44	54	Magni Ducatus Lithuaniae
mwin0104	india	1642	HONDIUS	750	37	50	Magni Mogolis Imperium (as Jansson but lacking his imprint)
mwat0106	atlantic bermuda	1633	HONDIUS	2000	40	53	Mappa Aestivarum Insularum, alias Barmudas Dictarum ... Accurate Descripta (illustrated is Jansson 1647 reprint)
mwaf0773	africa north morocco	1608	HONDIUS	200	15	19	Marocchi Regnum

AMPG REFERENCE	REGION	DATE	MAP MAKER	PRICE (UK£)	VERT. (cm.)	HOR. (cm.)	TITLE OF MAP (Comments by the editor in brackets)
mwe0703	europe danube	1633	HONDIUS	500	44	51	Maximi Totius Europae Fluminis Danubii Cursus per Germaniam Hungariamque Nova Delineatio (2 maps on 1 sheet)
mwit0486	italy lombardy	1641	HONDIUS	500	38	50	Mediolanum Ducatus
mwe1094	europe slovak republic (moravia)	1608	HONDIUS	180	15	19	Moravia (illustrated is the Jansson 1631 re-issue)
mwbh0230	belgium holland	1632	HONDIUS	320	39	50	Namurcum Comitatus 1632
mwme0937a	turkey etc	1608	HONDIUS	240	15	19	Natolia
mwit1053	italy naples	1627	HONDIUS	250	18	25	Neapolis (shown above left)
mwbh0237a	belgium holland	1634	HONDIUS	650	45	51	Nieuwe Caerte waerinne vertoont wordt de gantsche Vaert van Amsterdam over de Watten tot de stadt Hamborch toe
mwf0771	france normandy	1640	HONDIUS	350	38	53	Normandia Ducatus
mwaf0037	africa	1606	HONDIUS	2000	37	50	Nova Africae Tabula Auctore Jodoco Hondio
mwg0257a	baden-wurttemberg	1630	HONDIUS	400	38	49	Nova Alemanniae sive Sueviae Superioris
mwbh0222	belgium holland	1630	HONDIUS	4500	47	55	Nova Brabantiae Ducatus Tabula. Auctore Judoco Hondio. Dirck Gryp Sculpsit (carte-a-figure borders)
mwbh0281b	belgium holland	1641	HONDIUS	1200	39	49	Nova et Exacta Tabula Geographica Salae et Castellaniae Iprensis ... La Chastelenie D'Ipre ... MDCXXXXI
mwe0046	europe	1638	HONDIUS	3000	41	56	Nova Europae Descriptio Auctore I. Hondio (carte-a-figures on 3 borders, publ. by Jansson)
mwe0040	europe	1630	HONDIUS	1500	35	48	Nova Europae Descriptio Auctore Iodoco Hondio
mwg0479	mecklenburg	1631	HONDIUS	300	37	48	Nova Famigerabilis Insulae ac Ducatus Rugiae Descriptio
mwf0044c	france	1628	HONDIUS	7200	46	55	Nova Galliae tabula (4 carte-a-figure borders; re-issued by Cloppenburg and then by Danckerts, illustrated here, dated 1661.)
mwsw0039	switzerland	1608	HONDIUS	200	14	20	Nova Helvetia Tabula
mwsp0173b	spain	1611	HONDIUS	8000	42	57	Nova Hispaniae Descriptio (all borders with cartes-a-figures. Illustrated is the 1635 edition, publ. by Cloppenburg)
mwgm0154	mexico	1630	HONDIUS	720	36	49	Nova Hispania et Nova Galicia
mwit0076a	italy	1628	HONDIUS	1800	38	50	Nova Italiae Delineatio (re-issue of Hondius 1620, but lacking the four borders. Publ. by Jansson.
mwit0072	italy	1620	HONDIUS	9000	46	54	Nova Italiae Delineatio (4 carte-a-figure borders)
mwbp0226	poland	1620	HONDIUS	6000	42	56	Nova Poloniae Delineatio (carte-a-figure borders on 4 sides)
mww0142	world	1633	HONDIUS	9600	38	54	Nova Totius Terrarum Orbis Geographica ac Hydrographica Tabula (State 1: dated 1630 but first publ. 1633. Second state dated 1641.)
mwuss1603	virginia	1638	HONDIUS	2000	38	49	Nova Virginiae Tabula
mwuss1593	virginia	1618	HONDIUS	18000	38	48	Nova Virginiae Tabula. Ex Officina Judoci Hondij. D. Grijp. Sculpt. (first derivative of John Smith's 1612 map)
mwsp0425	spain regions	1639	HONDIUS	400	44	55	Novissima Arragoniae Regni Tabula Authore Ioanne Baptistae Labanna
mwbh0230b	belgium holland	1632	HONDIUS	200	21	28	Novissima Delflandiae
mwbh0230c	belgium holland	1632	HONDIUS	550	45	55	Novissima Delflandiae (shown above)
mwbh0250	belgium holland	1638	HONDIUS	800	39	50	Novissima et Accuratissima Brabantiae Ducatus Tabula ... 1629 (illustrated below)
mwru0038	russia	1638	HONDIUS	1200	47	56	Novissima Russiae Tabula Authore Isaaco Massa (Western Russia incl. Scandinavia)
mwuk0350	scotland	1650	HONDIUS	600	38	48	Orcadum et Schetlandiae Insularum Accuratissima Descriptio
mwg0593	saxony	1636	HONDIUS	400	37	48	Osnabrugensis Episcopatus. Auctore Ioanne Gigante
mwg0777	westphalia	1629	HONDIUS	800	38	50	Paderbornensis Episcopatus
mwme0064	holy land	1607	HONDIUS	240	15	19	Paradisus
mwsam0703	south america paraguay	1629	HONDIUS	900	37	48	Paraguay, o Prov. de Rio de la Plata cum Regionibus Adiacentibus Tucuman et Sta. Cruz de la Sierra (illustrated is the later re-issue by Blaeu. Also re-issued by Jansson.)
mwme0064a	holy land	1607	HONDIUS	240	15	19	Peregrinatio Israelitaru in Deserto
mwsam0737	south america peru	1629	HONDIUS	1000	38	49	Peru (illustrated is Jansson re-issue, with slightly changed cartouche. Same applies to Blaeu's re-issue.)
mwf0964	france poitou	1606	HONDIUS	350	38	50	Poictou Pictaviensis Comitatus
mwaa0083	arctic	1636	HONDIUS	2400	44	50	Poli Arctici, et Circumiacentium Terrarum Descriptio Novissima (Three editions during 1636, the third being the least rare and first to have a continuous border of whaling activities)
mwbp0216	poland	1613	HONDIUS	500	35	46	Polonia et Silesia
mwbp0215a	poland	1608	HONDIUS	180	15	18	Polonia et Silesia
mwaa0070	arctic	1607	HONDIUS	900	15	20	Polus Arcticus cum Vicinis Regionibus
mwsp0023	portugal	1620	HONDIUS	200	13	20	Portugallia olim Lusitania
mwbh0281a	belgium holland	1641	HONDIUS	2500	38	47	Praenobili Magnifico Amplissimoq Magistratui in clytae civitatis Gandavensis (Ghent)
mwg0596	saxony	1640	HONDIUS	400	39	49	Principatus Anhaldinus et Magdeburgensis Archiepiscopatus
mwbh0257	belgium holland	1639	HONDIUS	720	45	55	Rhinolandiae, Amstelandiae et Circumjacent aliquot Territorioru Accurata Desc.
mwgr0522	greece rhodes	1607	HONDIUS	200	10	13	Rhodi
mwit0569	italy north	1608	HONDIUS	150	14	18	Romandiola cum D. Parmensi
mwru0028	russia	1608	HONDIUS	200	14	18	Russia cum Confinijs

AMPG REFERENCE	REGION	DATE	MAP MAKER	PRICE (UK£)	VERT. (cm.)	HOR. (cm.)	TITLE OF MAP (Comments by the editor in brackets)
mwuk0324	scotland	1608	HONDIUS	240	15	19	Scotia
mwit0879	italy sicily	1608	HONDIUS	250	15	19	Sicilia
mwbp0240	poland	1636	HONDIUS	400	39	49	Silesiae Ducatus Accurata et Vera Delineatio
mwme0094	holy land	1633	HONDIUS	750	37	50	Situs Terrae Promissionis. S.S. Bibliorum Intelligentiam Exacte Aperiens per Chr. Adrichom
mwit0298	italy central	1635	HONDIUS	500	42	53	Stato della Chiesa. Dominium Ecclesiasticum in Italia
mwit1100	italy tuscany	1630	HONDIUS	400	38	50	Stato della Republica di Lucca
mwsc0053	scandinavia	1642	HONDIUS	675	48	55	Sueciae, Norvegiae, et Daniae, Nova Tabula
mwsc0050	scandinavia	1636	HONDIUS	1500	44	55	Tabula Exactissima Regnorum Sueciae et Norvegiae
mwsc0488	scandinavia iceland	1631	HONDIUS	720	38	49	Tabula Islandiae Auctore Georgio Carolo Flandro
mwit0062	italy	1608	HONDIUS	250	15	19	Tabula Italiae, Corsicae, Sardinae, et Adjacentium Regnorum
mwru0472	ukraine	1607	HONDIUS	200	14	22	Taurica Chersonesus nostra Aetate Przecopsca et Gazara Dicitur
mwru0473	ukraine	1609	HONDIUS	450	41	51	Taurica Chersonesus Nostra aetate Przecopsca et Gazara dicitur
mwit0276	italy campagna	1635	HONDIUS	550	38	48	Terra di Lavoro olim Campania Felix
mwsam0494	south america colombia	1639	HONDIUS	1000	38	49	Terra Firma et Novum Regnum Granatense et Popayan (re-issue of Blaeu 1630)
mwme0063	holy land	1606	HONDIUS	720	35	49	Terra Sancta quae in Sacris Terra Promissionis ol. Palestina
mwit1173	italy veneto	1633	HONDIUS	550	38	50	Territorio Padovano
mwit1172	italy veneto	1633	HONDIUS	400	38	50	Territorium Vicentinum
mwg0738a	thuringia	1608	HONDIUS	140	14	18	Thuringia
mwsc0270	scandinavia denmark	1647	HONDIUS	550	44	56	Totius Iutiae Generalis Accurata Delineatio
mwe0991	europe rhine	1633	HONDIUS	550	45	52	Totius Rheni, ab eius Capitibus ad Oceanu usque Germanicum in quem se Exonerat Novissima Descriptio
mwbh0819	luxembourg	1608	HONDIUS	250	14	18	Trier et Lutzeborg
mwsp0178	spain	1631	HONDIUS	720	36	50	Typus Hispaniae ab Hesselo Gerardo delineata
mww0115	world	1607	HONDIUS	1200	14	20	Typus Orbis Terrarum
mwuk0019	ireland	1610	HONDIUS	150	15	19	Ultonia Conatia et Media
mwuk0020	ireland	1610	HONDIUS	150	15	19	Ultonia Oriental
mwsc0673	scandinavia sweden	1640	HONDIUS	500	36	49	Uplandia
mwsam0820	south america venezuela	1629	HONDIUS	1200	38	49	Venezuela, cum Parte Australi Novae Andalusiae (illustration shows Blaeu re-issue. Also re-issued by Jansson)
mww0086	world	1595	HONDIUS	180000	39	55	Vera Totius Expeditionis Nauticae ... Iudocus Hondius
mwit1169a	italy veneto	1607	HONDIUS	150	15	18	Veronae Vicentiae et Patavii Dit.
mwuss1590	virginia	1607	HONDIUS	650	16	19	Virginia et Florida
mwuss1589	virginia	1606	HONDIUS	3200	34	49	Virginiae Item et Floridae Americae Provinciarum, Nova Descriptio
mwuk1353	england north	1610	HONDIUS	150	13	18	Westmorland, Castria, Cestria
mwbh0172	belgium holland	1608	HONDIUS	180	13	19	Zeelandia
mwsw0040	switzerland	1608	HONDIUS	150	14	20	Zuirchou
mwsw0046	switzerland	1619	HONDIUS	480	36	47	Zurichgow et Basiliensis Provincia
							SEE ALSO MERCATOR-HONDIUS (MERCATOR'S MAPS with HONDIUS'S ORNAMENTATION)
mwuk0695	uk	1630	HONDIUS-BLAEU	15000	46	55	Magnae Britanniae et Hiberniae Tabula (re-issue of Hondius' map of c1625 with Blaeu's imprint)
mwit0057	italy	1603	HONDIUS-CLUVER	850	36	50	Italia antiqua
mwp0225	pacific (all)	1589	HONDIUS-LE CLERC		33	46	Americae Novissima Descriptio
mwaf0354	africa east	1625	HONDIUS-PURCHAS	150	14	18	Abissinorum Regnu (in a page of text)
mwsp0407	spain regions	1625	HONDIUS-PURCHAS	150	13	19	Aragonia et Catalonia
mwgr0370	greece crete	1625	HONDIUS-PURCHAS	200	14	19	Candia
mwaf1098	africa west	1625	HONDIUS-PURCHAS	150	15	20	Congi Regnu
mwgm0150	mexico	1625	HONDIUS-PURCHAS	300	14	19	Hispania Nova
mwaf0041	africa	1625	HONDIUS-PURCHAS	280	15	19	Hondius his Map of Africa
mwgr0472	greece cyprus	1625	HONDIUS-PURCHAS	550	14	19	Hondius his Map of Cyprus
mwuss0391	florida	1625	HONDIUS-PURCHAS	500	15	18	Hondius his Map of Florida - Virginia et Florida
mwjk0013	japan	1625	HONDIUS-PURCHAS	400	13	17	Hondius his map of Japan.
mwsc0485	scandinavia iceland	1625	HONDIUS-PURCHAS	250	13	19	Hondius, his Map of Iceland (English edition of map first publ. 1608)
mwe0870	europe hungary	1625	HONDIUS-PURCHAS	200	15	18	Hungaria
mwgr0055	greece	1625	HONDIUS-PURCHAS	150	15	20	Morea
mwme0767	persia etc	1625	HONDIUS-PURCHAS	240	15	19	Persicum Regnum
mwbp0229	poland	1625	HONDIUS-PURCHAS	200	17	23	Polonia
mwit0881	italy sicily	1625	HONDIUS-PURCHAS	250	15	19	Sicilia
mwme0087	holy land	1625	HONDIUS-PURCHAS	240	15	19	Tabula Cananae
mwuk1088	england and ireland	1643	HONDIUS-STENT		51	76	Angliae Et Hiberniae Nova Descriptio Veteribus Et recentioribus (copy of Hondius' 1592 map)
mww0140	world	1630	HONDIUS-TAVERNIER	15000	39	58	Nova Totius Terrarum Orbis Geographica ac Hydrographica Tabula
mwuk1087	england and ireland	1629	HONDIUS-VISSCHER	15000	53	80	Angliae et Hiberniae Nova Descriptio (re-issue of Hondius' 1592 map)
mwgr0567	greece islands	1576	HONTER	240	13	24	(Carpathus) / (Rhodus) / (Lemnos)
mwgr0015	greece	1546	HONTER	600	13	16	(Greece)
mwme0024	holy land	1546	HONTER	600	13	16	(Holy Land)
mwat0237	atlantic madeira	1561	HONTER	480	12	16	(Madeira) / (Forteventura)
mwuk1090	england and scotland	1561	HONTER	900	13	8	(No title)
mwaf0002	africa north	1546	HONTER	720	12	16	(Africa)

AMPG REFERENCE	REGION	DATE	MAP MAKER	PRICE (UK£)	VERT. (cm.)	HOR. (cm.)	TITLE OF MAP (Comments by the editor in brackets)
mwme0908	turkey etc	1546	HONTER	480	12	16	Asia Minor
mwat0007	atlantic ocean (all)	1561	HONTER	800	12	16	Atlantici Maris Insulae
mwf0458	france corsica	1561	HONTER	480	12	8	Corsica
mwgr0340	greece crete	1561	HONTER	480	8	12	Creta
mwgr0453	greece cyprus	1571	HONTER	600	8	12	Cyprus
mwe1040	europe romania	1546	HONTER	480	12	16	Dacia
mwgr0568	greece islands	1576	HONTER	240	8	13	Euboea
mwf1089a	france pyrenees	1561	HONTER	480	12	15	Gallia Narbonensis
mwg0016	germany	1561	HONTER	480	12	15	Germania
mwsp0153	spain	1546	HONTER	480	12	16	Hispania
mwuk0008	ireland	1585	HONTER	650	13	9	Hybernia (shown below left)
mwin0088	india	1561	HONTER	480	12	15	Indiae Extra Gangem Tabula & Taprobana Insulae
mwin0089	india	1561	HONTER	480	12	16	Indiae intra Gangem Tabula
mwit0018	italy	1546	HONTER	600	12	16	Italia
mwit0774	italy sardinia	1561	HONTER	480	8	12	Sardinia
mwas0339	asia central	1573	HONTER	200	13	15	Scythia (Ptolemaic map)
mwsc0225	scandinavia denmark	1561	HONTER	480	12	8	Seelandia
mwit0860	italy sicily	1546	HONTER	480	13	8	Sicilia (on verso Sarmatia)
mwme0533	arabia etc	1561	HONTER	480	12	16	Sinus Persicus
mwas0873	asia south east sumatra	1561	HONTER	480	12	8	Taprobana
mwsc0474	scandinavia iceland	1561	HONTER	480	12	8	Thyle
mww0041	world	1546	HONTER	1800	12	16	Universalis Cosmographia
mww0032	world	1530	HONTER		13	18	Universalis Geographicae Typus
mwuss1330	oregon	1838	HOOD	350	44	51	Map of the United States Territory of Oregon West of the Rocky Mountains, Exhibiting the Various Trading Depots or Forts Occupied by the British Hudson Bay Company, Connected with the Western and Northwestern Fur Trade
mwam1358	america north (west)	1834	HOOD	450	44	47	Map of the Western Territory &c.
mwp0175	australia	1854	HOOD	1800	49	41	Plan of City of Hobart Town Compiled from Frankland's Map and Recent Surveys
mwuss1194	new york	1824	HOOKER	2400	31	38	Hooker's New Pocket Plan of the City of New York (at least 6 editions, some larger, until 1842)
mwuss1197	new york	1825	HOOKER	650	41	50	Map of the State of New York, with the Latest Improvements
mwuss0134b	california	1849	HOPPE	1200	43	25	Karte von Californien
mwme0157	holy land	1662	HORN	2600	90	181	Dimida Tribus Manasse Ultra Iordanem (based on Jansson's 1658 map)
mwin0392	india bay of bengal	1856	HORSBURGH	480	62	79	(Bay of Bengal)
mwin0334	india	1813	HORSBURGH	160	94	63	(from Calcutta to Hainan)
mwaf0425c	africa east	1816	HORSBURGH	480	97	62	(from Zanzibar to Oman)
mwas0602a	asia south east borneo	1820	HORSBURGH	350	95	64	(Kalimantan, Southwestern Coast)
mwat0312a	atlantic south	1815	HORSBURGH	1500	63	94	(Untitled chart)
mwin0346	india	1825	HORSBURGH	750	94	120	A General Map of India. Compiled from the Latest Authorities (from Kabul to Sumatra)
mwc0309a	china formosa	1810	HORSBURGH	450	47	30	Chart of the Channels, Islands and Dangers between Luzon and Formosa
mwas0292	asia burma	1842	HORSBURGH	350	93	66	Chart of the Coast of Arracan from Akyab to Lat. 17° 50'
mwin0457	indian ocean laccadive isl.	1830	HORSBURGH	450	86	68	Chart of the Islands and Reefs of the Laccadive Group by Lieutenant Moresby I.N. 1828 (now known as Laksadweep)
mwin0469	indian ocean maldives	1836	HORSBURGH	400	63	31	Chart of the Maldeeve, or Maldiva Islands; Reduced from the Large Scale in Three Sheets, Surveyed by Commander R. Moresby, and Lieutenant F.J. Powell, I.N. in 1836
mwc0236	china	1806	HORSBURGH	1250	64	90	China Sea Sheet 1
mwc0248	china	1823	HORSBURGH	1000	68	99	China Sea Sheet II
mwc0249	china	1823	HORSBURGH	1000	97	76	Eastern Passage to China Sheet III
mwp0095	australia	1830	HORSBURGH	480	29	50	Passages through the Barrier Reefs
mwas0708	asia south east malacca	1806	HORSBURGH	600	62	78	Strait of Malacca Sheet 1
mwin0349	india	1827	HORSBURGH	1800	81	53	The Triangulation of India. Plan of the Trigonometrical Operations Carried on in the Peninsula of India from the Year 1802 to 1814 Inclusive under the Superintendance of Lieut. Col. W. Lambton (in 8 sheets, each roughly 81x53cm.)
mwaf0427a	africa east	1819	HORSBURGH	480	94	64	To the Hon'ble the Court of Directors of the United East India Company. This Chart, Intended as an Accompaniment to the Book of Directions for Navigating to, from, and in the East Indies
mwin0391	india bay of bengal	1834	HORSBURGH	240	36	41	Trigonometrical Survey of the entrance to the Gulf of Cutch, with the Island and Harbour of Bate
mwuk0870	uk	1794	HORSLEY	320	53	49	Britanniae Antiquae Tabule Geographia ex Aevi Romani
mwuk1267	england london	1799	HORWOOD	20000	220	402	Plan of the Cities of London and Westminster the Borough of Southwark, and Parts Adjoining Shewing Every House by R. Horwood (issued as an atlas of 32 sheets in 1799, but some individual sheets dated from 1794. Four editions until 1819. Other editions have 40 sheets.)
mwgm0359	mexico	1847	HOUSE & BROWN	2750	45	59	Map of Mexico, Texas, Old and New California, and Yucatan
mwuss1290	ohio	1824	HOWARD	3000	60	42	Map of the District of Delaware in Ohio
mwuss1325	ohio	1847	HOWE	180	28	33	Ohio

AMPG REFERENCE	REGION	DATE	MAP MAKER	PRICE (UK£)	VERT. (cm.)	HOR. (cm.)	TITLE OF MAP (Comments by the editor in brackets)
mwuss1384	pennsylvania	1792	HOWELL	12000	96	162	A Map of the State of Pennsylvania ... MDCCXCII (in 4 sheets, mixed states. Size: if sheets joined together)
mwuss1321	ohio	1843	HOWELLS	1350	62	55	Map of the Politics and Statistics of Ohio, Exhibiting Counties with Their Seats of Justice
mwuss1399	pennsylvania	1811	HOWELL-VALLANCE	2000	55	87	A Map of Pennsylvania, & the Parts Connected therewith, Relating to the Roads and Inland Navigation (a reduced size edition of the 1792 map.)
mwit1056c	italy naples	1700	HUBERT	12000	91	69	(Naples)
mwit0671	italy piedmont	1710	HUCHTENBURGH	400	46	59	Plan de la Bateille de Turin
mww0418	world	1750	HUEBNER	300	19	23	Planisphaerium Terrestre
mww0396	world	1747	HUISSTEEN	350	24	12	Planiglobium Terrestre ou Mappe-Monde
mww0676a	world	1826	HULBERT	250	8	12	The World
mwsc0757	scandinavia sweden	1850	HULDBERG	450	23	238	Karta ofver segelleden fran Stockholm Kanalvagen till Gotheborg (illustration shows one end of the map)
mwam0921	america north (east)	1720	HULETT	1000	30	31	A New Accurate Map of the English Plantations in America and of the Louisiana and River Mississipi
mwf0358	france brittany	1760	HULETT	150	18	28	Plan of the City and Castles of St. Malo
mwaf0035	africa	1602	HULSIUS	3000	38	36	(no title, in 2 sheets)
mwsc0670	scandinavia sweden	1632	HULSIUS	450	9	17	Der Sundt
mww0099	world	1598	HULSIUS	1600	16	25	Descriptio Totius Orbis Terrae ex Varys Recentior
mwsam0559	south america ecuador	1603	HULSIUS	360	16	12	Insula Puna
mwas0378	asia south east	1615	HULSIUS	1200	16	26	Insulae Indiae Orientalis et Molucae
mwsam0278	south america brazil	1603	HULSIUS	320	16	12	Isola de S. Sebastian
mwam0851	america north (east)	1617	HULSIUS	12000	30	34	New England. Die Mercklichsten Dheile, also Genennet durch den Durchl: und Mechtigen Prinzen und H.H. Carolus, Prinzen von Gross Britannien (first version of John Smith's 1616 map with English translated into German)
mwsam0012	south america	1603	HULSIUS	2800	45	32	Nova et Exacta Delineatio Americae Partis Australis que est: Brasilia, Caribana, Guiana
mwat0297	atlantic south	1603	HULSIUS	900	16	37	Oceanus Aethiopicus
mwaa0072	arctic	1614	HULSIUS	1200	14	34	Vera Delineatio Totius Tractus ex Hollandia Septentrionem versus per Fretrum Nassovicum, ad Fluvium Oby Ducentes, ex Annotatione Iohannis Hugonis Lintschottani, de Annis 1594 et 1595
			HUMBOLDT: SEE 'VON HUMBOLDT'				
mwme0410	holy land	1831	HUNTINGTON	200	32	48	An Ancient or Bible Map, Designed for the Use of Bible Classes, Sunday Schools and Private Families
mwuss0321	connecticut	1837	HUNTINGTON	300	50	58	Map of Connecticut from Actual Survey
mwam0672	america north	1831	HUNTINGTON	900	33	51	Map of the United States
mwuss1228	new york	1834	HUNTINGTON	685	41	52	The State of New York from the Most Recent Surveys
mwam0698	america north	1835	HUNTINGTON	500	27	45	United States
mwam0717	america north	1838	HUNTINGTON	900	29	48	United States, Texas & ... The Canadas
mwam1194	america north (east)	1826	HUNTINGTON & WILLARD	2400	50	67	Map of the United States Compiled from the Most Authentic Sources (1st edition)
mwe0263	europe	1830	HUOT	350	31	44	Carte Geologique d'Europe
mwbp0136	baltic states	1775	HUPEL	875	53	60	Liefland, oder die Beyden Generalgouvernementer ... und Ehstland
mwg0256	baden-wurttemberg	1625	HURTER	2000	57	74	Alemanniae sive Sueviae Superioris
mwbh0531	belgium holland	1706	HUSSON	800	50	58	Carte Generale des Provinces Unies des Pais Bas des Terres Voisines qui en Dependent avec leurs Principales Divisions
mwsp0231	spain	1706	HUSSON	800	48	56	Carte Generale des Royaumes d'Espagne & de Portugal avec leur Divisions &c.
mwf0095	france	1708	HUSSON	800	48	59	Carte Nouvelle du Royaume de France Divise en Toutes ses Provinces et ses Acquisitions (title above map: Galliae Regnum. Illustrated is Ottens re-issue c1730)
mwuk0781	uk	1706	HUSSON	800	44	55	Les Isles Britanniques (close copy of De l'Isle)
mwsp0070a	portugal	1709	HUSSON	1500	42	52	Lisbona (view of English and Dutch fleets, 1704. Small inset map of Spain)
mwit0140	italy	1706	HUSSON	800	46	55	L'Italie
mwbh0870	luxembourg	1743	HUSSON	1500	43	55	Nouveau Plan de la Ville de Luxembourg avec Tous les Ouvrages ... depuis 1724
mwsp0695a	gibraltar	1709	HUSSON	1200	51	44	Plan de la Ville de Gibraltar
mwf0746	france nord pas-de-calais	1710	HUSSON	650	59	40	Plan du Siege de Lille avec ses Environs
mwbh0537a	belgium holland	1709	HUSSON	900			Plan du Siege et des Attaques de la Ville et Cittaddle de Gand ... 1708 (Ghent. Map by P. van Call)
mwuss1269	ohio	1766	HUTCHINS	1800	36	31	A Map of the Country on the Ohio and Muskinghum Rivers ... Bouquet / A Survey of that Part of the Indian Country ... 1764
mwam0808	america north (central)	1778	HUTCHINS	50000	92	112	A New Map of the Western Parts of Virginia, Pennsylvania, Maryland and North Carolina ... River Ohio ... River Mississippi ... Illinois River, Lake Erie; Part of the Lakes Huron, Michigan
mwuss0591	kentucky	1778	HUTCHINS	600	15	18	A Plan of the Rapids in the River Ohio by Thos. Hutchins

AMPG REFERENCE	REGION	DATE	MAP MAKER	PRICE (UK£)	VERT. (cm.)	HOR. (cm.)	TITLE OF MAP (Comments by the editor in brackets)
mwuss1270	ohio	1767	HUTCHINS	1800	24	30	Carte du Cours de l'Ohio & du Muskingum Representant la Position des Villes Indiennes par Rapport a l'Armee du Colonel Bouquet
mwuss1357	pennsylvania	1768	HUTCHINS	1650	22	16	Plan of the Battle near Bushy-Run, Gained by Colonel Bouquet, over the Delawares, Shawanese, Mingoes, Wyandots, Mohikons, Miamies, & Ottawas; on the 5th and 6th of August 1763
mwuk0829	uk	1747	HUTCHINSON	400	36	47	Great Britain And Ireland with ye Judges Circuits
mwe0599	europe czech republic (bohemia)	1760	HUTTER	600	49	54	Le Royaume de Boheme Divisee en ses Douze Cercles
			HYDROGRAPHIC OFFICE: See BRITISH ADMIRALTY				
mwuss0614	kentucky	1834	ILLMAN	400	26	32	Kentucky and Tennessee
mwca0558	canada quebec	1834	ILLMAN	100	32	27	Lower Canada
mwuss1232	new york	1836	ILLMAN	375	32	29	Map of the Country Twenty Five Miles round the City of New-York
mwuss0984	missouri	1834	ILLMAN	400	27	34	Missouri
mwam0689	america north	1834	ILLMAN	100	24	21	North America
mww0711	world	1836	ILLMAN	235	27		Northern Hemisphere / Southern Hemisphere (2 circular maps)
mwuss1329	oregon	1833	ILLMAN	550	27	33	Oregon Territory
mwca0481	canada ontario	1834	ILLMAN	200	26	32	Upper Canada
mwam1045	america north (east)	1777	IMBERT	3000	54	74	Carte des Possessions Angloises dans l'Amerique Septentrionale pour Servir d'Intelligence a la Guerre Presente Traduite de l'Anglois
mwgm0085	gulf of mexico and surrounding regions	1846	IMRAY	1000	99	183	A New Chart of the Gulfs of Mexico and Florida
mwaf1033a	africa south	1856	IMRAY	1350	100	180	Chart of Southern Africa, and of the Islands of Madagascar, Bourbon and Mauritius
mwin0381	india	1850	IMRAY	1200	102	171	Chart of the Bay of Bengal Including Plans of the Principal Harbours
mwuss0129	california	1849	IMRAY	4400	66	146	Chart of the Coast of California from San Blas to San Francisco Drawn Chiefly from the Spanish Surveys, the Charts of Vancouver &c.
mwit1127	italy tuscany	1830	INGHIRAMI	1500	146	112	Carte Geometrica della Toscana Ricavata dal Veo nella Proporzione di 1 a 200.000
mwuk0794	uk	1715	INSELIN	2800	64	85	Carte des Royaumes D'Angleterre D'Ecosse Et D'Irlande (incl. North Sea and Denmark)
mwe0153	europe	1735	INSELIN	1400	50	65	Carte Generale de L'Europe
mwe0720	europe danube	1704	INSELIN	3800	30	96	Le Theatre de la Guerre pour les Mouvements des Armees en Allemagne et en Alsace et dans le Royaume de Hongrie
mwaf0170a	africa	1735	INSELIN	1800	52	65	Carte Generale de l'Afrique
mwwi0178	west indies	1828	IRVING	480	44	61	Chart of the West Indies
mwam1362	america north (west)	1837	IRVING	685	43	42	Map of the Territory West of the Rocky Mountains
mwam1359	america north (west)	1836	IRVING	280	24	46	Sketch of the Routes of Hunt & Stuart
mwme0952	turkey etc	1662	ISAC	1400	39	53	La Ville de Constantinople
mww0001	world	1472	ISIDORE OF SEVILLE	60000	7		(Circular diagram, known as a T-O map. The first printed map)
mwru0264	russia	1777	ISLENYEV	800	47	56	Mappa Fluvii Irtisz Partem Meridionalem Gubernii Sibiriensis
mwru0554	ukraine	1779	ISLENYEV	1600	47	57	Mappa Generalis Gubernii Novae Russiae in Circulos Divisi (This map was also published with Cyrillic script)
mwg0216	germany north east	1802	JACK	600	65	101	General Karte von den Konig: Preussischen Staaten ... im Jahre 1799
mwg0544	rheinland-pfalz	1797	JACK	400	33	50	Plan von der Schlacht welche bey Pirmasens den 14ten September 1793 von dem Koniglich Preussischen Feldmarschal Herzog von Braunschweig uber die Franzosische Vosgen Armee Gewonnen worden ist
mwuss1480	rhode isl	1840	JACKSON	350	51	30	A Geological Map of Rhode Island
mwam0242	america continent	1795	JACKSON	480	52	51	America Divided into North and South with their Several Subdivisions and the Newest Discoveries
mwca0182	canada	1838	JACKSON	120	20	26	Canada and the other British Provinces in North America
mwuss0139	california	1850	JACKSON	9000	44	43	Map of the Mining District of California
mwaa0058	antarctic	1850	JACOBS	1250	60	85	Ocean Pacific Feuille 3 (S. Australia, New Zealand and fragments of the Antarctic continent)
mwwi0023	west indies	1666	JACOBSZ	1600	44	54	(Lesser Antilles)
mwsc0416	scandinavia finland	1662	JACOBSZ	1350	43	53	Caarte van 't Gat van Abbo / Caarte van Stockholmse Liet
mwsc0547	scandinavia norway	1650	JACOBSZ	785	43	53	Caerte van Finnmarcken van 't Eylandt Sanien tot Noord-Kyn
mwbp0268	poland	1660	JACOBSZ	550	43	53	Caerte van Pruyssen en Coerlandt, van Rygshooft tot der Winda
mwf0289	france bay of biscay	1666	JACOBSZ	550	42	53	Cust van Biscayen tussen Gatarya en Rio de Sella / Cust van Biscayen tusschen Villa Vicioca ende C. de Ortegael
mwuk1547	bristol channel	1676	JACOBSZ	720	42	53	Cust van Engelant van Lezard tot Engelands Eynd, de Sorlinges, ende Canael van Brestou

AMPG REFERENCE	REGION	DATE	MAP MAKER	PRICE (UK£)	VERT. (cm.)	HOR. (cm.)	TITLE OF MAP (Comments by the editor in brackets)
mwbh0397	belgium holland	1676	JACOBSZ	450	42	52	Cust van Hollant tusschen de Maes ende Texel
mwsp0434a	spain regions	1644	JACOBSZ	600	43	53	De Cust van Andaluzia en Algarve, van Capo de Spichel tot aen het Clif (map by J. Theunisz)
mwaf0688	africa north	1644	JACOBSZ	650	43	52	De Cust van Barbaryen
mwuk1530a	uk english channel (east)	1676	JACOBSZ	480	42	52	De Cust van Normandie en Picardie
mwbh0391	belgium holland	1674	JACOBSZ	1000	43	53	De Cust van Zeeland (copy of Goos 1666)
mwf0314	france brittany	1653	JACOBSZ	1000	42	52	De Custen van Bretaigne ... Caap de Hague en t'Eylant Heysant (south to the top)
mwec0172	uk england cornwall	1690	JACOBSZ	650	43	53	De Custen van Engelant tusschen de Tween Pointen van Poortlandt en Lezard
mwm0269	mediterranean west	1692	JACOBSZ	350	39	52	De Custen van Granada van Malaga tot Cabo de Gata, en de Custen van Barbarien van Penon de Veles tot C. de Hoone
mwsc0566	scandinavia norway	1663	JACOBSZ	900	43	55	De Custen van Noorwegen en Finmarcken van Wtweerclippen to aen de Noort-Caap
mwsc0568	scandinavia norway	1668	JACOBSZ	500	42	58	De Custen van Noorwegen en Laplandt, vande Noord-Kyn tot aen de Rivier van Kola
mwsc0548	scandinavia norway	1650	JACOBSZ	785	43	53	De Custen van Noorwegen tusschen der Neus en Schuitenes
mwsc0549	scandinavia norway	1650	JACOBSZ	785	43	53	De Custen van Noorwegen, en Laplandt, vande Noord-kyn tot aen de River van Kola
mwf0316	france brittany	1653	JACOBSZ	1000	42	52	De Custen van Saintoigne, Poictou, en een Gedeelte van Bretaigne
mwuk0415	scotland	1676	JACOBSZ	550	42	52	De Custen van Schotland met de Eylanden van Orcanese; van't Eyland Coket tot I. Sande
mwuk0072	ireland	1668	JACOBSZ	550	43	36	De Noord Ost Zyde van Yerlandt
mwuk0052	ireland	1644	JACOBSZ	720	53	53	De West Custen van Yerlandt Beginnende van Corckbeg tot aen Slynhooft
mwf0315	france brittany	1653	JACOBSZ	1000	43	52	De Zee-Custen van Bretaigne van Heysandt tot aen Boelyn
mwuk0073	ireland	1668	JACOBSZ	480	43	36	De Zuyd Oost Zyde van Yerlandt van Dublin
mwuk0051	ireland	1644	JACOBSZ	550	41	54	De Zuyd Oost Zyde van Yerlandt van Dublin tot aen t'Eylandt Corkbeg
mwuk0416	scotland	1676	JACOBSZ	550	42	52	Eylanden van Hitlant ofte Schetlant ... Eylanden van Hebrides ... Eylanden van Fero ...
mwbp0009a	baltic sea (east)	1644	JACOBSZ	2500	43	55	Pascaart Vande Oost-Zee Vertoonende in sich alle gelegentheden van de Custen va Denemarken en Sweden, Pomeren, Prusssen, Courlant, Lyflant, en Finlant (image courtesy of B. Ruderman)
mwuk0705	uk	1644	JACOBSZ	2500	43	55	Pascaart vant Canaal Begrypende in sich Engelandt, Schotlandt en Ierlandt als mede een Gedeelte van Francryck
mwuk0056	ireland	1650	JACOBSZ	1500	43	55	Pascaart Vant Canaal Tusschen Engelant en Vrancryck alsmede geheel Jerlant en Schotlant (illustrated is the Jansson re-issue, 1650)
mwuk1642	north sea	1644	JACOBSZ	2000	43	56	Pascaarte van de Noort Zee Vertonende van Caliz tot Dronten, als oock tusschen Doeveren en Hitlandt
mwsc0421	scandinavia finland	1680	JACOBSZ	1600	43	53	Pascaarte van Liiflandt ende Oost Finlandt
mwm0011	mediterranean	1663	JACOBSZ	3000	40	50	Pascaarte van 't Westelyckste Deel van de Middellandsche Zee / Pascaarte van 't Oostelyckste Deel van de Middellandsche Zee (2 charts)
mwbp0021a	baltic sea (east)	1663	JACOBSZ	2400	43	55	Pascaarte vande Oost Zee van t eylandt Rugen of van de hoeck van Valsterbon tot aen Wyborg
mwbp0010	baltic sea (east)	1644	JACOBSZ	1500	44	56	Pascaarte vande Oost-Zee van 't Eylandt Rugen, ofte Bornholm tot aen Wyborg
mwat0150	atlantic canary isl.	1680	JACOBSZ	785	43	54	Pascaarte voor een Gedeelte der Canarise Eylanden, als Canaria, Tenerifa, Forteventura etc.
mwe1191	europe west	1666	JACOBSZ	2000	43	53	Pascaer van Europa als mede een Gedeelt van Cust van Africa (copied from Goos 1666)
mwru0119	russia	1705	JACOBSZ	1000	43	55	Pascaert van Ruslant, Laplant, Finmarcken, Spitsbergen en Nova Zembla
mwat0337	atlantic west	1650	JACOBSZ	3000	43	55	Pascaert vande Carybes, Nieu Neder Landt, Brazil, de Flaemsche en Soute Eylanden, en de Landen daer Ontrent Gelegen
mwsam0298	south america brazil	1650	JACOBSZ	1600	42	54	Pascaerte van Brasil van Rio de Maranhaon tot Rio de la Plata
mwru0072	russia	1676	JACOBSZ	450	43	52	Pascaerte van de Mont van de Witte Zee, tot aen de Rivier van Archangel
mwam0861	america north (east)	1650	JACOBSZ	5500	43	53	Pascaerte van Nieu Nederlant, Virginies, Nieu Engelant en Nova Francia, van C. of Faire tot C. Forchu
mwsc0298	scandinavia denmark	1680	JACOBSZ	850	41	53	Pascaerte van Schager-Rack en de Sond
mwas0401	asia south east	1670	JACOBSZ	5000	43	54	Pascaerte van't Oostelyckste Deel van Oost-Indien (right-hand sheet only of a map of the Indian Ocean. Shown below left. For the complete map see AMPG 20)
mwin0416	indian ocean	1670	JACOBSZ	6500	54	86	Pascaerte Van't Oostelyckste deel van Oost-Indien met alle de Eylanden daer onder gelegen van Cubo Comorin tot aen Iapan / Pascaerte Van't Westelyckste deel van Oost Indien En De Eylanden daer onder Begrepen, van C. de Bona Esperanca tot C. Comorin (close copies of Doncker 1659)

AMPG REFERENCE	REGION	DATE	MAP MAKER	PRICE (UKE)	VERT. (cm.)	HOR. (cm.)	TITLE OF MAP (Comments by the editor in brackets)
mwin0478	indian ocean west	1681	JACOBSZ	1350	43	52	Pascaerte van 't Westelyckste Deel van Oost-Indien
mwwi0013	west indies	1650	JACOBSZ	9000	43	55	Pascaerte van West Indien van de Caribes tot aen de Golfo van Mexico
mwwi0227a	west indies (east)	1650	JACOBSZ	2000	43	55	Pascaerte vande Caribes S. Iuan de Porte Rico, de Oosthoeck van I. Spagnola als mede de Vaste Cust van Nueva Andalusia met de Eylanden daer Omtrent Gelegen
mwsc0265	scandinavia denmark	1644	JACOBSZ	1500	43	72	Pascaerte vande West en Oost-Zyde van Iutlandt
mwme0051a	holy land	1590	JACOBSZ	500	17	13	Tabula Geographica, in qua Iisraelitarum, ab Aegypto ad Kenahanaeam (shown above)
mwuk0737	uk	1679	JACOBSZ (LOOTSMAN)	2000	43	52	Pas-Caert van Engelandt Schotlandt Yrlandt
mwaf0554	africa egypt etc	1826	JACOTIN	4000			Carte Topographique de L'Egypte (in 41 sheets)
mwaf0548	africa egypt etc	1818	JACOTIN	1800	64	96	Le Kaire ... Plan Particulier de la Ville
mwaf0544	africa egypt etc	1809	JACOTIN	320	38	52	Plan General de Boulaq, du Kaire, de l'Ile de Roudah, du Vieux-Kaire et de Gyzeh
mwf1169	france lyon	1747	JACQUEMIN	500	44	57	Plan Geometral et Proportionel de la Ville de Lyon ou sont Designes ses 28 Quartiers ou Pennonages
mwru0541a	ukraine	1769	JAEGER	600	48	73	Carte exacte d'une partie de l'Empire de Russie et de la Pologne meridionale renfermant l'Ukraine, la Podolie
mwg0158	germany	1789	JAEGER		50	60	Carte Topographique d'Allemagne (in 81 sheets)
mwe0961a	europe hungary	1789	JAEGER	1200	90	64	Carte Topographique d'Allemagne contenant une partie du Royaume d'Hongrie
mwe0610b	europe czech republic (bohemia)	1790	JAEGER	500	46	61	Carte Topographique d'Allemagne contenant ... Royaume de Boheme ... (2 sheets, XLIII and XLIV of Jaeger's atlas of Germany.)
mwe0605	europe czech republic (bohemia)	1778	JAEGER	600	47	55	Le Royaume de Boheme Divisee en ses Douze Circles (A reduction of Muller's map. See also Covens & Mortier.)
mwru0295	russia	1788	JAEGER	1000	94	135	Le Theatre de la Guerre entre des Deux Puissans Empires l'Autriche, la Russie et la Turquie
mwam1033	america north (east)	1776	JAEGER	7200	64	76	Schauplatz des Kriegs zwischen Engelland und seinen Collonien in America nach Richtigen Carten Gezeichnet und in diese Form Gebracht von I:C: Iaeger
mwbh0677	belgium holland	1747	JAILLOT	720	49	67	(Antwerp) Carte Topographique des Forts, Ville, Citadelle d'Anvers et de ses Environs
mwg0534	rheinland-pfalz	1736	JAILLOT	785	47	66	(Mainz) Plan de Mayence de ses Nouvelles Fortifications
mwf0319	france brittany	1669	JAILLOT	875	46	67	(untitled chart of the 'Environs du Port de Brest')
mwsam0027	south america	1674	JAILLOT	1350	57	87	Amerique Meridionale Divisee en ses Principales Parties ou sont Distingues les uns des Autres les Estats Suivant qu'ils Appartienent Presentement, aux Francois, Castillans, Portugais, Hollandois, &c.
mwam0323	america north	1674	JAILLOT	6000	57	88	Amerique Septentrionale, Divisee en ses Principales Parties, ou sont Distingues les Uns des Autres les Estats Suivant qu'ils Appartiennent Presentemet aux Francois, Castillans, Anglois, Suedois, Danois, Hollandois
mwam0338	america north	1695	JAILLOT	2000	46	64	Amerique Septentrionale divisée en ses Principales Parties
mwg0811a	westphalia	1692	JAILLOT	380	57	43	Archevesscheet Eslectorat de Cologne (illustrated above left. Re-issued 1762)
mwuk1476	uk english channel (all)	1692	JAILLOT	1200	59	80	Carte de la Manche
mwbp0031	baltic sea (east)	1693	JAILLOT	1600	61	89	Carte de la Mer Baltique Contenant les Bancs, Isles et Costes Comprises entre l'Isle de Zelande et l'Extremite du Golfe du Finlande (inset of Dantzig. Also issued by Mortier)
mwsc0315	scandinavia denmark	1693	JAILLOT	1600	61	89	Carte de la Mer de Dannemark et des Entrees dans la Mer Baltique Contenant les Bancs, Passes, Isles et Costes Comprises depuis Norden et le Cap Der-Neus jusques a Rostock et Valsterbon
mwbh0467	belgium holland	1693	JAILLOT	950	60	88	Carte des Entrees du Suyder Zee et de l'Embs avec les Isles, Bancs et Costes Comprises entre la Hollande et la Frise Orientale
mwg0282	baden-wurttemberg	1735	JAILLOT	720	42	57	Carte des Environs de Philipsbourg (example seen printed in sepia ink)
mwbh0412	belgium holland	1680	JAILLOT	350	40	51	Carte Generalle de Flandre
mwsp0238	spain	1713	JAILLOT	1500	61	92	Carte Nouvelle et Curieuse de Royaume d'Espagne
mwf0476	france corsica	1700	JAILLOT	550	27	44	Carte Particuliere de l'Isle de Corse Divisee par ses Provinces ou Jurisdictions, & Fiefs
mwf0496	france corsica	1738	JAILLOT	1800	50	80	Carte Particuliere de L'Isle de Corse.
mwuk0115	ireland	1693	JAILLOT	1000	64	95	Carte Particuliere des Costes Occidentales d'Irlande qui comprend la Baye de Galloway et la Riviere de Lymerick Comme elles paroissent a Basse Mer dans les Grandes Marees (north to the left)
mwm0235	mediterranean malta	1734	JAILLOT	1200	43	73	Carte Particuliere des Isles de Malte du Goze
mwf0081	france	1693	JAILLOT	450	68	62	Carte Particuliere des Postes de France (re-issued by Covens & Mortier 1720)
mwf0788	france normandy	1736	JAILLOT	1200	74	50	Carte Topographique du Diocese de Bayeux (in 2 sheets, each 74x50cm.)
mwit1194	italy veneto	1706	JAILLOT	550	48	72	Estat de la Seigneurie et Republique de Venise en Italie les Evesches de Trente et de Brixen

AMPG REFERENCE	REGION	DATE	MAP MAKER	PRICE (UK£)	VERT. (cm.)	HOR. (cm.)	TITLE OF MAP (Comments by the editor in brackets)
mwe0551	europe czech republic (bohemia)	1693	JAILLOT	600	57	88	Estats de la Couronne de Boheme qui Comprenent le Royaume de Boheme, le Duche de Silesie et les Marquisats de Moravie et de Lusace
mwbp0353	poland	1708	JAILLOT	550	46	64	Estats de la Couronne de Pologne Subdivises Suivant l'Estendue des Palatinats
mwit0311	italy central	1721	JAILLOT	300	52	65	Estats de l'Eglise et de Toscane
mwe1144a	europe south east	1692	JAILLOT	750	58	88	Estats de l'Empire des Turqs en Europe
mwme0572	arabia etc	1686	JAILLOT	1350	58	88	Estats de l'Empire du Grand Seigneur des Turcs en Europe, en Asie, et en Afrique
mwme0573	arabia etc	1686	JAILLOT	850	46	61	Estats de l'Empire du Grand Seigneur des Turcs en Europe, en Asie, et en Afrique (title above map: 'Nova Imperii Turcarum Tabula...'. Illustrated is Ottens 1740 reprint. Also reprinted by Elwe 1788)
mwbp0322	poland	1692	JAILLOT	1500	54	86	Estats de Pologne Subdivises Suivant l'Estendue des Palatinats (re-issued by Mortier in 1693)
mwgr0142	greece	1705	JAILLOT	650	56	84	Etats De L'Empire Des Turqs En Europe
mwf0979	france poitou	1722	JAILLOT	450	51	70	Generalite de La Rochelle Divisee en Cinq Elections
mwf0952	france picardy	1692	JAILLOT	360	54	80	Gouvernement General de Picardie ou sont le Pays Reconquis
mwbh0477	belgium holland	1696	JAILLOT	875	42	55	Gueldre Espagnole ou Quartier du Ruremonde
mwg0804	westphalia	1681	JAILLOT	350	44	57	Haute Partie de l'Evesche de Munster
mwme0464	jerusalem	1678	JAILLOT	30000	118	188	Hierusalem Saincte Cite de Dieu
mwme0207	holy land	1690	JAILLOT	650	47	57	Iudaea seu Terra Sancta quae Hebraeorum sive Israelitarum
mwme0174	holy land	1677	JAILLOT	1500	58	84	Iudaea, seu Terra Sancta quae Hebraeorum sive Israelitarum in suas Duodecim Tribus Divisa
mwf0337c	france brittany	1696	JAILLOT	900	55	80	La Bretagne Divisee en ses Neuf Evesches qui sont aussi l'Estendue des Receptes de la Generalite de Nantes
mwsp0502	spain regions	1705	JAILLOT	875	58	88	La Catalogne, sous le Nom de laquelle sont Compris la Principaute de Catalogne, et les Comtes de Roussillon et de Cerdagne
mwf0101	france	1714	JAILLOT	400	51	66	La France Divisee par Provinces ou sont Exactement Remarquees Toutes les Routes des Postes du Royaume
mwf0099	france	1713	JAILLOT	1650	61	93	La France Dressee Suivant les Nouvelles Observations de Mrs. de l'Academie Royale des Sciences
mwf0844	france paris	1708	JAILLOT	900	42	65	La Generalite de Paris
mwgr0162	greece	1716	JAILLOT	500	46	55	La Grece Tiree des Memoires de Monsieur l'Abbe Baudrand (reprint of Baudrand's 1682 map)
mwf0679	france lorraine	1692	JAILLOT	600	55	88	La Lorraine, qui comprend Les Duches de Lorraine et de Bar et les Balliages des Evesches et des Villes de Metz, Toul, et Verdun
mwuk1480	uk english channel (all)	1695	JAILLOT	1200	51	60	La Manche ou le Canal entre la France et l'Angleterre (illustrated is Covens & Mortier reprint c1730)
mwm0026	mediterranean	1696	JAILLOT	1500	58	88	La Mer Mediterranee Divisee en ses Principales Parties ou Mers
mwgr0143	greece	1705	JAILLOT	900	57	85	La Moree et les Isles de Zante, Cefalonie, Ste Maure, Cerigo &c.
mwf1139	france rhone-alpes	1692	JAILLOT	685	64	46	La Principaute de Piemont les Marquisats de Saluce et de Suze, les Comtes de Nice et d'Ast, le Montferrat &c.
mwf1020	france provence	1685	JAILLOT	800	46	65	La Provence Divisee en ses Vigueries et Terres Adjacentes
mwru0074	russia	1679	JAILLOT	550	49	58	La Russie Blanche ou Moscovie (title above map: Nova Russiae Albae sive Moscoviae Delineatio Geographica. Illustrated is Schenk 1700 re-print)
mwru0107	russia	1700	JAILLOT	500	51	61	La Russie Blanche ou Moscovie (title above map: Nova Russiae Albae sive Moscoviae Tabula, ad usum Serenissimi Burgundiae Ducis)
mwru0070	russia	1674	JAILLOT	875	55	88	La Russie Blanche ou Moscovie Divisee Suivant l'Estendue des Royaumes, Duches
mwsc0092	scandinavia	1696	JAILLOT	1200	55	87	La Scandinavie et les Environs, ou sont les Royaumes de Suede de Danemarck et de Norwege
mwsc0089	scandinavia	1695	JAILLOT	750	46	65	La Scandinavie ou sont les Royaumes de Suede, Danemark et Norwege
mwbh0459	belgium holland	1692	JAILLOT	600	43	56	La Seigneurie d'Ouest-Frise
mwit0909	italy sicily	1693	JAILLOT	750	42	54	La Sicile divisees en ses trois Provinces ou Valees
mwsw0082	switzerland	1674	JAILLOT	1650	59	85	La Suisse Divisee en ses Treze Cantons, ses Alliez & ses Sujets (3 borders decorated with crests)
mwsw0084	switzerland	1680	JAILLOT	1350	47	60	La Suisse Divisee en ses Treze Cantons, ses Alliez & ses Sujets (3 borders decorated with crests)
mwaf0103	africa	1694	JAILLOT	960	46	59	L'Afrique Divisee en ses Empires, Royaumes et Etats
mwaf0149	africa	1719	JAILLOT	10000	113	132	L'Afrique Divisee en ses Principales Parties, et ses Isles
mwaf0083	africa	1674	JAILLOT	1500	58	88	L'Afrique Divisee Suivant l'Estendue de ses Principales Parties
mwaf0129	africa	1708	JAILLOT	650	46	64	L'Afrique Divisee Suivant l'Estendue de ses Principales Parties
mwf0228	france alsace	1692	JAILLOT	650	80	57	L'Alsace Divisee en ses Principales Parties
mwam0126	america continent	1719	JAILLOT	24000	116	131	L'Amerique Divisee en ses Principales Parties Savoir dans la Septentrionale

AMPG REFERENCE	REGION	DATE	MAP MAKER	PRICE (UK£)	VERT. (cm.)	HOR. (cm.)	TITLE OF MAP (Comments by the editor in brackets)
mwsam0036	south america	1694	JAILLOT	785	46	60	L'Amerique Meridionale
mwe0337	europe austria	1692	JAILLOT	480	55	87	Partie du Cercle d' Austriche scavoir l' Archduche d' Austriche divise en Haute et Basse
mwas0084a	asia continent	1692	JAILLOT	900	47	58	L'Asie Divisee en ses Empires, Royaumes, et Etats (title above map: 'Asia Divisa in Imperia Regna'. Illustrated is the Ottens re-issue)
mwas0089	asia continent	1696	JAILLOT	1400	58	87	L'Asie divisee en ses Principale Regions (title above map: L'Asie Distinguee en ses Principales Parties)
mwsp0191a	spain	1672	JAILLOT	600	60	90	L'Espagne Divisee en Tous ses Royaumes
mwe0103a	europe	1696	JAILLOT	750	48	58	L'Europe Divisée en ses Principaux Estats
mwbh0436	belgium holland	1684	JAILLOT	785	44	57	Le Brabant Espagnol qui Comprend les Quartiers de Brusselles, de Louvain et Partie de Celuy d'Anvers
mwg0351	bavaria	1692	JAILLOT	375	81	56	Le Cercle de Baviere
mwg0620	saxony	1692	JAILLOT	480	54	87	Le Cercle de la Basse Saxe ou sont les Evesches de Lubeck, et d'Hidelsheim, les Duches de Magdebourg, de Breme
mwg0624	saxony	1708	JAILLOT	450	46	65	Le Cercle de la Basse Saxe Subdivise en Tous les Estates et Principautes
mwg0264	baden-wurttemberg	1675	JAILLOT	400	58	88	Le Cercle de Souabe Subdivise en Touts les Estats que le Composent
mwg0811	westphalia	1692	JAILLOT	500	86	57	Le Cercle de Westphalie
mwbh0520	belgium holland	1705	JAILLOT	600	59	82	Le Comte de Flandre Divise en ses Chastellenies et Balliages &c, le Franc de Bruges, et le Pays de Waes
mwbh0521	belgium holland	1705	JAILLOT	250	53	62	Le Comte de Namur, Partie de l'Evesche de Liege, du Luxembourg, &c.
mwe0344	europe austria	1710	JAILLOT	875	49	70	Le Comte de Tirol
mwbh0522	belgium holland	1705	JAILLOT	900	57	81	Le Comte de Zeelande
mwbh0466	belgium holland	1692	JAILLOT	650	56	80	Le Comte de Zeelande
mwe1010	europe rhine	1696	JAILLOT	500	86	58	Le Cours de la Riviere du Rhein depuis sa Source jusques a son Embouchure
mwe0716	europe danube	1693	JAILLOT	2000	60	120	Le Cours du Danube depuis sa Source jusqu'a ses Embouchures
mwf1101	france pyrenees	1706	JAILLOT	350	45	67	Le Diocese de Toulouse
mwg0813	westphalia	1696	JAILLOT	300	43	56	Le Duche de Berg, le Comte de Homberg, les Seigneuries de Hardenberg, et de Wildenborg
mwbh0466a	belgium holland	1692	JAILLOT	650	47	78	Le Duche de Brabant qui comprend les Quartiers
mwg0810	westphalia	1692	JAILLOT	300	43	57	Le Duche de Cleves la Seigneurie de Ravenstein et le Comte de Meurs
mwbh0882	luxembourg	1785	JAILLOT	800	43	56	Le Duche de Luxembourg Divise en Francois, et Espagnol
mwbh0846	luxembourg	1692	JAILLOT	900	57	67	Le Duche de Luxembourg, Divisee en Quartier Walon, et Allemand
mwbh0853	luxembourg	1705	JAILLOT	1250	105	123	Le Duche de Luxembourg Divise en Quartier Walon, et Allemand
mwg0805	westphalia	1681	JAILLOT	350	44	58	Le Duche de Westphalie
mwf0782	france normandy	1695	JAILLOT	720	59	88	Le Duche et Gouvernement de Normandie Divisee en Haute et Basse Normandie, en Divers Pays, et par Evechez, avec le Gouvernement General du Havre de Grace
mwm0091	mediterranean adriatic	1693	JAILLOT	1600	55	74	Le Golfe de Venise avec ses Principaux Caps
mwf1038	france provence	1705	JAILLOT	950	58	84	Le Gouvernement de Provence Divise en ses Vigueries et Terres Adjacentes
mwf1189	france south west	1705	JAILLOT	400	49	60	Le Gouvernement General de Guienne et Gascogne
mwf0616	france languedoc	1720	JAILLOT	750	77	92	Le Gouvernement General de Languedoc
mwf0580a	france ile de france	1692	JAILLOT	400	42	65	Le Gouvernement General de L'Isle de France / Seconde Partie du Gouvernement General de L'Isle de France (2 maps, north and south)
mwg0414	brandenburg	1692	JAILLOT	685	54	89	Le Marquisat et Eslectorat de Brandebourg ... Par le S. Sanson
mwuk0957	england	1693	JAILLOT	1000	79	58	Le Royaume d'Angleterre ... Par le Sr. Sanson
mwsc0303	scandinavia denmark	1681	JAILLOT	650	60	89	Le Royaume de Danemark
mwsc0315a	scandinavia denmark	1695	JAILLOT	500	46	65	Le Royaume de Danemark
mwf0094	france	1705	JAILLOT	550	60	89	Le Royaume de France Distingue Suivant l'Estendue de Toutes ses Provinces, et ses Acquisitions dans l'Espagne, dans l'Italie, dans l'Allemagne, et dans la Flandre, l'Artois, le Haynaut, le Namur, et le Luxembourg, Provinces des Pays-Bas
mwf0106a	france	1720	JAILLOT	500	51	60	Le Royaume de France divisee en toutes ses Provinces et ses Acquisitions. (Title above map: Galliae Regnum ...)
mwf0112	france	1721	JAILLOT	4500	104	119	Le Royaume de France divisee en toutes ses Provinces (illustrated is the Covens & Mortier re-issue)
mwf0103	france	1717	JAILLOT	685	67	89	Le Royaume de France Dresse sur les Memoires et les Nouvelles Observations de Messieurs de l'Academie Royale des Sciences
mwe0914	europe hungary	1696	JAILLOT	785	59	88	Le Royaume de Hongrie et les Estats qui en ont este Sujets
mwe0786a	europe east	1717	JAILLOT	480	46	65	Le Royaume de Hongrie
mwit1018	italy south	1696	JAILLOT	480	45	55	Le Royaume de Naples Divise en Douze Provinces
mwit1023	italy south	1706	JAILLOT	800	89	75	Le Royaume de Naples Divise en Toutes ses Provinces
mwsp0060	portugal	1695	JAILLOT	1200	75	54	Le Royaume de Portugal et des Algarves

AMPG REFERENCE	REGION	DATE	MAP MAKER	PRICE (UK£)	VERT. (cm.)	HOR. (cm.)	TITLE OF MAP (Comments by the editor in brackets)
mwuk0439a	scotland	1693	JAILLOT	1200	88	58	Le Royaume d'Escosse
mwuk0122a	ireland	1696	JAILLOT	1200	91	62	Le Royaume d'Irlande Divise en ses Provinces. Subdivise en Shireries ou Comtes (inset: British Isles)
mwf0586	france ile de france	1718	JAILLOT	350	36	40	Le Vexin Francois, ou le Vicariat de Pontoise avec les Presentateurs aux Benefices qu'il Contient
mwg0086	germany	1692	JAILLOT	550	57	88	L'Empire D'Allemagne (also issued smaller, as below)
mwbh0524	belgium holland	1705	JAILLOT	400	47	57	Les Campemens des Armees du Roy de France & des Alliez aux Pays-Bas, depuis l'Annee 1690 jusques a Present
mwaf0491	africa egypt etc	1693	JAILLOT	1500	56	78	Les Deserts D'Egypte (large inset of the Nile)
mwbh0525	belgium holland	1705	JAILLOT	875	88	56	Les Dix-Sept Provinces des Pays Bas Distinguees Suivant quelles sont Possedees a Present par les Roys de France, et d'Espagne et les Estats Generaux des Provinces Unies
mwuk0760	uk	1695	JAILLOT	850	49	65	Les Isles Britanniques qui Contiennent les Royaumes d'Angleterre, Escosse, et Irlande
mwuk0730	uk	1673	JAILLOT	1600	59	89	Les Isles Britanniques; qui Contiennent les Royaumes d'Angleterre, Escosse, et Irlande
mwit0585	italy north	1692	JAILLOT	785	54	87	Les Montagnes des Alpes ou sont Remarques les Passages de France en Italie. Le Duche de Milan, et les Estats du Duc de Savoye &c.
mwf1096a	france pyrenees	1675	JAILLOT	800	57	88	Les Monts Pyrenees ou sont Remarques les Passages de France en Espagne (reissued by Mortier in 1700)
mwbh0465	belgium holland	1692	JAILLOT	750	58	88	Les Provinces de Pays-Bas Catholiques
mwit1191	italy veneto	1705	JAILLOT	600	48	73	Les Provinces du Veronese, du Vicentin, du Padouan, de Polesine de Rovigo et du Dogado ou Duche a la Republique de Venise. Les Duches de Mantoue, de la Mirandole &c.
mwsw0111	switzerland	1717	JAILLOT	4000	48	65	Les Suisses Leurs Sujets Et Leurs Alliez (in 4 sheets, each 48x65cm)
mwsp0210	spain	1696	JAILLOT	480	45	58	L'Espagne divisee ... a l'usage de Monseigneur le Duc de Bourgogne
mwsp0241	spain	1716	JAILLOT	1600	88	111	L'Espagne Suivant l'Etendue de Tous les Royaumes et Principautes Compris ... (4 sheets joined)
mwe0104	europe	1697	JAILLOT	1350	55	88	L'Europe Divisee Suivant l'Estendue de ses Principaux Estats
mwf0339	france brittany	1700	JAILLOT	550	45	58	L'Evesche de Vannes
mwit0118a	italy	1692	JAILLOT	1350	55	89	L'Italie Distinguee Suivant l'Estendue de Tous les Estats ... 1692 (different title above map)
mww0253	world	1695	JAILLOT	3500	44	65	Mappe-Monde Geo-Hydrographique, ou Description Generale Du Globe (smaller version of 1674 map)
mww0198	world	1674	JAILLOT	4500	54	89	Mappe-Monde Geo-Hydrographique, ou Description Generale du Globe Terrestre et Aquatique en Deux Plans-Hemispheres
mwf0846	france paris	1713	JAILLOT	2000	87	119	Nouveau Plan de la Ville et Faubourgs de Paris
mwe0139	europe	1720	JAILLOT	200	53	77	Nouvelle Carte Marine de Tous les Ports de l'Europe sur l'Ocean et sur la Mediterranee (after Berey)
mwaf0077	africa	1669	JAILLOT	40000	117	168	Nova Africae Geographica et Hydrographica Descriptio, Auct. G. Blaeu
mww0252	world	1694	JAILLOT	5000	49	61	Nova Orbis Tabula, Ad Usum Serenissima Burgundiae Ducis - Mappe Monde ou Description du Globe (shown is the Ottens c1740 re-issue)
mwam0070	america continent	1669	JAILLOT	80000	122	177	Nova Totius Americae sive Novi Orbis Tabula. Auct. G.I. Blaeu
mwg0621	saxony	1692	JAILLOT	600	43	56	Oost-Frise, ou le Comte d'Embden
mwca0034	canada	1685	JAILLOT	2500	45	64	Partie de la Nouvelle France
mwe0331	europe austria	1681	JAILLOT	480	57	88	Partie du Cercle d'Austriche, ou sont les Duches de Stirie, de Carinthie, de Carniole et autres Estates Hereditaires a la Maison d'Austriche par le Sr. Sanson
mwit0661	italy piedmont	1690	JAILLOT	500	46	64	Partie du Duche de Milan, la Principaute de Piemont, le Monferrat et la Republique de Genes
mwsp0074a	portugal	1715	JAILLOT	750	45	57	Partie Septentrionale du Royaume de Portugal / Partie Meridionale du Royaume de Portugal (2 maps, each 45x57cm. Titles outside maps)
mwg0540	rheinland-pfalz	1781	JAILLOT	600	42	55	Plan de Coblens et du Chateau d'Hermanstein
mwit0895	italy sicily	1675	JAILLOT	750	43	55	Plan de la Ville de Messine
mwe0418	europe austria vienna	1692	JAILLOT	960	46	65	Plan de la Ville de Vienne en Austriche et ses Environs
mwf0832	france paris	1686	JAILLOT	1500	47	61	Plan de la Ville, Cite, Universite, et Fauxbourgs de Paris avec les environs
mwbh0868	luxembourg	1741	JAILLOT	1350	38	50	Plan de Luxembourg
mwbh0867	luxembourg	1741	JAILLOT	1500	65	54	Plan de Luxembourg et de ses Environs
mwe0592	europe czech republic (bohemia)	1757	JAILLOT	1250	53	58	Plan de Prague et de se Environs
mwbh0663	belgium holland	1745	JAILLOT	350	51	62	Plan et Environs de Tournay
mwsp0506	spain regions	1706	JAILLOT	550	46	65	Principaute de Catalogne ou sont Compris les Comtes de Roussillon et de Cerdagne Divises en leurs Vigueries
mwe1045a	europe romania	1696	JAILLOT	550	48	61	Principauté de Transilvanie
mwbh0493	belgium holland	1700	JAILLOT	650	46	65	Provinces Unies des Pays-Bas
mwbh0464	belgium holland	1692	JAILLOT	750	57	76	Provinces-Unies des Pays-Bas
mwme0214	holy land	1697	JAILLOT		64	138	Theatre de la Terre Saincte qui represent les Lieux

AMPG REFERENCE	REGION	DATE	MAP MAKER	PRICE (UK£)	VERT. (cm.)	HOR. (cm.)	TITLE OF MAP (Comments by the editor in brackets)
mwas0434	asia south east	1705	JAILLOT	800	57	50	Troisieme Partie de l'Asie ou Partie de la Chine, les Isles de Borneo et Philippines &c.
mwas0199	asia continent	1782	JAILLOT-DESNOS	4000	117	134	L'Asie Divisee Suivant l'Estendue de ses Principales Parties. Revue Corrigee et Augmentee en 1782 (illustrated is the 1789 edition with a newly engraved inset top right showing the latest discoveries in Eastern Siberia)
mwam0905	america north (east)	1700	JAILLOT-MORTIER	5500	51	79	Carte Particuliere de Virginie, Maryland, Pennsilvanie, la Nouvelle Iarsey Orient et Occidentale
mwca0037	canada	1696	JAILLOT-MORTIER	1250	47	61	Le Canada ou Partie de la Nouvelle France dans l'Amerique Septentrionale, Contenant la Terre de Labrador, la Nouvelle France, les Isles de Terre Neuve (2nd state of map publ. in 1685)
mwam1381	america north (west)	1848	JAMES	320	33	24	A New Map of Mexico, California & Oregon
mwuss0770	maryland	1818	JAMES	975	34	39	Map of Maj. Gen. Ross's Route, with the British Column, from Benedict, on Patuxent River, to the City of Washington, August 1814
mwam0819	america north (central)	1823	JAMES	1500	38	52	Map of the Country Drained by the Mississippi
mwe1101	europe slovak republic (moravia)	1660	JANSSON	685	34	45	(Neutra) Nitria vulgo Neitra Superioris Hungariae Episcopatus et Oppidum
mwuss0665	louisiana	1818	JAMES	600	50	20	Plan of the Operations of the British & American Forces below New Orleans, on the 8th of January 1815
mwca0015	canada	1633	JAMES		31	40	The Platt of Sailing for the discoverye of a Passage into the South Sea. 1631. 1632.
mwru0476a	ukraine	1653	JANSSON	400	38	49	Pontus Euxinus
mwme0148	holy land	1658	JANSSON	3750	85	179	(The tribes of Israel, in 8 sheets, after Adrichom)
mwe1186a	europe west	1631	JANSSON		53	68	(Untitled sea chart, north to the right. Engraved by P. van den Keere)
mwec0814	uk england norfolk	1646	JANSSON	600	44	56	A General Plott and Description of the Fennes and Surounded Grounds in the six Counties of Norfolke, Suffolke, Cambridge, with in the Isle of Ely, Huntington, Northampton and Lincolne etc. (copied from Hondius)
mwit0260	italy abruzzo	1628	JANSSON	150	14	20	Abruzzo et Terra di Lavoro
mwsam0297	south america brazil	1648	JANSSON	1000	37	48	Accuratissima Brasiliae Tabula (re-issue of Hondius)
mwgr0074b	greece	1650	JANSSON	550	39	56	Achaiae Noua & accurata Descriptio Auctore I. Laurenbergio.
mwaf0477	africa egypt etc	1666	JANSSON	785	40	49	Aegypti Recentior Descriptio: Aegyptius & Turcis Elchibith; Arabibus Mesre & Misri, Hebraeis Mitsraim
mwaf0477a	africa egypt etc	1666	JANSSON	480	38	51	Aegyptus Antiqua
mwm0123	mediterranean east	1652	JANSSON	720	39	48	Aeneae Troiani Navigatio ad Virgilij Sex Priores Aeneidos
mwaf0860	africa south	1640	JANSSON	650	39	50	Aethiopia Inferior vel Exterior (as Blaeu 1635 but with 3 ships not 4.)
mwaf0359	africa east	1640	JANSSON	675	39	50	Aethiopie Superior vel Interior vulgo Abissinorum sive Presbiteri Ioannis Imperium (close copy of Blaeu)
mwf0732	france nord pas-de-calais	1653	JANSSON	450	43	51	Afbeeldinghe vande Vermaerde Seehaven ende Stadt van Duynkercken met der Omliggende Plaetsen Sanden ende Droochten (inset views of Dunkirk, Calais)
mwaf0690	africa north	1652	JANSSON	400	37	52	Africae Propriae Tabula. In qua, Punica Regna Vides, Tyrios, et Agenoris Urbem
mwas0340	asia central	1650	JANSSON	600	37	47	Alexandri Magni Macedonis Expeditio
mwaf0474	africa egypt etc	1657	JANSSON	1000	47	56	Alexandria Vetustissimum Aegypti Emporium
mwsw0062	switzerland	1639	JANSSON	400	38	50	Alpinae seu Foederatae Rhaetiae Subditarumque ei Terrarum Nova Descriptio
mwsam0018	south america	1631	JANSSON	280	14	19	America Meridionalis
mwam0046	america continent	1641	JANSSON	3000	38	50	America Noviter Delineata (by Hondius, with Jansson imprint)
mwam0314	america north	1641	JANSSON	3600	47	55	America Septentrionalis (re-issue of Hondius' map of 1636)
mwam0036	america continent	1628	JANSSON	720	15	20	Americae Descriptio (shows North America divided into two halves. Illustrated is Boisseau's 1643 re-issue with a changed title: 'Nouvelle description de l'Amerique'.)
mwsam0020	south america	1636	JANSSON	1000	46	54	Americae Pars Meridionalis
mwbh0189	belgium holland	1617	JANSSON	1000	27	39	Amstelodamum (based on Braun & Hogenberg, second state)
mwsp0409	spain regions	1628	JANSSON	150	13	19	Andalusia et Granada
mwsp0449	spain regions	1666	JANSSON	550	39	55	Andaluzia Continens Sevillam et Cordubam
mwuk0923	england	1646	JANSSON	750	39	50	Anglia Regnum
mwf0648	france loire	1628	JANSSON	150	14	19	Aniou
mwme0557	arabia etc	1658	JANSSON	2000	44	52	Arabiae Felicis, Petraeae et Desertae Nove et Accurata Delineatio
mwgr0583a	greece islands	1660	JANSSON	650	47	54	Archipelagi Meridionalis, seu Cycladum Insularum accurata Delineatio
mwf0221a	france alsace	1657	JANSSON	720	41	50	Argentina. Straßburg (enlarged copy of Merian)
mwm0122	mediterranean east	1652	JANSSON	720	38	50	Argonautica
mwsw0071	switzerland	1656	JANSSON	350	38	50	Argow cum Parte Merid. Zurichgow
mwsp0450	spain regions	1666	JANSSON	400	42	53	Arragonia Regnum
mwgr0063	greece	1639	JANSSON	550	36	49	Attica, Megarica, Corinthiaca, Boeotia, Phocis, Locri
mwe0321a	europe austria	1642	JANSSON	500	38	51	Austria Archiducatus Auctore Wolfgango Lazio

AMPG REFERENCE	REGION	DATE	MAP MAKER	PRICE (UK£)	VERT. (cm.)	HOR. (cm.)	TITLE OF MAP (Comments by the editor in brackets)
mwe0312	europe austria	1625	JANSSON	1650	39	51	Austria Archiducatus Nova Descriptio (dec. lower border with 4 town views. Map by Van Den Keere.)
mwg0333	bavaria	1639	JANSSON	300	38	47	Bavariae Superioris et Inferioris Nova Descriptio
mwam0862	america north (east)	1651	JANSSON	6500	44	51	Belgii Novi, Angliae Novae, et Partis Virginiae Novissima Delineatio (first of the Jansson-Visscher series)
mwsc0550	scandinavia norway	1657	JANSSON	1500	49	59	Berga Noorwegiae (re-issue of Braun & Hogenberg)
mwsc0536	scandinavia norway	1627	JANSSON	1600	25	55	Beschryvinge der Zeecusten van Noorweghen, Geleghen tusschen Berghen en Dronten
mwsp0451	spain regions	1666	JANSSON	480	38	50	Biscaia et Guipuscoa Cantabriae Veteris Pars. Amstelodami Apud Ioannem Ianssonium
mwsp0410	spain regions	1628	JANSSON	150	13	19	Biscaia, Guipiscoa, Navarra, et Asturias de Santillana
mwf0429	france central	1640	JANSSON	400	37	48	Bituricum Ducatus. Duche de Berri
mwe0538	europe czech republic (bohemia)	1647	JANSSON	600	38	50	Bohemia
mwe0532	europe czech republic (bohemia)	1628	JANSSON	150	14	19	Bohemia
mwe0536	europe czech republic (bohemia)	1636	JANSSON	720	41	47	Bohemia in suas Partes Geographice Distincta
mwe0528a	europe czech republic (bohemia)	1620	JANSSON	3000	48	56	Bohemia in suas Partes Geographice Distincta (3 carte-a-figure borders)
mwf0716	france nord pas-de-calais	1628	JANSSON	150	14	18	Bolonia et Guines Com
mwg0481	mecklenburg	1634	JANSSON	150	14	19	Brandeburg et Pomerania
mwg0202	germany north east	1633	JANSSON-BLAEU	500	39	52	Brandeburgum Marchionatus, cum Ducatibus Pomeraniae et Mekelenburgi
mwit0474	italy lombardy	1628	JANSSON	150	15	19	Brescia Episcopatus Mediolanum Ducatus
mwf1107	france rhone-alpes	1630	JANSSON	300	38	50	Bresse
mwuk1096	england and scotland	1646	JANSSON	3500	41	53	Britannia Prout Divisa fuit Temporibus Anglo-Saxonum, Praesertim Durante Illorum Heptarchia (based on Blaeu 1645)
mwec0062	uk england buckinghamshire	1646	JANSSON	785	41	51	Buckingamiae Comitatus cum Bedfordiensi; vulgo Buckinghamshire and Bedfordshire
mwf0402	france burgundy	1666	JANSSON	350	37	49	Burgundia Comitatus
mwit1005	italy south	1636	JANSSON	450	39	50	Calabria Citra olim Magna Graecia
mwit1014a	italy south	1652	JANSSON	350	39	49	Calabria Ultra, olim Altera Magnae Graeciae pars
mwuk1763a	wales	1647	JANSSON	785	36	49	Cambriae Typus (re-issue of Mercator 1607, shown above left)
mwec0606	uk england kent	1646	JANSSON	650	39	50	Cantium vernacule Kent
mwec0607	uk england kent	1657	JANSSON	800	29	43	Cantuarbury (Braun & Hogenberg's map with revised cartouche)
mwsam0299	south america brazil	1652	JANSSON	1000	44	54	Capitaniae de Cirii, et Parnambuco (north to the right)
mwsam0300	south america brazil	1652	JANSSON	1000	44	55	Capitaniarum de Phermanbuca, Itamaraca, Paraiba, et Rio Grande Nova Delineatio
mwf0391	france burgundy	1631	JANSSON	450	37	50	Carte Geometrique des Environs de l'Estang de Longpendu, d'ont leau Tombe dans l'Ocean et dans la Mediterranee Comprenant Grand Part du Comte du Charolois
mwg0450	hessen	1657	JANSSON	450	17	48	Cassel. - Cassula, Communiter Cassel, Florentissimu Lanigerae Oppidum (copy of Braun & Hogenberg 1572)
mwuk1758	wales	1646	JANSSON	480	39	50	Ceretica: sive Cardiganensis Comitatus; Anglia Cardigan shire (after Speed)
mwec0132	uk england cheshire	1646	JANSSON	785	41	51	Cestria Comitatus Palatinatus. The Countye Palatine of Chester
mwsam0448	south america chile	1666	JANSSON	600	37	48	Chili
mwc0019	china	1636	JANSSON	1400	41	50	China Veteribus Sinarum Regio nunc Incolis Tame Dicta (based on Blaeu)
mwg0788	westphalia	1647	JANSSON	300	38	50	Clivia Ducatus et Ravestein Dominium
mwg0522	rheinland-pfalz	1682	JANSSON	1400	39	50	Colonia Agrippina - Colln (Cologne)
mwg0789	westphalia	1647	JANSSON	300	38	49	Coloniensis Archiepiscopatus
mwec0090	uk england cambridgeshire	1646	JANSSON	720	41	51	Comitatis Cantabrigiensis; vernacule Cambridge shire
mwf0398	france burgundy	1656	JANSSON	400	42	53	Comitatus Burgundiae
mwec0257	uk england derbyshire	1646	JANSSON	600	39	49	Comitatus Darbiensis
mwec0325	uk england dorset	1646	JANSSON	785	41	51	Comitatus Dorcestria. vulgo Anglice Dorsetshire
mwuk0048	ireland	1638	JANSSON	480	39	49	Comitatus Lageniae. The Province of Leinster
mwec0677	uk england lancashire	1636	JANSSON	785	38	51	Comitatus Lancastrensis. The Countie Palatine of Lancaster
mwg0601	saxony	1647	JANSSON	375	38	48	Comitatus Mansfeldiae Descriptio
mwec0852	uk england northamptonshire	1646	JANSSON	500	41	51	Comitatus Northantonensis vernacule Northampton shire
mwec0879	uk england northumberland	1646	JANSSON	500	41	51	Comitatus Northumbria vernacule Northumberland
mwec0907	uk england nottinghamshire	1646	JANSSON	600	38	49	Comitatus Nottinghamiensis; sive Nottingham shire
mwuk1745	wales	1644	JANSSON	480	39	52	Comitatus Penbrochensis (incl. Caermarthenshire)
mwe0323b	europe austria	1647	JANSSON	500	40	52	Comitatus Tirolensis
mwg0263	baden-wurttemberg	1647	JANSSON	400	38	50	Comitatus Wertheimici Finitimarumque Regionum Nova et Exacta Descriptio
mwec0170	uk england cornwall	1646	JANSSON	800	37	49	Cornubia sive Cornwallia (8 coats of arms)

AMPG REFERENCE	REGION	DATE	MAP MAKER	PRICE (UK£)	VERT. (cm.)	HOR. (cm.)	TITLE OF MAP (Comments by the editor in brackets)
mwuk1382	england south	1628	JANSSON	150	14	20	Cornubia, Devonia, Somersetus, Dorcestria, Wiltonia, Glocestria, Monumetha, Glamorgan, Caermarden, Penbrok, Breknoke, et Herefordia
mwit0785	italy sardinia	1634	JANSSON	200	13	19	Corsica / Sardinia
mwbp0260	poland	1657	JANSSON	4000	37	106	Cracovia Metropolis Regni Poloniae (close copy of Braun & Hogenberg 1618)
mwgr0382a	greece crete	1652	JANSSON	400	38	49	Creta Iovis Magni, Medio Jacet Insula Ponto Ex Conatibus Geographicis Abrahami Ortely
mwec0223	uk england cumbria	1646	JANSSON	785	41	51	Cumbria & Westmoria, vulgo Cumberland & Westmorland
mwgr0473	greece cyprus	1628	JANSSON	560	18	25	Cyprus Insula
mwgr0478	greece cyprus	1640	JANSSON	1800	38	50	Cyprus Insula (copy of Blaeu)
mwgr0480	greece cyprus	1652	JANSSON	1200	35	48	Cyprus Insula Laeta Choris, Blandorum et Mater Amorum
mwme0864	syria etc	1657	JANSSON	1000	28	37	Damascus Urbs Nobilissima ad Libanu Montem, Syriae Metropols (based on Braun & Hogenberg)
mwsc0257	scandinavia denmark	1630	JANSSON	3000	47	54	Daniae Regni Typum (4 carte-a-figure borders)
mwsw0072	switzerland	1656	JANSSON	350	38	50	Das Wiflispurgergow
mwbh0285	belgium holland	1642	JANSSON	500	36	48	De Zype / Beemster / De Purmer / De Wormer / Caerte van Waterland
mwf0430	france central	1640	JANSSON	400	38	50	Description du Blaisois. Anno 1630
mwf0944	france picardy	1630	JANSSON	300	37	50	Description du Gouvernement de la Cappelle
mwec0286	uk england devon	1646	JANSSON	600	39	49	Devoniae Descriptio. The description of Devon-Shire
mwf0444	france champagne	1656	JANSSON	300	38	50	Diocese de Rheims, et le Pais de Rethel
mwsc0551	scandinavia norway	1658	JANSSON	600	43	53	Dioecesis Trundhemiensis Pars Australis
mwit1107	italy tuscany	1666	JANSSON	400	39	49	Dominio Fiorentino
mwit1184	italy veneto	1650	JANSSON	550	38	50	Dominium Venetum in Italia
mwit0348	italy emilia-romagna	1657	JANSSON	500	40	50	Piacenza
mwit0347a	italy emilia-romagna	1640	JANSSON	280	39	48	Ducato di Modena, Regio et Carpi, col Dominio della Carfagnana
mwit0476	italy lombardy	1635	JANSSON	320	38	49	Ducato, overo Territorio di Milano
mwbp0249	poland	1646	JANSSON	550	40	49	Ducatus Breslanus sive Wratislaviensis
mwec1305	uk england yorkshire	1646	JANSSON	785	41	51	Ducatus Eboracensis Pars borealis. The Northridinge of Yorke Shire
mwec1306	uk england yorkshire	1646	JANSSON	600	41	51	Ducatus Eboracensis pars Occidentalis; the Westriding of Yorke Shire
mwec1307	uk england yorkshire	1646	JANSSON	600	41	51	Ducatus Eboracensis pars orientalis. The Eastriding of Yorke Shire
mwec1308	uk england yorkshire	1646	JANSSON	1000	41	51	Ducatus Eboracensis. Anglice Yorkshire
mwg0703	schleswig-holstein	1650	JANSSON	500	38	51	Ducatus Holsatiae Nova Tabula (re-issue of Hondius 1629)
mwg0602	saxony	1647	JANSSON	375	38	48	Ducatus Lunebergensis
mwbh0837	luxembourg	1666	JANSSON	500	40	52	Ducatus Lutzenburgensis Nova et Accurata Descriptio
mwbh0824	luxembourg	1628	JANSSON	400	12	17	Ducatus Lutzenburgicus
mwbp0251	poland	1647	JANSSON	450	39	48	Ducatus Silesiae Ligniciensis
mwbp0246	poland	1640	JANSSON	400	39	48	Ducatus Silesiae Wolanus
mwru0042	russia	1645	JANSSON	500	47	55	Dwinae Fluvii, Nova Descriptio
mwgr0073a	greece	1650	JANSSON	785	39	51	Epirus, hodie vulgo Albania. Auctore J. Laurenbergio
mwsc0552	scandinavia norway	1658	JANSSON	600	44	53	Episcopatus Bergensis
mwec0363	uk england durham	1646	JANSSON	600	41	51	Episcopatus Dunelmensis Vulgo The Bishoprike of Durham
mwg0790	westphalia	1647	JANSSON	300	38	49	Episcopatus Paderbornensis Descriptio Nova
mwec0402	uk england essex	1646	JANSSON	600	39	50	Essexiae Descriptio. The Description of Essex
mwe0045	europe	1638	JANSSON	875	36	47	Europam sive Celticam Veterem. Sic Describere Conabar Abrahamus Ortelius (an apparently unrecorded Ortelius plate)
mwaf0779	africa north morocco	1647	JANSSON	500	38	50	Fezzae et Marocchi Regna Africae Celeberrima (re-issue of Blaeu)
mwbh0256	belgium holland	1639	JANSSON	400	38	48	Flandriae Pars Occidentalis Continens
mwit1132	italy florence	1657	JANSSON	2250	45	72	Florentia Pulcherrima Etruriae Civitas
mwg0451	hessen	1682	JANSSON	1400	40	51	Francofurtum - Franckfurt
mwg0338	bavaria	1645	JANSSON	400	42	54	Franconiae Nova Descriptio
mwsam0668	south america magellan	1640	JANSSON	720	38	51	Freti Magellanici ac Novi Freti vulgo Le Maire Exactissima Delineatio
mwf0048	france	1631	JANSSON	700	37	50	Gallia. Nova Galliae descriptio
mwf0049	france	1632	JANSSON	5000	46	56	Gallia. Nova Galliae descriptio (4 carte-a-figure borders)
mwf0057	france	1639	JANSSON	650	37	50	Galliae supra Omnes in hac Forma Editiones Locu Pletissima et Exactissima Descriptio (copy of Hondius 1639)
mwf0062	france	1650	JANSSON	550	45	56	Galliae, Nova et Accurata Descriptio vulgo Royaume de France
mwsp0417	spain regions	1631	JANSSON	150	14	19	Gallicia, Legio et Asturias de Oviedo
mwaf1123	africa west	1670	JANSSON	480	42	50	Genehoa, Jaloffi, et Sierraliones Regna
mwg0056	germany	1647	JANSSON	600	35	48	Germaniae Nova et Accurata Delineatio
mwg0058	germany	1650	JANSSON	300	38	47	Germaniae Veteris Nova Descriptio
mwec0436	uk england gloucestershire	1646	JANSSON	785	41	51	Glocestria Ducatus, cum Monumethensi Comitatu. Gloucester Shire & Monmouth Shire
mwsc0679b	scandinavia sweden	1666	JANSSON	600	39	49	Gothia
mwf0399	france burgundy	1656	JANSSON	350	42	52	Gouvernement General du Duche de Bourgogne, Comte de Bresse, Pays de Buge Valromey
mwsp0454	spain regions	1666	JANSSON	450	38	50	Granata, et Murcia Regna

AMPG REFERENCE	REGION	DATE	MAP MAKER	PRICE (UK£)	VERT. (cm.)	HOR. (cm.)	TITLE OF MAP (Comments by the editor in brackets)
mwbh0275	belgium holland	1640	JANSSON	550	38	50	Groninga Dominium. Auctore Bartholdo Wicheringe
mwaf1102	africa west	1636	JANSSON	600	38	52	Guinea
mwec0469	uk england hampshire	1646	JANSSON	785	41	51	Hantoniae Comitatus cum Bercheria
mwgr0083	greece	1666	JANSSON	950	36	50	Hellas seu Graecia Sophiani
mwgr0072	greece	1650	JANSSON	850	46	56	Hellas seu Graecia Universa Autore J. Laurenbergio
mwsw0079	switzerland	1666	JANSSON	600	41	52	Helvetiae Rhetiae & Valesiae cum Omnibus Finitimis Regionibus Tabula vulgo Schweitzerland
mwec0515	uk england herefordshire	1646	JANSSON	500	39	51	Herefordia comitatus vernacule Hereford Shire
mwsc0539	scandinavia norway	1634	JANSSON	1500	25	54	Het Niewe Landt van Spitzbergen (north to the left)
mwuk0046	ireland	1636	JANSSON	950	39	50	Hibernia Regnum vulgo Ireland. Amstelodami, Apud Ioannem Ianssonium (as Blaeu, except for 3 ships and 1 sea monster, shown above left)
mwgm0151	mexico	1628	JANSSON	300	13	18	Hispaniae Novae Nova Descriptio
mwuk1559	england islands	1646	JANSSON	650	41	51	Holy Iland / Garnsey / Farne / Jarsey
mwe0864a	europe hungary	1616	JANSSON	150	15	19	Hungaria (illustration below shows van der Aa re-issue of 1714 with changed title 'La Hongrie')
mwe0878b	europe hungary	1652	JANSSON	480	42	51	Hungaria Regnum (as Blaeu)
mwec0576	uk england huntingdonshire	1646	JANSSON	500	39	50	Huntingdonensis comitatus Huntingtonshire
mwjk0015	japan	1632	JANSSON	450	13	19	Iaponia
mwjk0021	japan	1651	JANSSON	480	15	19	Iaponia et Terra Esonis
mwjk0016	japan	1636	JANSSON	1500	34	44	Iaponiae Nova Descriptio
mwme0457a	jerusalem	1657	JANSSON	1400	36	47	Iherusalem Turcis Cusembareich (3 town views on one map)
mwc0047	china	1660	JANSSON	2000	47	52	Imperii Sinarum Nova Descriptio. Auctore, Joh. Van Loon
mwas0380	asia south east	1628	JANSSON	350	14	20	India Orientalis
mwas0386	asia south east	1644	JANSSON	1800	39	49	India quae Orientalis Dicitur, et Insulae Adiacentes (re-issue of Hondius)
mwas0383	asia south east	1634	JANSSON	2250	39	51	Indiae Orientalis Nova Descriptio
mwm0160a	mediterranean islands	1660	JANSSON	600	43	49	Insular Aliquot Aegaei Maris Antiqua Descrip (10 maps on one sheet)
mwas0582	asia south east borneo	1657	JANSSON	1500	42	53	Insula Borneo et Occidentalis Pars Celebis cum Adjacentibus Insulis
mwwi0015	west indies	1652	JANSSON	1500	40	51	Insula S. Juan de Puerto Rico Caribes, vel Canibalum Insulae
mwin0019	ceylon	1652	JANSSON	750	41	51	Insula Zeilan, olim Taprobana nunc Incolis Tenarisim
mwwi0012	west indies	1640	JANSSON	1500	38	53	Insulae Americanae in Oceano Septentrionali, cum Terris Adiacentibus. Amstelodami, Apud Ioannem Ianssonium (copied from Blaeu's map of 1635 and based on Gerritsz' map of 1631)
mwsp0646	balearic islands	1647	JANSSON	650	39	50	Insulae Balearides et Pytiusae
mwat0140	atlantic canary isl.	1657	JANSSON	850	42	53	Insulae Canariae, olim Fortunatae Dictae
mwf0472	france corsica	1669	JANSSON	800	39	51	Insulae Corsicae Nova & Accurata Descriptio
mwat0181	atlantic cape verde isl.	1652	JANSSON	550	43	53	Insulae de Cabo Verde, olim Hesperides, sive Gorgades: Belgice de Zoute Eylanden
mwas0630	asia south east java	1652	JANSSON	1000	42	51	Insulae Iavae cum Parte Insularum Borneo Sumatrae
mwsc0516	scandinavia jan mayen isl.	1657	JANSSON	700	44	55	Insulae Iohannis Mayen cum Universo Situ Sinuum et Promontoriorum Nova Descriptio
mwm0185	mediterranean malta	1650	JANSSON	2250	41	51	Insulae Melitae vulgo Malte Nova et Accurata Descriptio
mwit0788	italy sardinia	1644	JANSSON	1250	42	51	Insulae Sardiniae Nova & accurata descriptio (see Valk re-issue, 1700 for illustration)
mwgr0583	greece islands	1660	JANSSON	480	49	58	Insularum Archipelagi Septentrionalis seu Maris Aegaej Accurata Delineatio Auctore I. Laurenbergio
mwuk0706	uk	1646	JANSSON	650	39	51	Insularum Britannicarum Acurata Delineatio ex Geographicis Conatibus Abrahami Ortelii (based on Ortelius 1595)
mwwi0287	west indies (west)	1652	JANSSON	1200	41	53	Insularum Hispaniolae et Cubae cum Insulis Circumjacentibus Accurata Delineatio
mwas0712	asia south east moluccas	1640	JANSSON	550	38	50	Insularum Moluccarum Nova Descriptio. Amstelodami, Apud Ioannem Ianssonium
mwuk0047	ireland	1636	JANSSON	1200	33	41	Irlandiae Regnum (as Mercator-Hondius but with new cartouche and Mercator's signature removed)
mwit0280	italy campagna	1660	JANSSON	750	35	46	Ischia Isola olim Aenaria
mwme0778	persia etc	1657	JANSSON	1500	41	51	Isfahan (view)
mwit1008	italy south	1640	JANSSON	400	38	51	Italia Nam Tellus Graecia Maior Erat Ovid. IV. Fastor
mwit0587	italy north	1700	JANSSON	480	35	46	Italia Gallica sive Gallia Cisalpina
mwme0146	holy land	1652	JANSSON	1500	36	48	Iudaeae seu Terrae Israelis Tabula Geographica; in qua Locorum in Veteri et Novo Testamento Celebratissimorum Situs Accurate Descripti
mwg0791	westphalia	1647	JANSSON	300	38	50	Iuliacensis et Montensis Ducatus. De Hertoghdomen Gulick en Berghe
mwc0045	china	1658	JANSSON	1200	47	53	Iunnan, Queicheu, Quangsi et Quantung Provinciae Regni Sinensis (South West China)
mwf1112	france rhone-alpes	1631	JANSSON	300	35	46	La Principaute de Dombes
mwf0974	france poitou	1657	JANSSON	600	41	52	La Rochelle
mwf0973	france poitou	1645	JANSSON	500	45	56	La Saintonge vers le Septentrion avecq le Pays d'Aulnis et les Isles de Re et Oleron
mwsp0339	spain madrid	1657	JANSSON	4000	48	74	La Villa de Madrid Corte delos Reyes Catolicos de Espanna (re-issued by Van Der Aa in 1729)

AMPG REFERENCE	REGION	DATE	MAP MAKER	PRICE (UK£)	VERT. (cm.)	HOR. (cm.)	TITLE OF MAP (Comments by the editor in brackets)
mwe0495a	europe croatia	1654	JANSSON	450	38	50	Ladera, Sicum et Aenona Vulgo Zara, Sibenica et Nova cum Insula adjacentibus in Parte Dalmatiae Boreali
mwsc0266	scandinavia denmark	1645	JANSSON	480	41	53	Lalandiae et Falstriae Accurata Descriptio
mwec0679	uk england lancashire	1646	JANSSON	785	41	51	Lancastria Palatinus Anglis Lancaster & Lancasshire
mwit0399	italy lazio	1690	JANSSON	500	36	49	Latium
mwit0395	italy lazio	1628	JANSSON	150	15	20	Latium nunc Campagna di Roma
mwf0260	france aquitaine	1640	JANSSON	350	36	49	Le Comte de Perigort
mwf1185	france south west	1639	JANSSON	550	37	47	Le Diocese de Sarlat Dioccesis Sarlatensis
mwf0262	france aquitaine	1656	JANSSON	400	41	51	Le Duche d Aiguillon Trace par le Sr. du Vall
mwf0426	france central	1628	JANSSON	150	14	18	Le Duche d'Berry
mwf0281	france auvergne	1640	JANSSON	350	38	49	Le Duche de Auvergne
mwf0725	france nord pas-de-calais	1640	JANSSON	600	40	51	Le Gouvernement de Calais & Pais Reconquis
mwf0571	france ile de france	1633	JANSSON	450	38	50	Le Gouvernement de l'Isle de France
mwf1187	france south west	1645	JANSSON	350	38	50	Le Pais de Bearn
mwf0773	france normandy	1656	JANSSON	300	37	50	Le Pais de Caux
mwsp0455	spain regions	1666	JANSSON	400	38	49	Legionis Regnum et Asturiarum Principatus
mwec0714	uk england leicestershire	1646	JANSSON	600	41	51	Leicestrensis comitatus cum Rutlandiae
mwbh0213	belgium holland	1628	JANSSON	150	13	20	Leodiensis Dioecesis
mwec0739	uk england lincolnshire	1646	JANSSON	600	41	51	Lincolnia Comitatus Anglis Lyncolne shire
mwf1116	france rhone-alpes	1634	JANSSON	375	38	50	Lionnois, Forest, et Beaviolois
mwf1115	france rhone-alpes	1634	JANSSON	150	13	19	Lionnois, Forest, et Beaviolois
mwf0572	france ile de france	1634	JANSSON	150	13	19	L'Isle de France Parisiensis Agri Descriptio
mwuk0401	scotland	1659	JANSSON	675	44	53	Lochabria, omnesq Insulae versus Occidentem Sitae, ut Uisto, Mulla, aliaeque
mwuk1114	england london	1657	JANSSON	3000	34	49	Londinum Vulgo London (based on Braun & Hogenberg 1572)
mwuk0406	scotland	1664	JANSSON	500	45	54	Lorna, Knapdalia, Cantire, Iura, Ila, Glota, et Buthe Insulae
mwf0677	france lorraine	1666	JANSSON	350	42	54	Lotharingia Ducatus Nova descriptio
mwf0669	france lorraine	1634	JANSSON	150	13	20	Lotharingia Meridionalis
mwsw0075	switzerland	1657	JANSSON	1800	31	48	Lucerna Helvetiorum vulgo Lucernn (view)
mwm0032	mediterranean	1700	JANSSON	480	39	93	Lumen Historiarum per Occidentem ex Conatibus Fran. Haraei Antuerpiae / Lumen Historiarum per Orientem, Illustrandis Biblijs Sacris, Martyrologio, & alijs Multis a Fran. Hareio Concinnatum
mwf0826	france paris	1657	JANSSON	2400	43	53	Lutetia Parisiorum vulgo Paris
mwbh0828a	luxembourg	1640	JANSSON	600	37	47	Lutzenburg Ducatus (shown above left)
mwgr0074a	greece	1650	JANSSON	550	41	58	Macedonia Alexandri M. Patria Illustris Auctore I. Laurenbergio.
mwuk0707	uk	1646	JANSSON	1500	42	53	Magnae Britanniae et Hiberniae Nova Descriptio
mwsc0412	scandinavia finland	1658	JANSSON	1500	44	53	Magni Ducatus Finlandiae Nova et accurata delineatio
mwin0103	india	1641	JANSSON	750	37	50	Magni Mogolis Imperium (with Jansson's imprint)
mwat0106	atlantic bermuda	1633	JANSSON	2500	39	51	Mappa Aestivarum Insularum, alias Barmudas Dictarum ... Accurate Descripta
mwat0253	atlantic north	1650	JANSSON	1500	44	56	Mar del Nort
mwp0229	pacific (all)	1650	JANSSON	2500	44	54	Mar del Zur Hispanis Mare Pacificum
mwp0237	pacific (all)	1688	JANSSON	3500	44	54	Mar del Zur Hispanis Mare Pacificum (As 1650 but incl. Tasman's discoveries etc. Publ. by A. Wolfgang)
mwat0300	atlantic south	1652	JANSSON	650	44	56	Mar di Aethiopia vulgo Oceanus Aethiopicus
mwin0409	indian ocean	1650	JANSSON	2500	44	56	Mar di India
mwit0552	italy marches	1631	JANSSON	150	14	19	Marcha Anconitana cum Spoletano Ducatu
mwe1099	europe slovak republic (moravia)	1640	JANSSON	480	37	50	Marchionatus Moraviae Auct. I. A. Comenio
mwe0707	europe danube	1666	JANSSON	500	45	52	Maximi Totius Europae Fluminis Danubii Cursus per Germaniam Hungariamque Nova Delineatio
mwit0533	italy milan	1658	JANSSON	1650	41	51	Mediolanum vulgo Milanen (re-issued by De Wit, 1695)
mwuk1759	wales	1646	JANSSON	480	39	50	Mervina; et Montgomeria Comitatus (after Speed)
mwf0675a	france lorraine	1657	JANSSON	600	40	50	Metz
mwec0770	uk england middlesex	1646	JANSSON	1000	41	51	Middelsexiae cum Hertfordiae comitatu: Midlesex & Hertford Shire
mwuk0037	ireland	1628	JANSSON	150	13	19	Momonia et Lagenia
mwuk1560	england islands	1646	JANSSON	650	44	54	Mona Insula Vulgo Anglesey / Mona Insula: Vulgo The Isle of Man / Vectis Insula Anglice The Isle of Wight
mwg0792	westphalia	1647	JANSSON	300	37	48	Monasteriensis Episcopatus. Amstelodami, Apud Ioannem Ianssonium
mwgr0057	greece	1628	JANSSON	150	15	20	Morea olim Peloponensis
mwgr0064	greece	1639	JANSSON	400	34	41	Morea olim Peloponnesus. Per Gerardum Mercatorem
mwru0035	russia	1628	JANSSON	200	14	20	Moscovia
mwru0382	russia moscow	1657	JANSSON	1800	35	46	Moscovia Urbs Metropolis Totius Russiae Albae
mwme0945	turkey etc	1647	JANSSON	600	39	50	Natolia, quae olim Asia Minor
mwsp0456	spain regions	1666	JANSSON	400	43	53	Navarra Regnum
mwit1009	italy south	1640	JANSSON	600	43	52	Neapolitanum Regnum
mwaf1122a	africa west	1670	JANSSON	750	38	50	Nigritarum Regnum
mwg0187	elbe river	1650	JANSSON	960	37	52	Nobilis Fluvius Albis (inset view of Hamburg)
mwec0815	uk england norfolk	1657	JANSSON	650	29	42	Nordovicum (Braun & Hogenberg's map revised)
mwec0813	uk england norfolk	1646	JANSSON	600	41	51	Nortfolcia; vernacule Norfolke

AMPG REFERENCE	REGION	DATE	MAP MAKER	PRICE (UK£)	VERT. (cm.)	HOR. (cm.)	TITLE OF MAP (Comments by the editor in brackets)
mwuk1355	england north	1634	JANSSON	150	14	20	Northumbria, Cumberlandia, Dunelmesis, Episc. Westmorlandia, et Mania Ins.
mwsc0048	scandinavia	1634	JANSSON	240	13	19	Norvegia et Suecia
mwam0857	america north (east)	1636	JANSSON	2500	39	50	Nova Anglia Novum Belgium et Virginia
mwaf0687	africa north	1638	JANSSON	600	35	52	Nova Barbariae Descriptio
mwam0859	america north (east)	1647	JANSSON	2000	39	51	Nova Belgica et Anglia Nova
mwit1106a	italy tuscany	1654	JANSSON	550	35	49	Nova & accurata Tvsciae Antiquae Descriptio
mwsc0268a	scandinavia denmark	1646	JANSSON	350	40	51	Nova et Accurata descriptio totius Fioniae vulgo Funen (copied by Valk & Schenk 1700)
mwjk0026	japan	1658	JANSSON	1650	45	54	Nova et Accurata Japoniae Terrae Esonis.
mwaa0084	arctic	1637	JANSSON	1350	41	53	Nova et Accurata Poli Arctici et Terrarum Circum Iacentium Descriptio (later issue illustrated, c1700)
mwsc0540	scandinavia norway	1636	JANSSON	720	40	50	Nova et accurata tabula Episcopatuum Stavangriensis, Bergensis et Asloiensis Vicinarumque aliquot territoriorum
mwru0054	russia	1659	JANSSON	720	47	56	Nova et Accurata Wolgae Fluminis, olim Rha Dicti Delineatio (illustrated is Blaeu issue)
mwe0033	europe	1624	JANSSON		119	167	Nova et Acurata Totius Europae Tabula, Auct: Guil Ianssonio (map surrounded by text)
mwe0037	europe	1630	JANSSON	6000	41	56	Nova Europae Descriptio (4 carte-a-figure borders)
mwg0327	bavaria	1626	JANSSON	1600	45	55	Nova Franconiae Descriptio (4 carte-a-figure borders)
mwf0053	france	1634	JANSSON	180	14	19	Nova Galliae Tabulae
mwg0052	germany	1632	JANSSON	4500	47	56	Nova Germaniae Descriptio (4 carte-a-figure borders, mounted royalty in upper border)
mwg0052a	germany	1632	JANSSON	4000	42	55	Nova Germaniae Descriptio (4 carte-a-figure borders)
mwsw0054	switzerland	1630	JANSSON	2500	41	54	Nova Helvetiae Tabula (4 carte-a-figure borders. Map engraved by Hondius.)
mwsw0064	switzerland	1642	JANSSON	600	36	48	Nova Helvetiae Tabula (based on the previous map, but without the decorative borders)
mwgm0158	mexico	1636	JANSSON	875	35	48	Nova Hispania et Nova Galicia
mwsp0177	spain	1630	JANSSON	5500	46	56	Nova Hispaniae Descriptio (all borders with cartes-a-figures)
mwbp0252a	poland	1650	JANSSON	750	38	49	Nova Illustrissimi Ducatus Pomeraniae … Eilhardo Lubino edita
mwbh0377	belgium holland	1666	JANSSON	950	45	55	Nova Totius Belgii sive Germaniae Inferioris Accuratissima Delineatio
mwg0074	germany	1680	JANSSON	720	44	52	Nova Totius Germaniae Descriptio
mwgr0061	greece	1636	JANSSON	650	36	47	Nova Totius Graeciae Descriptio
mwbp0086	baltic states	1653	JANSSON	750	38	51	Nova Totius Livoniae Accurata Descriptio. Apud Joan Janssonium
mww0153	world	1641	JANSSON	8000	38	54	Nova Totius Terrarum Orbis Geographica ac Hydrographica Tabula (as Hondius but with Jansson imprint)
mwuss1607	virginia	1649	JANSSON	1500	38	49	Nova Virginiae Tabula
mwuss1596	virginia	1628	JANSSON	600	14	19	Nova Virginiae Tabula
mwru0046	russia	1650	JANSSON	960	41	51	Nova Zemla, Waygats, Fretum Nassovicum, et Terra Samoiedum
mwbp0252	poland	1650	JANSSON	900	44	54	Novissima Poloniae Regni Descriptio
mwsam0290	south america brazil	1640	JANSSON	1850	32	47	Olinda de Phernambuco
mwsp0036	portugal	1657	JANSSON	1200	40	50	Olisippo. Lisabona (view)
mwuk0402	scotland	1659	JANSSON	600	41	51	Orcadum et Schetlandiae Insularum Accuratissima Descriptio
mwec0943	uk england oxfordshire	1651	JANSSON	150	15	20	Oxoniensis Comitatus Descriptio
mwec0942	uk england oxfordshire	1646	JANSSON	1000	41	51	Oxonium Comitatus. Vulgo Oxford shire
mwg0330	bavaria	1631	JANSSON	150	14	19	Palatinatus Bavariae
mwbp0277	poland	1664	JANSSON	750	46	54	Palatinatus Posnaniensis, in Maiori Polonia Primarii Nova Delinatio per G.F.M.(copy of Blaeu 1664)
mwme0089	holy land	1630	JANSSON	2800	43	56	Palestina, sive Terrae Sanctae Descriptio (north to the left)
mwit0491	italy lombardy	1660	JANSSON	400	38	49	Parte Alpestre dello Stato di Milano con il Lago Maggiore di Lugano, e di Como
mwbp0016	baltic sea (east)	1650	JANSSON	1350	43	55	Pascaart van de Oost-Zee Vertoonende in sich, Alle Gelegentheden (based on Jacobsz 1644)
mwsp0042	portugal	1660	JANSSON	850	44	54	Pascaart vande Custen van Andaluzia, Portugal, Gallissien, en een Gedeelt van Vranckryck
mwuk1644	north sea	1650	JANSSON	2500	44	55	Pascaart vande Noort-Zee (north to the right)
mwuk0031	ireland	1625	JANSSON	1500	25	54	Pascaart vande Oostzyde van Yerlandt van Waterfoort tot Carlingfoord
mwaa0088	arctic	1650	JANSSON	1500	44	55	Pascaart vande Zee-Custen van Finmarcken, Laplant, Ruslant, Nova Zembla en Spitsbergen
mwuk0709	uk	1650	JANSSON	1500	43	55	Pascaart Vant Canaal Tusschen Engelant en Vrancryck, alsmede geheel Ierlant en Schotlant (4 editions in 1650)
mwaf1108	africa west	1650?	JANSSON	1000	41	54	Pascaart, waer in Men Claarlyck Zien can, Alle Havens Rivieren Droogten, Gelegen tusschen C.S. Vincent en C. Verde
mwm0004	mediterranean	1638	JANSSON	3000	42	97	Pascaarte … Middelandsche Zee … Tabula Hydrographica
mwat0250	atlantic north	1634	JANSSON	2000	25	54	Pascaarte van de Custen van Hitlandt Yslandt ende voort naer Oudt-Groenlandt en nade Straet Davies
mwuk0343	scotland	1634	JANSSON	1200	25	54	Pascaarte van de Eylanden van Fero ofte Farre / Eygentlycke afbeeldinghe vande Eylanden Hitlandt anders Scetlandt …

AMPG REFERENCE	REGION	DATE	MAP MAKER	PRICE (UK£)	VERT. (cm.)	HOR. (cm.)	TITLE OF MAP (Comments by the editor in brackets)
mwsc0537	scandinavia norway	1627	JANSSON	2000	25	54	Pascaarte van Noorweghen, Vertoonende de Zee-Custen Geleghen tusschen der Neus en Berghen
mwm0008	mediterranean	1652	JANSSON	4000	42	54	Pascaarte van 't Westelyckste Deel vande Middelandsche-Zee / Pascaarte van 't Oostelyckste Deel vande Middelandsche Zee (2 charts)
mwat0136	atlantic canary isl.	1625	JANSSON	1500	25	54	Pascaarte vande Eijlanden van Canarien (re-issue of Blaeu 1608)
mwat0239	atlantic madeira	1625	JANSSON	1500	25	54	Pascaarte vande Eylanden van Madera ende Porto Santo
mwbp0008	baltic sea (east)	1634	JANSSON	2000	25	54	Pascaarte vande Finlandsche Cust van Elsenvos tot Wyburgh (now the entrance to St Petersburg)
mwsc0538	scandinavia norway	1627	JANSSON	2000	25	54	Pascaarte vant Noordersche Deel van Noorwegen van Dronten aff Tot om de Noortcaap toe
mwuk1420	england thames	1634	JANSSON	1500	25	54	Pascaarte verthoonende de mont vande Teemse, die Rivier van London (North to the right. Inset: the Thames to London)
mwsp0408	spain regions	1625	JANSSON	1500	25	54	Pascaerte vande Zeecuste van Galissien tusschen de C. de Pinas, ende de C. de Finisterre
mwit0637	italy piedmont	1634	JANSSON	150	14	19	Pedemontana Regio cum Genvensium Territorio & Montisferrati Marchionatu
mwgr0073	greece	1650	JANSSON	785	46	55	Peloponnesus sive Morea
mwuk1760	wales	1646	JANSSON	480	39	50	Penbrochia Comitatus et Comitatus Caermardinum (after Speed)
mwme0775	persia etc	1647	JANSSON	720	38	49	Persia, sive Sophorum Regnum
mwme0769	persia etc	1631	JANSSON	200	13	19	Persici vel Sophorum Regni Typus
mwit1155	italy umbria	1657	JANSSON	750	36	44	Perusia (view)
mwf0945	france picardy	1634	JANSSON	150	14	20	Picardia
mwf0951a	france picardy	1666	JANSSON	320	40	55	Picardia Vera et Inferior
mwf1095	france pyrenees	1657	JANSSON	450	41	52	Plan de la Ville de Tholouse (copy of Tavernier 1631)
mwf0965	france poitou	1628	JANSSON	200	13	19	Poictou
mwbp0242	poland	1639	JANSSON	800	39	50	Poloniae Nova et Acurata Descriptio
mwaa0006	antarctic	1639	JANSSON	2800	44	49	Polus Antarcticus
mwsp0044	portugal	1666	JANSSON	450	39	50	Portugallia et Algarbia quae olim Lusitania. Auctore Vernando Alvaro Secco. Amstelodami Apud Joannem Janssonium (re-issue of Blaeu)
mwsp0024	portugal	1628	JANSSON	200	14	20	Portugallia et Algarve
mwbh0322	belgium holland	1650	JANSSON	600	41	53	Prima Pars Brabantiae cuius Caput Lovanium
mwit0282	italy campagna	1660	JANSSON	300	38	49	Principato Citra olim Picentia
mwit0644	italy piedmont	1660	JANSSON	400	42	53	Principatus Pedemontii
mwuk1761	wales	1646	JANSSON	480	39	50	Principatus Walliae borealis Vulgo North Wales (after Speed)
mwuk1762	wales	1646	JANSSON	550	39	50	Principatus Walliae pars australis: Vulgo South-Wales (after Speed)
mwf1006	france provence	1639	JANSSON	480	38	50	Provincia - La Provence
mwuk0064	ireland	1659	JANSSON	480	41	51	Provincia Connachtiae. The Province of Connaugt
mwec1299	uk england yorkshire	1636	JANSSON	800	39	50	Provincia Eboracensis. Yorkshire
mwuk0065	ireland	1659	JANSSON	600	41	51	Provincia Ultoniae. The Province of Ulster
mwf0999	france provence	1628	JANSSON	200	13	19	Provincia, la Provence
mwec0604	uk england kent	1644	JANSSON	1000	38	50	Provinciae Cantii Vulgo Kendt Nova Descriptio
mwuk0410	scotland	1666	JANSSON	500	37	54	Provinciae Lauden seu Lothien et Linlitouo
mwuk0066	ireland	1659	JANSSON	480	41	51	Provinciae Momoniae
mwbp0247	poland	1640	JANSSON	750	38	49	Prussia Accurate Descripta
mwit1004	italy south	1634	JANSSON	150	13	19	Puglia Piana Terra di Barri Otranto etc.
mwbh0297	belgium holland	1647	JANSSON	1200	41	52	Quarta Pars Brabantiae cujus Caput Sylvaducis
mwf1091	france pyrenees	1631	JANSSON	300	38	50	Quercy Cadurcium
mwuk1763	wales	1646	JANSSON	480	39	50	Radnoriensis Comitatus Vulgo The Countie of Radnor (after Blaeu)
mwaf1115	africa west	1666	JANSSON	675	41	50	Regna Congo et Angola (north to the left)
mwsc0293	scandinavia denmark	1666	JANSSON	500	46	57	Regni Daniae Accuratissima delineatio
mwsc0553	scandinavia norway	1658	JANSSON	1100	43	54	Regni Norvegiae Nova et Accurata Descriptio (north to the left)
mwsp0419	spain regions	1634	JANSSON	150	14	18	Regni Valentiae Typus
mwit0415	italy liguria	1630	JANSSON	700	37	49	Reipublicae Genuensis Ducatus et Dominii Nova Discrip.
mwe0996	europe rhine	1647	JANSSON	1200	42	94	Rhenus Fluviorum Europae Celeberrimus, cum Mosa, Mosella, et Reliquis, in illum se Exonerantibus Fluminibus
mwbp0089	baltic states	1660	JANSSON	1000	40	51	Riga (view)
mwit0419	italy liguria	1658	JANSSON	400	38	50	Riviera di Genova di Levante
mwit0420	italy liguria	1658	JANSSON	400	43	52	Riviera di Genova di Ponente
mwf0767	france normandy	1631	JANSSON	6600	62	205	Rotomagum vulgo Rouen, Emporium Galliae Celeberimum Opulentum, Amplum ac Vetustum (view of Rouen and text below)
mwf1122	france rhone-alpes	1644	JANSSON	480	38	50	Sabaudia Ducatus. Savoye
mwec1006	uk england shropshire	1646	JANSSON	675	41	51	Salopsiensis comitatus cum Staffordiensi. Shropshire & Staffordshire
mwe0325	europe austria	1657	JANSSON	1200	38	48	Saltzburg
mwe0323a	europe austria	1647	JANSSON	500	38	48	Saltzburg archiepiscopatus cum ducatu Carinthiae (shown below left)

AMPG REFERENCE	REGION	DATE	MAP MAKER	PRICE (UK£)	VERT. (cm.)	HOR. (cm.)	TITLE OF MAP (Comments by the editor in brackets)
mwe0314	europe austria	1628	JANSSON	150	13	18	Saltzburg et Carinthie
mwuk0338	scotland	1628	JANSSON	360	15	20	Schotia
mwe1122d	europe slovenia	1628	JANSSON	200	13	19	Sclavonia Croatia Bosnia cum Dalmatiae Parte
mw1122f	europe slovenia	1649	JANSSON	350	36	45	Sclavonia, Croatia, Bosnia cum Dalmatiae Parte (copy of Mercator)
mwuk0352	scotland	1650	JANSSON	900	35	40	Scotia Regnum (based on Mercator)
mwuk0411	scotland	1666	JANSSON	720	39	51	Scotia Regnum (close copy of Blaeu)
mwuk0351	scotland	1650	JANSSON	1200	35	45	Scotiae pars Septentrionalis / Pars Scotiae Australis (2 sheets, each 35x45cm.)
mwuk0403	scotland	1659	JANSSON	600	43	52	Scotiae Provinciae intra Flumen Taum, et Murra Fyrth Sitae, Utpote Moravia, Badenocha, Atholia, Aberdonia, Baneia et Mernis
mwsc0268	scandinavia denmark	1646	JANSSON	400	44	53	Selandiae in Regno Daniae Insulae Chorographica Descriptio
mwaa0080	arctic	1628	JANSSON	500	15	20	Septentrionalium Terrarum descript.
mwit0890	italy sicily	1650	JANSSON	1200	40	49	Sicilia Regnum
mwit0890a	italy sicily	1657	JANSSON	720	39	49	Siciliae Veteris Typus
mwit0642	italy piedmont	1647	JANSSON	480	38	50	Signoria di Vercelli
mwbp0279	poland	1666	JANSSON	450	39	49	Silesiae Ducatus Accurata et Vera Delineatio
mwbp0249a	poland	1646	JANSSON	650	39	50	Silesiae Ducatus Nova et accurata Descriptio
mwin0383	india bay of bengal	1657	JANSSON	1200	47	54	Sinus Gangeticus; vulgo Golfo de Bengala Nova Descriptio
mwec1034	uk england somerset	1646	JANSSON	600	38	50	Somersettensis comitatus. Somerset Shire
mwsc0550a	scandinavia norway	1657	JANSSON	1200	41	51	Spitzberga
mwit0300	italy central	1660	JANSSON	550	41	53	Stato della Chiesa con la Toscana
mwsc0065	scandinavia	1666	JANSSON	960	47	55	Sueciae, Norvegiae, et Daniae, Nova Tabula
mwec1097	uk england suffolk	1646	JANSSON	500	38	50	Suffolcia vernacula Suffolke
mwas0876	asia south east sumatra	1657	JANSSON	960	42	52	Sumatrae et Insularum Locorumque Nonnullorum Circumiacentium Tabula Nova
mwec1130	uk england surrey	1646	JANSSON	1500	41	51	Surria. vernacule Surrey
mwec1159	uk england sussex	1646	JANSSON	1000	39	51	Suthsexia vernacule Sussex
mwme0865	syria etc	1658	JANSSON	960	44	52	Syriae sive Soriae Nova et Accurata Descriptio
mwe0539	europe czech republic (bohemia)	1657	JANSSON	720	34	45	Tabor Civitas Anno 1621 Obsessa et Capta
mwsc0047	scandinavia	1631	JANSSON	900	45	56	Tabula Exactissima Regnorum Sueciae et Norvegiae (based on Veen's 1613 map)
mwsc0490	scandinavia iceland	1638	JANSSON	720	38	49	Tabula Islandiae Auctore Georgio Carolo Flandro
mwit0081	italy	1631	JANSSON	280	15	20	Tabula Italiae Corsicae, Sardiniae et Adjacentium Regnorum
mwit0087	italy	1640	JANSSON	5000	46	54	Tabula Italiae, Corsicae, Sardiniae, et Adjacentium Regnorum (4 carte-a-figure borders. First edition 1628. Close copy of Visscher 1625)
mwme0145a	holy land	1651	JANSSON	480	38	52	Tabula Itineraria Patriarcharum Abrahami, Isaaci et Jacobi
mwuk0404	scotland	1659	JANSSON	785	41	51	Tabula Leogi et Haraiae, ac Skive vel Skianae Insularum
mwsam0670	south america magellan	1657	JANSSON	1000	41	54	Tabula Magellanica, qua Tierrae del Fuego, cum Celeberrimis Fretis a F. Magellano et I. Le Maire Detectis Novissima et Accuratissima Descriptio Exhibetur
mwit0575	italy north	1628	JANSSON	150	14	19	Taravisina Marchia et Tirolis Comitatus
mwru0422	russia tartary	1634	JANSSON	200	14	19	Tartaria (first issued by Hondius in 1608)
mwru0424	russia tartary	1640	JANSSON	650	38	50	Tartaria sive Magni Chami Imperium
mwru0476	ukraine	1644	JANSSON	450	38	50	Taurica Chersonesus, hodie Przecopsca, et Gazara Dicitur
mwsam0498	south america colombia	1650	JANSSON	900	38	49	Terra Firma et Novum Regnum Granatense et Popayan
mwme0088	holy land	1628	JANSSON	240	13	19	Terra Sancta quae in Sacris Terra Promissionis ol. Palestina
mwg0518	rheinland-pfalz	1647	JANSSON	400	40	52	Territorii Novoforensis. In Superiore Palatinatu Accurata Descriptio
mwit0488	italy lombardy	1647	JANSSON	400	38	48	Territorio di Cremona
mwit1108	italy tuscany	1666	JANSSON	450	39	50	Territorio di Siena, con il Ducato di Castro
mwit1183	italy veneto	1647	JANSSON	500	38	49	Territorio di Verona
mwf0219	france alsace	1647	JANSSON	350	38	49	Territorium Argentoratense. Petrus Kaerius Caelavit
mwg0447	hessen	1640	JANSSON	500	38	49	Territorium Francofurtense
mwf0221	france alsace	1656	JANSSON	400	38	49	Territorium Metense Auctore AB. Fabert Consule Urbis Metensis. Le Pais Messin
mwsw0073	switzerland	1656	JANSSON	350	38	49	Territory Basiliensis Nova Descriptio
mwec0130	uk england cheshire	1636	JANSSON	785	38	50	The Countye Palatine of Chester. Comitatus Cestrensis
mwgr0074	greece	1650	JANSSON	550	39	51	Thessaliae Accurata Descriptio
mwgr0130	greece	1700	JANSSON	350	37	49	Thraciae Veteris Typus
mwg0740	thuringia	1640	JANSSON	280	38	48	Thuringiae Nova Descriptio
mwe0315	europe austria	1628	JANSSON	150	14	17	Tirolensis
mwg0342	bavaria	1647	JANSSON	400	39	49	Totius Sueviae Novissima Tabula. Amstelodami ex Officina Ioannis Ianssonii
mwf0431	france central	1640	JANSSON	400	38	49	Touraine - Turonensis Ducatus
mwru0045	russia	1646	JANSSON	400	41	49	Tractuum Borussiae, circa Gedanum et Elbingam, ab Incolis Werder Appellati, cum Adiuncta Neringia, Nova et Elaboratissima Delineatio
mwe0756	europe east	1628	JANSSON	150	15	20	Transylvania
mwme0549	arabia etc	1628	JANSSON	280	13	19	Turcici Imperii Imago
mwme0558	arabia etc	1658	JANSSON	800	42	52	Turcicum Imperium (almost an exact copy of Blaeu, lacking right-hand cartouche)
mwit1101	italy tuscany	1631	JANSSON	200	14	18	Tuscia

AMPG REFERENCE	REGION	DATE	MAP MAKER	PRICE (UK£)	VERT. (cm.)	HOR. (cm.)	TITLE OF MAP (Comments by the editor in brackets)
mwru0477	ukraine	1657	JANSSON	1250	42	54	Typus Generalis Ukrainae sive Palatinatuum Podoliae, Kioviensis et Braczlaviensis Terras Nova Delineatione Exhibens (illustrated is the Moses Pitt re-issue c1680)
mwsp0189	spain	1666	JANSSON	600	35	48	Typus Hispaniae (copy of Hondius 1631)
mwat0256	atlantic north	1659	JANSSON	1500	43	53	Typus Maritimus Groenlandiae, Islandiae, Freti Davidis, Insulae Iohannis Mayen
mww0135	world	1628	JANSSON	960	15	20	Typus Orbis Terrarum
mwuk0038	ireland	1628	JANSSON	150	14	20	Ultonia, Conatia, et Media
mwit1156	italy umbria	1658	JANSSON	400	38	49	Umbria overo Ducato di Spoleto
mwsc0675a	scandinavia sweden	1651	JANSSON	600	36	49	Uplandia
mwit0717	italy rome	1657	JANSSON	1350	38	51	Urbis Romae (after Braun & Hogenberg)
mwf0220	france alsace	1647	JANSSON	360	39	54	Utriusquae Alsatiae Superioris ac Inferioris Nova Tabula
mwsp0457	spain regions	1666	JANSSON	400	41	52	Utriusque Castiliae Nova Descriptio
mwsp0458	spain regions	1666	JANSSON	400	36	48	Valentia Regnum. Cotestani. Ptol. Edentani Plin.
mwsp0421	spain regions	1634	JANSSON	150	14	20	Valentia, Murcia cum Insulis Majorca, Minorca et Yvica
mwm0187	mediterranean malta	1657	JANSSON	1350	42	51	Valetta Civitas Nova Maltae olim Millitae
mwit1224	italy venice	1657	JANSSON	8000	46	102	Venetia
mwg0263a	baden-wurttemberg	1657	JANSSON	1200	45	80	Vera Totius Marchionatus Badensis, et Hochbergensis (illustrated is re-issue by M. Pitt 1680)
mwit1174	italy veneto	1634	JANSSON	150	15	19	Verona, Vicentiae et Pataviae Dit.
mwe0411	europe austria vienna	1657	JANSSON	1800	39	50	Vienna Austriae. Wien in Oostenreyk (illlustrated is c1695 re-issue by De Wit)
mwuss1606	virginia	1648	JANSSON	720	14	19	Virginia
mwuss1604	virginia	1639	JANSSON	1800	38	49	Virginiae Partis Australis, et Floridae Partis Orientalis, interjacentiumq. Regionum Nova Descriptio (copy of Blaeu's map of 1638)
mwsc0255	scandinavia denmark	1625	JANSSON	450	24	55	Waare Afbeeldinge der Zeecusten vant Noorder Deel van Jutlant
mwe0757	europe east	1628	JANSSON	150	15	20	Walachia Servia, Bulgaria et Romania
mwe0759	europe east	1642	JANSSON	550	34	46	Walachia, Servia, Bulgaria, Romania
mwuk1381	england south	1628	JANSSON	150	15	20	Warwicum Northamptonia, Huntingdonia, Cantabrigia, Suffolcia, Oxonium, Buckinghamia, Bedfordia, Hartfordia, Essexia, Berceria, Middelsexia, Southhamtonia, Surria, Catium, et Southsexia
mwec1274	uk england worcestershire	1646	JANSSON	700	41	51	Wigorniensis Comitatus cum Warwicensis, nec non Conventriae Libertas
mwec1242	uk england wiltshire	1646	JANSSON	785	41	51	Wiltonia sive comitatus Wiltoniensis. Anglis Wil Shire
mwbp0261	poland	1657	JANSSON	800	36	48	Wratislavia (Braun & Hogenberg's plate)
mwc0044	china	1657	JANSSON	1000	45	52	Xuntien alias Quinzay (view of Hang Chow, enlarged version of Merian 1638)
mwsw0074	switzerland	1656	JANSSON	350	38	50	Zurichgow et Basiliensis Provincia
mwaa0008	antarctic	1657	JANSSON-HONDIUS	2000	44	49	(Untitled re-issue of Jansson/Hondius 'Polus Antarcticus', with indications of Tasmania and New Zealand etc added. The two cartouches have been removed. Illustrated is the Valk? 1690 reprint. An intermediate stage also exists, with one cartouche removed.)
mwaa0007	antarctic	1641	JANSSON-HONDIUS	2500	44	49	Polus Antarcticus (signed by Hondius)
		JANSSON also used the name VAN LOON. See below.					
mwit1041	italy south	1776	JANVIER	240	30	45	(Southern Italy)
mwaf0223	africa	1769	JANVIER	785	48	66	L'Afrique (insets of the Cape and Mauritius)
mwaf0213	africa	1762	JANVIER	320	30	44	L'Afrique Divisee en ses Principaux Etats
mwam0184	america continent	1762	JANVIER	450	31	45	L'Amerique Divisee par Grands Etats par le Sr. Janvier (Illustrated is the 1783 edition showing New Zealand after Cook)
mwsam0080	south america	1762	JANVIER	280	31	45	L'Amerique Meridionale Divisee en ses Principaux Etats
mwam0428a	america north	1762	JANVIER	600	31	45	L'Amerique Septentrionale Divisee en ses Principaux Etats
mwas0177a	asia continent	1762	JANVIER	375	31	45	L'Asie Divisee en ses Principaux Etats
mwe0955	europe hungary	1771	JANVIER	200	30	44	Le Royaume de Hongrie Divise en Haute et Basse Hontrie Transilvanie Esclavonie et Croatie
mwsc0151	scandinavia	1762	JANVIER	280	31	44	Les Couronnes du Nord Comprenant les Royaumes de Suede Danemarck et Norwege Divise par Provinces et Gouvernements
mwsc0156	scandinavia	1769	JANVIER-LATTRE	480	47	65	Les Couronnes du Nord Comprenant les Royaumes de Suede Danemarck et Norwege Divise par Provinces et Gouvernements
mwuk0848	uk	1769	JANVIER-LATTRE	675	47	65	Les Isles Britanniques
mwuk0841	uk	1759	JANVIER	350	31	45	Les Isles Britanniques Comprenant les Royaumes d'Angleterre, d'Ecosse, et d'Irlande
mwbp0496	poland	1780	JANVIER	600	47	65	Les Royaumes de Pologne et de Prusse avec le Duche de Curlande Divises en Provinces et Palatinats
mwsc0142	scandinavia	1749	JANVIER	480	49	56	Les Royaumes de Suede, de Danemarck et de Norwege
mwsp0283	spain	1769	JANVIER	480	47	65	Les Royaumes d'Espagne et de Portugal Divisee par Grandes Provinces
mwsp0282	spain	1763	JANVIER	280	30	44	Les Royaumes d'Espagne et de Portugal, Divises par Grandes Provinces
mwe0184	europe	1762	JANVIER	320	32	46	L'Europe Divisee en ses Principaux Etats

AMPG REFERENCE	REGION	DATE	MAP MAKER	PRICE (UK£)	VERT. (cm.)	HOR. (cm.)	TITLE OF MAP (Comments by the editor in brackets)
mwit0192	italy	1762	JANVIER	250	32	45	L'Italie Divisee en ses Differents Etats, Royaumes et Republiques
mww0457	world	1762	JANVIER	1100	30	45	Mappe-Monde ou Description du Globe Terrestre
mww0575	world	1792	JANVIER	2000	48	66	Mappe-Monde ou Description du Globe Terrestre
mwbh0723	belgium holland	1771	JANVIER	200	30	44	Partie Meridionale des Pay Bas, Comprenant les Provinces de Brabant, Gueldre, Limbourg, Luxembourg, Haynaut, Namur, Flandre
mwbh0725	belgium holland	1773	JANVIER	400	48	66	Partie Meridionale des Pays Bas ... Brabant/Gueldre, Limbourg, Luxembourg
mwbh0747	belgium holland	1786	JANVIER	280	30	38	Partie Septentrionale des Pays Bas Comprenant les Etats Generaux des Provinces Unies
mwe1160	europe south east	1783	JANVIER	240	32	44	Turquie d'Europe et Partie de celle d'Asie Divisee par Grandes Provinces et Gouvernemts.
mwaf0200	africa	1754	JANVIER & LONGCHAMPS	13500	119	149	L'Afrique Divisee en Tous ses Etats
mwam0172	america continent	1754	JANVIER & LONGCHAMPS	20000	119	152	L'Amerique Divisee en Tous ses Pays et Etats
mwas0167	asia continent	1754	JANVIER & LONGCHAMPS	15000	119	149	L'Asie Divisee en Tous ses Etats
mwe0172	europe	1754	JANVIER & LONGCHAMPS	12000	119	149	L'Europe Divisee en Tous ses Etats
mww0430	world	1754	JANVIER & LONGCHAMPS	40000	120	149	Mappe Monde, Contenant les Parties Connues du Globe Terrestre (see revised re-issue without the decorative borders by Mondhare 1788.)
mwf0885a	france paris	1766	JANVIER & LONGCHAMPS	6000	115	136	Nouveau Plan de la Ville et Faubourgs de Paris par Elevation
mwuss0130	california	1849	JARVES	10000	37	30	A Correct Map of the Bay of San Francisco and the Gold Region from Actual Survey June 20th, 1849
mwsc0196	scandinavia	1810	JATTNIG	240	19	24	Karte von Norwegen und Schweden
mww0237	world	1688	JAUGEON	40000	71	121	Carte Generale Continente les Mondes Coeleste Terrestre et Civile. (Illustration shows the final updated re-issue with a different title by Desnos, 1786 and with 36 text panels surrounded by decorative columns below the map. The map was also reduced in size to 54x93cm, total size 103x93cm.)
mwgr0505	greece cyprus	1747	JAUNA	4800	37	49	Acamantis Insula nunc Cyprus
mwf0907	france paris	1807	JEAN	600	52	75	Carte des Environs de Paris Divises en Departements, Prefectures et Sous Prefectures
mwbp0518	poland	1790	JEAN	1200	32	51	Cracovie (view)
mwf0930	france paris	1841	JEAN	450	59	87	Nouveau Plan de la VIlle de Paris, Divise en 12 Arrondissemens et 48 Quartiers
mwf0200	france	1841	JEAN	400	67	54	Nouvelle Carte des Routes de France
mwf0276	france aquitaine	1805	JEAN	675	53	71	Plan de la Ville de Bourdeaux et de ses Faux-Bourgs
mwf0908	france paris	1807	JEAN	3600	102	175	Plan de Paris Divise en 12 Mairies Subdivisee chacune en 4 Parties
mwru0399	russia moscow	1801	JEAN	1800	47	72	Plan Geometral de la Ville de Moscow
mwf0904	france paris	1800	JEAN	960	57	82	Plan Routier de la Ville et Faubourg de Paris Divise en 12 Mairies
mwca0090	canada	1770	JEFFERYS	300	17	44	(Hudson Bay) A Draught of Nelson & Hayes's Rivers
mwuk0179	ireland	1759	JEFFERYS	720	64	59	A New and Accurate Map of the Kingdom of Ireland
mwam0171	america continent	1753	JEFFERYS		127	114	A Chart of North and South America, Including the Atlantic and Pacific Oceans, with the Nearest Coasts of Europe, Africa and Asia (in 6 sheets)
mwca0262	canada labrador	1770	JEFFERYS	800	55	46	A Chart of Part of the Coast of Labrador, from the Straights of Bell Isle to Cape Bluff, Surveyed by Joseph Gilbert in 1767
mwat0039a	atlantic ocean (all)	1775	JEFFERYS	2000	50	64	A Chart of the Atlantic Ocean
mwuk1512	uk english channel (all)	1794	JEFFERYS	2000	50	70	A Chart of the British Channel, Extending from Dover to the Isles of Scilly on the English Coast, and from Cape Gris-Nez to the Isle of Ouessant on the French Coast (6 sheets, each 50x70cm.)(1st edition 1776)
mwuss0428	florida	1770	JEFFERYS	2250	51	61	A Chart of the Entrance into St. Mary's River Taken by Captn. W. Fuller in Nov. 1769 / Plan of Amelia Island in East Florida / A Chart of the Mouth of Nassau River
mwca0614	canada st lawrence	1775	JEFFERYS	1250	50	61	A Chart of the Gulf of St. Laurence, Composed from a Great Number of Actual Surveys and Other Materials, Regulated and Connected by Astronomical Observations
mwin0432	indian ocean	1778	JEFFERYS	1650	60	98	A Chart of the Indian Sea and Eastern Ocean by Thos. Jefferys, Geographer to the King (incl. Australia)
mwca0617	canada st lawrence	1777	JEFFERYS	600	28	35	A Chart of the Magdalen Islands in the Gulf of St. Lawrence Surveyed in 1765
mwsam0690	south america magellan	1775	JEFFERYS	675	52	70	A Chart of the Straits of Magellan Inlarged from the Chart Published at Madrid in 1769 by Don Juan de la Cruz Cano y Olmedilla
mww0492	world	1775	JEFFERYS	1200	39	46	A Chart of the World upon Mercator's Projection Describing the Tracks of Capt. Cook in the Years 1768 ... -75 with the New Discoveries

AMPG REFERENCE	REGION	DATE	MAP MAKER	PRICE (UK£)	VERT. (cm.)	HOR. (cm.)	TITLE OF MAP (Comments by the editor in brackets)
mwca0511	canada quebec	1759	JEFFERYS	1500	88	41	A Correct Plan of the Environs of Quebec, and of the Battle Fought on the 13th September, 1759: Together with a Particular Detail of the French Lines and Batteries, and also the Encampments, Batteries and Attacks of the British Army
mwca0324	canada newfoundland	1775	JEFFERYS	1500	54	56	A General Chart of the Island of Newfoundland with the Rocks & Soundings Drawn from Surveys
mwca0266	canada new brunswick	1755	JEFFERYS	1750	34	58	A Large and Particular Plan of Shegnekto Bay, and the Circumjacent Country, with the Forts and Settlements of the French 'till Dispossess'd by the English in June 1755. Drawn on the Spot by an Officer
mwca0391	canada nova scotia	1768	JEFFERYS	800	19	22	A Map Exhibiting a View of the English Rights, Relative to the Ancient Limits of Acadia / Carte d'une Partie de l'Amerique Septentrionale pour Servie a l'Intellegence du Memoire sur les Pretentions des Anglois (2 maps, each 19x22cm)
mwme1012	turkey etc	1760	JEFFERYS	320	36	41	A Map of Asia Minor
mwca0079	canada	1760	JEFFERYS	900	32	54	A Map of Canada and the North Part of Louisiana with the Adjacent Countrys. By Thos. Jefferys, Geographer to His Royal Highness the Prince of Wales (in 1762 this map was re-issued with a pasted-on left-hand sheet, extending it to the West coast.)
mwca0081a	canada	1762	JEFFERYS	2500	32	76	A Map of Canada and the North Part of Louisiana with the Adjacent Countrys. By Thos. Jefferys, Geographer to His Royal Highness the Prince of Wales (see also 1760)
mwgr0503	greece cyprus	1745	JEFFERYS	720	29	22	A Map of Cyprus
mwca0086	canada	1766	JEFFERYS	400	15	21	A Map of Hudson's Bay & Straits
mwsam0091	south america	1775	JEFFERYS	2000	98	118	A Map of South America Containing Tierra-Firma, Guayana, New Granada, Amazonia, Brasil, Peru, Paraguay, Chaco, Tucuman, Chili and Patagonia. From Mr. D'Anville with Several Improvements and Additions, and the Newest Discoveries
mwp0413	pacific north	1761	JEFFERYS	1500	49	62	A Map of the Discoveries Made by the Russians on the North West Coast of America. Published by the Royal Academy of Sciences at Petersburg … Republished by Thomas Jefferys (English edition of 1758 Muller map)
mwuss0745	maryland	1753	JEFFERYS	100000	77	123	A Map of the Inhabited Part of Virginia Containing the Whole Province of Maryland with Part of Pensilvania, New Jersey and North Carolina Drawn by Joshua Fry & Peter Jefferson in 1751
mwwi0374	barbados	1750	JEFFERYS	750	42	35	A Map of the Island of Barbados … from the Observations of Mr. Griffith Hughes
mwwi0461	cuba	1774	JEFFERYS	650	35	40	A Map of the Isle of Cuba, with the Bahama Islands, Gulf of Florida, and Windward Passage: Drawn from English and Spanish Surveys
mwgm0414	panama	1762	JEFFERYS	480	22	30	A Map of the Isthmus of Panama, Drawn from Spanish Surveys
mwp0364	pacific marianas	1756	JEFFERYS	250	15	8	A Map of the Ladrone Islands
mwam1028	america north (east)	1774	JEFFERYS	6000	104	101	A Map of the Most Inhabited Part of New England, Containing the Provinces of Massachusets Bay and New Hampshire, with the Colonies of Conecticut and Rhode Island, Divided into Counties and Townships
mwuss0746	maryland	1755	JEFFERYS	50000	76	122	A Map of the Most Inhabited Part of Virginia Containing the Whole Province of Maryland with Part of Pensilvania, New Jersey and North Carolina Drawn by Joshua Fry & Peter Jefferson in 1751 (later state of 1753 map)
mwca0610	canada st lawrence	1768	JEFFERYS	1000	19	25	A Map of the Several Dispositions of the English Fleet & Army on the River St. Laurence, to the Taking of Quebec
mwuss1638	virginia	1758	JEFFERYS	320	15	20	A Map of Virginia and Maryland
mwuss0180	carolinas	1753	JEFFERYS	1500	39	32	A New and Exact Plan of Cape Fear River from the Bar to Brunswick, by Edward Hyrne 1749
mwwi0097	west indies	1762	JEFFERYS	250	16	29	A New Chart of the West Indies, Drawn from the Best Spanish Maps
mwuk0997	england	1750	JEFFERYS	3500	128	117	A New Map (Laid down from Surveys by ye Wheel) Of all the Great or Post Roads and principal Cross Roads throughout England and Wales
mwuk1001	england	1757	JEFFERYS	400	43	37	A New Map of England and Wales
mwca0376	canada nova scotia	1755	JEFFERYS	1250	47	61	A New Map of Nova Scotia and Cape Breton Island with the Adjacent Parts of New England and Canada (illustrated is the 1775 edition. This map was also issued with the title 'A New Map of Nova Scotia and Cape Britain …' and other minor changes)
mwuk1203	england london	1762	JEFFERYS	1250	46	94	A New Plan of the City and Liberty of Westminster / the City of London and Borough of Southwark, Exhibiting All the New Streets, Roads (2 maps on one sheet. 4 editions until 1772)

AMPG REFERENCE	REGION	DATE	MAP MAKER	PRICE (UK£)	VERT. (cm.)	HOR. (cm.)	TITLE OF MAP (Comments by the editor in brackets)
mwca0615	canada st lawrence	1775	JEFFERYS	1250	34	53	A Plan of Chaleur Bay in the Gulf of St. Lawrence. Surveyed by His Majesty's Ship Norwich in 1760 (publ. by Sayer & Bennett)
mwme0500	jerusalem	1745	JEFFERYS	400	38	38	A Plan of Jerusalem and the Adjacent Country
mwca0530	canada quebec	1775	JEFFERYS	600	34	52	A Plan of Ristigouche Harbour in Chaleur Bay Surveyed in 1760 by the King's Ship Norwich
mwf0356	france brittany	1758	JEFFERYS	200	20	27	A Plan of the City & Fortifications of St. Malo's
mwca0523	canada quebec	1760	JEFFERYS	1400	34	49	A Plan of the City of Quebec the Capital of Canada (3rd state ... after surrender to the British)
mwca0381	canada nova scotia	1758	JEFFERYS	800	39	63	A Plan of the City, and Fortifications of Louisburg, from a Survey Made by Richard Gridley, Lieut. Col. of the Train of Artillery in 1745 / A Plan of the City and Harbour of Louisburg, with the French Batteries
mwsam0520	south america colombia	1756	JEFFERYS	200	15	8	A Plan of the Harbour of Carthagena
mwec0751	uk england lincolnshire	1767	JEFFERYS	900	28	37	A Plan of the Haute Huntre, or Holland Fen
mwaf0578a	africa islands goree	1759	JEFFERYS	350	45	39	A Plan of the Island of Goree
mwit0441a	italy liguria	1750	JEFFERYS	400	21	38	A South View of the City of Genoa
mwaf0203	africa	1758	JEFFERYS	165	19	25	Africa
mwec1202	uk england warwickshire	1770	JEFFERYS	500	62	50	An Accurate Map of the County of Warwick
mwca0511a	canada quebec	1769	JEFFERYS	800	33	48	An Authentic Plan of the River St. Laurence from Sillery, to the Fall of Montmorenci, with the Operations of the Siege of Quebec under the Commander of Vice-Adml. Saunders & Major Genl. Wolfe down to the 5. Sepr. 1759
mwwi0621	hispaniola	1760	JEFFERYS	600	33	48	An Authentic Plan of the Town & Harbour of Cap Francois in the Isle of St. Domingo
mwuss1348	pennsylvania	1756	JEFFERYS	25000	49	91	An East Prospect of the City of Philadelphia; Taken by George Heap from the Jersey Shore, under the Direction of Nicolas Scull Surveyor General of the Province of Pennsylvania (incl. a street plan and 2 other views)
mwca0596	canada st lawrence	1757	JEFFERYS	1000	60	94	An Exact Chart of the River St. Laurence, from Fort Frontenac to the Island of Anticosti Shewing the Soundings, Rocks, Shoals, &c. with Views of the Lands and All Necessary Instructions for Navigating that River to Quebec
mwwi0105	west indies	1775	JEFFERYS	600	39	65	An Index Map to the Following Sixteen Sheets, Being a Compleat Chart of the West Indies
mwwi0302	antigua	1775	JEFFERYS	2000	50	65	Antigua Surveyed by Robert Baker, Surveyor General of that Island (Laurie & Whittle re-issue 1794 shown above left)
mwas0172	asia continent	1758	JEFFERYS	165	18	23	Asia
mwwi0377	barbados	1775	JEFFERYS	850	61	46	Barbadoes, Surveyed by William Mayo
mwwi0534	grenadines	1775	JEFFERYS	875	33	46	Bequia or Becouya, the Northernmost of the Grenadilles Surveyed in 1763
mwwi0523	grenada	1775	JEFFERYS	1500	49	63	Plan de L'Isle de la Grenade, ou sont marques dans leur juste position le Ports et mouillages les Ville et Bourgs
mwaa0145	arctic	1775	JEFFERYS	600	46	53	Chart Containing Part of the Icy Sea with the Adjacent Coast of Asia & America
mwp0183	new zealand	1775	JEFFERYS	300	42	52	Chart Containing the Greater Part of the South Sea to the South of the Line, with the Islands Dispersed thro' the Same (part of a 6-sheet map)
mwsam0076	south america	1753	JEFFERYS	720	53	60	Chart of South America, Comprehending the West Indies
mwam1318	america north (west)	1753	JEFFERYS	2000	46	52	Chart, Containing the Coasts of California, New Albion, and Russian Discoveries to the North, with the Peninsula of Kamchatka, in Asia, Opposite Thereto ... Feb. 19, 1753 by T. Jefferys
mwc0160	china	1758	JEFFERYS	165	18	22	China
mwgm0243	mexico	1777	JEFFERYS	600	48	64	Coast of Yucatan from Campeche to Bahia del Ascension with the West End Cuba
mwwi0506	dominica	1760	JEFFERYS	1250	62	48	Dominica from an Actual Survey Compleated in the Year 1773
mwuss0427	florida	1769	JEFFERYS	3000	42	35	East Florida from Surveys
mwas0483	asia south east	1758	JEFFERYS	200	18	29	East Indies
mwuk1014	england	1775	JEFFERYS	500	55	45	England and Wales
mwwi0524	grenada	1775	JEFFERYS	1250	47	63	Grenada Divided into its Parishes, Surveyed by Order of His Excellency Governor Scott and Engraved by Thomas Jefferys
mwwi0552	guadeloupe	1768	JEFFERYS	500	34	37	Guadaloupe one of the Caribbee Islands Subject to France in the West Indies, from the Best Authorities
mwwi0555	guadeloupe	1775	JEFFERYS	720	47	61	Guadeloupe Done from Actual Surveys and Observations of the English, whilst the Island was in their Possession
mwat0225a	atlantic falkland isl.	1773	JEFFERYS	750	26	36	Hawkins's Maiden-Land, called afterwards Falkland Islands ...
mwuk0200	ireland	1768	JEFFERYS	150	18	20	Ireland
mwit0197	italy	1768	JEFFERYS	135	18	23	Italy
mwwi0731	jamaica	1775	JEFFERYS	650	46	61	Jamaica from the Latest Surveys; Improved and Engraved by Thomas Jefferys
mwsp0101	portugal	1762	JEFFERYS	1500	169	91	Mappa ou Carta Geographica dos Reinos de Portugal e Algarve

AMPG REFERENCE	REGION	DATE	MAP MAKER	PRICE (UK£)	VERT. (cm.)	HOR. (cm.)	TITLE OF MAP (Comments by the editor in brackets)
mwwi0797	martinique	1775	JEFFERYS	1000	47	61	Martinico, Done from Actual Surveys and Observations, Made by English Engineers whilst the Island was in their Possession
mwuk1168	england london	1735	JEFFERYS	3000	86	121	New and Exact Plan of the City's of London and Westminster and the Borough of Southwark And the Additional New Buildings Churches &c to the present Year 1735 Laid down in such a manner, that any place may readily be found by inspection; the like not Extant
mwam0418	america north	1758	JEFFERYS	240	19	24	North America
mwam0973	america north (east)	1755	JEFFERYS	2400	46	52	North America from the French of Mr. d'Anville, Improved with the Back Settlements of Virginia and Course of Ohio, Illustrated with Geographical and Historical Remarks
mwuss0426	florida	1768	JEFFERYS	10000	49	64	Pais Cedes, Sheet Ist Containing the Coast of Louisiana and Florida / Pais Cedes, Sheet IId Containing the Peninsula & Gulf of Florida, with the Bahama Islands (2 maps, each 49x64cm.)
mwsam0720	south america paraguay	1766	JEFFERYS	200	15	9	Paraguay and the Rio del Plata
mwgm0097	costa rica	1775	JEFFERYS	600	47	63	Part of the Provinces of Costa Rica and Nicaragua with the Lagunas. by Thos. Jefferys
mwwi0436	cuba	1762	JEFFERYS	160	25	20	Plan de Puerto de Mariel
mwuss0429	florida	1770	JEFFERYS	1600	51	61	Plan of Amelia Island in East Florida / A Chart of the Entrance into St. Mary's River / A Chart of the Mouth of the Nassau River with the Bar and the Soundings on it Taken at Low Water
mwwi0437	cuba	1762	JEFFERYS	160	20	32	Plan of Bahia de Matanzas
mwwi0456	cuba	1768	JEFFERYS	160	18	25	Plan of Bahia Honda
mwwi0438	cuba	1762	JEFFERYS	200	27	20	Plan of Guantanimo, Called by the English Cumberland Harbour
mwuss1358	pennsylvania	1768	JEFFERYS	15000	30	33	Plan of Le Quesne, Built by the French at the Fork of the Ohio and Mononquahela in 1764
mwuss0635	louisiana	1760	JEFFERYS	480	18	23	Plan of New Orleans the Capital of Louisiana
mwuss0633	louisiana	1759	JEFFERYS	2250	33	48	Plan of New Orleans the Capital of Louisiana; with the Disposition of its Quarters and Canals / The Course of the Mississippi River / The East Mouth of the Mississipi
mwgm0232	mexico	1768	JEFFERYS	350	20	27	Plan of Port Royal Laguna, Commonly Called the Logwood Creeks
mwgm0415	panama	1762	JEFFERYS	400	20	26	Plan of Porto Belo
mwsam0834	south america venezuela	1762	JEFFERYS	200	19	29	Plan of Puerto Cavello on the Coast of the Caracas
mwwi0439	cuba	1762	JEFFERYS	160	18	25	Plan of Puerto de Baracoa
mwsam0835	south america venezuela	1762	JEFFERYS	200	21	28	Plan of Puerto de la Guaira on the Coast of the Caracas
mwwi0829	puerto rico	1768	JEFFERYS	480	24	18	Plan of the Aguada Nueva de Puerto Rico
mwwi0547	guadeloupe	1760	JEFFERYS	1200	33	47	Plan of the Attack Against Basseterre on the Island of Guadaloupe by a Squadron of His Majestys Ships of War Commanded by Commodore Moore on ye 22nd Jan. 1759. Also the Incampments of the British Army Commanded by Genl. Hopson
mwsam0521	south america colombia	1762	JEFFERYS	200	21	24	Plan of the Bay & Town of Sta Martha, on the Coast of Terra Firma
mwwi0457	cuba	1768	JEFFERYS	200	24	20	Plan of the City & Harbour of St. Jago de Cuba
mwwi0458	cuba	1768	JEFFERYS	480	22	27	Plan of the City and Harbour of the Havana
mwsam0763	south america peru	1756	JEFFERYS	200	14	17	Plan of the City of Lima, Capital of Peru
mwwi0622	hispaniola	1762	JEFFERYS	350	19	26	Plan of the City of San Domingo
mwwi0459	cuba	1768	JEFFERYS	160	20	25	Plan of the Colorado Rocks near the West end of Cuba
mwuss0415	florida	1762	JEFFERYS	600	18	26	Plan of the Harbour and Settlement of Pensacola
mwsam0522	south america colombia	1762	JEFFERYS	400	21	31	Plan of the Harbour of Carthagena (on a sheet with 'Plan of Zisapata Bay')
mwgm0118	honduras	1762	JEFFERYS	280	21	28	Plan of the Harbour of San Fernando de Omoa
mwgm0233	mexico	1768	JEFFERYS	300	20	31	Plan of the Road and Port of La Vera Cruz
mwwi0784	martinique	1760	JEFFERYS	400	30	36	Plan of the Town and Citidel of Fort Royal the Capital of Martinico. With the Bay of Cul de Sac Royal. By Mr. De Caylus
mwwi0519	grenada	1760	JEFFERYS	350	30	23	Plan of the Town and Fort of Grenada by Mr. de Caylus, Engineer General of the French Islands
mwca0571	canada quebec montreal	1758	JEFFERYS	1350	33	51	Plan of the Town and Fortifications of Montreal or Ville Marie in Canada
mwwi0830	puerto rico	1768	JEFFERYS	480	20	30	Plan of the Town and Harbour of San Juan de Puerto Rico
mwuss0416	florida	1762	JEFFERYS	550	20	28	Plan of the Town and Harbour of St. Augustine
mwwi0547a	guadeloupe	1760	JEFFERYS	350	33	23	Plan of the Town of Basse Terre the Capital of Guadaloupe from an Authentic Survey
mwsam0610	south america guyana	1760	JEFFERYS	200	32	35	Plan of the Town of Cayenne and Fort St Michael Drawn by the Chevalier de Mareechais
mwgm0416	panama	1762	JEFFERYS	250	27	20	Plan of the Town, Road and Harbour of Chagre
mwbp0463	poland	1760	JEFFERYS	120	18	20	Poland, Lithuania and Prussia
mwru0234	russia	1760	JEFFERYS	135	18	23	Russia or Moscovy in Europe
mwuk0504	scotland	1759	JEFFERYS	150	20	24	Scotland
mwwi0642	hispaniola	1775	JEFFERYS	600	49	60	South Part of St. Domingo, or Hispaniola

AMPG REFERENCE	REGION	DATE	MAP MAKER	PRICE (UK£)	VERT. (cm.)	HOR. (cm.)	TITLE OF MAP (Comments by the editor in brackets)
mwwi0863	st kitts	1775	JEFFERYS	1500	46	61	St. Christophers, or St. Kitts, Surveyed by Anthony Ravell Esqr. Surveyor General of the Islands of St. Christophers, Nevis & Montserrat.
mwwi0879	st lucia	1775	JEFFERYS	850	61	47	St. Lucia Done from Surveys and Observations Made by the English whilst in their Possession
mwwi0892	st vincent	1775	JEFFERYS	720	65	49	St. Vincent, from an Actual Survey made in the Year 1773, after the Treaty with the Caribs
mwgm0119	honduras	1775	JEFFERYS	650	47	63	The Bay of Honduras
mwwi0255b	west indies	1777	JEFFERYS	960	48	64	The Caribbee Islands, the Virgin Islands, and the Isle of Porto Rico. By Thomas Jefferys Geographer to His Majesty
mwgm0230	mexico	1766	JEFFERYS	200	14	16	The City of Mexico
mwsam0840	south america venezuela	1777	JEFFERYS	960	48	64	The Coast of Caracas, Cumana, Paria and the Mouths of Rio Orinoco with Islands Trinidad, Margarita, Tobago, Granada and St. Vincent
mwgm0236a	mexico	1775	JEFFERYS	600	47	62	The Coast of Mexico from Laguna de Esmotes to Punta Brava
mwgm0236	mexico	1775	JEFFERYS	600	48	63	The Coast of New Spain from Nueva Vera Cruz to Triste Island
mwsam0839	south america venezuela	1775	JEFFERYS	1250	48	63	The Coast of Tierra Firma from Cartagena to Golfo Triste
mwuss0433	florida	1775	JEFFERYS	3500	48	123	The Coast of West Florida and Louisiana / The Peninsula and Gulf of Florida or Channel of Bahama with the Bahama Islands
mwgm0237	mexico	1775	JEFFERYS	850	47	62	The Coast of Yucatan from Campeche to Bahia del Ascension; with the West End of Cuba
mwec0017	uk england bedfordshire	1765	JEFFERYS	2000	185	113	The County of Bedford, Surveyed Anno MDCCLXV, and Engraved by Thomas Jefferys
mwec0074	uk england buckinghamshire	1770	JEFFERYS	2000	131	85	The County of Buckingham, Surveyed in MDCCLXVI, VII and VIII and Engraved by Thomas Jefferys, Geographer to His Majesty, MDCCLXX
mwec0868	uk england northamptonshire	1791	JEFFERYS	1350	63	61	The County of Northampton as Surveyed and Planned by the Late Mr. Thomas Eyre of Kettering, Revised by the Late Mr. Thomas Jefferys, Geographer to the King and Engraved by William Faden, 1779 (on 4 sheets, each 63x61cm.)
mwec0959	uk england oxfordshire	1768	JEFFERYS	2500	63	47	The County of Oxford, Surveyed Anno MDCCLXVI & VII (in 4 sheets, each 63x47cm.)
mwec1341	uk england yorkshire	1772	JEFFERYS	5000	60	40	The County of York Survey'd in MDCCLXVII, VIII, IX and MDCCLXX (atlas of 20 sheets, each 60x40cm.)
mwaa0130	arctic	1748	JEFFERYS	350	30	44	The Geography of the Great Solar Eclipse of July, 14. MDCCXLVIII. Exhibiting an Accurate Map of All Parts of the Earth in which it will be Visible with the North Pole According to the Latest Discoveries. By G. Smith Esqr.
mwwi0440	cuba	1762	JEFFERYS	160	18	25	The Grand Bay of Nipe on the North Side of Cuba from Spanish Draughts
mwsam0609	south america guyana	1759	JEFFERYS	500	36	44	The Island and Colony of Cayenne Subject to the French
mwgr0430	greece crete	1780	JEFFERYS	150	29	22	The Island of Candia the Antient Crete
mwwi0462	cuba	1775	JEFFERYS	1500	48	63	The Island of Cuba with Part of the Bahama Banks & the Martyrs
mwwi0623	hispaniola	1762	JEFFERYS	750	35	40	The Island of Hispaniola Called by the French St. Domingo. Subject to France & Spain
mwwi0732	jamaica	1775	JEFFERYS	675	48	62	The Island of Jamaica and Cape Gracias a Dios with the Banks
mwca0395	canada nova scotia	1770	JEFFERYS	400	29	37	The Island of Sable
mwgm0428	panama	1775	JEFFERYS	1500	48	63	The Isthmus of Panama with the Coast from Great River on the Moskito Shore to Cartegena (illustration shows Laurie & Whittle re-issue of 1794)
mwe0612	europe czech republic (bohemia)	1794	JEFFERYS	450	48	57	The Kingdom of Bohemia with the Dutchy of Silesia and the Marquisates of Moravia and Lusatia
mwg0461	hessen	1760	JEFFERYS	1200	49	42	The Landgraviate of Hesse Cassel with Part of Wetteravia (4 sheets, each 49x42cm.)
mwwi0332	bahamas	1775	JEFFERYS	1500	48	62	The Peninsula and Gulf of Florida or Channel of Bahama with the Bahama Islands
mwuk1007	england	1765	JEFFERYS	900	57	48	The Post Roads through England and Wales
mwuss1102	new york	1775	JEFFERYS	5500	133	53	The Provinces of New York and New Jersey; with Part of Pensilvania, and the Governments of Trois Rivieres, and Montreal; Drawn by Capt. Holland (2nd state)
mwe0189	europe	1768	JEFFERYS	2000	51	68	The Royal Geographical Pastime or the Complete Tour of Europe
mwin0223	india	1754	JEFFERYS	350	47	37	The Seat of War on the Coast of Choromandel
mwe0593	europe czech republic (bohemia)	1757	JEFFERYS	450	48	56	The Theatre of War in the Kingdom of Bohemia, Drawn from the Survey of J.C. Muller
mwwi0928	virgin isl	1775	JEFFERYS	3500	46	61	The Virgin Islands from English and Danish Surveys
mwwi0091	west indies	1760	JEFFERYS	800	46	44	The West Indies Exhibiting the English, French, Spanish, Dutch & Danish Settlements
mwgm0037	gulf of mexico and surrounding regions	1775	JEFFERYS	2500	48	62	The Western Coast of Louisiana and the Coast of New Leon

AMPG REFERENCE	REGION	DATE	MAP MAKER	PRICE (UK£)	VERT. (cm.)	HOR. (cm.)	TITLE OF MAP (Comments by the editor in brackets)
mwwi0331	bahamas	1775	JEFFERYS	1200	05	63	The Windward Passage, with the Several Passages, from the East End of Cuba, and the North Part of St Domingo
mww0473	world	1768	JEFFERYS	400	15	27	The World
mwuss0496	georgia	1770	JEFFERYS	1200	51	61	To the Right Honourable John Earl of Egmont, &c. this Plate is Most Humbly Inscribed by ... Willm. Fuller (St. Mary's River)
mwwi0900	trinidad & tobago	1775	JEFFERYS	1350	48	61	Tobago from Actual Surveys and Observations
mwme1011	turkey etc	1758	JEFFERYS	135	18	24	Turkey in Asia
mwuss0193	carolinas	1776	JEFFERYS & FADEN	7200	71	58	A Plan of Port Royal in South Carolina. Survey'd by Capn. John Gascoigne
mwec1342	uk england yorkshire	1774	JEFFERYS & FADEN	500	31	58	A Plan of the Intended Navigable Canal from Cooper Bridge to Huddersfield, in the County of York Taken November the 6th 1773
mwec1343	uk england yorkshire	1774	JEFFERYS & FADEN	400	31	58	A Plan of the Intended Navigable Canal from Cooper Bridge to Huddersfield, in the County of York Taken November the 6th 1773
mwuss0192	carolinas	1776	JEFFERYS & FADEN	2500	66	47	A Plan of the River and Sound of D'Awfoskee, in South Carolina
mwuss0813	massachusetts	1775	JEFFERYS & FADEN	12000	66	75	A Sketch of the Action between the British Forces and the American Provincials on the Heights of the Peninsula of Charlestown, the 17th of June 1775
mwaa0146	arctic	1775	JEFFERYS & FADEN	400	36	34	Northern Hemisphere Engraved by Faden, and Jefferys
mwam0995	america north (east)	1757	JEFFERYS-ANON	2000	50	70	Amerique Septentrionale, suivant les Nouvelles Découvertes, Augmenté des Collonies qui sont derriere la Virginie et du Cour de l'Ohio
mwam1002	america north (east)	1758	JEFFERYS-EVANS	4400	48	67	A General Map of the Middle British Colonies in America: viz. Virginia, Maryland, Delaware, Pensilvania, New Jersey, New-York, Connecticut and Rhode Island
mwat0125	atlantic bermuda	1778	JEFFERYS-SAYER	4500	50	65	The Bermudas, or Summer's Islands from a Survey by C. Lempriere, Regulated by Astronomical Observations
mwgr0031	greece	1571	JENICHEN	20000	17	28	(Battle of Lepanto) Warhaffte Contrefactur der Grossen Schlacht zu Wasser welche die Venediger mit den Turckhen gethan haben, den 7 Tag Octobris in dem 1571 Jar
mwg0302	bavaria	1571	JENICHEN	1800	37	48	Chorographia Nova Franciae Orientalis vulgo Franckenlandt
mwme0037	holy land	1570	JENICHEN	20000	20	39	Nova Totius Palestinae seu Terrae Sanctae Descriptio / Newe unnd Deutliche Beschreibung des Gelobten Heyligen Lanndts Palestinae zu Besserem Verstanndt unnd Brauch der Bibel
mwit1210	italy venice	1570	JENICHEN	3500	24	36	Venetia
mwgr0444	greece cyprus	1570	JENICHEN	30000	24	28	Ware Contrafetung der Kueniglichen Haubtstat Nicosia in Cipern Gelegen ist von dem Turcken Erobert und Eingenomen worden. Geschen den 8. September im 1570
mwgr0295	greece corfu	1571	JENICHEN	10000	28	33	Warhafftige Contrafactur der Gewaltigen Festung Corfu. Den Venedigern Zugehorig, welche der Turck Niemals hat Gewinnen konnen ... 1571
mwuk1645	north sea	1653	JENNER	1500			(Untitled chart of the North Sea, north to the right. Inset: 'The River of Thames')
mwec0467	uk england hampshire	1643	JENNER	120	10	10	Hamshire (based on Simmons' 1635 map)
mwec0603	uk england kent	1643	JENNER	120	10	10	Kent (based on Simmons)
mwec1032	uk england somerset	1643	JENNER	100	11	11	Somerset (based on Simmons)
mwuk0922	england	1644	JENNER	5500	40	52	The Kingdome of England, & the Principality of Wales, Exactly Described (4 sheets, each 40x52cm, engraved by W. Hollar. Known as 'the Quarter-master's map'. Illustrated is a later edition with title: 'A New Map of the Kingdome of England and Principality of Wales ...')
mwuk0419	scotland	1679	JENNER	3600	41	51	The Kingdome of Scotland
mwru0574	ukraine	1817	JERVIS	6500	238	130	Military Topographical Map of the Krima Peninsula (title also in Russian)
mwam1204	america north (east)	1828	JOCELYN	6000	121	39	An Improved Reference Map of the Valley of the Connecticut and Western Section of New England
mwam1202	america north (east)	1828	JOCELYN	2750	117	39	Map Exhibiting the Farmington & Hampshire & Hampden Canals, Together with the Line of their Proposed Continuation through the Valley of the Connecticut River, to Canada
mwru0372	russia	1854	JOCELYN	1000	77	62	Mirror of the City of Sebastopol and Map of Crimea and Black Sea
mww0675	world	1825	JOCELYN	200	17	24	The World
mwam1337	america north (west)	1798	JOHNSON	200	22	18	A Chart of the Northwest Coast of America from California to Cook's River; Agreeable to the Discoveries Made in the Years 1786-1787 by French Frigates Boussole & Astrolabe
mww0502	world	1778	JOHNSON	500	28	44	A Map of the World in Three Sections: Describing the Polar Regions to the Tropic in which are Traced the Tracts of Lord Mulgrave and Captain Cook towards the North and South Poles and the Torrid Zone or Tropical Regions with the New Discoveries

AMPG REFERENCE	REGION	DATE	MAP MAKER	PRICE (UK£)	VERT. (cm.)	HOR. (cm.)	TITLE OF MAP (Comments by the editor in brackets)
mww0503a	world	1778	JOHNSON	720	30	52	The World; Comprising the New Discoveries in the Southern Hemisphere. (Illustrated is the updated 1787 edition with 'Islands discovered between the Continents of Asia and America in the Years 1778 &79'. Publ. by C. Stalker)
mww0743	world	1847	JOHNSON	4800	142	178	Johnson's Illustrated and Embellished Steel Plate Map of the World Mercator's Projection Compiled from the Latest and Most Authentic Sources Exhibiting the Recent Arctic and Antarctic Discoveries and Explorations
mwuss0996	missouri	1835	JOHNSON	350	30	38	Johnson's Nebraska and Kansas
mwuss1326	ohio	1850	JOHNSON	240	28	43	Map of the Frontiers of the Northern Colonies with the Boundary Line Established between them and the Indians at the Treaty Held by S. Will Johnson at Ft. Stanwix in Nov'r 1768.
mwwi0179	west indies	1828	JOHNSON	200	36	50	Map of the Route of Columbus on Arriving among the Bahama Islands
mwaf1032	africa south	1850	JOHNSTON	180	44	57	(Untitled map)
mwaf0336	africa	1843	JOHNSTON	200	60	49	Africa
mwas0256	asia continent	1844	JOHNSTON	240	48	61	Asia
mwp0151	australia	1844	JOHNSTON	450	50	61	Australia
mwca0195	canada	1844	JOHNSTON	360	50	60	Canada
mww0728	world	1844	JOHNSTON	250	48	60	Chart of the World on Mercator's Projection
mwc0279	china	1841	JOHNSTON	200	50	61	China
mwp0153	australia	1844	JOHNSTON	360	50	61	Colony of New South Wales and Australia Felix
mwsc0406	scandinavia denmark	1845	JOHNSTON	100	50	60	Denmark
mwaf0568	africa egypt etc	1850	JOHNSTON	100	58	50	Egypt and Arabia Petraea
mwuk1076	england	1848	JOHNSTON	180	61	51	England & Wales
mwe0274	europe	1849	JOHNSTON	100	50	59	Ethnographic Map of Europe According to Dr Gustaf Kombst
mwgr0263	greece	1846	JOHNSTON	100	36	53	Greece or Hellas, Ionian Islands and Crete
mwbh0804	belgium holland	1844	JOHNSTON	100	50	60	Holland
mwin0374	india	1846	JOHNSTON	240	60	51	India
mwuk0284	ireland	1843	JOHNSTON	100	60	49	Ireland
mwp0289	pacific (all)	1844	JOHNSTON	300	50	60	Islands in the Pacific Ocean
mwuk0644	scotland	1850	JOHNSTON	240	80	93	Johnston's Map of the Counties of Perth and Clackmannan with the Railways
mwuk0620	scotland	1837	JOHNSTON	180	67	52	Johnston's Map of the County of Caithness with the Railways
mwuk0621	scotland	1837	JOHNSTON	180	52	68	Johnston's Map of the County of Linlithgow with the Railways
mwuk0631	scotland	1840	JOHNSTON	180	69	53	Map of the County of Selkirk
mwgm0351	mexico	1844	JOHNSTON	100	23	30	Mexico, Guatimala and the Texas
mwp0220	new zealand	1844	JOHNSTON	650	60	50	New Zealand
mwam0761	america north	1844	JOHNSTON	300	60	50	North America
mwaf0433	africa east	1846	JOHNSTON	180	49	60	Nubia and Abyssinia
mwme0424	holy land	1843	JOHNSTON	180	60	50	Palestine
mwme0434	holy land	1850	JOHNSTON	180	57	44	Palestine or the Holy Land
mwme0854	persia etc	1846	JOHNSTON	180	43	61	Persia and Cabool
mwat0067	atlantic ocean (all)	1848	JOHNSTON	180	51	58	Physical Chart of the Atlantic Ocean, Shewing the Form & Selection of Currents: Distribution of Heat at the Surface Navigation and Trade Routes, Banks, Rocks &c.
mwp0294	pacific (all)	1849	JOHNSTON	180	51	58	Physical Chart of the Pacific Ocean or Great Sea (Mare Pacifico) Showing the Currents and Temperature of the Ocean, the Trade Routes &c.
mwbp0570	poland	1846	JOHNSTON	120	43	58	Prussia
mwru0369	russia	1846	JOHNSTON	100	61	50	Russia in Europe
mwas0554	asia south east	1849	JOHNSTON	720	127	152	S.E. Peninsula and Malaysia
mwsam0166	south america	1850	JOHNSTON	140	58	48	South America
mwsp0335	spain	1846	JOHNSTON	100	36	53	Spain & Portugal
mww0729	world	1844	JOHNSTON	250	50	58	Survey of the Geographical Distribution and Cultivation of the Most Important Plants
mwsc0219	scandinavia	1846	JOHNSTON	100	61	43	Sweden & Norway
mww0746	world	1849	JOHNSTON	400	52	60	The World in Hemispheres, with Comparative Views of the Heights of the Principal Mountains and Lengths of the Principal Rivers on the Globe
mwme0691	arabia etc	1846	JOHNSTON	100	43	61	Turkey in Asia
mwe1182	europe south east	1848	JOHNSTON	50	51	61	Turkey in Europe
mwam1248a	america north (east)	1843	JOHNSTON	900	49	61	United States and Texas (inset of Niagara river. Later issued as a 'Lithographed Edition', see below)
mwp0155	australia	1844	JOHNSTON	240	58	50	Van Dieman's Land or Tasmania
mwwi0211	west indies	1844	JOHNSTON	320	50	60	West India Islands
mwit1066	italy naples	1755	JOLIVET	1400	50	77	Pianta della Citta di Napoli
mwf0252	france alsace	1830	JOLLAIN	900	60	70	(Plan of Metz and its Environs)
mwf0403	france burgundy	1680	JOLLAIN	1350	35	48	Besanson (view)
mwf0735	france nord pas-de-calais	1667	JOLLAIN	1350	39	53	Carte de la Province de Lille

AMPG REFERENCE	REGION	DATE	MAP MAKER	PRICE (UK£)	VERT. (cm.)	HOR. (cm.)	TITLE OF MAP (Comments by the editor in brackets)
mwit0660	italy piedmont	1690	JOLLAIN	2750	41	51	Carte du Piemont et Monferrat, Ensemble la Marche de l'Armee de France, Commandee par Mr. de Catinat, en l'Annee 1690
mwf0222	france alsace	1675	JOLLAIN	2400	44	124	Carte Generalle de la Haute et Basse Alsace
mwme0460a	jerusalem	1570	JOLLAIN	2500	37	50	Jerusalem Comme elle estoit du temps que nostre Sauveur Jesus-Christ souffrit mort et passion pour nous.
mwf0445	france champagne	1670	JOLLAIN	600	37	48	La Champagne / Comitatus Campania
mwbh0461a	belgium holland	1692	JOLLAIN	1250	38	52	Le Comté de Namur, et partie des Duchez de Brabant, Limbourg et Luxembourg avec partie de l'Eveché et Seigneurie de Lyege
mwg0086a	germany	1699	JOLLAIN	3000	39	50	L'empire d'Allemagne Divisé en ses dix cercles
mwc0060	china	1672	JOLLAIN	4000	39	41	Le Roiaume de la Chine, et ses Provinces
mwbh0508	belgium holland	1702	JOLLAIN	750	45	58	Le Theatre de la Guerre dans la Hollande ou les Provinces Unies des Pays-Bas
mwf0678a	france lorraine	1680	JOLLAIN	800	36	50	Lotharingiae Ducatus Superioris vera delineatio - Description de la Haute et Superieure Lorraine (re-issue of Bussemacher 1590)
mwf1166	france lyon	1680	JOLLAIN	1350	38	51	Lyon (view)
mwit0534	italy milan	1660	JOLLAIN	3000	39	47	Milan
mwuk0751	uk	1689	JOLLAIN	5000	39	53	Nouvelle Carte D'Angleterre avec les Royaumes D'Ecosse et D'Irlande (4 carte-a-figure borders)
mww0187	world	1669	JOLLAIN	3750	38	56	Nova Totius Terrarum Orbis Geographica ac Hydpographica Tabula Auct: Iud Hondio (title misspelt)
mwuss1077	new york	1672	JOLLAIN	22500	31	50	Nowel Amsterdam en l'Amerique
mwf0827	france paris	1670	JOLLAIN	4000	40	51	Plan de la Ville Citte et Universite et Fauxbourgs de Paris (Copied from Bertrand. 3 borders with 65 portraits of kings of France)
mwe0543	europe czech republic (bohemia)	1667	JOLLAIN	1350	30	50	Prague (view)
mwf0321	france brittany	1680	JOLLAIN	1350	38	51	Rennes (view)
mwit1109	italy tuscany	1680	JOLLAIN	2400	31	43	Siena
mwme0182	holy land	1680	JOLLAIN	960	40	55	Terra Sancta Promissionis olim Palestina
mwf1097	france pyrenees	1680	JOLLAIN	1350	38	52	Tholose (plan)
mwe0413	europe austria vienna	1685	JOLLAIN	1350	30	55	Vienne en Austriche (view)
mwuss0940	mississippi	1689	JOLLIET	12000	18	38	Tabula Exhibens Regiones quasdam Recens Detectas in America Spetemtrionali, Anno 1673 (2nd edition)
mwme0674	arabia etc	1823	JOMARD	2000	42	54	Carte Comprenant le Pays de Nejd ou Arabie Centrale ... Occupees en 1820, par les Troupes de Mohammed-Aly
mwe0478	europe central	1810	JOMINI	600	125	153	Carte Generale de la Chaine des Alpes Contenant la Haute Italie, la Suisse et l'Allemagne Meridionale Dressee pour l'Intelligence de l'Histoire des Guerres de la Revolution
mww0442	world	1758	JONGE	550	17	25	Globus Terrestris, det er Jordens Klode, Forestillende Verdens IV Deele
mwsp0097	portugal	1760	JONGE	135	18	17	Landkort over Kongeriget Portugall og Algarbien
mwsp0278	spain	1760	JONGE	150	16	25	Landkort over Spanien og Portugal
mwf0377	france brittany	1845	JOUANNE	300	48	57	Plan de Nantes
mwf0203	france	1845	JOURNAL CHEMINS DE FER	320	55	83	Carte Generale des Chemins de Fer de France
mwf0911	france paris	1814	JOURNEAUX L'AINE	500	54	77	Nouveau Plan Routier de la Ville et Faubourgs de Paris Divise en Douze Mairies
mwf0635	france limousin	1680	JOUVIN DE ROCHEFORT	1350	52	62	Limoges
mwme0843	persia etc	1822	JUDD	150	20	25	Persia
mwe0486	europe central	1842	JUGEL	400	107	125	Carl Jugel's Post- u. Reise-Karte von Deutschland und den Nachbar-Staaten ... Bearbeitet von U. Hendschel
mwf0524	france corsica	1769	JULIEN	550	22	60	Carte de la Province de Capo Corso et Chemin de communication
mwf0525	france corsica	1769	JULIEN	1350	37	82	Carte Generale de l'Atlas topographique de l'Isle de Corse
mww0427	world	1753	JULIEN	3200	46	66	Nouvelle Mappe Monde Dediee au Progres de nos Connoissances
mwam1116	america north (east)	1795	JUNCKER	340	26	21	Die Funfzehn Vereinigten Staaten von Nord America
mwuss0339	washington DC	1796	JUNCKER	1250	22	27	Plan der Stadt Washington in America
mwg0334	bavaria	1639	JUNG	1500	55	43	Nova Delineatio Episcop Ducatus Herbip cum Locis Adiacentibus
mwe0615b	europe czech republic (bohemia)	1820	JUTTNER	5000	97	97	Grundriss der Königlichen Hauptstadt Prag
mwas0828	asia south east siam	1733	KAEMPFER	400	31	19	Carte du Cours de la Riviere de Meinam depuis Judia jusqu'a son Embouchure (French version of his 1727 map)
mwjk0083	japan	1729	KAEMPFER	2500	42	51	Het Koninkryk Japan (sl. reduced Dutch version of his 1727 map)
mwjk0072	japan	1727	KAEMPFER	400	42	30	Ichnographia Urbis Miaco
mwjk0073	japan	1727	KAEMPFER	3000	46	53	Imperium Japonicum in Sexaginta et Octo Provincias Divisum (1st edition, published in London)
mwas0826	asia south east siam	1727	KAEMPFER	400	31	19	Mappa Meinam Fluvij (course of the river around Bangkok)

AMPG REFERENCE	REGION	DATE	MAP MAKER	PRICE (UK£)	VERT. (cm.)	HOR. (cm.)	TITLE OF MAP (Comments by the editor in brackets)
mwjk0074	japan	1727	KAEMPFER	400	30	37	Particuliere Kaart van de Reys te Land van Fammamatz tot aan Farra
mwjk0075	japan	1727	KAEMPFER	500	30	37	Particuliere Kaart van de Reys te Land van Farra tot Jedo
mwjk0076	japan	1727	KAEMPFER	400	30	37	Particuliere Reis Kaart te Land Strekkende van Jokaitz tot aan het Dorp Fammamatz
mwjk0077	japan	1727	KAEMPFER	400	30	37	Particuliere Reis Kaart van Japan Strekkende van Khurissima tot Osaka
mwjk0078	japan	1727	KAEMPFER	400	30	37	Particuliere Reis Kaart van Japan Strekkende van Kokura tot Khurissima
mwjk0079	japan	1727	KAEMPFER	400	30	37	Particuliere Reis Kaart van Japan Strekkende van Nagasaki tot Kokura (north to the left)
mwjk0080	japan	1727	KAEMPFER	400	30	37	Particuliere Reyskaart over Land Strekkende van Osaka, tot Miaco
mwjk0152	japan tokyo	1727	KAEMPFER	1200	35	39	Plan de Jedo Capitale du Japon / Ichnographia Urbis Jedo, quae Japonici Imperiy Metropolis (1st western map of Tokyo)
mwjk0081	japan	1727	KAEMPFER	400	32	47	Urbs Nangasaki cum Porto & Agro Circumjacenti. Ex Ipsis Japonum Mappis Descripsit & E Koempferi Observationibus Illustratam Sistu J.G. Scheuchzer
mwam1022	america north (east)	1770	KALM	2500	57	76	A New and Accurate Map of Parts of North-America, comprehending the Provinces of New England, New York, Pensilvania (first publ. in Sweden)
mwam1026	america north (east)	1772	KALM	1800	56	76	Nieuwe en Nauwkeurige Kaart van een Gedeelte van Noord Amerika, Behelzende Nieuw Engeland, New York, Pensylvania, New Jersey, Connecticut, Rhode Island, een Stuk van Virginia, Kanada en Halifax
mwe0968	europe hungary	1798	KARACS	350	45	55	Magyar Orszagnak Foldkepe
mwe0510	europe croatia	1822	KARACS	7200	132	188	Mappa Diocesis Zagrabiensis
mwbp0230	poland	1625	KATSCHKER	960	28	32	(Untitled map of Glatz. North to the right.)
mwbp0357	poland	1710	KAUFFER	400	26	32	Nova Totius Regni Poloniae
mwuss1068	new jersey	1850	KEILY	1800	93	98	Map of Middlesex County, New Jersey
mww0398	world	1747	KEIZER	500	17	24	De Nieuwe en Ouden, Oppervlakke en Doorzigtkundige Aardryks Bollen
mww0399	world	1747	KEIZER	650	18	28	De Wareld in een Ronde Gedaante van de Noord Pool te Zien door G. De l'Isle en andere Auteuren / De Wareld Verbeeld in de Gedaante van een Hard en Geleege na de Stelling van de Hr. Guil de l'Isle (2 projections on one sheet)
mwru0450	russia tartary	1742	KEIZER	350	18	24	Het oosterdeel van de Moscoviesche Tarters
mww0397	world	1747	KEIZER	500	18	29	Kaart van de Geheele Wereld
mwam0399	america north	1747	KEIZER	500	18	24	Kaartje van het Noorder-Deel van America
mwca0589	canada st lawrence	1715	KEIZER	600	21	32	L'Ile de Terra Neuve et le Golfe de Saint Laurent, selon les Meilleurs Memoires
mww0369	world	1734	KEIZER	650	17	24	Schuine Ronde Aard Bolle / Waar van t'Middlepunt is Amsterdam en de Tegenvoeters van Amsterd. (polar double hemisphere map.)
mwit0814	italy sardinia	1750	KEIZER	350	24	18	T'Koninkryk Sardinien
mwsw0232	switzerland	1839	KELLER	800	116	175	Carte de la Suisse en 8 Feuilles
mwsw0215	switzerland	1799	KELLER	240	16	26	Die Schweitz oder Helvetien
mww0646a	world	1814	KELLER	960	60	100	Erd Charte nach der Bonneschen Projection
mwsw0237	switzerland	1849	KELLER	400	51	67	H. Keller's Erste Reisekarte der Schweiz, Premiere Carte Routiere de la Suisse, Road Map of Switzerland
mwsw0229	switzerland	1834	KELLER	450	50	66	H. Keller's Keilcharte der Schweis, Carte Routiere de la Suisse, Road Map of Switzerland
mww0714	world	1838	KELLER	2000	122		Keller's Wandkarte der Ostlichen / Westlichen Halbkugel der Erde (2 hemispheres, each 122cm. Diameter)
mwit1220	italy venice	1607	KELLER	750	8	11	Venetiae
mwgm0091	belize	1832	KELLY	75	10	17	(Belize)
mwaf0302	africa	1815	KELLY	75	24	19	Africa
mwca0187	canada	1840	KELLY	75	20	25	Canada
mwas0546	asia south east	1838	KELLY	75	19	24	East India Islands
mwwi0492	cuba	1837	KELLY	75	13	18	Harbour & City of Havannah
mwgm0326	mexico	1835	KELLY	200	20	24	Mexico & Guatemala
mwp0094	australia	1830	KELLY	100	20	25	New South Wales
mwam0600	america north	1815	KELLY	150	24	19	North America
mwp0284	pacific (all)	1835	KELLY	75	19	25	Pacific Ocean
mwme0517	jerusalem	1837	KELLY	75	24	19	Plan of the Ancient City of Jerusalem
mwsam0431	south america brazil	1837	KELLY	150	13	17	Rio de Janeiro
mwuk0611	scotland	1830	KELLY	75	24	18	Scotland
mww0699	world	1832	KELLY	235	24	40	The World on Mercator's Projection
mwam0550	america north	1800	KELLY	180	19	24	United States
mwwi0190	west indies	1834	KELLY	95	19	24	West Indies
mwuss1534	texas	1846	KEMBLE	1200	24	24	Texas in 1836
mwuss1524a	texas	1844	KENDALL	600	40	29	Texas and Part of Mexico & the United States Showing the Route of the First Santa Fe Expedition

AMPG REFERENCE	REGION	DATE	MAP MAKER	PRICE (UK£)	VERT. (cm.)	HOR. (cm.)	TITLE OF MAP (Comments by the editor in brackets)
mwuss0305	connecticut	1806	KENSETT	6000	67	49	A Plan of the Town of New Haven, with All the Buildings in 1748 Taken by the Hon. Gen. Wadsworth of Durham to which are Added the Names and Professions of the Inhabitants at the Period
mwam1298	great lakes	1812	KENSETT	4000	36	47	To the Officers of the Army and Citizens of the United States this Map of Upper and Lower Canada and United States Contiguous
mwam0830	america north (central)	1839	KEPOHONI	8000	25	42	Amerika Huipuia (Hawaiian language map for schools)
mwme0230	holy land	1702	KEUR	400	35	45	De Gelegentheyt van 't Paradys en 't Landt Canaan, Mitsgaders d'Eerst Bewoonde Landen der Patriarchen (5 inset scenes)
mwme0476	jerusalem	1702	KEUR	650	36	45	Ierusalem (12 scenes in borders)
mww0217	world	1682	KEUR	2500	35	45	Orbis Terrarum Tabula Recens Emendata in Lucem Edita
mwm0138	mediterranean east	1703	KEYSER	600	21	51	Een Tafla pa the landskap ock Stader the then helige Apostolen
mwuss1539	texas	1847	KIEPERT	6000	56	63	Mexico Texas und Californien
mwuss1287	ohio	1821	KILBOURN	400	31	30	A Map of Ohio, by John Kilbourn, Columbus, January 1821
mwam1005	america north (east)	1760	KILIAN	475	20	22	America Septentrionalis oder Mitternachtiger Theil von America, Bestehend, in Neu Brittania Canada, Neu Engeland, Neu Schotland, Neu Jorck, Pensylvania, Carolina Florida Georgien. Worinnen der Grosse S. Laurentius und Ohio Fluss Samt
mwam0183	america continent	1760	KILIAN	250	15	20	Americae Septentrionalis et Meridional Compendiosa Repraesentatio Compendiose Vorstellung des Ganzen Weltheils Nord und Sud Americce mit seinen Konigreichen und Provincien
mwit0363	italy emilia-romagna	1757	KILIAN	375	16	20	Bologna
mwe0597	europe czech republic (bohemia)	1760	KILIAN	350	18	28	Das Konigreich Bohmen mit seinen Zugehorigen Provintzien
mwg0495	mecklenburg	1760	KILIAN	300	16	24	Die Belagerung von Colberg Angegriffen durch den Russischen General v. Palmbach und Defendirt durch den Preussi. Obristen Bar v. Heyden von 3ten Oct. 1758
mwbp0464	poland	1760	KILIAN	300	16	222	Die Häfftige Belagerung und darauf den 12.Nov.1757 Erfolgte Eroberung der Festung Schweidnitz
mwwi0092	west indies	1760	KILIAN	300	14	27	Die Insulen in West America
mwit1137a	italy florence	1760	KILIAN	320	14	19	Florentia
mwg0832	westphalia	1760	KILIAN	300	16	26	Gegend am Rhein im Clevischen, wo die Alliirte Armee ... den 2. Juny 1758 Ubergangen
mwe0598	europe czech republic (bohemia)	1760	KILIAN	300	16	24	Gegend der Vestung Olmutz auf 4. bis 5. Stund Wie Solche den 27. Maj 1758 von den Koniglich-Preuss. Trouppen Berent, und den 2. July die Belagerung Wieder auf Gehoben Worden
mwam0383a	america north	1730	KILIAN	875	17	25	General Charte von dem Mitternacht America und Sonderlich denen darin Befindliche Franzos Colonien
mwit0441	italy liguria	1750	KILIAN	500	16	19	Genua
mwbp0465	poland	1760	KILIAN	300	18	28	Grund Riss und Kon. Preuss. Belagerung der Stadt Breslau vom 8. bis 20. Dec. 1757
mwwi0548	guadeloupe	1760	KILIAN	350	18	27	Inseln uber dem Winde. Karte von den Inseln Guadelupe und Grand Terre
mwru0230	russia	1757	KILIAN	350	17	20	Konigsberg die Haupt und Residenz-Statt des Konigreichs Preussen
mww0444	world	1760	KILIAN	800	27	34	Mappa Totius Mundi
mwaf0204	africa	1759	KILIAN	350	27	34	Nova Tabula Africae
mwam0179	america continent	1759	KILIAN	500	29	34	Nova Tabula Americae
mwbp0466	poland	1760	KILIAN	300	18	25	Plan der Bataille bey Breslau da die Kaysl. Kon. Armee den 22.Nov.1757 die Konigl. Preussische Armee aus ihren Verschanzten Dorffer und Retranchements zu Weichen u. zu Verlassen Forcirt
mwg0384	bavaria	1757	KILIAN	350	17	24	Regenspurg
mwe0373	europe austria	1757	KILIAN	350	16	21	Saltzburg
mwg0239c	berlin	1758	KILIAN	150	17	26	Überfall der Königl. Haupt Stadt Berlin ... 1758 (environs to the East of Berlin)
mwe0430	europe austria vienna	1757	KILIAN	450	15	17	Wien in Oesterreich
mwsw0182	switzerland	1780	KILIAN	800	15	19	Zurich (view)
mwp0452	pacific north	1799	KINCAID	200	18	29	A Chart of the North West Coast of America & the North East Coast of Asia
mwp0129	australia	1840	KINCAID	240	19	24	Australia New Zealand &c.
mwuss0024	alaska	1782	KINCAID	300	16	25	Bhering's Straits with the Adjacent Coasts of Asia and America
mwp0029a	australia	1790	KINCAID	1500	19	24	New Holland, & the Adjacent Islands, Agreeable to the Latest Discoveries
mwme0376	holy land	1791	KINCAID	100	21	14	Palestine or the Holy Land
mwsam0697	south america magellan	1790	KINCAID	200	18	22	Streights of Magellan from the Latest Authorities
mwe0509	europe croatia	1803	KINDERMANN	500	48	58	Charte von Kaernthen und Krain, nebst den Grafschaften Gorz und Gradiska und dem Gebiethe von Triest

AMPG REFERENCE	REGION	DATE	MAP MAKER	PRICE (UK£)	VERT. (cm.)	HOR. (cm.)	TITLE OF MAP (Comments by the editor in brackets)
mwe0614	europe czech republic (bohemia)	1802	KINDERMANN	500	48	59	Charte von Maehren und dem Oesterreichischen Anteile von Schlesien
mwe0390a	europe austria	1797	KINDERMANN	500	50	59	Der Noerdliche Theil von Untersteyermark … (from his atlas of Austria)
mwe0615	europe czech republic (bohemia)	1802	KINDERMANN	500	47	58	Nordoestlicher Theil von Boehmen, Enthaltend den Bunzlauer, Bidschower, Koenig, Graetzer, Chrudimer, Czaslauer, und Karuzimer Kreis
mwuss0654	louisiana	1806	KING	20000	21	71	Map of the Red River in Louisiana from the Spanish Camp where the Exploring Party of the U.S. was met by the Spanish Troops to where it Enters the Mississippi
mwuk1604	isle of man	1656	KING	800	17	24	The Isle of Man Exactly Described, and into Severall Parishes Divided with Every Towns, Village, Baye, Creke, and River Therein Conteyned
mwuss0590	kansas	1836	KINGSBURY	1000	50	89	(Western Territory)
mwbh0787	belgium holland	1816	KINNERSLEY	180	18	25	A Sketch of the Battle of Waterloo, Fought Sunday 18th June 1815
mwuss0079	california	1705	KINO	2000	24	21	Passage par Terre a la Californie Decouvert par le Rev. Pere Eusebe-Francois Kino Jesuite depuis 1698 jusqu'a 1701 (Kino was the first European to point out the fallacy of the 'island' theory)
mwuss0081	california	1726	KINO	1500	34	22	Tabula Californiae Anno 1702 ex Autoptica Observatione Delineata a R.P. Chino e S.I. (first publ. 1702)
mwru0551	ukraine	1776	KINSBERGEN	3000	80	90	Carte de la Crimee, Levee pendant la Derniere Guerre de 1772
mwru0555	ukraine	1780	KINSBERGEN	4000	57	173	Carte de la Mer Noire de la Mer d'Asow
mwbh0686	belgium holland	1748	KINTS	1500	114	82	Carte de la Principaute de Liege et de ses Environs Tiree des Observations Faites sur les Lieux par le R.P. Nicolas le Clerc
mwam0257	america continent	1806	KIPFERLING	200	44	33	America nach dem Neuesten Geographischen und Politischen Zustande zum Gebrauch der Oesterreichischen Schulen Entworfen
mwp0515a	pacific south	1806	KIPFERLING	550	33	43	Australien oder die Insel Welt
mwec1105a	uk england suffolk	1737	KIRBY	2500	51	73	A Survey of the County of Suffolk
mwgm0178	mexico	1682	KIRCHER	150	14	8	(Mexico City to Gulf. On sheet with text)
mwaf0090	africa	1682	KIRCHER	720	46	36	Chorographia Originis Nili iuxta Observationem / Chorographia Originis Nili … ex Arabum Geographia / Vera et Genvina Fontium Nili (3 maps on one sheet)
mwme0184	holy land	1682	KIRCHER	300	10	15	Communicatio Maris Mediterranei et quod Mortum dicuntum Mari Rubro
mwsc0077	scandinavia	1682	KIRCHER	280	20	19	Descriptio Vorticis Norvegiae et Bothniae
mww0202	world	1675	KIRCHER	960	34	48	Geographia Conjecturalis de Orbis Terrestris Post Diluvium Transformatione ex Variorum Geographorum Sententia cui Author Subscribit
mwaf0872	africa south	1678	KIRCHER	600	34	41	Hydrophylacium Africae Precipuum, in Montibus Lunae Situm, Lacus et Flumina Praecipua Fundens ubi et Nova Inventio Originis Nili Discribitur
mwc0052	china	1665	KIRCHER	1250	34	45	Imperium Sinicum Quindecupartitum
mwam0085	america continent	1682	KIRCHER	750	34	41	Mappa Fluxus et Refluxus Rationes in Isthmo Americano, in Freto Magellanico, caeterisque Americae Littoribus Exhibens
mwm0019	mediterranean	1678	KIRCHER	960	34	56	Mappa Maris Mediterranei Fluxus Currentes et Naturam Motionum Explicans
mwat0259a	atlantic ocean (all)	1682	KIRCHER	450	20	20	Tabula Fluxus et Refluxus, Rationes in Mari Anglico
mwas0055	asia continent	1667	KIRCHER	720	27	35	Tabula Geodoborica Itinerum a Varijs in Cataium
mwas0068	asia continent	1682	KIRCHER	1000	34	41	Tabula Geographica Hydrophylacium Asiae Majoris
mww0182	world	1665	KIRCHER	1800	36	55	Tabula Geographico-Hydrographica Motus Oceani, Currentes, Abyssos, Montes Igniuomus in Universo Orbe Indicans
mwsam0028	south america	1678	KIRCHER	720	34	20	Tabula qua Hydrophylacium Andium Exhibetur, quo Universa America Australis Innumeris Fluviis Lacubus q. Irrigatur
mwme0717	caucasus	1682	KIRCHER	200	16	16	Typus Communicationis Maris Caspii, cum Persico et Euxino (on sheet with text)
mwsw0239	alps	1682	KIRCHER	240	15	19	Typus Hydrophylacii intra Alpes Rhaeticas
mwru0171	russia	1734	KIRILOV	10000	56	86	Imperii Russici Tabula Generalis (1st map of Russia by a Russian. Title also in Cyrillic)
mwsc0434a	scandinavia finland	1745	KIRILOV	4000	48	56	Magnus Ducatus Finlandiae (place names in Latin and Cyrillic)
mwuk0570a	scotland	1804	KIRKWOOD	750	71	58	Travelling Map of Scotland
mwbp0479b	poland	1771	KISCHSHLAGER	1500	72	195	Plan des in Ober Schlesien gegen die Polnische Graenze Ano. 1771
mwec0642a	uk england kent	1769	KITCHIN	200	18	29	(Untitled map of Kent)
mwp0259	pacific (all)	1780	KITCHIN	400	43	36	A Chart of the Discoveries Made by the Late Capn. Cook & Other European Navigators in the Great Pacific Ocean
mwaf1215	africa west	1752	KITCHIN	150	20	25	A Chart of the Western Coast of Africa
mwuk0866	uk	1787	KITCHIN	480	64	50	A Compleat Map of the British Isles
mwe0173	europe	1755	KITCHIN	650	67	77	A Correct Map of Europe Divided into its Empires
mwwi0724	jamaica	1766	KITCHIN	150	11	19	A Correct Map of the Island of Jamaica

AMPG REFERENCE	REGION	DATE	MAP MAKER	PRICE (UK£)	VERT. (cm.)	HOR. (cm.)	TITLE OF MAP (Comments by the editor in brackets)
mwuk1008	england	1767	KITCHIN	400	62	53	A General Map of England & Wales Divided into its Counties, Corrected from the Best Surveys and Astronl. Observations
mwin0250	india	1773	KITCHIN	375	33	38	A General Map of India Including the Empire of Hindustan with the Kingdom of Bengal & its other Dependencies
mwam0988	america north (east)	1756	KITCHIN	8000	48	67	A General Map of the Middle British Colonies in America viz. Virginia, Maryland ... New York, Connecticut, and Rhode Island ... Publish'd by Lewis Evans
mwuk0996	england	1749	KITCHIN	150	18	14	A Map of England and Wales
mwec0295d	uk england devon	1749	KITCHIN	140	18	14	A Map of Devonshire (title above map. Size incl. text below map)
mwec0412	uk england essex	1749	KITCHIN	75	12	14	A Map of Essex
mwec0629a	uk england kent	1749	KITCHIN	140	12	14	A Map of Kent (title above map)
mwc0196	china	1780	KITCHIN	200	16	22	A Map of Kitay or Empire of the Kin adapted to the History of Jenghiz Khan
mwc0314a	china tibet	1750	KITCHIN	150	17	23	A Map of Little Bochara and the Adjacent Countrys Drawn from the Survey of the Jesuits and Mr. Kyrillow's Map
mwca0076	canada	1758	KITCHIN	320	27	34	A Map of New England, and Nova Scotia; with Part of New York, Canada, and New Britain & the Adjacent Islands of New Found Land Cape Breton &c. By Tho. Kitchin Geogr.
mwam1021	america north (east)	1768	KITCHIN	1200	42	58	A Map of North America from the Latest Surveys and Maps by John Blair LLD. & F.R.S. As a Supplement to his Tables of Chronology
mwjk0164	korea	1753	KITCHIN	750	28	22	A Map of Quan-Tong or Lea-Tonge Province and the Kingdom of Kau-Li or Corea
mwca0439	canada nova scotia	1780	KITCHIN	200	16	11	A Map of Royal or Cape Breton I.
mwsam0092	south america	1775	KITCHIN	1200	101	118	A Map of South America Containing Tierra-Firma, Guayana, New Granada, Amazonia, Brasil, Peru, Paraguay, Chaco, Tucuman, Chili and Patagonia. From Mr. D'Anville with Several Improvements and Additions, and the Newest Discoveries
mwuss0500	georgia	1780	KITCHIN	480	20	24	A Map of Such Parts of Georgia and South Carolina as Tend to Illustrate the Progress and Operations of the British Army, &c.
mwuss1452	rhode isl	1778	KITCHIN	480	19	24	A Map of the Colony of Rhode Island: with the Adjacent Parts of Connecticut, Massachusets Bay. &c. By Thos. Kitchen
mwuk1196	england london	1758	KITCHIN	500	45	51	A Map of the Countries Thirty Miles Round London. (5 editions until 1780)
mwas0487	asia south east	1770	KITCHIN	320	33	38	A Map of the East India Islands, Agreeable to the Most Approved Maps and Charts
mwuss1085	new york	1756	KITCHIN	350	18	22	A Map of the Eastern Part of the Province of New York; with Part of New Jersey, &c. Drawn from the Best Authorities
mwam0955	america north (east)	1747	KITCHIN	200	18	17	A Map of the French Settlements in North America by Thos. Kitchin Geogrr.
mwwi0618	hispaniola	1758	KITCHIN	250	19	26	A Map of the Island of Hispaniola or St. Domingo. Drawn from the Best Authorities by T. Kitchin Geo.
mwme0361	holy land	1772	KITCHIN	280	24	34	A Map of the Land of Canaan or Holy Land as Divided Among the Twelve Tribes
mwam0987	america north (east)	1756	KITCHIN	400	17	21	A Map of the Province of Pensilvania Drawn from the Best Authorities by T. Kitchin Gr.
mwuss0447	florida	1781	KITCHIN	350	19	24	A Map of the Province of West Florida
mwaf1202	africa west	1745	KITCHIN	150	20	32	A Map of the River Gambia from Eropina to Barrakunda by Captain John Leach in 1732
mwuss1650	virginia	1781	KITCHIN	500	28	34	A Map of the Seat of War in the Southern Part of Virginia
mwsam0086	south america	1772	KITCHIN	750	99	72	A Map of the Southern Parts of America
mwsc0741	scandinavia sweden	1781	KITCHIN	280	47	39	A Map of the Southern Provinces of Sweden
mwru0454	russia tartary	1750	KITCHIN	150	17	23	A Map of Western Tartary Drawn from the Survey of the Jesuits
mwec1282	uk england worcestershire	1749	KITCHIN	60	13	14	A Map of Worcestershire
mwc0168	china	1764	KITCHIN	400	34	41	A New & Accurate Map of China Drawn from Surveys Made by the Jesuit Missionaries, by Order of the Emperor
mwuss0419	florida	1763	KITCHIN	350	18	23	A New and Accurate Map of East and West Florida, Drawn from the Best Authorities
mwit0196	italy	1766	KITCHIN	320	43	39	A New and Accurate Map of Italy
mwsc0626	scandinavia norway	1762	KITCHIN	235	23	24	A New and Accurate Map of Norway, Drawn from the Best Authorities
mwam1018	america north (east)	1766	KITCHIN	2200	52	62	A New and Accurate Map of the British Dominions in America, According to the Treaty of 1763; Divided into the Several Provinces and Jurisdictions
mwam1069	america north (east)	1780	KITCHIN	400	18	22	A New and Accurate Map of the Cherokee Nation
mwru0252	russia	1775	KITCHIN	280	34	44	A New and Accurate Map of the Whole Russian Empire as Contained both in Europe and Asia
mww0449	world	1760	KITCHIN	1000	29	54	A New and Accurate Map of the World Drake & Anson

AMPG REFERENCE	REGION	DATE	MAP MAKER	PRICE (UK£)	VERT. (cm.)	HOR. (cm.)	TITLE OF MAP (Comments by the editor in brackets)
mwf0135	france	1763	KITCHIN	150	24	30	A New and Correct Chart of the Seat of War, on the Coasts of France, Spain, Portugal and Italy; with the Adjacent Coasts & Islands, in the Ocean and Mediterranean Sea: Drawn from Surveys, & Regulated by Astronomical Observations
mwuk0541	scotland	1783	KITCHIN	180	28	22	A New and Correct Map of Scotland
mwwi0098	west indies	1762	KITCHIN	250	29	36	A New and Correct Map of the American Islands, Now Called the West Indies, with the Whole Coast of the Neighbouring Continent
mwuk1232	england london	1775	KITCHIN	1400	44	68	A New and Correct Plan of the Cities of London, Westminster, and Southwark (12 editions until 1791)
mwca0602	canada st lawrence	1760	KITCHIN	200	18	25	A New Chart of the River St. Lawrence from the Island of Anticosti to Lake Ontario by T. Kitchin, Geogr.
mwec0551	uk england hertfordshire	1749	KITCHIN	720	53	65	A New Improved Map of Hertfordshire
mwec0016	uk england bedfordshire	1764	KITCHIN	80	26	20	A New Map of Bedfordshire
mwuk1846	wales	1764	KITCHIN	60	20	26	A New Map of Brecknock Shire, Drawn from the Best Authorities
mwec0103	uk england cambridgeshire	1764	KITCHIN	100	26	20	A New Map of Cambridgeshire &c.
mwuk1847	wales	1764	KITCHIN	60	20	26	A New Map of Carmarthen Shire, Drawn from the Best Authorities
mwec0145	uk england cheshire	1764	KITCHIN	120	20	25	A New Map of Cheshire
mwec0298	uk england devon	1764	KITCHIN	100	19	25	A New Map of Devon Shire
mwec0339	uk england dorset	1764	KITCHIN	100	20	25	A New Map of Dorset Shire
mwec0377	uk england durham	1764	KITCHIN	60	20	25	A New Map of Durham
mwuk1031	england	1794	KITCHIN	800	128	100	A New Map of England & Wales
mwec0485	uk england hampshire	1764	KITCHIN	100	19	25	A New Map of Hamp Shire Drawn from the Best Authorities
mwec0554	uk england hertfordshire	1764	KITCHIN	100	20	25	A New Map of Hartfordshire
mwec0525	uk england herefordshire	1764	KITCHIN	80	26	20	A New Map of Hereford Shire, Drawn from the Best Authorities
mwec0584	uk england huntingdonshire	1764	KITCHIN	60	25	19	A New Map of Huntingdon Shire
mwuk0207	ireland	1777	KITCHIN	550	64	56	A New Map of Ireland Divided into Provinces, Counties &c.
mwuk1848	wales	1764	KITCHIN	80	26	20	A New Map of Monmouth Shire, Drawn from the Best Authorities
mwec0831	uk england norfolk	1764	KITCHIN	80	20	25	A New Map of Norfolk
mwam0177	america continent	1759	KITCHIN	450	36	28	A New Map of North and South America
mwuss0187	carolinas	1765	KITCHIN	400	18	23	A New Map of North and South Carolina and Georgia. Drawn from the Best Authorities
mwuk1849	wales	1764	KITCHIN	80	20	26	A New Map of North Wales, Drawn from the Best Authorities
mwec0864	uk england northamptonshire	1764	KITCHIN	60	25	19	A New Map of Northhampton Shire
mwec0918	uk england nottinghamshire	1764	KITCHIN	60	25	20	A New Map of Nottingham Shire
mwuk1850	wales	1764	KITCHIN	100	20	26	A New Map of Pembroke Shire, Drawn from the Best Authorities
mwuk1851	wales	1764	KITCHIN	60	20	26	A New Map of Radnor Shire, Drawn from the Best Authorities
mwec0990	uk england rutland	1764	KITCHIN	60	26	20	A New Map of Rutland Shire, Drawn from the Best Authorities
mwec1017	uk england shropshire	1764	KITCHIN	80	25	20	A New Map of Shropshire
mwec1046	uk england somerset	1764	KITCHIN	150	20	26	A New Map of Somerset Shire, Drawn from the Best Authorities
mwsc0735a	scandinavia	1758	KITCHIN	235	23	18	A New Map of Sweden
mwuss0184	carolinas	1760	KITCHIN	480	17	22	A New Map of the Cherokee Nation with the Names of the Towns & Rivers. They are Situated on No. Lat. from 34 to 36
mwuk1184	england london	1747	KITCHIN	300	24	29	A New Map of the Countries Ten Miles round the Cities of London
mwec1111	uk england suffolk	1764	KITCHIN	80	20	26	A New Map of the County of Suffolk
mwf0506	france corsica	1760	KITCHIN	250	25	18	A New Map of the Island of Corsica
mwwi0723	jamaica	1764	KITCHIN	280	30	42	A New Map of the Island of Jamaica Divided into its Parishes Including the South End of Cuba and the West End of Hispaniola with the Trade Winds &c.
mwwi0899a	trinidad & tobago	1762	KITCHIN	2400	44	60	A New Map of the Island of Tobago
mwbp0509	poland	1787	KITCHIN	360	50	66	A New Map of the Kingdom of Poland
mwsc0176	scandinavia	1788	KITCHIN	360	50	66	A New Map of the Northern States Containing the Kingdoms of Sweden, Denmark, and Norway
mwca0312	canada newfoundland	1762	KITCHIN	250	18	26	A New Map of the Only Useful & Frequented Part of New Found Land
mwas0791	asia south east philippines	1769	KITCHIN	240	23	17	A New Map of the Philippine Islands, Drawn from the Best Authorities
mwca0522	canada quebec	1760	KITCHIN	320	18	22	A New Map of the Province of Quebec in North America; Drawn from the Best Authorities: By Thos. Kitchin, Geogr.
mwin0238	india	1763	KITCHIN	200	24	23	A New Map of the Seat of War on the Coast of Malabar & Coromandel, in the Empire of the Great Mogol

AMPG REFERENCE	REGION	DATE	MAP MAKER	PRICE (UK£)	VERT. (cm.)	HOR. (cm.)	TITLE OF MAP (Comments by the editor in brackets)
mww0580	world	1794	KITCHIN	6500	56	104	A New Map of the World. with All the New Discoveries. By Capt. Cook and Other Navigators Ornamented with the Solar System the Eclipses of the Sun Moon & Planets &c. by T. Kitchen Geographer
mwec1228	uk england westmorland	1764	KITCHIN	60	20	26	A New Map of Westmoreland, Drawn from the Best Authorities
mwec1253	uk england wiltshire	1764	KITCHIN	80	26	20	A New Map of Wiltshire
mwam1027	america north (east)	1772	KITCHIN	500	28	26	A Plan of Fort Edward and its Environs on Hudson's River
mwca0517	canada quebec	1759	KITCHIN	240	11	19	A Plan of Quebec, Metropolis of Canada in North America
mwca0362	canada nova scotia	1746	KITCHIN	280	19	10	A Plan of the City & Harbour of Louisburg
mwru0395	russia moscow	1784	KITCHIN	450	30	33	A Plan of the City of Moscow
mwru0274	russia	1784	KITCHIN	280	23	30	A Plan of the City of St. Petersburgh
mwuk1228	england london	1773	KITCHIN	800	32	49	A Pocket Plan of the Cities of London & Westminster, & Borough of Southwark (reprinted 1775)
mwaf0274	africa	1794	KITCHIN	480	43	53	Africa
mwaf0228	africa	1771	KITCHIN	300	34	37	Africa Drawn and Engraved from the Best Maps and Charts
mwaf0256	africa	1787	KITCHIN	250	34	39	Africa Drawn from the Latest and Best Authorities
mwaf0248	africa	1783	KITCHIN	240	23	29	Africa with the European Settlements &c.
mww0528	world	1783	KITCHIN	1000	31	44	An Accurate Chart of the World with the New Discoveries
mwuk1840	wales	1754	KITCHIN	300	34	51	An Accurate Map of Brecknock Shire. Drawn from an Actual Survey with Various Improvements
mwuk1838	wales	1754	KITCHIN	500	33	52	An Accurate Map of Cardigan Shire
mwuk1835	wales	1749	KITCHIN	500	35	52	An Accurate Map of Carmarthen Shire Drawn from an Actual Survey with Various Improvements
mwuk1002	england	1760	KITCHIN	500	59	50	An Accurate Map of England and Wales drawn from all the particular surveys
mwuk1841	wales	1754	KITCHIN	500	34	52	An Accurate Map of Glamorgan Shire
mwuk1839	wales	1754	KITCHIN	500	33	52	An Accurate Map of Radnor Shire
mwe0465	europe central	1763	KITCHIN	150	21	24	An Accurate Map of the Seat of War in the Kingdom of Prussia as also in Bohemia, Lusatia, Silesia, Saxony Westphalia &c. By Tho: Kitchin Geogr.
mwuk1212	england london	1765	KITCHIN	1000	28	50	An Improved Plan of the Cities of London and Westminster and Borough of Southwark
mwas0218	asia continent	1792	KITCHIN	375	43	53	Asia and its Several Islands and Regions
mwas0190	asia continent	1773	KITCHIN	250	35	37	Asia Drawn and Engraved from the Best Maps and Charts
mwas0206	asia continent	1787	KITCHIN	300	33	39	Asia Drawn from the Latest and Best Authorites
mwam1046	america north (east)	1777	KITCHIN	5000	44	54	British Dominions in America Agreeable to the Treaty of 1763
mwgm0040	gulf of mexico and surrounding regions	1777	KITCHIN	450	31	48	Carta del Golfo del Messico dell' Isole e Paesi Adjacenti
mwgm0245	mexico	1778	KITCHIN	280	29	38	Carte du Mexique ou de la Nouvelle Espagne, ou l'on peut Suivre les Mouvemens de Cortes pour l'Histoire de l'Amerique
mwsam0239	south america argentina	1760	KITCHIN	240	20	25	Chart of the Rio de la Plata in South America (inset of Buenos Aires)
mwc0161	china	1758	KITCHIN	150	17	22	China
mwc0171	china	1764	KITCHIN	265	28	30	China as Surveyed by the Jesuit Misionaries between the Years 1708 & 1717 with Korea & the Adjoining Parts of Tartary
mwec0267	uk england derbyshire	1764	KITCHIN	120	26	20	Derbyshire, Drawn from the Best Authorities
mwuk0212	ireland	1780	KITCHIN	350	38	34	Ireland Divided into its Provinces and Counties, Drawn from the latest Surveys
mwuk0187a	ireland	1762	KITCHIN	200	30	19	Ireland Divided into Provinces & Counties
mwuk0187	ireland	1762	KITCHIN	280	36	34	Ireland with the Roads from the Latest Surveys
mwuk0219	ireland	1783	KITCHIN	160	22	27	Ireland, Drawn from the Best Authorities
mwat0332	atlantic st helena	1756	KITCHIN	100	15	9	Island of St. Helena, Belonging to ye English East India Company
mwuk1608	isle of man	1749	KITCHIN	180	19	15	Isle of Man
mwit0203	italy	1786	KITCHIN	480	60	52	Italy
mwgm0043	gulf of mexico and surrounding regions	1778	KITCHIN	450	31	48	Kaart van de Golf van Mexico, de Eilanden en de Aangrenzende Landschappen
mwec0632	uk england kent	1751	KITCHIN	140	14	21	Kent Drawn from an Actual Survey
mwuk1005	england	1764	KITCHIN	350	35	35	Kitchin's Most Accurate Map of the Roads of England and Wales: With the Distances by the Mile Stones, and other Most Exact Admensurations between Town & Town
mwp0427	pacific north	1780	KITCHIN	480	20	59	Krenitzin's and Levasheff's Voyage to the Fox Islands in 1768 and 1769
mwgm0234	mexico	1768	KITCHIN	200	18	11	La Vera Cruz or St. Juan de Ulua
mwam1288	great lakes	1772	KITCHIN	650	22	25	Lake Ontario
mwec0689	uk england lancashire	1764	KITCHIN	100	25	20	Lancashire
mwuk1581	channel islands	1746	KITCHIN	180	26	20	Les Isles de Jersey, Guernsey, Alderney, &c.
mwuss0642	louisiana	1765	KITCHIN	240	18	23	Louisiana, as Formerly Claimed by France, Now Containing Part of British America to the East & Spanish America to the West of the Mississipi
mwe0206	europe	1783	KITCHIN	300	41	43	Map of Europe Divided into its Empires, Kingdoms, etc.

AMPG REFERENCE	REGION	DATE	MAP MAKER	PRICE (UK£)	VERT. (cm.)	HOR. (cm.)	TITLE OF MAP (Comments by the editor in brackets)
mwuss1128	new york	1778	KITCHIN	350	25	18	Map of New York I. with the Adjacent Rocks and other Remarkable Parts of Hell-Gate. By Thos. Kitchin, Senr. Hydrographer to His Majesty
mwgm0120	honduras	1779	KITCHIN	400	18	23	Map of the Bay of Honduras: Shewing the Situation of the Spanish Town and Fort of St. Fernando de Omoa, Taken by the Honble. John Luttrell & Wm. Dalrymple Esq Oct. 20th. 1779
mwsam0197	south america (north west)	1777	KITCHIN	235	38	24	Map of the Countries on the South Sea from Panama to Guayaquil
mwam0452	america north	1776	KITCHIN	240	33	26	Map of the European Settlements in North America
mwas0494	asia south east	1776	KITCHIN	320	32	46	Map of the European Settlements in the East Indies and on the Eastern Coast of Africa Including Part of Europe (inset S. India)
mwam1079	america north (east)	1783	KITCHIN	1000	41	51	Map of the United States in North America with the British, French and Spanish Dominions Adjoining, According to the Treaty of 1783
mww0529	world	1783	KITCHIN	1200	33	51	Map of the World with the New Discoveries on Mercator's Projection by T.J. Senr. Hydrographer to His Majesty
mwgm0249	mexico	1780	KITCHIN	300	28	37	Messico o Nuova Spagna
mwgm0244	mexico	1777	KITCHIN	480	29	38	Mexico or New Spain in which the Motions of Cortes may be Traced
mwec0787	uk england middlesex	1764	KITCHIN	100	21	26	Middlesex
mwme0831	persia etc	1782	KITCHIN	280	37	34	New Map of Persia Divided into its Provinces from the Latest Authorities
mwam0456	america north	1777	KITCHIN	400	33	37	North America Drawn & Engraved from the Best Maps & Charts
mwam0476	america north	1782	KITCHIN	280	19	23	North America Drawn from the Best Authorities
mwam0499	america north	1787	KITCHIN	300	33	39	North America Drawn from the Latest and Best Authorities
mwam0974	america north (east)	1755	KITCHIN	450	32	23	North America from Cape Florida to Baffins Bay with the Isles & Limits Conquer'd Ceded & Confirmed to Great Britain by Treaty
mwuk0518	scotland	1773	KITCHIN	650	68	55	North Britain or Scotland Divided into its Counties ... by Thos. Kitchen ... London. Printed for W. Faden Charing Cross ... Decr. 1st. 1778 by Wm. Faden
mwca0364	canada nova scotia	1749	KITCHIN	200	11	17	Nova Scotia, Drawn from Surveys by T Kitchin Gr.
mwme0345	holy land	1755	KITCHIN	500	42	57	Palestine seu Terra Promissionis in Duodecim Tribus Partitae Facies Antiqua
mwuss1360	pennsylvania	1772	KITCHIN	280	24	25	Plan of Fort Pitt or Pittsbourg
mwsc0743	scandinavia sweden	1784	KITCHIN	300	37	29	Plan of the City of Stockholm
mwuss1548	vermont	1772	KITCHIN	250	27	17	Plan of the Land between Lake Champlain and Fort Edward on the Hudson
mwbp0504	poland	1784	KITCHIN	280	41	51	Poland with its Dismember'd Provinces
mwsc0157	scandinavia	1770	KITCHIN	600	27	35	Schonlandia XIII Nova Tabula
mwuk0543	scotland	1785	KITCHIN	280	36	33	Scotland with the Roads, from the Latest Survey
mwsam0097	south america	1779	KITCHIN	320	45	55	South America
mwsam0111	south america	1790	KITCHIN	240	34	38	South America agreeable to the most approved Maps and Charts, by Mr Kitchen
mwsam0085	south america	1771	KITCHIN	250	34	37	South America, Drawn and Engrav'd from the Best Maps & Charts
mwwi0080	west indies	1744	KITCHIN	280	18	30	The British Islands and Privileges in the West Indies
mwc0138	china	1745	KITCHIN	240	15	22	The Empire of Hya, Including Great Part of Tangul Adapted to the History of Jenghis Kahn
mwuk1201	england london	1761	KITCHIN	500	46	53	The Environs or Countries Twenty Miles Round London.
mwca0576	canada quebec montreal	1761	KITCHIN	480	24	33	The Isles of Montreal, as they have been Survey'd by the French Engineers
mwf0167	france	1794	KITCHIN	350	42	57	The Republic of France
mwca0608	canada st lawrence	1764	KITCHIN	720	13	75	The River Saint Lawrence from Lake Ontario to the Island of Montreal, Engrav'd for Mr. Mante's History of the War in North America
mwuss1129	new york	1778	KITCHIN	350	25	18	The Southern Part of the Province of New York: With Part of the Adjoining Colonies
mww0472	world	1767	KITCHIN	480	18	37	The World from the Best Authorities
mwwi0093	west indies	1760	KITCHIN	235	18	29	West Indies
mwwi0116	west indies	1782	KITCHIN	300	34	38	West Indies Agreeable to the Most Approved Maps & Charts
mwuk0547	scotland	1787	KITCHIN-SAYER	1200	128	107	A New and Correct Map of Scotland or North Britain
mwc0250	china	1825	KLAPROTH	320	31	37	Carte de l'Ile de Hainan Formant le Department Chinois de Khioung Tcheou Fou
mwjk0171	korea	1832	KLAPROTH	960	71	49	Carte des Huit Provinces de Tchao Sian
mwc0238	china	1810	KLIEWER	350	18	24	Karte von China
mwuss1406	pennsylvania	1824	KLINCKOWSTROM	280	19	24	Plan of Philadelphia
mwsc0180	scandinavia	1789	KLINGER	650	85	60	Carte des Couronnes du Nord
mww0569	world	1791	KLINGER	1350	45	53	Die Zwo Halften der Erdkugel mit einige Astronomischen Zeichnungen (re-issued in 1812)
mwsc0393	scandinavia denmark	1808	KLINT	720	97	64	Karta ofver Kattegat och Bohus Bugten med en Del af Skagerrack

AMPG REFERENCE	REGION	DATE	MAP MAKER	PRICE (UK£)	VERT. (cm.)	HOR. (cm.)	TITLE OF MAP (Comments by the editor in brackets)
mwbp0063	baltic sea (east)	1810	KLINT	400	65	96	Karta ofver Syd Ostra Delen af Oster Sjon
mwsc0394	scandinavia denmark	1808	KLINT	720	65	96	Karta ofver Syd Westra Delen af Oster Sjon
mwsc0752	scandinavia sweden	1805	KLINT	500	95	66	Karta ofwer den Ostra Delen af Kattegat
mwam0211	america continent	1782	KLOCKHOFF	400	9	13	America, Volgens de Nieuwste Waarneminge (depicts the US flag)
mwsc0470	scandinavia greenland	1780	KLOCKHOFF	240	19	25	Groenland Dressee et Gravee pour l'Histoire Generale des Voijages
mwam0407	america north	1752	KNAPTON	3000	83	85	North America. Performed Under the Patronage of Louis Duke of Orleans, First Prince of the Blood; by the Sieur d'Anville. Improved by Mr Boulton
mwam1167	america north (east)	1812	KNEASS	280	20	26	A Map of the United States and Part of Louisiana
mwuk0133	ireland	1708	KNIGHT	1000	56	47	A New Mapp of the Kingdom of Ireland (large title above map: A New Mapp of Ireland)
mwuss0281	carolinas	1842	KNIGHT	200	38	33	Parts of North & South Carolina
mwf0744	france nord pas-de-calais	1709	KNIGHT	1500	56	90	The Seat of War in the Province of Artois and Country Adjacent According to the Observations of William de Isle and others as Communicated to ye Royal Academy of Sciences at Paris
mwam0680	america north	1832	KNIGHT	120	13	16	United States
mwuk1410	uk geological	1837	KNIPE	1600	151	127	Geological & Mineralogical Map of England and Wales with Parts of Scotland, Ireland & France Showing also the Inland Navigation by Means of Rivers & Canals ... Together with the Rail Roads & Principal Roads
mwuk0645	scotland	1859	KNIPE	900	107	81	Geological Map of Scotland, Lochs, Mountains, Islands
mwuk1412	uk geological	1843	KNIPE	2000	159	135	Geological Map of the British Isles and Part of France, Showing Also the Inland Navigation ... The Railways and Principal Roads, and Sites of the Minerals
mwru0332	russia	1812	KNITTEL	300	59	63	Neue Post-Karte von Russland Herausgegeben vom Moscowschen Oberpostamt
mwuk0637	scotland	1845	KNOR	1000	109	146	Map of the County of Edinburgh from Actual Survey by James Knor, New Edition with the Lines of Railway: New Roads with Distances of Miles from Edinburgh, Names of Land Owners and other Additions to 1845
mwuk0540	scotland	1782	KNOX	500	74	56	A Commercial Map of Scotland
mwuk0608	scotland	1828	KNOX	400	65	81	Map of the Basin of the Firth of Forth, Including the Lothians, Fife & Kinross with Parts of Adjoining Shires
mwuk0578	scotland	1812	KNOX	1800	123	155	Map of the Shire of Edinburgh or County of Midlothian, from Actual Survey
mwuk0588	scotland	1824	KNOX	500	51	62	Plan of Edinburgh and its Environs
mwme0735	caucasus	1850	KOCH	785	92	127	Karte von dem Kaukasischen Isthmus und von Armenien
mwp0529a	pacific south	1849	KOHLER	180	38	50	Australien oder Oceanien
mwe1181	europe south east	1848	KOHLER	200	48	39	Die Europaeische Turkei, Griechenland und die Ionischen Inseln
mwbh0756	belgium holland	1792	KOK	400	32	39	Nieuwe Kaart van de Provintie Zeeland
mwbh0736	belgium holland	1782	KOK	400	32	42	Nieuwe Kaart van Friesland
mwaf0902	africa south	1719	KOLBENS	1200	28	38	Accurate Voorstellung von Capo Bonae Spei in Africa (3 insets. Reprinted 1745)
mwaf0908	africa south	1727	KOLBENS	550	30	38	Caarte van de Beyde Afgelegenste Colonien Drakensteen
mwaf0911	africa south	1727	KOLBENS	650	30	38	Caarte van de Colonie van de Kaap (re-issued in 1741 with additional title in French, top left)
mwaf0909	africa south	1727	KOLBENS	550	30	38	Caarte van de Colonie van Stellenbosch
mwaf0912	africa south	1727	KOLBENS	750	30	38	Caarte van de Kaap de Goede Hoop Leggende in't Zuyder Gedeelte van Africa
mwaf0910	africa south	1727	KOLBENS	550	30	38	Caarte van de Oost-Kust van Africa van Mozambique to ... Kaap de Goede Hoop
mwaf0913	africa south	1727	KOLBENS	600	27	36	Gezigt van de Kaap de Goede Hoop. (view of Table Bay)
mwaf1048	africa south east	1727	KOLBENS	480	30	38	Kaarte van de Oost Cust van Africa
mwaf0920	africa south	1745	KOLBENS	200	13	19	Prospect von dem Vorgeburge der Guten Hoffnung (view of Cape Town)
mwbp0564a	poland	1827	KOLBERG	900	43	51	Plan Warszawy
mwme0304	holy land	1740	KOLLER	8000	59	120	Iudaea seu Terra Sancta quae Hebraeorum ... Israelitarum Terra
mwme0224	holy land	1700	KOLLER	4000	64	119	Judaea oder das Heilige Land in Welchem die Hebraeen oder Israeliten Gewohnet Haben in Seine Zwolff Stamme Eingetheilet
mwru0404c	russia moscow	1823	KOLPAKOV	2000	85	100	(Topographical map of the environs of Moscow, in Cyrillic. Military Topographical Dept, His Imperial Majesty, Moscow 1819.)
mwru0240	russia	1769	KONIGLICHE AKADEMIE BERLIN	1200	56	127	Totius Imperii Russici Tabula Generalis
mwe1034	europe rhine	1797	KOOPS	400	64	98	A Map of the River Rhine. From Basle to Strasburgh and Fort-Lewis
mwme0469	jerusalem	1685	KOPPMAYER	400	18	29	Jerusalem heutiges tags.
mwg0526	rheinland-pfalz	1690	KOPPMAYER	1800	42	104	Mosel-Strom

AMPG REFERENCE	REGION	DATE	MAP MAKER	PRICE (UK£)	VERT. (cm.)	HOR. (cm.)	TITLE OF MAP (Comments by the editor in brackets)
mwe0963	europe hungary	1791	KORABINSZKY	600	47	60	Novissima Regni Hungariae Potomographica et Telluris Productorum Tabula / Wasser und Producten Karte des Koenigreichs Ungarn / Magyarorszag Termeszeti Tulajdonsaganak Tukore
mwe0960	europe hungary	1786	KORABINSZKY	400	35	42	Vorstellung des Konigreichs Ungarn nach den Poststationen fur Reisende
mwsw0190	switzerland	1785	KORNER	500	37	49	Geographisches Vergeichnis der Merkwurdigsten Orte in der Schweiz
mwbh0781	belgium holland	1810	KRAYENHOFF	480	76	92	Carte Generale de la Hollande Avec Les Routes de Postes. 1810
mwbh0775	belgium holland	1805	KRAYENHOFF	300	49	59	Charte von der Batavischen Republik
mwbh0789	belgium holland	1820	KRAYENHOFF	2400	87	96	Choro-Topographische Kaart der Noordelyke Provincien van het Konigryk der Nederlanden, Uitgevoerd aan het Topographischen Bureau van Dezen Staat (map in 8 sheets, each 87x96cm, plus index sheet)
mwbh0094	belgium holland	1580	KREFFELDT	4000	14	36	Egentlicke Beschryvinge des Iselstrooms, sampt Ittelicke Omliggende Steeden unde Vlecken, door Mart. Karol Kreffeldt
mwe0457	europe central	1594	KRESS	7500	28	41	Der Rom: Kayserl. Mayestat Rudolphi II. Unsers Aller Gnadigsten Herrens, wie auch des Turggischen Keysers Amuraths III (broadsheet. Size is for map, not incl. text)
mwsam0626	south america guyana	1771	KREVELT	60	22	30	Carte de la Guiane
mwwi0864	st kitts	1775	KREVELT	200	20	30	Carte de l'Isle St. Christophle pour Servir a l'Histoire Gen. des Voyages
mwas0671	asia south east java	1785	KREVELT	800	64	37	Grundris der Stadt und Citadelle Batavia
mww0487	world	1773	KREVELT	235	25	38	Mappe-Monde ou Description du Globe Terrestre
mwe0558a	europe czech republic (bohemia)	1720	KRIEGER	960	24	68	Prospect der Welt-Berühmten Königl: Haupt Statt Prag in Böhmen wie solche jetziger Zeit anzusehen ist
mwme0859a	persia etc	1859	KRIZIZ	7500	80	97	(Plan of Teheran, with Arabic script.)
mwbh0544	belgium holland	1712	KRUIKIUS	8000	250	300	t'Hooge Heemradschap van Delfland met alle de Steden, Dorpen, Ambachten (Polder map in 25 sheets, joined)
mwas0356	asia north east	1807	KRUSENSTERN	1500	61	85	(Map in Cyrillic script)
mwjk0133	japan	1807	KRUSENSTERN	1500	46	44	(Map in Cyrillic script)
mwca0056	canada	1744	LA FRANCE	3000	33	48	A New Map of Part of North America from the Latitude of 40 to 68 Degrees. Including the Late Discoveries Made on Board the Furnace Bomb Ketch in 1742. And the Western Rivers & Lakes Falling into Nelson River in Hudson's Bay
mwp0189	new zealand	1785	LA HARPE	1200	29	23	Carta della Nuova Zelanda
mwme0644	arabia etc	1780	LA HARPE	180	29	24	Carte de l'Arabie
mwam1173	america north (east)	1816	LA HARPE	150	30	23	Etats Unis et Grandes Antilles
mwsam0082	south america	1770	LA HARPE	135	24	30	I.ere Feuille de l'Amerique Meridionale / II.eme Feuille de l'Amerique Meridionale (2 sheets)
mww0474	world	1769	LA LANDE	2500	48	66	Figure du Passage de Venus sur le Disque du Soleil ... 5 Juin 1769
mwit0366	italy emilia-romagna	1780	LA LANDE	200	25	39	Plan de Rimini
mwf0842	france paris	1705	LA MARE	5000	45	57	Traite de la Police (containing 8 plans of Paris over the past 2 millenia, each 45x57cm.)
mwit0290	italy campagna	1768	LA MARRA	800	33	91	Veduta Puteolani della Costa Litoris di Pozzuoli Prospectus
mwp0471	pacific samoa	1797	LA PEROUSE	600	50	68	Carte de l'Archipel des Navigateurs Decouvert par M. de Bougainville en 1768 et Reconnu par les Francaises en Dec. 1787 (first map of the Samoan Islands)
mwp0449	pacific north	1797	LA PEROUSE	785	50	68	Carte des Cotes de l'Amerique et de l'Asie depuis la Californie jusqu'a Macao d'Apres les Decouvertes Faites en 1786-7 par les Fregates Francaises la Boussole et l'Astrolabe
mwam0500a	america north	1788	LA PEROUSE	1500	57	52	Carte des Declinaisons et Inclinaisons de L'Aiguille Aimantee ... depuis l'Annee 1776 (2 sheets of a 4-sheet map of the Pacific 57x57cm and 57x52cm - publ. by Buffon, 9 years before its official release. It was the most accurate map of North America of its time.)
mwjk0125	japan	1797	LA PEROUSE	500	50	69	Carte des Decouvertes au Nord du Japon Faites en 1643 par les Vaisseaux Hollandais le Kastrikum et le Breskens, Comprenant la Terre de Jeso, Ile des Etats et la Terre de la Compagnie, dont Partie a ete Reconnue en 1787 (north to the right)
mwc0224a	china	1797	LA PEROUSE	1350	49	69	Carte des Decouvertes Faites en 1787 dans les Mers de Chine et de Tartarie par les Fregates Francaises la Boussole et l'Astrolabe depuis Leur Depart de Manille jusqu'a Leur Arrivee au Kamtschatka
mwp0334	pacific hawaii	1797	LA PEROUSE	2000	68	49	Carte des Parties de Iles Sandwich qui ont ete Visitees au Mois de Mai 1786 par les Fregates Francaises la Boussole et l'Astrolabe / Carte des Iles Sandwich
mwp0265	pacific (all)	1797	LA PEROUSE	800	50	69	Carte du Grand Ocean ou Mer du Sud
mwp0506	pacific south	1797	LA PEROUSE	800	34	50	Carte d'une Partie du Grande Ocean a l'E et S.E. de la Nouvelle Guinee (incl. N. Australia)

AMPG REFERENCE	REGION	DATE	MAP MAKER	PRICE (UK£)	VERT. (cm.)	HOR. (cm.)	TITLE OF MAP (Comments by the editor in brackets)
mwru0466	russia tartary	1797	LA PEROUSE	650	68	49	Carte Generale des Decouvertes Faites en 1787 dans les Mers de Chine et de Tartarie ou depuis Manille jusqu'a Avatscha
mwam1335	america north (west)	1797	LA PEROUSE	800	68	49	Carte Generale d'une Partie de la Cote du Nord-Ouest de l'Amerique Reconnue par les Fregates Francaises La Boussole et Astrolabe
mwp0335	pacific hawaii	1797	LA PEROUSE	240	50	68	Carte Plate de l'Isle Necker Situee par 23°34' de Latitude N, et 166°52' de Longitude a l'Ouest de Paris ... Decouvertes en Novembre 1786
mwc0225a	china	1798	LA PEROUSE	650	36	49	Chart of Discoveries made in 1787 in the seas of China and Tartary (English edition)
mww0597	world	1797	LA PEROUSE	2000	58	92	Mappemonde ou Carte Reduite des Parties Connues du Globe pour Servir au Voyages de La Perouse
mwru0462	russia tartary	1797	LA PEROUSE	400	49	68	Plan de la Baie de Castries Situee sur la Cote Orientale de Tartarie (later known as 'La Perouse Straits')
mwsam0469	south america chile	1797	LA PEROUSE	240	33	49	Plan de la Baie de la Conception
mwru0463	russia tartary	1797	LA PEROUSE	240	49	33	Plan de la Baie de Langle Situee a la Partie Ouest de l'Ile de Tchoka
mwuss0092	california	1797	LA PEROUSE	800	33	23	Plan de la Baie de Monterey Situee dans la Californie Septentrionale par 36°38' de Latitude Nord et 124°3' de Longitude Occidentale
mwru0464	russia tartary	1797	LA PEROUSE	240	49	34	Plan de la Baie de Ternai Situee sur la Cote de Tartarie ... Decouverte de 22 Juin 1787
mwru0465	russia tartary	1797	LA PEROUSE	240	49	34	Plan de la Baie d'Estaing Situee a la Cote de l'Ouest de Tchoka ... Prise du Mouillage de l'Astrolabe
mwjk0167	korea	1797	LA PEROUSE	250	49	34	Plan de la Partie de l'Ile de Quelpaert / Plan de l'Ile Hoapinsu / Plan de l'Ile Dagelet / Plan de la Partie de l'Ile de Botol / Plan de l'Ile de Kumi (5 maps on one sheet)
mwjk0166	korea	1797	LA PEROUSE	350	50	69	Plan de la Partie des Iles, ou Archipel de Coree, vue au Mois de Mai 1787 par les Fregates Francaises la Boussole et Astrolabe
mwuss0034	alaska	1797	LA PEROUSE	350	50	69	Plan de l'Entree du Port de Bucarelli sur la Cote du Nord-Ouest de l'Amerique, par 55°15' de Latitude Nord et 136°15' de Longitude a l'Ouest de Paris
mwp0310	pacific easter isl.	1797	LA PEROUSE	720	50	68	Plan de l'Ile de Paque / Plan de la Baie de Cook Situee a la Cote Occid. l'Ile de Paque / Vues de l'Ile de Paque
mwjk0127	japan	1797	LA PEROUSE	350	69	49	Plan des Iles Kuriles de des Terres Peu Connues Situees a la Suite de ces Iles: d'apres un Manuscrit Conserve dans les Archives d'Ochotsk qui a ete Communique a M. Lesseps. en 1788
mwuss0093	california	1797	LA PEROUSE	800	49	33	Plan du Port de St. Diego en Californie ... Leve en 1782 / Plan du Port et Departement de St. Blas ... Leve en Nov. 1777
mwuss0091	america north (west)	1797	LA PEROUSE	1500	49	33	Plan du Port de St. Francois, Situe sur la Cote de la California Septentrionale. La Pointe des Rois par 37°59' de Latitude Nord (1st printed chart of San Francisco)
mwuss0091	california	1797	LA PEROUSE	1500	49	33	Plan du Port de St. Francois, Situe sur la Cote de la California Septentrionale. La Pointe des Rois par 37°59' de Latitude Nord (1st printed chart of San Francisco. For illustration see 'America North [West])
mwuss0033	alaska	1797	LA PEROUSE	350	50	70	Plan du Port des Francais sur la Cote du Nord-Ouest de l'Amerique, par 58°37' de Latitude de Nord et 139°50' de Longitude Occidentale, Decouverte le 2 Juillet 1786, par les Fregates Francaise la Boussole et l'Astrolabe (Lituya Bay)
mwp0472	pacific samoa	1798	LA PEROUSE	240	36	24	Plan of Part of the Island of Maouna Visited by the Boussole & Astrolabe in Dec. 1787 / Plan of Massacre Cove at Time of the Massacre Dec. 11, 1787
mwc0225	china	1797	LA PEROUSE	300	25	40	Vue de Macao en Chine
							FOR OTHER MAPS BY LA PEROUSE SEE 'BUFFON', WHO PUBLISHED SOME OF HIS MAPS IN 1788.
mwsc0454	scandinavia greenland	1647	LA PEYRERE	1500	15	37	Carte de Groenland
mwam1130	america north (east)	1799	LA ROCHEFOUCAULT	550	33	51	Map of the Northern Provinces of the United States / Map of the Southern Provinces of the United States (2 maps)
mwam1129a	america north (east)	1799	LA ROCHEFOUCAULT	250	36	43	Map of the United States, Canada, Intended to Illustrate the Travels of the Duke (during 1795-7)
mwaf1176	africa west	1718	LABAT	140	23	38	A General Map of the River Sanaga; from the Falls of Govina to the Ocean; Taken by a French Engineer in 1718 / Map of ye Entrance of the Sanaga / Island of Sanaga or St. Louis
mwwi0855	st kitts	1722	LABAT	350	13	25	Carte de l'Isle de Saint Christophe Situee a 17 Degrez 30 Minutes de Lat. Septentrionale
mwwi0554	guadeloupe	1772	LABAT	200	13	19	Isle de la Guadeloupe Scituee a 16 Degres de Lat. Septentrionale
mwwi0768	martinique	1722	LABAT	250	22	30	Isle de la Martinique a 14 Degrez 30 Min. de Latit. Sept. et a 317 de Longitude

AMPG REFERENCE	REGION	DATE	MAP MAKER	PRICE (UK£)	VERT. (cm.)	HOR. (cm.)	TITLE OF MAP (Comments by the editor in brackets)
mwwi0769	martinique	1724	LABAT	200	13	19	Plan de la Ville et du Fort Royal de la Martinique
mwwi0773	martinique	1742	LABAT	200	13	21	Plan du Fort St. Pierre de la Martinique
mwec0626	uk england kent	1737	LABELYE	2000	66	90	A Mapp of the Downes Much More Correct than Any Hitherto Published Shewing the True Shape, & Situation of the Coast between the North & South Forelands, & of All the Adjacent Sands Together with the Soundings at Low Water
mwin0446	indian ocean	1800	LABILLARDIERE	1500	48	69	A Chart of the Indian Ocean and part of the South Sea, Exhibiting the Track of the Recherche and Esperance ... by J.D. Barbie du Bocage ... to Illustrate an Account of the Voyage in Search of La Perouse
mwin0191	india	1733	LAFITAU	180	18	14	La Ville de Calicut (view)
mwas0685	asia south east malacca	1733	LAFITAU	180	19	14	La Ville de Malaca (view)
mwaf1049	africa south east	1734	LAFITAU	180	19	14	L'Isle de Mosambique / Sofala
mwin0403	india goa	1734	LAFITAU	180	14	19	L'Isle et Ville de Goa
mww0370	world	1734	LAFITAU	785	24	45	Mappe-Monde pour Servir a l'Histoire des Decouvertes et Conquests des Portugais dans le Nouveau-Monde (oval projection)
mwsp0086	portugal	1734	LAFITAU	180	20	15	Ville de Lisbone et Flote des Indes (view)
mwit1048c	italy naples	1566	LAFRERI SCHOOL	12000	52	83	(untitled plan of Naples)
mwsc0473	scandinavia iceland	1558	LAFRERI	4000	25	19	Frisland (blank cartouche top right)
mwgr0445	greece cyprus	1570	LAFRERI	45000	56	43	L'Isola di Cypro
mwm0167	mediterranean malta	1565	LAFRERI	4000	36	52	Ultimo Disegno delli Forti di Malta
mwbh0016	belgium holland	1560	LAFRERI SCHOOL	4800	32	43	Antverpiae Civitatis Belgicae Toto Orbe Cogniti et Celebrati Simulacrum
mwe0280	europe austria	1559	LAFRERI SCHOOL	3000	29	42	Austria e Ungaria
mwf0456	france corsica	1560	LAFRERI SCHOOL	2500	30	20	Cirnus sive Corsica Insula (engraved by Licinio)
mwit0023	italy	1561	LAFRERI SCHOOL	15000	42	65	Della Italia la Vera, et Ultima Descriptione Riformata, et in Molti Luogi Diligentemente Ricoretta, et Apliata
mwbh0020	belgium holland	1563	LAFRERI SCHOOL	3000	37	48	Humanissimo Lectori Incisor S.P.D. Caelauissimus Descriptionem Galliae Belgicae
mwuk0003	ireland	1570	LAFRERI SCHOOL	8500	34	25	Hybernia nunc Irlant
mwbh0112	belgium holland	1585	LAFRERI SCHOOL	4800	38	50	Il Vero Disegno del Mirabile Assedio della Fortissima Cita de Anversa Fatto dal ... Alexandro Farnese ... del 27 Agosto 1585. G.R. Form.
mwf0017	france	1554	LAFRERI SCHOOL	1800	37	47	La Vera Descritione, di Tutta la Francia, & la Spagna, et la Fiandra
mwbh0022	belgium holland	1565	LAFRERI SCHOOL	2500	29	39	La Vera Descrittione della Gallia Belgica
mwit0703	italy rome	1568	LAFRERI SCHOOL	6850	52	94	Ne Prorsus Romae (view)
mwit0628	italy piedmont	1560	LAFRERI SCHOOL	3000	51	40	Regionis Subalpinae vulgo Piemonte Appellatae Discriptio, Aeneis nostris Formis Excussa
mwit0985	italy south	1557	LAFRERI SCHOOL	2800	33	43	Regno di Napoli
mwsam0576	south america guyana	1652	LAGNIET	1500	31	40	Carte de l'Isle Cayenne
mwsp0442	spain regions	1659	LAGNIET	800	34	41	Plan de la Rivière de Bidasso dans la quelle est l'isle où se fait la grande conférence pour la paix générale entre la France et l'Espagne, et la description des villes, et autres rivières adjacentes, tant de France, Espagne, que du Royaume de Navarre
mwme0153	holy land	1660	LAGNIET	1200	40	55	Terra Sancta Promissionis olim Palestina
mwca0041	canada	1703	LAHONTAN	960	23	29	Carte Generale de Canada
mwca0040a	canada	1703	LAHONTAN	2000	41	56	Carte Generale de Canada. Dediee au Roy de Danemark (larger version of previous map)
mwca0041a	canada	1704	LAHONTAN	400	10	17	Carte Generale de Canada en Petit Point (this and the previous map were publ. in the book 'Nouveaux Voyages de Mr le Baron de Lahontan, dans l'Amerique Septentrionale'. An edition in English with maps also exists.)
mwca0502	canada quebec	1703	LA HONTAN	450	10	20	Profil de la Ville de Quebec
mwme0695a	arabia etc	1853	LALLEMAND	300	61	67	Carte du Theatre de la Guerre dans l'Empire Ottoman
mwuk0098	ireland	1689	LAMB	300	22	18	A Generall Mapp of the Kingdom of Ireland
mwgm0007	gulf of mexico and surrounding regions	1677	LAMB	900	28	42	A New Mapp of the Empire of Mexico Describing the Continent to the Istmus of Panama
mwec0592a	uk england kent	1570	LAMBARDE		38	23	The Shyre of Kent, Divided into the Five Lathes (3 editions known before c1730)
mwam1169	america north (east)	1813	LAMBERT	480	38	38	Map of the British Settlements and the United States of North America, from the Coast of Labrador to Florida
mwca0547	canada quebec	1813	LAMBERT	200	11	17	Quebec and its Environs ... Operation of the Siege
mwme0483	jerusalem	1720	LAMY	450	34	41	Descriptio seu ichnographia veteris urbis Hieruslem et locorum adjacentium.
mwme0474	jerusalem	1699	LAMY	350	27	37	L'Ancienne Ville de Jerusalem
mwca0320	canada newfoundland	1774	LANE	1250	59	60	Chart of Part of the Coast of Newfoundland, from Point Lance to Cape Spear ... by Michael Lane, in 1773 (illustrated is the scarce 1st issue, published by Jeffreys and Faden, before it was issued with the Sayer & Bennett imprint. The map was part of the 1st British survey of Newfoundland carried out by James Cook R.N and Michael Lane).

AMPG REFERENCE	REGION	DATE	MAP MAKER	PRICE (UK£)	VERT. (cm.)	HOR. (cm.)	TITLE OF MAP (Comments by the editor in brackets)
mwca0222	canada arctic	1821	LANE W.	7500	69	47	Plan of Lancaster Sound, penetrated by Capt. Parry in July, 1819 (separately issued broadsheet compiled from Admiralty records)
mwuss1210	new york	1829	LANGDON	875	32	38	A New Map of the City of New York, Comprising All the Late Improvements
mwuss1211	new york	1829	LANGDON	875	31	39	A New Map of the City of New York, Comprising All the Late Improvements
mwe0825	europe east	1788	LANGE	1200	39	60	Neue Karte von den Gegenwartigen Kriegs-Schauplatze zwischen den Osterreichischen, Russisch Kayserl. und Turkischen Armeen, welche Vorzuglich den Grosten Theil der Europaischen Turkey, die Krim
mwbp0056	baltic sea (east)	1788	LANGE	600	41	47	Neue Karte von den gegenwartigen Kriegs-Schauplatze zwischen den Russisch Kayserl
mwe0394a	europe austria	1803	LANGE	550	31	39	Neue Karte von den Oesterreichischen teutschen Staaten (inset of Vienna)
mwbp0057	baltic sea (east)	1788	LANGE	500	26	22	Topographischer Plan von Riga
mwsp0388a	spain regions	1598	LANGENES	200	9	12	Calis Malis (Bay of Cadiz)
mwbh0678	belgium holland	1747	LANGEWEG	1200	46	67	(The Hague) Nieuwe Afbeelding van s Gravenhage
mwuk1867	wales	1818	LANGLEY	60	17	27	Anglesey
mwec0022	uk england bedfordshire	1818	LANGLEY	80	17	27	Bedfordshire
mwec0052	uk england berkshire	1818	LANGLEY	80	17	27	Berkshire
mwuk1868	wales	1818	LANGLEY	60	17	27	Brecknockshire
mwuk1869	wales	1818	LANGLEY	60	17	27	Cardiganshire
mwuss0145	california	1862	LANGLEY	1500	51	65	City and County of San Francisco. Compiled from Official Surveys, and Sectionized in Accordance with U.S. Surveys
mwuk1046	england	1818	LANGLEY	80	17	27	England & Wales
mwec0499	uk england hampshire	1818	LANGLEY	100	17	27	Hampshire
mwec0531	uk england herefordshire	1818	LANGLEY	80	17	27	Herefordshire
mwec0562	uk england hertfordshire	1817	LANGLEY	140	18	27	Hertfordshire
mwec0589	uk england huntingdonshire	1818	LANGLEY	80	17	27	Huntingdonshire
mwec0241	uk england cumbria	1819	LANGLEY	120	34	21	Langley's New Map of Cumberland
mwuk1868a	wales	1818	LANGLEY	75	17	26	Langley's new Map of Glamorganshire
mwec0660	uk england kent	1818	LANGLEY & BELCH	150	20	26	Langley's New Map of Kent
mwec0837	uk england norfolk	1818	LANGLEY	120	18	26	Langley's New Map of Norfolk
mwec1051	uk england somerset	1818	LANGLEY	130	20	26	Langley's New Map of Somersetshire
mwec0967	uk england oxfordshire	1818	LANGLEY	100	17	27	Oxfordshire
mwec0992	uk england rutland	1818	LANGLEY	80	17	27	Rutlandshire
mwec1020	uk england shropshire	1818	LANGLEY	80	17	27	Shropshire
mwuk1283	england london	1812	LANGLEY & BELCH	2800	53	79	Langley & Belch's New Map of London (7 editions until 1828)
mwuk1045	england	1817	LANGLEY & BELCH	480	48	67	Langley's New Travelling and Commercial Map of England and Wales
mwbp0253	poland	1650	LANGLOIS	675	41	52	Carte de Pologne
mwf0180	france	1812	LANGLOIS	180	53	55	Carte Routiere de la France
mwsc0281a	scandinavia denmark	1660	LANGLOIS	1500	38	54	Daniae Nova Descriptio - Description du Royme de Danemarck et des costes de la mer Baltiq.
mwe0244	europe	1815	LANGLOIS	375	61	78	Europe Dressee d'apres les Traites de Paris et du Congres de Vienne
mwbh0472	belgium holland	1695	LANGLOIS	1650	88	57	Le Bombardement de la Ville de Bruxelles Capitale des Pays-Bas par l'Armee du Roi Sous Mr. le Marechal Duc de Villeroy 1695
mwbh0378	belgium holland	1667	LANGLOIS	400	37	57	Le Duche de Brabant Divise en ses Quatre Grands Cartiers
mwit1229	italy venice	1699	LANSVELT	2000	31	47	Venise
mwaf0304	africa	1817	LAPIE	350	50	76	Afrique Dediee et Presentee au Roi
mwaf0991	africa south	1809	LAPIE	150	22	29	Afrique Meridionale
mwam0579	america north	1809	LAPIE	180	27	23	Amerique Septentrionale
mwaf0320	africa	1829	LAPIE	250	49	56	Carte d'Afrique
mwg0180	germany	1838	LAPIE	180	39	54	Carte d'Allemagne Comprenant la Confederation Germanique, l'Empire d'Autriche, le Royaume de Prusse et le Royaume de Pologne
mwsam0547	south america colombia	1828	LAPIE	240	41	55	Carte de Colombie et des Guyanes
mwbp0064	baltic sea (east)	1854	LAPIE	480	60	77	Carte de la Mer Baltique
mwm0078	mediterranean	1811	LAPIE	320	47	76	Carte de la Mer Mediterranee Dressee pour le Voyage de Mr. de Chateaubriand
mwme0411	holy land	1833	LAPIE	235	53	39	Carte de la Palestine ou Terre Sainte
mwsp0328	spain	1831	LAPIE	180	39	53	Carte de la Peninsule Comprenant l'Espagne et le Portugal
mwsam0256	south america argentina	1828	LAPIE	360	53	39	Carte de la Plata du Chili et de la Patagonie
mwru0335	russia	1812	LAPIE	960	162	166	Carte de la Russie d'Europe, avec l'Empire d'Autriche, la Suede, le Danemark et la Norwege, la Prusse, le Grand Duche de Varsovie, les Provinces Illyriennes, et une Partie de la Cofederation du Rhin et de la Turquie d'Europe
mwme0679	arabia etc	1829	LAPIE	250	40	54	Carte de la Turquie d'Asie, de la Perse, de l'Afghanistan et de l'Arabie
mwam0752	america north	1842	LAPIE	350	56	40	Carte de l'Amerique Septentrionale
mwas0250	asia continent	1832	LAPIE	235	39	53	Carte de l'Asie

AMPG REFERENCE	REGION	DATE	MAP MAKER	PRICE (UKE)	VERT. (cm.)	HOR. (cm.)	TITLE OF MAP (Comments by the editor in brackets)
mwaf0432	africa east	1842	LAPIE	180	54	39	Carte de l'Egypte, de la Nubie, de l'Abissinie, du Kourdofan, et d'une Partie de l'Arabie
mwc0271	china	1838	LAPIE	250	39	54	Carte de l'Empire Chinois et du Japon
mwme0851	persia etc	1832	LAPIE	235	39	53	Carte de l'Empire d'Alexandre
mwme1051a	turkey etc	1822	LAPIE	720	88	109	Carte de l'Empire Ottoman en Europe, en Asie et en Afrique, avec les Pays Limitrophes
mwe0243	europe	1815	LAPIE	1500	178	182	Carte de l'Europe ou sont Tracees les Limites des Empires, Royaumes et Etats Souverains, d'apres les Derniers Traites de Paix
mwwi0485	cuba	1826	LAPIE	360	32	64	Carte de l'Isle de Cuba
mwit0241	italy	1831	LAPIE	240	56	43	Carte de l'Italie
mwp0091	australia	1829	LAPIE	400	39	54	Carte de l'Oceanie Contenant l'Australie, la Polynesie et les Iles Asiatiques
mwwi0182	west indies	1829	LAPIE	400	40	55	Carte des Antilles du Golfe du Mexique et d'une Partie des Etats Voisins
mwsc0389a	scandinavia denmark	1802	LAPIE	240	50	60	Carte des Etats Danois … AN X (insets of Bengal, Mysore, Coromandel, Nicobar Isl, Antilles, Guinee, Greenland)
mwam0708a	america north	1837	LAPIE	350	40	55	Carte des Etats-Unis d'Amerique, du Canada, du Nouveau Brunswick et d'une Partie de la Nouvelle Bretagne
mwgm0315	mexico	1829	LAPIE	300	56	40	Carte des Etats-Unis du Mexique (inset: Central America)
mwuk0889	uk	1836	LAPIE	240	54	39	Carte des Iles Britanniques Comprenant l'Angleterre, l'Ecosse et l'Irlande
mwuk0881	uk	1812	LAPIE	960	146	151	Carte des Iles Britanniques ou Royaume-Uni de la Grande-Bretagne et d'Irlande
mwit0841a	italy sardinia and corsica	1805	LAPIE	180	43	49	Carte des Isles de Corse et de Sardaigne
mwsam0422	south america brazil	1829	LAPIE	240	53	39	Carte du Bresil Dressee par M. Lapie 1er. Geographe du Roi
mwsam0795	south america peru	1829	LAPIE	240	41	54	Carte du Perou et du Haut Perou
mwe1176	europe south east	1822	LAPIE	1800	217	165	Carte Generale de la Turquie d'Europe, en XV Feuilles, Dressee sur des Materiaux Recueillis par Mr. le Lieutenant Generale Guilleminot
mwe1178	europe south east	1827	LAPIE	240	64	52	Carte Generale de la Turquie d'Europe, et de la Grece
mwsam0156	south america	1838	LAPIE	180	54	39	Carte Generale de l'Amerique Meridionale
mwgr0248a	greece	1826	LAPIE	850	107	157	Carte Physique, Historique & Routiere de la Grece (re-issue by Ordnance Survey, 1878 illustrated)
mwm0085	mediterranean	1830	LAPIE	1800	80	198	Carte Reduit de la Mer Mediterranee et de la Mer Noire
mwca0666	canada west	1822	LAPIE	320	32	43	Charte von Einem Theile des Nordlichen Oceans und von Nord America
mwe0250	europe	1817	LAPIE	400	51	75	Europe Dediee et Presentee au Roi
mwgm0066	gulf of mexico and surrounding regions	1813	LAPIE	180	22	30	Golfe du Mexique et Archipel Des Antilles
mwin0340	india	1820	LAPIE	140	23	30	Inde en Deca et au dela du Gange
mww0694	world	1831	LAPIE	450	46	61	Mappe-Monde en Deux Hemispheres par Mr. Lapie Lieutenant Colonel et Lapie Fils Lieut. d'Etat Major. Paris 1831
mww0653	world	1816	LAPIE	250	28	41	Mappemonde Physique sur la Projection de Mercator
mww0700	world	1832	LAPIE	450	41	55	Mappe-Monde sur la Projection de Mercator
mwme0885	syria etc	1804	LAPIE	480	48	28	Neue Charte von Syrien
mwp0273	pacific (all)	1817	LAPIE	650	49	76	Oceanie ou Australasie et Polynesie Dediee et Presentee au Roi
mwsam0170a	south america (central)	1812	LAPIE	150	23	30	Perou et Brasil
mwru0572	ukraine	1809	LAPIE	360	28	41	Plan d'Odessa et d'une Partie de ses Environs
mwf0526	france corsica	1769	LAPIS	720	23	17	Isola di Corsica
mwp0208	new zealand	1833	LAPLACE	600	86	59	Plan de la Riviere Kawa-Kawa (Nouvelle Zeelande, Baie des Iles)
mwbh0371a	belgium holland	1665	LAPORT	2400	48	58	Bruga flandrorum Urbs et Emporium Mercatu Celebre
mwas0203	asia continent	1786	LAPORTE	200	18	23	Carte d'Asie, divisee en ses Principaux Etats (polar projection)
mwam1071	america north (east)	1781	LAPORTE	320	18	22	Carte de la Nouvelle Angleterre, Nouvelle York, Nouvelle Jersey et Pensilvanie
mwat0284	atlantic north	1781	LAPORTE	280	24	36	Carte de la Partie Septentrionale de la Mer du Sud
mwam1068	america north (east)	1781	LAPORTE	320	18	22	Carte de la Virginie et du Mariland
mwaf0524a	africa egypt etc	1786	LAPORTE	120	22	18	Carte de l'Egypte Ancienne et Moderne
mwe0209a	europe	1786	LAPORTE	80	18	23	Carte de l'Europe
mwbh0735	belgium holland	1781	LAPORTE	90	18	22	Carte des Pays Bas Comprenant le Brabant, Gueldre, Limbourg, Luxembourg, Haynant, Namur, Flandre, Cambresis et Artois
mwbh0742a	belgium holland	1786	LAPORTE	120	18	22	Carte des Pays Bas Comprenant Les Provinces Unies
mwme0374a	holy land	1786	LAPORTE	180	18	22	Carte des Regions et des Lieux dont il est parle dans le Nouveau Testament (insets of Jerusalem and Judee)
mwuk1023	england	1786	LAPORTE	140	18	22	Carte du Royaume d'Angleterre, Divise en ses principales Provinces
mwuk0535	scotland	1780	LAPORTE	160	18	22	Carte du Royaume d'Ecosse
mwuk0216	ireland	1781	LAPORTE	160	18	22	Carte du Royaume d'Irlande
mwbp0508a	poland	1786	LAPORTE	100	18	22	Carte Generale de la Pologne
mwgm0055	gulf of mexico and surrounding regions	1786	LAPORTE	200	18	22	Golfe du Mexique Assujetti aux Observations Astronomiques

AMPG REFERENCE	REGION	DATE	MAP MAKER	PRICE (UK£)	VERT. (cm.)	HOR. (cm.)	TITLE OF MAP (Comments by the editor in brackets)
mwwi0740	jamaica	1781	LAPORTE	235	18	22	Isle de la Jamaique
mwe1161a	europe south east	1786	LAPORTE	80	18	22	La Royaume de Hongrie et la Turquie D'Europe
mwru0268	russia	1781	LAPORTE	90	18	23	La Russie d'Europe
mwaf0253	africa	1786	LAPORTE	180	18	22	L'Afrique Divisee en ses Principaux Etats
mwg0155a	germany	1786	LAPORTE	80	18	22	L'Allemagne Divisee par Cercles
mwam0472	america north	1781	LAPORTE	350	18	22	L'Amerique Septentrionale Divisee en ses Principaux Etats
mwc0201	china	1781	LAPORTE	180	18	22	L'Empire de la Chine avec les Isles du Japon et la Coree
mwsc0165	scandinavia	1781	LAPORTE	160	18	22	Les Couronnes du Nord Comprenant les Royaumes du Suede, Norwege, et Danemarck (inset: Spitzbergen)
mwas0504	asia south east	1781	LAPORTE	180	18	23	Les Indes Orientales et leur Archipel
mwsp0300a	spain	1786	LAPORTE	80	18	22	L'Espagne et le Portugal
mwit0206	italy	1786	LAPORTE	120	18	22	L'Italie Divisee en ses differents Etats
mww0541	world	1786	LAPORTE	300	18	22	Mappe-Monde ou Description du Globe Terrestre
mwme1031a	turkey etc	1786	LAPORTE	100	18	22	Turquie D'Asie
mwg0672	saxony	1789	LASIUS	1000	53	81	Geographische Carte des Harz Gebirges
mwin0165	india	1711	LASO	120	13	16	Peninsula del Indo de Esta Parte del Golfo del Ganges / Peninsula del Indo de la Otra Parte del Golfo del Ganges
mwbh0546	belgium holland	1713	LASOR A VAREA	100	8	13	(Deventer)
mww0320	world	1713	LASOR A VAREA	350	11	15	(Untitled)
mwm0218	mediterranean malta	1713	LASOR A VAREA	300	12	18	(Valetta)
mwaf0496	africa egypt etc	1713	LASOR A VAREA	200	14	18	Aegyptus
mwaf0141	africa	1713	LASOR A VAREA	235	14	18	Africa
mwam0121	america continent	1713	LASOR A VAREA	400	13	17	America
mwf0956	france picardy	1713	LASOR A VAREA	100	9	13	Amiens (view)
mwbh0547	belgium holland	1713	LASOR A VAREA	100	9	13	Amorfortia Dioecesis Ultrarectensis Oppidum (view of Utrecht)
mwf0235	france alsace	1713	LASOR A VAREA	100	8	12	Argentina (view)
mwas0114	asia continent	1713	LASOR A VAREA	280	14	18	Asia
mwg0357	bavaria	1713	LASOR A VAREA	200	8	12	Augusta (view of Augsburg)
mwf0436	france central	1713	LASOR A VAREA	100	9	14	Aurelia Francie Civitas
mwbh0548	belgium holland	1713	LASOR A VAREA	250	13	17	Belgium, seu Germania Inferior
mwuk0791	uk	1713	LASOR A VAREA	280	14	18	Britanicae Insulae
mwbh0549	belgium holland	1713	LASOR A VAREA	200	8	12	Bruxeles
mwsp0517	spain regions	1713	LASOR A VAREA	100	9	13	Caliz (view of Cadiz)
mwgr0421	greece crete	1713	LASOR A VAREA	200	10	18	Candia
mwec0620	uk england kent	1713	LASOR A VAREA	100	9	14	Cantauria (view of Canterbury)
mwg0452	hessen	1713	LASOR A VAREA	100	9	13	Cassel (view)
mwgr0498	greece cyprus	1713	LASOR A VAREA	1200	18	10	Cipro
mwwi0420	cuba	1713	LASOR A VAREA	250	11	15	Cuba
mwsam0751	south america peru	1713	LASOR A VAREA	200	9	14	Cusco
mwsc0334	scandinavia denmark	1713	LASOR A VAREA	180	11	15	Danimarca
mwe0921	europe hungary	1713	LASOR A VAREA	200	14	20	Di Hungaria et Transilvania Tavola Novissima
mwe0129	europe	1713	LASOR A VAREA	280	14	18	Europa
mwg0452a	hessen	1713	LASOR A VAREA	100	9	14	Francfordia (view of Frankfort)
mwf0100	france	1713	LASOR A VAREA	180	14	18	Galliae Regnum
mwbh0550	belgium holland	1713	LASOR A VAREA	100	8	12	Gandt (view of Ghent)
mwsw0106	switzerland	1713	LASOR A VAREA	250	8	14	Genevra
mwg0100	germany	1713	LASOR A VAREA	150	12	17	Germania
mwsp0518	spain regions	1713	LASOR A VAREA	180	8	13	Granata
mwf1148	france rhone-alpes	1713	LASOR A VAREA	100	8	13	Grationapolis Acusia (view of Grenoble)
mwsc0335	scandinavia denmark	1713	LASOR A VAREA	250	9	13	Hafnia (view of Copenhagen)
mwsw0107	switzerland	1713	LASOR A VAREA	200	14	18	Helvetia
mwas0442	asia south east	1713	LASOR A VAREA	250	13	18	India Orientalis
mwuk0971	england	1713	LASOR A VAREA	240	11	15	Inghilterra
mwuk0139	ireland	1713	LASOR A VAREA	200	11	15	Irlandia
mwgr0618	greece islands	1713	LASOR A VAREA	100	21	16	Isola di Cerigo Cythera
mwgr0499	greece cyprus	1713	LASOR A VAREA	2250	21	16	Isola di Cipro (copy of Bonifacio 1570)
mwgr0315	greece corfu	1713	LASOR A VAREA	300	20	15	Isola di Corfu
mwuk0457	scotland	1713	LASOR A VAREA	200	10	14	Isole Hebride et Orcade
mwas0725	asia south east moluccas	1713	LASOR A VAREA	200	10	14	Isole Molucche
mwgr0421a	greece crete	1713	LASOR A VAREA	250	21	15	L'Isola di Candia Creta
mwit0403	italy lazio	1713	LASOR A VAREA	150	13	17	Latium seu Territorium Romae
mwit0500	italy lombardy	1713	LASOR A VAREA	150	14	18	Lombardia et Marchia Tarusina
mwuk1147	england london	1713	LASOR A VAREA	300	9	13	Londra (reprint of Valegia's 1595 map)
mwg0626	saxony	1713	LASOR A VAREA	100	8	13	Luneburgum Nobilis Saxonie Urbs (view)
mwgm0196	mexico	1713	LASOR A VAREA	240	9	13	Mexico (Mexico City)
mwbh0551	belgium holland	1713	LASOR A VAREA	100	8	13	Mons
mwgr0156	greece	1713	LASOR A VAREA	200	10	17	Morea
mwru0386	russia moscow	1713	LASOR A VAREA	300	9	14	Moscovia, Urbs, Regionis eius de Nominis Metropolitica (view)
mwe0345	europe austria	1713	LASOR A VAREA	300	9	13	Oenipons sive Enipontus vulgo Inspruch Tirolensis Urbs Amplissima (view of Innsbruck)
mww0321	world	1713	LASOR A VAREA	450	17	25	Orbis Terrae Compendiosa Descriptio (reprint of Rosaccio 1598)
mwe0721	europe danube	1713	LASOR A VAREA	150	10	12	Origine del Danubio
mwit0426	italy liguria	1713	LASOR A VAREA	200	14	18	Pedemontium Monsferratus et Liguria

AMPG REFERENCE	REGION	DATE	MAP MAKER	PRICE (UK£)	VERT. (cm.)	HOR. (cm.)	TITLE OF MAP (Comments by the editor in brackets)
mwru0502	ukraine	1713	LASOR A VAREA	140	10	15	Piccola Tartaria (Crimea)
mwbp0360	poland	1713	LASOR A VAREA	180	13	18	Poloniae Regnum
mwsp0072	portugal	1713	LASOR A VAREA	180	14	18	Portugalliae Regnum
mwme0247	holy land	1713	LASOR A VAREA	200	14	19	Questa Tavole e l'Antica Siria
mwit0357	italy emilia-romagna	1713	LASOR A VAREA	100	11	16	Ravenna
mwwi0825	puerto rico	1713	LASOR A VAREA	300	11	15	S. Giovanni
mwaf0598	africa islands madagascar	1713	LASOR A VAREA	250	11	15	S. Lorenzo
mwat0269	atlantic north	1713	LASOR A VAREA	280	14	18	Scandia, sive Regiones Septentrionales
mwgr0619	greece islands	1713	LASOR A VAREA	200	10	18	Sciro
mwuk0457a	scotland	1713	LASOR A VAREA	200	11	15	Scotia
mwit1116	italy tuscany	1713	LASOR A VAREA	250	9	12	Siena
mwwi0591	hispaniola	1713	LASOR A VAREA	250	28	18	Spagnuola
mwsc0706	scandinavia sweden	1713	LASOR A VAREA	150	9	12	Stockholm (view)
mwg0271	baden-wurttemberg	1713	LASOR A VAREA	300	9	14	Stucharth Metropololis Wirtembergiaci Regia Pulchra Ducis
mwg0817	westphalia	1713	LASOR A VAREA	180	9	13	Susatum Urbs Westphalie Opuleritissima (view of Soest)
mwin0034	ceylon	1713	LASOR A VAREA	250	10	14	Taprobana
mwit1026	italy south	1713	LASOR A VAREA	100	18	13	Taranto in Terra d'Otranto (view)
mwgr0620	greece islands	1713	LASOR A VAREA	150	10	18	Tenedo
mwsp0519	spain regions	1713	LASOR A VAREA	100	8	13	Toledo (view)
mwit0672	italy piedmont	1713	LASOR A VAREA	150	12	18	Torino Metropoli del Piamonte (view of Turin)
mwg0529	rheinland-pfalz	1713	LASOR A VAREA	100	9	13	Treveris (view of Trier)
mwme0598	arabia etc	1713	LASOR A VAREA	200	12	17	Turcici Imperii Descriptio
mwsw0108	switzerland	1713	LASOR A VAREA	300	9	13	Ursina Berna (view of Bern)
mwbp0110	baltic states	1713	LASOR A VAREA	200	9	14	Vera Designatio Urbis in Littauia Grodnae (map part of a page of text)
mwe0420	europe austria vienna	1713	LASOR A VAREA	250	8	24	Viena (view)
mwbp0111	baltic states	1713	LASOR A VAREA	300	8	13	Vilna Lituaniae Metropolis (view)
mwbp0361	poland	1713	LASOR A VAREA	300	9	13	Wratislavia Silesie Metropolis (view of Breslau)
mwgr0286	greece cefalonia	1713	LASOR A VAREA	300	10	18	Zafalonia
mwaf1227	africa west	1780	LATH	800	49	111	A Draught of the River Senegal
mwaf0999	africa south	1818	LATROBE	350	22	54	The Southern Division of the Cape of Good Hope Colony
mwsam0106	south america	1787	LATTRE	180	18	24	Amerique Meridionale
mwam0483	america north	1783	LATTRE	200	18	25	Amerique Septentrionale Divisee en ses Principaux Etats
mww0419	world	1750	LATTRE	400	23	41	Carte dans laquelle on Voit la Route que le Centurion a Tenu dans la Voiage au tour du Monde
mwme0742	iraq etc	1766	LATTRE	600	56	41	Carte de la Babylonie
mwuk1507	uk english channel (all)	1779	LATTRE	580	53	70	Carte de la Manche avec Tous les Bancs de Sables, les Profondeurs d'Eau, et l'Heure de la Maree
mwca0095	canada	1773	LATTRE	450	33	47	Carte De L'Amerique Septentrionale
mwaf0651	africa islands seychelles	1776	LATTRE	750	62	76	Carte de l'Archipel au Nord de l'Isle de France (incl. inset of Seychelles)
mwru0245	russia	1771	LATTRE	280	30	43	Carte de l'Empire de Russie en Europe et en Asie
mwf0518	france corsica	1768	LATTRE	875	65	46	Carte de l'Isle de Corse Divisee par Jurisdictions
mwaf0631a	africa islands mauritius	1753	LATTRE	1200	53	41	Carte de L'Isle de France ... 1753
mwat0050	atlantic ocean (all)	1780	LATTRE	480	50	63	Carte de l'Ocean Atlantique
mwuss0794	massachusetts	1750	LATTRE	750	29	23	Carte des Environs de Boston Capitale de la N.lle Angleterre en Amerique
mwam1085	america north (east)	1784	LATTRE	12000	54	76	Carte des Etats-Unis de l'Amerique Suivant le Traite de Paix ... Benjamin Franklin (with additional text side panels)
mwf0658	france loire	1771	LATTRE	180	41	30	Carte des Gouvernments d'Anjou et de Saumurois, de la Tourraine, du Poitou, de Pays d'Aunis, Saintonge-Angoumois
mwf0415	france burgundy	1771	LATTRE	180	41	29	Carte des Gouvernments de Bourgogne, de Franche Comte et de Lyonnois
mwgm0235	mexico	1771	LATTRE	280	30	42	Carte du Mexique ou de la Nlle. Espagne Contenant aussi le Nouveau Mexique, la Californie, avec une Partie des Pays Adjacents
mwf0141	france	1771	LATTRE	235	30	43	Carte Generale de France Divisee par Gouvernements
mwme0728	caucasus	1766	LATTRE	600	51	71	Carte Generale de la Georgie et de l'Armenie
mwme0884	syria etc	1764	LATTRE	720	56	42	Carte Particuliere de la Syrie
mwf0500	france corsica	1749	LATTRE	375	28	44	Carte Particuliere de l'Isle de Corse Divisee par ses Provinces ou Juridictions, & Fiefs
mwam1102	america north (east)	1790	LATTRE	200	25	18	Etats-Unis de l'Amerique Seple. avec le Canada et la Floride
mwwi0526	grenada	1779	LATTRE	675	44	59	La Grenade Divisee par Quartiers avec ses Ports et Mouillages d'apres cell Levee par Ordre du Gouverneur Scott
mwaf0257	africa	1787	LATTRE	235	18	24	L'Afrique Divisee en ses Principaux Etats
mwam0224	america continent	1787	LATTRE	235	18	24	L'Amerique
mwas0210	asia continent	1787	LATTRE	235	18	29	L'Asie
mwf0535	france corsica	1783	LATTRE	480	44	30	L'Isle de Corse divisee
mwwi0512	dominica	1779	LATTRE	960	62	48	L'Isle de la Dominique par M. J. M. Anglois ... Chez Lattre
mww0450	world	1760	LATTRE	300	14	20	Mappemonde pour la Concorde de la Geographie
mwme0364	holy land	1776	LATTRE	580	43	66	Paradisi Terrestris
mwru0278	russia	1785	LATTRE	580	43	62	Partie Occidental de l'Empire de Russie / Partie Orientale de l'Empire de Russie
mwf0274	france aquitaine	1780	LATTRE	785	52	64	Plan de la Ville de Bordeaux avec ses Environs

AMPG REFERENCE	REGION	DATE	MAP MAKER	PRICE (UK£)	VERT. (cm.)	HOR. (cm.)	TITLE OF MAP (Comments by the editor in brackets)
mwf0756	france nord pas-de-calais	1760	LATTRE	580	36	73	Plan de la Ville de Dunkerque
mwit0756	italy rome	1788	LATTRE	960	45	65	Plan de la Ville de Rome
mwsp0727	gibraltar	1765	LATTRE	650	40	55	Plan du Promontoire, de la Ville et du Port de Gibraltar
mwf0452	france champagne	1769	LATTRE	3000	110	140	Plan General de la Ville de Reims et des ses Environs (map by M Le Gendre)
mwf0454	france champagne	1810	LATTRE	580	43	54	Plan General de la Ville de Reims et de les Environs avec ses Projets et Embelissemens. Reduit d'apres celui Leve par M. Le Gendre Ecuyer et Inspecteur General des Ponts et Chaussees
mwf0270	france aquitaine	1755	LATTRE	2400	79	107	Plan Geometral de la Ville de Bordeaux et de Parties de ses Faubourgs Leve par les Ordres de M. de Tourny
mwf0413	france burgundy	1761	LATTRE	1500	80	108	Plan Geometral de la Ville de Dijon Leve en 1759
mwru0392	russia moscow	1771	LATTRE	650	48	73	Plan Geometral de la Ville de Moscow Ancienne Capitale de l'Empire de Russie
mwf0272	france aquitaine	1776	LATTRE	875	53	71	Plan Geometral de la Ville et Faubourg de Bordeaux
mwf0889	france paris	1774	LATTRE	675	53	75	Plan Routier de la Ville et Faubourg de Paris
mwg0644a	saxony	1740	LAUENSTEIN	480	49	55	Dioecesis Hildesheimensis medii aevi tabula (illustrated below left)
mwaf0173	africa	1738	LAUNAY	320	12	17	Africae emendata Descriptio
mww0374	world	1738	LAUNAY	450	12	20	Typus Orbis Terrarum
mwru0444	russia tartary	1705	LAURENT	500	52	30	Carte du Kamtchatka Dressee et Gravee par Laurent (re-issued by Bellin 1757 and in 1771 with title in German)
mwe0823	europe east	1788	LAURENT	580	74	71	Carte du Theatre de la Guerre Presente entre les Turcs, les Russes, et l'Empereur ou se Trouvent la Turquie d'Europe, la Pologne, la Hongrie, la Russie Meridionale, la Tartarie et la Georgie
mwme0398a	holy land	1820	LAURIE	200	35	42	A Map shewing ye situation of Paradise
mwuk1296a	england london	1820	LAURIE	1350	67	83	Laurie's New Plan of London and its Environs (10 editions to 1836. Illustrated is 1825 edition.)
mwwi0939	virgin isl	1821	LAURIE	3000	49	70	The Virgin Islands, Trigonometrically Surveyed and adjusted by accurate Astronomic Observations
mwin0302	india	1794	LAURIE & WHITTLE	240	52	23	(Pulicat / Fort St. David)
mwas0803	asia south east philippines	1794	LAURIE & WHITTLE	300	50	24	(Sorgoson / Bongo Bay. Two plans on one sheet)
mwca0344	canada newfoundland	1803	LAURIE & WHITTLE	300	37	50	A Chart of the Banks of Newfoundland Drawn from a Great Number of Hydrographical Surveys, Chiefly from those of Chabert, Cook, and Fleurieu, and Current Observations of Frans. Owen
mwec0200	uk england cornwall	1795	LAURIE & WHITTLE	400	51	68	A Chart of the Chops of the Channel to the South of Scilly Islands; Containing the West Coast of Cornwall, and Scilly Islands, Corrected from the Survey Made by Order of the Trinity House 1795
mwec0307	uk england devon	1799	LAURIE & WHITTLE	1350	64	79	A Chart of the Coast of Devonshire from Exmouth to Rame Head; Containing Tor Bay, Start Bay, Plymouth Sound, &ca.
mwin0303	india	1794	LAURIE & WHITTLE	375	62	60	A Chart of the Coast of India from Goa to Cape Cormorin, Exhibiting the Coasts of Canara and Malabar
mwin0439	indian ocean	1794	LAURIE & WHITTLE	200	43	46	A Chart of the Currents in the Indian Sea during the South West Monsoon, to the Northward of the Line by Msr. le Vicomte Grenier
mwec0652	uk england kent	1796	LAURIE & WHITTLE	750	52	70	A Chart of the Downs with the Flats of the North and South Forelands ... From the Observations etc. of the Trinity House Pilots and Surveyors
mwaf0622	africa islands madagascar	1797	LAURIE & WHITTLE	650	62	73	A Chart of the Inner Passage, between the Coast of Africa and the Isle of Madagascar from the Charts of D'Anville and D'Apres (re-issue of Sayer & Bennett, 1781. See under 'Africa South East')
mwuk1597a	channel islands	1794	LAURIE & WHITTLE	600	71	51	A Chart of the Islands of Jersey and Guernsey, Sark, Herm and Alderney (re-issue of Faden 1781)
mwec0345	uk england dorset	1794	LAURIE & WHITTLE	400	50	70	A Chart of the Isle, Roads, and Race of Portland with the Shambles &c.
mwat0170	atlantic canary isl.	1794	LAURIE & WHITTLE	650	60	47	A Chart of the Maderas and Canary Islands. According to the Surveys Published at Madrid in 1780, by Don Thomas Lopez
mwaf0657	africa islands seychelles	1803	LAURIE & WHITTLE	650	42	58	A Chart of the Mahe and Admirantes Islands with their Shoals
mwin0304	india	1794	LAURIE & WHITTLE	400	61	90	A Chart of the Northern Part of the Bay of Bengal between Point Palmiral and the Aragan Shore
mwin0442	indian ocean	1794	LAURIE & WHITTLE	785	58	89	A Chart of the Northern Part of the Indian Ocean, Containing a Part of the Coast of Africa from Magadasho River to the Straits of Bab-el-Mandeb, and the Coasts of Asia ... to the Mouths of the Ganges; with the Lakedivas, Maldivas and Ceylon
mwas0804	asia south east philippines	1794	LAURIE & WHITTLE	650	60	90	A Chart of the Passages between the Philippine and the Isles of Borneo and Mindanao with Those to the Southward of the Sooloo Archipelago and the Isle of Mindanao
mwme0662	arabia etc	1794	LAURIE & WHITTLE	600	48	65	A Chart of the Red Sea from Moka to Geddah

AMPG REFERENCE	REGION	DATE	MAP MAKER	PRICE (UK£)	VERT. (cm.)	HOR. (cm.)	TITLE OF MAP (Comments by the editor in brackets)
mwec0649	uk england kent	1794	LAURIE & WHITTLE	400	45	61	A Chart of the Sands and Channels from the Nore to Margate Road
mwas0897	asia south east sumatra	1794	LAURIE & WHITTLE	750	61	82	A Chart of the South Part of Sumatra
mwas0864	asia south east singapore	1794	LAURIE & WHITTLE	1800	61	83	A Chart of the Straits of Malacca and Sincapore
mwuk0237	ireland	1795	LAURIE & WHITTLE	685	79	127	A Chart of the West and South West Coast of Ireland, from the Mouth of the River Shannon to Waterford Haven on the Same Scale as the Chart of St. Georges Channel by Capt. Jos. Huddart
mww0581	world	1794	LAURIE & WHITTLE	2400	53	141	A Correct Chart of the Terraqueous Globe on which are Described Lines Shewing the Variation of the Magnetic Needle ... By the Celebrated Dr. Edmund Halley; Renewed by William Mountaine and James Dodson ... 1756 (between 60 degrees N and S)
mwsp0688	balearic islands	1794	LAURIE & WHITTLE	1200	44	56	A Correct Map of the Island of Minorca
mwaf0305	africa	1817	LAURIE & WHITTLE	1250	31	44	A Geographical Picture of Africa (Africa depicted as a cat - cartoon)
mwin0321	india	1798	LAURIE & WHITTLE	240	53	77	A Geohydrographic Draught of the Northern Circars
mwsam0115	south america	1794	LAURIE & WHITTLE	1500	98	118	A Map of South America Containing Tierra-Firma, Guayana, New Granada, Amazonia, Brasil, Peru, Paraguay, Chaco, Tucuman, Chili and Patagonia. From Mr. D'Anville with Several Improvements and Additions, and the Newest Discoveries
mwec0197	uk england cornwall	1794	LAURIE & WHITTLE	720	48	69	A Nautic Survey of Mounts Bay in Cornwall, with the Adjacent Coast from Cape Lizard to Cape Cornwall
mwam1159	america north (east)	1808	LAURIE & WHITTLE	7200	79	250	A New and Accurate Chart (from Captain Holland's Surveys) of the North American Coast, for Navigation between Philadelphia and Florida Respectfully Inscribed to his Excellency Thomas Jefferson, President
mwam1140	america north (east)	1800	LAURIE & WHITTLE	3600	81	310	A New and Accurate Chart ... Cape Cod ... Havanna
mwuk1442	england thames	1794	LAURIE & WHITTLE	600	67	100	A New and Accurate Chart of the Mouth of the Thames and its Entrances, viz: the Kings the Queens and South Channels &c from the Nore to Orford Ness and the North Foreland
mwwi0336	bahamas	1794	LAURIE & WHITTLE	2000	68	102	A New and Accurate Chart of the Windward Passage from Jamaica with the Several Passages Northward of Hispaniola, and Part of the Old channel of Bahama Drawn from Actual Surveys Made by the English and the French
mwgm0057	gulf of mexico and surrounding regions	1791	LAURIE & WHITTLE	785	46	86	A New and Complete Map of the West Indies Comprehending All the Coasts and Islands Known by that Name
mwat0055	atlantic ocean (all)	1794	LAURIE & WHITTLE	1200	71	104	A New and Correct Chart ... Exhibiting the Whole of the Atlantic or Western Ocean, and the Greatest Part of the Ethiopic or Southern Ocean; wherein the Respective Coasts of Europe, Africa, and America (2 sheets, each 71x104cm.)
mwuk1447	england thames	1800	LAURIE & WHITTLE	1250	89	95	A New and Correct Chart Extending from London Bridge to Orford Ness on the Essex and Suffolk Coast; & from the Nore to the North Foreland, the Downs, and South Foreland on the Kentish Coast
mwam0238a	america continent	1794	LAURIE & WHITTLE	6000	55	93	A New & Correct Map of America With The West India Islands
mwuk0560	scotland	1794	LAURIE & WHITTLE	1350	64	107	A New and Correct Map of Scotland or North Britain with All the Post and Military Roads, Divisions
mwca0120	canada	1794	LAURIE & WHITTLE	800	48	66	A New and Correct Map of the British Colonies in North America Comprehending Eastern Canada with the Province of Quebec, New Brunswick, Nova Scotia, ... Newfoundland: with the Adjacent States of New England, Vermont, New York, Pennsylvania and New Jersey
mwam1109	america north (east)	1794	LAURIE & WHITTLE	2000	48	65	A New and General Map of the Middle Dominions Belonging to the United States of America, viz. Virginia, Maryland, the Delaware-Counties, Pennsylvania, New Jersey &c. with the Addition of New York, & of the Greatest Part of New England (derived from Lewis Evans' map of 1781)
mwam1109a	america north (east)	1794	LAURIE & WHITTLE	1800	50	63	A New and General Map of the Southern Dominions Belonging to the United States of America, viz: North Carolina, South Carolina, and Georgia: with the Bordering Indian Countries, and the Spanish Possessions of Louisiana and Florida
mwuk0307a	irish sea	1794	LAURIE & WHITTLE	800	98	67	A New and Original Hydrographical Survey of the North and St. George's Channel Extending from Arran to Caldy Island on the British Coast and from Skerries Port Rush to Bannow on the Irish Coast By Capt. Joseph Huddart
mwas0865	asia south east singapore	1794	LAURIE & WHITTLE	1200	42	60	A New Chart containing the Southwest Part of the China Sea

AMPG REFERENCE	REGION	DATE	MAP MAKER	PRICE (UK£)	VERT. (cm.)	HOR. (cm.)	TITLE OF MAP (Comments by the editor in brackets)
mwec1115	uk england suffolk	1794	LAURIE & WHITTLE	600	49	49	A New Chart of Harwich Harbour ... Presented to the Hon:ble Capt: James Lutterell
mwin0453b	andaman/nicobar isl.	1799	LAURIE & WHITTLE	600	36	71	A New Chart of the Andaman and Nicobar Islands, with the Adjacent Islands, from the Draughts and Observations of Captn. Phins. Hunt, Captn. Mackay, Captn. John Ritchie, and Lieutt. Mc. Cluer, &c.
mwas0574	asia south east banda	1799	LAURIE & WHITTLE	480	44	62	A New Chart of the Banda Sea Including the Isles of Amboyna and Banda
mwsc0384	scandinavia denmark	1794	LAURIE & WHITTLE	500	104	64	A New Chart of the Cattegat Published at Copenhagen in the Year 1790 ... by Christian Charles Lous
mwsam0401	south america brazil	1794	LAURIE & WHITTLE	600	86	57	A New Chart of the Coast of Brazil from the Banks of St. Roque, to the Island of St. Sebastian
mwec0346	uk england dorset	1799	LAURIE & WHITTLE	400	64	80	A New Chart of the Coast of Dorsetshire and Devonshire from St. Alban's Head to Sidmouth
mwsam0643	south america guyana	1796	LAURIE & WHITTLE	850			A New Chart of the Coast of Guayana from River Berbice to Cape North, and the River of Amazons Containing the Dutch Colonies of Berbice and Surinam, with the French Colony of Cayenne
mwam1164	america north (east)	1809	LAURIE & WHITTLE	3500	53	72	A New Chart of the Coast of North America from Port Royal Entrance to Matanza Inlet Exhibiting the Coast of Georgia
mwam1111	america north (east)	1794	LAURIE & WHITTLE	4000	103	70	A New Chart of the Coast of North America, from New York to Cape Hatteras Including the Bays of Delaware and Chesapeak, with the Coasts of New Jersey, Maryland, Virginia and Part of the Coast of North Carolina
mwca0454	canada nova scotia	1798	LAURIE & WHITTLE	2400	71	153	A New Chart of the Coast of Nova Scotia with ... New Brunswick
mwuk1346	england east	1794	LAURIE & WHITTLE	400	69	50	A New Chart of the East Coast of England from Flamborough Head to the Entrance of Boston Deeps with the Course of the River Humber from Hull to the Sea
mwin0307	india	1794	LAURIE & WHITTLE	450	60	63	A New Chart of the Gulf or Bay of Bengal with Part of the Indian Ocean, as Far as the Line
mwuk1597	channel islands	1794	LAURIE & WHITTLE	1350	51	71	A New Chart of the Island of Guernsey with those of Sark, Herm and Jethou
mwuk1636	scilly isles	1794	LAURIE & WHITTLE	685	49	67	A New Chart of the Islands of Scilly with their Soundings, Channels and Sailing Marks
mwuk1626	isle of wight	1800	LAURIE & WHITTLE	1500	64	79	A New Chart of the Isle of Wight with the Adjacent Coast of Hampshire, wherein are Particularly Described the Roads of St. Helen's, Spithead, &c.
mwas0672	asia south east java	1794	LAURIE & WHITTLE	960	58	86	A New Chart of the Java Sea within the Isles of Sunda with its Straits and the Adjacent Seas
mwaf0972	africa south	1794	LAURIE & WHITTLE	1250	60	74	A New Chart of the Southern Coast of Africa from the Cape of Good Hope to Dalagoa Bay (re-issue of Sayer & Bennett 1781)
mwas0601	asia south east borneo	1799	LAURIE & WHITTLE	720	88	83	A New Chart of the Straits of Macassar between the Islands of Borneo and Celebes with the Adjacent Seas
mww0583	world	1794	LAURIE & WHITTLE	500	30	41	A New Chart of the World on Mercator's Projection
mww0615a	world	1800	LAURIE & WHITTLE	1200	72	91	A New Chart of the World on Wright's or Mercator's Projection... with the tracks of... Byron, Wallis, Carteret and Cook & ... La Pérouse
mwwi0133	west indies	1794	LAURIE & WHITTLE	6000	69	99	A New General Chart of the West Indies from the Latest Marine Journals and Surveys Regulated and Ascertained by Astronomical Observations. (Based on Carleton's map of 1789, which was first printed by J. Norman in 1790)
mwin0316	india	1794	LAURIE & WHITTLE	720	49	70	A New General Map of the East Indies (illustrated is the 1815 edition)
mwuk0235	ireland	1794	LAURIE & WHITTLE	720	52	80	A New Hydrographical Survey of the West Coast of Ireland from Sligo Bay to Tory Island and of the North Coast from Tory Island to Raughlan Island...being a Continuation of the Survey Made by Captn Joseph Huddart
mwme0663	arabia etc	1794	LAURIE & WHITTLE	1000	49	62	A New Map of Arabia Divided into its Several Regions and Districts from Mons. D'Anville
mwuk0248	ireland	1808	LAURIE & WHITTLE	375	64	50	A New Map of Ireland Compiled from Actual Surveys
mwit0217	italy	1794	LAURIE & WHITTLE	400	58	50	A New Map of Italy, with the Islands of Sicily, Sardinia & Corsica
mwuk1273	england london	1804	LAURIE & WHITTLE	2000	60	78	A New Map of London ... (12 editions until 1819. Title changed to 'Laurie & Whittle's New Map of London ...' in 1809)
mwam0522	america north	1794	LAURIE & WHITTLE	2000	102	116	A New Map of North America with the West India Islands ... the United States, and the Several Provinces, Governments &c. which Compose the British Dominions
mwuk0569	scotland	1803	LAURIE & WHITTLE	400	62	49	A New Map of Scotland Compiled from Actual Surveys & Regulated by the Latest Astronomical Observations
mwsw0203	switzerland	1794	LAURIE & WHITTLE	375	50	67	A New Map of Switzerland, Divided into the Thirteen Cantons with Their Allies & Their Subjects
mwit0821	italy sardinia	1794	LAURIE & WHITTLE	600	70	51	A New Map of the Dominions of the King of Sardinia
mwme0836	persia etc	1794	LAURIE & WHITTLE	400	53	60	A New Map of the Empire of Persia

AMPG REFERENCE	REGION	DATE	MAP MAKER	PRICE (UK£)	VERT. (cm.)	HOR. (cm.)	TITLE OF MAP (Comments by the editor in brackets)
mwf0540	france corsica	1794	LAURIE & WHITTLE	500	64	50	A New Map of the Island and Kingdom of Corsica by Thomas Jefferys
mwin0308	india	1794	LAURIE & WHITTLE	360	72	52	A New Map of the Jaghir Lands, on the Coast of Coromandel, or the Territory Belonging to the East India Company round Madras
mwbp0529	poland	1794	LAURIE & WHITTLE	600	48	65	A New Map of the Kingdom of Poland, with its Dismembered Provinces and the Kingdm. of Prussia
mwsp0308	spain	1794	LAURIE & WHITTLE	350	47	64	A New Map of the Kingdoms of Spain and Portugal
mwbh0766a	belgium holland	1796	LAURIE & WHITTLE	1000	94	117	A New Map of the Netherlands or Low Countries
mwsc0187	scandinavia	1794	LAURIE & WHITTLE	360	49	66	A New Map of the Northern States Containing the Kingdoms of Sweden, Denmark, and Norway; with the Western Parts of Russia, Livonia, Courland
mwbh0764	belgium holland	1794	LAURIE & WHITTLE	300	47	64	A New Map of the Seat of War in the Netherlands
mwe0477	europe central	1809	LAURIE & WHITTLE	1000	73	81	A New Map of the Seat of War, Comprehending Germany; Poland, with its Dismemberments, Prussia; Turkey in Europe, Italy &c.
mwam0238	america continent	1794	LAURIE & WHITTLE	1800	103	118	A New Map of the Whole Continent of America, Divided into North and South and West Indies, wherein are Exactly Described the United States of North America
mww0607	world	1799	LAURIE & WHITTLE	3000	48	71	A New Map of the World with Captain Cook's Tracks, his Discoveries and those of the Other Circumnavigators
mwme1040	turkey etc	1794	LAURIE & WHITTLE	320	51	70	A New Map of Turkey in Asia by Monsr. D'Anville First Geographer to the Most Christian King
mwe1166	europe south east	1794	LAURIE & WHITTLE	300	58	61	A New Map of Turkey in Europe Divided into All its Provinces; with the Adjacent Countries of Europe and Asia
mwuk1269	england london	1801	LAURIE & WHITTLE	1500	37	62	A New Plan of London, Westminster and Southwark (5 editions until 1815)
mwaf1239	africa west	1797	LAURIE & WHITTLE	600	98	66	A New Survey of the Coast of Africa from Senegal and Cape Verd to Cape St. Ann
mwuk1287	england london	1816	LAURIE & WHITTLE	450	54	67	A New Survey of the Environs of London, Extending Twenty Miles North & South from the Parallel of St. Pauls; and Twenty Six East & West from the Meridian of the Same Place
mwit1251a	italy venice	1795	LAURIE & WHITTLE	600	24	41	A Perspective View of the City of Venice
mwuss0453	florida	1794	LAURIE & WHITTLE	2400	60	41	A Plan of Amelia Harbour and Barr, in East Florida
mwin0326	india	1804	LAURIE & WHITTLE	1500	49	81	A Plan of Bombay - Harbour, on the Coast of Malabar
mwat0070	atlantic ascension isl.	1795	LAURIE & WHITTLE	720	27	44	A Plan of English Road in the Island of Ascension, and View of The Said Island from Where the Ship Appears at Anchor
mwuk1862	wales	1794	LAURIE & WHITTLE	400	51	69	A Plan of Milford Haven in Pembroke Shire, with the Fortifications Intended
mwca0276	canada new brunswick	1794	LAURIE & WHITTLE	480	34	51	A Plan of Ristagouche Harbour, in Chaleur Bay, Surveyed in 1760, by the King's Ship Norwich
mwaf0973	africa south	1794	LAURIE & WHITTLE	1500	48	55	A Plan of Table Bay, with the Road of the Cape of Good Hope (reprint of van Keulen's map of 1753)
mwec1177	uk england sussex	1794	LAURIE & WHITTLE	480	43	29	A Plan of the Harbour of Rye in Sussex
mwec0198	uk england cornwall	1794	LAURIE & WHITTLE	600	61	49	A Plan of the Road and Harbour of Fowey or Foy
mwin0309	india	1794	LAURIE & WHITTLE	240	69	48	A Sketch of Coringa Bay
mwuk0565	scotland	1797	LAURIE & WHITTLE	480	84	57	A Sketch of the Faro, Shetland & Orkney Isles
mwuss1555	vermont	1794	LAURIE & WHITTLE	2500	68	49	A Survey of Lake Champlain, Including Lake George, Crown Point and St. John. Surveyed by Order of His Excellency Major General Sr. Jeffery Amherst ... by William Brassier, Draughtsman. 1762
mwec0650	uk england kent	1794	LAURIE & WHITTLE	400	49	70	A Survey of the East Swale
mwc0214	china	1794	LAURIE & WHITTLE	500	64	52	A Survey of the Tigris, from Canton to the Island of Lankeet
mwaf0275	africa	1794	LAURIE & WHITTLE	300	31	44	Africa and its Several Regions (map by S. Dunn, first publ. 1774)
mwf0298	france bay of biscay	1794	LAURIE & WHITTLE	580	71	99	An Accurate Chart of the Bay of Biscay
mwwi0339	bahamas	1794	LAURIE & WHITTLE	1000	66	88	An Accurate Draught of the Gulph-Passage from Jamaica with the West End of Cuba (inset of Cayman Isl.)
mwwi0338	bahamas	1794	LAURIE & WHITTLE	800	63	48	An Accurate Draught of the Windward Passage from Jamaica with the French Part of Hispaniola (inset of Jamaica)
mwec0651	uk england kent	1794	LAURIE & WHITTLE	320	49	69	An Actual Survey of the Coast of Kent from Dim Church to Rye Harbour with the New Shoal to the Westward of Dungeness
mwec0648	uk england kent	1793	LAURIE & WHITTLE	280	51	69	An Actual Survey of Varne, & Ridge
mwaf0533	africa egypt etc	1798	LAURIE & WHITTLE	3000	32	42	An Exact Representation of the English & French Fleets under the Command of Rear Admiral Sr. Horatio Nelson K.B. & Admiral Brueys off the Mouth of the Nile on the 1st of August 1798
mwec0305	uk england devon	1795	LAURIE & WHITTLE	400	47	36	An Eye Sketch of the Entrance of Yealme River with the Depths of Water &c. &c.
mwec0304	uk england devon	1794	LAURIE & WHITTLE	480	69	51	An Hydrographical Survey of the Coast of Devonshire from Exmouth Bar to Stoke Point
mwas0227	asia continent	1799	LAURIE & WHITTLE	2000	102	119	Asia and its Islands

AMPG REFERENCE	REGION	DATE	MAP MAKER	PRICE (UK£)	VERT. (cm.)	HOR. (cm.)	TITLE OF MAP (Comments by the editor in brackets)
mwas0222	asia continent	1794	LAURIE & WHITTLE	300	48	52	Asia with its Islands and Different Regions According to their Modern Divisions; Also the Discoveries Made by Capt. Cook
mwwi0536	grenadines	1810	LAURIE & WHITTLE	600	33	46	Bequia or Becouya, the Northernmost of the Granadilles
mwuk1030a	uk england	1794	LAURIE & WHITTLE	240	54	49	Britanniae Antiquae
mwat0099	atlantic azores	1797	LAURIE & WHITTLE	720	46	61	Chart of the Acores (Hawks) Islands, Called also Flemish and Western Islands
mwuss1160	new york	1794	LAURIE & WHITTLE	2250	70	52	Chart of the Entrance to Hudson's River, from Sandy Hook to New York, with the Banks, Depths of Water, Sailing Marks &ca.
mwwi0850	st barts	1814	LAURIE & WHITTLE	1500	51	71	Chart of the Islands and Channels of St. Barholemew (copy of Fahlberg 1801)
mwam0266	america continent	1813	LAURIE & WHITTLE	960	60		Columbia, or the Western Hemisphere (circular map)
mwuss0951	mississippi	1794	LAURIE & WHITTLE	3000	112	34	Course of the River Mississippi, from the Balise to Fort Chartres; Taken on an Expedition to the Illinois, in the Latter End of the Year 1765
mwwi0503	curacao	1794	LAURIE & WHITTLE	1800	46	61	Curacao, from the Dutch Originals of Gerard van Keulen (copy of Sayer 1774)
mwaf0528	africa egypt etc	1794	LAURIE & WHITTLE	500	66	40	Egypt
mwaf0529	africa egypt etc	1794	LAURIE & WHITTLE	500	70	43	Egypt Called in the Country Missir
mwuk1032	england	1794	LAURIE & WHITTLE	500	58	98	England and Wales Drawn from the Most Accurate Surveys
mwe0236	europe	1805	LAURIE & WHITTLE	320	50	59	Europe Divided into its Several States
mwsp0617	spain regions	1805	LAURIE & WHITTLE	2000	28	43	Ever Memorable Battle off Cape Trafalgar: 21 October 1805
mwgr0231	greece	1794	LAURIE & WHITTLE	320	52	48	Graeciae Antiquae (based on Santini)
mwgr0232	greece	1794	LAURIE & WHITTLE	480	48	64	Graeciae pars Septentrionalis
mwgr0630	greece islands	1801	LAURIE & WHITTLE	120	19	25	Greece the Archipelago and Part of Anadoli
mwwi0530	grenada	1801	LAURIE & WHITTLE	1000	46	61	Grenada Divided into its Parishes, Surveyed by Order of His Excellency Governor Scott and Engraved by Thomas Jefferys
mwuk1523	uk english channel (all)	1815	LAURIE & WHITTLE	450	94	62	Harbours and Islands in the English Channel
mwin0325	india	1801	LAURIE & WHITTLE	120	24	20	Hindoostan with the Island of Ceylon Maldivas &c.
mwe0966	europe hungary	1794	LAURIE & WHITTLE	350	48	61	Kingdom of Hungary, Principality of Transylvania, Sclavonia, Croatia, with Part of Valakia, Bulgaria, Bosnia and Servia
mwam0255	america continent	1805	LAURIE & WHITTLE	450	48	58	Laurie & Whittle's New General Map of America
mwin0447	indian ocean	1800	LAURIE & WHITTLE	3000	74	109	Laurie and Whittle's New Chart of the Indian and Pacific Oceans between the Cape of Good Hope, New Holland, and Japan, Comprehending New Zealand, New Caledonia, New Britain, New Ireland, New Guinea, &c.
mwsc0753	scandinavia sweden	1807	LAURIE & WHITTLE	500	62	48	Laurie and Whittle's New Travelling Map of Sweden Proper, Gothland, &c. Exhibiting the Measured Distances, on All the Principal and Cross Roads, in Quarters of a Swedish Mile
mwg0163	germany	1794	LAURIE & WHITTLE	675	102	120	Map of the Empire of Germany, Including All the States Comprehended under that Name: with the Kingdom of Prussia, &c.
mwwi0804	martinique	1798	LAURIE & WHITTLE	960	46	61	Martinico, Done from Actual Surveys and Observations, Made by English Engineers whilst the Island was in their Possession
mwec0495	uk england hampshire	1801	LAURIE & WHITTLE	1350	76	61	New & Correct Chart of Spithead, from the East End of Hayling Island to Stokes Bay
mwsam0641	south america guyana	1795	LAURIE & WHITTLE	320	69	48	New Chart of Coast of Guayana from Orinoco to Berbice, Containing Dutch Colonies of Poumaron, Issequibo and Demerary
mwaa0158	arctic	1801	LAURIE & WHITTLE	120	19	19	North Pole; Extending to the Tropic of Cancer with the Addition of All the New Discoveries
mwm0074a	mediterranean	1794	LAURIE & WHITTLE	500	67	54	Orbis Romani Pars Orientalis / Pars Occidentalis (2 maps by D'Anville, each 67x54cm)
mwme0379	holy land	1794	LAURIE & WHITTLE	320	39	42	Palaestina by Mons. d'Anville of the Royal Academy
mwin0440	indian ocean	1794	LAURIE & WHITTLE	320	54	52	Particular Plans of Islands, Rocks and Shoals in the Indian Ocean
mwas0704	asia south east malacca	1796	LAURIE & WHITTLE	400	48	33	Plan of Salangor and Coast of Malaya from Point Caran to Parcelar Hill
mwas0807	asia south east philippines	1798	LAURIE & WHITTLE	580	48	33	Plan of the Bay of Manilla
mwec0199	uk england cornwall	1794	LAURIE & WHITTLE	400	66	47	Plan of the Bays of Polkerris and Mevagizey in Cornwall
mwsam0400	south america brazil	1794	LAURIE & WHITTLE	600	48	60	Plan of the Island of Fernand de Noronha
mwwi0905	trinidad & tobago	1800	LAURIE & WHITTLE	1800	50	65	Plan of the Isle of Trinidad, from Actual Surveys Made in the Year 1797
mwas0805	asia south east philippines	1794	LAURIE & WHITTLE	300	47	32	Plan of the Port of Subec ... Survey'd in the Year 1776
mwec0306	uk england devon	1798	LAURIE & WHITTLE	675	70	51	Plymouth Sound, Hamoaze and Catwater Surveyed in 1797
mwgm0124	honduras	1794	LAURIE & WHITTLE	1000	46	61	Ruatan or Rattan, Surveyed by Lieutenant Henry Barnsley with Improvements by Thomas Jefferys Geographer to the King
mwaf0970	africa south	1794	LAURIE & WHITTLE	360	43	27	Seamons Bay in the Bay of False (Simon's Bay)

AMPG REFERENCE	REGION	DATE	MAP MAKER	PRICE (UK£)	VERT. (cm.)	HOR. (cm.)	TITLE OF MAP (Comments by the editor in brackets)
mwbh0765	belgium holland	1794	LAURIE & WHITTLE	300	47	57	Seat of War in the Seven United Provinces, Comprehending Holland, Zeeland, Utrecht, Gelders, Over-Yssel, Frieseland and Groningen; with the Land of Drant; also Dutch Flanders and Dutch Brabant
mwas0624	asia south east gaspar	1794	LAURIE & WHITTLE	550	64	47	Sketch of the Straits of Gaspar
mwaa0043	antarctic	1801	LAURIE & WHITTLE	200	19	19	South Pole; from the Tropic of Capricorn with the Addition of All the New Discoveries
mwwi0871	st kitts	1794	LAURIE & WHITTLE	1200	46	61	St. Christophers, or St. Kitts, Surveyed by Anthony Ravell Esqr. Surveyor General of the Islands of St. Christophers, Nevis & Montserrat.
mwat0056	atlantic ocean (all)	1794	LAURIE & WHITTLE	400	49	65	The Atlantic Ocean by Governor Pownall F.R.S.
mwaf0971	africa south	1794	LAURIE & WHITTLE	450	58	26	The Bay of Algoa / Plan of Mossel Bay / Plan of Flesh Bay or Bay St. Bras, on the South Coast of Africa
mwf0299	france bay of biscay	1794	LAURIE & WHITTLE	400	54	69	The Bay of Biscay, with the Soundings, Taken by the Kings Order, from Ushant to Bayone, by Mr. de Perigny, Officer in the French Navy, from the French Chart, Composed by Mr. Bellin for Use of the King's Ships, with Several Additions and Improvements
mwgm0125	honduras	1794	LAURIE & WHITTLE	580	47	62	The Bay of Honduras
mwat0128	atlantic bermuda	1794	LAURIE & WHITTLE	2000	46	61	The Bermudas, or Summer's Islands from a Survey by C. Lempriere, Regulated by Astronomical Observations (copy of Le Rouge 1779)
mwuk1513	uk english channel (all)	1794	LAURIE & WHITTLE	2400	68	151	The British Channel with a Part of the Atlantic Ocean and of the Coast of Ireland ... with Numerous Improvements and Emendations to the Year 1788
mwat0204	atlantic cape verde isl.	1794	LAURIE & WHITTLE	400	53	29	The Cape Verd Islands
mwwi0264	west indies (east)	1794	LAURIE & WHITTLE	720	47	62	The Caribbee or Leeward Islands, the Virgin Islands, and the Isle of Porto Rico
mwin0311	india	1794	LAURIE & WHITTLE	240	58	43	The Coast of India between Calymere and Gordeware Points
mwin0322	india	1798	LAURIE & WHITTLE	600	58	88	The Coast of India from Mount Dilly to Pondichery, Comprehending the Coast of Malabar, Madura and Part of the Coast of Coromandel with the Isle of Ceylon
mwin0312	india	1794	LAURIE & WHITTLE	280	44	60	The Coast of India from Point Gordeware to the Ganges
mwin0313	india	1794	LAURIE & WHITTLE	240	61	44	The Coast of India from Point Jigat to Cape Ramas
mwgm0260	mexico	1794	LAURIE & WHITTLE	500	48	63	The Coast of Mexico from Laguna de Esmotes to Punta Brava
mwgm0261	mexico	1794	LAURIE & WHITTLE	500	48	64	The Coast of New Spain from Nueva Vera Cruz to Triste Island
mwuss0452	florida	1794	LAURIE & WHITTLE	2400	49	122	The Coast of West Florida and Louisiana and the Peninsula and Gulf of Florida of New Bahama Channel
mwgm0262	mexico	1794	LAURIE & WHITTLE	650	48	66	The Coast of Yucatan from Campeche to Ascension Bay with the West End of Cuba
mwc0216	china	1794	LAURIE & WHITTLE	800	48	62	The Empire of China with its Principal Divisions ... from the Maps of M. D'Anville
mwjk0123	japan	1794	LAURIE & WHITTLE	1000	48	64	The Empire of Japan ... with the Kindom of Corea from Kempfer and the Portuguese
mwit0965	italy sicily	1799	LAURIE & WHITTLE	875	49	69	The Island and Kingdom of Sicily, According to the Best Observations, & Improved; from the Map, of the Baron de Schmettau
mwwi0471	cuba	1794	LAURIE & WHITTLE	1200	48	61	The Island of Cuba with Part of the Bahama Banks & the Martyrs
mwwi0747	jamaica	1794	LAURIE & WHITTLE	480	47	62	The Island of Jamaica and Cape Gracias a Dios with the Banks
mwgm0436	panama	1794	LAURIE & WHITTLE	1200	48	63	The Isthmus of Panama with the Coast from Great River on the Moskito Shore to Cartegena. (Copy of Jefferys map of 1775)
mwsp0118	portugal	1794	LAURIE & WHITTLE	400	59	41	The Kingdoms of Portugal and Algarve from Zannoni's Map by J. Lodge
mwec0753	uk england lincolnshire	1780	LAURIE & WHITTLE	600	67	51	The Map of Lincolnshire
mwin0315	india	1794	LAURIE & WHITTLE	200	52	23	The Road of Palleacate / the Road of Tengepatnam
mwas0866	asia south east singapore	1798	LAURIE & WHITTLE	1250	44	70	The South Part of the Straits of Malacca Inscribed to Capt. G.G. Richardson, by Captn. J. Lindsey
mwas0867	asia south east singapore	1799	LAURIE & WHITTLE	1500	42	58	The Straits of Sincapore with those of Drion, Sabon, Mandol, &ca and South Part of Malacca Straits. Improved and Corrected from the Observations of Captn. John Hall ... and other Navigators
mwam1110	america north (east)	1794	LAURIE & WHITTLE	1200	47	52	The United States of America with the British Possessions of Canada, Nova Scotia, New Brunswick and Newfoundland Divided with the French, also the Spanish Territories of Louisiana and Florida According to the Preliminary Articles of Peace
mwwi0337	bahamas	1794	LAURIE & WHITTLE	800	48	63	The Windward Passage, with the Several Passages from the East End of Cuba & from the North Part of St. Domingo
mwuk1521	uk english channel (all)	1814	LAURIE & WHITTLE	1500	95	189	this Chart of the English Channel

AMPG REFERENCE	REGION	DATE	MAP MAKER	PRICE (UK£)	VERT. (cm.)	HOR. (cm.)	TITLE OF MAP (Comments by the editor in brackets)
mwin0441	indian ocean	1794	LAURIE & WHITTLE	785	48	61	To the King's Most Excellent Majesty George the Third; this Chart, with the Comparative Tracts of Ships, in the Different Monsoons
mwin0443	indian ocean	1794	LAURIE & WHITTLE	300	44	55	Track of the Calcutta East Indiaman over the Bassas de Chagas
mwit0259a	italy abruzzo	1600	LAURO	3000	39	52	Citta Dell' Aquila
mwru0380	russia moscow	1628	LAURO	1250	16	24	Moscovia Urbs Metropolis Totius Russiae Albae
mwit0882	italy sicily	1630	LAURO	800	16	24	Palermo
mwit0713a	italy rome	1630	LAURO	2500	48	73	Roma Antiqua Triumphatrix Abantiquis Monumentis et Rerum Gestarum
mwit1052b	italy naples	1616	LAURO	500	18	24	Topographica Puteolorum (Pozzuoli or ancient Naples)
mwf0188	france	1820	LAVOISNE	120	42	52	A New Map of France Conformable to the Treaty of Paris 1815; with the Netherlands, Switzerland and Part of Italy &c. (map incl. text panels)
mwaf0310	africa	1820	LAVOISNE	120	41	51	Africa Drawn from the Best Authorities (map incl. text panels)
mwas0247	asia continent	1828	LAVOISNE	120	42	53	Asia: Drawn from the Best Authorities, for Elucidation of Lavoisne's Genealogical, Historical, Chronological and Geographical Atlas. Revised 1828 (map incl. text panels)
mwme0397	holy land	1820	LAVOISNE	160	42	52	Canaan, with Part of Egypt, during the Residence of the Israelites in the Desert / Canaan, Subsequent to its Conquest by the Israelites, and its Division among the Tribes (maps incl. text panels)
mwc0245	china	1820	LAVOISNE	120	42	52	China and the Tributary Kingdom of Corea (map incl. text panels)
mwe0254	europe	1820	LAVOISNE	120	41	51	Europe Drawn from the Best Authorities (map incl. text panels)
mwaf0312	africa	1821	LAVOISNE	120	42	52	Geographical and Historical Map of Africa (map incl. text panels)
mwe0255	europe	1821	LAVOISNE	120	43	52	Geographical and Historical Map of the Incursions of the Barbarians (map incl. text panels)
mwme0399	holy land	1821	LAVOISNE	160	43	52	Geographical and Historical Maps, Illustrative of Sacred History (2 maps on one sheet)
mwuk1048	england	1820	LAVOISNE	120	42	52	Geographical and Statistical Map of England (map incl. text panels)
mwgr0241	greece	1813	LAVOISNE	120	42	52	Geographical and Statistical Map of Greece (map incl. text panels)
mwuk0260	ireland	1820	LAVOISNE	120	42	52	Geographical and Statistical Map of Ireland (map incl. text panels)
mwit0239	italy	1828	LAVOISNE	120	42	52	Geographical and Statistical Map of Italy (map incl. text panels)
mwbp0560	poland	1820	LAVOISNE	120	42	52	Geographical and Statistical Map of Poland (map incl. text panels)
mwe0839	europe east	1820	LAVOISNE	120	42	52	Geographical and Statistical Map of Poland and Hungary (map incl. text panels)
mwru0341	russia	1820	LAVOISNE	120	42	52	Geographical and Statistical Map of Russia (map incl. text panels)
mwuk0585	scotland	1820	LAVOISNE	120	42	52	Geographical and Statistical Map of Scotland (map incl. text panels)
mwsp0322	spain	1820	LAVOISNE	120	42	52	Geographical and Statistical Map of Spain and Portugal (map incl. text panels)
mww0666	world	1820	LAVOISNE	250	41	51	Geographical Map of the World, with the Tracks of the Most Celebrated Navigators (map incl. text panels)
mwam0277	america continent	1821	LAVOISNE	240	44	56	Geographical, Historical, and Statistical Map of America (map incl. text panels)
mwuk0884	uk	1820	LAVOISNE	120	36	51	Map of England, Scotland and Ireland Indicating the Places Rendered Celebrated by Battles and Sieges (map incl. text panels)
mwg0177	germany	1820	LAVOISNE	120	42	52	Map of Germany, Divided According to the Treaty of Paris, and the Acts of the Congress of Vienna (map incl. text panels)
mwe0840	europe east	1820	LAVOISNE	120	42	52	Map of Poland, Prussia and Hungary, Indicating the Places Rendered Celebrated by Sieges and Battles (map incl. text panels)
mwsam0138	south america	1820	LAVOISNE	120	41	52	Map of South America (map incl. text panels)
mwuss0624	louisiana	1720	LAW	875	18	16	Louisiana by de Rivier Mississippi
mwam0371	america north	1718	LAWSON	675	18	18	A Map of the English Plantations in America (1st edition 1709)
mwuss0167	carolinas	1712	LAWSON	2000	37	30	Die Vornehmste Eigenthums Herren und Besitzer von Carolina (German edition of the 1709 1st edition in English)
mwuss0131	california	1849	LAWSON	7500	37	52	Lawson's Map from Actual Survey of the Gold, Silver and Quicksilver Regions of Upper California
mwca0136	canada	1814	LAY	2800	55	86	A New Correct Map of the Seat of War in Lower Canada, Protracted from Holland's Large Map

AMPG REFERENCE	REGION	DATE	MAP MAKER	PRICE (UK£)	VERT. (cm.)	HOR. (cm.)	TITLE OF MAP (Comments by the editor in brackets)
mwam0659	america north	1827	LAY	8000	132	160	Lay's Map of the United States. Compiled from the Latest and Best Authorities and Actual Surveys by Amos Lay
mwuss1170	new york	1801	LAY	1200	67	76	Map of the Northern Part of the State of New York Compiled from Actual Survey
mwuss1198	new york	1825	LAY	2400	128	128	Map of the State of New York (later edition of 1817 map)
mwuss1185	new york	1817	LAY	3500	131	131	Map of the State of New York, with Part of the States of Pennsylvania, New Jersey &c.
mwe0278	europe austria	1545	LAZIUS	4000	32	45	Ducatus juraemontis / Marcha boiorum (2 maps on one sheet. Lazius was the author of the first atlas of Austria.)
mwg0503	rheinland-pfalz	1561	LAZIUS	9000	32	57	R. Autrasia ad Rhenum cu Edel
mwca0053	canada	1738	LE BEAU	350	16	23	Carte du Canada Dediee a son Altesse Serenissime Monseigneur E.J.G. de Biron Duc de Courlande et Semigalle &c.
mwe0234	europe	1803	LE BOUGE	2000	218	218	Carte de L'Europe
mwf0668	france lorraine	1617	LE CLERC	400	38	42	(Metz) Description Du Pays Messin et ses Confins
mwuk0913	england	1605	LE CLERC	1500	38	48	Anglia Regnum si quod Aliud in Toto Oceano Ditissimum et Florentissimum
mwas0025	asia continent	1602	LE CLERC	3200	37	48	Asiae Nova Descriptio (close copy of Ortelius 1570)
mwf0570	france ile de france	1617	LE CLERC	400	32	49	Carte du Gouvernement de Lile de France
mwf0710	france nord pas-de-calais	1602	LE CLERC	1250	33	43	Description du Pais de Caux
mwf0255	france aquitaine	1624	LE CLERC	300	36	47	Descrition du Diocese de Sarlat et Haut Perigord
mwe0026	europe	1602	LE CLERC	3000	34	46	Europa
mwsp0531	spain regions	1730	LE CLERC	200	25	33	Het Innemen van Cadix, Geschiedt in den Jaere 1596
mwru0500b	ukraine	1705	LE CLERC	120	16	20	La Mer Noire Commune aux Moscovites et aux Turcs
mwf1180	france south east	1619	LE CLERC	800	35	45	Le Daulphine, Languedoc, Gascoigne, Provence et Xaintonge
mwbh0823	luxembourg	1626	LE CLERC	720	39	47	Luxenburgicus Ducatus
mww0107	world	1602	LE CLERC	4800	34	52	Nova Universi Orbis Descriptio (oval projection)
mww0108	world	1602	LE CLERC	4800	34	52	Orbis Terrae Novissima Descriptio
mwf0632	france limousin	1620	LE CLERC	300	35	47	Totius Lemovici
mwf0738	france nord pas-de-calais	1680	LE CLERC	600	41	35	Valencienne Ville de Haynaut (small plan at top and 1677 siege)
mwbh0413	belgium holland	1680	LE CLERC	600	42	36	Ypres. Grand Ville Riche & Marchande
mwc0302a	china formosa	1727	LE GENTIL	550	13	18	(Untitled map showing part of Formosa extreme left. North to the left. Publ. by P. Mortier. Shown above left)
mwp0325	pacific guam	1727	LE GENTIL	375	13	18	Isle Guahan ou Mariamne (publ. by P. Mortier)
mwuk1599b	channel islands	1834	LE GROS	5000	84	70	This Geometrical Plan Of The Town, Fort & Harbour Of Saint Helier
mwuk1602a	channel islands	1856	LE LIEVRE	500	38	56	Map of the Island of Jersey
mwas0558	asia south east bali	1619	LE MAIRE	400	14	21	(Untitled map of Bali. South to the top.)
mwp0376	pacific new guinea	1619	LE MAIRE	400	15	27	Description de la Coste Setentrionale de Nova Guinea Nouvellement Decouvert par Guillaume Schouten de Hoorn (from Le Maire and Schouten's voyage publ. by van Keelkercken)
mwas0628	asia south east java	1619	LE MAIRE	350	14	21	Iava Maior
mwc0011	china	1619	LE MAIRE	160	16	20	Mont van der Rivier Chimcheo in China
mwat0322	atlantic st helena	1619	LE MAIRE	250	14	21	S. Helena
mwsam0656	south america magellan	1619	LE MAIRE	650	16	21	Suydsyde van tierra del Fuego Waergenomen ende afgebeelt door Joannem a Walbeek (1st map to focus on Le Maire Straits, publ. by van Geelkerken. Le Maire traveled with Schouten [see previous map] on their expedition but they split up en route)
mwsam0657	south america magellan	1619	LE MAIRE	1500	15	43	Typus Freti Magellantici (see comments on previous map)
mwaa0166	arctic	1821	LE MAITRE	160	30		Carte des Regions Polaires Boreales ou se Trouvent Tracees la Route et les Decouvertes du Cap. Parry en 1819 et 1820 (circular map)
mwuss0637	louisiana	1763	LE PAGE DU PRATZ	200	15	18	(Mobile Bay to Trinity river Texas)
mwuss0631	louisiana	1757	LE PAGE DU PRATZ	1000	25	34	Carte de la Louisiane Colonie Francaise avec le Cours du Fleuve St. Louis, les Rivieres Adjacentes, les Nations des Naturels, les Etablissems Francais, et les Mines
mwuss0632	louisiana	1758	LE PAGE DU PRATZ	180	13	19	Nouvelle Orleans Capitale de la Louisiane
mwe0186	europe	1764	LE PAUTE	1600	48	65	Passage de l'Ombre de la Lune au Travers l'Europe
mwf0917	france paris	1830	LE ROI	675	70	89	Nouveau Plan Routier de la Ville de Paris Revu et Corrige en 1830. Orne de ses Principaux Monuments
mwf0918	france paris	1832	LE ROI	550	55	81	Nouveau Plan Routier de la Ville de Paris, ou Guide du Voyageur dans cette Capitale
mwam1048	america north (east)	1777	LE ROUGE	4800	101	97	A Map of the Most Inhabited Part of New England. Containing the Provinces of Massachusets Bay and New Hampshire, with the Colonies of Conecticut and Rhode Island
mwsam0069	south america	1748	LE ROUGE	200	20	27	Amerique Meridionale
mwam0989	america north (east)	1756	LE ROUGE	25000	66	48	Amerique Septentrionale avec les Routes, Distances en Miles, Limites et Etablissements Francois et Anglois par le Docteur Mitchel (8 sheets, each 66x48cm.)
mwam0945	america north (east)	1742	LE ROUGE	2250	51	49	Amerique Septentrionale Suivant la Carte de Pople Faite a Londres en 20 Feuilles

AMPG REFERENCE	REGION	DATE	MAP MAKER	PRICE (UK£)	VERT. (cm.)	HOR. (cm.)	TITLE OF MAP (Comments by the editor in brackets)
mwuss0200	carolinas	1777	LE ROUGE	4800	49	138	An Accurate Map of North and South Carolina with their Indian Frontiers
mwwi0297	antigua	1746	LE ROUGE	240	20	27	Antigue une des Antilles aux Anglois
mwuss1111	new york	1776	LE ROUGE	960	36	35	Attaque de l'Armee des Provinciaux dans Long Island de 27 Aoust 1776. Dessin de l'Isle de New-York et des Etats Publie a Londres par Acte du Parlement du 24 8bre 1776
mwuss0204	carolinas	1778	LE ROUGE	3600	46	62	Barre et Port de Charles-Town leve en 1776
mwbp0457	poland	1758	LE ROUGE	1000	55	82	Basse Silesie
mwuss0753	maryland	1778	LE ROUGE	6000	91	134	Baye de Chesapeake en 4 feuilles
mwuss0366	delaware	1777	LE ROUGE	2250	47	64	Baye de la Deleware avec les Ports, Sondes, Dangers, Bancs, &c. depuis les Caps, jusqu'a Philadelphie d'apres la Carte de Joshua Fisher Publiee a Philadelphie
mwuss0795	massachusetts	1756	LE ROUGE	12000	46	33	Baye et Port de Boston Tire des Manuscrits de M. le Chevalier de la Rigaudiere Lieutenant de Vaisseau du Roy
mwam0976	america north (east)	1755	LE ROUGE	2500	61	50	Canada et Louisiane (title above map)
mwuss0202	carolinas	1778	LE ROUGE	6000	130	104	Caroline Meridionale et Partie de la Georgie / Course de la Riviere d'Hudson (reduced size version of De Brahm's map of 1757)
mwe0590	europe czech republic (bohemia)	1756	LE ROUGE	3600	148	171	Carte Chorographique de la Boheme Divisee en 12 Cercles (Reduced version of Muller's map of 1722)
mwe0451	europe bulgaria	1770	LE ROUGE	400	31	49	Carte de la Bulgarie et Romanie
mwuss0436	florida	1777	LE ROUGE	3000	47	60	Carte de la Floride Occidentale et Louisiane / La Peninsula et Golfe de la Floride ou Canal de Bahama avec les Isles de Bahama, Traduit de Gefferys (2 sheets, both 47x60cm.)
mwe0810	europe east	1770	LE ROUGE	1250	64	48	Carte de la Moldavie Sur celle de Prince Cantimir
mwuss1132	new york	1778	LE ROUGE	1800	71	52	Carte des Troubles de l'Amerique Levee par Ordre du Chevalier Tryon Capitaine General et Gouverneur de la Province de New-York Ensemble la Province de New-Jersey par Sauthier et Ratzer. Traduit de Anglaises ... 1778
mwin0278	india	1782	LE ROUGE	1000	96	138	Carte du Bengale, Bahar (copy of Rennell 1776)
mwjk0100	japan	1748	LE ROUGE	875	21	28	Carte du Japon et la Coree
mwru0291	russia	1788	LE ROUGE	400	61	38	Carte du Voyage de Sa Majeste Imperiale dans la Partie Meridio.le de la Russie en 1787
mwam1094	america north (east)	1787	LE ROUGE	1200	62	50	Carte d'une Partie de l'Amerique Septentrionale, pour Servir a l'Histoire de la Derniere Guerre
mwf0519	france corsica	1768	LE ROUGE	3500	65	124	Carte Militaire de l'Isle de Corse, ou sont Marquees Toutes les Paroisses et Tous les Principaux Hameaux de Chaque Pieve, Rectifiee en l'Annee 1740
mwbh0666	belgium holland	1746	LE ROUGE	480	63	48	Carte Topographique des Environs de Charleroy jusqu'a Philippeville. Par le Rouge, Ingr. Geographe
mwe1025	europe rhine	1745	LE ROUGE	720	49	125	Carte Topographique du Cours du Rhin de Philisbourg a Mayence
mwwi0502	curacao	1779	LE ROUGE	2000	46	61	Curacao (copy of Sayer 1774 in French)
mwe0688	europe dalmatia	1770	LE ROUGE	600	33	49	Dalmatie, Montenegrins et Partie du Golfe de Venise
mwbp0453	poland	1757	LE ROUGE	480	50	68	Duche de Pomeranie
mwaf0512	africa egypt etc	1748	LE ROUGE	200	21	28	Egypte
mwuss1131	new york	1778	LE ROUGE	3600	67	50	Entree de la Riviere d'Hudson ... 1778
mwuss0442	florida	1778	LE ROUGE	1200	50	60	Entrée de la Riviere S.te Marie: Isle Amelia en Floride
mwg0659	saxony	1759	LE ROUGE	180	21	22	Environs de Leipzig
mwg0394	bavaria	1780	LE ROUGE	180	22	29	Environs de Munich
mwuss1376	pennsylvania	1778	LE ROUGE	3600	57	45	Environs de Philadelphia. Par Scull et Heap ... 1778
mwuss1268	ohio	1757	LE ROUGE	960	20	30	Essay du Cours de l'Oyo avec les Forts Francois et Anglois
mwru0195	russia	1744	LE ROUGE	600	47	54	Etats de Moscovie
mwru0241	russia	1770	LE ROUGE	1200	53	46	Frontieres de Turquie et de Russie Entre la Mer Caspienne et la Mer d'Asof
mwme0729	caucasus	1770	LE ROUGE	720	52	46	Frontieres de Turquie et de Russie entre la Mer Caspienne et la Mer d'Asof
mwsp0713	gibraltar	1756	LE ROUGE	720	51	69	Gibraltar avec les Nouveaux Ouvrages Faits depuis le Dernier Siege. Les Lignes Espagnoles Leve Nouvellement sur les Lieux / Plan du Port et Ville de Mahon, du Fort St. Philippe et ses Fortifications (Gibraltar/Minorca)
mwbp0130	baltic states	1759	LE ROUGE	280	21	28	Grande Duche de Lithuanie, Divise en 9. Palatinats
mwg0657	saxony	1758	LE ROUGE	180	22	28	Haute Saxe, Bailliages de Doelitsch Bitterfeld Zoerbig
mwwi0774	martinique	1748	LE ROUGE	180	21	29	Isle de la Martinique
mwwi0607	hispaniola	1746	LE ROUGE	280	21	28	Isle de St. Domingue
mwwi0865	st kitts	1779	LE ROUGE	1250	48	61	Isle St. Christophe ou St. Kitts
mwwi0857b	st kitts	1746	LE ROUGE	150	27	20	Isle St. Christophle une des Antilles aux Anglois / La Barbade une des Antilles aux Anglois divisée par paroisses
mwwi0860	st kitts	1756	LE ROUGE	480	27	20	Isle St. Christophle une des Antilles aux Anglois. A Paris. Par le Sr. Le Rouge Rue des Grands Augustins [on sheet with] La Barbade une des Antilles aux Anglois Divisee par Paroisses
mwwi0894	st vincent	1778	LE ROUGE	650	58	46	Isle St. Vincent Levee en 1773 apres le Traite Fait avec les Caribes Traduite de l'Anglais
mwas0472	asia south east	1748	LE ROUGE	180	21	27	Isles de la Sonde
mwas0734	asia south east moluccas	1748	LE ROUGE	180	20	27	Isles Moluques

AMPG REFERENCE	REGION	DATE	MAP MAKER	PRICE (UK£)	VERT. (cm.)	HOR. (cm.)	TITLE OF MAP (Comments by the editor in brackets)
mwas0770	asia south east philippines	1743	LE ROUGE	600	20	28	Isles Philippines
mwwi0380	barbados	1779	LE ROUGE	1250	60	47	La Barbade
mwwi0375	barbados	1756	LE ROUGE	200	27	10	La Barbade / Isle St. Christophie
mwe0365	europe austria	1743	LE ROUGE	150	20	26	La Basse Austriche
mwg0391	bavaria	1767	LE ROUGE	180	25	19	La Baviere Dediee a S A Monseigr le Comte de Saxe
mwuss0441	florida	1778	LE ROUGE	960	33	35	La Baye de Spiritu Santo / S. Augustin Capitale de la Floride Orientale (2 maps on one sheet)
mwf0451	france champagne	1744	LE ROUGE	320	60	51	La Champagne Divisee par Elections Suivant les Dernieres Observations
mwc0140	china	1748	LE ROUGE	250	28	21	La Chine
mwwi0527	grenada	1779	LE ROUGE	850	46	60	La Grenade Divisee par Paroisses Levee par Ordre du Gouverneur Scott. Traduit de l'Anglais
mwwi0559	guadeloupe	1788	LE ROUGE	720	47	54	La Guadeloupe Dediee a Mgr. Charles Philippe D'Albert Duc de Luynes
mwe0369	europe austria	1748	LE ROUGE	150	20	26	La Haute Autriche
mwbh0688a	belgium holland	1748	LE ROUGE	3000	245	155	La Hollande en 12 Feuilles
mwbh0687	belgium holland	1748	LE ROUGE	180	28	22	La Hollande ou les Provinces Unies
mwbh0667	belgium holland	1746	LE ROUGE	685	49	58	La Hollande ou les VII Provinces Unies (inset of SE Asia)
mwwi0734	jamaica	1778	LE ROUGE	720	47	61	La Jamaique
mwat0121	atlantic bermuda	1746	LE ROUGE	400	20	27	La Jamaique aux Anglois dans le Golfe du Mexique a Paris. Chez le Sr. Le Rouge 1746 / La Bermude aux Anglois
mwit0607	italy north	1743	LE ROUGE	180	20	27	La Lombardie le Cours du Po &c. le Duche de Toscane
mwwi0776	martinique	1753	LE ROUGE	720	48	62	La Martinique une des Antilles Francoises de l'Amerique Dressee sur les Nouvelles Observations
mwm0062	mediterranean	1756	LE ROUGE	2250	53	66	La Mediterranee (2 charts, 53x66 and 53x63cm)
mwgr0200	greece	1770	LE ROUGE	550	32	47	La Moree
mwme0325	holy land	1748	LE ROUGE	240	28	20	La Palestine ou la Terre Sainte Divisee en Dix Tribus ... 1746
mwuss1377	pennsylvania	1778	LE ROUGE	7200	67	133	La Pennsylvanie en Trois Feuilles
mwf1070	france provence	1747	LE ROUGE	875	49	58	La Provence Suivant les Nouvelles Observations
mwf1155	france rhone-alpes	1743	LE ROUGE	180	20	26	La Savoye
mwsc0138	scandinavia	1743	LE ROUGE	280	20	26	La Scandinavie ou la Suede et Danemark
mwbh0694	belgium holland	1750	LE ROUGE	200	20	27	La Seigneurie d'Utrecht
mwsw0146	switzerland	1746	LE ROUGE	180	20	26	La Suisse
mwg0457b	hessen	1745	LE ROUGE	500	49	58	La Vederavie
mwbh0665a	belgium holland	1746	LE ROUGE	320	31	46	La Ville et Citadelle d'Anvers
mwbh0679	belgium holland	1747	LE ROUGE	685	47	56	La Zelande avec une Partie de la Flandre Hollandoise
mwaf0186	africa	1747	LE ROUGE	785	50	64	L'Afrique Suivant les Derniers Observations de Mr. Hass et des RRPP Jesuites
mwg0129	germany	1748	LE ROUGE	180	19	26	L'Allemagne
mwam0397	america north	1746	LE ROUGE	320	28	21	L'Amerique Septentrionale
mwam0159	america continent	1746	LE ROUGE	1000	49	64	L'Amerique Suivant le R.P. Charlevoix Jte. Mr. de la Condamine, et Plusieurs Autres Nouvle. Observations (shows discoveries up to 1742)
mwuk0994a	england	1748	LE ROUGE	175	29	22	L'Angleterre
mwas0159	asia continent	1748	LE ROUGE	320	22	28	L'Asie avec les Nouvelles Decouvertes
mwas0156	asia continent	1747	LE ROUGE	900	50	64	L'Asie Suivant les Dernres. Observons. des Moscovites
mwbh0668	belgium holland	1746	LE ROUGE	400	63	51	Le Brabant
mwe0366	europe austria	1743	LE ROUGE	150	20	26	Le Cercle d'Austriche
mwe0364	europe austria	1742	LE ROUGE	580	49	57	Le Comte du Tirol l'Eveche de Trente et de Brixen
mwe1026	europe rhine	1745	LE ROUGE	1500	71	252	Le Cours du Rhin de Bale a Hert pres Philisbourg Contenant l'Alsace et Partie du Brisgau
mwe1027	europe rhine	1745	LE ROUGE	550	49	125	Le Cours du Rhin de Constance a Bale en Deux Feuilles Contenant le Fricqthal les Quatre Villes Forrestieres et Partie de la Souabe
mwe1024	europe rhine	1744	LE ROUGE	720	114	49	Le Cours du Rhin dresse Sur les Nouvelles Observations
mwe0364b	europe austria	1742	LE ROUGE	500	49	55	Le Duche de Carinthie (shown above left)
mwbh0871	luxembourg	1743	LE ROUGE	720	47	54	Le Duche de Luxembourg divise
mwf1156	france rhone-alpes	1744	LE ROUGE	450	65	51	Le Duche de Savoye
mwe0364a	europe austria	1742	LE ROUGE	550	49	55	Le Duché de Stirie
mwf0244	france alsace	1743	LE ROUGE	280	55	48	Le Haute et Basse Alsace
mwuk0993	england	1745	LE ROUGE	480	57	49	Le Royaume d'Angleterre Divise en Comtez et Baronnies
mwe0942	europe hungary	1743	LE ROUGE	180	20	26	Le Royaume de Hongrie
mwe0797	europe east	1742	LE ROUGE	675	48	56	Le Royaume de Hongrie, la Transilvanie, l'Esclavonie, la Croatie et la Bosnie
mwbp0427	poland	1742	LE ROUGE	800	48	55	Le Royaume de Prusse
mwit0814	italy sardinia	1753	LE ROUGE	1100	69	40	Le Royaume de Sardaigne
mwit0812	italy sardinia	1744	LE ROUGE	960	71	42	Le Royaume de Sardaigne Dresse sur les Cartes Manuscrites Levees dans le Pays par les Ingenieurs Piemontois
mwuk0503	scotland	1756	LE ROUGE	240	27	21	Le Royaume d'Ecosse
mwuk0491	scotland	1748	LE ROUGE	250	27	20	Le Royaume d'Ecosse Divise en ses Parties Meridionale et Septentrionale
mwuk0166	ireland	1745	LE ROUGE	785	57	48	Le Royaume d'Irlande Divise en Provinces, Comtes et Baronies
mwe0370	europe austria	1748	LE ROUGE	150	21	28	Le Tirol

AMPG REFERENCE	REGION	DATE	MAP MAKER	PRICE (UK£)	VERT. (cm.)	HOR. (cm.)	TITLE OF MAP (Comments by the editor in brackets)
mwme0326	holy land	1748	LE ROUGE	200	20	28	L'Empire d'Alexandre et ses Expeditions
mwme0822	persia etc	1748	LE ROUGE	240	20	27	L'Empire de Perse
mwme0621	arabia etc	1748	LE ROUGE	240	21	28	L'Empire des Turcs
mwe0163b	europe	1747	LE ROUGE	480			L'Europe
mwe0163a	europe	1746	LE ROUGE	220	21	28	L'Europe Suivant les Nouvelles Observations
mwat0127	atlantic bermuda	1779	LE ROUGE	2400	46	61	Les Bermudes
mwuk1181	england london	1745	LE ROUGE	400	48	56	Les Environs de Londres a Sept Lieues a la Ronde
mwuk0821	uk	1744	LE ROUGE	580	49	63	Les Isles Britanniques ou les Royaumes d'Angleterre, d'Ecosse et d'Irlande, Divisees par Provinces
mwuk0829a	uk	1748	LE ROUGE	220	28	21	Les Isles Britanniques
mwuk1583	channel islands	1756	LE ROUGE	1000	48	67	Les Isles de Gersay, Guernesay et Aurigny
mwsc0618	scandinavia norway	1744	LE ROUGE	250	20	27	Les Isles du Spitsberg
mwwi0919	turks & caicos Isl.	1779	LE ROUGE	1250	46	31	Les Isles Turques
mwwi0930	virgin isl	1779	LE ROUGE	2000	46	60	Les Vierges, Levees par les Anglais, et par les Danois Traduit de l'Anglais
mwbh0654	belgium holland	1742	LE ROUGE	500	50	57	Les XVII Provinces Dites les Pays-Bas, par et Chez le Sr. Le Rouge
mwsp0270	spain	1748	LE ROUGE	150	20	26	L'Espagne Suivant les Nouvelles Observations (illustrated is the 1767 Crepy edition)
mwit0435	italy liguria	1747	LE ROUGE	1200	44	110	L'Etat de la Republique de Genes Tires des Meilleurs Cartes d'Italie Corrige sur les Lieux / Stato di Genova con Altri Adiacenti (close copy of Rossi 1697)
mwit1121a	italy tuscany	1744	LE ROUGE	550	49	57	L'État de l'Eglise et le Gd Duché de Toscane
mwuk0169	ireland	1748	LE ROUGE	200	28	21	L'Irlande (illustrated is 1767 edition, edited by Crepy)
mwca0328	canada newfoundland	1778	LE ROUGE	960	53	53	L'Isle de Terre Neuve
mwit0176a	italy	1743	LE ROUGE	480	50	63	L'Italie dressée sur les dern.res observations
mww0387	world	1744	LE ROUGE	4800	52	63	Mappe Monde Nouvelle
mww0404	world	1748	LE ROUGE	1100	23	30	Mappe Monde qui Comprend les Nouvelles Decouvertes Faites jusqua ce Jour
mwg0655	saxony	1757	LE ROUGE	960	49	57	Neinbourg une des Forteresses de l'Electorat de Hanover Capitale du Comte de Hoya
mwbh0875	luxembourg	1745	LE ROUGE	580	32	47	Nouveau Plan de Luxembourg
mwca0534	canada quebec	1777	LE ROUGE	960	48	65	Nouvelle Carte de la Province de Quebec
mwuss0196	carolinas	1777	LE ROUGE	2500	42	55	Nouvelle Carte des Cotes des Carolines Septentrionales et Meridionales du Cap Fear a Sud Edisto Levees et Sondees par N. Pocock en 1770. Traduites de l'Anglois ... 1777
mwca0377	canada nova scotia	1755	LE ROUGE	875	46	59	Nouvelle Ecosse ou Partie Orientale du Canada
mwat0283	atlantic north	1778	LE ROUGE	1500	96	137	Ocean Atlantique et Mers Adjacentes en Quatre Feuilles Contenant les Cotes de l'Europe, de l'Afrique et de l'Amerique ... Traduit de l'Anglois
mwru0544	ukraine	1770	LE ROUGE	400	20	29	Oczakow aux Tures
mwca0264	canada labrador	1778	LE ROUGE	900	49	56	Partie des Cotes de Labrador depuis le Cap Charles a la Baye de Sandwich ... par M. Lane (2 sheets, each 49x56cm)
mwca0072	canada	1755	LE ROUGE	1000	47	61	Partie Orientale du Canada
mwuss1364	pennsylvania	1776	LE ROUGE	2500	25	37	Philadelphie par Easburn
mwuss0829	massachusetts	1778	LE ROUGE	2000	54	89	Plan de Boston avec les Sondes et les Directions pour la Navigation. Traduit de l'Anglais
mwg0830	westphalia	1758	LE ROUGE	400	50	57	Plan de Dusseldorp, Capitale du Duche de Berg
mwit0442	italy liguria	1750	LE ROUGE	650	31	46	Plan de Genes
mwbh0668a	belgium holland	1746	LE ROUGE	500	51	59	Plan de la Ville de Bruxelles
mwf0873	france paris	1749	LE ROUGE	1200	52	68	Plan de Paris de de ses Faubourgs ... 1749
mwf0357	france brittany	1758	LE ROUGE	480	32	48	Plan de St. Malo
mwbp0476	poland	1768	LE ROUGE	1000	48	99	Plan de Varsovie
mwe0429a	europe austria vienna	1750	LE ROUGE	720	39	56	Plan de Vienne et de ses Environs
mwe0577	europe czech republic (bohemia)	1742	LE ROUGE	650	49	71	Plan des Environs ... la Defense de Prag
mwe0576	europe czech republic (bohemia)	1742	LE ROUGE	500	48	55	Plan des Environs de Prague et des Camps des Deux Armees
mwbh0695	belgium holland	1750	LE ROUGE	480	31	47	Plan d'Ostende & du Fort Philippe
mwaf0753	africa north algeria	1775	LE ROUGE	300	21	32	Plan du Port d'Alger
mwf0887	france paris	1767	LE ROUGE	550	53	69	Plan du Quartier de Ste. Genevieve avec le Plan de la Nouvelle Eglise et des Nouvelles Rues du Dessein de M. Souflos
mwca0423	canada nova scotia	1778	LE ROUGE	1500	49	56	Port de Halifax de la Nouvelle Ecosse avec les Recifs, Dangers, Bas Fonds et Sondes
mwca0361	canada nova scotia	1745	LE ROUGE	2250	50	60	Port de Louisbourg (Illustrated is updated 1758 edition)
mwuss1453	rhode isl	1778	LE ROUGE	3600	51	69	Port de Rhode Island et Narraganset Baye ... 1778 (2 sheets, each 51x69cm.)
mwuss0440	florida	1778	LE ROUGE	650	53	40	Port et Barre d'Amelia, de la Floride Orientale
mwuss0205	carolinas	1778	LE ROUGE	3000	61	57	Port Royal dans la Caroline Meridionale
mwg0386	bavaria	1759	LE ROUGE	400	22	21	Principaute d'Anspach (4 sheets, each 22x21cm.)
mwsw0155	switzerland	1759	LE ROUGE	180	22	28	Principaute de Neuchatel et Vallangin
mwuss1130	new york	1778	LE ROUGE	8000	140	90	Province de New-York en 4 Feuilles par Montresor (copy of Montressor's map of 1775)

AMPG REFERENCE	REGION	DATE	MAP MAKER	PRICE (UK£)	VERT. (cm.)	HOR. (cm.)	TITLE OF MAP (Comments by the editor in brackets)
mwat0284a	atlantic north west	1782	LE ROUGE	6000	34	38	Remarques sur la Navigation de Terre-Neuve a New York Afin d'Eviter les Courrants et las Bas-Fonds au Sud de Nantuckett et du Banc de George
mwit0438	italy liguria	1748	LE ROUGE	150	21	29	Republique de Genes
mwuss0203	carolinas	1778	LE ROUGE	1800	49	32	Riviere du Cap Fear de la Bare a Brunswick
mwuss0206	carolinas	1778	LE ROUGE	3000	58	36	Riviere et Detroit de D'Awfoskee en Caroline Merid.le
mwsp0093	portugal	1748	LE ROUGE	150	26	19	Royaume de Portugal
mwgm0121	honduras	1779	LE ROUGE	785	46	60	Ruatan or Rattan
mwgm0122	honduras	1779	LE ROUGE	1100	45	88	Ruatan ou Rattan Leve par Henry Barnsley Lieut. Augmente par Jefferys en 1775 Traduit de l'Anglais
mwit0514	italy lombardy	1742	LE ROUGE	500	51	65	Succession de Charles VI en Italie. Le Duché de Milan, de Mantoue, de Parme et de Plaisance, suivant les Nouvelles Observations
mwwi0902	trinidad & tobago	1779	LE ROUGE	1000	48	61	Tabago (French edition of Jefferys 1775)
mwin0229	india	1759	LE ROUGE	400	49	33	Theatre de la Guerre dans les Indes Orientales ou coste de Coromandel
mwam1047	america north (east)	1777	LE ROUGE	1800	62	50	Theatre de la Guerre en Amerique
mwe0571	europe czech republic (bohemia)	1741	LE ROUGE	750	50	64	Theatre de la Guerre en Boheme avec les principaux Postes de ce Royaume
mwsc0434	scandinavia finland	1742	LE ROUGE	1600	48	55	Theatre de la Guerre en Finland pour l'Intelligence des Mouvements des Trouppes Suedoises et Moscovites a Paris par et Chez le Sr. Le Rouge Ing'r Geographe du Roy Rue des Augustins A.P.D.R. 1742
mwbp0426	poland	1741	LE ROUGE	550	49	64	Theatre de la Guerre en Silesie
mwru0539	ukraine	1769	LE ROUGE	2000	49	135	Theatre de la Guerre entre les Russes, les Turcs et les Polonois (1736-1739)
mwbh0688	belgium holland	1748	LE ROUGE	2000	46	56	Topographie de la Zelande en 9 Feuilles. Paris, Rue des Grands Augustins, pres le Panier Fleury (9 sheets, each 46x56cm.)
mwuss1643	virginia	1777	LE ROUGE	8000	66	98	Virginie, Maryland en 2 Feuilles par Fry et Jefferson. Traduit, Corrige, Augmente
mwru0545	ukraine	1770	LE ROUGE	850	33	47	Volhinie (in 3 sheets)
mwf0216a	france alsace	1636	LE ROY	2500	44	124	Carte Generalle de la Havte et Basse Alsace (re-issued by J. Jollain in 1675)
mwm0004a	mediterranean	1640	LE ROY	1200	46	54	Romanum Imperium
mwam0681	america north	1832	LE SAGE	500	48	64	America Settentrionale Designata Dopo i Viaggi di Lewis, Clarke, Parry e Franklin
mwam0284	america continent	1826	LE SAGE	500	48	64	Amerique Historique, Physique et Politique en 1825
mwwi0191	west indies	1834	LE SAGE	200	48	64	Arcipelago Colombiano Cioe le Isole Lucaje le Grande e Piccole Antille
mwit0240	italy	1829	LE SAGE	200	47	64	Carte Geographique D'Italie
mwam0580	america north	1809	LE SAGE	600	49	66	Carte Speciale Historique et Geographique de la Republique des Etats-Unis
mwgm0327	mexico	1835	LE SAGE	500	48	64	Confederazione Messicana
mwwi0561	guadeloupe	1815	LE SAGE	200	48	64	Guadeloupe
mwwi0676	hispaniola	1815	LE SAGE	200	48	64	Hayti or Ile. St. Domingue
mwru0328	russia	1810	LE SAGE	200	48	64	L'Empire Russe en Europe et en Asie avec ses Acquisitions Graduelles et Caracterisees
mww0648	world	1814	LE SAGE	200	48	64	Mappemonde Historique
mwwi0809	martinique	1815	LE SAGE	200	48	64	Martinique
mwam0682	america north	1832	LE SAGE	500	48	64	Stati-Uniti dell-America Settentrionale dalle piu Recenti Mappe
mwm0084	mediterranean	1829	LE SAGE	250	48	64	Tableau De L'Empire Romain
mwaf0967	africa south	1792	LE VAILLANT	720	60	88	Carte de la Partie Meridionale de l'Afrique, pour Servir d'Intelligence aux Deux Voyages de Le Vaillant
mwaf0975	africa south	1796	LE VAILLANT	360	34	41	Map of M. Le Vaillant's two Journies in the Southern Part of Africa.
mwaf0966	africa south	1792	LE VAILLANT	200	16	24	Vue des Montagnes du Cap de Bonne-Esperance (view of Cape Town)
mwuk1428	england thames	1690	LEA	960	44	48	(Untitled map with inset plan of London)
mwec0613	uk england kent	1693	LEA	2400	42	54	This New Map of Kent (inset of Canterbury)
mwwi0701	jamaica	1687	LEA	4000	49	56	A Generall Mapp of the Continent and Islands which bee Adjacent to Jamaica / A New Mapp of the Island of Jamaica (2 maps on one sheet, each with an inset)
mwme0209	holy land	1692	LEA	1250	50	59	A Map of Canaan with the Adjacent Countries
mwuk1131	england london	1690	LEA	4000	53	57	A Mapp Containing the Townes Villages Gentlemens Houses Roads Rivers Woods and other Remarks for 20 Miles Round London (3 editions until 1730)
mwme0473	jerusalem	1690	LEA	1650	32	47	A Mapp of Jerusalem
mwjk0050	japan	1690	LEA	2800	36	52	A Mapp of the Isles of Iapon (re-issue of Pitt's 1680 map)
mwuk0944	england	1687	LEA	3000	48	51	A New Map of England and Wales with the Direct and Cross Roads (made in 4 strips, joined)
mwe1007	europe rhine	1691	LEA	1350	64	43	A New Map of the Courses of the Rhine and the Rhone from their Fountaines to their Runnings

AMPG REFERENCE	REGION	DATE	MAP MAKER	PRICE (UK£)	VERT. (cm.)	HOR. (cm.)	TITLE OF MAP (Comments by the editor in brackets)
mwe0088	europe	1680	LEA	1000	38	47	A New Mapp of Ancient Europe to All Historiographers but More Especially to the Most Worthy Clement Mayo Gnt.
mww0236	world	1687	LEA	6000	43	53	A New Mapp of the World
mwuk0099	ireland	1689	LEA	1600	48	55	An Epitome of Sr William Petty's Large Survey of Ireland
mwam0332	america north	1690	LEA	13500	51	57	North America divided into lll Principall Parts
mwuk0952	england	1690	LEA	4800	50	55	The Natural Shape of England with the Names of the Rivers, Seaports
mwe1197	europe west	1692	LEA	2000	61	50	This Mapp of the Sea Coast of Europe and ye Straits
mwf0073	france	1684	LEA	650	50	57	This New and Accurate Mapp of France
mwuss1620a	virginia	1696	LEA	5000	13	15	Virginia and Maryland
mwaf0095	africa	1687	LEA & OVERTON	750	48	56	A New Mapp of Africa, Divided into Kingdoms and Provinces (copy of De Wit 1680)
mwam0091	america continent	1690	LEA & OVERTON	6500	48	56	A New Mapp of America Devided According to the Best and Latest Observations and Discoveries wherein are Described by thear Proper Names the Seaverall Countries that Belong to ye English
mwas0075	asia continent	1687	LEA & OVERTON	750	48	55	A New Mapp of Asia, Divided into Kingdoms and Provinces (copy of De Wit 1680)
mwe0098	europe	1687	LEA & OVERTON	1600	48	55	A New Mapp of Europe. Divided into its Principall Kingdoms, and Provinces by Phillip Lea and by J. Overton
mwaf1191	africa west	1732	LEACH	240	20	32	Carte de la Riviere de Gambia ou Gambie depuis son Embouchure jusqu'a Eropina / ... depuis Eropina jusqu'a Barrakonda
mwuk1119a	england london	1667	LEAKE	6000	52	82	An Exact Surveigh of the Streets Lanes and Churches, Comprehended within the Ruins of the City of London First Described in Six Plats ... Reduced here into one intire plat by John Leake (Engraved by W. Hollar. Re-issued in 1669 and revised in 1723)
mwuk1160	england london	1723	LEAKE	2250	52	123	An Exact Surveigh of the Streets Lanes and Churches, Comprehended within the Ruins of the City of London ... for the Use of the Commissioners for the Regulation of Streets, Lanes &c. (based on the 1667 original)
mwuk0107	ireland	1690	LEA-MOLL	2400	92	62	A New Map of Ireland According to Sr. W. Petty (but Supplied with many Additions)
mwme1041a	turkey etc	1802	LECHEVALIER	360	40	56	Carte de La Troade (shows the environs of ancient Troy. North to the left.)
mwgr0289	greece cefalonia	1802	LECHEVALIER	350	22	19	Carte de Royaume d'Ulysse (incl. Ithaca)
mwgr0332	greece corfu	1802	LECHEVALIER	600	30	47	Plan de l'Ile de Corfou
mwgr0631	greece islands	1802	LECHEVALIER	300	26	36	Plan de L'Ile de Zante
mwgr0543	greece zante (zakynthos)	1802	LECHEVALIER	400	26	36	Plan de L'Ile de Zante (north to the right)
mwgr0272	greece athens	1802	LECHEVALIER	650	23	32	Plan des environs d'Athens
mwgr0273	greece athens	1802	LECHEVALIER	300	22	39	Vue D'Athenes (view)
mwaa0034	antarctic	1778	LECLERC	400	23	44	Carte des Deux Regions Polaires jusqu'au 45e Degre de Latitude
mwf0800	france normandy	1800	LECLERC	720	49	64	Plan de la Ville de Caen
mwuss0474a	florida	1837	LEE	2000	86	76	Map of Florida
mwca0604	canada st lawrence	1762	LEFEBURE	480			Cours du Fleuve St. Laurent depuis Montreal jusqu'a Tadoussac
mwca0082	canada	1762	LEFEBURE	480	22	34	Partie Orientale de l'Amerique Septentrionale (early survey by triangulation)
mwin0330	india	1807	LEGOUX DE FLAIX	320	53	46	Carte Hydro-Topographique de l'Indou-Stan
mwaf0314	africa	1822	LEGRAND	165	28	30	Afrique Physique et Division
mwp0277	pacific (all)	1822	LEGRAND	165	25	25	Oceanie ou Cinquieme Partie du Monde
mwuk1873	wales	1820	LEIGH	50	8	12	Anglesey
mwec0110	uk england cambridgeshire	1820	LEIGH	50	8	12	Cambridgeshire
mwec0242	uk england cumbria	1820	LEIGH	50	8	12	Cumberland
mwec0385	uk england durham	1820	LEIGH	50	8	12	Durham
mwuk1874	wales	1820	LEIGH	50	8	12	Glamorganshire
mwuk1628	isle of wight	1820	LEIGH	50	8	12	Isle of Wight
mwuk1292	england london	1818	LEIGH	600	43	56	Leigh's New Plan of London (3 editions until 1824)
mwuk1062	england	1834	LEIGH	500	100	77	Leigh's New Road Map of England, Wales and Scotland, Drawn ... by Sidney Hall
mwec0758	uk england lincolnshire	1820	LEIGH	50	8	12	Lincolnshire
mwec0895	uk england northumberland	1820	LEIGH	50	8	12	Northumberland
mwec0969	uk england oxfordshire	1820	LEIGH	50	8	12	Oxfordshire
mwg0469	hessen	1830	LEIGH	1350	90	22	Panorama of the Maine and adjacent country
mwec1178	uk england sussex	1820	LEIGH	50	8	12	Sussex
mwuss0144	california	1855	LEMERCIER	10000	27	87	San Francisco (view)
mwsp0663	balearic islands	1746	LEMPRIERE	1800	45	55	A New and Accurate Survey of the Island of Minorca, a Perticular Plan of the Harbour of Mahon and its Fortifications, with a Map of the Mediterranean Sea, Shewing the Situation of that Island and those of Majorca and Yvica
mwat0119	atlantic bermuda	1738	LEMPRIERE	7200	40	52	To His Excellency Alured Popple Esq. Governour of Bermuda or the Summer Islands. This map.
mwsp0470	spain regions	1687	LEONARDO	10000	79	108	Toletum, Hispanici Orbis Urbs

AMPG REFERENCE	REGION	DATE	MAP MAKER	PRICE (UK£)	VERT. (cm.)	HOR. (cm.)	TITLE OF MAP (Comments by the editor in brackets)
mwe1062b	europe serbia	1717	LEOPOLD	1200	49	56	Accuratester Plan und Grundriss, vorstellend... gloriöse Victorie... 1717... Belgrad
mwgr0322	greece corfu	1725	LEOPOLD	800	20	30	Corcyra. Corfu
mwin0401	india goa	1720	LEOPOLD	600	19	29	Goa (view)
mwru0501	ukraine	1709	LEOPOLD	960	45	59	Grundriss der Glorieusen Action welche in der Gegend Pultawa in d'Ucraine
mwbh0641	belgium holland	1740	LEOPOLD	240	16	29	Guda. Gaude (view of Gouda)
mwme0479	jerusalem	1711	LEOPOLD	600	20	30	Hierosolyma - Jerusalem (view)
mwsp0215	spain	1700	LEOPOLD	500	22	34	Hispaniae et Lusitaniae Regna quorum
mwsp0088	portugal	1735	LEOPOLD	960	20	30	Lisabona. Lisabon (view)
mwuk1146	england london	1711	LEOPOLD	1200	20	30	Londinum - London (view)
mwit0516	italy lombardy	1750	LEOPOLD	960	16	29	Mantua (view)
mwru0131	russia	1711	LEOPOLD	1000	42	53	Moscoviae seu Russiae Magnae Generalis Tabula (re-issue of Von Sandrart, 1688)
mwf0850a	france paris	1720	LEOPOLD	720	21	30	Parisii - Paris (view)
mwme0992	turkey etc	1720	LEOPOLD	2250	49	56	Plan de Constantinople de son Port Canal et Environs
mwit0491a	italy lombardy	1700	LEOPOLD	1200	46	56	Tabula Geographica in qua integri Ducatus Mediolanensis et Mantuanus item Ditio Veneta et Comitatus Tyrolensis
mwit0593	italy north	1702	LEOPOLD	450	32	50	Theatrum Belli Italici seu Novissima Tabula Geographica
mwf0579	france ile de france	1678	LEPINE	2800	126	135	Carte Particuliere des Environs de Paris
mwca0008	canada	1609	LESCARBOT	40000	18	44	Figure de la Terre Neuve, Grande Riviere de Canada, et Cotes de l'Ocean en la Nouvelle France
mwsam0280	south america brazil	1608	LESCARBOT	1500	11	18	Figure du Port de Ganabara au Brisil (plan of Rio de Janeiro harbour)
mwca0347	canada nova scotia	1609	LESCARBOT	3000	14	24	Figure du Port Royal en la Nouvelle France (1st map of Port Royal, now Annapolis Royal)
mwuk0316	scotland	1578	LESLIE	7000	18	27	Scotiae Regni Antiquissimi Accurata Descriptio
mwp0043	australia	1807	LESUEUR-BAUDIN	3000	20	46	Nouvelle Hollande: Nouvelle Galles du Sud - Vue de la Partie Meridionale de la Ville de Sydney Capitale des Colonies Anglaises aux Terres Australes, et de l'Embouchure de la Riviere de Paramatta (1803.)
mwsam0335	south america brazil	1690	LETI	2000	28	36	(View of Recife)
mwsam0332	south america brazil	1690	LETI	450	27	36	Afbeeldinghe van Pariba ende Forten (Paraibo)
mwme0973	turkey etc	1690	LETI	1800	33	48	Byzantium, nunc Constantinopolis
mwbp0315	poland	1689	LETI	450	42	52	Elbing (Elblag)
mwbh0449	belgium holland	1690	LETI	900	38	53	Haga Comitis, vulgo 's Graven-Hage (close copy of Blaeu 1649)
mwe0335	europe austria	1689	LETI	450	38	48	Saltzburg (view)
mwbp0319a	poland	1690	LETI	480	36	47	Silesia Ducatus
mwsam0333	south america brazil	1690	LETI	450	28	37	t Neemen van de Suyker Prysen in de Bay de Tode los Santos Anno 1627
mwsam0334	south america brazil	1690	LETI	650	28	37	Veroveringe van Rio Grande in Brasil (view of Natal)
mwas0632	asia south east java	1681	LETI	960	41	51	Waere Affbeeldinge Wegens het Casteel ende Stadt Batavia Gelegen opt Groot Eylant Java Anno 1681 (view)
mwas0530a	asia south east	1815	LEUTERMANN	240	30	36	Die Ostindischen Inseln
mwam0648	america north	1825	LEUTERMANN	150	20	25	Nord America
mwwi0425	cuba	1728	LEVAL	200	14	20	Carte de la Baye et Port de Matance dans l'Isle de Cube
mwme0954	turkey etc	1664	LEVANTO	600	40	52	Carta maritima che contiene come si posse vellegiare fra l'isola Tenedo e la Natolia
mwme0955	turkey etc	1664	LEVANTO	600	40	52	Carta maritima del Golfo di Smirne com' anche l'Isola Scio
mwm0130	mediterranean east	1664	LEVANTO	650	41	51	Carta Maritima del Levante
mwgr0589	greece islands	1664	LEVANTO	500	41	52	Carta Maritima del Mare Arcipelago / Negroponte (2 sea charts on one sheet)
mwgr0485	greece cyprus	1664	LEVANTO	2500	41	52	Carta Maritima dell' Isola Cypri (inset: coast of Egypt. Copy of Goos 1662)
mwgr0308	greece corfu	1664	LEVANTO	875	40	52	Carta Maritima dell' Isola di Corfu
mwm0103	mediterranean central	1664	LEVANTO	720	40	51	Carta Maritima della Costa Ligustica fra C. delle Melle e M. Argentato con l'Isola di Corsica et Altre Circonvicine
mwgr0081	greece	1664	LEVANTO	550	40	51	Carta Maritima della Meridionale Costa di Morea
mwgr0540	greece zante (zakynthos)	1664	LEVANTO	900	40	51	Carta Maritima Della parte Meridionale della Cefalonia com'anche l'Isola del Zante e la costa di Morea da C chiarese fin a C. Sapienza (map by P. Goos)
mwgr0588	greece islands	1664	LEVANTO	720	40	51	Carta Maritima di Tutto l'Arcipelago
mwsp0446	spain regions	1664	LEVANTO	1000	40	51	Costa di Spagna del Rio di Siviglia fino a Malaga et la Costa di Barbaria da Larache fino al Penon de Velez
mwgr0390	greece crete	1664	LEVANTO	1000	41	52	Coste Maritime dell'Isola di Candia (re-issued by Coronelli in 1696)
mwsp0447	spain regions	1664	LEVANTO	1000	39	51	La Costa di Granata ... Barbaria
mwgr0080	greece	1664	LEVANTO	2500	54	78	Tavola nova del Arcipelago Acresciutta in magiori forma
mwaf0339	africa	1845	LEVASSEUR	240	29	44	Afrique
mwaf0759	africa north algeria	1845	LEVASSEUR	200	29	43	Algerie Colonie Francaise
mwsam0162	south america	1845	LEVASSEUR	240	30	43	Amerique Meridionale
mwam0769	america north	1845	LEVASSEUR	450	30	43	Amerique Septentrionale (Texas shown as a separate country)
mwas0257	asia continent	1845	LEVASSEUR	280	29	43	Asie
mwaf1258	africa west	1845	LEVASSEUR	200	28	43	Colonies Francaises en Afrique (incl Madagascar)

AMPG REFERENCE	REGION	DATE	MAP MAKER	PRICE (UK£)	VERT. (cm.)	HOR. (cm.)	TITLE OF MAP (Comments by the editor in brackets)
mwwi0815	martinique	1845	LEVASSEUR	200	28	43	Colonies Francaises, Martinique
mwca0201	canada	1845	LEVASSEUR	180	29	43	Colonies Francaises. (incl. Ile St. Martin near Guadeloupe, and Guyana)
mwwi0567	guadeloupe	1845	LEVASSEUR	200	29	43	Colonies Francaises. L'Ile de la Guadeloupe l'une des Plus Considerables de l'Archipel des Petites Antilles
mwf0565	france corsica	1845	LEVASSEUR	200	43	29	Dept. de la Corse
mwf1102	france pyrenees	1845	LEVASSEUR	100	29	41	Dept de L'Ariege
mwf1102a	france pyrenees	1845	LEVASSEUR	100	43	29	Dept. de La H.te Garonne
mwf0595	france ile de france	1845	LEVASSEUR	150	42	29	Dept. de la Hte Marne
mwf1102b	france pyrenees	1845	LEVASSEUR	100	30	41	Dept. des B.ses Pyrenees
mwf1102c	france pyrenees	1845	LEVASSEUR	100	29	43	Dept. des H.tes Pyrenees
mwf1102d	france pyrenees	1845	LEVASSEUR	100	29	43	Dept. des Or.les Pyrenees
mwf1089	france provence	1845	LEVASSEUR	150	28	44	Dept. du Var
mwc0296	china	1850	LEVASSEUR	80	23	31	Empires Chinois et Japonnais
mwe0272	europe	1845	LEVASSEUR	240	29	43	Europe
mwaf0577	africa islands bourbon	1845	LEVASSEUR	280	29	43	Ile de la Reunion (also found with title 'Ile Bourbon')
mwp0289a	pacific (all)	1845	LEVASSEUR	300	28	42	Oceanie
mww0734	world	1845	LEVASSEUR	400	29	43	Planisphere
mwme0858	persia etc	1850	LEVASSEUR	80	23	31	Royaumes de Perse Herat & Kaboul
mwuk1069	england	1841	LEWIS	1500	104	87	A Map of England & Wales divided into Counties Parliamentary Divisions & Dioceses The Principal Roads Railways & Canals and The Seats of the Nobility and Gentry with the Distance of Each Town from the General Post Office, London (4 sheets, each 104x87cm.)
mwuss1466	rhode isl	1806	LEWIS	360	44	25	A Map of Part of Rhode Island Shewing the Positions of the American and British Armies at the Siege of Newport, and the Subsequent Action on the 29th of August 1778
mwuk0638	scotland	1845	LEWIS	1200	58	135	A Map of Scotland Divided into Counties Shewing the Principal Roads, Railways, Rivers, Canals, Lochs, Mountains, Islands, &c. (3 sheets, each 58x135cm.)
mwam1145	america north (east)	1803	LEWIS	2000	43	54	A Map of the United States of America
mwam1152	america north (east)	1806	LEWIS	360	37	27	A Map of those Parts of Virginia, North Carolina, South Carolina & Georgia which were the Scenes of the Most Important Operations of the Southern Armies
mwam1174	america north (east)	1816	LEWIS	20000	173	186	A New and Correct Map of the United States of North America. Exhibiting the Counties, Towns, Roads, &c. in each State
mwuk1323	england london	1840	LEWIS	1500	93	112	A Plan of London and its Environs
mwuk0291	ireland	1846	LEWIS	100	30	24	Carlow
mwuk0292	ireland	1846	LEWIS	100	30	24	Dublin
mwuk0293	ireland	1846	LEWIS	100	30	24	Galway
mwuk0294	ireland	1846	LEWIS	100	30	24	Kerry
mwuk0295	ireland	1846	LEWIS	100	30	24	Londonderry
mwuk1071	england	1842	LEWIS	150	47	38	Map of England & Wales ... showing the Principal Roads, Railways , Canals & the Rivers
mwca0119	canada	1794	LEWIS	350	40	46	The British Possessions in North America from the Best Authorities
mwuss0760	maryland	1795	LEWIS	600	28	41	The State of Maryland, from the Best Authorities
mwuss0849	massachusetts	1795	LEWIS	600	36	47	The State of Massachusetts. Compiled from the Best Authorities
mwuss1007	new hampshire	1795	LEWIS	600	45	28	The State of New Hampshire Compiled Chiefly from Actual Survey by Samuel Lewis
mwuss1388	pennsylvania	1795	LEWIS	600	29	46	The State of Pennsylvania. Reduced with Permission from Reading Howells Map
mwuss0240	carolinas	1795	LEWIS	850	39	44	The State of South Carolina: From the Best Authorities, by Samuel Lewis
mwuss1671	virginia	1799	LEWIS	280	19	25	The State of Virginia from the Best Authorities
mwam1181	america north (east)	1819	LEWIS	8000	75	105	The Travellers Guide A New and Correct Map of the United States, Including Great Portions of Missouri Territory, Upper & Lower Canada, Nova Scotia, New Brunswick, The Floridas, Spanish Provinces &c. ... by Samuel Lewis
mwuk0296	ireland	1846	LEWIS	100	30	24	Wexford
mwam1350	america north (west)	1814	LEWIS & CLARK	15000	30	69	A Map of Lewis and Clark's Track across the Western Portion of North America, from the Mississippi to the Pacific Ocean, by Order of the Executive of the United States in 1804, 5 & 6 (a restrike made from the original plate was published in 1979 in an edition of 150 copies)
mwuss1692	washington	1815	LEWIS & CLARK	2400	10	18	Great Falls of Columbia / Lower Falls of the Columbia / Mouth of Columbia River (3 maps)
mwsam0560a	south america ecuador	1646	L'HERMITE	350	16	21	Afteykeninghe van de Rivier van Guayaquil, en de Eylanden Puna en S.ta Clara (inset: Vertoning van de Ree onder I. Puna)
mwsam0736b	south america peru	1626	L'HERMITE	450	16	21	Pascaert van de Zeecust van By Suyen Callao de Lima tot by Noorden de Bay achter de Piscadores [inset at lower left] Vertoning van de Ree in de Bay achter de Piscadores

AMPG REFERENCE	REGION	DATE	MAP MAKER	PRICE (UK£)	VERT. (cm.)	HOR. (cm.)	TITLE OF MAP (Comments by the editor in brackets)
mwgm0159a	mexico	1646	L'HERMITE	650	16	21	Vertoning van de Haven van Acapulco (illustration is the 1646 re-issue by Commelin)
mwsam0736a	south america peru	1626	L'HERMITE	450	16	21	Vertoning van't Callao de Lima (publ. by Jansson 1646)
mwaf0188a	africa	1748	LIDL	1000	28	39	(Untitled map of Africa)
mwbp0471	poland	1760	LIDL	2500	46	112	Kriegs Schau-Platz in Preussischen Landen / Theatrum Belli Borussici
mwit0434	italy liguria	1747	LIDL	2000	35	56	Kriegs-Schau-Platz in Italien in der Republic Genua (insets: Genoa, Castello Di Savona)
mwe0591	europe czech republic (bohemia)	1756	LIDL	960	46	78	Neue und Accurat Verfaste Geographische Landt Karte dess Gantzen Konig Reichs Bohmen sambt der darzu Incorporirten Schlesischen Graffschafft Glatz
mwe0570	europe czech republic (bohemia)	1740	LIDL	1350	37	56	Neue und Accurate Geographische Post Land Karten des gantzen Konig Reichs Bohmen und Marggraffthum Lausitz sambt allen Angrantzenden Landern
mwbp0432	poland	1745	LIDL	1200	88	79	Novissimum Silesiae Theatrum id est Exactissimus Superioris et Inferioris Silesiae, Comitatus Glacensis
mwf0105	france	1719	LIEBAUX	675	48	64	La France Suivant les Nouveles Observations Divisee par Parlemens et en Toutes ses Provinces
mwf0581	france ile de france	1700	LIEBAUX	685	44	57	Le Plan de la Foret de Compiegne ou sont Marquees Toutes les Routes avec les Environs de la Ville de Compiegne
mwf0587	france ile de france	1720	LIEBAUX	685	42	61	Plan de la Foret de Halatte ou sont les Nouvelles Routes Faites par Ordre du Roy. Avec les Environs de Senlis
mwit0150	italy	1715	LIEBAUX	350	50	64	Tabula Italiae Antiquae
mwsp0664	balearic islands	1753	LIEBE	400	26	33	Die Insel Minorca Aufgenommen von Lempriere
	asia africa	1750	LIEBE	500	39	47	General Karte zur Erleuterung der Missions-Geschichte
mwg0670	saxony	1784	LIEBE	500	51	57	Grundriss von Halberstadt
mwuk1240	england london	1780	LIEBE	1500	36	67	Neuester Grundriss von London, Westminster, und Southwark
mwg0675	saxony	1801	LIEBE	500	60	54	Special Karte von dem zum Herzogthum Magdeburg Gehorigen Saal Kreis
mwin0209	india	1750	LIEBE	650	46	45	Special-Carte von der Halb-Insul Indiens diesseits dem Ganges
mwbh0814	luxembourg	1582	LIEFRINCK	720	23	32	Lutzenbourg. Lutzenburgum ... Urbs
mwuss1070	new jersey	1851	LIGHTFOOT	2000	94	139	Map of Monmouth County, New Jersey
mwme0198	holy land	1686	LIGHTFOOT	500	36	43	Tabula Canaanis ex Mente Ioannis Lightfooti
mwme0468	jerusalem	1684	LIGHTFOOT	600	36	52	The City of Jerusalem according to Dr. Lightfoot
mwwi0358	barbados	1657	LIGON	8000	37	52	A Topographicall Description and Admeasurement of the Yland of Barbados in the West Indyaes with the Mrs. Names of the Severall Plantacons (1st printed map of Barbados)
mwam0869	america north (east)	1674	LIGON	1400	19	25	Costes et Rivieres de Virginie, de Mariland et de Nouvelle Angleterre
mwwi0692	jamaica	1674	LIGON	1000	28	32	Isle de la Iamaique Divisee par Paroisses ou sont Exactement Remarques les Ports et les Bayes - Par le Sieur Modiford. R. Michault Scrip.
mwme0436a	jerusalem	1559	LIGORIO	2000	19	27	Civitas Hierusalem (illustrated is the c1570 re-issue engraved by Forlani, publ. by Camocio)
mwit0702a	italy rome	1561	LIGORIO		152	131	Effigies Antiquae Romae ... (text top left. Illustration shows re-print from the original plates, 1820)
mwit0984	italy south	1557	LIGORIO	6850	44	68	Nova Regno Neapolit. Descript.
mwit0701	italy rome	1552	LIGORIO	3000	40	54	Urbis Romae
mwbh0007a	belgium holland	1558	LIGORIO-TRAMEZINI	4000	38	49	La nova & vera descrittion della Gallia Belgica (shown above left)
mwuk0659	uk	1546	LILY	50000	54	75	Britanniae Insulae quae nunc Angliae et Scotiae Regna Continet cum Hibernia Adiacente Nova Descriptio (North to the right. 1st edition)
mwuk0663	uk	1558	LILY- DI RE	20000	40	54	Britanniae Insulae quae nunc Angliae et Scotiae Regna Continet cum Hibernia Adiacente Nova Descriptio (reduced size version of Lily's 1546 map)
mwuk0662	uk	1556	LILY-IHS	25000	49	35	Britannia Insula quae Duo Regna Continet Angliam Et Scotiam Cum Hibernia Adiacente (title top left. North at the top)
mwe1108	europe slovak republic (moravia)	1719	LINCK	960	44	112	Mappa des March-Flus, wie Solcher in Donau Lauft, und die so Grossen Nutzen Bringende Schiffart ... vom Teutschen bis in das Schwartze Meer Eingericht Werden
mwin0058	ceylon	1775	LINDEMAN	480	29	20	Kaart van 't Eyland Ceylon
mwas0665	asia south east java	1775	LINDEMAN	200	20	34	Kaart van 't Eyland Groot Java
mww0493	world	1775	LINDEMAN	600	19	47	Nieuwe en Nette Zee-Kaart van de Geheele Waareld. Toonende de Afwijkingen van het Kompas (reduced version of Halley's chart)
mwm0146	mediterranean east	1730	LINDENBERG	650	34	48	Description Geographique des Voyages de St. Paul et des Autres Apostres
mwec1146	uk england surrey	1793	LINDLEY & CROSLEY	1200	86	116	To the King's Most Excellent Majesty, this Map of the County of Surrey from a Survey Made in the Years 1789 and 1790

AMPG REFERENCE	REGION	DATE	MAP MAKER	PRICE (UK£)	VERT. (cm.)	HOR. (cm.)	TITLE OF MAP (Comments by the editor in brackets)
mwp0538	pacific tahiti	1816	LINDNER	280	27	38	Charte der Insel Otaheite nach der Messung des Capit. Cook im Jahre 1769, und dessen Spateren Astronomischen Beobachtungen Entworten von Capn. Will Wilson
mwp0061	australia	1815	LINDNER	1000	32	42	Karte von Neu Holland
mwuss1415	pennsylvania	1830	LINDSTROM	240	25	12	Nova Suecia Hodie dicta Pensylvania
			LINSCHOTEN. See VAN LINSCHOTEN				
mwe0970	europe hungary	1806	LIPSZKY	3500	135	210	Mappa Generalis Regni Hungariae (in 12 sheets, joined. Title cartouche illustrated below. Size does not include text panels below map.)
mww0538a	world	1786	LIRELLI	2000	59	70	Le Globe Terrestre presenté d'une maniere nouvelle (2 polar projections and a map of the equatorial latitudes. Reduced size version 1793, 37x45cm shown below)
mwuss0048	alaska	1837	LISIANSKY	650	22	17	Island of Cadiack with its environs, 1805
mwuss0050	alaska	1837	LISIANSKY	650	22	17	Sitka or Norfolk Sound, Alaska. Surveyed by Capt. Lisiansky 1805.
mwaf0331	africa	1840	LIZARS	350	75	88	Africa (4 sheets, joined)
mwam0301	america continent	1840	LIZARS	500	75	88	America (4 sheets, joined)
mwme0683	arabia etc	1837	LIZARS	240	39	49	Arabia
mwas0254	asia continent	1840	LIZARS	550	75	88	Asia (4 sheets, joined)
mwp0116	australia	1837	LIZARS	400	43	49	Australia &c
mwg0408	bavaria	1837	LIZARS	180	38	48	Bavaria
mwe0844	europe east	1837	LIZARS	180	39	49	Bohemia & Moravia
mwsam0148	south america	1828	LIZARS	200	24	41	Bolivia or Upper Peru; Chili and the United Provinces of South America, la Plata
mwp0523a	pacific south	1822	LIZARS	240	22	38	Chart Of Polynesia or Groups of Islands Spread over the North & South Pacific Oceans Between the Latitudes 30° N and 30' S and Longitudes 110° and 130' E
mwat0059	atlantic ocean (all)	1820	LIZARS	220	48	42	Chart of the Atlantic Ocean
mww0690	world	1830	LIZARS	450	53	80	Chart of the World on Mercator's Projection
mww0719	world	1840	LIZARS	280	41	53	Chart of the World on Mercator's Projection
mwc0260	china	1828	LIZARS	250	38	44	China
mwsc0399a	scandinavia	1837	LIZARS	180	47	37	Denmark
mwaf0563	africa egypt etc	1837	LIZARS	120	49	40	Egypt
mwe0269	europe	1837	LIZARS	450	75	88	Europe (4 sheets, joined)
mwf0198	france	1837	LIZARS	180	38	45	France in Departments
mwe0845	europe east	1837	LIZARS	180	37	46	Hungary Transilvania &c.
mwuk0276	ireland	1837	LIZARS	400	83	51	Ireland with all the Railways
mwg0678	saxony	1837	LIZARS	180	39	50	Lower Saxony
mwp0067	australia	1821	LIZARS	550	30	46	Map of Part of New South Wales / Map of Van Diemens Land
mwuk0605	scotland	1826	LIZARS	600	55	47	Map of the Highlands of Scotland
mwgm0070	gulf of mexico and surrounding regions	1831	LIZARS	400	41	49	Mexico & Guatimala
mwuss1508	texas	1838	LIZARS	960	41	49	Mexico & Guatimala with the Republic of Texas
mwme0853	persia etc	1837	LIZARS	200	39	48	Persia
mwuss0344	washington DC	1819	LIZARS	650	34	34	Plan of the City of Washington and the Territory of Columbia
mwaa0167	arctic	1822	LIZARS	240	40	38	Polar Regions
mwuk0632	scotland	1840	LIZARS	400	83	51	Scotland with all the Railways
mwsp0331	spain	1837	LIZARS	200	42	51	Spain and Portugal
mwsw0230	switzerland	1837	LIZARS	150	37	48	Switzerland
mwme1064	turkey etc	1837	LIZARS	200	39	49	Turkey in Asia
mwbh0802	belgium holland	1837	LIZARS	150	38	48	United Kingdom of the Netherlands Belgic Provinces
mwam1211	america north (east)	1831	LIZARS	500	41	51	United States
mwam1181a	america north (east)	1819	LIZARS	550	39	46	United States of America
mwam1242	america north (east)	1840	LIZARS	720	41	52	United States & Texas. With All the Railways & Canals
mwg0546	rheinland-pfalz	1837	LIZARS	180	38	49	Upper & Lower Rhine
mwg0679	saxony	1837	LIZARS	180	39	50	Upper Saxony
mwg0854	westphalia	1837	LIZARS	160	38	49	Westphalia
mwuk1407	uk geological	1831	LOADER	2400	134	108	T.B. Loader's Scientific and Commercial Map of England and Wales, in which are Delineated the Canals, Rail-Roads & Navigable Rivers ... Together with the Geology and Principal Situations of the Mineral Productions
mwaf0214	africa	1762	LOBECK	200	10	13	Africa
mwam0185	america continent	1762	LOBECK	300	10	13	America
mwe0601	europe czech republic (bohemia)	1762	LOBECK	160	10	13	Bohemia Regnum in Circulos suos Divisu
mwbp0472	poland	1762	LOBECK	160	10	13	Borussiae Regnum cum Adjacentibus Regionibus
mwe0182	europe	1762	LOBECK	200	10	13	Europa
mwg0140	germany	1762	LOBECK	100	10	13	Germania H. Romische Reich mit seinen X. Craissen
mwaa0196	arctic / antarctic	1762	LOBECK	275	10	13	Hemisphaerium Boreale. Hemisphaerium Australe
mwru0237	russia	1762	LOBECK	160	10	13	Imperium Russicum Omnisque Tartaria
mwuk0844	uk	1762	LOBECK	200	10	13	Magna Britannia Complectens Angliae, Scotiae et Hiberniae Regna

AMPG REFERENCE	REGION	DATE	MAP MAKER	PRICE (UK£)	VERT. (cm.)	HOR. (cm.)	TITLE OF MAP (Comments by the editor in brackets)
mwit0193	italy	1762	LOBECK	160	10	13	Nova Totius Italiae cum Adjacentibus Majoribus et Minoribus Insulis Tabula
mwe0378	europe austria	1762	LOBECK	160	10	13	Osterreichische Crais
mwbp0473	poland	1762	LOBECK	160	10	13	Poloniae Regnum, Ducatusq. Magnae Lithuaniae
mwsw0160	switzerland	1762	LOBECK	160	10	13	Potentissimae Helvetiorum Reipublicae Cantones Tredecim
mwe0953	europe hungary	1762	LOBECK	160	10	13	Regni Hungariae Tabula Generalis
mwsp0281	spain	1762	LOBECK	160	10	13	Regnorum Hispaniae et Portugalliae Tabula Generalis
mwsc0371	scandinavia denmark	1762	LOBECK	160	10	13	Regnum Daniae
mwsc0152	scandinavia	1762	LOBECK	200	10	13	Regnum Sueciae
mwit0444	italy liguria	1762	LOBECK	120	10	13	Republica di Genova
mwit0318	italy central	1762	LOBECK	120	10	13	Status Ecclesiastici Magni que Ducatus Florentini Tabula
mwe0727	europe danube	1762	LOBECK	120	10	13	Tabula Danubii, Graeciae et Archipelagi
mwbh0711	belgium holland	1762	LOBECK	200	10	13	Tabula Genera. Totius Belgii qua Provinciae XVII Infer. Germaniae olim sub S.R.I. Circulo Burgundiae
mwf0133	france	1762	LOBECK	160	10	13	Totius Regn. Galliae sive Franciae Tabula
mwas0177	asia continent	1762	LOBECK-LOTTER	200	10	13	Asia
mwf0855	france paris	1726	LOBINEAU	2800	63	86	Plan de Paris
mwam0611a	america north	1818	LOCARD	100	21	18	Amerique Septentrionale
mwru0101a	russia	1690	LOCHNER	1000	42	53	Moscau oder des grosen Russlands General-Tafel, in welcher Lappland, Norwegen, Schweden, Dennemarck, Poln, und … (close copy of Von Sandrart 1688)
mwe1005	europe rhine	1690	LOCHNER	2000	37	103	Neueste Beschreibung des Gantzen Rheinstroms
mwuss0082	california	1743	LOCKMAN	720	24	21	Passage by Land to California Discover'd by Father Eusebus Kino a Jesuit; between the Years 1698, & 1701
mwuss1469	rhode isl	1819	LOCKWOOD	400	25	18	Map of Rhode Island and Providence Plantations; Corrected and Enlarged with Many Additions, by Benoni Lockwood
mwuss1478	rhode isl	1835	LOCKWOOD	1600	53	74	Map of the City of Providence and the Town of North Providence
mwam1034	america north (east)	1776	LODGE	580	27	38	A General Map of North America from the Latest Observations
mwuss0369	delaware	1781	LODGE	600	25	37	A Map and Chart of those Parts of the Bay of Chesapeak York and James Rivers which are at Present the Seat of War
mwgm0107	guatemala	1778	LODGE	150	18	23	A Map of a Part of Mexico Comprehending the District or Audience of Guatimala, from the Best Authorities, by Mr. B.
mwec0647	uk england kent	1787	LODGE	200	25	31	A Map of Kent from the Best Authorities
mwuss0430	florida	1772	LODGE	400	19	34	A Map of Part of West Florida from Pensacola to the Mouth of the Iberville River with a View to Shew the Proper Spot for a Settlement on the Mississipi
mwam0990	america north (east)	1756	LODGE	500	22	33	A Map of that Part of America which was the Principal Seat of War, in 1756
mwwi0883	st lucia	1781	LODGE	350	38	27	A Map of the Islands of St. Lucia and Martinique, with Part of Dominica and St. Vincents; Shewing the Two Passages between Martinique and St. Lucia, and Martinique and Dominica, to Fort Royal Bay and Harbour, the Station of the French Fleets
mwgm0430	panama	1783	LODGE	300	18	24	A Map of the Isthmus of Panama, Drawn from Spanish Surveys
mwec1324	uk england yorkshire	1700	LODGE	900	29	41	A Mapp of ye 2 Wapentakes of Skirac and Agbridge and Morley within the Westriding of Yorkshire Famous for the Manufacture of Cloth
mwaf1229	africa west	1781	LODGE	200	28	37	A New and Accurate Map of the European Settlements on the Coast of Africa, from the River Senegal to that of Benin
mwam1066b	america north (east)	1780	LODGE	1000	37	28	A New and Accurate Map of the Province of New York and Part of the Jerseys, New England and Canada, Shewing the Scenes of Our Military Operations During the Present War. Also the New Erected State of Vermont
mwca0421	canada nova scotia	1778	LODGE	550	29	33	A New and Accurate Map of the Province of Nova Scotia, in North America; from the Latest Observations
mwwi0304	antigua	1782	LODGE	400	28	37	A New and Exact Map of the Island of Antigua in America, According to an Actual and Accurate Survey, with the Different Parishes, the Churches, Divisions, Boundaries; and a Plan of English Harbour
mwaf0252	africa	1785	LODGE	250	33	36	A New Map of Africa, from the Best Authorities
mwas0196	asia continent	1780	LODGE	300	34	37	A New Map of Asia from the Best Authorities
mwam0433	america north	1763	LODGE	580	34	35	A New Map of North America, from the Best Authorities
mwca0450	canada nova scotia	1785	LODGE	1000	46	60	A New Map of Nova Scotia, and Cape Britain, with the Adjacent Parts of New England and Canada from the Latest Authorities
mwsam0112	south america	1791	LODGE	235	33	36	A New Map of South America, from the Best Authorities
mwec1077	uk england staffordshire	1790	LODGE	250	32	26	A New Map of Staffordshire, from the Latest Authorities
mwuss0217	carolinas	1780	LODGE	550	14	28	A Plan of Charles Town the Capital of South Carolina, with the Harbour, Islands and Forts; the Attack on Fort Sulivan, by His Majesty's Ships under Sir Peter Parker, in 1776

AMPG REFERENCE	REGION	DATE	MAP MAKER	PRICE (UK£)	VERT. (cm.)	HOR. (cm.)	TITLE OF MAP (Comments by the editor in brackets)
mwuss1345	pennsylvania	1750	LODGE	150	8	10	A Plan of the City of Philadelphia, with the Country Adjacent
mwwi0382	barbados	1782	LODGE	650	29	37	An Accurate Map of the Island of Barbadoes. In which the Different Parishes are Laid Down; with a Plan of Bridge-Town and Carlisle Bay
mwwi0869	st kitts	1782	LODGE	400	28	37	An Accurate Map of the Island of St. Christophers, from an Actual Survey; Shewing the Parishes, Churches, and Rivers; also the Bays, Rocks, Shoals & Soundings that Surround the Whole
mwam1057	america north (east)	1778	LODGE	350	20	25	An Exact Map of New Jersey, Pensylvania, New York, Maryland & Virginia from the Latest Surveys
mwuss0209	carolinas	1778	LODGE	350	22	25	An Exact Map of North and South Carolina & Georgia, with East and West Florida from the Latest Discoveries
mwam1292	great lakes	1778	LODGE	350	21	25	An Exact Map of the Five Great Lakes, with Part of Pensilvania, New York, Canada and Hudsons Bay Territories from the Best Surveys
mwca0536	canada quebec	1778	LODGE	300	21	26	An Exact Map of the Province of Quebec with Part of New York & New England from the Latest Surveys
mwsam0841	south america venezuela	1783	LODGE	375	29	19	Gulf & Lake of Maracaibo
mwme0741	iraq etc	1752	LODGE	350	41	56	Mr Ives's Route from Bassora to Latichea
mwuss0430	florida	1772	LODGE	500	19	34	Part of West Florida from Pensacola to Iberville River with a View to Shew the Proper Spot for a Settlement on the Mississippi
mwuss0449	florida	1783	LODGE	350	18	24	Plan of the Town and Harbour of St. Augustin, in East Florida
mwuk1510	uk english channel (all)	1786	LODGE	120	17	30	The British Channel Including the Coasts of England and France
mwwi0258	west indies (east)	1781	LODGE	350	27	22	The Dutch Islands of St. Eustatia, Saba, and St. Martins; the French Island of St. Bartholomew; the English Islands of St. Christophers, Nevis and Anguila; with the Smaller Islands and Keys Adjoining
mwwi0644	hispaniola	1783	LODGE	400	34	48	The Island of St. Domingo, Called by the Spaniards, Hispaniola, Subject to France and Spain, from the Best Authorities
mww0494	world	1775	LODGE	400	28	51	The World with the Latest Discoveries, from the Best Authorities
mwaa0064	arctic	1598	LOEW	2000	21	24	Septentrionalium Terrarum Descriptio 1597 (based on Mercator 1595.)
mwru0305a	russia	1793	LOGAN	600	36	39	Plan de la Residence Imperiale de St: Petersbourg (map by G. Georgi, first publ. in German by Muller 1790)
mwf0927	france paris	1840	LOGEROT	800	74	108	Nouveau Plan de Paris Divise en 20 Arrondissements
mwec0948	uk england oxfordshire	1688	LOGGAN	1350	41	52	(Oxford) Nova & Accuratissima Celeberrimae Universitatis Oppidique Cantabrigiensis Ichnographia Ano. 1688
mwam1283	great lakes	1755	LONDON MAG.	320	22	27	(Separately-issued part of a three-sheet map with the title: 'A Map of the Five Great Lakes with Part of Pensilvania, New York, Canada and Hudsons Bay Territories &c.')
mwuss0899	michigan	1761	LONDON MAG.	650	24	32	(Straits of Mackinac)
mwas0787	asia south east philippines	1763	LONDON MAG.	350	25	21	A Chart of the Channel in the Philipine Islands, through which the Manila Galeon Passes, with a Map of Manila Island
mwuss0803	massachusetts	1774	LONDON MAG.	320	24	18	A Chart of the Coast of New England, from Beverly to Scituate Harbour, Including the Ports of Boston and Salem
mwsc0736	scandinavia sweden	1760	LONDON MAG.	200	10	18	A Chart of the Port of Stockholm, Capital of the Kingdom of Sweden
mwme1018	turkey etc	1770	LONDON MAG.	200	17	23	A Correct Plan of Constantinople, with the Adjacent Country, from an Actual Survey
mwf0372	france brittany	1790	LONDON MAG.	120	20	24	A Map of Bell'Isle, Divided into Parishes
mwe0589	europe czech republic (bohemia)	1756	LONDON MAG.	160	17	23	A Map of Bohemia Being the Present Seat of War in Germany.
mwwi0544	guadeloupe	1759	LONDON MAG.	135	12	18	A Map of Guadeloupe One of the Caribby Islands in the West Indies Subject to France
mwin0230	india	1760	LONDON MAG.	280	29	34	A Map of Indostan or the Great Mogol's Empire
mwuss0754	maryland	1778	LONDON MAG.	400	16	23	A Map of Maryland with the Delaware Counties and the Southern Part of New Jersey &c.
mwuss1372	pennsylvania	1778	LONDON MAG.	720	38	29	A Map of that Part of Pensylvania Now the Principle Seat of War in America wherein may be Seen the Situation of Philadelphia, Red Bank, Mud Island, & Germantown
mwam0977	america north (east)	1755	LONDON MAG.	240	21	27	A Map of the British & French Plantations in North America
mwuss0292	connecticut	1758	LONDON MAG.	400	17	22	A Map of the Colonies of Connecticut and Rhode Island, Divided into Counties & Townships, from the Best Authorities. By Tho. Kitchin Geogr.
mwaf1218	africa west	1759	LONDON MAG.	120	18	11	A Map of the Countries Bordering on the Rivers Sanagra & Gambia
mwin0247	india	1770	LONDON MAG.	140	19	26	A Map of the Countries round Surat and Bombay in the East Indies

AMPG REFERENCE	REGION	DATE	MAP MAKER	PRICE (UK£)	VERT. (cm.)	HOR. (cm.)	TITLE OF MAP (Comments by the editor in brackets)
mwsam0614	south america guyana	1763	LONDON MAG.	160	22	19	A Map of the Dutch Colonies of Surinam and Barbutius and the French Colony of Cayenne; between the Orinoko and Amazon Rivers, in South America
mwaf0795	africa north morocco	1760	LONDON MAG.	140	11	17	A Map of the Empire of Morocco, Comprehending the Kingdoms of Fez, Morocco, &c. by T. Kitchen
mwca0359	canada nova scotia	1745	LONDON MAG.	180	11	18	A Map of the Harbour of Louisburg and Parts Adjacent
mwg0393	bavaria	1778	LONDON MAG.	140	24	18	A Map of the Seat of War in Bavaria and Bohemia. By Thos. Kitchin Senr.
mwbp0460	poland	1759	LONDON MAG.	140	22	18	A Map of the Seat of War in the Western Part of the Kingdom of Poland. By T. Kitchin Geogr.
mwbh0680	belgium holland	1747	LONDON MAG.	150	19	24	A New & Exact Map of the Provinces of Holland, Utrecht, Gelderland, Zeeland, Dutch Flanders and Dutch Brabant &c. Exhibiting a View of the Parts Now Invaded by the French, & the Present Seat of War. Drawn from the Best Authorities
mwin0231	india	1760	LONDON MAG.	160	18	26	A New and Accurate Map of Bengal Drawn from the Best Authorities. By Thos. Kitchen
mwin0232a	india	1760	LONDON MAGAZINE	160	24	18	A New and Accurate map of the Northern Coast of Choramandel in the East Indies (map by T. Kitchin)
mwwi0441	cuba	1762	LONDON MAG.	480	27	37	A New Chart of the Seas, Surrounding the Island of Cuba, with the Soundings, Currents, Ships Courses &c. and a Map of the Island Itself, Lately Made by an Officer in the Navy
mwuk0510	scotland	1763	LONDON MAG.	200	17	22	A New Map of Edinburgh Shire Drawn from an Actual Survey by Thos. Kitchen Geogr.
mwuk0511	scotland	1763	LONDON MAG.	200	17	22	A New Map of Haddington Shire Drawn from an Actual Survey by Thos. Kitchen Geogr.
mwuk0512	scotland	1763	LONDON MAG.	200	17	22	A New Map of Linlithgow Shire Drawn from an Actual Survey by Thos. Kitchen Geogr.
mwuk1842	wales	1756	LONDON MAG.	140	17	21	A New Map of the Island of Anglesey Drawn from the Best Authorities. By T. Kitchin Geographr.
mwp0414	pacific north	1764	LONDON MAG.	350	17	23	A New Map of the North East Coast of Asia, and North West Coast of America, with the Late Russian Discoveries
mwuss0944	mississippi	1761	LONDON MAG.	500	18	24	A New Map of the River Mississipi from the Sea to Bayagoulas
mwuss1639	virginia	1761	LONDON MAG.	400	18	23	A New Map of Virginia, from the Best Authorities: By T. Kitchin, Geogr.
mwgm0402	panama	1740	LONDON MAG.	200	10	18	A Plan of Porto Bello
mwca0518a	canada quebec	1759	LONDON MAG.	200	11	18	A plan of Quebec, Metropolis of Canada
mwin0232	india	1760	LONDON MAG.	180	18	24	A Plan of the Battle of Plassey, Fought 23d. June, 1757, by Coll. Robt. Clive, against the Nabob of Bengal
mwwi0442	cuba	1762	LONDON MAG.	160	18	11	A Plan of the City and Harbour of Havanna, Capital of the Island of Cuba
mwg0240d	berlin	1760	LONDON MAG.	240	18	24	A Plan of the City of Berlin / A Prospect of the City of Berlin.
mwsp0095b	portugal	1756	LONDON MAG.	100	19	12	A Plan of the City of Lisbon …
mwca0519	canada quebec	1759	LONDON MAG.	350	18	24	A Plan of the River St. Lawrence, from the Falls of Montmorenci to Sillery; with the Operations of the Siege of Quebec
mwwi0321	bahamas	1763	LONDON MAG.	200	11	22	A Plan of the Straights of Bahama, through which the Expedition Fleet was Conducted in the Year 1762, Against the Havana
mwca0386	canada nova scotia	1760	LONDON MAG.	350	18	11	A Plan of the Town & Harbour of Halifax in Nova Scotia
mwwi0788	martinique	1762	LONDON MAG.	160	19	25	A Plan of the Town and Citadel of Fort Royal in Martinco; the Last Landing Place of our Army, and the Country through which it Marched to the Attack
mwgm0403	panama	1740	LONDON MAG.	160	11	18	A Plan of the Town Chagre, &c.
mwuk1215	england london	1766	LONDON MAG.	200	18	24	Aldersgate Ward with it's Divisions into Precincts and Parishes and the Liberty of St. Martins le Grand, According to a New Survey
mww0443	world	1758	LONDON MAG.	960	30	44	An Accurate Chart of the World, with the New Discoveries; also a View of the General & Coasting Trade Winds, Monsoons or Shifting Trade Winds, & the Variations of the Compass
mwwi0247	west indies (east)	1759	LONDON MAG.	200	25	19	An Accurate Map of the Caribby Islands, with the Crowns, &c. to which they Severally Belong. By T. Kitchin Geogr.
mwwi0779	martinique	1758	LONDON MAG.	180	19	25	An Accurate Map of the Island of Martinico
mwgr0201	greece	1770	LONDON MAG.	200	16	24	An Accurate Map of the Morea, and the Islands in the Archipelago. With the Neighboring Countries in Greece, being the Seat of War between the Russians and Turks.
mwec0188	uk england cornwall	1749	LONDON MAG.	200	20	24	Cornwall Drawn from an Actual Survey and Regulated by Astronl. Observatns. By T. Kitchin Geograpr.
mwec0235b	uk england cumbria	1786	LONDON MAGAZINE	80	21	15	Cumberland Drawn from the best Surveys
mwwi0279b	west indies (east)	1782	LONDON MAG.	280	25	19	Island of St. Lucia / Island of St. Vincent / Chart of Part of the Windward Is. By T. Kitchin Sen. / Island of Barbados

AMPG REFERENCE	REGION	DATE	MAP MAKER	PRICE (UK£)	VERT. (cm.)	HOR. (cm.)	TITLE OF MAP (Comments by the editor in brackets)
mwuss1133	new york	1778	LONDON MAG.	350	25	19	Part of the Counties of Charlotte and Albany, in the Province of New York; being the Seat of War between the King's Forces under Lieut. Gen. Burgoyne and the Rebel Army. By Thos. Kitchin Senr.
mwwi0545	guadeloupe	1759	LONDON MAG.	200	11	18	Plan of the General Attack upon the Island of Guadaloupe, January. 23d. 1759
mwca0575	canada quebec montreal	1760	LONDON MAG.	240	18	25	Plan of the Town & Fortifications of Montreal, or Ville Marie in Canada
mwsp0717	gibraltar	1760	LONDON MAG.	180	28	15	Plan of the Town and Fortifications of Gibraltar with All the New Works
mwuss1368	pennsylvania	1777	LONDON MAGAZINE	300	20	24	Seat of War in the Environs of Philadelphia: by Thos. Kitchin Senr. Hydrographer to His Majesty
mwsw0180	switzerland	1776	LONDON MAG.	180	19	24	Switzerland Divided into its Cantons with its Allies &c.
mwuk0536	scotland	1780	LONDON MAG.	120	23	18	The Island of Skye, Drawn from the Latest Authorities, by T. Kitchin & J. Barber, Geogrs.
mwuk1634	scilly isles	1753	LONDON MAG.	250	18	22	The Islands of Scilly Drawn from the Best Surveys, by T. Kitchin Geogr.
mwuk0533	scotland	1778	LONDON MAG.	120	18	23	The Isles of Orkney & Shetland which Compose One Shire or County of Orkney: By T. Kitchin & J. Barber
mwp0421	pacific north	1775	LONDON MAG.	250	17	24	The Northern Archipelago or New Discover'd Islands in the Seas of Kamtschatka & Anadir
mwuk0538	scotland	1781	LONDON MAG.	150	23	18	The Western Islands, Drawn from the Latest Authorities by T. Kitchin & J. Barber, Geographers
mwwi0730	jamaica	1774	LONG	480	29	44	A Draught of the Harbours of Port Royal and Kingston
mwf0527	france corsica	1769	LONGCHAMPS	675	72	51	Carte de l'Isle de Corse Dressee sur le Nouveaux Memoires et Suivant les Dernieres Observations par le Sr. Clermont Ingr. Geographe
mwam0991	america north (east)	1756	LONGCHAMPS	2000	54	75	Carte des Possessions Francoises et Angloises dans le Canada, et Partie de la Louisiane
mwf1162	france rhone-alpes	1795	LONGCHAMPS	320	64	50	Departement du Mont Blanc (cy-devant Savoie) Decrete par la Convention Nationale le 27 Novembre 1792
mwuk1582	channel islands	1754	LONGCHAMPS	500	46	71	Description Historique et Geographique des Isles de Gersay, Guernesay, Cers, Herms, Gethou et Aurigny
mwf0990	france poitou	1767	LONGCHAMPS	320	49	73	Gouvernement General et Militaire du Poitou Dresse sur les Dernieres Observations
mwru0540	ukraine	1769	LONGCHAMPS	785	52	76	Nouveau Theatre de la Guerre entre les Russes les Turcs et les Polonois Confederes
mwsp0730	gibraltar	1779	LONGCHAMPS	750	39	54	Plan des Ville, Chateau, Mole, et Baye de Gibraltar
mwaf0799	africa north morocco	1779	LONGCHAMPS	550	35	46	Pland de la Ville de Ceuta
mwaf0478a	africa egypt etc	1670	LONGHI	4500	36	95	Descrittione del Gran Cairo (view. Size excl. text below view)
mwsp0052	portugal	1680	LONGHI	5000	49	97	Lisbona (view)
mwit1106b	italy tuscany	1661	LONGHI	5500	32	81	Prospetiva della Bellissima Citta di Fiorenza Metropoli (size excl. text below)
mwaf0818a	africa north tunisia	1670	LONGHI	3000	37	100	Thunis (view)
mww0634	world	1808	LONGMAN	250	33	44	A General Chart of the World on Mercator's Projection Exhibiting All the New Discoveries and Tracks of the Different Circumnavigators
mwaf0300	africa	1813	LONGMAN	75	16	19	Africa
mwsam0796	south america peru	1829	LONGMAN	100	20	25	Batalla de Ayacucho
mwwi0164	west indies	1820	LONGMAN	320	31	51	Central America and the West Indies
mww0686	world	1829	LONGMAN	550	53	43	Eastern Hemisphere / Western Hemisphere (2 maps, each 53x43cm)
mwwi0748	jamaica	1803	LONGMAN	250	19	32	Jamaica. Exhibiting the Boundaries of each Parish and the Different Post Roads throughout the Island
mwam0590	america north	1813	LONGMAN	120	17	19	North America
mwec0974	uk england oxfordshire	1835	LONGMAN	350	39	33	Oxfordshire
mwgm0272	mexico	1810	LONGMAN	280	20	25	Plan of the Port of Vera Cruz
mwbp0561	poland	1823	LONGMAN	80	19	23	Poland
mwam0284a	mexico	1818	LONGMAN	350	25	39	Spanish North America
mwam1162	america north (east)	1808	LONGMAN	450	35	39	United States of America
mwuss1176	new york	1807	LONGWORTH	2000	38	53	Plan of the City of New York
mwbh0492a	belgium holland	1700	LOOTS	3000	49	57	Amstelodamum Vetus et Novissimum
mwuk0456a	scotland	1710	LOOTS	800	43	53	De Custen van Schotlant met de Eylanden van Oreaneße, van Eylandt Coket tot I. Sande
mwbp0039a	baltic sea (east)	1717	LOOTS	4000	61	102	Dese Nieuwe en Curieuze Paskaart van de Geheele Oost Zee (map by C. Middagten)
mwwi0057	west indies	1717	LOOTS	20000	58	89	Nieuwe groote en Seer Curieuse Paskaart Van Westindien de vaste Custen nevens de Caribische en deversche Eylanden
mwuk0767	uk	1700	LOOTS	1500	53	61	Nieuwe Paskaart van de Noort Zee Strekkende van Texel tot Aghter Yrland
mwg0816	westphalia	1710	LOOTS	1650	52	92	... Nieuwe verbeterde Wad en Buyten Kaart van het Vlie, tot Hamburg ...

AMPG REFERENCE	REGION	DATE	MAP MAKER	PRICE (UK£)	VERT. (cm.)	HOR. (cm.)	TITLE OF MAP (Comments by the editor in brackets)
mwat0217	atlantic east	1750	LOOTS	2500	59	102	Nieuwe Verbeeterde Wassende Graade Paskaart over een Gedeelte van de Spaanse Zee, Strekkende van Yrland Tot aan Caap Bayador (date of original issue unknown)
mwat0267	atlantic north	1707	LOOTS	960	54	61	Nieuwe Wassende Gradige Paskaart van een Groot deel der Noord Zee vertoonende de West Kust van Engeland, Schotland, en Vranckryck. Nevens geheel Yrland, en Ysland, met een gedeelte van Groenland, en Terra Nova
mwsc0699	scandinavia sweden	1697	LOOTS	2500	52	59	Pascaart vant Schager-Rack en.de.Belt. (north to the left)
mwaf1166	africa west	1710	LOOTS	1600	53	61	Paskaart van de West Kust van Africa van C. Bajador tot C. Tres Puntas
mwin0422	indian ocean	1695	LOOTS	12500	70	89	Wassende Grade Paskaert van Oost-Indien van Pieter Goos Werkelyk Verbetert door Verscheyde Ervaren Schippers en Stier Lieden
mwat0021	atlantic ocean (all)	1695	LOOTS	36000	84	101	West Indische Paskaert (state 4 of Blaeu's c1630 map)
mwam0572	america north	1806	LOPEZ	2000	89	76	A Map of the United States and Canada, New Scotland, New-Brunswick and New-Foundland / A Map of the West-Indies and of the Mexican-Gulph (2 maps on one sheet)
mwaf0269	africa	1792	LOPEZ	275	18	25	Africa
mwg0162	germany	1792	LOPEZ	120	18	25	Alemania Dividida En Circulos Con Los Estados De Bohemia
mwsam0114	south america	1792	LOPEZ	275	18	25	America Meridional
mwam0518	america north	1792	LOPEZ	300	19	25	America Septentrional
mwas0217	asia continent	1792	LOPEZ	280	18	25	Asia (size excl. text panel outside right-hand border)
mwwi0663b	hispaniola	1794	LOPEZ	300	21	33	Bahia y Ciudad de Bayaha, o Puerto del Delfin, en la Isla de Santo Domingo (map by J. Bellin)
mwsp0731	gibraltar	1779	LOPEZ	750	43	39	Carta de la Bahia de Gibraltar
mwwi0381	barbados	1780	LOPEZ	785	39	38	Carta de la Isla de Barbados
mwwi0303	antigua	1780	LOPEZ	600	39	38	Carta de la Isla de la Antigua Reducida y Grabada por D. Juan Lopez
mwwi0799	martinique	1781	LOPEZ	450	37	39	Carta de la Isla de la Martinica por D. Juan Lopez Pensionista de S.M.
mwwi0867	st kitts	1780	LOPEZ	500	37	39	Carta de la Isla de San Christoval Reducida y Gravada por D. Juan Lopez, Pensionista de S.M.
mwp0367	pacific marquesas	1797	LOPEZ	320	20	34	Carta de las Islas Llamadas las Marquesas / Isla de Pascuas
mwwi0259	west indies (east)	1781	LOPEZ	550	79	38	Carta General de las Islas Antillas Menores Llamadas de Barlovento y Tambien Caribes por Don Tomas Lopez
mwwi0466	cuba	1783	LOPEZ	1600	37	84	Carta Maritima de la Isla de Cuba, que Comprehende las Jurisdicciones de Filipina, la Havana ... Madrid, ano 1783
mwgm0431	panama	1785	LOPEZ	875	36	78	Carta Maritima del Reyno de Tierra Firme u Castilla del Oro
mwwi0333	bahamas	1782	LOPEZ	550	38	39	Carta Nautica que Comprehende los Desembocaderos al Mar del Norte
mwwi0334	bahamas	1782	LOPEZ	900	39	39	Carta Reducida de las Islas Lucayas, o de los Lucayos por D. Juan Lopez Pensinista de S.M. Ano de 1782
mwam1331a	america north (west)	1796	LOPEZ	4000	39	33	Carta Reducida que compréndé las costas septentrionales De La California, contenidas entre el grado 36 y el 61 de latitud norte, descubiertas el año de 1775 y el de 1779 en las expediciones que de órden del Soberano se dispusieron para dichos
mwat0096	atlantic azores	1781	LOPEZ	600	38	79	Carta Reducida y General de las Islas de los Azores ... 1781
mwsc0185	scandinavia	1792	LOPEZ	220	18	25	Coronas Del Norte
mwaf0723	africa north	1792	LOPEZ	100	18	25	Costas De Berbera
mwaf0527	africa egypt etc	1792	LOPEZ	150	25	18	Egypto Antiguo Y Moderno
mwam1104	america north (east)	1792	LOPEZ	320	25	18	Estados Unidos d'America, Terra Nova, Canada, Luiziana e Florida
mwwi0127	west indies	1792	LOPEZ	300	18	25	Golfe de Mexico Y Las Islas Anullas
mwc0212	china	1792	LOPEZ	300	18	25	Imperio De La China
mwit0212	italy	1792	LOPEZ	250	18	25	Italia
mwam0183a	america continent	1760	LOPEZ	800	46	52	La America Dispuesta segun las ultimas y nuevas observaciones
mwuss0636	louisiana	1762	LOPEZ	2400	40	40	La Luisiana (inset of New Orleans)
mwas0515	asia south east	1792	LOPEZ	300	18	25	Las Indias Orientales Y El Archipelago
mwbh0757	belgium holland	1792	LOPEZ	120	25	18	Los Paises Baxos Septentrionales Y Meridonales
mwuk0869	uk	1792	LOPEZ	200	18	25	Los Reynos De Inglaterra
mwsp0345b	spain madrid	1771	LOPEZ	300	11	7	Madrid
mwsp0314	spain	1808	LOPEZ	300	43	53	Map of Spain & Portugal
mwas0215a	asia continent	1790	LOPEZ	720	48	59	Mapa de Asia
mwsp0586	spain regions	1777	LOPEZ	720	66	75	Mapa de el Principado de Asturias (inset: Oviedo)
mwf0165	france	1792	LOPEZ	100	18	25	Mapa De La Francia
mwat0164	atlantic canary isl.	1779	LOPEZ	500	35	43	Mapa de la Isla de Fuerteventura
mwat0165	atlantic canary isl.	1779	LOPEZ	500	35	37	Mapa de la Isla de Lanzarote
mwat0165a	atlantic canary isl.	1779	LOPEZ	1000	36	38	Mapa de la Isla de la Palma / Gomera (illustrated below left)
mwat0166	atlantic canary isl.	1779	LOPEZ	1000	36	37	Mapa de la Isla de Teneriffe
mwsp0595	spain regions	1782	LOPEZ	480	63	37	Mapa Geografico de la Provincia de Palencia
mwsp0560	spain regions	1761	LOPEZ	280	38	38	Mapa de la Provincia de Toledo
mwsp0580	spain regions	1773	LOPEZ	240	38	38	Mapa de la Provincia de Zamora

AMPG REFERENCE	REGION	DATE	MAP MAKER	PRICE (UK£)	VERT. (cm.)	HOR. (cm.)	TITLE OF MAP (Comments by the editor in brackets)
mwsp0104	portugal	1762	LOPEZ	240	33	28	Mapa de la Provincia, de Entre Duero y Mino. Construido Segun las Mas Modernas Memorias
mwsp0105	portugal	1762	LOPEZ	240	33	28	Mapa de la Provincia, de Tras-Los-Montes Construido
mwgm0256	mexico	1785	LOPEZ	400	36	39	Mapa de las Cercanias de Mexico
mwam0175	america continent	1758	LOPEZ	750	48	60	Mapa de las Indias Occidentales Dedicada al Serenissimo Principe de Asturias Don Fernando Dispueta por Guillermo Delisle Geographo Mayor (Spanish edition of De L'Isle 1722)
mwsp0583	spain regions	1776	LOPEZ	650	78	82	Mapa del Principado de Cataluna
mwsp0106	portugal	1762	LOPEZ	240	33	28	Mapa del Reyno de Algarve Construido
mwsp0561	spain regions	1761	LOPEZ	400	40	39	Mapa del Reyno de Cordova
mwsp0562	spain regions	1761	LOPEZ	280	39	35	Mapa del Reyno de Granada
mwsp0578	spain regions	1767	LOPEZ	550	75	72	Mapa del Reyno de Sevilla
mwsp0107	portugal	1762	LOPEZ	240	40	30	Mapa del Reyno, de Portugal. Construido, Segun las Mas Modernas Memorias
mwsp0317	spain	1810	LOPEZ	1200	83	102	Mapa General de Espana, Dividido en sus Actuales Provincias, Islas Adyacentes, y Reyno de Portugal
mwsp0114	portugal	1778	LOPEZ	1000	138	79	Mapa General del Reyno de Portugal: Comprehende sus Provincias, Corregimientos, Oidorias, Proveedurias, Concejos, Cotos, &. Dedicado a Don Pedro Rodriguez Campomanes
mwam0239	america continent	1794	LOPEZ	1500	50	59	Mapa Generale de America o Hemispherio Occidental qui Contiene los Nuevos Descubrientes y Rectificaciones de los Anteriores por Dom Tomas Lopez Geografo ... en Madrid Calle de Atocha Frente la Casa Nueva de Los Grenues
mwsp0286	spain	1770	LOPEZ	550	49	60	Mapa Generale de Espana, Dedicado al Serenissimo Senor Don Carlos Antonio
mwgm0264a	mexico	1801	LOPEZ	4000	60	70	Mapa Geográfico de la Península y Provincia de Yucatán
mwsp0597	spain regions	1783	LOPEZ	580	79	90	Mapa Geografico de la Provincia de Salamanca
mwsam0245	south america argentina	1780	LOPEZ	480	24	33	Mapa Geografico de la Provincias, y Costas de Buenos Ayres
mwsp0601	spain regions	1786	LOPEZ	785	106	82	Mapa Geografico De Una Parte De La Provincia De Leon
mwuss1070a	new mexico	1795	LOPEZ	1500	30	39	Mapa Geográfico Del Gobierno De La Nueva Granada ó Nuevo México: Con Las Provincias De Nabajo Y Moqui...
mwgm0264b	mexico	1801	LOPEZ	1500	49	41	Mapa Geográfico Del Obispado De Mechoacan
mwsp0600	spain regions	1785	LOPEZ	350	36	38	Mapa Geografico del Partido de Carrion
mwsp0602	spain regions	1786	LOPEZ	550	61	44	Mapa Geografico del Partido de Ponferrada ... Vierzo
mwsp0598	spain regions	1784	LOPEZ	350	35	38	Mapa Geografico del Partido de Toro
mwsp0599	spain regions	1784	LOPEZ	720	76	82	Mapa Geografico del Reyno de Galicia
mwgm0438	panama	1802	LOPEZ	2500	33	44	Mapa Geografico del Reyno de Tierra Firma y ... Veragua y Darien
mwwi0087	west indies	1755	LOPEZ	10000	59	82	Mapa Maritimo Del Golfo de Mexico e Isles de la America para el uso de los navegantes en esta parte del mundo, construido sobre las mexores memorias, y observaciones astronomicas de longitudes, y latitudes
mwwi0832a	puerto rico	1791	LOPEZ	1500	36	64	Mapa topográfico de la Isla de San Juan de PuertoRico, y la de Bieque
mwsp0723	gibraltar	1762	LOPEZ	750	34	34	Mapa Topographico de los Payses, y Costas, que forman el Estrecho de Gibraltar
mwsp0564	spain regions	1762	LOPEZ	900	54	82	Parte Meridional de las Costas d'Espanas
mwgm0429	panama	1780	LOPEZ	675	42	38	Plano de la Bahia y Ciudad de Portobello / Puerto de Portobello
mwwi0741	jamaica	1782	LOPEZ	600	36	39	Plano de la Ciudad de Kingston / Plano de la Ciudad de Puerto Real / Carta del Puerto de Bluefields / Carta de Los Puertos de Kingston
mwgm0434	panama	1789	LOPEZ	600	38	41	Plano de la Ciudad de Panama, y Su Arribal
mwwi0469	cuba	1785	LOPEZ	960	35	37	Plano de la Ciudad y Puerto de la Havana
mwuss0450	florida	1783	LOPEZ	650	19	39	Plano de la Cuidad y Puerto de San Agustin de la Florida
mwsam0388	south america brazil	1777	LOPEZ	360	32	41	Plano de la Entrada del Rio Grande de San Pedro
mwsam0389	south america brazil	1777	LOPEZ	360	38	42	Plano de la Isla y Puerto de Santa Catalina
mwsam0811	south america uruguay	1777	LOPEZ	480	39	42	Plano de la Plaza de la Colonia del Sacremento
mwwi0832	puerto rico	1785	LOPEZ	750	36	37	Plano de Puerto Rico
mwgm0258	mexico	1786	LOPEZ	400	37	40	Plano del Puerto de Veracruz (2 maps on one sheet)
mwsp0603	spain regions	1788	LOPEZ	2000	86	106	Plano Geometrico de la Ciudad de Sevilla Dedicado al Excelentisimo Senor Don Pedro Lopez de Lerena
mwgm0256a	mexico	1785	LOPEZ		86	110	Plano Geometrico de la Imperial Noble y Leal Ciudad de Mexico
mwsp0346a	spain madrid	1785	LOPEZ	2500	53	80	Plano Geométrico de Madrid : dedicado y presentado al rey nuestro Señor Don Carlos III (north to the right)
mwsp0724	gibraltar	1762	LOPEZ	750	38	38	Plano Geometrico de la Cuidad de Gibraltar
mwe0965	europe hungary	1792	LOPEZ	100	18	25	Reyno De Hungaria
mwbp0524	poland	1792	LOPEZ	200	18	25	Reynos De Polonia
mwru0302	russia	1792	LOPEZ	240	25	18	Russia Europea (size excl. text panel below map)
mwe1165	europe south east	1792	LOPEZ	120	18	25	Turquia Europea
mwam0662	america north	1829	LORRAIN	280	28	38	Amerique Septentrionale
mwit0754	italy rome	1773	LOSI	650	52	86	Pianta di Roma come si Trova al Presente colle Alzate delle Fabriche piu Nobili cosi Antiche come Moderne

AMPG REFERENCE	REGION	DATE	MAP MAKER	PRICE (UK£)	VERT. (cm.)	HOR. (cm.)	TITLE OF MAP (Comments by the editor in brackets)
mwas0258	asia continent	1846	LOTHIAN	140	41	34	Asia
mwp0160	australia	1846	LOTHIAN	200	34	40	Australia with the British Settlements
mwca0202	canada	1846	LOTHIAN	120	38	32	British America
mwuk0297	ireland	1846	LOTHIAN	120	41	33	Ireland
mwuss1536	texas	1846	LOTHIAN	450	29	37	Mexico & Guatimala with Texas (shows Republic of Texas)
mww0739	world	1846	LOTHIAN	200	32	39	The World on Mercator's Projection
mwam1239	america north (east)	1838	LOTHIAN	240	28	33	United States
mwwi0216	west indies	1846	LOTHIAN	140	30	41	West Indies
mww0740	world	1846	LOTHIAN	240	42	34	Western Hemisphere / Eastern Hemisphere (2 maps)
mwbh0708	belgium holland	1760	LOTTER	720	49	58	XVII Provinciae Belgii sive Germaniae Inferioris (copy of Seutter 1740)
mwam1030	america north (east)	1775	LOTTER	5500	101	95	A Map of the Most Inhabited Part of New England, Containing the Provinces of Massachusets Bay and New Hampshire, with the Colonies of Conecticut and Rhode Island, Divided into Counties and Townships
mwuss1124	new york	1777	LOTTER	2000	75	56	A Map of the Provinces of New-York and New-Jersey, with a Part of Pennsylvania and the Province of Quebec. From the Topographical Observations of C.J. Sauthier
mwam0487	america north	1784	LOTTER	5500	100	113	A New and Correct Map of North America with the West India Islands, Divided According to the Last Treaty of Peace ... 20th of Jan. 1783 ... the Thirteen Provinces wich Compose the United States of North America
mwuss1369	pennsylvania	1777	LOTTER	2500	59	46	A Plan of the City and Environs of Philadelphia
mwg0459	hessen	1757	LOTTER	580	50	58	Abbatia Fuldensis alias Buchovia
mwsp0547	spain regions	1740	LOTTER	675	51	59	Accurata Designatio Celebris Freti Prope Andalusiae Castellum Gibraltar
mwaf0208	africa	1760	LOTTER	600	46	58	Africa Concinnata Secundum Observationes (re-issue of De L'Isle 1700)
mwaf0947	africa south	1770	LOTTER	900	46	55	Africae Pars Meridionalis cum Promontorio Bonae Spei
mwsam0087	south america	1772	LOTTER	650	47	59	America Meridionalis Concinnata Juxta Observationes ... per G. De L'Isle (copies De L'Isle's distorted 1700 map. See above)
mwam0416	america north	1758	LOTTER	785	46	57	America Septentrionalis, Concinnata juxta Observationes Dnn Academiae Regalis Scientiarum et Nunnullorum Aliorum, et juxta Annotationes Recentissimas, per G. De L'Isle
mwru0537	ukraine	1760	LOTTER	685	50	58	Amplissima Ucraniae Regio, Palatinatus Kioviensem et Braclaviensem (re-issue of Seutter)
mwg0390	bavaria	1764	LOTTER	350	38	46	Archidiaconatus Baumburgensis
mwas0185	asia continent	1770	LOTTER	500	49	58	Asia Concinnata Secundum Observationes Academiae Regalis
mwas0189a	asia continent	1772	LOTTER	750	48	57	Asia Secundum novas celeberrimi de l'Isle Proiectiones aliorumque recentissimorum Geographorum observationes concinnata
mwbh0718	belgium holland	1770	LOTTER	675	48	58	Belgica Foederata Complectens Septem Provincias, Ducatum Geldriae, Comitatus Hollandiae et Zeelandiae Dioec. Traject. Transisul. Groningam et Frisiam
mwme1021	turkey etc	1771	LOTTER	480	25	39	Beschreibung welche die Attaque der Russchischen mit der Turkischen Flotte vom 24. Jun: 1770
mwbp0467	poland	1760	LOTTER	600	49	57	Borussiae Regnum
mwru0552	ukraine	1777	LOTTER	1500	79	87	Carte de la Krimee
mwf0150a	france	1780	LOTTER	450	45	59	Carte de la France
mwam1050	america north (east)	1777	LOTTER	1350	50	58	Carte de la Nouvelle Republique de l'Amerique ou les Treize Provinces Unies
mwg0836	westphalia	1762	LOTTER	875	47	55	Carte de l'Eveche de Paderborn avec une Partie de Westphalie, du Princip. de Waldeck du Landgraviat de Hesse-Cassel, du Duche de Brounsvic de l'Abb. de Corvey et du Comte de Lippe
mwp0428	pacific north	1781	LOTTER	750	47	51	Carte de l'Ocean Pacifique au Nord de l'Equateur - Charte des Stillen Weltmeers im Nordlichen Aequator ... 1780
mwsp0671	balearic islands	1760	LOTTER	550	49	57	Carte des Isles de Maiorque Minorque et d'Yvice Gravee par Tobie Conrad Lotter, Geographe a Augsbourg (copy of Seutter 1741)
mwru0546	ukraine	1770	LOTTER	480	44	64	Carte du Gouvernement de Tauride Comprenenant la Krimee et les Pays Voisins
mwe0203	europe	1782	LOTTER	2000	108	139	Carte Generale de Toute l'Europe, Divisee selon l'Etendue des ses Principaux Etats, Subdivisee en leurs Principales Provinces. Representee sur Six Feuilles
mwru0235	russia	1760	LOTTER	400	49	106	Carte Geographique Contenant le Royaume de Siberie Divisee en Trois Departemens, Savoir Tobolskago, Ienisseiskago, Irkutskago, et quelques Autres Parties de la Tartarie (copy of D'Anville 1753)
mwg0828	westphalia	1757	LOTTER	600	50	58	Carte Geographique du Comte de la Marck
mwg0837	westphalia	1762	LOTTER	785	49	58	Carte Geographique du Comte de Lippe

AMPG REFERENCE	REGION	DATE	MAP MAKER	PRICE (UK£)	VERT. (cm.)	HOR. (cm.)	TITLE OF MAP (Comments by the editor in brackets)
mwe0812	europe east	1771	LOTTER	1200	94	116	Carte Geographique du Theatre de la Guerre en General Representant le Royaume de Hongarie, de Transylvanie, Croacie, Dalmacie, Esclavonie, Bosnie, Servie
mwm0067	mediterranean	1770	LOTTER	2400	53	131	Carte Geographique Representant la Mer Mediterranee ou la Seconde Partie du Theatre de la Guerre entre les Russes et les Turcs
mwe1030a	europe rhine	1784	LOTTER	1500	113	165	Carte Geographique representant le Cours Entier du Rhin, de la Moselle, de la Meuse et de l'Escaut
mwru0541	ukraine	1769	LOTTER	1400	49	147	Carte Geographique Representant le Theatre de la Guerre entre les Russes, les Turcs, et les Polonois Confederes (copied by Truskot 1776)
mwam1049	america north (east)	1777	LOTTER	800	59	49	Carte Nouvelle de l'Amerique Angloise Contenant Tout ce que les Anglois Possedent sur le Continent de l'Amerique Septentrionale Savior le Canada, la Nouvelle Ecosse ou Acadie, les Treize Provinces Unies
mwbp0468	poland	1760	LOTTER	800	49	60	Carte Nouvelle des Royaumes de Galizie et Lodomerie avec le Districe de Bukowine
mwsp0718	gibraltar	1760	LOTTER	875	48	58	Castellum Gibraltar in Andalusia Situm, cum Celebri Freto inter Europam et Africam, Annexis Circumjacentibus Portubus et Castelis
mwsp0579	spain regions	1770	LOTTER	550	50	58	Cataloniae Principatus et Ruscinonis ac Cerretaniae Comitatuum (copy of Seutter 1734)
mwin0051a	ceylon	1760	LOTTER	800	50	58	Ceylon
mwsc0737	scandinavia sweden	1770	LOTTER	800	55	46	Charta Nova Exhibens Regnum Sueciae et Gothiae
mwsc0738	scandinavia sweden	1770	LOTTER	675	55	47	Charta ofwer Sodra Delen af Swerige
mwin0259	india	1777	LOTTER	800	54	48	Charte von Ostindien
mwg0387	bavaria	1760	LOTTER	480	50	58	Circulus Franconicus
mwbh0719	belgium holland	1770	LOTTER	400	50	64	Comitatus Flandriae
mwit0518	italy lombardy	1770	LOTTER	1350	57	130	Cursus Padi per Longobardiam a Fonte usque ad Ostia (re-issue of map by Seutter, 1740)
mwe0375	europe austria	1760	LOTTER	400	47	47	Das Inn Viertel in dem Erzherzogthum Oesterreich ob der Enns
mwuk1199	england london	1760	LOTTER	480	50	57	Delineatio ac Finitima Regio Magnae Brittaniae Metropoleos Londini ad Novissimam Norman
mwuk1499	uk english channel (all)	1760	LOTTER	1200	48	59	Die durch die Engellaender Beunruhigte Franzosische Kusten Ao. 1758 / Brittische Ubermacht zur See (2 maps, 48x59cm and 48x48cm)
mwit0615	italy north	1770	LOTTER	550	50	57	Dominium Venetum cum Adjacentibus Mediolan. Mantuano, Mutinensi, Mirandolano, Parmensi, Placentino Ducatibus (copy of Seutter 1740)
mwg0242	berlin	1760	LOTTER	2000	50	114	Eigentliche Abbildung und Prospecte … Berlin (copy of Seutter 1740)
mwme0648	arabia etc	1780	LOTTER	500	49	57	Empire de la Porte Ottomane
mwe0175	europe	1758	LOTTER	600	47	57	Europa Delineata juxta Observationes
mwe0178	europe	1760	LOTTER	650	50	58	Europa Regnorum
mwit1138	italy florence	1770	LOTTER	1300	50	59	Firenza la Capitale di Toscana (copy of Seutter 1730)
mwbh0707	belgium holland	1760	LOTTER	400	50	59	Germaniae Inferioris sive Belgii Pars Meridionalis Exhibens X Provincias Catholic (copy of Seutter 1740)
mwf0366	france brittany	1770	LOTTER	600	50	58	Gouvernement General de Bretagne (copy of Seutter 1740)
mwgr0204	greece	1770	LOTTER	360	49	58	Graecia Pars Septentrionalis
mwgr0202	greece	1770	LOTTER	750	48	58	Graeciae Antiquae Designatio Nova (2 maps)
mwg0723	schleswig-holstein	1730	LOTTER	720	50	58	Grund-Riss der Kayserlichen und des Heil. Rom. Reichs Freyen Stadt Lubeck
mwsp0287	spain	1770	LOTTER	550	44	62	Hispania ex Archetypo Roderici Mendez Sylvae et Variis Relationibus et Chartis Manuscriptis … Per G De L'Isle
mwme0495	jerusalem	1740	LOTTER	720	58	50	Ierusalem, cum Suburbiis, Prout Tempore Christi Floruit (copy of Seutter 1740)
mwgr0429	greece crete	1770	LOTTER	850	49	58	Insula Creta nunc Candia (re-issue of Seutter 1730)
mwit0815	italy sardinia	1760	LOTTER	720	58	50	Insula et Regnum Sardiniae (copy of Seutter 1740)
mwsc0370	scandinavia denmark	1760	LOTTER	480	49	58	Insularum Danicarum ut Zeelandiae, Fionae, Langelandiae, Lalandiae, Falstriae, Fembriae Monae
mwit0189	italy	1758	LOTTER	450	48	57	Italia annexis insulis Sicilia, Sardinia et Corsica
mwe1076	europe serbia	1788	LOTTER	675	54	63	Kriegs Schauplatz zu Leichter Erklaerung der Zeitungsblaetter uber die Rustingen zu Wasser und zu Land zwischen Russland, Oesterreich und Polen, gegen die Turkey
mwuk0843	uk	1760	LOTTER	580	49	58	La Grande Bretagne ou les Royaumes d'Angleterre et d'Ecosse comme aussi le Royaume d'Irlande Divisee par Provinces
mwg0462	hessen	1761	LOTTER	960	97	83	Le Landgraviat de Hesse-Cassel Meridional et Septentr. avec une Partie du Landgraviat de Hesse-Darmstat et de la Vetteravie avec Autres Dependences
mwf0881	france paris	1758	LOTTER	850	50	58	Le Plan de Paris, ses Faubourgs et ses Environs (copy of Seutter 1740)
mwf0126	france	1750	LOTTER	900	47	57	Le Royaume de France et les Conquetes de Louis le Grand (1st publ. by J. Wolff c1715)

AMPG REFERENCE	REGION	DATE	MAP MAKER	PRICE (UK£)	VERT. (cm.)	HOR. (cm.)	TITLE OF MAP (Comments by the editor in brackets)
mwf0127	france	1750	LOTTER	400	48	60	Les Routes Exactes des Postes du Royaume de France (copy of Seutter 1730)
mwf0497	france corsica	1740	LOTTER	785	50	57	L'Isle de Corse avec les Differents Districts, Appartenante a la Republique de Genes, mais Divisee et Soulevee depuis Plusieurs Annees
mwit0199	italy	1770	LOTTER	480	49	57	L'Italia con le sue Poste e Strade Principali Descritta da Giacomo Cantelli da Vignola (copy of Seutter 1730)
mwbp0131	baltic states	1760	LOTTER	700	50	58	Livoniae et Curlandiae Ducatus cum Insulis Adjacentib. (copy of Seutter 1740)
mwit0446	italy liguria	1770	LOTTER	1200	50	58	Lo Stato della Repubblica di Genova (as Seutter 1730 but with sea decorations removed)
mwbh0878	luxembourg	1758	LOTTER	1350	49	57	Luxembourg, une Fortresse Tres-Celebre de la Duche de cette Nom (copy of Seutter 1730)
mwsc0438	scandinavia finland	1758	LOTTER	1200	50	58	Magni Ducatus Finlandiae Russiae Partim, Partim Sueciae Subjecti, Sinus Item Bothnici ac Finnici Nova et Accurata Delineatio (re-issue of Seutter's 1740 map)
mwme0618	arabia etc	1740	LOTTER	685	50	58	Magni Turcarum Dominatoris Imperium per Europam, Asiam, et Africam (copy of Seutter 1730)
mwbp0132	baltic states	1770	LOTTER	500	49	57	Magnus Ducatus Lithuania in suos Palatinatus et Castellanias Divisa
mwg0660a	saxony	1760	LOTTER	960	58	98	Mappa Geographica Circuli Metalliferi Electoratus Saxoniae
mwbp0482	poland	1772	LOTTER	900	49	58	Mappa Geographica, ex Novissimis Observationibus Repraesentans Regnum Poloniae et Magnum Ducatum Lithuaniae
mwg0419	brandenburg	1758	LOTTER	375	50	58	Mappa Geographica Exhibens Electoratum Brandenburgensem, sive Marchiam Veterem, Mediam et Novam, nec non Marchiam Ukeram
mwe0464	europe central	1760	LOTTER	400	49	58	Mappa Geographica Exhibens Postas Omnes ... Totius Germaniae
mwgm0038	gulf of mexico and surrounding regions	1775	LOTTER	1400	49	57	Mappa Geographica Regionem Mexicanam et Floridam Terrasque Adjacentes, ut et Anteriores Americae Insulas Cursus Itidem et Reditus Navigantium versus Flumen Missisipi et Alias Colonias (copy of Seutter 1740)
mwit0837a	italy sardinia and corsica	1764	LOTTER	720	56	49	Mappa Geographica exhibens Regna sive Insulas Sardiniae ac Corsicae (shown above left)
mwe1119	europe slovak republic (moravia)	1758	LOTTER	360	50	58	Mappa Geographica Specialis Marchionatus Moraviae in Sex Circulos Divisae
mwit0950	italy sicily	1760	LOTTER	800	50	58	Mappa Geographica Totius Insulae et Regni Siciliae (inset: Malta. Map by Seutter.)
mwe0587	europe czech republic (bohemia)	1750	LOTTER	550	48	53	Mappa Geographica Totius Regni Bohemiae in XII Circulos Divisae
mww0495	world	1775	LOTTER	2500	45	64	Mappa Totius Mundi Adornata juxta Observationes Dnn Academiae Regalis Scientarum ... Per G. De L'Isle Geographum Parisiis. Prostat Nunc in Officina Tobia Conradi Lotter Geogr
mww0503	world	1778	LOTTER	1800	47	95	Mappe Monde ou Carte Generale de l'Univers sur une Projection Nouvelle d'une Sphere Ovale pour Mieux Entendre les Distances entre l'Europe et Amerique avec le Tour du Monde du Lieut. Cook et Tous les Decouvertes Nouvelles (shown below is the 1782 updated version, incl. all three of Cook's voyages. See also Probst 1782)
mwit1037	italy south	1760	LOTTER	375	59	50	Neapolis Regnum quo Continentur Aprutium Ulterius et Citerius, Comitatus Molisius Terra Laboris, Capitaniata Principat. Ulterior et Citerior Barianus et Hydruntinus Ager Basilicata Calabria Citerior et Ulterior (copy of Seutter 1730)
mwe1163	europe south east	1788	LOTTER	600	49	57	Neue Graenzkarte zwischen Oesterreich, Russland und der Turkey
mwg0243	berlin	1772	LOTTER	1100	45	60	Neuer geometrischer Plan der gesammten ... Residenzstadt Berlin
mwg0151	germany	1780	LOTTER	600	43	46	Neueste Grenzkarte von Deutschland und Oberitalien (in 2 sheets, each 43x46cm)
mwbh0733b	belgium holland	1780	LOTTER	400	47	62	Nouvelle Carte du Cercle de Bourgogne... Maison d'Autriche
mwg0379	bavaria	1741	LOTTER	500	49	56	Nova et Accuratior Repraesentatio Geographica Sacr. Rom. Imperii Episcopatus Worceburgensis Franciae Orientalis Ducatus
mwg0287	baden-wurttemberg	1760	LOTTER	400	51	58	Nova et Accuratissima Ducatus Wurtenbergici
mwg0829	westphalia	1758	LOTTER	720	58	50	Nova et Exacta Mappa Geographica exhibitens Circulum Westphalicum
mwsc0739	scandinavia sweden	1770	LOTTER	675	50	57	Nova Mappa Geographica Sueciae ac Gothiae Regna ut et Finlandiae Ducatum ac Lapponiam (copy of Seutter 1735)
mwbp0458	poland	1758	LOTTER	600	48	57	Nova Mappa Geographica Totius Ducatus Silesiae (inset of Breslau)
mwru0536	ukraine	1760	LOTTER	400	50	58	Nova Mappa Maris Nigri et Freti Constantinopolitani (re-issue of Seutter 1730)
mwbh0720	belgium holland	1770	LOTTER	400	58	49	Nova Tabula Geographica Exhibens Ducatum Brabantiae

AMPG REFERENCE	REGION	DATE	MAP MAKER	PRICE (UK£)	VERT. (cm.)	HOR. (cm.)	TITLE OF MAP (Comments by the editor in brackets)
mwit0317	italy central	1760	LOTTER	400	50	58	Novissima et Accuratissima Delineatio Status Ecclesiae et Magni Ducatus Hetruriae (copy of Seutter 1730)
mwsw0149	switzerland	1750	LOTTER	550	49	58	Novissima et Accuratissima Helvetiae, Rhaetiae, Valesiae, et Partis Sabaudiae Tabula
mwme0824	persia etc	1770	LOTTER	480	50	58	Opulentissimi Regni Persiae (re-issue of Seutter 1730)
mwc0166	china	1760	LOTTER	850	49	58	Opulentissimum Sinarum Imperium (copy of Seutter 1744)
mwg0388	bavaria	1760	LOTTER	480	48	64	Pars Sueviae Borealior
mwca0074	canada	1756	LOTTER	1000	51	58	Partie Orientale de la Nouvelle France ou du Canada avec l'Isle de Terre-Neuve et de Nouvelle Escosse, Acadie et Nouv. Angleterre avec Fleuve de St Laurence (re-issue of Seutter 1740)
mwam0951	america north (east)	1745	SEUTTER	2000	59	51	Pensylvania Nova Jersey et Nova York cum Regionibus ad Fluvium Delaware in America Sitis, Nova Delineatione ob Oculos Posita (re-issued by T. Lotter)
mwbh0707a	belgium holland	1760	LOTTER	1250	50	58	Plan de la Haye en Hollande (updated edition of Homann Heirs 1739)
mwg0283	baden-wurttemberg	1740	LOTTER	480	49	57	Plan de Ville et Chateaux de Fribourg, dans le Brisgau sur le Rhin / Grund-Riss der Stadt und Vestungen Freiburg im Brisgau am obern Rhein
mwbp0505	poland	1784	LOTTER	875	55	44	Plan der Statd (!) und Gegend von Dantzig nebst dem Ausflus der Weichsel
mwme1019	turkey etc	1770	LOTTER	1600	49	55	Plan von Constantinopel, mit der Umliegenden Gegend, und des Canals vom Schwarzen Meer
mww0456	world	1762	LOTTER	300	10	13	Planisphaerium Globi Terrestris
mwbp0449	poland	1753	LOTTER	785	50	57	Polonia Seraphico Observans, juxta Domicilia Propriae, & Alienae Jurisdictionis Geographice Delineata
mwsp0102	portugal	1762	LOTTER	500	56	47	Regna Portugalliae et Algarbiae, cum Adjacentibus Hispaniae Provinciis (inset of Brazil)
mwuk0162	ireland	1740	LOTTER	750	57	49	Regnum Hiberniae, tam Secundum IV Provincias Principales Ultoniam, Connaciam, Lageniam, Momoniam (copy of Seutter 1735)
mwgr0203	greece	1770	LOTTER	480	50	58	Regnum Moreae Accuratissime Divisum in Provincias Saccaniam, Tzaconiam, Caliscopium et Ducatum Clarensae; una cum Insulis Cephalonia, Zacyntho Cythera, Aegina et Sidra
mwsc0629	scandinavia norway	1770	LOTTER	600	58	51	Regnum Norwegiae Accurata et Novissima Delineatione juxta V. Praefecturas Generales Aggerhusiensem, Bergensem, Nidrosiens, Wardhusiens, et Bahus (copy of Seutter 1731)
mwsc0633a	scandinavia norway	1780	LOTTER	900	55	48	Regnum Norwegiae Divisum in Quatuor Collegia quae Dicuntur Aggerhus, Christiansand, Bergen et Trontheim (close copy of Wangensteen 1761)
mwru0242	russia	1770	LOTTER	600	50	57	Spatiosissimum Imperium Russiae Magnae juxta Recentissimas Observationes Mappa Geographica (see also Seutter 1730)
mwe0376	europe austria	1760	LOTTER	400	50	58	Stiria Ducatus
mwf0247	france alsace	1760	LOTTER	480	56	49	Superioris atque Inferioris Alsatiae
mwbp0461	poland	1759	LOTTER	480	49	57	Tabula Generalis Totius Pomeraniae ... Ducatus Bardens. et Comit Gutzkoviensis, nec non Adjacens Insula Rugia, ad Posteriorem Ducatus Pomeraniae
mwru0243	russia	1770	LOTTER	800	44	61	Tabula Geographica Generalis Imperii Russici ad Normam Novissimarum Observationium (see also Truskot 1776)
mwe0952	europe hungary	1760	LOTTER	580	48	59	Tabula Hungaria et Regionum
mwuk0849	uk	1770	LOTTER	580	56	49	Tabula Novissima Accuratissima Regnorum Angliae, Scotiae Hiberniae (copy of Seutter 1720)
mwe0725	europe danube	1750	LOTTER	1200	49	170	Tabula Synoptica Totius Fluminis Danubii a Fontibus usque ad Ostia ... et Pontus Euxinus (copy of Seutter 1730)
mwme0349	holy land	1762	LOTTER	580	48	58	Terra Sancta sive Palaestina Exhibens non Solum Regnae Vetera Iuda et Israel
mwru0535	ukraine	1750	LOTTER	580	49	57	Theatrum Belli Russorum Victoriis Illustratum sive Nova et Accurata Turcicarum et Tartaricum (copy of Seutter 1739)
mwe0377	europe austria	1761	LOTTER	785	49	59	Tirolis Comitatus Continens Episcop. Tridentinum et Brixiensem nec non Comit. Brigantinum, Feldkirch Sonneberg et Pludentin
mwe0811	europe east	1770	LOTTER	480	49	58	Transylvaniae, Moldaviae, Walachiae, Bulgariae (see also Seutter 1738)
mwit1245	italy venice	1760	LOTTER	2000	50	58	Venetia Potentissima (re-issue of Seutter 1730)
				LOTTER: See also maps listed under SEUTTER			
mwuss1322	ohio	1844	LOVEJOY	180	24	18	Cincinnati
mww0462	world	1764	LOVERINGH	300	13	22	Nieuwe Kaart des Geheelen Aardbols
mwuss1112	new york	1776	LOW	785	18	11	A View of the Present State of War, at and near New-York
mwuss0514	georgia	1810	LOW	600	20	38	Georgia from the Latest Authorities
mwuss0598	kentucky	1800	LOW	280	19	22	The State of Kentucky with the Adjoining Territories, from the Best Authorities
mwuk1686	north sea	1814	LOWERNORN	1200	94	115	Kaart over Nord-Soen

AMPG REFERENCE	REGION	DATE	MAP MAKER	PRICE (UK£)	VERT. (cm.)	HOR. (cm.)	TITLE OF MAP (Comments by the editor in brackets)
mwbp0454	poland	1757	LUBBEN	20000	42	54	Nova Illustrissimi Principatus Pomeraniae Descriptio (In 12 sheets, each 42x54cm. Border of 46 town views. Map first publ. in 1617)
mwit0580	italy north	1659	LUBIN	200	13	17	Congregatio Lombardiae Ordinis Eremitarum Sancti Augustini
mwuk0067	ireland	1659	LUBIN	200	13	17	Provincia Hiberniae ordinis Eremitarum Sancti Augustini (southern two-thirds of Ireland only)
mwit0791	italy sardinia	1659	LUBIN	500	13	17	Provincia Sardiniae ordinis Eremitarum S.ti Augustini (central part only)
mwgr0582	greece islands	1659	LUBIN	4000	13	17	Provincia Terrae Sanctae Ordinis Eremitarum Sancti Augustini (4 maps on one sheet: Corfu, Rhodes, E. Cyprus, part of Crete)
mwuss1055	new jersey	1823	LUCAS	300	29	23	(New Jersey)
mwuss0384	delaware	1840	LUCAS	2000	102	72	A Chart of the Chesapeake and Delaware Bays. Compiled and Published by Fielding Lucas, Jr., Baltimore, in 1832. Corrected to 1840
mwuss0006	alabama	1822	LUCAS	250	29	23	Alabama
mwwi0308	antigua	1823	LUCAS	225	22	29	Antigua
mwuss0054	arkansas	1822	LUCAS	500	22	28	Arkansas Ter.
mwwi0346	bahamas	1824	LUCAS	400	25	29	Bahamas
mwwi0385	barbados	1823	LUCAS	240	29	23	Barbadoes
mwat0130	atlantic bermuda	1823	LUCAS	600	23	28	Bermudas
mwca0147	canada	1823	LUCAS	200	23	29	Canada
mwat0173	atlantic canary isl.	1823	LUCAS	400	28	21	Canary Ids.
mwuss0310	connecticut	1823	LUCAS	240	24	30	Connecticut
mwwi0482	cuba	1823	LUCAS	200	30	44	Cuba
mwwi0504	curacao	1823	LUCAS	480	21	29	Curacao
mwuss0378	delaware	1816	LUCAS	400	32	26	Delaware
mwuss0380	delaware	1823	LUCAS	375	38	30	Delaware
mwwi0516	dominica	1823	LUCAS	300	30	22	Dominica
mwuss0462	florida	1823	LUCAS	400	29	24	Florida
mwuss0516	georgia	1816	LUCAS	400	26	32	Georgia
mwwi0533	grenada	1823	LUCAS	225	22	33	Grenada
mwwi0564	guadeloupe	1823	LUCAS	225	23	29	Guadaloupe &c.
mwwi0679	hispaniola	1823	LUCAS	350	30	48	Hayti or Saint Domingo
mwuss0547	illinois	1823	LUCAS	400	31	23	Illinois
mwuss0568	indiana	1823	LUCAS	280	28	22	Indiana
mwwi0754	jamaica	1823	LUCAS	150	23	30	Jamaica
mwuss0605	kentucky	1823	LUCAS	600	29	49	Kentucky
mwuss0602	kentucky	1816	LUCAS	400	26	32	Kentucky
mwuss0668	louisiana	1823	LUCAS	550	28	44	Louisiana
mwuss0663	louisiana	1816	LUCAS	400	26	32	Louisiana
mwat0245	atlantic madeira	1823	LUCAS	400	21	27	Madeira Ids.
mwuss0717	maine	1823	LUCAS	300	30	25	Maine
mwwi0810	martinique	1823	LUCAS	225	24	31	Martinico
mwuss0772	maryland	1823	LUCAS	600	29	50	Maryland
mwuss0769	maryland	1816	LUCAS	400	26	32	Maryland
mwuss0863	massachusetts	1823	LUCAS	300	29	44	Massachusetts
mwgm0285	mexico	1819	LUCAS	500	20	25	Mexico
mwuss0905	michigan	1823	LUCAS	400	22	30	Michigan Ter.
mwuss0958	mississippi	1823	LUCAS	300	29	23	Mississippi
mwuss0955	mississippi	1816	LUCAS	400	26	32	Mississippi Territory
mwuss0975	missouri	1823	LUCAS	450	28	23	Missouri
mwwi0818	nevis	1823	LUCAS	450	29	23	Nevis
mwuss1018	new hampshire	1823	LUCAS	300	30	24	New Hampshire
mwuss1056	new jersey	1823	LUCAS	240	29	23	New Jersey
mwuss1192	new york	1823	LUCAS	320	30	47	New York
mwam0635	america north	1823	LUCAS	200	25	23	North America
mwuss0260	carolinas	1823	LUCAS	300	28	48	North Carolina
mwuss0903	michigan	1818	LUCAS	960	22	29	North Western and Michigan Territories (approx. date)
mwuss0261	carolinas	1823	LUCAS	720	28	50	Nth Carolina
mwuss1281	ohio	1816	LUCAS	400	26	32	Ohio
mwuss1289	ohio	1823	LUCAS	250	28	23	Ohio
mwuss1405	pennsylvania	1823	LUCAS	300	29	45	Pennsylvania
mwuss0787	maryland	1852	LUCAS	1800	53	69	Plan of the City of Baltimore
mwwi0839	puerto rico	1823	LUCAS	450	22	31	Porto Rico
mwuss1472	rhode isl	1823	LUCAS	250	23	29	Rhode Island
mwuss0262	carolinas	1823	LUCAS	300	23	29	South Carolina
mwwi0874	st kitts	1823	LUCAS	350	22	30	St. Christophers
mwwi0885	st lucia	1823	LUCAS	400	23	28	St. Lucia
mwwi0895	st vincent	1823	LUCAS	225	23	29	St. Vincent
mwuss1492	tennessee	1823	LUCAS	720	28	46	Tennessee
mwuss0779	maryland	1836	LUCAS	600	36	52	The Tourist's Guide through the States of Maryland, Delaware and Parts of Pennsylvania & Virginia, with the Routes to their Springs, &c.
mwwi0910	trinidad & tobago	1823	LUCAS	225	25	29	Tobago

AMPG REFERENCE	REGION	DATE	MAP MAKER	PRICE (UK£)	VERT. (cm.)	HOR. (cm.)	TITLE OF MAP (Comments by the editor in brackets)
mwwi0911	trinidad & tobago	1823	LUCAS	500	24	29	Trinidad
mwam0625	america north	1821	LUCAS	1250	30	48	United States
mwuss1282	ohio	1816	LUCAS	1000	28	22	Upper Territories of the United States
mwuss1568	vermont	1816	LUCAS	400	26	32	Vermont
mwuss1571	vermont	1823	LUCAS	240	28	22	Vermont
mwwi0941	virgin isl	1823	LUCAS	600	23	31	Virgin Islands &c.
mwuss1677	virginia	1816	LUCAS	400	26	32	Virginia
mwuss1679	virginia	1823	LUCAS	400	31	38	Virginia
mwwi0171	west indies	1823	LUCAS	160	28	38	West Indies
mwsp0157	spain	1559	LUCHINI	16000	45	57	Hispaniae Descriptio
mwsw0014	switzerland	1566	LUCHINI	3600	41	58	Iodoco a Meggen Lucernati Praetorianorum Praefecto Helvetios olim Vir Clariss. nunc Suiceros Gallorum
mwit0027	italy	1562	LUCHINI	12500	41	57	Italia Nuova (re-issue of the anonymous 1554 map)
mwit0459	italy lombardy	1558	LUCHINI	7200	31	48	Lombardia
mwit0862	italy sicily	1558	LUCHINI	6000	35	46	Sicilia seu Trinacria Insula (after Gastaldi)
mwaf0376	africa east	1683	LUDOLF	800	44	54	Jobi Ludolfi, Habessinia seu Abassia, Presbyteri Johannis Regio
mwsam0248	south america argentina	1806	LUFFMAN	720	19	33	A Chart of the Rio de la Plata and a Plan of the City of Buenos-Ayres
mwuk1082	england and france	1803	LUFFMAN	1000	40	34	A Complete Representation of the Coast of England, also France and Holland, from the Texel to Brest, with the Bearings from London, and the Distance, in Miles, from Port to Port
mwam0614	america north	1819	LUFFMAN	500	23	38	A Map Sketch of the United States of America, Including the Whole of the Immense Territory of Louisiana
mwm0080	mediterranean	1816	LUFFMAN	300	18	26	A New Map of the Mediterranean Sea, and the Countries adjacent (title above map)
mwe0475	europe central	1807	LUFFMAN	450	66	43	A New Map of the Seat of War between Russia and France Comprising All the Countries from the Baltic Sea in the North, to the Mediterranean Sea in the South, and from France in the West, to Russia, Poland, Hungary, Turkey in the East
mwec0021	uk england bedfordshire	1803	LUFFMAN	150	6	6	Bedfordshire (circular map)
mwp0454	pacific north	1802	LUFFMAN	120	15	13	Behring's Strait
mwca0342	canada newfoundland	1801	LUFFMAN	120	13	17	Belleisle
mwec0051	uk england berkshire	1803	LUFFMAN	150	6	6	Berkshire (circular map)
mwg0246	berlin	1814	LUFFMAN	120	29	24	Berlin
mwuss0859	massachusetts	1813	LUFFMAN	200	18	19	Boston
mwaf0980	africa south	1800	LUFFMAN	250	15	12	Cape of Good Hope
mwsam0537	south america colombia	1802	LUFFMAN	300	19	15	Cartagena, Capital of a Province of the Same Name in Terra Firma
mwin0066	ceylon	1801	LUFFMAN	150	17	13	Ceylon
mwuss0250	carolinas	1801	LUFFMAN	300	16	13	Charleston Harbour ... One of the Most Commodious Ports in N. America
mwru0573	ukraine	1813	LUFFMAN	120	13	20	Crimea (publ. in London by Gold)
mwuss0377	delaware	1815	LUFFMAN	350	37	18	Delaware River and Bay from Philadelphia to the Atlantic Ocean
mwec0417	uk england essex	1803	LUFFMAN	140	7	7	Essex
mwbh0770	belgium holland	1799	LUFFMAN	400	37	29	Grand Expedition. A Map of the Texel and Vlieter Roads with the Country of Holland as Far South as the Hague: Intended to Illustrate the Operations of the Grand Expedition
mwca0458	canada nova scotia	1815	LUFFMAN	300	21	18	Hallifax
mwec0588	uk england huntingdonshire	1803	LUFFMAN	150	6	6	Huntingdonshire (circular map)
mwsc0515	scandinavia iceland	1814	LUFFMAN	280	24	29	Iceland
mwuk0255	ireland	1814	LUFFMAN	120	24	29	Ireland
mwec0755	uk england lincolnshire	1803	LUFFMAN	150	6	6	Lincolnshire (circular map)
mwit0521	italy lombardy	1813	LUFFMAN	120	17	20	Mantua
mwbh0782	belgium holland	1810	LUFFMAN	250	23	19	Map of the Island of Walcheren with the Fortifications &c.
mwec0791	uk england middlesex	1803	LUFFMAN	120	7	7	Middlesex
mwec0869	uk england northamptonshire	1803	LUFFMAN	150	6	6	Northamptonshire (circular map)
mwec0893	uk england northumberland	1803	LUFFMAN	150	6	6	Northumberland (ciruular map)
mwec0923	uk england nottinghamshire	1803	LUFFMAN	150	6	6	Nottinghamshire (circular map)
mwuss0714	maine	1815	LUFFMAN	150	21	18	Penobscot
mwgm0437	panama	1801	LUFFMAN	200	17	12	Porto Bello
mwuss1468	rhode isl	1815	LUFFMAN	200	23	20	Rhode Island and Newport Harbor
mwaf0979	africa south	1800	LUFFMAN	120	16	12	Saldanha Bay
mwwi0669	hispaniola	1801	LUFFMAN	300	17	13	San Domingo
mwru0333	russia	1812	LUFFMAN	120	20	24	St. Petersburg
mwec1116	uk england suffolk	1803	LUFFMAN	180	6	6	Suffolk (circular map)

AMPG REFERENCE	REGION	DATE	MAP MAKER	PRICE (UK£)	VERT. (cm.)	HOR. (cm.)	TITLE OF MAP (Comments by the editor in brackets)
mwuss0376	delaware	1813	LUFFMAN	300	23	20	The Coast of America, from Sandy Hook, S.S.West, to the Capes of Virginia, Including the Delaware & Chesapeake Bays
mwuk1517	uk english channel (all)	1801	LUFFMAN	200	8	10	The Roads from London to Paris
mwec1205	uk england warwickshire	1803	LUFFMAN	180	6	6	Warwickshire (circular map)
mwec1349	uk england yorkshire	1803	LUFFMAN	180	6	6	Yorkshire N. Riding (circular map)
mww0033	world	1530	LUFFT	2500	13	18	(Woodblock illustration made for Martin Luther's book on Daniel. Semi-Ptolemaic.)
mwsc0647a	scandinavia norway	1830	LUND	2000	54	39	Veikart over Norge. Udarbeidet efter Foranstaltning af den Kogl: Norske Regjerings Justits og Politie Departement
mwuss0119a	california	1847	LUNDY	550	22	26	California, Texas, Mexico, and part of the United States
mwit0398a	italy lazio	1679	LUPARDI	850	41	53	Le Paludi Pontine
mwm0212	mediterranean malta	1692	LUYTS	450	20	31	Les Isles de Malte, Goze &c.
mwjk0052	japan	1692	LUYTS	650	19	25	Les Isles du Japon, par le Sr. Sanson d'Abbeville Geogr. du Roy
mwas0759	asia south east philippines	1692	LUYTS	450	20	25	Les Isles Philippines / Islas de los Ladrones ou Isle des Larrons
mww0246	world	1692	LUYTS	800	21	31	Mappe-Monde ou Carte Generale du Globe Terrestre, Representee en Deux Plan-Hemispheres
mwp0075	australia	1825	LYCETT	400	34	44	A Map of New South Wales from the Best Authorities. And from the Latest Discoveries. 1825
mwp0076	australia	1825	LYCETT	300	33	22	A New Map of Van Diemens Land, from the Best Authorities, and from the Most Recent Surveys
mwam0666	america north	1830	LYELL	360	39	50	Geological Map of the United States Canada &c. Compiled from the State Surveys of the U.S. and Other Sources
mwam0663	america north	1829	MAAS	480	41	48	United States of North America. Published for the Jackson Wreath
mwin0371	india	1845	MACDONALD	235	41	32	Hindoostan
mwjk0146	japan	1840	MACDONALD	280	32	39	Japan
mwit0946	italy sicily	1748	MACHENBAUER	300	17	24	Das Konigreich Sicilien
mww0404a	world	1748	MACHENBAUER	400	17	23	Mappemonde Planisphere ou Carte Generale Monde
mwuk0307	irish sea	1775	MACKENZIE	960	116	95	A General Chart of the Irish Channel
mwuk1552	bristol channel	1775	MACKENZIE	900	71	95	A General Chart of the St. George and Bristol Channels
mwca0130	canada	1801	MACKENZIE	1500	46	79	A Map of America, between Latitudes 40 and 70 North, and Longitudes 45 and 180 West, Exhibiting Mackenzie's Track from Montreal to Fort Chipewyan & from thence to the North Sea in 1789, & to the West Pacific Ocean in 1793
mwca0665	canada west	1801	MACKENZIE	800	57	61	A Map of Mackenzie's Track, from Fort Chipewyan to the Pacific Ocean in 1793
mwuk0309a	irish sea	1800	MACKENZIE	650	77	131	A New Mercator`s Chart of the Coast of Ireland from Drogheda to the Skerries
mwuk1853	wales	1775	MACKENZIE	600	95	103	Caernarvon Bay in Wales
mwuk1854	wales	1775	MACKENZIE	400	69	91	Carmarthen Bay on the South Coast of Wales
mwuk0522	scotland	1775	MACKENZIE	400	107	104	Part of Long Island from South-Uist to Harris
mwuk0494	scotland	1750	MACKENZIE	1500	48	77	Pomona or Main-Land with the Rocks, Tides, Soundings &c. Surveyed & Navigated by Murdoch Mackenzie (first sea charts produced by triangulation - mwuk0485-0489)
mwuk0526	scotland	1776	MACKENZIE	500	67	100	The Channel between Sky I. and the Lewis
mwec0147	uk england cheshire	1776	MACKENZIE	800	85	103	The Coast Adjacent to Chester and Liverpool from Orme's Head to Formby Point
mwuk0527	scotland	1776	MACKENZIE	400	76	126	The Firth of Clyde in Scotland
mwuk1610	isle of man	1775	MACKENZIE	650	70	99	The Isle of Man
mwuk0523	scotland	1775	MACKENZIE	400	85	103	The Lewis, or North Part of Long Island
mwuk0524	scotland	1775	MACKENZIE	800	72	133	The Mouth of Solway Firth
mwuk0528	scotland	1776	MACKENZIE	500	72	150	The Mouth of the Clyde and Loch Fyne
mwuk0205	ireland	1775	MACKENZIE	650	74	127	The North Coast of Ireland from Malin Head to Rathlin Island
mwuk1855	wales	1775	MACKENZIE	400	67	100	The North Coast of Wales from Holy-Head Island to Orme's Head
mwuk0495	scotland	1750	MACKENZIE	1500	64	50	The North East Coast of Orkney with the Rocks Tides Soundings etc. Surveyed and Navigated by Murdoch Mackenzie
mwuk1856	wales	1775	MACKENZIE	400	90	103	The North Part of Cardigan Bay in Wales
mwuk0496	scotland	1750	MACKENZIE	1500	46	50	The North West Coast of Orkney Surveyed & Navigated by Murdoch Mackenzie
mwec0693	uk england lancashire	1775	MACKENZIE	400	71	102	The North-West Coast of England from Walney Island to St. Bee's Head
mwuk0529	scotland	1776	MACKENZIE	400	103	96	The North-West Coast of Scotland, from Rurea in Ross Shire, to Cape Wrath in Strathnaver
mwuk1857	wales	1775	MACKENZIE	800	50	142	The South Coast of Cardigan Bay
mwuk0497	scotland	1750	MACKENZIE	1500	61	56	The South East Coast of Lewis
mwuk0498	scotland	1750	MACKENZIE	1500	60	66	The South Isles of Orkney with the Rocks, Tides, Soundings
mwuk0525	scotland	1775	MACKENZIE	400	72	105	The South Part of Long-Island, from Bara Head to Benbecula Island

AMPG REFERENCE	REGION	DATE	MAP MAKER	PRICE (UK£)	VERT. (cm.)	HOR. (cm.)	TITLE OF MAP (Comments by the editor in brackets)
mwuk1858	wales	1775	MACKENZIE	600	74	103	The South-West Coast of Wales from Tenby to Cardigan
mwuk0530	scotland	1776	MACKENZIE	400	105	100	The West Coast of Scotland from Ardnamurchan to the Island Sky
mwam0718	america north	1838	MACLURE MACDONALD	180	27	21	North America
mwca0158	canada	1829	MACPHERSON	140	19	25	British Possessions in North America
mwam0664	america north	1829	MACPHERSON	140	24	19	North America
mwgm0288	mexico	1820	MACPHERSON	160	20	25	Spanish Dominions in N. America
mwam0584	america north	1811	MACPHERSON	140	20	25	United States of North America
mwam0088	america continent	1685	MACQUART	180	18	14	L'Amerique Suivant les Dernieres Observations de l'Academie Royale des Sciences
mwam1195	america north (east)	1826	MACREDIE	200	52	43	United States
mww0008	world	1483	MACROBIUS	20000	14		(Circular map of the world according to Macrobius, who lived in the 5th century AD. Several reprints incl. a reversed white/black version were printed until c1640)
mwuss1675	virginia	1807	MADISON	48000	117	180	A Map of Virginia Formed from Actual Surveys, and the Latest as Well as Most Accurate Observations, by James Madison, D.D. President of Wm. & Mary College (9 sheet map. 1st state. Inset of Ohio, sometimes sold separately).
mww0076	world	1589	MAFFEI	4800	26	48	Indiarum Orientalium Occidentaliumque Descriptio, Pet. Maffei Historiae Harum Verissimae, Dedicata (based on Ortelius)
mwca0071	canada	1755	MAGAZINE OF MAG.	200	24	22	A Map of Hudsons Bay and Parts Adjacent, from the Latest Surveys and Best Authorities
mwam0960	america north (east)	1750	MAGAZINE OF MAG.	400	26	32	A Map of the British Empire in America, from the Head of Hudsons Bay to the Southern Bounds of Georgia, with the Intervention of Canada
mwca0366	canada nova scotia	1750	MAGAZINE OF MAG.	180	19	28	A Plan of Annapolis Royal.
mwca0507	canada quebec	1755	MAGAZINE OF MAG.	220	19	26	Plan of ye Town of Quebec
mwit0698	italy piedmont	1850	MAGGI	350	71	55	Carta Corografica delle Divisioni di Torino e di Aosta
mwam0738	america north	1840	MAGGI	160	33	28	Stati Uniti d'America Ridotta della Carta Pubblicata a Nuova York
mwaf0470	africa egypt etc	1608	MAGINI	140	13	17	Aegyptus
mwaf0024	africa	1596	MAGINI	250	14	18	Africa
mwas0016	asia continent	1597	MAGINI	280	13	17	Asia
mwbh0132	belgium holland	1596	MAGINI	200	14	18	Belgium, seu Germania Inferior
mwuk0681	uk	1597	MAGINI	300	13	18	Britanicae Insulae
mwit0999	italy south	1620	MAGINI	480	37	45	Calabria Citra, olim Magna Graecia
mwgr0361	greece crete	1596	MAGINI	240	13	18	Candia Insula olim Creta
mwit1000	italy south	1620	MAGINI	400	37	45	Capitanata Olim Mesapiae
mwit0259c	italy abruzzo	1620	MAGINI	400	37	45	Contado di Molise, & Principato Ultra
mwf0466	france corsica	1620	MAGINI	1000	35	45	Corsica Isola, olim Cyrnus
mwgr0465	greece cyprus	1596	MAGINI	500	13	17	Cypri Insula
mwit1170	italy veneto	1620	MAGINI	550	30	47	Dominio Veneto nell'Italia
mwit0573	italy north	1620	MAGINI	400	37	45	Ducato di Ferrara
mwit0574	italy north	1620	MAGINI	480	35	48	Ducato di Mantova All'ill'mo et Cec'mo Sig. Il Sig'r D Vicenzo Prencipe Gonzaga Fabio di Gio: Ant'o Magini
mwit0342	italy emilia-romagna	1620	MAGINI	400	33	44	Ducato di Parma et di Piacenza
mwit0327	italy elba	1598	MAGINI	350	17	23	Elba Isola olim Ilua
mwe0019	europe	1596	MAGINI	200	13	18	Europa
mwit0563	italy north	1596	MAGINI	140	13	18	Forum Iulii, et Histria
mwf0035	france	1597	MAGINI	200	13	16	Galliae Regnum
mwg0031	germany	1597	MAGINI	180	13	16	Germania
mwgr0044	greece	1597	MAGINI	240	13	16	Graecia
mwsw0029	switzerland	1597	MAGINI	240	13	16	Helvetia
mwsp0168	spain	1596	MAGINI	240	14	18	Hispaniae Regnum
mwe0750	europe east	1597	MAGINI	200	14	18	Hungaria et Transilvania
mwas0368	asia south east	1597	MAGINI	375	13	17	India Orientalis
mwit0275	italy campagna	1620	MAGINI	800	37	45	Ischia Isola, olim Aenaria
mwit0781a	italy sardinia	1620	MAGINI	650	34	44	Isola di Sardegna
mwas0366a	asia south east	1596	MAGINI	160	11	14	Isole Molucche (copy of Porcacchi 1576)
mwit0046	italy	1596	MAGINI	150	13	17	Italia
mwit0069	italy	1620	MAGINI	720	34	48	Italia antica di Cl. Tolomeo
mwit0061	italy	1608	MAGINI		89	112	Italia Nuova
mwit0390	italy lazio	1596	MAGINI	140	14	18	Latium, seu Territorium Romae
mwit0411a	italy liguria	1620	MAGINI	720	35	50	Liguria ò Stato della Repubblica di Genova
mwit0068	italy	1617	MAGINI		86	107	L'Italia nuovamente piu perfetta
mwit0564	italy north	1596	MAGINI	140	14	18	Marca Anconae
mwit0550	italy marches	1598	MAGINI	140	13	16	Marca Anconae, olim Picenum
mwru0029	russia	1608	MAGINI	140	13	17	Moscoviae Imperium
mwme0932	turkey etc	1598	MAGINI	240	13	17	Natolia olim Asia Minor
mwit0993	italy south	1596	MAGINI	140	13	18	Neapolitanum Regnum
mwit0067	italy	1616	MAGINI		109	125	Nova Descrittione d'Italia di Gioann. Antonio Magino. (title above map)
mww0100	world	1598	MAGINI	1000	18	25	Orbis Terrae Compendiosa Descriptio ex ... Rumold Mercator ... Forma Hieronymo Porro Redacta

AMPG REFERENCE	REGION	DATE	MAP MAKER	PRICE (UK£)	VERT. (cm.)	HOR. (cm.)	TITLE OF MAP (Comments by the editor in brackets)
mwme0056	holy land	1596	MAGINI	240	13	17	Palestinae sive Totius Terrae Promissionis
mwit0371a	italy friuli	1598	MAGINI	3500	36	46	Patria del Friuli olim Forum Iulii
mwit0394	italy lazio	1620	MAGINI	280	36	47	Patrimonio di S. Pietro, Sabina et Ducato di Castro
mwit0413	italy liguria	1608	MAGINI	140	13	17	Pedemontium, Monsferratus et Liguria
mwme0762	persia etc	1596	MAGINI	240	18	25	Persiae Regnum sive Sophorum Imperium
mwit0635	italy piedmont	1620	MAGINI	600	36	46	Piemonte, et Monferrato
mwit1171	italy veneto	1620	MAGINI	480	34	47	Polesino di Rovigo
mwbp0206	poland	1597	MAGINI	240	13	17	Poloniae Regnum
mwsp0014	portugal	1598	MAGINI	240	13	18	Portugalliae Regnum
mwit0880	italy sicily	1620	MAGINI	1100	38	48	Regno di Sicilia
mwit0414	italy liguria	1620	MAGINI	720	39	47	Riviera de Genova da Ponente / Riviera de Genova di Levante (2 maps)
mwit0856	italy sardinia and sicily	1596	MAGINI	300	14	18	Sardinia et Sicilia
mwsc0035	scandinavia	1596	MAGINI	350	14	18	Scandia, sive Regiones Septentrionales
mwit0296	italy central	1620	MAGINI	600	36	42	Stato della la Chiesa
mwru0417	russia tartary	1596	MAGINI	550	13	18	Tartariae Imperium
mwit1002	italy south	1620	MAGINI	400	37	45	Terra di Bari Et Basilicata
mwit1151	italy umbria	1620	MAGINI	400	35	39	Territorio di Orvieto
mwit0471	italy lombardy	1620	MAGINI	480	33	45	Territorio di Pavia, Lodi, Novarra, Tortona, Alessandria et Altri Vicini dello Stato di Milano
mwme0541	arabia etc	1598	MAGINI	350	13	18	Turcici Imperii Descriptio
mwit1095	italy tuscany	1598	MAGINI	350	13	17	Tuscia
mww0088a	world	1596	MAGINI	600	14	18	Universi Orbis Descriptio (reduced version of Ortelius)
mww0088b	world	1596	MAGINI	600	13	17	Universi Orbis Descriptio ad Usum Navigantium (reduced version of Mercator 1569)
mwit1139	italy florence	1783	MAGNELLI	12000	137	150	Pianta della Citta di Firenza Rileveta Esattamente nell Anno 1783
mwsc0020	scandinavia	1567	MAGNUS	9000	36	52	(Untitled 'trapezoid-shaped' map)
mwuss1265	new york	1850	MAGNUS	960	46	28	Map of the City of New-York, with Part of Brooklyn and Williamsburg
mwsc0012	scandinavia	1555	MAGNUS	4000	26	17	Regnorum Aquilonarum descriptio (same as 1554 woodblock map, but different title above the map)
mwsc0011	scandinavia	1554	MAGNUS	4500	26	17	Scandianae Insulae Index
mwf0936a	france paris	1849	MAILLARD	1000	75	95	Paris Illustre et ses Fortifications
mww0667	world	1820	MAILLART	200	15	27	Mappe-Monde Dessinee d'apres Toutes les Decouvertes qui ont ete Faites jusqu'en 1800
mwf0564	france corsica	1844	MAINA	480	54	36	Carta Antica dell'Isola di Corsica
mwf0555	france corsica	1828	MAINA & STANGHI	480	53	35	Carta Moderna dell'Isola di Corsica
mwe1042	europe romania	1596	MAIR	550	20	25	(Battle of Lipova in Temesvar)
mwe0693	europe dalmatia	1788	MAIRE	400	34	43	Carte de la Partie d'Albanie occupee par la Bacha de Scutari
mwit0225	italy	1810	MAIRE	800	60	92	Carte d'Italie Divisee en ses Divers Etats, avec les Plans des Principales Villes (6 city insets)
mwe1173	europe south east	1813	MAIRE	800	75	110	Carte Itineraire et Politique d'Europe d'apres les Dernies Traites de Paix, avec les Plans des Principales Villes d'Europe
mwf0916	france paris	1826	MAIRE	800	67	98	Carte Topographique des Environs de Paris
mwru0567	ukraine	1788	MAIRE	300	22	63	Confluent et Embouchure du Bog et du Dnieper pour Servir de Renseignmens a la Carte des Limites des Trois Empires ou Theatre de la Guerre de 1787 et 88 entre la Russie et les Turcs. 1788
mwe1162	europe south east	1788	MAIRE	2500	67	149	Geographische General Karte der Granzen zwischen denen Dreyen Kaiserthumern und ihren … Veranderungen vom Jahr 1718 bis Heutigen Tags oder Kriegs Schauplatz Gegenwartigen Kriegs
mwme1034	turkey etc	1788	MAIRE	360	29	58	Helespont ou Detroit des Dardanelles
mwit0316	italy central	1755	MAIRE	2000	119	65	Nuova Carta Geograifica dello Stato Ecclesiastico (illustration: top to the left)
mwme1035	turkey etc	1788	MAIRE	800	27	59	Plan de Constantinople et du Bosphore
mwf0912	france paris	1816	MAIRE	800	65	92	Plan de la Ville de Paris, Dedie et Presente au Roi
mwru0566	ukraine	1788	MAIRE	450	29	42	Post Karte von der Halbinsel Taurien oder Krim
mwe0432b	europe austria vienna	1788	MAIRE	2000	84	105	Topohydrographische Karte der Stadt Wien und ihren umligenden Gegenden
mwuk1174a	england london	1739	MAITLAND	350	23	34	A Plan of the City and Liberties of London after the Dreadful Conflagration in the year 1666 … (map by E. Bowen)
mwuk1173	england london	1738	MAITLAND	500	31	48	A View of London about the Year 1560 (reduced version of the Agar plan of 1633)
mwe1033	europe rhine	1794	MALAFISIDZ	2000	37	105	Karte des Ganzen Rheinstroms von seinem Doppelten Ursprung bis zu seinen Ausfluss (copy of Von Sandrart's map of 1688)
mwas0808	asia south east philippines	1808	MALASPINA	200	21	18	Baie de Manille
mwbp0058	baltic sea (east)	1797	MALHAM	120	23	19	A Correct Chart of the Baltic Sea
mwf0300	france bay of biscay	1797	MALHAM	120	24	19	A Correct Chart of the Bay of Biscay
mwsp0120	portugal	1797	MALHAM	120	24	18	A Correct Chart of the Coast of Portugal
mwin0317	india	1797	MALHAM	120	18	23	A Correct Chart of the Coasts of Hindostan

AMPG REFERENCE	REGION	DATE	MAP MAKER	PRICE (UK£)	VERT. (cm.)	HOR. (cm.)	TITLE OF MAP (Comments by the editor in brackets)
mwsam0121	south america	1797	MALHAM	120	23	19	A Correct Chart of the Coasts of South America from the Equator to Cape Horn
mwuk1515	uk english channel (all)	1797	MALHAM	120	19	31	A Correct Chart of the English Channel
mwuk1679	north sea	1797	MALHAM	120	19	23	A Correct Chart of the German Ocean
mwin0445	indian ocean	1797	MALHAM	120	18	23	A Correct Chart of the Indian Ocean
mwuk0309	irish sea	1797	MALHAM	120	24	19	A Correct Chart of the Irish Sea, with St. Georges Channel
mwm0075	mediterranean	1797	MALHAM	240	18	39	A Correct Chart of the Mediterranean Sea
mwuk1680	north sea	1797	MALHAM	120	23	19	A Correct Chart of the North Sea
mwaf0976	africa south	1797	MALHAM	120	19	23	A Correct Chart of the Southern Coasts of Africa, from the Equator to the Cape of Good Hope
mwaf1240	africa west	1797	MALHAM	120	23	19	A Correct Chart of the West Coast of Africa
mwuss0035	alaska	1797	MALHAM	480	19	23	A Correct Chart of the West Coast of North America from Bhering's Straits to Nootka Sound
mwam1336	america north (west)	1797	MALHAM	240	18	23	A Correct Chart of the West Coast of North America from Bhering's Straits to Nootka Sound
mwwi0142	west indies	1797	MALHAM	180	16	23	A Correct Chart of the West India Islands
mwas0263	asia (from turkey to india)	1683	MALLET	150	14	10	(Untitled map, incl. Australia)
mwaf0379	africa east	1683	MALLET	180	14	10	Abissinie
mwaf0091	africa	1683	MALLET	235	15	10	Afrique Moderne
mwaf0485	africa egypt etc	1683	MALLET	100	15	10	Alexandrie
mwg0080	germany	1685	MALLET	140	15	11	Allemagne en General
mwsam0031	south america	1685	MALLET	180	15	10	Amerique Meridionale
mwam0328	america north	1683	MALLET	220	15	11	Amerique Septentrionale
mwbh0438	belgium holland	1685	MALLET	140	14	10	Amsterdam (view)
mwuk0085a	ireland	1683	MALLET	200	15	10	Ancienne Isle d'Hibernie
mwin0028a	ceylon	1683	MALLET	200	15	10	Ancienne Isle Taprobane (shown above far left)
mwme0467	jerusalem	1684	MALLET	150	15	10	Ancienne Jerusalem
mwc0068a	china	1683	MALLET	120	15	10	Ancienne Region des Sines (illustrated above left)
mwuk0742	uk	1683	MALLET	180	15	10	Anciennes Isles Britanniques
mwat0086	atlantic azores	1685	MALLET	180	14	9	Angra
mwme0569	arabia etc	1683	MALLET	280	15	11	Arabie
mwas0070	asia continent	1683	MALLET	200	15	11	Asie Ancienne (illustrated right, above)
mwas0069	asia continent	1683	MALLET	240	15	11	Asie Moderne (illustrated left)
mwme0737	iraq etc	1683	MALLET	150	15	10	Bagdet
mwsw0089	switzerland	1685	MALLET	140	14	10	Basle (view)
mwas0634	asia south east java	1683	MALLET	100	14	11	Batavia
mwsc0588	scandinavia norway	1683	MALLET	180	14	10	Bergen (view)
mwsam0323	south america brazil	1683	MALLET	140	15	10	Bresil
mwf0322	france brittany	1683	MALLET	150	15	11	Bretagne
mwbh0439	belgium holland	1685	MALLET	140	14	10	Bruxelles (view)
mwsp0468	spain regions	1685	MALLET	100	15	10	Cadis
mwaf0486	africa egypt etc	1683	MALLET	140	15	10	Caire
mwc0067	china	1683	MALLET	240	14	9	Peking (view)
mwca0033	canada	1683	MALLET	280	14	10	Canada ou Nouvelle France
mwaf0878	africa south	1683	MALLET	240	15	10	Cap de Bone Esperance
mww0221	world	1683	MALLET	200	14	10	Carte du Monde de Marc Paul / Carte du Monde de Jacques Castaldo / Carte du Monde de Miguel Lopez
mww0222	world	1683	MALLET	150	14	10	Carte ou Planisphere General du Monde / Globe Terrestre
mwsam0504	south america colombia	1683	MALLET	120	15	11	Castille Neuve ou Castille D'Or
mwe0333	europe austria	1685	MALLET	140	14	11	Cercle d'Autriche
mwg0617	saxony	1685	MALLET	140	15	11	Cercle de Basse Saxe
mwin0027	ceylon	1683	MALLET	200	14	10	Columbo / Gale (2 views)
mwaf1143	africa west	1683	MALLET	140	14	11	Congo
mwme0966	turkey etc	1683	MALLET	180	15	10	Constantinople (view)
mwaa0012	antarctic	1683	MALLET	240	15	11	Continent Meridional Austral ou Antarctique
mwaa0098	arctic	1683	MALLET	150	14	10	Continent Septentrional
mwsc0308	scandinavia denmark	1683	MALLET	200	15	10	Copenhagen
mwaf0380	africa east	1683	MALLET	180	14	10	Costes d'Abex d'Aian et de Zanguebar
mwbp0308	poland	1683	MALLET	150	14	10	Cracovie (view)
mwme0790	persia etc	1683	MALLET	140	15	10	Curdistan, Diarbeck &c. 1682
mwsam0748	south america peru	1683	MALLET	140	15	10	Cusco
mwgr0602	greece islands	1685	MALLET	100	15	11	D'Amorgo et de Zinara
mwuk0424	scotland	1683	MALLET	140	14	10	De Fero, de Scheland, Orknay et Hebrides
mwat0260	atlantic north	1683	MALLET	150	15	10	Decowerte de la Groenlande
mwru0089	russia	1683	MALLET	140	15	10	Detroit de Waigats
mwas0620	asia south east cocos isl	1686	MALLET	75	15	11	Die Insel Cocos
mwwi0414	cuba	1685	MALLET	240	14	10	Die Stadt Havana (view)
mwuss1618	virginia	1686	MALLET	150	15	11	Die Stadt Pamejok
mwsam0676	south america magellan	1683	MALLET	200	15	10	Dt. de Magellan
mwuk0085	ireland	1683	MALLET	200	16	11	Dublin
mwuk0425	scotland	1683	MALLET	200	16	11	Edimbourg
mwme0195	holy land	1683	MALLET	150	15	10	Empire des Assyriens / Assyrie Chaldee et Mesopotamie selon les Anciens
mww0223	world	1683	MALLET	100	15	10	Equateur / Carte Generale du Monde (various spheres on one sheet)
mwme0718	caucasus	1683	MALLET	180	15	10	Erivan

AMPG REFERENCE	REGION	DATE	MAP MAKER	PRICE (UK£)	VERT. (cm.)	HOR. (cm.)	TITLE OF MAP (Comments by the editor in brackets)
mwuk0426	scotland	1683	MALLET	140	15	10	Escosse
mwit1186	italy veneto	1683	MALLET	140	15	11	Estat de la Republique de Venise
mwit1110	italy tuscany	1683	MALLET	200	15	11	Estat Ecclesiastique et Duche de Toscane
mwe0092	europe	1683	MALLET	200	20	15	Europe
mwuss0400	florida	1683	MALLET	350	15	11	Floride
mwme0719	caucasus	1683	MALLET	180	14	10	Georgie Armenie &c.
mww0224	world	1683	MALLET	150	14	10	Globe Terrestre
mwin0399	india goa	1683	MALLET	150	14	11	Goa
mwgr0097	greece	1683	MALLET	180	15	10	Grece Particuliere (Morea etc)
mwsc0461	scandinavia greenland	1683	MALLET	150	15	10	Groenlande
mwwi0316	bahamas	1685	MALLET	200	15	10	Guanahani ou de St. Salvador (Watling isl., the first island discovered by Christopher Columbus)
mwaf1142	africa west	1683	MALLET	140	14	10	Guinee
mwuk0941a	england	1683	MALLET	140	15	10	Heptarchie des Saxons (illustrated above)
mwe0894	europe hungary	1683	MALLET	120	15	11	Hongrie
mwat0327	atlantic st helena	1683	MALLET	180	15	10	I de St Helene
mwwi0585	hispaniola	1683	MALLET	250	15	10	I d'Hispaniola et P. Rico
mwf0473	france corsica	1683	MALLET	350	14	10	I. de Corse
mwas0623	asia south east futuna	1683	MALLET	75	15	11	Ie. d'Horn
mwjk0046	japan	1683	MALLET	200	15	10	Iedo (view of Tokyo)
mwme0466	jerusalem	1683	MALLET	150	15	11	Ierusalem Moderne
mwaf0569	africa islands bourbon	1683	MALLET	200	14	10	Ile Bourbon
mwin0128	india	1683	MALLET	140	14	10	Inde
mwuk1605a	isle of man	1683	MALLET	150	16	11	Is de Man et D'Anglese
mwgr0596	greece islands	1683	MALLET	100	15	10	Is de Nio, Nampho Sta. Erini
mwgr0597	greece islands	1683	MALLET	100	15	10	Is de Pelagnisi, Dromi, etc.
mwwi0410	cuba	1683	MALLET	200	15	11	Is. de Cuba et de Iamaica
mwuk1575	channel islands	1683	MALLET	200	15	10	Is. de Iersey et de Garnesey
mwuk1562	england islands	1686	MALLET	150	15	11	Is. de Man et d'Anglesey
mwgr0598	greece islands	1683	MALLET	100	15	10	Is. de Nicaria et Patmos
mwat0069	atlantic ascension isl.	1683	MALLET	140	15	10	Isle Ascension
mwuk0086	ireland	1683	MALLET	200	15	11	Isle D Irlande
mwuk1096a	uk	1686	MALLET	180	15	10	Isle d'Albion
mwsam0587	south america guyana	1683	MALLET	140	14	10	Isle de Cayenne
mwin0028	ceylon	1683	MALLET	200	15	10	Isle de Ceylan
mwgr0311	greece corfu	1683	MALLET	180	15	10	Isle de Corfou
mwgr0411	greece crete	1683	MALLET	180	14	10	Isle de Crete
mwaf0592	africa islands madagascar	1683	MALLET	180	15	10	Isle de Madagascar Dite de St Laurens ou Lisle Daufine
mwm0205	mediterranean malta	1684	MALLET	250	14	10	Isle de Malthe
mwgr0526	greece rhodes	1683	MALLET	150	15	10	Isle de Rhodes
mwgr0603	greece islands	1685	MALLET	100	15	11	Isle de Scarpanto
mwit0901	italy sicily	1683	MALLET	180	14	10	Isle de Sicile
mwgr0607	greece islands	1686	MALLET	100	15	10	Isle de Stalimene
mwgr0604	greece islands	1685	MALLET	100	15	11	Isle de Stampalia
mwca0284	canada newfoundland	1683	MALLET	240	14	10	Isle de Terre Neuve
mwuk1619	isle of wight	1686	MALLET	120	15	11	Isle de Wigh
mwsc0497	scandinavia iceland	1683	MALLET	280	16	11	Isle d'Islande
mwas0718	asia south east moluccas	1683	MALLET	200	14	10	Isle Molucques
mwgr0599	greece islands	1683	MALLET	100	15	10	Isle Ste. Maure, Cefalonie, Zante
mwat0085	atlantic azores	1683	MALLET	180	20	15	Isles Acores
mwuk0742a	uk	1683	MALLET	180	15	10	Isles Britanniques
mwat0152	atlantic canary isl.	1683	MALLET	150	15	11	Isles Canaries
mwwi0237	west indies (east)	1683	MALLET	250	15	10	Isles Caribes
mwgr0486	greece cyprus	1683	MALLET	300	14	10	Isles de Cypre
mwas0583	asia south east borneo	1683	MALLET	200	14	11	Isles de la Sonde vers l'Occident
mwas0609	asia south east celebes	1683	MALLET	200	14	11	Isles de la Sonde vers l'Orient
mwp0482	pacific solomon isl	1683	MALLET	250	15	10	Isles de Salomon (shown with a named New Zealand)
mwat0153	atlantic canary isl.	1683	MALLET	150	15	11	Isles des Canaries et du Cap Verd
mwp0360	pacific marianas	1683	MALLET	120	15	10	Isles des Larrons
mwin0461	indian ocean maldives	1683	MALLET	100	14	11	Isles des Maldives
mwat0192	atlantic cape verde isl.	1683	MALLET	140	15	10	Isles du Cap-Verd
mwjk0048	japan	1683	MALLET	250	14	10	Isles du Japon
mwwi0315	bahamas	1683	MALLET	240	15	11	Isles Lucayes
mwas0817	asia south east siam	1683	MALLET	140	17	13	Iudia ou Sian (view of Ayuthaya)
mwc0068	china	1683	MALLET	200	15	10	La Chine
mwme0569a	arabia etc	1683	MALLET	280	15	11	La Mecque
mwwi0586	hispaniola	1683	MALLET	200	15	11	Le Plan ... de la Ville de San-Domingo ou de St Dominique
mwaf0783a	africa north morocco	1683	MALLET	80	15	10	L'Empire du Cherif de Fez Maroc Sus &c (shown below left)
mwgr0600	greece islands	1683	MALLET	180	15	10	Les Isles de l'Archipel quisont de l'Europe
mwas0757	asia south east philippines	1684	MALLET	240	14	10	Les Isles Philippines 1684
mwuk1125	england london	1684	MALLET	200	14	10	Londres (view)
mwgr0098	greece	1683	MALLET	120	15	11	Macedoine Thessalie Epire
mwsp0340	spain madrid	1683	MALLET	150	14	10	Madrid
mwm0203	mediterranean malta	1683	MALLET	200	14	10	Malte (view of Valetta)
mwas0756	asia south east philippines	1683	MALLET	300	14	10	Manille (view of Manilla)
mwme0569b	arabia etc	1683	MALLET	180	15	11	Medine

AMPG REFERENCE	REGION	DATE	MAP MAKER	PRICE (UK£)	VERT. (cm.)	HOR. (cm.)	TITLE OF MAP (Comments by the editor in brackets)
mwm0020	mediterranean	1683	MALLET	120	15	10	Mer Mediterranee selon les Anciens / Partie Orientale de la Mer Mediterranee / Partie Occidentale de la Mer Mediterranee (3 maps on one sheet)
mwgm0179	mexico	1683	MALLET	150	14	10	Mexique (view of Mexico City)
mwgm0180	mexico	1683	MALLET	350	15	10	Mexique ou Nouvelle Espagne
mwjk0049	japan	1683	MALLET	150	15	10	Miaco (view of Kyoto)
mwaf0877	africa south	1683	MALLET	180	15	10	Monomotapa et la Cafrerie
mwru0384a	russia	1683	MALLET	240	14	10	Moscov (view)
mwru0091	russia	1683	MALLET	140	15	11	Moscovie
mwaf1043	africa south east	1683	MALLET	140	14	11	Mozambique
mwc0069	china	1683	MALLET	120	15	10	Nanking
mwme0964	turkey etc	1683	MALLET	120	14	10	Natolie
mwgr0605	greece islands	1685	MALLET	100	15	11	Nisaro et de Piscopia
mwsc0589	scandinavia norway	1683	MALLET	180	14	10	Norwege
mwam0086a	america continent	1683	MALLET	200	14	10	Nouveau Continent Avec plusieurs Isles et Mers
mwam0086	america continent	1683	MALLET	200	14	10	Nouveau Continent ou Amerique
mwuss0075	california	1683	MALLET	400	15	10	Nouveau Mexique et Californie
mwp0378	pacific new guinea	1683	MALLET	280	15	12	Nouvelle Guinee et Carpentarie
mwaf0377	africa east	1683	MALLET	140	14	10	Nubie
mwsam0221	south america argentina	1683	MALLET	140	15	10	Pais qui sont aux Environs de la Riviere de la Plata et du Pais de Patagonia
mwit0902	italy sicily	1683	MALLET	140	14	10	Palerme (view)
mwf0831	france paris	1683	MALLET	180	15	11	Paris (view)
mwin0129	india	1683	MALLET	140	14	10	Partie de la Terre Ferme de l'Inde ou l'Empire du Mogol
mwbh0434	belgium holland	1683	MALLET	140	16	11	Pays Bas Catholiques
mwaf1144	africa west	1683	MALLET	140	14	10	Pays des Negres
mwsam0749	south america peru	1683	MALLET	140	15	10	Perou
mwme0792	persia etc	1683	MALLET	140	15	11	Perse Moderne
mwru0495	ukraine	1683	MALLET	140	14	10	Petite Tartarie
mwme0965	turkey etc	1683	MALLET	180	15	10	Plan de Constantinople (illustrated is German edition)
mwf0833	france paris	1686	MALLET	150	14	10	Plan de Paris
mwit0726	italy rome	1686	MALLET	150	15	10	Plan et Profil de la Ville de Rome Moderne
mwgr0418a	greece crete	1692	MALLET	750	38	50	Plan Geometrique, et Topographique, tres exact, de la tres importante ville de Candie, au Royaume de Crete, assiegée depuis 25 ans, par les Turcs... 1669
mwbp0309	poland	1683	MALLET	180	15	12	Pologne
mwe0548	europe czech republic (bohemia)	1685	MALLET	150	15	10	Prague
mwe1104	europe slovak republic (moravia)	1683	MALLET	120	15	10	Presbourg (view of Bratislava)
mwin0129a	india	1683	MALLET	140	14	10	Presqu-Isle de l'Inde deca le Golfe de Bengala
mwuk1773	wales	1683	MALLET	140	15	10	Principaute de Galles
mwbh0435	belgium holland	1683	MALLET	140	16	11	Provinces Unies
mwca0499	canada quebec	1683	MALLET	200	14	10	Quebec
mwgr0527	greece rhodes	1683	MALLET	150	14	10	Rhodes
mwit0725	italy rome	1683	MALLET	150	15	11	Rome Ancienne
mwuk0941	england	1683	MALLET	160	16	11	Royaume d'Angleterre
mwsam0453	south america chile	1683	MALLET	140	16	11	Royaume de Chili
mwit1016	italy south	1686	MALLET	140	15	11	Royaume de Naples
mwsam0203	south america amazon	1683	MALLET	200	15	10	Royaume des Amazones
mwuk0087	ireland	1683	MALLET	200	15	11	Royaume d'Irlande
mwit0792	italy sardinia	1683	MALLET	240	15	10	Sardaigne
mwf1135	france rhone-alpes	1683	MALLET	150	15	11	Savoye
mwaf1042	africa south east	1683	MALLET	100	14	11	Sofala
mwaf0378	africa east	1683	MALLET	180	15	10	Source du Nil
mwuss0399	florida	1683	MALLET	200	15	11	St. Augus. de Floride (view)
mwaf1145	africa west	1683	MALLET	140	15	10	St. Thomas
mwsc0695	scandinavia sweden	1683	MALLET	200	15	11	Suede
mwme0869	syria etc	1683	MALLET	180	15	10	Syrie Moderne
mwjk0047	japan	1683	MALLET	200	15	10	Terre de Jesso
mwit1226	italy venice	1683	MALLET	200	14	10	Venise (view)
mwe0414	europe austria vienna	1686	MALLET	140	14	10	Vienne (view)
mwuss1617	virginia	1683	MALLET	350	15	10	Virginie (incl. Maryland)
mwin0133	india	1683	MALLET	140	14	11	Visapor
mwe0896	europe hungary	1683	MALLET	120	15	10	Waradin
mwaf0699	africa north	1684	MALLET	75	15	10	Zaara le Desert
mwsw018a	switzerland	1781	MALLET, H.	2000	67	53	Carte de la Suisse Romande qui comprend le Pays de Vaud et le Gouvernement d'Aigle, dépendant du Canton de Berne (in 4 sheets)
mwaf0325	africa	1837	MALTE-BRUN	200	33	41	Afrique
mwsam0151	south america	1832	MALTE-BRUN	80	30	22	Amerique Meridionale
mwca0180	canada	1836	MALTE-BRUN	200	22	32	Amerique Russe, Nouvelle Bretagne et Canada
mwam0699	america north	1835	MALTE-BRUN	150	22	30	Amerique Septentrionale (illustrated left)
mwam0754	america north	1842	MALTE-BRUN	250	22	30	Amerique Septentrionale (independent Texas)
mwme1057	turkey etc	1831	MALTE-BRUN	100	22	30	Asie Mineure Ancienne
mwaf0727	africa north	1834	MALTE-BRUN	80	22	30	Barbarie

AMPG REFERENCE	REGION	DATE	MAP MAKER	PRICE (UK£)	VERT. (cm.)	HOR. (cm.)	TITLE OF MAP (Comments by the editor in brackets)
mwg0179	germany	1834	MALTE-BRUN	100	32	41	Carte de la Confederation Germanique
mwgr0257	greece	1837	MALTE-BRUN	80	23	30	Carte de la Grece et de l'Archipel
mwas0326	asia caspian sea	1810	MALTE-BRUN	240	23	18	Carte de la Kharismie
mwas0543	asia south east	1835	MALTE-BRUN	120	22	30	Carte de la Malaisie ou Grand Archipel D'Asie
mwp0526a	pacific south	1837	MALTE-BRUN	200	23	30	Carte de la Melanesie ou Nouvelle Hollande
mwru0350	russia	1834	MALTE-BRUN	120	22	30	Carte de la Siberie ou Russie D'Asie
mwas0252	asia continent	1835	MALTE-BRUN	150	31	43	Carte de L'Asie
mwc0267	china	1835	MALTE-BRUN	120	22	30	Carte de l'Empire Chinois et du Japon
mwin0360	india	1835	MALTE-BRUN	120	22	30	Carte de L'Inde
mwp0527	pacific south	1837	MALTE-BRUN	200	30	43	Carte de l'Oceanie
mwwi0199	west indies	1837	MALTE-BRUN	150	23	31	Carte des Antilles, du Golfe du Mexique et du Guatemala
mwam0700	america north	1835	MALTE-BRUN	150	22	30	Carte des Etats-Unis (illustrated above)
mwbh0800	belgium holland	1833	MALTE-BRUN	80	30	22	Carte des Royaumes de Belgique et de Hollande
mwsam0428	south america brazil	1836	MALTE-BRUN	80	22	30	Carte du Bresil 1836
mwe0268	europe	1837	MALTE-BRUN	480	32	44	Carte Geologique d'Europe
mwbp0568	poland	1837	MALTE-BRUN	120	23	30	Carte Historique de la Pologne Presentment ses Divers Dismembremens en 1772, 1794, 1795, 1807 et 1815
mwf0195	france	1832	MALTE-BRUN	200	31	44	Carte Physique et Mineralogique De La France
mwsc0400	scandinavia denmark	1837	MALTE-BRUN	60	23	30	Danemark
mwuk0622	scotland	1837	MALTE-BRUN	80	23	30	Ecosse
mwaf0545a	africa egypt etc	1810	MALTE-BRUN	120	34	25	Egypte
mwaf0564	africa egypt etc	1837	MALTE-BRUN	50	23	30	Egypte Ancienne
mwaf0430	africa east	1837	MALTE-BRUN	80	23	30	Egypte Nubie & Abyssinie
mwe0403	europe austria	1834	MALTE-BRUN	80	22	30	Empire D'Autriche
mwc0262	china	1831	MALTE-BRUN	90	21	30	Empire des Mongols
mwm0086	mediterranean	1831	MALTE-BRUN	60	22	31	Empire Romain sous Constantin
mwsp0330	spain	1836	MALTE-BRUN	180	31	43	Espagne et Portugal
mwf0194	france	1832	MALTE-BRUN	120	31	43	France
mwme0416	holy land	1837	MALTE-BRUN	80	23	30	Geographie des Hebreux
mwuk0277	ireland	1837	MALTE-BRUN	60	23	30	Irlande
mwit0242	italy	1831	MALTE-BRUN	80	30	22	Italie
mww0703	world	1833	MALTE-BRUN	320	27	47	Mappemonde en deux Hemispheres
mww0641	world	1812	MALTE-BRUN	240	28	44	Mappe-Monde sur la Projection Reduite de Mercator
mww0642	world	1812	MALTE-BRUN	500	33	48	Mappe-Mondes sur Diverses Projections
mwgm0278	mexico	1812	MALTE-BRUN	240	23	30	Mexique
mwsam0185	south america (north)	1812	MALTE-BRUN	120	22	30	Nlle Grenade Caracas et Guyanes
mwp0517	pacific south	1812	MALTE-BRUN	550	22	29	Oceanique (map by Lapie, the first to show the Australian coast complete. See also his map of Australia, 1812.)
mwp0052	australia	1812	MALTE-BRUN	850	22	30	Oceanique Centrale (the first map of Australia to show all of Australia's coast, with the help of information obtained from Flinders while he was detained by the French.)
mwas0530	asia south east	1812	MALTE-BRUN	180	22	30	Oceanique Occidentale
mwme0392	holy land	1812	MALTE-BRUN	120	22	29	Palestine
mwsam0786	south america peru	1810	MALTE-BRUN	100	22	30	Perou et Bresil
mwru0348	russia	1833	MALTE-BRUN	120	43	33	Russie d'Europe
mwsc0211	scandinavia	1832	MALTE-BRUN	120	30	22	Suede et Norvege
mwsw0227	switzerland	1831	MALTE-BRUN	75	22	30	Suisse
mwuss0774	maryland	1828	MALTE-BRUN	140	24	20	The Middle States Maryland & Virginia
mwam1205	america north (east)	1828	MALTE-BRUN	120	24	20	The Middle States Maryland & Virginia
mwme1047	turkey etc	1812	MALTE-BRUN	140	22	30	Turquie d'Asie
mwam0582	america north	1810	MALTE-BRUN	240	28	32	United States
mwam1355	america north (west)	1828	MALTE-BRUN	240	24	20	Western States & Territories
mwit0377	italy friuli	1830	MALVOLTI	1200	110	77	Carta topografica della Provincia del Friuli
mwam1082	america north (east)	1784	MANDRILLON	1200	41	41	Carte Generale des Treize Etats-Unis & Independants de l'Amerique Septentrionale pour Servir ou Spectateur Americain
mwuss1172	new york	1803	MANGIN & GOERCK	40000	89	102	Plan of the City of New York, Drawn from Actual Survey
mwam0243a	america continent	1796	MANNERT	480	53	60	America nach der zweyten Ausgabe von Arrowsmiths Weltcharte
mwru0308	russia	1794	MANNERT	875	51	69	Imperii Russici Pars Orientem Spectans. Tab. IIda
mwru0309	russia	1794	MANNERT	580	50	68	Westlicher Theil des Russischen Reichs, aus der St. Petersburger Karte vom Jahr 1787 ... Entworfen
mwuss1100	new york	1772	MANTE	375	27	17	(Crown Point)
mwuss1101	new york	1772	MANTE	450	29	25	A Plan of Fort Edward and its Environs on Hudson's River
mwca0529	canada quebec	1772	MANTE	3850	43	89	Attack on Quebec. The Fleet Commanded by Admiral Saunders. The Army by Major Wolfe
mwuss1099	new york	1772	MANTE	960	37	47	The Attack of Ticonderoga; Major General Abercromby-Commander in Chief
mwp0339	pacific hawaii	1798	MARCHAND	500	13	26	Iles Sandwich d'Apres Cook / Groupe de la Mesa
mwin0243	india	1764	MARCHAND	650	31	59	Plan des Attaques de la Ville de Madure
mwru0396	russia moscow	1789	MARCHENKOV	5500	76	48	Stolichnago Goroda Moskvy (in Cyrillic)
mwit1146	italy umbria	1583	MARCUCCI	3500	41	53	Orvieto (view)
mwsc0740	scandinavia sweden	1778	MARELIUS	500	56	48	Charta ofwer Sodra Delen af Swerige
mwsc0731a	scandinavia sweden	1750	MARELIUS	600	43	33	Charta som Wisar Strackningen sa wal af Landryggen som Fiallryggen samt Riks Grantsen imellan Swerige och Norrige

AMPG REFERENCE	REGION	DATE	MAP MAKER	PRICE (UK£)	VERT. (cm.)	HOR. (cm.)	TITLE OF MAP (Comments by the editor in brackets)
mwme0957	turkey etc	1666	MARIETTE	550	41	53	Anaplus Bosphori Thracii
mwgr0379	greece crete	1650	MARIETTE	600	38	52	Candia olim Creta
mwaf0054	africa	1650	MARIETTE	1200	37	49	Carte de l'Afrique Corrigee et Augmentee dessus Toutes les Aultres cy devant Faictes
mwe0058	europe	1650	MARIETTE	875	37	48	Carte de l'Europe Corrigee et Augmentee dessus Toutes les Aultres cy devant Faictes l'Annee 1646
mwwi0853	st kitts	1645	MARIETTE	2000	31	43	Carte de Lisle de Sainct Christophle (1st map of St. Kitts, by P. Du Val.)
mwsp0433	spain regions	1641	MARIETTE	480	32	44	Catalogne et Arragon
mwsp0439	spain regions	1650	MARIETTE	600	37	47	Catalonia
mwbh0276	belgium holland	1640	MARIETTE	650	39	51	Comitatus Flandriae Nova Tabula. Paris, Pierre Mariette, Rue St-Jacques a l'Enseigne de Esperance
mwgr0481	greece cyprus	1660	MARIETTE	3000	38	49	Cyprus Insula
mwe0760a	europe east	1651	MARIETTE	550	38	53	La Partie Septentrionale de la Turquie en l'Europe
mwme0961b	turkey etc	1670	MARIETTE	400	33	46	Lycaonia in Minores Regiones (illustrated is Covens & Mortier re-issue, 1730)
mww0156	world	1643	MARIETTE	7000	38	56	Nova Totius Terrarum Orbis Geographica ac Hydpographica Tabula Auct: Iud Hondio
mwuk0710	uk	1650	MARIETTE	850	37	49	Novissima Descriptio Angliae Scotiae et Hiberniae.
mwme0105	holy land	1646	MARIETTE	720	41	55	Palestinae sive Terrae Sanctae quae et Promissionis Nova Tabula ad SS. Bibliorum Intelligentiam Delineata
mwme0961a	turkey etc	1670	MARIETTE	400	33	51	Pamphilia et Pisidia
mwit0643	italy piedmont	1650	MARIETTE	650	36	49	Piedmont Montferrat et Territoires de Gennes
mwe0419b	europe austria vienna	1704	MARINONI	1500			Accuratissima Viennae Austriae Ichnographica Delineatio (title above map)
mwp0528a	pacific south	1844	MARMOCCHI	200	22	33	L'Oceania Divisa Nelle Quattro Sue Magne Parti 1844
mwit0828a	italy sardinia	1845	MARMORA	1500	135	88	Carta dell'Isola e Regno di Sardegna
mwgr0309a	greece corfu	1672	MARMORA	600	18	28	Pianta Dell Isola Di Corfu con Parte Della Grecia
mwuss0478	florida	1839	MARRYAT	320	29	32	Portion of Middle Florida, Shewing the Seat of Hostilities between Seminole Indians, and United States
mwuss0307	connecticut	1819	MARSH	350	18	25	Connecticut
mwuss1052	new jersey	1807	MARSHALL	240	26	40	A Map of the Country from Rariton River in East Jersey, to Elk Head in Maryland, Shewing the Several Operations of the American & British Armies, in 1776 & 1777
mwam1154	america north (east)	1807	MARSHALL	180	37	27	A Map of those Parts of Virginia, North Carolina, South Carolina & Georgia which were the Scenes of the Most Important Operations of the Southern Armies
mwuss1051	new jersey	1806	MARSHALL	300	41	25	A Plan of the Northern Part of New Jersey, Shewing the Positions of the American and British Armies after Crossing the North River in 1776
mwuss0858	massachusetts	1806	MARSHALL	320	20	32	Boston, and its Environs (map by R. Phillips)
mwam1156	america north (east)	1807	MARSHALL	200	35	51	Carte des Provinces Meridionales des Etats-Unis
mwuss1177	new york	1807	MARSHALL	280	41	27	Ile de New-York. Partie de Long-Island ou de l'Ile Longue, et Positions des Armees Americaine et Britannique, apres le Combat Livre sur Hauteurs, le 27 Aout 1776
mwuss1674	virginia	1806	MARSHALL	240	21	23	Investment and Attack of York, in Virginia
mwuss1467	rhode isl	1807	MARSHALL	200	43	27	Partie de l'Etat de Rhode-Island, et Position des Armees Americaine et Britannique, au Siege de Newport, et a l'Affaire du 29 Aout 1778
mwca0545	canada quebec	1807	MARSHALL	150	27	22	Theatre des Operations de l'Armee du Nord, et Desert que le General Arnold Traversa en Marchant contre Quebec
mwam1155	america north (east)	1807	MARSHALL	300	36	26	Theatre des Operations les Plus Importantes de l'Armee du Sud, dans la Virginie, dans les Deux Carolines, et dans la Georgie
mwe0724a	europe danube	1743	MARSIGLI	1200	70	93	Mappa generalis in qua Danubii, Fl. Caetium montem inter et Bulgariae flumen Jantra
mwg0824	westphalia	1744	MARTELL	240	28	33	A New Plan of Fort Louis of ye Rhein
mwru0204	russia	1746	MARTELL	1200	30	49	A New Plan of Petersburg
mwsam0759b	south america peru	1748	MARTIN, A	300	25	37	El Puerto de el Callao en el Mar Pacyfyco o de el Sur
mwsam0759a	south america peru	1748	MARTIN, A	720	38	53	Plano Scenographico de la ciud.d delos Reyes o Lima Capital delos Reynos del Peru (south to the top)
mwca0496	canada prince edward isl.	1834	MARTIN	450	19	36	Prince Edward Island Divided into Counties & Parishes with Lots as Granted by Government, Exhibiting the New Settlements, Roads, Mills &c.
mwaf0704	africa north	1700	MARTINEAU DU PLESSIS	140	19	26	Barbarie (2 insets)
mwsc0327	scandinavia denmark	1700	MARTINEAU DU PLESSIS	140	20	25	Dannemarck
mwaf0385	africa east	1700	MARTINEAU DU PLESSIS	140	19	25	L'Abissinie
mwaf0118	africa	1700	MARTINEAU DU PLESSIS	150	16	22	L'Afrique Ancienne
mwe1144b	europe south east	1700	MARTINEAU DU PLESSIS	175	21	19	La Turquie en Europe, ou la Turquie en Europe ou font les Etats possedez par les Turcs Jusqu en l'An 1690.
mwwi0042	west indies	1700	MARTINEAU DU PLESSIS	300	19	26	Les Antilles (based on Cloppenburg 1630)

AMPG REFERENCE	REGION	DATE	MAP MAKER	PRICE (UK£)	VERT. (cm.)	HOR. (cm.)	TITLE OF MAP (Comments by the editor in brackets)
mwsam0750	south america peru	1700	MARTINEAU DU PLESSIS	180	19	26	Peru ou Perou
mwaa0016	antarctic	1700	MARTINEAU DU PLESSIS	500	18	25	Terres Antarctiques
mwaa0105	arctic	1700	MARTINEAU DU PLESSIS	250	18	25	Terres Arctiques
mwec0186	uk england cornwall	1748	MARTYN	4800	55	41	A New and Accurate Map of Cornwall (9 sheets, each 55x41cm.)
mwec0195	uk england cornwall	1784	MARTYN	1000	56	70	A New and Accurate Map of the County of Cornwall from an Actual Survey (reduced version of 1748 map)
mwwi0569	hispaniola	1534	MARTYR	3000	20	28	Isola Spagnuola
mwp0519	pacific south	1815	MARX	500	50	68	Generalcharte von Australien
mwg0292a	baden-wurttemberg	1825	MARX	720	43	63	Situationsplan der Stadt Baden
mwwi0222	west indies	1850	MARZOLLA	240	43	60	Arcipelago delle Antille Ossia Indie Occidentali (incl. large text panels)
mwp0168	australia	1848	MARZOLLA	400	43	50	Australia Occidentale ed Isola di Van-Diemen (2 maps on one sheet)
mwaa0053a	antarctic	1842	MARZOLLA	720	42	51	Carta Generale dell' Antartica
mwjk0148	japan	1847	MARZOLLA	675	58	43	Impero del Giappone
mwit0253	italy	1853	MARZOLLA	150	54	44	Italia
mwsam0817	south america uruguay	1850	MARZOLLA	400	61	45	Province Unite del Rio de la Plata ossia Republica Argentina, e Stati del Chili, Uruguay o Montevideo e Paraguay
mwsp0334a	spain	1844	MARZOLLA	150	41	59	Regni di Spagna e Portogallo, e Repubblica di Andorra
mwca0282	canada newfoundland	1626	MASON	2000	17	27	Insula olim vocata Nova Terra. The Island called of olde: Newfound Land
mwam1163	america north (east)	1808	MASON	5500	94	190	Steel's New and Correct Chart of the Coast from Cape Canaveral
mwuss0750	maryland	1769	MASON & DIXON	1200	18	10	A Map of that Part of America where a Degree of Latitude was Measured for the Royal Society: By Cha. Mason, & Jere. Dixon
mwam0718a	america north	1838	MASPERO	350	28	20	America Settentrionale
mww0535a	world	1785	MASSON-MOITHEY	3000	50	66	Esquisse d'un Tableau Generale du Genre Humain
mwwi0846	puerto rico	1845	MATENAS	785	60	89	Carte de l'Ile Espagnole de Porto-Rico
mwam0908	america north (east)	1702	MATHER	2500	31	38	An Exact Mapp of New England and New York
mwit0443	italy liguria	1757	MATTEO	2500	49	88	Stato della Serenissima Republica di Genova
mwaf0535	africa egypt etc	1799	MAUBORGNE	350	47	57	Carte D'Egypte
mwe0432a	europe austria vienna	1783	MAUER	2000	50	70	Neue Topograph Karte der K:K:Haupt und Residenz Stadt Wien
mwsp0719	gibraltar	1760	MAUGEIN	750	59	66	Plan de la Ville et des Forts de Gibraltar
mwf1164	france lyon	1625	MAUPIN	5000			Description de la Ville de Lyon
mww0509	world	1780	MAURO	650	37	35	Abbozzo del Mappamondo di F. Mauro (reduced version of Mauro's 1459 map)
mwuss1178	new york	1807	MAVERICK	2400	31	33	Plan of the City of New York, with Recent and Intended Improvements
mwgm0309	mexico	1827	MAWMAN	150	18	23	Mexico
mwam0615	america north	1819	MAWMAN	150	20	24	N. America. Published May 1, 1819 by J. Mawman and the other Proprietors
mwam0616	america north	1819	MAWMAN	150	19	24	United States. Published May 1, 1819
mwwi0163	west indies	1819	MAWMAN	120	19	24	West Indies
mwam0726	america north	1839	MAXIMILIAN	10000	43	81	Map to Illustrate the Route of Prince Maximilian of Wied in the Interior of North America from Boston to the Upper Missouri, etc, in 1832, 33, & 34
mwwi0497a	cuba	1850	MAY	2000	44	55	Plano Pintoresco de La Habana con los numeros de las casas (below is the 1853 re-issue with different border views etc.)
mwbp0442	poland	1750	MAYER	480	45	53	Carte des Estats de la Couronne de Pologne
mwg0494	mecklenburg	1757	MAYER	1500	48	57	Pomeraniae Anterioris Suedicae ac Principatus Rugiae Tabula Nova
mww0158	world	1648	MAYERNE-TURQUET	4800	45	45	La Nouvelle Maniere de Representer le Globe Terrestre (North polar azimuth projection)
mwwi0368a	barbados	1722	MAYO		94	111	A New & Exact Map of the Island of Barbadoes in America
mwaf0019	africa	1590	MAZZA	5000	36	47	Africa ex Magnae Orbis Terrae Descriptione
mwam0014	america continent	1590	MAZZA		34	46	Americae et Proximar Regionum Orae Descriptio Venetiis Donato Rascicotti formis
mwuss1317	ohio	1839	MCBRIDE	2500	66	86	Map of the Towns of Hamilton and Rossville, Butler County, State of Ohio
mwuss0358	washington DC	1846	McCLELLAND	280	35	45	Map of the City of Washington (inset plan of Capitol)
mww0752	world	1850	MCDOWALL	140	9	13	World
mwca0168	canada	1833	MCGREGOR	240	17	39	Chart Exhibiting the British Possessions in North America: The Atlantic, British Isles &c. with the Proposed Tracks of the Projected Trans-Atlantic Steam Navigation
mwca0465	canada nova scotia	1833	MCGREGOR	150	12	32	Map Exhibiting the Harbour of Halifax and the Shubenacadie Canal, for McGregor's British America
mwca0495	canada prince edward isl.	1833	MCGREGOR	150	11	17	Map of Prince Edward Island in the Gulf of St. Lawrence

AMPG REFERENCE	REGION	DATE	MAP MAKER	PRICE (UK£)	VERT. (cm.)	HOR. (cm.)	TITLE OF MAP (Comments by the editor in brackets)
mwam0963	america north (east)	1753	MEAD	1000	48	61	Chart of the Atlantic Ocean, with the British, French, & Spanish Settlements in North America (from a larger map by Jefferys)
mwca0116	canada	1790	MEARES	500	25	46	A Chart of the Interior Part of North America Demonstrating the Very Great Probability of an Inland Navigation from Hudsons Bay to the West Coast
mwca0661	canada west	1790	MEARES	360	19	23	A Plan of Port Effingham in Berkley's Sound
mwp0443	pacific north	1794	MEARES	750	43	61	Carte de la Cote N.O. d'Amerique et de la Cote N.E. d'Asie Reconnues en 1778 et 79. Par le Capitaine Cook et Plus Particulierement Encore en 1788. et 89. Par le Capne. J. Meares
mwp0445	pacific north	1794	MEARES	600	43	57	Carte de la Mer Pacifique du Nord, Contenant la Cote Nord-Est d'Asie et la Cote Nord-Ouest d'Amerique Reconnues en 1778 et 79 par le Capitne. Cook, et Plus Particulierement Encore en 1788 et 89 par le Capne. Jean Meares
mwam1330	america north (west)	1790	MEARES	400	25	46	Carte de la Partie Interieur de l'Amerique Septentrionale ... Navigation Interieur depuis la Baye d'Hudson jusqua la Cote Nord-Ouest
mwp0442	pacific north	1794	MEARES	400	27	39	Chart of Norton Sound and of Bherings Strait Made by the East Cape of Asia and the West Point of America
mwp0333	pacific hawaii	1790	MEARES	450	20	24	The New Discover'd Sandwich Island & Johnstone's Island
mwme0547	arabia etc	1610	MEGISER	1500	8	11	Arabia / Ormus (2 maps, Arabia and Persian Gulf)
mwec0920	uk england nottinghamshire	1768	MEIJER	120	19	11	(Nottinghamshire)
mwaf0222	africa	1768	MEIJER	150	18	23	Afrika, Volgen de Nieuwste Ontdekking
mwas0183	asia continent	1768	MEIJER	150	18	23	Asia, Volgens de Laatste Ontdekkingen
mwuk0199	ireland	1767	MEIJER	150	17	20	Naauwkeurige Kaart van Ierland
mwuk1009	england	1768	MEIJER	150	18	21	Nazuwkeurige Kaart van Engeland
mwam0441	america north	1768	MEIJER	240	18	23	Noord Amerika
mwc0012	china	1623	MEISNER	400	10	15	Amacao in Chyna (View of Macao)
mwec0220	uk england cumbria	1623	MEISNER	140	10	15	Carlile in Anglia
mwec0127	uk england cheshire	1623	MEISNER	140	10	14	Chester in Engelland
mwme0942	turkey etc	1638	MEISNER	400	10	15	Constantinopel
mwuk0344	scotland	1638	MEISNER	250	10	15	Edenburck in Schottl.
mwg0702	schleswig-holstein	1638	MEISNER	400	10	15	Hamburg
mwme0448	jerusalem	1638	MEISNER	400	10	15	Jerusalem
mwsw0060	switzerland	1638	MEISNER	400	10	15	Lucern in Schweitz
mwm0215	mediterranean malta	1701	MEISNER	400	7	15	Malts maris medit.Inf. (plan of Valetta)
mwit0531	italy milan	1627	MEISNER	400	10	15	Meylandt
mwaf0360	africa east	1642	MEISNER	200	8	14	Mombaza in Africa
mwe0531	europe czech republic (bohemia)	1623	MEISNER	200	10	15	Prag
mwaf1040	africa south east	1623	MEISNER	140	10	15	Quiloa in Africa (Quelimane)
mwbp0080	baltic states	1638	MEISNER	150	10	15	Riga In Lieflandt
mwin0404b	indian ocean	1538	MELA	3500	25	33	Asia Maior
mwas0260	asia (from turkey to india)	1550	MELA-ANON	12000	44	57	Orbis Situs Secundum Melam Pomponium Fideliter (Anonymous map, based on Mela, who lived during the 1st century AD)
mww0007	world	1482	MELA-ANONYMOUS	8000	14	19	Novellae Etati ad Geographie Umiculatos Calles Humano Viro Necessarios Flores Aspirati Votubnmereti Ponif (Anonymous map, based on Mela, who lived during the 1st century AD. Closely copied in 1498 , slightly smaller.)
mwam0816	america north (central)	1815	MELISH	120	17	30	A Map of the National Road between Cumberland and Wheeling
mwuss0457	florida	1813	MELISH	2250	43	55	A Map of the Southern Section of the United States Including the Floridas & Bahama Islands Shewing the Seat of War in that Department. Drawn by John Melish. Engraved by H.S. Tanner
mwaf0307	africa	1818	MELISH	180	34	23	Africa
mwuss0778	maryland	1834	MELISH	200	18	13	Baltimore, Annapolis and Adjacent Country
mwuss0347	washington DC	1822	MELISH	350	17	10	District of Columbia
mwam1301	great lakes	1815	MELISH	875	46	56	East End of Lake Ontario and River St. Lawrence from Kingston to French Mills, Reduced from an Original Drawing in the Naval Department
mwuss0601	kentucky	1812	MELISH	875	19	37	Kentucky
mwuss0901	michigan	1813	MELISH	600	58	43	Map of Detroit River and Adjacent Country, from an Original Drawing by a British Engineer
mwuss0661	louisiana	1815	MELISH	3000	38	53	Map of New Orleans and Adjacent Country
mwuss1404	pennsylvania	1822	MELISH	40000	129	189	Map of Pennsylvania, Constructed from the County Surveys Authorized by the State, and other Original Documents ... Engraved by B. Tanner
mwuss1416	pennsylvania	1830	MELISH	4500	49	54	Map of Philadelphia County. Constructed by Virtue of an Act of the Legislature of Pennsylvania by John Melish (2nd edition)
mwca0632	canada st lawrence	1824	MELISH	875	45	60	Map of the River St. Lawrence and Adjacent Country, from Williamsburg to Montreal, from an Original Drawing in the War Department

AMPG REFERENCE	REGION	DATE	MAP MAKER	PRICE (UK£)	VERT. (cm.)	HOR. (cm.)	TITLE OF MAP (Comments by the editor in brackets)
mwam1176	america north (east)	1817	MELISH	720	39	55	Map of the Seat of War in North America
mwam0603	america north	1816	MELISH	40000	91	150	Map of the United States with the Contiguous British & Spanish Possessions Compiled from the Latest & Best Authorities
mwuss1190	new york	1822	MELISH	120	17	10	New York and Adjacent Country
mwam0639	america north	1824	MELISH	960	38	53	Northern Section of the United States Including Canada (a Swedish edition)
mwuss1284	ohio	1818	MELISH	675	23	23	Ohio
mwuss1327	oregon	1822	MELISH	400	17	10	Outlet of Columbia River
mwuss1401	pennsylvania	1814	MELISH	200	18	13	Philadelphia and Adjacent Country
mwuss0974	missouri	1822	MELISH	180	17	10	St. Louis and Adjacent Country
mww0656	world	1818	MELISH	6000	96	128	The World on Mercator's Projection, Revised and Improved to 1818
mwam0619	america north	1820	MELISH	1600	43	53	United States of America
mwam1180	america north (east)	1818	MELISH	1500	41	50	United States of America Compiled from the Latest & Best Authorities by John Melish
mwf1167	france lyon	1696	MENESTRIER	2000	66	86	Carte de l'Ancienne Ville de Lyon
mwuss0246	carolinas	1798	MENTELLE	550	32	43	Carte de la Caroline Meridionale et Septentrionale et de la Virginie
mwuss0454	florida	1798	MENTELLE	675	32	42	Carte de la Floride et de la Georgie
mwam1123	america north (east)	1798	MENTELLE	600	32	43	Carte de la Partie Septentrionale des Etats Unis, & le Canada, la Nouvelle Escosse, New Hampshire, Massachusett's Bay, Rhode-Island, Connecticut, New Yorck, Etat de Vermont, avec Partie de Pensilvanie et de New-Jersey
mwbp0537	poland	1797	MENTELLE	300	42	62	Carte de l'Ancien Royaume de Pologne, Partage entre la Russie, la Prusse et l'Autriche par les Traites Successifs de 1772 1793 et 1795. Contenant aussi le Royaume de Prusse
mwc0233	china	1804	MENTELLE	300	33	43	Carte de l'Empire de la Chine
mwme0732a	caucasus	1799	MENTELLE	2000	84	88	Carte du Théâtre de la Guerre en Orient
mwam1124	america north (east)	1798	MENTELLE	450	33	43	Carte Generale des Etats Unis de L'Amerique Septentrionale
mwsc0167	scandinavia	1782	MENTELLE	280	31	42	Carte Generale et Physique du Royaume de Sweden
mwas0226	asia continent	1798	MENTELLE	400	32	42	Carte Generale et Politique de L'Asie
mwsw0209	switzerland	1798	MENTELLE	300	32	42	Carte Physique et Politique de la Suisse
mwaf0536	africa egypt etc	1799	MENTELLE	350	48	57	Carte Physique et Politique de L'Egypte
mwsp0296	spain	1782	MENTELLE	200	31	42	Espagne et Portugal Carte Physique
mwsp0297	spain	1782	MENTELLE	960	32	42	Espagne et Portugal en IX feuilles (in 9 sheets)
mwin0324	india	1800	MENTELLE	550	32	43	Inde Indostan Bengale &c / Partie Septentrionale (2 maps, each 32x43cm.)
mww0610	world	1800	MENTELLE	1800	60	104	Planisphere en Quatre Feuilles Reunies de Maniere a ne Point Diviser le Grand Ocean ou la Mer du Sud
mwsc0635	scandinavia norway	1782	MENTELLE	280	31	42	Royaume de Danemark Premiere Carte (incl. Iceland, Scotland)
mwsc0751	scandinavia sweden	1795	MENTELLE	250	33	43	Royaume de Suede, Suede Moderne
mwru0315	russia	1798	MENTELLE	250	32	42	Russie Europeene Partie Septentrionale
			SEE ALSO UNDER PUBLISHER 'CHANLAIRE'				
mwam0523	america north	1794	MENZIES	240	29	33	A New and Accurate Map of North America from the Best Authorities
mwuk0009	ireland	1595	MERCATOR	2000	34	47	(Untitled northern Ireland) / Irlandiae Regnum (southern Ireland, 2 sheets, each 34x47cm)
mwuk1338	england east	1636	MERCATOR-HONDIUS	500	44	55	A Generall Plat and Description of the Fenns and other Grounds with in the Isle of Ely and the Counties of Lincolne, Northampton, Huntingdon, Cambrig, Suffolke and Norfolke
mwit0258	italy abruzzo	1595	MERCATOR	600	35	48	Abruzzet et Terra di Lavoro
mwbp0293	poland	1680	MERCATOR-DE WIT?	1000	37	49	Accurata Prussiae Descriptio (printed from Mercator's original 1595 engraving with his signature but with a different title within a re-engraved cartouche after Blaeu, reversed left to right. Details in the sea area have also been changed and lines of latitude and longitude added. This example is from a De Wit atlas. Note the same colouring as the previous item.)
mwaf0023a	africa	1595	MERCATOR	3000	37	46	Africa ex Magna Orbis Terre Descriptione Gerardi Mercatoris Desumpta, Studio & Industria G.M. Iunioris
mwf0211	france alsace	1605	MERCATOR	400	37	44	Alsatia Inferior
mwf0212	france alsace	1605	MERCATOR	600	36	48	Alsatia Superior cu Suntgoia & Brisgoia
mwsam0013	south america	1606	MERCATOR-HONDIUS	2000	36	49	America Meridionalis
mwam0016	america continent	1595	MERCATOR	6500	37	46	America sive India Nova, ad Magnae Gerardi Mercatoris Avi Universalis Imitationem, in Compendium Redacta
mwuk1553	england islands	1595	MERCATOR	720	32	44	Anglesey / Wight Vectis olim / Garnesay / Jarsay
mwuk0910	england	1595	MERCATOR	1100	35	47	Anglia Regnum
mwuk0677	uk	1595	MERCATOR	1200	33	42	Anglia, Scotia et Hibernia
mwuk0668	uk	1564	MERCATOR		89	129	Angliae Scotiae & Hiberniae nova descriptio (reduced size re-issues by Ortelius, editions from 1570 to 1612)

AMPG REFERENCE	REGION	DATE	MAP MAKER	PRICE (UK£)	VERT. (cm.)	HOR. (cm.)	TITLE OF MAP (Comments by the editor in brackets)
mwf0647	france loire	1605	MERCATOR	500	35	46	Aniou
mwf1183	france south west	1605	MERCATOR	500	36	47	Aquitania Australis Regnu Arelatense cum Confinijs
mwg0514	rheinland-pfalz	1633	MERCATOR-HONDIUS	320	42	53	Archiepiscopatus Trevirensis Descriptio Nova
mwsp0416	spain regions	1630	MERCATOR-HONDIUS	500	35	47	Arragonia et Catalonia
mwf0711	france nord pas-de-calais	1605	MERCATOR	500	35	46	Artesia Comit.
mwas0014	asia continent	1595	MERCATOR	2500	38	46	Asia ex Magna Orbis Terre Descriptione Gerardi Mercatoris Desumpta
mwe0297a	europe austria	1594	MERCATOR	480	33	49	Austria archiducatus
mwg0321	bavaria	1605	MERCATOR	300	37	47	Bavaria Ducatus
mwbh0167	belgium holland	1605	MERCATOR	720	35	45	Belgii Inferioris Descriptio Emendata cum Circumiacentium Regionu Confinijs
mwg0770	westphalia	1605	MERCATOR	400	33	46	Berghe Ducatus Marck Comitatus et Coloniensis Dioecesis
mwf0425	france central	1605	MERCATOR	350	35	45	Berry Ducatus
mwe0525	europe czech republic (bohemia)	1605	MERCATOR	500	41	55	Bohemia
mwg0575	saxony	1605	MERCATOR	600	35	45	Braunswyck & Meydburg cum Ceteris Adiacentibus
mwit0469	italy lombardy	1609	MERCATOR	550	37	48	Brescia Episcopatus Mediolanu Ducatus
mwf1113	france rhone-alpes	1633	MERCATOR-HONDIUS	300	38	49	Bresse
mwf0801	france north	1605	MERCATOR	480	36	48	Britannia & Normandia cum Confinib Regionibus
mwf0390	france burgundy	1605	MERCATOR	350	35	45	Burgundia Ducatus
mwuk1704	wales	1607	MERCATOR-HONDIUS	875	35	50	Cambriae Typus Auctore Humfredo Lhuydo Denbigiense Cambrobritanno
mwgr0360	greece crete	1589	MERCATOR	785	34	48	Candia cum Insulis Aliquot circa Graeciam (6 insets of islands)
mwf1108	france rhone-alpes	1630	MERCATOR-HONDIUS	300	38	49	Carte et Description Generale de Dauphine avec les Confins des Pais et Provinces Voisines
mwsp0392	spain regions	1605	MERCATOR	350	35	45	Castiliae Veteris et Novae Descriptio
mwsp0394	spain regions	1606	MERCATOR	480	39	49	Cataloniae Principatus Descriptio Nova
mwf0439	france champagne	1605	MERCATOR	600	38	50	Champagne Comitatus Campania
mwsw0053	switzerland	1630	MERCATOR-HONDIUS	785	31	54	Chorographica Tabula Lacus Lemanni Locorumque Circumiacentium Auctore Iac. G. Genevensi (Lake Geneva)
mwsw0043	switzerland	1609	MERCATOR-HONDIUS	1800	38	54	Chorographica Tabula Lacus Lemanni (5 portraits in lower border)
mwf0394	france burgundy	1640	MERCATOR-HONDIUS	400	42	54	Comitatus Burgundiae
mwbh0239	belgium holland	1634	MERCATOR	480	38	49	Comitatus Drentiae
mwuk1384	england south	1650	MERCATOR-HONDIUS	500	37	46	Cornubia, Devonia, Somersetus, Dorcestria, Wiltonia, Glocestria Monumetha, Clamorga, Caermarden, Penbrok, Cardiga, Radnor, Breknoke, Herefordia et Wigornia
mwuk1378	england south	1595	MERCATOR	800	37	46	Cornubia, Devonia, Somersetus, Dorcestria, Wiltonia, Glocestria Monumetha, Glamorgan, Caermarden, Penbrok, Cardigan, Radnor, Breknoke, Herefordia, & Wigornia
mwit0830	italy sardinia and corsica	1595	MERCATOR	650	35	47	Corsica / Sardinia (2 maps on one sheet)
mwgr0468	greece cyprus	1605	MERCATOR	1800	35	49	Cyprus Ins. (6 insets of islands)
mwsc0243	scandinavia denmark	1595	MERCATOR	750	38	44	Daniae Regnu
mwsw0034	switzerland	1605	MERCATOR	350	36	48	Das Wiflispurgergou
mwf0718	france nord pas-de-calais	1630	MERCATOR-HONDIUS	300	38	52	Descriptio Boloniae Pontieu Comit. S. Pauli cum Adjacentibus
mwbh0232	belgium holland	1633	MERCATOR	400	46	54	Dioecesis Leodiensis Accurata Tabula
mwuk1337	england east	1595	MERCATOR	800	35	42	Eboracum, Lincolnia, Derbia, Staffordia, Notinghamia, Lecestria, Rutlandia, et Norfolcia
mwg0576	saxony	1605	MERCATOR	600	34	42	Emden & Oldenborch Comit.
mwbh0214	belgium holland	1628	MERCATOR	480	37	48	Episcop. Utraiectinus. Auct. Balthazaro Florentio a Berckenrode
mwe0027	europe	1605	MERCATOR	1500	38	47	Europa, ad Magnae Europae Gerardi Mercatoris P. Imitationem, Rumoldi Mercatoris F. Cura Edita, Seruato Tamen Initio Longitudinis ex Ratione Magnetis, quod Pater in Magna sua Universali Posuit
mwsc0253	scandinavia denmark	1619	MERCATOR	400	36	40	Fionia
mwbh0177	belgium holland	1609	MERCATOR	450	33	48	Flandria Comit.
mwbh0223	belgium holland	1630	MERCATOR	400	40	51	Flandria Gallica Continens Castellanias
mwbh0252	belgium holland	1638	MERCATOR	480	38	48	Flandriae Pars Occidentalis Continens
mwe0493c	europe croatia	1609	MERCATOR	675	35	47	Forum Iulium, Karstia, Carniola, Histria et Windorum Marchia
mwf0942a	france picardy	1595	MERCATOR	480	36	40	France Picardie Champaigne (shown above left)
mwg0323	bavaria	1605	MERCATOR	400	34	50	Franckenlandt Francia Orientalis
mwbh0165	belgium holland	1605	MERCATOR	800	36	46	Frisia Occidentalis
mwf0031a	france	1595	MERCATOR	785	36	41	Gallia
mwbh0186	belgium holland	1613	MERCATOR	480	35	46	Geldria et Transysulana
mwg0040	germany	1609	MERCATOR	300	36	49	Germania
mwgr0051	greece	1605	MERCATOR	550	37	47	Graecia (illustrated left. Below is the Mercator-Hondius re-issue with new title 'Nova Totius Graeciae descriptio' publ. after 1635)
mwgr0053	greece	1618	MERCATOR-HONDIUS	800	37	50	Graeciae Sophiani. Ex Conatibus Geographicis Abrahamus Ortelii (published for Bertius)

AMPG REFERENCE	REGION	DATE	MAP MAKER	PRICE (UK£)	VERT. (cm.)	HOR. (cm.)	TITLE OF MAP (Comments by the editor in brackets)
mwbh0166	belgium holland	1605	MERCATOR	785	38	52	Habes hic Novam & Accuratissimam Descriptionem Tractus Illius Flandriae
mwg0433a	hessen	1605	MERCATOR	400	35	45	Hassia Landtgraviatus (1st edition)
mwgr0049	greece	1605	MERCATOR	800	36	50	Hellas seu Graecia Sophiani
mwsw0028b	switzerland	1595	MERCATOR	785	35	47	Helvetia cum finitimis regionibus confoederatis
mwgm0145	mexico	1606	MERCATOR-HONDIUS	850	34	49	Hispaniae Novae Nova Descriptio
mwbh0113	belgium holland	1585	MERCATOR	1200	35	48	Hollandt Comitatus Utricht Episcop.
mwg0696	schleswig-holstein	1605	MERCATOR	350	35	48	Holsatia Ducatus
mwe0861a	europe hungary	1598	MERCATOR	600	37	45	Hungaria
mwe0874	europe hungary	1636	MERCATOR-HONDIUS	400	37	44	Hungaria Regnum Sumptibus Henrici Hondy per Gerardum Mercatorem
mwin0016	ceylon	1606	MERCATOR-HONDIUS	800	34	50	Ins. Ceilan quae Incolis Tenarisin Dicitur (illustrated is the first of 2 states of the cartouches. North to the left.)
mwuk0018A	ireland	1609	MERCATOR-HONDIUS	1000	35	47	Irlandiae regnum (north to the right)
mwsc0480	scandinavia iceland	1595	MERCATOR	1200	28	43	Islandia
mwit0040	italy	1589	MERCATOR	1000	37	47	Italia
mwsc0250	scandinavia denmark	1605	MERCATOR	400	29	40	Iutia Septentrionalis
mwf0721	france nord pas-de-calais	1633	MERCATOR-HONDIUS	400	38	50	L'Archivesche de Cambray
mwit0393	italy lazio	1609	MERCATOR	400	37	47	Latium nunc Campagna di Roma
mwf1184	france south west	1631	MERCATOR-HONDIUS	320	37	48	Le Diocese de Sarlat Dioccesis Sarlatensis
mwbh0200	belgium holland	1619	MERCATOR	550	35	45	Leodiensis Dioecesis Typus
mwf1114	france rhone-alpes	1633	MERCATOR-HONDIUS	400	38	50	Lionnois, Forest, et Beaviolois
mwf0568	france ile de france	1595	MERCATOR	400	35	45	L'Isle de France. Parisiesis Agri Descriptio
mwbp0072	baltic states	1595	MERCATOR	750	37	43	Lithuania
mwbp0079	baltic states	1636	MERCATOR	580	36	48	Livonia
mwit0470	italy lombardy	1613	MERCATOR	400	36	46	Lombardiae Alpestris pars Occidentalis cum Valesia
mwf0665	france lorraine	1605	MERCATOR	300	38	50	Lorraine, vers le Midy
mwf0666	france lorraine	1605	MERCATOR	400	35	45	Lotharingia Ducatus
mwbh0827	luxembourg	1638	MERCATOR	650	37	47	Lutzenburg Ducatus
mwgr0043	greece	1595	MERCATOR	320	37	43	Macedonia, Epirus et Achaia
mwuk0697	uk	1631	MERCATOR	1250	39	52	Magnae Britanniae et Hiberniae Tabula
mwg0201	germany north east	1609	MERCATOR	350	36	48	Marca Brandenburgensis & Pomerania (1st edition 1585)
mwit0551	italy marches	1605	MERCATOR	600	35	45	Marchia Anconitana cum Spoletano Ducatu
mwe1093	europe slovak republic (moravia)	1605	MERCATOR	400	35	45	Moravia
mwgr0050	greece	1605	MERCATOR	300	33	41	Morea olim Peloponnesus
mwg0772	westphalia	1609	MERCATOR-HONDIUS	450	36	50	Murs Comitatus / Regionum Urbium et Fluminum que Potissimu Comitatum Murs Ambiunt Brevis Descriptio (2 maps on one sheet)
mwme0937	turkey etc	1606	MERCATOR-HONDIUS	800	34	48	Natoliae sive Asia Minor
mwuk1352	england north	1595	MERCATOR	800	36	42	Northumbria, Cumberlandia et Dunelmensis Episcopatus.
mwuk1354b	england north	1630	MERCATOR-HONDIUS	500	35	46	Northumbria, Cumberlandia, et Dunelmensis Episcopatus
mwg0329	bavaria	1630	MERCATOR-HONDIUS	400	38	49	Nova Alemanniae sive Sueviae Superioris Tabula
mww0073	world	1587	MERCATOR	7500	29	52	Orbis Terrae Compendiosa Descriptio quam ex Magna Universali Gerardi Mercatoris Domino Richardo Gartho (1st edition, with 4 text columns below map.)
mwg0322	bavaria	1607	MERCATOR-HONDIUS	400	37	48	Palatinatus Bavariae
mwg0511	rheinland-pfalz	1605	MERCATOR	300	35	45	Palatinatus Rheni
mwit0634	italy piedmont	1607	MERCATOR	450	36	46	Pedemontana Regio cum Genvensium Territorio & Montisferrati Marchionatu
mwme0766	persia etc	1605	MERCATOR	800	35	51	Persici vel Sophorum Regni Typus
mwbp0199a	poland	1595	MERCATOR	720	35	46	Polonia et Silesia
mwsp0021	portugal	1605	MERCATOR	720	33	49	Portugalliae que olim Lusitania, Novissima et Exactissima Descriptio Auctore Vernando Alvaro Secco, et de Integro Emendata, Anno 1600
mwuk0340	scotland	1630	MERCATOR-HONDIUS	800	36	54	Provinciae Lauden seu Lothien et Linlitouo
mwf0995	france provence	1595	MERCATOR	600	36	51	Provinciae, Regionis Galliae, Vera Exactissimaq. Descriptio Petro Ioanne Bompario Auctore
mwbp0200	poland	1595	MERCATOR	900	37	49	Prussia
mwit0998	italy south	1609	MERCATOR	480	34	46	Puglia Piana, Terra di Barri, Terra di Otranto, Calabria et Basilicata
mwf1090	france pyrenees	1605	MERCATOR	300	38	50	Quercy Cadurcium
mwsp0395	spain regions	1606	MERCATOR-HONDIUS	585	36	48	Regni Valentiae Typus
mwit0571	italy north	1609	MERCATOR	400	36	44	Romandiola cum Parmensi Ducatu
mwru0036	russia	1633	MERCATOR	1200	35	47	Russia cum Confinijs
mwf1109	france rhone-alpes	1630	MERCATOR-HONDIUS	550	38	50	Sabaudia Ducatus. La Savoie
mwe0313	europe austria	1627	MERCATOR-HONDIUS	350	35	45	Saltzburg archiepiscopatus cum ducatu Carinthiae
mwit0781b	italy sardinia	1627	MERCATOR	450	23	35	Sardinia
mwg0577	saxony	1605	MERCATOR	300	35	45	Saxonia Inferior et Meklenborg Duc.
mwg0578	saxony	1605	MERCATOR	300	35	49	Saxoniae Superioris Lusatiae Misniaeque Descriptio
mwe1122b	europe slovenia	1606	MERCATOR	450	36	46	Sclavonia, Croatia, Bosnia cum Dalmatiae Parte
mwuk0325	scotland	1609	MERCATOR	800	35	45	Scotia Regnum (2 overlapping sheets, each 35x45cm. Title on Northern sheet.)
mwuk0322a	scotland	1606	MERCATOR	800	35	40	Scotia Regnum

AMPG REFERENCE	REGION	DATE	MAP MAKER	PRICE (UK£)	VERT. (cm.)	HOR. (cm.)	TITLE OF MAP (Comments by the editor in brackets)
mwaa0062	arctic	1595	MERCATOR	6000	37	39	Septentrionalium Terrarum Descriptio (Illustrated below is a detail from the second state of this map, with a revised Novaya Zemlya and new Spitzbergen added by Hondius)
mwit0884	italy sicily	1633	MERCATOR	800	34	48	Siciliae Regnum (first publ. 1589. Illustrated left is the Hondius re-issue)
mwe0307	europe austria	1605	MERCATOR	350	31	42	Stiria
mwsc0031	scandinavia	1595	MERCATOR	2000	36	47	Suecia et Norvegia cum confinijs
mwg0574	saxony	1604	MERCATOR	720	40	53	Tabula Geographica Amplissimae Ditionis Westphaliae Conterminarumq Provinciarum
mwru0421	russia tartary	1630	MERCATOR-HONDIUS	1200	34	49	Tartaria
mwit0568	italy north	1605	MERCATOR	550	36	43	Tarvisina Marchia et Tirolis Comitatus (also issued with the title: Comitatus Tirolis)
mwru0471	ukraine	1595	MERCATOR	785	31	40	Taurica Chersonesus, hodie Przecopsca, et Gazara Dicitur (illustrated is the Mercator-Hondius edition, with title 'Taurica Chersonesus VS Nostra aetate Przecopsca et Gazara dicitur')
mwg0738	thuringia	1605	MERCATOR	350	35	42	Thuringia
mwg0741	thuringia	1650	MERCATOR-HONDIUS	300	42	52	Thuringia Lantgraviatus
mwsc0261	scandinavia denmark	1638	MERCATOR-HONDIUS	400	38	45	Totius Daniae Nova Descriptio
mwe1042b	europe romania	1605	MERCATOR	480	34	43	Transylvania
mwbh0816	luxembourg	1595	MERCATOR	720	37	48	Trier & Lutzenburg
mwme0550	arabia etc	1630	MERCATOR-HONDIUS	800	37	49	Turcici Imperii Imago
mwit1099	italy tuscany	1609	MERCATOR	785	33	47	Tuscia
mwuk0049	ireland	1638	MERCATOR	400	34	28	Udrone Irlandiae in Catherlagh Baronia (Leinster)
mwuk0015	ireland	1605	MERCATOR	400	35	38	Ultoniae Orientalis Pars (Ulster. Revised Hondius re-issue of 1636 illustrated)
mwit1169	italy veneto	1606	MERCATOR	400	37	49	Veronae Vicentiae et Patavii Ditiones
mwe0748	europe east	1589	MERCATOR	750	35	47	Walachia, Servia, Bulgaria, Romania
mwg0436	hessen	1605	MERCATOR	600	36	46	Waldeck Comitatus
mwuk1377	england south	1595	MERCATOR	800	37	47	Warwicum, Northhamtonia, Huntingdonia, Cantabrigia, Suffolcia, Oxonium, Buckinghamia, Bedfordia, Hartfordia, Essexia, Berceria, Middelsexia, Southhatonia, Surria, Cantiu & Southsexia
mwuk1379	england south	1607	MERCATOR-HONDIUS	500	37	47	Warwicum, Northhamtonia, Huntingdonia, Cantabrigia, Suffolcia, Oxonium, Buckinghamia, Bedfordia, Hartfordia, Essexia, Berceria, Middelsexia, Southhatonia, Surria, Cantiu & Southsexia
mwg0771	westphalia	1605	MERCATOR	350	36	46	Westfalia cum Dioecesi Bremensi
mwuk1352a	england north east	1595	MERCATOR	800	36	42	Westmorlandia, Lancastria, Cestria, Caernarvan, Denbigh, Flint, Merionidh, Montgomery, Salopia cum Insulis Mania et Anglesey
mwg0255	baden-wurttemberg	1607	MERCATOR	400	37	44	Wirtenberg Ducatus
mwbh0251	belgium holland	1638	MERCATOR	600	35	49	Zelandia Comitatus
SEE 'HONDIUS' FOR MAPS INCORRECTLY DESCRIBED AS 'MERCATOR-HONDIUS'							
mwuss1208	new york	1828	MERCHANT	960	31	40	Map of the City of Albany
mwg0343	bavaria	1648	MERIAN	800	31	38	(Nuremberg)
mwsam0288	south america brazil	1637	MERIAN	600	26	35	Abbildung der Statt und Vestung Parayba in der Lanschaft Brasilia
mwf1195	monaco	1640	MERIAN	1350	21	38	Abriss der Dreijen … Vestungen Monaco
mwf1017	france provence	1680	MERIAN	350	22	38	Abriss die Dreijen Gegeneinander Correspondierenden Vestungen Monaco, Capo di Sant' Spirito, und Niza di Provenza (re-issued by Bodenehr c1720, 16x20cm)
mwaf0860a	africa south	1645	MERIAN	480	29	37	Aethiopia Inferior vel Exterior Monomotapa
mwaf0357	africa east	1630	MERIAN	400	28	37	Aethiopia Superior vel Interior vulgo Abissinorum sive Presbiteri Ioannis Imperium (reduced size copy of Blaeu)
mwam0040	america continent	1631	MERIAN	1800	35	44	America Noviter Delineata
mwbh0323	belgium holland	1650	MERIAN	550	28	35	Amsterdam
mwbh0253	belgium holland	1638	MERIAN	450	28	36	Antverpia
mwf0218	france alsace	1644	MERIAN	400	24	39	Argentina. Strassburg (view and inset)
mwsw0067	switzerland	1650	MERIAN	400	27	35	Basilea - Basel
mwg0337	bavaria	1644	MERIAN	300	28	36	Bavaria Ducatus
mwbh0253a	belgium holland	1638	MERIAN	500	30	36	Belgii sive Germania Inferioris. Nider-Teuschlandt (shown above left)
mwsc0542	scandinavia norway	1641	MERIAN	550	21	31	Bergen
mwsw0065a	switzerland	1644	MERIAN	1200	24	35	Bern de hooft Stadt in Nüchtlant …
mwgm0155	mexico	1631	MERIAN	350	20	18	Beschreibung des Statt Mexico
mwe0535	europe czech republic (bohemia)	1633	MERIAN	480	28	36	Bohemia
mwf0261a	france aquitaine	1646	MERIAN	400	22	57	Bordeaux (view)
mwe0877a	europe hungary	1646	MERIAN	400	20	33	Buda. Ofen
mwgr0376	greece crete	1642	MERIAN	400	30	39	Candia, cum Insulis (insets, of Corfu, Cefalonia, Zante. Another untitled version shown below)
mwc0020	china	1640	MERIAN	960	27	34	China Veteribus Sinarum Regio nunc Incolis Tame Dicta
mwwi0579	hispaniola	1640	MERIAN	550	20	33	Civitas S. Dominici in Hispaniola
mwf1008	france provence	1649	MERIAN	400	27	34	Civitatis Avenionis Omnimq Viarum et Aedificiorum eius Perfecta Delineatio. 1635 (view of Avignon)

AMPG REFERENCE	REGION	DATE	MAP MAKER	PRICE (UK£)	VERT. (cm.)	HOR. (cm.)	TITLE OF MAP (Comments by the editor in brackets)
mwit0579a	italy north	1650	MERIAN	350	32	29	Comitatus Tirolis
mwme0944a	turkey etc	1638	MERIAN	1200	23	70	Constantinopolis (view)
mwgr0305	greece corfu	1650	MERIAN	450	14	35	Corphu (view)
mwbp0254	poland	1650	MERIAN	650	21	39	Cracovia (view)
mwgr0476	greece cyprus	1640	MERIAN	960	29	38	Cyprus Insula
mwsc0271	scandinavia denmark	1650	MERIAN	375	28	33	Dania Regnum
mwbp0269a	poland	1660	MERIAN	600	20	48	Dantiscum - Dantzig
mwwi0405	cuba	1628	MERIAN	2000	32	40	Das Eylandt Cuba mit Derselben Gelegenheit (shows Matanzas Bay with Cuba as an inset. Also publ. by De Bry)
mwe0665	europe dalmatia	1652	MERIAN	350	29	38	Delineatio Situsue Provinciae circa Clissam & Spalatum
mwg0235a	berlin	1720	MERIAN		33	91	Die Churfürstle Brandenburgle Residentz Stätt Berlin, Cöln, und Friedrichs Werder
mwsw0061	switzerland	1638	MERIAN	400	27	32	Die Eydtgnoschafft Punten und Wallis Helvetia cum Confinijs. Hans Conr'd Geiger von Zurich. Fecit Anno 1637
mwg0261	baden-wurttemberg	1643	MERIAN	650	21	33	Die Fürst. Statt Stuetgart
mwg0483	mecklenburg	1682	MERIAN	200	31	37	Die Insel Rugen
mwf0772	france normandy	1650	MERIAN	480	28	36	Duche et Gouvernement de Normandie
mwg0262	baden-wurttemberg	1643	MERIAN	600	25	36	Eigentliche Contrafactur der Statt Costantz am Bodensee wie Solche Wahrender Belagerung Anno 1633 im Wesen Gestanden
mwf1018	france provence	1680	MERIAN	300	28	36	Eigentliche Delineation der Insulen S. Margarite und St. Honorat (Bay of Cannes)
mwe1063a	europe serbia	1717	MERIAN	400	24	39	Entwurff der Belagerung Belgrad und dabey vorgegangner Schlacht
mwsam0287	south america brazil	1637	MERIAN	300	27	35	Eroberung der Vestung Povacon zu Porto Calvo in Brasilia (view)
mwe0049	europe	1640	MERIAN	450	28	36	Europa Nova Delineatio
mwe0043	europe	1635	MERIAN	600	33	45	Europa Partium Orbic Terrae
mwgr0477	greece cyprus	1640	MERIAN	480	26	17	Famagusta
mwaf0778	africa north morocco	1646	MERIAN	300	25	33	Fezzae et Marocchi Regna Africae Celeberrima, Describebat Abrah: Ortelius
mwbh0324	belgium holland	1650	MERIAN	300	26	34	Flandria et Zeelandia Comitatus
mwg0449b	hessen	1657	MERIAN	1200	43	112	Francofurti ad Moenum Urbis Imperialis
mwg0438	hessen	1628	MERIAN	12500	74	104	Francofurti ad Moenum, Urbis Imperialis, Electioni Rom; Regum atq; Imperatorum Consecratae, Emporiique tam Germaniae quam Totius Europae Celeberrmi, Accurata Delineatio
mwg0449a	hessen	1650	MERIAN	500	28	35	Francofurtum. Franckfurt
mwbh0280	belgium holland	1640	MERIAN	280	27	33	Frisia Occidentalis
mwf0051	france	1633	MERIAN	320	28	36	Gallia. Le Royaume de France. Franckreych
mwsw0049	switzerland	1628	MERIAN	960	23	34	Geneve. Genff (view)
mwit0416a	italy liguria	1638	MERIAN	350	31	39	Genovesato. Serenissimae Reipublicae Genuensis Ducatus et Dominii Nova Descriptio (reduced copy of Blaeu 1634)
mwit0417	italy liguria	1638	MERIAN	600	21	39	Genua.
mwgr0380	greece crete	1650	MERIAN	1200	23	68	Genuina Delineatio Insulae Cretae
mwin0397	india goa	1650	MERIAN	450	27	36	Goa
mwg0232a	berlin	1652	MERIAN	750	28	36	Grundriss der Beyden Churf: Residentz Statte Berlin und Colln an der Spree (map by JG Memhardt)
mwuk1122	england london	1670	MERIAN	1200	31	42	Grundtriss der Statt London
mwsc0264	scandinavia denmark	1640	MERIAN	720	20	34	Hafnia Metropolis et Portus Celeberrimus Daniae - Coppenhagen
mwsp0179	spain	1638	MERIAN	480	28	36	Hispania Regnum
mwe0877	europe hungary	1646	MERIAN	300	27	33	Hungaria Regnum
mwme0454	jerusalem	1650	MERIAN	480	22	34	Ierusalem
mwas0385a	asia south east	1660	MERIAN	720	27	35	India Orientalis et Insulae Adiacentes
mwsp0647	balearic islands	1649	MERIAN	480	30	39	Insulae Balearides et Pytiusae
mwuk0050	ireland	1641	MERIAN	720	26	36	Irlandiae Mari Portus
mwme0776	persia etc	1650	MERIAN	600	29	38	Isfahan
mwg0517	rheinland-pfalz	1645	MERIAN	300	22	35	Keysers Lautern
mwsw0065	switzerland	1642	MERIAN	720	21	33	Lausanna
mwf0818b	france paris	1615	MERIAN	10000	53	74	Le Plan de la Ville, Cite, et Universite et Fauxbourgs de Paris (the engraver, M. Tavernier, re-issued this map in 1630, with a top border of recent additions, shown below in part)
mwbp0085a	baltic states	1652	MERIAN	350	29	38	Livonia vulgo Lyefland
mwuk1107a	england london	1638	MERIAN	4000	22	70	London (panorama)
mwf0675	france lorraine	1649	MERIAN	280	29	37	Lotharingia Ducatus, vulgo Lorraine
mwit1111	italy tuscany	1688	MERIAN	400	26	37	Luca (view of Lucca)
mwbh0832	luxembourg	1654	MERIAN	360	26	34	Lutzenburg Ducatus
mwuk0699	uk	1638	MERIAN	1000	27	36	Magnae Britanniae et Hiberniae Tabulae.
mwbp0083	baltic states	1640	MERIAN	300	31	37	Magni Ducatus Lithuaniae
mwit0490	italy lombardy	1650	MERIAN	280	28	37	Mantua Ducatus (reduced copy of Blaeu)
mwit0532	italy milan	1654	MERIAN	600	27	35	Mediolanum
mwg0343a	bavaria	1648	MERIAN	720	31	38	Monachium. Munchen
mwe1097	europe slovak republic (moravia)	1633	MERIAN	350	27	35	Moravia Marchionatus
mwru0381	russia moscow	1640	MERIAN	960	27	36	Moscva

AMPG REFERENCE	REGION	DATE	MAP MAKER	PRICE (UK£)	VERT. (cm.)	HOR. (cm.)	TITLE OF MAP (Comments by the editor in brackets)
mwit1055	italy naples	1650	MERIAN	480	28	36	Neapolis
mwg0337a	bavaria	1644	MERIAN	600	20	63	Norenberga - Nurnberg
mwaf0049a	africa	1640	MERIAN	800	27	36	Nova Descriptio Africae
mwit0086	italy	1640	MERIAN	550	28	36	Nova Italiae Delineatio
mwg0061	germany	1654	MERIAN	375	31	36	Nova Totius Germaniae Descriptio Teutschland
mww0146	world	1638	MERIAN	2000	26	35	Nova Totius Terrarum Orbis Geographica ac Hydrographica Tabula. Wahre Bildtnuss des Gantzen Erden Krayses mit Allen seinen Theilen
mwsp0033	portugal	1650	MERIAN	480	28	36	Olisippo. Lisabona. (view)
mwit0888	italy sicily	1650	MERIAN	550	30	38	Panormo (Palermo)
mwf0826a	france paris	1660	MERIAN	500	35	47	Paris ... 1620
mwf0819	france paris	1630	MERIAN	1250	26	69	Parys (view)
mwme0781	persia etc	1661	MERIAN	500	27	35	Persia sive Sophorum Regnum
mwit1106	italy tuscany	1646	MERIAN	550	20	27	Pisa
mwbp0255	poland	1650	MERIAN	400	27	36	Polonia Regnum, et Silesia Ducatus
mwsp0031	portugal	1646	MERIAN	375	28	37	Portugallia et Algarbia quae olim Lusitania
mwe0538b	europe czech republic (bohemia)	1649	MERIAN	2400	28	110	Praga
mwe0538c	europe czech republic (bohemia)	1650	MERIAN	1200	24	68	Praga
mwbh0396	belgium holland	1676	MERIAN	500	27	34	Prosp. der Belägrung Maestricht und Wyck, durch den Princen von Oranien. Anno 1676
mwf0826b	france paris	1660	MERIAN	1500	26	79	Prosp. der Statt Parys... 1654
mwbp0269	poland	1660	MERIAN	280	27	34	Prussiae Nova Tabula
mwit1005a	italy south	1638	MERIAN	350	28	36	Regno di Napoli
mwbp0085	baltic states	1652	MERIAN	785	22	26	Riga
mwuk1425	england thames	1667	MERIAN	350	22	35	Rivier oder gegent von London, mit der eroberung der Insul Schepey ... 1667 (inset of Isle of Sheppey)
mwit0716	italy rome	1650	MERIAN	1500	31	72	Roma
mwbh0325	belgium holland	1650	MERIAN	480	28	35	Rotterdam
mwf1123	france rhone-alpes	1650	MERIAN	350	27	36	Sabaudia Ducatus. Savoye
mwe0323	europe austria	1644	MERIAN	400	28	36	Saltzburg
mwit0789	italy sardinia	1649	MERIAN	400	28	18	Sardinia
mwit0886	italy sicily	1638	MERIAN	550	27	36	Sicilia Regnum
mwbp0256	poland	1650	MERIAN	300	28	35	Silesia Ducatus
mwe0666	europe dalmatia	1652	MERIAN	350	29	37	Situs Particularis Comitatus Sebenciani (view)
mwbp0257	poland	1650	MERIAN	400	21	33	Stetinum
mwsam0665	south america magellan	1630	MERIAN	350	15	17	Sud Seite des Landts Terra del Fuoco (copy of Le Maire 1619)
mwsc0052	scandinavia	1638	MERIAN	400	29	36	Tabula Exactissima Regnoru Sueciae et Norvegiae nec non Maris Universi Orientalis
mwuk1640	north sea	1641	MERIAN	480	26	35	Tabula Maris Septentrionalis (North Sea south)
mwbp0009	baltic sea (east)	1641	MERIAN	500	26	36	Tabula Navigatoria Maris Orientalis
mwuk1641	north sea	1641	MERIAN	480	26	36	Tabula Portuum Angliae, Belgii, Iutlandia in Norwegia, nec non Reliqui Maris Septentrionalis
mwat0211	atlantic east	1641	MERIAN	400	26	35	Tabula Portuum Barbariae, junctis Insulis Canariensibus
mwsp0027a	portugal	1641	MERIAN	400	26	35	Tabula Portuum Gallitiae, Portugaelliae et Andalusiae (based on Blaeu 1625)
mwaa0087	arctic	1641	MERIAN	550	26	36	Tabula Portuum Lappiae et Russiae, usq Novam Zembalam
mwsc0543	scandinavia norway	1641	MERIAN	800	25	56	Tabula Portuum Occidentalium Norwegiae et Spizbergi (north to the right)
mwru0047	russia	1650	MERIAN	500	28	36	Tabula Russiae ... alias dicta Moscovia
mwe1187	europe west	1644	MERIAN	650	26	36	Tabula Transeundi Maris Orientalis ...
mwat0251	atlantic north	1641	MERIAN	800	26	36	Tabula Transeundi Maris Orientalis, Septentrionalis, et Occidentalis
mwsp0434	spain regions	1641	MERIAN	400	26	35	Tabula Transitus Gibraltaris cum Portibus Hispanicis usq Malagam
mwe0667	europe dalmatia	1657	MERIAN	300	28	36	Tafel der Statte und Herschafften Zara und Sebenico in Dalmatia Gelegen, allwo die Venediger dem Turckhen Underschiedliche Veste Orther Abgenomen im Jahr 1646 und 47
mwru0425	russia tartary	1646	MERIAN	350	27	35	Tartaria sive Magni Chami Imperiorum
mwsw0070	switzerland	1654	MERIAN	720	27	36	Tigurum Zurych
mwe1098	europe slovak republic (moravia)	1638	MERIAN	400	24	35	Topographia Regiae Liberaeque Civitatis Posoniensis vulgo Pressburg (view of Bratislava)
mwe0707a	europe danube	1672	MERIAN	600	31	60	Totius Regni Hungariae
mwm0006	mediterranean	1647	MERIAN	500	20	35	Treffen Zwischen den Maltesern und Turcken in dem Mittellandischen Meer Ao 1648
mwme0554	arabia etc	1650	MERIAN	580	27	36	Turcicum Imperium. Turckische Reych
mww0154a	world	1641	MERIAN	1350	17	26	Typus Orbis Terrarum
mwm0186	mediterranean malta	1650	MERIAN	600	28	36	Valetta Citta Nova di Malta
mwit1222	italy venice	1638	MERIAN	3500	28	70	Venetia
mwe0410d	europe austria vienna	1648	MERIAN	600	19	33	Vienna Austria
mwuss1594	virginia	1627	MERIAN	3500	29	36	Virginia / Erforshet und Beschriben durch Capitain Iohan Schmidt

AMPG REFERENCE	REGION	DATE	MAP MAKER	PRICE (UK£)	VERT. (cm.)	HOR. (cm.)	TITLE OF MAP (Comments by the editor in brackets)
mwe0538a	europe czech republic (bohemia)	1648	MERIAN	1000	30	58	Wahrer Abriß der beyden Königlichen Haubt Alt und Newstatt Prag... belagert 1648
mwc0019a	china	1638	MERIAN	500	18	26	Xuntien alias Quinzay (view of Hang Chow. See also Valegio 1600.)
mwe0031	europe	1621	MERULA	280	10	13	Europa
mww0111	world	1605	MERULA	5500	30	50	Totius Orbis Cogniti Universalis Descriptio (engraved by J. van Doetecum)
mwsw0136	switzerland	1739	MERVEILLEUX	240	18	24	Carte der 13. Schweitzer Cantons
mwsw0093a	switzerland	1694	MERVEILLEUX	1600	53	83	Carte Geographique de la Souveraineté de Neufchâtel et Vallangin en Suisse
mwuk0013a	ireland	1600	METALUS?	500	15	20	Hibernia Irlandt Irlande (shown above left)
mwat0232	atlantic islands	1601	METELLUS	480	10	16	(Tercera / Bay of Cadiz / Madeira & environs / Canary Islands)
mwaf0025	africa	1597	METELLUS	1800	19	24	Africa
mwam0026	america continent	1602	METELLUS	8000	21	29	Americae sive Novi Orbis
mwuk0680	uk	1596	METELLUS	1200	20	21	Anglia Scotia et Hibernia
mwas0015	asia continent	1595	METELLUS	1200	20	24	Asia
mwe0300	europe austria	1596	METELLUS	500	19	24	Austria. Styria. Carinthia. Tyrol. Carina. Corithia Windorum Marchia
mwe0519c	europe czech republic (bohemia)	1597	METELLUS	400	14	20	Bohemia, Beheym, Boheme
mwsam0276	south america brazil	1598	METELLUS	1000	19	24	Brasilia
mwin0092	india	1596	METELLUS	500	15	22	Calecuty Regnum
mwsam0488	south america colombia	1598	METELLUS	850	18	23	Castilia Aurifera cum Vicinis Provinciis
mwaa0002	antarctic	1598	METELLUS	1500	18	23	Chica sive Patagonica et Australis Terra
mwsam0439	south america chile	1598	METELLUS	600	19	24	Chili Provincia Amplissima
mwca0005b	canada	1598	METELLUS	1500	17	22	Conibas Regio cum Vicinis Gentibus
mwwi0403	cuba	1598	METELLUS	750	19	23	Cuba Insula et Iamaica
mwsc0032	scandinavia	1596	METELLUS	1500	16	25	Dania et Norvegia (north to the right. Illustration below left)
mwca0006	canada	1598	METELLUS	850	18	23	Estotilandia et Laboratoris Terra
mwe0022	europe	1599	METELLUS	650	18	25	Europae
mwaf0771	africa north morocco	1596	METELLUS	600	15	20	Fessae et Marocchi Regna
mwaf0837	africa north west	1596	METELLUS	400	15	21	Fessae et Marocchi Regna (north to the right)
mwam0849	america north (east)	1598	METELLUS	4000	19	24	Florida et Apalche
mwf0033	france	1596	METELLUS	500	15	19	Francia - Franckreich
mwf0034	france	1596	METELLUS	500	14	19	Gallia Franza Franckreich France
mwg0030	germany	1596	METELLUS	350	16	21	Germania
mwgr0041	greece	1595	METELLUS	600	19	24	Graeciae universae secundum
mwuss0066	california	1598	METELLUS	1500	18	24	Granata Nova et California
mwsp0166	spain	1595	METELLUS	850	15	19	Hispania
mwjk0005	japan	1596	METELLUS	2000	15	21	Iaponia Regnum
mwit0047	italy	1596	METELLUS	1500	20	24	Italia
mwgm0141	mexico	1598	METELLUS	600	18	23	Iucatana Regio et Fondura
mwf0765	france normandy	1596	METELLUS	800	22	28	La Ville Dieppe (view)
mwam1312	america north (west)	1598	METELLUS	2000	18	22	Limes Occidentis et Quivira: Anian
mwru0418	russia tartary	1596	METELLUS	1200	15	21	Magni Chami Tartari Imperium
mwin0093	india	1596	METELLUS	500	16	23	Magni Mogori Imperium
mwp0227	pacific (all)	1598	METELLUS	3500	20	28	Maris Pacifici vulgo Mar del Zur - Terra Australis
mwru0019	russia	1596	METELLUS	1000	15	20	Moscovia
mwam0848	america north (east)	1598	METELLUS	2800	18	23	Norumbega et Virginia
mwca0007	canada	1598	METELLUS	1500	19	24	Nova Francia et Canada
mwf0818	france paris	1596	METELLUS	1200	22	28	Pareis vom Konig Navarro ... 1590
mwme0761	persia etc	1596	METELLUS	650	15	21	Persiae Regnum
mwsam0731a	south america peru	1598	METELLUS	600	18	24	Peruani Regni Descriptio
mwas0747a	asia south east philippines	1601	METELLUS	2000	18	24	Philippinae Insulae
mwsam0211a	south america argentina	1598	METELLUS	600	18	24	Plata Americae Provincia
mwbp0205	poland	1596	METELLUS	800	20	29	Polonia Lithania Livonia (north to right)
mwsp0013	portugal	1595	METELLUS	750	15	24	Portugallia
mwaf0351	africa east	1596	METELLUS	650	15	20	Presbiteri Iohannis Imperium (north to the right)
mwc0004	china	1596	METELLUS	1500	15	21	Regnum Chinae (north to the right)
mwaf0853	africa south	1596	METELLUS	1200	16	23	Regnum Monomotapae
mwin0094	india	1596	METELLUS	500	16	23	Regnum Narsingae (incl. Southern India and Bay of Bengal)
mwas0815	asia south east siam	1596	METELLUS	2500	16	23	Regnum Sian (first western map to use the name 'Sian')
mwwi0224	west indies (east)	1598	METELLUS	800	18	23	Residuum Continentis cum Adiacentibus Insulis
mwit0779a	italy sardinia	1601	METELLUS	650	18	26	Sardinia (see above left)
mwsc0033	scandinavia	1596	METELLUS	1500	15	19	Sueciae Regnum (north to the right)
mwme0539	arabia etc	1596	METELLUS	1200	20	25	Turcici Imperii Descriptio
mww0089	world	1596	METELLUS	2250	20	30	Typus Orbis Terrarum
mwe0383	europe austria	1782	METZBURG	1500	101	150	Post Charte der Kaiserl. Konigl. Erblanden
mwuk1121	england london	1668	MEYER, M.	3000	30	54	Platte Grondt der Verbrande Stadt London
mwbh0808	belgium holland	1847	MEYER	160	29	36	Antwerpen (Plan Topographique a d'Anvers) 1845
mwuss0063	arkansas	1845	MEYER	95	37	30	Arkansas
mwru0367	russia	1845	MEYER	95	29	36	Asiatisches Russland
mwp0161	australia	1846	MEYER	280	30	37	Australien
mwg0249	berlin	1845	MEYER	300	25	34	Berlin
mwbh0807	belgium holland	1845	MEYER	140	36	39	Brussel (Bruxelles)

AMPG REFERENCE	REGION	DATE	MAP MAKER	PRICE (UK£)	VERT. (cm.)	HOR. (cm.)	TITLE OF MAP (Comments by the editor in brackets)
mwuss0325	connecticut	1846	MEYER	150	30	38	Connecticut
mwc0290	china	1846	MEYER	100	29	38	Das Chinesische Reich mit seinen Schutzstaaten nebst dem Japanischen Inselreiche
mwam0841	america north (central)	1850	MEYER	150	20	27	Die Staaten von Arkansas, Mississippi, Louisiana & Alabama
mwam1265	america north (east)	1850	MEYER	95	27	20	Die Staaten von Maine, New Hampshire, Massachusetts, Vermont, Connecticut, & Rhode I.
mwam0840	america north (central)	1850	MEYER	150	28	20	Die Staaten von Missouri, Illinois, Indiana, Ohio, Kentucky & Tennessee
mwam1264	america north (east)	1850	MEYER	95	25	20	Die Staaten von N. & S. Carolina, Georgia & Florida
mwaa0057	antarctic	1849	MEYER	480	30	36	Erd-Karte in der Globular Projektion (shows discoveries of Weddell, Wilkes etc.)
mwe0849	europe east	1850	MEYER	75	19	25	Europ. Turkei: Rumelien, Bulgarien und Walachei 1850
mwuss0484	florida	1845	MEYER	225	37	30	Florida
mwg0471	hessen	1845	MEYER	160	34	41	Frankfurt (am Mayn)
mwf0204	france	1845	MEYER	95	29	36	Frankreich
mwme0855	persia etc	1846	MEYER	95	29	36	Iran Turan Persien Afghanistan Beludschistan Turkestan
mwsp0137	portugal	1844	MEYER	160	34	41	Lissabon (Lisboa) (close copy of S.D.U.K. 1833)
mwit1079	italy naples	1845	MEYER	160	34	41	Neapel
mwwi0212	west indies	1844	MEYER	120	30	37	Neueste Karte der Grossen Antillen
mwaa0175	arctic	1842	MEYER	120	30	30	Neueste Karte vom Nord Pol
mwaa0055	antarctic	1845	MEYER	400	30	32	Neueste Karte vom Sud-Pol
mwaf0338	africa	1844	MEYER	80	29	36	Neueste Karte von Africa
mwuss0019	alabama	1845	MEYER	200	37	31	Neueste Karte von Alabama mit Seinen Canaelen, Strassen, Eisenbahnen und Routen fur Dampfschiffe nach den Bessten Quellen Verbessert
mwme0688	arabia etc	1845	MEYER	240	30	37	Neueste Karte von Arabien
mwwi0208	west indies	1843	MEYER	95	29	36	Neueste Karte von Central America und West Indien
mwsc0407	scandinavia denmark	1846	MEYER	80	36	29	Neueste Karte von Danemark mit Holstein
mwe0270	europe	1843	MEYER	95	29	36	Neueste Karte von Europa
mwuss0535	georgia	1845	MEYER	200	30	37	Neueste Karte von Georgia
mwgr0261	greece	1844	MEYER	95	29	36	Neueste Karte von Griechenland
mwuk0897	uk	1844	MEYER	95	36	29	Neueste Karte von Grossbritannien und Ireland
mwas0855	asia south east siam	1844	MEYER	120	37	32	Neueste Karte von Hinter Indien
mwbh0805	belgium holland	1844	MEYER	95	29	36	Neueste Karte von Holland, Belgien und Luxemburg
mwuss0565	illinois	1845	MEYER	250	38	30	Neueste Karte von Illinois mit seinem Strassen Entfernung der Hauptpunkte
mwit0247	italy	1844	MEYER	95	36	29	Neueste Karte von Italien
mwuss0681	louisiana	1845	MEYER	150	30	38	Neueste Karte von Louisiana
mwca0197	canada	1844	MEYER	95	30	38	Neueste Karte von Lower Canada (Unter-Canada)
mwuss0737	maine	1845	MEYER	120	38	30	Neueste Karte von Maine nach den Bessten Quellen Verbessert
mwuss0785	maryland	1846	MEYER	150	30	38	Neueste Karte von Maryland und Delaware mit seinen Canaelen, Strassen und Entfernungen der Hauptpunkte
mwuss0895	massachusetts	1846	MEYER	120	29	38	Neueste Karte von Massachusetts und Rhode Island
mwgm0353	mexico	1845	MEYER	100	29	37	Neueste Karte von Mexico
mwuss0929	michigan	1845	MEYER	480	37	29	Neueste Karte von Michigan
mwuss0994	missouri	1845	MEYER	200	37	30	Neueste Karte von Missouri nach den Besten Quellen Verbessert
mwuss1029	new hampshire	1846	MEYER	200	37	30	Neueste Karte von New Hampshire und Vermont
mwuss1064	new jersey	1846	MEYER	150	37	30	Neueste Karte von New Jersey
mwuss1250	new york	1844	MEYER	200	30	37	Neueste Karte von New York
mwuss0285	carolinas	1845	MEYER	150	30	37	Neueste Karte von Nord Carolina mit seinen Canaelen, Strassen, Eisenbahnen, Entfernungen der Hauptpunkte und Routen fur Dampfschiffe
mwuss1323	ohio	1845	MEYER	200	37	30	Neueste Karte von Ohio mit seinen Canaelen, Strassen & Entfernungen der Hauptpunkte
mwuss1442	pennsylvania	1845	MEYER	150	31	37	Neueste Karte von Pennsylvania mit Seinen Canaelen, Eisenbahnen &c.
mwsp0138	portugal	1844	MEYER	95	36	29	Neueste Karte von Portugal
mwe0404	europe austria	1843	MEYER	95	29	36	Neueste Karte von Salzburg
mwsc0220	scandinavia	1846	MEYER	80	36	29	Neueste Karte von Schweden und Norwegen
mwsp0333	spain	1843	MEYER	95	29	36	Neueste Karte von Spanien und Portugal
mwuss0286	carolinas	1845	MEYER	150	30	38	Neueste Karte von Sud Carolina
mwaf1025	africa south	1846	MEYER	240	29	36	Neueste Karte von Sudafrica
mwaf0432b	africa north	1845	MEYER	120	29	36	Neueste Karte von Sudan und Guinea
mwuss1498	tennessee	1845	MEYER	300	30	37	Neueste Karte von Tennessee
mwe0848	europe east	1847	MEYER	95	30	36	Neueste Karte von Ungarn, Galizien, Slavonien und Croatien, Siebenburgen und dem Militairgrenzland
mwuss1690	virginia	1845	MEYER	150	30	37	Neueste Karte von Virginia
mwin0370	india	1844	MEYER	95	36	29	Neueste Karte von Vorder Indien oder Hindostan
mwsam0192	south america (north)	1847	MEYER	95	29	36	Neu-Granada, Venezuela, Ecuador und Guyana
mwam0304	america continent	1843	MEYER	95	38	30	Neuste Karte von America
mwam1266	america north (east)	1850	MEYER	95	27	20	New York, Pensylvania, Maryland, New Jersey, Delaware & Virginia
mwca0199	canada	1845	MEYER	95	30	38	Ober- (Upper-) Canada

AMPG REFERENCE	REGION	DATE	MAP MAKER	PRICE (UK£)	VERT. (cm.)	HOR. (cm.)	TITLE OF MAP (Comments by the editor in brackets)
mwf0934	france paris	1845	MEYER	375	41	56	Ostliche Halfte von Paris / Westliche Halfte von Paris
mwuss1441	pennsylvania	1845	MEYER	250	37	30	Philadelphia
mwbh0806	belgium holland	1844	MEYER	160	34	41	Plan von Amsterdam
mwuk0635	scotland	1844	MEYER	300	36	39	Plan von Edinburgh
mwsp0349	spain madrid	1844	MEYER	200	33	40	Plan von Madrid
mwg0409	bavaria	1844	MEYER	150	34	41	Plan von Munchen
mwuss1249	new york	1844	MEYER	450	36	29	Plan von New York
mwru0366	russia	1844	MEYER	350	36	49	Plan von St. Petersburg
mwuss0357	washington DC	1845	MEYER	480	31	37	Plan von Washington
mwuk1121	england london	1668	MEYER	2500	30	54	Platte Grondt der Verbrande Stadt London
mwru0371	russia	1850	MEYER	95	21	28	Pontus Euxinus et Regio
mwca0561	canada quebec	1838	MEYER	95	10	16	Quebeck in Canada
mwsc0651	scandinavia norway	1845	MEYER	95	36	29	Sudliches Norwegen nach Carpelan
mwsc0756	scandinavia sweden	1845	MEYER	80	36	29	Sudliches Schweden nach Forsell
mwuss1529	texas	1845	MEYER	1500	29	36	Texas nach den Besten Quellen (map by C. Radefeld)
mwf0937	france paris	1849	MEYER	95	23	28	Topographische Karte von Paris und Gegend
mwgm0082	gulf of mexico and surrounding regions	1845	MEYER	120	18	24	West Indien und Mittel America
mwe0442	europe austria vienna	1844	MEYER	160	42	33	Wien
mwit0523	italy lombardy	1846	MICHAELIS	320	43	29	Carta della Repubblica e Cantone del Ticino
mwme0210	holy land	1693	MICHALET	875	56	78	Les Deserts d'Egypte, de Thebaide d'Arabie, de Sirie, &c., ou sont Exactement Marques les Lieux Habitez par les Saincts Peres des Deserts
mwam0870	america north (east)	1674	MICHAULT	960	19	24	Costes et Rivieres de Virginie, de Mariland et de Nouvelle Angleterre
mwam1147	america north (east)	1804	MICHAUX	480	36	50	Carte des Etats du Centre, de l'Ouest et du Sud des Etat-Unis-An XII-1804
mwm0141	mediterranean east	1715	MICHELOT & BREMOND	2000	47	69	(Eastern Mediterranean)
mwm0107	mediterranean central	1726	MICHELOT & BREMOND	2000	47	68	(Untitled chart centred on Sicily)
mwm0275	mediterranean west	1723	MICHELOT & BREMOND	1500	48	69	Carte Particuliere des cotes d'Espagne et de Barbarie
mwm0272	mediterranean west	1718	MICHELOT & BREMOND	2500	49	135	Nouvelle Carte de Cotes de Catalogne, Roussillon, Languedoc, Provence, d'Italie et Partie de l'Isle de Corce
mwm0274	mediterranean west	1718	MICHELOT & BREMOND	2000	47	69	Nouvelle Carte de la Baye de Cadis et du Detroit de Gibraltar
mwgr0621	greece islands	1715	MICHELOT & BREMOND	1800	47	63	Nouvelle Carte de l'Archipel (north to the right)
mwm0219	mediterranean malta	1718	MICHELOT & BREMOND	2800	46	67	Nouvelle Carte de Lisle de Malthe
mwit0800	italy sardinia	1719	MICHELOT & BREMOND	2500	47	69	Nouvelle Carte de l'Isle de Sardaigne et Partie de celle de Corse
mwm0273	mediterranean west	1718	MICHELOT & BREMOND	2500	55	69	Nouvelle Carte Generalle de la Mer Mediterannee (1726 version 47x59cm shown below)
mwsp0659	balearic islands	1730	MICHELOT & BREMOND	300	18	25	Partie de l'Isle d'Yvice et des Isles Fromentieres
mwsp0532	spain regions	1730	MICHELOT & BREMOND	350	18	25	Plan de la Baye de Cadis et des Environs
mwsp0703	gibraltar	1730	MICHELOT & BREMOND	300	18	25	Plan de la Baye de Gibraltar
mwf1049	france provence	1723	MICHELOT & BREMOND	1200	48	69	Plan de la Baye et Rades de Marseille
mwf1050	france provence	1728	MICHELOT & BREMOND	300	18	25	Plan de la Ville et Port d'Antibe
mwsp0533	spain regions	1730	MICHELOT & BREMOND	450	18	25	Plan de la Ville et Port de Barcelona
mwit0935	italy sicily	1730	MICHELOT & BREMOND	300	18	25	Plan de la Ville et Port de Messine
mwit0936	italy sicily	1730	MICHELOT & BREMOND	300	18	25	Plan de la Ville, Port et Rades de Palerme
mwit0428	italy liguria	1730	MICHELOT & BREMOND	400	18	25	Plan de Port de Genes
mwf0484	france corsica	1730	MICHELOT & BREMOND	300	18	25	Plan de Porto Vecchio, en L'Isle de Corse
mwit1034	italy south	1730	MICHELOT & BREMOND	300	18	25	Plan du Golfe de Naples
mwsp0534	spain regions	1730	MICHELOT & BREMOND	350	18	25	Plan du Port de Cartagene
mwf1051	france provence	1728	MICHELOT & BREMOND	300	18	25	Plan de la Rade du Gourjan et des Isles Ste. Marguerite (environs of Cannes)
mwit1028	italy south	1718	MICHELOT & BREMOND	1400	48	70	Suite de la Carte d'Italie (south to the top)
mwru0391	russia moscow	1739	MICHURIN	4000	59	49	Plan Imperatorskago Stolicnago Goroda Moskvy (Russian script)
mwam0469	america north	1779	MIDDLETON	450	27	43	A New & Accurate Map of North America

AMPG REFERENCE	REGION	DATE	MAP MAKER	PRICE (UK£)	VERT. (cm.)	HOR. (cm.)	TITLE OF MAP (Comments by the editor in brackets)
mwas0499	asia south east	1779	MIDDLETON	235	20	29	An Accurate Map of the East Indies from the Latest Improvements and Regulated by Astronomical Observations
mww0584	world	1794	MIDDLETON	280	18	28	New & Complete Mercator Chart of the World
mwsam0098	south america	1779	MIDDLETON	150	19	29	South America ... Including the Latest Discoveries of the Most Eminent Navigators along the Coast and in the Seas Contiguous Thereto
mwwi0113	west indies	1780	MIDDLETON	250	18	28	The West Indies, Exhibiting the English, French, Spanish, Dutch & Danish Settlements, with the Adjacent Parts of North & South America
mwca0214a	canada arctic	1743	MIDDLETON	4000	48	67	To the King, this Chart of Hudson's Bay & Straits, Baffin's Bay, Strait Davis & Labrador Coast &c. is Most Humbly Dedicated
mwbh0809	belgium holland	1850	MIGEON	140	38	28	Hollande et Belgique.
mwuk0898	uk	1851	MIGEON	140	39	28	Iles Britanniques
mwp0295	pacific (all)	1851	MIGEON	150	30	37	Oceanie
mww0754	world	1851	MIGEON	280	29	37	Planisphere
mwaf0760	africa north algeria	1854	MIGEON	200	42	28	Province D'Alger
mwme1071	turkey etc	1851	MIGEON	180	28	37	Turquie D'Asie
mwam1196	america north (east)	1826	MILBERT	350	50	42	Carte pour Servir a l'Itineraire Pittoresque du Fleuve Hudson et des Parties Laterales de l'Amerique du Nord (2 maps on one sheet)
mww0523	world	1782	MILLAR	900	30	47	A New and Accurate Map of the World, Comprehending All the New Discoveries, in Both Hemispheres; Carefully Brought Down to the Present Year 1782
mwuk1020	england	1782	MILLAR	180	33	22	A New and Correct Map of England & Wales from the Latest & Best Improvements
mwg0669	saxony	1782	MILLAR	200	30	28	A New and Correct Plan of Hannover
mwuk0213	ireland	1780	MILLAR	150	17	25	A Prospect of Dublin, the Capital of Ireland
mwaf0242	africa	1780	MILLAR	280	34	38	Africa
mwe0431	europe austria vienna	1780	MILLAR	150	20	29	An Accurate Prospect of Vienne, the Capital of Germany
mwp0429	pacific north	1782	MILLAR	200	15	20	Chart of the New Northern Archipelago; Discover'd by the Russians in the Seas of Kamtschatka & Anadir
mww0524	world	1782	MILLAR	450	20	30	New & Complete Mercator Chart of the World
mwam0477	america north	1782	MILLAR	350	33	37	North America Agreeable to the Most Approved Maps and Charts
mwsc0636	scandinavia norway	1782	MILLAR	400	20	29	Perspective View of Bergen
mwuss1142	new york	1780	MILLAR	350	14	10	Plan of the Harbour of New-York and Parts Adjacent
mwam1077	america north (east)	1782	MILLAR	135	29	21	Various Plans and Draughts of Cities, Towns, Harbours &c.
mwuss0266	carolinas	1825	MILLS	3000	91	91	Charlestown District, South Carolina
mwgm0088	gulf of mexico and surrounding regions	1850	MILNAR	200	30	24	California, Mexico, Guatimala &c.
mwec0491	uk england hampshire	1791	MILNE	2000	150	142	Hampshire, or the County of Southampton, Including the Isle of Wight, Surveyed by Thos. Milne in the Years 1788, 89 & 90
mwuk0639	scotland	1845	MILNE	650	45	56	Milne's Pictorial Plan of Edinburgh
mwam0727	america north	1839	MILNE	160	23	19	North America
mwme0470	jerusalem	1687	MILONIUS	15000	58	90	Vera Deliniatio Hodierni Situs Almae Civitatis Ierusalem
mwec0481	uk england hampshire	1754	MILTON	2800	48	65	A Geometrical Plan & West Elevation of His Majesty's Dock Yard near Portsmouth with Part of the Common
mwwi0430	cuba	1739	MILTON	1250	41	57	Plan of the City and Harbour of Havana Situated on the Island of Cuba
mwg0183	germany	1844	MINSINGER	580	98	115	Post-Reise-Karte von Deutschland mit Spezieller Angabe der Eisenbahn- u. Dampfschiffahrt-Verbindungen
mwf0687	france lorraine	1775	MIQUE	360	29	32	Plan des Villes, Citadelle, Faubourgs, et Environs de Nancy
mwbh0233a	belgium holland	1633	MIRAEUS	2400	46	54	Galliae Belgicae
mww0727	world	1843	MITCHELL	3500	119	188	A Map of the World on Mercator's Projection Exhibiting the Researches of the Principal Modern Travellers and Navigators
mwuss0020	alabama	1849	MITCHELL	200	36	29	A New Map of Alabama with its Roads and Distances from place to place along the Stage and Steamboat Routes
mwuss0064	arkansas	1849	MITCHELL	80	37	30	A New Map of Arkansas with its Canals, Roads and Distances
mwuss0538	georgia	1849	MITCHELL	160	35	29	A New Map of Georgia with its Roads and Distances
mwuss0566	illinois	1849	MITCHELL	200	36	29	A New Map of Illinois with its Proposed Canals, Roads and Distances from place to place along the Steamboat Routes (inset: Lead Region)
mwuss0581	indiana	1849	MITCHELL	140	35	29	A New Map of Indiana with its Roads and Distances
mwuss0620	kentucky	1849	MITCHELL	200	29	35	A New Map of Kentucky with its Roads & Distances from place to place along the Stage & Steam Boat Routes (insets: Lexington, Falls of Ohio, Clarksburg)
mwuss0684	louisiana	1849	MITCHELL	160	29	36	A New Map of Louisiana with its Canals, Roads and Distances from place to place along the Stage and Steamboat Routes (inset: New Orleans)
mwuss0738	maine	1849	MITCHELL	120	38	30	A New Map of Maine

AMPG REFERENCE	REGION	DATE	MAP MAKER	PRICE (UK£)	VERT. (cm.)	HOR. (cm.)	TITLE OF MAP (Comments by the editor in brackets)
mwuss0786	maryland	1849	MITCHELL	200	29	37	A New Map of Maryland and Delaware with their Canals, Roads & Distances (inset of Baltimore)
mwuss0930	michigan	1849	MITCHELL	180	37	30	A New Map of Michigan with its Canals, Roads & Distances (inset: Western part of Michigan)
mwuss0971	mississippi	1849	MITCHELL	120	36	29	A New Map of Mississippi with its Roads and Distances
mwuss1260	new york	1849	MITCHELL	140	29	35	A New Map of New York with its Canals, Roads & Distances
mwuss0289	carolinas	1849	MITCHELL	300	29	36	A New Map of Nth. Carolina with its Canals, Roads, and Distances from place to place along the Stage & Steam Boat Routes (insets: Gold Region, Newbern)
mwuss1324	ohio	1849	MITCHELL	200	36	29	A New Map of Ohio with its Canals, Roads, and Distances
mwuss1446	pennsylvania	1847	MITCHELL	120	29	36	A New Map of Pennsylvania with its Canals, Rail-roads, &c.
mwuss0288	carolinas	1849	MITCHELL	300	29	36	A New Map of South Carolina with its Canals, Roads, and Distances from place to place along the Stage & Steam Boat Routes (inset: Charleston)
mwuss1499	tennessee	1849	MITCHELL	200	29	39	A New Map of Tennessee with its Roads and Distances from place to place along the Stage and Steamboat Routes (insets: Nashville, Knoxville)
mwam1374	america north (west)	1846	MITCHELL	8000	57	52	A New Map of Texas Oregon and California with the Regions Adjoining
mww0747	world	1849	MITCHELL	280	24	36	A New Map of the World on the Globular Projection
mwuss1691	virginia	1849	MITCHELL	200	29	36	A New Map of Virginia with its Canals, Roads & Distances from Place to Place, along the Stage & Steam Boat Routes
mwaf0341	africa	1849	MITCHELL	100	31	38	Africa (inset of Liberia)
mwas0259	asia continent	1849	MITCHELL	200	31	39	Asia (inset of Australia)
mwca0566	canada quebec	1849	MITCHELL	100	31	40	Canada East Formerly Lower Canada. (inset: Nova Scotia)
mwam1309	great lakes	1846	MITCHELL	250	32	40	Canada West Formerly Upper Canada. (inset: Lake Superior. For illustration, see 'Canada Ontario'.)
mwsam0266	south america argentina	1849	MITCHELL	150	39	32	Chili La Plata and Uruguay
mwc0293	china	1847	MITCHELL	120	29	37	China
mwuss1259	new york	1849	MITCHELL	280	39	31	City of New York
mwuss0359	washington DC	1849	MITCHELL	200	31	39	City of Washington
mwuss0328	connecticut	1849	MITCHELL	200	31	38	Connecticut (insets of Hartford and Newhaven)
mwaf0567	africa egypt etc	1846	MITCHELL	80	38	32	Egypt &c.
mwuss0486	florida	1849	MITCHELL	300	37	30	Florida (insets: Pensacola, Tallahassie, St. Augustine)
mwgr0265	greece	1849	MITCHELL	100	31	38	Greece.
mwin0373	india	1846	MITCHELL	140	32	38	Hindoostan
mwuss0589	iowa	1849	MITCHELL	250	41	33	Iowa.
mwuk0300	ireland	1849	MITCHELL	120	37	28	Ireland
mwit0829	italy sardinia	1849	MITCHELL	200	32	39	Kingdom of Sardinia (inset of Sardinia isl)
mwuss0468	florida	1831	MITCHELL	1000	41	24	Map of Florida According to the Latest Authorities / Comparative Elevation of the Principal Mountains Cities &c. in North & South America
mwuss0474	florida	1836	MITCHELL	1400	41	52	Map of Florida According to the Latest Authorities / The West Indies from the Best Authorities / Comparative Elevation of the Principal Mountains Cities &c. in North & South America.
mwam0822	america north (central)	1831	MITCHELL	2000	43	54	Map of Louisiana Mississippi and Alabama Constructed from the Latest Authorities
mwam1213	america north (east)	1831	MITCHELL	1000	43	55	Map of Maine New Hampshire and Vermont Compiled from the Latest Authorities
mwuss0870	massachusetts	1831	MITCHELL	1250	43	55	Map of Massachusetts Connecticut and Rhode Island Constructed from the Latest Authorities
mwgm0354a	mexico	1846	MITCHELL	5500	45	64	Map of Mexico, Including Yucatan & Upper California, Exhibiting the Chief Cities and Towns, the Principal Travelling Routes &c.
mwgm0358	mexico	1847	MITCHELL	5500	83	61	Map of Mexico, including Yucatan & Upper California, exhibiting the Chief Cities and Towns, The Principal Travelling Routes &c.(incl. Mexican road map below 1846 map)
mwuss0995	missouri	1849	MITCHELL	200	40	35	Map of Missouri
mwam0673	america north	1831	MITCHELL	900	54	43	Map of North America Including All the Recent Geographical Discoveries (copied from Finley 1826)
mwuss0271	carolinas	1831	MITCHELL	2000	43	55	Map of North and South Carolina and Georgia Constructed from the Latest Authorities
mwam1372	america north (west)	1846	MITCHELL	300	26	20	Map of Oregon and Upper California
mwam1212	america north (east)	1831	MITCHELL	1000	43	55	Map of Pennsylvania New Jersey and Delaware Constructed from the Latest Authorities
mwam0831	america north (central)	1839	MITCHELL	80	26	41	Map of the Chief Part of the Western States and Part of Virginia
mwam1387	america north (west)	1850	MITCHELL	750	39	33	Map of the State of California, the Territories of Oregon & Utah, and the Chief Part of New Mexico
mwuss0056	arkansas	1831	MITCHELL	2000	43	54	Map of the State of Missouri and Territory of Arkansas Compiled from the Latest Authorities
mwuss1216	new york	1831	MITCHELL	1250	43	55	Map of the State of New York

AMPG REFERENCE	REGION	DATE	MAP MAKER	PRICE (UK£)	VERT. (cm.)	HOR. (cm.)	TITLE OF MAP (Comments by the editor in brackets)
mwuss1309	ohio	1834	MITCHELL	960	38	32	Map of the State of Ohio Exhibiting its Internal Improvements Roads Distances etc.
mwuss1537	texas	1846	MITCHELL	600	27	20	Map of the State of Texas
mwuss0013	alabama	1835	MITCHELL	1500	45	55	Map of the States of Louisiana, Mississippi & Alabama
mwuss0927	michigan	1844	MITCHELL	80	23	28	Map of the States of Michigan & Wisconsin
mwam0823	america north (central)	1831	MITCHELL	1200	43	55	Map of the States of Ohio Indiana & Illinois and Part of Michigan Territory Compiled from the Latest Authorities
mwam1214	america north (east)	1831	MITCHELL	8000	112	89	Map of the United States
mwam0798	america north	1849	MITCHELL	200	26	43	Map of the United States (inset: gold regions)
mwuss0776	maryland	1831	MITCHELL	1800	43	55	Map of Virginia and Maryland Constructed from the Latest Authorities
mwuss0896	massachusetts	1846	MITCHELL	120	31	40	Massachusetts and Rhode Island
mwgm0354b	mexico	1846	MITCHELL	960	30	38	Mexico & Guatemala (2 insets, issued in pocket map format)
mwgm0369	mexico	1849	MITCHELL	180	31	38	Mexico & Guatemala: (insets: Guatemala, Valley of Mexico. Issued in 1846 in pocket map format before it appeared as an atlas map)
mwam1230	america north (east)	1835	MITCHELL	1000	49	60	Mitchell's Map of the United States; Showing the Principal Travelling, Turnpike and Common Roads; on which are Given the Distances in Miles from One Place to Another; also, the Courses of the Canals & Rail Roads
mwam1248	america north (east)	1843	MITCHELL	1850	93	114	Mitchell's National Map of the American Republic or United States of North America. Together with Maps of the Vicinities of Thirty-Two of the Principal Cities & Towns in the Union
mwam1224	america north (east)	1834	MITCHELL	6000	137	176	Mitchell's Reference & Distance Map of the United States
mwam1215	america north (east)	1832	MITCHELL	1200	44	56	Mitchell's Travellers Guide through the United States. A Map of the Roads, Distances, Steam Boat & Canal Routes &c.
mwam1223	america north (east)	1833	MITCHELL	1200	56	43	Mitchell's Traveller's Guide through the United States. A map of the Roads, Distances, Steam Boats and Canal Routes &c. by J.H. Young
mwuss1030	new hampshire	1849	MITCHELL	150	38	30	New Hampshire and Vermont
mwuss1065	new jersey	1849	MITCHELL	120	38	31	New Jersey Reduced from T. Gordon's Map
mww0723	world	1841	MITCHELL	1250	73	120	No. 1. Mitchell's Series of Outline Maps for the Use of Academies and Schools
mwam0728	america north	1839	MITCHELL	250	26	41	No.4. Map of the United States and Texas, Engraved to Illustrate Mitchell's School and Family Geography (inset) No. 5 Map of Mexico and Guatimala
mwp0290	pacific (all)	1846	MITCHELL	180	32	39	Oceania or Pacific Ocean (small inset shows Wilkes' discoveries in the Antarctic. Copy of Tanner 1835).
mwam1373	america north (west)	1846	MITCHELL	900	41	32	Oregon and Upper California
mwam1385a	oregon	1849	MITCHELL	2500	41	32	Oregon, Upper California & New Mexico (shows the gold region. Illustrated far left is an early-1849 issue, prior to the gold discoveries)
mwme0430	holy land	1846	MITCHELL	120	41	33	Palestine & Adjacent Countries (inset of Jerusalem)
mwme0856	persia etc	1849	MITCHELL	200	31	38	Persia Arabia &c
mwsam0803	south america peru	1847	MITCHELL	80	32	38	Peru and Bolivia
mwuss1445	pennsylvania	1849	MITCHELL	200	40	32	Philadelphia
mwsp0337	spain	1849	MITCHELL	120	32	39	Spain and Portugal (inset: Environs of Madrid)
mwsc0222	scandinavia	1849	MITCHELL	100	28	22	Sweden & Norway
mwuss1256	new york	1845	MITCHELL	1400	104	129	The Empire State New York, with its Counties, Towns, Cities, Villages
mwuss0916	michigan	1835	MITCHELL	1800	35	30	The Tourist's Pocket Map of Michigan Exhibiting its Internal Improvements, Roads, Distances, &c.
mwuss1420	pennsylvania	1831	MITCHELL	1500	32	38	The Tourist's Pocket Map of Pennsylvania Exhibiting its Internal Improvements Roads Distances &c by J.H. Young
mwuss0527	georgia	1834	MITCHELL	1500	39	32	The Tourist's Pocket Map of the State of Georgia Exhibiting its Internal Improvements Roads Distances &c.
mwuss0554	illinois	1834	MITCHELL	1200	38	32	The Tourist's Pocket Map of the State of Illinois Exhibiting its Internal Improvements, Roads, Distances &c.
mwuss0617	kentucky	1839	MITCHELL	720	33	40	The Tourist's Pocket Map of the State of Kentucky Exhibiting its Internal Improvements Roads Distances &c. By J.H. Young
mwuss1302	ohio	1831	MITCHELL	1350	39	32	The Tourist's Pocket Map of the State of Ohio Exhibiting its Internal Improvements, Roads, Distances, &c.
mwuss1497	tennessee	1839	MITCHELL	720	32	39	The Tourist's Pocket Map of the State of Tennessee
mwuss1685	virginia	1834	MITCHELL	1000	32	38	The Tourist's Pocket Map of the State of Virginia, Exhibiting its Internal Improvements Road Distances &c.
mwwi0186	west indies	1831	MITCHELL	280	24	41	The West Indies from the Best Authorities
mwam0787	america north	1847	MITCHELL	200	40	32	United States
mwsam0863	south america venezuela	1849	MITCHELL	100	32	39	Venezuela, New Granada & Ecuador (copy of Tanner 1836)
mwwi0219	west indies	1849	MITCHELL	150	31	38	West Indies.
mwuss1701	wisconsin	1849	MITCHELL	180	41	34	Wisconsin
mwuss1696	wisconsin	1838	MITCHELL-ABEL	2000	53	44	Map of the Settled Part of Wisconsin Territory Compiled from the Latest Authorities

AMPG REFERENCE	REGION	DATE	MAP MAKER	PRICE (UK£)	VERT. (cm.)	HOR. (cm.)	TITLE OF MAP (Comments by the editor in brackets)
mwca0170	canada	1833	MOFFAT	720	39	67	Map of the British North American Provinces and Adjoining States 1833
mwit0749a	italy rome	1763	MOGALLI	300	40	54	Carta Topografica delle Antichità di Roma
mwuk1272	england london	1803	MOGG	2400	46	90	An Entire New Plan of the Cities of London & Westminster; with the Borough of Southwark
mwuk1275	england london	1806	MOGG	2400	50	92	London in Miniature with the Surrounding Villages. An Entire New Plan (25 editions to 1846)
mwuk1329	england london	1845	MOGG	600	51	69	Modern London and its Environs (6 editions to 1849)
mwuk1328	england london	1843	MOGG	400	53	74	Mogg's Excursion Map of the Country Twenty Four Miles Round London
mwuk1297	england london	1821	MOGG	600	96	116	Mogg's Forty-Five Miles round London (8 editions to 1846)
mwuk1318	england london	1835	MOGG	1500	56	92	Mogg's New Plan of London (5 editions to 1843)
mwuk1330	england london	1845	MOGG	1500	85	117	Mogg's New Plan of London Improved
mwuk1274	england london	1805	MOGG	1000	54		Mogg's Twenty Four Miles round London (circular map, 11 editions to 1860)
mwuk1053	england	1823	MOGG	1000	132	105	New Map of England and Wales with Part of Scotland
mwuk1276	england london	1806	MOGG	1200	38	56	Strangers Guide to London and Westminster (23 editions to 1848)
mwam0494	america north	1785	MOITHEY	3000	72	100	Amerique Septentrionale par le Sr. Moithey / Amerique Meridionale
mwru0292	russia	1788	MOITHEY	1400	87	65	Carte Generale de l'Empire de Russie Comprise en Europe
mwam0192	america continent	1767	MOITHEY	800	27	39	Carte Nouvelle d'Amerique
mwbp0510	poland	1787	MOITHEY	150	27	37	Carte Nouvelle de la Pologne, avant son Demembrement
mwam1051	america north (east)	1777	MOITHEY	2400	49	69	Carte Nouvelle des Possessions Angloises en Amerique Dressee pour l'Intelligence de la Guerre Presente et Divisee Suivant les Pretentions des Anglois (inset of the N. Atlantic)
mwsc0172	scandinavia	1787	MOITHEY	280	27	42	Carte Nouvelle du Dannemarck, de la Norwege, et de la Suede
mww0484	world	1772	MOITHEY	960	29	42	Indication Nautique des Principaux Espaces de l'Ocean
mwaf0249a	africa	1785	MOITHEY	2500	71	98	L'Afrique revüe corrigée et publiée (illustrated is 1789 edition)
mwas0214	asia continent	1789	MOITHEY	2500	71	97	l'Asie divisee en ses Regions
mww0554	world	1788	MOITHEY	7500	72	102	Le Globe Terrestre Divise en ses Deux Hemispheres Oriental et Occidental
mwaa0198	arctic / antarctic	1769	MOITHEY	480	23	42	Le Globe Terrestre Vu en Convexe par les Deux Poles, l'Equateur Servant d'Horison
mwc0193	china	1779	MOITHEY	200	17	22	L'Empire de la Chine avec les Isles du Japon et la Coree
mwe0208	europe	1785	MOITHEY	1350	72	98	L'Europe divisee en tous les Royaumes
mww0553	world	1787	MOITHEY	240	26	36	Orbis Vetus. Le Monde Connu des Anciens
mwf0897	france paris	1787	MOITHEY	2500	28	42	Plan General de Paris en Quatre Divisions - Division Sud-Est de Paris / Division Sud-Ouest / Division Nord-Est / Division Nord-Ouest (5 sheets)
mwf0890	france paris	1774	MOITHEY	8000	113	146	Plan Historique de la Ville et Faubourgs de Paris son Accroissement depuis Philippe Auguste jusq'au Regne de Louis XV
mwf1172	france lyon	1780	MOITHEY	785	52	63	Plan Scenographique de la Ville de Lyon, sous les Regnes de Francois Ir et de Henri II
mwam0258	america continent	1806	MOLINI	480	51	66	(Untitled map with text at sides and bottom)
mwit1143	italy florence	1847	MOLINI	1200	51	68	Pianta Della Citta di Firenze
mww0627	world	1806	MOLINI, LANDI	960	46	64	Nouvelle Mappemonde (2 offset polar projections)
mwe0712	europe danube	1687	MOLITOR	1350	32	120	(Der Wegen des Hochst-Tapferen Kayser-Adlers Helden-Thaten Sieg-Beruhmte Donau-Fluss)
mwuk1667a	north sea	1740	MOLL	375	20	27	A Chart of Part of ye Sea Coast of England, Holland & Flanders &c
mwbp0035	baltic sea (east)	1710	MOLL	300	28	36	A Chart of the Baltick or East Sea, Gulf of Finland &c.
mwuk1492	uk english channel (all)	1740	MOLL	300	33	41	A Chart of the Channel Between England & France
mwas0456	asia south east	1730	MOLL	450	28	34	A Chart of the East-Indies, with the Coast of Persia, China
mwm0056	mediterranean	1740	MOLL	550	29	42	A Chart of the Mediterranean Sea According to Monsr. Berthelot &c
mwgr0131	greece	1700	MOLL	320	29	41	A Chart of the Sea Coast of Naples, Sicily, Greece and the Archipelago Islands
mwm0108	mediterranean central	1745	MOLL	275	29	42	A Chart of the Sea Coast of Naples, Sicily, Greece and the Archipelago Islands &c
mwsam0454	south america chile	1711	MOLL	140	18	31	A Chart of the South-Sea Coast from the Steights of Magellan to Arica
mwsam0682	south america magellan	1745	MOLL	240	18	27	A Chart of the Streights of Magellan
mwin0427	indian ocean	1745	MOLL	360	30	43	A Chart of ye East-Indies, with the Coast of Persia, China also the Philipina, Moluca and Sunda Islands &c.
mwwi0067a	west indies	1730	MOLL	550	28	35	A Chart of ye West-Indies or the Islands of America in the North Sea &c.
mwwi0072a	west indies	1740	MOLL	550	29	37	A Chart of ye West-Indies or the Islands of America in the North Sea &c. Being ye Present Seat of War (based on Moll 1730)

AMPG REFERENCE	REGION	DATE	MAP MAKER	PRICE (UK£)	VERT. (cm.)	HOR. (cm.)	TITLE OF MAP (Comments by the editor in brackets)
mwca0350	canada nova scotia	1729	MOLL	400	21	44	A Description of the Bay of Fundy Shewing ye Coast, Islands, Harbours, Creeks, Coves, Rocks, Sholes, Soundings & Anchorings &c. Observed by Nat Blackmore in ye Years 1711 & 1712
mwme0494	jerusalem	1739	MOLL	240	13	23	A Draught of the City of Jerusalem as it is Now, Taken from the South East by Corneille Le Bruyn
mwuss0170	carolinas	1715	MOLL	400	12	12	A Draught of ye Town and Harbour of Charles Town
mwas0086	asia continent	1695	MOLL	200	17	19	A General and Particular Description of Asia
mwat0035	atlantic ocean (all)	1730	MOLL	280	36	28	A General Chart of the Sea Coast of Europe, Africa & America. According to E. Wrights or Mercator's Projection. by H. Moll Geographer
mwuk0808	uk	1729	MOLL	200	20	26	A General Map of Great Britain and Ireland
mwam0909	america north (east)	1703	MOLL	1000	22	34	A General Map of New France Com. Call'd Canada
mwe1155	europe south east	1735	MOLL	280	25	31	A general map of Turkey in Europe, Hungary &c
mwsp0707	gibraltar	1739	MOLL	360	23	61	A Map of ... Gibraltar / An Exact Plan of Part of Gibraltar / (Western Mediterranean)
mwam0160	america continent	1746	MOLL	500	18	27	A Map of America According to ye Newest and Most Exact Observations
mwaf1189	africa west	1730	MOLL	160	18	26	A Map of Guinea, Loango, &c.
mwgm0198a	mexico	1717	MOLL	480	18	25	A Map of Mexico or New Spain Florida Now Called Louisiana and Part of California &c.
mwam0912	america north (east)	1711	MOLL	500	18	25	A Map of New France Containing Canada, Louisiana &c. in Nth. America. According to the Patent Granted by the King of France to Monsieur Crozat
mwsam0755	south america peru	1717	MOLL	140	25	18	A Map of Peru and the West Part of the Country of the Amazones
mwsam0051	south america	1711	MOLL	200	18	26	A Map of South America According to ye Newest & Most Exact Observations
mwsw0099	switzerland	1701	MOLL	180	19	25	A Map of Switzerland
mwsam0175	south america (north)	1716	MOLL	200	21	28	A Map of Terra Firma Peru, Amazone-Land, Brazil & the North P. of la Plata
mwsam0831	south america venezuela	1729	MOLL	300	18	26	A Map of Terra Firma, Guiana and the Antilles Islands
mwgm0198	mexico	1717	MOLL	150	15	28	A Map of the Bay of Campechy
mwam0340	america north	1704	MOLL	500	20	20	A Map of the British Plantations in America
mwin0426	indian ocean	1729	MOLL	180	22	44	A Map of the Continent of the East-Indies &c.
mwas0447	asia south east	1720	MOLL	300	15	28	A Map of the East Indies
mwas0448	asia south east	1720	MOLL	3000	61	102	A Map of the East-Indies and the Adjacent Countries; with the Settlements, Factories and Territories, Explaining what Belongs to England, Spain, France, Holland, Denmark, Portugal &c.
mwam0900	america north (east)	1695	MOLL	320	20	18	A Map of the English Plantations in America
mwuss0165	carolinas	1710	MOLL	240	24	33	A Map of the Improved Part of Carolina with the Settlements &c.
mwaa0123	arctic	1729	MOLL	400	20	27	A Map of the North Pole with All the Territories that Lye Near it Known to us &c. According to the Latest Discoveries and Most Exact Observations Agreeable to Modern History
mwuss0175	carolinas	1730	MOLL	960	36	39	A Map of the Province of Carolina Divided into its Parishes &c. According to the Latest Accounts
mwas0680	asia south east malacca	1697	MOLL	240	15	28	A Map of the Streights of Malacca
mwwi0065	west indies	1729	MOLL	375	20	26	A Map of the West Indies &c. Mexico or New Spain. Also ye Trade Winds, and ye Several Tracts Made by ye Galeons and Flota from Place to Place
mwwi0059	west indies	1720	MOLL	4000	59	101	A Map of the West-Indies or the Islands of America in the North Sea; with ye Adjacent Countries; Explaining what Belongs to Spain, England, France, Holland &c. also ye Trade Winds, and ye Several Tracts Made by ye Galeons and Flota from Place to Place
mww0267	world	1697	MOLL	675	16	30	A Map of the World Shewing the Course of Mr. Dampier's Voyage round it: From 1679 to 1691. H. Moll Fecit
mwat0115	atlantic bermuda	1708	MOLL	675	18	10	A Map of ye Island of Bermudos, Divided into its Tribes, with the Castles, Forts &c. / Carolina (2 maps on one sheet)
mwaf1159	africa west	1700	MOLL	240	18	25	A Map of Zaara or the Desart. Negroland & Cape Virde Islands
mww0333	world	1719	MOLL	8000	70	119	A New & Correct Map of the Whole World Shewing ye Situation of its Principal Parts ... with the Most Remarkable Tracks of the Bold Attempts which have been Made to Find Out the Northeast and Northwest Passages
mwsam0056	south america	1719	MOLL	1500	66	50	A New & Exact Map of the Coast, Countries and Islands within ye Limits of ye South Sea Company, from ye River Aranoca to Terra del Fuego, and from thence through ye South Sea, to ye North Part of California

AMPG REFERENCE	REGION	DATE	MAP MAKER	PRICE (UK£)	VERT. (cm.)	HOR. (cm.)	TITLE OF MAP (Comments by the editor in brackets)
mwg0627	saxony	1713	MOLL	785	59	103	A New & Exact Map of the Electorate of Brunswick-Lunenburg and ye Rest of ye Kings Dominion in Germany. Very Much Improved by ye Kind Assistance of Severall Curious Gentlemen, Natives of those Countries
mwuk0466a	scotland	1725	MOLL	280	31	28	A New and Correct Map of Scotland
mww0308a	world	1709	MOLL	7200	57	97	A New and Correct Map of the World. Laid Down According to the Newest Discoveries, and from the Most Exact Observations (illustrated is c1730 edition, with revised dedication)
mwf0098	france	1710	MOLL	1200	61	98	A New and Exact Map of France Dividid into All its Provinces and Acquisitions, According to the Newest Observations, and that Accurate Survey Made by the King's Command by Mr. Picar and De La Hire
mwsp0237	spain	1711	MOLL	960	61	98	A New and Exact Map of Spain and Portugal Divided into its Kingdoms and Principalities &c.
mwam0915	america north (east)	1715	MOLL	20000	107	64	A New and Exact Map of the Dominions of the King of Great Britain on ye Continent of North America Containing Newfoundland, New Scotland, New England, New York, New Jersey, Pensilvania Maryland, Virginia and Carolina.
mwbh0560	belgium holland	1715	MOLL	1800	60	101	A New and Exact Map of the United Provinces, or Netherlands, &c.
mwsp0697a	gibraltar	1727	MOLL	750	23	61	A New and Exact plan of Gibraltar
mwat0303	atlantic south	1720	MOLL	480	47	58	A New Generall Chart of the Coast of Guinea and Brasil. From C. Virde to C. de Bonne Esperance, and from the River of Amazons to Rio de la Plata &c
mwsc0599	scandinavia norway	1700	MOLL	800	50	63	A New Generall Chart of the Coast of ye Northern Ocean ...
mwuk1135	england london	1700	MOLL	600	26	29	A New Map Containing the Towns ... round London
mwsc0112	scandinavia	1710	MOLL	2000	60	102	A New Map of Denmark and Sweden According to the Newest and Most Exact Observations
mwg0099	germany	1712	MOLL	800	60	100	A New Map of Germany, Hungary, Transilvania & the Suisse Cantons, with Many Remarks Not Extant in any Map ... 1712
mwuk1097	england and scotland	1717	MOLL	2000	102	62	A New Map of Great Britain (illustrated is Bowles' re-issue, after 1732)
mwuk0140	ireland	1714	MOLL	2400	103	62	A New Map of Ireland Divided into its Counties, Provinces, and Baronies, wherein are Distinguished the Bishopricks, Borroughs, Barracks, Bogs, Passes, Bridges, &c., with the Principal Roads, and Common Reputed Miles (re-engraved sl. Smaller in 1733)
mwit0151	italy	1716	MOLL	2000	59	100	A New Map of Italy Distinguishing All the Sovereignties in it, Whether States, Kingdoms, Dutchies, Principalities, Republicks &c. with the Post Roads
mwca0296	canada newfoundland	1711	MOLL	350	18	26	A New Map of Newfoundland, New Scotland, the Isles of Breton, Anticoste, St. Johns &c. Together with the Fishing Bancks
mwam0394	america north	1745	MOLL	480	18	25	A New Map of North America According to the Newest Observations
mwuss1626a	virginia	1708	MOLL	550	26	18	A New Map of Virginia, and Maryland
mwbp0108	baltic states	1709	MOLL	720	51	62	A New Map of the Baltick &c. Shewing All the Dominions About it, with ye Great or Post Roads and Principal Cross-Roads
mwwi0367	barbados	1717	MOLL	280	18	26	A New Map of the Island of Barbadoes, Containing All ye Parishes and Principal Plantations; together with ye Forts, Lines, Batteries, Roads &c.
mwwi0707	jamaica	1720	MOLL	200	18	26	A New Map of the Island of Jamaica
mwsp0658a	balearic islands	1727	MOLL	900	16	29	A New Map of the Island of Minorca / A New and Exact Map of the City and Bay of Gibraltar
mwam0377	america north	1720	MOLL	5000	61	102	A New Map of the North Parts of America Claimed by France under ye Names of Louisiana, Mississipi, Canada and New France with ye Adjoining Territories of England and Spain
mwuk0766	uk	1699	MOLL	280	28	33	A New Map of the Sea Coasts of England, Scotland and Ireland also France
mwit0597	italy north	1719	MOLL	1400	62	102	A New Map of the Upper Part of Italy Containing ye Principality of Piemont ye Dutchies of Savoy, Milan, Parma, Mantua, Modena, Tuscany, the Dominions of ye Pope &c. The Republics of Venice, Genoa, Lucca &c.
mww0356	world	1729	MOLL	850	20	26	A New Map of the Whole World with the Trade Winds According to ye Latest and Most Exact Observations by H. Moll Geographer
mww0306	world	1707	MOLL	1800	30	54	A New Map of the World
mww0316	world	1711	MOLL	750	17	28	A New Map of the World

AMPG REFERENCE	REGION	DATE	MAP MAKER	PRICE (UK£)	VERT. (cm.)	HOR. (cm.)	TITLE OF MAP (Comments by the editor in brackets)
mww0304	world	1706	MOLL	3200	59	95	A New Map of the World According to Wright's alias Mercators Projection, &c. Drawn from the Newest and the Most Exact Observations Together with a View of the General and Coasting Trade Winds Monsoons, or the Shifting Trade Winds (publ. by Harris)
mwam0938	america north (east)	1735	MOLL	450	20	27	A New Map of ye North Parts of America Claimed by France under ye Names of Louisiana, Mississipi, Canada & New France, with the Adjoyning Territories of England & Spain
mwin0196	india	1739	MOLL	180	20	20	A Plan of Fort St. George, and the City of Madras
mwuss0174	carolinas	1729	MOLL	350	20	27	A Plan of Port Royal Harbour in Carolina with the Proposed Forts, Depth of Water &c. Latitude 32°-6 North
mwas0652	asia south east java	1735	MOLL	300	21	28	A Plan of the City and Castle of Batavia
mwuk0154a	ireland	1732	MOLL	250	31	28	A Pocket Companion of Ireland (slightly larger than Moll 1720)
mwuk0145	ireland	1720	MOLL	300	29	27	A Pocket Companion of ye Roads of Ireland
mwuk0976a	england	1717	MOLL	280	28	30	A Pocket Companion Of Ye Roads Of Ye South Part Of Great Britain (illustrated is the c1733 reprint by Bowles with a changed title 'The Roads Of Ye South Part Of Great Britain Called England')
mwgm0396	panama	1729	MOLL	120	22	20	A Scots Settlement in America Called New Caledonia A.D. 1699
mwp0245	pacific (all)	1720	MOLL	350	18	51	A View of ye General & Coasting Trade-Winds, Monsoons or ye Shifting Trade Winds through ye World
mwaf0396	africa east	1720	MOLL	200	18	26	Abissina and Anian &c.
mwaf0104	africa	1695	MOLL	240	15	20	Africa
mwaf0160	africa	1727	MOLL	240	20	27	Africa
mwaf0144	africa	1714	MOLL	250	22	26	Africa, Antiqua et Nova
mwam0116	america continent	1710	MOLL	450	17	19	America
mwme0616	arabia etc	1740	MOLL	240	18	25	Arabia According to the Newest and Most Exact Observations
mwme0602	arabia etc	1720	MOLL	350	20	26	Arabia Agreable to Modern History
mwas0087	asia continent	1695	MOLL	240	23	17	Asia
mwas0098	asia continent	1701	MOLL	240	20	26	Asia
mwme0291	holy land	1730	MOLL	150	30	39	Asiae Antiquissimae Tabula (the entire Middle East)
mwsw0094	switzerland	1695	MOLL	150	9	14	Basel
mwec0042	uk england berkshire	1724	MOLL	180	19	31	Berkshire
mwsam0355	south america brazil	1723	MOLL	280	17	18	Brasil, Divided into its Captainships
mwuk0801	uk	1720	MOLL	280	18	27	Britannia Saxonica
mwec0070	uk england buckinghamshire	1724	MOLL	140	30	19	Buckingham Shire
mwec0098	uk england cambridgeshire	1727	MOLL	200	26	20	Cambridgeshire
mwme0228	holy land	1701	MOLL	200	22	18	Canaan, Palestine or the Holy Land &c. Divided into the Twelve Tribes of Israel
mwuss0173	carolinas	1729	MOLL	400	20	27	Carolina
mwc0095	china	1720	MOLL	200	17	19	China
mwc0095a	china	1720	MOLL	300	18	26	China According to the Newest and most Exact Observations (shown above left)
mwg0527	rheinland-pfalz	1695	MOLL	120	16	13	Coblentz
mwec0180	uk england cornwall	1727	MOLL	280	19	26	Cornwall
mwit0835	italy sardinia and corsica	1717	MOLL	300	26	11	Corsicae Antiqua Descriptio / Sardinae Antiqua Descriptio
mwuk1825a	wales	1724	MOLL	200	21	34	Denbigh and Flintshire
mwsc0353	scandinavia denmark	1727	MOLL	100	18	26	Denmark According to the Newest Observations by H. Moll Geographer
mwsc0090	scandinavia	1695	MOLL	200	19	19	Denmark, Norway & Sweden
mwec0293	uk england devon	1724	MOLL	240	19	26	Devon Shire
mwec0334	uk england dorset	1724	MOLL	180	20	31	Dorset Shire
mwec0408	uk england essex	1724	MOLL	200	22	32	Essex
mwe0117	europe	1701	MOLL	200	16	19	Europe
mwbh0635	belgium holland	1739	MOLL	120	20	27	Flanders or the Austrian Netherlands, with ye Bishoprick of Liege
mwbh0586	belgium holland	1720	MOLL	120	17	19	Flanders or the Spanish Netherlands
mwuss0406	florida	1725	MOLL	550	20	27	Florida Called by ye French Louisiana &c.
mwuss0408	florida	1740	MOLL	600	20	28	Florida, the North Part of the Gulf of Mexico, with the Adjacent Territories Belonging to Great Britain & to France
mwuk0146	ireland	1720	MOLL	140	20	24	Galloway Containing the Shires of Wigton and Kirkcudbright
mwgr0182	greece	1736	MOLL	100	19	24	Graecia Antiqua Secundum Cornelium Nepotem, Cellarium &c.
mwas0342	asia central	1720	MOLL	180	20	26	Great or Asiatick Tartary (updated edition shown far left wth title 'Great Tartary')
mwru0447	russia tartary	1723	MOLL	200	17	19	Great Tartary, the Isle of Japon
mwgr0174	greece	1729	MOLL	320	20	26	Greece or the South Part of Turky in Europe
mwgm0117	honduras	1717	MOLL	250	17	21	Gulf of Amapalla Alias Fonseca
mwec0549	uk england hertfordshire	1724	MOLL	200	19	31	Hertfordshire
mwbh0504	belgium holland	1701	MOLL	200	18	18	Holland and the other Provinces
mwe0937	europe hungary	1736	MOLL	160	20	27	Hungary and Transilvania Agreeable to Modern History

AMPG REFERENCE	REGION	DATE	MAP MAKER	PRICE (UK£)	VERT. (cm.)	HOR. (cm.)	TITLE OF MAP (Comments by the editor in brackets)
mwe0925	europe hungary	1719	MOLL	2400	62	102	Hungary Corrected from ye Observations Communicated to the Royal Society in London & the Royal Academy at Paris (illustrated is Willdey re-issue)
mwjk0060	japan	1712	MOLL	350	13	17	Iapon or Niphon, the Land of Iesso and Straits of the Vries &c
mwin0142a	india	1701	MOLL	350	17	18	India or the Mogul's Empire
mwin0176a	india	1726	MOLL	800	26	19	India Proper or the Empire of the Great Mogul (first map to recognise the true borders of India. Illustrated is the 1745 re-issue. It was also re-engraved in slightly smaller format)
mwuk0126	ireland	1701	MOLL	200	18	17	Ireland
mwuk0134	ireland	1708	MOLL	250	26	18	Ireland Divided into its Provinces & Counties &c
mwit0134	italy	1701	MOLL	160	18	18	Italy
mwit0163	italy	1729	MOLL	160	21	27	Italy
mwec0625	uk england kent	1724	MOLL	240	22	32	Kent
mwec0721	uk england leicestershire	1724	MOLL	150	19	30	Leicestershire
mwbh0542	belgium holland	1710	MOLL	720	61	100	Les Provinces des Pay-Bas Catholiques ou a Most Exact Map of Flanders or ye Austrian Netherlands &c.
mwec0746	uk england lincolnshire	1727	MOLL	150	26	20	Lincolnshire
mwgm0026	gulf of mexico and surrounding regions	1723	MOLL	300	17	18	Mexico, or New Spain. Divided into the Audiance of Guadalayara, Mexico, and Guatimala. Florida
mwec0780	uk england middlesex	1727	MOLL	250	20	26	Middlesex
mwuk1826	wales	1724	MOLL	150	19	30	Monmouthshrire
mwru0156	russia	1727	MOLL	200	17	18	Moscovia or Russia
mwaf1228	africa west	1780	MOLL	200	27	28	Negroland and Guinea
mwaf1192	africa west	1732	MOLL	140	20	27	Negroland and Guinea, with the European Settlements, Explaining what Belongs to England, Holland, Denmark &c.
mwam0928	america north (east)	1729	MOLL	450	20	27	New England, New York, New Jersey, and Pensilvania
mwp0005a	australia	1712	MOLL	2000	14	19	New Guinea, New Britain and New Holland &c.
mwca0301	canada newfoundland	1729	MOLL	300	20	27	Newfoundland St. Laurence Bay, the Fishing Banks, Acadia, and Part of New Scotland ... 1729
mwec0827	uk england norfolk	1724	MOLL	130	20	32	Norfolk
mwuk1827	wales	1724	MOLL	150	20	32	North Wales
mwec0861	uk england northamptonshire	1727	MOLL	150	20	26	Northamptonshire
mwec0914	uk england nottinghamshire	1727	MOLL	180	26	19	Nottinghamshire
mwru0137	russia	1716	MOLL	450	32	47	Nouvelle Carte de l'Empire du Czar de la Grande-Russie
mwgm0199	mexico	1717	MOLL	150	16	21	Part of Mexico: The Gulf of Nicoya, by Some Called the Gulf of Salinas
mwwi0318	bahamas	1729	MOLL	280	10	27	Part of Providence Island
mwme0803	persia etc	1709	MOLL	280	23	18	Persia
mwme0814	persia etc	1730	MOLL	240	19	25	Persia According to the Newest and Most Exact Observations
mwme0813a	persia etc	1730	MOLL	300	24	26	Persia, The Caspian Sea Done by ye Czar (shown below left)
mwas0766	asia south east philippines	1730	MOLL	360	20	26	Philippine Islands Agreeable to Modern History
mwf0237	france alsace	1723	MOLL	120	9	13	Plan of Strasburg (plan of the fortifications)
mwbp0346a	poland	1701	MOLL	180	19	20	Poland
mwbp0389	poland	1729	MOLL	280	20	26	Poland subdivided into its several Palatinates &c.
mwsp0079	portugal	1720	MOLL	240	25	19	Portugal According to the Latest Observations
mwec0987	uk england rutland	1724	MOLL	100	20	31	Rutland Shire
mwit0601	italy north	1723	MOLL	100	21	18	Savoy and Piedmont
mwuk0442	scotland	1695	MOLL	180	18	18	Scotland
mwec1012	uk england shropshire	1724	MOLL	200	32	20	Shropshire
mwit0925	italy sicily	1717	MOLL	160	25	32	Siciliae Antiquae Descriptio
mwec1042	uk england somerset	1724	MOLL	160	19	31	Somerset Shire
mwuk1828	wales	1724	MOLL	150	20	32	South Wales
mwsp0248	spain	1720	MOLL	200	16	18	Spain and Portugal
mwsp0267	spain	1745	MOLL	200	18	24	Spain and Portugal
mwat0330	atlantic st helena	1729	MOLL	200	28	21	St. Helena / The Bay of Algoa de Saldanha (South Africa)
mwec1072	uk england staffordshire	1724	MOLL	200	32	19	Staffordshire
mwec1105	uk england suffolk	1724	MOLL	200	19	30	Suffolk
mwsw0124	switzerland	1726	MOLL	180	22	25	Suisse or Switzerland with their Allies and Subjects &c.
mwec1138	uk england surrey	1724	MOLL	300	19	30	Surrey
mwec1168	uk england sussex	1727	MOLL	250	20	26	Sussex
mwsam0174	south america (north)	1701	MOLL	200	16	19	Terra Firma and the Caribbe Islands &c.
mwas0319	asia caspian sea	1735	MOLL	350	27	21	The Caspian Sea Done by the Czar's Special Command by Carl van Verden in the Year 1719, 1720 and 1721. This Exact Copy is Done by H. Moll Geographer (see Van Verden 1722)
mwec0140	uk england cheshire	1724	MOLL	225	19	32	The Conty Palatine of Cheshire
mwec0370	uk england durham	1727	MOLL	200	19	26	The County Palatine of Durham
mwec0686	uk england lancashire	1724	MOLL	200	32	20	The County Palatine of Lancaster
mwas0440	asia south east	1711	MOLL	240	25	18	The East Part of India, or India beyond the R. Ganges
mwc0105	china	1727	MOLL	500	25	25	The Empire of China and Island of Japan, Agreeable to Modern History
mwam0911	america north (east)	1709	MOLL	400	21	18	The English Empire in America, Newfound-Land, Canada, Hudsons Bay. &c in Plano, Herman Moll Fecit

AMPG REFERENCE	REGION	DATE	MAP MAKER	PRICE (UK£)	VERT. (cm.)	HOR. (cm.)	TITLE OF MAP (Comments by the editor in brackets)
mwsam0566	south america galapagos	1717	MOLL	480	14	13	The Gallapagos Islands Discovered by Capt. John Eaton
mwsam0223	south america argentina	1701	MOLL	240	16	18	The Great Province of Rio de la Plata
mwsam0205	south america amazon	1716	MOLL	500	16	37	The Great River Maranon or of the Amazons Geographically Describ'd by Samuel Fritz Missioner on the Said River
mwsp0480	spain regions	1695	MOLL	150	16	14	The Island City & Port of Cadis
mwwi0296	antigua	1740	MOLL	480	29	37	The Island of Antego
mwwi0370	barbados	1729	MOLL	550	29	36	The Island of Barbadoes. Divided into its Parishes, with the Roads, Paths, &c. According to an Actual and Accurate Survey
mwat0118	atlantic bermuda	1730	MOLL	675	20	27	The Island of Bermudos Divided into its Tribes, with the Castles, Forts &c. / (New Providence Island, Bahamas)
mwas0610	asia south east celebes	1730	MOLL	240	20	25	The Island of Celebes, or Macassar with the Islands of Banda, Amboyna and the Moluccas
mwwi0278b	west indies (islands)	1736	MOLL	240	18	26	The Island of St. Christophers / Antego Island / Part of ye Islands of America &c.
mwwi0857	st kitts	1729	MOLL	280	20	27	The Island of St. Christophers alias St. Kitts
mwam1317	america north (west)	1709	MOLL	450	16	18	The Isle of California. New Mexico. Louisiane. The River Misisipi and the Lakes of Canada ...
mwbp0324	poland	1695	MOLL	140	17	18	The Kingdome of Poland with its Confines (part of a page of text)
mwf0335	france brittany	1695	MOLL	240	12	16	The Marquisate and Government of Bell-Isle Divided into its Four Parishes of the Palace Bangor Lomaria and Sauzon
mwg0212	germany north east	1714	MOLL	75	18	26	The North East Part of Germany
mwuk0470	scotland	1730	MOLL	2250	60	100	The North Part of Great Britain Called Scotland. With Considerable Improvements ... 1714
mwe0791	europe east	1732	MOLL	140	20	26	The North Part of Turky in Europe Slavonia &c.
mwg0219	germany north west	1714	MOLL	75	18	26	The North West Part of Germany
mwas0441	asia south east	1714	MOLL	300	18	26	The Philippine Islands and others of the East Indies
mwme1003	turkey etc	1739	MOLL	350	18	31	The Plan of Constantinople (view)
mwas0431	asia south east	1700	MOLL	200	17	19	The Principal Islands of the East Indies
mwgm0397	panama	1729	MOLL	280	25	20	The Scots Settlement in America Called New Caledonia. A.D. 1699. Lat. 8D.-30' North
mwg0225	germany north west	1707	MOLL	180	14	22	The Seat of War in Swabia &c.
mwwi0045	west indies	1702	MOLL-MORDEN	4000	60	102	The Seat of War in the West-Indies, or the Islands of America in the North Sea (left is a later edition with new title 'A New Mapp of the West Indies ...' and text removed upper right)
mwaf1044	africa south east	1700	MOLL	240	18	25	The South East Part of Africa. Containing Zanguebar, Sofala, Sabia, the Island Madagascar &c.
mwaf0917	africa south	1732	MOLL	280	20	27	The South Part of Africa, and the Island Madagascar. Here the Portugueze have Many Settlements and All the Trade
mwuk0968	england	1708	MOLL	200	18	26	The South Part of Great Britain Divided into its Counties, with ye Roads &c.
mwuk0969	england	1710	MOLL	2000	61	99	The South Part of Great Britain, Called, England and Wales. Containing All ye Cities, Market Towns, Boroughs: And whatever Places have ye Election of Members of Parliament ... A.D.1710
mwaf1077	africa south west	1732	MOLL	200	26	18	The South West Part of Africa Containing Congo, Benguela, Monomatapa, Caffers, Terra de Natal &c.
mwas0902	asia south east sunda	1739	MOLL	200	20	26	The Sunda Islands ... Borneo, Sumatra and Java &c.
mwme0600	arabia etc	1715	MOLL	2400	60	101	The Turkish Empire in Europe, Asia and Africa, Dividid into All its Governments, together with the other Territories that are Tributary to it as also the Dominions of ye Emperor of Marocco
mwin0165a	india	1712	MOLL	1000	26	19	The West Part of India, or the Empire of the Great Mogul (first map of India as it is known today. This was only recognised by Moll in 1726 and changed the title to 'India Proper')
mww0255	world	1695	MOLL	480	17	19	The World in Planisphere
mwaa0113	arctic	1705	MOLL	550	37	42	This Draught of the North Pole is to Shew All the Countries Near and Adjacent to it, as also the Most Remarkable Tracks of the Bold Discoverers of them, and Particularly the Attempts of our own Countrymen to find out the N.East and N.West Passages
mwe0126	europe	1708	MOLL	1400	58	96	To her Most Sacred Majesty Ann Queen of Great Britain, France & Ireland ... This Map of Europe (shows proposed canal between Black and Caspian Seas)
mwru0134	russia	1714	MOLL	2000	62	98	To His Most Serene and August Majesty Peter Alexovitz Absolute Lord of Russia, &c. this Map of Moscovy, Poland, Little Tartary and ye Black Sea &c.

AMPG REFERENCE	REGION	DATE	MAP MAKER	PRICE (UK£)	VERT. (cm.)	HOR. (cm.)	TITLE OF MAP (Comments by the editor in brackets)
mwsam0052	south america	1711	MOLL	2000	58	98	To the Right Honorable Charles Earl of Sunderland, and Baron Spencer of Wormleighton … this Map of South America, According to the Newest and Most Exact Observations is Most Humbly Dedicated (illustrated is Bowles re-issue, 1730)
mwaf0134	africa	1710	MOLL	2800	57	95	To the Right Honourable Charles Earl of Peterborow, and Monmouth, &c. This Map of Africa, According to ye Newest and Most Exact Observations is Most Humbly Dedicated by your Lordship's Most Humble Servant H:Moll Geographer
mwam0375	america north	1719	MOLL	6500	60	98	To the Right Honourable John Lord Sommers … This Map of North America According to ye Newest and Most Exact Observations
mwas0113	asia continent	1710	MOLL	2250	58	97	To the Right Honourable William Lord Cowper, Lord High Chancellor of Great Britain. This Map of Asia (illustrated is the 1725 re-issue)
mwme0246	holy land	1711	MOLL	200	26	20	Totius Terrae Sanctae Delineatio
mwme1002	turkey etc	1735	MOLL	160	20	25	Turkey in Asia or Asia Minor &c. Agreeable to Modern History
mwuss1631	virginia	1729	MOLL	550	27	20	Virginia and Maryland by H. Moll Geographer
mwec1197	uk england warwickshire	1724	MOLL	250	19	30	Warwickshire
mwaf0713	africa north	1732	MOLL	140	20	27	West Part of Barbary / East Part of Barbary
mwec1249	uk england wiltshire	1724	MOLL	180	32	19	Wilt Shire
mwec1328a	uk england yorkshire	1724	MOLL	750	20	25	The North Riding of York Shire … (etc. set of 4 maps of Yorkshire, each 20x25cm.)
mwec1340	uk england yorkshire	1753	MOLL	250	20	26	York Shire with the Post Roads &c.
mwg0424	brandenburg	1830	MOLLENDORF	1500	43	53	Plan von Potsdam und Umgegend, mit Benutzung des Gartenplane des Konigl: Garten-Directors Lenne Aufgenommen
mwam0248a	america continent	1799	MOLLO	600	52	76	Amerika - mit den Neuesten Entdeckungen und Cooks Reisen
mwru0334	russia	1812	MOLLO	800	150	135	Carte des Europaisch - und eines Theils des Asiatischrussischen Reichs, nach den Neuesten Astronomischen Ortsbestimungen
mwit0825b	italy sardinia	1824	MOLLO	250	33	45	Charte des Koenigreichs Sardinien
mwaf0994	africa south	1812	MOLLO	135	30	41	Charte der Suedspitze von Africa oder des Hottentotten und Caplands
mwam0614a	america north	1819	MOLLO	2000	86	118	Charte von Nord America nach Arrowsmith v. Humboldt … Joseph Dirwald
mwit0969	italy sicily	1821	MOLLO	235	30	41	Charte von Sicilien und Malta
mwsam0137a	south america	1819	MOLLO	800	89	115	Charte von Sud America nach Arrowsmith v. Humboldt … Joseph Dirwald
mwwi0153	west indies	1807	MOLLO	235	33	45	Charte von West-Indien nach den Besten Huelfsmitteln Verfast
mwg0195	germany north	1808	MOLLO	800	53	75	Die Konigreiche Sachsen und Westphalen
mww0612	world	1800	MOLLO	500	65	58	Die Obere oder Nordliche Halbkugel der Erde auf den Horizont von Wien (polar projection centred on Vienna)
mwe0436	europe austria vienna	1821	MOLLO	1500	97	117	Grundriss der Kais: Konig: Haupt und Residenzstadt Wien samp ihren Vorstadten
mwsc0197	scandinavia	1812	MOLLO	960	114	90	Karte der Konigreiche Schweden und Norwegen nach dem Schwedischen Atlas des Baron v: Hermelin und den Ponteppidanschen und Erichsenschen Karten
mwe1170	europe south east	1807	MOLLO	150	44	32	Karte von der Europaeischen Tuerkey
mwbh0797	belgium holland	1829	MOLLO	150	33	45	Karte von Holland nach der Letzten Granz Berichtigung Verfasst
mwe1058	europe romania	1807	MOLLO	150	33	45	Karte von Siebenburgen nach den Besten Huelfsmitteln Verfast
mwbh0798	belgium holland	1829	MOLLO	150	44	32	Konigreich Niederland nach der Letzten Grenz Berichtigung Verfasst
mwe1124b	europe slovenia	1820	MOLLO	250	33	44	Koenigreich Slavonien
mwe0437	europe austria vienna	1825	MOLLO	200	37	44	Plan de la Ville … Vienne (view)
mwe0482	europe central	1826	MOLLO	180	74	103	Post Reise Karte durch Deutschland und die Angraenzenden Staaten
mwsp0312	spain	1807	MOLLO	150	34	47	Spanien und Portugal nach de Lopez und den Neuesten Astronomischen Ortsbestimmungen
mwe0842	europe east	1822	MOLLO	800	106	139	Topographische Karte der Oesterreichischen Monarchie mit Angabe Aller Post-Strassen nach den Neuesten Astronomischen Ortsbestimmungen und den Neusten Karten
mwam0551	america north	1800	MOLLO	450	32	44	Vereinigte Staaten in Nord America
mwme1068	turkey etc	1849	MOLTKE	300	82	71	Karte des Nordlichen Befestigen Theils des Bosphorus von den Hissaren bis zu dem Leuchtthurmen am Schwarzen Meer in Auftrage Sr. Hoheit Sultan Mahmud II
mwit0768	italy rome	1843	MONALDINI	600	62	86	Nuova Pianta di Roma Moderna
mwit0760	italy rome	1824	MONALDINI	1800	76	112	Pianta della Citta di Roma con la Indicazione di Tutte le Antichita e Nuovi Abbellimenti (illustrated is 1837 edition)
mwf0478	france corsica	1710	MONATH	650	38	28	Corsica Insula et Regnum

AMPG REFERENCE	REGION	DATE	MAP MAKER	PRICE (UK£)	VERT. (cm.)	HOR. (cm.)	TITLE OF MAP (Comments by the editor in brackets)
mwe0682	europe dalmatia	1720	MONATH	800	47	55	Dalmatia et regiones adjacentes, Croatia, Bosnia, Slavonia, Servia, Albania accurate descriptae (inset: Corfu)
mwaf0150	africa	1720	MONATH	500	24	28	Novae Africae Delineatio
mwas0126	asia continent	1720	MONATH	500	24	28	Novae Asiae Delineatio
mwe0140	europe	1720	MONATH	400	24	29	Novae Europae Delineatio
mwme0267	holy land	1720	MONATH	350	24	29	Palaestina sive Terra Sancta
mwam0129	america continent	1720	MONATH	750	24	28	Totius Americae Descriptio Nova
mww0337	world	1720	MONATH	1500	25	29	Typus Orbis Terrarum
mwf0161	france	1790	MONDHARE	550	65	90	Carte de France Divisee en ses 83 Departements et Districts. Suivant les Decrets de l'Assemblee Nationale
mwf0419	france burgundy	1790	MONDHARE	600	68	49	Carte de Franche Comte
mwsw0181	switzerland	1777	MONDHARE	600	47	65	Carte de la Republique du Suisses
mwg0152a	germany	1783	MONDHARE	150	21	26	Carte de l'Empire de L'Allemagne
mwuk0861	uk	1780	MONDHARE	500	54	73	Carte des Isles Britanniques
mwsc0161	scandinavia	1780	MONDHARE	600	52	63	Carte des Royaumes de Suede et Norwege
mwwi0117a	west indies	1782	MONDHARE	2500	51	72	Carte Générale des Isles Antilles
mwsp0292	spain	1780	MONDHARE	1200	52	73	El Reyno de Espana Dividido en Dos Grandes Estados de Aragon y de Castilla Subdivido en Muchas Provincias, donde se halla Tambien el Reyno de Portugal (many medallion portraits of Spanish kings in side borders)
mww0530	world	1783	MONDHARE	600	23	19	Hemisphere Occidental ou Nouveau Monde / Hemisphere Oriental ou Ancien Monde (2 maps)
mwaf0209	africa	1760	MONDHARE	12000	118	147	L'Afrique Divisee en Tous ses Etats
mwam0184	america continent	1760	MONDHARE	15000	118	147	L'Amerique Divisee en Tous ses Etats
mwam0227a	america continent	1788	MONDHARE	2500	72	103	L'Amérique divisée en tous ses pays suivant les Nouvelles Observations des plus Celêbres Navigateurs ... 1788
mwas0176	asia continent	1760	MONDHARE	10000	118	145	L'Asie Divisee en Tous ses Etats
mwg0152	germany	1778	MONDHARE	1250	93	116	L'Empire Allemagne
mwsc0173	scandinavia	1787	MONDHARE	550	47	55	Les Royaumes de Suede de Danemarck et de Norwege
mwe0215	europe	1788	MONDHARE	1800	74	105	L'Europe divisee en tous ses etats
mwe0179	europe	1760	MONDHARE	10000	117	145	L'Europe Divisee en Tous ses Etats
mww0562	world	1788	MONDHARE	7200	73	104	Mappe Monde, Contenant les Parties Connues du Globe Terrestre (based on Janvier and Longchamps, 1754, but without the 4 decorative borders)
mwme0362	holy land	1772	MONDHARE	1350	92	61	Nouvelle Carte de la Terre Sainte
mwf0528	france corsica	1769	MONDHARE	875	48	64	Nouvelle Carte de l'Isle de Corse
mwf0899	france paris	1788	MONDHARE	1800	62	95	Plan de la Ville et Faubourg de Paris avec Tous ses Accroissemens et la Nouvelle Enciente de Barrieres de cette Capitale
mwf0901	france paris	1792	MONDHARE	1800	62	95	Plan de la Ville et Faubourg de Paris Divise en ses 48 Sections Decrete par l'Assemblee Nationale le 22 Juin 1790
mwwi0433	cuba	1760	MONDHARE	400	27	40	Vue de la Prise des Forts et Ville de Havane par les Anglois en 1762 (view d'optique)
mwsam0534	south america colombia	1782	MONDHARE	400	23	41	Vue de la Ville de Carthagene en Amerique, Prise par les Francois en 1667 (vue d'optique)
mwaf1023	africa south	1843	MONIN	100	22	28	Afrique Meridionale
mwaf0431	africa east	1837	MONIN	120	45	31	Afrique Orientale
mwam0739	america north	1840	MONIN	360	66	47	Amerique Septentrionale
mwsam0437	south america brazil	1850	MONIN	200	45	31	Bresil - Paraguay et Uruguay
mwf0563	france corsica	1835	MONIN	100	24	19	Corse
mwam0706	america north	1836	MONIN	300	32	46	Etats Unis et Canada Dresse par C.V. Monin
mwgr0260	greece	1843	MONIN	75	21	28	Grece ou Hellas
mwm0262	mediterranean malta	1844	MONIN	200	20	14	Ile de Malta & Plan de la Ville et du Port de Malte
mwsam0264	south america argentina	1845	MONIN	200	46	30	La Plata ou Etats Unis de l'Amerique Meridionale et Chili
mwp0526	pacific south	1835	MONIN	300	46	65	Oceanie Dressee par C.V. Monin. (incl. Australia)
mwf0920	france paris	1834	MONIN	280	33	45	Plan de Paris
mwgm0332	mexico	1837	MONIN	600	46	32	Republique des Etats Unis du Mexique (Texas shown as a republic)
mwsc0215	scandinavia	1834	MONIN	120	45	32	Suede Norvege et Danemark
mwat0081	atlantic azores	1671	MONTANUS	250	29	35	(Angra)
mwwi0820	puerto rico	1671	MONTANUS	250	29	34	(San Juan)
mwjk0032	japan	1669	MONTANUS	400	27	35	Afbeeldinge vant Maghtich Keyserlyck Casteel Osacca Geleegen int Groot Ryck Jappan Besuyden de Stadt Osacca inde Provinsie Qioo (view)
mwuss0149	carolinas	1671	MONTANUS	480	29	35	Arx Carolina
mww0062	world	1572	MONTANUS B.	10000	32	53	Benedict Arias Montanus Sacrae Geographiae Tabulam ex Antiquissimorum Cultor. Familii a Mose Recensitis
mwsam0314	south america brazil	1671	MONTANUS	900	29	37	Brasilia
mwsam0746	south america peru	1673	MONTANUS	300	29	36	Callao de Lima
mwjk0033	japan	1669	MONTANUS	650	27	57	Cangoxuma (Kagoshima view)
mwsam0500	south america colombia	1671	MONTANUS	300	27	35	Cartagena (view)
mwsam0450	south america chile	1671	MONTANUS	400	29	35	Chili
mwsam0743	south america peru	1671	MONTANUS	250	26	35	Cusco (view)
mwjk0034	japan	1669	MONTANUS	1250	42	43	De Land Reyse van Osacca tot Iedo / De Water Reyse van Nangasacqui to Osacca (2 maps on one sheet)
mwjk0035	japan	1669	MONTANUS	550	26	69	De Stadt Osacco (view)

AMPG REFERENCE	REGION	DATE	MAP MAKER	PRICE (UK£)	VERT. (cm.)	HOR. (cm.)	TITLE OF MAP (Comments by the editor in brackets)
mwaf0783	africa north morocco	1673	MONTANUS	350	27	35	Fezzae et Marocchi Regna Africae Celeberrima
mwsam0583	south america guyana	1673	MONTANUS	400	29	37	Guiana sive Amazonum Regio
mwjk0150a	japan tokyo	1670	MONTANUS	1500	29	88	Iedo (view)
mwwi0024	west indies	1671	MONTANUS	1200	28	37	Insulae Americanae in Oceano Septentrionali, cum Terris Adiacentibus
mwc0300	china formosa	1669	MONTANUS	1500	29	35	La Ville et le Chateau de Zelandia dans L'Ile de Tayovan (view of Dutch settlement)
mwin0114	india	1671	MONTANUS	450	29	35	Magni Mogolis Imperium
mwat0109	atlantic bermuda	1671	MONTANUS	1350	29	36	Mappa Aestivarum Insularum, alias Barmudas Dictarum ... Accurate Descripta
mwsam0317	south america brazil	1673	MONTANUS	550	26	53	Mauritiopolis (view)
mwjk0036	japan	1669	MONTANUS	950	29	79	Miako (view)
mwgm0174	mexico	1673	MONTANUS	720	29	36	Nova Hispania Nova Galicia Guatimala
mwgm0167	mexico	1671	MONTANUS	1000	29	54	Nova Mexico (view, one of the earliest to show the lay-out of the streets of Mexico City)
mwuss1611	virginia	1671	MONTANUS	2000	29	35	Nova Virginiae Tabula
mwam0868	america north (east)	1671	MONTANUS	1800	29	36	Novi Belgii, quod nunc Novi Jorck Vocatur, Novae qz. Angliae & Partis Virginiae Accuratissima et Novissima Delineatio
mwsam0709	south america paraguay	1673	MONTANUS	480	29	37	Paraquaria vulgo Paraguay cum Adjacentibus
mwme0785	persia etc	1672	MONTANUS	480	27	34	Persia sive Sophorum Regnum
mwsam0747	south america peru	1673	MONTANUS	450	29	35	Peru
mwwi0821	puerto rico	1671	MONTANUS	650	29	35	Porto Rico (city view)
mwgm0168	mexico	1671	MONTANUS	480	28	38	Portus Acapulco
mwsam0745	south america peru	1673	MONTANUS	250	28	36	Potosi (view)
mwgm0169	mexico	1671	MONTANUS	350	28	36	St. Francisco de Campeche (Yucatan)
mwsam0672	south america magellan	1671	MONTANUS	650	29	36	Tabula Magellanica, qua Tierrae del Fuego, cum Celeberrimis Fretis a F. Magellano et I. Le Maire Detectis Noviss et Accuratissim Descript. Exhibetur
mwsam0501	south america colombia	1671	MONTANUS	550	28	36	Terra Firma et Novum Regnum Granatense et Popayan
mwwi0581	hispaniola	1671	MONTANUS	400	29	35	Urbs Domingo in Hispaniola
mwsam0824	south america venezuela	1673	MONTANUS	675	29	37	Venezuela cum Parte Australi Novae Andalusiae
mwuss1610	virginia	1671	MONTANUS	960	29	36	Virginiae Partis Australis et Floridae Partis Orientalis interia centiumq Regionum Nova Descriptio
mwas0631	asia south east java	1669	MONTANUS	580	26	35	Ware Afbeeldinge Wegens het Casteel ende Stadt Batavia ... Plan de la Ville et du Chateau de Batavia
mwsp0180c	spain	1643	MONTECALERIO	800	22	33	(untitled map. Illustrated is the 1712 edition. Shown above left)
mwg0057	germany	1647	MONTECALERIO	400	22	32	Germania Continens Septem Provincias Capuci
mwit0090	italy	1643	MONTECALERIO	800	24	34	Italia (1712 edition illustrated)
mwf1031a	france provence	1700	MONTECALERIO	400	22	32	Provinca, Sancti Ludovici vel Provincia
mwsp0437	spain regions	1649	MONTECALERIO	280	22	33	Provincia Aragoniae
mwf0346	france brittany	1712	MONTECALERIO	480	22	32	Provincia Britanniae Armoricae
mwit0486a	italy lombardy	1642	MONTECALERIO	480	22	32	Provincia Brixiana cum Confinijs 1642
mwit0418a	italy liguria	1649	MONTECALERIO	550	21	31	Provincia Genuensis cum confinijs
mwf0479	france corsica	1712	MONTECALERIO	600	23	33	Provincia Insulae Corsicae
mwit0787	italy sardinia	1643	MONTECALERIO	800	23	32	Provincia Insulae Sardiniae
mwit0887	italy sicily	1643	MONTECALERIO	650	23	33	Provincia Messanensis Cum Confinjs
mwit0642a	italy piedmont	1649	MONTECALERIO	500	23	32	Provincia Pedemontana cum confinijs
mwit0715	italy rome	1649	MONTECALERIO	350	22	31	Provincia Romana cum Confiniis
mwit1154a	italy umbria	1649	MONTECALERIO	500	22	32	Provincia S. Francisci seu Umbriae Cum confinijs
mwit1183a	italy veneto	1649	MONTECALERIO	450	22	31	Provincia Venetiarum Cum Confinijs
mwit0797a	italy sardinia	1712	MONTECALERIO	675	23	33	Vera Provae Calaritanae Imago cum sua Turritana Contermina
mwsw0219	switzerland	1802	MONTI	450	41	56	Carte Generale de la Suisse et des ses Environs
mwuss0630	louisiana	1753	MONTIGNY	350	12	15	Plan de la Concession de M. Le Blanc et Associes aux Yazoux (Yazoo City)
mwuss1103	new york	1775	MONTRESOR	12000	145	92	A Map of the Province of New York, with Part of Pensilvania, and New England, from an Actual Survey by Captain Montresor
mwuss1113	new york	1776	MONTRESOR	10000	64	53	A Plan of the City of New York & its Environs to Greenwich on the North or Hudsons River ... Survey'd in the Winter, 1775
mwca0394	canada nova scotia	1768	MONTRESOR	1500	102	142	Map of Nova Scotia, or Acadia; with the Islands of Cape Breton and St. John's, from Actual Surveys
mwam1185	america north (east)	1821	MONTULE	500	34	26	Carte des Etats Units et des Iles du Golfe du Mexique (1st US lithographed map)
mwuk1017	england	1779	MOORE	200	33	23	A New & Accurate Map of England & Wales from the Latest & Best Improvements
mwuk0214	ireland	1780	MOORE	240	28	19	A New and Correct Map of Ireland from the Latest Surveys of that Kingdom
mwru0265	russia	1778	MOORE	200	20	28	A New and Correct Map of the Russian Empire as Comprehended in Europe and Asia from the Best Authorities and Latest Improvements
mww0753	world	1850	MOORE	1350	71	98	Chart Prepared by James B. Moore, to Accompany his Memorial to Congress Respecting the Subject of Steam Communication with China, Japan etc. 1850

AMPG REFERENCE	REGION	DATE	MAP MAKER	PRICE (UK£)	VERT. (cm.)	HOR. (cm.)	TITLE OF MAP (Comments by the editor in brackets)
mwuk0082	ireland	1681	MOORE	200	21	15	Ireland (engraved by Moll)
mwuss1481	rhode isl	1844	MOORE	200	18	22	Plan of the City of Providence
mwuss0207	carolinas	1778	MOORE	150	13	10	Plan of the Harbour of Charles Town, South Carolina
mwam1150	america north (east)	1805	MOORE	3000	81	122	To His Excellency Thomas Jefferson ... Chart of the United States
mwwi0111	west indies	1779	MOORE	320	34	39	West Indies, Agreeable to the Most Approved Maps and Charts
mwam0896	america north (east)	1693	MORDEN	550	13	13	A Map of Florida and ye Great Lakes of Canada by Robt. Morden
mwwi0043	west indies	1700	MORDEN	300	13	14	A Map of the Western Islands
mwru0435a	russia tartary	1687	MORDEN	150	11	13	A New Description of Tartarie
mwme0575	arabia etc	1688	MORDEN	480	11	13	A New Map of Arabia
mwuss0157	carolinas	1688	MORDEN	550	13	13	A New Map of Carolina
mwin0029	ceylon	1688	MORDEN	480	13	13	A New Map of Ceylon
mwuk0930	england	1676	MORDEN	4800	45	56	A New Map of England Containing the Adjacent Parts of Scotland, Ireland, France, Flanders and Holland
mwbh0450	belgium holland	1690	MORDEN	720	48	59	A New Map ... Flanders
mwsp0197	spain	1680	MORDEN	180	13	14	A New Map of Hispania and Portugallia
mwe0913	europe hungary	1693	MORDEN	150	12	14	A New Map of Hungary by Robt. Morden
mwas0413	asia south east	1687	MORDEN	375	13	10	A New Map of India beyond Ganges
mwam0897	america north (east)	1693	MORDEN	550	13	14	A New Map of New England and New York
mwme0794	persia etc	1687	MORDEN	160	11	13	A New Map of Persia
mwsp0055	portugal	1688	MORDEN	160	13	11	A New Map of Portugal
mwe1123b	europe slovenia	1700	MORDEN	160	13	14	A New Map of Sclavonia, Croatia, Dalmatia, Bosnia et Repur, Ragusa
mwam0901	america north (east)	1695	MORDEN	18000	50	58	A New Map of the English Empire in America viz Virginia, Maryland, Carolina, Pennsylvania, New York, New Iarsey, New England, Newfoundland, New France &c. (3rd state of this map illustrated. Final state publ. in 1719 by Senex.)
mwuk0953	england	1690	MORDEN	4800	40	54	A New Map of the Kingdome of England And Principality of Wales
mwaf0788	africa north morocco	1687	MORDEN	140	14	12	A New Map of the Kingdoms of Fez and Marocco
mwme0574	arabia etc	1687	MORDEN	200	13	11	A New Map of the Turkish Empire
mwuss0743	maryland	1688	MORDEN	550	13	12	A New Map of Virginia
mwam0887	america north (east)	1687	MORDEN	300	12	11	A New Map of Virginia, Maryland, Pensilvania, New Yarsey
mww0213	world	1680	MORDEN	550	10	16	A New Map of ye World by Robt. Morden
mwuk0747	uk	1685	MORDEN	6000	52	59	A New Mapp of England Scotland and Ireland (1st edition 1678)
mwbp0284	poland	1672	MORDEN	720	43	56	A New Mapp of the Estates of the Crown of Poland. Containing the Kingdom of Poland the Dutchies & Provinces of Prussia. Cuiavia. Mazovia. Russia Nigra. Lithuania. Podolia. Volhinia the Ukraine. &c.
mwuk1530b	uk english channel (east)	1679	MORDEN	1800	56	43	A New Mapp of the Sea Coasts of England, France & Holland
mwaf0488	africa egypt etc	1687	MORDEN	140	13	10	Aegypt
mwat0111	atlantic bermuda	1680	MORDEN	850	11	13	Aestivarum Insulae al Barmudas
mwaf0097	africa	1688	MORDEN	200	11	13	Africa
mwam0089	america continent	1688	MORDEN	300	12	13	America by R. Morden
mwuk0965	england	1703	MORDEN	30000	142	162	Angliae & Walliae Totius Tabula
mwme0721	caucasus	1688	MORDEN	160	11	13	Armenia & Georgia Comania &c by Robt. Morden
mwas0076	asia continent	1688	MORDEN	200	11	13	Asia. A New Description
mwec0039	uk england berkshire	1695	MORDEN	280	35	42	Bark Shire
mwec0040	uk england berkshire	1701	MORDEN	120	17	20	Barkshire
mwec0009	uk england bedfordshire	1695	MORDEN	350	32	40	Bedford Shire
mwec0010	uk england bedfordshire	1701	MORDEN	120	17	20	Bedford Shire
mwaf1137	africa west	1680	MORDEN	140	11	13	Biledulgerid Sarra Terra Nigritarum Guine Nova Descriptio
mwsam0331	south america brazil	1687	MORDEN	180	12	10	Brazile, a New Description
mwuk1805	wales	1701	MORDEN	120	17	20	Brecknock Shire
mwuk0960a	uk england	1695	MORDEN	240	36	43	Britannia Romana
mwuk0960b	uk england	1695	MORDEN	240	36	30	Britannia Saxonica
mwec0065	uk england buckinghamshire	1695	MORDEN	300	42	35	Buckingham Shire
mwec0067	uk england buckinghamshire	1701	MORDEN	120	17	20	Buckingham Shire
mwuk1800	wales	1701	MORDEN	120	17	20	Caernarvon Shire
mwec0093	uk england cambridgeshire	1695	MORDEN	300	42	36	Cambridge Shire
mwec0095	uk england cambridgeshire	1701	MORDEN	140	17	20	Cambridge Shire
mwme0220	holy land	1700	MORDEN	180	14	13	Canaan by Rob. Morden
mwuk1806	wales	1701	MORDEN	120	17	20	Cardigan Shire
mwuk1807	wales	1701	MORDEN	120	17	20	Carmarthenshire
mwsam0202	south america amazon	1680	MORDEN	160	11	12	Castilla del Or, Guiana, Peru, the Country of ye Amasones
mwec0138	uk england cheshire	1701	MORDEN	140	17	20	Cheshire
mwsam0222	south america argentina	1687	MORDEN	160	11	12	Chili and Paragay by Robt. Morden
mwc0072	china	1687	MORDEN	180	11	13	China, a New Description
mwec0984	uk england rutland	1695	MORDEN	200	29	36	Comitatus Rotelandiae Tabula Nova & Aucta
mwaf1147	africa west	1687	MORDEN	140	10	12	Congo

AMPG REFERENCE	REGION	DATE	MAP MAKER	PRICE (UK£)	VERT. (cm.)	HOR. (cm.)	TITLE OF MAP (Comments by the editor in brackets)
mwec0175	uk england cornwall	1695	MORDEN	400	37	42	Cornwall
mwec0176	uk england cornwall	1701	MORDEN	240	17	20	Cornwall
mwec0227	uk england cumbria	1695	MORDEN	225	36	43	Cumberland
mwec0228	uk england cumbria	1695	MORDEN	180	36	42	Cumberland
mwec0229	uk england cumbria	1701	MORDEN	100	17	20	Cumberland
mwgr0491	greece cyprus	1688	MORDEN	600	15	13	Cypri Insula
mwec0260	uk england derbyshire	1695	MORDEN	275	36	42	Darby Shire
mwec0262	uk england derbyshire	1701	MORDEN	120	17	20	Darby Shire
mwuk1801	wales	1701	MORDEN	120	17	20	Denbigh Shire
mwsc0299	scandinavia denmark	1680	MORDEN	150	11	13	Denmark
mwec0291	uk england devon	1701	MORDEN	120	18	22	Devon Shire
mwec0290	uk england devon	1695	MORDEN	320	36	42	Devonshire
mwec0330	uk england dorset	1695	MORDEN	240	36	42	Dorset Shire
mwec0332	uk england dorset	1701	MORDEN	130	17	20	Dorset Shire
mwec0368	uk england durham	1701	MORDEN	120	17	20	Durham
mwin0136	india	1688	MORDEN	160	11	13	Empire de Mogol by Robt. Morden
mwuk0960	england	1695	MORDEN	480	36	43	England
mwuk0959	england	1695	MORDEN	180	18	16	England
mwuk0739	uk	1680	MORDEN	280	10	13	England Scotland & Ireland
mwec0367	uk england durham	1695	MORDEN	250	36	42	Episcopatus Dunelmensis vulgo the Bishoprick of Durham by Robt. Morden
mwec0405	uk england essex	1695	MORDEN	300	35	42	Essex
mwec0406	uk england essex	1701	MORDEN	120	17	20	Essex
mwe0109	europe	1700	MORDEN	200	11	13	Europe
mwuk1802	wales	1701	MORDEN	120	17	20	Flintshire
mwuk1808	wales	1701	MORDEN	120	17	20	Glamorganshire
mwec0443	uk england gloucestershire	1695	MORDEN	280	35	42	Glocester Shire
mwec0444	uk england gloucestershire	1701	MORDEN	120	17	20	Glocester Shire
mwgr0104	greece	1688	MORDEN	180	11	13	Greciae Novae Descriptio
mwaf0381	africa east	1685	MORDEN	150	14	12	Habessinia seu Abassia at Ethiopia
mwec0475	uk england hampshire	1695	MORDEN	350	37	42	Hamp Shire
mwec0476	uk england hampshire	1701	MORDEN	130	17	20	Hampshire
mwec0519	uk england herefordshire	1695	MORDEN	200	36	42	Hereford Shire
mwec0520	uk england herefordshire	1701	MORDEN	100	17	20	Hereford Shire
mwec0545	uk england hertfordshire	1695	MORDEN	300	36	45	Hertford Shire
mwec0547	uk england hertfordshire	1701	MORDEN	120	17	20	Hertford Shire
mwec0579	uk england huntingdonshire	1695	MORDEN	180	29	36	Huntingdon Shire
mwec0580	uk england huntingdonshire	1701	MORDEN	100	17	20	Huntingdon Shire
mwin0122	india	1680	MORDEN	150	11	13	India on this Side Ganges
mwwi0702	jamaica	1688	MORDEN	320	13	15	Insula Jamaicae by Robt. Morden
mwuk0094	ireland	1688	MORDEN	200	14	12	Ireland
mwjk0045	japan	1680	MORDEN	350	11	13	Japonae ac Terrae Iessonis Novissima Descriptio
mwec0615	uk england kent	1695	MORDEN	450	35	63	Kent
mwec0618	uk england kent	1701	MORDEN	150	16	20	Kent
mwec0718	uk england leicestershire	1695	MORDEN	225	36	42	Leicester Shire
mwec0719	uk england leicestershire	1701	MORDEN	120	17	20	Leicester Shire
mwec0744	uk england lincolnshire	1701	MORDEN	120	17	20	Lincoln Shire
mwec0743	uk england lincolnshire	1695	MORDEN	240	37	42	Lincolnshire
mwaf0594	africa islands madagascar	1698	MORDEN	160	11	13	Madagascar or St. Laurance
mwm0200	mediterranean malta	1680	MORDEN	320	11	13	Maltha
mwuk1803	wales	1701	MORDEN	120	17	20	Merioneth Shire
mwgm0182	mexico	1688	MORDEN	280	11	13	Mexico or New Spaine
mwec0777	uk england middlesex	1701	MORDEN	130	17	20	Middlesex
mwec0775	uk england middlesex	1695	MORDEN	320	36	43	Midlesex
mwuk1798	wales	1701	MORDEN	120	17	20	Monmouth Shire
mwuk1804	wales	1701	MORDEN	120	17	20	Montgomery Shire
mwru0097	russia	1688	MORDEN	180	14	13	Moscovie or Russie
mwam0880	america north (east)	1680	MORDEN	900	11	13	New England and New York by Robt. Morden
mwuss0076	california	1688	MORDEN	720	11	13	New Mexico vel New Granata et Marata et California (for illustration, see under 'America North [West])
mwuss0076	america north (west)	1688	MORDEN	720	11	13	New Mexico vel New Granata et Marata et California
mwec0821	uk england norfolk	1695	MORDEN	300	37	58	Norfolk
mwec0824	uk england norfolk	1701	MORDEN	120	17	20	Norfolk.
mwuk1794	wales	1695	MORDEN	250	36	43	North Wales
mwec0858	uk england northamptonshire	1695	MORDEN	240	36	42	Northampton Shire
mwec0859	uk england northamptonshire	1701	MORDEN	100	17	20	Northampton Shire
mwec0885	uk england northumberland	1695	MORDEN	240	42	36	Northumberland
mwec0910	uk england nottinghamshire	1695	MORDEN	250	35	43	Nottingham Shire
mwec0911	uk england nottinghamshire	1701	MORDEN	120	17	20	Nottingham Shire
mwec0951	uk england oxfordshire	1695	MORDEN	300	42	37	Oxford Shire
mwec0952	uk england oxfordshire	1701	MORDEN	140	17	20	Oxford Shire
mwam0879	america north (east)	1680	MORDEN	550	11	13	Partie de l'Amerique Septentrionale
mwuk1809	wales	1701	MORDEN	120	17	20	Pembrockshire
mwbp0314	poland	1688	MORDEN	150	10	13	Poland by Robt. Morden

AMPG REFERENCE	REGION	DATE	MAP MAKER	PRICE (UK£)	VERT. (cm.)	HOR. (cm.)	TITLE OF MAP (Comments by the editor in brackets)
mwuk1810	wales	1701	MORDEN	120	17	20	Radnor Shire
mwec0985	uk england rutland	1701	MORDEN	100	17	20	Rutland Shire
mwuk0428	scotland	1688	MORDEN	200	14	13	Scotiae Nova Descriptio
mwuk0443	scotland	1695	MORDEN	400	44	35	Scotland
mwec1009	uk england shropshire	1695	MORDEN	240	36	42	Shropshire
mwec1010	uk england shropshire	1701	MORDEN	120	17	20	Shropshire.
mwit0904	italy sicily	1688	MORDEN	300	10	12	Sicilia
mwec1038	uk england somerset	1695	MORDEN	280	36	42	Somerset Shire
mwec1040	uk england somerset	1701	MORDEN	120	17	20	Somerset Shire
mwuk1795	wales	1695	MORDEN	250	35	43	South Wales
mwec1068	uk england staffordshire	1695	MORDEN	240	36	42	Stafford Shire
mwec1069	uk england staffordshire	1701	MORDEN	120	17	20	Stafford Shire
mwec1101	uk england suffolk	1695	MORDEN	300	36	42	Suffolk
mwec1102	uk england suffolk	1701	MORDEN	120	17	20	Suffolk
mwsw0085	switzerland	1680	MORDEN	180	11	13	Suisse
mwec1135	uk england surrey	1695	MORDEN	350	36	43	Surrey
mwec1136	uk england surrey	1701	MORDEN	130	17	20	Surrey
mwec1165	uk england sussex	1695	MORDEN	300	34	42	Sussex
mwec1166	uk england sussex	1701	MORDEN	130	17	20	Sussex.
mwsc0075	scandinavia	1680	MORDEN	180	9	12	Sweden & Norway
mwru0498a	ukraine	1700	MORDEN	180	11	13	Tartaria in Europe
mwsam0675	south america magellan	1680	MORDEN	150	13	11	Terra Magellanica
mwaf0386	africa east	1700	MORDEN	150	12	10	The Coast of Zanguebar and Aien
mwuk1796	wales	1695	MORDEN	225	39	44	The County of Monmouth
mwec0137	uk england cheshire	1695	MORDEN	350	35	42	The County Palatine of Chester
mwec0683	uk england lancashire	1695	MORDEN	300	42	36	The County Palatine of Lancaster
mwec0684	uk england lancashire	1701	MORDEN	120	17	20	The County Palatine of Lancaster
mwec1319	uk england yorkshire	1695	MORDEN	200	36	44	The East Riding of York Shire
mwaf0882	africa south	1688	MORDEN	160	10	13	The Empire of Monomotapa and ye Coast of Cafres
mwwi0365	barbados	1687	MORDEN	320	13	11	The Island of Barbados
mwuk1799	wales	1701	MORDEN	120	17	20	The Island of Mona, now Angelsey
mwat0089	atlantic azores	1700	MORDEN	150	10	13	The Isles of Azores
mwas0415	asia south east	1688	MORDEN	250	10	13	The Isles of Sonda
mwuk0121	ireland	1695	MORDEN	400	42	35	The Kingdom of Ireland
mwin0462	indian ocean maldives	1687	MORDEN	150	13	11	The Maldives and Ceylon Islands
mwas0719	asia south east moluccas	1687	MORDEN	180	10	13	The Mulucca Ilands &c.
mwec1323	uk england yorkshire	1701	MORDEN	130	17	20	The North & East Riding of Yorkshire
mwec1320	uk england yorkshire	1695	MORDEN	280	37	42	The North Riding of York Shire
mwam0888	america north (east)	1687	MORDEN	550	11	13	The North West Part of America by R. Morden at ye Atlas in Cornhill (North West?)
mwas0755	asia south east philippines	1680	MORDEN	480	10	13	The Philipine Isles
mwuk1564	england islands	1695	MORDEN	320	36	42	The Smaller Islands in the British Ocean
mwuk1566	england islands	1701	MORDEN	140	17	20	The Smaller Islands in the British Ocean
mwbh0494	belgium holland	1700	MORDEN	150	9	11	The Spanish Provinces vulgo Flanders
mwbh0414	belgium holland	1680	MORDEN	180	11	13	The United Provinces vulgo Holland
mwec1321	uk england yorkshire	1695	MORDEN	300	36	42	The West Riding of York Shire
mwec1322	uk england yorkshire	1701	MORDEN	140	17	20	The West Riding of York Shire
mwuk1129	england london	1690	MORDEN	8000	66	104	This Actuall Survey of London, Westminster & Southwark (5 editions to 1765)
mwe0898	europe hungary	1685	MORDEN	685	44	54	Totius Regni Hungariae
mwe0770	europe east	1680	MORDEN	150	10	13	Transilvania Moldavia Valachia Bulgaria &c.
mwec1194	uk england warwickshire	1695	MORDEN	250	37	42	Warwick Shire
mwec1195	uk england warwickshire	1701	MORDEN	130	17	20	Warwick Shire
mwaf0700	africa north	1687	MORDEN	120	11	12	West Barbarie / East Barbarie
mwec1224	uk england westmorland	1695	MORDEN	200	36	42	Westmoreland
mwec1225	uk england westmorland	1701	MORDEN	100	17	20	Westmoreland.
mwec1245	uk england wiltshire	1695	MORDEN	250	37	42	Wilt Shire
mwec1246	uk england wiltshire	1701	MORDEN	130	17	20	Wilt Shire
mwec1278	uk england worcestershire	1695	MORDEN	240	36	42	Worcester Shire
mwec1279	uk england worcestershire	1701	MORDEN	120	17	20	Worcester Shire
mwuk1136	england london	1700	MORDEN & LEA	4000	64	129	London Westminster and Southwark (4 editions until 1725)
mwru0436	russia tartary	1690	MORDEN & LEA	1200	43	55	Tartary
mwuk1132	england london	1691	MORDEN & LEA	7200	57	97	This Actual Survey of London, Westminster & Southwark (5 editions until 1765)
mwuss0156	carolinas	1685	MORDEN, THORNTON & LEA	24000	54	45	A New Map of Carolina by John Thornton at the Platt in the Minories. Robert Morden at ye Atlas in Cornhill. And by Phillip Lea a the Atlas O'Herculus in the Poultry
mwam0875	america north (east)	1676	MORDEN-BERRY	60000	45	53	A Map of New England New Yorke New Iersey Mary-Land & Virginia
mwam0868a	america north (east)	1673	MORDEN-BERRY	8000	44	54	A New Map of the English Plantations in America
mww0205	world	1676	MORDEN-BERRY	15000	49	101	To Capt. John Wood this Map of the World Drawn according to Mercators Projection is Humbly Dedicated
mwuk0100	ireland	1689	MORDEN-BROWNE	1350	87	61	A New Map of Ireland Drawn from the Survey made by Sr. William Petty
mwaf0122a	africa	1703	MORDEN-HEYLYN	500	36	43	Africa
mwam0109	america continent	1703	MORDEN-HEYLYN	650	36	42	America

AMPG REFERENCE	REGION	DATE	MAP MAKER	PRICE (UK£)	VERT. (cm.)	HOR. (cm.)	TITLE OF MAP (Comments by the editor in brackets)
mwas0098a	asia continent	1703	MORDEN-HEYLYN	650	36	39	Asia
mwe0120a	europe	1703	MORDEN-HEYLYN	400	36	41	Europe
mwuk0112	ireland	1691	MORDEN-OVERTON	875	59	51	A New Map of Ireland Sold by I.Overton
mwf0442	france champagne	1635	MOREAU	1600	34	48	Le Pourtraict au Naturel de la Ville Cite et Universite de Reims (view)
mwme0084	holy land	1622	MOREAU		38	54	Peregrinatio Israelitarum per Desertum
mwwi0652	hispaniola	1791	MOREAU	600	24	37	Plan de la Baye et de la Ville de St. Louis, dans la Partie du Sud de l'Isle de St. Domingue (publ. by Phelipeau)
mwwi0653	hispaniola	1791	MOREAU	400	25	38	Plan de la Baye et de la Ville du Mole St. Nicolas dans l'Isle St. Domingue (south to the top.)
mwwi0655	hispaniola	1791	MOREAU	400	24	38	Plan de la Baye et du Bourg de Jacmel dans l'Isle St. Domingue
mwwi0656	hispaniola	1791	MOREAU	400	24	37	Plan de la Baye et du Bourg de Tiburon dans l'Isle St. Domingue
mwwi0657	hispaniola	1791	MOREAU	400	24	38	Plan de la Ville de St. Marc, dans l'Isle St. Domingue
mwwi0658	hispaniola	1791	MOREAU	600	36	45	Plan de la Ville des Cayes, dans l'Isle St. Domingue
mwwi0659	hispaniola	1791	MOREAU	700	36	45	Plan de la Ville des Rades et des Environs de Port-au-Prince, dans l'Isle Saint Domingue
mwwi0660	hispaniola	1791	MOREAU	600	42	59	Plan de la Ville du Cap Francois et de ses Environs dans l'Isle St. Domingue
mwwi0661	hispaniola	1791	MOREAU	400	25	38	Plan de la Ville du Port de Paix dans l'Isle St. Domingue
mwwi0662	hispaniola	1791	MOREAU	400	25	38	Plan de la Ville et de la Rade du Petit Goave dans l'Isle St. Domingue
mwwi0663	hispaniola	1791	MOREAU	400	25	38	Plan de la Ville et des Environs de Leogane dans l'Isle St. Domingue (south to the top)
mwme0680c	arabia etc	1836	MORESBY	4000	195	65	A Chart of the Red Sea, Comprising the part above Jiddah, on Mercator's Projection, Compiled from A Stasimetric Survey, Executed in the Years 1830, 31, 32, & 33
mwme0680d	arabia etc	1836	MORESBY	4000	195	65	A Chart of the Red Sea, from Jiddah, to the Straits of Bab-el-Mandeb, Surveyed in the Years 1830, 31, 32, & 33
mwit1263	italy venice	1844	MORETTI	720	63	72	Pianta della Citta di Venezia Disegnata ed Incisa da Dionisio Moretti
mwuk1124	england london	1682	MORGAN		176	236	London &c Actually Survey'd by Wm. Morgan (only one copy of this map is known. The map was also issued without the 'Prospect of London and Westminster' along the bottom of the map. The map was re-issued in 1720 with Morgan's name replaced by Morden & Lea. An updated version was issued in 1732 by Thomas Jefferys.)
mwuss1188	new york	1820	MORGAN	12000	51	61	The City of New York in the State of New York in North America
mwit1068	italy naples	1765	MORGHEN-CARDON	2000	62	91	Icon Crateris Neapolitani (illustrated is 1772 edition)
mwit1040	italy south	1770	MORGHEN	240	28	36	Pianta Litorale e sue adiacenze di Napoli fin a Pesto
mwg0249a	berlin	1847	MORIN	1600			Plan von Berlin (in 4 sheets)
mwuk0519	scotland	1774	MORISON	2000	34	87	Plan of the Navigation Proposed upon the Rivers of Forth, Devon, and Gudie, Made under the Direction of the Lords Commissioners of Police
mwaf0052	africa	1643	MORISOT	500	13	17	Africae Litora Priscis Navigata (excl. the southern tip of Africa)
mwsam0021	south america	1643	MORISOT	350	14	17	Americae Meridionales Periplus
mwam0315	america north	1643	MORISOT	850	14	17	Americae Septentrionalis Circuitus
mwit1123a	italy tuscany	1769	MOROZZI	350	46	51	Porzione della Toscana Inferiore, che comprende i Territorii di Volterra, di Piombino, e di Massa
mwuk0304a	irish sea	1748	MORRIS	3000	51	71	A Chart of the Coast of Wales in St. George's Channel, drawn from an Actual Survey now lying at the Admiralty Office, and made between the Years 1737 & 1744 by Order and Encouragement of the Lords of the Admiralty (re-issued 1800, 78x89cm)
mwuk0245a	ireland	1801	MORRIS, W.	550	19	32	A Plan of the Bay & Harbour of Dublin
mwuss1417	pennsylvania	1830	MORRISON	2800	54	53	Map of Huntingdon County. Constructed by Virtue of an Act of the Legislature of Pennsylvania by John Morrison
mwam0583	america north	1810	MORRISON	180	25	20	North America
mwam1327	america north (west)	1785	MORSE	300	18	29	A Chart of the Nth. West Coast of America and the Nth. East Coast of Asia, Showing the Discoveries that have Lately been Made in those Parts
mwuss0002	alabama	1797	MORSE	500	18	15	A Correct Map of the Georgia Western Territory
mwuss0509	georgia	1796	MORSE	350	19	31	A Map of Georgia, Also the Two Floridas, from the Best Authorities
mwuss0852	massachusetts	1796	MORSE	360	18	24	A Map of Massachusetts from the Best Authorities by J. Denison
mwam0562	america north	1804	MORSE	160	19	22	A Map of North America Showing All the New Discoveries
mwuss0235	carolinas	1794	MORSE	320	23	43	A Map of North Carolina from the Best Authorities
mwuss1457	rhode isl	1794	MORSE	200	23	18	A Map of Rhode Island
mwam0811	america north (central)	1794	MORSE	400	19	22	A Map of the Back Settlements
mwuss0708	maine	1796	MORSE	240	18	23	A Map of the District of Maine with New Brunswick & Nova Scotia

AMPG REFERENCE	REGION	DATE	MAP MAKER	PRICE (UK£)	VERT. (cm.)	HOR. (cm.)	TITLE OF MAP (Comments by the editor in brackets)
mwam0836	america north (central)	1844	MORSE	550	32	38	A Map of the Indian Territory, Northern Texas and New Mexico Showing the Great Western Prairies by Josiah Gregg
mwuss0931	minnesota	1796	MORSE	450	19	24	A Map of the North Western Territory
mwam0519	america north	1792	MORSE	550	31	39	A Map of the Northern and Middle States; Comprehending the Western Territory and the British Dominions in North America, from the Best Authorities
mwuss0597	kentucky	1796	MORSE	550	19	29	A Map of the State of Kentucky and the Tennessee Government Compiled from the Best Authorities by Cyrus Harris
mwuss1009	new hampshire	1796	MORSE	280	18	24	A Map of the States of New Hampshire and Vermont by J. Denison
mwuss1484	tennessee	1794	MORSE	1400	17	23	A Map of the Tennessee Government
mwuss1556	vermont	1794	MORSE	300	23	17	A Map of Vermont
mwca0452	canada nova scotia	1794	MORSE	160	18	22	A New Map of Nova Scotia, New Brunswick and Cape Brunswick and Cape Breton
mwaf0265	africa	1790	MORSE	100	21	24	Africa from the Best Authorities
mwuss0010	alabama	1825	MORSE	160	19	24	Alabama, Mississippi and Louisiana
mwas0215	asia continent	1790	MORSE	120	19	23	Asia from the Best Authorities
mwp0512	pacific south	1798	MORSE	200	17	25	Chart of the New Discoveries East of New Holland and New Guinea
mwuss1247	new york	1843	MORSE	240	38	30	City of New York
mwuss0297	connecticut	1794	MORSE	200	18	23	Connecticut
mwp0351	pacific hawaii	1840	MORSE	400	23	25	Hawaiian Islands
mwuss0564	illinois	1844	MORSE	180	36	28	Illinois
mwuss0585	iowa	1842	MORSE	280	34	28	Iowa
mwuss0588	iowa	1844	MORSE	100	18	21	Iowa and Wisconsin
mwuss0587	iowa	1844	MORSE	320	32	38	Iowa and Wisconsin Chiefly from the Map of J.N. Nicollet
mwuss0719	maine	1825	MORSE	160	20	24	Maine, New Hampshire & Vermont
mwuss0245	carolinas	1796	MORSE	350	19	23	Map of North and South Carolina by J. Denison
mwuss0118	california	1845	MORSE	360	36	28	Map of the Californias by T.J. Farnham
mwam1125	america north (east)	1798	MORSE	360	22	41	Map of the Northern Part of the United States of America
mwuss1164	new york	1796	MORSE	400	19	24	Map of the State of New York
mwuss0763	maryland	1796	MORSE	300	19	24	Map of the States of Maryland and Delaware by J. Denison
mwuss1664	virginia	1792	MORSE	720	36	30	Map of the States of Virginia, North Carolina, South Carolina and Georgia ... Comprehending the Spanish Provinces of East and West Florida: Exhibiting the Boundaries as Fixed by the Late Treaty of Peace between the United States and the Spanish
mww0589	world	1795	MORSE	200	19	36	Map of the World from the Best Authorities
mwuss1665	virginia	1794	MORSE	720	25	47	Map of Virginia, Maryland and Delaware
mwuss0867	massachusetts	1827	MORSE	280	40	28	Massachusetts, Rhode Island & Connecticut
mwuss0970	mississippi	1844	MORSE	240	36	28	Mississippi
mwuss0993	missouri	1844	MORSE	180	28	36	Missouri
mwuss1047	new jersey	1796	MORSE	350	19	15	New Jersey
mwuss0268	carolinas	1825	MORSE	160	20	25	North Carolina, South Carolina and Georgia
mwuss1293	ohio	1825	MORSE	160	19	25	Ohio and Indiana
mwuss1334	oregon	1843	MORSE	400	28	36	Oregon
mwuss1390	pennsylvania	1796	MORSE	375	19	34	Pennsylvania Drawn from the Best Authorities
mwuss1461	rhode isl	1796	MORSE	400	19	33	Rhode-Island and Connecticut
mwuss0283	carolinas	1843	MORSE	150	30	38	South Carolina
mwuss1525	texas	1844	MORSE	400	39	31	Texas
mwuss0702	maine	1793	MORSE	580	27	20	The District of Main from the Latest Surveys
mwam0631	america north	1822	MORSE	550	26	42	United States
mwuss1668	virginia	1796	MORSE	480	15	19	Virginia
mwwi0139	west indies	1796	MORSE	100	18	30	West Indies from the Best Authorities
mwam0824	america north (central)	1832	MORSE	160	15	18	Western States
mwuss1699	wisconsin	1844	MORSE	280	32	39	Wisconsin, Southern Part
mwe0617	europe czech republic (bohemia)	1835	MORSTADT	1600	13	72	Panorama von Prag.
mwjk0087	japan	1736	MORTIER	320	19	28	(Kyoto) Plan de la Ville de Meaco
mwe0501	europe croatia	1704	MORTIER	500	44	53	(Split) Spalato. Ville des Venetiens
mwf0327	france brittany	1693	MORTIER	785	58	80	2me Carte Particuliere des Costes de Bretagne depuis le Cap de Frehel, jusques a Perros, & l'Isle Tome
mwf0328	france brittany	1693	MORTIER	785	59	80	3me Carte Particuliere des Costes de Bretagne qui Comprend Morlaix, Saint Paul de Leon, les Sept Isles, et l'Isle de Bas
mwf0329	france brittany	1693	MORTIER	785	59	80	4me Carte Particuliere des Costes de Bretagne depuis l'Anse de Goulven jusqu'a l'Isle d'Ouessant (south to the top)
mwf0330	france brittany	1693	MORTIER	785	61	81	5e Carte Particuliere des Costes de Bretagne Contenant les Environs de la Rade de Brest
mwf0331	france brittany	1693	MORTIER	785	57	81	6me. Carte Particuliere des Costes de Bretagne depuis la Baye d'Hodierne jusqu'a l'Isle de Groa, Contenant les Isles de Glenan comme Elles Paroissent a Basse Mer dans les Grandes Marees

AMPG REFERENCE	REGION	DATE	MAP MAKER	PRICE (UK£)	VERT. (cm.)	HOR. (cm.)	TITLE OF MAP (Comments by the editor in brackets)
mwf0332	france brittany	1693	MORTIER	785	59	79	7me Carte Particuliere des Costes de Bretagne depuis l'Isle de Groa jusqu'au Croisic Contenant le Port Louis, Bell'Isle et le Morbian
mwf0333	france brittany	1693	MORTIER	785	59	79	8eme Carte Particuliere des Costes de Bretagne qui Comprend l'Entree de la Loire et l'Isle de Noirmoustier
mwbh0510a	belgium holland	1705	MORTIER	960	60	61	A true & exact map of the Seat of War in Brabant & Flanders with ye Enemies Lines in their just dimensions
mwgr0132	greece	1700	MORTIER	580	45	56	Achaiae Descriptio (Peloponnesos)
mwsam0040	south america	1700	MORTIER	1250	57	86	Amerique Meridionale (re-issue of Jaillot 1674)
mwam0335	america north	1692	MORTIER	3600	57	88	Amerique Septentrionale Divisee en ses Principales Parties (re-issue of Jaillot 1674)
mwme0981	turkey etc	1700	MORTIER	450	41	51	Anaplus Bosphori Thracii Delineatus (re-issue of Mariette 1666)
mwit0556	italy marches	1704	MORTIER	800	48	61	Ascoli
mwam0104	america continent	1700	MORTIER	1000	39	55	Atlantis Insula (copy of Sanson 1669)
mwgm0384	panama	1692	MORTIER	580	21	31	Baye et Ville de Havana ou S. Christoval / Bay et Chateau de Porto Bello / (on verso) Cartegene avec ses Ports, et Fortresses (3 maps, each 21x31cm, on one sheet, one map on verso)
mwit0355	italy emilia-romagna	1704	MORTIER	960	44	50	Bononia Docet Mater Studiorum (Bologna, based on Blaeu)
mwme0219	holy land	1700	MORTIER	400	40	47	Byzondere Kaart van de Landen daar de Apostelen het Evangelium Gepredikt
mwgr0420	greece crete	1705	MORTIER	785	45	56	Candiae Urbis a Turca MDCXXXXVII (south to the top)
mwaf1160	africa west	1700	MORTIER	960	51	79	Carta Particuliere des Costes de l'Afrique qui Comprent une Partie de la Guinee et Partie de Mina
mwuk1482	uk english channel (all)	1700	MORTIER	1350	57	86	Carte de la Manche
mwuk0439	scotland	1693	MORTIER	1200	63	89	Carte de la Mer D'Ecosse Contendant les Isles et Costes Septentrionales et Occidentales D'Ecosse et les Costes Septentrionales D'Irlande (north to the left)
mwat0302	atlantic south	1700	MORTIER	600	47	60	Carte de la Mer Meridional
mwme0234	holy land	1705	MORTIER	480	40	47	Carte de la Terre Sainte Divisee selon les Douze Tribus d'Israel ou sont ... Jesus Christ
mwme0593	arabia etc	1710	MORTIER	720	47	58	Carte de la Turquie de l'Arabie et de la Perse
mwuk1430	england thames	1693	MORTIER	1000	45	89	Carte de l'Entree de la Tamise avec les Bancs (north to the right. Map by Jaillot. Re-issued by Bellin 1757)
mwaf1163	africa west	1705	MORTIER	675	58	44	Carte des Costes de l'Afrique depuis Cabo Corso jusques a Omorro
mwaf0387	africa east	1700	MORTIER	960	59	48	Carte des Costes de L'Afrique depuis Cap de Lopo jusques a l'Isle Mazira
mwaf1161	africa west	1700	MORTIER	960	54	77	Carte des Costes de l'Afrique ou est Compris une Partie de Guinee, le Royaume de Benin, l'Isle de St. Thomas &c.
mwas0420	asia south east	1696	MORTIER	3500	58	87	Carte des Costes de l'Asie sur l'Ocean Contenant les Bancs Isles et Costes &c.
mwf0977	france poitou	1693	MORTIER	1000	60	86	Carte des Costes de Poitou, d'Aunis et de Saintonge depuis l'Isle de Noirmoustier jusqu'a l'Embouchure de la Riviere de Bourdeaux
mwsp0478	spain regions	1693	MORTIER	720	58	85	Carte des Costes Septentrionales d'Espagne depuis Fontarabie jusqu'a Bayonne en Gallice
mwsc0098	scandinavia	1700	MORTIER	1200	45	59	Carte des Courones du Nord (2 maps, each 45x59cm)
mwat0088	atlantic azores	1700	MORTIER	785	50	54	Carte des Isles d'Acores
mwme0579	arabia etc	1700	MORTIER	480	51	43	Carte des Principales Ports ... la Mer Rouge (11 maps on one sheet and Suez, Sinai)
mwf0292	france bay of biscay	1693	MORTIER	1200	72	90	Carte du Golfe de Gascogne Contenant les Costes de France et d'Espagne depuis l'Isle d'Ouessant jusqu'au Cap Finistere
mwuss0163	carolinas	1705	MORTIER	2250	57	47	Carte General de la Caroline. Dresse sur les Memoires le Plus Nouveaux par le Sieur S
mwaf0117	africa	1700	MORTIER	1750	59	87	Carte Generale de l'Afrique
mww0249	world	1693	MORTIER	5500	59	90	Carte Generale de Toutes les Costes du Monde, et les Pays Nouvellement Decouvert (also issued with an extra title to left-hand sheet 'Carte Generale des Costes de L'Amerique ...')
mwe1198	europe west	1693	MORTIER	800	59	85	Carte Generale des Costes de l'Europe sur l'Ocean Comprises depuis Dronthem en Norvege jusques au Destroit de Gibraltar
mwuk0118b	ireland	1693	MORTIER	900	60	86	Carte Generale des Costes d'Irlande et des Costes Occidentales d'Angleterre avec une partie de celles d'Ecosse
mww0279	world	1700	MORTIER	1000	40	47	Carte Generale du Monde, ou Description du Monde Terrestre & Aquatique
mwf0780	france normandy	1693	MORTIER	850	58	47	Carte Maritime des Environs de Dieppe depuis Pont Asselane jusques au Havre de Grace ... 1693
mwru0441	russia tartary	1700	MORTIER	1000	55	99	Carte Nouvelle de la Grande Tartarie
mwm0030	mediterranean	1700	MORTIER	2250	53	105	Carte Nouvelle de la Mer Mediterranee
mwam0903	america north (east)	1698	MORTIER	2500	59	91	Carte Nouvelle de l'Amerique Angloise Contenant la Virginie, Mary-Land, Caroline, Pensilvania, Nouvelle Iorck, N. Iarsey N: France, et les Terres Nouvellement Decouverte

AMPG REFERENCE	REGION	DATE	MAP MAKER	PRICE (UK£)	VERT. (cm.)	HOR. (cm.)	TITLE OF MAP (Comments by the editor in brackets)
mwit0797	italy sardinia	1704	MORTIER	960	50	61	Carte Nouvelle de l'Isle et Royaume de Sardagne (also issued with sea decorations, as shown below)
mwgm0389	panama	1700	MORTIER	1350	60	86	Carte Particuliere de Isthmus ou Darien qui Comprend le Golfe de Panama &c. Cartagena, et les Isles aux Environs
mwuss0162	carolinas	1696	MORTIER	3500	48	59	Carte Particuliere de la Caroline Dresse sur les Memoires le Plus Nouveaux
mwme0580	arabia etc	1700	MORTIER	1000	52	76	Carte Particuliere de la Mer Rouge &c.
mwca0213	canada arctic	1696	MORTIER	1500	58	82	Carte Particuliere de l'Amerique Septentrionale, ou sont Compris le Detroit de Davids, le Detroit de Hudson, &c.
mwaf0596	africa islands madagascar	1705	MORTIER	900	57	85	Carte Particuliere de l'Isle Dauphine ou Madagascar et St. Laurens
mwaf1046	africa south east	1705	MORTIER	675	41	59	Carte Particuliere des Costes de l'Afrique depuis C. del Gado jusques Rio Mocambo, et les Isles aux Environs (incl. Comoro Isl.)
mwaf1045	africa south east	1700	MORTIER	720	57	82	Carte Particuliere des Costes de l'Afrique qui Comprend le Pays de Cafres &c. (Mozambique. North to the right.)
mwaf1162	africa west	1700	MORTIER	1600	55	76	Carte Particuliere des Costes de l'Afrique qui Comprend le Royaume de Cacheo, le Province de Gelofo &c.
mwaf1070	africa south west	1700	MORTIER	785	58	43	Carte Particuliere des Costes de L'Afrique, Depuis Cabo Ledo Jusques au Cap de Bone Esperance (inset of Saldanha Bay)
mwaf0886	africa south	1700	MORTIER	1500	57	81	Carte Particuliere des Costes du Cap de Bone Esperance &c.
mwuk1386	england south	1693	MORTIER	1250	59	80	Carte Particuliere des Costes Meridionales d'Angleterre qui Comprend l'Isle de Wicht
mwg0528	rheinland-pfalz	1705	MORTIER	1350	73	53	Carte Particuliere des Pays que sont Situez entre le Rhein, la Saare, la Moselle, et la Basse Alsace (4 sheets, each 73x53cm.)
mwf0086	france	1700	MORTIER	750	57	86	Carte Particuliere des Postes de France
mwin0423	indian ocean	1700	MORTIER	2500	60	88	Carte Particuliere d'une Partie d'Asie ou sont les Isles d'Andemaon, Ceylan, les Maldives / Partie Occidentale d'une Partie d'Asie ou sont les Isles de Zocotora, de l'Amirante (re-issued by Covens & Mortier in 1710)
mwit0920	italy sicily	1705	MORTIER	850	42	53	Catana (view, first publ. by Blaeu)
mwgr0314	greece corfu	1700	MORTIER	650	40	50	Corfu Ville dela Republique de Venise dans la Dalmatie
mwit0128	italy	1700	MORTIER	785	46	55	des Postes de l'Italie
mwit0307	italy central	1705	MORTIER	960	60	67	Estats de l'Eglise et de Toscane
mwme0984a	turkey etc	1700	MORTIER	300	35	58	Galatia cujus Populi Tolistobogi
mwit0425	italy liguria	1704	MORTIER	3000	44	100	Genoa (view)
mwf0448	france champagne	1700	MORTIER	450	77	54	Gouvernement Generale de Champagne
mwgr0114	greece	1690	MORTIER	875	40	52	Graecia Foederata sub Agamemnone ob Helenae Raptum in Troiam Coniurans ex Homaero Collecta Conatibus Geographicis
mwbh0495	belgium holland	1700	MORTIER	480	43	58	Gueldre Espagnol
mwf0781	france normandy	1693	MORTIER	1200	60	85	I. Carte Particuliere des Costes de Normandie depuis Dieppe jusqu'a la Pointe de la Percee en Bessin
mwf0326	france brittany	1693	MORTIER	785	57	80	Ire Carte Particuliere des Costes de Bretagne depuis Granville jusques au Cap de Frehel
mwf0680	france lorraine	1700	MORTIER	650	57	86	La Lorraine
mwru0112	russia	1700	MORTIER	750	55	89	La Russie Blanche ou Moscovie (re-issue of Jaillot 1674)
mwsc0099	scandinavia	1700	MORTIER	1200	57	86	La Scandinavie
mwit0912	italy sicily	1700	MORTIER	785	57	86	La Sicile
mwit0496a	italy lombardy	1704	MORTIER	480	38	52	La Ville de Como
mwit0496	italy lombardy	1704	MORTIER	720	42	61	La Ville de Mantoue (view)
mwf0232	france alsace	1700	MORTIER	650	57	86	L'Alsace
mwca0035	canada	1690	MORTIER	2000	55	78	Le Canada ou Partie de la Nouvelle France, Contenant la Terre de Labrador la Nouvelle France, les Isles de Terre Neuve, de Nostre Dame &c.
mwf1031	france provence	1696	MORTIER	580	48	56	Le Comte et Gouvernement de Provence
mwe1012	europe rhine	1700	MORTIER	400	86	57	Le Cours de la Riviere du Rhein
mwsp0694	gibraltar	1705	MORTIER	785	55	83	Le De Troit de Gibraltar ou sont Exactement Observee la Maree &c.
mwf0611	france languedoc	1700	MORTIER	650	45	60	Le Diocese de L'Eveche de Nismes (Nimes)
mwbh0497	belgium holland	1700	MORTIER	875	57	86	Le Duche de Brabant. Partie Meridionale
mwbh0498	belgium holland	1700	MORTIER	960	57	86	Le Duche de Brabant. Partie Septentrionale
mwbh0498a	belgium holland	1700	MORTIER	500	58	50	Le Duche de Brabant qui comprend les Quartiers (title above map: Ducatus Brabantiae Complectens …)
mwbh0850	luxembourg	1700	MORTIER	1350	57	86	Le Duche de Luxembourg
mwit0539	italy milan	1700	MORTIER	1350	54	66	Le Duche de Milan
mwgm0012	gulf of mexico and surrounding regions	1700	MORTIER	1850	60	85	Le Golfe de Mexique, et les Isles Voisine. Dresse sur les Relations les Plus Nouvelles. Archipelague du Mexique ou sont les Isles de Cuba, Espagnola, Jamaica, &c. Dresse sur les Relations les Plus Nouvelles (re-issued by Covens & Mortier in 1720)
mwit1231	italy venice	1700	MORTIER	2750	56	73	Le Golfe de Venise
mwf0266	france aquitaine	1700	MORTIER	650	48	60	Le Gouvernement General de Guienne et Gascogne
mwit0595	italy north	1705	MORTIER	2500	98	122	Le Grand Theatre de la Guerre en Italie
mwsc0328	scandinavia denmark	1700	MORTIER	650	59	87	Le Royaume de Danemark

AMPG REFERENCE	REGION	DATE	MAP MAKER	PRICE (UK£)	VERT. (cm.)	HOR. (cm.)	TITLE OF MAP (Comments by the editor in brackets)
mwf0087	france	1700	MORTIER	750	57	86	Le Royaume de France
mwas0429	asia south east	1700	MORTIER	2000	79	56	Le Royaume de Siam avec les Royaumes qui luy sont Tributaires, et les Isles de Sumatra, Andemaon, etc. et les Isles Voisines
mwuk0447	scotland	1700	MORTIER	1350	86	57	Le Royaume d'Ecosse
mwuk0123	ireland	1700	MORTIER	1350	86	57	Le Royaume d'Irland
mwf0608	france languedoc	1696	MORTIER	580	87	60	Le Theatre de la Guerre dans les Sevennes, le Languedoc ... ou sont Exactement Observes les Chemins &c. d'ou les Mecontents Font leurs Courses
mwme0581	arabia etc	1700	MORTIER	1350	57	86	L'Empire du Grand Seigneur des Turcs
mwaa0186a	arctic / antarctic	1690	MORTIER	4000	43	53	Les Deux Poles Arcticque ou Septentrional, et Antarcticque ou Meridional. (Copy of Sanson's map of 1657. Illustration shows Covens & Mortier re-issue of 1730)
mwuk1137	england london	1700	MORTIER	785	48	54	Les Environs de Londres
mwit1233	italy venice	1705	MORTIER	675	26	42	Les Environs de Venise
mwuk0786	uk	1708	MORTIER	785	46	58	Les Isles Britanniques ou sont les Royaumes (slightly reduced copy of De L'Isle)
mwbh0499	belgium holland	1700	MORTIER	675	57	86	Les Provinces des Pays-Bas Catholiques
mwit1192	italy veneto	1705	MORTIER	800	58	96	L'Etat de la Republique de Venise
mwe0110	europe	1700	MORTIER	960	57	86	L'Europe
mwit0285	italy campagna	1704	MORTIER	800	38	48	L'Isle d'Ischia dans le Voisinage de Naples
mwit0795	italy sardinia	1700	MORTIER	1350	57	86	L'Isle et Royaume de Sardagne
mwit0129	italy	1700	MORTIER	960	57	86	L'Italie
mwuk0101	ireland	1689	MORTIER	720	36	27	London-Derry soo als het nu Belegert is door Jacob de Tweede (Ulster)
mwit1114	italy tuscany	1704	MORTIER	675	41	52	Lucques ou Luca
mwg0484	mecklenburg	1700	MORTIER	250	49	56	Marchionatus Brandenburgi et Ducatus Pomerania Tabula
mwit0541	italy milan	1704	MORTIER	1500	49	61	Mediolanum Vulgo Milano
mwp0240	pacific (all)	1700	MORTIER	3500	60	74	Mer de Sud ou Pacifique, Contenant l'Isle de Californe, les Costes de Mexique, du Perou, Chili, et le Destroit de Magellanique &c. (re-issued by Covens & Mortier from 1711)
mwm0031	mediterranean	1700	MORTIER	1800	57	86	Mer Mediterrane
mwit0919	italy sicily	1704	MORTIER	850	42	52	Messina Ville de la Sicile (view, first publ. by Blaeu)
mwit0540	italy milan	1701	MORTIER	300	13	19	Milan - Capitale du Duche
mwit0353	italy emilia-romagna	1704	MORTIER	720	42	52	Modene ou Modena (view)
mwit1057	italy naples	1704	MORTIER	4800	42	100	Napoli
mwsp0492	spain regions	1702	MORTIER	1000	38	49	Nette Afteykeningh van het Veroveren der France en Spanse Scheepen inde Bay van Vigos door de Engelesche en Hallandse Vloot
mwme0592	arabia etc	1710	MORTIER	650	52	74	Nieuwe Platte Paskaart van de Roode Zee in Oostindien / Carte Particuliere de la Mer Rouge &c.
mwbh0429b	belgium holland	1700	MORTIER	5000	48	58	Novissima Amsterodami Tabula
mwuk1385a	uk england west	1680	MORTIER	785	58	48	Occidentalior Regni Angliae Districtus Comprehendens Principatum Walliae et Glocestriae Ducatum
mwat0266	atlantic ocean (north)	1700	MORTIER	960	48	59	Ocean Atlantique, ou Mer du Nord
mwme0984b	turkey etc	1700	MORTIER	300	38	51	Paphlagonia (shown above left)
mwit0354	italy emilia-romagna	1704	MORTIER	720	41	50	Parma (view)
mwin0479	indian ocean west	1700	MORTIER	875	59	88	Partie Occidentale d'une Partie d'Asie ou sont les Isles de Zocotora, de l'Amirante
mwf0435	france central	1696	MORTIER	550	92	61	Partie Septentrionale de l'Evesche de Chartres / Partie Meridionale de l'Evesche de Chartres
mwit1115	italy tuscany	1704	MORTIER	960	42	52	Pisa
mwe0419	europe austria vienna	1700	MORTIER	1350	57	86	Plan de la Ville de Vienne
mwgm0405	panama	1740	MORTIER	1200	42	58	Plan de la Ville Rade et Forts de Porto Bello (see also Toms)
mwf0836	france paris	1694	MORTIER	2250	60	89	Plan de la Ville, Cite, Universite et Faubourgs de Paris
mwaf0764a	africa north libya	1705	MORTIER	800	49	65	Plan de la Ville de Tripoli en Barbarie
mwsam0340	south america brazil	1700	MORTIER	1200	41	53	Praefecturae de Paraiba, et Rio Grande (copy of Blaeu 1662)
mwsam0339	south america brazil	1700	MORTIER	1200	42	53	Praefecturae Paranambucae Pars Borealis, una cum Praefectura de Itamaraca (copy of Blaeu 1662)
mwsp0490	spain regions	1700	MORTIER	1200	57	86	Principaute de Catalogne
mwit0286	italy campagna	1704	MORTIER	675	41	51	Puteolanus Ager. Le Golfe de Pouzol et une Partie du Golfe de Naples elle est vers la Ville de Pouzol, & les Ruines des Baies
mwsc0600	scandinavia norway	1700	MORTIER	1800	59	51	Regni Norvegia ... Aggerhusiensem, Bergensem, Nidrosiensem, Warhusiae, et Bahusiae
mwit0730	italy rome	1700	MORTIER	1650	57	86	Roma
mwit0921	italy sicily	1705	MORTIER	650	44	56	Siciliae Insulae
mwme0240	holy land	1708	MORTIER	960	40	94	Situs Terrae Canaan sive Terrae Promissionis
mwgm0018	gulf of mexico and surrounding regions	1705	MORTIER	7500	60	101	Teatre de la Guerre en Amerique, telle qu'elle est a Present Possedee par les Espagnols, Anglois, Francois, et Hollandois &c. - Archipelague du Mexique ou sont les Isles de Cuba, Espagnole, Iamaïque (a c1703 edition only had one inset, rather than four, as shown below)
mwit0589	italy north	1700	MORTIER	720	55	46	Teatre de la Guerre en Italie ou Partie de la Republique de Venise Verone, Mantoue, Modene Padoue

AMPG REFERENCE	REGION	DATE	MAP MAKER	PRICE (UK£)	VERT. (cm.)	HOR. (cm.)	TITLE OF MAP (Comments by the editor in brackets)
mwru0525a	ukraine	1740	MORTIER	1600	48	62	Theatre de la Guerre dans la Petite Tartarie, La Crimee, la Mer Noire (2 sheets, each 48x62cm)
mwe1012a	europe rhine	1700	MORTIER	720	95	59	Teatre de la Guerre sur le Rhein, Moessele, Mayn, & le Necker. Sur les Memoires du Sr. Sanson (see also Covens & Mortier 1725)
mwe0460	europe central	1705	MORTIER	450	47	59	Theatre de la Guerre des Couronnes du Nord
mwe0339	europe austria	1700	MORTIER	720	95	58	Theatre de la Guerre en Austriche, Baviere, Souabe, le Tirol
mwsp0234	spain	1710	MORTIER	4800	95	120	Theatre de la Guerre en Espagne et en Portugal
mwe0782	europe east	1705	MORTIER	1500	100	122	Theatre de la Guerre en Hongarie Transylvanie &c.
mwsp0069a	portugal	1690	MORTIER	1800	98	61	Theatre de la Guerre en Portugal, et dans les Algarves (2 sheets only of a 4-sheet map. See 'Spain 1710')
mwgr0144	greece	1705	MORTIER	675	43	53	Thracia Vetus
mwru0499	ukraine	1700	MORTIER	1600	41	57	Ukranae Pars quae Kiovia Palatinatus
mwm0216	mediterranean malta	1705	MORTIER	1500	52	57	Valletta ou Valete Ville Forte, de l'Isle de Malta
mwit1232	italy venice	1704	MORTIER	4000	45	100	Venetia
mwit0666b	italy piedmont	1704	MORTIER	1000	42	50	Veue de la Ville de Turin et de ses Environs
mwit1190	italy veneto	1704	MORTIER	900	39	53	Vicence, ou Vincence
mwme0235	holy land	1705	MORTIER	600	40	47	Voyage des Enfans d'Israel dans le Desert depuis leur Sortie d'Egypt ... au Pays de Canaan
mwgm0192	mexico	1706	MORTIER	785	41	52	Yucatan Conventus Iuridici Hispaniae Novae Pars Occidentalis, et Guatimala Conventus Iuridicus
mwe0501a	europe croatia	1704	MORTIER	375	41	51	Zara en Dalmatie
mwam1086	america north (east)	1784	MOSER	480	22	28	Karte des Oestliehe oder Ehemahlige Englischen Amerika nach den Besitzungen und Graenzen nach dem Frieden von 1783
mwec0027	uk england bedfordshire	1837	MOULE	100	27	21	Bedfordshire
mwec0055	uk england berkshire	1837	MOULE	160	21	27	Berkshire
mwec0116	uk england cambridgeshire	1839	MOULE	160	27	20	Cambridgeshire
mwec0158	uk england cheshire	1837	MOULE	160	21	27	Cheshire
mwec0975	uk england oxfordshire	1840	MOULE	160	25	18	City and University of Oxford
mwec0211	uk england cornwall	1836	MOULE	150	21	27	Cornwall
mwec0246	uk england cumbria	1837	MOULE	120	27	21	Cumberland
mwec0277	uk england derbyshire	1837	MOULE	140	27	21	Derbyshire
mwec0313	uk england devon	1837	MOULE	140	21	27	Devonshire
mwec0426	uk england essex	1836	MOULE	150	21	27	Essex
mwec0460	uk england gloucestershire	1845	MOULE	150	27	21	Gloucestershire
mwec0505	uk england hampshire	1837	MOULE	200	21	27	Hampshire
mwec0568	uk england hertfordshire	1836	MOULE	140	21	27	Hertfordshire
mwec0706	uk england lancashire	1837	MOULE	160	27	21	Lancashire
mwec0730	uk england leicestershire	1837	MOULE	120	27	21	Leicesterhire
mwec0760	uk england lincolnshire	1837	MOULE	140	27	21	Lincolnshire
mwec0799	uk england middlesex	1837	MOULE	235	20	26	Middlesex
mwuk1882	wales	1837	MOULE	100	27	21	Monmouthshire
mwec0898	uk england northumberland	1840	MOULE	120	27	20	Northumberland
mwec0931	uk england nottinghamshire	1840	MOULE	120	26	20	Nottinghamshire
mwec0994	uk england rutland	1840	MOULE	100	25	20	Rutlandshire
mwec1023	uk england shropshire	1837	MOULE	140	26	20	Shropshire
mwec1086	uk england staffordshire	1836	MOULE	140	26	20	Staffordshire
mwec1152	uk england surrey	1836	MOULE	200	21	27	Surrey
mwuk1615	isle of man	1843	MOULE	140	17	20	The Isle of Man
mwec1212	uk england warwickshire	1850	MOULE	150	27	20	Warwickshire
mwec1209	uk england warwickshire	1837	MOULE	140	25	20	Warwickshire
mwec1233	uk england westmorland	1837	MOULE	120	21	27	Westmoreland
mwec1264	uk england wiltshire	1837	MOULE	140	21	27	Wiltshire
mwec1289	uk england worcestershire	1836	MOULE	120	27	21	Worcestershire
mwec1362	uk england yorkshire	1836	MOULE	140	21	27	Yorkshire East Riding
mwec1363	uk england yorkshire	1836	MOULE	180	21	27	Yorkshire North Riding
mwec1364	uk england yorkshire	1836	MOULE	200	20	27	Yorkshire West Riding
mww0254	world	1695	MOULLARD-SANSON	1500	23	43	Hemisphere Occidental du Globe / Hemisphere Oriental du Globe (illustrated is a 1710 version of the same map, using mirror images of the two hemispheres)
mwat0117	atlantic bermuda	1728	MOUNT & PAGE	1800	22	29	(Bermuda. Text below map.)
mwaf0930	africa south	1750	MOUNT & PAGE	480	32	53	(Delagoa Bay / River English)
mwuk0776	uk	1702	MOUNT & PAGE	785	44	54	A Chart of England Scotland and Ireland (north to the left)
mwbp0041	baltic sea (east)	1740	MOUNT & PAGE	750	42	51	A Chart of Lyfland and East Fynland between der Winda and Revel with ye Island of Aland
mwuss1155	new york	1784	MOUNT & PAGE	3000	61	46	A Chart of New York Harbour with the Banks Soundings and Sailing Marks from the Most Accurate Surveys & Observations
mwbp0443	poland	1750	MOUNT & PAGE	550	42	52	A Chart of Prussia and Coerland, from Rygshead to der Winda
mwsc0732	scandinavia sweden	1750	MOUNT & PAGE	875	42	51	A Chart of Stockholm Leith / The Channell of Abbo or Uttoy
mwuss0172	carolinas	1724	MOUNT & PAGE	1800	49	59	A Chart of the Atlantick Ocean from Buttons Island to Port Royall
mwca0297	canada newfoundland	1713	MOUNT & PAGE	960	45	58	A Chart of the Banks and Harbours of Newfoundland
mwsc0358a	scandinavia denmark	1740	MOUNT & PAGE	900	43	80	A Chart of the Belt and Sound (north to the left)

AMPG REFERENCE	REGION	DATE	MAP MAKER	PRICE (UK£)	VERT. (cm.)	HOR. (cm.)	TITLE OF MAP (Comments by the editor in brackets)
mwuk1484	uk english channel (all)	1715	MOUNT & PAGE	750	42	52	A Chart of the Channell
mwaf1071	africa south west	1708	MOUNT & PAGE	550	43	55	A Chart of the Coast of Africa from Cape Virde to Cape Bona Esperanca
mwam0978	america north (east)	1755	MOUNT & PAGE	1600	45	58	A Chart of the Coast of New Foundland, New Scotland, New England, New York, New Jersey with Virginia and Maryland
mwuk0167	ireland	1747	MOUNT & PAGE	600	44	53	A Chart of the Coasts of Ireland and Part of England
mwbp0049	baltic sea (east)	1750	MOUNT & PAGE	2250	43	53	A Chart of the East Sea
mwaf1159a	africa west	1700	MOUNT & PAGE	650	43	52	A Chart of the Grain Ivory & Quaqua Coasts in Guinea from Cape St. Anne to Teen Pequene
mwat0198	atlantic cape verde isl.	1747	MOUNT & PAGE	450	44	54	A Chart of the Islands of Cape Verd
mwuk1668	north sea	1740	MOUNT & PAGE	900	44	52	A Chart of the North Sea (north to the right)
mwuk1664a	north sea	1715	MOUNT & PAGE	1000	44	54	A Chart of the North Sea from South Foreland...
mwuk1674	north sea	1777	MOUNT & PAGE	1500	88	100	A Chart of the North Sea from the Forelands to North Bergen, and from the Scaw to the Orkneys and Shetlands
mwuk0180	ireland	1760	MOUNT & PAGE	450	44	55	A Chart of the Northwest Coast of Ireland from Lough Swilly to Slyne Head
mwca0068	canada	1751	MOUNT & PAGE	875	43	55	A Chart of the Sea Coast of New Foundland New Scotland New England ...
mwam0904	america north (east)	1698	MOUNT & PAGE	1650	45	57	A Chart of the Sea Coast of New Foundland, New Scotland, New England, New York, New Jersey, with Virginia and Maryland
mwsp0557	spain regions	1760	MOUNT & PAGE	450	43	53	A Chart of the Sea Coasts of Biscay and Gallicia between Cape Machicaca and Cape de Pinas and from Cape de Pinas to Cape de Finisterre
mwsp0558	spain regions	1760	MOUNT & PAGE	500	43	52	A Chart of the Seacoasts of Algarve and Andalusia between Cape St. Vincent and the Strait of Gibraltar and C. Spartel
mwuk0181	ireland	1760	MOUNT & PAGE	480	43	53	A Chart of the Seacoasts of Ireland from Dublin to London-Derry
mwca0329	canada newfoundland	1780	MOUNT & PAGE	580	47	60	A Chart of the South-East Coast of Newfoundland. Printed for Mount & Page Tower Hill London
mwaf0391a	africa east	1708	MOUNT & PAGE	875	44	56	A Chart of the Western part of the East Indies With all the Adjacent Islands from Cape Bona Esperanca to the Island of Ceylon
mwaf1073	africa south west	1715	MOUNT & PAGE	300	43	53	A Chart of ye Coast of Angola from ye R. Ambris to Mount Negro
mwaf1169	africa west	1715	MOUNT & PAGE	480	43	53	A Chart of ye Coast of Biafra from Foche Island to Corisco Island
mwsc0719	scandinavia sweden	1730	MOUNT & PAGE	550	43	52	A Chart of ye Coast of Sweden from Oeland to Stockholm
mwaf0898	africa south	1715	MOUNT & PAGE	960	43	53	A Chart of ye Coasts of Cimbebas and Caffaria from Mt. Negro to ye C. of Good Hope
mwaf1074	africa south west	1715	MOUNT & PAGE	480	43	53	A Chart of ye Coasts of Gabon, Loango, and Congo from C. St. John to the River Ambris
mwca0298	canada newfoundland	1715	MOUNT & PAGE	960	46	56	A Chart Shewing Part of the Sea Coast of Newfoundland, from ye Bay of Bulls to Little Placentia Exactly and Carefully Lay'd Down by John Gaudy
mwwi0240	west indies (east)	1715	MOUNT & PAGE	1350	43	53	A Correct Chart of the Caribbee Islands
mwm0061	mediterranean	1753	MOUNT & PAGE	4000	48	118	A Correct Chart of the Mediterranean Sea from the Coast of Portugal to the Levant
mwam0933	america north (east)	1731	MOUNT & PAGE	2500	47	105	A Correct Map of the Coast of New England
mwsp0093a	portugal	1749	MOUNT & PAGE	750	48	59	A Correct Map of the Coast of Portugal & Barbaria (map by C. Price, north to the right)
mwsam0536	south america colombia	1789	MOUNT & PAGE	150	48	31	A Description of Carthagena (page of text incl. map)
mwca0318	canada newfoundland	1767	MOUNT & PAGE	350	41	23	A Description of Newfoundland. Thus Appears Kitty Vitty Lying between St. John's & Small Point
mwca0650	canada st pierre & miquelon	1753	MOUNT & PAGE	280	32	25	A Description of the Island of St. Peters
mwuss1083	new york	1729	MOUNT & PAGE	2000	45	56	A Draught of New York from the Hook to New York Town, by Mark Tiddeman (a pirated edition of this map was issued by G. Grierson c1749)
mwec0336	uk england dorset	1744	MOUNT & PAGE	400	41	61	A Draught of Portland the Shambles, and the Race of Portland
mwuss0497	georgia	1778	MOUNT & PAGE	3000	46	83	A Draught of South Carolina and Georgia from Sewee to St. Estaca
mwsam0596	south america guyana	1732	MOUNT & PAGE	875	44	56	A Draught of the Coast of Guiana from the River Oronoque, to the River Amazones
mwuk1390	england south	1760	MOUNT & PAGE	675	43	53	A Draught of the Sands, Shoals, Buoys, Beacons, & Sea Marks upon the Coast of England from the South Foreland to Orford
mwwi0826	puerto rico	1720	MOUNT & PAGE	600	49	61	A Draught of the West End of the Island of Porto Rico and the Island of Zachee
mwuss1645	virginia	1780	MOUNT & PAGE	1600	46	58	A Draught of Virginia from the Capes to York in York River and to Kuiquotan or Hamton in James River by Mark Tiddeman
mwat0043	atlantic ocean (all)	1759	MOUNT & PAGE	750	47	58	A General Chart of the Western Ocean
mwat0022	atlantic ocean (all)	1698	MOUNT & PAGE	1350	46	57	A Generall Chart for the West Indies According to Mr. Edw: Wrights Projection Commonly Called Mercator's Chart

AMPG REFERENCE	REGION	DATE	MAP MAKER	PRICE (UK£)	VERT. (cm.)	HOR. (cm.)	TITLE OF MAP (Comments by the editor in brackets)
mwaf1171	africa west	1715	MOUNT & PAGE	675	44	105	A Large Chart of the Coast of Guinea from Sherbro to Cape Lopas
mwec1173	uk england sussex	1781	MOUNT & PAGE	550	46	61	A Large Chart of the Downs Shewing the Sands, Shoals, Depths of Water & Anchorages, with All the Leading Marks to Avoid Dangers
mwaf1170	africa west	1715	MOUNT & PAGE	480	44	53	A Large Chart of the North Coast of Guinea from Cape de Verd to Sherbro
mwsc0358	scandinavia denmark	1740	MOUNT & PAGE	750	46	58	A Large Chart of the Sound Going into the Baltic Sea
mwru0219	russia	1751	MOUNT & PAGE	400	44	57	A Large Chart of the White Sea
mwuss0164	carolinas	1706	MOUNT & PAGE	1200	45	56	A Large Draft of South Carolina from Cape Roman to Port Royall
mwwi0295	antigua	1721	MOUNT & PAGE	450	27	33	A Large Draft of the Island Antegua (on a page of text)
mwas0612	asia south east celebes	1750	MOUNT & PAGE	875	44	54	A Large Draught from Benjar on the Island of Borneo to Macasser on the Island of Celebes Shewing the Streights of Bally
mwc0144	china	1750	MOUNT & PAGE	1200	53	43	A Large Draught of the Coast of China from Amoye to Chusan with ye Harbour of Amoye at Large
mwas0641	asia south east java	1716	MOUNT & PAGE	1200	44	104	A Large Draught of the Coast of Iava from Bantam Point to Batavia
mwas0590	asia south east borneo	1750	MOUNT & PAGE	720	43	53	A Large Draught of the South Part of Borneo
mwam1080	america north (east)	1783	MOUNT & PAGE	3600	61	80	A Map of the Coast of New England from Staten Island to the Island of Breton as it Was Actualy Survey'd by Capt. Cyprian Southack
mwwi0324	bahamas	1767	MOUNT & PAGE	1350	46	64	A New & Correct Chart of Cuba, Streights of Bahama, Windward Passage, the Current through the Gulf of Florida, with the Soundings &c.
mwwi0728	jamaica	1773	MOUNT & PAGE	650	46	69	A New & Correct Chart of the Island of Jamaica, with its Bays, Harbours, Rocks, Soundings, &c.
mwin0206	india	1750	MOUNT & PAGE	480	44	53	A New & Correct Chart Shewing the Goeing over the Braces with the Sands Shoals Depth of Water and Anchorage from Point Palmiras to Hughley in the Bay of Bengall
mwat0280	atlantic north	1774	MOUNT & PAGE	1100	60	78	A New and Accurate Chart of the Vast Atlantic or Western Ocean, Including ... from the Equator to 59 Degrees North Latitude
mwuk0835	uk	1750	MOUNT & PAGE	720	46	56	A New and Correct Chart of England Scotland and Ireland
mwas0282	asia burma	1740	MOUNT & PAGE	400	50	60	A New and Correct Chart of Mergui with the Islands Adjacent / A New and Correct Chart of Acheen Road
mwas0656	asia south east java	1745	MOUNT & PAGE	650	44	53	A New and Correct Chart of Part of the Island of Java from the West End to Batavia
mwuk1486	uk english channel (all)	1728	MOUNT & PAGE	1600	65	100	A New and Correct Chart of the Channel between England and France
mwaf1212a	africa west	1750	MOUNT & PAGE	450	43	52	A New & Correct Chart of the Coast of Guinea from Cape Verd to Cape Negro
mwca0310	canada newfoundland	1755	MOUNT & PAGE	1250	42	102	A New and Correct Chart of the Coast of New Foundland from Cape Raze to Cape Bonavista. With Chebucto Harbour in Nova Scotia
mwca0067	canada	1751	MOUNT & PAGE	875	43	55	A New and Correct Chart of the North Part of America from New Found Land to Hudsons Bay
mwam0961	america north (east)	1750	MOUNT & PAGE	2800	50	118	A New and Correct Chart of the Sea Coast of New-England from Cape Codd to Casco Bay
mwwi0072	west indies	1737	MOUNT & PAGE	1600	46	79	A New and Correct Chart of the Trading Part of the West Indies
mwat0040	atlantic ocean (all)	1755	MOUNT & PAGE	2000	58	71	A New and Correct Chart of the Western and Southern Oceans Showing the Variations of the Compass According to the Latest and Best Observations (map by E. Halley)
mwwi0455	cuba	1767	MOUNT & PAGE	400	23	30	A New and Correct Draught of the Bay of Matanzas, on ye North Side of ye Island Cuba. Done from a Survey in the Year 1729, by Robt. Pearson
mwuk0772	uk	1701	MOUNT & PAGE	785	45	56	A new Chart of England Scotland & Ireland
mwwi0317	bahamas	1706	MOUNT & PAGE	1250	42	53	A New Chart of the Bahama Islands and Windward Passage
mwm0047	mediterranean	1725	MOUNT & PAGE	2400	44	110	A New Chart of the Coast of the Mediterranean Sea
mwit0836c	italy sardinia and corsica	1745	MOUNT & PAGE	850	41	54	A New Chart of the Islands of Corsica & Sardinia by Michelot (north to the left)
mwuk1345	england east	1779	MOUNT & PAGE	550	51	103	A New Chart of the Newcastle Trade Describing the Sea Coast of England from the South Forelands to Newcastle with the Soundings, Shoals, Harbours, Buoys, Beacons and Seamarks upon the Said Coast
mwuk0458a	scotland	1715	MOUNT & PAGE	750	47	53	A New Chart of the Sea Coast of Scotland with the Islands thereof
mwwi0861a	st kitts	1761	MOUNT & PAGE	1200	43	54	New Map of the Island of St. Christophers being an Actual Survey taken by Mr. Andrew Norwood, Surveyr. Genll. / New Map of the Island of Guardalupa / New Map of the Island of Martineca.

AMPG REFERENCE	REGION	DATE	MAP MAKER	PRICE (UK£)	VERT. (cm.)	HOR. (cm.)	TITLE OF MAP (Comments by the editor in brackets)
mwam0926	america north (east)	1728	MOUNT & PAGE	50000	106	87	A New Map of Virginia. Maryland, Pensilvania, New Jersey, Part of New York, and Carolina. Sold by T: Page W: & F Mount on Tower Hill
mwuss0176	carolinas	1730	MOUNT & PAGE	2400	43	52	A New Mapp of Carolina
mwwi0859	st kitts	1755	MOUNT & PAGE	785	48	58	A New Mapp of the Island of St. Christophers Being an Actual Survey Taken by Mr. Andrew Norwood / A New Mapp of the Island Martineca / A New Mapp of the Island Guardalupa
mwin0031a	ceylon	1700	THORNTON	950	53	44	A New Mapp of the Island of Zeloan
mwuss0791	massachusetts	1708	MOUNT & PAGE	5500	42	54	A New Survey of the Harbour of Boston in New England
mwsp0559	spain regions	1760	MOUNT & PAGE	450	43	54	A Sea Chart of Part of the Coasts of Gallicia and Portugall from Cape de Finisterre to the Burlings and from the Burlings to Cape de St. Vincent
mwm0110	mediterranean central	1770	MOUNT & PAGE	650	40	51	A Sea Chart of the Gulph of Venice
mwgm0398	panama	1738	MOUNT & PAGE	1200	43	53	An Exact Draught of the Gulf of Darien & the Coast to Porto Bello with Panama in the South Sea & the Scotch Settlement in Caledonia
mwwi0368	barbados	1721	MOUNT & PAGE	480	29	27	Barbados
mwm0271a	mediterranean west	1716	MOUNT & PAGE	650	43	53	Barcelona / The Harbour of Malta / A Large Chart of Port Maon (re-issue of 1747 shown)
mwca0302	canada newfoundland	1732	MOUNT & PAGE	400	32	26	Port Bonavista (on verso:) Cattalina Harbour
mwsc0366	scandinavia denmark	1750	MOUNT & PAGE	785	42	51	The Coast of Denmark and Sweden from Falsterbon to Schanckenes & ye Coast of Pomeren from te Island of Rugen to Rygshead
mwaa0134	arctic	1751	MOUNT & PAGE	400	42	51	The Coast of Lapland from ye River of Kola to ye Islands of Swetnoes
mwca0299	canada newfoundland	1716	MOUNT & PAGE	1100	42	103	The Coast of New Found Land from Cape Raze to Cape St. Francis ... by Henry Southwood [joined with] The Coast of New Found Land Salmon Cove to Cape Bonavista ... by Henry Southwood
mwsc0601	scandinavia norway	1700	MOUNT & PAGE	300	41	51	The Coast of Norway and Lapland from North Kyn to the River Kola
mwsc0613	scandinavia norway	1730	MOUNT & PAGE	450	42	51	The Coast of Norway from ye Naze to ye Paternosters and Part of Iutland
mwsp0665	balearic islands	1755	MOUNT & PAGE	650	42	53	The Coast of Spain from Cape St. Martin to Cape St. Sebastian with the Islands of Majorca Minorca & Yvica
mwgr0629	greece islands	1764	MOUNT & PAGE	1600	56	81	The coast of the Mediterranean Sea from C. Doro and island of Scio to Constantinople
mwgr0197	greece	1764	MOUNT & PAGE	1500	56	82	The coast of the Mediterranean Sea from Island de la Cirico to Islands Rhodes, Scarpanto etc.
mwm0152a	mediterranean east	1764	MOUNT & PAGE	750	56	83	The Coast of the Mediterranean Sea from Cape Razatin to Alexandria, with part of the Island of Candia (map by G. Alagna)
mwm0152	mediterranean east	1764	MOUNT & PAGE	1500	81	56	The Coast of the Mediterranean Sea from Rusato and Gironda to Alexandreta Including the I. of Cyprus (map by G. Alagna)
mwwi0428	cuba	1732	MOUNT & PAGE	400	19	23	The Draught of the Bay of Honda
mwuss0688	maine	1759	MOUNT & PAGE	650	43	54	The Harbour of Casco Bay and Islands Adjacent by Capt. Cyprian Southicke
mwuk0155	ireland	1733	MOUNT & PAGE	850	43	51	The Harbour of Corke
mwaf0642	africa islands rodrigues	1734	MOUNT & PAGE	800	43	55	The Island of Diego Rays
mwuk1439	england thames	1779	MOUNT & PAGE	400	47	59	The River of Thames from London to the Buoy of ye Noure
mwf0359	france brittany	1760	MOUNT & PAGE	450	44	54	The Sea Coast of France from Ushent to Olone
mwit0612	italy north	1750	MOUNT & PAGE	675	40	52	The Sea Coast of Italy from Cape Delle Melle to Mount Argentato with the Island of Corsica
mwf1192	france south west	1760	MOUNT & PAGE	400	43	53	The Sea Coasts of France from Olone to Cape Machiacaca in Biscay
mwuk0182	ireland	1760	MOUNT & PAGE	450	43	52	The Southwest Coast of Ireland from Dungarvan to the River Shannon
mwat0091	atlantic azores	1715	MOUNT & PAGE	480	37	47	The Western Isles
mwam0946	america north (east)	1743	MOUNT & PAGE	5500	51	79	Virginia, Maryland, Pennsilvania, East & West New Jarsey (2nd edition)
mwuss0197	carolinas	1777	MOUZON	16000	98	137	An Accurate Map of North and South Carolina with their Indian Frontiers
mww0193	world	1671	MOXON	1600	32	45	A Map of All the Earth and How after the Flood it was Divided among the Sons of Noah
mwwi0695a	jamaica	1677	MOXON	2000	44	53	A New Mapp of Jamaica
mwuk0113	ireland	1691	MOXON	875	53	41	A New Mapp of the Kingdom of Ireland Collected from the actual Survey made by Sr. W. Petty
mww0164	world	1657	MOXON	60000	52	77	A Plat of All the World ... First Set Forth by Mr. Edw. Wright ... 1655 (updated version of Wright's map of 1610)
mwuk0716	uk	1657	MOXON	2000	43	53	A Plat of the Channel Discovering the Sea Coasts of England, Scotland, Ireland and Part of France
mwbp0018	baltic sea (east)	1657	MOXON	3000	43	54	A Plat of the East Sea Newly Corrected by Jospeh Moxon

AMPG REFERENCE	REGION	DATE	MAP MAKER	PRICE (UK£)	VERT. (cm.)	HOR. (cm.)	TITLE OF MAP (Comments by the editor in brackets)
mwme0167	holy land	1671	MOXON	500	31	46	Canaan or the Land of Promise, Possessed by the Children of Israel and Travelled through by our Saviour Jesus Christ; and His Apostles. Translated by Joseph Moxon
mwme0168	holy land	1671	MOXON	500	32	46	Israels Perigrinations, or the Forty Years Travel of the Children of Israel out of Egypt through the Red Sea ... into Canaan
mwme0461	jerusalem	1671	MOXON	500	32	46	Jerusalem to the Right Reverend Father in God John, Lord Bishop of Chester (based on Visscher 1643)
mwme0169	holy land	1671	MOXON	500	32	46	Paradise or the Garden of Eden. With the Countries Circumjacent Inhabited by the Patriarchs
mwme0170	holy land	1671	MOXON	500	32	47	The Travels of St. Paul and other Apostles or a Geographical Description of those Lands and Countries where in the Gospel of Christ was First Propagated
mww0194	world	1671	MOXON	875	21	33	Totius Orbis Terrarum Tabula, eiusque Post Diluvium Divisio inter Filios Noachi
mwec0421	uk england essex	1805	MUDGE	1200	122	181	(Essex)
mwat0155	atlantic canary isl.	1692	MUELLER (or MULLER)	180	7	8	(Canary Islands)
mwme0722	caucasus	1692	MUELLER	135	6	8	(Georgia & Dagastan)
mwaf0382a	africa east	1692	MUELLER	240	8	7	(Pair of untitled maps showing the East African coast south to Madagascar)
mwsam0711a	south america paraguay	1702	MUELLER	180	7	8	(Untitled map)
mwin0138a	india	1692	MUELLER	120	7	8	(Untitled map)
mwsam0223a	south america argentina	1702	MUELLER	180	7	8	(untitled map of Tucuman)
mwuss1623	virginia	1703	MUELLER	320	6	8	(Virginia & Carolina)
mwsam0335a	south america brazil	1692	MULLER	180	7	8	Brasilia
mwaf0382	africa east	1692	MUELLER	120	7	8	Das mitternachtige Zanguebar
mwaf1151	africa west	1692	MUELLER	120	7	8	Die Kuste von Congo (title below map)
mwaf1150	africa west	1692	MUELLER	120	7	8	Die Kuste von Guinea (title below map)
mwsam0035	south america	1692	MUELLER	180	6	8	America Meridionalis
mwam0336	america north	1692	MUELLER	320	7	8	America Septentrionalis
mwme0577	arabia etc	1692	MUELLER	280	7	8	Arabia
mwaf0840	africa north west	1692	MUELLER	120	7	8	Barbaria Occidentalis
mwaf0490	africa egypt etc	1692	MUELLER	100	7	8	Barbaria Orientalis
mwbh0460	belgium holland	1692	MUELLER	180	7	8	Belgium Hispanicum
mwaf0883	africa south	1692	MUELLER	240	17	10	Caffraria und Monomotapa (title and text incl. below map)
mwca0036	canada	1692	MUELLER	280	7	8	Canada
mwin0031	ceylon	1692	MUELLER	240	7	8	Ceilan
mwc0078	china	1692	MUELLER	320	8	7	China
mwsc0314	scandinavia denmark	1692	MUELLER	180	7	8	Dania
mwaa0015	antarctic	1692	MUELLER	300	15	9	Die Antarctischen Lande
mwin0463	indian ocean maldives	1692	MUELLER	150	7	8	Die Insula Maldivae. (title below map)
mwuss0402	florida	1692	MUELLER	350	6	8	Florida
mwf0079	france	1692	MUELLER	180	7	8	Gallia
mww0247	world	1692	MUELLER	360	7	13	Globi Terrestris Hemisphaerum Superius / Globi Terrestris Hemisphaerum Inferius
mwsam0590b	south america guyana	1702	MUELLER	140	7	8	Guaiana
mwuk0127	ireland	1702	MUELLER	180	8	7	Hibernia
mwas0419	asia south east	1692	MUELLER	320	8	6	India extra Gangem
mwin0138b	india	1692	MUELLER	180	7	8	India intra Gangem
mwwi0040	west indies	1692	MUELLER	240	7	8	Insulae Antilles
mwuk0756a	uk	1692	MUELLER	180	7	8	Insulae Britannicae
mwas0721	asia south east moluccas	1692	MUELLER	160	7	8	Insulae Molucce
mwas0901	asia south east sunda	1692	MUELLER	200	6	8	Insulae Sondae
mwas0758	asia south east philippines	1692	MUELLER	300	6	8	Isles Philippinae
mwit0117	italy	1692	MUELLER	200	7	8	Italia
mwgm0184	mexico	1692	MUELLER	240	6	8	Mexico sive Nova Hispania
mwaf1149	africa west	1692	MUELLER	120	7	8	Nigritien
mwjk0053	japan	1692	MUELLER	480	7	8	Niphon Ins. (title above map)
mwuss0077	california	1692	MUELLER	450	7	8	Nova Mexico
mwit0666	italy piedmont	1702	MUELLER	180	7	8	Pedmontum (north to the right)
mwsam0750a	south america peru	1702	MUELLER	160	7	8	Peru
mwbp0321	poland	1692	MUELLER	180	7	8	Pohlen
mwbh0461	belgium holland	1692	MUELLER	200	7	8	Provinciae Unitae
mwru0438	russia tartary	1692	MUELLER	135	7	8	Tartary
mwaa0102	arctic	1692	MUELLER	320	7	8	Terrae Arctica (illustrated is the slightly smaller format untitled c1793 edition)
mwe0405	europe austria	1844	MUGERAUER	785	74	58	Neueste Dioecesan Land und Postkarte der Viertel Oberwienerwald und Obermannhardsberg oder der Dioecese St. Poelten im Lande Oesterreich unter der Enns
mwsam0779	south america peru	1780	MULDER	875	37	52	Lima, Ciudad de los Reyes
mwp0419	pacific north	1773	MULLER	2000	46	64	(A map of the discoveries made by the Russians, in Cyrillic. Russian edition of Muller's map of 1754.)
mwme0877	syria etc	1720	MULLER	720	49	74	A Map of Part of Syria from an Actual Survey
mww0440	world	1757	MULLER	8000	43	65	Izobrazhenye Zemnago Globusa (Cyrillic: 'Mirror image of the Earth's Globe')
mwe0954a	europe hungary	1769	MULLER	6500	205	240	Mappa Geographica novissima Regni Hungariae

AMPG REFERENCE	REGION	DATE	MAP MAKER	PRICE (UK£)	VERT. (cm.)	HOR. (cm.)	TITLE OF MAP (Comments by the editor in brackets)
mwe0560	europe czech republic (bohemia)	1722	MULLER	6500	48	57	Mappa Geographica Regni Bohemiae in Duodecim Circulos Divisae (25 sheets, each 48x57cm)
mwe0385	europe austria	1787	MULLER	4000	183	212	Mappa von dem Land ob der Enns
mwp0407a	pacific north	1754	MULLER	5000	46	64	Nouvelle Carte des Decouvertes Faites par des Vaisseaux Russiens aux Cotes Inconnues de l'Amerique Septentrionale avec les Pais Adiacents ... a St. Petersbourg a l'Academie Imperiale des Sciences
mwe0561	europe czech republic (bohemia)	1726	MULLER-WIELAND	2400	30	35	Mappa Chorographica ... Totius Regni Bohemiae (reduced size version in 25 sheets of Muller's map)
mwsc0652	scandinavia norway	1845	MUNCH	3000	120	75	Kart over det Sydlige Norge, Efter de Bedste Forhaandenvaerende Kilder, Fornemmelig de ve Norges Topographiske og Hydrographiske Opmaaling Anstillede Astronomiske og Geodaetiske Iagttagelser
mwbh0772	belgium holland	1800	MUNRO	9600	126	165	Nieuwe Platte Grond der Stad Rotterdam Gelegen aan de Rivieren de Maas en de Rotte
mwam0770	america north	1845	MUNSON	2400	90	120	A New and Embellished Map of the United States Compiled from the Latest and Most Authentic Documents
mwbh0004	belgium holland	1544	MUNSTER	350	12	14	(Aach, Brabant)
mwgr0546	greece islands	1550	MUNSTER	200	11	15	(Aegean Islands)
mwbh0138	belgium holland	1598	MUNSTER	320	15	18	(Amsterdam)
mwe0988	europe rhine	1614	MUNSTER	960	31	108	(Course of the River Rhine on 3 sheets)
mwe0005a	europe	1548	MUNSTER	1350	26	16	(Europe as a Woman. Anthropomorphic map.)
mwit0411	italy liguria	1578	MUNSTER	200	27	33	(Genoa)
mwe0488	europe croatia	1561	MUNSTER	280	14	16	(Istria)
mwsw0024	switzerland	1580	MUNSTER	200	15	16	(Lake Geneva)
mwgm0136	mexico	1588	MUNSTER	240	17	16	(Mexico City)
mwaf0809	africa north tunisia	1544	MUNSTER	300	24	17	(Tunis)
mwgr0012a	greece	1538	MUNSTER	650	11	15	(untitled map, based on Mela)
mwit0557	italy north	1545	MUNSTER	240	30	20	(Untitled map with South to the top)
mwgr0014b	greece	1544	MUNSTER	480	15	13	(Untitled map in a page of text)
mwgr0516	greece rhodes	1550	MUNSTER	200	13	16	(Untitled map in a page of text)
mwit0017	italy	1545	MUNSTER	200	8	13	(Untitled map in a page of text)
mwbp0208	poland	1598	MUNSTER	150	10	14	(Untitled map of part of Prussia in a page of text)
mwbp0207	poland	1598	MUNSTER	100	9	14	(Untitled map of Poland in a page of text)
mwwi0395	cuba	1550	MUNSTER	320	8	13	(untitled map on page of text)
mwaf0455	africa egypt etc	1552	MUNSTER	180	17	16	(untitled map on sheet of text)
mwit0861	italy sicily	1550	MUNSTER	650	22	15	(Untitled map)
mwbh0017a	belgium holland	1560	MUNSTER	300	16	18	(Untitled plan of Rotterdam in a page of text)
mwe0852	europe hungary	1550	MUNSTER	160	9	18	(Untitled view of Buda in a page of text)
mwuk0319	scotland	1598	MUNSTER	180	10	19	(Untitled view of Edinburgh in page of text, south to the top)
mwsp0156b	spain	1558	MUNSTER	300	15	25	(Untitled wood cut, shown above)
mwme0759	persia etc	1580	MUNSTER	400	19	17	(Untitled wood block)
mwaf0735	africa north algeria	1550	MUNSTER	200	15	20	(View of Algiers)
mwbh0139	belgium holland	1598	MUNSTER	280	13	16	(View of Antwerp)
mwbp0217	poland	1614	MUNSTER	280	8	11	(View of Cracow)
mwsw0013	switzerland	1560	MUNSTER	280	12	17	(View of Zurich)
mwaf0015	africa	1580	MUNSTER	720	32	36	Affricae Tabula Nova (Munster's 2nd version of Africa, based on Ortelius, used for editions after 1578)
mwaf0002	africa	1540	MUNSTER	2000	26	34	Africa XVIII Nova Tabula (1st edition, which can be distinguished from later printings using the same wood block by its superior impression. Several re-engravings of this map until 1572 with different titles above the map and different texts in cartouche.)
mwe0984	europe rhine	1542	MUNSTER	450	25	34	Alsatia et Brisgoia II. Rheni et VII. Nova Tabula
mwuk0902	england	1540	MUNSTER	1500	27	34	Anglia II Nova Tabula (north to the left)
mwuk0903	england	1552	MUNSTER	1200	29	37	Anglia II Nova Tabula (only this edition with border grid)
mwuk0901	england	1538	MUNSTER	720	14	11	Anglie Triquetra Descriptio (reprinted in 1543)
mwe0408	europe austria vienna	1550	MUNSTER	875	25	71	Anno Domini 1548. Viena Austriae nunc Habuit Situm / Vienne Cite Metropolitaine d'Austriche (view)
mwsw0008	switzerland	1549	MUNSTER	400	21	30	Anno Domini 1549 Berna Helvetiae hunc Habuit Situm
mwme0931	turkey etc	1598	MUNSTER	300	14	19	Asia Minor
mwas0010a	asia continent	1588	MUNSTER	720	31	36	Asia wie es jetziger zeit nach... beschriben ist (several editions until 1628; based on Ortelius)
mwuk1092	england and scotland	1578	MUNSTER	240	25	17	Beschzeibrung Engellants und Schottlandts (1st edition)
mwe0516	europe czech republic (bohemia)	1572	MUNSTER	500	26	36	Bohemiae descriptio
mwe0511	europe czech republic (bohemia)	1545	MUNSTER	360	27	36	Bohemiae Nova Descriptio Tabula XVII
mwf0253	france aquitaine	1550	MUNSTER	375	23	30	Bourdeaux (size excl. key below map)
mwbh0002	belgium holland	1540	MUNSTER	600	27	34	Brabantia V Rheni Et X Nova Tabula (North to the top)
mwe0985	europe rhine	1542	MUNSTER	500	25	34	Brabantia V. Rheni et X. Nova Tabula
mwit0771	italy sardinia	1550	MUNSTER	300	19	18	Calaris Sardiniae Caput
mwgr0339	greece crete	1550	MUNSTER	200	8	16	Candia seu Creta insula
mwme0911	turkey etc	1550	MUNSTER	1500	26	38	Constantinopolitanae urbis (re-issued several times with different titles. Ilustrated is the 1580 edition).

AMPG REFERENCE	REGION	DATE	MAP MAKER	PRICE (UK£)	VERT. (cm.)	HOR. (cm.)	TITLE OF MAP (Comments by the editor in brackets)
mwsw0031	switzerland	1598	MUNSTER	350	18	39	Contrafactur der Statt Zurich Anno 1595
mwf0467	france corsica	1628	MUNSTER	280	12	8	Corsica
mwgr0339	greece crete	1550	MUNSTER	200	8	16	Creta seu Candia insula
mwgr0437	greece cyprus	1550	MUNSTER	250	10	15	Cyprus
mwme0860a	syria etc	1550	MUNSTER	650	27	35	Cyria, Cypern, Palestina, Mesopotamia
mwaf0850	africa south	1552	MUNSTER	750	12	16	De Affricae Regionibus (page of text below map)
mwbh0017	belgium holland	1560	MUNSTER	280	12	15	De Comitatus Flandriae
mwe0006	europe	1560	MUNSTER	280	8	14	De Europa, quae nostro Aevo Christianum Complectitur Orbem, & nonnihil de Turcica Ditione
mwit1131	italy florence	1580	MUNSTER	960	25	36	De la Cosmographie Florence
mwe0279	europe austria	1550	MUNSTER	150	31	21	De Pannonia Superiore, quae Hodie Austria
mwbp0172	poland	1559	MUNSTER	280	14	15	De Regno & Tota Regione Poloniae
mwe0740	europe east	1559	MUNSTER	180	15	19	De Ungaria Transsylvania Ungarici Regni Provincia
mwe0631	europe dalmatia	1545	MUNSTER	550	27	35	Descriptio Totius Illyridis XVI No. Tab. (south to the top)
mwsw0025	switzerland	1580	MUNSTER	1800	39	83	Die Loblich und weit berumpt Statt Basel
mwsam0736c	south america peru	1628	MUNSTER	650	27	35	Die Statt Cusco (title above map. Based on Ramusio's 1605 map)
mwf0214	france alsace	1614	MUNSTER	350	18	39	Die Statt Strasburg
mwe0512	europe czech republic (bohemia)	1550	MUNSTER	240	22	34	Egrana Civitas olim de Imperio Romanorum, hodie Vero Regno Bohemiae Subiecta (view of Eger)
mwuk0908	england	1588	MUNSTER	720	31	36	Engellandt mit dem anstossenden Reich Schottlandt (1st edition of Munster's revised map of England, north to the right)
mwit1128	italy florence	1550	MUNSTER	650	22	36	Florentia nobilissima Hethruriae civitas
mwg0425a	hessen	1544	MUNSTER	800	26	40	Franckfurt am Mayn
mwg0296	bavaria	1540	MUNSTER	500	27	35	Franconia XII Nova Tabula
mwf0013	france	1540	MUNSTER	550	27	34	Gallia IIII Nova Tabula
mwsc0029	scandinavia	1588	MUNSTER	960	26	35	Gemeine Beschreibung aller Mitnachtigen Lander Schweden, Gothen, Nordwegien, Denmarck (2nd edition of Munster's 1545 map)
mwg0011	germany	1540	MUNSTER	400	27	34	Germania VI, Nova Tabula (south to the top)
mwsc0021	scandinavia	1569	MUNSTER	200	10	14	Gotlandt oder Gothen
mwg0692	schleswig-holstein	1598	MUNSTER	200	13	16	Hamburg (view)
mwsw0010	switzerland	1550	MUNSTER	400	26	34	Helvetiae Moderna Descriptio
mwsw0004	switzerland	1540	MUNSTER	600	27	34	Helvetia Prima Rheni Et V Nova Tabula
mwsp0150	spain	1540	MUNSTER	650	27	34	Hispania III Nova Tabula
mwbh0007	belgium holland	1550	MUNSTER	400	21	14	Holand
mwit0015	italy	1540	MUNSTER	900	28	37	Italia XIIII Nova Tabula
mwme0436	jerusalem	1550	MUNSTER	1200	15	38	Jerusalem Civitas Sancta, olim Metropolis Regni Judaici, Hodie Uero Colonia Turcae
mwaf0003	africa	1550	MUNSTER	350	12	16	La description d'Affricque selon les divers pais, animaux et monstres horribles (title below map. Excludes southern tip of Africa)
mwsw0011	switzerland	1550	MUNSTER	350	25	35	La dipintura della citta di Basilea
mwg0251	baden-wurttemberg	1540	MUNSTER	1800	26	35	Lacus Constan XX Tab Nova
mwf1165	france lyon	1628	MUNSTER	200	25	33	Leon (view)
mwsp0015	portugal	1598	MUNSTER	350	22	37	Lisbona (view)
mwuk1102	england london	1573	MUNSTER	2000	30	38	Londinum Feracis Ang. Met. (reprinted until 1628)
mwf0813	france paris	1550	MUNSTER	750	27	36	Lutetia Parisiorum Urbs, Toto Orbe Celeberrima Notissimaque Caput Regni Franciae
mwm0165	mediterranean malta	1560	MUNSTER	400	12	8	Melita
mwuk0039	ireland	1628	MUNSTER	240	14	20	Momonia et Lagenia
mwru0017	russia	1571	MUNSTER	280	18	16	Moscovia
mwg0318	bavaria	1598	MUNSTER	200	12	15	Munchen (view)
mwit1048a	italy naples	1550	MUNSTER	400	27	33	Neapels (view. Close copy by De Belleforest 1575)
mwit1048b	italy naples	1550	MUNSTER	250	14	19	Neapolis (shown above left)
mwgr0014	greece	1540	MUNSTER	800	27	35	Nova Graecia XXII Nova Tabula (illustration, left, shows woodcut 1552 edition. Below: engraved 1580 edition.)
mwam0002	america continent	1540	MUNSTER	6500	27	34	Novae Insulae XVII Nova Tabula (Later editions may have different titles above the map, printed in Latin, French, Italian or German until 1578.)
mwf0814a	france paris	1572	MUNSTER	400	17	25	Paris (size excl. decorative border)
mwbp0164	poland	1540	MUNSTER	650	27	35	Polonia et Ungaria, XV Nova Tabula
mwbp0171	poland	1552	MUNSTER	450	29	38	Pomerania XIIII Nova Tabula
mwg0501	rheinland-pfalz	1540	MUNSTER	550	27	35	Quarta Rheni et IX Nova Tab. (south to the top)
mwit0994	italy south	1598	MUNSTER	150	16	13	Regn. Neapolit. Mare Mediterraneum
mwit0700	italy rome	1550	MUNSTER	750	24	36	Romanae Urbis Situs, quem hoc Christi Anno 1549 habet.
mwe0296	europe austria	1592	MUNSTER	250	13	16	Saltzburg (view)
mwit0772	italy sardinia	1550	MUNSTER	450	26	16	Sardinia Insula
mwsc0008	scandinavia	1540	MUNSTER	3500	27	35	Schonlandia XIII Nova Tabula (only publ. in 1540 and 1542)
mwe1120b	europe slovenia	1550	MUNSTER	550	25	34	Sclavonia oder Windisch Marck, Bossen, Crabaten (south to the top. Shown below is 1588 edition)
mwg0502	rheinland-pfalz	1552	MUNSTER	550	29	37	Secunda Rheni Et IX Nova Tabula (north to the right)
mwsc0009	scandinavia	1545	MUNSTER	1200	28	38	Septentrionales Regiones XVIII No. Tab. (illustrated is 1552 edition with grid around map)
mwbp0165	poland	1545	MUNSTER	450	26	33	Slesiae Descriptio XV Nova Tabula

AMPG REFERENCE	REGION	DATE	MAP MAKER	PRICE (UK£)	VERT. (cm.)	HOR. (cm.)	TITLE OF MAP (Comments by the editor in brackets)
mwg0297	bavaria	1540	MUNSTER	500	27	35	Suevia et Bavaria XI Nova Tabula (south to the top)
mwas0874	asia south east sumatra	1590	MUNSTER	750	31	36	Sumatra ein grosse Insel
mwme0863	syria etc	1588	MUNSTER	450	31	36	Syria, Cypern, Palestina ...
mwe0004	europe	1540	MUNSTER	1400	26	34	Tabula Nova Prima Europa (South to the top. Excl. northern regions. Early French edition illustrated.)
mwas0002	asia continent	1540	MUNSTER	1400	27	34	Tabula Orientalis Regionis, Asiae Scilicet Extremas Complectens Terras & Regna (different editions may have different titles. Illustrated is a c1550 edition. Includes Marco Polo's 'Archipelagus 7448 insularu' i.e. The Philipinnes)
mwe0633a	europe dalmatia	1550	MUNSTER	250	25	34	Tabula Rhaetiae et Vindeliciae
mwgr0014a	greece	1542	MUNSTER	400	25	33	Tabula Europa IX (Thrace)
mwme0022	holy land	1540	MUNSTER	720	27	35	Terra Sancta XVI Nova Tabula
mwe0986	europe rhine	1542	MUNSTER	500	25	34	Tertia Rheni Nova Tabula
mwbh0001	belgium holland	1540	MUNSTER	600	27	35	Tertia Rheni Nova Tabula (North to the right. 1552 edition illustrated, the only edition with a grid reference around the map).
mwe1039	europe romania	1542	MUNSTER	450	26	34	Transsylvania XXI Nova Tabula
mww0037	world	1540	MUNSTER	6000	26	34	Typus Orbis Universalis (1st issue. Different editions may have different titles)
mwsw0005	switzerland	1545	MUNSTER	550	27	34	Valesiae Altera et VII. Nova Tabula
mwsw0006	switzerland	1545	MUNSTER	550	27	34	Valesiae Charta Prior et VI. Nova Tabula
mwit1215	italy venice	1582	MUNSTER	650	27	41	(Venice) ... Statt Venedig
mwit1205	italy venice	1550	MUNSTER	850	27	38	Venetiarum amplissima & maritima urbs cum multis circumacientibus insulis
mwe0519a	europe czech republic (bohemia)	1588	MUNSTER	150	9	14	Von dem Konigreich Bohem
mww0035	world	1532	MUNSTER-HOLBEIN	35000	36	55	Typus Cosmographicus Universalis (1st state, with ASIA in small letters)
mwam0012	america continent	1588	MUNSTER-PETRI	1500	31	37	Americae sive Novi Orbis Nova Descriptio
mwsp0690	balearic islands	1833	MUNTANER	300			Mallorca (text in Spanish)
mwuk1411	uk geological	1842	MURCHISON	300	40	30	Geological Map of England & Wales
mwsw0080	switzerland	1670	MURER	12000	105	122	(Zurich) Eigentliche Verzeichnuss der Staetten Graffschafften und Herrschafften welche in der Statt Zuerich Gebiet und Landschafft Gehoerig seind (reprint of 1566 map)
mwas0777	asia south east philippines	1749	MURILLO	15000	51	34	Mapa delas Yslas Philipinas (reduced size version of Murillo's 1734 map)
mwgm0297	mexico	1824	MURRAY	200	30	36	A Plan of the City of Mexico by Lt. Col. Count Don Diego Garcia A.D. 1793
mwaf1019	africa south	1839	MURRAY	60	20	18	Africa North East of Cape Colony Exhibiting the Relative Postions of the Emigrant Farmers and the Native Tribes, May 1837
mwwi0180	west indies	1828	MURRAY	400	44	61	Chart of the West Indies, with the Adjacent Coast of South America Shewing the Tracks of Don Cristopher Columbus
mwuk0269	ireland	1830	MURRAY	240	69	46	Ireland
mwuss0830	massachusetts	1778	MURRAY	1200	29	13	Plan of the Town of Boston, with the Attack on Bunkers-Hill, in the Peninsula of Charlestown, the 17th of June, 1775
mwgr0254	greece	1830	MURRAY	400	56	68	Tabula qua Graecia Superior, qualis Tempore Belli Peloponnesiaci Ineuntis Fuit
mwam0709	america north	1837	MURRAY	140	22	27	United States of America
mwas0869	asia south east singapore	1830	MURRAY	2500	23	80	View of Singapore Town and Harbour Taken from the Government Hill
mwit0980	italy sicily	1834	MUSUMECI	1250	55	82	Pianta Geometrica della Citta di Palermo con suoi Sobborghi, Molo e Campagne
mwuss0343	washington DC	1818	MUTLOW	400	34	39	Map of Maj. Gen. Ross's Route, with the British Column, from Benedict, on Patuxent River, to the City of Washington, August 1814
mwec1361	uk england yorkshire	1835	MYERS	960	54	57	Map of the Parish of Halifax in the West Riding of the County of York, Shewing the Township Borough & Manorial Boundaries, from an Actual Survey Made in the Years, 1834 and 1835(4 sheets, each 54x57cm)
mwaf0508	africa egypt etc	1732	MYLLER	180	15	18	Alexandria.
mwaf0507	africa egypt etc	1732	MYLLER	200	15	18	Plan von gros Cairo
mwuk1415	uk geological	1848	N.SOC. EDU. POOR	240	51	37	Map Showing the Distribution of the Chief Mineral Deposits of England and Wales with Part of Scotland
mwuk1077	england	1848	N.SOC. EDU. POOR	200	52	37	Physical Map of England and Wales with Part of Scotland
mww0538	world	1785	NAGAKUBO	25000	107	150	(Revised map of the world - English transl. of title of Japanese folding map on oval projection.)
mwbp0050	baltic sea (east)	1757	NAGAYEV	1200	53	104	(Cyrillic script. Western part of Baltic Sea)
mwsc0368	scandinavia denmark	1757	NAGAYEV	750	53	72	(Title in Russian script. Map centred on Copenhagen.)
mwec1252	uk england wiltshire	1751	NAISH	1650	60	46	The City of Salisbury wth. the Adjacent Close, Church and River. Accurately Surveyed by William Naish
mwjk0114	japan	1776	NAKAMURA	2500	147	103	(Yamato no kuni saiken zu)
mwgr0533	greece zante (zakynthos)	1568	BONIFACIO	1200	21	16	Isola de Zante

AMPG REFERENCE	REGION	DATE	MAP MAKER	PRICE (UK£)	VERT. (cm.)	HOR. (cm.)	TITLE OF MAP (Comments by the editor in brackets)
mwe0387a	europe austria	1791	NAUMANN	750	31	56	Vue de la Ville Capitale de Salzbourg prise du Convent de Maria Plan coté de l'Orient
mwp0118	australia	1837	NAUTICAL MAG	200	19	23	Eastern Entrances to Torres Strait with the Tracks of H.M. Colonial Schr. Isabella and E.I. Company's Slp. Tigris in Search of the Survivors of the Charles Eaton 1836
mwgm0221a	mexico	1755	NAVA	5000	20	30	Mapa y Tabla Geografica de Leguas comunes, que ai de unos à otros Lugares, y Ciudades principales de la America septentrional
mwru0409a	russia moscow	1841	NAVAL ACADEMY ST. PETERSBURG	1500	74	93	(Plan of Moscow, in Cyrillic)
mwru0404b	russia moscow	1819	NAVAL ACADEMY ST. PETERSBURG	1800	77	104	(Plan of the City of Moscow, in Cyrillic)
mwp0433a	pacific north	1784	NAVAL ACADEMY ST. PETERSBURG	550	20	26	(Map in Russian script by I. Kobelev)
mwru0311a	russia	1795	NAVAL ACADEMY ST. PETERSBURG	3000	133	107	(Title in Russian: A New Map of the Russian Empire)
mwru0201a	russia	1745	NAVAL ACADEMY ST. PETERSBURG	800	49	55	Delineatio Fluvii Volgae a Samara usque ad Tsaricin
mwas0317b	asia caspian sea	1735	NAVAL ACADEMY ST. PETERSBURG	1000	50	39	Maris Caspii littori occidentali inter fluviorum Wolgae et Kur... descriptio simul ac in provinciis Schirwan et Lesgistan inter Russos et Turcas terrarum divisionis linea Anno 1727 determinata (first map prepared for the first Russian atlas. It was issued in Russian and Latin editions - 200 copies each. Map by J. Gerber.)
mwru0286	russia	1787	NAVAL ACADEMY ST. PETERSBURG	2400	81	178	Nova Tabula Geographica Imperii Russici in Gubernia Divisi (illustrated is version with Russian script publ. in 1786. See title cartouche below).
mwru0452	russia tartary	1745	NAVAL ACADEMY ST. PETERSBURG	785	52	56	Ostium Fluvii Amur cum Parte Australiori Terrae Kamtschatkae (from the 1st Russian atlas incl. 6 maps of Siberia.)
mwru0201	russia	1745	NAVAL ACADEMY ST. PETERSBURG	1200	49	55	Pars Sibiriae Tractum inter Salinas ad Camam et Tobolium comprehendens
mwru0202	russia	1745	NAVAL ACADEMY ST. PETERSBURG	1000	48	54	Partes Fluviorum Petschorae Obii et Ieniseae
mwru0203	russia	1745	NAVAL ACADEMY ST. PETERSBURG	2000	48	63	Plan der Kayserl. Residentz Stadt St. Petersburg wie solcher 1737 aufgenommen worden (title also in Russian script)
mwru0532	ukraine	1745	NAVAL ACADEMY ST. PETERSBURG	1200	47	54	Tartaria Minor cum Adiacentibus Kiovensi et Belgorodensi Gubernis
mwru0451	russia tartary	1745	NAVAL ACADEMY ST. PETERSBURG	960	51	56	Territorii Jakutensis Pars Orientalior cum Maxima Parte Terre Kamtschatke (from the 1st Russian atlas, incl. 6 maps of Siberia.)
mwru0203b	russia	1745	NAVAL ACADEMY ST. PETERSBURG	960	49	56	Territorium Archangelopolin inter Petroburgum et Vologdam
mwru0203	russia	1745	NAVAL ACADEMY ST. PETERSBURG	800	49	54	Territorium Mesenense
mwru0203a	russia	1745	NAVAL ACADEMY ST. PETERSBURG	800	48	55	Territorium Pontum Euxinum et Mare Caspium interiacens Cubanae et Georgiae
mwca0343	canada newfoundland	1801	NAVAL CHRONICLE	200	36	32	Chart of the Island of Newfoundland
mwaf0284	africa	1799	NAVAL CHRONICLE	235	23	30	Chart of the Lines of Magnetic Variation, in the Seas around Africa
mwat0286	atlantic north	1804	NAVAL CHRONICLE	280	16	39	Chart of the Supposed Course of the Florida Stream
mwsam0844	south america venezuela	1808	NAVAL CHRONICLE	200	14	23	De la Guayra on the Spanish Main (view)
mwwi0806	martinique	1805	NAVAL CHRONICLE	150	11	16	Martinico
mwwi0750	jamaica	1809	NAVAL CHRONICLE	120	12	16	Port Royal in Jamaica
mwgm0440	panama	1814	NAVAL CHRONICLE	280	14	23	Porto Bello on the Spanish Main
mwaf0995	africa south	1812	NAVAL CHRONICLE	100	15	12	Saldanha Bay
mwwi0817	nevis	1808	NAVAL CHRONICLE	200	14	23	The Islands Redonda and Nevis in the West Indies (view)
mwwi0341	bahamas	1799	NAVAL CHRONICLE	600	13	23	View of Nassau in the Bahamas
mwwi0515	dominica	1799	NAVAL CHRONICLE	240	15	23	View of Prince Rupert's Bay, Dominica
mwf0566	france corsica	1850	NAYMILLER	450	42	32	Corsica
mwam0922	america north (east)	1720	NEAL	960	24	36	A New Map of New England According to the Latest Observations 1720
mwam0610	america north	1818	NEELE	200	19	25	A Chart of the Route of His Majesty's Hired Armed Vessel 'The Alexander'. On a Voyage of Discovery to the Arctic Regions Performed in the Year 1818
mwaa0160	arctic	1808	NEELE	240	36	35	A Map of the Countries Thirty Degrees round the North Pole (enlarged version of Wilkes' 1807 map)
mwru0296	russia	1789	NEELE	200	20	20	A Plan of the City of St. Petersburgh
mwca0135	canada	1813	NEELE	280	23	29	Canada
mwsam0855	south america venezuela	1820	NEELE	100	19	24	Caraccas and Guyanas
mwam0233	america continent	1792	NEELE	240	20	23	Map of America with the Latest Discoveries
mwam0740	america north	1840	NEELE	400	44	53	North America
mwaf0230	africa	1773	NEELE	240	37	36	Present Africa
mwsam0118	south america	1796	NEELE	240	23	19	South America

AMPG REFERENCE	REGION	DATE	MAP MAKER	PRICE (UK£)	VERT. (cm.)	HOR. (cm.)	TITLE OF MAP (Comments by the editor in brackets)
mwuk0252	ireland	1811	NEELE	4800	133	225	The County of Cork, Surveyed by Order of the Grand Jury of the County
mwuk0269a	ireland	1830	NEELE	2000	174	176	...this Chart of the Coasts of Ireland and St George`s Channel (map by A. Nimmo)
mwam1170	america north (east)	1813	NEELE	450	22	28	United States (shows Franklinia)
mwam1175	america north (east)	1816	NEELE	200	25	34	United States of America, Exhibiting the Seat of War on the Canadian Frontier from 1812 to 1815
mwam0253	america continent	1804	NEELE	240	40		Western Hemisphere (circular map)
mwe0386	europe austria	1790	NEGGES	1800	69	45	Chronologia Imperatorum Romanorum ... Exhibens a Iulio Caesare ad Franciscum Semper Augustum: Catalogo
mwgr0345	greece crete	1570	NELLI	2000	19	14	(Untitled map based on Pagano, 1538. North to the left).
mwgr0294	greece corfu	1570	NELLI	2000	20	14	(Untitled map)
mwgr0446	greece cyprus	1570	NELLI	10000	19	14	Cipro
mwg0732	thuringia	1567	NELLI	2250	31	41	Gotta
mwm0166	mediterranean malta	1564	NELLI	2500	31	44	Il Porto di Malta (view of Valetta showing attack against the Turks)
mwgr0516a	greece rhodes	1570	NELLI	3500	32	25	Rhodi Insula nobilissima nel Mare
mwca0190	canada	1840	NELSON	600	48	67	North America. British Provinces of New Brunswick, Nova Scotia, & Part of Canada
mwe1077	europe serbia	1789	NEUBAUER	2250	28	40	Belagerung der Beruhmten Festung Belgrad unter dem Kayserlichen General-Feld-Marschal Laudon welcher solche durch seine Vortreffliche Anstalten am 8ten Octb 1789 zur Uebergabe Zwang
mwru0030	russia	1612	NEUGEBAUER	1000	34	40	Moscoviae Totius cum Regionibus Finitimus
mww0753a	world	1850	NEUREUTHER	1500	61	92	(Untitled map to illustrate Von Martius' botanical work on palms, 1823-1850. The map was engraved by E. Neureuther)
mwf1141	france rhone-alpes	1695	NEUVEGLISE	1500	57	64	Souverainete de Dombe (with 4 views of towns)
mwuk0120	ireland	1694	NEVILL	3000	115	90	A New Map of the City of Londonderry with its Confines: As it was Beseiged by the Irish Army in the Year 1689 Exactly Survey'd by Capt. Francis Nevill
mwuss1335	oregon	1845	NEW YORK SUN	320	16	23	Map of Oregon
mwuss1538	texas	1846	NEWMAN	2500	24	27	Texas & Mexico in 1846. Seat of War.
mwuk1577	channel islands	1694	NEWTON	960	30	39	A New & Accurate Map of their Majesties Island of Jersey. Drawn from the Survey of Philip Dumaresq Esqr. Seigneur of Samares, by Tho: Lempriere Philomat. London Printed for John Newton at the 3 Pigeons ... 1694
mwgr0617	greece islands	1709	NICHOLLS	600	51	37	A New Map of the Islands of the Aegean Sea, together with the Island of Crete, and the Adjoining Isles
mwsp0733	gibraltar	1780	NICHOLLS	1200	46	56	An Exact Plan of the Town, Castle, Mole and Bay of Gibraltar likewise the Approaches of ye Spaniards in the Last War
mwsp0696	gibraltar	1712	NICHOLLS	1500	49	57	Several Prospects of the Rock, Town, Castle, Fortifications, & Bay of Gibraltar, also a Plan of ye Same with ye Approaches of the Spaniards in ye Last War, & ye Additions of the New Works (re-issued by Bowles in 1727)
mwuk0985	england	1732	NICHOLLS	450	30	28	The Roads of England According to Ogilby's Survey
mwc0176	china	1769	NICOL	360	67	50	(Shantung Peninsula)
mwas0268	asia (from turkey to india)	1796	NICOL	480	58	93	A General Chart on Mercators Projection to Shew the Track of the Lion and Hindostan from England to the Gulph of Pekin in China ... also the Limits of the Chinese Empire as Extended by the Conquests of the Present Emperor Tchien-Lung.
mwgm0267	mexico	1806	NICOL	180	15	10	St. Iago - Se Lagues - Natavidaet
mwme0661	arabia etc	1791	NICOLAS & VARIN	6000	40	86	(View of Mecca. Title in Arabic script below)
mwaf0066	africa	1660	NICOLOSIO	1800	80	93	Africa (in 4 sheets. Total size given. Large inset of France)
mwas0048	asia continent	1660	NICOLOSIO	3000	80	93	Asia (in 4 sheets. Total size given)
mww0172	world	1660	NICOLOSIO	2800	44	85	Continentem Dudum Notam / Continentem Noviter Detectam (2 circular maps with separate titles)
mwe0066	europe	1660	NICOLOSIO	1600	80	93	Europa (in 4 sheets. Total size given)
mwg0064	germany	1660	NICOLOSIO	480	40	46	Imperium Romano-Germanicum Secundum (large inset of N. Norway)
mwit0096	italy	1660	NICOLOSIO	875	40	46	Italia Secundum Dominatus Descripta per Ioannem Baptistam Nicolosium (Large inset of part of Siberia)
mwam0319	america north	1660	NICOLOSIO	8000	80	93	Mexicum in hac Forma in Lucem Edebat Ioannes Baptista Nicolosius S.T.D. (in 4 sheets. Total size given)
mwsam0024	south america	1660	NICOLOSIO	2500	80	93	Peru Descriptore / (Inset of Spain:) Hispania Descripta Secundum Tres Coronas Auctore Joanne Baptista Nicolosio (in 4 sheets. Total size given)
mwme0654	arabia etc	1787	NIEBUHR	850	80	22	Mare Rubrum seu Sinus Arabicus
mwaf0523	africa egypt etc	1780	NIEBUHR	300	29	24	Nili Brachia Ambo Majora
mwme0631	arabia etc	1763	NIEBUHR	400	46	39	Tabula Itineraria Sistens Illam Partem Terrae Yemen
mwme0614	arabia etc	1733	NIEBUHR	240	20	19	Terrae Oman
mwme0635	arabia etc	1774	NIEBUHR-LOTTER	750	56	37	Terrae Yemen Maxima Pars, seu Imperii Imami, Principatus Kaukeban nec non Ditionum Haschid u Bekil, Nehhm, Chaulan, Abu Arisch et Aden Tabula

AMPG REFERENCE	REGION	DATE	MAP MAKER	PRICE (UK£)	VERT. (cm.)	HOR. (cm.)	TITLE OF MAP (Comments by the editor in brackets)
mwg0849	westphalia	1786	NIEHAUSEN	1600	53	60	Grafschaft Lippe sowohl Schaumburg-Lippische als Lippe-Dettmoldische Antheile (re-issued 1806)
mwaf0876	africa south	1682	NIEUHOFF	720	28	36	Caerte vande Cabo de Bona Esperanca en haer Gelegenheyt daer Omtrent
mwin0125	india	1682	NIEUHOFF	200	27	35	Coylang (view of this Portuguese colony under attack)
mwc0053	china	1665	NIEUHOFF	650	28	36	Kanton in Platte Grondt
mwin0127	india	1682	NIEUHOFF	280	28	35	Landt Caert vande Cust van Malabaer, Madura en Cormendel
mwas0633	asia south east java	1682	NIEUHOFF	500	28	35	Landt Caerte van Batavia met haer onder Hoorende Forten
mwc0054	china	1665	NIEUHOFF	2000	43	52	Reys-Kaerte van de Ambassade der Nederlantse Oost Indise Comagnie, door China (illustrated is 1671 English re-issue with different title cartouche)
mwuss1074	new york	1656	NIEUWENHOF	12500	31	19	Nova Belgica sive Nieuw Nederlandt (incl. view of New York by van der Donck)
mwsam0660	south america magellan	1621	NODAL	30000	40	34	Reconocimiento de los Estrechos de Magellanes y San Vicente Mandado (The Nodal brothers completed the 1st circumnavigation of Terra del Fuego. This map was part of their book of sailing instructions, publ. Madrid.)
mwaf0199	africa	1754	NOLIN	720	47	65	Afrique divisee en ses Grandes Regions (illustrated is the Denis 1817 edition)
mwaf0098	africa	1689	NOLIN	1200	45	60	Afrique selon les Relations les plus Nouvelles Dressee et Dediee par le P. Coronelli
mwme0831a	persia etc	1783	NOLIN	200	21	26	Alexandri Magni Imperium et Expeditio ... JB Nolin (publ. by Mondhare)
mwsam0064	south america	1743	NOLIN	160	20	29	Amerique Meridionale Divisee en ses Grandes Regions et Possessions
mwam0178	america continent	1759	NOLIN	1500	50	69	Amerique ou le Nouveau Continent Dressee sur les Nouvelles Relations
mwam0378	america north	1720	NOLIN	480	22	24	Amerique Septentrionale avec les Nouvelles Decouvertes Fait au Nord, par les Russes et les Anglois
mwf0799	france normandy	1777	NOLIN	480	49	66	Carte de la Province de Normandie
mwf0614a	france languedoc	1703	NOLIN	500	60	45	Carte de Diocese d'Uzes
mwam0993	america north (east)	1756	NOLIN	2250	37	48	Carte des Colonies Anglaises dans l'Amerique Septentrionale
mwru0128	russia	1711	NOLIN	960	86	56	Carte des Empires de Moscovia et Turquie
mwuk0838	uk	1756	NOLIN	550	45	64	Carte des Isles Britanniques (with text side borders)
mwf0958	france picardy	1777	NOLIN	360	49	67	Carte des Provinces de Picardie et d'Artois
mwam0992	america north (east)	1756	NOLIN	1500	50	71	Carte du Canada et de la Louisiane qui Forment la Nouvelle France et des Colonies Angloises ou sont Representez les Pays Contestez
mwf0589a	france ile de france	1746	NOLIN	250	44	70	Carte du Gouvernement Militaire de l'Isle de France
mwin0423a	india	1701	NOLIN	1800	48	72	Carte Marine depuis Suratte jusqu'au Detroit de Malaca Dressee par le R.P. Tachard de la Compagnie de Jesus Missionaire et Mathematicien du Roy dans les Indes
mwf0268a	france aquitaine	1727	NOLIN	650			Direction de Bordeaux, Comprenant La Seneschaussee de Bordeaux
mwsp0235	spain	1710	NOLIN	960	48	61	El Reyno de Espana Dividido en Dos Grandes Estados de Aragon y de Castilla Subdivido en Muchas Provincias, donde se halla Tambien el Reyno de Portugal
mwit0592	italy north	1701	NOLIN	450	31	45	Fond du Golfe de Venise
mwf1046a	france provence	1716	NOLIN	600	41	48	Galliae Christianae Provincia Ecclesiastica Arelatensis
mwit0799	italy sardinia	1717	NOLIN	500	43	29	Isle et Royaume de Sardaigne
mwf0978	france poitou	1704	NOLIN	1000	74	66	La Generalite de La Rochelle Comprenant le Pays d'Aunis, la Saintonge, &c., Divisee en Cinq Elections
mwgr0124	greece	1699	NOLIN	785	44	61	La Grece Ancienne et Moderne
mwbh0451	belgium holland	1690	NOLIN	480	45	60	La Partie Meridionale des Pays-Bas, Connue sous le Nom de Flandre ... par le P. Coronelli, Corrigee Par le Sr. de Tillemont
mwsp0477	spain regions	1691	NOLIN	750	46	57	La Principaute de Catalogne avec les Comtez de Roussillon et de Cerdagne
mwsp0494	spain regions	1703	NOLIN	2400	58	86	La Principaute de Catalogne et le Comte de Roussillon
mwf0342	france brittany	1703	NOLIN	400	45	60	La Province ou Duche de Bretagne Divisee en Deux Grandes Parties, qui sont la Haute, et la Basse Bretagne
mwme0346	holy land	1756	NOLIN	550	46	66	La Terre Sainte Divisee en ses Douze Tribus (size incl. text panels in side borders)
mwam1073	america north (east)	1781	NOLIN	400	20	26	La Virginie, Pennsilvanie, Nouvelle Angleterre et Autres Pays ... Partie des Possessions Angloises
mwaf0176	africa	1740	NOLIN	13500	122	136	L'Afrique Dressee sur les Relations les Plus Recentes et Rectifices sur les Dernieres Observations Dediee et Presentee a Sa Majesti Tre Chrestienne Louis XV
mwg0091	germany	1706	NOLIN	450	46	61	L'Allemagne divisee
mwam0132a	america continent	1720	NOLIN	30000	123	138	L'Amerique Dressee sur les Relations les Plus Recentes Rectifiees sur les Derniers Observations (re-issued in 1740, and in 1755 publ. by Crepy, illustrated here)
mwam0130	america continent	1720	NOLIN	1500	45	60	L'Amerique ou le Nouveau Continent Dressee sur les Memoires les Plus Nouveaux
mwe0363b	europe austria	1742	NOLIN	500	44	57	L'Archi Duché d'Autriche ... avec Partie de la Moravie ...

AMPG REFERENCE	REGION	DATE	MAP MAKER	PRICE (UK£)	VERT. (cm.)	HOR. (cm.)	TITLE OF MAP (Comments by the editor in brackets)
mwas0169	asia continent	1754	NOLIN	600	47	52	L'Asie Divisee en ses Grandes Regions et Empires Subdivisee en ses Principaux Estats
mwas0150	asia continent	1740	NOLIN	12000	126	140	L'Asie Dressee sur les Nouvelles Observations Faites en Touttes les Parties de la Terre
mwas0082	asia continent	1690	NOLIN	900	45	60	L'Asie selon les Memoires les plus Nouveaux Dressee par le P. Coronelli
mwf0609a	france languedoc	1697	NOLIN	650	60	48	Le Canal Royal de Languedoc
mwf0609	france languedoc	1697	NOLIN	8000	58	144	Le Canal Royal de Languedoc, pour la Jonction de l'Ocean et de la Mer Mediterranee
mwbh0478	belgium holland	1696	NOLIN	400	46	57	Le Comte de Haynaut … Le Comte de Cambresis
mwbh0654a	belgium holland	1742	NOLIN	320	45	60	Le Comté de Namur
mwf1041	france provence	1707	NOLIN	650	43	58	Le Comte et Gouvernement de Provence
mwe0714	europe danube	1688	NOLIN	2000	46	119	Le Cours du Danube depuis sa Source jusqu'a ses Embouchures, ou sont Partie de l'Empire d'Allemagne; et des Estats qui ont este, ou qui sont encore de l'Empire des Turcs en Europe … Dresse par le P. Coronelli
mwf0636	france limousin	1742	NOLIN	300	50	54	Le Diocese de Limoges
mww0307	world	1708	NOLIN	72000	118	150	Le Globe Terrestre Represente en Deux Plans-Hemispheres Dresse sur la Projection de Mr de la Hyre … 1708 (1st edition 1700. Illustration shows 1784 updated re-issue.)
mww0338	world	1720	NOLIN	4800	46	60	Le Globe Terrestre Represente en Deux Plans-Hemispheres, et en Diverses autres Figures
mwf0612	france languedoc	1700	NOLIN	550	45	60	Le Gouvernement General de Languedoc
mwf1142	france rhone-alpes	1696	NOLIN	500	80	62	Le Gouvernement General et Militaire du Lyonnois
mwgm0182a	mexico	1688	NOLIN	8000	44	59	Le Nouveau Mexique Appele aussi Nouvelle Grenade et Marata. Avec Partie de Californie. Selon les Memoires les Plus Nouveaux. Par le Pere Coronelli
mwuk0949	england	1689	NOLIN	875	45	59	Le Royaume d'Angleterre Divise en Plusieurs Parties
mwe0575a	europe czech republic (bohemia)	1742	NOLIN	500	45	56	Le Royaume de Boheme
mwe0674	europe dalmatia	1689	NOLIN	785	45	60	Le Royaume de Dalmacie, Divise en ses Comtez, Territoires etc. La Morlaquie, et la Bosnie
mwf0085	france	1698	NOLIN	875	43	58	Le Royaume de France avec ses Acquisitions suivant le Traite de Paix de Ryswick 1697 (below is another version with 'Roy' instead of 'Louis le Grand' in title)
mwf0082	france	1693	NOLIN	6000	95	129	Le Royaume de France divisé en Provinces, et en Gouvernemens
mwsp0565	spain regions	1762	NOLIN	600	44	71	Le Royaume de Galice Divise en Plusieurs Territoires et les Asturies
mwe0941a	europe hungary	1742	NOLIN	750	45	60	Le Royaume de Hongrie
mwbp0333	poland	1697	NOLIN	1200	46	59	Le Royaume de Pologne
mwsp0065	portugal	1704	NOLIN	875	64	46	Le Royaume de Portugal Divise en Cinq Grandes Provinces … avec le Royaume des Algarves
mwuk0429	scotland	1689	NOLIN	1200	49	61	Le Royaume d'Escosse Divisee en Deux Parties, Subdivisee en Provinces etc.
mwe1014a	europe rhine	1702	NOLIN	800	62	46	Le Theatre de la Guerre sur le Haut Rhein contenant l'Alsace divisée en Haute et Basse…Soüabe
mwc0100	china	1720	NOLIN	360	20	26	L'Empire de la Chine avec les Isles du Japon et la Coree
mwbh0869	luxembourg	1742	NOLIN	685	45	57	Les Courans des Riviers de Meuse … Luxembourg
mwf0679b	france lorraine	1696	NOLIN	550	48	61	Les Duchez de Lorraine et de Bar
mwg0268	baden-wurttemberg	1695	NOLIN	400	23	30	Les Environs d'Hailbron
mwf1137	france rhone-alpes	1691	NOLIN	1350	81	62	Les Etats de Savoye et de Piemont
mwuk0774	uk	1701	NOLIN	900	60	49	Les Isles Britanniques ou sont les Royaumes d'Angleterre d'Escosse et d'Irlande &c.
mwf0614	france languedoc	1703	NOLIN	600	43	50	Les Montagnes des Sevennes ou se Retirent les Fanatiques de Languedoc et les Plaines des Environs ou ils Font leur Courses avec les Grands Chemins Royaux
mwbh0452	belgium holland	1690	NOLIN	650	46	60	Les Provinces Unies ou la Partie Septentrionale des Pays-Bas Connue sous le Nom de Hollande. Paris, Nolin, 1690. H. Van Loon Sculpt.
mwsc0087	scandinavia	1691	NOLIN	800	50	57	Les Royaumes de Suede, de Danemarck et de Norwege
mwsp0494b	spain regions	1703	NOLIN	720	57	44	Les Royaumes de Valence et Murcie tirez de Cantel … Los Reynos de Valencia y de Murcia
mwsp0299	spain	1784	NOLIN	160	21	26	Les Royaumes d'Espagne et de Portugal
mwsw0097	switzerland	1700	NOLIN	500	46	58	Les Suisses, leurs Alliez
mwsp0219	spain	1701	NOLIN	1200	45	59	L'Espagne divisee en plusiers estats … P. Coronelli
mwit0590	italy north	1701	NOLIN	1650	47	118	L'Etat de Milan Divise en ses Principales Parties: avec Parties des Etats de Venise et des Duches de Mantoue et de Parme et Modene / Le cours du Po depuis Turin … Venise (2 maps joined)
mwe0118	europe	1701	NOLIN	1200	44	58	L'Europe divisee en ses Grands Etats
mwe0120b	europe	1704	NOLIN	20000	124	138	L'Europe Dressee sur les Nouvelles Observations Faites en Toute les Parties de la Terre
mwe0105a	europe	1696	NOLIN	1200	45	60	L'Europe selon les memoires
mwbh0473	belgium holland	1695	NOLIN	600	21	47	Liege et Partie de l'Evesche de Liege
mwm0201	mediterranean malta	1680	NOLIN	720	19	27	L'Isle de Malthe Possedee par les Chevaliers

AMPG REFERENCE	REGION	DATE	MAP MAKER	PRICE (UK£)	VERT. (cm.)	HOR. (cm.)	TITLE OF MAP (Comments by the editor in brackets)
mwit0916	italy sicily	1702	NOLIN	1250	44	55	L'Isle et Royaume de Sicile
mwit0131	italy	1700	NOLIN	280	20	26	L'Italie Divisee en ses Differents Etats Royaumes et Republiques
mwit0137	italy	1705	NOLIN	1250	46	61	L'Italie divisee en ses estats
mww0434	world	1755	NOLIN	5600	48	65	Mappe-Monde Carte Universelle de la Terre (updated in 1779 with Capt. Cook's discoveries and in 1791, illustrated here)
mwf0830	france paris	1680	NOLIN	400	22	28	Paris
mwsp0494a	spain regions	1703	NOLIN	1200	55	86	Partie Meridionale des Costes D'Espagne ou sont les Royaume de Granade et d'Andalousie
mwam1080a	america north (east)	1783	NOLIN	375	21	26	Partie Meridionale des Possessions Angloises en Amerique
mwe0575	europe czech republic	1742	NOLIN	1000	52	40	Plan de Prague
mwm0202	mediterranean malta	1680	NOLIN	720	21	27	Plan Des Vieilles et Nouvelles Fortifications de Malthe
mwf0838	france paris	1698	NOLIN	1250	49	82	Plan Routier de la Ville de Paris et de ses Faubourgs
mwf1035	france provence	1700	NOLIN	600	36	44	Provinciae Ecclesiastica Arelatensis (Camargue)
mwit0745	italy rome	1748	NOLLI	3000	46	68	La Topografia di Roma
mwit0744	italy rome	1748	NOLLI	15000	169	201	Nuova Pianta di Roma Data in Luce (12-sheet map)
mwit0746	italy rome	1748	NOLLI	2000	45	69	Urbis Ichinographiam
mwuk1227	england london	1772	NOORTHOUCK	875	39	66	A New and Accurate Plan of the Cities of London and Westminster, Including the New Roads & New Buildings
mwuk1103a	england london	1593	NORDEN	3000	16	26	London
mwuk1112	england london	1653	NORDEN-STENT	2000	16	26	London. A Guide for Countrey Men. In the Famous Cittey of London by the Help of which Plot they shall be Able to Know how Farr it is to any Street (3rd state of Norden's map of 1593)
mwaf0515a	africa egypt etc	1755	NORDEN, F.L.	480	42	26	Premiere Partie de la Carte du cours du Nil (in 2 parts. South to the top. Title below map. Price is for both parts.)
mwbp0060	baltic sea (east)	1801	NORDENANKAR	720	63	95	Charta ofver Medlersta Delen af Ostersjon
mwsc0443	scandinavia finland	1791	NORDENANKAR	800	63	95	Pass Charta ofver Finska Wiken
mwsc0749	scandinavia sweden	1791	NORDENANKAR	600	63	95	Pass Charta ofver Nra. Delen af Ostersjon, Alands Haf med Sdra. Delen af Botten-Hafwet
mwsc0727	scandinavia sweden	1739	NORDENCREUTZ	2500	51	97	Charta ofwer Malaren
mwaf1006a	africa south	1827	NORIE	1200	97	65	A Chart of False Bay surveyed … to which is added Table Bay … (1st edition 1819 68x65cm. This edition with another map on the same sheet showing the southern coast)
mwam1231	america north (east)	1835	NORIE	1800	78	240	A Chart of the Coast of North America, from Cape Canso to Halifax and from thence to Philadelphia
mwsc0648	scandinavia norway	1844	NORIE	550	78	122	A Chart of the Coast of Norway, Including the White Sea
mwgm0328	mexico	1835	NORIE	550	99	73	A Chart of the East Coast of Yucatan and the Bay of Honduras
mwaf1253	africa west	1834	NORIE	1000	81	201	A Chart of the Western Coast of Africa Extending from Sierra Leone and the Isles de Los to the Cape of Good Hope with Enlarged Plans of the Principal Islands, Harbours and Roadsteads
mwsam0422a	south america brazil	1830	NORIE	1800	77	190	A New and Complete Chart of the Coast of Brazil from Maranham, to the Entrance of the River Plate
mwat0061	atlantic ocean (all)	1834	NORIE	1350	126	91	A New and Correct Chart of the Atlantic Ocean
mwin0454	andaman/nicobar isl	1817	NORIE	480	64	93	A New Chart of the Andaman and Nicobar Islands with the Adjacent Continent
mwaf1010	africa south	1831	NORIE	1400	54	156	A New Chart of the Cape of Good Hope, to the Islands of Madagascar, Mauritius, &c. Showing the Mozambique Passage
mwwi0181	west indies	1828	NORIE	600	63	93	A New Chart of the Carribean Isles, Called also the Windward & Leeward Islands from Porto Rico to Trinidad
mwc0272a	china	1840	NORIE	2000	60	79	A New Chart of the Coast of China from Pedra Branca to St. John's Island Exhibiting the Entrances to, and Course of The River Tigris. Drawn from the latest surveys by J. W. Norie. Stephenson Engraver. A New Edition 1840.
mwsam0647	south america guyana	1828	NORIE	450	64	80	A New Chart of the Coast of Guayana Comprehending the Colonies of Demerary, Surinam, Cayenne and the Island of Trinidad
mwuk1524	uk english channel (all)	1819	NORIE	1200	79	65	A New Chart of the Coasts of England and Holland from Dungeness to Flamborough Head and from Calais to the Elbe and Weser (2 sheets, each 79x65cm)
mwp0463a	pacific north	1825	NORIE	1800	79	182	A New Chart of the Pacific Ocean, exhibiting the Western Coast of Amerika from Cape Horn to Beerings Strait, the eastern shores of Asia including Japan, China and Australia (illustration shows revised edition until 1850)
mwsc0408	scandinavia denmark	1850	NORIE	875	81	122	A New Chart of the Skager Rak or Sleeve Including the Coasts of Norway and Sweden, from the Naze to Christiana & Gothenborg with Part of the Coast of Jutland
mwas0618	asia south east celebes	1832	NORIE	600	95	64	A New Chart of the Straits of Macassar with Various Additions & Improvements
mwwi0493	cuba	1840	NORIE	750	64	93	A Survey of the Island of Cuba
mww0673	world	1824	NORIE	480	53	142	Chart of the Variations of the Magnetic Needle for All the Known Seas

AMPG REFERENCE	REGION	DATE	MAP MAKER	PRICE (UK£)	VERT. (cm.)	HOR. (cm.)	TITLE OF MAP (Comments by the editor in brackets)
mwuk1636a	scilly isles	1815	NORIE	550	65	78	JW Norie's New and Improved Chart of the Isles of Scilly
mwin0450	indian ocean	1832	NORIE	1500	111	199	Steel's New Chart of the Indian and Pacific Oceans; from the Cape of Good Hope Canton and New Zealand; Including All the Passages to India and China
mwwi0309	antigua	1827	NORIE	750	46	67	The Island of Antigua
mwwi0386	barbados	1828	NORIE	750	64	47	The Island of Barbadoes, Revised by J.W. Norie
mwwi0886	st lucia	1827	NORIE	750	65	46	The Island of St. Lucia
mwsc0396	scandinavia denmark	1813	NORIE	800	62	77	To John Wilson Crocker ... This Chart of the Sound and Grounds
mwin0448	indian ocean	1812	NORIE	1500	66	122	To the Officers in the Honourable East India Company's Service this Outline Chart Intended for their Use to Pick off a Ship's Track
mwam1143	america north (east)	1803	NORMAN	6000	54	43	A Chart of South Carolina and Georgia
mww0596a	world	1797	NORMAN	500	36	46	A General Chart of the World on Mercator's Projection, exhibiting all the New Discoveries (publ. in Boston USA)
mwam1091	america north (east)	1785	NORMAN		154	156	An Accurate Map of the Four New England States Shewing in a Distinct Manner All the Mountains, Forts, Rivers
mwuss0236	carolinas	1794	NORMAN	20000	53	82	Chart of the Coast of America from Cape Hateras to Cape Roman.
mwuss0682	louisiana	1845	NORMAN	5000	47	65	Norman's Plan of New Orleans & Environs, 1845 By Henry Moellhausen Civil Engineer
mwuss0841	massachusetts	1781	NORMAN	7500	29	13	Plan of the Town of Boston, with the Attack on Bunkers-Hill, in the Peninsula of Charlestown, the 17th of June, 1775
mwg0298	bavaria	1559	NOTTELEIN	3000	70	71	Das Nurnbergische Territorium
mwuk1535	uk english channel (east)	1745	NUNN	600	43	56	A Large Draught of the Downes, Showing the Sands, Shoals, Depths of Water
mwuk0580	scotland	1814	NUTTALL, FISHER, DIXON	90	23	18	Scotland
mwam0595	america north	1814	NUTTALL, FISHER, DIXON	150	18	23	States of America
mwca0516	canada quebec	1759	OAKLEY	2200	31	35	A Plan of Quebec ... by E. Oakley & Sold by J. Rocque
mwf0985	france poitou	1757	OAKLEY	750	29	42	A Plan of the City, and the Harbour of Rochefort, a Place Remarkable for its Fine Docks, & Surprizing Magazines for Warlike Stores
mwf0753	france nord pas-de-calais	1750	OAKLEY	750	43	67	Exact Plan of the Town Port & Citadel of Calais
mwuss0166	carolinas	1711	OCHS	1800	27	22	Die Provintz Nord und Sud Carolina
mwuk0208	ireland	1777	O'CONOR	650	62	58	Ortelius Improved or a New Map of Ireland Wherein are inserted, the Principal Families of Irish and English Extraction
mwit0555	italy marches	1680	ODOARDI	1800	27	44	Topografia del Stato d'Ascoli della Marca con suoi Confini
mwg0244	berlin	1778	OESFELD	580	32	40	Gegend bey Berlin und Potsdam
mwbp0508	poland	1786	OESFELD	2000	99	94	Magna Mappa Geographica Borussiae Regnum (in 4 sheets)
mwme0452	jerusalem	1648	OFFERMANS	500	30	42	De Heylige en Wytvermaerde Stadt Ierusalem, Eerst Genaemt Salem (close copy of Visscher 1643)
mwf0368	france brittany	1771	OGEE	1600	112	155	Carte Geometrique de la Province de Bretagne
mwam0349	america north	1702	OGIER	400	14	19	L'Amerique Septentrionale
mwuss0150	carolinas	1672	OGILBY	7200	47	57	A New Description of Carolina by Order of the Lords Proprietors
mwas0058	asia continent	1673	OGILBY	1400	42	54	A New Map of Asia
mwuk0949a	england	1689	OGILBY	960	37	49	A New Map Of England With A Table Readily To Find The Townes
mwec0609	uk england kent	1672	OGILBY	2800	43	55	A New Map of Kent
mwuk0929	england	1675	OGILBY	1000	38	50	A New Map of the Kingdom of England & Dominion of Wales. Whereon are Projected All ye Principal Roads Actually Measured & Delineated by John Ogilby Esq.
mwaf0868	africa south	1670	OGILBY	480	28	36	Aethiopia Inferior vel Exterior
mwaf0368	africa east	1670	OGILBY	450	29	37	Aethiopia Superior vel Interior vulgo Abissinorum sive Presbiteri Ioannis Imperior
mwec0773	uk england middlesex	1673	OGILBY	1200	42	53	An Actual Survey of Midlesex (Ogilby only produced three county maps, the other being Kent, publ. 1673 and Essex, publ. 1678 after his death)
mwat0082	atlantic azores	1671	OGILBY	300	30	35	Angra op Tercera
mwaf0869	africa south	1670	OGILBY	650	24	33	Cabo de Bone Esperanse (view of Table Bay)
mwaf1124	africa west	1670	OGILBY	340	23	32	Castel del Mina
mwaf0740	africa north algeria	1670	OGILBY	450	26	36	De Stadt Alger
mwwi0889	st martin	1670	OGILBY	423	28	36	De Stadt St. Martin (view)
mwsam0744	south america peru	1671	OGILBY	250	34	18	Expugnatio Paytae
mwaf0768	africa north marocco	1670	OGILBY	350	27	36	Fezzae et Marocchi Regna Africae Celeberrima
mwwi0408	cuba	1671	OGILBY	650	29	35	Havana (view)
mwc0059	china	1671	OGILBY	350	28	70	Hocsieu with its Suburbs (view, English re-issue of Nieuhoff)
mwaf0590	africa islands madagascar	1670	OGILBY	400	28	37	Insula S. Laurentii vulgo Madagascar
mwat0187	atlantic cape verde isl.	1668	OGILBY	250	25	31	Insulae Promontorii Viridis, Hispanis Islas de Cabo Verde, Belgis de Soute Eylanden

AMPG REFERENCE	REGION	DATE	MAP MAKER	PRICE (UK£)	VERT. (cm.)	HOR. (cm.)	TITLE OF MAP (Comments by the editor in brackets)
mwme0784	persia etc	1671	OGILBY	480	29	36	Isfahan
mwm0194	mediterranean malta	1670	OGILBY	1000	28	36	Melite Insula vulgo Malta
mwaf1126	africa west	1670	OGILBY	500	27	37	Nigritarum Regio
mwgm0170	mexico	1671	OGILBY	650	29	36	Nova Hispania Nova Galicia Guatimala
mwuss0740	maryland	1671	OGILBY	6500	29	37	Nova Terrae-Mariae Tabula
mwuss1613	virginia	1671	OGILBY	1100	29	35	Nova Virginiae Tabula
mwwi0689	jamaica	1671	OGILBY	1800	43	53	Novissima et Accuratissima Jamaicae Descriptio per Johannem Ogilvium. Cosmographum Regium
mwam0073	america continent	1671	OGILBY	1800	44	54	Novissima et Accuratissima Totius Americae Descriptio per Johanem Ogilvium
mwwi0359	barbados	1670	OGILBY	1100	29	36	Novissima et Acuratissima Barbados
mwuss1076	new york	1671	OGILBY	450	13	17	Novum Amsterodamum (view, on page of text)
mwsam0315	south america brazil	1671	OGILBY	550	28	35	Olinda de Phernambuco
mwuss0395	florida	1671	OGILBY	489	28	36	Pagus Hispanorum in Florida
mwaf1125	africa west	1670	OGILBY	450	29	35	Regna Congo et Angola
mwat0324	atlantic st helena	1671	OGILBY	480	25	32	St. Helena
mwsam0502	south america colombia	1671	OGILBY	500	29	36	Terra Firma et Novum Regnum Granatense et Popayan
mwaf0769	africa north marocco	1670	OGILBY	500	28	45	The Citty of Tanger
mwaf0479	africa egypt etc	1670	OGILBY	400	23	34	The City Cairus
mwaf0480	africa egypt etc	1670	OGILBY	400	37	35	The City of Alexandria or Scanderik (view)
mwat0146	atlantic canary isl.	1668	OGILBY	300	24	32	The Pike Mountaine upon the Island Tenerieto / De Piek-Bergh op het Eilant Tenerieto
mwaf0818	africa north tunisia	1668	OGILBY	300	26	35	Thunis
mwgm0116	honduras	1671	OGILBY	320	29	36	Truxillo
mwsam0316	south america brazil	1671	OGILBY	550	29	36	Urbs Salvador (view)
mwm0195	mediterranean malta	1670	OGILBY	600	28	37	Valetta Civitas Nova Maltae olim Milittae
mwgm0171	mexico	1671	OGILBY	350	30	36	Vetus Mexico
mwuss1612	virginia	1671	OGILBY	960	29	36	Virginiae Partis Australis et Floridae Partis Orientalis interia centiumq Regionum Nova Descriptio
mwgm0172	mexico	1671	OGILBY	550	29	36	Yucatan Conventus Iuridici Hispaniae Novae Pars Occidentalis, et Guatimala Conventus Iuridicus
mwec0612	uk england kent	1690	OGILBY-OVERTON	2000	36	55	The North Prospect of Canterbury / The Groundplott of Canterbury / A Prospect of Christ Church the Cathedral of Canterbury
mwuss0492	georgia	1735	OGLETHORPE	12000	40	37	A Map of the County of Savannah
mwwi0256	west indies (east)	1777	OLDENDORP	800	35	37	Caraibische Inseln
mwwi0928a	virgin isl	1777	OLDENDORP	600	17	32	Die Insel Sainte Croix mit den Namen der Plantagen die Bestaendig sind
mwwi0928b	virgin isl	1777	OLDENDORP	600	17	32	Die Insel Sanct Thomas mit den Mehresten Plantagen 1767
mwc0026	china	1655	OLEARIUS	1500	29	35	An Exact Mapp of China, Being Faithfully Copied from One Brought from Peking by a Father Lately Resident in that Citty (based on Purchas 1625)
mwas0304	asia caspian sea	1656	OLEARIUS	350	27	33	D.D. Georgio Melbourne - A Map of ye Province of Kilan as it lies on ye Caspian Sea.
mwbp0087	baltic states	1656	OLEARIUS	900	29	37	D.D. Joanni Berkenhead ... A New Map of Liefland
mwru0055	russia	1659	OLEARIUS	2000	38	111	Le Cours de la Riviere de Wolga
mwme0777	persia etc	1656	OLEARIUS	1350	39	55	Nova Delineatio Persiae et Confinorum Deteri Longe Accuratior Edita. Anno 1655
mwec0546	uk england hertfordshire	1695	OLIVER	3000	58	76	The Actual Survey of the County of Hertford Containing the Miles, Furlongs and Poles between Place and Place on All the Roads in the Survey Exactly Measured
mwam0741	america north	1840	OLIVER & BOYD	140	18	22	N. America
mwuk1033	england	1800	OLIVER & BOYD	580	69	56	Oliver & Boyd's New Travelling Map of England & Wales
mwgr0627a	greece islands	1746	OLIVIER	3000	80	57	Carte de l'Archipel
mwm0058a	mediterranean	1746	OLIVIER	5500	58	81	Nouvelle Carte de la Mer Mediterranee (2 sheets each 58x81cm)
mwsp0323a	spain	1823	OLIVIERI	90	14	18	Li Regni di Spagna e Portogallo
mwuss1312	ohio	1835	OLNEY	875	45	54	A Map of the Towns of Perrysburg, Maumee and Port Miami
mwam1219	america north (east)	1833	OLNEY	100	27	23	Environs of New York / Philadelphia and Trenton / Portland / Charleston / Boston / Baltimore and Washington
mwuss0928	michigan	1844	OLNEY	180	22	27	Map of Michigan & Wisconsin
mwuss1541	texas	1849	OLNEY	500	27	22	Map of Texas to Illustrate Olney's New School Geography
mwam1207	america north (east)	1829	OLNEY	100	24	20	Map of the Eastern States
mwam0762	america north	1844	OLNEY	300	27	44	Map of the United States Canada and a Part of Mexico
mwam0742	america north	1840	OLNEY	300	25	42	Map of the United States to Illustrate Olney's School Geography
mwam1377	america north (west)	1847	OLNEY	200	28	44	Western Territories of the United States
mwgm0274a	mexico	1811	OLTMANNS		39	46	Map of the Valley of Mexico And Neighbouring Mountains Sketched on the Spot in 1804, by Don Louis Martin (publ. by Von Humboldt)
mwbh0726	belgium holland	1775	OOSTWOUDT	1400	48	58	Nieuwe Kaart van het Dykgraafscahp van Dregterland (4 sheets, each 48x58cm. First publ. 1732 by H. de Leth)

AMPG REFERENCE	REGION	DATE	MAP MAKER	PRICE (UK£)	VERT. (cm.)	HOR. (cm.)	TITLE OF MAP (Comments by the editor in brackets)
mwuss0121a	california	1848	ORD	1500	54	39	Topographical Sketch of the Gold & Quicksilver District of California July 25th., 1848. E.O.C.O. Lt. U.S.A.
mwme0673	arabia etc	1822	ORGIAZZI	600	93	111	Carte de l'Empire Ottoman en Europe, en Asie et en Afrique, avec les Pays Limitrophes; Dressee par le Chevalier Lapie (Inset of Constantinople)
mwit0231	italy	1816	ORGIAZZI	875	123	73	Carte Statistique, Politique, et Minerologique de l'Italie, ou sont Tracee Toutes les Routes, Relais, et Distances de Postes (re-printed in English in 1822)
mwme0936	turkey etc	1602	ORLANDI	2500	29	44	Costatinopoli (re-issue of Ducheto's 1570 map)
mwit0412	italy liguria	1600	ORLANDI	2500	41	54	Genova
mwit0056	italy	1602	ORLANDI	8000	39	50	Geographia moderna de tutta la Italia con le sue (copy of Ducheto's 1582 map)
mwg0036	germany	1602	ORLANDI	2250	37	53	Germania
mwit1211	italy venice	1570	ORLANDI	7500	37	57	Venetia
mww0034	world	1531	ORONCE FINE	75000	33	43	Nova, et Integra Universi Orbis Descriptio
mww0712	world	1836	ORR & SMITH	200	21		Eastern Hemisphere / Western Hemisphere (2 circular maps)
mwp0285	pacific (all)	1836	ORR & SMITH	75	21	26	Pacific Ocean
mwit0766	italy rome	1836	ORR & SMITH	135	21	26	Rome
mwsp0366	spain regions	1579	ORTELIUS	550	35	46	(Andalusia) Hispalensis Conventus Delineatio Auctore Hieronymo Chiaves
mwf0642	france loire	1579	ORTELIUS	300	35	47	(Anjou) Andegavensium Ditionis Vera et Integra Desciptio
mwsp0370	spain regions	1584	ORTELIUS	480	39	48	(Cadiz) Carpetaniae Partis Descr. 1584 / Vardusorum, sive Guipuscoae Regionis Typus / Hanc Insulam Perlustrabat, et sua Manu Depingebat Georgius Hoefnaglius Antverpian. Belga
mwit0558	italy north	1570	ORTELIUS	800	34	49	(Como) Larii Lacus vulgo Comensis Descriptio / Territorii Romani Descrip. / Fori Iulii vulgo Friuli Typus (3 maps on one sheet)
mwme0050	holy land	1590	ORTELIUS	3000	36	46	Abrahami Patriarchae Peregrinatio, et Vita
mwat0073	atlantic azores	1584	ORTELIUS	1000	33	47	Acores Insulae
mwaf0464	africa egypt etc	1584	ORTELIUS	3200	79	49	Aegyptus Antiqua
mwaf0468	africa egypt etc	1601	ORTELIUS	800	36	52	Aegyptus Antiqua
mwm0114	mediterranean east	1595	ORTELIUS	750	35	50	Aeneae Troiani Navigatio (incl. Italy)
mww0078	world	1590	ORTELIUS	1200	31	44	Aevi Veteris, Typus Geographicus
mwaf0763	africa north tunisia	1590	ORTELIUS	875	34	49	Africae Propriae Tabula, in qua, Punica Regna Vides; Tyrios, et Agenoris Urbem
mwaf0763	africa north libya	1590	ORTELIUS	875	34	49	Africae Propriae Tabula
mwaf0009	africa	1570	ORTELIUS	3500	37	50	Africae Tabula Nova
mwit0464	italy lombardy	1579	ORTELIUS	500	35	50	Agri Cremonensis Typus
mwme0760	persia etc	1595	ORTELIUS	800	36	47	Alexandri Magni Macedonis Expeditio
mwam0007	america continent	1570	ORTELIUS	6000	36	50	Americae sive Novi Orbis, Nova Descriptio (illustrated are 1st state and 3rd state)
mwuk0912	england	1602	ORTELIUS	2500	39	48	Anglia Regnum...Christophorus Saxton Describebat. 1579 (this map replaced Ortelius' 1570 map, being based on Saxton's 1579 map. It was in turn replaced in 1606; see 'England and Ireland' below).
mwuk1085	england and ireland	1606	ORTELIUS	5500	44	58	Angliae et Hiberniae Accurata Descriptio Veteribus et Recentioribus (derived from Hondius 1592)
mwuk0904	england	1573	ORTELIUS	1250	38	47	Angliae Regni Florentissimi Nova Descriptio, Auctore Humfredo Lhuyd Denbygiense
mwuk0669	uk	1570	ORTELIUS	1500	34	50	Angliae, Scotiae et Hiberniae, sive Britannicar: Insularum Descriptio
mwit0257	italy abruzzo	1590	ORTELIUS	750	33	43	Aprutii Ulterioris Descriptio 1590
mwm0115	mediterranean east	1598	ORTELIUS	960	35	50	Argonautica.
mwf0697	france nord pas-de-calais	1587	ORTELIUS	450	37	49	Artois - Artesia
mwf0693	france nord pas-de-calais	1579	ORTELIUS	500	38	49	Artois - Atrebatum Regionis Vera Descriptio. Johanne Surhonio Montensi Auctore
mwas0005	asia continent	1570	ORTELIUS	3000	37	49	Asiae Nova Descriptio
mwe0298	europe austria	1595	ORTELIUS	600	35	48	Austriae Descrip. per Wolfgangum Lazium
mwe0281	europe austria	1570	ORTELIUS	785	34	47	Austriae Ducatus Chorographia, Wolfgango Lazio Auctore
mwaf0835	africa north west	1570	ORTELIUS	650	34	50	Barbariae et Biledulgerid, Nova Descriptio
mwsw0018	switzerland	1573	ORTELIUS	500	33	50	Basiliensis Territorii Descriptio Nova, Auctore Sebastiano Munstero / Circulus sive Liga Sveviae
mwg0305	bavaria	1573	ORTELIUS	600	38	49	Bavariae olim Vindeliciae, Delineationis Compendium ex Tabula Philippi Apiani Math.
mwbh0109	belgium holland	1584	ORTELIUS	800	38	49	Belgii Veteris Typus
mwf0630	france limousin	1598	ORTELIUS	300	34	47	Blaisois. Blesiensis Territorii / Lemovicum Totius et Confinium Provinciarum Quantum
mwit0340	italy emilia-romagna	1608	ORTELIUS	2250	36	50	Bononiense Territorium / Ioanni Delphino
mwbh0129	belgium holland	1592	ORTELIUS	960	37	48	Brabantiae Descriptio
mwbh0036	belgium holland	1570	ORTELIUS	650	36	50	Brabantiae, Germaniae Inferioris Nobilissimae Provinciae Descriptio
mwg0410	brandenburg	1590	ORTELIUS	400	36	48	Brandenburgensis Marchae Descriptio
mwg0569	saxony	1590	ORTELIUS	400	31	47	Braunsvicensis, et Luneburgensis Ducatuum Vera Delineat / Norimberg. Agri, Fidissima Descrip.

AMPG REFERENCE	REGION	DATE	MAP MAKER	PRICE (UK£)	VERT. (cm.)	HOR. (cm.)	TITLE OF MAP (Comments by the editor in brackets)
mwuk0678	uk	1595	ORTELIUS	900	37	51	Britannicarum Insularum Typus. Ex Canatibus Geographicis Abrah. Ortelij.
mwuk0676	uk	1590	ORTELIUS	3500	72	49	Britannicarum Insularum Vetus Descriptio
mwit0465	italy lombardy	1590	ORTELIUS	900	33	47	Brixiani Agri Typus. Brixia, Cygnea Supposita in Specula
mwg0432	hessen	1579	ORTELIUS	650	31	47	Buchaviae, sive Fuldensis Ditionis Typus / Waldeccensis Comitatus Descriptio Accuratissima
mwf0384	france burgundy	1589	ORTELIUS	1100	37	49	Burgundiae Comitatus (only 1 re-issue, in 1603)
mwf0381	france burgundy	1579	ORTELIUS	375	37	51	Burgundiae Comitatus Recentiss, Descriptio Dno Ferdinando Lannoyo Auctore
mwf0389	france burgundy	1602	ORTELIUS	750	36	50	Burgundiae Ducatus / Burgundiae Comitatus
mwf0383	france burgundy	1584	ORTELIUS	500	37	46	Burgundiae Inferioris, quae Ducatus Nomine Censetur, Des. 1584
mwf0690	france nord pas-de-calais	1570	ORTELIUS	400	44	53	Caletensium et Bononiensium Ditionis Accurata Delinatio / Veromanduorum Eorumque Confinium Exactissima Discript. Iohanne Surhonio Auctore
mwuk1690	wales	1573	ORTELIUS	1000	37	50	Cambriae Typus Auctore Humfredo Lhuydo Denbigiense Cambrobritano
mwgr0356	greece crete	1584	ORTELIUS	950	36	51	Candia Insula - Archipelagi Insularum Aliquot Descrip. (10 insets)
mwe0492b	europe croatia	1573	ORTELIUS	400	33	48	Carinthiae Ducatus, et Goritiae Palatinus / Histriae Tabula / Zarae et Sebenici Descriptio
mwsp0397	spain regions	1608	ORTELIUS	960	39	49	Cataloniae Principatus Novissima et Accurata Descriptio
mwf0305b	france brittany	1595	ORTELIUS	450	37	51	Cenomanorum Galliae Regionis, Typus. Auctore Mattheo Ogerio. La Mans. / Neustria. Britanniae, et Normandiae Typus. 1594
mwc0002	china	1584	ORTELIUS	4200	37	48	Chinae, olim Sinarum Regionis, Nova Descriptio. Auctore Ludovico Georgio (north to the right)
mwgr0357	greece crete	1584	ORTELIUS	650	34	49	Creta Iovis Magni, Medio Iacet Insula Ponto / Corsica / Insulae Maris Ionii / Sardinia
mwwi0002	west indies	1579	ORTELIUS	2000	36	50	Culiacanae, Americae Regionis Descriptio / Hispanoliae, Cubae, Aliarumque Insularum Circumiacientium, Delineato
mwgr0455	greece cyprus	1573	ORTELIUS	2000	35	49	Cypri Insulae Nova Descript. 1573
mwgr0449	greece cyprus	1570	ORTELIUS	1800	37	44	Cyprus Insula / Candia, olim Creta (2 maps on one sheet)
mwe0749	europe east	1595	ORTELIUS	450	36	46	Daciarum, Moesiarumque, Vetus Descriptio
mwsc0226	scandinavia denmark	1570	ORTELIUS	750	32	42	Daniae Regni Typus
mwsc0244	scandinavia denmark	1595	ORTELIUS	720	35	49	Daniae Regni Typus / Cimbricae Chersonesi Nunc Iutiae
mwsc0229	scandinavia denmark	1584	ORTELIUS	600	35	50	Daniae Regni Typus / Oldenburg Comit
mwsp0396	spain regions	1606	ORTELIUS	960	38	49	Descripcion del Reyno de Galizia
mwbh0042	belgium holland	1570	ORTELIUS	1600	39	51	Descriptio Germaniae Inferioris (oval map in decorative border)
mwit0341	italy emilia-romagna	1608	ORTELIUS	2500	45	52	Ducatus Ferrariensis,
mwit0559	italy north	1570	ORTELIUS	720	36	48	Ducatus Mediolanensis
mwit0551a	italy marches	1608	ORTELIUS	1650	38	49	Ducatus Urbini Nova Exacta Descriptio
mwuk0004	ireland	1570	ORTELIUS	2800	35	48	Eryn. Hiberniae, Britannicae Insulae, Nova Descriptio. Irlandt
mwin0405	indian ocean	1598	ORTELIUS	800	36	47	Erythraei sive Rubri Maris Periplus (Historical map, inset: Mediterranean)
mwe0008	europe	1570	ORTELIUS	1750	34	46	Europae
mwe0018	europe	1595	ORTELIUS	1100	36	48	Europam, sive Celticam Veterem
mwaf0770	africa north morocco	1595	ORTELIUS	1000	40	51	Fessae et Marocchi Regna Afrucae Celeberr. (inset of Congo)
mwbh0041	belgium holland	1570	ORTELIUS	1600	39	51	Flandria (oval map in decorative border)
mwbh0130	belgium holland	1592	ORTELIUS	1000	39	51	Flandriae Comitatus Descriptio
mwit1094	italy tuscany	1595	ORTELIUS	850	37	48	Florentini Dominii, Fidelissima et Nova Descriptio
mwit0369	italy friuli	1573	ORTELIUS	960	36	48	Fori Iulii Accurata Descriptio
mwg0300	bavaria	1570	ORTELIUS	400	36	51	Franciae Orientalis (vulgo Franckenlant) Descriptio / Monesteriensis et Osnaburgensis Episcopatus Descriptio
mwbh0087	belgium holland	1579	ORTELIUS	550	37	50	Frisia Occidentalis (inset: Antiquae Frisiae)
mwg0573	saxony	1595	ORTELIUS	700	38	50	Frisia Orientalis (inset:) Riderae Portionis
mwg0557	saxony	1579	ORTELIUS	400	32	45	Frisiae Orientalis Descriptio
mwf0035a	france	1598	ORTELIUS	5000	35	50	Gallia (shown below left)
mwf0029	france	1590	ORTELIUS	600	36	46	Gallia Vetus
mwf0040	france	1606	ORTELIUS	1600	40	49	Gallia. Geographica Galliae descriptio,
mwf1089b	france pyrenees	1570	ORTELIUS	350	30	45	Gallia Narbonensis Ora Marittima Recenter descripta / Sabaudiae Et Burgundiae Comitatus descriptio
mwf0020	france	1570	ORTELIUS	1200	34	50	Galliae Regni Potentiss. Nova Descriptio, Ioanne Ioliveto Auctore
mwf0032	france	1595	ORTELIUS	400	40	50	Galliae Veteris Typus
mwbh0040	belgium holland	1570	ORTELIUS	650	37	50	Gelriae, Cliviae, Finitimorumque Locorum Verissima Descriptio Christiano Schrot. Auctore (north to the left)
mwme0542	arabia etc	1598	ORTELIUS	1200	36	47	Geographia Sacra
mwg0020	germany	1570	ORTELIUS	600	37	51	Germania
mwg0027	germany	1590	ORTELIUS	500	37	46	Germaniae Veteris typus
mwgr0040	greece	1579	ORTELIUS	750	35	50	Graecia Sophiani
mwgr0028	greece	1570	ORTELIUS	850	35	50	Graeciae Universae Secundum Hodiernum Situm Neoterica Descriptio
mwg0687	schleswig-holstein	1579	ORTELIUS	350	34	49	Hassiae Descriptio, Ioanne Drynadro Auctore. 1579 / Holsatiae Descrip.

AMPG REFERENCE	REGION	DATE	MAP MAKER	PRICE (UK£)	VERT. (cm.)	HOR. (cm.)	TITLE OF MAP (Comments by the editor in brackets)
mwsw0016	switzerland	1570	ORTELIUS	800	34	44	Helvetiae Descriptio Aegidio Tschudo Auct. (south to the top)
mwg0433	hessen	1595	ORTELIUS	550	35	48	Hennebergensis Ditionis / Hassiae Descriptio
mwgm0135	mexico	1579	ORTELIUS	850	35	51	Hispaniae Novae sivae Magnae, Recens et Vera Descriptio. 1579
mwsp0165	spain	1590	ORTELIUS	600	38	50	Hispaniae Veteris Descriptio
mwbh0039	belgium holland	1570	ORTELIUS	1000	36	49	Hollandiae Antiquorum Catthorum Sedis Nova Descriptio, Auctore Iacobo a Daventria
mwe0854	europe hungary	1570	ORTELIUS	875	36	50	Hungariae Descriptio, Wolfgango Lazio Auct.
mwjk0004	japan	1595	ORTELIUS	3500	36	49	Iaponiae Insulae Descriptio. Ludoico Teisera Auctore
mwe0492a	europe dalmatia	1573	ORTELIUS	650	37	48	Illyricum
mwas0364	asia south east	1570	ORTELIUS	2500	35	50	Indiae Orientalis Insularumque Adiacientium Typus
mwbh0184	belgium holland	1612	ORTELIUS	5000	42	56	Inferioris Germaniae Provinciarum Nova Descriptio
mwgr0460	greece cyprus	1584	ORTELIUS	1800	36	48	Insular. aliquot Aegaei Maris Antiqua Descrip. (10 island maps on one sheet, the largest map Cyprus)
mwm0158	mediterranean islands	1570	ORTELIUS	1000	36	48	Insularum Aliquot Maris Mediterranei Descriptio (Sardinia, Sicily, Corfu, Djerba, Elba, Malta)
mwuk0018	ireland	1609	ORTELIUS	6000	44	58	Irlandiae Accurata Descriptio Auctore Baptista Boazio
mwit0271	italy campagna	1590	ORTELIUS	1000	36	48	Ischia, quae olim Aenaria. Ab Aeneae Classe hic Appulsa sic Nominata
mwsc0479	scandinavia iceland	1587	ORTELIUS	7500	34	49	Islandia
mwit0992	italy south	1595	ORTELIUS	720	34	48	Itala nam Tellus Graecia Maior
mwit0562	italy north	1590	ORTELIUS	600	35	47	Italia Gallica, sive Gallia Cisalpina
mwit0031	italy	1570	ORTELIUS	1800	36	52	Italiae Novissima Descriptio Auctore Iacobo Castaldo Pedemontano
mwit0039	italy	1584	ORTELIUS	1350	35	48	Italiae Veteris Specimen
mwsw0041	switzerland	1608	ORTELIUS	800	38	51	Lacus Lemani Vicinorumq. Locorum Nova et Accurata Descriptio
mwit0389	italy lazio	1595	ORTELIUS	550	36	46	Latium. Ex Conatibus Geographicis Abrah. Ortelij Antverp
mwbh0109a	belgium holland	1584	ORTELIUS	650	38	50	Leodiensis Dioecesis Typus
mwbh0168a	belgium holland	1606	ORTELIUS	1400	40	49	Limburgensis Ducatus Tabula Nova, Exusa Sumptibus Ioan. Baptistae Vrints
mwf0569	france ile de france	1598	ORTELIUS	300	34	46	L'Isle de France - Parisiensis Agri Descrip.
mwf0662	france lorraine	1590	ORTELIUS	550	34	50	Lorraine. Lotharingiae Nova Descriptio
mwm0265a	mediterranean west	1624	ORTELIUS	1000	27	35	Lumen Historiarum per Occidentem ex Conatibus Fran. Haraei Antverpiae
mwbh0811	luxembourg	1579	ORTELIUS	750	37	49	Lutzenburgensis Ducatus Veriss Descript. Iacobo Surhonio Montano Auctore
mwg0552	saxony	1573	ORTELIUS	400	37	43	Mansfeldiae Comitatus Descriptio Auctore, Tilemanno Stella Sig.
mwp0226	pacific (all)	1590	ORTELIUS	8000	35	50	Maris Pacifici, (quod vulgo Mar del Zur) cum Regionibus Circumiacentibus, Insulisque in Codem Passim Sparsis, Novissima Descriptio
mwe1086	europe slovak republic (moravia)	1573	ORTELIUS	480	36	47	Moraviae, quae olim Marcomannoarum Sedes, Corographia
mwbh0086	belgium holland	1579	ORTELIUS	350	39	51	Namurcum. Comitatus
mwme0921	turkey etc	1570	ORTELIUS	500	32	49	Natoliae, quae olim Asia Minor Nova Descriptio / Aegypti Recentior Descriptio / Carthaginis Celeberrimi Sinus Typus
mwbh0053	belgium holland	1573	ORTELIUS	450	37	49	Nobilis Hannoniae Comitatus Descrip. Auctore Iacobo Surhonio Montano
mwbh0037	belgium holland	1570	ORTELIUS	650	35	51	Oost ende West Vrieslandts Beschryvinghe utriusque Frisiorum Regionis Noviss: Descriptio
mwg0314	bavaria	1584	ORTELIUS	600	31	49	Palatinatus Bavariae Descriptio, Erhardo Reych Tirolense Auctore / Argentoratensis Agri Descriptio
mwg0301	bavaria	1570	ORTELIUS	350	31	49	Palatinatus Bavariae Descriptio, Erhardo Reych Tirolense Auctore / Wirtenbergensis Ducatus
mwme0038	holy land	1570	ORTELIUS	1800	35	49	Palestinae sive Totius Terrae Promissionis Nova Descriptio Auctore Tilemanno Stella Sigenens
mwe0650	europe dalmatia	1590	ORTELIUS	650	36	46	Pannoniae, et Illyrici Veteris Tabula
mwit0339	italy emilia-romagna	1608	ORTELIUS	2000	37	48	Parmae et Placentiae Ducatus
mwit0988	italy south	1573	ORTELIUS	480	31	46	Patavini Territorii Corographia. Iac Castaldo Auct. / Apuliae quae olim Iapygia. Nova Corographia.
mwit1164a	italy veneto	1595	ORTELIUS	500	31	50	Patavini Territorii Corographia. Iac Castaldo Auct. / Tarvisini Agri Typus
mwit0631	italy piedmont	1573	ORTELIUS	700	37	50	Pedemontanae Vicinorumque Regionum Auctore Iacobo Castaldo Descrip.
mwm0111	mediterranean east	1579	ORTELIUS	950	35	50	Peregrinationis Divi Pauli Typus Chorographicus
mwme0757	persia etc	1570	ORTELIUS	800	35	50	Persici sive Sophorum Regni Typus
mwit1147	italy umbria	1584	ORTELIUS	900	34	46	Perusini Agri; Exactissima Novissimaque Descriptio: Auctore Egnatio Dante
mwsam0486	south america colombia	1584	ORTELIUS	2500	34	47	Peruviae Auriferae Regionis Typus. Didaco Mendezio / La Florida. Auctore Hieron. Chiaves / Guastecan Reg.
mwf0942	france picardy	1579	ORTELIUS	400	33	52	Picardiae Belgicae Regionis Descriptio. Joanne Surhonio Auctore
mwf0961	france poitou	1579	ORTELIUS	500	36	50	Poictou. Pictonum Vicinarumque Regionum Fidiss Descriptio

AMPG REFERENCE	REGION	DATE	MAP MAKER	PRICE (UK£)	VERT. (cm.)	HOR. (cm.)	TITLE OF MAP (Comments by the editor in brackets)
mwbp0177	poland	1570	ORTELIUS	1200	37	50	Poloniae Finitimarumque Locorum Descriptio Auctore Wenceslao Godreccio Polono
mwbp0203	poland	1595	ORTELIUS	1200	37	48	Poloniae, Lituaniaeq. Descriptio. Auctore Wenceslao Godreccio; et Correctore Andrea Pograbio Pilsnensi
mwbp0183	poland	1573	ORTELIUS	500	39	50	Pomeraniae, Wandalicae Regionis, Typ. / Livoniae Nova Descriptio / Ducatus Oswieczensis, et Zatoriensis, Descriptio
mwru0469	ukraine	1590	ORTELIUS	750	36	50	Pontus Euxinus. Aequor Iasonis Pulsatum Remige Primum (shown below left is the Jansson 1650 version)
mwsp0002	portugal	1570	ORTELIUS	800	34	51	Portugalliae que olim Lusitania, Novissima & Exactissima Descriptio
mwaf0346	africa east	1573	ORTELIUS	1450	37	43	Presbiteri Iohannis, sive, Abissinorum Imperii Descriptio
mwf0994	france provence	1595	ORTELIUS	600	35	51	Provinciae Regionis Galliae Vera Exactissimaque Descriptio
mwbp0193	poland	1584	ORTELIUS	1000	37	43	Prussiae Regionis Sarmatiae Europae Nobiliss. Vera et Nova Descriptio
mwbp0204	poland	1595	ORTELIUS	800	37	47	Prussiae Vera Descriptio
mwme0085	holy land	1624	ORTELIUS	550	27	35	Rdo. Dno. D. Adr. Stalpartio Abb. Togerlesi Disniso.d. Lumen Historiarum per Orientem. Illustrandis Biblijs Sacris, Martyro-Logio, et Alijs Multis. Concinn. Fran. Hareio Antverpiae (2 insets: World, Judea. Map surrounded by text. An accompanying left-hand sheet shows the remainder of the Mediterranean sea)
mwf0421	france central	1570	ORTELIUS	350	31	48	Regionis Biturigum - Limaniae
mwe0514	europe czech republic (bohemia)	1570	ORTELIUS	500	34	51	Regni Bohemiae Descriptio
mwsp0161	spain	1570	ORTELIUS	800	38	50	Regni Hispaniae Post Omnium Editiones Locuplettissima Descriptio
mwit0987	italy south	1570	ORTELIUS	550	37	50	Regni Neapolitani Verissima Secundum Antiquorum et Recentiorum Traditionem Descriptio, Pyrrho Ligorio Auct.
mwe0299	europe austria	1595	ORTELIUS	500	34	50	Rhetiae Alpestris Descriptio, in qua hodie Tirolis Comitatus / Goritiae, Karstii, Chaczeolae, Carniolae, Histriae, et Windorum Marchae Descrip
mwit0341a	italy emilia-romagna	1608	ORTELIUS	2250	38	49	Romagna olim Flaminia (inset: Rhodiginae)
mwm0003	mediterranean	1579	ORTELIUS	1050	35	50	Romani Imperii Imago
mwe1041	europe romania	1584	ORTELIUS	650	36	50	Romaniae, (quae olim Thracia Dicta) Vicinorumq3 Regionum, uti Bulgariae, Walachiae, Syrfiae, etc. Descriptio
mwru0016	russia	1570	ORTELIUS	2000	36	44	Russiae, Moscoviae et Tartariae Descriptio. Auctore Antonio Ienkensono Anglo, Edita Londini Anno 1562
mwe0295	europe austria	1592	ORTELIUS	480	39	46	Salisburgensis Iurisdictionis
mwe0282	europe austria	1570	ORTELIUS	720	34	44	Salisburgensis Iurisdictionis (inset view:) Urbis Salisburgensis Genuina Descriptio
mwg0547	saxony	1570	ORTELIUS	400	35	51	Saxoniae, Misniae, Thuringiae, Nova Exactissimaq. Descriptio
mwe1121	europe slovenia	1570	ORTELIUS	720	34	46	Schlavoniae, Croatiae, Carniae, Istriae, Bosniae, Finitimarumque Regionum Nova Descriptio, Auctore Augustino Hirsuogelio
mwuk0313	scotland	1573	ORTELIUS	2000	36	48	Scotiae Tabula
mwit1091	italy tuscany	1573	ORTELIUS	550	33	49	Senensis Ditionis Accurata Descriptio / Corsica / Marcha Anconae
mwsc0022	scandinavia	1570	ORTELIUS	2800	36	49	Septentrionalium Regionum Descrip.
mwit0570	italy north	1608	ORTELIUS	4800	39	54	Serenissimae Reipublicae Genuensis Ducatus et Dominii Nova Descriptio
mwit0873	italy sicily	1584	ORTELIUS	1250	37	49	Siciliae Veteris Typus
mwbp0179	poland	1570	ORTELIUS	600	28	38	Silesiae Typus Descriptus et Editus a Martino Heilwig Neisense, et Nobili Viro Nicolao Rhedinger Dedicatus. Anno 1561
mwbp0201	poland	1595	ORTELIUS	600	35	42	Silesiae Typus, a Martino Heilwig Nissense Descriptus, et Nobili Doctoque Viro Domino Nicolao Rhedingero Ded.
mwru0414	russia tartary	1570	ORTELIUS	1800	36	47	Tartariae sive Magni Chami Regni Typus
mwme0049	holy land	1584	ORTELIUS	1250	37	50	Terra Sancta, a Petro Laicstain Perlustrata, et ab eius Ore et Schedis a Christiano Schrot in Tabulam Redacta
mwbp0202	poland	1595	ORTELIUS	550	31	44	Thietmarsiae, Holsaticae Regionis Partis Typus / Oldenburg
mwbp0178	poland	1570	ORTELIUS	500	31	44	Thietmarsiae, Holsaticae Regionis Partis Typus / Prussiae Descriptio ante aliquot Annos ab Henrico Zellio
mwg0693	schleswig-holstein	1598	ORTELIUS	450	31	44	Thietmarsiae, Holsaticae Regionis Partis Typus / Rugiae
mwgr0040a	greece	1590	ORTELIUS	550	36	48	Thraciae Veteris Typus
mwit1088	italy tuscany	1570	ORTELIUS	850	32	50	Thusciae Descriptio Auctore Hieronymo Bellarmato
mwg0299	bavaria	1570	ORTELIUS	400	33	43	Tipus Vindeliciae sive utriusque, Bavariae, Secundum Antiquum & Recentiorum Situm
mwf0423	france central	1598	ORTELIUS	550	36	46	Touraine. Turonensis Ducatus et Confinium Galliae Celticae Descriptio
mwe1040b	europe east	1573	ORTELIUS	400	31	43	Transilvania
mwme0535	arabia etc	1570	ORTELIUS	1800	37	49	Turcici Imperii Descriptio
mwg0733	thuringia	1573	ORTELIUS	320	30	45	Turingiae Noviss. Descript. / Misniae et Lusati: Ae Tabula
mwit1093	italy tuscany	1584	ORTELIUS	850	32	49	Tusciae Antiquae Typus. Ex Conatibus Geographicis Ab. Ortelij.

AMPG REFERENCE	REGION	DATE	MAP MAKER	PRICE (UK£)	VERT. (cm.)	HOR. (cm.)	TITLE OF MAP (Comments by the editor in brackets)
mwme0051	holy land	1590	ORTELIUS	900	36	46	Typus Chorographicus, Celebrium Locorum in Regno Iudae et Israel Arte Factus a Tilemanno Stella Sigenensi
mww0060	world	1570	ORTELIUS	8000	34	49	Typus Orbis Terrarum (first of 3 states of this map. 3rd state illustrated below, 36x49cm.)
mwe0857a	europe hungary	1579	ORTELIUS	720	35	50	Ungariae Loca Praecipua
mwsp0371	spain regions	1584	ORTELIUS	1200	35	50	Valentiae Regni, olim Contestanorum si Ptolomaeo, Edetanorum si Plinio Credimus Typus
mwit1162	italy veneto	1579	ORTELIUS	675	33	47	Veronae Urbis Territorium, a Bernardo Brognolo Descriptum
mwg0760	westphalia	1579	ORTELIUS	800	34	50	Westphaliae Totius, Finitimarumque Regionum Accurata Descriptio
mwg0253	baden-wurttemberg	1579	ORTELIUS	550	39	44	Wirtenberg Ducatus Accurata Descriptio; in qua Omnio eius Opida, Monasteria, Pagi Nemora
mwbh0038	belgium holland	1570	ORTELIUS	1650	34	47	Zelandicarum Insularum Exactissima et Nova Descriptio, Auctore D. Iacobo a Daventria (1575 edition illustrated)
mwsp0391	spain regions	1603	ORTELIUS (MINIATURE)	140	8	11	(Cadiz) Gades
mwit0561	italy north	1577	ORTELIUS (MINIATURE)	200	8	11	(Como) Larii Lacus vulgo Comensis
mwaa0069	arctic	1604	ORTELIUS (MINIATURE)	160	10	13	(Kola, Lappland)
mww0105a	world	1601	ORTELIUS (MINIATURE)	750	9	13	(Untitled map by Vrients, illustrated above left)
mwaf0462	africa egypt etc	1577	ORTELIUS (MINIATURE)	160	8	11	Aegiipti recentior descriptio
mwaf0012	africa	1577	ORTELIUS (MINIATURE)	350	8	11	Africae tabula nova (illustrated is c1598 edition)
mwam0010	america continent	1577	ORTELIUS (MINIATURE)	500	8	11	Americae sive novi orbis nova descriptio
mwsp0381	spain regions	1588	ORTELIUS (MINIATURE)	140	8	11	Andaluzia
mwuk0905	england	1577	ORTELIUS (MINIATURE)	300	8	11	Anglia. (title above map)
mwit0259	italy abruzzo	1598	ORTELIUS (MINIATURE)	120	8	11	Aprutium (shown below far left)
mwas0024	asia continent	1602	ORTELIUS (MINIATURE)	350	9	13	Asia
mwas0007	asia continent	1577	ORTELIUS (MINIATURE)	1000	16	21	Asiae nova descr.
mwe0286	europe austria	1577	ORTELIUS (MINIATURE)	200	8	11	Austriae Descriptio
mwaf0682	africa north	1603	ORTELIUS (MINIATURE)	160	8	10	Barbaria, et Biledulgerid
mwaf0678	africa north	1577	ORTELIUS (MINIATURE)	200	8	11	Barbariae et biledulgerid nova descriptio
mwe0524	europe czech republic (bohemia)	1601	ORTELIUS (MINIATURE)	180	8	12	Bohemia
mwbh0073	belgium holland	1577	ORTELIUS (MINIATURE)	180	8	11	Brabantiae
mwg0409a	brandenburg	1577	ORTELIUS (MINIATURE)	200	8	11	Brandeburgens. Marcha (shown is the 1593 Italian edition)
mwit0467	italy lombardy	1602	ORTELIUS (MINIATURE)	180	8	11	Bresciano
mwf0306a	france brittany	1601	ORTELIUS (MINIATURE)	180	8	11	Britannia
mwf0385	france burgundy	1590	ORTELIUS (MINIATURE)	175	8	11	Burgundiae Ducatus
mwf0691	france nord pas-de-calais	1577	ORTELIUS (MINIATURE)	200	8	11	Caletensium bononien (north to the left)
mwgr0365	greece crete	1602	ORTELIUS (MINIATURE)	200	8	10	Candia
mwgr0354	greece crete	1577	ORTELIUS (MINIATURE)	250	8	11	Candia olim Creta
mww0101	world	1598	ORTELIUS (MINIATURE)	600	8	10	Carta Marina (reduced size re-issue of Porcacchi's 1572 map)
mwaf0814	africa north tunisia	1577	ORTELIUS (MINIATURE)	140	8	11	Carthaginis celeberrimi Sinus typus
mwc0008	china	1601	ORTELIUS (MINIATURE)	350	8	11	China Regio Asie (English edition)
mwgr0300	greece corfu	1577	ORTELIUS (MINIATURE)	350	8	11	Corfu
mwf0465	france corsica	1601	ORTELIUS (MINIATURE)	250	8	11	Corsica
mwit0567	italy north	1601	ORTELIUS (MINIATURE)	140	8	11	Cremonensis Ager
mwgr0458	greece cyprus	1577	ORTELIUS (MINIATURE)	800	8	11	Cyprus Insula (illustrated is the 1598 Italian edition)
mwsc0233a	scandinavia denmark	1588	ORTELIUS (MINIATURE)	250	8	11	Daniae regni typus
mwbh0071	belgium holland	1577	ORTELIUS (MINIATURE)	180	8	11	Descript. Frisiae
mwf0025	france	1577	ORTELIUS (MINIATURE)	375	17	22	Descriptio Galliae
mwbh0070	belgium holland	1577	ORTELIUS (MINIATURE)	450	16	21	Descriptio Germaniae Infer.
mwit0560	italy north	1577	ORTELIUS (MINIATURE)	200	8	11	Ducatus Mediolanensis
mwe0014a	europe	1588	ORTELIUS (MINIATURE)	320	8	11	Europa (a later issue shown left)
mwe0011	europe	1577	ORTELIUS (MINIATURE)	600	16	21	Europae
mwaf0772	africa north morocco	1602	ORTELIUS (MINIATURE)	140	9	13	Fessae, et Marocci Regna
mwbh0074	belgium holland	1577	ORTELIUS (MINIATURE)	180	8	11	Flandria
mwit0370	italy friuli	1577	ORTELIUS (MINIATURE)	200	8	11	Fori Iuly vulgo fruili typus
mwg0309	bavaria	1577	ORTELIUS (MINIATURE)	200	8	11	Franciae Orientalis
mwf0027	france	1588	ORTELIUS (MINIATURE)	200	8	11	Gallia (shown below left)
mwbh0163	belgium holland	1603	ORTELIUS (MINIATURE)	200	8	11	Gallia Belgica
mwf1089c	france pyrenees	1577	ORTELIUS (MINIATURE)	200	8	11	Galliae Narbonensis
mwbh0072	belgium holland	1577	ORTELIUS (MINIATURE)	180	8	11	Gelria (north to the right)
mwg0022	germany	1577	ORTELIUS (MINIATURE)	350	16	21	Germania
mwgr0038	greece	1577	ORTELIUS (MINIATURE)	200	8	11	Graecia
mwsw0019	switzerland	1577	ORTELIUS (MINIATURE)	200	8	11	Helvetiae descriptio
mwbh0075	belgium holland	1577	ORTELIUS (MINIATURE)	350	8	11	Hollande (north to the right)
mwe0856	europe hungary	1577	ORTELIUS (MINIATURE)	160	8	11	Hungariae descriptio
mwjk0006	japan	1598	ORTELIUS (MINIATURE)	550	8	10	Iaponia Insula (publ. by Galle. Illustrated below is the 1601 slightly larger edition 9x12cm publ. by Vrients)
mwe0493f	europe croatia	1602	ORTELIUS (MINIATURE)	160	8	11	Illyricum
mwas0373	asia south east	1602	ORTELIUS (MINIATURE)	350	8	12	India Orient
mwuk0007	ireland	1577	ORTELIUS (MINIATURE)	400	8	11	Irlandia (shown left is 1593 version, far left 1604)
mwit0272	italy campagna	1598	ORTELIUS (MINIATURE)	120	8	12	Ischia Ins
mwsc0482	scandinavia iceland	1602	ORTELIUS (MINIATURE)	250	9	13	Islandia
mwit0033	italy	1577	ORTELIUS (MINIATURE)	750	16	21	Italiae Novissim. Descriptio
mwit0048	italy	1598	ORTELIUS (MINIATURE)	240	8	10	Italiae Typus

AMPG REFERENCE	REGION	DATE	MAP MAKER	PRICE (UK£)	VERT. (cm.)	HOR. (cm.)	TITLE OF MAP (Comments by the editor in brackets)
mwsw0042	switzerland	1609	ORTELIUS (MINIATURE)	120	8	13	Lacus Lemani Vicinorumque Locorum Descrip.
mwf0596	france languedoc	1593	ORTELIUS (MINIATURE)	180	8	13	Languedoc
mwf0629	france limousin	1577	ORTELIUS (MINIATURE)	250	8	11	Limaniae Descriptio (North to the right)
mwbp0068	baltic states	1577	ORTELIUS (MINIATURE)	250	8	11	Livoniae Nova Descriptio Ioanne Portantio Autore (illustrated is c1610 edition)
mwbh0816a	luxembourg	1598	ORTELIUS (MINIATURE)	200	9	11	Lutzeburg
mwm0172	mediterranean malta	1577	ORTELIUS (MINIATURE)	400	8	11	Malta olim. Melita Insula
mwg0757a	westphalia	1577	ORTELIUS (MINIATURE)	160	8	11	Monasteriensis et Osnaburgensis Episcopatus Descriptio (south at the top)
mwe1087	europe slovak republic (moravi	1577	ORTELIUS (MINIATURE)	180	8	11	Moraviae pars
mwme0928	turkey etc	1577	ORTELIUS (MINIATURE)	180	8	11	Natioliae quae oli asia minor nova descriptio (south to the top)
mwf0764	france normandy	1588	ORTELIUS (MINIATURE)	140	8	10	Normandia
mwbp0215	poland	1603	ORTELIUS (MINIATURE)	180	8	11	Oswiecz, et Zator
mwg0308	bavaria	1577	ORTELIUS (MINIATURE)	200	8	11	Palatinatus Bavariae
mwme0043	holy land	1577	ORTELIUS (MINIATURE)	400	8	11	Palestinae sive Totius Terrae Promissionis Nova Descriptio
mwit1168	italy veneto	1600	ORTELIUS (MINIATURE)	160	8	10	Patavinum Teritor.
mwit0632	italy piedmont	1577	ORTELIUS (MINIATURE)	200	8	11	Pedemontiae
mwme0758	persia etc	1577	ORTELIUS (MINIATURE)	180	8	11	Persici sive Sophorum Regni Tipus
mwbp0188	poland	1577	ORTELIUS (MINIATURE)	280	8	11	Poloniae Descrip.
mwbp0185	poland	1577	ORTELIUS (MINIATURE)	160	8	11	Pomeraniae
mwsp0004	portugal	1577	ORTELIUS (MINIATURE)	200	8	11	Portugalliae que olim Lusitania novissima
mwaf0347	africa east	1577	ORTELIUS (MINIATURE)	200	8	11	Presbiteri Johannis
mwf0997	france provence	1612	ORTELIUS (MINIATURE)	200	8	11	Provincia
mwbp0186	poland	1577	ORTELIUS (MINIATURE)	160	8	11	Prussiae descrip. (north to the left)
mwf0422	france central	1577	ORTELIUS (MINIATURE)	200	8	11	Regionis Biturigum
mwe0517	europe czech republic (bohemi	1577	ORTELIUS (MINIATURE)	250	8	11	Regni Bohemiae descriptio
mwsp0163	spain	1577	ORTELIUS (MINIATURE)	200	8	11	Regni Hispaniae post omnium editi
mwit0989	italy south	1577	ORTELIUS (MINIATURE)	200	8	11	Regni Neapolitani verissima secundu
mwe0753	europe east	1609	ORTELIUS (MINIATURE)	180	9	12	Romania, Bulgaria, Walachia et Syrfia
mwru0018	russia	1577	ORTELIUS (MINIATURE)	280	8	11	Russiae moscovia et tartariae
mwf1103	france rhone-alpes	1577	ORTELIUS (MINIATURE)	300	8	11	Sabaudiae et Burgudiae (north to the left)
mwe0287	europe austria	1577	ORTELIUS (MINIATURE)	180	8	11	Salisburgensis Iurisdictio
mwit0776	italy sardinia	1577	ORTELIUS (MINIATURE)	250	8	11	Sardinia (also issued with the title 'Sardigna')
mwg0554	saxony	1577	ORTELIUS (MINIATURE)	160	8	11	Saxoniae misniae
mwuk0315	scotland	1577	ORTELIUS (MINIATURE)	450	8	11	Scotia. (title above map)
mwsc0023	scandinavia	1577	ORTELIUS (MINIATURE)	450	8	11	Septentronalium regionum descriptio
mwit0867	italy sicily	1577	ORTELIUS (MINIATURE)	250	8	11	Siciliae descriptio
mwbp0187	poland	1577	ORTELIUS (MINIATURE)	160	8	11	Silesiae typus
mwe1122	europe slovenia	1577	ORTELIUS (MINIATURE)	200	8	11	Slavoniae Croatiae Carniae Istriae Bosniae descrip
mwru0415	russia tartary	1577	ORTELIUS (MINIATURE)	300	8	11	Tartariae sive Magni Chami regni typus
mwat0077	atlantic azores	1612	ORTELIUS (MINIATURE)	140	8	11	Tercera
mwg0686	schleswig-holstein	1577	ORTELIUS (MINIATURE)	150	8	11	Thietmarsia (north to the left)
mwit1092	italy tuscany	1577	ORTELIUS (MINIATURE)	200	8	11	Thusciae
mww0066	world	1577	ORTELIUS (MINIATURE)	1800	16	22	Tiipus orbis Terrarum ... 1574
mwg0307	bavaria	1577	ORTELIUS (MINIATURE)	200	8	11	Tipus Vindeliciae
mwit0572	italy north	1612	ORTELIUS (MINIATURE)	140	8	11	Tirolis Comitat.
mwe0747	europe east	1577	ORTELIUS (MINIATURE)	140	8	11	Transilvania
mwme0537	arabia etc	1577	ORTELIUS (MINIATURE)	250	8	11	Turcici Imperii descriptio
mww0074	world	1588	ORTELIUS (MINIATURE)	600	8	11	Typus Orbis Terrarum (replaces his 1577 map)
mww0105b	world	1601	ORTELIUS (MINIATURE)	750	8	12	Typus Orbis Terrarum (Mercator's Projection)
mwsp0382	spain regions	1588	ORTELIUS (MINIATURE)	140	8	11	Valentia Regnum
mwf0692	france nord pas-de-calais	1577	ORTELIUS (MINIATURE)	200	8	11	Veromaduorum (north to the left)
mwg0769	westphalia	1601	ORTELIUS (MINIATURE)	140	8	11	Westfalia
mwg0252	baden-wurttemberg	1577	ORTELIUS (MINIATURE)	160	8	11	Wirtenbergiensis
mwe0493g	europe dalmatia	1602	ORTELIUS (MINIATURE)	160	8	11	Zara, & Sebenic
mwbh0076	belgium holland	1577	ORTELIUS (MINIATURE)	180	8	11	Zelandicarum Insularum descrip.
mwjk0134a	japan	1808	(OSAKA)	5000	144	242	(Dai Nippon Saiken Shisho Zenzu)
mwec0295b	uk england devon	1748	OSBORNE	140	14	17	A Correct Map of Devon Shire
mwam0952	america north (east)	1745	OSBORNE	600	34	30	A Map of the Brittish Plantations on the Continent of America
mwe0400	europe austria	1823	OSTELL	50	20	25	Austria
mww0671	world	1823	OSTELL	250	22	35	Chart of the World
mwbh0792	belgium holland	1823	OSTELL	60	25	20	Netherlands.
mwsw0225	switzerland	1823	OSTELL	60	19	25	Switzerland
mwuk1370	england north east	1818	OTLEY	350	31	26	A New Map of the Lakes in Cumberland, Westmorland
mwuk0476	scotland	1739	OTTENS	750	49	57	(Shetland Isl.) Nieuwe Paskaard van Hitland met de daar Omleggende Eylanden
mwgm0106	guatemala	1740	OTTENS	675	41	56	(untitled map of Guatemala etc with 2 large insets: Acapulco harbour and Vera-Cruz. From the six-sheet map 'Grand Theatre de la Guerre en Amerique'. See 'West Indies', 1740)
mwe0137	europe	1720	OTTENS	750	48	57	Accuratissima Europae Tabula
mwf0108	france	1720	OTTENS	480	48	57	Accuratissima Galliae Tabula Gallis vulgo Dicta le Royaume de France
mwbp0387	poland	1725	OTTENS	960	48	87	Accuratissima Regni Poloniae Nova Tabula

AMPG REFERENCE	REGION	DATE	MAP MAKER	PRICE (UK£)	VERT. (cm.)	HOR. (cm.)	TITLE OF MAP (Comments by the editor in brackets)
mwbh0642	belgium holland	1740	OTTENS	3600	50	144	Afbeeldinge van de Maes van de Stadt Rotterdam tot in Zee
mwam0150	america continent	1740	OTTENS	24000	136	170	America Gedruckt tot Amsterdam by R and J Ottens op den Niewe Druk uit der Wereldt Kaart
mwam0384	america north	1730	OTTENS	1600	48	58	Amerique Septentrionale Divisee en ses Principales Parties. Presente a Monseigneur le Duc de Bourgogne
mwas0135	asia continent	1730	OTTENS	18000	100	240	Asia
mwbh0664	belgium holland	1745	OTTENS	580	52	60	Belgii Regii ... Auctore Fredericum De Witt
mwgr0184	greece	1745	OTTENS	400	48	58	Carte de la Grece (also issued with border plans and view 58x86cm)
mwam0923	america north (east)	1720	OTTENS	2500	50	55	Carte de la Nouvelle France, ou se Voit le Cours des Grandes Rivieres de S. Laurens & de Mississipi ... de la Floride, de la Louisiane, de la Virginie, de la Marie-Lande, de la Pensilvanie, du Nouveau Jersay, de la Nouvelle Yorck (based on De Fer 1719)
mwru0509	ukraine	1725	OTTENS	875	50	59	Carte de la Petite Tartarie et la Mer Noire
mwit1200	italy veneto	1765	OTTENS	720	39	44	Carte de Territoire de Padouan, et le Dogado de le Repub. de Venise (3 insets)
mwm0098	mediterranean adriatic	1745	OTTENS	300	27	40	Carte du Golfe de Venise (also issued with 3 insets in extended lower border)
mwsp0262	spain	1740	OTTENS	650	48	58	Carte Generale des Royaumes d'Espagne & de Portugal (close copy of Schenk 1706)
mwsc0131	scandinavia	1730	OTTENS	685	51	58	Carte la Plus Nouvelle de la Scandinavie ou les Couronnes du Nord (inset: Iceland)
mwas0315	asia caspian sea	1723	OTTENS	1500	89	60	Carte Marine de la Mer Caspiene (based on De L'isle but incl. 4 inset views.)
mwru0163	russia	1730	OTTENS	480	82	55	Carte Nouvelle de Moscovie Represente la Partie Septentrionale / Partie Meridionale de Moscovie Dressee par G. De L'Isle (2 maps, joined)
mwru0153	russia	1724	OTTENS	960	47	65	Carte Nouvelle de Tout l'Empire de la Grande Russie dans l'Estat ou il s'est Trouve a la Mort de Pierre le Grand
mwbh0876	luxembourg	1750	OTTENS	350	48	60	Carte Nouvelle du Duche de Luxembourg
mwaf0921	africa south	1745	OTTENS	900	42	53	Cimbebas et Caffariae Littora a Catenbela ad Promontorium Bonae Spei - Pascaerte van Cimbebas en Caffares Streckende van Catembela tot Cabo de Bona Esperanca (inset of Cape Peninsula)
mwe0363a	europe austria	1740	OTTENS	500	49	58	Circuli Austriaci
mwg0648a	saxony	1745	OTTENS	550	49	57	Circulis Saxoniae Inferioris
mwsc0349	scandinavia denmark	1720	OTTENS	675	51	58	Daniae Regnum in quo sunt Ducatus Holsatia et Slesvicum Insulae Danicae et Provinciae Iutia Scania Blekingia et Hallandia
mwsc0361	scandinavia denmark	1745	OTTENS	1200	49	57	Daniae, Frisiae, Groningae et Orientalis Frisiae Littora (re-issue of de Wit's chart)
mwbh0588	belgium holland	1720	OTTENS	480	59	50	Ducatus Geldriae nova tabula
mwbp0396	poland	1730	OTTENS	960	50	58	Ducatus Poloniae, Ducatus Mazoviae et Province Cujaviae Descriptio Emendata
mwbp0118	baltic states	1730	OTTENS	650	46	56	Ducatuum Livoniae et Curlandiae Novissima Tabula in quibus sunt Estonia Litlandia et aliae Minores Provinciae
mwas0148	asia continent	1740	OTTENS	600	50	58	Exactissima Asiae Delineatio (re-issue of De Wit 1680)
mwsc0619	scandinavia norway	1745	OTTENS	900	49	57	Finmarchiae et Laplandiae Maritimae
mwbh0696	belgium holland	1750	OTTENS	320	33	42	Friesland
mwf0295	france bay of biscay	1745	OTTENS	875	48	56	Galliae, Biscajae et Gallissiae Sinus
mwbh0689	belgium holland	1748	OTTENS	1800	114	157	Generale Kaart van Zuyd Holland, Utrecht en het Meerder Deel van Gelderland
mwwi0078	west indies	1740	OTTENS	12000	85	159	Grand Theatre de la Guerre en Amerique
mwaa0192	arctic / antarctic	1745	OTTENS	2000	46	46	Hemisphere Meridional pour Voir Plus Distinctement les Terres Australes / ... les Terres Arctiques (2 maps)
mwaa0192	antarctic	1745	OTTENS	1600	46		Hemisphere Meridional pour Voir Plus Distinctement les Terres Australes (based on De L'Isle. Incl. Bouvet's discoveries in 1739, lower right. As the southern half of the previous item, but with a right-hand text panel added)
mwme0303	holy land	1740	OTTENS	650	50	59	Het Beloofde Landt Israels. Terra Sancta, sive Promissionis, olim Palestina (close copy of Visscher 1659)
mwsp0268	spain	1745	OTTENS	900	49	56	Hispaniae et Portugalliae Maritimi Tractus, a' S. Andero, ad Malagam - Pascaert van Spangiae, en Portugal
mwsc0705a	scandinavia sweden	1710	OTTENS	3000	52	60	Holmia, Regia Sedes et Caput Totius Sueciae, cum Omnium Suburbis (title also in Dutch. North to the left)
mwjk0096	japan	1745	OTTENS	3000	47	60	Imperium Japonicum
mwwi0081	west indies	1745	OTTENS	2250	48	56	Indiarum Occidentalium Tractus Littorales cum Insulis Caribicis - Pascaert van Westindien ende Caribise Eylanden
mwin0038	ceylon	1725	OTTENS	675	56	58	Insula Ceilon et Madura
mwwi0062	west indies	1726	OTTENS	1600	49	58	Insulae Americanae, Nempe: Cuba, Hispaniola, Jamaica, Pto Rico, Lucania, Antillae vulgo Caribae, Barlo-et Sotto-Vento, etc.
mwit0941	italy sicily	1740	OTTENS	650	51	58	Insulae et Regni Siciliae Novissima Tabula - Carte de L'Isle et Royaume de Sicilie (inset of Malta. Map by De L'Isle)

AMPG REFERENCE	REGION	DATE	MAP MAKER	PRICE (UK£)	VERT. (cm.)	HOR. (cm.)	TITLE OF MAP (Comments by the editor in brackets)
mwf0341	france brittany	1700	OTTENS	580	46	62	La Bretagne Divisee en ses Neuf Evesches
mwuk1580	channel islands	1740	OTTENS	480	50	60	La Plus Grande Partie de la Manche (excl. western part)
mwf1048	france provence	1720	OTTENS	450	46	61	La Provence Divisee en ses Vigueries et Terres Adjacentes
mwaf0177	africa	1740	OTTENS	750	46	59	L'Afrique Divisee en ses Empires, Royaumes et Etats
mwsam0054	south america	1715	OTTENS	785	48	60	L'Amerique Meridionale Divisee en ses Principales Parties
mwam0388	america north	1740	OTTENS	1600	45	59	L'Amerique Septentrionale Dressee sur les Observations de Mrs. de l'Academie Royale des Sciences ... Par G. de l'Isle
mwbh0597	belgium holland	1725	OTTENS	600	51	58	Land Caerte van 't Verenigde Nederland, met 'tgene daer Onderhoort, Verdeelt in sijn Provincien
mwf0786	france normandy	1720	OTTENS	675	50	59	Le Gouvernement de Normandie & une Partie de l'Isle de France (2 sheets, each 50x59cm)
mwsc0356a	scandinavia denmark	1740	OTTENS	450	49	60	Le Royaume de Danemark (title above map: Nova Daniae Regni ...)
mwas0460	asia south east	1740	OTTENS	2400	77	55	Le Royaume de Siam avec les Royaumes qui luy sont Tributaires, et les Isles de Sumatra, Andemaon, etc. et les Isles Voisine (2 sheets joined)
mwg0114	germany	1725	OTTENS	500	48	61	L'Empire d'Allemagne Divise en Tous ses Estats
mwuk0817	uk	1740	OTTENS	750	47	59	Les Isles Britanniques qui Contiennent les Royaumes d'Angleterre, Escosse, et Irlande
mwsp0249	spain	1720	OTTENS	675	45	58	L'Espagne Divisee en Tous ses Royaumes et Principautes, &c.
mwe0160	europe	1740	OTTENS	450	52	62	L'Europe representee par la Geographie Naturelle et Historique
mwit0172	italy	1740	OTTENS	500	50	63	L'Italie Dressee sur les Observations de l'Academie Royale des Sciences sur celles du R.P. Riccoli (re-issue of De L'Isle, 1700)
mwsam0366	south america brazil	1745	OTTENS	960	48	56	Littora Brasiliae. Pascaert van Brasil (re-issue of De Wit 1675)
mwbp0115	baltic states	1726	OTTENS	720	49	57	Magni Ducatus Lithuaniae
mwp0249	pacific (all)	1745	OTTENS	1800	50	57	Magnum Mare del Zur cum Insula California. De Groote Zuyd-Zee en 't Eylandt California (re-issue of De Wit 1675)
mwuk1669	north sea	1745	OTTENS	1500	49	57	Mare Germanicum ac Tractus Maritimus retro Hiberniam et Scotiam - Pascaert vande Noort Zee om Achter Yrland en Schotland om te Seylen
mwaf0746	africa north algeria	1732	OTTENS	500	42	55	Nette Aftekening der Stad Oran &c. Gelegen in Barbaryen Opgedragen aan den Ed. Heer Cornelis Schryver (inset coastal view)
mwaf0903	africa south	1725	OTTENS	960	44	55	Nieuwe Caarte van Kaap de Goede Hoop en't Zuyderdeel van Africa (copied by Lakeman in 1727)
mwsp0549	spain regions	1740	OTTENS	875	49	58	Nieuwe en naukeurige kaart van het zuidelijkste gedeelte van Spanje genaant Andalusie
mwsam0599	south america guyana	1740	OTTENS	2250	49	96	Nieuwe Gemeten Kaart van de Colonie de Berbice (inset of Surinam)
mwbh0643	belgium holland	1740	OTTENS	785	58	51	Nieuwe Kaart van de XVII Nederlandsche Provincien
mwwi0851	st eustatia	1775	OTTENS	1250	37	49	Nieuwe Kaart van het Eyland St. Eustatius
mwsam0591	south america guyana	1710	OTTENS	875	41	52	Nieuwe Kaart van Suriname Vertonende de Stromen en Landstreken van Suriname Comowini, Cottica, en Marawini
mwsc0622	scandinavia norway	1745	OTTENS	800	49	57	Nieuwe Pascaert vande kusten Finmarcken en Lapland (revised version of De Wit)
mwbp0398	poland	1730	OTTENS	1250	102	59	Nieuwe zeer ... Caart vande River de Don
mwru0158	russia	1729	OTTENS	1500	104	61	Nieuwe Zeer Accurate, en Naauwkeurige Caarte vande Rivier de Don of Tanais ... te Amsterdam by R. & J. Ottens op den Nieuwen Dyk in de Werelt Kaart
mwsc0613a	scandinavia norway	1730	OTTENS	650	59	51	Norvegia Regnum Divisum in suos Dioeceses Nidrosiensem, Bergensem, Opsloensem, et Stavangriensem et Praefecturam Bahusiae (close copy of Homann 1720)
mwit0431	italy liguria	1740	OTTENS	1250	36	45	Nouvelle Carte de l'Etat et de la Republique de Genes (3 insets incl. Corsica)
mwf0516	france corsica	1765	OTTENS	875	51	59	Nouvelle Carte de l'Isle de Corse
mwaf0751	africa north algeria	1765	OTTENS	600	43	56	Nouvelle Carte du Roiaume d'Alger, Divisee en Toutes ses Provinces (inset: Bay of Algiers)
mwe0684	europe dalmatia	1740	OTTENS	550	46	58	Nouvelle Carte du Royaume de Dalmacie Divise en ses Comtes, Territoires etc. La Morlaquie, la Bosnie, et la Servie, Partie de la Hongrie, Croatie, Albanie, Istrie, & du Roye. de Naples
mwas0453	asia south east	1725	OTTENS	4000	49	59	Nouvelle Grande Carte des Indes Orientales (in 4 sheets, each 49x59cm)
mww0363	world	1730	OTTENS	12000	51	143	Nova & Accuratissima Totius Terrarum Orbis Tabula Nautica Variatum Magneticarum Index Juxta Observationes Anno 1700 Habitas Constructa per Edm: Halley (as Halley's chart of 1701 but with small changes)
mwas0309	asia caspian sea	1719	OTTENS	675	49	61	Nova ac Verissima Maris Caspii ... ac Regionum Adjacentium Delineatio
mwru0155	russia	1725	OTTENS	2500	50	59	Nova ac Verissima Urbis St. Petersburg ab Imperatore Russico Petro Alexii (large inset of environs)

AMPG REFERENCE	REGION	DATE	MAP MAKER	PRICE (UK£)	VERT. (cm.)	HOR. (cm.)	TITLE OF MAP (Comments by the editor in brackets)
mwgr0319	greece corfu	1717	OTTENS	1650	52	41	Nova et Accurata Geographica Tabula Insula Corfu (2 large insets)
mwaf0891a	africa south	1702	OTTENS?	4000	57	48	Nova et Accurata Tabula Promontorii Bonae Speii, Vulgo Cabo de Bona Esperanca. Nieuwe Naaukeurige Land-en Zee-Kaart, van het voornaamste Gedeelte der Kaffersche Kust, Begrypende de Sardanje-Bay en de Caap de Bonne Esperanca met alle des Zelfs Plantazien.
mww0390	world	1745	OTTENS	1500	52	60	Nova et Accuratissima Totius Terrarum Orbis Tabula
mwg0127	germany	1745	OTTENS	550	50	59	Nova et prae caeteris aliis Correcta Germaniae
mwgm0397a	panama	1730	OTTENS	960	41	54	Nova Isthmi Americani, qui et Panamiensis Item Dariensis, Tabula in qua Urbes Porto Bello, Panama et Carthagena (part of a six-sheet map, under 'West Indies')
mwme0611	arabia etc	1730	OTTENS	650	47	56	Nova Persiae Armeniae Natoliae et Arabiae per Fred: De Witt
mwsp0083	portugal	1725	OTTENS	750	49	58	Nova Regni Portugalliae et Algarbiae Descriptio
mwwi0318a	bahamas	1730	OTTENS	2000	46	54	Nova Tabula Exhibens Insulas Cubam et Hispaniolam vulgo S. Domingo Dictam Insulas Lucaias seu Bahamanas ac Peninsulam Floridae (title under insets. Part of a six-sheet map, under 'West Indies')
mww0391	world	1745	OTTENS	5500	48	55	Nova Totius Terrarum Orbis Tabula (re-issue of De Wit's map of c1670)
mwe1050	europe romania	1745	OTTENS	580	50	59	Nova Transilvaniae Principatus Tabula
mwsw0138	switzerland	1740	OTTENS	600	48	56	Novissima et Accuratissima Helvetiae, Rhaetiae, Valesiae, et Partis Sabaudiae Tabula ex Officina R. & I. Ottens Amst: Cum Privil. Ordin. Hollandiae et Westensfrisiae
mwsp0263	spain	1740	OTTENS	1800	91	116	Novissima et Accuratissima Tabula qua Gallaeciae et Legionis Regna, Asturiarum / Regnorum Arragoniae et Navarrae, Principatus Cataloniae (4 maps joined. Top 2 titles visible. Updated version of Allard 1700)
mwe0799a	europe east	1745	OTTENS	750	50	88	Novissima Tabula Regni Hungariae et Regionum quondam ei unitarum
mwin0483	indian ocean west	1745	OTTENS	1000	44	54	Occidentalior Tractus Indiarum Orientalium a Promontorio Bonae Spei ad C. Comorin
mwm0059	mediterranean	1747	OTTENS	3200	47	59	Orientalior Districtus Maris Mediterranei. t'Ooster Gedeelte van de Middelandse Zee / Occidentalior Tractus (2 maps, each 47x59cm)
mwas0466	asia south east	1745	OTTENS	2000	44	53	Orientaliora Indiarum Orientalium cum Insulis Adjacentibus a Promontorio C. Comorin ad Iapan - Pascaert van t'Ooster Gedeelte van Oost Indien van C. Comorin tot Iapan (re-issue of De Wit 1680)
mwuk1670	north sea	1745	OTTENS	900	47	58	Pascaert van de Noord Zee van Ameland tot de Hoofden - Mare Germanicum ab Amelandia ad Promontoria Caleti et Doverae
mwsc0621	scandinavia norway	1745	OTTENS	950	49	56	Pascaert van Noorwegen Streckende van Els-Burg tot Dronten (revised version of De Wit 1675)
mwru0533	ukraine	1745	OTTENS	800	42	59	Pontus Euxinus of Niewe en Naaukeurige Paskaart van de Zwarte Zee
mwam0139	america continent	1727	OTTENS	1200	50	57	Recentissima Novi Orbis sive Americae Septentrionalis et Meridionalis Tabula
mwuk0987a	england	1735	OTTENS	720	50	58	Regni Angliae Nova Tabula (revised edition of De Ram c1689)
mwbp0397	poland	1730	OTTENS	720	49	57	Regni Poloniae et Ducatus Lithuaniae
mwme0819a	persia etc	1740	OTTENS	1000	50	88	Regnum Persicum Imperium Turcicum in Asia, Russorum Provinciae ad Maris Caspium
mwbp0447	poland	1752	OTTENS	580	51	64	Reipublicae et Status Generalis Poloniae Nova Tabula, Comprehendens Maioris et Minoris Poloniae Regni Magni Ducatus Lithuaniae Ducatus Prussiae, Curlandiae ... Amstelodami Apud R. et J. Ottens
mwg0126	germany	1745	OTTENS	650	50	69	Routes des Postes et des Voitures pour les Marchandises et pour les Voyages par l'Empire
mwru0216	russia	1750	OTTENS	650	49	56	Russiae et Novae Zemlae Maritimae (re-issue of Renard 1715)
mwsc0711	scandinavia sweden	1720	OTTENS	300	16	20	Saltholm und Drako mit den Zeichen aus der See (6 maps on one sheet)
mwit0365	italy emilia-romagna	1765	OTTENS	550	57	48	Sedes Belli in Italia; in qua sunt, Ducatus Mantuensis, Modenensis
mwca0061	canada	1745	OTTENS	2400	48	119	Septemtrionaliora Americae a Groenlandia, per Freta Davidis et Hudson, ad Terram Novam / Nieuwe Algemeene Kaart van Groenland en Straet Davids naar de Allernieuwst Ondekkingen int Licht Gebracht (2 maps, sometimes joined)
mwsp0547a	spain regions	1740	OTTENS	875	34	50	Sevillia (shown below left)
mwwi0245	west indies (east)	1740	OTTENS	720	60	50	Tabula novissima atque accuratissima Caraibicarum insularum sive Cannibalum

AMPG REFERENCE	REGION	DATE	MAP MAKER	PRICE (UK£)	VERT. (cm.)	HOR. (cm.)	TITLE OF MAP (Comments by the editor in brackets)
mwwi0060	west indies	1720	OTTENS	1000	57	50	Tabula Novissima atque Accuratissima Caraibicarum Insularum sive Cannibalum quae etiam Antille Gallicae Dicuntur Item Insulae Supraventum, et in Archipelago Mexicano (inset: Martinique)
mwat0345	atlantic west	1745	OTTENS	1100	48	56	Terra Neuf, en de Custen van Nieuw Vranckryck, Nieu Engeland, Nieu Nederland, Nieu Andalusia, Guiana en Venezuela (based on De Wit 1680)
mwru0180	russia	1737	OTTENS	720	48	67	Theatre de la Guerre contre les Turcs & les Tartares
mwe1051	europe romania	1756	OTTENS	875	51	53	Theatre de la Guerre dans le Bannat de Temeswar Divise dans Tout ses Districts Mesure sur les Lieux
mwe0163	europe	1745	OTTENS	5500	50	88	Totius Europae Littora Novissime Edita
mwuss1082	new york	1725	OTTENS	6000	47	55	Totius Neobelgii Nova et Accuratissima Tabula
mwsam0234	south america argentina	1745	OTTENS	1000	48	55	Tractus Australior Americae Meridionalis, a Rio de la Plata per Fretum Magellanicum ad Toraltum - Nieuwe Perfecte Pascaert van 't Suyderlyckste Deel van Suyt America, van Rio de la Plata door de Straet Magellaen tot Toral (re-issue of De Wit 1675)
mwaf1203	africa west	1745	OTTENS	750	49	56	Tractus Littorales Guineae a Promontorio Verde usque ad Sinum Catenbelae (re-issue of De Wit 1680)
mww0368	world	1733	OTTENS-PANSER	2000	47	64	Vertoning van de merkwaardige zons-verduistering ofte groot zon-eclips …1733
mwsw0101a	switzerland	1707	OTTO	1200	52	81	Carte Geographique de la Souverainete de Neufchâtel et Vallangin en Suisse (copy of De Merveilleux's map of 1694)
mwsc0729	scandinavia sweden	1746	OUTHIER	250	16	18	Plan de la Ville de Falun
mwsc0730	scandinavia sweden	1746	OUTHIER	500	23	19	Plan de la Ville de Stockhom
mwsc0435	scandinavia finland	1746	OUTHIER	400	16	24	Veue de la Ville et des Environs de Tornea
mwit0049	italy	1598	OVERADT	15000	53	74	Italia Totius Europae Brachiu (map surrounded by text on 3 sides)
mwg0033	germany	1598	OVERRADT	2500	37	49	Germania Totius Europae Regnum Amplissimum ac Florentissimum Sedes Imperatoria
mwsp0700a	gibraltar	1727	OVERTON	1250	40	47	A Map of the Coast of Spain, from the Streights of Gibralter to the Gulf of Cartagena / A New Plan of the Garrison of Gibralter, with its Fortifications &c. 1726
mwuk0978	england	1719	OVERTON	4800	58	98	A New & Correct Map of England & Wales Now Called South Britain
mww0192	world	1670	OVERTON	15000	39	51	A New and Accurate Map of the World Drawne According to the Best and Late Discoveries Anno Dom 1670
mwam0389	america north	1741	OVERTON	24000	56	100	A New and Correct Map of the Trading Part of the West Indies (10 views of ports in side borders incl. New York and Boston. California shown as an island)
mwuk1153	england london	1720	OVERTON	1800	63	95	A New and Correct Map of Thirty Miles round London
mww0339	world	1720	OVERTON	9850	58	95	A New and Correct Map of ye World
mwe0134	europe	1719	OVERTON	2000	61	99	A New and Correct Mapp of Europe
mwuk0726a	uk	1667	OVERTON	5000	42	53	A new and Exact Map of Great Britannie (insets incl. the Fire of London 1666)
mwbh0538	belgium holland	1709	OVERTON	875	58	85	A New and Exact Map of the Theatre of War in Flanders & Holland Commonly Called the 17 Provinces
mwuk0796	uk	1716	OVERTON	7200	57	96	A New And Exact Mapp Of Great Britain And Ireland … 1716 (12 side border insets of ports)
mwuk0459a	scotland	1715	OVERTON	1650	88	51	A New and Exact Mapp of Scotland or North-Britain Described by N. Sanson
mwuk1154	england london	1720	OVERTON	6000	58	97	A New and Exact Plan of the City of London and Suburbs thereto (5 editions until 1739. From the 1730 edition the map was extended to 58x145cm).
mwaf0079	africa	1671	OVERTON	6500	43	53	A New and Most Exact Map of Africa Described by N.I. Vischer and Don into English Enlarged and Corrected According to I. Blaeu and Others with ye Habits of ye People & ye Manner of ye Cheife Sitties ye Like Never Before (4 carte-a-figure borders)
mwam0074	america continent	1671	OVERTON	15000	43	55	A New and Most Exact Map of America Described by N.I. Visscher and Don into English Enlarged and Corrected According to I. Bleau and Others
mwe0080a	europe	1671	OVERTON	5500	43	55	A New and most Exact map of Europe Described by NI Vischer and don into English and corected according to I. Bleau and Others with ye Habits of ye people & ye manner of ye cheife citties the like never before (shown above left)
mwuk1122a	england london	1676	OVERTON	4800	44	58	A New And Plaine Mapp Of The City Of London
mwec0036	uk england berkshire	1670	OVERTON	1200	27	50	A New Map of Barkshire
mwuk0114	ireland	1691	OVERTON	875	60	51	A New Map of Ireland
mwec1161	uk england sussex	1672	OVERTON	1600	31	48	A New Map of Sussex Corrected and Amended with all the Hundred
mwuk1187	england london	1749	OVERTON	4500	57	98	A New Map of the Cities of London and Westminster (reprinted 1756)

AMPG REFERENCE	REGION	DATE	MAP MAKER	PRICE (UK£)	VERT. (cm.)	HOR. (cm.)	TITLE OF MAP (Comments by the editor in brackets)
mwec1329	uk england yorkshire	1728	OVERTON	2400	56	95	A New Map of the County of York Laid Down from an Actual Survey
mwm0015	mediterranean	1670	OVERTON	3000	50	86	A New Map of the Mediterranean Sea
mwec0740	uk england lincolnshire	1670	OVERTON	1200	39	48	A New Mapp of Lincoln Shire with the Post & Cross Roads, & Other Remarks,
mwec0912	uk england nottinghamshire	1714	OVERTON	875	35	49	A New Mapp of Nottingham Shire with the Post & Cross Roads, & other Remarks, According to ye Latest & Best Observations
mwuk1140	england london	1706	OVERTON	3000	64	99	A New Mapp of the Citty of London Much Inlarged
mwec0178	uk england cornwall	1712	OVERTON	1800	37	49	A New Mapp of the County of Cornwall, with the Post & Cross Roads, & other Remarks, According to the Latest & Best Observations 1712
mwec0393	uk england essex	1603	OVERTON	1600	41	52	A New Mapp of the County of Essex, with the Post and Cross Roads, &c. other Remarks According to the Latest and Best Observations
mwec0825	uk england norfolk	1713	OVERTON	1200	33	48	A New Mapp of the County of Norfolk, with the Post and Cross Roads
mwec1103	uk england suffolk	1713	OVERTON	1200	33	47	A New Mapp of the County of Suffolk; with the Post ... Roads
mwsp0045	portugal	1675	OVERTON	785	58	48	A New Mapp of the Kingdom of Portugal and Algarve Divided into its Archbishopricks, Bishopricks and Territory's
mwas0057	asia continent	1671	OVERTON	5000	43	54	A New Plaine and Exact Map of Asia Described by N. I. Vischer and Rendered into English with the Habits of the Countries and Manner of the Cheife Citties (4 carte-a-figure borders)
mwuk1165	england london	1731	OVERTON	1350	26	51	A Pocket Map of London, Westminster and Southwark (5 editions to 1741)
mwme0502	jerusalem	1752	OVERTON	6000	47	74	An Exact Draught of the City of Jerusalem and the Appurtenances Belonging to the Temple with the Genealogy of Jesus Christ our Saviour in the Border thereof
mwme0255	holy land	1715	OVERTON	2000	60	102	Geographia Sacra, or New & Compendious Maps of the Holy Land
mwec0445	uk england gloucestershire	1712	OVERTON	650	40	50	Glocester Shire and Monmouth Shire
mwec0470	uk england hampshire	1670	OVERTON	2500	40	42	Hamshire (map by Norden, c1603)
mwuk0141	ireland	1715	OVERTON	2000	100	59	Ireland Corrected From The Latest Observations (inset of the UK)
mwec0855	uk england northamptonshire	1675	OVERTON	1400	36	48	Northamptoniae Comitatus Descriptio
mwec0953	uk england oxfordshire	1715	OVERTON	2400	58	89	Oxfordshire Actualy Survey'd &c
mwec1064	uk england staffordshire	1670	OVERTON	1400	34	47	Staffordiae Comitatus
mwec1131	uk england surrey	1670	OVERTON	1800	38	48	Surriae Comitatus Continens in se Oppida Mercatoria
mwuk0970	england	1712	OVERTON	900	28	27	The Roads of England According to Ogilby's Survey
mwaf0161	africa	1727	OVERTON	2500	57	97	To Her Most Sacret Majesty Caroline ... this Mapp of Africa (13 insets in side borders)
mwas0132	asia continent	1727	OVERTON	2800	56	97	To Her Most Sacret Majesty Caroline ... this Mapp of Asia
mwec1330	uk england yorkshire	1728	OVERTON & BOWLES	1250	56	95	A New Map of the County of York Laid Down from an Actual Survey
mwuk1816	wales	1720	OWEN & BOWEN	100	19	12	(Radnor)
mwuk1817	wales	1720	OWEN & BOWEN	100	19	12	A Map of Brecknock Shire
mwec0096	uk england cambridgeshire	1720	OWEN & BOWEN	100	18	12	A Map of Cambridge Shire
mwuk1818	wales	1720	OWEN & BOWEN	100	19	12	A Map of Cardiganshire
mwuk1819	wales	1720	OWEN & BOWEN	100	19	12	A Map of Carmarthen Shire
mwec0139	uk england cheshire	1720	OWEN & BOWEN	100	18	12	A Map of Che-shire
mwec0179	uk england cornwall	1720	OWEN & BOWEN	120	18	12	A Map of Cornwall
mwec0263	uk england derbyshire	1720	OWEN & BOWEN	100	18	12	A Map of Darby Shire
mwuk1820	wales	1720	OWEN & BOWEN	100	19	12	A Map of Denbigh-Shire
mwec0369	uk england durham	1720	OWEN & BOWEN	100	18	12	A Map of Durham
mwec0407	uk england essex	1720	OWEN & BOWEN	100	18	12	A Map of Essex
mwec0477	uk england hampshire	1720	OWEN & BOWEN	100	18	12	A Map of Hamp Shire
mwec0521	uk england herefordshire	1720	OWEN & BOWEN	100	18	12	A Map of Hereford Shire
mwec0623	uk england kent	1720	OWEN & BOWEN	100	18	12	A Map of Kent
mwec0720	uk england leicestershire	1720	OWEN & BOWEN	100	18	12	A Map of Leicester Shire
mwec0745	uk england lincolnshire	1720	OWEN & BOWEN	100	18	12	A Map of Lincoln Shire
mwec0778	uk england middlesex	1720	OWEN & BOWEN	100	18	12	A Map of Middlesex
mwec0826	uk england norfolk	1720	OWEN & BOWEN	100	18	12	A Map of Norfolk
mwec0860	uk england northamptonshire	1720	OWEN & BOWEN	100	18	12	A Map of Northampton Shire
mwec0887	uk england northumberland	1720	OWEN & BOWEN	100	18	12	A Map of Northumberland
mwec0954	uk england oxfordshire	1720	OWEN & BOWEN	100	18	12	A Map of Oxford Shire
mwec0986	uk england rutland	1720	OWEN & BOWEN	100	18	12	A Map of Rutland Shire
mwec1041	uk england somerset	1720	OWEN & BOWEN	100	18	12	A Map of Somerset Shire
mwec1071	uk england staffordshire	1720	OWEN & BOWEN	100	18	12	A Map of Stafford Shire
mwec1104	uk england suffolk	1720	OWEN & BOWEN	100	18	12	A Map of Suffolk
mwec1137	uk england surrey	1720	OWEN & BOWEN	100	18	12	A Map of Surrey

AMPG REFERENCE	REGION	DATE	MAP MAKER	PRICE (UK£)	VERT. (cm.)	HOR. (cm.)	TITLE OF MAP (Comments by the editor in brackets)
mwec1167	uk england sussex	1720	OWEN & BOWEN	100	18	12	A Map of Sussex
mwec1226	uk england westmorland	1720	OWEN & BOWEN	100	18	12	A Map of Westmorland
mwec1247	uk england wiltshire	1720	OWEN & BOWEN	100	18	12	A Map of Wilt Shire
mwec1280	uk england worcestershire	1720	OWEN & BOWEN	100	18	12	A Map of Worcester Shire
mwec0011	uk england bedfordshire	1720	OWEN & BOWEN	100	18	12	Bedford Shire
mwec0041	uk england berkshire	1720	OWEN & BOWEN	100	18	12	Berkshire
mwec0069	uk england buckinghamshire	1720	OWEN & BOWEN	100	18	12	Buckingham Shire
mwec0097	uk england cambridgeshire	1720	OWEN & BOWEN	100	18	11	Cambridgeshire
mwuk1821	wales	1720	OWEN & BOWEN	100	18	13	Carnarvan Shire
mwec0230	uk england cumbria	1720	OWEN & BOWEN	100	18	12	Cumberland
mwuk1822	wales	1720	OWEN & BOWEN	100	18	12	Denbighshire
mwec0292	uk england devon	1720	OWEN & BOWEN	100	18	12	Devon Shire
mwec0333	uk england dorset	1720	OWEN & BOWEN	100	18	12	Dorset Shire
mwuk1823	wales	1720	OWEN & BOWEN	100	18	12	Flint Shire
mwec0447	uk england gloucestershire	1720	OWEN & BOWEN	100	18	12	Glocester Shire
mwec0548	uk england hertfordshire	1720	OWEN & BOWEN	100	18	12	Hertford Shire
mwec0581	uk england huntingdonshire	1720	OWEN & BOWEN	100	18	12	Huntingdon Shire
mwec0685	uk england lancashire	1720	OWEN & BOWEN	100	18	12	Lanca Shire
mwuk1824	wales	1720	OWEN & BOWEN	100	18	12	Merioneth Shire
mwec0913	uk england nottinghamshire	1720	OWEN & BOWEN	100	18	12	Nottingham Shire
mwuk1825	wales	1720	OWEN & BOWEN	100	18	11	Radnorshire
mwec1011	uk england shropshire	1720	OWEN & BOWEN	100	18	12	Shrop Shire
mwec1326	uk england yorkshire	1720	OWEN & BOWEN	100	18	12	The North & East Riding of Yorkshire
mwuk1569	england islands	1720	OWEN & BOWEN	100	18	12	The Smaller Islands in the British Ocean
mwec1327	uk england yorkshire	1720	OWEN & BOWEN	100	18	12	The West Riding of York-Shire
mwec1196	uk england warwickshire	1720	OWEN & BOWEN	100	18	12	Warwick Shire
mwwi0933	virgin isl	1799	OXHOLM	12000	66	172	Charte over den Danske Oe St. Croix i America
mwgr0140	greece	1704	PACIFICO	6000	47	63	Penisola e Regno della Morea (10 fortress insets in side borders)
mwgr0338	greece crete	1538	PAGANO		26	40	Il vero disegno di tutta la isola de Candia
mwgr0436	greece cyprus	1538	PAGANO		26	41	Questa e la vera descriptione et geographia de tutta Linsula de Cypre
mwf0777	france normandy	1689	PAGERIE	1500	84	110	Diocese de Coutances, Divise en ses Quatre Archidiacones, et Vint-Deux Doiennes Ruraux avec les Isles de Iersay, Grenesey, Cers, Herms, Aurigny etc.
mwuk1000	england	1754	PALAIRET	120	52	52	1e. Carte d'Angleterre (student study map)
mww0431a	world	1755	PALAIRET	1500	56	75	3e Mappe-Monde
mwam0208	america continent	1780	PALAIRET	650	42	49	A General Map of America
mwaf0232	africa	1775	PALAIRET	350	49	57	A Map of Africa by J. Palairet According to d'Anville
mwam0979	america north (east)	1755	PALAIRET	1500	42	57	Carte des Possessions Angloises & Francoises du Continent de l'Amerique Septentrionale - Kaart van de Engelsche en Fransche Bezittingen in het Vaste Land van Noord America (Illustrated is the Ottens issue of the same year)
mwam0171a	america continent	1754	PALAIRET	500	49	51	Carte Générale de l'Amérique 1754
mwru0288b	russia	1787	PALLAS	300	37	44	Carte des Landes Situees Entre le Volga et L'Oural
mwru0288c	russia	1787	PALLAS	200	27	39	Carte D'une Partie des Gouvernemens de Tobolsk et D'Irkoutsk
mwru0288a	russia	1787	PALLAS	1200	55	117	Carte Generale de L'Empire de Russie 1787
mwe1172	europe south east	1811	PALMA	960	76	111	Carte de la Plus Grande Partie de la Turquie d'Europe Dressee sur d'Anciens Materiaux Rectifies par les Observations Astronomiques Faites Recements sur les Cotes et sur les Nombreux Renseignements Fournis par Divers Voyageurs
mwuk0270	ireland	1830	PALMER	600	77	64	A New and Improved Map of Ireland, Exhibiting the Mail, Coach and Turnpike Roads, the Lakes, Rivers & Canals, the Principal Ranges of Mountains
mwe0899	europe hungary	1686	PALMER	1800	49	57	A New Mapp of the Kingdom of Hungary and the States that have been Subject to it, which are at Present the Northern Parts of Turkey in Europe
mwaa0144	arctic	1774	PALMER	500	44	21	Chart shewing the tracks of His Majesty's sloops Racehorse and Carcass during the Expedition to the North Pole
mwru0467	russia tartary	1848	PALMER	400	57	88	Outline Map of North Eastern Asia ... to his Excellency James K. Polk, President of the United States.
mwm0168	mediterranean malta	1565	PALOMBO?	4000	40	51	Nuovo et Ultimo Disegno di Malta Havuto da li Avisi delli XIIJ et XIX Settembre
mwit0708	italy rome	1580	PANVINIO	650	34	45	Antique Urbis Imago
mwme0492	jerusalem	1733	PAOLI	2000	47	47	Regno di Gerusalemme in Tempo delle Guerre Sagre ... Giovanni Petroschi Incise in Roma
mwg0680	saxony	1840	PAPEN	720	91	115	(East Friesland) Statistische Ubersichtskarte des Bezirks der Landdrostei Aurich
mwsam0210	south america amazon	1780	PARCAR	720	47	55	Maragnonii sive Amazonum Fluminis
mwuk0983	england	1727	PARKER	500	45	37	A New and Correct Map of England & Wales

AMPG REFERENCE	REGION	DATE	MAP MAKER	PRICE (UK£)	VERT. (cm.)	HOR. (cm.)	TITLE OF MAP (Comments by the editor in brackets)
mwec0622	uk england kent	1719	PARKER-HARRIS	2800	58	84	A Map of the County of Kent (4 borders consist of 118 coats-of-arms)
mwuk1155	england london	1720	PARKER-SENEX	2000	50	59	A Plan of the City's of London, Westminster and Borough of Southwark; with the New Additional Buildings: Anno 1720
mwit1062a	italy naples	1725	PARRINO	400	12	54	Napoli
mwca0229	canada arctic	1824	PARRY	400	56	80	Chart of a Part of the North Eastern Coast of America and its Adjacent Islands
mwca0217	canada arctic	1821	PARRY	300	52	39	Chart of a Part of the Western Coast of Baffins Bay
mwca0239	canada arctic	1825	PARRY	300	18	37	Chart of Hudson's Strait & Sir Thos. Rowe's Welcome, Shewing the Track & Discoveries of H.M.S. Griper
mwat0290	atlantic north	1821	PARRY	350	25	61	General Chart Showing the Track of H.M. Ships Hecla & Griper, from the Orkneys to Melville Island, North Georgia, A.D. 1819 and Return in 1820
mwuk0488	scotland	1746	PATERSON	2250	36	45	A Survey of Old & New Aberdeen, with ye Adjacent Country between ye Rivers Dee and Don
mwaf0963	africa south	1789	PATERSON	750	33	56	Carte De L'Extremite Meridionale De L'Afrique, (inset of Cape Peninsula and False Bay)
mwuk1504	uk english channel (all)	1772	PATRY	1200	85	81	Le Ponant (north to the left)
mwaf0291	africa	1804	PATTESON	90	21	25	Africa, Antient & Modern
mwuss1400	pennsylvania	1811	PAXTON	960	48	50	To the Citizens of Philadelphia, this New Plan of the City and its Environs
mwp0270	pacific (all)	1799	PAYNE	300	25	20	A Chart Shewing the Tract of Capt. Cook's Last Voyage
mwam0548	america north	1799	PAYNE	200	19	24	A Map of North America from the Latest Authorities
mwaf0968	africa south	1793	PAYNE	250	21	38	A Map of the Southern Extremity of the Continent of Africa Comprehending the Cape of Good Hope, the Dutch Colonies & the Hottentot Settlements
mwuss1487	tennessee	1799	PAYNE	960	18	38	A Map of the Tennessee Government from the Latest Surveys 1799
mwuss0303	connecticut	1799	PAYNE	235	19	24	A New Map of Connecticut from the Best Authorities, 1799
mwuk0234	ireland	1793	PAYNE	580	30	46	A Plan of Dublin
mwaf0270	africa	1792	PAYNE	235	33	36	Africa
mwaf0285	africa	1799	PAYNE	100	18	22	Africa from the Best Authorities
mww0599	world	1798	PAYNE	100	18	23	General Chart on Mercator's Projection
mwuss0511	georgia	1799	PAYNE	480	19	38	Georgia from the Latest Authorities
mwin0310	india	1794	PAYNE	150	33	36	India in General
mwit0216	italy	1793	PAYNE	180	33	36	Italy and Sardinia
mwam1297	great lakes	1799	PAYNE	480	19	25	N.W. Territory
mwam0515	america north	1791	PAYNE	400	34	36	North America with the Boundaries of the Thirteen United States as Settled by the Treaty of 1783
mwuss0248	carolinas	1800	PAYNE	280	20	34	North Carolina
mwuss1463	rhode isl	1799	PAYNE	235	24	19	Rhode Island
mwuss1053	new jersey	1807	PAYNE	180	27	19	State of New Jersey
mwsw0202	switzerland	1793	PAYNE	80	19	28	Switzerland, Containing the Thirteen Cantons .
mwuss0710	maine	1799	PAYNE	200	27	19	The Province of Maine
mwaf0724	africa north	1793	PAYNE	150	18	39	The State of Barbary Comprehending the Northern Parts of Africa
mwuss1012	new hampshire	1799	PAYNE	200	30	19	The State of New Hampshire Compiled Chiefly from Actual Surveys
mwuss1169	new york	1800	PAYNE	235	19	22	The State of New York from the Best Information 1800
mwuss1398	pennsylvania	1810	PAYNE	180	18	27	The State of Pennsylvania from the Latest Surveys
mwuss0247	carolinas	1799	PAYNE	300	19	22	The State of South Carolina from the Best Authorities 1799
mwuss0765	maryland	1799	PAYNE	280	19	24	The States of Maryland and Delaware from the Latest Surveys
mwam1157	america north (east)	1807	PAYNE	300	24	31	The United States of America
mww0600	world	1798	PAYNE	150	19	19	The World from the Best Authorities
mwuss1564	vermont	1799	PAYNE	235	23	18	Vermont from the Latest Authorities, 1799
mwam0212	america continent	1782	PAYNE	360	39	34	Western Hemisphere or the New World
mwbp0513a	poland	1789	PAZZINI	240	23	32	Il Regno di Prussia diviso ...
mwuss1229	new york	1834	PEABODY	350	39	30	Map of the City of New York
mwam1216	america north (east)	1832	PEABODY	875	48	66	Map of the United States Compiled from the Most Authoritative Sources and Most Respectfully Inscribed to the Citizens of the United States by the Publisher
mwwi0425a	cuba	1729	PEARSON	250	23	31	A New and Correct Draught of the Bay of Matanzas, on ye North side of ye Island Cuba
mwuss1470	rhode isl	1819	PEASE	480	27	18	Map of Rhode Island and Providence Plantations
mwsp0629	spain regions	1815	PEDEMONTE	675	43	84	Plan de Lerida Assiege et Pris d'Assaut le 13 Mai 1810 par l'Armee Francaise d'Aragon
mww0248	world	1692	PEETERS	785	15	27	(Untitled double-hemisphere map)
mwaf0101	africa	1692	PEETERS	280	15	18	Africae
mwaf0743	africa north algeria	1690	PEETERS	240	11	27	Algiers
mwam0094	america continent	1692	PEETERS	400	14	18	Americae
mwme0737a	iraq etc	1690	PEETERS	300	12	23	Bagdad in Babylonie oft Chaldea nu Irak
mwgr0417b	greece crete	1690	PEETERS	200	15	20	Candia
mwgr0312a	greece corfu	1690	PEETERS	300	13	21	Corphu

AMPG REFERENCE	REGION	DATE	MAP MAKER	PRICE (UK£)	VERT. (cm.)	HOR. (cm.)	TITLE OF MAP (Comments by the editor in brackets)
mwme0869a	syria etc	1690	PEETERS	300	13	24	Damaskus in Syrien
mwme0180	holy land	1680	PEETERS	2500	34	51	Descriptio et Situs Terrae Sanctae alio Nomine Palestina Multis Preclaris Historys et Miraculis utriusq, Testameti a Christo Salvatore Nobilitata (almost identical to De Jode, 1593)
mwsp0208	spain	1692	PEETERS	240	14	18	Espagne
mwsp0692	gibraltar	1692	PEETERS	240	10	26	Gibralter
mwru0103	russia	1692	PEETERS	200	13	16	Grande Tartarie
mwe0675	europe dalmatia	1690	PEETERS	350	28	39	Il Disenio d'Zara et Sebenico con sui Castelli Vecini
mwgr0387	greece crete	1690	PEETERS	350	11	27	Insula di Candia del Mare Mediteranea
mwgr0312b	greece corfu	1690	PEETERS	300	13	24	Isle de Corfu
mwgr0541a	greece zante (zakynthos)	1690	PEETERS	250	13	21	Isle de Zante
mwuk0756	uk	1692	PEETERS	240	13	15	Isles Britaniques ou sont les Royaumes d'Angleterre d'Escosse et d Irlande
mwc0080	china	1692	PEETERS	280	13	16	La Chine
mwas0760	asia south east philippines	1692	PEETERS	375	14	17	Les Isles Philippines Molucques et de la Sonde (inset of Japan)
mwbh0462	belgium holland	1692	PEETERS	240	14	18	Les Pays Bas ou sont Remarquees les Aquisitions de la France
mwsc0088	scandinavia	1692	PEETERS	240	14	17	Les Royaumes de Suede et Norwege
mwit0118	italy	1692	PEETERS	240	13	15	L'Italie
mwbh0846a	luxembourg	1692	PEETERS	240	13	15	Lutzenburgi
mwm0210	mediterranean malta	1690	PEETERS	360	11	27	Malta
mwin0138	india	1692	PEETERS	240	13	16	Mogol
mwme0796	persia etc	1692	PEETERS	240	13	16	Perse
mwgr0528a	greece rhodes	1690	PEETERS	200	15	21	Rhode
mwgr0268a	greece athens	1690	PEETERS	200	13	20	Ville d'Athènes
mwe1036	europe rhine	1836	PELET	960	53	77	Cours du Rhin depuis Constance jusqu'a Nimegue (11 sheets, each 53x77cm)
mwuss0826	massachusetts	1777	PELHAM	30000	98	71	A Plan of Boston in New England with its Environs, Including Milton, Dorchester, Roxbury, Brooklin, Cambridge, Medford, Charlestown, Parts of Malden and Chelsea; with the Military Works Constructed in those Places in the Years 1775 and 1776
mwuss0039	alaska	1808	PELHAM	100	14	20	Snug Corner Cove in Prince William's Sound
mwat0313	atlantic south	1843	PELTON	1200	167	208	Pelton's Outline Map of South America - Pelton's Outline Map of Africa (incl. South Atlantic Ocean)
mww0613	world	1800	PENNANT	1350	50	59	Map for Mr. Pennant's Outline of the Globe
mwuss1550	vermont	1775	PENNSYLVANIA MAG.	900	16	36	A Map of the Present Seat of War on the Border of Canada
mwuss0814	massachusetts	1775	PENNSYLVANIA MAG.	1000	26	18	A New and Correct Plan of the Town of Boston and Provincial Camp
mwf1019	france provence	1680	PERELLE	1250	48	74	Carte d'une Partie des Costes Maritime de Provence de la Terre, Seigneurie, Golfe, et Dependances de la Napoule (near Cannes)
mwuss1266	new york	1851	PERRIS	20000	92	125	Map of the City of New York
mwuk0589	scotland	1824	PERROT	100	11	7	Aberdeen - Kincardine
mwuk0590	scotland	1824	PERROT	80	11	7	Angus - Fife
mwuk0591	scotland	1824	PERROT	70	11	7	Argyle
mwuk0262	ireland	1823	PERROT	120	11	7	Armagh - Down
mwuk0265	ireland	1828	PERROT	90	11	7	Donegal
mwuk0266	ireland	1828	PERROT	90	11	7	Galway
mwuk0592	scotland	1824	PERROT	80	11	7	Haddington, Edimbourg. Berwick
mwaf0576	africa islands bourbon	1827	PERROT	400	29	34	Ile Bourbon
mwwi0681	hispaniola	1825	PERROT	375	30	49	Ile de St. Domingue ou d'Haiti
mwuk0887a	uk	1828	PERROT	200	13	15	Iles Britanniques
mwuk0593	scotland	1824	PERROT	100	11	7	Iles Hebrides
mwuk0594	scotland	1824	PERROT	100	11	7	Iles Shetland
mwuk0595	scotland	1824	PERROT	85	11	7	Inverness
mwuk0596	scotland	1824	PERROT	100	11	7	Is Orcades. Caithness
mwuk0267	ireland	1828	PERROT	90	11	7	Kerry
mwuk0597	scotland	1824	PERROT	80	11	7	Nairn Elgin Banff
mwuk0598	scotland	1824	PERROT	70	11	7	Peebles, Selkirk, Roxburgh
mwuk0599	scotland	1824	PERROT	100	11	7	Perth. Kinross
mwuk0600	scotland	1824	PERROT	70	11	7	Ross
mwuk0601	scotland	1824	PERROT	80	11	7	Stirling Dumbarton Linlithgow, Clackmanan
mwuk0602	scotland	1824	PERROT	80	11	7	Sutherland
mwuk0603	scotland	1824	PERROT	70	11	7	Wigtown Kircudb
mwp0065	australia	1819	PERRY	675	36	78	An Outline Map of the Settlements in New South Wales
mwc0311	china formosa	1856	PERRY	500	23	16	The Island of Formosa
mwg0812	westphalia	1692	PERSON	800	19	28	Accurata Territorii Coloniensis Descriptio
mwf0334	france brittany	1694	PERSOY	750	47	56	Nobme Prudmoo Viro Joanni Six Wimnae Toparchae Vronmadae Domino Consuli et Senatori Amstelaedamensi Hanc Novissimam Britanniae
mwf0783	france normandy	1695	PERSOY	500	47	56	Nova et Accurata Normandiae Ducatus Tabula
mwf0740	france nord pas-de-calais	1700	PERSOY	800	49	53	Plan en Profil van Duynkerken, met sijn Sterktens en Zee-Kasteelen ... op den 9 Augustus, 1695

AMPG REFERENCE	REGION	DATE	MAP MAKER	PRICE (UK£)	VERT. (cm.)	HOR. (cm.)	TITLE OF MAP (Comments by the editor in brackets)
mwme0682	arabia etc	1835	PERTHES	2400	60	84	Arabia und das Nil-Land
mwme0734	caucasus	1848	PERTHES	80	40	34	Armenia, Mesopotamia, Babylonia et Assyria cum Adjacentibus Regionibus
mwam0755	america north	1842	PERTHES	160	33	39	Bergketten in Nord Amerika (shows mountain ranges)
mwbp0552	poland	1809	PERTHES	360	64	79	Carte Hydrographique de Pologne
mwc0265	china	1833	PERTHES	140	29	38	Das Chinesische Reich mit seinen Schutzstaaten nebst dem Japanischen Inselreiche
mwp0088	australia	1828	PERTHES	280	28	37	Das Innere von Neu-Sud-Wales nach John Oxley 1822
mwas0537	asia south east	1830	PERTHES	120	32	41	Die Ostindischen Inseln
mwam0779	america north	1846	PERTHES	280	29	39	Ethnographische Karte von Nordamerika
mwin0362	india	1836	PERTHES	480	85	58	General Karte von Vorderindien sur Ulberisch der Haupterhaltnisse den Manen James Rennell Dargebracht
mww0744	world	1848	PERTHES	480	33	40	Geographische Verbreitung der Menschen-Rassen
mwwi0213	west indies	1845	PERTHES	100	19	24	Indie Occidentali e America-Centrale
mwas0290	asia burma	1834	PERTHES	480	60	92	Karte van Assam
mwru0357	russia	1837	PERTHES	350	54	73	Karte vom Ural Gebirge
mwme0413	holy land	1835	PERTHES	500	85	58	Karte von Syrien den Manen Jacotin's und Burckhardt's Gewidmet
mwgm0331	mexico	1836	PERTHES	600	29	35	Mexico und Centro-America
mwas0270	asia (from turkey to india)	1850	PERTHES	80	32	29	Oestliche Halbkugel
mwas0706	asia south east malacca	1835	PERTHES	960	60	88	Reduzirte Karte vom Chinesischen Meere; 1stes oder Sudliches Blatt
mwme0850	persia etc	1832	PERTHES	480	41	59	Reduzirte Karte vom Persischen Golf
mwas0907a	asia south east sunda	1835	PERTHES	720	61	89	Reduzirte Karte vom Sunda oder Borneo-Meere
mwas0812	asia south east philippines	1832	PERTHES	1600	86	60	Reduzirte Karte von den Philippinen und den Sulu Inseln
mwc0319	china tibet	1835	PERTHES	600	57	81	Spezial Karte vom Himalaya in Kumaon, Gurhwal, Sirmur &c.&c.
mww0712a	world	1836	PERTHES	200	18	20	Westliche HalbKugel / Oestliche HalbKugel
mwit1056a	italy naples	1685	PESCHE	900	21	33	Fidelissimae Urbis Neapolitanae (closely copied by Coronelli c1690 with title 'La Citta di Napoli')
mwe0398a	europe austria	1818	PETER	800	42	59	Uibersicht des Taxen-Systems bey der Oesterreichischen k.k. Briefpost
mwuss0231	carolinas	1790	PETRIE	30000	49	69	Ichnography of Charleston ... for the Use of the Phoenix Fire Company of London (1st printed fire insurance map)
mwit0501	italy lombardy	1717	PETRINI	450	45	62	Alta et Bassa Lombardi
mwsam0038	south america	1700	PETRINI	720	40	55	America Meridionale
mwam0344	america north	1700	PETRINI	2400	38	53	America Settentrionale ... Corretta, et Aumentata, Secondo le Relatione Piu Moderne, da N. Sanson d'Abbevile (close copy of Sanson's 1690 update of his 1650 map)
mwru0140	russia	1717	PETRINI	450	42	56	Bianco Moscovia
mwf0091	france	1704	PETRINI	785	44	58	Il Regno di Francia con li Paesi di Conquista, Diviso in Governi di Provincia
mwf0092	france	1704	PETRINI	2800	92	120	Il Regno di Francia Diviso in Provincie e Governi
mwit1027	italy south	1717	PETRINI	400	58	46	Il Regno di Napoli
mwg0082	germany	1690	PETRINI	720	46	61	Imperio d'Allemagna Diviso
mwm0211	mediterranean malta	1690	PETRINI	2400	42	55	Isola di Malta
mwru0445c	russia tartary	1717	PETRINI	785	40	59	La Grande Tartaria Descritta Secondo le Relation Piu Moderne de Nicolo de Fer ... Paulo Petrini ... In Napoli ... 1717
mwgr0115	greece	1690	PETRINI	875	44	57	La Grecia Descritta dal Abate Baudrand in Parigi e Novamente Data in Luce da Paulo Petrini in Napoli (Italian version of Baudrand's 1682 map)
mwsc0085	scandinavia	1690	PETRINI	600	41	55	La Scandinavia
mwaf0119	africa	1700	PETRINI	1350	40	55	L'Africa
mwaf0118a	africa	1700	PETRINI	12000	94	116	L'Africa, Divisa Secondo l'Estenzione delle sue Principali Parti (close copy of De Fer 1696, with title cartouche within map)
mwam0105	america continent	1700	PETRINI	25000	45	58	L'America (4 sheets, each 45x58cm. Italian version of De Fer's 1698 map, lacking 3 text borders)
mwas0095	asia continent	1700	PETRINI	15000	100	128	L'Asia (close copy of De Fer 1696 but lacking the text borders)
mwas0096	asia continent	1700	PETRINI	675	41	55	L'Asia (close copy of Rossi 1677)
mwe0132	europe	1717	PETRINI	960	39	54	L'Europa
mwuk0798	uk	1717	PETRINI	900	55	44	L'Inghilterra ... La Scotia ... L'Irlanda
mwit0125a	italy	1700	PETRINI	950	45	55	L'Italia
mww0280	world	1700	PETRINI	2500	36	56	Mappa Mondo o Vero Carta Generale del Globo Terestre
mwme0987	turkey etc	1717	PETRINI	500	40	54	Natolia detta Anticamenta Asia Minor
mwbp0341	poland	1700	PETRINI	650	43	55	Stati della Corona di Polonia
mwbh0563	belgium holland	1717	PETRINI	550	44	67	Teatro de la Guerra sule Frontiere de Paesi Bassi Spagnoli et Olande ... 1703
mwit0289	italy campagna	1750	PETRINI, N.	550	46	64	Mappa di Pozzuoli Secondo lo Stato Presente Anno 1750
mwme0344	holy land	1754	PETROSCHI	450	18	22	Carta Topographica Judeae quae Complectitur ea Loca Tantum quorum Mentio Fit in Evangelio
mwsam0713	south america paraguay	1732	PETROSCHI	3000	66	53	Neueste Vorstellung und Beschreibung der, der Gesellschafft Iesu zugehoerigen Provinz Paraquay (shown above left)

AMPG REFERENCE	REGION	DATE	MAP MAKER	PRICE (UK£)	VERT. (cm.)	HOR. (cm.)	TITLE OF MAP (Comments by the editor in brackets)
mwsam0718a	south america argentina	1760	PETROSCHI-MACHONI	2400	72	54	Paraquariae Provinciae Soc. Jesu cum Adiacentib Novissima Descriptio
mwme0550b	arabia etc	1640	PETRUCCI	1000	41	52	Turcicum Imperium (almost an exact copy of Blaeu)
mwuk0089	ireland	1685	PETTY	1800	49	38	A General Mapp of Ireland
mwuk0090a	ireland	1685	PETTY	600	38	48	The County of Slego
mwuk0090	ireland	1685	PETTY	800	38	49	The Province of Munster
mwe0384	europe austria	1783	PFAUNDLER	875	118	67	Provincia Arlbergica ... Accuratissime Delineata per Joannem Antonium Pfaundler
mwsam0513a	south america colombia	1741	PFEFFEL	600	33	37	Nouveau Plan de Cartagéne avec les dernieres attaques des forts par l'Amiral Vernon. Suivant l'original Anglois, 1741
mwg0317	bavaria	1596	PFINZING	2500	78	73	Das Ampt Herrspruck sampt den Dreij darin Ligunden Empter Reicheneck, Engelthal und Hohenstain
mwit0530	italy milan	1625	PFLAUMERN	450	16	20	Mediolanum
mwam1081	america north (east)	1783	PHELIPEAU	4000	51	71	Carte Generale des Colonies Angloises dans l'Amerique Septentrionale pour l'Intelligence de la Guerre Presente. D'apres des Manuscrit Anglais par J.B. Nolin, Geographe, Corrige, Augmente des Indications des Principaux Evenemens de la Guerre
mwwi0645a	hispaniola	1786	PHELIPEAU	400	24	37	Plan de la Baye et de la Ville de St. Louis
mwwi0646	hispaniola	1786	PHELIPEAU	1200	85	109	Plan de la Plaine du Cap Francois en l'Isle St. Domingue, Redige d'apres les Dernieres Operations Geometriques des Ingenieurs du Roy
mwwi0647	hispaniola	1786	PHELIPEAU	1200	100	73	Plan de la Ville des Cayes, dans l'Isle St. Domingue
mwuss1220	new york	1832	PHELPS	1500	43	50	Map of the City of New York, with the Latest Improvements ... Corrected to 1832
mwuss1216a	new york	1831	PHELPS	720	43	51	Map of the State of New York, with the Latest Improvements
mwam0683	america north	1832	PHELPS	3000	62	88	Map of the United States
mwam0686	america north	1833	PHELPS	2850	76	104	Phelps' Map of the United States from the Best Authorities
mwam0771	america north	1845	PHELPS	1500	52	65	Phelps's National Map of the United States, a Travellers Guide
mww0741	world	1846	PHELPS	650	71	53	Pictorial View of the World
mwuss1251	new york	1844	PHELPS	500	43	51	Strangers Guide through the City of New York with the Latest Improvements
mwuss1258	new york	1847	PHELPS & ENSIGN	600	44	53	Map of the City of New York with the Adjacent Cities of Brooklyn & Jersey City and the Village of Williamsburg
mwam0789	america north	1847	PHELPS & ENSIGN	2500	114	146	Map of the United States with the Recent Counties, Cities, Villages and Internal Improvements in the Western States
mwuss1242	new york	1841	PHELPS & ENSIGN	960	42	51	Phelps & Ensign's Map of the City of New York
mwam0719	america north	1838	PHELPS & ENSIGN	960	43	55	Phelps & Ensign's Traveller's Guide through the United States Containing Stage, Steamboat, Canal & Rail Road Routes, with the Distances from Place to Place, Illustrated by a New and Accurate Map of the United States
mwam0710	america north	1837	PHELPS & ENSIGN	2000	66	103	Phelps & Ensign's Traveller's Guide, and Map of the United States
mwam1375	america north (west)	1846	PHELPS & ENSIGN	1500	40	53	Traveller's Map of Michigan, Illinois, Indiana & Ohio
mwp0224	new zealand	1853	PHILIP	350	29	22	New Zealand (inset of the 'New Settlement of Canterbury')
mwp0182	new zealand	1774	PHILIPP	1500	49	38	Carte de la Nouvelle-Zelande - Carte von Neu-Seeland
mwp0186	new zealand	1780	PHILIPP	375	27	43	Riviere Tamise et Baye Mercure a la Nle. Zelande - Die Themse nebst Abbildung der Mercurius Bay in Neu Seeland
mwgm0222	mexico	1757	PHILIPPIN	450	31	20	Carte de la Californie Levee par la Societe des Jesuites
mwuk0249a	ireland	1808	PHILIPS	180	36	21	Ireland (2 sheets joined)
mwec0239b	uk england cumbria	1808	PHILLIPS	50	10	18	Cumberland (later editions publ. by Whitaker)
mwuk1414	uk geological	1847	PHILLIPS	800	80	62	Geological Map of the British Isles, and Adjacent Coast of France
mwuk1049	england	1820	PHILLIPS	960	102	183	Grand Southern Tour of England Including Principal Part of East, West, and Inland Counties
mwec1083	uk england staffordshire	1832	PHILLIPS-TEESDALE	875	137	100	A Map of the County of Stafford, Divided into Hundreds & Parishes, from an Accurate Survey Made in the Years 1831 and 1832
mwf0520	france corsica	1768	PHINN	720	27	45	A New and Accurate Map of the Island of Corsica
mwca0539	canada quebec	1780	PHINN	240	11	18	A Plan of Quebec, Metropolis of Canada
mwf0521	france corsica	1768	PHINN	685	27	44	Carte Nouvelle et Exacte de l'Isle de Corse
mww0498a	world	1776	PHIPPS	600	23	42	Geography. A Map of the World in Three Sections Describing the Polar Regions to the Tropics (2 polar part-hemispheres and tropical strip map)
mwsc0631	scandinavia norway	1774	PHIPPS	8000	17	21	Spitzbergen or New Greenland. (On this voyage towards the North Pole was midshipman Horatio Nelson).
mwgr0492	greece cyprus	1688	PIACENZA	1500	14	19	Cipro
mwru0346a	russia	1829	PIADYSHEV	2000	36	36	Carte générale de l'Empire de Russie les états incorporés: le Royaume de Pologne et le Grand Duche de Finlande (in 6 sheets, each 36x36cm. Title also in Russian. Inset of Alaskan coast.)
mwit1140	italy florence	1800	PIATTI	450	35	47	Pianta della Citta di Firenze

AMPG REFERENCE	REGION	DATE	MAP MAKER	PRICE (UK£)	VERT. (cm.)	HOR. (cm.)	TITLE OF MAP (Comments by the editor in brackets)
mwaf0053	africa	1644	PICART	3200	41	55	Africa Nova Tabula Auct Jud. Hondio (3 carte-a-figure borders. Close copy of Hondius).
mwam0049	america continent	1644	PICART	5000	42	55	America Noviter Delineata Auct: Judoco Hondio (3 carte-a-figure borders. Close copy of Hondius 1632)
mwas0037	asia continent	1644	PICART	3600	41	55	Asia Recens Summa Cura Delineata (3 carte-a-figure borders. Close copy of Hondius).
mwsc0067	scandinavia	1667	PICART	450	13	17	Norvege et Suede
mwaf0074	africa	1667	PICART	350	14	19	Nouvelle Description d'Afrique
mwam0069	america continent	1667	PICART	675	17	20	Nouvelle Description de l'Amerique
mwe0079	europe	1667	PICART	300	14	19	Nouvelle Description de l'Europe
mwas0054	asia continent	1667	PICART	450	14	19	Nouvelle Description de l'Asie
mwe0055	europe	1644	PICART	2800	42	55	Nova Europae Descriptio (3 carte-a-figure borders. Close copy of Hondius).
mwaa0089	arctic	1657	PICART	450	14	19	Pole Arctique ou Terre du Septentrion (1st edition c1651)
mww0460	world	1763	PICAUD	675	50	121	Carte pour l'Histoire Generale ou se Peuvent Representer Toutes les Revolutions de l'Univers depuis les plus Anciennes Monarchies jusqu'a celles qui Subsistent a Present (Europe and Asia only)
mwjk0003	japan	1589	PICCAGLIA		55	43	Descrittione E Sito Del Giapone (text above and below map)
mwf0896	france paris	1784	PICHON	5000	99	142	Nouveau Plan Routier de la Ville et Faubourg de Paris
mwuss0222	carolinas	1782	PICQUET	685	37	42	Caroline Meridionale, avec les Parties Adjacentes, pour Servir a l'Intelligence des Mouvements des Armees Americaines et Britanniques
mwf0812	france north	1813	PICQUET	375	69	79	Carte de la France No. 2
mwaf0726	africa north	1816	PICQUET	600	62	92	Carte des Cotes de Barbare Comprenant les Etats de Maroc, Fez, Alger, Tunis et Tripoli
mwf0186	france	1816	PICQUET	2500	196	185	Carte Routiere de la France
mwit0235	italy	1824	PICQUET	375	81	64	Carte Routiere, Physique et Politique de l'Italie, de la Suisse, et de Parties des Etats Voisins
mwuss0226	carolinas	1787	PICQUET	650	36	28	Esquisse des Operations du Siege de Charleston, Capitole de la Caroline Meridionale, en 1780
mwam0758	america north	1843	PICQUET	750	63	92	Nouvelle Carte des Etats-Unis, des Haut et Bas-Canada, de la Nouvle. Ecosse, du Nouvau-Brunswick, de Terre-Neuve &c.
mwaa0152	arctic	1785	PICQUET	300	18	20	Nouvelle Carte du Pole Artique
mwf0906	france paris	1804	PICQUET	2000	80	108	Plan Routier de la Ville de Paris et de ses Faubourgs (the map comes with a large key sheet, 150x54cm.)
mwf0924	france paris	1837	PICQUET	800	61	93	Plan Routier de la Ville de Paris, ou Guide des Etrangers dans cette Capitale, Divise en XII Arrondissements ou Mairies et en 48 Quatiers, Offrant Paris Tel qu'il est Aujourd'hui, avec les Noms des Rues, Quais,
mwuss1175	new york	1806	PICQUET	350	20	24	State of New York
mwit1125	italy tuscany	1796	PIEMONTESI	2000	51	68	Pianta della Citta e Porto di Livorno
mwuss1217	new york	1831	PIERCE	1600	75	51	A Reference & Distance Map of the State of New York
mwuss0315	connecticut	1828	PIERCE	2000	118	38	An Improved Reference Map of the Valley of the Connecticut and Western Section of New England
mwme0519b	jerusalem	1864	PIEROTTI	1250	26	73	Panorama of Jerusalem (shown above left)
mwme0519a	jerusalem	1860	PIEROTTI	2500	55	91	Plan de Jerusalem Ancienne et Moderne
mwme0519a	jerusalem	1864	PIEROTTI	800	49	35	Plan of Modern Jerusalem
mwf0277	france aquitaine	1823	PIERRUGUES	600	55	72	Plan de la Ville de Bordeaux
mwe0718	europe danube	1700	PIETRASANTA	1650	38	58	Ostia Danubii in Mare Nigro
mwit0981	italy sicily	1834	PIETRASANTA	280	35	47	Sicilia Antiqua
mwaf0020	africa	1591	PIGAFETTA	10000	62	43	(Untitled map of the whole continent but excl. West Africa, publ. in Rome.)
mwf0817	france paris	1591	PIGAFETTA	7200	41	55	Parigi
mwaf0030	africa	1598	PIGAFETTA-DE BRY	4000	56	40	(Untitled map of the whole continent but excl. West Africa. Reduced size version of Pigafetta, 1591.)
mwaf1091	africa west	1598	PIGAFETTA-DE BRY	1600	31	38	Tabula Geogra: Regni Congo
mwaf0026	africa	1597	PIGAFETTA-WOLFE	5500	63	43	A Description of Aegypt ... printed in London by Iohn Wolfe Graven by William Rogers (close copy of Pigafetta's untitled map of 1591)
mwaf1092	africa west	1598	PIGAFETTA-WOLFE	650	9	12	The Kingdome of Congo
mwec0025	uk england bedfordshire	1830	PIGOT	85	36	22	Bedfordshire
mwec0054	uk england berkshire	1830	PIGOT	120	22	36	Berkshire
mwec0078	uk england buckinghamshire	1830	PIGOT	120	36	22	Buckinghamshire
mwec0114	uk england cambridgeshire	1830	PIGOT	100	36	22	Cambridgeshire
mwec0154	uk england cheshire	1830	PIGOT	140	22	36	Cheshire
mwec0208	uk england cornwall	1830	PIGOT	140	22	36	Cornwall
mwec0210	uk england cornwall	1835	PIGOT	100	11	17	Cornwall
mwec0244	uk england cumbria	1830	PIGOT	100	37	25	Cumberland
mwec0274	uk england derbyshire	1830	PIGOT	100	36	22	Derbyshire
mwec0312	uk england devon	1830	PIGOT	120	22	36	Devonshire
mwec0349	uk england dorset	1830	PIGOT	100	22	36	Dorsetshire
mwec0425	uk england essex	1830	PIGOT	120	22	36	Essex

AMPG REFERENCE	REGION	DATE	MAP MAKER	PRICE (UK£)	VERT. (cm.)	HOR. (cm.)	TITLE OF MAP (Comments by the editor in brackets)
mwec0455	uk england gloucestershire	1830	PIGOT	100	36	22	Gloucestershire
mwec0503	uk england hampshire	1830	PIGOT	140	36	22	Hampshire
mwec0532	uk england herefordshire	1830	PIGOT	85	36	22	Herefordshire
mwec0565	uk england hertfordshire	1830	PIGOT	140	23	38	Hertfordshire
mwec0591	uk england huntingdonshire	1830	PIGOT	85	36	22	Huntingdonshire
mwec0665	uk england kent	1830	PIGOT	140	22	36	Kent
mwec0702	uk england lancashire	1830	PIGOT	140	36	22	Lancashire
mwec0729	uk england leicestershire	1830	PIGOT	120	22	36	Leicestershire & Rutlandshire
mwec0759	uk england lincolnshire	1830	PIGOT	85	36	22	Lincolnshire
mwec0798	uk england middlesex	1830	PIGOT	140	22	36	Middlesex
mwuk1875	wales	1830	PIGOT	85	36	22	Monmouthshire
mwuk0633	scotland	1840	PIGOT	350	67	53	New Map of Scotland with the Latest Improvements
mwec0840	uk england norfolk	1830	PIGOT	120	22	36	Norfolk
mwec0871	uk england northamptonshire	1830	PIGOT	85	36	22	Northamptonshire
mwec0896	uk england northumberland	1830	PIGOT	100	36	22	Northumberland
mwec0927	uk england nottinghamshire	1830	PIGOT	85	36	22	Nottinghamshire
mwec0972	uk england oxfordshire	1830	PIGOT	120	36	22	Oxfordshire
mwec1022	uk england shropshire	1830	PIGOT	100	36	24	Shropshire
mwec1053	uk england somerset	1830	PIGOT	100	22	36	Somersetshire
mwec1082	uk england staffordshire	1830	PIGOT	100	36	22	Staffordshire
mwec1120	uk england suffolk	1830	PIGOT	100	22	36	Suffolk
mwec1150	uk england surrey	1830	PIGOT	160	22	36	Surrey
mwec1179	uk england sussex	1830	PIGOT	140	22	36	Sussex
mwec1208	uk england warwickshire	1830	PIGOT	100	36	22	Warwickshire
mwec1232	uk england westmorland	1830	PIGOT	85	22	36	Westmorland
mwec1262	uk england wiltshire	1830	PIGOT	100	36	22	Wiltshire
mwec1288	uk england worcestershire	1830	PIGOT	85	36	22	Worcestershire
mwec1358	uk england yorkshire	1830	PIGOT	240	22	36	Yorkshire
mwuss0655	louisiana	1810	PIKE	2500	44	39	A Chart of the Internal Part of Louisiana
mwuss0683	louisiana	1847	PIKE	4000	201	21	Coast Directory
mwam0814	america north (central)	1810	PIKE	720	25	34	Map of the Interior or Lousiana with a Part of New Mexico
mwuss0656	louisiana	1810	PIKE	1800	23	76	Map of the Mississippi River, from its Source to the Mouth of the Missouri
mwuss0657	louisiana	1810	PIKE	960	45	46	The First Part of Captn. Pike's Chart of the Internal Part of Louisiana
mwg0182	germany	1843	PILOTY & LOEHLE	675	98	116	Post Reise Karte von Deutschland mit Spezieller Angabe der Eisenbahn- und Dampschiffart- Verbindungen, unter der Leitung der Generaladministration der Konigl. Bayer. Posten nach Amtlichen Mittheilungen Bearbeitet
mwwi0421	cuba	1717	PIMENTEL	200	13	15	B:de Matancas
mwwi0422	cuba	1717	PIMENTEL	450	14	15	Havana
mwwi0827	puerto rico	1762	PIMENTEL	500	23	15	P. Rico / B. Hondo (Cuba)
mwit0701a	italy rome	1555	PINARD	10000	55	89	Urbis Romae Descriptio
mwgr0298	greece corfu	1573	PINARGENTI	1000	20	14	(Untitled map)
mwgr0559	greece islands	1573	PINARGENTI	600	23	15	(Untitled map. Southern Archipelago incl. Crete)
mwgr0278	greece cefalonia	1573	PINARGENTI	1000	21	16	Zafalonia
mwgr0535	greece zante (zakynthos)	1573	PINARGENTI	600	21	16	Zante
mwit0625	italy north	1848	PINCHETTI	580	81	137	Carta Geographia Postale del Regno Lombardo-Veneto (insets of 17 cities)
mwuk1534a	uk english channel (east)	1739	PINE	1200	38	61	(Spanish Armada in the English Channel. One of 10 engravings by J. Pine of tapestries in the House of Lords depicting the Spanish Armada of 1588. The tapestries were destroyed in the fire of 1834)
mwuk1542a	uk english channel (west)	1739	PINE	1200	37	61	(Spanish Armada in the English Channel. One of 10 engravings by J. Pine of tapestries in the House of Lords depicting the Spanish Armada of 1588. The tapestries were destroyed in the fire of 1834)
mwuk0814	uk	1739	PINE	1600	39	62	A Chart Shewing the Several Places of Action between the English and Spanish Fleets (refer note above)
mwec0182	uk england cornwall	1739	PINE	1200	65	30	A Plott of All the Coast of Cornwall and Devonshire, as they were to be Fortified in 1588 against the Landing of any Enemy
mwuk1434	england thames	1739	PINE	750	37	67	Thamesis Descriptio Anno 1588
mwit0234	italy	1821	PINETTI	400	74	79	Carta Postale e Stradale dell'Italia, Correcta e Aumentata dietro la Carta Publicata dall'Instituto Geografico del I.R. Stato Maggiore 1821 ed altri Documenti Geografici
mwbp0428	poland	1744	PINGELING	800	39	47	(Torun) Vorstellung von der Belagerung der Stadt Thorn, welche den 14. October 1703 von dem Konige in Schweden Erobert Worden
mwam1035	america north (east)	1776	PINGELING	1200	26	37	Allgemeine Charte von Nord America als den Sitz des Krieges zwischen den Konigl. Engl. Truppen u: den Provinzialen (text under map. Total size: 58x39cm.)
mwg0187c	elbe river	1751	PINGELING	600	32	43	Der Mund der Elbe

AMPG REFERENCE	REGION	DATE	MAP MAKER	PRICE (UK£)	VERT. (cm.)	HOR. (cm.)	TITLE OF MAP (Comments by the editor in brackets)
mwg0846	westphalia	1770	PINGELING	800	72	92	Mappa Specialis Episcopatus Paderbornensis et Teritorii Secularis Abbatiae Corbeensis cum Adiacentibus Lippe, Ravensberg
mwg0673	saxony	1792	PINGELING	1500	99	65	Plan von Oldenburg
mwam1059	america north (east)	1778	PINGELING	1800	38	30	Special Karte von den Mittleren Brittishen Colonien in Nord Amerika
mww0657	world	1818	PINKERTON	875	69	51	(Mercator's projection - Western Part / Eastern part. 2 maps, each 69x51cm.)
mwaf0427	africa east	1818	PINKERTON	240	51	70	Abyssinia Nubia &c.
mwaf0301	africa	1814	PINKERTON	400	70	50	Africa
mwme0671	arabia etc	1818	PINKERTON	500	51	70	Arabia
mwp0064	australia	1818	PINKERTON	600	54	71	Australasia (incl. New Zealand)
mwca0137	canada	1814	PINKERTON	900	50	69	British Possessions in North America
mwsam0473	south america chile	1809	PINKERTON	300	70	50	Chili
mwas0533	asia south east	1818	PINKERTON	500	51	70	East India Isles
mwin0337	india	1814	PINKERTON	320	60	50	Hindostan
mwbh0783	belgium holland	1810	PINKERTON	250	52	57	Holland
mwuk0256	ireland	1814	PINKERTON	350	71	50	Ireland
mwjk0135	japan	1809	PINKERTON	600	50	66	Japan
mwsam0170	south america (central)	1810	PINKERTON	400	70	51	La Plata
mwsam0542	south america colombia	1818	PINKERTON	400	70	50	New Granada
mwam0587	america north	1812	PINKERTON	550	50	70	North America
mww0643	world	1812	PINKERTON	750	48		Northern Hemisphere / Southern Hemisphere (2 circular maps)
mwsam0789	south america peru	1815	PINKERTON	300	52	70	Peru
mwp0518	pacific south	1813	PINKERTON	300	51	70	Polynesia (incl. North-East Australia)
mwsp0130	portugal	1813	PINKERTON	300	70	49	Portugal
mwuk1570	england islands	1814	PINKERTON	350	71	51	Remote British Isles (Scilly Is., Shetland Isl, Jersey & Guernsey)
mwru0330	russia	1811	PINKERTON	250	61	50	Russia in Europe
mwsam0133	south america	1811	PINKERTON	350	70	50	South America
mwaf0992	africa south	1809	PINKERTON	450	50	69	Southern Africa
mwsp0318	spain	1810	PINKERTON	320	51	42	Spain and Portugal
mwgm0065	gulf of mexico and surrounding regions	1811	PINKERTON	2000	50	71	Spanish Dominions in North America Northern Part / Middle Part / Southern Part (3 maps, each 50x71cm. Northern map illustrated.)
mwgm0275	mexico	1811	PINKERTON	450	51	70	Spanish Dominions in North America. Middle Part
mwuss0658	louisiana	1811	PINKERTON	950	51	70	Spanish Dominions in North America. Northern Part
mwsw0221	switzerland	1809	PINKERTON	300	50	70	Swisserland
mwsam0845	south america venezuela	1810	PINKERTON	400	51	69	The Caracas
mwme1049	turkey etc	1813	PINKERTON	250	50	70	Turkey in Asia
mwam1166	america north (east)	1810	PINKERTON	950	51	69	United States of America Northern Part
mwam1165	america north (east)	1809	PINKERTON	500	51	71	United States of America Southern Part
mwwi0157	west indies	1809	PINKERTON	450	51	71	West Indies
mwaf1243	africa west	1813	PINKERTON	300	55	77	Western Africa
mwec0450	uk england gloucestershire	1780	PINNELL	500	70	63	A Plan of the City of Gloucester
mwuk0876a	uk	1800	PIQUET	450	68	53	Nouv.le Carte Géo-Hydrographique des Isles Britanniques
mwit0749	italy rome	1756	PIRANESI	1500			Pianta di Roma disegnata colla situazione
mwit0751a	italy rome	1770	PIRANESI	2000	135	75	Pianta di Roma e del Campo Marzo
mwaa0095	arctic	1680	PITT	2850	46	58	A Map of the North-Pole and the Parts Adioining. Oxon at the Theatre MDCLXXX
mwjk0044	japan	1680	PITT	3000	36	52	A Mapp of the Isles of Japan (close copy of Tavernier's 1679 map)
mwf0737	france nord pas-de-calais	1680	PITT	360	38	49	Arciepiscopatus Cameracensis. Archevesche de Cambray
mwe0549	europe czech republic (bohemia)	1690	PITT	300	41	47	Bohemia
mwg0803	westphalia	1680	PITT	300	38	50	Clivia Ducatus et Ravestein Dominium
mwg0615	saxony	1680	PITT	300	38	50	Comitatus Bentheim et Steinfurt
mwbp0294	poland	1680	PITT	360	45	38	Comitatus Glatz
mwg0613	saxony	1680	PITT	300	41	50	Comitatus Mansfeldiae Descriptio
mwe0330	europe austria	1680	PITT	300	40	52	Comitatus Tirolensis (copy of Jansson 1647)
mwsc0580	scandinavia norway	1680	PITT	500	43	53	Dioecesis Trundhemiensis Pars Australis
mwbp0295	poland	1680	PITT	450	40	49	Ducatus Breslanus sive Wratislaviensis
mwbh0415	belgium holland	1680	PITT	400	39	52	Ducatus Geldriae Novissima Descriptio
mwg0614	saxony	1680	PITT	300	38	48	Ducatus Luneburgensis
mwbp0296	poland	1680	PITT	300	42	51	Ducatus Silesiae Glogani Vera Delineatio
mwbp0297	poland	1680	PITT	400	50	39	Ducatus Silesiae Grotganus cum Districtu Episcopali Nissensi
mwbp0298	poland	1680	PITT	400	39	48	Ducatus Silesiae Ligniciensis
mwbp0299	poland	1680	PITT	350	41	38	Ducatus Silesiae Wolanus
mwru0078	russia	1680	PITT	350	46	53	Dwinae Fluvii nova descriptio (copy of Jansson 1645)
mwbh0416	belgium holland	1680	PITT	360	38	49	Episcop. Utraiectinus. Auct. Balthazaro Florentio a Berckenrode
mwsc0581	scandinavia norway	1680	PITT	500	43	53	Episcopatus Bergensis
mwbh0417	belgium holland	1680	PITT	400	48	56	Flandria Nova Descriptio
mwbh0418	belgium holland	1680	PITT	300	40	49	Flandriae Pars Occidentalis Continens

AMPG REFERENCE	REGION	DATE	MAP MAKER	PRICE (UK£)	VERT. (cm.)	HOR. (cm.)	TITLE OF MAP (Comments by the editor in brackets)
mwbh0419	belgium holland	1680	PITT	450	39	50	Frisia Propria
mwsc0689	scandinavia sweden	1680	PITT	450	39	49	Gothia
mwbh0430	belgium holland	1682	PITT	450	45	54	Hollandiae Meridionalis Pars II Continens Novissimam Insularum Dordracensis Alblasser, Crimper et Clundert
mwbh0431	belgium holland	1682	PITT	450	45	55	Hollandiae Pars Septentrionalis, vulgo Westvriesland en 't Noorder Quartier
mwe0890	europe hungary	1680	PITT	400	42	51	Hungariae Regnum
mwsc0300	scandinavia denmark	1680	PITT	400	41	53	Lalandiae et Falstriae Accurata Descriptio
mwg0616	saxony	1680	PITT	360	38	48	Lusatia Superior
mwbp0095	baltic states	1680	PITT	675	44	54	Magni Ducatus Lithuaniae
mwsc0422	scandinavia finland	1680	PITT	960	43	51	Magnus Ducatus Finlandiae Nova et Accurata Delineatio
mwg0208	germany north east	1680	PITT	360	50	38	Marchia Nova vulgo New Marck in March Brandenburg
mwe1103	europe slovak republic (moravia)	1680	PITT	360	39	53	Marchionatus Moraviae Auct. I. Comenio
mwbh0420	belgium holland	1680	PITT	360	40	50	Mechlinia Dominium et Aerschot Ducatus
mwru0079	russia	1680	PITT	400	38	50	Moscoviae Pars Australis Auctore Isacco Massa
mwsc0582	scandinavia norway	1680	PITT	720	40	49	Nova et Accurata Tabula Episcopatuum Stavangriensis, Bergensis et Asloiensis Vicinarumque aliquot Territoriorum
mwru0080	russia	1680	PITT	400	47	55	Nova et Accurata Wolgae Fluminis, olim Rha Dicti Delineatio
mwbp0096	baltic states	1680	PITT	720	39	51	Nova Totius Livoniae accurata Descriptio. Apud Joan Janssonium
mww0214	world	1680	PITT	13500	45	54	Nova Totius Terrarum Orbis Geographica ac Hydrographica Tabula (4 carte-a-figure borders. Revision of van den Keere's map of 1608)
mww0214a	world	1680	PITT	1250	31	45	Nova Totius Terrarum Orbis Geographica ac Hydrographica Tabula (close copy of Merian 1638)
mwsc0494	scandinavia iceland	1680	PITT	900	38	49	Novissima Islandiae Tabula
mwru0081	russia	1680	PITT	785	47	56	Novissima Russiae Tabula Authore Isaaco Massa (re-issue of Hondius)
mww0215	world	1680	PITT	8500	45	53	Orbis Terrarum Nova et Accuratissima Tabula. Auctore Ioanne a Loon (based on van Loon's map of 1666)
mwg0520	rheinland-pfalz	1680	PITT	360	40	50	Palatinatus ad Rhenum
mwbp0300	poland	1680	PITT	480	46	53	Palatinatus Posnaniensis, in Maiori Polonia Primarii Nova Delinatio per G.F.M. (copy of Jansson 1664)
mwbp0301	poland	1680	PITT	450	38	49	Prussia Accurate Descripta
mwsc0583	scandinavia norway	1680	PITT	875	54	43	Regni Norvegiae Nova et Accurata Descriptio
mwru0085	russia	1681	PITT	360	42	53	Russiae, vulgo Moscovia Dictae, Partes Septentrionalis et Orientalis. Auctore Isacco Massa.
mwsc0690	scandinavia sweden	1680	PITT	450	45	54	Scania, vulgo Schonen (first publ. by Jansson 1656)
mwe0671	europe slovenia	1680	PITT	480	39	50	Sclavonia, Croatia, Bosnia cum Dalmatiae Parte (based on Mercator and Blaeu)
mwbp0302	poland	1680	PITT	300	42	41	Silesia Inferior
mwbp0303	poland	1680	PITT	350	38	48	Silesiae Ducatus Accurata et Vera Delineatio
mwsc0076	scandinavia	1680	PITT	720	47	54	Sueciae, Norvegiae, et Daniae, Nova Tabula
mwg0714	schleswig-holstein	1681	PITT	360	44	53	Tabula Geographica Novissima Ducatus Stormariae, in Meridionli Parte Holsatiae
mwbh0421	belgium holland	1680	PITT	300	43	52	Tertia Pars Brabantiae qua Continetur Marchionat. S.R.I. Horum Urbs Primaria Antverpia
mwg0743	thuringia	1680	PITT	250	38	48	Thuringia Lantgraviatus
mwru0490	ukraine	1680	PITT	400	46	54	Tractus Borysthenis vulgo Dniepr et Niepr Dicti, a Kiovia ad Urbum Oczakow Ubi in Pontum Euxinum se Exonerat
mwbp0304	poland	1680	PITT	480	42	48	Tractuum Borussiae, circa Gedanum et Elbingam, ab Incolis Werder Appellati, cum Adiuncta Neringia
mwsc0689a	scandinavia sweden	1680	PITT	450	36	49	Uplandia (shown below left)
mwbh0432	belgium holland	1682	PITT	600	38	48	Zeelandia Comitatus
mwf0531a	france corsica	1780	PITTARELLI	1200	40	41	Carte de la Sicile Moderne
mwe0459	europe central	1689	PLACIDE	375	43	45	Carte des Confins de la France et des Principales Postes, de Paris aux Pais Estrangers
mwas0819	asia south east siam	1686	PLACIDE	14000	47	33	Carte du Royaume de Siam et des Pays Circonvoisins
mwsp0509	spain regions	1707	PLACIDE	1200	69	100	La Catalogne, Dediee au Roy
mwf1160	france rhone-alpes	1782	PLACIDE	480	58	43	La Savoye, Dediee au Roy
mwit0511	italy lombardy	1734	PLACIDE	1500	41	49	Le Cours du Po (in 5 sheets, each 41x49cm. First publ. 1703. Here publ. by Ottens, and in 1735 by Covens & Mortier)
mwsp0059a	portugal	1695	PLACIDE	900	69	47	Le Portugal (publ. by M. Du Val)
mwbh0467a	belgium holland	1693	PLACIDE	1200	56	91	Les Provinces Unies des Païs-Bas (publ. by Du Val)
mwe0016	europe	1594	PLANCIUS	9000	40	55	Europam ab Asia et Africa Segregant Mare Mediterraneum
mwf0030a	france	1593	PLANCIUS	3000	39	48	Gallia
mww0084	world	1594	PLANCIUS	16000	41	58	Orbis Terrarum Typus de Integro Multis in Locis Emendatus Auctore Petro Plancio 1594
mwme0067	holy land	1609	PLANCIUS	1500	30	50	Tabula Geographica, in qua Israelitarum, ab Aegypto ad Kenahanaeam

AMPG REFERENCE	REGION	DATE	MAP MAKER	PRICE (UK£)	VERT. (cm.)	HOR. (cm.)	TITLE OF MAP (Comments by the editor in brackets)
mwm0117	mediterranean east	1609	PLANCIUS	1200	29	48	Tabula Geographica, in qua Omnes Regiones, Urbes Oppida, et Loca Describuntur, Quarum Mentio Fit in Actis et Epistoli Apostolorum, et Apocalypri
mwme0066	holy land	1609	PLANCIUS	1500	30	50	Tabula Geographica, in qua omnes regiones, urbes, oppida
mwme0065	holy land	1609	PLANCIUS	1500	30	50	Tabula Geographica, in qua Paradisus, nec non Regiones, Urbes, oppida
mwme0068	holy land	1609	PLANCIUS	1500	30	50	Tabula Geographica, in qua regiones Cananaeae, et locorum situs prout ea tempore Christi
mwit0044	italy	1595	PLANCIUS		39	55	Tabula Hydrographica ac Geographica in qua Italia
mwme0445a	jerusalem	1609	PLANCIUS	2000	30	50	Waerachtige beschrijvinge vande wijdvermaerde Conincklicke Hooft Stadt Ierusalem (illustrated is 1643 edition)
mwit0107	italy	1680	PLANCIUS-GARRETT	2000	39	55	Italiae, Illirici, Sardiniae, Corsicae, et Confinium Regionum (UK reprint of Plancius' 1620 map)
mwas0379	asia south east	1617	PLANCIUS-VISSCHER	40000	39	55	Insulae Moluccae Celeberrimae sunt ob Maximam Aromatum Copiam quam per Totum Terrarum Orbem Mittunt (3rd state of Plancius' 1594 map. The 2nd state was produced by Wolfe in 1598.)
mwam1253	america north (east)	1847	PLATT	1000	72	94	General-Karte der Vereinigten Staaten von Nord-Amerika ... Canada & Tejas
mwuk0257	ireland	1814	PLAYFAIR	160	52	43	Ancient and Modern Ireland
mwam0626	america north	1821	PLAYFAIR	360	44	53	North America
mwsam0135	south america	1814	PLAYFAIR	140	53	43	South America
mwp0069	australia	1821	PLAYFAIR	675	44	54	The Asiatic Islands (incl. Australia and New Zealand)
mww0654	world	1816	PLAYFAIR	400	44	51	The World on Mercator's Projection
mwwi0160	west indies	1814	PLAYFAIR	240	46	56	West Indies
mwam0278	america continent	1821	PLAYFAIR	250	46	46	Western Hemisphere
mwec1066	uk england staffordshire	1686	PLOT	1500	65	54	(Staffordshire)
mwec0946	uk england oxfordshire	1677	PLOT	1350	51	49	To the Right Reverend Father in God by Divine Permission Ld Bishop Oxon the Map of Oxfordshire Being his Lordship's Diocess, Newly Delineated, and after a New Manner (172 coats of arms in borders)
mwbp0544a	poland	1804	POGGIOLI	180	25	30	La Polonia ... Roma 1804 (Vincenzo Poggioli was a publisher based in Rome)
mwam0994	america north (east)	1756	POILLY	3600	39	47	Carte des Colonies Anglaises dans l'Amerique Septentrionale Terminee par la Re. Ohio (enlarged version of 1755 map)
mwam0981	america north (east)	1755	POILLY	3600	35	30	Carte des Colonies Anglaises dans l'Amerique Septentrionale Terminee par la Re. Ohio (French version of Overton's 1754 map)
mwuk0259a	ireland	1820	POIRET	350			(Untitled map of the north coast of Antrim)
mwsam0124	south america	1803	POIRSON	160	43	35	Amerique Meridionale
mwam0560	america north	1803	POIRSON	350	34	42	Amerique Septentrionale
mwaf0290	africa	1803	POIRSON	180	36	43	Carte d'Afrique
mwam0259	america continent	1808	POIRSON	480	52	69	Carte d'Amerique
mwf0172	france	1803	POIRSON	400	76	92	Carte de la France Divisee en Prefectures et Sous Prefectures, Archeveches et Eveches, et en 27 Divisions Militaires
mwwi0672	hispaniola	1803	POIRSON	350	34	42	Carte de St. Domingue
mwf0799a	france normandy	1793	POIRSON	720	77	105	Carte des Départemens de la Manche, du Calvados, de la Seine infér.re, de l'Eure et de l'Orne (insets of Cherbourg, Channel Is.)
mwam1158	america north (east)	1807	POIRSON	875	41	66	Carte des Deux Florides et de la Louisiane Inferieure
mwwi0268	west indies (east)	1803	POIRSON	350	34	42	Carte des Iles Antilles
mwsp0324	spain	1823	POIRSON	320	49	65	Carte d'Espagne et de Portugal Divisee en Tous ses Royaumes et Principautes (insets: 10 city plans)
mwgm0276	mexico	1811	POIRSON	1350	42	72	Carte du Mexique et des Pays Limitrophes Situes au Nord et a l'Est Dressee d'apres la Grande Carte de la Nouvelle Espagne de Mr. A. de Humboldt
mwm0157	mediterranean east	1801	POIRSON	580	93	99	Carte Generale du Levant ... pour Servir au Voyage de C.S. Sonnini, en Grece et en Turquie
mwin0447b	pacific south	1803	POIRSON	1350	35	46	Carte Reduite de la Mer des Indes et de la Partie Occidentale du Grand Ocean.
mwe1032a	europe rhine	1794	POIRSON	720	101	70	Cours du Rhin
mwam0813	america north (central)	1803	POIRSON	1200	54	41	Cours du Mississipi Comprenant la Lousiane, les 2 Florides, une Partie des Etats-Unis, et Pays Adjacents
mwp0455a	pacific north	1803	POIRSON	550	35	46	Partie Septentrionale de l'Ocean Pacifique ou l'on a Marque les Descouvertes et les Routes de Mrs. de la Perouse et Cook. Par J.B. Poirson Ingenieur Geographe
mww0636	world	1810	POIRSON	500	46	70	Planisphere ou Carte General du Globe
mwru0398a	russia moscow	1796	POLEZHAYEV	4000	49	76	(Plan of Moscow, Cyrillic script)
mwf0529	france corsica	1769	POLICARDI	6000	78	165	Carta dell'Isola di Corsica
mwsam0842	south america venezuela	1783	POLITICAL MAG.	350	28	19	(Maracaibo)
mwwi0739	jamaica	1780	POLITICAL MAG.	450	26	38	A Chart of the Island of Jamaica, with its Bays, Harbours, Rocks, Soundings, &c.

AMPG REFERENCE	REGION	DATE	MAP MAKER	PRICE (UK£)	VERT. (cm.)	HOR. (cm.)	TITLE OF MAP (Comments by the editor in brackets)
mwbp0053	baltic sea (east)	1782	POLITICAL MAG.	240	27	37	A Correct Map and Chart of the Catagatte and the Baltic Sea, from the Scawe up to Petersburgh, with the Surrounding Countries of Norway, Sweden, Russia, Poland, Prussia, Pomerania, Holstein, and Denmark
mwwi0742	jamaica	1782	POLITICAL MAG.	350	26	38	A Draught of the Harbours of Port Royal and Kingston, in Jamaica. With the Fortifications Correctly Laid Down; also All the Keys and Shoals Adjacent
mwuss1651	virginia	1781	POLITICAL MAG.	450	25	37	A Map and Chart of those Parts of the Bay of Chesapeak York and James Rivers which are at Present the Seat of War
mwsam0099	south america	1780	POLITICAL MAG.	160	27	29	A Map of South America, Drawn from the Latest and Best Authorities
mwas0500	asia south east	1780	POLITICAL MAG.	200	28	38	A Map of the East Indies, from the Best Authorities
mwuk1624	isle of wight	1787	POLITICAL MAG.	160	19	25	A Map of the Isle of Wight, from the Best Authorities.
mwca0107	canada	1782	POLITICAL MAG.	600	26	34	A New & Accurate Map of the Province of Canada, in North America; from the Latest and Best Authorities
mwuss0218	carolinas	1780	POLITICAL MAG.	500	27	38	A New and Accurate Map of North Carolina, and Part of South Carolina, with the Field of Battle between Earl Cornwallis and General Gates
mwuss0217a	carolinas	1780	POLITICAL MAG.	500	28	38	A New and Accurate Map of the Chief Parts of South Carolina, and Georgia (map by J. Lodge)
mwam1071	america north (east)	1780	POLITICAL MAG.	500	37	27	A New and Accurate Map of the Province of New York and Part of the Jerseys, New England and Canada, Shewing the Scenes of our Military Operations during the Present War. Also The New Erected State of Vermont
mwuss1646	virginia	1780	POLITICAL MAG.	360	27	38	A New and Accurate Map of Virginia, and Part of Maryland and Pennsylvania
mwam0484	america north	1783	POLITICAL MAG.	400	28	38	A New and Correct Map of North America in which the Places of the Principal Engagements during the Present War, are Accurately Inserted. And the Boundaries as Settled by Treaty in 1783, Clearly Marked
mwat0051	atlantic ocean (all)	1781	POLITICAL MAG.	600	39	52	A New Map or Chart in Mercators Projection, of the Western or Atlantic Ocean, with Part of Europe, Africa and America
mwam1072	america north (east)	1780	POLITICAL MAG.	250	27	38	An Accurate Map of Rhode Island, Part of Connecticut and Massachusetts, Shewing Admiral Arbuthnot's Station in Blocking up Admiral Ternay
mwit1042	italy south	1783	POLITICAL MAG.	160	32	24	An Accurate Map of the Two Sicilies, Particularly Shewing the Places Destroyed by the Late Earthquakes
mwuss0221	carolinas	1781	POLITICAL MAG.	180	24	18	Cape Fear River, with the Counties Adjacent, and the Towns of Brunswick and Wilmington, against which Lord Cornwallis, Detached Part of his Army, the 17th. of January Last
mwuss1149	new york	1781	POLITICAL MAG.	1100	43	25	Chart and Plan of the Harbour of New York & the Couny. Adjacent, from Sandy Hook to Kingsbridge, Comprehending the Whole of New York and Staten Islands, and Part of Long Island & the Jersey Shore: and Shewing the Defences of New York
mwwi0800	martinique	1782	POLITICAL MAG.	500	24	28	Map of the Islands of Martinico, Dominico, Guardalupe, St. Christophers &c. Shewing the Place of Adml: Rodney's Late Victory over the French Fleet
mwca0108	canada	1782	POLITICAL MAG.	375	18	23	New and Accurate Chart of Hudson's Bay, in North America
mwin0062	ceylon	1782	POLITICAL MAG.	160	26	18	The Island of Ceylon, with Part of the Coromandel Coast.
mwwi0114	west indies	1780	POLITICAL MAG.	400	29	64	West Indies, with the Harbour & Fort of Omoa. From the Best Authorities
mwe0230	europe	1798	PONGRATZ	1800	117	222	Neueste Allgemeine Postkarte durch Alle Europaeische Staaten (inset of Moscow)
mwit0899	italy sicily	1682	PONT	1500	55	44	Isolae Regno di Sicilia
mwbh0182	belgium holland	1611	PONTANUS	650	26	34	Amstelodamum Emporium
mwaa0071	arctic	1611	PONTANUS	1000	27	36	Tabula Geogr. in qua Admiranda Navigationis Cursus et Recursus Designatur
mwin0407	indian ocean	1611	PONTANUS	2400	28	42	Tabula Geograph in qua Europa, Africa, Asiaq. et Circumiacentium Insularum Ora Maritima Accurata Describuntur
mwsc0637	scandinavia norway	1785	PONTOPPIDAN	1650	106	72	Det Sydlige Norge (shown left)/ Det Nordlige Norge (55x72cm, shown below)
mwsc0170	scandinavia	1785	PONTOPPIDAN	480	54	58	Mappa Daniae Norvegiae et Sueciae ex optimis
mwuss0937	minnesota	1849	POPE	360	62	71	Map of the Territory of Minnesota Exhibiting the Route of the Expedition to the Red River of the North, in the Summer of 1849 by Captn. John Pope
mwam0934	america north (east)	1733	POPPLE	75000	237	246	A Map of the British Empire in America with the French and Spanish Settlements Adjacent thereto. By Henry Popple (20 sheets, joined. State 6.)

AMPG REFERENCE	REGION	DATE	MAP MAKER	PRICE (UK£)	VERT. (cm.)	HOR. (cm.)	TITLE OF MAP (Comments by the editor in brackets)
mwam0935	america north (east)	1733	POPPLE	7500	50	49	America Septentrionalis. A Map of the British Empire in America with the French and Spanish Settlements Adjacent thereto by Hen. Popple (index map for Popple's 20-sheet map)
mwgr0557	greece islands	1572	PORCACCHI	300	11	15	Arcipelago
mwgr0347	greece crete	1572	PORCACCHI	400	11	14	Candia
mwgr0279	greece cefalonia	1576	PORCACCHI	350	11	14	Cefalonia
mwgr0569	greece islands	1576	PORCACCHI	300	10	14	Cerigo (Kythera)
mwgr0454	greece cyprus	1572	PORCACCHI	720	11	15	Cipro
mwgr0297	greece corfu	1572	PORCACCHI	450	11	15	Corfu
mwf0459	france corsica	1572	PORCACCHI	300	11	15	Corsica
mwme0926	turkey etc	1576	PORCACCHI	350	10	14	Costantinopoli (view)
mwwi0399	cuba	1572	PORCACCHI	500	11	15	Cuba
mww0063	world	1572	PORCACCHI	1200	7	14	Descrittione del Mappamondo (oval projection after Camocio 1567. Illustration taken from c1590 edition.)
mww0064	world	1572	PORCACCHI	800	11	15	Discorso Intorno Alla Carta Da Navigare (nautical map lacking SE Asia)
mwit0324	italy elba	1572	PORCACCHI	350	11	14	Elba
mwsc0656	scandinavia sweden	1572	PORCACCHI	400	11	15	Gotlandia (north to the left)
mwbh0052	belgium holland	1572	PORCACCHI	300	11	14	Hollanda
mwwi0688	jamaica	1576	PORCACCHI	300	11	15	Iamaica
mwme0927	turkey etc	1576	PORCACCHI	200	11	14	Il sito de Curzotari (Dardanelles region)
mwuk0670	uk	1572	PORCACCHI	360	11	15	Inghilterra
mwuk0006	ireland	1572	PORCACCHI	450	11	14	Irlanda
mwsc0478	scandinavia iceland	1576	PORCACCHI	400	11	15	Islanda (re-issued by Magini 1597 and Lasor a Varea 1713)
mwuk0312a	scotland	1572	PORCACCHI	400	11	14	Isole Hebride, et Orcade (north to the right)
mwas0365	asia south east	1576	PORCACCHI	450	11	15	Isole Molucche (Malacca etc)
mwbh0069	belgium holland	1576	PORCACCHI	250	11	14	Isole Selandie
mwe0492d	europe croatia	1576	PORCACCHI	300	15	18	Istria
mwsp0641	balearic islands	1572	PORCACCHI	400	11	15	Maiorica
mwm0171	mediterranean malta	1572	PORCACCHI	500	11	15	Malta
mwgr0570	greece islands	1576	PORCACCHI	300	10	14	Metellino (Lesbos)
mwgr0572	greece islands	1576	PORCACCHI	300	11	15	Milo (Melos)
mwsp0642	balearic islands	1572	PORCACCHI	400	11	14	Minorica
mwam0307	america north	1572	PORCACCHI	900	11	14	Mondo Nuovo. (Reduced size version of Forlani's 1565 map).
mwgr0036	greece	1572	PORCACCHI	300	11	14	Morea Penisola
mwgr0558	greece islands	1572	PORCACCHI	300	11	15	Negroponte
mwgr0573	greece islands	1576	PORCACCHI	300	10	14	Nicsia (Naxos)
mwgr0519	greece rhodes	1572	PORCACCHI	400	11	14	Rhodi
mwwi0819	puerto rico	1576	PORCACCHI	450	10	14	S. Giovanni (map in page of text)
mwaf0580	africa islands madagascar	1572	PORCACCHI	400	11	15	S. Lorenzo
mwgr0574	greece islands	1576	PORCACCHI	300	10	14	Santorini (Thera)
mwit0775	italy sardinia	1572	PORCACCHI	400	11	14	Sardegna
mwgr0575	greece islands	1576	PORCACCHI	200	11	14	Scarpanto (Karpathos)
mwgr0571	greece islands	1576	PORCACCHI	300	11	15	Scio (Chios)
mwuk0312	scotland	1572	PORCACCHI	600	11	15	Scotia (north to the right)
mwit0865	italy sicily	1572	PORCACCHI	450	11	15	Sicilia
mwwi0575	hispaniola	1572	PORCACCHI	400	11	15	Spagnuola
mwgr0576	greece islands	1576	PORCACCHI	200	10	14	Stalimene (Limnos)
mwin0012	ceylon	1572	PORCACCHI	400	11	15	Taprobana (positioned west of India. North to the right)
mwgm0134	mexico	1576	PORCACCHI	400	11	15	Temistitan (Mexico City)
mwit1213	italy venice	1572	PORCACCHI	600	11	15	Venetia
mwgr0536	greece zante (zakynthos)	1576	PORCACCHI	400	11	14	Zante
mwsam0570	south america galapagos	1822	PORTER	200	32	27	Gallapagos Islands
mwuk1113	england london	1655	PORTER	30000	29	76	The Newest & Exactest Mapp of the most Famous Citties London and Westminster with their Suburbs; and the manner of their Streets: With the Names of the Chiefest of them
mwam1329	america north (west)	1789	PORTLOCK	480	50	92	A Chart of the North West Coast of America with the Tracks of the King George and Queen Charlotte in 1786 & 1787
mwme0029	holy land	1562	POSTEL	720	16	21	(Map showing the Exodus and the wandering of the Jews as far north as Jericho)
mwme0032	holy land	1566	POSTEL	480	12	17	Le partage de la terre de Chanaan fait aux enfants d'Israel:
mwme0036	holy land	1569	POSTEL	675	17	21	Terrae Sanctae Descriptio
mwme0047	holy land	1583	POSTEL	675	17	22	The description of the countreys mentioned in the Actes of the Apostles
mwme0034	holy land	1568	POSTEL	720	16	21	The description of the holy lande (title and list of places below the map)
mwbp0541a	poland	1800	POSTILLON	720	18	30	Cracau, die Haupt Stadt in Pohlen
mwaf1222	africa west	1774	POSTLETHWAIT	300	39	48	A New and Correct Map of the Coast of Africa from Cape Blanco to the Coast of Angola with the Explanatory Notes of All the Forts and Settlements Belonging to the Several European Powers (inset of Gold Coast)

AMPG REFERENCE	REGION	DATE	MAP MAKER	PRICE (UK£)	VERT. (cm.)	HOR. (cm.)	TITLE OF MAP (Comments by the editor in brackets)
mwgm0214	mexico	1752	POSTLETHWAIT	480	41	32	North America, Plate III for Mr. Postlethwayte's Dictionary of Commerce (inset of Hudson's Bay)
mwsam0093	south america	1775	POSTLETHWAIT	875	122	71	South America. Performed under the Patronage of Louis Duke of Orleans First Prince of the Blood, by the Sieur d'Anville Improved by Mr. Bolton for Mr. Postelthwayt's Dictionary of Commerce
mwit1078	italy naples	1842	POTEL	450	45	60	Plan de la Ville de Naples et ses Indications (inset: Bay of Naples)
mwam1228	america north (east)	1834	POUSSIN	375	48	58	Carte Generale des Etats-Unis d'Amerique avec l'Indication de Partie Navigable de Chaque Riviere
mwm0260a	mediterranean malta	1840	POZZI	720	33	51	Gruppo delle Isole di Malta
mwsc0753f	scandinavia sweden	1836	PRAHL	300	52	34	Kart over Kongeriget Sverige
mwsc0653	scandinavia norway	1845	PRAHL	1350	70	48	Norge, et Historisk-Geografisk of Statistisk Erindringsblad (broadsheet with map 25x19cm, surrounded by historical scenes)
mwuk0135	ireland	1708	PRATT		122	97	A Mapp Of The Kingdom Of Ireland Newly Corrected & Improvd (Another title above cartouche: Tabula Hiberniae Novissima Et Emendatissima. Side border insets with 16 towns and ports.)
mwin0055	ceylon	1765	PREVOST	150	28	36	Carte de la Baye de Trinquemale
mwc0153	china	1754	PREVOST	180	20	28	Carte de la Baye d'Hoesieu et des Entrees de la Riviere de Chang
mwuss0089	california	1777	PREVOST	550	31	20	Carte de la Californie d'Apres les Observations le Plus Exactes
mwsam0564	south america ecuador	1756	PREVOST	400	59	35	Carte de la Province de Quito au Perou (reprint of De La Condamine's map of 1751)
mwc0154	china	1754	PREVOST	200	22	32	Carte de la Tartarie Orientale, pour Servir a l'Histoire Generale des Voyages
mwsam0604	south america guyana	1753	PREVOST	180	22	28	Carte de l'Isle de Cayenne
mwp0302	pacific caroline isl.	1757	PREVOST	285	23	34	Carte des Isles Carolines et des Marianes ou Isles des Larons
mwsam0372	south america brazil	1753	PREVOST	280	24	33	Carte du Bresil depuis la Riviere des Amazones jusqu'a la Baye de Tous les Saintes pour Servir l'Histoire Generale des Voyages
mwc0155	china	1754	PREVOST	250	21	32	Carte du Katay, ou Empire de Kin, pour Servir a l'Historie de Jenghiz Khan
mwin0049	ceylon	1750	PREVOST	200	18	26	Grundriss der Festung Ceylon
mwas0657a	asia south east java	1750	PREVOST	200	21	44	Idee de l'Isle de Java (map by Bellin. See also 1760)
mwuss0747	maryland	1756	PREVOST	250	19	29	Karte von der Bay Chesapeack und den Benachbarten Landen zur Allgemeinen ...
mwsam0605	south america guyana	1753	PREVOST	180	22	28	La Ville de Cayenne pour Servir a l'Histoire General des Voyages 1753
mwjk0155	japan tokyo	1752	PREVOST	300	25	25	Plan de la Ville de Jedo
mwin0212	india	1751	PREVOST	235	19	15	Plan de Pondicheri en 1741 (map by J. Bellin. Re-issued by Bellin in 1764 with the title 'Plan de la Ville de Pondicheri')
mwc0147	china	1750	PREVOST	180	20	30	Plan de Quelques Villes de la Province de Hou-Quang
mwin0236	india	1761	PREVOST	235	18	27	Plan de Ville de Cochin
mww0422	world	1752	PREVOST	400	21	32	Planisphere General pour Servir a l'Intelligence de la Navigation et du Commerce des Europeans entre les Deux Indes
mwwi0616	hispaniola	1756	PREVOST	180	18	26	Stadt St Domingo (view)
mwsam0371	south america brazil	1753	PREVOST	200	24	18	Suite du Bresil pour Servir a l'Histoire Generale des Voyages
mwf0501	france corsica	1749	PREVOST-DEZAUCHE	785	50	67	Carte Particuliere de l'Isle de Corse
mwwi0597	hispaniola	1730	PRICE	2500	47	59	A Correct Chart of Hispaniola with the Windward Passage
mwuk0137	ireland	1711	PRICE	1600	95	67	A Correct Map of Ireland Divided into it's Provinces, Counties, and Baronies,
mwru0129	russia	1711	PRICE	960	96	64	A Correct Map of Muscovy
mww0317	world	1711	PRICE	6500	69	99	A New and Correct Map of the World Projected upon the Plane of the Horizon Laid Down from the Newest Discoveries and Most Exact Observations (2 polar projections)
mwuk0788	uk	1708	PRICE	1400	94	65	A New Map of Great Britain, Corrected from the Observations Communicated to the Royal Society at London
mwaf0140	africa	1711	PRICE-SENEX	2800	66	95	Africa Corrected from Observations of Mess. of ye Royal Societies at London and Paris
mwgr0155	greece	1711	PRICE	785	48	64	Graecia Pars Meridionalis
mwaf0170	africa	1732	PRICE-WILLDEY	2400	65	95	Africa Corrected from Observations of Mess. of ye Royal Societies at London and Paris by C. Price
mwaf0337	africa	1843	PRICHARD	200	48	60	Ethnographical Map of Asia, in the Earliest Times, Illustrative of Dr. Prichard's Natural History of Man and his Researches into the Physical History of Mankind
mwme0285	holy land	1725	PRIDEAUX	900	39	45	Delineatio und Beschreibung Palestinae oder des Gelobten Landes (size incl. text panel below map)

AMPG REFERENCE	REGION	DATE	MAP MAKER	PRICE (UK£)	VERT. (cm.)	HOR. (cm.)	TITLE OF MAP (Comments by the editor in brackets)
mwme0286	holy land	1725	PRIDEAUX	750	29	45	Delineatio und Beschreibung des Gelobten Landes (different inset and cartouche from previous map)
mwuk0183	ireland	1760	PRINALD	235	28	19	A New Map of Ireland
mwuk0499	scotland	1750	PRINALD	235	29	19	A New Map of Scotland or North Britain
mww0469	world	1766	PRINALD	480	19	28	A New Map of the World on Mercator's Projection
mwec0724	uk england leicestershire	1779	PRIOR	2800	117	127	A Map of Leicestershire from an Actual Survey, Begun in the Year 1775, and Finished in the Year 1777
mwbp0281a	poland	1670	PRIORATO	550	36	47	Silesia Ducatus
mwaf0189	africa	1748	PROBST	785	28	39	(Untitled map illustrating a voyage to Goa)
mwam1052	america north (east)	1777	PROBST	3500	100	97	A Map of the Most Inhabited Part of New England, Containing the Provinces of Massachusets Bay and New Hampshire, with the Colonies of Conecticut and Rhode Island
mwaf0262	africa	1789	PROBST	320	16	24	Africa
mwaf0243	africa	1780	PROBST	650	50	57	Africa iuxta Navigationes et Observationes (re-issue of Seutter 1730)
mwam0228	america continent	1788	PROBST	450	17	20	America
mwam1078a	america north	1782	PROBST	300	17	20	America Septentrionalis Coloniis in Interiorem Virginiam Deductis &c. (close copy of Schreibern 1755)
mwas0197	asia continent	1780	PROBST	750	50	58	Asia cum Omnibus Imperiis Provinciis Statibus et Insulis
mwbh0732a	belgium holland	1780	PROBST	300	50	58	Belgium Catholicum seu Decem Provinciae Germaniae Inferioris
mwuk1508a	uk english channel (all)	1782	PROBST	650	53	75	Carte de la Manche
mwf0590a	france ile de france	1770	PROBST	400	49	58	Carte de la Prevoste et Vicomte de Paris (map by Seutter)
mwbp0497	poland	1780	PROBST	720	49	57	Carte Nouvelle des Royaumes de Galizie et Lodomerie avec le Districe de Bukowine
mwru0293	russia	1788	PROBST	180	17	20	Charte das Russische Reich
mwme1015a	turkey etc	1760	PROBST	960	28	41	Constantinopolis (view)
mwsc0377	scandinavia denmark	1786	PROBST	140	16	24	Das Koenigreich Daennemarck nebst denen Angraentzenden Laendern
mwit1036	italy south	1750	PROBST	480	44	54	Das Konigreich Napoli in dessen XII Hauptprovincien
mwbp0511	poland	1787	PROBST	160	17	20	Das Konigreich Preussen nebst dem Polnischen Antheil
mwe0961	europe hungary	1789	PROBST	140	16	24	Das Konigreich Ungarn mit Angraenzenden Kayserlichen Landern
mwg0396	bavaria	1787	PROBST	140	17	20	Der Schwabische Creis
mwme1037	turkey etc	1789	PROBST	160	17	25	Die Asiatische Turkey Begreift in sich Natolien, Georgien, Armenien, Mesopotamien, Syrien und Arabien
mwru0570	ukraine	1789	PROBST	160	15	24	Die Europaische oder Kleine Tartarey
mwbh0742	belgium holland	1785	PROBST	160	17	20	Die Oestereichische Niederlande
mwas0802	asia south east philippines	1782	PROBST	480	17	20	Die Philippinische Inselen
mwit0517	italy lombardy	1759	PROBST	400	36	43	Ducatus Mediolanus, Placentini et Parmensis Nova Tabula
mwme0623	arabia etc	1750	PROBST	675	46	56	Estats de l'Empire du Grand Seigneur des Turcs (title above map: 'Imperium Turcicum Complectens ...')
mwe0200	europe	1780	PROBST	550	50	57	Europa Religionis Christianae Morum et Pacis ac Belli Artium Cultu
mwe0216	europe	1788	PROBST	180	17	20	Europe
mww0543	world	1786	PROBST	300	17	24	Globus Terrestris
mwuk0863	uk	1785	PROBST	180	17	20	Gros Britan
mwsw0195	switzerland	1788	PROBST	200	17	20	Helvetia Foederata
mwme0507	jerusalem	1760	PROBST	5500	37	102	Ierusalema Hodierna
mwf0150	france	1780	PROBST	480	49	57	Le Royaume de France
mwsp0111a	portugal	1776	PROBST	3500	39	104	Lisabona
mwsp0098	portugal	1760	PROBST	3000	32	112	LissBona (view)
mwe0830a	europe east	1789	PROBST	720	46	57	Mappa nova Principatus Moldaviae & Bucovinae cum finitimis regionibus
mww0525	world	1782	PROBST	3000	47	95	Mappe Monde ou Carte Generale de l'Univers sur une Projection Nouvelle d'une Sphere Ovale pour Mieux Entendre les Distances entre l'Europe et Amerique avec le Tour du Monde du Lieut. Cook et Tous les Decouvertes Nouvelles Dessinee et gravee par Jean Michel Probst a Augsbourg MDCCLXXXII (updated version of Lotter's 1778 map)
mww0543a	world	1786	PROBST	950	53	77	Mappe-Monde ou sont marquées les nouvelles Découvertes
mwe0467	europe central	1785	PROBST	450	61	74	Neue und Vollstandige Post Charte durch Gantz Deutschland nach Italien ... und Ungarn
mwe0814	europe east	1771	PROBST	600	50	59	Nova et Accurata Tabula Regnorum Sup. et Inf. Hungariae It. Sclavoniae, Bosniae, Serviae, Albaniae. Bessarabiae Ut et Princip. Transilvaniae, Moldaviae, Walachiae, Bulgar et Romaniae
mwru0558	ukraine	1784	PROBST	550	46	56	Nova et Accurata Tartariae Europae seu Minoris et in Specie Crimeae ... cum Omnibus Circa Pontium Euxinum
mwam1078	america north (east)	1782	PROBST	2000	50	49	Nova Mappa Geographica Americae Septentrionalis ... Sumptibus Ioh: Mich: Probst, Aug: Vind: Ao MDCCLXXXII (Probst's version of Popple's index map of 1733)
mwbh0733	belgium holland	1780	PROBST	480	51	57	Nova Mappa Geographica Belgii Universi
mwru0559	ukraine	1784	PROBST	750	45	54	Nova Mappa Geographica Tartariae Europaeae

AMPG REFERENCE	REGION	DATE	MAP MAKER	PRICE (UK£)	VERT. (cm.)	HOR. (cm.)	TITLE OF MAP (Comments by the editor in brackets)
mwe1057	europe romania	1789	PROBST	500	46	57	Nova Mappa Principatus Walachiae MDCCLXXXIX - Neue Landkarte von dem Furstenthum Walachey
mwuk0840	uk	1758	PROBST	650	47	55	Nova Totius Angliae, Scotiae et Hiberniae Tab:
mwsw0183	switzerland	1780	PROBST	480	50	57	Nova Totius Helvetiae
mwme0375	holy land	1788	PROBST	200	17	20	Palestina in XII Tribus Divisa
mwbp0455	poland	1757	PROBST	550	50	58	Poloniae Regnum ut et Magni Ducatus Lithuaniae
mwe0606	europe czech republic (bohemia)	1779	PROBST	785	39	49	Regnum Bohemiae iuxta XII Circulos Divisum (unusual decorative border)
mwg0156	germany	1788	PROBST	160	17	20	Reise Charte durch Deutschland
mwf0158	france	1789	PROBST	140	17	24	Reise Charte durch Franckreich
mwbp0128	baltic states	1750	PROBST	2500	35	111	Riga, metropolis Livoniae
mwsc0177	scandinavia	1788	PROBST	280	17	20	Scandinavia
mwit1249a	italy venice	1780	PROBST	5500	30	101	Venetia (also issued without the text panels, top)
mwbh0738	belgium holland	1782	PROBST	240	17	20	VII. Provintiae seu Belgiu Foederatum
mwsp0735	gibraltar	1782	PROBST	720	36	55	Vue de la Montagne de Gibraltar et de la Ligne Espagnole (size excl. text panel below map)
mwuss0424	florida	1765	PROCKTER	280	19	20	A New and Accurate Map of East and West Florida, Drawn from the Best Authorities
mwwi0094	west indies	1760	PROCKTER-SAYER	650	56	59	The West Indies Exhibiting the English, French, Spanish, Dutch, and Danish Settlements, with the Adjacent Parts of North & South America (based on De Vaugondy 1750)
mwgr0001	greece	1477	PTOLEMY (BOLOGNA)		30	48	(Untitled 1st printed map of Greece)
mwit0001	italy	1477	PTOLEMY (BOLOGNA)		40	55	(Untitled 1st printed map of Italy)
mwaf0663	africa north	1477	PTOLEMY (BOLOGNA)		32	52	(Untitled 1st printed map of the northern half of Africa)
mww0003	world	1477	PTOLEMY (BOLOGNA)	300000	35	53	(Untitled conical projection. 1st printed geographical map of the world, based on Ptolemy, who lived in the 1st century AD.)
mwuk0646	uk	1477	PTOLEMY (BOLOGNA)		40	48	Prima Tabula (1st printed map of the UK. Illustrated is an early proof copy lacking the engraved wave effect in the sea areas and the scrolls surrounding the names of the oceans.)
mwg0001	germany	1477	PTOLEMY (BOLOGNA)		42	42	Quarta Tabula (1st printed map of Germany)
mwaf0825	africa north west	1477	PTOLEMY (BOLOGNA)		30	49	Tabula 11 (1st printed map of Morocco and Algeria)
mwaf0802	africa north tunisia	1477	PTOLEMY (BOLOGNA)		37	52	Tabula 12 (1st printed map of Tunisia)
mwaf0445	africa egypt etc	1477	PTOLEMY (BOLOGNA)		31	47	Tabula 13 (1st printed map of Egypt)
mwme0697	caucasus	1477	PTOLEMY (BOLOGNA)		40	40	Tabula 16 (1st printed map of Armenia etc)
mwme0897	turkey etc	1477	PTOLEMY (BOLOGNA)		34	50	Tabula 17 (1st printed map of Turkey)
mwme0002	holy land	1477	PTOLEMY (BOLOGNA)		34	53	Tabula 18
mwme0747	persia etc	1477	PTOLEMY (BOLOGNA)		38	52	Tabula 19 (1st printed map of Persia/Iran)
mwsp0139	spain	1477	PTOLEMY (BOLOGNA)		35	47	Tabula 2 (1st printed map of Spain)
mwme0520	arabia etc	1477	PTOLEMY (BOLOGNA)		31	50	Tabula 20 (1st printed map of Arabia)
mwas0295	asia caspian sea	1477	PTOLEMY (BOLOGNA)		32	52	Tabula 21 (1st printed map of this region)
mwas0328	asia central	1477	PTOLEMY (BOLOGNA)		32	38	Tabula 22 (1st printed map of this region)
mwin0488	pakistan etc.	1477	PTOLEMY (BOLOGNA)		36	33	Tabula 23 (1st printed map of this region)
mwin0074	india	1477	PTOLEMY (BOLOGNA)		37	51	Tabula 24 (1st printed map of India)
mwas0271	asia burma	1477	PTOLEMY (BOLOGNA)		35	45	Tabula 25 (1st printed map of this region)
mwin0001	ceylon	1477	PTOLEMY (BOLOGNA)		28	28	Tabula 26 (1st printed map of Taprobana/Ceylon)
mwru0001	russia	1477	PTOLEMY (BOLOGNA)		37	45	Tabula 8 (1st printed map of Sarmatia/Western Russia)
mwe1125	europe south east	1477	PTOLEMY (BOLOGNA)		30	33	Tabula 9 (1st printed map of South Eastern Europe)
mwe0621	europe dalmatia	1477	PTOLEMY (BOLOGNA)		27	42	Tabula Quinta (1st printed map of Dalmatia)
mwit0843	italy sardinia and sicily	1477	PTOLEMY (BOLOGNA)		23	34	Tabula Sete (1st printed map of Sicily and Sardinia)
mwf0001	france	1477	PTOLEMY (BOLOGNA)		40	34	Tabula Tercia (1st printed map of France)
mwuk0900	england	1528	PTOLEMY (BORDONE)	900	23	16	Tavola secondo Tolomeo (title below map. Incl. Scotland.)
mww0005	world	1482	PTOLEMY (FLORENCE)	150000	41	57	Caelestem hic Terram Inspicias Terrestre q' Caelum (atlas by Francesco Berlinghieri. World map includes curved lines of longitude implying a three-dimensional curvature of the earth, which was commonly believed to be flat at the time.)
mwg0002	germany	1482	PTOLEMY (FLORENCE)	8000	36	31	Quarta Tabula D Europa
mwin0075	india	1482	PTOLEMY (FLORENCE)	12000	35	50	Tabula Decima d Asia
mwgr0002	greece	1482	PTOLEMY (FLORENCE)	9000	36	42	Tabula Decima De Europa
mwaf0803	africa north tunisia	1482	PTOLEMY (FLORENCE)	3000	28	43	Tabula di Libya Seconda
mwin0002	ceylon	1482	PTOLEMY (FLORENCE)	8000	32	30	Tabula Duodecima Dasia.
mwin0490	pakistan etc.	1482	PTOLEMY (FLORENCE)	3000	34	25	Tabula Nona de Asia
mwe1126	europe south east	1482	PTOLEMY (FLORENCE)	6000	35	46	Tabula Nona De Uarsopa
mwas0330	asia central	1482	PTOLEMY (FLORENCE)	4000	27	25	Tabula Octava Dasia.
mwe0728	europe east	1482	PTOLEMY (FLORENCE)	8000	39	43	Tabula Octava de Europe
mwbp0155	poland	1482	PTOLEMY (FLORENCE)	8000	39	43	Tabula Octava de Europe
mwuk0647	uk	1482	PTOLEMY (FLORENCE)	15000	38	45	Tabula Prima d Europa
mwme0898	turkey etc	1482	PTOLEMY (FLORENCE)	8000	35	49	Tabula Prima de Asia
mwaf0826	africa north west	1482	PTOLEMY (FLORENCE)	6500	32	48	Tabula Prima di Libya quale et Aphrica
mwme0004	holy land	1482	PTOLEMY (FLORENCE)	9000	33	49	Tabula Quarta de Asia
mwaf0664	africa north	1482	PTOLEMY (FLORENCE)	9000	34	51	Tabula Quarta di Libya
mwme0748	persia etc	1482	PTOLEMY (FLORENCE)	10000	33	46	Tabula Quinta De Asia
mwe0622	europe dalmatia	1482	PTOLEMY (FLORENCE)	6000	30	49	Tabula Quinta de Europa
mwru0002	russia	1482	PTOLEMY (FLORENCE)	18000	37	41	Tabula Seconda De Asia (note triangular-shaped Black Sea)

AMPG REFERENCE	REGION	DATE	MAP MAKER	PRICE (UK£)	VERT. (cm.)	HOR. (cm.)	TITLE OF MAP (Comments by the editor in brackets)
mwsp0141	spain	1482	PTOLEMY (FLORENCE)	7500	38	50	Tabula Secunda de Europa
mwas0297	asia caspian sea	1482	PTOLEMY (FLORENCE)	6000	33	48	Tabula Septima de Asia
mwit0844	italy sardinia and sicily	1482	PTOLEMY (FLORENCE)	5000	24	43	Tabula Septima De Europa
mwme0521	arabia etc	1482	PTOLEMY (FLORENCE)	15000	31	50	Tabula Sexta de Asia
mwit0004	italy	1482	PTOLEMY (FLORENCE)	15000	33	46	Tabula Sexta De Vropa
mwme0699	caucasus	1482	PTOLEMY (FLORENCE)	6000	34	46	Tabula Tertia d Asia
mwf0003	france	1482	PTOLEMY (FLORENCE)	6000	35	30	Tabula Tertia de Europa
mwaf0446	africa egypt etc	1482	PTOLEMY (FLORENCE)	6000	28	48	Tabula Tertia di Libya
mwas0272	asia burma	1482	PTOLEMY (FLORENCE)	6000	39	40	Tabula Undecima de Asia
FOR 'MODERN' MAPS IN THE PTOLEMY (FLORENCE) SEE UNDER 'BERLINGHIERI'							
mww0029	world	1522	PTOLEMY (FRIES)	3000	30	46	Generale Ptho. (reprinted with changes 1525, 1535 and 1541. Title above map)
mwme0752	persia etc	1522	PTOLEMY (FRIES)	1500	37	54	Quinta Asie Tabula. (reprinted 1525, 1535 and 1541)
mwg0010	germany	1522	PTOLEMY (FRIES)	1500	33	37	Tabu. III Europ. (reprinted 1525, 1535 and 1541)
mwin0495	pakistan etc.	1522	PTOLEMY (FRIES)	1200	30	28	Tabu. IX Asiae (reprinted 1525, 1535 and 1541)
mwas0335	asia central	1522	PTOLEMY (FRIES)	2000	31	36	Tabu. VIII. Asiae. (reprinted 1525, 1535 and 1541)
mwaf0831	africa north west	1522	PTOLEMY (FRIES)	1500	33	48	Tabula I Affri. (reprinted 1525, 1535 and 1541)
mwaf0808	africa north tunisia	1522	PTOLEMY (FRIES)	1000	28	46	Tabula II. Affri (reprinted 1525, 1535 and 1541)
mwme0704	caucasus	1522	PTOLEMY (FRIES)	1200	34	42	Tabula III Asiae (reprinted 1525, 1535 and 1541)
mwf0011	france	1522	PTOLEMY (FRIES)	1200	35	47	Tabula III Euro. (reprinted 1525, 1535 and 1541)
mwaf0669	africa north	1522	PTOLEMY (FRIES)	2400	33	47	Tabula IIII Affri. (reprinted 1525, 1535 and 1541)
mwe1131	europe south east	1522	PTOLEMY (FRIES)	1250	34	51	Tabula IX Euro. (reprinted 1525, 1535 and 1541)
mwsp0149	spain	1522	PTOLEMY (FRIES)	2000	35	45	Tabula II Europae (reprinted 1525, 1535 and 1541)
mwru0007	russia	1522	PTOLEMY (FRIES)	3500	35	43	Tabula II. Asiae. (reprinted 1525, 1535 and 1541)
mwit0849	italy sardinia and sicily	1522	PTOLEMY (FRIES)	1200	39	57	Tabula VII Euro. (reprinted 1525, 1535 and 1541)
mwe0735	europe east	1522	PTOLEMY (FRIES)	1500	33	47	Tabula VIII. Europ (reprinted 1525, 1535 and 1541)
mwbp0162	poland	1522	PTOLEMY (FRIES)	1500	33	47	Tabula VIII. Europ (reprinted 1525, 1535 and 1541)
mwin0082	india	1522	PTOLEMY (FRIES)	2000	34	49	Tabula X Asiae (reprinted 1525, 1535 and 1541)
mwas0277	asia burma	1522	PTOLEMY (FRIES)	1000	28	32	Tabula XI Asia (reprinted 1525, 1535 and 1541)
mwuk0655	uk	1522	PTOLEMY (FRIES)	2500	33	44	Tabula. I Euro. (reprinted 1525, 1535 and 1541)
mwme0905	turkey etc	1522	PTOLEMY (FRIES)	1500	33	52	Tabula. I. Asiae. (reprinted 1525, 1535 and 1541. Illustrated is 1541 edition.)
mwaf0451	africa egypt etc	1522	PTOLEMY (FRIES)	1500	34	53	Tabula. III. Affri. (reprinted 1525, 1535 and 1541)
mwme0015	holy land	1522	PTOLEMY (FRIES)	1500	35	51	Tabula. IIII. Asiae (reprinted 1525, 1535 and 1541)
mwe0627	europe dalmatia	1522	PTOLEMY (FRIES)	1500	33	53	Tabula. V. Europ. (reprinted 1525, 1535 and 1541)
mwit0012	italy	1522	PTOLEMY (FRIES)	2000	28	43	Tabula. VI Europ. (reprinted 1525, 1535 and 1541)
mwme0527	arabia etc	1522	PTOLEMY (FRIES)	3500	28	46	Tabula. VI. Asiae. (reprinted 1525, 1535 and 1541)
mwas0302	asia caspian sea	1522	PTOLEMY (FRIES)	2000	28	45	Tabula. VII. Asiae. (reprinted 1525, 1535 and 1541)
mwgr0008	greece	1522	PTOLEMY (FRIES)	2000	36	52	Tabula. X. Euro. (reprinted 1525, 1535 and 1541)
mwin0007	ceylon	1522	PTOLEMY (FRIES)	2000	28	36	Tabula. XII. Asiae (reprinted 1525, 1535 and 1541)
FOR MODERN MAPS BY FRIES, SEE UNDER 'FRIES' ETC.							
mwaf0832	africa north west	1548	PTOLEMY (GASTALDI)	550	13	17	Tabula Aphricae I
mwaf0673	africa north	1548	PTOLEMY (GASTALDI)	350	13	17	Tabula Aphricae II
mwaf0453	africa egypt etc	1548	PTOLEMY (GASTALDI)	300	13	17	Tabula Aphricae III
mwme0910	turkey etc	1548	PTOLEMY (GASTALDI)	450	13	17	Tabula Asiae I
mwme0708	caucasus	1548	PTOLEMY (GASTALDI)	400	13	17	Tabula Asiae III
mwme0025	holy land	1548	PTOLEMY (GASTALDI)	650	14	18	Tabula Asiae IIII
mwin0497	pakistan etc.	1548	PTOLEMY (GASTALDI)	400	13	17	Tabula Asiae IX
mwme0755	persia etc	1548	PTOLEMY (GASTALDI)	350	14	17	Tabula Asiae V
mwme0530	arabia etc	1548	PTOLEMY (GASTALDI)	500	13	18	Tabula Asiae VI
mwru0413	russia tartary	1548	PTOLEMY (GASTALDI)	450	13	17	Tabula Asiae VII
mwas0337	asia central	1548	PTOLEMY (GASTALDI)	1000	13	17	Tabula Asiae VIII
mwin0085	india	1548	PTOLEMY (GASTALDI)	400	12	17	Tabula Asiae X
mwas0279	asia burma	1548	PTOLEMY (GASTALDI)	500	13	17	Tabula Asiae XI
mwin0010	ceylon	1548	PTOLEMY (GASTALDI)	400	13	17	Tabula Asiae XII
mwuk0661	uk	1548	PTOLEMY (GASTALDI)	500	12	17	Tabula Europae I
mwsp0155	spain	1548	PTOLEMY (GASTALDI)	350	13	17	Tabula Europae II
mwf0014	france	1548	PTOLEMY (GASTALDI)	300	13	17	Tabula Europae III
mwg0013	germany	1548	PTOLEMY (GASTALDI)	300	13	17	Tabula Europae IIII
mwe1132a	europe south east	1548	PTOLEMY (GASTALDI)	300	13	17	Tabula Europae IX
mwe0633	europe dalmatia	1548	PTOLEMY (GASTALDI)	300	13	17	Tabula Europae V
mwit0021	italy	1548	PTOLEMY (GASTALDI)	400	13	17	Tabula Europae VI
mwit0852	italy sardinia and sicily	1548	PTOLEMY (GASTALDI)	350	13	17	Tabula Europae VII
mwe0738	europe east	1548	PTOLEMY (GASTALDI)	450	13	18	Tabula Europae VIII
mwbp0167	poland	1548	PTOLEMY (GASTALDI)	450	13	18	Tabula Europae VIII
mwuk0658	uk	1541	PTOLEMY (HONTER)	720	13	16	(Untitled map. Honter's modern map of the UK first appeared in 1561)
mwit0035	italy	1578	PTOLEMY (MERCATOR)	2000	34	48	Eur: VI Tab:
mwuk0672	uk	1578	PTOLEMY (MERCATOR)	1100	34	41	Europae 1 Tab:
mww0069	world	1578	PTOLEMY (MERCATOR)	2500	34	49	Universalis Tabula iuxta Ptolemaeum (1st edition, no text on verso)
mwaf0452	africa egypt etc	1545	PTOLEMY (MUNSTER)	450	26	35	Africae Tabula III
mwaf0833	africa north west	1540	PTOLEMY (MUNSTER)	500	27	33	Aphricae Tabula I
mwaf0672	africa north	1540	PTOLEMY (MUNSTER)	550	27	34	Aphricae Tabula II (shows St Paul's shipwreck.)
mwaf0671	africa north	1540	PTOLEMY (MUNSTER)	550	27	35	Tabula Africae IIII
mwme0907	turkey etc	1542	PTOLEMY (MUNSTER)	600	26	34	Tabula Asiae I

AMPG REFERENCE	REGION	DATE	MAP MAKER	PRICE (UK£)	VERT. (cm.)	HOR. (cm.)	TITLE OF MAP (Comments by the editor in brackets)
mwru0008	russia	1540	PTOLEMY (MUNSTER)	600	27	34	Tabula Asiae II
mwme0705	caucasus	1540	PTOLEMY (MUNSTER)	450	26	33	Tabula Asiae III
mwme0021	holy land	1540	PTOLEMY (MUNSTER)	720	27	35	Tabula Asiae IIII
mwme0753	persia etc	1540	PTOLEMY (MUNSTER)	450	25	34	Tabula Asiae V
mwme0528	arabia etc	1540	PTOLEMY (MUNSTER)	1000	27	35	Tabula Asiae VI
mwru0412	russia tartary	1540	PTOLEMY (MUNSTER)	450	26	34	Tabula Asiae VII
mwas0336	asia central	1542	PTOLEMY (MUNSTER)	650	25	34	Tabula Asiae VIII
mwin0496	pakistan etc.	1540	PTOLEMY (MUNSTER)	400	25	34	Tabula Asiae IX
mwin0083	india	1540	PTOLEMY (MUNSTER)	400	27	33	Tabula Asiae X (re-issued in 1571 with title 'Tabula Indiae X')
mwas0278	asia burma	1540	PTOLEMY (MUNSTER)	550	27	35	Tabula Asiae XI
mwin0009	ceylon	1540	PTOLEMY (MUNSTER)	400	25	34	Tabula Asiae XII
mwuk0657	uk	1540	PTOLEMY (MUNSTER)	1200	26	33	Tabula Europae I
mwsp0151	spain	1540	PTOLEMY (MUNSTER)	550	28	35	Tabula Europae II
mwf0012	france	1540	PTOLEMY (MUNSTER)	450	27	33	Tabula Europae III
	germany	1540	PTOLEMY (MUNSTER)	450	27	34	Tabula Europae IIII
mwe0630	europe dalmatia	1540	PTOLEMY (MUNSTER)	480	26	33	Tabula Europae V
mwit0016	italy	1540	PTOLEMY (MUNSTER)	750	27	34	Tabula Europae VI (illustrated is the 1552 Strabo edition with title 'Tabula Italiae')
mwit0850	italy sardinia and sicily	1540	PTOLEMY (MUNSTER)	400	27	35	Tabula Europae VII
mwbp0163	poland	1540	PTOLEMY (MUNSTER)	600	27	34	Tabula Europae VIII
mwe0736	europe east	1540	PTOLEMY (MUNSTER)	450	28	34	Tabula Europae VIII
mwgr0013	greece	1540	PTOLEMY (MUNSTER)	675	27	32	Tabula Europae X
mwg0012	germany	1540	PTOLEMY (MUNSTER)	400	28	33	Tabula Germaniae
mww0038	world	1540	PTOLEMY (MUNSTER)	1350	27	34	Typus Orbis A Ptol Descriptus
mww0014	world	1503	PTOLEMY (REISCH)	12500	28	41	(Untitled map with 12 windheads)
mww0015	world	1504	PTOLEMY (REISCH)	12000	27	40	(Untitled map with 4 windheads)
mww0004	world	1478	PTOLEMY (ROME)	150000	32	54	(Untitled conical projection, 1st edition of the Rome Ptolemy, reprinted in 1490 and 1507.)
mwin0077	india	1490	PTOLEMY (ROME)	8000	34	48	Decima Asiae Tabula (1st edition 1478, 2nd 1490, 3rd 1507, 4th 1508)
mwgr0004	greece	1490	PTOLEMY (ROME)	7200	37	52	Decima et Ultima Europe Tabula (1st edition 1478, 2nd 1490, 3rd 1507, 4th 1508)
mwin0004	ceylon	1490	PTOLEMY (ROME)	4800	35	32	Duodecima et Ultima Asiae Tabula (1st edition 1478, 2nd 1490, 3rd 1507, 4th 1508)
mwin0492	pakistan etc.	1490	PTOLEMY (ROME)	2500	37	30	Nona Asiae Tabula (1st edition 1478, 2nd 1490, 3rd 1507, 4th 1508)
mwe1128	europe south east	1490	PTOLEMY (ROME)	5000	36	53	Nona Europae Tabula (1st edition 1478, 2nd 1490, 3rd 1507, 4th 1508)
mwas0329	asia central	1478	PTOLEMY (ROME)	8000	37	42	Octava Asiae Tabula (1st edition 1478, 2nd 1490, 3rd 1507, 4th 1508)
mwe0730	europe east	1490	PTOLEMY (ROME)	4500	37	54	Octava Europe Tabula (1st edition 1478, 2nd 1490, 3rd 1507, 4th 1508)
mwbp0157	poland	1490	PTOLEMY (ROME)	4500	37	54	Octava Europe Tabula (1st edition 1478, 2nd 1490, 3rd 1507, 4th 1508)
mwaf0828	africa north west	1490	PTOLEMY (ROME)	4500	34	54	Prima Africae Tabula (1st edition 1478, 2nd 1490, 3rd 1507, 4th 1508)
mwme0900	turkey etc	1490	PTOLEMY (ROME)	5000	38	55	Prima Asiae Tabula (1st edition 1478, 2nd 1490, 3rd 1507, 4th 1508)
mwuk0650	uk	1490	PTOLEMY (ROME)	10000	34	55	Prima Europe Tabula (1st edition 1478, 2nd 1490, 3rd 1507, 4th 1508)
mwaf0666	africa north	1490	PTOLEMY (ROME)	6000	29	56	Quarta Africae Tabula (1st edition 1478, 2nd 1490, 3rd 1507, 4th 1508)
mwme0008	holy land	1490	PTOLEMY (ROME)	6000	37	54	Quarta Asiae Tabula (1st Rome edition 1478, 2nd 1490, 3rd 1507, 4th 1508)
mwg0005	germany	1490	PTOLEMY (ROME)	5000	37	46	Quarta Europe Tabula (1st edition 1478, 2nd 1490, 3rd 1507, 4th 1508)
mwme0750	persia etc	1490	PTOLEMY (ROME)	4000	36	55	Quinta Asiae Tabula (1st edition 1478, 2nd 1490, 3rd 1507, 4th 1508)
mwe0624	europe dalmatia	1490	PTOLEMY (ROME)	4000	27	54	Quinta Europe Tabula (1st edition 1478, 2nd 1490, 3rd 1507, 4th 1508)
mwaf0805	africa north tunisia	1490	PTOLEMY (ROME)	2000	28	54	Secunda Africae Tabula (1st edition 1478, 2nd 1490, 3rd 1507, 4th 1508)
mwru0004	russia	1490	PTOLEMY (ROME)	9000	36	50	Secunda Asiae Tabula (1st edition 1478, 2nd 1490, 3rd 1507, 4th 1508)
mwsp0144	spain	1490	PTOLEMY (ROME)	5000	36	52	Secunda Europe Tabula (1st Rome edition 1478, 2nd 1490, 3rd 1507, 4th 1508)
mwas0299	asia caspian sea	1490	PTOLEMY (ROME)	6000	30	55	Septima Asiae Tabula (1st edition 1478, 2nd 1490, 3rd 1507, 4th 1508)
mwit0846	italy sardinia and sicily	1490	PTOLEMY (ROME)	3000	27	47	Septima Europe Tabula (1st edition 1478, 2nd 1490, 3rd 1507, 4th 1508)
mwme0524	arabia etc	1490	PTOLEMY (ROME)	9000	28	50	Sexta Asiae Tabula (1st edition 1478, 2nd 1490, 3rd 1507, 4th 1508)
mwit0002	italy	1478	PTOLEMY (ROME)	25000	33	54	Sexta Europe Tabula (reprinted 1490, 1507, 1508)

AMPG REFERENCE	REGION	DATE	MAP MAKER	PRICE (UK£)	VERT. (cm.)	HOR. (cm.)	TITLE OF MAP (Comments by the editor in brackets)
mwsc0003	scandinavia	1507	PTOLEMY (ROME)	18000	32	56	Tabula Moderna Prussie, Livonie, Norvegie et Gottie (One of 6 modern maps in the 1507 and 1508 editions of Rome Ptolemy atlas)
mwme0010	holy land	1507	PTOLEMY (ROME)	8000	31	53	Tabula Moderna Terre Sancte (one of 6 modern maps in the 1507 and 1508 editions of the Rome Ptolemy atlas)
mwaf0448	africa egypt etc	1490	PTOLEMY (ROME)	3000	28	54	Tertia Africae Tabula (1st edition 1478, 2nd 1490, 3rd 1507, 4th 1508)
mwme0701	caucasus	1490	PTOLEMY (ROME)	4000	37	50	Tertia Asiae Tabula (1st edition 1478, 2nd 1490, 3rd 1507, 4th 1508)
mwf0006	france	1490	PTOLEMY (ROME)	4000	39	43	Tertia Europe Tabula (1st Rome edition 1478, 2nd 1490, 3rd 1507, 4th 1508)
mwas0274	asia burma	1490	PTOLEMY (ROME)	5000	38	56	Undecima Asiae Tabula (1st edition 1478, 2nd 1490, 3rd 1507, 4th 1508)
mwit0854	italy sardinia and sicily	1561	PTOLEMY (RUSCELLI)	250	18	25	Euopae Tabula VII
mwe0634	europe dalmatia	1561	PTOLEMY (RUSCELLI)	300	18	26	Europae Tabula V
mwit0024	italy	1561	PTOLEMY (RUSCELLI)	300	18	25	Europae Tabula VI
mwe0743	europe east	1564	PTOLEMY (RUSCELLI)	200	18	25	Europae Tabula VIII
mwbp0184	poland	1574	PTOLEMY (RUSCELLI)	200	18	25	Europae Tabula VIII (the sea lower right is the Black Sea)
mww0051	world	1561	PTOLEMY (RUSCELLI)	720	14	26	Ptolemaei Typus
mwaf0456	africa egypt etc	1561	PTOLEMY (RUSCELLI)	200	18	25	Tabula Africae III
mwaf0677	africa north	1574	PTOLEMY (RUSCELLI)	250	19	26	Tabula Africae IIII
mwaf0834	africa north west	1561	PTOLEMY (RUSCELLI)	200	18	25	Tabula Aphricae I
mwme0913	turkey etc	1561	PTOLEMY (RUSCELLI)	200	18	25	Tabula Asiae I
mwru0013	russia	1561	PTOLEMY (RUSCELLI)	200	18	25	Tabula Asiae II
mwme0709	caucasus	1561	PTOLEMY (RUSCELLI)	250	18	24	Tabula Asiae III
mwme0028	holy land	1561	PTOLEMY (RUSCELLI)	500	18	25	Tabula Asiae IIII
mwin0498	pakistan etc.	1561	PTOLEMY (RUSCELLI)	200	18	24	Tabula Asiae IX
mwme0763	persia etc	1596	PTOLEMY (RUSCELLI)	200	19	25	Tabula Asiae V
mwme0534	arabia etc	1561	PTOLEMY (RUSCELLI)	300	18	24	Tabula Asiae VI
mwas0303	asia caspian sea	1561	PTOLEMY (RUSCELLI)	350	18	25	Tabula Asiae VII
mwas0338	asia central	1561	PTOLEMY (RUSCELLI)	500	18	24	Tabula Asiae VIII
mwin0090	india	1561	PTOLEMY (RUSCELLI)	200	18	23	Tabula Asiae X
mwas0281	asia burma	1561	PTOLEMY (RUSCELLI)	250	19	26	Tabula Asiae XI
mwin0011	ceylon	1561	PTOLEMY (RUSCELLI)	250	18	24	Tabula Asiae XII
mwuk0665	uk	1561	PTOLEMY (RUSCELLI)	500	19	27	Tabula Europae I
mwsp0159	spain	1561	PTOLEMY (RUSCELLI)	250	20	28	Tabula Europae II
mwf0018	france	1561	PTOLEMY (RUSCELLI)	200	18	24	Tabula Europae III
mwg0017	germany	1561	PTOLEMY (RUSCELLI)	250	20	24	Tabula Europae IIII
mwe1134	europe south east	1561	PTOLEMY (RUSCELLI)	200	19	25	Tabula Europae IX
mwgr0018	greece	1561	PTOLEMY (RUSCELLI)	250	18	25	Tabula Europae X
mww0012	world	1493	PTOLEMY (SCHEDEL)	18000	37	52	Secunda Etas Mundi (2 editions in 1493)
mww0013	world	1496	PTOLEMY (SCHEDEL)	4500	10	15	Secunda Etas Mundi (publ. by Schonsperger on text page)
mww0019	world	1511	PTOLEMY (SYLVANUS)	9000	27	57	(Untitled map)
mwin0078	india	1511	PTOLEMY (SYLVANUS)	5000	37	56	Decima Asiae Tabula
mwgr0005	greece	1511	PTOLEMY (SYLVANUS)	6000			Decima Europae Tabula
mwin0005	ceylon	1511	PTOLEMY (SYLVANUS)	4000	38	38	Duodecima et Ultima Asiae Tabula
mwin0493	pakistan etc.	1511	PTOLEMY (SYLVANUS)	2000	41	51	Nona Asiae Tabula
mwe1129	europe south east	1511	PTOLEMY (SYLVANUS)	3000	39	48	Nona Europae Tabula
mwas0333	asia central	1511	PTOLEMY (SYLVANUS)	3000	41	51	Octava Asiae Tabula
mwe0731	europe east	1511	PTOLEMY (SYLVANUS)	3500	39	48	Octava Europae Tabula
mwbp0158	poland	1511	PTOLEMY (SYLVANUS)	3500	39	48	Octava Europae Tabula
mwaf0829	africa north west	1511	PTOLEMY (SYLVANUS)	3500	41	56	Prima Africae Tabula
mwme0901	turkey etc	1511	PTOLEMY (SYLVANUS)	4500	41	56	Prima Asiae Tabula
mwme0011	holy land	1511	PTOLEMY (SYLVANUS)	4500	38	56	Quarta Asiae Tabula
mwg0006	germany	1511	PTOLEMY (SYLVANUS)	3500	37	48	Quarta Europae Tabula
mwe0625	europe dalmatia	1511	PTOLEMY (SYLVANUS)	2500	41	51	Quinta Europae Tabula
mwaf0806	africa north tunisia	1511	PTOLEMY (SYLVANUS)	1500	41	56	Secunda Africae Tabula
mwru0005	russia	1511	PTOLEMY (SYLVANUS)	6000	41	51	Secunda Asiae Tabula
mwsp0145	spain	1511	PTOLEMY (SYLVANUS)		41	57	Secunda Europae Tabula (Printed on 2 sheets, one of which has on the verso part of the UK and the other sheet, the Ptolemaic world. Hence no estimated price.)
mwas0300	asia caspian sea	1511	PTOLEMY (SYLVANUS)	3000	38	53	Septima Asiae Tabula
mwme0525	arabia etc	1511	PTOLEMY (SYLVANUS)	7500	34	56	Sexta Asiae Tabula (incl. part of India, Ceylon)
mwit0007	italy	1511	PTOLEMY (SYLVANUS)	9000	41	56	Sexta Europae Tabula
mwaf0449	africa egypt etc	1511	PTOLEMY (SYLVANUS)	2500	41	51	Tertia Africa Tabula
mwme0702	caucasus	1511	PTOLEMY (SYLVANUS)	2500	41	56	Tertia Asiae Tabula
mwf0007	france	1511	PTOLEMY (SYLVANUS)	2500	41	51	Tertia Europae Tabula
mwas0275	asia burma	1511	PTOLEMY (SYLVANUS)	3000	41	46	Undecima Asiae Tabula
mwin0489	pakistan etc.	1482	PTOLEMY (ULM)	6000	40	37	(Nona Asie Tabula)
mwg0003	germany	1482	PTOLEMY (ULM)	8000	38	50	(Quarta Europe Tabula)
mwas0296	asia caspian sea	1482	PTOLEMY (ULM)	9000	30	50	(Septima Asie Tabula)
mwme0698	caucasus	1482	PTOLEMY (ULM)	8000	37	53	(Tertia Asie Tabula)
mwsc0001	scandinavia	1482	PTOLEMY (ULM)	45000	31	56	(Title on verso: 'Tabula Moderna Prussie Livonie Norbegie Et Gottie'. 1st printed map of Scandinavia on its own.)
mwme0522	arabia etc	1482	PTOLEMY (ULM)	24000	29	56	(Untitled map)
mwas0331	asia central	1482	PTOLEMY (ULM)	6000	37	45	(Untitled map)

AMPG REFERENCE	REGION	DATE	MAP MAKER	PRICE (UK£)	VERT. (cm.)	HOR. (cm.)	TITLE OF MAP (Comments by the editor in brackets)
mwin0003	ceylon	1482	PTOLEMY (ULM)	10000	29	26	(untitled map. 1486 edition has the title 'Duodecima Asie Tabula')
mwsp0142	spain	1482	PTOLEMY (ULM)	18000	39	53	(Untitled map, reprinted in 1486 with the title: Secunda Europe Tabula.)
mwuk0648	uk	1482	PTOLEMY (ULM)	25000	38	56	(Untitled map, reprinted in 1486 with title. See below.)
mww0006	world	1482	PTOLEMY (ULM)	150000	40	55	(Untitled map, reprinted in 1486. Includes Scandinavia for the first time. Copies previous map's curved lines of longitude.)
mwit0005	italy	1482	PTOLEMY (ULM)	20000	38	57	(Untitled map. Reprinted in 1486 with title 'Sexta Europe Tabula'. Illustrated is 1486 edition.)
mwme0005	holy land	1482	PTOLEMY (ULM)	18000	32	53	(Untitled 'modern' map. Also appears in the 1486 Ulm edition with the title 'Tabula Moderna Terre Sancte', illustrated here. However, the geographic details are copied from the Ptolemaic map.)
mwin0076	india	1482	PTOLEMY (ULM)	12000	36	51	Decima Asie Tabula (reprinted 1486)
mwgr0003	greece	1486	PTOLEMY (ULM)	9000	38	46	Decima Europe Tabula (1st edition 1482)
mwin0491	pakistan etc.	1486	PTOLEMY (ULM)	3000	41	55	Nona Asie Tabula (1st edition 1482)
mwe1127	europe south east	1482	PTOLEMY (ULM)	6500	38	56	Nona Europae Tabula (2nd edition 1486)
mwas0332	asia central	1486	PTOLEMY (ULM)	4500	33	55	Octava Asie Tabula
mwe0729	europe east	1482	PTOLEMY (ULM)	15000	40	57	Octava Europe Tabula (2nd edition 1486)
mwaf0827	africa north west	1482	PTOLEMY (ULM)	7500	36	54	Prima Affrice Tabula (2nd edition 1486)
mwme0899	turkey etc	1486	PTOLEMY (ULM)	9000	36	55	Prima Asie Tabula (1st edition 1482, untitled)
mwuk0649	uk	1486	PTOLEMY (ULM)	16000	37	56	Prima Europe Tabula
mwaf0665	africa north	1482	PTOLEMY (ULM)	15000	42	57	Quarta Affrice Tabula (2nd edition 1486)
mwme0006	holy land	1486	PTOLEMY (ULM)	12000	37	53	Quarta Asie Tabula (also in the 1482 Ulm edition, untitled.)
mwg0004	germany	1486	PTOLEMY (ULM)	6500	39	50	Quarta Europe Tabula (1st Ulm edition 1482)
mwme0749	persia etc	1486	PTOLEMY (ULM)	6000	39	56	Quinta Asie Tabula (1st edition 1482, untitled)
mwe0623	europe dalmatia	1486	PTOLEMY (ULM)	6000	29	58	Quinta Europe Tabula (1st edition 1482)
mwaf0804	africa north tunisia	1482	PTOLEMY (ULM)	5000	33	57	Secunda Affrice Tabula (2nd edition 1486)
mwru0003	russia	1482	PTOLEMY (ULM)	24000	39	51	Secunda Asie Tabula (title on verso)
mwas0298	asia caspian sea	1486	PTOLEMY (ULM)	6000	33	55	Septima Asie Tabula (1st edition 1482)
mwit0845	italy sardinia and sicily	1486	PTOLEMY (ULM)	5000	28	49	Septima Europe Tabula (1st edition 1482, untitled)
mwme0523	arabia etc	1486	PTOLEMY (ULM)	12000	29	55	Sexta Asie Tabula (1st edition 1482)
mwf0005	france	1486	PTOLEMY (ULM)	8000	39	55	Tabula Moderna Francie ('modern' map of France included in both Ulm Ptolemy editions of 1482 and 1486. The map is 'modern' as far as place names etc. are concerned, but it retains Ptolemy's coastline.)
mwsp0143	spain	1486	PTOLEMY (ULM)	12000	39	53	Tabula Moderna Hispanie ('modern' map of Spain included in both the Ulm Ptolemy atlases of 1482 and 1486, using modern names but retaining Ptolemy's coastline.)
mwit0006	italy	1486	PTOLEMY (ULM)	13500	35	54	Tabula Moderna Italie ('modern' map of Italy included in both the Ulm Ptolemy atlases of 1482 and 1486. The map is 'modern' as far as place names are concerned, but it retains Ptolemy's coastline.)
mwsc0002	scandinavia	1486	PTOLEMY (ULM)	30000	31	56	Tabula Moderna Prussie Livonie Norbegie et Gottie (2nd Ulm edition)
mwaf0447	africa egypt etc	1482	PTOLEMY (ULM)	6000	33	57	Tercia Affrice Tabula (2nd edition 1486)
mwme0700	caucasus	1486	PTOLEMY (ULM)	4500	39	55	Tercia Asie Tabula (1st edition 1482)
mwf0004	france	1482	PTOLEMY (ULM)	6000	40	50	Tercia Europe Tabula (1st Ulm edition 1482, untitled)
mwas0273	asia burma	1482	PTOLEMY (ULM)	14000	40	52	Undecima Asie Tabula (2nd edition 1486)
mwin0079	india	1513	PTOLEMY (WALDSEEMULLER)	4000	37	55	Decima Asiae Tabula (reprinted 1520)
mwgr0006	greece	1513	PTOLEMY (WALDSEEMULLER)	3600	41	55	Decima et Ultima Tabula Europae
mwin0006	ceylon	1513	PTOLEMY (WALDSEEMULLER)	3000	30	25	Duodecima Asiae Tabula (reprinted 1520)
mww0021	world	1513	PTOLEMY (WALDSEEMULLER)	18000	44	55	Generale Ptholemei
mwin0494	pakistan etc.	1513	PTOLEMY (WALDSEEMULLER)	2000	40	37	Nona Asiae Tabula
mwe1130	europe south east	1513	PTOLEMY (WALDSEEMULLER)	2500	41	57	Nona Europe Tabula (reprinted 1520)
mwas0334	asia central	1513	PTOLEMY (WALDSEEMULLER)	4000	37	52	Octava Asie Tabula
mwe0732	europe east	1513	PTOLEMY (WALDSEEMULLER)	2400	40	58	Octava Europe Tabula (reprinted 1520)
mwbp0159	poland	1513	PTOLEMY (WALDSEEMULLER)	2400	40	58	Octava Europe Tabula (reprinted 1520)
mwme0012	holy land	1513	PTOLEMY (WALDSEEMULLER)	3600	39	53	Quarta Asiae Tabula (reprinted 1520)
mwg0007	germany	1513	PTOLEMY (WALDSEEMULLER)	3000	38	48	Quarta Europae Tabula (reprinted 1520)
mwme0751	persia etc	1513	PTOLEMY (WALDSEEMULLER)	3000	38	55	Quinta Asie Tabula
mwe0626	europe dalmatia	1513	PTOLEMY (WALDSEEMULLER)	2250	34	53	Quinta EuropaeTabula (reprinted 1520)

AMPG REFERENCE	REGION	DATE	MAP MAKER	PRICE (UK£)	VERT. (cm.)	HOR. (cm.)	TITLE OF MAP (Comments by the editor in brackets)
mwru0006	russia	1513	PTOLEMY (WALDSEEMULLER)	6000	38	49	Secunda Asiae Tabula (reprinted 1520. Note Caspian Sea lower right.)
mwas0301	asia caspian sea	1513	PTOLEMY (WALDSEEMULLER)	3000	34	53	Septima Asie Tabula
mwit0847	italy sardinia and sicily	1513	PTOLEMY (WALDSEEMULLER)	2500	33	59	Septima Europe Tabula
mwme0526	arabia etc	1513	PTOLEMY (WALDSEEMULLER)	7500	31	54	Sexta Asie Tabula
mwit0008	italy	1513	PTOLEMY (WALDSEEMULLER)	6000	37	59	Tabula Europ. Sexta Italiae (reprinted 1520)
mwaf0830	africa north west	1513	PTOLEMY (WALDSEEMULLER)	3000	34	52	Tabula Prima Africae
mwme0903	turkey etc	1513	PTOLEMY (WALDSEEMULLER)	2500	39	53	Tabula Prima Asie (reprinted 1520)
mwuk0652	uk	1513	PTOLEMY (WALDSEEMULLER)	6000	41	59	Tabula Prima Europae (reprinted 1520)
mwaf0668	africa north	1513	PTOLEMY (WALDSEEMULLER)	4000	34	50	Tabula Quarta Africae (reprinted 1520)
mwaf0807	africa north tunisia	1513	PTOLEMY (WALDSEEMULLER)	1500	35	53	Tabula Secunda Africae
mwsp0146	spain	1513	PTOLEMY (WALDSEEMULLER)	3000	39	59	Tabula Secunda Europe (reprinted 1520)
mwme0703	caucasus	1513	PTOLEMY (WALDSEEMULLER)	2400	39	56	Tercia Asiae Tabula (reprinted 1520)
mwf0008	france	1513	PTOLEMY (WALDSEEMULLER)	2500	38	46	Tercia Europe Tabula (reprinted 1520)
mwaf0450	africa egypt etc	1513	PTOLEMY (WALDSEEMULLER)	2400	34	53	Tertia Africae Tabula (Reprinted 1520)
mwas0276	asia burma	1513	PTOLEMY (WALDSEEMULLER)	2500	39	51	Undecima Asiae Tabula
mwe0683	europe dalmatia	1737	PUJADIES	2500	43	144	(Untitled map. Text reads: Haec Mappa Interibitur. Exhib et illa Praecipue Regiones)
mwme0087a	holy land	1625	PURCHAS	500			(Untitled map)
mwam0852	america north (east)	1625	PURCHAS	3000	25	35	(Untitled map containing regions called New England and New France)
mwsc0451	scandinavia greenland	1625	PURCHAS	1200	29	33	(Untitled map of Greenland, surrounded by whaling scenes)
mwca0586	canada st lawrence	1625	PURCHAS	5000	25	35	Golfe of Canada
mwc0014	china	1625	PURCHAS	3000	30	36	The Map of China (illustration below shows the De Bry 1628 same-size version with title 'Descriptio Chorographica Regni Chinae')
mwsp0334	spain	1844	PURDY	375	93	100	A New Chart of the Coasts of Spain, Portugal, and Barbary, from St. Sebastian to Cape Blanco North; with Part of the Mediterranean Sea
mwca0143	canada	1821	PURDY	3600	122	156	Map of Cabotia; Comprehending the Provinces of Upper and Lower Canada, New Brunswick, and Nova Scotia, with Breton Island, Newfoundland, &c., and Including the Adjacent Parts of the United States
mwg0656	saxony	1757	PUSCHEL	1250	44	56	Aucta et Emendata Anhaltini Principatus Tabula
mwuss1274	ohio	1798	PUTNAM	3500	36	66	Plat of that Tract of Country in the Territory Northwest of the Ohio Appropriated for Military Services
mwuss1040	new jersey	1777	PYLE	2500			An Accurate Plan of the Country between New York and Philadelphia … 1777
mwaf0352	africa east	1600	QUAD	400	22	29	Abyssinorum sive Magni Regis Davidis, quem vulgo Presbyterum Joannem Vocant, Imperium
mwf0210	france alsace	1600	QUAD	200	20	27	Alsatia Inferior. Under Elsas
mwuk0909	england	1592	QUAD	720	18	27	Angliae Regni Florentissimi Nova Descriptio, Auctore Humfredo Lhuyd Denbygiense
mwaf0033	africa	1600	QUAD	650	21	30	Aphrica
mwf0705	france nord pas-de-calais	1600	QUAD	200	21	30	Artesia
mwas0023	asia continent	1600	QUAD	650	21	30	Asia Partiu Orbis Maxima MDXCVIII
mwe0303	europe austria	1600	QUAD	250	21	28	Austria Archiducatus
mwaf0683	africa north	1603	QUAD	250	20	28	Barbaria Africana, et Biledulgerid
mwbh0174	belgium holland	1608	QUAD	450	23	31	Belgium
mwe0523	europe czech republic (bohemia)	1600	QUAD	350	18	26	Bohemia
mwbh0157	belgium holland	1600	QUAD	250	18	27	Brabantiae Belgarum Provinciae Recens Exactaque Descriptio
mwg0571	saxony	1593	QUAD	140	21	30	Braunswick Ducatus, Hildesheim Episcop. & Halberstat Episcop. cum Coeteris Adiacentib.
mwf0386	france burgundy	1592	QUAD	240	19	26	Burgundiae Inferioris quae Ducatus Nomine Censetur Desc.
mwe0702a	europe danube	1596	QUAD	12000	48	115	Celeberrimi Tractus Danubiani pars Praecipua ab Austrie Vienna Constantinopolim
mwaa0003	antarctic	1600	QUAD	1250	22	28	Chica sive Patagonica et Australis Terra. MDC
mwg0766	westphalia	1600	QUAD	240	22	27	Cliviae Ducatus
mwg0434	hessen	1600	QUAD	200	21	27	Comitatus Waldeck Accurate Descriptus

AMPG REFERENCE	REGION	DATE	MAP MAKER	PRICE (UK£)	VERT. (cm.)	HOR. (cm.)	TITLE OF MAP (Comments by the editor in brackets)
mwf0464	france corsica	1600	QUAD	550	23	32	Corsica
mwgr0367	greece crete	1608	QUAD	450	23	31	Creta Iovis Magni Medio Iacet Insula Ponto
mwgr0469	greece cyprus	1608	QUAD	1500	22	30	Cyprus Insula
mwsc0248	scandinavia denmark	1600	QUAD	500	18	26	Daniae Regni Typus
mwg0767	westphalia	1600	QUAD	240	22	31	Diocesis Coloniensis
mwbp0197	poland	1592	QUAD	250	19	27	Ducatus Oswieczensis & Zatoriensis Descriptio
mwe0021	europe	1598	QUAD	500	22	30	Europa
mwbh0158	belgium holland	1600	QUAD	250	20	27	Flandriae Descriptio
mwg0510	rheinland-pfalz	1600	QUAD	250	21	28	Florentissimus Rheni Palatinatus
mwg0315	bavaria	1592	QUAD	240	23	30	Francia Orientalis, vulgo Franconia
mwf0039	france	1600	QUAD	350	20	27	Franciae Accurata Descriptio / Franckreich mit seinen Grentzen
mwbh0159	belgium holland	1600	QUAD	250	18	27	Frisiae Antiquissimae Trans Rhenu Provinc. et Adiacentium Regionum Nova et Exacta Descriptio
mwg0026	germany	1589	QUAD	350	22	29	Germaniae non vera minus quam Compendiosa Descriptio. Deutschlandt
mwgr0048	greece	1600	QUAD	480	20	28	Graeciae Universae Secundum Hodiernum Situm Neoterica Descriptio
mwsw0030	switzerland	1597	QUAD	450	22	31	Helvetia
mwuk0013	ireland	1600	QUAD	650	22	30	Hiberniae Britanicae Insulae Nova Descriptio. Eryn, Irlandt
mwgm0144	mexico	1600	QUAD	400	21	29	Hispaniae Novae sive Magnae Vera Descriptio
mwbh0160	belgium holland	1600	QUAD	400	18	27	Hollandia quae olim Batavia
mwe0863	europe hungary	1600	QUAD	350	18	27	Hungariae Loca Precipua Recens Emendata
mwas0371	asia south east	1600	QUAD	1250	21	29	India Orientalis (incl. all of India)
mwsc0484	scandinavia iceland	1608	QUAD	1500	22	29	Islandia
mwit0042	italy	1592	QUAD	600	21	27	Italia
mwg0773	westphalia	1610	QUAD	3000	29	43	Iuliae & Cliviae Ducatum Nov. Ac Verus Typus Geographicus
mwbh0161	belgium holland	1600	QUAD	160	20	26	Leodiensis Episcopat
mwf0664	france lorraine	1600	QUAD	240	20	28	Lotharingiae Ducatus Superioris Vera Delineatio
mwg0572	saxony	1593	QUAD	140	21	27	Lunaeburgensis Ducatus
mwbh0815	luxembourg	1589	QUAD	400	21	28	Lutzenburgensis Montuosissimi
mwg0199	germany north east	1600	QUAD	300	20	30	Marca Brandenburgensis & Pomerania
mwit0468	italy lombardy	1608	QUAD	300	21	29	Mediolanum Lombardiae Ducatus
mwg0768	westphalia	1600	QUAD	180	18	27	Monasteriensis Episcopatus
mwe1092	europe slovak republic (moravia)	1600	QUAD	300	21	28	Moravia
mwru0024	russia	1600	QUAD	675	22	29	Moscoviae Imperium
mwbh0125	belgium holland	1589	QUAD	200	20	27	Namurcum cum Adiacentibus Regionibus Descr. Namen. Colonie Exc. Iohan Bussm
mwme0935	turkey etc	1600	QUAD	350	22	28	Natolia olim Asia Minor
mwbh0133	belgium holland	1596	QUAD	160	23	30	Nobilis Hannonie Comitatus Descriptio
mwam0309	america north	1600	QUAD	2400	23	29	Novi Orbis Pars Borealis, America Scilicet, Complectens Floridam, Baccalaon, Canadam, Terram Corterialem, Virginiam, Norombecam, Pluresque alias Provincias
mwme0058	holy land	1600	QUAD	550	20	29	Palaestina quae et Terra Sancta vel Terra Promisionis
mwg0319	bavaria	1600	QUAD	300	21	28	Palatinatus Bavariae 1596
mwme0765a	persia etc	1600	QUAD	300	20	26	Persiae Regnum sive Sophorum Imperium
mwsam0010	south america	1600	QUAD	1100	21	28	Peruvia id est, Novi Orbis Pars Meridionalis a Praestantissima eius in Occidetem Regione sic Appellata. 1598
mwbp0212	poland	1600	QUAD	450	18	27	Poloniae Finitimarumque Locarum Descriptio Auctore Wenceslao Grodreccio Polono Johann Bussemacher Exc.
mwaa0067	arctic	1600	QUAD	800	22	28	Polus Arcticus sive Tract. Septentrionalis. Coloniae, ex Officina Typographica Jani Bussemechers
mwsp0018	portugal	1600	QUAD	375	18	27	Portugalliae que olim Lusitania, Novissima et Exactissima
mwsp0170	spain	1600	QUAD	300	21	28	Regni Hispaniae Post Omnium Editiones Locupletissima Descriptio (excl. Southern Spain)
mwit0996	italy south	1608	QUAD	300	22	28	Regni Neapolitani Verissi
mwe0294	europe austria	1590	QUAD	240	18	26	Salisburgensis Jurisdictionis Locorumque Vicinorum Vera Descriptio
mwit0781	italy sardinia	1608	QUAD	600	20	29	Sardinia
mwe1122	europe slovenia	1600	QUAD	400	18	27	Sclavonia Croatia, Bosnia & Dalmatiae Pars Maior
mwuk0321	scotland	1600	QUAD	550	19	27	Scotiae Tabula
mwsc0034	scandinavia	1596	QUAD	960	21	30	Septentrionalium Regionum Suetiae Gothiae Norvegiae Daniae &c (north to the left)
mwit0878	italy sicily	1600	QUAD	550	21	30	Sicilia
mwbp0213	poland	1600	QUAD	250	22	29	Silesiae Ducatus Accuratissima Descriptus
mwg0320	bavaria	1600	QUAD	350	21	28	Sueviae
mwe0449	europe bulgaria	1596	QUAD	300	23	31	Thracia et Bulgaria cum Viciniis
mww0091	world	1596	QUAD	2000	22	32	Typus Orbis Terrarum ad Imitationem Universalis Gerhardi Mercatoris
mwg0254	baden-wurttemberg	1600	QUAD	250	22	31	Wirtenbergensis Ducatus
mwbh0175	belgium holland	1608	QUAD	350	18	27	Zelandicarum Insularum Exactissima et Nova Descriptio
mwme0449	jerusalem	1639	QUARESMIUS	2000	28	39	Novae Ierosolymae et Locorum Circumiacentium Accurata Imago (engraved by P. Verbiest)

AMPG REFERENCE	REGION	DATE	MAP MAKER	PRICE (UK£)	VERT. (cm.)	HOR. (cm.)	TITLE OF MAP (Comments by the editor in brackets)
mwf0412	france burgundy	1748	QUERRET	2500	110	176	Carte du Comte de Bourgogne. Levee par Ordre de la Cour par le Sieur Jean Querret Ingenieur des Ponts et Chaussees. Vue et Verifiee par Mrs. Cassini et Maraldi de l'Academie Royale des Sciences (publ. by Lattre)
mwsam0438	south america brazil	1850	RADEFELD	80	25	20	(Brazil)
mwp0293	pacific (all)	1849	RADEFELD	95	22	26	Der Grosse Ozean und Australien
mwme0694	arabia etc	1850	RADEFELD	150	30	36	General Karte des Osmanischen Reichs
mwuk0299	ireland	1849	RADEFELD	95	24	19	Ireland
mwuk0640	scotland	1847	RADEFELD	120	37	30	Neueste Karte von Schotland nach den Besten Quellen Entworfen und Gezeichnet
mwe1059	europe romania	1843	RADEFELD	150	30	36	Neueste Karte von Siebenburgen. Nach den Besten Quellen Entworf. u. Gezeichn. von Hauptm. Radefeld
mwam0772	america north	1845	RADEFELD	400	29	35	Nord-Americanische Freistaaten 1845
mwe0407	europe austria	1850	RADEFELD	80	20	26	Oesterreich
mwg0425	brandenburg	1847	RADEFELD	150	26	35	Potsdam
mwbp0571	poland	1847	RADEFELD	120	30	36	Provinz Pommern 1845
mwsc0223	scandinavia	1850	RADEFELD	75	24	18	Schweden, Norwegen und Danemark
mwsp0338	spain	1849	RADEFELD	80	21	27	Spanien und Portugal
mwg0294	baden-wurttemberg	1850	RADEFELD	95	27	22	Sudostlicher Theil vom Donau-Kreis im Konigreich Wurtemberg
mwwi0223	west indies	1850	RADEFELD	95	18	24	West Indien und Mittel America
mwe1047	europe romania	1720	RAD	785	40	44	(Timisoara) Temeswar ist die Haubtstatt der Graffschafft Temeswar
mwsp0630	spain regions	1820	RADOS	650	56	83	Plan de la Ville de Cadix, sa Baie, et ses Environs
mwas0673	asia south east java	1817	RAFFLES	960	41	113	A Map of Java
mww0621	world	1804	RAIF	1800	37	70	(Double-hemisphere map with Turkish script)
mwwi0269	west indies (east)	1803	RAIF	1500	58	51	(Lesser Antilles. Turkish script)
mwm0077	mediterranean	1803	RAIF	2000	70	90	(Turkish script)
mww0622	world	1804	RAIF	3000	58	88	A General Chart Exhibiting the Discoveries Made by Capt. James Cook (Turkish script)
mwam0254	america continent	1804	RAIF	2800	52	57	A Map of America or the New World (Turkish script)
mwas0233	asia continent	1803	RAIF	2000	48	55	Asia (Turkish script)
mwuk1036	england	1803	RAIF	720	59	52	England and Wales (Turkish script)
mwe0233	europe	1803	RAIF	960	51	64	Europa (Turkish script)
mwme1043	turkey etc	1804	RAIF	960	53	68	European Dominions of the Ottomans or Turkey in Europe (Turkish script)
mwf0173	france	1803	RAIF	650	52	60	France Divided into Metropolitan Circles Departments (Turkish script)
mwbp0544	poland	1803	RAIF	1500	53	58	Kadimi Memalik-i Leh (Turkish script. Small inset plan of Warsaw)
mwm0179	mediterranean malta	1629	RAIGNAULD	720	20	14	Description de la Cite, Valette
mwgr0474	greece cyprus	1629	RAIGNAULD	4000	19	26	Isle de Cipre (illustrated map publ. 1643)
mwm0180	mediterranean malta	1629	RAIGNAULD	960	20	26	Isle et Siege de Malta
mwm0181	mediterranean malta	1629	RAIGNAULD	2250	20	27	Valletta Citta Nova di Malta
mwec0028	uk england bedfordshire	1844	RAMBLE	80	19	15	Bedfordshire
mwec0056	uk england berkshire	1844	RAMBLE	120	19	15	Berkshire
mwec0079	uk england buckinghamshire	1844	RAMBLE	100	19	15	Buckinghamshire
mwec0117	uk england cambridgeshire	1844	RAMBLE	120	19	15	Cambridgeshire
mwec0159	uk england cheshire	1844	RAMBLE	120	19	15	Cheshire
mwec0214	uk england cornwall	1844	RAMBLE	120	19	15	Cornwall
mwec0248	uk england cumbria	1844	RAMBLE	60	19	15	Cumberland
mwec0278	uk england derbyshire	1844	RAMBLE	100	19	15	Derbysh.
mwec0316	uk england devon	1844	RAMBLE	120	19	15	Devonshire
mwec0351	uk england dorset	1844	RAMBLE	80	19	15	Dorsetsh.
mwec0388	uk england durham	1844	RAMBLE	80	19	15	Durham
mwec0427	uk england essex	1844	RAMBLE	100	19	15	Essex
mwec0459	uk england gloucestershire	1844	RAMBLE	100	19	15	Glocestersh.
mwec0506	uk england hampshire	1844	RAMBLE	120	19	15	Hampshire
mwec0533	uk england herefordshire	1844	RAMBLE	100	19	15	Herefordshire
mwec0569	uk england hertfordshire	1844	RAMBLE	100	19	15	Hertfordsh.
mwec0666	uk england kent	1844	RAMBLE	120	19	15	Kent
mwec0707	uk england lancashire	1844	RAMBLE	120	19	15	Lancashire
mwec0762	uk england lincolnshire	1844	RAMBLE	80	19	15	Lincolnshire
mwec0800	uk england middlesex	1844	RAMBLE	120	19	15	Middlesex
mwec0842	uk england norfolk	1844	RAMBLE	100	19	15	Norfolk
mwec0899	uk england northumberland	1845	RAMBLE	100	19	15	Northumberland
mwec0932	uk england nottinghamshire	1844	RAMBLE	80	19	15	Nottinghamshire
mwec0976	uk england oxfordshire	1844	RAMBLE	120	19	15	Oxfordshire
mwec1054	uk england somerset	1844	RAMBLE	100	19	15	Somersetshire
mwec1087	uk england staffordshire	1844	RAMBLE	120	19	15	Staffordshire
mwec1121	uk england suffolk	1844	RAMBLE	100	19	15	Suffolk
mwec1153	uk england surrey	1843	RAMBLE	180	16	21	Surrey (Map surrounded by vignettes)
mwec1181	uk england sussex	1844	RAMBLE	100	19	15	Sussex
mwec1211	uk england warwickshire	1844	RAMBLE	100	19	15	Warwickshire
mwec1234	uk england westmorland	1844	RAMBLE	80	19	15	Westmoreland

AMPG REFERENCE	REGION	DATE	MAP MAKER	PRICE (UK£)	VERT. (cm.)	HOR. (cm.)	TITLE OF MAP (Comments by the editor in brackets)
mwec1265	uk england wiltshire	1844	RAMBLE	120	19	15	Wiltshire
mwec1369	uk england yorkshire	1844	RAMBLE	120	19	15	Yorkshire
mwgm0234a	mexico	1768	RAMIREZ	20000	53	65	Nuevo Mapa Geográfico de la América Septentrional, Perteneciente al Virreynato de Mexico (publ. Madrid/Paris)
mwgm0247	mexico	1779	RAMIREZ-DEZAUCHE	3000	53	65	Nuevo Mapa Geographico de la America Septentrional, Perteneciente al Virreynato de Mexico (publ. by Dezauche)
mwgm0234b	mexico	1770	RAMIREZ-LORENZANA	3500	31	41	Plano de la Nueva España en que se señalan los Viages que hizo el Capitán Hernan Cortés assi antes como despues de conquistado el Imperio Mexicano: dispuesto por D$^{n.}$ Jph. Ant$^{o.}$ de Alzate y Ramírez año de 1769
mwsc0646	scandinavia norway	1827	RAMM & MUNTHE	450	62	46	Kart over Agershuus Amt (inset plan of Oslo)
mwsc0647	scandinavia norway	1829	RAMM & MUNTHE	450	61	79	Kart over Hedemarkens Amt
mwsc0645	scandinavia norway	1826	RAMM & MUNTHE	450	60	45	Kart over Smaalehnenes Amt (environs of Oslo)
mwuss0252	carolinas	1802	RAMSAY	900	42	48	(Untitled map of South Carolina)
mwuss0223	carolinas	1785	RAMSAY	320	16	29	A Sketch of Charleston Harbour Shewing the Disposition of the British Fleet under the Command of Vice Adml. Mariot Arbuthnot upon the Attack on Fort Moultrie on Sulivan Island in 1780
mwuss0227	carolinas	1787	RAMSAY	675	37	42	Caroline Meridionale, avec les Parties Adjacentes, pour Servir a l'Intelligence des Mouvements des Armees Americaines et Britanniques
mwuss0229	carolinas	1787	RAMSAY	675	37	29	Equisse des Operations du Siege de Charleston Capitale de la Carolina Meridionale, en 1780
mwuss0228	carolinas	1787	RAMSAY	675	16	30	Plan du Havre de Charleston, Montrant la Disposition de la Flotte Britannique
mwuss1641	virginia	1775	RAMSAY	320	22	19	Plan of the Investment of York & Gloucester, by the Allied Armies: in Septr. & Octr. 1781
mwuss0224	carolinas	1785	RAMSAY	900	50	58	South-Carolina and Parts Adjacent; Shewing the Movements of the American and British Armies
mwgm0131	mexico	1563	RAMUSIO	720	27	17	(Mexico City, south to the top)
mwaf1086	africa west	1556	RAMUSIO	2500	28	38	(Parte Del Africa)
mwsam0273	south america brazil	1556	RAMUSIO	3000	27	37	Brasil (illustrated is the 1565 re-engraving of the original 1556 woodblock, which was destroyed in a fire. The first map to show Brazil on its own. North to the right.)
mwsam0734	south america peru	1606	RAMUSIO	785	28	37	Il Cuscho Citta Principale della Provincia del Peru
mwwi0571	hispaniola	1556	RAMUSIO	650	19	27	Isola Spagnuola
mwat0003	atlantic ocean (all)	1534	RAMUSIO		53	43	La carta universale della terra firma
mwam0844	america north (east)	1556	RAMUSIO	5500	27	37	La Nuova Francia (map by G. Gastaldi)
mwca0567	canada quebec montreal	1606	RAMUSIO	2250	27	36	La Terra de Hochelaga nella Nova Francia (Includes 'Monte Real'. Hochelaga was disbanded before 1613, but occupied the site of Montreal)
mwaf0459	africa egypt etc	1563	RAMUSIO	400	22	14	Mezzo Di (The Nile River, south to the top).
mwaf0004	africa	1554	RAMUSIO	3000	28	40	Prima Tavola (south to the top. Woodblock. Later re-issues were engraved, with two monsters in the top right corner of the map. First 'reasonably accurate' coastline of Africa.)
mwin0086	india	1554	RAMUSIO	3500	29	39	Seconda Tavola (Illustrated is the 1565 edition by Bertelli. South to the top)
mwas0872	asia south east sumatra	1556	RAMUSIO	1500	27	37	Sumatra - Taprobana (south to the top)
mwas0361	asia south east	1554	RAMUSIO	3500	28	38	Terza Tavola (south to the top)
mwam0005	america continent	1556	RAMUSIO	4000	27		Universale della Parte del Mondo Nuovamente Ritrovata
mwuss1188a	new york	1821	RANDEL	20000	73	117	The City of New York as laid out by the Commissioners with the Surrounding Countryside (This map was first issued in 1811 by William Bridges, based on Randel's survey, but before it was completed. Randel's name does not appear on the earlier map.)
mwuk0173	ireland	1750	RAPIN	360	40	50	(Untitled map consisting of 16 city plans)
mwuk1494	uk english channel (all)	1743	RAPIN	480	38	48	A Correct Chart of the English Channel from the No. Foreland to the Lands End
mwuk1671	north sea	1745	RAPIN	480	48	38	A Correct Chart of the German Ocean from the North of Scotland to the Start Point on the Coast of Great Britain
mwbh0614	belgium holland	1730	RAPIN	580	39	48	Antwerp a Strong, Large, and Beautiful City on ye River Scheld, in the Dutchy of Brabant, Subject to ye Queen of Hungary
mwbh0644	belgium holland	1740	RAPIN	300	36	47	Bruges, one of the Principal Cities of Flanders
mwbh0645	belgium holland	1740	RAPIN	580	38	48	Brussels, a Large and Beautiful City ... Subject to the Queen of Hungary
mwbh0658	belgium holland	1744	RAPIN	300	36	48	Ghent a Large City and Castle in Flanders, Twice Taken by ye Duke of Marlborough viz. in ye Year 1706 & 1708
mwbh0656	belgium holland	1743	RAPIN	300	39	48	Mechlin, or Malines the Capital of One of the Ten Provinces of the Netherlands in Brabant an Archbishoprick, Situated on ye Dyle
mwsp0551	spain regions	1745	RAPIN	250	38	46	Plan of the City and Castle of Alicant, Besieged by the Chevalier d'Asfeldt Nov. 30th 1708
mwsp0548	spain regions	1740	RAPIN	300	36	48	Plan of the City of Barcelona

AMPG REFERENCE	REGION	DATE	MAP MAKER	PRICE (UK£)	VERT. (cm.)	HOR. (cm.)	TITLE OF MAP (Comments by the editor in brackets)
mwaf1204	africa west	1745	RAPIN	200	24	35	Plan of the Island of Goree
mwit0943	italy sicily	1744	RAPIN	300	36	48	Plan of the Works of the City of Messina, One of the Strongest and Most Considerable Cities of Sicily, and a Fine Sea-Port
			SEE ALSO UNDER 'TINDAL' AND 'BASIRE' (engraver)				
mwit0528	italy milan	1598	RASCICOTTI	2500	40	54	La Gran Citta di Milano
mwit0050	italy	1599	RASCIOTTI		40	52	(No title. Text in cartouche begins: 'L'Italia nobilisima provincia della Europa')
mwf0363	france brittany	1764	RASPE	180	23	38	Ao. 1762 den 6 Junii wurde diese Stadt St. Malo von einer Englaendischen Flotte unter Befehl des Chef d'Escadre Howe Eingeschlossen, Alle Schiffe im Hafen Verbrandt
mwca0311a	canada newfoundland	1762	RASPE	320	24	25	Carte von der Insel Terre-Neuve entworfen von Bellin
mwca0598	canada st lawrence	1757	RASPE	300	22	35	Grund Riss der Americanischen Insuln Cape Breton, St. Jean und Anticosti im Flusse S. Laurencii
mwas0786	asia south east philippines	1760	RASPE	600	19	26	Isles Philippines
mwwi0521	grenada	1762	RASPE	320	20	29	Karte von der Insel Grenada und den Grenadillen in Nord America, unter den Zwolften Grad der Breite
mwca0578	canada quebec montreal	1764	RASPE	450	22	29	Karte von der Insel Montreal und den Gegenden Umher
mwam0424	america north	1760	RASPE	400	27	20	L'Amerique Septentrionale
mwg0665	saxony	1764	RASPE	180	22	37	Plan der Bataille bey Freyberg d. 29 Oct. 1762 zwischen den Konigl. Preussischen Trouppen ... und der Combinirten Kayserl. und Reichs Armee
mwwi0454	cuba	1764	RASPE	450	22	36	Plan der Insel Cuba (2 insets of Havana)
mwru0236	russia	1760	RASPE	200	20	35	Plan der Konigl: Preussischen Haupt und Residenz Stadt Konigsberg in Preussen (inset view of Konigsberg/Kaliningrad)
mwg0389	bavaria	1760	RASPE	200	22	37	Plan der Stadt Bamberg
mwca0526	canada quebec	1764	RASPE	400	21	34	Plan der Stadt Quebec Hauptstadt in Neu Franckreich oder Canada
mwg0496	mecklenburg	1760	RASPE	240	22	37	Plan der Stadt und Vestung Stralsund in Pommern (inset view of Stralsund)
mwg0661	saxony	1760	RASPE	200	21	36	Plan der Stadt Zelle (inset view of Celle)
mwca0379	canada nova scotia	1757	RASPE	350	22	36	Plan des Hafens und Festung Louisbourg auf der Insul Cap Breton
mwuss1125	new york	1777	RASPE	360	38	27	Plan von den Operationen der Koeniglichen Armee
mwg0660	saxony	1759	RASPE	180	24	38	Plan von der Retraite der Franzosischen Armee, durch die Defilees bey Oberscheden zwischen Dransfeld und Munden
mwsp0734	gibraltar	1781	RATINO	675	30	44	Veduta della Citta e Rocca di Gibilterra (view. Illustrated is French edition)
mwuss1114	new york	1776	RATZER	68500	117	88	Plan of the City of New York, in North America: Surveyed in the Years 1766 & 1767
mwuss1097	new york	1767	RATZER	24000	58	88	To His Excellency Sr. Henry Moore, Bart ... This Plan of the City of New York and its Environs
mwam1112	america north (east)	1794	RAYNAL	360	32	21	Carte de la Louisiane, et de la Floride
mwsam0394	south america brazil	1784	RAYNAL	200	20	32	Carte de la Partie Meridionale du Bresil, avec les Possessions Espagnoles Voisines qui en sont a l'Ouest
mwsam0395	south america brazil	1784	RAYNAL	240	20	31	Carte de la Partie Septentrionale du Bresil
mwwi0645	hispaniola	1784	RAYNAL	240	21	32	Carte de l'Isle de St. Domingue une des Grandes Antilles. Colonie Francoise et Espagnole
mwsam0780	south america peru	1784	RAYNAL	200	32	21	Carte du Perou avec une Partie des Pays qui en sont a l'Est
mwsam0636	south america guyana	1784	RAYNAL	200	32	21	La Guyane Francoise, avec Partie de la Guyane Hollandoise: Suivant les Operations et les Cartes Recentes des Ingenieurs-Geographes Francois
mwam1323	america north (west)	1784	RAYNAL	240	21	32	Le Nouveau Mexique, avec la Partie Septentrionale de l'Ancien, ou de la Nouvelle Espagne
mwgm0050	gulf of mexico and surrounding regions	1783	RAYNAL	875	30	51	Map of the European Settlements in Mexico or New Spain and the West Indies
mwsam0122	south america	1798	RAYNAL	350	46	34	Map of the European Settlements in South America
mwsam0152a	south america	1833	RAYNAUD	350	52	73	Carte de l'Amérique Méridionale
mwf1066	france provence	1743	RAZAUD	900	72	115	Plan Geometral de la Ville, Citadelles, Port et Arcenaux de Marseille
mwec0629	uk england kent	1745	READ	140	16	20	Kent
mwat0334	atlantic st helena	1816	READ	1200	45	60	This Geographical Plan of the Island & Forts of Saint Helena
mwit1076	italy naples	1828	REALE OFFICIO	1650	68	95	Pianta della Citta di Napoli e de' suoi Contorni Delineata ed Incisa nel Reale Officio Topografico della Guerra
mwuss0541	illinois	1809	RECTOR	400	38	43	Map of the Village Tract Common Field Lands & Part of the Village of Cahokia
mwuss0542	illinois	1809	RECTOR	400	34	20	Plat of the Claims within the Tract Called Grand Prairie
mwuss0543	illinois	1809	RECTOR	450	41	39	Reservations for the Mitchegamia Indians by the French Government
mwuss1361	pennsylvania	1774	REED		75	150	To the Honourable House of Representatives of the Freemen of Pennsylvania this Map of the City and Liberties of Philadelphia

AMPG REFERENCE	REGION	DATE	MAP MAKER	PRICE (UK£)	VERT. (cm.)	HOR. (cm.)	TITLE OF MAP (Comments by the editor in brackets)
mwam0720	america north	1838	REGNIER	400	50	39	America do Norte (Portuguese map)
mwam0268	america continent	1816	REICHARD	360	34	28	America 1816
mwp0271a	pacific (all)	1803	REICHARD	250	43	42	Atlas des ganzen Erdkreises in der Central-Projektion. Dritte Tafel
mwam0558	america north	1802	REICHARD	850	58	51	Charte von Nordamerica nach den Neuesten Bestimmungen und Entdeckungen (publ. by Weimar)
mwp0457	pacific north	1804	REICHARD	480	51	67	Der Noerdliche Theil des Grossenwelt Meeres
mwam1164a	america north (east)	1809	REICHARD	1500	59	72	Die Vereinigten Staaten von Nordamerika nach den sichersten Bestimmungen (uses an 'equal area' projection invented by Albers in 1805)
mwam1177	america north (east)	1817	REICHARD	480	28	33	Nordlicher Theil der Vereinigten Staaten
mwam0527	america north	1795	REID	300	36	46	A General Map of North America Drawn from the Best Surveys (copy of Russell 1794)
mwuss1486	tennessee	1796	REID	960	18	38	A Map of the Tennessee Government Formerly Part of North Carolina from the Latest Surveys. 1795
mwam1120	america north (east)	1796	REID	450	36	46	An Accurate Map of the United States of America, According to the Treaty of Peace of 1783
mwwi0140	west indies	1796	REID	675	35	45	An Accurate Map of the West Indies with the Adjacent Coast of America
mwuss0301	connecticut	1796	REID	600	35	43	Connecticut from the Best Authorities
mwuss0508	georgia	1796	REID	960	23	41	Georgia from the Latest Authorities
mwuss0596	kentucky	1796	REID	960	37	43	Map of the State of Kentucky with the Adjoining Territories 1795
mwuss0340	washington DC	1796	REID	2000	41	52	Plan of the City of Washington
mwuss0705	maine	1795	REID	600	36	24	The Province of Maine from the Best Authorities. 1795
mwuss0853	massachusetts	1796	REID	600	36	43	The State of Massachusetts from the Best Information
mwuss1010	new hampshire	1796	REID	500	43	27	The State of New Hampshire, Compiled Chiefly from Actual Surveys
mwuss1048	new jersey	1796	REID	450	44	35	The State of New Jersey, Compiled from the Most Accurate Surveys
mwuss1165	new york	1796	REID	500	39	46	The State of New York, Compiled from the Most Authentic Information
mwuss0244	carolinas	1796	REID	600	28	46	The State of North Carolina: From the Best Authorities
mwuss1391	pennsylvania	1796	REID	600	32	45	The State of Pennsylvania from the Latest Surveys
mwuss1460	rhode isl	1796	REID	500	35	23	The State of Rhode Island, from the Latest Surveys
mwuss0243	carolinas	1796	REID	600	38	43	The State of South Carolina: From the Best Authorities
mwuss1669	virginia	1796	REID	900	34	46	The State of Virginia from the Best Authorities
mwuss0761	maryland	1795	REID	800	35	43	The States of Maryland and Delaware, from the Latest Surveys
mwuss1560	vermont	1796	REID	500	42	34	Vermont from the latest Authorities
mwe0340	europe austria	1701	REIFFENSTUELL	600	26	33	Comitatus Tyrolis Tabula
mwme0733	caucasus	1802	REINECKE	300	44	56	Charte der Laender am Caucasus
mwaf0998	africa south	1817	REINECKE	480	40	60	Charte der Sudspitze Africa's
mwam0250	america continent	1800	REINECKE	675	51	61	Charte von America, nach den Neuesten Entdeckungen und Astronomischen Ortsbestimmungen Berichliget und Geseichnet (inset: Cook's discoveries in N. Pacific)
mwp0518a	pacific (south)	1813	REINECKE	350	30	41	Charte von Australien Berichtigt im November 1812 (based on his 1803 map. Publ. by Weimar)
mwsc0514	scandinavia iceland	1808	REINECKE	280	29	39	Charte von Island und den Faroer Inseln (inset: Faroe isl.)
mwsc0191	scandinavia	1800	REINECKE	650	48	47	Charte von Schweden und Norwegen
mwsc0512a	scandinavia iceland	1800	REINECKE	150	16	22	Doppel-Charte von Island
mwp0514	pacific south	1803	REINECKE	800	46	61	General Charte von Australien nach den neuesten Entdeckungs-Reisens
mwsc0512	scandinavia iceland	1800	REINECKE	480	47	54	Island nach Murdochischer Projection
mwbp0542	poland	1800	REINECKE	480	38	45	Reise Charte von Leipzig nach St. Petersburg (road map in 13 vertical strips)
			SEE ALSO 'WEIMAR', REINECKE'S PUBLISHER				
mwgr0513	greece cyprus	1768	REINHARD	1500	24	33	Cypri facies antiqua
mwgr0512	greece cyprus	1768	REINHARD	3000	37	48	Cypri facies hodierna
mwg0406a	bavaria	1829	REINHARD, F.	720	52	66	Plan der Koniglichen Residenzstadt Munchen
mwg0667	saxony	1767	REINHOLD	960	43	63	Plan der Stadt Osnabruck. Gemessen und im Riss Gebracht 1767
mww0544	world	1786	REINHOLD	480	19	33	Plan von der Ganzen Erdkugel Entworfen von C.L. Reinhold, D. 1786 (Oval projection showing Cook's 3 voyages)
mww0024	world	1515	REISCH	15000	18	44	Typus Univeralis Terrae, iuxta Modernorum Distinctionem et Extensionem per Regna et Provincias
mww0022	world	1513	REISCH	20000	19	29	Typus Univeralis Terrae, iuxta Modernorum Distinctionem et Extensionem per Regna et Provincias (size incl. key below map)
mwme0250	holy land	1714	RELAND	200	18	14	Conspectus Palaestinae uti divisa fuit a Mose et Josua
mwme0252	holy land	1714	RELAND	800	56	50	Facies Palaestinae ex Monumentis Veteribus Descripta ab Hadriano Relando
mwjk0063	japan	1715	RELAND	1875	47	60	Imperium Japonicum (inset of Nagasaki Bay)
mwme0253	holy land	1714	RELAND	450	48	29	Intervalla Locorum Palaestinae Digesta per Millaria Romana (shows distances between locations)

AMPG REFERENCE	REGION	DATE	MAP MAKER	PRICE (UK£)	VERT. (cm.)	HOR. (cm.)	TITLE OF MAP (Comments by the editor in brackets)
mwjk0064	japan	1715	RELAND	1875	31	46	Le Japon Divise en Soissante et Six Provinces (inset of Nagasaki Bay)
mwaf0244	africa	1780	REMONDINI	800	100	97	Afrique (close copy of D'Anville 1749)
mwru0550a	ukraine	1774	REMONDINI	2000	87	153	Carte De La Partie Septentrionale De L'Empire Otoman Contentant la Crimee, la Moldavie, la Valakie, la Bulgarie, avec la Nouvelle Russie, les Gouvernement d'Astracan, et de Voronez, les Tartares, Cosques &c. (in 6 sheets)
mwbp0543	poland	1802	REMONDINI	480	48	65	La Pologne Divisee en ses Palatinats selon la Derniere Condivision des Trois Puisances Savoir l'Autriche, la Russie, la Prusse
mwru0269	russia	1782	REMONDINI	785	63	94	Tabula Geographica Generalis Imperii Russici
mwam0302	america continent	1841	REMQUET	450	50	65	Amerique Historique et Politique Actuelle
mwaf1172	africa west	1715	RENARD	720	49	57	Barbariae et Guineae Maritimi a Freto Gibraltar ad Fluvium Gambiae (based on De Wit 1675)
mwbh0526	belgium holland	1705	RENARD	785	63	64	Carte du Brabant
mwsc0341	scandinavia denmark	1715	RENARD	1350	48	57	Daniae, Frisiae, Groningae et Orientalis Frisiae Littora
mwsc0605	scandinavia norway	1715	RENARD	1000	49	58	Finmarchiae et Laplandiae Maritimae
mwf0293	france bay of biscay	1715	RENARD	960	49	57	Galliae, Biscajae et Gallissiae Sinus
mwsp0240	spain	1715	RENARD	1000	50	57	Hispaniae et Portugalliae Maritimi Tractus, a' S. Andero, ad Malagam - Pascaert van Spangiae, en Portugal
mwwi0056	west indies	1715	RENARD	2500	48	56	Indiarum Occidentalium Tractus Littorales cum Insulis Caribicis / Pascaert van Westindien ende Caribise Eylanden
mwsam0348	south america brazil	1715	RENARD	1200	49	57	Littora Brasiliae. Pascaert van Brasil (re-issue of De Wit 1675)
mwp0244	pacific (all)	1715	RENARD	2000	49	57	Magnum Mare del Zur cum Insula California. De Groote Zuyd-Zee en 't Eylandt California (re-issue of De Wit 1675)
mww0325	world	1715	RENARD	6000	48	56	Nova Totius Terrarum Orbis Tabula ex Officina L. Renard Amstelodami
mwsam0196	south america (north west)	1715	RENARD	900	50	57	Novae Hispaniae, Chili, Peruviae, et Guatimalae Littorae (re-issue of De Wit 1675. Also copied by Ottens 1745)
mwin0481	indian ocean west	1715	RENARD	1200	45	54	Occidentalior Tractus Indiarum Orientalium a Promontorio Bonae Spei ad C. Comorin
mwm0038	mediterranean	1715	RENARD	4000	48	58	Orientalior Districtus Maris Mediterranei. t'Ooster Gedeelte van de Middelandse Zee / Occidentalior Tractus (2 charts, each 48x58cm)
mwas0445	asia south east	1715	RENARD	2500	44	54	Orientaliora Indiarum Orientalium cum Insulis Adjacentibus a Promontorio C. Comorin ad Iapan - Pascaert van t'Ooster Gedeelte van Oost Indien van C. Comorin tot Iapan (re-issue of De Wit 1680)
mwuk1664	north sea	1715	RENARD	1000	47	58	Pascaert van de Noord Zee van Ameland tot de Hoofden - Mare Germanicum ab Amelandia ad Promontoria Caleti et Doverae
mwaf1079	africa south west	1739	RENARD	785	43	54	Pascaerte van Cimbebas en Caffares
mwru0518	ukraine	1739	RENARD	960	42	60	Paskaart van de Zwarte Zee
mww0326	world	1715	RENARD	1500	43	27	Planisphere Represent Toute l'Etendue du Monde (north polar projection - frontispiece of atlas)
mwaa0117	arctic	1715	RENARD	1850	43	49	Poli Arctici, et Circumiacentium Terrarum Descriptio Novissima (updated version of De Wit 1675)
mwru0504	ukraine	1715	RENARD	1000	42	60	Pontus Euxinus of Niewe en Naaukeurige Paskaart van de Zwarte Zee
mwru0136	russia	1715	RENARD	720	49	57	Russiae et Novae Zemlae Maritimae (update of De Wit 1675)
mwat0343	atlantic west	1715	RENARD	1300	48	57	Terra Nova, ac Maris Tractus circa Novam Franciam, Angliam, Belgium, Venezuelam Novam Andalusiam, Guianam et Brasiliam - Terra Neuf, en de Custen van Nieuw Vranckryck, Nieu Engeland, Nieu Nederland, Nieu Andalusia, Guiana en Venezuela (copy of De Wit's map of 1680)
mwe1201	europe west	1715	RENARD	6000	48	90	Totius Europae Littora Novissime edita. Pascaert vertoonende alle de See-custen van Europa (based on De Wit 1675)
mwsam0227	south america argentina	1715	RENARD	1200	49	57	Tractus Australior Americae Meridionalis, a Rio de la Plata per Fretum Magellanicum ad Toraltum - Nieuwe Perfecte Pascaert van 't Suyderlyckste Deel van Suyt America, van Rio de la Plata door de Straet Magellaen tot Toral (re-issue of De Wit 1675)
mwaf1173	africa west	1715	RENARD	850	49	57	Tractus Littorales Guineae a Promontorio Verde usque ad Sinum Catenbelae (re-issue of De Wit 1680)
mwin0291	india	1788	RENNELL	1200	103	121	A Map of Hindoostan, or the Mogul Empire: from the Latest Authorities
mwin0305	india	1794	RENNELL	650	73	105	A Map of the North Part of Hindostan, or a Geographical Survey of the Provinces of Bengal, Bahar, Awd, Ellahabad, Agrah and Delhi
mwin0306	india	1794	RENNELL	720	108	107	A Map of the Provinces of Delhi, Agrah, Oude, and Ellahabad, Comprehending the Countries Lying between Dehi, and the Bengal-Provinces

AMPG REFERENCE	REGION	DATE	MAP MAKER	PRICE (UK£)	VERT. (cm.)	HOR. (cm.)	TITLE OF MAP (Comments by the editor in brackets)
mwaf0725	africa north	1798	RENNELL	240	41	71	A Map Shewing the Progress of Discovery & Improvement in the Geography of North Africa
mwin0354	india	1831	RENNELL	360	91	56	A New and Improved Map of India
mwin0258	india	1776	RENNELL	1200	99	148	An Actual Survey of the Provinces of Bengal, Bahar &c. By Major James Rennell, Engineer, Surveyor General to the Honourable East-India Company
mwaf0283	africa	1798	RENNELL	200	23	30	Chart of … Magnetic Variation in the Seas around Africa (Africa in outline only)
mwaf0722a	africa north	1790	RENNELL	240			Sketch of the Northern Part of Africa … collected by The Africa Association
mwin0276	india	1781	RENNELL	300	26	59	The Burrampooter, from the Head of the Luckia or Bannar River to Assam
mwin0268	india	1779	RENNELL	100	41	38	The Conquered Provinces on the South of Bahar; Containing Ramgur, Palamow &c. Chuta-Nagpour
mwin0300	india	1792	RENNELL	160	30	46	The Countries Situated between Delhi and Candahar, Including Cashmere, and the Heads of the Indus, Drawn Chiefly from Materials Collected by Captain William Kirkpatrick of the Bengal Establishment
mwas0345	asia central	1792	RENNELL	160	27	53	The Countries Situated between the Source of the Ganges and Caspian Sea
mwin0275	india	1781	RENNELL	300	26	64	The River Ganges from Patna to Surdah with Plans of Surdah and Monghir
mwaf1242	africa west	1798	RENNELL	200	26	65	The Route of Mr. Mungo Park
mwec0761	uk england lincolnshire	1840	RENNIE & FULTON	200	65	51	East Coast Railway through Lincolnshire and Norfolk
mwg0248	berlin	1836	RENOUARD	150	19	25	Berlin
mwin0361	india	1836	RENOUARD	150	20	25	Calcutta
mwam0756	america north	1842	RENOUARD	650	49	66	Carte Speciale, Historique et Geographique de la Republique des Etats-Unis de l'Amerique du Nord (Map surrounded by text, incl. Texas Republic)
mwuk1321	england london	1836	RENOUARD	150	19	26	Londres
mwgm0292	mexico	1822	RENOUARD	960	28	48	Mapa de Megico y de los Paises Confinantes Situados al Norte y al Este
mww0678	world	1827	RENOUARD	200	28	57	Mappe Monde Historique
mwf0922	france paris	1836	RENOUARD	150	20	26	Paris
mwf0941	france paris	1850	RENOUARD	400	44	58	Plan et Panoramas de Paris
mwru0356	russia	1836	RENOUARD	150	20	26	St. Petersbourg
mwsam0118a	south america	1796	REQUENA	2500	125	96	Mapa Geografico de la mayor parte de la América Meridional que contiene los paises por donde debe trazarse la linea divisoira que divida los dominios de Espana y Portugal (only publ. in 1876)
mwg0246a	berlin	1822	REYMANN	550	37	50	Neuester Grundriss von Berlin
mwbp0449a	poland	1753	RHODE	550	30	41	Borussia Regia et Ducalis
mwgr0208	greece	1777	RHODE	350	37	32	Graecia Antiqua (title above map. Inset: environs of Athens)
mwgr0209	greece	1778	RHODE	350	32	37	Graeciae Antiquae Pars Meridionalis (title above map. Inset: environs of Sparta)
mwme1028	turkey etc	1780	RHODE	200	38	39	Mappa Geographica Asiae Minoris Antiquae
mww0428	world	1753	RHODE	480	32	37	Mappa Mundi Generalis
mwbp0474	poland	1763	RHODE	1850	45	56	Regnum Borussiae … et Culmensis cum Territorio Dantiscano (in 6 sheets, each 45x56cm)
mwaf0522	africa egypt etc	1771	RHODE	200	32	21	Succincta Antiquoris Aegypti et Palaestinae Delineatio
mwaa0024	antarctic	1753	RHODE	600	32		Tabula Geographica Hemisphaerii Australis
mwaa0135	arctic	1753	RHODE	350	30		Tabula Geographica Hemisphaerii Borealis (circular map)
mwg0142	germany	1762	RHODE	480	62	74	Tabula Geographica Imperii Germanici
mwam0982	america north (east)	1755	RHODE	7200	57	80	Theatrum Belli in America Septentrionali (2nd edition c1761)
mwit0409	italy lazio	1824	RICCARDI	850	79	63	Nuova Carta Geografica dello stato Pontificio
mwwi0257	west indies (east)	1779	RICHMOND	5000	82	61	A Map of the Caribbee, Granadilles and Virgin Isles
mww0380	world	1741	RICHTER	650	20	23	Planisphaer
mwam1019	america north (east)	1766	RIDGE	480	27	38	A Map of the British Dominions in North America as Settled by the Late Treaty of Peace 1763.
mwam0434	america north	1763	RIDGE	480	27	38	A New Map of North America from the Latest Discoveries
mwuss1090	new york	1758	RIDGE	480	11	19	A Plan of the Country from the Landing Place with the Encampments and Marches of the Troops under Major General Abercrombie to the Attack of Ticonderoga
mwaf0952	africa south	1780	RIEDEL	1350	27	40	Prospect des Vorgeburges der guten Hoffnung, nebst dem Castell und Haafen (Vue d'optique of Cape Town)
mwbp0043	baltic sea (east)	1743	RIEGEL	1350	42	59	Accurate Geographische Vorstellung der Ost-See (6 insets)
mwg0350	bavaria	1690	RIEGEL	450	46	55	Chur-Bairn samt Demselben Incorporirten und Angrenzenden Landen so Accurat als Jemals mit Sondern Fleiss auf Jezige Lauften Gemacht
mwit0910a	italy sicily	1700	RIEGEL	600	38	38	Die Königreich Sicilien u: Neapolis
mwe0574	europe czech republic (bohemia)	1742	RIEGEL	785	58	49	Grundriss der … Stadt Prag mit der Konigl. Ungarschen Belagerung und Attaquen 1742
mwit0143a	italy	1710	RIEGEL	550	49	56	Land=Karte von Italien oder Welschland
mwit0535	italy milan	1692	RIEGEL	350	6	11	Mediolanum

AMPG REFERENCE	REGION	DATE	MAP MAKER	PRICE (UK£)	VERT. (cm.)	HOR. (cm.)	TITLE OF MAP (Comments by the editor in brackets)
mwit0607a	italy north	1744	RIEGEL	400	31	44	Neueröffnetes Kriegs Theatrum von Anno 1743 u 1744, oder der Obere Theil von Italien, und Lombardie
mwit0908	italy sicily	1692	RIEGEL	200	15	19	Palermo
mwe0346a	europe austria	1715	RIEGEL	300	22	31	Provincia Tyrolensis Cum confinijs
mwe0338a	europe austria	1700	RIEGEL	720	46	54	Tirol samt denen angrenzend und einverleibten Ländern nach möglichster Richtigkeit
mwuk1011a	england	1771	RIGHINI	450	18	25	Tabula Topographica Omnium Locor ... Anglia
mwsp0676b	balearic islands	1771	RIGHINI	500	18	25	Tabula Topographica ... Aragoniae (north to the left)
mwit1040b	italy south	1771	RIGHINI	550	18	25	Tabula Topographica ... Calabriae (north to the right. Illustration above left)
mwsp0579b	spain regions	1771	RIGHINI	250	18	25	Tabula Topographica ... Castilliae
mwuk0203a	ireland	1771	RIGHINI	550	18	25	Tabula Topographica ... Hiberniae (incl. Scotland, north to the right)
mwbp0134a	baltic states	1771	RIGHINI	450	18	25	Tabula Topographica ... Lithuaniae
mwbp0479a	poland	1771	RIGHINI	500	18	25	Tabula Topographica ... Poloniae
mwgr0206a	greece	1771	RIGHINI	350	18	25	Tabula Topographica ... Romaniae
mwru0548a	ukraine	1771	RIGHINI	550	18	25	Tabula Topographica ... Russiae
mwit1040a	italy south	1771	RIGHINI	500	18	25	Tabula Topographica ... S. Angeli
mwit0264	italy abruzzo	1771	RIGHINI	500	18	25	Tabula Topographica ... S. Bernardini
mwsp0579a	spain regions	1771	RIGHINI	500	18	25	Tabula Topographica ... S. Jacobi (W Spain/Portugal)
mwit1123b	italy tuscany	1771	RIGHINI	550	18	25	Tabula Topographica ... Tusciae
mwuss0140	california	1850	RINGGOLD	500	50	77	Chart of Suisun & Vallejo Bays with the Confluence of the Rivers Sacramento and San Joaquin
mwuss0907	michigan	1825	RISDON	6000	108	70	Map of the Surveyed Part of the Territory of Michigan
mww0121	world	1610	RITTER	10000	30	35	(Untitled map with a 'sundial' projection. 1st edition 1610)
mwme0687	arabia etc	1844	RITTER	480	44	50	Skizze einer Karte von Asyr und einem Theile von Hejas und Nedjd (SW Arabia)
mwaf0425b	africa east	1814	RIVINGTON	500	70	51	General Chart of the East Coast of Africa ... Henry Salt Esq. (2 insets: Aden Back Bay, Mozambique coast)
mwit0959	italy sicily	1780	RIZZI-ZANNONI	280	30	45	(Untitled map of southern Italy, Sicily and most of Sardinia)
mwit1044a	italy south	1807	RIZZI-ZANNONI	1500			Atlante del Regno di Napoli Ridotto in VI Fogli
mwru0251	russia	1774	RIZZI-ZANNONI	1500	73	154	Carte de la Partie Septentrionale de l'Empire Otoman
mwbp0484	poland	1772	RIZZI-ZANNONI	6000	188	204	Carte de la Pologne divisee par Provinces et Palatinats (in 24 sheets)
mwbp0475	poland	1765	RIZZI-ZANNONI	235	30	45	Carte Generale de la Pologne
mwwi0099	west indies	1762	RIZZI-ZANNONI	280	31	44	Carte Geo-Hydrographique du Golfe du Mexique et de ses Isles
mwf0145	france	1776	RIZZI-ZANNONI	200	34	43	Galliae Veteris Tabula Populos, Civitates, Pagos, nec non Provincias, Municipia Colonias
mwit1046	italy south	1820	RIZZI-ZANNONI	720	60	42	General-Karte von dem Koenigreiche Neapel in 4 Blattern (in 4 sheets)
mwg0136	germany	1759	RIZZI-ZANNONI	650	76	118	Germaniae Universiae
mwit0229	italy	1814	RIZZI-ZANNONI	480	102	41	Italy (touring map publ. by Mawman, London)
mwf0134	france	1762	RIZZI-ZANNONI	250	58	51	La France, Divisee par Gouvernements Militaires (2 sheets joined)
mwsw0161	switzerland	1762	RIZZI-ZANNONI	235	33	47	La Suisse Divisee en ses XIII Cantons et ses Allies
mwg0141	germany	1762	RIZZI-ZANNONI	180	30	44	L'Alemagne Divisee par Cercles
mwit0211	italy	1791	RIZZI-ZANNONI	320	30	44	L'Italie Divisee en ses Differens Etats (2 sheets, together forming an irregular shape)
mwsp0103	portugal	1762	RIZZI-ZANNONI	480	57	41	Mapa dos Reynos de Portugal e Algarve
mwit0620	italy north	1799	RIZZI-ZANNONI	1100	88	148	Nova Carta dell' Italia Settentrionale delle Alpi. che la Circoscrivono
mwit0223	italy	1802	RIZZI-ZANNONI	1500	122	92	Nuova Carta dell'Italia Eseqita a Suese di Giuseppe Molini Librajo in Forenze
mwit1071	italy naples	1790	RIZZI-ZANNONI	2400	55	81	Pianta della Citta di Napoli come Esiste nel Presente Anno MDCCXC
mwbp0483	poland	1772	RIZZI-ZANNONI	5000	38	56	Plan de Varsovie (this map is a single sheet, issued with Rizzi-Zannoni's 24-sheet map of Poland)
mwit0291	italy campagna	1793	RIZZI-ZANNONI	900	59	88	Topografia dell'Agro Napoletano con le sue Adacenze
mwbp0485	poland	1772	RIZZI-ZANNONI	650	34	54	Wizerunek Powszechny Polski y Litwy: Sluzacy do Zrozumienia Zbioru XXIV Karta (inset of Warsaw. This map is an overview sheet issued with Rizzi-Zannoni's 24-sheet map of Poland)
mwec0241a	uk england cumbria	1819	ROBBINS	60	24	19	Cumberland
mwam0601	america north	1815	ROBERTS	320	18	22	Gogledd-Barth America (in Welsh language)
mwuss1429	pennsylvania	1838	ROBERTS	3000	114	126	Plan of the City of Philadelphia and Adjoining Districts Originally Drawn by W. Allen. Enlarged with Numerous Additions & Corrections by F.J. Roberts
mwc0191	china	1778	ROBERTS	600	48	63	The Empire of China with its Principal Divisions Drawn from the Surveys Made by the Jesuits
mwuss0178	carolinas	1739	ROBERTS	30000	44	53	The Ichnography of Charles-Town at High Water
mwwi0748a	jamaica	1804	ROBERTSON	7200	90	189	To the King's Most Excellent Majesty, this Map of the Island of Jamaica, constructed from actual surveys, under the authority of the Hon. House of Assembly;

AMPG REFERENCE	REGION	DATE	MAP MAKER	PRICE (UK£)	VERT. (cm.)	HOR. (cm.)	TITLE OF MAP (Comments by the editor in brackets)
mwaf1147a	africa west	1690	ROBIJN	650	36	48	Pas-caert vertoonende alle de Zee Custen van Biafra. Fernando Poo en Ilha de Prince (north to the left)
mwaa0154	arctic	1799	ROBINSON	375	37	34	A Chart of the Countries Thirty Degrees Round the North Pole
mwam1341	america north (west)	1798	ROBINSON	300	22	18	A Chart of the Northwest Coast of America from California to Cook's River; Agreeable to the Discoveries Made in the Years 1786-1787 by French Frigates Boussole & Astrolabe
mwam1188	america north (east)	1825	ROBINSON	1100	42	48	An Improved Map of the United States
mwuss1579	vermont	1840	ROBINSON	1650	61	44	An Improved Map of Vermont Compiled from the Latest Authorities
mwca0127	canada	1799	ROBINSON	450	34	39	British America, Comprehending Canada, Labrador, New-Foundland, Nova Scotia &c.
mwp0337	pacific hawaii	1798	ROBINSON	180	38	50	Chart of Necker Island
mwam1322	america north (west)	1778	ROBINSON	800	50	38	Chart of Part of the North West Coast of America Explored by the Boussole and Astrolabe Laid Down Conformably to the Situation of the Boussole Every Day at Noon as Determined Astronomically by Mr. Dagelet
mwam1340	america north (west)	1798	ROBINSON	400	49	38	Chart of Part of the North West Coast of America Explored by the Boussole and Astrolabe Laid Down Conformably to the Situation of the Boussole Every Day at Noon as Determined Astronomically by Mr. Dagelet
mwjk0128	japan	1798	ROBINSON	450	38	50	Chart of the Discoveries to the North of Japan, in 1643 by the Dutch Ships, the Kastrikum & the Breskens, Including the Land of Jeso, Staten Island, & Company's Land of which Part was Explored in 1787, by the Boussole and Astrolabe (English version of La Perouse's 1797 map)
mwam1339	america north (west)	1798	ROBINSON	300	38	50	Chart of the North West Coast of America Explored by the Boussole & Astrolabe in 1786
mwam1338	america north (west)	1798	ROBINSON	550	38	49	Chart of the North West Cost of America Explored by the Boussole & Astrolabe in 1786. - 3rd Sheet (Cap Rond, Oregon to Port of Monterey)
mwp0338	pacific hawaii	1798	ROBINSON	1200	50	38	Chart of the parts of the Sandwich Islands / Chart of the Sandwich Islands (2 maps on one sheet)
mww0618	world	1801	ROBINSON	375	33	48	Chart of the World, According to Mercators Projection Shewing the Tracks & Discoveries of Captn. Cook
mwuss0540	illinois	1808	ROBINSON	300	36	22	District of Kaskaskia
mwuss1575	vermont	1834	ROBINSON	2000	61	44	Improved Map of Vermont
mwuss0559	illinois	1838	ROBINSON	3000	57	42	Map of Illinois Compiled from the Latest Authorities (inset: lead mine region)
mwuss1031	new hampshire	1850	ROBINSON	1650	60	39	Map of New Hampshire, Compiled from the Latest Authorities
mwuss1318	ohio	1840	ROBINSON	1500	66	57	Map of Ohio Compiled from the Latest Authorities
mwuss0739	maine	1850	ROBINSON	1250	38	111	Map of the Bangor, Orono, & Oldtown Railroad
mwam1232	america north (east)	1835	ROBINSON	3000	101	121	Map of the United States
mwam0759a	america north	1844	ROBINSON	650	28	44	Map of the United States Canada, Texas & Part of Mexico. To Illustrate Olney's School Geography
mwam1240	america north (east)	1838	ROBINSON	3500	97	121	Map of the United States Compiled from the Latest Authorities
mwuss1574	vermont	1828	ROBINSON	1500	71	57	Map of Vermont & New Hampshire
mwuss1585	vermont	1849	ROBINSON	1400	73	58	Map of Vermont & New Hampshire (1st publ. 1828)
mwam0528	america north	1795	ROBINSON	300	33	36	New & Accurate Map of North America
mwuss1301	ohio	1830	ROBINSON	180	19	24	Ohio & Indiana
mwp0513	pacific south	1798	ROBINSON	300	24	38	Part of the Great Pacific Ocean Shewing the Route of the Spanish Frigate La Princesa Commanded by D. Franc Antonio Maurelle in 1781 (reduced copy of La Perouse 1797)
mwru0317	russia	1798	ROBINSON	180	37	22	Plan of Baie de Ternai Situate on the Coast of Tartary
mwp0310a	pacific easter isl.	1799	ROBINSON	450	38	50	Plan of Easter Island taken in April 1786 (reduced size version of La Perouse 1797)
mwru0318	russia	1798	ROBINSON	180	37	24	Plan of la Baie de Langle on the West Side of the Isle of Tehoka
mwru0319	russia	1798	ROBINSON	180	37	24	Plan of la Baie d'Estaing
mwam1342	america north (west)	1798	ROBINSON	300	37	37	Plan of Port des Francais on the North West Coast of America
mwuss0094	california	1798	ROBINSON	850	36	24	Plan of Port St. Francisco, in California, Point de Reyes in 37°59' of Latitude North & 124°54' Longitude West
mwsam0471	south america chile	1798	ROBINSON	280	25	37	Plan of the Bay of Conception in Chili
mwuss0038	alaska	1798	ROBINSON	300	38	48	Plan of the Entrance of the Port of Bucarelli on the North West Coast of America
mwjk0129	japan	1798	ROBINSON	235	48	38	Plan of the Kurile Islands, and Lands Little Known Situate in their Vicinity, from a Manuscript Chart in the Archives of Ochotsk Communicated to Mr. Lesseps in 1788 (English version of La Perouse's 1797 map)
mwca0451	canada nova scotia	1789	ROBINSON	300	25	44	Plan of the Town of Louisbourg and Fort Louis. With the Habitation on the Opposite Side of the River

AMPG REFERENCE	REGION	DATE	MAP MAKER	PRICE (UK£)	VERT. (cm.)	HOR. (cm.)	TITLE OF MAP (Comments by the editor in brackets)
mwjk0121	japan	1789	ROBINSON	160	24	40	Plans of the Bay of Usilpatchar, Sound of Usmay Ligon and Island and Harbour of Tacasima in Japan
mwwi0147	west indies	1799	ROBINSON	450	36	48	The West Indies
mww0687	world	1829	ROBINSON	280	29	46	The World on a Globular Projection
mwam1367	america north (west)	1844	ROBINSON	200	27	44	Western Territories of the United States
mwp0451	pacific north	1798	ROBINSON, G.G.	500	38	50	Chart of the Coasts of America & Asia from California to Macao According to the Discoveries Made in 1786 & 1787 by the Boussole & Astrolabe
mwp0267	pacific (all)	1798	ROBINSON, G.G.	450	35	49	Chart of the Great Pacific Ocean or South Sea, to Illustrate the Voyage of Discovery Made by the Boussole and Astrolabe (map by La Perouse 1797)
mwp0513	pacific (all)	1798	ROBINSON, G.G.	300	25	38	Part of the Great Pacific Ocean Shewing the Route of the Spanish Frigate La Princesa Commanded by D. Franc Antonio Maurelle in 1781 (copy of La Perouse)
mwuss0095	california	1798	ROBINSON, G.G.	400	25	37	Plan of the Bay of Monterey Situate in North California in 36°38' of Latitude North and 124°3' of Longitude West
mwuss0096	california	1798	ROBINSON, G.G.	400	28	42	Plan of the Port S. Diego in California ... Survey in 1782 / Plan of the Port & Department of S. Blas ... Survey in November 1777
mwat0028	atlantic ocean (all)	1711	ROBINSON, T.	320	26	26	A Chart of the Western and Southern Oceans Describing the Course of Sir John Narbrough's Voyage to the South Sea
mwsam0438a	south america brazil	1851	ROBIQUET	800	98	68	Carte de la Côte du Brésil comprise entre la Rivière du Para et l'Ile S. Catherine (6 insets)
mwm0088	mediterranean	1854	ROBIQUET	2800	68	178	Carte Generale de la Mer Mediterranee et de la Mer Noire Partie Occidentale (26 insets)
mww0262	world	1696	ROBYN	18000	60	52	Nieuw Aerdsch Pleyn (north polar projection. Illustrated is Danckerts re-issue, c1700)
mww0225	world	1683	ROBYN	7000	43	52	Nova Totius Terrarum Orbis Tabula
mwuk1658	north sea	1685	ROBYN	2000	51	58	Pascaartte van een Gedeelte vande Noort Zee
mwaf0879	africa south	1683	ROBYN	2000	43	50	Paskaart Vertoonende van Cambebas en Caffaria Streckende van Monte Negro tot Beooste Cabo de Bona Esperanca (inset of Table Bay)
mwat0261	atlantic north	1683	ROBYN	1200	51	58	Paskaert waer in Vertoont wert de Spaense Zee; en een Gedeelte der Custen van Europa: Africa: en America
mwgr0373	greece crete	1630	ROCCHETTA	300	9	12	Candia (close copy of Zvallart's map of 1587)
mwaf0621b	africa isl. madagascar	1791	ROCHON	480			Ancienne Carte Topographique de L'Isle de Madagascar
mwuk1188	england london	1749	ROCQUE	4500	51	92	... this Plan of the Cities of London and Westminster and Borough of Southwark, with the Contiguous Buildings (reduced version of Rocque's 24-sheet map. Three editions until 1769)
mwam0427	america north	1762	ROCQUE	7200	86	90	A General Map of North America
mwuk1185	england london	1748	ROCQUE	1600	49	63	A Map of London and the Adjacent Country 10 Miles Round,
mwec0048	uk england berkshire	1762	ROCQUE	1200	44	67	A Map of the County of Berks. Reduced from an Actual Survey in 18 Sheets, by the Late John Rocque (Inset: Oxford. Title also in French)
mwec0786	uk england middlesex	1757	ROCQUE	1200	51	68	A Map of the County of Middlesex Reduced from an Actual Survey (his 1754 map)
mwuk0184	ireland	1760	ROCQUE	1800	121	99	A Map of the Kingdom of Ireland, Divided into Provinces Counties and Baronies
mwuk1004	england	1761	ROCQUE	480	52	51	A New Map of England and Wales
mwec0047	uk england berkshire	1761	ROCQUE	4000	163	273	A New Map of the County of Berks (in 24 sheets, joined)
mwec0750	uk england lincolnshire	1764	ROCQUE	235	10	13	A Plan of Boston in the County of Lincoln
mwuk1191	england london	1754	ROCQUE	6000	50	64	A Plan of London on the Same Scale as that of Paris (6 editions to 1769)
mwuk1219	england london	1769	ROCQUE	2000	49	73	A Plan of London, with All the New Streets, Lanes, Roads &c to this Present Year (centre sheet of Rocque's 16-sheet 1746 map, sold separately)
mwin0210	india	1751	ROCQUE	400	32	47	A Plan of Madras and Fort St. George
mwf1073	france provence	1750	ROCQUE	480	26	44	A Plan of Marseilles by Peter Martel Engineer
mwf0877	france paris	1754	ROCQUE	1600	50	71	A Plan of Paris &c. Reduced to the Same Scale as that of London (environs of Paris)
mwf0872	france paris	1748	ROCQUE	4800	136	140	A Plan of Paris and the Adjacent Country
mwf0878	france paris	1754	ROCQUE	1400	42	66	A Plan of Paris. This Survey has been reduced to the same Scale as that of London
mwit0747	italy rome	1750	ROCQUE	2400	45	53	A Plan of Rome, Surveyed & Publish'd by Mr. G.B. Nolli (reduced version of Nolli's 1748 plan)
mwuk1209	england london	1764	ROCQUE	450	10	13	A Plan of the Cities of London & Westminster and the Borough of Southwark, &c. (2 sheets, each 10x13cm)
mwuk1182	england london	1746	ROCQUE	40000	213	269	A Plan of the Cities of London and Westminster, and Borough of Southwark; with the Contiguous Buildings (24 sheets, each 69x51cm, joined. 6 editions until 1775)

AMPG REFERENCE	REGION	DATE	MAP MAKER	PRICE (UK£)	VERT. (cm.)	HOR. (cm.)	TITLE OF MAP (Comments by the editor in brackets)
mwuk1192	england london	1755	ROCQUE	25000	115	190	A Plan of the Cities of London and Westminster, the Borough of Southwark, and the Contiguous Buildings; with all the New Roads that have been made on account of Westminster Bridge, and the New Buildings and Alterations to the present year MDCCLV
mwsp0566	spain regions	1762	ROCQUE	500	48	53	A Plan of the City of Cadis and the Environs
mwuk0203b	ireland	1773	ROCQUE	10000	101	140	A Survey of the City Harbour Bay and Environs of Dublin on the same scale as those of London Paris & Rome By John Rocque Chorographer to his Royal Highness the Prince of Wales / Plan de la Ville, Havre, Baye & Environs de Dublin sur la meme Echelle que ceux de Londres, Paris & Rome par Jean Rocque chorographer du Roi avec des additions jusq a l'année 1773 par Mr Bernard Scalé
mwuk0185	ireland	1760	ROCQUE	1350	94	131	A Topographical Map of the County of Armagh to which is Anex'd the Plans of Newry and Armagh
mwec0045	uk england berkshire	1750	ROCQUE	2000	64	48	A Topographical Map of the County of Berks (4 sheets, each 64x48cm)
mwec1143	uk england surrey	1768	ROCQUE	3000	174	205	A Topographical Map of the County of Surrey in which is Expressed All the Roads, Lanes, Churches, Noblemen and Gentlemen's Seats
mwec1015	uk england shropshire	1752	ROCQUE	2400	122	103	Actual Survey of the County of Salop (title also in French)
mwec1340a	uk england yorkshire	1769	ROCQUE	100	16	20	An Accurate Map of Yorkshire (first publ. in 1746)
mwuk1183	england london	1746	ROCQUE	15000	145	180	An Exact Survey of the City's of London, Westminster ye Borough of Southwark and the Country near Ten Miles round (16 sheets, joined. 8 editions until 1769.)
mwec0785	uk england middlesex	1754	ROCQUE	3600	98	136	Carte Topographique de la Comte de Middlesex = A Topgraphical Map of the County of Middlesex
mwec0185	uk england cornwall	1746	ROCQUE	200	16	20	Cornwall
mwec0232a	uk england cumbria	1746	ROCQUE	80	21	16	Cumberland
mwec0294a	uk england devon	1743	ROCQUE	150	15	19	Devon Shire
mwec0374	uk england durham	1750	ROCQUE	60	17	21	Durham
mwuk1027	england	1790	ROCQUE	1500	118	99	England and Wales Drawn from the Most Accurate Surveys
mwec0633	uk england kent	1753	ROCQUE	180	17	21	Kent
mwf1168	france lyon	1746	ROCQUE	875	47	68	Plan de Lion (views in side and lower borders)
mwca0523b	canada quebec	1763	ROCQUE	300	12	17	Plan of Quebec, reduc'd from an Actual Survey
mwsp0715a	gibraltar	1758	ROCQUE	650	27	71	Plan of the Peninsula and part of the Isthmus of Gibralar
mwec1170	uk england sussex	1746	ROCQUE	100	16	20	Sussex
mwuk1205	england london	1763	ROCQUE	9500	90	130	The Environs of London Reduced from an Actual Survey in 16 Sheets. By the Late John Rocque (3 editions to 1769)
mwca0370	canada nova scotia	1750	ROCQUE	2250	56	44	This Chart of Chibucto Harbour ... Halifax
mwec1014	uk england shropshire	1746	ROCQUE	960	44	62	To the Right Honourable William ... This Plan of Shrewsbury
mwp0410	pacific north	1757	RODRIGUEZ	1500	30	36	Mapa de la America Septent.l. Asia Oriental y Mar del Sur Intermedio Formado Sobre las Memorias Mas Recientes Yexactas Hasta el Ano de 1754
mwbh0760	belgium holland	1793	ROEDER	960	90	62	Groot Toneel des Tegenwoordigen Oorlogs in Verscheiden Gewesten
mwaf0343a	africa	1850	ROELANDSZ	240	51	58	Afrika naar de beste bronnen
mwgr0447	greece cyprus	1570	ROGEL	75000	26	39	Insola Cipern (title outside border: 'Zupern Insel und Konigreich ... Anno 1570')
mwuk0014a	ireland	1600	ROGERS	500	20	15	Hibernia Antiqua (shown below left)
mwuss0151	carolinas	1675	ROGGEVEEN	22500	41	52	Caerte vande Cust van Florida tot de Verginis Streckende van Cabo de Canaveral tot Baya de la Madalena
mwgm0006	gulf of mexico and surrounding regions	1675	ROGGEVEEN	20000	42	53	De Cust van West Indien, van la Desconoscida tot C. Escondido (north to the right)
mwgm0382b	panama	1675	ROGGEVEEN	2500	43	54	De Cust van Westindien ... Punta d Naes (south to the top)
mwsam0584a	south america guyana	1675	ROGGEVEEN	2250	43	54	De Zeekusten van Westindien (north to the right)
mwwi0035	west indies	1681	ROGGEVEEN	5000	44	53	Generaele Kaert van West Indien vande Linie Aequinoctiael
mwp0246	pacific (all)	1724	ROGGEVEEN	480	20	35	Kaart der Reyze van drie Schepen
mwat0110	atlantic bermuda	1675	ROGGEVEEN	16000	42	52	Pascaert van 't Eylandt la Bermuda of Sommer Ilands en de Andere Eylanden daer by Geleeghen (1st printed map of Bermuda)
mwwi0409	cuba	1675	ROGGEVEEN	8000	43	54	Pascaerte van de Eylanden Cuba en Jamaica en de Andere Eylanden daer Ontrent Gelegen
mwgm0372	nicaragua	1675	ROGGEVEEN	2000	43	54	Paskaerte vande Cust van West-Indien... C. de Honduras
mwuss0291	connecticut	1675	ROGGEVEEN	45000	41	51	Pascaerte van Nieu Nederland Streckende vande Noordt Revier tot Hendrick Christiaens Eylandt
mwwi0314	bahamas	1680	ROGGEVEEN	20000	42	52	Pascaerte van 't Canael de Bahama, en de Eylanden Gelegen Benoorden Cuba (first publ. by P. Goos in 1675. Later publ. by J. Robijn)
mwwi0822	puerto rico	1675	ROGGEVEEN	5000	42	52	Pascaerte van 't Eylandt St. Juan de Puerto Rico en de Andere Resterende Caribes Eylanden van Anguilla tot Spagnola

AMPG REFERENCE	REGION	DATE	MAP MAKER	PRICE (UK£)	VERT. (cm.)	HOR. (cm.)	TITLE OF MAP (Comments by the editor in brackets)
mwam0871	america north (east)	1675	ROGGEVEEN	7200	44	54	Pascaerte van Terra Nova Nova Francia Nieuw Engeland en de Groote Revier van Canada
mwwi0234	west indies (east)	1675	ROGGEVEEN	3500	43	54	Pascaerte vande Caribes Eylanden, van 't Eylant Granadillos, tot 't Eylandt Anguilla (north to the right)
mwuss1615	virginia	1675	ROGGEVEEN	28500	42	52	Pascaerte vande Virginies van Baya de la Madelena tot de Zuydt Revier
mwsam0583a	south america guyana	1675	ROGGEVEEN	2500	43	54	Paskaert vande Cust van Westindien... Soronama (mouth of the Surinam river, south to the top)
mwsam0584	south america guyana	1675	ROGGEVEEN	2250	41	51	Paskaert vande Cust van West Indien tusschen Rio Soronama en Rio Demerary
mwsam0502a	south america colombia	1675	ROGGEVEEN	3000	43	54	Paskaerte vande Cust van West-Indien Tusschen St Martha en Ilha Cares (south to the top)
mwwi0897	trinidad & tobago	1675	ROGGEVEEN	2500	41	51	Paskaerte van 't Eylandt Trinidad en de Eijlanden daer Ontrent Gelegen, Mitsgaders de Vaste Cust van Cabo Salines tot Commonagod Bay (south to the top)
mwwi0498	curacao	1675	ROGGEVEEN	7500	42	52	t Eylandt Curacao ende de Afbeeldinghe van t Fort Amsterdam Groot Besteck
mwit0542	italy milan	1706	ROGISSART	350	12	15	Milan
mwit1058a	italy naples	1706	ROGISSART	200	12	15	Naples
mwwi0940	virgin isl	1822	ROHDE	1200	48	61	Sydside af Oen St. Thomas
mww0314	world	1710	ROKASHI	30000	114	144	(Map of the Universe - English transl. of the Japanese title. Folding map.)
mwme1010	turkey etc	1750	ROLFFSEN	600	35	43	Plan von Constantinopel und den Angraenzenden Oertern nebst dem Canal des Schwarzen Meeres
mwru0555a	ukraine	1780	ROLFFSEN	900	41	50	Theatre de la Guerre entre les Russes et les Turcs, dans les anneés 1736, 1737, &c.
mwwi0786	martinique	1761	ROLLOS	140	18	25	A Map of the Island of Martinico Drawn from the Best Authorities
mwam0420	america north	1759	ROLLOS	480	17	22	A New and Accurate Map of the Present Seat of War in North America
mwg0147	germany	1770	ROLLOS	120	20	29	A New Map of Germany Divided into Circles
mwas0184	asia continent	1770	ROLLOS	200	19	30	An Accurate Map of Asia Drawn from the Sieur Robert. Geogr. to the French King with Improvements
mwf0139	france	1770	ROLLOS	140	20	25	An Accurate Map of France Drawn from the Sieur Robert
mwit0198	italy	1770	ROLLOS	200	19	28	An Accurate Map of Italy
mwam1007	america north (east)	1760	ROLLOS	320	18	22	An Accurate Map of Louisiana and the Territory in Dispute between the English & French
mwam0428	america north	1762	ROLLOS	240	19	29	An Accurate Map of North America Drawn from the Sieur Robert, with Improvements
mwsam0083	south america	1770	ROLLOS	140	19	30	An Accurate Map of South America Drawn from the Sieur Robert, Geogr. to the French King with Improvements
mwc0169	china	1764	ROLLOS	480	27	34	An Accurate Map of the Empire of China
mwe0604	europe czech republic (bohemia)	1770	ROLLOS	140	23	28	An Accurate Map of the Kingdom of Bohemia
mwbh0721	belgium holland	1770	ROLLOS	140	19	29	An Accurate Map of the Netherlands
mww0451	world	1760	ROLLOS	480	15	28	An Accurate Map of the World Drawn from the Best Authorities
mwme1020	turkey etc	1770	ROLLOS	140	20	28	Turky in Europe
mwam1036	america north (east)	1776	ROMANS	4800	27	67	A General Map of the Southern British Colonies in America, Comprehending North and South Carolina, Georgia, East and West Florida, with the Neighbouring Indian Countries
mwec0108	uk england cambridgeshire	1804	ROPER	140	24	19	Cambridge (town plan)
mwec0793	uk england middlesex	1807	ROPER	120	20	25	Middlesex
mwg0401	bavaria	1801	ROPPELT	1400	75	75	Karte von dem Hochstift und Furstenthum Bamberg nebst Verschiedenen Angraenzenden Gegenden (4 sheets, each 75x75cm)
mwgm0333	mexico	1837	ROSA	25000	58	72	Mapa de los Estados Unidos Mejicanos Arreglado a la Distribucion que en Diversos Decretos ha hecho del Territorio el Congreso General Mejicano (unauthorised copy in Spanish of the 1834 edition of Tanner's 1826 map, with additional changes. Illustrated is the 1851 re-issue.)
mww0080	world	1592	ROSACCIO	750	6		(Untitled circular projection)
mww0109a	world	1604	ROSACCIO	600	6	8	(Untitled crude woodblock on title page).
mwit0855	italy sardinia and sicily	1595	ROSACCIO	400	13	17	(Untitled map consisting of two woodblocks. Illustration shows reprint of 1688 recut as one woodblock, size 9x13cm).
mwaf0023	africa	1594	ROSACCIO	500	13	17	(Untitled map made from 2 wood blocks)
mwe0017	europe	1595	ROSACCIO	450	13	17	(Untitled map made from 2 wood blocks)
mwru0470	ukraine	1594	ROSACCIO	400	13	17	(Untitled map made from 2 wood blocks)
mwf0031	france	1594	ROSACCIO	350	13	17	(Untitled map made from 2 wood blocks)
mwsp0167	spain	1595	ROSACCIO	350	13	17	(Untitled map made from 2 wood blocks)
mwg0029	germany	1595	ROSACCIO	300	13	17	(Untitled map made from 2 wood blocks)
mwgr0042	greece	1595	ROSACCIO	400	13	17	(Untitled map made from 2 wood blocks. Illustrated is 1688 edition, now made from one woodblock.)
mwit0043	italy	1595	ROSACCIO	480	13	17	(Untitled map of Italy)

AMPG REFERENCE	REGION	DATE	MAP MAKER	PRICE (UK£)	VERT. (cm.)	HOR. (cm.)	TITLE OF MAP (Comments by the editor in brackets)
mww0087	world	1595	ROSACCIO	1200	13	17	(Untitled oblong projection)
mww0081	world	1592	ROSACCIO	750	6	8	(Untitled oblong projection)
mwit0060	italy	1607	ROSACCIO		114	153	Abiti Antichi et Moderni D'Italia
mwas0011	asia continent	1592	ROSACCIO	500	13	17	Asia (map made from 2 wood blocks)
mwgr0363	greece crete	1598	ROSACCIO	400	10	17	Candia
mwgr0466	greece cyprus	1598	ROSACCIO	1200	10	17	Cipro
mwgr0301	greece corfu	1598	ROSACCIO	500	10	18	Corfu
mwam0015	america continent	1594	ROSACCIO	750	8	8	Figura dell America (title above map)
mwam0017	america continent	1595	ROSACCIO	750	13	17	Figura della America (made from 2 wood blocks)
mwme0442	jerusalem	1598	ROSACCIO	650	10	17	Ierusalem
mwuk0679	uk	1595	ROSACCIO	420	13	8	Inghilterra (title above map)
mwit0058	italy	1604	ROSACCIO	480	13	18	Italia (title above map)
mwgr0045	greece	1598	ROSACCIO	400	10	17	Morea
mww0102	world	1598	ROSACCIO	1600	17	24	Orbis Terrae Compendiosa Descriptio (double-hemisphere map based on Mercator)
mwme0863a	syria etc.	1598	ROSACCIO	650	14	19	Questa tavola e l'Antica Siria
mww0092	world	1596	ROSACCIO	15000	21	25	Universale Descritione de Tuto il Mondo
mww0119	world	1610	ROSACCIO	5000	27	32	Universale Descrittione di Tutto il Mondo (double-hemisphere map and Ptolemaic map below)
mwit1217	italy venice	1598	ROSACCIO	550	10	18	Venetia (plan and view)
mwgr0280	greece cefalonia	1598	ROSACCIO	500	10	18	Zafalonia
mwca0251	canada arctic	1847	ROSS	500	20	96	A Copy of the Tracing of the Icy Barrier Attached to the Arctic Continent Discovered by the United States Exploring Expedition 1840
mwec0692	uk england lancashire	1773	ROSS	2400	60	48	A Map of the Shire of Lanark Taken from an Actual Survey and Laid down from a Scale of One Inch to a Mile (4 sheets, each 60x48cm)
mwaa0056	antarctic	1847	ROSS	600	40	40	South Polar Chart showing the discoveries and track of H.M.S. Erebus and Terror
mwca0246	canada arctic	1834	ROSS	500	46	61	To His Most Excellent Majesty William IVth King of Great Britain Ireland &c. this Chart of the Discoveries Made in the Arctic Regions in 1829, 30, 31, 32 & 33
mwca0250	canada arctic	1835	ROSS	100	21	13	Victoria Harbour
mwf0925	france paris	1837	ROSSELIN	875	73	102	Nouveau Plan Routier de la Ville de Paris ou Guide Exact de cette Capitale Divisee en XII Arrondissemens avec leurs Mairies et en 48 Quartiers par (28 views in borders)
mwe0411b	europe austria vienna	1683	ROSSETTI	1000	61	49	Vienna à Turcis obsessa & Deo Dante a Christianis eliberata
mwe0275	europe albania	1689	ROSSI	875	54	44	Albania Propria Overo Superiore della Anche Macedonia Occidentale Descritta
mwe0332	europe austria	1684	ROSSI	580	41	57	Archiducato d'Austria
mwgr0606	greece islands	1685	ROSSI	1500	55	45	Arcipelago Mar Aegeo con le coste del Medesimo
mwme0969	turkey etc	1686	ROSSI	875	41	57	Asiae Minoris
mwe0496	europe croatia	1687	ROSSI	875	37	52	Battaglia e Rotta dell'Esercito Turco nelle Vicinanze di Darda ... 12. Agosto 1687
mwas0534	asia south east	1820	ROSSI	140	20	25	Carta dell Archipelago delle Indie Orientali
mwam1144	america north (east)	1802	ROSSI	240	25	18	Carta della Florida, Luigiana e Laghi del Canada
mwsam0645	south america guyana	1821	ROSSI	200	36	41	Carta della Gujana Francese ed Olandese
mwwi0271	west indies (east)	1821	ROSSI	320	34	42	Carta della Isole Antille
mwam1352	america north (west)	1820	ROSSI	720	27	22	Carta della Parte della Costa Nord-Ouest dell'America Riconosciuta nelle Estati del 1792. 1793, 1794 ... dal Capito. Giorgio Vancouver
mwwi0678	hispaniola	1821	ROSSI	320	34	42	Carta di S. Domingo Guista quella di Poirson
mwaf1001	africa south	1820	ROSSI	140	20	25	Colonia del Capo di Bona Speranza
mwme0968	turkey etc	1684	ROSSI	2000	39	52	Constantinopoli (view) / Stretto de Dardanelli
mwe0709	europe danube	1684	ROSSI	500	42	55	Corso del Danubio da Belgrado Fino al Mar Nero
mwe0671a	europe dalmatia	1684	ROSSI	720	42	55	Dalmatia Istria Bosnia Servia Croatia e parte di Schiavonia
mwe0673	europe dalmatia	1689	ROSSI	1000	56	80	Dalmatia Maritima Occidentale e Dalmatia Maritime Orientale Descritta
mwe0771a	europe east	1686	ROSSI	650	42	54	Descritione delli Principati della Moldavia, e Valachia
mwe0497	europe croatia	1687	ROSSI	875	39	52	Disegno del Famoso Ponte e Fortezza di Essech / Verowitiza
mwe0902	europe hungary	1687	ROSSI	1350	39	52	Dissegno delle Segnalate Vittorie de Christiani contro il Turco con la Presa de Parcan e Strigonia l'Anno MDCLXXXIII
mwca0142	canada	1820	ROSSI	240	20	25	Dominj Inglesi in America
mwsam0336	south america brazil	1698	ROSSI	875	34	51	Geografia della Marina della Citta della Baia [di San Salvador]
mwjk0137	japan	1820	ROSSI	280	20	25	Giappone
mwf0580	france ile de france	1692	ROSSI	500	58	46	Governo Generale dell Isola di Francia
mwf0655	france loire	1692	ROSSI	900	57	85	Governo Generale d'Orleans
mwf0325	france brittany	1692	ROSSI	400	43	57	Governo Gnale del Ducato di Bretagna
mwp0275	pacific (all)	1820	ROSSI	100	20	25	Grande Oceano ouvero Quinta Parte del Mondo
mwe0903	europe hungary	1687	ROSSI	1500	39	52	Gyula / Tokay / Dissegno delle Segnalate Vittorie de Christiani contro il Turco con la Presa di Parcan e Strigonia l'Anno MDCLXXXIII
mwg0807	westphalia	1687	ROSSI	320	56	43	Il Circolo di Westfalia

AMPG REFERENCE	REGION	DATE	MAP MAKER	PRICE (UK£)	VERT. (cm.)	HOR. (cm.)	TITLE OF MAP (Comments by the editor in brackets)
mwe1003	europe rhine	1689	ROSSI	1000	82	56	Il Corso del Fiume Reno dalle sue Fonti sino al Mare con Tutti li Fiumi, che si Scaricano in Esso Tanto a Destra
mwe1105a	europe slovak republic (moravia)	1692	ROSSI	550	41	58	Il Ducato di Sllesia Il Marchesato di Moravia
mwit0664	italy piedmont	1691	ROSSI	2400	102	84	Il Piemonte
mwsp0482	spain regions	1696	ROSSI	720	38	51	Il Principato delle Asturie
mwsp0476	spain regions	1690	ROSSI	750	45	59	Il Principato di Catalogna
mwsp0483	spain regions	1696	ROSSI	675	56	41	Il Regno de Leone
mwe0443	europe bosnia	1689	ROSSI	800	41	53	Il Regno della Bossina
mwc0079	china	1682	ROSSI	2000	44	55	Il Regno della China detto Presentemente Catay, e Mangin
mwe1061	europe serbia	1689	ROSSI	720	41	55	Il Regno della Servia detta Altrimenti Rascia
mwsp0484	spain regions	1696	ROSSI	675	42	55	Il Regno di Aragona Descritto da D. Nicolo Cantelli Geografo
mwsp0485	spain regions	1696	ROSSI	675	43	55	Il Regno di Castiglia Vecchia Descritto da Giacomo Cantelli da Viga Geografo del Sereniss Sigr. Duca di Modena
mwsp0486	spain regions	1696	ROSSI	675	42	55	Il Regno di Galicia Descritta da Giacomo da Vignola Geografo
mwe0895a	europe hungary	1683	ROSSI	600	43	55	Il Regno d'Ungaria Transilvania, Schiavonia, Bosnia, Croatia, Dalmatia
mwe1148	europe south east	1715	ROSSI	360	41	52	Illyricum Orientis in quo Partes II. Moesia et Thracia. Provinciae XI
mwc0246	china	1820	ROSSI	200	25	20	Impero della Cina
mwin0341	india	1820	ROSSI	140	18	21	Indostan o siano l'Indie
mwm0207	mediterranean malta	1686	ROSSI	3500	41	55	Isola di Malta Gozzo Comino e Cominotto (large inset: Valletta)
mwas0410	asia south east	1683	ROSSI	2000	45	58	Isole dell'India cioe le Molucche le Filippine e della Sonda
mwit0900	italy sicily	1682	ROSSI	900	44	55	Isole e Regno di Sicilia
mwit0116	italy	1691	ROSSI	1500	55	84	Italia Ecclesiastica in suas Viginti Distincta Provincias sive Italiae Episcopales Ecclesiae
mwf0223	france alsace	1680	ROSSI	280	42	57	La Bassa Alsazia e l'Ortnavia Divise ne Dominy che in esse e ne Confini d'esse si Ritrovano
mwe0449a	europe bulgaria	1689	ROSSI	800	41	56	La Bulgaria e la Romania con parte di Macedonia
mwf1027	france provence	1691	ROSSI	650	56	45	La Contea di Nizza divisa ne suoi quattro Vicariati
mwf1098	france pyrenees	1690	ROSSI	480	40	57	La Contea di Rossilone
mwe0497a	europe croatia	1690	ROSSI	875	42	56	La Croatia e Contea di Zara
mwru0435	russia tartary	1683	ROSSI	800	43	53	La Gran Tartaria Divisa nelle sue Parte Principali da Giacomo Cantelli da Vignola
mwgr0098a	greece	1689	ROSSI	900	44	55	La Grecia Universale Antica Paragonnata con la Moderna
mwit0423a	italy liguria	1697	ROSSI	1600	44	105	La Liguria o Stato della Republica di Genova con altri Stati adiacenti
mwgr0107	greece	1689	ROSSI	600	44	57	La Macedonia
mwgr0099	greece	1685	ROSSI	750	43	55	La Morea Ridatta dal' Esemplare antico nella moderna divisione
mwbp0316	poland	1689	ROSSI	320	43	56	La Pomerania
mwg0210	germany north east	1689	ROSSI	500	43	58	La Prussia Divisa in Reale che Appartiene al Re di Polonia et in Ducale che Spetta all'Elettore di Brandeburgo
mwf1140	france rhone-alpes	1692	ROSSI	800	78	58	La Savoia Divisa nelle sue Principali Provincie
mwf1137a	france rhone-alpes	1691	ROSSI	400	43	58	La Savoia La Bressa e Bugey
mwsc0073	scandinavia	1679	ROSSI	875	41	55	La Scandinavia Divisa nelli suoi Regni di Svezia, Danemarca, Norvegia, e Paese de Lapponi
mwsp0192	spain	1677	ROSSI	480	41	53	La Spagna
mwe1044	europe romania	1686	ROSSI	480	42	57	La Transylvania
mwaf0093a	africa	1677	ROSSI	720	40	55	L'Africa Nuovamente corretta (Italian copy of Sanson 1650)
mwsam0139	south america	1821	ROSSI	320	77	70	L'America Meridionale
mwsam0032	south america	1687	ROSSI	875	39	54	L'America Meridionale Nuovamente Coretta, et Accresciuta Secondo le Relationi pui da Guglielmo Sansone Geografo di S.M. Christianissima e Data in Luce da Giacomo de Rossi
mwam0324	america north	1677	ROSSI	2000	39	54	L'America Settentrionale Nuovamente Corretta et Accresciuta Secondo le Relationi Piu Moderne da Guglielmo Sansone Geografo di S.M. Christianisa. e Data in Luce da Gio. Giacomo de Rossi, in Roma nella sua Stamperia alla Pace, l'Anno 1677
mwas0063	asia continent	1677	ROSSI	720	40	56	l'Asia (copy of Sanson 1650 with different cartouche)
mwbh0444	belgium holland	1689	ROSSI	1200	107	90	Le Diecisette Provincie de Paesi Bassi
mwg0083	germany	1690	ROSSI	550	46	57	Le Poste con le sue Strade Principali dell'Alta e Bassa Germania e de Paesi Adiacenti
mwf0083	france	1697	ROSSI	480	67	54	Le Poste della Francia con le sue Strade Principali
mwit0555a	italy marches	1697	ROSSI	400	43	55	Legatione del Ducato d'Urbino con la Diocesi, e Governo di Citta di Castello el Altri Governi, e Stati Confinanti
mwit0356	italy emilia-romagna	1710	ROSSI	480	55	44	Legazione di Bologna Descritta da ... Magini
mwsw0091	switzerland	1686	ROSSI	675	42	55	L'Helvetia o' Paese de Svizzeri
mwit0400	italy lazio	1696	ROSSI	2000	84	113	Il Lazio (map by Ameti)
mwsp0487	spain regions	1696	ROSSI	1000	53	86	Il Regni di Granata, e d'Andalucia
mwsp0058	portugal	1690	ROSSI	900	87	55	Il Regno di Portogallo
mwsp0488	spain regions	1696	ROSSI	675	54	41	Li Regni di Valenza, e di Murcia
mwin0131	india	1683	ROSSI	675	43	53	L'India di qua e di la dal Gange oue sono li Stati del G. Mogol

AMPG REFERENCE	REGION	DATE	MAP MAKER	PRICE (UK£)	VERT. (cm.)	HOR. (cm.)	TITLE OF MAP (Comments by the editor in brackets)
mwuk0102	ireland	1689	ROSSI	1200	58	44	L'Irlanda o' uero Hibernia
mwuk0734	uk	1677	ROSSI	875	41	51	L'Isole Britanniche overo l'Inghilterra ... la Scotia ... l'Irlanda
mwit0122	italy	1695	ROSSI	900	44	57	L'Italia con le sue Poste e Strade Principali
mwit0120	italy	1694	ROSSI	875	45	58	L'Italia dedicata
mwe0900	europe hungary	1686	ROSSI	900	58	89	L'Ungaria
mwgr0113	europe albania	1689	ROSSI	600	44	56	Macedonia Epiro Livadia Albania et Ianna divise nelle sue parti principali
mwgr0108	greece	1689	ROSSI	600	44	56	Macedonia Epiro Livadia Albania et Ianna divise nelle sue parti principali
mww0199	world	1674	ROSSI	2800	33	56	Mappa Mondo o Vero Carta Generale del Globo Terestre Rapresentato in Due Planisferi
mww0668	world	1820	ROSSI	600	41	69	Mappa-Mondo in Due Emisferi
mww0669	world	1820	ROSSI	200	18	25	Mappamondo Ridotto
mwme0970	turkey etc	1686	ROSSI	875	42	56	Natolia detta Anticamente Asia Minore
mwas0314	asia caspian sea	1723	ROSSI-OTTENS	550	45	58	Novissima et accurata Maris Caspij
mwe1060	europe serbia	1687	ROSSI	1350	43	55	Orientis Porta Taurunum (vulgo Belgrado) ... Expugnatum die 6. Septembris 1688
mwg0525	rheinland-pfalz	1689	ROSSI	875	41	54	Paese d'Eiffel
mwe1123a	europe slovenia	1690	ROSSI	600	43	56	Parte della Schiavonia, Overo Slavonia, aggiuntavi la Contea di Cillea, e Windisch Mark
mwf1188	france south west	1692	ROSSI	600	57	43	Parte Occidentale / Parte Meridionale del Governo Generale d'Orleans nella quale sono Comprese le Provincie Particulari (2 maps)
mwit1111a	italy tuscany	1693	ROSSI	2000	84	113	Patrimonio di S. Pietro olim Tusca Suburbicaria con le sue più cospicue strade antiche
mwgr0099a	greece	1685	ROSSI	750	44	55	Peloponnesus ad Antiquor
mwas0818	asia south east siam	1683	ROSSI	2000	53	41	Penisola dell'India di la dal Gange
mwin0130	india	1683	ROSSI	900	53	42	Penisola dell'India di qua dal Gange
mwe0412	europe austria vienna	1683	ROSSI	2000	39	55	Pianta Della Cesarea Citta Di Vienna
mwe0904	europe hungary	1687	ROSSI	1500	45	57	Pianta della Real Citta e Fortezza di Buda Capitale del Regno d'Ungaria
mwgr0109	greece	1689	ROSSI	875	40	55	Pianta e Elevazione della Citta e Famoso Porto di Napoli di Romania nella Morea Assediata
mwgr0268	greece athens	1687	ROSSI	1000	39	53	Pianta e Prospetto dell' Antica Citta e Fortezza Athene
mwe0905	europe hungary	1687	ROSSI	1500	41	54	Pianta et Elevatione della Reale Citta e Fortezza di Buda
mwgr0101	greece	1687	ROSSI	875	40	53	Pianta et Elevatione delle Fortezze di Navarino e suo Famoso Porto Posto in Morea
mwe0906	europe hungary	1687	ROSSI	1500	39	53	Pianta, et Assedio delle Citta di Buda, e Pest ... 1684
mwgm0289	mexico	1820	ROSSI	140	20	25	Possessioni della Spagna nell'America Settentrionale
mwsam0338	south america brazil	1698	ROSSI	750	39	51	Provincia di Paraiba (by Santa Teresa)
mwit0287	italy campagna	1714	ROSSI	580	54	43	Provincia di Terra di Lavoro
mwbh0463	belgium holland	1692	ROSSI	480	37	51	Provincie Meridionali de Paesi Bassi, Intese Sotto Nome di Flandra, overo li Paesi Bassi Cattolici, con li Confini di Francia, di Allemagna, et di Hollanda
mwaa0208	arctic / antarctic	1820	ROSSI	300	22	39	Regioni Polari Paragonate Secondo gli Ultimi Viaggi (2 polar maps on one sheet)
mwsc0297	scandinavia denmark	1677	ROSSI	480	41	53	Regno di Danimarca Diviso nelle sue Due Jutlandie cioe Settentrionale in Quattro Diocesi et Australe
mwme0787a	persia etc	1679	ROSSI	675	45	56	Regno di Persia (shown below left)
mwsam0337	south america brazil	1698	ROSSI	1350	37	51	Rio di Gennaro (view)
mwit0723	italy rome	1676	ROSSI	1800	48	73	Roma Antiqua Triumphatrix Abantiquis Monumentis et Rerum Gestarum (first publ. by Lauro c1630)
mwm0019a	mediterranean	1679	ROSSI	960	40	102	Romani Imperii qua Occidens /Oriens est Descriptio (2 sheets. Re-issue of Sanson 1637)
mwru0098	russia	1688	ROSSI	875	43	55	Russia Bianca e Moscovia
mwgr0608	greece islands	1687	ROSSI	1500	39	53	Situatione e Prospetto della Fortezza di S. Maura / Citta di Scio
mwsp0323	spain	1820	ROSSI	140	18	23	Spagna e Portogallo
mwme0566a	arabia etc	1679	ROSSI	720	43	57	Stato del Gran Turco
mwbp0288	poland	1678	ROSSI	685	43	57	Stati della Corona di Polonia
mwam1183	america north (east)	1820	ROSSI	200	19	20	Stati Uniti di America
mwe0907	europe hungary	1687	ROSSI	785	39	53	Strigonia Liberata / Esech e suo Pont Bruggiata
mwru0496	ukraine	1684	ROSSI	875	44	55	Tartaria d'Europa overo Piccola Tartaria
mwme0177	holy land	1679	ROSSI	875	43	55	Terra Sancta sive Promissionis, olim Palestina, in Duo Divisa Regna, Israel et Iuda, et in Sex Sub Divisa Provincias Scilicet Iudaea, Samaria, Galilaea, Trachonitide, Peraea, et Idumaea
mwaf0086	africa	1679	ROSSI	13500	57	91	Totius Africae Nova et Exacta Tabula ex Optimis tum Geographorum tum Aliorum Scriptis Collecta et ad Hodiernam Regnorum Principatuum et Maiorum Partium Distinctionem Accommodata per Gulielmu Blaew Amstelodami MDCLXXIX

AMPG REFERENCE	REGION	DATE	MAP MAKER	PRICE (UK£)	VERT. (cm.)	HOR. (cm.)	TITLE OF MAP (Comments by the editor in brackets)
mwam0083	america continent	1679	ROSSI		57	91	Totius Americae Nova et Exacta Tabula ex Optimis tum Geographorum tum Aliorum Scriptis Collecta et ad Hodiernam Regnorum Principatuum et Maiorum Partium Distinctionem Accommodata per Gulielmu Blaew Amstelodami MDCLXXIX
mwas0065	asia continent	1679	ROSSI	13500	57	91	Totius Asiae Nova et Exacta Tabula ex Optimis tum Geographorum tum Aliorum Scriptis Collecta et ad Hodiernam Regnorum Principatuum et Maiorum Partium Distinctionem Accommodata per Gulielmu Blaew Amstelodami MDCLXXIX
mwe0085	europe	1679	ROSSI	8000	57	91	Totius Europae Nova et Exacta Tabula ex Optimis tum Geographorum tum Aliorum Scriptis Collecta et ad Hodiernam Regnorum Principatuum et Maiorum Partium Distinctionem Accommodata per Gulielmu Blaew Amstelodami MDCLXXIX
mwe0895	europe hungary	1683	ROSSI	720	56	40	Ungaria Occidentale / Ungaria Orientale (2 sheets, each 56x40cm)
mwme0971	turkey etc	1687	ROSSI	1500	41	54	Veduta e Prospetto de' Dardanelli nello Stretto del Golfo di Lepanto con la Citta di Patrasso / Prospetto della Citta e Fortezza di Lepanto in Livadia
mwe0415	europe austria vienna	1687	ROSSI	875	42	55	Vienna Assediata dalle Armi Ottomane gli 12 Luglio 1683 Soccorsa, e Liberata gli 12 Settembre
mwe0813	europe east	1771	ROTH	875	68	85	Carte Speciale de la Principaute de Moldavie Divisee en ses Districts
mwru0257	russia	1776	ROTH	2000	45	70	Novoj Plan Stolicnago Goroda Dreposti Sanktpetersburga (St. Petersburg)
mwm0153	mediterranean east	1771	ROTH	1350	51	93	Theatre de la Guerre entre les Russiens et les Turcs
mwru0547	ukraine	1770	ROTH	1200	51	95	Theatre de la Guerre entre les Russiens et les Turcs
mwuss0352	washington DC	1836	ROTHWELL	2400	39	53	Map of the City of Washington
mwf1100	france pyrenees	1703	ROUSSEL	2000	115	180	Carte Generale des Monts Pyrenees, et Parties des Royaumes de France et d'Espagne
mwf0902	france paris	1795	ROUSSEL	2400	130	178	Paris, ses Fauxbourgs et ses Environs (1st publ. 1730. Illustrated is Chardon's reduced size copy 82x107cm publ. 1860)
mwme0881a	syria etc	1764	ROUX	200	13	20	(Untitled chart of Acre and Haifa)
mwgr0328	greece corfu	1764	ROUX	240	14	20	(Untitled map of Corfu. See illustration above left)
mwgr0508	greece cyprus	1764	ROUX	2000	81	56	(Untitled map of Cyprus from Roux's 12-sheet map. See Mediterranean.)
mwsp0674	balearic islands	1764	ROUX	100	13	20	(Untitled map of the environs of Palma)
mwe0503	europe croatia	1764	ROUX	100	20	14	(Untitled map of the fortifications of Split)
mwsp0577	spain regions	1764	ROUX	200	14	21	Barcelone
mwit0815a	italy sardinia	1764	ROUX	150	13	20	Baye de Cagliari
mwsp0725	gibraltar	1764	ROUX	100	13	20	Baye de Gibraltar
mwaf0798	africa north morocco	1764	ROUX	100	13	20	Baye de Tanger
mwit0837b	italy sardinia and corsica	1764	ROUX	150	13	20	Bouches de Boniface
mwm0064	mediterranean	1764	ROUX	800	56	64	Carte de la Mediterranee
mwm0065	mediterranean	1764	ROUX	6000	56	81	Carte de la Mer Mediterranee en Douze Feuilles (in 12 sheets, each 56x81cm)
mwsp0674a	balearic islands	1764	ROUX	960	81	55	Carte de la Mer Mediterranee en Douze Feuilles (sheet 2 only)
mwgr0287	greece cefalonia	1764	ROUX	200	13	18	Carte des isles St. Maure, Cefallonie et Zante
mwgr0327	greece corfu	1764	ROUX	240	14	20	Carte du Mouillage de Corfou
mwit0445	italy liguria	1764	ROUX	200	14	21	Genes
mwgr0288	greece cefalonia	1764	ROUX	150	20	15	Isola di Cefalonia
mwit0951	italy sicily	1764	ROUX	120	14	21	Palerme
mwm0247	mediterranean malta	1764	ROUX	200	13	18	Plan du Port de Malte
mwgr0532	greece rhodes	1764	ROUX	200	15	20	Port de Rhode
mwgr0509	greece cyprus	1764	ROUX	200	20	15	Rada di Limassol
mwgr0542	greece zante (zakynthos)	1764	ROUX	200	15	20	Ville et Port de Zante
mwe0232	europe	1803	ROWE	650	72	85	A New Map of Europe with its Modern Divisions
mwuk1286	england london	1814	ROWE	1350	41	79	London, Westminster and Southwark, Exhibiting the Various Improvements to the Year ... (9 editions to 1820)
mwuk1277	england london	1806	ROWE	960	51		Rowe's Map of the Country Twenty-One Miles round London (circular map, 7 editions to 1825)
mwaa0022	antarctic	1740	ROYAL ACAD. PRUSSIA	1200	31	32	Tabula Geographica Hemisphaeri Australis
mwwi0943	virgin isl	1832	ROYAL GEOGRAPHIC SOCIETY	240	18	23	Anegada with its Reefs by R. Schomburgh / Virgin Islands
mwgm0075	gulf of mexico and surrounding regions	1841	ROYAL GEOGRAPHIC SOCIETY	250	42	37	Map of Central America to Illustrate the Papers of Captn. Bird Allen, R.N., Alonso de Escober and Chevr. Emanuel Friedrichstal
mwsam0649	south america guyana	1840	ROYAL GEOGRAPHIC SOCIETY	200	28	39	Map of Guayana to Illustrate the Route of R.H. Schomburgk Esq. 1840
mwaf1082	africa south west	1838	ROYAL GEOGRAPHIC SOCIETY	300	38	24	Map to illustrate Capt. Alexander's Route in South Africa.
mwp0107	australia	1834	ROYAL GEOGRAPHIC SOCIETY	200	18	44	Melville & Bathurst Island with Coburg Peninsula, Northern Australia

AMPG REFERENCE	REGION	DATE	MAP MAKER	PRICE (UK£)	VERT. (cm.)	HOR. (cm.)	TITLE OF MAP (Comments by the editor in brackets)
mwin0359	india	1834	ROYAL GEOGRAPHIC SOCIETY	80	20	16	Sketch of Part of the Himma-Leh Mountains to Illustrate the Paper by Capt. Johnson
mwgm0100	costa rica	1836	ROYAL GEOGRAPHIC SOCIETY	250	20	25	Sketch of the state of Costarricca
mwca0247	canada arctic	1835	ROYAL GEOGRAPHIC SOCIETY	360	16	23	Sketch Shewing the Route of the Recent Arctic Land Expedition
mwwi0944	virgin isl	1835	ROYAL GEOGRAPHIC SOCIETY	360	19	43	The Virgin Islands Shewing the Set of the Tide amongst them (map by R. Schombergh)
mwuss0105	california	1835	ROYAL GEOGRAPHIC SOCIETY	160	25	11	Upper California to Illustrate the Paper by Dr. Coulter
mwp0102	australia	1832	ROYAL GEOGRAPHIC SOCIETY	1500	37	33	Western Australia, from the Latest Documents Received in the Colonial Office 1832
mwam1004	america north (east)	1759	ROYAL MAG.	400	17	22	A New and Accurate Map of the Present Seat of War in North America
mwam1015	america north (east)	1763	ROYAL MAG.	300	19	24	A New Map of North America: Shewing the Advantages Obtain'd therein to England, by the Peace
mwwi0443	cuba	1762	ROYAL MAG.	360	18	27	A Plan of the Siege of the Havana, Drawn by an Officer on the Spot. 1762
mwwi0444	cuba	1762	ROYAL MAG.	200	18	25	An Accurate Map of Cuba, and the Adjacent Islands; by G. Rollos, Geogr.
mwca0511b	canada quebec	1759	ROYAL MAG.	300	19	24	An Authentic Plan of the River St. Lawrence, from Sillery to the Fall of Montmerenci. With the Operations of the Siege of Quebec, under the Command of Vice-Adml. Saunders & Majr. Genl. Wolfe down to the 5 Sepr. 1759
mwuk1589	channel islands	1770	ROYCE	280	23	17	A Map of the Islands of Guernsey, Jersey, Isle of Man, Isle of Wight
mwbp0154	baltic states	1839	RUCKER	1500	162	141	Specialcharte von Livland in 6 Blattern
mwe0084	europe	1679	RUDBECK	320	45	55	(Europe)
mwsc0074	scandinavia	1679	RUDBECK	500	44	55	(Scandinavia)
mwsc0687	scandinavia sweden	1679	RUDBECK	400	45	58	(Sueonia)
mwsc0688	scandinavia sweden	1679	RUDBECK	960	33	41	(Uppsala and environs)
mwam0286	america continent	1827	RUGA	250	33	46	L'Amerique Secondo le Ultime Osservazioni Divisa ne'suoi Stati Principali
mwit0760a	italy rome	1829	RUGA	600	63	80	Pianta Topografica della Città di Roma dell'anno 1829
mwit1136	italy florence	1731	RUGGIERI	1500	50	68	Pianta della Citta di Firenze
mwuss0864	massachusetts	1824	RUGGLES	4500	75	93	A Map of Massachusetts, Connecticut, & Rhodeisland. Humbly Submitted to the Citizens thereof
mwuss1016	new hampshire	1817	RUGGLES	3500	77	47	New-Hampshire, from Late Survey; to the Citizens of which, this Map is Most Respectfully Dedicated
mwaf0027	africa	1597	RUGHESI	20000	53	69	Africa
mwam0021	america continent	1597	RUGHESI		53	70	America
mwas0017	asia continent	1597	RUGHESI		53	69	Asia
mwe0020	europe	1597	RUGHESI	15000	53	70	Europa
mww0095	world	1597	RUGHESI	200000	53	70	Novissima Orbis Universi Descriptio Romae Accuratissime Delineata
mwe1054	europe romania	1788	RUHEDORF	960	39	69	Mappa Specialis Walachiae ... Delineata
mwaf0761a	africa north libya	1561	RUSCELLI	200	18	24	Africa Minor Nuova Tavola
mwaf0851	africa south	1574	RUSCELLI	400	19	26	Africa Nuova Tavola
mwuk0664	uk	1561	RUSCELLI	500	19	25	Anglia et Hibernia Nova (1574 edition illustrated)
mwme0532	arabia etc	1561	RUSCELLI	600	18	25	Arabia Felice Nuova Tavola
mwsam0274	south america brazil	1561	RUSCELLI	600	18	25	Brasil Nuova Tavola
mwin0087	india	1561	RUSCELLI	300	18	24	Calecut Nuova Tavola
mww0054	world	1562	RUSCELLI	960	18	25	Carta Marina Nuova Tavola
mwaf0457	africa egypt etc	1561	RUSCELLI	250	18	24	Egitto Nuova Tavola
mwbh0018	belgium holland	1561	RUSCELLI	400	18	25	Flandria, Brabantia, et Holanda Nuova (1574 edition illustrated)
mwf0022	france	1574	RUSCELLI	250	19	26	Gallia Nova Tabula (1st publ. 1561)
mwgr0019	greece	1561	RUSCELLI	350	18	24	Graetia Nuova Tabula
mwsp0162	spain	1574	RUSCELLI	350	19	26	Hispania Nova Tabula
mwas0363	asia south east	1561	RUSCELLI	600	19	26	India Tercera Nuova Tavola
mwwi0396	cuba	1561	RUSCELLI	600	19	25	Isola Cuba Nova
mwwi0572	hispaniola	1561	RUSCELLI	500	20	25	Isola Spagnola Nova
mwaf0458	africa egypt etc	1561	RUSCELLI	200	18	24	Marmarica Nuova Tavola
mwaf1087	africa west	1574	RUSCELLI	350	19	26	Mauritania Nuova Tavola
mwru0014	russia	1561	RUSCELLI	350	19	25	Moschovia Nuova Tavola
mwme0912	turkey etc	1561	RUSCELLI	350	18	25	Natolia Nuova Tavola
mwgm0130	mexico	1561	RUSCELLI	1200	19	25	Nueva Hispania Tabula Nova (enlarged version of Gastaldi 1548)
mww0052	world	1561	RUSCELLI	960	13	25	Orbis Descriptio
mwme0756	persia etc	1561	RUSCELLI	300	18	25	Persia Nuova Tavola
mwe0746	europe east	1575	RUSCELLI	450	20	27	Polonia et Hungaria Nuova Tavola
mwsc0015	scandinavia	1561	RUSCELLI	850	19	25	Schonladia Nuova (based on Gastaldi's 1548 map.)
mwsc0016	scandinavia	1561	RUSCELLI	850	19	25	Septentrionalium Partium Nova Tabula (Based on Zeno's 1558 map.)
mwme0861	syria etc	1561	RUSCELLI	500	20	26	Soria et Terra Santa Nuova Tavola

AMPG REFERENCE	REGION	DATE	MAP MAKER	PRICE (UK£)	VERT. (cm.)	HOR. (cm.)	TITLE OF MAP (Comments by the editor in brackets)
mwit0547	italy marches	1561	RUSCELLI	280	18	25	Tavola Nuova della Marca d'Ancona
mwit1159	italy veneto	1561	RUSCELLI	200	18	25	Tavola Nuova della Marca Trivigiana
mwg0018	germany	1561	RUSCELLI	300	18	25	Tavola Nuova di Germania
mwit0629	italy piedmont	1561	RUSCELLI	200	18	24	Tavola Nuova di Piemonte
mwbp0065	baltic states	1561	RUSCELLI	300	18	25	Tavola Nuova di Prussia et di Livonia
mwit0853	italy sardinia and sicily	1561	RUSCELLI	350	19	25	Tavola Nuova di Sardigna et di Sicilia
mwe0635	europe dalmatia	1561	RUSCELLI	300	18	24	Tavola Nuova di Schiavonia
mwit0026	italy	1561	RUSCELLI	600	18	24	Tavola Nuova d'Italia
mwit0379	italy lazio	1561	RUSCELLI	250	19	25	Territorio di Roma (1574 edition illustrated)
mwsam0002	south america	1561	RUSCELLI	600	19	25	Tierra Nova (enlargement of Gastaldi's 1548 map)
mwca0002	canada	1561	RUSCELLI	1500	19	24	Tierra Nueva (Enlargement of Gastaldi's map)
mwit1084	italy tuscany	1561	RUSCELLI	320	17	25	Toscana Nuova Tabula
mwam0524a	america north	1794	RUSSELL	350	38	48	A General Map of North America Drawn from the Best Surveys
mwam0464	america north	1778	RUSSELL	400	28	41	A General Map of North America; from the Latest Observations. Engrav'd by Jn. Lodge, from the Late Mr. Jefferys
mwsam0119	south america	1796	RUSSELL	150	36	46	A General Map of South America from the Best Surveys
mwgm0246	mexico	1778	RUSSELL	150	15	24	A Map of the Province of Mexico in New Spain from the Best Authorities
mwaf0297	africa	1811	RUSSELL	240	39	45	Africa Drawn from the Best Authorities
mwam1114	america north (east)	1794	RUSSELL	450	37	47	An Accurate Map of the United States of America, According to the Treaty of Peace of 1783
mwam0463	america north	1778	RUSSELL	375	25	38	An Exact Map of North America from the Best Authorities
mwca0415	canada nova scotia	1777	RUSSELL	180	21	25	An Exact Map of Nova Scotia Newfoundland ... 1777
mwas0240	asia continent	1810	RUSSELL	75	18	22	Asia.
mwca0126	canada	1799	RUSSELL	600	40	46	British Colonies in North America Drawn from the Best Authorities
mwc0239	china	1811	RUSSELL	240	39	46	China Divided into Provinces Drawn from the Best Authorities
mwsc0381	scandinavia denmark	1790	RUSSELL	240	41	32	Denmark, Divided into Dioceses and Prefectures Compiled from the Best Authorities
mwsam0569	south america galapagos	1798	RUSSELL	200	18	16	Gallapagos Islands, Described by Ambrose Cowley in 1684
mwin0333	india	1811	RUSSELL	240	40	45	Hindoostan or India
mwuk0246	ireland	1802	RUSSELL	280	40	32	Ireland Divided into Provinces and Counties from the Best Authorities by J. Russell 1802
mwsam0478	south america chile	1825	RUSSELL	200	41	18	Map of Chile, Including Indian Chile
mwam1113	america north (east)	1794	RUSSELL	450	36	46	Map of the Middle States of America, Comprehends New-York, New-Jersey, Pennsylvania, Delaware and the Territory N.W. of Ohio
mwam1142	america north (east)	1801	RUSSELL	500	32	51	Map of the Northern Provinces of the United States
mwam1118	america north (east)	1795	RUSSELL	500	37	46	Map of the Northern, or, New England States of America, Comprehending Vermont, New Hampshire, District of Main, Massachusetts, Rhode-Island, and Connecticut
mwam1117	america north (east)	1795	RUSSELL	500	37	51	Map of the Southern States of America, Comprehending Maryland, Virginia, Kentucky, Territory Sth of the Ohio, North Carolina, Tennessee Governmt. South Carolina, & Georgia
mwuss0593	kentucky	1794	RUSSELL	750	38	44	Map of the State of Kentucky; with the Adjoining Territories
mww0628	world	1806	RUSSELL	300	23	43	Map of the World Including the Most Recent Tracts and Discoveries of the Latest Navigators
mwam0585	america north	1811	RUSSELL	400	39	45	North America
mwuss0338	washington DC	1795	RUSSELL	3000	40	53	Plan of the City of Washington
mwam1134	america north (east)	1799	RUSSELL	500	39	45	States of America, Drawn from the Best Authorities by J. Russell
mwwi0110	west indies	1778	RUSSELL	350	23	36	The West Indies and Gulf of Mexico from the Latest Discoveries and Best Observations
mww0590	world	1795	RUSSELL	100	8	15	The World. 1795
mwru0326	russia	1809	RUSSIAN GOV.	1200	118	112	Carte de la Partie Europeenne de l'Empire de Russie, avec l'Indication des Chemins de Poste, ainsi que des Douanes Frontieres
mwgm0073	gulf of mexico and surrounding regions	1836	RUSSO	280	33	42	Messico, America Centrale ed Antille. 1836
mwuk0487	scotland	1745	RUTHERFORD	6000	58	37	An Exact Plan of His Majesty's Great Roads through the Highlands of Scotland (inset: battle of Prestonpans)
mww0016	world	1507	RUYSCH	200000	41	54	Universalior Cogniti Orbis Tabula ex Recentibus Confecta Orbservationibus (fan-shaped projection. 1st 'available' printed map to show America and 'modern' Africa.)
mwp0530	pacific south	1850	S.P.C.K.	480	49	58	Australasia
			For SDUK, see SOCIETY D.U.K.				
mwit0721a	italy rome	1668	SABADINI	6000	51	82	Descrittione dell'Alma Citta di Roma
mwe0846	europe east	1842	SAFARIK	400	49	61	Slovanksy Zemevid (publ. in Prague)
mwam1376	america north (west)	1846	SAGE	2500	46	60	Map of Oregon, California, New Mexico, N.W. Texas, & the Proposed Territory of Ne-Bras-Ka

AMPG REFERENCE	REGION	DATE	MAP MAKER	PRICE (UK£)	VERT. (cm.)	HOR. (cm.)	TITLE OF MAP (Comments by the editor in brackets)
mwaa0126a	arctic	1739	SAINT-ALBIN	1500	60	81	Horizon de Paris (polar projection incl. most of the world. Text side borders.)
mww0044	world	1550	SALAMANCA	75000	33	52	(Untitled double-cordiform projection. Based on Fine, 1531 and Mercator 1538)
mwsw0012	switzerland	1555	SALAMANCA	8000	44	62	(Untitled map)
mwgr0346	greece crete	1570	SALAMANCA	5000	43	64	El vero disegno di Candia (also issued without title)
mwgr0017	greece	1558	SALAMANCA	20000	41	62	Graeciae Chorographia (title above map. Also issued without title)
mwit1083a	italy tuscany	1558	SALAMANCA	10000	41	54	Sacra Tuscia (Salamanca also produced a later? version of this map, with more ships etc. but lacking the scroll title)
mwe0739	europe east	1548	SALAMANCA	5000	41	53	Tabula Moderna Poloniae, Ungariae, Bohemiae, Germaniae, Russiae, Lithuae
mwme0026	holy land	1548	SALAMANCA	8000	26	51	Tabula Moderna Terrae Sanctae
mwsam0479a	south america chile	1827	SALLUSTI	400	50	32	Mapa del Pais que Habitan Los Araucanos en Chile de Poncho Chileno, y De Las Misiones Apostolicas
mwam0940	america north (east)	1739	SALMON	600	34	30	A Map of the Brittish Plantations on the Continent of America
mwas0653	asia south east java	1735	SALMON	250	32	42	A Plan of the City and Castle of Batavia
mwaf0218	africa	1765	SALMON	180	18	24	Africa
mwbh0636	belgium holland	1739	SALMON	140	15	19	Amsterdam / Rotterdam
mwas0173	asia continent	1760	SALMON	180	18	23	Asia
mwat0218	atlantic falkland isl.	1750	SALMON	350	23	33	Carta delle Isole Malouine dette dagl'Inglesi Isole Falkland
mwgr0171	greece	1725	SALMON	400	34	44	Carta Geografica del Levanto Veneto o sia delle isole del Mar Ionio nella Grecia
mwuk0177	ireland	1758	SALMON	180	19	18	Ireland (engraved by T. Jefferys)
mwgr0326	greece corfu	1750	SALMON	400	16	37	La Citta di Corfu Capitale dell' Isola di Corfu
mwas0458	asia south east	1732	SALMON	400	29	34	Neue Charte von den Philippinischen und Moluckischen Insuln, Insulis Latronum, wie auch Celebes etc.
mwam0188	america continent	1765	SALMON	300	18	23	North America / South America (2 maps)
mwas0477	asia south east	1752	SALMON	240	18	29	The East Indies
mwme0620	arabia etc	1745	SALMON	480	47	45	The Whole Turkish Empire with the Countries and Territories Bordering upon it Agreable to Modern History
mwaf0543b	africa egypt etc	1809	SALT	600	48	79	A Geometrical Survey of the City of Alexandria
mwec0929	uk england nottinghamshire	1835	SANDERSON	675	114	114	To the Nobility, Clergy, Gentry ... This Map of the Country Twenty Miles round Mansfield
			FOR SANDRART, SEE VON SANDRART				
mwe0619	europe czech republic (bohemia)	1844	SANDTNER	720	42	51	General Karte von der Hochfurstlich von Metternich'schen Herrschaft Plass
mwuk0129	ireland	1706	SANDYS	1500	90	63	A General Map of the Kingdom of Ireland (inset: British Isles)
mwme0447	jerusalem	1615	SANDYS	300	10	10	Ierusalem
mwm0177	mediterranean malta	1615	SANDYS	280	10	12	Malta (view of Valetta)
mwaf0057	africa	1650	SANSON	600	39	55	Africa Vetus
mwaf0055	africa	1650	SANSON	1200	39	55	Afrique (illustrated left is the revised 1669 edition)
mwaf0060	africa	1656	SANSON	400	20	28	Afrique
mwaf1140	africa west	1682	SANSON	180	18	28	Afrique ou Libie Ulterieure ou sont le Saara ou Desert, le Pays des Negres, la Guinee, &c.
mwg0076	germany	1683	SANSON	150	19	24	Allemagne
mwam0317	america north	1657	SANSON	750	20	28	Americque Septentrionale
mwsam0026	south america	1662	SANSON	350	20	25	Amerique Meridionale
mwsam0022	south america	1650	SANSON	960	40	54	Amerique Meridionale par N. Sanson
mwam0321	america north	1669	SANSON	2400	39	56	Amerique Septentrionale par N. Sanson (cartouche top left instead of top right, as in 1651 map)
mwam0316	america north	1650	SANSON	3500	39	56	Amerique Septentrionale par N. Sanson d'Abbeville Geog. du Roy (1st map to show the 5 Great Lakes in recognizable form. Illustrated is the 1690 edition.)
mwme0948a	turkey etc	1652	SANSON	240	18	24	Anatolie (later edition shown left)
mwuk1529	uk english channel (east)	1654	SANSON	250	37	48	Anciens Royaumes de Kent, d'Essex, et de Sussex ... Normandie
mwuk1355a	england north	1654	SANSON	150	38	51	Anciens Royaumes de Northumberland aujourdhuy Provinces de Nort: ou sont les Comtés de Northumberland, Cumberland, Durham, Westmorland, Lancaster et York...
mwas0040	asia continent	1650	SANSON	500	40	56	Asia Vetus
mwas0039	asia continent	1650	SANSON	960	39	55	Asie. Par N. Sanson d'Abbeville Geog. du Roy (see also 1703 updated re-issue 'L'Asie')
mwam0071	america continent	1669	SANSON	1100	39	56	Atlantis Insula, a Nicolao Sanson Antiquitati Restituta; nunc demum Majori Forma Delineata, et in Decem Regna, iuxta Decem Neptuni Filios Distributa ... ex Conatibus Geographicis Gulielmi Sanson Nicolai Filii
mwuss0069	california	1656	SANSON	1200	20	24	Audience de Guadalajara, Nouveau Mexique, Californie, &c. (1st printed map 'concentrating on' California as an island)
mwgm0102	guatemala	1657	SANSON	200	18	27	Audience de Guatimala
mwgm0163	mexico	1657	SANSON	300	17	28	Audience de Mexico
mwsc0068	scandinavia	1667	SANSON	650	40	52	Baltia, quae et Scandia, Finningia Cimbrica Chersonesuss
mwsc0056a	scandinavia	1654	SANSON	500	33	33	Baltia, quae et Scandia, Finningia Cimbrica Chersonesuss

AMPG REFERENCE	REGION	DATE	MAP MAKER	PRICE (UK£)	VERT. (cm.)	HOR. (cm.)	TITLE OF MAP (Comments by the editor in brackets)
mwaf0864	africa south	1655	SANSON	1000	42	56	Basse Aethiopie (after Sanuto, 1588)
mwg0188a	germany north	1652	SANSON	350	39	54	Basse Allemaigne
mwbp0285	poland	1674	SANSON	650	42	56	Basse ou Grande Pologne; ou sont les Palatinats de Posna, Calisch, Sirad, Lencici, Rava, Brest, et Inowlocz
mwg0707	schleswig-holstein	1657	SANSON	300	38	53	Basse Partie de la Basse Saxe, ou sont les Duches de Sleswick, Holsace, Meckelenbourg, et Lauwenbroug; Subdivises en leurs Principales Parties
mwru0480	ukraine	1665	SANSON	960	34	52	Basse Podolie, ou Palatinat de Braclaw
mwg0343b	bavaria	1655	SANSON	300	42	42	Bayern Baviere
mwbh0334	belgium holland	1659	SANSON	450	41	48	Belgica in Provincias Quatuor
mwbh0833	luxembourg	1657	SANSON	675	40	54	Caeraesi in Treveris. Partie du Dioecese del' Archev.che de Treves. Partie Meridionale du Duche de Luxembourg
mwsc0417	scandinavia finland	1666	SANSON	480	44	58	Cajanie, ou Bothnie Orientale
mwit1013	italy south	1648	SANSON	350	41	59	Calabre Citerieure et Ulterieure la Far de Messine &c.
mww0329	world	1716	SANSON	480	41	55	Carte de la Geographie Sacree pour l'Ancien Testament
mwf0061a	france	1643	SANSON	550	41	52	Carte des Rivieres de la France
mwme0555	arabia etc	1654	SANSON	2000	41	50	Carte des Trois Arabies. Tiree en Partie de l'Arabe de Nubie, en Partie de Divers Autres Autheurs (apparently the first large-scale modern printed map of Arabia on its own)
mwas0390	asia south east	1654	SANSON	1500	39	48	Carte Generale des Indes Orientales et des Isles Adiacentes
mwuk0407	scotland	1665	SANSON	720	41	54	Carte Generale des Royaume d'Angleterre L'Escosse dela le Tay / ... L'Escosse deca le Tay (2 maps, each 41x54cm)
mwf0061	france	1643	SANSON	550	41	52	Carte Generale du Royaume de France
mwg0345	bavaria	1667	SANSON	480	40	49	Cercle de Franconie
mwg0809	westphalia	1690	SANSON	350	52	39	Cercle de Westphalie
mwin0458a	indian ocean maldives	1660	SANSON	300	19	24	Ceylan, et les Maldives
mwme0804a	persia etc	1712	SANSON	550	41	57	Chodorlahomoris Aelamitarum ... Imperium (also issued with title: 'Alexandri Magni Imperium', shown left, and other changes)
mwru0478	ukraine	1658	SANSON	400	40	50	Cimmeria quae Postea Scythia Europaea
mwme0713	caucasus	1667	SANSON	400	36	48	Colchis Iberia, Albania, quaeq; Caucasiae Gentes Istmum quod Pontum Eriximum Aspinma. Mar Interjacet Incolunt, ex Conatibus Geograficis
mwf1012	france provence	1667	SANSON	685	43	54	Comte et Gouvernement de Provence
mwe0668	europe dalmatia	1664	SANSON	600	41	56	Coste de Dalmatie
mwe0706	europe danube	1667	SANSON	480	45	55	Cours du Danube, depuis Belgrade jusques au Pont Euxin
mwgr0405	greece crete	1676	SANSON	500	40	54	Creta Insula pleriumq. Deum Natalibus, Iovis Incunabulis Sepulchroq. Inclyta
mwgr0502	greece cyprus	1720	SANSON	2000	38	49	Cyprus - autrefois Royaume de Chypre (close copy of previous map, in French)
mwgr0501a	greece cyprus	1718	SANSON	2500	38	49	Cyprus Praestantia nulli cedens Insulae (with acknowledgment to Maria Iacovou)
mwru0427	russia tartary	1654	SANSON	785	37	57	Description de la Tartarie Tiree en Partie de Plusieurs Cartes, qui en ont este Faictes en Partie
mwme0779a	persia etc	1658	SANSON	550	39	52	Description de L'Empire du Sophi des Perses
mwjk0022	japan	1652	SANSON	720	18	27	Description des Isles du Japon en Sept Principales Parties
mwme0244a	holy land	1700	SANSON	500	40	36	Description Geographique de la Terre Promise, Terre des Hebreux, et des Israelites Partagee selon l'Ordre de Dieu, aux Douze Tribus Descendantes des Douze Fils de Jacob
mwsam0671	south america magellan	1662	SANSON	275	20	25	Destroit de Magellan, Terre et Isles Magellanicques, &c.
mwf0313	france brittany	1650	SANSON	600	37	50	Duche et Gouvernement de Bretagne
mwf0775	france normandy	1667	SANSON	600	39	52	Duche et Gouvernement de Normandie
mwaf0487	africa egypt etc	1683	SANSON	180	28	20	Egypte Divisee en ses Douze Cassilifs ou Gouvernemens
mwg0069	germany	1665	SANSON	400	40	52	Empire d'Allemagne Divise en ses Dix Circles, les Cercles en leurs Principaux Estats, Royaume de Boheme (extended right-hand margin text leaf)
mwe0327	europe austria	1667	SANSON	550	30	51	Ertz-Hertzogthumb Oesterreich - Archiduche d'Austriche
mwsp0200	spain	1683	SANSON	180	18	24	Espagne
mwbp0310	poland	1683	SANSON	240	20	26	Estats de la Couronne de Pologne
mwbp0287	poland	1676	SANSON	2500	92	121	Estats de la Couronne de Pologne ou sont les Royaume de Pologne, Duches et Provinces de Prusse, Cuivaie, Mazovie, Russie Noire &c. Duches de Lithuanie, Volhynie Podolie &c. de l'Ukraine &c.
mwbp0274	poland	1663	SANSON	800	43	57	Estats de la Couronne de Pologne ou sont les Royaume de Pologne, Duches et Provinces de Prusse, Cuivaie, Mazovie, Russie Noire &c. Duches de Lithuanie, Volhynie Podolie &c. de l'Ukraine &c.
mwsc0685	scandinavia sweden	1669	SANSON	800	44	48	Estats de la Couronne de Suede dans la Scandinavie
mwit0299	italy central	1648	SANSON	450	43	57	Estats de l'Eglise et de Toscane
mwe1137	europe south east	1655	SANSON	450	40	50	Estats de l'Empire des Turqs en Europe, et Pays circomvoisins; entre lesquels sont Hongrie, Transilvanie, Valaquie, Moldavie 1655
mwme0556	arabia etc	1654	SANSON	720	41	55	Estats de l'Empire du Grand Seigneur des Turqs ou Sultan des Ottomans en Asie, en Afrique; et en Europe
mwru0046a	russia	1650	SANSON	350	41	47	Estats du Czar ou Grand Duc de la Russie Blanche ou Moscovie (left border incompleted)

AMPG REFERENCE	REGION	DATE	MAP MAKER	PRICE (UK£)	VERT. (cm.)	HOR. (cm.)	TITLE OF MAP (Comments by the editor in brackets)
mwit0645	italy piedmont	1665	SANSON	550	54	43	Estats du Duc de Savoye au dela des Alpes, et vers l'Italie; qui Passent Communement sous le Nom de Piemont
mwaf0781	africa north morocco	1667	SANSON	450	36	52	Estats et Royaumes de Fez et Maroc, Darha et Segelmesse
mwe0059a	europe	1650	SANSON	480	40	56	Europa Vetus
mwe0093	europe	1683	SANSON	280	18	23	Europe par N. Sanson le Fils
mwsc0418	scandinavia finland	1666	SANSON	960	43	57	Finlande Septentr.le et Merid.le Nylande et Tavasthus
mwf0072	france	1682	SANSON	180	18	24	France
mwme0158	holy land	1662	SANSON	300	39	50	Geographiae Sacrae ex Veteri ... MDCLXII
mwme0215	holy land	1699	SANSON	200	20	25	Geographiae Sacrae Tabula in qua Terra Promissa in sua Tribus Partesq Distincta
mwm0019b	mediterranean	1680	SANSON	350	43	56	Geographica Synodica
mwg0054a	germany	1641	SANSON	300	41	54	Germania Antiqua
mwbh0353	belgium holland	1660	SANSON	200	21	22	Germanie Inferieure ou les Dix-Sept Provinces des Pays-Bas
mwbp0258a	poland	1655	SANSON	550	39	56	Germano-Sarmatia in qua Populi maiores Venedi, et Peucini, et Bastarnae
mwsc0570	scandinavia norway	1668	SANSON	750	57	43	Gouvernement D'Aggerhus (Oslo and environs)
mwsc0571	scandinavia norway	1668	SANSON	750	57	43	Gouvernement De Berghenhus
mwsc0572	scandinavia norway	1668	SANSON	750	40	58	Gouvernement de Wardhus
mwgr0062	greece	1636	SANSON	750	42	56	Graecia
mwgr0117	greece	1690	SANSON	600	39	50	Graeciae Foederata (Ancient Greece)
mwgr0076	greece	1658	SANSON	720	40	51	Grece Moderne ou Partie Meridionale de la Turquie en Europe
mwsam0579	south america guyana	1662	SANSON	225	20	25	Guiane Divisee en Guiane et Caribane (incl. Trinidad)
mwg0224	germany north west	1650	SANSON	500	39	54	Haute Allemagne
mwaf0364	africa east	1655	SANSON	720	40	50	Haute Ethiopie, ou sont l'Empire des Abissins, la Nubie, et le Zanguebar
mwbp0278a	poland	1666	SANSON	685	43	56	Haute, ou Petite Pologne, ou sont les Palatinats de Cracow, Sandomirie, et Lublin
mwru0483	ukraine	1665	SANSON	960	39	51	Haute volhynie, ou Palatinat de Kamieniec / Basse Partie de la Basse Podolie (2 maps on one sheet)
mwru0482	ukraine	1665	SANSON	960	38	56	Haute Volhynie, ou Palatinat de Lusuc
mwsc0683	scandinavia sweden	1667	SANSON	500	42	56	Helsinge, Medelpadie Angermannie, Iemptie, Dalecarlie
mww0257	world	1695	SANSON	1600	32	60	Hemisphere Occidental du Globe Terrestre / Hemisphere Oriental du Globe Terrestre
mwaa0112	arctic	1704	SANSON	250	24	21	Hemisphere Septentrional du Globe Terrestre
mwaa0109	arctic	1704	SANSON	250	24	21	Hemisphere Superieur du Globe Terrestre (shown below far left)
mwbp0322a	poland	1694	SANSON	400	32	50	Hertzogthumb Pommern - Duche de Pomeranie
mwe0889	europe hungary	1680	SANSON	150	18	26	Hongrie
mwe0884	europe hungary	1665	SANSON	480	43	55	Hongrie, Transilvanie, Esclavonie ...
mwe0878a	europe hungary	1652	SANSON	480	42	51	Hungaria Regnum
mwe0778a	europe east	1700	SANSON	600	42	53	Illyricum Orientis in quo Partes II Moesia et Thracia (left is 'Illyricum Occidentalis')
mwin0411a	indian ocean	1655	SANSON	240	20	29	Indiae Veteris
mwwi0033	west indies	1680	SANSON	320	21	30	Insulae Americanae
mwjk0043	japan	1679	SANSON	350	18	27	Insularum Iaponiae in VII. Partes & LXVI. Regna Antiqua Divisae (publ. by Zunner)
mwuk0070	ireland	1665	SANSON	875	37	48	Irlande Royaume divise en ses quatre Provinces, et ces Provces en leurs Comtes
mwaf0588	africa islands madagascar	1667	SANSON	785	58	45	Isle Dauphine ... Madagascar
mwit0831b	italy sardinia and corsica	1658	SANSON	650	39	56	Isle de Corse / Isle et Royme. de Sardaigne
mwwi0538	guadeloupe	1667	SANSON	785	32	43	Isle de la Guadeloupe Scituee a 16 Degrez de Lat. Septentrionale
mwaf0595	africa islands madagascar	1699	SANSON	280	19	24	Isle de Madagascar ou de St. Laurens
mwat0182	atlantic cape verde isl.	1656	SANSON	180	19	28	Isle du Cap Verd. Coste et Pays des Negres aux Environs du Cap Verd (1705 Dutch edition illustrated)
mwgr0385	greece crete	1658	SANSON	720	39	55	Isle et Royaume de Candie Tiree de Divers Memoires
mwit0892	italy sicily	1663	SANSON	685	39	56	Isle et Royaume de Sicile
mwuk0708	uk	1648	SANSON	320	24	18	Isles Britanniques
mwuk0798a	uk	1718	SANSON	200	14	16	Isles Britanniques (north to the right)
mwat0139	atlantic canary isl.	1656	SANSON	350	18	25	Isles Canaries
mwit0108	italy	1682	SANSON	280	20	24	Italie
mwe0542	europe czech republic (bohemia)	1667	SANSON	480	40	52	Konigreich Boheim Royaume de Boheme. Divise en ses Quinze Cercles ou Provinces &c.
mwc0043	china	1656	SANSON	2000	41	53	La Chine Royaume
mwbp0107	baltic states	1703	SANSON	500	42	55	La Curlande Duche et Semigalle autrefois de la Livonie - La Samogitie Duche en Lituanie
mwuss0394	florida	1657	SANSON	1500	18	26	La Floride
mwru0431	russia tartary	1670	SANSON	280	17	29	La Grande Tartarie
mwaf1112	africa west	1662	SANSON	200	17	31	La Guinee et Pays Circomvoisins, Tires de Mercator, de Blommart &c.
mwbp0091	baltic states	1663	SANSON	750	41	53	La Livonie Duche Divisee en ses Principles. Parties Esten, et Letten &c.

AMPG REFERENCE		REGION	DATE	MAP MAKER	PRICE (UK£)	VERT. (cm.)	HOR. (cm.)	TITLE OF MAP (Comments by the editor in brackets)
mwme0259		holy land	1717	SANSON	400	35	40	La Monarchie des Hebreux sous Salomon, ou le Roiaume d'Israel Distingue en Douze Prefectures ou Gouvernements ce Royaume a Dure 120 Ans, depuis l'An du Monde 2909 jusqu'en 3029
mwru0488		ukraine	1674	SANSON	960	43	57	La Russie Noire ou Polonoise ... Connues sous le Nom d'Ukraine ou Pays des Cosaques
mwsc0055		scandinavia	1647	SANSON	600	33	33	La Scandinavie et les Environs ou sont les Estats et Royaumes de Danemarck Norwegue et Suede par N. Sanson le Fils ... 1647 (illustrated below is a proof state of this map, without complete borders)
mwsc0058		scandinavia	1658	SANSON	960	41	56	La Scandinavie ou sont les Estats de Svede, Norwegue et Danemarck. A Paris Chez Mariette, Rue S. Jacques a l'Esperance
mwit0910		italy sicily	1699	SANSON	240	19	24	La Sicile Divisee en ses Trois Vallees
mwsam0671a	south america magellan		1668	SANSON	800	37	49	La Terre et les Isles Magelaniques Tirees des Relations les Plus Recentes
mwaf0125		africa	1704	SANSON	900	46	54	L'Afrique Divisee en ses Principales Parties, ou sont les Empires les Monarchies les Royaumes les Estats et Peuples
mwaf1110		africa west	1656	SANSON	500	35	56	L'Afrique ou Lybie Ulterieure ou sont le Saara, ou Desert, le Pays des Negres, la Guinee
mwam0339		america north	1695	SANSON	675	20	27	L'Amerique Septentrionale
mwme0567		arabia etc	1680	SANSON	350	19	24	L'Arabie Petree, Deserte et Heureuse
mwas0071		asia continent	1683	SANSON	300	19	27	L'Asie
mwin0107		india	1652	SANSON	400	19	24	L'Empire du Grand Mogol
mwme0776a		persia etc	1652	SANSON	180	19	24	L'Empire du Sophy des Perses
mwuk0408		scotland	1665	SANSON	500	40	50	L'Escosse Royaume en ses Deux Principales Parties qui sont deca et dela le Tay
mwsp0188		spain	1663	SANSON	550	41	53	L'Espagne Subdivisee en Tous ses Royaumes, Principtes, Seignries, &c.
mwe0059		europe	1650	SANSON	900	41	55	L'Europe
mww0161		world	1652	SANSON	1800	40	53	L'Hydrographie ou Description de l'Eau c'est a Dire des Mers, Golfes, Lacs, Destroits et Rivieres Principales qui sont dans la Surface du Globe Terrestre
mwin0108		india	1654	SANSON	785	34	54	L'Inde deca et dela le Gange, ou est l'Empire du Grand Mogol
mwwi0765		martinique	1645	SANSON	785	32	44	L'Isle de la Martinique Scituee a 14 Degrez 30 Minutes de Latitude Septentrionale
mwit0102		italy	1665	SANSON	875	43	53	L'Italie et les Isles Circomvoisines Sicile, Sardaigne, Corse, &c.
mwsam0323a	south america brazil		1683	SANSON	300	20	27	Le Bresil
mwsam0301	south america brazil		1656	SANSON	1000	40	54	Le Bresil, dont la Coste est Possedee par les Portugais et Divisee en Quatorze Capitanieries. Le Milieu du Pays est Habite par un Tres Grand Nombre de Peuples Presque Tous Incogneus ... par N. Sanson d'Abbeville
mwsam0311	south america brazil		1662	SANSON	275	20	27	Le Bresil, dont la Coste est Possedee par les Portugais, et Divisee en Quatorze Capitanieries
mwca0020		canada	1656	SANSON	4000	40	54	Le Canada, ou Nouvelle France, &c.
mwca0021		canada	1657	SANSON	600	21	30	Le Canada, ou Nouvelle France, &c. Tiree de Diverses Relations des Francois, Anglois, Hollandois, &c.
mwsam0449	south america chile		1667	SANSON	600	40	46	Le Chili Divise en ses Treize Iurisdictions
mwsam0446	south america chile		1660	SANSON	200	27	19	Le Chili Tire de Alf de Ovalle de la C de J et Divise en Treize Iurisdictions par N. Sanson d'Abb Geogr Ordre du Roy
mwbh0468	belgium holland		1693	SANSON	650	43	57	Le Comte de Zeelande
mwam0318	america north		1658	SANSON	5500	31	55	Le Nouveau Mexique et La Floride ... 1656
mwsam0705	south america paraguay		1650	SANSON	250	20	25	Le Paraguay Subdivise en ses Principales Parties Suivant les Dernieres Relaons par N. Sanson d'Abbeville Geographe Ordre. du Roy
mwsam0708	south america paraguay		1668	SANSON	450	41	55	Le Paraguay Tire des Relations les Plus Recentes.
mwsam0214	south america argentina		1656	SANSON	650	40	50	Le Paraguayr, le Chili, la Terre, et les Isles Magellanicques
mwsam0741	south america peru		1656	SANSON	685	41	55	Le Perou et le Cours de la Riviere Amazone, depuis ses Sources jusques a la Mer
mwsam0740	south america peru		1650	SANSON	200	19	28	Le Perou et le Cours de la Rivre. Amazone par N. Sanson d'Abbeville Geographe
mwuk0925		england	1665	SANSON	600	40	51	Le Royaume D'Angleterre ... Heptarchie des Saxons
mwuk0446		scotland	1699	SANSON	180	27	21	Le Royaume d'Escosse Divisee en ses Parties Meridionale et Septentrionale
mwuk0122		ireland	1695	SANSON	1000	40	44	Le Royaume D'Irlande
mwuk0124		ireland	1700	SANSON	280	27	21	Le Royaume d'Irlande Divisee en ses Grandes Provinces
mwe0324		europe austria	1654	SANSON	400	36	47	Le Tirol
mwaf0362a		africa east	1648	SANSON	250	18	30	Le Zanguebar / Partie du Zanguebar ou sont les Costes d'Ajan et d'Abex
mwaa0186		arctic / antarctic	1657	SANSON	2500	39	53	Les Deux Poles Arcticque ou Septentrional, et Antarcticque ou Meridional
mwsp0440a		spain regions	1652	SANSON	450	41	52	Les Estats de la Couronne d'Arragon en Espagne ou sont l'Arragon Royaume, la Catalogne Principte, la Valence Royaume, et les Isles de Maiorque

AMPG REFERENCE	REGION	DATE	MAP MAKER	PRICE (UK£)	VERT. (cm.)	HOR. (cm.)	TITLE OF MAP (Comments by the editor in brackets)
mwsp0459	spain regions	1667	SANSON	450	40	52	Les Estats de la Couronne de Castille ... Andalousie, Granade, et Murcie
mwsp0441	spain regions	1652	SANSON	450	41	54	Les Estats de la Couronne de Castille, dans les parties plus Septentrionales de l'Espagne, et la ou sont les Royaumes de Castille Vielle, Leon, Galice, Asturie, Biscaie, Seign, Navarra
mwe0768	europe east	1676	SANSON	2800	93	122	Les Estats de la Couronne de Pologne, ou sont les Royaume de Pologne, Duches de Prusse, Mazovie, Russie Noire & Duches de Lithuanie, Volhynie Podolie &c. de l'Ukraine &c.
mwe0760b	europe east	1655	SANSON	720	43	57	Les Estats de la Couronne de Pologne, ou sont les Royaume de Pologne, Duches de Prusse, Mazovie, Russie Noire & Duches de Lithuanie, Volhynie Podolie &c. de l'Ukraine &c. (shown above left)
mwsp0034	portugal	1653	SANSON	550	41	43	Les Estats de la Couronne de Portugal en Espagne
mwme0946	turkey etc	1650	SANSON	450	40	51	Les Estats de l'Empire des Turqs en Asie
mwwi0017	west indies	1656	SANSON	900	39	55	Les Isles Antilles &c. entre lesquelles sont les Lucayes, et les Caribes. Par N Sanson d'Abbeville
mwwi0018	west indies	1657	SANSON	300	22	32	Les Isles Antilles, &c. entre lesquelles sont les Lucayes, et les Caribes
mwuk0726	uk	1665	SANSON	850	41	53	Les Isles Britannicques
mwat0138	atlantic canary isl.	1653	SANSON	600	35	53	Les Isles Canaries par P. du Val d'Abbeville Geographe Ordinaire du Roy. A Paris Chez Pierre Mariette Rue St. Jacques a l'Esperance avec Privilege
mwas0389	asia south east	1652	SANSON	320	19	25	Les Isles de la Sonde entre lesquelles sont Sumatra, Java Borneo &c.
mwm0204	mediterranean malta	1683	SANSON	400	20	29	Les Isles de Malte, Goze &c.
mwjk0023	japan	1652	SANSON	675	19	24	Les Isles du Iapon (1705 Dutch edition illustrated)
mwas0714	asia south east moluccas	1652	SANSON	280	19	25	Les Isles Molucques; Celebes Gilolo &c.
mwuk0409	scotland	1665	SANSON	500	43	55	Les Isles Orcadney, ou Orkney
mwas0751	asia south east philippines	1652	SANSON	500	19	25	Les Isles Philippines / Islas de los Ladrones ou Isle des Larrons (2 maps on one sheet)
mwas0391	asia south east	1654	SANSON	1500	40	56	Les Isles Philippines Molucques et de la Sonde
mwf0075	france	1690	SANSON	550	41	53	Les Postes qui Traversent la France. Corrigees et Augmentees Suivant les Derniers Establisements
mwbh0453	belgium holland	1690	SANSON	450	44	59	Les Provinces des Pay-Bas Catholiques Vulgairement Connues sous le Nom Flandre
mwsw0066	switzerland	1648	SANSON	450	37	54	Les Suisses, les Allies des Suisses et leurs Sujets; qui Peuvent Passer sous le Nom des Suisses
mww0173	world	1660	SANSON	1500	43	57	Mappe-Monde ou Carte Generale du Globe Terrestre Representee en Deux Plan-Hemispheres
mww0258	world	1695	SANSON	4000	46	48	Mappemonde ou Carte Marine Universelle Reduite
mwbp0278	poland	1665	SANSON	685	40	53	Masovie Duche, et Polaquie; ou sont les Palatinats de Czersk, Bielsk, et Plocsko
mwru0494	ukraine	1682	SANSON	200	18	24	Mer Noire ou Mer Maieure
mwgm0162	mexico	1656	SANSON	1500	37	55	Mexicque, ou Nouvelle Espagne, Nouvlle. Gallice, Iucatan &c. et autres Provinces jusques a l'Isthme de Panama; ou sont les Audiences de Mexico, de Guadalaiara, et de Guatimala
mwme0950	turkey etc	1658	SANSON	720	47	58	Natolia quae olim Asia Minor
mwsc0271a	scandinavia denmark	1650	SANSON	400	40	53	Nort-Iutlande ... et Provinces du Royaume de Danemarck
mwsc0680	scandinavia sweden	1666	SANSON	500	40	57	Ostro-Gothlande
mwe0996a	europe rhine	1648	SANSON	250	37	48	Palatinat du Rhein Alsace, et Partie de Souabe de Franconie
mwsp0035	portugal	1654	SANSON	500	40	54	Parte Septentrional do Reyno de Portugal / Parte Meridional do Reyno de Portugal (2 maps)
mwaf0820	africa north tunisia	1683	SANSON	150	20	25	Partie de Barbarie ou sont les Royaumes de Tunis, et Tripoli
mwaf0789	africa north morocco	1699	SANSON	180	17	28	Partie de Biledulgerid ou sont Tesset, Darha et Segelmesse
mwaf0817a	africa north tunisia	1655	SANSON	450	39	54	Partie de la Barbarie ou est le Royaume d'Alger Divise en ses Provinces
mwaf0822	africa north tunisia	1699	SANSON	100	19	26	Partie de la Barbarie ou est le Royaume d'Alger Divise en ses Provinces
mwaf0817b	africa north tunisia	1655	SANSON	450	37	53	Partie de la Coste de Barbarie en Africque ou Sont les Royaumes de Tunis, et Tripoli
mwaf0363	africa east	1652	SANSON	200	30	22	Partie de la Haute Aethiopie ou sont l'Empire des Abissins et la Nubie &c.
mwas0423	asia south east	1699	SANSON	200	19	25	Partie de l'Inde au dela du Gange / Presqu'Isle de l'Inde au dela du Gange (2 maps on one sheet; Siam / Malacca)
mwbp0092	baltic states	1665	SANSON	900	40	55	Partie de Lithuanie ... Minsk (3 maps)
mwru0067	russia	1667	SANSON	300	43	55	Partie de Lithuanie ou sont les Palatinats de Poloczk, Witepsk, Mseislaw, et Partie de Minsk. Avec le Duche de Smolensko
mwsam0576a	south america guyana	1656	SANSON	600	40	54	Partie de Terre Ferme ou sont Guiane et Caribane. Augmentee et Corrigee Suivant les Dernieres Relations. Par N Sanson d'Abbeville
mwgr0075	greece	1656	SANSON	240	19	24	Partie de Turquie en Europe
mwas0392	asia south east	1654	SANSON	850	38	52	Partie Meridionale de l'Inde en Deux Presqu'Isles, l'une deca et l'autre dela le Gange
mwsc0573	scandinavia norway	1668	SANSON	750	57	43	Partie Meridionale Du Gouvernement De Dronthemhus

AMPG REFERENCE	REGION	DATE	MAP MAKER	PRICE (UK£)	VERT. (cm.)	HOR. (cm.)	TITLE OF MAP (Comments by the editor in brackets)
mwsc0684	scandinavia sweden	1667	SANSON	500	42	54	Partie Orientale de la Lapponie Suedoise
mwsc0574	scandinavia norway	1668	SANSON	750	57	43	Partie Septentrionale Du Gouvernement De Dronthemhus
mwe0883	europe hungary	1664	SANSON	785	36	58	Partie Septentrionale du Royme. de Hongrie / Partie Meridionale du Rme de Hongrie (2 maps)
mwm0003c	mediterranean	1637	SANSON	1100	40	102	Romani Imperii qua Occidens /Oriens est Descriptio (re-issued by Rossi 1679)
mwuk0071	ireland	1665	SANSON	1350	40	49	Partie Septentrle. du Royaume d'Irlande / Partie Meridiole. du Royaume d'Irlande (2 maps, each 40x49cm)
mwf1124	france rhone-alpes	1663	SANSON	450	42	57	Partie Septentrnale. des Estats de Savoye ou sont les Duches de Genevois, de Chablais et le Faussigny &c.
mwaf0884	africa south	1699	SANSON	280	20	29	Pays, et Coste de Cafres: Empires de Monomotapa Monoemugi, &c.
mwme0809	persia etc	1721	SANSON	400	41	58	Persarum Imperium in Viginti Satrapias Vectigales Distributum
mwf0950	france picardy	1648	SANSON	300	37	52	Picardie et les Pays Bas Catholiques &c.
mwsp0034a	portugal	1653	SANSON	600			Portugallia et Algarbia quae olim Lusitania
mwin0139	india	1699	SANSON	200	19	25	Presqu'Isle de l'Inde deca la Gange (inset: Malabar)
mwin0107a	india	1652	SANSON	300	19	25	Presqu'isle de l'Inde deça le Gange où sont les Royaumes de Decan, de Golconde, de Bisnagar, et le Malabar
mwsp0443	spain regions	1660	SANSON	550	38	46	Principaute de Catalogne, Divisee en Neuf Dioeceses; et en Dix-Sept Vegueries, &c.
mwuk1764	wales	1658	SANSON	600	37	44	Principaute de Galles
mwe1043	europe romania	1664	SANSON	480	38	56	Principaute de Transilvanie
mwuk1384a	uk england south	1654	SANSON	500	37	53	Provinces d'West
mwbh0300	belgium holland	1648	SANSON	785	40	51	Provinces Unies des Pays-Bas
mwm0032a	mediterranean	1700	SANSON	800			Romani Imperii Quae Occidens / Oriens (2 sheets)
mwe0766	europe east	1670	SANSON	600	48	60	Romanie, Bulgarie et Partie de Moldavie
mwas0910	asia south east vietnam	1650	SANSON	900	43	31	Royaume d'Annan Comprenant les Royaumes de Tumkin et de la Cocinchine
mwaf0784	africa north morocco	1683	SANSON	150	20	25	Royaume de Fez
mwc0025	china	1652	SANSON	360	24	20	Royaume de la Chine
mwaf0780	africa north morocco	1657	SANSON	150	20	25	Royaume de Maroc
mwit1014	italy south	1648	SANSON	350	41	59	Royaume de Naples
mwsp0440	spain regions	1652	SANSON	400	54	41	Royaume de Navarre Divise en Six Merindades
mwsc0575	scandinavia norway	1668	SANSON	900	55	45	Royaume de Norwege Subdivise en ses Principaux Gouvernements
mwjk0028	japan	1658	SANSON	2500	37	52	Royaume du Iapon Designe par le Pere Ph. Briet de la Compagnie de Jesus
mwaf0492	africa egypt etc	1699	SANSON	150	17	27	Royaume et Desert de Barca et l'Aegypte Divisee en ses Principales Parties
mwaf0483	africa egypt etc	1679	SANSON	300	33	51	Royme. et Desert de Barca et l'Egypte
mwru0092	russia	1683	SANSON	280	18	24	Russie Blanche
mwru0057a	russia	1660	SANSON	450	41	47	Sarmatia Utraque Europaea et Asiatica
mwsc0419	scandinavia finland	1669	SANSON	785	45	53	Savolax et Kexholm
mwsc0078	scandinavia	1682	SANSON	200	18	24	Scandinavie ou sont les Estats de Danemark de Suede &c.
mwme0871	syria etc	1699	SANSON	180	19	26	Sorie et Diarbeck
mwsc0676	scandinavia sweden	1659	SANSON	450	41	53	Sud-Gotlande, et Pays Circomvoisins ou sont les Provinces de Schonen ou Scanie, Hallande, et Bleckinge
mwsc0681	scandinavia sweden	1666	SANSON	500	43	58	Sueonie ou Suede, ou sont les Provinces de Uplande, Sudermannie, Westmannie Noricie, Dalecarlie, Gestricie et les Isles d'Aland
mwru0481	ukraine	1665	SANSON	600	40	50	Tartarie Europeene ou Petite Tartarie
mwme0163	holy land	1667	SANSON	600	39	52	Terra Promissa in Sortes seu Tribus XII
mwsam0823	south america venezuela	1662	SANSON	275	20	25	Terre Ferme Nouveau Royme. de Grenade &c.
mwsam0172	south america (north)	1656	SANSON	685	39	53	Terre Ferme ou sont les Governations, ou Gouvernemens de Terre Ferme, Cartagene, Ste. Marthe, Rio de la Hache, Venezuela, Nouvelle Andalusie, Popayan, Nouveau Royme. de Grenade
mwme0711	caucasus	1653	SANSON	200	19	23	Turcomanie, Georgie, Commanie
mwme0967	turkey etc	1683	SANSON	180	19	25	Turquie en Asie
mwsc0682	scandinavia sweden	1666	SANSON	500	44	55	Westro-Goth-Lande
mwgr0138	greece	1700	SANSON-MORTIER	720	37	51	Antiquorum Illyrici Orientalis Episcopatuum Geographica Descriptio
mwaa0017	antarctic	1704	SANSON-MOULLART	500	26	21	Hemisphere Inferieur du Globe Terrestre
mwf0050	france	1632	SANSON-TAVERNIER	960	40	52	Carte Geographique des Postes qui Traversent la France (engraved by Tavernier)
mwuk0702	uk	1641	SANSON-TAVERNIER	875	40	53	Brtiannicae Insulae in quibus Albium sive Britannia Maior Ivernia sive Britannia Minor tum et Orcades, Ebudes, Cassiterides (Britannia misspelt, rh border not engraved)
mwuk0701	uk	1640	SANSON-TAVERNIER	800	41	53	Carte Generale des Royaume d'Angleterre Escosse Et Irlande
mwaf1069	africa south west	1698	SANTA TERESA	550	38	51	Pianta della Citta di Loanda O S. Paolo Metrop del ... d'Angola
mwme0046	holy land	1583	SANTANDREANYS	720	20	21	Terrae Sanctae Descriptio, atque Locorum Omnium quae in Evangelistis Quatuor Reperiuntur
mwas0498	asia south east	1778	SANTINI	720	49	61	Archipel des Indes Orientales qui Comprend les Isles de la Sonde, Moluques et Philippines

AMPG REFERENCE	REGION	DATE	MAP MAKER	PRICE (UK£)	VERT. (cm.)	HOR. (cm.)	TITLE OF MAP (Comments by the editor in brackets)
mwme1025	turkey etc	1772	SANTINI	480	47	61	Asia Minor
mwme0829	persia etc	1779	SANTINI	500	47	60	Carte d L'Empire de Perse
mwaf0845	africa north west	1775	SANTINI	450	46	55	Carte de la Barbarie Contenant les Royaumes de Maroc, de Fez, d'Alger, de Tunis et de Tripoli
mwme0730	caucasus	1775	SANTINI	400	48	66	Carte de la Georgie et des Pays Situes entre la Mer Noire et la Mer Caspienne
mwaf1223	africa west	1776	SANTINI	500	45	60	Carte de la Guinee Contenant les Isles du Cap Verd, le Senegal (inset: Gold Coast)
mwru0258	russia	1776	SANTINI	450	57	46	Carte de la Lithuanie Russienne
mwe1161	europe south east	1784	SANTINI	1500	41	54	Carte de la Partie Septentrionale de l'Empire Otoman (6 sheets, each 41x54cm, from Romania to the Caucasus)
mwbp0495	poland	1776	SANTINI	375	45	59	Carte de la Pologne Autrichienne Contenant la Russie Rouge et la Partie Meridionale du Palatinat de Cracovie
mwit0958	italy sicily	1780	SANTINI	650	46	64	Carte de l'Isle et Royaume de Sicile (inset: Malta)
mwru0560	ukraine	1784	SANTINI	650	50	64	Carte des Environs de la Mer-Noire ou se Trouvent l'Ukrayne la Petite Tartrie, et les Confins de la Russie Europeene ... par le Sr. Robert de Vaugondy
mwf1078	france provence	1777	SANTINI	450	58	44	Carte des Gouvernements de Dauphine et de Provence
mwsp0680	balearic islands	1780	SANTINI	650	44	56	Carte des Isles de Maiorque Minorque et Yvice (2 insets)
mwp0422	pacific north	1776	SANTINI	1500	47	63	Carte des Nouvelles Decouvertes au Nord de la Mer du Sud, tant a l'Est de la Siberie et du Kamtchatka, qu'a l'Ouest de la Nouvelle France. Dressee sur les Memoires de Mr. Del'Isle
mwsam0244	south america argentina	1779	SANTINI	480	45	54	Carte du Chili Meridional, du Rio de la Plata, des Patagons, et du Detroit de Magellan ... de l'Amerique Meridle.
mwf0370	france brittany	1776	SANTINI	400	44	58	Carte du Gouvernement de Bretagne
mwit1124	italy tuscany	1776	SANTINI	500	48	57	Carte du Grand Duche de Toscane
mwgm0044	gulf of mexico and surrounding regions	1779	SANTINI	450	46	59	Carte du Mexique et de la Nouvelle Espagne, Contenant la Partie Australe de l'Amerique Septentle. Par Mr. d'Anville
mwca0098	canada	1776	SANTINI	785	46	65	Carte Generale du Canada, de la Louisiane, de la Floride, de la Caroline, de la Virginie, de la Nouvelle Angleterre etc. par le Sr. d'Anville (inset: Hudson Bay, Baffin Bay etc)
mwf0532	france corsica	1780	SANTINI	785	48	66	Carte Particuliere de l'Isle de Corse. Divisee par ses Dix Provinces ou Jurisdictions et ses Quatre Fiefs (inset: Capo Corso)
mwit0690	italy piedmont	1779	SANTINI	450	64	48	Carte qui Contient la Principaute de Piemont le Monferrat et la Comte de Nice
mwsam0169	south america (central)	1779	SANTINI	480	48	67	Carte qui Represente la Partie Meridionale du Bresil et du Perou, le Chili Septentrional, et le Paraguay, ce qui Fait la Partie de Milieu de l'Amerique Meridionale, par le Sr. d'Anville
mwit1201	italy veneto	1776	SANTINI	400	47	66	Estat de la Seigneurie et Republique de Venise en Terre Ferme
mwit0448	italy liguria	1776	SANTINI	450	47	68	Etats de la Seigneurie et Republique de Genes
mwme0731	caucasus	1779	SANTINI	400	43	55	L'Armenia, la Georgie et le Daghistan
mwgr0210	greece	1778	SANTINI	200	55	48	Graeciae Antiquae Specimen Geographicum
mwru0553	ukraine	1777	SANTINI	650	41	65	La Crimee, la Nouvelle Russie, les Tatares Nugay
mwe0819	europe east	1784	SANTINI	500	41	54	La Romelie et les Environs de Constantinople
mwsw0184	switzerland	1780	SANTINI	480	44	55	La Suisse Divisee en ses Treize Cantons et ses Allies
mwaf0245	africa	1780	SANTINI	675	47	64	L'Afrique Divisee en ses Principaux Etats (re-issue of Janvier 1769)
mwam0209	america continent	1780	SANTINI	650	47	65	L'Amerique Divisee en ses Principaux Etats Assujettie aux Observations Astronomiqes. Par le Sr. Janvier Geographe
mwas0201	asia continent	1784	SANTINI	500	49	66	L'Asie Divisee en ses Principaux Etats
mwuk1037	england	1803	SANTINI	300	48	51	Le Royaume d'Angleterre, Divise Selon les Sept Royaumes, ou Heptarchie des Saxons, avec la Principaute de Galles et Subdivise en Shires ou Comtes
mwbp0506	poland	1784	SANTINI	480	48	52	Le Royaume de Pologne
mwit0820	italy sardinia	1776	SANTINI	720	69	47	Le Royaume de Sardaigne
mwg0154	germany	1784	SANTINI	350	47	64	L'Empire d'Allemagne
mwc0194	china	1779	SANTINI	650	47	54	L'Empire de la Chine, avec la Tartarie Chinoise (map by M. Bonne. Based on De Vaugondy 1757)
mwjk0115	japan	1778	SANTINI	800	46	53	L'Empire du Japon Divise en Sept. Principales Parties, Savoir, Ochio, Quanto, Jetsegen, Jetsen, Jamaisoit, Xicoco et Ximo (copy of De Vaugondy's 1750 map)
mwwi0112	west indies	1779	SANTINI	500	49	60	Les Grandes et Petites Isles Antilles, et les Isles Lucayes avec une Partie de la Mer du Nord (close copy of De Vaugondy 1750)
mwin0269	india	1779	SANTINI	550	48	57	Les Indes Orientales
mwuk0853	uk	1776	SANTINI	580	46	64	Les Isles Britanniques
mwsc0163	scandinavia	1780	SANTINI	500	46	64	Les Royaumes de Suede et Norwege Divises par Provinces et Gouvernements (inset: Iceland. Map by Janvier)
mwe0207	europe	1784	SANTINI	675	48	65	L'Europe Divisee en ses Principaux Etats
mww0499	world	1776	SANTINI	2500	47	65	Mappe Monde ou Description du Globe Terrestre Assujettie aux Observations Astronomiques par le Sr. Janvier Geographe

AMPG REFERENCE	REGION	DATE	MAP MAKER	PRICE (UK£)	VERT. (cm.)	HOR. (cm.)	TITLE OF MAP (Comments by the editor in brackets)
mwe0690	europe dalmatia	1780	SANTINI	800	46	62	Nouvelle Carte de la Partie Occidentale de Dalmatie / Nouvelle Carte de la Partie Orientale de Dalmatie (2 maps)
mwe0505a	europe croatia	1790	SANTINI	400	33	22	Nouvelle Carte de l'Istrie
mwp0430	pacific north	1784	SANTINI	960	49	64	Nouvelle Carte des Decouvertes Faites par des Vaisseaux Russiens aux Cotes Inconnues de l'Amerique Septentrionale avec les Pais Adiacents ... a St. Petersbourg a l'Academie Imperiale des Sciences (based on Muller's 1758 map)
mwsp0729	gibraltar	1776	SANTINI	450	57	48	Nouvelle Carte du Detroit de Gibraltar et de l'Isle de Cadix
mww0533	world	1784	SANTINI	2250	46	64	Nouvelle Mappe Monde Dediee au Progres de nos Connoissances (2 offset polar projections. Size incl. text panels below map. Copy of Julien's 1753 map)
mwam1087	america north (east)	1784	SANTINI	1000	48	57	Partie Meridionale de la Louisiane, avec la Floride, la Caroline et la Virginie. Par le Sr. d'Anville (first publ. 1776)
mwe0382	europe austria	1777	SANTINI	375	48	62	Partie Meridionale du Cercle d'Autriche
mwit0957	italy sicily	1779	SANTINI	375	47	58	Partie Meridionale du Royaume de Naples (incl. Calabria)
mwam1290	great lakes	1775	SANTINI	1250	48	57	Partie Occidentale du Canada et Septentrionale de la Louisiane avec une Partie de la Pensilvanie par le Sr. D'Anville
mwca0099	canada	1776	SANTINI	650	48	58	Partie Orientale du Canada, avec la Nouvelle Angleterre, l'Acadie, et la Terre-Neuve, par le S. D'Anville
mwe0959	europe hungary	1786	SANTINI	280	48	55	Royaume de Hongrie
mwuk0210	ireland	1778	SANTINI	500	48	54	Royaume d'Irlande
mwru0263	russia	1776	SANTINI	1200	64	140	Tabula Geographica Generalis Imperii Russia (copy of Truskot 1776)
mwgr0221	greece	1784	SANTINI	480	48	63	Turquie d'Europe
mwaf1088	africa west	1588	SANUTO	2000	39	52	Africae Tabula I (the numbering of Sanuto's 11 regional maps of Africa begins and ends with West Africa, moving clockwise. The general map of Africa is no. XII)
mwaf0767	africa north marocco	1588	SANUTO	1250	39	54	Africae Tabula II (see also Sanuto: Africa North West)
mwaf0836	africa north west	1588	SANUTO	1500	39	52	Africae Tabula III
mwaf0815	africa north tunisia	1588	SANUTO	1000	39	52	Africae Tabula IIII
mwaf0762	africa north libya	1588	SANUTO	2500	39	52	Africae Tabula V
mwaf0465a	africa egypt etc	1588	SANUTO	2500	39	51	Africae Tabula VI (illustrated above left)
mwaf0465	africa egypt etc	1588	SANUTO	2500	39	52	Africae Tabula VII.
mwaf0349	africa east	1588	SANUTO	2000	40	52	Africae Tabula VIII (Abyssinia)
mwaf0350	africa east	1588	SANUTO	2000	40	53	Africae Tabula VIIII (Horn of Africa)
mwaf0852	africa south	1588	SANUTO	6000	39	52	Africae Tabula X.
mwaf1089	africa west	1588	SANUTO	2000	40	53	Africae Tabula XI
mwaf0018	africa	1588	SANUTO	12000	40	52	Africae Tabula XII.
mwp0457a	pacific north	1808	SARYCHEV	1000	38	73	Kaart Van Het Noordoostelijke Gedeelte Van Siberie, De Ijs-Zee, Den Ooster-Oceaan in de Noordwestelijke Kust van America, Met aanwuzing van de vaart der Schepen, onder get bevel van Kapitein Billings; ontworpen door Sarytschew (publ. in Amsterdam; 1st publ. in Russian 1802)
mwgr0304	greece corfu	1623	SARZINA	200	8	11	(Untitled map, north to the left)
mwgr0369	greece crete	1623	SARZINA	240	8	11	Candia olim Creta
mwjk0145	japan	1836	SASUKE	1800	17	670	(Route map of Japan, accordion folded) Dai Nihon Kairiku Koutei Zukan
mwjk0156	japan tokyo	1761	SASUKE	2250	60	90	(Tokyo) Edo Ezu
mwp0455	pacific north	1802	SAUER	600	40	61	Carte du Detroit qui Separe l'Asie de l'Amerique, avec la Cote des Tschoutskis, Tracee d'apres les Observations Faites dans la Mer Glaciale depuis 1786 jusqu'en 1794
mwuk1104	england london	1595	SAUR	720	9	11	Die Stadt Londen
mwit1221	italy venice	1608	SAUR	650	7	10	Venetia
mwsp0637	spain regions	1849	SAURI & MATAS	550	43	58	Plano de la Ciudad de Barcelona
mwme0107	holy land	1648	SAVERY	650	33	47	De Gelegentheyt van 't Paradys ende 't Landt Canaan Mitsgaders de Eerst Bewoonde Landen der Patriarchen
mwme0109	holy land	1648	SAVERY	785	32	48	Geographische Beschryvinge van t'Beloofde-Landt Canaan, door Wandelt van onsen Heere ende Salichmaecker Iesu Christo neffens syne Apostelen van Nieus Gecorigeert ende Seer Verbetert
mwme0110	holy land	1648	SAVERY	320	32	48	Perigrinatie ofte Veertich-Iarige Reyse
mww0328	world	1715	SAVRY-PUTTE	2500	31	47	Werreldt Kaert (Savry's map of 1672 reissed by Putte)
mwru0405b	russia moscow	1827	SAVINKOW	5000	64	66	(Plan of Moscow in Cyrillic and French. Size is for map only) Планъ Столичнаго Города Москвы, изданный Надв. Сов. Савинковымъ 1827 года - Plan De La Ville Kapitale de Moskou 1827
mwme0680a	arabia etc	1835	SAVINKOW	450	29	29	Карта Азиатск: Турции, Персии, Аравии и Туркестана
mwru0329	russia	1810	SAVINKOW	3200	62	92	Plan de la Ville Capitale S. Petersbourg (in French and Cyrillic script)
mwuk0906	england	1579	SAXTON	12000	38	50	Anglia ... 1579 (1st map of England by an Englishman. State 2 publ. 1583 etc.)
mwuk0907	england	1583	SAXTON		140	173	Britannia Insularum In Oceano Maximo (illustrated is c1720 re-issue with different ornamentation and title 'The Travellers Guide', publ. by Anne Lea)

AMPG REFERENCE	REGION	DATE	MAP MAKER	PRICE (UK£)	VERT. (cm.)	HOR. (cm.)	TITLE OF MAP (Comments by the editor in brackets)
mwec0593	uk england kent	1579	SAXTON	7200	38	50	Cantii, Southsexiae, Surriae et Middelsexiae comitat ... Descriptio ... 1575.
mwec0119	uk england cheshire	1579	SAXTON	6000	39	50	Cestriae comitatus ... effigies ... 1577.
mwuk1691	wales	1579	SAXTON	2000	38	50	Denbigh ac Flint ... comitatuum descriptio. 1577.
mwec0279	uk england devon	1579	SAXTON	5000	38	50	Deuoniae comitat' ... descriptio ... 1575.
mwec0317	uk england dorset	1579	SAXTON	5000	37	53	Dorcestriae comitatus ... descriptio ... 1575.
mwec0355	uk england durham	1579	SAXTON	3000	38	50	Dunelmensis episcopatus (qui comitatus est palatinus) ... descriptio ...1576
mwec1290	uk england yorkshire	1579	SAXTON	7850	72	53	Eboracensis comitatus ... 1577.
mwec0391	uk england essex	1579	SAXTON	3600	39	50	Essexiae comitat' ... descriptio ... 1576.
mwec0507	uk england herefordshire	1579	SAXTON	2500	38	50	Frugiferi ac ameni Herefordiae comitatus deliniatio ... 1577.
mwuk1692	wales	1579	SAXTON	3600	38	50	Glamorga comitatus ... descriptio ... 1578.
mwec0428	uk england gloucestershire	1579	SAXTON	5000	39	50	Glocestriae ... comitat' ... tipus atq effigies ... 1577.
mwec0534	uk england hertfordshire	1579	SAXTON	5000	39	50	Hartfordiae comitatus ... descriptio ... 1577.
mwec0669	uk england lancashire	1579	SAXTON	5500	40	48	Lancastriae comitatus ... descriptio ... 1577.
mwec0731	uk england lincolnshire	1579	SAXTON	3600	41	53	Lincolniae Nottinghamiaeq Comiatuu ... descriptio ... 1576.
mwuk1693	wales	1579	SAXTON	3000	38	50	Mone Insulae modo Anglesey, et Caernaruan ... 15778
mwuk1694	wales	1579	SAXTON	2000	34	46	Montgomeri ac Merionidh ... comitatuum ... descriptio ... 1578
mwuk1695	wales	1579	SAXTON	3600	39	48	Monumenthensis comitatus ... 1577.
mwec0802	uk england norfolk	1579	SAXTON	5000	34	49	Norfolciae comitatus ...descriptio ... 1574.
mwec0844	uk england northamptonshire	1579	SAXTON	6000	40	52	Northamton Bedfordiae, Cantabrigiae, Huntingdoniae et Rutlandiae ... descriptio ... 1576.
mwec0873	uk england northumberland	1579	SAXTON	3600	38	46	Northumbriae comitatus ... descriptio. (no date)
mwec0934	uk england oxfordshire	1579	SAXTON	6000	39	44	Oxonii buckinghamiae et berceriae comitatuum ... descriptio ... 1574
mwuk1696	wales	1579	SAXTON	3600	35	46	Penbrok comitat' ... descriptio ... 1578.
mwuk1539	uk english channel (west)	1579	SAXTON	12000	38	50	Promontorium hoc in mare projectum Cornubia dicitur
mwec0160	uk england cornwall	1579	SAXTON	12000	38	50	Promontorium hoc in mare projectum Cornubia dicitur ... 1576.
mwuk1697	wales	1579	SAXTON	3600	38	50	Radnor Breknok Cardigan et Caermarden ... comitatum ... descriptio ... 1578.
mwec0996	uk england shropshire	1579	SAXTON	3000	39	51	Salopiae comitatus ... descriptionem haec tibi tabula refert ... 1577.
mwec1025	uk england somerset	1579	SAXTON	4000	39	51	Somersetensem Comitat' ... haec ob oculos ponit tabula ... 1575.
mwec0461	uk england hampshire	1579	SAXTON	6000	38	50	Southamtoniae comitatus ... descriptio ... 1575.
mwec1055	uk england staffordshire	1579	SAXTON	5000	39	50	Staffordiae comitatus ... haec tibi tabula exhibet ... 1577.
mwec1088	uk england suffolk	1579	SAXTON	4000	38	50	Suffolciae comitatus ... 1575.
mwec0250	uk england derbyshire	1579	SAXTON	3600	38	50	Vniuersi Derbiensis comitatus graphica desciptio 1577.
mwec1184	uk england warwickshire	1579	SAXTON	3000	40	45	Warwic, Lecestriaeq. comitat' ... descriptio ... 1576.
mwec1214	uk england westmorland	1579	SAXTON	5000	39	50	Westmorlandiae et Cumberlandiae comit ... descriptio ... 1576.
mwec1266	uk england worcestershire	1579	SAXTON	5000	39	50	Wigorniensis comitatus ... descriptio ... 1577.
mwec1235	uk england wiltshire	1579	SAXTON	3600	39	50	Wiltoniae comitatus ... hic ob oculos proponitur ... 1576.
mwuk0950	england	1689	SAXTON-LEA	3000	38	50	Anglia. The Kingdome of England and Principality of Wales exactly Described.
mwec0173	uk england cornwall	1694	SAXTON-LEA	3500	37	49	Cornwall Described by C. Saxton Corrected & Many Additions as the Roads &c
mwec0327	uk england dorset	1689	SAXTON-LEA	1650	38	54	Dorsetshire Described by C. Saxton. Corrected and Amended with Many Additions as Roads &c by P. Lea
mwuk1776	wales	1693	SAXTON-LEA	850	35	47	Glamorga Shire Discribed by C.S. Corrected and Amended by P. Lea.
mwec0440	uk england gloucestershire	1689	SAXTON-LEA	1500	39	50	Glocester-Shire Described by C. S. Corrected and Amended with Many Additions
mwuk1777	wales	1693	SAXTON-LEA	850	35	47	Merioneth and Montgomery Discribed by C.S. Corrected ... P. Lea
mwuk1778	wales	1693	SAXTON-LEA	850	35	47	Mona Insula alias Anglesea and Caernarvan Shire Discribed by C.S. Corrected and Amended with Many Additions by P. Lea
mwuk1779	wales	1693	SAXTON-LEA	850	35	47	Monmouthshire ... by C.S. Corrected & Amended by P. Lea
mwec0819	uk england norfolk	1693	SAXTON-LEA	1600	34	50	Norfolk Described by C: Saxton.
mwec0949	uk england oxfordshire	1693	SAXTON-LEA	2000	39	48	Oxford, Buckingham & Bark Shire
mwec0856a	uk england northamptonshire	1689	SAXTON-LEA	1500	39	53	The County of Northampton togeather with ye Three Small Counties of Bedford Huntingdon and Rutland Exactly Drawen by one Scale by C.S. Corrected & Amended with Many Additions by P. Lea
mwec0365	uk england durham	1693	SAXTON-LEA	1000	38	49	The County Palatine and Bishoprick of Durham, Described by C. Saxton. Corrected and Amended with Additions by P. Lea.
mwec1317	uk england yorkshire	1693	SAXTON-LEA	2750	72	53	York-Shire Described by C. Saxton. Many Additions and Corrections as ye Roads, Wapentakes &c. by P Lea
mwec1304	uk england yorkshire	1645	SAXTON-WEB	3200	72	53	(1st edition title erased, 1579, and a view of Hull substituted)

AMPG REFERENCE	REGION	DATE	MAP MAKER	PRICE (UK£)	VERT. (cm.)	HOR. (cm.)	TITLE OF MAP (Comments by the editor in brackets)
mwec0605	uk england kent	1645	SAXTON-WEB	4500	41	54	Cantii, Southsexiae, Surriae et Middelsexiae comitat' ... Descriptio. 1642.
mwec0401	uk england essex	1645	SAXTON-WEB	2250	42	53	Essexiae Comitat' Nova Vera ac Absoluta Descriptio ... 1642.
mwec0514	uk england herefordshire	1645	SAXTON-WEB	1500	37	50	Frugiferi ac Ameni Herefordiae Comitatus Deliniatio ... 1642.
mwec0435	uk england gloucestershire	1645	SAXTON-WEB	2800	39	50	Glocestriae ... comitat' ... tipus ... 1642
mwuk1747	wales	1645	SAXTON-WEB	2250	39	48	Monumenthensis comitatus ... 1642.
mwec0850a	uk england northamptonshire	1645	SAXTON-WEB	3500	40	52	Northamton Bedfordiae, Cantabrigiae, Huntingdoniae et Rutlandiae ... descriptio ... 1642.
mwec1005	uk england shropshire	1645	SAXTON-WEB	1800	39	50	Salopiae Comitatus, Summa cum Fide cum et Diligentia Descriptionem haec Tibi Tabula Refert ... 1642
mwec1096	uk england suffolk	1645	SAXTON-WEB	2750	42	47	Suffolciae Comitatus ... Pagos et Villas 464 una cum Singulis Hundredis & Fluminibus in Eodam Vera Descriptio ... 1642.
mwec0362	uk england durham	1645	SAXTON-WEB	2000	37	48	The County Palatine of Durisme Exactly Drawne 1642. (The date 1576 remains).
mwec1241	uk england wiltshire	1645	SAXTON-WEB	2350	42	47	Wiltoniae Comitatus (Herbida Planitie Nobilis) hic ob Oculos Proponitur ... 1642.
mwec1331	uk england yorkshire	1732	SAXTON-WILLDEY	2400	72	53	York-Shire Described by C. Saxton. Many Additions and Corrections as ye Roads, Wapentakes &c. by P Lea
mwas0892a	asia south east sumatra	1780	SAYER	300	45	44	(Untitled chart of the south west coast)
mwin0059	ceylon	1778	SAYER	250	71	51	A Chart of Palk's Straits and Bay
mwuk1544	uk english channel (west)	1789	SAYER	720	51	69	A Chart of the Chops of the Channel, to the South of the Scilly Islands; containing the West Coast of Cornwall and Scilly Islands.
mwin0290	india	1788	SAYER	250	47	32	A Chart of the Eastern Coast of the Gulf of Bengal from Mr. D'Apres de Mannevillette
mwuk1633	scilly isles	1779	SAYER	500	52	71	A Chart of the Entrance into the Channel Containing the West Coast of Cornwall, and Scilly Islands, with All the Soundings
mwat0168a	atlantic canary isl.	1787	SAYER	720	60	47	A Chart of the Maderas and Canary Islands. According to the Surveys Published at Madrid in 1780, by Don Thomas Lopez
mwas0895	asia south east sumatra	1788	SAYER	300	48	65	A Chart of the Western Coast of Sumatra from Touroumane to Indrapour with the Adjacent Islands from the Neptune Oriental: with Considerable Additions and Improvements
mwuk0851	uk	1772	SAYER	480	64	50	A Compleat Map of the British Isles, or Great Britain and Ireland; with their Respective Roads and Divisions
mwgm0432	panama	1788	SAYER	400	18	23	A Draught of the Bahias del Almirante Named by the Buccaniers Bocatoro
mwe0195	europe	1772	SAYER	1500	101	122	A New and Accurate Map of Europe ... drawn by the Sieur Robert De Vaugondy ... by Thos. Kitchin (inset of Iceland)
mwaf0201	africa	1754	SAYER	2000	54	93	A New and Correct Map of Africa (based on Moll)
mwuk0556	scotland	1790	SAYER	900	117	101	A New and Correct Map of Scotland (re-issue of Armstrong's map)
mwam1098	america north (east)	1788	SAYER	785	50	68	A New and Correct Map of the British Colonies in North America Comprehending Eastern Canada with the Province of Quebec, New Brunswick, Nova Scotia, ... Newfoundland: with the Adjacent States of New England, Vermont, New York, Pennsylvania and New Jersey
mww0499a	world	1777	SAYER	7500	58	95	A New and Correct Map of Ye World laid down according to ye latest and best observations (based on Overton 1720)
mwin0281	india	1785	SAYER	450	58	43	A New Chart of the Braces and Sea Reefs at the Entrance of Hoogly River, with the Course of that River up to the Town of Hoogly
mwuss0504	georgia	1792	SAYER	4000	53	72	A New Chart of the Coast of North America from Port Royal Entrance to Matanza Inlet Exhibiting the Coast of Georgia
mwp0025	australia	1787	SAYER		102	136	A New Chart of the Eastern Coast of New Holland, from South Cape to Cape York ... (shown is the 1790 edition with extra insets)
mwas0170	asia continent	1757	SAYER	900	57	48	A New Map of Asia Divided into its Empires and Kingdoms (separately issued. 2 sheets, each 57x48cm.)
mwam0435	america north	1763	SAYER	3500	58	96	A New Map of North America, with the British, French, Spanish, Dutch & Danish Dominions ... and the West India Islands, According to the Definitive Treaty, Concluded at Paris 10th February 1763
mwam0497	america north	1786	SAYER	3500	102	116	A New Map of North America, with the West India Islands, Divided According to the Preliminary Articles of Peace Signed at Versailles 20 Jan. 1783, wherein are Particularly Distinguished the United States and the Several Provinces, Governments
mwam1092	america north (east)	1786	SAYER	960	48	30	A New Map of the United States of North America with the British Dominions on that Continent. by Samuel Dunn, Mathematician; Improved from the Surveys of Capt. Carver

AMPG REFERENCE	REGION	DATE	MAP MAKER	PRICE (UK£)	VERT. (cm.)	HOR. (cm.)	TITLE OF MAP (Comments by the editor in brackets)
mww0435	world	1755	SAYER	3600	55	96	A New Map of the World in Two Hemispheres
mwec0635	uk england kent	1758	SAYER	800	47	60	A Plan of the City of Canterbury
mwwi0651	hispaniola	1788	SAYER	400	26	31	A Plan of the Town and Harbour of Cap Francois in the Island of St. Domingo
mwc0206	china	1786	SAYER	600	60	49	A Survey of the Tigris from Canton to the Island of Lankeet
mwsp0681	balearic islands	1780	SAYER	2400	60	98	A Topographical Map of the Isle of Minorca Geometrically Surveyd
mwaf0229	africa	1772	SAYER	3500	104	123	Africa According to Mr. D'Anville with Several Additions, & Improvements with a Particular Chart of the Gold Coast, wherein are Distinguished All the European Forts and Factories, the Whole Illustrated with a Summary Description (map by S. Boulton)
mwaf0263	africa	1789	SAYER	500	46	57	Africa and its Several Regions and Islands
mwam0220	america continent	1786	SAYER	550	31	44	America North and South and the West Indies; with the Atlantic, Aethiopic and Pacific Ocean: wherein are Distinguished All the Discoveries Lately Made
mwuk0226a	ireland	1787	SAYER	1250	57	73	An Actual Survey of the Harbour and River of Waterford and of the Bay of Tramor
mwme0509	jerusalem	1770	SAYER	2400	58	90	An Exact Draught of the City of Jerusalem
mwuss0233	carolinas	1791	SAYER	9000	51	70	An Exact Plan of Charleston Bar and Harbour. From an Actual Survey (2nd state incl. attack on Fort Sullivan)
mwas0061	asia continent	1676	SAYER	200	9	6	Asia
mwas0205	asia continent	1787	SAYER	960	103	120	Asia and its Islands According to d'Anville
mwsam0084	south america	1770	SAYER	350	53	61	Chart of South America
mwuss0948	mississippi	1773	SAYER	4500	112	34	Course of the River Mississippi, from the Balise to Fort Chartres; Taken on an Expedition to the Illinois, in the Latter End of the Year 1765
mwwi0501	curacao	1774	SAYER	3000	47	62	Curacao from The Dutch Originals of Gerard van Keulen
mwuk1018a	england	1780	SAYER	2000	162	155	England and Wales. Laid down from all the Surveys of Particular Counties hitherto published
mwuk1028	england	1790	SAYER	850	58	98	England & Wales
mwe0083	europe	1676	SAYER	240	9	6	Europe
mwuk1026a	england	1789	SAYER	500	55	46	Kitchin's Enlarged Map of the Roads of England & Wales
mwam0983	america north (east)	1755	SAYER	2400	45	51	North America from the French of Mr. d'Anville, Improved with the Back Settlements of Virginia and Course of Ohio, Illustrated with Geographical and Historical Remarks
mwin0063	ceylon	1785	SAYER	500	53	69	Plan of the Bay and Harbour of Trincomalay, on the Island of Ceylon, Surveyed in 1762. By the Order of Admiral Cornish. From Mr. D'Apres de Mannevillette
mwgm0433	panama	1788	SAYER	300	23	18	Plan of the Road and Harbour of Chagre with the Town and Castle
mwas0567	asia south east banca	1791	SAYER	350	47	33	Plan of the Straits of Banca
mwbh0739	belgium holland	1783	SAYER	800	54	80	Plan Routier de la Ville de Bruxelles
mwaf0953	africa south	1781	SAYER	575	43	28	Seamons Bay in the Bay False (Simon's Bay)
mwaf0939	africa south	1754	SAYER	450	26	40	The Cape of Good Hope - Le Cap de bonne Esperance (view of Cape Town. Illustrated is Laurie & Whittle 1794 reprint)
mwwi0255	west indies (east)	1775	SAYER	1350	47	63	The Caribbee Islands, the Virgin Islands, and the Isle of Porto Rico. By Thomas Jefferys Geographer to His Majesty
mwbh0724	belgium holland	1772	SAYER	200	33	48	The Catholic Netherlands, Divided into their Several Provinces with the Roads
mwin0284	india	1785	SAYER	450	58	43	The Coast of India between Calymere and Gordeware Points including the Coast of Coromandel and Part of the Coast of Golconda
mwas0914	asia south east vietnam	1780	SAYER	750	59	44	The Coast of India and China from the point and river of Camboja to Canton comprehending the coasts of Tsiompa and Cochinchina ... with the isle of Hai-Nan
mwin0249a	india	1772	SAYER	1200	106	136	The East Indies with the Roads by Thomas Jefferys Geog. to the King MDCCLXVIII
mwru0294	russia	1788	SAYER	1200	48	128	The European Part of the Russian Empire from the Maps Published by the Imperial Academy at St. Petersburg, with the New Provinces of the Black Sea / The Asiatic Part of the Russian Empire .. .with the New Discoveries of Captn. Cook, &c. (illustrated is the Laurie & Whittle 1794 re-issue).
mwuk0225	ireland	1785	SAYER	785	60	97	The Kingdom of Ireland, Divided into its Provinces, Counties and Baronies
mwbp0486	poland	1772	SAYER	350	33	48	The Kingdom of Poland and Great Duchy of Lithuania with All their Divisions
mwbp0515b	poland	1789	SAYER	500	47	62	The Kingdom of Prussia, and its newly incorporated Province of Polish Prussia (map by J. Roberts)
mwsp0301	spain	1787	SAYER	400	50	67	The Kingdoms of Spain and Portugal
mwsp0288	spain	1772	SAYER	180	33	48	The Kingdoms of Spain and Portugal Divided into their Great Provinces
mwuk1213	england london	1765	SAYER	960	41	51	The London Directory, or a New & Improved Plan of London (15 editions to 1792)

AMPG REFERENCE	REGION	DATE	MAP MAKER	PRICE (UK£)	VERT. (cm.)	HOR. (cm.)	TITLE OF MAP (Comments by the editor in brackets)
mwme0509a	jerusalem	1773	SAYER	1200	61	46	The New City of Jerusalem
mwsc0174	scandinavia	1787	SAYER	350	47	64	The Northern States, Containing the Kingdoms of Sweden, Denmark, and Norway
mwbh0761	belgium holland	1793	SAYER	350	48	59	The Seven United Provinces Comprehending Holland, Zeeland, Utrecht, Gelders, Over-Yssel, Frieseland and Groningen; with the Land of Drent; also Dutch Flanders and Dutch Brabant
mwru0246	russia	1772	SAYER	960	48	127	The Whole Russian Empire
mwwi0918	turks & caicos Isl.	1778	SAYER	1500	46	31	Turks Islands, from a Survey Made in 1753, by the Sloops l'Aigle and l'Emeraude … Improvements from Observations Made in 1770 in the Sr Edward Hawke (illustrated is Laurie & Whittle 1794 re-issue)
mwaf1238	africa west	1789	SAYER	785	71	52	Western Coast of Africa from Cape Blanco to Cape Virga Exhibiting Senegambia Proper
mwuss0365	delaware	1776	SAYER & BENNETT	3500	47	71	A Chart of Delaware Bay and River; Containing a Full and Exact Description of the Shores, Creeks, Harbours, Soundings, Shoals, Sands and Bearings, of the Most Considerable Land Marks … by Joshua Fisher
mwsam0094	south america	1775	SAYER & BENNETT	2000	46	112	A Chart of North and South America, Including the Atlantic and Pacific Oceans, with the Nearest Coasts of Europe, Africa, and Asia (2 sheets only of 6)
mwca0218	canada arctic	1775	SAYER & BENNETT	2000	44	112	A Chart of North and South America … (2 sheets only of 6)
mwca0263	canada labrador	1770	SAYER & BENNETT	800	51	52	A Chart of Part of the Coast of Labradore, from Grand Point to Shecatica. Surveyed by Michael Lane in 1768. And Engraved by Thomas Jefferys
mwca0322	canada newfoundland	1775	SAYER & BENNETT	800	49	67	A Chart of the Banks of Newfoundland Drawn from a Great Number of Hydrographical Surveys, Chiefly from those of Chabert, Cook, and Fleurieu, Connected and Ascertained by Astronomical Observations
mwc0195	china	1780	SAYER & BENNETT	3000	61	79	A Chart of the China Sea from the Island of Sanciam to Pedra Branca with the Course of the River Tigris from Canton to Macao from a Portuguese Draught Communicated by Captain Hayter and Compared with the Chinese Chart of the Macao Pilots (Illustrated is the c1795 revised edition, publ. by Sayer on his own. It was also reprinted by Laurie & Whittle in 1794 and by Norie 1840)
mwas0285	asia burma	1778	SAYER & BENNETT	720	79	56	A Chart of the Coasts of Pegu with the Adjacent Coast of Arakan and Tanasserim (shown far left. Centre is Laurie & Whittle 1794 edition and below, 1798 edition)
mwin0431	indian ocean	1778	SAYER & BENNETT	650	43	46	A Chart of the Currents in the Indian Sea during the South West Monsoon, to the Northward of the Line by Msr. le Vicomte Grenier
mwas0496	asia south east	1778	SAYER & BENNETT	1400	57	80	A Chart of the East India Islands with the Coasts of the Continent … Drawn from the Best Journals and Remarks of Navigators … and Improved from the Last Edition of the Neptune Oriental of Mons. d'Apres de Mannevillette
mwuss1116	new york	1776	SAYER & BENNETT	7200	70	52	A Chart of the Entrance of Hudsons River, from Sandy Hook to New York, with the Banks, Depths of Water, Sailing Marks, &c.
mwme0640	arabia etc	1778	SAYER & BENNETT	275	34	65	A Chart of the Entrance of the Red Sea
mwme0642	arabia etc	1780	SAYER & BENNETT	675	48	70	A Chart of the Gulf of Persia from Basra to Cape Rosalgate … from Cpt Neibuhr One of the Travellers Sent to Arabia by the King of Denmark
mwuss0827	massachusetts	1777	SAYER & BENNETT	7200	53	87	A Chart of the Harbour of Boston with the Soundings, Sailing Mark's and other Directions
mwca0402	canada nova scotia	1775	SAYER & BENNETT	2000	40	60	A Chart of the Harbour of Halifax in Nova Scotia with Jebucto Bay and Cape Sambro
mwin0437	indian ocean	1780	SAYER & BENNETT	1500	50	99	A Chart of the Indian Sea and Eastern Ocean by Thos. Jefferys, Geographer to the King (incl. Australia)
mwaf1056	africa south east	1781	SAYER & BENNETT	800	62	73	A Chart of the Inner Passage, between the Coast of Africa and the Isle of Madagascar, from d'Anville and d'Apres's Charts Compared with the English Journals (for illustration see under 'Madagascar', Laurie & Whittle 1797 re-issue)
mwaf0653	africa islands seychelles	1778	SAYER & BENNETT	750	44	58	A Chart of the Mahe and Amirantes Islands with their Shoals
mwas0599	asia south east borneo	1778	SAYER & BENNETT	450	52	46	A Chart of the North West Coast of Borneo from Balambangan to Borneo Proper Surveyed in the Sloop Endeavour by James Barton
mwc0192	china	1778	SAYER & BENNETT	1200	56	57	A Chart of the Northern Part of the China Sea Showing the Passage from Formosa to Japan with the Eastern Coast of China and the Lekeyo Islands by Van Keulen from the Maps Drawn in China by Father Gaubil

AMPG REFERENCE	REGION	DATE	MAP MAKER	PRICE (UK£)	VERT. (cm.)	HOR. (cm.)	TITLE OF MAP (Comments by the editor in brackets)
mwin0433	indian ocean	1778	SAYER & BENNETT	650	59	90	A Chart of the Northern Part of the Indian Ocean, Containing a Part of the Coast of Africa from Magadasho River to the Straits of Bab-el-Mandeb, and the Coasts of Asia ... to the Mouths of the Ganges; with the Lakedivas, Maldivas and Ceylon
mwas0698	asia south east malacca	1778	SAYER & BENNETT	450	47	69	A Chart of the Northern Part of the Straits of Malacca from the Road of Achen to Malacca by Mr. d'Apres de Mannevillette
mwat0311	atlantic south	1778	SAYER & BENNETT	785	50	65	A Chart of the Oceans between the Western Part of the Old World and the Eastern Part of the New World ... by Thomas Jefferys
mwme0650	arabia etc	1781	SAYER & BENNETT	500	49	68	A Chart of the Red Sea from Geddah to Suez According to the General Chart of Mr d'Apres Mannevillette
mwc0199	china	1781	SAYER & BENNETT	250	36	76	A Chart of the South Coast of Hay-Nan from Tinhosa to Guichou Survey'd in 1776 and 77 by Capt. Haldane
mwca0318a	canada newfoundland	1770	SAYER & BENNETT	5000	61	111	A Chart of the Straights of Bellisle with Part of the Coast of Newfoundland and Labradore from Actual Surveys, Published by Permission ... Surveyed by James Cook in 1766 and Michael Lane in 1769
mwas0861	asia south east singapore	1778	SAYER & BENNETT	2250	62	84	A Chart of the Straits of Malacca and Sincapore by Thomas Jefferys
mwas0904	asia south east sunda	1778	SAYER & BENNETT	500	61	88	A Chart of the Straits of Sunda from the Manuscript Draught of the Dutch East India Company
mwuk0212a	ireland	1780	SAYER & BENNETT	900	79	127	A Chart of the West and South-West Coast of Ireland from the Mouth of the River Shannon to Waterford Haven
mwas0887	asia south east sumatra	1778	SAYER & BENNETT	300	52	61	A Chart of the West Coast of Sumatra from Old Bencoolen to Buffaloe Point Containing the Road to Bencoolen and Poolo Bay by Joseph Huddart
mwaf0616	africa islands madagascar	1778	SAYER & BENNETT	200	48	33	A Chart of the Western Coast of Madagascar from St. Augustin's Bay to Cape St. Andrew
mwuss0439	florida	1777	SAYER & BENNETT	6000	102	127	A Chart of the Whole Gulf of Florida, with All the Shoals, Channels, Soundings, Islands, &c. Including the Coasts of Both the Floridas, as Far as the Mississippi, or the River of New Orleans, the Bahama Islands, Coasts of Cuba, &c.
mwas0905	asia south east sunda	1778	SAYER & BENNETT	960	66	48	A Chart to Sail from the Straits of Sunda or Batavia, to the Straits of Banca, by Mr. d'Apres de Mannevillette
mwc0190	china	1778	SAYER & BENNETT	1650	83	61	A General Chart of the China Sea, Drawn from the Journals of the European Navigators, Particularly from those Collected by Capt Hayter
mwas0497	asia south east	1778	SAYER & BENNETT	1200	57	71	A General Map of the East Indies Exhibiting in the Peninsula on this Side of the Ganges or Indostan. The Several Partitions of the Mogul's Empire and the Dominions of the English East India Company
mwam1037	america north (east)	1776	SAYER & BENNETT	1400	48	65	A General Map of the Northern British Colonies in America, which Comprehends the Province of Quebec, the Government of Newfoundland, Nova-Scotia, New-England and New-York
mwam1040	america north (east)	1776	SAYER & BENNETT	4500	51	64	A General Map of the Southern British Colonies, in America. Comprehending North and South Carolina, Georgia, East and West Florida, with the Neighboring Indian Countries ... By B. Romans (2 insets)
mwuss1362	pennsylvania	1775	SAYER & BENNETT	4000	68	134	A Map of Pennsylvania Exhibiting not only the Improved Parts of that Province but also its Extensive Frontiers ... from the Late Map of W Scull, Published 1770
mwca0488a	canada prince edward isl.	1776	SAYER & BENNETT	800	36	69	A Map of St. John in the Gulf of St. Lawrence
mww0514	world	1781	SAYER & BENNETT	1100	33	50	A Map of the World with The Latest Discoveries By Samuel Dunn
mwin0260	india	1778	SAYER & BENNETT	400	44	53	A New & Correct Chart Shewing the Goeing over the Braces with the Sands Shoals Depth of Water and Anchorage from Point Palmiras to Hughley in the Bay of Bengall
mwuss0751	maryland	1777	SAYER & BENNETT	7200	102	152	A New and Accurate Chart of the Bay of Chesapeake, with All the Shoals, Channels, Islands, Entrances, Soundings, and Sailing Marks, as Far as the Navigable Parts of the Rivers Patomack, Patapsco, and North-East
mwuk1441	england thames	1785	SAYER & BENNETT	720	68	101	A New and Accurate Chart of the Mouth of the Thames and its Entrances, viz: the Kings the Queens and South Channels &c from the Nore to Orford Ness and the North Foreland
mwuk0532	scotland	1777	SAYER & BENNETT	960	59	98	A New and Complete Map of Scotland, and Islands thereto Belonging (2 sections, each 59x98cm)
mwaf0957	africa south	1781	SAYER & BENNETT	1650	60	72	A New Chart of the Southern Coast of Africa from the Cape of Good Hope to Dalagoa Bay
mwat0048	atlantic ocean (all)	1777	SAYER & BENNETT	1200	99	151	A New General Chart of the Atlantic or Western Ocean and Adjacent Seas (illustrated is a later variant, 1788, courtesy Barry Ruderman. Original title top left, as shown below)

AMPG REFERENCE	REGION	DATE	MAP MAKER	PRICE (UK£)	VERT. (cm.)	HOR. (cm.)	TITLE OF MAP (Comments by the editor in brackets)
mwca0532	canada quebec	1776	SAYER & BENNETT	1200	50	67	A New Map of the Province of Quebec, According to the Royal Proclamation, of the 7th of October, 1763, from the French Surveys (4 insets)
mwam0204	america continent	1777	SAYER & BENNETT	2000	52	120	A New Map of the Whole Continent of America Divided into North and South and West Indies. With a Descriptive Account of the European Possessions (2 sheets, each 52x120cm)
mwas0562	asia south east bali	1778	SAYER & BENNETT	350	48	33	A New Plan of the Straits, Situated to the East of Java and Madura Commonly Called the Straits of Bali
mwuss0438	florida	1777	SAYER & BENNETT	2000	71	53	A Plan of Amelia Harbour and Bar, in East Florida, Surveyed by Jacob Blamey, Master of His Majesty's Schooner St. John
mwin0293	india	1788	SAYER & BENNETT	960	48	81	A Plan of Bombay Harbour, on the Coast of Malabar. Shewing the True Situation of All the Rocks, Sands & Shoals (inset: Bombay)
mwaf0955	africa south	1781	SAYER & BENNETT	960	67	46	A Plan of Capa Bona Esperance with False Bay
mwuss0199	carolinas	1777	SAYER & BENNETT	2800	71	53	A Plan of Port Royal in South Carolina. Survey'd by Capn. John Gascoigne
mwaf0949a	africa south	1778	SAYER & BENNETT	2000	48	55	A Plan of Table Bay with the Road of the Cape of Good Hope, from the Dutch Survey Published by Joannes van Keulen
mwuss0815	massachusetts	1775	SAYER & BENNETT	27500	48	35	A Plan of the Battle, on Bunkers Hill, Fought on the 17th of June 1775. By an Officer on the Spot (text at bottom of map)
mwuss0198	carolinas	1777	SAYER & BENNETT	1500	71	53	A Plan of the Cape Fear River, from the Bar to Brunswick
mwas0699	asia south east malacca	1778	SAYER & BENNETT	300	33	48	A Plan of the Isles of Merguy on the Coast of Tanasserim / Plan of Junkseylon Island and its Harbour on the Coast of Queda (2 maps on one sheet)
mwsp0735a	gibraltar	1782	SAYER & BENNETT	1350	35	52	A Plan of the Town and Fortifications of Gibraltar
mwuss1551	vermont	1776	SAYER & BENNETT	4800	66	48	A Survey of Lake Champlain, Including Lake George, Crown Point and St. John. Surveyed by Order of His Excellency Major General Sr. Jeffery Amherst ... by William Brassier, Draughtsman. 1762
mwuss0190	carolinas	1775	SAYER & BENNETT	15000	101	142	An Accurate Map of North and South Carolina with their Indian Frontiers Shewing in a Distinct Manner All the Mountains, Rivers, Swamps, Marshes, Bays, Harbours, Sandbanks, and Soundings on the Coasts with the Roads and Indian Paths
mwgm0039	gulf of mexico and surrounding regions	1775	SAYER & BENNETT	500	38	63	An Index Map ... of the West Indies
mwme0641	arabia etc	1778	SAYER & BENNETT	200	46	33	Appearances of the Capes of Aden, St Anthony and Bab-el-Mandeb / Appearances of Socotra Island
mwaf0954	africa south	1781	SAYER & BENNETT	400	58	27	Bay of Algoa / Plan of Mossel Bay / Plan of Flesh Bay (3 maps on one sheet)
mwin0064	ceylon	1788	SAYER & BENNETT	320	51	28	Calpertyn Road on the West Coast of Ceylon / East Coast of Ceylon from Venlos Bay to Batecalo (2 maps on one sheet)
mwaf1224	africa west	1778	SAYER & BENNETT	300	49	68	Chart of the Coast of Africa between Cape Blanco and River Gambia
mwam0449	america north	1775	SAYER & BENNETT	2000	46	110	Chart, Containing the Coasts of California, New Albion, and Russian Discoveries to the North; with the Peninsula of Kamtschatka, in Asia, Opposite thereto - North America and the West Indies, with the Opposite Coasts of Europe and Africa (2 sheets of 6 showing the whole of North and South America)
mwam0453	america north	1776	SAYER & BENNETT	400	30	46	North America, as Divided amongst the European Powers. By Samuel Dunn ... 10 Jany. 1774
mwc0198a	china	1781	SAYER & BENNETT	1200	52	63	Plan of Galloon Bay On The Island of Hay-Nan
mwaf0646	africa islands rodrigues	1778	SAYER & BENNETT	350	50	65	Plan of Mathurin Bay on the North Side of the Island of Diego Rays, Called by the French Isle Rodriguez ... Surveyed by Wm Nichelson in 1761 (re-issued by Laurie & Whittle in 1794)
mwas0697	asia south east malacca	1777	SAYER & BENNETT	450	48	32	Plan of Salangor, and of the Coast of Malaya from Point Caran to Parcelar Hill. By Monsr d'Apres de Mannevillette
mwas0797	asia south east philippines	1778	SAYER & BENNETT	280	49	24	Plan of Solsogon Harbour on the South Coast of Luconia / Chart of the Eastern Coast of Bongo Bay in the Island of Mindanao
mwas0798	asia south east philippines	1778	SAYER & BENNETT	650	48	33	Plan of the Bay and City of Manilla, Capital of the Philippine Islands Situated on the Island of Luconia
mwsam0390	south america brazil	1777	SAYER & BENNETT	1200	49	32	Plan of the Bay and Harbour of Rio-Janeiro on the Coast of Brasil (illustrated is Laurie & Whittle 1794 re-issue)
mwec0194	uk england cornwall	1779	SAYER & BENNETT	500	66	47	Plan of the Bays of Polkerris and Mevagizey in Cornwall
mwin0065	ceylon	1788	SAYER & BENNETT	500	41	30	Plan of the Harbour of Colombo on the West Coast of Ceylon
mwaf0645	africa islands rodrigues	1778	SAYER & BENNETT	400	33	48	Plan of the Isle Rodrigues, Commonly Called Diego Rays Island (re-issue of De Mannevillette's map of 1775)

AMPG REFERENCE	REGION	DATE	MAP MAKER	PRICE (UK£)	VERT. (cm.)	HOR. (cm.)	TITLE OF MAP (Comments by the editor in brackets)
mwas0862	asia south east singapore	1778	SAYER & BENNETT	500	51	41	Plan of the Port of Rhio on the Island of Bintang in the Straits of Sincapore from a Draught Published by Mr. de Mannevillette
mwas0799	asia south east philippines	1778	SAYER & BENNETT	250	47	33	Plan of the Port of Subec in the Island of Luconia ... from Mr. d'Apres de Mannevillette
mwas0668	asia south east java	1778	SAYER & BENNETT	450	51	59	Plan of the Road and City of Batavia on the North Coast of the Island by Gerard Van Keulen
mwin0060	ceylon	1778	SAYER & BENNETT	400	59	30	The Bay of Trincomale or Trinkilli-Mele on the East Coast of Ceylon / Plan of Venica Bay
mwaf0617	africa islands madagascar	1778	SAYER & BENNETT	300	60	43	The Bays of St. Augustine and Tullea on the Western Coasts of Madagascar, Surveyed in 1755 and 1768
mwat0203	atlantic cape verde isl.	1788	SAYER & BENNETT	480	52	29	The Cape Verd Islands
mwc0198	china	1780	SAYER & BENNETT	450	59	44	The Coast of India and China from the Point and River of Camboja to Canton Comprehending the Coasts of Tsiompa and Cochinchina with the Coast of Tonkin and the Coast of Koen-Ton with the Isle of Hai-Nan
mwin0261	india	1778	SAYER & BENNETT	300	61	61	The Coast of India from Goa to Cape Comorin Comprehending the Coasts of Canara and Malabar
mwin0262	india	1778	SAYER & BENNETT	250	61	46	The Coast of India from Gyants Point to Cape Rama
mwin0263	india	1778	SAYER & BENNETT	480	56	87	The Coast of India from Mount Dilly to Pondichery, Comprehending the Coast of Malabar, Madura and Part of the Coast of Coromandel with the Isle of Ceylon
mwas0842a	asia south east siam	1778	SAYER & BENNETT	600	54	67	The Coast of India from Pulo Timon to Pulo Cambir Comprehending the Malayan Coast, the Gulf of Siam, the Coasts of Tsiampa and Cochinchina with the Adjacent Islands and Part of the Isle of Borneo
mwc0188	china	1775	SAYER & BENNETT	600	48	63	The Empire of China with its Principal Divisions
mwjk0116	japan	1778	SAYER & BENNETT	300	57	51	The Entrance to Nagasacqui the Chief Port of the Island of Kiusiu in the Kingdom of Japan from the Manuscript Chart of the Dutch East India Company
mwaf0652	africa islands seychelles	1778	SAYER & BENNETT	750	55	50	The Mahe Islands in the Indian Ocean ... Geometrically Surveyed in the Year 1768 by l'Abbe Rochon
mwuss1115	new york	1776	SAYER & BENNETT	9000	46	41	The Seat of Action, between the British and American Forces, or an Authentic Plan of the Western Part of Long Island, with the Engagement of the 27th. August 1776
mwuss0816	massachusetts	1775	SAYER & BENNETT	25000	61	53	The Seat of War in New England, by an American Volunteer, with the Marches of the Several Corps Sent by the Colonies towards Boston, with the Attack on Bunker's Hill
mwas0863	asia south east singapore	1778	SAYER & BENNETT	2000	43	59	The Straits of Sincapore with those of Drion, Sabon, Mandol, &ca and South Part of Malacca Straits. Improved and Corrected from the Observations of Captn. John Hall ... and other Navigators
mwam1039	america north (east)	1776	SAYER & BENNETT	11000	73	54	The Theatre of War in North America, with the Roads and a Table of the Distances (1st edition)
mwec0725	uk england leicestershire	1780	SAYER & BENNETT	500	52	64	To the Nobility, Gentry and All the Subscribers for the County of Rutland
mwuk0230	ireland	1788	SCALE	240	20	15	A Map of Ireland
mww0576	world	1792	SCHALEKAMP	400	21	41	de Oude en Nieuwe Waereld, Ontwerpen door den Heer Bonne
mwe0273a	europe	1848	SCHEDA	2400	200	250	General-Karte von Europa (in 25 sheets. Insets of St. Petersburg, Vienna and environs, Rome)
mwe0405a	europe austria	1847	SCHEDA	280	41	50	Geognostische Karte des Oesterreichischen Kaiserstaates
mwru0368	russia	1845	SCHEDA	350	40	49	Grundriss von St. Petersburg und den Nachsten Umgebungen (this map is an inset from his 25-sheet map of Europe)
mwuk1332	england london	1846	SCHEDA	720	40	49	London (circular map)
mwg0295	bavaria	1493	SCHEDEL	1000	20	52	(Munich) Monacum (size excl. text)
mwe0001	europe	1493	SCHEDEL	2500	39	57	(Untitled map of central and northern Europe)
mwsw0001	switzerland	1493	SCHEDEL	2000	26	52	(View of Basle. Size excl. text)
mwf0206a	france alsace	1493	SCHEDEL	800	33	52	Argentina (view of Strasbourg)
mwe0849a	europe hungary	1493	SCHEDEL	1600	24	52	Buda (view)
mwme0900a	turkey etc	1493	SCHEDEL	1800	24	53	Constantinopolis (size excl. text above the view)
mwbp0157a	poland	1493	SCHEDEL	2000	20	52	Cracovia
mwme0435	jerusalem	1493	SCHEDEL	2000	38	54	Destruccio Iherosolime
mwe0510a	europe czech republic (bohemia)	1493	SCHEDEL	1200	19	52	Praga (view)
mwit0699	italy rome	1493	SCHEDEL	1600	23	54	Roma (view)
mwit1203	italy venice	1493	SCHEDEL	2400	19	52	Venecie (view)
mwg0293	baden-wurttemberg	1845	SCHEDLER	1000	38	51	Plan der Grossh. Badischen Kreis-Stadt Constanz nebst Ansichten
mwgm0187	mexico	1700	SCHENK	300	22	26	Acapulco (view)
mwe0594	europe slovak republic (moravia)	1757	SCHENK	400	46	41	Accurate Geograph. Delineation ... Boehmen (size excl. text side borders)
mwsp0202	spain	1686	SCHENK	850	46	57	Accuratissima totius Regni Hispaniae et Portugalliae Tabula
mwaf0139	africa	1710	SCHENK		83	95	Africa - Nova Totius Africae Tabula

AMPG REFERENCE	REGION	DATE	MAP MAKER	PRICE (UK£)	VERT. (cm.)	HOR. (cm.)	TITLE OF MAP (Comments by the editor in brackets)
mwaf0127	africa	1705	SCHENK	900	49	58	Africa Elaboratissima
mwaf0120	africa	1700	SCHENK	900	50	58	Africae in Tabula Geographica Delineatio
mwaf0489	africa egypt etc	1690	SCHENK	240	21	26	Alexandria (view)
mwam0095	america continent	1695	SCHENK	2000	46	57	America Septentrionalis Novissima - America Meridionalis Accuratissima
mwbh0500	belgium holland	1700	SCHENK	3000	38	48	Amstelaedami Novissima Delineatio per Petrum Schenk
mwuk0954	england	1690	SCHENK	650	54	48	Anglia in Septem Anglo-Saxonum Regna
mwas0088	asia continent	1695	SCHENK	850	48	58	Asia Accuratissime Descripta
mwas0094	asia continent	1700	SCHENK	900	50	58	Asiae in Tabula Geographica Delineatio
mwbh0501	belgium holland	1700	SCHENK	1250	48	60	Belgii Pars Septentrionalis Communi Nomine vulgo Hollandia (insets: NE America with New Amsterdam view / SE Asia)
mwbh0646	belgium holland	1740	SCHENK	480	51	59	Brabantiae Batavae Pars Orientalis, Comprehendens Tetrachiam sive Majoratum Sylvaeducensem in ejusdem Subjacentes Ditiones (1st edition by Visscher c1709)
mwin0176	india	1725	SCHENK	500	44	57	Carte des Cotes de Malabar et de Coromandel
mwsc0108	scandinavia	1708	SCHENK	650	89	60	Carte des Courones du Nord
mwg0284	baden-wurttemberg	1743	SCHENK	1350	27	89	Carte des Operations sur le Rhin (Breisach)
mwbp0405	poland	1733	SCHENK	1100	87	72	Carte du Teatre de la Guerre dans la Pologne, Moscovie & Turquie
mwg0650b	saxony	1750	SCHENK	960	59	98	Carte von Ertzgebürgischen Creysse in Churfürstenthum Sachsen
mwf0404	france burgundy	1686	SCHENK	400	57	47	Comitatus Burgundiae tam in Praecipuas ejus Praefacturas quam in Minores Earundem Balliviatus
mwit0917	italy sicily	1703	SCHENK	785	59	49	Continentis Italiae Pars Australior; sive Regnum Neapolitanum
mwsp0063	portugal	1703	SCHENK	720	58	49	Corona Portugalliae et Algarbiae
mwbp0342a	poland	1700	SCHENK	950	49	58	Ducatus Silesiae Iauranus
mwg0715a	schleswig-holstein	1700	SCHENK	400	43	53	Ducatus Slesvicensis Australis
mwe0122	europe	1706	SCHENK	1500	47	57	Eclipseos Solis Totalis ... 12 Maji 1706 ... in Europa
mwbp0342	poland	1700	SCHENK	650	46	59	Estats de Pologne Subdivises Suivant l'Estendue des Palatinats
mwe0096	europe	1686	SCHENK	1200	48	57	Europa Excultissima
mwbp0359	poland	1711	SCHENK	960	49	59	Friderico Augusto Vero Augusto Polon. Lithua. Borus. (inset: Saxony)
mwf0096	france	1709	SCHENK	650	48	59	Galliae Regnum in Omnes suas Provincias Accurate Divisum (copy of Husson 1708)
mwwi0418	cuba	1702	SCHENK	350	20	26	Havana een Vermaerde Haven in 't Noorder Amerika, op 't Eilant Kuba (view)
mwuk0195	ireland	1765	SCHENK	1250	57	48	Hiberniae Regnum tam in Praecipuas Ultoniae, Connaciae, Lageniae, et Momoniae
mwbh0580	belgium holland	1720	SCHENK	600	45	55	Hollandiae pars Meridionalis vulgo Zuydt Holland
mwg0716a	schleswig-holstein	1700	SCHENK	550	50	88	Holsatiae Ducatus (copy of Visscher)
mwme0810	persia etc	1722	SCHENK	675	48	57	Imperii Persici Delineatio ex Scriptus Potissimum Geographicis Arabum et Persarum Tentata ab Adriano Relando (shown left is an updated edition)
mwme0578	arabia etc	1700	SCHENK	800	48	56	Imperium Turcicum Complectens Europae, Asiae et Africae. Arabiae (title above map)
mwas0417	asia south east	1690	SCHENK	1200	46	56	Indiae Orientalis nec non Insularum Adiacentium Nova Descriptio
mwgr0625	greece islands	1730	SCHENK	2400	48	60	Insula Samos, Polycratis Reg. et Pythagorae Phil.
mwwi0046	west indies	1702	SCHENK	1250	46	56	Insulae Americanae in Oceano Septentrionali ac Regiones Adiacentes (re-issue of Visscher 1677. See above for illustration.)
mwe0460a	europe central	1705	SCHENK	480	48	58	Invictissimis ... Victoria XIII. Aug. 1704, inclytis Hanc Germaniae Austriacae Generalem Tabulam
mwit0797a	italy sardinia	1708	SCHENK	600	15	18	Isle et Royaume de Sardagne (shown below left)
mwme0476a	jerusalem	1702	SCHENK	500	22	27	Jerusalem midden in het Joodsche lant
mwme0223	holy land	1700	SCHENK	600	47	58	Iudea, seu Terra Sancta quae Hebraeorum sive Israelitarum
mwaf0889	africa south	1702	SCHENK	400	21	26	Kabo de Bona Esperanca (view)
mwsam0508	south america colombia	1702	SCHENK	300	21	26	Kartagena, een Stedeken in Zuidamerika, in de Promintie Zuinbaya (view)
mwsc0100	scandinavia	1700	SCHENK	960	46	59	La Scandinavie et les Environs ou sont les Royaumes de Suede, de Danmark, et de Norwege
mwaf0130	africa	1708	SCHENK	875	44	57	L'Afrique Dresee sur les Observations de Mrs de l'Academie Royal des Sciences (re-issue of De L'Isle 1700)
mwg0649	saxony	1745	SCHENK	480	47	58	Lagers der Konigliege Pohlnische ... Armee in der Gegend Leipzig
mwsam0047	south america	1708	SCHENK	675	49	59	L'Amerique Meridionale Dressee sur les Observations de Mrs. de l'Academie Royale des Sciences ... Par G. de l'Isle (updated South American coastline)
mwas0108	asia continent	1708	SCHENK	875	45	58	L'Asie Dressee sur les Observations de l'Academie Royale des Sciences et quelques Autres
mwe0500a	europe croatia	1700	SCHENK	800	29	50	Le Gouvernement de Raguse /Cherso et Ossoro
mwe0586	europe czech republic (bohemia)	1745	SCHENK	600	51	63	Le Royaume de Boheme Divisee en ses Douze Cercles

AMPG REFERENCE	REGION	DATE	MAP MAKER	PRICE (UK£)	VERT. (cm.)	HOR. (cm.)	TITLE OF MAP (Comments by the editor in brackets)
mwe0124	europe	1708	SCHENK	800	46	60	L'Europe Dressee sur les Observations de Mrs. de l'Academie Royale des Sciences
mwbh0854	luxembourg	1706	SCHENK	280	15	19	Luxemburg, in het Landschap van die Naam, aan den Abritz … door Crequi de Spaansche Ontnoomen 1684
mwbp0379	poland	1720	SCHENK	600	44	53	Magnae Prussiae Ducatus Tabula
mwme0607	arabia etc	1720	SCHENK	1200	51	85	Magni Turcarum Domini Imperium in Europa, Asia, et Africa
mww0308		1708	SCHENK	1600	44	58	Mappe-Monde Dresse sur les Observations de Mrs. de l'Academie Royale des Sciences et quelques Autres (copy of De L'Isle 1700)
mwin0410	indian ocean	1650	SCHENK	2000	43	55	Mar di India (update of Jansson's map of 1650)
mwg0638a	saxony	1720	SCHENK	600	50	59	Neue Sächsische Post-Charte
mwuss1081	new york	1702	SCHENK	9600	22	26	Nieu Amsterdam, een Stedeken in Noord Amerikaes Nieu Hollant, op het Eilant Mankattan: Namaels Nieu Jork Genaemt, toen het Geraekte in 't Gebiet der Engelschen (view of New York city)
mwru0114	russia	1700	SCHENK	650	49	58	Nouvelle Carte de la Mer Noire, et du Canal de Constantinople
mwg0625	saxony	1710	SCHENK	450	45	58	Nova Anhaltini Principatus Tabula
mwe1045	europe romania	1695	SCHENK	360	39	49	Nova et Accurata Transylvaniae Descriptio
mwam0953	america north (east)	1745	SCHENK	2000	60	90	Nova Tabula Geographica Complectens Borealiorem Americae Partem: in qua Exacte Delineatae sunt Canada sive Nova Francia, Nova Scotia, Nova Anglia, Novum Belgium, Pensylvania - Carte Nouvelle Contenant la Partie d'Amerique la Plus Septentrionale (inset: Louisbourg)
mwam0929	america north (east)	1729	SCHENK	5200	46	55	Novi Belgii Novaeque Angliae nec non Partis Virginiae Tabula (inset: view of New York)
mwsp0231a	spain	1706	SCHENK	720	48	58	Novissima et Accuratissima Regnorum Hispaniae et Portugalliae
mwuk0754	uk	1690	SCHENK	900	57	48	Novissima Prae Caeteris aliis Accuratissima Regnorum Angliae, Scotiae, Hiberniae (close copy of previous map)
mwuk0448	scotland	1700	SCHENK	900	58	49	Novissima Regni Scotiae Septentrionalis et Meridionalis Tabula
mwgm0391	panama	1702	SCHENK	500	22	26	Panama een Koopstadt in Zuid-Amerika, Gelegen aen de Zuidzee (view of Panama city)
mwf1042	france provence	1707	SCHENK	500	49	59	Pars Inferior Principatus Languedoc, Provinciae, Delphinatus
mwe1146	europe south east	1700	SCHENK	500	46	58	Regni Hungariae, Graeciae et Moreae. Regionumque Finitimarum, Nova Polita, Fide Delineatio: Per Petrum Schenck (title in cartouche: 'Estats de L'Empire des Turqs en Europe')
mwe0788	europe east	1720	SCHENK	500	47	56	Regnorum Hungariae, Dalmatiae, Croatiae, Scalvoniae, Bosniae, Serviae, et Transylvaniae Typus Accuratior
mwsp0493	spain regions	1702	SCHENK	250	21	26	Seville, een Oude en Mactige Stadt (view)
mwme0984	turkey etc	1702	SCHENK	240	21	26	Smyrne (view)
mwf0231	france alsace	1700	SCHENK	300	56	49	Superioris atque Inferioris Alsatiae
mwbh0536	belgium holland	1708	SCHENK	750	57	49	Tabula Hollandiae Borealis, Cognitae olim sub Nomine Kennemariae et Westfrisiae (below is the 1720 re-issue with title: 'Kennemaria et Westfrisia vulgo et vernacule Noord-Holland')
mwgm0021a	gulf of mexico and surrounding regions	1710	SCHENK	1800	48	61	Tabula Mexicae et Floridae, Terrarum Anglicarum, et Anteriorum Americae Insularum; Item Cursuum et Circuituum Fluminis Mississipi Dicti
mwru0148	russia	1720	SCHENK	550	98	62	Tabula Moscoviae nunc Accuratius Concinnata et Edita … per G. De L'Isle
mwg0815	westphalia	1700	SCHENK	480	57	48	Tabula Nova atque Exacta Westphaliae
mwbh0562	belgium holland	1716	SCHENK	400	48	57	Tafel Vande XVII Nederlandze Provincien … 1705
mwe0938	europe hungary	1737	SCHENK	550	45	55	Theatre de la Guerre Ouvert en Hongrie & dans la Tartarie Crimee
mwit1189	italy veneto	1700	SCHENK	600	55	47	Venet. Reip. Dominium nec non Pontificii
			See also VALK & SCHENK				
mwru0406	russia moscow	1836	SCHEPKIN	2500			(Plan of Moscow, Cyrillic script) План Столичного города Москвы
mwaf0137	africa	1710	SCHERER	480	22	35	Africa ab Auctore Naturae suis Dotibus Instructa Geographice Exhibita
mwaf0111	africa	1699	SCHERER	500	23	35	Africae Dei Mater Alicubi Nota & haec ibidem Benificia 1699
mwaf0890	africa south	1702	SCHERER	350	23	35	Africae Pars Australis
mwaf0710	africa north	1710	SCHERER	250	23	36	Africae Pars Borealis 1699
mwsam0043a	south america	1703	SCHERER	450	23	35	America Australis. 1699
mwsam0042	south america	1702	SCHERER	450	22	36	America Australis Dei Parae
mwam0119	america continent	1710	SCHERER	600	24	18	America Borealis / America Australis
mwam0350a	america north	1702	SCHERER	960	22	35	America Borealis Multis in Locis Dei Matrem Colit & Honorat, et haec suis Cultoribus Multos Favores & Beneficia Praestat 1699
mwam0353	america north	1702	SCHERER	1250	23	35	America Borealis. 1699
mwuk0768	uk	1700	SCHERER	450	23	35	Anglia Scotia Hibernia 1699
mwwi0047	west indies	1702	SCHERER	650	23	34	Archipelagi Americani Delineatio Geographica

AMPG REFERENCE	REGION	DATE	MAP MAKER	PRICE (UK£)	VERT. (cm.)	HOR. (cm.)	TITLE OF MAP (Comments by the editor in brackets)
mwgr0152	greece	1710	SCHERER	350	23	35	Archipelagi Graeciae sive Maris Aegei
mwaf1166a	africa west	1710	SCHERER	400	23	34	Archipelagus Atlanticus
mwas0437	asia south east	1710	SCHERER	960	22	35	Asiae Pars Australis. Insulae Indicae cum suis Naturae Dotibus (incl. large compass rose)
mwas0109	asia continent	1710	SCHERER	685	22	35	Asiae Status Naturalis Dextera Dei Omnipotentis Perfect. Geographice Designat.
mww0288	world	1702	SCHERER	1800	23	35	Beatam Medicent Omnes Generationes
mwbh0509	belgium holland	1702	SCHERER	400	23	35	Belgium Regium
mwam1316	america north (west)	1703	SCHERER	550	23	34	Delineatio Nova et Vera Partis Australis Novi Mexici cum Australi Parte Insulae Californiae
mwit0144	italy	1710	SCHERER	400	22	34	Dominium Temporali Pontificis Romani in Italiae
mwe0119	europe	1702	SCHERER	450	22	36	Europae Situs Naturalis sive Structura Naturae Artificio Elaborata et Geographice Repraesentata
mwe0120	europe	1702	SCHERER	450	23	36	Europe Orbis Christiani Domina
mwsam0041	south america	1702	SCHERER	450	22	35	Figura Naturalis Americae Australis
mwsp0220	spain	1703	SCHERER	400	23	34	Hispania cum Fimitimis Regionibus Novissime Delineata. Anno MDCCIII
mwsp0221	spain	1703	SCHERER	400	29	36	Hispaniae et Lusitaniae Complura Pia Loca Immaculatae Virginae Dicata ... 1699
mwam0350	america north	1702	SCHERER	1500	22	35	Idea Naturalis Americae Borealis Digito Dei Formata Geographice Proposita
mwgr0151	greece	1710	SCHERER	350	23	35	Illyricum sive Magna Graecia
mww0289	world	1702	SCHERER	1250	24	35	Imago Totius Orbis Terraquei cum suo Apparatu ab Auctore Naturae in suas Partes Distributi. Geographica Exhibita
mwas0438	asia south east	1710	SCHERER	400	23	35	Insulae Indicae cum Terris Circumvicinis
mwit0146	italy	1710	SCHERER	400	24	35	Italiae complectens statum Pontificium Hispanicum
mww0290	world	1702	SCHERER	1650	24	35	Iter S. Francisci Xaverii ex Europa in India, & Japoniam (oval projection)
mwit0402	italy lazio	1710	SCHERER	350	23	35	Latii Moderni
mwaf0135	africa	1710	SCHERER	480	23	35	Mappa Geographica Exhibens Religionem Catholi cum Alicubi per Africam Sparsam
mww0291	world	1702	SCHERER	1650	22	34	Navigationes Praecipuae Europaeorum ad Exteras Nationes (oval projection)
mwam0907	america north (east)	1700	SCHERER	875	23	35	Nova Anglia Gaudet Bonis Purimis de est Tame adhuc Angelorum Regina / Mna. Britannia Dei Matris Cultu & Beneficiis olim hodieq. Celebrata (2 maps on one sheet: US/UK)
mwp0361	pacific marianas	1710	SCHERER	720	23	34	Nova et Vera Exhibitio Geographica Insularum Marianarum cum Insulis de Pais
mwgm0188	mexico	1700	SCHERER	1250	23	36	Novi Mexici cum Australi Parte Insulae Californiae
mwme0243	holy land	1710	SCHERER	600	22	35	Paradisi Terrestris Vera et Sacris Literis Conformis Exhibitio Geographica
mwme0986	turkey etc	1710	SCHERER	480	23	36	Patriarchat Constantinopolitanus
mwme0244	holy land	1710	SCHERER	500	23	36	Patriarchatus Ierosolymitanus Comprehendebat Tres Provincias
mwam0355	america north	1703	SCHERER	1500	23	35	Provinciae Borealis Americae non ita Pridem Detectae aut Magis ab Europaeis Excultae
mwaa0108	arctic	1701	SCHERER	750	23	35	Regionum Circum Polarium Lapponiae Islandiae et Groenlandiae, Novae et Veteris Nova Descriptio Geographica 1701
mwsam0042a	south america	1702	SCHERER	800	23	35	Religionis Catholicae Australi Americae implantatae Descripitio Geographica
mwam0351	america north	1702	SCHERER	960	22	34	Religionis Catholicae in Americae Boreali Disseminatae Repraesentatio Geographica
mwas0101a	asia continent	1703	SCHERER	400	22	35	Religionis Catholocae per Totam Asiam Dis Seminatae Exhibito Geographica
mwsam0043	south america	1702	SCHERER	450	23	35	Repraesentatio Americae Australis cuius Provinciae Luce Verae Fidei Imbutae Inumbres sunt Reliquae Umbra Copertae, & Vera Fide Destitutae
mwam0352	america north	1702	SCHERER	1250	24	35	Repraesentatio Americae Borealis cuius Provinciae Vera Fide Illuminatae Umbram non Habent, Reliquae Umbris Immersae sunt
mww0293	world	1703	SCHERER	1400	24	35	Repraesentatio Geographica Itineris Maritimi Navis Victoriae
mww0292	world	1702	SCHERER	1250	24	35	Repraesentatio Totius Orbis Terraquei cuius Partes, quae Umbra Carent, Fide Catholica Imbutae sunt, Reliquae Omnes Inumbrate Religionis Catholicae Expertes sunt
mwaf0136	africa	1710	SCHERER	650	22	34	Representatio Totius Africae
mww0294	world	1702	SCHERER	960	23	35	Societas Iesu per Universum Mundum Diffusa Praedicat Christi Evangelium (north polar projection)
mwsc0102	scandinavia	1700	SCHERER	450	23	33	Suecia Noruegia Russia Moscove Tica 1699
mwm0138a	mediterranean east	1703	SCHERER	300	23	35	Terra Sancta ... (shown above left)
mwsw0100a	switzerland	1703	SCHERER	200	24	36	Tirolis - Helvetia & Rhaetia
mwas0101	asia continent	1703	SCHERER	400	23	35	Totius Asiae Continens cum Praecipuis Insulis Eidem Annexis

AMPG REFERENCE	REGION	DATE	MAP MAKER	PRICE (UK£)	VERT. (cm.)	HOR. (cm.)	TITLE OF MAP (Comments by the editor in brackets)
mwf0090	france	1702	SCHERER	450	22	34	Totius Galliae cum Provinciis Finitimis et Partibus in America
mww0311	world	1710	SCHERER	960	25	20	Totius Terrarum Orbis Beneficys Dei Pare Repletus (north polar projection)
mwru0443	russia tartary	1703	SCHERER	480	23	35	Utriusq Tartariae Asiaticae Nova Descriptio Geographica
mwaf0891	africa south	1702	SCHERER	450	23	34	Utriusque Nili Albi et Atri Fons et Origo ex Veris Relationibus Geograhice Exhibetur
mwsw0129	switzerland	1730	SCHEUCHZER	250	22	28	Nouvelle Carte Géographique de la Suisse, contenant les Terres de Genève, d'Eschalens, de Schwartzburg et du Wallais
mwsw0128	switzerland	1730	SCHEUCHZER	650	22	28	Nouvelle Carte Geographique de la Suisse, Contenant les Cantons de Zurich, Lucerne, Schwitz, Zug, Glaris, Schaffhouse, Underwald, Appelzell & le Comte de Baden (2 sheets, each 22x28cm. 46 coats of arms.)
mwsw0105	switzerland	1712	SCHEUCHZER	12000	110	148	Nova Helvetiae Tabula Geographica
mwsw0110	switzerland	1715	SCHEUCHZER	5000	93	113	Nova Helvetiae Tabula Geographica (reduced size copy of his 1712 map)
mwsw0130	switzerland	1730	SCHEUCHZER	200	12	25	Plan du Lac des IV. Cantons (view)
mwru0403	russia moscow	1812	SCHLEICH	4000	116	104	Plan de Moscou - Plan von Moskau nach der Neuesten Russichen Original Aufnahme samt einer Erklaerung in Rusischer, Franzosischer und Deutscher Sprache
mwe0600	europe czech republic (bohemia)	1760	SCHLEUEN	875	42	61	Plan der Battaille bey Prag, den 6 ten May. 1757
mwg0241	berlin	1760	SCHLEUEN	1350	37	47	Abriss der Koniglichen Preussischen Residentzstadt Berlin
mwbp0424a	poland	1741	SCHLEUEN	1400	42	56	Accurater Abriss der Stadt Breslau im Hertzogthum Schlesien (title above map)
mwbp0469	poland	1760	SCHLEUEN	650	31	24	Das Furstenhum Wohlau in Nieder-Schlesien (view of Wolow at top)
mwg0238a	berlin	1739	SCHLEUEN	2000	41	57	Die Konigl. Preussl: Residentz Berlin Die Konigl. Preussl: Residentz Berlin
mwg0239b	berlin	1754	SCHLEUEN	6000	79	84	Die Konigl. Residenz Berlin
mwe0585	europe czech republic (bohemia)	1745	SCHLEUEN	875	43	34	Eigentliche Abbildung des Harten Treffens, und Erfochtenen Gloriosen Victorie, welche mit Gottes Hulfe durch Sr. Konigl. Maj. von Pruessen ... uber die Vereinigte Osterreich-Und Sachsische Armee ... den 30 September 1745
mwg0190	germany north	1760	SCHLEUEN	2400	58	70	General-Carte der Gesamten Koniglichen Preussischen Lander
mwg0729a	schleswig-holstein	1801	SCHLEUEN	600	46	57	Karte vom Herzogthum Holstein den Gebiethen der Reichs:Staedte Hamburg und Lübek, und des Bisthums Lübek
mwg0653	saxony	1756	SCHLEUEN	960	69	83	Situations-Plan des Lagers der Sachsischen Armee bey Pirna, und dessen Einschliessung durch die Konigl. Preussische Armee den 10 7tbr 1756
mwat0335a	atlantic st helena	1830	SCHLICHT	500	41	51	Plan von der Insel St. Helena (2 insets and examples of Napoleon's signature)
mwit0827	italy sardinia	1830	SCHLIEBEN	175	20	26	Il Kon. Sardinien - Savoyen / Sardinien
	SCHMETTAU: SEE 'VON SCHMETTAU'.						
mwbp0051	baltic sea (east)	1770	SCHMIDT	1200	56	150	(Map of the Gulf of Finland , Cyrillic title)
mwg0192	germany north	1782	SCHMIDT	785	50	59	Carte Topographique d'Allemagne Contenant une Partie du Duche de Holstein Stormaringen, du Duche de Bremen et de la Ville Libre Imperial de Hambourg
mwru0550	ukraine	1774	SCHMIDT	960	46	58	Crimeae seu Chersonesus Tauricae item Tartariae Nogayae Europaeae Tabula Geographica
mwe0266	europe	1831	SCHMIDT	875	67	84	Post-Reise-Karte durch Deutschland und die Angraenzenden Staaten. Zwischen London und Lublin, Koppenhagen und Mantua
mwbp0133	baltic states	1770	SCHMIDT	1500	45	112	Provincia Revaliensis sive Estlandia (Estonia)
mwru0249	russia	1773	SCHMIDT	650	46	57	Tabula Geographica Generalis Gubernii Archangelopolitani in suas Provincias Divisi
mwbp0137	baltic states	1777	SCHMIDT	720	46	56	Tabula Geographica Gubernii Mohileviensis
mwbp0127	baltic states	1750	SCHMIDT	900	46	56	Tabula Geographica Gubernii Rigensis
mwam0793	america north	1848	SCHMOLDER	1500	43	56	Neueste Special-Karte der Westlichen u. Sudlichen Theile von Nord Amerik. Die Neuesten Gebiete der Union und die Vereinigten Staaten von Mexico aus deu Neuesten Quellen Verostentlicht durch, Mo Landrath Capt. B. Schmolder
mwe0472	europe central	1803	SCHNEIDER	480	70	49	Charte von Ungarn ... Croatien, Slavonien, Dalmatien (2 sheets, each 70x49cm)
mwe0830	europe east	1789	SCHNEIDER	480	58	51	Charte von Ungarn, Polen, Russland und der Turkey
mwam1135	america north (east)	1799	SCHNEIDER	2000	54	65	Die Vereinigten Staaten von Nordamerika nach Arrowsmiths und Lewis Karten vom Jahre 1795 und 1796
mwg0421	brandenburg	1798	SCHNEIDER	400	50	77	Karte von der Mark Brandenburg nach den Besten Spezialkarten Neu Entworfen
mwbp0525	poland	1792	SCHNEIDER	480	45	71	Special Charte vom Herzogthum Pommern nebst den Angranzenden Landern

AMPG REFERENCE	REGION	DATE	MAP MAKER	PRICE (UK£)	VERT. (cm.)	HOR. (cm.)	TITLE OF MAP (Comments by the editor in brackets)
mwbh0750	belgium holland	1787	SCHNEIDER	875	103	126	Special-Karte von den VII. Provinzen der Vereinigten Niederlanden nebst dem Generalitaets Lande
mwe0226a	europe	1794	SCHNEIDER & WEIGEL	300	39	49	Charte von Europa
mwin0318	india	1797	SCHNEIDER & WEIGEL	550	52	69	Charte von Hindostand und der Habinsel
mwg0165	germany	1797	SCHNEIDER & WEIGEL	400	52	60	Das Deutsche Reich
mwas0224a	asia continent	1797	SCHNEIDER & WEIGEL	600	52	57	Die Oestliche Halbkugel (eastern hemisphere)
mwsw0223a	switzerland	1817	SCHNEIDER & WEIGEL	350	52	57	Die Schweiz (shown above left)
mwam0247	america continent	1797	SCHNEIDER & WEIGEL	500	52	57	Die Westliche Halbkugel (western hemisphere)
mwuk0872	uk	1795	SCHNEIDER & WEIGEL	480	72	52	Grosz-Britannien und Ireland
mwbp0526	poland	1793	SCHNEIDER & WEIGEL	1350	87	102	Nova Mappa Geographica Regni Poloniae, Magni Ducatus Lituaniae Regni
mwit0822a	italy sardinia	1800	SCHNEIDER & WEIGEL	400	50	30	Sardinien
mwsc0632	scandinavia norway	1778	SCHOENING	400	51	37	Norvegia Antiqua
mwwi0388	barbados	1846	SCHOMBURGH	6000	121	92	A Topographical Map of the Island of Barbados Based upon Mayo's Original Survey in 1721 and Corrected to the Year 1846
mwsam0651	south america guyana	1847	SCHOMBURGK	400	47	52	Map of the Settled Districts of the Colony of British Guiana, Comprising the Counties of Demerara, Essequibo and Berbice, Shewing the Line of Railway
mww0259	world	1695	SCHOONEBECK		119	170	(Title in Armenian in large letters below map)
mwbh0421a	belgium holland	1680	SCHOTANUS	500	48	39	Typus Frisiae Veteris
mwp0375	pacific new guinea	1618	SCHOUTEN	650	15	27	Caarte van Nova Guinea, Nieulijck inden Iare 1616
mwsam0655	south america magellan	1618	SCHOUTEN	650	17	21	Caerte vande Nieuwe Passagie Bezuyden de Strate Magellani
mwam1197	america north (east)	1826	SCHOYER	960	41	51	Map of the United States Drawn from the Most Approved Surveys
mwgm0056a	gulf of mexico and surrounding regions	1788	SCHRAEMBL	450	51	58	(Untitled map. Inset: Southern California)
mwuk0879	uk	1805	SCHRAEMBL	350	60	49	Charte der Vereinigten Konigreiche Grossbritannien und Irland
mwe0447	europe bosnia	1788	SCHRAEMBL	800	67	107	Das Koenigreich Bosnien, und die Herzegovina (Rama)
mwaf0964	africa south	1789	SCHRAEMBL	550	50	33	Das Vorgebirg der Guten Hofnung Verfasst von Herrn L.S. de la Rochette (copy of Faden's 1782 map)
mwru0287	russia	1787	SCHRAEMBL	1350	51	53	Dritter Theil der Karte von Asien welcher Sibirien und Einige Andere Theile der Tatarei (2 sheets, each 51x53cm)
mwaf0525	africa egypt etc	1787	SCHRAEMBL	320	66	40	Egypten oder Misir
mwme0745a	iraq etc	1786	SHRAEMBL	300	43	51	Euphrat und Tigris (based on D'Anville)
mwe0210	europe	1787	SCHRAEMBL	720	55	71	Europa
mwaf0845a	africa north west	1789	SCHRAEMBL	280	37	80	General Karte der Koenigreiche Marokko, Fez, Algier, und Tunis.
mwru0303	russia	1792	SCHRAEMBL	1500	78	170	Generalkarte des Russischen Reichs mit der Eintheilung in die Neu Errichteten Statthalterschaften und Kreise (3 sheets, each 78x57cm)
mww0563	world	1789	SCHRAEMBL	1500	60	93	Generalkarte Saemtlicher Entdeckungen auf den Drei Grossen Weltreisen des Kapit. Jacob Cook (in 2 sheets)
mwam0504	america north	1788	SCHRAEMBL	2000	102	117	GeneralKarte von Nord America samt den Westindischen Inseln Verfasst von Herrn Pownall
mwbp0512	poland	1788	SCHRAEMBL	1250	84	97	Generalkarte von Polen, Litauen und den Angraenzenden Laendern
mwe1056	europe romania	1789	SCHRAEMBL	785	68	112	Generalkarte von Siebenburgen
mwaf1232	africa west	1786	SCHRAEMBL	280	30	66	Guinea Zwischen Sierra-Leona und dem Aequator (Gold Coast inset)
mwsam0696	south america magellan	1787	SCHRAEMBL	675	52	68	Karte der Magellanischen Strasse
mwme0660a	arabia etc	1789	SCHRAEMBL	450	68	48	Karte des Arabischen Meerbusens oder des Rothen Meeres
mwat0053	atlantic ocean (all)	1788	SCHRAEMBL	600	48	62	Karte des Atlantischen Oceans
mwm0074	mediterranean	1787	SCHRAEMBL	650	37	72	Karte des Mittellaendischen Meers
mwru0563	ukraine	1787	SCHRAEMBL	600	46	58	Karte Tauriens oder der Halbinsel Krim und der Westlichen Nogayischen Tartarei
mwaf0258	africa	1787	SCHRAEMBL	1500	97	108	Karte von Africa Verfasst von Herrn Robert Vaugondy
mwbp0513	poland	1789	SCHRAEMBL	785	47	56	Karte von Danzig, Elbing, und Marienburg oder Erstes Blat von Westpreussen / Karte von Ermeland oder Zweites Blat von Westpreussen (2 sheets, each 47x56cm)
mwas0325b	asia caspian sea	1787	SCHRAEMBL	320	48	26	Karte von dem Caspischen Meer
mwme0660	arabia etc	1789	SCHRAEMBL	960	56	37	Karte von dem Groessten Theil des Landes Jemen Imame, Kaukaban &c. (Yemen)
mwp0439	pacific north	1788	SCHRAEMBL	750	40	68	Karte von den N.W. Amerikanischen und N.OE. Asiatischen Kusten nach den Untersuchungen des Kapit. Cook in den Jah. 1778 und 1779 (copy of Cook-Roberts 1784)
mwuk1024	england	1787	SCHRAEMBL	1500	64	54	Karte von England und Wallis ... von Herrn Thomas Kitchin (4 sheets, each 64x54cm)
mwgr0230	greece	1791	SCHRAEMBL	720	48	65	Karte von Griechenland
mwuk0228	ireland	1787	SCHRAEMBL	675	64	57	Karte von Ireland Verfasst von Herrn Thomas Kitchin
mwuk0548	scotland	1787	SCHRAEMBL	480	55	51	Karte von Schottland Verfasst von J. Dorret
mwsam0107	south america	1787	SCHRAEMBL	850	123	76	Karte von Sud-America (re-issue of D'Anville 1748 with added inset: Falkland Isl.)

AMPG REFERENCE	REGION	DATE	MAP MAKER	PRICE (UK£)	VERT. (cm.)	HOR. (cm.)	TITLE OF MAP (Comments by the editor in brackets)
mwe0213	europe	1787	SCHRAEMBL	450	55	71	Neue Carte von Europa welche die Merkwurdigsten Producte und Vornehmsten Handelslatze ... Enthalt (text side borders)
mwsw0196	switzerland	1789	SCHRAEMBL	800	61	83	Neue Karte von der Schweiz oder Helvetien
mwf0162	france	1790	SCHRAEMBL	1200	52	75	Neueste General Karte von Frankreich (6 sheets, each 52x75cm)
mwsp0305	spain	1790	SCHRAEMBL	1600	132	140	Neueste General Karte von Portugal und Spanien nach den Astronomischen Beobachtungen und Karten des Herrn Thomas Lopez
mwbh0754	belgium holland	1790	SCHRAEMBL	785	100	124	Neueste Generalkarte von den Saemtlichen Oestreichischen Niederlanden nebst dem Ausfluss der Schelde
mwe0387	europe austria	1790	SCHRAEMBL	785	68	72	Neueste Generalkarte von Tyrol nach den Vortreflichen Karten Peter Anichs und Blasius Huebers
mwin0296	india	1788	SCHRAEMBL	1800	115	141	Neueste Karte von Hindostan, Bengalen etc. Mit der Anzeige der Strasen, Paesse und Genauester Eintheilung der Britischen Besitzungen in Ostindien
mwru0568	ukraine	1788	SCHRAEMBL	300	22	31	Odessa
mwe0468	europe central	1792	SCHRAEMBL	480	100	74	Ostreichisch-Franzosischer Kriegsschauplatz
mwp0505	pacific south	1789	SCHRAEMBL	1200	47	72	Polynesien (Inselwelt) oder der Funfte Weltheil Verfasst von Herrn Daniel Djurberg
mwsc0178	scandinavia	1788	SCHRAEMBL	1200	67	99	Schauplatz des Schwedisch Russischen Kriegs
mwaf1233	africa west	1786	SCHRAEMBL	580	101	69	Specialkarte der West-Kuste von Africa von Cabo Blanco bis Cabo Verga
mwe1206	europe west	1791	SCHRAEMBL	900	67	54	Ubersicht der Europaeischen Seekusten (inset: East Mediterranean Sea)
mww0545	world	1786	SCHRAEMBL	1800	66	62	Westliche Halb-Kugel / Oestliche Halb-Kugel (2 circular maps, each 66x62cm.)
mwaf0193	africa	1750	SCHREIBERN	300	16	24	Africa
mwam0143	america continent	1732	SCHREIBERN	450	17	23	America Verfertiget
mwas0160	asia continent	1749	SCHREIBERN	300	16	25	Asia Verferliget von Joh. George Schreibem in Leipzig
mwam0985	america north (east)	1755	SCHREIBERN	500	18	24	Charte von dem Engellandischen u. Franzoesischen Besitzungen in Nord America
mwru0196	russia	1744	SCHREIBERN	250	18	28	Das Gantze Russische Kaeyserthum mit Allen Seinen Laendern
mwme0328	holy land	1749	SCHREIBERN	275	18	25	Das Gelobte Land Sammt der 40 Iahrigen Reise der Kinder Israel aus Egypten
mwsc0430	scandinavia finland	1740	SCHREIBERN	350	17	24	Das Gros Hertzogthum Finland
mwit0687	italy piedmont	1750	SCHREIBERN	165	17	25	Das Hertzogthum Piemont nebst dem Hertzogthum Montferat
mwbp0429a	poland	1744	SCHREIBERN	235	18	28	Das Hertzogthum Pommern (1780 edition illustrated)
mwe0586a	europe czech republic (bohemia)	1749	SCHREIBERN	150	17	24	Das Königreich Böhmen
mwsc0360	scandinavia denmark	1744	SCHREIBERN	235	18	28	Das Konigreich Dannemarck nebst denen Angrantzenden Lendem
mwsc0139	scandinavia	1744	SCHREIBERN	280	18	28	Das Konigreich Schwegen und Norwegen
mwe0943	europe hungary	1744	SCHREIBERN	250	18	28	Das Konigreich Ungarn nebst den Angrantzenden Keyserlichen Landem
mwsw0144	switzerland	1744	SCHREIBERN	250	18	28	De Republic Schweitz mit Ihren Unterthanen und Bundsgenossen
mwbp0429	poland	1744	SCHREIBERN	235	18	28	Der Konigreich Preussen nebst dem Polnischen Antheil
mwwi0279a	west indies (islands)	1761	SCHREIBERN	200	19	25	Die Caribischen Insuln in Nord America - Guadaloupe, Martinique, Maria Galanta, Dominique u. Desiderade
mwe0798	europe east	1744	SCHREIBERN	250	18	28	Die Europeasche oder Kleine Tartary nebst den Angrantzenden Landem
mwe0580	europe czech republic (bohemia)	1744	SCHREIBERN	250	18	28	Die Gegend um Dia Hauft Stadt Prag im Konigreich Bohmen
mwbp0122	baltic states	1741	SCHREIBERN	200	16	24	Die Hertzogthumer Curland und Liefland
mwf0502	france corsica	1749	SCHREIBERN	400	16	23	Die Insul Corsica mit dessen Districten und Aemtern Abgetheilet
mwit0812b	italy sardinia	1749	SCHREIBERN	400	26	18	Die Insel und Königreich Sardinien (shown below left)
mwbh0698	belgium holland	1750	SCHREIBERN	200	16	25	Die Oesterreichische Niederlande verfertig von JG Schreibe - in Leipzig (Belgium)
mwbh0697	belgium holland	1750	SCHREIBERN	250	16	25	Die Republic Holland oder die Vereinigte Niederlande
mwe0162	europe	1744	SCHREIBERN	300	18	28	Europa Verferliget von J.G. Scheibern in Leipzig
mwgr0188	greece	1749	SCHREIBERN	280	17	25	Gantz Griechenland
mww0410	world	1750	SCHREIBERN	400	17	24	Globus Terrestris ex probatissimus recentiorum
mwuk0810	uk	1730	SCHREIBERN	300	16	25	Gros Britannien oder Engelland, Schottland und Irrland
mwit0177	italy	1744	SCHREIBERN	250	18	28	Italien in sein Unterscheide ne Lander
mwg0644	saxony	1732	SCHREIBERN	500	45	57	Ober Lausitz Entworfen
mwe0584	europe czech republic (bohemia)	1744	SCHREIBERN	250	18	28	Reise Charte durch das Konigreich Bohmen Hertzzogthum Schlesien Marggrafthum Maehren und Lausitz
mwbp0380	poland	1720	SCHREIBERN	250	17	27	Reise Charte durch das Konigreich Polen
mwg0124	germany	1744	SCHREIBERN	200	18	28	Reise Charte durch Deutschland
mwf0123	france	1744	SCHREIBERN	250	18	28	Reise Charte durch Frankreich in seine 12 Provintzien
mwe0367	europe austria	1744	SCHREIBERN	250	18	28	Reise Charte durch Oesterreich
mwsp0265	spain	1741	SCHREIBERN	250	17	24	Spanien und Portugal

AMPG REFERENCE	REGION	DATE	MAP MAKER	PRICE (UK£)	VERT. (cm.)	HOR. (cm.)	TITLE OF MAP (Comments by the editor in brackets)
mwas0241a	asia continent	1817	SCHREIBERS ERBEN	160	19	26	Karte von Asien - Leipzig bei Schreibers Erben 1817
mwp0513a	pacific south	1799	SCHREIBERS ERBEN	250	19	26	Karte von Australien oder Polynesien
mwam0275	america continent	1820	SCHROPP	350	60	45	America
mwp0522	pacific south	1820	SCHROPP	480	43	58	Australien
mwe0256	europe	1822	SCHROPP	200	49	55	Europa
mwg0175	germany	1818	SCHROPP	350	56	80	Neueste Post-Karte von Deutschland und dessen Angrenzenden Lander
mwg0249b	berlin	1848	SCHROPP	600	44	61	Topographische Karte Der Gegend Um Berlin
mwe0479	europe central	1814	SCHROPP	550	114	127	Wege-Karte durch den Grosten und Wichtigsten Theil Europa's von London bis Moscau, und von Stockholm bis Neapel
mwwi0613	hispaniola	1752	SCHROTER	300	22	29	Der Insel Hispaniola, oder San Domingo, Vorgestellet nach den Alten Niederlasfungen der Spanien
mwru0411	russia moscow	1850	SCHUBERT	1000	72	93	Plan Stolitschnago Goroda Moskwy
mwe0829	europe east	1788	SCHULTZ	675	41	66	Kriegstheater oder Graenzkarte Oesterreiches, Russlands, und der Turkey
mwat0039	atlantic ocean (all)	1751	SCHWEBEL	300	36	48	Carte Generale des Royaumes, Etats et Domaines … la Grande Bretagne …
mwgr0394	greece crete	1668	SCOLARI	1500	39	49	Candia per la Terza Volta Attacatta dall'Armi Ottomane …. 1667 et 1668
mwe0664	europe dalmatia	1650	SCOLARI	1200	51	55	Dalmatia et Albania et Altri Stati Confinanti
mwit0576	italy north	1640	SCOLARI	2000	39	102	Descritione del Polesene, con suoi Confini
mwgr0395	greece crete	1668	SCOLARI	1650	40	34	Disegno del Combattimento Glorioso Seguito tra le Galere della Sereniss.ma Republica di Venetia et le Galere de Bei … 8 Marzo 1668
mwgr0392	greece crete	1666	SCOLARI	1650	39	57	La Piaza di Candia
mwgr0085	greece	1670	SCOLARI	12000	79	106	Le Otto Provincie della Morea Cavate dalli Atlanti et Altri Autori con' Diligenze Acresciute
mwbh0354	belgium holland	1660	SCOLARI	2000	39	53	Novo disegno delle Province Unite delli Stati di Olanda
mwgr0086	greece	1670	SCOLARI	5000	78	102	Tavola Nova dell' Arcipelago Accresciuta in Magior Forma (based on Levanto, 1664)
mwit1221a	italy venice	1627	SCOLARI	3500	39	53	Venetia
mwit1224a	italy venice	1660	SCOLARI	40000	77	159	Vero e Real Disegno Della Inclita Cita di Venetia
mwe0411a	europe austria vienna	1680	SCOLARI	1200	41	49	Viena D'Austria
mwit0053	italy	1600	SCOTO	2500	25	33	Italia (borders consist of 12 inset city views)
mwit1056b	italy naples	1699	SCOTO	175	13	18	Napoli (shown below left)
mwit1184a	italy veneto	1670	SCOTO	150	14	13	Verona (re-issue of first edition, publ. 1600)
mwit0055	italy	1601	SCOTO-BERTELLI	300	13	19	Italia
mwuk1202	england london	1761	SCOTS MAG.	875	22	40	A Correct Plan of the Cities of London & Westminster & Borough of Southwark Including the Bills of Mortality with the Additional Buildings
mwp0384	pacific new guinea	1763	SCOTS MAG.	400	11	18	A Curious Map of some Late Discoveries in Terra Australis Comprehending New Guinea & New Britain
mwuss0756	maryland	1781	SCOTS MAG.	350	16	17	A Map of Maryland with Part of Virginia and Pensylvania
mwam0962	america north (east)	1750	SCOTS MAG.	450	29	39	A Map of the British and French Settlements in North America
mwuss1365	pennsylvania	1776	SCOTS MAG.	275	18	23	A Map of the Country round Philadelphia Including Part of New Jersey, New York, Staten Island & Long Island
mwuk0505	scotland	1759	SCOTS MAG.	200	20	19	A Plan of the City of Edinburgh with the Adjacent Grounds
mwca0518	canada quebec	1759	SCOTS MAG.	200	11	19	A Plan of the Operations at the Taking of Quebec, and the Battle Fought near that City, Septr: 13. 1759
mwuss1091	new york	1758	SCOTS MAG.	275	19	11	The Country between Crown Point and Albany being the Great Pass from the English to the French Settlements in North America
mwuss0817	massachusetts	1775	SCOTS MAG.	750	26	26	Thirty-Miles round Boston, by M. Armstrong Geo. 14th Augt. 1775
mwuss1386	pennsylvania	1794	SCOTT	1750	31	51	A Map of the State of Pennsylvania from Mr. Howell's Large Map
mwam0529	america north	1795	SCOTT	375	27	37	A Map of the United States
mwuss0300	connecticut	1795	SCOTT	160	15	18	Connecticut
mwuss0372	delaware	1795	SCOTT	160	18	15	Delaware
mwuss0595	kentucky	1795	SCOTT	240	15	18	Kentucky
mwuss0706	maine	1795	SCOTT	160	19	15	Maine
mwuss0762	maryland	1795	SCOTT	200	17	19	Maryland
mwuss0850	massachusetts	1795	SCOTT	160	15	18	Massachusetts
mwam0812	america north (central)	1795	SCOTT	450	18	16	N.W. Territory
mwuss1008	new hampshire	1795	SCOTT	160	19	15	New Hampshire
mwuss1046	new jersey	1795	SCOTT	160	19	15	New Jersey
mwuss1163	new york	1795	SCOTT	160	15	18	New York
mwuss0241	carolinas	1795	SCOTT	200	15	19	North-Carolina
mwuss1389	pennsylvania	1795	SCOTT	160	16	18	Pennsylvania
mwuss1458	rhode isl	1795	SCOTT	160	18	15	Rhode Island
mwuss1485	tennessee	1795	SCOTT	450	15	18	S.W. Territory
mwuss0242	carolinas	1795	SCOTT	200	16	18	South Carolina
mwuss1559	vermont	1795	SCOTT	160	19	16	State of Vermont
mwuss1667	virginia	1795	SCOTT	200	15	19	Virginia

AMPG REFERENCE	REGION	DATE	MAP MAKER	PRICE (UK£)	VERT. (cm.)	HOR. (cm.)	TITLE OF MAP (Comments by the editor in brackets)
mwwi0149	west indies	1800	SCOTT	120	20	25	West Indies
mwuss1351	pennsylvania	1759	SCULL	50000	153	76	To the Honourable Thomas Penn ... this Map of the Improved Part of the Province of Pennsylvania Is Humbly Dedicated
mwuss1347	pennsylvania	1753	SCULL & HEAP	800	35	30	A Map of Philadelphia, and Parts Adjacent (from Gentleman's Magazine)
mwuss1346	pennsylvania	1752	SCULL & HEAP	72000	31	53	A Map of Philadelphia, and Parts Adjacent. With a Perspective View of the State-House (separate publication printed on silk)
mwuss1370	pennsylvania	1777	SCULL & HEAP	6500	46	62	A Plan of the City and Environs of Philadelphia. Survey'd by N. Scull and G. Heap. Engraved by Willm. Faden. 1777
mwuk0304	irish sea	1732	SEALE	350	47	38	A Correct Chart of St. George's Channel and the Irish Sea, Including all the Coast of Ireland and ye West Coast of Great Britain from Cantire to Portland Isle
mwbp0044	baltic sea (east)	1744	SEALE	375	39	49	A Correct Chart of the Baltick or East Sea from ye Sound to Petersburg (inset of St. Petersburg)
mwuk1496	uk english channel (all)	1745	SEALE	350	38	47	A Correct Chart of the English Channel from the No. Foreland to the Lands End
mwaf0182	africa	1744	SEALE	350	31	40	A Map of Africa from the Latest and Best Observations
mwam0151	america continent	1740	SEALE	900	40	30	A Map of America from the Latest and Best Observations
mwaf0518	africa egypt etc	1764	SEALE	100	24	21	A Map of Antient Egypt
mwas0145	asia continent	1740	SEALE	350	30	39	A Map of Asia from the Latest and Best Observations
mwe0156	europe	1740	SEALE	350	30	39	A Map of Europe from the Latest & Best Observations
mwam0395	america north	1745	SEALE	1200	38	47	A Map of North America with the European Settlements & Whatever Else is Remarkable in ye West Indies
mwsp0266	spain	1744	SEALE	375	37	47	A Map of the Kingdoms of Spain and Portugal
mwme0300	holy land	1739	SEALE	450	36	43	A Map Shewing ye Situation of Paradice and ye Country Inhabited by ye Patriarchs Design'd for the Better Understanding of ye Sacred History
mwam1025	america north (east)	1771	SEALE	1500	47	51	A New and Accurate Map of North America, Drawn from the Famous Mr. D'Anville with Improvements from the Best English Maps; and Engraved by R.W. Seale; also the New Divisions According to the Late Treaty of Peace, by Peter Bell (publ. by Bowles)
mwam1053	america north (east)	1777	SEALE	580	36	28	A New and Accurate Map of the Present Seat of War in North America, Comprehending New Jersey, Philadelphia, Pensylvania, New-York &c.
mwaf1213	africa west	1750	SEALE	400	39	48	A New and Correct Map of the Coast of Africa from Cape Blanco to the Coast of Angola with the Explanatory Notes of All the Forts and Settlements Belonging to the Several European Powers (inset: Gold Coast)
mwm0256	mediterranean malta	1804	SEALE	2800	56	132	A New Map & Land Chart of the Sovereign Principality of Malta
mwsam0760	south america peru	1749	SEALE	100	22	38	A Plan of the Town of Payta in the Kingdom of Santa Fee
mwe0167	europe	1750	SEALE	2800	61	104	An Accurate Map of Europe with its Empires, Kingdoms
mwme0622a	arabia etc	1750	SEALE	1100	33	36	Arabia (inset: 'The Temple of Mecca'. Illustrated is a later French edition of unknown origin)
mwec0293a	uk england devon	1732	SEALE	240	19	26	Devon Shire
mwas0788	asia south east philippines	1763	SEALE	550	47	34	The Philippin, Carolin, Molucka, and Spice Islands
mwec0784	uk england middlesex	1751	SEALE	1400	52	73	To the Most Noble Thomas Holles Pelham, Duke of Newcastle ... this Map of the County of Middlesex (92 crests of livery companies)
mwm0057	mediterranean	1745	SEALE-BASIRE	875	36	72	A Correct Chart of the Mediterranean Sea, from the Straits of Gibraltar to the Levant
mwme0414	holy land	1835	SEATON	800	84	93	Seaton's Map of Palestine or the Holy Land, with Part of Egypt. Compiled from Surveys Made for the French and English Governments
mwuk1058	england	1830	SEATON	800	117	94	This New Map of England & Wales Compiled from the Latest Surveys
mwsp0001	portugal	1561	SECO	8000	36	67	(Untitled map, north to the right.)
mwit1199	italy veneto	1745	SEGUIER	1500	61	35	Territorio Veronese Anno MDCCXLV
mwaf0058	africa	1652	SEILE	800	36	42	Africae Descriptio Nova
mwam0055	america continent	1652	SEILE	1000	36	42	Americae Descriptio Nova (shown is 1663 edition, with title 'Americae Nova descriptio')
mwas0041	asia continent	1652	SEILE	800	36	42	Asiae Descriptio Nova
mwe0060	europe	1652	SEILE	600	36	42	Europae Descriptio Nova
mwru0404a	russia moscow	1819	SELIVANOVSKAYA	2000	61	61	(Plan of the Capital City of Moscow, in Cyrillic)
mwuk0735	uk	1678	SELLER	2000	44	53	A Chart of England Scotland and Ireland with the Channell
mwaf1141	africa west	1682	SELLER	160	11	14	A Chart of Guinea by John Seller
mwaf1135	africa west	1679	SELLER	1000	44	53	A Chart of Guinea Describing the Seacoast from Cape de Verde to Cape Bona Esperanca
mwbp0025	baltic sea (east)	1670	SELLER	2000	44	54	A Chart of the Baltick Sea with the North Bodom & Lading
mwf0291	france bay of biscay	1679	SELLER	550	43	53	A Chart of the Bay of Biscaia
mwuk1464	uk english channel (all)	1675	SELLER	2250	43	54	A Chart of the Brittish Chanel (shown left is the 1701 edition with title 'Chart of the Channell')

AMPG REFERENCE	REGION	DATE	MAP MAKER	PRICE (UK£)	VERT. (cm.)	HOR. (cm.)	TITLE OF MAP (Comments by the editor in brackets)
mwsc0420	scandinavia finland	1670	SELLER	1800	43	53	A Chart of the Coast of Sweden / A Chart of the Gat of Abbo or Uttoy
mwuk0075a	ireland	1672	SELLER	900	46	55	A Chart of the East side of Ireland, from Waterford to Carlingford, shewing all the havens, Bayes, harbours, sands, depths and dangers / A Discription of the West side of Ireland from Cape Clere to the River of Waterford, shewing all the Roads and Harbors (2 plates printed on one sheet)
mwas0402	asia south east	1670	SELLER	5500	44	55	A Chart of the Easternmost Part of the East Indies
mwgr0310	greece corfu	1677	SELLER	1200	40	52	A Chart of the Islands Corfu, Pachsu and Antipachsus
mwm0133	mediterranean east	1677	SELLER	1600	40	52	A chart of the Levant or the sea coast of Egypt, Syria, Caramania and the island Cyprus
mwuk0733	uk	1675	SELLER	2000	44	54	A Chart of the Narrow Seas Extending Northerly as far as Iceland (north to the left)
mwca0211c	canada arctic	1673	SELLER	2750	43	52	A Chart of the North Part of America. Describing the Sea Coasts of Groenland Davies Streights Baffins Bay Hudsons Streights Buttons Bay and James Bay
mwuk1652	north sea	1672	SELLER	2500	44	55	A Chart of the North Sea (north to the right)
mwam0872	america north (east)	1675	SELLER	15000	43	54	A Chart of the Sea Coasts of New England New Jarsey Virginia Maryland and Carolina from C. Cod to C. Hatteras
mwaa0093	arctic	1675	SELLER	2500	44	54	A Chart of the Sea Coasts of Russia Lapland Finmarke Nova Zembla and Greenland
mwat0215	atlantic east	1690	SELLER	180	11	14	A Chart of the Seacoast from the Lands End of England to Cape Bona Esperanca
mwat0214	atlantic east	1675	SELLER	2500	46	58	A Chart of the Seacoasts from the Landsend of England to Cape Bona Esperanca
mwuk1653	north sea	1675	SELLER	2000	43	53	A Chart of the Seacoasts of England, Flanders & Holland
mwp0233	pacific (all)	1675	SELLER	6000	43	53	A Chart of the South Sea
mwsp0691a	gibraltar	1677	SELLER	1000	43	53	A Chart of the Straits of Gibralter (illustrated is the 1747 re-issue by Mount & Page)
mwgm0008	gulf of mexico and surrounding regions	1682	SELLER	500	11	14	A Chart of the West Indias from Cape Cod to ye River Orinoque
mwwi0026	west indies	1673	SELLER	10000	43	52	A Chart of the West Indies from Cape Cod to the River Oronoque, by John Seller
mwat0015	atlantic ocean (all)	1677	SELLER	2000	43	54	A Chart of the Western Ocean
mwin0421	indian ocean	1690	SELLER	180	11	15	A Chart of the Western Part of the East Indies
mwin0477a	indian ocean	1679	SELLER	2400	43	55	A Chart of the Western Part of the East Indies with All the Adjacent Islands from Cape Bona Esperanca to Cape Comorin
mwuk0729	uk	1671	SELLER	2000	43	53	A Chart of ye Narrow Seas Newly Corrected by John Seller Hydrographer to the Kings Most Excellent Majestie (north to the right)
mwuk0075b	ireland	1672	SELLER	900	49	55	A Description of the North Coast of Ireland between Banhaven and Cabo Moye, shewing all the Bayes, havens and harbors / A Chart of the Southwest side of Ireland, from Cape Cleare to the River Shannon, Describeing all the Bayes, havens, Roads and Harbors (2 plates printed on one sheet)
mwaf0870	africa south	1675	SELLER	3500	44	54	A Draught of Cape Bona Esperanca (view of Table Bay above)
mwuk1426	england thames	1671	SELLER	1800	44	55	A Draught of the Sands, Channels, Buoyes, Beacons and Sea Marks upon the Coast of England from the Southforeland to Orfordness
mwat0016	atlantic ocean (all)	1678	SELLER	4000	43	52	A General Chart of the West India's
mwat0259	atlantic north	1676	SELLER	2400	44	55	A Generall Chart of the Northerne Navigation
mwec0947	uk england oxfordshire	1680	SELLER	1500	37	48	A Map of Oxford Shire
mwuk1472	uk english channel (all)	1680	SELLER	180	12	14	A Map of the Channel by John Seller
mwit0894	italy sicily	1675	SELLER	2500	43	53	A Mapp Containing the Island & Kingdome of Sicily (3 insets)
mww0207	world	1678	SELLER	720	10	13	A Mapp Of All The World
mwec0331	uk england dorset	1695	SELLER	130	12	15	A Mapp of Dorsetshire.
mwam0876	america north (east)	1676	SELLER		44	55	A Mapp of New England (2nd state has dedication)
mwuss1034	new jersey	1675	SELLER	45000	43	54	A Mapp of New Jersey
mwaf0763c	africa north libya	1675	SELLER	1500	44	53	A Mapp of the Citie and Port of Tripoli in Barbary
mwaa0101	arctic	1690	SELLER	300	11	15	A Mapp of the North Pole by John Seller
mwaa0094	arctic	1675	SELLER	3000	43	54	A Mapp of the Regions & Countreyes under and about the North Pole
mwaa0013	antarctic	1685	SELLER	850	12	14	A Mapp of the South Pole
mww0229	world	1685	SELLER	750	13	15	A Mapp of the World Shewing what a Clock it is ... (size does not incl. clock page)
mwgr0589a	greece islands	1675	SELLER	750	53	44	A New Chart of the Archipelago
mwuk0958	england	1694	SELLER	200	12	15	A New Mapp of England and Wales.
mwuk0757	uk	1694	SELLER	250	12	15	A New Mapp of Great Britain and Ireland.
mwat0326	atlantic st helena	1675	SELLER	2250	43	53	A New Mapp of the Island of Saint Hellena
mwe1193	europe west	1670	SELLER	2000	54	43	A New Mapp of the Sea Coasts of England, France and Holland
mwuk0736	uk	1678	SELLER	2000	44	53	A Plat of the Channel Discovering the Sea Coasts of England, Scotland, Ireland and Part of France.

AMPG REFERENCE	REGION	DATE	MAP MAKER	PRICE (UK£)	VERT. (cm.)	HOR. (cm.)	TITLE OF MAP (Comments by the editor in brackets)
mwm0089b	mediterranean adriatic	1677	SELLER	1000	40	52	A Sea Chart of the Gulph of Venice (illustrated is the 1738 issue by Thornton)
mwaf0482	africa egypt etc	1678	SELLER	180	9	6	Aegyptus
mwaf0084	africa	1676	SELLER	240	9	6	Africa
mwaf0093	africa	1685	SELLER	240	12	15	Africa
mwam0079	america continent	1678	SELLER	360	9	6	America
mwuk1780	wales	1694	SELLER	140	12	14	Anglesey Island
mwme0566	arabia etc	1678	SELLER	350	9	6	Arabia
mwaf0696	africa north	1678	SELLER	160	9	6	Barbaria
mwec0038	uk england berkshire	1694	SELLER	130	12	14	Barkshire.
mwec0008	uk england bedfordshire	1694	SELLER	130	12	14	Bedford Shire.
mwaf0697	africa north	1678	SELLER	160	9	6	Biledulgerid
mwsam0319	south america brazil	1678	SELLER	240	9	6	Brazil
mwuk1781	wales	1694	SELLER	140	12	14	Breknoke Shire.
mwec0064	uk england buckinghamshire	1694	SELLER	130	12	14	Buckingham Shire.
mwec0092	uk england cambridgeshire	1694	SELLER	160	11	14	Cambridge Shire
mwca0030	canada	1678	SELLER	360	9	6	Canada or New France
mwuk1782	wales	1694	SELLER	140	12	14	Cardigan Shire.
mwuk1783	wales	1694	SELLER	140	12	14	Carmarden Shire.
mwuk1784	wales	1694	SELLER	140	12	14	Carnarvan Shire.
mwuss0160	carolinas	1694	SELLER	720	11	15	Carolina Newly Described by John Seller
mwsam0453a	south america chile	1685	SELLER	180	12	15	Chili
mwaf1131	africa west	1678	SELLER	180	9	6	Congo
mwec0174	uk england cornwall	1694	SELLER	200	12	15	Cornwall.
mwec0226	uk england cumbria	1694	SELLER	130	14	12	Cumberland.
mwuk1785	wales	1694	SELLER	140	12	14	Denbigh Shire.
mwsc0310	scandinavia denmark	1685	SELLER	100	12	15	Denmark
mwec0289	uk england devon	1694	SELLER	130	12	14	Devon Shire.
mwec0404	uk england essex	1694	SELLER	140	12	14	Essex.
mwuk1786	wales	1694	SELLER	140	12	14	Flint-Shire.
mwam0878	america north (east)	1678	SELLER	500	9	6	Florida
mwf0069	france	1678	SELLER	160	9	6	France
mwme0715	caucasus	1678	SELLER	200	9	6	Georgia
mwg0072	germany	1678	SELLER	160	9	6	Germany
mwuk1787	wales	1694	SELLER	140	12	14	Glamorgan Shire.
mwec0442	uk england gloucestershire	1694	SELLER	130	12	14	Glocester Shire.
mwru0432	russia tartary	1678	SELLER	120	9	6	Great Tartaria
mwaf1132	africa west	1678	SELLER	180	9	6	Guinea
mwec0474	uk england hampshire	1694	SELLER	160	12	14	Hant Shire.
mwec0544	uk england hertfordshire	1694	SELLER	140	12	14	Hartford Shire.
mwec0518	uk england herefordshire	1694	SELLER	140	12	14	Hereford Shire.
mwe0908a	europe hungary	1689	SELLER	180	12	14	Hungaria and Sclavonia (shown above)
mwec0578	uk england huntingdonshire	1694	SELLER	120	12	14	Huntingdon Shire.
mwwi0700	jamaica	1685	SELLER	175	13	15	Insulae Iamaicae
mwuk0091	ireland	1685	SELLER	250	12	14	Ireland
mwit0106	italy	1678	SELLER	280	9	6	Italia
mwit0111	italy	1685	SELLER	160	12	15	Italy
mwec0614	uk england kent	1694	SELLER	160	12	14	Kent.
mwec0682	uk england lancashire	1694	SELLER	140	12	14	Lancashire by John Seller.
mwec0717	uk england leicestershire	1694	SELLER	140	12	14	Leicester Shire.
mwru0094	russia	1685	SELLER	120	12	15	Lesser Tartaria
mwec0742	uk england lincolnshire	1694	SELLER	120	12	14	Lincolne Shire.
mwbp0097	baltic states	1685	SELLER	140	12	15	Lithuania
mwuk1788	wales	1694	SELLER	140	12	14	Merioneth Shire.
mwgm0177	mexico	1678	SELLER	220	9	6	Mexico or New Spain
mwgm0181a	mexico	1685	SELLER	350	12	15	Mexico or New Spaine (shown above)
mwec0776	uk england middlesex	1695	SELLER	1800	43	53	Middlesex Actually Surveyed and Deliniated by John Seller Hydrographer to ye King cum Previligio Regis
mwec0774	uk england middlesex	1694	SELLER	150	12	14	Midlesex.
mwuk1789	wales	1694	SELLER	140	12	14	Monmouth Shire.
mwuk1790	wales	1694	SELLER	140	12	14	Montgomery Shire.
mwgr0088	greece	1675	SELLER	160	13	15	Morea olim Peloponnesus
mwru0073a	russia	1678	SELLER	120	9	6	Moscovia
mwam0884	america north (east)	1685	SELLER	750	11	14	New England and New York
mwuss1079	new york	1679	SELLER	600	15	16	New England and New York
mwuss1035	new jersey	1682	SELLER	600	13	14	New Iarsey
mwam1315	america north (west)	1678	SELLER	500	9	6	New Mexico
mwec0820	uk england norfolk	1694	SELLER	120	12	14	Norfolk.
mwam0333	america north	1690	SELLER	600	12	14	North America
mwec0857	uk england northamptonshire	1694	SELLER	120	12	14	Northampton Shire.
mwec0884	uk england northumberland	1694	SELLER	120	12	14	Northumberland.
mwec0909	uk england nottinghamshire	1694	SELLER	120	12	14	Nottingham Shire.
mwwi0691	jamaica	1672	SELLER	2250	43	55	Novissima et Accuratissima Insulae Jamaicae Descriptio
mww0195	world	1673	SELLER	8500	44	55	Novissima Totius Terrarum Orbis Tabula

AMPG REFERENCE	REGION	DATE	MAP MAKER	PRICE (UK£)	VERT. (cm.)	HOR. (cm.)	TITLE OF MAP (Comments by the editor in brackets)
mwaf0370	africa east	1678	SELLER	180	9	6	Nubia
mwec0950	uk england oxfordshire	1694	SELLER	160	12	14	Oxford Shire.
mwsam0710	south america paraguay	1678	SELLER	180	9	6	Paragua
mwsam0710a	south america paraguay	1689	SELLER	180	12	15	Paraguay
mwuk1791	wales	1694	SELLER	140	12	14	Pembrook Shire.
mwuss1340	pennsylvania	1685	SELLER	900	12	14	Pensilvania
mwme0787	persia etc	1678	SELLER	180	9	6	Persia
mwme0793	persia etc	1685	SELLER	220	12	15	Persia (shown above left)
mwbp0289	poland	1678	SELLER	180	9	6	Poland
mwsp0054	portugal	1685	SELLER	140	12	15	Portugal
mwuk1792	wales	1694	SELLER	140	12	14	Radnor Shire.
mwec0983	uk england rutland	1694	SELLER	120	12	14	Rutland.
mwuk0444	scotland	1695	SELLER	180	11	15	Scotland
mwec1008	uk england shropshire	1694	SELLER	120	12	14	Shrop-Shire.
mwec1039	uk england somerset	1695	SELLER	130	13	15	Somerset Shire
mwsp0201	spain	1685	SELLER	100	12	15	Spaine
mwec1067	uk england staffordshire	1694	SELLER	140	12	14	Stafford Shire.
mwec1135a	uk england surrey	1700	SELLER-LEA	1800	42	52	Surrey Actually Survey'd and Delineated
mwec1134	uk england surrey	1694	SELLER	160	12	14	Surrey.
mwsc0081	scandinavia	1685	SELLER	140	12	15	Swedeland and Norway
mwsam0173	south america (north)	1678	SELLER	180	9	6	Terra Firma
mwsam0202a	south america amazon	1683	SELLER	180	12	14	The Amazones Country
mwec0366	uk england durham	1694	SELLER	130	12	14	The Bishoprick of Durham.
mwwi0029	west indies	1678	SELLER	300	9	6	The Chief Islands of ye Antilles and Lucayes
mwbh0388	belgium holland	1672	SELLER	800	40	52	The City of Maestricht. With the Present Fortifications
mwuk1540c	uk english channel (west)	1678	SELLER	850	44	53	The Coast of England & France ; from the Start, to the Isles of Silly, & from Isle de Bass, to Ushant (shown below left)
mwaf1067	africa south west	1678	SELLER	180	9	6	The Country of the Negro's or Blacks
mwec0261	uk england derbyshire	1695	SELLER	130	13	15	The County of Darby.
mwec1100	uk england suffolk	1694	SELLER	140	12	14	The County of Suffolke.
mwec0136	uk england cheshire	1694	SELLER	130	12	14	The Countye Palatine of Chester.
mwin0117	india	1678	SELLER	200	9	6	The Empire of the Great Mogul
mwam0325	america north	1678	SELLER	600	9	6	The English Empire in America
mwaf0873	africa south	1678	SELLER	240	9	6	The Higher and Lower Ethiopia
mwaf0371	africa east	1678	SELLER	200	9	6	The Higher Ethiopia
mwwi0364	barbados	1685	SELLER	650	12	14	The Island of Barbados
mwuk1578	channel islands	1694	SELLER	160	12	14	The Island of Garnsey.
mwuk1579	channel islands	1694	SELLER	180	12	14	The Island of Jarsey
mwuk1607	isle of man	1694	SELLER	240	13	15	The Island of Man
mwwi0899	trinidad & tobago	1684	SELLER	800	10	14	The Island of Tobago
mwuk1621	isle of wight	1694	SELLER	180	12	14	The Island of Wight
mwm0267	mediterranean west	1678	SELLER	200	9	6	The IX Chiefe Islands in ye Mediterranean Counted in Europe
mwc0061	china	1678	SELLER	360	9	6	The Kingdom of China
mwsc0686	scandinavia sweden	1678	SELLER	200	9	6	The Kingdom of Sweaden
mwin0118	india	1678	SELLER	200	9	6	The Main Land of India within the Ganges
mwin0119	india	1678	SELLER	200	9	6	The Peninsula of India without ye Ganges
mwuk1793	wales	1694	SELLER	160	12	14	The Principality of Wales.
mwuk1356	england north	1671	SELLER	1250	43	52	The River of Humber / The River of Tyne
mwit0833a	italy sardinia and corsica	1675	SELLER	1400	39	52	The Sea Coast of the Island of Sardinia and Corsica
mwe1141	europe south east	1685	SELLER	120	13	15	The South Part of Turky in Europe
mwgr0485a	greece cyprus	1678	SELLER	1200	9	6	The two chief Islands in ye Mediterranean Reckon'd in Asia (Cyprus and Rhodes)
mwsam0193a	south america (north west)	1678	SELLER	240	9	6	The West Coast of South America
mwwi0696	jamaica	1679	SELLER	1000	43	50	The Windward Passage from Jamaica Betwene the East End of Cuba and the West End of Hispaniola
mwbh0440	belgium holland	1685	SELLER	100	12	15	The XVII Provinces
mwme0178	holy land	1678	SELLER	200	9	6	Turkey in Asia
mwe1139	europe south east	1678	SELLER	160	9	6	Turkey in Europe
mwe1142	europe south east	1685	SELLER	100	13	15	Turky in Europe
mwec1193	uk england warwickshire	1694	SELLER	140	12	14	Warwick Shire.
mwec1223	uk england westmorland	1694	SELLER	130	12	14	Westmoreland County.
mwec1244	uk england wiltshire	1694	SELLER	140	12	14	Wiltshire.
mwec1277	uk england worcestershire	1694	SELLER	130	12	14	Worcester Shire.
mwec1318	uk england yorkshire	1694	SELLER	150	12	14	York Shire.
mwaf1133	africa west	1678	SELLER	180	9	6	Zaara
mwm0142	mediterranean east	1716	SELLER-GAUDY	1350	40	52	A Chart of the Levant or the Sea Coast of Egypt Syria Caramania and the Island Cyprus (Seller's chart of 1677 'corrected')
mwec0624	uk england kent	1720	SELLER-MOLL	3000	59	89	Kent Actually Survey'd and Delineated (re-issue of Seller's c1681 map)
mwuk1483	uk english channel (all)	1701	SELLER-PRICE	1500	45	58	A New Chart of the Channell between England and France, Shewing the Sands and Depth of Water with the Flowing of the Tydes ... Observed in the Year 1701. By Cap't Edm: Halley

AMPG REFERENCE	REGION	DATE	MAP MAKER	PRICE (UK£)	VERT. (cm.)	HOR. (cm.)	TITLE OF MAP (Comments by the editor in brackets)
mwat0025	atlantic ocean (all)	1703	SELLER-PRICE	960	46	58	A New Generall Chart for the West Indies of E. Wrights Projection (map engraved by H. Moll)
mwam0702a	america north	1836	SELVES	200	42	34	Amerique Septentrionale
mwat0344	atlantic west	1728	SENEX	1000	50	116	A Chart of the Atlantick Ocean from Oronoque River to the River May with the Caribbee & Bahama Is.
mwin0182	india	1728	SENEX	650	48	57	A Chart of the Coast of Cormandel and the Great Bay of Bengal
mwsp0693a	gibraltar	1705	SENEX	720	30	38	A Compleat Plan of the Town Castle and Bay of Gibralter
mwsp0250	spain	1720	SENEX	960	63	93	A Correct Map of Spain & Portugal (1760 Bowles edition illustrated)
mwgm0024	gulf of mexico and surrounding regions	1721	SENEX	1500	59	48	A Draft of the Golden & Adjacent Islands, with Part of ye Isthmus of Darien as it was Taken by Capt. Ienefer where ye Scots West India Company were Settled / A New Map of ye Isthmus of Darien in America, the Bay of Panama (2 maps on one sheet)
mwgr0169	greece	1721	SENEX	875	48	56	A Map of Greece with Part of Anatolia. Revis'd by I. Senex (inset: view of Constantinople)
mwe0929	europe hungary	1721	SENEX	650	48	59	A Map of Hungary and Countries adjacent
mwam0804	america north (central)	1721	SENEX	2400	49	58	A Map of Louisiana and of the River Mississipi by Iohn Senex
mwsp0516	spain regions	1711	SENEX	580	45	55	A Map of Old & New Castile from the Observations of Rodrigo Mendes Silva and Others
mww0318	world	1711	SENEX	5000	59	109	A Map of the World Corrected from the Observations Communicated to the Royal Societys of London and Paris (illustrated is 1725 edition)
mwme0597	arabia etc	1711	SENEX	750	48	60	A Map of Turky, Arabia and Persia. Corrected from the Latest Travels & from ye Observations of ye Royal Societys of London & Paris by G. de l'Isle. Revis'd by I. Senex
mwme0265	holy land	1720	SENEX	450	36	44	A Map Shewing ye Situation of Paradice and ye Country Inhabited by ye Patriarchs Design'd for the Better Understanding of ye Sacred History
mwbh0598	belgium holland	1725	SENEX	960	63	94	A New and Correct Map of the Ten Spanish Provinces
mwaf0153	africa	1721	SENEX	800	49	56	A New Map of Africa from the Latest Observations
mwam0127	america continent	1719	SENEX	1800	49	57	A New Map of America from the Latest Observations Revis'd by I. Senex
mwas0128	asia continent	1721	SENEX	900	48	56	A New Map of Asia from the Latest Observations ... Revis'd by I. Senex
mwuk0982	england	1721	SENEX	785	50	60	A New Map of England; from the Latest Observations, by Iohn Senex
mwe0136	europe	1720	SENEX	785	48	57	A New Map of Europe from the Latest Observations
mwe0154	europe	1738	SENEX	1200	49	58	A New Map of Europe from the Latest Observations with Mr. Whiston's Delineation of the Paths of the Centers of VIII Famous Eclipses of the Sun: and the Breadths of their Total Shadows & Annular Penumbrae
mwf0110	france	1721	SENEX	450	41	58	A New Map of France Agreeable to the Observations of the Royal Academy of Paris
mwf0106	france	1719	SENEX	500	51	58	A New Map of France, Shewing the Roads & Post Stages Thro:out that Kingdom, as also the Errors of Sanson's Map Compared wth ye Survey Made by Order of ye Late French King (inset; part of Catalonia)
mwas0449	asia south east	1720	SENEX	1200	50	59	A New Map of India & China from the Latest Observations by J. Senex
mwuk0147	ireland	1720	SENEX	750	58	49	A New Map of Ireland from the Latest Observations by John Senex
mwit0142	italy	1708	SENEX	1200	65	94	A New Map of Italy
mwf1151	france rhone-alpes	1721	SENEX	600	56	42	A New Map of Savoy and Piedmont
mwuk0465	scotland	1721	SENEX	785	56	47	A New Map of Scotland According to Gordon of Straloch (re-issue of Browne's map of 1708)
mwbh0589	belgium holland	1720	SENEX	1200	50	59	A New Map of the City of Amsterdam
mwwi0708	jamaica	1721	SENEX	750	51	61	A New Map of the English Empire in the Ocean of America or West Indies (7 maps on one sheet)
mwit0932	italy sicily	1721	SENEX	750	48	57	A New Map of the Island and Kingdom of Sicily (inset of Malta)
mwsc0350	scandinavia denmark	1721	SENEX	675	49	56	A New Map of the Kingdom of Denmark with the Duchy of Holstein
mwe0930	europe hungary	1725	SENEX	900	65	95	A New Map of the Kingdom of Hungary and of the Countries, Provinces &c. Bordering thereupon; with their Respective Bannats, Countries, Sanjiacships, Mountains, Passes, Post Roads, Cities &c.
mwru0186	russia	1740	SENEX	1200	57	72	A New Map of the Seat of War between ye Moscovite and the Turk
mww0344a	world	1721	SENEX	3200	42	52	A New Map of the World from the Latest Observations
mwam0919	america north (east)	1719	SENEX	4200	48	55	A New Map of Virginia Mary:Land and the Improved Parts of Pennsylvania & New Jersey. Most Humbly Inscrib'd to the Right Hon. the Earl of Orkney ... 1719 Revised by I. Senex

AMPG REFERENCE	REGION	DATE	MAP MAKER	PRICE (UK£)	VERT. (cm.)	HOR. (cm.)	TITLE OF MAP (Comments by the editor in brackets)
mwuss1629	virginia	1719	SENEX	4200	48	55	A New Map of Virginia Mary:Land and the Improved Parts of Pennsylvania & New Jersey. Most Humbly Inscrib'd to the Right Hon. the Earl of Orkney ... 1719 Revised by I. Senex
mwm0055	mediterranean	1738	SENEX	5000	52	58	A New Map, or Chart of the Mediterranean Sea (in 3 sheets, each 52x58cm. Insets: 9 harbours)
mwit0740	italy rome	1721	SENEX	1200	49	58	A New Mapp of Rome Shewing its Antient and Present Situation
mwas0128a	asia continent	1721	SENEX	4000	49	59	A New Plaine and Exact Map of Asia Described by N. I. Vischer and Rendered into English ... (4 carte-a-figure borders. Based on Visscher 1652. See also Overton 1671)
mwe0558	europe czech republic (bohemia)	1720	SENEX	400	30	37	A Plan of the City of Prague with the French Camp, and the Disposition of the Austrian Army to Attack the Same in their Trenches
mwaf0151	africa	1720	SENEX	1800	67	94	Africa Corrected from the Observations of the Royal Society of London & Paris
mwas0115	asia continent	1714	SENEX	1200	64	93	Asia Corrected from the Observation Communicated to the Royal Society at London and the Royal Academy at Paris
mwas0317a	asia caspian sea	1732	SENEX	650	52	62	Charta, in qua eruditis spectanda exhibetur pars Asiae (map surrounded by text)
mwsc0339	scandinavia denmark	1714	SENEX	875	66	97	Denmark Corrected from the Newest Observations of the Royal Societies at London and Paris
mwe0123	europe	1708	SENEX	1200	64	94	Europe Corrected from the Observations Communicated to the Royal Society at London
mwg0115	germany	1725	SENEX	650	65	96	Germany
mwe0917a	europe hungary	1709	SENEX	1000	64	94	Hungary
mwuk0138	ireland	1712	SENEX	1350	97	67	Ireland Corrected from the Latest Observations Divided into its Provinces, Counties & Baronies. Shewing the Principal Roads, and the Distances of Places, in Common Reputed Miles, by Inspection, where Barracks are Erected &c. (copied from Price's map of 1711)
mwit0153	italy	1719	SENEX	650	48	55	Italy Distinguished According to the Extent of All the States, Kingdomes, Republicks, Dukedoms, Principalities &c. and All that do at Present Divide it. Revised by I. Senex, 1719
mwru0149	russia	1721	SENEX	450	60	50	Moscovey in Europe
mwru0132	russia	1712	SENEX	650	95	64	Moscovy Corrected from ye Observations Communicated to the Royal Society of London and Paris
mwam0367	america north	1711	SENEX	3500	96	65	North America Corrected from the Observations Communicated to the Royal Society
mwbp0370	poland	1719	SENEX	785	48	54	Poland and other the Countries Belonging to that Crowne According to the Newest Observations 1719 Revised by I. Senex
mwbp0381	poland	1720	SENEX	875	65	95	Poland Corrected from the Observations Communicated to the Royal Society of London and the Royal Academy at Paris
mwsc0119	scandinavia	1719	SENEX	785	48	55	Scandinavia and its Confines in which are the Kingdom's of Sweden, Norway &c.
mwsam0050	south america	1710	SENEX	950	97	65	South America Corrected from the Observations Communicated to the Royal Society's of London & Paris
mwsp0254	spain	1721	SENEX	600	49	56	Spain and Portugall Distinguish't into their Kingdoms and Principalities &c.
mwsc0715	scandinavia sweden	1725	SENEX	960	95	67	Sweden Corrected from the Observations Communicated to the Royal Society at London and the Royal Academy at Paris. By John Senex F.R.S.
mwsw0119	switzerland	1721	SENEX	960	54	41	Switzerland and the Country of the Grisons
mwbh0593	belgium holland	1721	SENEX	960	46	55	The Dutch Netherlands or the Seven United Provinces Commonly Called Holland ... Revis'd by Ion. Senex
mwg0112	germany	1721	SENEX	400	42	54	The Empire of Germany
mwbh0594	belgium holland	1721	SENEX	480	41	54	The Spanish Netherlands Commonly Called Flanders ... 1719
mwbh0537b	belgium holland	1709	SENEX	1200	64	94	The VII United Provinces
mwe1150	europe south east	1721	SENEX	650	96	68	Turky in Europe, corrected
mwme0283	holy land	1725	SENEX & TAYLOR	960	44	29	Sacred Geography, Contained in Six Maps (set of 6 maps, each 44x29cm)
mwg0521	rheinland-pfalz	1680	SENGRE	480	42	59	Estats Situes pres du Rhin & du Mein / Estats Situes pres & sur le Rhin & le Necre (2 maps, each 42x59cm)
mwru0250	russia	1774	SERGEEV	1000	41	59	Vorstellung des Plans von Astrachan
mwam1267	america north (east)	1850	SERZ	1500	54	74	Neueste Eisenbahn-Kanal-u. Post-Karte fur Reisende in den Vereinigten Staaten von Nord-Amerika Canada, Texas u. Californien
mwg0645	saxony	1740	SEUTTER	800	47	58	(Leipzig) Lipsia, florentissimum ac permumitium et Academia celeberrima
mwam0942	america north (east)	1740	SEUTTER	2600	49	57	Accurata Delineatio Celeberrimae Regionis Ludovicianae vel Gallice Louisiane ol. Canadae et Floridae Adpellatione in Septemtrionali America Descriptae quae Hodie Nomine Fluminis Mississipi vel St. Louis

AMPG REFERENCE	REGION	DATE	MAP MAKER	PRICE (UK£)	VERT. (cm.)	HOR. (cm.)	TITLE OF MAP (Comments by the editor in brackets)
mwru0177	russia	1735	SEUTTER	1350	50	58	Accurata Delineatio Sinus Finnici Cronstadio Petropolin usque (inset: view of St. Petersburg. Title also in Russian.)
mwsp0700	gibraltar	1727	SEUTTER	675	50	58	Accurata Designatio Celebris Freti Prope Andalusiae Castellum Gibraltar
mwg0650	saxony	1747	SEUTTER	600	49	57	Accurata et Novissima Repraesentatio Ichnographica Hannoverae ... Haupt u: Residentz Stadt an der Leine Gelegen (plan and fortifications of Hanover)
mwg0372a	bavaria	1730	SEUTTER	600	49	58	Accurata recens delineata Ichnographia...Auspurg...
mwe0565	europe czech republic (bohemia)	1730	SEUTTER	800	49	57	Accurate abbildung der Statt Kayser Carlsbad
mwin0201	india	1745	SEUTTER	960	49	56	Accurater Geographischer Entwurf der ... Stadt und Vestung Trankenbar
mwuk0802	uk	1720	SEUTTER	250	20	26	Accuratissima Angliae Scotiae et Hiberniae Tab.
mwg0646a	saxony	1740	SEUTTER	600	49	58	Accuratissima Delineatio Geographica Dioecesis ac Praefecturae Dresdensis
mwaf0509	africa egypt etc	1740	SEUTTER	550	56	47	Aegypta Hodierna (copy of Homann 1720)
mwaf0167	africa	1730	SEUTTER	900	50	57	Africa iuxta Navigationes et Observationes Recentissimas Aucta, Correcta et in sua Regna et Status Divisa in Lucem Edita
mwaf0178	africa	1740	SEUTTER	300	20	26	Africa juxta Navigationes et Observationes Recentissimas Aucta, Correcta et in sua Regna et Status Divisa in Lucem Edita
mwaf0712	africa north	1730	SEUTTER	350	49	58	Africae Magna Pars as Illustrationem Historiae Ecclesiasticae Imprimis Faciens (from Morocco to Tripoli)
mwaf0744	africa north algeria	1730	SEUTTER	600	50	56	Algercurm Munita Metropolis Regni Algeriani in Littore Africano Barbariae
mwf0242	france alsace	1735	SEUTTER	1400	60	176	Alsatia Superioribus et Interior III. Tabulis Delineata
mwsam0065	south america	1744	SEUTTER	300	19	25	America Meridionalis per sua Regna Provinc: et Ins: juxta Observation: et Descript Recentis: Divisa et Adornata Cura et Opera Matth: Seutter
mwru0530	ukraine	1742	SEUTTER	875	50	58	Amplissima Ucraniae Regio, Palatinatus Kioviensem et Braclaviensem
mwbh0647	belgium holland	1740	SEUTTER	1200	49	57	Amsterdam die Weltberuhmte Haupt- und Handel Statt in Holland
mwe0357b	europe austria	1730	SEUTTER	375	49	57	Archiducatus Austriae Inferioris (shown above left)
mwas0146	asia continent	1740	SEUTTER	750	49	57	Asia cum Omnibus Imperiis Provinciis Statibus et Insulis
mwsp0535	spain regions	1730	SEUTTER	1350	50	57	Barcino Metropolis Hispanici Principatus Cataloniae - Barcellona die Haupt Statt des Spanischen Furstenthums Catalonien (titles above map)
mwbh0615	belgium holland	1730	SEUTTER	785	50	57	Belgium Foederatum (inset: south east asia)
mwe1072	europe serbia	1735	SEUTTER	1100	49	57	Belgradum sive Alba Graeca
mwg0237	berlin	1737	SEUTTER	1650	50	57	Berlin die praechtigst u: maechtigste Haupstatt
mwe0564	europe czech republic (bohemia)	1730	SEUTTER	400	49	57	Bohemia Regnum
mwe0583a	europe czech republic (bohemia)	1744	SEUTTER	200	19	26	Bohemiae Regnum accuratiss (close copy of Le Rouge 1742)
mwbp0388	poland	1725	SEUTTER	650	49	57	Borussiae Regnum (inset: Neufchatel)
mwbp0422b	poland	1740	SEUTTER	235	20	26	Borussiae Regnum (shown above)
mwbh0590	belgium holland	1720	SEUTTER	320	57	50	Brabantiae Ducatus cum Adjacentibus Provinciis Studio et Impensis
mwuk0988	england	1735	SEUTTER	720	57	49	Britanniae sive Angliae Regnum
mwbh0616	belgium holland	1730	SEUTTER	1000	48	56	Bruxeliae Belgii Cathol. Ornamentum et Ducatus Brabantiae Metropolis
mwru0197a	russia	1745	SEUTTER	4000	50	58	"Canalis Ladogensis" - "Accurata delineatio Sinus Finnici" - "Fluvius Newa e lacu Ladoga Petropolin versus procurrens" (illustrated) - "Conspectus recens et accuratus magnae partis Lacus Ladogae et Sinus Finnici" (set of 4 maps, based on Grimmel, 1741. Titles also in Russian.)
mwsw0156	switzerland	1760	SEUTTER	400	50	58	Canton ... Respublica Lucernensis
mwe0358	europe austria	1730	SEUTTER	480	49	58	Carinthia Ducatus (illustration shows Lotter 1760 re-issue)
mwsw0145	switzerland	1745	SEUTTER	600	49	57	Carte de la Souverainete de Neuchatel et Vallangin
mwsp0661	balearic islands	1741	SEUTTER	650	48	57	Carte des Isles de Maiorque Minorque et d'Yvice (based on Bellin)
mwsp0543	spain regions	1734	SEUTTER	650	50	58	Cataloniae Principatus et Ruscinonis ac Cerretaniae Comitatuum
mwin0043	ceylon	1730	SEUTTER	750	49	57	Ceylon olim Taprobana
mwru0514	ukraine	1736	SEUTTER	900	53	63	Charte der Kriegs Operationen am Donn u. Dnieper (map surrounded on 3 sides by text)
mwe1023	europe rhine	1734	SEUTTER	850	49	114	Charte Geographique de la Campagne du Haut Rhin
mwg0382	bavaria	1746	SEUTTER	450	57	49	Circulus Bavariae
mwe0361	europe austria	1740	SEUTTER	720	48	56	Clagenfurtum Ducatus Carinthiae Metropolis - Clagenfurt die Haupt Stadt des Herzogthums Karnthen
mwme0998	turkey etc	1730	SEUTTER	2000	49	57	Constantinopolis Amplissima, Potentissima, et Magnificentissima - Constantinopel, die grossest, machtigst u. Prachtigste Residenz Stadt des Turck. Kaysers

AMPG REFERENCE	REGION	DATE	MAP MAKER	PRICE (UK£)	VERT. (cm.)	HOR. (cm.)	TITLE OF MAP (Comments by the editor in brackets)
mwsc0359	scandinavia denmark	1740	SEUTTER	800	49	57	Coppenhagen die Konigl. Danische Haupt und Residenz Stadt / Plan de Coppenhague (illustrated is Lotter 1772 re-issue)
mwit0510a	italy lombardy	1730	SEUTTER	1800	57	130	Cursus Padi per Longobardiam a Fonte usque ad Ostia (in 3 sheets joined)
mwsc0367	scandinavia denmark	1750	SEUTTER	550	50	58	Daniae Regnum cum Ducatu Holsatiae et Slesvici, nec non Insulae Danicae, et Iutia cum Parte Scaniae
mwbp0399	poland	1730	SEUTTER	875	48	56	Dantiscum s. Gedanum ... in Polonia Borussica in Provincia Pomerellia Sita - Dantzig eine Beruhmte
mwbp0422	poland	1740	SEUTTER	800	49	57	Dantzig eine berühmte, sehr grosse auch seste Handel ư Hansee=Statt
mwg0372	bavaria	1730	SEUTTER	720	49	58	Das Nurenbergische Gebiet mit Allen Nurnbergischen Hauptmannschafften
mwuk1167	england london	1734	SEUTTER	600	50	57	Delineatio ac Finitima Regio Magnae Britanniae Metropoleos Londini
mwsw0140	switzerland	1740	SEUTTER	600	50	59	Delineatio Pagi Tigurini (environs of Zurich)
mwsc0728	scandinavia sweden	1740	SEUTTER	450	49	58	Descriptio Nova et Accurata Scaniae Blekingae et Hallandiae
mwme0302	holy land	1740	SEUTTER	650	50	58	Deserta Aegypti, Thebaidis, Arabiae, Syriae, etc. ubi Accurate Notata sunt Loca Inhabita per Sanctos Patres Anachoretas (based on Michalet 1693)
mwe0362	europe austria	1740	SEUTTER	480	49	57	Die vornehmste Prospect Der weltberühmten... Statt Salzburg (title also in Latin)
mwsw0132	switzerland	1730	SEUTTER	500	49	57	Ditionis pagi Scaphusiani (Schaffhausen)
mww0377	world	1740	SEUTTER	800	21	26	Diversi Globi Terr-Aquei Statione Variante Et Visu Intercedente Pe Coluros Tropicorum
mww0378	world	1740	SEUTTER	3600	49	57	Diversi Globi Terr-Aquei Statione Variante et Visu Intercedente
mwit1198a	italy veneto	1740	SEUTTER	675	48	56	Dominium Venetum cum Adjacentibus Mediolan. Mantuano, Mutinensi, Mirandolano, Parmensi, Placentino Ducatibus
mwg0646	saxony	1740	SEUTTER	850	49	56	Dresda ad Albim, Saxoniae Superioris Metropolis - Dresden an der Elb, eine Haupt-Statt des Obern Sachsen
mwbh0866	luxembourg	1740	SEUTTER	675	51	59	Ducatus Luxemburg Distinctis Limitibus Majorum et Minorum Ditionum Exacte Designatus et in Lucem Editus
mwit0513	italy lombardy	1740	SEUTTER	600	50	58	Ducatus Mantuani
mwit0606a	italy north	1740	SEUTTER	400	49	56	Ducatus Mediolanensis
mwbp0470	poland	1760	SEUTTER	2500	95	167	Ducatus Pomeraniae Citerioris et Ulterioris ... Nova et Ampla Descriptio Geographica
mwf0787	france normandy	1730	SEUTTER	750	50	59	Duche et Gouvernem. General de Normandie Divise en Haut et Bas en Divers Pays et Bailliages avec le Gouvernement General de Havre de Grace (inset: Channel Isl.)
mwe0426	europe austria vienna	1740	SEUTTER	785	57	49	Eigentlich und Neuester Prospect der Kayserl. Residenz Stadt Wien (10 plans on one sheet)
mwg0239a	berlin	1750	SEUTTER	2500	50	112	Eigentliche Abbildung und Prospecte ... Berlin
mwg0641a	saxony	1730	SEUTTER	300	57	49	Electoratus Hanoverani
mwe0147	europe	1730	SEUTTER	600	50	58	Europa Religionis Christianae Morum et Pacis ac Belli Artium Cultu Omnium Terrarum Orbis Partium Praestantiss
mwe0502	europe croatia	1740	SEUTTER	480	49	57	Exactissima Ducatus Carniolae ...
mwit1134	italy florence	1730	SEUTTER	1500	48	56	Firenza la Capitale di Toscana - Florenz die Haupt Statt in Toscana
mwg0456a	hessen	1740	SEUTTER	900	49	57	Francofurtum - Franckfurt am Mayn
mwbh0648	belgium holland	1740	SEUTTER	450	49	57	Germaniae inferioris sive Belgii pars meridionalis
mwf0351	france brittany	1740	SEUTTER	600	49	58	Gouvernement General de Bretagne
mwgr0183	greece	1740	SEUTTER	400	50	56	Graecia Nova et Mare Aegeum ... Macedonia, Albania, Epiris, Thessalia et Morea (illustrated is the Lotter re-issue)
mwg0726	schleswig-holstein	1740	SEUTTER	1350	50	58	Hamburgum Celeberrima Libera Imperii et Hanseatica Civitas ac Opulentissimum Emporium, circa Ostium Albis ad Mare Septentr.
mwsp0277	spain	1758	SEUTTER	400	48	55	Hispania Augustiniana
mwsp0257	spain	1730	SEUTTER	550	49	62	Hispania ex Archetypo Roderici Mendez Sylvae et Variis Relationibus ... Per Guill. De L'Isle
mwsc0724a	scandinavia sweden	1735	SEUTTER	1600	49	56	Holmia Celeberrima Metropolis et Sedes Regia Regni Sueciae - Stockholm die Vortreffliche Haupt und Residenz Stadt des Konig Reichs Schweden
mwg0119a	germany	1730	SEUTTER	500	49	57	Hydrographica Germaniae (Shown above left. See also Homann 1720)
mwru0517	ukraine	1737	SEUTTER	400	51	58	Ichnographia Munitissimae Arcis Otzakoff
mwme0498	jerusalem	1740	SEUTTER	850	58	50	Ierusalem, cum Suburbiis, Prout Tempore Christi Floruit / Abriss der Weltberuhmten Statt Ierusalem
mwin0202	india	1745	SEUTTER	600	50	57	Imperii Magni Mogolis sive Indici Padschach
mwjk0094	japan	1740	SEUTTER	1500	49	58	Imperium Japonicum per Sexaginta et Sex Regiones Digestum atque ex Ipsorum Japonensium Mappis Descriptum (close copy of Reland 1715)
mwru0198	russia	1745	SEUTTER	280	20	26	Imperium Russiae Magnae

AMPG REFERENCE	REGION	DATE	MAP MAKER	PRICE (UK£)	VERT. (cm.)	HOR. (cm.)	TITLE OF MAP (Comments by the editor in brackets)
mwme0613	arabia etc	1730	SEUTTER	550	55	47	Imperium Turcicum per Europam, Asiam, et Africam. (Incl. two genealogical trees: Ottoman Sultans and Tsars of Russia)
mwas0459	asia south east	1740	SEUTTER	1350	48	57	India Orientalis, cum Adjacentibus Insulis Nova Delineatione ob Oculos Posita
mwf0483	france corsica	1730	SEUTTER	1500	57	49	Insula Corsica olim Regni Titulo Insignis
mwgr0427	greece crete	1730	SEUTTER	1100	49	58	Insula Creta nunc Candia
mwit0811	italy sardinia	1740	SEUTTER	800	58	50	Insula et Regnum Sardiniae
mwit0155	italy	1720	SEUTTER	400	49	58	Italia Augustiniana in suas Provinces una cum Conventibus Distributa
mwit0171	italy	1740	SEUTTER	500	47	55	Italiae Antiquae item Insularum Siciliae
mwe1071	europe serbia	1730	SEUTTER	550	50	58	Iustissimae Causae … Accurata delineatio Provinciarum …. (environs of Belgrade)
mwuk1534	uk english channel (east)	1730	SEUTTER	720	50	57	La Plus Grande Partie de la Manche, qui Contient les Cotes d'Angleterre et celles de France les Bords Maritimes de Picardie (re-issued by Lotter 1760)
mwg0283a	baden-wurttemberg	1741	SEUTTER	1000	49	57	Lacus Bodamicus vel Acronius cum regionibus circumjacentibus recens delineatus à Matthaeo Seuttero
mwsam0062	south america	1740	SEUTTER	785	50	58	Le Pays de Perou et Chili (Spanish South America i.e. excl. Brazil)
mwf0867	france paris	1740	SEUTTER	960	50	58	Le Plan de Paris, ses Faubourgs et ses Environs
mwf0117	france	1734	SEUTTER	480	48	56	Gallia Concinnata ad magnum numerum mapparum particularum manuscriptarum
mwf0982	france poitou	1750	SEUTTER	550	49	55	Les Environs de Rochelle et Rochefort avec les Isles d'Oleron et de Re
mwf0115	france	1730	SEUTTER	450	46	58	Les Routes Exactes des Postes du Royaume de France
mwsp0085	portugal	1730	SEUTTER	1350	49	58	Lisabona Magnificentisima Regia Sedes Portugalliae
mwit0164	italy	1730	SEUTTER	550	49	57	L'Italia con le sue Poste e Strade Principali Descritta da Giacomo Cantelli da Vignola
mwbp0121	baltic states	1740	SEUTTER	785	48	56	Livoniae et Curlandiae Ducatus cum Insulis Adjacentib.
mwit0430	italy liguria	1730	SEUTTER	1350	49	58	Lo Stato della Repubblica di Genova (shown left is the revised edition with title 'Reipublicae Genuensis Dominium'. See also Lotter 1770)
mwuk1164	england london	1730	SEUTTER	2000	50	57	Londinum Celeberrima Metropolis, Splendissima Regia et Opulentissimum Angliae Emporium, Accuratissime Delineata
mwbh0858	luxembourg	1730	SEUTTER	1600	49	57	Luxembourg, une Fortresse tres-celebre de la Duche de cette Nom
mwsp0345	spain madrid	1730	SEUTTER	1200	50	58	Madritum sive Mantua Carpetanorum Celeberrima Castiliae Novae Civitas - Madrit la Plus Celebre Ville dans la Castille Nouvelle (illustrated is the Lotter re-issue of c1744)
mwsc0431	scandinavia finland	1740	SEUTTER	1350	49	57	Magni Ducatus Finlandiae Russiae Partim, Partim Sueciae Subjecti, Sinus Item Bothnici ac Finnici Nova et Accurata Delineatio (see also Lotter 1758)
mwme0612	arabia etc	1730	SEUTTER	875	50	58	Magni Turcarum Dominatoris Imperium per Europam, Asiam, et Africam
mwe0357a	europe austria	1730	SEUTTER	480	49	58	Maiestas Austriaca
mwit0510	italy lombardy	1730	SEUTTER	1200	48	57	Mantua la Citta Principale et Fortezza Incomparabile, del Ducato Medesino in Italia - Mantua, die Haupt-Stadt u. Unvergleichliche Festung
mwsw0134	switzerland	1730	SEUTTER	600	49	57	Mappa Geographica illustris Helvetiorum Reipublicae Bernensis
mwg0119	germany	1730	SEUTTER	550	49	57	Mappa Geographica indicans … bello tricenalli
mwgm0030a	gulf of mexico and surrounding regions	1740	SEUTTER	1650	49	58	Mappa Geographica Regionem Mexicanam et Floridam Terrasque Adjacentes, ut et Anteriores Americae Insulas Cursus Itidem et Reditus Navigantium versus Flumen Missisipi et Alias Colonias
mwe0563	europe czech republic (bohemia)	1730	SEUTTER	400	49	57	Mappa Geographica Regnum Bohemiae cum Adiunctis Ducatu Silesiae et Marcionatib. Moraviae et Lusatiae Repraesentans
mwru0164	russia	1730	SEUTTER	450	50	58	Mappae Imperii Moscovitici Pars Septentrionalis / Imperii Moscovitici Pars Australis (2 sheets, each 50x58cm)
mwg0214	germany north east	1740	SEUTTER	650	49	56	Marchia sive Electoratus Brandenburgicus nec non Ducatus Pomeraniae
mwg0417	brandenburg	1740	SEUTTER	480	49	56	Marchionatus Brandenburgensis
mwe1115	europe slovak republic (moravia)	1744	SEUTTER	180	19	25	Marchionatus Moravia Accurate Designatus
mwm0276	mediterranean west	1730	SEUTTER	400	51	58	Mare Mediterraneum, juxta Regna et Provincias, quas Alluit Distinctum et Cognominatum (Gibraltar to Greece)
mwe1021a	europe rhine	1730	SEUTTER	400	57	49	Martis Area et Alea per Tractum Rheni, Mosellae, ac Mosae
mwm0237	mediterranean malta	1740	SEUTTER	1800	50	57	Melite vulgo Malta cum Vicinis Goza, quae olim Gaulos, et Comino Insulis

AMPG REFERENCE	REGION	DATE	MAP MAKER	PRICE (UK£)	VERT. (cm.)	HOR. (cm.)	TITLE OF MAP (Comments by the editor in brackets)
mwit0544	italy milan	1740	SEUTTER	2000	50	57	Milano, la Citta Principale et Fortezza Reale del Ducato Medesimo in Italia - Mailand, die Haupt-Statt und Real Festung
mwit0937	italy sicily	1730	SEUTTER	1350	48	57	Milazzo, olim Mylae Munitissimum Siciliae Castellum adversus Hispanos
mwg0536	rheinland-pfalz	1740	SEUTTER	720	50	58	Moguntia - Mayntz
mwe1112	europe slovak republic (moravia)	1730	SEUTTER	500	50	59	Moravia Marchionatus in Sex Circulos Divisus (inset view of Brno)
mwru0167a	russia	1730	SEUTTER	500	42	54	Moscoviae seu Russiae Magnae Generalis Tabula (shown above left)
mwg0377	bavaria	1740	SEUTTER	950	49	57	Munchen, die weit beruhmt ... Haupt u: Residenz Stadt
mwme0999	turkey etc	1730	SEUTTER	600	47	54	Natoliae, olim Asiae Minoris Tabula
mwit1032	italy south	1730	SEUTTER	400	58	50	Neapolis Regnum quo Continentur Aprutium Ulterius et Citerius
mwit1064	italy naples	1740	SEUTTER	1200	49	58	Neapolis, Regni hujus maxima, ornatissima
mwe1072c	europe serbia	1745	SEUTTER	200	19	26	Neu und verbessertes Ungarisches Kriegs-Theatrum in Servien und dem Bannat Temesvar
mwbh0733a	belgium holland	1780	SEUTTER	2000	48	57	Nouveau et exact dessein de la Ville de Gent ... 1780 (Map made in conjunction with Probst, copied from Hondius?)
mwam0391	america north	1744	SEUTTER	550	20	26	Nov. Orbis sive America Septentrionalis. Divisa per sua Regna Provinc: et Insul: Cura et Opera
mwwi0709	jamaica	1730	SEUTTER	800	50	56	Nova Designatio Insulae Jamaicae ex Antillanis Americae Septentrion
mwe0685	europe dalmatia	1740	SEUTTER	480	50	57	Nova et Accurata Dalmatiae, Croatiae, Sclavoniae, Bosniae
mwru0187	russia	1740	SEUTTER	1100	58	50	Nova et Accurata Delineatio Ingriae et Careliae cum Magna Parte Sinus Finnici et Lacus Ladogae, nec non Insularum Adjacentium
mwbp0422a	poland	1740	SEUTTER	500	49	58	Nova et accurata Geographica Delineatio Ducatus Teschenensis
mwe0941	europe hungary	1740	SEUTTER	550	50	57	Nova et accurata Hungariae
mwru0528	ukraine	1740	SEUTTER	750	49	57	Nova et Accurata Tartariae Europaeae seu Minoris
mwuk0479	scotland	1740	SEUTTER	875	58	49	Nova et Accurata Totius Regni Scotiae
mwru0531	ukraine	1744	SEUTTER	200	19	25	Nova et Accurata Turcicarum et Tartaricum
mwru0165	russia	1730	SEUTTER	2000	48	56	Nova et Accuratissima Urbis St. Petersburg - Neue u. Accurate Abbildung der ... Ao 1703 Erbaueten Statt St. Petersburg (copy of Ottens 1725)
mwgr0325	greece corfu	1740	SEUTTER	2000	49	56	Nova et Exactissima Geographica Delineatio Insulae Corfu
mwit0166	italy	1730	SEUTTER	650	50	57	Nova et Exactissima Totius Italiae, Sardiniae et Corsicae Delineatio
mwme0819	persia etc	1740	SEUTTER	675	49	58	Nova Imperii Persici Delineatio
mwru0166	russia	1730	SEUTTER	650	48	57	Nova Mappa Geographica Maris Assoviensis vel de Zabache, et Paludis Maeotidis (Asov Sea)
mwsc0725	scandinavia sweden	1735	SEUTTER	550	49	56	Nova Mappa Geographica Sueciae ac Gothiae Regna ut et Finlandiae Ducatum ac Lapponiam
mwru0511	ukraine	1730	SEUTTER	500	49	57	Nova Mappa Maris Nigri et Freti Constantinopolitani
mwsw0139	switzerland	1740	SEUTTER	240	20	25	Nova Totius Helvetiae
mwsw0131	switzerland	1730	SEUTTER	720	49	57	Nova Totius Helvetiae cum suis Subditis
mwit0173	italy	1740	SEUTTER	550	49	57	Nova Totius Italiae cum Adjacentibus Majoribus et Minoribus Insulis
mwit1121	italy tuscany	1740	SEUTTER	675	50	57	Novissima et Accuratior Tabella Magni Ducatus Hetruriae ... Florentinum Pisanum et Senense cum Insula Elba
mwit0313	italy central	1730	SEUTTER	550	47	56	Novissima et Accuratissima Delineatio Status Ecclesiae et Magni Ducatus Hetruriae
mwe0946	europe hungary	1745	SEUTTER	480	50	58	Novissima et accuratissima Hungariae
mwbp0119	baltic states	1731	SEUTTER	960	50	57	Novissima et Accuratissima Magni Ducatus Lithuaniae
mwsp0264	spain	1740	SEUTTER	600	49	57	Novissima et Accuratissima Regnorum Hispaniae et Portugalliae (copy of Schenk 1706)
mwbh0617	belgium holland	1730	SEUTTER	800	50	58	Novissima Ichnographica Delineatio Munitissimae Urbis et Celeberrimi Emporii Ostendae, in Comitatu Flandriae Austriacae Sitae, Cur et Coela Matthaei Seutteri
mwam0152	america continent	1740	SEUTTER	1600	48	57	Novus Orbis sive America Meridionalis et Septentrionalis, per sua Regna, Provincias, et Insulas iuxta Observationes et Descriptiones Recentiss. Divisa et Adornata
mwme0814a	persia etc	1730	SEUTTER	600	50	58	Opulentissimi Regni Persiae (shown above left)
mwc0136	china	1744	SEUTTER	960	50	58	Opulentissimum Sinarum Imperium
mwaf0749	africa north algeria	1740	SEUTTER	500	48	54	Oran Munita Urbs et Comodus Porta in Ora Maritima Barbariae
mwsw0132a	switzerland	1730	SEUTTER	500	49	57	Pagi Basileensis qui Pars est Reipublicae Helvetiorum cum Adjacentibus Terrarum Tractibus
mwsw0157	switzerland	1760	SEUTTER	600	50	57	Pagus Helvetiae Abbatiscellanus cum Comunitatibus Interioribus et Exterioribus, ac Adjacente Valle Rhenana Accurate Delineatus
mwsw0141	switzerland	1740	SEUTTER	600	57	50	Pagus Helvetiae Glaronensis cum Satrapia Werdenberg
mwsw0154	switzerland	1757	SEUTTER	500	50	58	Pagus Helvetiae Suitensis
mwsw0133	switzerland	1730	SEUTTER	600	57	50	Pagus Helvetiae Uriensis

AMPG REFERENCE	REGION	DATE	MAP MAKER	PRICE (UK£)	VERT. (cm.)	HOR. (cm.)	TITLE OF MAP (Comments by the editor in brackets)
mwme0308	holy land	1741	SEUTTER	675	50	57	Palaestinae Accurata Descriptio Geographica, ita Adornata, ut Diversarum Aetatum Regna
mwsam0712	south america paraguay	1730	SEUTTER	650	59	50	Paraquariae Provinciae Soc. Iesu cum Adjacentibus Novissima Descriptio
mwca0066	canada	1740	SEUTTER	1500	57	49	Partie Orientale de la Nouvelle France ou du Canada avec l'Isle de Terre-Neuve et de Nouvelle Escosse, Acadie et Nouv. Angleterre avec Fleuve de St Laurence (re-issued by Lotter)
mwgr0180	greece	1730	SEUTTER	500	49	57	Peloponnesus hodie Morea
mwme1000	turkey etc	1730	SEUTTER	2000	49	56	Plan de Constantinople de son Port Canal et Environs (copied from Leopold c1720)
mwbh0615a	belgium holland	1730	SEUTTER	1500	50	58	Plan de la Ville et Citadelle d'Anvers
mwg0538	rheinland-pfalz	1750	SEUTTER	850	46	54	Plan de Mayence
mwbh0642a	belgium holland	1740	SEUTTER	750	50	57	Plan du Project de Fortification sur la Ville de Maastrick et sur la Fortification de Wyck
mwsp0720	gibraltar	1760	SEUTTER	1200	49	57	Plan Tres Exact et Vue de la Ville, Baye, et des Nouvelles Fortifications de Gibraltar
mwuss0493	georgia	1747	SEUTTER	6000	58	50	Plan von Neu Ebenezer Verlegt von Matth. Seutter (incl. St. Simons and Jekyl's isl. and view / plan of mill)
mwbp0404	poland	1731	SEUTTER	675	50	58	Poloniae Regnum ut et Magni Ducatus Lithuaniae
mwsp0084	portugal	1725	SEUTTER	785	49	57	Portugalliae et Algarbiae Regna (inset: Brazil)
mwg0110	germany	1720	SEUTTER	480	48	56	Postarum seu Cursorum Publicorum ... Germanicam
mwg0641b	saxony	1730	SEUTTER	450	49	49	Praefectura Lipsiensis
mwe0562	europe czech republic (bohemia)	1730	SEUTTER	1350	49	57	Praga Celeberrima et Maxima Totius Bohemiae Metropolis et Universitatis Florentissima
mwe0360	europe austria	1740	SEUTTER	500	50	58	Principat. Et Archiepiscopatus Salisburgensis delineatio
mwme0491	jerusalem	1730	SEUTTER	1500	49	57	Prospectus Sanctae olim et Celeberrimae Urbis Hierosolymae
mwf1052	france provence	1728	SEUTTER	480	50	58	Provincia Gallis La Provence dicta
mwam0932	america north (east)	1730	SEUTTER	4500	51	59	Recens Edita Totius Novi Belgii, in America Septentrionali Siti, Delineatio Cura et Sumtibus Matthaei Seutteri (illustrated is Lotter 1760 re-issue)
mwsam0361	south america brazil	1735	SEUTTER	875	49	56	Recens Elaborata Mappa Geographica Regni Brasiliae in America Meridionali
mwg0820	westphalia	1725	SEUTTER	720	50	55	Recens et Accurata Designatio Episcopatus Paderbornensis
mwme0282	holy land	1725	SEUTTER	785	50	58	Regio Canaan seu Terra Promissionis Postea Judaea vel Palaestina Nominata Hodie Terra Sancta
mwe0945	europe hungary	1744	SEUTTER	180	20	26	Regni Hungariae Delineatio Studio
mwjk0085	japan	1730	SEUTTER	3000	48	55	Regni Japoniae Nova Mappa Geographica
mwe0583	europe czech republic (bohemia)	1744	SEUTTER	200	19	25	Regnum Bohemiae cum Adiunctis Ducatu Silesiae et Marchionat: Moraviae et Lusatiae
mwuk0158	ireland	1735	SEUTTER	850	58	50	Regnum Hiberniae, tam Secundum IV Provincias Principales Ultoniam, Connaciam, Lageniam, Momoniam
mwsc0617	scandinavia norway	1731	SEUTTER	650	58	51	Regnum Norwegiae Accurata et Novissima Delineatione juxta V. Praefecturas Generales Aggerhusiensem, Bergensem, Nidrosiens, Wardhusiens, et Bahus
mwwi0770	martinique	1728	SEUTTER	960	49	56	Representation la plus nouvelle et exacte de l'Ile Martinique, la Premiere des Iles de l'Amerique Antilles
mwsw0142	switzerland	1740	SEUTTER	600	49	57	Rhaetiae Foederata cum confinibus et Subditis suis Valle Tellina, Comitatu Clavennensis et Bormiensi
mwbh0699	belgium holland	1750	SEUTTER	1200	49	57	Roterodami Delineatio
mwg0647	saxony	1740	SEUTTER	500	37	49	Saxoniae Inferioris Circulus (left is shown the lotter 1761 version)
mwit0949	italy sicily	1750	SEUTTER	300	21	27	Siciliae Regnum cum adiacente Insula Sardinia
mwit0939	italy sicily	1730	SEUTTER	960	49	58	Siciliae Regnum, cum Adjacente Insula Sardinia et Maxima Parte Regni Neapolitani Accuratissime Delineat. (insets of Catania and Messina. Issued later with a different cartouche)
mwbp0400	poland	1730	SEUTTER	600	50	58	Silesiae Ducatus tam Superior quam Inferior
mwru0167	russia	1730	SEUTTER	875	50	57	Spatiosissimum Imperium Russiae Magnae juxta Recentissimas Observationes Mappa Geographica (see also Lotter 1770)
mwe0360	europe austria	1740	SEUTTER	500	50	58	S.R.I. Principat. Et Archiepiscopatus Salisburgensis delineatio
mwbp0403	poland	1730	SEUTTER	1350	49	57	Stetinum Celeberrima et Munitissima Pomeraniae Citerioris Metropolis ac Emporium Florentissimum - Stettin die Weitberuhmtest und Uberaus Feste Haupt Stadt
mwf0239b	france alsace	1740	SEUTTER	1000	49	57	Strasbourg, ville ancienne celebre et tres fortifiee (title also in German)
mwg0277	baden-wurttemberg	1730	SEUTTER	850	49	57	Stutgardia
mwg0278	baden-wurttemberg	1730	SEUTTER	3000	51	53	Suevia Universa IX. Tabulis Delineata (in 9 sheets, each 51x53cm)
mwsc0123	scandinavia	1720	SEUTTER	600	48	57	Synopsis Plagae Septentrionalis, sive Sueciae Daniae et Norwegiae Regn. (also issued with a different cartouche, as below)

AMPG REFERENCE	REGION	DATE	MAP MAKER	PRICE (UK£)	VERT. (cm.)	HOR. (cm.)	TITLE OF MAP (Comments by the editor in brackets)
mwbh0649	belgium holland	1740	SEUTTER	785	50	56	Tabula Comitatus Hollandiae ... cui Adjuncta est Provinc. Ultraiectina et Maxima Pars Geldriae Delin.
mwg0381	bavaria	1746	SEUTTER	550	50	58	Tabula Geographica Novissima Principalis Episcopatus Bambergensis
mwin0198	india	1740	SEUTTER	960	50	56	Tabula Ichnographica ... Trankenbar et castellum Danoburgum
mwg0641	saxony	1730	SEUTTER	300	50	58	Tabula Ichnographica Accuratissima Brunsuigae ... Accurate Ichnographische Vorstellung der Haupt-Stadt und Vestung Braunschweig nebst der um Dieselbe Liegenden Gegend
mwuk0803	uk	1720	SEUTTER	720	58	50	Tabula Novissima Accuratissima Regnorum Angliae, Scotiae Hiberniae
mwe0723	europe danube	1730	SEUTTER	1350	49	171	Tabula Synoptica Totius Fluminis Danubii a Fontibus usque ad Ostia ... et Pontus Euxinus
mwe1049a	europe romania	1740	SEUTTER	1250	51	59	Temeswaria Oppidum Superioris Hungariae
mwme0313	holy land	1744	SEUTTER	240	20	25	Terra Sancta Vocata, quae olim XII Tribus hoc Autem Aevo in VI Provinc.
mwg0456b	hessen	1740	SEUTTER	675	49	57	Territorium Sac. Rom. Imp. Lib. Civitatis Francofurti (shown above left)
mwit0599	italy north	1720	SEUTTER	875	55	89	Theatrum Belli per Italiam A. MDCCXXXIV. Recentissima et Accuratissima Designatio (9 inset maps, top and bottom. Additional page of fortification plans not included in size.)
mwru0519	ukraine	1739	SEUTTER	785	49	57	Theatrum Belli Russorum Victoriis Illustratum sive Nova et Accurata Turcicarum et Tartaricum
mwe1151	europe south east	1725	SEUTTER	580	50	58	Theatrum Belli sive Novissima Tabula qua Maxima Pars Danubii et Praesentim Hungaria ... nec non Graecia Morea et Archipelagi Insulae
mwru0197	russia	1744	SEUTTER	1350	50	58	Topographia Sedis Imperatoriae Moscovitarum Petropolis - Plan der Kayserl. Residentz Stadt St. Petersburg
mwbh0618	belgium holland	1730	SEUTTER	1200	50	58	Traiecti ad Rhenum Delineatio (Utrecht)
mwe1048	europe romania	1728	SEUTTER	400	50	57	Transylvaniae Principatus in Quinque Nationes Divisus
mwe0792a	europe east	1738	SEUTTER	550	49	58	Transylvaniae, Moldaviae, Walachiae, Bulgariae
mwit0682	italy piedmont	1740	SEUTTER	900	48	57	Turin Ville Superbe et Forte, la Capitale du Piemont - Turin die so Prachtig als Feste Haupt Statt in Piemont
mwe0424	europe austria vienna	1730	SEUTTER	480	47	53	Typus choro-topographicus ... urbis Viennae Austriacae
mwf0859	france paris	1730	SEUTTER	960	49	57	Typus Choro-Topographicus Regiae et Totius Orbis Celeberrimae Urbis Lutetiae Parisiorum
mwg0279	baden-wurttemberg	1730	SEUTTER	600	50	58	Ulm eine considerable Freye Reichs Statt in Schwaben
mwit1243	italy venice	1730	SEUTTER	2400	50	58	Venetia Potentissima – Venedig die Mächtig u. Prächtigst Florisant u Reicheste Haupt Stadt
mwit0743	italy rome	1740	SEUTTER	1600	50	57	Veteris et Modernae Urbis Romae Ichnographia et Accurata Designatio
mwe0423	europe austria vienna	1730	SEUTTER	875	49	57	Vienna Metropolis Austriae Inferioris
mwe0425	europe austria vienna	1740	SEUTTER	800	50	58	Wien die Welt beruhmte Kayserl. Resid. Stadt
mwbp0401	poland	1730	SEUTTER	900	50	58	Wratislavia Antiquissima et Celeberrima Ducat. Silesiaci Metropolis - Breslau
mwbh0650	belgium holland	1740	SEUTTER	600	47	57	Zeelandiae Comitatus novißima et accuratißima delineatione (shown above left)
mwbh0651	belgium holland	1740	SEUTTER	480	50	58	XVII Provinciae Belgii sive Germaniae Inferioris
mwit0374	italy friuli	1760	SEUTTER-LOTTER	1800	49	54	Prospetto vero della citta di Trieste
mwm0021	mediterranean	1685	SEYFRIED	675	45	64	Entwurff derer dem Turckische Reich Unterworffenen Landen und daran Angranzenden Provincien
mww0208	world	1679	SEYFRIED	960	25	35	Tabula Geographico-Hydrographica. Motus Oceani Currentes in Universo Orbe Indicans
mwp0167	australia	1848	SHARPE	250	32	42	Australia and New Zealand
mwam0604	america north	1816	SHELTON & KENSETT	20000	122	140	A Map of the United States and British Provinces of Upper and Lower Canada with other Parts Adjacent
mwam0592	america north	1813	SHELTON & KENSETT	2400	47	54	An Improved Map of the United States
mwca0203	canada	1846	SHERMAN & SMITH	3000	118	222	Map of the Provinces of Canada, New Brunswick, Nova Scotia, Newfoundland and Prince Edward Island, with a Large Section of the United States and Exhibiting the Boundary of the British Dominions in North America (revised edition of Bouchette 1831)
mwam1250	america north (east)	1845	SHERMAN & SMITH	8000	165	205	Map of the United States of America Including Canada and a Large Portion of Texas: Showing the Base Meridians and Township Lines of the U.S. Surveys
mwp0068	australia	1821	SHERWOOD	250	19	24	New Holland and its Dependencies (3 insets)
mwaa0044	antarctic	1809	SHERWOOD	200	25	20	Southern Hemisphere Corrected from the Latest Voyages
mwe1083	europe serbia	1810	SHROPP	900	72	133	Charte von Servien Bosnien und dem Grossten Theile von Illyrien
mwuk1313	england london	1832	SHURY	3500	55	80	Plan of London from Actual Survey (33 views of buildings forming ornamental borders. 8 editions to 1851)
mwit0764	italy rome	1832	SICKLER	600	56	87	Plan Topographique de la Campagne de Rome ... a l'Usage des Voyageurs
mwuss1261	new york	1849	SIDNEY	1500	84		Sidney's Map of Twelve Miles around New York, with Names of Property Owners (circular map)

AMPG REFERENCE	REGION	DATE	MAP MAKER	PRICE (UK£)	VERT. (cm.)	HOR. (cm.)	TITLE OF MAP (Comments by the editor in brackets)
mwme0515	jerusalem	1823	SIEBER	650	45	60	Karte von Jerusalem ... 1818
mwe0493a	europe croatia	1593	SIEBMACHER	1200	19	26	Croatia cum finitimis locis versus Turcarum ditionem (north to the right; shown below left)
mwe0265	europe	1831	SIEGMEYER	1600	131	154	Neue Poste und Reise Karte durch Gan Europa
mwgm0319	mexico	1831	SIGUENZA	375	16	21	Mapa de las Aguas que pr. el Circulo de 90. Leguas Vienen a la Laguna de Tesuco y la Ytencion qe esta y la de Chalco Tienen Deliniado pr. D. Carlos Zaguen (re-printed from a 17th century map by Siguenza)
mwf1010	france provence	1660	SILVESTRE	960	20	81	Massiliam hic cernimus gimnasio (view of Marseille)
mwec0034	uk england berkshire	1635	SIMMONS	160	10	10	Barke Shire
mwec0004	uk england bedfordshire	1635	SIMMONS	160	10	10	Bedford Shire
mwec0360	uk england durham	1635	SIMMONS	160	10	10	Bishoprick of Durham
mwec0061	uk england buckinghamshire	1635	SIMMONS	160	10	10	Buckingham Shire
mwec0087	uk england cambridgeshire	1635	SIMMONS	160	10	10	Cambridgeshire
mwec0129	uk england cheshire	1635	SIMMONS	160	10	10	Cheshire
mwec0168	uk england cornwall	1635	SIMMONS	160	10	10	Cornewall
mwec0221	uk england cumbria	1635	SIMMONS	160	10	10	Cuberland
mwec0255	uk england derbyshire	1635	SIMMONS	160	10	10	Darbyshire
mwec0284	uk england devon	1635	SIMMONS	160	10	10	Devonshire
mwec0323	uk england dorset	1635	SIMMONS	160	10	10	Dorsetshire
mwec0399	uk england essex	1635	SIMMONS	160	10	10	Essex
mwec0433	uk england gloucestershire	1635	SIMMONS	160	10	10	Gloucestershire
mwec0466	uk england hampshire	1635	SIMMONS	180	10	10	Hamshire
mwec0541	uk england hertfordshire	1635	SIMMONS	160	10	10	Hartforde shire
mwec0512	uk england herefordshire	1635	SIMMONS	160	10	10	Hereford Shire
mwec0573	uk england huntingdonshire	1635	SIMMONS	160	10	10	Huntingdon shire
mwec0602	uk england kent	1635	SIMMONS	160	10	10	Kent
mwec0676	uk england lancashire	1635	SIMMONS	160	10	10	Lancashire
mwec0711	uk england leicestershire	1635	SIMMONS	160	10	10	Leicester and Rutland
mwec0737	uk england lincolnshire	1635	SIMMONS	160	10	10	Lincoln shire
mwec0768	uk england middlesex	1635	SIMMONS	160	10	10	Midlesex
mwec0849	uk england northamptonshire	1635	SIMMONS	160	10	10	Northapto
mwec0811	uk england norfolk	1635	SIMMONS	160	10	10	Northfolke
mwec0877	uk england northumberland	1635	SIMMONS	160	10	10	Northumberland
mwec0905	uk england nottinghamshire	1635	SIMMONS	160	10	10	Nottingha: shire
mwec0939	uk england oxfordshire	1635	SIMMONS	160	10	10	Oxford shire
mwec1003	uk england shropshire	1635	SIMMONS	160	10	10	Shropshire
mwec1030	uk england somerset	1635	SIMMONS	160	10	10	Somerset
mwec1062	uk england staffordshire	1635	SIMMONS	160	10	10	Stafford shire
mwec1094	uk england suffolk	1635	SIMMONS	160	10	10	Suffolke
mwec1127	uk england surrey	1635	SIMMONS	160	10	10	Surrey
mwec1156	uk england sussex	1635	SIMMONS	160	10	10	Sussex
mwec1190	uk england warwickshire	1635	SIMMONS	160	10	10	Warwick shire
mwec1219	uk england westmorland	1635	SIMMONS	160	10	10	Westmerland
mwec1239	uk england wiltshire	1635	SIMMONS	160	10	10	Wiltshire
mwec1272	uk england worcestershire	1635	SIMMONS	160	10	10	Worcester shire
mwec0044	uk england berkshire	1746	SIMPSON	160	16	20	Berk Shire
mwec0072	uk england buckinghamshire	1746	SIMPSON	160	20	16	Buckingham Shire
mwec0184	uk england cornwall	1746	SIMPSON	240	16	20	Cornwal
mwec0233	uk england cumbria	1746	SIMPSON	150	20	16	Cumberland (inset of the Isle of Man)
mwec0265	uk england derbyshire	1746	SIMPSON	160	20	16	Derby Shire
mwec0295	uk england devon	1744	SIMPSON	160	16	20	Devon Shire
mwec0337	uk england dorset	1746	SIMPSON	160	16	20	Dorset Shire
mwec0373	uk england durham	1746	SIMPSON	160	16	20	Durham
mwec0411	uk england essex	1746	SIMPSON	160	16	20	Essex
mwec0143	uk england cheshire	1746	SIMPSON	160	16	20	The County Palatine of Chester
mwuk1059a	england	1830	SLATER	360	68	53	I.Slater's Map of England and Wales with part of Scotland
mwec0971	uk england oxfordshire	1824	SLATTER	550	45	44	Slatter's New Map of the Country Twenty-Five Miles round Oxford
mwuk1161	england london	1724	SMITH	4000	58	97	A New and Exact Plan of the Cities of London & Westminster, and the Borough of Southwark (illustrated is 1725 edition)
mwca0134a	canada	1812	SMITH	4000	50	78	A Map Exhibiting the Frontiers of Canada and the United States, intended to illustrate the operations of the British & American armies
mwam0780	america north	1846	SMITH	900	53	68	A New Map for Travelers through the United States of America, Showing the Railroads, Canals & Stage Roads
mwuk1050	england	1821	SMITH	400	57	46	A New Map of England and Wales, Comprehending the Whole of the Turnpike Roads, with the Great Rivers, and Navigable Canals
mwuk0980	england	1720	SMITH	675	43	43	A New Map of South Britain or England and Wales
mwec0112	uk england cambridgeshire	1821	SMITH	240	50	45	A New Map of the County of Cambridge, Divided into Hundreds

AMPG REFERENCE	REGION	DATE	MAP MAKER	PRICE (UK£)	VERT. (cm.)	HOR. (cm.)	TITLE OF MAP (Comments by the editor in brackets)
mwec0239	uk england cumbria	1804	SMITH	200	49	44	A New Map of the County of Cumberland divided into Wards
mwec0382	uk england durham	1804	SMITH	200	44	49	A New Map of the County of Durham divided into Wards
mwec0420	uk england essex	1804	SMITH	200	45	51	A New Map of the County of Essex divided into Hundreds
mwec0529	uk england herefordshire	1804	SMITH	200	51	45	A New Map of the County of Hereford divided into Hundreds
mwec0658	uk england kent	1804	SMITH	280	42	47	A New Map of the County of Kent
mwec0756	uk england lincolnshire	1804	SMITH	200	49	44	A New Map of the County of Lincoln divided into Wapontakes
mwec0792	uk england middlesex	1804	SMITH	300	45	51	A New Map of the County of Middlesex divided into Hundreds
mwec0894	uk england northumberland	1804	SMITH	250	50	44	A New Map of the County of Northumberland divided into Wards
mwec0965	uk england oxfordshire	1801	SMITH	240	51	46	A New Map of the County of Oxford Divided into Hundreds
mwec1050	uk england somerset	1804	SMITH	240	44	51	A New Map of the County of Somerset divided into Hundreds
mwec1079	uk england staffordshire	1804	SMITH	300	49	45	A New Map of the County of Stafford divided into Hundreds
mwec0698	uk england lancashire	1804	SMITH	300	50	45	A New Map of the County Palatine of Lancaster divided into Hundreds
mwe0476	europe central	1807	SMITH	375	101	87	A New Map Showing the Seat of the War between the Allied Powers & France
mwuk0174	ireland	1750	SMITH	550	41	54	A New Plan of the City of Cork
mwec0122	uk england cheshire	1603	SMITH		37	49	Cestriae comitatus palatinus.
mwsam0549	south america colombia	1832	SMITH	140	27	38	Colombia
mwec0239c	uk england cumbria	1808	SMITH	90	24	19	Cumberland
mwec0392	uk england essex	1602	SMITH	12000	41	52	Essexiae comitatus descriptio. 1602 (close copy of Saxton with roads added)
mwgr0238	greece	1808	SMITH	135	27	36	Greece
mwam0837	america north (central)	1844	SMITH	750	50	61	Guide through Ohio, Michigan, Indiana, Illinois, Missouri, Wisconsin & Iowa. Showing the Township Lines of the United States Surveys
mwec0535	uk england hertfordshire	1602	SMITH	12000	39	48	Hartfordiae comitatus nova descriptio (based on Norden's map)
mwuk0249	ireland	1808	SMITH	180	34	25	Ireland
mwec0670	uk england lancashire	1603	SMITH		37	49	Lancastriae comitatus palatinus.
mwec0709	uk england leicestershire	1602	SMITH	10000	36	50	Lecestria Rutlandiaeq. comitatum delineatio ... Anno 1602
mwaf0327	africa	1839	SMITH	80	22	27	Map of Africa
mwuss1444	pennsylvania	1848	SMITH	1500	105	142	Map of Delaware County, Pennsylvania
mwit0255	italy and switzerland	1818	SMITH	400	84	82	Map of Italy and Switzerland Particulary Distinguishing the Different Travelling Roads and the Post Stations with the Number of Posts between Each Station (illustrated is 1859 edition)
mwuss1447	pennsylvania	1849	SMITH	1500	95	138	Map of Montgomery County, Pennsylvania, from Original Surveys
mwuss1069	new jersey	1850	SMITH	1200	93	75	Map of Morristown, New Jersey
mwam0802	america north	1850	SMITH	720	57	49	Map of North America
mwam0721	america north	1838	SMITH	600	77	64	Map of North America, Including Part of the West India Islands
mwsam0144	south america	1825	SMITH	375	77	59	Map of South America
mwuss0330	connecticut	1850	SMITH	1350	113	80	Map of the City of Hartford, Connecticut
mwaa0168	arctic	1823	SMITH	200	29	28	Map of the Countries round the North Pole
mwuss1244	new york	1842	SMITH	350	48	61	Map of the State of New York, Showing the Boundaries of Counties & Townships, Cities, Towns and Villages
mwam0759	america north	1843	SMITH	3500	163	206	Map of the United States of America Including Canada and a Large Portion of Texas: Showing the Base Meridians and Township Lines of the U.S. Surveys
mww0730	world	1844	SMITH	280	27	46	Map of the World on a Globular Projection (double hemisphere projection)
mwam1247	america north (east)	1842	SMITH	350	42	55	Map Shewing the Rail Roads between Lake Erie, New York, & Boston; Intended to Illustrate the Importance of the N. York & Erie Rail Road
mwwi0166	west indies	1820	SMITH	300	37	58	Mexico and West Indies
mwp0110	australia	1835	SMITH	280	25	34	New Holland, and New Zealand
mwuss1238	new york	1839	SMITH	875	34	29	New Map of the City of New York, with Part of Brooklyn & Williamsburg
mwe0483	europe central	1834	SMITH	250	105	85	New Post Map of the Northern Parts of France and Germany
mwec0804	uk england norfolk	1602	SMITH	9000	33	49	Norfolciae comitatus descriptio ... Auctore Christophoro Saxton (re-engraved after Saxton)
mwam0575	america north	1808	SMITH	175	27	35	North America
mwec0845	uk england northamptonshire	1602	SMITH	10000	36	48	Northamptoniae comitatus descriptio
mwme0391	holy land	1809	SMITH	250	57	36	Palaestina
mwme0841	persia etc	1809	SMITH	280	26	35	Persia

AMPG REFERENCE	REGION	DATE	MAP MAKER	PRICE (UK£)	VERT. (cm.)	HOR. (cm.)	TITLE OF MAP (Comments by the editor in brackets)
mwme0846	persia etc	1830	SMITH	100	26	35	Persia, Arabia, and Cabul
mwuss0881	massachusetts	1835	SMITH	1200	53	53	Plan of Boston Comprising a Part of Charlestown and Cambridge
mwsp0126	portugal	1808	SMITH	140	34	27	Portugal
mwuk0575	scotland	1808	SMITH	140	34	25	Scotland
mwec0238	uk england cumbria	1802	SMITH	500	60	48	Smith's New and Accurate Map of the Lakes, in the Counties of Cumberland, Westmoreland and Lancaster
mwam0267	america continent	1814	SMITH	600	71	75	Smith's New Map of America with the Recent Explorations
mwuk1055	england	1827	SMITH	900	114	69	Smith's New Map of England and Wales with Part of Scotland
mwuk1035	england	1801	SMITH	400	63	53	Smith's New Map of the Inland Navigation of England and Wales
mwuk1282	england london	1811	SMITH	785	42	63	Smith's New Plan of London, Westminster & Southwark: Comprehending All the New Buildings and 350 References to the Principal Streets (28 editions to 1843)
mwsam0141	south america	1824	SMITH	80	36	25	South America
mwec1056	uk england staffordshire	1603	SMITH	10000	35	48	Staffordiae comitatus.
mwec1089	uk england suffolk	1602	SMITH	9000	33	48	Suffolciae comitatus accurata descriptio ... Auctore Christophoro Saxton (re-engraved after Saxton)
mwec1122	uk england surrey	1603	SMITH	15000	41	50	Surriae comitatus.
mwuss1512	texas	1839	SMITH		36	42	Texas as Settled by Congress 1839
mwec0781	uk england middlesex	1732	SMITH	2400	59	90	The County of Middlesex Actually Survey'd and Delineated ...
mwuss0880	massachusetts	1835	SMITH	720	42	59	The Town of Boston in New England (reproduction of state 3 of Bonner's map of 1722)
mww0716	world	1839	SMITH	1800	82	125	The World on Mercator's Projection
mwec1267	uk england worcestershire	1603	SMITH		37	48	Vigorneiensis (vulgo Worcestershire) comitatus descriptio.
mwec1185	uk england warwickshire	1603	SMITH	10000	41	46	Warwici comitatus descriptio ... Anno 1603
mwwi0155	west indies	1808	SMITH	160	27	34	West Indies
mwam0850	america north (east)	1616	SMITH, JOHN		30	35	New England the Most Remarqueable Parts thus Named by the High and Mighty Prince Charles, Prince of Great Britaine
mwat0101	atlantic bermuda	1624	SMITH, JOHN	12000	28	36	The Summer Ils
mwuss1600	virginia	1632	SMITH, JOHN	22500	33	42	Virginia (state 10 of map originally publ. in 1612)
mwam0832	america north (central)	1839	SMITH, ROSWELL	100	28	46	Map of the Western States
mwuk1406	uk geological	1816	SMITH, WILLIAM		270	185	A Delineation of the Strata of England and Wales, with Part of Scotland (1st printed geological map of a country)
mwuk1406b	uk geological	1824	SMITH, WILLIAM	5000	51	60	Geological Map of Durham
mwec1132	uk england surrey	1670	SMITH-OVERTON	2500	39	49	Surriae Comitatus Continens in se Oppida Mercatoria (3rd state of Smith's map. 1st publ. 1603, 2nd issue c1641)
mwuss1595	virginia	1627	SMITH-VAUGHAN	5000	27	36	Ould Virginia - A description of part of the adventures of Cap: Smith in Virginia ... by Robert Vaughan (4th state of map first publ. in 1624)
mwca0468	canada ontario	1800	SMYTH	1500	58	88	A Map of the Province of Upper Canada, Describing All the New Settlements, Townships, &c. with the Countries Adjacent, from Quebec to Lake Huron. Compiled from the Original Documents in the Surveyor General's Office
mwuss0108	california	1840	SMYTH	250	11	20	Mission of San Carlos, and Bay of Carmel, Upper California
mwuss0106	california	1840	SMYTH	250	11	18	Santa Barbara-Upper California
mwit0978	italy sicily	1824	SMYTH	800	48	63	Sicily. Von Schmettau's Map Corrected
mwuss0107	california	1840	SMYTH	250	11	18	The Mission of San Francisco, Upper California
mwsam0784	south america peru	1791	SOBREVIELA	2400	42	30	Plan del Curso de los Rios Huallaga y Ucayali, y de la Pampa del Sacramento ... 1791 (shown below left is the revised 1830 edition)
mwam1220	america north (east)	1833	SOC. OF FRIENDS	480	44	27	Map of the Yearly Meeting of Friends for New England
mwca0278	canada new brunswick	1843	SOC.P.G.	200	27	21	Diocese of New Brunswick
mwca0565	canada quebec	1843	SOC.P.G.	200	21	27	Diocese of Quebec
mwf0544	france corsica	1803	SOCIETA CALCOGRAFICA	2500	48	66	L'Isle de Corse divisee (the society was formed by Zatta and Remondini)
mwaf0328	africa	1839	SOCIETY D.U.K. (SDUK)	80	33	39	Africa
mwbh0801	belgium holland	1835	SOCIETY D.U.K.	150	31	39	Amsterdam
mwaf0766	africa north libya	1831	SOCIETY D.U.K.	100	32	39	Ancient Africa or Libya Part 11
mwgr0252	greece	1829	SOCIETY D.U.K.	80	24	35	Ancient Greece Northern Part
mwgr0253	greece	1829	SOCIETY D.U.K.	80	29	38	Ancient Greece Southern Part
mwme0896	syria etc	1843	SOCIETY D.U.K.	120	40	31	Ancient Syria
mwme1056	turkey etc	1830	SOCIETY D.U.K.	120	30	40	Asia Minor
mwgr0274	greece athens	1832	SOCIETY D.U.K.	150	34	39	Athens
mwp0128	australia	1840	SOCIETY D.U.K.	200	32	40	Australia in 1839
mwg0247	berlin	1833	SOCIETY D.U.K.	150	31	38	Berlin
mwin0500	pakistan etc.	1838	SOCIETY D.U.K.	150	40	32	Bokhara, Cabool, Beloochistan &c.
mwf0278	france aquitaine	1832	SOCIETY D.U.K.	80	31	38	Bordeaux
mwuss0889	massachusetts	1842	SOCIETY D.U.K.	250	36	30	Boston with Charlestown and Roxbury
mwca0172	canada	1834	SOCIETY D.U.K.	150	32	39	British North America
mwbh0803	belgium holland	1837	SOCIETY D.U.K.	120	33	38	Brussels (Bruxelles)
mwin0367	india	1842	SOCIETY D.U.K.	200	31	41	Calcutta

AMPG REFERENCE	REGION	DATE	MAP MAKER	PRICE (UK£)	VERT. (cm.)	HOR. (cm.)	TITLE OF MAP (Comments by the editor in brackets)
mwc0284	china	1844	SOCIETY D.U.K.	750	31	38	Canton and its Approaches, Macao and Hong Kong (4 maps on one sheet)
mwgm0076	gulf of mexico and surrounding regions	1842	SOCIETY D.U.K.	450	30	38	Central America I. Including Yucatan, Belize, Guatemala, Salvador, Honduras, Nicaragua ... & Southern States of Mexico / Central America II. Including Texas, California and the Northern States of Mexico (2 maps)
mwc0283	china	1843	SOCIETY D.U.K.	200	40	32	China - the Interior Chiefly from Du Halde and the Jesuits 1710 to 1718 and the Sea Coasts from Modern Authorities
mwas0853	asia south east siam	1834	SOCIETY D.U.K.	120	30	37	China and the Birman Empire with Parts of Cochin-China and Siam
mwaa0172	arctic	1831	SOCIETY D.U.K.	120	28	28	Circumjacent the North Pole
mwaa0050	antarctic	1831	SOCIETY D.U.K.	300	28	28	Circumjacent the South Pole
mwme1066	turkey etc	1840	SOCIETY D.U.K.	150	32	38	Constantinople (Stambool)
mwsc0402	scandinavia denmark	1837	SOCIETY D.U.K.	150	32	39	Copenhagen. (Kiobenhaven)
mwm0164	mediterranean islands	1831	SOCIETY D.U.K.	100	31	36	Corsica and Sardinia / Balearic Islands / Valetta
mwuk0287	ireland	1844	SOCIETY D.U.K.	200	31	39	Dublin
mww0720	world	1840	SOCIETY D.U.K.	250	33	33	Eastern Hemisphere / Western Hemisphere (2 maps)
mwas0544	asia south east	1836	SOCIETY D.U.K.	280	32	39	Eastern Islands or Malay Archipelago
mwru0358	russia	1838	SOCIETY D.U.K.	120	33	39	Eastern Siberia
mwuk0617	scotland	1834	SOCIETY D.U.K.	120	30	39	Edinburgh
mwaf0560	africa egypt etc	1831	SOCIETY D.U.K.	150	37	30	Egypt
mwjk0144	japan	1835	SOCIETY D.U.K.	250	39	32	Empire of Japan
mwuk1066	england	1837	SOCIETY D.U.K.	200	39	30	England with its Canals and Railways
mwsam0190	south america (north)	1842	SOCIETY D.U.K.	100	32	41	Equador, Granada, Venezuela & Parts of Brazil
mwit1142	italy florence	1835	SOCIETY D.U.K.	150	30	39	Florence. Firenze
mwg0470	hessen	1837	SOCIETY D.U.K.	150	30	38	Frankfort (Frankfurt) (Am Mayn)
mwsw0234	switzerland	1841	SOCIETY D.U.K.	150	28	38	Geneva (Geneve)
mwit0456	italy liguria	1836	SOCIETY D.U.K.	150	28	38	Genoa (Genova. Genes)
mwuk1413	uk geological	1843	SOCIETY D.U.K.	200	38	31	Geological Map of England and Wales
mwe0402	europe austria	1833	SOCIETY D.U.K.	200	40	32	Germany Austrian Dominions 1 / Austrian Dominions 2 (2 maps)
mwg0731	schleswig-holstein	1841	SOCIETY D.U.K.	150	31	39	Hamburg
mwin0355	india	1831	SOCIETY D.U.K.	100	36	26	India - Bengal Presidency
mwin0356	india	1832	SOCIETY D.U.K.	500	27	36	India (10 sheets, each roughly 27x36cm)
mwuk0280	ireland	1838	SOCIETY D.U.K.	200	60	47	Ireland
mwuk0288	ireland	1844	SOCIETY D.U.K.	100	39	33	Ireland
mwat0235	atlantic islands	1836	SOCIETY D.U.K.	150	40	33	Islands in the Atlantic
mwsp0135	portugal	1833	SOCIETY D.U.K.	150	31	38	Lisbon (Lisboa)
mwuk1319	england london	1835	SOCIETY D.U.K.	650	40	65	London (reprinted in 1836)
mwca0162	canada	1832	SOCIETY D.U.K.	150	33	38	Lower Canada, New Brunswick with Part of New York, Vermont & Maine
mwsp0348	spain madrid	1831	SOCIETY D.U.K.	200	33	40	Madrid
mwf1087	france provence	1840	SOCIETY D.U.K.	80	32	40	Marseille
mwit0545	italy milan	1832	SOCIETY D.U.K.	150	32	38	Milan
mwru0408	russia moscow	1836	SOCIETY D.U.K.	320	32	36	Moscow
mwg0407	bavaria	1832	SOCIETY D.U.K.	150	31	39	Munich (Munchen)
mwit1077	italy naples	1835	SOCIETY D.U.K.	180	32	40	Naples (Napoli)
mwp0104	australia	1833	SOCIETY D.U.K.	200	40	33	New South Wales (inset: Sydney)
mwuss1239	new york	1840	SOCIETY D.U.K.	300	30	37	New York
mwaf0800	africa north morocco	1836	SOCIETY D.U.K.	100	32	39	North Africa or Barbary I Marocco
mwaf0824	africa north tunisia	1836	SOCIETY D.U.K.	140	32	39	North Africa or Barbary III Tunis and part of Tripoli
mwam0743	america north	1840	SOCIETY D.U.K.	350	38	31	North America (independent Texas)
mwam0690	america north	1834	SOCIETY D.U.K.	200	36	31	North America Index Map to Canada and the United States
mwca0163	canada nova scotia	1832	SOCIETY D.U.K.	100	39	31	North America sheet I Nova-Scotia
mwca0164	canada	1832	SOCIETY D.U.K.	200	32	43	North America sheet III Upper Canada
mwam1307	great lakes	1832	SOCIETY D.U.K.	150	31	38	North America Sheet IV Lake Superior
mwam1357	america north (west)	1833	SOCIETY D.U.K.	150	31	38	North America Sheet V The Northwest and Michigan Territories
mwam1217	america north (east)	1832	SOCIETY D.U.K.	250	34	32	North America Sheet VI New-York, Vermont, Maine, New-Hampshire, Massachusetts, Connecticut, Rhode-Island, and New-Jersey
mwam1221	america north (east)	1833	SOCIETY D.U.K.	175	37	32	North America Sheet VII Pennsylvania, New Jersey, Maryland, Delaware, Columbia and Part of Virginia
mwuss1308	ohio	1833	SOCIETY D.U.K.	150	39	30	North America Sheet VIII Ohio, with Parts of Kentucky and Virginia
mwuss0983	missouri	1833	SOCIETY D.U.K.	150	31	39	North America Sheet X Parts of Missouri, Illinois, Kentucky, Tennessee, Alabama, Mississippi and Arkansas
mwuss0274	carolinas	1833	SOCIETY D.U.K.	150	38	34	North America Sheet XI Parts of North and South Carolina
mwuss0526	georgia	1833	SOCIETY D.U.K.	150	41	31	North America Sheet XII Georgia with Parts of North & South Carolina, Tennessee, Alabama & Florida
mwuss0675	louisiana	1833	SOCIETY D.U.K.	350	33	41	North America Sheet XIII Parts of Louisiana, Arkansas, Mississippi, Alabama & Florida
mwuss1546	utah etc	1836	SOCIETY D.U.K.	500	31	39	North America Sheet XV Utah, New Mexico, Texas, California &c. and the Northern States of Mexico
mwuss0472	florida	1834	SOCIETY D.U.K.	300	40	30	North America XIV Florida
mwsp0134	portugal	1833	SOCIETY D.U.K.	150	31	38	Oporto (Porto)

AMPG REFERENCE	REGION	DATE	MAP MAKER	PRICE (UK£)	VERT. (cm.)	HOR. (cm.)	TITLE OF MAP (Comments by the editor in brackets)
mwme0426	holy land	1843	SOCIETY D.U.K.	100	40	32	Palestine with the Hauran and the Adjacent Districts
mwit0367	italy emilia-romagna	1840	SOCIETY D.U.K.	150	32	38	Parma
mwuss1700	wisconsin	1844	SOCIETY D.U.K.	150	32	38	Parts of Wisconsin and Michigan
mwsam0261	south america argentina	1838	SOCIETY D.U.K.	150	32	40	Patagonia (sheet V. incl. 2 insets: Isle of Georgia / South Shetland and Orkneys)
mwme0847	persia etc	1831	SOCIETY D.U.K.	100	30	36	Persia with part of the Ottoman Empire
mwuss1433	pennsylvania	1840	SOCIETY D.U.K.	150	39	31	Philadelphia
mwit0761	italy rome	1830	SOCIETY D.U.K.	120	30	39	Plan of Ancient Rome
mwit0762	italy rome	1830	SOCIETY D.U.K.	150	30	39	Plan of Modern Rome
mwbp0565	poland	1831	SOCIETY D.U.K.	80	37	32	Poland (Polska)
mwp0286	pacific (all)	1840	SOCIETY D.U.K.	150	30	39	Polynesia or Islands in the Pacific Ocean
mwit0293	italy campagna	1832	SOCIETY D.U.K.	120	30	39	Pompeii
mwsp0132a	portugal	1831	SOCIETY D.U.K.	100	38	27	Portugal
mwru0351	russia	1834	SOCIETY D.U.K.	80	33	40	Russia (part 4)
mwru0354	russia	1835	SOCIETY D.U.K.	80	33	39	Russia in Europe (part 2)
mwru0355	russia	1835	SOCIETY D.U.K.	120	33	39	Russia in Europe part IX and Georgia
mwru0360	russia	1840	SOCIETY D.U.K.	120	40	31	Russia in Europe part X. General Map
mwbp0153	baltic states	1834	SOCIETY D.U.K.	140	32	39	Russia part III
mwuk0636	scotland	1844	SOCIETY D.U.K.	150	39	31	Scotland
mwuk0618	scotland	1834	SOCIETY D.U.K.	200	28	39	Scotland I / II / III (3 sheets: North/South/Orkneys-Shetlands)
mwaf1013	africa south	1834	SOCIETY D.U.K.	250	34	40	South Africa (insets of Cape, George, Grahamstown, Cape Town)
mwsam0430	south america brazil	1837	SOCIETY D.U.K.	150	41	34	South America Sheet 3 South Brazil with Paraguay and Uruguay
mwru0352	russia	1834	SOCIETY D.U.K.	250	31	39	St. Petersburg
mwsc0754	scandinavia sweden	1836	SOCIETY D.U.K.	150	33	41	Stockholm
mwsw0231	switzerland	1838	SOCIETY D.U.K.	90	31	40	Switzerland Schweiz La Suisse
mwit0982	italy sicily	1839	SOCIETY D.U.K.	100	32	40	Syracuse
mwme0895	syria etc	1843	SOCIETY D.U.K.	120	40	31	Syria
mwwi0196	west indies	1835	SOCIETY D.U.K.	200	31	38	The Antilles or West-India Islands
mwwi0286a	west indies (islands)	1835	SOCIETY D.U.K.	150	32	39	The British Islands in the West Indies
mwme0849	persia etc	1831	SOCIETY D.U.K.	100	30	36	The Eastern Part of the Ancient Persian Empire
mwuk0278	ireland	1837	SOCIETY D.U.K.	120	31	39	The Environs of Dublin
mwuk0624	scotland	1838	SOCIETY D.U.K.	80	30	39	The Environs of Edinburgh
mwf0919	france paris	1832	SOCIETY D.U.K.	100	31	38	The Environs of Paris
mwp0209	new zealand	1833	SOCIETY D.U.K.	350	40	31	The Islands of New Zealand
mww0724	world	1841	SOCIETY D.U.K.	250	39	64	The World on Mercator's Projection
mwit0695	italy piedmont	1837	SOCIETY D.U.K.	150	31	37	Turin (Torino)
mwme1055	turkey etc	1830	SOCIETY D.U.K.	120	30	40	Turkey containing the Provinces in Asia Minor
mwit1261	italy venice	1838	SOCIETY D.U.K.	350	40	59	Venice. Venezia. Venedig
mwe0441	europe austria vienna	1833	SOCIETY D.U.K.	140	34	37	Vienna (Wien)
mwbp0566	poland	1831	SOCIETY D.U.K.	300	30	37	Warsaw (Warszawa)
mwaf1254	africa west	1839	SOCIETY D.U.K.	80	31	39	West Africa II
mwp0099	australia	1831	SOCIETY D.U.K.	500	32	42	Western Australia / Van Diemen Island (1st printed map to name Perth)
mwf0921	france paris	1834	SOCIETY D.U.K.	350	39	53	Western Division of Paris / Eastern Division of Paris
mwru0359	russia	1838	SOCIETY D.U.K.	120	40	32	Western Siberia
mwit0014	italy	1538	SOLINUS	1000	13	17	(Unitled map of Italy with South to the top)
mwaf0670	africa north	1538	SOLINUS	600	16	23	(Untitled map based on Mela - all of Africa except southern Africa)
mwas0001	asia continent	1538	SOLINUS	2000	25	33	(Untitled map by Munster, based on Mela)
mwe0003a	europe	1538	SOLINUS-MUNSTER	1000	18	25	Europa (shown above left)
mwit0778a	italy sardinia	1595	SOLINUS	300	13	8	Sardinia
mwgr0333	greece crete	1485	SONETTI		19	28	Candia (reprinted in 1532)
mwgr0434	greece cyprus	1485	SONETTI		19	28	Cipro (reprinted in 1532)
mwgr0544	greece islands	1485	SONETTI	130000	23	17	Isolario (Book containing 49 charts of islands in the Greek Archipelago. Reprinted 1532. Based on a manuscript c1450 by Christopher Buondelmonte entitled 'Liber insularum Arcipelagi')
mwgr0029	greece	1570	SOPHIANOS	120000	74	109	Descriptio Nova Totius Graeciae per Nicolaum Sophianum
mwgm0361	mexico	1847	SOTO	280	27	38	Plan of the Campaign of the American Army in the Valley of Mexico in the Months of August and September of the Year 1847
mwbp0545	poland	1804	SOTZMANN	300	48	59	Charte vom Konigreiche Preussen oder Ost-West-Sud und Neu Ost-Preussen
mwru0569	ukraine	1788	SOTZMANN	875	51	63	Charte von den Oberhalb und Seitwarts dem Schwarzen Meere
mwuss0302	connecticut	1796	SOTZMANN	2000	36	44	Connecticut
mwam0563	america north	1804	SOTZMANN	1500	53	66	Die Vereinigten Staaten von Nordamerika
mwg0671	saxony	1788	SOTZMANN	550	43	47	Generalcharte von der Altemarck
mwg0217	germany north east	1804	SOTZMANN	250	56	67	Generalkarte vom Konigreich Preussen
mwg0215	germany north east	1798	SOTZMANN	960	17	23	Generalkarte von dem Samtlichen Konigl. Preussischen Staaten (in 20 sheets, each 17x23cm)

AMPG REFERENCE	REGION	DATE	MAP MAKER	PRICE (UK£)	VERT. (cm.)	HOR. (cm.)	TITLE OF MAP (Comments by the editor in brackets)
mwg0168	germany	1803	SOTZMANN	450	104	74	Generalkarte von Deutschland, der Batavischen und Helvetischen Republik, Ober und Mittel Italien und dem Ostlichen Theil der Franzosischen Republik
mwbp0532	poland	1796	SOTZMANN	960	96	118	Grenzkarte der Preussischen Russischen und Oesterreichischen Monarchien in XVI Blattern
mwuk0874	uk	1796	SOTZMANN	280	30	25	Grossbritannien und Irland
mwg0245a	berlin	1803	SOTZMANN	720	33	43	Grundriss der Königlichen Haupt und Residenzstadt Berlin
mwbp0515a	poland	1789	SOTZMANN	2000	98	209	Karte des Königl. Preuß. Herzogthums Vor- und Hinter-Pommern
mwca0118	canada	1791	SOTZMANN	1500	39	48	Karte des Nordlichsten America, nach den Zweiten Ausgabe von Arrowsmith's Grosser Mercators-Karte in Acht Blatt
mwsp0117	portugal	1791	SOTZMANN	550	50	33	Karte von den Konigreichen Portugal und Algarbien
mwit0820f	italy sardinia	1793	SOTZMANN	375	37	43	Karte von den Staaten des Königs von Sardinien
mwg0422	brandenburg	1798	SOTZMANN	450	78	50	Karte von der Mark Brandenburg nach den Besten Spezialkarten Neu Entworfen
mwg0159	germany	1789	SOTZMANN	960	96	114	Karte von Deutschland in XVI. Blatt
mwam1345	america north (west)	1800	SOTZMANN	750	51	41	Karte von einem Theil der Nordwestlichen Kuste von America zu der Reise des Capit George Vancouver
mwe0226	europe	1792	SOTZMANN	1800	96	128	Karte von Europa in XVI Blattern
mwf0168	france	1795	SOTZMANN	960	26	30	Karte von Frankreich in XVI Blattern: nach Cassini, und dem Atlas National (in 16 sheets, each 26x30cm)
mwbp0527	poland	1793	SOTZMANN	1600	97	117	Karte von Polen und den Angranzenden Provinzen in XVI Blattern
mwp0035	australia	1794	SOTZMANN	400	21	24	Lauf des Transport-Schiffes Waaksamheyd von Port Jackson in Neu Sud Wallis, nach Batavia, im Jahre 1792 (inset: Norfolk Isl.)
mwuss1011	new hampshire	1796	SOTZMANN	3600	67	45	New Hampshire Entworfen von D.F. Sotzmann (inset: Northern tip of state)
mwuss1166	new york	1797	SOTZMANN	5500	65	46	New Jersey Entworfen von D.F. Sotzmann
mwuss1167	new york	1799	SOTZMANN	3600	54	76	New York
mwuss1394	pennsylvania	1797	SOTZMANN	3600	41	70	Pennsylvania ... Entworfen von D.F. Sotzman
mwuss1462	rhode isl	1797	SOTZMANN	2000	48	36	Rhode Island ... Entworfen von D.F. Sotzmann
mwsc0188	scandinavia	1796	SOTZMANN	300	26	30	Schweden und Norwegen
mwg0850	westphalia	1790	SOTZMANN	675	66	88	Special Charte von den Westphalschen Provinzen Cleve Geldern Meurs Marck Ravensberg Minden Lingen und Tecklenburg nebst den Angrenzenden Landern
mwg0423	brandenburg	1807	SOTZMANN	2000	144	128	Special Karte von der Neumark
mwbp0549	poland	1808	SOTZMANN	1800	41	55	Topographische-Militarische-Karte vom Vormaligen Neu Ostpreussen ... Warschau (in 16 sheets, each 41x55cm)
mwru0323	russia	1803	SOTZMANN	150	23	34	Umriss des Schwarzen Meeres ... des Archipelagus nebst den Kusten, nach den Neuesten Berichtigungen
mwuss1561	vermont	1796	SOTZMANN	3600	69	46	Vermont ... entworfen von D.F. Sotzmann
mwam1095	america north (east)	1787	SOULES	1200	28	93	(Untitled map of the coast between Boston and Roanoke River)
mwuss1659	virginia	1787	SOULES	480	29	38	Plan d' York en Virginie avec les Attaques et les Campemes de l'Armee Combinee de France et d'Amerique
mwe0397a	europe austria	1810	SPAETH	400	56	72	General Charte von den Kaiserlich=Oestreichischen Erb Staaten Nach dem Wiener Friedenschluss den neuen Gränzen... neu entworfen
mwbh0741b	belgium holland	1785	SPANOGHE	900	66	80	Carte des XVII Provinces des Pays Bas
mwuk1557	england islands	1635	SPARKE	150	13	17	Anglesey Ins. / Wight ol. Vectis / Ins. Garnesey / Ins. Iarsey
mwc0018	china	1635	SPARKE	450	15	19	China
mwsp0424	spain regions	1635	SPARKE	150	17	24	Gallicia
mwaf1101	africa west	1635	SPARKE	200	14	18	Guinea
mwe0873	europe hungary	1635	SPARKE	200	15	18	Hungaria
mwsc0489	scandinavia iceland	1635	SPARKE	320	13	19	Island
mwgr0060b	greece	1635	SPARKE	250	14	17	Macedonia, Epir, et Achaia (illustrated above)
mwat0107	atlantic bermuda	1635	SPARKE	950	17	24	Mappa Aestivarum Insularum alias Bermudas Dictarum
mwgr0060a	greece	1635	SPARKE	250	14	17	Morea
mwm0121	mediterranean east	1635	SPARKE	240	14	19	Peregrinatio Pauli in qua & Omnia Loca Quorum Fit Mentio in Actis et Epistolis Apostolorum et Apocalypsi, Describuntur
mwsam0019	south america	1635	SPARKE	240	14	19	Southerne America
mwf1193	france west	1635	SPARKE	150	17	24	The Archbishoprick and County of Burdigala
mwsam0493	south america colombia	1635	SPARKE	300	16	24	The Description of the Firme Land
mwme0771	persia etc	1635	SPARKE	240	14	18	The Kingdome of Persia
mwm0120	mediterranean east	1635	SPARKE	240	14	19	The Lesser Asia
mwwi0011	west indies	1635	SPARKE	500	17	23	The Ylandes of the West Indies
mwaf0959	africa south	1784	SPARRMAN	600	32	52	Geographische Karte vom Vorgebirge der Guten Hoffnung (2nd edition. First publ. in Swedish in 1783)
mwbh0512	belgium holland	1703	SPECHT	400	52	61	Theatre de la Guerre in de 17 Nederlandse Provintien
mwf0207	france alsace	1576	SPECKEL	2000	38	114	Elsass
mwwi0362	barbados	1676	SPEED	1350	38	50	A Map of Jamaica / Barbados
mwwi0695	jamaica	1676	SPEED	1350	38	50	A Map of Jamaica / Barbados
mwam0874	america north (east)	1676	SPEED	4500	38	51	A Map of New England and New York
mwru0073	russia	1676	SPEED	1500	39	51	A Map of Russia (copy of Visscher 1651)

AMPG REFERENCE	REGION	DATE	MAP MAKER	PRICE (UK£)	VERT. (cm.)	HOR. (cm.)	TITLE OF MAP (Comments by the editor in brackets)
mwuss0741	maryland	1676	SPEED	4200	37	49	A Map of Virginia and Maryland
mwat0102	atlantic bermuda	1627	SPEED	2500	40	53	A Mapp of the Sommer Ilands Once Called the Bermudas
mww0157	world	1646	SPEED	675	9	12	A New and Accurat Map of the World
mww0130	world	1627	SPEED	15000	31	52	A New and Accurat Map of the World Drawne According to ye Truest Descriptions Latest Discoveries & Best Observations yt have beene Made by English or Strangers
mwuss0152	carolinas	1676	SPEED	3750	37	50	A New Description of Carolina
mwas0404	asia south east	1676	SPEED	2000	39	51	A New Map of East India
mwbh0229	belgium holland	1631	SPEED	1800	39	51	A New Mape of ye XVII Provinces of Low Germanie, Mended a New in Manie Places (3 carte-a-figure borders)
mwm0003a	mediterranean	1627	SPEED	2000	40	52	A New Mappe of the Romane Empire Newly Described by John Speede (3 carte-a-figure borders)
mwg0047	germany	1631	SPEED	2000	39	51	A Newe Mape of Germany Newly Augmented by Iohn Speed. Ano Dom. 1626 (3 carte-a-figure borders)
mwbp0235	poland	1631	SPEED	3200	39	51	A Newe Mape of Poland Done into English by I. Speede (3 carte-a-figure borders)
mwru0420	russia tartary	1627	SPEED	2000	39	50	A Newe Mape of Tartary Augmented by Iohn Speede
mwaf0043	africa	1627	SPEED	3200	39	51	Africae, Described, the Manners of their Habits, and Buildings: Newly Done into English by I.S. (3 carte-a-figure borders)
mwam0050	america continent	1646	VAN DEN KEERE-SPEED	400	9	13	America
mwam0035	america continent	1627	SPEED	5000	40	52	America with those Known Parts in that Unknowne World both People and Manner of Buildings Discribed and Inlarged by I.S. Ano. 1626 (3 carte-a-figure borders)
mwuk1726	wales	1627	SPEED	150	9	12	Anglesey and Carnarvan
mwuk1705	wales	1610	SPEED	800	38	51	Anglesey, Antiently Called Mona. Described 1610
mwas0030	asia continent	1627	SPEED	3500	38	51	Asia with the Islands Adioyning Described, the Atire of the People, & Townes of Importance, All of them Newly Augmented by I.S. Ano. Dom. 1626 (3 carte-a-figure borders)
mwwi0361	barbados	1676	SPEED	300	9	13	Barbados
mwec0032	uk england berkshire	1627	SPEED	150	9	12	Barkshire
mwec0033	uk england berkshire	1631	SPEED	1250	38	51	Barkshire Described
mwec0003	uk england bedfordshire	1627	SPEED	140	9	12	Bedford Shire
mwec0001	uk england bedfordshire	1610	SPEED	850	39	52	Bedford Shire and the Situation of Bedford Described with the Arms of thos Honorable Familyes that have Borne ye Titles of Dukes and Earls thereof
mwe0534	europe czech republic (bohemia)	1631	SPEED	2000	39	51	Bohemia Newly Described (3 carte-a-figure borders)
mwuk1706	wales	1610	SPEED	650	38	51	Breknoke Both Shyre and Towne Described
mwuk1094	england and scotland	1612	SPEED	3500	38	51	Britain as it was Devided in the Tyme of the Englishe-Saxons Especially during their Heptarchy (14 inset scenes in side borders)
mwec0058	uk england buckinghamshire	1610	SPEED	1250	38	51	Buckingham both Shyre, and Shire Towne Describ.
mwec0060	uk england buckinghamshire	1627	SPEED	150	9	12	Buckingham Shire
mwuk1707	wales	1610	SPEED	350	39	51	Caermarden both Shyre and Towne Described
mwuk1768	wales	1676	SPEED	550	38	51	Caernarvon both Shyre and Shire-Towne with the Ancient Citie Bangor Described
mwec0085	uk england cambridgeshire	1627	SPEED	160	9	12	Cambridge Shire
mwec0086	uk england cambridgeshire	1627	SPEED	2400	38	51	Cambridgshire Described with the Devision of the Hundreds, the Townes Situation, with the Armes of the Colleges of that Famous Universiti (25 college coats of arms)
mwme0055	holy land	1595	SPEED		75	96	Canaan As It Was Possessed Both In Abraham and Israels Dayes With The Stations And Bordering Nations.
mwme0087b	holy land	1611	SPEED	3000	39	52	Canaan. Begun by Mr. John More Continued and Finished by John Speede
mwgr0371	greece crete	1627	SPEED	180	8	11	Candia olim Creta
mwuk1717	wales	1612	SPEED	500	38	50	Cardigan Shyre Described with the Due Forme of the Shiretown as it was Surveyed by J.S. Anno 1610
mwuss0153	carolinas	1676	SPEED	650	8	13	Carolina
mwuk0334	scotland	1627	SPEED	120	9	12	Cathanes. and Orknay. Ins.
mwec0128	uk england cheshire	1627	SPEED	140	9	12	Chester
mwc0022	china	1646	SPEED	320	9	12	China
mwuk0032	ireland	1627	SPEED	120	9	12	Connack
mwec0167	uk england cornwall	1627	SPEED	160	9	12	Cornwaile
mwec0164	uk england cornwall	1612	SPEED	2400	37	49	Cornwall
mwec0218	uk england cumbria	1610	SPEED	680	39	52	Cumberland and the Ancient Citie Carlile Described with Many Memorable Antiquities therein Found Observed
mwsc0269	scandinavia denmark	1646	SPEED	120	9	12	Dania
mwec0259	uk england derbyshire	1676	SPEED	950	38	51	Darbieshire Described
mwec0254	uk england derbyshire	1627	SPEED	140	9	12	Darby Shire
mwuk1727	wales	1627	SPEED	120	9	12	Denbigh and Flint Discribed
mwuk1708	wales	1610	SPEED	500	38	51	Denbigh Shire

AMPG REFERENCE	REGION	DATE	MAP MAKER	PRICE (UK£)	VERT. (cm.)	HOR. (cm.)	TITLE OF MAP (Comments by the editor in brackets)
mwec0283	uk england devon	1627	SPEED	150	9	12	Devonshire
mwec0281	uk england devon	1612	SPEED	1500	38	51	Devonshire with Excester Described and the Armes of such Nobles as have Borne the Titles of them
mwec0321	uk england dorset	1627	SPEED	140	8	12	Dorcet Shire
mwec0322	uk england dorset	1631	SPEED	1000	38	51	Dorsetshyre with the Shyre-Towne Dorchester Described
mwuk0693	uk	1627	SPEED	350	12	16	England, Scotland and Ireland
mwec0397	uk england essex	1627	SPEED	150	9	12	Essex County
mwec0398	uk england essex	1631	SPEED	1100	38	51	Essex, Devided into Hundreds, with the Most Antient and Fayre Towne Colchester Described and Other Memorable Monuments Observed
mwe0034	europe	1626	SPEED	3000	39	51	Europ, and the Cheife Cities Contaned therein Described; with the Habits of Most Kingdoms Now in Use. by Io: Speed 1626 (3 carte-a-figure borders)
mwuk1769	wales	1676	SPEED	450	38	51	Flint-Shire
mwf0047	france	1631	SPEED	2000	39	51	France, Revised and Augmented, the Attires of the French and Situations of their Chieftest Cityes Observed by John Speed (3 carte-a-figure borders)
mwg0055	germany	1646	SPEED	120	9	12	Germania
mwuk1728	wales	1627	SPEED	120	9	12	Glamorgan Shire
mwuk1709	wales	1610	SPEED	850	38	51	Glamorgan Shyre with the Sittuations of the Chiefe Towne Cardyff and Ancient Llandaffe Described
mwec0432	uk england gloucestershire	1627	SPEED	140	9	12	Glocester Shire
mwec0439	uk england gloucestershire	1676	SPEED	1400	38	51	Glocestershire Contrived into Thirty Three Severall Hundreds ... the Citie of Glocester & Bristowe Discribed with the Armes of ... Earles & Dukes thereof
mwgr0059	greece	1631	SPEED	1200	39	51	Greece
mwec0473	uk england hampshire	1676	SPEED	1400	38	51	Hantshire, Described and Devided
mwec0540	uk england hertfordshire	1631	SPEED	950	38	51	Hartford Shire Described the Sittuations of Hartford, and the Most Ancient Towne S Albons with such Memorable Actions as have Happened
mwec0539	uk england hertfordshire	1627	SPEED	140	9	12	Hartforde Shire
mwec0511	uk england herefordshire	1631	SPEED	850	38	51	Herefordshire Described with the True Plot of the Citie Hereford as also the Armes of thos Nobles that have been Intituled with that Dignity
mwuk1554	england islands	1611	SPEED	850	38	51	Holy Iland / Garnsey / Farne / Iarsey ... 1610
mwe0876	europe hungary	1646	SPEED	150	9	12	Hungaria
mwec0570	uk england huntingdonshire	1610	SPEED	650	39	52	Huntington both Shire and Shire Towne with the Ancient Citie Ely Described
mwec0572	uk england huntingdonshire	1627	SPEED	120	9	12	Huntington Shire
mwit0091	italy	1646	SPEED	300	9	12	Italia
mwit0074	italy	1626	SPEED	3000	39	52	Italia Newly Augmented by I. Speede (3 carte-a-figure borders)
mwwi0694	jamaica	1676	SPEED	300	8	13	Jamaica
mwec0601	uk england kent	1627	SPEED	160	9	13	Kent
mwec0597	uk england kent	1611	SPEED	1600	38	51	Kent with her Cities and Earles Described and Observed
mwec0674	uk england lancashire	1627	SPEED	140	9	12	Lancaster
mwec0716	uk england leicestershire	1676	SPEED	960	38	51	Leicester both Countye and Citie Described, the Honorable Famiylies that have had the Titles of Earls thereof with other Accidents therein Observed
mwec0710	uk england leicestershire	1627	SPEED	130	9	13	Leicester Shire
mwec0735	uk england lincolnshire	1627	SPEED	120	8	12	Lincolne Shire
mwuk0033	ireland	1627	SPEED	120	9	12	Linster
mwuk1770	wales	1676	SPEED	500	38	51	Merioneth Shire Described
mwec0767	uk england middlesex	1627	SPEED	160	8	12	Midle-Sex
mwec0765	uk england middlesex	1612	SPEED	1800	39	52	Midle-Sex Described with the Most Famous Cities of London and Westminster
mwuk1729	wales	1627	SPEED	120	9	12	Monmouth Shire
mwuk1730	wales	1627	SPEED	120	9	12	Montgomeri e Merionidh Shires
mwuk1718	wales	1612	SPEED	650	38	51	Montgomery Shire
mwuk0034	ireland	1627	SPEED	120	9	12	Mounster
mwam0873	america north (east)	1676	SPEED	500	8	12	New England and New York
mwec0809	uk england norfolk	1627	SPEED	120	9	12	Norfolcke
mwec0806	uk england norfolk	1612	SPEED	1200	38	50	Norfolk a Countie Florishing & Populous Described and Devided with the Armes of such Noble Families as have Borne the Titles therof
mwec0848	uk england northamptonshire	1627	SPEED	120	9	12	Northampton Shire
mwec0856	uk england northamptonshire	1676	SPEED	800	38	51	Northamton Shire
mwec0881	uk england northumberland	1676	SPEED	800	38	51	Northumberland
mwec0904	uk england nottinghamshire	1627	SPEED	120	8	12	Nottingham Shire
mwec0938	uk england oxfordshire	1627	SPEED	160	9	12	Oxfordshire
mwec0945	uk england oxfordshire	1676	SPEED	2400	38	51	Oxfordshire Described with ye Citie and the Armes of the Colledges of ye Famous University (17 college coats of arms)

AMPG REFERENCE	REGION	DATE	MAP MAKER	PRICE (UK£)	VERT. (cm.)	HOR. (cm.)	TITLE OF MAP (Comments by the editor in brackets)
mwuk0335	scotland	1627	SPEED	120	9	12	Part of Scotland it is Called of the Inhabitance Stranaverne with his Borderers
mwuk1731	wales	1627	SPEED	120	9	12	Pembrok Shire
mwuk1710	wales	1610	SPEED	750	39	52	Penbrokshyre Described and the Sittuations Both of Penbroke and St. Davids Showed in Due Form as they were Taken by John Speed
mwme0774	persia etc	1646	SPEED	200	8	12	Persia
mwbp0250	poland	1646	SPEED	150	9	12	Polonia
mwuk1732	wales	1627	SPEED	120	9	12	Radnor Breknok Cardigan and Caermarthen Described
mwec0980	uk england rutland	1627	SPEED	120	9	12	Rutlandshire
mwec0978	uk england rutland	1610	SPEED	480	39	52	Rutlandshire with Oukham and Stanford her Bordering Neighbour Newly Described
mwec1001	uk england shropshire	1627	SPEED	140	9	12	Shropshire
mwec1002	uk england shropshire	1631	SPEED	800	38	51	Shropshyre Described the Sittuation of Shrowesbury Shewed with the Armes of thos Earles, and other Memorable Things Observed
mwec1029	uk england somerset	1627	SPEED	150	9	12	Somersetia
mwec1026	uk england somerset	1611	SPEED	1400	38	51	Somerset-Shire Described ad into Hundreds Devided, with the Plott of the Famous and Most Wholsom Waters and Citie of the Bathe
mwec0465	uk england hampshire	1627	SPEED	150	9	12	Southampton
mwsp0174	spain	1626	SPEED	2000	41	53	Spaine Newly Described with Many Adictions, both in the Attires of the People & the Setuations of their Cheifest Cityes (3 carte-a-figure borders)
mwec1061	uk england staffordshire	1631	SPEED	950	38	51	Stafford Countie and Towne with the Ancient Citie Lichfeild Described
mwec1060	uk england staffordshire	1627	SPEED	140	9	12	Staffordshir
mwec1093	uk england suffolk	1627	SPEED	140	9	12	Suffolck
mwec1091	uk england suffolk	1610	SPEED	1000	39	52	Suffolke Described and Divided into Hundreds
mwec1126	uk england surrey	1627	SPEED	180	9	12	Surrey
mwec1124	uk england surrey	1616	SPEED	2400	39	51	Surrey Described and Divided into Hundreds
mwec1155	uk england sussex	1627	SPEED	160	9	12	Sussex
mwec1163	uk england sussex	1676	SPEED	2000	39	51	Sussex Described and Divided into Rapes with the Situation of Chichester the Cheife Citie thereof
mwru0426	russia tartary	1646	SPEED	180	8	12	Tartaria
mwec0359	uk england durham	1627	SPEED	140	9	12	The Bishopprick of Durham
mwec0357	uk england durham	1611	SPEED	800	39	52	The Bishoprick and Citie of Durham
mwec1192	uk england warwickshire	1676	SPEED	900	38	51	The Counti of Warwick the Shire Towne and Citie of Coventre Described
mwec0736	uk england lincolnshire	1631	SPEED	1250	38	51	The Countie and Citie of Lyncolne Described with the Armes of them that have been Earles thereof since the Conquest
mwuk0041	ireland	1631	SPEED	1500	38	51	The Countie of Leinster with the Citie Dublin Described
mwec0903	uk england nottinghamshire	1612	SPEED	580	39	52	The Countie of Nottingham Described, the Shire Townes Situation and the Earls thereof Observed
mwuk1771	wales	1676	SPEED	450	39	51	The Countie of Radnor Described and the Shiretownes Sittuatione
mwec0675	uk england lancashire	1631	SPEED	2000	38	51	The Countie Palatine of Lancaster Described and Divided into Hundreds 1610
mwec1215	uk england westmorland	1610	SPEED	560	39	51	The Countie Westmorland and Kendale the Cheif Towne Described
mwuk1733	wales	1627	SPEED	850	39	51	The Countye of Monmouth with the Sittuation of the Shire-Town Described Ann. 1610
mwec0124	uk england cheshire	1610	SPEED	1300	39	51	The Countye Palatine of Chester with that Most Ancient Citie Described
mwuk0336	scotland	1627	SPEED	120	9	12	The Eastern Part of Scotland
mwuk1086	england and ireland	1627	SPEED	2500	39	52	The Invasions of England and Ireland with Al their Civill Wars since the Conquest
mwuk1603	isle of man	1627	SPEED	300	9	12	The Isle of Man
mwuk1605	isle of man	1676	SPEED	800	39	51	The Isle of Man Exactly Described, and into Several Parishes Divided ... Described by Tho Durham Ano. 1595 ... Performed by Iohn Speed Anno. 1610
mwuk1617	isle of wight	1627	SPEED	180	8	13	The Isle of Wight
mwc0015	china	1627	SPEED	4000	39	51	The Kingdome of China Newly Augmented by I.S. (3 carte-a-figure borders)
mwsc0256	scandinavia denmark	1627	SPEED	1750	39	51	The Kingdome of Denmarke (3 carte-a-figure borders)
mwuk0916	england	1612	SPEED	2000	39	52	The Kingdome of England
mwuk0687	uk	1612	SPEED	3500	38	51	The Kingdome of Great Britaine and Ireland (inset views of London, Edinburgh)
mwuk0035	ireland	1627	SPEED	240	8	13	The Kingdome of Ireland
mwuk0021	ireland	1612	SPEED	2800	39	51	The Kingdome of Irland Divided into Severall Provinces, and the Againe Divided into Counties Newly Described
mwme0770	persia etc	1631	SPEED	2000	39	51	The Kingdome of Persia with the Cheef Citties and Habites Described (3 carte-a-figure borders)
mwuk0326	scotland	1612	SPEED	3500	38	51	The Kingdome of Scotland

AMPG REFERENCE	REGION	DATE	MAP MAKER	PRICE (UK£)	VERT. (cm.)	HOR. (cm.)	TITLE OF MAP (Comments by the editor in brackets)
mwe0871	europe hungary	1626	SPEED	2000	39	51	The Mape of Hungari Newly Augmented by John Speede (3 carte-a-figure borders)
mwec1296	uk england yorkshire	1631	SPEED	1200	38	51	The North and East Riding of Yorkshire
mwuk0042	ireland	1631	SPEED	1500	38	51	The Province of Connaugh with the Citie of Galawaye Described
mwuk0043	ireland	1631	SPEED	1500	38	51	The Province of Mounster
mwuk0022	ireland	1612	SPEED	1500	38	51	The Province Ulster Described
mwuk0337	scotland	1627	SPEED	120	9	12	The Southren Parte of Scotland
mwme0552	arabia etc	1646	SPEED	240	8	12	The Turkish Empire
mwme0548	arabia etc	1626	SPEED	2800	38	51	The Turkish Empire. Newly Augmented by Iohn Speed. 1626 (3 carte-a-figure borders)
mwec1297	uk england yorkshire	1631	SPEED	1500	38	51	The West Ridinge of Yorkeshyre with the Most Famous and Fayre Citie Yorke Described
mwuk0036	ireland	1627	SPEED	120	9	12	Ulster
mwuss0742	maryland	1676	SPEED	600	9	13	Virginia and Maryland
mwuk1772	wales	1676	SPEED	2250	38	51	Wales (16 town view insets in borders)
mwec1189	uk england warwickshire	1627	SPEED	150	10	13	Warwicke Shire
mwec1218	uk england westmorland	1627	SPEED	140	9	12	Westmorland and Comberlad
mwuk1616	isle of wight	1610	SPEED	960	39	51	Wight Island
mwec1238	uk england wiltshire	1631	SPEED	1000	38	51	Wilshire
mwec1270	uk england worcestershire	1627	SPEED	140	9	12	Worcestershir
mwec1271	uk england worcestershire	1631	SPEED	1000	38	51	Worcestershire Described
mwec1298	uk england yorkshire	1631	SPEED	1500	38	51	York Shire
mwwi0639	hispaniola	1771	SPEER	280	25	25	A Plan of Cape Nicholas Mole at the N.W. End of the Island of Hispaniola, Lat. 19°58'N.
mwwi0104	west indies	1774	SPEER	10000	73	115	To His Royal Highness George Augustus Frederick Prince of Wales … This Chart of the West Indies (engr. By T. Bowen)
mwgm0300	mexico	1825	SPEHR	800	32	41	Der Freistaat Mexico
mwit0375	italy friuli	1790	SPERGS	2500	91	103	Tyrolis pars meridionalis Episcopatum Tridentinum
			SPILBERGEN: SEE 'VAN SPILBERGEN'				
mwam0248	america continent	1799	SPILSBURY	300	39	33	A New Map of America According to the Method of Abbe Gaultier
mwam1008	america north (east)	1761	SPILSBURY	650	28	38	A New Map of North America from the Latest Discoveries
mwit0160a	italy	1725	SPINELLI	1200	51	71	Tabula Italiae medii aevi Graeco Langobardico francici. Accurante Societate Palatina
mwuss0219	carolinas	1780	SPROULE	2750	51	72	A Sketch of the Environs of Charlestown in South Carolina
mwme0311	holy land	1744	STACKHOUSE	150	30	20	A Map of Canaan Divided among ye XII Tribes
mwaf0247	africa	1782	STACKHOUSE	120	36	36	Africa Antiqua
mwme1029	turkey etc	1783	STACKHOUSE	240	37	37	Anatolia Syria &c.
mwsc0374a	scandinavia denmark	1783	STACKHOUSE	150	38	38	Denmark
mwe0958	europe hungary	1786	STACKHOUSE	150	37	37	Hungary with part of Turkey
mwme0388	holy land	1798	STACKHOUSE	240	38	37	Judea or the Holy Land
mwam0485	america north	1783	STACKHOUSE	750	38	36	North America in its Present Divisions Agreeable to the Peace
mwaf0246	africa	1782	STACKHOUSE	240	38	37	Present Africa
mwas0200a	asia continent	1783	STACKHOUSE	300	37	37	Present Asia
mwe0206a	europe	1783	STACKHOUSE	300	37	37	Present Europe
mwuk0218	ireland	1782	STACKHOUSE	320	41	37	Present Ireland
mwbp0519	poland	1790	STACKHOUSE	180	38	41	Present Poland Prussia &c.
mwsc0168	scandinavia	1782	STACKHOUSE	240	41	37	Present Sweden & Norway
mwru0276	russia	1784	STACKHOUSE	150	38	36	Russia in Europe
mwsam0100	south america	1782	STACKHOUSE	200	37	36	South America
mwgr0629a	greece islands	1783	STACKHOUSE	250	37	37	The Islands in the Aegaean Sea
mwam0234	america continent	1792	STACKHOUSE	300	38	36	Western Hemisphere Engraved by S. Neele
mwit0692	italy piedmont	1790	STAGNON	960	72	47	Pianta della Citta di Torino
mwbh0704	belgium holland	1758	STAMPIOEN	12000	108	173	Onderwys in 't Regte Gebruyk van het Hemels-Plyn, Strekkende tot nut en Vermaak der Liefhebbers
mwin0382a	india	1859	STANFORD	750	166	127	Stanford's Map of India (shown above left)
mwam1149	america north (east)	1805	STANSBURY	500	41	33	America
mwam1199	america north (east)	1827	STANSBURY	1800	97	44	Map of the Country Embracing the Several Routes Examined with a View to a National Road from Washington to Lake Ontario
mwuss1066	new jersey	1849	STANSBY, KEILY & REA	4500	97	137	Map of the Counties of Salem and Gloucester, New Jersey
mwme0726a	caucasus	1730	STARCKMAN	180	23	20	Kaarte van het Aardsche Paradys, Volgens het Ontwerp van den Schryver
mwaf0322	africa	1831	STARLING	75	9	15	Africa
mwas0248	asia continent	1831	STARLING	80	9	13	Asia
mwp0093	australia	1830	STARLING	200	10	15	Australia
mwe0401	europe austria	1833	STARLING	50	9	14	Austrian Dominions
mwas0289	asia burma	1831	STARLING	80	15	10	Birman Empire
mwsam0424	south america brazil	1833	STARLING	100	14	9	Brazil, with Guiana & Paraguay, by Thos. Starling
mwca0166	canada	1833	STARLING	150	9	14	British Possessions in North America
mwca0167	canada	1833	STARLING	120	9	14	Canada with New Brunswick, Nova Scotia & Newfoundland
mwsam0551	south america colombia	1833	STARLING	80	9	14	Colombia
mwas0542	asia south east	1833	STARLING	100	9	14	East India Islands

AMPG REFERENCE	REGION	DATE	MAP MAKER	PRICE (UK£)	VERT. (cm.)	HOR. (cm.)	TITLE OF MAP (Comments by the editor in brackets)
mwaf0561	africa egypt etc	1833	STARLING	60	14	9	Egypt
mwit0243	italy	1833	STARLING	80	14	9	Italian States.
mwgm0321	mexico	1833	STARLING	80	9	14	Mexico and Guatimala
mwam0687	america north	1833	STARLING	120	14	9	North America
mwsp0133	portugal	1833	STARLING	60	14	9	Portugal
mwru0349	russia	1833	STARLING	80	9	14	Russian Empire
mwsam0153	south america	1833	STARLING	80	14	9	South America by T. Starling
mwsp0329	spain	1833	STARLING	80	9	15	Spain
mwsw0228	switzerland	1833	STARLING	75	9	14	Switzerland
mww0702	world	1833	STARLING	150	9	15	The World
mwam0667	america north	1830	STARLING	100	9	14	United States
mwwi0189	west indies	1833	STARLING	90	9	14	West Indies
mww0590a	world	1795	STASI	300	16	30	Il Mappamondo
mwec0928	uk england nottinghamshire	1830	STAVELEY & WOOD	2000	114	116	Plan of the Town and County of the Town of Nottingham and of the Several Extra Parochial Places within the Liberties of Lenton, Redford, and Sneinton, in the County of Nottingham. From Surveys Made in the Years 1827, 1828 and 1829
mwaf0969	africa south	1793	STAVORINUS	1000	21	41	Schetz der ligging van de Saldanha, Tafel, Hout en Fals Baai aan Caap de Goede Hoop.
mwgm0362	mexico	1847	STEALEY	25000	58	86	Map of Mexico Showing the Seat of the War Compiled from the Latest Authorities by Geo. Stealey, Civ. Eng.
mwsam0639	south america guyana	1791	STEDMAN	300	20	44	A Map of Surinam
mwuss1161	new york	1794	STEDMAN	2000	69	50	A Plan of the Operations of the King's Army under the Command of General Sr. William Howe, K.B. in New York and East New Jersey, against the American Forces Commanded by General Washington, from the 12th of October to the 28th of November 1776
mwuss1157	new york	1793	STEDMAN	650	65	51	Plan of the Attack of the Forts Clinton & Montgomery upon Hudsons River, which were Stormed by His Majestys Forces under the Command of Sir Henry Clinton, K.B. on the 6th of Octr. 1777
mwuss0237	carolinas	1794	STEDMAN	600	25	29	Plan of the Siege of Charlestown in South Carolina
mwuss0505	georgia	1794	STEDMAN	1200	41	57	Plan of the Siege of Savannah, with the Joint Attack of the French and Americans on the 9th October 1779 (reduced size version of Faden, 1784)
mwsam0640	south america guyana	1794	STEDMAN	400	16	41	View of the Town of Paramaribo, with the Road & Shipping; from the Opposite Shore
mwuk1447a	england thames	1802	STEEL	550	63	72	A Survey of the River Thames
mwf0301	france bay of biscay	1813	STEEL	720	69	83	The Bay of Biscay, from the Latest Original Executed at the French Depot Marine. Embellished with Views Taken by Admiral Knight. Second Edition. Revised and Corrected Octr. 25th, 1813
mwuss0912	michigan	1834	STEELE	300	36	33	A New & Correct Map of Michigan from the Latest Surveys Published by O.G. Steele Buffalo
mwe1124d	europe slovenia	1843	STEIN	1350	106	88	General-Karte des Konigreichs Illyrien nebst dem Koniglich Ungarischen Littorale (shown above left)
mwe1124c	europe slovenia	1832	STEIN	800	56	68	Karte vom Herzogthume Krain
mwe0618	europe czech republic (bohemia)	1841	STEIN	250	32	38	Neuester Situations-Plan von Prag
mww0216	world	1680	STEINBERGER	1200	19	23	Tab.I Geographia et Astronomia (illustrated is 1741 re-issue by Richter)
mwsw0090	switzerland	1685	STEINER	750	28	39	Helvetiae Rhaetiae et Valesiae Nova Tabula MDCLXXXV
mwe0419b	europe austria vienna	1710	STEINHAUSEN	2500			Josepho Augusto … Vienna Austria
mwg0664	saxony	1763	STEINMETZ	2250	42	37	Mappe der Wulfter Burgfreyheit
mww0180	world	1663	STENT	20000	38	51	A New and Accurat Map of the World Drawne According to the Best and Late Discoveries: Anno Dom: 1663
mwuk0074	ireland	1669	STENT	5500	37	48	A New and Exact Mapp of Ireland with an Addition of the Foure Chieffe Citties Belonging to the Several Provinces thereof (first published 1653)
mwuk0924	england	1662	STENT	7500	40	51	A New Map of the Kingdome of England and Principality of Wales
mwme0451	jerusalem	1647	STENT	10000	50	74	Ierusalem with her Suburbes, and the Most Princapall Places thereof, as it Florished in Christ his Tyme, Most Trewly Described
mwgr0330	greece corfu	1800	STEPHENSON	200	16	20	(Untitled chart, incl. neighbouring Albanian coast)
mwgr0331	greece corfu	1800	STEPHENSON	200	16	20	The Harbour of Corfu
mwme0081	holy land	1620	STERN	1200	31	51	Peregrination der Apostolen und das Leben Pauli
mwme0082	holy land	1620	STERN	1200	31	49	Peregrination Ihesu Christi
mwme0083	holy land	1620	STERN	1200	31	49	Peregrination. Die Reise der Kindern Israel
mwgm0202a	mexico	1725	STEVENS	650	18	22	An Hidrographical Draught of Mexico as it Lies in its Lakes (English translation of De Herrera's map of 1601. The illustration here is from a re-issue by Careri in 1728 'Hydrocoaphicame lo Mexicano rappresentato nelle sue Lacune')

AMPG REFERENCE	REGION	DATE	MAP MAKER	PRICE (UK£)	VERT. (cm.)	HOR. (cm.)	TITLE OF MAP (Comments by the editor in brackets)
mwuss1477	rhode isl	1831	STEVENS	3600	112	74	A Topographical Map of the State of Rhode Island and Providence Plantations
mwca0494	canada prince edward isl.	1798	STEWART	960	19	35	Prince Edward Island Divided into Counties and Parishes
mwbh0505	belgium holland	1701	STEYAART	1750	51	88	Caarte ende Afbeeldinge der Stede en Vrye Heerlykheit van Heenvliet. No. XVII (Polder map)
mwit0824	italy sardinia	1805	STIELER	400	48	28	(Untitled map)
mwaf0332	africa	1840	STIELER	80	29	36	Afrika
mwp0111	australia	1835	STIELER	150	30	38	Australien
mwc0234	china	1804	STIELER	300	47	52	Charte von China nach Murdochischer Projektion Entworfen
mwf0545	france corsica	1805	STIELER	650	48	58	Charte von Corsica und Sardinien (2 maps on one sheet)
mwe0485	europe central	1840	STIELER	360	89	111	Deutschland Konigr. der Niederlande, Kgr. Belgien und die Schweiz, nebst Theilen der Angranzenden Lander
mwaf1021	africa south	1841	STIELER	200	32	41	Karte von Sud-Afrika
mwam0744	america north	1840	STIELER	240	19	23	Nord-America und West-Indien (independent Texas)
mwas0539	asia south east	1831	STIELER	140	30	39	Ost-Indien mit den Inseln
mwam0269	america continent	1816	STIELER	280	31	36	Planiglob der Antipoden
mwaa0171	arctic	1830	STIELER	120	32	38	Polar-Karte Enthaltend: die Lander u. Meere vom Nord-Pol bis 50° N. Br. u. Weiter, mit der Ubersicht des Russischen Reichs in Eur., As. Ame. und des Brittischen Nord-America entw. v Ad. St. 1823
mwsc0218	scandinavia	1837	STIELER	100	34	40	schweden und norvegen
mwam0649	america north	1825	STIELER	200	33	39	Vereinigte Staaten von Nord-America (illustrated is 1848 edition)
mwam1254	america north (east)	1847	STIELER	180	34	40	Verein-Staaten von Nord-America mit Ausnahme Florida's und der Westlichen Territorien
mwwi0200	west indies	1837	STIELER	100	30	38	West-Indien mit Florida, d. Landenge v. Panama
mwam0293	america continent	1832	STIELER	100	31	30	Westliche Halbkugel
mww0695	world	1831	STIELER	200	31	34	Zur Uebersicht der Erd-Flaeche und der Grossen Seerisen
mwuss0874	massachusetts	1832	STIMPSON	350	22	36	Plan of the City of Boston
mwp0090	australia	1829	STIRLING	15000	28	63	Chart of Swan River (publ. by Hansard)
mwit0874	italy sicily	1592	STIZZIA	675	38	52	La Clarissima citta di Catania (close copy of Braun & Hogenberg)
mwuk0515	scotland	1770	STOBIE	1250	106	100	A Map of Roxburgh Shire or Tiviotdale
mwam0001	america continent	1512	STOBNICZA		27	38	(Untitled map, the first to focus on the Americas, based on Waldseemuller's world map of 1507)
mwp0039b	australia	1801	STOCKDALE	650	27	38	A Chart Showing Part of the SW Coast of New Holland (reduced version of Vancouver's 1798 map)
mww0601	world	1798	STOCKDALE	400	36	61	A Chart of the World Exhibiting the Track of M. de La Perouse and the Route of M. Lesseps across the Continent
mww0536	world	1785	STOCKDALE	960	41	58	A General Chart Exhibiting Discoveries Made by Capt. James Cook
mwuss0298	connecticut	1794	STOCKDALE	320	19	17	A Map of Connecticut
mwuss1006	new hampshire	1794	STOCKDALE	400	23	18	A Map of New Hampshire
mwca0341	canada newfoundland	1794	STOCKDALE	240	23	17	A Map of Newfoundland
mwaa0157	arctic	1800	STOCKDALE	350	36	34	A Map of the Countries Thirty Degrees round the North Pole
mwam1097	america north (east)	1787	STOCKDALE	10000	59	59	A Map of the Country between Albemarle Sound and Lake Erie, Comprehending the Whole of Virginia, Maryland, Delaware and Pennsylvania
mwwi0673	hispaniola	1806	STOCKDALE	450	46	73	A Map of the Island of St. Domingo
mwam0810a	america north (central)	1792	STOCKDALE	480	31	39	A Map of the Northern and Middle States; Comprehending the Western Territory and the British Dominions in North America, from the Best Authorities
mwam1106	america north (east)	1792	STOCKDALE	650	31	37	A Map of the States of Virginia, North Carolina, South Carolina and Georgia, Comprehending the Spanish Provinces of East and West Florida: Exhibiting the Boundaries as Fixed by the Late Treaty of Peace
mwwi0134	west indies	1794	STOCKDALE	250	25	41	A Map of the West Indies from the Best Authorities
mwsp0129	portugal	1812	STOCKDALE	650	142	81	A New General Military Map of the Kingdom of Portugal. The Roads are Laid down from the Carta Militar, Published by the French at Lisbon, 1808, and the Principal Military Features from the Best Authorities
mwca0128	canada	1800	STOCKDALE	200	17	23	A New Map of Upper & Lower Canada
mwbh0758	belgium holland	1792	STOCKDALE	400	41	52	A New Map of Zealand; with the Rivers Schelde, part of Halland, Flanders & Brabant; Shewing the Situation of the Schelde the Present Subject of Dispute
mwuk1261	england london	1797	STOCKDALE	8000	105	150	A New Plan of London XXIX Miles in Circumference
mwg0245	berlin	1800	STOCKDALE	240	17	25	A Plan of the City of Berlin
mwsw0216	switzerland	1800	STOCKDALE	200	16	25	A Plan of the City of Bern
mwsw0217	switzerland	1800	STOCKDALE	200	17	24	A Plan of the City of Geneva
mwit0455	italy liguria	1800	STOCKDALE	150	18	25	A Plan of the City of Genoa
mwg0729	schleswig-holstein	1800	STOCKDALE	200	17	24	A Plan of the City of Hamburg.
mwg0400	bavaria	1800	STOCKDALE	150	16	23	A Plan of the City of Munich
mwit1073	italy naples	1800	STOCKDALE	150	16	25	A Plan of the City of Naples
mwf0905	france paris	1800	STOCKDALE	200	23	26	A Plan of the City of Paris
mwca0544	canada quebec	1798	STOCKDALE	280	18	24	A Plan of the City of Quebec

AMPG REFERENCE	REGION	DATE	MAP MAKER	PRICE (UK£)	VERT. (cm.)	HOR. (cm.)	TITLE OF MAP (Comments by the editor in brackets)
mwit0758	italy rome	1800	STOCKDALE	200	24	26	A Plan of the City of Rome
mwit0694	italy piedmont	1800	STOCKDALE	150	17	25	A Plan of the City of Turin
mwit1253	italy venice	1800	STOCKDALE	200	17	25	A Plan of the City of Venice
mwe0432c	europe austria vienna	1800	STOCKDALE	200	17	25	A Plan of the City of Vienna.
mwe0471	europe central	1800	STOCKDALE	400	47	81	A Reduced Map of the Empire of Germany, Holland, the Netherlands, Switzerland, the Grisons, Italy, Sicily, Corsica and Sardinia (3 sheets, each 47x81cm)
mwuk1041	england	1809	STOCKDALE	1800	61	68	Map of England & Wales from the Latest Surveys (20 sheets, each 61x68cm)
mwuk0571	scotland	1806	STOCKDALE	1650	61	67	Map of Scotland, from the Latest Surveys (12 sheets, each 61x67cm)
mwwi0384	barbados	1794	STOCKDALE	200	24	18	Map of the Island of Barbadoes
mwuk1445	england thames	1796	STOCKDALE	350	23	84	Map of the River Thames
mwuss0370	delaware	1794	STOCKDALE	400	25	48	Map of Virginia, Maryland and Delaware
mwuk1042	england	1809	STOCKDALE	1350	133	162	New Physical, Historical ... Map of England & Wales
mwam1126	america north (east)	1798	STOCKDALE	450	41	47	Part of the United States of North America
mwam1141	america north (east)	1800	STOCKDALE	400	41	46	Part of the United States of North America (illustrated is German edition 'Theil der Vereinigten Staaten von Nord America')
mwuss0341	washington DC	1798	STOCKDALE	350	17	22	Plan of the City of Washington
mwuss0031	alaska	1789	STOCKDALE	200	32	30	Sketch of McLeod's Harbour on the West Side of Montagu I.
mwuss0029	alaska	1789	STOCKDALE	200	22	30	Sketch of Port Etches, Situated 5 Leagues NNE of Cape Hinchingbrook; together with a Sketch of Brooks Harbour
mwuss0030	alaska	1789	STOCKDALE	200	32	33	Sketch of Portlock's & Goulding's Harbours on the North West Coast of America
mwp0027	australia	1788	STOCKDALE	2000	45	52	Sketch of Sydney Cove, Port Jackson in the County of Cumberland, New South Wales, July 1788
mwam0552	america north	1800	STOCKDALE	300	33	39	United States of America
mwaf0505a	africa egypt etc	1728	STOCKLEIN	300	23	18	A. Insula S. Claudii in qua arx Imperatoris Aethiopiae. Iter Cl. Viri Caroli Iacobi Poncet, Medici Galli per Aegyptum, Nubiam, Abyssinum et Arabiam. 1700
mwc0303	china formosa	1728	STOCKLEIN	785	18	23	Die Insel Formosa Neu Abgemessen aus Besehl Kaysers Kamhi
mwc0103	china	1726	STOCKLEIN	450	31	21	Grab-Statt des Heiligen Franc. Xaverij auf der Insel Sanciano / Land-Taffel der Insel Sanciano (Macao environs)
mwin0180	india	1726	STOCKLEIN	80	11	20	Iter R. Patris Mauduit Galli e S.I. ab Ora Coromandeli per Regnum Carnate a 3. Sept. 1701
mwc0107	china	1729	STOCKLEIN	300	21	31	Land-Taffel de Insel Sanciano (Pearl River Delta, Macao)
mwsam0269	south america bolivia	1726	STOCKLEIN	350	19	13	Mission bey den Moschen durch die Jesuiter von Peru Gestisst
mwjk0084	japan	1730	STOCKLEIN	350	13	24	Nangasak Call'd by the Chinese Tchangk
mwjk0071	japan	1726	STOCKLEIN	400	14	24	Nangasaki, so die Sineser Tchangki nennen
mwuss0346	washington DC	1820	STONE	1500	40	54	A Correct Map of the City of Washington Capital of the United States of America. Lat. 38°53' N. Long. 0°0'
mwec0616	uk england kent	1700	STOOPENDAAL	350	24	34	Afbeelding van de Stad en Revier van Rochester, Chattam
mwm0144	mediterranean east	1729	STOOPENDAAL	500	35	45	De Beschryvingh van de Reysen Pauli en van de Andere Apostelen
mwme0251	holy land	1714	STOOPENDAAL	300	35	46	De Gelegentheyt van 't Paradys en 't Landt Canaan, Mitsgaders de Eerst Bewoonde Landen der Patriarchen
mwsc0329	scandinavia denmark	1700	STOOPENDAAL	400	25	34	De Stadt Nyborg Veroverdt door de Hr. Michiel de Ruiter, en 't Slaan der Zweeden
mwme0233	holy land	1704	STOOPENDAAL	400	31	45	Perigrinatie ofte Veertich-Iarige Reyse der Kinderen Israels, uyt Egypten door de Roode Zee, ende de Woestyne, tot in't Beloofde Landt Canaan
mwbh0231	belgium holland	1632	STRADA	2500	31	22	(Leo Belgicus) De Bello Belgico Decas Prima Famiani Stradae Rom Soc. Jesu
mwbh0632	belgium holland	1736	STRADA	600	10	8	(Leo Belgicus) Famiani Stradae Romani e Societate Iesu Decas Secunda
mwbh0286	belgium holland	1643	STRADA	1200	19	13	(Leo Belgicus) Novus XVII. Inferioris Germaniae Provinciarum
mwbh0327	belgium holland	1651	STRADA	1200	19	14	(Leo Belgicus. Title page of book) De Bello Belgico Decades Duae Auctores et Correctiores
mwbh0302	belgium holland	1648	STRADA	500	13	7	De Bello Belgico
mwru0447a	russia tartary	1730	STRAHLENBERG	5000	65	99	Nova Descriptio Geographica Tattariae Magnae (re-engraved by R. Seale in 1736)
mwaf0321	africa	1829	STREIT	200	39	47	Afrika
mwsc0209	scandinavia	1830	STREIT	240	48	40	Charte der Drey Nordischen Reiche Schweden, Norwegen und Daenemark
mwme0680	arabia etc	1830	STREIT	240	39	48	Charte des Osmanischen Reiches in Europa u. Asien
mwam0264	america continent	1810	STREIT	480	57	47	Charte von America nach den Neuesten Materialen
mwas0242	asia continent	1817	STREIT	400	50	62	Charte von Asien
mwp0063	australia	1817	STREIT	1800	48	65	Charte von Australien (2 Sydney insets)

AMPG REFERENCE	REGION	DATE	MAP MAKER	PRICE (UK£)	VERT. (cm.)	HOR. (cm.)	TITLE OF MAP (Comments by the editor in brackets)
mwam0627	america north	1821	STREIT	400	39	47	Charte von dem Nordamericanischen Staatenbunde, nach den Neuesten Vorhandenen Hulfsmitteln Entworfen und Gezeichnet
mwit0238	italy	1828	STREIT	240	49	40	Charte von Italien
mwam1243	america north (east)	1840	STREIT	350	38	47	Die Vereinigten Staaten von Nord-Amerika
mwg0176	germany	1818	STREIT	400	116	103	General-Charte von Teutschland in Vier Blattern
mwam0668	america north	1830	STREIT	300	40	47	Nord-America und West-Indien
mww0691	world	1830	STREIT	400	25	50	Planiglobien
mwsam0149	south america	1830	STREIT	200	47	39	Sud-America
mwf0233	france alsace	1700	STRIDBECK	1200	32	58	Argentina versus Septentr. (6 plans of Strassbourg and view)
mwsp0536	spain regions	1730	STRIDBECK	350	15	31	Barcelona (view)
mwbh0542a	belgium holland	1710	STRIDBECK	250	16	20	Die Graffschaft Flandern
mwit0930	italy sicily	1720	STRIDBECK	275	15	19	Messina
mwit0665	italy piedmont	1700	STRIDBECK	375	63	80	Piemont und Monferrat mitt Angraenzenden Staaten Laendern und Provincien
mwg0354	bavaria	1710	STRIDBECK	650	74	92	Theatrum des Krieges in der Marggrafschaft Burgau u. Angraenzenden Laendern
mwsc0221	scandinavia	1846	STROM	500	88	63	Karta ofver Landsvagarne uti Sverige och Norrige samt en Del af Dannemark
mwsc0726	scandinavia sweden	1737	STROMERONA	1200	54	64	Special Hydrographik Charta ofwer Sandehamn
mwam1229	america north (east)	1834	STRONG	960	32	51	Map of the United States Corrected from the Most Authentic Surveys
mwuss0556	illinois	1835	STRONG	1600	40	53	The States of Ohio Indiana & Illinois and Michigan Territory
mwam0701	america north	1835	STRONG	2000	61	79	United States, from the Latest Authorities
mwbp0071	baltic states	1589	STRUBICZ	1600	32	40	Magni Ducatus Lithuaniae Livoniae et Moscoviae Descriptio
mwuk1156	england london	1720	STRYPE	2400	50	68	A New Plan of the City of London, Westminster and Southwark
mwas0305	asia caspian sea	1668	STRUYS	600	29	35	Carte Marine ou est Decrite la Mer Caspienne
mwam0650	america north	1825	STUCCHI	750	54	71	America Settentrionale o Colombia (illustrated is 1856 edition)
mwit0622	italy north	1818	STUCCHI	400	53	71	Nuova Carta Geografica, Statistica e Stradale degli Stati di Terraferma di S.M. il Re di Sardegna
mwbp0166	poland	1548	STUMPF	400	13	18	(Untitled map in page of text. Size is for map only)
mwit0019	italy	1548	STUMPF	600	12	16	(Unitled map showing Italy and the Adriatic running east-west)
mwsw0007	switzerland	1548	STUMPF	500	28	18	(Untitled maps of parts of Switzerland, south at top, from 'Schweytzer Chronick'. Price for each.)
mwe0005	europe	1548	STUMPF	1000	28	38	Europa / Die Erste Tafel dieser Chronicken so im Ersten Buch Begriffen
mwsp0156	spain	1548	STUMPF	400	12	17	Form und Gestalt Hispanie
mwf0016	france	1548	STUMPF	1000	30	42	Gallia oder Franckreych / Die Landtafel dess Dritten Buchs
mwg0025	germany	1586	STUMPF	800	28	39	Germania
mwf0378	france burgundy	1548	STUMPF	500	19	29	Graffschaffe Burgund (also part of Switzerland as mwe0007 above)
mwas0897a	asia south east sumatra	1839	STURLER	960	154	139	Figurative Kaart van het zuid oostelijk gedeelte van Sumatra bevattende Palenbang, Benkoelen en de Lampongs
mwsp0622	spain regions	1814	SUCHET	300	43	59	Plan de Mequinenza Pris le 8 Juin 1810 par l'Armee Francaise d'Aragon
mwsp0623	spain regions	1814	SUCHET	300	46	61	Plan de Peniscola Pris le 4 Fevrier 1812 par l'Armee Francaise d'Aragon
mwsp0628	spain regions	1814	SUCHET	300	44	58	Plan de Sagonte
mwsp0626	spain regions	1814	SUCHET	300	44	58	Plan de Tortose
mwsp0624	spain regions	1814	SUCHET	300	45	59	Plan de Valence
mwsp0627	spain regions	1814	SUCHET	300	60	44	Plan des Attaques de Tarragone
mwsp0625	spain regions	1814	SUCHET	300	42	50	Plan du Fort D'Oropesa
mww0560	world	1788	SUDLOW	250	15	26	The World with All the Late Discoveries
mww0591	world	1795	SUDLOW	1200	25	50	The World with the Latest Discoveries (Botany Bay noted as convict destination)
mww0537	world	1785	SUDLOW	400	27	44	Universalis Tabula iuxta Ptolemaeum
mwuss0728	maine	1834	SUMNER	675	38	50	Map of Maine, New Hampshire, and Vermont, from the Most Authentic Sources
mwuss0319	connecticut	1833	SUMNER	675	38	48	Map of Massachusetts, Connecticut and Rhode Island
mwam0691	america north	1834	SUMNER	960	37	53	Map of the United States, Compiled from the Latest Authorities
mwuss1297	ohio	1826	SUMNER	6000	30	51	Map of the Western Reserve, Including the Fire Lands in Ohio
mwca0215	canada arctic	1749	SWAINE	240	34	29	A Chart of Hudson's Straits and Bay, According to the Discoveries Made between the Years 1610 & 1743
mwuss0132	california	1849	SWANSTON	200	23	14	Map of California
mwam1382	america north (west)	1848	SWANSTON	180	23	14	Oregon and California
mwbh0382a	belgium holland	1670	SWART	4000	44	57	Amstelredam Anno 1623

AMPG REFERENCE	REGION	DATE	MAP MAKER	PRICE (UK£)	VERT. (cm.)	HOR. (cm.)	TITLE OF MAP (Comments by the editor in brackets)
mwru0448b	russia tartary	1734	SWEDENBORG	800	48	64	Charta ofwer Siberiskae... som och Tobolska... och Faedkowska Iernbruk
mwuss0467	florida	1829	SWIFT	1500	70	169	Map of the Territory of Florida, from its Northern Boundary to Lat: 27°30' N. Connected with the Delta of the Mississippi
mwec0155	uk england cheshire	1830	SWIRE	1000	99	133	A Map of the County Palatine of Chester Divided into Hundreds & Parishes, From an Accurate Survey, Made in the Years 1828 & 1829. By W. Swire & W. F. Hutchings, London.
mwp0515	pacific south	1805	SWOBODA & HARTL	1500	50	67	Generalcharte von Australien nach dem entwurfe des H.Joseph Marx Freiherrn v. Liechtenstern (depicts the belief that Australia was two land masses split 'vertically')
mww0020	world	1511	SYLVANUS	72000	41	55	(Untitled heart-shape projection printed in black and red lettering. Illustrated example also has early hand colouring.)
mwuk0651	uk	1511	SYLVANUS	15000	41	56	Prima Europae Tabula (1st 'modern' map focussing on the British Isles. The map was printed in two colours.)
mwaf0667	africa north	1511	SYLVANUS	4800	41	51	Quarta Africae Tabula (printed in 2 colours, red and black)
mwec0595	uk england kent	1596	SYMONDSON		54	80	A New Description of Kent (only one example of this 1st state known)
mwp0426	pacific north	1780	SYND	500	43	43	Chart of Synd's Voyage towards Tschukotskoi Noss
mwru0405a	russia moscow	1825	SYROEZHIN	5000	73	87	(Plan of the City of Moscow, in Cyrillic)
mwf0529a	france corsica	1769	SYSANG	1000	27	43	Neue und Accurate Carte von der Insel Corsica
mwaf0881a	africa south	1686	TACHARD	400	17	17	Carte des Pays et des Peuples du Cap de Bonne Esperance Nouvellement Decouvertes par les Hollandais
mwaf0881	africa south	1686	TACHARD	400	18	30	La Baye du Cap De Bonne Esperance. (view)
mwjk0157b	japan tokyo	1848	TAKASHIBA	2000	69	90	Shoei on Edo ezu
mwuk1333	england london	1851	TALLIS	3000	55	75	Tallis's Illustrated Plan of London and its Environs in Commemoration of the Great Exhibition if Industry of All Nations, 1851
mwuss0664	louisiana	1817	TANESSE	8000	54	84	Plan of the City and Suburbs of New Orleans (views in borders)
mwam0636	america north	1823	TANNER	10000	112	149	A Map of North America, Constructed According to the Latest Information
mwuss1436	pennsylvania	1841	TANNER	500	51	69	A Map of the Canals & Rail Roads of Pennsylvania and New Jersey and the Adjoining States
mwam1245	america north (east)	1841	TANNER	9000	121	161	A Map of the United States Including Every County Enumerated in the Census of 1840 (1st edition 1829)
mwam0684	america north	1832	TANNER	2000	42	68	A Map of the United States of America
mwgm0305	mexico	1826	TANNER	35000	58	74	A Map of the United States of Mexico, as Organized and Defined by the Several Acts of the Congress of that Republic. Constructed from a Great Variety of Printed and Manuscript Documents ... 1825 (other editions in 1826, 1834, 1837)
mwuss0059	arkansas	1836	TANNER	280	35	28	A New Map of Arkansas with its Canals, Roads and Distances
mwuss0531	georgia	1839	TANNER	240	34	28	A New Map of Georgia with its Roads & Distances
mwuss0553	illinois	1833	TANNER	280	36	30	A New Map of Illinois with its Proposed Canals, Roads & Distances from Place to Place along the Stage and Steam Boat Routes
mwuss0573	indiana	1833	TANNER	280	36	30	A New Map of Indiana with its Roads & Distances
mwuss0613	kentucky	1833	TANNER	250	30	36	A New Map of Kentucky with its Roads & Distances from Place to Place along the Stage & Steam Boat Routes
mwuss0678	louisiana	1839	TANNER	400	28	36	A New Map of Louisiana with its Canals, Roads and Distances from Place to Place along the Stage and Steamboat Routes
mwuss0731	maine	1840	TANNER	240	36	29	A New Map of Maine
mwuss0965	mississippi	1836	TANNER	240	33	27	A New Map of Mississippi with its Roads and Distances
mwuss0989	missouri	1839	TANNER	240	36	30	A New Map of Missouri with its Roads & Distances
mwuss1240	new york	1840	TANNER	200	27	33	A New Map of New York with its Canals, Roads & Distances from Place to Place along the Stage & Steam-Boat Routes
mwuss1305	ohio	1833	TANNER	600	33	27	A New Map of Ohio with its Canals, Roads, & Distances
mwuss0060a	arkansas	1839	TANNER	5000	51	60	A New Map of the State of Arkansas, Constructed principally from United States Surveys, Exhibiting Countries, Townships & Sections.
mwaf0308	africa	1818	TANNER	250	50	55	Africa
mwam0282	america continent	1823	TANNER	650	50	62	America
mwsam0429	south america brazil	1836	TANNER	120	38	30	Brazil
mwp0280	pacific (all)	1830	TANNER	120	23	36	Chart of the Pacific Ocean (Library of Congress puts date as c1830 but outline of Australia is c1800)
mwc0287	china	1845	TANNER	120	27	33	China
mwuss1231	new york	1835	TANNER	300	38	33	City of New York
mwuss0353	washington DC	1836	TANNER	240	30	39	City of Washington
mwjk0136	japan	1810	TANNER	280	24	40	Empire of Japan
mwe0252	europe	1818	TANNER	120	48	54	Europe

AMPG REFERENCE	REGION	DATE	MAP MAKER	PRICE (UK£)	VERT. (cm.)	HOR. (cm.)	TITLE OF MAP (Comments by the editor in brackets)
mwuss0007	alabama	1823	TANNER	2000	54	71	Georgia and Alabama
mwuss0548	illinois	1823	TANNER	1400	71	57	Illinois and Missouri
mwuss0586	iowa	1843	TANNER	350	38	33	Iowa
mwuk0285	ireland	1843	TANNER	120	28	22	Ireland
mwuss0606	kentucky	1823	TANNER	2250	53	70	Kentucky and Tennessee
mwuss0666	louisiana	1820	TANNER	1400	69	56	Louisiana and Mississippi
mwuss1421	pennsylvania	1831	TANNER	5500	59	46	Map of Bucks County, Pennsylvania
mwuss1418	pennsylvania	1830	TANNER	3000	46	57	Map of Chester County. Constructed by Virtue of an Act of the Legislature of Pennsylvania by James Hindman (1st edition 1822)
mwuss0463	florida	1823	TANNER	1200	69	53	Map of Florida
mwuss0263	carolinas	1823	TANNER	1000	55	75	Map of North & South Carolina
mwuss1408	pennsylvania	1825	TANNER	550	52	69	Map of Pennsylvania and New Jersey
mwuss1530	texas	1845	TANNER	1500	31	38	Map of Texas from the most recent authorities ... 1845
mwam1184	america north (east)	1820	TANNER	750	63	52	Map of the States of Maine, New Hampshire, Vermont, Massachusetts, Connecticut & Rhode Island
mwgm0329	mexico	1835	TANNER	400	31	38	Mexico & Guatemala
mwuss0913	michigan	1834	TANNER	240	13	17	Michigan (inset: Detroit)
mwuss1023	new hampshire	1833	TANNER	240	36	29	New Hampshire & Vermont
mwuss1199	new york	1825	TANNER	2400	60	76	New York
mwp0284a	pacific (all)	1835	TANNER	200	32	39	Oceana or Pacific Ocean (small inset shows Wilkes' discoveries in the Antarctic)
mwuss0569	indiana	1823	TANNER	2400	51	67	Ohio and Indiana
mwme0425	holy land	1843	TANNER	120	37	31	Palestine & Adjacent Countries
mwuss1439	pennsylvania	1845	TANNER	350	25	30	Pennsylvania
mwsc0216	scandinavia	1836	TANNER	120	28	22	Sweden & Norway
mwam1189	america north (east)	1825	TANNER	2000	45	56	The Traveller's Guide, A Map of the Roads, Canals and Steam Boat Routes of the United States; with the Distances from Place to Place Carefully Noticed; Including a Series of Tables Showing the Routes Pursued by the Various Steam Boats
mwww0672	world	1823	TANNER	800	50	62	The World on Mercator's Projection
mwam1252	america north (east)	1846	TANNER	200	39	31	United States
mwam1210	america north (east)	1830	TANNER	9600	116	153	United States of America (1st edition 1829)
mwsam0861	south america venezuela	1836	TANNER	150	30	37	Venezuela, New Granada & Equador (inset of Panama Canal proposal)
mwuss0782	maryland	1838	TANNER	900	51	73	Virginia, Maryland and Delaware
mwwi0192	west indies	1834	TANNER	140	28	36	West Indies
mwuss1698	wisconsin	1843	TANNER	350	38	32	Wisconsin
mwe0221	europe	1790	TAPALDOU	12000	167	226	(Map in Arabic)
mwam1352a	america north (west)	1820	TARDIEU	2500	107	79	A Map of Louisiana and Mexico / Carte de la Louisiane et du Mexique
mwaf1016	africa south	1838	TARDIEU	150	24	21	Afrique au Nord-Est de la Colonie du Cap ... Capitaine W.C. Harris
mwam0577	america north	1808	TARDIEU	220	28	23	Amerique Septentrionale
mwas0325a	asia caspian sea	1785	TARDIEU	500	63	47	Carte de la Mer Caspienne 1785
mwwi0670	hispaniola	1802	TARDIEU	300	37	46	Carte de la Partie Francaise de St. Domingue
mwe0841	europe east	1821	TARDIEU	400	83	85	Carte de la Turquie d'Europe
mwam0623a	america north	1821	TARDIEU	400	40	54	Carte de l'Amerique Septentrionale
mwme0646	arabia etc	1780	TARDIEU	400	34	44	Carte de l'Arabie et d'apres les Differents Morceaux qu'a Donnes M. Niebuh de cette Partie de l'Asia; et d'apres M. Danville pour l'Interieur des Terres
mwgr0431	greece crete	1785	TARDIEU	550	50	69	Carte de l'Isle de Candie, Nommee par les Turcs, Icriti
mwp0276	pacific (all)	1820	TARDIEU	450	39	52	Carte de L'Oceanie ou Cinquieme partie du Monde
mwwi0266	west indies (east)	1797	TARDIEU	400	33	42	Carte des Antilles
mwp0438	pacific north	1788	TARDIEU	750	50	69	Carte des Cotes de l'Amerique et de l'Asie Depuis la Californie
mwwi0666	hispaniola	1798	TARDIEU	400	33	43	Carte des Isles de la Jamaique et de St. Domingue
mwgm0067	gulf of mexico and surrounding regions	1821	TARDIEU	500	41	55	Carte du Golfe du Mexique
mwgm0290	mexico	1821	TARDIEU	250	43	30	Carte du Mexique
mwgr0220	greece	1782	TARDIEU	300	32	42	Carte du Peloponese
mwaf0428	africa east	1820	TARDIEU	250	42	31	Carte du Zanguebar
mwwi0563	guadeloupe	1821	TARDIEU	450	37	46	Carte Generale de la Guadeloupe. Dessinee et Gravee par Ambroise Tardieu
mwru0276a	russia	1785	TARDIEU	1250	53	122	Carte Générale de l'Empire de Russie 1785
mwam0620	america north	1820	TARDIEU	1800	50	76	Carte Generale du Theatre de la Guerre dans les Etats-Unis de l'Amerique avec une Carte du Mexique pour Suivre les Operations Militaires
mwsc0440	scandinavia finland	1785	TARDIEU	850	50	128	Carte Hydrographique du Golfe de Finlande
mwww0637	world	1810	TARDIEU	350	18	35	Carte Magnetique des Deux Hemispheres Grave par Tardieu (double polar hemispheres)
mwam1348	america north (west)	1810	TARDIEU	500	24	19	Carte Pour Servir au Voyage des Cap.es Lewis et Clark
mwgr0629b	greece islands	1795	TARDIEU	800	59	93	Carte Reduite des Cotes de la Grece et de L'Archipel

AMPG REFERENCE	REGION	DATE	MAP MAKER	PRICE (UK£)	VERT. (cm.)	HOR. (cm.)	TITLE OF MAP (Comments by the editor in brackets)
mwc0228	china	1800	TARDIEU	250	65	46	Carte sur laquelle est Trace la Route qu'a Suivie l'Ambassade Anglaise, depuis Zhe-Hol en Tartarie jusqu'a Pekin, et de Pekin a Han-Choo-Foo, en Chine
mwsp0676a	balearic islands	1770	TARDIEU	960	33	51	Carte Topographique et Militaire de L'Isle Minorque
mwme1038	turkey etc	1790	TARDIEU	450	39	47	Constantinople
mwsw0164	switzerland	1765	TARDIEU	250	35	45	Gouvernement de Bearn
mwit0233	italy	1820	TARDIEU	75	8	10	Italie
mwsp0115	portugal	1780	TARDIEU	350	34	44	Lisbonne
mwuk1241	england london	1780	TARDIEU	600	33	45	Londres
mwuk1214	england london	1765	TARDIEU	750	32	45	Londres … avec le Bourg de Southwark
mwsp0346	spain madrid	1780	TARDIEU	350	33	43	Madrid
mww0661	world	1819	TARDIEU	500	52	71	Mappe-Monde Divise en Deux Hemispheres avec les Decouvertes Faites dans les Derniers Voyages
mww0638	world	1810	TARDIEU	350	22	40	Mappe-Monde en deux Hemispheres
mwgm0279	mexico	1812	TARDIEU	200	23	30	Mexique
mwru0409	russia moscow	1840	TARDIEU	250	23	36	Moskou
mwg0728	schleswig-holstein	1800	TARDIEU	275	30	40	Plan de l'Ile Helgoland
mwbp0519a	poland	1790	TARDIEU	900	35	45	Plan de Varsovie
mwuss1272	ohio	1787	TARDIEU	2750	45	35	Plan des Achats des Compagnies de l'Ohio et du Scioto
mwf0914	france paris	1820	TARDIEU	120	24	37	Plan General du Siege de la Ville de Paris. Par les Troupes Alliees dans la Journee du 30 Mars 1814, et Relation de Divers Combats qui eurent Lieu dans les Environs de Paris en Juin 1815, apres la Defaite de Buonaparte a Mont-St.-Jean
mwit0755	italy rome	1780	TARDIEU	400	33	44	Rome
mwsc0162	scandinavia	1780	TARDIEU	300	32	43	Royaume de Danemarck: Premiere Carte. Danemarck, Norwege et Island
mwru0272	russia	1783	TARDIEU	1500	47	77	St. Petersbourg
mwam0578	america north	1808	TARDIEU	4000	122	140	United States of Nth. America Carte des Etats-Unis de l'Amerique Septentrionale. Copiee et Gravee sur celle d'Arrowsmith (copied from Arrowsmith's 1796 map)
mwbp0507	poland	1785	TARDIEU	750	34	44	Varsovie
mwe0432	europe austria vienna	1780	TARDIEU	350	33	42	Vienne
mwuss0230	carolinas	1787	TARLETON	720	25	30	Plan of the Siege of Charlestown in South Carolina
mwuss1660	virginia	1787	TARLETON	1000	29	32	Plan of the Siege of York Town in Virginia
mwuss1661	virginia	1787	TARLETON	2500	64	49	The Marches of Lord Cornwallis in the Southern Provinces, Now States of North America; Comprehending the Two Carolinas, with Virginia and Maryland and the Delaware Counties
mwin0363	india	1837	TASSIN	6500	148	123	Anglo-Persian Map of India (In English and Persian)
mwf1003a	france provence	1635	TASSIN	140	11	16	Antibes (from his miniature atlas)
mwf0283	france auvergne	1643	TASSIN	350	37	50	Carte d'Auvergne
mwf0310	france brittany	1634	TASSIN	675	37	51	Carte de Bretagne
mwf1117	france rhone-alpes	1634	TASSIN	400	37	52	Carte de Dauphine
mwf0392	france burgundy	1634	TASSIN	350	37	52	Carte de la Franche Comte et du Duche de Montbeliart
mwf0768	france normandy	1634	TASSIN	500	37	52	Carte de Normandie
mwf1001	france provence	1634	TASSIN	600	37	52	Carte de Provence
mwbh0826a	luxembourg	1637	TASSIN	720	37	52	Carte des Duches de Luxembourg Iuliers et Partie de Brabant et Comte de Namur (re-issued 1660)
mwe0992	europe rhine	1634	TASSIN	2000	42	165	Carte des Haute et Basse Elsace avec le Palatinat du Rhein
mwf0427	france central	1634	TASSIN	350	37	51	Carte du Duche d'Orleans
mwf1118	france rhone-alpes	1634	TASSIN	280	37	51	Carte du Lionnois Forest et Beauielois
mwf0440	france champagne	1634	TASSIN	400	37	51	Carte Generale de Champagne
mwf0946	france picardy	1634	TASSIN	280	37	51	Carte Generale de Picardie et Artois
mwbh0240	belgium holland	1634	TASSIN	500	37	52	Carte Generale des Dix et Sept Provinces des Pays Bas
mwsw0057	switzerland	1634	TASSIN	600	36	52	Carte Generale des Treize Cantons de Suisse
mwf1002a	france provence	1634	TASSIN	960	53	38	Description du Cap de la Croix Isles Ste. Marguerite et St. Honorat
mwf1002	france provence	1634	TASSIN	720	31	51	Golphe du Grimaut (St. Tropez)
mwit1102	italy tuscany	1634	TASSIN	900	37	52	Patrimoine St Pierre et Florentin
mwf0767a	france normandy	1631	TASSIN	500	37	52	Rouen
mwf1003	france provence	1634	TASSIN	600	37	52	Seigneurie de Genes, Comte de Nice et Partie de l'Isle de Corsse
mwgm0338	mexico	1840	TASSO	240	24	24	Antigo Impero Messicano (size excl. text below map)
mwuk0894	uk	1840	TASSO	150	34	46	La Gran Brettagne
mwsp0180	spain	1640	TAVERNIER	750	37	51	Antiquorum Hispaniae Espiscopatuum Geographica
mwit0088a	italy	1642	TAVERNIER	600	37	51	Antiquorum Italiae & Illyrici Occidentalis Episcopatuum (Halma 1704 re-issue shown below)
mwgr0065	greece	1640	TAVERNIER	480	37	51	Antiquorum Illyrici Orientalis Episcopatuum Geographica Descriptio
mwf0969	france poitou	1632	TAVERNIER	900	39	52	Carte de la Coste de la Rochelle a Brouiage et de l'Isle Oleron … 1627
mwsw0047	switzerland	1625	TAVERNIER	1800	39	51	Carte de la Suisse
mww0148	world	1639	TAVERNIER	4000	30		Carte de L'Amerique / Carte Nouvelle de Europe … (illustrated is the second edition, 1661, each hemisphere printed on a separate sheet)

AMPG REFERENCE	REGION	DATE	MAP MAKER	PRICE (UK£)	VERT. (cm.)	HOR. (cm.)	TITLE OF MAP (Comments by the editor in brackets)
mwe0053	europe	1643	TAVERNIER	1200	38	50	Carte de l'Europe (copy of Bertius 1627)
mwjk0040	japan	1679	TAVERNIER	3500	52	77	Carte des Isles du Iapon Esquelles est Remarque la Route tant par Mer que par Terre que Tiennent les Hollandois
mwjk0041	japan	1679	TAVERNIER	850	22	32	Carte des Isles du Iapon Esquelles est Remarque la Route tant par Mer que par Terre que Tiennent les Hollandois
mwf1094	france pyrenees	1643	TAVERNIER	300	39	53	Carte du Diocese d'Alby
mwf0967	france poitou	1632	TAVERNIER	750	38	43	Carte du Pais d'Aunis Ville & Gouverment de la Rochelle
mwit0472	italy lombardy	1625	TAVERNIER	2250	53	35	Carte et Description Generale de la Valtoline
mwas0911	asia south east vietnam	1679	TAVERNIER	1500	49	40	Carte Faite sur les Lieux par Daniel Tavernier en Plusieurs Voiages quil a Fait au Tonquin
mwf0257	france aquitaine	1634	TAVERNIER	500	37	52	Carte Generale de Guyenne (engraved by Tassin)
mwit0089	italy	1643	TAVERNIER	1350	41	56	Carte Generale de l'Italie et des Isles et Pays Circonvoisins Nouvellement Dressee sur les Cartes de Magin
mwbh0281	belgium holland	1640	TAVERNIER	600	53	42	Carte Generale des Dixsept Provinces des Pais-Bas ... par M. Tavernier, Graveur et Imprimeur du Roy ... a la Sphere Royalle, 1640
mwsp0180a	spain	1641	TAVERNIER	800	41	56	Carte Generale d'Espagne (separately issued)
mwf1110	france rhone-alpes	1630	TAVERNIER	2400	72	59	Carte Generalle de la Savoye du Piemont Duche de Montferrat
mwf0968	france poitou	1632	TAVERNIER	1000	39	52	Carte Particuliere des Costes de Poittou Aunis
mwf1004	france provence	1637	TAVERNIER	1250	41	53	Description des Isles de Ste. Margrite & St. Honorat
mwg0053a	germany	1638	TAVERNIER	2800	60	92	Generalis Exactissima et Novissima Germaniae Descriptio
mwsp0179a	spain	1638	TAVERNIER	3000	60	92	Generalis Exactissima et Novissima Hispaniae Descriptio
mwit0083	italy	1638	TAVERNIER	4000	60	92	Generalis Exactissima et Novissima Italiae Descriptio
mwsp0180b	spain	1641	TAVERNIER	600	41	52	Hispaniae Antiquae
mwit0088	italy	1641	TAVERNIER	785	36	50	Italia Antiqua cum insulis
mwf0055	france	1637	TAVERNIER	850	38	49	L'Empire Francois
mwf0672	france lorraine	1640	TAVERNIER	600	41	47	Nanci
mww0156a	world	1643	TAVERNIER	4000	38	53	Nova Totius Terrarum Orbis Geographica
mwaf0471	africa egypt etc	1640	TAVERNIER	480	36	50	Patriarchatus Alexandrini
mwme0098	holy land	1640	TAVERNIER	600	37	50	Patriarchatus Antiocheni Geographica Descriptio Tabularum Geographicarum Hydrographicarum (re-issued by Vailant in 1711)
mwme0961c	turkey etc	1677	TAVERNIER c	450	37	50	Patriarchatus Constantinopolitani Geographica Descriptio (re-issued by Covens & Mortier c1720)
mwme0099	holy land	1640	TAVERNIER	600	35	50	Patriarchatus Hierosolymitani Geographica Descriptio Parisiis aput M. Tavernier (re-issued by Vailant in 1711)
mwuss1306	ohio	1833	TAYLOR	5000	32	51	A Map of the Western Reserve Including the Fire Lands in Ohio, August, 1832 (1st publ. by Sumner 1826)
mwuk0975	england	1715	TAYLOR	3000	59	54	A New Map of England and Wales or South Britain 1715.
mwec0524	uk england herefordshire	1754	TAYLOR	2000	142	142	A New Map of the County of Hereford
mwuk0472	scotland	1733	TAYLOR	3000	58	100	A New Mapp of Scotland or North Britain with Considerable Improvements According to the Newest Observations 1731
mwuk1149	england london	1716	TAYLOR	3500	62	103	A New Mapp of the City of London (4 editions to 1745)
mwec1078	uk england staffordshire	1790	TAYLOR	650	47	60	A Plan of Wolverhampton Surveyed in 1750 by Isaac Taylor and Engraved by Thomas Jefferys
mwec0340	uk england dorset	1765	TAYLOR	2400	110	153	Dorset ... This Map of the County of Dorset
mwec0483	uk england hampshire	1759	TAYLOR	3200	160	138	Map of Hampshire, including the Isle of Wight
mwca0176	canada	1834	TAYLOR	2000	81	124	New Travelling and Commercial Map of the Canadas, from the Sault of St. Marie to the River Saguenay; and a Large Section of the United States of America (2 sheets, each 78x60cm)
mwme0386	holy land	1797	TAYLOR	150	20	34	Plan Explanatory of the Passage of the Red-Sea, by the Israelites
mwru0405	russia moscow	1824	TCHELIEF	2000	88	95	Plan Projete de la Ville Capitale Moscou et des Edifices Ajoutes en 1824
mwec0156	uk england cheshire	1830	TEESDALE	875	100	134	A Map of the County Palatine of Chester
mwme0417a	holy land	1838	TEESDALE	800	83	105	A New Historical Map of Palestine (map by Creighton)
mwe0261	europe	1829	TEESDALE	400	77	89	A New Map of Europe Corrected & Revised from the Best and Latest Authorities
mwaf0333	africa	1840	TEESDALE	100	38	34	Africa
mwme0412	holy land	1834	TEESDALE	120	41	34	Ancient Palestine
mwas0253	asia continent	1840	TEESDALE	120	34	41	Asia
mwsam0423	south america brazil	1831	TEESDALE	280	41	34	Brazil. Drawn & Engraved by J. Dower
mwca0198	canada	1845	TEESDALE	120	34	42	Canada, New Brunswick and Nova Scotia (inset: Niagara river)
mwc0270	china	1835	TEESDALE	200	35	43	China and Japan (map by J. Dower)
mwsam0555	south america colombia	1838	TEESDALE	100	34	41	Columbia
mwsc0399	scandinavia denmark	1831	TEESDALE	60	42	34	Denmark
mwuk0268	ireland	1828	TEESDALE	240	64	52	Ireland
mwgm0086	gulf of mexico and surrounding regions	1848	TEESDALE	240	34	42	Mexico and Guatimala
mww0735	world	1845	TEESDALE	5000	127	191	New Chart of the World on Mercator Projection with the Tracks of the Most Celebrated & Recent Navigators (With discoveries in the Antarctic to 1840 and Texas shown as an independent state. First edition 1836.)

AMPG REFERENCE	REGION	DATE	MAP MAKER	PRICE (UK£)	VERT. (cm.)	HOR. (cm.)	TITLE OF MAP (Comments by the editor in brackets)
mwsam0798	south america peru	1831	TEESDALE	100	41	34	Peru and Bolivia
mww0696	world	1831	TEESDALE	200	34	41	The World on Mercator's Projection
mwam0692	america north	1834	TEESDALE	200	33	41	United States
mwp0159	australia	1845	TEESDALE	240	42	33	Van Diemens Land
mwwi0214	west indies	1845	TEESDALE	240	34	52	West Indies
mwam0303	america continent	1842	TEESDALE	150	34	34	Western Hemisphere
mwaf0318	africa	1826	TEGG	80	21	26	Africa
mwas0251	asia continent	1833	TEGG	100	20	25	Asia
mwuk0886	uk	1827	TEGG	120	26	21	British Islands.
mwuk1688	north sea	1828	TEGG	120	20	25	Chart of the North Sea or German Ocean
mwit0237	italy	1826	TEGG	80	26	21	Italy
mwjk0140	japan	1829	TEGG	200	20	25	Japan
mwgm0069	gulf of mexico and surrounding regions	1829	TEGG	180	20	26	Mexico and Guatimala
mwp0278	pacific (all)	1829	TEGG	80	21	26	Pacific Ocean and South Sea Islands
mwca0159	canada	1829	TEGG	180	21	25	Polar Regions Including British Nth. America. &c.
mwuk0606	scotland	1827	TEGG	100	26	21	Scotland
mwme0890	syria etc	1829	TEGG	120	26	21	Syria and Palestine.
mwuk1309	england london	1829	TEGG	850	44	62	Tegg's New Plan of London &c. with 360 References to the Principal Streets, &c. 1829
mww0684	world	1828	TEGG	180	21	26	The World, on Mercator's Projection
mwam1206	america north (east)	1828	TEGG	180	21	26	United States
mwwi0176	west indies	1827	TEGG	120	21	26	West Indies.
mwuk0625	scotland	1838	TELFORD	200	42	34	A Chart of the Bay of Ardrossan with a Plan of the Harbour (2 maps on one sheet)
mwuk0281	ireland	1838	TELFORD	180	40	33	Howth Harbour (Dublin)
mwsc0755	scandinavia sweden	1838	TELFORD	450	40	90	Map and Section of the Gotha Canal (Telford was the designer of the canal)
mwec0157	uk england cheshire	1830	TELFORD	500	41	65	Map of the Canals in the District between Liverpool, Manchester and Birmingham
mwit0711	italy rome	1593	TEMPESTA		109	239	Disegno et Prospetto dell'alma Citta di Roma
mwp0033	australia	1793	TENCH	1200	24	30	A Map of the hitherto explored Country, Contiguous to Port Jackson: Laid Down from Actual Survey
mwm0099	mediterranean adriatic	1750	TENTIVO	350	37	51	Carta Marittima, nella quale si Contiene la Navigazione dal Capo della Linguetta al Capo d'Otranto
mwuss1267	new york	1851	THAYER, BRIDGEMAN	750	54	70	The Empire State
mwsam0581	south america guyana	1669	THELOTT	720	37	48	Guiana sive Amazonum Regio
					THEUNISZ: SEE MAPS PUBLISHED BY JACOBSZ		
mwp0003	australia	1663	THEVENOT	10000	39	60	(Untitled map, the first to show Australia on its own incl. Tasman's discoveries in 1642. First edition 1644).
mwas0398	asia south east	1664	THEVENOT	6000	51	67	(Untitled sea chart based on Teixeira's manuscript chart)
mwme0719a	caucasus	1683	THEVENOT	500	27	38	Carte de la Colchide Appelee Maintenant Mengrelie et par ceux du Pays, Odisci
mwin0110	india	1663	THEVENOT	800	28	36	Description de la Partie des Indes Orientales qui est sous la Dominations du Grand Mogol (based on Baffin's map of 1619)
mwc0050	china	1663	THEVENOT	2400	46	64	Imperii Sinarum Nova Descriptio
mwaf0366	africa east	1664	THEVENOT	5500	74	51	Ioao Teixeira Cosmographo de sue Magestade (after Teixeira's manuscript chart of 1649)
mwc0065	china	1681	THEVENOT	600	19	64	Route du Voyage de Canton a Peking
mwme0736	iraq etc	1663	THEVENOT	350	30	39	Vera Delineatio Civitatis Bassorae
mwgr0564	greece islands	1575	THEVET	350	13	15	(Chios)
mwgr0565	greece islands	1575	THEVET	350	13	11	(Rhodes)
mwin0013	ceylon	1575	THEVET	350	14	16	(Taprobana)
mwas0006	asia continent	1575	THEVET	5500	35	45	Asie
mwe0009	europe	1575	THEVET	3000	35	45	Europe
mwaf0581	africa islands madagascar	1575	THEVET	350	9	13	Ile Madagascar
mwgr0566	greece islands	1575	THEVET	350	14	16	Isle de Negrepont
mwam0009	america continent	1575	THEVET	5500	38	47	Quarte Partie du Monde
mwaf0011	africa	1575	THEVET	3500	35	45	Table d'Afrique
mwru0409c	russia moscow	1845	THIEME	2000	58	75	(Plan of Moscow, Cyrillic script)
mwm0260	mediterranean malta	1840	THIERS	240	20	33	(Malte)
mwru0288	russia	1787	THOMAS	350	40	51	Carte von der Reise Ihro Russisch Kaiserlichen Maiestat
mwg0467	hessen	1790	THOMAS	600	40	66	Geometrischer Plan von der Gegend der Stadt Franckfurth am Mayn
mwuss1392	pennsylvania	1796	THOMAS & ANDREWS	300	19	33	Pennsylvania, Drawn from the Best Authorities
mwwi0129	west indies	1793	THOMAS & ANDREWS	150	20	30	West Indies According to the Best Authorities
mwit1150	italy umbria	1613	THOMASSIN	3000	40	54	Spoletum Umbriae Caput (plan of Spoleto. Illustrated map damaged.)
mwjk0173	korea	1952	THOMPSON, A.	250	40	32	(Map of Korea, printed in Hong Kong for HMS Ceylon)
mwaf1004	africa south	1827	THOMPSON	950	23	33	George Thompson's Plan of Cape Town and its Environs (1st plan of 'modern' Cape Town)
mwme0380a	holy land	1795	THOMPSON	4000	57	139	A New Map of the Land of Promise and the Holy City of Jerusalem with the Principal Scripture Histories
mww0602	world	1798	THOMPSON, G.	5000	64	95	A New Map of the World. with All the New Discoveries (updated version of Willdey 1732)

AMPG REFERENCE	REGION	DATE	MAP MAKER	PRICE (UK£)	VERT. (cm.)	HOR. (cm.)	TITLE OF MAP (Comments by the editor in brackets)
mwuss1582	vermont	1842	THOMPSON, Z.	480	28	18	Map of the State of Vermont
mwp0066	australia	1821	THOMSON	1000	50	60	A Chart of New South Wales, Van Diemen's Land &c.
mwca0225	canada arctic	1822	THOMSON	960	50	58	A Chart of the Discoveries of Captains Ross, Parry & Franklin in the Arctic Regions in the Years 1818, 1819, 1820, 1821 & 1822 (re-issued 1827 with an additional inset top left)
mwe0245	europe	1816	THOMSON	1000	102	118	A Map of Europe with the Political Divisions after the Peace of Paris and Congress of Vienna
mwaf0306	africa	1817	THOMSON	300	47	52	Africa
mwam0270	america continent	1817	THOMSON	300	51	61	America
mwwi0280	west indies islands	1814	THOMSON	250	50	60	Antigua / Guadaloupe / Mariegalante
mwme0669	arabia etc	1815	THOMSON	280	50	58	Arabia, Egypt, Abyssinia, Red Sea, &c.
mwas0241	asia continent	1817	THOMSON	180	52	58	Asia
mwme1050	turkey etc	1814	THOMSON	240	51	59	Asiatic Turkey
mwat0234	atlantic islands	1814	THOMSON	400	51	59	Atlantic Islands (Cape Verde, Canary, Azores, Madeira)
mwat0058	atlantic ocean (all)	1820	THOMSON	300	50	62	Atlantic or Western Ocean
mwe1174	europe south east	1814	THOMSON	150	46	33	Attica / Turkish Dominions in Europe
mwe0397	europe austria	1816	THOMSON	180	50	59	Austrian Dominions
mwbh0785	belgium holland	1815	THOMSON	180	47	59	Belgium or the Netherlands
mwin0339	india	1817	THOMSON	400	52	60	British India, Northern Part / British India, Southern Part (2 maps, each 52x60cm. The first state of these maps, 1817, had the titles 'Northern Hindostan' and 'Southern Hindostan'.)
mwuk0882	uk	1815	THOMSON	200	58	44	British Isles
mwuk0613	scotland	1831	THOMSON	250	67	53	Caithness Shire
mwca0141	canada	1819	THOMSON	450	48	60	Canada and Nova Scotia
mwsam0847	south america venezuela	1814	THOMSON	350	50	58	Caraccas and Guiana
mwwi0284	west indies islands	1816	THOMSON	400	50	60	Chart of the Bahama Islands / The Bermudas or Summer Islands / Island of Cuba
mwm0081	mediterranean	1817	THOMSON	400	52	65	Chart of the Mediterranean Sea
mwuk1687	north sea	1816	THOMSON	450	50	61	Chart of the North and Baltic Seas &c. (3 insets incl. St. Petersburg)
mwat0288	atlantic north	1814	THOMSON	400	50	62	Chart of the North Atlantic Ocean with Tracks of the Shipping to West Indies, North America &c.
mwp0458	pacific north	1816	THOMSON	350	49	58	Chart of the Northern Passage between Asia & America
mwp0071	australia	1824	THOMSON	600	84	61	Chart of Van Dieman's Land from the Best Authorities and from Actual Surveys and Measurements
mwc0241	china	1815	THOMSON	300	58	51	China
mwjk0169	korea	1815	THOMSON	500	49	62	Corea and Japan
mwsc0397	scandinavia denmark	1814	THOMSON	200	53	62	Denmark
mwas0531	asia south east	1817	THOMSON	300	44	52	East India Isles
mwaf0426	africa east	1817	THOMSON	240	50	60	Egypt / Abyssinia
mwe0246	europe	1816	THOMSON	180	45	53	Europe
mwe0249	europe	1817	THOMSON	1000	104	124	Europe after the Congress of Vienna
mwru0339	russia	1815	THOMSON	180	59	50	European Russia
mwf0184	france	1814	THOMSON	150	50	57	France in Provinces
mwg0172	germany	1816	THOMSON	400	50	60	Germany North of the Mayne / Germany South of the Mayne (2 maps, each 50x60cm.)
mwwi0281	west indies islands	1814	THOMSON	450	50	60	Grenada / Tobago / Curacao / Trinidad
mwin0336	india	1814	THOMSON	300	45	61	Hindoostan
mwbh0784	belgium holland	1814	THOMSON	180	59	50	Holland
mww0649	world	1814	THOMSON	400	46	51	Hydrographical Chart of the World on Wright or Mercator's Projection with Tracts of the Last Circumnavigators
mwuk0258	ireland	1815	THOMSON	180	60	50	Ireland
mwit0227	italy	1814	THOMSON	240	58	48	Italy
mwwi0751	jamaica	1814	THOMSON	240	42	60	Jamaica
mwp0551	pacific west	1817	THOMSON	280	50	60	Map of the Islands in the Pacific Ocean (Incl. east coast of Australia, 4 insets)
mwwi0285	west indies islands	1817	THOMSON	240	50	60	Martinico / Dominica
mwp0059	australia	1814	THOMSON	1200	50	61	New Holland and Asiatic Isles
mwam0596	america north	1814	THOMSON	320	51	60	North America
mwuk0614	scotland	1831	THOMSON	400	51	65	North West Part of Perthshire / North East Part of Perthshire / South West Part of Perthshire / South East Part of Perthshire with Clackmannan (4 sheets, each 51x65cm)
mwaa0162	arctic	1814	THOMSON	200	53	46	Northern Hemisphere
mwuk0615	scotland	1831	THOMSON	360	50	66	Northern Part of Ayrshire / Southern Part (4 sheets, each 50x66cm)
mwuk0259	ireland	1817	THOMSON	400	53	62	Northern Part of Ireland / Southern Part of Ireland (2maps)
mwme0398	holy land	1820	THOMSON	160	48	66	Palaestina / Aegyptus Antiqua
mwme0842	persia etc	1817	THOMSON	200	45	50	Persia
mwsam0251	south america argentina	1816	THOMSON	150	61	50	Peru, Chili and La Plata
mwbp0559	poland	1814	THOMSON	200	44	49	Poland as divided
mwwi0286	west indies islands	1817	THOMSON	400	51	60	Porto Rico and Virgin Isles / Haiti, Hispaniola or St. Domingo

AMPG REFERENCE	REGION	DATE	MAP MAKER	PRICE (UK£)	VERT. (cm.)	HOR. (cm.)	TITLE OF MAP (Comments by the editor in brackets)
mwuk1571	england islands	1821	THOMSON	300	49	59	Remote British Islands (Wight, Mann, Guernsey, Jersey, Scilly)
mwru0337	russia	1814	THOMSON	400	51	61	Russian Empire
mwsc0202	scandinavia	1817	THOMSON	180	54	46	Scandinavia. Or Sweden, Denmark & Norway
mwuk0581	scotland	1815	THOMSON	180	60	50	Scotland
mwsam0136	south america	1814	THOMSON	200	58	50	South America
mwaa0045	antarctic	1814	THOMSON	400	51		Southern Hemisphere
mwaa0046	antarctic	1816	THOMSON	480	57	50	Southern Hemisphere Projected on the Plane of the Horizon of London
mwam1178	america north (east)	1817	THOMSON	550	50	59	Southern Provinces of the United States
mwsp0320	spain	1815	THOMSON	180	53	74	Spain and Portugal
mwgm0281	mexico	1814	THOMSON	600	51	62	Spanish North America
mwgm0108	guatemala	1816	THOMSON	300	51	62	Spanish North America, Southern Part (from Guatemala to Panama)
mwwi0872	st kitts	1817	THOMSON	400	50	60	St. Christophers
mwwi0282	west indies islands	1814	THOMSON	400	50	59	St. Christophers / St. Lucia / Nevis
mwwi0283	west indies islands	1814	THOMSON	200	50	58	St. Vincent / Barbadoes
mwsw0223	switzerland	1814	THOMSON	375	57	49	Swisserland (large view of Mont Blanc below)
mwc0240	china	1814	THOMSON	300	49	58	Tartary
mwuk1522	uk english channel (all)	1814	THOMSON	450	51	64	The British Channel
mwam0622	america north	1820	THOMSON	500	50	60	United States and Additions
mwam1171	america north (east)	1814	THOMSON	550	41	61	United States of America / The Course of the River St. Laurence, from Lake Ontario, to Manicouagan Point
mwit1202	italy veneto	1817	THOMSON	150	50	60	Venetian States
mwwi0162	west indies	1817	THOMSON	450	55	71	West Indies
mwuk0616	scotland	1831	THOMSON	400	68	50	Western Part of Fife with Kinross-Sh. / East Part of Fife-Sh. (2 maps, each 68x50cm)
mwuk0769	uk	1700	THORNTON	2000	43	53	A Chart of England, Scotland, France, And Ireland.
mwwi0235	west indies (east)	1689	THORNTON	1250	45	55	A Chart of the Caribe Ilands
mwaf0842	africa north west	1711	THORNTON	875	44	53	A Chart of the Coast of Barbaria with the Western, Canaria, & Cape de Verd, Isles
mwas0411	asia south east	1685	THORNTON	3000	43	52	A Chart of the Easternmost Part of the East Indies and China from Cape Comorin to Japan
mwwi0411	cuba	1689	THORNTON	2000	42	52	A Chart of the Iland of Cuba …
mwwi0587	hispaniola	1689	THORNTON	2000	42	53	A Chart of the Iland of Hispaniola.
mwaf0627	africa islands mauritius	1711	THORNTON	2500	45	53	A Chart of the Island of Mauritius
mwme0594	arabia etc	1711	THORNTON	550	44	55	A Chart of the Straits of Babelmandell and Moha (The Red Sea)
mwas0403	asia south east	1672	THORNTON	8500	43	54	A chart of the Tradeing Part of the East Indies and China
mwin0480	indian ocean west	1711	THORNTON	1800	43	54	A Chart of the Western Part of the East-Indies. With All the Adjacent Islands from Cape Bona Esperanca to the Island of Zelone
mwca0261	canada labrador	1689	THORNTON	12500	43	52	A Chart of ye North part of America. For Hudsons Bay Commonly called ye North West Passage (north to the right. Below is the 1753 edition publ. by Mount & Page entitled: 'A New and Correct Chart of the North Part of America from New Found Land to Hudsons Bay')
mwp0005	australia	1703	THORNTON	8000	40	20	A Draft of the Coast of New Holland and Parts Adjacent (inset of Shark's Bay)
mwaf0896	africa south	1711	THORNTON	2800	43	53	A Draught of Cape Bona Esperanca
mwuk1385	england south	1667	THORNTON	960	44	53	A Draught of the Sands, Shoals, Buoys, Beacons, & Sea Marks upon the Coast of England from South Foreland to Orfordness
mwat0216	atlantic east	1711	THORNTON	1200	53	44	A General Chart from England to Cape Bona Esperanca with the Coast of Brasile
mwat0263	atlantic north	1689	THORNTON	1250	47	56	A General Chart from England to Guinea with All the Trading Part of the West Indies
mwwi0037	west indies	1689	THORNTON	4000	44	54	A General Chart of the West India.
mwp0241	pacific (all)	1705	THORNTON	7200	43	57	A Generall Chart of the South Sea from the River of Plate to Dampiers Streights on ye Coast of New Guinea
mwat0020	atlantic ocean (all)	1689	THORNTON	2000	44	54	A Generall Chart of the West Indies
mwas0857	asia south east singapore	1716	THORNTON	2500	44	54	A Large Chart Describing ye Streights of Malacca and Sincapore
mwin0156	india	1711	THORNTON	550	44	53	A Large Chart of Part of the Coast of Coremandell from Point Pedro to Armegon (north to the right. The 1745 edition illustrated.)
mwwi0293	antigua	1701	THORNTON	1250	43	52	A Large Chart of the Island of Antegua
mwin0164	india	1711	THORNTON	800	44	53	A Large Chart of the Part of the Coast of Guzaratt & India from Diu Head to Bombay
mwas0439a	asia south east	1711	THORNTON	1000	45	55	A Large Draught from Benjar on the Island of Borneo to Macasser on the Island of Celebes Shewing the Streights of Bally
mwin0157	india	1711	THORNTON	875	43	53	A Large Draught of Part of the Coast of India from Bombay to Bassalore (The 1745 edition illustrated)
mwme0595	arabia etc	1711	THORNTON	900	43	53	A Large Draught of the Coast of Arabia from Maculla to Dofar

AMPG REFERENCE	REGION	DATE	MAP MAKER	PRICE (UK£)	VERT. (cm.)	HOR. (cm.)	TITLE OF MAP (Comments by the editor in brackets)
mwc0093	china	1711	THORNTON	2000	53	44	A Large Draught of the Coast of China from Amoye to Chusan with ye Harbour of Amoye at Large (includes part of Formosa)
mwas0639	asia south east java	1711	THORNTON	1350	44	53	A Large Draught of the East End of Java and Madura Shewing the Streights of Bally (north to the right)
mwme0596	arabia etc	1711	THORNTON	1600	43	54	A Large Draught of the Golf of Persia
mwin0158	india	1711	THORNTON	550	44	53	A Large Draught of the Mallabar Coast from Bassalore to Cape Comaroone
mwc0094	china	1711	THORNTON	2000	54	87	A Large Draught of the North Part of China: Shewing All the Passages of and Chanells into the Harbour of Chusan (this map forms a left-hand sheet when added to his 1689 map, as illustrated here. North to the right.)
mwas0585	asia south east borneo	1711	THORNTON	400	44	53	A Large Draught of the South Part of Borneo
mwin0159	india	1711	THORNTON	800	44	54	A Mapp of the Greate River Ganges, as it Emptieth itselfe into the Bay of Bengala. Taken from a Draught Made upon the Place
mwuk0128	ireland	1703	THORNTON	1200	43	53	A New and Correct Chart of the Coast of Ireland (insets of Cork Harbour, Dublin Bay in the centre of the map)
mwas0640	asia south east java	1711	THORNTON	1350	44	53	A New and Correct Chart of the Part of the Island of Java from the West End to Batavia with the Streights of Sunda
mwuk0776a	uk	1703	THORNTON	1200	43	53	A New and Correct Chart of the Sea Coast of England Scotland & Ireland
mwin0160	india	1711	THORNTON	550	44	54	A New and Correct Chart Shewing the Goeing over the Braces with Sands Shoals Depth of Water and Anchorage from Point Palmiras to Hughley in the Bay of Bengal
mww0319	world	1711	THORNTON	6000	52	85	A New and Correct Mapp of the World, According to Mr. Edward Wright Commonly Called Mercator's Projection with a View of the Winds and Variation (updated issue of 1685, incl. 'and Correct' in the title)
mwin0161	india	1711	THORNTON	550	43	53	A New Chart of Part of the Coast of Coremandell from Armegon to Bimlepatam
mwin0163	india	1711	THORNTON	500	44	53	A New Chart of the Coast of Orixa and Galconda
mwam0883	america north (east)	1685	THORNTON	18000	44	52	A New Chart of the Sea Coast of Newfoundland, New Scotland, New England, New Jersey, Virginia, Maryland, Pennsilvania, and Part of Carolina
mwaf0597	africa islands madagascar	1711	THORNTON	1250	43	53	A New Draught of the Island of Madagascar als. St. Lorenzo with Augustin Bay and the Island of Mombass at Large
mwam0885	america north (east)	1685	THORNTON-MORDEN-LEA	20000	45	54	A New Map of New England New York New Iarsey Pensilvania Maryland and Virginia
mwuss0159	carolinas	1689	THORNTON	3000	43	52	A New Mapp of Carolina (inset of Charlestowne and environs)
mwuk0301c	irish sea	1685	THORNTON	900	43	53	A New Chart of the Irish Sea (illustrated below left is the 1760 re-issue)
mwin0162	india	1711	THORNTON	1500	44	52	A New Mapp of the Island of Bombay and Sallset
mwat0328	atlantic st helena	1703	THORNTON	1500	43	52	A New Mapp of the Island of Saint Hellena (inset of Trinidada I.)
mwin0031a	ceylon	1700	THORNTON	950	53	44	A New Mapp of the Island of Zeloan
mww0230	world	1685	THORNTON	8000	42	67	A New Mapp of the World According to Mr. Edward Wright Commonly Called Mercator's Projection
mwaf1167	africa west	1711	THORNTON	1000	43	53	A New Mapp of ye Coast of Guinea from Cape de Verd to Cape Bona Esperance
mwca0289	canada newfoundland	1689	THORNTON	200	34	25	Bay Bulls.
mwuss0790	massachusetts	1689	THORNTON		41	24	Boston Harbor in New-England
mwca0290	canada newfoundland	1689	THORNTON	200	34	26	Cattalina Harbour.
mwca0291a	canada newfoundland	1689	THORNTON	2400	43	53	Chart of Ye Iland of New Found Land with ye Particular Harbors
mwca0288	canada newfoundland	1689	THORNTON	200	34	25	Harbor Grace.
mwam0891	america north (east)	1689	THORNTON	20000	43	52	Part of New England New York East New Iarsey and Long Iland
mwam0892	america north (east)	1689	THORNTON		43	48	Part of New England. (Centred on 'Marthas Vinyard')
mwca0291	canada newfoundland	1689	THORNTON	200	32	26	Port Bonavista.
mwat0113	atlantic bermuda	1689	THORNTON	2000	42	52	The Iland of Bermudas / The Iland of Barbados (2 maps on one sheet)
mwwi0703	jamaica	1689	THORNTON	960	41	53	The Island of Jamaica
mwc0073	china	1689	THORNTON	1200	54	43	To the Honourable the Court of Mannagers for the United Trade to the East Indies this Map of Chusan & Parts Adjacent (see also mwc0094)
mwuss0161	carolinas	1695	THORNTON	25000	48	57	To the Right Honorable William Earl of Craven ... This New Map of the Cheif Rivers, Bayes, Creeks, Harbours, and Settlements, in South Carolina. Actually Surveyed
mwam0890	america north (east)	1689	THORNTON	4500	52	81	Virginia, Maryland, Pennsilvania, East & West New Jarsey
mwuss1344	pennsylvania	1715	THORNTON-WILLDEY	15000	39	54	A Mapp of ye Improved Part of Pensilvania in America, Divided into Countyes Townships and Lotts Surveyed by Thomas Holme. Sold by Geo. Willdey (first publ. 1687)
mwuss0729	maine	1834	THRALL	400	38	53	Maine New Hampshire and Vermont
mwuss0317	connecticut	1831	THRALL	2000	49	56	Map of Connecticut from Actual Survey

AMPG REFERENCE	REGION	DATE	MAP MAKER	PRICE (UK£)	VERT. (cm.)	HOR. (cm.)	TITLE OF MAP (Comments by the editor in brackets)
mwuss1307	ohio	1833	THRALL	1800	57	54	Map of Ohio, Compiled from the Latest and Most Authentic Information
mwam0660	america north	1828	THRALL	1800	50	67	Map of the United States. Compiled from the Most Authentic Sources (2nd edition)
mwsc0723	scandinavia sweden	1733	TILLAEUS	3600	155	192	General Charta ofwer Stockholm med Malmarne Ahr
mwg0228	germany north west	1750	TINDAL	300	35	43	A Correct Map of the South East Part of Germany
mwuk0483	scotland	1744	TINDAL	350	48	39	A Map of the Kingdom of Scotland from the Latest and Best Observations for Mr. Tindal's Continuation of Mr. Rapin's History
mwg0231	germany north west	1750	TINDAL	350	35	43	A New and Correct Map of the South West Part of Germany
mwuss0701	maine	1785	TINDAL	1200	37	38	Attack of the Rebels upon Fort Penobscot in the Province of New England in which their Fleet was Totally Destroyed and their Army Dispersed the 14th August 1779
mwbh0652	belgium holland	1740	TINDAL	180	35	42	Belgium a New and Correct Map of the Netherlands or Low Countries (map by E. Bowen)
mwbh0659	belgium holland	1744	TINDAL	300	38	48	Plan of the City and Citadel of Antwerp
mwru0529	ukraine	1740	TINNEY	1500	48	56	A New Map of the Ukrain ... Crim Tartary, &c.
mwme0093	holy land	1632	TIRINUS	1500	32	85	Chorographia Terrae Sanctae in Angustiorem Formam Redacta, et ex Variis Auctoribus a Multis Erroribus Expurgata (reprinted several times until 1785)
mwsam0528	south america colombia	1766	TIRION	350	18	26	Carthagena in de Spaansche West-Indien
mwwi0831	puerto rico	1769	TIRION	300	18	26	De Hoofdstad en Haven, van 't Eiland Porto Rico in de Westindien
mwsam0241	south america argentina	1769	TIRION	240	19	31	De Ingang van Rio de la Plata, waar aan de Stad Buenos Ayres Legt, in Zuid-Amerika
mwbh0709	belgium holland	1760	TIRION	300	32	43	De Provincie van Utrecht
mwgm0413	panama	1754	TIRION	240	18	25	De Stad en Haven van Porto-Bello
mwgm0231	mexico	1766	TIRION	200	18	25	De Stad Vera Cruz in Nieuw Spanje
mwgm0426	panama	1765	TIRION	120	26	17	De Stad, Reede, Haven en Rivier van Chagres
mwsw0158	switzerland	1760	TIRION	280	18	19	Grondtekening van de Stad Geneve
mwuss0641	louisiana	1764	TIRION	600	33	44	Grondvlakte van Nieuw Orleans, de Hoofdstad van Louisiana / De Uitloop van de Rivier Missisippi / De Oostelyke Ingang van de Missisippi, met een Plan van het Fort, 't Welk het Kanaal Beheerscht
mwuk1011	england	1770	TIRION	240	33	37	Het Koninkryk Engeland
mwaf0717	africa north	1762	TIRION	240	33	63	Het Noordelykste deel van Afrika
mwwi0785	martinique	1760	TIRION	240	31	37	Het Westindisch Eiland Martenique Volgens de Nieuwste Waarneemingen in Kaart Gebragt. 't Amsterdam by I. Tirion
mwit0187	italy	1755	TIRION	280	38	43	Italie
mwit0191	italy	1761	TIRION	400	39	44	Italie volgens de Allernieuwste Uitgave van den Heere d'Anville
mwaf0216	africa	1763	TIRION	280	35	35	Kaart van Afrika door den Heer d'Anville
mwsam0376	south america brazil	1760	TIRION	500	35	41	Kaart van de Aller-Heiligen Baay (inset of San Salvador)
mwgm0427	panama	1769	TIRION	280	27	30	Kaart van de Landengte van Panama, Volgens de Spaansche Aftekeninge Opgemaakt
mwwi0102	west indies	1765	TIRION	300	30	48	Kaart van de Onderkoningschappen van Mexico en Nieuw Granada in de Spaansche West-Indien
mwp0382	pacific new guinea	1753	TIRION	300	32	36	Kaart van de Papoasche Eilanden
mwbh0703b	belgium holland	1757	TIRION	200	16	29	Kaart van de Stad Utrecht
mwsam0622	south america guyana	1765	TIRION	300	33	40	Kaart van Geheel Guajana of de Wilden-Kust, en die der Spaansche Westindien, op het Noord-End van Zuid-Amerika
mwgm0229	mexico	1765	TIRION	720	32	34	Kaart van het Westelyk Gedeelte van Nieuw Mexico en van California Volgens de Laatste Ontdekkingen der Jesuiten en Anderen ... MDCCLXV
mwaf0945	africa south	1769	TIRION	240	32	37	Kaart van het Zuidelykste Gedeelte van Afrika of het Land der Hottentotten
mwuk1190	england london	1754	TIRION	450	28	41	Kaart van Londen Enz. en van het Naby Gelegen Land (London and its environs which today form part of London)
mwsam0602	south america guyana	1750	TIRION	300	33	40	Landkaart van de Volkplantingen Suriname en Berbice (inset: Paramaribo)
mwsam0625	south america guyana	1770	TIRION	300	35	41	Landkaart van het Eiland en de Volkplanting van Cayenne aan de Kust van Zuid-Amerika
mwjk0082	japan	1728	TIRION	500	25	33	Naauw-Keurige Kaart van't Keizerryk Japan
mwf0129	france	1757	TIRION	250	31	45	Nieuwe en Naaukeurige Kaart van het Zuidelykste Gedeelte van Frankryk / Nieuwe en Naaukeurige Kaart van het Noordelykste Gedeelte van Frankryk (2 maps, each 31x45cm.)
mwf0880	france paris	1756	TIRION	550	31	37	Nieuwe Kaart der Platte Grond van de Stad Parys
mwaf0210	africa	1760	TIRION	240	28	32	Nieuwe Kaart van Africa na de Alderlaatste Ontdekking int Licht Gebracht
mwam0193	america continent	1769	TIRION	350	28	32	Nieuwe Kaart van America
mwme0619	arabia etc	1744	TIRION	750	29	36	Nieuwe Kaart van Arabia

AMPG REFERENCE	REGION	DATE	MAP MAKER	PRICE (UK£)	VERT. (cm.)	HOR. (cm.)	TITLE OF MAP (Comments by the editor in brackets)
mwas0152	asia continent	1740	TIRION	400	28	35	Nieuwe Kaart van Asia (Italian issue by Albrizzi, 1740 illustrated)
mwuk0822	uk	1744	TIRION	280	33	38	Nieuwe Kaart van de Eilanden van Groot Brittannien
mwas0462	asia south east	1744	TIRION	450	29	33	Nieuwe Kaart van de Filippynsche, Ladrones, Moluccos of Specery Eilanded als mede Celebes, etc.
mwam0986	america north (east)	1755	TIRION	550	36	45	Nieuwe Kaart van de Grootbrittannische Volkplantingen in Noord America waar in Tevens de Fransche Bezittingen en de Landen tuschen die Beide Volken in Geschil Staande en de Wederzydsche Pretensien Duidelyk Aangewezen worden
mwaf0943	africa south	1763	TIRION	240	32	22	Nieuwe Kaart van de Kaap der Goede Hoope en der na by Gelegen Landen Volgens de Afmeetingen van den Abt de la Caille in 1752
mwaa0124	arctic	1735	TIRION	320	29	33	Nieuwe Kaart van de Noord Pool
mwme0354	holy land	1766	TIRION	240	30	38	Nieuwe Kaart van de Reizen der Israeliten uit Egipte naa Kanaan
mwas0485	asia south east	1765	TIRION	450	28	38	Nieuwe Kaart van de Sundasche Eilanden als Borneo, Sumatra en Gooot Iava &c.
mwg0145	germany	1765	TIRION	180	28	34	Nieuwe Kaart van Duitsland Verdeelt in zyn Thien Kreitzen
mwe0151	europe	1733	TIRION	250	33	36	Nieuwe Kaart van Europa na de Alderlaatste Ondekking int licht gebracht
mwe1154	europe south east	1733	TIRION	240	30	36	Nieuwe Kaart van Europisch Turkyen
mwsc0356	scandinavia denmark	1734	TIRION	200	28	34	Nieuwe Kaart van het Koninkryk van Deenemarken
mwsc0133	scandinavia	1734	TIRION	300	28	34	Nieuwe Kaart van het Koninkryk Zweden, na de Laatste Ondekkinge int Licht Gebracht
mwas0166	asia continent	1753	TIRION	450	32	36	Nieuwe Kaart van het Oostelykste Deel der Weereld, Dienende tot Aanwyzing van de Scheepstogten der Nederlanderen naar Oostindie Volgens de Laatste Ontdekkingen (incl. Australia)
mwme0633	arabia etc	1769	TIRION	280	29	35	Nieuwe Kaart van het Turksche Ryk Gelegen in Europa, Asia en Africa
mwam0173	america continent	1754	TIRION	450	34	36	Nieuwe Kaart van het Westelykste Deel der Weereld
mwbh0681	belgium holland	1747	TIRION	240	32	36	Nieuwe Kaart van het Westelykste Gedeelte van Staats-Vlaanderen
mwuk0165	ireland	1744	TIRION	280	34	28	Nieuwe Kaart van Ierland
mwas0827	asia south east siam	1730	TIRION	500	28	37	Nieuwe Kaart van India over de Ganges, of van Malakka, Siam, Cambodia, Chiampa, Kochinchina, Laos, Pegu, Ava, enz.
mwme0297	holy land	1732	TIRION	240	28	34	Nieuwe Kaart van Irak Arabi Kurdistan, Diarbek, Turkomannia, Syrie en het Heilige Land
mwca0088	canada	1769	TIRION	500	31	44	Nieuwe Kaart van Kanada, de Landen aan de Hudsons-Baay en de Noordwestelyke Deelen van Noord-Amerika
mwru0172	russia	1734	TIRION	200	28	35	Nieuwe Kaart van Muskovie of Rusland
mwsp0280	spain	1760	TIRION	280	33	38	Nieuwe Kaart van Spanje en Portugal
mwin0045	ceylon	1740	TIRION	350	28	36	Nieuwe Kaart van t Eiland Ceilon
mwin0185	india	1730	TIRION	600	28	36	Nieuwe Kaart van t Keyzer Ryk van den Grooten Mogol
mwe0807	europe east	1765	TIRION	200	28	33	Nieuwe Kaart van 't Koninkryk Bohemen t Hertogdom Silesien Markgraafschap Moravien en Lusatien
mwe0953a	europe hungary	1765	TIRION	180	28	33	Nieuwe Kaart van t Koninkryk Hongaryen en Zevenbergen
mwbp0406	poland	1733	TIRION	400	29	34	Nieuwe Kaart van 't Koninkryk Poolen Verdeelt in zyn Byzondere Waywoodschappen na de Nieuwste Stelling in t' Ligt Gebragt
mwuk0502	scotland	1754	TIRION	240	33	36	Nieuwe Kaart van 't Noorder Gedeelte van Groot Britannie Behelzende het Koningryk Schotland
mwme0823	persia etc	1750	TIRION	240	30	37	Nieuwe Kaart van 't Ryk van Persie
mwru0448a	russia tartary	1732	TIRION	350	28	35	Nieuwe Kaart van Tartarie, Na de alderlaaste ondekking int ligt gebragt
mwf0118	france	1734	TIRION	150	33	38	Nieuwe Kaart van Vrankryk
mwsw0159	switzerland	1760	TIRION	240	33	37	Nieuwe Kaart van Zwitserland
mwm0245	mediterranean malta	1761	TIRION	650	28	46	Nieuwe Kaart van't Eiland Maltha met Gozo en Comino (west to the top)
mwjk0095	japan	1740	TIRION	720	28	32	Nieuwe Kaart van't Keizerryk Japan
mww0431	world	1754	TIRION	550	23	40	Nieuwe Wereld Kaart waar in de Reizen van den Hr. Anson rondsom de Wereld met een Gestipte Linie worden Aangewezen
mwsp0716	gibraltar	1759	TIRION	240	39	42	Nieuwe Zeekaart van de Straat van Gibraltar
mwbh0710	belgium holland	1760	TIRION	180	27	32	Niewe Kaart van het Graafschap Vlaanderen Artois en Henegouwen
mwc0133	china	1740	TIRION	450	25	33	Nouvelle Carte de L'Empire de la Chine
mwuk0818	uk	1740	TIRION	350	27	35	Nuova Carta dell'Isole Britannische
mwsam0530	south america colombia	1768	TIRION	300	18	30	Plan van de Haven van Carthagena
mwbp0411	poland	1734	TIRION	200	16	19	Platte Grond van de Stadt Dantzik
mwca0521	canada quebec	1759	TIRION	450	33	43	Quebek, de Hoofdstad van Kanada; aan de Rivier van St. Laurens: door de Engelschen Belegerd en by Verdrag Bemagtigd, in 't Jaar 1759

AMPG REFERENCE	REGION	DATE	MAP MAKER	PRICE (UK£)	VERT. (cm.)	HOR. (cm.)	TITLE OF MAP (Comments by the editor in brackets)
mwjk0093	japan	1736	TIRION	450	18	20	t Eilandje Desima Verblyf Plaats der Hollanders in Japan (view of Deshima)
mww0388	world	1744	TIRION	800	33	42	Wereld Kaart na de Alderlaatste Ontdekking in't Licht Gebracht
mwit1109a	italy tuscany	1680	TODESCHI	1500	36	47	Carta del Stato del Papa et del Duca di Toscana (close copy of Blaeu)
mwaf0082	africa	1673	TODESCHI	35000	121	170	Nova et Acurata Totius Africae Tabula auct G.I. Blaeu (size incl. text panels at sides. Copy of Jaillot 1669)
mwam0077	america continent	1673	TODESCHI	80000	121	170	Nova et Acurata Totius Americae Tabula auct: G.I. Blaeu (size incl. text side panels)
mwas0059	asia continent	1673	TODESCHI	40000	121	170	Nova et Acurata Totius Asiae Tabula, Auct: G.I. Blaeu (size incl. side text panels)
mwe0081	europe	1673	TODESCHI	30000	121	170	Nova et Acurata Totius Europae Tabula auct G.I. Blaeu (size incl. text side panels)
mwsp0685	balearic islands	1786	TOFINO	960	81	56	Carta Esferica de la Isla de Mallorca y sus Adyacentes
mwsp0684	balearic islands	1786	TOFINO	960	56	81	Carta Esferica de la Isla de Menorca
mwsp0739	gibraltar	1786	TOFINO	720	82	56	Plano Geometrico de la Bahia de Algeciras y Gibraltar
mwuk1448	england thames	1840	TOMBLESON	900	127	25	Tombleson's Panoramic Map of the Thames and Medway
mwf1069	france provence	1745	TOMS	1500	35	72	The Situation of the English, French and Spanish Fleets, when they Begun the Engagement in the Mediterranean, on the Eleventh of Feby. 1743/4 (Battle of Toulon)
mwsam0513	south america colombia	1740	TOMS	1500	43	58	This Plan of the Harbour, Town, and Forts, of Cartagena
mwgm0407	panama	1740	TOMS	1500	42	58	This Plan of the Harbours, Towns and Forts of Porto Bello Taken by Edward Vernon Esqu. Vice Admiral of the Blue on the 22nd. November 1739 with Six Men of War Only (see also Mortier)
mwuk0937	england	1680	TOOKER	1500	42	52	A New Map, Shewing the Naturall face of England.
mwuk0938	england	1680	TOOKER	1500	55	45	A Travelling Mapp of England Containing the Principall Roads
			TORDESILLAS: See under DE HERRERA Y TORDESILLAS				
mwme0445	jerusalem	1609	TORNIELLO	480	32	43	Hierosolymae, Cura Neemiae Ducis Instauratae Descriptio (2 plans on one sheet)
mww0118	world	1609	TORNIELLO	1600	19	38	Situs Partium Praecipuarum Totius Orbis Terrarum (based on Ortelius)
mwme0078	holy land	1615	TORNIELLO	750	34	41	Terrae Chanaan inter XII Tribuus Isrel Distributae Orthographia
mwsam0859	south america venezuela	1831	TORRENTE	280	25	32	Mapa de las Provincias de Venezuela y del Reino de Santa Fe
mwf0931	france paris	1841	TOUSSAINT	600	76	108	Nouveau Plan Itineraire de la Ville de Paris
mwf0915	france paris	1820	TOUSSAINT	850	74	112	Paris, Divise en 12 Arondissements, et 48 Quatiers, Dresse par Toussaint, Architecte
mwjk0148a	japan	1849	TOYOJIRO	3000	144	235	(Zotei Nihon Yochi Zenzu)
mww0047	world	1554	TRAMEZZINI	150000	75		(Two untitled hemispheres)
mwsc0655	scandinavia sweden	1558	TRAMEZINI	2500	25	19	Gotlandia
mwe0853	europe hungary	1559	TRAMEZINI	4800	47	39	Nova Descriptio Totius Hungariae (reduced size version of Lazius' 1556 map in 10 sheets)
mwg0015	germany	1553	TRAMEZINI	6000	47	71	Nova Germaniae Descriptio cum Adiacentibus Italiae, Galliae, Britanniae, Poloniae, et Pannoniae Partibus
mwsp0158	spain	1559	TRAMEZINI	9000	40	53	Nova totius Hispaniae descriptio
mwsc0224	scandinavia denmark	1558	TRAMEZINI	2500	29	19	Selandia, Vel Sialandia sive Zelandia
mwsc0013	scandinavia	1556	TRAMEZINI	20000	39	53	Septentrionalium Regionum Suetiae, Gothiae, Norvegiae, Daniae et Terrarum (southern parts of Scandinavia)
mwgr0020	greece	1561	TRAMEZINI	9000	48	69	Vedrai Divisi i Termini di Tutta la Grecia
mwit0752	italy rome	1773	TRAMEZINI-LOSI	4000	127	147	Anteiquae Urbis Imago Accuratissime ex Vetusteis Monumenteis Formata (Title above map. Restrike of the 1561 original by Tramezini)
mwe0251	europe	1818	TRAUX	1500	150	186	Carte Generale et Itineraire de l'Europe Divisee en Tous ses Etats, d'apres le Congres de Vienne
mwe0697	europe dalmatia	1810	TRAUX	3000	84	222	Carte von Dalmatien und dem Gebieth von Ragusa aux Achten Quellen Gezogen und Bearbeitet (view)
mwe0480	europe central	1821	TRAUX	650	121	110	Neueste General und Post-Karte von Ganz Deutschland und Italien mit Inbegiff Aller Provinzen der Oesterreichischen Monarchie, des Grossten Theils von Preussen, der Niederlande, Frankreich, Russland, der Turkey, England und Danemark
mwme0732	caucasus	1790	TREUTTEL	785	46	57	General Charte der Laender Zwischen dem Schwarzen und Caspisschen Meere, Circassien, Georgien, Armenien, Wuste von Astrachan und Caucusus Hauptsechlich die Grosse und Kleine Kabarda
mwf0199	france	1838	TRIBOUT	650	90	91	Nouvelle Carte Routiere (size excl. side borders, each with 7 town views)
mwuss0090	california	1787	TRONCOSO	3000	26	35	Californias: Antigua y Nueva (publ. in Mexico)
mwbp0478	poland	1769	TRUSKOT	960	109	74	Karta Predstavljajuscaja Pol'su (Cyrillic)
mwru0253	russia	1775	TRUSKOT	500	46	57	Mappa Gubernii Astrachanesis
mwru0260	russia	1776	TRUSKOT	500	46	57	Mappa Gubernii Irkutensis, Complectens Provincias Irkutensem, Jakutensem et Udinensem

AMPG REFERENCE	REGION	DATE	MAP MAKER	PRICE (UK£)	VERT. (cm.)	HOR. (cm.)	TITLE OF MAP (Comments by the editor in brackets)
mwru0247	russia	1772	TRUSKOT	500	46	58	Mappa Gubernii Orenburgensis Geographica Exhibita a Iohanne Truskotio
mwru0254	russia	1775	TRUSKOT	500	46	56	Mappa Gubernii Sibiriensis, Continens Provincias Toboliensem et Jenisejenesem
mwru0255	russia	1775	TRUSKOT	650	58	71	Mappa Representans Partem Septentrionalem Imperii Russici ab Ostio Ieniseae Fluvii usque ad Mare Album (size incl. ornate border)
mwru0248	russia	1772	TRUSKOT	500	45	57	Mare Baikal cum Partibus Fluviorum Lenae Argun Selengae et Angarae ac Circumjacentibus Territoriis
mwbp0134	baltic states	1770	TRUSKOT	550	46	56	Nova Descriptio Insulae Oseliae
mwru0256	russia	1775	TRUSKOT	500	46	58	Pars Territorii Mangaseiensis et Iakutensis Ostiaque Fluviorum Ienisseae et Lenae
mwru0223	russia	1753	TRUSKOT	15000	114	159	Plan Stolicnago Goroda Sanktpeterburga (in 9 sheets, joined, in Cyrillic)
mwru0261	russia	1776	TRUSKOT & SCHMIDT	8750	54	75	(Map of Russia in 23 sheets, each 54x75cm in Cyrillic)
mwru0262	russia	1776	TRUSKOT & SCHMIDT	2000	64	140	Tabula Geographica Generalis Imperii Russici (map by Tobias Lotter. Re-issued 1784)
mwca0117	canada	1790	TRUSLER	180	16	23	A Map of Part of North America from Lat. 40 to Lat 62 N
mwc0317	china tibet	1790	TRUSLER	120	19	23	A Map of Tibet, with the Adjacent Country
mwm0252	mediterranean malta	1793	TRUSLER	240	18	23	A Plan of the City of Malta
mwam0236	america continent	1793	TRUSLER	180	19	18	Map of America with the New Discovered Islands
mwca0543	canada quebec	1792	TRUSLER	180	20	21	Map of the City of Quebec
mwit0822	italy sardinia	1796	TRUSLER	120	22	16	Map of the Island of Sardinia
mwit0453	italy liguria	1794	TRUSLER	180	18	25	Plan of the City of Genoa
mwsp0121	portugal	1797	TRUSLER	180	18	25	Plan of the City of Lisbon
mwsp0347	spain madrid	1796	TRUSLER	180	18	23	Plan of the City of Madrid
mwru0398	russia moscow	1794	TRUSLER	240	20	22	Plan of the City of Moscow
mwit0757	italy rome	1795	TRUSLER	180	18	23	Plan of the City of Rome
mwbh0759	belgium holland	1792	TRUSLER	200	15	20	Plan of the City of Rotterdam
mwsc0748	scandinavia sweden	1790	TRUSLER	180	20	18	Plan of the City of Stockholm
mwit1251	italy venice	1794	TRUSLER	200	18	23	Plan of the City of Venice
mww0585	world	1794	TRUXTON	2000	47	91	A General Chart of the Globe, Shewing the Course of the Gulph Stream, and Various Tracks to and from the East Indies, China, Europe, &c.
mwec1343a	uk england yorkshire	1787	TUKE	5500	119	141	Map of the County of York
mwec0492	uk england hampshire	1791	TUNNICLIFF	300	53	48	A New Map of Hampshire
mwec1049	uk england somerset	1791	TUNNICLIFF	200	40	54	A New Map of Somersetshire
mwec1260	uk england wiltshire	1791	TUNNICLIFF	240	50	37	A New Map of Wiltshire
mwuk0892	uk	1838	TURNBULL	350	80	42	Map of Great Britain ... in Mr Telford's Narrative (details canals, roads and high tides etc)
mwaf0215	africa	1762	TURNER	200	16	21	Africa
mwas0178	asia continent	1762	TURNER	200	16	21	Asia
mwe0183	europe	1762	TURNER	220	16	21	Europe
mwam0429	america north	1762	TURNER	400	16	21	Nth.America
mwsam0081	south america	1762	TURNER	200	16	21	Sth.America
mww0458	world	1762	TURNER	500	16	29	The World agreeable to the latest Discoveries (map by J. Gibson)
mwam0707	america north	1836	US ANTIQUARIAN SOC	1200	38	41	Map of the Indian Tribes of North America about 1600 A.D. along the Atlantic; & about 1800 A.D. Westwardly (by Albert Gallatin)
mwam0794	america north	1848	US ETHNOLOGICAL SOC	900	37	41	Map of the Sites of the Indian Tribes of North America when First Known to the Europeans about 1600 A.D. along the Atlantic and about 1800 A.D. on the Pacific
mwp0157	australia	1845	U.S. EXPL. EXPED.	180	22	29	(Untitled map of New South Wales)
mwaa0051	antarctic	1840	U.S. EXPL. EXPED.	1600	60	87	Chart of the Antarctic Continent Shewing the Icy Barrier Attached to it. Discovered by ... Charles Wilkes
mwp0314	pacific fiji	1840	U.S. EXPL. EXPED.	600	60	88	Chart of the Viti Group or Feejee Islands
mww0736	world	1845	U.S. EXPL. EXPED.	720	60	86	Chart of the World Shewing the Tracks of the U.S. Exploring Expedition in 1838, 39, 40, 41, & 42
mwp0540	pacific tuamotu	1841	U.S. EXPL. EXPED.	100	22	29	Low Archipelago or Paumotu Group
mwp0353	pacific hawaii	1844	U.S. EXPL. EXPED.	960	39	60	Map of Part of the Island of Hawaii Sandwich Islands Shewing the Craters and Eruption of May and June 1840
mwuss1334a	oregon	1845	U.S. EXPL. EXPED.	960	58	88	Map of the Oregon Territory by the U.S. Ex. Ex. Charles Wilkes ... 1841 (inset: Columbia River)
mwuss1338	oregon	1849	U.S. EXPL. EXPED.	240	22	33	Map of the Oregon Territory from the Best Authorities
mwuss0109	california	1841	U.S. EXPL. EXPED.	280	21	28	Map of Upper California by the U.S. Ex. Ex. and Best Authorities
mwp0473	pacific samoa	1850	U.S. EXPL. EXPED.	160	20	29	Samoan or Navigator Islands by U.S. Ex. Ex. ... 1839
mwam0827	america north (central)	1835	U.S. GOVERNMENT	350	67	97	A Map of a Portion of the Indian Country Lying East and West of the Mississippi River to the Forty Sixth Degree of North Latitude from Personal Observation Made in the Autumn of 1835 ...
mwuss0878	massachusetts	1835	U.S. GOVERNMENT	720	74	89	A Map of the Extremity of Cape Cod Including the Townships of Provincetown & Truro: With a Chart of their Sea Coast and of Cape Cod Harbour, State of Massachusetts ... 1833, 34, 35

AMPG REFERENCE	REGION	DATE	MAP MAKER	PRICE (UK£)	VERT. (cm.)	HOR. (cm.)	TITLE OF MAP (Comments by the editor in brackets)
mwuss0479	florida	1839	U.S. GOVERNMENT	1000	113	79	A Map of the Seat of War in Florida 1836
mwuss0919	michigan	1836	U.S. GOVERNMENT	400	17	17	A Map, Exhibiting the Relative Positions of Lake Erie & Michigan According to Recent Surveys / A Map Exhibiting the Relative Position of Lake Erie & Michigan, According to Mitchell's Map, Published in the Year 1755
mwuss0560	illinois	1839	U.S. GOVERNMENT	1200	29	37	A Plan of Chicago Harbor Lake Michigan
mwuss0278	carolinas	1838	U.S. GOVERNMENT	4000	155	127	Charleston Harbor and the Adjacent Coast and Country; of South Carolina. Surveyed at Intervals in 1823, 1824, and 1825
mwam0818	america north (central)	1822	U.S. GOVERNMENT	1250	42	27	Country Drained by the Mississippi Western Section
mwam0835	america north (central)	1842	U.S. GOVERNMENT	1250	93	78	Hydrographical Basin of the Upper Mississippi River from Astronomical and Barometrical Observations Surveys and Information, by J.N. Nicollet in the years 1836, 37, 38 and 40
mwuss0561	illinois	1839	U.S. GOVERNMENT	450	28	28	Map of Chicago River
mwuss0557	illinois	1836	U.S. GOVERNMENT	250	50	36	Map of Illinois with Parts of Indiana, Ouisconsin, &c by David H. Burr
mwgm0382	nicaragua	1849	U.S. GOVERNMENT	160	36	44	Map of Nicaragua
mwuss1525	texas	1844	U.S. GOVERNMENT	7500	54	84	Map of Texas and the Countries Adjacent: Compiled in the Bureau of the Corps of Topographical Engineers (map by W. Emory)
mwuss1526	texas	1844	U.S. GOVERNMENT	3000	36	55	Map of Texas and the Countries Adjacent: Compiled in the Bureau of the Corps of Topographical Engineers
mwuss0987	missouri	1837	U.S. GOVERNMENT	300	33	102	Map of the Harbor of St. Louis, Mississippi River, Oct. 1837. Surveyed by Lt. R.E. Lee, Corps of Engineers
mwam0834	america north (central)	1842	U.S. GOVERNMENT	35000	242	204	Map of the Hydrographical Basin of the Upper Mississippi River: from Astronomical and Barometrical Observations, Surveys and Information, by J.N. Nicollet, made in the years 1836, 37, 38 39 & 40; assisted in 1838, 39 & 40 by Lieut. J.C. Fremont
mwuss0935	minnesota	1834	U.S. GOVERNMENT	450	40	49	Map of the Route Passed over by an Expedition into the Indian Country in 1832 to the Source of the Mississippi, by Lieut. J. Allen
mwuss1071	new mexico	1847	U.S. GOVERNMENT	320	65	50	Map of the Territory of New Mexico … 1846-7
mwam0828	america north (central)	1836	U.S. GOVERNMENT	200	47	44	Map Showing the Lands Assigned to Emigrant Indians West of Arkansas & Missouri
mwuss0910	michigan	1831	U.S. GOVERNMENT	600	36	46	Plan of Detroit
mwuss0487	florida	1846	U.S. GOVERNMENT	400	107	102	The State of Florida Compiled in the Bureau of Topographical Engineers from the Best Authorities
mwam0829	america north (central)	1836	U.S. GOVERNMENT	1250	50	89	Western Territory
mwuss1359	pennsylvania	1771	US PHILOSOPHICAL SOC	1000	32	42	A Map of Part of Pennsylvania & Maryland Intended to Show, at One View, the Several Places Proposed for Opening a Communication between the Waters of the Delaware & Chesopeak Bays
mwuss0544	illinois	1815	U.S. STATE SURVEY	3500	46	38	Map of the Bounty Lands in Illinois Territory
mwuss0016	alabama	1840	U.S. STATE SURVEYS	150	57	30	A Diagram of the State of Alabama
mwuss0475	florida	1837	U.S. STATE SURVEYS	130	22	60	A Plat Exhibiting the State of the Surveys in the Territory of Florida
mwuss0967	mississippi	1838	U.S. STATE SURVEYS	100	41	29	Diagram of the Surveying District South of Tennessee
mwuss0057	arkansas	1832	U.S. STATE SURVEYS	150	53	58	Map of Arkansas
mwuss0674	louisiana	1828	U.S. STATE SURVEYS	150	28	30	Map of Part of Louisiana North of the Base Line
mwuss1694	wisconsin	1835	U.S. STATE SURVEYS	300	57	43	Map of the Surveyed Part of Wisconsin Territory Compiled from Public Surveys as Returned to the Surveyor Generals Office
mwuss0576	indiana	1835	U.S. STATE SURVEYS	200	29	23	Plat of the Ancient Possessions of Upper Prairie Confirmed by the Governors
mwuss0939	minnesota	1849	U.S. STATE SURVEYS	150	46	56	Public Surveys in the State of Wisconsin and Territory of Minnesota
mwuss0921	michigan	1839	U.S. STATE SURVEYS	200	58	33	Sketch of the Public Surveys in the North Part of Michigan
mwuss0986	missouri	1836	U.S. STATE SURVEYS	130	38	42	South West Land District of Missouri
mwuss0529	georgia	1837	U.S. WAR DEPT	300	28	33	A Sketch of the Harbour of Brunswick
mwuss0925	michigan	1842	U.S. WAR DEPT	600	118	76	Chart of Detroit River. From Lake Erie to Lake St. Clair. Surveyed in 1840, '41, '42 … W.G. Williams
mwuss0356	washington DC	1838	U.S. WAR DEPT	600	48	91	Chart of the Head of Navigation of the Potomac River Shewing the Route of the Alexandria Canal Made in Pursuance of a Resolution of the Alex'a Canal Company Oct. 1838
mwam1198	america north (east)	1826	U.S. WAR DEPT	800	43	64	Map of the Country between Washington and Pittsburg Referring to the Contemplated Chesapeake & Ohio Canal and its General Route and Profile, October 1826
mwuss0480	florida	1839	U.S. WAR DEPT	960	107	74	Map of the Seat of War in Florida … By Capt. John Mackay and Lieut. J. E. Blake
mwuss1072	new mexico	1848	U.S. WAR DEPT	130	10	18	Santa Fe
mwit1241	italy venice	1730	UGHI	3500	63	67	(Untitled plan of Venice, a reduced version of Ughi's 1725 map. Illustration shows 1747 edition.)
mwit1238a	italy venice	1725	UGHI	15000	149	205	Iconografica rappresentatione della inclita città di Venezia

AMPG REFERENCE	REGION	DATE	MAP MAKER	PRICE (UK£)	VERT. (cm.)	HOR. (cm.)	TITLE OF MAP (Comments by the editor in brackets)
mwaf1235	africa west	1787	ULLOA	550	64	55	Carta Esferica de la Costa de Africa desde C. Bojador hasta C. Verde e Yslas Adjacentes; Presentada al Rey nuestro Senor por Dn. Antonio Valdes, Jefe del Rl. Armada
mwgm0408	panama	1748	ULLOA	720	43	69	Plan de la Baye et Ville de Portobelo en 1736 (large inset of the west coast of America)
mwsam0483	south america juan fernandez	1748	ULLOA	300	25	31	Plano de la Isla d. Tra. de Juan Fernandez en el Mar de Sur (shown above left)
mwsam0806	south america uruguay	1752	ULLOA	550	17	24	Plan de la Ville de Montevideo
mwec0233a	uk england cumbria	1748	UNIVERSAL MAG.	150	21	17	A Correct Map of Cumberland from the best Surveys
mwru0543	ukraine	1769	UNIVERSAL MAG.	140	25	36	A Map of the Present Seat of War between the Russians, Poles, and Turks
mwaf1217	africa west	1757	UNIVERSAL MAG.	80	28	37	A New & Correct Map of the Coast of Africa, from Cape Blanco, to the Coast of Angola: Exhibiting All the European Forts and Settlements
mwuss0295	connecticut	1780	UNIVERSAL MAG.	450	26	34	A New and Accurate Map of Connecticut and Rhode Island, from the Best Authorities
mwin0224	india	1756	UNIVERSAL MAG.	200	27	36	A New and Accurate Map of Cormandel, Malabar, Bengal &c. Exhibiting the Principal European Settlements in the East Indies
mwuss1042	new jersey	1780	UNIVERSAL MAG.	400	32	27	A New and Accurate Map of New Jersey, from the Best Authorities
mwam0436	america north	1763	UNIVERSAL MAG.	720	26	34	A New and Accurate Map of North America, Laid Down According to the Latest, and Most Approved Observations, and Discoveries
mwuss0210	carolinas	1779	UNIVERSAL MAG.	650	27	36	A New and Accurate Map of North Carolina, in North America
mwca0541	canada quebec	1781	UNIVERSAL MAG.	400	27	32	A New and Accurate Map of Quebec and its Boundaries; from a Late Survey
mwuss0834	massachusetts	1780	UNIVERSAL MAG.	600	26	33	A New and Accurate Map of the Colony of Massachusetts Bay, in North America from a Late Survey
mwbp0456	poland	1757	UNIVERSAL MAG.	140	27	37	A New and Accurate Map of the Kingdom of Prussia, Pomerania, Courland, & the Adjacent Parts Bordering on the Baltick Sea
mwuss1041	new jersey	1777	UNIVERSAL MAG.	650	36	29	A New and Accurate Map of the Present Seat of War in North America, Comprehending New Jersey, Philadelphia, Pensylvania, New-York &c.
mwam1028a	america north (east)	1775	UNIVERSAL MAG.	650	29	38	A New and Accurate Map of the Present Seat of War in North America, from a Late Survey (shown above)
mwam0999	america north (east)	1757	UNIVERSAL MAG.	600	28	37	A New and Accurate Map of the Present War in North America
mwuss0498	georgia	1779	UNIVERSAL MAG.	600	33	28	A New and Accurate Map of the Province of Georgia in North America
mwca0445	canada nova scotia	1781	UNIVERSAL MAG.	350	28	34	A New and Accurate Map of the Province of Nova Scotia, in North America
mwuss1380	pennsylvania	1780	UNIVERSAL MAG.	400	27	33	A New and Accurate Map of the Province of Pennsylvania in North America, from the Best Authorities
mwuss0211	carolinas	1779	UNIVERSAL MAG.	550	34	23	A New and Accurate Map of the Province of South Carolina in North America
mwuss1644	virginia	1779	UNIVERSAL MAG.	720	28	34	A New and Accurate Map of the Province of Virginia, in North America
mwuss0805	massachusetts	1774	UNIVERSAL MAG.	750	27	35	A New and Accurate Plan of the Town of Boston, in New England / A New Plan of Boston Harbour, from an Actual Survey
mwuss0755	maryland	1780	UNIVERSAL MAG.	550	28	33	A New Map of the Province of Maryland in North America
mwuss0804	massachusetts	1774	UNIVERSAL MAG.	300	27	19	A New Plan of Boston Harbour, from an Actual Survey
mwca0514	canada quebec	1759	UNIVERSAL MAG.	200	19	23	A Plan of Quebec
mwca0382	canada nova scotia	1758	UNIVERSAL MAG.	350	27	36	A Plan of the City & Fortifications of Louisburg, from a Survey Made by Richard Gridley, Lieut. Col. of the Train of Artillery in 1745 / A Plan of the City and Harbour of Louisburg, with the French Batteries
mwuss1117	new york	1776	UNIVERSAL MAG.	1200	29	37	A Plan of the City and Environs of New York in North America
mwca0080	canada	1761	UNIVERSAL MAG.	350	26	34	An Accurate Map of Canada, with the Adjacent Countries; Exhibiting the Late Seat of War between the English & French in those Parts
mwuss1001	new hampshire	1781	UNIVERSAL MAG.	400	32	28	An Accurate Map of New Hampshire in New England, from a Late Survey
mwuss1143	new york	1780	UNIVERSAL MAG.	450	33	27	An Accurate Map of New York in North America, from a Late Survey
mwuk1344	england east	1760	UNIVERSAL MAG.	200	36	27	An Accurate Map of the East Part of England, with the Parts of Holland and Flanders Bordering on the German Ocean (map by J. Hinton)
mwam0966	america north (east)	1754	UNIVERSAL MAG.	350	20	24	An Accurate Map of the English Colonies in North America Bordering on the River Ohio
mwam1041	america north (east)	1776	UNIVERSAL MAG.	375	27	35	An Accurate Map of the Present Seat of War between Great-Britain and her Colonies in North America

AMPG REFERENCE	REGION	DATE	MAP MAKER	PRICE (UK£)	VERT. (cm.)	HOR. (cm.)	TITLE OF MAP (Comments by the editor in brackets)
mwm0244	mediterranean malta	1761	UNIVERSAL MAG.	450	26	17	An exact plan of the Capital City and Port of Malta / An Accurate Map of the Islands of Malta and Goza
mwwi0445	cuba	1762	UNIVERSAL MAG.	350	26	34	An Exact Plan of the City, Fortifications & Harbour of Havana in the Island of Cuba: From an Original Drawing Taken on the Spot
mwp0504a	pacific south	1787	UNIVERSAL MAG.	450	16	26	Chart of New Holland with the Adjacent Countries and New Discover'd Islands. 1787 (inset: Botany Bay)
mwec0237b	uk england cumbria	1791	UNIVERSAL MAGAZINE	60	23	18	Cumberland
mwec0523	uk england herefordshire	1750	UNIVERSAL MAG.	60	18	20	Hereford Shire Drawn from the Best Authorities
mwwi0781	martinique	1759	UNIVERSAL MAG.	250	37	35	Martinico, one of the Caribbee Islands in the West Indies; Subject to the French
mwca0573	canada quebec montreal	1759	UNIVERSAL MAG.	650	24	36	Plan of the Town and Fortifications of Montreal or Ville Marie in Canada
mwec0989	uk england rutland	1756	UNIVERSAL MAG.	50	17	19	Rutland Shire Drawn from the Best Authorities. By Eman: Bowen
mwec1045	uk england somerset	1758	UNIVERSAL MAG.	50	17	20	Somerset Shire Drawn from the Best Authorities by E. Bowen
mwat0161	atlantic canary isl.	1748	UNIVERSAL MAG.	350	19	23	The Canary Islands; & a Draught of the Fountain-Tree in the Island of Ferro
mwsp0682	balearic islands	1781	UNIVERSAL MAG.	100	18	23	The Island of Minorca from the Best Authorities.
mwec0187	uk england cornwall	1748	UNIVERSAL MAGAZINE	200	19	21	Cornwall from the Best Surveys (Map by J. Hinton, who founded the Universal Magazine)
mwbh0164	belgium holland	1603	VALDOR	1200	29	39	(Liege) Vera et Exacta Dexcriptio Spa Vici Arduenne cum Vicinis Montibus Sylvis et Pratis J. Valdor Fecit 1603
mwsp0390b	spain regions	1600	VALEGIO	720	9	12	Barcelona
mwit0777	italy sardinia	1580	VALEGIO	450	9	13	Caliari
mwsam0729	south america peru	1595	VALEGIO	300	8	13	Cusco (view)
mwgr0464	greece cyprus	1590	VALEGIO	1350	9	13	Famagusta, Civitas Cypri
mwit0063	italy	1610	VALEGIO	8000	53	77	Geografia della Italia di Giacomo Gastaldo (copy of Forlani 1568)
mwsw0028a	switzerland	1595	VALEGIO	275	9	14	Ginevra
mwit0070	italy	1620	VALEGIO	6000	45	55	Italiae, Sardiniae, Corsicae et Confinium Regionum Nova Tabula, Effigies Praeciparum Urbiu et Habituum Inibi Final Complectens (Carte-a-figure borders on four sides)
mwit0526a	italy milan	1580	VALEGIO	280	8	13	La Gran Citta di Milano
mwuk1105	england london	1600	VALEGIO	600	9	12	Londra
mwe0519b	europe czech republic (bohemia)	1597	VALEGIO	450	9	12	Pragha (shown above left)
mwc0007	china	1600	VALEGIO	550	9	13	Quinzai Metropolis Asia Orientalis (Hang Chow)
mwit1218	italy venice	1600	VALEGIO	4500	39	53	Venetia (text key and 2 insets below map)
mwas0824	asia south east siam	1724	VALENTYN	720	27	36	(Ayutthaya) Judia, de Hoofd-Stad van Siam
mwas0730	asia south east moluccas	1726	VALENTYN	150	30	38	(Buru and Ambelou)
mwas0726	asia south east moluccas	1724	VALENTYN	240	29	38	(Buru and Western Ceram)
mwin0179	india	1726	VALENTYN	240	30	37	(Malabar Coast)
mwas0606	asia south east cambodia	1724	VALENTYN	350	27	36	(Phnom Phenh) Eauweck, Hoofd-Stad van Cambodia
mwin0175	india	1725	VALENTYN	150	29	37	(Surat)
mwaf0907	africa south	1726	VALENTYN	750	27	35	(Untitled plan of Cape Town, incl. background view)
mwme0811	persia etc	1724	VALENTYN	350	30	38	(Untitled map of Persia)
mwp0006	australia	1724	VALENTYN	200	15	17	(Untitled map of south east Tasmania, west at the top, showing Boreels Eylanden.)
mwp0007	australia	1724	VALENTYN	200	13	16	(Untitled map of south east Tasmania, west at the top, showing Frederik Hendrikx Bay.)
mwaf0905	africa south	1726	VALENTYN	650	30	38	(Untitled sea chart: Saldanha Bay, Taafel Bay, Sout Bay and Bay falso)
mwp0008	australia	1724	VALENTYN	800	29	18	Anthony Van Diemans Land / Het Vaste Landt Bezuyden den Klippigen Hoek / Het Staten Landt Bezuyden den Klippigen Hoek (map of Tasmania and 2 views of New Zealand)
mwas0880	asia south east sumatra	1726	VALENTYN	300	27	36	Atsjien
mwin0040	ceylon	1728	VALENTYN	150	27	36	Baay van Tricoen Male
mwas0727	asia south east moluccas	1724	VALENTYN	160	44	56	Caart van het Eyland Manipa / Caart van het Eyland Noessa-Laoet / Caart van het Eyland Honimoa / Caart van het Eyland Oma
mwas0824a	asia south east siam	1724	VALENTYN	720	23	74	De Groote Siamse Rievier Me - Nam
mwas0728	asia south east moluccas	1724	VALENTYN	1500	46	58	De Landvoogdy der Moluccos met de Aangrenzende Eylanden
mwas0729	asia south east moluccas	1724	VALENTYN	300	28	37	De Platte Grond van Amboina, zoo als het was inden Jaare 1718
mwas0645	asia south east java	1726	VALENTYN	300	28	36	De Stad Bantam
mwc0102	china	1726	VALENTYN	750	27	36	De Stad Macao
mwas0762	asia south east philippines	1724	VALENTYN	1500	29	38	De Stad Manilha
mwas0683	asia south east malacca	1726	VALENTYN	650	27	54	De Stadt Malacka (view)
mwaf0906	africa south	1726	VALENTYN	650	27	36	Gezichte van Kaap der Goede Hope, als Men op de Reede Legt.
mwgm0202	mexico	1724	VALENTYN	720	27	36	Haven van Aquapulco in t Coninkryk van Nova Spagnien in de Zuyd Zee

AMPG REFERENCE	REGION	DATE	MAP MAKER	PRICE (UK£)	VERT. (cm.)	HOR. (cm.)	TITLE OF MAP (Comments by the editor in brackets)
mwin0041	ceylon	1728	VALENTYN	150	28	36	Jaffenapatnam
mwp0009	australia	1726	VALENTYN	6000	31	47	Kaart der Reyse van Abel Tasman Volgens syn eygen Opstel
mwas0571	asia south east banda	1726	VALENTYN	960	34	47	Kaart der Zuid-Wester Eylanden van Banda
mwas0570	asia south east banda	1724	VALENTYN	960	44	55	Kaart van de Zuyd-Ooster Eylanden van Banda
mwas0559	asia south east bali	1724	VALENTYN	1250	46	56	Kaart van het Eyland Bali
mwas0589	asia south east borneo	1726	VALENTYN	800	44	54	Kaart van het Eyland Borneo
mwc0302	china formosa	1726	VALENTYN	4800	44	56	Kaart van het Eyland Formosa en de Eylanden van Piscadores
mwaf0628	africa islands mauritius	1726	VALENTYN	2000	43	54	Kaart van het Eyland Mauritius
mwas0646	asia south east java	1726	VALENTYN	3200	46	182	Nieuwe en Zeer Naaukeurige Kaart van t Eyland Java Major of Groot Java Verdeeld in Seven Byzondere Bestekken
mwaf0906a	africa south	1726	VALENTYN	2000	44	56	Nieuwe Kaart van Caap der Goede Hoop (Inset: Cape Peninsula)
mwin0177	india	1726	VALENTYN	720	50	58	Nieuwe Kaart van Choromandel ende Malabar
mwin0039	ceylon	1726	VALENTYN	1100	44	55	Nieuwe Kaart van het Eyland Ceylon
mwjk0070	japan	1724	VALENTYN	2800	44	56	Nieuwe Kaart van het Eyland Japan Verbeterd door Francois Valentyn
mwas0879	asia south east sumatra	1725	VALENTYN	1500	51	61	Nieuwe Kaart van het Eyland Sumatra
mwin0178	india	1726	VALENTYN	500	45	54	Nieuwe Kaarte van't Koninckryk Bengale
mwc0104	china	1726	VALENTYN	900	28	37	Platte Grond vande Stadt Macao
mwin0425	indian ocean	1724	VALENTYN	2500	50	66	Tabula Indiae Orientalis et Regnorum Adiacentium. J.van Braam et G. onder de Linden
mwec0081	uk england cambridgeshire	1600	VALESO	300	13	8	Cantebrigia Opulentissimum Regni Anglie Celebris
mwec0121	uk england cheshire	1600	VALESO	300	9	13	Cestria, vulgo Chester, Anglie Civitas
mwit1257a	italy venice	1830	VALLARDI	1350	61	78	Pianta Topografica
mwaf0151a	africa	1720	VALK	1000	49	59	Africa Mauro Percussa Oceano, Niloque admota (revised version of Allard 1696)
mwam0107	america continent	1700	VALK	1650	49	60	America Aurea Pars Altera Mundi
mwas0105a	asia continent	1706	VALK	1200	48	59	Asia Qua nulla beatior Ora
mwe0450	europe bulgaria	1705	VALK	400	60	48	Bulgaria et Romania divisa
mwbh0856	luxembourg	1720	VALK	720	48	59	Ducatus Luceburgii, divisus in Regionem Germanicam et Wallonicam
mwe0121a	europe	1706	VALK	750	49	59	Europae Pars tenet Haec Mundi
mwgr0145	greece	1705	VALK	900	56	48	Graeciae et Archipelago divisus
mwsw0101	switzerland	1705	VALK	800	47	58	Helvetiorum Divisa in Tredecim Cantones
mwsw0081	switzerland	1670	VALK	800	49	57	Helvetiorum Republicae Cantones XIII
mwsp0203	spain	1686	VALK	850	48	59	Hispaniarum Portugalliaeque Coronarum Typus Novus
mwe0777a	europe east	1700	VALK	750	50	58	Hungaria Generalis ...
mwm0022	mediterranean	1686	VALK	1250	48	86	La Mer Mediterranee Divisee en ses Principales Parties ou Mers
mwam0094a	america continent	1695	VALK	2000	50	59	L'Amerique Septentrionale & Meridionale divisée en ses principales parties
mwuk0764	uk	1695	VALK	720	48	58	Les Isles Britanniques
mwe0097	europe	1686	VALK	1000	46	57	L'Europe Divisee Suivant l'Estendue de ses Principaux Estats
mwuk0780	uk	1705	VALK	720	49	60	Magna Britannia, aut Anglia, Scotia et Hibernia
mww0233	world	1686	VALK	7200	48	58	Mappe-Monde Geo-Hydrographique, ou Description Generale du Globe
mwm0033	mediterranean	1705	VALK	2000	48	116	Mare Mediterraneum
mwf1036c	france provence	1702	VALK	650	50	60	Provincia Supremarum Galliae ... Provence
mwsp0222	spain	1704	VALK	2500	97	114	Regnum Hispaniarum, atque Portugalliae
mwgr0146	greece	1705	VALK	400	50	60	Regnum Moreae Accuratissime Divisum in Provincias Saccaniam, Tzaconiam, Caliscopium et Ducatum Clarensem; una cum Insulis Cephalonia, Zacyntho Cythera, Aegina et Sidra
mwsc0104	scandinavia	1705	VALK	850	56	48	Scandinavia, vel Regna Septentrionalia
mwsc0703	scandinavia sweden	1705	VALK	800	59	48	Sueciae Magnae, Totius Orbis
mwbp0101	baltic states	1690	VALK	650	48	58	Tabula Ducatuum Livoniae et Curlandiae
mwam0092	america continent	1690	VALK	60000	110	148	Totius Americae Novior Accura Tabula
mwas0083a	asia continent	1690	VALK	30000	110	147	Totius Asiae Novior Accura Tabula
mwec0822	uk england norfolk	1700	VALK & SCHENK	500	43	55	A General Plott and Description of the Fennes and Surounded Grounds in the Six Counties of Norfolke, Suffolke, Cambridge, with in the Isle of Ely, Huntington, Northampton and Lincolne etc.
mwit0262	italy abruzzo	1700	VALK & SCHENK	400	38	49	Abruzzo Citra et Ultra
mwsam0342	south america brazil	1700	VALK & SCHENK	720	37	48	Accuratissima Brasiliae Tabula. Amstelodami P. Schenk et G. Valk C. Priv. (re-issue of Hondius 1638)
mwaf0502	africa egypt etc	1720	VALK & SCHENK	720	41	50	Aegypti Recentior Descriptio: Aegyptius & Turcis Elchibith; Arabibus Mesre & Misri, Hebraeis Mitsraim
mwaf0893	africa south	1705	VALK & SCHENK	650	38	50	Aethiopia Inferior vel Exterior
mwaf0391	africa east	1708	VALK & SCHENK	600	38	49	Aethiopie Superior vel Interior vulgo Abissinorum sive Presbiteri Ioannis Imperium (close copy of Jansson 1640)
mwsp0491	spain regions	1700	VALK & SCHENK	450	38	49	Andaluzia Continens Sevillam et Cordubam
mwuk0451	scotland	1700	VALK & SCHENK	480	43	51	Angusia Provincia Scotiae sive the Shire of Angus
mwme0570	arabia etc	1685	VALK & SCHENK	2000	42	50	Arabiae Felicis, Petraeae et Desertae Nove et Accurata Delineatio (re-issue of Jansson)
mwsp0491d	spain regions	1700	VALK & SCHENK	400	41	49	Arragonia Regnum

AMPG REFERENCE	REGION	DATE	MAP MAKER	PRICE (UK£)	VERT. (cm.)	HOR. (cm.)	TITLE OF MAP (Comments by the editor in brackets)
mwam0898	america north (east)	1694	VALK & SCHENK	5500	44	51	Belgii Novi, Angliae Novae, et Partis Virginiae Novissima Delineatio (re-issue of Jansson's 1651 map)
mwec0066	uk england buckinghamshire	1700	VALK & SCHENK	550	40	50	Buckingamiae Comitatus cum Bedfordiensi; vulgo Buckinghamshire and Bedfordshire
mwgm0014	gulf of mexico and surrounding regions	1700	VALK & SCHENK	4800	50	70	Caarte van Westindien (re-issue of Vingboons map of c1655)
mwit0401	italy lazio	1700	VALK & SCHENK	375	39	50	Campagna di Roma, olim Latium: Patrimonio di S. Pietro; et Sabina
mwec0617	uk england kent	1700	VALK & SCHENK	720	38	50	Cantium vernacule Kent
mwec0133	uk england cheshire	1670	VALK & SCHENK	500	37	48	Cestria Comitatus Palatinus.
mwec0094	uk england cambridgeshire	1700	VALK & SCHENK	800	41	51	Comitatis Cantabrigiensis; vernacule Cambridgeshire
mwuk0125	ireland	1700	VALK & SCHENK	360	38	48	Comitatus Lageniae - The Countie of Leinster
mwec0853	uk england northamptonshire	1670	VALK & SCHENK	480	38	49	Comitatus Northantonensis vernacule Northampton shire
mwec0886	uk england northumberland	1700	VALK & SCHENK	540	41	49	Comitatus Northumbria. Vernacule Northumberland
mwec0224	uk england cumbria	1670	VALK & SCHENK	550	42	52	Cumbria & Westmoria, vulgo Cumberland & Westmorland
mwgr0497	greece cyprus	1705	VALK & SCHENK	1600	38	49	Cyprus Insula
mwsc0701	scandinavia sweden	1700	VALK & SCHENK	450	39	49	Dalecarliae et Westmanniae
mwit0352	italy emilia-romagna	1700	VALK & SCHENK	280	37	48	Ducato di Ferrara
mwit0351	italy emilia-romagna	1700	VALK & SCHENK	280	39	50	Ducato di Parma et di Piacenza
mwec1310	uk england yorkshire	1670	VALK & SCHENK	650	40	48	Ducatus Eboracensis pars Occidentalis - The Westriding of Yorke Shire
mwec1311	uk england yorkshire	1670	VALK & SCHENK	650	37	48	Ducatus Eboracensis pars Orientalis - The Eastriding of Yorke Shire
mwec1309	uk england yorkshire	1670	VALK & SCHENK	650	38	50	Ducatus Eboracensis. Anglice Yorkshire
mwbh0840	luxembourg	1686	VALK & SCHENK	800	38	49	Ducatus Lutzenburgensis Nova et Accurata Descriptio
mwsc0592	scandinavia norway	1694	VALK & SCHENK	500	43	51	Episcopatus Bergensis
mwuk0450	scotland	1700	VALK & SCHENK	480	44	52	Extimae Scotiae Pars Septentrionalis, in qua Provinciae Rossia, Sutherlandia, Cathenesia, et Strath-Naverniae
mwsp0491a	spain regions	1700	VALK & SCHENK	650	38	49	Gallaecia Regnum
mwaf1181	africa west	1720	VALK & SCHENK	450	41	49	Genehoa Jaloffi et Sierraliones Regna (north to the left)
mwec0437	uk england gloucestershire	1670	VALK & SCHENK	720	40	50	Glocestria Ducatus, Monumenthensi Comitatu
mwsp0491b	spain regions	1700	VALK & SCHENK	450	37	49	Granata et Murcia Regna
mwec0471	uk england hampshire	1670	VALK & SCHENK	550	43	53	Hantoniae Comitatus cum Bercheria
mwec0517	uk england herefordshire	1683	VALK & SCHENK	480	38	50	Herefordia Comitatus vernacule Hereford Shire
mwuk1568	england islands	1705	VALK & SCHENK	720	40	51	Holy Iland / Garnsey / Farne / Iarsey (4 maps on one sheet)
mwc0056	china	1670	VALK & SCHENK	900	46	52	Huquang, Kiangsi, Che Kiang, ac Fokien, Provin: sivae Praefecturae Regni Sinen:s
mwc0088	china	1700	VALK & SCHENK	1350	47	52	Imperii Sinarum Nova Descriptio. Auctore, Joh. Van Loon
mwas0426	asia south east	1700	VALK & SCHENK	1350	39	49	India quae Orientalis Dicitur, et Insulae Adiacentes (re-issue of Hondius)
mwas0584	asia south east borneo	1690	VALK & SCHENK	960	42	52	Insula Borneo et Occidentalis Pars Celebis cum Adjacentibus Insulis
mwin0044	ceylon	1730	VALK & SCHENK	685	41	50	Insula Zeilan, olim Taprobana nunc Incolis Tenarisim
mwwi0044	west indies	1700	VALK & SCHENK	1200	38	53	Insulae Americanae in Oceano Septentrionali
mwat0157	atlantic canary isl.	1702	VALK & SCHENK	720	41	52	Insulae Canariae, olim Fortunatae Dictae
mwat0196	atlantic cape verde isl.	1720	VALK & SCHENK	400	43	55	Insulae de Cabo Verde, olim Hesperides, sive Gorgades: Belgice de Zoute Eylanden
mwat0090	atlantic azores	1710	VALK & SCHENK	720	42	53	Insulae Flandricae, olim Asores Dicta
mwas0643	asia south east java	1720	VALK & SCHENK	800	42	52	Insulae Iavae cum Parte Insularum Borneo Sumatrae
mwm0214	mediterranean malta	1700	VALK & SCHENK	2000	41	51	Insulae Melitae vulgo Malte Nova et Accurata Descriptio
mwit0796	italy sardinia	1700	VALK & SCHENK	960	41	51	Insulae Sardiniae Nova
mwwi0288	west indies	1700	VALK & SCHENK	1000	41	52	Insularum Hispaniolae et Cubae cum Insulis Circumjacentibus Accurata Delineatio (copy of Jansson 1652)
mwas0427	asia south east	1700	VALK & SCHENK	1500	38	50	Insularum Indiae Orientalis Nova Descriptio (re-issue of Jansson 1634)
mwc0097	china	1720	VALK & SCHENK	900	46	52	Iunnan, Queicheu, Quangsi et Quantung Provinciae Regni Sinensis (copy of Jansson 1658)
mwaf0392	africa east	1710	VALK & SCHENK	600	44	56	Jobi Ludolfi Habessinia seu Abassia Presbyteri Johannis Regio
mwsc0328a	scandinavia denmark	1700	VALK & SCHENK	300	43	53	Jutia Australis
mwsc0328b	scandinavia denmark	1700	VALK & SCHENK	300	43	53	Jutia Septentrionalis (shown above left)
mwf0610	france languedoc	1700	VALK & SCHENK	350	38	49	La Partie Meridionale du Languedoc
mwsw0098	switzerland	1700	VALK & SCHENK	875	42	51	Lacus Lemanni Locorumque Circumiacentium Accuratissima Descriptio
mwec0680	uk england lancashire	1670	VALK & SCHENK	650	37	49	Lancastria Palatinus Anglis
mwuk0459	scotland	1715	VALK & SCHENK	480	44	53	Lochabria, omnesq Insulae versus Occidentem Sitae, ut Uisto, Mulla, aliaeque
mwuk0452	scotland	1700	VALK & SCHENK	480	45	52	Lorna, Knapdalia, Cantire, Iura, Ila, Glota, et Buthe Insulae
mwgr0100a	greece	1686	VALK & SCHENK	400	35	42	Macedonia, Epirus et Achaia
mwbp0106	baltic states	1700	VALK & SCHENK	720	43	53	Magni Ducatus Lithuaniae Caeterarum Regionum Illi Adjacentium
mwin0141	india	1700	VALK & SCHENK	600	37	49	Magni Mogolis Imperium (close copy of Jansson 1641)
mwsc0425	scandinavia finland	1700	VALK & SCHENK	960	44	53	Magnus Ducatus Finlandiae Nova et Accurata Delineatio

AMPG REFERENCE	REGION	DATE	MAP MAKER	PRICE (UK£)	VERT. (cm.)	HOR. (cm.)	TITLE OF MAP (Comments by the editor in brackets)
mwat0116	atlantic bermuda	1720	VALK & SCHENK	1500	38	51	Mappa Aestivarum Insularum, alias Barmudas Dictarum ... Accurate Descripta
mwec0771	uk england middlesex	1646	VALK & SCHENK	750	43	54	Middelsexiae cum Hertfordiae Comitatu; Midlesex & Hertford Shire
mwuk1565	england islands	1700	VALK & SCHENK	500	44	54	Mona Insula vulgo Anglesey / Mona Insula: vulgo the Isle of Man / Vectis Insula Anglice the Isle of Wight (copy of Jansson)
mwru0125	russia	1710	VALK & SCHENK	400	39	52	Moscoviae Pars Australis Auctore Isacco Massa
mwme0982	turkey etc	1700	VALK & SCHENK	500	38	49	Natolia, quae olim Asia Minor (close copy of Blaeu/Jansson)
mwsp0491c	spain regions	1700	VALK & SCHENK	400	41	49	Navarra Regnum
mwaf1162a	africa west	1700	VALK & SCHENK	600	43	57	Nigritarum Regnum
mwaf1187	africa west	1729	VALK & SCHENK	600	44	57	Nigritarum Regnum
mwec0816	uk england norfolk	1670	VALK & SCHENK	550	37	47	Norfolcia vernacule Norfolke
mwam0899	america north (east)	1694	VALK & SCHENK	2500	39	50	Nova Belgica et Anglia Nova (updated Jansson map of 1636)
mwsam0341	south america brazil	1700	VALK & SCHENK	960	50	59	Nova et Accurata Brasiliae Totius Tabula (re-issue of Blaeu 1667)
mwjk0056	japan	1700	VALK & SCHENK	2000	45	55	Nova et Accurata Japoniae, Terrae Esonis, ac Insularum Adjacentium ex Novissima Detectione Descriptio
mwaa0106	arctic	1700	VALK & SCHENK	875	40	52	Nova et Accurata Poli Arctici et Terrarum Circum Iacentium Descriptio
mwe1045b	europe romania	1700	VALK & SCHENK	400	39	49	Nova et Accurata Transylvaniae Descriptio
mwru0115	russia	1700	VALK & SCHENK	400	46	54	Nova et Accurata Wolgae Fluminis (copy of Jansson 1659 / Pitt 1680)
mwuss1621	virginia	1700	VALK & SCHENK	1350	38	49	Nova Virginiae Tabula
mwsc0500	scandinavia iceland	1695	VALK & SCHENK	960	37	48	Novissima Islandiae Tabula
mwru0126	russia	1710	VALK & SCHENK	450	46	54	Novissima Russiae Tabula Authore Isaaco Massa (copy of Hondius 1638)
mwec0940	uk england oxfordshire	1644	VALK & SCHENK	800	38	50	Oxonium Comitatus vulgo Oxfordshire
mwbp0343	poland	1700	VALK & SCHENK	480	45	52	Palatinatus Posnaniensis, in Maiori Polonia Primarii Nova Delinatio per G.F.M.
mwc0057	china	1670	VALK & SCHENK	1000	46	52	Pecheli, Xansi, Xantung, Honan, Nanking, in Plaga Regni Sinensis inter Septentrionem ac Orientem Ceciam versus Sitae Provinciae
mwaf1072	africa south west	1710	VALK & SCHENK	480	41	49	Regna Congo et Angola
mwsc0593	scandinavia norway	1694	VALK & SCHENK	875	43	54	Regni Norvegiae Nova et Accurata Descriptio
mwsc0702	scandinavia sweden	1700	VALK & SCHENK	450	46	54	Scania, vulgo Schonen
mwuk0449	scotland	1700	VALK & SCHENK	480	44	52	Scotiae Provinciae intra Flumen Taum, et Murra Fyrth Sitae, Utpote Moravia, Badenocha, Atholia, Aberdonia, Baneia et Mernis
mwuk0456	scotland	1710	VALK & SCHENK	480	45	54	Scotiae Provintiae inter Taum Fluvium, et Septentrionales Oras Angliae
mwin0383	india bay of bengal	1700	VALK & SCHENK	960	47	54	Sinus Gangeticus; vulgo Golfo de Bengala Nova Descriptio (north to the right)
mwec1035	uk england somerset	1646	VALK & SCHENK	600	37	48	Somersettensis Comitatus: Somerset Shire
mwsc0602	scandinavia norway	1700	VALK & SCHENK	580	41	51	Spitzberga
mwc0058	china	1670	VALK & SCHENK	700	46	52	Suchuen; et Xensi, Provinciae seu Praefecturae Regni Sinensis, versus Caurum id est inter Occidentem et Septentrionem Sitae
mwec1098	uk england suffolk	1670	VALK & SCHENK	600	37	47	Suffolcia vernacula Suffolke
mwas0877	asia south east sumatra	1700	VALK & SCHENK	785	43	52	Sumatrae et Insularum Locorumque Nonnullorum Circumiacentium Tabula Nova
mwec1160	uk england sussex	1670	VALK & SCHENK	650	37	50	Suthsexia vernacule Sussex
mwme0869b	syria etc	1690	VALK & SCHENK	875	43	51	Syriae, sive Soriae nova et accurata descriptio (re-issue of Jansson 1658)
mwsam0681	south america magellan	1740	VALK & SCHENK	750	41	52	Tabula Magellanica qua Tierrae del Fuego
mwsp0490a	spain regions	1700	VALK & SCHENK	400	36	49	Tarraconensis Episcopatus (shown below left)
mwbp0344	poland	1700	VALK & SCHENK	1250	45	53	Tractus Borysthenis vulgo Dniepr et Niepr dicti, a Kiovia ad Urbum Oczakow
mwbp0345	poland	1700	VALK & SCHENK	480	41	48	Tractuum Borussiae, circa Gedanum et Elbingam, ab Incolis Werder Appellati, cum Adiuncta Neringia
mwru0500	ukraine	1700	VALK & SCHENK	785	42	53	Typus Generalis Ukrainae sive Palatinatuum Podoliae, Kioviensis et Braczlaviensis Terras Nova Delineatione Exhibens (re-issue of Jansson 1657)
mwsp0511	spain regions	1708	VALK & SCHENK	360	41	50	Utriusque Castiliae Nova Descriptio
mwsp0491e	spain regions	1700	VALK & SCHENK	650	36	48	Valentia Regnum. Cotestani. Ptol. Edentani plin.
mwsam0829	south america venezuela	1710	VALK & SCHENK	650	37	48	Venezuela, cum Parte Australi Novae Andalusiae
mwuss1619	virginia	1694	VALK & SCHENK	1350	38	49	Virginiae Partis Australis, et Floridae Partis Orientalis, interjacentiumq; Regionum Nova Descriptio (update of Jansson's map of 1639)
mwec1275	uk england worcestershire	1670	VALK & SCHENK	500	44	53	Wigorniensis Comitatus cum Warwicensis, nec non Conventriae Libertas
mwec1248	uk england wiltshire	1720	VALK & SCHENK	650	40	50	Wiltonia sive Comitatus Wiltoniensis Anglis Wil Shire
mwe1182a	europe south east	1850	VALLARDI	400	48	66	La Turchia d'Europa
mwbp0152b	baltic states	1813	VALLARDI	650	59	92	Nuova Carta del Teatro della Guerra
mwe0506a	europe croatia	1792	VALLE	900	63	44	Carta dell'Istria

AMPG REFERENCE	REGION	DATE	MAP MAKER	PRICE (UK£)	VERT. (cm.)	HOR. (cm.)	TITLE OF MAP (Comments by the editor in brackets)
mwit1202b	italy veneto	1793	VALLE	750	44	65	Il Polesine di Rovigo, il Ducato di Ferrara e la parte Meridionale del Dogado
mwe1123	europe slovenia	1689	VALVASOR	1800	25	93	(View of Ljubljana) Die Haubt Stadt Laybach in dem Hertzogthumb Crain
mww0174	world	1660	VAN ALPHEN	5500	41	56	Nova Totius Terrarum Orbis Geographica ac Hydrographica Tabula
mwuk0718	uk	1660	VAN ALPHEN	1500	43	54	Paskaart vant Canaal Tusschen englelant en Vrancryck alsmede geheel Jerlant en Schotlant
mwas0519	asia south east	1795	VAN BAARSEL	280	34	52	Kaart der Nederlandsche Beziltingen in Oost-Inde
mwsam0691	south america magellan	1775	VAN BAARSEL	480	41	49	Kaart van het Zuidlijk Eind van Amerika 1775
mwbh0794	belgium holland	1825	VAN BAARSEL	240	53	41	Nouvelle Carte Routiere du Royaume des Pays-Bas, de la France et l'Allemagne
mwbh0209a	belgium holland	1625	VAN BERCKENRODE		139	157	Amstelredamum Emporium Hollandiae Primarium Totiusque Europae Celiberrimum
mww0177	world	1661	VAN CAMPEN	800	43	74	De Grondt en Vloor de Groote Burger Sael (copy of the floor of Amsterdam Town Hall)
mwme0431	holy land	1847	VAN DE COTTE	950	90	74	Carte Topographique de la Palestine
mwme0199	holy land	1687	VAN DEN AVELEN	500	36	46	Beschryvinge van den Oorsprong der Volkeren, uyt de Drie Sonen van Noah na den Sondvloed, en Voorts vande Reysen der Eerste Vaderen in Canaan
mwme0202	holy land	1687	VAN DEN AVELEN	500	36	46	De Beschryving van de Reysen Pauli, en van de Andere Apostelen
mwme0203	holy land	1687	VAN DEN AVELEN	500	35	46	Het Beloofde Landt Canaan door Wandelt van onsen Salichmaaker Iesu Christo, neffens syne Apostelen
mwsc0704a	scandinavia sweden	1707	VAN DEN AVELEN	400	26	33	Ichonographica Delineatio Pervetustae Anse-aticae Urbis Wisyae in Gothlandia / Urbs Wisbya, et Arx Wisburgum, Prout
mwc0063	china	1680	VAN DEN AVELEN	300	16	20	Imperium Sinicum Quindecupartitum
mwp0001	australia	1625	VAN DEN ENDE?		56	32	(Fragment of a revised version of Van Den Ende's world map of c1604, including names used by Carstensz, 1623 to describe parts of Cape York peninsula in Australia, but which on the map are shown as parts of New Guinea.)
mwuk1108	england london	1638	VAN DEN HOEYE	7500	41	51	Londinum Celeberrimum Angliae Emporium. London (view)
mwbh0202	belgium holland	1620	VAN DEN KEERE	720	13	18	(Leo Belgicus untitled)
mwbh0190	belgium holland	1617	VAN DEN KEERE	800	37	49	(Overijssel) Ditio Transisulana
mwaf0040	africa	1614	VAN DEN KEERE	8000	45	58	Africae Nova Descr. (4 carte-a-figure borders)
mwam0031	america continent	1614	VAN DEN KEERE	20000	44	56	Americae Nova Descriptio (4 carte-a-figure borders)
mwuk0684	uk	1604	VAN DEN KEERE	2500	35	50	Angliae, Scotiae, Et Hiberniae, Sive Britannicar: Insularum Descriptio (based on Ortelius. Re-issued by Jansson in 1621)
mwf0715	france nord pas-de-calais	1624	VAN DEN KEERE	800	37	48	Artesia Descriptio (inset view of Arras)
mwas0029	asia continent	1614	VAN DEN KEERE	9000	45	58	Asiae Nova Descriptio (4 carte-a-figure borders)
mwbh0199	belgium holland	1617	VAN DEN KEERE	650	38	49	Belgii Veteris Typus
mwbh0191	belgium holland	1617	VAN DEN KEERE	1500	35	50	Brabantia Ducatus, Machliniae Urbis Dominium
mwbh0176	belgium holland	1608	VAN DEN KEERE	1600	33	48	Celeberrimi Flandriae Comitatus Typus
mwbh0181b	belgium holland	1610	VAN DEN KEERE	10000	44	56	Comitatus Hollandia. T'Graefschap Holland
mwsc0259	scandinavia denmark	1631	VAN DEN KEERE	2000	38	49	Daniae Regni Typus
mwf0041	france	1608	VAN DEN KEERE	8000	45	56	Gallia. Nova Galliae descriptio (4 carte-a-figure borders)
mwbh0192	belgium holland	1617	VAN DEN KEERE	3000	38	52	Hollandiae Comitatus. Hollandia ... Anno 1617
mwit0066	italy	1607	VAN DEN KEERE	10000	41	56	Italiae Sardiniae, Corsicae, & Confinium Regionum (4 carte-a-figure borders. Re-issued by Jansson in 1616)
mwbh0193	belgium holland	1617	VAN DEN KEERE	10000	37	46	Leo Belgicus
mwbh0198a	belgium holland	1617	VAN DEN KEERE	800	37	49	Limburgensis Ducatus Nova Descriptio
mwme0175	holy land	1677	VAN DEN KEERE	300	38	47	Lumen Historiarum per Orientem, Illustrandis Biblijs Sacris, Martyrologio, & alijs Multis a Fran. Hareio Concinnatum
mwf0818b	france paris	1617	VAN DEN KEERE	30000	59	224	Lutetia Parisiorum Urbs Regia Academia Toto Orbe Celeberrima Totius Galliae Metropolis
mwbh0194	belgium holland	1617	VAN DEN KEERE	1200	38	49	Marchionatus Sacri Romani Imperii (inset view of Antwerp)
mwe1094a	europe slovak republic (moravia)	1625	VAN DEN KEERE	2400	39	50	Moravia Marchionatus. Merhern (engraved by Abrahamus Janssonius, 1625)
mwbh0195	belgium holland	1617	VAN DEN KEERE	900	38	49	Namurcum Comitatus (inset view)
mwe0990	europe rhine	1621	VAN DEN KEERE	3500	34	98	Nieuwe en Warachtighe Beschryvinghe van den Rhynstroom en Alle de Steden
mwbh0181a	belgium holland	1610	VAN DEN KEERE	6000	44	57	Nova descriptio Orientalis & Occidentalis Frisiae
mwe0868	europe hungary	1620	VAN DEN KEERE	1200	35	53	Nova et Recens Emendata Totius Regni Ungariae una cum Adiacentibus et Finitimis Regionibus Delineatio (illustrated is CJ Visscher version 1624. See also Danckerts 1657)
mwe0029	europe	1614	VAN DEN KEERE	8000	45	58	Nova Europae Descriptio (4 carte-a-figure borders)
mww0129a	world	1622	VAN DEN KEERE	35000	46	57	Nova Totius Terrrarum Orbis Geographica ac Hydrographica Tabula
mww0117	world	1608	VAN DEN KEERE	20000	40	53	Nova Totius Terrarum Orbis Geographica Ac Hydrographica Tabula. A Pet. Kaerio (A close copy of Blaeu's map of 1606, with revisions. The illustration shows a later state of this map with Joannes Janssonius imprint added in the lower cartouche, c1675. See also Blaeu 1630 below and Shirley's 'The Mapping of the World', entry 264.)

AMPG REFERENCE	REGION	DATE	MAP MAKER	PRICE (UK£)	VERT. (cm.)	HOR. (cm.)	TITLE OF MAP (Comments by the editor in brackets)
mwbh0196	belgium holland	1617	VAN DEN KEERE	1200	39	50	Novus XVII Inferioris Germaniae Provinciarum Typus. De Integro Multis in Locis Emendatus a Petro Kaerio. Anno 1617
mww0116	world	1607	VAN DEN KEERE	15000	40	57	Orbis Terrarum Typus de Integro Multis in Locis Emendatus Auctore Petro Kaerio Anno 1607 (1st edition 1604, after Plancius 1594)
mwe0528	europe czech republic (bohemia)	1618	VAN DEN KEERE	1200	38	50	Regni Bohemiae Nova Descriptio
mwbp0227	poland	1621	VAN DEN KEERE	1200	39	51	Silesiae Ducatus Nova Descripto
mwg0218b	germany north west	1617	VAN DEN KEERE	1500	40	50	Typus Frisiae Orientalis (Title text lower left. Inset of Embden)
mwbh019b	belgium holland	1617	VAN DEN KEERE	1500	37	48	Ultraiectum Dominium (illustrated above left)
mwbh0197	belgium holland	1617	VAN DEN KEERE	1200	35	47	Zelandiae Comitatus (title on verso)
mwbh0198	belgium holland	1617	VAN DEN KEERE	1200	38	49	Zipa. Agri Zupani Nova Descriptio. 1617
mwuk0688	uk	1617	VAN DEN KEERE / BLAEU	400	12	16	Anglia Scotia et Hibernia
mwec0599	uk england kent	1617	VAN DEN KEERE / BLAEU	150	9	12	Cantii, Southsexiae
mwuk0327	scotland	1617	VAN DEN KEERE / BLAEU	120	9	12	Cathnes. et Orcades. In.
mwec0125	uk england cheshire	1617	VAN DEN KEERE / BLAEU	140	9	12	Cestriae
mwuk0025	ireland	1617	VAN DEN KEERE / BLAEU	120	9	12	Connacia
mwec0165	uk england cornwall	1617	VAN DEN KEERE / BLAEU	160	9	12	Cornuwallia
mwuk1719	wales	1617	VAN DEN KEERE / BLAEU	120	9	12	Denbigh ac Flint
mwec0252	uk england derbyshire	1617	VAN DEN KEERE / BLAEU	140	9	12	Derbiensis Comitatus
mwec0282	uk england devon	1617	VAN DEN KEERE / BLAEU	140	9	12	Devonia
mwec0320	uk england dorset	1617	VAN DEN KEERE / BLAEU	140	9	12	Dorcestria
mwec0358	uk england durham	1617	VAN DEN KEERE / BLAEU	140	9	12	Dunelmesis Episcopatus
mwec1294	uk england yorkshire	1617	VAN DEN KEERE / BLAEU	300	12	16	Eboracensis comitatus
mwec0395	uk england essex	1617	VAN DEN KEERE / BLAEU	160	9	12	Essexiae Comitat.
mwuk1720	wales	1617	VAN DEN KEERE / BLAEU	120	9	12	Glamorgan
mwec0430	uk england gloucestershire	1617	VAN DEN KEERE / BLAEU	140	9	12	Glocestria
mwec0538	uk england hertfordshire	1617	VAN DEN KEERE / BLAEU	160	9	12	Hartfordia Comitatus
mwuk0328	scotland	1617	VAN DEN KEERE / BLAEU	120	9	12	Hebrides Insulae
mwec0509	uk england herefordshire	1617	VAN DEN KEERE / BLAEU	120	9	12	Herefordia Comitatus
mwuk0026	ireland	1617	VAN DEN KEERE / BLAEU	120	9	12	Lagenia
mwec0672	uk england lancashire	1617	VAN DEN KEERE / BLAEU	160	9	12	Lancastria
mwec0733	uk england lincolnshire	1617	VAN DEN KEERE / BLAEU	140	9	12	Lincolnia et Notingham
mwuk0027	ireland	1617	VAN DEN KEERE / BLAEU	120	9	12	Midia
mwuk0028	ireland	1617	VAN DEN KEERE / BLAEU	120	9	12	Momonia
mwuk1721	wales	1617	VAN DEN KEERE / BLAEU	120	9	12	Mone Ins. Et Carnavan
mwuk1722	wales	1617	VAN DEN KEERE / BLAEU	120	9	12	Montgomeri ac Merionidh
mwuk1723	wales	1617	VAN DEN KEERE / BLAEU	120	9	12	Monumethensis comitatus
mwec0807	uk england norfolk	1617	VAN DEN KEERE / BLAEU	140	9	12	Norfolcia
mwec0846	uk england northamptonshire	1617	VAN DEN KEERE / BLAEU	140	9	12	Northamtoniae Bedfordiae Cantabrigae Hutigdoniae et Rutlandiae
mwec0875	uk england northumberland	1617	VAN DEN KEERE / BLAEU	140	9	12	Northumbria
mwec0937	uk england oxfordshire	1617	VAN DEN KEERE / BLAEU	150	9	12	Oxonij
mwuk1724	wales	1617	VAN DEN KEERE / BLAEU	120	9	12	Penbrok

AMPG REFERENCE	REGION	DATE	MAP MAKER	PRICE (UK£)	VERT. (cm.)	HOR. (cm.)	TITLE OF MAP (Comments by the editor in brackets)
mwuk1725	wales	1617	VAN DEN KEERE / BLAEU	120	9	12	Radnor
mwec0999	uk england shropshire	1617	VAN DEN KEERE / BLAEU	140	9	12	Salopia
mwuk0329	scotland	1617	VAN DEN KEERE / BLAEU	120	9	12	Scotiae pars Australior
mwuk0330	scotland	1617	VAN DEN KEERE / BLAEU	120	9	12	Scotiae pars australissima
mwuk0331	scotland	1617	VAN DEN KEERE / BLAEU	120	9	12	Scotiae pars Orientalior
mwuk0332	scotland	1617	VAN DEN KEERE / BLAEU	120	9	12	Scotiae pars quae incolis Stratnahern vocatur
mwec1028	uk england somerset	1617	VAN DEN KEERE / BLAEU	140	9	12	Somersetia
mwec0464	uk england hampshire	1617	VAN DEN KEERE / BLAEU	140	9	12	Southamtioniae
mwec1059	uk england staffordshire	1617	VAN DEN KEERE / BLAEU	140	9	12	Staffordia
mwec1092	uk england suffolk	1617	VAN DEN KEERE / BLAEU	160	9	12	Suffolcia
mwuk0029	ireland	1617	VAN DEN KEERE / BLAEU	120	9	12	Ultonia
mwec1188	uk england warwickshire	1617	VAN DEN KEERE / BLAEU	140	9	12	Warwic. & Lecestria
mwec1216	uk england westmorland	1617	VAN DEN KEERE / BLAEU	120	9	12	Westmorlandia et Comberladia
mwec1269	uk england worcestershire	1617	VAN DEN KEERE / BLAEU	140	9	12	Wigorniensis Comitatus
mwec1237	uk england wiltshire	1617	VAN DEN KEERE / BLAEU	140	9	12	Wiltonia
mww0141	world	1632	VAN DEN KEERE-JANSSON	25000	45	56	Nova Totius Terrarum Orbis Geographica ac Hydrographica Tabula (4 carte-a-figure borders in the style of Visscher 1614)
mwjk0061	japan	1715	VAN DER AA	400	19	16	(Hirado, Nagasaki) Les Ports et Havres de Firando et Nangesaque
mwsam0045	south america	1706	VAN DER AA	350	16	23	A. Knivets zeldzame Reystogt door de Straat Magellaan na de Zuyd Zee
mwat0027	atlantic ocean (all)	1706	VAN DER AA	300	18	23	A. Knivets Zeldzame Reystogt door de Straat Magellaan na de Zuyd Zee
mwaf0390	africa east	1707	VAN DER AA	200	15	23	Aethiopie of Abissine in't Gemeen 't Land van Preste Ian Genoemd
mwaf0138	africa	1710	VAN DER AA	235	15	18	Africa
mwaf0128	africa	1707	VAN DER AA	350	20	30	Africa Volgens de Alder-Eerste Scheeps-Togten der Portugysen ter Ontdekking Uytgesonden Ao. 1419 enz.
mwam0112	america continent	1706	VAN DER AA	650	15	23	America, of Nieuw-Ontdekte Weereld, tot de Beschryving van Joseph d'Acosta Afgebakend
mwam0113	america continent	1707	VAN DER AA	400	15	23	Amerika, of de Nieuwe Weerld Aller Eerst door C. Kolumbus ... 1492
mwgr0157	greece	1713	VAN DER AA	1800	38	52	Antiquorum Illyrici episcopaatum orientalis geographica
mwas0106	asia continent	1706	VAN DER AA	235	15	23	Babylonie en Balsara van Aleppo tot in Pegu Bereyet
mwme0738	iraq etc	1706	VAN DER AA	250	15	24	Bassora en de Landschappen tussen de Eufrat en Tiger Stroom, een Gedeelte van Persien, de Indiaanze Zee en Kusten, tot aan de Straat Zunda
mwgm0390	panama	1700	VAN DER AA	200	22	31	Bay et Chateau de Porto Bello
mwwi0426	cuba	1729	VAN DER AA	250	21	31	Baye et Ville de Havana ou St. Christoval (copy of Bernard 1722)
mwat0113a	atlantic bermuda	1700	VAN DER AA	1200	29	36	Bermudes, ou Iles de Sommer dans l'Amerique Septentrionale avec le Regitre des departments de ce Pays aux peuplades Angloises
mwsp0519c	spain regions	1714	VAN DER AA	400	16	20	Biscaie, Guipiscoa, Navarre Et L'Asturie De Santillana (illustration above extreme left)
mwsam0345	south america brazil	1707	VAN DER AA	250	15	23	Brasiliaanze Scheepvaard, door Johan Lerius Gedaan uit Vrankryk in't Iaar 1556
mwf0350	france brittany	1728	VAN DER AA	120	26	38	Bretagne
mwaf1047	africa south east	1718	VAN DER AA	200	15	19	Caarte van de Oost-Kust van Africa (title also in French)
mwca0051	canada	1729	VAN DER AA	500	23	30	Canada ou Nouvelle France, Suivant les Nouvelles Observations de Messrs. de l'Academie Royale des Sciences
mwat0158	atlantic canary isl.	1720	VAN DER AA	500	26	34	Canaries ou Iles Fortunees
mwf0587a	france ile de france	1728	VAN DER AA	120	26	38	Carte de l'Isle de France
mwf0683	france lorraine	1714	VAN DER AA	150	22	29	Carte de Lorraine
mwbh0552	belgium holland	1714	VAN DER AA	150	22	29	Carte du Brabant
mwbh0602	belgium holland	1728	VAN DER AA	235	22	30	Carte du Comte de Flandre
mwin0187	india	1732	VAN DER AA	450	28	36	Carte du Golfe de Bengale, Mer des Indes, et Riviere du Gange

AMPG REFERENCE	REGION	DATE	MAP MAKER	PRICE (UK£)	VERT. (cm.)	HOR. (cm.)	TITLE OF MAP (Comments by the editor in brackets)
mwf0348	france brittany	1720	VAN DER AA	120	23	31	Carte du Gouvernement de Bretagne Suivant les Nouvelles Observations
mwf0449	france champagne	1715	VAN DER AA	120	26	38	Carte du Gouvernement de Champagne
mwf1153	france rhone-alpes	1728	VAN DER AA	120	26	38	Carte du Gouvernement de Dauphine
mwf1053	france provence	1728	VAN DER AA	280	26	38	Carte du Gouvernement du Provence
mwf1154	france rhone-alpes	1728	VAN DER AA	120	26	38	Carte du Lyonnois
mwf0957	france picardy	1728	VAN DER AA	120	26	38	Carte du Picardie
mwgm0191	mexico	1704	VAN DER AA	2500	42	51	Carte d'un Tres Grand Pays entre le Nouveau Mexique
mwc0108	china	1730	VAN DER AA	850	43	52	Carte Exacte ... de la Chine
mwme0805	persia etc	1719	VAN DER AA	350	29	34	Carte la Plus-Nouvelle & Plus-Exacte du Royaume de Perse
mwas0307	asia caspian sea	1710	VAN DER AA	600	29	36	Carte Marine de la Mer Caspienne (copy of Dapper)
mwme0804	persia etc	1710	VAN DER AA	450	29	35	Carte Marine de la Mer Caspienne
mwit0427	italy liguria	1729	VAN DER AA	235	34	41	Carte Nouvelle et Exacte de la Gaule Cisalpine et sur Tout de la Ligurie de l'Insubrie
mwit0678	italy piedmont	1729	VAN DER AA	280	34	43	Carte Particuliere a Toute Nouvelle de Milianois, avec Tous ses Confins
mwbh0603	belgium holland	1728	VAN DER AA	120	26	38	Cartes des Comtez de Hainaut de Namur et de Cambresis
mwbh0604	belgium holland	1728	VAN DER AA	120	26	38	Cartes des Pays Bas Catholiques
mwit1239	italy venice	1729	VAN DER AA	4000	41	102	Celeberrima Urbs Venetiae
mwg0370	bavaria	1720	VAN DER AA	235	34	41	Cercle de Baviere
mwg0628	saxony	1714	VAN DER AA	150	22	29	Cercle de la Haute Saxe
mwme0985	turkey etc	1705	VAN DER AA	450	33	41	Constantinople, Ville de la Turquie en Europe
mwsc0330	scandinavia denmark	1705	VAN DER AA	280	33	41	Coppenhague Capitale de Danemarc
mwuk0151	ireland	1729	VAN DER AA	120	12	13	Corcahia. Corcke. Corcach
mwwi0419	cuba	1707	VAN DER AA	300	15	23	Cuba en Iamaica soo als die door Kolumbus Ontdekt en by de Kastilianen Bevolkt syn
mwsc0501	scandinavia iceland	1706	VAN DER AA	480	15	23	D. Blefkenius Scheeps-Togt Gedaan na Ysland en Kusten van Groenland
mwm0035	mediterranean	1707	VAN DER AA	250	15	23	d'Avontuurlyke Reystogt van Johan Smith, uit Engeland
mwas0451	asia south east	1720	VAN DER AA	235	15	23	De Agste Oostindize Reys voor d'Engelse Maatschappie
mwat0114	atlantic bermuda	1707	VAN DER AA	850	15	23	De Bermudes of Summer Eylanden tot de Reystogten Afgepeyld, door de Engelzen derwards Gedaan
mwin0464	indian ocean maldives	1707	VAN DER AA	280	15	28	De Eilanden Maldives (incl. Ceylon and Sumatra)
mwat0024	atlantic ocean (all)	1700	VAN DER AA	300	15	22	De Graaf van Cumberlands Verscheyde Reysen na de Kusten van Africa na Porto Rico en Andere Gesesten van America
mwaf0708	africa north	1707	VAN DER AA	235	15	23	De Koninkryken van Fez en Marocco in een Elfjarige Slaver Nye door den Heer Mouette
mwme0588	arabia etc	1707	VAN DER AA	350	16	23	De Kusten van Arabie, het Roode Meer, en Persize Zee van Bassora voorby 't Nau van Ormus tot aan den Indus, Guzaratte en Kaap Comorin
mwin0147	india	1706	VAN DER AA	250	15	24	De Kusten van Guzaratte, Malabaar, Bengale en Malacca, med die van't Magtig Koninkryk Siam tot aan China Bestevend
mwin0148	india	1706	VAN DER AA	250	15	23	De Land-Reyes, door Benedictus Goes, van Lahor Gedaan, door Tartaryen na China
mwgm0193	mexico	1706	VAN DER AA	250	15	23	De Landschappen Tabasco en Iucatan tussen de Golf van Mexico en de Zuyd Zee Gelegen
mwgm0194	mexico	1706	VAN DER AA	250	15	24	De Land-Togt door Ferdinand Cortes Gedaan uyt Mexico, na las Ybueras
mwas0761	asia south east philippines	1700	VAN DER AA	235	23	30	De Manilles of Philippines Eylanden Benevens de Moluccos, Macassar, Tymor, en Andere
mwas0724	asia south east moluccas	1707	VAN DER AA	235	16	23	De Moluccos en andere Speceri-Eilanden in d'Oost-Indien
mwas0723	asia south east moluccas	1707	VAN DER AA	235	15	24	De Moluccos, of Speceri-dragende Eilanden tussen Gilolo en Celebes Gelegen
mwme0585	arabia etc	1706	VAN DER AA	280	17	24	De Persiaanze Zee met de Eylanden Baharem, Queixome en Ormus, tussen Arabie en Persie, tot aan Dio en Suratte
mwme0589	arabia etc	1707	VAN DER AA	550	15	23	De Roode Zee in een Zesde Scheepstogt der Engelze Maatschappie onder H. Middleton, tot aan Mocha
mwme0590	arabia etc	1707	VAN DER AA	550	16	22	De Roode Zee met de Kusten van Arabien
mwaf0493	africa egypt etc	1705	VAN DER AA	250	24	34	De Stadt Cairus. La Ville de Caire, en Egypte
mwsam0678	south america magellan	1706	VAN DER AA	235	15	23	De Straat van Magellaen Sedert Desselfs Eerste Ondekker, F. Magellaen A. 1520
mwsam0828	south america venezuela	1706	VAN DER AA	265	17	24	De Vaste Kust van Cheribichi door Alonzo d'Ojeda van 't Eyland Cubagua Besogt
mwwi0288a	west indies (west)	1706	VAN DER AA	450	15	24	De Vaste Kust van Chicora
mwuss0404	florida	1706	VAN DER AA	450	18	23	De Vaste Kust van Chicora tussen Florida en Virginie door Lucas Vasquez d'Ayllon en Andere, van Hispaniola Bestevend
mwme0221	holy land	1700	VAN DER AA	960	29	77	De Veertig-Jaarige Reys-Togten der Kinderen Israels Num. XXXIII. in welkze onder 't Geley van Moses en Aaron uyt het Diensthuys van Aegypten Uytgetoogen
mwwi0051	west indies	1706	VAN DER AA	400	15	22	De Voor Eylanden van America tegens de Vaste Kusten van Florida, Mexico, Nieuw Spanje, Cartagena, Iucatan en Darien met de Grenzen aande Zuyd Zee Gelegen

AMPG REFERENCE	REGION	DATE	MAP MAKER	PRICE (UK£)	VERT. (cm.)	HOR. (cm.)	TITLE OF MAP (Comments by the editor in brackets)
mwme0802	persia etc	1707	VAN DER AA	265	15	23	De Zee en Land-Reyse, van Ioh Mildenhal en Cartwright na Persien en Mogol, op 't Spoor Gevolgd
mwsam0592	south america guyana	1710	VAN DER AA	350	15	23	D'Engelze Volkplanting in 't Amerikaans Gewest Gujana, en Rio de las Amazones. Door de Scheeps-Togt van Charles Leig Begonnen
mwuss1626	virginia	1707	VAN DER AA	450	15	23	D'Engelze Volkplanting in Virginie door Iohan Smith Bezogt en Verder Uytgeset
mwme0610	arabia etc	1729	VAN DER AA	400	30	36	Description Exacte de l'Arabie Heureuse, Petree et Deserte
mwjk0054	japan	1696	VAN DER AA	280	43	53	Description Exacte et Fidele des Villes, Bourgs et Villages qui les Ambassadeurs de Holande ont Recontrez dans leur Voyage par Terre de la Ville d'Osaca jusqu'a Jedo Capitale du Japon / Voyage des Ambassadeurs de Hollande
mwaf0394	africa east	1714	VAN DER AA	235	16	23	d'Ethiopie au Roi de Gingiro
mwas0435	asia south east	1707	VAN DER AA	235	16	28	D'Oost-Indize Landschappen, Zeen en Eylanden
mwas0107	asia continent	1707	VAN DER AA	235	15	23	D'OostIndize Voyagien door Johan Davis Tweemaal
mwit0672a	italy piedmont	1714	VAN DER AA	300	16	21	Duche de Monferrat
mwe0130	europe	1713	VAN DER AA	1400	50	66	Europa praecipiuas ipsius partes (title above map)
mww0305	world	1706	VAN DER AA	400	16	23	F. Draakx Schip-Vaart door de Straat en Zuyd Zee Gedaan om de Gantsen Aard Kloot
mwit0359	italy emilia-romagna	1730	VAN DER AA	280	36	46	Ferrara
mwuk0152	ireland	1729	VAN DER AA	120	13	13	Galwaia. Galway. Gallive
mwin0402	india goa	1720	VAN DER AA	450	32	46	Goa Indiae Orientalis Metropolis
mwm0092	mediterranean adriatic	1700	VAN DER AA	1250	44	50	Golfe de Venise avec les Cotes Maritimes
mwgr0175	greece	1729	VAN DER AA	480	35	49	Graecia Sophiani per Abrahamum Ortelium
mwbp0364	poland	1714	VAN DER AA	550	29	37	Grande Pologne et Prusse
mwaf1180	africa west	1719	VAN DER AA	360	26	37	Guinee, Grand Pays de l'Afrique, avec Toutes ses Cotes, Havres et Rivieres, Suivant les Memoires les Plus Recens des Voyageurs
mwwi0053	west indies	1707	VAN DER AA	250	16	23	H. Benzos Scheep-Togt uit Italie over Spanje na de Westindize Eylanden, en Kusten van't Zuider America
mwbh0606	belgium holland	1729	VAN DER AA	1500	39	54	Haga Comitatus, vulgo 's-Graven-Hage (revised version of Blaeu)
mwwi0427	cuba	1729	VAN DER AA	500	29	36	Havana, Ville Capital de l'Isle de Cuba en Amerique
mwgm0203	mexico	1729	VAN DER AA	400	29	36	Havre de la Ville d'Acapulco dans d'Amerique, Portus Acapulco
mwas0637	asia south east java	1707	VAN DER AA	250	15	24	het Eiland Java zoo als het Sederd de Tyden der Portugysen by de Ed. Oost-Indize Maatschappye Bekend Geworden en Bevarenis
mwas0878	asia south east sumatra	1707	VAN DER AA	280	15	22	Het Eiland Sumatra; hoe ten Aansien van Malacca
mwgr0531	greece rhodes	1707	VAN DER AA	300	12	16	Het Eylant Rhodus
mwsam0588	south america guyana	1700	VAN DER AA	200	15	23	Het Goudryk Gewest Guiana tot de Drywerfze Scheepstogten van den Ridder Walter Ralegh Afgebakend
mwin0152	india	1707	VAN DER AA	250	15	23	Het Koninkryk van Bengale
mwin0149	india	1706	VAN DER AA	250	15	23	Het Koninkryk van Guzaratte met d'Engte van Cambaya en der Selver Vloeden, Volgens de Kundschap der Portugysen
mwuk0148	ireland	1720	VAN DER AA	250	13	16	Hibernia (north to the left)
mwwi0589	hispaniola	1707	VAN DER AA	300	15	22	Hispaniola soo als het door Kolumbus Ontdekt, en by de Kastilianen Bevolkt is
mwgr0501	greece cyprus	1714	VAN DER AA	600	14	19	Ile de Chypre (Hondius-Jansson reprint with changed title)
mwaf0600	africa islands madagascar	1720	VAN DER AA	360	28	37	Ile de S. Laurens ou Madagascar
mwwi0066	west indies	1729	VAN DER AA	750	28	36	Iles de l'Amerique, Situees dans l'Ocean Septentrional
mwin0150	india	1706	VAN DER AA	250	17	24	Indien binnen de Ganges Vert Oonende de Koninkryken van Golconda, Decan, Bisnaga en Grenzen van Mogol
mwf0480	france corsica	1720	VAN DER AA	480	32	38	Insula Corsica
mwit0802	italy sardinia	1720	VAN DER AA	500	30	38	Insula et Regnum Sardiniae
mwm0232	mediterranean malta	1729	VAN DER AA	350	18	21	Insulae Melita & Gozo
mwat0329	atlantic st helena	1719	VAN DER AA	400	25	31	Isle St. Helene
mwas0443	asia south east	1714	VAN DER AA	220	15	19	Isles des Indes Orientales
mwgm0019	gulf of mexico and surrounding regions	1706	VAN DER AA	400	15	23	Iukatan en Vaste Kusten van Nieuw Spanje, met de Landschappen en Eylanden, ten Oosten Noorden en Zuiden Bezogt
mwsam0343	south america brazil	1706	VAN DER AA	235	15	22	Jan Stadens Scheepstogten ... na Rio de Janeiro
mwat0026	atlantic ocean (all)	1706	VAN DER AA	250	15	23	Jan Stadens Scheepstogten over Portugal en Spanje, na Rio de Janeiro en Elders in Brasil Gedaan 1547
mwjk0058	japan	1707	VAN DER AA	400	15	23	Japan
mwuss1343	pennsylvania	1714	VAN DER AA	500	15	23	Jonathan Dickenson Ramspoedige Reystogt van Jamaika na Pensylvania Nagespoord
mwas0444	asia south east	1714	VAN DER AA	400	22	28	Joris van Spilbergens Eerste Voyagie Gedaan na Oost Indien
mwru0445b	russia tartary	1714	VAN DER AA	200	15	22	Kaart van Tartaryen. Volgens de Voyagien Gedann door Johan du Plan Carpin en Aseelin
mwc0101a	china	1720	VAN DER AA	550	28	36	Kanton (based on Nieuhoff 1665)
mwaf0389	africa east	1706	VAN DER AA	200	15	22	Keyserlynk Gezandschap, door de eerw. Vader A. Fernandez en Tecur Egzy uyt Aethiopien
mwsc0355	scandinavia denmark	1730	VAN DER AA	280	19	25	Koppenhaven
mwme0873	syria etc	1714	VAN DER AA	200	15	22	L. Rouwolf Land-Reysen, Gedaan van Aleppo, door Babylonien, Syrien en Palestina

AMPG REFERENCE	REGION	DATE	MAP MAKER	PRICE (UK£)	VERT. (cm.)	HOR. (cm.)	TITLE OF MAP (Comments by the editor in brackets)
mwm0139	mediterranean east	1707	VAN DER AA	200	15	22	L. Rouwolfs Reys-Togten
mwas0761a	asia south east philippines	1719	VAN DER AA	450	19	18	La Baie de Manille
mwaf0915	africa south	1729	VAN DER AA	720	28	36	La Basse Ethiopie en Afrique
mwe0557	europe czech republic (bohemia)	1714	VAN DER AA	300	22	29	La Boheme (illustrated below is a smaller - 15x19cm - map by van der Aa, a Hondius-Jansson reprint also dated 1714)
mwc0099	china	1720	VAN DER AA	350	23	30	La Chine, Suivant les Nouvelles Observations
mwuss0405	florida	1713	VAN DER AA	650	23	30	La Floride Suivant les Nouvelles Observations de Messrs. de l'Academie Royale des Sciences
mwbh0553	belgium holland	1714	VAN DER AA	150	23	29	La Frise
mwru0445a	russia tartary	1713	VAN DER AA	300	22	29	La Grande Tartarie Suivant les Nouvelles Observations
mwgr0158	greece	1713	VAN DER AA	240	23	30	La Grece Suivant les Nouvelles Observations
mwbh0554	belgium holland	1714	VAN DER AA	150	22	29	La Gueldre
mwe0927	europe hungary	1720	VAN DER AA	200	26	38	La Hongrie
mwe0931	europe hungary	1729	VAN DER AA	200	22	29	La Hongrie Suivant les Nouvelles Observations
mwg0117	germany	1729	VAN DER AA	200	31	41	L'Allemagne (size excl. printed borders)
mwgr0159	greece	1713	VAN DER AA	750	46	50	La Moree, autrefois le Peloponnese
mwru0135	russia	1714	VAN DER AA	400	23	30	La Moscovie Septentrionale Suivant les Nouvelles Observations / La Moscovie Meridionale ... (2 maps, printed separately. Sizes do not include printed borders. Also publ. without the borders.)
mwru0135	russia	1714	VAN DER AA	180	23	30	La Moscovie Septentrionale Suivant les Nouvelles Observations
mwbh0619	belgium holland	1730	VAN DER AA	265	22	30	La Nord-Holland (and) La Sud-Holland (2 maps)
mwsc0612	scandinavia norway	1729	VAN DER AA	650	34	40	La Norvegue
mwg0096	germany	1710	VAN DER AA	2400	121	137	La Plus Nouvelle, la plus Exacte et la plus Grande Carte de L'Empire d'Allemagne
mwbp0390	poland	1729	VAN DER AA	480	22	29	La Pologne Suivant les Nouvelles Observations
mwbp0391	poland	1729	VAN DER AA	280	22	29	La Prusse Suivant les Nouvelles Observations
mwas0576	asia south east bantam	1732	VAN DER AA	150	16	16	La Rade de Bantam
mwas0650	asia south east java	1732	VAN DER AA	150	16	16	La Rade de Batavia
mwme0812	persia etc	1729	VAN DER AA	200	19	16	La Rade de Gammeron
mwit1116a	italy tuscany	1714	VAN DER AA	375	15	19	La Republique de Lucques
mwit0677	italy piedmont	1728	VAN DER AA	120	28	36	La Savoye
mwsc0711a	scandinavia sweden	1714	VAN DER AA	350	25	34	La Suede, Suivant les Nouvelles Observations
mwaa0114	arctic	1710	VAN DER AA	350	23	39	La Terre du Nord (copy of Jansson 1628)
mwas0731	asia south east moluccas	1732	VAN DER AA	180	27	35	La Ville de Amboine (view)
mwas0577	asia south east bantam	1732	VAN DER AA	300	27	35	La Ville de Bantam (view)
mwme0815	persia etc	1732	VAN DER AA	300	28	35	La Ville de Gamron en Perse (view)
mwru0388	russia moscow	1720	VAN DER AA	650	28	50	La Ville de Moscou, Capitale de la Moscovie
mwsc0704	scandinavia sweden	1705	VAN DER AA	350	23	40	La Ville de Stockholme, Capitale de la Suede
mwuss0407	florida	1729	VAN DER AA	850	27	35	La Ville, le Chateau et le Village de St. Augustin, en Amerique
mwuss1628	virginia	1714	VAN DER AA	2000	13	19	La Virginie (reprint of Hondius-Jansson derivative of John Smith's map)
mwbh0555	belgium holland	1714	VAN DER AA	150	23	29	La Zelande
mwaf0143	africa	1713	VAN DER AA	1500	49	65	L'Afrique selon les Nouvelles Observations (title above map 'Afrika in Praecipuas Ipsius Partes Distributa ad Observationes Academiae Regiae Scientarum')
mwaf0145	africa	1714	VAN DER AA	350	22	30	L'Afrique Suivant les Nouvelles Observations de Messrs. de l'Academie Royale des Sciences, etc.
mwf0238	france alsace	1728	VAN DER AA	120	26	38	L'Alsace
mwf0239	france alsace	1728	VAN DER AA	120	26	38	L'Alsace
mwam0123	america continent	1714	VAN DER AA	550	14	20	L'Amerique (based on Jansson 1628)
mwsam0057	south america	1720	VAN DER AA	320	33	41	L'Amerique Meridionale
mwam0122	america continent	1713	VAN DER AA	2800	50	67	L'Amerique selon les Nouvelles Observations de Messrs. de l'Academie des Science, etc. (title above map: America in Praecipuas)
mwam0379	america north	1720	VAN DER AA	450	22	30	L'Amerique Septentrionale Suivant les Nouvelles Observations
mwam0111	america continent	1705	VAN DER AA	875	42	30	L'Amerique Septentrionale Suivant les Nouvelles Observations / L'Amerique Meridionale (2 maps joined)
mwsp0519a	spain regions	1714	VAN DER AA	400	15	20	L'Andalousie Et Grenade
mwam0363	america north	1707	VAN DER AA	400	15	23	Land en Volk-Ontdekking in't Noorder Gedeelte van America. door P. Marquette en Joliet; daan in't Jaar 1673
mwgm0195	mexico	1706	VAN DER AA	250	15	24	Land Togten door Ferdinando Cortes aan de Golf van Nieuw Spanje
mwuk0981	england	1720	VAN DER AA	265	23	30	L'Angleterre Suivant les Nouvelles Observations
mwgr0160	greece	1713	VAN DER AA	900	45	52	L'Archipel avec toutes ses Iles et les Cotes les environs
mwas0114a	asia continent	1714	VAN DER AA	300	15	21	L'Asie
mwas0111	asia continent	1710	VAN DER AA	1500	49	66	L'Asie Selon les Nouvelle Observations - Asia in Praecipuas Ipsius
mwas0134	asia continent	1729	VAN DER AA	400	23	29	L'Asie Suivant les Nouvelles Observations
mwsam0346	south america brazil	1714	VAN DER AA	450	23	30	Le Bresil
mwaf0914	africa south	1727	VAN DER AA	600	29	35	Le Cap de Bonne Esperance (view)
mwaf0897	africa south	1713	VAN DER AA	480	22	30	Le Cap de Bonne Esperance Suivant les Nouvelles Observations

AMPG REFERENCE	REGION	DATE	MAP MAKER	PRICE (UK£)	VERT. (cm.)	HOR. (cm.)	TITLE OF MAP (Comments by the editor in brackets)
mwf0746a	france nord pas-de-calais	1714	VAN DER AA	250	16	21	Le Comté D'Artois
mwru0157a	russia	1729	VAN DER AA	900	24	59	Le Cours De La Riviere De Wolga. Anciennement appellée Rha. Selon la Relation D' Olearius (north to the left. See Olearius 1659.)
mwsc0340	scandinavia denmark	1714	VAN DER AA	200	23	30	Le Danemarc
mwas0684	asia south east malacca	1729	VAN DER AA	250	27	16	Le Detroit de Malacca, Dressee sur les Memoires des plus Savans Voyageurs Moderns
mwbh0556	belgium holland	1714	VAN DER AA	150	22	29	Le Duche de Limbourg
mwbh0854a	luxembourg	1713	VAN DER AA	300	27	40	Le Duche de Luxembourg (size incl. printed frame. Also issued without the frame)
mwit1119	italy tuscany	1720	VAN DER AA	250	23	30	Le Grand Duche de Toscane
mwit1117	italy tuscany	1714	VAN DER AA	250	22	29	Le Grand Duche de Toscane Suivant les Nouvelles Observations
mwbh0556a	belgium holland	1714	VAN DER AA	400	15	19	Le Marquisat Du St. Empire (Antwerp)
mwjk0065	japan	1715	VAN DER AA	550	16	16	Le Pais d'Eso avec les Baies, Bancs de Sables &c.
mwsp0080	portugal	1720	VAN DER AA	250	23	23	Le Portugal Suivant les Nouvelles Observations
mwsp0519b	spain regions	1714	VAN DER AA	250	16	20	Le Royaume d'Arragon (illustration above left)
mwsc0336	scandinavia denmark	1713	VAN DER AA	235	31	39	Le Royaume de Danemark, avec une Partie de la Suede
mwit1059	italy naples	1714	VAN DER AA	150	22	29	Le Royaume de Naples
mwuk0458	scotland	1714	VAN DER AA	280	22	30	L'Ecosse
mwam0362	america north	1706	VAN DER AA	450	15	22	Les Cotes de la Virginie les Detroits de Forbisher et de Hudson
mwas0572	asia south east banda	1727	VAN DER AA	250	28	35	Les Iles de Banda Suivant les Meilleures Cartes Levees sur les Lieux
mwas0457	asia south east	1732	VAN DER AA	800	28	33	Les Indes Orientales
mwuk0793	uk	1714	VAN DER AA	300	23	30	Les Isles Britanniques Suivant les Nouvelles Observations (also issued without printed border. Size excl. border)
mwsam0347	south america brazil	1714	VAN DER AA	350	14	19	Les Provinces de Rio de la Plata
mwbh0557	belgium holland	1714	VAN DER AA	150	22	28	Les Provinces Unies des Pays Bas
mwaf0793	africa north morocco	1721	VAN DER AA	300	26	34	Les Royaumes de Fez et de Maroc
mwbp0365	poland	1714	VAN DER AA	600	29	36	Les Trois Iles, Appellees en Allemand Werders, ou sont les Territoires de Dantzic, Marienbourg et Elbing dans la Prusse Royale
mwsp0255	spain	1728	VAN DER AA	320	28	36	L'Espagne
mwsp0258	spain	1730	VAN DER AA	500	52	38	L'Espagne - Le Portugal Suivant les Nouvelles Observations
mwit0308	italy central	1713	VAN DER AA	200	22	30	L'Etat de l'Eglise
mwit1194a	italy veneto	1714	VAN DER AA	350	16	21	L'Etat de Venise
mwbh0605	belgium holland	1728	VAN DER AA	95	26	38	L'Eveche de Liege
mwas0587	asia south east borneo	1720	VAN DER AA	200	19	17	L'Ile de Borneo
mwgr0426	greece crete	1729	VAN DER AA	450	25	34	L'Ile de Candie, anciennement Crete
mwc0300a	china formosa	1720	VAN DER AA	1500	29	35	L'Ile de Formosa
mwas0644	asia south east java	1720	VAN DER AA	235	27	17	L'Ile de Java (north to the right)
mwm0233	mediterranean malta	1729	VAN DER AA	650	28	37	L'Ile de Malte, Anciennement Melita
mwit0927	italy sicily	1720	VAN DER AA	350	24	31	L'Ile de Sicile
mwgr0614	greece islands	1700	VAN DER AA	240	23	40	L'Ile Dromi, ou Dromo, dans la Partie Septentrionale de l'Archipel / L'Ile Amorgo, dans la Partie Meridionale de l'Archipel (2 maps on one sheet)
mwaf0629	africa islands mauritius	1732	VAN DER AA	250	19	16	L'Ile Maurice Suivant les nouvelles Observations
mwuk0153	ireland	1729	VAN DER AA	120	13	13	Limmericum. Limrich
mwin0166	india	1713	VAN DER AA	400	23	29	L'Inde de ca le Gange Suivant les Nouvelles Observations (illustration shows 1729 edition with printed frame)
mwas0451a	asia south east	1720	VAN DER AA	400	22	30	L'Inde de la de Gange
mwuk0154	ireland	1729	VAN DER AA	375	25	38	L'Irlande Suivant les Nouvelles Observations (size incl. ornate frame border. 1st edition 1713 without ornate border.)
mwsp0069	portugal	1705	VAN DER AA	250	33	41	Lisbonne Capitale du Royaume de Portugal
mwas0881	asia south east sumatra	1732	VAN DER AA	150	27	16	L'Isle de Sumatra
mwit0148	italy	1714	VAN DER AA	220	22	29	L'Italie Suivant les Nouvelles Observations
mwuk1163	england london	1729	VAN DER AA	2000	50	59	Londini Angliae Regni Metropolis Delineatio Accuratissima
mwbh0558	belgium holland	1714	VAN DER AA	150	22	29	L'Over-Issel
mwbh0559	belgium holland	1714	VAN DER AA	150	22	29	L'Utrecht
mwsc0463	scandinavia greenland	1707	VAN DER AA	350	15	22	M. Frobichers Scheeps Togt, Gedaan om de Noort, ter Ontdekking van een Straat na Cataya en China
mwm0140	mediterranean east	1707	VAN DER AA	200	15	23	M. Herberers Ongelukkige Voyagie
mwas0611	asia south east celebes	1732	VAN DER AA	350	27	35	Macassar (view of the town)
mww0340	world	1720	VAN DER AA	1500	22	29	Mappe-Monde, Suivant les Nouvelles Observations
mwit0933	italy sicily	1725	VAN DER AA	750	42	52	Messana Urbs Sicilia
mwgm0197	mexico	1713	VAN DER AA	450	23	30	Mexique ou Nouvelle Espagne Suivant les Nouvelles Observations de Messrs. de l'Academie Royale des Sciences
mwme0723a	caucasus	1713	VAN DER AA	300	29	35	Mingrelie, autrefois Colchis... Mer Noire
mwsp0526	spain regions	1729	VAN DER AA	200	33	41	Mont-Serrat / Plan de Rosel / Habits & Croix des Chevaliers Espagnols / Procession des Disciplinans
mwru0390	russia moscow	1729	VAN DER AA	500	29	36	Moscou, Capitale de la Moscovie Suivant Olearius
mwru0444a	russia tartary	1706	VAN DER AA	235	15	22	Naaukeurige Kaart van Tartaryen
mwit1058	italy naples	1705	VAN DER AA	250	22	33	Naples

AMPG REFERENCE	REGION	DATE	MAP MAKER	PRICE (UK£)	VERT. (cm.)	HOR. (cm.)	TITLE OF MAP (Comments by the editor in brackets)
mwit1062	italy naples	1720	VAN DER AA	350	39	49	Neapolis
mwgm0374	nicaragua	1707	VAN DER AA	250	15	22	Nicaragua en de Kusten der Zuyd-Zee Noordwaard von Panama
mwam0910	america north (east)	1707	VAN DER AA	800	15	23	Nieuw Engeland in Twee Scheeptogten door Kapitein Johan Smith inde Iaren 1614 er 1615 Bestevend
mwaf1184	africa west	1728	VAN DER AA	400	27	37	Nigritie ou le Pays des Negres, en Afrique
mwsp0527	spain regions	1729	VAN DER AA	235	22	33	Nouvelle Carte d'Aragon et Navarre
mwas0310	asia caspian sea	1720	VAN DER AA	200	29	34	Nouvelle Carte de la Province de Kilan en Perse
mwam0131	america continent	1720	VAN DER AA	1800	43	54	Nouvelle Carte de l'Amerique
mwas0112	asia continent	1710	VAN DER AA	500	29	34	Nouvelle Carte de l'Asie
mwit0147	italy	1713	VAN DER AA	850	50	66	Nouvelle Carte de l'Italie ou sont Exactement Marquez les Postes et les Chemins , par Jaques Cantelli da Vignola
mwsp0528	spain regions	1729	VAN DER AA	235	21	33	Nouvelle Carte du Castille Vieille
mwam0914	america north (east)	1714	VAN DER AA	1500	29	37	Nouvelle Hollande, (a Present Nouvelle-York) Nouvelle-Angleterre, et une Partie de la Virginie
mww0341	world	1720	VAN DER AA	2500	26	34	Nouvelle Mappe-Monde Recemment Mise en Lumiere
mww0312	world	1710	VAN DER AA	1500	26	34	Nova Delineatio Totius Orbis Terrarum per Petrum Van der Aa (reduced version of Colom 1655, first publ. by J. Gottfried in 1660)
mwit1238	italy venice	1715	VAN DER AA	2250	42	52	Nova et Accuratissima Venetiarum Urbis Tabula Topographica
mww0322	world	1713	VAN DER AA	6000	50	63	Nova Orbis Terraquei Tabula Accuratissime Delineata - Mappe-Monde ou Description Generale de Globe Terrestre et Aquatique
mwsp0251	spain	1720	VAN DER AA	750	48	61	Novissima et Accuratissima Tabula Regnorum Hispaniae et Portugalliae
mwg0628a	saxony	1716	VAN DER AA	500	35	47	Oldenbourg, Capitale du même nom
mwin0153	india	1707	VAN DER AA	450	16	24	Oost-Indize Voyagie door William Hawkins van Suratte gedaan na't Hof van den Grooten Mogol
mwaf0393	africa east	1714	VAN DER AA	200	15	23	Opper-Ethiopien of 't Ryk der Abyssinen door de E. Vaders H. Lobo en M. Almeida Bereyst en met de Nyle en Roode Zee Beschreven
mww0327	world	1715	VAN DER AA	750	17	29	Orbis Terrarum Nova et Accuratissima Tabula
mwsam0344	south america brazil	1706	VAN DER AA	235	15	23	P. Carders Zee en Land Reyse na Brasil, Rio de la Plata en de Zuyd Zee
mwit0923	italy sicily	1713	VAN DER AA	580	32	48	Palermo (copy of Braun & Hogenberg)
mwf0847	france paris	1715	VAN DER AA	580	35	42	Paris, Capitale de France
mwuss1625	virginia	1706	VAN DER AA	850	29	36	Partie Meridionale de la Virginie, et la Partie Orientale de la Floride dans l'Amerique Septentrionale
mwit0742	italy rome	1729	VAN DER AA	350	23	29	Plan de la Ville de Rome
mwas0649	asia south east java	1729	VAN DER AA	350	27	36	Plan de la Ville et du Chateau de Batavia en l'Isle de Iava
mwf0848	france paris	1715	VAN DER AA	480	24	30	Plan de la Ville, Cite Universite et Fauxbourgs de Paris
mww0323	world	1713	VAN DER AA	6000	53	65	Planisphere Terrestre, Suivant les Nouvelles Observations des Astronomes. Dressee Presente au Roy Tres Chretien par Mr. Cassini le Fils, de l'Academie Royale des Sciences.
mwsam0268	south america bolivia	1708	VAN DER AA	235	29	36	Potosi
mwwi0052	west indies	1706	VAN DER AA	400	16	23	Reys Togt door Gil Gonzales van't Eyland St. Dominica Gedaan na de Honduras en Nicaragua
mwme0801	persia etc	1707	VAN DER AA	235	15	23	Reys Togt van A. Sherley te Land Gedaan van Aleppo over Babylonien
mwme0591	arabia etc	1707	VAN DER AA	260	22	29	Reystogt door Thomas Coryat, van Jerusalem ... Grooten Mogols
mwme0586	arabia etc	1706	VAN DER AA	280	15	22	Reys-Togt van Aleppo, over Ormus, door Indien tot in Pegu en Siam Gedaan
mwm0271	mediterranean west	1707	VAN DER AA	200	15	22	Reys-Weg uit Brabant ... tot aan Fez en Marocco.
mwin0184	india	1729	VAN DER AA	250	22	29	Robert Covertes Swerf-Reysen na Gelede Schipbreuk, van Cambaya te land door Opper Indien, Persien en Arabie
mwit0731	italy rome	1705	VAN DER AA	550	33	41	Rome, Capitale de l'Etat de l'Eglise
mwme0816	persia etc	1732	VAN DER AA	350	28	35	Royaume de Perse
mwit0923a	italy sicily	1714	VAN DER AA	450	15	20	Royaume de Sicile
mwin0188	india	1732	VAN DER AA	450	29	35	Royaume du Grand Mogol
mwaf1183	africa west	1727	VAN DER AA	360	28	36	Royaumes de Congo et Angola
mwit0836b	italy sardinia and corsica	1725	VAN DER AA	400	28	35	Sardiniae Antiquae Descriptio / Corsicae
mwsc0113	scandinavia	1713	VAN DER AA	350	51	38	Scandinavie Septentrionale ou Couronnes du Nord - Scandinavie Meridionale ou Couronnes du Nord (the 'frame' is a printed border of the maps)
mwsc0114	scandinavia	1713	VAN DER AA	550	52	38	Scandinavie Septentrionale ou Couronnes du Nord (and) Scandinavie Meridionale ou Couronnes du Nord
mwwi0054	west indies	1707	VAN DER AA	245	15	23	Scheeps Togt van Iamaica Gedaan na Panuco en Rio de las Palmas aan de Golf van Mexico Gelegen
mwme0587	arabia etc	1707	VAN DER AA	300	15	22	Scheeps-Togt door Don Henrique de Menezes van Couchin na Panama
mwp0242	pacific (all)	1707	VAN DER AA	550	15	22	Scheeps-Togt door Ferdinand Magellaan uit Kastilien Gedaan na R. de la Plata en van daar door zyn Ontdekte Straat tot aan de Moluccas

AMPG REFERENCE	REGION	DATE	MAP MAKER	PRICE (UK£)	VERT. (cm.)	HOR. (cm.)	TITLE OF MAP (Comments by the editor in brackets)
mwwi0238a	west indies (east)	1707	VAN DER AA	300	15	23	Scheeps-Togt door Rodrigue de Bastides en P. Alvares Polomina uyt de Haven van St. Domingo op Hispaniola, Gedaan na St. Martha
mwaf0127a	africa	1706	VAN DER AA	235	15	23	Scheepstogt nad' Africaanze Kusten van Congo en Angola tot Agter om Beoosten Caap de Bonne Esperance
mwas0682	asia south east malacca	1714	VAN DER AA	400	22	33	Scheeps-Togt van Malacca na de Golf van Bengale, en de Kusten van Siam tot in China
mwas0439	asia south east	1710	VAN DER AA	400	22	28	Scheeptogt onder den Ammiraal Wybrand van Warwyk, van Bantam na China Gedaan
mwit1237	italy venice	1714	VAN DER AA	150	22	29	Seigneurie de Venise
mwsp0503	spain regions	1705	VAN DER AA	400	34	41	Seville, Capitale de l'Andalousie
mwsw0123	switzerland	1725	VAN DER AA	300	36	47	Solothurn
mwgr0615	greece islands	1700	VAN DER AA	240	33	41	Stampalia / Zanara e Levit / Stalimine / Pelagnis
mwuss0403	florida	1706	VAN DER AA	450	15	23	t Amerikaans Gewest van Florida door Ferdinand de Soto Nader Ontdekt en Groot Deels Bemagtigd
mwin0400	india goa	1702	VAN DER AA	150	12	17	t Eyland Goa
mwas0638	asia south east java	1707	VAN DER AA	250	15	23	t Koninkryk Sunda met dat van Iava, by d'Inwoonderen voor een Eiland Gehouden en door den Hr. I.B. de Lavanha
mwc0101	china	1720	VAN DER AA	750	22	34	t Koninkryk van China met d'Aangrenzende Landen van Siam en Bengale
mwsam0830	south america venezuela	1714	VAN DER AA	350	22	33	t Landschap Cumana tussen Golfo de Venezuela en Rio de Paria Gelegen
mwgm0104	guatemala	1728	VAN DER AA	235	15	23	t Landschap Guatimala door Pedro d'Alvarado in een Land-Togt uyt Mexico Bevolkt, 1523
mwam0345	america north	1700	VAN DER AA	800	20	30	t Noorder Deel van Amerika door C. Kolumbus in zyn Eerste Togt Ontdekt en Desselfs Kusten en Voor-Eylanden een en Andermaal Bevaaren
mwuss1624	virginia	1706	VAN DER AA	400	15	23	t Noorder Gedeelte van Virginie door Bartholomeus Gosnol en Martin Pringe uyt Engeland Bevaaren
mwin0151	india	1706	VAN DER AA	250	15	24	t Ryk van den Grooten Mogol met de Grenzen van Cambaya en't Koninkryk Deli
mwsam0509	south america colombia	1706	VAN DER AA	250	16	23	t Vaste Land van Darien ten Zuyden Cuba en Hispaniola Gelegen
mwsam0046	south america	1706	VAN DER AA	400	20	30	t Zuider America van Terra Firma ou Gujana voor by Rio de la Plata, tot an de Straat Magellen en Kusten tegen de Zuid Zee
mwm0037	mediterranean	1710	VAN DER AA	750	38	83	Tabula Geographica quae Continet Totam Fere Europam et Proxima Africae -Tabula Altera quae Continet Potissima Asiae et Reliqua Europae ac Africae
mwsam0175a	south america north	1700	VAN DER AA	240	15	23	Terra Firma oft Vaste Land van Darien, Veragua, Cartagena en Nieuw Andalusie etc.
mwme0290	holy land	1729	VAN DER AA	280	23	29	Terre Sainte Suivant les Nouvelles Observations
mwsw0111a	switzerland	1720	VAN DER AA	750	39	51	Tigurum. Zurych (first publ. by De Wit)
mwit1120	italy tuscany	1728	VAN DER AA	250	28	36	Toscane Grand Duche
mwme0995	turkey etc	1727	VAN DER AA	250	23	29	Turquie en Asie
mwm0224	mediterranean malta	1720	VAN DER AA	650	17	37	Typus Insularum Melitae, Comini et Gauli
mwru0503	ukraine	1714	VAN DER AA	400	29	36	Ukraine, Grand Pays de la Russie Rouge
mwm0225	mediterranean malta	1720	VAN DER AA	1600	42	51	Valetta Civitas Nova Maltae olim Millitae
mwit1193	italy veneto	1705	VAN DER AA	265	23	39	Verone, Ville de l'Etat de Venise
mwsp0529	spain regions	1729	VAN DER AA	235	23	28	Vigo
mwuss1630	virginia	1729	VAN DER AA	1000	29	36	Virginie, Grande Region de l'Amerique Septentrionale, avec Tous ses Bourgs, Hameaux, Rivieres et Bayes, Suivant les Recherches Exactes de ceux qui l'ont Decouverte
mwit1118	italy tuscany	1720	VAN DER AA	235	22	29	Vue de la Ville de Pise, et le Combat pour Gagner le Pont
mwg0492	mecklenburg	1720	VAN DER AA	120	26	50	Wiismaria
mwjk0057	japan	1706	VAN DER AA	900	15	23	William Adams Reystogt na Oost-Indien; Avontuurlyk door de Straat Magellaan, in't Keyzerryk van Japan Voleyndigd
mwgm0105	guatemala	1729	VAN DER AA	360	28	36	Yucatan (Partie de la Nouvelle Espagne) et Guatimala
mwsam0194	south america (north west)	1714	VAN DER AA	300	15	21	Zee en Land Togt door Fr. Pizarrus en D. Almagrus Van Panama Gedaan na Peru.
mwuss0169	carolinas	1714	VAN DER AA	650	15	23	Zee en Land Togten der Franszen Gedann na, en in't Americaans Gewest van Florida, Aller-Eerst door Ioh. Pontius Ontdekt
mwuss0168	carolinas	1729	VAN DER AA	800	22	30	Zee en Land Togten der Franszen Gedann na, en in't Americaans Gewest van Florida, Aller-Eerst door Ioh. Pontius Ontdekt (with picture frame border)
mwru0124	russia	1707	VAN DER AA	200	14	22	Zee en Landtogt door A. Jenkinson van Astracan Gedaan na Tartarien en te Rug tot in Moscow
mwas0436	asia south east	1707	VAN DER AA	235	15	23	Zee Togt van Alfonso d'Albuquerque (shows his route through SE Asia)
mwme0236	holy land	1706	VAN DER AA	300	15	24	Zee-Togt van den Grooten Turk uyt het Roode Meyr tegen de Portugysen na Indien tot aan Kaap Comorin Ondernomen
mwit0728	italy rome	1695	VAN DER AA /HALMA	950	49	63	Novissima et Accuratissima Romae Veteris et Novae Tabula Topographica
mwas0836a	asia south east siam	1765	VAN DER SCHLEY	300	19	28	(Ayutthaya) Judia, Capitale de Siam - Hoofd-Stad van Siam

AMPG REFERENCE	REGION	DATE	MAP MAKER	PRICE (UK£)	VERT. (cm.)	HOR. (cm.)	TITLE OF MAP (Comments by the editor in brackets)
mwg0460	hessen	1759	VAN DER SCHLEY	120	27	24	Bataille de Bergen, pres Francfort ... le 13 Avril 1759
mwat0310	atlantic south	1760	VAN DER SCHLEY	240	34	45	Carte de L'Ocean Meridional ... par M. Bellin - Kaart van de Zuid-Zee ... door den Hr. Bellin
mwg0662	saxony	1760	VAN DER SCHLEY	320	24	54	Carte d'une Partie du Cours du Weser Contenant les Camps de Corvey, Luttringen, Holtzminden et Bevern ... Juillet 1757
mwas0732	asia south east moluccas	1750	VAN DER SCHLEY	140	20	29	Carte Particuliere de l'Isle Amboine
mwgm0411	panama	1753	VAN DER SCHLEY	240	21	36	Grond-Tekening van den Uitersten Oost Hoek van t'Eiland Quibo
mwsam0621	south america guyana	1764	VAN DER SCHLEY	240	22	28	La Ville de Cayenne
mwaf1219	africa west	1760	VAN DER SCHLEY	180	20	36	Plan de l'Isle de Goree, sur les Desseins du Sr. Compagnon / Plan de l'Isle de Gore avec ses Fortifications (2 sheets)
mwsam0384	south america brazil	1771	VAN DER SCHLEY	100	18	24	Suite du Bresil, depuis la Baie de Tous les Saints jusqu'a a St. Paul
mwc0167	china	1760	VAN DER SCHLEY	240	17	26	Vue de Peking tiree de Nieuhof
mwbh0030	belgium holland	1567	VAN DEVENTER-CAMOCIO	5000	49	39	Gelriae, Cliviae, nee non aliarum regionum
mwbh0008	belgium holland	1558	VAN DEVENTER-TRAMEZINI	7200	52	40	Brabantia Belgarum Provinciae Recens Exactique Descriptio
mwbh0009	belgium holland	1558	VAN DEVENTER-TRAMEZINI	8000	38	49	Descriptio Totius Galliae Belgicae. Pyrrho Ligorio Neapolit. Auctore. Romae MDLVIII. Michaelis Tramezine Formis ... Sebastianus de Regibus Clodiensis Incidebat
mwbh0010	belgium holland	1558	VAN DEVENTER-TRAMEZINI	3600	38	52	Flandriae Recent Exactq. Descriptio
mwbh0011	belgium holland	1558	VAN DEVENTER-TRAMEZINI	3600	49	39	Frisiae Antiquissimae trans Rhenum Provinc. et Adiacentium Regionem Nova et Exacta Descriptio
mwbh0012	belgium holland	1558	VAN DEVENTER-TRAMEZINI	3600	49	39	Gelriae Cliviae Iuliae nec non Aliarum Regionum Adiacentium Nova Descriptio
mwbh0013	belgium holland	1558	VAN DEVENTER-TRAMEZINI	9000	52	38	Hollandiae Batavor Veteris Insulae et Locorum Adiacentium Exacta Descriptio Michaelis Tramezine Formis ... MDLVIII (closely copied in 1563 by Forlani)
mwbh0031	belgium holland	1567	VAN DEVENTER-ZALTIERI	5000	51	40	Brabantia Belgarum Provinciae Recens Exactique Descriptio (copy of Camocio 1566)
mwbh0032	belgium holland	1567	VAN DEVENTER-ZALTIERI	7200	52	38	Hollandia - Hollandiae Batavoru. Veteris Insulae et Locorum Adiacentum Exacta Descriptio (close copy of Tremazini 1558)
mwru0021	russia	1598	VAN DOETECUM	800	18	25	Caerte van Nova Zembla, de Weygats, de Custe van Tartarien en Ruslandt
mwsam0166a	south america central	1602	VAN DOETECUM	600	16	23	Deliniatio Orarum Peru; cujus Metropolis Lima
mwe0028	europe	1605	VAN DOETECUM	6000	40	57	Europam ab Asia et Africa Segregant Mare Mediterraneum (re-issue of Plancius 1594)
mwf0039a	france	1605	VAN DOETECUM	960	24	34	Galliae Nova et Exacta Descriptio (publ. by P. Merula; shown below left)
mwsp0188a	spain	1666	VAN DOETECUM		81	102	Hispaniae Nova Descriptio Ceteus Castigatior
mwit0051	italy	1600	VAN DOETECUM	1500	23	32	Italae nova et exacta descriptio
mwbh0161a	belgium holland	1600	VAN DOETECUM	2500	41	56	Nova Descriptio Orientalis et Occidentalis Frisiae
mwbh0168	belgium holland	1606	VAN DOETECUM	1400	25	35	Tabella, Isellae Fluvij Cursum / Contrefaicture du Fleuve Isel, del la Diocese Trans Isulane, & Conte de Zutphen (battle plan)
mwsw0044	switzerland	1618	VAN GEELKERKEN	2000	40	53	Alpinae seu Foederatae Rhaetiae Subditarumque ei Terrarum Nova Descriptio
mwg0773a	westphalia	1610	VAN GEELKERKEN	3000	33	53	Ducatus Iuliace(n)sis Clivensis et Bergensis cum Comitatu Marckensi et Rauenspergensi
mww0126	world	1618	VAN GEELKERKEN	18000	42	56	Orbis Terrarum Descriptio Duobis Planis Hemisphaeriis Comprehesa (updated version of 1610 edition)
mww0120	world	1610	VAN GEELKERKEN	25000	42	56	Universi Orbis Tabula De-integro Delineata
mwwi0880	st lucia	1777	VAN HARREVELDT	360	20	30	Carte de l'Isle de Sainte Lucie
mwas0913	asia south east vietnam	1749	VAN HARREVELDT	250	21	14	Carte des Costes de Cochinchine, Tunquin, et Partie de celles de la Chine
mwat0243	atlantic madeira	1773	VAN HARREVELDT	250	22	29	Carte des Isles de Madere et Porto Santo
mwin0465	indian ocean maldives	1750	VAN HARREVELDT	150	22	15	Carte des Isles Maldives pour Servir a l'Histoire des Etablissemens Europeens
mww0407	world	1750	VAN JAGEN	1500	31	46	(Untitled map)
mwme0331	holy land	1750	VAN JAGEN	480	50	39	Afbeelding van Egypte, de Woestyne der Schelf-Zee, en 't Land Kanaan
mwme0323	holy land	1748	VAN JAGEN	480	30	44	De Gelegentheyd van 't Paradys en 't Landt Canaan, Mitsgaders d'Eerst Bewoonde Landen der Patriarchen
mwm0151	mediterranean east	1748	VAN JAGEN	300	30	44	Geographische Beschryvinghe van de Wandeling der Apostelen ende de Reysen Pauli
mwme0324	holy land	1748	VAN JAGEN	480	30	44	Het Beloofde Landt Canaan Doorwandelt van onsen Saligmaker Jesu Christo, neffens syne Apostelen
mwbh0735a	belgium holland	1781	VAN JAGEN	1400	86	112	T Hoog-Heemraetschap vande Uytwaterende Sluysen in Kennemerlant ende West-Frieslant (1st publ. 1730 by H. de Leth)
mwru0498	ukraine	1695	VAN KEULEN	4000	53	99	(Black Sea) Nieuwe Paskaart van de Geheele Swarte Zee van Constantinopolen tot Azak
mwg0623	saxony	1700	VAN KEULEN	1250	52	59	(East Friesland)

AMPG REFERENCE	REGION	DATE	MAP MAKER	PRICE (UK£)	VERT. (cm.)	HOR. (cm.)	TITLE OF MAP (Comments by the editor in brackets)
mwsp0654	balearic islands	1710	VAN KEULEN	2000	39	58	(Minorca) Nieuwe Afteekening van de Rivier of Port Mahon
mwsc0086	scandinavia	1690	VAN KEULEN	375	51	30	(Scandinavian harbours)
mwit0928a	italy sicily	1720	VAN KEULEN	800	52	30	(Sicily - 9 views of ports, shown above left)
mwas0883	asia south east sumatra	1753	VAN KEULEN	400	50	56	(Southwest Coast of Sumatra)
mwas0903	asia south east sunda	1753	VAN KEULEN	1650	50	58	De Straat Sunda (title in centre)
mwaf1052	africa south east	1753	VAN KEULEN	1250	50	57	(Untitled map. North to the right.)
mwam0889	america north (east)	1688	VAN KEULEN	4500	52	59	A Chart of the Sea Coasts of New Neder Land, Virginia, New-England, and Penn-Silvania, with the City of Philadelphia, from Boston to Cabo Karrik
mwaf0748	africa north algeria	1734	VAN KEULEN	1200	32	61	Aftbeelding van Algiers (view)
mwme0626	arabia etc	1753	VAN KEULEN	1650	54	57	Afteekening van de Persische Golf
mwsam0597	south america guyana	1734	VAN KEULEN	1350	59	99	Afteekening van de Rivier Barbice en Courantin
mwuk1433	england thames	1734	VAN KEULEN	600	50	58	Afteekening van de Rivier van London of River Thames / Afteekening van de Iarmouthse Banken Geleegen voor Iarmouth ann de Ooost Kust van Engeland in de Noord Zee
mwas0283	asia burma	1753	VAN KEULEN	3500	51	59	Afteekening van een gedeelte van de kust van Arracam, Pegu en Siam ... (north to the left)
mwuk1610a	isle of man	1780	VAN KEULEN	1000	51	59	Afteekening van het Eyland Man in St. Georges Channell tussen Irland en Engeland
mwas0736	asia south east moluccas	1755	VAN KEULEN	400	46	28	Caart van het Eyland Manipa / Caart van het Eyland Honimoa (2 maps on one sheet)
mwas0737	asia south east moluccas	1755	VAN KEULEN	400	44	28	Caart van het Eyland Noessa-Laoet / Caart van het Eyland Oma (2 maps on one sheet)
mwme0625	arabia etc	1753	VAN KEULEN	1650	49	57	Caarte van het inkomen van de Roode Zee
mwam0924	america north (east)	1720	VAN KEULEN	13500	57	97	Carte de la Nouvelle France ou se Voit le Cours des Grandes Rivieres de S. Laurens & de Mississipi Aujour d'hui S. Louis, aux Environs des quelles se Trouvent les Etats Pais Nations Peuples &c. de la Floride, de la Louisiane, de la Virginie
mwca0300a	canada newfoundland	1728	VAN KEULEN	1200	52	58	Carte Nouvelle Contenant la Partie d'Amerique le plus Septentrionale (see also 1684)
mwsp0691b	gibraltar	1681	VAN KEULEN	1200	52	62	De Baayen Stadt van Gibralter (north to the left)
mwc0308	china formosa	1753	VAN KEULEN	1500	28	48	De Eylanden van Pehou
mwf0617	france languedoc	1720	VAN KEULEN	500	46	58	De Haven van Cette in de Middelandse Zee (shows port of Sete)
mwuk0156	ireland	1734	VAN KEULEN	900	51	59	De Haven van Corke Geleegen aan de Zuyd Kust van Ireland
mwsc0614	scandinavia norway	1730	VAN KEULEN	2400	52	59	De Kust van Noorwegen of 't Land van Noord Oosten: van de Langesond tot Gottenborg Vertoonende Frederiks Stad Frederiks Hall en de Swynsond int Groot
mwsc0615	scandinavia norway	1730	VAN KEULEN	1200	51	57	De Kust van Noorwegen, Beginnende van Bommelsondt tot aan de Uutweer Klippen
mwas0738	asia south east moluccas	1755	VAN KEULEN	1200	46	58	De Landvoogdy der Moluccos, met de Aangrenzende Eylanden
mwaf0934	africa south	1753	VAN KEULEN	900	55	28	De Mossel Baay / Pas-caart van de Baay de Lagoa (2 maps on one sheet)
mwsc0716	scandinavia sweden	1728	VAN KEULEN	960	52	91	De Oost Zee of Oster Sioon Vertoonende de Kust van Blekingen van Christianopel tot Sandhammer
mwas0658	asia south east java	1753	VAN KEULEN	2000	50	58	De Reede en Stadt Batavia
mwuk1549b	bristol channel	1734	VAN KEULEN	650	51	60	De Rivier van Kingsale (Ireland) / Afteenkening van de Rivier Avon of Bristoll, is geleegen Agter in T`Verkeerde Canaal Aan de West Kust van Engeland of Cornwal
mwaf0755	africa north algeria	1780	VAN KEULEN	800	51	58	De Stad Haven en Mouillie van Algiers neven desselfs Kasteelen (view of Algiers)
mwas0739	asia south east moluccas	1755	VAN KEULEN	400	46	28	De Talautse Eylanden
mwaa0097	arctic	1681	VAN KEULEN	1200	51	60	De Zee Custen van Noorwegen, Finmarcken, Laplant, Ruslant, Nova Zemla, Spitsbergen en Yslant
mwbp0029	baltic sea (east)	1686	VAN KEULEN	1350	42	52	De Zee kusten van Liiflandt ende Oost Finlandt, van Wolfs-oort tot Wyborgh.
mwm0039	mediterranean	1720	VAN KEULEN	500	51	58	Haaven-Kaart van Eenige Voornaamste Haavens Leggende in de Middel-Landsche Zee en Archipelago (29 small harbours)
mwwi0292	antigua	1680	VAN KEULEN	2800	42	57	Het Eyland Antigua Antego of Santa Maria el Antigua Geleegen in Westindia onder de Caribis Eylanden
mwaf0631	africa islands mauritius	1753	VAN KEULEN	900	51	28	Het Eyland Diego Rais / Mauritius
mwuk0468	scotland	1728	VAN KEULEN	1200	51	58	Het Eyland Hitland Met Zyn Onderhoorige Eylandem (north to the right)
mwas0735	asia south east moluccas	1752	VAN KEULEN	500	29	57	Het Eyland Neira en het Casteel Nassau Mitsgaders Belgica
mwas0740	asia south east moluccas	1755	VAN KEULEN	400	46	29	Het Eyland Sangir
mwwi0767a	martinique	1720	VAN KEULEN	2000	52	60	Het Eylandt Martanico of Isle de la Martenique
mwc0149	china	1753	VAN KEULEN	1800	49	29	Het Inkomen van de Haven van Aimoey van Rio Chinchew af tot de Erasmus Baay onder Quemoey
mwsc0717	scandinavia sweden	1728	VAN KEULEN	3500	51	93	Het Inkoomen en Reeden van Gotten Borg
mwin0219	india	1753	VAN KEULEN	1250	50	58	Het Opkomen en Vervolg van de Riever de Ganges (Calcutta)
mwp0013	australia	1753	VAN KEULEN		59	100	Het Westelykste Gedeelte van 't Land vande Eendragt of Nova Hollandia (North to the left. Inset: Het Eyland genaamt Rottenest)

AMPG REFERENCE	REGION	DATE	MAP MAKER	PRICE (UK£)	VERT. (cm.)	HOR. (cm.)	TITLE OF MAP (Comments by the editor in brackets)
mwaf0933	africa south	1753	VAN KEULEN	900	50	27	In de Baay Falso/ Robben Eyland (2 maps on one sheet)
mwas0648	asia south east java	1728	VAN KEULEN	5000	52	116	Insulae Iavae Pars Occidentalis Edente Hadriano Relando / Insulae Iavae Pars Orientalis Edente Hadriano Relando (eastern sheet illustrated)
mwas0659	asia south east java	1753	VAN KEULEN	3000	51	120	Insulae Javae Pars Occidentalis / Pars Orientalis
mwas0573	asia south east banda	1753	VAN KEULEN	875	34	47	Kaart der Zuyd-Wester Eylanden van Banda
mwsp0465	spain regions	1682	VAN KEULEN	1200	50	56	Kaart van de Baay van Cadix met de Plans der Fortifcatien
mwaf0935	africa south	1753	VAN KEULEN	3000	49	57	Kaart van de Tafel Baay vertoonende De Reede van C. de Goede Hoop
mwwi0504a	curacao	1838	VAN KEULEN	1000	40	47	Kaart van het Eiland Curacao
mwas0833a	asia south east siam	1753?	VAN KEULEN	350	23	27	Kaarte van het Eiland Junkseilon (north to the right. First map of Phuket, Thailand)
mwg0194	germany north	1793	VAN KEULEN	960	60	69	Kaart van het inkommen, van de Weser, Jade - en Elve-Stroomen ...
mwca0299a	canada newfoundland	1720	VAN KEULEN	800	51	59	New Foundland of Nieuw Vrankryk, of anders genaamt Terra Neuf
mwe0924	europe hungary	1716	VAN KEULEN	500	51	59	Nieuwe Accurate Kaert van een Gedeelte van Hongarie en Donau Stroom Vertonende Belgrado en Peter Wardein, alwaer de Batalje ... 1716
mwbh0701	belgium holland	1750	VAN KEULEN	1200	51	59	Nieuwe Afteekening van Alle de Banken, Canaalen, Tonnen en Dieptens, Geleegen voor de Stad Enkhuyzen in de Zuyder Zee
mwin0220	india	1753	VAN KEULEN	1250	44	52	Nieuwe Afteekening van Bombay, en Omliggende Eylanden Gelegen aan de Kust van Decam, op de Noorder Breedte van 19 gr. O.
mwuk0157	ireland	1734	VAN KEULEN	500	52	29	Nieuwe Afteekening van de Bay van Dublin / Afteekening van der Rivier of Haven van Carlingford (2 maps on one sheet)
mwat0233a	atlantic islands	1709	VAN KEULEN	720	51	58	Nieuwe Afteekening van de Eylanden van Fero
mwm0236	mediterranean malta	1734	VAN KEULEN	3000	51	58	Nieuwe Afteekening van de Eylanden van Gozo en Melite of Malta
mwg0485	mecklenburg	1716	VAN KEULEN	800	51	89	Nieuwe Afteekening van de Haven en Stad Wismar met Desselfs Inkomende Zee Gaaten soo Beoosten als Beweste Poel Eyland en Beleegering van Dito Stad
mwin0222	india	1753	VAN KEULEN	960	50	58	Nieuwe afteekening van de Kust van Coromandel
mwec0181	uk england cornwall	1734	VAN KEULEN	1200	50	59	Nieuwe Afteekening van de River van Fowey
mwsc0355a	scandinavia denmark	1734	VAN KEULEN	1500	51	89	Nieuwe Afteekening van de Sond
mwwi0499	curacao	1720	VAN KEULEN	4800	52	60	Nieuwe Afteekening van het Eijland Curacao Vertoonende Desselfs Gelegentheeden Mitsgaders de Haven van St. Anna en 't Fort Amsterdam
mwit0922a	italy sicily	1710	VAN KEULEN	2500	51	91	Nieuwe Afteekening van het Eyland en Koninkryk Sicilia ...
mwsp0655	balearic islands	1710	VAN KEULEN	2000	48	60	Nieuwe Afteekening van het Eyland Maiorca
mwsp0655a	balearic islands	1710	VAN KEULEN	2000	40	58	Nieuwe Afteekening van het Eyland Minorca
mwbp0036	baltic sea (east)	1710	VAN KEULEN	785	53	61	Nieuwe Afteekening van het Eyland Rugen en de Straal Sond Als mede de Stad Strallsond
mwsc0610	scandinavia norway	1728	VAN KEULEN	2400	52	59	Nieuwe Afteekening van het Eyland Spits-Bergen
mwe1069	europe serbia	1720	VAN KEULEN	1600	49	59	Nieuwe Afteenkening van de Sterke Stad Belgrado
mwas0767	asia south east philippines	1735	VAN KEULEN	1500	50	27	Nieuwe Aftekening van de Baay Manilla in de Oostindische Zee, op de Plaats Zelfs Afgetekent in't Iaar 1735 te Amsterdam / Kaart van de baay van Bongo onder 't Eilandt Mindanao (2 maps on one sheet, shown above)
mwas0479	asia south east	1753	VAN KEULEN	3000	51	58	Nieuwe Caart strekkende van Banca, langs de kusten van Malacca, Siam, Cambodia, CochinChina
mwas0308	asia caspian sea	1712?	VAN KEULEN	1800	52	74	Nieuwe Caart van de Caspische Zee (North to the left. At top, panoramic view of Astrakan)
mwwi0921	virgin isl	1719	VAN KEULEN	4800	52	99	Nieuwe en Aldereerste Afteekening van 't Eyland St. Thomas. Met All desselfs Havenen, Anker Plaatse (this map was also issued with coastal profiles in lower border, size 57x99cm)
mwwi0597a	hispaniola	1730	VAN KEULEN	3000	60	102	Nieuwe en Naaukeurige Paskaart van het Eyland Hispaniola of St. Domingo, met Alle desselfs Havanen, Dieptens en Ankergronden, als Meede de door Passeeringe tusschen de Caiques, en andere Eylanden, naer de Opservatien van Monsr. Frezier
mwwi0319	bahamas	1734	VAN KEULEN	4000	59	100	Nieuwe en Naeukerige Afteekening van't Canaal van Bahama
mwit0835a	italy sardinia and corsica	1720	VAN KEULEN	1350	53	89	Nieuwe en Nette Afteekening van het Eyland Corsica - Sardinia
mwsc0503	scandinavia iceland	1750	VAN KEULEN	3000	52	60	Nieuwe en seer Accurate Paskaart van het Eyland Yslandt
mwgr0322a	greece corfu	1730	VAN KEULEN	5000	51	59	Nieuwe en seer Naauwkeurige Kaart van t Eylant Corfu of Corcyra
mwuk0462	scotland	1720	VAN KEULEN	1500	52	61	Nieuwe en Seer Perfecte Paskaart van Schotlandt ... van Berwyk tot Bokannais / A New and Pertinent Map of the Eastern Sea-Coasts of Scotland
mwuk0246a	ireland	1803	VAN KEULEN	480	53	30	Nieuwe en Zeer Acurate Kaart van de Haven van Cork

AMPG REFERENCE	REGION	DATE	MAP MAKER	PRICE (UK£)	VERT. (cm.)	HOR. (cm.)	TITLE OF MAP (Comments by the editor in brackets)
mwwi0243	west indies (east)	1720	VAN KEULEN	2250	59	102	Nieuwe en Zeer Naaukeurige Paskaart van der Kusten van West Indien Strekkende van Rio Oronoque tot Beneede Cartagena
mwaa0107	arctic	1700	VAN KEULEN	1000	59	100	Nieuwe Gelijk Gradige of Platte Zekaart van het Noorder Deel van Europa Vertoonende de Geheele Groenlandse en Moskovise Scheepvaard Waer in Elk de Miswijsinge van het Compas Selver Moet Verbeeteren
mwf0294	france bay of biscay	1720	VAN KEULEN	1500	59	100	Nieuwe Generale Paskaart van de Bocht van Vrankryk Biscaia en Gallissia tussen I. de Ouessant en C. de Finisterre
mwsp0071	portugal	1710	VAN KEULEN	1000	59	100	Nieuwe Generale Paskaart van de Cust van Portugal tusschen C. de Finisterre en C. St. Vincent
mwsc0606	scandinavia norway	1716	VAN KEULEN	7500	57	89	Nieuwe Groote en Curieuse Paskaart van het Zoen Water, met al zen Droogtens, Dieptens, en Omleggende Landen en Steden in Noorwegen, Geteekend door Ian Heyteman Matematicus in Christiania
mwwi0061	west indies	1720	VAN KEULEN	4000	59	99	Nieuwe Groote en Seer Curieuse Paskaart van Geheel-West Indien
mwin0216	india	1752	VAN KEULEN	650	50	58	Nieuwe Kaart van Choromandel ende Malabar
mwwi0539	guadeloupe	1680	VAN KEULEN	2800	50	57	Nieuwe Land en Zee Kaart van de Eylanden Guadaloupe en Mariegalande &c Gelegen in Westindia onder de Caribisse Eylanden
mwwi0369	barbados	1728	VAN KEULEN	2500	51	60	Nieuwe Land en Zeekaart van het Eyland Barbados
mwc0150	china	1753	VAN KEULEN	8000	51	57	Nieuwe Pas-Caart Strekkende van Pta. Cataon tot Pta. Lamtaon, langs de Kusten van Cochinchina, Tonquin, Quangsi en Quantung (Island of Hainan and surrounding region)
mwuk1665	north sea	1720	VAN KEULEN	4000	58	99	Nieuwe Pascaart van de Geheele Noord-Zee
mwf0656	france loire	1709	VAN KEULEN	960	50	59	Nieuwe Pascaart van de Zeekusten van Bretangne, en Poictou / Carte Marine des Costes de Bretangne et Poictou
mwf0336	france brittany	1695	VAN KEULEN	785	51	58	Nieuwe Pascaart van een Gedeelte van Bretagne Beginnende van 't Eylandt Groa tot aande Penmarck
mwat0216a	atlantic east	1720	VAN KEULEN	1000	52	59	Nieuwe Pascaart van het Canaal tot de custen van Barbarien, en Canarische en Flaemsche eylanden
mwuk1543	uk english channel (west)	1750	VAN KEULEN	1200	72	101	Nieuwe Pascaart Van het Westelykste Gedeelte van Het Kanaal
mwuk1663a	north sea	1710	VAN KEULEN	1500	59	99	Nieuwe Paskaart van Het Zuyderste Gedeelte der Noord-Zee Strekkende van Texel tot aande Hoofden Begrypende in Sigh de Zeekusten van Vriesland, Holland, Zeeland, Vlaanderen ook een Gedeelte van d'Oostkust van Engeland.
mwm0214a	mediterranean malta	1700	VAN KEULEN	800	51	59	Nieuwe Pascaart voor een Gedeelte van Barbaria beginnende van Susa tot Caap Mesurata als mede t'Eylandt Malta
mwaf0698	africa north	1681	VAN KEULEN	1200	51	58	Nieuwe Pascaart voor een Gedeelte van de Zeekusten van Barbaria Beginnende van C. Rusato tot Alexandria als Mede t' Meeste Gedeelte van't Eylandt Candia (2 sheets)
mwsp0513a	spain regions	1709	VAN KEULEN	1200	51	58	Nieuwe Pascaart Waar in Vertoont Wert de Baÿ van Cadix
mwat0151	atlantic canary isl.	1682	VAN KEULEN	1350	51	59	Nieuwe Pascaert van Al de Carnarisse Eylande. Met Al Hunne Diepten en Drooghte Dus ver Naeukeurig op Gestelt (north to the left)
mwat0084	atlantic azores	1681	VAN KEULEN	1200	51	58	Nieuwe Pascaert van Alle de Vlaemse Eylanden
mwaf0785	africa north morocco	1685	VAN KEULEN	800	50	58	Nieuwe Pascaert van de Kuste van Maroca en Zanhaga van C. Cantin tot C. Bajador … (Incl. Canary Islands, north to the left)
mwuk0422	scotland	1681	VAN KEULEN	960	52	58	Nieuwe Pascaert van de Oost Cust van Schotlandt Beginnende van Barwyck tot aen de Orcades Ylanden (north to the right)
mwsc0309	scandinavia denmark	1684	VAN KEULEN	900	51	59	Nieuwe Pascaert van de Sond ende Beldt met de Onder Behoorende Eylanden
mwsc0304	scandinavia denmark	1681	VAN KEULEN	960	51	59	Nieuwe Pascaert van Jutlandt van't Jutsche Riff: Tot aen de Hoeck van Schagen als Mede een Gedeelte van de Cust van Noorwegen Beginnende van der Neus, tot aen Oxefoort
mwin0418	indian ocean	1680	VAN KEULEN	12000	51	59	Nieuwe Pascaert van Oost Indien Verthoonende hen van C. De Bona Esperanca tot aen het Landt van Eso
mwsc0305	scandinavia denmark	1681	VAN KEULEN	1250	51	57	Nieuwe Pascaert van Schager-Rack en een Gedeelte van de Sont van Gottenburgh tot aen Coppenhaven
mwuk0082a	ireland	1682	VAN KEULEN	785	50	56	Nieuwe Pascaert, vande Suyt Syde van Yrlandt Beginnende van Blasques tot ande Hoeck van Waterfoort
mwsc0131a	scandinavia	1730	VAN KEULEN	3000	59	101	Nieuwe Paskaard Inhoudende t'Noorder Deel van Europa Sijnde Seer Dienstigh voor de Groenlandse en Moskovise Scheepvaard
mwm0147	mediterranean east	1734	VAN KEULEN	3200	59	100	Nieuwe Paskaard van 't Tweede Gedeelte der Middelansche-Zee
mwsc0584	scandinavia norway	1681	VAN KEULEN	1350	52	59	Nieuwe Paskaart van de Kusst van Noorwegen Beginnende van Bommelsondt tot aan de Wtweer Klippen

AMPG REFERENCE	REGION	DATE	MAP MAKER	PRICE (UK£)	VERT. (cm.)	HOR. (cm.)	TITLE OF MAP (Comments by the editor in brackets)
mwsp0464	spain regions	1680	VAN KEULEN	1200	51	57	Nieuwe Paskaart van de Kust van Hispania van't Klif tot aan Velez Malaga als mede de Kust van Barbaria van Larache tot Belis (north to the left)
mwsp0053a	portugal	1681	VAN KEULEN	720	51	60	Nieuwe Paskaart van de Kust van Portugal Beginnende 3 a 4 Myl Benoorde C. Roxent, tot aen C.d. S. Vincente (north to the left)
mwsc0426	scandinavia finland	1709	VAN KEULEN	700	51	59	Nieuwe Paskaart van de Noord Bodem (north to the right)
mwuk0445	scotland	1695	VAN KEULEN	1000	51	59	Nieuwe Paskaart van de Orcades Eylanden
mwas0566	asia south east banca	1753	VAN KEULEN	2500	58	50	Nieuwe Paskaart van de Straaten Sunda en Banca
mwuk0470a	scotland	1730	VAN KEULEN	1500	61	101	Nieuwe Paskaart van de Westkust van Schotland, de Lewys Eylanden en de Noord Kust van Yrland
mwaf1076	africa south west	1720	VAN KEULEN	875	51	58	Nieuwe Paskaart van de Zee Kusten van Gunea van Cabo Verde tot Cabo de Bona Esperanca
mwf0337a	france brittany	1695	VAN KEULEN	650	52	59	Nieuwe Paskaart van de Zeekusten van Bretagne Beginnende van t'Incoomen van de Rivier de Loire tot aant' Eylandt Groa
mwf0337b	france brittany	1695	VAN KEULEN	650	52	59	Nieuwe Paskaart van de Zeekusten van Bretagne en Poictou
mwat0194	atlantic cape verde isl.	1717	VAN KEULEN	650	50	58	Nieuwe Paskaart van de Zoute Eylanden
mwuk0303	irish sea	1718	VAN KEULEN	1000	59	98	Nieuwe Paskaart van Ierland en de West Kust van Engeland ... The New Sea Map of Ireland and the West Coast of England, containing St. George and the Channel of Bristol
mwm0276a	mediterranean west	1730	VAN KEULEN	2500	60	100	Nieuwe Paskaart van't Eerste Gedeelte der Middelansche-Zee tusschen t' I. Cadix en 't I. Malta
mwsp0692a	gibraltar	1700	VAN KEULEN	720	52	60	Nieuwe Paskaart van t'opkomen der Straat Gibralter besloten tussen de kusten van Algarve, Andalusia, Barbaria en Marocco van C. S. Vincent tot C. Cantin (North to the left)
mwf0337	france brittany	1695	VAN KEULEN	650	52	59	Nieuwe Paskaart vant' Ras van Conquest en Fonteny Behelsende de West Cust van Bretaigne met de Byleggende Eylanden (north to the left)
mwbp0039	baltic sea (east)	1716	VAN KEULEN	5000	60	100	Nieuwe Paskaart voor een Gedeelte van de Oost Zee (2 charts, each 60x100cm.)
mwsp0053	portugal	1681	VAN KEULEN	720	51	60	Nieuwe Paskaart, van de Kust van Reino do Algarve
mwsc0079	scandinavia	1682	VAN KEULEN	1500	51	58	Nieuwe Paskaart, vande Geheele Oosterze en Noortze Schip-Vaart
mwaf1165	africa west	1709	VAN KEULEN	675	50	57	Nieuwe Paskaert van de Custen Zee Loango en Angoy van C. de Lopo Gonzalves tot R. de Zaire of Congo Vertoonende Alle desselfs Gelegentheden
mwbh0429	belgium holland	1681	VAN KEULEN	800	51	58	Nieuwe Paskaert van de Kust van Hollandt tussen Texel en de Maes
mwuk0301b	irish sea	1682	VAN KEULEN	1200	51	58	Nieuwe Pas-kaert vande Oost Kust van Yrland. Beginnende van de hoeck van Waterfoort tot aen de Mayds, Als mede de west Kust van Engeland (part of a set of 4 maps of the coasts of Ireland)
mwf0477	france corsica	1700	VAN KEULEN	2500	51	59	Nieuwe Paskaert van de Zee Kusten van Provence en Italiae ... de Zee Kusten van t'Eylandt Corsica
mwit0928	italy sicily	1720	VAN KEULEN	1350	52	59	Nieuwe Paskaart van de Zee Kusten van't Eylandt Sicilia
mwuk1427	england thames	1682	VAN KEULEN	1350	50	58	Nieuwe Paskaart van d'Oost Kust van Engelandt van Dover tot Dunwich als mede de Teems
mwsc0705	scandinavia sweden	1709	VAN KEULEN	1200	52	59	Nieuwe Paskaert van het Stockholmse Liet
mwat0215b	atlantic east	1700	VAN KEULEN	1200	51	59	Nieuwe Paskaert vande gheheele Westersche Scheep-Vaert
mwat0266	atlantic north	1700	VAN KEULEN	2000	51	56	Nieuwe Paskaert vande Gheheele Westersche Scheep-Vaert, op Nieus uyt Ondervindinghe van Schrandre Stierlieden Naaukeurigh Geteeckent en Samen Gebracht
mwuk1548	bristol channel	1681	VAN KEULEN	900	51	59	Nieuwe Paskaert vande Verkeerde Canael of de Kust Van Engelant Beginnende van Montsbay tot an S. David Hoeck
mwaf1153	africa west	1695	VAN KEULEN	675	50	58	Nieuwe Paskaert, van de Kust van Genehoa als mede een Gedeelte van Gambia
mwbp0027	baltic sea (east)	1680	VAN KEULEN	3000	51	115	Nieuwe Perfecte Paskaart van de Oost-Zee
mwsc0460	scandinavia greenland	1680	VAN KEULEN	4000	59	100	Nieuwe Platte Pas Kaart van de Noord Occiaan van Hitland tot in de Straat Davids
mwca0214	canada arctic	1727	VAN KEULEN	2400	60	100	Nieuwe Platte Paskaart van de Straat Davids, van 67 Graade tot 73 Graade Noorder Breeten, of van de Zuyd Bay tot verby de Vrouwe Eylanden: Alles Naawkeurig Afgeteekent door Schipper Laurens Feykes Haan
mwbp0033	baltic sea (east)	1709	VAN KEULEN	1250	52	60	Nieuwe Wassende Graade Paskaart over de Geeheele Oost-Zee Nieuwelijcks Opgestelt door Nicolaas de Vries
mwat0271	atlantic north	1728	VAN KEULEN	2400	60	100	Nieuwe Wassende Graade Zee Kaart over de Spaanse Zee vant Kanaal tot 't Eyland Cuba in Westindia
mwsc0325a	scandinavia denmark	1700	VAN KEULEN	1200	52	60	Nieuwe Wassende Graaden Paskaart van het Schagerak de Sond ende Beld beginnende van de Hoek van Schagen tot Bornholm
mww0353	world	1728	VAN KEULEN	12000	58	99	Nieuwe Wassende Graaden Paskaart Vertoonende Alle de Bekende Zeekusten en Landen op den Geheelen Aard Boodem of Werelt door Gerard Van Keulen

AMPG REFERENCE	REGION	DATE	MAP MAKER	PRICE (UK£)	VERT. (cm.)	HOR. (cm.)	TITLE OF MAP (Comments by the editor in brackets)
mwat0304	atlantic south	1720	VAN KEULEN	1500	60	98	Nieuwe Wassende Graadige Pas-Kaart van de Kust van Guinea en Brasilia Strekkende van Cap Verde tot de Cap de Bon-Esperance en Verders van Rio de Berbice tot Rio de la Plata
mwuk1485	uk english channel (all)	1720	VAN KEULEN	960	51	59	Nieuwe Wassende Gradige Pas-Kaart van het Inkomen van het Canaal op de Hoofden
mwat0270	atlantic north	1720	VAN KEULEN	4000	60	99	Nieuwe Wassende Graeden Kaert van de Noord Occiaen van Hitland tot inde Straet Davids
mwe1203	europe west	1720	VAN KEULEN	1200	59	99	Nieuwe Wassende Pas-Caart van de Westelykste Zee Custen van Europa
mwbp0057a	baltic sea (east)	1793	VAN KEULEN	1200	64	96	Nieuwe wassende zeekart van de Oost-Zee. Bevattende de Westkust van Calmar tot Stockholm, de oostkust van Libau tot Dago, met de eilanden Gotland , Ösel en Dago.
mwuk1531	uk english channel (east)	1684	VAN KEULEN	650	51	61	Nieuwe Zeekaart ... van't Canaal tuschen Engelend et Vrankryk
mwuk1576	channel islands	1690	VAN KEULEN	1200	51	61	Nieuwe Zeekaart van het Tweede gedeelte van't Canaal (north to the right)
mwuk1542	uk english channel (west)	1720	VAN KEULEN	675	50	58	Nieuwe Zeekaart van t' derde Gedeelte van't Canaal (north to the right)
mwsc0438a	scandinavia finland	1770	VAN KEULEN	1000	52	60	Nieuwe. Paskaart Van De. Noord. Bodem. (North to the right.)
mwm0105	mediterranean central	1690	VAN KEULEN	875	50	58	Niewe Pascaart ... Barbaria ... Malta
mwsp0466	spain regions	1684	VAN KEULEN	1200	53	61	Niewe Pascaart van t' Opkomen der Straat Gibralter Bestode tuschen de Kusten van Algarve, Andalusia Barbaria en Marocco van C.S. Vincent tot C. Cantin
mwsp0467	spain regions	1684	VAN KEULEN	1200	51	58	Niewe Pascaart war in Vertoont wert de Bay van Cadix
mwin0387	india bay of bengal	1753	VAN KEULEN	1500	52	59	Niewe Paskaart van het Noordelijkste Gedeelte van de Golf van Bengalen
mwca0589a	canada st lawrence	1717	VAN KEULEN	1200	52	60	Nouvelle Carte de la Riviere de Canada ou St. Laurens de l'Isle de Anticoste jusqua Quebec
mwwi0064	west indies	1728	VAN KEULEN	5000	58	100	Nouvelle Carte Marine de Toute les Cotes de l'Amerique Montrant Toutes les Isles Bayes et Rivieres / Nieuwe Groote en Seer Curieuse Paskaart van Geheel-Westindien. Vertoonende
mwf1078a	france provence	1780	VAN KEULEN	500	52	60	Nouvelle Carte Marine des Côtes Maritimes de Provence
mwca0304	canada newfoundland	1734	VAN KEULEN	1200	52	58	Nouvelle Carte Marine du Grand Banq de Terra Neuff a Grand Point sur la quelle Outes les Profoundeurs par Brasses sont Marquees (updated re-issue of 1684 edition)
mwin0186	india	1730	VAN KEULEN	675	49	61	Nova Tabula Terrarum Cucan, Canara Malabaria, Madurs & Coromandelia cum Parte Septentrionale Insulae Ceylon, in Mari Indico Orientali
mwin0420	indian ocean	1680	VAN KEULEN		62	89	Oost Indien / Wassende-Graade Paskaart, Vertoonende nevens het Oostelykste van Africa, meede de Zeekusten van Asia (Illustrated map lacks top section).
mwas0454	asia south east	1728	VAN KEULEN	4000	61	53	Oosterdeel van Oost Indien Streckende van Cilon tot Iapon en tot de Landrones Ilanden (close copy of Colom 1658)
mwin0183a	india	1728	VAN KEULEN	650	50	58	Pas Caart van een Gedeelte van de Kusten van Cuncancanara en Malabar met het Noortlykste van de Maldivische Eylanden in de Oostindische Zee
mwaf1154	africa west	1695	VAN KEULEN	800	49	57	Pas Caarte van Rio Gambia van C. Verde tot Rio de Serraliones (north to the left)
mwaf1175	africa west	1715	VAN KEULEN	720	50	86	Pas Caarte vande Gryen Cust en Adaows qua Quaas ... C. de Tres Puntas
mwaf1155	africa west	1695	VAN KEULEN	675	49	57	Pas Caarte vande Gryen-Cust en Adaows qua Quaas tuhessen de Serraliones en C. de Puntas
mwaf1075	africa south west	1719	VAN KEULEN	600	51	58	Pas Caert vande Custen van Angola van Rio de Zaire tot C. Negro
mwaf0404b	africa east	1750	VAN KEULEN	1200	50	57	Pas Kaart van ... de Aethiopische Zee (extends east to the Maldive Isl.)
mwgm0009	gulf of mexico and surrounding regions	1684	VAN KEULEN	4500	51	58	Pas Kaart van de Boght van Florida met de Canaal tusschen Florida en Cuba
mwwi0238	west indies (east)	1684	VAN KEULEN	1000	50	58	Pas Kaart van de Caribes tusschen I. Barbados en I.S. Martin
mwgm0010	gulf of mexico and surrounding regions	1684	VAN KEULEN	4500	51	59	Pas Kaart van de Golff van Mexico (north to the right)
mwuss0158	carolinas	1688	VAN KEULEN	4000	51	58	Pas Kaart van de Kust van Carolina tusschen C de Canaveral en C Henry
mwwi0583	hispaniola	1682	VAN KEULEN	1350	52	58	Pas Kaart van de Noord Kust van Espaniola met d'Eylanden daar Benoorden door Voogt (south to the top)
mwuss1620	virginia	1695	VAN KEULEN	9600	51	58	Pas Kaart van de Zee Kusten van Virginia tusschen C. Henry en t Hooge Land van Renselaars Hoek
mwc0148a	china	1753	VAN KEULEN	5000	51	58	Pas Kaart van het in-en opkomen van de Rivier van Quantong (the Pearl River estuary and environs of today's Hong Kong)
mwat0112	atlantic bermuda	1682	VAN KEULEN	6000	52	61	Pas Kaart van I. la Barmuda anders Sommer Ilands int Groot door C.J. Vooght

AMPG REFERENCE	REGION	DATE	MAP MAKER	PRICE (UK£)	VERT. (cm.)	HOR. (cm.)	TITLE OF MAP (Comments by the editor in brackets)
mwwi0898	trinidad & tobago	1683	VAN KEULEN	1500	51	58	Pas Kaart van Rio Oronoque Golfo de Paria met d'Eylanden Trinidad, Tabago, Granada, Granadillos, en Bequia
mwwi0824	puerto rico	1700	VAN KEULEN	1500	52	59	Pas kaart van t Eyland S. luan de Porto Rico met d Eylanden daar beoosten
mwat0342	atlantic west	1682	VAN KEULEN	5500	51	58	Pas kaart van West Indien Behelsende soo Deszelffs Vaste Kusten als d'onder Behoorende Eylanden aan de Noord Oceaan (north to the right)
mwsam0590	south america guyana	1700	VAN KEULEN	900	51	58	Pas Kaart vande Kust van Guiana tusschen R. Courantin en R. Oronoque (Georgetown)
mwsam0590a	south america guyana	1700	VAN KEULEN	900	51	58	Pas kaart vande Kust van Guiana tusschen R. Cupanama en R. Oronoque (south to the top)
mwwi0413	cuba	1684	VAN KEULEN	3000	51	58	Pas Kaart vande Noord Oost Kust van Cuba en d'Oost Kust van Florida
mwgr0626	greece islands	1734	VAN KEULEN	1000	52	60	Pas kaart vande Zee-kusten van Cicilia, Calabria, Graetia en Morea
mwwi0416	cuba	1695	VAN KEULEN	2000	52	58	Pas Kaart vande Zuyd Kust van Cuba en van Geheel Yamaica en and're Bygeleegen Plaatsen
mwsc0331	scandinavia denmark	1706	VAN KEULEN	1100	52	60	Pascaart om Door de Sond en de Droogen te Seylen Strekkende van Kol tot Meun
mwaf1053	africa south east	1753	VAN KEULEN	600	25	28	Pas-Caart van de Baay de Lagoa
mwm0036	mediterranean	1710	VAN KEULEN	2000	52	59	Pas-Caart van de Middellandsche Zee (2 maps on one sheet)
mwuk0083	ireland	1682	VAN KEULEN	785	51	58	Pascaart van de Noortcust van Yrland als meede de Westcust van Schotland (south to the top)
mwm0095	mediterranean adriatic	1708	VAN KEULEN	1600	52	59	Pas-Caart van de Weder Zytsche Zeekusten soo van Italia als Dalmatia en Griecken inde Golff van Venetien (1st edition 1681)
mwsp0512	spain regions	1708	VAN KEULEN	500	51	59	Pascaart van de Zee Kusten van Granada en Murcia tusschen Velez Malaga en C.S Martin als meede de Barbarische Zee-Kusten tusschen Penon de Veles en C. Ivy
mwit0793	italy sardinia	1685	VAN KEULEN	800	51	59	Pas-Caart van de Zee kusten van 't Eylandt Sardinia met de tegen over geleegene Zee Kusten van Barbaria, Tusschen C. de Ferro en C. Bona
mwsp0467a	spain regions	1684	VAN KEULEN	1500	51	59	Pascaart van de Zeekusten van Galissen
mwf0267a	france aquitaine	1709	VAN KEULEN	600	52	58	Pascaart vande Zeekusten van Aunis en Saintonge beginnende van Ollone toot aande Rievier van Bordeaux
mwwi0236	west indies (east)	1681	VAN KEULEN	1200	49	58	Pascaarte vande Caribes, S. Juan de Porto Rico, de Oosthoeck van I. Espangnola als Mede de Vaste Cust van Nueva Andalusia met de Eylanden Daer Omtrent Ghelegen, Nieulyckx Uytgegeven en van Veel Fouten Verbetert
mwru0433a	russia tartary	1681	VAN KEULEN	1350	52	60	Pascaarte vande Noord Oost Cust van Asia. Verthoonende in sich Alle de Zee-Custen van Tartarien van Japan tot Nova Zemla
mwca0032	canada	1680	VAN KEULEN	1250	51	59	Pascaarte vande Noorder Zee Custen van America, vande West-Hoeck van Ysland doorde Straet Davis en Hudson, tot aen Terra Neuf (illustrated is the 1687 edition, with additions taken from Doncker's chart of the same year)
mwat0301	atlantic south	1681	VAN KEULEN	1200	52	59	Pascaarte vande Zee Custen van Guinea, en Brasilia: van Cabo de Verde, tot C. de Bona Esperanca: en van R. de Amazones tot Rio de la Plata
mwuk1541	uk english channel (west)	1680	VAN KEULEN	675	50	58	Pas-Caert van de Canael, tusschen Engelandt en Vranckryck, van Pleymuyen tot aen de Sorlinges (north to the left)
mwaf1068	africa south west	1684	VAN KEULEN	875	51	59	Pascaert van de Costa de Caffres, tusschen Cabo Negro en Cabo de Bona Esperanca
mwsc0463a	scandinavia greenland	1720	VAN KEULEN	1250	51	61	Pascaert van Groen-landt Yslandt Straet Davidts Ian Mayen Eylandt
mwsc0306	scandinavia denmark	1681	VAN KEULEN	1250	51	63	Pascaert van Schager-Rack, de Belt, en de Orisondt tot in de Oost Zee
mwuk1655	north sea	1680	VAN KEULEN	1200	51	59	Pascaert van Texel tot aen Bergen als Mede de Belt, Schagerrack, Hitland en de Cust van Engeland
mwaf1156	africa west	1695	VAN KEULEN	675	50	57	Pascaert vande Bocht van Benin, Tary Ardra en Rio de Lagos, van Acra tot C. Formosa (variant shown left)
mwaf1157a	africa west	1695	VAN KEULEN	675	51	58	Pascaert vande Bocht van Gabon (north to the left)
mwuk0740	uk	1680	VAN KEULEN	1350	52	61	Pascaert vande Canaal Engeland, Schotland, en Yrland (north to the right)
mwaf1157	africa west	1695	VAN KEULEN	675	50	57	Pas-Caert vande Goud Cust en Guinea van C. Tres Puntas tot Acara
mwuk1340	england east	1685	VAN KEULEN	1800	51	58	Pas-Caert vande Zee-Custen van Engeland van Orfordness tot aen Flamborger Hoof
mwuk1657a	north sea	1684	VAN KEULEN	1350	52	59	Pas Caerte van Texel tot aende Hoofden
mwp0236	pacific (all)	1680	VAN KEULEN	8000	52	59	Pascaert vande Zuyd Zee en een Gedeelte van Brasil van Ilhas de Ladrones tot R. de la Plata
mwin0042	ceylon	1728	VAN KEULEN	2500	52	60	Pascaert van't Eylandt Ceylon, Voordefen Taprobana; by de Inwoonders Genaemt Lankaun. By Joannes Van Keulen
mwuk0423	scotland	1681	VAN KEULEN	960	51	58	Pascaert, vande Westkust van Schotlant, als mede een Gedeelte vande Lewys Eylanden

AMPG REFERENCE	REGION	DATE	MAP MAKER	PRICE (UK£)	VERT. (cm.)	HOR. (cm.)	TITLE OF MAP (Comments by the editor in brackets)
mwwi0034	west indies	1680	VAN KEULEN	3000	51	59	Pascaerte van Westindien Begrypende in zich de Vaste Kusten en Eylanden
mwaf1074a	africa south west	1719	VAN KEULEN	600	51	58	Pascaerte vande Custen van Loango, Angoy als mede een gedeelte van Angola, van C. de Lopo Gonçalves tot aen R. de Zaire
mwp0405	pacific north	1726	VAN KEULEN	1500	53	60	Pascaerte vande Noord Oost Cust van Asia Verthoonende in Sich Alle de Zee-Custen van Tartarien van Japan tot Nova Zemla
mwsc0080	scandinavia	1685	VAN KEULEN	2000	52	59	Pascaerte van't Noordlyckste Deel van Europa
mwm0106	mediterranean central	1720	VAN KEULEN	1350	51	58	Paskaart der Zeekusten van Italien tusschen Piombino en C. dell Arme met de Noord-Kust van 't Eylandt Sicilia
mwin0484	indian ocean west	1753	VAN KEULEN	2000	48	57	Paskaart Strekkende van Dofar, Langs de Kusten van Arabien, Persien, Guzuratte en Decam
mwaf0649	africa islands seychelles	1753	VAN KEULEN	1500	49	57	Paskaart van de Aethiopische Zee
mwgr0623	greece islands	1720	VAN KEULEN	4000	51	59	Paskaart van de Archipelagusche Eylanden (4 sheets, each 51x59cm.)
mwuk1541a	uk english channel (west)	1693	VAN KEULEN	720	52	53	Pas-Kaart van de Bocht van Vrankryk Biscaien en Galissen 't Inkomen van't Canaal
mwc0151a	china	1753	VAN KEULEN	5500	51	58	Pas-Kaart van de Chineesche Kust langs Quantung en Fokien, alsook Formosa
mwat0216b	atlantic east	1720	VAN KEULEN	1000	51	57	Paskaart Van de Cust van Portugal, Barbaria, en Genehoa Beginnende van d'Barlenges tot aan C. Verde (shown above left)
mwc0151	china	1753	VAN KEULEN	5000	41	54	Paskaart van de Eylanden Cheuxan Lowang ... de kust van China (South of Shanghai)
mwf0267	france aquitaine	1709	VAN KEULEN	600	52	58	Paskaart van de Garonne, of Rivier van Bordeaux (south to the top)
mwgm0181	mexico	1684	VAN KEULEN	1250	51	58	Pas-Kaart van de Golff de Guanaios. Met 't Canaal tusschen Yucatan en I. Cuba (south to the top)
mwca0286	canada newfoundland	1684	VAN KEULEN	1500	51	59	Pas-Kaart van de Grand Banq by Terra Neuff met Alle syn Diepten op Vaademen door J.C. Vooght Geometra
mwjk0108	japan	1753	VAN KEULEN	12000	39	52	Pas-Kaart van de Haven van Nangasequi (the only Dutch sea chart focussed on this region)
mwsc0585	scandinavia norway	1681	VAN KEULEN	960	51	58	Paskaart van de Kust van Finmarken van Heyligerlander Leen tot C. Tromsondt
mwaf0785a	africa north morocco	1685	VAN KEULEN	600	50	58	Paskaart van de Kust van Maroca beginnende van Larache tot aan C. Cantin (shown above left)
mwsc0586	scandinavia norway	1681	VAN KEULEN	960	51	58	Paskaart van de Kust van Noorwegen Beginnende van Swarten Os tot aan Heyligelander Leen
mwaf1174	africa west	1715	VAN KEULEN	675	51	58	Paskaart van de Kuste van Gualate en Arguyn
mwin0467	indian ocean maldives	1753	VAN KEULEN	3000	57	50	Paskaart van de Maldivische Eylanden
mwru0101	russia	1689	VAN KEULEN	800	51	59	Paskaart van de Mont van de Witte Zee Beginnende van Tiepena tot Pelitza
mwbp0028	baltic sea (east)	1681	VAN KEULEN	1500	52	58	Paskaart van de Oost Zee Verthoonende Al de Gelegentheyt tuschen Rostok, en Wyborg
mwru0104a	russia	1697	VAN KEULEN	1000	51	58	Paskaart van de Rivier de Dwina of Archangel
mwuk0084	ireland	1682	VAN KEULEN	785	50	58	Paskaart van de West Cust van Yrlandt Beginnende van Klady tot aen de Blasques
mwru0100	russia	1689	VAN KEULEN	800	51	59	Paskaart van de Witte Zee Beginnende van Pelitza tot Kandalox
mwas0689	asia south east malacca	1753	VAN KEULEN	12000	58	50	Pas-Kaart van de Vaar-Weg van Straat Banca af tot aan Pulo Temaon, Inhoudende de Straaten Drioens, Sabon, Brouwer en Sincapoera
mwsam0505a	south america colombia	1700	VAN KEULEN	960	51	59	Pas-kaart van de Zee Kusten van Carthagena Tierra Firma Costa Rica ende Honduras
mwgm0373	nicaragua	1687	VAN KEULEN	1350	51	58	Pas-Kaart van de Zee Kusten van Carthagena Tierra Firma Costa Rica ende Honduras
mwsam0324	south america brazil	1684	VAN KEULEN	960	51	58	Pas-Kaart van de Zee-Kusten van Brazilia, tusschen Bahia Baxa en Punto de Lucena
mwsam0325	south america brazil	1684	VAN KEULEN	960	51	58	Pas-Kaart van de Zee-Kusten van Brazilia, tusschen Cabo de Cuma en Bahia Baxa
mwsam0326	south america brazil	1684	VAN KEULEN	960	51	58	Pas-Kaart van de Zee-Kusten van Brazilia, tusschen Cabo S. Agostino en Rio Coroipo
mwsam0329	south america brazil	1684	VAN KEULEN	960	51	58	Pas-Kaart van de Zee-Kusten van Brazilia, tusschen I.S. Catharina en C.S. Anthonio
mwsam0330	south america brazil	1684	VAN KEULEN	960	51	58	Pas-Kaart van de Zee-Kusten van Brazilia, tusschen Punto de Lucena en Cabo S. Augustino
mwsam0327	south america brazil	1684	VAN KEULEN	960	51	58	Pas-Kaart van de Zee-Kusten van Brazilia, tusschen Rio Coroipo en Rio Ponica
mwsam0328	south america brazil	1684	VAN KEULEN	960	51	58	Pas-Kaart van de Zee-Kusten van Brazilia, tusschen Rio das Contas en Cabo S. Thome
mwsam0589	south america guyana	1700	VAN KEULEN	550	51	58	Pas-Kaart van de Zee-Kusten van Guiana tusschen Cabo Noord en Rio Amano
mwca0285	canada newfoundland	1684	VAN KEULEN	1800	51	58	Pas-Kaart van de Zee-Kusten van Terra Nova, met de Byleggende Zee-Kusten van Francia Nova, Canada en Accadie

AMPG REFERENCE	REGION	DATE	MAP MAKER	PRICE (UK£)	VERT. (cm.)	HOR. (cm.)	TITLE OF MAP (Comments by the editor in brackets)
mwsp0513	spain regions	1708	VAN KEULEN	1500	52	59	Paskaart van de Zee-kusten van Valence, Catalonien, Languedocq en Provence
mwwi0584	hispaniola	1682	VAN KEULEN	1200	51	58	Pas-Kaart van de Zuyd-Kust van Espanjola met de Zee Kust van Nuevo Reyne de Granada
mwc0308a	china formosa	1753	VAN KEULEN	5000	51	58	Paskaart van den Vaarweg tusschen Formosa en Japan
mwuk1666	north sea	1720	VAN KEULEN	1200	52	59	Paskaart van een Gedeelte der Noort Zee Beginnende van de Maas tot Dronte
mwaf0604	africa islands madagascar	1753	VAN KEULEN	1350	50	57	Paskaart van een Gedeelte van de Aethiopische-Zee, Strekkende van R. Sta. Lucia tot C. del Gado, Langs de Kusten van Suffalo en Mocambique, Bevattende Insgelyks 't Eiland Madagascar met Desselfs Onderhorige Eilanden
mwsp0077	portugal	1720	VAN KEULEN	720	52	58	Paskaart van een gedeelte van de Kust van Portugal van Zurara de Barlenges (north to the left)
mwbh0422	belgium holland	1680	VAN KEULEN	900	50	58	Paskaart van een Gedeelte van Vriesland, Groeningen, en Emderland. Met zyn Onderhoorige Eylanden; Strekkende van't Eylant der Schelling, tot aan Wanger Oog
mwsp0467b	spain regions	1684	VAN KEULEN	1000	51	57	Paskaart van Gallissien van C. de Finisterre tot aen Zurara
mwaf0936	africa south	1753	VAN KEULEN	3000	51	58	Paskaart van het Zuydelykste Gedeelte van Africa
mwuk0741	uk	1681	VAN KEULEN	1350	51	58	Paskaart van 't Canaal Engelandt Schotlandt en Yrland (north to the left)
mwm0134	mediterranean east	1680	VAN KEULEN	1800	51	58	Pas-Kaart van t' Oosterste Deel vande Middellantsche Zee Vervattende de Zee-Kusten van Caramania, Cyprus, Soria en Aegiptia
mwgr0488	greece cyprus	1688	VAN KEULEN	4000	51	58	Pas-Kaart van t' Oosterste Deel vande Middellantsche Zee Vervattende de Zee-Kusten van Caramania, Cyprus, Soria en Aegiptia (north to the left)
mwaf0937	africa south	1753	VAN KEULEN	12000	59	101	Paskaart van 't Zuydelykste gedeelte van Africa vertoonende de Saldanha Bay de Bay de Goede Hoop en de Bay Falso (north to the left)
mwbh0424	belgium holland	1680	VAN KEULEN	1000	50	58	Paskaart vande Iade, Weser en Elve. Met een Gedeelte van Emderland, Keydingerland, Holsatia en Ditmarschen (south to the top)
mwuk0421	scotland	1681	VAN KEULEN	960	51	58	Paskaart vande Noord Cust van Schotland als mede de Eylanden van Hitlandt en Fero
mwsam0593a	south america guyana	1720	VAN KEULEN	1200	51	58	Pas-Kaart vande Rivieren Commewini Suriname en Cupanama (as the next map but without the right-hand section and slightly different title)
mwsam0593	south america guyana	1720	VAN KEULEN	1800	51	87	Pas-Kaart vande Rivieren Commewini Suriname Suramaca Cupanama
mwsc0307	scandinavia denmark	1682	VAN KEULEN	750	51	59	Paskaart vande West Kust van Jutland van Busem tot aen 't Jutsche Riff met Alle syn Eylanden daer onder Begrepen (north to the left)
mwam0881	america north (east)	1684	VAN KEULEN	4000	51	58	Pas-Kaart vande Zee Kusten inde Boght van Niew Engeland tusschen de Staaten Hoek en C. de Sable. Door Vooght Geometra t' Amsterdam by Johannes Van Keulen Boek en Zee Kaart Verkoper aande Niewe Brug inde Gekroonde Lootsman met Privilegie voor 15 Iaaren
mwam0882	america north (east)	1685	VAN KEULEN	12000	51	58	Pas-Kaart vande Zee Kusten van Niew Nederland (insets of the Hudson, Connecticut rivers)
mwca0039	canada	1700	VAN KEULEN	1200	51	58	Pas-Kaart vande Zee-Custen van Terra Nova
mwsam0827	south america venezuela	1700	VAN KEULEN	1800	52	59	Pas-Kaart vande Zee-Kusten van Venecuela (south to the top)
mwaf0630	africa islands mauritius	1753	VAN KEULEN	2500	49	57	Paskaart van't Eyland Mauritius
mwsc0082	scandinavia	1685	VAN KEULEN	2500	52	59	Paskaart van't Noordelykste deel der Noort Zee beginnende van der Neus. tot Nova Zemla
mwsc0722	scandinavia sweden	1730	VAN KEULEN	960	52	60	Paskaart van't Schager-Rak Soo 't
mwbp0034	baltic sea (east)	1709	VAN KEULEN	900	51	58	Paskaart voor een Gedeelte der Oost Zee Beginnende van Lemsaal, tot Beooste Kok als mede de Kust van Oost Finlandt. Van 't Alandse Haff, tot Parna, waar in ook vervat is, d' Eylande Oesel, en Dagho (north to the left)
mwsc0696	scandinavia sweden	1684	VAN KEULEN	1500	51	58	Paskaart voor een Gedeelte der Oost Zee Beginnende van Schenkkenes, tot aan Stokholm
mwsc0694	scandinavia sweden	1681	VAN KEULEN	1500	51	58	Paskaart voor een Gedeelte van de Oost Zee. Beginnede van Valsterbon tot Schenkkenes
mwbp0030	baltic sea (east)	1690	VAN KEULEN	720	51	58	Paskaart voor een Gedelte van de Oost Zee. Beginnende van Sernevisse, tot aan Parnout, Waar in noch in een Bysonder Tafelne Vervat is de Revier van Dantzigk
mwsam0328a	south america brazil	1684	VAN KEULEN	960	51	58	Paskaart, van de Zee Kusten ... tusschen, C. S. Thome en I. S. Catharina
mwsam0330a	south america brazil	1684	VAN KEULEN	960	51	58	Pas-Kaart, van de Zee-Kusten, van, Brazilia, tusschen Cabo Noord, en Cabo de Cum
mwsp0652	balearic islands	1708	VAN KEULEN	1500	51	59	Paskaart, voor een Gedeelte der Kust van, Barbaria, van C. Ivi, tot Bona. En de Kust van, Catalonia, van, Peniscola, tot Mataro. Als mede de Eylanden, Yvica, Majorca, en Minorca (south to the top)

AMPG REFERENCE	REGION	DATE	MAP MAKER	PRICE (UK£)	VERT. (cm.)	HOR. (cm.)	TITLE OF MAP (Comments by the editor in brackets)
mwsam0327a	south america brazil	1684	VAN KEULEN	960	51	58	Pas-kaart... tusschen Rio Ponica, en Rio das Contas (north to the right)
mwbh0423	belgium holland	1680	VAN KEULEN	1800	51	57	Paskaarte van de Zuyder Zee met Alle des Zelfs Inkoomende Gaaten Ao 1771
mwsc0495	scandinavia iceland	1681	VAN KEULEN	1500	51	58	Paskaarte van Ysland, Spitsberge, en Ian Mayen Eyland (3 maps on one sheet)
mwat0215a	atlantic east	1690	VAN KEULEN	1000	52	61	Paskaert van Cales tot Cadix als mede een gedeelte van Engelandt (north to the left. Re-issued with redesigned cartouches etc., as below)
mwsc0603	scandinavia norway	1700	VAN KEULEN	1000	51	58	Pas-Kaert van de Cust van Noorwegen Beginnende van Der Neus tot aen Bommel Sond (north to the left)
mwin0482	indian ocean west	1728	VAN KEULEN	1600	52	62	Paskaert van t Westerdeel van Oost Indien Streckende van Cabo de Bona Esperance tot het Eyland van Cilon, met al syn Omleggende Eylande daar ontrent (incl. Arabia)
mwsc0587	scandinavia norway	1681	VAN KEULEN	1800	52	58	Paskaert voor een Gedeelte van de Cust van Noorwegen Beginnende van Oxefoort tot aen Gottenborg
mwat0017	atlantic ocean (all)	1680	VAN KEULEN	3000	52	57	Paskaert waer in de Graden der Breedde over Weder Zyden vande Middellyn Wassende ... Vertonende (Behalve Europaes Zuijdelijkste) een Gedeelte van de Custen van Africa en America (north to the right)
mwbh0425	belgium holland	1680	VAN KEULEN	2000	49	109	Paskaerte van het inkoomen van de Maes
mwgr0616a	greece islands	1700	VAN KEULEN	1750	51	59	Paskaerte vande Archipel en de Eylanden daer omtrent gelegen, als Candia Serigo en Rodus, tusschen Golfo de Lepanto Constantinopolen en C. Serdeni in Natolia
mwsp0738	gibraltar	1783	VAN KEULEN	875	38	49	Plan van de Baay van Gibraltar
mwwi0856	st kitts	1728	VAN KEULEN	3750	52	59	t Eyland St. Christofal / I. Isle de St. Croix
mwin0221	india	1753	VAN KEULEN	450	28	47	t Inkoomen van de Rivier van Suratte
mwuk1532	uk english channel (east)	1689	VAN KEULEN	720	52	60	The New Sea Map of the First Part of the Channel Betwext England et France
mwm0140a	mediterranean east	1710	VAN KEULEN	3000	59	101	The New Sea Map of the second part of the Mid-Land Sea (title in 4 languages)
mww0218	world	1682	VAN KEULEN	6000	52	60	Wassende Graade Kaart van Alle Bekende Zeekusten op den Geheelen Aardbodem door C.J. Voogt Geometra. T'Amsterdam by Johannes Van Keulen. Boekverkoper aande Niewen-Brug inde Gekroonde Loots-Man
mwat0264	atlantic north	1692	VAN KEULEN	1500	52	59	Wassende Graade Kaart van de Noord Oceaan van Terra Nova en de Straat Davids en Hudson tot Hidland en de Westkust van Schotland en Engeland en Bretagne Begrypende ook Yrland en Ysland. Door C.J. Vooght Geometra
mwaa0096	arctic	1681	VAN KEULEN	1350	52	60	Wassende Graade Kaart van de Noord Ys Zee. Behelsende de Kusten v. Finmarken, Lapland, Rusland, Nova Zembla en Spitsbergen
mwuk1656	north sea	1681	VAN KEULEN	3000	52	89	Wassende Graade Kaart van de Noort Zee Beginnende van de Hoofden tot t'Land Stadt in Noorwegen met de Gantse Oostkust van Engeland en Schotland als ook met d'Orcades Hitland Fero en Lewys eylanden
mwuk1657	north sea	1681	VAN KEULEN	2000	53	60	Wassende Graade Kaart van 't Noordelykste Deel der Noord Zee tussen Schotland, Ysland Noorwegen en Finmarken tot Booven de Noord Caap
mwsp0066	portugal	1704	VAN KEULEN	1000	50	57	Wassende Graade Kart vande Geheele Cust van Portugaal
mwat0309a	atlantic south	1753	VAN KEULEN	600	51	59	Wassende-Grade-Kaart van de Aetiopische Ocean beslooten met de kusten van Guinea, Angola, de Caffers en Brasilia
mwat0018	atlantic ocean (all)	1680	VAN KEULEN	50000	79	95	West Indische Paskaert waerin de Graden der Breedde over Weder Zijden vande Middellijn Wassende (derived from Blaeu c1630)
mwas0884	asia south east sumatra	1753	VAN KEULEN	3000	50	113	Zee-Caart van het Eyland Sumatra, met de Straaten Malacca, Sincapoera, Banca en Sunda
mww0085	world	1594	VAN LANGREN	8750	30	46	Typus Orbis Terrarum (based on Ortelius)
mwat0074	atlantic azores	1596	VAN LINSCHOTEN	2400	48	84	A Cidade de Angra na Ilha de Iesu Xpo da Tercera
mwsam0007	south america	1596	VAN LINSCHOTEN	6750	38	54	Delineatio Omnium Orarum Totius Australis Partis Americae, Dictae Peruvianae, a R. de la Plata, Brasiliam, Pariam, & Castellam
mwme0540	arabia etc	1596	VAN LINSCHOTEN	6000	39	54	Deliniantur in hac tabula, Orae maritimae Abexiae ... (re-engraved and closely copied by Wolfe, London in 1598)
mwaf0031a	africa	1599	VAN LINSCHOTEN	7500	35	67	Descriptio Hydrographica Accomodata ad Battavorum Navagatione in Javam Insulam Indiae Orientalis
mwas0367	asia south east	1596	VAN LINSCHOTEN	10000	38	52	Exacta & Accurata Delineatio cum Orarum Maritimarum tum etiam Locorum Terrestrium quae in Regionibus China, Cauchinchina, Camboja sive Champa, Syao, Malacca, Arracan & Pegu (north to the left)
mwin0395	india goa	1595	VAN LINSCHOTEN	4000	57	79	Goae Indiae Orientalis Metropolis
mwat0318	atlantic st helena	1598	VAN LINSCHOTEN	1350	37	50	Insula D. Helenae Sacra Coeli Clementia et Aequabilitate
mwaf1035	africa south east	1596	VAN LINSCHOTEN	650	25	32	Insulae et Arcis Mocambique Descriptio ad Fines Melinde

AMPG REFERENCE	REGION	DATE	MAP MAKER	PRICE (UK£)	VERT. (cm.)	HOR. (cm.)	TITLE OF MAP (Comments by the editor in brackets)
mwaf0854	africa south	1596	VAN LINSCHOTEN	9000	39	53	Typus Orarum Maritimarum Guineae, Manicongo, & Angolae ultra Promontorium Bonae Spei / Delineatio Orarum Maritimarum, Terrae vulgo Indigetatae Terra do Natal, item Sofalae, Mozambicae, & Melindae (2 maps, SE and SW Africa, each 39x53cm. Re-issued by Wolfe 1598)
mwru0025	russia	1601	VAN LINSCHOTEN	2800	28	54	Vera Delineatio Maris Insularum Portuum et Littorum Septentrionalium ab Insula Toxar per Fretum Nassoviacum seu Arcticum in Mare Tartaricum ultra Flumen Obi
mwat0067a	atlantic ascension isl.	1596	LINSCHOTEN	960	24	35	Vera effigies et delineatio Insulae Ascenscio
mwat0320	atlantic st helena	1599	VAN LINSCHOTEN	1250	30	48	Vera Effigies et Delineatio Insulae Sanctae Helenae, qua Ortum Occasum, et Septentrionem Spectat, Sitae in Altitudine 16 Graduum ad Austrum Linea Aequinoctialis (shows 3 views)
mwaf1038	africa south east	1598	VAN LINSCHOTEN-WOLFE	350	19	24	The Description of the Islandes, and Castles of Mozambique, lyeing upon the Borders of Melinde ... printed in London by Iohn Wolfe Graven by William Rogers
mwsam0008	south america	1598	VAN LINSCHOTEN-WOLFE	6000	38	54	The Description of the Whole Coast Lying in the South Seas of Americae Called Peru, beginning at Rio de Plata ... to the Cape of Florida ... Imprinted at London by Iohn Wolfe and Graven by Robert Beckit (English edition of 1596 map)
mwaf0050	africa	1640	VAN LOCHOM	1200	38	50	Carte de L'Afrique (French edition of Hondius 1631)
mwe0048	europe	1640	VAN LOCHOM	1500	38	50	Carte de l'Europe
mwit0090a	italy	1646	VAN LOCHOM	800	37	47	Carte d'Italie Corsique Sardegne et Royaumes Circumvoisines (reduced version of Magini 1608)
mwf0284	france auvergne	1645	VAN LOCHOM	375	43	55	Carte du Pais d'Auvergne
mwf0432	france central	1653	VAN LOCHOM	375	34	50	Description Generalle du Pais et Viconte de Turenne, avec les Confins des Provinces qui l'Avoisinent
mwe0067	europe	1660	VAN LOCHOM	600	38	50	L'Europe Nouvellement Tracee, et Rendue Plus Claire
mwsp0180c	spain	1641	VAN LOCHOM	875	37	47	Nova Hispaniae Descriptio 1641
mww0144	world	1636	VAN LOCHOM	12000	39	57	Nova Totius Terrarum Orbis Geographica ac Hydrographica Tabula. Auct Iud Hondio (based on Hondius' 1617 map)
mwuk0700	uk	1639	VAN LOCHOM	785	39	51	Novissima Descriptio Angliae Scotiae et Hiberniae (copy of Hondius' map of 1631)
mwg0053	germany	1637	VAN LOCHOM	960	35	46	Novissima Germania
mwme0097	holy land	1640	VAN LOCHOM	960	39	54	Palestinae Delineatio ad Geographica Canones Revocata (map by P. Briet)
mwsp0027	portugal	1640	VAN LOCHOM	875	38	49	Portugallia et Algarbia quae olim Lusitania (based on Secco's map of 1560)
mwit0714	italy rome	1640	VAN LOCHOM	1800	31	50	Roma, Gentium Domina
mwas0264	asia (from turkey to india)	1691	VAN LOOCK	1800	50	50	Eevwighen Kalendier oste Almanack (perpetual calender)
mwm0093	mediterranean adriatic	1700	VAN LOON	550	44	51	Caarte vaande Golf van Venetien ... Italien Dalmatien et Griekenlant
mwuk1662	north sea	1693	VAN LOON	1350	61	86	Carte de la Mer d'Allemagne ... depuis Bergen et les Isles Schetland jusques au Pas de Calais (north to the left)
mwsp0051	portugal	1680	VAN LOON	1200	58	86	Carte des Costes de Portugal et de Partie d'Espagne depuis le Cap de Finisterre jusques au Detroit de Gibraltar
mwbh0623	belgium holland	1734	VAN LOON	280	37	38	Landkaart Verbeeldende de Twee Romeynsche Heirbaanen
mwuk0722	uk	1661	VAN LOON	800	49	63	Pascaerte van Engeland, Schotlandt, Yerlant
mww0184	world	1666	VAN LOON	9750	45	53	Orbis Terrarum Nova et Accuratissima Tabula. Auctore Ioanne a Loon
mwsam0305	south america brazil	1661	VAN LOON	1200	43	55	Pascaarte van Brasil
mwca0211b	canada arctic	1666	VAN LOON	3000	44	54	Pascaarte vande Noorder Zeekusten van America van Groenland door de Straet Davis en Hudson tot aen Terra Neuf (almost the same as Goos' 1666 map)
mwbh0358	belgium holland	1661	VAN LOON	960	42	54	Pascaarte vande Zuyder-Zee, Texel ende Vlie-Stroom, als mede het Amelander-Gat
mwsam0578	south america guyana	1661	VAN LOON	550	42	55	Pascaerte van de Cust van Guaiana Oste de Wilde Cust; en't Noorder Deel van Brazil ... tusschen villa d'Olinda de Pernambuco en R. Oronoque
mwat0183	atlantic cape verde isl.	1661	VAN LOON	950	42	55	Pascaerte van de Soute Eylanden, oste Ilhas de Cabo Verde
mwsc0458	scandinavia greenland	1666	VAN LOON	1800	43	53	Pas-caerte van GroenLand
mwuss0070	california	1661	VAN LOON		43	55	Pascaerte van Nova Granada en t'Eylandt California
mwsam0192a	south america (north west)	1661	VAN LOON	1800	43	54	Pascaerte van Nova Hispania, Peru en Chili
mwsc0413	scandinavia finland	1661	VAN LOON	1800	43	55	Pascaerte van Sueden en Een Gedeelte van Finlandt en Lyflandt
mwca0022a	canada	1661	VAN LOON	5000	44	53	Pas-Caerte van Terra Nova, Nova Francia, Niew-Engeland en de Groote Rivier van Canada. t'Amsterdam (see Doncker 1669 for illustration)
mwm0266	mediterranean west	1660	VAN LOON	2400	30	46	Pascaerte van 't Westelyckste Deel vande Middelandsche Zee
mwuk1650	north sea	1666	VAN LOON	2500	43	55	Pascaerte vande Noort Zee, Vertonende van Cales tot Dronten
mwuk1540	uk english channel (west)	1666	VAN LOON	875	42	53	Pas-Caerte vant in Comen van de Canael

AMPG REFERENCE	REGION	DATE	MAP MAKER	PRICE (UK£)	VERT. (cm.)	HOR. (cm.)	TITLE OF MAP (Comments by the editor in brackets)
mwaf0364a	africa east	1661	VAN LOON	1800	43	53	Pascaerte van't Westelyckste Deel van Oost Indien, en de Eylanded daer Onder Begrepen van C. de Bona Esperanca tot C. Comorin
			The name VAN LOON was used by JANSSON				
mwsam0281	south america brazil	1629	VAN METEREN	800	29	44	Warhafftige Abbildung von Einnehmung der Statt S. Salvator in der Baya de Todos los Santos (view)
mww0175	world	1660	VAN MEURS	2500	26	34	Nova Delineatio Totius Orbis Terrarum
mwam0075	america continent	1671	VAN MEURS	2000	43	53	Novissima et Accuratissima Totius Americae Descriptio
mwc0023	china	1650	VAN MEURS	280	20	32	Peking
mwme0181	holy land	1680	VAN MEURS	675	39	47	Terra Sancta
mwe0100	europe	1690	VAN SCHAGEN	875	44	54	Europa Delineata et Recens Edita
mww0219	world	1682	VAN SCHAGEN	8000	49	56	Nova Totius Terrarum Orbis
mwe0769	europe east	1680	VAN SCHAGEN	720	45	58	Theater des Oorlogs in Hongarye tussen de Keyerlyke en de Turken (illustrated is the 1729 re-issue with slightly different titles in Dutch/French)
mwam0030	america continent	1609	VAN SCHOEL		37	50	America - Il Mondo Nuovo su Chiamato America da Amerigo Vespucci Fiorentino
mwf0706	france nord pas-de-calais	1600	VAN SCHOEL	2000	29	44	Bologna in Francia (view of Boulogne)
mwp0489	pacific south	1619	VAN SPILBERGEN	1100	16	43	(Unitled map with 2 insets: New Guinea / Magellan)
mwas0749	asia south east philippines	1619	VAN SPILBERGEN	1800	16	43	(Untitled map of the Manila region)
mww0129	world	1619	VAN SPILBERGEN	5000	32	45	Nova Totius Orbis Terrarum Descriptio
mwas0311	asia caspian sea	1722	VAN VERDEN	960	40	27	Carte Marine De La Mer Caspiene levée suivant les ordres de S.M.Cz. En 1719, 1720 et 1721 (first survey of the Caspian Sea)
mwuss1200	new york	1825	VANCE	4000	83	187	Map of the Western Part of the State of New York
mwp0039a	australia	1798	VANCOUVER	4000	60	77	A Chart Showing part of the SW Coast of New Holland
mwp0336	pacific hawaii	1798	VANCOUVER	2000	56	78	A Chart of the Sandwich Islands as Surveyed During the Visits of His Majesty's Sloop Discovery and the Armed Tender Chatham Commanded by George Vancouver Esq. in the Years 1792 1793 & 1794 (insets: part of Galapagos Isl, Cocos Isl.)
mwca0666	canada west	1798	VANCOUVER	2000	79	62	A Chart Shewing Part of the Coast of N.W. America with the Tracks of His Majesty's Sloop Discovery ... from Lat. of 45°30' N. & Long. 236°12' E. to Lat. 52°15' N. & Long. 232°40' E. (3 insets. Reduced size version publ. 1801 in French)
mwam1343	america north (west)	1798	VANCOUVER	1400	75	61	Cote Nord-Ouest de l'Amerique Reconnue par le Cape. Vancouver. 1e. Partie (insets: San Diego, San Francisco)
mwsam0472	south america chile	1798	VANCOUVER	160	18	23	The Town of Valparaiso on the Coast of Chili
mwaf1005	africa south	1827	VANDERMAELEN	400	47	53	Afrique No. 53 Colonie du Cap de Bonne Esperance / Afrique No. 54 Colonie du Cap de Bonne Esperance (2 maps, east and west, each 47x53cm.)
mwat0230	atlantic falkland isl.	1825	VANDERMAELEN	200	47	57	Amer. Mer. Iles Malouines ou Falkland No. 41
mwat0316	atlantic south shetland isl.	1825	VANDERMAELEN	250	47	57	Amer. Mer. No.43 Iles Shetland Meridionale
mwsam0699	south america magellan	1827	VANDERMAELEN	240	47	57	Amer. Merid. No. 42 Terre de Feu (La Maire Strait)
mwsam0646	south america guyana	1825	VANDERMAELEN	250	47	57	Amer. Merid. No. 7 Guyanes
mwca0238	canada arctic	1825	VANDERMAELEN	400	50	57	Amer. Sep. No. 3 Baie de Baffin
mwca0240	canada arctic	1827	VANDERMAELEN	300	47	53	Amer. Sep. No. 10 Detroit de Davis (Canada-Greenland)
mwca0241	canada arctic	1827	VANDERMAELEN	250	48	56	Amer. Sep. No. 17 Ile Southampton (Hudson Bay)
mwca0242	canada arctic	1827	VANDERMAELEN	300	48	56	Amer. Sep. No. 18 Detroit d'Hudson (Hudson Strait)
mwuss0044	alaska	1827	VANDERMAELEN	400	48	58	Amer. Sep. No. 21 Presqu'Il d'Alaska
mwuss0043	alaska	1827	VANDERMAELEN	400	48	58	Amer. Sep. No. 22 Partie de l'Amerique Russe (Kodiak Isl.)
mwuss0045	alaska	1827	VANDERMAELEN	400	48	58	Amer. Sep. No. 23 Partie de l'Amerique Russe
mwca0670	canada west	1825	VANDERMAELEN	600	48	57	Amer. Sep. No. 30 Isle de la Reine Charlotte
mwca0671	canada west	1825	VANDERMAELEN	800	47	57	Amer. Sep. No. 31 Partie de la Nouvelle Hanovre (incl. Vancouver Isl.)
mwca0211	canada alberta saskatchewan	1827	VANDERMAELEN	960	47	56	Amer. Sep. No. 32 Partie de la Nouvelle Bretagne
mwca0265	canada manitoba	1827	VANDERMAELEN	500	47	56	Amer. Sep. No. 33 Partie de la Nouvelle Bretagne (Lake Winnipeg area)
mwca0475	canada ontario	1825	VANDERMAELEN	400	47	57	Amer. Sep. No.34 Partie de la Nouvelle Bretagne
mwca0552	canada quebec	1825	VANDERMAELEN	400	47	57	Amer. Sep. No. 35 Partie de la Nouvelle Bretagne
mwuss1328	oregon	1827	VANDERMAELEN	550	47	52	Amer. Sep. No. 38 Partie des Etats-Unis
mwuss0331	connecticut	1825	VANDERMAELEN	550	47	51	Amer. Sep. No. 40 Partie des Etats-Unis
mwuss0934	minnesota	1827	VANDERMAELEN	600	47	52	Amer. Sep. No. 41 Partie des Etats-Unis
mwam1302	great lakes	1825	VANDERMAELEN	960	47	51	Amer. Sep. No. 42 Haut Canada et Michigan
mwam1190	america north (east)	1825	VANDERMAELEN	450	47	49	Amer. Sep. No. 43 Partie des Etats-Unis
mwuss0103	california	1827	VANDERMAELEN	500	47	57	Amer. Sep. No. 46 Nouvelle Californie
mwuss0997	nevada utah	1831	VANDERMAELEN	250	46	56	Amer. Sep. No. 47 Partie du Mexique
mwuss0290	colorado	1825	VANDERMAELEN	720	47	56	Amer. Sep. No. 48 Parties des Etats-Unis et du Nouveau Mexique
mwuss0552	illinois	1827	VANDERMAELEN	420	47	57	Amer. Sep. No. 49 Partie des Etats-Unis
mwuss0104	california	1827	VANDERMAELEN	350	47	49	Amer. Sep. No. 52 Partie de la Nouvle. Californie
mwgm0309	mexico	1827	VANDERMAELEN	500	47	53	Amer. Sep. No. 53 Partie de la Vieille Californie
mwuss0051	arizona	1827	VANDERMAELEN	500	47	49	Amer. Sep. No. 54 Partie du Mexique

AMPG REFERENCE	REGION	DATE	MAP MAKER	PRICE (UK£)	VERT. (cm.)	HOR. (cm.)	TITLE OF MAP (Comments by the editor in brackets)
mwuss0960	mississippi	1825	VANDERMAELEN	550	47	49	Amer. Sep. No. 56 Partie des Etats Unis (Mississippi and surrounding states)
mwuss0521	georgia	1827	VANDERMAELEN	550	47	49	Amer. Sep. No. 57 Partie des Etats Unis
mwuss0104b	california	1827	VANDERMAELEN	350	47	53	Amer. Sep. No. 58 Partie de la Vieille Californie
mwuss0466	florida	1827	VANDERMAELEN	900	47	49	Amer. Sep. No. 62 Florides et Iles Lucayes
mwuss0104c	california	1827	VANDERMAELEN	150	47	53	Amer. Sep. No. 63 Partie de la Vieille Californie
mwwi0486	cuba	1827	VANDERMAELEN	300	47	55	Amer. Sep. No. 67 Ile de Cuba
mwwi0682	hispaniola	1827	VANDERMAELEN	800	47	54	Amer. Sep. No. 68 Haiti ou St. Domingue
mwwi0842	puerto rico	1825	VANDERMAELEN	300	47	53	Amer. Sep. No. 69 Porto-Rico
mwgm0112	guatemala	1827	VANDERMAELEN	300	47	55	Amer. Sep. No. 71 Partie du Mexique et de Guatemala
mwas0287	asia burma	1827	VANDERMAELEN	160	47	57	Asie No. 104 Partie de l'Empire Birman
mwjk0170	korea	1827	VANDERMAELEN	400	48	57	Asie No. 60 Coree (northern part)
mwc0258	china	1827	VANDERMAELEN	600	47	53	Asie No. 98 Partie de la Chine (Hainan, Canton, Macao)
mwam0656a	america north	1827	VANDERMAELEN	220	48	57	Carte D'Assemblage De L'Amerique Septen.le (key to 76 N. American maps)
mwru0343a	russia	1825	VANDERMAELEN	300	66	54	Carte de la Russie
mwe1179a	europe south east	1830	VANDERMAELEN	350	65	55	Carte générale de la Turquie d'Europe et de la Grèce
mwin0350	india	1827	VANDERMAELEN	180	49	56	Hyderabad et Mysore
mwas0909	asia south east timor	1827	VANDERMAELEN	350	47	56	Ile Timor
mwp0322	pacific friendly isl.	1827	VANDERMAELEN	200	47	54	Iles des Amis
mwin0468	indian ocean maldives	1825	VANDERMAELEN	150	51	55	Iles Maldives et Laquedives
mwp0365	pacific marianas	1827	VANDERMAELEN	400	47	56	Iles Mariannes No. 2 / No. 5 (2 charts, no. 5 illustrated)
mwp0348	pacific hawaii	1827	VANDERMAELEN	600	49	55	Iles Sandwich
mwp0312	pacific fiji	1825	VANDERMAELEN	200	47	57	Isles Fidji
mww0697	world	1831	VANDERMAELEN	2500	104	104	Mappe-Monde en Huit Feuilles
mwaf1002	africa south	1825	VANDERMAELEN	240	51	55	Monomatapa
mwsam0571	south america galapagos	1827	VANDERMAELEN	400	49	55	Oceanique No. 17 Iles Galapagos
mwp0079	australia	1827	VANDERMAELEN	450	48	56	Oceanique No. 37 Partie de la Nouvelle Hollande (north)
mwp0080	australia	1827	VANDERMAELEN	350	48	56	Oceanique No. 38 Partie de la Nouvelle Hollande (Queensland)
mwp0081	australia	1827	VANDERMAELEN	600	48	56	Oceanique No. 45 Partie de la Nouvelle Hollande (Queensland)
mwp0082	australia	1827	VANDERMAELEN	450	47	54	Oceanique No. 54 Partie de la Nouvelle Hollande (South Australia)
mwp0083	australia	1827	VANDERMAELEN	960	48	56	Oceanique No. 55 Partie de la Nlle Galles du Sud (New South Wales)
mwp0084	australia	1827	VANDERMAELEN	600	48	58	Oceanique No. 57 Partie de la Nouvelle Hollande (Victoria and northern Tasmania)
mwp0085	australia	1827	VANDERMAELEN	450	48	53	Oceanique No. 58 Ile de Dieman (southern Tasmania)
mwru0575	ukraine	1827	VANDERMAELEN	300	48	53	Partie de la Russie No. 22
mwme0677	arabia etc	1827	VANDERMAELEN	4000	47	53	Partie de L'Arabia No. 90 (Centred on Mecca.)
mwas0673a	asia south east java	1827	VANDERMAELEN	480	47	60	Partie de L'Ile de Java (2 sheets, 46x60 and 46x56cm)
mwp0304	pacific caroline isl.	1827	VANDERMAELEN	300	47	56	Partie des Iles Carolines No. 8 / No. 9 (2 charts)
mwas0743	asia south east moluccas	1827	VANDERMAELEN	240	48	57	Partie des Isles Moluques No. 21
mwas0811	asia south east philippines	1827	VANDERMAELEN	900	48	57	Partie des Isles Philippines (in 3 sheets, each 48x57cm, nos 4,6,7. Illustrated is sheet 6.)
mwjk0138	japan	1827	VANDERMAELEN	750	48	49	Partie du Japon (3 sheets, each 48x49cm. Illustration shows environs of Jedo.)
mwuss1501	texas	1827	VANDERMAELEN	2000	47	57	Partie du Mexique (parts of Texas in 5 sheets, each 47x57cm. Nos 48,54,55,59,60)
mwsam0793b	south america peru	1827	VANDERMAELEN	200	47	54	Partie du Perou - No. 20 (shown above left)
mwsam0793a	south america peru	1827	VANDERMAELEN	200	47	54	Partie du Perou - No. 25
mwc0318	china tibet	1827	VANDERMAELEN	800	48	55	Partie du Thibet (nos 68-71. Price is for set of 4 maps)
mwaf1003	africa south	1825	VANDERMAELEN	360	47	51	Pays de Hottentots
mwas0868	asia south east singapore	1827	VANDERMAELEN	450	48	57	Presqu'Ile de Malacca No.2
mwin0487	nepal	1825	VANDERMAELEN	240	47	52	Territoire de Nepaul
mwaf1248	africa west	1827	VANDERMAELEN	120	47	53	Timbouctou
mwm0249	mediterranean malta	1784	VARIN	720	28	34	Plan Geometral de la Ville & du Port de Malte
mwam1179	america north (east)	1817	VARLE	8000	109	145	Map of the United States Partly from New Surveys Dedicated to the Citizens thereof
mwuss1393	pennsylvania	1796	VARLE	22500	46	62	To the Citizens of Philadelphia this Plan of the City and its Environs is Respectfully Dedicated
mwit0751	italy rome	1770	VASI	180	13	16	Planum Novae Urbis
mwit0750	italy rome	1765	VASI		100	256	Prospetto dell'alma Città di Roma visto dal monte Gianicolo
mwe0438a	europe austria vienna	1830	VASQUEZ	1500			Grundriss ... Wien
mwas0343	asia central	1732	VATATZIS	3000	34	39	Kharta, de is Tois Filomathesi Parekhetai Eidein Meros ti tes Asias - Charta, in qua Eruditis Spectanda Exhibetur Pars Asiae (Title in Greek script and Latin. Publ. by J. Senex)
mww0136	world	1628	VAUGHAN	1500	16	24	A New and Accurate Mappe of the World, drawn according to the best and latest discoveries that have beene made
mwas0550	asia south east	1843	VEELWAARD	280	33	65	Kaart van Nederlands Oostindische Bezittingen
mwsc0041	scandinavia	1613	VEEN	2400	44	57	Nativus Sueciae Adiacentiumque Regnorum Typus (engraved by J. Hondius)
mwg0248a	berlin	1840	VEIT	400			Grundriss von Berlin

AMPG REFERENCE	REGION	DATE	MAP MAKER	PRICE (UK£)	VERT. (cm.)	HOR. (cm.)	TITLE OF MAP (Comments by the editor in brackets)
mwas0766a	asia south east philippines	1734	VELARDE	30000	112	120	Carta Hydrographica y Chorographica de las Yslas Filipinnas (title above map. Based on a map by F. Romero and A. de Chandia, 1727)
mwgr0235a	greece	1797	VELESTINLIS	30000	200	210	(SE Europe, in Greek script, in 12 sheets. Publ. by Muller, Vienna)
mwam0287	america continent	1828	VELTEN	250	49	66	Amerika Historisch, Physisch und Politisch vom Jahr 1828
mwam0665	america north	1829	VELTEN	280	51	66	Historisch-Geographische Carte der Nordamerikanischen Freistaaten (map surrounded by text)
mwuk1120	england london	1667	VENCKEL	2000	21	29	Platte Grondt der Verbrande Stadt London
mwp0409	pacific north	1757	VENEGAS	300	23	24	Carta de la Mar del Sur, o Mar Pacifico, entre el Equador, y 39½ de Latitud Septentrional Hallada por el Almirante Jorge Anson en el Galeon de Philipinas, que Apreso
mwuss0084	california	1757	VENEGAS	3000	37	31	Mapa de la California su Golfo, y Provincias Fronteras en el Continente de Nueva Espana
mwe0610a	europe czech republic (bohemia)	1790	VENUTO	1000	96	82	Mappa Dioeceseos Reginaehradecensis in usum et commodum Venerabilis Cleridioecesani delineata
mww0138	world	1630	VERBIEST		46	57	Ampla Et Accuratissima Universi Orbis Terrarum Tabula
mwbh0257a	belgium holland	1639	VERBIEST	12500	46	56	Belgium, Sive Inferior Germania Post Omnes in hac Forma, Exactissime Descriptia … Anno. 1639 (3 carte-a-figure borders. 17 crests in lower border.)
mwbh0299	belgium holland	1648	VERBIEST	2000	44	55	Caerte figuerative van t'Ueurne Ambacht (north to the right)
mwbh0247	belgium holland	1637	VERBIEST	3000	47	55	Comitatus Flandria (carte-a-figures on all 4 borders)
mwbh0246	belgium holland	1636	VERBIEST	1000	35	40	Diocesis Episcopatus Antverpiensis
mwbh0223a	belgium holland	1630	VERBIEST	4000	47	39	Eigentlijck Beschryvinghe van de Hertogdommen van Brabant
mwbh0287	belgium holland	1644	VERBIEST	1350	40	48	Het Noorder Deel van t'Graefschap Vleandren … t'Antwerpen, Gedruckt bij Peeter Verbist op de Lombaerde Vest in America. Anno 1644
mwit0082	italy	1634	VERBIEST		41	55	Italiae Sardiniae, Corsicae, & confinium Regionum nova Tabula (3 carte-a-figure borders)
mwsp0174a	spain	1629	VERBIEST	10000	45	55	Nova Carte del Muy Podroso Reyno D'Espania
mwf0044a	france	1628	VERBIEST	9000	46	57	Nova Totius Geographica Regni Galliae Descriptio
mwf0044b	france	1628	VERBIEST	1500	36	47	Nova Totius Geographica Regni Galliae Descriptio (as previous map but with borders removed. Shown above left)
mww0145	world	1636	VERBIEST		41	56	Nova Totius Terrarum Orbis Geographica ac Hydrographi Emendata auct. I. Verbist
mwaa0005	antarctic	1637	VERBIEST		110	110	Octavii Pisani Globus Terrestris Projectus (South polar projection based on Pisani)
mwwi0254a	west indies (east)	1775	VERDUN DE LA CRENNE	685	88	55	Carte Reduite des Iles Antilles au Nord du 13me Degre de Latitude … Publiee par Ordre de Roi. Par M'rs de Verdun de la Crenne, le Chevalier de Borda, et Pingre 1775 / Carte Reduite des Debouquements de St. Domingue
mwat0282	atlantic north	1776	VERDUN DE LA CRENNE	900	56	79	Carte Reduite des Mers du Nord (size excl. right-hand text border. Also found without the 3 ships.)
mwam0354	america north	1702	VERDUSSEN	960	32	41	L'Amerique Septentrionale
mwbh0567	belgium holland	1718	VERMEY	800	46	54	Naeukeurige Nieuwe Land-Caert des Graefschaps Zeeland
mwf0239a	france alsace	1730	WERNER-WOLFF	1200	30	104	Strasburg (panoramic view)
mwwi0511	dominica	1778	VERRIER	550	60	47	La Dominique Prise pas les Francois le 8 Septembre 1778
mwam1060	america north (east)	1778	VERRIER	4000	51	72	Partie Septentrionale des Possessions Angloise en Amerique, pour Servire d'Intelligence a la Guerre Presente entre les Anglois et leur Colonies … Traduite de l'Angloise / Partie Meridionale des Possessions Angloise en Amerique (2 maps, each 51x72cm.)
mwme0070	holy land	1611	VESCONTE-BONGARS	450	14	20	Civitas Acon sive Ptolomayda (copy of Vesconti's c1320 manuscript plan of Acre)
mww0122	world	1611	VESCONTE-BONGARS	3500	33		(Untitled circular map reproduced from Vesconte's c1320 manuscript atlas.)
mwm0118	mediterranean east	1611	VESCONTE-WECHELIUS	960	31	26	(Untitled map reproduced from Vesconte's manuscript map of c1320)
mwme0069	holy land	1611	VESCONTE-WECHELIUS	2000	16	38	(Untitled map reproduced from Vesconte's manuscript map of c1320, the forerunner of modern maps of Palestine)
mwme0446	jerusalem	1611	VESCONTE-WECHELIUS	785	26	19	(Untitled plan of Jerusalem, copied from Vesconte's drawing of c1320)
mwaa0177	arctic / antarctic	1524	VESPUCCI		28	38	Totius Orbis Descriptio … 1524 (only one example known)
mwf0201	france	1844	VIARD	400	60	67	Carte speciale des Postes de France
mwsc0649	scandinavia norway	1844	VIBE & IRGENS	3000	61	56	(Oslo) Kart over Christiania med en Kvadratmiil af Omegnen Sammendraget efter de Nyeste og Paalideligste Materialer
mwgm0302	mexico	1825	VICTORIA	900	89	56	Carta Esferica de las Costas y Golfo de Californias Llamado Mar de Cortes (Publ. in Mexico City)
mwp0463	pacific north	1825	VICTORIA	1200	65	142	Carta General para las Navegaciones a la India Oriental por el Mar del Sur y el Grande Oceano que Separa el Continente Americano de Asiatico (Publ. in Mexico City)
mwuss0100	california	1825	VICTORIA	750	33	47	Plano de la Bahia de Montery Situado en la California Septentrional (Publ. in Mexico City)

AMPG REFERENCE	REGION	DATE	MAP MAKER	PRICE (UK£)	VERT. (cm.)	HOR. (cm.)	TITLE OF MAP (Comments by the editor in brackets)
mwuss0101	california	1825	VICTORIA	750	47	33	Plano del Puerto de San Diego de la California Septentrional / Plano del Puerto de St. Blas (Publ. in Mexico City)
mwgm0303	mexico	1825	VICTORIA	550	57	91	Plano del Puerto de Vera-Cruz (Publ. in Mexico City)
mwit1252	italy venice	1799	VIERO	1600	48	63	La Veneta Laguna antica e moderna
mwit1257	italy venice	1816	VIERO	450	54	60	Nuova Pianta Iconografica dell'Inclita Citta di Venezia
mwf0162a	france	1790	VIGNON	650	122	115	Carte de la France suivant sa nouvelle division en departements et districts. Dediée a l'Assemblée Nationale
mwme0453	jerusalem	1650	VILLALPANDO	4000	35	41	Andere Abriess der Stadt Jerusalem
mwme0443	jerusalem	1604	VILLALPANDO	3500	69	75	Vera Hierosolymae Veteris Imago
mwm0176	mediterranean malta	1600	VILLAMENA	2000	33	44	Valletta Citta Nova di Malta
mwf0923	france paris	1836	VILLEDIEU	750	59	78	Nouveau Plan de la Ville de Paris Divise en Douze Arrondissements avec Tous les Changemens et Edifices Publics
mwit0437	italy liguria	1747	VINZONI	2000	59	44	Tipo Dimostrativo di Genova Assediata dalle Truppe Austro-Sarde, e Dalle Navi Inglesi. L'Anno MDCCXLVII
mwp0127	australia	1840	VIRTUE	200	20	24	Australia
mwca0188	canada	1840	VIRTUE	80	19	25	Canada
mwwi0218	west indies	1848	VIRTUE	80	23	30	Central America, and the West Indies
mwuk1315	england london	1833	VIRTUE	480	42	66	Improved Map of London for 1833, from Actual Survey (4 editions until 1843)
mwam1244	america north (east)	1840	VIRTUE	120	18	24	The North Eastern Part of the United States
mwe0328	europe austria	1669	VISCHER G.M.	8000	184	174	Archiducatus Austriae Superioris Geographica Descriptio facta Anno 1667 (12-sheet map. A smaller 16-sheet map of Lower Austria was issued in 1669, size 122x175cm).
mwbh0489a	belgium holland	1700	VISSCHER, F.	650	28	40	Plan de Bruxelles (date unknown)
mwbh0224	belgium holland	1630	VISSCHER	1200	46	55	(Antwerp) Marchionatus Sacri Romani Imperii
mwbh0202b	belgium holland	1620	VISSCHER	3500	44	55	XVII Provinciarum Inferior Germaniae
mwuk0943	england	1685	VISSCHER	850	58	50	A New Mapp of the Kingdome of England ... Princedome of Wales ... other Provinces, Cities, Market Towns, with the Roads from Town to Town (publ. by Overton)
mwe1062a	europe serbia	1716	VISSCHER	900	48	77	Accurate Kaart van't Land Belgrado, Temeswar en Peterwardein... 1716
mwuk1424	england thames	1667	VISSCHER	1500	20	29	Afbeeldinge vande Rivieren van London en Rochester (size excl. text panel below map)
mwgr0404	greece crete	1670	VISSCHER	720	42	50	Afbeeldinghe der Stercke Stadt Candia, voor de Derdemael van 't Ottomannische Heyr Belegert, en Verweert door die vande Doorlucht: Rep: van Venetien (Plan of Candia-Heraklion)
mwaf0063	africa	1658	VISSCHER	1500	44	55	Africae Accurata Tabula ex Officina Nic. Visscher
mwaf0047	africa	1631	VISSCHER	7200	45	57	Africae Nova Descr. per Nicolaum Io. Visscher (re-issue of Van Den Keere's 1614 map. Four carte-a-figure borders.)
mwsw0048	switzerland	1625	VISSCHER	1600	41	53	Alpinae seu Foederatae Rhaetiae Subditarumque ei Terrarum Nova Descriptio
mwam0056	america continent	1652	VISSCHER	16000	44	56	Americae Nova Descriptio (re-issue of Van Den Keere's 1614 map)
mwbh0383	belgium holland	1670	VISSCHER	1350	49	57	Amstelodami Veteris et Novissimae Urbis Accuratissima Delineatio
mwbh0199a	belgium holland	1618	VISSCHER	40000	94	83	Amstelodamum Urbs Hollandiae Primaria (bird's eye plan in 4 sheets. Revised version of Pieter Bast's map of 1597).
mwuk0961	england	1695	VISSCHER	720	56	49	Angliae Regnum Tam in Septem Antiqua Anglo-Saxonum Regna
mwas0067	asia continent	1680	VISSCHER	1000	43	54	Asiae Nova Delineatio
mwas0043	asia continent	1652	VISSCHER	6000	45	57	Asiae Nova Descriptio (re-issue of Van Den Keere's 1614 map)
mwe0329a	europe austria	1680	VISSCHER	400	46	59	Austriae Archiducatus Pars Inferior
mwe0326	europe austria	1660	VISSCHER	300	47	57	Austriae Archiducatus Pars Superior
mwbh0208	belgium holland	1624	VISSCHER	450	38	50	Belgii Veteris Typus. Ex Conatibus Geographicis Abrahami Ortelij
mwbh0426	belgium holland	1680	VISSCHER	480	47	56	Belgium Foederatum
mwbh0207	belgium holland	1622	VISSCHER	3500	47	56	Brabantia Ducatus (4 carte-a-figure borders)
mwbh0454	belgium holland	1690	VISSCHER	450	58	46	Bruxellensis Tetrarchia
mwbh0207a	belgium holland	1622	VISSCHER	1500	38	42	Caerte van t'Vrye sijnde een Gedeelte en Lidt van Vlaenderen (illustrated above left)
mwaf0895	africa south	1710	VISSCHER	1350	51	58	Carte de l'Afrique Meridionale ou Pays entre la Ligne & le Cap de Bonne Esperance et l'Isle de Madagascar
mwsam0226	south america argentina	1710	VISSCHER	750	52	60	Carte du Paraguay, du Chili, Detroit de Magellan, & Terre de Feu: Dans l'Amerique Meridionale (2 insets: Antarctic, Magellan)
mwf0582	france ile de france	1700	VISSCHER	500	58	49	Carte Particuliere du Terroir et des Environs des Paris
mwbh0202a	belgium holland	1620	VISSCHER	6000	44	54	Carte vande Vereenichde Nederlanden Mitsgaders de Landen
mwsp0463	spain regions	1680	VISSCHER	580	48	58	Cataloniae Principatus, nec non Ruscinonensis et Cerretanae Comitatus
mwbh0204a	belgium holland	1621	VISSCHER	4000	46	56	Comitatus Flandria. t'Amsterdam Gedruckt by Claes Janss Visscher inde Calverstraet in de Visscher (4 carte-a-figure borders)

AMPG REFERENCE	REGION	DATE	MAP MAKER	PRICE (UK£)	VERT. (cm.)	HOR. (cm.)	TITLE OF MAP (Comments by the editor in brackets)
mwbh0331a	belgium holland	1656	VISSCHER	15000	165	216	Comitatus Flandriae Summa Cura Recens Delineatus
mwbh0223b	belgium holland	1630	VISSCHER	6000	47	57	Comitatus Hollandia
mwbh0204b	belgium holland	1622	VISSCHER	60000	47	56	Comitatus Hollandiae Denuo Forma Leonis Curiose Editus (Leo Belgicus)
mwbh0245a	belgium holland	1636	VISSCHER	5000	47	57	Comitatus Zelandiae
mwbh0384a	belgium holland	1670	VISSCHER	650	46	54	Comitatus Zelandiae Novissima (illustrated is Covens & Mortier re-issue, with title below cartouche 'Comitatus Zelandiae Tabula')
mwme0961	turkey etc	1680	VISSCHER	350	22	28	Constantinopel (view)
mwbp0263	poland	1659	VISSCHER	400	22	28	Cracov (view)
mwgr0418	greece crete	1690	VISSCHER	960	50	58	Cretae seu Candiae Insula et Regnum, cum Diversis aliis Archipelagi Insulis
mwsc0258	scandinavia denmark	1630	VISSCHER	3000	47	55	Daniae Regni Typum (4 carte-a-figure borders. Except for a different cartouche, copied from Jansson 1630)
mwbp0258	poland	1650	VISSCHER	200	21	28	Dantzig (view)
mwme0102	holy land	1642	VISSCHER	500	31	48	De Gelegentheyt van t'Paradys ende t'Landt Canaan, Mitsgaders de Eerst Bewoonde Landen der Patriarchen (from a Dutch bible)
mwme0449a	jerusalem	1643	VISSCHER	800	32	48	De Heylige en Wytvermaerde Stadt Ierusalem Eerst Genaemt Salem Genesis 14, Vers 18 (from a Dutch bible)
mwit0583	italy north	1690	VISSCHER	600	59	74	De Stoel des Oorlogs in Italien Waar in Vertoont Werden de Staat van Milano
mwme0299	holy land	1736	VISSCHER	450	38	50	Die Gegend des Irdischen Paradieses und des Landes Canaan
mwbh0211	belgium holland	1627	VISSCHER	5000	47	56	Ducatus Geldriae nec non Comitatus Zutphaniae (4 carte-a-figure borders)
mwg0699	schleswig-holstein	1630	VISSCHER	2500	45	55	Ducatus Holsatiae, Summa Diligentia Accurataq Censura Noviter Editus (4 carte-a-figure borders)
mwbh0835	luxembourg	1660	VISSCHER	850	46	56	Ducatus Lutzenburgi Novissima et accuratissima Delineatio
mwgr0093	greece	1680	VISSCHER	1200	46	56	Ellas seu Graecia Universa
mwe0080	europe	1670	VISSCHER	850	43	54	Europa Delineata et Recens Edita
mwaf0089a	africa	1681	VISSCHER		150	180	Exacta Totius Africae Tabula
mwsw0076	switzerland	1658	VISSCHER	400	46	56	Exactissima Helvetiae, Rhaetiae, Valesiae
mwuk0453	scotland	1700	VISSCHER	875	58	48	Exactissima Regni Scotiae Tabula tam in Septentrionalem et Meridionalem
mwe0708	europe danube	1680	VISSCHER	1350	48	58	Exactissima Tabula qua tam Danubii Fluvii Pars Inferior / Pars Media / Pars Superior (3 sheets, each 48c58cm. Sheet 1 illustrated)
mwgr0094	greece	1680	VISSCHER	1500	47	57	Exactissima Totius Archipelagi nec non Graeciae Tabula in qua Omnes Subjacentes Regiones
mwsc0072	scandinavia	1677	VISSCHER	800	43	53	Exactissima Totius Scandinaviae Tabula, qua tam Sueciae, Daniae, et Norvegiae Regna
mwbh0426b	belgium holland	1680	VISSCHER	480	49	55	Flandriae Comitatus Pars Batava
mwbh0426a	belgium holland	1680	VISSCHER	480	49	55	Flandriae Comitatus Pars Occidentalis
mwf0043	france	1625	VISSCHER	8000	47	55	France - Nova Haec Tabula Galliae (some later editions had changed borders. See 1660)
mwf0071	france	1680	VISSCHER	450	47	57	Gallia vulgo la France
mwm0124	mediterranean east	1650	VISSCHER	600	30	48	Geographische Beschryvinge van de Wandeling der Apostelen ende de Reysen Pauli (from a Dutch bible)
mwme0101	holy land	1642	VISSCHER	500	30	47	Geographische Beschryvinge van t'Beloofde-Landt Canaan (from a Dutch bible)
mwg0084	germany	1690	VISSCHER	550	48	55	Germaniae Generalis Tabula
mwg0042	germany	1621	VISSCHER		46	56	Germaniae Nova ac accurata descriptio (4 carte-a-figure decorative borders. See Hondius 1625)
mwbp0233	poland	1630	VISSCHER	5500	47	54	Haec Tabula Nova Poloniae et Silesiae
mwsam0284	south america brazil	1630	VISSCHER	3000	36	47	Hanc Tabulam Continens Laetam Pharnambuci Victoriam
mwme0147	holy land	1657	VISSCHER	400	32	47	Het Beloofde Landt Canaan door Wandelt van onsen Salichmaecker Iesu Christo, neffens syne Apostelen
mwuk0109	ireland	1690	VISSCHER	1500	56	47	Hiberniae Regnum tam in Praecipuas Ultoniae, Connaciae, Lageniae, et Momoniae
mwsp0198	spain	1680	VISSCHER	650	46	56	Hispaniae et Portugalliae Regna
mwbh0384	belgium holland	1670	VISSCHER	480	46	57	Hollandiae Pars Meridionalior vulgo Zuyd-Holland
mwas0400a	asia south east	1670	VISSCHER	1350	47	57	Indiae Orientalis nec non Insularum Adiacentium Nova Descriptio (illustration shows second state c1690)
mwgr0409	greece crete	1680	VISSCHER	1000	41	51	Insula Candia olim Creta (view of Candia and map of the Island on one sheet)
mwin0024	ceylon	1680	VISSCHER	1100	50	59	Insula Ceilon olim Taprobana Incolis Tenarisin et Lankawn Exactissime Delineata (illustrated is Schenk re-issue)
mwwi0766	martinique	1657	VISSCHER	800	47	57	Insula Matanino vulgo Martanico in Lucem Edita
mwwi0028	west indies	1677	VISSCHER	1800	46	56	Insulae Americanae in Oceano Septentrionali
mwm0196	mediterranean malta	1670	VISSCHER	1500	53	63	Insularum Melitae vulgo Maltae et Gozae Novissima Delineatio
mwwi0698	jamaica	1680	VISSCHER	950	52	60	Jamaica, Americae Septentrionalis Ampla Insula, Christophoro Columbo Detecta, in suas Gubernationes Peraccuratae Distincta
mwbh0215	belgium holland	1629	VISSCHER	875	27	36	Kaerte van Bergen op zoom

AMPG REFERENCE	REGION	DATE	MAP MAKER	PRICE (UK£)	VERT. (cm.)	HOR. (cm.)	TITLE OF MAP (Comments by the editor in brackets)
mwsc0106	scandinavia	1706	VISSCHER	2500	59	73	La Scandie. Ou les Trois Royaumes du Nord Suede, Danemarc & Norvege … la Veuve de Nicolas Visscher (publ. by Elizabeth Visscher)
mwf1033	france provence	1700	VISSCHER	550	47	56	La Ville et Havre de Toulon avec ses Forts - De Stadt Toulon
mwsp0495	spain regions	1704	VISSCHER	785	40	53	Le Plan de Barcelonne et de ses Environs
mwf0851	france paris	1720	VISSCHER	1200	55	75	Le Plan de Paris ses Faubourgs et ses Environs
mwbh0426c	belgium holland	1680	VISSCHER	400	46	57	Leodiensis Episcopatus
mwbh0822	luxembourg	1625	VISSCHER	2000	37	48	Lutzenburgensis Ducatus Veriss. Descript. Iacobo Suhonio Montano Auct (engraved by P. Kaerius)
mwbh0841	luxembourg	1688	VISSCHER	600	48	58	Luxemburgensis Ducatus, tam in Ejusdem Minores
mwuk0728	uk	1670	VISSCHER	1250	45	53	Magnae Britanniae Tabula, Angliam, Scotiam, Et Hiberniam continens
mwuk0758	uk	1694	VISSCHER	960	46	56	Magnae Britanniae Tabula; Comprehendens Angliae, Scotiae, ac Hiberniae Regna
mwbp0320	poland	1690	VISSCHER	600	43	52	Magnae Prussiae Ducatus Tabula
mwme0565	arabia etc	1677	VISSCHER	1650	51	85	Magni Turcarum Domini Imperium in Europa, Asia, et Africa
mwuk1473	uk english channel (all)	1680	VISSCHER	875	48	57	Manica, Gallis la Manche, et Belgis het Canaal, Pars Oceani inter Angliam et Galliam
mwbh0209	belgium holland	1624	VISSCHER	650	37	49	Mechlinia
mwe1106	europe slovak republic (moravia)	1692	VISSCHER	2800	104	126	Moravia Marchionatus Perlustratus & Delineatus
mwe1096a	europe slovak republic (moravia)	1633	VISSCHER	2000	45	55	Moraviae Nova et Post Omnes Priores Accuratissima Delineatio, Auctore J.A. Comenio (4 city views along top border)
mwru0083	russia	1680	VISSCHER	650	42	53	Moscoviae seu Russiae Magnae Generalis Tabula (incl. Scandinavia)
mwbh0620	belgium holland	1730	VISSCHER	2250	48	58	Nieuwe Kaart van t' Baljuwschap van Kennemerland met de Bannen van Westsaanen, Assendelft, Heemskerk, Wyk aan Duyn, Velsen, Spaarwoude &c.
mwg0356	bavaria	1710	VISSCHER	480	39	48	Nieuwe Kaart, van t'Land Donawert, en Hochstett &c. alwaar de Roemwaardige Battaille, Zyn voor Gevallen door den Hartog van Marlebourg
mwaf1127	africa west	1670	VISSCHER	785	43	57	Nigritarum Regnum
mwru0488a	ukraine	1680	VISSCHER	600	48	58	Nouvelle Carte de la Mer Noire, et du Canal de Constantinople (inset: Constantinople)
mwru0488b	ukraine	1680	VISSCHER	450	48	58	Nouvelle Carte Geographique de la Mer d'Asof ou de Zebache; & des Palus Meotides
mwru0127	russia	1710	VISSCHER	960	50	70	Nouvelle Carte Geographique du Grande Royaume de Moscovie
mwsp0184	spain	1660	VISSCHER	4000	47	57	Nova et Accurata Tabula Hispaniae (4 carte-a-figure borders)
mwe0061	europe	1652	VISSCHER	5500	44	56	Nova Europae Descriptio (re-issue of Van Den Keere's 1614 map with minor decorative changes)
mwf0065	france	1660	VISSCHER	4800	46	55	Nova Haec Tabula Galliae (4 carte-a-figure borders)
mwsw0137	switzerland	1739	VISSCHER	3200	93	113	Nova Helvetiae Tabula Geographica: Illustrissimis et Potentissimis Cantonibus et Rebuspublicis Reformatae Religionis (re-issue of Scheuchzer's 1711 map)
mwam0886	america north (east)	1685	VISSCHER	2250	59	47	Nova Tabula Geographica Complectens Borealiorem Americae Partem: in qua Exacte Delineatae sunt Canada sive Nova Francia, Nova Scotia, Nova Anglia, Novum Belgium, Pensylvania / Carte Nouvelle Contenant la Partie d'Amerique la Plus Septentrionale (2 sheets, each 59x47cm. Illustrated joined.)
mww0149	world	1639	VISSCHER	30000	45	57	Nova Totius Terrarum Orbis Geographica Ac Hydrographica Tabula … N.L. Piscator (4 carte-a-figure borders)
mwg0798	westphalia	1656	VISSCHER	350	41	56	Nova Totius Westphaliae
mwam0895	america north (east)	1690	VISSCHER	8500	46	55	Novi Belgii Novaeque Angliae nec non Partis Virginiae Tabula Multis in Locis Emendata
mwbh0182a	belgium holland	1611	VISSCHER	65000	48	58	Novissima et Accuratissima Leonis Belgici
mwam0060	america continent	1658	VISSCHER	2000	43	54	Novissima et Accuratissima Totius Americae Descriptio per N. Visscher (later state illustrated)
mwbh0355	belgium holland	1660	VISSCHER	650	47	57	Novissima et Accuratissima XVII Provinciarum Germaniae Inferioris Delineatio
mww0209	world	1679	VISSCHER	6000	43	53	Novissima Totius Terrarum Orbis Tabula, Auctore Nicolao Visscher
mww0169	world	1658	VISSCHER	6500	47	56	Orbis Terrarum Nova et Accuratissima Tabula
mww0181	world	1663	VISSCHER	2500	31	47	Orbis Terrarum Tabula Recens Emendata et in Lucem Edita Per N. Visscher (California as a peninsula)
mww0423	world	1752	VISSCHER	1500	31	47	Orbis Terrarum Tabula Recens Emendata et in Lucem Edita Per N. Visscher (re-issue of Visscher 1663)
mww0124	world	1614	VISSCHER		51	62	Orbis Terrarum Typus de Integro in Plurimis Emendatus, Auctus, et Icunculis Illustratus
mww0165	world	1657	VISSCHER	3500	31	48	Orbis Terrarum Typus de Integro in Plurimus Emendatus, Auctus, et Icunculis Illustratus (from a Dutch bible)

AMPG REFERENCE	REGION	DATE	MAP MAKER	PRICE (UK£)	VERT. (cm.)	HOR. (cm.)	TITLE OF MAP (Comments by the editor in brackets)
mww0146a	world	1638	VISSCHER	35000	44	56	Orbis Terrarum Typus De Integro Multis in Locis (illustrated is the close copy by A. de Fer, 1645)
mwg0519	rheinland-pfalz	1652	VISSCHER	1500	45	56	Palatinatus Rheni Nova et Accurata Descriptio (4 carte-a-figure borders)
mwsam0286	south america brazil	1634	VISSCHER	500	14	36	Pascaert van Ghelegentheyt van Parnambuc Betrocken door Hessel Gerritsz.
mwgr0129	greece	1700	VISSCHER	650	46	55	Peloponnesus hodie Morea
mwgr0090	greece	1677	VISSCHER	4000	55	83	Peloponnesus hodie Morea (with 16 town views/plans along 3 borders)
mwme0104	holy land	1645	VISSCHER	500	33	48	Perigrinatie ofte Veertich-Iarige Reyse der Kinderen Israels, uyt Egypten door de Roode Zee, ende de Woestyne tot in't Beloofde Landt Canaan
mwme0151	holy land	1660	VISSCHER	450	33	48	Perigrinatie ofte Veertich-Iarige Reyse der Kinderen Israels, uyt Egypten door de Roode Zee, ende de Woestyne tot in't Beloofde Landt Canaan
mwbh0543	belgium holland	1710	VISSCHER	960	66	96	Plan de la Grande & Fameuse Ville Machande d'Amsterdam
mwf1044	france provence	1710	VISSCHER	785	56	89	Plan Geometral de la Ville ... de Marseille
mwsp0059	portugal	1690	VISSCHER	650	46	56	Portugalliae et Algarbiae Regna
mwf1142a	france rhone-alpes	1698	VISSCHER	600	58	49	Regiae Celsitudinis Sabaudicae Status
mwsc0301	scandinavia denmark	1680	VISSCHER	600	46	55	Regni Daniae Novissima et Accuratissima Tabula
mwsc0697	scandinavia sweden	1696	VISSCHER	650	42	53	Regni Gothiae Tabula
mwsp0496	spain regions	1704	VISSCHER	1800	98	122	Regnorum Castilliae Veteris Legionis et Gallaeciae Principatuumq Biscaiae et Asturiarum - Regnorum Castelliae Novae Andalusiae Granadae Valentiae
mwsp0060a	portugal	1698	VISSCHER	900	68	50	Regnorum Portugalliae et Algarbiae (close copy of Placide 1695)
mwe0555	europe czech republic (bohemia)	1710	VISSCHER	550	50	58	Regnum Bohemia etque Annexae Provinciae ut Ducatus Silesiae Marchionatus Moraviae et Lusatiae vulgo die Erb-Landeren
mwe0915	europe hungary	1700	VISSCHER	480	48	57	Regnum Hungariae in Omnes suos Comitatus Accurate Divisum et Editum
mwit0898	italy sicily	1680	VISSCHER	750	46	56	Regnum Siciliae cum Circumjacentibus Regnis et Insulis
mwbh0425a	belgium holland	1680	VISSCHER	480	46	56	Rhenolandia, Amstelandia
mwg0084a	germany	1690	VISSCHER	240	47	56	S. Imperium Romano-Germanicum oder Teutschland mit seinen angräntzenden Königreichen und Provincien
mwg0345d	bavaria	1680	VISSCHER	350	57	46	S.R.I. Bavariae Circulus atq. Electoratus
mwbp0305	poland	1682	VISSCHER	450	47	57	Serenissimo, Celsissimo ac Invictissimo Principi, Frederico Guilielmo ... Pomeraniae Ducatus Tabulam
mwf0224a	france alsace	1680	VISSCHER	500	47	56	Superioris Alsatiae nec non Brisigaviae
mwbh0331	belgium holland	1656	VISSCHER	875	47	63	t Meerderdeel van 't Oost-Vrye in Vlaenderen
mwg0411a	brandenburg	1633	VISSCHER	1000	45	55	Tabula Electoratus Brandenburgici, Meckelenburgi et Maximae Partis Pomeraniae (4 city views, top and bottom)
mwsc0046	scandinavia	1630	VISSCHER	1200	46	55	Tabula Exactissima Regnorum Sueciae et Norvegiae
mwbh211a	belgium holland	1628	VISSCHER	5000	46	56	Tabula Frisiae, Groninghae, et Territory Embdensis (city views, top and bottom)
mwg0054	germany	1640	VISSCHER	600	48	55	Tabula Germaniae
mwit0073a	italy	1625	VISSCHER	7200	46	55	Tabula Italiae, Corsicae, Sardinae, et Adjacentium Regnorum (4 carte-a-figure borders. Re-issued 1630, 1633 and 1652)
mwuk0690	uk	1623	VISSCHER	20000	47	55	Tabula Magnae Britanniae continens Angliam Scotiam et Hiberniam (Carte-a-figures on all borders)
mwuk1474	uk english channel (all)	1680	VISSCHER	720	47	56	Tabula Nova Complectens Praefecturas Normanniae et Britanniae
mwme0983	turkey etc	1700	VISSCHER	785	44	55	Tabula Nova Geographica Natoliae et Asiae Minoris, Accuratissime Composita per Jacobum Cantelli
mwbp0306	poland	1682	VISSCHER	800	42	56	Tabula Nova Totius Regni Poloniae.
mwbp0235a	poland	1633	VISSCHER	1000	45	54	Tabula Prussiae (inset of Konigsberg)
mwru0050	russia	1651	VISSCHER	1500	43	54	Tabula Russiae ex Mandato Foedor Borissowits Delineata (5 insets)
mwme0150	holy land	1659	VISSCHER	785	46	55	Terra Sancta, sive Promissionis, olim Palestina Recens Delineata, et in Lucem Edita
mwg0065	germany	1660	VISSCHER		123	140	Totius Germaniae Accuratissima Tabula
mwit0100	italy	1664	VISSCHER	800	46	56	Totius Italiae Tabula
mwe0768b	europe east	1680	VISSCHER	900	43	80	Totius Regni Hungariae et Adjacentium Regionum Tabula (below is the same map with the title 'Totius Regni Hungariae, Maxim aeque Partis ...')
mwg0218c	germany north west	1622	VISSCHER	1500	39	49	Typus Frisiae Orientalis (Title text lower left. Revised version of Van Den Keere 1617. Shown above left)
mwsp0695	gibraltar	1706	VISSCHER-SCHENK	960	43	52	Plan de la Ville de Gibraltar
mwca0150	canada	1825	VIVIEN	160	27	46	Carte de la Partie Septentrionale du Nouveau Monde ou sont Comprises les Possessions Anglaises de l'Amerique du Nord
mwsam0553	south america colombia	1834	VIVIEN	140	32	46	Carte de la Republique de Colombie Gravee par Giraldon Bovinet
mwe1177a	europe south east	1826	VIVIEN	240	50	40	Carte de la Turquie d'Europe et de la Grece
mwsam0145	south america	1825	VIVIEN	100	40	30	Carte de l'Amerique Meridionale

AMPG REFERENCE	REGION	DATE	MAP MAKER	PRICE (UK£)	VERT. (cm.)	HOR. (cm.)	TITLE OF MAP (Comments by the editor in brackets)
mwbp0562	poland	1824	VIVIEN	80	28	34	Carte du Nouveau Royaume de Pologne
mwaf0728	africa north	1834	VIVIEN	100	25	44	Carte d'une Partie de l'Afrique Septentrionale
mwme0675	arabia etc	1824	VIVIEN	200	46	58	Carte Generale de la Turquie d'Asie
mwc0256	china	1826	VIVIEN	160	29	46	Carte Generale de l'Empire Chinois
mwsam0425	south america brazil	1834	VIVIEN	140	36	30	Carte Generale de l'Empire du Bresil
mwit0244	italy	1834	VIVIEN	160	48	43	Carte Generale de l'Italie
mwgm0324	mexico	1834	VIVIEN	200	31	41	Carte Generale des Etats Unis de l'Amerique Septentrionale
mwgm0325	mexico	1834	VIVIEN	200	30	41	Carte Generale du Mexique et des Provinces-Unies de l'Amerique Centrale ou Guatemala
mwaf0562	africa egypt etc	1834	VIVIEN	100	43	29	Carte Particular de l'Egypte
mwwi0193	west indies	1834	VIVIEN	140	29	41	Carte Particuliere des Antilles et du Golfe du Mexique avec l'Isthme de Panama
mwgr0256	greece	1834	VIVIEN	100	30	38	Graecia Antiqua
mwe0556	europe czech republic (bohemia)	1712	VOGT	2000	68	88	Nova Totius Regni Boemiae Tabula
mwit0903	italy sicily	1683	VOLCKAMER	720	19	28	Sicilia
mwf0898	france paris	1787	VOLKMANN	800	53	76	Neuester Grundris der Stadt und Vorstaedte von Paris 1787
mwme0884a	syria etc	1787	VOLNEY	300			Carte de la Syrie apellee en Arabe Bar-El-Cham
mwaf0525a	africa egypt etc	1787	VOLNEY	180			Carte de L'Egypte appellee en Arabe Barr Masr
mwam1146	america north (east)	1803	VOLNEY	350	42	55	Carte des Etats-Unis de l'Amerique-Nord pour Servir au Tableau du Climat et du Sol par C.F. Volney
mwbh0108	belgium holland	1583	VON AITZING	12000	37	44	(Leo Belgicus) Leo Belg IC V S (Von Aitzing or Aitzinger created the Leo Belgicus)
mwbh0134	belgium holland	1596	VON AITZING	300	22	31	(Nijmegen view) Novo Magum
mwbh0135	belgium holland	1596	VON AITZING	400	23	29	Antwerpiae Nobiliss Totius Orbis Terrarum (view)
mwbh0087a	belgium holland	1580	VON AITZING	400	15	19	Flandria
mwe0229	europe	1797	VON BERKEN	3000	203	225	Carte de l'Europe Dediee a son Altesse Royale Monseigneur Charles Louis Archiduc d'Austriche, Prince Royal de Hongrie, et de Boheme (in 25 sheets)
mwe0487	europe croatia	1486	VON BREYDENBACH	1200	27	40	(Porec) Parenzo
mwme0007	holy land	1486	VON BREYDENBACH	45000	28	128	(Untitled modern map of the Holy Land. Inset: Jerusalem. North to the left.)
mwit1202a	italy venice	1486	VON BREYDENBACH	15000	27	164	(wood cut view)
mwgr0334	greece crete	1486	VON BREYDENBACH	3000	25	78	Candia (view)
mwgr0290	greece corfu	1486	VON BREYDENBACH	4000	25	41	Corfun (view of the city)
mwgr0515	greece rhodes	1486	VON BREYDENBACH	3000	25	78	Rhodis
mwaf0577a	africa islands bourbon	1849	VON CLOUE	800	60	88	Carte des Côtes de l'Ile de la Réunion
mwm0143a	mediterranean east	1721	VON ERLACH	400	30	41	Allgemeine Landcarte
mwbp0550	poland	1808	VON HELDENSFELD	960	198	178	Carte von West-Gallizien
mwgm0273	mexico	1810	VON HUMBOLDT	750	41	29	A Map of New Spain from 16.° to 38.° North Latitude Reduced from the Large Map Drawn from Astronomical Observations at Mexico in the Year 1804, by Alexandre de Humboldt, and Comprehending the Whole of that Information Contained in the Original Map
mwgm0280	mexico	1812	VON HUMBOLDT	1000	55	47	Carte de la Route qui Mene depuis la Capitale de la Nouvelle Espagne jusqu'a S. Fe du Nouveau Mexique
mwsam0188	south america (north)	1817	VON HUMBOLDT	360	23	50	Carte du Cours de Rio Meta et d'une Partie de la Chaine Orientale des Montagnes de la Nouvelle Grenade
mwsam0186	south america (north)	1813	VON HUMBOLDT	480	30	61	Carte du Cours du Rio Apure et d'une Partie de la Chaine des Montagnes de la Nouvelle Grenade
mwsam0187	south america (north)	1816	VON HUMBOLDT	280	27	20	Carte du Rio Caura et des Missions qui ont ete Etablies sur ses Bords
mwgm0274	mexico	1810	VON HUMBOLDT	10000	100	69	Carte Generale du Royaume de la Nouvelle Espagne depuis le Paralleles de 16 jusqu'au Parallele de 38 (Latitude Nord) Dressee sur des Observations Astronomique et sur l'Ensemble des Materiaux qui Existoient a Mexico...l'Annee 1804 (in 2 sheets)
mwgm0269	mexico	1807	VON HUMBOLDT	875	22	62	Carte Reduite de la Partie Orientale de la Nouvelle-Espagne depuis le Plateau de la Ville de Mexico jusqu'au Port de la Veracruz
mwgm0280a	mexico	1812	VON HUMBOLDT	500	17	19	Plan du Port d'Acapulco ... 1791
mwgm0270	mexico	1807	VON HUMBOLDT	400	22	29	Plan du Port de Veracruz
mwp0274	pacific (all)	1820	VON KOTZEBUE	1000	53	44	Carte du Grand Ocean pour Servir au Voyage de M.O. de Kotzebue autour du Monde de 1815 a 1818
mwp0461	pacific north	1821	VON KOTZEBUE	300	20	20	Chart of Behring's Strait, upon Mercator's Projection
mwp0462	pacific north	1825	VON KOTZEBUE	1000	38	39	Charte von der Behrings Strasse
mwp0371	pacific marshall isl	1820	VON KOTZEBUE	550	43	69	Plan der Insel-Gruppe Romanzoff
mwp0341	pacific hawaii	1823	VON KOTZEBUE	6000	65	116	Ploskaio Karta ... Ganaruru (first printed plan of Honolulu harbour)
mwam0640	america north	1824	VON LILIENSTERN	300	34	45	Freistaat von Nordamerica
mww0675a	world	1825	VON LILIENSTERN	500	45	49	Hemisphaere des Atlantischen Oceans / Hemisphaere des Stillen Oceans (2 maps)
mww0716a	world	1839	VON MANNERT	600	44	60	Die Erde in Zwey Halbkugeln
mwru0549a	ukraine	1772	VON MANSTEIN	400	35	45	Nouvelle Carte de la Crimmee ... 1737

AMPG REFERENCE	REGION	DATE	MAP MAKER	PRICE (UK£)	VERT. (cm.)	HOR. (cm.)	TITLE OF MAP (Comments by the editor in brackets)
mwbp0149	baltic states	1796	VON MELLIN	785	69	49	Der Dorptsche Kreis
mwbp0145	baltic states	1791	VON MELLIN	785	48	70	Der Fellinsche Kreis
mwbp0150a	baltic states	1798	VON MELLIN	1200	51	71	Der Rigische Kreis - Le Cercle de Riga
mwbp0150	baltic states	1798	VON MELLIN	850	50	70	Der Walcksche Kreis
mwbp0146	baltic states	1791	VON MELLIN	675	48	69	Der Wendensche Kreis (Latvia)
mwbp0147	baltic states	1791	VON MELLIN	785	48	69	Der Werrosche Kreis (Estonia)
mwbp0150a	baltic states	1798	VON MELLIN	500	50	70	Der Wolmarsche Kreis - Le Cercle de Wolmar
mwbp0148	baltic states	1791	VON MELLIN	1200	49	70	Livland nach der Eintheilung des Letten
mwme1079	turkey etc	1852	VON MOLTKE	4000	72	78	(Plan of Constantinople in Turkish script)
mwsc0698	scandinavia sweden	1696	VON PUFENDORF	500	25	31	(Bohus view) Bahusia Arx Norwegiae Regi Sueciae Carolo Gustavo
mwsc0317	scandinavia denmark	1697	VON PUFENDORF	250	30	38	(Copenhagen) Castra Suedica ad Haffniam
mwbp0327	poland	1696	VON PUFENDORF	300	30	39	(Danzig) Dantiscum
mwsc0318	scandinavia denmark	1697	VON PUFENDORF	250	27	34	(Fredericia) Accurata Delineatio Geometrica in Iuthia Septentrionali nuper Conditae Urbis et Fortalitij Friderici Oddae
mwbp0334	poland	1697	VON PUFENDORF	250	27	34	(Gulf of Gdansk) Tabula Geographica Exhibens Districtum inter Weichselmundam et Promontorium Reesehoeft
mwsc0595	scandinavia norway	1696	VON PUFENDORF	500	25	31	(Hallden) Delineatio Oppidi Halldae in Norwegia
mwsc0319	scandinavia denmark	1697	VON PUFENDORF	200	28	34	(NW coast of Funen) Tabula Exibens Situm Focorum Ubi Sercniss et Polentiss
mwsc0320	scandinavia denmark	1697	VON PUFENDORF	200	24	30	(Nyborg) Situs Locurm circa Neoburgum in Fionia
mwbp0102	baltic states	1697	VON PUFENDORF	900	29	54	(Riga) Delineatio Regiae Urbis Rigae et Obsidionis
mwsc0321	scandinavia denmark	1697	VON PUFENDORF	200	25	31	(Rudkobing) Ichnographis Rutcopiae Langelandiae Oppdid
mwbp0328	poland	1696	VON PUFENDORF	600	25	46	(Torun) Delineatio Schenographica Urbis Thoruniensis
mwsc0596	scandinavia norway	1696	VON PUFENDORF	400	28	34	(Trondheim) Delineatio Urbis Nidrosiae vulgo Dronheem ... 1658 (Another view with title 'Ichnographia Urbis Nidrosiae vulgo Dronheem In Norwegiae eo statu' shown left)
mwsc0322	scandinavia denmark	1697	VON PUFENDORF	150	27	34	Accurata Delineatio Geometrica in Iuthia Septentrionali nuper Conditae Urbis et Fortalitij Friderici Oddae
mwbp0329	poland	1696	VON PUFENDORF	600	29	38	Auctior et Correctior Tabula Chorographica Regni Poloniae Vicinarumque Regionum
mwbp0336	poland	1697	VON PUFENDORF	250	25	31	Ichnographia Castelli Pillau ... 1656
mwsc0323	scandinavia denmark	1697	VON PUFENDORF	200	25	30	Ichnographia Helsingorae et Arcis Croneburgensis
mwg0715	schleswig-holstein	1697	VON PUFENDORF	250	28	34	Ichnographia Oppidi Itzehoae in Stormaria ad Fluvium Storam
mww0381	world	1743	VON PUFENDORF	600	14	17	Mappe-Monde ou Carte Generale du Globe Terrestre, Representee en Deux Plan-Hemispheres
mwbp0335	poland	1697	VON PUFENDORF	250	27	34	Oppidum Neumarck ad Fluvium Drebnitz in Borussia a Suecis Occupatum / Oppidum et Arx Gollup (2 town plans on one sheet)
mwsc0315b	scandinavia denmark	1696	VON PUFENDORF	1200	29	107	Obsidium Haffniense ... Ao. 1658
mwbp0334a	poland	1697	VON PUFENDORF	1200	29	54	Praelii. Ad Warsaviaum ... 1616 (map by E. Dahlberg)
mwsc0324	scandinavia denmark	1697	VON PUFENDORF	200	25	31	Situs Ahlborger Fiordt
mwsc0325	scandinavia denmark	1697	VON PUFENDORF	200	25	31	Sonderburgum Sedes Principis cui Sueci Praesidium
mwbp0330	poland	1696	VON PUFENDORF	1500	25	63	Urbs Warsovia Sedes Ordinaria Regnum Poloniae ... 1656 (view)
mwsp0608	spain regions	1799	VON REILLY	180	24	29	(Andalusia) Des Koenigreichs Granada Oestlicher Theil
mwuk0566	scotland	1799	VON REILLY	150	33	20	(Hebrides) Die Insel Lewis
mwuk0567	scotland	1799	VON REILLY	150	32	20	(Hebrides) Die Insel Vist
mwsp0609	spain regions	1799	VON REILLY	400	22	25	(Province of Castille in 4 sheets, each 22x25cm)
mwe0962	europe hungary	1790	VON REILLY	350	34	49	Allgemeine Postkarte von Ungarn Kroatien, Sklavonien und Siebenburgen
mwat0169a	atlantic canary isl.	1790	VON REILLY	200	21	27	Carta dell' Isole Canarie
mwgr0629c	greece islands	1789	VON REILLY	200	32	25	Das Aegaeische Meer heute der Archipelagus oder das Insel=Meer Nro. 18
mwuk1860	wales	1789	VON REILLY	180	20	27	Das Furstenthum Wales
mwbp0143	baltic states	1789	VON REILLY	250	20	28	Das Herzogthum Kurland u. Semgallen
mwbh0885	luxembourg	1792	VON REILLY	280	28	30	Das Herzogthum Luxemburg
mwe0448	europe bosnia	1789	VON REILLY	280	21	28	Das Koenigreich Bosnien
mwf0537a	france corsica	1791	VON REILLY	235	27	32	Das Koenigreich Corsica
mwit0820d	italy sardinia	1790	VON REILLY	235	24	32	Das Koenigreich Sardinien
mwe1079	europe serbia	1789	VON REILLY	250	21	28	Das Koenigreich Serwien
mwe1082	europe serbia	1791	VON REILLY	200	20	29	Das Koenigreich Sklavonien und Herzogthum Syrmien
mwuk0240	ireland	1796	VON REILLY	240	21	28	Das Konigreich Ireland
mwsp0610	spain regions	1799	VON REILLY	150	28	28	Das Konigreich Murcia
mwsc0639	scandinavia norway	1790	VON REILLY	280	23	28	Das Konigreich Norwegen
mwuk0561	scotland	1794	VON REILLY	200	23	29	Das Konigreich Scotland
mwsp0611	spain regions	1799	VON REILLY	150	22	25	Das Konigreich Valencia
mwsc0745	scandinavia sweden	1789	VON REILLY	400	22	36	Das Konigreichs Schweden Mittlere Provincen
mwsc0746	scandinavia sweden	1789	VON REILLY	300	22	27	Das Konigreichs Schweden Nordliche Provincen
mwbp0144	baltic states	1789	VON REILLY	800	22	28	Der Grosherzogthums Litauen Ostsudlicher / Nordostlicher / Westsudliche / Nordwestlicher (4 maps, each 22x28cm)
mwsp0686a	balearic islands	1790	VON REILLY	300	21	26	Der Insel Majorca Noerdlicher / Südlicher Theil (2 maps)
mwsw0205	switzerland	1796	VON REILLY	280	23	30	Der Kanton Bern

AMPG REFERENCE	REGION	DATE	MAP MAKER	PRICE (UK£)	VERT. (cm.)	HOR. (cm.)	TITLE OF MAP (Comments by the editor in brackets)
mwsw0206	switzerland	1796	VON REILLY	200	21	26	Der Kanton Schweiz
mwbp0514	poland	1789	VON REILLY	235	21	29	Der Koniglichen Republik Polen Woiwodschaften Posen, Kalilsz, Gnesen, Brzesc, u: Inowroclaw
mwit0454	italy liguria	1797	VON REILLY	200	22	26	Der Ligurischen Republick order Genua Westerlicher Theil / Genua Oestlicher Theil (2 maps, each 22x25cm)
mwe0277	europe albania	1789	VON REILLY	375	22	30	Der Noerdliche Theil des Koenigreichs Albanien mit dem Distrikte Montenegro / Der Sudliche Theil des Koenigreichs Albanien (2 maps, each 22x30cm)
mwe0694	europe dalmatia	1789	VON REILLY	240	22	28	Der Noerdliche Theil des Koenigreichs Dalmatien
mwe0695	europe dalmatia	1789	VON REILLY	240	22	28	Der Sudlich Theil des Koenigreichs Dalmatien
mwsw0207	switzerland	1796	VON REILLY	400	24	31	Des Kantons Zurch Sudlicher Theil / Des Kantons Zurch Nordlicher Theil (2 maps)
mwe0454	europe bulgaria	1789	VON REILLY	100	22	28	Des Koenigreichs Bulgarien Oestliche Haelfte
mwe0453	europe bulgaria	1789	VON REILLY	100	22	29	Des Koenigreichs Bulgarien Westliche Haelfte
mwe0972	europe hungary	1810	VON REILLY	150	24	32	Des Koenigreichs Ungarn Nordwestlicher Theil
mwf0537	france corsica	1791	VON REILLY	580	27	32	Des Koenigsreichs Corsica Noerdlicher Theil / Mittlerer Theil / Sudlicher Theil (3 maps, each roughly 27x32cm)
mwe0611	europe czech republic (bohemia)	1791	VON REILLY	200	21	29	Des Konigreichs Boheim Kreise Klattau und Parchin mit den Koniglichen Freydorfern
mwuk1029	england	1791	VON REILLY	200	20	27	Des Konigreichs England
mwuk1359	england north	1795	VON REILLY	150	22	28	Des Konigreichs England Nordlicher Theil, oder York Shire, das Bisthum Durham, Northumberland, Cumberland, Westmoreland, und Lancashire
mwuk1392	england south	1789	VON REILLY	150	21	28	Des Konigreichs England Sudlicher Theil oder Cornwall, Devon Shire, Derset S., Somerset S., Bristol, Wilt S., Hamp S., Berk S., Buckingham S., Oxford S., Gloucester S. und Monmouth S.
mwit0820e	italy sardinia	1790	VON REILLY	400	23	32	Des Koenigreichs Sardinien Südlicher Theil/Des Koenigreichs Sardinien Noerdlicher Theil (2 maps)
mwe0961b	europe hungary	1789	VON REILLY	150	23	31	Des Königreichs Ungarn nordwestlicher Theil Nro. 28
mwe0961a	europe hungary	1789	VON REILLY	150	20	31	Des Königreichs Ungarn nordöstlicher Theil Nro. 31.
mwsc0181	scandinavia	1789	VON REILLY	150	22	27	Des Konigreichs Schweden Nordliche Provinzen
mwuk0551	scotland	1789	VON REILLY	320	22	28	Des Konigreichs Scotland Nordlicher Theil / Der Konigsreichs Scotland sudlicher Theil (2 maps)
mwe0388	europe austria	1791	VON REILLY	200	28	31	Des Landes unter der Enns Viertel unter dem Wiener Walde
mwbp0142	baltic states	1789	VON REILLY	280	20	27	Des Russischen Reiches Stattalterschaft Riga
mwru0298	russia	1789	VON REILLY	240	20	27	Des Russischen Reiches Statthalterschaften ... Moskau
mwru0297	russia	1789	VON REILLY	240	20	27	Des Russischen Reiches Statthalterschaften Archangel
mwru0571	ukraine	1789	VON REILLY	300	20	27	Des Russischen Reiches Statthalterschaften Woronesch, Belgorod, Kiow o. Kleinrussland und Charkow od. d. Russische Ukraine
mwuk1516	uk english channel (all)	1799	VON REILLY	150	21	32	Die Englische Kuste dem Nordlichen Frankreich Gegenuber
mwuk1594	channel islands	1791	VON REILLY	250	24	31	Die Englischen Inseln an der Kuste von Frankreich
mww0568	world	1790	VON REILLY	600	28	40	Die Funf Theile der Erde
mwuk1255	england london	1791	VON REILLY	300	21	28	Die Gegend um London (environs of London)
mwuk1861	wales	1789	VON REILLY	200	22	34	Die Insel Anglesey
mwuk1595	channel islands	1791	VON REILLY	250	19	33	Die Insel Guernsey
mwsc0511	scandinavia iceland	1791	VON REILLY	300	23	28	Die Insel Island Nro. 76
mwuk1596	channel islands	1791	VON REILLY	250	20	34	Die Insel Jersey
mwm0251	mediterranean malta	1790	VON REILLY	450	22	30	Die Insel Malta
mwuk1612	isle of man	1789	VON REILLY	250	34	22	Die Insel Man
mwgr0432	greece crete	1789	VON REILLY	200	22	29	Die Insel und das Konigreich Kandien
mwgr0226	greece	1789	VON REILLY	180	23	30	Die Insel und Halbinsel Morea
mwuk1625	isle of wight	1790	VON REILLY	150	23	29	Die Insel Wight
mwe0832	europe east	1789	VON REILLY	200	22	29	Die Landschaft Bessarabien
mwe1055	europe romania	1789	VON REILLY	200	22	28	Die Landschaft Bukowina
mwgr0227	greece	1789	VON REILLY	200	21	33	Die Landschaft Livadien einst Hellas
mwgr0228	greece	1789	VON REILLY	150	21	28	Die Landschaft Macedonien
mwe0831	europe east	1789	VON REILLY	200	22	33	Die Landschaft Romanien
mwsw0208	switzerland	1796	VON REILLY	200	20	26	Die Schweizer Landvogteyen in Italien
mwit0962	italy sicily	1791	VON REILLY	250	27	32	Die Sicilianische Landschaft Val di Mazarra
mwit0963	italy sicily	1791	VON REILLY	250	27	32	Die Sicilianische Landschaft Val di Noto
mwe0223	europe	1791	VON REILLY	200	22	28	Europa
mwsc0378	scandinavia denmark	1789	VON REILLY	150	24	30	General Kaart von dem Konigreichs Daenemark Halbinsel Jutland (north to the right)
mwru0299	russia	1789	VON REILLY	240	20	27	General Karte von dem Russischen Reiche in Europa
mwuk0867	uk	1789	VON REILLY	180	24	28	General-Karte von Grossbritannien und Ireland
mwsc0471	scandinavia greenland	1789	VON REILLY	280	23	28	Gronland so Weit es Bekant ist mit den Inseln Faeroer
mwe0506	europe croatia	1791	VON REILLY	200	25	28	Inner Krain mit der Windischen Mark und dem Triester Gebiethe
mwaf0278	africa	1795	VON REILLY	450	50	53	Karte von Afrika nach Vaugondy
mwam0243	america continent	1795	VON REILLY	950	58	76	Karte von Amerika nach D'Anville und Pownall
mwas0224	asia continent	1795	VON REILLY	550	47	63	Karte von Asien nach d'Anville (inset: NE Siberia)
mwbh0766	belgium holland	1795	VON REILLY	600	58	73	Karte von de Republik der Vereinigten Niederlande (inset S. Netherlands)
mwsc0189	scandinavia	1796	VON REILLY	650	57	75	Karte von dem Koenigreiche Schweden

AMPG REFERENCE	REGION	DATE	MAP MAKER	PRICE (UK£)	VERT. (cm.)	HOR. (cm.)	TITLE OF MAP (Comments by the editor in brackets)
mwsc0642	scandinavia norway	1796	VON REILLY	600	59	73	Karte von dem Konigreiche Norwegen nach O.A. Wangensteen und I.N. Wilse
mwbp0533	poland	1796	VON REILLY	600	59	74	Karte von dem Konigreiche Preussen
mwe0967	europe hungary	1796	VON REILLY	400	61	80	Karte von dem Konigreiche Ungarn … Kroatien und Sklavonien
mwe1167	europe south east	1794	VON REILLY	400	57	73	Karte von dem Oschmanischen Reiche in Europa
mwru0313	russia	1796	VON REILLY	500	56	75	Karte von dem Russischen Reiche in Europa
mww0592	world	1795	VON REILLY	1350	40	65	Karte von der Erde Ostlicher und Westlicher Halbkugel nach d'Anville
mwp0508a	pacific south	1795	VON REILLY	950	46	64	Karte von der Inselwelt Polynesien oder der Funften Weltheile nach Djurberg und Roberts … 1795
mwf0169	france	1796	VON REILLY	450	55	69	Karte von Frankreich
mwuk0238	ireland	1795	VON REILLY	580	48	64	Karte von Ireland nach Jefferys Neu Verzeichnet
mwbp0534	poland	1796	VON REILLY	720	58	72	Karte von Polen nach Sotzmann
mwuk0564	scotland	1795	VON REILLY	550	46	63	Karte von Scotland.
mwgr0228a	greece	1789	VON REILLY	600	35	42	Macedonia, Epirus et Achaia
mwe0389	europe austria	1791	VON REILLY	180	22	31	Ober Kaernten mit den Salzburgischen Antheilen
mwit0964	italy sicily	1791	VON REILLY	200	36	45	Poltkarte von Calabrien und Sicilien
mwbp0515	poland	1789	VON REILLY	180	21	31	Spezial Karte von des Koenigreichs Galizien und Lodomerien Westlichen Kreisen
mwsc0747	scandinavia sweden	1789	VON REILLY	300	22	26	Spezial Karte von des Konigreichs Schweden Sudlichen Provincen
mwaf0108	africa	1697	VON SANDRART	960	49	57	Accuratissima Totius Africae Tabula in Lucem Producta
mwe0541a	europe czech republic (bohemia)	1666	VON SANDRART	1800	56	76	Bohemia in suas partes geograph: distinc:
mwg0211	germany north east	1690	VON SANDRART	400	28	38	Brandeburgum Marchionatus, cum Ducatibus Pomeraniae et Mekelenburgi
mwgr0412	greece crete	1687	VON SANDRART	875	12	7	Candia Insula
mwgr0487	greece cyprus	1687	VON SANDRART	2000	12	7	Cyprus Insula
mwme0287	holy land	1728	VON SANDRART	300	32	47	Das Gelobte Landt Canaan Durchwandelt von unserm Seeligmacher Iesu Christo und seinen Aposteln
mwme0159	holy land	1662	VON SANDRART	1200	40	52	Das Land Canaan
mwme0196	holy land	1685	VON SANDRART	785	38	51	Die Reise der Kinder Israel aus Egypten
mwuk0092	ireland	1685	VON SANDRART	1500	47	54	Hiberniae Brevis Tabula, Iuxta Ampliorem Delineationem D. Wilhelmi Petty
mwgr0312	greece corfu	1687	VON SANDRART	875	12	7	Insula Corfu
mwgr0609	greece islands	1687	VON SANDRART	750	12	7	Insula Scharpanto
mwgr0284	greece cefalonia	1687	VON SANDRART	875	12	7	Insula Zafalonia
mwgr0102	greece	1687	VON SANDRART	900	12	15	Morea Peninsula provincia principale della Grecia
mwru0099	russia	1688	VON SANDRART	1250	42	53	Moscoviae seu Russiae Magnae Generalis Tabula
mwe0881	europe hungary	1664	VON SANDRART	960	35	54	Neue Land Tafel von Hungarn
mwam0098	america continent	1697	VON SANDRART	2750	48	57	Nova Tabula Americae … sic Dictae ab Americo Vesputio Florentino (one of the earliest maps engraved by J. Homann)
mwe1140	europe south east	1680	VON SANDRART	960	41	52	Nova Totius Graecia, Italiae, Natolae, Hungarie nec non Danubii Fluminis
mwbp0283	poland	1670	VON SANDRART	1800	40	51	Nova Totius Regni Poloniae Magniq. Ducatus Lithuaniae
mwe0775b	europe east	1695	VON SANDRART	1000	42	81	Novissima et accuratissima toti Regni Hungariae, Dalmatiae, Croatiae, Sclavoniae… Tabula
mwit0724	italy rome	1677	VON SANDRART	2500	67	87	Recensis Romae Ichnographia (close copy of Falda 1667)
mwg0345a	bavaria	1680	VON SANDRART	600	54	44	S. R. Imperii Circuli Et Electoratus Bavariae Cum Finitimis Accurata Delineatio
mwe1001	europe rhine	1680	VON SANDRART	3000	38	103	Totius Fluminis Rheni Novissima Descriptio (20 views/plans in borders)
mwgr0541	greece zante (zakynthos)	1687	VON SANDRART	750	12	7	Zante insula posta nel mare Mediterraneo longi dala Morea
mwsam0189	south america (north)	1830	VON SCHLIEBEN	120	20	26	Die Rep. Columbia Department; Orinoco, Venezuela, Maturin, Zulia, Boyaca
mwam0820	america north (central)	1830	VON SCHLIEBEN	150	20	26	Die Vereinigten Staaten von Nord Amerika. XIV Gebiet Michigan. XV Das Nordwestliche Gebiet
mwam0821	america north (central)	1830	VON SCHLIEBEN	150	20	27	Die Vereinigten Staaten von Staat Mississippi, Louisiana, Gebiet Arkansas
mwm0230a	mediterranean malta	1724	VON SCHMETTAU	1600	52	65	(Untitled map of Valletta and environs)
mwg0497	mecklenburg	1780	VON SCHMETTAU	1500	270	230	Carte Chorographique et Militaire du Duche de Meklenburg-Strehlitz en 9 Sections 1780
mwit0682a	italy piedmont	1740	VON SCHMETTAU	400	35	48	Carte d'une Partie du Piemont
mwm0230	mediterranean malta	1724	VON SCHMETTAU	1500	22	60	Carte Particuliere de l'Isle de Malte de Goze et Cuming dans l'Etat qui Estoients l'Anne 1724
mwit0961	italy sicily	1784	VON SCHMETTAU	550	40	51	Carte de la Sicile et des Isles Adjacentes
mwit0955	italy sicily	1779	VON SCHMETTAU	3500	91	121	Descrizione Geografica del Regno di Sicilia e sue Isole Adiacenti (map by G. Orcel)
mwg0239	berlin	1749	VON SCHMETTAU	1500	52	73	Plan de la Ville de Berlin
mwg0499	mecklenburg	1788	VON SCHMETTAU	2500	61	89	Topographisch Oeconomisch und Militaerische Charte des Herzogthums Mecklenburg Schwerin und des Furstenthums Ratzeburg (16 sheets, each 61x89cm)

AMPG REFERENCE	REGION	DATE	MAP MAKER	PRICE (UK£)	VERT. (cm.)	HOR. (cm.)	TITLE OF MAP (Comments by the editor in brackets)
mwe0610	europe czech republic (bohemia)	1789	VON SCHMETTAU	1200	96	145	Topographische und Militarische Carte Desienigen Theils von Boehmen welcher zwischen Hohenelbe Pless und der Schlesischen Grentze Gelegen ist nebst den Laegern von der Campagne 1778
mwjk0141	japan	1832	VON SIEBOLD	650	16	17	(Deshima) Nederlandsche Factorij Dezima 1828
mwjk0139	japan	1828	VON SIEBOLD	650	44	60	De Baai van Nagasaki
mwjk0143	japan	1832	VON SIEBOLD	480	67	49	Die Insel Krafto Seghalien und die Mündung des Mankô (Amur)
mwjk0142	japan	1832	VON SIEBOLD	3000	33	54	Gezigt op de Haven en de Baai van Nagasaki (view)
mwjk0150	japan	1852	VON SIEBOLD	650	23	26	Japan ten Tyde van Zin-Mu-Ten-Woo 660 V.C. Genaamd Jama-To v. Aki-Tsu-Sima
mwjk0157a	japan tokyo	1832	VON SIEBOLD	4000	42	58	Panorama Van Jedo (title below map)
mww0036	world	1534	VON WATTE	7200	24	38	Typus Cosmographicus Universalis (This mapmaker's Latin name: Vadianus)
			VON WERDEN: SEE VAN VERDEN				
mwe1004a	europe rhine	1689	VON WIERING	12000	83	123	Entwurff des edlen Rhein-Strohms
mwit1201c	italy veneto	1810	VON ZACH	1200	91	122	Il Ducato di Venezia
mwam0669	america north	1830	VOSGIEN	150	20	23	Amerique Septentrionale Corrige et Augmentee
mwwi0854	st kitts	1667	VOUILLEMONT	2000	53	38	La Representation de l'Isle St. Christophe des Antilles et des Combats Donnez-Entre les Francois et les Angois / L'Isle de Cayenne Occupee par Messieurs de la Compagnie des Indes Occidentales (view of a sugar mill at the centre)
mwbh0114	belgium holland	1585	VRIENTS	2500	38	44	(Antwerp) Vraije Description de l'Assiegement d'Anvers par le … Prince de Parme etc. sur la Riviere de l'Escault entre Calloo et Oirdam l'An 1585. Ioannes Baptista Vrints Excudit
mwbh0181	belgium holland	1610	VRIENTS	2500	37	49	(Flanders) Tornaci Nervorum Episcopatus Perantiquus Totaq. Tornacesii Ditio … Ioan. Baptista Vrientius
mww0093	world	1596	VRIENTS	14000	39	57	Orbis Terrae Compendiosa Descriptio ex peritissimorum totius orbis Gaeographorum operibus desumta Antverpiae, apud Joanem Baptistam Vrient
mwam0722	america north	1838	VUILLEMIN	100	26	19	Amerique du Nord
mwru0576	ukraine	1840	VUILLEMIN	200	27	40	Carte de la Crimee (shown above left)
mwe0271	europe	1845	VUILLEMIN	800	81	107	Carte Pittoresque & Maritime de l'Europe
mwgr0259	greece	1841	VUILLEMIN	60	19	26	Etat de la Grece
mww0721	world	1840	VUILLEMIN	500	44	75	Mappemonde
mwf0935	france paris	1845	VUILLEMIN	600	84	107	Nouveau Plan Illustre de la Ville de Paris avec le Systeme Complet de ses Fortifications et Forts Detache, et des Communes de la Banlieue (part of 1857 edition illustrated)
mwf0928	france paris	1840	VUILLEMIN	600	86	110	Plan Pittoresque de la Ville de Paris
mwbh0427	belgium holland	1680	WAESBERGEN	480	40	53	Naeuwkeurige Afbeeldinge, van alle de Posten en Vastigheden by dese Weerende Oorlogh Gemaeckt, in Holland, Utrecht en Gedeelte van Gelderlandt
mwsc0237	scandinavia denmark	1588	WAGHENAER	1800	33	53	A Carde of the Beldt, with All the Sea Coastes, Bounds, and Site of the Countries Called Laland, unto Stevens Head
mwbh0123	belgium holland	1588	WAGHENAER	3000	32	50	A Description of the Iles of Sealand as they Lie upon all ye Rivers & Chanells with a Part of the Sea Coastes of Holland and Flaundres
mwsc0238	scandinavia denmark	1588	WAGHENAER	1500	34	51	A Description of the Outermost Coastes of Jutland Both of the Belt Side & of the North Sea Side as they are Situated between Aelburger Diep or Haven and Rijncopen
mwg0691	schleswig-holstein	1588	WAGHENAER	2500	32	50	A Description of the Sea Coastes of Eyder Ditmerst & a Part of Jeverland with the Rivers of Weser, Elve, Eyder, Heuer and other Entrees Sandes and Shoaldes, Lienge Alongest thes Sea Coaste of Germany
mwbh0124	belgium holland	1588	WAGHENAER	3000	32	50	A Description of the Twoo Famous Rivers Streames or Channells the Flie & the Maersdeepe Streaching up in to the Sowther Sea before Enchuysen unto Amsterdam
mwbp0005	baltic sea (east)	1588	WAGHENAER	1800	32	50	A Dilligent Description of the Sea Coastes of Lyffland
mwe1184	europe west	1588	WAGHENAER	18000	55	39	A Generall Carde & discription of the Sea Coastes of Europe, and navigation in this book conteyned (English edition of the previous map)
mwg0475	mecklenburg	1588	WAGHENAER	1800	32	50	A True and Perfect Pourtraicte of the Duchie of Mekelenburghe from Iasmunde to Femeren
mwuk1375	england south	1585	WAGHENAER	2800	32	50	Angliae Orae Maritimae inter Plemoutham t Portlandum
mwuk0318	scotland	1585	WAGHENAER	2500	33	51	Beschrijvinge van een deel vann Schottlandt van Bambourg tot Aberdein daer Edenburg de Princepaele Copestat in is (north to the right)
mwuk0322	scotland	1602	WAGHENAER	2800	19	55	Beschrijvinge vande Noortcosten van Engelant ende Scotland, ende Ghelegentheit van dien Mitsgaders de Monden vande Rivieren, ende Havenen, ende waer Voren, men hem moet Wachten
mwbh0115	belgium holland	1585	WAGHENAER	6000	33	51	Beschrijvinge vande Vermaerde Stroemen, Tvlie ende Tmaersdiep; Opstreckende inde Zuijder Zee voer bij Enchuijsen tot Amstelredam (north to the left)

AMPG REFERENCE	REGION	DATE	MAP MAKER	PRICE (UK£)	VERT. (cm.)	HOR. (cm.)	TITLE OF MAP (Comments by the editor in brackets)
mwsc0232	scandinavia denmark	1585	WAGHENAER	1500	33	51	Beschrijvinge vande Wterste omlopende custe van Jutlandt (south to the top)
mwsp0008	portugal	1585	WAGHENAER	1500	33	51	Beschrijvinghe der Zee Custen van Algarbe, en een Deel vande Condado soe hem Tlandt Aldaer Verthoont en in Gedaente en Wesen is
mwuk1372	england south	1584	WAGHENAER	1900	33	50	Beschrijvinghe der Zee Custen van Engelandt tusschen Wicht ende Doveren met die Principale Havenen
mwsp0007	portugal	1584	WAGHENAER	1500	33	51	Beschrijvinghe der Zee Custen vant Landt va Argarbe (north to the top. The directions in the compass rose are inconsistent!)
mwuk1373	england south	1584	WAGHENAER	1900	33	51	Beschrijvinghe der Zee-Custen van Engelandt, tusschen Pleijmouth en Porthlandt, met zijne Principale Havenen
mwsc0242	scandinavia denmark	1590	WAGHENAER	1350	19	55	Beschrijvinghe van de Westcosten van Iuitlant, Holsten, Exderlant Mitsgaders de Elbe, ende Meer Ander Rivire ende Stroomen, mits oock de Iuitsche Eylanden
mwuk0011	ireland	1596	WAGHENAER	5000	19	54	Beschrijvinghe vande Suijt-Custe van Irlandt, die Eijlanden voor Capo de Claro, ende Hoemen in die Havenen Seylen Sal, met Noch een Gedeelte van Walsch-Engelandt (shown is French edition 1601)
mwsp0375	spain regions	1584	WAGHENAER	1800	33	51	Beschryvinge der Zee custen van Galissien beginnende van Capo de finisterre tot Camino (north to the left)
mwbh0116	belgium holland	1585	WAGHENAER	1500	33	52	Beschryvinghe van de zee Custen va Vlanderen en Picardien
mwg0566	saxony	1585	WAGHENAER	2000	33	52	Beschryvinghe van de zee Custen van Ost Vriesslandt (south to the top)
mwuk1336	england east	1585	WAGHENAER	2000	33	51	Beschrijvinghe vande Zee Custen van Engelandt tusschen Blaigney en Scharenburch
mwbh0117	belgium holland	1585	WAGHENAER	3000	33	52	Beschryvinghe vande Zeeusche Eylanden (north to the left)
mwuk1335	england east	1585	WAGHENAER	2000	33	51	Caerte der Noordt Custe va Engelandt, Beginnende van Robinhodes Baij tot Cocket Eijlandt, alsoe Tzelve Landt Aldaer in zijn Gedaente is. Doer Lucas Iansz Wagenaer van Enchuijsen (north to the right)
mwbp0194	poland	1585	WAGHENAER	2000	33	52	Caerte van de Zee Custe vant Landt te Pomere also tselfde in zijn Weesen en Gedaente is
mwsp0377	spain regions	1584	WAGHENAER	1800	33	50	Caerte vande Zee Custen van Acason en Biscaie (south to the top)
mwsp0372	spain regions	1584	WAGHENAER	1800	33	51	Caerte vande Zee Custen van Galissien, va Ortugal tot voer bij C. de Finisterre
mwuk1545a	bristol channel	1588	WAGHENAER	2000	37	53	Canalis Celebris vel Navigationis a Bristovio
mwbp0214	poland	1600	WAGHENAER	1800	32	50	Carte de la Coste Maritime du Pays de Pomere, selon sa Forme & Situation
mwf0305	france brittany	1585	WAGHENAER	3000	33	51	Chartae orarum marinarum partim Normandiae, partim Britanniae, et Insularu cira eas Sitarum. Caerte vanden zee Custen, eensdeels Normandien en Brittangen (incl. Channel Islands; south to the top)
mwru0020	russia	1596	WAGHENAER	1800	19	55	Cotes Marine de Russie - Zee Custen van Mezin
mwsc0525	scandinavia norway	1590	WAGHENAER	2250	33	52	Custe van Noorweghen, tusschen Berghen, ende de Iedder, soe dat Landt al Daer in sijn Wesen is, Alsmen dat Lie op Ende off Zeijlt
mwg0198	germany north east	1585	WAGHENAER	2000	33	52	De Caerte Ofte Zee Custen van Pruijssen, met zijne haffen ofte Groote Rivieren, vander Memel off tot Heel tho, alsoe Tlant Aldaer in zijn Wesen is (north to the left)
mwsc0521	scandinavia norway	1585	WAGHENAER	3200	33	51	De Custe van Noorweghen, met dat Landt van Noordt Oosten in Zijne Wesen en Gedaente soe Hem dat Verhoont en op Doet van Mardou tot Akersondt
mwsc0658	scandinavia sweden	1585	WAGHENAER	1800	33	51	De Custen van Een Deel van Denmarken en Swederijk, Beginnede va Vuijtste tot Calmer
mwg0474	mecklenburg	1585	WAGHENAER	2000	33	52	De Kuste van Lalandt (south to the top)
mwf0304	france brittany	1585	WAGHENAER	1200	33	51	De Zee Custe met de Eylande van Britaignen, tuschenn Blauet en Picqueliers
mwf0254	france aquitaine	1585	WAGHENAER	1250	34	51	De Zee Custe van tLandt van Poictou ende Bordeaux
mwuk1417a	england thames	1584	WAGHENAER	1600	33	51	De Zee Custen tusschen Dovere en Orfordts Ness, daer de Teemse de Vermaerde Rivire va Lonen
mwsp0383	spain regions	1590	WAGHENAER	1500	33	52	De Zee Custen van Galissien, van Capo Daviles off; tot Ortegal tho ... 1583
mwbp0001	baltic sea (east)	1585	WAGHENAER	2000	33	51	De zee kuste Rontomme Oesel en een Deel van Curlandt Beginnende va Dagher Oort tot Derwinde, also hem Tlandt daer Verthoont, en in zijn Ghedaente is (north to the left)
mwsc0657	scandinavia sweden	1585	WAGHENAER	1800	33	51	De zee Kuste vant Landt te Noortoosten Sorterende onder Norweghen en Eendeels onder Sweden ... Distelberch tot Waersberghe
mwbh0118	belgium holland	1585	WAGHENAER	1350	33	51	Descriptio ditionum littorialium maris Germanici
mwsp0385	spain regions	1596	WAGHENAER	1500	19	55	Description de Galice
mwsp0376	spain regions	1584	WAGHENAER	1800	33	51	Die Caerte vande Zeekusten van Biscaien, Zeer Quade Havens voer Groote Schepen tussche Rio de Sella e Aviles

AMPG REFERENCE	REGION	DATE	MAP MAKER	PRICE (UK£)	VERT. (cm.)	HOR. (cm.)	TITLE OF MAP (Comments by the editor in brackets)
mwbp0004	baltic sea (east)	1585	WAGHENAER	2000	33	51	Die Custe va Lyfflandt, met de Eylanden daer Beneffens, also hem dat Landt Aldaer Verthoont en in Zijn Ghedaente is (south towards the top)
mwsp0009	portugal	1585	WAGHENAER	1500	33	52	Die Zee Caerte van Portugal, tusschen Camino en Montego, alsoe dat Landt Alt daer in sijn Ghedaente is, met alle sijne Haeven enn Ondipten (north to the left)
mwsc0522	scandinavia norway	1585	WAGHENAER	1750	33	50	Die zee Custe van Noorweghen tusschen der Noess en Mardou
mwsp0373	spain regions	1583	WAGHENAER	1800	33	51	Die Zee Custen va Biscaijen tusschen Laredo en Sentillana
mwsp0374	spain regions	1584	WAGHENAER	1800	33	51	Die Zee Custen van Galissien, van Capo Dauiles off tot Ortegal tho Doer
mwuk1450	uk english channel (all)	1584	WAGHENAER	2000	33	50	Het Canael tusschen Engeland en Vranckryk / The Channell betweene England and Fraunce
mwsc0409	scandinavia finland	1585	WAGHENAER	3000	33	51	Het wterste ofte Oosterste Deel van de Oster Zee, Beslooten tegens Ruslandt Lijfflandt, Oost Finlandt (north to the left)
mwbp0002	baltic sea (east)	1585	WAGHENAER	2000	33	51	Het wterste ofte Oosterste Deel van de Oster Zee, Beslooten tegens Ruslandt Lijfflandt, Oost Finlandt (north to the left)
mwsc0526	scandinavia norway	1596	WAGHENAER	12000	33	51	Hydrographica Septentrionalis Norvegiae Partis Descriptio / Beschrijvinghe der Zeecusten vant Nordelicxste Deel van Norweghen ... 1596
mwg0200	germany north east	1601	WAGHENAER	1400	19	55	Prusse, Pomeranie et Meckelburg
mwec0803	uk england norfolk	1585	WAGHENAER	1800	34	53	See Caerte vande Noordt Custe van Engelandt
mwsc0233	scandinavia denmark	1585	WAGHENAER	1500	35	54	Situs Iuttiae - De Gelegentheijt van Jutlandt ... van Boeuenbergen Tot dat Eijlandt Silt
mwbp0196	poland	1588	WAGHENAER	2000	33	51	The Carde of the Sea Coastes of the Land of Prusia (illustration has Dutch title 'De Caerte ofte Zee Custen van Pruijssen')
mwbp0006	baltic sea (east)	1588	WAGHENAER	1800	32	50	The Outtermost or the Fartheste Parte of the Easterne Sea East Wardly, the which Lyeth Inclosed with in the Coastes of East Finland, Rusland, & Lyffland, and wherin Lye the Narue and Wyburgh
mwuk1376	england south	1588	WAGHENAER	2800	32	49	The Sea Coastes of England betweene the Ile of Wight & Dover, with the Principal Havens thereof According to their Situation and Appearing
mwsc0524	scandinavia norway	1588	WAGHENAER	2750	32	50	The Sea Coastes of Norway as they doo Appeare According to their Situation betweene der Noess & Mardou
mwsc0239	scandinavia denmark	1588	WAGHENAER	1800	32	50	The Sea Coastes of Part of Denmarke and Swedeland from Vuytste to Calmer
mwsc0663	scandinavia sweden	1588	WAGHENAER	2000	32	50	The Sea Coasts of Swedeland, about the Coastes of Westerwijck and the Entrance of Stockholm, Beginning from Kalmar unto the Wigstone and the Redde Kowe
mwsc0240	scandinavia denmark	1588	WAGHENAER	1500	32	50	The Situation of Jutland with the Havens, Rivers, Shoalds, and Bankes of the Iles thereof, from Boeuenbergen unto the Ile of Silt
mwe1183	europe west	1583	WAGHENAER	20000	55	39	Universae Europae maritime ... navigationis descriptio. Generale Paschaerte van Europa (1586 edition shown below)
mwf0302	france brittany	1584	WAGHENAER	1200	33	51	Verthoninghe van de Zee Custen van Bretaignen ... tusschen S: Malo en Rouscou
mwec0161	uk england cornwall	1583	WAGHENAER	2800	33	52	Zee Caerte van Engelants Eijndt, alsoe hem Tselfde Landt Verthoont Beginnede van Sorlinges tot Pleijmondt
mwsp0010	portugal	1585	WAGHENAER	2000	33	51	Zee Caerte van Portugal ... Coopstadt van Lisbone
mwbp0003	baltic sea (east)	1585	WAGHENAER	2000	33	51	Zee Caerte vande Custe va Lyfflant begrepen Rontsome de Grooten Inham vande Rijgsche Zee, soe Tselfe hem Verthoent en op Doet
mwuk1334	england east	1585	WAGHENAER	2000	33	51	Zee Caerte vande Noordt Custe van Engelandt, alsoe Tzelffde Landt Aldaer in sijn Gedaente en Wesen is, met Alle sijnen Ondieptenn (north to the right)
mwsc0230	scandinavia denmark	1585	WAGHENAER	1500	33	51	Zee Caerte vande Sondt Tvermaerste van Denemarcke (north to the left)
mwsc0659	scandinavia sweden	1585	WAGHENAER	2400	33	52	Zee Custe van Sweeden Otrent de Westerwijk en Tgatt vann Stockholm Beginnende va Kalmar Tot sen Wigsteen en Rookoe Gelegen bijnnen Tgatt va Stockholm
mwsp0384	spain regions	1590	WAGHENAER	1500	33	51	Zee Custen van Andaluzien
mwf0303	france brittany	1585	WAGHENAER	1200	34	52	Zee Kaerte van Britaigne
mwe0901a	europe hungary	1686	WAGNER	120	15	22	(untitled map)
mwaf0172	africa	1737	WAGNER	240	17	21	Africa Nova
mwe0711	europe danube	1685	WAGNER	2500	41	137	Danubius Fluminum Europaeorum Princeps
mwit1198b	italy veneto	1742	WAGNER	650	46	55	Il Corso del Po dal Mantovano fino al Mare
mwme0837	persia etc	1795	WAHL	180	45	67	Neue Karte des Persishen Reichs
mwsp0325	spain	1824	WAHLEN	150	12	14	Espagne et Portugal
mwf0188a	france	1824	WAHLEN	130	12	14	France
mwam0553	america north	1800	WALCH	850	44	56	(Untitled map of North America, with 'Isles de Sandwich' shown close to Californian coast)
mwp0519b	pacific south	1818	WALCH	600	49	62	Australien (Sudland) auch Polynesien oder Inselwelt, Insgemein der Funfte Welttheil Genannt

AMPG REFERENCE	REGION	DATE	MAP MAKER	PRICE (UK£)	VERT. (cm.)	HOR. (cm.)	TITLE OF MAP (Comments by the editor in brackets)
mwe0237	europe	1805	WALCH	1200	103	129	Carte Generale de Toute l'Europe
mwaf0286	africa	1800	WALCH	400	47	55	Charte de l'Afrique
mwas0215b	asia continent	1790	WALCH	600	50	58	Charte de l'Asie
mww0677	world	1826	WALCH	500	47	60	Charte der Erde … Professor Fishchers Methode
mwsw0236a	switzerland	1845	WALCH	350	48	65	Charte der Schweiz in seine Cantone eingetheilt
mwam0255a	america continent	1805	WALCH	400	59	50	Charte von America
mwe0696	europe dalmatia	1807	WALCH	480	56	46	Charte von Dalmatien
mwuk1038	england	1803	WALCH	750	124	107	Charte von England und Wallis (map by Kitchin)
mwam0574	america north	1807	WALCH	650	56	48	Charte von Nordamerica
mwam0605	america north	1816	WALCH	500	57	49	Charte von Nordamerica nach den Neuesten Entdeckungen und Zuverlagsigsten Astronomischen Ortsbestimmungen Entworfen (incl. Franklin State)
mwas0527	asia south east	1805	WALCH	400	46	63	Charte von Ostindien dies- und jenseits des Ganges
mwe1175	europe south east	1822	WALCH	280	49	58	Das Osmanische Reich in Europa
mww0658	world	1818	WALCH	300	18	23	Der Erde Nordl. Halbkugel / Der Erde Sudl. Halbkugel (2 polar maps)
mwe0227	europe	1795	WALCH	650	47	55	Europa Secundum Recentissimas Clarissimorum Geographorum
mwsc0194	scandinavia	1801	WALCH	550	64	48	General Karte von Koenig Schweden nebst Daenemark u Norwegen
mwgr0239	greece	1810	WALCH	300	64	58	Graeciae Pars Borealis Hellas Peloponnesus et Insulae
mww0619	world	1803	WALCH	800	48	64	Karte der Erde, nach ihrer oestlich, westlich, noerdlich und sudlichen Halbkugel
mwg0402	bavaria	1806	WALCH	800	76	58	Karte vom Konigreich Baiern
mwru0331a	russia	1812	WALCH	600	59	47	Karte von dem Russischen Reiche in Europa Nach der Karte der Gesellschaft der Kunste und Wissenschaften in Petersburg
mwe0390	europe austria	1797	WALCH	375	48	57	Karte von der Gefursteten Grafschaft Tyrol
mwaf0534	africa egypt etc	1798	WALCH	235	49	55	Karte von Egypten
mwf1162a	france rhone-alpes	1800	WALCH	300	50	59	Kriegstheater oder Graenzkarte zwischen Frankreich und Italien
mwam0229	america continent	1790	WALCH	1350	50	60	L'Amerique selon l'Etendue de ses Principales Parties et dont les Points Principaux sont Placez sur les Dernieres Observations des Geographes (2 sheets, each 50x60cm.)
mwuk0875	uk	1797	WALCH	450	55	46	Magna Britannia et Hibernia
mww0614	world	1800	WALCH	800	46	64	Mappa Totius Mundi (after Lotter)
mwsam0138a	south america	1820	WALCH	300	62	48	Neueste Carte von Süd-Amerika… Westindien
mwbh0788	belgium holland	1818	WALCH	200	50	61	Nouvelle Carte de la Province de Flandre
mwbp0535	poland	1796	WALCH	235	47	59	Polen nach seiner Ersten, und Letzen, oder Gaenzlichen Theilung
mwwi0146	west indies	1798	WALCH	450	49	60	Tabula Geographica Maximae Partis Americae Mediae sive Indiae Occidentalis / Karte des Betraechtlichsten Theils von Mittel-America oder Westindien Entworfen nach der Grossen Karte des B. Edwards
mww0017	world	1507	WALDSEEMULLER	550000	18	34	(Set of globe gores.)
mww0025	world	1516	WALDSEEMULLER		134	248	Carta Marina Navigatoria Portugallen Navigationes Atque Tocius Cogniti Orbis Terra Maris (title above map.)
mwf0659	france lorraine	1513	WALDSEEMULLER	500	37	26	Ducatus Lotharingie (reprinted 1520)
mww0023	world	1513	WALDSEEMULLER	40000	44	57	Orbis Typus Universalis iuxta Hydrographorum Traditionem
mwuk0653	uk	1513	WALDSEEMULLER	10000	38	51	Tabuia Nova Hibernie Anglie et Scotie (reprinted 1520)
mwgr0007	greece	1513	WALDSEEMULLER	8000	42	54	Tabula Moderna Bossine Servie Gretiae et Sclavonie (1st 'modern' map of Greece)
mwsp0147	spain	1513	WALDSEEMULLER	4500	41	58	Tabula Moderna et Nova Hispanie (reprinted 1520)
mwit0010	italy	1513	WALDSEEMULLER	12000	42	55	Tabula Moderna Et Nova Italie Ac Sicilie
mwf0009	france	1513	WALDSEEMULLER	5000	44	57	Tabula Moderna Gallie (reprinted 1520)
mwg0008	germany	1513	WALDSEEMULLER	5000	40	53	Tabula Moderna Germanie (reprinted 1520)
mwin0080	india	1513	WALDSEEMULLER	15000	42	54	Tabula Moderna Indiae (reprinted 1520. First 'modern' map of India.)
mwit0009	italy	1513	WALDSEEMULLER	10000	39	57	Tabula Moderna Italie (reprinted 1520)
mwsc0004	scandinavia	1513	WALDSEEMULLER	13500	31	57	Tabula Moderna Norbegie et Gottie (re-issued 1520)
mwaf1083	africa west	1513	WALDSEEMULLER	4500	44	57	Tabula Moderna Prime Partis Aphricae
mwe0733	europe east	1513	WALDSEEMULLER	4000	40	55	Tabula Moderna Sarmatie Eur. sive Hungarie Polonie Russie Prussie et Walachie (reprinted 1520)
mwbp0160	poland	1513	WALDSEEMULLER	4000	40	55	Tabula Moderna Sarmatie Eur. sive Hungarie Polonie Russie Prussie et Walachie (reprinted 1520)
mwaf0847	africa south	1513	WALDSEEMULLER	6000	38	50	Tabula Moderna Secunde Porcionis Aphrice (1st printed map of Southern Africa, reprinted 1520)
mwme0013	holy land	1513	WALDSEEMULLER	8000	38	55	Tabula Moderna Terra Sancte (reprinted 1520)
mwgr0335	greece crete	1513	WALDSEEMULLER	4000	39	53	Tabula Neoterica Crete sive Candie Insule (reprinted 1520)
mwme0902	turkey etc	1513	WALDSEEMULLER	3500	37	49	Tabula Nova Asie Minoris (reprinted 1520. First map of 'modern' Turkey.)
mwsw0002	switzerland	1513	WALDSEEMULLER	5000	42	54	Tabula Nova Heremi Helvetiorum (re-issued 1520)
mwg0250	baden-wurttemberg	1513	WALDSEEMULLER	1800	33	54	Tabula Nova Particularis Provincie Rheni Superioris (reprinted 1520)
mwat0001	atlantic ocean (all)	1513	WALDSEEMULLER	60000	39	45	Tabula Ter re Nove

AMPG REFERENCE	REGION	DATE	MAP MAKER	PRICE (UK£)	VERT. (cm.)	HOR. (cm.)	TITLE OF MAP (Comments by the editor in brackets)
mww0018	world	1507	WALDSEEMULLER	6000000	132	236	Universalis Cosmographia Secundum Ptholemaei Traditionem Et Americi Vespucii Alioruque Lustrationes (title below map, woodcut in 12 sheets. Probably the only example of this map. The 'birth certificate' map, because it was the first to name 'America'. Acquired in 2007 by the US Library of Congress, as also Waldseemuller's 1516 map.)
mww0028	world	1522	WALDSEEMULLER-FRIES	5000	29	46	Diefert Situs Orbis Hydrographorum ab eo quem Ptolomeus Posuit (reprinted 1525, 1535 and 1541)
mwsc0654	scandinavia norway	1847	WALIGORSKI	785	110	77	Veikart over Norge. Udarbeidet efter Foranstaltning af den Kogl: Norske Regjerings Justits og Politie Departement
mwec1183	uk england sussex	1850	WALKER	65	32	40	(Untitled)
mwec0030	uk england bedfordshire	1850	WALKER	60	32	40	(Untitled)
mwec0872	uk england northamptonshire	1850	WALKER	60	32	40	(Untitled)
mwec0763	uk england lincolnshire	1850	WALKER	50	32	40	(Untitled)
mww0561	world	1788	WALKER	150	18	30	A General Chart on Mercator's Projection Representing the World as Diversified by Different Natural Productions and as Inhabited by Man and Brute under Large and General Divisions
mwuk1408	uk geological	1835	WALKER	1600	144	99	A Geological Map of England, Wales and Part of Scotland
mwme0419	holy land	1840	WALKER	800	84	93	A Map of Palestine or the Holy Land with Egypt and the Wilderness of Mount Sinai, to Illustrate the Geography of the Holy Scriptures by Peter Graham
mwin0343	india	1822	WALKER	450	92	64	A New and Improved Map of India
mwaf0279	africa	1795	WALKER	75	19	21	Africa
mww0659	world	1818	WALKER	800	60	88	Allgemeine Welt Charte nach Mercators Projection Entworfen von Krusenstern Capitain der Russischen Marine London 1815 (engraved by J.Walker)
mwec0029	uk england bedfordshire	1846	WALKER	60	43	34	Bedfordshire
mwca0173	canada	1834	WALKER	200	32	43	British Possessions in North America
mwec0118	uk england cambridgeshire	1850	WALKER	80	39	33	Cambridgeshire (from Hobson's Fox Hunting atlas)
mwat0314	atlantic south	1846	WALKER	1200	93	121	Chart of the South Atlantic Ocean and West Coast of South America
mwca0584	canada quebec montreal	1830	WALKER	400	20	23	City of Montreal 1830
mwca0555	canada quebec	1830	WALKER	250	19	23	City of Quebec 1830 (map by J. Bouchette)
mwec0215	uk england cornwall	1844	WALKER	240	33	39	Cornwall
mwec0249	uk england cumbria	1850	WALKER	80	32	40	Cumberland (from Hobson's Fox Hunting Atlas)
mwec0386	uk england durham	1836	WALKER	60	34	42	Durham
mwec1370	uk england yorkshire	1845	WALKER	80	32	40	East Riding of Yorkshire
mww0646	world	1813	WALKER	375	40	51	Geographical Map of the World with the Tracts of the Most Celebrated Navigators
mwuk1409	uk geological	1835	WALKER	1200	127	98	Geological Map of England & Wales, Showing also the Inland Navigation by Means of Rivers and Canals
mwec0458	uk england gloucestershire	1840	WALKER	60	41	34	Gloucestershire
mwuk1600	channel islands	1840	WALKER	150	18	23	Guernsey and its Dependent Isles
mwec0504	uk england hampshire	1835	WALKER	65	42	34	Hampshire
mwec0567	uk england hertfordshire	1835	WALKER	60	35	41	Hertfordshire
mwec0592	uk england huntingdonshire	1837	WALKER	50	39	32	Huntingdonshire
mwuk1614	isle of man	1840	WALKER	150	24	18	Isle of Man
mwuk1601	channel islands	1840	WALKER	150	18	23	Jersey
mwec0668	uk england kent	1850	WALKER	65	35	42	Kent
mwin0501	pakistan etc.	1844	WALKER	400	80	64	Map of Afghanistan and the Adjacent Countries
mwin0372	india	1845	WALKER	450	98	84	Map of India from the Most Recent Authorities
mwas0346	asia central	1841	WALKER	1000	131	102	Map of the Countries on the North West Frontier of India
mwin0375	india	1846	WALKER	675	110	106	Map of the East India Railway, Shewing the Line Proposed to be Constructed to Connect Calcutta with the North West Provinces and the Intermediate Civilian and Military Stations
mwca0346	canada newfoundland	1840	WALKER	300	60	53	Map of the Island of Newfoundland
mwca0189	canada	1840	WALKER	280	42	50	Map of the Northern Parts of America
mwam1200	america north (east)	1827	WALKER	9600	127	193	Map of the United States; and the Provinces of Upper & Lower Canada, New Brunswick, and Nova Scotia
mwec0843	uk england norfolk	1850	WALKER	80	33	39	Norfolk (from Hobson's Fox Hunting Atlas)
mwam0542	america north	1798	WALKER	150	19	22	North America
mwec1365	uk england yorkshire	1840	WALKER	60	35	41	North Riding of Yorkshire
mwec0930	uk england nottinghamshire	1836	WALKER	60	41	34	Nottinghamshire
mwca0631	canada st lawrence	1818	WALKER	250	25	60	Part of Lake Ontario and of the River St. Lawrence from an Actual Survey by Captn. W.F.W. Owen R.N. 1816
mwuss1425	pennsylvania	1834	WALKER	150	16	20	Philadelphia
mwec0995	uk england rutland	1850	WALKER	80	34	39	Rutlandshire (from Hobson's Fox Hunting atlas)
mwuk0612	scotland	1830	WALKER	60	24	19	Scotland
mwec1024	uk england shropshire	1850	WALKER	80	40	33	Shropshire (from Hobson's Fox Hunting atlas)
mwec1151	uk england surrey	1835	WALKER	65	32	39	Surrey
mwuk1070	england	1841	WALKER	480	128	99	This New Map of England & Wales, Compiled from the Latest Surveys

AMPG REFERENCE	REGION	DATE	MAP MAKER	PRICE (UK£)	VERT. (cm.)	HOR. (cm.)	TITLE OF MAP (Comments by the editor in brackets)
mwin0351	india	1827	WALKER	1250	158	127	This Newly Constructed and Extended Map of India from the Latest Surveys of the Best Authorities Published Principally for Use of the Officers of the Army in India
mwec1213	uk england warwickshire	1850	WALKER	80	39	33	Warwickshire (from Hobson's Fox Hunting atlas)
mwwi0194	west indies	1834	WALKER	175	32	48	West India Islands and Adjacent Coast
mwec1366	uk england yorkshire	1840	WALKER	60	41	34	West Riding of Yorkshire
mwuk1300	england london	1824	WALLIS	2000	54	75	(Untitled map. 10 editions to 1843)
mwec0151	uk england cheshire	1812	WALLIS	135	21	30	Cheshire
mwec0383	uk england durham	1812	WALLIS	100	21	30	Durham
mwec0563	uk england hertfordshire	1819	WALLIS	50	14	10	Hertfordshire
mwec0794	uk england middlesex	1812	WALLIS	140	21	30	Middlesex
mwuk1245	england london	1783	WALLIS	1250	58		The Country Twenty-Two Miles round London (circular map. 6 editions to 1845)
mwam0588	america north	1812	WALLIS	100	26	22	United States of America
mwuk1279	england london	1808	WALLIS	1000	30	58	Wallis's Guide for Strangers through London and Westminster 1808 (4 editions to 1821)
mwuk1259	england london	1795	WALLIS	2000	42	86	Wallis's New and Correct Plan of London And Westminster
mwuk1264	england london	1798	WALLIS	1200	30	58	Wallis's Plan of the Cities of London and Westminster 1797 (5 editions to 1806)
mwuk1262	england london	1797	WALLIS	2000	42	85	Wallis's Plan of the Cities of London and Westminster 1797 (8 editions to 1819)
mwme0370	holy land	1784	WALPOOLE	300	31	43	A Plan of Nazareth - According to Modern Travellers
mwgm0041	gulf of mexico and surrounding regions	1777	WALTHARD	350	17	36	West Indien
mwuk0714	uk	1654	WALTON	3000	65	52	A Curious New and Plaine Mapp of England, Ireland, Scotland and Wales
mww0163	world	1656	WALTON	10000	39	52	A New and Accurat Map of the World Drawne According to ye Truest Descriptions Latest Discoveries & Best Observations yt have beene Made by English or Strangers (close copy of Speed's 1627 map)
mwuk0934	england	1679	WALTON	2250	59	51	A New Map Containing All the Citties, Market Townes, Rivers, Bridges & other Considerable Places in England & Wales wherin are Delineated ye Roads from Towne to Towne ...
mwuk0928	england	1668	WALTON	4500	40	50	A New Map of England and Wales In Which the Roads or highways are playnly layd forth
mwaf0070	africa	1662	WALTON	5500	42	53	A New, Plaine & Exact Map of Africa Described by: N:I: Visscher and Done into English, Enlarged and Corrected According to: I: Blaeu (4 carte-a-figure borders)
mwe0078	europe	1666	WALTON	5500	43	54	A New, Plaine & Exact Map of Europe Described by N:I: Visscher and Done into English Enlarged & Corrected According to I. Blaeu (4 borders with carte-a-figures)
mwam0058	america continent	1658	WALTON	15000	42	53	A New, Plaine, and Exact Map of America (4 borders with carte-a-figures)
mwas0047	asia continent	1660	WALTON	5500	42	53	A New, Plaine, and Exact Map of Asia (4 carte-a-figure borders)
mwuk1123	england london	1676	WALTON	12000	43	55	England's Glory or The Glory of England, Being a New Mapp of the City of London Shewing the remarkable streets Lanes Alleyes Churches Halls Courts and other places as they are now rebuilt the which will therefore be a guide to Strangers
mwsc0627	scandinavia norway	1763	WANGENSTEEN	2000	57	48	Aggershuus Stift, Afdelet i sine Amter og Fogderier med Kongelig Allernaadigst Tillatelse og Bevilling 1762 (1st map to focus on the environs of Oslo)
mwsc0625	scandinavia norway	1761	WANGENSTEEN	1600	57	48	Kongeriget Norge Afdeelet i sine Fiire Stifter, Nemlig Aggershuus, Christiansand, Bergenhuus og Tronhjem samt Underligende Provstier (1st map of Norway by a Norwegian)
mwe1053a	europe romania	1780	WAPPLER	800	44	56	Geographische Mappe des Gross=Fürstenthums Siebenbürgen
mwec1328	uk england yorkshire	1720	WARBURTON	2400	99	127	(Unitled map of Yorkshire)
mwec0779	uk england middlesex	1724	WARBURTON	2500	116	182	A New and Correct Mapp of Middlesex, Essex, and Hertfordshire, with the Roads Rivers and Sea-Coast etc., Actually Surveyed by John Warburton Esq. (incl. 738 coats of arms)
mwec0552	uk england hertfordshire	1749	WARBURTON	1500	62	78	Hertfordshire
mwec0783	uk england middlesex	1749	WARBURTON	1500	61	77	Middlesex
mwec0409	uk england essex	1726	WARBURTON	1500	61	95	The Counties of Essex Middlesex & Hertfordshire Actualy Survey'd by Several Hands, Corrected and Amended & Humbly Dedicated to the Nobility of the Said Counties
mwuss0345	washington DC	1819	WARDEN	400	34	35	Plan of the City of Washington and Territory of Columbia
mwuk0062	ireland	1654	WARE	200	15	10	Hiberniae Veteris Typus.
mwme0487	jerusalem	1725	WARE	400	35	39	Ierusalem. Sold by Richd. Ware and Will. Taylor
mwam0616a	america north	1820	WARNER	1500	42	64	United States of America Corrected and Improved from the Best Authorities

AMPG REFERENCE	REGION	DATE	MAP MAKER	PRICE (UK£)	VERT. (cm.)	HOR. (cm.)	TITLE OF MAP (Comments by the editor in brackets)
mwuss0766	maryland	1801	WARNER & HANNA	4800	48	74	Warner & Hanna's Plan of the City and Environs of Baltimore
mwec1108	uk england suffolk	1747	WARREN	2000	63	94	Survey of the Borough of St. Edmundsbury
mwuss1522	texas	1843	WARREN	300	27	22	Territories and Texas
mwuss0306	connecticut	1812	WARREN & GILLET	6000	91	110	Connecticut, from Actual Survey, Made in 1811
mwuk0506	scotland	1759	WATT	6000	51	72	The River of Clyde Surveyed by John Watt
mwru0150	russia	1721	WEBER	400	32	40	Grundriss der Festung Stadt u: Situation St. Petersburg
mwam1237	america north (east)	1834	WEBSTER	800	42	51	Map of the United States (illustrated is 1836 edition)
mwaa0049	antarctic	1825	WEDDELL	800	38	30	Chart of the tracks of the vessels Jane & Beaufoy
mwuk0877	uk	1801	WEIDNER	450	60	48	Charte der Vereinigten Konigreiche Grossbritannien und Irland
mwuss0337	washington DC	1794	WEIDNER	720	16	20	Plan de la Ville de Washington en Amerique
mwg0371	bavaria	1721	WEIGEL	240	28	35	(Augsburg) Augspurg mit umligender Gegend
mwgr0153	greece	1710	WEIGEL	300	31	39	Accurata Moreae
mwaf0504	africa egypt etc	1720	WEIGEL	240	39	32	Aegyptus Antiqua in suas Partes et Nomos Divisa, cum Troglodytice Marmarica et Aethiopia supra Aegyptum
mwaf0503	africa egypt etc	1720	WEIGEL	150	31	40	Aegyptus Inferior sive Delta
mwaf0152	africa	1720	WEIGEL	300	33	41	Africa Vetus
mwaf0844	africa north west	1720	WEIGEL	400	32	41	Africae Pars Superior Occidentalis
mwaf0157	africa	1724	WEIGEL	450	28	34	Africae Tabula
mwam0380	america north	1725	WEIGEL	1000	32	41	America Septentrionalis
mwuk0977	england	1718	WEIGEL	275	41	34	Anglia Cambdeni
mwuk0799	uk	1718	WEIGEL	375	28	34	Anglia, Scotia & Hibernia cum Insulis Vicinis
mwuk0804	uk	1720	WEIGEL	150	14	18	Angliae, Scotiae et Hiberniae Regna
mwme0603	arabia etc	1720	WEIGEL	350	31	37	Arabiae Veteris Typus
mwme0725	caucasus	1720	WEIGEL	300	31	39	Armenia Utraque
mwme0725a	caucasus	1720	WEIGEL	300	31	39	Asia intra Maeotim Pontum et Mare Caspium
mwas0127	asia continent	1720	WEIGEL	300	33	41	Asia Vetus
mwe0354	europe austria	1724	WEIGEL	180	28	34	Austria Inf.
mwe0355	europe austria	1724	WEIGEL	180	28	34	Austria Superior
mwbh0595	belgium holland	1724	WEIGEL	240	34	39	Belgium Regium Accuratissime Descriptum, cum Permutationibus Cursus Publici Curante
mwbh0596	belgium holland	1724	WEIGEL	240	34	39	Belgium sive Inferior Germania
mwbp0385	poland	1724	WEIGEL	350	32	37	Borussia Integra Accuratiori Stylo Delineata
mwg0371c	bavaria	1724	WEIGEL	250	40	32	Circulus Bavaricus
mwg0371b	bavaria	1724	WEIGEL	400	38	33	Circulus Franconicus ad Orientem / ad Occidentem (2 maps)
mwg0276a	baden-wurttemberg	1724	WEIGEL	200	33	39	Circulus Suevicus
mwgr0321	greece corfu	1720	WEIGEL	900	31	37	Corcyrae Insulae vulgo Corfu Planities unacum Parte Greciae
mwsc0351	scandinavia denmark	1724	WEIGEL	250	28	34	Dania Iutia, Holsatia, Scandia
mwe0356	europe austria	1724	WEIGEL	180	31	37	Ducatus Corinthiae
mwit0602	italy north	1724	WEIGEL	240	34	39	Ducatus Mediolanensis
mwf1152	france rhone-alpes	1724	WEIGEL	240	32	37	Ducatus Sabaudiae
mwg0272	baden-wurttemberg	1719	WEIGEL	180	34	41	Ducatus Wurtembergiae Curculi imo Suevici Pars Maximatus March et Badensis uterque
mwe1065a	europe serbia	1718	WEIGEL	420	41	34	Eigentliche Entwurf der Weltberuhmtem Stadt und Vestung Belgrad
mwe0138	europe	1720	WEIGEL	300	32	40	Europa Vetus
mwme0278	holy land	1724	WEIGEL	320	40	32	Facies Palaestinae ex Monumentis Veteribus Descripta ab Hadriano Relando (reduced version of Relands's 1714 map)
mwaa0019	antarctic	1720	WEIGEL	400	32	36	Facies Poli Antarctici ex Recentissimis Itinerariis Descripta a Christophori Weigelio (See also Arctic)
mwaa0120	arctic	1724	WEIGEL	300	32	36	Facies Poli Arctici (See also Antarctic)
mwf0109	france	1720	WEIGEL	200	28	35	Gallia cum Provinciis Insertis et Adsitis
mwgr0168	greece	1720	WEIGEL	480	55	40	Graeciae Antiquae Tabula Nova (2 sheets, joined)
mwgr0154	greece	1710	WEIGEL	480	31	38	Graeciae Nova Tabula
mwgr0165	greece	1720	WEIGEL	240	30	41	Graeciae Septentrionalis Pars
mwsw0121	switzerland	1724	WEIGEL	240	29	33	Helvetia cum subditis
mwsp0252	spain	1720	WEIGEL	375	26	33	Hispaniae et Portugaliae Regna
mwsp0253	spain	1720	WEIGEL	275	31	38	Hispaniae Vetus
mwg0722	schleswig-holstein	1724	WEIGEL	280	33	39	Holsatiae Dithmarsiae Stormariae et Vagriae Ducatus
mwe0923	europe hungary	1715	WEIGEL	650	41	61	Hungaria cum Adiacentibus Provinciis Nova et Accuratiori Forma Exhibetur (2 maps, joined)
mwg0116	germany	1725	WEIGEL	300	35	40	Imperium Germanicum
mwru0154	russia	1724	WEIGEL	200	28	34	Imperium Moscovia cum Regionibus Amplissimis huc Pertineutibus
mwin0170	india	1720	WEIGEL	480	31	39	India Intra et Extra Gangem
mwin0036	ceylon	1720	WEIGEL	300	40	33	Insula Ceylon
mwwi0242	west indies (east)	1720	WEIGEL	550	33	36	Insulae Antillae Franciae Superiores cum Vicinis Insulis / Insulae Antillae Francicae Inferiores (2 maps, each 33x36cm.)
mwm0220	mediterranean malta	1718	WEIGEL	900	33	39	Insulae Maltae Nova et Accurata Tabula
mwit0926	italy sicily	1720	WEIGEL	400	33	42	Insulae sive Regni Siciliae (inset: Corsica)
mwm0161	mediterranean islands	1720	WEIGEL	250	40	32	Insularum Corsicae Sardinae Melitae Accurata Descriptio ex Mente Veterum Geographorum
mwit0836	italy sardinia and corsica	1720	WEIGEL	350	42	33	Insularum Corsicae Sardiniae Melitae ... veterum
mwit0160	italy	1724	WEIGEL	120	14	18	Italia cum Insulis

AMPG REFERENCE	REGION	DATE	MAP MAKER	PRICE (UK£)	VERT. (cm.)	HOR. (cm.)	TITLE OF MAP (Comments by the editor in brackets)
mwit0310	italy central	1720	WEIGEL	300	30	40	Italia Media Lectioni Auctorum Classicorum (inset: Urbs Septicollis)
mwf0684	france lorraine	1719	WEIGEL	150	34	40	Lotharingia cum Contiguis
mwit1031	italy south	1720	WEIGEL	240	33	41	Magnae Graeciae Descriptio
mwe0918	europe hungary	1710	WEIGEL	250	30	38	Mappa der zu Carlovitz Geschlossenen und Hernach durch Zwey Gevollmachtigte Commisarios Vollzogenen Kaiserlich-Turkischen Grantz-Scheidung, so in dem Fruh-Jahr 1699 Angefangen
mwaf0844a	africa north west	1720	WEIGEL	300	32	37	Mauretania et Numidia
mwme0739	iraq etc	1720	WEIGEL	320	32	39	Mesopotamiae Assyriae et Babyloniae Tabula
mwas0125	asia continent	1720	WEIGEL	450	28	34	Nova Tabula Asiae
mwam0132	america continent	1720	WEIGEL	960	27	34	Novi Orbis sive Totius Americae cum Adiacentibus Insulis Nova Exhibitio
mwsw0122	switzerland	1724	WEIGEL	120	14	19	Novissima Foederatorum Helvetiorum Tabula
mwam0936	america north (east)	1734	WEIGEL	1100	32	41	Novissima Tabula Regionis Ludovicianae Gallice dictae la Louisiane
mwe0143	europe	1724	WEIGEL	400	27	33	Novissima totius Europae
mwg0532a	rheinland-pfalz	1724	WEIGEL	200	33	40	Palatinus Rheni
mww0344	world	1720	WEIGEL	1500	28	35	Planiglobium Terrestre Minus in hanc Formam Reductam
mwbp0382	poland	1720	WEIGEL	300	28	34	Poloniae & Lithuania Accurante Curatius
mwg0213a	germany north east	1720	WEIGEL	240	28	34	Pomerania
mwme0608	arabia etc	1720	WEIGEL	400	29	36	Portae Ottomanicae Regna & Ditiones per Europam, Asiam & Africam
mwsp0081	portugal	1720	WEIGEL	300	40	34	Portugallia ex Descriptione Exactissima Eduardi Nonii Verandi Alvari Secci et Antonii Vasconcelli Delineata
mwuk0142	ireland	1720	WEIGEL	400	39	33	Regni Hiberniae Accurata Tabula per Hermanum Moll
mwit0801	italy sardinia	1720	WEIGEL	500	40	32	Regni Sardiniae Descriptio
mwsc0427	scandinavia finland	1712	WEIGEL	350	32	39	Regnum Sueciae
mwg0639	saxony	1720	WEIGEL	180	33	38	Saxonia Superior
mwsc0129	scandinavia	1724	WEIGEL	320	32	37	Scandinavia complectens Sueciae, Daniae, Norvegiae Regna
mwm0043	mediterranean	1720	WEIGEL	400	32	41	Scena Historiarum Occidentalis Quinti / Scena Historiarum Orientalis Quinti (2 maps, showing the Roman Empire. Insets: 2 world hemispheres)
mwuk0464	scotland	1720	WEIGEL	320	37	31	Scotia Cambdeni et Sibbaldi
mwbp0386	poland	1724	WEIGEL	250	32	37	Silesia Ducatus
mwme0879	syria etc	1720	WEIGEL	350	32	41	Syria Propria cum Phoenice
mwgr0270	greece athens	1719	WEIGEL	350	32	41	Tabula Topographica Athenarum Veterum et Novarum. Auctore Fr. Vincentino Coronelli, Ord. Min. et Cosmograph Veneto (view)
mwme0279	holy land	1724	WEIGEL	250	33	40	Terra Sancta in XII olim Tribus nunc VI Provincias Dispertita
mwe0789	europe east	1720	WEIGEL	240	31	38	Thracia Antiqua
mwgr0164	greece	1719	WEIGEL	150	32	39	Thracia Antiqua
mwit1030	italy south	1720	WEIGEL	240	39	33	Typus Regni Neapolitani
mwru0508	ukraine	1720	WEIGEL	450	33	39	Ukrania seu Cosacorum Regio Walachia item Moldavia et Tartaria
mwe1065	europe serbia	1717	WEIGEL	420	33	42	Umstandliche Orts-Gelegen heit … Belgrad.
mwe0419a	europe austria vienna	1702	WIEGEL	1000	24	69	Vienna Austriae, 1683 (view)
mwg0819	westphalia	1724	WEIGEL	250	38	33	Westfaliae Ordines Secundum
mwf0893	france paris	1780	WEIGEL-SCHNEIDER	320	30	37	Grundriss von Paris
mwp0508	pacific south	1792	WEIGEL-SCHNEIDER	850	47	66	Karte von Australien oder Polynesien, nach den Zeichnungen, Reisebeschreibungen und Tagebucher der Vorzuglichsten Seefahrer bis 1789 Entworffen im Jahr 1792 (shows explorer routes in the western Pacific)
mwaf0335	africa	1841	WEILAND	200	51	60	Africa Entworfen und Gezeichnet
mwam0295	america continent	1835	WEILAND	240	62	50	America Entworfen und Gezeichnet
mwp0524	pacific south	1830	WEILAND	350	44	62	Australien nach Krusenstern, Flinders, Freycinet, Oxley, Cross
mwaf0556	africa egypt etc	1827	WEILAND	180	60	49	Das Nordoestliche Africa oder Aegypten
mwam1238	america north (east)	1837	WEILAND	450	62	52	Der Oestliche Theil der Vereinigten Staaten von Nord America
mwas0347	asia central	1845	WEILAND	450	47	62	Der westliche Theil von Mittel-Asien oder Turan
mww0687a	world	1829	WEILAND	450	42	59	Die Nördliche und Südliche Halbkugel der Erde
mww0701	world	1833	WEILAND	350	34	45	Die Oestlich und Westliche Halbkugel der Erde
mwam0711	america north	1837	WEILAND	600	48	64	Die Vereinigten Staaten von Nord-America (illustrated is 1846 issue)
mwuss0009	alabama	1825	WEILAND	350	29	23	Geographisch - Statistiche und Historische Chate von Alabama
mwuss1292	ohio	1825	WEILAND	350	40	46	Geographisch-Statistiche und Historische Charte des Staates Ohio
mwas0541	asia south east	1832	WEILAND	240	49	56	Hinterindien nebst den Hinterindischen Inseln
mwme0844a	persia etc	1828	WEILAND	350	45	59	Iran Afghanistan und Beludschistan
mwam0623	america north	1820	WEILAND	650	58	54	Nord America
mww0662	world	1819	WEILAND	500	50	66	Oestliche und Westliche Halbkugel der Erde
mwuss0267	carolinas	1825	WEILAND	480	34	36	Sud Carolina
mwwi0165	west indies	1820	WEILAND	240	51	58	West Indien

AMPG REFERENCE	REGION	DATE	MAP MAKER	PRICE (UK£)	VERT. (cm.)	HOR. (cm.)	TITLE OF MAP (Comments by the editor in brackets)
mwaf0545	africa egypt etc	1809	WEIMAR	500	29	49	(Cairo) Plan von Kahira nebst Fostat oder Alt-Kahira, Bulak und Dschise
mwme1054a	turkey etc	1813	WEIMAR	400	23	37	Ansicht der Meerenge der Dardanellen…
mwme0685	arabia etc	1839	WEIMAR	300	53	53	Arabien
mwwi0272	west indies (east)	1828	WEIMAR	200	48	55	Caraibisches Meer Die Inseln ueber dem Winde
mwca0471	canada ontario	1814	WEIMAR	200	20	31	Charte de Neuen Nieder Lassungen in Ober Canada nach der Smythschen Chart
mwca0345	canada newfoundland	1821	WEIMAR	150	32	30	Charte der Insel Newfoundland und eines Theils der Kuste von Labrador
mwwi0837	puerto rico	1814	WEIMAR	350	22	32	Charte der Insel Puerto Rico und der Insel Beique nach Don Tomas Lopez von Ledru
mwsam0788	south america peru	1814	WEIMAR	150	42	30	Charte der Provinz oder Audiencia von Lima oder des Alten Konigreichs Peru
mwaf0981	africa south	1804	WEIMAR	150	39	59	Charte der Sudspitze Africas und der Colonie vom Vorgebirge der Guten Hoffnung
mwru0321	russia	1800	WEIMAR	720	48	102	Charte des Ganzen Russischen-Reichs in Europa und Asien
mwbh0778	belgium holland	1808	WEIMAR	180	47	57	Charte des Konigreichs Holland
mwaf0982	africa south	1804	WEIMAR	500	53	24	Charte van der Halbinsel des Vorgebirge der Guten Hoffnung
mwaf0292	africa	1804	WEIMAR	350	50	57	Charte von Africa
mwas0235	asia continent	1805	WEIMAR	400	51	62	Charte von Asien
mwbp0564c	poland	1831	WEIMAR	300	61	56	Charte von dem Königreiche Polen
mwp0456	pacific north	1803	WEIMAR	480	38	45	Charte von dem Meer von Kamtschatka
mwwi0908	trinidad & tobago	1814	WEIMAR	400	23	41	Charte von den Inseln Trinidad, Tabago und Margaretha
mwwi0560	guadeloupe	1814	WEIMAR	120	17	20	Charte von der Insel Guadeloupe
mwat0172	atlantic canary isl.	1803	WEIMAR	120	16	21	Charte von der Insel Teneriffa
mwam1346	america north (west)	1804	WEIMAR	150	25	20	Charte von der Nordwestkuste Americas nach Vancouver
mwam1153a	america north (east)	1806	WEIMAR	240	30	41	Charte von der Vereinigten Staaten von Nord-America mit Luisiana
mwwi0805	martinique	1804	WEIMAR	120	17	19	Charte von der Westindischen Insel Martinique
mwwi0749	jamaica	1804	WEIMAR	140	17	31	Charte von Jamaica in Kirchspiele Eingetheilt, und mit den Poststrassen
mwam0608a	america north	1817	WEIMAR	750	59	54	Charte Von Nord America Entworfen und gezeichnet von C.G. Reichard
mwam0611	america north	1818	WEIMAR	350	42	30	Charte von Nord-America Prag … 1818
mwas0525	asia south east	1800	WEIMAR	750	47	86	Charte von Ostindien (in 2 sheets, joined)
mwsam0726a	south america paraguay	1812	WEIMAR	800	66	25	Charte von Paraguay und Buenos-Ayres.
mwit0823	italy sardinia	1801	WEIMAR	400	42	55	Charte von Sardinien
mwit0966	italy sicily	1801	WEIMAR	450	44	56	Charte von Sicilien und Malta
mwwi0169	west indies	1822	WEIMAR	350	30	41	Charte von West Indien oder den Antillischen Inseln
mwc0264	china	1832	WEIMAR	300	45	65	Das Chinesische Reich und das Kaiserthum Japan
mwe0406	europe austria	1849	WEIMAR	400	59	47	Das Konigreich Illyrien und das Herzoghum Steyermark
mwp0459	pacific north	1820	WEIMAR	500	54	70	Der Noerdliche Theil des Grossen Welt Meeres nach den Neuesten Bestimmungen und Entdeckungen
mwam1354	america north (west)	1826	WEIMAR	350	40	56	Die Gebiete Missouri und Oregan
mwwi0907	trinidad & tobago	1806	WEIMAR	400	16	22	Die Insel Trinidad
mwuk0573	scotland	1807	WEIMAR	160	24	19	Die Orkney's oder die Orkadischen Inseln
mwaf1059	africa south east	1827	WEIMAR	180	63	54	Die Ostkuste Sud Africa's nebst der Insel Madagascar, den Comoren, Sechellen, Amiranten und Mascarenischen Inseln
mwaf1006	africa south	1827	WEIMAR	400	50	63	Die Sudspitze von Africa mit der Colonie vom Vorgebirge der Guten Hoffnung mit Besonderer Berucksichtigung von Burchell's Reisen
mwam0794a	america north	1848	WEIMAR	300	27	38	Die Vereinigten Staaten von Nordamerica und deren Teritorien nebst Canada 1848 (map based on Fremont)
mwuk1064	england	1836	WEIMAR	180	54	46	England
mwp0040	australia	1804	WEIMAR	1200	45	62	General Charte von Australien
mwe0395	europe austria	1808	WEIMAR	150	48	59	Generalcharte des Osterreichischen Kaisertums
mwuss0348	washington DC	1823	WEIMAR	480	33	47	Geographisch-Statistische und Historische Charte von Columbia
mwwi0679a	hispaniola	1824	WEIMAR	300	45	49	Geographisch-statistische und historische Charte von Hayti
mwuss0551	illinois	1826	WEIMAR	350	41	45	Illinois
mwit0250	italy	1847	WEIMAR	250			Italien
mwbp0572	poland	1848	WEIMAR	180	55	50	Karte von den Konigl. Preussischen Provincen
mwuss0610	kentucky	1826	WEIMAR	350	46	52	Kentucky
mwgm0305	mexico	1826	WEIMAR	600	48	55	Mexico
mwgm0365a	mexico	1848	WEIMAR	1500	54	63	Mexico Texas und Californien (map by H. Kiepert)
mwuss0978	missouri	1826	WEIMAR	350	38	44	Missuri
mwgm0282	mexico	1814	WEIMAR	200	44	33	Neue Charte des Thales von Mexico und der Benachbarten Gebirge (environs of Mexico City)
mwam1153	america north (east)	1806	WEIMAR	300	34	47	Neue Charte von den mitteren, westlichen und sudliched Lande
mwwi0675	hispaniola	1814	WEIMAR	350	30	42	Neue Charte von S. Domingo Entworfen von Leyritz Levassor und Bourjolly Colonisten
mwuss1285	ohio	1819	WEIMAR	240	23	21	Ohio
mwme1048	turkey etc	1812	WEIMAR	300	45	61	Plan de Constantinople
mwru0323a	russia	1804	WEIMAR	450	35	42	Plan de la Ville de St. Petersbourg

AMPG REFERENCE	REGION	DATE	MAP MAKER	PRICE (UK£)	VERT. (cm.)	HOR. (cm.)	TITLE OF MAP (Comments by the editor in brackets)
mwru0344a	russia	1826	WEIMAR	320	26	35	Plan der Residenzstadt St. Petersburg
mwuk1271	england london	1802	WEIMAR	650	25	49	Plan des Villes de Londres et Westminster et du Bourg de Southwark
mwru0400	russia moscow	1807	WEIMAR	720	60	48	Plan von Moskwa - Plan de Moskwa
mwp0053	australia	1808	WEIMAR	2000	17	21	Plan von Sydney (by C. Lesueur)
mwit1254	italy venice	1807	WEIMAR	280	23	24	Plan von Venedig
mwsc0214	scandinavia	1833	WEIMAR	180	60	45	Schweden und Norwegen
mwuk0623	scotland	1837	WEIMAR	180	54	46	Scotland
mwg0676	saxony	1807	WEIMAR	480	33	41	Special-Charte des Furstenthums Schaumburg Lippe, und der Umliegenden Gegend
mwsam0126	south america	1804	WEIMAR	350	70	52	Sud America
mww0622a	world	1804	WEIMAR	600	47	60	Sudliche und Noerdliche Halbkugel der Erde nach den Neuesten Entdeckungen nach den Vulkanischen-Linien nach Herrn Dr. Sicklers Theorie Entworfen (2 polar projections)
mwit0960	italy sicily	1783	WEIS	300	26	41	La Sicile et Partie du Royaume de Naples (inset: Malta)
mwe1179	europe south east	1829	WEISS	1000	295	190	Carte der Europaeischen Turkey nebst einem Theile von Kleinasien
mwf0418	france burgundy	1786	WEISS	140	53	45	Carte du Comte de Montbeliard et Terres Limitrophes ... a la Convention Signee a Paris le 21 May 1786
mwsw0218	switzerland	1800	WEISS	400	56	85	Nouvelle Carte Hydrographique et Routiere de la Suisse Levee et Executee par J.H. Weiss, Ingr. Geophe. a l'Etat Major General de l'Armee du Rhin. a Strasbourg, An 8eme.
mwsw0210	switzerland	1798	WEISS	350	53	71	Partie des Grisons du Haut Rheinthal et ... d'Arlberg et Tyrol (from 'Atlas Suisse' in 16 sheets)
mwaf0121	africa	1700	WELLS	720	37	51	A New Map of Africk Shewing its Present General Divisions Cheif Cities or Towns, Rivers, Mountains &c.
mwas0093	asia continent	1700	WELLS	480	37	51	A New Map of Ancient Asia
mwf0089	france	1700	WELLS	240	36	50	A New Map of Ancient Gaul
mwsc0101	scandinavia	1700	WELLS	240	36	49	A New Map of Ancient Scandinavia together with as Much More of ye Northern Part of Ancient Europe as Answers to Present Denmark & Moscovia
mwg0090	germany	1700	WELLS	240	36	48	A New Map of Antient Germany, Rhaetia, Vindelicia, and Noricum, Shewing their Principal People, Tribes, Cities, Towns, Rivers, Mountains, &c.
mwgr0133	greece	1700	WELLS	480	36	48	A New Map of Antient Greece
mwit0126	italy	1700	WELLS	480	37	49	A New Map of Antient Italy
mwgr0134	greece	1700	WELLS	250	36	47	A New Map of Antient Thrace
mwru0116	russia	1700	WELLS	400	37	50	A New Map of Denmark, Norway, Sweden, & Moscovy
mwe0111	europe	1700	WELLS	400	39	49	A New Map of Europe According to its Ancient General Divisions
mwe0107	europe	1700	WELLS	500	37	49	A New Map of Europe according to the Present General Divisions
mwf0088	france	1700	WELLS	500	37	50	A New Map of France (incl. 'Sansons Coast', showing earlier inaccuracies)
mwit1020	italy south	1700	WELLS	200	47	36	A New Map of Gallia Cisalpina & Graecia Magna
mwru0439a	russia tartary	1700	WELLS	550	36	50	A New Map of Great Tartary, and China with the Adjoining Part of Asia
mwsp0217	spain	1700	WELLS	350	37	49	A New Map of Iberia, Europaea Aloas Celtiberia or Ancient Spain
mwit0401a	italy lazio	1700	WELLS	280	36	48	A New Map of Latium
mwaf0122	africa	1700	WELLS	480	36	48	A New Map of Libya or Old Africk Shewing its General Divisions, Most Remarkable Countries or People, Cities, Townes, Rivers, Mountains &c.
mwam0346	america north	1700	WELLS	2000	37	49	A New Map of North America Shewing its Principal Divisions, Chief Cities, Townes, Rivers, Mountains &c.
mwas0092	asia continent	1700	WELLS	600	37	51	A New Map of Present Asia Dedicated to His Highness William Duke of Gloucester
mwg0089	germany	1700	WELLS	375	37	48	A New Map of Present Germany Showing its Principal Divisions, Cities, Towns, Rivers, Mountains &c.
mwit0127	italy	1700	WELLS	600	37	49	A New Map of Present Italy, together with the Adjoyning Islands of Sicily, Sardinia, Corsica
mwbp0346	poland	1700	WELLS	600	36	50	A New Map of Present Poland
mwe0777	europe east	1700	WELLS	480	36	50	A New Map of Present Poland, Hungary, Walachia, Moldavia, Little Tartary
mwsp0216	spain	1700	WELLS	480	37	50	A New Map of Present Spain & Portugal
mwru0117	russia	1700	WELLS	400	37	50	A New Map of Sarmatia Europaea
mwsam0039	south america	1700	WELLS	675	38	51	A New Map of South America, Shewing it's General Divisions, Chief Cities & Towns; Rivers, Mountains &c.
mwuk0770	uk	1700	WELLS	720	37	49	A New Map of the British Isles, Shewing their Antient People, Cities, and Towns of Note, in the Time of the Romans
mwuk0771	uk	1700	WELLS	785	38	50	A New Map of the British Isles, Shewing their Present Genl. Divisions
mwas0425	asia south east	1700	WELLS	1250	35	48	A New Map of the East Indies, Taken from Mr. de Fer's Map of Asia, Shewing their Chief Divisions, Cities, Towns, Ports, Rivers, Mountains &c.

AMPG REFERENCE	REGION	DATE	MAP MAKER	PRICE (UK£)	VERT. (cm.)	HOR. (cm.)	TITLE OF MAP (Comments by the editor in brackets)
mwme0980	turkey etc	1700	WELLS	480	37	48	A New Map of the Eastern Parts of Asia Minor Largely Taken: as also Syria, Armenia, Mesopotamia &c.
mwgr0616	greece islands	1700	WELLS	480	50	37	A New Map of the Islands of the Aegean Sea, together with the Island of Crete, and the Adjoining Isles
mwme0217	holy land	1700	WELLS	480	36	48	A New Map of the Land of Canaan and Parts Adjoining Shewing the Division thereof among the Twelve Tribes of Israel
mwam0906	america north (east)	1700	WELLS	1350	35	48	A New Map of the Most Considerable Plantations of the English in America
mwbh0503	belgium holland	1700	WELLS	480	36	48	A New Map of the Netherlands, or Low Countries, Showing their Principal Divisions, Cities, Towns, Rivers etc.
mwaf0705	africa north	1700	WELLS	240	37	49	A New Map of the North Part of Antient Africa Shewing the Chiefe People, Cities, Towns, Rivers, Mountains &c. in Mauritania, Numidia, Africa Propria, Lybia Propria, and Egypt (2 maps on one sheet. The map on the left with north to the left).
mwgr0135	greece	1700	WELLS	480	38	50	A New Map of the So. & Mid. Parts of Antient Greece viz. Epirus, Hellas, or Graecia Propria, and Peloponnesus, together with the Adjoyning Islands
mww0281	world	1700	WELLS	1600	36	50	A New Map of the Terraqueous Globe according to the Ancient Discoveries and most general Divisions of it into Continents and Oceans
mww0282	world	1700	WELLS	2000	36	50	A New Map of the Terraqueous Globe according to the latest Discoveries and most general Divisions of it into Continents and Oceans
mwme0979	turkey etc	1700	WELLS	600	37	49	A New Map of the Western Parts of Asia Minor, Shewing their Antient Divisions, Countries or People
mwe1145	europe south east	1700	WELLS	480	37	49	A New Map of Turkey in Europe and Parts Adjoyning Shewing their Principal Divisions and Cheife Cities, Towns, Rivers, Mountains, &c.
mwgr0136	greece	1700	WELLS	480	36	48	A New Map of Turky in Europe
mwme0218	holy land	1700	WELLS	480	36	48	A New Map Shewing All the Severall Countries, Cities, Towns, and other Places Mentioned in the New Testament
mwme0275	holy land	1722	WELLS	480	36	48	A New Map Shewing the Travels of the Patriarchs. As also of the Children of Israel from Egypt through the Wilderness to the Land of Canaan
mwsam0058	south america	1726	WELLS	200	9	16	Americae Australis Tabula
mwam0381	america north	1726	WELLS	400	9	16	Americae Septentrionalis Tabula
mwaf0158	africa	1726	WELLS	180	10	16	Antiquae Africae Tabula
mwme0997	turkey etc	1726	WELLS	180	10	17	Antiquae Asiae Minoris &c Tabula
mwas0131	asia continent	1726	WELLS	180	9	16	Antiquae Asiae Tabula
mwe0145	europe	1726	WELLS	180	9	14	Antiquae Europae Tabula
mwgr0173	greece	1726	WELLS	250	11	16	Antiquae Graeciae Tabula
mwit0161	italy	1726	WELLS	180	9	16	Antiquae Italiae Tabula
mwaf0159	africa	1726	WELLS	280	9	16	Hodiernae Africae Tabula
mwas0130	asia continent	1726	WELLS	200	9	16	Hodiernae Asiae Tabula
mwe0144	europe	1726	WELLS	200	9	14	Hodiernae Europae Tabula
mwit0162	italy	1726	WELLS	180	9	16	Hodiernae Italiae Tabula
mwuk0806	uk	1726	WELLS	200	16	9	Insularum Britannicarum Tabula
mwuss1419	pennsylvania	1830	WELLS	2500	45	56	Map of Somerset County. Constructed by Virtue of an Act of the Legislature of Pennsylvania by John Wells
mwm0049	mediterranean	1726	WELLS	240	10	16	Maris Mediterranei Tabula
mww0351	world	1726	WELLS	400	8	16	Orbis Terrarum Cognitus Hodiernis Europaeis
mww0352	world	1726	WELLS	280	9	16	Orbis Terrarum Cognitus Veteribus Graecis et Latinis
mwas0137	asia continent	1730	WELLS	600	37	50	Present Asia Distinguisht into its General Divisions or Countries together with their Capital Cities
mwec0644a	uk england kent	1782	WELLS, T.	800	52	69	A Parochial Map of the Diocese of Canterbury (incl. gazetteer in side borders)
mwme0680b	arabia etc	1835	WELLSTED	600	19	20	Map of Oman in Arabia
mwgm0318	mexico	1830	WERNER	180	19	26	Das Reich Mexico
mwam1356	america north (west)	1830	WERNER	200	20	27	Die Vereinigten Staaten von Nord Amerika. Gebiet Missouri, Gebeit Oregan
mww0364	world	1730	WETSTEIN	1500	36	51	De Werelt Caart (re-issue of 1700 map by Danckerts. Shirley 615)
mwp0501	pacific south	1777	WHITCHURCH	1200	36	66	Chart of Part of the South Seas Shewing the Tracts & Discoveries Made by His Majesty's Ships (incl. Australia)
mwuk1602	channel islands	1840	WHITE	800	63	95	A Survey of the Islands of Guernsey, Sercq and Herm, with the Surrounding Dangers
mwuss1032	new hampshire	1850	WHITE	450	30	19	Map of New Hampshire
mwuss1587	vermont	1850	WHITE	450	27	18	Map of Vermont
mwgm0313	mexico	1828	WHITE	35000	74	104	Mapa de los Estados Unidos de Mejico, Segun lo Organizado y Definido por las Varias Actas del Congreso de dicha Republica: y Construido por las Mejores Autoridades (copy in Spanish of Tanner's updated 1826 map with incorrect US/Mexico border)
mwuss1566	vermont	1807	WHITELAW	800	44	29	A Map of the State of Vermont

AMPG REFERENCE	REGION	DATE	MAP MAKER	PRICE (UK£)	VERT. (cm.)	HOR. (cm.)	TITLE OF MAP (Comments by the editor in brackets)
mwuss1557	vermont	1794	WHITELAW	960	35	29	A Map of the State of Vermont by J. Whitelaw
mwuss1569	vermont	1821	WHITELAW	3500	112	75	Vermont from Actual Surveys, with All the Late Additions and Improvements
mwg0543	rheinland-pfalz	1797	WIEBEKING	960	31	318	Hydrographisch-hybrotechnische Karte von dem Nieder Rhein von Linz bis unter Arnheim in X Blatt
mwme1042	turkey etc	1803	WIEIMAR	550	46	61	Plan de Constantinople
mwme0477	jerusalem	1703	WIJKMAN	650	43	50	Jerusalems Grundrifning och Belagenhet
mwru0324	russia	1804	WILBRECHT	960	69	98	(Black Sea - title in Cyrillic)
mwp0453	pacific north	1802	WILBRECHT	6000	75	100	(Karta Morskykh Otkrytii Rossiiskimi Moreplavatelimi na Tikhom ... in Cyrillic)
mwbp0151	baltic states	1800	WILBRECHT	875			(Title in Russian script. Estlyandskaya Province.)
mwbp0152	baltic states	1800	WILBRECHT	875			(Title in Russian script. Liflyandskaya Province.)
mwp0441a	pacific north	1792	WILBRECHT	1500	47	59	(Title in Russian: Eastern Part of the Irkutsk Province with the adjacent islands and West Coast of America)
mwru0305	russia	1792	WILBRECHT	4000	74	147	(Title in Russian script: General'naia karta Rossiiskoi Imperii na sorok odnu guberniiu razdielennoi. Inset of Alaska.)
mwp0436	pacific north	1787	WILBRECHT	2500	55	81	Carte des Decouvertes Faites par les Russes et par le Capitaine Anglois Jacques Cook dans la Mer du Sud (illustrated is edition with Russian script)
mwru0304	russia	1792	WILBRECHT	800	47	60	Carte des Environs de St. Petersbourg 1792
mwsam0249	south america argentina	1807	WILCOCKE	240	19	11	Plan of the City of Buenos Ayres
mwuss0134	california	1849	WILKES	800	60	43	A Correct Map from Actual Surveys and Examinations Embracing a Portion of California between Monterey and the Prairie Butes in the Valley of the Sacramento
mwca0125	canada	1797	WILKES	160	23	18	British Colonies in North America
mwaa0159	arctic	1807	WILKES	140	20	21	Countries Surrounding the North Pole
mwp0354	pacific hawaii	1845	WILKES	400	40	60	Map of the Hawaiian Group or Sandwich Islands ... 1841 (illustrated is the 1845 reduced version 22x28cm)
mwuss0135	california	1849	WILKES	160	21	29	Map of Upper California
mwam0534	america north	1796	WILKES	180	23	19	North America
mwam1122	america north (east)	1797	WILKES	240	19	24	United States of America
mww0631	world	1807	WILKES	280	20	38	Western Hemisphere, or New World - Eastern Hemisphere, or Old World
mwam1115	america north (east)	1794	WILKINSON	200	21	27	A Map of the United States of America with Part of the Adjoining Provinces from the Latest Authorities
mwaf0276	africa	1794	WILKINSON	120	23	25	A New and Accurate Map of Africa
mwp0032	australia	1792	WILKINSON	350	27	23	A New and Accurate Map of New South Wales, also Norfolk and Ld. Howes Islands, from Actual Surveys (insets of New Norfolk and Lord Howe Islands)
mww0630	world	1807	WILKINSON	5000	62	104	A New and Correct Map of the World, wherein Besides what is to be Met with in ye Common Maps Such as the Three Systems of the World, the Magnetical Variations, Trade Winds &c. are Incerted an Abstract of ye First Principles of Geography
mwsc0391	scandinavia denmark	1806	WILKINSON	60	22	28	A New Map of Denmark and Holstein
mwg0170	germany	1806	WILKINSON	60	22	28	A New Map of Germany Divided into Circles from the Best Authorities
mwam0524	america north	1794	WILKINSON	240	21	25	A New Map of North America, Agreeable to the Latest Discoveries
mwbp0530	poland	1794	WILKINSON	140	23	29	A New Map of Prussia
mww0615	world	1800	WILKINSON	280	27	44	A New Mercator's Chart Drawn from the Latest Discoveries
mwaf0287	africa	1800	WILKINSON	120	28	25	Africa including the Mediterranean
mwam0251	america continent	1803	WILKINSON	480	55	68	America
mwas0518	asia south east	1794	WILKINSON	135	22	28	An Accurate Map of the Islands and Channels between China and New Holland
mwwi0135	west indies	1794	WILKINSON	135	23	33	An Accurate Map of the West Indies from the Latest Improvements
mwgr0233	greece	1794	WILKINSON	90	19	24	Antient Greece
mwas0238	asia continent	1808	WILKINSON	135	23	29	Asia Drawn from the Latest Astronomical Observations (incl. Australia)
mwe0394	europe austria	1807	WILKINSON	60	23	29	Austria
mwg0403	bavaria	1806	WILKINSON	70	23	28	Bavaria Divided into its Respective Sovereign States
mwe1169	europe south east	1800	WILKINSON	70	23	29	Bohemia Including Moravia, Austrian Silesia, Eger and Glatz
mwme0387	holy land	1798	WILKINSON	135	44	28	Canaan from the Time of Joshua to the Babylonish Captivity
mwsam0642	south america guyana	1795	WILKINSON	850	61	95	Chart of the River and Sea Coast of the Colony of Demerary
mwc0230	china	1801	WILKINSON	100	23	28	China, Contains 15 Subject Provinces Including the 2 Islands of Hainan, Formosa and the Tributary Kingdoms of Corea, Tonkin
mwit0825	italy sardinia	1808	WILKINSON	100	29	23	Dominions of the King of Sardinia
mwuk1043	england	1813	WILKINSON	100	29	23	England and Wales

AMPG REFERENCE	REGION	DATE	MAP MAKER	PRICE (UK£)	VERT. (cm.)	HOR. (cm.)	TITLE OF MAP (Comments by the editor in brackets)
mwit0322	italy central	1809	WILKINSON	100	29	23	Estates of the Church, Grand Duchy of Tuscany, Republic of Lucca, &c.
mwe0238	europe	1806	WILKINSON	70	22	28	Europe
mwf0179	france	1810	WILKINSON	50	23	29	France Divided into Governments, as it was before the Revolution MDCCXC
mwf0177	france	1806	WILKINSON	60	22	28	France Divided into Provinces
mwin0329	india	1806	WILKINSON	100	33	27	Hindoostan Divided into Soubahs According to the Ayin Acbaree
mwe0971	europe hungary	1806	WILKINSON	70	23	28	Hungary and Transilvania Drawn from the Latest Authorities
mwuk0247	ireland	1806	WILKINSON	100	29	23	Ireland as Represented in the Imperial Parliament
mwit0224	italy	1806	WILKINSON	70	22	28	Italy with the Islands of Sicily, Sardinia, & Corsica, Drawn from the Best Authorities
mwme0514	jerusalem	1814	WILKINSON	200	28	23	Land of Moriah or Jerusalem
mww0546	world	1786	WILKINSON	400	19	36	Map of the World from the Best Authorities
mwit1045	italy south	1809	WILKINSON	70	29	23	Naples and Sicily from the Latest Observations
mwp0045	australia	1810	WILKINSON	135	29	23	New South Wales, New Zealand, New Hebrides and the Islands Adjacent
mwam0608b	america north	1817	WILKINSON	220	23	29	North America
mwam0564	america north	1804	WILKINSON	4800	52	61	North America, Published the 12th. of August 1804 (1st map to show Louisiana part of US)
mwgr0234	greece	1794	WILKINSON	120	32	33	Peloponnesus, cum insulae circumjacentibus
mwuk0574	scotland	1807	WILKINSON	100	29	23	Scotland
mwsam0125	south america	1803	WILKINSON	70	28	23	South America
mwsam0127	south america	1806	WILKINSON	280	52	61	South America with its Political Divisions Compiled from State Papers and Observations Astronomical, Nautical and Historical
mwsp0315	spain	1808	WILKINSON	90	23	29	Spain and Portugal
mwc0257	china	1826	WILKINSON	480	50	60	The Chinese Empire and the Islands of Japan Compiled from the Most Authentic Documents
mwbh0779	belgium holland	1809	WILKINSON	70	22	29	The Netherlands including Liege
mwit0618	italy north	1794	WILKINSON	70	23	28	The North East Part of Italy Comprising the Estates of Venice the Dutchies of Milan, Mantua, Modena & Parma; with Part of the Estate of Genoa
mwru0322	russia	1801	WILKINSON	120	23	29	The Russian Empire in Europe and Asia
mwin0332	india	1808	WILKINSON	90	33	27	The Southern Provinces of Hindoostan
mwaf0558	africa egypt etc	1830	WILKINSON	1200	146	164	Topographical Survey of Thebes, Tape, Thaba or Diosopolis Magna
mwme1045	turkey etc	1808	WILKINSON	70	23	29	Turkey in Asia
mwme1052	turkey etc	1824	WILKINSON	280	51	61	Turkey in Asia from Recent Authorities Regulated by Astronomical Observations
mwe1171	europe south east	1809	WILKINSON	70	29	23	Turkey in Europe
mww0620	world	1803	WILKINSON	720	55	64	World … Published by Robr. Wilkinson, June 4th 1803
mwsp0742	gibraltar	1800	WILL	400	21	32	Abriss der Stadt Gibraltar
mwsp0743	gibraltar	1800	WILL	400	21	32	Caerte van de Baey van Gibraltar (inset of Gibraltar)
mwe1157	europe south east	1770	WILL	720	52	59	Kriegs Schauplatz (concentric circles centred on Belgrade)
mwe1080	europe serbia	1790	WILL	500	38	44	Kriegskarte bey der Stadt … Belgrad (illustrated left)
mwam0230	america continent	1790	WILL	800	89	57	L'Amerique
mwsam0123	south america	1800	WILL	480	43	55	L'Amerique selon l'etendue de ses principales parties
mwe1081	europe serbia	1790	WILL	400	35	29	Neuer und genaur Abriss … Vestung Belgrade (illustrated above)
mwsp0736	gibraltar	1782	WILL	720	34	24	Plan de Gibraltaar attaque par Terre et par Mer (2 maps on one sheet)
mwuss0316	connecticut	1829	WILLARD	960	46	54	Connecticut, from Actual Surveys of Warren & Gillet, with the Addition of New Towns, Turnpikes, Roads, &c. by George Gillet, Esq. (re-issue of 1812 map)
mwam1203	america north (east)	1828	WILLARD	2400	99	120	Map of the United States
mwuss0313	connecticut	1824	WILLARD	4000	54	46	Plan of the City of Hartford from a Survey Made in 1824
mwbh0682	belgium holland	1747	WILLCOCK	875	46	33	A New Plan of the City of Bergen-op-Zoom; with the Forts
mwuk0489	scotland	1746	WILLDEY	3500	46	38	A Map of the King's Roads, Made by his Excellency General Wade in the Highlands of Scotland; from Sterling to Inverness, with the Adjacent Countries &c.
mwuk0976	england	1715	WILLDEY	4500	61	99	A New & Correct Map of England and Wales, Now Called South Britain (18 views of ports in side borders)
mww0366	world	1732	WILLDEY	10000	65	96	A New & Correct Map of the World Laid down according to the Newest Observations & Discoveries in several different Projections (first edition 1702?)
mwuk1157	england london	1720	WILLDEY	2500	64	97	A New & Correct Map of Thirty Miles round London, Shewing all the Towns, Villages, Roads &c with the Seats of the Nobility & Gentry & whatever else is Remarkable (circular map. Size incl. text references in side borders)
mwuk1158	england london	1721	WILLDEY	1350	36	36	A New & Correct Map of Twenty Miles round London (circular map)
mwg0101	germany	1715	WILLDEY	750	64	93	A New & Exact Map of Germany According to the Newest Observations
mwbh0564	belgium holland	1717	WILLDEY	800	61	89	A New and Correct Map of the X Spanish Provinces According to the Newest Observations Communicated

AMPG REFERENCE	REGION	DATE	MAP MAKER	PRICE (UK£)	VERT. (cm.)	HOR. (cm.)	TITLE OF MAP (Comments by the editor in brackets)
mwsp0244	spain	1717	WILLDEY	1400	60	95	A New and Exact Map of Spain & Portugal Corrected According to the Best Observations
mwec0099	uk england cambridgeshire	1730	WILLDEY	1800	42	51	Cambridge Shire Actually Surveyed and Delineated
mwec0550	uk england hertfordshire	1730	WILLDEY	1500	42	51	Hertford Shire Actually Surveyed and Delineated
mwuk0136	ireland	1710	WILLDEY	720	44	36	Ireland according to the latest Improvements
mwuk0973	england	1713	WILLDEY	2500	52	53	The Roads of England According to Mr Ogilby's Survey (circular map)
mwam0369	america north	1717	WILLDEY	4500	97	65	To His Sacred & Most Excellent Majesty George by the Grace of God King of Great Britain France and Ireland etc. this Map of North America (Corrected from the Latest Discoveries and Observations) is Most Humbly Dedicated
mwuk0795	uk	1715	WILLDEY	4800	95	66	To His Sacred and Most Excellent Majesty George ... Great Britain and Ireland, Corrected from the Newest and Most Exact Observations
mwe1152	europe south east	1725	WILLDEY	675	43	35	Turkey in Europe.
mwuss1184	new york	1815	WILLETTS	2250	61	73	Map of the State of New York with Parts Adjacent
mwuk1551	bristol channel	1760	WILLIAMS	675	62	112	A New and Exact Draught of the Channell of Bristoll from Hartland Poynt to the River Avon & from Caldy Isle to Red Cliff
mwuss0471	florida	1832	WILLIAMS	300	25	20	Florida
mwuss0476	florida	1837	WILLIAMS	1800	86	76	Map of Florida
mwuss1531	texas	1845	WILLIAMS	1000	31	38	Map of Texas from the most recent authorities (inset: Texas north of Red River)
mwuss0938	minnesota	1849	WILLIAMS	300	31	40	Map of the North-Western States Including Minnesota and the Copper Region of Lake Superior
mwam1222	america north (east)	1833	WILLIAMS	1200	55	42	Map of the United States Constructed from the Latest Authorities
mwuss1206	new york	1827	WILLIAMS	400	49	74	The Tourist's Map of the State of New York
mwuk0306	irish sea	1767	WILLIAMSON	3500	127	193	A General Chart of the Saint George's Channel, containing a Particular Description Of the bearings of each Point of Land by the Common Compass
mwuk1538	uk english channel (east)	1849	WILSON	960	90	238	A Chart of the East Coast of England from Dungeness to Newcastle Including the Entrances of the Thames and the Coast of France &c. from Boulogne to Flushing
mwp0465	pacific pelew isl.	1788	WILSON	120	28	53	A Chart of the Pelew Islands and Adjacent Seas
mwin0453	indian ocean	1850	WILSON	450	113	198	A General Chart of the Indian and Part of the Pacific Oceans, Shewing the Various Passages to & from China, Australia, New Zealand, &c.
mwuss0259	carolinas	1822	WILSON	17500	117	150	A Map of South Carolina, Constructed and Drawn from the District Surveys
mwuk0609	scotland	1829	WILSON	240	22		A Map of the Country 8 Miles round Glasgow (circular map surrounded by views)
mwuk0193	ireland	1764	WILSON	320	25	34	A New Plan of Dublin
mwp0324	pacific gambier isl.	1799	WILSON	200	22	28	Chart of Gambier's Islands, Discovered by Capt. James Wilson in the Ship Duff
mwp0513b	pacific south	1799	WILSON	750	36	55	Chart of the Duff's Track in the Pacific Ocean 1797
mwp0321	pacific friendly isl.	1799	WILSON	300	25	38	Chart of the Island and Harbour of Tongataboo by Wm. Wilson
mwp0369	pacific marquesas	1799	WILSON	150	28	20	Chart of the Marquesas by Capt. James Wilson, in the Ship Duff 1797
mwuk1599	channel islands	1814	WILSON	320	33	38	Island of Guernsey
mwp0513c	pacific south	1799	WILSON	200	24	38	Sketch of the Duff's Groupe, Discovered September 25, 1797 by Capt. James Wilson
mwp0536	pacific tahiti	1799	WILSON	250	28	38	The Island of Otaheite, According to the Survey Taken by Cap. Cook 1769
mwuk0220	ireland	1783	WILSON	320	35	34	Wilson's New & Accurate Map of the Roads of Ireland.
mwbp0383	poland	1720	WINCKLER	800	41	57	Ducatus in Silesia Inferiore Olsnensis Novissima Delineatio
mwme0508	jerusalem	1760	WINNKLER	600	38	53	Neuer und Wahrer Abriss der Stadt Ierusalem
mwam0530	america north	1795	WINTERBOTHAM	320	35	44	A General Map of North America, Drawn from the Best Surveys
mwsam0116	south america	1794	WINTERBOTHAM	200	36	45	A General Map of South America Drawn from the Best Surveys
mwuss0342a	washington DC	1800	WINTERBOTHAM	3000	40	53	Plan of the City of Washington in the Territory of Columbia, Ceded by the States of Virginia and Maryland to the United States of America, and by them Established as the Seat of their Government, after the Year 1800 (reduced size version of Ellicot's 1792 map, with additions)
mwru0542	ukraine	1769	WISGER	500	28	38	Vorstellung der Bataille zwischen denen Russen und Turken, de 13ten Julli 1769
mwgm0366	mexico	1848	WISLIZENUS	450	50	41	Map of a Tour from Independence to Santa Fe, Chihuahua, Monterey and Matamoros ... in 1846 and 1847
mwru0095	russia	1687	WITSEN	2000	52	69	Nova Tabula Imperii Russici (illustration shows Covens & Mortier re-issue c1720)
mwbh0545	belgium holland	1712	WITSEN	2500	57	97	Texel en Flie Stroom.
mwat0285	atlantic north	1784	WOHLERS	4800	63	130	See, und Land Carte eines Theils von Europa, Africa und Nord-America von der Nord-See an, zur Aequinoctial Linie

AMPG REFERENCE	REGION	DATE	MAP MAKER	PRICE (UK£)	VERT. (cm.)	HOR. (cm.)	TITLE OF MAP (Comments by the editor in brackets)
mwg0236a	berlin	1730	WOLFF	1500	27	31	Berlin
mwsp0090	portugal	1740	WOLFF	3000	34	106	LissBona (view)
mwsw0086	switzerland	1680	WOLFF	800	48	56	Novissima et Accuratissima Helvetiae
mwam0855	america north (east)	1634	WOOD	27500	30	18	The South part of New-England, as it is Planted this Yeare, 1634
mwam0674	america north	1831	WOODBRIDGE	120	26	42	Geographical & Statistical Map of the United States
mww0679	world	1827	WOODBRIDGE	240	27	46	Moral & Political Chart of the World
mwam0629	america north	1821	WOODBRIDGE	120	27	21	North America and the West Indies
mww0670	world	1821	WOODBRIDGE	250	10	13	The World (shows the Antarctic discoveries of N. Palmer)
mwam0628	america north	1821	WOODBRIDGE	350	30	46	United States
mwuss1505	texas	1835	WOODMAN	10000	23	30	Map of the Colonization Grants to Zavala, Behlein & Burnet in Texas (inset plan of Galveston)
mwam0559	america north	1802	WOOTEN	150	21	29	A Correct Map of North America
mwas0569	asia south east banda	1611	WRIGHT	400	9	13	(Untitled map by Pontanus)
mwas0578	asia south east borneo	1600	WRIGHT	600	14	22	(Untitled map of Borneo)
mwca0629	canada st lawrence	1807	WRIGHT	1800	54	73	A New Geographical and Nautical Chart of the Gulf ... St. Lawrence (in 6 sheets, each 54x73cm.)
mwme0381	holy land	1796	WRIGHT	300	23	33	Accurate Map of the Holy Land
mwuss1193	new york	1823	WRIGHT	160	29	30	Map of the State of New York Engraved for Prest. Dwight's Travels
mwuk1418	england thames	1600	WRIGHT	1500	19	54	Vray Pourtraict de la Riviere Tres Renomde de Londres, auetrement Nomed, la Tamihe
mwru0231	russia	1757	WYBORG	2000	55	71	Karta Morskaja Okuratnaja tschast Kareli
mwme0692	arabia etc	1849	WYLD	280	38	51	(Untitled map of Arabia)
mwuk0271	ireland	1830	WYLD	360	70	53	A Map of Ireland Divided into Provinces and Counties Shewing the Great and Cross Roads with the Distances of the Principal Towns from Dublin. Also the Steam Communications from the out Ports and the Average Time of Passage
mwca0483	canada ontario	1838	WYLD	500	57	88	A Map of the Province of Upper Canada, Describing All the New Settlements, Townships &c. with the Countries Adjacent, from Quebec to Lake Huron
mwuk1072	england	1844	WYLD	100	44	36	A map shewing the places in England and Wales, Sending Members to Parliament with the numbers returned. Divisions of Counties and Population, places of election, polling places and Borough Disfranchised
mwc0281a	china	1842	WYLD	2000	35	84	A Map to Ilustrate the War in China (north to the right)
mww0674	world	1824	WYLD	400	41	56	A New General Chart of the World Exhibiting the Whole of Discoveries Made by Cook, with Tracks of Ships under his Command, also Phipps, Ross and Parry in their Expeditions to North Polar Seas
mwuk1059	england	1830	WYLD	600	126	99	A New Map of England and Wales, Projected upon the Trigonometrical Operations Made for the General Survey of the Kingdom
mwuk0891	uk	1838	WYLD	360	74	58	A New Map of Great Britain Particularly Shewing the Inland Navigation by the Canals; and Principal Rivers, with the Railways, Finished and in Progress
mwgr0250	greece	1827	WYLD	280	91	61	A New Map of Greece, Constructed Chiefly from Original Materials, in which it has Been Attempted to Improve the Ancient and Modern Geography of that Country
mwuk0274	ireland	1832	WYLD	360	76	62	A New Map of Ireland Having the Great Features of the Country Described in a Manner Highly Expressive. and the Distances between the Towns & Stages Marked in Miles and Furlongs for the Use of Travellers by Alexander Taylor
mwec0276	uk england derbyshire	1832	WYLD	100	51	45	A New Map of the County of Derby Divided into Hundreds and the Parlaimentary Divisions
mwwi0914	trinidad & tobago	1850	WYLD	3000	129	153	A New Map of the Island of Trinidad, Divided into Countries and Parishes, under the Instruction of his Excellency the Right Honble. Lord Harris, K.C.B., Kch. &c. from the Original Surveys of Capt. Mallet
mwca0554	canada quebec	1829	WYLD	720	58	88	A New Map of the Province of Lower Canada, Describing All the Seigneuries, Townships, Grants of Land, &c ... by Samuel Holland ... Surveyed in 1796, 97, and 98
mwuk1301	england london	1824	WYLD	550	40	66	A New Plan of London and Westminster with the Borough of Southwark (9 editions to 1841)
mwaf0553	africa egypt etc	1825	WYLD	75	13	11	Aegyptus antiqua (inset: Pyramid)
mwaf0315	africa	1823	WYLD	320	54	60	Africa
mwaf0311	africa	1820	WYLD	90	29	23	Africa
mwas0552	asia south east	1848	WYLD	100	23	28	Archipelago of the Indian Ocean
mwas0245	asia continent	1823	WYLD	200	52	64	Asia
mwas0246	asia continent	1825	WYLD	75	11	12	Asia with the latest Discoveries
mwme1053	turkey etc	1825	WYLD	75	10	13	Brevis Asiae Minoris Descriptio
mwaf1017	africa south	1838	WYLD	350	50	32	Cape District Cape of Good Hope
mwc0281	china	1842	WYLD	2800	42	56	Chart of the Canton River with the Entrances & Islands
mwc0272	china	1840	WYLD	300	27	37	Chart of the Chu-San Archipelago

AMPG REFERENCE	REGION	DATE	MAP MAKER	PRICE (UK£)	VERT. (cm.)	HOR. (cm.)	TITLE OF MAP (Comments by the editor in brackets)
mwsp0136	portugal	1838	WYLD	300	73	51	Chorographical Map of the Kingdom of Portugal Divided into its Grand Provinces
mwsam0142	south america	1824	WYLD	550	116	80	Colombia Prima or South America Drawn from the Large Map in Eight Sheets by Louis Stanislas d'Arcy Delarochette
mwsc0398	scandinavia denmark	1825	WYLD	80	12	11	Denmark and Holstein
mwca0226	canada arctic	1822	WYLD	500	30	45	Discoveries of Capts. Ross, Parry & Franklin in the Arctic Regions. 1818. 1819. 1820. 1821 & 1822. (Either this or the previous map could have been the first printed map to report these discoveries. Re-issued 1823 same size, with the coast-line made clearer, as shown left)
mwp0074	australia	1824	WYLD	200	22	30	East India Isles & Australia
mwaf0552	africa egypt etc	1825	WYLD	75	14	11	Egypt - 1819 (inset: Alexandria)
mwuk1051	england	1822	WYLD	75	30	23	England and Wales
mwe0257	europe	1825	WYLD	75	11	12	Europe According to the Treaty of Paris
mwe1180	europe south east	1837	WYLD	200	55	72	European Dominions of the Ottomans, or Turkey in Europe
mwm0087	mediterranean	1838	WYLD	720	47	91	General Chart of the Mediterranean Sea Including the Gulf of Venice, Archipelago and Part of the Black Sea Reduced from the Large Chart in Four Sheets by J.F. Dessiou
mwat0246	atlantic madeira	1835	WYLD	720	59	76	Geo-Hydrographic Survey of the Island of Madeira
mwuss0133	california	1849	WYLD	480	28	22	Gold Regions of California
mwgr0248	greece	1825	WYLD	80	10	12	Graeciae Antiquae et Aegaei Maris Tabula
mwgr0247	greece	1825	WYLD	80	10	12	Greece and Archipelago with Part of Anadoli
mwgr0246	greece	1824	WYLD	500	53	76	Greece, Archipelago and Part of Anadoli. By L.S. de la Rochette
mwgm0115	guatemala	1847	WYLD	100	22	28	Guatemala or United States of Central America
mwsp0327	spain	1825	WYLD	60	10	12	Hispania Vetus
mwit0979	italy sicily	1828	WYLD	1250	45	70	Historical & Topographical Map of the Eruptions of Etna from the Aera of the Sicani to the Present Time, Intended to Show the Origin, the Direction & the Age of each Eruption
mwbh0791	belgium holland	1822	WYLD	60	22	29	Holland
mwin0378	india	1849	WYLD	280	76	52	India Showing the Post Roads & Dawk Stations
mwuk0264	ireland	1825	WYLD	80	13	11	Ireland Divided into Provinces and Counties
mwit0236	italy	1825	WYLD	75	12	11	Italy Divided into its Respective States
mwsc0206	scandinavia	1825	WYLD	75	12	10	Kingdom of Sweden including Norway
mwaf0550	africa egypt etc	1824	WYLD	180	53	75	Lower Egypt and the Adjacent Deserts, with a Part of Palestine
mwin0368	india	1842	WYLD	400	61	81	Map of Afghaunistan, Caubul, the Punjab, Rajpootana, and the River Indus
mwaf0342	africa	1849	WYLD	350	55	80	Map of Africa with the Latest Discoveries
mwam0296	america continent	1835	WYLD	375	54	60	Map of America
mwp0112	australia	1835	WYLD	1500	59	85	Map of Australia, Compiled from the Nautical Surveys, Made by Order of the Admiralty, and other Authentic Documents
mwme0433	holy land	1850	WYLD	750	89	130	Map of Canaan According to God's Covenant with Abraham, Isaac & Jacob
mwgm0089	gulf of mexico and surrounding regions	1850	WYLD	400	58	81	Map of Central America, Shewing the Different Lines of Atlantic & Pacific Communication
mwc0276	china	1840	WYLD	500	65	83	Map of China Compiled from Original Surveys & Sketches
mwsam0191	south america (north)	1842	WYLD	90	23	28	Map of Colombia, and British Guyana, Including the States of New Granada, Venezuela and Ecuador. London James Wyld
mwaf0559	africa egypt etc	1830	WYLD	300	62	76	Map of Egypt
mwin0366	india	1841	WYLD	320	94	67	Map of India, Constructed with Great Care and Research from All the Latest Authorities ... to Facilitate a Reference to the Civil and Military Actions
mwam0637	america north	1823	WYLD	3500	130	160	Map of North America, Exhibiting the Recent Discoveries
mwaf1245	africa west	1825	WYLD	300	65	92	Map of Part of the Western Coast of Africa Extending from the Isles de Loss to Sherboro Island. Particularly Exhibiting the Discoveries Lately Made to the N.E. of Sierra Leone by Surgeon O'Beirne and Major Laing
mwp0105	australia	1834	WYLD	750	61	92	Map of South Australia, New South Wales, Van Diemen's Land and Settled Parts of Australia (illustrated is the updated 1881 edition)
mwme0891	syria etc	1837	WYLD	720	97	62	Map of Syria, Ancient and Modern
mwas0288	asia burma	1832	WYLD	320	42	34	Map of the Burman Empire Including also Siam, Cochin-China, Ton-King and Malaya from Calcutta to Hong Kong
mwg0181	germany	1842	WYLD	200	64	76	Map of the Germanic Confederated States, Including the Kingdom of Prussia
mwsc0404	scandinavia denmark	1842	WYLD	280	76	57	Map of the Kingdom of Denmark Including the Duchies of Holstein & Lauenburg
mwsp0336	spain	1848	WYLD	1500	135	193	Map of the Kingdoms of Spain and Portugal, Including Algarve. Describing the Post Roads their Stations and Distances, Chains of Mountains and Military Passes, likewise the Places of the Principal Actions during the Campaigns in the Peninsula

AMPG REFERENCE	REGION	DATE	MAP MAKER	PRICE (UK£)	VERT. (cm.)	HOR. (cm.)	TITLE OF MAP (Comments by the editor in brackets)
mwme0684	arabia etc	1837	WYLD	280	52	71	Map of the Ottoman Dominions in Asia with the Adjacent Frontiers of the Russian and Persian Empires
mwme0690	arabia etc	1846	WYLD	280	41	57	Map of the Ottoman Empire, the Black Sea and the Frontiers of Russia and Persia
mwin0364	india	1838	WYLD	280	50	81	Map of the Peninsula of India, from the 19th Degree of North Latitude to Cape Comorin
mwsw0235	switzerland	1841	WYLD	200	59	86	Map of the Republic of Switzerland Describing the Twenty-Two Cantons
mwuk1416	uk geological	1848	WYLD	1100	132	101	Map of the Superficial Geology of the British Isles, with the Physical and Topographical Features, the Line of the Railways
mwuk1417	uk geological	1850	WYLD	350	48	36	Map of the United Kingdom of Great Britain and Ireland
mwwi0215	west indies	1845	WYLD	100	23	27	Map of the West India Islands
mwca0194	canada	1843	WYLD	350	33	38	Map to Illustrate the Boundary Line Established by the Treaty of Washington ... August, 1842 between Her Majestys Colonies of New Brunswick and Canada and the United States of America
mwgm0304	mexico	1825	WYLD	150	11	12	Mexico and Adjacent Territories in North America
mwgm0111	guatemala	1825	WYLD	200	34	79	Mexico and Guatemala, Shewing the Position of the Mines
mwam0781	america north	1846	WYLD	6000	131	141	Mexico the British Possessions in North America and the United States
mwe0455	europe bulgaria	1830	WYLD	675	97	63	Military Sketch of the Country between the Danube and Constantinople. Compiled by the King of Prussia's General Staff
mwp0172	australia	1849	WYLD	280	55	39	New South Wales
mwaf1244	africa west	1825	WYLD	75	11	12	Nigritia and Guinea with the Adjacent Coast from Cape Blanco to Cape Lopo-Gonsalves
mwaa0170	arctic	1824	WYLD	300	58	58	Northern Hemisphere
mwme0422	holy land	1841	WYLD	100	29	22	Palestine
mwaf0758	africa north algeria	1830	WYLD	240	36	49	Plan of the Bay, City and Environs of Algiers
mwca0563	canada quebec	1841	WYLD	480	66	84	Plan of the Military & Naval Operations under the Command of the Immortal Wolfe & Vice Admiral Saunders before Quebec
mwme0893	syria etc	1840	WYLD	300	21	27	Plan of the Town & Harbour of Beirout, Ancient Berytus
mwe1207	europe west	1845	WYLD	250	91	138	Post Map of Europe Comprehending England, France, Germany, Italy, &c. with the Posts, Distances, Roads, Railways, Packet Routes, &c.
mwgm0368	mexico	1849	WYLD	100	23	28	Republic of Mexico and Texas
mwsw0226	switzerland	1825	WYLD	60	11	15	Republic of Switzerland with the New Limits
mwru0344	russia	1825	WYLD	100	10	13	Russian Dominions in Asia
mwsc0205	scandinavia	1823	WYLD	240	74	52	Scandia or Scandinavia Comprehending the Kingdom of Sweden including Norway
mwuk0619	scotland	1835	WYLD	320	76	53	Scotland with its Islands, Drawn from the Topographical Surveys
mwuk0604	scotland	1825	WYLD	80	13	11	Scotland, or North Britain
mwwi0887	st lucia	1829	WYLD	300	38	48	Sketch of Part of the Island of Ste. Lucie
mwuss0734	maine	1842	WYLD	480	24	33	Sketch of the North Eastern Boundary Disputed between Great Britain and the United States as Settled by Treaty Augt. 9th 1842
mwaf1026	africa south	1846	WYLD	480	50	81	South Africa
mwaa0048	antarctic	1824	WYLD	600	58	58	Southern Hemisphere (revised in 1836)
mwsp0326	spain	1825	WYLD	60	11	12	Spain and Portugal
mwp0131	australia	1840	WYLD	350	54	39	Tasmania or Van Diemen's Land
mwat0292	atlantic north	1840	WYLD	600	56	83	The Atlantic Steam Packet Chart Shewing the Line of Communication with North America and the West Indies
mwp0291	pacific (all)	1846	WYLD	480	57	85	The Basin of the Pacific
mwsp0634	spain regions	1830	WYLD	320	22	47	The Country between St. Sebastian and the French Frontier
mwin0348	india	1825	WYLD	100	11	12	The East Indies according to the General Acceptation (incl. Cambodia etc)
mwg0178	germany	1825	WYLD	60	10	13	The Germanic States or Empire of Germany as in 1800
mwwi0760	jamaica	1843	WYLD	300	35	68	The Island of Jamaica
mwp0222	new zealand	1846	WYLD	2000	117	83	The Islands of New Zealand from the Admiralty Surveys of the English and French Marine, from the Observations of the Officers of the New Zealand Company and from Private Surveys & Sketches
mwf0189	france	1825	WYLD	80	11	13	The Kingdom of France According to the Treaty of Paris ... 1815
mwbp0563	poland	1825	WYLD	60	11	13	The Kingdom of Poland
mwbp0564	poland	1825	WYLD	60	10	15	The Kingdom of Prussia
mwp0223	new zealand	1849	WYLD	1000			The North Island of New Zealand embracing the country round Auckland, Wellington & New Plymouth
mwme0859	persia etc	1850	WYLD	280	50	68	The Persian Gulf, Persia with the Adjacent Countries of Russia, India & Turkey
mwca0210	canada	1850	WYLD	500	68	99	The Province of Canada

AMPG REFERENCE	REGION	DATE	MAP MAKER	PRICE (UK£)	VERT. (cm.)	HOR. (cm.)	TITLE OF MAP (Comments by the editor in brackets)
mwru0361	russia	1840	WYLD	480	54	93	The Russian Dominions in Europe ... with the Post Roads & New Governments from the Russian Atlas of 1806 by Jasper Nantiat (2 sheets, each 54x93cm.)
mwit0623	italy north	1825	WYLD	75	10	12	The States of Upper Italy
mwam0773	america north	1845	WYLD	960	38	56	The United States & the Relative Position of the Oregon & Texas
mww0725	world	1841	WYLD	550	64	92	The World on Mercator's Projection
mww0715	world	1838	WYLD	600	88	128	The World, Designed to Show the Languages and Dialects into which the British and Foreign Bible Society, has Translated the Scriptures
mwp0214	new zealand	1840	WYLD	960	76	54	To the Right Honourable the Secretary of State for the Colonies, &c. &c. &c., This Chart of New Zealand (6 insets)
mwe1177	europe south east	1825	WYLD	75	13	11	Turkish Dominions in Europe, or European Turkey
mwam0774	america north	1845	WYLD	400	38	55	United States of America (inset: UK)
mwuk1328a	england london	1844	WYLD	720	62	77	Wyld's New Plan of London for 1844
mwuk1326	england london	1842	WYLD	2400	64	133	Wyld's Plan of the City of London
mwuk1065	england	1836	WYLD	200	68	51	Wyld's Road Director through England and Wales being a New and Comprehensive Display of the Roads and Distances from Town to Town and of each Remarkable Place from London
mwin0380	india	1849	WYLD	240	42	44	Wyld's Theatre of War in the Punjaub
mwsam0275	south america brazil	1597	WYTFLIET	600	23	29	Brasilia
mwsam0487	south america colombia	1597	WYTFLIET	650	23	29	Castilia Aurifera cum Vicinis Provinciis
mwaa0001	antarctic	1597	WYTFLIET	2000	23	29	Chica sive Patagonica et Australis Terra
mwsam0440	south america chile	1598	WYTFLIET	480	23	29	Chili Provincia Amplissima
mwc0010	china	1611	WYTFLIET	500	9	12	Chinae Regnum*
mwca0005a	canada	1597	WYTFLIET	1200	22	27	Conibas Regio cum Vicinis Gentibus
mwwi0402	cuba	1597	WYTFLIET	750	23	29	Cuba Insula et Iamaica
mwca0004	canada	1597	WYTFLIET	800	23	29	Estotilandia et Laboratoris Terra
mwam0846	america north (east)	1597	WYTFLIET	2500	23	29	Florida et Apalche
mwuss0065	california	1597	WYTFLIET	2500	24	29	Granata Nova et California
mwgm0139	mexico	1597	WYTFLIET	1000	23	29	Hispania Nova
mwwi0576	hispaniola	1597	WYTFLIET	650	24	29	Hispaniola Insula
mwas0368a	asia south east	1605	WYTFLIET	500	10	12	India Orientalis * (*these 4 maps publ. on one sheet)
mwas0748	asia south east philippines	1611	WYTFLIET	750	9	12	Insulae Philippinae *
mwgm0140	mexico	1597	WYTFLIET	1000	23	29	Iucatana Regio et Fondura
mwjk0009	japan	1605	WYTFLIET	650	10	13	Japaniae Regnum*
mwca0657	canada west	1597	WYTFLIET	1200	24	29	Limes Occidentis et Quivira: Anian. 1597
mwam1311	america north (west)	1597	WYTFLIET	1200	24	29	Limes Occidentis Quivira et Anian. 1597
mwam0847	america north (east)	1597	WYTFLIET	2250	23	29	Norumbega et Virginia
mwca0005	canada	1597	WYTFLIET	1350	23	29	Nova Francia et Canada
mwsam0731	south america peru	1597	WYTFLIET	480	23	29	Peruani Regni Descriptio
mwsam0211	south america argentina	1597	WYTFLIET	480	23	28	Plata Americae Provincia
mwsam0171	south america (north)	1597	WYTFLIET	600	23	29	Residuum Continentis cum Adiacentibus Insulis
mww0096	world	1597	WYTFLIET	2000	23	29	Utriusque Hemispherii Delineatio
mwuk1865	wales	1799	YATES	850	95	142	A Map of the County of Glamorgan; from an Actual Survey, Made by George Yates of Liverpool. On which are Delineated the Course of the Rivers and Navigable Canals; with the Roads, Parks, Gentlemens Seats, Castles, Woods, &c. &c.
mwec0696	uk england lancashire	1786	YATES	2500	52	66	The County Palatine of Lancaster (in 8 sheets, each 52x66cm.)
mwec1172a	uk england sussex	1778	YEAKELL & GARDNER		80	97	An Actual Topographical Survey of the County of Sussex (in 4 horizontal sheets, each 80x97cm; size includes separately printed borders of subscribers, one for each sheet. Title above map, obscured by borders. The map was re-issued by Faden in 1794).
mwec1172b	uk england sussex	1779	YEAKELL & GARDNER	2000	51	47	Brighthelmston (Brighton)
mww0655a	world	1817	YEATS	6000	55	150	Chart of the Variation of the Magnetic Needle
mwuss1438	pennsylvania	1843	YOUNG	2000	86	150	A Map of the County of Philadelphia from Actual Survey Made under the Direction of Charles Ellet, Jr. Civil Engineer and in Accordance with the Act of Assembly Passed June 30th 1839
mwuss1544	texas	1850	YOUNG	600	35	41	Map of the State of Texas from the Latest Authorities
mwuss1532	texas	1845	YOUNG	5500	30	37	Map of the State of Texas from the Most Recent Authorities (pocket version)
mwgm0320	mexico	1832	YOUNG	150	20	25	Mexico and Guatimala
mwam0632	america north	1822	YOUNG	150	25	20	North America
mwuss1440	pennsylvania	1845	YOUNG	300	32	38	The Tourist's Pocket Map of Pennsylvania
mwuss0574	indiana	1833	YOUNG	300	39	32	The Tourist's Pocket Map of the State of Indiana, Exhibiting its Internal Improvements, Roads, Distances, &c.
mwuss1303	ohio	1832	YOUNG	300	40	33	The Tourist's Pocket Map of the State of Ohio Exhibiting its Internal Improvements
mwuss0015	alabama	1838	YOUNG & WILLIAMS	2000	101	126	A New Map of the City of Mobile with its Environs, Including Jacksonville, Summerville, and Lasmandville ... 1836

AMPG REFERENCE	REGION	DATE	MAP MAKER	PRICE (UK£)	VERT. (cm.)	HOR. (cm.)	TITLE OF MAP (Comments by the editor in brackets)
mww0264	world	1696	ZAHN	3600	36	84	Facies una Hemisphaerii Terrestris / Facies altera Hemisphaerii Terrestris
mww0263	world	1696	ZAHN	1500	35	42	Tabula Geographico-Hydrographica Motus Oceani Currentes, Abyssos, Montes Ignivomos in Universo Orbe Indicans, Notat haec Fig. Abyssos Montes Vucanios
mwe0513	europe czech republic (bohemia)	1566	ZALTIERI	9000	47	64	(Untitled map of Bohemia)
mwaf0810	africa north tunisia	1566	ZALTIERI	1600	27	38	Benigni lettori, per rappresentarvi piu particulari della Città di Tunisi (illustrated is the Orlandi 1602 re-issue)
mwuk0002	ireland	1566	ZALTIERI	6000	33	25	Hibernia Insula non Longe a Britania in Oceano Sita est
mwf1127	france rhone-alpes	1680	ZAPPATA	5000	196	166	Carta Generale de Stati di Sva Altezza Reale
mwsam0095	south america	1776	ZATTA	320	33	42	America Meridionale Divisa ne' suoi Principali Stati
mwam0495	america north	1785	ZATTA	500	33	43	America Settentrionale Divisa ne' suoi Principali Stati
mwsp0584	spain regions	1776	ZATTA	180	30	39	Andalusia e Granada di Novissima Projezione
mwme1031	turkey etc	1785	ZATTA	235	33	42	Asia Minor in suas Parte seu Provincias Divisa
mwuk0864	uk	1785	ZATTA	280	30	40	Britannicae Insulae
mwit0407	italy lazio	1798	ZATTA	180	31	41	Campagna di Roma di Nuova Projezione
mwp0448	pacific north	1796	ZATTA	480	46	58	Carta del Mar Pacifico del Nord che Comprende la Costa Nord-Est d'Asia e la Costa Nord Ouest d'America
mwaa0141	arctic	1770	ZATTA	200	23	23	Carta delle due Regioni Polari
mwsam0467	south america chile	1783	ZATTA	250	43	33	Chili la Terra Magellanica coll'Isola della Terra del Fuoco
mwbp0141	baltic states	1782	ZATTA	300	43	32	Ducati di Livonia e di Estonia e Governi di Nowogorod, Bielogorod e. Kiowia
mwaa0035	antarctic	1779	ZATTA	450	33	42	Emisfero Terrestre Meridionale Tagliato su l'Equatore
mwaa0147	arctic	1778	ZATTA	500	32	41	Emisfero Terrestre Settentrionale Tagliato su l'Equatore
mwru0270	russia	1782	ZATTA	180	42	33	Governi di Moscovia e Woronez Colle loro Provincie nella Russia Europea
mwgr0219	greece	1782	ZATTA	200	42	33	Graecia Antiqua
mwca0103	canada	1778	ZATTA	450	30	41	Il Canada, le Colonie Inglesi con la Luigiana e Florida. Di Nuova Projezione
mwit0519	italy lombardy	1779	ZATTA	150	32	41	Il Ducato di Mantova di Nuova Projezione
mwf0371	france brittany	1777	ZATTA	150	32	41	Il Governo di Bretagna di Nuova Projezione
mww0489	world	1774	ZATTA	1250	30	43	Il Mappamondo o sia Descrizione Generale del Globo
mww0490	world	1774	ZATTA	1250	33	43	Il Mappamondo o sia Descrizione Generale del Globo Ridotto in Quadro
mwam1063	america north (east)	1778	ZATTA	300	32	43	Il Maryland, il Jersey Meridionale, la Delaware, e la Parte Orientale della Virginia, e Carolina Settentrionale
mwam1293	great lakes	1778	ZATTA	350	30	42	Il Paese de' Selvaggi Outagamiani, Mascoutensi, Illinesi, e Parte delle VI Nazioni
mwam1294	great lakes	1778	ZATTA	350	30	42	Il Paese de' Selvaggi Outauacesi, e Kilistinesi Intorno al Lago Superiore (inset of Florida. Title above map.)
mwsam0722	south america paraguay	1785	ZATTA	200	39	32	Il Paraguai e Parti dei Paesi Adiacenti
mwit0408	italy lazio	1798	ZATTA	180	31	40	Il Patrimonio di S. Pietro e la Sabina di Nuova Projezione
mwsam0782	south america peru	1785	ZATTA	200	41	31	Il Peru ove si Trovano le Udienze di Quito, Lima, e Plata
mwsp0111	portugal	1776	ZATTA	160	32	42	Il Portogallo cioe le Provincie di Entre Douro, e Minho, Traz-Os-Montes, e Beira di Nuova Projezione
mwsc0374	scandinavia denmark	1781	ZATTA	200	42	33	Il Regno di Danimarca con il Ducato di Sleswik di Nuova Projezioni
mwbp0498	poland	1780	ZATTA	240	26	33	Il Regno di Polonia con le Provincie ora Possedute dalle Tre Confinati Potenze Prussia Russia e Casa d'Austria
mwbp0499	poland	1781	ZATTA	250	31	40	Il Regno di Prussia con la Prussia Polacca
mwuk0531	scotland	1776	ZATTA	280	32	41	Il Regno di Scozia di Nuova Projezione
mwe0957	europe hungary	1781	ZATTA	250	32	41	Il Regno di Ungheria di Nuova Projezione
mwas0509	asia south east	1784	ZATTA	1000	33	42	Indie Orientali di Quà e di la Dal Gange col Loro Arcipelago (in 4 sheets)
mwc0203	china	1784	ZATTA	400	33	42	Impero della China colle Isole della Giappone
mwsp0678	balearic islands	1778	ZATTA	400	32	42	Isola di Minorca di Nuova Projezione (inset: Environs of Mahon)
mwsp0679	balearic islands	1778	ZATTA	500	32	42	Isole di Majorca, d'Ivica e di Formentera di Nuova Projezione
mwas0796	asia south east philippines	1776	ZATTA	720	41	31	Isole Filippine
mwbp0139	baltic states	1781	ZATTA	480	32	42	L Palatinati di Nowogrodek Podlachia e Brzesk Littew
mwca0219	canada	1778	ZATTA	450	31	42	La Baja d'Hudson Terra di Labrador e Groenlandia con le Isole Adiacenti di Nuova Projezione
mwsp0581	spain regions	1775	ZATTA	160	29	39	La Catalogna li Regni di Aragona ed Alta Navarra
mwe0505	europe croatia	1782	ZATTA	300	31	40	La Croazia, Bosnia, e Servia di Nuova Projezione
mwf0808a	france north	1794	ZATTA	235	52	60	La Francia cioe le Regioni dell' Occidente del Centro e del Levante
mwg0150	germany	1776	ZATTA	240	30	40	La Germania divisa
mwwi0735	jamaica	1778	ZATTA	250	34	44	La Giammaica
mwgr0215	greece	1781	ZATTA	350	42	33	La Grecia Divisa nelle sue Provincie
mwaf1231	africa west	1784	ZATTA	350	41	31	La Guinea Occidentale/Orientale (2 maps)
mwru0271	russia	1782	ZATTA	240	42	33	La Lapponia Russa con Governa Olonechoi, Carelia, Bielozero, ed Ingria
mwsc0634	scandinavia norway	1781	ZATTA	300	42	33	La Norvegia Divisa nelle sue Provincie
mwaf0415	africa east	1784	ZATTA	300	33	42	La Nubia et Abissinia

AMPG REFERENCE	REGION	DATE	MAP MAKER	PRICE (UK£)	VERT. (cm.)	HOR. (cm.)	TITLE OF MAP (Comments by the editor in brackets)
mwp0184	new zealand	1778	ZATTA	2000	44	36	La Nuova Zelanda Trascorsa nel 1769 e 1770 dal Cook Commandante dell'Endeavour Vascello di S.M. Britannica
mwca0537	canada quebec	1778	ZATTA	250	33	44	La Parte Occidentale della Nuova Francia o Canada (title above map)
mwam1295	great lakes	1778	ZATTA	650	30	42	La Pensilvania, la Nuova York …
mwbp0502	poland	1782	ZATTA	240	33	42	La Polonia Divisa ne' suoi Palatinati
mwbh0728	belgium holland	1776	ZATTA	240	42	32	La Repubblica d'Ollanda Divisa nelle sue Provincie di Nuova Projezione
mwit1124a	italy tuscany	1783	ZATTA	350	40	31	La Republicca di Lucca
mwuk0534	scotland	1779	ZATTA	375	32	42	La Scozia Settentrionale Divisa nelle sue Contee Particolari / La Scozia Meridionale Divisa nelle sue Contee Particolari di Nuova Projezione (2 maps)
mwe1120a	europe slovak republic (moravia)	1785	ZATTA	200	35	44	La Slesia Infer. divisa ne Suoi Principati di Nuova Proiezione
mwsc0742	scandinavia sweden	1781	ZATTA	280	42	33	La Suezia Divisa ne suoi Regni di Nuova Projezioni
mwc0204	china	1784	ZATTA	240	31	40	La Tartaria Chinese
mwru0459	russia tartary	1784	ZATTA	400	31	40	La Tartaria Indipendente che Comprende il Paese de' Calmuchi quello degli Usbeks, e il Turkestan co le loro Dipendenze
mwsam0184	south america (north)	1785	ZATTA	240	32	42	La Terra Ferma la Gujana Spagnola, Olandese, Francese, e Portughese e la Parte Settentrle. del Bresil
mwme1030	turkey etc	1784	ZATTA	235	33	42	La Turchia d'Asia che Comprende l'Anatolia, la Giorgia, l'Armenia, il Curdistan, il Diarbec, l'Irak-Arabi, la Siria &c.
mwca0423a	canada nova scotia	1778	ZATTA	400	33	44	L'Acadia, le Provincie di Sagadahook e Main, la Nuova Hampshire, la Rhode Island, e Parte di Massachusset e Connecticut
mwaf0235	africa	1776	ZATTA	350	31	41	L'Africa Divisa ne suoi Principali Stati di Nuova Projection
mwam0231	america continent	1790	ZATTA	150	17	19	L'America
mwam0203	america continent	1776	ZATTA	450	31	40	L'America Divisa ne suoi Principali Stati di Nuova Projezione (incl. New Zealand after Cook)
mwme0651	arabia etc	1784	ZATTA	450	30	39	L'Arabia Divisa in Petrea, Deserta e Felice
mwas0194	asia continent	1777	ZATTA	280	30	40	L'Asia Divisa ne' suoi Principali Stati di Nuova Projezione
mwam1061	america north (east)	1778	ZATTA	3750	34	45	Le Colonie Unite dell' America Settentrle. di Nuova Projezione a Ss.Ee. li Signori Riformatori dello Studio di Padova. Venezia, 1778 (in 12 sheets, each 34x45cm)
mwme0372	holy land	1784	ZATTA	200	32	41	Le Dodeci Tribu d'Israele / Terra di Canaan ou Terra Promessa ad Abramo, e a suoi Posteri
mwat0126	atlantic bermuda	1778	ZATTA	1500	33	43	Le Isole Bermude (from Zatta's 12 sheet map of North-East America)
mwca0327	canada newfoundland	1778	ZATTA	350	43	33	Le Isole di Terra Nuova e Capo Breton di Nuova Projezione
mwe0452	europe bulgaria	1781	ZATTA	300	42	33	Le Provincie di Bulgaria, e Rumelia Tratte dalla Carte dell' Impero Ottomano del Sig Rizzi Zanoni
mwsw0191	switzerland	1785	ZATTA	360	32	41	L'Elvezia
mwsp0109	portugal	1775	ZATTA	240	32	34	L'Estremadura di Portogallo Alentejo, ed Algarve di Nuova Projezione
mwe0197	europe	1776	ZATTA	280	29	40	L'Europa Divisa ne' suoi Principali Stati
mwf0892	france paris	1776	ZATTA	140	27	42	Li Contorni di Parigi (environs of Paris)
mwf0249	france alsace	1776	ZATTA	160	32	42	Li Governo di Lorena, Barr ed Alsazia
mwru0557	ukraine	1781	ZATTA	950	41	31	Li Palatinati de Braclaw, e Kiowia
mwru0556	ukraine	1781	ZATTA	875	32	42	Li Palatinati della Russia Rossa Podolia e Wolhynia
mwbp0500	poland	1781	ZATTA	235	32	41	Li Palatinati di Cracowia, Lekzyca, Sieradz, Sandomir, e Lublino
mwbp0138	baltic states	1781	ZATTA	480	41	31	Li Palatinati di Minsk, Mscislaw, e Witebsk nella Littuania
mwbp0140	baltic states	1781	ZATTA	240	40	31	Li Palatinati di Wilna, Troki, Inflant coi Ducati di Kurlandia e Smudz
mwsp0585	spain regions	1776	ZATTA	160	29	40	Li Regni di Galizia, Asturies, Leon, Castiglia Vecchia con la Biscaglia di Nuova Projezione
mwsp0289	spain	1775	ZATTA	280	30	42	Li Regni di Spagna e Portogallo Divisi nelle sue Provincie di Nuova Projezione
mwsc0166	scandinavia	1781	ZATTA	280	30	41	Li Regni di Suezia, Danimarca e Norvegia
mwsp0677	balearic islands	1775	ZATTA	450	29	39	Li Regni di Valenza, e Murcia
mwsp0582	spain regions	1775	ZATTA	280	32	42	Li Regni di Valenza, e Murcia con l'Isole Baleari, e Pitiuse
mwuk1089	england and ireland	1776	ZATTA	250	31	40	Li Regni d'Inghilterra e d'Irlanda di Nuova Projezione
mwjk0117	japan	1785	ZATTA	1000	32	41	L'Impero del Giapon Diviso in Sette Principali Parti
mwme0832	persia etc	1784	ZATTA	320	32	42	L'Impero della Persia Diviso ne suoi Stati
mwf0533	france corsica	1782	ZATTA	550	40	31	L'Isola di Corsica Divisa nelle sue Provincie di Nuova Projezione
mwit0820c	italy sardinia	1784	ZATTA	400	41	32	L'isola di Sardegna divisa ne' suoi Distretti (shown above)
mwsc0510	scandinavia iceland	1781	ZATTA	240	33	41	L'Isola d'Islanda Divisa ne suoi Distretti
mwam0809	america north (central)	1778	ZATTA	280	32	42	Luigiana Inglese, colla Parte Occidentale della Florida, della Giorgia, e Carolina Meridionale
mwgm0257	mexico	1785	ZATTA	480	32	41	Messico ouvero Nuova Spagna che Contiene il Nuovo Messico la California con una Parte de' Paesi Adjacenti
mwp0185	new zealand	1779	ZATTA	1100	29	39	Nuova Guinea e Nuova Galles ed Isole Adjacenti
mwp0424	pacific north	1776	ZATTA	500	30	40	Nuove Scoperte de' Russi al Nord del Mare del Sud si nell' Asia, che nell' America (close copy of Boudet 1774)

AMPG REFERENCE	REGION	DATE	MAP MAKER	PRICE (UK£)	VERT. (cm.)	HOR. (cm.)	TITLE OF MAP (Comments by the editor in brackets)
mwp0500	pacific south	1776	ZATTA	1200	32	42	Nuove Scoperte Fatte nel 1765, 67, e 69 nel Mare del Sud
mwit0691	italy piedmont	1782	ZATTA	240	31	41	Parte del Piemonte che Contiene il Distretto di Torino, il Contado d'Asti ... e il Pavese oltre Po
mwuk0211	ireland	1778	ZATTA	480	42	33	Parte del Regno d'Irlanda ... di Nuova Projezione (2 sheets, west/east)
mwaf0621a	africa islands madagascar	1784	ZATTA	300	31	40	Parte della Costa Orientale dell' Africa con l'Isola di Madagascar (insets: Mauritius, Bourbon)
mwe0607	europe czech republic (bohemia)	1780	ZATTA	375	40	31	Parte Occidentale del Regno di Boemia / Parte Orientale del Regno di Boemia (2 sheets)
mwsw0188	switzerland	1781	ZATTA	400	42	33	Parte Occidentale dell'Elvezia / Parte Orientale dell'Elvezia (2 sheets)
mwca0617a	canada	1778	ZATTA	350	34	44	Parte Orientale del Canada, Nuova Scozia Settentrionale, e Parte di Labrador
mwuk1016	england	1778	ZATTA	350	59	42	Parte Settentrionale dell'Inghilterra, e del Principato di Galles / Parte Meridionale (2 sheets)
mwaf0416	africa east	1784	ZATTA	300	32	41	Partie della Costa Orientale del' Africa
mwgr0271	greece athens	1781	ZATTA	200	19	28	Pianta D'Atene Del Viaggio d'Anacarsi il Giovane
mwit1202a	italy veneto	1782	ZATTA	350	31	40	Polesine di Rovigo
mwe0818	europe east	1782	ZATTA	150	32	42	Principati di Moldavia, e Vallachia Tratti dalle Carte dell' Impero Ottomano del Sig. Rizzi Zanoni
mwec0415	uk england essex	1779	ZATTA	150	21	32	Provincia di Essex di Nuova Projezione
mwec0644	uk england kent	1775	ZATTA	180	20	31	Provincia di Kent
mwec0788	uk england middlesex	1776	ZATTA	180	21	32	Provincia di Middlesex di Nuova Projezione
mwec1144	uk england surrey	1779	ZATTA	150	21	32	Provincia di Surrey di Nuova Projezione
mwas0508	asia south east	1783	ZATTA	480	40	32	Regni d'Aracan del Pegu di Siam di Camboge e di Laos
mwe0815	europe east	1779	ZATTA	180	32	42	Regno di Boemia, Ducato di Silesia, e Marchesati di Moravia, e Lusazia
mwf0144	france	1776	ZATTA	240	31	40	Regno di Francia Diviso ne suoi Governi
mwsp0110	portugal	1775	ZATTA	280	29	41	Regno di Portogallo
mwgr0216	greece	1781	ZATTA	180	28	20	Saggio Su La Topografia Di Sparta
mwgr0217	greece	1781	ZATTA	180	18	28	Saggio Sulla Topografia D'Olimpia
mwwi0122	west indies	1785	ZATTA	350	32	41	Stabilimenti de Francesi, Inglesi, e Spagnuoli nelle Isole Antille di Nuova Projezione
mwin0283	india	1785	ZATTA	250	42	33	Stato del Mogol con l'Isole di Ceilan e Maldive
mwit0448a	italy liguria	1779	ZATTA	200	33	42	Stato della Repubblica di Genova di nuova proiezione (shown below left)
mwru0565	ukraine	1788	ZATTA	1800	65	97	Teatro della Guerra Presente tra la Russia e la Porta Ottomana
mwgr0218	greece	1782	ZATTA	250	42	32	Turchia d'Europa Divisa
mwe1159	europe south east	1780	ZATTA	200	41	31	Turchia d'Europa Divisa nelle sue Provincie, e Governi. Di Nuova Projezione
mwgr0433	greece crete	1814	ZENNER	600	24	20	Plan de Candie
mwsc0014	scandinavia	1558	ZENO	3000	28	38	Carta Da Navegar De Nicolo Et Antonio Zeni
mwit0029	italy	1567	ZENOI	16000	40	52	(Untitled map. Beginning of text reads: Il Golfo di Venetia ... Map by Donato Bertelli)
mwe0280a	europe austria	1567	ZENOI	2000	34	47	Descritione dell'Austria ... Dalmatia
mwbh0014	belgium holland	1559	ZENOI	4800	50	42	Exactissima Flandriae Descriptio ... Ad Cordatum Lectorem N. Stopius. Venetijs, 1559
mwit0031a	italy	1570	ZENOI	2000	21	27	Italia con la Descritione Delle Provincie Regni, Città, Castelli, Monti, Mari, Fiumi Laghi che sono in essa (shown above)
mwsc0007	scandinavia	1532	ZIEGLER	7500	23	35	(Title on verso: Octava tabula continet Cheronessum Schondiam)
mwme0016	holy land	1532	ZIEGLER	1500	24	35	(Title on verso: Quarto tabula continet Judeam)
mwme0017	holy land	1532	ZIEGLER	1500	24	35	(Title on verso: Quinta tabula universalis Palaestinae)
mwme0018	holy land	1532	ZIEGLER	1500	23	36	(Title on verso: Secunda tabula continet Partem Phoeniciae)
mwme0019	holy land	1532	ZIEGLER	1500	23	35	(Title on verso: Septima tabula continet Tribum Iuda)
mwme0020	holy land	1532	ZIEGLER	1500	23	36	(Title on verso: Tercia tabula continet Samariam)
mwme0689	arabia etc	1846	ZIMMERMANN	400	57	95	Jemen. Hadramaut.
mww0510	world	1780	ZIMMERMANN	720	49	68	Tabula Mundi Geographico Zoologica sistens Quadrupedes (names of animals. Kangaroos shown in Australia)
mwsw0088a	switzerland	1684	ZOLLINGER	2500	45	56	Inclytae Urbis et Ditionis Bernensis cum locis finitimus (inset of Bern)
mwme0440b	jerusalem	1587	ZUALLARDO	800	9	13	Hierusalem C.D. (shown above)
mwf1086	france provence	1835	ZUCCAGNI-ORLANDINI	500	34	53	Carta Corografica ... di Nizza
mwit0696	italy piedmont	1845	ZUCCAGNI-ORLANDINI	300	34	53	Carta Corografica della Divisione Militare di Aosta
mwf1198	monaco	1845	ZUCCAGNI-ORLANDINI	800	52	34	Carta Topografica del Principato di Monaco
mwit0697	italy piedmont	1845	ZUCCAGNI-ORLANDINI	300	34	53	Divisione Militare di Cuneo
mwit0828	italy sardinia	1840	ZUCCAGNI-ORLANDINI	300	36	57	Pianta della Citta di Cagliari
mwit1080	italy naples	1845	ZUCCAGNI-ORLANDINI	300	67	57	Pianta della Citta di Napoli
mwit1262	italy venice	1840	ZUCCAGNI-ORLANDINI	550	48	60	Pianta della Citta di Venezia
mwgr0450	greece cyprus	1570	ZUNDT	150000	29	39	Die Insel Cypern den Venedigern Zugeherig ... Gott Well Ine Genedig bey Sten Wyder den Thiran
mwgr0549	greece islands	1571	ZUNDT	2500	26	36	Die Victoria ist Geschehe 1571 ... zwische Leponto, Ceffalonia beij Cuzolari

AMPG REFERENCE	REGION	DATE	MAP MAKER	PRICE (UK£)	VERT. (cm.)	HOR. (cm.)	TITLE OF MAP (Comments by the editor in brackets)
mwm0168a	mediterranean malta	1566	ZUNDT	2500	27	19	Ioannes de Valeta Magnus Magister Hospitalis Hierosolimitani. Vera effigies a dil Gran Magistro effigurata. Abconterfectung des grosen Maijsters zu Malta.
mwbh0034	belgium holland	1568	ZUNDT	3500	31	48	Tabula Complectens totam Belgicam, Flandriam, Brabantiam, Selandiam ...
mwaf0132	africa	1709	ZURNER	900	50	58	Africae in Tabula Geographica Delineatio (copy of Schenk 1700)
mwam0114a	america continent	1709	ZURNER	2000	50	58	Americae in Tabula Geographica Delineatio (publ. by P. Schenk)
mwas0117	asia continent	1719	ZURNER	1200	50	58	Asiae in Tabula Geographica Delineato
mwe0108	europe	1700	ZURNER	1200	50	58	Europae in Tabula Geographica Delineatio
mwe0557a	europe czech republic (bohemia)	1715	ZURNER-SCHENK	1200	51	59	Geographischer Entwurff der Stadt und Gegend des... Carlsbades
mww0283	world	1700	ZURNER	5500	50	58	Planisphaerium Terrestre cum utroque Coelesti Hemisphaerio, sive Diversa Orbis Terraquei
mwgr0359	greece crete	1587	ZVALLART	450	9	13	Candia
mwgr0463	greece cyprus	1587	ZVALLART	850	9	13	Cipro
mwm0089a	mediterranean adriatic	1587	ZVALLART	500	9	13	Colfoco e Italia
mwm0113	mediterranean east	1587	ZVALLART	600	9	13	Mediteraneo. E' Colpho De Setelia - Palestina
mwgr0538	greece zante (zakynthos)	1587	ZVALLART	450	9	12	Zante

Made in the USA
Charleston, SC
31 May 2016